ENGLISH DICTIONARY

FOR ADVANCED LEARNERS

ARABIC ENGLISH DICTIONARY

FOR ADVANCED LEARNERS

الفرائِد الدّرّيّة

J.G. HAVA

Goodword
BOOKS

First Published by Goodword Books 2001

Reprinted 2002, 2003, 2004, 2006

Goodword Books Pvt. Ltd.
1, Nizamuddin West Market
New Delhi - 110 013
e-mail: info@goodwordbooks.com
www.goodwordbooks.com

Printed in India

EXPLANATORY REMARKS.

I. ORDER OF WORDS.

1° The order followed in the Dictionary is the same as is generally adopted by European Orientalists, viz. the radicals, marked thus (✱) are given in alphabetical order, each one followed by all the derivative forms.

2° The foreign words introduced into Arabic, although they do not belong to any radical, have been assimilated to Arabic words, being considered as arabicised and as such connected with a radical really existing or supposed to exist. Therefore they are to be sought in the Dictionary, without taking into account the augmentative letters included in the paradigm سألتموني , exactly as would be done for Arabic words. For instance استنبول is to be found under the root نبل (paradigm استفعل). بازار in بزر , بيكار in بكر , بيرامون in برم , انكليز in كلز , انجيل in نجل etc.

3° Whenever a ن occurs in the second letter of a quadriliteral noun or verb, it is to be referred to the triliteral root. the letter ن being then augmentative ; thus عنقود is to be found in عقد , عنكبوت in عكب , عنبس in عبس , خنزير in خزر , حندس in حدس , and so on. The reason lies in this, that this letter is added to give an intensive form to the original meaning of the triliteral form, and this kind of words has been so classed in the Arabic Lexicons. But when ن is considered as radical, the words are left in the ordinary alphabetical order. Even as a rule we repeat them, in order to save too much trouble to the students.

4° Quasi-quadriliteral forms having a و or ي in the second or third letter are to be found in the corresponding triliteral form. to which they are supposed to belong, بيقر in بقر , جوهر in جهر , بروز in برز .

5° Reduplicative verbs such as زلزل , فرفر always follow the biliteral verb to which they correspond, زلزل to زلّ , فرفر to فرّ ; and they are placed in the same order even if the biliteral root is wanting : thus زعزع is mentioned immediately after زطّ .

6° Quadriliteral words beginning by ي are to be referred to a triliteral noun, as يحمور to حمر , يربوع to ربع , ينبوع to نبع , يبراق to برق .

II. ETYMOLOGY.

We give in an appendix a list of Arabic words derived from foreign languages. Those borrowed from Turkish or Persian are mentioned only when they have undergone a change in the Arabic transcription. For the others the orthography being the same, there is no need of repeating them. We refer these words to their primitive origin, although the foreign words used in common language may be said, almost without exception, to belong to Turkish, and have been introduced through its medium ; as كرنتينه , لوكندة , سكورته , استريديا , سناموره ; and especially all the Persian words as وشنة , ششمة , ششمر.

We give the etymology of the words as they are to be found in Arabic, Persian, or Turkish Lexicons, such as Lane, Freytag, Dozy, Barbier de Meynard, Meninski, etc ; but we cannot vouch for the accuracy of all, as some of them are obviously doubtful, especially some Persian words, the etymology of which is variously explained. In that case we quote the form that appeared to us more consistent with analogy. The words derived from Coptic are not included in the list ; they are very few and they chiefly pertain to names of months, which are only used in Egypt.

To the words derived from foreign languages we have prefixed some letters indicating their origin :

F = French ; G = Greek ; H = Hebrew
I = Italian ; L = Latin ; P = Persian
S = Syriac ; T = Turkish.

III. CONVENTIONAL SIGNS.

1. * Indication of a new Arabic root.
✧ Used in the dialect of Syria.
▫ In that of Egypt.

a) It must be remarked that if the two preceding signs are placed before an Arabic root, it means that the Arabic word and its meaning pertain to that dialect ; if placed before the English sense, it affects only the special meaning given, the word being good Arabic in its form.

b) It must be noted that most of the vulgar meanings marked with the sign ✦ are common to both dialects, while those marked ▫ are only used in Egypt.

2. The sign (—), in the beginning of a line, stands for the repetition of the preceding word :

E. g. تَرَّس ة

— وتَتَرَّس is for تَرَّس وتَتَرَّس

جَعَل

— لهُ ة و ه stands for جَعَل لهُ ة و ه

3. A comma (,), intervening between nouns or verbs following in a sequel, indicates a new form having the same meaning as the former :

E. g. حُبَاشَة ج حُبَاشَات , وأُحْبُوشَة ج أحَابِيش

means that a حُبَاشَات is the plural of حُبَاشَة and that أُحْبُوشَة is a new form in the singular, retaining the same meaning as حُبَاشَة .

حَبَض i حَبْضًا , وحبِض a حَبَضًا

means that (a حَبِض) is another form of the same verb, having the same meaning as (i حَبَض).

4. A semicolon (;) is put for distinguishing words that have a common meaning, without being synonymous.

5. A colon (:) placed between two nouns separates the object from the subject of a verb.

E. g. To blast (the plants : hoar-frost) شَفْشَف ه

To miss (the butt : shooter) أَخْبَى

6. The words included in a parenthesis ( ) are either given as an explanation. or to complete the meaning of a verb or noun, which is not mentioned explicitly in Arabic. Thus a parenthesis explains the sense understood by the letters ه or ة in Arabic.

7. (ه , ة) These letters show a verb to be transitive ; and when they are wanting, the verb is intransitive.

ة stands for animate beings ;

ه for inanimate things.

When both signs are found together without being separated by , they mean that the verb has a double object

8. The letters a, i, o, following an Arabic verb show that the aorist has its second radical in ـَـ, ـِـ, or ـُـ:

a stands for ـَـ as دَغَرَ a يَدْغَرُ

o — — ـُـ as جَبَرَ o يَجْبُرُ

i — — ـِـ as خَفَّ i يَخِفُّ

Two letters following the same verb indicate that the same may have two forms, as : i o جَفَلَ means that the aorist is يَجْفِلُ or يَجْفُلُ.

IV. NUMERICAL VALUE OF THE ARABIC LETTERS

disposed in the following order :

أَبْجَدْ هَوَّزْ حُطِّي كَلَمَنْ سَعْفَصْ قَرَشَتْ ثَخَذْ ضَظَغْ

ا is equal to	1	س	60
ب	2	ع	70
ج	3	ف	80
د	4	ص	90
ه	5	ق	100
و	6	ر	200
ز	7	ش	300
ح	8	ت	400
ط	9	ث	500
ي	10	خ	600
ك	20	ذ	700
ل	30	ض	800
م	40	ظ	900
ن	50	غ	1000

V. SOME PARTICULARS ABOUT GENDER.

A. Feminine nouns having a masculine termination.

Pick-axe	فأس	Foot	رِجْل	Ear	أذُن
Thigh	فخذ	Womb	رَحِم	Earth	أرْض
Ship	فُلْك	Wind	رِيح	Hare	أرْنَب
Bow	قوس	Hell	سَقَر	Buttocks	إسْت
Foot	قدم	Year, age	سِنّ	Finger	إصْبَع
Cup	كأس	Leg	سَاق	Viper	أفعى
Shoulder	كَتِف	Sun	شَمْس	Pit	بِئْر
Ventricle	كرش	Left hand	شِمَال	Hell	جَحِيم
Palm of the hand	كَفّ	Hyena	ضَبُع	Hell	جَهَنَّم
Fire	نار	Poetical metre	عَرُوض	War	حَرْب
Shoe	نَعْل	Stick, staff	عَصَا	Bucket	دَلْو
Hip. haunch	وَرِك	Heel	عَقِب	House	دَار
Hand	يَد	Eye ; spring	عَيْن	Arm, cubit	ذِراع
Right hand, oath	يَمِين				

All the winds such as جَنُوب , قَبُول , صَبَا , حَرُور , سَمُوم , هَيْف , شَمَال , دَبُور etc.

N. B. The adjectives having a common termination for both genders or numbers have been specially mentioned in the dictionary throughout.

B. Nouns admitting both the masculine and feminine gender.

Back of the neck	قَفَا	Road	طَرِيق	Arm-pit	إبط
Liver	كَبِد	Posteriors	عَجُز ; عَجْز	State, condition	حال
Tongue	لِسَان	Upper-arm	عَضُد	Wine	خَمْر
Musk	مِسْك	Eagle, orfrey	عُقَاب	Shirt, coat-of-mail	دِرْع
Salt	مِلْح	Scorpion	عَقْرَب	Gold	ذَهَب
Ballista	مَنْجَنِيق	Neck	عُنُق	Ample trousers	سَرَاوِيل
Razor	مُوسَى	Spider	عَنْكَبُوت	Knife	سِكِّين
Soul, individual	نَفْس	Garden, heaven	فِرْدَوْس	Power, might	سُلْطَان
Hind-part	وَرَاء	Horse, mare	فَرَس	Peace	سِلْم
All the letters of the alphabet.		Iron-pestle	فِهْر	Heaven, sky	سَمَاء
		Cooking-pot	قِدْر	Morning	ضُحَى

VI. PARADIGMS OF THE VERBS.

A. Paradigm of the triliteral verbs.

Participle: Passive	Participle: Active		Aorist	Preterite
		ضَرَبَ يَضْرِبُ as	يَفْعِلُ	فَعَلَ i
		نَصَرَ يَنْصُرُ	يَفْعُلُ	فَعَلَ o
مَفْعُولٌ	فَاعِلٌ	مَنَعَ يَمْنَعُ	يَفْعَلُ	فَعَلَ a
		عَلِمَ يَعْلَمُ	يَفْعَلُ	فَعِلَ a
		حَسِبَ يَحْسِبُ	يَفْعِلُ	فَعِلَ i
		فَضُلَ يَفْضُلُ	يَفْعُلُ	فَعُلَ o

N. B. The nouns of action of the triliteral verb have no regular form.

B. Derivatives of the triliteral verb.

Participle: Passive	Participle: Active	Noun of action	Aorist	Preterite
مُفَعَّلٌ	مُفَعِّلٌ	تَفْعِلَةً وتَفْعِيلًا	يُفَعِّلُ	فَعَّلَ
مُفَاعَلٌ	مُفَاعِلٌ	مُفَاعَلَةً وفِعَالًا	يُفَاعِلُ	فَاعَلَ
مُفْعَلٌ	مُفْعِلٌ	إِفْعَالًا	يُفْعِلُ	أَفْعَلَ
مُتَفَعَّلٌ	مُتَفَعِّلٌ	تَفَعُّلًا	يَتَفَعَّلُ	تَفَعَّلَ
مُتَفَاعَلٌ	مُتَفَاعِلٌ	تَفَاعُلًا	يَتَفَاعَلُ	تَفَاعَلَ
مُنْفَعَلٌ	مُنْفَعِلٌ	إِنْفِعَالًا	يَنْفَعِلُ	إِنْفَعَلَ
مُفْتَعَلٌ	مُفْتَعِلٌ	إِفْتِعَالًا	يَفْتَعِلُ	إِفْتَعَلَ
	مُفْعَلٌّ	إِفْعِلَالًا	يَفْعَلُّ	إِفْعَلَّ
مُسْتَفْعَلٌ	مُسْتَفْعِلٌ	إِسْتِفْعَالًا	يَسْتَفْعِلُ	إِسْتَفْعَلَ
	مُفْعَالٌّ	إِفْعِيلَالًا	يَفْعَالُّ	إِفْعَالَّ
مُفْعَوْعَلٌ	مُفْعَوْعِلٌ	إِفْعِيعَالًا	يَفْعَوْعِلُ	إِفْعَوْعَلَ
مُفْعَوَّلٌ	مُفْعَوِّلٌ	إِفْعِوَّالًا	يَفْعَوِّلُ	إِفْعَوَّلَ

C. Quadriliteral verb and its derivatives.

Participle: Passive	Participle: Active	Noun of action	Aorist	Preterite
مُفَعْلَلٌ	مُفَعْلِلٌ	فَعْلَلَةً وفِعْلَالًا	يُفَعْلِلُ	فَعْلَلَ
مُتَفَعْلَلٌ	مُتَفَعْلِلٌ	تَفَعْلُلًا	يَتَفَعْلَلُ	تَفَعْلَلَ
مُفْعَنْلَلٌ	مُفْعَنْلِلٌ	إِفْعِنْلَالًا	يَفْعَنْلِلُ	إِفْعَنْلَلَ
مُفْعَلَلٌّ	مُفْعَلِلٌّ	إِفْعِلَّالًا	يَفْعَلِلُّ	إِفْعَلَلَّ

VII. ENGLISH ABBREVIATIONS.

a	shows the accent of the aorist —
anat.	anatomy
a. o.	any one
arch.	architecture
arithm.	arithmetic
astron.	astronomy
a. th.	any thing
C	Coptic
Ch	Chaldaic
coll.	collective noun
e. g	(*exempli gratia*) for instance
e. o.	each other
F	French
F. or *fem.*	feminine
G	Greek
Ge	German
Gr. or *gram.*	grammar
H	Hebrew
I	Italian
i	shows the accent of the aorist —
i. e.	(*id est*) that is
imp.	imperative
ins.	insect
int. or *interj.*	interjection
L	Latin
lit.	literally
m.	masculine
med.	medicine
o	shows the accent of the aorist —
o. a.	one another
o. 's	one's
P	Persian
p. or *pl.*	plural
pers.	person
pla.	plant
pron.	pronoun
pros.	prosody
Prov.	proverb
Rhet.	rhetoric
S	Syriac
s. or *sing.*	singular
Sp	Spanish
T	Turkish
un.	noun of unity
viz.	(*videlicet*) namely

ARABIC

Plural	ج = جمع
Plural of a plural	جج = جمع الجمع
Feminine	م = مؤنث
Dual	مث = مثنى
Animate being	ع
Inanimate object	

N. B. A smaller E or S following any of the capital letters used for indicating languages means that the word is used in Egypt or Syria. Thus CE must be read : Coptic word used in Egypt ; and TS is for Turkish word used in Syria.

كتاب

الفرائد الدرّية

في اللغتين العربيّة والانكليزيّة

ARABIC-ENGLISH DICTIONARY.

ا

To prick a. o. ٭ أبَر i o أبرًا وإبارًا ه
with a needle. To spur. To give to a.o. to eat a needle (in his food). To backbite.

To fecundate ; أبَر o i أبرًا وإبارةً ه
to graft (a palm tree, etc).

Needle ; sting. Sea-compass. إبرة ج إبر

Geranium, crane's bill (plant) إبرة الراعي

Needle-case. Grafting-knife. مِئبَر ومِئبار

Slander, backbiting. مِئبَرة ج مآبِر

Pricked ; grafted. Sharp-pointed. مأبور

To dart forth, to rush, to leap (gazelle). ٭ أبَز i أبزًا وأبوزًا

To insult a. o. — ب أبزًا

To reprove, to despise, to humiliate a. o. ٭ أبَس i أبسًا , وأبَّس ه

To pick up, to gather a. th. ٭ أبَش o أبشًا , وأبَّش ه

Crowd. أباشة

To fasteu the foot of a camel to (his thigh). ٭ أبَض o i أبضًا , وتأبَّض ه

Rope for fastening the foot of a camel. Hock, hamstring. إباض ج أبُض

Man's or camel's ham. أبْض ج آباض ومَأبِض ج مآبِض

Armpit. إبْط ج آباط وباط ج باطات

To carry a. th. under the armpit. تأبَّط ه

Nickname of an Arabian poet, *lit*.: he carries evil under his arm. تأبَّط شرًّا

Anything put under the armpit. إباط

I put it benes.th my armpit. جَعلتُهُ إباطًا

Hey, *interr. part.*, I say, is it ? ٭ أ

Is (he, she, it)... not ? ألَمْ وألا

Is (he, she, it)... not... yet ? ألمّا

٭ أب see أبو

To desire a. th. ٭ أبَّ o أبًّا وأبابةً وإبابةً الى

To prepare oneself to, for. — i o أبًّا وأبيبًا وأبابًا وأبابةً ل

Meadow, grazing. أبّ ج أُؤُبّ

Eleventh month of the Coptic year. July. أبيب ĈE

To be burning, hot (day). ٭ أبَت o i وأبِت a أبْتًا وأبوتًا

Burning, hot (day). أبِت وأبِت وأبْت

To speak ill of, to slander. ٭ أبَث i أبْثًا ه وعلى

The alphabet. ٭ ابجَد والحُرُوف الأبْجَدِيّة

To last. ٭ أبَد i أبودًا

To settle, to abide in a place. — ب

To become wild (cattle) ; to take fright. — o i أبودًا

To irritate o.'s self with. أبِد a أبَدًا على

To perpetuate a. th. To scare a. o. أبَّد ه وه

To become everlasting. To become wild (place). تأبَّد

Perpetuity ; eternity. أبَد ج آباد وأبود

Always, ever. never. أبدًا وأبَد الأبِدين وأبد الأبَد

For ever. على لأبد والى الأبد

An extraordinary event. A wild beast. آبِدة ج أوابِد

Perpetual ; eternal. أبدِيّ ومُؤبَّد

Perpetuity ; eternity. أبدِيّة

✱ أبق i o أبقًا وإباقًا إلى To run away, to flee, to take flight (slave).

أبَق Flax.

آبِق وأبُوق ج أُبَّق وأبَّاق Who has run away, who has fled.

✱ أبِل a أبَلًا وأبِل o أبالةً To be a skilled manager of camels.

— i o أبلا وأبولًا , وأبِل أبَلًا To go from the water to a fresh pasturage (cattle).

إبِل ج آبال وأبيل Camels.

أبِيل وأبيلي وأيْبُلِيّ ج آبال وأُبل Sexton, monk, bell-ringer.

إبالة وإبَّالة Large fagot of wood. Management of property, of goods.

أبابِيل Troop (of camels or birds) following each other in a file.

مَأبَلة Place full of camels, where many camels are to be found.

✱ أبَن i o أبْنًا ه ب To accuse, to charge a. o. with (a fault).

أبَّن ه To compose the elegy of, to praise a dead person.

إبَّان Beginning. Propitious time.

أُبْنة ج أُبَن Knot. Hatred, enmity.

مَأبُون Blameworthy. Suspicious. Unmanly, effeminate.

✱ أبِه a أبهًا ب او ل To remember a. th.

لا يُؤْبَهُ لهُ No one pays attention to it, unheeded.

أبَّه ه ب To suspect a. o. of.

تأبَّه على To show pride to.

— عن To turn aside with scorn from.

أُبَّهة Beauty, brightness. Pride.

✱ أبا o إباوةً وأبُوًّا وأبُوَّةً To be a father.

أبَّى ه To swear by one's father, to say : بِأبي أنت, may I ransom thee with my father.

تأبَّى ه To consider a. o. as a father.

أبٌ (for ابو) ج آباء Father. *Pl.* Ancestors, forefathers ; patriarchs.

أبو و ✧ بُو Father. *Word meaning causality or possession.*

الآب The Heavenly Father.

أبَتِ ويا أبَتِ ويا أبَتَ ويا أبتاه O my father !

أبو جابِر Bread.

أبو جَعْدة Wolf.

أبو الحارث Lion.

أبو الحُصَين Fox.

أبو النَّوم Poppy.

أبو الهَوْل Sphynx.

أبو اليَقْظان Cock.

أبو النَّظَّارة The man wearing spectacles.

أبُوَّة وأباوة Paternity.

أبَوِيّ Fatherly, belonging to a father.

أبَويَّة Fatherly. ✧ Paternity.

أباتي I Abbot.

✱ أبَى i a إباءً وإباءةً , وتأبَّى ه او عَن To refuse, to disdain a. th.

— ه على To refuse a. th. to a. o.

إباء Refusal. Scorn

آبٍ Who refuses, who scorns.

أبِيّ Haughty.

✱ إتْب ج آتاب وإتاب Shirt. Shift. Coat of mail.

تأتَّب بالإتب To put on a shift, a coat of mail.

مُؤْتَّب الظُّفر Having crooked nails.

✱ إتاد ج آتِدة وأُتُد Rope to fasten the feet of a cow, when milked.

Tε آتَشجي ج آتَشجيّة Stoker.

✱ أتَل i أتْلًا وأتَلانًا To walk at a quick pace.

✱ أتم — مأتم ج مآتِم Meeting at a dead person's house, funeral meeting.

✱ أتان ج أُتُن وآتُن وأتْن She-ass.

إستأتن To buy a she-ass. To fall, to decline.

كان حمارًا فاستأتن *Prov.* The ass became a she-ass, *i.e.* He was honoured and fell into contempt.

أتُون ج أُتُن وأتاتين Limekiln, brickkiln. Furnace.

✱ أتا o أتوًا وإتاء To produce (ground). To grow up abundantly (corn).

أتْو *N. of act.* Straight path. Manner.

إتاء Abundant produce.

إتاوة ج أتاوَى Tribute, tax. Bribe.

✱ أتى i إتيانًا وأتْيًا وإتْيانةً ومأتاةً ه وه To come to a.o.'s (house) or to (a place). To happen to a. o. To give as a gift. To undertake (a thing), to make it.

أتى على To ruin a. o. (fate). To accomplish a. th.

— ب To bring a. o. or a. th.

— ه ب To present, to offer a. th. to a. o.

أتَّى تأتيةً وتأتّيًا ه To make a passage

What remains of a lost science. أَثَارَة وأَثْرَة مِن عِلْمٍ ج أُثَر
Inheritance. ◘ أَثْرِيَّة
Choice. Preference. Selfishness. أَثَرَة
Who wears traces of. Excellent. Ethereal atmosphere. أَثِير ج أُثَرَاء
Influence. Impression. تأْثِير
Memorable fact, brilliant action. Benefit. مَأْثَرَة ومَأْثُرَة ج مَآثِر
Transmitted by tradition. مَأْثُور
Moving, pathetic. مُؤَثِّر
To prop (a pot) on a trivet. ✻ أَثَّف تَأْثِيفًا ه
Support of a pot. أُثْفِيَّة ج أَثَافِيّ
To take root, ✻ أَثَل i أُثُولًا وأَثْل o أَثَالَة
To become wealthy. أَثَّل وتأَثَّل مَالَهُ
To become, to get firm. تأَثَّل
Tamarisk. أَثْل ج أَثَلات وآثَال وأُثُول
A tamarisk. أَثْلَة ج أَثَلات
Furniture of a house. أَثْلَة وأُثْلَة ج إِثَال
Nobility of origin. أَثْلَة وأَثَال
Rooted. Noble. أَثِيل ومُؤَثَّل
To commit a sin, a crime. ✻ أَثِم a إِثْمًا وأَثَمًا ومَأْثَمًا
To accuse a. o. of a crime أَثَّم ه
To incite a. o. to a crime. آثَم إِيثَامًا ه
To abstain from iniquity. تأَثَّم مِن
Sin, crime, felony. إِثْم ج آثَام
Guilty. أَثِيم ج أُثَمَاء وآثِم ج أَثَمَة
Sin, crime. مَأْثَمَة ومَأْثَم ج مَآثِم
✻ أَثَا o أَثْوًا إِثَاوَة, أَثَى أَثْيًا وإِثَاوَةً ب
To slander, to backbite a. o.
Slander. مَأْثِيَة ومَأْثَاة
To burn, to blaze (fire). ✻ أَجَّ o أَجِيجًا
To run (ostrich). — i o أَجِيجًا
To be brackish (water). — o أُجُوجًا
To light, to kindle (the fire). To charge (the enemy). أَجَّج ه وه
To render water bitter and brackish. آجَّ ه
To burn fiercely, to become hot. تأَجَّج وإِئْتَجَّ وتَأَجَّ
Ardour, heat. أَجَّة ج إِجَاج
Brackish, bitter (water). أُجَاج
Ardent. Bright. أَجُوج
Sound of falling water. أَجِيج المَاء
Gog and Magog, two powerful nations mentioned in the Bible. H يأْجُوج ومأْجُوج

for (water).
To comply with the wishes of, to obey a. o. آتَى مُؤَاتَاةً ه على
✧ To suit a. o. (dress, climate). — ه
To give a. th. to a. o. آتَى إِيتَاء ه ه
To proceed, to derive from. تأَتَّى مِن او عَن
To be prepared, disposed to. — ل
To happen unexpectedly (mishap).
To become easy to a. o.
To urge a. o. to come. إِستأْتَى ه
To deem a. o. to be slow.
Who arrives, comer. آتٍ م آتِيَة
The future, time to come. الآتِي
Front, opposite side. Place to which one goes or comes from. مَأْتَى
To be thick, ✻ أَثَّ a i o أَثَاثًا وأُثُوثًا وأَثَاثَة close (hair, grass).
✧ To furnish (a house). أَثَّثَ ه
To become rich. To live in a comfortable way, to have a good living. تأَثَّث
✧ To be furnished (house).
Household furniture, moveable goods, utensils. أَثَاث
Luxuriant (head — of hair), tufted (hair). أَثّ وأَثِيث
✧ Furnished, supplied with furniture. مُؤَثَّث
To relate (a fact). ✻ أَثَر o i أَثْرًا وأَثَارَةً ه
To begin. To choose. أَثِرَ a أَثَرًا
He began to do. — يَفْعَل
To propose a. th. — عَلَى
He appropriated it in preference to his friends. — عَلَى أَصْحَابِهِ
To imprint, to leave marks upon. To impress, to move. أَثَّر في
To choose, to prefer a. th. آثَر إِيثَارًا ه
To prefer a. o. to. — ه على
To follow a. o. تأَثَّر وإِئْتَثَر ه
To be wounded, moved by. — وإِئْتَثَر ب ومِن
To appropriate a. th. exclusively to o.'s self. إِستأْثَر بِشَيْءٍ عَلَى
To call a. o. to Him (God). — ب
Trace, track, print, foot-step. Mark. Tradition. إِثْر وأَثَر ج آثَار
Scar, cicatrix. أُثْر وأُثُر ج آثَار وأُثُور
Glitter of a sword. أَثْر ج أُثُور
The old monuments, ruins of old monuments. الآثَارُ القَدِيمَة

✱ أجر o i أجرًا وإجارةً ه على To reward, to hire a. o.

أجر o أجرًا وأجارًا وأجورًا To be set (bone).

أُجرت يَدُهُ His hand has been set.

أجّر ه To burn (bricks).

آجر مُؤاجرةً ه على او في To pay the wages of. To hire a. o.

آجر إيجارًا ه To reward a. o.

— ه و ه To hire ; to rent.

إئتجر To give alms. To be hired.

إستأجر ه و ه ب To hire a. o. To let a. th. at (such a price).

أجر ج أجور وآجار Remuneration.

✧ إجر Foot, paw.

أجرَّة وأُجرَّة ج آجُرّ A baked brick.

أجرة وإجارة Salary, hire.

إجّار وإجّارة ج أجاجير Flat roof.

إيجار Lease of house, farm.

أجير ج أجراء و✧ أجري Servant, hireling.

مُستأجِر Tenant.

مُستأجَر Workman, hireling, hired labourer. Hired (house).

✱ اجز — إستأجز To recline on a pillow without leaning the back.

✱ إجّاص و✧ إنجاص Plum ✧ Pear.

✱ إجْطِ Cry for chiding (sheep).

✱ أجِل a أجلاً To be delayed, postponed.

أجل o ه على To cause (evil) to a. o.

أجّل ه To give delay to a. o.

تأجّل To ask for a delay. ✧ To be postponed.

إستأجل ه To request a delay of a. o.

أجَلْ Yes, no doubt ; of course.

أجل ج آجال Fixed term. Death. Maturity, expiration.

أجْل Cause, reason.

مِن أجلِك For thee, on account of thee, for thy sake.

إجِل Pain on the neck.

— ج آجال A herd of oxen.

الآجل والآجلة The future life, the life to come.

آجلاً او عاجلاً Sooner or later.

مَأجِل الماء ج مآجل Swamp.

مُؤجّل That has a fixed limit.

✱ أجم i أجمًا وأجيمًا , وتأجّم To be violent, intense (fire). To become tainted (water). To be hot (day) To be disgusted (with a food)

تأجّم على To be angry with a. o.

أجمة ج أجم وأجمات وآجام Brush-wood, thicket. Den of a lion.

أجم Any flat-roofed and square house.

أُجُم ج آجام Asylum, stronghold, fort.

✱ أجن o i أجنًا وأُجونًا , وأجِن a أجنًا To become corrupted, tainted (water).

أجن أجنًا To beat cloth (dyer).

إجّانة ج أجاجين Urn. Amphora. Washing-tub.

مِئجنة ج مآجن Dyer's mallet.

✱ أحّ o أحًّا To cough.

أُحاح Thirst. Anger.

أحاح وأحيح وأحيحة Shriek of pain.

✱ أحد (See وحد) One. Sunday.

✱ أحِن a أحنًا على To hate a. o.

إحْنة ج إحَن Anger. Inveterate hatred.

✱ أخّ و✧ آخ *Interj. expressing disgust, sorrow.* Alas ! poh !

أخّ وإخّ Dirt.

أخيخة Flour mixed with butter or oil.

✱ أخذ o أخذًا وتأخاذًا ه او ب من To take a. th. from a. o.

✧ أخذ على خاطره He was offended. grieved.

✧ أخذ وأعطى مع فلان To frequent a. o.

— يقول He began to say.

— في To begin by.

أخذ ب To seize, to r[illegible]ish a. th. or a. o.

— ه عن To learn, to quote a.th.from.

أخذ ه To bewitch a. o.

آخذ مؤاخذةً ه ب او على To blame, to reprehend a. o. on, to punish a. o. for.

إتّخذ ه و ه To take a. th. chosen amongst many.

إستأخذ To bow the head as a sign of sadness.

أخذ Chastisement. Use, custom.

أُخُذ وأُخذة Blearedness.

أُخذة Benumbing.

إخاذة ج إخاذات Land given as fee. Fish-pool. Shield-handle.

تأخيذ Witchcraft, witchery.

أخيذ ج أخذى Prisoner, captive.

أخيذة Spoils, booty.

مأخذ ج مآخذ Place from which some-

horse-lock, stake to which a beast is tied.
Brotherly. أَخَوِيّ
Confraternity, congregation. ✧ أَخَوِيَّة
Viper's bugloss (*bot.*). G أَخِيُون
To happen unexpectedly; to overwhelm a. o. (evil). ✱ أَدَّ o i أَدًّا ه
To behave resolutely. تَأَدَّدَ
Misfortune, adversity. إِدّ وإِدَّة ج إِدَد
Difficult, serious (affair). أَدِيد
To be well brought up, to be or become civilized. ✱ أَدُبَ o أَدَبًا
To invite a. o. to a banquet. To prepare a banquet. أَدَبَ i أَدْبًا , وآدَبَ إِيدَابًا ه
To give a good beeding to a.o. To punish, to correct. a. o. أَدَّبَ ه
To receive a good bringing up. To be well disciplined. تَأَدَّبَ
To study literature. — وإِسْتَأْدَبَ
Good breeding. Politeness. Literature. Culture of mind. أَدَب ج آدَاب
✧ Water-closet. بَيْت الأَدَب و✧ أَدَبْتَا
Literature, letters. عِلْمُ الأَدَب
Meal, feast. أَدْبَة ومَأْدُبَة ومَأْدَبَة ج مَآدِب
Punishment, chastisement, correction. تَأْدِيب
Ecclesiastical censures. تَأْدِيبات كَنائِسِيَّة
Of good morals, honest, polite. أَدَبِيّ م أَدَبِيَّة
Morals, ethics. العِلْم الأَدَبِيّ
Moral theology. اللَّاهُوت الأَدَبِيّ
Learned. Polite, honest. أَدِيب ج أُدَبَاء
Tutor, teacher. مُؤَدِّب
To have a rupture, a hernia. ✱ أَدِرَ a أَدَرًا
Hernia, rupture. أَدَرَة وأُدْرَة
To heal (wound). ✱ أَدَلَ i أَدْلًا
To beat (the milk). — ه
Beaten (milk). إِدْل
To season the bread with a condiment. ✱ أَدَمَ i أَدْمًا , وائْتَدَمَ
To reconcile a.o. أَدَمَ i وآدَمَ إِيدَامًا بَيْن
To be brown. أَدِمَ a أَدَمًا وأَدُمَ o أُدْمَة
Daily subsistence. Condiment. Chief. أُدْم وإِدَام
Human skin, derm. أَدَم وأَدَمَة
Adam (the first man). آدَم
Men. Human kind. بَنُو آدَم
Of Adam, human. آدَمِيّ ج أَوَادِم

thing is extracted. Source, mine. Manner.
Taken, seized. Drawn, extracted. مَأْخُوذ
To delay. To put at the end. To leave behind, to abandon a. th. ✱ أَخَّرَ تَأْخِيرًا ه و ه
To remain behind, to be late. To be in bad business. تَأَخَّرَ وإِسْتَأْخَرَ
Other, else, *masc.* آخَر م أُخْرَى ج آخَرُون
Other, else, *fem.* أُخْرَى ج أُخَر وأُخْرَيَات
Back, backside, hind part. أُخُر
Delay. أَخَرَة
With delays; at last, at the end. أَخَرَةً وبِأَخَرَةٍ
End. Last. آخِر ج أَوَاخِر
At the end, in the last. فِي الآخِر
Till the last. عَن آخِرِهِم
Extremity, end. Desinence. آخِرَة ج أَوَاخِر
The other life, the life to come. الآخِر والآخِرَة والأُخْرَى
Belonging to the life to come. أُخْرَوِيّ
Stable. P أَخُور و✧ يَاخُور
Equerry, shield-bearer. أَمِير أَخُور
Last, extreme. أَخِير ج أَخِيرُون
At last, at the end, finally. أَخِيرًا
Back part, hinder part, back, croup. Exterior angle (of the eye). Stern (of a ship). مُؤَخَّر
Delayed, late. مُؤَخَّر
Remained behind; late. مُتَأَخِّر
Palm-tree that keeps its fruit till winter. نَخْلَة مِئْخَار ج مَآخِير
To fraternise with. ✱ أَخَا o أُخُوَّة ه
To tie up (an animal). أَخَّى ه
To fraternise with, to take as a brother; to become intimately acquainted, to act in a brotherly way with. آخَى مُؤَاخَاةً وإِخَاء ه
To restore friendship between. — بَيْن
To act as a brother and friend of. تَآخَى ه
To adapt a. th. — وتَوَخَّى ه
Brotherhood; friendship, union. إِخَاء وإِخَاوَة ومُؤَاخَاة وأُخُوَّة و✧ خُوَّة
أَخ (for اخو) ✧ خَيّ ج إِخْوَة وإِخْوَان
Brother. Friend. Companion. Match, fellow of a pair.
Sister. أُخْت ج أَخَوَات ✧ خَيَّة ج خَيَّات
Female friend. Female companion.
Tie, band. أَخِيَّة وآخِيَّة ج أَوَاخِيّ وأَوَاخٍ

✧ Honest, polite.
Women. ¤ آدَمِيَّات
Brown. أَدَمُ جـ أُدْم وَأُدْمَان م أَدْمَاءُ وأُدْمَانَة جـ أُدْم
Tanner. أَدَّام
✧ Honesty, politeness. أَدَمِيَّة
Skin. Terrestrial surface. أَدِيم جـ أُدُم
A hard, stoneless ground. إِيدَامَة جـ أَيَادِيم
To ripen. ✱ أَنَا o أُدُوًّا
To lay in ambush for a. o. — لِفُلَانٍ أَدُوًّا
To be supplied with tools, to be ready for a. th. تَأَدَّى بِ
Tool, implement, instrument. Particle (*gram.*). أَدَاة جـ أَدَوَات
To transmit, to pay, to restitute a. th. to a. o. ✱ أَدَّى i أَدْيًا , وأَدَّى تَأْدِيَةً ه إلى
To help, to assist a. o. against. آدَى إِيدَاءً ه على
To pay, to settle to a. o. a. th. تَأَدَّى ه لَهُ
To reach to. — إلى
To exact, to take a. th. from a. o. إِسْتَأْدَى ه ه
To implore the help of a. o. against. إِسْتَأْدَى ه على
Payment of a debt. Performance of a duty. أَدَاء
Then, at that time, when, as, while ; since. ✱ إِذْ وإِذْ ذَاكَ
Here... is, there... is ; on a sudden. When, if. إِذَا
On a sudden. (*with a genitive*) إِذَا بِ
When, whereupon. إِذَا مَا
In that case, then, thus. إِذًا وإِذَن
March (month). S أَذَار وآذَار
A kind of anemone. P آذَرْيُون
To listen, to hearken to. ✱ أَذِن a أَذَنًا الى
To permit a. th. to a. o. — لَهُ إِذْنًا في
To know a. th. — إِذْنًا وأَذَنًا وأَذَانَةً بِ
To call out to prayer (amongst Moslems). أَذَّنَ تَأْذِينًا , وآذَن إِيذَانًا
To inform a. o. of. آذَن إِيذَانًا ه ه وب
To ask from a. o. permission to. إِسْتَأْذَن ه في
To ask leave of entering in. — على
To take leave of. — من
Permission, leave. ✧ Order (of a bill) إِذْن

Ear. أُذْن وأُذُن جـ آذَان و ¤ وُدْن وَ✧ دَيْنَة
Handle.
Izan, call to prayer. آذَان
Chamberlain. آذِن
Long-eared. آذَن وأُذَانِيّ
Muezzin (crier to prayer). مُؤَذِّن وأَذِين
Minaret, turret of a mosque. مِئْذَنَة جـ مَآذِن مَأْذَنَة
To suffer damage from. ✱ أَذِيَ a أَذًى وأَذَاةً بِ
To injure, to harm a. o. آذَى إِيذَاءً ه
To suffer damage from. تَأَذَّى من
Damage, harm done. أَذًى وأَذِيَّة وأَذَاة
Who suffers or causes damage. أَذٍ وأَذِيّ
Noxious, harmful, prejudicial. مُؤْذٍ
To be skilful, ingenious in. ✱ أَرِب a أَرَبًا , وأَرُب o أَرَابَةً وإِرْبًا في
To achieve, to better a. th. أَرَّب ه وه
To render a. o. intelligent, sharp.
To cut up a. th.
To try to deceive a. o. آرَب مُؤَارَبَةً ه
To win, to overcome a. o. آرَب إِيرَابًا على
To be tightened (knot). تَأَرَّب
To strive for. — في
To be hard towards a. o. in. تَأَرَّب على في
End prosecuted, aim. أَرَب جـ آرَاب
Cunning. Limb. Anything necessary إِرْب جـ آرَاب
In small pieces. إِرْبًا إِرْبًا
Gordian knot. أُرْبَة جـ أُرَب
The upper part of the thigh-bone. ✧ Tumour. أُرْبِيَّة
Clever, able. Artful. أَرِيب وأَرِب
End, aim, thing wanted. مَأْرَب ومَأْرَبَة جـ مَآرِب
Europe. أُورُبًّا , أُرُبًّا
European. أُورُبَّاوِيّ وَأُرُبِّيّ
Inheritance. Ashes. (*See* ورث) ✱ إِرْث
Old thing. Boot.
To light (the fire). أَرَّث ه
To excite discord between. — بَيْن
Combustible, tinder. أُرْثَة وإِرَاث
To exhale a perfume, to smell fragrant. ✱ أَرِج a أَرَجًا وأَرِيجًا , وتَأَرَّج
To excite a. o., to excite dissension. أَرَّج ه وه

Organ. G ✧ أُرْغُن
To set limits to. ✱ أَرَّف تَأْرِيفًا ه
Boundaries, limit. أُرْفَة ج أُرَف
To be sleepless, wakeful. ✱ أَرِق a أَرَقًا
To slumber.
To cause a. o. أَرَّقَ تَأْرِيقًا , وآرَقَ إِيرَاقًا ه
to slumber.
Partial insomnia, sleeplessness. أَرَق
A kind of thorny tree. ✱ أَرَاك
To eat the leaves of that أَرَكَ o i أُرُوكًا
tree (camel).
To be seized with أَرِكَ a أَرَكًا , وأُرِكَ
colic for having eaten it (camel).
To cicatrize (wound). أَرِكَ
Throne, seat. Ottoman. أَرِيكَة ج أَرَائِك
To eat all (the food). ✱ أَرَمَ i أَرْمًا ه
To devour the whole harvest,
to destroy the crops (of the land).
He reduced people — القَوْمَ وبِأَمْوَالِهِم
to misery, wretchedness.
Tooth. آرِمَة ج أَوَارِم
Stone set up in the إِرَم ج آرَام وأُرُوم
desert.
Iram (name of a place). إِرَم
There is nobody, مَا بِهَا أَرِمٌ أَوْ أَيْرَم
no one.
Molar teeth. أُرَّم
To gnash the teeth يُحَرِّقُ الأُرَّمَ عَلَى فُلَان
against.
Wasted (land). أَرْمَاء ومَأْرُومَة
Root, origin. أُرُوم وأَرُومَة وأُرُومَة
To be lively, ✱ أَرِنَ a أَرَنًا وأَرِينًا وإِرَانًا
quick.
Litter, coffin. إِرَان ج أُرُن
Den. — ومِئْرَان ج مَآرِن
Lively, quick. أَرِن وأَرُون
To produce honey (bee). ✱ أَرَى i أَرْيًا
To remain in the stable, — ه
to be accustomed to it (beast).
To prepare a stable for أَرَّى ه ول
(a beast); to fasten (a beast) to
(a pole).
Honey. أَرْي
Pole to which آرِيّ وآرِيَة ج أَوَارِيّ
a beast is fastened. Stable.
To produce ✱ أَزَّ o أَزًّا وأَزَازًا وأَزِيزًا
a noise (e. g. pot on the fire).
To incite a. o. to. — ه إِلَى
Confusion, press, pell-mell. أَزَّة

Perfume, good smell, أَرِيج وأَرِيجَة
scent.
Odoriferous, sweet-smelling. أَرِج
Intriguer, intriguing. أَرَّاج
To put the date ✱ أَرَّخ وآرَخ إِيرَاخًا ه
to. To write the history of.
Date of a fact, of a تَأْرِيخ ج تَوَارِيخ
letter. History, chronology.
Historical. تَأْرِيخِيّ
Date of coins. تَأْرِيخ المُعَامَلَة
Chronicler, historian. مُؤَرِّخ
Dated; of such a date. مُؤَرَّخ
Ardab (*weight of* P إِرْدَبّ
about 2. 500 *pounds*).
To cower, ✱ أَرَزَ o i وأَرِزَ a أَرْزًا وأُرُوزًا
to squat, to roll up (reptile).
To be cold (night).
Cold. أَرِز
Sustainer of a tribe. — القَوْم
Cedar. أَرْز
A cedar-tree. أَرْزَة
Rice. أَرُزّ ورُزّ
To practice agricul- ✱ أَرَسَ i أَرْسًا
ture, to be a tiller, a husbandman.
Prince. إِرِّيس
— وأَرِيس ج إِرِّيسُون وأَرِيسُون وأَرَارِس
Agriculturist, tiller. وأَرَارِيس وأَرَارِسَة
He was asked the price ✱ أُرِشَ فُلَان
of blood.
To make mischief amongst, أَرَّشَ بَيْن
to set at variance.
To light (the fire). To kindle (war). — ه
Price of blood. Gift. Price أَرْش
given for damage. Incitement
to discord.
To bring forth herbs ✱ أَرَضَ o أَرْضًا
abundanty (soil).
To become luxuriant and أَرُضَ o أَرَاضَة
covered with green (soil).
أَرْض ج أَرَضُون وأُرُوض وأَرَاضٍ وآرَاض
Earth, terrestrial globe. Soil,
ground. Country, land.
A tree-worm, wood-fretter. أَرَضَة ج أَرَض
Terrestrial, earthly. أَرْضِيّ
Artichoke. ✧ أَرْضِيّ شَوْكِيّ
Bottom of a vase; ground of ✧ أَرْضِيَّة
a stuff. Ground of a house. ✧ Urinal.
Course of the week. ✧ أَرْضِيَّة الجُمْعَة
Fruitful. Broad. أَرِيض

To be opposite to.
To be opposite to, to front تَآزَى تَآزِيًا o. anoth.
Before, opposite, in front. إِزَاءَ
Before him, opposite to him. بِإِزَائِهِ
✱ إِسّ وأُسّ ج إِسَاس، أَسَاس ج أُسُس
Foundation, principle, basis.
To lay the foundation, أَسَّسَ ه to ground a. th.
To be founded (building). تَأَسَّسَ
Small quantity of ashes. أَسّ
Foundation of أَسَس ج آسَاس وأَسَاسَات a building.
Foundation, principle, establishment. تَأْسِيس
Fundamental, principal. أَسَاسِيّ
Founder. مُؤَسِّس
Founded upon, established, مُؤَسَّس عَلَى grounded on.
Buttock. (*See* سَتَه) ✱ إِسْت
Surname of Constantinople. P أَلإِسْتَانَة العَلِيَّة
To ✱ أَسَدَ i أَسْدًا ، وأَسَّدَ وآسَدَ إِيسَادًا ه set (a dog). To encourage a. o.
To be as courageons as تَأَسَّدَ وإِسْتَأْسَدَ a lion. To become strong, tall or dry.
Lion. أَسَد ج أُسُود وأُسَاد وأُسْد وأُسُد
Lioness. أَسَدَة
Place full of lions. مَأْسَدَة ج مَآسِد
To tie, to bind ✱ أَسَرَ i أَسْرًا وإِسَارَةً ه a. o., to take captive.
To bring a.o. — أَسْرًا وإِسَارًا وإِسْتَأْسَرَ ه away as a captive.
To fasten tighly, أَسَّرَ ه وه to squeeze a. o. or a. th.
To surrender to a. o. as إِسْتَأْسَرَ ل a prisoner.
Leather-strap. Captivity. أَسْر وإِسَار
All, the whole of them, بِأَسْرِهِم without exception.
All, entirely. بِأَسْرِهِ
Retention of urine. أُسْر
He suffers from بِهِ أُسْر مِن البَوْل ischury.
Relationship, kindred, أُسْرَة ج أُسَر affinity. Family. Strong breast-plate
Strong leather-strap. إِسَار ج أُسُر
Left side. (for يَسَار) —
Prisoner, أَسِير ج أُسَرَاء وأُسَارَى وأَسْرَى

✱ أَزَأَ a أَزْأً ه To feed to the full, to satiate (sheep).
— عَن To renounce, to give up a. th.
✱ أَزَبَ i أَزْبًا To flow (water).
إِزْب Little man, despised man.
مِئْزَاب ج مَآزِيب Drain, sewer. Leaden pipe.
✱ أَزَج ج آزُج وآزَاج وإِزَجَة A prolate vault.
أَزَّجَ ه To build a prolate vault.
✱ أَزِجَ i أُزُوجًا ، وتَأَزَّجَ To be late.
أَرُوج Person in arrears, late.
P آزَادِرَخْت وأَزْدِرَخْت Lilac of Persia.
✱ أَزَاذ Very good dates.
✱ أَزَرَ i أَزْرًا ه To surround a. th.
— وأَزَّرَ تَأْزِيرًا ه ب To strengthen. To wrap a. o. in a veil. To clothe a. o. with a waist-wrapper.
آزَرَ ه مُؤَازَرَةً To strengthen, to assist a. o.
تَأَزَّرَ وإِتَّزَرَ وإِئْتَزَرَ ب To girdle; to wrap o.'s self in a veil, a mantle.
أَزْر Strength; weakness. Back. Middle part of the body.
إِزْر Veil. Root.
إِزَار وإِزَارَة ج أُزُر وآزِرَة A very ample veil. Waist-wrapper.
مِئْزَر ومِئْزَرَة ج مَآزِر Waist-wrapper. Veil. Clothing. Mantle.
مُؤَازَرَة Help, assistance.
✱ أَزِفَ a أَزَفًا وأُزُوفًا إِلَى To arrive suddenly. To draw near, to approach.
تَآزَفَ To draw near (one to the other).
أَزَفَى Quick step.
آزِفَة Day, hour of the last judgment.
✱ أَزِقَ i أَزَقًا ، وتَأَزَّقَ To be straitened.
مَأْزِق ج مَآزِق Narrow place. Battlefield.
✱ أَزَلَ i أَزْلًا ، وتَأَزَّلَ To be in a strait.
أَزَل وأَزَلِيَّة Eternity.
أَزَلِيّ Eternal.
أَزْل Anguish; narrow circumstances.
أَزِل Uncomfortable, under constraint.
✱ أَزَمَ i أَزْمًا وأُزُومًا ه وه To bite.
— ه To ruin a. o. (dearth).
— عَلَى To be unfruitful (year) for.
آزِم وآزِمَة ج أُزَّم وأَوَازِم Canine tooth.
أَزْمَة ج إِزَم Scarcity, dearth. Poverty.
✱ آزَى مُؤَازَاةً ه To correspond to.

Doctoress.
To leave a. th. to a. o. ✻ أَسَى i أَسْيًا مِن ل
Honey that remains in the hive. آسِيّ
Base, column. آسِيَة ج أَوَاسٍ
To be sad, afflicted. ✻ أَسِيَ a أَسًى عَلَى
Sadness, pain, sorrow. أَسًى وَأَسًا
Dry bread. ✻ أَشّ
To be intertwisted (tree). To be entangled. ✻ أَشِبَ a أَشَبًا . وَتَأَشَّبَ
To be mixed (crowd). أَشَّبَ وَائْتَشَبَ
Intertwisted (tree). Confused. أَشِب
Thicket. أَشَب
Rabble. أُشَابَة ج أَشَائِب
To be cheerful, merry. ✻ أَشِرَ a أَشَرًا
Joy, sprightliness. أَشَر
To saw (wood). ✻ أَشَرَ i أَشْرًا ه
To sharpen (teeth). — i أَشْرًا وَأَشَّرَ ه
To annotate. To put a visa upon. □ أَشَّرَ
Denticulation. أَشْرَة ج أَشَر وَأُشُر
Leg of a grass-hopper. مِئْشَر
Saw. مِئْشَار ج مَآشِير وَمَوَاشِير
White moss that grows on oak- and pine-trees. ✻ أُشْنَة
Alkali. Potash. أُشْنَان وَإِشْنَان
To break or soften a. th. ✻ أَصَّ o أَصًّا ه
To strengthen a. th. أَصَّصَ ه
Earthenware, earthen pan, vessel. أَصِيص
Adjoining houses. أَصِيصَة
To stop, to shut a. th. ✻ أَصَدَ وَآصَدَ ه
To clothe a. o. with a chemisette, a short dress. أَصَّدَ ه
Chemisette, tucker, a kind of short dress. أُصْدَة ج أُصَد وإِصَاد
To provide (a tent) with a stake. ✻ أَصَرَ i أَصْرًا ه
To render a. o. kind towards. — ه عَلَى
To be near, contiguous, adjacent to. آصَرَ مُؤَاصَرَةً ه
Burden. Compact. Crime. إِصْر ج آصَار
Stake of a tent. إِصَار ج أُصُر وَآصِرَة
Tie. band. Relationship. Favour. آصِرَة ج أَوَاصِر
Caper-bush. ✻ أَصَف
To be rooted. ✻ أَصُلَ o أَصَالَة
To state the origin of. To consolidate. To consider a. o. as أَصَّلَ ه وه

captive.
Tube. ✧ Shank of a tobacco-pipe. ✧ Gun-barrel. مَاسُورَة ج مَوَاسِير
Israel. إِسْرَائِيل H
To be afflicted with. ✻ أَسِفَ a أَسَفًا عَلَى
To afflict; to irritate a. o. آسَفَ إِيسَافًا ه
To regret, to be sorry for, to lament on. تَأَسَّفَ عَلَى
Sadness, affliction. أَسَف وأَسَافَة
Alas! What a pity! يَا أَسَفِي وَوَاأَسَفَاه
Regret. تَأَسُّف
Sorry, angry. أَسِف
Sad, afflicted. أَسِيف وأَسِيفٌ عَلَى
Barren soil. أَسَفَة وأَرْض أَسِيفَة
Sad. Nervous, touchy. أَسُوف
To be oblong, full and smooth (face). ✻ أَسُلَ o أَسَالَةً , وأَسِلَ a أَسَلًا
To sharpen, to point a. th. أَسَّلَ ه
He is like his father. أَسَّلَ أَبَاهُ
Reed used for making lances, arrows. Spear, blade. أَسَل
Tip of the tongue. Fore-arm. أَسَلَة
Oval-shaped, full and smooth (face). أَسِيل
Noun, name. ✻ إِسْم ج أَسْمَاء وأَسَامٍ
See سمو.
Lion. ✻ أُسَامَة
Ismael. إِسْمَعِيل H
✻ أَسَنَ o i أَسْنًا وأُسُونًا , وأَسِنَ a أَسَنًا , وتَأَسَّنَ
To be corrupted, to stink (water).
Corrupted, putrid (water). آسِن
To nurse, to cure a. o. To console a. o. ✻ أَسَا o أَسْوًا وأَسًا ه وه
To make peace between. — بَيْن
To console a. o., to nurse him. أَسَّى تَأْسِيَةً ه
He gave him a part of his goods; he was munificent to him. آسَاهُ مُؤَاسَاةً
To console o.'s self. To bear with patience. تَأَسَّى
To imitate a. o. — وائْتَسَى ب
To console o. a. تَآسَى ه
Imitation; model. Relief; consolation. أُسْوَة ج أُسًى وإِسًى
Medicine. أَسُوّ وإِسَاء ج آسِيَة
Physician. آسٍ ج إِسَاء وأُسَاة
A medical woman. آسِيَة ج آسِيَات وأَوَاسٍ

noble. To classify (things) according to a common origin.
To take a footing, to take root in. تَأَصَّل في
To originate in, to descend from. — مِن
To extirpate. To root out, to uproot a. th. إِسْتَأْصَل ه
Origin. Race. Principle. Lineage. Root. أَصْل ج أُصُول
Of noble origin. شَرِيفُ الأَصْل
Capital, stock. أَصْلُ المَال
Firmness of will, decision of character. أَصَالَة
Extirpation. Extermination. إِسْتِئْصَال
Original, radical. أَصْلِيّ
On no account, not at all, by no means. لَا . . أَصْلًا
The rudiments, the principles. الأُصُول
Fundamental, regular. أُصُولِيّ
Solid, well rooted. Gifted with a firm temper. Noble; of good breed (horse). أَصِيل ج أُصَلَاء
Time before sunset, evening. أَصِيل ج آصَال وأُصُل وأُصْلَان وأَصَائِل
They came all of them. جَاءُوا بِأَصِيلَتِهِم
To compel a. o. to. ✱ أَضَّ o i أَضًّا ه إِلى
Shelter, refuge, asylum. إِضَاض
To crack (saddle). To groan (camel). ✱ أَطَّ i أَطِيطًا
He was moved with pity. أَطَّت بِهِ الرَّحِم
To arch, to curve an arch. To bend a. th.; to bow a. th. ✱ أَطَر o أَطْرًا ، وأَطَّر ه
To surround (a house). أَطَر o i ه
Fault, misdemeanor. أَطِير
Circumference. Hoop, circle, ring. ✧ Frame. إِطَار ج أُطُر
Side, flank. ✱ إِطْل ج آطَال ، وأَيْطَل ج أَيَاطِل
Fort, fortlet, stronghold. ✱ أُطُم ج أُطُوم وآطَام
To swell (waves). To rise up (flame). تَأَطَّم
To become irritated with. — على
Sea-turtle. أُطُوم ج آطِمَة وأُطُم
Chimney-piece. Hearth, fire-place. أَطِيمَة
Agha (a Turkish officer). Ts آغَا ج آغَاوَات

Dirt of the ears or nails. ✱ أُفّ
Fie, for shame! أُفٍّ
Time. ✱ إِفَّان وأَفَّان وإِفّ وإِفَف
At the time of that. على إِفِّ ذَلِك
To hurry. ✱ أَفَد a أَفَدًا
To be active, nimble. ✱ أَفَر i أَفْرًا وأُفُورًا
Quick, active, sprightly. أَفَّار ومِئْفَر
Wormwood. Absinth. G إِفْسَنْتِين
To tan (hides, skins). ✱ أَفَق i أَفْقًا ه
To excell in science, generosity, etc. أَفِق a أَفَقًا
Liberal, learned. آفِق وأَفِيق
Tanned (hide, skin). أَفِيق
Horizon. Country. أُفْق وأُفُق ج آفَاق
Horizontal. أُفُقِيّ
Great traveller. Adventurer. أَفَّاق
To lie. ✱ أَفَك i أَفْكًا وأُفُوكًا ، وأَفِك a أَفَكًا
To deter a. o. from. — أَفَكًا ه عَن
To be in want of rain and barren (soil). To be weak-minded. أُفِك
Lie, falsehood. إِفْك وإِفْكَة وأَفِيكَة ج أَفَائِك
Liar. أَفِك وأَفَّاك
Good for nothing. Weak-minded. أَفِيك ومَأْفُوك
Wild and destructive winds; hurricanes, storms. المُؤْتَفِكَات
To set (star). ✱ أَفَل i o أُفُولًا
To dry up, to have no more milk (woman). أَفَل o أُفُولًا ، وأَفِل a أَفَلًا
To milk a (she-camel) out of time. ✱ أَفَن i أَفْنًا ه
To be weak-minded. أَفِن a وأُفِن أَفَنًا
To have very little milk (she-camel). أَفِن a
To decrease (th.). To boast of what one has not. تَأَفَّن
Weak-minded. أَفِين ومَأْفُون
Opium. P أَفْيُون
Laudanum. خَمْر الأَفْيُون
To prepare (a dish) with sour cheese. ✱ أَقَط i أَقْطًا ه
To give to a. o. sour cheese to eat. — ه
أَقِط وأَقْط وإِقِط وأَقُط وإِقْط وأُقْط ج أُقْطَان
Cheese made with sour milk.
Heavy and indigestible (food). أَقِط وأَقِيط
Battlefield. مَأْقِط

To sharpen the point of. أَلَّ هـ
Compact. Relationship. Rancour, hatred. إِلّ
State of a mother who has lost her children. أَلِيل
September. S أَيْلُول
Title-deed. ◘ أَيْلُولَة
A broad-headed spear, weapon. أَلَّة ج أَلّ
Lest... That he... not. أَلَّا (أَنْ لَا)
In order not to... For fear that he... not. Lest. لِئَلَّا
If not, unless, except, save, besides, otherwise. Less. إِلَّا
Or else, nevertheless. وَإِلَّا
Is (he, she, it)... not? أَلَا
To meet with. ✱ أَلَب o أَلْبًا , وتَأَلَّب إِلَى
To gather (dispersed people). أَلَب o i أَلْبًا , وأَلَّب ه
To excite a. o. against. أَلَّب ه عَلَى
They are all united against me. هُمْ عَلَيَّ إِلْبٌ وَاحِد
Ambassador. Ts إِلْجِيّ ج إِلْجِيَّة
Gloves. Tᴇ إِلْدِزَان
Who, whose, whom; that (*rel. pron. masc.*). ✱ أَلَّذِي ج أَلَّذِين ✧ إِلَي
Who, whose, whom; that (*rel. pron. fem.*). أَلَّتِي ج اللَّوَاتِي وَاللَّائِي
Et cetera. (*abbrev. for.* إِلَى آخِرِهِ) إِلَخ
To deceive, to circumvent a. o. ✱ أَلَس i أَلْسًا , وآلَس مُؤَالَسَةً ه
To become insane. أُلِسَ
Lie. Madness. Treachery. أَلْس
Insane. مَأْلُوس
To become tame. ✱ أَلِفَ a أَلْفًا
To get accustomed to a. o. or to a. th. — وآلَف إِيلَافًا ه وهـ
To join, to unite, to bring together. أَلَّف بَيْن
To compose (a book). — هـ
To frequent the society of. آلَف مُؤَالَفَةً وإِيلَافًا ه
To accustom a. o. to. — إِيلَافًا ه هـ
To be intimately acquainted with. تَأَلَّف ه
To be composed of. — مِن
To have relations of friendship, to keep up a friendly connexion wih. إِئْتَلَف وتَآلَف مَع

✱ أَلَّ o أَلًّا To be hot and windless (day).
Hot and windless (day). أَلِيك
✱ أَكَّد ووَكَّد هـ To strengthen a. th. To assert, to certify a. th.
To ascertain. To be verified. To be confirmed. تَأَكَّد
Firm. Certain. أَكِيد
Reliance. Certainty. تَأْكِيد
Consolidation. (*cf.* وَكَّد) تَوْكِيد
✱ أَكَرَ i أَكْرًا , وتَأَكَّر هـ To till (the ground), to dig.
Tiller, husbandman. أَكَّار ج أَكَرَة وأَكَّارُون
Ball, bowl. Ditch, hole. أُكْرَة ج أُكَر
✱ إِكَاف وأُكَاف ج أُكُف وآكِفَة Pack-saddle (for asses, mules).
To put a pack-saddle (on an ass, a mule). أَكَّف تَأْكِيفًا , وآكَف إِيكَافًا ه
✱ أَكَل o أَكْلًا ومَأْكَلًا هـ To eat. To gnaw, to nibble, to corrode a. th.
To itch (head). أَكَل o إِكْلَةً وأُكَالًا وأَكَالًا
To be corroded, rotten. أَكِل a أَكَلًا
To give to a. o. a. th. to eat. أَكَّل تَأْكِيلًا , وآكَل إِيكَالًا ه هـ
To eat together, to take one's meals at a friend's. آكَل مُؤَاكَلَةً ه
To be eaten. To feel an itching. To be rotten (tooth). تَأَكَّل
To become incensed. To put o.'s self into a passion. إِئْتَكَل
Food, eatable. أُكْل وأُكُل
Piece, mouthful. أُكْلَة
Meal, repast. أَكْلَة
Canker. Itching. Rust. آكِلَة
Great eater, glutton. أَكَّال وأَكِيل وأَكُول
Food, victuals. مَأْكَل ج مَآكِل
Porringer for 3 persons. مِئْكَلَة
Spoon. مِئْكَال ج مَآكِيل
Edible, eatable. Victuals. مَأْكُول ج مَآكِيل ومَأْكُولَات
✱ أَكَمَة ج أَكَم وأَكَمَات وإِكَام وأُكُم وآكَام Hill, hillock. Rising ground.
The (*article*). (*m. f. s. pl.*). ✱ أَل
To hurry, To be restless. ✱ أَلَّ o i أَلًّا To be clear and bright (colour).
To strike a. o. with a spear. — ه
To moan (sick person). — i أَلًّا وأَلَلًا وأَلِيلًا
To be decayed (tooth), أَلِل a أَلَلًا

To seek the friendship of, to court. إستألف ه
Friendship. Company. إلف وألفة
Thousand. ألف ج أُلوف وآلاف
Friend, companion. إلف ج آلاف , وأليف ج ألائف
Familiar, companion. آلِف ج أُلّاف
More familiar than. آلف من
Very familiar, very intimate. Tame. ألوف ج أُلُف
Compact, alliance إيلاف
Agreement, friendship. إئتلاف
Book. Collection. تأليف ج تآليف
Usual, familiar. مألوف
Familiarity. Friendship مؤالفة
Author (of a book). مؤلِّف
Composed. Book. مؤلَّف
Dwelling, continuance in one place. مألف ج مآلف
To flash (lightning), to lighten. ✻ ألق i ألقًا , وتألّق وائتلق
To be mad. To lie. ألِق a ألقًا
Madness, lunacy. أولَق
Seized with madness. مألق ومألوق
To send ه to a. o. To champ (the bit horse). ✻ ألك o i ألكًا , وألك إلاكة ه
To bear (a letter) إستألك ه
Letter, missive ألوكة ومألكة
To suffer, to be in pain. ✻ ألِم a ألمًا
To cause suffering a. o. To affect, to grieve a o. ألّم وآلم إيلامًا ه
To suffer. To be grieved. ✧ To be irritated. تألّم
Pain, suffering, ache. Irritation. Passion, violent commotion of the mind. ألم ج آلام
The passion of Jesus-Christ آلام المسيح
Sufferer. ألِم
That causes suffering. مؤلِم
Painful. ✧ Rancorous. أليم
Diamond : adamant. G ألماس
To adore a. o. ; to worship a. o. ✻ أله a إلاهة وألوهة ه
To deify a. o. To call a. o. a god. ألّه
To be deified. تألّه
To adore a. o. ; to worship. — ه
To be like God. إستأله
A god. Deity. إله ج آلهة

God (the true and only one). الله
O my God ! Good God ! اللّهمّ
Goddess. إلاهة
The goddess of poetry ; muse. إلاهة الشعر
Deification, apotheosis. تأليه
Divinity. ألاهة وألوهة وألوهيّة وإلهانيّة
Divine ; theological (virtue). إلهي
Theology. Metaphysics. علم الإلهيّات
To be unable to do a. th. To be late in. ✻ ألا o ألوًا وألوًّا وأليًّا في
To neglect, to leave a. th. — ه
He spared no pains. لم يألُ جهدًا وجهدًا
He does not cease to warn, to admonish thee. لا يألوك نصحًا
Nevertheless, for all that, he continues. لا يألو إلّا يفعل
To be unable. To neglect a. th. ألّى وائتلى
Do not cease to claim what thou hast not obtained (*prov.*). إلّا حظيّة فلا أليّة
To swear, to take an oath. آلى إيلاء وتألّى وائتلى
Gift, benefit. **Dung**. ألو
Aloes. ألوّ وألوّة وإليّة ج ألاوية
Swearing, oath. ألوة وأليّة
Possessors, possessed of (*pl. of* ذو) ✻ أولو
Men gifted with strength. أولو القوّة
These (*pl. of* ذا , ذه). (*m. f.*) ألى وأولى وأولاء
Those (*pl. of* ذلك , ذاك). (*m. f.*) أولئك وأولائك
The ancient Arabs. العرب الأولى والألى
To have big buttocks. ✻ ألِي a أليًا
Fat tail. Buttocks. أليّة ج ألايا وأليات
Benefit, favour, grace. إلي وإلى ج آلاء
A green-leaved and bitter fruit-tree. ألاء وألى
Large, fat in the tail, buttocks (sheep, men). ألي ج أليانة وأليا. وآلى مر أليات
Regiment. Ts آلاي ج آلايات
Handkerchief used by hired mourners. مئلاة ج مآل
To. Till. Towards. At o.'s. ✻ إلى
To me, to thee, to him. إليّ , إليك , إليه
And so on, et cetera. إلى آخره
To what quantity ? إلى كم
Go away ; withdraw, be off ! إليك عنّي
How long ? إلى متى
Till, until. إلى أن

To become irritated with a. o. أَمِدَ a أَمَدًا على

To fix the limits of. أَمَّدَ ه

Laden ship. آمِدَ وآمِدَة

Amida (town), i. e. Diarbekir. آمِدُ

To command to a. o. a. th. ✻ أَمَرَ o أَمْرًا ه ب

To become a prince, chief, amir. أَمِرَ a أَمْرًا , وأَمُرَ o إِمْرَةً وإِمَارَةً على

To be in good quantity (th.) To have numerous flocks. أَمِرَ a أَمَرًا وأَمَرَةً

To invest a. o. with power. أَمَّرَ ه

To consult a. o. on. آمَرَ مُؤَامَرَةً ه في

To command a. th. to a.o.; to order. To render a.o. wealthy (God). آمَرَ إِيمَارًا ه

To be invested with power; to reign upon تَأَمَّرَ على

To make a common deliberation; to consult a. o. To plot. تَآمَرَ و ائْتَمَرَ

To consult a. o. on. إِئْتَمَرَ ه في او ب

To be actively engaged, busied about. To obey (a command). — ب

To consult a. o. إِسْتَأْمَرَ ه

Commandment, order, decree. Power, authority. أَمْر ج أَوَامِر

Thing, business, subject. أَمْر ج أُمُور

Sign, indication. أَمَارَة ج أَمَارَات

Opened, trodden road. أَمَارَات الطَّرِيق

Prefecture, power, empire. إِمْرَة وإِمَارَة

Foolish, silly. إِمَّر وإِمَّرَة

He does not possess a farthing. مَا لَهُ إِمَّرٌ ولَا إِمَّرَة

Serious, painful affair. أَمْرٌ إِمْرٌ

Soul. Vital spirits. The heart's blood. تَأْمُور ج تَآمِير

Convent of monks. تَأْمُور وتَأْمُورَة

Man. تَأْمُرِيّ وتَأْمُورِيّ وتُؤْمُرِيّ

Chief. Prince, amir. أَمِير ج أُمَرَاء

Civil title equal to that of a colonel. أَمِير الأُمَرَاء

The Commander of the faithful, the Caliph. أَمِير المُؤْمِنِين

Admiral. أَمِير البَحْر

✦ Colonel. أَمِير آلَاي و✧ مِير أَلَاي

Belonging to a prince. Public treasury. Duty paid to a prince. أَمِيرِيّ و✧ مِيرِي

Passions. ✧ أَمَارَات

To direct a. o.'s steps towards (a place). To propose a. th. ✻ أَمَّ o أَمًّا , وأَأْمَمَ وتَأَمَّمَ وائْتَمَّ ه

To wound a. o. in the brain. أَمَّ o ه

To become a mother. — أُمُومَة

To walk ahead. To be at the head (of an army). — إِمَامَة ه وه

To adopt as a mother. تَأَمَّمَ

To imitate a. o. إِئْتَمَّ ب

To follow a. o. as a leader. — واسْتَأَمَّ ه

Mother. Source, principle, prototype. أُمّ ج أُمَّات وأُمَّهَات

O my mother! Mother! يَا أُمَّتِ وأُمَّاهُ وأُمَّتَاهُ

Fire. *Lit.*: the mother of hospitality. أُمّ اقِرى

Mecca. *Lit.*: the mother of the towns. أُمّ القُرَى

✧ The Virgin Mary. *Lit.*: the mother of light. أُمّ النُّور

Pia mater, the brain. أُمّ الدِّمَاغ و أُمّ الرَّأْس

Milleped, polypode (*ins.*). أُمّ أَرْبَع وأَرْبَعِين

The milky way. أُمّ النُّجُوم

Situated near or opposite to. A trifle. أَمَم

Before, in front of. أَمَام

Imam. Leader. President. Highway. String-course (*arch.*). إِمَام ج أَئِمَّة

Dignity, rank of an imam. إِمَامَة

People. Nation. أُمَّة ج أُمَم

The gentiles, idolaters. الأُمَم

Motherly. Ignorant, illiterate. أُمِّيّ

Gentile, idolater. ✧ أُمَمِيّ

Maternity. أُمِّيَّة وأُمُومَة

Wounded in the brain. أَمِيم ومَأْمُوم

A *conj. part.* Either, or. ✻ أَمْ

Is (he, she, it).., not? Is there not? أَمَا

But; as to; however. أَمَّا

When. If. (*for* إن ما) إِمَّا

Either.... or. Whether.... or. إِمَّا ... وإِمَّا

To conjecture, to determine a. th. ✻ أَمَتَ i أَمْتًا وأَمَّتَ ه

Weakness. Emptiness. inequality. Doubt. أَمْت ج إِمَات وأُمُوت

To be thirsty. ✻ أَمِجَ a أَمَجًا

Very hot summer. صَيْفٌ أَمَجٌ

Extreme point. Starting-place or goal in a race. Anger. ✻ أَمَد ج آمَاد

Eternally. عَلَى الأَمَد

Trustee, attorney, plenipotentiary. مُؤْتَمَن
Congress. Council. Conference. مُؤْتَمَر
Commanded ; proxy. ✧ Public officer. مَأْمُور
Mission, power of attorney. Office in the government. مَأْمُورِيَّة
Yesterday. ✱ أَمْس ج آمُس وآمَاس وأُمُوس
Lately, time not long past. الأَمْس
Silly. Parasite. ✱ إِمَّع وإِمَّعَة ج إِمَّعُون
To hope a. th. ✱ أَمَل o أَمَلًا وأَمَلًا ، وأَمَّل ه
To trust in, to set o.'s hope on. ه —
To give hope to a. o. أَمَّل ه
To meditate, to reflect on a. th. To consider, to contemplate. تَأَمَّل في وه
Hope, expectation. أَمَل وأَمْل ج آمَال
Meditation, reflection. تَأَمُّل ج تَأَمُّلَات
Who hopes. مُؤَمِّل
Hope, expectation. مَأْمَل ج مَآمِل
Hope, that which is hoped. مَأْمُول
To be true, loyal, faithful. ✱ أَمُنَ o أَمَانَةً
To be secure, in safety. أَمِنَ a أَمْنًا وأَمَنًا وأَمَانًا وأَمَنَةً
To be in safety against. — ه ومن
To trust to, to confide in. أَمِن ه
To intrust a. o. with, to commit a.th. to. — ه ب وعلى
To put o.'s self under a. o.'s protection or safekeeping. — الى
To intrust a. o. with. أَمَّن وإِئْتَمَن ه على
To reassure, to tranquillise a. o. أَمَّن تَأْمِينًا ، وآمَن إِيمَانًا ه
To say : Amen. أَمَّن
To believe, to have faith in. آمَن إِيمَانًا ب
To protect a. o. — ه
To put a. o. under shelter, to shelter him from (danger). — ه من
To confide in. إِئْتَمَن ه
To seek protection from. إِسْتَأْمَن الى
Safety. Safe-conduct, security. Protection. أَمْن وأَمَان
Mercy! Alas ! ✧ Well ! beautiful! أَمَان
Loyalty. Security. Fidelity, faithfulness. أَمَانَة
Deposit; thing intrusted to a. o.'s care. — ج أَمَانَات
Good faith ; sincerity. أَمَنَة

Trusted by all. أَمَنَة
Belief. Religious faith. إِيمَان
Faithful. Loyal. Steadfast. أَمِين ج أُمَنَاء
Treasurer. أَمِين الصُّنْدُوق
Amen, be it so. Yes. آمِين وأَمِين
Lime-kiln. ◻ أَمِينَة
Safe, sheltered. أَمِن وأَمِين
The best part. آمَن
Trustworthy. مَأْمُون
Place of safety. مَأْمَن
Believer, faithful. مُؤْمِن
Trusted upon. مُؤْتَمَن
He whose safety is guaranteed. مُسْتَأْمَن
To forget a. th. ✱ أَمِه a أَمَهًا ه
To have the mind disturbed, disordered. أُمِه
To become a maid-servant, a female slave. ✱ أَمِيَ a وأَمَا o وأَمَى i أُمُوَّة
To use (a female) as a servant, a slave. أَمَّى ه
To take a female servant or slave. تَأَمَّى واسْتَأْمَى ه
emale servant, bondwoman ; handmaid. أَمَة ج إِمَاء وأَمَوَات وآمٍ
Name of a tribe of Quraish. أُمَيَّة
The Ommiads بَنُو أُمَيَّة
That (*conjunctive*). ✱ أَنْ وأَنَّ
Until. إِلَى أَنْ
But, provided that. عَلَى أَنْ
If. إِنْ
Unless, except. إِنْ لَمْ
Indeed if, that if. لَئِنْ
Certainly, indeed. إِنَّ
How ? Whence ? Where ? أَنَّى
To moan. ✱ أَنَّ i أَنِينًا وأَنًّا وأُنَانًا وتَأْنَانًا
To spill (water). — ه
I will not do it as long as a star appears in the sky. مَا أَفْعَلُهُ مَا أَنَّ نَجْمٌ فِي السَّمَاءِ
Groan, moan. أَنِين وأَنَّة وأَنَان
Groan. Lamenting continually. أَنَّان
I. We. ✱ أَنَا ج نَحْنُ
Selfishness, egotism. أَنَانِيَّة
To reprehend a. o. energetically. ✱ أَنَّب ه
Thou, you. ✱ أَنْتَ ج أَنْتُمْ م أَنْتِ ج أَنْتُنَّ
You both. (*dual*) أَنْتُمَا
To lament. ✱ أَنَت i أَنِيتًا
To measure a. th. To grudge a. o. — ه وه

Moan. Envy. أنيت
To be soft (iron). ✱ أنث o أنوثة
To be effeminate (pers.).
To render feminine, to effeminate a. o. أنّث ه وه
To become of the feminine gender. To become effeminate. تأنّث
Female. أنثى ج إناث وأناثى ◘ نِثاية و✧ إنثاية
Soft, tender. Sweet, affectuous. أنيث
Feminine ; effeminate. مؤنّث
To be polite, kind, social. ✱ أنِس a وأنُس o أنسًا وأنَسًا وأنَسَة
To have an intimate connection with a. o. — ب
To become acquainted and familiar with. — إلى
To render familiar. To tame. أنّس ه
To be sociable, friendly, familiar with. آنس مؤانسة ه
To delight a. o. by good manners. To perceive a. th. from afar. آنس إيناسًا ه وه
To become a man (Son of God). To show kindness. تأنّس
To act as a social man. إستأنس
To get accustomed to. — ب
Social life ; kindness, politeness. أُنس
Crowd. Familiar. أنَس ج آناس
Man, mankind. إنس ج أناس وأناسِيّ وأناس، وأنَسِيَّة وآناس
People, mankind. ناس
Humanity. Mankind. نَسُوت
A human being. إنسِيّ وأنَسِيّ
Thy intimate friend. إبن إنسِك
Man. إنسان ج أناس وأناسِي
Apple of the eye. إنسان العَيْن
Human. Polite. إنسانِيّ
Humanity, manliness. Politeness, good breeding. إنسانيّة
Friendly. Meek, kind. أنِيس ومؤنِس ومؤانِس
Social life. Friendly relations. إستئناس
Incarnate (the Verb). متأنِّس
Accustomed. Familiar. مستأنِس
To be insufficiently cooked (meat). ✱ أنض o أناضة
To cook insufficiently (the meat). آنض إيناضًا ه
Insufficiently cooked (meat). أنِيض
To abstain from a. th. ✱ أنِف a أنفًا من

out of modesty, of shame.
To knock a. o. on his nose ; to mortify. أنف i أنفًا ه
To begin or to commence anew. إئتنف واستأنف ه
To go to appeal : to institute new proceedings. إستأنف ه
Nose. Forepart of anything. Extremity, point. أنف ج آناف وأنوف وآنف
In the first place. Above. Before, afore. آنِفًا
Bashfulness, shame. Scorn. أنَفَة
New. Harmless, unhurt. أُنُف
First of all, in the first place. مِن ذِي أنُف
He who rates himself high ; piqued, disdainful. أنُوف
Beginning. Appeal (in law). إئتِناف واستِئناف
Initial. إستِئنافِيّ
Future. مُستأنَف
For the future, henceforth. مُستأنَفًا
To admire a. th. ✱ أنِق a أنَقًا ه
To delight in. — ب
To do a. th. carefully. تأنّق ب او في
Elegance, grace. Beauty. أناقة
Fine, pretty ; pleasing. أنِق وأنِيق ومؤنِق
Vulture. Carrion-kite. أنُوق
Scarcer than a vulture's eggs (*said of a. th. difficult to be found*). أعَزّ مِن بَيض الأنُوق
To be gross, coarse (th.). ✱ أنك o أنكًا
To be ill-tempered (pers.).
Lead. آنُك
Creatures. Mankind. ✱ أنام وآنام
To become mature, to ripen. ✱ أنى i أنيًا وإنًى وأناء
To procrastinate, to delay a. th. أنّى ه
✧ To acquiesce in, to come to an a agreement with. أنّى مع
To hinder a. o. آنى إيناء ه
To act slowly. To procrastinate. تأنّى واستأنى في او ب
To treat a. o. with meekness. — ه
To wait for, to expect a. o. استأنى ه
Patience. Meekness. Staidness. Expectation. أناة
Time. Point of maturity. أناء وأنًى وإنًى
Time, space of time. أنًى ج آناء وأنِيّ
Day and night. آناء اللَّيل وأطراف النَّهار

Vase, vessel. إناء ج آنية وجمع أوانٍ

Slowness. Meekness. تَأَنٍ

Slow. Meek, patient. مُتَأَنٍّ

Ah! Alas! * آه وآهًا

To groan, to sigh. أَهَّ o أَهَّة , وتأهّه

To get ready, to prepare to. * أَهَب وتأهَّب ل

Skin, hide, raw leather. إهاب ج آهِبة وأُهُب

Provision. Ammunition, apparatus. أُهْبَة ج أُهَب

Ready. Prepared, fitted out. مُتَأَهِّب

Movables, chattels. * أَهَر — أَهَرة ج أَهَر وأَهَرات

To marry. * أَهَل o i أَهْلًا وأُهُولًا ه

To get accustomed to (a place). To welcome a. o. أَهِل a أَهَلًا ب

To be inhabited (house, town). أَهِل

To believe or to render a. o. worthy of, able to. أَهَّل وآهَل إيهالًا ه ل

To welcome a. o. — ب

To marry a. o. آهَل إيهالًا ه

To marry. تأهَّل واتَّهَل ه

To be qualified, to be fitted out for. تأهَّل ل

To deserve, to be worthy of, entitled to. إستأهَل ه وه

Be welcome! أهلًا وسهلًا

Family, house, household, (as father, wife, children); people belonging to a community or locality. أهل ج أهلون وآهال وأهالٍ

Household. — الدار

The superiors. — الأمر

The blessed, the inhabitants of Paradise. — الجنّة

Wife. أهل الرَّجُل

Scholars, learned men. أهل العِلم

Domestic. National, civil. Tame. أهليّ

Worthy of, entitled to. أهل ل

Ability, aptitude. Relationship. أهليّة

Inhabited. Crowded. آهِل ومأهول

Who deserves, worthy of. مُستأهِل

Hereditary goods. Home-born slave, cattle. * أهن — آهِن مِن المال

Whether, or. Unless. * أوْ

To come back from, to repent. To set (star). * آب o أوبًا وإيابًا مِن

He came back to God. — إلى الله

He came back from. أوّب وأيّب عن

To walk the whole day. أوّب وآوب مُؤاوبة

To arrive at (the water), at (a. o.'s house), during the night. تأوّب وائتاب ه وه

August (month). S آب

Return. أوب وأوبة وإياب

Shore. Use. Custom. أوْب

From all sides. من كلّ أوب

Crowd of friends. أوَبة

Who comes back to God, contrite for sin, penitent. أوّاب ج أوّابون

Place to which one comes back. مآب ج مآوِب

The highest point of the sky. Summit. Apogee. * أوج

White of eggs. * أوح — آح

To complain, to express grief. * اوخ ✧ تأوّخ

To overwhelm a. o. (affair). * آد o أوْدًا وأُوُودًا ه

To decline, to incline towards its end (day). آد o أوْدًا

To be bent, curved, crooked. أوِد a أوَدًا , وتأوّد

To bend, to curve a. th. — أوْدًا , وأوّد ه

To overcharge a. o. (work). تأوّد ه

Bend, inclination. Work. أوَد

To supply the wants of a. o. قوّم أوَد فلان

Burden, weight. أوْدة ج أوْدات

Ardour of fire, thirst. * أوار ج أُوُر

Goose. * إوزّة ج إوزّ

To bestow a. th. upon a. o.: to reward. * آس o أوْسًا وإياسًا ه

Gift. أوْس

Wolf. — وأُوَيس

Myrtle. آس

Holly. آس بَرّيّ

Room, apartment. Ts أوضة ج أوَض

Waiter, footman. Ts أوضجي

To cause damage to a. o. or a. th. * آف o أوفًا ه وه

Damage. Misfortune. Infirmity, bane, evil. آفة ج آفات

Damaged, affected. مَؤوف

To draw an evil upon a. o. * آق o أوْقًا على

To burden a. o. أوّق ه

To be gentle to. — (ه) عَلَى
Calmness, tranquillity. أَوْن
Time, moment. Season آن وأَوان ج آوِنَة of the year. Opportunity.
Now, now-a-days. أَلآنَ
Henceforward. مِن الآنَ وصاعِدًا
Till this day, till now. إلى الآنَ
P إِيوان ج إِيوانات وأَوَاوِين ✦ لِيوان ج لَوَاوِين
Palace. Arched hall.
✱ آه o أَوْهًا , وأَوَّه وتَأَوَّه ! To exclaim ah ! To weep.
He who sighs and cries أَوَّاه
Ah ! Alas ! آه وآهًا وأَوَّه وأَوْه
✱ أَوَى i أُوِيًّا ه او إِلى To retire anywhere, to take shelter in, to alight at.
أَوَى وآوَى وأَوَّى ه إِلى To receive a. o. at o.'s own house, to give hospitality to.
أَوَى i أَوْيَة وإِيَّة ومَأْوِيَة ومَأْوَاة ل To be moved with pity for.
To flock together. تأَوَّى وتآوَى
To settle somewhere. إِئْتَوَى إِتَّوَى ه وإلى
To pity. — ل
Mansion, settlement. مَأْوًى ومَأْوَاة ج مَآوٍ
Jackal. إِبْنُ آوَى ج بَنَات آوَى ✦ وَاوِي
Sign. Wonder. Miracle. آيَة ج آيَات وآيٌ Verse (of a sacred book). Example.
That is..., viz. Hey ! ✱ أَيْ
Yes, of course. إِي
O ! Ho ! Holloa ! أَيْ
Which ? What ? Which one ? ✱ أَيٌّ م أَيَّة
Whosoever. أَيُّ مَن
What ? أَيُّ شَيْءٍ
Particle prefixed to the objective case of pronouns. ✱ إِيَّا
إِيَّايَ وإِيَّاكَ وإِيَّاهُ وإِيَّانَا وإِيَّاكُم وإِيَّاهُم
Me, thee, him, us, you, them.
It is thee we worship. إِيَّاكَ نَعْبُدُ
Beware of. إِيَّاكَ مِن
Take care not to do. إِيَّاكَ أَن تَفْعَل
Particle prefixed to ها *before the vocative.* أَيٌ م أَيَّة
أَيُّهَا الرَّجُل , أَيَّتُهَا المَرْأَة — أَيُّهَا الرِجَال
O man! O woman ! O men !
When ? Wheresoever. أَيَّان
Interj. used in calling. Holloa ! ✱ أَيَا
Sunlight. ✱ إِيَا وإِيَاة وأَيَاء
To be strong, firm. ✱ آدَ i أَيْدًا وآدًا
To strengthen. To help. أَيَّدَ ه وه

Burden. Sorrow, misfortune. أَوْق
Ounce. أُوقِيَّة ج أَوَاقٍ
G أُوقَة وأُقَّة ج أُقَّات Okka (a weight of about two pounds and a half).
✱ آل o أَوْلًا ومَآلًا إِلى To reach a. th. To come back to. To be reduced to.
To abandon a. c. — عَن
To govern (subjects). — أَوْلًا وإِيَالًا ه
To be a chief : to be set over. — إِيَالًا وإِيَالَة عَلَى
To get a.o. back to. أَوَّل ه إِلى
To interpret, to explain a.th. — وتأَوَّل ه
Family. Race, dynasty. Vapour that rises morning and evening. mirage. آل
Instrument, tool. Organ. آلَة ج آلَات
War-apparel ; weapons, arms. آلَات الحَرْب
Coffin. أَلآلَة الحَدْبَاء
Musical instruments. آلَات الطَّرَب
Instrumental. Musician. آلَاتِيّ
Organic, organized bodies (animal or vegetal). آلِيّ
Principle, principal. أَوَّل ج أَوَائِل وأَوَال
Firstly, at first. أَوَّلًا وفي الأَوَّل وفي أَوَّل الأَمْر
Successively, by turns. أَوَّلًا فأَوَّلًا
First. Old. Preceding. Anterior. أَوَّل ج أَوَّلُون م أُولى ج أُوَل وأُولَيَات
The day before yesterday. أَوَّل البَارِحَة
The ancients and the moderns. أَلأَوَّلُون والآخِرُون
Anterior, primitive. أَوَّلِيّ م أَوَّلِيَّة
Priority, anteriority. Axiom. أَوَّلِيَّة
Interpretation, commentary. Spectre, apparition. تأْوِيل
Government. Province. إِيَالَة ج إِيَالَات
Deer, stag, mountain-goat. أُيَّل وإِيَّل وأَيِّل ج أَيَائِل
End, result. Return to a place, retreat. Event. Meaning (of a writing). مَآل
✱ آمَ o أَوْمًا To thirst.
To smoke out (the bees). — أَوْمًا وأُيَامًا وإِيَامًا عَلَى
To excite the thirst of a.o. To fatten (the cattle). أَوَّم ه
Burning thirst. Giddiness. أُوَام
✱ آنَ o أَوْنًا عَلَى نَفْسِهِ To go, to act at ease.

To authorize, to confirm a. o. or a. th.
To help, to succour, to strengthen a. o. – وآيد مُؤايَدَةً ه
To be strengthened. To be helped. تأيَّد
Force. Support. Authority. أيْد وإياد
Help. Authorisation. تأييد
In support, in confirmation of. تأييدًا ل
Strong, mighty. أيِّد
Serious affair. Monster. مُؤيِد ج مَوائِد ومآوِد
The North wind. The East wind. Membrum virile. ✧ أيْر ج أيُور وآيار
May (month). S أيّار ✧ نُوّار
To despair of. ✻ أيِس a إياسًا مِن
To make a. o. to despair of. أيَّس وآيَس إياسًا ه مِن
Despair. إياس
Disheartening, hopeless. آيِس
What? (*for* أيّ شيء) ✧ أيْش
To reiterate a. th ✻ آض i أيضًا ه
To come back to. – إلى
Again. Too, also. أيضًا

Wood, forest of bushy trees. ✻ أيك
God. H إيل
Ambassador, envoy. P إيلَچي
September. S أيلول
To be a widower. To be a widow. To be unmarried. ✻ آم i أيْمَة وأيْمًا وأيُومًا
To widow a. o. (God). أيَّم ه
To remain unmarried or a widower, a widow. تأيَّم
Who lives in celibacy. Widower; widow. أيِّم ج أيايِم وأيامى
Snake. Male viper. أيْم
By God! (*see* يمن) أيْمُ الله
To draw near (time). ✻ آن i أيْنًا
To be tired, fatigued.
Weariness, fatigue. أيْن
Where? ✻ أيْنَ
Wheresoever, wherever. أينما
Always and everywhere. في كلّ أينٍ وآنٍ
Whereabout? Where? How far? إلى أين
Wherefrom? مِن أين
Tell me. Go on! (*imper. particle*). ✻ إيهِ
Yes. So. ✧ أيْواه وأيوا

ب

✱ ب. At. During. In. With. For. By.
مَرَرْتُ بِهِ I passed by him.
بِسَحَرٍ وبِالسَّحَرِ Early in the morning.
سَارَ بِاللَّيْلِ He has walked during the night.
أَهْبُطْ بِسَلَامٍ Go down in pace.
ضَرَبَهُ بِالسَّيْفِ He struck him with the sword.
لَقِيتُ بِهِ أَسَدًا I found him to be lion-hearted.
العَيْنُ بِالْعَيْنِ Eye for eye.
بِاللهِ. بِحَيَاتِي By God! By my life!
بِلَا (ب and لا) In want of. Without.
✧ بَلَاش (for بِلَا شَيْءٍ) Free of charge. Uselessly.
بِمَ What? How?
بِمَا أَنَّ وبِمَا أَنَّ Since. For the reason that. Because.
Ts بَابَا Papa, old man.
L — ج بَابَاوَات Pope. the Holy Father.
بَابَوِيّ وبَابَاوِيّ Papal.
Cκ بَابَة Second month of the Coptic year, October.
P بَابُوج ج بَوَابِيج Slipper.
P. بَابُونَج Camomile.
✱ بَأْبَأَ To say father.
— ٥ : بِأَبِي أَنْتَ To say to a. o.: I will ransom thee with my father.
بُؤْبُؤ Root, origin, middle of a. th.
بُؤْبُؤُ الْعَيْنِ Apple of the eye.
✱ بَأْج Kind; way. The best head of a flock.
✧ Duty upon importation, town-due.
✱ بَأَرَ a بَأْرًا هـ To sink a well.
— وابْتَأَرَ هـ To conceal, to keep in store.
أَبْأَرَ ٥ To ensnare a. o.
بِئْر ج آبَار وبِئَار ✧ بِيَارَة Well, pit.
بُؤْرَة Hollow. Deposit, treasure. Fire-pit dug in the open.
Ts بَارَة ج بَارَات Para, farthing (money).
P بَاز و✧ بَاز ج بُؤُوز وبِيزَان Falcon, hawk.

✱ بَئِسَ a بُؤْسًا وبُؤُوسًا وبُؤْسَى To be unhappy. To be destitute.
بِئْسَ الرَّجُلُ What a bad man!
بَؤُسَ o بَأْسًا To be strong. To be brave.
أَبْأَسَ To be crushed by misfortune.
تَبَاءَسَ To pretend poverty.
إِبْتَأَسَ ب To be afflicted, sad of.
بَأْس Courage, strength, boldness.
بُؤْس وبَأْس وبَأْسَاء وبُؤْسَى Misfortune. adversity. Sorrow, harm.
لَا بَأْسَ No matter! Never mind!
لَا بَأْسَ فِي ذٰلِكَ No harm in it.
لَا بَأْسَ بِذٰلِكَ No objection to it.
لَا بَأْسَ عَلَيْكَ Be fearless. No fear.
بَنَاتُ بِئْسٍ Misfortunes.
بَائِس ج بُؤْس Unhappy. Poor.
بَئِيس Unhappy. Poor. Brave, gallant.
Is بَاسَابُورط Passaport.
✱ بَأَشَ a بَأْشًا، وبَاءَشَ ٥ To throw a. o. down unexpectedly.
Ts بَاش Head, chief, first.
Ts بَاش كَاتِب Head-clerk.
Ts بَاشَا ج بَاشَاوَات Pasha.
Ts بَاشِي بُوزُوق Irregular troops.
Ts أُون بَاشِي Corporal in the army.
Ts يُوزْ بَاشِي Captain
Ts بِيكْبَاشِي Major (in the army).
✱ بَأَطَ — تَبَنَّأَطَ To recline quietly on the side.
— عن To neglect a. th.
✱ بَأَقَ o بُؤُوقًا To surprise a. o.
إِنْبَاقَ عَلَى To fall on (misfortune).
بَامِيَا *Ochrea* (leguminous plant), bamia
✱ بَؤُلَ o بَآلَةً وبُؤُولَةً To be small, wretched.
بَئِيل وضَئِيل بَئِيل Small, wretched, paltry.
✱ بَأَى a بَأْوًا وبَأْوَاء عَلَى To boast of, to glory in.
أَبْأَى More glorious.
✱ بَبّ وبَبَّان Kind; way. Fat baby.

They have the same temper, the same manners. هُمْ بَبَّان وَاحِد
P بَابُوج ج بَوَابِيج Turkish slippers.
P بَبْر ج بُبُور A kind of hunting leopard.
L بَابُور ج بَابُورَات وبَوَابِير Steamer, engine, stove.
✧ بَبْغَاء وبَبَّغَاء ج بَبْغَاوَات Parrot.
✧ بَابِل Babel. Babylon.
بَابِلِيّ From Babel. Babylonian; Magical.
P بَابُونَج Camomile (plant).
✻ بَتّ o بَتًّا وأَبَتّ ٥ وه To cut. To decide. To give up. To achieve a. o. or a. th. To exhaust (a beast).
بَتّت ٥ وه To furnish a. o. with travelling provisions, apparel. To take (a promise) as certain.
تَبَتّت To provide o.'s self with provisions.
إِنْبَتّ To be cut off. To be decided.
بَتّ ج بُتُوت A coarse garment.
بَتَّة A cutting, a cut.
البَتَّة وبَتَّة وبَتَاتًا Decidedly. Irrevocably.
لَا بَتَّة . . والبَتَّة Not at all, by no means.
✧ بَتِّيَّة ج بَتَاتِي Cask.
بَتَات ج أَبِتَّة Travelling provisions, apparel.
بَتِّي وبَتَّات Manufacturer or seller of coarse garments.
بَتَّات Who cuts, settles, decides.
مَبْتُوت ومُنْبَتّ Cut off. Decided.
✻ بَتَر o بَتْرًا ه To curtail, to bob.
بَتِر a بَتَرًا ، وانْبَتَر To be cut.
بَاتِر وبَتَّار Sharp-edged (sword).
أَبْتَر Maimed. Bob-tailed.
✧ بَاتُور ج بَوَاتِير Rush-mat.
✻ بَتِع i بَتَعًا To be obstinate, stubborn. To have strong articulations (man).
بَتِع a بَتَعًا وبُتُوعًا بِأَمْرِهِ To have o.'s own way, to take nobody's advice.
بِتْع Intoxicating drink made of honey and dates.
أَبْتَع م بَتْعَاء ج بُتْع Whole, complete.
القَبِيلَة بَتْعَاء بَصْعَاء The whole tribe.
✧ بَتَاع (for مَتَاع) Means possession: belonging to.
✻ بَتَك i o بَتْكًا ، وبَتَّك ه To detach violently, to cut off a. th.
تَبَتَّك وانْبَتَك To be cut.

بِتْكَة ج بِتَك A part cut, torn off.
بَاتِك وبَتُوك Sharp (sword).
✻ بَتَل i o بَتْلًا ، وبَتَّل ه To cut, to cut off a. th.
بَتَّل وتَبَتَّل إلى To devote o.'s self to God's service. To live in celibacy.
إِنْبَتَل To be curtailed, cut off.
تَبْتِيل Disengagement from all worldly things.
بَتُول Virgin, maid. Nun.
أَلْبَتُول The blessed Virgin.
بَتُولِيَّة Maidenhood, virginity.
بَتِيل Depressed bed (of a river). With dependent branches (tree).
بَتِيلَة Separated from the world for God's service.
بَتِيلَة Shoot of a palm-tree cut off.
✻ بَثّ o بَثًّا وبَثّث ه و ٥ To divulge. a. th. To scatter, to disseminate.
— وبَاثّ وأَبَثّ ٥ ه To communicate (a secret) to a. o. To open one's heart to.
تَبَاثّ ه To confide (secrets) one to another.
إِنْبَثّ To be divulged. To be scattered.
إِسْتَبَثّ ه To ask from a. o. to reveal a secret.
بَثّ State. Great sorrow. Scatter.
بَثّ وانْبِثَاث Matter divulged, disclosure.
مَبْثُوث ومُنْبَثّ Published, divulged.
✻ بَثْبَث ه To divulge a. th. To raise and scatter (the dust etc.).
✻ بَثَر i وبَثِر a بَثْرًا وبَثَرًا وبُثُورًا ، وتَبَثَّر To be covered with blotches, carbuncles, tubercles.
بَثْر ج بُثُور Pimple, blotch, tubercle.
بَثِير وكَثِير بَثِير Numerous, much, many.
✻ بَثِم a بَثَمًا وتَبَثَّم To be red and swollen with blood (lip).
أَبْثَم م بَثْمَاء ج بُثْم Red-lipped.
✻ بَثَق o بَثْقًا ، وتَبْثَاقًا To overflow (river).
إِنْبَثَق To emanate, to derive.
إِنْبَثَق عَلَى To break its dams and overflow (water).
— مِن To pour from. To proceed from (Holy Ghost).
إِنْبِثَاق Procession (of the Holy Ghost).
مُنْبَثِق Overflowing. Proceeding (Holy Ghost).

well off.
To be glad, merry.
To be respected. بَجُلَ o بَجَالَةً وبُجُولاً
To honour a. o. To applaud, بَجَّلَ ﻫ to commend a. o.
Wonder. بَجَلٌ
Enough, sufficient. بَجَلْ
Yes, certainly. (*adv.*). بَجَلْ
Honoured. Respected. بَجِيل ومُبَجَّل
✻ بَجَمَ i بَجْمًا وبُجُومًا To be silent out of fear or stupidity. To stare. To shrink. To delay.
Numerous party. بَجْم وقَوْم بَجْم
✧ Simpletons, fools.
To inculcate a. th. ✧ بَجَّنَ ﻫ في (in the mind). To rivet, to clinch (a nail).
To be inculcated. ✧ تَبَجَّنَ
✻ بَحَّ a بَحًّا وبَحَحًا وبُحُوحًا وبَحَاحًا وبُحُوحَة وبَحَاحَة To be hoarse, husky.
To render a. o. hoarse. أَبَحَّ وبَحَّحَ ﻫ
Hoarseness. Rough, harsh voice. بُحَّة
Hoarse. أَبَحُّ م بَحَّاء و✧ مَبْحُوح
To remain firm in. ✻ بَحْبَحَ وتَبَحْبَحَ في To enjoy (glory).
✧ To give a. th. generously. تَبَحْبَحَ ﻫ
✧ To render a. th. plentiful, abundant.
He went in the middle تَبَحْبَحَ الدَّارَ of a house.
He spent life in grandeur — في المَجْد and glory.
Company. ✧ Comfortable life, بَحْبَحَة comfort.
Middle-part, centre. بُحْبُوحَة
✧ Considerable, plentiful. مُبَحْبَح
To be pure, unalloyed. ✻ بَحُتَ o بُحُوتَة
To show a cordial, true بَاحَتَ ﻫ الوُدَّ love to a. o.
Pure, unmingled. بَحْت
A true born Arab. عَرَبِيٌّ بَحْت
Stout and short. ✻ بُحْتُر وبُحْتُرِيّ
To scrape (the earth). ✻ بَحَثَ a بَحْثًا في
To be in quest of, to search — عن a. th.
To contend, to enter بَاحَثَ ﻫ وتَبَاحَثَ مَعَهُ into discussion with.
To investigate, تَبَحَّثَ واسْتَبْحَثَ وابْتَحَثَ عن to scrutinize a. th.

Piece of ground even and ✻ بَثْنَة ج بِثَن smooth.
Wheat growing in it. بَثْنِيَّة
To sweat. ✻ بَثَا o بَثْوًا
Sycophant, flatterer, fawner. بَثِيّ
To lance, to prick. ✻ بَجَّ o بَجًّا ﻫ
To fatten (cattle : pasture-land).
To strike a. o. with. — ﻫ ب
To make mischief to a. o.
To be lanced. To be struck. إِنْبَجَّ
Pimple on the eye. بَجَّة
To quiet, to dandle (a child). ✻ بَجْبَجَ ﻫ
To be fat. ✧ To be swollen. تَبَجْبَجَ
To rejoice at. ✻ بَجِحَ a بَجَحًا, وتَبَجَّحَ ب
To cheer, to rejoice a. o. بَجَّحَ ﻫ
Cheerfulness, joy. بَجَح
To stay in. ✻ بَجَدَ o بُجُودًا, وبَجَّدَ ب
Crowd, multitude. بَجْد
Bottom. Root, origin, بَجْدَة وبُجْدَة وبُجُدَة real state of a thing.
He knows thy هُوَ عَالِمٌ بِبَجْدَةِ أَمْرِك concerns, thy business.
He is aware of the هُوَ ابْنُ بَجْدَةِ الأَمْر thing.
Clothing made with striped بِجَاد ج بُجُد stuff.
Precious garnet ; carbuncle. بِجَادِيّ
To have an umbilical ✻ بَجِرَ a بَجَرًا hernia.
To be paunchy, to bulge out.
Swelling of the navel. بُجْرَة ج بُجَر
He mentioned his ذَكَرَ عُجَرَهُ وبُجَرَهُ apparent and hidden defects.
بُجْر ج أَبَاجِر وأَبَاجِير, وبُجْرِيّ ج بَجَارِيّ Misfortune.
Paunchy, أَبْجَر م بَجْرَاء ج بُجْر وبُجْرَان big-bellied.
Misfortunes. ✻ بَجْرَم — البَجَارِم
To cause ✻ بَجَسَ o i بَجْسًا, وبَجَّسَ ﻫ (water) to flow, to gush.
To spring, to gush. تَبَجَّسَ وانْبَجَسَ
Abundant (spring). بَجْس وبَجِيس ومُنْبَجِس
Filled with water (clouds). بَاجِس ج بُجَّس
To cut a. th. with ✻ بَجَعَ a بَجْعًا ﻫ a sword.
To eat to surfeit. بَجَمَ a بَجْمًا وابْتَجَمَ
Pelican. Stork. بَجَع
✧ Knave (at cards). بَجَق T
To be prosperous, ✻ بَجَلَ o بُجُولاً وبَجَلاً

Research. Examination. بَحث ج أَبحاث
Mine.
Scope for search, for investigation. مَبحث ج مَباحِث
Dispute, discussion. مُباحثة
To scatter, to separate. To find out a. th. ✧ بَحثَر ه
To be squandered, wasted. تَبحثَر
Wastefulness. Lavishness. بَحثَرة
Lavisher. Squanderer. مُبحثِر
To be confused, seized with fear. To be very thirsty. ✧ بَحِر a بَحَرًا
To till (the earth). بَحَر بَحرًا ه
To slit, to cut open (a she-camel's ear). — ه
To be salty (water). أَبحر
To voyage upon the sea. To be swampy (land).
To examine a. th. thoroughly, to go deep into. تَبحّر في
To expand. To widen. to stretch forth. إِستبحر
Sea. Any great river ; brine. A generous man. Man of extensive knowledge. Swift horse. Fruitful land. ✧ Course (of the year, of the week). بَحر ج أَبحُر وبُحور وبِحار
The Caspian sea. بَحر الخَزَر
The Ocean. البَحر المُحِيط
The Mediterranean sea. البَحر المُتَوَسِّط وبَحر الرُّوم
The Atlantic Ocean. بَحر الظُّلُمات
Mirage. ◻ بَحر الشَّيْطان
The river Nile. بَحر النِّيل
Clouds rising from the sea. بَنات بَحر
Province of Arabia. البَحرَين
Basin. Fish-pond. Haven, pool. Land, country. بَحرة ج بِحار
Lop-eared and set free (she-camel). بَحِيرة ج بُحُر وبَحائر
Lake. بُحَيرة ج بُحَيرات
Belonging to the sea. marine. (opp. to بَرّيّ) بَحرِيّ
Sailor. بَحرِيّ وبَحّار ج بَحّارون وبَحرِيُّون
Depressed place, hollow. ◻ بَحراة
Forbidden. Inquisitive. prying. باحِر
Canicular, dog-days. باحُور وباحُوراء
To be in a fit. To be delirious. ✧ بَحرَن
Delirious, raving. ✧ مُبَحرَن

Crisis of (an illness). Delirium. بُحران
To prick a. o. ✱ بَحَز a ه بَحزًا
To dig. To excavate a. th. (for بحث) ✧ بَحَش ه
Flint, pebble. (for حَصَبة) ✧ بَحصة ج بَحص
To be empty-handed. ✱ بَحلَس — تَبحلَس
Idle, unemployed. مُتَبحلِس
To snore. ✧ To drizzle. ✱ بَخّ o بَخًّا
✧ To sprinkle a. th.. To eject its (venom : snake). — ه
Exclamation of praise, admiration. Bravo ! بَخْ وبَخٍ بَخٍ
✧ Aspersion. Drizzling rain. بَخّة
To groan (camel). To snore. To approve. ✱ بَخبَخ
To cool (heat). — وتَبَخبَخ
Drizzling rain. ✧ بَخبُوخة
Happiness, good chance, luck. بَخت P
Happy, lucky, fortunate. بَخِيت ومَبخُوت
Camels of Bactriana. بُخت
To waddle. To walk in a stately gait. ✧ To become proud. ✱ بَختَر — تَبختَر
Elegant bearing. بَختَرة
To scatter a. th. ✱ بَخثَر ه
To steam (pot). ✱ بَخَر a بَخَرًا
To have a foul breath. بَخِر
To perfume a. o. with incense. ✧ To emit vapours. بَخَّر
To perfume with incense. — ه وعلى
To perfume one's self with incense, to be incensed. تَبَخَّر ب
Nettle. بَخرة وبَخر
Foul-breathed. أَبخَر
Vapour ; effluvium. بُخار ج أَبخِرة
Frankincense. بَخُور ج أَبخِرة وبَخُورات
Cyclamen (plant). ✧ بَخُور مَريَم
✧ Steamer, steamboat. باخِرة ج بَواخِر
Steamer. مَركَب بُخاريّ
Censer, thurible. مِبخَرة ج مَباخِر
Perfuming with incense, thurifer. مُبَخِّر
To put out (the eye) of a. o. ✱ بَخَز a بَخزًا ه
To cause damage to a. o. To put out a. o.'s eye. ✧ بَخَس a بَخسًا ه و ه
To wrong a. o. in his (rights). — ه ه
To be diminished. بَخِس وتَبخَّس
To do mischief, to wrong one another. تَباخَس
Deficient Low (price). Tax. بَخس

To bore a. th. ✧ بَخَش o بَخْشًا , وبَخَّش ه
Hole, eyelet. ✧ بُخْش ج أَبْخَاش وبَخْوِيش
Bodkin. ✧ مِبْخَش
Gratuity, gift. bribe. ✧ بَخْشِيش ج بَخَاشِيش
To give a gratuity, to a. o. ✧ بَخْشَش ه
To put out the eye of. ✻ بَخَص a بَخْصًا ه
To have the eyelids fleshy, بَخِص a بَخَصًا swollen.
To have the eyelids inverted. تَبَخَّص
To look steadfastly.
Having fleshy ey lids. أَبْخَص م بَخْصَاء
To slaughter (a sheep). ✻ بَخَع a بُخُوعًا ه
To commit suicide from – نَفْسَهُ grief or passion.
To sink (a well). – بَخْعًا ه
✧ To reprehend a. o. publicly. – وبَخَّع ه
He gave him friendly advice. بَخَع لَهُ النُّصْح
To بَخَع a بُخُوعًا وبَخِع a بَخَاعَةً وبُخُوعًا ب recognize (the right) of.
✧ Public reproof. Confusion, بَخْعَة shame.
✧ Reprehended. Covered with مَبْخُوع shame.
To put out ✻ بَخَق a بَخْقًا , وأَبْخَق ه (the eye).
His eye was put out. بَخِقَت عَيْنُهُ a بَخَقًا
One-eyed. بَاخِق وأَبْخَق وبَخِيق ومَبْخُوق
To be ✻ بَخِل a بَخَلًا , وبَخُل o بُخْلًا ب عَلَى miserly, avaricious of, towards a. o.
To charge a. o. with avarice. بَخَّل ه
To find a. o. avaricious. أَبْخَل ه
To give reluctantly to. تَبَاخَل ب وعَلَى
Avarice, stinginess. بُخْل وبَخَل
Avaricious. بَاخِل وبَخِيل ج بُخَّل وبُخَلَاء stingy.
Niggard, very avaricious. بَخَّال
Inducement to avarice. مَبْخَلَة
Veil. Head-covering. ✻ البُخْنُق والبُخْنَق
To subside (anger). ✻ بَخَا o بَخْوًا
To separate, to remove ✻ بَدَّ o بَدًّا ه و ه a. o. or a. th.
To scatter, to th. w بَدَّد تَبْدِيدًا ه away. To squander a. th.
To remove a. th. from. – عَن
To barter a. th. بَادَّ مُبَادَّةً وبِدَادًا ه
To share a. th. between. أَبَدَّ ه بَيْن
To be scattered, lavished. تَبَدَّد
To rush against o. a. (fighters). تَبَادَّ
To apply o.'s self solely to. إِسْتَبَدَّ ب

To appropriate. To use a. th. freely. To be despotic.
They went away. أَسْتُبِدَّ بِهِم
Equal, similar. بِدّ
Flight, escape. بُدّ
Certainly. Necessarily. لَا بُدَّ
Assuredly ; unavoidably. ✧ مِن كُلِّ بُدّ
Idol ; temple of P بُدّ ج بِدَدَة وأَبْدَاد idols. Buddha. Veda.
Part of a thing. – وبُدَّة وبُدَاد
Power, strength. Want. بَدَد
Battle, fight. Equal number of بَدَاد fighters.
They have dis- ذَهَبُوا أَبَادِيد وتَبَادِيد persed.
Stout, large and big. أَبَدّ م بَدَّاء
Having parted thighs.
Scattered. Spent recklessly. مُبَدَّد
Despotism. إِسْتِبْدَاد
I will, (for ✧ بَدِّي وبُدِّي وبِدِّي (بِوُدِّي) I desire. I wish.
To begin a. th. ✻ بَدَأ a بَدْءًا ه او ب
To create (God).
To start from (a country). – مِن
To make to begin. بَدَّأ ه
✧ To admit as a novice in a religious order.
✧ To make a. th. before – ه عَلَى another, to begin with.
To create, to find out a. th. أَبْدَأ ه
To cut new teeth (child). –
To begin a. th. أَبْتَدَأ ه او ب
✧ To become a novice.
Beginning بَدْء وبَدْأَة وبَدَاءَة وبَدِيئَة و✧ بِدَايَة principle.
In the beginning. أَوَّلَ بَدْءٍ وبَادِئَ بَدْءٍ
He رَجَع عَوْدَهُ عَلَى بَدْئِهِ او فِي عَوْدَتِهِ وبَدْأَتِهِ went back by the same way.
Beginning. ✧ Novitiate. إِبْتِدَاء
Initial, primordial. إِبْتِدَائِي
Preferable, more urgent. ✧ أَبْدَأ
Principle. Origin. مَبْدَأ ج مَبَادِئ
Begun. A beginning. مَبْدُوء
Founder. Creator. مُبْدِئ وبَادِئ
A beginning. Inchoative. مُبْتَدَأ Subject (*gram.*).
Beginner. ✧ Novice. مُبْتَدِئ
He فَعَلَهُ بَدْءًا وبَدْءَ بَدْءٍ وبَادِئَ بَدْءٍ وبَدِيءٍ has done it first of all.

✻ بَدَحَ a بَدْحًا ه ب To strike a.o. with a stick ; to surprise a. o. with.
بَدَاحٌ ج بُدُحٌ Extensive field.
✻ بَدِخَ a ، بَدُخَ o ، بَدْخًا وَبَدَاخَةً To be raised in dignity.
تَبَدَّخَ عَلَى To be exalted above a. o.
بَدَخَ a بَدْخًا ✧ To squander. To lavish, to throw away.
بَدْخٌ ✧Lavishness, prodigality.
بَدِيخٌ ج بُدَخَاءُ Invested with dignity, raised to dignity.
✻ بَدَرَ o بُدُورًا ه To fall unexpectedly upon a. o. (accident); to surprise a.o. To have a face like the full moon. To ripen (fruit).
بَدَرَ ه وإلى To hurry towards a. o. To hasten forward.
بَادَرَ مُبَادَرَةً وبِدَارًا ه To run up to. To lose no time in.
— إلى وفي To hasten to do a. th.
أَبْدَرَ To walk by moonlight.
إِبْتَدَرَ ه To outrun. to forestall a. o.
إِبْتَدَرَ إلى To run up to.
إِبْتَدَرَتْ عَيْنَاهُ His eyes flowed with tears.
بَدْرٌ ج بُدُورٌ Full moon. Disk.
البَدْرَى Advance, motion forward.
بَدْرِيٌّ Rain before winter. Small fat camel. ◻ Early, soon.
بَدْرَةٌ ج بِدَرٌ وبُدُورٌ Sum of money equal to 10 000 dirhems (*about 20 pounds sterling*). Bag that contains it.
بَادِرٌ Hastening. Shining in all its splendour (full moon).
بَادِرَةٌ ج بَوَادِرُ Point, edge of a sword. Fit of passion.
بَدَارِ بَدَارِ Make haste ! (*interj.*).
◻ بَدَارَةٌ Basket.
◻ بَدَارَى Chickens.
Is. بَادْرِي ج بَادْرِيَّةٌ European priest.
✻ بَيْدَرَ ه To heap up (provisions)
بَيْدَرٌ ج بَيَادِرُ Threshing floor.
✻ بَدْرَقَ ه وه To protect a. o. ✧ To waste, to squander (money).
✧ تَبَدْرَقَ To be wasted, squandered.
✧ تَبَدْرُقٌ Lavishness, wastefulness.
✧ مُبَدْرِقٌ Spendthrift. Lavisher, squanderer.
P بَادْزَهْر Bezoar (stone).
✻ بَدَعَ a بَدْعًا ه To begin a. th
To produce, to find out a new th.
بَدُعَ o بَدْعًا وبَدَاعَةً وبُدُوعًا To be matchless, unequalled.
بَدِعَ a بَدَعًا To become fat.
بَدَّعَ ه To consider a. o. as an innovator, a heretic.
✧ بَدَّعَ To have a strange behaviour.
أَبْدَعَ وابْتَدَعَ ه To find out, to create a. th.
أَبْدَعَ فِي To excel in doing a. th. To be an heresiarch.
— بِفُلَانٍ To forsake, to abandon a. o.
إِسْتَبْدَعَ ه To look at a. th. as strange, as new.
بِدْعٌ ج أَبْدَاعٌ Inventor. New.
بِدْعَةٌ ج بِدَعٌ Novelty. New doctrine. Heresy. Sect.
إِبْدَاعٌ وابْتِدَاعٌ Invention, innovation.
بَدِيعٌ ج بُدُعٌ Contriver of a new thing. Strange, extraordinary. Floweriness of style. New water-skin.
عِلْمُ البَدِيعِ Rhetoric, elocution.
✧ تَبْدِيعٌ ج تَبَادِيعُ Strange things ; uproar, theft, fight, etc.
مُبْدِعٌ ومُبْتَدِعٌ Creator. Contriver. Heresiarch.
✻ بَدِغَ a بَدَغًا To be defiled with defection. To be stained with a crime. To hobble like a cripple.
بَدَغَ a بَدْغًا ه To crack (walnuts).
بِدْغٌ وبَدِغٌ Corpulent, fat.
✻ بَدَلَ o بَدْلًا ، وبَدَّلَ ه To change a. th.
— ه مِن أو بِ To substitute o. th. for another.
بَدَّلَ وأَبْدَلَ ه مِن To receive a. th. in exchange (of).
بَدَّلَ ه ه To change a. th. for another, to interchange.
بَادَلَ مُبَادَلَةً وبِدَالًا ه ب To give in exchange for ; to barter.
تَبَدَّلَ To be changed, exchanged. ✧ To change clothes. ✧ To put on fine clothes.
تَبَدَّلَ ه وب To receive a. th. in exchange for another.
— في ✧ To work by turns (workmen).
تَبَادَلَ ه To exchange things, to permute.
إِسْتَبْدَلَ ه وب To receive, to ask a. th. in exchange for another.

To manifest a. th. to a. o.	— ه ل
To appear. To come forth.	تَبَدَّى ه وه
To manifest a reciprocal (hatred).	تَبَادَى ب
Desert of nomads.	بَدْو وبَادِيَة
Nomads, bedouins.	بَادِيَة ج بَوَادٍ
Nomadism. Desert.	بَدَاوَة وبِدَاوَة
Bedouin. Nomad.	بَدَوِيّ , بَدْوِيّ
Clear, evident, manifest.	بَادٍ ج بَادُون وبُدًى وبُدَّى
Caprice, fancy, freak.	بَدَاة ج بَدَوَات
Fanciful, whimsical, freakish.	ذُو م ذَات بَدَوَات
Encampment in the desert.	مَبْدًى ج مَبَادٍ
To be decayed, to be old, worn out.	✻ بَذَّ a بَذَذًا وبَذَاذًا وبَذَاذَة وبُذُوذَة
To subdue, to tame, to humiliate a. o.; to overcome a. o.	بَذَّ o بَذًّا وبَذِيذَة ه
Worn out, decayed.	بَاذّ وبَذّ م بَاذَّة وبَذَّة
To despise, to loathe a. o. or a. th.	✻ بَذَأَ i بَذْءًا ه وه وعلى
To be dissolute, wicked.	بَذَأَ o وبَذِيَ a وبَذُوَ o بَذَاء وبَذَاءَة
To abuse a. o. in words. To quarrel. To blame a. o.	بَاذَأَ ه
Of bad morals, profligate. Foul-mouthed.	بَذِيّ م بَذِيئَة
Lamb.	✻ بَذَج ج بِذْجَان
To split a. th. To rub off (a skin).	✻ بَذَح a بَذْحًا ه
Fissure; rent. Chap on the skin.	بَذْح ج بُذُوح
To be high, great. To be proud.	✻ بَذِخ a بَذَخًا , وتَبَذَّخ
To vie with a. o. in fastuousness.	بَاذَخ ه
Pride, haughtiness.	بَذَخ
High. Proud.	بَذَّاخ وبَاذِخ ج بَوَاذِخ
To sow, to scatter a. th.	✻ بَذَر o بَذْرًا ه
He diffused talk among the people.	بَذَر كَلَامًا بَيْنَ النَّاس
To scatter. To squander, to waste a. th.	بَذَّر وبَاذَر ه
Seed. Grain for sowing.	بَذْر ج بِذَار وبُذُور
Here and there, to and fro.	شَذَر بَذَر
Great talker.	بَذِر وبَيْذَار وبَيْذَارَة
Slanderer.	بَذُور وبَذِير
Wastefulness. Prodigality.	تَبْذِير

A thing given or received in exchange. Change, substitution.	بِدْل وبَدَل , وبَدِيل ج أَبْدَال وبُدَلَاء
Generous, noble man.	رَجُل بِدْل وبَدَل
Apposition (*gram.*). Price, value.	بَدَل
Instead of.	بَدَل أَن
In exchange for. Instead of.	بَدَلًا مِن
✧ Suit of clothes. Chasuble.	بَدْلَة
Change, permutation. Exchange.	تَبْدِيل وتَبَدُّل
Reciprocity.	تَبَادُل
Reciprocally.	تَبَادُلًا
Reciprocal, mutual (agreement).	مُتَبَادَل
✻ بَدَن o بَدْنًا وبُدْنًا , وبَدُن o بَدَانَة وبَدَانًا	
To grow big, stout.	
To grow old. ✧ To become wealthy.	بَدَّن
To clothe a. o. with a coat of mail.	— ه
Stoutness, obesity,	بَدَانَة
Body (especially the trunk). Short coat or cuirass. Of noble descent (man).	بَدَن ج أَبْدَان
Old (man). Old chamois.	بَدَن ج أَبْدُن وبُدُن
Sleeveless corselet. Victim offered in Mecca.	بَدَنَة ج بَدَنَات وبُدُن
Big, stout.	بَادِن ج بُدْن , وبَدِين ج بُدُن
To overtake a. o. suddenly (event)). To accost a. o. unexpectedly, to surprise.	✻ بَدَه a بَدْهًا , وبَادَه ه
To overtake a. o. by.	— وبَادَه ه ب
To extemporize (a speech).	إِبْتَدَه ه
Extempore speaking. Extempore, production without previous notice. Surprise.	بَدَاهَة وبُدَاهَة
Extemporaneously, without premeditation, unaware.	بَدِيهًا وعلى البَدِيه
Beginning. Extemporaneous action, intuition.	بَدِيهَة
Extempore speaker. Extemporizer.	مِبْدَه ومُبْتَدِه
To appear, to become manifest. To seem good, fit.	✻ بَدَا o بُدُوًّا
To live in the desert, to lead a nomadic life.	بَدَى o , وتَبَدَّى
To manifest a. th. or a.o.	بَادَى ه وه
To manifest openly to a.o. (hatred). To reward a.o. with.	بَادَى ه ب
To do a. th. for the first time.	أَبْدَى ه

To keep (an oath). To intend — ه وهـ (alms-giving). To take a. o. along to (the desert).
To exceed ; to overcome a. o. — على
To justify o.'s self, to be cleared تَبَرَّر from a charge. To become just, pious.
To do good o. to another. تبارّ
Innocence. Good faith. Beneficence. بِرّ Filial piety. Good work. Rat.
He cannot distinguish لا يَعرِفُ هِرًّا مِن بِرٍّ anything. (*lit* : a cat from a rat).
Wheat. بُرّ
Inland, continent. Province. بَرّ ج بُرُور
By land and by sea. بَرًّا وبَحْرًا
Just. Pious. بَرّ وبارّ ج أبرار وبررة Innocent.
He shows filial piety هو بَرٌّ وبارٌّ بِوالدَيْهِ to his parents.
Out, outside (*adv. and interj.*). ✧ بَرّا
Savage (animal). Not grafted بَرّيّ (tree). Continental, inland.
Desert, waste. بَرّيّة ج بَرارِي
Exterior, outward, بَرّانِيّ ج بَرّانِيُّون external. ✧ Foreign. Base, counterfeit(coin).
First fruit of the tree called بَرِير . أراك
More pious. More beneficent. أبَرّ
Justification. تَبْرِير
Filial piety. Beneficence. مَبَرّة ج مَبارّ
Good, pious. accepted (work). مَبْرُور
To make a noise. ✧ To mutter. ✻ بَرْبَرَ
Berbers. Nubians. بَرْبَر ج بَرابِر وبَرابِرة
Noise-maker. بَرْبار
Barbarous, barbarian. بَرْبَرِيّ
Berberry, sorrel (*pla.*). ✧ بَرْبَرِيس
To create, ✻ بَرَأَ a بَرْءًا ه وهـ to form out of nothing (God).
To get free of, freed بَرِئَ a بَراءة مِن from.
To recover from بَرِئَ a بُرْءًا مِن (disease).
To absolve, to clear a. o. بَرَّأَ تَبْرِئة ه مِن from (guilt).
To recover. أبرأ
To free. To cure a. o. from. أبرأ ه مِن
To be cleared from. تَبَرَّأ مِن
To part from o. a. تَبارَأ
To ask to be freed from a.th. إستبرأ مِن
To abstain from. To cleanse the

Spendthrift. Talkative. تِبْذار وتِبذارة
Spendthrift, squanderer. مُبَذِّر
To protect. ✻ بَذْرَقَ ه وهـ a o. or a. th.
To frighten. ✻ بَذَعَ بَذْعًا وأبذَعَ ه وهـ To drip (a liquid).
To be scared, ✻ بذعر — إبذعرّ frightened away. To disperse in the pursuit of a. th.
Drink made from the juice P بَاذَق of grapes slightly boiled.
Pawn(chess). Pedestrian. P بَيْذَق ج بَيَاذِق
To bestow, ✻ بَذَلَ i o بَذْلًا وبَاذَل ه to give generously to.
To devote o.'s self to. بَذَلَ نَفسَهُ دُون او عَن
He did his best. — جُهدَهُ
To make a daily use of إبتذل هـ (clothes).
To be in daily use (clothes). أُبتُذِل
Valuable present, donation. بَذْل
Strenuous exertion, بَذْل الجُهد endeavour.
Devotedness, self- بَذل الذات وبَذل النفس devotion.
Generous giver. باذِل ومِبذال
Given, delivered, spent. مَبذُول
Shabby بِذْلة . مِبذَل ومِبذَلة ج مَباذِل , ومُبتَذَل clothes, in daily use.
Common word, common style كلام مُبتَذَل
To be considerate and ✻ بَذُمَ o بَذامة self-possessed.
Generosity. Firmness. Patience. بُذْم
Self-possessed, reflecting. بَذِيم
Egg-plant. P باذِنجان و✧ بادِنجان
To speak ✻ بَذا o بَذْوًا , وأبذَى عَن obscenely about.
To be bad, dissolute بَذُوَ o بَذاء (in language).
Of bad morals. بَذِيّ م بَذِيّة ج أبذِياء
To be truthful(man); ✻ بَرَّ i بِرًّا وبُرُورًا inviolate (oath).
To do good. To have mercy on. بَرَّ ه To bestow bountiful gifts upon.
To show filial piety to ه — بِرًّا ومَبَرّة i o
To obey a. o. — ه بِرًّا وبَرارة
To justify, to clear a. o. بَرَّرَ ه
To be beneficent towards. بارَّ ه To show kindness to.
To travel by land. To multiply. أبَرّ

Man-of-war. ✧ Inn. بَارِجَة ج بَوَارِج
Having beautiful eyes. أَبْرَج م بَرْجَاء ج بُرْج
A streaky woollen garment. ✻ بُرْجُد
Target put on the point of a spear. Heap of stones. P بُرْجَاس ج بَرَاجِيس
Jupiter (planet). البِرْجِيس
Finger-joints. ✻ بُرْجُمَة ج بَرَاجِم
To leave (a place). To cease. ✻ بَرِح a بَرَاحًا وبَرَحًا ه ومن
He is still rich. مَا بَرِح غَنِيًّا
I do not cease doing it. لَا أَبْرَح أَفْعَل ذٰلِكَ
To come over the left side (game). بَرَح o بُرُوحًا
To become irritated with. بَرَح o بَرَحًا عَلَى
To afflict, to trouble a. o. بَرَّح ب
To exceed (in praise or blame). أَبْرَح
To please, to honour a. o. To cause a. o. to depart. أَبْرَح ه
Evil, pain, sorrow. بَرْح ج أَبْرَاح , وتَبْرِيح وبُرَحَاء
Choice part of a. th. بُرْحَة ج بُرَح
Desert plain. Sun. Wonderful thing. بَرَاح
Past, spent (time). بَارِح
Yesterday. البَارِح والبَارِحَة
The day before yesterday. البَارِحة الأُولَى
Strong (wind). بَارِح ج بَوَارِح
Great pain, great distress. بَرْح بَارِح
Crossing on the left side (beast). — وبَرُوح وبَرِيح
Misfortunes. بَنَات بَرْح
Fit, becoming word. قَوْل بَرِيح •
Exclamation in missing the target to express a failure. بَرْحَى
Root of the mandrake. S يَبْرُوح
Misfortunes. Eager desire. تَبَارِيح
To subdue a.o. or a.th. To bruise the (head or back). ✻ بَرَخ i بَرْخًا ه وه
To be cold. To cool (ardour). ✻ بَرَد o بَرْدًا وبَرُد o بَرْدًا وبُرُودًا
To file (iron). To cool the eyes with collyrium بُرُود. — بَرَد ه
To be just, unquestionable (right). بَرَد الحَقّ عَلَى
To cool, to chill a. th. To soothe, to alleviate a. th. بَرَد o وبَرَّد ه
To be devastated by hail. بُرِد
✦ He confirmed his claim. بَرَّد حَقَّهُ

body from (dirt).
Cure, recovery. بُرْء وبُرُوء
First night in a month. البَرَاء
Last night in a month. ابن البَرَاء
Shed, hut for hunters. بُرْأَة ج بُرَأ
Immunity. ✧ Privilege. Diploma. Permit. Passport. بَرَاءَة
✧ A Pope's bull. بَرَاءة ألبَابَا
Franchise. Exemption. Sentence of liberation, of discharge. تَبْرِئَة
Receipt in full, acquittance. تَبْرِئَة ذِمَّة
Creator (God). Cured. بَارِئ
Free, exempted. Innocent. Cured. بَرِيّ ج بُرَاء وأَبْرِيَاء وبَرِيئُون
Creature. بَرِيَّة ج بَرَايَا
Cured. Freed. مُبْرَأ
To bristle up. ✻ بَرْأَل وأبْرَأَلّ
Fine feathers on a cock's neck. بُرَائِل وبُرَائِلَى
The herbage of the land. بُرَائِل الأرض
Cock. أبو بُرَائِل
Pipe. Aqueduct. Sewer. ✻ بَرْبَخ ج بَرَابِخ
Kind of spinage. Blite. ✻ بَرْبُوز
To mumble, to mutter. ✧ بَرْبَس
A deep well. بِرْبَاس
Guitar. G بَرْبَط
To deceive a. o. ✧ بَرْبَك بَرْبَكَة على
Deceit, imposition. Romance. ✧ بَرْبُوكَة ج بَرَابِيك
Ancient Egyptian temple. CE بِرْبَة
To cut a. th. ✻ بَرَت i بَرْتًا ه
To be stupefied at. بَرِت a بَرَتًا ه
To be skilful in an art. أَبْرَت
White sugar. بُرْت ومِبْرَت
Orange. Orange-tree. Ts بُرْتُقَان ✧ بُرْدُقَان
Jar. ¤ بَرْتَمَان
Beyrouth. town in Syria. بَيْرُوت
Soft ground. ✻ بَرْث ج بِرَاث وأبْرَاث وبُرُوث
Clutches. claws, paws. ✻ بُرْثُن ج بَرَاثِن
To have good fare, to fare well. ✻ بَرِج a بَرَجًا
To appear. To ascend (stars). o بَرَج
To build a tower. بَرَّج وأَبْرَج
✧ To augur a. th. by the course of the stars. بَرَّج ه
To array herself (woman). تَبَرَّج
Tower. Castle. بُرْج ج بُرُوج وأَبْرَاج وأَبْرِجَة
Signs of the Zodiac. بُرُوج الأفلاك
Able sailor. Liberal (man). بَارِج

To enter upon the cold season. أَبْرَدَ
To weaken a. o. (illness). أَبْرَدَ ه
To send off (a messenger).
He served him up a cooling drink. أَبْرَدَ لَهُ
To take the fresh air. ✧ بَوْرَدَ
To be cooled. To be soothed (pain). تَبَرَّدَ
To show coldness; to act slowly. تَبَارَدَ ✧ To be dull (man).
To find a. th. cold. إِسْتَبْرَدَ ه
Cold. Coldness. Coolness. Sleep. بَرْد
Morning and evening. البَرْدَانِ والأَبْرَدَانِ
Hail. بَرَد
Hail-stone. Indigestion. بَرَدَة
Cooling eye-water, collyrium. بَرُود
Coldness. coolness. بُرُودَة
Coldness, slowness. ✧ بُرُودِيَّة
Streaky cloth garment. بُرْد ج أَبْرَاد وأَبْرُد وبُرُود
A streaky garment. بُرْدَة
Papyrus. Paper-rush. بَرْدِيّ
Barada, river of Damascus. بَرَدَى
Curtain. Ts بُرْدَايَة
Filings. بُرَادَة
Ague, intermittent fever. بُرَدَاء و ✧ بَرْدِيَّة
A porous earthen cooler. بَرَّادَة
Messenger, courier. بَرِيد ج بُرُد
Mailpost. Distance of twelve miles.
Mail-horses. خَيْل البَرِيد
Messenger, courier. بَرِيدِيّ
Cold, cool. Easy (life). Weak (argument). ✧ Dull. Slow. بَارِد
Gunpowder. Ts بَارُود
Nitre. ✧ بَارُود أَبْيَض
Gun, musket. ✧ بَارُودَة ج بَوَارِيد
Easy booty. غَنِيمَة بَارِدَة
Feeling cold. ✧ بَرْدَان
Colder. ✧ Slower. أَبْرَد
Leopard. أَبْرَد م أَبْرَدَة ج أَبَارِد
File. مِبْرَد ج مَبَارِد
Cooling. Refreshment. مُبَرِّد ج مُبَرِّدَات
Cooled. Filed. Ruined with hail. مَبْرُود
Captivity. P بَرْدَج
To polish, to give a gloss to a.th. To civilize a. o. ✧ بَرْدَخَ ه و ه
To be polished, civilized. ✧ تَبَرْدَخَ
Polish. finish of a. th. ✧ بَرْدَاخ
Varnish. Glosser, polisher.
Pitcher, jug. TE بَرْدَاق ج بَرَادِيق

Orange Ts بُرْذُقَان وَبُرْذُقَال
Likewise, too, also. TE بَرْذُو وبَرْذُه
Pack-saddle for asses. Cloth put under a pack-saddle. P بَرْذَعَة وبَرْدَعَة ج بَرَاذِع
Pack-saddle maker. بَرْذَعِيّ وبَرَاذِعِيّ
Hackney. Jade. P بِرْذَوْن ج بَرَاذِين
To appear. To issue. ✱ بَرَزَ o بُرُوزًا
To appear, to show o.'s self to. — وبَرِزَ a بَرَزًا ل
To overcome, to surpass a. o.; to excel. بَرُزَ o بَرَازَةً عَلَى
To publish, to bring out. بَرَّزَ وأَبْرَزَ وإِسْتَبْرَزَ ه
To outrun, to get ahead (horse). بَرَّزَ
To secure the flight (of his rider: horse). بَرَّزَ ه
To excel in science. — في العِلْم
To take the field against. To fight a duel. بَارَزَ مُبَارَزَةً وبِرَازًا ه
To set off. أَبْرَزَ
To bring out a. th. To publish a (book). — ه
To go out for a natural want. تَبَرَّزَ
To raise a contest (champions). تَبَارَزَ
Going out, egress. Appearance in broad daylight. بُرُوز
Human excrement. بَرَاز
Fight. Duel. بِرَاز ومُبَارَزَة
Publication. إِبْرَاز
Large field. بَرَاز
Coming forth. Projecting. بَارِز
Champion; fighter; duellist. مُبَارِز
✧ Frame. P بِرْوَاز ج بَرَاوِيز
To put a frame to. ✧ بَرْوَزَ
To be framed (picture). ✧ تَبَرْوَزَ
Pure gold. G إِبْرِيز وذَهَب إِبْرِيزِيّ
Trumpeter. TE بُورُزُون
Interstice. Isthmus. ✱ بَرْزَخ ج بَرَازِخ
Lively, full-grown youth. ✱ بُرْزُع وبُرْزُوع وبِرْزَاع
To act harshly towards (a debtor). ✱ بَرَسَ a بَرْسًا ه
Lock of cotton. بِرْس
A kind of dates. بِرْسِيَان
To suffer from pleurisy. ✱ بُرْسِمَ
Pleurisy. P بِرْسَام
Pleuritic. مُبَرْسَم
Silk. P إِبْرِيسَم
Clover. Trefoil. □ بَرْسِيم

Squanderer. بَرَّاض ومُبَرِّض
To hire (a beast) to. ✱ بَرْطَس ة
To be a broker, a middle man. ✱ بَرْطَش
Auctioneer. مُبَرْطِش
Threshold (of a door), window-sill. ✧ بُرْطَاش ج بَرَاطِيش
To be restless, to fret about. ✧ بَرْطَم بَرْطَمَة
To bribe a. o. ✱ بَرْطَل بَرْطَلَة ة
To be corrupted by presents. تَبَرْطَل
Present, bribe. بِرْطِيل ج بَرَاطِيل
Oblong stone.
To be dark, obscure (night). ✱ بَرْظَم
To anger a. o. — ة
To become swollen with anger. — وتَبَرْظَم وابْرَنْظَم
Large-lipped. بِرْظَام وبُرَاظِم
Elephant's trunk. ✧ بَرْظُوم
To ascend (a mountain). ✱ بَرَعَ ٥ بُرُوعًا ه
He excelled his companion. بَرَعَ صَاحِبَهُ
To be accomplished in every excellence. بَرِعَ a وبَرُعَ ٥ وبَرُعَ a بَرَاعًا
To give a. th. as a free gift. تَبَرَّعَ ب
He has done so gratuitously, spontaneously. فَعَلَ كَذَا مُتَبَرِّعًا او تَبَرُّعًا
Excellency ; merit, perfection. بَرَاعَة
Free gift. alms. تَبَرُّع ج تَبَرُّعَات
Excellent. distinguished. Beautiful. بَارِع
Giving freely. مُتَبَرِّع
To bud (plant). ✱ بَرْعَم وتَبَرْعَم
بُرْعُم وبُرْعُمَة ج بَرَاعِم ، وبُرْعُوم وبُرْعُومَة ج
Calyx, flower-cup. Unblown flower-bud. بَرَاعِيم
To be full of fleas. ✱ بَرْغَث
Flea. ✧ Silver coin, (equal to one piastre). بُرْغُوث ج بَرَاغِيث
Shrimp, prawn. ◻ بُرْغُوث البَحْر
✱ بُرْغُز وبُرْغُز وبُرْغُوز وبِرْغَاز ج بَرَاغِز
Calf. وبَرَاغِيز
Gnat. A gnat ✱ بَرْغَش ، بَرْغَشَة
Country, villages little remote from water. ✱ بِرْغِيل ج بَرَاغِيل
Crushed wheat. Pearl-wheat. ✧ بُرْغُل
Screw. Gimlet. ✧ بُرْغِي ج بَرَاغِي
Purple, scarlet. G بِرْفِير ج بَرَافِير
To lighten (sky). To flash (lightning). To ascend (star). ✱ بَرَقَ ٥ بَرْقًا وبُرُوقًا وبَرَقَانًا

To be variegated. ✱ بَرِش a بَرَشًا وابْرَشَّ
speckled.
To pare (cheese). ✧ بَرَش ٥ بَرْشًا (for بَشَر)
Opium-paste for smoking. بَرْش
Datura stramonium, thorn-apple.
Motley. Spot on the skin. بَرَش وبُرْشَة
Partly coloured, spotted, dappled. بَرِيش وأَبْرَش م بَرْشَاء ج بُرْش
Parish. Diocese. G أَبْرَشِيَّة
Rasp (for cheese). Brush. ✧ مِبْرَشَة
Soft-boiled (egg). Ps بِرِشْت (for نِيمْبِرِشْت)
To carve (meat). ✱ بَرْشَق ه
To lash a. o. with. — ة بِ
To feel and show grief ✧ To brush. ✱ بَرْشَم بَرْشَمَة وبِرْشَامًا
Sharp-sighted. بُرَاشِم وبُرَاشِن
✧ Brush. ✧ بُرْشِيمَة
Host, wafer. ✧ بُرْشَان
To make wafers, hosts. ✧ بَرْشَن
To be leprous. ✱ بَرِص a بَرَصًا
To shave (the head). بَرَّص ه
To beget a leprous child. أَبْرَص
To strike a. o. with leprosy (God). أَبْرَص ة
Sandy. barren ground. بُرْصَة ج بِرَاص
Leprosy. بَرَص
A leper, leprous. أَبْرَص م بَرْصَاء ج بُرْص
✧ Albino ; freckled.
سَامّ أَبْرَص ج سَوَامّ أَبْرَص ✧ وأَبُو بُرَيْص ج
Gecko. أَبَارِص
The moon. الأَبْرَص
Land cropped by cattle. أَرْض بَرْصَاء
Gleaming. بَرِيص
To gush out in a small stream. ✱ بَرَض ٥ بَرْضًا وابْتَرَض
To give a part of. — ٥ مِن
To send forth its first sprouts (plant). — ٥ بُرُوضًا
To produce the first shoots of plants (soil). بَرَّض وابْرَض
To take little of a thing. to take little by little. To suck in. تَبَرَّض
بَرْض وبَرَاض ج بِرَاض وبُرُوض وأَبْرَاض
Small quantity.
Abundant water. مَاء بَرْض
Barren soil. بُرْضَة
First shoot of a plant. بَارِض ومُبَارِض

To glitter, to gleam. — برقا وبريقا
To attire herself (woman). — برقا ، وبرّق وأبرق
To be astounded, dazzled. برِق a برَقًا
To undertake a long journey. برّق
To glare at a. o. برّق ة
To send forth lightning (cloud). أبرق
To threaten. To be thunderstruck. To walk in the direction of lightning.
To be illumined by lightning (place). إستبرق
Lightning. Brightness. برق ج بروق
Light.
✧ Lumbago. برقة
Dread, fright. Ram, sheep. برق
Hard ground. بُرقة ج بُرَق
Lightning. Brightness. Brilliancy. بريق ج برائق
Sending forth lightning (cloud). Bright. بارق م بارقة
Wearing a mixture of white and black. أبرق م برقاء
Hard soil. أبرق ج أبارق
Borak (a fantastical horse mentioned in the Coran). بُراق
Cowardly (man). برُوق
Daybreak. مَبرَق ج مبارق ومباريق
Silk garment embroidered with gold. إستبرق
Ewer. Water-jug. ✧ Kettle. P إبريق ✧ بريق ج أباريق
Asphodel (plant). برَوق
Borax. Nitre. Ps بورق
Flag, banner. Ts بيرق ج بيارق
Flag-bearer. Ts بيرقدار
Vine-leaves stuffed. Ts يبرق
To take flight. ✻ برقش
To paint in various colours. برقش ه
To speak confusedly. – في الكلام
To paint (her face: woman). تبرقش
To be variegated (land).
To cheer up (man). إبرنقش
Motley. Confusion, disorder. برقشة
Chaffinch (bird). برقش
Finch. Fickle, unsteady. أبو براقش
To walk at a short and quick pace. To depart whilst looking back. To squat by parting the knees. ✻ برقط
To scatter a. th. برقط ه

To speak at random. – الكلام
To fall on the back (man). تبرقط
To feed on various foods (camel).
To veil the face of a. o. with. ✻ برقع ة ب
To veil o.'s face with. تبرقع ب
Veil. برقع ج براقع
Apricot, yellow plum. P برقوق
To lie. ✻ برقل
Balista. ✧ Deadly snake, aspic. برقيل
To kneel (camel). ✧ To sit, to lie down. ✻ برك o بروكا وتبراكا ، وبرّك واستبرك
To stand firm, to dwell in. برك ب
To sit upon. – على
To make kneel down: to bend the knees. برّك
✧ To congratulate a. o. برّك ل
To bless, to ask God's blessing on. برّك على او في
To bless, to invoke benediction upon. بارك ة ول او في او على
To compel (a camel) to kneel. أبرك ة
To bode well of. تبرّك ب
To be blessed by. To delight in.
To be exalted. تبارك
May God be blessed and exalted! تبارك الله وتعالى
To augure good from. – ب
To apply o.'s self to. إبترك في
To attack a. o. or a. th. – ة وفي وعلى
To bode well of. إستبرك ب
Upper part of the chest. برك ج بروك
Herd of camels kneeling.
Blessing. Abundance. بركة ج بركات
Pool. Tank, pond, puddle. بِركة ج بِرك
Way of kneeling (of camels). بِركة
Price for grinding, miller's fee. بُركة ج بُرك وأبراك وبُركان
Cowardly: slothful. باروك
Hedgehog. بَرُوكة
Happy. Fresh dates with cream. بريك
Miller. برّاك
Happier. Bolder. إبرك
Kneeling-place for camels. مبرك
Blessed. مبارك
Abundant, prosperous (crops). ✧ مبروك
P بركار و✧ بيكار ◻ برجل وبرجار
Compasses.
To rise on his legs (horse). To fall on the knees (camel). ✻ بركم بركمة

Burnoose.
To wrap o.'s self in a burnoose. بَرْنَس
A small earthenware vessel. Dates of good quality. * بَرْنِيَّة ج بَرَانِيّ
Hat. Is بُرْنَيْطَة ج بَرَانِيط
Bonnet. — النِّسَاء
(*Indecl.*) People, men. S بَرْنَسَاء بَرْنَاسَاء بَرَاسَاء
To be convalescent. * بَرِهَ a بَرَهًا بَرَهَانًا
To prove a. th.; to afford arguments. To overcome a. o. by feats of dexterity. — أَبْرَهَ ه و ه
Space of time. بُرْهَة وبَرْهَة ج بُرَه وبُرْهَات
Bulk, freshness. Bulky, fresh (woman). * بَرَهْرَهَة
To look steadfastly at. * بَرْهَمَ إلى
Brahmin. * بَرْهَمِن ج بَرَاهِمَة
To prove a. th., to demonstrate a. th. * بَرْهَنَ ه
To argue against a. o. بَرْهَنَ على
To be proved. تَبَرْهَنَ
Argument. Proof. بُرْهَان ج بَرَاهِين
To put a ring in (a camel's) nostril; to smooth, to fashion a. th. * بَرَا o بَرْوًا وبَرَاء وأَبْرَى ه
Brass-ring in a camel's nostril. Ring, ringlet used as an ornament by women. بُرَة ج بُرًى وبُرَات وبُرِين
Rubbish; residue. ✧ بَرْوَة
To dress, to trim (wood). To make (an arrow). To cut (a pen). To exhaust a.o. (journey). To wear out. * بَرَى i بَرْيًا ه
To imitate a. o. To vie with a. o. in. بَارَى ه ه
To be covered with dust. أَبْرَى
To oppose a. o.: to venture upon, to attempt a. th. تَبَرَّى ل
To compete for a prize, an office. تَبَارَى
To be cut, to be smoothed. إِنْبَرَى
To offer o.'s services for. To oppose a. o. إِنْبَرَى ل
To trim, to cut a. th. إِبْتَرَى ه
Earth, dust. بَرًى
Cutting of a pen. a reed. بِرْيَة
Splinter, chip. Rubbish. بُرَايَة وبُرَاء
Dandruff. إِبْرِيَة وتَبْرِيَة

To fall on the buttocks. تَبَرْكَمَ
Volcano. I بُرْكَان ج بَرَاكِين
To twist, to plait, to turn round. a. th. To manage a. th. well. * بَرَمَ o بَرْمًا وبَرَّمَ , وأَبْرَمَ ه
✧ To ramble. to prowl about. o بَرَمَ
To be annoyed, weary; to feel pain or sorrow at. بَرِمَ a بَرَمًا وتَبَرَّمَ ب
To strengthen a. th. أَبْرَمَ ه
To manage well a. th.
To annoy, to weary a. o. أَبْرَمَ ه
He caught him in words. — عليهِ في الكلام
To be strengthened, well managed. To be twisted, woven. إِنْبَرَمَ
Weariness. Fruit of a kind of acacia *called* عِضَاه. بَرَم
Sealing of a contract. إِبْرَام
A stone-pot. بُرْمَة ج بُرَم وبِرَام
✧ Twist of sweetmeats.
Turn. round, circuit. ✧ بَرْمَة
Spoke of a wheel.
Weaver; rope-weaver. بَرَّام
String. Twisted cord. Vestment made of silk and linen. Mixed flock of calves and goats. Mixed army of Arabs and Persians. بَرِيم وبِرَام
Gimlet, drill. Cork-screw. Worm-screw (for extracting shots). بَرِيمَة ✧ وبَرِّيمَة
Confirmed (contract, peace). Twisted (thread). مُبْرَم
Ineluctable fate, inevitable doom. قَضَاء مُبْرَم
Spindle. مِبْرَم ج مَبَارِم
Twisted, woven. Wound, rounded. مَبْرُوم وبَرِيم
Bodkin. Feast at the close of Ramadan, *Bairam*. ✧ بَيْرَم
Eve (of a feast), vigil. G بَرَامُون وبَارَامُون
Eighth month of the Coptic year: April. Cв بَرْمُودَة
Certain sweetmeat. Ts بُرْمَا
Barmecide. بَرْمَكِيّ ج بَرَامِكَة
Cask. Barrel. * بِرْمِيل و✧ بَرْمِيل ج بَرَامِيل
Seventh month of the Coptic year: March. Cв بَرْمَهَات
Lace, crape. Ts بُرُنْجُك
Balance-sheet. Budget. P بَرْنَامَج
Mantle. * بُرْنُس ج بَرَانِس

Arrow maker. بَرَّاء
Drawing-knife. Pen-knife. بَرَّاءَة ومِبْرَاة
Cut (reed, pen). مَبْرِيّ وبَرِيّ
To ravish, to take away a. o. or a. th. ✱ بَزَّ o بَزًّا وبِزِّيزَى , إِبْتَزَّ ه وه
To get the better of, to overcome a. o. To rob, to plunder a. o. To withhold a. o. — ه
To strip a. o. of (his clothes). إِبْتَزَّ ه
Breast, nipple, teat. Mouth-piece (of a pipe). ✧ بَزّ ج بِزَاز وأَبْزَاز
Cloth, linen. بَزّ ج بُزُوز
Weapons, arms. — وبِزَّة وبَزَز وبِزِّيزَى
Shape, figure. بِزَّة
Cloth-merchant. بَزَّاز
Cloth-business, linen-trade. بِزَازَة
To walk quickly. ✱ بَزْبَزَ
To constrain a. o. To perform (a work) skillfully. — ه وه
Strong and faint-hearted. Well-tempered (man). بُزَابِز
Walking quickly. بَزْبَاز
To boast of. ✱ بَزَجَ o بَزْجًا , وبَازَجَ في
To incite a. o. against. — ه على
To embellish a. th., to adorn. بَزَّجَ ه
To vie with a. o. in merits. تَبَازَجَ
To have a hollow back and a prominent chest. ✱ بَزِخَ a بَزَخًا وانْبَزَخَ
To strike a. o. or a. th. with (a stick). بَزَخَ ه وه ب
To submit to. بَزَخَ ل
To assume the manners of a hollow-backed man. تَبَازَخَ
To retire from (business). تَبَازَخَ عن
Having a hollow back and a prominent chest. أَبْزَخُ م بَزْخَاء
To sow (seeds). ✱ بَزَرَ i بَزْرًا ه
To strew (seed or grain) To amplify (a subject). — ه
To season the potful. بَزَرَ القِدْرَ
✧ To seed (plant). To lay eggs (silk-moth, locust). بَزَّرَ
To season (food) with spices. بَزَّرَ ه
Seeds. ✧ Silkworms' eggs. بِزْر ج بُزُور
Spices, seasoning. — ج أَبْزَار جمع أَبَازِير
A seed. بِزْرَة
Plant or dry fruit full of seeds. ✧ بِزْرَايَة
Retail seedsman. Seedsman بَزَّار
✧ Dealer in silkworms' eggs.
Beetle, mallet of dyers. بَيْزَر ومِبْزَر
✧ Full of seeds (plant). مُبَزِّر
Bazaar, bargain. Ps بَازَار ج بَازَارَات
Petty trader. Ps بَازَرْكَان
To be gracious, well educated. ✱ بَزُعَ o بَزَاعَة
To look gracious. To be momentous; tremendous (evil). تَبَزَّعَ
Gracious, candid. بَزِيع وبُزَّاع
Unbecoming (young man). بُزَّاع
To rise (sun). To scarify (cupper). To grow (tooth). ✱ بَزَغَ o بَزْغًا وبُزُوغًا
To shed (blood). — ه
To scarify (a beast : farrier). بَزَّغَ ه
To peep forth (*v. g.* spring). إِنْبَزَغَ
Star. بَازِغَة ج بَوَازِغ
Sunrise. بُزُوغ
Lancet. مِبْزَغ
To spit. To reject. a. th. ✱ بَزَقَ o بَزْقًا ه
Spittle, saliva. بُزَاق
Snail. Slug. ✧ بَزَّاقَة
Spittoon. ✧ مِبْزَقَة ج مَبَازِق
To cleave, to split a. th. ✧ To puncture (a dropsical man). ✱ بَزَلَ o بَزْلًا وبَزَّلَ
To cut its first teeth (camel). بَزَلَ بُزُولًا
To broach (a cask of) wine. — الخَمْرَ
To clarify, to filter (a liquid). — الشَّرَابَ
To be sound, true (opinion). — الرَّأْيُ بَزَالَةً
To be broached. To be split. To ooze (liquid). تَبَزَّلَ وانْبَزَلَ
To split, to tap a. th. إِبْتَزَلَ ه
To pierce, to split; to filter. اِسْتَبْزَلَ ه
Drill used to broach casks. بَزَّال
Hole made in a wine-cask. بُزَال
Cutting its first teeth (animal). بَازِل ج بَوَازِل وبُزَّل وبُزُل
Tooth growing. Experienced man. بَازِل
Great misfortune. بَزْلَاء
Drill. Water-filter, strainer. Bung-hole. مِبْزَل ومِبْزَلَة
To bite a. th. ✧ To speak. To utter a word. ✱ بَزَمَ i بَزْمًا على
To bear (a burden). — ب
To strip a. o. of. — ه وه
A misfortune befell him. بَزَمَتْهُ البَازِمَة
✧ A single word. بَزْمَة
Leaf rolled up to be used as a band. Necklace. بَزِيم

a frowning look.
To approach maturity (dates). بَسَّرَ
To do out of time, unsea- ـ وأَبْسَرَ ه sonably. To make wine of (dates).
To become cold (day). تَبَسَّرَ
To do a. th. unsea- تَبَسَّرَ وابْتَسَرَ ه sonably. To be benumbed (foot).
Frowning (face). بَسِر وباسِر
Fresh (fruit). بُسْر ج بِسَار
Dates beginning to ripen. ـ النَّخْل
Lion. بَسُور
Piles, hemorrhoids. بَاسُور ج بَوَاسِير
Hemorrhoidal flux. سَيَلَان بَاسُورِيّ
Who suffers from hemorrhoids. مَبْسُور
To spread a. th. ✱ بَسَطَ o بَسْطًا ه
To widen ; to dilate. To stretch (the (arm). To draw (a sword).
To enliven, to cheer up. ـ ه
To prefer a. o. to. ـ ه عَلَى
To be simple. To be بَسُطَ o بَسَاطَة frank, open (man).
To unfold (a mat). To spread ه بَسَّطَ (clothes, a carpet, etc.).
To receive a. o. with a smiling بَاسَطَ ه face, to be at ease with.
To be spread, unfold تَبَسَّطَ وانْبَسَطَ (carpet). To grow longer (day). To be at ease.
To stretch o.'s self To enter- إِنْبَسَطَ tain o.'s self. To brighten up.
To stretch (the arms) إِبْتَسَطَ ه in lying along.
Open hand. يَد بَسْط وبُسُط
Fine-bodied. بَسْط م بَسْطَة
Extent. Capacity. بَسْطَة
✧ A piece of cloth.
▫ Landing-place at a staircase.
Extended ground. بَسَاط وبَسِيط
Very large carpet. بِسَاط ج بُسُط
Area, the terrestrial بَسِيطَة ج بَسَائِط surface. Earth.
Elements. Constituents of البَسَائِط a body. Simples, medicinal plants.
Simplicity ; ingenuousness, ✧ بَسَاطَة openness.
Joy, cheerfulness, enter- إِنْبِسَاط tainment.
Extending, Embracing. بَاسِط
Simple, not compound. بَسِيط ج بُسَطَاء

Buckle, clasp, lock. إِبْزِيم ج أَبَازِيم P
To become proud. ✱ بَزْمَخَ
Copper-basin. أَبْزَن ج أَبَازِن P
To be kind. ✱ بَزَا o بَزْوًا
To subdue, to overcome ـ ه وأَبْزَى بِ a. o.
To equal ; to raise o.'s self ـ عَلَى above a. o.
To be hollow-backed ـ o وبَزِيَ a بَزًا and broad-breasted.
Hollow-backed and أَبْزَى م بَزْوَاء broad-breasted.
Haughtiness. بَزَاء
Equivalent, equal. بَزْو
Foster-brother. بَزِيّ
Kind of hawk or falcon. بَازٍ ج بُوَاز وبِيزَان
To drive on (an ✱ بَسَّ o بَسًّا , وأَبَسَّ animal) gently.
To prepare a dish made of ـ بَسِيسَة (flour and oil).
To send (a spy) after a. o. ـ ه لِ
To drive a. o. away from. ـ ه عن
To crumble a. th. ـ ه
To send off a. th. in. ـ ه في
To collect a. th. To call (cattle), أَبَسَّ بِ to gather it.
Cat. بَسّ بَسَّة ج بِسَاس
Kitten. ✧ بُسَيْن م بُسَيْنَة
Enough, it is enough. ✧ بَسّ
Small quantity of food. بَسِيس
Flour mixed with butter or oil. بَسِيسَة
She-camel which does not بَسُوس ج بُسُس yield to be milked, till she is called.
To say (بَسّ) enough. ✱ بَسْبَسَ
To flow (water). تَبَسْبَسَ
Desert, waste. بَسْبَس ج بَسَابِس
Trifles, idle words. تُرَّهَات البَسَابِس
Mace, spice. بَسْبَاسَة
To be fami- ✱ بَسَأَ a وبَسِئَ بُسُوءًا وبَسْأً بِ liar, friendly with. To cheer a. o. To become accustomed to. To make little of a. th
Garden. Fruit-garden. بُسْتَان ج بَسَاتِين P
Gardener. بُسْتَانِيّ و✧ بُسْتَنْجِي
Spade (at cards). ✧ بِسْتُونِي
To anticipate, ✱ بَسَرَ o بَسْرًا ه to accelerate a. th. To make a. th. out of season.
To become cross ; to wear ـ بُسُورًا

To smile. بَسَمَ i بَسْمًا ✱
To have a smiling air. تَبَسَّمَ وَٱبْتَسَمَ
Smile. تَبَسُّم وٱبْتِسَام
Smiling. بَاسِم ومُبْتَسِم وبَسَّام ومِبْسَام
Mouth. ◻ Mouth-piece. مَبْسِم ج مَبَاسِم
To say : in the name of God. To make the sign of the cross. بَسْمَلَ بَسْمَلَة ✱
Invocation of the name of God. أَلْبَسْمَلَة
To be fine. gracious. بَسُنَ — أَبْسَن ✱
Plough-share. Workmen's tools. بَاسِنَة ج بَوَاسِن
To be affable, cheerful. To have a cheerful. smiling face. بَشَّ a بَشًّا وبَشَاشَة ✱
To smile at a. o. To be kind, gentle to. To undertake a. th. joyfully. بَشَّ لِ
To rejoice at. بَشَّ بِ
To become covered with plants (land). أَبَشَّ
Kindness, meekness. بَشَاشَة
Kind. Smiling. بَشّ وبَاشّ وبَشُوش وبَشَّاش
Face. cheerful countenance. بَشِيش
To show regard, to welcome a. o. تَبَشْبَشَ بِ ✱
Ward-robe, closet for clothes. Case, coffer. Ts بُشْخَتَة
To peel. To take off the bark. To grate. a. th. To devour the crops (locusts). بَشَرَ o بَشْرًا ه ✱
To rejoice at a. th. بَشِرَ a وبَشَرَ i بِ
To bring good news to a. o. ✧ To preach. بَشَّرَ وأَبْشَرَ وٱسْتَبْشَرَ ه بِ
To be busied about a. th. ; to practice (an art). To set to work. بَاشَرَ ه او بِ
To know (a woman). — ه
To grow its plants (soil). أَبْشَرَ
To rejoice at a. th. — بِ
To enliven a. o.'s face (news). — ه
To communicate good news one to another. تَبَاشَرَ بِ
To bark, to peel a. th. أَبْشَرَ وٱبْتَشَرَ ه
To rejoice in hearing (good news). To rejoice at. ✧ To draw a good omen from. إِسْتَبْشَرَ بِ
Joyful countenance. بِشْر
Good news. بُشْر

✧ Simple, guileless.
Open-handed. generous. بَسِيط ٱلْيَدَيْن ج بُسُط
Dilated. Stretched. مَبْسُوط
✧ Well off : comfortable, in good health.
Post-office. mail. Is بُوسْطَة وبُوسْتَة
To spit. بَسَقَ o بَسْقًا ✱
To be lofty, tall (tree). بَسَقَ o بُسُوقًا
To obtain superiority over. — ه وعَلَى
To be clever in. — فِي
To put off a. o. or a. th. : to protract a. th. بَسَّقَ ه وه
Spittle. بُسَاق
Tall, lofty (tree). Goodly yellow fruit. Noble-minded. بَاسِق
A white cloud. Misfortune. Tree with lofty branches. بَاسِقَة ج بَوَاسِق
Whose milk flows prematurely (female). بَسُوق
To be gallant, brave. بَسُلَ o بَسَالَة ✱
To become sour and strong (wine). To be weakened (vinegar). To stink (meat). بَسَلَ o بَسْلًا وبُسُولًا
To assume a severe look. بَسَلَ o بُسُولًا
To anathematize a. o. بَسَلَ o بَسْلًا ه
To prohibit a. th., to forbid. To anathematize a. o. or a. th. أَبْسَلَ ه وه
To offer, to give a. th. as a pledge to a. o. — ه ه
He devoted himself to death, he laid down his life. — وٱبْتَسَلَ نَفْسَهُ لِلْمَوْت
To assume a severe mien. a frightful appearance. تَبَسَّلَ
To face danger. To rush to certain death (in a battle). إِسْتَبْسَلَ
Permitted or forbidden things. بَسْل
Cross-looking. بَسْل وبَسِيل
Woe to him ! بَسْلًا لَهُ
Prohibition ; anathema. بُسْل وإِبْسَال
Courage, gallantry, heroism بَسَالَة
Brave, gallant, warrior, hero. strong. بَاسِل ج بُسْل وبُسَلَاء
Lion. — ج بَوَاسِل
Gallant, courageous. Lion. بَسُول
Forbidden. بَسِيل
Wine remaining in a bottle. —
The basilic vein (in the arm). G بَاسِلِيق
✧ Peas. Is ✧ بِسِلَّة وبِزِلَّة

To lie. الكَذِبَ —
To stitch (clothes). ه —
He did amiss, he botched his work. في عَمَلِهِ —
To lie. إِبْتَشَكَ
To extemporize a. th. ه —
Liar. بَشَّاك
Towel. بَشْكِير ج بَشَاكِير Pe
Silver coin worth 5 piastres. بِشْلِك Ts
To trouble a. o.; to entangle (a business). ✧ بَشْلَل ه وه
To be entangled in. ✧ تَبَشْلَل ب او في
Obstruction, perplexity, intricacy. ✧ بَشْلَلَة وتَبَشْلُل
To have an indigestion from. To feel disgust at. ✱ بَشِم a بَشَمًا من
To rivet, to clinch (a nail). ✧ بَشَّم ه
To cause an indigestion to a.o. أَبْشَم ه
Indigestion. Disgust. بَشَم
Balsam of Mecca. بَشَام
Kind of millet. ✱ بِشْنَة
Cash, ready money. بَشِين Te
Ninth month of the Coptic year: May. بَشَنْس Ce
A kind of water-lily: lotus. ✧ بَشْنِين
To shine, to gleam. To ooze (water). ✱ بَصَّ i بَصِيصًا وبَصًّا
To give a. th. بَصَّ ب
To open the eyes (whelp). To show first signs of verdure (soil), its first leaves (tree). بَصَّص
✧ Burning coal, spark. بَصَّة
Eye. ✧ Watch. Spy. بَصَاصَة
Brightness, glaring light. Bright, shining. بَصِيص
To wag the tail (dog). To open the eyes (whelp). ▫ To court, to search. ✱ بَصْبَص بَصْبَصَة
To wag the tail. تَبَصْبَص
To caress, to pat. ه —
Apple of the eye. ✧ بَصْبُوص
To see a. th. To understand a.th. ✱ بَصُر o وبَصِر a بَصَرًا وبَصَارَةً ب
To make a.o. understand a. th.; to enlighten, to initiate. بَصَّر ه ه
To open the eyes (whelp). بَصَّر
✧ To divine, to soothsay. ل —
To see a. th. from afar. باصَر ه
To observe, to see, أَبْصَر ه وب

Good news. ✧ Gospel. بُشْرَى
Fine-looking appearance. بَشَارَة
Good news. ✧ Gospel. Lady-day. بِشَارَة ج بِشَارَات وبَشَائِر
Present received by a messenger of good news. بُشَارَة
Man, mankind. men. بَشَر
Mankind. البَشَر
Human. بَشَرِيّ
Epidermis. Exterior shape (human). بَشَرَة ج بَشَر
✧ Butterfly. بَشَّارَة
Good tidings. Preaching of the Gospel. تَبْشِير
✧ The Angelus. التَّبْشِير
Day-break. Beginning of a thing. تَبَاشِير
Messenger. ✧ Evangelist. بَشِير ج بُشَرَاء
Good news. البَشَائِر
The musical instruments have conveyed good tidings. دُقَّت البَشَائِر
Fine features. بَشَائِر الوَجْه
First gleam of dawnlight. بَشَائِر الصُّبْح
Announcer of good news. ✧ Preacher. مُبَشِّر
To be distasteful (food). To be ugly, deformed. To have a foul breath (person). ✱ بَشِع a بَشَعًا وبَشَاعَة
He dashed and smashed it. بَشَعَ بِهِ
To give a bad taste to. To disfigure a. o. or a. th. To blacken a. o.'s character. to disparage. ✧ بَشَّع ه وه
To commit abominable (deeds). ✧ تَبَشَّع في
To find (a place) to be uncomfortable. إِبْتَشَع ه
To find a. th. ugly. frightful. إِسْتَبْشَع ه
Bad taste (of a dish). Deformity. بَشَاعَة
Unpalatable (dish). Having a foul breath (person). بَشِع وبَشِيع
Ugly, deformed, hideous, unsightly. — الخَلْق أَوِ المَنْظَر
Unpleasing word. كَلَام بَشِع
To strike a. o. with. To tear off (clothes). ✱ بَشَق i وبَشِق a بَشْقًا ه ب
Entangled in an affair, perplexed. بَشِق
Buzzard, sparrow-hawk. بَاشِق ج بَوَاشِق
Different, other. بَشْقَه Ts
To walk quickly. ✱ بَشَك o i بَشْكًا

to perceive a. th. ; to make a. o. to understand.
To consider, to observe a. th. تبصّر ه
To reflect on a. th. — في
To observe o. a. تباصر
To observe attentively. إستبصر ه
To investigate a hidden thing.
To reflect on a. th. — في
Sight. Perspicacity. بَصَر ج أبصار
As far as the eye can reach. على مَدَى البَصَر
Soft and whitish stone. بَصِر وبَصْر
Clay mixed with pebbles. بَصْرَة ج بِصَار
Basrah (town in Iraq). البَصْرَة
Bosra (town in Syria). بُصْرَى
Acuteness, perspicacity. بَصَارَة
Intelligence, clear-sight. Caution. Proof. بَصِيرَة ج بَصَائِر
Seeing. باصِر م باصِرَة
Eye. باصِرَة ج بَوَاصِر
Any sight-giving, or demonstrative thing. تَبْصِرَة
Consideration, reflection. تَبَصُّر
More clear-sighted. ◻ Perhaps. أبْصَر
Perspicacious. Intelligent. Piercing (eye, look). بَصِير ج بُصَرَاء
Evident proof. مَبْصَر ومَبْصَرَة
Diviner. Sorcerer. ✧ مُبَصِّر
Seeing. Understanding. مُبْصِر
To flow. To ooze (water). ✱ بَصَع a بَصْعًا
To gather, to pick up a. th. — ه
Perspiration. بَصِيع ج بُصْع
Stupid. أبْصَع م بَصْعَاء
To spit. ✱ بَصَق o بَصْقًا
Saliva, spittle. بُصَاق
To strip a. o. of his clothes ; a (tree) of its bark. ✱ بَصَّل — بَصَّل وتبصّل ه وه
To weary a.o. by questions. تبصّل ه
Onion : an onion, a bulb. بَصَل , بَصَلَة
Shallot. بَصَل صَغِير
Squill. Scallion. بَصَل أخْضَر
Wild onion. بَصَل الفَأر و✧ بُصَيْلَة
Distance between the ring and the little finger. ✱ بُصْم
Compact (clothes). Thick (man). ذو بُصْم
To print cloth. To stamp. ✧ بَصَم o بَصْمًا
Print made on cloth. Stamp. Ts بَصْمَة
To take off the property of ; to strip a debtor of his possess- ✱ بَصَا o بَصْوًا

ion.
Embers. بَصْوَة و✧ بَصَّة
To be thin-skinned. ✱ بَضّ a i بَضَاضَة وبُضُوضَة
To ooze, to leak. — i بَضًّا وبُضُوضًا وبَضِيضًا
To flow scantily (water) o —
to ooze out, to ooze from ; to weep (eye).
To give scantily to a. o. — لهُ وأبَضّ
To pinch (the chords of a lyre). — بَضِيضًا وبَضًّا ه
To collect debts from a. o. little by little. تبضّض حَقَّهُ مِن
Thin-skinned. بَضّ وباض
Sour milk. بَضّ وبَضَّة
Small quantity of water. بَضَض وبُضَاضَة وبَضِيضَة
Uselessness of a. th. ✱ بَضْر — بَضْرَة
His blood is still unavenged. ذَهَب دَمُهُ بِضْرًا مِضْرًا
To split a. th. ; to lance. To cut. To carve (meat). To elucidate a. th. ✱ بَضَع a بَضْعًا , وبَضَّع ه
To be clear, plain (speech). —
To understand (a speech). — ه بُضُوعًا
To know (a woman). باضَع ه
To explain a. th. to a. o. To deliver goods to. أبْضَع ه ه وعن
✧ To purchase goods. بَضَّع
To carry on business, to practice trade. تبضّع واستبضع ه
To be clear, plain (speech). إبْتَضَع
بَضْعَة وبِضْعَة ج بَضْع وبِضَع وبِضَاع وبَضَعَات
Piece, bit.
Small number, few. بِضْع وبِضْعَة
Portion of the night.
Few days, some days. بِضْعَة أيّام
Dowry. Divorce. بُضْع
Goods, wares. بِضَاعَة ج بَضَائِع
Partner. بَضِيع
Knife, lancet. مِبْضَع ج مَبَاضِع
Merchant, trader. مُسْتَبْضِع
To cut off a. th. ✱ بَضَك i بَضْكًا ه
To run to seed (corn). ✱ بَضَر o بَضْرًا
Soul. Ear of corn. بُضْر
To lance (an abscess). To cut open a. th. ✱ بَطّ o بَطًّا ه
Ducks. A duck. بَطّ . بَطَّة

To render a. o. sprightly, or insolent. To fatigue a. o. أَبْطَر ه
Uselessly. Saucily. بَطَرًا
Sprightliness, insolence. Carelessness. بَطَر
Pert. Hot (horse). بَطِر و ✧ بَطْرَان
To practice farriery ✻ بَيْطَرَ
To shoe (animals). ه —
To be shod (horse). تَبَيْطَر
Veterinary medicine, farriery. بَيْطَرَة
Veterinary surgeon, farrier. بَيْطَار ج بَيَاطِرَة , ومُبَيْطِر ✧ بِيطَار
Shod (horse). مُبَيْطَر
Boisterous, stubborn man. Termagant. Foul-tongued woman. ✻ بِطْرِير
Deck of a ship. Electrical battery. Gun battery. Is بَطَّارِيَّة
Roe. ✧ بَطْرَخ ج بَطَارِخ
Stole. Gs بَطْرَشِيل ج بَطَارِش
G بِطْرِيق ج بَطَارِق وبَطَارِيق وبَطَارِقَة General of a Christian army. Patrician.
Tall (man). بُطَارِق
Patriarch. G بَطْرَك وبَطْرِيَرْك ج بَطَارِكَة
Patriarchate. Dignity of a patriarch. بَطْرِيَرْكِيَّة وبَطْرَكِيَّة
To snatch a.th. To overwhelm a. o. (terror). ✻ بَطَش i o بَطْشًا ب
To assault a. o. — عَلَى
To recover from (fever). — مِن
To seize a. o. forcibly. To begin a struggle with. بَاطَش ه
Strength. Courage, violence. بَطْش
Man in the prime of life. Gallant, vigorous. بَاطِش وبَطَّاش وبَطِيش
Who has lost his lower teeth. ✻ بطم — أَبْطَم
Letter. Billet. Card. Label. GE بِطَاقَة ج بَطَائِق
To be corrupted, to be reduced to nothing. To be of no avail. ✻ بَطَل o بُطْلًا وبُطُولًا وبُطْلَانًا
To relate a. th. jestingly. — بَطَالَةً فِي
To be workless, idle. To cease. بَطَل o بَطَالَةً
To be brave ; to behave as a hero. بَطُل o بَطَالَةً وبُطُولَةً
To annul. to cancel (a deed). To render a. th. worthless, بَطَّل وأَبْطَل ه

Leather-bottle. بَطَّة ج بُطُوط وبِطَاط
✧ Calf of the leg. بَطَّة السَّاق
Drill, dissecting-knife. مِبَطَّة ومِبَطّ ج مَبَاطّ
Potato. Is بَطَاطَا
To dabble. To caw (duck). To have a weak judgment (man). ✻ بَطْبَط
To injure (the head, skin). ه —
To be slow. to walk slowly. ✻ بَطُؤ بُطْأً وبِطَاء , وأَبْطَأ
To detain a. o. with a. th. To procrastinate. بَطَّأ عَلَى فُلَان ب
To be slow in doing a. th. تَبَطَّأ وتَبَاطَأ فِي
To find a. o. to be slow. إِسْتَبْطَأ ه
Slowness, delay. بِطْء وبِطَاء وبُطُوء
Slow, straggle, tardy. بَطِيء ج بِطَاء
Slower, later. أَبْطَأ
Acting slowly. مُتَبَاطِئ
To spread. To flatten a. th. ✻ بَطَح a بَطْحًا ه
To throw a. o. down. ه —
To be seized with malignant fever. بُطِح
To spread out in a valley (torrent). تَبَطَّح واسْتَبْطَح
✧ To undertake a. th. تَبَطَّح ل
To spread (torrent). To tumble down. إِنْبَطَح
بَطْحَاء ج بِطَاح وبَطْحَاوَات , وأَبْطَح ج أَبَاطِح Large bed of a torrent.
Large bed of a torrent. بَطِيحَة ج بَطَائِح
✧ Female butterfly. بَطِيحَة ج بِطَاح وبَطَائِح
A kind of pleurisy. بُطَاح وبُطَاحِيّ
Laying flat on the belly. Depressed, flattened. أَبْطَح ومُنْبَطِح
To lick a. th. ✻ بَطَخ o بَطْخًا
To abound with melons. أَبْطَخ
Stout. بَطِخ وبُطَاخِيّ
Melon. Pumpkin. بِطِّيخ ✧ وبَطِّيخ
Melon. بِطِّيخ أَصْفَر
Water-melon. بِطِّيخ أَحْمَر
Field full of melons, melon-bed. مَبْطَخَة ج مَبَاطِخ
To incise a. th. ✻ بَطَر i o بَطْرًا ه
To be sprightly, merry ; to be bewildered. To be ungodly. بَطِر a بَطَرًا
To contemn a. th. To undervalue (a grace). ه —

Gluttony, surfeit. بِطْنَة
Repletion banishes intelligence (*prov.*). البِطْنَة تُذْهِبُ الفِطْنَة
Strap, girth. بِطَان ج أَبْطِنَة وبُطُن
Thriving (man). عَرِيض البِطَان
Lining of clothes. بِطَانَة الثَّوب ج بَطَائِن
Familiars. Courtiers. — الرَّجُل
Large woollen blanket. ◻ بَطَّانِيَّة ج بَطَاطِين وبَطَّانِيَّات
Interior. Intimate, hidden. The Hidden (God). بَاطِن ج بَوَاطِن
Depressed (ground). بَاطِن ج أَبْطِنَة وبُطْنَان
Sole of the foot. بَاطِن القَدَم
Interiorly. بَاطِنًا وبَاطِنَةً
Big-bellied. Glutton. بَطِن وبَطِين ج بِطَان, ومِبْطَان
Full (bag, purse). كِيس بَطِين
Feeling a pain in the belly. مَبْطُون
Slender and thin-bellied. مُبَطَّن
✧ Felucca, small sailing vessel. مُبَطَّنَة
Jar. ✧ Swamp. ✲ بَطِي — بَاطِيَة ج بَوَاطٍ
To tune (a musical instrument). ✲ بَطَّ o بَطًّا ه
To be fat, corpulent. أَبَطَّ
Harsh-tempered. فَظّ بَظّ
Fat, corpulent. بَظِيظ وفَظِيظ بَظِيظ
To be compact in flesh. ✲ بَظَا o بُظُوًّا
To be uncircumcised. ✲ بَظِر a بَظَرًا
Big-lipped; uncircumcised. أَبْظَر
To pour down a continual (rain · cloud). ✲ بَعَّ o بَعًّا ه
To fall from a cloud (rain). To send forth spring-herbage (land). بَعَّ بَعًّا وبَعَاعًا
Furniture, possession. Water contained in a cloud. بَعَاع
Gurgling. Fluency of speech. ✲ بَعْبَعَة
To tickle. ◻ بَعْبَص
To send, to delegate, to consign a. o. or a. th. to. ✲ بَعَثَ a بَعْثًا ه ه او ب إلى او على
To awake a. o. To raise (the dead). — بَعْثًا وَتَبْعَاثًا ه
To incite a. o. — ه على
To be awake, to wake. بَعِثَ a بَعَثًا
To be sent. To flow. تَبَعَّثَ
To be sent. To be raised (from the dead). To flow (water). To hasten. إِنْبَعَثَ

of no avail. To stop, to break an (habit). To give up. ✧ To stop (work) on a feast day.
To be gallant. To busy o.'s self about trifles. To be in quest of vain things. ✧ To be kept as a holiday (feast). تَبَطَّلَ
Vanity. Falsehood. Trifle, groundlessness بُطْل وبُطْلَان
In mere waste. بُطْلًا
Idleness, stoppage, leisure, rest time. ✧ Holiday; leave of absence. بِطَالَة
Bravery, heroism. بَطَالَة وبُطُولَة
Abolition, abrogation; cancelling, rescission. إِبْطَال
Vanity. Falsehood. Useless. Delusive. بَاطِل ج أَبَاطِيل
Wizard. Devil. — ج بَطَلَة
Vanities, trifles. أَبَاطِيل
Hero, gallant man. بَطَل ج أَبْطَال
Worthless. Workless. Hero. بَطَّال
Rescinding. Trifler. مُبْطِل
Turpentine-tree. Turpentine. Ulcer on the shank. ✲ بُطْم وبُطُم
To be inside. To conceal o.'s self. ✲ بَطَنَ o بُطُونًا وبَطْنًا
To penetrate, to engage in the middle of. — ه
To strike a. o. on the belly. — ه ولهُ
To be surfeited and distended (belly). بَطِن a بَطَنًا
To be big-bellied. بَطُنَ o بَطَانَةً
To have a belly-ache. بُطِنَ بَطْنًا
To choose a. o. as an intimate friend. To line (clothing). To strap (a beast). To conceal a. th. بَطَّنَ وأَبْطَنَ ه وه
To confide a secret to a. o. بَاطَنَ ه
To be lined (clothing). تَبَطَّنَ
To penetrate, to fathom a. th.; to explore a. o.'s designs. — واسْتَبْطَنَ ه
Belly. Interior. بَطْن ج بُطُون وأَبْطُن وبُطْنَان
Under-tribe, smaller than a قَبِيلَة بَطْن ج بُطُون وأَبْطُن
The longest part of a feather. بَطْن ج بُطْنَان
She brought forth but once (woman). وَلَدَتْ بَطْنًا وَاحِدًا

After. بَعْدَ مَا ومن بَعْدِ أن
Immediately after, soon after. بُعَيْد ذلك
Remote. Damned. باعِد ج بعد
Far away, remote. بعيد ج بُعَداء وبُعْد وبُعْدان
Farther. Foreigner. أبْعَد
✧ Far be it from thee! الأبْعَد
Farm, country-house. ◻ أبْعادِيَّة
Remote, distant from. مُتَبَعِّد عن
To dung (cattle). ✱ بَعَر a بَعْرًا
To throw dung at a. o. بَعَر ه ب
To purge. بَعَّر وأبْعَر وتَبَعَّر ه
Dung of hoofed animals. بَعْر وبَعَر
Extreme destitution.
Dung. بَعْرَة ج بَعَرات
Camel. بَعِير ج بُعْران وأبْعِرَة وجج أباعِر
(*m. f.*).
Stand, stable for cattle. مَبْعَر
To palpitate (member cut off). ✱ بَعْرَض — تَبَعْرَض
To scatter (people, goods). ✱ بَعْزَق ه وه
Dispersion, scattering. بَعْزَقَة
Disperser, lavisher, spendthrift. مُبَعْزِق
To be startled. ✱ بَعَص a بَعْصًا
To become emaciated.
To sting a. o. (mosquito). ✱ بَعَضَ a بَعْضًا ه
To be stung by mosquitoes. بُعِض
To share, to divide a. th. into lots, parts. بَعَّض ه
To have many mosquitoes. أبْعَض
To be divided, dissected. تَبَعَّض
Part, share, portion. بَعْض ج أبْعاض
Some, any, certain.
During a certain night, one night. بَعْض الليالي
Between them. بَعْضُهُم بَعْضًا
Each other, one another.
Gnat, mosquito. بَعُوض
Full of mosquitoes. بَعِض ومَبْعُوض
Division, distinction. تَبْعِيض
Partly, in part. بالتَّبْعِيض
Place full of mosquitoes. مَبْعَضَة
To go beyond. ✱ بَعَط a بَعْطًا, وأبْعَط في
To exceed in.
To slaughter (a beast). — ه
To overburden a. o. أبْعَط ه
To soak (the soil: ✱ بَعَق o a بُعاقًا ه
rain). To dig (a well).
✧ To yell, to shout. —
To slaughter (a camel). — بَعْقًا ه

To send a. o. إنْبَعَث ه
Sending. Resurrection. بَعْث
Army. Envoy. بَعْث وبَعَث ج بُعُوث
Easter. S باعُوث ج بَواعِيث
Prayers said on Easter Monday.
Army. بَعِيث ج بُعُث
Mission of a prophet. بَعْثَة ومَبْعَث
Sender, impulsive. Cause. باعِث
Cause. Impulsion. باعِثَة ج بَواعِث
Motive.
Awake, waker, watcher. بَعِث
Sent. Raised, risen. بَعِيث ومَبْعُوث ومُنْبَعِث
To upset (furniture) ✱ بَعْثَر بَعْثَرَة
and to jumble it together. To scatter (things). To turn a. th. upside down.
To rip up. ✱ بَعَج a بَعْجًا ه
✧ To dent (metallic vessels).
To dig (the earth). — وبَعَّج ه
To burst with rain (cloud). تَبَعَّج وانْبَعَج
To be ripped up. ✧ To be dented.
He broke out into words. إنْبَعَج بالكلام
Large valley. باعِجَة ج بَواعِج
Ripped open. بَعِيج وباعِج ومَبْعُوج
To go ✱ بَعُد o بُعْدًا . وبَعِدَ a بَعَدًا عن
away, to be afar off from. To die.
To remove to a distance, بَعَّد وأبْعَد ه وه
to take away. To drive off a. o. or a. th.
To keep a. o. away, off. باعَد مُباعَدَة وبِعادًا ه
To be remote. To send far away. أبْعَد
May God curse him! أبْعَدَهُ الله
To be distant from o. a. تَباعَد
To part from. To quit. — وتَبَعَّد وابْتَعَد عن
To consider a. th. as distant. إسْتَبْعَد ه
remote.
To go away from. — عن
Distance, remoteness. بُعْد وبَعَد وبُعْدَة
Very great distance. بُعْد باعِد
Wariness. بُعْد وبُعْدَة
May he be afar off! بُعْدًا
May he perish!
After, later on. بَعْد وبَعْدًا
He is not come yet. لَمْ يَأْتِ بَعْد
Now after.... أمّا بَعْد ....
Usual beginning of a letter or of a book meaning: After compliments or the invocation of God's name, *I begin.*

Bagdad (town). ✻ بَغْدَاد وبَغْدَاذ
To pretend to be from Bagdad, to assume the manners of the people of Bagdad. To go to Bagdad. ✧ To flaunt. تَبَغْدَد
To drink without quenching its thirst (camel). ✻ بَغَر a بَغْرًا , وبَغِر a بَغَرًا
To rain abundantly. — o النَّوْءُ او السَّمَاءُ بُغُورًا
To be well soaked (soil). بُغِر
Shower. بَغْر وبَغَر
Unquenchable thirst. بَغَر
Who feels an unquenchable thirst. بَغِر وبَغِير ج بَغَارَى وبُغَارَى
Sweepingness of water, rain. بَغْرَة
To kick, to strike a. o. ✻ بَغَز a بَغْزًا ه
To cut.
Swiftness, sprightliness. بَغَز
Lively, sprightly. Libertine. — وباغِز
Channel, strait. The Bosphorus. Ts بُوغَاز ج بَوَاغِيز
To pour down a fine rain (clouds). ✻ بَغَش a بَغْشًا
To be watered by a fine rain (soil). بُغِش
Fine rain. بَغْشَة
To be hated; loathed. ✧ To hate, execrate. ✻ بَغَضَ وبَغُضَ o وبَغِضَ a بَغَاضَة
To render a. o. or a. th. hateful, to cause a. o. to loathe a. th. بَغَّض ه وه إلى
To hate, to detest a. o. or a. th. أَبْغَض ه وه
To show coldness to. تَبَغَّض إلى
To hate one another. تَبَاغَض
Hatred, dislike, disgust. بُغْض وبَغَاضَة
Detestation. بِغْضَة وبَغْضَاء
Hating, loathful. مُبْغِض
Odious, loathsome. بَغِيض ومُبْغَض و✧ مَبْغُوض
More hateful. أَبْغَض
To beget degenerate children through a misalliance. ✻ بَغَل a بَغْلًا , وبَغَّل ه
To be slow, weary. To walk at the pace of a mule. بَغَّل
Mule. بَغْل ج بِغَال وأَبْغَال
✧ Spur, projection.
She-mule. بَغْلَة ج بَغْلَات وبِغَال
Mule-driver, muleteer. بَغَّال
To ✻ بَغَم i o وبَغِم a بُغُومًا وبُغَامًا , وتَبَغَّم

To crack (a water-skin, a vessel). بَعَّق ه
To burst (cloud). تَبَعَّق وانْبَعَق
He burst out into big, high words. — وانْبَعَق وابْتَعَق في الكَلَام
Cloud pouring down an abundant rain. Shriek, vociferation. بُعَاق
To be hard (body). ✻ بَعِك a بَعَكًا
To cut off the extremities of... with. بَعَك o بَعْكًا ه ب
Fool. بَاعِك
Heat. Intenseness of a. th. Meeting-place. بَعْكُوكَة
To marry a. o. ✻ بَعَل o بَعَالَة وبُعُولَة ل
To be astonished, amazed at. بَعِل a بَعَلًا ب
They allied by marriage (tribes). بَاعَل القَوْمُ قَوْمًا
To obey her husband (wife). تَبَعَّل
To become the husband of. إِسْتَبْعَل ل
Consort, husband. Owner. Lord. The god Baal. بَعْل م بَعْلَة ج بُعُول وبِعَال
Unwatered land or plant; or land. plant that is only watered by rain. بَعْل
Balbeck (town). ✻ بَعْلَبَكّ
Idol, wooden statue. ✻ بَعِيم
To commit an offense. ✻ بَعَا o a بَعْوًا , وبَعِيَ i بَعْيًا
To borrow a. th. بَعَا واسْتَبْعَى
Loan. بَعْو
To be stirred (bood). ✻ بَغَّ o بَغًّا
To tread a. th. under foot. ✻ بَغْبَغ ه
Snorting, bellow. بَغْبَغَة
Eager, forward. مُبَغْبِغ
To happen unexpectedly. To surprise. ✻ بَغَت a بَغْتًا
To fall suddenly upon. To break unexpectedly on. — وباغَت ه
To be surprised; to remain speechless, amazed. إِنْبَغَت
Unexpected event. Surprise. بَغْتَة ج بَغَتَات
Unexpectedly. Suddenly, abruptly. بَغْتَةً وعلى بَغْتَة
Surprised: speechless. مَبْغُوت
To be spotted, speckled. ✻ بَغِث a بَغَثًا
Mixture of black and white. بُغْثَة
A lot of people. بَغْثَاء
Rabble. أَبْغَث م بَغْثَاء
Any innoxious bird. بُغَاث ج بِغْثَان

✧ Of no avail, wastefully. بالبُقّ
Old furniture, old wares. بَقَّاق
Loquacious, talkative. بقاق وبقاقة ومِبَقّ
To gurgle (bottle plunged into water). To prattle. To have blisters on the hands. To rise in bubbles (boiling water). ✧ To be swollen, to swell. ✻ بَقْبَق
Bubble. ✧ Blister, bladder on the skin. بَقْبُوقَة
Gurgling. Prattle, gossip. ✧ Blister ; swelling of the hands. بَقْبَقَة
Loquacious, garrulous. بَقْبَاق وبَقْبَاقَة
To mix up (food, talks, business). ✻ بَقَّ o بَقًّا
Bundle (of linen or clothes). بُقْجَة ج بُقَج Ts
Parsley. بَقْدُونِس Ts
To cut open, to split. ✻ بَقَر a بَقْرًا وأَبْقَرَ ه
To take information about. — عن
To be rich, learned. تَبَقَّر
To be cr cked in the middle. إِبْتَقَر
Oxen and cows, the bovine kind. بَقَر
Bulimia, violent hunger. جُوع البَقَر
Untruth. Misfortune. بُقَر وبُقَّارَى
A children's play. بُقَّيْرَى
Cow. Numerous family, people. بَقَرَة ج بَقَرَات
Ox-driver, neat-herd. بَقَّار
A herd of oxen. بَاقِر وبَاقُور وبَيْقُور
Bodice without sleeves بَقِيرَة
Relating to the bull family. بَقَرِي
Leathern shields. بَقَرِيَّات
To settle in a town and leave o.'s tribe in the desert. To go at random. To migrate. To walk in stooping the head. To be corrupted. To die. ✻ بَيْقَر
Box-tree. بَقْس وبَقْش T
To gather and pack (things). ✻ بَقَط o بَقْطًا ه
To farm out (a field) to. — ه ه
To scatter a. th. بَقَّط ه
✧ *Imprecation* : May his food be unsound ! تَبَقَّط
To receive, to perceive a. th. little by little. — ه
Bit, broken piece. بَقْط
To be spotted white and ✻ بَقِع a بَقَعًا

groan (gazelle). To sing sweetly. ·
To speak to a. o. with a sweet and agreable voice. بَاغَم ه
Groaning of a gazelle. بُغَام
Groaning (gazelle). Sweet-voiced. بَاغِم وبَغُوم
Necklace (of pearls). بُغْمَة ج بُغَم Ts
To swell (wound). ✻ بَغَا o بَغْوًا
To observe, to consider a. th. — ه
Fruit ; green, unripe. بَغْو
To covet, to request, to desire a. th. ✻ بَغَى i بَغْيٌ وبُغَاء وبُغْيَة وبِغْيَة ه
To lie. - بَغْيًا
To oppress a. o. To act wrongfully, to treat a. o. unjustly. — عَلَى
To help a. o. in attaining a. th. بَغَى ه ه
To wish, to desire a. th. To request a. th. بَغَّى وانْبَغَى ه
To hate, to wrong o. a. تَبَاغَى
It must, it is convenient, fit to. يَنْبَغِي ان
He wants, he must. — لَهُ
To desire a. th. إِسْتَبْغَى ه
Trespass. Injustice. Iniquity. بَغْي
Wish (thing desired). بُغْيَة وبِغْيَة وبُغَاء وبُغَايَة
Earnest desire, wish. Request. بُغَاء وابْتِغَاء
Wisher. Unjust, oppressor. بَاغٍ ج بُغَاة وبُغْيَان
Harlot, prostitute. بَغِيّ ج بَغَايَا
Place where a. th. is searched. مَبْغًى ومَبْغَاة
Things coveted. مَبَاغِي
Desired, requested, coveted. Object of desire. مُبْتَغًى
White cloth. Calico. بَفْتَة Pe
To pour an abundant rain (cloud). To make a display of wealth. To point out (defects). To spread (news). ✻ بَقَّ o بَقًّا وبُقُوقًا ه
To prate about a. o. — بَقًّا وبَقَاقًا, وأَبَقَّ عَلَى
To scatter (goods). ✧ To blot (the ink : paper). — وبَقَّق ه
To be full of bugs (place). To have many children (woman). To pour an abundant rain (cloud). — وأَبَقَّ
Gnat. Bug. Stout, broad. بَقّ
Elm-tree ; plane-tree. شَجَرَة البَقّ

To look ✻ بَقَا o بَقَاوَة , وبَقَى i وبَقْيًا ة وهـ at a. o. ; to expect a. th.
To remain, to live, بَقِيَ a بَقَاء to be redundant. To last, to continue. To persevere. To watch, to look after. بَقِيَ a ة
He continued striking. بَقِيَ يَضْرِب
To keep, to hold a. o. back. بَقَّى ة وهـ To preserve a. th.
To put in store, to preserve أَبْقَى ة وهـ a. th. To keep a. o. alive. To allow a. o. to live ◘ To become.
To have pity on ; to spare a. th. — عَلَى
To preserve a. th. تَبَقَّى واسْتَبْقَى هـ وة To allow a. o. to live.
To keep a. th. from : إِسْتَبْقَى مِن to store up.
Duration, continuance. بَقَاء
Remainder, بَقْوَى وبُقْيَا وبَقِيَّة ج بَقَايَا remains. That outlasts, outlives.
Lasting, surviving. بَاقٍ ج بَاقُون
The remainder. The Everlasting البَاقِي Almighty God.
Providence of God. بَاقِيَة Obedience to God.
Mercy ! Spare us ! البَاقِيَة
More lasting. أَبْقَى
Good works. البَاقِيَات الصَّالِحَات
Preserved, kept in store. مُسْتَبْقًى
Bey, prince. Ts بَك و✧ بَيْك
To squeeze a. o. ✧ بَكَّ o بَكًّا ة وهـ To press, to break, to tear a. th. To tire (a beast).
To crowd, to throng. تَبَاكَّ
Foolish. بَاكٌّ وأَحْمَق بَاكّ
To crowd (people). ✻ بَكْبَكَ
To ✻ بَكَأَ a بَكْأً , وبَكُوَ o بُكُوءًا وبَكَاءَة have little milk (ewe, she-camel). To have little water (well) ; few tears (eye).
That has few tears (eye). بَكِيئَة ج بِكَاء Holding little water (well).
Water-cress. بَكْء وبَكْأ
To address ✻ بَكَتَ o بَكْتًا وبَكَّتَ ة a. o. rudely. To ill-treat a. o.
Reproof, rebuke. تَبْكِيت
Remorse of conscience. — الضَّمِير
Reprover, rebuker. مُبَكِّت
To rise up ✻ بَكَرَ o بُكُورًا , وبَكَّرَ وتَبَكَّرَ black. ✧ To be stained.
To befall a. o. (misfortune). — ة
To go away. بَقِمَ a بَقَمًا , وبَقَّم
To be disgraced, abused by. بُقِمَ بِ
To make white and black بَقَّم هـ spots (on cloth : dyer). To stain (clothes). ✧To wet here and there.
To be spotted. تَبَقَّم ✧ To be wet here and there.
To hurry back. إِنْبَقَم
To lose o.'s fair complexion اِبْتَقَم (from sorrow).
Depressed land, swamp. بُقْعَة ج بِقَاع وبُقَع ✧ Stain.
Upland, plain in a hilly country. بِقَاع وبُقَع
Place full of roots of various trees. بَقِيم
A very cautious bird. بَاقِعَة ج بَوَاقِع Keen, intelligent man. Calamity.
Spotted. Droughty أَبْقَع م بَقْعَاء ج بُقْع (year). Leprous. Crow.
Medley. ✧ Stained (garment). مُبَقَّع
To appear, to come ✻ بَقَلَ o بَقْلًا , وأَبْقَلَ out (plant, tooth).
To be covered بَقَلَ o بُقُولًا , وبَقَّلَ وأَبْقَلَ with down (face).
To become green with plants بَقَلَ وأَبْقَلَ (ground).
To fatten from feeding تَبَقَّلَ وابْتَقَلَ upon green herbs (cattle).
To search for herbage (cattle). تَبَقَّلَ
Vegetable, herbage ; بَقْل ج بُقُول وأَبْقَال green.
Purslain. بَقْلَة وبَقْلَة الحَمْقَاء
Cauliflower. بَقْلَة الأَنْصَار
Endive, succory. أَلْبَقْلَةُ المُبَارَكَة
Large boat. ◘ بَقْلَة
Broad-bean. بَاقِلَاء وبَاقِلَّى وبَاقِلَى
Abundant in herbs, بَقِل وبَقِيل ومُبْقِل vegetables (soil).
Green-grocer. بَقَّال
Kitchen-garden. مَبْقَلَة
A handleless Sp بُوقَال وبَاقُول ج بَوَاقِيل vessel. Earthenware, glass-jar.
Cod-fish. Is بَقَلَا
Kind of almond cake. Ts بَقْلَاوَا
To dye a. th. red. ✻ بَقَّم هـ
Logwood, red dye. بَقَّم
Undressed wool. Weak-minded. بُقَامَة
Dyed red. مُبَقَّم

To mix a. th. ✱ بَكَل o بَكْلًا ه
To prepare (a mess) of flour, dates and oil.
To mix, to mingle a. th. بَكَّل ه
✧ To buckle. To button up.
He spoke in unconnected phrases. تَبَكَّل في الكَلَام
To get the upper hand by blows and invectives. — ٥ وعلى
To prey upon a. th. إِبْتَكَل ه
Shape. Nature. State. بِكْلَة ج بِكَل
✧ Buckle. Fs بُكْلَة ج بُكَل
Food made of flour, dates, oil, etc. بَكَالة وبَكِيلة
Buckled. Buttoned (coat). ✧ مُبَكَّل
Treasury. Principality. State. government. Ts بَكْلِيك
To confiscate a. th. (state). ✧ بَكْلَك
To be dumb, mute. ✱ بَكِم a بَكَمًا
To be silent. بَكُم o بَكَامَة
To render a. o. dumb. أَبْكَم ٥
He was unable to speak. تَبَكَّم عَلَيْهِ الكَلَامُ
Dumb, mute. أَبْكَم ج بُكْم ، وبَكِيم ج بُكْمَاء
To shed tears, to weep. ✱ بَكَى i بُكَاء وبُكًى
To weep over a. o. To lament on. — وبَكَّى ٥
To move a. o. to tears. بَكَّى وأَبْكَى واسْتَبْكَى ٥
To make a. o. to weep over. — ٥ على
To sham weeping. تَبَاكَى
Weeping, tears. بُكَاء وبُكًى
Weeping, shedding tears. بَاكٍ ج بُكَاة
Weeping (woman). بَاكِيَة ج بَوَاكٍ
Mourner hired at a funeral. ✧ Shed.
Shedding tears; weeping bitterly. بَكِيّ وبَكَّاء م بَكِيَّة وبَكَّاءَة
Causing a. o. to weep. مُبَكٍّ ومُبْكٍ
Weeping-place. مَبْكًى ج مَبَاكٍ
But: on the contrary, besides, much more, rather; no, nay. ✱ بَلْ
To wet, to moisten a. th. ✱ بَلَّ o بَلًّا وبِلَّة ه
To give a. th. To be benficent. — o بَلًّا وبِلَالًا ٥ او يَدَهُ ب
To enjoy a. th. To obtain. To know a. th. بَلَّ a بَلَلًا وبِلَالًا ب

early in the morning.
To do a. th. early in the morning. — في
To go towards a. o. early in the morning. — وبَكَّر وأَبْكَر وابْتَكَر إلى وعلى
To hasten towards. بَكِر a وأَبْكَر إلى
To attend prayer from the beginning. — بِالصلاة
To visit a.o. early in the morning. بَكَّر وبَاكَر ٥
To hasten to. بَكَّر وأَبْكَر على
To send a. o. early. أَبْكَر ٥
To hasten towards. أَبْكَر الى
To accost a. o. first of all. To eat the first (fruits). To deflower (a virgin). ابْتَكَر ٥ وه
First-born. First-fruits. Inviolate. Virgin. بِكْر ج أَبْكَار
Young (camel). بَكْر ج أَبْكُر وبُكْرَان
Daybreak. ✧ To-morrow. بُكْرَة ج بُكَر
Early in the morning. بُكْرَة وبَاكِرًا
Morning and evening. البُكَر والآصَال
Pulley. Wheel of a watering-engine. بَكَرَة ج بَكَر وبَكَرَات
All without exception. على بَكْرَة أَبِيهِم
Virginity. بَكَارَة
Primogeniture. Birth-right. Precocious. بَكْرِيَّة وبُكُورَة و✧ بُكُورِيَّة
First fruits. بَكِيرَة وبَاكُورَة
✧ A small crooked staff. بَاكُور
Early. rising early. بَاكِر وبَكِير
Precocious. بَكِير وبَاكُور وبَكُور ج بُكُر
First rain in the spring. بَاكُور وبَكُور
Precocious. Very early. soon. ✧ بَكِّير
First rain in the spring. مِبْكَار
Early, early comer. riser. مُبَكِّر
Compass. (for بركار) P بِيكَار
To measure with compasses. ✧ بَيْكَر وبَرْكَر ه
Hackney. (for بار كير) Te بَيْكِير
Kettle, coffee-pot. Te بَكْرَج وبَقْرَاج
To overcome a. o. ✱ بَكَس o بَكْسًا ٥
Biscuit. Te بَكْسِمَاد وبَكْسِمَاط و✧ بَقْسَمَاط
To receive a.o. rudely. To rebuke a. o. To strike a. o. on several parts of the body. ✱ بَكَع a بَكْعًا ٥
To reprove a. o. To cut off a. th. بَكَّع ٥ وه
✧ Large sum of money. بَكْعَة
One-armed. أَبْكَع

بَلَّ i فِي الأرض To go away.

بَلَّ i بَلًّا وبَلَلًا وبُلُولًا, وأَبَلَّ مِن To recover from.

بَلَّ بهِ بَلَلًا وبَلَالَةً وبُلُولًا To enjoy the company of a. o.

بَلَّت يَدَاكَ بهِ Thou hast obtained it.

بَلَّل ه To wet, to drench, to moisten.

أَبَلَّ To be sappy (tree); to bear fruit.

— عَلَيْهِ To overcome a. o.

تَبَلَّل وابْتَلَّ To be drenched, to be wet. To be soaked.

— وابْتَلَّ واسْتَبَلَّ من To be cured of.

بَلّ Wetting. Wetness.

بَلّ وبَلِيل Moan.

بِلّ Allowance. Recovery.

بِلَّة Freshness of youth.

مَا أَصَابَ هَلَّةً وَلَا بَلَّةً He has not got a. th.

بِلَّة وبَلَل وبُلَالَة Dampness, moisture.

بَلَال وبُلَال Water ; milk. Meeting-place.

بَلِيل وبَلِيلَة Cold and damp wind.

ذَهَبَ بِذِي بِلِّيَان وبِذِي بِلَّى وبِذِي بِلِّي He went nobody knows where.

أَبَلّ م بَلَّاء ج بُلّ Wicked, hypocrite, unjust.

بَلَّان ج بَلَّانَات ✧ Warm bath. A kind of fern.

بَلَّان م بَلَّانَة Waiter at baths.

مَبْلُول ومُبْتَلّ Drenched, wet,

✱ بَلْبَل بَلْبَلَةً وبِلْبَالًا ه وه To trouble. a. o. to throw a. th. into disorder.

تَبَلْبَل To be entangled. To be restless, troubled.

بَلْبَلَة ج بَلَابِل Trouble, confusion, disorder, restlessness.

بَلَابِل Anxieties, sorrows.

بُلْبُل ج بَلَابِل Nightingale (bird). ✧ Spinning-top.

مُبَلْبِل Disturber, revolutionary.

✱ بَلَأَز وبَلَأَص To escape.

✱ بَلَتَ o بَلْتًا, وبَلِتَ a بَلَتًا To be cut. To swear.

— i بَلْتًا ه To sever a. th. ; to cut

أَبْلَت To stop short (in speaking).

أَبْلَت ه ه To swear a. o.

بَلِيت Taciturn, reserved. Prudent. Eloquent.

✱ بلتم — تَبَلْتَم To be vain-glorious.

بَلْتَم Cunning. Boisterous (woman).

بَلْتَعِيّ وبَلْتَعَانِيّ ومُتَبَلْتِع Eloquent and bold in speech.

✱ بَلَج o بُلُوجًا, وأَبْلَج وتَبَلَّج وانْبَلَج وابْتَلَج To dawn, to break (dawn).

بَلِج a بَلَجًا To be merry. To have parted eyebrows.

أَبْلَج To shine (sun).

تَبَلَّج To be cheerful, merry, smiling.

إِنْبَلَج To be clear, evident.

بَلْجَة وبُلْجَة Dawn, day-break.

بَلَج وبُلْجَة Separation between the eyebrows. Day-light.

بُلْجَة Whiteness, brightness.

بَلْج وبَلِج Bright. Evident. Jovial, open-faced.

بَلِيج Shining, gleaming.

أَبْلَج م بَلْجَاء Bright. Serene. Smiling. Having parted eyebrows. Munificent.

✱ بَلَح a بَلْحًا To be dry (soil).

— بُلُوحًا, وبَلَّح وتَبَلَّح To be weary, fatigued. To fail.

أَبْلَح To bring forth unripe dates (palm-tree).

بَلَح Unripe date. ✧ Date

بَالِح ج بَوَالِح Barren, dry (ground).

بَالِح ومُبَالِح Stubborn, indomitable (man).

✱ بَلِخ a بَلَخًا, وتَبَلَّخ To be haughty.

بَلِخ وأَبْلَخ م بَلْخَاء Haughty.

بَلْخ وبُلَّاخ Evergreen, oak-tree.

✱ بَلَخْش Hyacinth (gem).

✱ بَلَدَ o بُلُودًا وبَلِدَ a بَلَدًا ب To settle. to remain in. To occupy (a country).

بَلُدَ o بَلَادَةً To be foolish, dull, lazy.

بَلَّد To be undetermined, to lay idle.

بَلَّد ه ✧ To naturalize a.o. ; to accustom a. o. to a country. ✧ To acclimatize (a plant).

أَبْلَد To cling to a country, a place. To be perplexed.

أَبْلَد ه وه To settle a. o. in a country. To colonize (a country). To conquer it.

تَبَلَّد To show stupidity. To settle in a country. ✧ To be accustomed, naturalized. ▫ To run ashore (ship).

بَلْدَة وبَلَد ج بِلَاد وبُلْدَان City. town. Country, Land. Village.

Countryman, citizen; indigenous. بَلَدِيّ
Town-council مَجْلِس بَلَدِيّ
✧ Municipal council or district. بَلَدِيَّة
Stupidity. Dullness. Spiritlessness. بَلَادَة
Silly, foolish. بَلِيد وأَبْلَد
Steel. Razor. (*for* فولاذ) بُولاد Ps
✱ بَلْدَح To recline on the ground.
To break a promise. To be dull.
Silly. Breaking his promise. بَلَنْدَح
✱ بَلْدَم To stand mute from fear.
Beryl. Crystal. بِلَّور وبَلُّور P
✧ تَبَلْوَر To crystallize.
Crystalline, crystal. بَلُّورِيّ
▫ إِبْلِيز Black and thick slime left by the Nile.
✱ بلس — أَبْلَس To remain disheartened, sad and gloomy. To be desperate, stupefied. To remain speechless.
To despair of. — مِن
To drive a. o. to despair. — ه
Ficus morifolia. Whitefig-tree بَلَس وبُلْس
Sack-cloth. بَلَاس
Silent, gloomy. بَلِس وبَلَس ومُبْلِس
Constabulary. Policeman. بُولِيس Fs
Devil, demon. إِبْلِيس ج أَبَالِسَة
✱ بَلَسْكَاء وبَلِسِكَاء Burdock (*pla.*).
✱ بَلْسَم ه ✧ To anoint with balm. To embalm.
Amyris opobalsamum. Balsam. بَلَسَم
✧ Embalming. بَلْسَمَة
Embalmed. مُبَلْسَم
✱ بَلَسَان Balm-tree.
✱ بَيْلَسَان Elder-tree.
✧ بَلَّش وابْتَلَش ه او ب To begin. to undertake a. th.
✱ بَلَشُون Heron.
✧ بَلَص o بَلْصًا وبَلَّص ه مِن To exact a. th. from, to despoil a. o. of.
تَبَلَّص ه To seek secretly after.
✧ بَلْص وبَلَصَة Exaction. Extortion, oppression.
✧ مَبْلُوص Ground down by taxes.
▫ بَلَاصِيّ وبَلَاص ج بَلَالِيص Earthenware jar.
Is بُولِيصَة Bill of exchange, draft.
✱ بَلَط o بَلْطًا, وبَلَّط وأَبْلَط ه To pave (a. th).
✧ بَلَّط To tack (sailor). ▫ To run aground (ship). To cheat. To stop work.
To plunder a. o. (thief). أَبْلَط ه
To weary a. o. with requests.
To come to poverty. أَبْلَط وأُبْلِط
To fight with a sword. بَالَط وتَبَالَط
✧ To behave foolishly. To play the devil. تَبَالَط
Heedless, giddy, frolicsome. ✧ بِلْط وبَلِيط
Pavement. Paving-stone. Even ground. ✧ Palace. بَلَاط
A flag-stone. A paving-tile. بَلَاطَة
Axe, hatchet. بَلْطَة Ts
Labrus niloticus, a fish of the Nile. بُلْطِي
Sapper. Executioner. بَلْطَجِيّ Ts
✧ Pavement, paving. Altar-stone. ▫ Stoppage. تَبْلِيط ج تَبَالِيط
Paver. Paviour. مُبَلِّط
Paved with stones or tiles. مُبَلَّط
Oak. Acorn. بَلُّوط
Germander, *diuretic herb*. بَلُّوط الأَرْض
Sweet acorn of the ash-tree. — المَلِك
Chestnut-tree. شاه بَلُّوط P
✱ بَلْطَح To lay o.'s self down on the ground.
✧ To flatten (a. th. round). — ه
✱ بَلِع a بَلْعًا, وابْتَلَع ه To swallow a. th. To swallow up. To absorb a. th.
Hoariness began to appear upon his head. بَلَّع وتَبَلَّع الشَّيْبُ فِي رَأْسِهِ
To get a. o. to swallow a. th. بَلَّع وأَبْلَع ه ه
Swallowing. Absorption. بَلْع وابْتِلَاع
Mouthful. Draught, gulp. بَلْعَة
Draught. Hole of a mill-stone. بُلْعَة ج بُلَع
Glutton, voracious. بَلَّاع وبُلَعَة وبَلُوع وبَوْلَع
✧ بَالُوع ج بَوَالِيع Gulf, whirlpool.
Drain. Sewer. Underground pipe. بَالُوعَة وبَلَّاعَة وبَلُّوعَة ج بَوَالِيع وبَلَالِيع
✧ Sink-hole. بَلُّوعَة المَطْبَخ
Throat, gullet. مَبْلَع
Swallowed. Absorbed. مَبْلُوع ومُبْتَلَع
✱ بَلْعَم To swallow greedily.
Oesophagus, gullet. بُلْعُم وبُلْعُوم ج بَلَاعِم
Very greedy, gluttonous. بَلْعَم
✱ بَلَغ o بُلُوغًا وبَلَاغًا ه وه To reach a. place.
To ripen (fruit). To grow of age. To increase (decease). —
Thy words have moved — عَنِّي مَا قُلْتَ

me, have hurt me.
He attained the utmost degree in science. بَلَغَ في العِلْمِ وَمِنْهُ مَبْلَغًا
To be exhausted. بَلِغَ
To be eloquent. بَلُغَ o بَلَاغَةً
To forward a. th. to a. o. بَلَّغَ ه ۵
To inform a.o. of a. th.
To strive, to use every possible exertion for. To exaggerate in. بَالَغَ في
To lead, to bring a. o. or a. th. up to, as far as. أَبْلَغَ ۵ وه إلى
To live on, to be satisfied with. تَبَلَّغَ ب
To increase (evil). تَبَالَغَ فِيهِ الـ
He affected eloquence. تَبَالَغَ في كَلَامِهِ
Very foolish. أَحْمَقُ بَلْغٌ وبِلْغٌ م بِلْغَةٌ
Means of subsistence, living. بُلْغَةٌ وبَلَاغٌ وبُلَاغٌ
Coming to, as far as. Coming of age. Nubility. Maturity. Perfection. بُلُوغٌ
Legal summons. Delivery of a message. Sufficiency. بَلَاغٌ
Ultimatum. — أَخِيرٌ
False statements. Slanders. بَلَاغَاتٌ
Eloquence. بَلَاغَةٌ
Rhetoric. عِلْمُ البَلَاغَةِ
Reaching. Attaining (*m. f.*) an aim. Mature, of age. Marriageable. بَالِغٌ
Inviolable oath يَمِينٌ بَالِغَةٌ
Eloquent. Efficient. Chaste in speech. بَلْغٌ وبَلِيغٌ وبَلَاغِيٌّ
✧ Sum of money. Limit, farthest end attained. مَبْلَغٌ ج مَبَالِغُ
Exaggeration, hyperbole. Utmost care, striving. مُبَالَغَةٌ
Chanter in a mosque. مُبَلِّغٌ
Bugloss, ox-tongue (*pla.*). بَلْغُصُونُ G
Phlegm. Pituite. ✻ بَلْغَمٌ ، بَلَاغِمُ
Phlegmatic. Pituitous. بَلْغَمِيٌّ
To hurry on. ✻ بَلَقَ o بُلُوقًا
To open (a door) wholly. To open or shut it (abruptly). — وأَبْلَقَ ه
To be spotted white and black. بَلِقَ a وبَلُقَ o بَلَقًا وأَبْلَقَّ وابْلَوْلَقَ
To be stupefied, amazed. بَلِقَ a بَلَقًا
To repair (a well) with plane-boards. بَلَّقَ ه
To be opened wholly (door). إِنْبَلَقَ
Camel-hair tent. Marble. Door. بَلَقٌ

Motley. بَلَقٌ وبُلْقَةٌ
Variegated. Piebald (horse). Famous castle. أَبْلَقُ م بَلْقَاءُ ج بُلْقٌ
Plain of Balka. بَلْقَاءُ
To be waste and uninhabited. ✻ بَلْقَمَ
Waste country. بَلْقَمٌ وبَلْقَمَةٌ ج بَلَاقِمُ
Company of infantry, squadron of cavalry. بُلُوكٌ ج بُلُوكَاتٌ Ts
Perhaps. ✧ بَلْكِهِ بَلْكِي . بَرْكِهِ Ts
He may come. ✧ بَلْكِي يَجِي
To mar a. o. or a. th. ✻ بَلَمَ — بَلَّمَ ۵ وه
To be silent. To have swollen lips. أَبْلَمَ
Having swollen lips. أَبْلَمُ
A kind of broad-bean. Berry of the lote-tree. أَبْلَمُ وإِبْلِمٌ وأُبْلُمٌ وأَبْلَمَةٌ
Small fishes. ✧ Foolish, stupid. بَلَمٌ
Tumour on the lips. بَلَمَةٌ
Ambergris. Honey. إِبْلِيمٌ
Tar. ✻ بَلَنْسَرٌ
Kind of marble, or ivory. ✻ بَلَنْطٌ
To be foolish. To be a cipher, a simpleton. ✻ بَلِهَ a بَلَهًا وبَلَاهَةً وابْتَلَهَ
To behave as a simpleton. تَبَلَّهَ
To pretend simplicity. تَبَالَهَ
Silliness, tom-foolery. بَلَهٌ وبَلَاهَةٌ
Tom-fool, silly, stupid. أَبْلَهُ م بَلْهَاءُ ج بُلْهٌ
Do not mind. Do abstain. Put it off. بَلْهَ
To walk at a quick step. ✻ بَلْهَسَ
Ampleness of circumstances. ✻ بُلَهْنِيَةٌ
To try, to experiment a. o. in. To afflict, to put a.o. to the test. ✻ بَلَا o بَلْوًا وبَلَاءً ۵ ب
To be worn out (clothes). To be consumed (corpse). بَلِيَ a بِلًى وبَلَاءً
To be affected with fear. To be smitten by (a disease, a calamity). بُلِيَ وابْتُلِيَ
To wear out. To waste (clothes). بَلَّى تَبْلِيَةً وأَبْلَى إِبْلَاءً ه
To pay attention to. To take care of. To esteem, to be anxious about. To vie in splendour with o. a. To contradict. بَالَى مُبَالَاةً وبِلَاءً ه او ب
To put a. o. or a. th. to trial. أَبْلَى ۵ ه
He showed gallantry in war. أَبْلَى في الحَرْبِ بَلَاءً حَسَنًا
To try, to test, to afflict a. o. تَبَالَى وابْتَلَى ۵

Merchant. بُنْدار ج بَنادِرَة
Syndic of merchants. Consul. شاه بَنْدَر P
Flag, banner, colours. بَنْدِيرَة Is
Love-apple, tomato. بَنادُورَة Is
Nut, hazel-nut. Bullet-shot. بُنْدُقَة ج بُنْدُق وبَنادِق P
Venice (town). ◻ Rifle, gun. بُنْدُقِيَّة G
Gun-stock. ✧ خَشَب البُنْدُقِيَّة
Bastard, spurious. ✧ بُنْدُوق ج بَنادِيق
To debase, to render a. o. degenerate. ✧ بَنْدَق ه
To shun a. o. or a. th. ✱ بَنِس a بَنَسًا وأَبْنَس ه وه
To retrace o.'s steps. To draw back. بَنَّس
Ebony (wood). آبَنُوس وآبَنُس وآبِنُس وأَبْنُس G
A cloth upper-garment with very full sleeves. بُنُش Ts
Ring-finger. ✱ بِنْصِر
Violet (flower). بَنَفْسَج P
Violet (colour), violet-coloured. بَنَفْسَجِي
Amethyst. بَنَفْش و بَنَفْش P
To come towards, to arrive at. ✱ بَنَق o بَنَقًا إِلى
To put a triangular piece on (a shirt). To make (a quiver) of a triangular shape. To set (a discourse). To trump up (a lie). بَنَّق ه
To sojourn in (a place). — ب
Gore of a shirt. بِنَقَة وبَنِيقَة ج بَنائِق
To communicate family secrets (girls). ✱ بَنَك — بَنَّك
To settle in (a place). بَنَّك وتَبَنَّك ب
Pith. Aromatic plant. Root, bottom. بُنْك P
Bloom of youth. بُنْك العُمْر
Bench. Banking-house. بَنْك ج بُنُوك Is
Clepsydra. Water or sand-clock. بَنْكام P
✱ بَنَى i بَنْيًا وبِناء وبُنْيانًا وبِنْيَة وبِنايَة ه
To construct, to build, to erect (a house).
He went into his wife (man). بَنَى بأَهْلِهِ وابْتَنَى
To build up (a building). To give (a house). بَنَّى ه

To put a. o. to the test. إِبْتَلَى ه
Consumption. Rottenness. Decay. بِلًى
Pressure of calamity. Trial. Sorrow. بَلْوَى وبِلْوَة ج بَلَايَا
Trial, test. Misfortune. بَلَاء
Trial. Misfortune, affliction. بَلِيَّة ج بَلَايَا
Overfatigued Worn out. بِلْو وبِلْي ج أَبْلَاء
Worn out, consumed, rotten. بَالٍ وبَلٍ
Afflicted. Tried. مُبْتَلِي ومَبْلُو
Anxiety, care, attentiveness. مُبَالَاة
Intent on. Mindful of. Who takes account of. مُبَالٍ
Yes, no doubt. Ay, yea. So. ✱ بَلَى
The thickest string of a musical instrument. Bass (in music). بَم ج بُمُوم P
Ochrea bamia, (leguminous plant). بَامِيَا Gs
To remain in (a place). ✱ بَنَّ i بَنًّا وأَبَنَّ ب
To tie (a sheep) in order to fatten it. بَنَّن ه
Fingers, tip of the fingers. بَنَان
One finger. بَنَانَة ج بَنَانَات
Verdant garden, meadow. Finger-joint. بُنَانَة
Coffee (berry). Coffee-tree. بُنّ
Coffee-coloured. بُنِّي
Good or bad smell. بَنَّة ج بِنَان
Prudent, steady. بَنِين
A kind of shark. ✱ بِنْبِك
Gold coin worth 20 francs. بِنْتُو IE
To come back to o.'s origin. ✱ بَنَج o
To put a. o. under chloroform. بَنَّج ه
To claim a noble origin. إِبْتَنَج
Hyosciamus niger. Henbane, (soporific plant). Chloroform. بَنْج
✧ To chloroform. بَنَّج
Origin, source. بِنْج
Beet-root. بَنْجَر TE
Hole. Cannon-bore; gun-barrel. Window. بَنْجَرَة ج بَنَاجِر Ts
Clove-pink. Clove. بَنْجَكُشْت P
Standard, flag. Lake. Deceit. ✧ Cross-belt. Part. Chapter. بَنْد ج بُنُود P
Sword-belt. ✧ بَنْد السَّيْف
Crafty man. كَثِير البُنُود
To enlist (soldiers). ✧ To divide (a book) into chapters. بَنَّد ه وه
Sea-town. Commercial town. بَنْدَر ج بَنَادِر P

To have a. th. built, erected. أبنى ه
To adopt a. o. as a son. تبنّى ه
To build, to have (a house) built. إبتنى ه
To want repair (house). إستبنى
Structure, fabric. بِناء وبِناية وبُنيان
Building, edifice. بِناء ج أبنية
From that, accordingly. بِناء عليه
✧ Good example, edification. بُنيان صالح
Adoption, adopting. تبنٍّ
Building, structure. بِنية وبُنية ج بِنى وبُنى
Shape, frame of the body. بِنية
Strongly built (man), healthy. صحيح البنية
Son, child. إبن ج بنون وأبناء
Man. *Pl.* men. إبن آدم ج بنو آدم
The man of perdition, damned. إبن الهلاك
Traveller, wanderer. إبن السبيل
Jackal. إبن آوى
Weasel. إبن عرس
Mindless of the morrow. إبن يومه
Relatives. بنو عمّه
Citizens. بنو المدينة
Thieves, robbers. بنو الليل
Daughter ; girl. إبنة وبنت ج بنات
✧ Queen (at cards).
Word. بنت الشفة
Tear. بنت العين
Wine. بنت العنب والعنقود والكرم
Thought, design. بنت الفكر
Arrow. بنت الكنائن
Siren. بنت الماء والبحر
Small rivers. بنات الأرض
Misfortunes, calamities. بنات الدهر
Cares, troubles. بنات الليل والصدر
My little son. بُنيّ
Sonship, filiation. بُنوّة
Belonging to a son, filial. بُنويّ
Builder. Founder, constructor. بانٍ ج بُناة
Wrist. Blow. ▫ بُنية
Foundations of a house. بانية ج بوانٍ
Architect. Mason, builder. بنّاء ج بنّاءون
Pigeon-hole. ▫ بُناني
Foundation, basis. مَبنى
Constructed. Indeclinable (noun). مَبنيّ
The public buildings. المباني
Letters of the Alphabet. حروف المباني
Adopting as a son, adopter. مُتبنٍّ
Adopted, adoptive (child). مُتبنًّى
✻ بها a وبهي a وبهُو o بهْئًا وبهاء وبهُوًّا ب

To show kindness to a. o.
To mind a. th. — ل
To empty (a house). بهّأ a بهأ وأبهأ ه
To be astonished, to remain speechless. ✻ بهت a وبهُت o وبُهت بهتًا
✧ To be of a faint colour. بهت a بهتًا
To surprise a. o. بهت a بهتًا ه
To slander a. o. — بهتًا وبهتانًا ه
To lie. باهت
To shock a. o. by slander. — ه
Astonishment, amazement. بهتة
Lie. Calumny. بُهت وبُهتان وبهيتة
✧ Dull, dead (colour). باهت
Calumniator. بهّات ، وبهوت ج بُهُت وبُهْت
Anæmia. ▫ بهاتة
Falsely charged. Stupefied مبهوت
To cheer up, to enliven a. o. ✻ بهج a بهجًا وأبهج ه
To rejoice in, to gladden at. بهج a بهجًا ب
To be fine, elegant. بهُج o بهاجة وبهجانًا
To embellish. To cheer up a. o. بهّج ه وه
To be luxuriant (garden, soil). أبهج وتباهج
To be merry. تبهّج وابتهج
To marvel. ✧ إنبهج
To rejoice at. إستبهج ب
Joy, cheerfulness. Beauty. بهجة
Joyful, cheerful. Fine-looking. بهِج وبهيج
Cheering, enlivening. مُبهِج
To squander, to waste. ✧ بهدر بهدرة ه
Hero. P بهادور ج بهادورية
To walk quickly. ✻ بهدل
✧ To insult, to scoff at. بهدل ه
✧ To be reviled. تبهدل
Agility. بهدلة
✧ Insult.
To overcome a. o. in beauty, merit. To slander a. o. To overburden. To grieve a. o. ✻ بهر a بهرًا ه
To shine. بهر a بهرًا وبهورًا
To outstrip a. o. in a. th. — ه
To be out of breath. بُهر
✧ To be dazzled (by sunshine). بهر وتبهّر
To pepper, to season (a dish) with pepper. ✧ بهّر ه

Gravity of a. th.
Heavy, crushing. Important, serious (affair). باهظ
Overwhelmed. مَبْهُوظ
To come forth, to emerge from a cloud (sun). ✧ بَهِق a بَهَقًا
Dandruff. ◻ Leprosy. بَهَق
Lichen. — الحجر
Soft, full of vigour (youth). ✻ بَهْكَن وبَهْكَنَة وبَهْكَل وبَهْكَلَة
To curse a. o. ✻ بَهَل a بَهْلًا ه
To let a. o. act at pleasure. To let a. o. to himself. — وأَبْهَل ه
To abandon a. o. ✧ To render stupid, to stultify. أَبْهَل ه
To curse o. a. بَاهَل بَعْضُهُم بَعْضًا وتَبَهَّل وتَبَاهَل
To grow stupid, silly. إِنْبَهَل
To implore, to beseech. to supplicate (God). إِبْتَهَل إلى
To call (upon God) against. To curse, to imprecate upon a. o. — على
To let a. o. do what he would. ✧ To find a. o. foolish, stupid. إِسْتَبْهَل ه
Curse, imprecation. بَهْلَة
✧ Stupidity, silliness. بَهْلَة وبَهْلَنَة
Supplication, earnest prayer; call for help from God. إِبْتِهَال
Indecisive, wavering. Staffless (shepherd). Untied (she-camel). Unarmed (man). باهِل ج بُهْل وبُهَّل
Good chief. Laugher. ✧ Fool, stupid. بُهْلُول ج بَهَالِيل
Imprecation. مُبَاهَلَة
✧ Silly, simple. مَبْهُول
To come suddenly from a country without any luggage. ✻ بَهْلَس – تَبَهْلَس
To lie. ✻ بَهْلَق وتَبَهْلَق
Fool. Rope-dancer, juggler, tumbler. Ps بَهْلَوَان ج بَهَالِين
To wean (lambs, etc.). ✻ بَهَم – بَهَم البَهْم
To conceal a. th. To use uncertain, ambiguous terms. أَبْهَم ه
To be concealed, equivocal, uncertain, unknown to. أَبْهَم وتَبَهَّم على
To divert a. o. from a. th. أَبْهَم ه على
To be concealed, vague, equivocal, unknown to. إِسْتَبْهَم عن
Hordeum murinum, common بُهْمَى

To vie with a.o. in. باهَر مُبَاهَرَة وبِهَارًا ه
To make a fortune. To bring forth a. th. astounding. To be exposed to heat. أَبْهَر
✧ To dazzle a. o. (sun). — ه
To be breathless. ✦ To be dazzled. إِنْبَهَر
To use every endeavour on behalf of, or against. إِبْتَهَر في ول
He repeated his prayer. إِبْتَهَر في الدُّعَاء
Beauty, splendour, victory. بَهْر
Publicly. بَهْرًا
Breathlessness, short-breathing. بُهْر
He exhausted himself in endeavours. جَهَدَت نَفْسَهُ بُهْرَهَا
Centre. Extensive field. بُهْرَة
Beauty. Pepper, spice. بَهَار
Idol. Swallow. Devil. بُهَار
Short-breathed, breathless. بَهِير ومَبْهُور
Splendid. Wonderful, magnificent. باهِر
A slender, delicate woman. بَهِيرَة ج بَهَائِر
Artery. Back. Jugular vein. ✧ Aorta. أَبْهَر
The two arteries of the heart. الأَبْهَرَان
Dazzling. ✧ مُبْهِر
To allow (blood) to be shed with impunity. ✻ بَهْرَج ه
To be shed with impunity (blood). بُهْرِج
To sweep, to pass with pomp. تَبَهْرَج
Vain, trifling. Vanity, trifle, worthless. Tinsel. Counterfeit (coin). P بَهْرَج
To dye (the beard) yellow. ✻ بَهْرَم ه
Mars (planet). P بَهْرَام وبَهْرَامَج
Yellow dye. P بَهْرَمَان
Ruby, carbuncle. — وياقوت بَهْرَمَانِيّ
Braminism. بَهْرَمَة
To push a. o. back from. ✻ بَهَز a بَهْزًا , وأَبْهَز ه من
To prepare to. ✻ بَهَش a بَهْشًا ل
To search. to scrutinize a. th. — عن
To hurry towards. — إلى
To meet, to gather. — وتَبَهَّش
To rejoice, to be glad. إِبْتَهَش
A kind, smiling man. رَجُل بَهْش
To take off o.'s clothes and stake them (gambler). ✻ بَهْصَل
To overwhelm, to overburden a. o. (work, weight). ✻ بَهَظ a بَهْظًا , وأَبْهَظ ه
Weight. Heinousness of a crime. بَهْظ

wall barley-grass.
بَهْمَة وبَهَمَة ج بَهْم وبَهَم وبِهَام وجج بِهَامَات Lamb, kid, calf.
بُهْمَة ج بُهَم Brave, hero. Difficult task.
إِبْهَام Uncertainty, doubt. Ambiguity.
بَهِيم ج بُهْم وبُهُم Black. Of one colour. Rumbling (sound, noise). Thumb.
بَهِيمَة ج بَهَائِم Beast, quadruped. ✧ She-ass.
بَهِيمِيّ Bestial, brutish.
بَهِيمِيَّة Bestiality. Brutishness.
أَبْهَم ج بُهْم Speaking an unknown language. Barbarian, stranger.
إِبْهَام ج أَبَاهِم وأَبَاهِيم و ✧ بَاهِم ج بَوَاهِم Thumb. Great toe.
مُبْهَم Ambiguous, unknown, vague.
✱ تَبَهْنَس To walk with a haughty gait.
بَهْنَس Stout and heavy. Lion.
✱ بَهَا ه وبَهِيَ a وبَهُوَ ه بَهَاء To be fine. To shine.
بَهَا ه ه To exceed a. o. in beauty.
بَهَّى ه To enlarge (a house).
بَاهَى To boast, to get proud.
بَاهَى ه To vie with a. o. in beauty.
أَبْهَى To have a handsome face.
— ه To empty (a vessel, a house).
إِبْتَهَى ب To boast of.
تَبَاهَى To vie with a.o. in beauty, elegance.
بَهَاء Beauty. Elegance. Splendour.
بَهْو ج أَبْهَاء وبُهُوّ وبُهِيّ House situated foremost. Court-yard. Hollow of the chest. Extended plain.
بَهِيّ Fine, pretty. Bright.
✱ بَوّ Young camel, stuffed camel-hide for deceiving a she-camel when milked.
بَوّ م بَوَّاء وبَوِّيّ م بَوِّيَّة Stupid.
✱ بَاءَ ه بَوْءًا الى To come back to.
— ب الى To bring back a. o. to.
— بِذَنْبِهِ To acknowledge o.'s fault.
— بَوْءًا وبَوَاء ب To be equal with a. o. in retaliation.
بُؤْ بِهِ Do die, do atone for his death.
بَوَّأَ وأَبَاءَ ه To come and stay in (a place).
بَوَّأَ ه نَحْوَ To point (a spear) towards.
بَوَّأَ وأَبَاءَ ه ول ه To prepare (a lodging) for.

أَبَاءَ إِبَاءَةً ه او بِهِ الى وعلى To bring, to lead back a. o. to.
في أَبَاءِ القَاتِلَ بالقَتِيل He slew him in retaliation.
— ه ب To receive a. o. as a guest, in.
تَبَوَّأَ ه او ب To enter, to go in. To take possession of.
تَبَاوَأَ To be equal.
إِسْتَبَاءَ ه To take lodging in.
— ه To kill a man in order to compensate for the murder of another.
بَوَاء Tantamount. Equality.
دَم بَوَاء دَم Blood. Retaliation.
بَاءَة وبِيئَة ومَبْوَأ ومَبَاءَة Home. Dwelling. Inn.
رَحِيب المَبَاءَة Bountiful.
✱ بَابَ ه لِفُلَان To serve a. o. as a door-keeper.
بَوَّبَ ه وه To divide (a book) into chapters. ✧ To direct a. o.
تَبَوَّبَ ه To take a. o. for a door-keeper.
بَاب ج أَبْوَاب وبِيبَان Gate, door. Chapter. Article. Class.
البَاب العَالِي The Sublime Porte.
بَابُ البَدَن ✧ Anus.
✧ على بَاب الله At random. Carelessly.
بَابَة ج بَابَات Boundary, farthest end. Kind, sort. Class. Way. Making.
هٰذَا مِن بَابَتِكَ It suits thee.
بَوَّاب ج بَوَّابُون Door-keeper, porter.
بَوَّابَة Portress. ✧ Main-gate.
بِوَابَة Door-keeping, porterage.
P بُوتَقَة وبُوطَة و✧ بُودَقَة Melting-pot for goldsmiths. Crucible.
✱ بَاثَ ه بَوْثًا وأَبَاثَ وإِنْبَاثَ ه وعن To examine, to look for. To scatter a. th.
إِسْتَبَاثَ ه وه To rouse a.o. To take out a. th.
✱ بَاحَ ه ه, وإنباح على To come upon a. o. (misfortune).
بَوْح وبَوَّاح Traveller.
بَاحَتْهُم البَائِحَة Misfortunes have overwhelmed them.
تَبَوَّحَ وإنْبَاحَ To flash all over the sky (lightning).
P بَاج • بَاجَ Permit, way-leave.
✧ بَوَّجَ ه To deliver a permit to.
✱ بَاحَ ه بَوْحًا وبُؤُوحًا وبُؤُوحَة To appear in broad light.
— ب الى To reveal, to communicate

Gudgeon. Whiting.
Bower, anchor. ◘ بَوَّرَة
Bugle, trumpet. ✧ بُورِي
A rush-mat. P بُورِيَّة وبُورِيَاء
Mat-seller. بَوَّارِي
P بَاز وبَازِي ج بَوَاز, وبُزَاة وبِيزَان وأَبْوَاز
Falcon. Bird of prey.
Falconer. P بَازْدَار وبَازْيَار ج بَيَادِرَة
Ice-cream. Ts بُوز وبُوزَة
Snout, muzzle. ✧ بُوز
To be sullen, sulky. To frown, ✧ بَوَّز to look angry. ◘ To spoil a. th.
To kiss a. o. ✻ بَاس o بَوْسًا ة
To make a. o. to kiss a. o. ة و ه ✧ بَوَّس or a. th. To smack.
Kiss. بَوْس . بَوْسَة
To mix. To vociferate. ✻ بَاش o بَوْشًا To be noisy, disorderly (rabble).
To assail o. a.; to come to blows. تَبَاوَش
Mob, (for أَهْوَاش) بَوْش وبُوش ج أَوْبَاش riotous assembly. Flock. Uproar.
Useless, vain. Vainly, in Ts بُوش mere waste, to no purpose. Nonsense, bosh.
To precede a. o. ✻ بَاص o بَوْصًا ة To escape from a. o.
To outrun the others (horse). بَوَّص To be gaudy, bright-coloured.
Colour. Complexion. بَوْص وبُوص Buttocks. Thatch.
Flat boat. Sailor. S بُوصِيّ
To recover o.'s complexion. ✧ بَاض o بَوْضًا
To stay in (a place). – ب
To sink into contempt ✻ بَاط o بَوْطًا or misery.
Crucible. ✧ Rose-shaped P بُوطَة ج بُوط design on cloth.
Arm-pit. ✧ بَاط (see إِبْط)
To become plump ✻ بَاظ o i بَوْظًا وبَيْظًا (emaciated person).
To stretch the hand in ✻ بَاع o بَوْعًا order to offer a. th. To make rapid strides.
To measure a. th. by the – وتَبَوَّع ه fathom.
To rush. إِنْبَاع
To inveigh against a. o. – بِالْكَلَام عَلَى

(a secret) to a. o.
To give to a. o. information أَبَاح ة ه about a. th. To reveal (a secret). To declare a. th. to be permitted to.
To profess openly (a religion, – ب a doctrine).
To allow a. th. إِسْتَبَاح ه To consider a. th. as permitted. To permit a. th.
To destroy (a tribe). – ة و ه
Revelation of a secret. Permission to do anything. License. إِبَاحَة
Dissolute. Free-thinker. إِبَاحِيّ ج إِبَاحِيُّون ✧ Radical (in politics).
Great quantity of water. بَاحَة ج بُوح Entrance-hall.
Sun. بُوح
Openly, publicly. بَوَاحًا
Revealer of a secret. بَائِح ومُبِيح Traitor. ✧ Shameless, barefaced.
Allowed, declared lawful, common. What is used at will, at pleasure by all. مُبَاح
To be weary. To abate ✻ بَاخ o بَوْخًا (heat); to remit (fever). To subside (anger).
To die out fire. To be – بُؤُوخًا tainted (meat). ✧ To lose its lustre, its dye, its glaze (textile fabric).
To extinguish (fire); to appease أَبَاخ ه (hatred).
Trouble, disturbance. بُوخ
To perish, to be ✻ بَار o بَوْرًا وبَوَارًا lost. To be void (deed). To remain uncultivated (ground).
To put a. o. to trial. بَار وابْتَار ة و ه To know a. th. by experience.
To let a ground untilled. بَوَّر ة ه ✧ To let a girl unmarried.
To cause a. o. to perish. أَبَار ة
Worthless fellow, (m. f. s. pl.) بُور rogue. قَوْم بُور امْرَأَة بُور
Uncultivated, waste land. بُور وبُورَة
Ruin, perdition. بَوَار
Hell. دَار الْبَوَار
Uncultivated soil. بَائِر وبَائِرَة
Wretch, forlorn man. – ج بُور
Lost, led astray, wayless. حَائِر بَائِر
Mullet, mugil. PE بُورِيّ ج بَوَارِي

To lower the price of... for a. o. — لهُ في

Fathom, measure of the two arms extended. High rank. — باع ج أبواع

Generous. Powerful. — طويل الباع

Stingy. Unable. — ضيّق او قصير الباع

Toe-bone. — بُوع

He is a dunce. — لا يَعرِف كُوعَهُ مِن بُوعِهِ

To overcome ; to equal a. o. — ✱ باغ o بَوْغًا ه

To boil (blood). — تبوّغ

To overcome a. o. — على —

Fine dust. Smell. Medley. Mob. — بَوْغاء

To perish (wealth). To be missed (th.). — ✱ باق o بَوْقًا وبُؤُوقًا

To fall upon a. o. (misfortune). To ill-treat, to embezzle a. o. To harm a. o. — ه —

To assault a. o. — على —

To sound the bugle. — بوّق

✧ To tie or put a. th. into a bundle. — ه —

To lie. — تبوّق

A calamity befell them. — إنباقت عليهم بائقة

Trumpet. Bugle. Horn. Indiscrete man. — بُوق ج أبواق وبِيقان وبُوقات

He told a story. — نفخ بالبُوق

Bugler. — بوّاق

Shower. Calamity. — بوقة ج بُوق

Bundle, bunch. Nosegay. — باقة ج باقات

Injustice. Calamity, disaster. — بائقة ج بوائق

To be fat (camel). — ✱ باك o بُؤُوكًا

To be entangled (business). — بَوْكًا —

To mix and press in (a crowd). — ه —

To purchase or sell a. th. — ه —

Big (camel). — بائك ج بُوك وبيّك

First of all. — أوّل بائك وبائكة وبوك

To urine. — ✱ بال o بَوْلًا ومَبالًا , و✧ بوّل

To cause a. o. to discharge urine. — بوّل وأبال واستبال ه

Heart, mind, state. Attention. Boldness. Welfare. ✧ Whale. — بال

What is the matter with thee? Why? — ما بالك

Attention, mindfulness. — ✧ إعطاء البال

Important, serious affair. — أمر ذو بال

Scent-bag. Bottle, phial. — Ps بالة

Bale, bundle. — Is بالة

Postage-stamp. — Ts بُول ووَرَق بُول

Urine. Matrimony. Offspring. — بَوْل ج أبوال

Diabetes. — بَوْل سُكَّرِي

Albuminuria, Bright's disease — بَوْل زُلالي

Great abundance of urine. Diabetes. — بُوال

Urinal. — مِبْوَلة

Owl. An owl. — ✱ بُوم وبُومة ج أبوام

To surpass a. o. in virtue, merit — ✱ بان o ه بَوْنًا

Ben-tree, a species of *moringa*. *Salix ægyptia*, Egyptian willow — بان وبانة

Interval. Difference. Distance. Merit, virtue. — بُون وبَوْن

Tenth Coptic month : June. — Ce بَؤُونة

To remember, to understand a. th. To think of. — ✱ باه o ه بَوْهًا وبَيْهًا ل

Matrimony. — باه

Court-yard. — باحة

Curse. Malediction. — بَوْه

Hawk. Owl. — بُوه

Owl. Fool, stupid. Wool (before it is soaked in the inkstand). — بُوهة

To act in the same way as another. — ✱ بوى i ه بَيًّا

Imitation. Counterfeiting. — بَوَى

✧ Varnish, blacking. — Ts بُويا

Shoe-black. — Ts بُوياجي

Conduit, sink-hole of a tank. — ✱ بيب

To spend the night. To marry. — ✱ بات i بَيْتًا وبَيْتُوتةً ومَبِيتًا ومَباتًا

To spend the night in (a place). — ب او عِند —

To be busy about a. th. during the night. To build (a house). To brood over (a design). — بيّت ه

To attack the enemy by night. — العدوّ —

To let a. o. spend the night. — وأبات ه —

To prepare provisions for one night. — إستبات

بَيْت ج بُيُوت وأبيات وبُيُوتات وأبابيت

House; dwelling. Room, apartments. Household, family. Case. Strophe. Stanza. Verse.

He is a man of good family. — هُوَ مِن أهل البُيُوتات

To be white, to get white. إِبْيَضَّ
Whiteness. Milk. ✧ Milk-food بَيَاض (butter, cheese, eggs). ✧ Albugo.
White of eggs. بَيَاض البَيْض
White of the eye. بَيَاض العَيْن
Day-light. بَيَاض النَّهار
Good character. بَيَاض الوجه
The whole day. بَيَاض اليَوْم
Carte-blanche. خَتْم عَلَى بَيَاض
Eggs. بَيْض ج بُيُوض
An egg. Heart. Middle- بَيْضَة ج بَيْضَات part. Helmet of iron. Testicle.
Cock's egg (*said of a. th. impossible to be got*). بَيْضَة الدِّيك
The foremost man of a place. بَيْضَة البَلَد
Woman. بَيْضَة الخِدْر
Oval, egg-shaped. بَيْضِيّ
Whiteness. بَيَاضَة
Egg-seller. ✧ White clay. بَيَّاض
بَائِض ج بَوَائِض , وبَيُوض ج بُيُض وبِيض
Bringing forth eggs, oviparous.
Good layer (hen). بَيَّاضَة
White. Whiter. أَبْيَض م بَيْضَاء ج بِيض Sword.
Happy days. الأَيَّام البِيض
Moon-lighted nights. اللَّيَالِي البِيض
Silver. Wheat. Sun. Paper. البَيْضَاء
He has not مَا رَدَّ عَلَيَّ بَيْضَاء وَلَا سَوْدَاء returned to me any answer whether good or bad (*lit.* black or white).
The first gleam of dawn. الخَيْط الأَبْيَض
Milk and water. الأَبْيَضَان
Sudden death. المَوْت الأَبْيَض
Beneficence. Power. Favour, اليَد البَيْضَاء merit, glory.
The white race (*opp. to* البِيضَان (السُّودَان the black.
Washing. Tinning. Fair copy. تَبْيِيض
Ovary. مَبِيض
Copier. Tinner. Fuller. Bleacher. مُبَيِّض
To trade. ✱ بَاعَ i بَيْعًا ومَبِيعًا ه ه To buy or to sell a. th. to a. o.
To sell a. th. to a. o.; to make بَايَع ه a contract, a covenant with a. o.
To acknowledge a. o. as — ه ب (a chief).
He was recognized as بُويِع لَهُ بِالخِلَافَة Caliph.

Arsenal. بَيْت السِّلَاح
Temple of البَيْت العَتِيق والبَيْت الحَرَام Mecca, the Caaba.
Cobweb. بَيْت العَنْكَبُوت
Water-closet. بَيْت المَاء وبَيْت الخَلَاء
Public treasury. بَيْت المَال
Food for one night. بَيْت لَيْلَة
Jerusalem. بَيْت المَقْدِس والبَيْت المُقَدَّس
Small house, small room. بُيَيْت
Nightly raid. بَيَات
Being by night. بَائِت
Stale (bread, food). بَائِت وبَيُّوت
Shelter for the night. مَبِيت
To ✱ بَادَ i بَيْدًا وبَيَادًا وبُيُودًا وبَيْدُودَة cease, to finish. To perish, to be lost.
To set (sun). — بُيُودًا
To cause a. o. to perish; أَبَاد ه وه to destroy, to annihilate a. o. or a. th.
If not, except that. On account بَيْدَ أَنْ of. However, besides.
Dangerous desert. بَيْدَاء ج بِيد وبَيْدَاوَات
Perishing, perishable. بَائِد
Foot-soldier. Infantry. Ps بَيَادِيّ ج بَيَادَة
Ale, beer. Is بِيرَة
To raise o.'s self above ✱ بَاسَ i بَيْسًا (people) and oppress them.
To beautify (a. o.'s face: ✱ بَاشَ — بَيَّش God).
To produce, to germinate a. th. أَبَاش ه
Hole for planting a tree. ✧ بِيش ج أَبْيَاش
To make a hole for planting ✧ بَيَّش a tree.
Wolf's bane, aconite. بِيش
Misfortune. Confusion. ✱ بَيْص وبِيص Strait, distress.
He was وَقَع فِي حِيص بَيْص وحِيص بِيص involved in a hopeless affair.
To lay eggs (hen). ✱ بَاضَ i بَيْضًا
To excede a. o. in white- — وبَايَض ه ness.
To remain in (a place, — ب
To bleach. To tin. a. th. بَيَّض ه ✧ To copy fair. To whitewash (a house).
May God cheer him! بَيَّض الله وَجْهَهُ
To be bleached. ✧ To be copied تَبَيَّض fair.
To put on an iron helmet. إِبْتَاض
To destroy (a tribe). — ه

To contrast.
To be clear, manifest. إِسْتَبَان
To recognize a. th. as evident. ه —
To manifest a. th.
Meeting or separation. Tie. بَيْن
Interval. Difference.
Friendship, concord. Enmity. ذَات البَيْن
Between, amongst, in the midst of. بَيْن
Before him, in his presence. بَيْن يَدَيْهِ
Meanwhile. بَيْن ذٰلِكَ
Equally distant from بَيْن بَيْن
the extreme points, average.
Middling.
Amongst, between them. فِيمَا بَيْنَهُمْ
When, whilst, while, as. بَيْنَمَا وبَيْنَا
Tract of land. Boundary. بَيْن ج بُيُون
Separation.
Tract of land. Division between بَيْن
two lands.
Declaration. Explanation. بَيَان
Argument. Rhetoric, Clear meaning
of a word.
Explanation, clear demonstration تَبْيِين
Evidence. Clear explanation. تِبْيَان
Interstice, interval, gap. بَيْنُونَة
Divorced woman. Deep well. بَائِن
Clear, evident, manifest. بَائِن وبَيِّن
Obvious, clear. بَيِّن ج أَبْيِنَاء
Eloquent, expres- — ج أَبْيِنَاء وأَبْيَان وبَيْنَا
sing himself clearly.
Evidence, clear proof, ar- بَيِّنَة ج بَيِّنَات
gument. Witness, precise testimony.
Clearer. أَبْيَن
Explaining clearly. Clear, beyond مُبِين
doubt, obvious.
Parting. Contrast. Difference تَبَايُن
between two things.
Relation of two numbers — ومُبَايَنَة
that cannot have any other common divisor but a unit. Contradiction.
The Imperial Ante- ✧ المَابَيْن الهُمَايُونِي
chamber.
God keep you. God ✻ بِيّ — بَيَّاكَ الله
help you!
Unknown man; هَيّ بن بَيّ وهَيَّان بن بَيَّان
Mr so and so.
Firman بُيُورُدِي وبُيُورُلْدِي و✧ بُيُورُلْدِي Ts
of the Sultan.

To exhibit, to offer goods for أَبَاعَ ه
sale.
To draw up a contract. To agree تَبَايَعَ
together on a. th.
To be sold. To find a ready إِنْبَاعَ
market (goods).
To buy a. th. of To pur- إِبْتَاعَ ه مِن
chase.
To try to buy a. th. from a. o. إِسْتَبَاعَ ه ه
Sale or purchase. Investiture بَيْع وبَيْعَة
of a caliph, a king.
Church. Jewish S بِيعَة ج بِيَع وبِيعَات
synagogue.
Wares. Goods; things بِيَاعَة ج بِيَاعَات
offered for sale.
Seller of, dealer in. بَائِع ج بَاعَة
The two transactors (pur- البَائِعَان
chaser and seller).
Seller, buyer. بَيِّع ج بَيْعَاء وأَبْيِعَاء
Merchant, seller, بَيَّاع وبَيُّوع وبَيِّع
Deed of sale. Crowning of a مُبَايَعَة
king, a caliph.
Sold, Mart, market. مَبِيع
Offered for sale. Saleable. مُبَاع
Bought. Buyer. مُبْتَاع
To perish. ✻ بَاغَ i بَيْغًا
Major, officer commanding Ts بِيكْبَاشِي
1000 men.
Hospital. Lunatic asylum. P بِيمَارِسْتَان
To be sepa- ✻ بَانَ i بَيْنًا وبُيُونًا وبَيْنُونَة عَن
rated, far away, remote from; to be divorced from (woman).
To be married (girl). —
To be clear, obvious. — بَيَانًا وتِبْيَانًا
To appear, to be within sight.
To be divorced (woman). بَيَّن
To come forth, to appear. — وأَبَان
To give a. o. in marriage. — وأَبَان ه
To separate a. o. To mani- — وأَبَان ه
fest. To explain a. th.
To part from, to forsake a. o. بَايَن ه
To set a. o. apart. أَبَان إِبَانَة ه وه
To pronounce distinctly. To declare a. th.
To be clear, easily understood. تَبَيَّن
To appear.
To make a. th. clear, obvious. ه —
To explain. To understand a. th.
To be dissimilar, unlike. تَبَايَن

ت

ت 1 Pronoun postfixed to the verbs at the first and second as well as the third feminine person of the past فَعلْتُ فَعلْتَ فَعلْتِ.
2° Particle prefixed to the verbs at the second person as well as the third feminine of the future تَفْعَلُ تَفْعَلُ تَفْعَلِينَ.
3° Particle used in swearing.
By God, I swear by God. تَاللهِ
✻ تَا or تِي , ذِي , ذِهِ , (fem. of ذَا) ; This. تَانِ ; d. أُلَاءِ ,pl.
Sometimes ها is prefixed to the pronoun. هٰذِهِ , d. هٰتَانِ , pl. هٰؤُلَاءِ
Sometimes also كَ is postfixed to the pronoun:
That. تَاكَ or تِيكَ , d. تَانِكَ , pl. أُولَائِكَ
✻ تَأْتَأَ تَأْتَأَةً وتَأْتَاءً To stutter in pronouncing the T. To crawl (child).
Stammering. تَأْتَأَة
✻ تَأَرَ a تَأْرًا ه To scold a. o.
— ه ب To strike a. o. with.
أَتْأَرَ إِتْآرًا ه وأَتْأَرَ البَصَرَ إِلَيْهِ To look steadfastly at; to stare at.
تَارَة ج تَارَات وتِيَر وتِئَر Time (*in regard to repetition*).
تَارَةً ... تَارَةً Sometimes, now ... then.
Ps تَازًا وتَازَه Fresh, tender.
✻ تَئِقَ a تَأَقًا To be filled up (vessel). To sob (child). To be filled with anger, prone to evil (man).
تَأَقَة Irascibility, hot temper.
تَئِق ومِتْآق Passionate; hot-headed. Fiery (horse).
تَأَمَ — تَاءَمَ ه وه To be twin-born with a. o. To weave (a stuff) with double threads. To fetch two runs (horse).
أَتْأَمَ إِتْآمًا To give birth to twins (woman).

Twin-born. تِئْم وتُؤْم وتَتْئِيم
Twin. تَوْأَم م تَوْأَمَة ج تَوَائِم وتُؤَام
— Twin (thing). Match, fellow of a pair
Bringing forth twins (female). مِتْآم ج مَتَائِم
Woven of two threads (garment). ثَوْب مِتْآم
✻ تَبَّ o تَبًّا ه To cut off, to curtail o. th.
— تَبًّا وتَبَبًا وتَبَابًا وتَبِيبًا To perish. to be lost. To suffer loss.
— ه To lose a. o.
تَبَّبَ ه To utter the curse: «*Woe to thee* !» To destroy a. o.
أَتَبَّ ه To weaken, to enervate a. o.
إِسْتَتَبَّ To be set in order, to be in a fair way (affair). To be trodden (road).
Weakness, deficiency. Loss. تَبَاب وتَبِيب
Woe, loss, damage. تَبّ وتَبَّة
Woe to thee! Mayest thou perish! تَبًّا لَكَ
Old man. Aged. تَابّ م تَابَّة
Set in order, strengthened. مُسْتَتَبّ
✻ تَابُوت ج تَوَابِيت Coffin, wooden case. Ark of the Covenant.
✻ تَبِرَ a تَبَرًا , وتَبَرَ o i تَبْرًا To perish.
تَبَّرَ ه وه To ruin, to lose, to destroy a. o. or a. th. To smash, to crumble a. th.
Ruin, perdition. تَبَار
Gold. silver-sand or particle. Native ore. تِبْر
A gold or silver particle. تِبْرَة
Perishing. Deficient. مُتَبَّر
✻ تَبِعَ a تَبَعًا وتَبَاعًا وتَبَاعَةً , واتَّبَعَهُ ه To follow a. o., to come with. To imitate, to obey a. o. To be the follower of.

— تُبُوعًا ه To prosecute (an affair).
تَبِعَ ه وهـ To pursue unremittingly. To follow the scent of, to trak a. o.
تابع مُتابَعَة وتِباعًا ه على To follow a. o. in (his opinions).
— ه To fulfil a. th. ; to carry on, to get through. To trace back (a tradition) to its source.
أتبع ه ه وهـ To make a. o. or a. th. to follow another. To put. a. th. next to.
— ه وهـ To prosecute ; to attain. To overtake a. o. or a. th.
تتبّع هـ To observe a. th. in its growth. To study thoroughly (a science). To make repeated endeavours. To ask consecutively, to examine successively a. th.
تتابع To come one after the other, to arrive successively.
إستتبع ه To ask a.o. to follow ; to get a. o. to follow.
تَبَع ج أتباع (s. and pl.) Follower. ✧ Belonging to ; property of. Subject of a power.
تَبِعَة ج تَبِعات Consequence, result of a good or bad action. Chastisement. Prosecution.
تُبَّع ج تَبابِعَة Surname of the ancient kings of Yemen.
تِباعَة ج تِباعات Sequel, issue. Penalty, chastisement.
✧ تَبَعِيَّة Nationality. Succession.
✧ بالتَّبَعِيَّة Following, in succession, gradually, at the heels of.
تَبِيع ج تِباع Follower, attendant. Votary.
تَبِيع ج أتبِعَة Creditor. Debtor.
تابع وتَبِيع م تَبِيعَة ج تِباع وتَبائِع وتَبِع Helper. Adept. Votary. Zealot. Follower of women.
تابع ج تَبَع وتَبَعَة وتَوابِع وتُبَّاع Following, coming next. Follower, domestic servant. Amenable to. Appositive, (Gram.)
تابِعَة ج تَوابِع Female attendant, follower. Consequence, issue.
إتباع Imitative pleonasm *used for corroborating a word as* كثير بَثِير . وحَسَن بَسَن.
بالتَّتابُع Successively, one after the other, in turn.
مُتَتابِع Uninterrupted, successive. Uniform, symmetrical.
مَتْبُوع Followed. Obeyed. Sovereign. Antecedent of an appositive (*Gram.*)
P تِنْبَغ Smoking-tobacco.
✱ تَبَل i تَبْلًا ه To show hostility to.
— وأتبل ه To weaken. To make sick, to bewilder a. o. (love). To destroy a. o
تَبَّل وتابَل و✧ تَوْبَل هـ To season (a dish).
تَبْل ج أتبال وتُبُول Illness. Weakness. Hatred. Revenge.
تَتْبِيل Seasoning.
تابَل و تابِل ج تَوابِل Pickle, spices.
مُتَبَّل Seasoned (food).
مَتْبُول ومُتْبَل Weakened, enervated. Mad.
P تَوْبال Dross of iron, copper.
✱ تَبَن i تَبْنًا ه To feed (an animal) with straw.
تَبِن a تَبَنًا To be intelligent, prudent.
تَبَّن To gather straw in a granary.
إتَّبَن To put on small drawers.
تِبْن Straw. Large cup.
تِبْنَة Straw.
تَبانَة Intelligence.
P تُبان Breeches of sailors, wrestlers.
مَتْبَن وتَبانَة Barn for storing straw, heap of straw.
تَبَّان Dealer in straw.
مُتَبَّن ومَتْبُون وتِبْنِيّ Straw-coloured (garment, beast).
✧ دَرْب التَّبَّانَة وه سِكَّة التَّبَّانَة ✧ The milky way.
✱ تَبا o تَبْوًا To make a raid.
✱ تَتَر وتَتار Tartars (nation).
تَتَرِيّ A tartar. ✧ Courier, postman.
Ts تُتُن Smoking-tobacco.
✱ تَجَر o تَجْرًا وتِجارَة , وتاجَر وأتْجَر واتَّجَر To trade, to be in business.
تِجارَة Trade, mercantile affairs, business.
تاجِر ج تِجار وتُجّار Merchant, commercial man, dealer, trader. Wine-merchant.
تاجِرَة ج تَواجِر Tradeswoman. Merchantable (goods).

to settle the limits of.
To have (see وَخِم)(for اتّخم) an indigestion. تَخِم a تُخَمَة
To confine, to border upon a. th. تاخم ه
To cause an indigestion to. أتخم ه
Land-mark, limit, boundaries. borders. تَخْم وتُخْم ج تُخُوم
Indigestion. تُخَمَة وتُخْمَة ج تُخَمَات وتُخَم
Heavy, indigestible food. مَتْخَمَة
Suffering indigestion. ✧ مَتْخُوم
To be severed (limb). ✻ تَرَّ i o تَرًّا وتُرُورًا
To go away. To retire apart form. — عن
To become fat, fleshy and fresh. — وتَرَّ a تَرَارَة
To drive a. o. away. To cut off a. th. — ه وه
Architect's string. تُرّ
I will set thee right. أُقِيمُكَ عَلَى التُّرّ
Fat. Solitary. Tall. تارّ م تارَّة
Lustiness. تَرَارَة
Boy. أُتْرُورٌ
To chatter. ✧ To utter idle words. ✻ تَرْتَر
To shake, to stir a. o. — ه
To be shaken, bustled. تَتَرْتَر
✧ Mill-clack. تَرْتَار
Talkativeness. Hurry, shock. تَرْتَرَة
Misfortunes, bad circumstances. تَرَاتِر
To be full of earth (place). To have dust in the hands. To be destitute. ✻ تَرِب a تَرَبًا ومَتْرَبًا
To be rich. To be destitute. تَرَّب وأتْرَب
✧ To become dust (corpse). To assume an earth-like appearance. تَرَّب
He sank from wealth into destitution. تَرَّب بَعْدَ مَا أتْرَب
To soil a. o. with dust. To cover with earth. To throw earth upon a. th. To sprinkle (a letter) with sand. تَرَّب وأتْرَب ه
To be contemporary, coeval with, friend of a. o. تارَب ه
To be soiled with earth. To crumble to dust. تَتَرَّب
Contemporary. Friend. Companion. Match. تِرْب ج أتْرَاب

Goods, merchandise. مَتْجَر ج مَتَاجِر
Provost of merchants. Pe سر تُجّار
Commercial. مَتْجَرِيّ
Market. Trading country. مَتْجَرَة
Before, in front of. (see وجه) ✻ تُجَاه
Opposite to thee. تُجَاهَكَ
Under, beneath. Below. ✻ تَحْت
Men of the lowest class. التُّحُوت
Inferior. Situated underneath. تَحْتَانِيّ
Scaffold, shop-counter. Ts تَحْتَا بُوش
Movement. ✻ تَحْتَحَة
To present a. o. with a very precious gift. ✻ تحف – أتحف ه ب
Any fine, rare, and precious object. Masterpiece. Gift. Present. تُحْفَة وتُحَفَة ج تُحَف وتَحَائِف
Museum. مَتْحَف ودَار التُّحَف
To shade (a stuff). ✻ تَخِر o تَخْرًا ه
Weaver. تاخِر
Black colour. Black. تُخْمَة
To become sour; to transform into leaven (paste). To be moistened too much (dough, mud). ✧ To be worm-eaten (wood). ✻ تَخَّ o تُخُوخَة
To render sour. To leaven (the dough). أتَخَّ ه
Sesame-dregs. Leavened paste. تَخّ
✧ Rotten part (of a tree). تُخَاخ
Loathing food (man). تاخّ
To stammer. ✧ To be rotten, worm-eaten. ✻ تَخْتَخ
To be bruised by a blow (man). ▫ تَتَخْتَخ
Stammering. Inarticulate sound. تَخْتَخَة
Fat (man). ▫ مُتَخْتِخ
Stammerer. Foreigner having a bad Arabic pronounciation. تَخْتَاخ
Bedstead. Throne, sofa-bed. Seat. Ward-robe. ▫ Meeting-place. Music-hall. P تَخْت ج تُخُوت
To make a ceiling. To board (a room). ▫ To sit on a soft bed. تَخَّت
Litter. Palanquin. P تَخْت رُوَان وتَخْتَرْوَان
Capital of a kingdom. تَخْت المُلْك
Gallery, raised platform. ✧ مُتَخَّت
To take. (see اخذ) (for اتّخذ) ✻ تَخِذ
Dolphin (fish). ✻ تُخَس
To set boundaries, ✻ تَخَم i تَخْمًا ه

ترب وتُرْب وتُرَاب وتَرِيب وتَيْرَب وتَيْرَاب

Earth, dust. وتَوْرَب ﺟ أتْرِبَة وتِرْبَان

Destitute. Full of earth. تَرِب

A piece of land. تُرَابَة

Earth. Terrestrial globe. تُرْبَاء

Earth. Grave-yard. Tomb. تُرْبَة ﺟ تُرَب

Dusty (place). Bringing dust (wind). Soiled with dust. تَرِب م تَرِبَة

Thlaspi, leguminous plant. تَرِبَة وتَرِب

End of the fingers. — ﺟ تَرِبَات

Grave-diggers, navvies. ▫ تُرَابِيَّة

Breast; upper-part of the breast. Ribs. تَرِيبَة ﺟ تَرَائِب

Poverty, destitution. مَتْرَبَة

Bolt of a door. ▫ تِرْبَاس

Inheritance. (*see* ورث). ✻ تُرَاث

To be veiled, concealed. ✻ تَرِجَ o تَرَجًا

To find difficulties in (a science). تَرِجَ a تَرَجًا عَلَى

Place full of lions. تَرِج

Large lemon. Citron. أُتْرُجّ وتُرُنْج وأُتْرُنْج

Muscular. تُرِيج

To interpret, to translate from (one language) to (another). ✻ تَرْجَمَ ه عن ... إلى

To write the biography of. — ه

Interpretation, translation. Biography. تَرْجَمَة ﺟ تَرَاجِم

Condition (of a citizen). تَرْجَمَة حال

Introduction. Preface of a book. — الكِتَاب

The Septuagint. التَّرْجَمَة السَّبْعِينِيَّة

Interpreter. dragoman. تُرْجُمَان ﺟ تَرَاجِمَة وتَرَاجِم

Interpreter. Biographer. مُتَرْجِم

Interpreted, translated. Dubious. مُتَرْجَم

To be grieved, afflicted. ✻ تَرِحَ a تَرَحًا، وتَتَرَّحَ

To sadden, to grieve a. o. تَرَّحَ وأَتْرَحَ ه

Sadness, sorrow. تَرَح ﺟ أَتْرَاح

Scanty (stream). Painful (life). مُتَرَّح

To scarify (cupper). ✻ تَرَخَ a تَرْخًا

Slight incision on the skin. تَرْخ

To be thick, hard, dry. ✻ تَرَزَ i o وتَرِزَ a تَرَزًا وتُرُوزًا

To freeze (water). تَرِزَ a تَرَزًا

To harden, to dessicate a. th. أَتْرَزَ ه

Sudden death. تُرَاز

Dead, dried up. Hard and thick. تَارِز

Scales, balance. Pe تَرَازِي

▫ To fill (a vessel). ✻ تَرَسَ o ه

To provide a. o. with a shield. تَرَّسَ ه

To arm o.'s self with a shield. To protect o.'s self with. — وتَتَرَّسَ

تُرْس ﺟ أَتْرَاس وتُرُوس وتِرَاس وتِرَسَة

Shield. Disk (of the sun).

✧ The reverse, the wrong way. Ts بِالتَّرْس

Libertine. Ts تَرَس

Art of making shields. تِرَاسَة

Shield-bearer. تَارِس وتَرَّاس

Shield-maker. ▫ Hirer of donkeys. تَرَّاس

Wooden bar. مِتْرَس ومِتْرَسَة ﺟ مَتَارِس

Intrenchment, rampart, bulwark. Barricade. مِتْرَاس ﺟ مَتَارِيس

To intrench themselves (army). ✧ تَمَتْرَسَ

Arsenal. (*for* دار الصناعة) Ts تَرْسَانَة وتَرْسَخَانَة

To be wicked, stingy. ✻ تَرِشَ a تَرَشًا

Wicked, stingy. تَرِش وتَارِش

To be straightened, fastened. ✻ تَرُصَ o تَرَاصَة

To straighten, to fasten a. th. To rectify (the weight in a balance). تَرَّصَ وأَتْرَصَ ه

Right, accurate (balance). Strong, hardy. تَرِيص ومُتْرَص

To rush into peril. To be filled (vessel). ✻ تَرِعَ a تَرَعًا

To avert a. o. from. — ه عن

To close (a door). تَرَّعَ ه

To fill up (a vessel). أَتْرَعَ ه

To hasten to do (evil). تَتَرَّعَ إلى وب

To be full (vessel). إِتَّرَعَ

Door. Flood-gate. Flight of stairs. Channel between two seas. Canal of irrigation. Mouth of a stream. Garden. تُرْعَة ﺟ تُرَع

Sappy (plant). Prone to evil, mischievous. Light-minded. تَرِع

Ordnance survey. ▫ تَارِع ﺟ تَوَارِع

Door-keeper. تَرَّاع

Flooding a valley (stream). — وأَتْرَع

To lead a delicate life. ✻ تَرِفَ a تَرَفًا

Pl. Clouds. Misfortunes.
Bridle, rein. تِزْكِين ودِزْكِين Ts
To be the ninth. ✻ تَسَع a i تَسْعًا
To take the ninth part of. — ه و ه
To make a. th. nine.
To become nine in number. أَتْسَع
Nine. تِسْعَة م تِسْع
The ninth, ninth part. تَسِيع وتُسْع ج أَتْسَاء
Ninth. تَاسِع
Nineteen. تِسْعَة عَشَر م تِسْعَ عَشْرَة
Nineteenth. تَاسِع عَشَر م تَاسِعَة عَشْرَة
Ninety. Ninetieth. تِسْعُون
Nine and nine. تُسَاع
Compound of nine. تُسَاعِيّ
Novena. تُسَاعِيَّة و ✧ تِسْعَوِيَّة
Woven of nine threads (rope). مُتْسُوء
Slipper, sandal, shoe. ✧ تَاسُومَة ج تَوَاسِيم
October. تِشْرِين الأَوَّل Ch
November. تِشْرِين الثَّانِي Ch
Autumn. Mulberry leaves gathered in October and November. ✧ تَشَارِين
To be languid. ✻ تَمّ o تَمًّا وأَتَمّ
To vomit. — وانْتَمّ
Languor. Vomiting. تَمّ وتَمَّة
To compel a. o. to do a. th. unwillingly. To ill-treat, to shake a. o. To make a. o. to stammer (confusion). ◻ To pull out (a tooth, a stone). ✻ تَعْتَع ه
To sink down in the sand (beast). تَعْتَع
To reiterate words. To be unable to express o.'s self. — في الكَلَام
To be tired, exhausted. ✻ تَعِب a تَعَبًا
To exhaust a. o. — ه
To weary, to tire a. o. To break (a bone) anew. To fill (a vessel). أَتْعَب ه و ه
Weariness, toil, fatigue. تَعَب ج أَتْعَاب
Tired, fatigued. تَعِب وتَعْبَان
Fees. ◻ أَتْعَاب
Fatigue. Toil. Place and cause of fatigue. مَتْعَب ومَتْعَبَة ج مَتَاعِب
Toilsome (work), tiring. مُتْعِب
Fatigued. Worn out by care, remorse or sorrow. مُتْعَب و ✧ مَتْعُوب
To cry out, to vociferate. ✻ تَعَر a تَعْرًا
Bleeding abundantly (wound). تَعَّار

To be luxuriant (plant).
To effeminate, to render a. o. inordinate (pleasures). تَرَّف وأَتْرَف ه
To persevere in a. th.
To behave inordinately. إِسْتَتْرَف
Effeminacy. Well-being تَرَف
Wealth. Welfare. Relish. تُرْفَة
Comfortable, easy (life). تَرِف وتَرِيف
Ungrateful, given to excess, softened by delights. Delicate (boy). مُتَرَّف ومُتْرَف
Truffle. ✧ تِرْفَاس وتِرْفَاش
To hit a man on the collar-bone. ✻ تَرْقَى ه
Clavicle, collar-bone. تَرْقُوَة ج تَرَاقٍ
Theriac, antidote. Wine. تِرْيَاق G
To forsake a. o., to abandon, to leave off. To give up a. th. To neglect, to omit a. th. ✻ تَرَك o تَرْكًا وتِرْكَانًا, واتَّرَك ه و ه
To bequeath a. th. to a. o. — ه ل
To forsake, to dismiss a. o. To let a. o. quiet. To grant a truce to a. o. تَارَك مُتَارَكَة وتِرَاكًا ه
To agree on leaving a. th. تَتَارَك ه
Forsaking, abandonment. تَرْك
Heirloom, inheritance, bequest. تَرِكَة وتِرْكَة
Branch stripped of its dates. تَرِيك
Middle-aged unmarried woman. Empty egg. Water left by a torrent. Iron helmet. تَرِيكَة ج تَرَائِك
Truce. مُتَارَكَة وتِرَاك
Turk. تُرْك ج أَتْرَاك
A Turk. Turkish. Turkish language. تُرْكِيّ
Turkmans. T تُرْكُمَان وتُرْكُمَانِيّ
Leathern socks. Ts تَرَلِك
To appoint a time, a term to a. o. ✧ تَرَّم ه ل
✧ Appointed time. Termination. Fs تِرْم ج أَتْرَام
To withdraw from fight. ✻ تَرْمَس
Lupine (kitchen-plant). Gs تُرْمُس
Underground passage. تُرْمُسَة وتُرْنُسَة
Persian manna. P تَرَنْجَبِين
To busy o.'s self about trifles. To utter idle words. ✻ تَرِه a تَرَهًا
Desert. Trifle. تُرَّهَة ج تُرَّهَات

To perish. To stumble. تعس a تعسا *
To render unhappy تعس وأتعس ه
To destroy a. o. (God).
Evil, unhappiness. Doss, ill-luck. تعس وتعاسة
Stumble. Fall. تعسة
Unhappy, miserable, wretched. Stumbling (horse). تعس وتعيس
Stumbling-block. Ill-luck. متعسة
To conceal laughter. To speak confusedly from want of teeth (old man). تعتع *
To perish. تغب a تغبا *
To lose, to cause the loss of a. o. or a. th. أتغب ه و ه
Destruction. Dearth. Hunger. Filth. تغب
Ugly, hideous. تغب
To burst with rain (cloud). تغر a تغورا *
To spurt from a vein (blood). To burst out (skin). — تغرا
To boil (pot). تغر تغرانا
✧ To spit (blood). ◻ To spit. To drivel in speaking. تف a تفا *
To show contempt by the word: تف, fie, tush! تفف
Dirt under the nails. تف ج تففة
Fie! For shame! تفا لك
Opportunity. تفان
Trifles. Rubbish. تفاتف
To be angry. تفي a تفا *
Seasonable time. تفيئة وتفية
To leave off the care of o.'s body, to become dirty. تفث a تفثا *
To stain (a place) with blood. تفث ه
Dirt. تفث
Apple. Apple-tree. تفاح ج تفافيح *
An apple. The haunch-bone. تفاحة
Apple-grove. متفحة
To bud, to put forth shoots (tree). تفر – أتفر و✧ طفر *
Sloven. Filthy (man). تافر وتفر وتفران
Dimple on the upper-lip. تفرة وتفرة وتفرة
Buds. Sprout. Carbuncled face. تفرة و✧ طفرة
To spit a fine saliva. تفل o i تفلا *
To leave off the use of تفل a تفلا

perfume and smell bad. To perfume o.'s self. To have a foul odour.
To make (odour) to be bad. أتفل ه
Spittle of fine saliva. Foam of the sea. تفل وتفال
Ill-smelling, unperfumed. تفل م تفلة ومتفال
Spittoon. متفلة
Fox. Dry grass. تتفل وتتفل
Gun, musket. تفنكة Ts
Musketeer, rifleman. تفنكجي Ts
To be small, mean, little, stupid. To be tasteless (food). تفه a تفها وتفها وتفاهة وتفوها *
To make a paltry gift. أتفهه في العطاء
Tastelessness of a dish. تفاهة
Tasteless (food). Very small, little. تفه وتافه
Badger (animal). تفه
Coriander-seed. Caraway-seed. تقدة *
To fatten (a land) by watering it with muddy water. تقن – تقن ه *
To improve a. th. To set in good order; to dispose with art. To arrange, to settle, to fasten a. th. To bring to perfection. أتقن ه
To study a science thoroughly. أتقن العلم
Inborn disposition. Sediment of water. Slime of a well. تقن ج أتقان
Skilful, clever (man). تقن وتقن
Perfection of a work. تقانة
Steadfastness. Improvement (of a work). إتقان
Strong. Perfect. Finished up, improved. متقن و✧ متقون
See وقى . ه (*for* اتقى) i a تقى *
To fear, to honour (God). To guard against.
To sow (corn-seeds). تقى ◻
Corn-seed. تقاوى ◻
Fat (man). متقي ◻
To cut, to tread upon, to crush a. th. ◻ To load (a gun). تك o تكا ه *
To inebriate a. o. (wine). ه —
To be meagre, weak-minded. i تكوكا —
To slib a running-lace into (trousers). إستتك ب

Small coin or about a half-penny. ✧ تِكّ وأبو تِكّ

Trousers-band. تِكَّة ج تِكَك و✧ دِكَّة

Second of time. ✧ تَكَّة ج تَكَّات

Monastery of dervishes. تَكَّة وتَكِيَّة TE

Bodkin. مِتَكّ

To trample a. th. under foot and break it. ◘ To boil fiercely (cooking-pot). To shiver from cold or fever. ✱ تَكْتَكَ ه

Ticking of a watch. تَكْتَكَة

To trust in, to rely upon. *See* وكل. ✱ تَكَل (*for* اتّكل)

To throw a. o. down. ✱ تَلّ o تَلًّا ٥ وه
To lead (a beast) behind o.'s back. ◘ To lift, to carry (a weight). ✧ To fill (a jar).

To let down (a rope) in (a well) — ه في

He charged him with a foul deed. تَلَّهُ بِتَلَّة سُوء

To fall down. To leak (tank). — o i تَلًّا

To exude (sweat). — i تَلًّا

To beseech a. o. To throw a. th. to a. o. To let down (a bucket) in a well. تَلّ إلى

To tie (a beast) and drive it. To make (a liquid) to drop. أَتَلّ ٥ وه

Hill of rubbish. Pillow. ◘ Ruins. تَلّ ج تِلَال وتُلُول وأَتْلَال

Way of lying down. Laziness. تِلَّة وتَلَّة

Neck. تَلِيل ج أَتِلَّة وتُلُل وتَلَائِل

Strong (man). Erect (spear). مِتَلّ

To shake a. th. violently. To drive (a beast) vehemently. ✱ تَلْتَلَ ه

To be in a good state (business, road). ✱ تَلَأَبَّ — اتْلَأَبَّ

Perdition, loss. ✱ تَلْب

May he perish! تَلْبًا لَهُ

Ass, she-ass one year old. Cub of the fox. تَوْلَب ج تَوَالِب

To be home-born, long in possession (cattle, slaves, *etc.*). ✱ تَلَدَ i o تُلُودًا

To stay, to dwell in a place. — o وتَلِدَ a ب

To gather property. تَلَّدَ

To possess property by inheritance. To acquire home-born property. أَتْلَدَ ه

Hereditary, long-possessed **goods**. Home-born slaves, cattle. تَلْد وتُلْد وتَلَد وتِلَاد , وتَالِد ج تَوَالِد

Hereditary, or acquired when young (cattle, slaves). Child. تَلِيد ومُتْلَد

Original possessor of a th. مُتْلِد

Palm-leaves basket. Portfolio. ✱ تلس — تِلِّيس ج تَلَالِيس

To erect, to lift the head (pers., gazelle). ✱ تَلَعَ a تَلْعًا

To break (day). — تُلُوعًا

To be long (neck). To be filled (vessel). تَلِعَ a تَلَعًا وتَلَاعَة

To stretch the neck and raise the head. أَتْلَعَ وتَتَالَعَ

Length of the neck. تَلَع

Height. Stream coming down a valley. تَلْعَة ج تِلَاع وتَلَع وتَلَعَات

Long-necked, tall (man, steed). Of high rank. تَلِيع وأَتْلَع

Erecting his head. مُتَتَالِع

To perish. To be spoiled. To be worn out, wasted. ✱ تَلِفَ a تَلَفًا

To destroy, to lose a. o. To ruin, to spoil a. th. أَتْلَفَ ٥ وه

Destruction. Unavenged (blood-shed). تَلَف

In a desperate state (sick pers.). في حال التَّلَف

A loss, a waste. تَلِيفَة

Dying (sick pers.). Worn out (knife). ✧ تَلْفَان

Spoiler, destroyer. تَلَّاف

Spoiling, ruining. مُتْلِف

Lavisher. Spendthrift. مِتْلَاف

Lost. Wasted. مُتْلَف و✧ مَتْلُوف

Dangerous spot. Desert. مَتْلَف ومَتْلَفَة

(*f. of* ذلك) This, that. ✱ تِلْكَ مث تَانِكَ وتَانِّكَ ج أُولَائِكَ

To furrow a. th. ✧ تَلَمَ ه

Furrow of the ploughshare. تَلَم ج أَتْلَام

Help-boy. Jeweller. تِلْم ج تِلَام

Brazen-faced, shameless. ◘ وَجْه تِلِم

To take a. o. as a disciple. ✱ تَلْمَذَ ٥

To become the disciple of a. o. تَلْمَذَ وتَتَلْمَذَ لِ

Pupil, disciple, student. ✧ Penitent (of a confessor). S تِلْمِيذ ج تَلَامِيذ وتَلَامِذَة

To perish. To be astonished. ✱ تَلِهَ a تَلَهًا

To give the finishing stroke to (a wounded man). تَمَّم عَلَى
To attain full growth. To be full (moon). To be near to bring forth. أَتَمَّ
To complete. To perform a. th. ه —
To be completed. To come one and all. تَتَامَّ
To ask a. o. to complete (a favour). إِسْتَتَمَّ ه
End. Term. Completion, complement. تَمّ وتِمّ وتُمّ وتَمَامَة
Mouth. ✧ تُمّ
Spade. Hatchet. Full moon. تِمّ
Performance. Completion. Full moon. تِمَام
The longest night of the year. لَيْلَة التِّمَام
Completely, entirely. تَمَامًا وبالتَّمَام
Remainder. Supplement. تُمَامَة
Complement, supplement. تَتِمَّة
Name of a tribe. Strong, tall. تَمِيم
Amulet. تَمِيمَة ج تَمَائِم وتَمِيمَات
Perfect; entire, complete. تَامّ م تَامَّة
Near to bring forth (female). Full moon. مُتِمّ
To mispronounce, to stammer. ✱ تَمْتَم
Stammerer. تَمْتَام م تَمْتَامَة
To feed a. o. with dates. ✱ تَمَر o تَمْرًا، وتَمَّر ه
To dry (dates). تَمَّر ه
To bear many dates (palm-tree). To have a large stock of dates (man). أَتْمَر
To be hard, stiff (spear, staff). إِتْمَارَّ
Dry dates. Dates of all sorts. تَمْر ج تُمُور وتُمْرَان
Tamarind. تَمْر هِنْدِيّ
A date. تَمْرَة ج تَمَرَات
Knot at the end of a whip.
Fond of dates. Relating to dates. تَمْرِيّ
Full of dates. تَامِر ومُتْمُور
Dealer in dates. تَمَّار
Nursing of the sick. Pe تِيمَار
Hospital servant. Pe تِيمَارْجِيّ
July. Adonis (the god of beauty). S تَمُّوز وتَمُوز
To gather, to collect a. th. ✱ تَمَش o تَمْشًا ه
To be high ✱ تَمَك o i تَمْكًا وتُمُوكًا

— ه وعن To forget a. th.
أَتْلَه ه To destroy a. o. (man: sickness).
✱ تَلَا o تُلُوًّا ه To follow. To walk behind a. o., to imitate a. o.
— عن To leave off, to forsake a. th.
— تِلَاوَة ه To read (a book). To recite a. th.
تَلِيَ a تَلِيَّة وتَلى To remain (debt, time).
تَلَّى ه وه To follow a. o. To ask the remnant of (a debt). To make a supererogatory prayer. To accomplish (a vow). ✧ To draw (water). To fill (a jar).
أَتْلَى ه ه To make a. o. to follow another.
— ه وه To precede a. o. To put off the payment of (a debt).
— ه على To transfer a debt from one to another.
تَتَلَّى ه وه To follow, to prosecute. To seek to obtain a. th.
تَتَالَى To come consecutively.
إِسْتَتْلَى ه ه To ask a. o. to follow a. th.
— ه To look for a. o.
تَلَا. Protection. Neighbourhood.
تِلَاوَة Reading. Recital.
تُلُوّ Follower, adept, votary.
تِلْو ج أَتْلَاء Young one following his mother. Trace, footstep. Consequent. Corollary.
تَالٍ م تَالِيَة ج تَوَالٍ Following. Consequence.
التَّوَالِي Hinder parts. Rumps, tail of a horse. Posteriors.
بِالتَّالِي Then. At the end. Afterwards. Consequently. At last.
تُلَاوَة وتَلِيَّة Residue of a debt. Remainder of time.
مُتَالٍ Relieving a. o. in singing.
✱ تَمّ i تَمًّا وتُمًّا وتَمَامًا وتِمَامًا وتُمَامَة To be complete, accomplished. To be elapsed (month).
— ب او على To achieve, to accomplish. To execute (an order). To persevere in a. th.
— إلى To aim at, to repair towards.
تَمَّم ه وه To finish, to fulfil. To improve a. th. To put an amulet upon (a child).

To find (a country) unwholesome. ه —
Stink. تُهَمَة
Ill-smelling. تَهِمٌ وتَهِمَة
Suspicion. *See* وَهم . تُهْمَة وتُهَمَة
Tihamah, coast of Arabia. تِهَامَة
Suspicious, charging with. ✧ تَاهِم ب
Suspected, charged with. ✧ مَتْهُوم ب
To sleep. ✻ تَهِن a تَهَنًا
To be neglectful. ✻ تَهَا o تَهْوًا
Single (fold, knot). ✻ تَوٌّ ج أَتْوَاء
He came directly. جَاءَ تَوًّا
▫ Just now, directly. تَوّه
To ✻ تَابَ o تَوْبًا وتَوْبَةً وتَابَةً ومَتَابًا إلى الله
come back to God. To repent.
To forgive a. o. (God). — عَلَى
To incite a. o. to return إسْتَتَابَ ه
to God.
Repentance, contrition, atonement. تَوْبَة
Repenter, contrite, penitent. تَائِب
Repenting (man). Forgiving تَوَّاب
(God).
Mulberry tree, mulberry. ✻ تُوت
▫ First Coptic month : September.
Raspberry. ▫ تُوت شَوْكِيّ
Strawberry. ▫ تُوت أَرْضِي و✧ تُوت فَرَنْجِي
Wild mulberry. Raspberry. تُوت العُلَّيْق
Tutty. Sulphate of zinc. تُوتِيَا وتُوتِيَاء
Oxid of copper. تُوتِيَا حَمْرَاء
Sulphate of copper. تُوتِيَا زَرْقَاء
Zinc. Antimony. تُوتِيَا مَعْدِنِيَّة
To put on a crown. ✻ تَاجَ o تَوْجًا
To crown a. o. تَوَّجَ ه
To be crowned. To be made تَتَوَّجَ
a prince.
Wearing a crown. تَائِج ومُتَوَّج
Crown. Mitre. Turban. تَاج ج تِيجَان
Bronze. TE تُوج وتُونْج
To befall a. o. (event). ✻ تَاحَ o تَوْحًا ل
To be prepared for a. o. (th.).
To dip into a soft ✻ تَاخَ o تَوْخًا وتَوَخًا
substance (finger).
To flow (water). ✻ تَارَ o تَوْرًا
To repeat (an action). أَتَارَ إتَارَةً ه
To look intently at. — إلى
N. of act. Small vessel. Transactor. تَوْر
Mosaic law. Bible. H تَوْرَاة وتَوْرِيَة
To dip bread in ✻ تَامَ o تَوْمًا ه
(butter).

(camel's hump). To be fully-developed, tall, big (camel).
To fatten (cattle). أَتْمَكَ ه
Camel's hump. Tall, fat تَامِك ج تَوَامِك
(hump). Lofty (building).
Basis. ▫ تَمَل
Betel, a pepper-plant. تَامُول وتَانْبُول
Compound used for chewing.
To be altered ✻ تَمِهَ a تَمَهًا وتَمَاهَةً
(food).
To compare (things) ✻ تَنَّ — تَانَّ بَيْن
together.
To be remote. أَتَنَّ
To stunt (a child : sickness). — ه
He is still sitting, ▫ تَنُّهُ قَاعِد , تَنُّهُ مَاشِي
going.
Similar. Equal. Companion. تِنّ
Tanny (fish). ✧ تُنّ
Enormous snake. Draco تِنِّين ج تَنَانِين
(*const.*). Sea-monster. Water-spout.
To inhabit (a country). ✻ تَنَأَ a تُنُوءًا ب
Having a fixed abode. تَانِئ ج تُنَّاء
Rich.
Persian tobacco for the nar- P تُنْبَك
ghileh.
Cone-bearing fir. ✻ تَنُّوب
Ts تِنْبَل وتِنْبَال وتُنْبُول ج تَنَابِيل وتَنَابِلَة
Short. Dwarf. ✧ Effeminate. Lazy.
Betel. تَانْبُول
To stop ✻ تَنَخَ o تُنُوخًا . وتَنَّخَ وتَتَنَّخَ ب
in (a place), to inhabit it.
To have an indigestion. تَنِخَ a تَنَخًا
A circular earthen ✻ تَنُّور ج تَنَانِير
oven.
Unslit dress. Petticoat. ✧ تَنُّورَة وتَنُّورِيَّة
Desert. ✻ تَنُوفَة وتَنُوفِيَّة ج تَنَائِف
Tin-plate. Ts تَنَك
Tinman. Tinker Ts تَنَكْجِي
Tree of the desert. ✻ تَنُّوم
Turnsol, heliotrope تُنُّوم
To repeat idle talks. ✻ تَهْتَهَ
Impediment in speech. تَهْتَهَة
Nonsense, false, vain, (actions, تَهَاتِه
words).
To be tainted, ✻ تَهِمَ a تَهَمًا وتَهَامَةً
to stink (meat). To be exhausted
(camel).
To go to Tihamah. To afford أَتْهَمَ
matter to suspicion.

A milky plant. تَيُّوع وتَيْتُوع ج تَيْتُوعات

To be dim (sight). ✻ تاف o تَوْف

Fault, mistake. تَافَة وتَوْفَة وتُوفَة

To long for, to desire earnestly a. th. To purpose a. th. To hasten towards. ✻ تاق o تَوْقًا وتُوُوقًا وتَوَقَانًا وتِيَاقَةً إلى

He is dying, in the agony of death. تاق بنفسِهِ

To show a craving for. تَشَوَّق ه

Desire; propensity. تَوْق وتَوَقَان

Earnest, eager to obtain. تَائِق وتَوَّاق

To practise witchcraft. ✻ تال o تَوْلًا

Sorrow, fatigue. Misfortune. تُوَلَة وتُولَة ج تُوَلَات

Witchcraft. Love-philter. تُوَلَة وتِوَلَة

Pearl. Ear-ring. Necklace. Silver-bead. Ostrich-egg. ✻ تُومَة ج تُوم وتُوَم

Pearl-shell. أُمّ تُومَة

Wearing a necklace. مُتَوَّم

Garlic. ✧ تُوم (for ثُوم)

Ten thousand. Persian coin equal to 9 piastres. P تُومَان

To pursue game in all directions. ✻ تان – تَتَاوَن وتَتَاءَن لِلصَّيْد

To wander, to go astray. To be disordered in mind. To be proud. ✧ To be absent-minded. ✻ تاه o تَوْهًا

To lead astray, to destroy. To perplex a. o. ✧ To distract a. o. تَوَّه وأَتَاه ه

Waterless desert. فَلَاة تَيْه وتُوه ج أَتْوَاه وأَتَاوِيه

✧ Absence of mind. Bewilderment. تَوْهَان

To pass away (wealth). ✻ تَوِي a تَوًى

To destroy (wealth). أَتْوَى ه

Lost, passed away (wealth). تَوٍ وتَاوٍ

To become easy to a. o. (affair). To be decreed, fixed to a. o. (good or evil). ✻ تاح i تَيْحًا ل

To predetermine, to preordain a. th. to a. o. (God). To facilitate a. th. أَتَاح ه ل

Intruder. Forward, interfering in what is not of his concern. تَيَّاح وتِيِّحان وتَيِّحان ومِتْيَح

Ordained, decreed. مُتَاح

To strike a. o. with (a stick). ✻ تاخ i تَيْخًا ه

Kindness, meekness. ✻ تَيْد

Go on gently! تَيْدَكَ يا هٰذا

To swell, to dash together (waves). ✻ تار i تَيَرَانًا

Dashing waves. Proud. Haughty. Vehement current. تَيَّار

Now...now... *See* (تَار) تَارَةً...تَارَةً

To win a. o. ✻ تار i تَيَرَانًا , وتَايَر ه

Of short stature. Severe. تَيْأَز

To become a buck. ✻ تاس i تَيْسًا

To dash together (waves). تَتَايَس

The she-goat became a buck, *i. e*: a vile man became mighty. إِسْتَتْيَسَتِ العَنْز

Roe-buck. Goat-buck. Stupid, fool. تَيْس ج تُيُوس وأَتْيَاس وتِيَسَة

Roe-buck. ✧ تَيْس جَبَلِيّ

Buck-like nature. Stubbornness, obstinacy. تَيْسِيَّة وتَيْسُوسِيَّة و✧ تَيْسَنَة

Buck-shepherd. تَيَّاس

Buck-like. أَتْيَس م تَيْسَاء

To flow and spread (water). ✻ تاع i تَيْعًا وتَيَعَانًا

To take, to carry a. th. away. – وتَيَّع ه وبه

To vomit. – وأَتَاع

To run headlong (into evil). To embark rashly in. تَتَيَّع إلى وتَتَايَع في

Prone to evil. تَيِّع وتَيِّعَان

To be a fool, stupid. ✻ تاك i تُيُوكًا

To pluck (the hair). أَتَاك ه

A great fool. أَحْمَق تائِك

This, that. (f. of ذٰلِك) تِيك

To be enslaved by (passion). ✻ تام i تَيْمًا

To enslave a. o. (love). To abase a. o. تَيَّم ه

To slaughter a home-bred ewe (from want). إِتَّام ه

Slave. Name of a tribe. Bewilderment, madness caused by love. تَيْم

Home-bred ewe. Amulet. تِيمَة

Wayless desert. Name of a place. تَيْمَاء

Enslaved by love, disordered in mind. مُتَيَّم

Fig-tree, fig. ✻ تِين

Indian fig. ✧ تِين هِنْدِيّ

A fig-tree, a fig. تِينَة

Fig-garden. مَتْيَنَة

✻ تاه i تِيهًا To be proud, haughty.
— تَيْهًا وتَيَهَانًا To go astray. To be perplexed. ✧ To be absent-minded.
تيّه وأتاه ه To render a. o. haughty. To perplex, to lead a. o. astray. ✧ To distract a. o.
تِيه ج أتياه وأتاوِيه Pride, haughtiness. Waterless desert. Mistake.
تائِه Proud, bewildered. ✧ Distracted. Wandering.
— وتَيَّهَان Proud.
تَيَّاه وتَيْهَان Stray, wandering.
أرض تَيْهَاء ومَتِيهَة ومُتِيهَة ومَتْيَهَة Wayless land.

ث

Scar of a wound. ثأى

To sit down comfortably. ✻ ثَبَّ o ثَبَابًا

To be finished (affair).

To be steady, resolute, brave. ✻ ثَبُتَ o ثَبَاتَةً وثُبُوتَةً

To be fast, firm. ثبت o ثَبَاتًا وثُبُوتًا

To fast, to continue.

To dwell, to remain in (a place). — في

To persevere in doing a. th. To be proved against a. o. (affair). To be incumbent upon a. o. (duty, affair). — على ه وه

He held it for certain. — عِنْدَهُ

To strengthen, to consolidate, to fasten. To prove, to demonstrate a. th. ✧ To administer the Sacrament of Confirmation to a. o. ثَبَّتَ ه وه

He knows the Koran by heart. ▫ ثَبَّتَ القُرْآنَ

To have a true knowledge of. ثَابَتَ وأَثْبَتَ

To confirm, to ascertain a. th. To declare a. th. necessary. To disable a. o. (wound). To transfix a. o. with (a spear). To establish (a proof). To recognize a. th. To confine a. o. to bed (disease). To write down (a name). أَثْبَتَ ه وه

To act deliberately. To be proved, ascertained. ✧ To receive the Sacrament of Confirmation. تَثَبَّتَ

To act slowly, prudently. إِسْتَثْبَتَ

To ask for (proofs). — ه

To persevere in. To keep to a. th. — في

Steady. Brave. Self-possessed. Firm. ثَبْت وثَابِت وثَبِيت

Steadfastness. Steadiness. Constancy, persistence. ثَبْت وثَبَات وثُبُوت

Spider. ▫ أَبُو ثَبَات

Certification, demonstration. Proof, forcible argument. Index of a book. *Pl.* Trustworthy men. ثَبَت ج أَثْبَات

Disease confining to bed. دَاء ثُبَات

To water (animals). ✻ ثَأْثَأَ ه وه

To keep them thirsty. To quench (the fire, anger). To remove a. th. from its place.

To withhold a. o. from. — ه عن

To fear a. o. — مَن

✻ ثَئِبَ a وثُئِبَ ثَأْبًا وثَأَبًا ، وتَثَأَّبَ وتَثَاءَبَ

To yawn. To become sluggish, drowsy. و✧ وَتَثَاوَبَ

To be upon the watch (for news). تَثَاءَبَ ه

Yawning. ثَأَب وثُؤَاب وتَثَاؤُب وتَثَاوُب

Heaviness, languor. ثُؤَبَاء

Gigantic tree. أَثْأَب

Gaper. مُتَثَئِّب ومُتَثَائِب ✧ مُتَثَاوِب

To bleat (sheep). ✻ ثَأَجَ a ثَأْجًا وثُؤَاجًا

To be covered with dew (plant). To feel cold (man). ✻ ثَئِدَ a ثَأَدًا

Dew. Encampment. Foul action. ثَأْد

Damp, dewy (place, night). ثَئِد م ثَئِدَة

To seek blood-revenge. To retaliate a murder upon. ✻ ثَأَرَ a ثَأْرًا وأَثْأَرَ ه ب

To avenge a. o. — ه وب

To obtain revenge from. أَثْأَرَ واثَّأَرَ من

To call for help in order to retaliate; to seek revenge. إِسْتَثْأَرَ

Blood-revenge, retaliation. ثَأْر ج أَثْآر وآثَار

To take revenge, to avenge o.'s self. أَخَذَ او أَدْرَكَ ثَأْرَهُ

Revengeful, vindictive. ثَائِر م ثَائِرَة

To be altered (meat). To smell bad (mud). ✻ ثَئِطَ a ثَأَطًا

To have a rheum. ثُئِطَ

Cold in the head, rheum. ثُؤَاط

Black and fetid mud. ثَأْطَة ج ثَأْط

To be warty. ✻ ثُؤْلِلَ وتَثَأْلَلَ

Nipple of the breast. Wart. ثُؤْلُول ج ثَآلِيل

To tear (a skin), to perforate it. ✻ ثَأَى a ثَأْيًا

To be bored (cowry). تَثَيَّ a ثَأًى

To wound (people). أَثْأَى في

Weakness. Momentous event. ثَأْي وثَأًى

تثبيت Strengthening. ✧ Sacrament of Confirmation.
ثابتة ج ثوابت Fixed star. (*opp. to* سَيَّارة)
مُثبَت Disabled. Unable to move.
✱ ثبج o ثَبجًا, وثبّج الكلام والخطّ To speak, to write confusedly.
ثبج i ثَبجًا وثُبوجًا To sit on the heels, to squat (man).
ثبّج وتثبّج ب To hold (a stick) on the back with the arms bent (shepherd).
ثَبَج ج أثباج وثُبوج Midst. Main-part of the back. Obscurity in speech.
أثباج البحر Middle of the sea.
أثبج Crook-backed.
✱ ثبجر – إثبجرّ إثبجرارًا To be terror-stricken. To waver, to be perplexed. To flow (water).
✱ ثبر o ثَبرًا ه To disappoint, to expel, to curse a. o. To destroy a. o. (God).
– ه عن To hinder a. o. from.
– ثُبورًا To perish.
ثبر a ثَبَرًا To reopen (wound).
ثابر على To be assiduous in, applied to.
تثابر To rush upon o. a.
ثُبرة Sinking ground. Hollow, cavity.
ثَبير ج أثبرة Name of various mountains.
ثُبور Loss, damage, destruction.
مثابرة وثِبار Application, assiduity.
✱ ثبط o ثَبطًا, وثبّط ه عن To prevent from. To divert, to delay a. o.
أثبط ه To hold a. o. without respite (illness).
تثبّط عن To linger, to be dilatory in. To be withheld from.
ثبط ج أثباط وثِباط Heavy, clumsy. Weak, foolish
✱ ثبق i ثَبقًا وثَبقانًا To drop tears (eye). To be swollen, to run high (river).
ثِبق ج ثُبوق Flooded ground.
✱ ثُبل وثبل Sediment in a vessel, dregs.
✱ ثبن i ثَبنًا وثِبانًا ه To tuck up (a garment) in order to sew it.
– وتثبّن ه To put and carry a. th. in the fold of the clothes.
ثُبنة ج ثُبَن, وثِبان ج ثُبُن Hollow formed by folded clothes.
مَثبنة ج مَثابن Dressing-bag.
✱ ثبى i ثَبيًا ه To gather, to collect a. th.
ثبّى ه وه To put together. To complete, to improve a. th. To praise a. o.
– على To be incessantly busied about.
ثُبة ج ثُبات وثُبون Troop of horsemen.
أُثبيّة ج أثابيّ Numerous company.
✱ ثيتل Wild goat, ibex. Effeminate.
✱ ثجّ o ثجًّا وثجوجًا, وانثجّ وتثجثج To flow.
– ه To let flow (water, blood).
ثجّاج Falling very thick (rain).
ثجيج Torrent.
مِثجّ Voluble (orator).
✱ ثجر o ثَجرًا ه To mix (dates) with the dregs.
ثجّر ه To extend, to enlarge a. th.
ثُجرة ج ثُجَر Upper part of the back. Midst of a valley.
ثَجر وثَجِر وأثجر Thick and broad.
ثجير Dregs of pressed dates.
✱ ثجل a ثَجَلًا To be big-bellied.
ثُجلة Ampleness of the belly.
أثجل م ثجلاء Big-bellied (person). Large (bag).
✱ ثجم i ثَجمًا, وأثجم To discharge rain suddenly (sky).
✱ ثجا o ثُجوًا To be silent, speechless.
أثجى ه To hush a. o.
✱ ثخن o ثِخَنًا وثَخانة وثُخونة To become coarse, stiff, thick.
أثخن ه To render a. o. thick, rude. To distress a. o.
– في To beat a. o. unmercifully. To make a great slaughter among. To exceed the bounds in. To apply o's self energetically to.
إثّخن To be covered with wounds.
إستثخن من To crush, to overcome a. o. (evil. sleep).
ثِخَن وثُخونة Thickness, heaviness.
ثخانة ✧ ثخانيّة Rudeness, roughness. ✧ Calibre.
ثَخين ج ثُخناء Thick, stiff, coarse.
مُثخَن Fleshy (woman).
✱ ثدق o ثَدقًا To fall thickly (rain). To flow (valley).
ثادق Abundant (stream).
✱ ثدم Unable to answer. Sv.
ثِدام Filter, strainer.
✱ ثدن a ثَدَنًا To smell bad (meat).
– وثُدِّن To become stout.

Fleshy. Heavy, thick. ثَدِن ومُثَدَّن
To water, to moisten a. th. ✻ ثَدَا o ثَدْوًا ه
To be wet, moist. ثَدِيَ a ثَدًى
To feed a. o. ثَدَّى تَثْدِيَةً ه
Breast (of woman), pap, mamma. ثَدْي وثَدًى ج أَثْدَاء وأَثْدٍ
Breast of man. ثُنْدُوَة وثَنْدُؤَة ج ثَنَادٍ
Big-breasted (woman). ثَدْيَاء
To give plentiful (water: spring) (milk: she-camel); (tears: eye). ✻ ثَرَّ i ثَرًّا , ثُرُورًا وثُرُورَةً وثَرَارَةً
To scatter a. th. To pour down rain (sky). — o ثَرًّا ه
To wet a. th. To water (a field). ثَرَّر ه
Holding much water (cloud, spring). Full of milk (ewe) ثَرّ م ثَرَّة ج ثِرَار وثُرُور
Loquacious, garrulous. — وثَارّ
To mix (food). To scatter a. th. To multiply (words). ✻ ثَرْثَر ه
Loquacity, talkativeness. ثَرْثَرَة
Prater. ✧ Mill-clack. ثَرْثَار
To undress (a sick man). ✻ ثَرَب i ثَرْبًا ه
To find fault with. To upbraid a. o. — وثَرَّب ه وعلى , وأَثْرَب ه
Fat of the intestines. ثَرْب ج ثُرُوب وأَثْرُب
Fat (ewe). ثَرْبَاء
Ancient name of Medinah in Arabia. يَثْرِب
To crumble and soak (bread) into broth. To dip (cloth) in dye. ✻ ثَرَد o ثَرْدًا , وأَثْرَد وإِثَّرَد ه
To kill (a beast) without cutting its throat. ثَرَّد ه
Chap on the lips. Weak rain. ثَرْد
Panada, soup. ثَرِيد وثَرِيدَة ج ثَرَائِد وثُرود
Glue. ✻ ثَرِط a
To come to dinner uninvited. ✻ ثَرِع a ثَرَعًا
Feathers on a cock's neck. ✻ ثُرْعُلَة
She-fox. ✻ ثُرْمُل
To break the teeth of. ✻ ثَرَم i ثَرْمًا , وأَثْرَم ه
To have the teeth broken or fallen. ثَرِم a ثَرَمًا , وانْثَرَم
To pull out the teeth of (a snake). ثَرَّم ه

Having an incisor tooth broken or fallen. أَثْرَم م ثَرْمَاء ج ثُرْم
To cook (meat) insufficiently. ✻ ثَرْمَد ه
Mire. ✻ ثُرْمُطَة
To patch up (a work), to do a. th. amiss. ✻ ثَرْمَل ه
To be considerable, to increase (wealth, tribe). ✻ ثَرَا o ثَرَاء , وثَرِيَ a ثَرًى
To multiply (wealth, people: God). — ه و ه
To be rich, wealthy. أَثْرَى إِثْرَاء
Wealth, opulence. ثَرَاء وثَرْوَة
Numerous (goods, company). Rich (man). ثَرِيّ ومُثْرٍ , وأَثْرَى م ثَرْوَاء
Opulent (man). ثَرْوَان م ثَرْوَى
Pleiades. Lustre, candlestick. ثُرَيَّا
To be softened by rain (ground). ✻ ثَرِيَ a ثَرًى , وأَثْرَى
To moisten, to wet (the earth). ثَرَّى ه
Earth. Moist earth. Goods. ثَرًى ج أَثْرَاء
The earth has been dried between them, *i. e.* from friends they became foes (*prov.*). يَبِس الثَّرَى بَيْنَهُم
Watery ground. ثَرِيّ م ثَرِيَّة , وأَثْرَى م ثَرْيَاء
To have a thin beard, scanty hair. ✻ ثَطّ i ثَطَطًا وثَطَاطَة وثُطُوطَة
Thin-bearded. ثَطّ ج أَثْطَاط وثُطَّان , وأَثَطّ ج ثُطّ
Having thin eye-brows. ثَطّ الحَاجِبَيْن
Spider. أَثَطّ وثَطَّأ
To have a cold. ✻ ثُطِع
Cold in the head. ثُطَاع
To vomit. ✻ ثَعّ i ثَعًّا
To bleed (wound, nose). إِنْثَعّ
To give vent to (water) ✻ ثَعَب a ثَعْبًا ه
To make a raid against. — الغَارَة عَلَى
To flow forth (water, blood). إِنْثَعَب
Stream of water. Torrent. ثَعْب ج ثُعْبَان
Long and thick snake. Winged dragon. ▫ Snake (*in general*). ثُعْبَان ج ثَعَابِين
Water-course. مَثْعَب ج مَثَاعِب
Fresh dates. Fresh (vegetable). ✻ ثَعْد
To become warty. ✻ ثَعِر a ثَعَرًا
To try to know (news) in lying. أَثْعَر
Venomous juice of the Egyptian thorn سَمُر. ثَعْر وثُعْر وثَعَر
To become tainted (meat, water). To stink and split (hide). To be swollen and chapped (lips). ✻ ثَعِط a ثَعَطًا

✱ ثَفَر – ثَفْر وأَثْفَر ه To drive (a beast) from behind.
أَثْفَر To crupper (a beast).
ثَفَر وثَفْر ج أَثْفَار Crupper.
✱ ما لهُ ثُفْرُوق He does not possess a. th.
✱ ثَفَل o ثَفْلًا ه To put a skin beneath an (arm-mill). To cast off, to scatter things.
أَثْفَل To settle, to form a sediment (liquids).
تَثَفَّل To be little generous.
ثُفْل وثَافِل Dregs, sediment. Dry food as dates, corn (except milk).
ثُفْل وثُفَال Lower mill-stone.
ثَفَال Slow-paced.
ثِفَال وثُفْل Skin put under an arm-mill.
✱ ثَفَن i ثَفْنًا To strike with the knees (she-camel).
ثَفِن a ثَفَنًا To become hardened by work (hand).
ثَافَن وأَثْفَن ه To enter into private conversation with a. o.
أَثْفَن ه To harden (the hands : work).
ثَفِنَة ج ثَفِنَات Callous parts of a camel. Knee of man.
✱ ثَفَا o ثَفْوًا ه To follow a. o.
ثَفَّى وأَثْفَى ه To supply (a pot) with a trivet.
أَثْفَى To take three wives.
أُثْفِيَّة ج أَثَافِيّ وأَثَافٍ Support of a cooking pot.
رَمَاهُ بِثَالِثَةِ الأَثَافِي He has reduced him to extreme destitution.
مُثَفًّى Who has lost many wives.
✱ ثَقَب o ثَقْبًا ه To pierce, to bore a. th. To make a hole in.
– ثُقُوبًا To shine (star). To burn (fire). To be penetrative (mind). To spread (odour). To soar aloft (bird).
ثَقِب o ثَقَابَة To be red-faced (man).
ثَقَّب وثَقَّب ه To perforate, to pierce a. th. through.
ثَقَّب ه وفِيهِ To appear on the head (white hair).
– وأَثْقَب ه To kindle (the fire). To strike (fire).
تَثَقَّب وانْثَقَب To be pierced, bored.
ثَقْب ج ثُقُوب وأَثْقَاب Bore. Hole. Orifice. Piercing, opening..

✱ ثَعِل a ثَعَلًا To have irregular teeth.
أَثْعَل To flock (guests). To become serious (affair).
ثَعَل على To disagree with. To thwart a. o.
ثَعْل وثَعَل وثُعْل وثُعْلُول Superfluous tooth. Excess.
أَثْعَل م ثَعْلَاء ج ثُعْل Who has one tooth more than usual.
ثُعَال م ثُعَالَة Fox. Tick corroding hides.
✱ ثَعْلَب وتَثَعْلَب To shift, to elude a. o. cunningly (from fear).
ثَعْلَب ج ثَعَالِب Fox. ◻ Jackal.
ثَعْلَب المَاء Otter.
دَاء الثَّعْلَب Fox-evil (fall of the hair).
ثُعْلُبَان Male fox.
✱ ثَغْثَغَة Confused speech.
✱ ثَغَب i ثَغْبًا ه To slaughter (a sheep).
– ه ب To pierce a. o. with (a spear).
ثَغِب a ثَغَبًا To melt (ice, grease).
ثَغْب وثَغَب ج ثُغْبَان Torrent never exposed to sunlight.
✱ ثَغَر a ثَغْرًا ه To break, to dent (a vessel). To stop up (a breach). To make a breach in (a wall).
– ه To break the front-teeth of.
– على To stop all access to (a pass).
ثُغِر وأُثْغِر واثَّغَر واتَّغَر To shed the milk-teeth (boy).
ثَغْر ج ثُغُور Frontiers. Mouth. Front-teeth.
ثُغْرَة ج ثُغَر Mountain-pass. Chink, crevice. Gap; breach. Pit of the neck.
ثُغُرُور Frontier of a hostile country.
مَثْغَر ج مَثَاغِر Gum of the teeth.
✱ ثَغَم – أَثْغَم To produce the plant called ثَغَامَة (valley). To be as white as that plant (head).
ثَاغِم Very white.
ثَغَامَة Mountain-plant whitening when dry. Hyssop. Wormwood.
✱ ثَغَا o ثُغَاء To bleat (sheep, goat).
أَثْغَى ه To make (a goat) to bleat.
ما لهُ ثَاغِيَة ولا رَاغِيَة He has no sheep nor she-camel, *i. e.* nothing.
✱ ثُفَّاء وثُفَا Mustard. Nasturtium. Indian cress.
✱ ثَفَد – ثَفَّد ه To line (a breast-plate).
ثَفَارِيد White clouds superposed
– وثَفَافِيد Lining (of clothes).

Hole. Canal, pipe, tube. ثقبة ج ثُقَب
Fuel, tinder. ✧ Matches. ثِقَاب وثُقُوب
Piercing through. Penetrative (mind). Shining (star). ثاقِب م ثاقِبة
Red-faced (man). ثقيب م ثقيبة
Drill. Tunnel, narrow-pass. Sagacious. مِثقَب ج مَثاقِب
To ثقِف a ثقفًا, وثقُف o ثقفًا وثقافة وثقوفة ✱
be intelligent, clever, skilled.
To percieve quickly, ثقِف a ثقفًا ه وه
to be skilled in(an art). To meet a.o. To overtake, to find. To overcome a. o. or a. th.
To become acid ثقف o, وثقِف a ثقفًا (vinegar).
To surpass a. o. in skill. — ه
To strike a. o. with a spear.
To straighten a. th. ثقّف ه و ه
To rear, to bring up a. o.
To vie with a. o. in ثاقف مُثاقفة وثقافًا ه
cleverness. To surpass a. o. in skill.
To become well educated, improved, disciplined. تثقّف
To struggle, to contend. تثاقف
Very intelligent woman. ثقاف
Struggle. Instrument for straightening lances. Skill. ثِقاف
Intelligence. penetrative mind. ثقافة
Intelligent, clever. Sharp. ثقف وثقِف
Very clever. Very strong (vinegar). ثقيف وثِقّيف
Brought up, well bred. مُثقّف
To be heavy, ثقُل o ثِقلًا وثقالة ✱
weighty. To be momentous (business). To be slow, dull (man). To be hard (ear, word).
To be very seriously ill. — ثقلًا
To weigh a. th. with ثقل o ثقلًا ه
the hand. To outweigh a. th.
To make a. th. heavy, ثقّل ه وه
weighty. To burden, to overcharge. To fold (a letter).
To load, to overcharge a. o. ثقّل على
To crush a.o. To be troublesome for.
To eat heavy dishes. ثاقل
To overburden a. o. (weight, أثقل ه
debt). To oppress. To crush a. o. (illness, sleep).
To be sluggish, dull. تثاقل
To be heavy, weighty. إستثقل
To find a. th. heavy, painful, — ه
difficult, hard.
Weightiness. Gravitation. ثقل
Hardness of hearing.
Charge of a household. ثقل ج أثقال
Luggage. Valuables
Men and genii. الثقلان
Weight, burden, loan. ثِقل ج أثقال
Gravity. Crime. Importance.
Treasures of the soil. The dead الأثقال
buried in the earth.
Weight, load. ثِقلة وثِقَلة وثقلة
Heaviness, weight. Slug- ثقلة وثقلة
gishness. Numbness. ✧ Tediousness, troublesomeness.
Heavy, of full weight(coin). ثاقِل ج ثواقِل
ثقيل ج ثُقلاء وثِقال , وثقال وثُقال ج ثِقال
Burdensome, difficult. Tedious. وثقل
Serious (illness). Important (th.). Dull (man). Grave, sedate. Slow (horse).
Crushed under a burden. مُثقل
Overweighed. Dull. Drowsy.
Piece of marble used to fasten مُثقّلة
carpets.
Weight of a balance. مِثقال ج مَثاقِيل
Weight equal to one dirhem and half. Gold coin.
To lose (her ثكِل a ثُكلًا وثكلًا ه ✱
child : mother).
To deprive (a mother) of أثكل ه ه
(her child).
Loss of a child; state of a ثُكل وثكل
mother bereft of her children.
Deprived of a child, ثاكِل وثكلان ج ثكالى
of a friend.
ثاكِل وثاكِلة. وثكلى ج ثكالى وثواكِل. ومُثكلة
Deprived of her child ج مَثاكِل
(mother).
Deprived of ثكول , ومِثكال ج مَثاكِيل
children.
Any cause depriving a mother مَثكلة
(of her child).
To be incessantly ثكِم o ثكمًا ه وه ✱
occupied about. To track a. o.
To remain (a place). — ثكِم a ثكمًا ب
Middle of a way; track of a road. ثكم
Flight of ثكن — ثكنة ج ثُكن ✱

pigeons. Barracks. Colours. Flock.
✻ ثلّ o ثلاً ه To drain off (a well). To fill up (a well).
— ثلا , وثللا ه وة To overthrow (a wall), to scatter. To destroy (people).
ثلّ عَرشُهُم They are ruined; their power has been destroyed.
أثلّ To have plenty of wool.
— ه To repair, to mend a. th.
تثلّل To be decayed, to fall in ruins.
انثلّ To be poured forth.
— على To rush upon.
ثلل , ثِلّة ج ثِلَل Decay, ruin.
ثلّة ج ثِلَل وثِلال Flock of sheep. Wool. Mud extracted from a well.
ثُلّة Multitude of men.
✧ ثالول Wart.
✻ ثلب i ثلبًا ة To rebuke, to blame a. o. To disparage, to slander, to calumniate. To expel a. o.
— ه To notch, to dent, to turn a. th. upside down.
ثلِب a ثلبًا To be dirty, broken.
ثلب Slander, backbiting. Calumny.
ثِلب ج أثلاب Worn out (old man).
— وثَلِب Dishonoured, blamed (person).
أثلب وإثلب ج أثالب Stones and earth.
ثالب Detractor, slanderer, calumniator.
ثلّاب ومِثلب Calumniator. Demon.
مَثلبة ج مَثالِب Cause of blame. Vice.
✻ ثلث o ثلثًا ة وه To take the third part of a. th. or from a. o.
— i ثلثًا To become the third. To arrive third in a race (horse).
ثلّث ه To triplicate. To make a. th. triangular. To do a. th. thrice. To reduce (liquids) to the third (by boiling). To mark (a letter) with three points. To hold the doctrine of the Trinity.
أثلث To become three, thirty in number.
ثلاثة م ثلاث Three.
ثلاثة عشر م ثلاث عشرة ✧ ثلاثعش Thirteen.
ثُلث وثُلُث ج أثلاث وثليث Third part.
ثلاثًا Thrice, three times.
الثلاثاء والثُلاثاء Tuesday.
ثلثي Large ornamental writing.
ثلاث ومَثلث Three and three.

ثلاثيّ Triliteral (verb).
ثِلثان وثُلثان Night-shade (plant).
ثلاثون Thirty.
تثليث Trinity (three Persons in one God). Doctrine of the Trinity.
ثالوث (The Holy) Trinity.
ثالث م ثالثة Third.
ثالثًا Thirdly.
مُثلَّث Trebled. Tertian (fever). Triangular. Triangle. Reduced to the third (wine). Three-pointed (letter).
مُثلَّث قائم Right-angled triangle.
مُثلَّث حادّ Acute-angled triangle.
مُثلَّثات Trigonometry.
مَثلوث Composed of three. Three-angled. Reduced to the third part.
✻ ثلج o ثلجًا , وأثلجتِ السَّماء To snow (sky).
ثلج o ثلوجًا ب وإلى To trust in.
ثُلِج To be covered with snow (earth). To lose o.'s wits.
ثلِج a ثلجًا وأثلج To be refreshed, calm (mind).
✧ ثلّج To be benumbed with cold. To become frozen, cold.
✧ — ه To cool, to ice (a drink).
— ة To cool, to cheer a. o.
أثلج To become snowy (day). To reach the snow (traveller).
أثلج ة To cool, to cheer a. o.
ثلِج Cold as snow (water).
ثلج ج ثلوج Snow.
ثلّاج Ice ; dealer in snow.
ثلاجيّ Snow-white.
مَثلجة ج مَثالج Ice-house. Snow-drift.
مَثلوج Covered with snow. ✧ Cooled with ice.
— الفؤاد Apathetic. Dull.
✻ ثلم a ثلمًا ه وثلّم ه a ثلمًا ه To break (the head).
مُنثلم Fallen to the ground and split (date).
✻ ثلم i ثلمًا , وثلّم ه To notch (a blade, a vessel). To make a breach in (a wall).
ثلِم a ثلمًا , وتثلّم وانثلم To be dented. To be blunted (sword); to be water-worn (brink of a river).
ثلم وثُلمة Notch (in a blade, vessel).

A fruit. Knot at the end ثَمَرَة ج ثَمَرَات of a whip. Tip (of the tongue). Skin of (the head). Child, progeny.
Fruit-bearing (tree). Kidney-bean. Fruit of the sorrel. ثَامِر
✧ Usufruct, use. إِسْتِثْمَار
Productive, numerous. ثَمِر ومَثْمُور
Productive, fruitful. Useful. مُثْمِر
To saturate (cloth) with dye. To shade (a stuff). To break a. th. ✻ ثَمَغَ o ثَمْغًا ه
To dye (the hair) with (henna). — ه ب
To get drunk, intoxicated. ✻ ثَمِلَ a ثَمَلًا
To stay, to abide. To remain (water). ثَمَلَ i o ثَمْلًا وثُمُولًا
To assist a. o. To feed (orphans). To leave (a remainder). — ه وه
To froth, to foam (milk). أَثْمَلَ
To inebriate a o. (drink). — ه
Remainder of water (in a vessel). ثَمْلَة وثُمْلَة وثَمِيلَة وثُمَالَة
Froth of milk. ثُمَالَة
Manager of a tribe's business. ثِمَال القَوْم
Intoxication. Abode. Shadow. ثَمَل
Intoxicated. ثَمِل وثَمِيل
Prone to, fond of, in love with. — إلى
Sour milk. ثَمِيل
Large cistern. مَثْمَلَة
Basket of palm leaves. Shepherd's bag. Slime, soft mud of a well. مِثْمَلَة
To take the eighth part of a. o.'s goods. ✻ ثَمَنَ o ثَمْنًا ه
To become the eighth. — i ثَمْنًا
To be precious valuable (th). ثَمُنَ o ثَمَانَةً وأَثْمَنَ
To value, to appraise a. th., to assign the price of. To render a. th. octangular. To increase a. th. to the number of eight. ثَمَّنَ ه
To discuss the price of ثَامَنَ ه
To be eight in number أَثْمَنَ
To give to a o. the price of a. th. — ه ول ه
Value, price. ثَمَن ج أَثْمَان وأَثْمُن وأَثْمِنَة
Eight. ثَمَانِيَة م ثَمَانٍ

Breach (in a wall).
Calumny. Backbiting. ثَلْم الصِّيت
Nick, indentation. ثُلْمَة
To pick up. To collect. To heap up (things). To repair a.th. ✻ ثَمَّ o ثَمًّا ه
To pluck up (the grass: ewe). — ه بِفِيهِ
To grow old, weak (body). إِثْمَثَّ
Repair, restoration. ثَمّ
Here, over there. ثَمَّ
Therefore, on that account. مِن ثَمَّ
His good and bad qualities. ثَمُّهُ ورَمُّهُ
He does not possess a farthing. لا يَملك ثَمًّا ولا رَمًّا
Then, afterwards. Moreover. ثُمَّ وثُمَّتَ
Handful of dried herbs. ثُمَّة
Old man. ثِمَّة
Picking up every thing, good or bad, little or much. مِثَمّ ومِثَمَّة
Panic-grass. Plant used for stopping holes. ثُمَام ويَثْمُوم
To feed a. o. with greasy dishes. To break up a. th. ✻ ثَمَأَ a ثَمْأً ه وه
To be smashed, broken. إِنْثَمَأَ
To mix a. th. ✻ ثَمَجَ i ثَمْجًا ه
Manufacturer of variegated cloth. مُثَمِّج
To dig up (a hole for water). ✻ ثَمَدَ i o ثَمْدًا وأَثْمَدَ واسْتَثْمَدَ ه
To exhaust a. o. (expenses): a she-camel (milking). ثَمَدَ ه
To go to a water-hole. إِثَّمَدَ وثَمَّدَ
To request a favour from a.o. إِسْتَثْمَدَ ه
Puddle drying up during summer. ثَمْد وثَمَد ج ثِمَاد
Thamoud, tribe of ancient Arabs. ثَمُود
Drained (water). Ruined through his prodigality (man). مَثْمُود
Antimony used as collyrium. إِثْمِد وأُثْمُد
To fructify, to bear fruit (tree). To get rich (man). ✻ ثَمَرَ o ثُمُورًا، وأَثْمَرَ
To increase (wealth). ثَمَّرَ ه
To find or to render a. th. fruitful. ✧ To enjoy the use of property. إِسْتَثْمَرَ ه
Fruit. Property, profit, income. ثَمَر ج ثِمَار جج ثُمُر وأَثْمَار

Eighteen. ثمانية عشر م ثماني عشرة
Eighteenth. ثامن عشر م ثامنة عشرة
The eighth part. ثمن وثمن ج أثمان
Eight and eight. ثمان ومثمن
Eighth. ثامن م ثامنة
Eighty. Eightieth. ثمانون
Valuation, estimation, appraisement. تثمين
Eighth part. ثمين
Precious, valuable (th.). ثمين ✧ مثمن
Appraiser, valuer, estimator. مثمن
Octagonal. Poisoned. Fevered. Of eight feet (verse). Appraised. مثمن
To be worn out (old man). ✻ ثن — اثن
Dry herbage. ثن
Fetlock on a horse's foot. — ثنة ج ثنن
To smell bad (meat). ✻ ثنت a ثنتا
To fold, to bend a. th. To bind a. th. To conceal (hatred). ✻ ثنى i ثنيا ه
To deter a. o. from doing a. th. To avert a. th. from. — ه وه عن
He has struck him a second time. — عليه بصفعة ثانية
He is unable to walk any more. لا يثني ولا يثلث
To bear rancour. ثنى صدره
To double a. th. To put (a noun) in the dual number. To repeat, to reiterate (an action). To mark (a letter) with two points. ثنى ه
To praise. To blame a. o. ثنى وأثنى على
To be doubled, folded, reiterated. تثنى
To strut about. To incline the body in walking. — في مشيه
To be doubled. To be bent down. To bow down. إثنى واثنى
To deviate, to swerve from a. th. إثنى عن
To except. To exclude, to set a. th. aside. إستثنى ه
To make an exception for. — ه او على
Fold (of clothes). Bend. Winding (of a river). Coils (of a snake). ثني ج أثناء
In the meantime, meanwhile. في أثناء ذلك
Reiterated, repeated action. ثني ج ثنية
Second in rank : — وثنيان ج ثنية
secondary. Unsound, wrong.
Praise, encomium. Dispraise. ثناء ج أثنية
Two and two. ثناء ومثنى
Cutting his first teeth when three years old (cloven-hoofed animal); when six years old (camel). ثني م ثنية ج ثناء وثنيان وأثناء
Eulogy. Praise. Panegyric. Action of praise. Central incisor. Path, narrow-pass in a mountain. ثنية ج ثنايا
Repetition. Praise. Putting (of a noun) to the dual number; dual. تثنية
Deuteronomy تثنية الاشتراع
Biliteral (noun). ثنائي
Two. إثنان م ثنتان واثنتان ✧ ثنين م ثنتين
Twelve. إثنا عشر م إثنتا عشرة ✧ ثنعش
Other, the others. ◻ ثاني ج ثانيين
Monday. الاثنين
Second. ثان م ثانية
Secondly. ثانيا وثانية
Second (of time). ✧ Joist, stop-plank. ثانية ج ثوان
Exception, exclusion. إستثناء
Exceptional. إستثنائي
Second string of a lute. Winding (of valleys, rivers). Knees. مثنى ج مثان
Bent. Folded double. مثني
Doubled. The dual number. مثنى
Marked with two points (letter). — م مثناة
Verses of the Koran. Windings of a valley. مثان
Excepted. Exceptional. مستثنى
To gather (people). To collect (water.) To rise (dust). ✻ ثاب o ثوبا وثؤوبا ، وثوب
To return. To turn back to (God). — إلى
To recover health. To be cured. — ثوبانا ، وأثاب وأثوب إثوابا
To recover o.'s senses, wits. — إليه عقله
To requite, to reward a. o. ثوب ه
To call to prayer. — تثويبا
To repay, to compensate a. o. To restore a. o. to health (God). To fill (a trough). أثاب إثابة ل وه
To add a supererogatory prayer (man). ✧ To gain a reward. تثوب

To ask a reward from a. o. إستثاب ه
To recover (health). — ه
To claim o.'s (goods) back.
Clothed. Garment. Morals. Behaviour. ¤ Woman's gown. ثوب ج ثياب وأثواب وأثوب
Pure-hearted, of good character. طاهر الثياب
Vicious, of bad morals. دنس الثياب
✧ Scapular of Our Lady. ثوب السيّدة
Reward (especially for good works). Honey. Bees. Rain. ثواب
Retribution. تثويب وإثابة
Call to prayer. تثويب
Dealer in clothes. Outfitter. ثوّاب
Meeting-place. مثاب ومثابة
Reward. مثوبة ومثوبة
Basket for carrying earth. ✻ ثوج
To sink in the mud (foot); in a soft body (finger). ✻ ثاخ o ثوخًا وثيخًا
To rise, and spread in the air (dust, locust). To take his flight (bird). To be shaken (th.). To be moved (soul). To be roused (anger). To be stirred (quarrel). To be kindled (war). To break out (disease, pimple). ✻ ثار o ثورًا وثؤورًا وثورانًا
To rush on. To assault a. o. — ب او إلى
To raise (the dust). To stir (war). To start (a wild beast) from its den. To investigate, to inquire after a. th. To till (the ground). ثوّر وأثار واستثار ه وه
To attack a. o. ثاور مثاورة وثوارًا ه
To be raised, stirred (dust). تثوّر
Whirlwind of dust. ثور ن
Dawn-light. — وثور الشفق
Bull. Taurus (zodiacal sign). Stupid, dull man. Pimple. ثور ج أثوار وثيران وثيار وثيرة
Cow. Excitement. Revolution. ثورة
Multitude of men. ثورة الرجال
Raised (dust). Fit of anger. ثائر
He has lost his temper. ثار ثائره
Uproar. ثائرة ج ثوائر
Country abounding in oxen. مثورة
To flow (water). ✻ ثاع o ثوعًا

To be seized with staggers (sheep). ✻ ثول a ثولًا, وأثول إثوالًا
To be crack-brained, mad, possessed by a devil, giddy. ثول a ثولًا, وثال o ثولًا
To swarm (bees). تثوّل
To gather against and ill-treat a. o. (people). تثوّل على
To accumulate and cover a. o. (dust). To rush and surround a. o. (crowd). إنثال على
To be giddy. To be taken with vertigo. ✧ إنثول
Vertigo, giddiness. Swimming in the head. Disease of sheep. Staggers. ثول وثول
Swarm of bees. ثول
Throng, rabble. ثويلة
Seized with staggers (sheep). Giddy, dizzy, sluggish (man). أثول م ثولاء ج ثول جج أثاولة
Garlic. ✻ ثوم
A head of garlic. Sword-hilt. ثومة
To halt, to settle (in a place). ✻ ثوى i ثواء وثويًّا ه وب وفي
To be buried. ثوي
To detain a. o. in (a place). ثوّى تثوية ه في
To stay in (a place). أثوى إثواء ب
To lodge, to entertain a. o. in (a house). — ه في
Furniture. House utensils. Stones set up as a way-mark. ثوّة ج ثوّى
Enclosure for cattle. ثاوة وثاية وثويّة
Inhabitant. Host. ثاوٍ م ثاوية
Guest. Captive. Guest-room. ثويّ
Dwelling, lodging; inn. مثوى ج مثاوٍ
To be separated from her husband (woman). ✻ ثيّب وتثيّب
Separated from her husband through divorce or death (woman). Married man. Any woman not virgin. ثيّب ومتثيّب ج ثيّبات
Dog's grass. ✻ ثيل وثيّل
Hemp, flax. Whip. — وه ثيل
Pearl-borer. Pearl-fishery. ✻ ثين

ج

To call camels to water by uttering the cry جِئْ جِئْ . ❋ جَأْجَأَ ب

To abstain from. تَجَأْجَأَ عَن

Breast of a bird. Stern of a ship. جُؤْجُؤ ج جَآجِئ

To acquire (wealth). To sell ochre. ❋ جَأَب a جَأْبًا

Onager. Thick and rough. Red ochre. Earning, gain. Lion. جَأْب

Navel. جَأْبَة البَطن

To walk sluggishly under a burden. To carry about news. ❋ جَأَث a جَأْثًا

To be overburdened. جَئِث a جَأَثًا

To be terror-stricken. جُئِث

To overburden (a camel : load). أَجْأَث ة

To low (bull). ❋ جَأَر a جَأْرًا وجُؤُورًا

To beseech, to entreat a. o. – إلى

To grow, to spread (grass). – a جَأَرًا

Tall (grass); luxuriant (vegetation). Copious rain. جَأْر

Fat, stout. جَئِر وجَأّار

Call for help. جُؤَار

To be choked by. ❋ جَئِز a جَأَزًا ب

To heave from fear, sorrow (soul). To be restless. ❋ جَأَش a جَأْشًا

Commotion of the mind. Soul. Firmness. Fear. جَأْش

Breast. Thick (man). Party of men. Portion of the night. جُؤْشُوش ج جَآشِيش

To throw down. To frighten a. o. To uproot (a tree). جَأَف a جَأْفًا ة وه

To halt, to be lame. ❋ جَأَل a جَأَلًا

Hyena. Wolf. Bulky. جَيْأَل جَيْأَلَة

To be bay (horse). ❋ جَأَى a جُؤْوَة وجُؤَّة

To mend (clothes). To hold back a. th. To watch over (a flock). To cover, to conceal a. th. – جَأْوًا ه

To be of a brownish colour. جَئِيَ a جَأًى

Brown colour; dark red, dun. جُؤْوَة

Brown, bay. أَجْأَى م جَأْوَاء

To cut off a. th. To emasculate a. o. To overcome a. o. ❋ جَبَّ o جَبًّا ة وه

To impregnate (a palm-tree). – جِبَابًا ه

To escape, to fly. To shrink. To be white-footed (horse). جَبِّب

To vie with a. o. in beauty, etc. جَابَّ مُجَابَّة وجِبَابًا ة

To marry one another's sister (two men). تَجَابَّ

To put on an upper-gown. تَجَبَّب واجْتَبَّ

Well. Cistern. Pit. ✧ Bush, shrub. جُبّ ج جِبَاب وأَجْبَاب وجِبَبَة

Upper-gown with very full sleeves. Eye-bone. جُبَّة ج جُبَب وجِبَاب

White hair from the feet to the knees of a horse. جَبَب وتَجْبِيب

Dearth. جَبَاب وجُبَاب

Having white hair from his feet to his knees (horse). مُجَبَّب

Eunuch. مَجْبُوب

To travel. To become fat. ❋ جَبْجَب

Stomach of ruminants used as a bag. Tripe. Leather-basket for navvies. *Pl.* Drum. جُبْجُبَة ج جَبَاجِب

To conceal o.'s self. ❋ جَبَأ a جَبْأً وجِبَاء وجُبُوءَة

To come upon a. o. of a sudden. To come out against a. o. (snake, wild beast). – عَلَى

To shrink, to desist from. To draw back in fear. To recoil from a. th. (eye, sword). – جَبْأً وجُبُوءًا عَن

To bring forth truffles (soil). أَجْبَأ

To conceal a. th. To extinguish (a fire). – ه

Red truffles. Hollow of stagnating water. جَبْء ج جَبْأَة وجِبَأَة وأَجْبُؤ

Red truffles. جَبَأ

Cowardly, dastardly man. جُبَّأ وجُبَّأَة

Land full of truffles. أَرض مَجْبَأَة

Idol. Witchcraft. Wizard. ❋ جِبْت

Powder magazine. War ammunition. Cartridge-box. Ts جَبْخَانَة

Gunpowder-room in a ship. جبخانة المركب

✻ جبر جبرًا وجبورًا وجبارة ، وجبّر هـ وه To set (a broken bone). To restore a. o.'s business.

To compel a. o. to do a. th. forcibly. — وأجبره على

To be reduced (broken bone). To be restored to a former state. جبر o جبورًا وجبرًا ، وانجبر

To converse kindly with a. o. جبر خاطره

✧ To oblige a. o. جابر ه

To consider a. o. as honest أجبر ه
To accuse a. o. of being proud.

To be set (bone). To become green again (tree). تجبّر وانجبر

To recover from illness; to recover from destitution, to regain wealth. To be reinstated in a former state. — واجتبر

To behave insolently, proudly. تجبّر

To show pride, haughtiness towards a. o. — على

To recover wealth. إستجبر

Setting of a bone. Constraint. Pride. King. Slave. Aloes-wood. جبر

Algebra. — وعلم الجبر

Art of setting broken bones. جبارة

Bandage. Truss. Splints. Silver bracelet. جبارة وجبيرة ✻ جبائر

Might. Power. Pride. Greatness. جبروت وجبروت وجبروت

✧ جبيرة (for جبيرة) Leather bag. Portfolio.

Setter of broken bones. Compulsory. Urging on forcibly. Tyrant. جابر م جابرة

Bread. أبو جابر و جابر بن حبّة

Powerful. Proud. Giant. Pitiless (heart). The Most Powerful (God). Tyrant. Young and lofty palm-tree. جبّار ✻ جبابرة

Sect of fatalists. Insolence. جبريّة

✧ إلجباري (for رنج ✻) Middling in wealth. talents. Simple. good (man).

Surgeon. Setter of bones. مجبّر

Set (bone). Compelled. مجبور

H جبرائيل وجبرائيل وجبرئيل Gabriel (the Archangel).

✻ جبز o جبزًا هـ To cut, to sever a. th.

جبز o جبازة To become dry (bread).

Thick. Hard. Avaricious. Vile. جبز

Dry bread. Unleavened bread. جبيز

✻ جبس — تجبّس To go on proudly.

Piaster. Gypsum. Sulphate of calcium. Bear's cub. جبس

Thick, hard. Wicked. Coward. جبس أجباس وجبوس ، وأجبس

✧ A kind of water-melon. جبس

◻ جباسة Lime-kiln.

Worthless fellow. Bad chap. جبوس

Bear's whelp. جبيس

Ill-famed. مجبوس وأجبس وجبيس

✻ جبل i o جبلًا ه وهـ To form, to create a. th. To mix (clay with water).

To give to a. o. inborn dispositions for a. th. (God) — على

To go, to come to a mountain. To be thick in make. To reach the rock by digging. To be spiritless (poet). To be disappointed. أجبل

To enter a mountain تجبّل

Thick. Court-yard. Blunt (sword). Large bowl. Numerous tribe. جبل

Natural disposition. Complexion of the body. جبلة وجبلة وجبلة ، وجبلة ✻ جبلات

Dry tree. جبل

Numerous company. — وجبلة وجبل

Mountain. Miser. Chief. جبل ✻ أجبال وجبال

The Pyrenees (mountain) جبل الأبواب

Fabulous mountain around the inhabited world. جبل قاف

Gibraltar. جبل طارق

Mount Hermon. جبل الشيخ

Echo. Snake. Calamity. إبنة الجبل

Mountaineer. Highlander. Relating to a mountain. جبلي

Inborn, implanted by nature. Essential. جبلي

Body of man. جبال

✻ جبن o جبنًا وجبانة To be low-spirited. faint-hearted.

To accuse a. o. of cowardice. جبّن ه وهـ

locust. Envelope of a date. Hillock.
Person. Corpse. جُثّة ج جُثَث وأجثاث
Grove of palm-trees. Shoot of palm-tree. جَثِيث
Gardener's **trowel.** مِجَثّة ومِجثاث
To drive (the **clouds** : wind). ✻ جَثَل i جَثلاً ه
To be tangled and soft (hair); dense (tree). جَثِل a وجَثُل o جَثالةً وجُثولةً
To ruffle its feathers from cold (bird). To become tall and tangled (plant). To become irritated and ready to fight (man). إجثألّ
Tufty, thick. Dark. جَثل وجَثِيل
Big ant. Bushy tree. جَثلة ج جَثَل
Fallen leaves. جُثالة
Catholicos, Patriarch of Eastern Christians. G جَثَلِيق وجاثَلِيق ج جَثالقة
To recline on the chest (man, beast). **To perch** (bird). To become tall (corn). To be half-spent (night). ✻ جَثَم o i جَثماً وجُثوماً
Hare. جُثَوم
Night-mare. جاثوم وجُثام
Reclining on the chest. — وجاثِم ج جُثَّم
Keeping at home (man). جاثِمة
Sedentary. Sluggish, dull (man). جَثّامة وجُثَم وجُثَمة وجاثوم
Body, the whole person. جُثمان
Resting-place of a bird. مَجثِم ج مَجاثِم
To kneel. to squat upon the toes. ✻ جَثا o جُثُوًّا، وجَثَى i جِثِيًّا
To sit knee to knee with a. o. ه جاثَى
To make a. o. to kneel. ه أجثَى
To sit upon the knees, to squat one opposite the other. تَجاثَى
Kneeling. Squatting. جُثُوّ
Hillock; heap of stones. Tomb. The whole body. جُثوة وجِثوة ج جُثًى
Person. Requital. Amount. جُثاء
Kneeling. Squatting. Hercules (*constell.*). جاثٍ ج جُثِيّ وجِثِيّ
To scrutinise a. th. ✻ جَحجَح ه
To hasten towards a. th.
To abstain from. — عن
Perdition. جَحجَحة
Chief. Generous lord. جَحجاح ج جَحاجِح

To curdle (milk).
To find, to hold a. o. to be a coward. جَبَّن وأجبَن واجتَبَن ه
To curd (milk). To become stout (man). تَجبَّن
Cowardice, faint-heartedness. جُبن وجَبانة
Cheese. جُبن وجُبُن وجُبُنّ
Forehead. Side of the forehead. جَبِين ج أجبُن وأجبِنة وجُبُن
Coward, dastard. جَبان ج جُبَناء وجَبِين
Cowardly fellow. Cheesemonger. جَبّان
Desert. Plain of great extent. Cemetery. جَبّانة
Dairy. Place full of cheese. Cause of cowardice. ✧ Curd. مَجبَنة
To strike a. o. on the forehead. To take (people) unawares (winter). To come to (water) without means for drawing it. ✻ جَبَه a جَبهاً ه وه
To receive a. o. harshly. — ه ب
To lower (the head). جَبَّه ه
To dislike (water). إجتَبَه ه
Broadness and beauty of the forehead. جَبَه
Forehead. Chief. Insult. Mansion of the moon. Ignominy. جَبهة ج جَبَهات وجِباه
Chief of a tribe. — القوم
Coming in front (beast). جابِه
Who has a broad and fine forehead. Lion. أجبَه م جَبهاء
To collect (taxes). To collect (water in a reservoir). ✻ جَبا o جَبوةً وجِباوةً وجَبا، وجَبَى i جِبايةً ه
To fall prostrate (in prayer). جَبَّى تَجبِيةً
To sell seed-produce (before maturity). أجبَى
To choose a. o. To find out. To extemporize a. th. اجتَبَى ه وه
Reservoir, tank. Watering-trough. جَبأ ج أجباء، وجابِية ج جَوابٍ
Tax, duties. جِباية ج جِبايات
Tax-gatherer. Locust. جابٍ م جابية
To cut off. To pull out (a tree). ✻ جَثّ o جَثًّا، واجتَثّ ه
Remains of bees mixed with honey. Wax. جُثّ
Remains of bees in honey. Dead جُثّ

To become poor (man). ✱ جحِد a جَحَدًا
To be avaricious. To be scar
(plant). To become strait (circumstances). To be dry (earth).
To abjure o'.s faith. To deny (a right). To disown (a benefit). جَحَد a جَحْدًا وجُحُودًا ه وب
To contradict a. o. — ١
Scantiness, poverty. جحد وجُحد وجحد
Denial. Negation. Disowning. جُحُود
Barren (soil). Dry year. جَحْد وجَحْدَة وجحِد
Of little value. Stingy. — وجَحِد وأَجْحَد
Denier, disowner, apostate. جَاحِد
Disowner. Ungrateful. جَحَّاد
Lusty youth. ✱ جَحْدَل
To hide in its hole (lizard, snake). To sink in the head (eye). To draw back (man). ✱ جَحَر a جَحْرًا وتجَحَّر وانْجَحَر
To force up (a beast) into its hole. To drive a. o. away. To put (people) in narrow circumstances (unfruitful year). — وأَجْحَر ه
To be rainless (sky). To be in a time of dearth. — وأَجْحَر
To make its burrow (beast). إِجْتَحَر ه
Cavern, deep hole. جَحْر
Unfruitful year. جَحْرَة
Hole of a reptile. Burrow. Womb. Buttocks. جُحْر ج أَجْحار وجِحَرَة جُحْرَان وجُحْر
Refuge. Lurking-place. مَجْحَر ج مَجَاحِر
To skin, to scratch (the skin). To kill a. o. To make a mark on (a wall). ✱ جَحَس a جَحْسًا ه وه
To repel a. o. from. جَاحَس مُجَاحَسَة وجِحَاسًا ه عن
To excoriate. To scratch (the skin). ✱ جَحَش a جَحْشًا ه
To drive a. o. back. To defend o.'s self against a. o. جَاحَش ه
Young ass, colt. Gazelle. Thickness, roughness. ✧ Ass; fool, stupid. جَحْش ج جِحَاش وجِحْشَان وجِحَشَة
Trestle. ✧ — ج جُحُوش وجُحُوشَة
Filly of the ass. جَحْشَة
Little donkey. جُحَيْش
Headstrong, self-willed. — وَحْدِهِ
To have a prominent cornea (eye). ✱ جَحَظ a جُحُوظًا

To gaze at. جَحَّظ إلى
To sweep away. To carry a. th. To strip off. To strike (the ball: player). ✱ جَحَف a جَحْفًا ه
To incline towards. — مع
To wash away, to waste a. th. (torrent). To ruin (people: fate). To approach. To overburden a. o. أَجْحَف ب
To fight with the sword. To return (the ball: players). تَجَاحَف
To destroy, to carry away a. th. To exhaust (a well). إِجْتَحَف ه
To ruin (people: fate). — ه
Torrent. Diarrhea. Death. جُحَاف
To throw a. o. down. To scold a. o. ✱ جَحْفَل ه
To meet in great numbers. تَجَحْفَل
Numerous army. Man of high rank. جَحْفَل ج جَحَافِل
Lip (of hoofed animals). جَحْفَلَة ج جَحَافِل
To throw a. o. down. ✱ جَحَل a جَحْلًا , وجَحَّل ه
Large water-skin. جَحْل ج جِحَال
Lizard. Queen-bee. Beetle. Chief. — ج جُحُول وجُحْلَان
Poison, venom. جُحَال
To light and stir up (the fire). To open (the eyes). ✱ جَحَم a جَحْمًا ه
جَحِم a جَحْمًا وجَحَمًا وجُحُومًا , وجَحُم o جُحُومًا
To be intense (fire).
To cast a piercing look at. جَحَّم ب
To abstain. To depart from. أَجْحَم عن
To burn with desires. To be in pangs (heart). تَجَحَّم
Ardent fire. Hell-fire. Hell. Intensely hot (place). جَحِيم
Swelling of the eyes. جُحَام
Burning (coal). Affray. Thick of a fight. Hot (place). جَاحِم
Having red eyes. أَجْحَم م جَحْمَاء
Old woman. Termagant. ✱ جَحْمَرِش
To be scantily fed. ✱ جَحِن a جَحَنًا
To feed (o.'s family) scantily ✱ جَحَن a جَحْنًا , وجَحَّن وأَجْحَن ه
Ill-fed. Mean. Weak (plant). Tick. جَحِن
Gihon (river). جَيْحُون
To walk. ✱ جَحَا o جَحْوًا

a. th. anew.
Good luck; chance. Wealth. جَدّ
Greatness. Brink of a river.
Serious endeavour. Pains-taking. جِدّ
Earnestness. Haste. Unavoidable (punishment).
Extremely learned man. عَالِمٌ جِدُّ عَالِمٍ
Much. Extremely. Seriously. جِدًّا
Grandfather; جَدّ ج جُدُود وجُدُودَة وأجْدَاد sire.
Ancestors, forefathers. أَجْدَاد
Happy, lucky. جِدّ وجَدِيد ومَجْدُود
Shore. Abundant or scanty جُدّ (well).
Very lucky man. — وجُدِّيّ
Smooth and hard ground. جَدَد ج أَجْدَاد
Thin sand.
Grandmother. Brink. جَدَّة ج جَدَّات
Mark. Streak on the back جُدَّة ج جُدَد of asses. Way, manner. Djeddah (town).
Shore. Bank of a river. جِدَّة ج جُدَد
Dog-brake. Rag.
Main road. Thoroughfare. جَادَّة ج جَوَادّ
Intertwisted boughs. P جُدَّاد
Rags.
New. Newly made. Mo- جَدِيد ج جُدُد dern, recent. Unexpected (death). Great (man). Fat (she-ass). Old coin worth 9 paras. Surface of the earth.
The day and the night. الجَدِيدَان والأَجَدَّان
Applying himself جَادّ ومُجِدّ في zealously to. In earnest, serious.
Happier. Dry (breast, udder). أَجَدّ
Lop-eared (ewe).
Waterless (desert). Small- جَدَّاء breasted (female).
Cricket. ✻ جُنْدُب ج جَنَادِب
Hard and even ground. جَنْجَد
✻ جَدُبَ o جَدْبًا, وجَدُبَ o جُدُوبَةً, وأَجْدَبَ
To be struck with barrenness وتَجَدَّبَ (soil).
To dispraise, جَدَبَ i o جَدْبًا ه وه to disapprove a. o. or a. th
To suffer from dearth (people). أَجْدَبَ
To be droughty (year). To find no hospitality (people).

To remain in (a place). — ب
To pull off a. th. إِجْتَحَى ه
Name of a celebrated wit. جُحَى
✻ جَحَّ i جَحًّا To lie on the ground from fatigue. To go from one place to another. ✧ To be luxuriously attired. ▫ To boast vainly, to humbug.
✧ Luxury. Sumptuousness. جَخَّة
✻ جَخَرَ a جَخْرًا, وجَخَّرَ وأَجْخَرَ ه To widen the orifice of (a well).
Large valley. جَاخِر
✻ جَخَفَ o i جَخْفًا وجَخِيفًا, وجَخِفَ a جَخَفًا To boast. To snore.
Snoring. Boasting. جَخْف وجَخِيف
Proud. Braggart. جَخَّاف وجَخِيف
✻ جَخَا o جَخْوًا ه To upset (a vessel).
To be crooked (old man). جَخَّى
To be upset (vessel). — وتَجَخَّى
✻ جَدَّ i جَدًّا To be respectable, important (man). To be serious, grievous (affair).
To cut out (a garment) To cut ه — off (a fruit).
To be new, newly جِدَّةً, واسْتَجَدَّ i — made (coat).
To endeavour to. To exert جِدًّا في o i — o.'s self in. To acquire credit (amongst). To act in earnest. To hasten (the pace). To ascertain a. th.
To succeed in جَدَّ a جَدًّا وجُدَّ ب (an affair).
To restore, to renew; جَدَّدَ ه to do a. th. up like new. ✧ To repeat, to reiterate. To commence a. th. anew.
To bring a law-suit against جَادَّ ه في a. o. on.
To become smooth (road). أَجَدَّ
To restore, to make a. th. anew. ه — To put on (a new garment). To settle a. th. To renew (a compact).
To perform a. th. zealously في — and assiduously.
To be renewed (compact). تَجَدَّدَ
To dry (udder). To be made new (garment).
To renew a. th. To undertake ه إِسْتَجَدَّ

To find (a land) barren. — ه
To find it shameful. أجدب أن
Drought. Droughty year. Vice. جدب
Barren (land). جَدْب وجَدِيب وجَدُوب ومُجْدِب
Barren, *f.* ✧ Stupidity. Madness. جَدْبَة
Barren, bare (soil). أجدب م جدباء
Unfruitful, unprofitable (land). مِجْداب
Barren (ground). ✧ Mad. crazy. مَجْدُوب
Cricket. Small locust. جُنْدَب وجُنْدُب
Grave. Tomb. ✻ جَدَث ج أجداث وأجْدُث
To mix, to beat (flour, a medicine). ✻ جَدَح a جَدْحًا , وأجدح واجتدح ه
Instrument for mixing. Name of a star. مِجْدَح
Setting stars foreboding rain. مجاديح السماء
To bloom (tree). To sprout (plant). To be covered with blisters (hand). To conceal o.'s self behind a wall. ✻ جَدَر o جَدْرًا
To wall, to inclose a. th. in walls. - جدرًا ه
To sprout (plant). جَدُر o جَدَارَة , وجدّر وأجدر
To become fit, suited for, able to. — ب و ل
To form its grains and sprout (vine). جَدِر a جَدَرًا
To have the small-pox. جُدِر و✧ جُدِّر وتجدّر
To raise (a building). جدّر واجتدر ه
To have young trees (land). To shoot forth (tree). أجدر
Natural tumour, swelling caused by a wound. Bite on an animal's neck. Sprout. جَدَر ج أجدار
Wall. Inclosure, fence. ✧ Manure, dung-hill. جدر ج جُدران . وجِدار ج جُدُر وجُدْر
Small-pox. جَدَرِيّ وجُدَرِيّ و✧ جِدْرِي
Measles. ✧ جَدَرِيّ المُوَيّ
Worthy of, suited for, able to جدير ج جَدِيرُون وجُدَراء ب او ل
Inclosure for cattle. Walled garden. — وجديرة ج جَدائِر
Country where small-pox is raging. مَجْدَرَة

Becoming a. o., suitable to. — ومَجْدُور ل
Seized with small-pox. Pock-marked (face). مَجْدُور و✧ مُجَدَّر
✧ Rice and lentils (dish). مُجَدَّرَة
Rye. جَاوَدَار
Spurred rye. جاودار قَرْنِيّ
Hard, firm. Dry blood. ✻ جدس — جادِس
Uncultivated ground. جادِسَة ج جَوادِس
To mutilate the nose, lips. To cut off (a limb). To withhold a. o. ✻ جَدَع a جَدْعًا ه
To nourish a. o. scantily. — وجدّع وأجدع ه
To be poorly nourished; to be mangled. To have the nose cut off. جَدِع a جَدَعًا
To wish a. o. to be maimed. جدّع ه
To insult a. o. جادع مُجادَعَة وجِداعًا ه
To quarrel, to abuse o. a. تَجادَع
Mutilation (of the nose, *etc.*). جَدْع
Poorly fed (child). جَدِع
Stump of amputated member. جَدَعَة
Bad year. جَدَاع
Bad, unwholesome (pasturage). جُدَاع
Mangled (nose, ears). أجدع م جدعاء ج جُدْع
Scalpel. مِجْدَع ج مَجادِع
Lop-eared (ass). Cropped by the cattle (plant). مُجَدَّع
To walk quickly (man). To walk with short steps (woman, gazelle). ✻ جَدَف i جَدْفًا
To propel (a boat) with oars. To cut off a. th. — جَدْفًا ه
To try to fly with its wings cut (bird). — o جُدُوفًا
To send down (snow: sky). — بِ
To row (a boat). جدّف ه
To disown benefits. To be ungrateful. — بالنِّعَم
To blaspheme against. جدّف على
To shout, to clamour. أجدف
Bustle and clamour, uproar. جَدَفَة
Blasphemy. تَجْدِيف ج تَجادِيف
Blasphemer. Ungrateful. مُجَدِّف
Oar. Wing of a bird. Whip. مِجْدَاف ج مَجَادِيف

To rise from destitution to wealth. ✻ جدن — أجدن
Fineness of the voice. جَدَن
To ask (a gift, or a thing wanted). ✻ جدا o جَدْوًا , واجْتَدَى واسْتَجدَى ه
To make a gift to. To bring (an evil) upon. — ه وعلى
To obtain a gift, a. th. wanted. أجدَى
To be of use to. To profit. To suffice a. o. — على
It is of no avail to thee. مَا يُجدِي عَنكَ هٰذَا
Gift. General rain. جَدًا
Utility. Profit. جَدَاء
Gift, present. جَدْوَى
More useful, more advantageous. أجدَى
To request of a. o. a donation. ✻ جَدَى i جَدْيًا ه
To bleed (wound). أجدَى
Square number. Product of a multiplication. (*Arith.*) جِدَاء
Kid. Capricorn (*zodiacal sign*). جَدي ج أجْدٍ وجِداء وجِديَان
Saddle-cushion. جَدية ج جَدَى وجَدَيَات
To cut. To break to pieces. To extirpate. To snatch a. th. ✻ جَذَّ o جَذًّا ه
To be cut off, plucked away. إنجَذَّ
Cut. أجَذّ م جَذّاء
Bit, fragment. Piece of a garment. جُذَّة
Bit, piece, fragment. جُذاذ وجِذاذ
Silver cuttings, clippings. جُذاذات
To draw, to attract. To bring over. To extend a. th. To wean (a boy). ✻ جَذَبَ i جَذْبًا ه و ه
To contend with a. o. in pulling. To remove a. th. from its place. جاذَبَ مُجاذَبَة وجِذابًا ه وه
✧ To stretch out the arms from weariness. To grow weary. تَجَذَّبَ
To drink (milk). — ه
To pull a th. in a contrary direction. To protract (a conversation). تَجاذَبَ ه
To be attracted, dragged. إنجَذَبَ
He went far away. — في السَّيْر
To drag, to snatch off, إجتَذَبَ ه

Having the legs cut off. مَجذُوف
To twist strongly (a rope). ✻ جَدَل o i جَدْلًا ه
To grow (grain). To become strong (gazelle). To be quarrelsome, contentious (man). — وجَدِل a جَدَلًا
To knock a. o. down. To plait (the hair). جَدَل وجَدَّل ه وه
To dispute, to contend with. جادَل ه
To be thrown down. To fall down. ✧ To be twisted. To be strongly wound (rope). تجَدَّل وانجَدَل
To discuss, to dispute together. تَجادَل
Hard. Strong. Whip. جَدْل وجَدِل وجُدَال
Member, sinew. *Pl.* Bones of the legs. جِدْل ج جُدُول
Sharpness, acrimony in dispute. Ripe (corn, grain). جَدَل
Well-made syllogism. جَدَل ج جُدُول وأجدَال
Polemics. جَدَل وعِلم الجَدَل
Pestle. جَدَلَة
The earth, the soil. الجَدَالَة
Contest, quarrel, discussion. Scientific debate. جِدَال ومُجادَلَة
Twisted rope. جَدِيل ج جُدُل
Way, mood. Country. State. Tribe. ✧ Plait of hair. جَديلَة ج جَدَائِل
A kind of hawk. أجدَل ج أجادِل
Breast-plate strongly made. دِرْع جَدلاء ج أدْرُع جُدْل
Quarrelsome (man). Liable to be discussed, litigable (matter). Syllogistic. جَدَلِيّ وجِدَالِيّ
Caviller, disputer. جَدَّال وجِدِيل
Disputative man. Castle. مِجْدَل ج مَجادِل
Disputatious person. مِجْدَال ج مَجادِل
Woven. twisted. Thin, slender. مَجْدُول
To make (a list. a table. a catalogue). ✻ جَدْوَل
Brook. trench. Rubric of a register, table of a book, framing of a page. List. catalogue. Table, sheet. جَدْوَل ج جَدَاوِل
Provided with a framing. rubrics. مُجَدْوَل
To bear fruit and become dry (palm-tree). ✻ جَدَم o جَدْمًا
To curtail, to cut off a. th. — ه

to carry a. th. by force.
Dragging. Attraction. جَذْب واجْتِذاب
✧ Ecstasy, rapture, ravishment. جَذْب وجَذْبَة
Distance. Thread spun at one revolution of the spindle. جَذْبَة ج جَذَبات
He fell into the valley of Jozabat, (*Prov.*) *to mean* : He missed his aim. أَخَذ في وادِي جَذَبات
Death ! *Imprecation.* جَذَاب
Attractive force. Attraction. جاذِبِيَّة وقُوَّة جاذِبَة
Attracting. dragging. Having scanty milk ; having a protracted pregnancy (she-camel). جاذِب و جَذّاب
Net of entangled hair for catching larks. جَذَّابَة
Dragged. مَجْذُوب
To cut off, to trench. To extirpate. To snatch. To root out a. th. ✱ جَذَر o جَذْرًا ه
To extract the square or cube root of a number. جَذَّر
To eradicate. To draw out a. th. — واَجْذَر ه
To be cut off, uprooted. إِنْجَذَر
Root of (the tongue). Foot (of a tree). Origin. Horn (of a cow). Square or cube root of a number. جَذْر وجِذْر ج جُذُور
Wild calf. جَوْذَر وجُوذَر وجُوذُر ج جَوَاذِر وجآذِر
To cut off (an animal's) food. ✱ جَذَع a جَذْعًا ه
To become two years old (sheep). أَجْذَع
Young, novice. Young sheep. ◻ Strong youth. Lively young man. جَذَع ج جِذَاع وجُذْعان
Palm-tree stock. Beam of a roof. ◻ Trunk of the body. جِذْع ج جُذُوع وأَجْذَاع
They dispersed on all sides. ذَهَبُوا جِذَعَ مِذَعَ
To fly swiftly (bird). To walk with short and quick steps. ✱ جَذَف i جَذْفًا , وأَجْذَف
To cut off, to curtail a. th. — ه
To propel (a boat) with (oars). — ب ه

Oar. Wing. مِجْذاف ج مَجاذِيف
To be glad, joyful. ✱ جَذِل a جَذَلًا , واجْتَذَل
To stand upright. — o جُذُولًا , واسْتَجْذَل
To cheer a. o. أَجْذَل ه
Stump of a tree. Summit of a mountain. جِذْل ج أَجْذال وجُذُول
Cheerful, gay. جَذِل وجَذْلان ج جُذْلان
To mangle. To cut off a. th ✱ جَذَم i جَذْمًا , وجَذَّم ه
To be affected witn elephantiasis. جُذِم و✧ تَجَذَّم
To be mangled. To havo one hand cut off. جَذِم a جَذَمًا
To be cut off. تَجَذَّم وانْجَذَم
Root, trunk Stock of a family. Root of a tooth. جِذْم ج جُذُوم وأَجْذام
Fragment of a. th. cut off. Whip. جِذْمَة ج جِذَم
Stump of a hand cut off. جُذْمَة
Corn-oars left by the reapers, gleanings. جُذامَة
Name of a tribe and of a king. جَذِيمَة
Elephantiasis (kind of leprosy). جُذام
Affected with elephantiasis. أَجْذَم ومَجْذُوم ومُجَذَّم
Having his hand mutilated. أَجْذَم ج جَذْمَى
Stump of a hand, of a tree cut off. Root, beginning. ✱ جُذْمُور وجِذْمار
To stand erect, firm. ✱ جَذَا o جَذْوًا وجُذُوًّا , وأَجْذَى
Burning coal, firebrand. جَذْوَة وجِذْوَة وجُذْوَة ج جِذاء وجِذًى وجُذًى
To prevent a. o. from. ✱ جَذَى i جَذْيًا , وأَجْذَى ه عَن
To drag the tail round his (mate : pigeon). تَجَذَّى ب
Root of a tree. جِذْي وجِذْيَة
To pull, to drag a. th. along . To induce a. o. To lead (a beast) gently. To draw, to attract a. th. To put (a noun) in the genitive case. ✱ جَرَّ o جَرًّا ه وه
To commit (a crime). — o a جَرِيرَةً عَلَى
To pull a. th. violently. جَرْجَر ه
He granted a delay to his debtor. جارَّ وأَجَرَّ ه الدَّيْن

◘ Death-rattle.
Olives very ripe. ✧ جُرْجُر وجَرْجار
Water-cress. Rocket. جِرْجِير
To be courageous, bold-spirited. ✻ جَرُؤَ ٥ جَراءة وجُرأة وجَرايَة
To render a. o. courageous, to inspirit. To embolden a. o. جَرَّأ ٥
To assume boldness; to take heart. To dare. إجْتَرَأ و ✧ تَجَرَّأ
To attempt a. th. against. To venture upon. — بِ على
To show courage, boldness. إسْتَجْرَأ
Boldness, daring; bravery, courage. جُرأة وجَراءة
Go-ahead. Bold. Lion. جَرِيء ج أَجْراء
F. Trap for wild beasts. جَرِيئة ج جَراء
Audacious, hardy. مُجْتَرِئ
To be scabby. To become rusty (sword). ✻ جَرِبَ a جَرَبًا
To tempt a. o. To try, to prove, to experience a. th. جَرَّب ٥ وه
To have cattle affected with scab. أجْرَب
To be tried. To be tempted. ✧ تَجَرَّب
Scab. Rust. Blemish. جَرَب
Ciliary blepharitis. Disease of the eyelids. جَرَب العَيْن
Leather bag. Cricket. Cavity of a well. جِراب ج أجْرِبَة وجُرُب وجُرْب
Socks, stockings. Ps جَوْرَب ج جَوارِب و ✧ جَوْرَبات
To put stockings on a. o. جَوْرَب ٥
Troop of men, of animals. جَرَبَّة
Experiment. trial, temptation. تَجْرِبَة ج تَجارِب
Scabbard of a sword. Collar of a shirt. جِرِبان وجُرُبان وجُرُبّان وجِرِبّان
جَرِب وجَرْبان، وأجْرَب م جَرْباء ج جُرْب
Scabby. وجِراب وجَرْبَى وأجارِب
Dry (land). Sky. Beautiful (girl). جَرْباء
Cultivated field. Measure for wheat. Measure of superficy. جَرِيب ج أجْرِبَة وجُرْبان
Tempter. Lion. ✧ The Devil. مُجَرِّب
Tempted. Experienced (man). Assayed (money). مُجَرَّب
Deceiver. ✻ جُرْبُز ج جَرابِزَة
Knapsack. Pe جَرابَنْدِيَّة

To drag along. To prevent a.o. from speaking. To slit the tongue of (a youngling). To leave (the spear) in the wound. To join a. o. in singing. To let (a beast) pasture freely. أجَرَّ ٥
To be drawn, dragged, pulled. إنْجَرَّ
To ruminate (animal). إجْتَرَّ
To draw, to drag a. th. — ه
To pull, to draw a. th. ✧ To contract (a debt) little by little. إسْتَجَرَّ ه
To submit to a. o. — لِ
Foot of a mountain. Basket. Burrow of (a beast). Genitive case. جَرّ
And so on, so forth. هَلُمَّ جَرًّا
Prepositions governing the genitive. حُرُوف الجَرّ
Mechanics. جَرّ الأثْقال
Way of pulling. Tribe, emigrating people. Cud. جِرَّة
Earthenware jar. Cud. جَرَّة ج جِرار وجَرّ
Snare for gazelles. Perforated plate of iron used to sow wheat. جُرَّة ج جُرَر
Eel. جِرِّيّ
Crop of a bird. جِرِّيَّة و جِرِّيئة
Stream of water, brook. ✧ Peg. Drawer. Flat bolt. جارُور ج جَوارِير
Restive (horse). Deep (well). جَرُور
Rope, camel's halter. جَرِيرَة ج أجِرَّة
Sin, crime. جَرِيرَة ج جَرائِر
Numerous army fully equipped. Potter. ◘ Pole of a carriage. ✧ Drawer of a table. جَرّار
A small and deadly yellow scorpion. جَرّارَة
The milky way. Quail. مَجَرَّة
Drawn along. In the genitive case (noun). ◘ Drain, channel. مَجْرُور
To gurgle (water). To growl (beast). To crepitate (fire). ✻ جَرْجَر
To drag a th. ◘ — ه
To produce a gurgling noise in swallowing water. — وتَجَرْجَر الماء
Thrashing-machine. جَرْجَر
Broad-bean. جِرْجِر
Gurgling of water. جَرْجَرَة

Eel. * جِرِّيث

To gather, to meet together. To fall down from a high place (man). * جَرْثَمَ — تَجَرْثَمَ واجْرَنْثَمَ

To take the greatest part of. ه —

Root. Origin. Clod sticking to a root. جُرْثُومَة

Ant-hill. جُرْثُومَة النَّمْل

To be loose (finger-ring). To walk upon a hard ground. * جَرِجَ a جَرَجًا

Sealing-clay. Mud. Gnat. * جِرْجِس

To profit. * جَرَحَ a جَرْحًا

To wound, to offend a. o. ه —

To disparage a witness and quash his evidence. — الشَّاهِدَ والشَّهَادَةَ

To be wounded. To be impaired, made void (testimony). جُرِحَ a جَرْحًا

To inflict severe wounds on a. o. جَرَّحَ ه

To be wounded. ✧ إِنْجَرَحَ

To procure, to obtain a th. To perpetrate (a crime). إِجْتَرَحَ ه

To be annulled (witness). إِسْتَجْرَحَ

Wound. Cut. sore. جُرْح ج جُرُوح وأَجْرَاح ; وجِرَاح و جِرَاحَات

Peremptory argument. جُرْحَة

N. *of un.* A wound. جِرَاحَة

Surgery. عِلْم الجِرَاحَة

Surgeon. جَرَّاح وجِرَاحِيّ . ✧ جَرَائِحِيّ

Productive member (*as the foot, hand*). Mare. Flesh-eating animals. Birds of prey. Blade. Calamity. جَارِحَة ج جَوَارِح

Wounded. جَرِيح ج جَرْحَى (*m. and f*).

Wounded (pers. animals). Made void (testimony). مَجْرُوح ج مَجَارِيح

Covered with wounds. مُجَرَّح

To become ill from eating locusts. To be smitten by locusts (land). To be threadbare (clothes). To be bare, without grass (soil, field). To be worn out, shabby (clothes). To lose o.'s hair, (man. animal). * جَرِدَ a جَرَدًا

To strib (a branch of its leaves; a tree of its bark; a skin of its hair). To induce a. o. to give a. th. against his will. To make a land bare (drought, locusts). To unsheath (a sword). ✧ To inventory. to reckon up a. th. جَرَدَ o جَرْدًا ه

To strip a. o. from. و جَرَّدَ ه مِن

To peal. To bark a. th. To strip a. o. of (his clothes). To bare (the ground). To write without marking the points. To shave. To abstract a. th. جَرَّدَ ه و ه

To be denuded. To come forth from its sheath (spike). To outstrip the others (horse). ✧ To be taken abstractively (th). تَجَرَّدَ

To disentangle o.'s self. To get rid of a. o. — عَن

To throw off (o.'s clothes). — مِن

To apply o.'s self exclusively, to devote o.'s self to. — لِ

To be isolated, separated. To be stripped. To be barked. To be worn out, threadbare. To cast his hair (camel). إِنْجَرَدَ

We had a very long way, we are wayworn. إِنْجَرَدَ بِنَا السَّيْر

To comb (wool) إِجْتَرَدَ ه

Smooth. even. Shaved. Shabby (clothes). Shield. ✧ Inventory. جَرْد

Troop of horsemen. ✧ High and bare mountains. جُرْد

Field bare, without vegetation. Baldness. جَرَد

Bare, without vegetation. أَجْرَد م جَرْدَاء

Unclad part of the body. جُرْدَة

Shabby dress. جِرْدَة

Locusts. (*Coll*). جَرَاد

A locust. جَرَادَة

Bark. جُرَادَة

Palm-bough stripped off. Mock fight, tilt. Whole (day, month). جَرِيد

Detachment of cavalry. Catalogue. Account-book. Register. ✧ Newspaper. ◻ Palm-branch. — و جَرِيدَة ج جَرَائِد

Bad (year). Unlucky (man). جَارُود

Separation. Abstraction. Isolation. Spoliation. Privation, disengagement from all worldly things. تَجْرِيد

تَجَرُّد Independence; unworldliness. Abstraction. Isolation. ◇ Indifference. Impartiality, fairness.

أَجْرَد م جَرْدَاء ج جُرْد Naked, flat, even. Bare (field). Free from hatred (heart). Short-haired. Without hair (man); without froth (milk). Pure from clouds (sky). Pure (wine). Complete (day, month).

◇ أَجْرُودِيّ Beardless. Thin-haired (man).

مِجْرَد ج مَجَارِد Surgical instrument for cleansing the teeth.

مَجْرُود Stripped off. Barked. Fleshless (bone). Abounding in locusts (country). ◇ Shovel.

مُجَرَّد Separated. Naked. Abstracted. Incorporeal. Alone, unique.

بِمُجَرَّد مَا For the sole reason that.

مُجَرَّدًا لِ Only for.

مُجَرَّدَات Abstracted matters.

✻ جَرْدَب To eat greedily at the expense of another.

P جَرْدَبَان ومُجَرْدِب , وجَرْدَبِيل Eating greedily. Spunger.

P جَرْدَق Cake of bread.

◇ جَرْدَل Bucket.

✻ جَرْدَم To eat (man). To speak much and volubly.

جَرْدَم Loquacious. Black green-headed locust.

✻ جَرِذَ ٥ جَرَذًا To turn into a tumour (wound).

جَرَّذَ ه و ٥ To cut away (the knots of a tree). To train a. o.

أَجْرَذَ ٥ To put a. o. out. To separate.

جَرَذ Tumour on the hock.

جُرَذ ج جِرْذَان , و◇ جَرْذَوْن Large rat. ◇ Field-rat. Mole.

أُمّ الجِرْذَان Kind of date.

أَرْض جَرِذَة Earth abounding in rats.

✻ جَرَزَ ٥ جَرْزًا ٥ To cut. To goad a. o.

جَرُزَ ٥ جَرَازَة To be voracious.

جَارَزَ ٥ مُجَارَزَة وجِرَازًا To joke maliciously with.

أَجْرَزَ To be barren (female). To become lean (she-camel).

تَجَارَزَ To revile o. another.

جُرُز وجُرْز ج أَجْرَاز Barren year. Body. Breast of man.

P جُرْز ج أَجْرَاز وجِرَزَة Iron rod. Fangs of a viper.

جَرْزَة Loss, destruction.

جُرْزَة ج جُرَز Bundle of trefoil.

جُرَاز Sharp sword.

جَرُوز Glutton.

مُجَارَزَة Abusive joke.

مِجْرَاز Barren ground.

✻ جَرَسَ i جَرْسًا , وأَجْرَسَ وتَجَرَّسَ To emit a gentle sound. To speak gently.

— ه To utter (a word). To lick a. th. (cattle).

جَرَّسَ ٥ To render a. o. experienced (business). ◇ To disgrace, to bring shame upon a. o.

جَرَّسَ بِفُلَان To render a. o. infamous. To publish a. o.'s misdoings.

أَجْرَسَ To produce a ringing sound (jewels). To produce a rustling sound in flying (bird). To be scared away at the voice of man (wild beast).

— ه To ring a bell.

تَجَرَّسَ To whisper. To speak gently.

جَرْس وجِرْس Gentle sound, hum.

مَا سَمِعْتُ لَهُ حِسًّا وَلَا جِرْسًا I have not perceived the slightest sound.

جَرَس ج أَجْرَاس Bell.

◇ جَرْسَة Shame, scandal.

جَارِسَة ج جَوَارِس Plant-devouring (insect). *Pl.* Bees.

جَرِيسَة ج جَرَائِس Head of cattle stolen during the night.

✻ جَرَشَ ٥ جَرْشًا ه To bray, to bruise (wheat, salt). To take away (the scurf of the head with a comb). To throw off its slough (viper).

أَجْرَشَ ٥ To steal a. th.

جَارُشَة ج جَوَارِيش Hand-mill for groats.

جُرَاشَة Wheat coarsely ground. Female comber.

جَرِيش ومَجْرُوش Coarsely ground. Roughly milled (wheat). Groats.

P جَوَارِش و◇ جَوَارِيش Sweets.

✻ جَرِضَ a جَرَضًا ب To swallow (saliva) difficultly from grief or anger.

To be oppressed by grief. To be to the pangs of death.
To strangle a. o. جَرَضَ o جَرْضًا
To suffocate a. o. with. أَجْرَضَ ه ب
Suffocation. Suffocating saliva. Death-rattle. Grief. جَرَضٌ وجَرِيضٌ
At the point of death. Oppressed by grief. Choked by saliva. جَرِيضٌ ج جَرْضَى
He escaped half-dead. أَفْلَتَ جَرِيضًا
He died broken-hearted. مَاتَ جَرِيضًا
Big-bellied. Glutton. ✻ جُرَاضِمٌ
To swallow in one draught. ✻ جَرَعَ a جَرْعًا وجَرِعَ a جَرَعًا . واجْتَرَعَ
To make a. o. to swallow (water). To make a. o. to restrain his rage. ✧ To embolden a. o. جَرَّعَ ه
✧ To dare, to assume boldness. ✧ تَجَرَّعَ (for تَجَرَّأَ)
To drink a. th. by draughts. To repress (anger). تَجَرَّعَ ه
Rope. Bow-string. جِرْعٌ
Draught. Mouthful. جَرْعَةٌ وجُرْعَةٌ
Small draught. جُرَيْعَةٌ
Sandy ground. جَرَعَةٌ وجَرْعَاءُ . وأَجْرَعُ ج أَجَارِعُ
Boldness, courage. ✧ جَرَاعَةٌ
To take the greatest part of. To sweep sway. To shovel. ✧ To rake up a. th. ✻ جَرَفَ o جَرْفًا , وجَرَّفَ وتَجَرَّفَ واجْتَرَفَ ه
To reduce a.o. to destitution. جَرَّفَ ه
To be flooded (place). أَجْرَفَ
Goods of all description. Harvest. جَرَفٌ
Bank undermined by water. جُرُفٌ ج جِرَفَةٌ , وجُرْفٌ ج أَجْرُفٌ
Piece of bread. جِرْفَةٌ
Stream of water washing a land away. Greedy. جُرَافٌ
Measure of capacity. — وجِرَافٌ
Scooping. Sweeping away. Mortality. Plague. جَارِفٌ
Glutton. Unhappy. جَارُوفٌ م جَارُوفَةٌ
Broom. Scoop. Shovel. ✧ Rake, hoe. مِجْرَفَةٌ و✧ جَارُوفَةٌ و✧ جَرَّافَةٌ
Sweeping torrent. Swift (hackney). جَرْوَفٌ
To throw a. o. down. ✻ جَرْفَسَ ه

To bind tightly.
Lion. جِرْفَاسٌ وجُرَافِسٌ
To be hard, stony. ✻ جَرِلَ a جَرَلًا
Stony ground. جَرَلٌ وجَرِلٌ ج أَجْرَالٌ , وجَرْوَلٌ ج جَرَاوِلُ
Golden redcolour. Wine. Pure (colour). جِرْيَالٌ
To cut, to lop off (a palm-tree). To complete a. th. To shear (sheep). ✧ To bone (the meat). ✻ جَرَمَ i جَرْمًا ه
To acquire a. th. for o.'s. family, to earn. — واجْتَرَمَ ل
To commit a crime against a. o. — وأَجْرَمَ واجْتَرَمَ عَلَى وإِلَى
To gather the fruit of (a tree). جَرَمَ i جَرْمًا وجِرَامًا ه
To cut a. th. short. جَرَّمَ ه
To charge a. o. falsely with a crime. — ه وتَجَرَّمَ عَلَى
To be elapsed (night, year). To be guilty. To abstain from sin. تَجَرَّمَ
Crime, sin, misdemeanour. جَرْمٌ , وجُرْمٌ ج جُرُومٌ أَو أَجْرَامٌ
Certainly. Indeed. Undoubtedly. لَا جَرَمَ ولَا جُرْمَ
Hot (country). ◇ Penalty. Large boat, barge on the Nile. جَرْمٌ ج جُرُومٌ
Body of animal. Throat. جِرْمٌ ج أَجْرَامٌ وجُرُمٌ
The hot countries (opp. to the cold الطُّرُودُ). الجُرُومُ
The celestial bodies. الأَجْرَامُ الفَلَكِيَّةُ
Sustainer of a family. Gatherer of dates. جَارِمٌ ج جُرَّمٌ وجُرَّامٌ
Dry dates. جَرَامٌ وجُرَامٌ وجَرِيمٌ
Gleanings. جُرَامَةٌ
Thick-bodied. Cut (tree). Culprit. جَرِيمٌ
Last descendant. Fruitstone. Crime, fault. ◻ Fine, penalty. جَرِيمَةٌ ج جَرَائِمُ
Loading and unloading of a ship. تَجْرِيمٌ وتَفْرِيغٌ
Elementary grammar. أَجْرُومِيَّةٌ
Culprit, guilty. ◻ Rogue, beggar. مُجْرِمٌ
To contract o.'s self. To shift. To shun an answer. To answer faultily. ✻ جَرْمَزَ

current (money).
To hasten to. To purpose a. th. إلى —
To follow the same course, جَرَى مَجْرَاه rules. To act in the same way.
To give vent جَرَّى وأَجْرَى ه وه (to water). To send (a deputy). To launch a.th. To start(a horse).
To compete with. جَارَى د وتجارَى To run with a. o.
To agree with a. o. in. د وتجارَى في —
To sign, to execute (a decree). أَجْرَى ه To close (an account). To decline (a noun).
To render alike. أَجْرَى ه مَجْرَاه To subject to the same rules.
To entrust a. o. with (a business). ه إلى —
To inflict a penalty on a. o. ه على — ✧ To grant (a pension) to. To carry a. th. to (the debit of).
To introduce a custom. العَادَة —
To appoint, to send (a deputy). To start (a horse). إِسْتَجْرَى ه
Course. Current, stream of water. ✧ Diarrhea. جَرْي وجَرَيَان
According to custom. على جَرْيِ العَادَة
For thee, on account of thee, for thy sake. مِن جَرَاك ومِن جَرائِك
Girlhood. Daily wages. Allowance for soldiers. ✧ Pension. جِرَايَة وجِراء
Mission. Commission. جِرَايَة
Running. Custom. Natural disposition. جِرِيَّاء وإجْرِيَّة وإجْرِيًا وإجْرِيَّاء
Procurator. Agent. Surety. Messenger, hiredman. جَرِيّ ج أَجْرِيَاء
Eel. جِرِّيّ
Flowing. Running. Continuous. Instant (month, year). جَارٍ م جارِيَة
Young woman, female slave. Girl. Maid-servant Ship. Viper. Wind. Sun. Eye of animal. جارِيَة ج جارِيَات وجَوَار
Usher of a Court. مَأمور الإجراء
Executive. اجرائِي
Occurrences, events. مَاجَرِيَات(ماجَرى)
Wate course, channel. Course of affairs. ✧Bed of a river. Track of a ship. *Pl.* Means. مَجْرَى ج مَجَارٍ
Zodiacal circle. مَجْرَى الشَّمس

To pass away(night). To gather (people). تَجَرْمَزَ
Small house. Lake in a depressed place. جُرْمُوز
Body of man. Legs of (wild beasts). جَرَامِز وجَرَامِيز
To scamper off. ضَمَّ جَرَامِيزَه
Overshoe, galoche. جُرْمُوق P
To be worn out (clothes). ✻ جَرَنَ ـُ جُرُونًا
To grind (wheat). ه —
To be trained (man, beast). على —
Young one of the serpent. Effaced (track). Worn out (garment). جَارِن
Floor. Pestle. Stone-basin. ✧ Stonemortar. جُرْن ج أَجْرَان
✧ Baptismal Font. جُرْن المَعْمُودِيَّة
Upper part of a camel's neck. جِرَان ج جُرُن وأَجْرِنَة
He threw off his burden upon him. He became accustomed to it. أَلْقَى عَلَيْهِ جِرَانَهُ
Thrashing-floor. Drying-place for dates. جَرِين
To proclaim. To publish a.th. ✻ جَرَّهَ ه
To be proclaimed, made notorious. جَرَّهَ
Clamour, shriek. Steeds. Company of men. جِرَاهِيَة
Side, flank. جَرْهَة
To hasten. To walk at a quick pace. ✻ جَرْهَدَ واجْرَهَدَّ
Great walker. جَرْهَد وجُرْهُد
Large, enormous lion. ✻ جِرْهَاس
Ancient tribe of Arabia. ✻ جُرْهُم
Lion. Huge camel. جِرْهَام وجُرَاهِم
Acting vigorously. جِرْهَام
To have whelps (bitch). ✻ أَجْرَى
جَرْو وجُرْو ج أَجْرٍ وجِرَاء وجج أَجْرِيَة
Whelp. Cub. Young one. Small colocynth. Pomegranate.
He bore the thing patiently (*Prov*). أَلْقَى او ضَرَبَ جِرْوَتَهُ على الأَمْرِ وعَنْهُ
Having whelps (wild beast). مُجْرٍ ومُجْرِيَة و✧ مُجَرِّايَة
To flow (water) To run, to be current. To be executed (order). To happen (event). To move (stars). To be ✻ جَرَى ـِ جَرْيًا وجَرَيَانًا وجِرْيَة

He gave him a part of his لَهُ مِن مالِهِ — wealth.
Present, gift. جُزْء
Portfolio. Case. Ps جزدان
To slaughter (a head of cattle). To cut off (fruit). ✱ جَزَر o جَزْرًا, واجْتَزَر هـ و
To go down (tide). To flow away (water). جَزَر o i
To be fit to be slaughtered. أَجْزَر
To be cut off (dates). To die (man). To be at the point of death (old man).
To insult one another. تَجازَر
To fight desperately. To leave a prey for wild beasts (fighters). تَجَزَّر واجْتَزَر
Ebbing tide, ebb. (*opp. to* مدّ) جَزْر
Slaughtered head of cattle. Prey. جَزَر
Carrot. Parsnip. P جَزَر وجِزَر
Butcher. Tyrant; cruel man. جَزّار
Fit to be slaughtered (camel). جَزُور ج جُزُر
Remains of a slaughtered beast, *as the head, feet.* جُزارة
Butchery. جِزارة
Island. Peninsula. جَزِيرة ج جَزائِر
Peninsula of Arabia. جَزِيرة العَرَب
Mesopotamia. Andalusia. الجَزِيرة
Algeria. Algiers (town). الجَزائِر
The Ionian islands. الجَزائِر السَّبع
The fortunate Islands, the Canaries. الجَزائِر الخالِدات
The Ottoman archipelago. جَزائِر بَحْر سَفِيد
Slaughter-house, butchery. مَجْزِر ج مَجازِر
To cut, to cross (a river). ✱ جَزَع a جَزْعًا هـ
To give to a. o. a part of. لَهُ جَزْعَة مِن —
To grow impatient, anxious about a. th. To show grief at. جَزِع a جَزَعًا وجُزُوعًا مِن
To compassionate a. o. عَلَى —
To be half-ripe (dates). To have little water left (pond). جَزَّع
To cut a. th. in two pieces. هـ و ه —
To afflict a. o. To leave (a remainder). أَجْزَع ه و هـ

Course of affairs. ◇ Bed of a river. Track of a ship. *Pl.* Means.
Zodiacal circle. مَجْرَى الشَّمْس
To cut, to shear, to crop (wool, herbs). ✱ جَزّ o جَزًّا, وجَزَّز واجْتَزّ واجْتَذّ هـ
To attain the proper season for being shorn, cut (tree, crops, wool). أَجَزّ واسْتَجَزّ
A sheep-shearing. Clipped wool. جَزَّة
Wool clipped at one time; fleece. جِزَّة ج جِزاز وجَزائِز وجِزَز
◇ Refuse of mulberry leaves eaten by silkworms. جَزَّة
Cuttings of leather. Clippings. Portion of the night. جُزاز وجُزازة
Crops, harvest-time. جَزاز وجِزاز
Cut off. Shorn. جَزِيز وجَزُوز ومَجْزُوز
Shearer. جَزّاز
Shears. Scythe. مِجَزّ
To divide into lots. ✱ جَزَأ a جَزْءًا هـ
To take a part of. To curtail (a verse). To strengthen a. th.
To be satiated with a. th. (camels). To be satisfied with. جَزِئ وتَجَزَّأ واجْتَزَأ بِ
To make a handle to. To allot, to partake a. th. جَزَّأ هـ
To satisfy a. o. (object). — هـ
To bring forth (female). أَجْزَأ
To put (a ring) on the finger: a (handle) to a knife. To suffice a. o. — ه و هـ
To satisfy a. o. and to do instead of. To stand instead of. — ه عن
To be allotted (portions). تَجَزَّأ
Some. Part, particle. Lot. جُزْء ج أَجْزاء
Awl-handle. Vine-prop. جُزْأة
Partial. (*opp. to* كُلِّيّ) special. ◇ In small quantity (th.). جُزْئِيّ م جُزْئِيَّة
Particles. Particulars. Atoms. جُزْئِيّات
Chemist. ◇ أَجْزاجِي وأَجْزاجِي وأَزاجِي
Chemistry. Pharmacy. ◇ أَجْزاجِيَّة وأَزاجِيَّة
Sufficiency, substitute. مَجْزَأ ومَجْزَأة ومُجْزَأ ومُجْزَأة
Satiating (food). جَزِيّ ومُجْزِئ
Lot; portion. ✱ جِزْب ج أَجْزاب
To go to business. To enter her retreat (gazelle). ✱ جَزَح a جَزْحًا

guage).
Very respectable. جزيل الاحترام
Young pigeon. Youth. جوزل ج جوازل
Asthma. Exhausted camel.
To eat one meal ✻ جزم i جزمًا
a day. To be watered (camels).
To cut off a. th. To decide a.th. ه —
irrevocably. To make (an oath)
without condition. To put (a verb)
in the conditional mood. To fill
(a skin). To trim (a palm-tree).
To write an even hand.
To determine. To resolve upon. على —
To impose a. th. on a. o. ه على —
To appraise roughly (واجتزم ه —
a palm-tree).
To refrain from. وجزّم عن —
To be afraid and unable to.
To remain silent about a.th. جزّم على —
To be cut. To be broken (bone). إنجزم
To be in the conditional mood (verb).
Decisive affair. Premature. Cut جزم
evenly (pen). Conditional mood,
jezm.
Sign of quiescence. جزمة ج جزمات
Single meal a day. ✧ Boots.
Part of a flock. جزمة
Deciding. Particle جازم ج جوازم
commanding the conditional mood.
Filled (skin). Watered (camel).
To reward, ✻ جزى i جزاء ه ب او على
to requite a. o. for (good or evil).
To pay (a debt). To satisfy a. o. ه وه —
To do instead of, to perform عن —
the office of.
To requite a.o. جازى مجازاة وجزاء ه ب
for.
To suffice. أجزى
To stand instead of. عن —
To claim تجازى دينه او بدينه على فلان
from a. o. the payment of a debt.
To claim a salary from إجتزى ه
a. o.
Requital, compensation. جزاء
✧ Criminal law.
✧ Fine, penalty. جزاء نقدي
✧ Penal code. قانون الجزاء
Capitation, poll-tax. جزية ج جزى
Remunerator. مجاز

To afflict a. o. To leave أجزع ه ه
(a remainder).
To break asunder (rope, إنجزع وتجزّع
stick).
To divide (spoils). تجزّع ه
To break, to cut (a branch). إجتزع
Violent outburst of im- جزع وجزوع
patience, grief.
Shell of Venus ✧ Onyx. جزع
Winding of a valley. جزع ج أجزاع
Encampment of a tribe.
Axis of watering-engine. Yellow جزع
dye.
Impatient. جزع وجزوع وجازع وجزيعة
Fretting.
Small quantity. جزعة وجزعة وجزيعة
Portion of a flock. Handle of a knife.
Medley of white and black. مجزّع
Halfripe (date). Holding little
water (pond).
Tesselated. Variega- مجزّع بأنواع الرخام
ted.
Very anxious. Restless. مجزاع ج مجازيع
To buy or ✻ جزف o جزفًا , واجتزف ه
sell (without weighing nor measu-
ring).
To buy or جازف ه في البيع جزافًا ومجازفة
sell a. th. to a. o. in a lump.
To speak on conjecture. في الكلام —
Sale or purchase in a lump. جزاف
Wholesale purchase or sale. بيع جزيف
Fisher. جزّاف
Fishing-net. مجزفة
To be thick (wood). ✻ جزل o جزالة
To be chaste, strong (language).
To be important, great (th.). To be
prudent, wise (man).
To cut (a stick) in جزل i جزلًا وجزّله ه
two pieces.
To be galled in the withers أجزل
(camel).
To bestow a generous gift له ه —
upon a. o.
To find (an advice) to be إستجزل ه
excellent.
Sound judgment. Chasteness جزالة
of speech. Firmness.
Considerable (gift). جزل وجزيل ج جزال
Generous. Correct. chaste (lan-

Remunerator. مُجَازٍ

To feel with ✻ جَسَّ o جَسًّا ، واجْتَسَّ ه وة the hand. To stare a. o. in the face.

To ascertain (news). جَسَّ وتَجَسَّس ه To scrutinise (hidden things).

To inquire after a. th. اجْتَسَّ ه

جَسِيس ج أَجِسَّة ، وجَاسُوس ج جَوَاسِيس . وجَسَّاس Spy.

Pulse. Chest. مَجَسّ ومُجَسَّة

To become ✻ جَسَأَ o جُسُوًّا وجُسْأَةً hardened (hand).

To show hostility to. جَاسَأَ ة

Hard skin. Frozen water. جَسْء

Hardness ; callosity. جُسْأَة وجَاسِيَاء

To coagulate (blood). ✻ جَسِدَ a جَسَدًا

To dye a. th. with saffron. جَسَّد ه

To assume consistency. تَجَسَّد ✧ To become man (Son of God).

Body (animated). Flesh. جَسَد ج أَجْسَاد

Clotted blood. جَسَد وجَسِيد

Corporal. Material. جَسَدِيّ وجُسْدَانِيّ

Saffron. جَسَد وجِسَاد

Incarnation (of the Verb). تَجَسُّد

Shirt. chemise. مُجْسَد ج مَجَاسِد

To dare, ✻ جَسَرَ o جَسَارَةً وجُسُورًا عَلَى to venture upon. To undertake (a business).

To be rash. bold. To dare. — وتَجَاسَرَ

To cross (a desert, the sea). — واجْتَسَرَ ه

To build a bridge. — جَسْرًا

To embolden a. o. جَسَّرَ ة

To make a dam. ◻ جَسَّرَ

Tall and strong (camel). جَسْر م جَسْرَة Tall and brave (man).

Courage. Daring. جَسَرَة وجَسَارَة

Bridge. جِسْر وجَسْر ج أَجْسُر وجُسُور Embankment. Pontoon. ✧ Beam upholding joists. ◻ Dam.

Axle-tree ✧ جِسْر الكَرُّوسَة ج جُسُورَة of a carriage.

Rashness. Daring. تَجَاسُر

جَاسِر ج جَاسِرُون وجُسَّار ، وجَسُور ج جُسُر وجُسْر وجَسَّار Tall and courageous, rash.

Daring, fool-hardy. مُتَجَاسِر

To decline (an offer). ✻ جَسَمَ a جُسُوعًا عَن

To be stout, bulky. ✻ جَسُمَ o جَسَامَة

To render a. o. stout, bulky. جَسَّمَ ه To give consistency to a. th.; to embody. To exaggerate a. th.

To become stout ; to increase تَجَسَّمَ in volume. To take consistency. ✧ To become momentous (affair).

To choose a.o. amongst many. — ة وفي To embark in a grave (affair). To repair to (a country).

Bulk. Body, جِسْم ج أَجْسَام وجُسُوم وأَجْسُم solid substance.

Bigness, grievousness. جَسَامَة enormity.

Body. bulk, mass. جُسْمَان

Corporal, material. جِسْمِيّ وجِسْمَانِيّ

Corpulent. lusty. جُسَام وجَسِيم ج جِسَام

Solid ; cubic. square (body). مُجَسَّم

To dry up. ✻ جَسَا o جَسْوًا وجُسُوًّا to become hard (hand). To freeze (water).

Hardness, stiffness. جَسَاوَة

Hard, dry, solid. جَاسٍ

To smash. To grind. ✻ جَشَّ o جَشًّا ه To sweep. To clean a. th.

To strike a. o. with (a stick). — ة ب

To break. To mill (corn). أَجَشَّ ة

To be covered with أَجَشَّ واجْتَشَّ clusters of herbs (soil).

Stony place. Middle part of an جَشّ animal's body.

Hoarseness. Disturbance. جُشَّة Clamorous party.

Having a harsh voice, أَجَشّ م جَشَّاء hoarse. Rumbling (cloud, thunder).

Hoarseness. جَشَش

Coarse flour. Pounded جَشِيش وجَشِيشَة and boiled wheat.

Hand-mill. مِجَشّ ومِجَشَّة

To be ✻ جَشَأَ a جُشُوءًا وجُشْأً وجَشَأً convulsed, to heave (from fear or grief : soul). To bring forth plants (soil). To rush forth (wild beast). To bleat (sheep). To rush on (sea).

To emigrate towards. — مِن بَلَدٍ إِلَى

To belch. جَشَّأَ وتَجَشَّأَ

Belch. (*n. of un* . جُشْأَة) جُشَأَة وجُشَاء

Swelling (of the sea). Darkness جُشَاء (of the night).

✻ جَشَبَ o وجَشِبَ a جَشْبًا ، وجَشُبَ o جَشَابَة To be unwholesome, coarse (food).

To live on unwholesome جَشُبَ o جُشُوبَة

To throw o.s'self on the ground out of grief. تَجَعْجَع
Grumbling of camels flocking together. Mill-clack. جَعْجَعَة
Narrow space. Battle-field. Unwholesome climate. Earth. Grumbling (camel). جَعْجَاع
To fell a. o. ✱ جَعَب a جَعْبًا , وجَعْب رِجَعْبَى ه
To manufacture (quivers). جَعَّب i ه
To throng and press together (army). تَجَعَّب والْجَعَب وتَجَعْبَى
Cartridge-box : quiver. Large bowl. جَعْبَة ج جِعَاب
Short and stout. ✱ جَعْبَر
To roll up, to be contracted. ✱ جَعْثَم – تَجَعْثَم وتَجَعْثَن
Stem of a tree. جِعْثِنَة ج جِعْثِن وجَعَاثِن
To be curled (hair). ✱ جَعُد o جَعَادَة وجُعُودَة
To curl (the hair). جَعَّد ه
To be curled (hair). To be crisped, contracted (th.). تَجَعَّد
Woolly, curled, (hair). Niggardly. Generous. Stout and strong (man). جَعْد ج جِعَاد . ومُجَعَّد
Avaricious. جَعْد اليَد والكَفّ والأَنَامِل
Worthless man. جَعْد القَفَا
Wolf. أَبُو جَعْدَة وأَبُو جَعَادَة
Foul-mouthed man. Stingy. ✧ جُعَيْدِي
To use foul language. ✧ جَعْدَن
✧ To bellow. (*for* جَأَر) ✱ جَعَر a جَعْرًا
To dung (wild beast). – وانْجَعَر
Dung of wild beasts. جَعْر ج جُعُور
Rope for tying a well-cleanser. جِعَار
Hyena. جَعَار وأَبُو جَعَار
Black-beetle. أَبُو جِعْرَان
Buttocks. جَاعِرَة ج جَوَاعِر وجَعْرَاء . ومَجْعَر
To relieve o.'s bowels. ✱ جَعَس a جَعْسًا
To utter bad words. تَجَعَّس
To drive a. o. away. ✱ جَعَظ a جَعْظًا , وأَجْعَظ ه
To escape. أَجْعَظ
Small and lusty. جِعْظَايَة
To prostrate a. o. ✱ جَعَف a جَعْفًا , وأَجْعَف ه
To uproot (a tree). – واجْتَعَف ه
To be uprooted (tree). إِنْجَعَف
Sweeping (torrent). جَاعِف وجُعَاف
Large stream. Small river. ✱ جَعْفَر

food.
طَعَام جَشْب وجَشِب وجَشِيب ومِجْشَاب ومَجْشُوب Coarse, unpalatable food.
Coarse, gross. جَشِيب
To take (cattle) to a pasture. To give up a. th. ✱ جَشَر o جَشْرًا . وجَشَّر ه وه
To break (dawn). To depart. – جُشُورًا
To be hardened (mud). To be hoarse (man). To cough (camel). جَشِر a جَشَرًا
To empty (a vessel). جَشَّر ه
N. of act. Cattle grazing freely. جَشْر
Cattle. جَشَار
Herdsman. جَشَارِي
Owner of a pasture-land. جَشَّار
Cough. Hoarseness. جُشْرَة
Hoarse, coughing. أَجْشَر م جَشْرَاء ج جُشْر
Tank from which water is not drawn. مِجْشَر
To covet, to desire earnestly a. th.; to thirst for. ✱ جَشِم a جَشَمًا ه وتَجَشَّم عَلَى
Very covetous. أَجْشَم وجَشِم ج جَشِمُون
To assume a painful (duty). ✱ جَشِم a جَشْمًا وجَشَامَة . وتَجَشَّم ه
To entrust a. o. with a difficult (affair). جَشَّم وأَجْشَم ه وه
Burden, difficult duty. جُشْم وجَشَم
Thick. Big. جَشِيم
Chest. Arm. Midnight. ✱ جَشْن – جَوْشَن
To moan (fettered captive). جَصَّ i جَصًّا
To sprout (plant). To open the eyes (puppy). جَصَّص
To whitewash, to plaster (a house). – ه
To be adjacent (neighbour). اجْتَصّ
Gypsum. Sulphate of calcium. جِصّ
Plasterer. ✧ Sage (plant). جَصَّاص
Plaster kiln. جَصَّاصَة
Gathering of men living close together. جَصِيصَة
To dart on a. o. with (a sword). ✱ جَضّ o جَضًّا عَلَى ب
✧ To scream, to shout. جَضّ
To kneel (camel). ✱ جَعْجَع
To make (a camel) to kneel. To slaughter (a beast). – ه
To proceed against (a debtor). – ب

of mail.
Numerous company. جَفّ وجُفّ وجفّة وجُفّة
Spathe of palm-tree. Any hollow tube. Old man. جُفّ
Coat of mail. تِجْفاف ج تجافيف
Dry, dried up, desiccated. جافّ وجَفِيف
Desiccative, drying. مُجَفِّف
To collect (camels). To pursue (ostriches). ✻ جَفْجَفَ ه وه
To bristle its feathers (bird). To be half-dry (moistened garment). تجفجف
To throw a. o. down. To upset a. th. To remove the scum (of a cooking-pot). To sweep off (the rubbish brought down by a torrent). ✻ جَفَأَ a جَفْأً ه وه
To cast forth froth (cooking-pot). To cast forth refuse on the shore (torrent). جَفَأَ
To jade (beasts) in a journey. To throw a. o. down. أَجْفَأَ ه
Sweepings of a torrent. Vanity. Empty ship. Useless. جُفاء
Double-barrelled gun. ◘ Pincers. Ts جِفت
Estate of the Sultan let out to tenants; farm. Ts جِفتلك
To be proud, haughty. ✻ جَفَخَ a جَفْخًا
To vie in merits with a. o. جافَخَ ه
Proud, boastful. جَفّاخ
To grow up (lamb). To be widened. ✻ جَفِرَ o جَفَرًا ، وتجفّر واستجفر
He recovered from illness. جَفَرَ مِن المَرَض
To cast off a. th. To break with a. o. أَجْفَرَ ه وه
Large well. جَفْر ج جِفار
Divination. عِلْم الجَفْر
Wide cavity in the ground. جُفْرَة ج جُفَر
Wooden or leather quiver. جَفِير
N. of un. Portfolio, leather bag جَفِيرَة
✧ White, waxed (yarns). مُجَفَّر
To suffer from indigestion. ✻ جَفِسَ a جَفَسًا وجَفاسَة
Mean, base. جَفْس وجِفْس وجِفِّيس
To be sharp, sour. ✧ جفص o جُفُوصة
Intruder. Tedious (man). Sour, harsh. Disobedient (child). ✧ جفص
To fill up (a vessel). ✻ جَفَظَ o جَفْظًا ه

Abundant sheep. Name of a celebrated vizier.
To swarm with black-beetles (water). ✻ جَعِلَ a جَعَلًا . وأَجْعَلَ
To put. to make, to appoint. To render a.o. or. a. th. *such*. To establish a. o. as. جَعَلَ a جَعْلًا ه وه
To appoint a. o. governor. — ه حاكمًا
To make a. th. to become *such*. To change a. th. in. to substitute a. th. To use a. th. instead of. — ه ه
He used it as a capital-stock. جَعَلَهُ رَأْسَ مالٍ
He took Basrah for Bagdad: *i. e.* He committed a gross blunder. (*Prov*). جَعَلَ البَصْرَة بَغْداد
To impose a condition upon a. o. To stipulate with a. o. (the amount of a salary). — لهُ ه وعلى
He began to do. — يفعل
He began to shed tears. جعل يَبْكِي
To bribe a. o. جاعَلَ ه
To give a. th. to a. o. أَجْعَلَ ه ل
To make a. th. together. تَجاعَلَ ه
To receive; to do a. th. إِجْتَعَلَ ه
Black-beetle (*ins.*). Overseer جُعَل ج جِعْلان
Stagnating water full of black-beetles. جَعِل ومُجْعِل
Price agreed upon: salary, wages. جِعال ج جُعُل . وجُعْل ج أجعال
Bribe. ✧ Pension. جِعالة وجَعالة ج جعائل
Stipulated price. ✧ Flocks of sheep with shepherds. جَعِيلة ج جعائل
To have no appetite. ✻ جَعِمَ a جَعَمًا . وجَعِمَ جَعَمًا
To muzzle (a camel). — ه
To covet. to long for a. th. جَعَمَ a جَعَمًا في وإلى ، وتَجَعَّمَ في
To eat up (a tree) to the root (camel). To pluck, to eradicate a. th. أَجْعَمَ ه
To pick up dung. ✻ جَعا o جَعْوًا
Beer (drink). ✻ جِعَة
To dry. to be dried. ✻ جَفَّ i جَفافًا وجُفُوفًا
To pick up and take a. th. away. — جَفًّا ه o
To dry up a. th. To fit a (horse) with a coat جَفَّفَ تجفيفًا وتَجْفافًا ه وه

✧ To use abusive language.
To remove a. th. from its place. إجتفى ه
Hardness; churlish, unkind behaviour; ill-treatment. جَفْوَة وجَفاء
جافٍ ج جُفاة م جافِيَة ج جافِيات وجَوافٍ
Harsh, rough, uncivil (man). Coarse (dress).
Rude, rough (man). جافي الخُلُق
To dung (bird). ✱ جقّ o جقًّا
To behave saucily towards a. o. ✧ جقِر – تجاقر على
Insolent, pert. Obstinate. ✧ جقِر
Clank of iron. ✱ جكجكة
To offer obtrusively goods for sale (merchant). ✱ جكر a جكرًا , وأجكر في البَيْع
To be offended, vexed by. To be despited by. ✧ جكِر مِن
To tease, to thwart a. o. ✧ جاكر ه
In spite of.... vexingly. ✧ جكارة وجكاريّة في
Offended. Vexed at. ✧ جكران مِن
To be high, great, imposing. To be illustrious. ✱ جلّ i جلالًا وجلالة
God who is great and mighty. الله عزّ وجلّ
To be aged, of a mature age. – جلالًا وجلالة
To scorn at. To abstain from. – وتجالّ عن
To be free from (defect). – عن
To put a horse-cloth to. – جلًّا , وجلّل ه
To emigrate from. جلّ o i جُلولًا عن
To pick up dung with the hand as fuel. – o جلًّا , واجتلّ
To be general, common to all. جلّل
The rain has been general. جلّل المطرُ الأرضَ
To honour, to respect a. o. جلّل ه وه
To be strong, hardy. To be weak. أجلّ
To respect, to honour; to load a. o. with gifts. – ه
To be exalted, great. تجلّل
To clothe o.'self in. – ب
To exalt o.'self above. تجالّ على
To take the main part of. – واجتلّ ه
Horse-cloth. جُلّ ج أجلال وجِلال
✧ Pack-saddle.

To swell (corpse). إجفاظ
Swollen (corpse). جَفيظ
To take fright, to be scared away. ✱ جفل o i جفولًا . جفلًا , وأجفل
To run away in a panic (people). – وأجفل وانجفل وتجفّل
To carry away (the clouds: wind). To cast (fish) upon the shore (sea). – i جفلًا ه
To sweep away (the mud), to scrape off a. tn. – وجفّل ه
To be disordered (hair). جفل o جُفولًا
To scare a. o. away. جفّل ه
To bristle his feathers (cock). تجفّل
To go away (shade). To run away in a panic. إنجفل
Fright. Ship. Driven away (cloud). جفل وجُفول
Dung of the elephant. جفل وجِفل ج أجفال
Leafy (tree). جَفِلة
A fleece of wool. جفلة
Foam of milk. Rubbish, scum cast forth by a torrent. Abundant (wool). جُفال
Scale of (a boiler). جفالة
Clearing off the clouds (wind). جَفُول ج جُفُل
General invitation to dinner. جفلى وإجفلى
Swift (wind). – ومُجفِل ومِجفال
Fearful, disquieted, flurried. إجفيل
To slaughter (a she-camel) and give her flesh for food. ✱ جفن o جفنًا ه
Eyelid. Apple of the eye. Vine-stock. Sheath. جفن ج جُفون وأجفان وأجفُن
Large porringer. Deep dish. A vine-stock. Generous man. جَفنة ج جِفان وجَفَنات
To be coarse (garment). To be restless. ✱ جفا o جفوًا وجفاء
To treat harshly, to tyrannise a. o. – ه وعلى
To slide from (the back: horse-saddle). – عن
To take, to send away a. o. جافى ه
✧ To behave rudely towards a. o.
To ill-treat (cattle). أجفى ه وه
To unsaddle (a horse).
To withdraw. To slide (saddle). تجافى

(blood).
To gather, to meet (people). جَلِبَ a جَلَبًا
To scream, to stir about. To flock in. جَلَّبَ وأَجْلَبَ
To be brought. To be imported. إِنْجَلَبَ
To bring (goods, cattle) from one place to another). إِجْتَلَبَ ه وه
To import (goods). To ask a. th. to be brought. إِسْتَجْلَبَ ه
Importation. Crime. جَلْب
Uproar, confused voices. جَلَب وجَلَبَة
Imported goods. — ج أَجْلَاب
A kind of upper-garment. ✧ جَلَبِيَّة
Cloud having a rounded outline. جُلْب
Wood of a camel's saddle. جِلْب الرَّحْل
Skin formed on a healing wound. جُلْبَة
جَلِيب ج جَلْبَى وجُلَبَاء م جَلِيبَة (m. and f.)
Imported (slave). ج جَلَائِب
Imported merchandise; camel bringing it. جَلُوبَة وجَلِيبَة ج جَلَائِب
Negro or slave-driver. Bringer. جَلَّاب
Rose-water. Gum-mixture. P جُلَاب وجُلَّاب
Peas. Vetch. جُلْبَان وجُلُبَّان
Boisterous, clamorous. جُلُبَّان وجَلَبَّان
Termagant woman. جُلُبَّانَة ومُجَلِّبَة
Resounding afar off (thunder). مُجَلِّب
Impulsive, attractive. مَجْلَبَة
Talisman, love-charm. يَنْجَلِب
Smock. Woman's gown. ✱ جِلْبَاب ج جَلَابِيب
To clothe a. o. in a smock. جَلْبَبَ ه
To put on a gown. تَجَلْبَبَ
Newly hatched bird. ✧ جُلْبُوط ج جَلَابِيط
To strike a. o. ✱ جَلَتَ i جَلْتًا, واجْتَلَتَ ه
To drink up the whole of. إِجْتَلَتَ ه
The giant Goliath. H جَالُوت
To lose o.'s hair on both sides of the head. ✱ جَلِحَ a جَلَحًا
To rush on. جَلَحَ عَلَى
To show open enmity to a. o. جَالَحَ ه
Baldness on both sides of the head. جَلَح
Temples stripped of hair. جَلَحَة
Bald on both sides of the head. Hornless (ox). أَجْلَح م جَلْحَاء ج جُلْح
Barren ground. جَلْحَاء
Unfruitful year. جَالِحَة ج جَوَالِح

Main part of a. th. جُلّ وجَلَال
Jasmine. Rose. P جُلّ وجُلّ
Sail of a ship. — ج جُلُول
Great, illustrious, aged. Bulky. جِلّ وجَلّ
The chief men of a place. قَوْمٌ جِلَّة
Emigrating party. Tax. جَالَّة
Serious, momentous or important thing. جَلَل
He has done it for thy sake. فَعَلَهُ مِن جَلَلِكَ
Majesty. Highness. جَلَال وجَلَالَة
Dung of sheep, goats, camels. جِلَّة وجَلَّة
Basket of palm-leaves (for dates). جُلَّة ج جُلَل وجِلَال
✧ Pack-saddle maker. جَلَّالِي و✧ جَلَايِلِي
F. of أَجَلّ Important affair. جُلَّى ج جُلَل
Saving your reverence. ✧ أَجَلَّكَ
Consideration, veneration. إِجْلَال وتَجِلَّة
For thy sake. مِن إِجْلَالِكَ ومِن تَجِلَّتِكَ
High, great. Strong. Big. Respectable, venerable. جَلِيل ج أَجِلَّاء وأَجِلَّة وجِلَّة
General, universal (rain). مُجَلِّل
Book. Code. ✧ Periodical review. مَجَلَّة
To scream. To thunder. ✱ جَلْجَلَ
To threaten a.o. To toss a.th. To hang bells to (a horse's neck). — ه وه
To be tossed, shaken. To sink in the earth. To be restless (mind). تَجَلْجَلَ
Bells hanged to the neck of beasts of burden. جُلْجُل ج جَلَاجِل
Resounding (thunder, rain). جَلْجَال
Sound of a bell, of thunder. جَلْجَلَة
✧ Mount Calvary.
Grain of coriander, of sesame. جُلْجُلَان
Black poppy. — الحَبَشَة
Egyptian lotus. — مِصْرِي
The heart's core. — القَلْب
Great number. عَدَد مُجَلْجِل
To throw a. o. down. ✱ جَلَأَ a جَلْأً وجَلَاء وجَلَاءَة ه
To import (goods). To assemble (a crowd). To threaten a. o. ✱ جَلَبَ o i جَلْبًا وجَلَبًا ه وه
To procure a. th. for a. o. — ه ل
To urge on (a horse) with the voice. — عَلَى وجَلَّبَ ه
To be cured (wound). To dry — جُلُوبًا

To be long (night). To be over (rain).
Mole. جُلَذ ج مَنَاجِذ
Mechanic. Monk. Priest. جُلَذِيّ وجُلَاذِيّ ج جَلَاذِيّ
To fasten (a sword-hilt) with a nerve. To tie up a. th. around the head. ✱ جلز i جَلْزًا ، وجَلَّز ه
To go quickly. جَلَّز
Quickness in walking. جَلْوَزَة
Leather strap. جِلَاز وجِلَازَة ج جَلَائِز
Soldier. Tax-collector. جِلْوَاز ج جَلَاوِزَة
Filbert. Pine-pitch. جِلَّوْز
Careful. steady in his work. مُجَلْوِز العَمَل
To sit down. ✱ جَلَس i جُلُوسًا ومَجْلَسًا
To sit (assembly). ✧ To be straight.
To grant an audience to. — وتَجَلَّس لـ وإلى
✧ To straighten a. th. جَلَّس ه
To sit in company with. جَالَس ه
To make a. o. to sit. أَجْلَس ه
To sit down. تَجَلَّس
To be sitting ; to hold a meeting. تَجَالَس
To allow a. o. to sit. إِسْتَجْلَس ه
Sitting of a Court. جَلْسَة
Way of sitting. جِلْسَة
Seating. Company of men sitting together. Society, company. جُلُوس
Feast of the enthronement. عِيدُ الجُلُوسِ المَأْنُوس
Companion. Friend. جَلِيس ج جُلَسَاء
Seated. جَالِس ج جُلُوس وجُلَّاس
✧ Straight.
Company. Tribunal, Court of Law, council, ministry. Parliament. مَجْلِس ج مَجَالِس
Martial law. مجلِس عسكرِي
Privy-council. مَجْلِس خاصّ
White rose. Basil (plant). P جُلَّسَان
To swear. To lie. ✱ جلط i جَلْطًا
To shave (the head). To draw (a sword). — ه
To contend with a. o. in cunning. جَالَط ه
To take away a. th. To absorb up. اجتلط ه
Unbecoming, shameless (wom.). جِلْوط
To be disclosed (teeth). ✱ جَلِع a جَلَعًا
To be shameless (woman). جَلِع a جُلُوعًا

Pl. Particles flying in the air from the heads of reeds, etc.
To flood (a valley). ✱ جَلَخ a جَلْخًا ه
To wash away (its banks : stream).
To cut off (a limb). ✧ To sharpen (a knife).
To throw a. o. down. — بـ
To be destroyed. To fall down and be unable to rise up. إِجْلَنْخَى
✧ Whetstone. جَلْخ
Overflowing torrent. جُلَاخ
To meet. To show pride. ✱ جلخم — اجْلَخَمّ
To lash, to flog a. o. ✱ جَلَد i جَلْدًا ه
To constrain a. o. to. — ه على
To be steady, patient, sturdy. جَلُد o جَلَدًا وجَلَادَة وجُلُودَة ومَجْلُودًا
To be frozen (ground). جَلِد a جَلَدًا ، وجُلِد وأُجْلِد
To bind (books). To skin (a beast). جَلَّد ه وه
To fight a. o. with (a sword). جَالَد مُجَالَدَة وجِلَادًا ه بـ
To compel a. o. to. — ه إلى
To be covered with ice (soil). أَجْلَد
To show endurance, hardiness. تَجَلَّد
To fight together. تَجَالَد
To strike with (a sword). إِجْتَلَد بـ
To empty (a cup). — ه
Flogging. جَلْد
Firm, strong. Robust. جَلْد ج أَجْلَاد
The whole person ; body and limbs. أَجْلَاد الإِنْسَان وتَجَالِيدُهُ
Firmament. Patience. Firmness. جَلَد
Smooth and hard ground. — وجَلَدَة
Skin. Hide. Leather. جِلْد ج جُلُود وأَجْلَاد
A skin, a piece of skin. جِلْدَة
✧ Avaricious.
Thy countryman. Thy kinsfolk. إِبْن جِلْدَتِك
Patience. Firmness جَلَادَة وجُلُودَة
Steadfast. Frost. Ice. جَلِيد ج جُلَدَاء
Skinner. ✧ جُلُودِي
Executioner. Seller of hides. جَلَّاد
Whip. Lash. مِجْلَدَة ج مَجَالِد
Book-binder. Enduring (horse). مُجَلِّد
Bound in leather (tome, volume). Volume, tome. مُجَلَّد
To walk fast. ✱ جلذ — اجْلَوَّذ

To take off a. th. ✱ جَلَه a جَلْهًا ه
To discard. To remove — ه و ٤ عن (pebbles) from (a place). To deter a. o. from.
To be bald on the forepart جَلِه a جَلَهًا ه of the head.
Opposite side of a valley. جَلْهَة ج جِلاه
The two brinks of a valley. جَلْهَتَا الوَادِي
Bald (man). Hornless (ox). أَجْلَه
Black rhamnus. ✱ جُلْهُم
To rub ✱ جَلَا o جَلاء وجَلْوًا، وجَلَى i جَلْيًا ه up, to polish (a blade, a mirror). To scour.
To become clear to a.o. (news). — جَلَاء ل
To show a. th. To display the — عَلَى bride to (her husband).
To emigrate from. — عن
To expel a. o. To dispel (grief) — ٤ عَن from. To disclose a. th. to.
To make (a present) جَلَا o وجَلَى ٤ ه to (his bride) on the wedding-day (bridegroom).
To have the forepart of the جَلِيَ a جَلًى head without hair.
To manifest a. th. جَلَّى ٤ ه و٤ عن to a. o.
He disclosed his sentiments. — عَن نَفْسِهِ
To manifest, to reveal جَالَى ٤ ب a. th. to.
To emigrate. أَجْلَى عَن بَلَدِهِ
To cause a. o. to emigrate — ٤ عن from (dearth).
To reveal Himself to man (God). تَجَلَّى ل
To disclose the mutual condition تَجَالَى of o. a.
To reveal Himself to man (God). إِنْجَلَى To be elucidated (affair). To be polished. To clear off (clouds. sadness).
To clear off, to result from. — عَن
To consider, to observe a. th. إِجْتَلَى ه
To unveil (a spouse) for the — ٤ عَلَى first time before (her husband).
To be presented to her إِسْتَجْلَى husband (spouse).
To ask a. o. to disclose a. th. — ٤ ه
Clearness, brightness. Emigration. جَلَاء
Baldness on the half of the head. جَلًى

To hold bad talks (people). جَالَم
To quarrel at play
Shameless, barefaced. Traveller. جَالِم
Showing his جَلِم وأَجْلَم م جَلِمَة وجَلْمَاء teeth.
To rest on the ground ✱ جَلْعَب — اِجْلَعَبَّ (horse). To increase. To hurry on.
To spread o.'s self ✱ جلعد — اِجْلَعَدَّ on the ground.
To make cuts to ✱ جَلَغ a جَلْغًا ه و٤ ب a. o. with (a sword). To trim a. th. with.
To fight with sword. جَالَغ
To disclose the teeth in laughing.
To take away (the ✱ جَلَف o جَلْفًا ه mud). To bark a. th. To cut off, to destroy a. th.
To strike a. o. with (a sword). — ٤ ب
To be rough, rude. جَلِف a جَلَفًا وجَلَافَةً
To reduce to nothing. جَلَّف ه to destroy (goods: dearth).
To uproot. To destroy a. th. إِجْتَلَف ه
Hard and dry bread. Empty jar. جِلْف
Water-skin. — جُلُوف وأَجْلَاف
Scratch on the skin. جَلْفَة
Piece of dry bread. جِلْفَة
Mud. Clay. جُلَاف
Cut of a pen. جِلْفَة وجِلْفَة
Rude, uncivil. جِلْف وجَلِيف
Taken away. Scratched. جَلِيف مَجْلُوف
Darnel-grass. جَلِيف
Impaired, curtailed. مُجَلَّف
To calk (a ship). ✱ جَلْفَط وجَلْفَظ ه
Calker. جِلْفَاط وجِلْفَاظ
To shave (the head). ✱ جَلَق i جَلْقًا ه
To throw (projectiles) on. — ٤ ب
To show the teeth in laughing. تَجَلَّق
Particle, piece of meat. جَلَاقَة
Damascus (town). جِلِّق وجِلَّق
Sack. P جُوَالِق ج جَوَالِيق
Ballista. G مَنْجَلِيق ومَنْجَنِيق
To shear a. th. ✱ جَلَم i جَلْمًا واجْتَلَم ه
Shears. جَلَم وجَلَمَان
Clipped wool. جُلَامَة
Large ✱ جَلْمَد وجُلْمُود ج جَلَامِد وجَلَامِيد stone, rock. Strong man.
Rose-preserve. P جُلَنْجَبِين
Pomegranate-blossom. P جُلَّنَار
Wild briar. Dog-rose. P جُلَّنْسَرِين

Luxuriant plant.	جَمِيم ج اجِمَّآء
Hornless (buck).	أجَمّ م جَمَّاء ج جُمّ
Spearless (warrior).	
Chest.	مَجَم
Long-haired, hairy.	مُجَمَّم
To articulate ه جَمْجَمَ وتَجَمْجَمَ *	
(words) confusedly.	
To avoid (an affair).	تَجَمْجَمَ عن
Wild parsnip.	جُمْجُم
Confused pronounciation.	جَمْجَمَة
Skull. Wooden cup.	جُمْجُمَة ج جَمَاجِم
Chief. Well sunk in a saline ground.	
To be angry with. جِمِيَ a جَمًا عَلَى *	
To wrap o.'s self in.	تَجَمَّا فِي
Person, individual.	جَمَا وجَمَا
To be جَمَحَ a جَمْحًا وجِمَاحًا وجُمُوحًا *	
ungovernable. to run away (horse).	
To indulge a fancy. To have o.'s	
own way. To forsake her husband	
and go to her family (wife).	
To hurry on.	
Restive, stubborn.	جَامِح وجَمُوح
Headless arrow.	جُمَّاح ج جَمَامِيح
To be proud, vain. جَمَخَ a جَمْخًا *	
To vie in merits with a. o. ه جَامَخَ	
Proud, vain.	جَامِخ ج جُمَّخ
To thicken جَمَدَ وجَمُدَ o جَمْدًا وجُمُودًا *	
(blood). To freeze (water). To be	
stingy.	
To freeze (liquids : cold). ه جَمَّدَ وأجْمَدَ	
To be contiguous to. جَامَدَ s	
To be stingy, poor.	أجْمَدَ
Ice. snow.	جَمْد وجَمَد
High and dry soil.	جَمَد وجُمُد وجَمَد
Tearless (eye).	جُمُود
Dry (soil).Rainless (year).	جَمَاد ج جُمُد
Solid body. Mineral.	جَمَادَات —
Name of two months	جَمَادَى ج جَمَادِيَات
of the Arabian year.	
Thickened, frozen.	جَامِد ج جَوَامِد، وجُمَّد
Solid, firm. Defective (verb) (Gr.)	
◊ Dull (man).	
Hard. Tearless eye.	جَامِد العَيْن
Niggardly.	اليَد —
Solid bodies. Minerals.	الجَوَامِد
جَمَرَ o جَمْرًا، وأجْمَرَ واسْتَجْمَرَ عَلَى *	
To meet for (business).	
To give live coals to a. o. د جَمَّرَ	
To twist her hair on the back	جَمَّرَ

Brilliancy. Splendour.	
Man of good fame. Moon.	ابْنُ جَلَا
Gift presented by the husband	جِلْوَة
to his spouse. Wedding-party.	
Apocalypse (of St. John).	جِلْيَان
Captivity of the Hebrews.	الجَالُوت ◊
Tribute paid by non-	جَالِيَة ج جَوَالٍ
Moslems. Exiled people. Colony.	
Clear, evident, manifest.	جَلِيّ
Polished.	
Garret-window.	جِلِّي
Obvious thing ; true report.	جِلِّيَّة
Exact statement.	
Clearly, evidently.	جَلِيًّا
Brighter. Handsome.	أجْلَى م جَلْوَاء
Bald on the forehead. Clear (sky).	
Revelation (of God to man).	تَجَلٍّ
Transfiguration (of Jesus=Christ).	
Forepart of the head.	مَجْلًى ج مَجَالٍ
◊ The horse ahead in a race.	مُجَلٍّ
To be filled up (well): جَمَّ i o جُمُومًا *	
crammed (measure). To be abun-	
dant. To collect in a well (water).	
◊ To prune.	
To heap (a measure). ه جَمَّ وجِمَامًا —	
To let (water) collect.	
To be left at rest (horse). وأجَمَّ وأجَمَّ —	
To cram (a measure), to fill it ه جَمَّ	
to excess.	
To grow, to multiply (plant). وتَجَمَّمَ —	
To be coming on (affair).	أجَمَّ
To leave (a horse) at rest. s —	
To let (water) flow. ه أجَمَّ	
To become tangled (plant).	تَجَمَّمَ
◊ To be heaped (measure).	
To be plentiful, to collect	اسْتَجَمَّ
(water). To be covered with plants	
(soil). To rest (man).	
Great number.	جَمّ ج جِمَام وجُمُوم
Noon-tide. Abundance of water.	
All together.	جَمًّا غَفِيرًا وجَمُّ الغَفِير
Filling up, heaping. Rest.	جَمَام
To the full.	بِجَمَام
Excess (of a	جَمّ وجَمَام وجِمَام
measure).	
Well full of water.	جَمّة
Numerous party.	جَمّة وجِمَّة
Luxuriant hair.	جُمّة ج جُمَم
Filled with water (well).	جَمُوم

of the head (woman).
To collect, to join a. th. جَمَّرَ ه وه
To gather the marrow (of a palm-tree). To canton (an army) in the enemy's country. To roast (meat) upon live coals. To fumigate (a garment). ✧ To char a. th.
To walk quickly (camel). أَجْمَرَ
To meet for a common (affair). — على
To prepare (a fire, race-horses). — ه
To fortify themselves in a hostile country (army). جَمَّرَ واسْتَجْمَرَ
To perfume o.'s self with. إِجْتَمَرَ بِ
Burning-coal. Stone. ✧ Carbuncle. جَمْرَة ج جَمْر
Benign carbuncle. جَمْرَة الحَمِيدَة
Malignant carbuncle. — الخَبِيثَة
Anthrax, carbuncle. — فارِسِيَّة
Party of horsemen. United tribe. — جَمَرَات وجِمَار
Men collected together. جُمَّار
Pith of palm-tree. Head of a mast. ◻ Head. جُمَّار وجَامُور
Meeting-place. جَمِير
Plait of hair. جَمِيرَة
Censer. Fire-place. Aloes-wood. مِجْمَرَة ج مَجَامِر
To walk at a quick pace. To jump. ✱ جَمَزَ i جَمْزًا
Quick walk. Trot. جَمَزَى
Swift-footed (ass). جَمَّاز
Sycomore-tree. Sycomore-fig. جُمَّيز وجُمَّيزَى
To congeal (grease). ✱ جَمَسَ o جُمُوسًا
Ill-bred, vulgar man. ◻ جَمِيس
Buffalo. P جَامُوس ج جَوَامِيس
Amethyst (precious stone). P جَمَسْت
To shave (the hair, the head). ✱ جَمَشَ o جَمْشًا ه
Depilatory paste. جَمُوش وجَمِيش
To connect, to collect a. th. To comprise, to include a. th. To put (a noun) in the plural. ✱ جَمَعَ a جَمْعًا ه
To unite, to reconcile (people). — بَيْنَ
To gather, to store up carefully. جَمَّعَ ه
To fit, to suit a. o. جَامَعَ مُجَامَعَةً وجِمَاعًا على
To go unto (his wife : man). — ٥

To agree on. To resolve unanimously upon (an affair). أَجْمَعَ ه وعلى
To drench (the soil : rain). — ه
To come together, to combine. تَجَمَّعَ واجْتَمَعَ
To reach manhood. إِجْتَمَعَ
They agreed unanimously upon. They united together against. إِجْتَمَعُوا على
His business goes on well. إِسْتَجْمَعَ لَهُ أُمُورُهُ
Crowd. Multitude of men. Army. Flock. Gathering. Addition. Plural of a noun. جَمْع ج جُمُوع
Recollection of thoughts. جَمْع الأَفْكار
The day of the meeting (last Judgment). يَوْم الجَمْع
Fist. جُمْع الكَفّ ج أَجْمَاع
Reunion, concourse of people. Week. Friendship. جُمْعَة ج جُمَع وجُمُعَات
Friday. يَوْم الجُمُعَة وجُمْعَة ج جُمُعَات
Party of men, society. جَمَاعَة ج جَمَاعَات
Congregation. Religious confraternity. جَمْعِيَّة
Reunion. Social life. إِجْتِمَاع
Comprehensive. General. جَامِع
Synagogue. Mosque. جَامِع ج جَوَامِع
Substantial discourse. الكَلَام الجَامِع
F. of جامِع. Tie. جَامِعَة ج جَوَامِع
The catholic church. الكَنِيسَة الجَامِعَة
Meeting. All, the whole. جَمِيع
All of them. Entirely, together. جَمِيعًا
All together, the whole. أَجْمَع ج أَجْمَعُون
Collection. Sum total. مَجْمُوع ج مَجَامِيع
Agreed upon. مُجْمَع عَلَيْه
Confluence. Meeting-room. Convocation. Council. Museum. ✧ Censer. مَجْمَع ج مَجَامِع
In the strength of life. Hurrying. مُجْتَمِع
P جَامَكِيَّة وجَوْمَك ج جَامَكِيَّات وجَوَامِك
Allowance, civil and military pay.
To gather (things). To melt (grease). ✧ To join, to unite. ✱ جَمَلَ o جَمْلًا ه
To be elegant, beautiful, kind, pleasing. جَمُلَ o وجَمِلَ a جَمَالًا
To embellish a. o. or a. th. جَمَّلَ ٥ وه

The public. Multitude, جُمْهُور ج جَمَاهِير people. Throng. Heap of sand.
Popular, vulgar. Heady جُمْهُوريّ (wine).
✧ Republic. جُمْهُورِيَّة
Volume. Prominent ✱ جمو — جما وجُما part.
Body. Bulk. جماء وجماءة
To be dark ✱ جَنَّ o جَنًّا وجُنُونًا وجَنَانًا (night).
To cover, — جَنًّا وجُنُونًا ه او على to wrap, to conceal a. th.
To be mad. To be جُنَّ جَنًّا وجُنُونًا possessed by the devil. To be covered with plants (soil). To buzz (insect). To be in a fit of passion, furious. ✧ To be mad with joy or anger.
To be hidden to. جُنَّ وأَجَنَّ عَن
✧ To overexcite a. o. جَنَّن ه
To render a. o. To insane (God). أَجَنَّ ه
To conceal, to veil a. th. or أَجَنَّ ه و ه a. o. To bury (a dead person).
To show symptoms of تَجَنَّن وتَجانَّ madness.
To play the insane before. — وتَجانَّ على
To be concealed. إِجْتَنَّ واسْتَجَنَّ عَن To veil o.'s self from.
The Genii (*opp. to* جِنّ وجانّ وجِنَّة *men*).
A genius, a demon. جِنِّي م جِنِّيَّة
Garden. Paradise. جَنَّة ج جَنَّات وجِنَان
Covering, protective. جُنَّة ج جُنَن
Shield: armour. — ومِجَنّ ومِجَنَّة ج مَجَانّ
Harmless serpent. جانّ ج جِوَانّ
Tomb. Corpse. جَنَن
Shroud. — ج أَجْنان
Veil. Darkness of the جَنَان وجُنُون night.
Shield. جُنَان وجُنانَة
Heart. جَنَان ج أَجْنان
Madness; diabolical fury. جُنّ وجُنُون
Possession, insanity. جُنُون ✧ Paroxysm of rage, passion.
Anything hidden. جَنِين ج أَجِنَّة وأَجْنُن Embryo. Fœtus.
Small garden. جُنَيْنَة ج جَنَائِن
Gardener. ✧ جُنَيْنَاتِي و ◻ جَنَائِنِيّ
Country haunted by demons. مَجَنَّة

To treat a. o. kindly. جامَل ه To blandish a. o.
To collect, to sum up a. th. اجمل ه To carry on (business) skillfully.
To behave decently, politely in. — في
To be embellished. To adorn o.'s تَجَمَّل self. To affect kindness, courtesy. To show self-restraint. To eat melted grease.
Camel. Cable. جَمَل ج جِمَال وأَجْمَال ship-cordage.
Sword-fish. Whale. جَمَل البَحْر
◻ Pelican.
Chameleon. جَمَل اليَهُود
Ship-rope. جُمَل وجُمَل وجُمَّل
Use of the alphabetical حِسَاب الجُمَّل letters according to their numerical value.
Beauty, elegance. Fine جَمال behaviour; good manners. Patience.
Camel-driver. جَمَّال ج جَمَّالَة
Whole, summing up. جُمْلَة ج جُمَل Proposition (*Gram*).
In short; upon the بِالجُمْلَة وفي الجُمْلَة whole, in a word.
Herd of جَمَالَة وجِمَالَة ج جَمَائِل وجُمَالات camels or she-camels.
Summary. (*opp. to* تفصيل) إِجْمال General way of speaking.
In short. In general. بالإِجْمال وفي الإِجْمال
The collective note المُذَكِّرَة الإِجْمَالِيَّة (diplomatical).
Splendour, brightness, تَجَمُّل grandeur. Fine behaviour. Courtesy, kindness.
Fine, handsome. Good service. جَمِيل Good deed. Grace, favour. Melted grease.
Finer. Better. أَجْمَل
Whole. Sum total. Summing up. مُجْمَل
Ridged roof. ✧ Dome. جَمَلُون ج جَمَالِين Garret.
Pearl. Silver-bead. Jewel. P جُمَان
To gather. To heap up ✱ جَمْهَر ه (earth). To cover (a grave) with earth. To take off the main part of.
To relate to a. o. part of — إلى وعلَى a news.
To exalt o.'s self above. تَجَمْهَر على

Madness. Hiding-place.
Mad. Possessed. مَجنُون ج مَجَانِين
Luxuriant (plant).
To be crook-backed. * جَنِئَ a جَنَأً
To bend on. To fall upon a. o. or a. th. جَنَأَ a جُنُوءًا , وتَجانَأَ على
Hump-backed. أَجْنَأُ م جَنْآءُ
To send a. o. away; to put a. th. aside. * جَنَبَ o جَنْبًا ه او ه
To make a. o. to avoid. to discard a. th. – وجَنَّبَ ه ه
To lead (a horse) by the side. – ه جَنَبًا ومَجْنَبًا
To blow from the south (wind). – جُنُوبًا
To be anxious about. To long for. جَنَبَ o جَنْبًا . وجَنِبَ a جَنَبًا إلى
To suffer from pleurisy. جُنِبَ
To be overtaken by the southwind. To be in a state of legal impurity (moslem). – وأَجْنَبَ
To avoid, to shun a. o. or a. th. جَنَّبَ وتَجَنَّبَ وتَجانَبَ واجْتَنَبَ ه او ه
To stand by the side of. To avoid a. o. جانَبَ ه مُجانَبَةً وجِنابًا
To send a. o. away. أَجْنَبَ ه
Side of a man's body. Region. Flank. جَنْب ج جُنُوب وأَجْناب
Side. ◻ Basket for dates, greens. جَنْبَة وجَنَبَة
✧ By your side. Beware! جَنْبَك
What one avoids. جُنْبَة
Polluted (moslem). جُنُب
Flank, side of the body. Declivity (of a mountain). ◻ Few, some. جانِب ج جَوانِب
Tractable. Compliant. لَيِّن الجانِب
(Forwarded) to the provincial authorities. إلى جانِب الوِلاية
(Issued) from the Foreign Office. إلى جانِب نظارة الخارِجيَّة
Neighbourhood. Abode, court-yard. ✧ Excellency (*title given to influential men*). جَناب
Horse-leash. جِناب
Manageable (horse). طَوْع الجِناب
Pleurisy. جُناب وذات الجَنْب و✧ داء الجَنْب
Legal impurity. Gross term. جَنابة
Led by the side (horse). Pleuritic (man). جَنِيب ومُجَنَّب ومَجْنُوب م جَنِيبَة

South. جَنُوب
South wind. – ج جَنائِب
Southern, meridional. جَنُوبِيّ
Foreigner. Stranger. أَجْنَب ج أَجَانِب, وأَجْنَبِيّ ج أَجْنَبِيُّون
Unmanageable. Foreigner. أَجْنَب وجُنُب
Shield. Veil. Border-province. مِجْنَب
Vanguard. مُجَنِّبَة
The two wings (of an army). مُجَنِّبَتان
Pomegranate-blossom. * جُنْبُذ
To overcharge (merchant). To quack. ✧ جَنْبَزَ وتَجَنْبَزَ
Acrobat. Quack. Ps جَنْباز ج جَنابِزَة
To alight with extended wings (bird). To pretend to descend from a noble race (man). To conceal o.'s self in a garment. * جَنَثَ – تَجَنَّثَ
To feel sympathy for. – على
Race, lineage. Stock of a tree. جِنْث
Polygonum. Knotgrass. * جُنْجُر
Asparagus. ✧ Sty (on the eye). * جُنْجُل
To be at hand (night). * جَنَحَ a جُنُوحًا
To stoop, to incline towards. – إلى
To break the wing of (a bird). – ه
To give wings to. جَنَّحَ ه
To lean towards. أَجْنَحَ واجْتَنَحَ إلى
To make a. o. to lean. To incline a. o. towards. أَجْنَحَ واستَجْنَحَ ه
To bow down in prayer. تَجَنَّحَ واجْتَنَحَ
Part of the night. Night. جِنْح وجُنْح
Side of a road. Shelter. جَنْح الطَّرِيق
Arm, armpit. Wing. Wing of an army, of a building. Fin of a fish. Shelter. Protection. جَناح ج أَجْنِحَة وأَجْنُح
Sin, crime. جُناح
Leaning on one side. جانِح
Rib. جانِحَة ج جَوانِح
To levy troops. * جَنَّدَ ه
To volunteer (soldier). تَجَنَّدَ
Army, troops, soldiers. ✧ City, province. جُنْد ج جُنُود وأَجْناد
A soldier. جُنْدِيّ
Military service. جُنْدِيَّة
Kind of locust. * جُنْدَب وجُنْدُب ج جَنادِب
Life-guard. F جَنْدار ج جَنادِرَة
Bubble formed on * جُنْدُعَة ج جَنادِع

A kind of cymbal. Chinese junk. جُنْك ج جُنوك P
Cymbal-player. جُنكي م جُنكيّة
To gather (fruits). To collect, to pick up a. th. ✻ جَنَى i جَنْيًا وجَنَى ه
To commit an offense, a crime. — جِنَايَة
To have ripe fruit (tree). To be rich in produce (soil). أَجْنَى
To charge a. o. falsely with a crime. تَجَنَّى على
To gather (fruit) from. — واجْتَنَى مِن
Gathered fruit. Harvest. جَنًى ج أَجْنَاء وجَنَاة
Freshly plucked (fruit). جَنِيّ
Arbute. Strawberry-tree. جِنًا
Crime, fault, guilt. جِنَايَة
Crime. ✧ Blood-price. جَنِيَّة
Gatherer. Criminal, culprit. جَانٍ ج جُنَاة وجُنَّاء وأَجْنَاء
To shout. ✧ To shine. ✻ جهجه
Man of sound judgment. Able critic. جِهْبَذ ج جَهَابِذَة P
To toil, to exert o.'s self strenuously in. ✻ جَهَد a جَهْدًا في
To try a. o. — ب
To overload (a camel). To distress, to weary, to exhaust a. o. — وأَجْهَد ه
He suffered from thirst. جُهِد عَطَشًا
To be hard, distressful (life). جَهِد a جَهْدًا
To struggle against a. o. To wage a holy war against (unbelievers). جَاهَد مُجَاهَدَة وجِهَادًا ه
To appear to a. o. (truth). To become within (sight : man). To become possible to a. o. (th.). أَجْهَد ل
To urge, to press a. o. To desire. To squander (goods). أَجْهَد ه وه
To strive after. To struggle against (difficulties). تَجَاهَد واجْتَهَد في
To meditate upon a th. إِسْتَجْهَد في
Zeal, exertion. Power. Fatigue. جَهْد
He exerted his utmost endeavours. أَفْرَغ جَهْدَهُ
Ability. Power, energy. Painstaking. Fatigue. جُهْد
Fight. Holy war. جِهَاد ومُجَاهَدَة
▫ War-office. دِيوَان الجِهَادِيَّة

water by rain drops. Evil. Worthless man.
Forerunners of evil. جَنَادِع الشَّرّ
To throw a. o. down. ✻ جَنْدَل ه
Stone. Water-fall. جَنْدَل ج جَنَادِل
Plane-tree. ✻ جُنَّار
To cover, to conceal a. th. ✻ جَنَز i جَنْزًا ه
To put (a dead person) on a litter. ✧ To make the funeral of. جَنَّز ه
Bier. Corpse. Funeral. جَنَازَة وجِنَازَة ج جَنَائِز
Funeral. obsequies. ✧ جُنَّاز ج جَنَانِيز
To be covered with verdigris. ✧ جَنْزَر (for زنجر)
To fetter a. o. ✧ جَنْزَر
To be in irons. ✧ تَجَنْزَر
Verdigris. جِنْزَار P
Chains. (for زنجير) جِنْزِير ج جَنَازِير P
Yellowish blue. جِنْزَارِيّ
To ripen (date). ✻ جَنَس o جَنْسًا
To specify, to classify a. th. ✧ To assort (goods). جَنَّس ه وه
To resemble a. o. To be homogeneous with. جَانَس مُجَانَسَة وجِنَاسًا ه وه
Kind, species. Genus. Class. Sex. Family. Race. جِنْس ج أَجْنَاس
Belonging to a sex, a kind. جِنْسِيّ
Common race, origin. جِنْسِيَّة
Affinity, likeness. مُجَانَسَة وجِنَاس
Homogeneous, similar. مُجَانِس
To go astray from (the right way). ✻ جَنَف i جُنُوفًا . وجَنِف a جَنَفًا عن
To act wrongfully (in a will). — وأَجْنَف في
✧ To overcharge a. o. (seller). To harass a. o. جَنَف على
To break off in anger with. جَانَف ه
He premeditated sin. تَجَانَف لِلإِثْم
Injustice. جَنَف
Astray. Wrong-doer. Crook-backed. جَنِف م جَنِفَة . وأَجْنَف م جَنْفَاء ج جُنْف
Canvass. Awning. Coarse cloth. ✧ جِنْفَاص وجِنْفِيص
To hurl (stones) with a ballista. ✻ جَنَق i جَنْقًا . وجَنَّق ه
Ballista. مَنْجَنِيق ج مَجَانِق ومَجَانِيق G
To become hot (fight). ✧ جَنَّك
War. fight. جَنْك Ts

Pasture-land much sought by cattle. جَهِيد

Utmost limit. uttermost. جُهَادَى

The utmost of thy ability is to do so. جُهَادَاكَ أَنْ تَفْعَلَ كَذَا

Zeal, exertion. مَجْهُود

He has exerted himself to the utmost of his power. بَذَلَ مَجْهُودَهُ

To be known, published, divulged (event). * جَهَرَ a جَهْرًا وجِهَارًا

To make a. th. notorious, to reveal a. th. To journey in an unknown (land). To see a. th. without veil. To discover. to disclose a. th. To cleanse (a well). To magnify a. o. To dazzle a. o. (sun). — ه و ﺩ

To speak aloud to a. o. — ﺩ بِالقَوْل

To be dazzled by the (sun). جَهِرَ a جَهَرًا

To be loud (voice). To become illustrious (man). جَهُرَ o جَهَارَةً

To declare a. th. openly to a. o. To overcome a. o. in. جَاهَرَ مُجَاهَرَةً وجِهَارًا ﺩ ب

To show open enmity to. — ﺩ بِالعَدَاوَة

To read aloud. — وأَجْهَرَ بِالقِرَاءَة

To divulge a. th. أَجْهَرَ ﺩ او ب

To appear in broad light. تَجَاهَرَ

To find (people) to be numerous. To see a. o. plainly. إِجْتَهَرَ ﺩ

Notoriousness. جَهْر وجِهَار وجَهْرَة

Openly, publicly. جَهْرًا وجِهَارًا وجَهْرَةً

Secretly and openly. سِرًّا وجَهْرًا

Exterior appearance. Pleasingness. جَهْر

Plain voice. Fair appearance. جَهْرَة

Fine-looking. Dazzled. أَجْهَر م جَهْرَاء

Bare soil. أَرْض جَهْرَاء

Beautiful. Striking. Loud, strong (voice). جَهِر وجَهِير ج جُهَرَاء

Having a loud voice (horse). جَهُور

Speaking aloud. مِجْهَر ومِجْهَار

Substance. essence. nature. Jewel. Gem. Pearl. P جَوْهَر ج جَوَاهِر

Essential. Jeweller. جَوْهَرِيّ

To give the last stroke to (a wounded man). * جَهَزَ a جَهْزًا، وأَجْهَزَ عَلَى

To supply a. o. with. To equip (a ship). To prepare. to fit out. To bury (the dead). جَهَّزَ ﺩ وه

To supply o.'s self with travelling apparatus. تَجَهَّزَ

To be prepared for a. th. — واجْهَازَّ ل

Provisions. equipment. Set of tools. Funeral apparatus. Outfitting of a bride. Rigging of a ship. Household furniture. Organs of the human body. جِهَاز وجَهَاز ج أَجْهِزَة

Urinary passages جِهَاز بَوْلِيّ

Puncta lachrymalis. — دَمْعِيّ

Biliary duct. — صَفْرَاوِيّ

Digestive apparatus. — هَضْمِيّ

Quick death. Light-footed (horse). جَهِيز

Wolf. Name of a woman. جَهِيزَة

Quick (death). مُجْهِز

* جَهَشَ a جَهْشًا وجُهُوشًا وجَهَشَانًا ، وأَجْهَشَ

To betake o.'s self to a. o. in weeping (frightened child). إِلَى

To fear a. o. To escape from. جَهِشَ a جَهَشَانًا مِن

To be about to weep. أَجْهَشَ بِالبُكَاء

Tears. Crowd. جَهْشَة

To prevent a. o. from. * جَهَضَ a جَهْضًا، وأَجْهَضَ ﺩ عن

To overcome a. o. To discard a. o. — ﺩ

To outstrip, to precede a. o. جَاهَضَ ﺩ

Abortive fœtus. مُجْهَض وجَهِيض

Casting forth her young one. مُجْهِض

To be ignorant; to be unlearned, to be foolish. * جَهِلَ a جَهْلًا وجَهَالَةً

To be unaware of a. th. — ه

To show ignorance to. — عَلَى

To attribute ignorance to. جَهَّلَ ﺩ

To undervalue a. o. جَاهَلَ ﺩ

To feign ignorance. تَجَاهَلَ

To deem a. o. ignorant or stupid. To despise a. o. To shake (a plant : wind). إِسْتَجْهَلَ ﺩ وه

Ignorance. Foolishness. جَهْل وجَهَالَة

State of infidelity amongst the pagan Arabs before Islamism. جَاهِلِيَّة

Feigned ignorance. تَجَاهُل

Ignorant. Foolish. جَاهِل ج جُهَّل وجُهَّال وجُهَلَاء

Ignorant, illiterate. Simple. جَهُول

Wayless desert. مَجْهَل ج مَجَاهِل

Passive (verb). مَجْهُول ج مَجَاهِيل

To converse together : تجاوب
to reply one to another.
To clear away (fog, mist). إنجاب
To be rent (clothes). To stretch the neck (camel).
To sink (a well). To tear إجتاب ه
a. th. To put on (a shirt). To cross (a country).
To answer a. o. To hear إستجاب ٥ او ل
(a prayer : God).
To ask a question. ○ إستجوب
Journey. Large bucket. Fire- جَوْب
place. Woman's shift. Shield.
Hollow, جَوْبَة ج جَوْبَات وجُوَب
excavation. Smooth tract between two lands.
Answer. ◻ Letter. جَوَاب
He brought a letter. ◻ رَفَع جَوَاب
Answer, reply. جَابَة , جَوَاب ج أَجْوِبَة
Way of answering. جِيبَة
Traveller in the desert. جَوَّاب
Circulating news. جَائِبَة ج جَوَائِب
Answer. Reply. مَجُوبَة
To go astray. ✱ جاح ٥ جَوْحًا
To destroy a. o. — واجتاح ٥
To extirpate.
To bare (the feet). جَوَّح ه
Water-melon of Damascus. جَوْح
Calamity, dearth. جَائِحَة ج جَوَائِح
Droughty year. سَنَة جَائِحَة
Wide. أَجْوَح م جَوْحَاء ج جُوح
To wash away ✱ جاخ ٥ جَوْخًا , وجَوَّخ ه
(a bank : torrent, river).
To prostrate a. o. جَوَّخ ٥ وه
To snatch off a. th.
To fall in (well). To burst تَجَوَّخ
(abscess).
Cloth. Ps جُوخ ج أَجْوَاخ
Ditch, hollow. ✧ Piece of cloth. جُوخَة
Cloth-gown with full sleeves.
To be excellent. ✱ جاد ٥ جُودَة وجَوْدَة
To make a. th. well.
To be swift (horse). — وأَجْوَد
To bestow a. th. — جُودًا على فُلان ب
bountifully upon a. o.
To offer o.'s self to death. — بِنَفْسِهِ
To shed abundant tears — جَوْدًا وجُوُودًا
(eye). To be copious (rain).
To render good. To better a. th. جَوَّد ه

Anonymous.
To ✱ جَهِم وجَهُم ٥ جَهْمًا ٥ وتَجَهَّم ٥ ول
meet a. o. with a frowning face.
To have a stern جَهُم ٥ جَهَامَة وجُهُومَة
look.
To look at a. o. with — تجهَّم ل و٥
a severe, morose face.
To have rainless clouds (sky). أَجْهَم
Stern, contracted face. جَهْم
The darkest part of the جُهْمَة وجَهْمَة
night.
Waterless cloud جَهَام
Impotent, weak. جَهُوم
To draw near. ✱ جَهَن ٥ جُهُونًا
Hell. Hell-fire. Gehenna. H جَهَنَّم
Infernal. جَهَنَّمِي
To be ruined (house). ✱ جَهِي a جَهًى
To widen (a wound). جَهَّى ه
To contend with a. o. for جَاهَى ه
glory.
To become serene (sky). أَجْهَى
To be conspicuous (road).
To show avarice towards a. o. — على
To contend with a. o. for تَجَاهَى على
superiority.
Bald. Roofless (house). أَجْهَى م جَهْوَاء
Serene (sky). Bald (man).
Tent without curtain. خِبَاء مُجْهٍ
Atmosphere. Wild ✱ جَوّ ج جِوَاء
pigeon.
The inside of a house. جَوّ البَيْت
Depressed ground. جَوّ ج جِوَاء
Interior, intimate, inside. جَوَّانِيّ
The atmospheric state. الحالة الجَوِّيَّة
Inside (*adv.*). ✧ جَوَّا وجُوَّا
Indoor. ✧ جُوَّاة البَيْت
Domestic (animal). (*opp. to* بَرِّيّ) ✧ جَوِّيّ
To ✱ جاب ٥ جَوْبًا وتَجْوَابًا , واجتاب ه
cross, to ramble in (a country).
To cut out (clothes). To bore ٥ جَوْبًا —
(a rock).
To cut an opening in a — وجَوَّب
shift, in a shirt.
To answer (a question). جَاوَب ٥ وه
To converse with a. o. ✧ To resound (vault, church). To correspond to (God's grace).
To answer a. o. on أَجَاب ٥ إلى او عن
a. th.

Female neighbour. جارَة ج جارَات
Spouse.
Deviating. جائِر ج جَوَرَة وجُوَّارَة
Unjust, tyrannical. Large bucket.
❉ جاز o جَوْزًا وجُوُوزًا وجَوَازًا ومَجازًا ه وفِ
To cross, to pass along (a place).
To outpass a. o.   s —
To be lawful. To be allowable. جَوَازًا —
To make, to declare a. th. جَوَّز ه
lawful. To execute a (design).
To give currency to money.
To marry a. o. (for زَوَّج) ♦ جَوَّز
To transgress جاوَز مُجَاوَزَة ه وه
(a limit). To outpass a. o.
To overlook (a sin). جاوَز عن
To consider as lawful. أجاز إجازَة ه وه
To allow a. th. To go beyond (a
place). To execute (an order). To
confirm (a sate). To water (the
land and cattle) of.
He used poetic license. — وأجاز بَيْتًا
To bear patiently. To let a. o. تَجَوَّز فِ
pass. To shorten (prayer).
To exceed the bounds in. تَجَاوَز فِ
To let (an offense) without عن —
punishment. To shut the eyes upon.
To cross, to pass along. إجْتَاز
To pass through (a place). ب —
To consider a. th. إسْتَجَاز إسْتِجَازَة ه وه
as lawful. To approve. To ask per-
mission from a. o.
Middle of a desert. جَوْز ج أَجْوَاز
Husband. (for زَوْج) ♦ جَوْز
Walnut, walnut-tree. ♦ Pair. جَوْز
Earth-nut. جَوْز أَرْقَم
Rock-moss. Lichenous جَوْز جُنْدُم
plant.
Fir-cone. جَوْز صَنَوْبَر
Nutmeg. جَوْز الطِّيب
Amomum. Grana جَوْز الشَّرْك والحَبَّة
Paradisi.
Nux vomica, vomic-nut. جَوْز القَيّ
Alkekengi. جَوْز المَرْج
Cocoa-nut. جَوْز هِنْدِي
A walnut. A single جَوْزَة ج جَوْزَات
watering. Excellent grapes.
Gemini (sign of the Zodiac). الجَوْزَاء
Transit. Passport. جَوَاز ج أَجْوِزَة
Licence.

To vie with a. o. in جاوَد ه
generosity.
To speak or to do a. th. اجاد وأَجْوَد ه
well. To make a. th. excellent.
He paid in good money. أَجَاد النَّقْد
To select a. th. good. تَجَوَّد
To vie in bounty with a. o. تَجَاوَد
To esteem a. th. good, إسْتَجَاد ه وه
excellent. To ask the bounty of.
To ask a. o. to lend a courser.
Vanity. جاد
Copious rain. جَوْد ومَطَر جَوْد
Yielding rain (sky). سَماء جَوْد
Excessive thirst. جُوَاد وجَوَاد وجُودَة
Saffron. جَادِي
Bounty. Good qualities. جُودَة
Liberality. Generosity. جُود
Generous. (m. f.) جَوَاد وجُود ج أَجْوَاد
جَوَاد ج جِيَاد وأَجْيَاد وأَجَاوِيد وأَجَاوِد وجُود
Fleet (horse). Courser. وجُودَة
Excellent. جَيِّد ج جِيَاد وجِيَادَات وجِيَائِد
Excellent poet. مَجِيد ومِجْوَاد
To go astray from. ❉ جار o جَوْرًا عن
To act wrongfully towards a. o. عَلَى —
To charge a. o. with unjust جَوَّر ه وه
conduct. To throw a. o. down.
To destroy a. th. ♦ To dig, to
hollow. a. th.
To live close جاوَر مُجَاوَرَة وجِوَارًا ه وه
by a. o. To repair to (a place).
To protect a. o. أجار إجارَة ه
To rescue a. o. from. — مِن
To put a. o. out of (the way) عَن — ه
To be prostrated. To lay down. تَجَوَّر
To be demolished (house). ♦ To be
hollowed, concave.
To live near together. تَجَاوَر واجْتَوَر
To ask the help of. إسْتَجَار ب
To ask protection from a. o. مِن — ه
against.
Wrong-doing. Tyranny. جَوْر
Injustice.
Hollow, excavation. ♦ جُورَة ج جُوَر
gap.
Neighbourhood. Safe-conduct. جِوَار
Protection.
Bengal rose. جُورِي ووَرْد جُورِي
Neighbour. جار ج جِيرَان وجِيرَة
Partner. Protestor. Claimant.

Side of a valley. جيزة ج جِيَز و جِيَز
A draught. ✧ (*for* زِيجَة) Marriage.
Permission. Licence. Degree of a licentiate. Diploma. إِجَازَة
Law-ful. Thirsty (traveller). Beam. جائز ج جوائز وجُوزان وجِيزان وأَجْوِزة
Provisions for the road. Gift made to travellers, poets. Draught of water. ✧ Prize. جائزة ج جوائز
Trope, metaphor. Bridge. مَجاز
Grove of walnuts. Path. Bridge. مَجازة
Metaphorical (*opp. to* حَقِيقِيّ) (sense). مَجازِيّ
Friend. Tutor of an orphan. مُجِيز
✱ جاس o جَوْسًا , واجتاس ه و ه To spy a. o. To search (a place).
Scrutinizer, inquisitive. جَوَّاس
✱ جاش o جَوْشًا To walk the whole night.
To be partly spent (night). تَجَوَّش
Breast. Portion of the night. جَوْش
Ser-geant. جاويش و ✧ شاوِيش وشاوِيشِيَّة Te
Sergeant-major. باش جاويش
✱ جَوْشَن ج جَواشِن Breast. Coat of mail.
— اللَّيل Middle of the night.
✱ جاظ o جَوْظًا وجَوَظانًا To walk with a haughty demeanour.
— ه ب To trouble a. o. by.
Anxiety. Weariness. جَوْظ وجُواظ
Walking haughtily. Weary. جَوّاظ
✱ جاع o جَوْعًا ومَجاعة To be or become hungry.
— إلى To long after a. th.
جَوَّع وأجاع ه To debar a. o. from food, to make a. o. hungry.
أَجِع كَلْبَك يَتْبَعْك Starve thy dog, it will follow thee (*prov.*) *i. e.* Unless you compel a vile man to serve you. he will not do it.
To bear hunger. تَجَوَّع
To be insatiable. إِسْتَجاع
Hunger. جُوع ومَجاعة
Bulimia. جُوع كَلْبِيّ وجُوع بَقَرِيّ
جائِع وجَوْعان م جائعة وجَوْعَى ج جِياع وجُوَّع Hungry, starved.
✱ جَوِف a جَوَفًا To be hollow. empty.
جاف o جَوْفًا ه ب . وأجاف ه ه او ب To pierce the abdomen (with a spear).

— وجَوَّف ه To render a. th. hollow, concave. To extract the bowels.
To be hollow. To be empty. تَجَوَّف
— واجتاف ه To enter the inside of.
إِسْتَجاف واستَجْوَف To become wide. spacious.
— ه To find a. th. spacious, deep, hollow.
جَوْف ج أجواف Hollow. Inside of a house. Belly.
Spaciousness, amplitude جَوَف
Penetrating (thrust). جائفة ج جوائف
أَجْوَف م جَوْفاء ج جُوف Hollow. Defective in its medial letter (verb). Belly. Enormous lion.
Big-bellied. مَجُوف وجُوفِيّ
Hollow. (*opp. to* مُحَدَّب) مُجَوَّف Concave. Faint-hearted.
✱ جَوِق a جَوَقًا To have a wry face.
جَوَّق ه To muster (a crowd).
To meet in large numbers. تَجَوَّق
Crowd, numerous party. جَوْقة ج جَوْقات
أَجْوَق م جَوْقاء ج جُوق Wry-mouthed. Big-necked.
✱ جال o جَوْلًا وجَوْلة وجَوَلانًا في To ramble over (a country). To run across (a race course : horse).
جال o جَوَلانًا , وجَوَّل في To ramble about in a country. To occur to (the mind: thought).
— واجتال ه مِن To select a. th. amongst.
جاوَل ه To turn away, to drive a. o. back.
أجال إجالة ه وه او ب To make a. o. or a. th. to turn round.
— ه To wheel (a sword).
✧ To make a turn. تَجَوَّل
تَجاوَل في To wheel about in (a battle).
Lateral part of a grave. Side. Well. Sea. Hill. جال
جَوْل وجُول ج جِوال وجِوالة وأجوال Troop of horses, herd of camels. Rope.
ما لَهُ جال او جُول He has no under-standing.
A turn, one time. جَوْلة
Dust, pebbles swept by the wind. جَوَلان

Runner, great traveller. جَوَّان وجَوَّالَة
Circus. Space, field. Passage. مَجَال
Amulet. Shield. Anklet. Good money. Silver crescent in a necklace. Wild ass. Short garment for a girl. مِجْوَال
To ask a. th. good or bad. ✻ جَامَ o جَوْمًا
P جَام ج أَجْوُم وأَجْوَام وجامات وجُوم Silver cup.
To become black (face). ✻ جَانَ o جَوْنًا
To whiten (a bride's door). تَجَوَّنَ ه
To blacken (a dead person's door).
Black, white. Light red. Day. Intensely black (horse). جَوْن ج جُون
Disk of the sun when setting. جَوْنَة
Bay, gulf, haven. ✧ جُون
A small leather scent-bag. Sun. Cooking-pot. Black camel. Jar smeared with tar. جُونَة ج جُوَن
Black-winged partridge. جُونِيّ ج جُون
To meet a. o. with an unwelcome face. ✻ جَاهَ o جَوْهًا ه بِالْمَكْرُوه
To raise a. o. to a dignity. جَوَّهَ وأَجَاهَ ه
Influence. High rank. جَاه وجَاهَة
To be heart-broken (from love, grief). To stink, (water). ✻ جَوِيَ a جَوًى
To dislike (a country). – مِن او عن , واجْتَوَى ه
To become, to be tamed. ✧ جَوَّى وتَجَوَّى
To loathe (a food). إِسْتَجْوَى ه
Valley. Shepherd's bag. Trivet. جِوَاء
Violent passion of grief, love. Chronical disease. Consumption. جَوًى
Rottenness. ✧ جَوًى
Stinking, fetid (water). جَوٍ
Altered water. Marsh. جِيَّة
Stink. ✧ جِيَّة
Rotten. Stinking. ✧ مَجْوِيّ وجِيَّة
To come, to arrive. To fall (rain). ✻ جَاءَ i جَيْئًا وجَيْئَةً ومَجِيئًا
To do a. th. – ه
To go towards. – ه وإلى
To bring a. o. in. جَاءَ ب إلى , وأَجَاءَ ه
Pus and blood. Patch. جِيئَة
Invitation to dinner. جِيءٌ
To cut out the collar (of a shirt). ✻ جَابَ i جَيْبًا وجَيَّبَ ه
To bring a. o. or a. th. To bring forth (a child). ✧ جَابَ i (for جَاءَ ب) ه او ه
Collar of a shirt, of a shift. Heart. جَيْب ج جُيُوب
Sine (*trigonom.*). – وجَيْبَة ج جِيَاب
✧ Pocket, bag.
Privy purse of a sovereign. الجَيْب الخاص , الجَيْب الهمايوني
Sincere. نَاصِح الجَيْب
To have a long and beautiful neck. ✻ جَادَ a جَيَدًا , وجَيِد
Neck. Coat of mail. جِيد ج أَجْيَاد وجُيُود
Fine-necked. أَجْيَد م جَيْدَاء وجَيْدَانَة ج جُود
Truly, verily. ✻ جَيْرِ
Gypsum, lime. جِيْر
To endorse (a bill). ✧ جَيَّرَ ه
Heat in the chest caused by hunger, anger. جَائِر وجَيَّار
Quick lime. جَيَّار
Lime-kiln. ◘ جَيَّارَة
Grass-hopper. ✧ جِيز (for زيز)
To swell (sea). To boil (cooking-pot). To be flurried (mind). To shed tears (eye). To burn with anger (heart). To become hot (fight). To be swollen and spread (river). To be frightened away (coward). ✻ جَاشَ i جَيْشًا وجَيَشَانًا وجُيُوشًا
To summon troops. جَيَّشَ ه
To be mustered (troops). تَجَيَّشَ
To be restless (soul).
To demand a military force of a. o. To collect soldiers. إِسْتَجَاشَ ه
Military force. army. جَيْش ج جُيُوش
✧ Shriek, voice.
Excitement. Agitation of the sea. جَيَشَان
Soul. جَائِشَة
Horse easily excited by the spur. جَيَّاش
To shun, to avoid a. o. ✻ جَاصَ i جَيْصًا , وجَيَّصَ عن
To vie in splendour with. جَايَصَ ه
Inclination to the right and left. جَيْصَة
Proud demeanour. جِيَص وجِيَصَى
To groan under (a ✻ جَاطَ i جَيَطَانًا ب

weight)

✧ جَافَ i جَيفًا, وجَيَّف, وتَجَيَّف, واجْتَاف
To stink (corpse).

جِيفَة ج جِيَف , أَجْيَاف Corpse ; carcass

◻ جَايِف Filthy

※ جِيل ج أَجْيَال Nation. Tribe
✧ Century . Generation.

جِيلًا بَعْدَ جِيل From age to age.

※ جِيم The letter ج

ح

A grain. Weight of two حَبَّة ج حَبَّات grains of barley. A seed. A berry. A pill. ✧ A pimple.

Aniseed. الحَبَّة الحُلْوَة

Fruit of the terebinth. الحَبَّة الخَضْرَاء

Nigella-seed. الحَبَّة السَّوْدَاء وحَبَّة البَرَكَة

Hail-stone. حَبَّة الغَمَام والقُرّ

✧ Pupil, apple of the eye. حَبَّة العَيْن

To flow scantily (water). ✻ حَبْحَب To blaze (fire).

✧ To pick (grains, grapes). — ه

Unsightly. Short in حَبْحَاب ج حَبَاحِب body.

Scanty flow of water. Weak- حَبْحَبَة ness. Ardour of fire. Water-melon.

Fire-fly. Sparks. حُبَاحِب

To appear on a sudden. ✻ حَبْجَ i حَبْجًا To approach. To walk quickly.

To strike a. o. with a stick. — ه

To be variegated ✻ حَبِرَ o حَبْرًا ه (cloth). To embellish a. th.

To cheer a. o. — o حَبْرًا وحَبْرَة , وأحْبَر ه

To rejoice, to be glad. حَبِرَ a حُبُورًا وحَبْرًا

To be cicatrised (wound). حَبِرَ a حَبَرًا To be luxuriant (land). To become yellow (tooth).

To adorn (speech). To put ink حَبَّرَ ه in (an inkstand).

To deck, to array o.'s self. تَحَبَّر To overspread the sky (cloud).

Learned man. Doctor حَبْر وحِبْر ج أحْبَار (amongst the Jews). Pontiff. Bishop. Joy. Favour.

The Sovereign Pontiff ; الحَبْر الأعظم the Pope. High Priest or [illegible] Jews.

Book of the Judges. سِفْر الأ[illegible]

Ink. Scar. Beaut[illegible] حِبْر ج حُبُور Likeness.

Seller of ink. حِبْرِيّ وحَبَّار

✻ حَبَّ أحِبّ حُبًّا وحِبًّا ه وه To love a. o. or a. th. ◻ To kiss a. o.

To like, to wish that. — أن

To be freckled (face). ◻ حَبَّ

To become the friend of. — وحَبُبَ إلى

To make a. o. to be حَبَّبَ ه إلى وه إيَّاه loved by.

To run to seed (plant). — وأحَبّ

To court the حَابَّ مُحَابَّة وحِبَابًا ه friendship of a. o. To behave in a friendly manner with a. o.

To love a. o. or a. th. أحَبَّ ه وه

To show love towards. تَحَبَّبَ إلى

To have mutual love. تَحَابَّ

To like, to be pleased with. إسْتَحَبَّ ه

To prefer a. o. to. — ه وه على

✻ حَبَّذَا ويَا حَبَّذَا (حَبَّ وذَا) *Word of praise.* Bravo !

To praise a. o. *by saying* : حَبَّذَ ه Bravo ! Very well !

Love, fondness. حِبّ وحُبّ ومَحَبَّة

Loved. Lover. حِبّ ج أحْبَاب وحِبَاب

Aim, end in view حِبَاب

Love. Friend. Snake. حُبَاب

Friend. Beloved. حَبِيب ج أحِبَّاء وأحْبَاب

Old gold coin (*about* 14 *sh.*). مَحْبُوب

The allied Powers. الدُّوَل المُتَحَابَّة

✻ حَبّ ج حُبُوب Grain. Corn-seed, fruit-seed. Bead. ✧ Pill. Speckle. Pimples.

Chaste-tree. حَبّ الفَقْد

Night-shade. حَبّ الهَنَا

Anagyris fetida, bean. حَبّ الكُلَى trefoil.

Convolvulus Nil., bind-weed. حَبّ النِّيل

Acme, (disease of the skin). حَبّ الصِّبَا

Large jar. P حُبّ ج حِبَاب وحِبَبَة وأحْبَاب

Row of teeth. Water-bubble. حَبَب Drop of dew.

To be made void (right).
To run (man). To miss the butt (arrow). أَحْبَض
To annul (a right). — ه
To exhaust (a well).
Irregular throbbing, palpitation. حَبَض
To be of no avail, useless (work, action). ✱ حَبِطَ i حَبْطًا وحُبُوطًا ، وحَبِطَ a حَبَطًا
To bring (a work) to perfection ¤ حَبَّطَ
To render a. th. useless. أَحْبَطَ ه و ة
To leave a scar upon a. o. (blow).
To go away from. — عن
Scar of a wound. Swelling. حَبَط
To strike a. o. with a rod. To lash, to flog a. o. ✱ حَبَقَ i حَبْقًا ة
To break wind (goat). — i حَبْقًا وحَبِقًا وحُبَاقًا
To make up a. th. To settle a business. حَبَّقَ ه
To become compliant. أَحْبَقَ
To abuse a. o. تَحَابَقَ على
Basil, penny-royal. حَبَق
Chamomile. حَبَق البَقَر
Artemisia. Wormwood. حَبَق الرَّاعِي
Marum. Cat-thyme. حَبَق الشُّيُوخ
Sweet marjoram. حَبَق الفَتَى او الفِيل
Acinus. حَبَق قُرُنْفُلِيّ
Water-mint. حَبَق المَاء وحَبَق التِّمْسَاح
Narrow-minded. حُبَّق ج حُبَقَة
Hail-stone. ✱ حَبْقُر
To weave (a stuff) well. ✧ To bind (a book). ✱ حَبَكَ o i حَبْكًا ه
To fasten, to tie a. th. tightly. ✧ To twist (a thread). حَبَّكَ ه
To make a work (carefully). أَحْبَكَ ه
To gird o.'s self. To wrap o.'s self in clothes. ✧ To be thrown into gear (cogs). تَحَبَّكَ
To weave carefully (a stuff). إِحْتَبَكَ ه
To gird o.'s self with. — ب
Girdle, girth. حُبْكَة ج حُبَك
Waist-band. Streak on the sand. Enclosure. حِبَاك ج حُبُك وحُبُك
Hosier. Bookbinder. ✧ حَبَّاك
Twisted. ✧ In gear. حَبِيك ومُحَبَّك
Trail of stars. Iron breast-plate. حَبِيكَة ج حَبِيك وحَبَائِك وحُبُك

Yellow colour of the teeth. حِبْر وحَبْر وحَبْرَة وحُبْرَة وحِبْرَة
Striped garment. حِبَرَة ج حِبَرَات وحِبَر
Newly made (garment). Soft (bed). Spotted (cloud). Variegated garment. حَبِير ج حُبُر
Assembly of the wicked. حَابُور ج حَوَابِير
Bustard (bird). حُبَارَى ج حُبَارَيَات
Small bustard. حُبُّور ج حَبَابِير ، وحُبْرُور وحِبْرِير ج حَبَارِير
Inkstand. Writing-desk. مِحْبَر ومِحْبَرَة ومَحْبَرَة ومَحْبُرَة ج مَحَابِر
To confine, to hold in custody. To detain a. o. ✱ حَبَسَ i حَبْسًا ومَحْبِسًا ة
To veil a. th. with. حَبَسَ ه ب
To withhold a. o. from. — ة عن
To give a. th. as mortmain. — ه
To veil a. o. or th. حَبَّسَ ة وه
To apply the produce of a. th. to pious works. — واحْبَسَ ه
To keep a. o. in custody. حَابَسَ ة
To confine o.'s self to. تَحَبَّسَ على
To keep a. o. in custody. To keep a. th. back. إِحْتَبَسَ ة وه
He was impeded in speech. — في الكلام
To become a hermit. ✧ اسْتَحْبَسَ
Dam of wood or stone. حِبْس ج أَحْبَاس
Prison. حَبْس ج حُبُوس ، و✧ حَبْسخانَة
Impediment in speech. حُبْسَة
Mortmain. حَبِيس وحُبْس ومُحَبَّس ومَحْبُوس
Hermit. Solitary. ✧ حَبِيس ج حُبَسَاء
Convict-prison. Dungeon. Manger of a beast. مَحْبَس ومَحْبِس ج مَحَابِس
✧ Hermitage. مَحْبَسَة
To collect a. th. for a. o. ✱ حَبَشَ o حَبْشًا وحُبَاشَة ، وحَبَّشَ ه ل
To bring forth a negro. أَحْبَشَ
To collect together (people). تَحَبَّشَ
Company of men from various tribes. حُبَاشَة ج حُبَاشَات ، وأُحْبُوش وأُحْبُوشَة ج أَحَابِيش
The Abyssinians. Abyssinia. حَبَش وحَبَشَة
An Abyssinian. حَبَشِيّ
Kosso (helminthic herb). حَشِيشَة حَبَشِيَّة
Pintado. Turkey-cock. ✧ حُبَيْش
To throb. To palpitate irregularly (heart). ✱ حَبَضَ i حَبْضًا ، وحَبِضَ a حَبَضًا
To twang (a bow-string). — وحَبِضَ ب
To be exhausted (well). — حُبُوضًا

To fall off (leaves, plaster). تحاتّ وانحتّ
To be cankered (tooth).
Fleet (horse). Ancient. Noble. حتّ ج أحتات
Bit, fragment. A little. ¤ حِتّة ج حِتَت
Rubbish, remains, crumbs. حُتات
To, till, until. Included. Even. In order that. ✧ That he... حتّى
How long, till when? حتّى متى وحتّام
To sew (a garment). ✱ حتأ a حتأً, وأحتأ ه
To tighten (a knot). To strengthen (a wall). To tuck up (a garment). To put down (a load).
To be pure, genuine. ✱ حتِد a حتَدًا
To live in (a place) (*obsolete*). حتَد i حُتودًا ب
To select a. th. pure. حتّد
Inexhaustible spring. حُتُد
Origin, race, lineage. محتِد
To tighten (a knot). ✱ حتر o i حترًا ه
To look steadfastly at.
To give, or to nourish a. o. scantily. To hinder a. o. — ه
Trifle. Small gift. حتر وحِتر وحُترة
Rim, circuit of a. th. حِتار
Banquet given at the completion of a building. حتيرة
To produce a sound in eating (locust). ✱ حترش
To meet together. تحترش
Small-sized. Sprightly (child). حُتروش
To displace a. th. ✱ حترف ه
Death. ✱ حتف ج حُتوف
He departed from life. مات حتفَ أنفهِ
Remainder of meat, grease. Rabble. ✱ حُتفُل
To walk at a quick and short pace. ✱ حتك i حتكًا وحتكانًا
To render a. th. obligatory to a. o. ✧ To make up o.'s mind to. ✱ حتم i حتمًا ه على
To improve a. th. — ه
To decide, to finish up a. th. — ب
To eat the remains of (a meal). تحتّم ه
✧ To be obligatory to a. o. تحتّم على
To be irreversible (decree). — وانحتم
Decree; judicial decision. حتم ج حُتوم
Blackness. حُتمة
Remainder of a meal. حُتامة

To ensnare a. o. ✱ حبل o حبلًا ه وه ب
in. To tie with (a rope).
To conceive (a child: woman). حبل a حبلًا ب
To swell with (wine, anger). — من
To be conceived (fœtus). حبل به
To render (a female) pregnant. حبّل وأحبل ه
To become pregnant. To entangle its legs in a rope (beast). تحبّل
To catch a. o. in a snare. إحتبل ه
Rope. Halter. Treaty. Vein of the neck. حبل ج حِبال وأحبل وحُبول وأحبال
Ivy. حبل المساكين
Conception. Fœtus. Fruit. Anger. Sadness. حبل
Shrewd, cunning. حِبل ج حُبول وأحبال
Hunter. Wizard. حابل
Snare, trap. أحبولة وحِبالة ج أحابيل وحبائل
Seasonable time. حِبالة
Pregnant (woman). حُبلى ج حَبالى
Filled. Swollen by anger. حبلان
An angry woman. إمرأة حبلانة
Beans. أحبل
To swell in dropsy. ✱ حبِن a حبنًا, وحُبِن
To be angry with a. o. حبِن a حبنًا على
Oleander. Laurel-tree. حبن وحبين
Dropsy. حبن
Dropsical. محبون وأحبن م حبناء
Chameleon. أمّ حبين وأمّ الحُبين وحُبينة
Purulent sore. Monkey. حِبن ج حُبون
To draw near. To creep (child). To glide along the soil (arrow). ✱ حبا o حبوًا
To give a. th. to a. o. — ه او ب ه
To protect a. o. حبّى ه
To show partiality in (a suit: judge). To show favor to a. o. in (a sale: merchant). حابى مُحاباة وحِباء ه في
To miss the butt (shooter). أحبى
To use (a garment) as a support, when sitting on the heels. إحتبى ب
Piece of cloth used as a support when sitting. حُبوة ج حُبى
Gift, present. حِباء وحِبوة وحَبوة وحُبوة
Respect of persons, unfairness, partiality. محاباة الوجوه
To rub off (mud). To bark (a tree). ✱ حتّ o حتًّا ه

To adduce (an argument). إحتجّ ب
To undertake the pilgrimage. إستحجّ
Pilgrimage. حجّ وحِجّة
Ear-ring. Lobe of the ear. حَجَّة
A pilgrimage. حِجَّة ج حِجّات وحِجَج
Last month of the Arabs. ذُو الحِجَّة
Argument, plea. حُجَّة ج حُجَج
✧ Title-deed. Protest.
He protested against. اقام الحجة على
Bone of the brow. حِجاج ج حِجاج وأحِجَّة
Pilgrim. حاجّ ج حُجّاج وحَجِيج وحُجّ
Female pilgrim. Polite term of address to a woman. حاجَّة
✧ Butt, aim. مَحَجّ
High road, thoroughfare. مَحَجَّة
Litigious. Surgeon's probe. مِحجاج
To refrain from speaking. ✱ حَجْحَج
To fall back after an attack (army).
To rejoice at. ✱ حجأ a حَجأً ب
To stick to. حَجِئ a حَجأً, وتَحَجَّأ ب
Refuge, protection. مَحْجَأ
To veil a. th. To hinder a. o. from access. ✱ حَجَب o حَجْبًا وحِجابًا, وحَجَّب ه وه
To be veiled, precluded. تَحَجَّب واحتجب
✧ To be modest, timid.
To appoint a. o. chamberlain. إستحجب ه
Veil, screen. ✧ Amulet. حِجاب ج حُجُب
Diaphragm, midriff. حِجاب الحاجز
Cupping-glasses. ✧ حِجابات هَوَاء
Office of chamberlain. حِجابَة
Chamberlain. حاجِب ج حُجّاب وحَجَبَة
Eye-brow. حاجِب ج حَوَاجِب
Veiled. Blind (man). مَحجُوب
To deprive a. o. from. To prohibit access to. ✱ حَجَر o حِجرًا وحُجرًا وحُجرانًا ه عن
To interdict access (to a place) to. — حَجرًا ومَحجَرًا ه على
To deprive a. o. of civil rights. حَجَر على
To be surrounded by a halo (moon). To be petrified (mud). حَجَّر
To cover, to hide a. th. أحجر ه
To harden, to petrify. تَحَجَّر واستحجر
To straiten a. o. — على
To make a cell for o.'s self. To retire to a cell. — واحتجر واستحجر

Black. Inauspicious. أحتم م. حَتماء ج حُتم
To be intense (heat). ✱ حَتِن a حَتَنًا
To be equal in. تحاتن في
To suit. To agree together. إحتتن
Companion. Alike. حَتْن وحِتن
To sew. to fasten a. th. To twist (a rope). ✱ حَتَى i حَتْيًا, وأحتى ه
To incite, to instigate, to urge a. o. to ✱ حَثّ o حَثًّا ه على, وحَثّث وأحثّ وأحتثّ واستحثّ ه على
To excite one another to. تحاثّ على
To be incited, impelled to. إحتثّ على
Incitement. حَثّ وإحثاث واحتثاث واستحثاث
Bits of straw. Unseasoned bread. حُثّ
Quick. Hasty. Greedy. حَثِيث وحَثُوث
To be covered with pustules (skin). To granulate (honey). To be widened. ✱ حَثِر a حَثَرًا
To make (a medicine) into pills. حَثّر ه
To bear fruit (palm-tree). أحثر
Particles of straw. حُثارة
To be turbid (water, well). ✱ حَثْرَب
Foul water. حُثْرُب
To feed (a child) badly. To straiten a. o. (fate). ✱ حثل — أحثل ه
Ill-fed (child). Short. Lazy. حَثِيل
Rubbish of grains. Sediment. حُثالة
To polish a. th. ✱ حَثَم o حَثمًا ه
To give a. th. to a. o. — ه ل
Reddish hillock. Lobe of the nose. حَثَمَة
To pour (dust) upon. ✱ حَثَا o حَثوًا وحَثَى i حَثيًا ه على وفي
He put him to shame. حثى في وَجهِهِ الرَّماد
lit. he poured ashes upon his face.
He outstripped him, حثى في وَجهِهِ التُّراب
lit. he poured dust on his face.
To give a. th. in small quantity. — ل
Bits of straw. Dust poured. حَثِيّ
To repair to a. o. To make a pilgrimage. ✱ حَجّ o حَجًّا ه وه
To overcome a. o. in dispute. — ه
To probe (a wound). حَجّ ه
To argue against. حاجّ حِجاجًا ومُحاجَّة ه
To plead in behalf of a. o. ✧ — عن
To send a. o. on a pilgrimage. حَجّ وأحجّ ه
To afford arguments. تحاجّ

To seek a refuge towards. — ب
To trespass upon. إستحجر على
Prohibition. Protection. Bosom, breast. Deprivation of civil rights. حجر
To reinstate a. o. in his civil rights. رفع الحجر عن
Quarantine. ✧ حجر صحّي
Forbidden. Unlawful. حِجر وحُجر
Bosom. Hole of snakes. Mind. — ج أحجار
To revoke on interdiction. رفع الحِجر عن
Mare. حِجر ج حُجور وحُجورة وأحجار
Stone. ✧ Man (*at chess*). حَجَر ج أحجار وحِجارة وحِجار
Lunar caustic. حجر جهنّم
Stumbling-block. حجر عثرة
The black stone of the Caaba. الحجر الأسود
Siderite. حجر حديديّ
Ostracite. حجر خزفي
Pumice-stone. حجر شفّاف
Mellite. حجر عسلي
Avanturine (quartz). حجرة البرق
Macadamisation. ✧ حجريّة
Side, quarter. حجرة ج حجر وحجرات وحواجر
His property has become extensive. إنتشرت حجرته
Cell, chamber. Enclosure for cattle. Grave. Side, region. حُجرة ج حُجَر
Chamber of commerce. حُجرة التّجارة
Stony (ground). حجر وحجير ومُتحجّر
Wall. Upland. Cell. حاجر ج حُجران
Dam. Refuge. — وحاجور
Stone-cutter. حجّار ج حجّارون
▫ Slate. حجر مُطبّق
Prohibited. Suburbs (of a town). ✧ Quarantine. مَحجَر ج محاجر
Orbit of the eye. Tract surrounding a village. ▫ Stone-quarry. مَحجِر ومحجَر ج مَحاجر
Windpipe. Larynx. ✱ حنجرة ج حناجر
Throat. Small basket. Flask for spices. ✧ Scent-bottle. حنجور ج حناجير
To withhold. ✱ حجز i o حجزًا و حِجازة ه
✧ To detain a. o. — على
To interpose between (fighters). — بين
✧ To sequester (the property) of. — ه على

To prevent a. o. from fighting. حاجز ه
To go to Hedjaz. أحجز واحتجز وانحجز
To abstain from fighting. تحاجز
To be refrained, restrained. إنحجز
To girdle o.'s self with a waist-wrapper. إحتجز
To carry a. th. in the bosom. — ه
Seizure, execution. حَجز
Root, Tribe. Shore. حُجز
Arabia Petræa, Hedjaz. Waist-wrapper. Girdle. Musical tune. Rope for tying a camel's feet. حِجاز
Tuck of trousers. Waistband. Waist. حُجزة ج حُجَز
Patient. شديد الحُجزة
Fence, screen. Isthmus. Edge of a sword. Hindrance. Dam. حاجز ج حَجَزة
Partition, barrier. Railing. — ج حواجز
To oppose. to repel a. o. ✱ حَجَف — حاجف ه
To pray, to beseech. إنحجف
To take hold of. to obtain. إحتجف ه
Leather-shield. حَجَفة ج حَجَف
Head of the hip-bone. حُنجف وحُنجُف
To limp (crow). To hop (shackled man). ✱ حَجَل o i حجلًا وحَجَلانًا
To intervene between. حُجِل حجلًا بين
To prepare the nuptial chamber for (a bride). To dye her fingers (woman). To shackle a. o. حجّل ه
To have one or more legs white on the lower part (horse). To put on anklets (woman). حُجّل
Partridge. حَجَل وحَجَلة ج حِجلان وحِجلى
White hair on a horse's legs. حِجل ج حُجول
Silver anklet. Ring of a shackle. Shackles. حَجل وحِجل وحِجِل ج حُجول وأحجال
Pavilion for a bride. حَجَلة ج حَجَل وحِجال
Whiteness on the legs of a horse. تحجيل
Having three legs white (horse). مُحجّل
Crow. حاجل ج حواجل
Bottle with a large bottom. Flagon. حَوجلة وحَوجلّة ج حواجل وحواجيل
To scarify a. o. To muzzle (a camel). To bite (a beast: stallion). To sting a. o. (snake). ✱ حَجَم o حَجمًا ه
To suck (the breasts : child). — o i ه

a. o. from. To forbid a. th. to. a. o.

To avert (an evil) حَدًّا وحَدَدَا ه عن —
from a. o. (God). To distinguish a.
th. from.

To put on حَدَّ٥ i حَدًّا وحِدَادًا , وأَحَدَّ
mourning garments (woman).

To sharpen حَدَّ٥ i حَدًّا , وحَدَّد وأَحَدَّ ه —
(a knife).

حَدَّ i حَدًّا وحَدَدًا وحِدَّة , وحَدَّدَ واحْتَدَّ واسْتَحَدَّ
To become angry with. على

To be edged (knife) ; sharp حِدَّة i —
(sword).

To be hindered by want of rain حدد
(vegetation). ✧ To work iron.

To set limits. To define a. th. ه —

To repair to a. o. إلى ول —

To counteract a. o. حَادَّ ٥ وه

To be contiguous to (land).

To look intently at. أَحَدَّ النَّظَرَ إلى

To provoke, to threaten a. o. ٥ تَحَدَّد

To be exasperated against o. a. تحَادَّ

To become intense. To be احْتَدَّ
sharpened (knife). ✧ To get into
a rage.

To shave o.'s self with اسْتَحَدَّ
a razor.

Hot tempered man. **Pungent** حَدّ ✧
(acid). Hot (sun).

Limit. End. Intensity. حَدّ ج حُدُود
Vehemence of anger. Bravery.
Strength of wine. Edge. ✧ Penalty.

Bounds set by God to human حُدُود الله
freedom. Law of God.

Contiguous. حَدّ وحَدِيد

Close to me. ✧ حَدِّي وحَدّ مَتِّي

Hastiness of temper. حِدَّة وحِ جِدَّة

Anything forbidden. Impossible. حَدَد
False (news).

God forbid that it حَدَدًا أَنْ يَكُونَ كَذَا
be so.

The utmost of حَدَادَك أَنْ يَكُونَ هذَا
thy power is to do so.

Mourning, black garments. حِدَاد

Craft of a blacksmith. حِدَادَة

حَدِيد وحَدِيدَة ج حِدَاد وحَدَائِد وحَدِيدَات
Iron. ✧ Iron-bar, rail.

Railway. ✧ سِكَّة حَدِيد

Iron-work. تَلْبِيس حَدِيد

Sharp حَدِيد وحَادّ ج أَحِدَّا وأَحِدَّة وحِدَاد

To stare at. حَجَمَ إلى

To swell (woman's breast). حَجَمَ

To suckle (a new-born child) for ل —
the first time.

To refrain. To draw back in عن —
fear from.

To ask to be cupped. اِحْتَجَمَ

Art of the cupper. حِجَامَة
Scarification.

Protuberance. ✧ Bulk. حَجْم ج حُجُوم

Camel's muzzle. حِجَام

Pink rose. حَوْجَمَة ج حَوْجَم

Cupper. حَجَّام وحَاجِم ج حُجَّام وحَجَمَة

Wont to shrink in fear (man). مِحْجَام

Cupping-glass. مِحْجَم ومِحْجَمَة ج مَحَاجِم

To bend, حَجَنَ i حَجْنًا , وحَجَّن ه ✧
to crook (a staff).

To draw a. th. with a ه واحْتَجَنَ —
hook.

To be hooked, crooked. تَحَجَّن

Crookedness. Hook. حَجَن وحُجْنَة

Lazy. Of long stage (raid). حَجُون

Crooked, hooked. أَحْجَن م حَجْنَاء ج حُجْن

Crooked staff. Hook. مِحْجَن ج مَحَاجِن

To remain in (a place). حَجَا ٥ حَجْوًا ب ✧
To be avaricious of.

To think, to deem a. th. بِهِ خَيْرًا —
good.

To keep (a secret). To propel وه ٥ —
(a boat : wind). To suppose, to
guess a. th. To reward. To withhold a. o.

To be enamoured حَجِيَ a حَجًى , وتَحَجَّى ب
of. To be attached to.

To outwit a. o. To vie حَاجَى مُحَاجَاةً ٥
with a. o. in sagacity.

Verb of wonder : How مَا أَحْجَاهُ وأَحْجِ بِهِ
worthy, how fit he is !

To remain in (a place). تَحَجَّى ب

To propose enigmas to one تَحَاجَى
another.

Sagacity, wit. حِجًى ج أَحْجَاء

Country, region. حِجًى ج أَحْجَاء

Enigma. Riddle. أُحْجِيَّة ج أَحَاجِيّ وأَحَاجٍ

Enigmatic word. كَلِمَة مُحْجِيَة

To define (a limit). حَدَّ ٥ حَدًّا ه وه ✧
To determine a. th. To punish
(a culprit).

To thrust back, to prevent عن ٥ وه —

To find (news). To produce a. th. new. To find out a. th. إِسْتَحْدَثَ هـ
Story-teller. حِدْث وحَدِث وحِدِّيث
Excrement. Unprecedented case of law. Novelty. Event. حَدَث ج أَحْدَاث
Young man. حَدَث ج أَحْدَاث وحُدْثَان
Man of agreeable conversation. رَجُل حَدِث وحَدُث
Novelty. Youth. Beginning. Freshness. حَدَاثَة
Beginning. حِدْثَان
The accidents of fortune. — وحَوَادِث الدَّهْر
Occurrence. Creation. حُدُوث
News. Story. أُحْدُوثَة ج أَحَادِيث
New. Novelty. حَادِث م حَادِثَة ج حَوَادِث
✧ Accident. Phenomenon. Case.
New. حَدِيث ج حِدَاث وحُدَثَاء
Young. — السِّنّ
Relation of an event. Tradition. News. Talk. — ج أَحَادِيث وحِدْثَان
Relater of traditions, stories. مُحَدِّث
New case of law. مُحْدَث ج مُحْدَثَات
To strike a. o. ✻ حَدَج i حَدْجًا . وأَحْدَج ه
To load (a mule). To strap (a beast).
To shoot (an arrow) at a. o. — ه ب
To throw (a fault) upon (another).
To circumvent a. o. in (a sale).
To impose a difficult (task) upon a. o.
To look intently at. — وحَدَّج ب
Colocynth. Load of water-melons. حَدَج
Load, burden. حِدْج ج حُدُوج وأَحْدَاج
Vehicle for women. حِدَاجَة ج حَدَائِج
To be thick and stout (man). ✻ حَدَر وحَدُر o حَدْرًا وحَدَارَة
To swell from beating (skin). To go down. — i o حَدْرًا
To send or let down. — حُدُورًا هـ
To let (tears) drop. To make a fold in (a garment). To discard (a muffler). To relax (the bowels: medicine).
To hasten (in reading, in walking). — وأَحْدَر هـ
To make (the skin) to swell (blow). — o حَدْرًا , وأَحْدَر هـ

(man, knife). Pungent (odour).
Sharp-tongued. — اللِّسَان
Iron plough-share. حَدِيدَة الحَرْث
Blacksmith ; ironmonger. Prison-keeper. Door-keeper. حَدَّاد
Impossible, unlawful thing. مَحْدُود
To dispel a. th. from. ✻ حَدَا a حَدْأً هـ عن
To help a. o. against. حَدِئَ a حَدَأً على
To rescue a. o. from (tyranny).
To be angry with a. o. To fondle (her child : woman).
To seek a refuge towards. — إلى
To stick to (a place). — ب
Double-headed axe. حَدَأَة ج حَدَأ وحِدَاء
A kite حِدَأَة وه حِدَايَة ج حِدَأ وحِدَاء وحِدْآن
To be protuberant. convex, humpbacked. ✻ حَدِب a حَدَبًا , وتَحَادَب
To show kindness to a. o. — على
To take care of her child (woman).
To render a. th. protuberant, convex. حَدَّب وأَحْدَب هـ وه
To become humpbacked, convex. تَحَدَّب
To devote herself to the care of her children (widow).
To show benevolence towards. — على
To be attached to a. o. — ب
To be humpbacked. إِحْدَوْدَب
Sand-drift. Wave. Scar on the skin. Severity of winter. حَدَب
Hump. Convexity. حَدَبَة
Humpbacked. Sword. Difficult undertaking. Vein of the arms. أَحْدَب
Unfruitful year. Difficult affair. Surname of Mossul. حَدْبَاء
To happen (event). ✻ حَدَث o حُدُوثًا
To be new, young. حَدُث o حَدَاثَة وحُدُوثًا
To relate a. th. to a. o. حَدَّث ه هـ وب
To relate dependently upon a. o. — عن
✧ I had a presentiment of. حَدَّثَتْنِي نَفْسِي ب
To converse with. حَادَث مُحَادَثَة ه وهـ
To furbish (a sword).
To create a. th. (God). أَحْدَث هـ
To cause, to occasion a. th.
To void ordure. أَحْدَث
To relate a. th. To speak of. تَحَدَّث ب او عن
To converse together. تَحَادَث

To have one shoulder higher than the other. حَدِلَ a حَدَلًا
To act cunningly towards a. o. حَادَلَ ه
To lean on the bow in shooting. تَحَادَلَ
Having one shoulder higher than the other. حَدِل ج حَدَالَى , وأَحْدَل ج حُدْل
Hill. حَوْدَلَة
✧ Stone-roller. مِحْدَلَة ج مَحَادِل
To be vehemently hot (day, fire) ; intense (heat). To boil fiercely (pot). ✻ حدم — إِحْتَدَمَ
To burn with anger against. تَحَدَّمَ واحْتَدَمَ عَلَى
To be intensely red (blood). To be strong (wine). إِحْتَدَمَ
Ardour of (fire). حَدْم وحَدَم
Sound of a blazing fire. حَدَمَة
To urge (camels) in singing. To drive (the clouds) along (wind). ✻ حَدَا o حَدْوًا وحُدَاء وحِدَاء ه وب
To follow (the day : night). — واحْتَدَى ه
Driving camels in singing. حَادٍ ج حُدَاة
Horse-shoe. ✧ حَذْوَة
Camel-driver. حَدَّاء
North-wind. حَدْوَاء
Song of camel-drivers. أُحْدُوَّة وأُحْدِيَّة
To settle in (a place). ✻ حَدِيَ a حَدًى ب
To purpose. a. th. حَدَّى وتَحَدَّى ه
To emulate a. o. تَحَدَّى ه
Emulation, struggle, battle. حُدَيَّا
To cut off, to curtail. ✻ حَذَّ o حَذًّا ه
Light-handedness. Lightness in wagging the tail. حَذَذ
Light-handed. Light-tailed. Having scanty hair (horse) ; scanty feathers (bird). Lean, slender. أَحَذّ م حَذَّاء ج حُذّ
To beware of. To caution o.'s self against a. o. ✻ حَذِرَ a حَذَرًا وحِذْرًا ه
To warn, to caution a. o. حَذَّرَ ه
To guard against a. o. حَاذَرَ ه
To be wary, cautious of. To guard against. — وتَحَذَّرَ مِن واحْتَذَرَ ه
Caution. Warning. حِذْر وحَذَر
Beware of. (Verbal name.) حَذَارِ
Cautious, prudent. حَذِر ج حَذِرُون
Ready. حَاذِر ج حَاذِرُون

To come down ; to fall down (tears, rain). تَحَدَّرَ وتَحَادَرَ
To go down a declivity. To be swollen (skin). إِنْحَدَرَ
Slope, declivity. حُدُور وحَدْرَاء وحَادُور وأُحْدُور وحَدَر ومُنْحَدَر
Flow of tears. حَدُورَة
Swelling at the corner of the eye. حَدْرَة
Fat, comely (youth). Thick (spear). Great (number). Lofty (mountain). Populated (district). Strongly woven (rope). حَادِر م حَادِرَة
Strong in the thighs and lank in the belly (horse). أَحْدَر م حَدْرَاء
Apple of the eye. حُنْدُر وحُنْدُور وحُنْدُورَة
Short. Lion. Hard. Pebbles. حَيْدَر
Lion. Perdition. حَيْدَرَة
To surmise. To guess a. th. To speak conjecturally of. To hasten (the walk). ✻ حَدَسَ i o حَدْسًا فِي
To go at random. — فِي الأَرْض
To throw a. o. down. — ه
To tread a. th. under foot. — ه وه بِرِجْلِهِ
To inquire stealthily about (news). تَحَدَّسَ ه وعَن
Conjectures. Hypotheses. حَدْسِيَّات
Prostrated. حَدِيس ومَحْدُوس
Object of inquiries. Aim in view. مَحْدِس
To be intensely dark (night). ✻ حَنْدَسَ وتَحَنْدَسَ
To throw, to fling a. th. (for حَذَفَ ه) ✧ حَدَفَ ه
To surround, to encompass. a. o. or a. th. ✻ حَدَقَ i حَدْقًا , وأَحْدَقَ وإِحْدَوْدَقَ ب
To look at a. o. — ه بِعَيْنِهِ
To gaze at. حَدَّقَ إِلَى
Pupil of the eye. حَدَقَة ج حَدَق وحَدَقَات وأَحْدَاق وحِدَاق
Walled garden. Solanum. حَدَق ج حَدَقَة
Fruit-garden. حَدِيقَة ج حَدَائِق
Sour, acid. ◻ حَدُوق
Wild lotus. خَنْدَقُوق وحَنْدَقُوقَى بَرِّيّ
Melilot (*plant*). — بُسْتَانِيّ
To wrong a. o. ✻ حَدَلَ i حَدْلًا وحُدُولًا عَلَى
✧ To roll (a terrace). — ه

To break in (a horse). ه —
To hurry on. وتحذلم —
To cut a. th. ✻ حذم i حذمًا ه
To hurry in (a work). في —
Cutting (sword). حذِم وحِذيَم
Name of a keen-sighted woman حَذَامِ surnamed زَرْقَاء اليَمَامَة.
Sluggish, lazy. حذام
Sharp sword. مِحذَم
To make (shoes) for a. o. ✻ حذا o حَذوًا وحِذاء ه ل
To put, to give (shoes) to a. o. وأحذى ه ه —
To make (shoes) on measure. ه ب —
To imitate a. o. حَذوَ فلان —
To be over against, opposite to a. th. or. a. o. وحاذى مُحاذاة وحِذاء ه وه —
To sit opposite to one another. تحاذى
To put on sandals. إحتذى
To imitate a. o. إحتذى مِثال فلان
To ask sandals from. إستحذى ه
Opposite to, over against. حِذاء وحِذة وحَذو وحُذوة
Gift. Piece of flesh. حِذوة
Sandals, shoes. Sole of a horse. حِذاء ج أحذية
In front of, opposite to. مُحاذٍ
To burn (the tongue : vinegar). To tear a. th. to pieces. To cut (the hand). ✻ حذى i حذيًا ه
To speak (evil) of a. o. ه ب —
To give a. o. a share of. أحذى ه ه
To thrust a. o. with (a spear).
To share a. th. with. تحاذى ه
Allotment of booty. حُذيا وحُذيا وحُذاية وحذية
Share of spoils. Gratuity given to a bringer of good news. حُذيا
To be freed (slave). ✻ حرّ a حرارًا
To be free-born (man). حُرّية —
To be thirsty. حَرّة —
To be hot, (day, fight). حرّ o i حرّ وحُرورًا وحَرارة
To be feverish. ✧ حُر
To free (a slave). To devote a. o. to (God's service). To compose (a writing) accurately. To write a. th. elegantly. To render (a balance, an account) accurate. حرّر ه وه

Cautioner. حذِير
I caution thee against him. أنا حذيرك منه
Reciprocal fear and caution. مُحاذرة
Danger. Dread. Inconvenience. مَحذور
Fear. Evil dreaded. War. مَحذورة
To take off, to curtail, to strike off a. th. ✻ حذف i حذفًا ه
To strike a. o. with (a sword). ه ب —
To perform (a work) cleverly. To trim (verses). حذّف ه
To put off. To act dilatorily with a. o. ✧ حاذف ه
Elision, curtailment. حذف
Leather clippings. Remainder of a meal. حُذافة
Side. ✻ حِذفار وحُذفور ج حذافير
Prepare thyself. اشدُد حذافيرك
He took it altogether. أخذه بحذفاره وبحُذفوره وبحذافيره
To be clever, skilled in (an art). To perform a. th. cleverly. To know a. th. thoroughly. ✻ حذق i وحذِق a حِذقًا وحَذاقة ه وفي
To bite the tongue (vinegar). حذق o حُذوقًا
To cut a. th. حذقًا ه i —
To render a. o. skilful. حذّق ه
To be cut, broken. إنحذق
Skilfulness, cleverness. حِذق وحَذاقة
Broken piece, fragment. حُذقة ج حُذاق
Mouthful. حُذاقة
Clever, skilled. Pungent (vinegar). Penetrating (mind). حاذق ج حُذّاق
To lose the eyelash. To have red eyelids (eye). ✻ حذِل a حذلًا
To cause (the eyes) to swell and (the eyelash) to fall (tears, heat). أحذل ه
Inclination, propensity. حذل
Skirt of a garment. وحِذل وحُذل —
Fall of the eyelash. Red tumour on the eye. حذل
Red gum. Remains of straw. حُذالة
Losing the eyelash (eye). حاذلة ج حُذّال
To show skill. To make a show of skilfulness. ✻ حذلق وتحذلق
To cut out (wood) in a pointed shape. ✻ حذلم ه

legs. To be widened (place).

War, battle, fight. حَرْب ج حُرُوب
Enemy. Warrior.

Seat of the war. دَار الحَرْب
The enemy's country.

Pertaining to war. حَرْبِيّ

Javelin Bayonet. Spear-head. حَرْبَة ج حِرَاب

Corruption of belief. — ج حَرْبَات وحَرَبَات
Spear-thrust. Plunder. Friday.

Alas! What a pity! وَاحَرَبَاه

Chameleon. حِرْبَاء م حِرْبَاءَة ج حَرَابِيّ

Easily excited; angered. حَرِب ج حَرْبَى

Spoiled. Plundered. حَرِيب ج حَرْبَى حُرَبَاء

Warrior, warlike. مِحْرَب ومِحْرَاب و✧ حَرْبَجِي

Upper end of a house. مِحْرَاب ج مَحَارِيب
First seat in a place. Palace. Direction of Mecca. Covert of a lion. Niche in a mosque. Private apartments of a prince. Synagogue.

To rub a. th. energetically. ✧ To work hard. ❋ حَرَت o حَرْتًا ه

To be ill-tempered. حَرِت a حَرَتًا

To till and sow (the earth). ❋ حَرَث o i حَرْثًا

To cut a. th. round. To acquire (goods). To study a. th. thoroughly. To stir (the fire). To crumble (bread). — ه

To exhaust (a beast: rider). — وأَحْرَث

To cultivate, to plough (the land). حَرَّث واحْتَرَث ه

To earn wealth. إِحْتَرَث ه

Land prepared for sowing. حَرْث
Tillage. Track of a road.

The land and its produces. الحَرْث والنَّسْل

Gain, earning. حَرِيثَة ج حَرَائِث

Tillage; cultivation. حِرَاثَة

Cultivator, plougher, tiller. حَارِث وحَرَّاث

Plough. مِحْرَث ومِحْرَاث ج مَحَارِث ومَحَارِيث
Poker for stirring the fire.

To be contracted (heart). To be narrow (place). To be guilty. To be dazzled (eye). To heap up (dust). ❋ حَرِج a حَرَجًا

To gnash the teeth. — o حَرْجًا

✧ To write (a letter). To straighten (a board). To point (a gun).

To become hot (day). أَحَرّ

To be freed (slave). تَحَرَّر

To be hot, vehement (fight). إِسْتَحَرّ

Hot (pepper, sun). ✧ حَرّ

Heat. حَرّ ج حُرُور

Heat of the sun. Hot wind in the night. حَرُور

Heat. Ardour, inflammation. حَرَارَة

Thermometer. مِيزَان الحَرَارَة

Freedom (*opp. to slavery*). Freedom from passions. Political liberty. ✧ Unrestraint. حُرُورَة وحُرِّيَّة وحُرُورِيَّة

Silk; silk-cloth. حَرِير

A piece of silk-cloth. A soup made of flour and milk. حَرِيرَة

Manufacturer of silk stuff. حَرِيرِيّ

Free-born. Blood-horse. حُرّ ج أَحْرَار
Generous. Choice part. Pure, unmixed. ✧ Frank, speaking plainly.

Middle of the house. — الدَّار

Cheek; cheek-bone. — الوَجْه

Stony tract. حَرَّة ج حَرّ وحِرَار وحَرَّات

Free; well-born (woman). حُرَّة ج حَرَائِر

A burning thirst. حِرَّة

The liberal party. الأَحْرَار

Hot, ardent. Hard (work). حَارّ

Thirsty. حَرَّان م حَرَّى

Enfranchisement. تَحْرِير ج تَحَارِير
✧ Letter. Redaction.

Chief clerk. Chief editor. مُدِير التَّحْرِيرَات

Heated by anger. Feverish. مَحْرُور

To prick the tongue (pepper). ✧ حَرْحَر

To be bitten (tongue). ✧ تَحَرْحَر

To plunder a. o. ❋ حَرَب o حَرْبًا ه

To ask a. th. importunately. ▫ — عَلَى

To be vehemently angry. حَرِب a حَرَبًا
To be affected with canine madness.

To provoke; to excite a. o. حَرَّب ه وه
To sharpen (an arrow-head).

To wage war with; to battle with. حَارَب مُحَارَبَة وحِرَابًا ه

To stir up (war). أَحْرَب ه

To lead (an army). — ه

To wage war one with another. تَحَارَب واحْتَرَب

To be ready to do mischief. إِحْرَنْبَى
To lay on the back in raising the

To be prohibited to a.o. (prayer). — على
To make a. th. difficult : to forbid it. حرّج ه
To ask a. th. importunately. — في
✧ To put up for auction.
✧ To urge ; to insist upon. حرّج على
To incite a. o. to crime. أحرج ه
To put a. o. in a strait. To force up (a beast) to a strait.
To forbid (prayer) to a. o. — ه على
To keep aloof from sin. تحرّج
Narrow space. Sin. Crime. حرج
Litter. Thicket.
Thou art not guilty. لا حرج عليك
Crime. Snare for wild beasts. Linen set on a rope for drying. حرج ج حراج
Cowry. Quarry given to the hounds. Flock. — ج أحراج
Thicket of impenetrable trees. حرج
Fighting incessantly.
Herd of camels. حرجة ج حرج وحرجات
Thicket of trees.
✧ Public sale, sale by auction. حراج
He swore by the most sacred things. حلف بالمُحرّجات
✱ Thin and swift she-camel. Cold wind. حُرجُوج ج حراجيج
✱ To become tall. To run fast ; to run to and fro. حرجل
Large wingless locust. حرجل
Troop of horses. Swarm of locusts. Lameness. حرجلة
✱ To drive back (camels). حرجم ه
To gather and press (crowd, beasts). To swerve from (a resolution). إحرنجم
✱ To be enraged against. To bear rancour to. ✧ To pout at. حرد a حردًا على
To purpose a. th. To pierce (wood) حرد i حردًا ه
To withhold a. o. — ه
To seclude o.'s self from. — i حرودًا عن
To betake o.'s self to a hut. حرّد
To hinder, to restrain a. o. — ه
To twist (a rope). — ه
To set a. th. apart. أحرد ه
To yield little حارد مُحاردة وحِرادًا
milk (she-camel) ; little rain (year).
To remain. To shoot (star). إنحرد
Anger, rancour. حرد
Roof of reeds. حرديّ ج حراديّ
Angry, exasperated. حارد وحرد وحردان
Apart. حرد وحريد ج حِراد , ومُنحرد
✱ Stellion (lizard). حِرذون ج حراذين
✱ To keep a. o. or a. th. حرز o حرزًا ه وه
To be on the watch. حرز a حرزًا
✧ To be important (affair).
It is not worth while. ✧ هذا لا يحرز
To be well fortified (place). حرز o حرازة
To preserve a. th. حرّز ه وه
To afford a safe refuge to a. o. (place).
To guard (property) carefully. أحرز ه
To afford a safe refuge to. أحرز ه
To guard against. تحرّز واحترز من
Safe refuge. Amulet. حِرز ج أحراز
Die for gaming. حَرز ج أحراز
Choice part of goods. حرزة
Well fortified, secure. حريز
✱ To guard, to watch over. حرس o حرسًا وحراسة
To steal (a ewe). — حرسًا , واحترس ه
✧ To keep a. th. carefully. حرس على
To live long. حرس a حرسًا
To guard against. تحرّس واحترس من
Watch, caution. حرس واحتراس
Time, century. حرس ج أحراس
Life-guards. حرس السّلطان
A life-guard. حرسيّ ج حرسيّة
The day and the night. الحرسان
✧ Careful of. حريس على
Enclosure. Ewe stolen during the night. حريسة ج حرائس
Keeper. Robber. حارس ج حُرّاس وحرسة
The Guardian Angel. الملاك الحارس
Very old. أحرس
Kept. ✧ Son. محروس
Kept, *fem.* ✧ Capital town. محروسة
The Ottoman Empire. الممالك المحروسة
✱ To hunt (lizards). To scratch a. o. حرش i حرشًا وتحراشًا , واحترش ه
To be rough to the skin. حرش a حرشًا
To beguile a. o. — ه
To provoke, to set (men حرّش بين

dogs) one against another.
To fight with. حارَش ه
To oppose a. o. تحرَّش ب
To earn for (o.'s family). إحتَرَش ل
Mark. Company. حَرْش ج حِرَاش
¤ Species of cucumber.
Wood, forest. ✧ حُرْش ج أحرَاش وحُرُوش
Roughness, coarseness. حُرْشة وحُرَاش
Ear-wig, myriapod. حَرِيش ج حُرُش
Rough to the skin. Lizard. New coin. أحرَش م حَرشاء
Black lizard-hunting snake. حُرَّاش
Swarm of locusts. Young ones of animals. Fish-scales. ✱ حَرشَف ج حَرَاشِف
To rend (a stuff) in beating it (dyer). ✱ حَرَص o حَرصًا ه
To covet a. th. حَرَص i وحَرِص a حِرصًا على
To be eaten up (pasture). حُرِص
To render a. o. eager of. To urge, to incite a. o. to. حَرَّص ه على
Wound tearing the skin. Hole in a garment. حَرصة وحارِصة
Hankering, covetous. Greedy. Niggardly. حَرِيص ج حُرَصاء وحِرَاص
Cloud pouring a heavy rain. حَرِيصة
To become emaciated. To be disordered, profligate. ✱ حَرَض i o حُرُوضًا ، وحَرِض a حَرَضًا
To be worn out by anxiety, grief, debauchery. حَرُض o حَرَاضة
To urge, to instigate a. o. to. حَرَّض ه على
To do a. th. perseveringly. حارَض على
To bring a. o. to the point of death (sorrow). To disorder a. o. (love). أحرَض ه
Disorder in body, mind, morals. Emaciated by love, grief. Wicked. حَرَض
Diseased and vicious. Debauchee. حَرَض وحَرِض وحارِض
Kali. Potash. حُرُض وحُرْض
Fallen and unable to rise. حَرِيض ومُحرَض
Disordered by grief, debauchery. Shameful (speech). مُحَرَّض
To turn away. To discard a. o. from. ✱ حَرَف i حَرفًا ه عن
To earn for (o.'s family). — ل
To change a. th. To alter (a word, a book). To tamper with. To cut (a writing-reed) obliquely. حَرَّف ه
To repay evil to a. o. حارَف ه بِسُوء
To probe (a wound). — ه
To become rich. أحرَف
To ill-treat a. o. — ه
To turn away from. تحرَّف وانحَرَف عن
✧ To use shifts for a livelihood. تحارَف
To deviate, to swerve from. إنحَرَف عن
To practice a craft. To be crafty. إحتَرَف
Margin. Extremity, end. Border. Summit (of a mountain). Edge (of a blade). حَرْف ج حِرَف
Letter (of the alphabet). Word. Particle (one of the three divisions of the Arabic grammar). حَرْف ج حُرُوف وأحرُف
Litteral (meaning). حَرْفِي
Litterally, word by word. حَرْفِيًّا
Craft, profession. ✧ Shift. حِرْفة ج حِرَف
Nasturtium (*plant*). حُرْف
Thlaspi (*plant*). حُرْف السُّطوح وه حُرفُوف
Water-cress. حُرْف الماء
Bad luck. حُرْفة
Fellow-worker. Artisan. حَرِيف ج حُرَفاء
Acritude of a dish. حَرَافة
Biting the tongue (dish). حِرِّيف
Altered. ✧ Angular (body). مُحَرَّف
Unlucky. Using shifts. مُحارَف
Surgeon's probe. مِحرَاف ج مَحَارِيف
Oblique. Trapezoid. ✧ Indisposed. مُنحَرِف
To file. To rub a. th. ✱ حَرَق o حَرْقًا ه
✧ To heat (the blood). To scorch a. o. (sun).
To burn down a. th. — ه بالنار
✧ To distress a. o. حرَق قلبَه
To gnash the teeth at. حَرَق o i نابَه على
To fall off (hair). حَرِق a حَرَقًا
To burn down a th. حَرَّق وأحرَق ه وه
To be burnt down. تحرَّق واحتَرَق
Combustion. Hole in a garment. حَرَق
Inflammation (of a limb). حُرْقة وحَرَقة
Sharp (sword). حُرْقة وحارُوقة وحُرَّاقة
Upper part of the uvula. الحَرقُوة
Burning. حِرَاق وحُرَاق
Brine. Salt water. حُرَاق وحُرَاق
✧ Fire-ship. Bomb. حَرَّاقة ج حَرَّاقات

Blister.

Gruel of flour and water. حَرُوقَة ج حَرَائِق

Fire, conflagration. حَرِيق ج حَرْقَى

Heat. Gruel. ✧ Combustion. حَرِيقَة

Stinging nettle. حُرَّيق

Holocaust, burnt-offering. مُحْرَقَة ج مُحْرَقَات

Root of the tongue. ✱ حِرْقِد ج حَرَاقِد

Pomum Adami. حَرْقَدَة

✧ To fry (meat). ✧ حَرْقَص ه و ة
 To vex, to enrage a. o.

Winged insect. حُرْقُوص ج حَرَاقِيص
 ✧ Piece of fried meat.

Head of the haunch-bone. ✱ حَرْقَفَة ج حَرَاقِف

To move about. ✱ حَرُكَ o حَرْكًا وحَرَكَةً

To wound (a horse) on the withers. حَرَكَ o حَرْكًا ة

To set in motion. To rouse, to excite a. o. To move a. o. to pity. To mark (a letter) with a vowel. حَرَّكَ ة وه

To be set in motion. تَحَرَّكَ
 ✧ To intrigue. To set off. To be moved (heart). To be marked with a vowel.

Upper part of the back. Horse's withers. حَارِك

Movement. Gesture. حَرَكَة ج حَرَكَات
 Vowel. ✧ Proceedings. Emotion. Revolution. Nimbleness.

Light-handed. Nimble. ذو , صاحِب حَرَكَة

Movement, accentuation. حَرَاك

Light, lively, sprightly (child). حَرِك

Weak-waisted, impotent. حَرِيك

Wooden poker. ✧ Agitator. مِحْرَاك

Upper extremity of the neck. مَحْرَك

The mover (of the world) (God). المُحَرِّك

To rummage, to stir up a. th. ✧ حَرْكَش ه

✧ حركَث — حرْكَثَة ج حَرَاكِث وحَرَاكِيث
Head of the haunch-bone.

✱ حَرَمَ i حِرْمًا وحَرِيمًا وحِرْمَانًا وحِرْمًا وحِرْمَة وحَرِمَةً وحَرِيمَةً

To prevent a. o. from. To deprive a. o. of a. th. To forbid a. th. to. ة ه

To forbid a. th. — ة وه
 ✧ To excommunicate a. o.

حَرِمَ a حَرَمًا وحَرَامًا , وحَرُمَ o حُرْمًا وحُرُمًا وحُرْمَةً وحَرَامًا على

To be forbidden.

To lose at play. حَرِمَ a حَرَمًا

To forbid, to declare a. th. to be unlawful, sacred, inviolable. حَرَّمَ ه

To win a. o. at play. — وأحْرَمَ ة

To go to the pilgrimage. أَحْرَمَ
 To seek refuge in a sacred place.
 To commit a. th. unlawful.

To render a. th. sacred, unlawful. — ه

To be forbidden, sacred. تَحَرَّمَ

To seek protection from. — ب

To show regard to. اِحْتَرَمَ ة وه
 To hold a. th. as sacred.

Prohibition. حِرْم ج حُرُوم
 ✧ Anathema.

Thing sacred. Harem. Wife. Sanctuary. حَرَم ج أَحْرَام

Unluckiness. ✧ Privation. حِرْمَان

Mecca and Medinah. الحَرَمَان

Protection. Reverence. Luck. Inviolable thing. Respectable woman. ✧ Wife. حُرْمَة ج حُرَم

✧ For the sake of. بِحُرْمَة فُلَان

حَرِيم ج حُرُم وأحَارِيم , وحَرَم ج أحْرَام

Apartments of women. Women subject to one man. ✧ Moslem women (*generally*).

Unattainable thing. حَرِيمَة

Sin, unlawful thing. Sacred. Venerable. حَرَام (*opp. to* حَلَال) ج حُرُم

✧ It is a shame for thee. حَرَام عَلَيْكَ

Rascal. Bastard. إِبْن حَرَام

Mecca. بِلَاد الحَرَام

The Caaba. أَلْبَيْت الحَرَام

Blanket used as a garment. ✧ حِرَام

Rites of the pilgrimage to Mecca. إِحْرَام

✧ Thief. Dishonest man. حَرَامِيّ ج حَرَامِيَّة

First month of the Mohammedan year, (inviolable). مُحَرَّم والشَّهْر الحَرَام

Illicit action. Crime. مَحْرَم ج مَحَارِم

✧ Pocket handkerchief. مَحْرَمَة ج مَحَارِم

Black and fetid slime. ✱ حَرْمَد

Unfruitful year. ✱ حِرْمِس ج حَرَامِس

Rue (*medicinal plant*). ✱ حَرْمَل

To stop on a sudden. To be restive (beast). ✱ حَرَنَ وحَرُنَ o حِرَانًا وحِرَانًا وحُرُونًا

He sold at the right price. حَرَنَ في البَيْع
Restiveness of a horse. حِرَان وحُرُون
Restive (horse). حَرُون و ◻ حَرْنَان ج حُرُن
Burning in the throat. ✱ حرو — حَرْوَة
Sparkling of fire. Rustling of trees shaken by the wind. حَرَاة
Pungency of mustard. حرَاوَة
To decrease. ✱ حَرَى i حَرْيًا
To cause a. th. to wane (time). أَحْرَى ه
How worthy of it he is. مَا أَحْرَاهُ بِهِ
To select the best of. تَحَرَّى في
To choose a. th. To propose a. th. — ه
To remain in (a place). — ب
Rather, more likely. بِالحَرِيّ
Convenient. Suitable. Fit to. Worthy of. حَرِيّ ج أَحْرِيَاء ب
Noise, sound. Twittering (of birds). Area of a house. Retreat of gazelles. Becoming, fit. حَرًى ج أَحْرَاء
I stopped in his neighbourhood. نَزَلْتُ بِحَرَاهُ
A short viper. حَارِيَة
More adapted; more suited. أَحْرَى
How much more. A fortiori. بِالأَحْرَى و ✧ بِالحَرِيّ
It is better for thee to. الأَحْرَى بِكَ أَن
To cut, to make an incision in a th. ✱ حَزَّ o حَزًّا , وحَزَّز واحْتَزَّ ه
To examine a. th. حَازَّ مُحَازَّةً وحِزَازًا ه
To be notched, cut. تَحَزَّز
To cut (the head). إِحْتَزَّ ه
Incision. Season. Speaking roughly. حَزّ ج حُزُوز
Pain in the heard. Painful state. حَزَّة
Slice (of melon). ✧ حِزَّة
Scurf of the head. Herpes. Violent impression of anger or grief. Eczema, humid scall. حَزَاز وحَزَازَة
Liver-wort (*plant*). حَزَاز الصَّخْر
Acidity of the stomach. حُزَّاز
Active and haughty man. حَزِيز ج حُزَّان وأَحِزَّة وحُزُز
Scruples, perplexing affairs. حَوَازّ القُلُوب
Notch. مَحَزّ
Knife for making notches. Rough (man). مِحَزّ ج مَحَازّ
To gather and ✱ حَزَأَ a حَزْءًا ه وة

drive (camels).
To befall and distress a. o. (misfortune). To divide (a book) into sections. ✱ حَزَبَ o حَزْبًا ة وه
To muster (people), to form (a party). حَزَّبَ ة
To become the partisan of. حَازَبَ ة
To form into parties, federation. تَحَزَّبَ
حَازِب ج حَوَازِب , وحَزِيب ج حُزْب وحُزُب Distressing event.
Party of men. Confederacy. Division. حِزْب ج أَحْزَاب
Accomplice. Partisan. مُتَحَزِّب
Bulky and short. Cock. Wild carrots. حِنْزَاب
To measure. To guess, to conjecture a. th. ✱ حَزَرَ i o حَزْرًا ومَحْزَرَةً ه
To become sour (milk). — حَزْرًا وحُزُورًا
✧ To propose an enigma to. ✧ حَزَّرَ ة
Diviner. Sour (milk, wine). حَازِر
Conjecture. Divination. حَزْر ومَحْزَرَة
Choice part of a. th. حَزْرَة ج حَزَرَات
Enigma, riddle. ✧ حَزُّورَة
June (month). S حَزِيرَان و ✧ حُزَيْرَان
To break wind (ass). ✱ حَزَقَ i حَزْقًا ه
To tighten (a rope). To compress a. th. To press out. — ه
To bind a. o. with (a rope). — ة ب
To hinder a. o. أَحْزَقَ ة
To be contracted. تَحَزَّقَ
Pinched by narrow boots. حَازِق
Party of men. Flight of (birds). Swarm of bees. حِزْق وحِزْقَة وحَازِقَة وحَزَاقَة
Party of men. حَزِيقَة ج حَزَائِق وحَزِيق وحُزُق
Walking at a short pace. حُزُقّ وحُزُقّ وحُزُقَّة وحُزُقَّة
Tenacious. حُزُقّ ومُتَحَزِّق
✧ Prone to anger. حُزُقَّة
Hiccough. ✧ حَازُوقَة وحَزُوقَة و ◻ حَزْقَة
Narrow-necked (ewer). مَحْزُوق العُنُق
To rise above the mirage (mountain). To be contracted (heart). To be gathered. ✱ حزل — إِحْزَأَلَّ
Short. حَوْزَل وحَوْزَلَة
To pack up, to bundle up (goods). To strap ✱ حَزَمَ i حَزْمًا , وحَزَّمَ ه وة

Physiognomist. حازٍ
To blast (the plants : cold). To slaughter (people). To curry (a beast). To put (meat) on burning coals. To cover (bread) with burning coals. ✻ حَسَّ o حَسًّا ه وه
To feel, to perceive a. th. ✧ To have a presentiment of. — i حَسًّا وأَحَسَّ ه
To be certain of. حَسَّ a حَسًّا ب
To make a. o. to feel. حسّس ه وهـ
To awake ; to rouse a. o. ✧ To feel with the hand, to grope.
To know, to perceive a. th. To feel a. th. أَحَسَّ وأَحَسَى ه ب و✧ إِسْتَحَسَّ
To listen to (news). To seek. To perceive a. th. by the senses. تَحَسَّسَ ه
To inquire about a. th. — مِن
To be pulled out (tooth). إِنْحَسَّ
Feeling ; presentiment. Voice. حِسّ
Currying of a horse. Cunning. حَسّ
State. حِسَّة
Sense, faculty of feeling. Locust. Wind. حَاسَّة ج حَوَاسّ
The five senses. الحَوَاسّ
Slight noise. حَسِيس
Small dry fishes. Cuttings of stones. Inauspicious. حُسَاس
Currycomb. مِحَسَّة
✧ To grope. To act waveringly. ✻ حَسْحَسَ
To roast (meat) on coals. — ه
To pity, to compassionate a. o. — ل
✻ حَسَب o حَسْبًا وحِسَابًا وحُسْبَانًا وحِسْبَة وحِسَابَة ه
To number, to reckon a. th. ✧ To mind a. th.
✧ To take a. th. into account, to foresee a. th. حَسَب حِسَابًا
To think, to suppose a. o. or a. th. *to be such or so.* حَسِبَ a i حِسْبَانًا ومَحْسَبَة ومَحْسِبَة ه وه
To be noble-born. حَسُبَ o حَسَبًا وحَسَابَة
To place a pillow for a. o. To give to a. o. food and drink to satiety. To bury a. o. حَسَّبَ ه
To settle an account with. حَاسَبَ مُحَاسَبَة ه
To be tawny (camel). To satisfy a. o. To satiate a. o. ✧ To take a. o. for. أَحْسَبَ

(a beast).
To be choked. حَزِمَ a حَزَمًا
To be resolute, self-confident. حَزُمَ o حَزْمًا وحَزَامَة وحُزُومَة
To strap (a horse). أَحْزَمَ ه
To be girt. To girdle o.'s self. تَحَزَّمَ واحْتَزَمَ
To be collected (things). To become big-bellied. To be rugged (place). إِحْزَوْزَمَ
Resolution. حَزْم وحَزَامَة وحُزُومَة
Strap, girth of a saddle. Silk or cotton girdle. حِزَامَة وحِزَام ج حَزَائِم وحُزُم
Obstruction in the throat. حَزَم
Bundle. Ball. ✧ Bunch of flowers. حُزْمَة
Resolute. حَازِم ج حَزَمَة ، وحَزِيم ج حُزَمَاء
Waist. Middle of the breast. حَزِيم ج حُزُم وأَحْزِمَة
Broad-breasted. أَحْزَم
Chest. Middle of the chest. حَيْزُوم ج حَيَازِيم وحَيَازِم
Part of the body covered by the girth. Waist. مَحْزِم
Girth. ✧ Apron, wrapper. مِحْزَم ج مَحَازِم
To grieve a. o. ✻ حَزَنَ o حُزْنًا ، وحَزَّنَ وأَحْزَنَ ه
To be grieved about. حَزِنَ a حَزَنًا وحُزْنًا عَلَى او ل
To walk upon a hard ground. أَحْزَنَ
To be sad, sorry. تَحَزَّنَ وتَحَازَنَ واحْتَزَنَ
Sorrow. Grief. حُزْن وحَزَن ج أَحْزَان
Mourning. ✧ حُزْن
Rugged and hard ground. حَزْن ج حُزُون
Charge of a household, family cares. حُزَانَة
Ruggedness of the soil. حُزُونَة
Grieved. حَزِن وحَزِين ج حُزَنَاء وحِزَان وحَزَانَى
Wearing, mourning. ✧ حَزِين وحَزْنَان
To augur a. th. from the flight of birds. To guess ; to conjecture. ✻ حَزَا o حَزْوًا ، وحَزَى i حَزْيًا ، وتَحَزَّى ه
To raise (figures) in the air (looming). حَزَا o وحَزَّى ه
To be lofty, prominent. أَحْزَى
To know a. th. — ب
Umbelliferous plant. حَزًى وحَزَاء (un. حَزَاة)

To be jaded (camel). — حَسَرًا ، وحَسِر حَسَرًا
To disclose a. th. — o i حَسْرًا ه
To bark (a bough). To jade (a camel). To sweep (a house).
To sigh for. حَسِر a حَسَرًا وحَسْرَةً على
To lose its feathers (bird). حَسَّر
To make a. o. to sigh. — ه
To harm a. o. To despise a. o.
To tire out (a beast). أَحْسَر ه
To sigh for, to regret a. th. تَحَسَّر على
To be disclosed. ✧ To be sorry. إِنْحَسَر
To be tired (man, beast). إِسْتَحْسَر
Presbyopie. حَسَر
Sigh, regret. Sorrow. حَسْرَة ج حَسَرات
✧ Reluctantly. بِحَسْرَة
Alas! What a pity! يا حَسْرَتي ، واحَسْرَتاه
Tired. Weak. Regretful. حَسِير ج حَسْرَى
Presbyope, for-sighted. حَسِير وأَحْسَر
Without helmet nor coat of mail or turban. حاسِر ج حَوَاسِر
Misfortune, calamity. تَحْسِير ج تَحَاسِير
Fatigued, sad, regretful.
Weak-sighted. حَسِير ومَحْسُور البَصَر
Known state. Face. Nature. مَحْسِر ج مَحَاسِر
To hiss (snake). ✻ حَسَف i حَسْفًا وحَسِيفًا
To pick out, to cull (dates). To tend (a flock). To take off (the crust of a wound). — حَسْفًا ه و ه
To reap (corn). — حَسْفًا وحُسَافًا ه
To be angered with. حَسِف a حَسَفًا ل
To pick out (dates). حَسَّف ه
To mix (dates) with their dregs. أَحْسَف ه
To be scratched (skin). تَحَسَّف
To fall off (hair).
To be smashed. إِنْحَسَف
Hissing of snakes. حَسْف وحَسِيف
Enmity, anger. حَسِيفَة وحُسَافَة
Refuse of dates. Scanty water. حُسَافَة
To be angry with. ✻ حَسِك a حَسَكًا على
To eat barley (beast). حَسِك
✧ To be choked with a fish-bone. حَسَّك
To store the remainder of. — ه
To give barley to (a beast). أَحْسَك ه
Star-thistle. Grappling iron. حَسَك
Prickly hedge. ✧ Fish-bone.

He gave bountifully. أَعْطَى فَأَحْسَب
To recline upon a pillow. تَحَسَّب
✧ To caution o.'s self.
To inquire about (news). — ه
To know and befriend a. o.
To settle accounts together. تَحَاسَب
To think, to believe a. th. إِحْتَسَب ه
To be content with. — ه وب
To disapprove a. o. for a. th. — ه على
He lost his elder son. — وَلَدًا لَهُ
Sufficiency. Burial. حَسْب
A dirhem is sufficient for thee. حَسْبُكَ وبِحَسْبِكَ دِرْهَم
Quantity, amount. حَسَب ج أَحْسَاب
Personal merit. Noble descent.
This is equal, tantamount to that. هٰذَا بِحَسَبِ ذٰلِكَ
Reckoning. Sufficiency. حِسَاب ج حُسْبَان
Great number of people.
Running-account. حِسَاب جَارٍ
Old style (Julian). حِسَاب شَرْقِيّ
New style (Gregorian). حِسَاب غَرْبِيّ
Arithmetic. عِلْم الحِسَاب
The day of judgment. يَوْم الحِسَاب
Account. Burying of the dead. Reward. حِسْبَة ج حِسَب
Honourable, noble. حَسِيب ج حُسَبَاء
Thou shalt account with God. حَسْبُكَ وحَسِيبُكَ الله
God alone is sufficient. كَفَى بِاللهِ حَسِيبًا
Opinion, conjecture. حِسْبَان
Punishment. Small arrow. حُسْبَان
Small pillow. Small ant. حُسْبَانَة
Thunderbolt. Cloud. Hailstone.
Accountant. حَاسِب ج حَسَبَة
Tawny camel. Red-haired (man). White from disease (skin). أَحْسَب
Audit-office. Book-keeping. مُحَاسَبَة
Inspector of weights and measures. مُحْتَسِب
To envy, to grudge a. o. for. ✻ حَسَد o i حَسَدًا ، وحَسَّد ه ه او على
To find a. o. envious. أَحْسَد ه
To grudge one another. تَحَاسَد
Grudge, envy. حَسَد
حَاسِد ج حُسَّاد وحُسَّد وحَسَدَة ، وحَسُود ج حُسُد
Grudging, envious.
Incentive to envy. مَحْسَدَة
To be tired (sight). ✻ حَسَر a حُسُورًا

Barley. Urchin. حَسِيكَة
Rancour, ill-will. حَسِيكَة وَحَسَكَة وَحُسَاكَة
Rubbish. ✻ حِسْكِل ج حَسَاكِل وحِسْكِلَة
Shatters of iron.
To urge on ✻ حَسَل o حَسْلًا ة وه
(a beast). To cast off a. th.
To leave the refuse of a. th. — مِن
To be reviled. حُسِل بِهِ
To revile o.'s self. حَسَّل بِنَفْسِهِ
To hunt lizards. تَحَسَّل واحْتَسَل
Lizard newly hatched. حِسْل ج حُسُول وأَحْسَال وحِسْلَان وحِسَلَة
Lizard. أَبُو حِسْل وأَبُو حُسَيْل
Silver filings. حُسَالَة
Refuse, rabble. — وحَسِيلَة
Calves. Oxen. Refuse. حَسِيل ج حُسُل
Refuse of dates. حَسِيلَة ج حَسِيل
To cut off. To cut ✻ حَسَم i حَسْمًا ه
(an artery) open and cauterize it.
To stop (a disease).
To deprive a. o. from. — ة ه
To be cut off. إِنْحَسَم
Unhappy (days). حُسُوم
Sharp sword. Edge (of a sword). حُسَام
Long (night).
Specific (of a disease). مَحْسَمَة
To be comely. ✻ حَسُن وحَسَن o حُسْنًا
To better, to embellish حَسَّن ة وه
a. o. or a. th.
To surpass a. o. in beauty. حَاسَن ة
To treat a. o. kindly.
To behave well. ✧ To be able to. أَحْسَن
To know. To do a. th. well. أَحْسَن ه
To embellish a. th.
To do good, to give alms to — إِلى وب
a. o.
To be able to do. ✧ أَحْسَن أن يَفْعَل
To be beautiful, to adorn o.'s تَحَسَّن
self. To be shaven.
To find a. o. or a. th. إِسْتَحْسَن ه وة
well, pleasing. To approve of.
Beauty. Goodness. حُسْن ج مَحَاسِن
Pleasingness.
✧ Kind of moss found حُسْن يُوسُف
on the sea-shore.
Goodly, حَسَن ج حِسَان, وحُسَان ج حُسَّانُون
fine. New.
Good-looking woman. حَسَنَة وحَسْنَاء ج حِسَان وحَسَنَات

Very fine, very handsome. حُسَّان م حُسَّانَة ج حُسَّانُون وحُسَّانَات
Well. All right. حَسَنًا
Good work. Benefit. حَسَنَة ج حَسَنَات
✧ Alms.
Better. ✧ More. أَحْسَن ج أَحَاسِن م حُسْنَى ج حُسَن وحُسْنَيَات
The best men. أَحَاسِن القَوْم
How pleasing is Zeid! مَا أَحْسَنَ زَيْدًا
Benefit, gift. إِحْسَان
Good action. حُسْنَى ج حُسْنَيَات وحُسَن
Good result. Benefit. Victory. Contemplation of God.
The 99 Names of God amongst Moslems. الأَسْمَاء الحُسْنَى
Victory and martyrdom. الحُسْنَيَان
The best he can do is to... حُسَيْنَاهُ أَن
Gold-finch. ✧ حَسُّون
Beneficent. مِحْسَان, ومُحْسِن ج مُحْسِنُون
Good works. Good qualities. المَحَاسِن
Charms, beauty.
To sip ✻ حَسَا o حَسْوًا, وتَحَسَّى واحْتَسَى ه
(broth) little by little.
To give to a. o. حَسَّى وأَحْسَى وحَاسَى ة ه
(broth) to sip.
Food made of flour and water. حَسْو وحَسَاء وحَسُوّ
A draught, a mouthful (absorbed). حَسْوَة ج حَسَوَات
Mouthful (*quantity*). حُسْوَة ج أَحْسُوَة وأَحْسِيَة وجج أَحَاسٍ
To dig a sandy ground. ✻ حَسَى i حَسْيًا, واحْتَسَى
To put a. o. to the test. حَسِيَ a واحْتَسَى ة
Swampy ground covered with sand. حِسْي وحَسْي ج أَحْسَاء وحِسَاء
To dry up (hand, valley). ✻ حَشَّ o حَشًّا
To hurry on (horse).
To kindle (a fire). To poke — ه وة
(the fire). To cut (herbage). To stir (war). To increase (wealth). To give herbs to (a horse).
To smoke hemp. ✧ حَشَّش
To be dried (hand). To have أَحَشّ
abundant herbage (land).
To help a. o. in gathering herbs. ة —
To seek for, to gather herbs. إِحْتَشَّ ه
To be thirsty (man). To be- اِسْتَحَشّ

come tall (branch). To dry (hand).

حَشِيش ج حَشَائِش Dry herbage. Still-born fœtus. ✧ Hashish.

حَشِيشَة الأَسَد Broom-rape, orobanche.

— الأَفْعَى Galium aparine, goose-grass.

✧ — البَزَّاز Lapsana, nipple-wort.

◻ — الثُّومِيَّة Alliaria, hedge-garlic.

◻ — الحَجَل Fritillaria, liliaceous plant.

◻ — الحَلِيب Glaucium, horn-poppy.

— الحَمْرَاء Belladona, deadly night-shade.

— الدِّينَار Hop (plant).

الحَشِيشَة القَرْبِيَّة Sarsaparilla root.

حَشِيشَة الهِرّ Valerian (plant).

حُشَاش وحُشَاشَة Last breath of life.

حُشَاشَتُكَ أَن تَفْعَلَ كَذَا The utmost of thy power is to do so.

✧ يَا حُشَاشَةَ قَلْبِي Portion of my heart i. e. my beloved.

حِشّ وحُشّ وحَشّ ج حُشُوش Fruit-garden. Collection of palm-trees. Privy.

حَشَّاش ج حَشَّاشُون Seller of dry herbage. ✧ Smoker of hashish. Dotard.

مَحَشّ Place abounding in dry herbage.

مِحَشّ ومِحَشَّة Reaping-hook. Poker.

✧ مَحْشَشَة Tavern for smoking hemp.

✱ حَشْحَش وتَحَشْحَش To stir about (men).

✱ حَشَأَ a حَشْأً ه To kindle (the fire).

— ه ب To lash a. o. with (a whip). To hit the belly with (an arrow).

مِحْشَأ ومِحْشَاء ج مَحَاشِئ Waist-wrapper.

✱ حَشِب — أَحْشَب ه To irritate a. o.

إِحْتَشَب To muster (people).

حَوْشَب Hare. Calf. Male fox. Big-bellied. Company of men.

✱ حَشَد o i حَشْدًا To bud out (plant).

✧ — ل To take the part. To side with.

— حُشُودًا To rush to the rescue.

— وحَشَّد ه وه To collect (men, things). To muster (troops).

أَحْشَد وتَحَاشَد واحْتَشَد To assemble (party).

إِحْتَشَد ل To answer the call of a. o. To exert o.'s self for (a guest).

حَشْد وحَشَد ج حُشُود Party of men.

حَشِيد Inexhaustible (spring).

✱ حَشَر i o حَشْرًا ه To assemble (people). To exile a. o. To expel a. o. To destroy (cattle : draught).

— ه To make (a spear-head) thin. ✧ To press a. o. To cram a. th.

حَشِر To be big-bodied. To die (wild beast).

✧ تَحَشَّر فِي To interfere, to intrude in.

حَشْر Congregation, swarm.

— ج حُشْر Thin (ear); pointed (spear).

يَوْم الحَشْر Day of the resurrection.

حَاشِر ج حُشَّار Tax-gatherer.

✧ حِشْرِيّ Intruder. Inquisitive.

حَشَرَة ج حَشَرَات Small reptiles. Insects.

✧ حُشْرِيَّة Inquisitiveness.

مَحْشِر ومَحْشَر ج مَحَاشِر Gathering-place, crowd.

✱ حَشْرَج To have the death-rattle (man). To bray (ass).

حَشْرَج Death-rattle.

حَشْرَج Small mug. Hollow in which water remains.

✱ حَشَف — حَشَّف ه To wink (the eyes).

أَحْشَف To bear bad dates (palm-tree). To be contracted (udder).

تَحَشَّف To wear shabby clothes. To fall off (hair).

حَشَف Dates of bad quality.

حَشِيف Worn out garment.

✱ حَشَك i حَشْكًا To be filled (udder). To be loaded with fruit (tree). To let fall a shower (sky). To have much water (cloud). To throng (crowd). To veer (wind). To become strong *and* to abate (wind).

✧ — وحَشَّك ه To cram up (a bag).

حَشَك a حَشْكًا To eat barley (horse). To collect in the udder (milk).

أَحْشَك ه To give barley to (a horse).

تَحَشَّك To be swollen with milk (udder).

حَشْكَة Shower; heavy rain.

حَشَكَة Numerous troop.

حَشِيكَة Barley.

حَاشِك Filled of (milk). Loaded (with fruit) Successive. Uninterrupted.

حَاشِكَة ج حَوَاشِك Winds blowing from various sides.

Muzzle for preventing a kid from sucking. حَشَاكَة وحِشَاك
Noise in the quarter of a house. حوشكة
✻ حَشَل o حَشْلًا ه To make little of. To revile a. o.
✻ حَشَم i حَشْمًا ه وه To put a. o. to the blush. To seek a. th.
مَا حَشَمَ الصَّيْدَ He has caught no game.
مَا حَشَمَ مِن To abstain from.
حَشِم i o إلى To abash a. o. by addressing him rudely.
حَشِم a حَشَمًا To be in a rage.
— وحَشَّم وأَحْشَم ه To irritate, to put a. o. to the blush; to harm a. o.
تَحَشَّم مِن To blush at. To refrain from.
إِحْتَشَم عَن ومِن وه To be angry at. To refrain from. To be ashamed of.
حَشَم وحَشْمَة وحَشَمَة Servants, household, family.
حِشْمَة Bashfulness, self-restraint. Politeness. Anger.
إِحْتِشَام Modesty. Respect.
حَشِيم ج حُشَمَاء Venerable. Neighbour. Guest.
مَحَاشِم Pudenda.
✻ حَشِن a حَشَنًا To smell bad (water-skin).
أَحْشَن ه To use a stinking (skin).
حَاشَن ه To abuse a. o., to revile a. o.
تَحَشَّن To make earnings.
حَشَن Filthiness of a vessel.
حِشْنَة Hatred, malevolence.
✻ حَشَا o حَشْوًا ه ب To fill up, to stuff (a cushion) with.
— ه To hit a. o. in the bowels.
حَاشَى ه To make a gift to a. o.
إِحْتَشَى To be filled with grains (pomegranate). To be stuffed.
حَاشِيَة وحَشْو The meanest of camels, men.
حَشًا ج أَحْشَاء Bowels, intestines.
حَشْو Stuffing of food, cloth. Stuffed garment. Soul. Redundant part of a speech. Refuse of men.
حُشْوَة وحِشْوَة Bowels, intestines.
— الأَرْض Forest, thicket.
حَشِيَّة ج حَشَايَا Stuffed bed. Bustle worn by women. Pad.

The rectum المُحَشَّاة
✻ حَشِي a حَشًى To suffer from asthma.
حَشَّى ه To border (a garment). To write marginal notes. ✧ To interpolate (a book).
حَاشَى ه مِن To exclude a. o. from (a number). To except a. o. from.
تَحَشَّى ه To shun a. o.
— مِن To except a. o. from.
— مِن وتَحَاشَى عَن To keep aloof from, to avoid, to guard against a. th.
حَشًى Asthma, short breathing.
حَاشَ وحَشَى وحَاشَا Except. Far from.
◻ حَاشَا Smallage (*plant*).
حَاشَا اللهُ عَن God forbid that.
✧ حَاشَا مِن التَّشْبِيه Excuse the comparison.
حَاشَا زَيْدٍ Save Zeid.
حَاشَاكَ وحَاشَا لَكَ أَن Far from thee. Excuse such a mention.
حَاشَاكَ أَن تَنْسَى Thou art far from forgetting.
حَاشِيَة ج حَوَاشٍ Side. Selvage of a garment. Margin (of a book). Marginal note. Followers. ✧ Postcript.
مُحَشًّى Covered with notes (book).
✻ حَصَّ o حَصًّا ه To shave (the hair). To destroy a. th.
— ه To be allotted to a. o. (share).
حَصْحَصَ To be clear, evident.
حَاصَّ ه To share a. th. with.
أَحَصَّ ه To allot a share to a. o.
تَحَاصَّ ه To divide a. th. together.
تَحَصَّصَ To lose its hair (beast).
إِنْحَصَّ To fall out (hair, leaves). To be curtailed (tail).
حَصَص Scantiness of hair on the head.
حِصَّة ج حِصَص Portion. ✧ A bit.
حُصّ ج أَحْصَاص وحُصُوص Saffron. Pearl. ✧ Kernel.
حُصَاص Quick running (of an ass).
حُصَاصَة Bunches remaining on the vine.
حَاصَّة Disease causing the hair to fall.
أَحَصّ م حَصَّاء Having little or no hair (man); having scanty feathers on the wings (bird).
يَوْم أَحَصّ Cloudless and cold (day).
✻ حَصْحَص To appear in broad light

Reaper. حَاصِد وَحَصَّاد
Scythe, sickle. مِحْصَد ج مَحَاصِد
To surround, ✻ حَصَرَ o i حَصْرًا ه وه to put a. o. in a strait. To withhold a. o. To put a cushion upon (a camel) To hold a. th. (vessel). ✧ To inconvenience a. o. To limit. a. th.
To encompass a. o. — ب
To be costive. حُصِرَ وأُحْصِرَ
To feel an oppression حَصِرَ a حَصَرًا of the heart. To be niggardly. To be tired. To falter in speech.
To conceal (a secret). — ب
To encompass. a. o. To invest (a town). حَاصَرَ مُحَاصَرَةً وحِصَارًا ه وه
To crush a. o. (disease). أَحْصَرَ ه
To hinder a. o. from. — ه عن
To be in a strait. To be besieged. ✧ To be annoyed. إِنْحَصَرَ
✧ To be restrained to. — في
To strap a pad on (a camel). إِحْتَصَرَ ه
Constipation. Ischury. حُصْر
Oppression of heart. Faltering in speech. Avarice. حَصَر
Hinderance. Restriction. ✧ Anguish. حَصْر
✧ Control of tobacco. حَصْر الدُّخَان
In a strict sense. بالحَصْر
Pad used as a saddle. حِصَار ومِحْصَرَة
Siege. Blockhouse. ✧ Fortress. حِصَار ومُحَاصَرَة
He raised the siege. رَفَعَ الحِصَار
Oppressed. Avaricious. Faltering in speech حَصِر وحَصُور وحَصِير
Discreet. Surname of John the Baptist. حَصُور
Prison. Surface of the earth. Side of the body. Road. Meeting. Row of people. Handle. Woven stuff. حَصِير ج حُصُر وأَحْصِرَة
Drying-floor for dates. ✧ Mat. حَصِيرَة ج حَصَائِر
To brace (a bow) strongly. To twist (a rope) strongly. To fill(a water-skin).To cut (a pen). ✻ حَضْرَمَ ه
To be sordid, miserly. ✧ To become sour (grape) تَحَضْرَمَ
Any green fruit. Verjuice. Miser. حِصْرِم و✧ حُصْرُم

(truth). To limp in walking (man).
To be fixed on the ground. تَحَصْحَصَ
Dust. Quick walk. حَصْحَاص
To suck milk to his fill (child). To eat or drink greedily (camel). ✻ حَصَأَ وحَصِيَ a حَصْأً
To quench o.'s thirst with. — مِن
To quench the thirst of. أَحْصَأَ ه
To throw pebbles at. ✻ حَصَبَ o i حَصْبًا ه
To pave (the soil) with pebbles. — وحَصَّبَ ه
To have the measles. حَصِبَ a حَصَبًا , وحُصِبَ
To strike up pebbles in running (horse). أَحْصَبَ
To take his flight to the country (pigeon). تَحَصَّبَ
To pelt one another with pebbles. تَحَاصَبَ
Stones. Fuel. Firewood. حَصَب
Scarlet fever. حَصْبَة وحَصَبَة و✧ حُمَّى حَصْبِيَّة
Small pebbles. حَصْبَاء
Strong wind scattering pebbles. Cloud casting down snow, hail. Numerous company of men. حَاصِب ج حَوَاصِب
Soil covered with pebbles. أَرض مَحْصَبَة وحَصِبَة
Seized with scarlet fever. مَحْصُوب
To reap (corn-crops). ✻ حَصَدَ o i حَصْدًا وحَصَادًا وحِصَادًا , واحْتَصَدَ ه
To destroy a. o. with the sword. حَصَدَ ه ب
He died. حُصِدَ فُلَان
To be strongly woven (rope, coat of mail). حَصِدَ a حَصَدًا
To be mature (corn-crops). أَحْصَدَ واسْتَحْصَدَ
To form a league (people). To be strongly made (rope). To be angry. إِسْتَحْصَدَ
Harvest-time. حَصَاد وحِصَاد
Crops. Gathered harvest. حَصَد وحَصِيد وحَصِيدَة
Stalks of reaped crops. حَصِيدَة ج حَصَائِد
Slanderous talks. حَصَائِد الأَلْسِنَة

To have a sound judgment. ✱ حَصُفَ o حَصَافَةً
To be mangy. حَصِفَ a حَصَفًا
To remove a. th. To weave a. th. compactly. To twist a rope (strongly). To settle (an affair). حَصَفَ o حَصْفًا , وأَحْصَفَ ة وه
To run swiftly. أَحْصَفَ
To be strongly made. إِسْتَحْصَفَ
Dry mange. حَصَفٌ
Gifted with a sound judgment. حَصِفٌ وحَصِيفٌ
Swift in running. مُحْصِفٌ ومِحْصَفٌ ومِحْصَافٌ
To remain. ✱ حَصَلَ o حُصُولًا ومَحْصُولًا
To be left. To result. To happen (event).
To befall a. o. (evil). حَصَلَ لِ
To be realised (profit).
To happen to a. o. (event). حَصَلَ عَلَى
To collect (a debt). ✧ To get a. th.
To eat (earth : beast). حَصِلَ o حَصَلًا
To have a pain in the belly from having eaten earth (horse).
To attain (an aim). To sum up (a speech). ✧ To recover (money). To acquire (science). حَصَّلَ ه
To produce unripe (dates). — وأَحْصَلَ
To result. To be obtained. To be realised. تَحَصَّلَ
Remainder. Result, product, quotient. Produce of land. Purified silver. ✧ Warehouse. حَاصِلٌ ج حَوَاصِلُ
Sum total. In short, in a word. الحَاصِلُ
Siftings of wheat. حُصَالَةٌ
Remainder. Produce. حَصِيلَةٌ ج حَصَائِلُ
Crop of a bird. Wheat. حَوْصَلٌ وحَوْصَلَةٌ
Vesicle on the skin. حُوَيْصِلَةٌ
Aubergine, egg-plant. حَيْصَلٌ
Success. Scientific attainment. ✧ Tax-gathering. تَحْصِيلٌ
Tax-gatherer. Ts تَحْصِيلْدَار
Result. ✧ Seed-produce. Income. مَحْصُولٌ ج مَحَاصِيلُ و✧ مَحْصُولَاتٌ
To break wind (horse). ✱ حَصَمَ i حَصْمًا بِ
To be broken (wood). إِنْحَصَمَ
To be inaccessible (place). ✱ حَصُنَ o حَصَانَةً

To be chaste (woman). حَصُنَ o حُصْنًا وحِصْنًا وحَصَانَةً
To fortify (a place). To surround (a village) with a wall. حَصَّنَ وأَحْصَنَ ه
To be chaste, virtuous (woman). To marry (man or woman). أَحْصَنَ
To keep herself chaste (woman). ه —
To give (a woman) in marriage. ة —
To fortify, to entrench o.'s self. To be chaste (woman). To become a stallion (horse). تَحَصَّنَ
Stronghold, fortress. Weapons. Horses. Crescent. حِصْنٌ ج حُصُونٌ
Chaste woman. Lawful wife. Pearl. حَصَانٌ ج حُصُنٌ وحَصَانَاتٌ
Stallion. Blood-horse. حِصَانٌ ج حُصُنٌ وأَحْصِنَةٌ
Hippopotamus. ✧ حِصَانُ البَحْرِ
حَاصِنٌ وحَاصِنَةٌ وحَصْنَاءُ ج حَوَاصِنُ وحَاصِنَاتٌ
Pudical woman. Lawful wife.
Strong, difficult of access. حَصِينٌ
Fox. أَبُو الحُصَيْنِ
Freedom. Marriage. Mind. إِحْصَانٌ
Entrenchment. تَحْصِينٌ ج تَحْصِينَاتٌ
Basket. Lock. مِحْصَنٌ ج مَحَاصِنُ
Virtuous woman. مُحْصَنَةٌ ومُحْصِنَةٌ
To hinder a. o. ✱ حَصَا o حَصْوًا ة
To abound in pebbles (land). حَصِيَ a حَصًا
To strike a. o. with pebbles. حَصَى i حَصْيًا ة
To have a stone in the bladder. حُصِيَ
To protect a. o. حَصَّى ة تَحْصِيَةً
To reckon, to number. To understand a. th. أَحْصَى إِحْصَاءً ه
To be on the watch. تَحَصَّى
Number. Small stones. حَصًى
حَصَاةٌ و✧ حَصْوَةٌ ج حَصَيَاتٌ وحُصِيٌّ وحِصِيٌّ
Calculus. Pebbles. Prudence.
Very prudent. حَصِيٌّ
Statistics. إِحْصَاءٌ
Soil abounding in pebbles. أَرْضٌ مَحْصَاةٌ
Innumerable. غَيْرُ مُحْصًى
To incite a. o. to. ✱ حَضَّ o حَضًّا , وحَضَّضَ ة عَلَى
To excite one another to. حَاضَّ ة عَلَى
To rouse o. another. تَحَاضَّ
Lycium. Box-thorn. حُضَضٌ
Foot of a حَضِيضٌ ج حُضُضٌ وأَحِضَّةٌ

city. Dwelling by water. Cultivated district. Settlement. ✧ Ready.

Party of men. حَضِيرَة ج حَضِير وحَضَائِر Matter in a wound. Vanguard. Drying-floor for dates.

✧ Summons sub pœna, writ. مُذَكِّرَة إِحْضَار

✧ Pharmaceutics. إِسْتِحْضَارَات

Colloquy, conference. مُحَاضَرَة

Fixed dwelling. مَحْضَر ج مَحَاضِر Presence. Return to water. Record signed by witnesses. ✧ Assembly.

Speaking well of the absent. حُسْنُ المَحْضَر

✧ Official record. عَرْضُ مَحْضَر

At the point of death. مُحْتَضَر

Coming to a settled country. مُحْتَضِر

Fleet (horse). مِحْضِير ج مَحَاضِير

He was indistinct in speech, he mispronounced. ✱ حَضْرَمَ في الكَلَام

To bark (a tree). To mix a. th. ه –

Name of a province and of a tribe of Yemen. حَضْرَمَوت وحَضْرُمُوت

To take in the bosom. To bring up (a child). To embrace (a child). ✱ حَضَن o حَضْنًا وحِضَانَة , واحْتَضَن ه

To brood upon its eggs (bird). – o بَيْضَهُ حَضْنًا وحِضَانًا وحِضَانَةً وحُضُونًا

To debar a. o. from. – حَضْنًا وحَضَانَة , واحْتَضَن ه عن

To have unequal breasts. حَضِن o حِضَانًا

To despise, to wrong a. o. أَحْضَن ه وب

To deprive a. o. of a right. – ه بِحَقِّهِ

Breast. Bosom. حِضْن ج حُضُون وأَحْضَان Clasp. Side. Foot of a mountain.

Fostering. ✧ Right and pension of tutorship, granted to the mother. حِضَانَة

Brood. ✧ Embrace. حُضْنَة

He felt the grasp of misfortune. أَصْبَحَ بِحُضْنَةِ سُوء

Nurse, dry nurse. حَاضِنَة ج حَوَاضِن

Having unequal breasts, teats. حَضُون

To stir (the fire). ✱ حَضَا o حَضْوًا ه

Wooden poker. مِحْضَاء

To go down; to alight. ✱ حَطَّ o حَطًّا

To abate (price). – o حَطًّا وحُطُوطًا

To be pimpled (face). – o حَطَاطًا , وأَحَطَّ

To put. To leave off a. th. – o حَطًّا ه

mountain. Perigee.

To be kindled (fire). ✱ حَضَأ o حَضْأً

To kindle (the fire). – وأَحْضَأ واحْتَضَأ ه

Wooden poker. مِحْضَأ ومِحْضَاء

To put wood (in the fire). ✱ حَضَب i حَضْبًا ه

To take a rugged by-way. تَحَضَّب

Twang of a bow. Side. حِضْب ج أَحْضَاب Foot of a mountain. Big snake.

Poker. Firebrand. مِحْضَب

To kindle (the fire). ✱ حَضَج o حَضْجًا ه

To throw a. o. down – ه وب ه

To unload (a camel). To stir (the fire).

To be roused to anger. إِنْحَضَج To spread o.'s self on the ground.

Fire-poker. مِحْضَج

✱ حَضَر o حُضُورًا وحَضَارَة (opp. to غَاب) To be present. To be at hand (time).

To settle in a country. – حَضَارَة

To occur to a. o. (thought). – ه وه To witness a. th. To present o.'s self before a. o.

To turn away from. – عن

To bring in حَضَّر وأَحْضَر واسْتَحْضَر ه وه a. o. or a. th. To get a. th. ready.

To give a ready حَاضَر مُحَاضَرَة وحِضَارًا ه (answer). To witness a. th. To contend with a. o. To run with a. o.

To run (horse). أَحْضَر واحْتَضَر

To attend (a meeting). – ه

To present o.'s self. تَحَضَّر واحْتَضَر ✧ To prepare o.'s self.

To be at the point of death. أُحْتُضِر

To send for a. o. To occur to the mind (thought). To make (a horse) to run. إِسْتَحْضَر ه

حَضَر وحَضَارَة وحَاضِرَة (opp. to بَادِيَة) Cultivated country.

Inhabitant of a village. حَضَرِيّ

Presence. Vicinity. حَضَر وحَضْرَة وحُضُور ✧ Majesty, Excellency (titles of honour).

In his presence. بِحَضَرِهِ وبِحَضْرَتِهِ و✧ بِحُضُورِهِ

Intruder. Spunger. حَضِر وحَضُر

Always ready to reply. Quick. حَضِر

حَاضِر ج حُضَّر وحُضَّار وحُضُور وحَضَرَة Present. Large tribe. Coming to a

To put a string to (a bow). ✱ حظر o حظرًا ه
To break a. th. ✱ حطم i حطمًا, وحطّم ه
To be broken by age. حطم a حطمًا
To be smashed (dry things). تحطّم وانحطم
Fragment, piece. حِطمة وحُطامة وحُطام
The vanities of the world. حُطام الدُّنيا
Unfruitful year. حطمة وحُطمة
Vehement fire. Gluttonous. حُطمة
Bad year. Digestible. حاطوم
Lion. حَطوم وحطّام وحِطَم
Wall of the Caaba. Plant of the precedent year. حطيم
To toss, to shake a. th. about. ✱ حظا o حظوًا ه
Big lice. حظًا
To be lucky. ✱ حظّ a حظًّا, وحظّ
To become rich. أحظّ
To enjoy a. th. ✧ إحتظّ ب
To be favoured with.
Luck. Portion, lot. حظّ ج حُظوظ
Happiness. ✧ Enjoyment. Favour.
Happy, lucky. حظي وحظيظ ومحظوظ
Pleasure, gladness. ✧ محظوظيّة
To be fat, fleshy. ✱ حظب i وحظب a حظبًا
Short and big-bellied. حظب م حظِبة
To prevent the access of (a place) to a. o. To enclose (cattle) in. ✱ حظر o حظرًا ه على
To make an enclosure for o.'s self. أحظر
To build an enclosure. إحتظر
Enclosure for cattle, sheepfold. Fence. حظيرة ج حظائر وحِظار
Paradise. حظيرة القُدس
Unlucky. Stingy. نَكِد الحظيرة
Forbidden. Unapproachable. محظور
To brace strongly (a bow). ✱ حظرب ه
To fill up (a skin).
To be filled (skin). تحظرب
To be surfeited. To be full of hatred (man).
Strong. Courageous. Stern. مُحظرِب
To prevent a. o. from acting. ✱ حظل o i حظلًا وحظلانًا وحَظلانًا على
To stop in walking. — o حظلانًا
Parsimonious man. حَظِل وحظّال

To polish, to figure (leather).
✧ To pay a. th. To lower a. th.
To eat much. — في الطعام
To put down (a burden). حطّط ه
✧ To make a. o. to pay, to put a. th.
To put a. th. down. أحطّ وانحطّ ه
To be put down. To sink (strength). To be humbled. To abate (price). إنحطّ
To ask a. o. to put down a. th. إستحطّ ه ه
To ask a lowering of price. — من الثمن شيئًا
Unloading, relief. حِطّة وحِطّيطى
Abatement of price. حطيطة
Carbuncled face. Froth of milk. حُطاط
Stink. حُطاط
Short. حطيط وحُطائط
Station. مَحَطّ ومحطّة ج محاطّ
✧ Fullstop. Pause.
Instrument for polishing. مِحطّ ومِحطّة
To prostrate a. o. ✱ حطأ a حطأ الأرض به
To turn a. o. back from. — به عن
To slap a. o. on the back. — ه
To cast forth froth (boiler). — بزَبَدها
Ugly, mean, small in body. حُطيئة
Dregs of the people. حطيّ
To pick up fire-wood. ✱ حطب i حطبًا, واحتطب
To bring wood to a. o. حطب ه وه
To prune (the vine). To wash away (roots : rain).
To abound in firewood. حطب وأحطب
To speak ill or well of. حطب على و ب
He came to his rescue. حطب في حبله
To want to be pruned (vine). أحطب واستحطب
Firewood. Slander. حطب ج أحطاب
✧ *Guiacum, lignum vitæ.* حطب القِدِّيسين
Very lean. حطِب وأحطب
Collector of firewood. حاطب
Great talker, mixing good and evil in his speech. — ليل
Wood-cutter. حطّاب م حطّابة
Abounding in firewood. حطيب
Pruning-knife. مِحطب

To walk slowly. ✱ حَظَا o حَظْوًا
To obtain a. th. حَظِيَ a حُظْوَة وحِظْوَة وحِظَّة ب
To enjoy the favour of. — واحْتَظَى عند
To procure a. th. to. أَحْظَى إحْظَاء ه ب
To render happy : to favour a. o. — ه
To prefer (one) to (another). — ه على
High estimation, regard. Favour, happiness. حِظَّة وحُظْوَة ج حِظًى وحُظًى
Small arrow. Small rod. حُظْوَة ج حِظَاء وحُظُوات
Slow walk. حُظَيًّا
Favourite slave. حَظِيَّة . حَظَا . ✧ مَحْظِيَّة
To pluck (the hair). To shave (the head); to clip (the beard): to bark a. th. ✧ To rub out a. th. ✱ حَفَّ o حَفًّا وحِفَافًا , واحْتَفَّ ه
To surround a. th. — حَفًّا وحَفَفًا ه وبه وحَوْلَهُ
To encompass a. o. or a. th. with. — ه وه ب
To produce a rustling sound (leaves, snake, horse, bird, shower). — i حَفِيفًا
To become dry (earth, food, stomach). To become deaf (ear). To be smitten by the evil eye. To speak evil of a. o. — i حُفُوفًا
He had shaggy, undressed (hair). أَحَفَّ رَأْسَهُ
To speak evil of a. o. — ه
To have (the hair) plucked out of the face. To eat up a th. احْتَفَّ ه
To encompass a. o. — حَوْلَ
To take the whole of. اسْتَحَفَّ ه
Surrounding. Evil-eyed. حَافّ م حَافَّة
Unkneaded flour. ✧ سَوِيق حَافّ
Dry, unseasoned bread. ✧ خُبْز حَافّ
✧ Margin. Border. Side. Wall breast-high in a field. حَافَّة
Side. Trace. Border of hair around a bald head. حِفَاف ج أَحِفَّة
Track, trace. حَفّ وحَفَف
He came upon his track. جَاءَ على حَفِّهِ وحَفَفِهِ
Servants. Young ostrich. حَفَّان
Generosity. Weaver. Robber. حَفَّة
Confused sound of the wind, of birds. Buzzing. حَفِيف
Litter for women flat on the top. مِحَفَّة
Surrounded. Poor. مَحْفُوف
To produce a rustling (with the wings : bird). ✱ حَفْحَفَ
To throw a. o. down. ✱ حَفَا a حَفْأً ه
To pull out papyrus. احْتَفَأ
Papyrus. حَفَأ
To crush, to destroy a. th. ✱ حَفَتَ o حَفْتًا ه
Large harmless snake. ✱ حِفْت وحَفْث ج أَحْفَاث
To do a. th. speedily ; to be nimble in work. ✱ حَفَدَ i حَفْدًا وحَفَدَانًا , واحْتَفَدَ
To serve a. o. speedily. — ه
To hurry, to hasten a. o. أَحْفَدَ ه
Quick pace. حَفْد وحَفَدَان
Grandson ; grandchild. حَفِيد ج حَفَدَة
Servant. Helper. حَافِد ج حَفَد وحَفَدَة
Origin of a man. Base of the hump. مَحْفِد ج مَحَافِد
Sharp (sword). مُحْتَفِد
To dig (the earth). ✱ حَفَرَ i حَفْرًا , واحْتَفَرَ ه
To scrutinize a. th. ✧ To engrave (a metal). حَفَرَ ه
To become cankered (teeth). — i حَفْرًا وحَفِرَ a حَفَرًا , وحُفِرَ
To shed his first teeth (child). حَفَرَ i وأَحْفَرَ
To go deep in his burrow (jerboa). حَافَرَ
To furrow (the earth : torrent). تَحَفَّرَ
Large well. Cankering of the teeth. حَفَر
Large well. Earth taken forth from a well. حَفَر ج أَحْفَار
Hollow, ditch, cavity. حُفْرَة ج حُفَر وحَفِيرَة ج حَفَائِر
Pit. Grave. Mussel (shell-fish). حَفِير
Digger. Hoof. حَافِر ج حَوَافِر
Beginning, original state. — وحَافِرَة
Directly. At first. عِنْد الحَافِرَة
He came back to his former state. رَجَعَ إلى حَافِرَتِهِ
Tartar of the teeth. ✧ حَافُور
Grave-digger. حَفَّار
Spade. مِحْفَر ومِحْفَرَة ومِحْفَار ج مَحَافِر ومَحَافِير

✧ مِحفَارَة Sand-bed.

✱ حَفَز i حَفزًا ه وهـ To push a. th. from behind. To urge on (the day : night).

— ه ب To pierce a. o. with (a spear).

— عن To hurry (an affair).

حَافَز ه To be seated opposite to.

تَحَفَّز واحتَفَز To be on the watch, to be ready to act.

احتَفَز في مَشيِهِ To press forward.

حَفَز Limit.

✱ حَفَس i حَفسًا To eat (man).

✱ حَفَش i حَفشًا To collect (water). To meet (tribe). To run two heats consecutively (horse).

— ه وهـ To expel a. o. To extract a. th. To bark a. th. To fill (a valley : flood).

— في To apply o.'s self to.

حَفِش a حَفَشًا To pour down showers (cloud).

حَفَّش وتَحَفَّش To remain in his tent (man).

حَفِشَة Place in which water abounds.

حِفش ج أَحفَاش. Receptacle, vessel, sack. Small tent of hair. Paltry articles of furniture.

أَحفَاش الأَرض Lizards, hedgehogs and jerboas.

✱ حَفَص i حَفصًا هـ To collect a. th.

حُفَاصَة Collection.

حَفص ج حُفُوص وأَحفَاص Leather-basket for cleansing wells. Tent. Lion's whelp.

✱ حَفَض i حَفضًا هـ To bend, to crook (a stick). To throw a. th.

— وحَفَّض ه To throw a. th. back. To dry (the earth).

حَفَض ج حِفَاض وأَحفَاض House furniture ready to be carried. Camel bearing it. Tent. Flag-bearer. Weak camel. Pole of a tent.

✱ حَفِظ a حِفظًا ه وهـ To put a. th. in store. To preserve a. th. To learn a. th. by heart. ✧ To observe (a feast ; o.'s conduct). To keep (a secret). To reserve (a sin).

حَفَّظ ه وهـ To make a. o. to learn a. th. by heart.

حَافَظ مُحَافَظَة وحِفَاظًا على To persevere in. To observe a. th. carefully.

أَحفَظ ه To put a. o. out of temper.

تَحَفَّظ To learn by heart.

— عَن To caution o.'s self against.

احتَفَظ ب وهـ To keep, to preserve a. th.

— هـ لِنَفسِهِ To appropriate a. th.

استَحفَظ ه وهـ To ask a. o. to keep a secret or a. th.

حِفظ Attention, watchfulness. Care. Keeping. Memory.

حِفظَة، وحَفِيظَة ج حَفَائِظ Anger, zeal to defend a. o. or a. th.

✧ تَحَفُّظ بَطَّال واحتِفَاظ بَاطِل Superstition. False worship.

حَافِظ ج حُفَّاظ وحَفَظَة Keeper. Knowing by heart. Conspicuous road.

الحَافِظ والحَفِيظ The Preserver (God).

حَافِظ العَين Watchful.

الحَافِظَة و✧ الحَافِظِيَّة Memory.

المَلَك الحَفِيظ The recording Angel of men.

الحَافِظُون والحَفَظَة The Angels.

مَع التَحَفُّظ Reservedly, cautiously.

مُحَافِظ Governor (at a town).

✧ المُحَافِظِين The conservatives, the Tories, the conservative party.

مُستَحفِظ Army of reserve.

✱ حَفَل i حَفلًا وحُفُولًا وحَفِيلًا To be copious (milk, water).

— i حَفلًا To meet (people). To pour torrents of rain (sky). To flow abundantly (tears).

— بِالسَّيل To be filled to the brink (river).

— هـ وب To apply o.'s self to. To mind a. th.

حَفَّل هـ To collect (water). To embellish a. th.

تَحَفَّل To leave (cattle) unmilked. To throng in (people). To be adorned. To collect in the udder (milk).

احتَفَل To flock in (people). To become conspicuous (road).

— ب To be flooded by (a stream : valley). ✧ To celebrate (a feast).

— ب و في To take care of.

Importune.
To overcome a. o. ✻ حَقّ o حَقًّا ه in contending for a right. To strike a. o. on the back of the neck.
To realize the fear of. — حَذَرَهُ
To prove a. th. To make a. th. ه — necessary. To be sure of. To ascertain (news).
To be suitable, حَقّ i على وحُقّ ل necessary, incumbent upon a. o.
Thou must, حَقّ عَلَيْكَ وحُقّ لَكَ أن تَفْعَل it is thy duty to do.
To become certain, حَقّ o i حَقًّا وحَقَّة necessary.
To ascertain, to prove a. th. حَقَّق ه To render necessary. To believe (a statement). ✧ To hold an inquest.
To contest with حاقّ مُحاقَّة وحِقاقًا a. o. for a right.
To obtain (a right) from أَحَقّ ه وه a. o. To render a. th. necessary. To kill (game) on the spot. To make a. th. certain.
To be ascertained (news). تحقّق
To verify a. th. ه —
To render a. th. binding.
To contend with a. o. تحاقّ واحتقّ for a right.
To be tightened (knot). انحقّ
To be slender (horse). احتقّ
To quarrel together about a right. To become fat (cattle).
To be due (payment). اسْتحقّ
To deserve a punishment (culprit).
To have a claim to; ه — to deserve a. th. To render a. th. necessary.
Right. Truth. Duty. حَقّ ج حُقُوق Justice. Certitude. Cattle. Authentic. The True, one of the Names of God.
✧ Civil court. مَجْلِس الحُقُوق
✧ Thou art right. الحَقّ مَعَكَ وبِيَدِك
✧ Thou art wrong. الحَقّ عَلَيْكَ
✧ I conjure thee by. أَسْأَلُكَ بِحَقّ
✧ Against, on the subject of. — في حَقّ
Worthy of. Fitted for. حَقّ ومَحْقُوق ب
Truly. Verily. حَقًّا وبالحَقّ
Camel three years old. حِقّ

To exaggerate a. th.
Crowd. Numerous. Care. حَفْل و حَفْلَة
Large crowd. Milk collected. حُفَال
Refuse of dates, of men. حُفَالَة
Froth of milk.
Solemnity of a feast; ceremony. احْتِفَال
Solemn, grand. احْتِفَالِيّ
Filled (river, حافِل ج حُفَّل وحَوافِل room, udder). Giving much milk (she-camel).
Assiduous. Numerous. حَفِيل م حَفِيلَة
They came all جاؤُوا بِحَفْلَتِهِم وبِحَفِيلَتِهِم of them.
Gathering. مَحْفِل ج مَحافِل ومُحْتَفَل
Meeting-place.
Nuisance. ◻ حَنْلَطَة
To scoop up (sand, ✻ حَفَن o حَفْنًا ه flour) with both hands.
To give to a. o. a handful of. ل —
To pull up (a tree). احْتَفَن ه
To appropriate a. th. ه لِنَفْسِهِ —
Handful of حَفْنَة ج حَفَنَات، وحُفْنَة ج حُفَن (sand). Rubbish. Hollow. A little.
To honour a. o. (God). ✻ حَفَا o حَفْوًا ب
To make a gift to. ه —
To deprive a. o. of. ه عن —
To walk barefoot. حَفِيَ i حَفًا وحَفَاء
To have the feet or hoofs worn by walking.
— o حَفَاوَة وحِفَاوَة وحِفَايَة وتَحْفَايَة، وتحفّى
To show honour to (a واحتفى ب guest).
To quarrel with a. o. حافاه
To let a. o. walk أَحْفَى إحْفَاء ه barefoot. To press a. o. with questions.
To clip (the mustaches). ه —
To repeat (a question).
To bare o.'s feet. ✧ تَحَفَّى
To strive after. تحفّى في
To take off. To walk barefoot. احتفى
To pick (a vegetable). ه —
To exhaust (a pasturage).
To inquire about a. th. of. استحفى ه عن
Barefootedness, abrasion حَفًا of the feet, hoofs. Shoe.
Welcome. حَفَاوَة وحِفَاوَة
Barefooted. Shoeless حافٍ ج حُفَاة (horse). Welcoming. Judge. Learned.

Upper part of the حُقّ ج أَحْقَاق وحِقَاق arm. Socket of the hip. Spider's web. Stone. Round piece of land. Small box. ✧ Pyx.

Casket; small حُقّة ج حُقّ وحُقَق وحِقَاق box. Calamity.

Right, duty. حِقّة

Worthy of. حَقِيق ج أَحِقّاء ب او أن

Truth. Reality. Essence. حَقِيقة ج حَقَائِق Proper sense (of a word).

Really, in truth. حَقِيقَةً وفي الحَقِيقَة Verily.

True, real. Proper (sense). حَقِيقِيّ

True. Perfect (man). Middle حاقّ م حاقّة (of the neck, of the winter).

Calamity. Resurrection. حاقّة Perfect.

Quarrel, dispute. حِقَاق ومُحَاقّة

Quarrelling about trifles. نَزَق الحِقَاق

Worthier of... than. أَحَقّ ب مِن

✧ Official inquest. تَحْقِيق ج تَحْقِيقات

Who is right. مُحِقّ

Who is wrong. مَحْقُوق

Merit. Dignity. إِسْتِحْقَاق ج إِسْتِحْقَاقَات Maturity. Due (of a bill).

To be suppressed ✱ حَقِبَ a حَقَبًا, وأَحْقَبَ (urine). To be rainless (year). To be unproductive (mine).

To convey a. th. in croup أَحْقَبَ ه (rider). To perpetrate (a crime).

To store up a. th. — واسْتَحْقَبَ ه و٥ To make a. o. to ride behind (rider).

A حُقْب ج حِقَاب, وحُقُب ج أَحْقَاب وأَحْقُب year. A long time. Space of eighty years.

Ornamented woman's girdle. حَقَب Girth of a camel.

Long space of time. حِقْبة ج حِقَب وحُقُوب Year.

Ornamented woman's حِقَاب ج حُقُب girdle. Amulet. Whiteness at the root of the nail.

Following. Riding behind. حَقِيب

Provision-bag, حَقِيبة ج حَقَائِب clothes carried behind the saddle. Posteriors.

Wild ass. أَحْقَب م حَقْبَاء

✱ حَقَدَ وحَقِدَ حِقْدًا وحَقَدًا وحَقِيدةً, وتَحَقَّدَ To brood a secret hatred واحْتَقَدَ عَلَى against a. o. To bear rancour to.

To fail totally (rain). حَقِدَ a حَقَدًا To withhold rain (sky). To be exhausted (mine). To become fat (she-camel).

To excite a. o. to rancour. أَحْقَدَ ٥ وه To seek without finding in (a mine).

To bear mutual hatred to o. a. تَحَاقَدَ

To fail (rain). احْتَقَدَ

Secret حِقْد ج أَحْقَاد, وحَقِيدة ج حَقَائِد hatred. Rancour.

Rancorous, malevolent. حاقِد وحَقُود

To despise a. o. ✱ حَقَرَ i حَقْرًا ٥ وه or a. th. To think slightly of.

To be mean, حَقُرَ a حَقْرًا وحَقُرَ o حَقَارةً despicable.

To look scornfully at. حَقَّرَ ٥ وه To use the diminutive form of (a noun).

To hold a. o. أَحْقَرَ واحْتَقَرَ واسْتَحْقَرَ ٥ وه or a. th. to be despicable, paltry, mean.

He held himself تَحَاقَرَتْ إِلَيْهِ نَفْسُهُ in little estimation.

Base, weak, vile. حَقِر وحَقِير

Degradation, lowness. حَقَارة ومَحْقَرة

Contempt, disdain. تَحْقِير Use of the diminutive form.

Mean, vile, paltry. ✧ Humble. حَقِير

Trifles. Things of small المُحَقَّرَات value.

Francolin (bird). ✱ حَيْقُط وحَيْقُطان

To be curved. To lie ✱ حَقَفَ o حُقُوفًا on the side, with the body bent (gazelle).

To be long and curved احْقَوْقَفَ (crescent, tract of sand).

Long حِقْف ج أَحْقَاف وحِقَاف وحُقُوف وحِقَفَة and winding tract of sand.

To be seized with ✱ حَقِلَ a حَقَلًا وحَقْلَةً belly-fretting (horse, camel).

To sell to a. o. seed-produce حاقَلَ ٥ while in growth. To make a bargain with a. o. for land-labour, on the condition of receiving the half, or third, of the produce.

To show ears (corn). أَحْقَلَ To become fertile (field).

the belly.
To rub a. th. with. To scrape off (gold) with. ✻ حَكَّ o حَكًّا ه ب او على
To busy the mind (cares). حَكَّ وأَحَكَّ واحْتَكَّ في صَدْرِهِ
To itch (head). – وأَحَكَّ واحْتَكَّ واسْتَحَكَّ ه
To imitate a. o. حاكَّ مُحاكَّةً وحِكاكًا ه
To prepare to do (mischief). تَحَكَّكَ ب
The scorpion prepared to do evil to the viper, (*proverb applied to him who struggles with one stronger than himself*). تَحَكَّكَت العَقْرَبُ بِالأَفْعَى
To rub, to scratch one another. تَحاكَّ
To rub o.'s self against. إِحْتَكَّ ب
Mischief-maker. حِكّ وحِكاكُ شرّ
Gulf. ◻ حَكَّة
Evil suggestions; doubts. حُكاكات
Sea-compass. ✧ حُكّ
White marbled stone. Jerking gait. حَكَك
Itch. Doubt in a point of faith. حِكَّة
Tooth. حاكَّة
Borax. Itch. حُكاك
Scrapings. Rubbings. Powder for ophtalmia. حُكاكَة
Prurigo, itching. ✧ حَكّه وحَكاك
Pumice-stone. ◻ حَجَر الحاكوك
Familiar, dependents. أَحْكاك
Rubber. Assayer of gold. حَكّاك
Touch-stone. مِحَكّ
To tighten (a knot). ✻ حَكَأَ a حَكْأً, وأَحْكَأَ واحْتَكَأَ ه
To be tightened (knot). To be fastened (necklace). To be convinced. احْتَكَأَ
To come back to o.'s origin. ✻ حَكَدَ i حَكْدًا
To rely upon a. o. حاكَدَ وأَحْكَدَ على
To wrong a. o. To ill-treat (o.'s people). ✻ حَكَرَ i حَكْرًا ه
To be obstinate, contentious. حَكِرَ a حَكَرًا
To monopolize (goods). – ب
✧ To prevent a. o. from building (on a ground). ◻ حَكَّرَ ه
To contend with a. o. حاكَرَ ه
To monopolize a. th. till it becomes scarce. تَحَكَّرَ واحْتَكَرَ ه

Fertile field. Corn-crops when green. ✧ Column of a page. حَقْل ج حُقُول
Litter for women. حِقْل
Belly-fretting (caused in horses, camels, by their eating earth). – وحَقْلَة
Fertile field. حَقْلَة
Remainder of water, milk. حَقْلَة وحُقْلَة
Sown field. مَحْقَلَة ج مَحاقِل
To be broken. weary (old man). To sleep. To decline. To walk with short steps. ✻ حَوْقَلَ حَوْقَلَةً وحِيقالًا
Impotent, aged man. حَوْقَل
Long-necked bottle. حَوْقَلَة
A kind of pigeon. ✻ حَقْم
Exterior angle of the eye. حَقِيم مث حَقِيمان
To withhold a. th. To collect (milk. in a skin: water, in a tank). To keep in (urine). To prevent (bloodshed). ✻ حَقَنَ o i ه
To administer a clyster to a. o. – ه
To mix various kinds of milk. أَحْقَنَ
To take a clyster. To suffer from strangury. To collect in a wound (blood). احْتَقَنَ
Clyster. حُقْنَة ج حُقَن
Pain in the belly. حَقْنَة ج أَحْقان
Suffering from retention of urine. Decumbent (new moon). حاقِن
Stomach. حاقِنَة ج حَواقِن
Collected in a tank (water). Poured into a skin (milk). حَقِين ومَحْقُون
Congestion of blood. إِحْتِقان دَمَوِيّ
Lymphatic congestion. – مَفْصِلِيّ
Milk-skin. مِحْقَن
Syringe. مِحْقَن ومِحْقَنَة
Retaining his urine. Tank. Fish-pond. Funnel. مِحْقان ج مَحاقِين
To hit a. o. on the loins. ✻ حَقا o حَقْوًا ه
To feel a pain on the loins. حَقِيَ حَقًا وتَحَقَّى
Waist-wrapper. Loins, waist. Foot of a mountain. حَقْو ج حِقاء وأَحْقٍ وأَحْقاء وحُقِيّ
Waist-wrapper. Pain in the belly. حِقْوَة وحَقْوَة
Having a complaint of مَحْقُوّ ومَحْقِيّ

To regret a. th. — تحكّر على
Wrongful behaviour. — حُكْر
Drinking cup. Little of water. — وحُكْر —
Monopolized (corn, goods). — حُكْر وحُكُر
Withholding of corn. — حُكْرَة
Withholder of corn. — حَكِر
✧ Kitchen-garden. — ✧ حاكورة
To make up (things). To detain. To wrong a. o. ✧ To draw (a wick). To stir (the fire). — ✱ حَكَش i حَكْشًا ه وه
Wick-holder. — ✧ مِحْكاش
To be remiss in work. — ✱ حَكَف i حُكُوفًا
To be confused, doubtful to a. o. (news). — ✱ حَكِل o حَكَلًا ، وأحْكَل واحْتَكَل على
✧ To be obliged to. — احْتَكَل إلى
A voiceless insect. — حُكْل
To speak inaudibly. — تكلّم كلام الحُكْل
Barbarous pronunciation. ✧ Great need. — حُكْلَة
To give judgment on. — ✱ حَكَم o حُكْمًا وحُكُومَةً ب
✧ To practice fencing. — حَكَم
✧ To overtake a. o. (rain, mishap). — ه —
To judge between (two parties). — بَيْن —
To pass sentence in favour of or against a. o. — ل او على —
To check (a horse) with a curb-bit. — وأحْكَم ه —
To come back. — حَكِم o حَكَمًا
To withhold a. o. To counteract a. o. — حَكَّم وحاكَم وأحْكَم ه
To be prudent, wise. — حَكُم o حِكْمَةً
✧ To practice medicine. — حَكَّم
To appoint a. o. as governor. — ه —
To choose a. o. as judge in. — حَكَّم ه في
To summon a. o. — حاكَم ه
To do a. th. well. To attach a ring to (a horse's bridle). — أحْكَم ه
To teach a. o. (trials). — ه —
To pass judgment on. To give a decision without regard to justice. To have o.'s own way. — تَحَكَّم واحْتَكَم في
To summon a. o. to. — تحاكَم واحْتَكَم إلى
To prevail upon a. o. — احْتَكَم على
To be thoroughly made, strong (work). — اسْتَحْكَم
To fortify (a place). — ه —
Sentence. Authority. Order. Law. Wisdom. — حُكْم ج أحْكام
✧ Judgment in presence of the adverse parties. — حُكْم وَجاهِيّ
✧ Judgment by default. — حُكْم غِيابِيّ
Judge. Aged man. ✧ Fencing. — حَكَم
Justice. Wisdom. Science. Philosophy. Forbearance. Prophecy. ✧ Medical knowledge. — حِكْمَة ج حِكَم
Martingale. Ring of a bridle. Head. State of a man. — حَكَمَة ج حَكَمات
Judicial authority. ✧ Government. — حُكُومَة
The local Authorities. — الحُكُومَة المَحَلِّيَّة
The turkish Government. — الحُكُومَة السَّنِيَّة
Governor. Judge. — حاكِم ج حُكّام وحاكِمُون
Name of Mansour, one of the Fatimite Caliphs. — الحاكِم بأمْرِهِ
Wise, learned man. Philosopher. ✧ Medical man. — حَكِيم ج حُكَماء
✧ Arbitration. — تَحْكِيم
✧ Compromise. — صَكّ التَّحْكِيم
Condemned (man). — المَحْكُوم عَلَيْهِ
Point at issue (*in law*). — المَحْكُوم بِهِ
✧ Tribunal. Court. — مَحْكَمَة ج مَحاكِم
Court of first instance. — مَحْكَمَة ابتِدائيَّة
Court of appeal. — مَحْكَمَة الإسْتِئناف
Proceedings of error. — مَحْكَمَة التَّمْيِيز
Judging o.'s self rightly. — مُحْكِم
✧ Arbitrator. Umpire. — مُحَكَّم
✧ Award. — حُكْم المُحَكَّمِين
Trial. Hearing of a case. — مُحاكَمَة
Law proceedings. — أُصول المُحاكَمات
Fortifications. — ✧ استِحْكامات ومُسْتَحْكَمات
To relate (a fact). — ✱ حَكَى i حِكايَةً ه
✧ To speak. — حَكَى
To relate a. th. on the authority of. — ه عن —
To backbite a. o. — على —
To speak or act like a. o. — ه وه —
To be alike to. To imitate (an action). ✧ To converse with. — حاكَى ه وه
To overcome a. o. — أحْكَى على

✧ حَكِي Word, speech.
حِكَايَة Narrative, story, tale.
✱ حَلَّ o حَلًّا ه وه To untie (a knot). To remit (sins). To solve (a difficulty). To wind off (cocoons). To unbend (a bow). ✧ To absolve a. o. To dilute a. th.
حَلَّ i o حُلُولًا وحَلًّا ه وب To alight at. ✧ To become (time). To come off (colour).
حَلَّكَ أن تَفعَل كَذَا ✧ It is time for thee to do so.
— عَلَى To befall a. o. (punishment).
حَلَّ مَحَلَّهُ He is the right man in the right place.
— حِلَّة To become free from marriage.
— o i حُلُولًا عَلَى To be obligatory on.
حَلَّ i حِلًّا To become lawful. To become due (debt).
حُلَّ To melt (ice). To dissolve. To be inhabited (place).
حَلَّ a حَلَلًا To have weak legs (horse). To feel a pain in the knees.
حَلَّل تحليلًا وتَحِلَّةً وتَحِلًّا ه To annul (an oath). To dispense with.
— تحليلًا ه To permit a. th. (God). To legitimize a. th. To expiate a. th.
— ه ب To make a. o. alight at.
أَحَلَّ To become free from obligation.
أَحَلَّ ه To make a. th. lawful (God).
— ه وه ب To let a. o. or a. th. down in.
— عَلَى To impose an obligation upon a. o.
تَحَلَّل في يَمِينِهِ He swore in making an exception.
اِنْحَلَّ To be loosened (knot).
اِحْتَلَّ ه وب To alight in (a place). To occupy (a country : army).
اِسْتَحَلَّ ه To consider a. th. as lawful.
— ه ه To ask a. o. to allow a. th.
حَلّ Loosening. Solution of difficulties. Dissolution. ✧ Absolution. Poetry turned into prose.
حِلّ Lawful thing. Absolution of an oath. Butt.
الحِلّ والرَّبْط Supreme authority.
عَلَى الحِلّ ✧ Pure, unmixed.

حَلَل Laxness of the hocks. Pain in the knees.
حَلَّة Large basket made of reeds.
Hamlet. Quarter of a town. Direction. ✧ Copper saucepan.
حَيٌّ حِلَال Nomadic tribe.
حُلَّة ج حُلَل وحِلَال Set of clothes. ✧ Sacerdotal vestments.
حَلَال (*opp. to* حَرَام) Lawful thing.
اِبْن حَلَال ✧ Honest man.
حَلَّالَة ✧ Instrument for winding silk.
حَلِيل ج أَحِلَّاء م حَلِيل وحَلِيلَة ج حَلَائِل Fellow-lodger, husband, wife.
إِحْلَال Fulfilling of the rites of the pilgrimage.
إِحْلَال ج أَحَالِيل Orifice of the udder.
أَحَلّ م حَلَّاء ج حُلّ Weak-legged.
تَحْلِيل Dispensation. ✧ Resolution of a tumour.
اِحْتِلَال Military occupation.
مَحَلّ ج مَحَالّ Halting-place. Station. Place. ✧ Firm. Funeral meeting. Liable to.
مَحَلَّة Inn. Station. Encampment. District. Quarter of a town.
مَحَلِّيّ Local.
✱ حَلْحَل ه To startle, to turn a. o. out.
تَحَلْحَل To be shaken, turned out.
حَلْحَل Bulbus esculentus (*plant*).
حُلَاحِل ج حَلَاحِل Chief of a tribe. Mighty.
✱ حَلَأ a حَلْأً ه ب To strike a. o with (a sword).
— بِهِ الأرضَ To prostrate a. o. on the ground.
— ه To apply collyrium to a. o.
— ل To prepare collyrium for a. o.
— حَلْأً وحَلَاءَةً ه To rub off (the skin). To bark. a. th.
— وحَلَّأَ تَحْلِيئًا وتَحْلِئَةً ه ه To give money to a. o.
حَلِئَ a حَلَأً To become covered with pustules.
حَلَأ Pustules upon the lips.
حَلُوء وحَلَاءَة Collyrium for ophtalmia.
حَلَاءَة وتِحْلِئ وتِحْلِئَة Hair and dirt shaven off by a currier.
تِحْلِئَة Troublesome (man).

مِحْلَأ ومِحْلَأَة Currier's knife.

✻ حَلَب o i حَلْبًا وحَلَبًا وحِلَابًا ه To milk (a female). ✧ To gull a. o. and take his money.

.. وأَحْلَبَ ه To allow a. o. to milk (a sheep).

.. وأَحْلَبَ واسْتَحْلَبَ To come to the rescue (party).

حَلِبَ a حَلَبًا To be black (hair).

حَالَبَ ه To milk in company of.

— وأَحْلَبَ ه To assist a. o.

أَحْلَبَ إِحْلَابًا وإِحْلَابَةً ل To draw milk for.

تَحَلَّبَ وانْحَلَبَ To flow with (sweat: body; with tears: eyes).

احْتَلَبَ واسْتَحْلَبَ ه To draw milk from.

حَلَب Fresh milk. Date-wine. Tax. Aleppo (town).

حَلَبُ الكَرْم وحَلَبُ العَصِير Wine.

حَلْبَة ج حَلَائِب One milking. Horses assembled for a race. ▫ Anchor.

الحَلْبَتَان Morning and evening.

حُلْبَة Fenugreek (*plant*). Food given to a confined woman.

حُلَّب A milky, evergreen plant much sought by sheep, gazelles.

حَلْبَانَة Storax.

حَالِب مث حَالِبَان Vein on the two sides of the navel.

حِلَاب ومِحْلَب Milking-vessel.

حَلِيب Fresh milk. Fresh (blood).

حَلَّاب Milker. Damp (day).

حَلُوب وحَلُوبَة ج حُلُب وحَلَائِب Milch camel. She-camel yielding milk.

مَحْلَب Prunus mahaleb (*plant*).

مُحْلَب ج مَحَالِب Groin, inguinal fold.

مُحْلِب Assistant, helper.

مَحْلَبِيَّة ✧ Food made of milk and flour.

مُسْتَحْلَب ✧ Emulsion, milk of (almonds).

حُلْبُوب Mercury (*plant*). Intensely black.

حِلِبْلَاب وحَلَبْلُوب Ivy. Euphorbia.

✻ حَلَتَ i حَلْتًا ه وه To shave (the head). To pluck (wool). To pay (a debt). To remain (on horseback). To flog a. o.

حُلَاتَة Flake of wool.

حَلِيت Ice. Frost. Hail.

حِلْتِيت وحِلِتِّيت Assafœtida.

✻ حَلَجَ o i حَلْجًا ه To card cotton. To round (a cake). To twist (a rope).

حَلَجَ To walk slowly.

— لَيْلًا To walk (the whole night).

— (for حَجَلَ) ✧ To limp. To hop.

تَحَلَّجَ To send forth lightnings (cloud).

— في صَدْرِهِ To be troubled by cares.

حَلْجَة Distance.

حَلُوج Cloud sending forth lightnings.

حَلَّاج Cotton-dresser.

مِحْلَج ومِحْلَاج Carding-machine.

مِحْلَج ومِحْلَجَة Table for dressing cotton.

مِحْلَاج ج مَحَالِيج Rolling-pin for dough. Card.

✻ حَلَزَ o حَلْزًا ه To pluck (the hair of a hide). To bark (wood).

تَحَلَّزَ To remain. To be in pangs (heart).

— ل To get ready for.

تَحَالَزَ بالكَلَام He held a conversation.

احْتَلَزَ ه مِن To take o.'s due from.

حِلِزّ م حِلِزَّة Ill-natured. Short. Avaricious.

✧ حَلَزُون Snail, shell.

✻ حَلَسَ i حَلْسًا . وأَحْلَسَ To let down a continuous rain (sky).

— ه To cover a horse with (a blanket).

حَلِسَ a حَلَسًا , وتَحَلَّسَ ب To remain in (a place).

— في وتَحَلَّسَ ل To apply o.'s self to.

حَالَسَ ه To become attached to. To cover (a camel) with a blanket.

أَحْلَسَ To become green with plants (soil).

— واسْتَحْلَسَ ه To hold a. o. continually (fear).

اِحْلَسَّ To be bay, chestnut-coloured (horse).

اسْتَحْلَسَ To become green (land). To cover the soil (plant).

حِلْس ج أَحْلَاس وحُلُوس وحِلَسَة Horse-cloth. Under-garment.

أَحْلَاس الخَيْل People living on horseback.

حَلْس وحَلِس Fourth arrow of a game.

Keeping to his tent. حَلِس بَيْتِهِ
Courageous. Greedy. حَلِس
Bay, chestnut-coloured (horse). أحلس م حَلْساء
Land covered with plants. أرض مُحْلِسة
To pluck out (grass). To reap pulse. ✧ حَلَش i حَلْشًا ه
Sickle. ✧ حالُوش
Reaping of pulse. ✧ حليشة
To be angered. To swear. To insist. To hurry. * حلط i حَلْطًا , وأحلط
To get angry with. حَلِط a حَلَطًا , واحتلط على
To anger a. o. أحلط ه
To take (an oath) with zeal and eagerness. — في
To be weary from. احتلط من
Bald and beardless. ✧ أحلط
To swear by (God). * حلف i حَلْفًا وحَلِفًا ومَحْلُوفًا ومَحْلُوفَة ب
To swear to a. o. by. — ل على
To give an oath to. To bind a. o. by an oath. حلّف وأحلف واستحلف ه
To make a covenant with. To keep to a. th. حالف مُحالَفَة ه وه
To attain puberty (boy). أحلف
To make a confederation. تحالف
Oath. Sworn agreement. Sworn treaty. حَلْف وحَلِف وأُحلوفة ✧ حِلْفان وحَلَف
League, covenant. Friendship. Confederate. حِلْف ج أحلاف
Alfa (*plant*). حَلْفاء
Abounding in alfa-grass. حُلافِيّ
Wont to swear. حَلّاف
Ally. Cleaving to a. th. حَلِيف ج حُلَفاء
Wild boar. □ حَلُّوف
Eloquent. حَليف اللِّسان
Uncertain, dubious. مُحْلِف
Oath. مَحْلُوف ومَحْلُوفة
To shave (the head). * حلق i حَلْقًا وتِحلاقًا , واحتلق ه
To hit a. o. on the throat. — o حَلْقًا ه
To fill up (a tank). To conjecture. — ه
To have a complaint of the throat. حَلِق a حَلَقًا
To soar and circle in the air (bird). To become swollen with milk (udder). To be surrounded with a halo (moon). حلّق
They met round the table. حلّقوا على الخِوان
To shave (the head). To pluck (the hair). To round a. th. — ه
To be surrounded with a halo (moon). To sit in a ring (people). تحلّق
Throat. Gullet. Strait, valley. حَلْق ج أحلاق وحُلُوق
Circle of persons. Ring of metal. Coat of mail. Rope. Buckle. Ferrel. ✧ Ear-ring. □ A thrashing. حَلْقَة ج حَلَق وحَلَقات
✧ Lock of hair. حَلْقة شَعر
The guttural letters. الحُرُوف الحَلْقِيَّة
Death. حَلاقِ والحَلاق
Pain in the throat. حُلاق وحَوْلَق
Shorn hair of a goat. حُلاقَة
Craft of a shaver. حِلاقَة
Barber, hair-dresser. حَلّاق
Bryony (*plant*). حالِق الشَّعر
Udder full of milk. Lofty and bare mountain. حالِق ج حُلُق وحَوالِق
Woman shaving her head in mourning. Unlucky. Bad year. Death. حالِقَة ج حَوالِق
Sharp (sword). Severe (man). حالُوقَة
Calamity, bad luck. حَوْلَق وحَيْلَق
Razor. Coarse garment. مِحْلَق
Shaven. حَلِيق ج حَلْقَى , ومَحْلُوق
To cut the throat of a. o. * حَلْقَمَ ه
Gullet. ✧ Neck of bottles. حُلْقُوم ج حَلاقِيم
✧ Turkish delight. راحة الحُلْقُوم
To become intensely black. * حلك a حَلَكًا واستحلك، واحلولك
Intense blackness. حُلْكَة وحَلَك
Species of lizard. حُلَكَة وحُلُكًا وحَلَكًا وحُلَكًا وحُلَكَى
Intensely black. حالك وحَلِك
Atrocious action. فِعل حالك
Miserable life. عُمر حالك
To dream a. th. * حلم o حُلْمًا وحُلُمًا ه او ب
To be forbearing. حَلُم o حِلْمًا
To be perforated by ticks. حَلِم a حَلَمًا
To render a. o. forbearing. حلّم تحليمًا وحِلامًا ه
To pluck the ticks (from a skin). — ه

○ *Solanum dulcamara*, deadly night-shade (*plant*). حُلْوَة مُرَّة	To bring forth forbearing sons. أحلمت
Sweet, kind (word). حَلِيّ م حَلِيَّة	To affect forbearance. تَحَلَّم
Sweet peas. ✧ حَالِيَة	To relate false dreams. To attain to puberty (boy). To become fat (cattle).
To adorn (a woman, a sword). ✱ حَلَى i حَلْيًا ه وهـ	To affect forbearance. تَحَالَم
To be attired (woman). حَلِيَ a حَلْيًا	To see evil dreams. إِنْحَلَم واحْتَلَم
To deck a. o. or a. th. حَلَّى ه وهـ	Forbearance. Mind. حِلْم ج حُلُوم وأَحْلَام
To describe (a man).	Dream. حُلْم ج أَحْلَام
To gild a. th. — هـ بِذَهَب	Evil dreams. Night-mare. أَضْغَاث أَحْلَام
To be adorned with jewels. تَحَلَّى	False hope. أَحْلَام نَائِم
To be embellished.	Coarse garment.
Ornaments of (a sword or a woman). حَلْي ج حُلِيّ , وحِلْيَة ج حِلًى وحُلًى	Nipple of the breast. حَلَمَة ج حَلَم
Exterior qualities of a man. حِلْيَة	Worm, tick. ✧ Mouth-piece.
The thistle نَصِيّ when dry. حَلِيّ ج أَحْلِيَة	Full of ticks. حَلِم م حَلِمَة
Asparagus. ○ حَلْيُون	*Anchusa*, alkanet (plant). حَالُوم
To heat (water, a bath, a stove). ✱ حَمَّ o حَمًّا , وحَمَّم وأَحَمَّ هـ	Salt cheese. ○ جُبْن حَالُوم
To urge on (a beast). To busy the mind of a. o. (affair). حَمَّ ه	Forbearing. *God*. Fat camel. حَلِيم ج حُلَمَاء
To melt (the grease). — هـ	Devoured by vermin. تَحْلِمَة ج تَحَالِم
To decree a. th. to a. o. (God). — وأَحَمَّ هـ ل	✱ حَلَا o وحَلُوَ o وحَلِيَ a حَلَاوَة وحُلْوَانًا To be sweet. To be ripe (fruit). To be delicious (th.).
To be accomplished (thing). To be at hand. To be seized with fever. حُمَّ	To be agreeable, pleasing to the sight, to the mind. حَلِيَ a ب او في
To become black. حَمَّ a حَمَمًا	To marry (a sister, a daughter) to a. o. on the condition of having a part or the whole of the dowry. حَلَا o حَلْوًا وحُلْوَانًا ه ه
To be hot (water).	To give (a gratuity) to. — حَلْوًا ه هـ وب
To appear (beard of a youth; hair on the head). To come forth (bird's plumage; plants). حَمَّم	To sweeten (a. th.). — وحَلَّى تَحْلِيَة هـ
✧ To give a hot bath.	To render a. th. pleasing.
To blacken (the face) with charcoal. — وأَحَمَّ ه	To show kindness to. حَالَى ه
To approach. a. o. حَامَّ ه مُحَامَّة	To find, or to render a. th. sweet, pleasing. أَحْلَى هـ
To seek a. o.	To find a. th. sweet, pleasing. تَحَلَّى واحْلَوْلَى واسْتَحْلَى هـ
To be imminent (event). أَحَمَّ	To show meekness, kindness. تَحَالَى
To be feverous (country).	To be sweet, pleasing. إِحْلَوْلَى
To wash o.'s self with cold water. To render a. o. black (God). — ه	Sweetness. ✧ Gratuity. حَلَاوَة
To afflict a. o. with fever.	Fee. Gratuity. Dowry. حُلْوَان
To be black. ✧ To take a bath. تَحَمَّم	Middlepart of the back of the head. حَلَاة وحَلَاوَة وحُلَاوَاء وحُلَاوَى
To be anxious (man). اِحْتَمَّ	حَلْوَاء وحَلْوَى ج حَلَاوَى و✧ حَلَاوِيَات , ومَحْلِي Sweetmeats.
To be sleepless (eye).	Seller of sweetmeats. حَلْوَانِي
To take a hot bath. اِسْتَحَمَّ	Sweet. Nice. حُلْو م حُلْوَة
To take any bath. To sweat.	Pleasing (person).
Vehemence of heat. حَمّ	
It is his ineluctable مَا لَهُ حَمٌّ عَنْهُ ومِنْهُ	

To cleanse (a well).	✻ حَمَا a حَمْأً ه
To be muddy (water).	حَمِئَ a حَمَأً ، حَمَاءً
To become angry with a. o.	— على
To throw mud in (a well).	أحْمَأَ ه
Black slime; filth.	حَمَأ و حَمْأَة
Slough.	حَمِيُّ و حَمِيٌّ
Evil-eyed (man).	
Muddy, slimy.	حَمِئَة
To become rancid (walnut).	✻ حَمِتَ a حَمَتًا
To be intensely hot (day).	حَمُتَ o حُمُوتَةً
To be clear, pure (colour).	تَحَمَّتَ
Hot (day).	حَمْت
Very sweet (date).	
Firm. Violent (anger).	حَمِيت
Sweet (dates). Skin for butter.	
To sink (eye).	✻ حَمَّجَ
To be altered from passion (face).	
To wink (the eyes).	— ه
To turn the eyes about a. th.	
A young antelope.	حَمُوج
To praise a. o. for.	✻ حَمِدَ a حَمْدًا، مَحْمَدًا مَحْمَدَةً ه على
To requite a. o. for.	
To praise God much, or repeatedly.	حَمَّدَ الله
To make a. th. praiseworthy.	أحْمَدَ
To deserve praise.	
To find a. o. or a. th. to be praiseworthy.	— ه و ه
To affect praise.	تَحَمَّدَ
To praise one's self.	
To prevail one's self upon a. o. for.	تَحَمَّدَ بِ و على
To praise a. th. one to another.	تَحَامَدَ ه
For اِحْتَمَدَ.	اِحْتَمَدَ
To require praise of a. o.	اِسْتَحْمَدَ الى
Praise, eulogy.	حَمْد
Praiseworthy.	
Praise be to God.	الحَمْدُ لله
Thanks to him.	حَمَادِ لَهُ
Sound of the flaming (for حَدَمَة).	حَمْدَة
Aim, utmost exertion.	حُمَاد
The utmost	حُمَادَكَ وحُمَادَاكَ ان تَفْعَل

fate.	
Main part of a thing.	حُمّ وحُمّ وحُمَّة الشي
Fever. Feverish heat.	حُمَّى ج حُمَّيَات
Tertian ague.	حُمَّى ثَالِثَة
Ague.	حُمَّى بَارِدَة و نَافِضَة
Inflammatory fever.	— إِلْتِهَابِيَّة
Hectic, continued fever.	— لازِمَة ودَائِمَة
✧ Malignant fever.	— خَبِيثَة
Putrid fever.	— عُفُونِيَّة
Hot spring. Thermal spring.	حَمَّة
Dark colour. Fever.	حُمَّة
The chief part of the heat.	
Venom, poison.	
Decree of God.	حُمَّة ج حُمَم
Charcoal, ashes.	حُمَم
Sweat. Death.	حِمَّة
Pigeon, any ringed bird.	حَمَام
Burdock (*plant*).	رَاعِي الحَمَام
A pigeon.	حَمَامَة ج حَمَامَات وحَمَائِم
Middle part of the breast. Beautiful woman. Choice part of a flock.	
Fever of horses or camels.	حُمَام
A noble chief.	
Fate. Death.	حِمَام
Warm bath.	حَمَّام ج حَمَّامَات
Turkish bath. Bath.	
Keeper of a bath.	حَمَّامِي و ✧ حَمَّامْجِي
Special friends. Choice camels.	حَامَّة
Hot or cold water.	حَمِيم ج حَمَائِم
Sweat. Midsummer. Midsummer rain.	
Relation, friend.	— ج أحِمَّاء
Hot water.	حَمِيمَة ج حَمَائِم
Warmed milk. Valuable camel.	
Black. White	ألأحَمّ ج حُمّ
A most beloved friend (or like).	
Feverish. Afflicted with fever.	مَحْمُوم
Decreed, or appointed.	
Any thing black. Smoke.	يَحْمُوم
Copper-boiler.	مِحَمّ
Keeping steadily to an affair.	مُحَامّ على
To neigh with a yearning sound (horse).	✻ حَمْحَمَ و تَحَمْحَمَ
Bugloss, ox-tongue (*plant*).	حِمْحِمَة ج حِمْحِم
Sweet basil (*plant*).	حَمَاحِم

of thy ability is to do....
Who praises much. حَمَّاد وحُمَدَة
Praiseworthy. حَمِيد وحَمُود
Spoken well of. Praised.
Commendable (deed).
✧ Scammony (*plant*). مَحْمُودَة
Praiseworthy action. مَحْمَدَة ج مَحَامِد
Praiseworthy. مُحَمَّد و مَحْمُود
Much praised.
To say الحَمْدُ لله ✽ حَمْدَل
i. e. Praise be to God.
Name of action. حَمْدَلَة
The formula الحَمْدُ لله.
To flay (a sheep). ✽ حَمَر o حَمْرًا ه وه
To strip a. th. of his superficial part, viz. peel, bark.
To excoriate a. th.
To shave (the head).
To become diseased حَمِر a حَمَرًا
(from overfeeding : horse).
To burn with anger (man). حَمِر على
To degenerate,
to become like an ass.
To excoriate a. th. حَمَّر ه
To cut a. th. in pieces. — ه
To dye a. th. red. — ه
To call a. o. an ass. — ه
✧ To roast a. th. — ه
To ride a jade. حَمَّر
To speak Hymiaritic.
To assert o.'s self تَحَمَّر
to be related to Hymiar.
To speak the dialect of Hymiar. تَحَمْيَر
To become red. احْمَرّ
To become hot (war).
To become accidentally red. إحْمَارّ
Inflammation caused to horses حَمَر
by eating too much barley,
or by prolonged thirst.
Tamarind. Jew's pitch. حُمَّر
Red-headed sparrow.
Choice part of a flock. حُمْر النَّعَم
Red colour. حُمْرَة
Red dye (for the face).
Erysipelas; anthrax.
✧ Pounded bricks.
Violent rain ; حَمِير
Violence, intenseness of a. th.
حِمَار ج حَمِير وأَحْمِرَة وحُمُر وحُمُور وحُمُرَات

Ass. Polisher for iron.
Wild ass. حِمَار الوَحْش وحِمَار وَحْش
She-ass. حِمَارَة ج حَمَائِر
Large rock. Tombstone.
Ass-driver. حَمَّار ج حَمَّارَة
✧ Measles. حُمَيْرَة
Pigeon-foot, *anchusa* (plant) حُمَيْرَاء
Hymiarites (ancient tribe حِمْيَر
of Yemen).
Red. أَحْمَر م حَمْرَاء ج حُمْر
Gold and silver. الأَحْمَر والأَبْيَض
Flesh-meat and wine. الأَحْمَرَان
Gold and saffron.
Bloody death. المَوْت الأَحْمَر
The red-faced (the foreigners). الحَمْرَاء
A recent footprint. وَطْأَة حَمْرَاء
A severe year. سَنَة حَمْرَاء
Granada (town). الحَمْرَاء
Intensely red. أَحْمَرِيّ
Suffering indigestion (horse). مَحْمُور
Red. Onager. يَحْمُور
To bite the tongue ✽ حَمَز i حَمْزًا ه
(acid). To sharpen (a blade).
To impress the mind (speech).
To become thick, hard. حَمُز o حَمَازَة
Acrid (drink). Sour (milk). حَامِز
Of a lively temper.... حَامِز الفُؤَاد وحَمِيز
Strong-hearted.
Pungency, acritude. حَمْز
Digestive. Tenacious. حَمُوز
To fry (meat). ✽ حَمَس o حَمْسًا ه وه
To irritate a. o.
To be rigorous حَمِس a حَمَسًا
(in religion); to be firm (in war).
To be courageous. — حَمَاسَة
To irritate a. o. حَمَّس وأَحْمَس ه وه
To excite a. o.
To heat (a machine upon the fire).
To feign rebellion, rigour. تَحَمَّس
To act with forced hardness.
To defend one's self.
To contend for superiority تَحَامَس
with o. another.
To be angry. احْمَوْمَس
Tortoise. حَمْسَة ج حَمَس
Bravery. Energy (in action). حَمَاسَة
Heroical poem. Enthusiam.
Brave, energetic. Oven. حَمِيس
Rigorous أَحْمَس م حَمْسَاء ج حُمْس وأَحَامِس

upon acid plants (camel).
To render a. th. sour, acid. حَمَّض وأحمَض ه
To discard a. th. from. حَمَّض ه عن
To reach acid plants. To be abundant in acid plants (soil). أحمَض
To pasture (camels) upon acid plants. — ه
To discard a. th. from. — ه عن
To relate interesting discourse, poetry. —
To turn from o. th. to another. تَحَمَّض
Salt or bitter plants. Glasswort. Soda. حَمْض ج حُمُوض
Eager desire. حَمْضَة
Acidity, sourness, pungency. حُمُوضَة
Sorrel. ✧ Species of citron. حُمَّاض و✧ حُمَّيض وحُمَّيْضَة
Pulp of the cedrat. حُمَّاض الأُتْرُجّ
Wild sorrel. حُمَّاض البَقَر
Dodder (*plant*). — الأرنب
Rumex aquatica, water-dock. — الماء
Sour, acid. ✧ Peevish (man) Chemical acid. حامِض و✧ حامِض
Bad-hearted (man). حامِض الفُؤاد
Camels pasturing acid plants. إبل حامِضة
Land full of acid plants. حَمِيضَة ج حُمُض — ومَحمَض ومُحمِض
To take off the skin of. ✲ حَمَط i حَمْطًا ه
To plant a tree in order to shade. To diminish a. th. To strike a. o. gently. حَمَّط ه وه
Bottom of the heart. Straw of indian corn. Heart's blood. حَماطَة
Burning in the throat. Wild fig-tree. — ج حَماط وحَمائِط
To be stupid, foolish. ✲ حَمِق a وحَمُق o حُمْقًا وحُمُقًا وحَماقَةً
To be dull (market, trade). حَمِقَت السُّوق
✧ To be in a rage. (for حَنِق) حَمِق
To ascribe foolishness to. حَمَّق ه وه
To find a. o. stupid. To bring forth a fool. أحمَق ه
How stupid or foolish is he! ما أحمَقَهُ
To feign stupidity. تَحامَق
To be stupid. To act like a fool. انحَمَق

(in religion). Brave. Firm in war. Severe (year).
A pious man. أحمَس ومُتَحَمِّس
Unfruitful year. سَنَة حَمْساء ج سِنُون حُمْس
A sterile land. أرض أحامِس
To collect a o. To stir a. o To irritate a. o. To repel (people) in anger. ✲ حَمَش حَمْشًا ه وه
To be thin (shank). حَمِش وحَمُش o حُمُوشَة
To become angry (man). To become hot (war). — حَمْشًا وحَمْشَة
To be thin-legged (man). حَمِش a حَمْشًا وحَمَشًا
To collect a. th. To stir, to anger a. o. To put fuel (in the fire). To rouse (people). حَمَّش ه وه
To be angered. تَحَمَّش واستَحمَش
To become slender (bow-ring). استَحمَش
Thin-legged (man). Or better أحمَش الساقين حَمْش وأحمَش ج حِماش
Slender in make. حَمْش الخِلقَة
To be reduced (swelling of a wound). To stop (swing). To swing (boy). To be dried (sweating beast of burden). ✲ حَمَص o حَمْصًا وحُمُوصًا
To extract (a straw) from the eye. حَمَّص ه
To roast (coffee); to toast a. th. حَمَّص ه
To hunt in the midst of day. —
To contract o.'s self. To be shrivelled (dry meat). تَحَمَّص
To be reduced (swelling). To become emaciated (she-camel). انحَمَص
Homs. *Emesa, town in Syria.* حِمْص
Peas. Chick-peas. حِمَّص وحِمِّص و✧ حُمُّص
Who ceases to be swollen. حَمِيص
Sheep stolen حَمِيصَة ومَحمُوصَة ج حَمائِص
✧ Cautery. حَمْصَة
Coffee-roaster. Gridiron. مِحمَصَة
✲ حَمَض o حَمْضًا — وحَمِض a حَمَضًا — وحَمُض o حُمُوضَة To be or become sour (plant, milk, wine).
To dislike a. th. حَمَض o حَمْضًا عن
To desire a. th. — ب
To graze — o حَمْضًا وحُمُوضًا , وحَمَّض

To become impotent to do a thing.
To be dull (market).
To be worn out (clothes).
To become stupid, to act like a fool. اِستحمق
To hold a. o. to be stupid. ه —
Weakness of judgment; Stagnancy. Dulness. حُمق وحَماقة
Rage, fit of passion. (*for* حَنَق) ✧ حَمَق
Small-pox. حُمَاق م وحُمَاق وحَمِيق وحُمَيْقَى وحُمَيْقَاء
Stupid, weak-minded. أحمَق م حَمْقاء ج حِماق وحُمُق وحُمْقَى وحَماقَى
Id. حَمِق وحَمْقان
Comparative. More stupid. أحمَق
Out of temper. ✧ حَمْقان
Garden purslane (*plant*). بَقلة الحَمْقاء
A foolish action أُحموقة
Affected with small-pox. مَحْمُوق
To lead the way (guide). ✻ حَمِك a حَمْكًا في الدَّلالة
Anything small. Lice. Lamp. Refuse of men. Essence. Guide. حَمَك
To carry, to bear a. th. ✻ حَمَل i حَمْلًا وحُمْلانًا ه
To constrain a. o. to bear. — ه على
To mount a. o. upon (a beast). — ه على
To be pregnant with (woman). To produce fruit (tree). — حَمْلًا (n.) او — ه
To bear the responsibility for (a debt). — ب حَمالةً وحَمَل الحَمالة
To take the responsibility *for* such a one, *to* such a one. — كذا عن فلان لفلان
To treat a. o. with forbearance. — عن
To know by heart (a book). — ه
To show (anger).
To relate (a tradition).
To rely upon a. o. in. — ه في وعلى
To charge (the enemy). — حَمْلة على
To incite a. o. to. — ه على
To make a word to accord with another. — لفظًا على لفظ
To charge (a mistake) upon the copyist. حَمَل ه على الناسخ
To load a. o. with. To impose a burden upon. To charge a. o. with. حَمَّل تحميلًا وحِمالًا ه ه
To help a. o. in bearing. حامَل ه

To reward, to requite a. o.
To help a. o. to carry a. th. أحمَل ه ه
To take upon o.'self the bearing of. To endure. To load beasts for setting off. تَحَمَّل تَحَمُّلًا وتحمالًا ه
To rely upon a. o. in. تَحَمَّل ه في وعلى
To become responsible for (a debt, a bloodwit). — بهِ
To bear the responsibility. — الحَمالة
To go away, to depart. —
To take upon o.'s self a duty. To constrain o.'s self to. تَحامَل في أمرٍ او بهِ او على نفسهِ
To press heavily upon. تَحامَل على
To treat a. o. wrongfully, unfairly. تَحامَل على وعن
To be favourable to. — الى
To be incited. instigated, induced to. انحَمل على
To carry a. th. اِحتمَل ه
To bear a. th. patiently.
To forgive. To carry a. th. away.
To mount a. o. upon (a beast). — ه على
To go away from. — مِن
To be susceptible of different meanings; to be equivocal. —
Anger disquieted him. اِحتمَل ه الغضب
يَحتمِلُ او يُحتمَل ان يكون هكذا
It it supposable that it may be thus; it may be thus.
To become angry. أُحْتُمِل
✧ To be likely possible.
To ask a. o. to carry a. th. اِستحمَل ه ه
Portage. حَمْل ج حِمال وأحمال
Gestation. Fœtus. Fruit (of a tree).
Load, burden. حِمْل ج أحمال وحُمولة
Litter. حِمْل ج حُمُول
Lamb. حَمَل ج حُملان وأحمال
Young ram. Aries (*Zodiacal sign*).
Cloud containing much water.
Charge at war. حَمْلة
What is carried at one time.
Transport. حُمْلة وحِمْلة
Porterage. Beast of burden. Adulterating alloy. حُمْلان
Debt taken upon o.'s self by a person. Responsibility taken by a person. Bloodwit. Tax. حَمال ج حُمُل وحَمالة

حِمَالَة وَحَمِيلَة ج حَمَائِل , ومِحْمَل ج مَحَامِل Sword-belt.

حِمَالَة Portage.

حَمَّال م حَمَّالَة Porter. Carrier.

حَمُول Meek.

حَمُولَة Beast of burden. ✧ Porterage.

حَمِيل Conveyed. Stranger. A surety. Rubbish. Foundling.

حَامِل ج حَمَلَة Pregnant (woman). ✧ Swollen (river). Bearer of a bill.

حَامِلَة ج حَوَامِل Basket for carrying grapes. Pregnant (woman).

حَوَامِل Sinews of the arms and legs. Legs.

إِحْتِمَال Patience. Opinion. ✧ Likeliness.

مَحْمِل ج مَحَامِل Litter on a camel. Basket for grapes. ✧ Litter for the dead.

مِحْمَل ج مَحَامِل Caravan of the pilgrims to Mecca.

مَحْمُول Borne. Predicate.

مَحْمُولَة Wheat dust-coloured and large-eared.

مُحْتَمَل ✧ Admissible. Possible.

✱ حَوْمَل حَوْمَلَة To carry (water). To be a water-carrier.

حَوْمَل Clear torrent. Beginning. Black cloud full of water.

✱ حَمْلَج ه To twist (a rope) strongly.

حِمْلَاج Bellows of a smith.

✱ حَمْلَق To open widely the eyes and stare at.

حُمْلَاق وحُمْلُوق ج حَمَالِيق Inner part of the eyelids.

✱ حَمْن وحَمْنَان Small ticks.

حَوْمَان Plant of the desert.

✱ حَمُو وحَمْو وحَمًا وحَمْءٌ وحَم ج أَحْمَاء

Father-in-law. Any male relation on the side of the husband.

حَمَاة ج حَمَوَات Mother-in-law. Any female relation on the side of the wife. Muscle of the shank. Hama, town of Syria.

حَمْو وحَمِي Heat of the sun.

✱ حَمَى i حَمْيًا وحِمْيَة وحِمَايَة ومَحْمِيَة ه وه

To protect a. o. against. ✧ To heat a. th.

— ه ه To interdict a noxious food to a sick man.

حَمِيَ a حَمِيَّة ومَحْمِيَة مِن To scorn to do a. th.

حَمِيَ a حَمْيًا وحُمِيًّا وحُمُوًّا To become hot (fire, sun, horse, iron).

— على To be angered with.

حَمَّى تَحْمِيَة ه وه To heat a. th. To excite a. o.

حَامَى مُحَامَاة وحِمَاء عن To defend a. o. against.

— على ضَيْفِهِ To welcome a (guest).

أَحْمَى إِحْمَاء ه To render (a place) inaccessible.

تَحَمَّى واحْتَمَى مِن To abstain from.

تَحَامَى ه To keep aloof from a. th.

إِحْمَوْمَى To become black (cloud, night).

حِمَايَة Protection. ✧ Person under the protectorate of a foreign Power.

حِمًى Inaccessible. Interdicted.

حِمَاء Protective.

حِمْيَة Defended. Diet imposed to (a sick man).

حَمِيَّة Scorn. Enthusiasm, zeal.

حُمَيَّا Outburst of anger. Strength (of wine). Wine. Intensity. Flush (of youth).

حُمَة ج حُمَات وحُمًى Venom, sting of scorpions, hornets. Vehemence (of fire).

حَامٍ ج حُمَاة وحَامِيَة Protector. Hot.

الحَامِي The dog. The lion.

حَامِيَة Defender. Garrison. Rear-guard.

مُحَامٍ ✧ Lawyer. Solicitor.

✱ حَنَّ i حَنِينًا To long for her child (woman). To produce a sound (bow, wand).

— إلى To yearn towards.

— i حَنَّة وحَنَانًا على To incline towards.

— o حَنًّا ه To dispel (an evil).

حَنَّن To blossom (tree) ✧ To be rotten (cheese).

أَحَنَّ ه To twang (a bow).

تَحَنَّنَ على To compassionate, to pity a. o.

تَحَانَّ واسْتَحَنَّ إلى To desire eagerly.

حِنّ Tribe of genii.

حَنَّة Wife. Likeness.

حَنَان و ✧ حِنِّيَّة Mercy. Prosperity. Blessing. Tenderness of heart. Long misfortune. ✧ Force of kindred.

حَنَانَك وحَنَانَيْك I beg thy mercy.

Plaintive wind. Yearning desire. حَنِين
Compassionate. Moaning wind. حَنُون
Woman remarrying for the sake of her children.
Tender-hearted. Sympathetic. حَنَّان
Conspicuous road.
The All-merciful (God). الحَنَّان
Name of a proverbial cobbler. حُنَيْن
He came back with رَجَعَ بِخُفَّيْ حُنَيْن
empty hands.
Merciful to. مُتَحَنِّن على
✻ حَنَا a حَنْوًا To be green (field).
To dye (a. th) red. حَنَّأَ تَحْنِيئًا وتَحْنِئَةً ه
Te be dyed with henna. تَحَنَّأَ تَحَنُّؤًا
Henna. *Lawsonia* حِنَّاء و✧ تَمْر حِنَّاء
inermis used as a red dye.
Arbute, strawberry-tree. الحِنَّاء الأَحْمَر
Lichen. حِنَّاء قُرَيْش
Anchusa tinctoria, alkanet. حِنَّاء الغُولَة
Indigo-plant. حِنَّا مَجْنُون
Withy-tree. حَطَب الحِنَّا
Privet (shrub). شَجَر الحِنَّا
✻ حَنِبَ a حَنَبًا, وحَنَّبَ To be curved
in the backbone (horse). To bend a. o. (old age).
To be bent, crooked (old man). تَحَنَّبَ
To feel pity for. — على
Bent with age. Having curved مُحَنَّب
bones (horse).
✻ حَنْبَشَ To dance. To jump (man). To walk. To clap the hands. To laugh in conversing. To play (boy).
✻ حَنْبَلَ To eat French beans. To put on a fur-garment.
Stout and big-bellied. Worn out حَنْبَل
shoe or skin-garment. Fur. Sea. Flowers of the Egyptian thorn (*acacia vera*). Fruit of the lote-tree. One of the four orthodox Imams.
French beans. حُنْبُل
Following the rite of Hanbal. حَنْبَلِي
✻ حَنْتَم ج حَنَاتِم Green jar. Colocynth-tree. Black clouds.
✻ حَنِثَ a حِنْثًا في To violate (an oath).
To incite a. o. to perjury. أَحْنَثَ ه
To avoid (sin). تَحَنَّثَ مِن
Sin. Perjury حِنْث ج أَحْنَاث
Perjurer ; violator of an oath. حَانِث
Place, occasion of sin. مَحْنَث ج مَحَانِث

✻ حَنَجَ i حَنْجًا ه To incline a. th. To twist (a rope) strongly.
To incline. To be still. To hurry أَحْنَجَ
on in looking back.
To incline a. th. To conceal — ه
(news). To pronounce indistinct speech.
Root, origin. حِنْج
✻ حَنْجَرَ To sink in the head (eye).
To cut open the throat to. — ه
Larynx. (*See* حجر). حَنْجَرَة وحُنْجُور
✻ حِنْجَف وحُنْجُف Head of the haunch.
✧ حَنْجَلَ حَنْجَلَةً وتَحَنْجَلَ ✧ To prance
(horse). To hop. ▫ To dance.
✻ حَنْدَسَ وتَحَنْدَسَ To be intensely dark
(night). To be weakened by a fall.
Very dark night. حِنْدِس ج حَنَادِس
✻ حِنْدَقُوق وحِنْدَقُوقَى Lotus. Sweet trefoil.
✻ حَنْدَل Very short ; dwarf.
✻ حَنَذَ i حَنْذًا وتَحْنَاذًا ه وه To roast (a lamb) with heated stones. To scorch (a traveller : sun).
To make (a horse) — حَنْذًا وحِنَاذًا ه
to sweat.
To promote sweat by lying in إِسْتَحْنَذَ
the sun.
Intense heat. حُنْذَة
Sun. حَنَاذِ
Roasted (meat). Heated حَنِيذ
(water). Perfumed ointment.
✻ حَنَرَ i حَنْرًا ه To build (a vault).
Vault. Crown of an حَنِيرَة ج حَنِير وحَنَائِر
arch. Bow. Carder, instrument used for dressing cotton.
✻ حَنِسَ a حَنْسًا To remain in the thick
of a fight (warrior).
Godly people. حُنُس
✻ حَنَشَ i حَنْشًا ه وه To hunt (a beast).
To deceive a. o. To drive a. o. away. To anger a. o. To bite a. o. (snake).
To remove a. o. from. — وأَحْنَشَ ه عَن
Serpent. Viper. Insect. حَنَش ج أَحْنَاش
Any game of the chase.
✻ حَنَطَ o حُنُوطًا, وأَحْنَطَ To become
mature (wheat, fruit-tree). To become white and mature (shrub *called* رِمْث).
To sigh. To become red — i حَنْطًا
(skin).
To embalm (a dead حَنَّطَ وأَحْنَطَ ه
person).

To die. To be embalmed (dead person). أَخنط

To be embalmed (dead person). تَحنّط

To be angry with a. o. تَحنّط ل

To face death. To be angry. إِستحنط

Wheat. حِنطة ج حِنط

✧ Buckwheat. حِنطة سَوداء

Art of embalming. حِناطة

Aromatics used for embalming. حَناط وحَنوط

Dealer in wheat. حَناط وحَناطيّ

Wheat-seller. Fruit of the spurge. Fruit-bearing (tree). Intense (red). حانِط

He bears rancour towards me. هُوَ حانط ومُستحنِط عليّ

Colocynth (*plant*). ✱ حَنظَل وحَمظَل

To lean on one side. ✱ حَنَف i حَنفًا

To be crook-legged. حَنِف a حَنَفًا, وحَنُف o حَنافَةً

To distort (the foot). حنَّف ه

To act like a Hanefite. To be cirumcised. To devote o.'s self to God's service. To forsake the worship of idols. تحنَّف

✧ To do a. th. accurately. — في

Bow. Razor. Chameleon. Tortoise. Sea-tortoise. حَنفاء

Sincere Moslem. Short. Boot-maker. Straightforward. حَنيف ج حُنَفاء

One of the four orthodox Imams. أَبو حَنيفَة

The Hanefites (*un.* حَنَفيّ) حَنَفيّة وأَحناف

✧ Water-tap. حَنفيّة

Crook-footed. أَحنَف م حَنفاء

To enrage against. ✱ حَنِق a حَنَقًا من وعلى

To spread forth its awn (corn). To bear rancour. To become lean (beast). To be fat (camel). أَحنَق

To enrage a. o. أَحنَق ه

Rage. Rancour. حَنَق ج حِناق

Enraged, angry. حَنِق وحَنيق

To bridle (a horse). ✱ حَنَك o i حَنكًا, واحتنك ه

To understand To fasten a. th. حنك ه

To chew a. th. and rub the palate with it (child). — وحنَّك

To teach, to break a. o. (trials, age). — حَنكًا وحَنَكًا, وحَنَّك وأَحنَك واحتنك ه

To rub the palate (of a beast). حَنَّك ه

To debar a. o. from. أَحنَك ه

To bring a turban under the chin. تحنَّك

To consume a country (locusts). To take the mastery over a. o. To take the whole of a o.'s property. إِحتنك ه وه

To eat much after having eaten little. To be pulled up (root). إِستحنك

Soundness of judgment. Experience. حُنك وحِنك وحُنكة

Palate, lower-jaw. Part beneath the chin. Beak and blackness of the raven. ✧ Mouth. حَنَك ج أَحناك

Taught by experience. حُنك وحَنيك ومُحنَك ومُحنَّك ومُحتنَك

Bridle, head-rope. حِناك ج حُنُك, ومِحنَك

Owl. ✱ حَنمَة ج حَنم

To bend (the back, a stick). To twist (the arm). To make a bow. ✱ حَنا o حَنوًا, وحَنَى i حِنايةً ه

To remain affectionately with her children without remarrying (widow). To lean to. حَنا o حُنُوًّا, وأَحنَى على

To bend, to curve a. th. حنَّى ه

To be bent, crooked. تحنَّى وانحنَى

To feel sympathy for. تحنَّى على

Shop. Tavern. Vintner. حانَاة وحانِيَة, وحانُوت ج حَوانِيت

Shop-keeper. Vintner. حانُوتيّ وحانيّ

Crookedness, curvature. حَنو وحِناية

Any curved member, as rib, jaw. Crooked. حِنو ج أَحناء وحِنيّ وحُنِيّ

Side. Bow of a saddle. حِنو ج أَحناء

Intricate business. أَحناء الأُمور

Wine. Wine-merchant. حانِيَة

Vault. Bow. حَنِيَّة ج حَنايا وحُنيّ

Croock-backed. Bowed (structure). أَحنَى م حَنواء وحَنياء

Sympathising with. أَحنَى ضُلوعًا على

Winding of (a valley). مَحنِيَة ومَحنُوَة ومَحناة ج مَحانٍ ومُنحنَى

To commit (a sin). ✱ حاب o حَوبًا وحُوبًا وحابًا ب

To chide a camel by the cry حَوبِ or حَوبُ. حوَّب

To pursue a sinful course. أَحوب إِحوابًا

To abstain from crime. To pray earnestly. تَحَوَّبَ
To lament, to express grief. — واسْتَحْوَبَ
Sin, crime, fault. حَوْب وحُوب وحَوْبَة وحُوبَة
Grief. Distress; affliction. حَوْب وحُوب
Maternal love. Want. Wife. حُوبَة
Relationship on the mother's side. Need. State. — وحَوْبَة
Soul. حَوْبَاء ج حَوْبَاوَات
To fly about. To prowl about a. th. (bird, beast). ✡ حَاتَ o حَوْتًا وحَوَتَانًا على
To take counsel with. To entice a. o. حَاوَتَ ه
To circumvent a. o. by. ب ه
To dissuade a. o. from. — عن ه
Fish. Large fish. Whale. Pisces (*Zodiacal sign*). حُوت ج حِيتَان وحِوَتَة وأَحْوَات
Salmon-fish. ◻ حُوت سُلَيْمَان
Fomelhaut, star in the Pisces. فَم الحُوت
Surname of the prophet Jonas. صَاحِب الحُوت
Cheater. ◻ حَوِيت
To scatter the earth (horse). To move and scatter a. th. To search (the ground). ✡ حَوَّثَ — أَحَاثَ ه
To extract a. th. إِسْتَحَاثَ ه
He left them scattered about. تَرَكَهُم حَوْثَ بَوْثَ وحِيثَ بِيثَ وحَاثِ بَاثِ وحَوْثًا بَوْثًا
Vein in the liver. حَوْث
✧ Over hill and dale, up and down. حَوْث بَوْث
Liver and the surrounding part. Fat woman. حَوْثَاء
To need, to require a. th. ✡ حَاجَ o حَوْجًا, وأَحْوَجَ واحْتَاجَ إلى
To lead a. o. astray from. حَوَّجَ ب عن
To put a. o. in want of. أَحْوَجَ ه
To seek a. th. wanted, ✧ To purchase goods (merchant). تَحَوَّجَ
Destitution. Need. حُوج
Necessity. Want. حَوْجَاء
I do not want it. مَا لِي فِيهِ حَوْجَاء ولَا لَوْجَاء
Want. Need. Affair. Natural want. ✧ Clothes, things. Luggage. Enough. حَاجَة ج حَاج وحِوَج وحَاجَات وحَوَائِج
Want. Poverty. Need. إِحْتِيَاج
To turn away from. To shun a. th. ✡ حَادَ o حَوْدًا عَن

To seize a. o. repeatedly (fever). حَاوَدَ ه
To drive (a beast) quickly. ✡ حَاذَ o حَوْذًا, وأَحْوَذَ ه
To keep a. th. with care. حَاذَ على
To gather (o.'s clothes). To walk quickly. To pare (an arrow). To trim (verses). أَحْوَذَ
To overcome a. o. To gain the mastery over. إِسْتَحْوَذَ على
Back. Styrax (tree). حَاذ ج آحَاذ
Having little property, little charge *lit*: light-backed. خَفِيف الحَاذ
Nenuphar, water-lily. حَوْذَان
Coachman, driver. حُوذِيّ
Quick in work. Clever manager. أَحْوَذِيّ
To return. To go down (mouthful). To be unsaleable (goods). To be perplexed (man). ✡ حَارَ o حَوْرًا
He passed from abundance to deficiency. حَارَ بَعْدَ مَا كَارَ
He does not increase nor augment. مَا يَحُور ومَا يَبُور
To have its white and its black strongly delineated (eye). حَوِرَ a حَوَرًا, و إِحْوَرَّ
To prepare and spread (dough) with a roller. To whiten (cloth). To disappoint a. o. (God). To cauterise (a camel) around the eye. حَوَّرَ ه وه
To hold a conference with a. o. حَاوَرَ مُحَاوَرَةً وحِوَارًا ه
To return (an answer). To give (a result). أَحَارَ إِحَارَةً ه
To hold a conference together. تَحَاوَرَ
To be intensely white. إِحْوَرَّ
To question a. o. إِسْتَحَارَ ه
Quarter of a town. Street. ✧ Large house. حَارَة ج حَارَات
Deficiency. Perdition. Result. حُور
Ox. White leather. Poplar. حَوَر ج أَحْوَار و✧ حَوْر ج حُوْرَان
White poplar. ✧ حَوْر رُومِي
Black poplar. ✧ حَوْر فَارِسِي
Aspen-tree. حَوْر الزَّجْزَج
Brand. District of Syria. حَوْرَان
Answer. حِوَار وحَوَار وحَوِير
Young unweaned camel. حُوَار · أَحْوِرَة وحِيرَان
Chalk. Tuff, sand-rock. ✧ حُوَارَة

✡ حَاش ٥ حَوْشًا, وأحْوَش وأحاش واسْتَحْوَش ه
To track (a beast) into a snare. To collect and drive (camels).
To collect a. th. ✧ To spare ه وه حَوَّش
(money). To pick up. To park (cattle).
To incite a. o. to. حَاوَش ه على
To remove from. تَحَوَّش عَن
To feel shame at. To be forlorn — مِن
of her husband (wife).
To be tracked (beast). To be collected (camels). إنحاش
To be frightened away. — عَن
To encompass a. o. إحتَوَش وتحَاوَش على
To track (a beast) one party to another. ه —
Enclosure for cattle. Court-yard. Back-yard. ✧ Cloister (in a convent). Hamlet. حَوْش ج أحْوَاش وحِيشَان
Rabble. ✧ حَوْش
Holy week. ✧ جُمْعَة الحَاش
Cause of shame. Relationship. Friend. حُوَاشَة
Grove of palm-trees. حَائِش
Hot-tempered (man). حُوش الفُؤَاد
Odd (expression). Unsociable (man). Dark. حُـوشِيّ
✡ To sew up حَاص ٥ حَوصًا وحِيَاصَةً ه
(a garment). To repair (a skin).
To flutter around a. th. — حَوْل
✧ To be anxious, restless. حَاص
To have an eye contracted حَوِص a حَوَصًا
in its outer angle.
To look at a. o. from the corner of the eye. حَاوَص ه
To act cautiously in. إحتَاص في
Stitching far apart. Colic. حَوْص
Wooden instrument for sewing. حِوَاص
Girth-strap. حِيَاصَة
Narrow-eyed. أحْوَص م حَوْصَاء ج حُوص وأحَاوِص
✡ To collect (water). To build a tank. حَاض ٥ حَوْضًا, وحَوَّض واحتَوَض ه
To make a tank for o.'s self. — واحتَوَض واستَحْوَض
To collect (water) in a tank. إستَحْوَض
Watering-trough. Tank. Dock. Basin. حَوْض و✧ حَاوُز ج أحْوَاض وحِيَاض
✡ حَاط ٥ حَوْطًا وحِيطَةً وحِيَاطَةً وتَحَوَّط ه
To guard, to protect a. th.

Jupiter (planet). Intellect. أحْوَر ج حُور
Fair and black-eyed.
Fair black-eyed (*un.* حُورِيَّة) ✧ و حُور العَيْن
women. Houris, nymphs of paradise.
White; of a fair complexion. أحْوَرِيّ
White flour. ✧ White clay, whiting. حُوَّارَى
Disciple of Jesus-Christ. حَوَارِيّ ج حَوَارِيُّون
Iron pin of a pulley. Ring of the buckle in a waist-belt. Rolling-pin. Axis of a sphere. Axle-tree. مِحْوَر ج مَحَاوِر
His affairs are unsettled. قَلِقَت مَحَاوِرُهُ
Return. Decrease. Litter. Cavity of the ear. Shell, mother-of-pearl. Palate. مَحَارَة
Conference. مُحَاوَرَة وحِوَار
Crooked stick. مِيحَار
✡ To gather a. th. To take a. th. for o.'s self. To possess (an estate). حَاز ٥ حَوْزًا وحِيَازَةً, واحتَاز ه
To brace strongly (a bow). حَاز ه
To drive (camels) to water gently. — وحَوَّز ه
To frequent a. o. حَاوَز ه
To writhe and twist about (serpent). To turn aside (man). تَحَوَّز
To part one from the other. تحَاوَز
To fly away (from the enemy). إنحَاز
Side. Seat of a king. Nature. Grapes. ✧ Enclosure. حَوْزَة
Fenced place. ✧ Styrax (tree). حَوْز
Solitary. Good manager. Black. حُوزِيّ وأحْوَزِيّ
Space. Spot. حَيِّز
Heart-alluring (evil). حَوَّاز القُلُوب
✡ To search. To prowl about. To rove amongst (the sheep: wolf). حَاس ٥ حَوْسًا ه وه
To be brave, daring. حَوِس a حَوَسًا
To assume courage. تَحَوَّس
To be detained. إستَحْوَس
Misfortunes, calamities. خُطُوب حُوس
Society, acquaintances. ✧ حَوْسَة
Want. Booty. حُوَاسَة
Relationship. حُوَيْسَاء
Night-walker. Herald at war. حَوَّاس
Bold, undaunted. Unsatiable. Wolf. أحْوَس ج حُوس

To protect. To surround a. th. حَوَّط ه
To make a wall around a. th. To enclose a. th. (in a wall).
To monopolise a. th. حَوَّط وأحاط على
To be destroyed. أُحِيط بِهِ
To try to circumvent a. o. حاوَط ه
To encompass a. o. ✧ To besiege (a place). To block (a country). أحاط ب
To have a thorough knowledge of. أحاط ب عِلمًا
To take care of. إحتاط على
To encircle, to hem a. o in. — ب
To be on the watch. — لِنفسِهِ
Wariness, prudence. حَوْطة وحَيْطة
Bicoloured string worn as an amulet. Silver-crescent. حَوط
Wall. Garden. حائِط ج حِيطان وحِياط
Tax-gatherer in a village. حَوَّاط
Wariness. Means of success. إحتِياط
✧ By way of security. على سَبِيلِ الاحتِياط
✧ Execution by way of security (*in law*). حَجز احتِياطِيّ
Year of dearth. تَحُوط وتَحِيط وتُحِيط
Enclosure, fence. مَحاط
The Ocean. البَحر المُحِيط
✱ To put a. th. on the side of. حاف o حَوْفًا, وحَوَّف ه
To surround a country (rain). حَوَّف ه
To curtail a. th. by the sides. تَحَوَّف ه
Leather-belt. Litter. Skin. حَوف
Two veins beneath the tongue. الحافانِ
Side, border. Destitution. حافَة ج حافات
✱ To encompass a. o. حاق o حَوْقًا ب
To sweep (a house). To rub and polish a. th. — ه
To hold unconnected speech to a. o. To efface (a word). حَوَّق على
Crowd. حَوْق وحَوْقة
Sweepings. حُواقة
Broom. مِحْوَقة ومِحْيَقة ج مَحاوِق
✱ To weave (a garment). To compose (poetry). To make (plants) to spring up (rain). حاك o حَوْكًا وحِياكًا وحِياكةً ه
✧ To distinguish a. th. حَوَّك
✧ To weave, to knit a. th. حَيَّك
To leave a mark upon (sword). أحاك في
Weaver. حائِك و✧ حَيّاك ج حاكة وحَوَكة
A female weaver. حائِكة ج حائِكات وحَوائِك
Purslain (*plant*). ✧ Colour. Shape. حَوك
Weaver's shop. مَحاكة
✱ To be finished. elapsed. To change, to pass from a state to another. To become crooked (bow). To shift (person). حال o حَوْلًا وحُؤُولًا
To be barren (female). To produce every second year (tree). — حُؤُولًا وحَيْلُولةً
To intervene between. — حَيْلُولةً بَين
To be elapsed over a. o. (year). — على
To leap and seat firmly on (horseback). — وأحوَل في
To withdraw (from a compact). — حُؤُولًا عن
To shift, to remove to. — إلى
To use deceit. — مَحالًا وحِيلةً
To squint (eye). حوِل a حَوَلًا
To change a. th. into. To give a new shape to. To convey a. th. to. حَوَّل ه إلى
To sow a land every second year. — الأرض
To make (the eye) to squint. — وأحوَل ه
To render a. th. absurd. حَوَّل ه
✧ To alight from a horse. To turn away (the eyes) from. حَوَّل عَن
✧ To send soldiers to a. o. حَوَّل على
To alight from (a carriage). — مِن
✧ To endorse (a bill) to the order of. — لِأمر فُلان
To desire a. th. To seek a. th by deceit. حاوَل مُحاوَلةً وحِوالًا ه
To look fixedly at. — البَصر ل
To be one year old. To say unconsistent things. To have barren camels. أحال
To spend (one year) in (a place). — ب
To hold absurd talk. To be one year old (child). أحوَل إحوالًا
To transfer (a debt) to another. أحال واحتال بِدَيْنِهِ على
To hold a. o. to be weak. — على
To fall upon a. o. with (a whip). — عَلَيهِ ب
To transmit (an affair) to. — ه على
To shift from one to another. تَحَوَّل تَحَوُّلًا عَن . . . إلى
To go from (a place) to. — مِن . . . إلى

pulley. Middle of the back.
There is no doubt about it. لا مَحَالَةَ مِنهُ It is unavoidable.
Artful, shrewd. مُحْتَال
Absurd, nonsensical. مِحْوَال
Full. Absurd. ✧ Impossible. مُسْتَحِيل
To be thirsty. To pursue (a design). ✲ حَامَ o حَوْمًا وحَوَمَانًا
To hover round about a. th. (bird). — على او حول
To long for (o.'s people). — حَوْمًا وحِيَامًا وحُؤُومًا على
To prosecute a. th. carefully. حَوَّمَ في
Ham, son of Noah. حَام
Thick of a fight; main part of the sea. حَوْمَة ج حَوْمَات
Crystal. حُومَة
To be humbled. To perish. ✲ حون — تَحَوَّنَ
To be or become of a dark green. ✲ حَوِيَ a حَوًى وحُوَّةً, واحْوَوَى واحْوَاوَى
Dark green or dark red colour. حُوَّة
Of a dark green colour. Side of a valley. أَحْوَى م حَوَّاء ج حُوّ
A dark-coloured vegetable. Sedentary (man). حُوَّاءَة
Eva, our first mother. حَوَّاء
To gather a. th. ✲ حَوَى i حَوَايَةً وحَيًّا ه
To get possession of. To preserve a. th. — واحْتَوَى
To grasp a. th. حَوَّى ه
To enter in possession of a. th. forcibly. أَحْوَى
To be contracted. To coil itself (serpent). تَحَوَّى
To include, to comprise a. To preserve a. th. إِحْتَوَى ه وعلى
Sound, noise. حَوَاء وحَوَاة
Worthy possessor. Small pond. حَوِيّ
Intestines. Cushion put around a camel's hump. حَوِيَّة ج حَوَايَا
Collection of houses close together. حِوَاء ج أَحْوِيَة
Collecting. Serpent-charmer. حَاوٍ ومُحْتَوٍ
F. Winding guts. حَاوِيَة وحَاوِيَاء
To live. ✲ حَيِيَ a حَيَاة
To be conspicuous (road). — حَيَاء
To be ashamed of. — مِن
To keep a. o. alive (God). To say to a. o. May God keep حَيَّا تَحِيَّةً ه وه

To seize the opportunity of (giving advice). — ه ب
To use deceit. إِحْتَالَ احْتِيَالًا و✧ تَحَايَل
To encompass a. o. إِحْتَوَلَ ه
To squint (eye). To become green and luxuriant (land). إِحْوَلَّ
To pass from a state to another. To be absurd. To become crooked (bow). ✧ To be transubstiated (element). إِسْتَحَال
Hot ashes. Black mud. ✧ One's self. حَال
✧ He committed suicide. قَتَلَ حَالَهُ
State, circumstance. Go-cart. Bundle, load. حَال (*m. f.*) ج أَحْوَال وأَحْوِلَة
The changes of time. حَالَات وأَحْوَال الدَّهْر
Immediately, at once. حَالًا وفي الحَال
As soon as. حَالَمَا
Actual, present. حَالِيّ
State, circumstance. حَالَة ج حَالَات
Year. Ability. Power. حَوْل ج أَحْوَال وحُؤُول
There is neither might nor strength but in God. لا حَوْلَ ولا قُوَّةَ إِلَّا بِالله
Perspicacity. Keen sight. Removal. — وحِوَل وحَوْلَة
There is no escape from it. لا حِوَلَ عَنْهُ
Around. حَوْلَ وحَوْلَى وحَوَالَ وحَوَالَى
Strabismus. حَوَل
Squint-eyed. حَوِل وأَحْوَل م حَوْلَاء ج حُول
Change. Around. حَوَال وحَوَلَان وحُوَلَان
The vicissitudes of time. حَوَلَان الدَّهْر وحُوَلَانُهُ
Obstruction, obstacle. حِوَال
Transfer. ✧ Soldiers sent to a debtor. Money-order. Bill of exchange. حَوَالَة
One year old (beast). حَوْلِيّ ج حَوَالِيّ
Shrewd. Skilful. حَوَالِيّ وحُوَّل وحُوَّلِيّ
In front of, opposite. حِيَال
Art, cunning. Perspicaity. Good sight. Ability. حِيلَة ج حِيَل, وحَائِلَة
Altered in colour. Barren (female). حَائِل ج حُوَّل وحُول وحِيَال وحَوَائِل
More skilful, more artful. أَحْوَل وأَحْيَل
✧ Fraudulent bankruptcy. إِفْلَاس احْتِيَالِيّ
✧ Check. Endorsement. تَحْوِيل
Absurd (speech). Crooked. ✧ Impossible. مُحَال
Good sight. Perspicacity. مَحَالَة
Water-wheel. Large — ج مَحَال ومَحَاوِل

Whereas, at the place where. ✱ حَيْثُ
✧ Wherever, whenever. حَيْثُمَا
✧ So... as. So... that. بِحَيْثُ وَمِن حَيْثُ
In respect of. Because.
✧ At any rate, of course. ✧ حَيْثُ كَان
Respect, relation. حَيْثِيَّة
To become destitute. ✱ حَاجَ i حَيْجًا
To produce thorns (ground). أَحَاجَ وأَحْيَجَ
Thorn. Thorny plant. حَاجٌ
✱ حَادَ i حَيْدًا وحَيَدَانًا ومَحِيدًا وحَيْدَةً وحُيُودًا
To stray from (the road). وحَيْدُودَةً عَن
To turn aside from.
To cut (a skin) in slices. To put a. th. aside. حَيَّدَ ه
To shun a. o. To be partial against. حَايَدَ مُحَايَدَةً وحِيَادًا ه و✧ تَحَايَدَ ه
Protuberant part of a. th. Rib. Knot on the horn of a mountain-goat. حَيَد ج حُيُود وأَحْيَاد وحِيَد
Evil look. Knot on a horn. حَيْدَة
Proud demeanour. Shy (ass). حَيَدَى
Pebbles thrown aside by the feet of a beast. حَيْدَان
To be dazzled. To lose the way. To fluctuate (water). ✱ حَارَ a حَيْرًا وحَيْرَةً وحَيَرًا وحَيَرَانًا
To be perplexed in. — في
To perplex a. o. حَيَّرَ ه
To be perplexed. To collect and whirl round (water). To be motionless (cloud). To become full of (food: bowl). تَحَيَّرَ
To be confused. To be in its bloom (youth). — واسْتَحَارَ
To be filled with water (place). — واسْتَحَارَ ب
Garden. Enclosure. حَيْر
Perplexity. حَيْرَة وتَحَيُّر ✧ حِيرَة
Cistern. Garden. حَائِر ج حُورَان وحِيرَان
Perplexed. حَيْرَان م حَيْرَى ج حَيَارَى وحُيَارَى
The planets. الكَوَاكِب المُتَحَيِّرَة
Way leading to the desert. Heavy motionless clouds. مُسْتَحِير
To urge (camels). To drive (camels) gently. ✱ حَازَ i حَيْزًا ه
To draw lines, streaks. ✧ حَيَّزَ
To roll up (snake). تَحَيَّزَ
To be overrun, subdued by a. o. (country). — ل

thee alive. To greet a. o. To approach the age of fifty.
To put (a child) to blush. To nourish (a child). حَايَا ه وه
To enliven (the fire). To spend (the night) awake. — وأَحْيَا ه
To fertilise the earth. (God). To find (the earth) fertile. أَحْيَا ه
To quicken (the dead : God). — ه
To have a fertile land. أَحْيَا
To spare a. o. To let a. o. alive. — واسْتَحْيَا ه
To feel ashamed of. To shrink. To abstain from. ✧ To veil her face (woman). إِسْتَحْيَا واسْتَحَى مِن
Repentance. Pudency, bashfulness. Vulva (of animals). حَيَاء
Rain. Abundance. Plant. أَحْيَا
Life. حَيَاة وحِيّ
Tar. حَيَاة المَوْتَى
Alive: in the bonds of life. في قَيْد الحَيَاة
Alive. Tribe. Quarter of a town. حَيّ ج أَحْيَاء
He cannot distinguish truth from falsehood. لَا يَعْرِف الحَيَّ مِن اللَّيِّ
Sempervivum, everlasting (*plant*). حَيّ العَالَم
✧ It does not matter. حَيّ الله
Make haste. حَيَّ هَـلًا وحَيَّ هَلَا وحَيْهَل
Come to prayer! حَيَّ على الصَّلَاة
Bring us such a one. حَيَّ هَل بِفُلَان
To call out to prayer (crier). حَيْهَل
Solanum (*plant*). P حَيْهَل وحَيَّهَل وحَيْهَل
Viper. ✧ Serpent. Mischievous man. حَيَّة ج حَيَّات
The lion. حَيَّة الوَادِي
Cerastes, horned snake. ✧ حَيَّة بِالقُرُون
Fertile land. أَرض حَيَّة
Serpentine, ophite. حَجَر الحَيَّة
Male serpent. حَيُّوت
Modest. Chaste. حَيِيّ وحَيّ
Animal, beast. Life. حَيَوَان ج حَيَوَانَات
Animal (being). حَيَوَانِيّ
Vital. Belonging to a tribe. حَيَوِيّ
Greeting. Security. Duration. Dominion. تَحِيَّة ج تَحِيَّات وتَحَايَا
Children's food. مُحَايَاة
Life-time. Place of life. مَحْيَا ج مَحَايِي
Countenance, face. مُحَيَّا

To hate, to grudge a. o. حَايَق ه
To surround. To cause (an evil) to befall a. o. أَحَاق إِحَاقَةً ه ب
Effects of an evil deed befalling the doer. حَيْق
☆ حَاكَ i حَيْكًا وحَيَكَانًا To flaunt, to waddle. To cut (knife).
— وأحاك في To impress a. o. (speech). To wound a. o. (sword).
إِحْتَاكَ ب To wrap o.'s self (in clothes).
☆ حَالَ i حُيُولًا To be changed. ✧ To be in heat (mare).
حَيْل ج أَحْيَال وحُيُول Strength. Water stagnating in the bottom of a valley.
على حَيْلِهِ ✧ Upright, standing.
حَيْلَة Flock of goats.
☆ حَانَ i حَيْنًا وحَيْنُونَةً To come, to be at hand (season). To experience a trial. To be fit to be reaped (spike).
حَانَ لَهُ ان The time comes for him to.
حَيَّنَ ه To appoint a time to a. o. To render a. o. unsuccessful.
— تَحَيَّنَ ه To milk (a she-camel) on fixed times.
حَايَنَ ه To appoint a time to a. o.
أَحَانَ ه To destroy a. o. (God).
أَحْيَنَ ب To remain in (a place).
تَحَيَّنَ To be unsuccessful (man).
إِسْتَحَانَ To look for an opportunity.
حَان وحَانَة وحَانُوت Wine-shop.
حَيْن Trial. Perdition. Death.
حِين ج أَحْيَان جج أَحَايِين Time, space of time. Opportunity.
حِينَة ومِحْيَان Once a day.
✧ يا حَيْنَهُ What a loss!
إلى حِين For a time.
حِينًا Sometime, awhile.
أَحْيَانًا Till, until.
✧ لِحِينِمَا Then, at that time.
حِينَئِذٍ Sometimes.
حَايِن Foolish, stupid.
حَايِنَة ج حَوَايِن Foolish woman. Calamity.

حَيْز ج أَحْيَاز ✧ Streak, line.
☆ حَاسَ i حَيْسًا ه To mix, a. th. To mix dates with curd and butter. To twist a (rope).
حِيس حَيْسُهُ He is on the brink of ruin.
حَيْس Meal of dates mixed with butter and curd. Bad business.
مَحْيُوس Slave-born.
☆ حَاشَ i حَيْشًا To be frightened. To hasten.
حَاشَ ه To frighten a. o.
تَحَيَّشَت نَفْسُهُ To shrink in fear.
حَيْشَان Fearful.
☆ حَاصَ i حَيْصًا وحَيْصَةً وحُيُوصًا ومَحِيصًا وحَيَصَانًا, وانحاص عَن To turn away from; to shun a. th.
حَايَصَ ه To endeavour to overcome, or to deceive a. o.
حِيَاصَة Ornamented waist-belt.
مَحِيص Escape, shelter.
☆ حَاضَ i حَيْضًا ومَحِيضًا ومَحَاضًا To menstruate (woman). To flow with gum (acacia).
حَيَّضَ المَاء To give vent to water.
حَائِض ج حُيَّض, وحَائِضَة ج حَوَائِض Menstruating (woman).
حِيَاض Menses.
☆ حَافَ i حَيْفًا على To act wrongfully towards.
تَحَيَّفَ ه To take a. th. from the side of.
حَيْف Injustice. Edge of a stone.
حَيْفَ عَلَيْهِ ✧ What a pity! What a shame!
حِيفَة ج حِيَف Side. Patch added to a shirt.
حَائِف ج حَافَة وحُيَّف Tyrannical.
— الجَبَل Side of a mountain.
أَحْيَف م حَيْفَاء Rainless (land).
☆ حَاقَ i حَيْقًا وحُيُوقًا وحَيَقَانًا ب To surround a. o. To be unavoidable for a. o. To come down upon a. o. (punishment).
— في To penetrate (the body : sword).

خ

Jewish rabbi. Hs خاخام

To become tall (plant). To defend o.'s property. To be deceitful. خبّ o خبّا

To rage, to dash (sea). – خِبًّا وخِبابًا

To amble (horse). – خبًّا وخَبِيبًا وخَبَبًا, واختبّ

To be crafty, mischievous. خبّ a خبًّا

✧ To sink down (in the sand). – في

To deceive, to corrupt a. o. خبّب ه

To make (a horse) to amble. أخبّ ه

Deceiver. خبّ ج خُبُوب

Commotion of the sea. خِبّ وخبّ وخِباب

Bark of trees. Depressed (ground). ✧ Wild artichoke. خبّ

Amble, soft trot. خَبِيب

Deceiving. Ambler (horse). خابّ

Relationship, affinity. – ج خوابّ

Tract of sand. Clouds. خِبّة وخُبّة

Rag, tatters. خِبّة ج خِبَب

Ragged garment. ثوب خِبَب وخبائب وأخباب

Slice of meat. Bottom of a valley. خبيبة ج خبائب

To have the bowels relaxed. ✱ خَبْخَب

To abate (heat). To become flaccid. To become lean after fatness. تخبخب

To conceal a. th. ✧ To preserve a. th. ✱ خبأ a خَبْأً وخَبًّا (و✧ خَبّى i) واختبأ ه

To propose an enigma to. خابأ ه

To conceal o.'s self. إختبأ و✧ تخبّأ

Hidden thing. خَبْء وخَبِيّ

Plants, herbage. خَبْء الأرض

Rain-drops. – السماء

In secret, hiddenly. بالخَبْء

Secret mark upon an excellent she-camel. خِباء ج أخبية

Seeds put in store. خبيئة ج خبايا

Large jar, vat. خابئة ج خوابي

Concealed, hidden. مَخْبُوء ومُخْبًأ

Hiding-place in a house. مَخْبَأ ج مخابئ

✧ Hidden treasure. ✧ مَخْبايَة

To come to a depressed land. ✱ خبت – أخبت

To humble o.'s self before (God). – إلى

Depressed tract of land. خَبْت ج أخبات وخُبُوت

Lowliness. Humility. خِبْتة وإخبات

Anything contemptible. خَبِيت

To be unproductive (land). To heave (stomach). ✱ خَبُث o خُبْثًا وخَباثة وخَباثِيَة

To be wicked, mischievous. خَبُث o خُبْثًا

To frequent bad companions. – وأخبث

To corrupt, to teach evil to a. o. – ه
To impute wickedness to a. o.

To show wickedness. تخابث

To affect wickedness. تخبّث

To act wickedly. إستخبث

To deem a. o. bad. To find (language) bad. – ه

Allay. Iron-dross. خَبَث

Wickedness. Abomination. Impurity. Deceit. Malice. Hypocrisy. خُبْث وخَباثة

O wicked man! يا خُبَث

O wicked woman. (*only used in the vocative*). يا خَباثِ

Impure food. Foul, abominable actions. خبائث

Impure. Mischievous. Abominable (talk, food). ✧ Scoffer. خبيث ج خُبُث وخُبَثاء وأخبات وخَبَثة

Urine and excrement. الأخبثان

Pernicious thing. مَخْبَثة

To know, to try a. th. ✱ خَبَر o خُبْرًا وخِبْرة ه

خَبُر o وخَبِر a خِبْرًا وخُبْرًا وخِبْرة وخُبْرة

To have a full knowlege of. ومَخْبَرة ومَخْبُرة ه وب

To inform a. o. of. To bring news to a. o. خبّر وأخبر ه ه او ب

To till the ground for a share of its produce. ✧ To manage (an affair). خابر ه

To be fully aware of. تخبّر ه

To ask news from a. o. – واستخبر ه

To give mutual information. تخابر

Lion. Plunderer. الخَابِس والخَبَّاس والخَبُوس
To pick up (scattered things). ✲ خَبَش o خَبْشًا وتَخَبَّش ه
To mix a. th. with. ✲ خَبَص i خَبْصًا ه ب
To make a mess with dates, cream and starch. — وخَبَّص وتَخَبَّص واختبص
✧ To squander recklessly; to act extravagantly. — وخَبَّص
✧ To entangle a. th. To squash (fruits). To do a. th. amiss. خَبَّص ه
✧ To eat slovenly. To dabble in mire. To botch (a work). — في
Sweet made of dates, cream and starch. خَبِيص وخَبِيصَة
Mess, work done amiss. Confusion. ✧ Quarrel. Vainly expense. خَبْصَة
Spoon for stirring up a mess. مِخْبَصَة
To knock a. o. or a. th. To trample upon a. th. ✲ خَبَط i خَبْطًا, و✧ خَبَّط ة وه
To strike a. o. with the sword. — بِسَيْفِهِ
To request a favour from a. o. To render a. o. insane (devil). — واختَبَط ة
To grant a favour to a. o. — ة بِخَيْر
To beat down (leaves). — واختَبَط ه
To strike the ground with (the foot : camel). خَبَط ه ب
He acts in a reckless manner. He goes at random (*lit* : He stamps the ground like a blind she-camel. يَخْبِط خَبْط عَشْوَاء
To journey at random by night. — اللَّيْل
To be affected with a rheum. خُبِط
To be disordered (country). تَخَبَّط
To knock a. o. or a. th. تَخَبَّط ة وه
To stamp vehemently (the ground).
To do harm to a. o. (devil).
✧ To writhe (in agony). إختَبَط
To strike a. th. strongly. — ه
To request a favour from. — ة
Leaves beaten off. Anything trampled upon. خَبَط
Rheum. Remainder of water in a vessel. Trifle. Knock. ✧ Noise. خَبْطَة ج خِبَط وخُبَط
Portion of (the night). Party of men. Draught of water in a skin. خِبْطَة ج خِبَط

To experience, to test a. o. or a. th. To know a. th. well. إختَبَر ة وه
She-camel yielding much milk. Lote-tree. Large water-skin. خَبْر ج خُبُور
Knowledge. Experience. خُبْر وخِبْرَة وإختِبَار ومَخْبَرَة
Sheep bought for being slaughtered. Large bowl. Provisions. Food. Share. خُبْرَة
Information. News. Notice. Predicate. (*log*). خَبَر ج أخبَار
✧ Do not mention it; it is unimportant. مَا تَحت خَبَر
Experience has confirmed science. صَدَّق الخَبَرَ الخُبْر
Elder-tree. ✧ Wooden peg. خَابُور
Soft soil. Roots. Burrow of a mole. خَبَار
Mantilla. ◘ خَبَّارَة
The lion. الخَبُور
News, story. ✧ خَبَرِيَّة
Aware. The Omniscient (God) Seed-produce. Camel's hair. Foam of the mouth of a camel. خَبِير ج خُبَرَاء
Black snake. خَيْبَرِي
Historian. Chronicler. أخبَارِيّ
Experience. (*opp to* مَنْظَر) مَخْبَرَة ومَخْبُرَة
Crane (bird). ✲ خَرْجَل
To make (bread). ✲ خَبَز i خَبْزًا ه
To feed a. o. with bread. To strike a. o. To urge (a beast). — ة
To tread the herbs (camels). تَخَبَّز
To be depressed (soil). إنخَبَز
To be baked (bread). إختَبَز ه
Bread; cake of bread. خُبْز وخُبْزَة
Large and flat mushroom. خُبْز الغُرَاب و✧ خُبْز القَعْق
Cyclamen. خُبْز المَشَايِخ
Flat and depressed ground. خَبْز
Anything baked. Mess. خَبِيز
Art of baking. خِبَازَة
Possessing bread. خَابِز
Baker. خَبَّاز م خَبَّازَة
Mallow (plant). خُبَّازَى وخُبَّاز وخُبَّازَة وخُبَّيْزَة
To take hold of a. th. ✲ خَبَس o خَبْسًا, واختَبَس ه
To wrong a. o. craftily. خَبَس فُلَانًا حَقَّهُ
To seize (booty). تَخَبَّس
Prey, booty. خُبَاسَاء وخُبَاسَة

carried in the folds of the clothes.
To be extinguished ✲ خبا o خبوًا وخبوًا
(fire). To subside (war, anger).
To extinguish (the fire). أخبى ه
To make, to pitch خبّى وأخبى وتخبّى ه
(a tent).
To pitch a tent and enter it. إستخبى ه
Tent of wool or camel's خباء ج أخبية
hair. Husk of wheat, barley.
To hit a. o with a ✲ ختّ ختًّا ه الى
spear.
To lessen the portion of. — وأختّ ه
To be ashamed of a. o. — من
Avaricious. Defective. ختيت
To prevent a. o. ✲ ختأ a ختأً ه عن
from.
To conceal o.'s self from fear إختتأ
or shame.
To carry away a. th. — وأختتى ه
To blush at. To dread a. o. — من
To deceive a. o. — ل
To act treacherously ✲ ختر i خترًا ه
towards.
To be wicked. — i o خترًا
To be confused by ختر a خترًا , وتختّر
drink.
To be weak, languid. تختّر
Perfidy, foulest treachery. ختر وختور
Treacherous. خاتر وختّار وختور وختير
To remain silent from fear ✲ ختارم
or weariness.
To set out. To ✲ ختع a ختعًا وختوعًا
lead the way in darkness (guide).
To fade away (mirage). To limp
(hyena).
To attack a. o. — على
Excellent guide. ختع وختوع وختوتع
Hyena. ختع
To vanish (mirage). ✲ ختعر
Mirage. Anything that passes ختيعور
away. Gossamer. Traitor. Ogre.
Wolf. Calamity.
To deceive ✲ ختل i o ختلًا وختلانًا , وخاتل ه
a. o. To lay in wait for (a prey).
To approach stealthily (hunter). خاتل
To deceive o. another. تخاتل
To listen stealthily to (the إختتل ل
secret of a. o).
✧ Corner of a wall. ختلة

Dust. خباط
Diabolical madness. خباط
Stamping خبوط وخبيط رأخبط ج خبط
the ground (horse).
Watering-trough tramp- خبيط ج خبط
led upon. Curd. Little of water.
Ink-fish. ✧ أخطبوط
Staff for beating off مخبط ج مخابط
leaves.
Beetle. Mallet. مخبط ج مخابيط
To be choked by sobbing ✲ خبع a خبوعًا
(child).
To enter (a place). خبع a خبعًا ب
To tot about. ✲ خبعل
To contemn a. o. ✲ خبق i خبقًا ه
To corrupt a. th. ✲ خبل o خبلًا , وخبّل
To disorder the brain (grief, love).
To cripple a. o.
To withhold a. o. — واختبل ه
To be crack-brained. خبل a خبلًا وخبالًا
To be dried up (limb).
To lend (cattle) to a. o. أخبل ه ه
To be crippled, dried up (limb). تخبّل
To ask of a. o. the loan إستخبل ه ه
of a (she-camel).
Palsy. Cripple. Cutting of a خبل
member. Loan, debt.
Crippling of the خبل وخبل ج خبول
limbs. Palsy. Madness. Large skin.
Bird crying the whole night.
Insane, demoniac. خبل وأخبل ومخبّل
Unsoundness of mind, body or خبال
action. Deadly poison. Ruin. Defect.
Seducer. The devil. خابل
The time. المخبّل
Insane. Crippled. مخبّل
Overwearied. ✧ Weakened. مخبول
To hem, to tuck ✲ خبن i خبنًا وخبانًا ه
and sew (a garment) for shortening
it. To put (provisions) in store for
a time of dearth.
To elide a syllable in — في الشعر
poetry.
He died. خبنته خبون
To tuck a. th. in a أخبن و✧ غبن ه
garment.
To conceal a. th. in the bosom. إختبن ه
Elision of a quiescent syllable. خبن
Folded skirt. Tuck. Food خبنة ج خبن

Ragged clothes. مَخْتُوّ

To collect, to pick up a. th. ✡ خَتَّ – خَتْخَتَ ﻫ

To be moved with awe, shame. إِخْتَتَّ

Faggot of fire-wood. خَتَّة وخُتَّة

✡ خَثَرَ o خَثْرًا وخُثُورًا وخَثَرَانًا خَثَرًا, وتَخَثَّرَ To thicken (milk).

To heave (stomach). خَثِرَ i خَثَرًا

To thicken (the milk). خَثَّرَ وأَخْثَرَ ﻫ

Body of men. خَاثِرَة

Remains of a meal. خُثَار

Remainder of clotted milk. خُثَارَة

To be stained with blood. ✡ خَثْعَمَ – تَخَثْعَمَ

Lion. الخَثْعَم والمُخَثْعِم

Abdomen. ✡ خَثْلَة وخَثَلَة ج خَثَلَات

To have a flat nose. ✡ خَثِمَ a خَثَمًا

Flatness of the nose, ears. خَثَم

Flat-nosed. خَثِم, وأَخْثَم م خَثْمَاء

To dung (cattle). ✡ خَثَى i خَثْيًا

To kindle dry dung. أَخْثَى إِخْثَاء

Dung of cattle (used as fuel). خِثْي ج أَخْثَاء وخُثِيّ

To push a. th. To split (wood). To help a. o. ✡ خَجَّ o خَجًّا ه و ﻫ

To hurry on in bending the body (camel). إِخْتَجَّ

Gale ; strong wind. خَجُوج

To draw towards its end (night). To enter (a house) stealthily. ✡ خَجَأَ a خَجْأً

To be ashamed. خَجِئَ a خَجَأً

To urge a question upon a. o. أَخْجَأَ ه

Levity, unsteadiness. ✡ خَجَف وخَجِيف

To be ashamed, confounded. To become tall and tangled (plant). To be covered with herbage (valley). To stick in mire (camel). ✡ خَجِلَ a خَجَلًا

To be overburdened by. To be entangled in (an affair). – ب

To abash a. o. خَجَّلَ وأَخْجَلَ ه

To be ashamed. ✧ إِنْخَجَلَ

Confusion. Perplexity. خَجَل و ✧ خَجَالَة

Ashamed. Perplexed. خَجِل وخَجْلَان و ✧ مَخْجُول

Tangled (plant). Luxuriant valley. Full (garment). مُخْجِل

Furrow of a hare. خَتَل

✧ Cozenage, fraud. مُخَاتَلَة

To seal, to put a signet upon (a writing). To stamp a. th. ✡ خَتَمَ i خَتْمًا وخِتَامًا وخَتَّمَ ﻫ وعلى

✧ To cicatrise (wound). ✧ خَتَمَ الجُرْحُ

To seal the heart *i. e.* To harden it. – على قلبه

To finish a. th. To read over (a book). To plaster (a vessel). – خَتْمًا ﻫ

God made his end to be good. خَتَمَ لَهُ اللهُ بالخَيْرِ

To finish (a book). خَتَّمَ ﻫ

To put a ring on (o.'s own finger). تَخَتَّمَ ﻫ و ب

To conceal a. th. – ب

To pass over, to be silent about. – عن

To complete a. th. إِخْتَتَمَ ﻫ

Seal, stamp. Honey. خَتْم ج خُتُوم وأَخْتَام

Reading of the whole Coran. خَتْمَة

Seal, signet-ring. Stamp. ✧ Anus. خَاتِم ج خَوَاتِم, وخَاتَام ج خَوَاتِيم

✧ Salomon 's seal (*plant*). خَاتِم سُلَيْمَان

Completion. Result. (*opp to* فَاتِحَة) خَاتِمَة ج خَوَاتِيم

Conclusion. Sealing-clay. خِتَام ج خُتُم

Sealed. Stamped ✧ Cicatrised (wound). مَخْتُوم

✧ Rock-salt. مُلْح مَخْتُوم

Measure for corn of about five pints and a third. مَخْتُوم ج مَخَاتِيم

End. مُخْتَتَم

To cut a. th. To circumcise (a boy). ✡ خَتَنَ i خَتْنًا ه

To ally by marriage to a. o. (man). – o خُتُونًا وخُتُونَة وخَاتَنَ ه

To be circumcised. إِخْتَتَنَ

Circumcision. خِتَان وخِتَانَة

Art of circumcising. خِتَانَة

Affinity on the wife's side. خُتُون وخُتُونَة

Any relation on the side of the wife. ✧ Son-in law. Bridegroom. خَتَن م خَتَنَة ج أَخْتَان

Noble lady. Queen. Ts خَاتُون ج خَوَاتِين

Circumcised. خَتِين ومَخْتُون

To be heart-broken from (grief, fear). ✡ خَتَا o خَتْوًا, واخْتَتَى

To hinder a. o. from. – o ه عن

To sell (clothes) one by one. خَتَّى إِخْتَاء ﻫ

To stupefy a. o. (narcotic).
To lie in his lair (lion). أَخدَرَ
To remain amongst (o.'s people). — مع
To be concealed in doors (girl). تَخَدَّرَ واختَدَرَ
Curtain. Inside of apartments of women. Lair. Darkness of the night. خِدْر جِ خُدُور وأَخْدَار وجج أخادير
Numbness (of the limbs). Sluggishness. Rain. Dark place. Narcotism. خَدَر
Darkness. — وخُدْرَة
Lair of a lion. خِدَار
Benumbed (limb). Obscure (place, night). Slothful. خَدِر
Sluggish. Perplexed. Hidden in his lair (lion). خَادِر
Cramp-fish. خَدَّارَة
Black ass. خُدرِيّ م خُدرِيَّة
Intensely black. خُدَارِيّ
The eagle. الخُدَارِيَّة
Dark night. Black cloud. الأَخْدَر والخُدَارِيّ
Wild ass. الأَخدَرِيّ
Narcotic, soporific. مُخَدِّر
Girl kept in doors. مُخَدَّرَة ومُخْدَرَة ومَخْدُورَة
To tear off (the skin). To scratch. To mar a. th. ✡ خَدَش i خَدشًا, وخَدَّش ه
✧ To wound the ears (offensive language). خَدَّش الآذان
To scratch o. another's face. خَادَش ه
Scratch. Bloodless wound. خِدَاش وأخداش
Flee. Fly. خَدُوش
Cat. مُخَادِش ومُخَدِّش
To deceive, to circumvent a. o. ✡ خَدَع a خَدعًا وخِدعًا, واختَدَع ه
To be dull (market). To be brisk (market). To be scanty (rain). To refrain from giving. To dry (saliva). To be changing (affair). To be reduced (wealth). To conceal o.'s temper. To sink (eye). To be sleepless (eye). To disappear (disk of the sun). To be corrupt. خَدَع
To hide in its hole (lizard). — في
To fold (a vestment). — ه
To try to out- خَادَع مُخَادَعَة وخِدَاعًا ه

To leave marks upon a. o. (stroke). ✡ خَدَّ o خَدًّا في
To furrow (the ground). — ه
To be wrinkled, lean (skin). خَدَّدَ
To wrinkle (the skin); to make it lean. — ه
To counteract a. o. خَادَّ ه
To oppose o. a. تَخَادَّ
To be cleft. To become lean. To be wrinkled (flesh). To part (people). تَخَدَّدَ
Rivulet. خَدّ جِ أَخِدَّة و خِدَاد وخِدَّان
Cheek. Side. Party of men. خَدّ جِ خُدُود
Trench. Furrow. — وخُدَّة جِ خُدَد
The two cheeks. الخَدَّان والخَدَّتَان
Furrow. Mark of a whip. أُخدُود جِ أخاديد
Blow leaving a mark. ضَربة أُخدُود
Martyrs of Nejran. أَصحاب الأُخدُود
Pillow, bolster. Ploughshare. مِخَدَّة و✧ خُدَيدِيَّة
To lie. ✡ خَدَب o خَدبًا
To bite a. o (serpent). — ه
To smite a. o. with (the sword). — ه ب
To walk at a middling pace. تَخَدَّب
Tallness. Stupidity. خَدَب
Tall and stupid. خَدِب, وأَخدَب م خَدبَاء ومُتَخَدِّب
Blow or arrow causing a large wound. ضَربة وحَربة خَدِبَة وخَدبَاء
To cast her young one before the time (she-camel). ✡ خَدَج i o خِدَاجًا
To bring forth a fœtus incompletely formed. To have little rain (season). To be defective (th). To fail to give fire (steel and flint). أَخدَج
Imperfection (of a work). خِدَاج
Abortive camel. خَدِيج
To be benumbed (limb). To be languid (eye). To be intense (cold, heat). To be sullen (day). ✡ خَدِر a خَدَرًا
To be perplexed. To remain behind the herd (gazelle). خَدَر o خَدْرًا
To remain and keep to (a place). — ب
To keep (a girl) in doors. — وخَدَّر وأَخدَر ه
To benumb (a limb). خَدَّر وأَخدَر ه وه

خَادِمٌ ج خَدَم وخُدَّام, وخُدَّام ج خَدَّامَة
Domestic servant. Slave.
Female servant. خَادِمَة و ✧ خَدِيمَة
Service, servitude (*opposed to mastership* مَخْدُومِيَّة). خَادِمِيَّة
Male slave, servant. خَدِيم و ✧ خَدِيم
Having a white spot on the feet (horse). أَخْدَم
Lower band of trousers on the leg of a woman. Garter. مُخَدَّم ومُخَدَّمَة
Master. ✧ Son. مَخْدُوم
✧ An official. مُسْتَخْدَم
To show friendliness to. ☆ خدن – خَادَنَ ه
Friend, companion. خِدْن وخَدِين ج أَخْدَان
To go at a quick pace (horse). ☆ خَدَى i خَدْيًا, وخَدَيَانًا
To go on gently. أَخْدَى
Vice-roy of Egypt. P خُدَيْوِيّ
To submit to a. o. ☆ خَذَأَ وخَذِيَ a خَذْأً وخُذُوءًا وخَذَاءً ل
To humble a. o. أَخْذَأَ ه
To submit to a. o. إِسْتَخْذَأَ ل
To hasten. To strike up pebbles (camel). ☆ خَذْرَف
To fill (a vessel). To sharpen (a sword). – ه
To cut the extremities of the body with (a sword.) – ه ب
To be rent (garment). تَخَذْرَف
Swift. Spinning-top. خُذْرُوف ج خَذَارِيف
Spring-plant drying in summer. خِذْرَاف
To cut (a fruit) in slices. To carve (meat). ☆ خَذَعَ a خَذْعًا ه
They dispersed in all directions. ذَهَبُوا خِذَعَ مِذَعَ
Kind of mince-pie. خَذِيعَة
Knife. مِخْذَعَة
To sling (pebbles, fruit-stones). ☆ خَذَفَ i خَذْفًا ب
Quick pace of camesl. خَذَفَان
Walking quickly. خَذُوف
Kind of sling. مِخْذَفَة
To desert, to forsake a. o. To separate from the herd (gazelle). ☆ خَذَلَ o خَذْلًا وخِذْلَانًا ه وعَن
To induce a. o. to forsake another. خَذَّلَ ه

wit a. o. To give up a. th. To deceive (the eye). ✧ To fawn a. o.
To act deceitfully with. To incite a. o. to deceit. أَخْدَعَ ه
To practice deceit. تَخَدَّعَ
To feign to be deceived. تَخَادَعَ
To be deceived. To be dull (market). إِنْخَدَعَ
Deceit. Imposture. Prohibition. خُدْعَة وخِدَاع
Deceit. Dupe. خُدْعَة
Impostor. خُدَعَة وخَيْدَع وخَدَّاع, وخَدُوع ج خُدُع
Craft, cheat. Meal of the Arabs. خَدِيعَة ج خَدَائِع
Deficient (coin). Variable (market). Unsteady (man). خَادِع
Misleading (road). – وخَدُوع
Small door in a large one. Wicket. خَادِعَة
House inside another. أَخْدَع
Vein of the neck. – ج أَخَادِع
Strong-necked. Daring. شَدِيد الأَخْدَع
Small room, closet. مُخْدَع ومِخْدَع ج مَخَادِع
Experienced. مُخَدَّع
To walk at a short and quick step. To lead an easy life. ☆ خَدَفَ i خَدْفًا
To rend (clothes). – واخْتَدَفَ ه
To carry away a. th. إِخْتَدَفَ ه
Helm. خَدَف
To serve, to minister to a. o. ✧ To last (garment). ☆ خَدَمَ i o خِدْمَة وخَدْمَة ه
To have a white spot on the feet (horse). خَدِمَ
To take a. o into service. ✧ خَدَّمَ ه
To give a servant to a. o. أَخْدَمَ ه
To serve o.'s self. إِخْتَدَمَ
To ask a servant from. – ه
To take a. o as servant. To ask a servant from a. o. ✧ To give civil employment to. إِسْتَخْدَمَ ه
✧ To be employed in. – في
Service. Civil service. ✧ Pay. Respect. Work. Liturgy. خِدْمَة ج خِدَم
Anklet. Leg. Ring, circle of people. خَدَمَة ج خَدَم وخِدَام وخَدَمَات
Thong tied to the pastern of a camel. – وخِدَمَة
Service. ✧ خَدَامَة

Awl. ◻ مَخْرُور
To purr (cat). To snore (man). ✡ خَرْخَر
Murmur of water. Rustling. خَرْخَر
Water flowing abundantly. خَرْخَار
To relieve o.'s bowels. ✡ خَرِئَ a خَرْءًا وخِرَاءَة وخُرُوءًا
Excrement. خُرْء ج خُرُوء و✧ خَرَاء وخَرْيَة
Mango-steen (tree). خُرْء الحَمَام
Arenaria, sand-wort. خُرْء الدَّجَاجَة
Water-closet. مَخْرَأ ومَخْرَأَة ومَخْرُأَة ج مَخَارِى
To be ruined, wasted (country). ✡ خَرِب a خَرَبًا وخَرَابًا
To have the ears pierced. — خَرَبًا
To ruin (a house). To pierce, to split a. th. خَرَب i خَرْبًا ه
To wound a. o. in the orifice of the ear. ✧ To ruin a. o. — ه
To become a robber. خَرَب o خِرَابَة
To carry off (flocks). — i خِرَابَة وخَرَابَة وخَرْبًا وخُرُوبًا ب
✧ To make havock. To make an uproar. To leave no stone unturned. خَرَب الدُّنيَا
To lay waste. To demolish a. th. ✧ To damage a. th. خَرَّب وأَخْرَب ه
To eat up (a tree: worm.) تَخَرَّب ه
To be crushed by adversity. To be split (water-skin). إِسْتَخْرَب
To long for a. th. — إِلى
Eye of a needle, hole of an axe. Anus. خَرْب وخُرْب وخُرَابَة
Shepherd's bag. Unsoundness in religion. خِرْب وخُرْب وخُرْبَة ج خُرَب
Hole of the ear; eye of a needle. Handle. خُرْبَة ج خُرَب
Sieve. Vice. Pudenda. خَرْبَة ج خَرَبَات
Wasted place. Ruins. خِرْبَة ج خِرَب
Male bustard. خَرَب ج خِرْبَان
Wasted, out of order. خَرِب و✧ خِرْبَان
Ruined place. Coward. خَرِب
Wasted place. خَرِبَة ج خَرَائِب وخَرِبَات وخَرَب
Ruin, devastation. خَرَاب ج أَخْرِبَة وخِرَاب
Carob. Carob-tree. خَرُّوب وخُرْنُوب
Thorny carob. خُرْنُوب الشَّوْك و✧ خُرْنُوب المَعْز
Anagyris fœtida, bean-trefoil. خَرُّوب الخِنْزِير

To incite (people) to forsake a. o. ه عن
To leave a. o. helpless. خَاذَل ه
To forsake o. a. To become weak (feet). تَخَاذَل
Forsaking. Fugitive. خَاذِل وخَذَّال ج خُذَّال
Holding back (from the herd: gazelle). — ج خَوَاذِل
To trench off a. th. To strike with its talons (hawk). ✡ خَذَم i خَذْمًا, وخَذَّم وتَخَذَّم ه
To hasten, to go quickly. خَذِم a خَذَمًا
To be trenched. To be drunk (man). — a خَذَمًا وتَخَذَّم
To confess a misdeed and remain silent. أَخْذَم
To intoxicate a. o. (drink). — ه
Cutting (sword). خَذِم
Generous (man). — ج خَذِمُون
Piece cut off. خُذَامَة
Cutting well (sword). Swift in running. خَذُوم ج خُذُم
Intoxicated. خَذِيم
Knife. Sharp sword. مِخْذَم
To hang down (ear). ✡ خَذَا o خَذْوًا وخَذِي i خَذًى
To submit. إِسْتَخْذَى
Lop-eared. أَخْذَى م خَذْوَاء
Dependant (ear). خَذِيّ
To murmur (water). To snore (sleeper). To produce a rustling (wind, flying bird). ✡ خَرَّ o i خَرِيرًا
To fall down from a (terrace). خَرَّ o i خَرًّا وخُرُورًا
To prostrate o.'s self to (God). — ل
To attack a. o. — على
To cut a. th. down. أَخَرَّ ه
To be flabby (man). إِنْخَرَّ
Mouth of a mill. Round grain. Base of the ear. خُرّ ج خِرَرَة
Gimlet. ✧ خِرّ بِرّ
Prostration. خُرُور
Purring (cat). خِرُور
Murmur of water. Rustling. Snoring. Upland. خَرِير ج أَخِرَّة
Murmuring (water). Snoring. خَرَّار
Spinning-top. Water-fall. ✧ Death-rattle. خَرَّارَة

To take out a. th. ✧ To spend (money). To let (blood). — ه
He made him solemn funerals. أخرجه خرجة عظيمة
To be well-bred, gentlemanlike. تخرّج في الأدب
To become clever in (an art). — في
To divide (an estate). تخارج ه
To extract (a meaning). To draw (water). إختَرج ه
To be coloured with white and black (horse, ostrich). إخرَجّ
To draw out a. th. To ask a. o. to go out. To extract (a mineral). To elucidate (a question). ✧ To translate (a book). To distillate a. th. إستخرج ه وه
Land-tax. Expenditure. خَرج ج أخراج
✧ Materials. Suitable. — ج خُروجة
✧ Waste. Refuse. Rubbish. خرج الكُبّ
✧ Privy purse; pocket-money. خرج الجَيب او العُب
✧ That is what just suits thee. هذا خَرجك
Deserving of the gallows. خِرج المَشنقة
Saddle-bag. خُرج ج خِرَجة
Sally of troops. ✧ Balcony. خَرجة
Living. Expenditure, pocket-money. ✧خَرجيّة
Poll-tax. Income. خَراج
Pimples, boils, abscess. خُراج (un خُراجة) ج خُراجات
✧ Relief of the bowels. Boil. خُروج
The day of Resurrection. Feast-day. يوم الخُروج
The book of Exodus. سِفر الخُروج
Clever, shrewd. خَرّاج ولّاج
Exterior, outside. ✧ Quotient. خارج
From without. مِن خارج
Abroad. Outside. في الخارج
External, exterior. خارِجيّ
Heretics, rebellious (people). الخوارج
Foreign-office. وِزارة الخارجيّة
Well'bred. Clever in an art. خِرّيج
Bicoloured. أخرج م خَرجاء
Outlet; place of exit. Result (of a calculation). Way of escape, shift. Orifice of the anus. مَخرَج

Robber. Camel-stealer. خارِب ج خُرّاب
Having his ear pierced. أخرَب م خَرباء ج خُرب
Nest of hornets. Hives. تخاريب
Sour milk. ✲ خَربد
Water-melon. Ts خِربِز
To spoil (a book). ✧ To scrawl, to scribble. ✲ خَربَش
Hen scratchings on the ground. خَرابيش الدَّجاج
To raffle a. th. To set th. apart. ✧ To mix up everything. To entangle (threads). To complicate a. th. ✲ خَربَص ه
Medley, intricacy. خَربَصة
To disorder, to impair a. th. ✧ خَربَط ه
To be impaired, spoiled. ✧ تخربط
To tear off a garment, to spoil, to corrupt a. th. ✲ خَربَق ه
Hellebore (*plant*). خَربَق
To pierce, (the ear, lips). ✲ خَرت o خَرتًا
To be a clever guide. خرِت a خَرتًا
Hole of the ear. Eye of a needle. خَرت وخِرت ج خُروت وأخرات
Ring of a saddle-girth. خُرتة وخُرتة
Skilful guide. خِرِّيت ج خَراريت وخَرارت
Direct road. مَخرَت
Having the lips perforated. مَخرُوت
Reddish ant. ✲ خِرت — خِرتاء
Rubbish, old furniture. خُرتيّ
To go out from. to depart from (a place). ✲ خَرج o خُروجًا ومَخرجًا من
✧ To relieve o.'s bowels. To spend money. خَرج
To be clever in (an art, a science). — في
To bring a. o. out. — ب
To attack a. o. To rebel against. — على
✧ To part with a. th. عن
To take, to send a. o. or a. th. out from. خرّج وأخرج ه وه من
To bring up, to breed (a child). خرّج ه
To train a. o. in (an art). — ه في
To impose a land-tax on. To elucidate (a question). To diversify (a work). — ه
To pay a tax. أخرج

✱ خَرِد a خَرَدًا, وتَخَرَّد To be a virgin (girl). To remain silent.
أَخْرَد To be bashful (boy). To keep silent.
— إلى To be fond of (sport, play).
خَرِيد وخَرُود Virgin, bashful woman.
خَرِيدَة ج خَرَائد وخُرَّد وخُرُد Unbored pearl. Maid.
صَوت خَرِيد Soft, low voice.
Ts خُرْدَة ✧ Small shot. Ironmongery. Petty money.
Ts خُرْدَجِيّ ج خُرْدَجِيَّة Ironmonger, haberdasher.
Ts خُرْدَق Small shot.
عِنَب مُخَرْدَق ✧ Small-grained grapes.
أَمر مُخَرْدَق ✧ Disordered (affair).
✱ خَرْدَل ه To parcel (meat). To eat the best part of a. th.
خَرَادِل Large pieces of meat.
خَرْدَل Mustard, charlock.
خَرْدَل فَارِسِيّ Thlaspi (*plant*).
خَرْدَلَة Mustard-seed.
✱ خَرَز o i خَرْزًا ه To sew (leather) with an awl ✧ To bore a. th.
خَرِز a خَرَزًا Te set o.'s affairs in order.
خَرَز (*un.* خَرَزَة) Shells, glass-wares, beads strung in a necklace. Bezel.
خَرَزَة الرَّقَبَة Pomum Adami.
خَرَزَة العَيْن Lens of the eye.
خَرِيز ✧ Tingling in the limbs.
خَرَز الظَّهر Vertebræ of the back.
خَرَزَة ج خَرَزَات A gem, a glass-bead or cowry set in a string.
خَرَزَة البِئر ✧ Curb of a well.
خَرَزَات المَلِك Jewels of the crown.
خُرْزَة ج خُرَز Stitch-hole.
خَرَّاز Cobbler.
خِرَازَة Art of a cobbler.
مُخَرَّز Having its wings perforated (bird).
مِخْرَز ج مَخَارِز Awl, needle.
✱ خَرِس a خَرَسًا To be dumb. To walk silently (army). To be sleepless.
خَرَّس على النُّفَسَاء To prepare food for a woman in childbirth.
أَخْرَس ه To render a. o. dumb (God).
تَخَرَّسَت النُّفَسَاء To prepare food for herself; (confined woman).
خَرَس Dumbness.

خُرْس وخِرَاس Feast on the birth of a child.
خُرْسَة Food for a confined woman.
خَرْس وخِرْس ج خُرُوس Wine-jar.
خَرَّاس Maker, seller of jars.
خُرَاسَان Khorassan (Persian province).
خُرَاسَانِيّ وخُرَاسِينِيّ وخُرَاسِيّ وخُرَسَنِيّ وخُرَسِيّ From Khorassan.
✧ بِزر خُرَيْسَانِيّ Semen-contra; worm-seed.
أَخْرَس م خَرْسَاء ج خُرْس Dumb. Still (echo, cloud, army).
✧ خُرْسْتَان Cupboard in a wall. Closet.
✱ خَرَش i خَرْشًا, وخَرَّش وخَارَش واخْتَرَش ه
وه To scratch a. o. To scrape a. th.
خَرَش ه وه To draw (a bough) with a crooked stick towards o.'s self. To sting a. o (fly).
خَارَش مُخَارَشَة وخِرَاشًا To be surly (dog).
تَخَارَش To attack and scratch o. a. (cats, dogs).
إِخْتَرَش ه من To snatch a. th. To scratch a. o. (cat).
خَرَش ج خُرُوش Flies. Old furniture (*coll*).
كَلْب خِرَاش Surly dog.
خُرَاشَة Filings. Trifles.
خِرْشَاء ج خَرَاشِيّ Slough of serpents. Broken egg-shell. Skin upon the cream. Dust.
مِخْرَش ومِخْرَاش Crooked stick. ✧ Awl.
✱ خَرْشَب ه To botch (a work).
✱ خَرْشَفَة Stir. Uncouth speech.
— وخِرْشَاف Hard and rugged ground
◻ خُرْشُوف ج خَرَاشِيف Artichoke.
✱ خُرْشُوم ج خَرَاشِيم Huge mountain. Peak. Canal from the nose to the mouth.
✱ خَرَص o خَرْصًا To lie.
— في To guess, to appraise a. th.
خَرَص o خِرَاصَة To repair a. th. To appraise (dates).
خَرِص a خَرَصًا To be hungry and cold.
خَرَّص ه ✧ To repair (plate).
خَارَص ه To barter a. th.
تَخَرَّص واخْتَرَص على To forge a lie against a. o.
خُرْص ج خِرْصَان و✧ خُرُوصَة Gold or silver ring. Ear-ring.
— ج أَخْرَاص وخِرَاص Palm-branch.

Rhinoceros. ☐ خَرتِيط
Oats. ✡ خَرطَال
To lift the nose. To become proud. To be angry. ✡ خَرطَم اخرَنطَم
Nose. Trunk of an elephant. Pig's snout. Heady wine. Khartoum, town of the Soudan. خُرطُوم ج خَرَاطِيم
Red and long earth-worms. ✡ خَرَاطِين
To split a. th. ✡ خَرَع a خَرعًا, واختَرَع ه
To be broken. To become weak in mind or body. خَرِع a خَرَعًا, وانخَرَع
To have flaccid limbs. خَرُع o خَرَاعَة وخُرعًا وخُرُوعًا
To become flaccid, weak, soft. To be dislocated (limb). تَخَرَّع
To split a. th. To create a. th. (God). To forge (a story). إختَرَع ه
To embezzle a. o. To squander away (goods). To break (a branch). — ه وه
Incision in a sheep's ear used as a mark. Weakness of the limbs. خَرع
Weak. Flaccid. خَرِع وخَرِيع
Weak man. Fine woman. Big-lipped. Soft lip. Pendulous (camel's lip). خَرِيع
Palma-Christi, castor-oil plant. خِروَع
Discovery. Creation. إختِرَاع ج اختِرَاعَات
✡ خَرعَب ج خَرَاعِب وخَرعُوب وخُرعُوبَة ج خَرَاعِيب
Soft twig of one year. Young girl. Soft woman. Tall and lusty man.
To become weak-minded. To dote (old man). ✡ خَرِف a خَرَفًا, وخَرُف o خَرَافَة
خَرَف o خَرفًا وخِرَافًا ومَخرَفًا واختَرَف ه وه
To pluck (a fruit). To gather fruit for a. o.
To be watered by autumnal rain (earth, men). To produce autumnal herbage. خُرِف
To hold a. o. to be a dotard. خَرَّف ه
To transact an affair with a. o. during autumn. خَارَف ه
To bring forth in autumn. (she-goat). To have ripe fruit (palm-tree). To enter upon the autumn. To become tall (Indian-corn). أخرَف

Conjecture. Valuation. Spear-head. Basket. خِرص
Instrument for collecting honey. خُرص وخُرص وخُرص ج أخرَاص
Share. Food for a woman confined. خُرصَة
Cold water. Stagnating water. Outflow of a river. Sea-gulf. خَرِيص
Liar. خَرَّاص ج خَرَّاصُون
Spear. مِخرَص ج مَخَارِص
To beat off the (leaves of a tree). To pick (grapes with the hand). ✧ To plane, to turn wood in a lathe. To brag. To crack a joke. ✡ خَرَط i o خَرطًا ه
To purge a. o (medicine). — o وخَرَّط ه
To have a disease of the udder (sheep). خَرِط a خَرَطًا, وأخرَط
To be slender (body). ✧ To be lathed. إنخَرَط
To be strung in : (bead). To embark rashly (in an affair). To break in (a place). To rush upon (the enemy). — في
To unsheathe (a sword). إختَرَط ه
To become long (beard). To hurry on. إخرَوَّط
To protract (a journey). To be entangled in a snare (hunter). — ب
It is a difficult thing. دُونَهُ خَرط القَتَاد
Coagulation of the milk in the udder. Weakening of the body. خَرَط
Restive (animal). Blunderer ✧ Humbug. خَرُوط ج خُرُط
Craft of a turner. ✧ Moulding. خِرَاطَة
Parings falling from a lathe. خُرَاطَة
Leathern bag for silk-worms' eggs. ✧ Map. خَرِيطَة ج خَرَائِط
Turner. ✧ Humbug. خَرَّاط
Petticoat. ✧ خَرَّاطَة
Lathe. مِخرَطَة ج مَخَارِط
Suffering from coagulation of the milk (beast). مُخرِط ج مَخَارِيط
Long (face). A cone. مَخرُوط
Conical. مَخرُوطِيّ
To scrawl. To strike off a. th. ✧ خَربَش
Waste-book. ✧ خَرطُوش
Butterfly brightly coloured. ✡ خِرطِيط ج خَرَاطِيط

hole. Open country. ✧ *Pl.* Openings as doors, windows.
✧ He has increased the evil *lit*; he has widened the hole. زَاد الخَرق ووسَّع الخَرقَة
Bountiful, profuse. خِرق ج أخراق وخُرّاق
Awkwardness. Misuse. Stupidity. خُرق وخَرَق وخُرقة
Hole. ✧ خُرق ج خُرَق
Coarse cloak worn by the Sofis. Rag, tatter. خِرقَة ج خِرَق
Cloak of Mohammed. الخِرقة الشَّرِيفة
Duster, rag. خَرقة وم خَرَّاقة وخَلَّاقة
Purslain (*plant*). خَرقة
Unskilful. Clumsy. خَرِق وخَرُق
Wonderful. ✧ First rate. خَارِق
Extraordinary. خارق العادة
Violent wind. Soft wind. خَرِيق وخَرُوق ج خَرائق
Plain rich in plants. — ج خُرَق
Bountiful. خِرِّيق
Clumsy. Foolish. أخرق م خَرقاء ج خُرق
Desert. مَخرَق ج مَخارِق
Holes of the body, *as* the mouth, nose. المَخارِق
Fine man. Experienced, generous man. Wild bull. Kerchief twisted for striking. مِخراق ج مَخارِيق
Swift. مُنخَرِق
In tatters (man). — ومُتخَرِّق السِّربَال
Passage. مُختَرَق
Windward place. — الرِّياح
Unfrequented (place). خَاوِي المُختَرَق
To shot (an arrow) carefully. ✱ خَرقَل في رَميِهِ
To slit a. th. To crack (a gem, the eye of a needle). To sweep away (its bank : water). ✱ خَرَم i خَرمًا ه
To perforate the nostrils of. — ه
To turn aside from (the road). — عن
✧ To forfeit o's promise. — في
He died. خَرَمَتهُ الخَوارِم
To have the partition of the nose perforated. خَرِم a خَرَمًا
To lead a dissolute life. خَرُم o خَرامة
To split (a gem). ✧ To embroider, to chisel a. th. خَرَّم ه
To be broken. ✧ To be embroidered. تَخَرَّم

Harvest-time. Fruit-season. خَراف وخِراف
Witticism, humourous talk. Dotage. خَرافة
Gathered fruits. Dotage, nonsense. خُرافة ج خُرافات
Lamb. Calf. Colt six months old. خَرُوف ج أخرِفة وخِرفان وخِراف
She-lamb. Palm-tree bearing fruit. خَرُوفة ج خَرائف
Autumn. Autumnal rain. Year. خَرِيف
Fresh dates. Water-wheel. Streamlet.
Palm tree farmed out. خَرِيفة ج خَرائف
Autumnal. خَرِيفِيّ وَخَرفِيّ وخَرَفِيّ
Dotard. خَرِف و✧ خَرفان
Basket for picking out the best dates. مِخرَف ج مَخارِف
Dotage. Avenue between two rows of palm-trees. مَخرَفة
To mix a. th. ✱ خَرفَش ه
✧ To speak confusedly. — في الكلام
Worthless furniture. Rubbish. Playing-cards from two to six. ✧ خِرفِيش
To rend (clothes). To traverse (a desert). To make a hole through (a wall). To ooze through (oil, water). To infringe (a custom). To forge (a lie). To pierce, to perforate a. th. ✱ خَرَق o i خَرقًا ه
✧ To violate, to desecrate (a sacred place). To dishonour a. o. خرق حُرمَتهُ
To remain continually in doors. — o خُرُوقًا و✧ خَرَّق في
To be confounded by fear or shame. To be unable to fly (bird). To be foolish. خَرِق a خَرَقًا
To be unskilful (in work). — وخَرُق o خَرَاقة ب
To lie impudently. خَرَّق
To tear off a. th. — ه
To bewilder a. o (fear). أخرق ه
To be torn off, pierced through. تَخَرَّق وانخَرَق واخرَورَق
To be profuse in. تَخَرَّق في
To forge (a lie). — واختَرَق ه
To blow violently (wind). إنخَرَق
To cross, to pass through a. th. إختَرَق ه
Desert. Crack, خَرق ج خُرُوق و✧ خُرُوقات

To wink the eyes. تَخَازَرَ
Small-eyed tribe on the shores of the Caspian Sea. خَزَر
The Caspian Sea. بَحْرِ الخَزَر
Pain in the spine of the back. خَزْرَة وخُزْرَة
Food made of minced meat and flour. خَزِير وخَزِيرَة
Pig, swine. خِنْزِير ج خَنَازِير
✧ Scrofula, king's evil. خَنَازِير
Dolphin. خِنْزِير البَحْر
Wild boar. خِنْزِير بَرِّي
Sow. خِنْزِيرَة
Unsteady gait. خَوْزَرَى وخَيْزَرَى
Bamboo. Stick, cane. خَيْزُرَان ج خَيَازِر
Spear. Tiller of the rudder. Knee-holly (*plant*).
Small-eyed. أَخْزَر م خَزْرَاء ج خُزْر
To waddle in walking. ✲ خَزْرَف
To remain behind; to part from. ✲ خَزَعَ a خَزْعًا, وتَخَزَّعَ عَن
To cut, to sever a. th. — وخَزَّعَ ه
To prevent a. o. from walking (lameness). خَزَعَ عَن فُلَان
To divide a. th. between. تَخَزَّعَ ه بَيْن
To be cut in the middle (rope). To be bent by (age). إِنْخَزَعَ
To separate a. o. from. إِخْتَزَعَ ه عَن
Death. خُزَاع
Piece, fragment. خُزَاعَة
Tales, amusive stories. ✲ خَزْعَبَل وخُزَعْبِل
Joke, witticism. خُزَعْبَلَة
To limp in walking. ✲ خَزْعَل
To walk haughtily. ✲ خَزَفَ i خَزْفًا في مَشْيِهِ
To rend (a garment). To split a. th. — ه
Earthenware, pottery. خَزَف
Earthen, made of clay. خَزَفِيّ
Pottery. — وخَزَّاف
To pass through (the target: arrow). ✧ To tear off a. th. ✲ خَزَقَ i خَزْقًا ه وه
To pierce a. o. with (a spear). To hit (the target) with an arrow. To cast (the eyes) at. — ه ب
To be pierced through. ✧ To be rent (garment). تَخَزَّقَ وانْخَزَقَ

To destroy, (a tribe). — واخْتَزَمَ ه
To be pierced (nose, ear) إِنْخَزَمَ
To cut off a. o. (death). To weaken a. o. (sickness.) إِخْتَزَمَ ه
He was taken away from us (by death). أُخْتُرِمَ عَنَّا
Peak of a mountain. خُرْم ج خُرُوم
Pros. Retrenchment of a syllable.
Lie. خُرْمَان
Pierced (ear). Inaccessible (hill). خَرْمَاء
Dissolute. خَرِيم
Leaves and branches of a tree. Kind of bean. Star-wort. خَزَم
Licentious sect admitting metempsychosis. خُرَمِيَّة
Impious, dissolute. Cold wind. خَارِم ج خُرَّام
Cloven rocks. خَوْرَم
Tip of the nose. خَوْرَمَة
Corn-cockle (weed). خَزُومَانَة
Having the nose perforated. أَخْرَم م خَرْمَاء
Lace-work. Lace. ✧ تَخْرِيم وتَخْرِيمَة
Projecting (peak). Point of a sword. مَخْرِم ج مَخَارِم
To alter (a book). ✧ To scratch, to tear a. th. with the nails. ✲ خَرْمَش ه
Hermaphrodite. ▫ خَرْنَتِي
Young hare. ✲ خِرْنِق ج خَرَانِق
Palace of king Naman at Coofah. خَوَرْنَق P
To cover (a wall) with pricks and thorns. ✲ خَزَّ o خَزًّا ه
To pierce a. o. through with (a lance). — واخْتَزَّ ه ب
Silk. Tissue of silk and wool. ✧ Duck-weed. خَزّ ج خُزُوز
Male hare. خُزَز ج خِزَّان وأَخِزَّة
Bramble dried up. خَزَز
Silk merchant. خَزَّاز
Burrow of a hare. المَخَزَّة
To be swollen (skin). To have the udders swollen (she-camel). ✲ خَزِبَ a خَزَبًا. وتَخَزَّبَ
Gold mine. خَزِيبَة
Garden flies; their buzzing. ✲ خَزْبَاز وخَازِبَاز
To wink the eyes. ✲ خَزَرَ o خَزْرًا
To be contracted (eye). خَزِرَ a خَزَرًا

To ask a. o. to store up a. th. إستخزن ه
Treasure. ✧ Safe for money. خزنة
Chamber. Inner cabin.
Treasurership. خِزانة ج خزائن
Treasury. ✧ Cupboard. Magazine, warehouse. Ward-robe. Closet.
Library. — الكُتُب
Arsenal. — السِلاح
Treasurer. خازن ج خزنة وخُزّان
Treasurer, secretary. P خزندار
Tongue. خازن وخُزّان
Property laid up. ✧ Treasury. خزينة
Magazine, cellar. مَخزن ج مَخازن
✧ Office of a merchant.
The nearest roads. مَخازن الطَّريق
To overcome, to rule ✱ خزا o خزوًا ه a. o. To treat as an enemy. To restrain a. o. To slit (the tongue of a young beast).
To fall into disgrace, to be lowered. ✱ خزي a خِزيًا وخزى
To be ashamed of. — خزاية وخزى من, ره
To disgrace خزى i خِزيًا وخازى وأخزى ه a. o (God). To confound. To disappoint a. o.
To feel shame. إستخزى
Confusion. Punishment. خِزي وخزاية Remoteness. Repentance.
Disgrace, misfortune. خزية وخِزية
Abased, reviled. خزِم خزية
Ashamed. خزيان م خزيا ج خزايا
Disgrace. Cause of shame. مَخزاة ج مَخازٍ
Confounded. ✧ The Devil. مُخزى
To be vile. ✱ خسّ a خساسة وخِسّة
✧ To decrease (value).
To diminish the — o خسًّا, وخسّس ه portion of.
He came to no harm ; he was unhurt. ✧ ما خسّه
To commit a felony. أخسّ إخساسًا
To find a. o. vile. To contemn — ه وه a. o. To render a. o. unlucky.
To make a. th. by turns. تخاسّ ه
To reckon a. o. mean, vile. إستخسّ ه
To hold a. o. to be stingy.
Lettuce. خسّ
Wild lettuce. خسّ البقر
Anchusa, alkanet (*plant*). خسّ الحِمار
Dipsachus, teasel (*plant*). خسّ الكَلْب

To be unsheathed (sword). إختزق
✧ Rent, hole in a garment. خزق
Spear-head. ✧ Tearing. خازق
Pale, pole. Pointed stick. ✧ خازوق ج خوازيق
To impale (a man). ✧ خوزق ه
To have a fracture in the back. ✱ خزل a خزلًا
To cut, to sever a. th. خزل i خزلًا ه
To hinder a. o. from — ه عن
To walk heavily. تخزّل وانخزل
To be alone to hold (an opinion). إختزل ب
To cut a. o. off from (his relatives). — ه عن
Fracture, in the back. خزلة
Hinderance, obstacle. خُزلة
Sluggish gait. خيزلى وخوزلى
Whose hump is gone away (camel). أخزل ومَخزول
To pass a ✱ خزم i خزمًا وخزّم ه وه ring through (a camel's nostril). To string (pearls).
To abash, to humble a. o. خزم أنفه
To meet with a. o. in taking a different road. خازم ه
To enter the foot (thorn) تخزّم
To oppose each other (armies). تخازم
Kind of palm used for twisting ropes. خزم
Tulip. ✧ خُزام
Hair-ring خِزام وخِزامة ج خزائم put in a camel's nostril. Nose-ring of (women).
Lavender. (*plant*). خزامى وخزام
Hyacinth (*plant*). خزامى صفراء
Male serpent. الأخزم
Having the nose pierced (camel). Having his beak pierced (bird). مَخزوم
To store up (goods). ✱ خزن o خزنًا ه
To keep (a secret). To prevent (speaking).
— خزنًا وخزونًا وخزِن a خزنًا وخزُن o خزانة
To be altered, to stink (meat).
To become rich (poor man). ن
To lay up (goods). To take (the shortest way). To keep (a secret). إختزن

land to be swallowed up with its inhabitants (God).
To sink in its orbit (eye). — i خَسْفًا
To become emaciated. To be in the way of recovery. To fall in (roof). To be deficient.
To tare a. th. ✧ خَسَّف ه
To be deprived of sight (eye). أَخْسَف
To be eclipsed (moon). To be blinded (eye). To be swallowed up (land). To be perforated (roof). To be decayed (well). إِنْخَسَف
Deficiency. Issue of water. خَسْف
Ignominy. Clouds rising in the West.
Walnut. — وخُسْف
He has humbled him. سَامَهُ خَسْفًا
He spent the night in hunger. بَاتَ فِي خِسْفَة او الخَسِيف
Eclipse of the moon. خُسُوف
خَسِيف ج أَخْسِفَة وخُسُف وخُسُوف ج خُسُف
Unexhaustible well sunk in the rock.
Emaciated. Sunk (eye). خَاسِف ج خُسُف
Altered in complexion. Light boy.
Soft tracts of land. أَخَاسِف وأَخَاسِيف
The lion. المُخَسِّف
To pierce a. th. through (arrow). ✱ خَسَق i خَسْقًا ه وه
Forger of lies. خَسَّاق
To cast a. th. away. To exile a. o. ✱ خَسَل o خَسْلًا ه وه
Refuse, rubbish. خُسَالَة
Of low quality, inferior. خَسِيل ج خِسَال وخَسَائِل
To settle (a difference). ✧ خَسَم ه
To sink into contempt. ✱ خسن — أَخْسَن
To play with a. o. at the game of odd and even. ✱ خسو — خَسًا تَخْسِيَة وخَاسَا وأَخْسَا ه
Odd number. خَسًا ج أَخَاس
To throw pebbles at o. a. خسى — تَخَاسَيَا
Woollen garment or tent. خَسِيّ
✧ To enter (a house). ✱ خَشَّ o i خَشًّا فِي
✧ To produce a rustling. To clink (jewel). خَشَّ
To insert a wooden bit into the nose of a camel. To give a. th. stealthily to. — ه
To bring a fine rain (cloud). — وانْخَشّ
To pass through (man).

Thing made by turns. خِسَاس
Lowliness, vileness. ✧ Sordidness. خَسَاسَة وخِسَّة وخَسِيسَة
Fixed stars that never set. خُسَّان
Vile. ✧ Stingy, ungrateful. خَسِيس
Ugly. خَسِيس الوَجْه
To be weakened (sight). ✱ خَسَأَ a خَسْأً وخُسُوءًا
To drive away (a dog). — ه
To be driven away (dog). — وخَسِئَ a خَسْأً, وانْخَسَأَ
To throw stones one at another. خَاسَأَ وتَخَاسَأَ
Indisposed, unwell. مُخَشْتَك Ts
✱ خَسِر a خَسْرًا وخَسَرًا و خُسْرًا وخَسَارًا وخَسَارَة وخُسْرًا وخُسْرَانًا
To lose (in trade). To perish. To go astray. ◻ To become a rascal.
To alter (a balance). To lose wealth. خَسَر i خَسْرًا وخُسْرَانًا ه
To cause a loss to. To impute an error, a loss to a. o. To mislead. To destroy a. o. ◻ To demoralise a. o. To misuse a. th. خَسَّر ه
To experience a loss. أَخْسَر هُو نَفْسَهُ
To make a (balance) deficient. To cause a loss to. أَخْسَر ه
To give a. th. unwillingly to a. o. إِسْتَخْسَر عَلَى الشَّيْء
Loss, error. خَسْر وخَسَارَة وخُسْرَان
✧ What a pity! يَا خَسَارَة
Losses and profits. الأَرْبَاح والخَسَائِر
Losing (at play, in trade). ◻ Rascal. Spoiled (child). خَاسِر
خَاسِر وخَسِير وخَيْسَرَى وخَنْسَر وخَنْسَرِيّ
Vile, misled. Lost.
Vileness. Calamities. Blame. خَنَاسِير
To be banished. ✱ خُسِم
Man of the lowest class. خَاسِم وخَسِيم القَوْم
Weak. ✧ خَسِيم
To sink down, (country). To be eclipsed (moon). ✱ خَسَف i خُسُوفًا
To put out the eyes of. — i خَسْفًا ه
To sink (an unexhaustible well) in the rock. To cut a. th. To humble and vex a. o. To tear off a. th. To confine (a beast) without food.
To cause a — وأَخْسَف الأَرْض ب

Anything hard. Black. Passer-by. Crack. Little rain. خَشّ
Hill. خُشّ
Passer, foot-passenger. خَاشّ ج خُشّ
Creeping insects. Small birds. Wood inserted in the nose of a camel. Sack. Anger. Side. Mountain-snake. خِشَاش ج أَخِشَّة
Brave. Bad. خُشَاش
Ground covered with mud and pebbles. Nest of bees. Posteriors. خَشَّاء ج خَشَّاوَات وخَشَاشِيّ
Protuberant bone behind the ear. خُشَشَاء
Dog-hole, paltry place. ✧ خُشَّايَة
To clink, to clash, to rustle (weapons, jewels, dry things). ✱ خَشْخَش وتَخَشْخَش
Rustling of a new garment. Clashing, clinking. خَشْخَشَة
Poppy. ✧ Rocky soil. خَشْخَاش ج خَشَاخِيش
Corn poppy, red poppy. خَشْخَاش بَرِّيّ
Garden poppy, white poppy. — بُسْتَانِيّ
Papaver cornutum, horned poppy. — مُقَرَّن
Papaver Rhœas, wild Egyptian poppy. — مَنْثُور
A poppy. ✧ Charnel-house. Depository for the corpses. خَشْخَاشَة
To mix a. th. with. ✱ خَشَب i خَشْبًا ه ب
To pick out a. th. To shape out (a bow). To polish (a sword). To roughen a. th. — ه
To compose (verses) unrefined. — واخْتَشَب ه
To become like wood. خَشُب
✧ To put a culprit in the stocks. — ه
✧ To wainscoat, to ceil a. th — ه
To pasture upon twigs or dry herbage (cattle). تَخَشَّب ه
To be inured to hardship and privation. To be rude, coarse in manners, food. إِخْشَوْشَب
خَشَب ج خُشْب وخُشُب وخُشْبَان و✧ أَخْشَاب وخَشَبَات
Wood, timber.
Gaiacum. ◻ خَشَب الأَنْبِيَا
A piece of wood, timber. خَشَبَة ج خُشُب
Rough to the touch. Hard (life). خَشِيب

Tall and vigorously framed (man). خَشِب وخَشِيب وخَشِبِيّ
Shaped out, trimmed. Polished. Corrupt. خَشِيب ج خُشُب وخَشَائِب
Wood-seller. Timber-merchant. خَشَّاب ج خَشَّابَة
Coarse, hard. Severe. High and rugged mountain. أَخْشَب
Hard, dry ground. خَشْبَاء
خَشْتَق ج حشَاتِق و✧ خَشْتَك ج خَشَاتِك Ps
Fob, waist-pocket.
To leave the refuse of a dish. ✱ خَشَر i خَشْرًا
To pick out, to cull a. th. — ه
To escape in fear. خَشِر a خَشَرًا
Rabble, refuse of mankind. خَاشِر
Refuse. Rabble. Remainder of a meal. خُشَار وخُشَارَة
To do a. th. amiss. ✱ خَشْرَب في العَمَل
Swarm of bees and hornets. Bee-hive. Queen-bee. Soft plaster-stones. ✱ خَشْرَم ج خَشَارِمَة
To be humble, submissive. To incline to setting (sun). To be cast down (eyes). To be faint (voice). To wither (leaves). To disappear (hump). To be dry, rainless (earth). ✱ خَشَع a خُشُوعًا
To cast down the eyes. — بِبَصَرِهِ
To humble o'self before a. o — ل
To humble, to lower a. o. أَخْشَع ه
To show humility. To make entreaties. ✧ To be moved, affected. تَخَشَّع
To lower the eyes, the voice before a. o. إِخْتَشَع ل
Humility. Faintness of the voice. Casting down of the eyes. ✧ Emotion. خُشُوع
✧ Moving, affecting the feelings. خُشُوعِيّ
Flattened hill. خُشْعَة ج خُشَع
Lowly. Low (voice). Depressed and wayless (place). Cast down (looks). Kneeling. Fallen down (wall). Withered and fallen (plant). خَاشِع ج خَاشِعُون وخَشَعَة وخُشَّع
Humble entreaty. ✧ Emotion. تَخَشُّع
To cross (a country). To be frozen (water). To be intense (cold). To be concealed. ✱ خَشَف i o خُشُوفًا وخَشَفَانًا

To enter, to penetrate into. — وانخشف في
To lead a. o. (guide). خشف خشافة ب
To crackle under the feet (snow). — خشفا وخشفة
To wound the head with (a stone). — ه ب
To pass along hastily. — في السَّير
To be infected with mange (camel). خَشِف a خَشَفًا
To lead the way (guide). خشّف
To resound (on the butt : arrow). خاشف
To break a compact. خاشف في ذمّتهِ
To hasten to do evil. — الى
Rapid walk. Rustling. Movement. Lowliness. Flattened hill. خَشْف
Hardened snow. Soft ice. خَشَف وخَشِيف
Young of a gazelle. خِشْف ج خِشَفة
Green fly.
Beverage made of raisins soaked into water. خُشاف P
Misfortune. خَشَّاف
Bat (night-bird). خُشَّاف
Travelling by night. Penetrating (sword). خَشُوف
Acute (sword). Frozen (water). خاشِف
Infected with mange. أخشف
Ice-house. مَخْشَف
Guide. Lion. مِخْشَف
To inveigh against. ¤ خشّك على
Bran mixed with flour. Brown bread. خُشْكار P
To revile a. o. ✲ خَشَل o خَشْلًا وخَشَّل ه
To be worn out (clothes). خَشِل a خَشَلًا
To be vile. To be depressed (earth). تخشّل
Empty egg. Date-stone. خَشْل
Head of an anklet, a bracelet. Fruit of the doom-palm. — وخَشَل
Refuse, base. خَشَل
Weak (man). خَشْل فَشْل وخَشِل فَشِل
To break the nose of. ✲ خَشَم i خَشْمًا ه
To become large (nose). To stink (nose). خَشِم a خَشَمًا وخُشُومًا
To be altered, to stink (meat). خَشِم a خَشَمًا وخشّم وأخشم وتخشّم
To intoxicate a. o. (wine). خشّم ه
✧ Nose. Mouth. Snout. ✧ خِشْم
To humble, to confound a. o. ✧ كسر خِشْمَهُ

Intoxication. خُشْمة
Lion. Huge (nose, mountain). خُشَام
Big-nosed.
Cartilage of the nose. خَيْشُوم ج خَياشِيم
Pl. ✧ Fish-gills.
Large-nosed. Stinking. أخشم ج خُشْم
Deprived of smell (man).
Drunk, intoxicated. مُخَشَّم ومَخْشُوم ومُتَخَشِّم
To be hard, rough to the touch. To be coarse. ✲ خَشُن o خُشْنة وخَشَانة وخُشُونة
To render a. th. hard. coarse. خَشَّن ه
✧ To thicken a. th. To wear (a garment); to inhabit (a house) for the first time.
He exasperated him. — صَدْرَهُ
To treat a. o. harshly. خاشن و✧ خشّن ل ه
To be coarse, uneven. To act rudely. To wear a coarse (garment). تخشّن
To find a. th. to be rough, coarse. إستخشن ه
To be harsh, rough to the hand. To be rude, rough (man). إخشوشن
Harshness, roughness. Rudeness. خُشْنة وخَشَانة وخُشُونة
خَشِن ج خِشَان, وأخشن م خَشْناء ج خُشْن
Harsh, rough to the touch.
Untractable (man). خَشِن وأخشن الجانِب
Thick-headed, rough. خَشِين
Kind of purslain. خَشْناء ✧ خُشَّينة
✲ خَشِيَ a خَشْيًا وخَشْيَة وخَشَيَانًا ومَخْشِيَة ه
To dread, to fear a. o. or a. th. وه
To fear that. — أن أو بأن
To frighten, to awe a. o. خشّى ه
To dread a. o. or a. th تخشّى ه وه
To be ashamed. ✧ إختشى
Dread, fear. خَشْيَة وخَشْيان ومَخْشاة
Lest, for fear that. خَشْيَة أن
Dry plant. خَشِي وخَشِيّ
خاشٍ وخَشٍ وخَشْيان م خَشْيَة وخاشِيَة, وخَشْيا
Spiritless, faint-hearted. ج خَشَايا
More dreadful (place). أخشى
✲ خَصَّ o خَصًّا وخُصُوصًا وخُصُوصَة وخَصُوصِيَّة
To attribute a. th. exclusively to. وتَخِصَّة ه ب
To be special, proper. To concern a. o. — خُصُوصًا
✧ It is not of my concern. هذا لا يخصُّني

To belong to. خَصَّ ه ول
To appropriate a. th. — ه لِنَفْسِهِ
To become destitute. خَصَّ a خَصَاصَةً وخَصَاصًا
To design a. o. for. To render a. th. special to. خَصَّصَ ه ب و ه ب
To attribute a. th. exclusively to. — واختصّ ه ب
To scorn at. أَخَصَّ ب
To be special, peculiar, proper to. To concern a. o. تَخَصَّصَ واختصّ ب
To claim the property of. ✧ To assign a. th. exclusively to. إستخصّ ه
Hut, booth of reeds. Tavern. ✧ Silk-worm nursery. خُصّ ج خِصَاص وأخصاص وخُصُوص
Proper, special, worthy, celebrated. Apart. ✧ First rate, superfine (goods). خاصّ (*opp. to* عامّ)
Property (of a plant). خاصّة ج خَوَاصّ
The chief men (of a tribe). The special officers (of a king). الخاصّة والخَوَاصّ والخُصَّان
Property, virtue (of a medicine). ✧ Self-restraint. خاصِيَّة ج خاصِيَّات وخَصَائِص
Interstice, hole, gap. Short garment. خَصَاص
Small bunches remaining on the vine after the gathering. Little of wine. خُصَاصَة ج خُصَاص
Poverty, destitution. خَصَاصَة وخَصَاص
Peculiarity, particularity. خَصُوص وخُصُوص
Most of all, specially. على الخُصُوص وخُصُوصًا
✧ On the subject of, about. مِن و بِخُصُوص
Special. ✧ An express. مَخْصُوص
To be fruitful (land). ✱ خَصَبَ i و خَصِبَ a خِصْبًا
To possess abundance of seed-produce. To find pasturage (man, cattle). أخصب
To render (a country) fruitful (God). أخصب ه
Side. White mountain-snake. خُصْب
Abundance of herbage. Life of plenty. Fertile (land). خِصْب ج أخصاب
Fertile, fruitful (land). خَصِب وخَصِيب
Fruit-bearing palm-tree. خِصَاب

Wealthy, bountiful (man). خَصِيب
Abounding with seed-produce (country). مُخْصِب و مِخْصَاب
To be cold. (day). To be seized by cold (limb). To suffer from cold (in the hands, feet). ✱ خَصِرَ a خَصَرًا
To walk hand in hand with a. o. or by his side. To meet with a. o in taking a different way. خاصَرَ ه
To take (a sceptre) in hand (king). تَخَصَّرَ ب
To put the hands upon the flanks. — واختصر
To walk together hand in hand. تَخاصَرَ
To abridge (a discourse). To take the shortest away. To shorten (prayer). إختصر ه
To curtail a. th. To cut off a. th. — في
To lean upon a stick. — ب
Middle of the body. Waist. Road crossing a heap of sand. Hollow of the sole. Encampment of nomads. خَصْر ج خُصُور
Cold (day). الخَصِر
Bitterly cold. خَصِر
Waist, flank. Pain in the flanks. خاصِرَة ج خَوَاصِر
Waist-wrapper. خِصَار
Curtailment, elision. إختصار وخُصَّيْرَى
Rod. Staff. Sceptre. مِخْصَرَة ج مَخَاصِر
The nearest ways. مَخاصِر الطَّرِيق
Slender in the waist (man); in the wrist (hand). Tight (sandal). مُخَصَّر
Summary, conpendium. مُختَصَر
To sew (a sole). To patch (a sandal). To walk in the footprints of. To exceed a. o. in reviling. ✱ خَصَفَ i خَصْفًا ه و ه
To apply a. th. upon. To cover (the body) with. — وأخصف واختصف ه على
To cast her young one in the seventh month (she-camel). — خِصَافًا
To be tracked by. خُصِفَ ب
To be ill-tempered. To do a. th. reluctantly. خَصَّفَ
To render a. o grey (hoariness). — ه
To hurry on. أخصف
Sandal. خَصَف
Colour mixed of white and black. خُصْف

✧ Subtraction, discount. خَصْم
Adversary, antagonist. خَصْم ج خُصُوم (m. f. s. pl.)
Side. Edge, corner. خُصْم ج خُصُوم وأخصام
Contentious. Quarreller. خَصِم وخَصُوم
Contention, quarrel. خِصَام وخُصُومَة ومُخَاصَمَة
Adversary. Litigant (in law). خَصِيم ج خُصَمَاء وخُصمَان وأخصام
To geld a. o. ☆ خَصَى i خِصَاء
To learn one science only. أخصى
Testicle. خُصْيَة ج خُصًى
Castoreum. خُصْيَة البَحْر
Satyrion (*plant*). خُصَى الثَّعْلَب
Round and white berries alike to the morell. — الدِّيك
Orchis (plant). — الكَلْب
Mercurialis annua, mercury (*plant*). — هِرْمِس
Gelded. Eunuch. خَصِيّ ج خِصْيَان وخِصْيَة
To stir (water). To jolt (his rider: horse). To frighten a. o. ✧ To shake a. th. To try a. o. ☆ خَضّ ه وه
✧ To be shaken, stirred. إنْخَضّ
To adorn (a girl) with a set of shells. خَضَّض ه
To barter a. th with. خَاضّ ه مُخَاضَّة
✧ Jolt, shock. Fright. خَضَّة
White shells. Dishes of a repast. Sophism. خَضَض
Ornament of little value. Collar for gazelles, cats. Ink. Fetters. خَضَاض
Foolish (man). Rained upon (land). خَضِيض
To stir (water). To dash a. th. about. To turn up (the earth). ☆ خَضْخَض ه
✧ To jolt (horse). خَضْخَض
To move about (a dagger) in a wound. — ه في
To be shaken, dashed about. تَخَضْخَض
Shock, jolt. خَضْخَضَة
Stout, fat (camel). خُضَاخِض
Abounding in water, in plants (land). Black liquid pitch for besmearing camels. خَضْخَاض
To colour, to tinge, to dye a. th. ☆ خَضَب i خَضْبًا وخَضَّب ه

Basket made of palm-leaves. Coarse garment. خَصَفَة ج خَصَف وخِصَاف
Eye of an awl. خُصْفَة
Names of a celebrated horse. خَصَاف وخِصَاف
Liar. Cobbler. خَصَّاف
Ashes. Sandal. Fresh milk mixed with curdled milk. خَصِيف
White in the flanks (horse). White and black. — وأخْصَف
Awl. مِخْصَف ج مَخَاصِف
To cut, to curtail a. th. ☆ خَصَل o خَصْلًا ه
To excel a. o. in shooting. — خَصْلًا وخِصَالًا ه
To cut off a. th. To lop (a tree). To cut (the forelock). خَصَّل ه وه
✧ To render (a horse) vicious. — ه
To shoot with a. o for a wager. خَاصَل مُخَاصَلَة وخِصَالًا ه
To hit the target (arrow). أخصَل
To contend in shooting for stakes. تَخَاصَل
Hitting of the target. Wager. خَصْل ج خُصُول
He attained his aim. أحرز او اصاب خَصْلَة
Good quality. Bad habit. Hitting of the target. Soft branch of mimosa. Any tender branch. ✧ Vice in a horse. خَصْلَة ج خِصَال
Bunch of grapes. Thorny branch. Lock of hair. — وخُصْلَة ج خُصَل
Dependant hair, branches. خُصَل
Losing the wager in shooting. Tail. خَصِيل
Flesh with its muscles. Complete limb of flesh. Tuft of hair. خَصِيلَة ج خَصَائِل
Scythe, reaping-hook. مِخْصَال
To overcome a. o. in dispute. ✧ To solve (a difficulty). To discount. To subtract a. th. To counteract a. o. ☆ خَصَم i خَصْمًا ه وه
To contend, to quarrel with. خَاصَم خِصَامًا ومُخَاصَمَة
To afford an argument against. أخصَم ه
To quarrel together. تَخَاصَم واختَصَم
✧ To be deducted (sum). To be solved (difficulty). إنْخَصَم

– وخَضِب a خُضُوبًا, وخُضِب وأَخضَب To become green (tree, land).
تَخَضَّب واختضب ب To dye o's self (with henna).
إِخضَوضَب To be green (tree).
خَضِب ج خُضُوب Green. New sprouts, off-shoots.
خِضَاب Dye (for the hair, hands).
خَضِيب ومَخضُوب ومُخَضَّب Dyed (hand, beard).
مِخضَب Trough, wash-house.
✡ خَضَد i خَضدًا ه To crack a. th. To bend (a branch) without breaking it. To cut off (the thorns of a tree). To craunch (a cucumber).
– وخَضَّد ه To cut a. th.
تَخَضَّد وانخضد To be broken (wood). To be shrivelled (fruit).
خَضَد Part broken or cut off (from a tree). Bruise, pain in the limbs. Shrivelled fruit.
خَضِد ومَخضُود Weak. Unable to rise.
خَضَاد Bruise of a limb. Tree without thorns.
أَخضَد ومُتَخَضِّد Bent, crooked.
مِخضَد Voracious.
✡ خَضِر a خَضَرًا To be green. To become verdant (plant).
خَضَر o خَضرًا ه To cut (a palm-tree).
خَضَّر ه To render a. th. green.
خُضِّر لهُ فِيهِ He was blessed in it.
خَاضَر ه To sell to a. o. green fruits.
أَخضَر ه To render (a land) green: (rain).
إِخضَرَّ واخضَوضَر To be green, of a green colour. To be verdant.
إِخضَرَّ To be dark (night).
إِختَضَر ه To cut herbage, while green. To bear (a burden). To eat green fruits. To cut off (the ear).
أُختُضِر To be cut green (herbs). To die young.
خِضر وخِضِر Surname of St George or the Prophet Elias.
خِضرًا مِضرًا وخَضِرًا مَضِرًا Without price. Unrevenged (blood).
خَضَر Green. Verdant aspect of seed-produce.
خَضِر Green-coloured. Branch. Seed-produce. Green vegetable. Verdant meadow.
خُضرَة ج خُضَر وخُضر Green colour. Softness of a branch. Cucumber. Greens. Herbs. Ash-colour (in horses). Blackish colour (in men).
خَضَار Milk mixed with much water. First greens.
الخُضَارَة والأَخضَر والخُضَيْر The sea.
خَضِير Verdant. Verdure. Green herbs. ✧ Fresh dung of cows.
خَضِيرَة Daphne, an evergreen laurel.
خَضَّار ✧ خُضَرِيّ وخَضَرجِيّ Green-grocer.
خُضَارِيّ ✧ خُضَرِيّ ج خَضَارِيّ Wild duck.
أَخضَر م خَضرَاء ج خُضر Recent. Green-coloured. Auspicious (man). Black-coloured. Greens. Fine woman. ✧ Fox-coloured (horse).
خَضرَاء القَوم The chief men of a tribe.
الخَضرَاء The sky, the firmament. Army clad in armour.
الأَخَاضِر Gold, meat and wine.
يَخضُور ومَخضَرَة Grass. Verdant meadow.
✡ خِضْرَم ج خَضَارِم وخَضَارِمَة وخِضرِمُون Numerous, plentiful. Generous lord. Holding much water (well). Immense (sea).
خِضرِمِيّ ج خَضَارِمَة Persians settled in Syria in the beginning of Islamism.
مُخَضرَم Living in the beginnimg of Islamism. Of mixed breed. Uncircumcised.
✡ خَضَع a خُضُوعًا خَضعًا وخَضَاعًا To be lowly. To set (star).
– أَخضَع ✧ انخضع ل To obey, to submit to a. o.
– ه To soothe, to soften a. o.
– ه إلى To incite a. o. (to evil).
– وأَخضَع ه To bend a. o. (age).
خَضَّع وأَخضَع ه وه To render a. o. humble and submissive. To cut up (meat).
خَاضَع ه To speak gently to a. o.
تَخَضَّع واختضع واخضَوضَع و✧ انخضع To humble o.'s self. To submit.
إِختَضَع To pass along rapidly (man, horse). To dash upon its prey (falcon).
خَضَع Depression of the neck.
خَضعَة Whips. Swords. Sound of a whip.

To appropriate a. th by making a mark upon it. خطَّ ه لِنَفْسِهِ
To draw lines. To register a. th. ✧ To groove (a column). ✧ To survey (a road). To lay colours (on her face woman). خطّط ه
✧ To paint o.'s brows. تَخَطَّط
To be streaked (face). To be tattooed. To grow forth (down of a youth). إِخْتَطَّ
To trace the boundaries of. To make the survey (of a town). — ه
Line, streak. Sword. Hand-writing. Furrow. ✧ Chiromancy. Geomancy. Paint for the face. خَطّ ج خُطُوط
Firman, autograph of the Sultan. Ts خَطّ شَرِيف وخَطّ هُمَايُون
Arbute-tree. ☐ خَطّ الأَدِيب
The equator. خَطّ الإِسْتِوَاء
Equinoctial line. خَطّ الإِعْتِدَال
Meridian. خَطّ نِصْف النَّهَار
Quarter of a town. Thoroughfare, street. خُطّ
Ground first occupied by a settler. خِطّ وخِطَّة ج خِطَط
Affair. Relation. Quality. Ignorance. Course, way of acting. خُطَّة ج خُطَط
Spear. خَطِّيّ ج خَطِّيَّة
Drawing lines. Sorcerer. خاطّ
Leaving footprints on the sand. ✧ Paint for the eyebrows. خَطُوط
Unwatered ground lying between two lands rained upon. خَطِيطَة ج خَطَائِط
Drawing lines. Calligraphist. خَطَّاط
Weaver's ruler for marking cloth. مِخَطّ ومِخْطَاط
Handsome (boy). Streaked. مُخَطَّط
Wooden ruler. مِخْطَاط
To swagger. ✧ To tattoo. ✲ خَطْخَط
✧ To paint her brows (woman). To tattoo o.'s self. تَخَطْخَط
To send forth foam (boiling pot). ✲ خَطَأَ a ب
To fail. To make a mistake. خَطِئَ a خَطَاء وخَطأ
To commit a fault, a sin. To do wrong. — خِطأ وخِطأَة
To charge a. o. with an error. خطّأ تَخْطِئَة وتَخْطِيئًا ه

Submitted to every one. Subduing his equals. خُضَمَة ج خُضَم
Submissiveness, obedience. خَضُوع
Gurgling of the bowels of a horse. Murmur of a torrent. خَضِيعَة
Lowly, tractable, obedient. خاضِع ج خُضَّع, وخَضُوع ج خُضَع
Bustle of a fight. Battle. Dust raised in a battle. خَيْضَعَة
Lowly, submitted. Having a depressed neck (horse). أَخْضَع م خَضْعَاء ج خُضْع
To break wind. ✲ خَضَف i خَضْفًا وخُضَافًا
Small water-melon. خَضَف
The serpent. الأَخْضَف
Wine. المُخْضِفَة
To be moist, wet. ✲ خَضِل a خَضَلًا, وأَخْضَل واخْضَلّ واخْضَوْضَل
To moist, to wet a. th. خَضَّل وأَخْضَل ه
To be moistened. To be tufty (tree). إِخْضَالّ واخْضَالّ
Lustrous pearl. Kind of beads. خَضْل وخَضَل
Moist, wet (body). خَضِل وخاضِل
Juicy (roast meat). Dripping with blood (sword). خَضِل
Abundance. Comforts of life. Rainbow. خُضْلَة
Easy, luxurious (life). مُخْضَل ومُخْضَل
To cut a. th. ✲ خَضَم i خَضْمًا, واخْتَضَم ه
To give a part of goods to. — لِفُلَان من
To eat a. th. — وخَضِم a خَضْمًا ه
To cut a. th. To stop (the way: robber). To wear out (its scabbard: sword). إِخْتَضَم ه
Bountiful (man). Large crowd. Sea. Sharp dagger. Hone. خِضَمّ ج خِضَمُّون
Green plant. Boiled wheat. Luxurious land. خَضِيمَة
Middle. Main part. خُضُمَّة
Leading a luxurious life. مُخْضَم ومُخْتَضَم
To crumble (dry things). ✲ خَضَا o خُضُوًا
To put marks on a. th. ✲ خَطّ o خَطًّا على
To write with (a pen). — ب
To write a. th. To streak (the sand: wind). To eat (little of food). To dig (a grave). — ه
His hair begins to become grey. خَطَّهُ الشَّيْب

أخطأ إخطاء وخاطئة To commit a mistake, a fault.

— ﻫ To miss (the butt, the way).

— وتخطّأ وتخاطأ ﻩ To lead a. o. into error, sin.

تخطّأ To be wrong, to make a mistake.

تخاطأ ﻫ To go beyond (the mark: arrow).

خِطْء Wrong, intentional fault.

خَطأ وخطاء Sin, error, mistake.

خطيئة ج خطايا و خطيئات Sin. Little of.

✧ خطيّة It is a pity.

خاطئ و✧ خاطي ج خطأة Sinner. Mistaken.

خاطئة ج خواطئ Sinful woman. Missing the mark (arrow).

مُخطئ Wrong, mistaken. Missing the mark.

✱ خطب o خُطبة و خَطابة To preach; to deliver an exhortation.

خَطُب o خَطابة To be, to become a preacher.

خَطب o خِطبًا وخِطبة ﻩ To ask (a woman) in marriage. To ally by marriage to (a tribe).

— إليه أختهُ He asked of him his sister in marriage.

— وخطّب ﻩ على ✧ To give (a woman) in marriage to.

خَطِب a خطبًا To be streaked with white or black. To be of a dusky colour.

خاطب ﻩ خِطابًا ومُخاطبة To converse with. To address a. o.

— في To discourse on.

— ﻩ To come within reach of: (game).

أخطب To become yellow. To be streaked with green. To assume colour (wheat).

تخاطب To converse together.

إختطب To be affianced. To ask a woman in marriage.

خَطْب ج خُطوب Thing, affair important or not. Cause of an affair.

ما خطبك What do you want? What is the cause of your affair?

خِطْب ج أخطاب Bride, bridegroom.

خِطاب ج أخطبة وخِطابات Discourse. ✧ Letter.

فصل الخِطاب Sentence delivered on proofs and oaths. Opening of a discourse. Rhetorics. Legal jurisprudence.

خُطْبة Dusky yellow. Dusty green.

خُطبة ج خُطَب Speech, sermon. Preface of a book.

خِطب وخِطّيب و✧ خَطيب Betrothing. Bridegroom.

خِطبة Betrothal. ✧ Betrothal-present.

خِطب وخِطبة وخِطّيبة و✧ خَطيبة Bride, betrothed woman.

خَطّاب Transactor of a marriage. Preacher.

خَطيب ج خُطباء Orator, preacher.

خاطِب ج خُطباء Asking a woman in marriage. Betrothed.

خُطبان Bitter plant resembling asparagus. Green leaves of the acacia-tree.

أخطب وخُطبان، وخُطبانة ج خُطبان Yellow colocynth striped with green.

أخطب م خَطباء ج خُطب Dusky yellow. Green wood-pecker. Hawk.

مُخاطَب Second person (*in grammar*).

✱ خطر i خطرانًا To quiver, to vibrate (spear). To happen (event).

— و✧ تخطّر في To shake o.'s self in walking. To waddle.

— خطرًا و خطرانًا وخطيرًا ب To wag the tail (camel). To raise (the hands, the fingers).

— خطرانًا ب To brandish (a spear).

خطَر o i خطورًا ببالِه او على او في بالِه To come back to the mind (thought). To remember a. th.

— لهُ To occur to a. o. (thought).

✧ تخوطر To change o.'s mind.

خطُر o خطورة To be eminent, high in rank, important.

خاطر بنفسه To risk o.'s self. To jeopardise o.'s life.

— ﻩ على To bet with a. o for.

أخطر To be in danger (sick man).

أخطر ﻩ To be the equal, the rival of. ✧ To warn a. o.

أخطر ﻫ ببالِه او على وفي بالِه To bring back a. th. to the mind (God).

— ﻫ To lay (a wager), to risk a. th.

To ✲ خَطِف a خَطْفًا و✧ خَطِيفَة ه snatch a. th. away. To deafen (the ear).
To dazzle. To blind a. o. (lightning). — البَصَر
To ravish the mind. — العَقْل
To walk quickly (camel). — a i خَطَفَانًا
To snatch a. th. stealthily. خَطَّف ه وه
To leave a. o. (fever). أَخْطَف ه
To miss game (shooter). — ه
To snatch away a. th. To ravish a. o. تَخَطَّف واختَطَف ه وه
To be rapt in ecstasy. ✧ إنخَطَف بالرُّوح
Snatching, elopement, rapine. خَطْف
Recovery. خُطْف
Theft. Limb torn off. خُطْفَة
Rapid walk. خَطْفَى و خَيْطَفَى
Skipping (arrow). خَاطِف ج خَوَاطِف
The wolf. الخَاطِف
Snare to catch gazelles. خَاطُوف
Hound. خَطَّاف
Ravisher. Satan. خَطَّاف
Swift, kind of swallow. Grapnel, iron-hook. خُطَّاف و✧ خَطِّيف ج خَطَاطِيف
Walking quickly. خَطِيف وخَيْطَف
Food made of flour and milk cooked. ✧ Snatching. خَطِيفَة
To ✲ خَطِل a خَطَلًا، وأَخطَل في كَلَامِهِ speak much, to utter foul language. To reason falsely.
To waddle. تَخَطَّل
Lightness. Quickness. Stupidity. Sophism. Idle talk. Length. Over-long (garment). خَطَل
Loquacious. Foolish. Lost (arrow). Coarse (clothes, body). خَطِل
Cat. Dog. Misfortune. Perfumer. Swarm of locusts. خَيْطَل
Having pendulous ears (ewe). Loquacious. أَخْطَل
Name of a christian poet. الأَخْطَل
To bridle, ✲ خَطَم i خَطْمًا، وخَطَّم ه ب to muzzle (a camel) with. To silence a. o by.
To strike the nose of. To disgrace a. o. To sew up the edges (of a skin). — ه
To put (a string) to (a bow). — خَطْمًا وخِطَامًا ه ب

To make a bet on. تَخَاطَر على
Large measure of Syria. Dirt agglomerated on a camel's flanks. خَطْر
Milk mixed with water. Branch. Large number of camels. Woad (*plant*). خِطْر ج أخطار
Danger. خَطَر ج أخطار
Elevation, nobility, rank, wealth. Equal in dignity. Stake at a race-course. — ج خِطَار
Strutting. Dangerous. خَطِر م خَطِرَة
Once, one time. ✧ Journey. خَطْرَة
Suggestion (of Satan). — ج خَطَرَات
Swaddling. Occurring (thought). Heart. ✧ Good pleasure, fancy, sake. خَاطِر ج خَوَاطِر
✧ Passer by, comer. — ج خُطَّار
✧ He got his consent. أخذ خَاطِرَهُ
✧ He condoled him. — بِخَاطِرِهِ
✧ He was offended at. — على خَاطِرِهِ مِن
✧ He consoled him. جَبَر خَاطِرَهُ
✧ He showed regard to him. رَاعَى خَاطِرَهُ
✧ He gave spontaneously. أَعطَى مِن خَاطِرِهِ
✧ He disobliged him. كَسَر خَاطِرَهُ
✧ Be good enough to. كَلِّف خَاطِرَك
✧ Important (man). واجِب خَاطِرُهُ
✧ Heart-broken. مَكْسُور الخَاطِر
✧ Good bye. خَاطِرَك
✧ As it pleases thee. بِخَاطِرِك وعلى خَاطِرِك
◻ On account of. على خَاطِر
For thy sake. من شَان ولأَجل خَاطِرِك
Sling. Ballista. Lion. Perfumer. Spear. Oily ointment. خَطَّار
Enclosure for camels. Moving the tail (she-camel). خَطَّارَة
✧ Warning given to a newspaper. إِخْطَار
Noble, eminent. Momentous. Dangerous. Pair, equal. Rope, halter. Threat. Darkness of night. Gossamer. خَطِير ج خُطَر
Dangers, risks, jeopardy. مَخَاطِر
To relate false news. ✲ خَطْرَب
To walk quickly. To become flaccid (skin). ◻ To be delirious. ✲ خَطْرَف وتَخَطْرَف
Walking quickly. خَطْرِيف و خُطْرُوف

Foot of a camel or ostrich. Sole of the foot. خُفّ ج أخفاف
Boots in yellow leather. — ج خِفاف
Lightness. Nimbleness, unsteadiness. Slightness. خِفَّة
Swiftness, sprightliness. خُفُوف
Light. Unimportant. خَفِيف ج خِفاف
Light-hearted. Brisk. Poetical metre.
Scanty-bearded. خفيف العارِضَين
Foolish. — العَقل
Gracious, kind. — الرُّوح و✧ الدَّم
Having little charge. — الظَّهر
Sharp-minded, sagacious. — القَلب
Light-handed, nimble. — اليَد
Pumice-stone. خَفَّاف وخُفَّان
Boot-maker. خَفَّاف
Swamp full of lions near Coofah. خَفَّان
Hyena. خَفُوف
✧ Undress, deshabille. تَخفِيفَة
To cry (bustard, hyena, pig). ✱ خَفخَف
To produce a rustling (paper, new garment).
Cry of the hyena. Rustling of new clothes. خَفخَفَة
To snatch and throw a. th. down. To destroy (a house). To split (a water-skin). ✱ خَفَأَ a خَفأً ﻫ
To become still, silent (voice). To cease speaking (dying man). ✱ خَفَت o خُفُوتًا
To die suddenly. — o خُفاتًا
To lower the voice, to read silently. — o خَفتًا, وخافَت وتَخافَت بِكَلامِهِ
Rue (*plant*). خُفت
Speechless (dying man). Waterless cloud. Weak (plant). خافِت
To be affected with trembling of the knees (camel). ✱ خَفِج a خَفَجًا
To incline, to lean. تَخَفَّج
Trembling of the knees (in camels). *Lapsana*, nipple-wort (*plant*). خَفَج
Affected with trembling of the knees (camel). Crooked. أَخفَج
To walk at a quick pace. ✱ خَفَد o خَفدًا و خَفَدانًا وخَفِد a خَفَدًا
To protect, to defend, to escort a. o. ✱ خَفَر o خَفرًا ه وب وعلى

To bind a halter on a camel's nose. إختطم ﻫ
Beak (of a bird). Muzzle (of a beast). Nose (of man). Momentous affair. خَطم
Nose-rein of a camel. خطام ج خُطُم
Mark on a camel's nose. Bow-string.
Marsh-mallow. خِطمِيّ (*un.* خِطمِيَّة)
Long-nosed. Black. أخطم ج خُطم
Nose. Bill. مَخطِم ومِخطَم ج مَخاطِم
To step, to make steps ✧ To trespass upon (a limit). ✱ خَطا o خَطوًا, واختطى
To make a. o. to walk. خَطًا وأخطى ﻫ
To overreach a. o. or a. th. تَخَطَّى ه وﻫ
Step, space between two footsteps. خُطوَة ج خُطًى وخُطُوات وخُطَوات وخُطْوات
Step. Time. Measure of 6 feet. خَطوَة ج خَطَوات وخِطاء
To be compact (flesh). ✱ خَظا o خُظُوًّا
To become fat (man). أخظى
To fatten a. o. — ه
Fat, fleshy. خَظٍ م خَظِيَة
Sleeveless shirt. Wolf. Ogre. Debauchee. ✱ خَيعَل
To be (*opp to* ثَقُل) light. To be light-minded. To be brisk, active. To fail (rain). To decrease (wealth). ✧ To relax (disease). ✱ خَفّ i خَفًّا وَخِفَّة
✧ To be light-handed. To be nimble in work. خَفّ يَدُهُ
✧ To be light-footed, swift. — رِجلُهُ
To rush on. — خَفًّا وخِفَّة وخُفُوفًا إلى
To alleviate, to lighten a. th. خَفَّف وأخَفّ ﻫ
To be in an easy condition. To have light beasts. To travel without encumbrance. أَخَفّ
To relieve a. o. To blame a. o. — ه
To wear boots. To hasten. ✧To wear an undress. تَخَفَّف
To act briskly. تَخافّ
To find (a burden) light. To render a. o. light-witted. To enliven a. o. إستَخَفّ ﻫ
To make little account of. To disregard a. th. إستَخَفّ ب
Light, unimportant. Small troop. خِفّ

To abash, to humble a. o. To circumcise (a female). — ه
To remain in a place. — ب
To be easy (life). خَفُض o خفضًا
To soften (the voice). To facilitate a. th. To lower (a camel's head) for riding. ✧ To abate (the price of). To end (a word) with a kesra. خَفَّض ه
To become easy (affair). ✧ To be lowered (price). تَخَفَّض
To be lowered (voice). To be humbled. إنخفض
To abate (price of goods). إختفض
Easy (life). Depressed place. Kesra, vowel-accent. خفض
The Humbler (God). Easy (life). Particle commanding a kesra. خافِض
Compliant, quiet. — الطَّير والجَناح
Easy, quiet (life). — وخَفِيض
Ground easily watered. أرض خافِضَة السُّقيا
Easy (life). خَفِيض ومَخفوض
Lowered (voice). خَفِيض
To fall in a swoon. To wave (curtain). ✲ خَفَم a خَفمًا
To be flaccid (joints). — خَفمًا وخَفمانًا
To have the liver contracted through hunger. خُفِم
To deject a. o. (hunger). أخفَم ه
To be contracted (liver). To be near to swoon. To be uprooted (tree). To be perforated (lung). إنخفم
To throb (heart). To flash (lightning). To flutter, to wave (flag). To quiver (sword). To move about (mirage). To blow (wind). ✲ خَفَق i o خفقًا وخفقانًا وخُفوقًا وأخفق
To patter (sandals). To fly (bird). To be nearly over (night). To break wind (beast). — i o خَفقًا
To slap a. o. with a. th. broad. ✧ To beat up (eggs). — ه وه
To set (sun, star). To be empty (place). — خُفُوقًا
To incline to setting (stars). To shine brightly (stars). To nod (the head in drowsiness). To fail. To be disappointed (hunter). To become أخفق

To ask for his hire (guardian). To break (a covenant). — ه
To fulfil (a compact). خَفَر ب
To circumvent a. o. — خفرًا وخُفورًا ب
To be shy, confused (maid). خَفِر a خفرًا وخَفارَة, وتَخَفَّر
To protect, to defend a. o. To wall (a town). خَفَّر ه وه
To betray a. o. To send an escort with a. o. أخفر ه
To have recoursn to a. o. for protection. تخفّر ب
Bashfulness, shyness. خَفَر وخفارَة
Escort. Sentry. خَفَر و✧ غَفَر
Protection, defence. خُفرَة وخِفارَة وخُفارَة
Hire of a watchman. خُفارَة وخِفارَة
Defender, protector. خُفرَة, وخَفِير ج خُفَراء
Bashful, modest (woman). ـر وخَفِرة ومِخفار ج مَخافِير
Wild oats. خافور
To scoff, to laugh at. ✲ خَفَس o خفسًا ه
To sink down. (*for* خسَف) ✧ — وانخفس
To destroy (a building). To eat little of. — ه
To hold foul language to. — ه
To hold foul, shocking speech. — i خفسًا وأخفس
To drink little or much water. خَفَس وأخفس من
To be thrown prostrate on the ground. تخفّس
To be altered (water). إنخفس
Blackbeetle. خَنفَساء
Wine mixed with much water. خَفِيس
To throw a. th. ✲ خَفَش o خفشًا ب
To be small-eyed. To be weak-sighted. To see only by night. To be contracted (hump). خَفِش a خَفَشًا
To prostrate and trample upon a. o. To pull down (a building). خَفَّش ه وه
Bat, night-bird. خُفَّاش ج خَفافِيش
Weak-sighted. Small-eyed. Nyctalops. أخفَش م خَفشاء ج خُفش
To lower a. th. To soften (the voice). To inflect (a word) with a kesra. ✲ خَفَض i خفضًا ه
To walk gently (camels). To be still *i. e.* to die (man). خَفَض

destitute (man). To flap its wings (bird). To have o.'s provisions consumed.

To prostrate a. o. — ه

To quiver (looming). To flutter (flag). اختفق

Palpitation (of the heart). خفقان

Thong, strap for striking. خفقة

خفقة وخفقة ج خفقات وخفقات وخفاق

Lank in the belly (horse).

Flags, banners. الخافقات والخوافق

Broad in the fore-part of the foot. ✧ Humbug. خفاق

The East and the West. الخافقان

The four cardinals points. الخوافق

Wide delusive desert. Swift-running (horse). خيفق

Fleet (she-camel). Light and bold woman. Confused run of horses. Calamity. خنفقيق

Setting points (of the stars). مخافق

Broad sword. مخفق

Insane. مخفوق

✲ خفا o خفوًا وخفوًّا To flash (lightning). To appear.

✲ خفى i خفيًا وخفيًّا ه To show, to bring out a. th. To conceal a. th.

To be concealed, to be latent. خفي a خفاء

To conceal o.'s self ; to disappear. — خفية وخفية

To disclose, to unveil a. th. أخفى ه

To conceal o.'s self; to lay hid. ✧ To disguise o.'s self. تخفى واستخفى و✧ اختفى

To make a. th. apparent. To kill a. o. (in secret). To dig (a well). إختفى ه

Secrecy. Veil, covering. خفاء ج أخفية

The eyes. أخفية الكرى

The calyxes of flowers. أخفية النور

The genii, the devils. الخافي والخافياء

Secret. Secrecy. Genii. خافية ج خوافٍ

Feathers of a bird concealed under the wing. خوافٍ

Secret. Thicket. Well. Touch of insanity. خفية ج خفيات وخفايا

The secrets of the hearts. خفايا القلوب

Robber of graves. المختفي

✲ خق i خقًا وخقيقًا وخقيقًا To boil fast (cooking-pot). To be loose (pulley).

خق ج خقوق وأخقاق , وأخقوق وإخقيق

Crack, gap in the ground. ج أخاقيق

Bed of a torrent. خقق

To elect a. o as an emperor. ✧ خقّن

Sultan of the Turks. خاقان ج خواقين Ts

✲ خلّ o i خلًّا وخلولًا وتخلّل To be lean. To become destitute.

To give sweet herbage to (camels). To pierce a. th. To slit (the tongue). To pin the skirts (of a garment). ✧ To apply a seton to. — o خلًّا ه

To specify a. th. (in prayer). ✧ To fail in a. th. — في

To become poor. خلّ وأخلّ

To become sour (wine). خلّل

To turn (wine) into vinegar. To pickle (dates). To pick (the tooth). To let (water) flow in the interstice of the beard, fingers. ✧ To pickle a. th. خلّل ه

To act friendly towards. خالّ مخالّة وخلالًا ه

To injure a. o: to disorder a. th. To be remiss in. To leave off a. th. To forsake (a place). أخلّ ب

To render a. o. poor (God). — ه

To want a. o. أخلّ ب

To be circumscribed (rain). To use a tooth-pick. ✧ To become sour. تخلّل

To mix in a crowd. — القوم

To penetrate in. — في

To become friends. تخالّ

To become sour (wine). To be disordered (mind). To be entangled (business). إختلّ

To make vinegar with. — ه

To pierce a. o. with (a spear). — ه ب

To be in want of. — إلى

Vinegar. Path in the sand. Crack-brained. Shabby garment. Vein in the neck. Lean. Fat. Weaned camel. Evil. Rent in a garment. خلّ ج أخلّ وخلال

There is neither evil nor good in him. ما عنده خلّ وخمر

Intimate friend. خِلّ ج أخلال

Interstice, gap. Unsoundness. Disorder. Defect. ✧ Seton. خلل ج خلال

Hole. Need. Destitution. Inborn quality. Acid wine. خلّة ج خلل وخلال

Rainless (cloud). خُلَّب
Ligthning without rain. بَرْق خُلَّب
Said of a promise without effect.
Wheedle, coaxing. خِلَابَة
Foolish (woman). خَلْبَاء وخَلْبَن
Deceiver. خَالِب وخِلَّبِيّ
Deceitful. خَلُوب وخَلَّاب وخَلَبُوت
Claws, clutches, talons. مِخْلَب ج مَخَالِب
Reaping-hook.
Orobus tuberosus, heath-pea. مِخْلَب العُقَاب الأَبْيَض
Variegated. مُخَلَّب
To entice a. o. by soft words. ✲ خَلْبَس ه وقَلْبَهُ
Lie. Wheedling. خُلَابِس
Vanities. Medley. Falsehoods. Unsuccessful business. خَلَابِيس
Flint-stone. خَلَنْبُوس
To make low tricks, jokes. ◻ تَخَلْبَص
Mischievous child. Mountebank, fool. ◻ خَلْبُوص ج خَلَابِيص وخلابِصَة
To drag, to pull out a. o. or a. th. To wean (a beast). ✲ خَلَج i خَلْجًا واخْتَلَج ه وه
To move, to stir a. th. — ه
To strike a. o. with (a sword). — ه ب
To wink to a. o. — ه بِعَيْنِهِ
To busy the mind (affair). — وخَالَج ه
To be spoiled. To be broken with fatigue. خَلِج a خَلَجًا
To contract the eyebrows. أَخْلَج ه عَن
To be shaken. To drag himself along (paralytic). To branch off (river). تَخَلَّج
To busy the mind (business). تَخَالَج واخْتَلَج في صَدْرِهِ
Strait of the sea. خَلِيج ج خُلُج وخُلْجَان
Canal. River. Rope. Eye-lid. Bank of a river. Schooner. ✧ Great canal of Cairo.
Fleet horse. إِخْلِيج
To last long, to remain for ever. ✲ خَلَد o خُلُودًا
To retain a youthful appearance (old man). — خَلْدًا وخُلُودًا
To abide in (a place). — وخَلَّد وأَخْلَد ب وإلى
✧ To reach a very old age (man). خَلَّد

Sweet herbage used as the staple food of camels. Thorny tree. Sincere love. Female friend. خُلَّة ج خُلَل
Scabbard of a sword. Friendship. Gap in a tank. خِلَّة ج خِلَل وخِلَال جج أَخِلَّة
Unripe dates. Between. خَلَال
Instrument for piercing. Wooden pin. Muzzle of a young camel. خِلَال ج أَخِلَّة
Tooth-pick. — وخِلَالَة
Remains of food between the teeth. — وخُلَالَة
Surroundings of a country. Inside of a house. خِلَال الدِّيَار
Sincere friendship. خَلَالَة وخُلَالَة
True friend. The friend (of God) *i. e.* the Patriarch Abraham. Lean and crack-brained. Destitute. Pierced. خَلِيل ج أَخِلَّاء وخُلَّان
Wretched, poor. Poorer. أَخَلّ
Species of thistle. ◻ أُخْلَة
✧ Pickles. مُخَلَّل
Vehemently thirsty. Destitute. Unsound of mind. Disordered (affair). مُخْتَلّ
To bare (a bone). ✧ To shake, to stir a. th. ✲ خَلْخَل ه
To put on an anklet. To be shaken. To be scattered (army). To be disjointed. تَخَلْخَل
Silver anklet. ✧ Ankle. خَلْخَال ج خَلَاخِيل
Unsteadiness. تَخَلْخُل
Uncompact (army). مُتَخَلْخِل
To kneel without moving, to be refractory (camel). ✲ خَلَأ a خَلْأً وخِلَاءً وخُلُوءًا
To keep to a place (man). — خُلُوءًا
To leave a. th. for another. خَالَأَ مُخَالَأَةً
Food and drink. تِخْلِئ
To wound a. o. with the claws (beast). To clutch its prey (lion). To captivate (a youth: woman). ✲ خَلَب o i خَلْبًا، واسْتَخْلَب ه
To wheedle a. o. — o خَلْبًا وخِلَابًا وخِلَابَةً ه
To be silly (woman). To be miry (water). خَلِب a خَلَبًا
To deceive a. o. خَلَّب وخَالَب واخْتَلَب ه
Membrane of the liver. Claw. Vine-leaf. Radish. Enticer. خِلْب ج أَخْلَاب
Pith of palm-tree. Palm-rope. Mire. خُلْب وخُلُب

خَلَّد وأَخْلَد ه وه To render a. o. everlasting (God). To perpetuate a. th.

أَخْلَد ب وإلى To lean towards. To stick faithfully to (a friend).

خُلْد وخُلُود Continuity. Eternity. Paradise.

خُلْد ج مَنَاجِذ ✧ وخُلُود Mole, field-rat. Lark (bird). ◻ Scrofula.

– وخَلَدَة ج خِلَدَة Earring. Bracelet.

خَلَد Thought. Mind; soul.

مُخَلَّد, Eternal, lasting. Vigorous (old man). Keeping to a place.

خِلْد Dog.

الجزائر الخالِدات The Canary Islands.

الخَوالِد The mountains. The rocks. Supports of a pot.

مُخْلَد ومُخْلِد Vigorous (old man).

مُخَلَّدًا For ever.

✡ خُلَّر Pea. Bean. Lentil.

✡ خَلَس i خَلْسًا وخِلِّيسَى, وخالَس واختَلَس ه To carry off a. th. by force. To take a. th. by deceit.

خالَس ه ه To snatch a. th. away from.

أَخْلَس To become hoary (head). To be partly green and partly dry (plant).

تَخالَس ه To contend together for stealing a. th.

إِخْتَلَس To cheat, to defraud.

– ه To embezzle a. th.

خَلْس وخَلِيس Herbage partly fresh and partly dry. Theft, embezzlement.

خُلْسَة ج خُلَس Flying opportunity. Mixture of white and black.

خِلاسِيّ Mulatto. Cock of mixed breed.

خَلِيس Hoary (hair). Faded (plant).

مُخْتَلِس Swindler.

✡ خَلَص o خُلُوصًا To be pure, unmixed. ✧ To be finished.

– o خَلاصًا من To be saved from (danger). To part from o.'s people. To be cleared from (the dregs). ✧ To be free from.

– o خُلوصًا إلى وب To reach a. o.

– خَلَصًا To be broken in the flesh (bone).

خَلَّص ه وه To save, to free a. o. To clear a. th. To refine a. th. To extract the best of. ✧ To save o.'s soul. To pay a. th. To discharge (o.'s conscience). To suit a. o. (affair).

خَلِّصْنِي ✧ Let me alone.

خَلَّص حَقَّهُ ✧ To retaliate. To recover a debt.

– على ✧ To pay postage on (a letter); duty on (goods).

خالَص ه To act sincerely with. ✧ To give a discharge to.

أَخْلَص ه To extract the best part of. To select a. th. To elect a. o. (God).

– لله دِينَهُ To worship God sincerely.

– لَهُ ه و ه ه To give sincere (advice) to. To have (sincere love) for.

تَخَلَّص من To be saved, freed from. To get rid of.

تَخالَص To act sincerely with o. a. ✧ To release o. a. from obligation.

إِسْتَخْلَص ه To claim, to appropriate a. th. To select a. th. ✧ To extract a. th.

– ه من To get a. th. back from.

خِلاص Refined, purified (gold, silver).

خَلاص Salvation. Redemption. ✧ End. Receipt.

خُلاصة وخِلاصة Purified (gold, butter). Choice part. ✧ Final sentence of a court. Discharge of an account. Medicinal extract.

خِلاصة الكلام Substance of a discourse.

خُلُوص وإخلاص Sincerity, devotedness. Rob of dates.

خِلْص وخُلْصان (s. pl). Sincere friend.

خالِص ج خُلَّص Pure (colour). White. Sincere. Free. Genuine. ✧ Down-right.

مُخْلِص Sincere, devoted (friend).

مُخْلَص ومُسْتَخْلَص Pure, unmixed.

المُخَلِّص The Saviour Jesus-Christ.

✡ خَلَط i خَلْطًا, وخَلَّط ه ب To mix, to mingle a. th. with.

خَلَّط To eat noxious food (sick man).

– في كلامِهِ To be delirious.

خالَط مُخالَطة وخِلاطًا ه وه To be blended with. To have intercourse with. To mix (cattle). To infect a. o. (disease). To fall upon a. o. (wolf).

خُولِط في عقلِهِ To be disordered in mind.

أَخْلَط واخْتَلَط To be slack (horse).

To be relaxed (nerve). تَخَلَّم و✧ تَخَلوَّء
To depart secretly. To be intoxicated.
To break a compact. To divorce. تَخَالَم
To be displaced. To be luxated (limb). To be removed from office. To be stripped of o.'s wealth. إِنخَلَم
To be divorced for a dowry (woman). إِختَلَم
To take the property of. — ة
Divorce. Meat cooked with aromatics. خَلْم
Robe of honour received as a gift. خِلْعَة ج خِلَع
The best part of goods. — وخُلْعَة
Wolf. Ogre. Gambler. Cast off (garment). خِلَعَة
Disorderly, immoral life. خَلَاعَة
Shameless. Debauchee. خَالِع العِذَار
Repudiated (son). Profligate. Deposed. خَلِيع ج خُلَعَاء
Constant fear. Foolish. Preserved colocynth. Pickled meat. خَوْلَم
Luxated. Loosened (limb). ✧ Paralytic. مُخَلَّم
To succeed a. o. To take the place of. To be the agent, subtitute of. ✫ خَلَف o خِلَافَةً وخِلِّيفَى ة
New fruits replace others. خَلَفَت الفَاكِهَة بَعْضُهَا بَعْضًا
To be stupid (young man). — خَلَافَةً وخُلُوفًا
He has not his father's worth. خَلَف عَن خُلُق أَبِيهِ
To be altered in (taste, odour: milk). To be corrupt (man). To ascend a mountain. — خُلُوفًا وخُلُوفَةً وأَخْلَف
To remain behind a. o. — خَلْفًا عَن
To cause a. o. to retrieve (a loss: God). — ه ل وعلى
To repair (clothes). — ه خَلْفَةً
To put a pole (to a tent). To replace o.'s (father). To seize a. o. from behind. — i خَلْفًا ه وة
To be left-handed, squint-eyed, foolish. To be pregnant (she-camel). خَلِف a خَلَفًا
To leave (luggage) behind. To appoint a. o. as a suc-

To be mingled. To become fat (camel). To be disordered in mind. To be intense (darkness). إِختَلَط
To leap the female (camel). إِستَخلَط
Flatterer, intriguer. Foolish. Mixture of dates. خَلْط وخِلَاط
Any mixture. Mixed dates. Intriguer. Crooked bow. خِلْط ج أَخْلَاط
Promiscuous multitude. Medley. — وأَخْلَاط وُخْلَيْطَى وخُلَّيْطَى
Man of mixed race. خِلْط مِلْط
✧ Pell-mell. — و✧ وخِلَاط بِلَاط
The four humours of the body. أَخْلَاط الإِنْسَان
Partnership. Society. خِلْطَة
Confused crowd of men and cattle. Deceit practised in the tithe of cattle. خِلَاط
Disorder of mind. خَلَاطَة
Medley. Insinuating man. Companion. Partner. Husband. First cousin. Friend. Neighbour. Mixture of clay and straw; of two kinds of milk. خَلِيط ج خُلُط وخُلَطَاء
Confusion. Rabble. خُلَيْطَى
Intriguer, interfering man. مِخْلَط ومِخْلَاط
Mixed food. ✧ Mess. مَخْلُوطَة
To pull off a. th. To take off (clothes, shoes). To release (a beast). To luxate (a limb). ✫ خَلَع a خَلْعًا ه
To disown, to repudiate (a son). — ة
To depose a. o. from (office). — ة من
To throw off all restraint. To act profligately. — عِذَارَهُ
✧ To lose the mind. To become ungodly. خَلَم
To clothe a. o. with a robe of honour. — ه على
To divorce (o.'s wife). خَلَع a خَلْعًا ة
To be cast off by his family (son). خَلُع o خَلَاعَةً
To be dismissed from office. To be stripped of its shroud (corpse). خَلِم
To snatch off a. th. To dislocate (a limb). خَلَّم و✧ خَلوَّء ه
To divorce (o.'s wife). خَالَم ة
To send forth leaves. To seed (corn-plants). أَخْلَم

خَلَف Substitute, replacer. Compensation. Good son. ✧ Off-shoot.
خالِف وخالِفَة Foolish, silly. Water-drawer. Spoiled (wine).
— وخالِفَة أهل بَيْتِهِ Good for nothing, worthless fellow.
خالِفَة Remainder of a tribe. Pole in the hinder part of a tent.
الخَوَالِف Women.
خِلَاف Diversity. Sleeve of a shirt. *Salix ægyptia*, Egyptian willow. ✧ Other, else.
من غَيْر خِلَاف Uncontrovertibly.
بِخِلَاف ذَلِك Contrarily to that.
خِلَافَة Vicariate, caliphate. ✧ Childbirth.
حَيّ خَلُوف Tribe deprived of her warriors.
خَلِيف Road between two mountains.
خَلِيفَة ج خُلَفَاء وخَلَائِف Vicar. Caliph, the supreme chief of Islam.
أَخْلَف Left-handed. Squint-eyed. Foolish. Torrent. Male serpent.
مِخْلَاف ج مَخَالِيف Delusive in his promises. Province.
مِتْلَاف مِخْلَاف ومُتْلِف مُخْلِف Bountiful without losing his wealth.
مَخْلَفَة Encampment of a tribe. Road. Willow-plot.
✧ مُخَالِف وَالدَيْه *Delphinium*, lark-spur (*plant*).
✧ خَوْلَفَت To travail (woman).
✡ خَلَق o خَلْقًا وخِلْقَة ه وه To create, to form a. th. out of nothing.
— خَلْقًا وخَلْقَة ه To forge (a lie). To polish (wood). To compose (a discourse). To take the measure of.
خَلِق a خَلَقًا وخَلُق o خُلُوقًا وخُلُوقَة وخَلَاقَة To be even, smooth (wood).
خَلِق وخَلُق o خُلُوقَة وخَلَقًا, وأَخْلَق To be shabby (clothes).
خَلُق o خَلَاقَة To be fine, goodly in make (woman).
خَلُق ل To be fit, apt to a. th.
خَلَّق ه To polish (wood). To aromatise a. th.
خالَق ه To behave kindly with.
أَخْلَق ه To wear out (a garment).
أَخْلَق وَجْهَهُ To disgrace o.'s self.

cessor. ✧ To leave an inheritance. To bring forth (a child : woman).
خالَف ه وه To disobey a. o. ✧ To transgress (a law). To forfeit o.'s word.
— مُخَالَفَة وخِلَافًا ه في To disagree with a. o. upon (an affair).
— ه إلى To go to (a place) during the absence of a. o.
أَخْلَف مَوْعِدَهُ To break a promise.
— ه To repair (a garment).
— ل To draw water for a. o.
— لِنَفْسِهِ To retrieve a loss.
— ه To send behind. To replace a. o.
أَخْلَفَت الشَّجَرَة The tree has put forth fruit.
تَخَلَّف عن To remain behind a. o.
تَخَالَف واخْتَلَف To disagree together.
إِخْتَلَف To branch off, to be diversified.
— ه To succeed. To replace a. o. To leave a. o. behind. To seize a. o. from behind.
— إلى الخَلَاء To return repeatedly to the privy.
إِسْتَخْلَف ه وه To appoint a. o. as successor, agent. To draw water. To find (water) to be sweet.
— ه من To substitute one for another.
خَلَف ج خُلُوف Coming in succession (time, people). Wrong saying. Edge of an axe.
فَأْس ذات خَلْفَيْن A two-headed axe.
خَلْفُ Behind, afterwards.
خُلْف ج أَخْلَاف Breach of promise. False prediction.
خِلْف ج أَخْلَاف وخِلْفَة Different, contrarious.
خِلْف ج أَخْلَاف Udder, or teat of a she-camel. The shortest rib.
خِلْفَان Two things contrasting, as short and long.
ذات الخِلْفَيْن ج ذوات الخِلْفَيْن Axe.
خِلْفَة Disagreement. Difference. Patch on clothes. Diarrhea. Succession of times, plants.
خُلْف واخْتِلَاف Disagreement, dissent.
خُلْفَة ج خُلَف Vice, blemish. Last taste of food

used for making bowls.
Galanga, aromatic root. خُلنجان وخُولنجان P
Wild thyme. خلندرة P
To be vacant (place); empty (vessel). To be alone in a place. To elapse (time). ✱ خَلَا o خُلوًا وخَلاء
He is free from troubles. خلا بالُه
He is dead. He is gone. خَلَا وخَلى مَكَانُهُ
To be free from. To send a. th. — عن
To be lonely in (a place). —ب وإلى
To apply o.'s self exclusively to. To keep to (a place). — ب
To speak in private with a. o. خلا o خلوة وخلوًا وخَلاء ب وإلى ومع
To retire apart by o.'s self. — بنفسِهِ
To devote o.'s self to an affair. — لِأمرٍ
To let a. o or a. th. To allow a. th. To make a. th. pairless. ✧ To preserve a. th. خَلّى تَخْلِيَةً ه
To cease to. To discard a. th. — عن
✧ I beseech thee (*lit.* May God preserve thee). الله يُخَلّيك
To let a. o. go. To release (a prisoner). خَلّى سَبِيلَهُ
To leave people alone. — بَيْنَهُمَا
To quit a. th. or a. o. خَالى ه وه
To be lonely, (man, place). أَخلى إِخلاء
To clear a (place). To find (a place) vacant. — ه
To be alone with a. o. — ه او ب
To deprive o.'s self of. — عن
To get rid of, to part from a. o. or a. th. تَخلّى عن ومن
✧ To retire in private with. — مع
To retire apart with a. o. — ب
To be lonely. To lead a solitary life. إِختلى
To be lonely, empty (place). إِستخلى
To ask an interview from. — ه
To have a private audience of. — ب
Lonely place. Empty space. Solitude. ✧ Open country. خَلاء
I am clear from it. أنا مِنْهُ خَلاء (*m. f. s. p.*) وأنا خالي منهُ
Prviy. خَلاء وبَيْت الخَلاء
Except, save. خلا وما خلا ✧ خلا عن
Quite alone. خِلو ج أخلاء
Emptiness. خُلُوّ

To clothe a. o. with shabby clothes. — ه ثوبًا
To disclose a. th. to a. o. — ه ل
To be perfumed. تَخلّق
To forge (a lie). — واختلق ه
To assume (the temper, manners of). — ب
✧ To get angry with a. o. — على
To become smooth (back of a horse, cloud). To become even with the earth (ruined house). إِخلولق
It may be, it is likely that. إِخلولق أن
Creation. Creatures. People. خَلق
✧ Crowd.
Constitution creation. خِلقة ج خِلَق
✧ Countenance. Birth.
Moral character, nature. Temper. Bravery. Habit. Religion. ✧ Anger. خُلق وخُلُق ج أخلاق
✧ He lost his temper. طلع خلقهُ
Moral science, ethics. عِلم الأخلاق
Shabby (garment). خلق (*m. f.*) ج أخلاق وخلقان
Share of happiness. خَلاق
Polish, shining. خُلاق
Yellow perfume, compound of saffron. خِلاق وخلوق
Suitable, able to... Worthy of... خليق ج خُلقاء وخُلق ب
Nature. Creatures, men and beasts. ✧ (*Pl.*) Female slaves. خليقة ج خلائق
The Creator (God). خالق وخلّاق
Praise to God the best Worker, the most Powerful! تبارك الله أحسن الخالقين
Even, smooth. Poor. More suitable, fitter. أخلق م خلقاء
Inner part of the hoof. Interior of the palate. Smooth part of the forehead. خلقاء وخليقاء
Smooth. Well proportioned. Aromatised (wine). مُخلّق
Generous, good-natured. مُختلق
Large copper caldron. خالقين ج خلاقين G
To choose a. th. ✱ خام — خلم واختلم ه
To treat a. o friendly. خالم ه
Friend. Covert of a gazelle. Grease of sheep. خِلم ج أخلام وخُلماء
Kind of heath خلنج ج خلانج P

Sluggish. Milk just drawn. Praised. خَوِيرٌ
Broom. Heart free from hatred. مِخَمَّةٌ
To snuffle, to speak, to sing through the nose. ✲ خَنْخَمَ
Argemone, prickly poppy. خِمْخِمٌ
To be exhausted through fatigue or disease. To be corrupt (meat). To become corrupt (morals). ✲ خَمِجَ a خَمَجًا
To speak ill of a. o. — ه
Of bad morals, dissolute. مُخَمَّجُ الأَخْلَاقِ
To die away (blazing). To abate (fever). To subside (anger). To faint (sick person). ✧ To be disheartened. ✲ خَمَدَ o وخَمِدَ a خَمْدًا وخُمُودًا
To be quiet and still. أَخْمَدَ
To allay (the flame). ✧ To dishearten a. o. — ه و ه
To cause a. o. to die (God). — أَنْفَاسَهُ
Dying away (fire). خَامِدٌ
Hole for covering embers. خَمُّودٌ
To conceal, to hide a. th. To withhold (a testimony). To leaven (the dough). ✲ خَمَرَ o i خَمْرًا ه
To give wine to a. o. — ه
To be c[illegible]. To absco[illegible] خَمِرَ a خَمَرًا
To be u[illegible] of (news). To be ashamed at. — مِن
To veil o.'s face. To leaven (the dough). خَمَّرَ ه
To mingle with a. th. To pervade a. th. To cleave to o.'s house. To be near to. خَامَرَ ه
To deceive a. o. in a sale. To infect a. o. (disease). — ه
✧ To plot against. خَامَرَ على
To abscond. To bear rancour. To veil o.'s self. أَخْمَرَ
To feel hatred against a. o. — لِ
To veil a. th. To take a. o. unawares. To keep (a secret). To leaven the (dough). To brood (a design). To give a. th. to a. o. as a gift. — ه و ه
To put on a muffler (woman). تَخَمَّرَ واخْتَمَرَ بِ

Without. خُلُوًّا من
Recess, retired place. Temple (amongst Druses). Solitude. Privy. خَلْوَةٌ ج خَلَوَاتٌ
Out of the way, apart. على خَلْوَةٍ
Bee-hive. Large ship. Milch-camel. Divorced. خَلِيَّةٌ ج خَلَايَا
Free, careless. Bachelor. خَلِيٌّ ج خَلِيُّونَ وأَخْلِيَاءُ
Empty. Free from. Elapsed. خَالٍ
Bachelor. Spinster. (m. f.) خَالٍ ج أَخْلَاءٌ
The centuries elapsed. القُرُونُ الخَالِيَةُ والخَوَالِي
To cut off a. th. To put firewood under a cooking-pot. To cut herbs (for cattle). To bridle (a horse). ✲ خَلَى i خَلْيًا ه
To unbridle (a horse). — عن
To put (barley) in a'bag. — ه في
To prostrate a. o. To deceive a. o. خَالَى ه
To abound in herbage (land). أَخْلَى
To cut (herbage). إِخْتَلَى ه
To be cut (herbs). إِنْخَلَى
To keep to milk-food. إِخْلَوْلَى
Fresh herbs. Vegetables. خَلًى
Scythe. مِخْلًى
Bag for green herbage. Nose-bag. مِخْلَاةٌ و✧ مِخْلَايَةٌ
To stink (meat); to be altered (milk). ✧ To eat slovenly; to glut. ✲ خَمَّ o i خَمًّا وخُمُومًا وأَخَمَّ
To sweep (a house). To cleanse (a well). To milk (a she-camel). ✧ To explore (a country). — خَمًّا ه
To praise a. o. — ثِيَابَ فُلَانٍ
The hens have been confined in their coop. خُمَّ الدَّجَاجُ
To eat the remains of a meal. تَخَمَّمَ
To sweep (a house). To cut a. th. إِخْتَمَّ ه
Stinking, corrupt. خَمٌّ وخَامٌّ ومُخِمٌّ
Garden without trees. خِمٌّ
Hen-coop. خُمٌّ و◻ خُنٌّ ج خِمَمَةٌ
Remains of foad eaten in hope of heavenly recompense. خُمَامَةٌ
Refuse of the people. Rubbish, old furniture. خُمَّانٌ وخَمَّانٌ

✧ To conspire secretly together. ✧ تخامر وتخمّر

To be fermented (beverage). To be leavened (dough). To be turned into wine. إختمر

Wine. Any intoxicating and fermented drink. Grapes. خَمر وخَمرَة

Screen. Crowd. Thicket. خَمَر

Stealthily, secretly. على خَمرٍ وعلى خَمرَةٍ

Sweet wine. خُمرَة

Intoxicated, giddy. خَمِر

Press, crowd of men. — وخُمار النّاس

Way of wearing a veil. خِمرَة

Vessel for leaven. Dregs of wine. Mat of palm-trees. Yeast. خُمرَة

Sweet odour. خُمرَة وخَمرَة

Brown, wine-coloured. خَمْرِيّ

Screen. Muffler. خِمار ج خُمُر وخُمر وأخمِرة

Remains of intoxication. خُمار

Ferment. Leavened bread. ✧ Dough. خَمِير وخَمِيرَة

Wine merchant. Vintner. خَمّار و✧ خُمّارجي

Public-house, tavern, inn. خَمّارة

Addicted to drink. خِمِّير ومُستخمِر

Affected with the vapours of wine. مَخمُور

Fermented. White-headed (beast). مُخمَّر ومُختمِر

Sea-shell, cowry (*un.* يَخمُورَة). يَخمُور

To take the fifth part of a. o.'s goods. ✲ خَمَس o خَمسًا ه او مالَهُ

To be the fifth; to complete the number five. To twist a rope with five strands. — i خَمسًا ه وهم

To make a. th. pentagonal, five-cornered. To amplify (verses). خَمَّس ه

To be in the number five. To have camels watered every fifth day. أخمَس

Five. خَمسة م خَمس

Fifteen. خَمسَة عَشَر ✧ خَمستَعش

Fifth part, a fifth. خُمس وخُمُس ج أخماس

To use deceit. To make a false pretence. ضَرَب أخماسًا لِأَسداس

They are both closely united. هُما في بُردَة أخماس

Watering of camels every five days. خِمس

Five and five, five together. خُماس ومَخمَس

Formed of five letters (noun). Five spans high (boy); five years old (girl). خُماسيّ

Fifty. خَمسُون

✧ Pentecost, Whitsunday. Golden jubilee. عِيد الخَمسِين

Hot wind of Egypt. Sirocco. ◻ الخَماسِين والخَمسِين

Fifth. خامِس م خامِسَة

Fifteenth. خامِس عشر م خامِسَة عَشرَة

Thursday. الخَمِيس ويَوم الخَمِيس ج أخمِسَة وأخمِساء

Army composed of five parts: the van and rear-guard, the main body and the two wings. ✧ A swine. خَمِيس

Five cubits long (spear). خَمِيس ومَخمُوس

Company of men. خَمِيس النّاس

Pentagon. ✧ Magical figure. مُخَمَّس

To scratch, to slap (the face). ✲ خَمَش o i خَمشًا وخُمُوشًا ه

To cut off (a limb). To beat a. o. — ه

Mark left on the face by scratching. خَمش ج خُمُوش

Small brook. خامِشَة ج خَوامِش

Slight wound not mulcted. خُماشَة ج خُماشات

Musquitoes, gnats. خَمُوش

To be reduced (swelling of a wound). ✲ خَمَص o خَمصًا وخُمُوصًا وانخَمص

To render the belly lank (hunger). — o خَمصًا ومَخمَصَة ه

To be empty (stomach). To be hungry. — وخَمِص a خَمَصًا

To dissipate (darkness of the night). تَخامَص

To shrink from. — عن

Hunger. Upland. خَمصَة

Suffering from hunger. خَمِيص الحَشَى ج خِماص الحَشَى

Empty-bellied. خَمصان وخُمصان الحَشَى ج خِماص الحَشَو

They (*the camels*) leave in the morning hungry and return in the evening satiated. تَغدُو خِماصًا وتَرُوح بِطانًا

Black-bordered cloak worn by men and women. خَمِيصَة ج خَمائِص

Hollow part of the sole. أخمَص ج أخامِص

Amaranth, velvet-flower. ✧ مُخَمَّنِيَّة
To guess, to ✱ خَمَن o خمنًا وخَمَّن ه conjecture approximatively. ✧ To think, to surmise.
To appraise a. th. roughly. — على
Stink. خَمَن
Elder-tree. ✧ خُمَّان
Weak (lance). خَمَّان
Rabble, refuse of the people. — النّاس
Appraisement, survey. تخمين
Nearly ; perhaps تخمينًا وعلى التَّخمين
Appraiser. ✧ Surveyor. مُخَمِّن
To thicken (milk). ✱ خَمأ o خموءًا
To speak, laugh or weep ✱ خَنَّ i خنينًا with a nasal sound.
To empty (a basket) gradually. To cut (the trunk of a tree). To take the property of. — o خَنا ه
To bereave a. o. of reason (God). أخَنَّ ه
To stink (well). إستخَنَ
Nasal voice. Twang. خُنَّة ومَخَنَّة
Laugh or tears uttered through the nose. خَنِين
Comfort of life. خَنان
Glanders in camels. خُنان
Snuffling, speaking through the nose. أخَنّ م خَنَّاء ج خُنّ
Nose. Narrow of a valley. Entrance of a road. Middle of a house. Destruction. مَخَنَّة
To snuffle. To speak indistinctly. ✱ خَنْخَن
Indistinct speech. Nasal voice. خَنْخَنَة
To cut (a tree-stock). ✱ خَنَأ a خَنأ ه
To be weak (foot). To be lame. To perish (man). ✱ خَنِب a خَنَبًا
To cut off a. th. To weaken. To destroy a. o. أخنَب ه
To become haughty. تَخَنَّب
Inner part of the knee. Interstice of the ribs, fingers. خِنب ج أخناب
Glanders of camels. خُنَّب
Treacherous. ذُو خُنُبات وَ ذُو خَنَبات
Tall, long. Bobby. خَنَاب وخِنَّاب
Brand of infamy. Evil. خَنابَة
Haughtiness. خِنابَة
The two wings of the nose. الخَنَّابَتان والخِنَّابَتان

Middle of the body. — البَدَن
✱ خَمَط o خَمطًا وخُموطًا . وخَمِط a خَمَطًا To have a good flavour. To be altered (wine, milk).
To roast (meat). — i خَمطًا ه
To skin and roast (a kid). — ه
To put (milk) in a skin. — i o خَمطًا ه
To be in anger. To growl (stallion). To roar (sea). To magnify o.'s self. خَمِط وتَخَمَّط
Acid, bitter. Bitter plant. Any thornless tree. Fruit of the *capparis sodata* (اراك). Good or bad-flavoured (wine, milk). خَمْط
Flavour, taste of wine, milk. خَمطة وخَمَطة
Skinned and roasted (kid). خَمِيط
To limp (hyena). ✱ خَمَع a خُمُوعًا وخَمعًا وخَمَعانًا
Hyena. خامِعَة ج خَوامِع
To be obscure, fameless (man). To be faint (voice). ✱ خَمَل o خُمُولًا
✧ To forsake a. o. (God). — ه
To have a defect in the joints. خَمِل
To reduce a. o. to obscurity. To make nappy (cloth). To fringe (a carpet). أخمَل ه وه
✧ To wander (mind). To be forsaken by God (man). إنخَمَل
Ostrich feathers. Fringes of a carpet. خَمْل
Nappy and fringy carpet, cloth. خَمْلَة
Mucous membrane of the stomach. خَمل المِعدة
Carpet. Hidden vices, secret habits. خَمْلَة ج خَمَلات
Obscurity, want of reputation. ✧ Dereliction from God. خُمُول
Defect in the joints. Sincere friend. خُمَال
Ostrich feathers. Varicose vein. خُمَالَة وخَمِيلَة
Fringy and nappy vestment. Soft food. Thick cloud. خَمِيل
Thicket, dense trees. Ostrich feathers. Soft, depressed ground fit for culture. Velvet. خَمِيلَة ج خَمائِل
Obscure, reputeless. خامِل ج خَمَل
Nappy silk or wool fabric. Velvet. مُخمَل

Lion. الأَخْنَس والخِنَّوْس
Satan. الخَنَّاس
Fern (*plant*). ✱ خِنْشَار
Suckling-pig. ✱ خِنَّوْص ج خَنَانِيص
Any young beast.
✱ خِنصِر وخِنصَر و✧ خُنصُر ج خَنَاصِر
The little finger. ◻ Pen-knife.
To insult a. o. ✱ خَنظَى خَنظَيَةً ب
To sow discord between. — بَيْنَ
To submit to a. o. To pray (God). ✱ خَنَع a خُنُوعًا ل وإلى
To be prone to evil. — إلى السُّوءِ
To constrain a. o. to a. th. (necessity). أَخنَع ه إلى
Baseness, lowness. خَنَع
Suspicion. Empty place. خَنعَة
Profligate. Inducing suspicion. خَانِع ج خَنَعَة
Perfidious, profligate. خَنُوع ج خُنُع
To turn back in walking. To turn its hoof outside in walking (camel). To strike her breast (woman). ✱ خَنَف i خِنَافًا
To be irritated. — i خُنُوفًا
To have a rib broken. خَنِف a خَنَفًا
Cause of shame. خَنفَة وخُنفَة
Haughty. خَانِف
Turning back its head (beast). Road. Liveliness. — وخَنُوف
Flax of bad quality. خَنِيف ج خُنُف
Having a bone broken (back). ◻ Speaking through the nose. أَخنَف ج خُنف
✱ خُنفُس وخِنفِس وخُنفَس وخُنفَسَاء وخُنفُسَاءَة
Buprestes, blackbeetle. ج خَنَافِس
To strangle, to throttle a. o. ✱ خَنَق o خَنقًا وخَنِقًا, وخَنَّق ه
To put a flag half-mast high. ✧ — البَندَيرَة
To cover a place (mirage). To fill (a vessel). To choke a. o. (sobs). To approach (the age of). ✧ To choke (silkworms) in their cocoons. خَنَّق ه
To quarrel together. ✧ تَخَانَق
To be throttled, strangled. إِختَنَق وانخَنَق
Carpus, wrist. ✧ خَنقَة اليَد
خُنَاق وخُنَّاق و✧ خَانُوق ج خَوَانِيق و◻ خُنَّاقَة
Quinsy, diphteria. ج خَنَانِيق

To scoff at. To fold (the mouth of a skin) for drinking. ✱ خَنَث i خَنثًا ه و ه
To be languid, flaccid, effeminate. خَنِث a خَنَثًا وأَخنَث وتَخَنَّث وانخَنَث
To bend a. th. To effeminate a. o. To soften the voice. ✧ To spoil (a child). خَنَّث ه وه
To be folded. ✧ To be spoiled (child). تَخَنَّث
Languid, unmanly, effeminate. ✧ Spoiled (child). خَنِث ومُخَنَّث, ومِخنَاث ج مَخَانِيث
Folds of a garment, of a skin. خِنَاث وأَخنَاث
Hermaphrodite. Asphodel (*plant*). خُنثَى ج خِنَاث وخَنَاثَى
Dagger. Large knife. Milch-camel. ✱ خَنجَر وخِنجِر ج خَنَاجِر
Old wine. Old wheat. G خَندَرِيس
To walk with the toes turned in. ✱ خَندَف
To surround (a place) with a moat. ✧ خَندَق ه
Moat. Ditch, sewer. P خَندَق ج خَنَادِق
To make a. o. to swerve from a resolution. ✧ خَندَل ه
Waterfalls of the Nile. خَنَادِل
Peak of a mountain. Eloquent speaker. Forbearing lord. Generous. Gallant. Whirlwind. ✱ خِنذِيذ ج خَنَاذِيذ
Female hyena. Cow. Misfortune. Abundance. Surname of Egypt. ✱ خنر — أُمّ خَنُّور وأُمّ خِنَّوْر
To stink (meat). ✱ خَنِز a خَنَزًا وخُنُوزًا
Stinking. خَنِز وخَنَز
Pride, self-conceitedness. خُنزُوان وخُنزُوانَة وخُنزُوانِيَّة وخُنزُوَّة
Pig (*See* خزر).
✱ خَنَس o i خَنسًا وخُنُوسًا وخِنَاسًا, وانخَنَس
To hold back. To hide herself (gazelle). عن
To delay. To keep a. o. or a. th. back. خَنَّس وأَخنَس ه
To conceal a. o. To hide a. th. — ه و ب, وخَنَّس ه, وتَخَنَّس ب
To be camous (nose). خَنِس a خَنَسًا
The planets, the stars. الخُنَّس
Camous-nosed. أَخنَس مـ خَنسَاء
Wild cow. Name of a poetess. الخَنسَاء

Disease of the throat in horses, birds. خُنَاقِيَّة
Cord for strangling. Quarrel. خِنَاق
Narrow pass in a mountain. خَانِق ج خَوَانِق
Narrow street, lane.
Aconitum lycoctonon, wolfsbane. خَانِق الكَلْب
Aconitum pardalianches, kind of wolfsbane. خَانِق النَّمِر
Colchicum, dogsbane. خَانِق الكَلْب
Orobanches, strangle-weed. خَانِق الكِرِسَنَّة
Throttled. خَنِيق وخَنِق ومُخَنَّق ومَخْنُوق
Asphyxia, strangulation. اِخْتِنَاق
Slender-waisted (young man). مُخْتَنَق الخَصْر
Necklace, collar. مِخْنَقَة ج مَخَانِق
Stove for choking silkworms. ✧ مَخْنَق ج مَخَانِق
Prince. خُنْكَار Ps
✻ خَنَا o خَنْوًا وخَنِيَ a خَنًى على, وأَخْنَى في كَلَامِهِ To hold foul talks against.
To cut (a root). خَنَى i خَنْيًا ه
To lay many eggs (locust). To abound with herbs (meadow). أَخْنَى
To cause the loss of. To deceive a. o. (fortune). To wrong a. o. To be long for a. o. (time). أَخْنَى على
Obscenity of speech. خَنًى
Calamities of time. خَنَى الدَّهْر
To fall into destitution. ✻ خَابَ o خَوْبًا
Hunger. Barren land. Unwatered land. خَوْبَة
To forfeit o.'s word. To break a covenant. ✻ خَاتَ o خَوْتًا وخَوَتَانًا
To pounce down upon its prey (hawk). — وانْخَاتَ واخْتَاتَ على
To experience a loss. — وتَخَوَّتَ مَالَهُ
To produce a rustling with its wings (eagle). — خَوَاتًا
✧ To be crack-brained. خَوِت
✧ To madden, to annoy a. o. خَوَّتَ ه
He glanced stealthily at me. خَاوَتَ طَرْفَهُ دُونِي
To steal a. th. To keep a. th. in memory. تَخَوَّتَ واخْتَاتَ ه
Bold. Eating little and often. خَوَّات

Idiot, crack-brained. ✧ أَخْوَت ج خُوتَان وخُوت
To be flabby (belly). To be full of food (belly). ✻ خَوِثَ a خَوَثًا
Flaccid, flabby. أَخْوَث م خَوْثَاء
Mr (*title given to Christians*). School-master. خَوَاجَا وخَوَاجَة ج خَوَاجَات P
✧ Plum, plum-tree. ▫ Nectarine, nectarine tree. ✻ خَوْخ (*un.* خَوْخَة)
Aperture in a wall. Wicket. Anus. ▫ Lane. خَوْخَة
To walk at a quick pace. ✻ خَوَّدَ
To incline, to bend (branch). تَخَوَّدَ
To promit a. th. To come unexpectedly upon a. o. (fever). — ه و ه
Soft girl, young woman. خَوْد ج خُود وخَوْدَات
To disagree with a. o. on. To agree on a. th. with. ✻ خَاذَ — خَاوَذَ ه على
To make a compact. تَخَاوَذ
Helmet. خُوذَة ج خُوَذ P
Servants, followers. خُوذَان
To bellow (ox). ✻ خَارَ o خُوَارًا
To be weak (man). To abate (heat). To soften (snow). To be strengthless (sick person). — خُؤُورًا وخَوِرَ a خَوَرًا
To be weak (man). ✧ To be hungry. خَوَّرَ
To incline a. th. أَخَارَ ه
To seek to incline a. o. To interrogate a. o. إِسْتَخَارَ ه
Gulf. Mouth of a river. Tract of land between two hills. خَوْر ج أَخْوَار
The best, the choice (camels). خُورَة
Bellowing, bleating. Whizzing of arrows. خُوَار
Rectum. Anus of the horse. خَوْرَان
Weak. Slender and fine she-camel. خَوَّار ج خَوَّارَات
Parish-priest, vicar. خُورِيّ ج خَوَارِنَة Gs
Wife of a priest. ✧ خُورِيَّة ج خُورِيَّات
Parish. Vicarage. ✧ خَوْرَنِيَّة
Choir of a church. خُورُس Gs
To cheat a. o. in. ✧ خَوزَ — خَاوَزَه على وعن
Treachery. ✧ مُخَاوَزَة
To be unsaleable (goods). To stink (carcass). ✻ خَاسَ o خَوْسًا

and sprightly man.
To diminish a. th. ٭ خَوَء من
To bruise a. o. by blows. — ة ب
To pay (a debt). To weaken a. o. ه —
To eat away (a bank: torrent).
To be secure. تَخَوَّء
To diminish a. th. gradually. — ه
٭ خَافَ a خَوْفًا وخِيفًا ومَخَافَةً وخِيفَةً, وتخوّف
To fear, to be cautious. To know.
To fear, to dread a. o. or a. th. — ه ومن
To fear for a. o. — وتَخَوَّف على
To frighten, to threaten ة خَوَّف وأخاف a. o. To render a. o. dreaded.
To be dangerous, unsecure (road). أخاف
To diminish a. th. gradually. تَخَوَّف ه To send (sheep) one by one.
Fear. Slaughter. Fighting. خَوْف Ornamented skin.
Bustle, confused noise. خَوَاف
Shy, fearful. خَائِف ج خُوَّف وخُيَّف وخائفون
Cowardly. خَاف و٭ خَوِّيف وخَوَّاف
Leather-garment worn by collectors of honey. Leather-bag for honey. خَافَة
More dreaful. أخوَف
Dangerous (road). Threatening (wall). مَخُوف
Terrible, frightful. مُخِيف
The lion. المُخِيف
Dangerous places. Dangers. مَخَاوِف
To be wide, broad. ٭ خَوِق a خَوَقًا
To adorn (a girl) with earrings. To snatch and carry away a. th. — ة وه
To widen, to expand a. th. خَوَّق ه
To go over (a country). أخاق
To be far-extending, remote. تخوَّق
Gold earring. خَوْق
One-eyed. Scabby. Far-extending. أخوَق م خَوقاء ج خُوق
To manage (the business) of. ٭ خَالَ o خَوْلًا وخِيَالًا ه
To take care of. — على
To grant, to confer a. th. upon a. o. خَوَّل ة وه
To have many uncles. أخوَل وأخوِل

To break a (promise). — ه وب
To betray a. o. — ب
To send (camels) to water one by one. To lessen a. th. خَوَّش ة وه
To pierce a. o. with (a spear). ٭ خَاش o خَوْشًا ة ب
To take a. th. — ه
To sprinkle a. th. in. — في
To diminish a. th. خَوَّش وتَخَوَّش ه
To be frightened. ٭ تَخَوَّش
House furniture. خَاش مَاش وخَاشِ مَاشِ
Old furniture.
٭ Well, so. Moreover. Ps خوش
Flank, side. خَوْش
Brown, blotting-paper. ¤ وَرَق خُوشِق
To have sunken eyes. ٭ خَوِص a خَوَصًا
To adorn (a crown) with plates of gold. خَوَّص ه
To make a. o. hoary (white hair). — ة
To propose a bargain to. خاوَص ة البَيْع
To blink. — وتَخاوَص
To become covered with leaves (palm-tree). أخوَص
Leaves of a palm-tree. خُوصَة ج خُوص
¤ Palm-Sunday. أحَد الخُوص
Papyrus. خُوص بَرْدَى
Hot wind; hot time of noon. خَوْصَاء
Deep well.
Seller of palm-leaves. خَوَّاص
Having sunken eyes. أخوَص م خَوْصاء ج خُوص
To wade through (water). To mix (a beverage). To embark in (an affair). ٭ خَاض o خَوْضًا وخِيَاضًا ه
To face death. — المَنَايَا
To engage in conversation. — في الحَدِيث
To move about a sword in (the wound). — ه بالسَّيْف
To bring (a horse) to water. To make (a beast) to ford through (water). خاوَض وأخاض ة وب
To enter in conversation (people). خاوَض في الحَدِيث
To enter into (water). إختاض وتَخَوَّض ه
Ford. Pearl. خُوضَة
Rash, go ahead. خَوَّاض
Ford. People, beasts fording. مَخَاضَة ج مَخَاض ومَخَاوِض ومَخَاضَات
Green bough. Stout ٭ خُوط ج خِيطَان

To bode well of a. th. أخَال وتَخَوَّل فِيهِ خَالًا من الخَيْر

To have or to adopt a. o. as an uncle. تَخَوَّل وتَخَيَّل خَالًا

To pay (frequent attention) to. – ه ب

To have uncles amongst. إستَخوَل في

To engage a. o. as servant, slave. – ه

Property. Servants. Lower part of the bit. ◻ Dancer. خَوَل ج خُوَل

خَال ج أخوَال وأخوِلَة وخُؤُول وخُؤُولَة

Maternal uncle. Good token. Colours of an army. Black stallion-camel. Owner of a. th.

Maternal aunt. ✧ Step-mother. خَالَة ج خَالَات

Relationship of maternal uncle. خُؤُولَة

Manager. Gardener, farmer. خَوَلِيّ ج خَوَل و✧ خُوَلِيَّة

Box-thorn. ◻ عَوْد الخَوْلَان

Manager of property. خَائِل ج خَوَل

Scattered on all sides. أخوَل أخوَل

Having many maternal uncles. مُخوِل ومُخوَل

To be unhealthy (ground). ✲ خَام o خَوَمَانًا

Unhealthy (country) (*See* خيم). خَامَة ج خَام

✲ خَان o خَوْنًا وخِيَانَةً وخَانَةً ومَخَانَةً ه و ب

To betray a. o. To embezzle a. o. To be unfaithful to (her husband : wife).

To break (a compact). – ه

To feel a weakening of the sight. – خَوْنًا

To charge a. o. with treachery. ✧ To betray a. o. To distrust a. o. To come repeatedly to. خَوَّن ه

To impair (a right). – ه ومن، وتَخَوَّن ه

To deceive, to betray a. o. إختَان ه

To seek to deceive a. o. إستَخَان ه

Khan, shop. Caravan-sary; inn. Sultan of the Tartars. P خَان ج خَانَات

Landlord of an inn. خَانِيّ وخَانَاتِيّ و◻ خَانجِي

Tune (in music). Square of (chess). Cook-shop. P خَانَة ج خَانَات

Unfaithfulness. Weak-sightedness. خَوَن

P خُوَان وخِوَان ج أخوِنَة وخُون وأخَاوِين

Footed tray for serving food.

Distrustful. ✧ خَوَّان

Perfidy, breach of trust خِيَانَة

Treacherous, deceiver. خَائِن ج خُوَّان وخَانَة وخَوَنَة

Lion. Languid-eyed. خَائِن العَيْن

Surreptitious glance, hint. خَائِنَة الأعْيُن

Faithless, full of treachery. خَؤُون وخَوَّان وخَائِنَة وخَوَان

To be ruined (house). To be empty-bellied, hungry. To give no rain (stars). To give no fire (flint). To bring forth (woman). To set (star). To be terror-stricken. ✲ خَوَى i خَوَاء، وأخوَى

To be uninhabited (house); empty (place). خَوِي a خَيًّا وخُوِيًّا وخَوَايَةً

To be delivered (woman). – a خَوَاء

To snatch away (the whole property). – وخَوِي خَوًى وخَوَايَةً، وأخوَى واختَوَى ه

To let an interstice in crouching (camel); in prostrating (man). To hang down (bird's wings). To be fat (cattle). خَوَّى

To prepare food for a confined woman. – ه و ل

To be very fat (cattle). To fail (rain, flint). To be hungry (man). أخوَى

To lose the reason. إختَوَى

To cross (a country). – ه

To pierce a (horse's) flanks with a spear. To devour (a calf : wild beast). – ه

Empty-bellied; hollow; hungry. خَوٍ

Emptiness of the belly. Gap, interstice. خَوَاء

Hunger. Steady. Soft ground. Upland. Bleeding of the nose. خَوًى وخَوٌ

Empty. Wasted. ✧ Uncompact (cloth). ◻ Mountebank. خَاوٍ وخَوَّة م خَاوِيَة

✧ Chaos. Abyss. خَاوِيَة

Depressed, low (land). خَوِيّ

Food given to a woman in childbirth. خَوِيَّة

Out of mind. أخوَى م خَيَّاء وخَوْيَاء

Brother. (*Diminutive* of أخ) ✧ *Interjection* of joy. ✧ خَيّ

✲ خَاب i خَيْبَةً، وتَخَيَّب (*opp. to* أصَاب)

To be disappointed (man). To be deceived (hope). To become an unbeliever.

To miss, to fail in. – عن

His endeavours have been frustrated. خَاب سَعْيُهُ

Cassia fistula (tree). خِيَار شَنْبَر P
Yellow gilliflower, viola alba. خِيرِيّ P
Old Turkish coin.
Excellent. خَيْرَى وَخَوْرَى وَخُورَى وخِيرَى
Goodness. Happiness. ✧ Happily; so much the better. خَيْرِيَّة
Generous. Pretty fine. Very religious. ✧ Mohair (stuff). خَيِّر م خَيِّرَة
Better. أَخْيَر م خِيرَى وخُورَى ج أَخَايِر
Option. Free will. إِخْتِيَار
Old man. إِخْتِيَار ج اختيارِيَّة Ts
Free, arbitrary. Spontaneous. إِخْتِيَارِيّ
Elected. ✧ Mayor of a village. مُخْتَار
Zinc (metal). خَارْصِينِيّ P
To be altered (meat, walnut). To be dull (sale). To lie (man). To decrease (value). To waste (goods). ✱ خَاسَ i خَيْسًا
To be subdued reluctantly. خِيسَ أَنْفُهُ
To break (a promise). To act treacherously in. — خَيْسًا وخَيْسَانًا ب
To humble a. o. To confine in prison. ✧ To diminish a. th. خَيَّسَ ه وه
Sorrow, grief. Fault. Mistake. Lie. Goods. خَيْس
Brush-wood. Milk. خِيس ج أَخْيَاس
Den of lions. — وخِيسَة ج خِيَس
Gaol, prison. مُخَيِّس ومُخَيَّس
Coarse cloth made of the worst of flax. Ignoble man. ✱ خَيْش ج خُيُوش وأَخْيَاش
✧ Coarse tent, sack; canvass. خَيْش ج خِيَش
Sack of straw being half a camel's load. ✧ خَيْشَة
To make brocade, to embroider. ◘ خَيَّش
To be in small quantity. ✱ خَاصَ i خَيْصًا
To have one eye larger than the other. خَيِصَ a خَيَصًا
Trifle, small quantity. خَيْص وخَائِص وخَيْصَى
Having an eye larger than the other. Having one horn broken (ram). أَخْيَص م خَيْصَاء
To sew up (a garment). ✱ خَاطَ i خَيْطًا, وخَيَّطَ ه
To call once only at; to pass along quickly. خَاطَ خَيْطَةً, واخْتَاطَ واخْتَطَى إِلى

To balk, to disappoint a. o. خَيَّبَ وأَخَابَ ه
Failure, disappointment. خَيْبَة
Faint-heartedness is always disappointed. الهَيْبَة خَيْبَة
Steel failing to produce fire. خَيَّاب
His endeavours have been to no avail. ذَهَبَ سَعْيُهُ في خَيَّاب بن هَيَّاب
He fell in a hopeless affair. وَقَع في وَادِي تُخَيِّب وتُخَيِّب
To make a sound. ✱ خَاتَ i خَيْتًا وخُيُوتًا
To earn wealth. ✱ خَارَ i خَيْرًا
May God be propitious to thee in the affair. خَارَ الله لكَ في الأَمْر
To prefer a. o. before. — خِيرَةً وخِيَرَةً وخَيْرًا, وخَيَّرَه على
To select a. th. — ه
To give to a. o. the option between. خَيَّرَ وخَايَرَ ه في او بَيْن
To overcome a. o. in science or a. th. خَايَرَ ه في
To choose a. th. To elect a. o. To put a. th. in store. تَخَيَّرَ واخْتَارَ ه وه
To ask a. th. good. ✧ To consult a wizard. إِسْتَخَار
To consult God by divination. — الله
Good (man). Excellent. Better, the best. خَيِّر ج خِيَار وأَخْيَار
He is better than thee. هُوَ خَيْر وأَخْيَر مِنكَ
The best of man, of women. خَيْرُ النَّاسِ وخَيْرُ النِّسَاءِ أو خَيْرَتُهُنَّ
Thank you. كَثَّرَ الله خَيْرَكَ و✧ كَتَّر خَيْرَك
Moral or physical good. Wealth. Horses. Welfare. Virtue. خَيْر ج خُيُور (*opp. to* شَرّ)
✧ There is a long time since. خَيْر الله
Hare's ear (*plant*). خَيْر الله
Lesser cardamom (small grain). خَيْر بَوًّا
F. Good, the best. Good deed. خَيْرَة ج خَيْرَات
✧ At the grace of God; as it pleases God. على خِيرَة الله
Nobility, generosity. Origin. Appearance. خِير
Choice, option. The best of. *Cucumis sativus*, cucumber. خِيَار
Thou hast the option. أَنتَ بِالخِيَار وبِالمُخْتَار

To appear on (hoariness). خيّط وتخيّط في
✧ To be sewed up. تخيّط
خيط ج خُيوط وأخياط وخُيوطة و✧ خيطان
Thread, string.
The first gleam of dawn. الخيط الأبيض
Twilight at sunset. الخيط الأسود
Gossamer. Atoms seen in the sunrays. خيط باطل
Flock of ostriches; swarm of locusts. خيط ج خيطان, وخيط وخيطى
Needle. خياط ومِخيط
Needlework. Art of sewing. خياطة
Tailor, seamster. خيّاط
Sebesten-plum. ☐ مُخيّط ونبق مُخيّط
Sebesten-tree. ☐ مُخيّطة
To have one eye blue and the other black (horse). ✲ خيف a خيفًا
To come down and settle in a plain. خيّف
To withdraw from a fight. — عن
To be shared, allotted amongst. — بين
To make a station at Mineh (pilgrim). أخاف وأخيف واختاف
To be diversified in colour. تخيّف ألوانًا
Declivity of a mountain. Side. Skin of the udder. خيف
Knife. Den of a lion. خيفة
Locusts having wings streaked of different colours. Multitude of men. خيفان
Having one eye blue and the other black (horse). أخيف م خيفاء ج خيف
Men of different shape, state. أخياف
Uterine brothers إخوة أخياف وبنو أخياف
Sultan, prince. T خاقان ج خواقين
✲ خال a خيلًا وخالًا وخيلة وخيلة وخيلانًا وخيلولة ومخيلة ومخالة ه أو ان To think to imagine a. th. or that.
To thunder over a. o. (cloud). To form a suspicion upon a. o. خيّل تخييلًا وتخيّلًا على
To put up a scarecrow for (wild beasts). — تخييلًا, وخيّل وخايل ل
To forebode rain (cloud). — وخايل وتخيّل
To perceive good symptoms in. To bode well of. — وتخيّل فيه الخير
✧ To gallop; to ride on horseback. خيّل
✧ To manage a horse well. — ه

To imagine a. th. To seem to a. o. خيّل إلى ول
To vie in pride with a. o. — ه
To have milk in the udder (she-camel). أخيل
To be dubious to a. o. — على
To be adorned with verdure (soil). أخال
To magnify o.'s self. ✧ To fancy, to imagine. تخيّل
To seem to a. o. — ه ول وعلى
✧ To feign. تخايل
To have a haughty deportment. To be self-conceited. تخايل واختال
Huge mountain. Big camel. Banner of a prince. Shroud. Fancy. Black stallion. Owner of a. th. Self-magnified. Caliphate. Lonely place. Opinion. Suspicion. Bachelor. Good manager. Horse's bit. Liberal man. Weak-bodied, weak-hearted man. Free from suspicion. Imaginative man. خال
Mole on the face; spot on the skin. Cloud giving no rain. Haughtiness. Lightning. — ج خيلان
Horses; horsemen. خيل ج أخيال وخيول
Rue. Asafœtida (*plants*). — وخيل
Haughty. Self-admirer. خايل وخال ج خالة وأخايل, ومختال
Phantasm, spectre. Human shape. Scarecrow. Opinion, suspicion. خيال ج أخيلة
Phantom. Human shape. خيالة ج خيالات
Imagination, fancy. قوّة خياليّة ومُخيّلة
Horseman. *Pl.* ✧ Cavalry. خيّال ج خيّالة
Siren (fabulous nymph). خيلان
Vanity, self-conceit. خيلاء وخيلة وخيل
Bird of bad omen. Green wood-pecker. Roller (bird). أخيل ج خيل وأخايل
Having moles on the face. أخيل مخيل ومخيول
Pride. Opinion. Symptom, sign. مخيلة ج مخايل
سحابة مخيلة ومُخيلة ومُختالة ومُخيّلة ومخيّل
Cloud giving no rain.
He is apt to do good. إنّهُ لمُخيّل الخير
✲ خام i خيمًا وخيمانًا وخيومًا وخيومة وخياما
To recoil cowardly from. وخيموميّة عن
To stand on three legs (horse. أخام

To pitch, to enter a tent. To cling (odour). خَيَّم

To camp, to pitch a tent (in a place). ب - وتَخَيَّم في وب

To pitch (a tent). خام وأخْيَم ه

Nature, inborn disposition. خِيم

Radish. Untanned skin. Unbleached cloth. Unpolished stone. Cotton-cloth. ✧ Inexperienced (man). خام

Ambergris. ✧ عَنْبَر خام

Tender stalk of a plant. خامَة ج خام وخامات

Tent. خَيْم وخَيْمَة ج خِيام وخِيَم وخَيْمات Booth. ✧ Arbour. Awning.

Dwelling under a tent. Nomad. خَيَّام

Manufacturer, seller of tents. - وخَيْمِيّ

Place for pitching a tent. Encampment. ✧ Cobwebbed. مُخَيَّم

د

✡ دَأْدَأَ دَأْدَأَةً ودِئْدَاءً To run fast (camel). To hasten. ✧ To begin to walk (child).

— ه To cover a. th. To stir a. th. To still a. th.

— في إِثْرِهِ To track a. o.

تَدَأْدَأَ To be moved. To be still. To be covered. To chew the cud (camel). To incline (load). To roll down (stone). To throng (crowd).

T دَادَاة Wet nurse. Dry nurse.

دَأْدَاة ج دَآدِئ Sound of the rocking of a cradle. Sound of a stone falling into water. Dark night.

✡ دَأَب a دَأْبًا ودَأَبًا ودُؤُوبًا في To strive steadily in.

— دَأْبًا ودَأَبًا ه To urge (a beast). To drive a. o. away.

أَدْأَب ه وه To weary a. o. To pursue (a journey).

دَأْب ودَأَب ج أَدْؤُب Affair. Work. Habit.

دَأْبُهُ أَن يَقْرَأَ او القِرَاءَة ✧ He reads continually.

أَلدَّائِبَان The day and the night.

✡ دَأَث a دَأْثًا To be heavy. To be unclean (dress).

— ه To eat (food). To stain (a dress).

✡ دَأْدَر To play (child).

✡ دَئِص a دَأَصًا To be mischievous. To become fat (cattle).

✡ دَأَظ a دَأْظًا ه وه To fill up (a vessel). To squeeze (an ulcer). To anger a. o. To strangle a. o

✡ دَأَل a دَأْلًا ودَأَلًا ودَأَلَى To walk sluggishly. To run with short steps.

— دَأْلًا ودَأَلَانًا ل, ودَاءَل ه To deceive a. o.

دُؤَالَة Fox.

دَأْل ودُئِل ودُؤُل ودَأَلَان Jackal. Weasel.

دُؤْلُول ج دَآلِيل Calamity.

✡ دَأَم a دَأْمًا ه To stay (a wall).

تَدَأَّم ه To wash a. th. (waves).

تَدَاءَم ه To crush a. o. (affair).

دَأْمَا Sea. Ocean.

✡ دَأَى o دَأْيًا, ودَأَى a دَأْيًا ل To delude (its prey: wolf). To deceive a. o.

دَأْي ج دَأْيَات Ribs of the breast.

إِبْن دَأْيَة Crow.

P دَايَة ج دَايَات Nurse. ✧ Midwife.

✡ دَبّ i دَبًّا ودَبِيبًا To walk slowly (animal). To creep (reptile). To crawl (child). To flow (brook).

— ه ✧ To throw a. th.

— في To pervade a. o. (poison, disease).

أَدَبَّ ه To make (a child) to walk.

— على To spread (slanders about) a. o. To rule (a country) with justice.

دَبَّت عَقَارِبُهُ His slanders (*lit*: his scorpions) crept along.

دُبّ ج أَدْبَاب ودِبَبَة Bear. ✧ Ruffian.

الدُّبّ الأَكْبَر والدُّبّ الأَصْغَر Major and Minor Ursa.

دُبّ البَحْر Manatee, sea-cow.

◘ حَشِيشَة الدُّبّ *Anthyllis vulneraria*, woundwort.

مِن شُبَّ إِلى دُبَّ او مِن شَبٍّ إِلى دَبٍّ From youth to old age.

دُبَّة She-bear. Way of acting.

دَبَّة ودُبّ ج دِبَاب Vessel for oil. Sandy hill. Down on the cheeks. Glass bottle. ◘ Hernia.

دَبَب Young calf. Down on the face.

✧ دُبَاب Wild mint.

دَبَّاب م دَبَّابَة ج دَبَّابَات Crawling. Quadruped.

دَبَّابَة ج دَبَّابَات Testudo, besieging machine.

دَبِيب Creeping. Reptile, insect.

دَبُوب ودَيْبُوب Slanderer. Bloody wound. Deep cavern. Fat.

دَابَّة ج دَوَابّ Beast of burden, hackney, mule. Reptile. ✧ She-ass.

دَابَّة الأَرْض The beast of the earth *said* to appear near the end of the world.

دُوَيْبَّة Small beast. Reptile.

دُبَّاء (*un.* دُبَّاءَة) *Cucurbita*, gourd.

أَدَبّ م دَبَّاء Downy on the face. Thick-haired camel.

مَدَبّ Bed of a torrent.

Country abounding in bears. أرضٌ مَدَبَّة
To resound (trampling). ✡ دَبْدَبَ
✧ To crawl (child).
Trampling of horses. دَبْدَبَة
Drum. دَبْدَاب ج دَبَادِب
To variegate ✡ دَبَجَ o دَبْجًا, ودَبَّجَ ه
(cloth).
To adorn (the ground) with — ودَبَّجَ ه
plants (rain). To embellish a. th.
P دِيبَاج ج دَبَابِج ودَبَابِيج (دِيبَاجَة .un)
Garment of silk. Brocade.
Face. Preface of a book. دِيبَاجَة
He keeps his honour stainless. يَصُون دِيبَاجَتَهُ
He disgraces himself. يَبْذُل ويُخْلِق دِيبَاجَتَهُ
The two cheeks. الدِّيبَاجَتَان
Silk-brocade seller. دَبَّاج
To stoopdown ✡ دبح — دَبَّح واندَبَح
in lowering the head.
Scorzonera, viper's grass. ✧ دَبَح
To turn the back. ✡ دَبَرَ o دَبْرًا ودُبُورًا
To become old.
To take a. th. away. — ب
To relate a. th. on the — ه عن فُلَان
authority of a dead person.
To fall beyond (the — o دَبْرًا ه وه
butt: arrow). To write (a book). To follow a. o.
To veer to the west (wind). — o دُبُورًا
To elapse (day, night).
To be overtaken by west wind. دُبِرَ
To be covered with دَبِرَ a دَبَرًا, وأَدْبَرَ
sores (camel).
To forecast a. th. To manage, دَبَّرَ ه وه
to settle (an affair). To rule well (his subjects: prince).
To relate a tradition. ✧ To — الحَدِيثَ
threaten a. o. with a punishment.
To exert o.'s self in. To cause دَبَّرَ على
the loss of.
To die. دَابَرَ مُدَابَرَةً ودِبَارًا
To oppose a. o. — ه
To be exposed to west wind. To أَدْبَرَ
turn the back. To retreat. To become wealthy. To set (star). To be adverse (fortune). To journey on Wednesday. To be ended (prayer).
To gall (a beast: saddle). — ه

To reflect on the results of. تَدَبَّرَ ه
To turn back one upon another: تَدَابَرَ
To be at variance.
To see the consequence of اِسْتَدْبَرَ ه وه
a. th. To track. To turn the back to. To look back at.
Swarm of دَبْر ج أَدْبُر ودُبُور (دَبْرَة .un)
bees, hornets. Mountain. Young locusts. Behind. Wealth. Death.
Great wealth. دِبْر (s. pl.)
Back. Posteriors. دُبْر ودُبُر ج أَدْبَار
Hinder, latter part. Angle of a house. End of prayer, of a month, of an affair.
To turn back (in fight). وَلَّى دُبُرَهُ
Defeat (in a fight). Con- دَبْرَة ج دِبَار
sequence. Adversity. Sown land.
Western part of دَبْرَة (opp to قَبْلَة)
the sky.
Sore, gall (of camels). دَبَرَة ج دَبَر وأَدْبَار
Ulcered (beast). دَبِر م دَبِرَة
Loss, ruin. دَبَار
Channels of irrigation. Events. دِبَار
Defeats.
Ancient name of Wednesday. دِبَار ودُبَار
Westerly wind. دَبُور
Shape, manner. دَبُّور ج دَبَابِير
✧ Hornet, wasp. Blindman's buff (play).
Mason's hammer. دَبُّورَة
Aldebaran, five stars in Taurus. الدَّبَرَان
Domestic economy. تَدْبِير المَنْزِل
Follower. Consequence. Root. دَابِر
Going beyond the mark (arrow). Last remains of a people. Elapsed (time).
They were exterminated. قُطِعَ دَابِرُ القَوْمِ
Hinder part of the hoof. Defeat. دَابِرَة
Back spur of hawks.
Late (prayer). دَبَرِيّ
Late, latest time. دَبْرِيّ
Twist of thread. Disobedience. دِبِير
He is grossly ignorant. لَا يَعْرِف قَبِيلَهُ من دَبِيرِهِ
✧ Trick, craft. String, Ps دُبَارَة ودُوبَارَة
thread.
The Ruler (God). Counsel of a مُدَبِّر
prince. ✧ Assistant (in a religious order).

ماء مُدَبَّر ◆ Infusion, diluent.
مُدَابِر Unlucky in the game of arrows.
المُقَابَل والمُدَابَر Noble of both parents. Lucky and unlucky.
✱ دبس – دَبَّس To conceal o'self. To become sweet (grapes). To be blunted (awl). ◆ To inspissate the juice of grapes.
ه – To conceal a. th. To mend (boots).
أَدْبَس To be of a reddish brown colour. To send forth off-shoots (earth).
دَبَس Black. Much.
دِبْس Treacle. Bee-honey. Crowd.
دُبْسِيّ ج دَبَاسِيّ Honey-guide (bird).
أَدْبَس م دَبْسَاء ج دُبْس Of a reddish brown colour.
دَبَّاس Seller of treacle, honey.
دَبُّوس ج دَبَابِيس Mace, club, ◆ Pin.
✱ دَبَش o دَبْشًا ه To peel a. th. To eat a. th.
دَبَش Furniture of a house. Rubbish. ◆ Ashlar, rubble. (un. دَبْشَة ◆) Clot of earth.
مَدْبُوش Eaten up by locusts (land).
✱ دَبَغ i a o دَبْغًا ودِبَاغًا ودِبَاغَة ه To tan (a skin).
إِنْدَبَغ To be tanned (hide). ◆ To be stained.
دِبْغ ودِبَاغ ودِبْغَة Ooze, tan. ◆ Stain.
دَبِيغ Tanned hide.
دَبَّاغ Tanner.
مَدْبَغَة ج مَدَابِغ, و◆ دَبَّاغَة Tannery. Hides in the ooze.
دَبِق a دَبَقًا وأَدْبَق وتَدَبَّق ب To stick to a. th. (glue). To cling to a. o. ◆ To be enamoured of.
◆ دُبِق To be gluey, sticky.
– ودَبَّق ه To catch (birds) with bird-lime.
أَدْبَق ه وه To stick a. th. To make a. o. to stick to a. o.
تَدَبَّق To be caught with bird-lime. To be stuck.
دِبْق ودَابُوق Bird-lime. Glue. Mistletoe.
دَبُوقَاء Dung. Glue. Viscous matter.
◆ دَبَك o دَبْكًا, ودَبَّك To trample. To make noise by trampling.
◆ دَبْكَة Trampling. Cadenced dance.

✱ دَبَل o دَبْلًا ودُبُولًا ه To manure (a land). To improve a. th.
– o i دَبْلًا ه وه To collect a. th. with the fingers. To take large mouthfuls. To beat a. o. with a stick. To befall a. o. (misfortune). ◆ To crush a. o.
دَبَلَتْهُ الدُّبُول Misfortunes have befallen him.
دَبْل ج دُبُول Plague. Streamlet. Mishap.
دَبْلَة ودُبْلَة ودُبَيْلَة Pain in the belly.
دَبْلَة ج دَبَل ◘ Finger-ring.
دُبْلَة ج دُبَل ودُبُل Tumour. Large mouthful. Hole of an adze.
دُبَال Manure.
دَبُول Bereft of her son (mother).
– ودُبَيْلَة Misfortune. Disease of the belly.
◆ دُبَّان (for ذُبَّان) Flies.
✱ دبي – دَبِيَ To be stripped by locusts (land).
دَبَّى ه To work a. th.
أَدْبَى To swarm with locusts (land).
دَبًى (un. دَبَاة) Small locusts. Ants. Gentle walk.
مَدْبِيّ Place wasted by locusts.
✱ دَثّ o دَثًّا ب To hit (game: hunter).
ه – To pain a. o. by striking. To drive away a. o. To overtake a. o. (rain). To distress a. o. (fever).
دَثّ ودِثَاث Slight rain.
الدُّثَّاث Shooters of birds.
✱ دَثَر o دُثُورًا To be obliterated (trace). To be exhausted by old age. To become unknown (man). To be rusty (sword). To be unclean, dirty (clothes). To put forth dense foliage (tree).
دَثَّر To prepare its nest (bird).
ه – To cause a. o. to perish. To cover (a sleeper) with a blanket.
تَدَثَّر وادَّثَر ب To wrap o.'s self in (vestments).
تَدَثَّر فَرَسَهُ To ride o.'s horse.
إِنْدَثَر To be erased.
إِدَّثَر To acquire wealth.
دَثْر (s. pl.) ودُثُور Abundant (goods).
دِثْر مَال Good manager of property.
دَاثِر Unclean (garment). Numerous (soldiers).

To be obscure, dark. ✡ دَجِيَ o دُجًا

To be sad. دَجِيَ a ودَجِيَ دَجًا

Darkness. دُجْمَة ج دُجَم ودُجْم

Friend, companion. دِجْمَة ج دِجَم

Impetuous torrent. غدير دَيْجَم

To be gloomy (day). To rain continually (sky). ✡ دَجَن o دَجْنًا ودُجُونًا ، وأَدْجَن

To remain in (a place). — o دُجُونًا ب
To keep to a house; to become familiar to a. o. (pigeons, dog).

To wheedle a. o. داجَن ه

To last (rain, fever). To have rainy weather. To be dark (night). أَدْجَن

Shadow of the clouds. Abundant rain. دَجْن ج دُجُون ودِجَان وأَدْجَان

Gloomy, dark weather. دُجْنَة ج دُجَن ودُجُنَات ، ودُجُنَّة ج دُجُنَّات

Domesticated animal. داجِنَة ومُدْجِنَة

Over-spreading (rain). دَجُون وداجِن م داجِنَة ج دَواجِن

Intensely dark. Black. أَدْجَن م دَجْنَاء ج دُجْن

To lie down in a covert (hunter). ✡ دجه — دَجَّه

To overspread (night). To spread everywhere. To be full (clothes). To be thick (hair). ✡ دَجَا o دَجْوًا ودُجُوًّا

To conceal hatred against a. o. To dissemble with. داجَى ه

To be obscure (night). أَدْجَى وتَدَجَّى وادْجَوْجَى

To let down (a curtain). — ه

The three first fingers. Mouthful. Button of a shirt. دُجَة ج دُجَات ودُجًى

Darkness, starless night. Lurking-place of a hunter. دُجْيَة ج دُجًى

Spreading over. Dark (night). داجٍ م داجِيَة

Easy life. عَيْش داجٍ

Darkness. دَيَاجٍ

Dissembling, hypocrisy. مُداجَاة

To fill (the belly: food). To enlarge (a house). To repel a. o. ✡ دَحَّ o دَحًّا ه وه

To conceal a. th. in the earth. — ه في
To slap a. o. in

To be swollen (belly). إِنْدَحَّ

To become luxuriant (ground). — كَلَأً

Upper garment. Blanket. دِثار

Lazy. Obscure (man). دَثُور

Perishing. Neglectful. Rusty (sword). داثِر ج دَوَاثِر

To alight suddenly in the neighbourhood (bird). ✡ دثن — دَثَّن

To make its nest on a tree (bird). — في

To advance slowly (crowd). ✡ دَجَّ i دَجِيجًا ودَجَجَانًا

To be overcast (sky). دَجَّج

To accoutre a. o. with weapons. — ه

To be fully armed. تَدَجَّج

Partridge. ✧ Thrush. ▫ Chaffinch. دُجّ

Amaranth (*plant*). دُجّ الأمير

Intense darkness. دُجَّة

Walking slowly داجّ (*s. pl.*) ج داجُّون وداجَّة

Domestic fowls: cocks, hens, chickens. دَجاج ج ودُجاج دُجُج (*un.* دَجاجَة)

Woodcock. دَجاج الأرض والغابَة

Coot (bird). دَجاج الماء

A fowl. Family. Cygnus (*constellation*). دَجاجَة

Fowler. دَجاجِيّ

Intensely dark (night). دُجُوجِيّ ودَيْجُوج ودَيَاجِيج

Fully armed. Hedgehog. مُدَجِّج ومُدَجَّج

To be amazed. To be intoxicated. To be lively (people). ✡ دَجِر a دَجَرًا

Wood of the plough fixed to the share. دَجْر ودِجْر ودُجْر

French bean. — ودُجْر ودُجُر

Stupefied. Inebriated. دَجِر ودَجْرَان ج دَجْرَى ودَجَارَى

Dust. Darkness. Dense (herbage). Dust-colour. دَيْجُور ج دَيَاجِير ودَيَاجِر

To lie, to quack. ✡ دَجَل o دَجْلًا

To smear (a camel) with tar. To journey through (a land). — ه وه

To cover a. th. To tar (a camel). To gild (a vessel). To manure (a land). دَجَّل ه

Manure, dung. دَجَال

Gold. Gold-wash. دُجَال

Tar. دُجَالَة ودَجِيل

Quack, impostor. دَجَّال ج دَجَّالُون ودَجَاجِلَة

Antichrist. المَسِيح الدَّجَّال

The Tigris (river). دِجْلَة

Numerous party. دَجَّالَة

* دَحْدَحٍ وَدَحْدَحَة, وَدَحْدَاحٍ وَدَحْدَاحَة وَدُحَادِحٍ وَدَحَيْدِحَة وَدَرْدَحٍ Short and stout.
* دَحَبَ a دَحْبًا ة To repel a. o.
* دَحَجَ a دَحْجًا ه To drag a. th. along.
* دَحْدَرَ ه To reol a. th. along.
تَدَحْدَرَ To roll along. ◻ To be declivous (ground).
* دَحَرَ a دَحْرًا وَدُحُورًا وَمَدْحَرَة To drive away, to discard a. o. To banish a. o.
دَاحِر وَدَحُور Driving away.
* دَحْرَجَ ه To upset a. th. To roll down a. th.
تَدَحْرَجَ To roll down. To become round.
مُدَحْرَج Rounded, globular.
دُحْرُوجَة ج دَحَارِيج Dung-ball rolled by black beetles.
* دَحَسَ a دَحْسًا بَيْنَ To set (people) at variance.
— ه To fill (a house: crowd). To learn (a tradition) by heart.
— بِ To throw about (the feet: slaughtered beast).
— بِالشَّرّ To cause evil in secret.
— وَأَدْحَسَ To become full of seeds (spike).
دَحِسَ a دَحْسًا To be affected by a whitlow (finger).
دَحْس Spike full of seeds.
دَحَّاس وَدُحَّاس ج دَحَاحِيس Insect used as a bait.
دَاحِس وَدَاحُوس و✧ دُوحَاس Whitlow
مَدْحُوس و✧ مُدَوَّحِس Affected by a whitlow (finger). Filled (house).
✧ دَحَشَ To thrust, to poke a. th. in.
✧ إِنْدَحَشَ To intrude.
* دَحَصَ a دَحْصًا بِرِجْلَيْهِ To agitate the feet (slaughtered beast).
* دَحَضَ a دَحْضًا بِرِجْلَيْهِ To jerk (slaughtered beast). To search the ground with the feet.
— a دُحُوضًا وَدَحْضًا To decline to the West (sun). To slip (foot).
— a دُحُوضًا وَانْدَحَضَ To be made void (argument).
— a دُحُوضًا, وَدَحَّضَ وَأَدْحَضَ ه To refute (an argument).

أَدْحَضَ ه To make a. o. to slip.
دَحْض وَدَحَض ج دِحَاض Slippery (place).
مَزَلَّة مِدْحَاض Slippery place; stumbling-block.
مَدْحَضَة Slippery place.
* دَحَقَ a دَحْقًا, وَأَدْحَقَ ة وه To drive away. To remove a. o.
دَاحِق ج دَوَاحِق Angry. Foolish. Yellow date.
دَحِيق Expelled (people).
* دَحَلَ a دَحْلًا To dig the sides of a well. To lie hid in the corner of a tent. To conceal o.'s self.
— وَادَّحَلَ فِي To enter the recess of a tent, well.
دَحِلَ a دَحَلًا To be crafty, deceitful.
دَاحَلَ ة To use deceit towards. To circumvent a. o.
دَحْل وَدُحْل ج دِحَال وَأَدْحَال وَأَدْحُل وَدُحُول وَدُحْلَان Large at bottom and narrow-mouthed well. Corner of a tent. Reservoir.
دَحُول A broad-sided well.
دَاحُول ج دَوَاحِيل Palisade set up for scaring gazelles.
دَحِل م دَحِلَة Flabby-bellied. Calamity. Treacherer. Short and fat.
دَحَّال Hunter.
* دَحَمَ a دَحْمًا ة To thrust a. o. back violently.
* دَحْمَس وَدِحَمِيس وَدُحْمُس وَدَحَامِس Dark (night). Black.
* دَحَا o دَحْوًا ه To extend (the earth: God). To drive along (pebbles: rain).
إِدْحَوَى To be spread, expanded.
أُدْحِيّ وإِدْحِيّ وأُدْحِيَّة وأُدْحُوَّة وَمَدْحَى Hatching-place of ostriches in the sand.
* دَحَى a دَحْيًا ه To spread out (a carpet).
تَدَحَّى To stretch down (man).
دَحْيَة She-ape.
دِحْيَة ج دِحَاء Chief of an army.
* دَخّ وَدُخّ Smoke.
* دَخْدَرَ ه To gild (an earring).
P دَخْدَار Black and white garment kept in a wardrobe. Gold.
P دِخْرِيص ج دَخَارِيص Patch for widening a shirt.

Secret thought of man. دَخِيل الرَّجُل
Interior disease. دَاء دَخِيل
Inside of. Intimate thought. دَخِيلَة
✧ Home Office. وِزَارَة الدَّاخِلِيَّة
Basket for dates. دَوْخَلَة ودَوْخَلَّة
✧ Ear-wig. دَخَّال الأُذُن
Entrance. Means of beginning, prelude. مَدْخَل ج مَدَاخِل
Emaciated. Weak-minded. Rotten (palm-tree). مَدْخُول
✧ Revenue, income. مَدْخُول ج مَدَاخِيل
Special love. Ash-coloured bird. ✲ دُخْلُل
To deceive a. o. ✲ دَخْمَس ✧ دَغْمَش ه
To conceal o.'s mind from. — على
Deceit, craft. دَخْمَسَة
To become altered by smoke (food). To smoke much (fire). To be ill-natured. To be smoky. ✲ دَخِنَ a دَخَنًا
To be dust-coloured (plant, beast). دَخُنَ o دُخْنَة
دَخَنَ a o دَخْنًا ودُخُونًا، ودَخَّنَ وأَدْخَنَ وادَّخَنَ
To send up (smoke). To rise (smoke, dust).
To fumigate a. th. ✧ To smoke (tobacco). دَخَّنَ ه
To be fumigated. تَدَخَّنَ
Millet (plant). دُخْن
Smoke. Malevolence, ill-nature. Unsoundness of mind, belief, origin. دَخَن
Dusky colour. *Calamus aromaticus*, incense for fumigating houses. دُخْنَة
Dust-coloured sparrow. دُخْنَاء ودُخْنَان
Smoke. ✧ Smoking-tobacco. دُخَان ودُخَّان ج دَوَاخِن
Chimney. Hole for smoke. دَاخِنَة ج دَوَاخِن
Tobacconist. دُخَّانِيّ و✧ دُخَّانْجِي ودُخَاخِي
Intensily hot (day). دَخْنَان
Of a dark, dusky colour. أَدْخَن م دَخْنَاء ج دُخْن
Chimney, hole for smoke. ✧ Room for smoking silk-worms-eggs. مَدْخَن و✧ مَدْخَنَة
Fumigatory censer. ✧ Red herrings. مِدْخَنَة ج مَدَاخِن
Play, sport. Space of time. ✲ دَد
Joking. دَدِد

To be lowered, humbled. دَخِرَ ودَخِرَ a دَخَرًا ودُخُورًا
To humble. To abash a. o. أَدْخَرَ ه
To stick a (trivet) in (the ashes). ✲ دَخَسَ a دَخْسًا، وأَدْخَسَ ه في
Dolphin (fish). دَخْس ودُخَس
Trivet. دُخَّس ج دَوَاخِس
To go in. to enter (a place). ✲ دَخَلَ o دُخُولًا ومَدْخَلًا ه او في
To bring in a. o or a. th. — ب
To visit a. o. To be introduced before (a king). — على
To enter in (an affair, a religion). — في
To intrude, to meddle in (an affair). دَخَلَ وتَدَخَّلَ وتَدَاخَلَ في
To be attacked by an evil, in body or mind. دَخِلَ في عَقْلِهِ او في جِسْمِهِ، ودَخِلَ a دَخَلًا
To be corrupt (affair). To be unsaleable (goods). دُخِلَ
To introduce a. o. To insert a. th. دَخَّلَ وأَدْخَلَ ه وه
To enter upon; to have intercourse with. To be seized with wonder. دَاخَلَ ه
To come apon a. o. To go in to o.'s wife. — على
To slip in, to enter gradually. تَدَخَّلَ
✧ To beseech, to make an entreaty. — على
To be commingled. To intrigue. تَدَاخَلَ
To go in, to penetrate. إِنْدَخَلَ وادَّخَلَ
Unsoundness of mind. Guile, deceit. Disease. Baseness of origin. Dense tree. دَخَل
Intention. Thought. Way of acting. دَخْل ودِخْلَة ودُخْلَة ودِخَال
Hive of wild bees. دَخْلَة
Income, revenue. دَخْل
Please, I beseech thee. ✧ دَخْلَك
Small bird. Herbs mixed with the roots. دُخَّل ج دَخَاخِيل
Inside, interior, inward. دَاخِل م دَاخِلَة
Within. From within. Inwards. في دَاخِل ومن دَاخِل وإلى دَاخِل
Inner part. Intention, mind, belief. Hidden part. دَاخِلَة ج دَوَاخِل
Guest. Intruder. Adventitious (word). دَخِيل ج دُخَلَاء

Watchman, sentry. Wild ass. — P ديدب وديدبان

Pilot of a ship. — ديدبان

To be on the watch, to keep guard (sentry). — ✧ ديدب

Play, joke. — ✲ ددن

Blunted sword. Sharp word. Poor man. — ددان

Custom, wont. — ديدن وديدان

To flow abundantly (milk). To become luxuriant (plant). — ✲ درّ o i درًّا

To yield much (milk: she-camel). — ب —

To stream (sweat). To shine brightly (lamp). To become brisk (market). To be full of blood (vein). To become soft. — o i درًّا ودرورًا —

To pour down (an abundant rain) (sky). To give of (o.'s property). — ب —

To recover o.'s complexion (after disease). — a i درًّا —

To run swiftly (horse). — i دريرًا -

To let flow milk (she-camel). — أدرّ

To draw forth (a shower of rain : wind). To whirl (the spindle) quickly. To move a. th. To whirl (an arrow upon the nail). To render a. th. plentiful (God). — ه —

To stream (milk). To give much milk. To draw forth rain from the clouds (wind). — إستدرّ

Milk. Abundance of milk. Soul. — درّ

What a generous man! *lit*: His abundance comes from God. — لله درّه

What a bad action! *lit*: May God withhold his blessings upon him. — لا درّ درّه

Pearls. — (*coll*). درّ

A pearl. ✧ Female parrot. — درّة ج درر ودرّات

Milk. Abundance of milk. Flow of milk. Blood. Whip, scourge. Flow of a cloud. Briskness (of a market). — درّة ج درر

Milk-fever. — حمّى المدرّة

Windward. Straight path. — درر

My house is opposite thine. — داري درر دارك

They have the same design. — هم على درر واحد

Flowing abundantly (milk). Lighted lamp. — دارّ ج درور ودرّر ودرّار

Milch-female, yielding much milk. — دارّة ودرور ومدرار

Brisk market. — سوق دارّة

Spindle. — درّارة

Shining brightly (star). — دُرّيّ ودَرّيّ ودِرّيّ ج دراري

Bloody (war). — درور

Lighted (lamp). Swift (horse). — درير

Plenty of milk. — تدرّة

Causing milk to flow. Revolving the spindle quickly. — مُدِرّ

Shedding abundant tears (eye). Pouring a copious rain (sky). — مدرار

Frequently, abundantly. — مدرارًا

To chew a date (old man). To scatter a. th. about. — ✲ دردر ه

Sound of drums. Elm-tree. Plant sought by camels. ✧ Ash-tree. — دردار

Toothless gum. — دردر ج درادر

Abyss, whirlpool. — دردور

Small tray of straw. — ✧ دردورة

To rush (torrent). To glow. (fire). — ✲ درأ a درءًا ودرأة

To thrust back a. o. To urge (a beast). To spread (a carpet). — درأ ه وه

To rush suddenly on a. o. — على —

To shine brightly (star). To have pestilential pustules (camel). — دروءًا —

To repel a. o. To flatter a. o. To treat kindly. To cheat a. o. — دارأ مدارأة ه

To lie in wait for game (hunter). — تدرّأ

To look scornfully at a. o. — على —

To repel o. a. in a quarrel. To disagree. — تدارأ وادّارأ

To rush on fiercely (torrent). To spread (fire). — إندرأ

To dart on a. o. — على —

To lurk for (game : hunter). — إدّرأ ل

Crookedness. Quarrel. Extremity of a. th. Projecting part. — درء

Pestilential tumour (on camels). — داريّ

Unevenness, furrows, rugged parts of a road. — درء ج دروء

Shining (star). *Pl.* Large stars. — دريّ ودرّيّ ج دراريّ

Camel. Lurking-place of a — دريئة

hunter. Ring for learning arrow-shooting, spear-thrusting.
Means of defence. تُدَرَأ وتُدْرَاة
✱ دَرِب a دَرَبًا ودُرْبَة ب To get used, accustomed to.
دَرَّب دُرْبَاة ه To throw a. o. into (a disagreable affair).
دَرِب To be steady (in a defeat).
دَرَّب ه ب وعلى وفي To train (soldiers, hounds) to (war, chase).
أَدْرَب To invade a Greek province (Moslems). To beat the drum.
تَدَرَّب ب To be trained, inured to.
دَرْب ج دِرَاب Large gate. Street-gate.
دَرْب ج أَدْرَاب Drying-floor for dates.
دَرْب ج دُرُوب Entrance of a country. Mountain-pass. ✧ By-street.
دُرْبَة Practice, training. Custom, habit.
دَرِبَة Skilled (woman). Female drummer.
دَارِب Skilful. Hunting (dog, hawk).
دَرَّابَة Very skilful (woman).
مُدَرَّب Experienced (man). Well trained (riding-camel). Lion.
دَرُوب ودَرَبُوت وتَرَبُوت Submissive (camel).
P دَرْبَان ج دَرَابِنَة Door-keeper
✱ دَرْبَج To become mild, tractable.
✱ دَرْبَح To be scared away. To stoop the back. To be lowly.
P دَرَبْزِين ودَرَابْزُون ج دَرَابْزُونَات Wooden or iron rail, fence. Balustrade.
✱ دِرْبَاس ج دَرَابِيس Lion. Biting dog. ✧ Bolt, bar.
✧ دَرْبَس ه To bolt (a door).
✱ دَرْبَص To remain silent from fear.
دَرَابُكَّة ✧ دِرْبَكَّة و دَرْبُوكَّة ج دَرَابِك Earthen kettle-drum.
✧ دَرْبَكَة Kind of walk. Beating of a drum. Noise.
Pe دُرْبِين Spy-glass, telescope,
P دَرْبَنْد و✧ دَرْوَنْد Shop-bolt.
Te دُرْتْشَغْل At full speed, at full gallop.
✱ دَرَج i o دُرُوجًا ودَرَجَانًا To walk (man, lizard). To die childless. To be destroyed (tribe). ✧ To be in general use; to be current (fashion).
— دَرْجًا, ودَرَّج وأَدْرَج ه To fold (a book, a garment). ✧ To give currency to.
— ودَرَّج ه To build a storied house.
دَرِج a دَرَجًا To follow o.'s course. To rise by degrees.
— في To keep to (the true religion). To feed on partridges.
✧ دَرَّج ه To graduate a. th.
دَرَّج ه إلى To bring a. o. by degrees to.
أَدْرَج To pass one year of pregnancy without bringing forth (she-camel).
— ه To draw up (a bucket) gently.
— ه في To insert a. th. into; to inwrap. ✧ To publish a. th. in (a paper).
تَدَرَّج إلى To come gradually to.
إِنْدَرَج To be destroyed. ✧ To be published.
— في وتحت كذا To be classed, implied in a. th.
إِسْتَدْرَج ه إلى To bring a. o. gradually to.
— ه To deceive a. o. To show forbearance to (a sinner: God).
— ه To roll pebbles (wind).
دَرْج ج أَدْرَاج Scroll of paper (for writing). Fold. Fluent reading.
دُرْج ج أَدْرَاج ودُرْجَة Case for articles of women, chest.
دَرَج ج أَدْرَاج ودِرَاج Road. Mediator. Track of a torrent.
✧ دِرْج ج دُرُوج Drawer of a table.
ذَهَب دَمُهُ أَدْرَاجَ او دَرَجَ الرِّيَاح His blood has been shed uselessly.
دَرَجَة ج دَرَج Ladder. Step. Flight of stairs.
— ج دَرَج ودَرَجَات Stair, step. Rank, dignity, office. Degree of a circle; four minutes of time. Story, stage.
✧ دَرَجَات الكَهَنُوت Holy orders.
دَرَجَةً دَرَجَةً و بالتَّدْرِيج Gradually, step by step.
دَارِج Growing (child). Spreading everywhere (dust). In general use (term). Current (article). Trilling of a song.
دَارِجَة ج دَوَارِج Foot of a beast. Extinguished (tribe).
دَرُوج Swift (arrow, wind).
دُرَّج Hardships, hopeless affairs.
دِرِّج Kind of drum.
دَرَّاج Runner. Slanderer. Hedgehog.

Go-cart. Testudo, besieging-machine. دَرَّاجَة
Heath-cock. (*un.* دَرَّاجَة) دُرَّاج ج دَرَارِيج Francolin, rail.
Hazel-hen. Quail, partridge, pheasant. تُدْرُج وتَدْرُجَة
Religious belief. Course. Folded book. مَدْرَج ج مَدَارِج
Roll of paper, of cloth. مُدْرَج ومُدْرَجَة ج مَدَارِج
Road. Scroll of paper. Wrapper of a writing. Main part. مَدْرَجَة
To drive a. o away. ✲ دَرَحَ a دَرْحًا ه
To be broken, decrepit. دَرِحَ a دَرَحًا
To lay a vine-layer. ✧ دَرَّخَ
To recline on the side (man). ✧ إِنْدَرَخَ
Loop-hole in a wall. ✧ دَرْخُوس ج دَرَاخِيس
To lose the teeth. ✲ دَرِدَ a دَرَدًا
Toothless (man). أَدْرَد م دَرْدَاء ج دُرْد
Toil, trouble. Ps دَرْد
Dregs, sediment, tartar. دُرْدِيّ
To become accustomed, trained to. ✲ دَرْدَب ب
Calamity. Old man. Old woman. Love-charm. ✲ دَرْدَبِيس
To mutter. To talk nonsense. ▫ دَرْدَش
Gossip, nonsense. دُرْدِيش
To live comfortably. ✲ دَرِزَ a دَرَزًا
To sew up (a garment). ▫ To cram a. th. دَرَزَ o دَرْزًا ه
Luxuriant life. Seam of a garment. Suture of the skull. دَرْز ج دُرُوز
Lice, nits. بَنَات الدُّرُوز
People of a low class. Tailors. Weavers. أَوْلَاد دَرْزَة
Druse. دَرْزِيّ ودَرَزِيّ ج دُرُوز
Elm-tree. دَرْزَن
To make amulets. ✲ دَرْوَز
To disappear (trace). To be effaced. To be scabby and smeared with tar (camel). To be worn out (clothes). To become old (book). ✲ دَرَسَ o دُرُوسًا
To erase (a trace). — ه
To study (a book). — o i دَرْسًا ودِرَاسَة, ودَارَسَ ه
To thrash (wheat) on the floor. To wear out (clothing). — دَرْسًا ودِرَاسًا ه

To lecture a. o.: to teach a. th. دَرَّسَ وأَدْرَسَ ه وه
To study under a. o. دَارَسَ ه وادَّارَسَ ه
To study (a book) together. تَدَارَسَ
To be obliterated (trace). To be dissipated (news). إِنْدَرَسَ
Study. Lesson. Lecture. Effaced road. دَرْس ج دُرُوس
Thrashing of corn. دَرْس ودِرَاس
Camel's tail. Shabby clothes. دِرْس ج أَدْرَاس ودِرْسَان
Practice, exercise. دُرْسَة
Erased, worn out. Learned. دَارِس ج دَوَارِس
Student. Thrasher. دَرَّاس
Shabby clothes. Tail of a camel. Dry Alexandrian trefoil. Straw, clover. دَرِيس
Bull-dog. Lion. Strong-necked camel. دِرْوَاس ج دَرَاوِيس
The Prophet Henoch. إِدْرِيس
Coran-school. College, university. مَدْرَسَة ج مَدَارِس
School; book studied. مِدْرَس
Bible-school of Jews. مِدْرَاس
Learned. Teacher. Shabby. مُدَرِّس
Shabby. Mad. Beaten (road). مَدْرُوس
Dervish. ✧ Careless man. P دَرْوِيش ج دَرَاوِيش
To live like a dervish. دَرْوَش وتَدَرْوَش
To have the teeth broken from old age (she-camel). ✲ دَرِصَ a دَرَصًا
Young of rats, jerboas, hedgehogs, hares. دَرْص ودُرْص ج دِرَصَة وأَدْرَاص
Misfortune. Jerboa أُمّ أَدْرَاص
Young cat, young rat. دُرَيْص
To be black-headed and white-bodied (sheep) ✲ دَرِعَ a دَرَعًا
To skin (a sheep). To bone (the joints of a sheep). دَرَعَ a دَرْعًا ه
To be stripped (corn-crops). دُرِعَ
To clothe a. o. with an armour. To clothe (a woman) with a shift. To strangle a. o. To manifest a. th. دَرَّعَ ه
To insert a. th. in. To enter its second half (month). To set off in darkness (traveller). أَدْرَعَ ه
To put on a breast-plate. To put on a shift (woman). أَدْرَعَ وتَدَرَّعَ وادَّرَعَ
To be stripped of its flesh (bone). إِنْدَرَعَ

horse). To make a. th. follow another uninterruptedly. To emit (a sound. To thrust (a spear) consecutively. To ward off a. th.

May لَا بَارَكَ اللهُ فِيكَ وَلَا تَارَكَ وَلَا دَارَكَ God not bless thee nor preserve thee!

To reach the age of reason أَدْرَكَ (child). To reach maturity (fruit).

To overtake a. o. — ه وه To reach (an epoch). To obtain a. th. To seize (a question).

To perceive a. th. with (the sen- — ب ses). To take (revenge).

To come up together. تَدَارَكَ

To obviate a. th. To continue (a — ه journey). To follow a. th. closely. To realise (the truth of).

(God) overtook him with — ه بِرَحْمَتِهِ his mercy.

To attain a. th. إِدَّرَكَ ه

To rectify (a mistake). To إِسْتَدْرَكَ ه ward off a. th. ✧ To remedy (an evil).

To amend (a fault) by. — ه ب

To correct a. o.'s words. — عَلَيْهِ قَوْلًا

Overtaking, obtention. دَرَك ج دَرَكَات Responsibility ✧ Police.

Watchmen, overseers. أَصْحَاب الدَّرَك

Result of an action. دَرَك ج أَدْرَاك Bottom of (the sea). Piece added to a bucket-rope.

دَرَكَة ج دَرَك وَدَرَكَات (opp. to دَرَجَة) Step downwards. Abyss. ✧ Patrol.

Step of descent. Hell-fire. Degrees of hell. دَرَكَات النَّار

Catch, overtake! دَرَاكِ

Uninterrupted journey. Dog. دِرَاك

Successful, sagacious. دَرَّاك

Game, tracked beast. دَرِيكَة

Restrictive particle حَرْف الاسْتِدْرَاك as rather; إِلَّا أَنَّ, غَيْر أَنَّ, لٰكِن but; بَل except. إِلَّا

Sharp-minded رَجُل مُدْرِك

Faculty of perception, intellect. القُوَّة المُدْرِكَة

The five senses. المُدْرِكَات وَالمَدَارِك الخَمْس

Tenth metre of verse. مُتَدَارِك

To roll a th. along. ✧ دَرْكَب وَدَرْكَل ه وه

To go forward. To be full (belly).

To emerge from the (clouds: — مِن moon).

He was hindered from doing. — يَفْعَل

To walk by a dark night. إِدَّرَعَ لَيْلًا

Breast-plate, coat of mail. دِرْع ج دِرَاع وَدُرُوع وَأَدْرُع

Woman's shift. Small garment of a girl. — ج أَدْرَاع

Whiteness of the head and blackness of the thighs (in sheep, horses). دَرَع وَدُرْعَة

Night lighted by the moon at dawn. دَرْعَاء ج دُرْع وَدُرَع

Piercing through a coat of mail (arrow). دِرْعِيَّة ج دَرَاعِي

Clad in armour (man). دَارِع وَمُدَرَّع

Woollen shift slit in the forepart. دُرَّاعَة ج دَرَارِيع, وَمِدْرَعَة ج مَدَارِع

Black-headed and white-bodied (horse, ewe). Of a mixed race (man). أَدْرَع م دَرْعَاء ج دُرْع

Long garment of the Jews. مِدْرَعَة

✧ Ironclads, men-of-war. مَرَاكِب مُدَرَّعَة

Side, flank. Shadow. Shield. ✱ دَرَف

Leaf of a door; window-shutter. دَرْفَة ج دِرَف

To drive a. o away. ✧ دَرَف ه

To bear a large standard. ✱ دَرْفَس

Large standard. Bulky lion. Silk. دِرَفْس

To hurry on. ✱ دَرَق o دَرْقًا

To soften a. o. دَرَّق ه

Leather shield. Sluice of a rivulet. دَرَقَة ج دَرَق وَأَدْرَاق

Thyriac. Wine. (for تِرْيَاق) دَرَّاق وَدِرْيَاق

✧ Peach (fruit). Apricot. G دَرَّاق وَ✧ دُرَّاقِن وَدَرَّاقِن

Jar having a loop-shaped handle. ✧ Narrow-necked cooler. Measure for wine. P دَوْرَق ج دَوَارِق

Lower part, mat of a room. P دُرْقَاعَة

To go on quickly (man). To dance. To waddle. ✱ دَرْقَل

To obey a. o. — ل

To drop closely (rain). ✱ درك — دَرَّكَ

✧ He holds him liable to damages. دَرَّكَهُ بِالعُطْل وَالضَّرَر

To overtake (game: دَارَكَ مُدَارَكَة ه وه

✡ تَدَرْكَل To roll (ship)
P دِرْكَاه ج دِرْكَاوَات Portico, court of a palace.
✡ دَرَمَ i دَرْمًا ودَرِمًا ودَرَمًا ودَرَمَانًا ودَرَامَةً To run with short steps (hedgehog).
دَرِمَ a دَرَمًا To be plump, sleek (limb). To fall out (teeth). To lose its teeth (camel).
دَرَّمَ ه To round the nails.
أَدْرَمَ To grow new teeth (child)
دَارِم ودَرِم ودَرِيم Fleshy, plump. Tree.
دَرُوم (m. f.) Roving by night.
دَرَّام Hedgehog. Ugly gait.
دَرَّامَة Hare. Hedgehog.
أَدْرَم م دَرْمَاء Toothless. Fleshy, sleek.
دَرْمَاء Toothless. Hare. Red-leaved plant. Plump (woman).
✡ دَرْمَق ودَرْمَك White and refined floor.
✡ دَرِنَ a دَرَنًا, وأَدْرَنَ To be dirty, soiled (clothes).
أَدْرَنَ ه وه To defile a. o or a. th.
✧ تَدَرَّنَ To be tuberculous.
دَرَن ج أَدْرَان Dirt, filthiness. Tumour on the body. ✧ Tubercle.
أُمّ دَرَن This lowly world
دَرِن ومِدْرَان Dirty, shabby (clothes).
دَرِين ودُرَانَة Dry and withered parts of bitter plants, trees.
أُمّ دَرِين Barren ground.
إِدْرَوْن Manger. Rope of a beast. Dirtiness. Fatherland. Origin.
دَرُونَج ودَرْنَج *Doronicum*, leopard's bane.
✧ مَنْدَرُونَة Roller, cylinder.
✡ دَرَهَ a دَرْهًا على To come up of a sudden to a. o.
— عن To defend, to protect a. o.
دَرَّهَ To disown a. o. To meet a. o. morosely.
— على To exceed a. th.
دَارِهَات الدَّهْر The strokes of fortune.
مِدْرَه ج مَدَارِه Noble lord. Spokesman, foremost man of a party.
دَرْهَرَهَة Shining star. Curved (knife).
✡ دَرْهَمَ To produce round leaves (mallow).
دُرْهِمَ To become wealthy (man).
إِدْرَهَمَّ To become old. To become toothless (man). To become dim (sight).

G دِرْهَم ودِرْهَام ودِرْهِم ج دَرَاهِم ودَرَاهِيم Silver coin weighing the eight of an ounce. Weight of one drachm ✧ *Pl.* Money, cash.
مُدَرْهِم Decrepit (old man).
✡ دَرَى i دَرْيًا ودِرْيَةً ودَرَيَانًا ودِرْيَانًا ودُرْيًا ودِرَايَةً ه وب To know a. th. To know by skill.
— دَرْيًا ة وه To delude (game). To comb (the hair).
دَارَى مُدَارَاةً ة To blandish a. o. To act deceitfully towards. ✧ To take care of.
أَدْرَى ة ب To acquaint a. o. with (news).
تَدَرَّى وادَّرَى ة وه To lurk for (prey). To comb (the hair).
✧ مِدْرِي (مَن يَدْرِي) Who knows? It may be; perhaps.
دِرَايَة Science. Taffeta. ✧ Prudence.
عِلْم الدِّرَايَة Jurisprudence.
مِدْرَى ومِدْرَاة ج مَدَارٍ Iron-comb. Horn of a bull. Iron-fork of winnowers. ✧ Mast of a boat.
✡ دَزَرَ o دَزْرًا ة To repel a. o.
Ts دَوْزَنَ ه To tune (an instrument). To prelude.
Ps دَزْكَاه Desk, stall.
Ts دِزْكِين Rein, bridle.
Is دَزِينَة A dozen.
✡ دَسَّ o دَسًّا ودِسِّيسَى ه To conceal a. th. ✧ To feel with the hand. To spy a. o. To insinuate a. th.
— ة To smear a camel with tar (in the armpits).
— على To plot, to machinate secretly against a. o.
دَسَّس ودَاسَّ ه To conceal a. th. To thrust a. th.
إِنْدَسَّ To be buried in the earth (th). To be inserted. To slip in stealthily.
— إلى To intrigue with. To bring calumnies to a. o.
✧ بِالدَّسّ Gropingly. Stealthily.
دَسِيس ج دُسُس Intriguer, intruder.
دَسِيسَة ج دَسَائِس Secret hatred. ✧ Underhand machination.
العِرق دَسَّاس The origin spreads: *said of the effects of atavism.*
دَسَّاس Eryx, red venomous snake.

Limpid stream.
Large village. دَسْكَرَة ج دَسَاكِر P
Hermit's cell. Plain. Tavern.
To stop (a flask). دَسَمَ o دَسْمًا ه *
To shut (a door). To sprinkle the ground (rain). To lay lint on (a wound).
To smear a (camel) with tar. دَسْمًا ه i —
To be greasy (food). دَسِمَ a دَسَمًا
To be unclean (clothes). To be dust-coloured. تَدَسَّمَ
To put grease in (a dish). To moisten (the ground : rain). To blacken (a child's dimple). دَسَّمَ ه
To stop (a flask). أَدْسَمَ ه
To eat dainties. To be defiled (clothes). تَدَسَّمَ
I am free from the affair. أَنَا عَلَى دَسَمِ الأَمْر
Dripping. Greasiness of food. Dirt. دَسَم وَدُسُومَة
Greasy (dish). Dirty. دَسِم
Cork, stopper. دِسَام وَدِسْمَة
Greyish-black colour. Stopper of a water-skin. Corrupt (man). دُسْمَة
Abyssinian. أَبُو دُسْمَة
Greasy. Dirty, black. أَدْسَم م دَسْمَاء ج دُسْم وَدُسْم
Young bees. Bear cubs. Fox. Blackness. Amaranth, anemone (flowers). دَيْسَم
To be stunted. دَسَا o دَسْوًا, وَدَسِيَ a دَسْيًا *
To seduce, to corrupt a. o. دَسَّى تَدْسِيَة ه
To relate the (words) of a. o. — ه عن
To prepare porridge. دَشَّ o دَشًّا *
✧ To see.
To crush, to grind. (for جَشَّ) دَشَّ ✧
To travel in (a country). — في
Porridge of pounded wheat. ✧ Measles. دَشِيشَة
Desert plain. ✧ Trash, lumber. دَشْت P
To be abandoned (woman, property). دَشَرَ o ✧
To leave. To put aside a. th. To dismiss (a servant). دَشَّرَ ه وه ✧
Foe, enemy. دُشْمَان TE

Earth-worm. دَسَّاسَة
Spy. دَاسُوس ج دَوَاسِيس
Spy, sycophant. Baked under the ashes (bread). دَسِيس ج دُسُس
Buried in the earth. Anointed with tar (camel). Perceived by the touch. مَدْسُوس
To grope. ✧ To plot secretly. دَسْدَسَ *
Plain. Seat of honour ; upper-end of a room. Court, council. Cushion. Ruse, craft. Suit of clothes. Game of chess. Quire of paper. ✦ Lot of things. Washing-tub. Copper-trough. Pack of cards. دَسْت ج دُسُوت P
I am the winner. الدَّسْتُ لِي
I have lost the game. الدَّسْتُ عَلَيَّ
Bundle. Handful. Large glass-vessel. دَسْتَجَة ج دَسَاتِج P
Military roll. Register. Pattern. ✧ Leave, permission. Minister. Digest of laws. دُسْتُور ج دَسَاتِير P
Key of a keyboard. دَسْتَان ج دَسَاتِين P
To spear a. o. To throw back a. th. To calk (a ship). To nail a. th. دَسَرَ o دَسْرًا ه *
Oakum for calking ships. Nail for planks. دِسَار ج دُسُر وَدُسْر
Skiff, ship. دَسْرَاء ج دُسْر
Bulky camel. Lion. Darnel-weed. دَوْسَر
Proverbial troop of horses belonging to king Naman.
To vomit. To bestow generously. دَسَعَ a دَسْعًا *
To drive a. th. away. To fill (a vessel). To stop (a hole). ه —
To ruminate (camel). — بِجِرَّتِهِ
Base of the neck. دَسِيع
Generous gift. Nature. Large basin. Table well dressed. Strength. دَسِيعَة ج دَسَائِع
Ruminating much. دَيْسَع
To overflow (tank). To be limpid (water). دَسِقَ a دَسَقًا *
To fill (a vessel) to overflowing. أَدْسَقَ ه
Silver-tray. Long road. Old man. Bull. Basin filled up. White appearance of looming. Whiteness. Silver trinkets. Beauty. White bread. دَيْسَق P

Bed, mattress. دَوْشَك Ts

✱ دَشَن o دَشْنًا ه To give a. th.

✧ دَشَّن ه To put on new clothes. To inaugurate a. th.

تَدَشَّن ه To receive a. th.

تَدْشِين Dedication; inauguration.

دَاشِن New (house, garment).

✱ دَشَا o دَشْوًا To rush into the thick of a fight.

✧ تَدَشَّى (for تَجَشَّأ) To belch.

✧ دَشَاة وتَدَشٍّ (for تَجَشُّؤ) Belch.

✱ دَصْدَص ه To shake (a sieve).

✱ دَصَق o دَصْقًا ه To smash (glass).

✱ دَعَّ o دَعًّا ه وه To repel (an orphan) roughly.

دُعَاع Isolated palm-trees. Black winged ants.

✱ دَعْدَع دَعْدَعَة ودَعْدَاعًا To run at a heavy pace.

— ه To fill up (a vessel). To shake (a measure) for filling it.

تَدَعْدَع To have a tottering gait.

دَعْدَعَة Sluggish and heavy demeanour.

دُعَادِع Watery summer-plants sought by oxen.

✱ دَعَب a دَعْبًا ودَعَابَة ه To repel a. o. To joke with a. o. ✧ To vex a. o.

دَاعَب ه To joke with a. o. To tire a. o. (child).

تَدَعَّب عَلَى To behave affectedly with.

تَدَاعَب To sport together.

دُعَابَة ومُدَاعَبَة Joke, sport. Witticism. Foolishness. Black ant.

دَعِب ودَاعِب Jolly, facetious. Violent wind. Playing (water).

دَعَّاب ودَعَّابَة Lively, jolly.

دُعْبُب Excellent singer. Playful. Thin-skinned youth. Fruit of the solanum.

دُعْبُوب Foolish. Weak. Lively. Tall (horse). Black (night). Trodden (road).

□ دَعْبَس ه To look for a. th.

دُعْبُوس Foolish.

✱ دِعْبِل Frog's egg.

دِعْبِل ودِعْبِلَة Strong she-camel.

✧ دَعْبَل To round with the hand (clay, wax). To rumple a. th.

دَعْبَلَة Crease. Slight indisposition.

✱ دَعَت a دَعْتًا ه وه To push violently a. o. or a. th.

✱ دَعَث a دَعْثًا ه To pulverise (the earth) by stamping.

دُعِث To feel a chill of fever.

أَدْعَث ه To put in store. To rob a. th.

تَدَعَّث To brood rancour (heart).

إِنْدَعَث على To be trodden upon

دُعْث Beginning of an illness.

دِعْث ج أَدْعَاث ودِعَاث Hatred. Remainder of water.

✱ دَعْثَر ه To waste (a water-trough).

دُعْثُور Wasted water-trough.

✱ دَعِج a دَعَجًا To be large, black and fine (eye).

دَعَج ودُعْجَة Width and blackness of the eyes.

أَدْعَج م دَعْجَاء ج دُعْج Wide and black-eyed. Black (night).

✱ دَعِر a دَعَرًا To smoke without blaze (wood). To fail to produce fire (flint). To be immoral, lewd.

تَدَعَّر To be spotted (face). To be wicked, lewd (man).

دَعَر ودَعَارَة ودِعَارَة Wickedness. Rottenness. Lewdness.

دُعَر Wood-fretter.

دُعَر Smoking without blaze (wood). Worm-eaten. ✧ Harsh (man).

دَاعِر ج دُعَّار Bad. Corrupt. Lewd. Generous camel-stallion.

أَدْعَر Giving no fire (flint).

مُدَعَّر Colour of the elephant. Ugly colour.

✱ دَعَس a دَعْسًا ه To tread upon, to press a. o. To repel a. o. To dishonour a (woman). ✧ To stumble.

— ودَعَّس ه ب To pierce a. o. with a spear.

دَاعَس ه To pierce on another.

✧ تَدَعَّس واندَعَس To be trampled upon, contemned.

دَعْس Trace, track. Beaten road.

دَعْسَة Even (land). Ceremony of trampling upon dervishes. ✧ Foot-print.

مِدْعَس ومِدْعَاس Spear. Beaten road.

✱ دَعَص a دَعْصًا, وأَدْعَص ه To kill a. o.

دَاعَص ه To thrust a spear into.

أَدْعَص ه To kill a. o. (heat).

تَدَعَّص To be rotten (meat).

To swarm with animalcules ✱ دَغْمَصَ (pond).
Black water-insect. Roamer. دُعْمُوص ج دَعَامِيص ودَعَامِص
To be light-minded. ✱ دَعِن a دَعَانَة
What a thoughtless man! مَا أَدْعَنَهُ
Palm-leaves tied together. دَعَن
Ill-natured. Ill-fed. دَعِن ومُدْعَن
To long after a. o. To help a. o. To call out a. o. To pray (God). ✱ دَعَا o دُعَاء ودَعْوَى ه
To induce, to urge a. o. to. — ه إلى
To invite a. o. to dinner. — ه دَعْوَة ومَدْعَاة
To call a. o. by a name. To send down (an evil) upon a. o. (God). — ه ه و ب
To wish good to. — ل
To swear against, to wish evil to. — على
To propose a riddle to a. o. ✧ To raise a contest with a. o. دَاعَى ه
To destroy (a wall). — ه
To induce a. o. to claim a spurious father. أَدْعَى ه
To weep (hired mourner). تَدَعَّى
To call one another. To draw near (enemy). To crumble down; to be cracked (wall). ✧ To be at law. تَدَاعَى
To claim a. th. — ه وب
To unite together against. — على
To answer a call. إِنْدَعَى ل
To pretend that. — كذا أو أن
To claim as a right. To demand a. th. إِدَّعَى ب
To enter an action against. — على
To claim (a genealogy). — إلى
To declare o.'s name (in war). — في
To call out a. o. To exact. to ask, a. th. ✧ To beseech, to invoke a. o. إِسْتَدْعَى ه وه
Call. Invocations. Call for help. Prayer to God. Invitation. دُعَاء ج أَدْعِيَة (*un.* دَعَاوَة)
A call. Convocation. Invitation to a repast; dinner-party. ✧ Business, thing. دَعْوَة
Claim, assertion. دَعْوَة ودَعَاوَة ودِعَاوَة
Call. Prayer. دَعْوَة ج دَعَوَات و✧ دَوَاعِي

Sandy and rounded hillock. دِعْص ج أَدْعَاص ودِعَصَة
Hard and hot plain. دَعْصَاء
To beat (a road). To waste (a watering-trough: camel). To make (a raid). ✱ دَعَق a دَعْقًا ه
To start (a horse). — وأَدْعَق ه
Beaten (road). دَعِق ومَدْعُوق
Troop of camels. Shower. دُعْقَة
Horses treading upon the enemy. خَيْل مَدَاعِيق
Wren (bird). ✧ دِعْوَيْقَة الطَّيُّون
To rub up (a skin). To soothe (an antagonist). To take the newness out of (clothes). To rumple a. th. ✧ To train a. o. ✱ دَعَك a دَعْكًا ه وه
To be foolish, insane. دَعِك a دَعَكًا
To contend pertinaciously with. دَاعَك ه
✧ To practice, to exercise (a profession). دَاعَك ه
To contend together in war. تَدَاعَك
Fight. ✧ Practice. مُدَاعَكَة
Desperate antagonist. ✧ Experienced. مُدَاعِك
Beaten *i. e.* populated country. ✧ Worn out (garment). مَدْعُوك
To coax a. o. ✱ دَعَل i دَعْلًا, ودَاعَل ه
To go about. To frisk (rat). To be dark (night). To be multicoloured. ✱ دَعْلَج
Filled sack. Clothes of various colours. Rambling at random. Voracious. Intertwisted plant. Soft and beautiful youth. Darkness. Wolf. Ass. Sluggish she-camel. Foot-prints. دَعْلَج
To prop (a wall). To hearten, to help a. o. ✱ دَعَم a دَعْمًا ه
To be propped upon. To rely upon a. o. إِدَّعَم على
دِعْمَة ج دِعَم, ودِعَام ج دُعُم, ودِعَامَة ج
Pillar of a house. Column, support of an affair. Lattice of an arbour. دَعَائِم
The chief of a tribe. دِعَامَة القَوْم
Carpenter. Main part of a road. Well supported. دُعْمِيّ
White-breasted (horse). دَعْمِيّ وأَدْعَم
Dim-sighted. ✧ دَعْمِيش ودَعْمِيص

Curse, imprecation.
Claim, action, law-suit. دَعْوَى ج دَعَاوٍ و دَعَاوَى
Praying earnestly. دَعَّاء
F. Fore-finger. دَعَّاءَة
Point at issue. Summons. Riddle. أُدْعِيَّة وأُدْعُوَّة
Surname of the Prophet of the Moslems. دَعِيّ الله
Adoptive son. Spurious son; claiming a false father. دَعِيّ ج أَدْعِيَاء
Calling to a religion. Muezzin. Motive. ✧ Humble. دَاعٍ ج دُعَاة
Clamours of horsemen. Motive, impulsive. دَاعِيَة ج دَوَاعٍ
Circumstances, vicissitudes of time. دَوَاعِي الدَّهر
Cares, anxieties. — الصَّدر
Invitation to a repast. مَدعَاة ج مَدَاعٍ
Plaintiff, claimant (*at law*). مُدَّعِي
✧ Attorney-general. المُدَّعِي العُمُومِي
Claimed (property, right). مُدَّعًى
Defendant (*at law*). — عَلَيْهِ
✧ Petition to a court. إِستِدعَاء
To tickle a. o. ✧ To bruise a. th. ✱ دَغدَغ ه
To wound a. o. (by words). — ه ب
Tickling. دَغدَغَة
To strangle a. o. ✱ دَغَت a دَغتًا ه
To repel a. o. To compress (the throat of a child). ✱ دَغَر a دَغرًا ه و ه
To ill-feed (a child). To choke a. o. — ه
To mix a. th. To squeeze a. o. to death. — ه
To break into (a house). — في
To rush inconsiderately upon. — على
To be ill-tempered. To put on a coat of mail. دَغِر a دَغَرًا
To rush on. — a دَغرًا ودَغرَى واندَغر على
To be thrust back, upset down. To be squeezed. إِندَغر
Furtive snatching. دَغرَة
Charge the enemy, in a body, not in ranks! دَغرَى لَا صَفَّى ودَغرًا لَا صَفًّا
Reviled, contemptible. Wicked. دَاغِر
✧ Straight on. Straightforwardly, directly. True. دُغرِي ودُوغرِي Ts
✧ Walk straight on. Behave in a straightforward way. ✧ إِمشِ دُغرِي

To be overtaken by (darkness). ✱ دَغَش a دَغشًا, وأَدغَش في
To rush on. دَغَش على
To throng near (the water). دَاغَش حَوْل
To drink (water) hastily. — ه
✧ Darkness is setting in. أَدغَشَت الدُّنيَا
To mix together (fighters). تَدَاغَش
Obscurity, darkness. Dusk. دَغَش ودُغشَة ودَغِيشَة و✧ دُغُوش
To dazzle a. o. ✧ دَغشَش
To be choked by (food or anger). ✱ دَغِص a دَغَصًا
To hurry in doing a. th. دَاغَص في
To irritate a. o. To snatch a. o. (death). أَدغَص ه
Knee-pan. Pure water. دَاغِصَة ج دَوَاغِص
To take in a lump. To overcome a. o. (heat). ✱ دَغَف a دَغفًا ه وه
Foolish. أَبُو دَغفَاء
Young of the wolf, elephant. Thick plumage. Easy life. ✱ دَغفَل
To slip in unperceived. ✱ دَغَل a دَغلًا في
✧ To fester (wound). دَغَل الجُرح
To be bushy (land). To glide in (a place). أَدغَل
To mar (a business). — في
To deceive, to slander a. o. — ب
Confusedness, unsoundness of an affair. Thicket. ✧ Secret hatred. دَغَل ج دِغَال وأَدغَال دَغِيلَة
Bushy, secret place. مَكَان دَغِل
Secret hatred. دَاغِلَة
Misfortunes, ill-luck. دَغَاوِل
Bottoms of valleys. مَدغَل ج مَدَاغِل
To cause a. o. to swoon (heat, cold). ✱ دَغَم ودَغِم a دَغمًا, وأَدغَم ه
To stop (a vessel). To crush (the nose of). دَغَم ه
To insert a. th. into. أَدغَم ه في
To bridle (a horse). To blacken (the face: God); to abash a. o. To glut (food). — ه
To contract (two letters) into one. أَدغَم وادَّغَم ه في
To be brown-coloured (horse). إِدغَامّ
Colour of the face blacker than the body (in beasts). دَغَم ودُغمَة
Willingly or not. In spite of. رَاغِم دَاغِم
Pain in the throat. دُغَام

To clothe a. o. with warm clothes; to warm a. o. To give much. أدفأ ه

To warm o.'s self with (clothes, fire). تدفّأ وادّفأ واستدفأ

Warmth. Produce of camels as (fur, milk etc). Shelter of a wall. Gift. Profitable (goods). دِفء ج أدفاء

Warm clothes. Warming. دِفاء ج أدفئة

Warm (day, house, clothes). Clothed warmly. دَفِئٌ ودَفِيء و ✧ دافي

Rain between spring and summer. دَفَئي

Summer-provisions. دَفَئيّة

Warm. دَفآن ومُستدفِي، و ✧ دَفيان م دَفآى

Stove, hearth. ◻ دفّاية

Crook-backed. أدفأ م دفآء

Register, account-book, writing-book. دفتر ج دفاتر

✧ Journal. Dayly book. P دفتر يومي

✧ Letter book; copy-book. دفتر نقل التحارير

✧ Inventory-book. دفتر تقويم الموجودات

Accountant-general. P دفتردار

Archives. P دفترخانة

To strike a. o. on the breast. ✧ To push a. o. ✡ دفر o دفرًا ه

To become maggotty (food). To be vile, despicable. دفِر o دفرًا

To stink. — دفَرًا ودفرًا

The world. Female slave. دفار

The world. أمّ دفر وأمّ دفار

Stinking. دفِر وأدفر م دفِرة ودفراء

Fie, what a stench! وادفراه

To jostle, to push, to elbow a. o. ✧ دفش o دفشًا ه وه

Screw-steamer. ✧ مركب دفّاش

To repel, to discard a. o. or a. th. ✧ To pay a. th. ✡ دفع a دفعًا ومَدفعًا ه وه

To refute (an argument) by. — ه ب

To quit (a place). To plead on behalf of. ✧ To pay for a. o. — عن

To lead to (way). To compel to. — إلى

To avert an evil from a. o. — ه عن

To deliver up a. th. to. ✧ To pay (a sum) to a. o. — ه إلى ول

To put off a. o. دافع مُدافعة ودِفاعًا ه

To avert an evil from. — عنه الأذى

To dash (torrent). تدفّع واندفع

To struggle together. To be contradictory. تدافع

Black-nosed (horse). Snuffling. أدغم م دغماء ج دغم

To mix a. th. To upbraid a. o. ✡ دغمر ه

To bring (news) confusedly to a. o. — ه على

Malice, obstinacy. دغمرة

Confused (mind). دغمري ودغموري

People of a low class; scoundrels. دغامر

To be dark, gloomy (day). ✡ دغش a دغشا

Darkness. Cloud. دغشة

Ill-nature. ✡ دغو — دغوة ج دغوات

To go on at leisure (camels). ✡ دفّ i دفًّا ودفيفًا

To hurry on. دفف

To flutter, to hover (bird). — i دفيفًا, وأدفّ

To root out, to snatch a. th. — i دفًّا ه

To despatch a wounded man. دفّف وداف ه

To come consecutively upon a. o. (affairs). أدفّ عليه

To press, to crowd together. — وتداف

To skim along the ground (hawk). To be well arranged (affair). استدفّ

To be possible, to be within the reach of. — ل

Side, flank. Bank of sand. Leaf of a door. دفّ ج دفوف

Tambourine. — ودَفّ ج دفوف

A side. A leaf, a shutter. Board, plank. ✧ Rudder. دفّة

✧ Tiller of a ship. يد الدفّة

The two leaves of a door. The two skins of a drum. The two faces of a book. الدفّتان

Army advancing slowly. Migrating nomads. Emigrants. دافّة

Pouncing in skimming the ground (vulture). دفوف

Drummer. Drum-maker. دفّاف

To flutter in skimming the ground (bird). To hurry (man). ✡ دفدف

To be warm. ✡ دفِي، a دفأ ودفوءًا, ودفُؤ o دفاءة

To warm, to keep warm (clothes, fire). دفّأ وأدفأ ه

Laurel-bay, oleander. Rhododendron. — ودِفْلَى

To fill up (a well) ه with earth. To conceal (news). ✡ دَفَن i دَفْنًا, وادَّفَن ه

To bury (the dead: a treasure). ه —

To be buried (dead; treasure). To hasten (beast). To be filled up (well). تَدَفَّن وانْدَفَن

To escape (slave). إدَّفَن

Burial. Fameless (man). دَفْن

Latent disease breaking out. دَاء دِفْن ودَفِين

Inside of an affair. دَافِنَاء الأَمْر

Buried treasure. Modest woman. دَفِينَة ج دَفَائِن

Concealed. Buried. دَفِين ج دُفَنَاء وأَدْفَان Filled up (well). Breaking out (latent evil).

Running at random (slave, camel). دَفُون

Burial-ground. مَدْفِن و✧ مَدْفَن ج مَدَافِن

Fool, insane. Sluggish (*m. f.*) woman. ✡ دِفْنِس

Fool. Avaricious. Lazy (shepherd). دِفْنَاس

To despatch ه (a wounded man). ✡ دَفَا o دَفْوًا, ودَافَى وأَدْفَى

To be long-horned (buck). أَدْفَى
To waggle in walking (camel).

To continue a. th. uninterruptedly. تَدَافَى

To attain a. th. ه —

Inclined, stooping. أَدْفَى م دَفْوَاء

Long-necked she-camel. Great tree. Crook-beaked (eagle). دَفْوَاء

To be abstruse (question). ✡ دَقَّ i دِقَّة To be small, paltry. To be fine, minute. ✧ To strike (clock).

To break, to bruise a. th. ه دَقَّ o دَقًّا To knock at (a door). To manifest a. th. ✧ To tattoo (the face). / To play on (an instrument). To coin (money). To send (a telegram).

To ring a bell. — الجَرَس

To bruise a. th. fine. دَقَّق وأَدَقَّ ه ✧ To refine (hemp). To examine minutely a. th.

To be minute, particular in. دَقَّق في

He exacted from him the particulars of the account. دَاقَّهُ في الحِسَاب

To examine a. th. minutely. دَاقَّ النَّظَر في

✧To pay a. th. to one another. ه تدافع

To be repelled, driven back. To launch forth (horse). To come all at once. To be dispelled (evil). إندَفع

To be profuse in speech. — في الحَدِيث

He began to sing. — يُغَنِّي

To pray (God) to avert ه ه (an evil). إستَدفع

A push. ✧ A time. A reaction. A payment. دَفْعَة ج دَفَعَات

Shower. A rush, a pouring. دُفْعَة ج دُفَع

Secreting (milk) before bringing forth (ewe). دَافِع

Propulsive force. قُوَّة دَافِعَة

Ravines of a valley. دَوَافِع

Kicking (camel). دَفُوع

Impetus of a torrent. Rush of people. دُفَّاع

Channel of a torrent. مَدْفَع ج مَدَافِع

Means of defense. ✧ Cannon. مِدْفَع ج مَدَافِع

✧ To load a cannon. دَكَّ المَدْفَع

✧ To fire a cannon. ضَرَب وَرَمَى المَدْفَع

Spanish crown *used in Egypt* (*about* 4 *sh.*). ◘ بُو مَدْفَع

Repulsed (poor man). مُدَفَّع

To pour forth (water). ✡ دَفَق o i دَفْقًا ✧ To vomit.

To cause a. o. to die (God). — الله رُوحَهُ

To be poured (water); to be shed (tears). — o دَفْقًا ودُفُوقًا واستَدفَق

To have the teeth standing out (camel). دَفِق a دَفَقًا

To bestow a. th. profusely. دَفَّق ه

To empty (a vessel) all at once. ه — وأَدْفَق

To be poured forth. To go briskly (ass). تَدَفَّق وانْدَفَق

A pouring, a rush. دُفْقَة

Filling a valley (stream). دُفَاق

Swift. Hurrying. دُفَاق ودَفُوق ودِفِق ودِفَق

Rapid walk. Fleet and generous she-camel. دِفِقَّى ودِفَقَّى

He hastened in his walk. مَشَى الدِفِقَّى

Oblique. Bent (old man). أَدْفَق م دَفْقَاء Rapid walk.

Rushing (water). Having the teeth standing out. Walking quickly (camel). مُتَدَفِّق

Tar, liquid pitch. ✱ دِفْل

Slanderer, Calamity. Short drawers. Quarrel.

Barren plain between two mountains. دَوْقَرَة

To penetrate into (a country). To be far-extending in the earth (marsh). ✱ دَقَسَ o دَقْسًا ودُقُوسًا في

To fall upon the enemy. — خلف العَدُوّ

To fill (a well). — ه

To content with a mean sustenance. To bear poverty impatiently. To cleave to the dust. To loathe milk (young camel). ✱ دَقِمَ a دَقَمًا

To reduce a. o. to misery. أَدْقَمَ ه

To revile a. o. with foul words. — ل وإلى

Dust. Stripped land. Bad Indian-corn. دَقْعَاء

Seeking, content with what is mean. دَاقِع ومِدْقَاع

Extreme destitution. Abasement. دَرْقَعَة

Black (poverty). Flying away. Emaciated. مُدْقِع

Vehement (hunger). دَيْقُوع وجوع أَدْقَم

To withhold a. o. To strike a. o. on the nose. ✱ دَقَلَ o دَقْلًا ه

To abscond (man). — دُقُولًا

To produce bad dates (palm-tree). To be small (sheep). أَدْقَلَ

Dates of inferior quality. دَقَل

Lateen-yard of a ship. — ودَوْقَل

Small ewe. دَقَلَة ودَقِلَة ودَقِيلَة ج دِقَال

To break the teeth of. To beat off. To strike a. o. on the chest. ✱ دَقَمَ i o دَقْمًا ه

To lose the front-teeth. دَقِمَ a دَقَمًا

To overtake a. o. (wind). إِنْدَقَمَ على

Embarrassment, perplexity. دَقَم

Having the front-teeth broken. دَقِم وأَدْقَم

Hammer. Nut-cracker. Tᴇ دِقْمَاق ج دَقَامِيق

To strike a. o. (on the chin). ✱ دَقَنَ o دَقْنًا في

Chin, beard. ✧ دَقْن

To open (a road). To destroy (a wall). To fill up (a well). ✧ To load (fire-arms). To pound, to crush a. th. To level a. th. To flatten (the earth). To cheat. To drink a great deal. ✱ دَكَّ o دَكًّا ه

To give little. To give sheep to. أَدَقَّ ه

He has given me neither little nor much. مَا أَدَقَّنِي ومَا أَجَلَّنِي

To be pounded fine. To be broken (neck). ✧ To be knocked (door). اِنْدَقَّ

To act minutely together. تَدَاقَّ

To become thin, fine. To become hollow (moon-crescent). اِسْتَدَقَّ

Fine, minute. Consumption. دِقّ

Hectic fever. حُمَّى الدِّقّ

A stroke. ✧ Performance of music. دَقَّة

✧ Step by step; gently. دَقَّة ودَقَّة

Minuteness. Smallness. Meanness. Abstruseness. دِقَّة

Fine dust swept by the wind. Pounded perfumes. Salt. Beauty. دُقَّة ج دُقَق

Fine. Flour. Crumbs. ✧ Powder. دُقَاق

Powder for the eyes. دَقُوق

Slender, thin. Abstruse (question). Man of little good. Flour. ✧ The small (intestine). دَقِيق ج أَدِقَّة وأَدِقَّاء

Grass-hopper. ✧ نو دَقِيق

Minute, degree of a circle; minute of time. Ewe. دَقِيقَة ج دَقَائِق

Particular (man). Flour-merchant. ✧ Performer of music. دَقَّاق

Pestle for pounding rice. دَقَّاقَة

Wooden mallet. Pestle. Stone-hammer. مِدَقّ ومِدَقّ ومِدَقَّة ج مَدَاقّ

✧ Minced meat in balls. مُدَقَّقَة

Pounded. Consumptive مَدْقُوق

Fore-arm near the wrist. مُسْتَدَقّ

To patter (horse). To clamour (man). ✧ To be exact, minute. To knock repeatedly. To mumble. ✱ دَقْدَقَ

Pattering of hoofs. Clamour. دَقْدَقَة

To scrutinise a. th. ✧ دَقْدَسَ ه

To be surfeited. To vomit. To be verdant (field, plants). ✱ دَقِرَ a دَقَرًا

✧ To wound the feelings of. To tap, to touch a. o. دَقَرَ a دَقْرًا

✧ To bar (a door). To delay, to detain a. o. دَقَّرَ ه

Luxuriant, verdant garden. دَقَر ودَقْرَة ودَقِيرَة ودَقَرَى

✧ Wooden bolt. Obstacle. دِقْر

Lattice supporting a vine. دُقْرَان

Slander. Opposition. Bad habit. دِقْرَارَة

To weaken a. o (illness). To exhaust (a beast). — ه

To be ill. دُكّ

To mix a. th. ✧ To run a string into trousers. دَكَّكَ ه

To press upon a. o. تَدَاكّ على

To be beaten. To be compact (sand). To be depressed (hump). ✧ To be loaded (gun). إِنْدَكّ

Even (ground). Plain. دَكّ ج دُكُوك

دَكّ ج دِكَاك ودُكّ ج دَكَّكَة, ودَكَّاء ج دَكَّاوَات

Flattened hill, surface.

Flattened sand-hill. Stone-bench ✧ Gun-charge. دَكَّة ج دِكَاك

✧ Running string for trousers. دِكَّة (for تِكَّة)

Bench, seat. Shop. دُكَّان ج دَكَاكِين

Grinder; pounder. Wily. دَكَّاك

Complete day. يَوم دَكِيك

Flat-backed (horse). Humpless (camel). أَدَكّ م دَكَّاء ج دُكّ, ومَدْكُوك

Strong, hard worker. مِدَكّ م مِدَكَّة

✧ Ramrod. Gunstick. Bodkin. مِدَكّ

Colocynth mixed with dates. مُدَكَّك

To fill up (a well). To run a string into trousers. To stop a crack (in a wall). ☐ To tickle a. o. ✧ دَكْدَكَ ه و ه —

To become levelled (hill). تَدَكْدَكَ

دَكْدَك ودِكْدِك ودَكْدَاك ج دَكَادِك ودَكَادِيك

Sandy and even land.

To spur (a horse). To push a. o. ✧ دَكَزَ ه

To heap up (earth). ✧ دَكَسَ o دَكْساً

To be heaped up. دَكِسَ a دَكَساً

To grow forth plants (soil). أَدْكَسَ

To relapse (sick person). ✧ إِنْدَكَسَ (for انتكس)

Crowd. دَكِيسَة

Of bad omen. دَاكِس

Sleepiness. دُكَاس

Relapse (in a disease). ✧ دَكْسَة واندِكَاس

Numerous flock. دِيَكْسَاء

Very numerous. Hard, difficult. Unmanageable. دَوْكَس ودَيْكَس ودِيَكْس ومُتَدَاكِس

To barter, to exchange a. th. ✧ دَكَشَ — دَاكَشَ ه وفي

Barter, exchange. ✧ دَكِيش ودَكِيشَة

Weak-sighted. ✧ أَدْكَش م دَكْشَاء ج دُكْش

Disagreeable thing. ✧ دَكْش ودُكْش

Oven-poker. ✧ دِكْش

To have a cold on the chest (horse). ✲ دَكِمَ — دُكِمَ

Cold on the chest of horses. دُكَاء

To pick up (mud). To trample upon a. th. ✲ دَكَلَ o i دَكْلاً ه

To let (a beast) wallow. دَكَّلَ ه

To be affected, proud. تَدَكَّلَ

To treat a. o. haughtily. — على

Blackish mud. Rebellious people. دَكَلَة

To drive a. o. away by striking his breast. To beat a. th. ✲ دَكَمَ o دَكْماً ه

To insert a. th. into. دَكَمَ ه في

To butt a. o. on the throat. — ه ب

To repulse one another. تَدَاكَمَ

To heap up (furniture). ✲ دَكَنَ o دَكْناً, ودَكَّنَ ه

To be blackish. دَكِنَ a دَكَناً

Blackish colour. دُكْنَة

Shop. P دُكَّان ج دَكَاكِين

Shop-keeper. دُكَّانِيّ و✧ دُكَانجِي

Blackish. أَدْكَن م دَكْنَاء ج دُكْن

To direct a. o. To indicate a. th. to a. o. ✲ دَلَّ o دَلَالَة ودِلِّيلَى ودُلُولَة ه على وإلى

He showed him the way. دَلَّهُ الطَّرِيقَ و✧ بالطَّرِيق

To behave boldly with a. o. To be lackdaisical, coquettish with. دَلَّ i دَلًّا ودَلَالاً, ودَلَّ a دَلَلاً, وتَدَلَّلَ على

What has emboldened thee against me. مَا دَلَّكَ عَلَيَّ

To cocker a child. To blandish a. o. دَلَّلَ ه

To put up a. th. to auction. — على

To pounce upon its prey (falcon). To overpower a. o. أَدَلَّ على

To behave boldly, familiarly towards. — على فُلَانٍ

To rely upon. — ب

To be directed. To be poured (water). انْدَلّ

To ask indications about. اسْتَدَلّ على

To infer a. th. from. — على ب

Boldness, coquetry, unrestraint. دَلّ, دَالَّة و دَلَال وتَدَلُّل

Fat. دَلِخ ودَلُوخ ج دُلَّخ ودَوَالِخ

To conceal the defects of goods (seller). To lean on apocryphal authority. ✱ دلس — دَلَّس

To cheat. To wrong a. o. دَلَّس ه

To become green at the end of summer (plant, land). أَدْلَس

To conceal o'self. To graze. تَدَلَّس واندَلَس

To eat a. th. little by little. — ه

Deceit. دَلْس

Darkness. دَلَس ودُلْسَة

Land, plant becoming green at the end of summer. — ج أَدْلَاس

Spain, Andalousia. بِلَاد الأَنْدَلُس

Spaniard. أَنْدَلُسِيّ

To throw a. th. ם دَلَش ه

To glisten. ✱ دَلَص o دَلِيصًا

To be polished (armour). To be worn out (incisor). دَلِص a دَلَاصَة

To smooth a. th. To furbish (an armour). To scatter (pebbles). To pluck (the hair of the forehead). دَلَّص ه

To drop from the hands, to slip out. إِنْدَلَص

Even ground. دَلِص ودَلَصَة ج دِلَاص

Smooth, glossy. دَلِص ودَلِيص ومُدَلَّص

Smooth. Shiny (star). Polished (armour). دِلَاص

Even (ground). Shiny (stone). دَلَّاص

Wabbling. دِلْوَص

Hairless. Worn out (tooth). أَدْلَص م دَلْصَاء

Shining. دُمَلِص ودُمَالِص

To push a. o. on the breast. ✱ دَلَظ i دَلْظًا, ودَالَظ دِلَاظًا ه

To dash (waves). إِنْدَلَظ

To hurry forward. To become fat, thick. إِدْلَنْظَى

Hardy wrestler. دَلَظَى

To loll out (wolf). ✱ دَلَع a دَلْعًا, وأَدْلَع ه

To loll (tongue). دَلَع a o دَلْعًا ودُلُوعًا, واندَلَع وادَّلَع

✧ To cocker, to pet (a child). دَلَّع ه

To be drawn (sword). To be big and flabby (belly). ✧ To be cockered (child). إِنْدَلَع

Idiotic fellow. أَحْمَق دَالِع

Broad, even road. دَلِيع ج دَلَائِع

Good manners. Mind, heart. دَلّ

Salary and craft of a broker. Bidding by auction. دِلَالَة ودَلَالَة

Broker. Auctioneer. دَلَّال

Indication, sign. Proof. Prognostic, symptom of a disease; inference. دِلَالَة ودَلِيلَة ج دَلَائِل وأَدِلَّة

Guide, direction. Pilot. دَلِيل ج أَدِلَّاء

Self-confident. مُدِلّ

To swing the arms in walking. To dangle a. th. ✱ دَلْدَل ه ✧ دَنْدَل

To dangle, to swing. تَدَلْدَل و✧ تَدَنْدَل

Hedgehog. دُلْدُل

Wavering. Motion, bustle. دَلْدَال

Plane-tree. Race of negroes. ✱ دُلْب

Unextinguished coal. دَالِب

Water-wheel. ✧ Cup-board. Trick, craft. Workshop. Any rotary machine. P دَوْلَاب ودُولَاب ج دَوَالِيب

Grove of plane-trees. مَدْلَبَة

Gladiolus, corn-flag (*plant*). ✱ دلبث — دَلْبُوث

To walk with short steps. ✱ دَلَث i دَلِيثًا

To rush towards. تَدَلَّث إلى

To cover; to wrap a. th. in. إِدَّلَث ه

To burst into high words against. إِندَلَث على

Swift-walking. دِلَاث ج دُلُث ودُلُث

Battle-fields. مَدَالِث

To carry water to a tank. To carry milk. ✱ دَلَج i دُلُوجًا

To set forward at night-fall. أَدْلَج

To begin a journey before day-break. إِدَّلَج

Journey undertaken at day-break. Portion of the night. دَلْجَة ودُلْجَة

Swarm of locusts. دَلَجَان

Underground. Lair of beasts. دَوْلَج ومَدْلَجَة

Intrigue, plotting. ✧ دَوْلَج

Hedgehog. مُدْلِج وأبو مُدْلِج

To walk sluggishly under a burden. ✱ دَلَح a دَلْحًا

To carry together (a burden) on a stick. تَدَالَح ه

دَالِح ج دُلَّح ودَوَالِح, ودَلُوح ج دُلُح

Giving much rain (cloud).

To be fat. ✱ دَلِخ a دَلَخًا

دَلُوع Outstripping camels (she-camel).
✧ دَالُوع Lark (bird).
دُلَّاع Sea-shell. Water-melon.
✧ دِلْغَانَة Clay, potter's earth.
✻ دَلَفَ i دَلْفًا ودَلَفًا ودُلُوفًا ودَلِيفًا ودَلَفَانًا To walk heavily. To move on slowly (army).
— وأَدْلَفَ ✧ To ooze through (water).
أَدْلَفَ لَهُ القَوْلَ He spoke to him harshly.
تَدَلَّفَ إِلَى To advance towards.
إِنْدَلَفَ عَلَى To be poured upon.
دَلِف Courageous. ✧ Oozing, chink.
دَالِف ج دُلَّف ودُلُف Walking heavily. Broken by age. Arrow glancing off short of the mark.
دَلُوف ج دُلُف Swift eagle. Fat camel. Fruitful palm-tree.
G. دُلْفِين ج دَلَافِين Dolphin-fish.
✻ دَلَقَ o دَلْقًا, وأَدْلَقَ ه To unsheathe (a sword). To open (a door) abruptly. ✧ To pour (a liquid).
دَلَقَ o دُلُوقًا ه على To make a raid upon.
دَلَقَ o دُلُوقًا, واندَلَقَ To slip forth (sword). To rush successively.
تَدَلَّقَ وانْدَلَقَ To pour forth (torrent).
إِنْدَلَقَ To slip out (sword). To fall back (door). To be launched (horseman).
إِسْتَدْلَقَ ه To draw (the sword).
P دَلَق Weasel, ichneumon.
✧ بُو دَلَاق Ash-tree.
دَالِق ودَلِق ودَلُوق ج دُلُق Slipping forth (sword). Rushing (horsemen, torrent).
ɑ دِلْوَقْت (for هٰذَا الوَقْت) Now, presently.
✻ دَلَكَ o دَلْكًا ه ب To rub a. th. with the hand. ✧ To polish a. th.
— ه To break, to train a. o. (time, trial). To anoint o.'s self with.
— ه To wrong a. o. (of his due).
— دُلُوكًا To decline; to set (sun).
دَالَكَ ه To put off (a creditor).
تَدَلَّكَ To rub o.'s self in a bath.
— ب To perfume o.'s self with.
دَلَك Weakening of the knees.
دَلُوك Depilatory paste: ointment.
دَلِيك Dust swept off. Food of fresh and sour milk. Fruit of the sweet-brier.

— ج دُلُك Experienced.
دُؤْلُوك ج دَآلِيك Momentous affair.
مِدْلَك ومِدْلَكَة Foot-rasp. Rubbing-stone.
مَدْلُوك Worn out. Intruded upon. Weak in the knees (camel). ✧ Glossy.
✻ دَلِمَ a دَلَمًا, وادْلَامَّ To be intensely black. To hang (lip).
✧ دَلَم (un. دَلَمَة) Wood pigeons.
إِدْلَامَّ To be black-coloured. To be obscure (night).
دُلَم Elephant.
دُلَام Black. Black colour.
أَدْلَم م دَلْمَاء ج دُلْم Very black. Black dye. Hang-lipped. Lion. Heath-cock. Male sand-grouse.
الدَّلْمَاء The last night of a lunar month.
دَيْلَم Tribe of Kurdes, of Turks. Misfortune. Foes. Cluster of ants.
✻ دَلْمَزَ To take a large mouthful.
تَدَلْمَزَ على To agree upon, to decide a. th.
دُلَامِز ج دَلَامِز The devil. Glistening (man). Clever (guide).
✻ إِدْلَمَّسَ To be intensely dark (night).
دُلْمِس ودُلَامِس Intense darkness. Calamity.
دِلْمِس Misfortune.
✻ دُلَامِص Shining (gold); glistening.
دَلِهَ a دَلَهًا ودَلْهًا ودُلُوهًا وتَدَلَّهَ To be absent-minded by love. To be bewildered.
دَلِهَ عن To be diverted from.
دَلَّهَ ه To bewilder a. o. (love).
دَالِه ودَالِهَة Weak-minded.
دَلْهًا Uselessly, to no avail.
مُدَلَّه Speechless, confounded. Absent-minded (lover).
✻ دَلْهَمَ — إِدْلَهَمَّ To be intensely dark (night). To become old (man).
دِلْهَم Dark. Absent-minded. Wolf. Male sand-grouse.
مُدْلَهِمّ Intensely dark.
✻ دَلَا o دَلْوًا, ودَلَّى ه To let down; to draw up (a bucket).
دَلَا ه To treat a. o kindly. To urge (a camel) gently.
— بِفُلَان إِلَى To ask the intercession of a. o. to

To be mild (temper). ✱ دَمُثَ o دَمَاثَةً
To be even and soft (ground). دَمِثَ a دَمَثًا
✧ To soften the manners. دَمَّثَ الأَخْلَاقَ
To soften and smooth (a bed). دَمَّثَ هُ
To mention (a tradition) to. — هُ لِ
Meekness. دَمَاثَةٌ
دَمْثٌ ودَمَثٌ ودَمِثٌ ودَمِيثٌ ج دِمَاثٌ وأَدْمَاثٌ
Soft and sandy land. Meek (man).
To be inserted fast. ✱ دَمَجَ o دُمُوجًا, واندَمَجَ وادَّمَجَ
To be in good state (affair). To hurry to its hole (rat). دَمَجَ
✧ To set a. th. aright. دَمَجَ هُ
To insert a. th. دَمَّجَ هُ
To agree with a. o. upon. دَامَجَ هُ عَلَى
To wrap a. th. in (o.'s clothes). أَدْمَجَ هُ فِي
To correct (speech). To render (a horse) slender. To plait (the locks). To twist (a rope). — هُ
To wrap o.'s self in clothes. تَدَمَّجَ
To league together against. تَدَامَجَ عَلَى
Plait of hair. دَمَجٌ
Dark (night). دَامِجٌ
Clandestine: firm (peace). دِمَاجٌ ودُمَاجٌ
Rounded (spear-head). Arrow of a game. مُدَمَّجٌ
✧ Demi-john. Is دَامِجَانَةٌ ج دَامِجَانَاتٌ
To stoop the head. ✱ دَمَحَ — دَمَّحَ هُ
To be high. ✱ دَمَخَ a دُمُوخًا
To break (the head). — هُ
To perish. To be ruined. ✱ دَمَرَ o دُمُورًا ودَمَارًا ودَمَارَةً
To intrude, to break upon. — دُمُورًا عَلَى
To destroy (people). دَمَّرَ هُ وعَلَى
To burn hair in his hut (hunter). دَمَّرَ
To spend (the night) awake. دَامَرَ هُ
To grumble against. ✧ تَدَمَّرَ (for تَذَمَّرَ) عَلَى
Flood-season of the Nile. ◘ دِمِيرَةٌ
Palmyre, *town of Syria*. تَدْمُرُ
Some one. تَدْمُرِيٌّ ✧ دُومَرِيٌّ
A small ear. أُذُنٌ تَدْمُرِيَّةٌ
To be intense. To be obscure (night), ✱ دَمَسَ o i دُمُوسًا
To defile o.'s self. دَمِسَ a دَمَسًا وتَدَمَّسَ
To cover, to conceal a. th. — o دَمْسًا, ودَمَّسَ هُ و هُ
To conceal (a secret) from. — هُ عَلَى

To let down a. th. with. دَلَّى هُ بِ
To delude a. o. — هُ بِغُرُورٍ
To blandish a. o. دَالَى هُ
To let down (a bucket). أَدْلَى هُ
To backbite a. o. — فِي فُلَانٍ
To offer a bribe to (a judge). — بِ إِلَى
To afford an argument. — بِحُجَّتِهِ
To ally by marriage with. — بِرَحِمِهِ
To hang (fruit, bucket). تَدَلَّى
To come down to a. o. from. — عَلَى هُ
To get down from a horse. — مِنَ الخَيْلِ
He gave himself up to evil. تَدَلَّى عَلَى الشَّرِّ
To hurry on. إِدْلَوْلَى
Bucket. Aquarius (*Zodiacal sign*). Misfortune. Brand of camels. دَلْوٌ ج أَدْلٍ ودِلَاءٌ ودُلِيٌّ
Small bucket. دَلَاةٌ ج دَلَوَاتٌ ودُلًى
Watch-chain, trinket. ◘ دَلَّايَةٌ
Black grapes. دَالِي
Water-wheel. Field watered by a water-wheel ✧ Grape-vine. دَالِيَةٌ ج دَوَالٍ
✧ Clematis, virgin's bower. دَالِيَةٌ سَوْدَاءُ
To be perplexed. ✱ دَلِيَ a دَلًى
To be near to. تَدَلَّى بِ
To submit to. — لِ
To smear a. th with. ✱ دَمَّ o دَمًّا هُ بِ
To whitewash (a house). To tar (a ship). To level (the ground). To stop up (a hole). — هُ
To torment a. o. To break (the head). To exterminate (a tribe). — هُ
To be foul, vile. دَمَّ i o دَمَامَةً
To anoint (the eyes) with collyrium. ودَمَّمَ هُ
To behave badly. To have a foul son. To be ugly. أَدَمَّ
Liniment, collyrium. دَمٌّ ودِمَمٌ ودِمَامٌ
دُمَّةٌ ودُمْمَةٌ ودُمَمَاءُ ج دُمَمٌ, ودَامَّاءُ ج دَوَامُّ
Hole of a jerboa.
Dung. Louse. Cat. Ant. دِمَّةٌ
Ugly and short. دَمِيمٌ ج دِمَامٌ
Broad desert. دَيْمُومٌ ودَيْمُومَةٌ ج دَيَامِيمُ
Hoe-rake. مِدَمَّةٌ
Red. Loaded with fat. مُدَمْمُومٌ
To mumble. To snarl (beast). To rumble (thunder). To hum. دَمْدَمَ
To speak in anger to a. o. To crush, to detroy a. o. ✱ دَمْدَمَ عَلَى

To bury a. o. alive or dead. – ة في الأرض
✧ To kill a. o. secretly دَمَسَ ة
To hide a. th. دَامَسَ ه
To anoint o.'s self. تَدَمَّسَ
To enter a cavern. إِنْدَمَسَ
Object, person seen from afar. دَمْس
Important business. دُمْس
Covered, concealed. دَمْس ودَمِيس
Obscure, dark (night). دَامِس وأَدْمُوس
Hunter's hut. دَامُوس ج دَوَامِيس
Secret place ✧ Underground, catacombs. Gaol. دِيمَاس ج دَيَامِيس ودَمَامِيس ودِيمَاس
Ambrosia, hog-weed. دُمْسِيسَة
General of army *in the Greek Empire.* L دُمُسْتُق ج دَمَاسِق
To fret from excessive heat. ✱ دَمِشَ a دَمَشًا
To despatch a. th. quickly. ✱ دَمْشَقَ ه
✧ To train, to break a. o. – ة
Speedy, light-handed. دَمْشَق اليَدَيْن
Damascus. دِمَشْق ودِمِشْق
✧ *Damasonium*, bastard hellebore. دِمَشْقِيَّة
To hasten in a. th. To bring forth before term. ✱ دَمَصَ o دَمْصًا في
To hatch (her eggs : hen). – ه و ب
To have the hair shaven off. To have eyebrows thin at the end and thick in the middle. دَمِصَ a دَمَصًا
Range of stones in a wall. دِمْص
Scanty-haired. أَدْمَص
To shed tears (eyes). To issue blood (wound). To shed a fine rain (cloud). ✱ دَمَعَ a دَمْعًا ودَمِعَ a دَمَعًا
To fill up a. th. to overflowing. أَدْمَعَ ه
Tears. دَمْع ج دُمُوع وأَدْمُع
A tear. ✧ A drop. دَمْعَة
Wine. دَمْعَة الكَرْم
Hard, shining seeds of a medicinal plant. دَمْع دَاوُد
Coix-lachryma, Job's tears. دَمْع أَيُّوب
Ready to shed tears (woman). دَمِعَة ودَمِيعَة ج دَمْعَى ودَمَائِع
Issuing blood (wound). دَامِعَة
Liquor oozing from the vine. دُمَّاع
Tears of old age or disease.
Tearful (eye, man). دَمَّاع ودَمُوع
Rainy. Dewy. دَمَّاع

Full to overflowing. دَمْعَان
Lachrymal glands. Tears. مَدْمَع ج مَدَامِع
To damage the brain (blow, sun). ✱ دَمَغَ a o دَمْغًا ة
To overcome a. o. To prevail upon (error : truth). – ه
✧ To brand (a beast). To stamp a. th. To disgrace a. o. – ة وه
To put grease (in food). دَمَّغَ ه
To constrain a. o. to. أَدْمَغَ ة إلى
To enter (a place). To swallow (food). – ه
✧ Brand. Stamp, seal. Ts دَمْغَة
✧ Stamped paper. وَرَق دَمْغَة
Wound reaching the brain. Spadix of a palm-tree coming forth. دَامِغَة
✧ Irrefutable argument. حُجَّة دَامِغَة
Brain, skull. دِمَاغ ج أَدْمِغَة
Meninges, pia mater. أُمّ الدِمَاغ
To intrude upon a. o. ✱ دَمَقَ o دُمُوقًا, واندَمَقَ على
To break the teeth. To steal a. th. – ه
To insert a. th. into. – i o دَمْقًا, ودَمَّقَ وأَدْمَقَ ه في
To sprinkle (dough) with flour. دَمَّقَ ه
✧ It drizzles. دَمَّقَت السَّمَاء بِالمَطَر
Snow-storm. P دَمَق
Hateful. دَامِق ودَمُوق
Entrance, way in. مُنْدَمَق
Raw silk. White silk-cloth. ✱ دِمَقْس ودِمَقْسَاس
To run quickly (hare). To be even, smooth. ✱ دَمَكَ o دُمُوكًا
To grind, (wheat). To twist (a rope). ✧ To compact a. th. – دَمْكًا ه
To rise in the sky (sun). – في الجوّ
Misfortune. دَامِكَة ج دَوَامِك
Quick. Great. دَمُوك ج دُمُك
Rolling-pin. مِدْمَك
Mason's level. Row of stones. مِدْمَاك ج مَدَامِيك
To manure (a land). ✱ دَمَلَ o دَمْلًا ودَمَلَانًا ه
To improve a. th. To heal (a tumour). – دَمْلًا ه
To make peace between. – ودَمَّلَ بَيْن
To be healed (wound). دَمِلَ a دَمَلًا, واندَمَلَ
To act gently with. دَامَلَ ة

To shed the blood of.
Treat thy debtor kindly. إستدمِر من غريمك ما دمي لك
دم (for دمى) ودمٌ مث دمان ودموان ودميان ج دماء ودُمِيّ Blood.
دم الأخوين ودم التِّنِّين ودم الثُّعبان Andemon; dragon's blood; red juice of several trees.
✧ Red cotton-cloth. دم العِفريت
Bloodstone, hematite. حجر الدم
He is the slayer of such a person. دمُهُ من ثوب فلان
Bleeding. دامٍ م دامِيَة
Poor. Cupid. دامي الشفة
Bloody. Sanguineous. دميّ ودمَوِي
Statue of red marble or ivory; figure. Idol. دمية ج دُمًى
Happiness, blessing. داماء
Hectic fever. ✧ دموِيَّة
Bloody arrow. Gilded bay(horse). مُدمّى
Stooping when bleeding from the nose. Kind to a debtor. مُستدمِر
To buzz (insect). ✱ دنّ o دنًّا, ودنّن
To mutter, to mumble. دنّ دنينًا
To be crook-backed (man). دنّ a دنَنًا
To be short in the forelegs (horse).
To stay in (a place). أدنّ ب
Buzzing. Mutter. دنين
Earther jar with a tapering bottom. دنّ ج دنان
Depression of the back, neck. دنَن
Tapering cap of judges. دنِّيَّة
Crook-backed (man). أدنّ م دنّاء ج دُنّ
Short-legged (horse). Low-roofed.
To dangle, to hang down. ✧ دنتش
Necklace; frog, tassel. ✧ دنتش
To buzz (wasp). To mutter. ✱ دندن
✧ To hum (man).
Mutter. Black and rotten plant. دِندن
To be mean. ✱ دنأ a ودنوء o دُنوءة ودناءة
To be crook-backed. دنِئ a دنأ
To ride a jade. ادنأ
To render a. o. vile. دنّأ ه
To incite a. o. to foul deeds. تدنّأ ه
Baseness. Weakness. دناءة ودنوءة
Ignoble. Cowardly. دنِيء ج دُنآء وأدنِئاء
Vice, defect. دنِيئة
Hump-backed. Vile. أدنأ م دنأى
Dwarf, short. ✱ دِنّب ودنّبة ودنّابة

To be manured (land). تدمّل
To reconcile together. تدامل
Gentleness. دمل
دمّل ودُمّل ج دمامل ودماميل (un. دُمّلة) Boil, imposthume.
Manure, dung. Rotten and black dates. Scum of the sea. دمال
To work a. th well. To round a. th. ✱ دملج دملجة ودِملاجًا ه
دُملج ودِملج ج دمالج, دُملوج ج دماليج Armlet, bracelet. Smooth stone.
Smooth (hoof, stone). ✱ دملق ودُمالق ومُدملق
Sort of truffle. دُملوق
To round, to smooth a. th. ✱ دملك ه
Rounded black stone. دُملوك ومُدملك
To manure (a field). ✱ دمن o دمنًا ه
To brood hatred against. دمِن a دمنًا على
To become rotten and black (palm-tree). دمّن
To stale in (a place: cattle). — ه و ه
To grant a. th. to a. o.
To cleave to the door of. — وأدمن ه
To be addicted, accustomed to. أدمن ه وعلى
To be defiled with dung (place, water). ✧ To become callous. تدمّن
خضراء الدِمن وخضرة الدِمن Verdure growing in manure; *said of* a beautiful woman of bad origin.
Rottenness of a palm-tree. دمن وأدمان
Dung. Manure. دِمن ودمان
Manager of property. دِمن ودِمنة مال
Heap of manure. دِمنة ج دِمن ودِمن
Traces of encampment. Dung-heap.
Deep-rooted hatred.
Rudder, tiller. Te دُمان
Blister, callosity, corn. دِمان
Plants becoming green after summer. Canker of palm-trees. أدمان
To be burning hot (sand). ✱ دمِه a دمهًا
To become boiling hot. To fall in a swoon. إدموّمه
To bleed. To be stained with blood. ✱ دمِي a دمًا ودُميًا
To make (a wound) to bleed. دمّى ه
To near a. th. to.
To open the way to. — ل
To make a. o. to bleed. أدمى ه

✡ دَنَجَ o دِنَاجًا ه To strengthen a. th.
دُنُج (pl.) Intelligent men.
✡ دَنَحَ o دُنُوحًا, ودَنَّحَ To stoop the head ; to humble o.'s self.
S دِنْح Feast of the Epiphany.
✡ دَنَخَ a دَنَخَانًا To walk heavily.
دَنَّخَ To humble o'self ; to stoop the head. To remain at home.
Ts دُنْدُرْمَة Ice-cream.
✧ دَنْدَلَ To hang down, to dangle.
دُنْدُل *Croton variegatum* (tree).
✡ دنر – دَنَّرَ To glisten (face).
دَنَّرَ ه To strike (money).
دُنِّرَ To be rich.
دِينَار ج دَنَانِير و دَنَانِير Old gold coin.
✧ دُنُورَة Gold-finch (bird).
✧ دِينَارِيّ Diamond (at cards).
مُدَنَّر Figured, brocaded (cloth). Dapple (horse).
✡ دَنِسَ a دَنَسًا ودَنَاسَةً To be stained (clothes, honour).
دَنَّسَ ه To defile (clothes). To sully (the character) ✧ To profane a. th.
تَدَنَّسَ To be defiled (clothes, honour) ✧ To be profaned.
دَنَس ج أَدْنَاس Impurity, stain.
دَنِس ج أَدْنَاس ومَدَانِيس Defiled. ✧ Rascal.
– الثِّيَاب Disgracing himself.
مَدَانِس Foul deeds, places.
✡ دَنَعَ a دُنُوعًا ودَنَاعَةً To be ignoble.
دَنِعَ a دَنَعًا To be hungry. To submit. To be vile, base. To be cupid.
أَدْنَعَ To follow a righteous course. To follow an ignoble course.
دَنَع Refuse of a butcher's shop.
دَنِع ودَنِيع ودَنِيعَة Heartless, mindless man, brute.
✡ دَنِفَ a دَنَفًا, وأَدْنَفَ To be at the point of death. To be about to set (sun). To be at hand (affair).
أَدْنَفَ ه و ه To crush a. o. (illness). To be near to a. th.
دَنَف Heavy and protracted illness. Setting of the sun.
دَنِف (m. f. s. pl.), ودَنِف ج أَدْنَاف Seriously ill.
✡ دَنْفَشَ To look askance, to ogle.
✡ دَنَقَ o دُنُوقًا To be minute, exact.
دَنِقَ a دَنَقًا ودَنِيقًا ✧ To die of cold.
دَنَّقَ To wane from grief or illness. To sink (eye). To near its setting (sun).
– ه To examine a. th. minutely.
– إلى To gaze at.
دَنَقَة Darnel-grass.
دَانِق Foolish. Thief. Lean.
P. دَانِق ودَانَق ج دَوَانِق ودَوَانِيق Weight of two carob-grains. Sixth part of a dirhem; small silver coin.
دَنِيق ج دُنُق Ignoble, unhospitable. ✧ Bitter cold.
✡ دَنْقَسَ To look askew.
– بَيْن To sow discord between.
✡ دَنْكَسَ To keep at home mindless of o.'s family. ✧ To raise the head conceitedly.
◻ دَنْكِل ج دَنَاكِل Axle-tree of a wheel.
✧ دَنْكَلَة Heron (bird).
Ts دُونُم Turkish acre of one hundred feet square.
Te دُونَانْمَة Squadron, fleet.
✡ دَنَا o دُنُوًّا ودَنَاوَةً وادَّنَى إلى ومن ول To be, to draw near. To be akin to.
دَنِيَ a دَنًا ودَنَايَةً To be vile.
دَنَّى وأَدْنَى ه To bring a. th. near.
دَنَّى في الأُمُور To mind trifles.
دَانَى القَيْد To tighten (shackles).
– بَيْن To be intermediate between.
أَدْنَى To live straitly.
تَدَنَّى To advance gradually.
تَدَانَى To draw near to one another.
إِسْتَدْنَى ه To ask a. o. to come nearer.
دَنَاوَة Proximity. Kindred.
دَنَايَة Baseness. Cowardice.
دَنِيّ ج أَدْنِيَاء Near, akin. Weak. Low.
أَدْنَى ج أَدَانٍ وأَدْنُون م دُنْيَا ج دُنًى Nearer. Baser. Worse. More. Less.
لَقِيتُهُ أَدْنَى دَنًى وأَدْنَى دَنًا I met him first of all.
هُوَ ابن عَمِّي دِنْيٍ ودِنْيَا ودُنْيَا He is my cousin closely related.
دُنْيَا ج دُنًى World. ✧ Weather. Much.
Te يَكِي دُنْيَا The New World, America. ✧ Medlar.
✧ حَشِيشَة الدُّنْيَا Hop (plant).
بَاعَ الدُّنْيَا بِالآخِرَة He bought this world in exchange of the other.
دُنْيَوِيّ ودُنْيَاوِيّ ودُنْيِيّ Worldly.
مُدْنٍ Near, Worthless man. About to bring forth.

To astound a. o. دَهَّش وأَدْهَش ه
Bewilderment, astonishment. دَهْشَة
To botch (a work). ✲ دَهْشَر ه
To fill up (a cup). To pour forth (a cup). ✲ دَهَق a دَهْقًا وأَدْهَق ه
To strike a. o. To cut up a. th. دَهَّق ه
To hurry a. o. أَدْهَق ه
To cohere (stones). ادَّهَق
Stocks for the feet of criminals. دَهَق
Plentiful (water). Overfilled (cup.) دِهَاق
To establish a. o. as mayor. ✧ To delay, to hinder a. o. ✲ دَهْقَن ه
To be appointed mayor ✧ To be delayed. تَدَهْقَن
Mayorship ✧ Delay. دَهْقَنَة
Mayor, chief of a district. Sharp and energetic man. Merchant. P دُهْقَان ج دَهَاقِنَة ودَهَاقِين
To grind a. th. To smash a. th. To tramp over (the ground) ✧ To consume a. o. (illness). To waste (wealth). ✲ دَهَك a دَهْكًا ه
Hour. Small quantity. ✲ دَهْل
Hall. Passage. ✧ Ante-chamber. Catacombs. P دِهْلِيز ج دَهَالِيز
Foundlings. أَبْنَاء الدَّهَالِيز
To crush a. o. (event). ✲ دَهَم a ودَهِم a دَهْمًا ه
To blacken (a pot: fire) دَهَّم ه
To grieve a. o. أَدْهَم ه
To be roan, dark bay (horse). إِدْهَمَّ
To be black. إِدْهَامَّ
Roan (horse). أَدْهَم أَخْضَر
Dark bay. أَحْمَر أَدْهَم
Sorrel (horse). أَشْقَر أَدْهَم
Large number. دَهْم ج دُهُوم
The last three nights of a lunar month. Creation. دُهْم
Black colour. دُهْمَة
Black or dark green. Fresh or effaced foot-prints. Black horse. أَدْهَم م دَهْمَاء ج دُهْم
Fetter, chain. أَدْهَم ج أَدَاهِم
Blackened-pot. Crowd. Last night of a month. Traces of en-campment. Herb for tanning. Brown (ewe). Gait of a man. Dark green (garden) دَهْمَاء
Misfortune. دُهَيْم بِدُهَيْمَاء وأُمّ الدُّهَيْم

To roll down (a stone). دَهْدَه , ودَهْدَى دَهْدَاة ودِهْدَاء ه
To break (dawn). To roll (stone). تَدَهْدَه وتَدَهْدَى
Troop of one hundred camels and more. دَهْدَهَة ودَهْدَهَان ودُهَيْدِهَان
I do not know what sort of man he is. مَا أَدْرِي أَيُّ الدَّهْدَاء والدَّهْدَاء هُو
Routed army. ✲ دَهْب
To take large mouthfuls. ✲ دَهْبَل ر
False, lie; liar. ✲ دُهْدُرّ ودُهْدُرِّين
To bob up (boiled meat). ✲ دَهْدَق دَهْدَقَة ودِهْدَاقًا
To smash a. th. To cut up (meat). ه —
Bubbling up of water. دَهْدَقَة ودَهْدَاق
To overthrow (a building). ✲ دَهْدَم ه
To crumble away (building). تَدَهْدَم
To befall a. o. (mishap). ✲ دَهَر a دَهْرًا ه وب
Time, long or short; beginning of time; year. Care. Custom. Event. Intention. دَهْر ج أَدْهُر ودُهُور
Lifetime of a man. دَهْر الإِنْسَان
Sect of materialists. ✧ Lasting very long (garment). دَهْرِيّ
Very old. دُهْرِيّ
Long space of time. دِهَار
Endless time. Severe epoch. دَهْر دَاهِر ودَهْر دَهِير
I will never go to him. لَا آتِيه دَهْرَ الدَّاهِرِين
By-gone times. دَهَارِير
Various or long times. دَهَارِير
To hurl a. th. into an abyss. To pull down (a wall). To gulp (mouthfuls). ✲ دَهْوَر ه
To be over (night). To be hurled down. To crumble away (wall). تَدَهْوَر
Misfortune. ✲ دَهْرَس ج دَهَارِس ودَهَارِيس
To be even (ground). ✲ دَهِس a دَهَسًا
✧ To trample, to crush. (*for* دَعَس) —
To walk upon a soft ground. أَدْهَس
To be reddish (ground, plant). إِدْهَاسّ
Reddish plant. Even place. دَهْس ج أَدْهَاس
Reddish colour. دُهْسَة
Reddish. أَدْهَس م دَهْسَاء ج دُهْس
Meek. دَهَّاس
To be bewildered. To be astonished. ✲ دَهِش a دَهَشًا , ودُهِش ر ✧ انْدَهَش

To totter (old man). ✱ دَهْمَجَ
Two humped (camel). Tottering. Huge. دُهَامِج
To break, to cut a. th. ✱ دَهْمَقَ ه
To make (food) soft, delicate.
To anoint (the head). ✱ دَهَنَ o دَهْنًا ه
To strike a. o. with a stick. To moisten the (ground: rain). ✧ To blandish a. o.
To dissemble with. — رداهن وأدهن ه
To coax, to circumvent a. o.
دَهَن o ودَهِن a ودَهُن o دِهَانًا ودَهَانَة
To yield little milk (she-camel).
To anoint a. o. ✧ To varnish a. th. دَهَّن ه وه
To be anointed. تَدَهَّن وادَّهَن
Grease. ✧ Balm, resin. دُهْن ج أدهان
✧ Butterwort, self-heal. حشيشة الدُّهن
✧ Tincture of opium. دُهْن الأفْيُون
Desert. Red plant. دَهْنَاء
Poisonous tree دِهْن
Oil-merchant. ✧ House-painter. دَهَّان
Red leather. Slippery place. دِهَان
Ointment. Paint, varnish. Dregs of oil.
Anointed (head). Giving little milk (she-camel). دَهِين
Flask, brush for pomade. Pool, marsh. مُدْهُن ج مَدَاهِن
Hypocrisy. Treason. ✧ Flattery. مُدَاهَنَة
Malachite. Jasper. P دَهْنَج
✧ Emery.
To overtake ✱ دَهَى a دَهْيًا ودَهِيَ ه
a. o. (calamity). ▫ To astound a. o.
To charge a. o. with deceit. — ه
To be shrewd, دَهِيَ a دَهْيًا ودَهَاءَةً ودَهَاءً
wily.
To be crafty. To be clever. تَدَهَّى
Sagacity. Shrewdness. Good manners. دَهَاء
Misfortune. Momentous event. دَاهِيَة ج دَوَاهٍ
Great calamity. دَاهِيَة دَهْيَاء
Cunning, shrewd man. دَاهِيَة
Lion. دَاهٍ ج دُهَاة
Skilful. Wily. دهٍ ج دَهُون
Wise, prudent. دَهِيّ ج أدْهِيَة ودُهَوَاء
✱ دَاءَ a دَاءً ودَوْءًا ، وأدْوَأَ إدْوَاءً وإدَاءً وإدَاءَة
To be ill, diseased.

To render a. o sick. أدْوَأَ ه
To suspect a. o. — وأدَاءَ ه
Illness, disease. دَاء ج أدْوَاء
Falling-sickness. دَاء الأرض
Fox-evil. دَاء الحَيَّة ودَاء الثَّعلب
Hunger. دَاء الذئب
Fever. دَاء الأسد
Elephantiasis. دَاء الفيل
Canine madness, hydrophobia. دَاء الكَلْب
He is in splendid health. بِهِ دَاءُ ظَبْيٍ
Gout. — المُلُوك
Diseased. دَاءٍ ودَيِّئٌ ومُدِيءٌ
Almost, scarcely. ✧ يا دُوب
Book-keeping by double entry. ✧ دُوبِيَا
To serve as a footman. ✱ دَاجَ o دَوْجًا
Followers of an army. دَاجَة
To be big (belly). To be lofty (tree). ✱ دَاحَ o دَوْحًا
To squander o.'s wealth. دَوَّحَ ه
To be distented (belly). تَدَوَّحَ واندَاحَ
To be expanded. إنْدَاحَ
Great and lofty tree. دَوْحَة ج دَوْح, ودَائِحَة ج دَوَائِح
Showy toy. Hair-bracelet. Embroidered cloth. Perfume. دَاح
This world is a gewgaw الدُّنيا دَاحَة
To be abashed. ✧ To feel giddy, sea-sick. ✱ دَاخَ o دَوْخًا
To subdue (a country). — ودَوَّخَ ه
To humble a. o. To explore (a country). To weaken a. o. (heat). دَوَّخَ وأدَاخَ ه
To stun. ✧ To bother a. o. — رَأْسَهُ
✧ Vertigo, giddiness. دَوْخَة
Obscure (night) ✧ Giddy. دَائِخ
To be maggoted (food). ✱ دَادَ a دَوْدًا, ودَوَّدَ وأدَادَ
Worm دُود (un. دُودَة) ج دِيدَان
✧ Fancy, prank. دُودَة
Silk-worms. دُودُ القَزّ
Ascarides, thread-worms. دُود القرع ودُود قَرْعِي
Tansy (*plant*). حَشِيشَة الدُّود
Hardstongue (*plant*). حَشِيشَة الدُّودِيَّة
Sea-saw, swing. دَوْدَاة
Grub, worm. دُوَيْد
Vermin. Sprightly man. دُوَاد
Intense red. ✧ دُودَى وأحْمَر دُودِي

Turn, movement. Change of fortune. Fit of fever. ✧ Stanza of a song. ◻ Floor, story. دَوْر ج أَدْوَار (un. دَوْرَة)
By turns. بِالدَّوْر
Revolution of a star. Circulation of blood. Procession. دَوَرَان
Vertigo, giddiness. دُوَار ودُوَار
Going about. Anklet. ✧ Pedlar, vagrant. ◻ Round village. دَوَّار
Sun-flower, turnsol. — الشَّمْس
✧ Whirlpool. دَوَّار المَاء
Sea-compass. دَوَّارَة
F. Circle. Ring, curl of hair. Shaft of a pulley. Change of fortune. ✧ Public administration. Retenue. Surroundings. دَائِرَة ج دَوَائِر
✧ Municipal council. دَائِرَة بَلَدِيَّة
✧ The priviledged Egyptian debt. الدَّائِرَة السَّنِيَّة
✧ Cyclopedia. — المَعَارِف
Convent, monastery. دَيْر ج أَدْيَار و✧ دُيُورَة وأَدْيِرَة
Round about. ✧ دَايِر مِن دَار
Inhabitant of a convent. دَيَّار ودَيْرَانِيّ
Board of administration. مَجْلِس الإِدَارَة
Axis, pivot. Point at issue. ✧ Tropic. مَدَار
Round water-skin. Embroidered veil. مُدَارَة ج مُدَارَات
Governor. Manager. مُدِير
✧ Treasurer of a district. مُدِير المَال
✧ Government of a district. مُدِيرِيَّة
Round, circular. مُدَوَّر ومُسْتَدِير
To tread on (the ground). To lower a. o. To polish (a blade). ✧ To trespass upon. ✫ دَاس o دَوْسًا ودِيَاسًا ودِيَاسَةً ه و ٥
To tread (corn-crops). — دِيَاسَة، وأَدَاس ه
To be trampled upon. To be foot-trodden (crops). إِنْدَاس
Ceremony of trampling upon dervishes. ✧ دَوْسَة
Colt's foot (*plant*). ✧ دَوْسَة الحِمَار
Thick forest. دِيسَة ج دِيَس ودِيس
Troop of men. دُوَاسَة ودَوِيسَة
Furbisher. دَائِس ج دُوس
Walking in a file (horsemen). دَاسَة ودَوَائِس

To turn. To elapse (time). To revolve (wheel). ✫ دَار o دَوْرًا ودَوَرَانًا
To turn round a. th. — حَوْل وب وعلى
✧ He went over the town. دَار المَدِينَة
✧ Pay attention. دِير بَالَك
To go about with a. o. To cause changes in (time). دار ب
To feel vertiginous. دِير رَأْدِير بِهِ
To whirl a. th. To take a. o. about. To work (a machine). دَوَّر ب او ٥ وه
✧ To search for a. th. ✧ دَوَّر على
✧ To addle the brain of. — وأَدَار رَأْسَهُ
✧ To wind up (a watch). — سَاعَة
To round a. th. — ه
To ramble about with a. o. To circumvent a. o. دَاوَر مُدَاوَرَة ودِوَارًا ٥
To perform a. th. To control (an affair). — ه وعلى
To look stealthily at. — ٥
To revolve (a wheel); to work (a machine). To hand round (a cup). To manage, to govern a. th. أَدَار ه و ب
To induce a. o. to. — ٥ على
To avert a. o. from. — ٥ عن
To be round-shaped. تَدَوَّر واسْتَدَار
To take an abode in. تَدَيَّر ه
To turn around a. th. إِسْتَدَار ه و ب
Mansion, seat. House. Court. Tribe. Year. Province. دَار ج دُور ودِيَار وأَدْوُر وأَدْؤُر ودِيَارَة وأَدْوَار ودُورَات ودِيَارَات
Christian countries (*for Moslems*). *lit*: seat of war دَار الحَرْب
The perishable and the lasting abode. دَار الفَنَاء ودَار البَقَاء
Islamitic countries. Surname of Bagdad. دَار السَّلَام
Arsenal. دَار الصِّنَاعَة
Cinnamon. دَار صِينِي
Bastard cinnamon. دَار صُوص
Long-pepper. دَار فُلْفُل
Aspalathus. Bistort-root. دَار شِيشَعَان
Dolphin, sea-hog. دَار فِيل
Capital town of a country. ✧ دَار الوِلَايَة
House, court. Upland. Tribe. Circle. Halo. دَارَة ج دُور ودَارَات
Round sand-hill. — ودِيرَة ودَوَّارَة وتَدْوِرَة
Seller of perfumes. دَارِيّ
Some one. دَارِيّ ودُورِيّ ودَيَّار
Sparrow. دُورِيّ وعُصْفُور دُورِيّ

Brave, Lion. دَوَّاس
Blind. دَوَّاس الكِلاب
Nose ✧ Weaver's treadle. دَوَّاسَة
Shoe, sandal. مَداس
Polishing-stone. Beater. مِدْوَس ومِدْوَاس
To be altered (eye). ✱ دَوِش a دَوَشًا
Dim-sightedness, squint. دَوَش
Altered (eye). أَدْوَش م دَوْشَاء ج دُوش
Quoit (for playing). Uproar. ✧ دَوْشَة
To spread amongst a tribe (disease). To be cheap (corn). ✱ داغ o دَوْغًا
To crush a. o. (heat). — ه وه
Whey, watery part of milk. P دُوغ
Cold. Foolishness. Epidemic. دَوْغَة
To mix (perfumes). To dilute (a medicine). ✱ داف o دَوْفًا ه
Nightmare. دَوْفان
Diluted (medicine). Pounded (musk). مَدُوف ومَدْوُوف
✱ داق o دَوْقًا ودُؤُوقًا ودُوُوقَة ودَوَاقَة
To be insane. To be lean (cattle)
To surround a. o. or a. th. أداق ب
To be swollen (belly). إنداق
Worthless furniture. دَايِق تَايِق
Foolishness. Corruptedness. دَوْقَة ودَوْقَانِيَّة
To be ill (people). ✱ داك o دَوْكًا ومَدَاكًا
To bruise (perfumes, colours). To smash a. th. (camel). To dip a. th. in (water, sand). — ه
To press together (riders). تَداوَك
Evil, disturbance, quarrel. دَوْكَة ودُوكَة
Stone pounded upon. مَداك
Pounding-stone. مِدْوَك
To elapse (time). To change (season). To be flabby (belly). To be shabby (clothes). ✱ دال o دَوْلَة
To become famous (man). — دَالَة ودَوْلًا
✧ To deliberate with. داوَل
To alternate (seasons, fortune : God). داوَل مُداوَلَة ه
To transfer, to hand a. th. أَدال ه
To make a. o. to prevail over. — ه من وعلى
To hand by turns. ✧ To confer together. To be current (coin). تَداوَل
To emigrate (people). To be flabby (belly). To dangle. إندال
Notoriousness. دَالَة ج دال
Revolution of time. دَوْلَة ج دُوَل
Change. Victory ✧ Government, state.
They have been prevailed upon. الدَّوْلَة عَلَيْهِم
The chief men of the state. وُجوه الدَّوْلَة
Adversity. دُولَة ج دُوَلات
Excellency (title of a vizir). Ts دَوْلَتْلو
Victory. إدالَة
By turns, alternatively. دَوَالَيْك
Reddish grapes. دَوَالِيّ
✧ Conference. تَداوُل ومُداوَلَة
To last. To continue. To stand still. To be filled (bucket). ✱ دام o دَوْمًا ودَوَامًا ودَيْمُومَة
As long as he remains standing. ما دام قائمًا
To pour a continuous rain (sky) دام دَيْمًا, ودَوَّم ودَيَّم
To move in the sky (sun). To circle in the air (bird). To turn in its orbit (eye). دَوَّم
To confuse a. o. (wine). — ه
To moisten a. th. To sprinkle (a boiling-pot) with cold water. — ه
To spin (a top). — ب
To ask or grant a respite to a. o. داوَم ه
To persevere in. — على
To continue a. th. To make a. th. to last. To fill (a bucket). To keep a. o. alive. أدام ه وه
To wait for. تَدَوَّم
To circle in the air (bird). إستدام
To act slowly in an affair. — أمرًا
To grant delays to (a debtor). — ه
Sea. دَأْماء
Continuous. Duration. *Theban palm*, doom-palm. Lote-tree. دَوْم
Duration, continuance. دَوَام ودَيْمُومَة
For ever. على الدَّوَام
Continuous rain without lightning nor thunder. دِيمَة ج دِيَم ودُيُوم
Continuous. The Everlasting (God). دائم ودَيُّوم
Always. دائمًا ✧ ودَوْم ومِدْوَم
Spinning-top. ✧ Whirlpool. دُوَّامَة
Rotatory motion. تَدْوَام وتَدْوِيم
Wine. مُدَام ومُدَامَة
Bleeding from the nose. مُدِيم
Piece of wood thrown مِدْوَم ومِدْوَام

To nurse (the sick). دَارَى مُدَارَاةً ه
To make a. o. sick. أَدْرَى إِدْرَاء ه
To treat o.'s self medically. تَدَاوَى
To eat the skin of milk. إِدَّرَى
Disease. دَرًى ج أَدْوَاء
Medicine, remedy. دَوَاء ج أَدْوِيَة
Gentian (*plant*). دَوَاء الحَيَّة
دَوَاة و✧ دَوَايَة ج دَوًى ودُوِيّ ودَوَيَات
Inkstand.
Secretary, clerk. P دَوَادَار ودَوِيدَار
Pellicle of milk. دُوَايَة ودِوَايَة
Ill. Foolish. Keeping in doors. دَوًى ودَوِيّ
Echo, sound. Rustling of wind, wings. Buzz. دَوِيّ
Wholesome (land). أَرْض دَوِيَّة
There is nobody in. مَا بِالدَّار دَوِيّ او دُوِيّ او دَوِيّ
Abundant (food). Hidden (affair). Thundering (cloud). مُدَوّ
Hand. (*dim. of* يَد) ✧ دَيّ ج دَيَّات
Thanks. Bravo. God preserve thy hands. ✧ سَلِم دَيَّاتَك
Blood-money *See* ودى. (*for* دِيَة) دِيَّة
Cloth with double woof. ✲ دَيْبُوذ ج دَيَابِيذ ودَيَابُوذ
To abase, to revile a. o. ✲ ديث – دَيَّث ه
Warbler (bird). طَيْر الدَّيُّوث
Reviled. Beaten (road). مُدَيَّث
To walk gently. ✲ دَاج i دَيْجًا ودَيَجَانًا
To stray. To move under the hand (gland). ✲ دَاص i دَيْصَانًا
To fall into abasement. To shun a fight. – i دَيْصًا
To drop from the hand. إِنْدَاص
To fall unexpectedly on. – على
Thief. دَائِص ج دَاصَة
Unruled. Muscular. دَيَّاص م دَيَّاصَة
Diving-place. مَدَاص
Two-handled jug. ✧ دُوَيْك
Flower of the cyclamen, sowbread. ✧ دُوَيْك الجَبَل
Cock. Compassionate. Spring. ✧ Cock of a gun. ✲ دِيك ج دُيُوك وأَدْيَاك ودِيَكَة
Turkey fowl. دِيك الحَبَش و ✧ دِيك رُومِي
Pheasant. ✧ دِيك بَرِّي
Fresh ripe dates. ✧ صُرْم الدِّيك
Land abounding in cocks. مَدَاكَة
To borrow, to be indebted. ✲ دَان i دَيْنًا

into a pot for allaying its boiling.
To be mean, weak, despised. ✲ دَان o دَوْنًا
To make a selection of works. To register a. th. دَوَّن ه
To be low, vile, weak. أَدْوَن
To become wealthy. To be registered. تَدَوَّن
Beneath, below,. Before. Besides, near. Without. Against. دُون
He is inferior to him. هُوَ دُونَهُ
He walked before him. مَشَى دُونَهُ
He sat behind him. قَعَدَ دُونَهُ
Preferably to another. دُون غَيْرِهِ
I admire thy virtue more than thy science. أَنَا مُتَعَجِّب مِن فَضْلِك دُون عِلْمِك
He interposed between. حَال دُون الشَّيْء
Without, unless he... دُون أَن
Behold! Beware. دُونَك
Do act as thou wishest. دُونَك ومَا تُرِيد
Inferior. Noble. Superior. دُون
Important thing. شَيْء دُون
Vile, despicable man. رَجُل دُون
Bad, wicked. ◘ دُونِي
Ear. ◘ دَان و✧ دَيْن ج دَيْنَات
Betony (*plant*). ✧ دَانِين الجِدَى
Register of soldiers. Collection of poetry, traditions. Council of state, divan. ✧ Saloon, sofa; parlour. P دِيوَان ج دَوَاوِين
✧ Court of referendaries. دِيوَان الآمِدِي
◘ Treasury department. دِيوَان الخَزْنَة
◘ War department. – الجِهَادِيَّة
◘ Home department. – المَشُورَة
Ministers of state. أَرْبَاب الدِّيوَان
Turkish official hand-writing. خَطّ دِيوَانِي
To call (she-camels) to their young ones. دره – دَوَّه ب
Cry for calling she-camels. دَهْ دَهْ ودَاهٍ دَاهٍ
To walk across a desert. ✲ دَوَّى
Desert. دَوّ ودَوِّيّ ودَوِّيَّة
To be diseased. To be rancorous (heart). To resound. دَوِي a دَوًى
To be overspread with a skin (milk); with scum (water). To move round (cloud). To go about (dog). To hum (bees). To snort (stallion). To resound (echo). دَوَّى تَدْوِيَة

To lend, to give a loan to. دَان ه
To requite a. o. for. — ه ه
Thou shalt be treated as thou hadst treated. كَمَا تَدِين تُدَان
To be honoured. To be reviled. To comply. To rebel. To have a good or bad habit. To be attacked by a disease. دَان دِينًا ودِيَانَةً
To serve a. o. To do good to a. o. To possess a. th. To constrain a. o. To judge a. o. To revile. To enslave a. o. — ه وه
To profess (a religion). — وتَدَيَّنَ ب
To submit to. دَان ل
To let a. o. profess his religion. ✧ To lend (money) to. دَيَّنَ ه
To give to, or to receive a loan from a. o. To sell to a. o. upon credit. دَايَنَ ه
To borrow. أَدَان إِدَانَةً
To lend money to a. o. To sell upon credit to. To summon a. o. to (a judge). — وادَّان ه
To contract debts. تَدَيَّنَ
To sell or buy upon credit. To be mutually indebted. تَدَايَنَ
To borrow a. th. from إِدَّان واسْتَدَان ه ه

Debt; loan. Death. دَيْن ج دُيُون وأَدْيُن
Active debt, credit. دَيْن ل
Passive debt, due. دَيْن عَلَى
Ear. (*dim. of* أُذُن) ✧ دَيْن ودَيْنَة ج دَيْنَات
He died. قَضَى دَيْنَهُ
Upon credit. بِالدَّيْن
Creditors. أَرْبَاب الدُّيُون
Requital. Custom. Condition. Affair. Religion; religious law; sect. Godliness. Rebellion. Revilement. Disease. Compulsion. Victory. Power, authority. Management. ✧ Kind, sort. دِين ج أَدْيَان
Judgment-day. يَوْم الدِّين او الدَّيْنُونَة
Worship. Religion, sect. دِيَانَة ج دِيَانَات
Maturity of a debt. Continuous rain. Obedience. دِينَة
Religious, godly. دَيِّن
The Rewarder (God). Judge. دَيَّان
Debtor. Creditor, debtee. دَائِن
Judged. Slave. مَدِين
Lender; borrower. مِدْيَان ج مَدَايِين
Debtor; indebted. مَدْيُون
Slave-maid. Town, country. مَدِينَة ج مُدُن ومَدَائِن
He is well aware of it. هُوَ ابْن مَدِينَتِنَا
Citizen. مَدَنِيّ

ذ

ذَا م ذِي وذِهِ ج أولاء وه دِه م دِي ج دُول (*postponed*). This, these (*near*). Who.
To-day. ه نهار ده
ذَاك م تَاك وتِيك ج أولائك وه دَاك م دِكْهَا ودِيكْهَا ج دَوْك That, those. (*middling*).
That (*far*). ذٰلِك م تِلْك أولائك ج ✧ هَدَوْلِيك
So. ✧ Too, also. كَذٰلِك
Such. Thus. كَذَا ه كِدَا وكِدِي
Interrogative particle. How? مَاذَا
Why? لِمَاذَا
This. هٰذَا وهٰذِه وهٰذِي و✧ هَل ج هٰؤُلاء و✧ هَدَوْل
That. هٰذَاك م هٰذِيك ج هٰؤلائك ه هدَوْك ودَوْك
So, thus. هٰكَذَا و✧ هيك
To totter, to waver. ✲ ذَأْذَأَ وتَذَأْذَأَ
To urge (asses). To frighten a. o. To despise. To blame. To expel a. o. ✲ ذَأَب a ذَأْبًا ه
To gather (things). — ه
To plait the locks of a. o. ذَأَب وأَذْأَب ه
To be as wicked as a wolf. To be frightened by wolves. ذَئِب a ذَأَبًا, وذُؤِب o ذَآبَةً
To be haunted by wolves (land). To fear (wolves). أَذْأَب
To veer (wind). تَذَأَّب وتَذَاءَب
To make a. th. by turns. — ه
To be wolfish, wicked. تَذَأَّب
To imitate a wolf, for frightening (a she-camel). — وتَذَاءَب ل
The sheep became wolf; *said of* a vile man who rebels. إِسْتَذْأَبَ النَقَد
Wolf. ذِئب و✧ ديب ج أَذْؤُب وذِئَاب وذُؤْبَان
Sea-wolf. ذِيب البَحْر
Small stars in *Draco*. أَظْفَار الذِيب
Brigands, thieves. ذُؤْبَان العَرَب
She-wolf. Throat-disease in cattle ✧ Croup of children. ذِئْبَة
Forelock. Hanging locks. ذُؤَابَة ج ذَوَائِب
Summit, apex of glory and power. ذُؤَابَة العِزّ والشَرَف

Country full of wolves. أرض مَذْأَبَة
To throttle a. o. ✲ ذَأَت a ذَأْتًا ه
To quaff (water). To tear (a water-skin). To kill (a sparrow). ✲ ذَأَج a وذَئِج a ذَأْجًا ه
To become pink (rose). ذَئِج a ذَأَجًا
To be torn off (skin). إِنْذَأَج
To fear, to shun a. o. ✲ ذَئِر a ذَأَرًا عن
To get accustomed to. — ب
To dare. To rebel against her husband (wife). — وذَاءَر على
To anger a. o. To seduce a. o. أَذْأَر ه
To embolden a. o. against. — ه على
To compel a. o. to seek refuge towards. — ه إلى
Manure mixed with earth. ذِئَار
To slaughter. To strangle a. o. To fill (a vessel). ذَأَط a ذَأْطًا
To die. ✲ ذَأَف a ذَأْفًا, وانْذَأَف
Quick death. مَوت ذُؤَاف
Death. Deadly (poison). ذَأْفَان
Deadly. ذَأْفَان وذِئْفَان وذُؤْفَان
To walk lightly. ✲ ذَأَل a ذَأْلًا وذَأَلَانًا
To become little. تَذَاءَل
Jackal. Wolf. ذَأْلَان وذُؤْلَان
Wolf. ذُؤَالَة ج ذِئْلَان وذُؤْلَان
To blame, to despise a. o. To drive away. To disgrace a. o. ✲ ذَأَم a ذَأْمًا ه
To frighten a. o. أَذْأَم ه
Vice, shameful action. ذَأْم وذَأَم
Bitter plant. Kind of fungus. ذُؤْنُون ج ذَآنِين
To remove a. o. To drive away (flies). To eject a. o. ✲ ذَبَّ o ذَبًّا ه
To protect a. th. or a. o. — وذَبَّب عن
To be parched (lips). To wane. To be faded (plant). To draw to its end (day). — i ذَبًّا وذَبَبًا وذُبُوبًا
To be full of flies (place). ذَبَّب وأَذَبّ
Restless. ذَبّ
Buffalo, wild bull. — وأَذَبّ وذِبَّب
Flies. Bees, breezes. ذُبَاب ج أَذِبَّة وذِبَّان وذُبّ و✧ دِبَّان

Madness. Plague. Consumption. Sharp edge. ذُبَاب
Cantharides. Blistering plaster. الذُّبَاب الهِنْدِي
A fly. Remainder of a debt. ذُبَابَة ج ذُبَابَات
Defender of women. ذَبَّاب وَمِذَبّ
Full of flies (place). أَرْض مَذْبُوبَة وَمَذَبَّة وَذَبُوبَة
Protracted (thirst). Hurrying. مُذَبِّب
Fly-whisk. مِذَبَّة
To dangle. ✱ ذَبْذَبَ
To protect. To annoy a. o. To move a. th. — ه و ه
Tongue. Dangling. ذَبْذَبَة ج ذَبَاذِب
Tassels of a litter ; fringes of a garment. ذَبَاذِب
Wavering (man). مُذَبْذَب
To rip open. To slaughter, to strangle a. o. To cover the chin (beard). ✱ ذَبَحَ a ذَبْحًا وذَبَاحًا ه وه
To slaughter, to massacre (people). ذَبَّحَ ه
To slay one another. تَذَابَحَ
To choose (a victim). إِذَّبَحَ ه
White truffles. Wild carrots. ذُبَّح
Slaughtered victim. ذِبْح
Two bright stars *in Capricornus*. سَعْد الذَّابِح
Diphteria. ذُبَاح وذِبَاح وذِبْحَة وذُبْحَة
Slaughtered. Victim. Surname of Ismael (*amongst Moslems*). ذَبِيح
Sacrifice, victim. ذَبِيحَة ج ذَبَائِح
Slaughter-place. Altar. مَذْبَح ج مَذَابِح
✧ Carnage, butchery. مَذْبَحَة
To write ; to dot (a book). To read over. ✱ ذَبَرَ i o ذَبْرًا وذَبَّرَ ه
To be good-sighted. ذَبِرَ i ذَبْرًا وذَبَارَة
To understand (news). To recite (verses). — ه
To get angry with. ذَبِرَ a ذَبَرًا على
Book. ذَبْر ج ذُبُور
Thoroughly learned. ذَابِر
To wither (plant). To dry up (skin); to be parched (lips). To be lean (horse). ✱ ذَبَلَ وذَبُلَ o ذُبُولًا وذَبَلًا
To cause a. th. to lose its freshness. To rumple a. th. ✧ ذَبَّلَ ه
To blight fruits (cold, heat). أَذْبَلَ ه

To waddle. To have a manly gait (woman). تَذَبَّلَ
Sea-turtle, tortoise-shell. ذَبْل
Dung. Withering wind. ذَبْلَة
Languid (eye). Weak. Lean. ذَابِل ج ذُبُل وذُبَّل
Spears. الذَّوَابِل
Wick. ذُبَالَة ج ذُبَال
To come from a journey. ✱ ذَجَّ o ذَجًّا
To slap a. o. To split (wood). To pound (pepper). ✱ ذَحَّ o ذَحًّا ه وه
To peel a. th. To sweep a. th. along (wind). To move a. th. ✱ ذَحَجَ o ذَحْجًا ه
To take care of (her son : widow). أَذْحَجَ على
To tot about quickly. ✱ ذَحْذَحَ
To sweep (the dust : wind). — ه
Revenge, hatred. ✱ ذَحْل ج أَذْحَال وذُحُول
To card (wool). To lash a. o. (wind). ✱ ذَحَى i ذَحْيًا ه وه
Treeless ground. مَذْحَاة
To put a. th. in store. ✱ ذَخَرَ a ذُخْرًا ه
To lay up a. th. To supply a. o. with stores. To prime (a gun). ✧ ذَخَّرَ ه
To put (goods) in store ✧ To adopt (a child). إِذَّخَرَ وادَّخَرَ ه وه
Stores, supply. ذُخْر ج أَذْخَار
Treasure. Stores. ذَخِيرَة ج ذَخَائِر
✧ Mouth and war ammunition. Relic. Priming of a gun.
✧ Adoptive child. اِبْن بِالذَّخِيرَة
Schœnantum, oderiferous rush. إِذْخِر ج أَذَاخِر
Magazine, store-house. مَذْخَر
Intestines. Veins. مَذَاخِر
To sprinkle a. th. with (salt, powder). To multiply (his faithful : God). ✱ ذَرَّ o ذَرًّا ه
To come forth (horn, herbage). To rise (sun). — o ذُرُورًا
To become hoary (man). — o وذَرَّ a
Atoms. Small ants, grubs. ذَرّ (*un.* ذَرَّة)
Aromatics, collyrium, perfume in powder. ذَرُور وذَرِيرَة ج أَذِرَّة وذَرَائِر
Calamus aromaticus, sweet rush. قَصَب الذَّرِيرَة

To swing the arms in walk. ذَرَّع في
To raise the arms. To stretch forth in (swimming).
To break (news) to. — لهُ شَيْئًا من
To sell to a. o. by the cubit. ذَارَع ة
To mingle with a. o.
To seize a. th. with the arm. أَذْرَع ه
To take out the arms from a cloak. — ه من تَحت الجُبَّة, واذَّرَع ه من الجُبَّة
To be profuse in speech. أَذْرَع وتَذَرَّع في الكَلَام
To measure with the arms. تَذَرَّع ه
To make long strides. إِنْذَرَع في
To screen o.'s self behind a. th. (hunter). إِسْتَذْرَع ب
Measure, length. Power. ذَرْع
Covetousness. Wild calf. ذَرَع ج ذِرْعَان
Fore-arm, fore-foot. ذِرَاع ج أَذْرُع وذُرْعَان
Cubit. Rod of cubit. Power.
ذِرَاع تُركي وإِسْتَانبُولي ومِعْمَاري
✧ Standard cubit of 29 1/2 inches.
✧ Common cubit of 22 3/4 inches. ذِرَاع بَلَدِي وعَرَبِي وهَاشِمِي
▫ Skein of thread, silk. ✧ ذِرَاع خَيط
Powerful, able. وَاسِع الذَّرْع او الذِرَاع
ضَاق بِالأَمر ذَرْعُهُ وذِرَاعُهُ وضَاق بِهِ ذَرْعًا
He fell short of the affair.
Walking by day and night ذَرِع م ذَرِعَة
Long-tongued. Good companion.
Means, ability. ذُرْعَة ج ذُرَع
Long-paced (horse, camel). ذَرُوع
Wide. Swift. Quick (death). ذَرِيع
Intercessor.
Camel used as a screen by a hunter. Means of. ذَرِيعَة ج ذَرَائِع
Mulatto. More eloquent. أَذْرَع
He has killed them quickly. قَتَلَهُم أَذْرَع قَتْل
Legs of a beast. Towns on the confines of the desert. مَذَارِع ومَذَارِيع
✡ ذَرَف i ذَرْفًا وذَرِيفًا وذُرُوفًا وذَرَفَانًا
To flow. To drop (tears). وتَذْرَافًا
To shed tears (eyes). ذَرَف العَيْن
To shed (tears : man). ذَرَّف تَذْرِيفًا وتَذْرَافًا وتَذْرِفَةً ه
To exceed a (number). — على
To make a. o. to be at the point of death. — فُلَانًا المَوْتَ
Flowing (tears). ذَرِيف ومَذْرُوف

Offspring. ذُرِّيَّة ج ذَرَارِيّ وذُرِّيَّات
Women.
Violent anger. ذِرَار
Sprinkler, drill-box. مُذَرَّة
To sow, to scatter (powder). ✡ ذَرْذَر ه
Babbler, loquacious. ذَرْذَار
To create. To multiply a. th. To sow (the ground). ✡ ذَرَأ a ذَرْءًا ة وه
To become grey on the forehead (hair). — وذَرِئ a ذَرَأً
To anger. To upbraid a. o. To shed (tears). أَذْرَأ ة وه
To compel a. o. to. — ة إلى
Little, a trifle, a rush. ذَرْء
They are created for hell-fire. هُم ذَرْء النَّار
Hoariness on the forehead. ذُرْأَة
Snow-white (salt). ذَرْآنِي وذَرَآنِي
White-headed (ram). أَذْرَأ م ذَرْءَاء
To be sharp (sword, tongue). To corrupt (wound). ✡ ذَرِب a ذَرَبًا وذَرَابَةً
To be in a good or corrupt state (stomach). — a ذَرَبًا وذَرَابَةً وذُرُوبَةً
To sharpen (a sword). ذَرَب o a ذَرْبًا وذَرَّب, وأَذْرَب ه
Tongue. Foul tongue. ذَرَب ج أَذْرَاب
Incurable disease. Rust. ▫ Diarrhea.
Ganglion on the neck. ذِرْب
Shoemaker's knife. ذَرِب ج ذُرُب
Sharp (man, sword).
Sharp-tongued. — اللِّسَان
Poison. ذُرَاب
To poison (food) with cantharides. ✡ ذَرَح a ذَرْحًا, وذَرَّح ه
To winnow a. th. ذَرَح ه
ذُرَاح وذُرُوح وذُرَّاح وذُرُّوح وذِرِّيح وذُرَح
وذُرُّوح وذَرِيحَة وذُرْنُوح ج ذَرَارِيح
Cantharides, spanish flies.
Purple red. أَحمَر ذَرِيحِيّ
To measure a. th. by the cubit. To stretch the fore-feet in walk (camel). To lower (a camel) for riding. To overcome a. o. (vomit). ✡ ذَرَع a ذَرْعًا ه
To strangle a. o. from behind. — وذَرَّع ة
To intercede with a. o. ذَرَع a ذَرْعًا عِند, وذَرِع a ذَرَعًا إلى

Inner corners of the eyes. مَذَارِف
To dung (bird). ✱ ذَرَق i o ذَرْقًا, وأَذْرَق
To produce trefoil (ground). أَذْرَق
Loranthus, mistletoe. ذَرَق الطَيْر
Sweet trefoil, melilot. ذُرَق
✱ ذَرَى o ذَرْوًا, وذَرَى i ذَرْيًا , وذَرَّى
To raise (the dust : wind). وأَذْرَى ه
To winnow, to scatter a. th. ذَرَى i وذَرَّى
To hasten. ذَرَا o ذَرْوًا
To praise o.'s origin. ذَرَّى حَسَبَهُ
To throw a. o. down (horse) أَذْرَى ه
To scatter (seeds). To shed (tears).
To be winnowed. تَذَرَّى
To ascend on the top of. To ally by marriage to (a noble tribe). — ه و ه
To shade o.'s self under a tree. To seek the protection of. إِسْتَذْرَى ب
Particles raised by the wind. ذَرًى
Poured tears. Shelter. Protection. Court-yard.
Broken particles of plants, straw. ذُرَاوَة
Apex, top. ذُرْوَة وذِرْوَة ج ذُرًى وذِرًى
Sweeping winds. (*un*. ذَارِيَة) ذَارِيَات
Prolific women.
Indian corn, maize. ذُرَة و✧ ذُرَا
Holcus sorghum, millet. ذُرَة و✧ ذُرَا صَيفِيّ وقَيْظِيّ وبَيْضَا
Zea mays, Indian corn. ✧ ذُرَة شَامِيّ وذُرَا وكَيْزَان
Yellow maize. ✧ ذُرَا مِصْرِيّ
Winnower's fork. مِذْرًى ومِذْرَاة ج مَذَارٍ
The two sides of the head. The two ends of a bow. The two buttocks. مِذْرَوَان
To appal a. o. (ghost). ✱ ذَعَب — تَذَعَّب
To run into a river (stream). إِنْذَعَب
To strangle a. o. ✱ ذَعَت a ذَعْتًا
To rub with dust. To repel forcibly.
To repel a. o. forcibly. ✱ ذَعَج a ذَعْجًا ه
To squander (wealth). ✱ ذَعْذَع ه
To divulge (a secret). To shake (the trees : wind).
To be scattered (hair). تَذَعْذَع
They dispersed on all sides. تَفَرَّقُوا ذَعَاذِع
To terrify a. o. ✱ ذَعَر a ذَعْرًا, وأَذْعَر ه
To be frightened. ذُعِر وتَذَعَّر وانْذَعَر
To be astounded. ذَعِر a ذَعَرًا
Panic, fear. ذُعْر
Wagtail (bird). ذُعَرَة
Hard (year). ذُعْرِيَّة
Vicious man. ذَاعِر وذُعْرَة وذُعَرَة وذُعُور
Frightened. ذُعُور
To kill a. o. unawares. ✱ ذَعَط a ذَعْطًا ه
Quick death. مَوْت ذَاعِط وذُعُوط
To poison a. o. ✱ ذَعَف a ذَعْفًا ه
To die. ذَعِف a ذَعَفًا
To kill a. o. suddenly. أَذْعَف ه
To be dazzled. To be broken (heart). إِنْذَعَف
Deadly (poison). ذَعْف وذُعَاف ج ذُعُف
Sudden death. ذَعَفَان
Poisoned food. طَعَام مَذْعُوف
To frighten a. o. by shrieking. ✱ ذَعَق a ذَعْقًا ه
Deadly disease. دَاء ذُعَاق
To acknowledge after denial. ✱ ذَعَل a ذَعْلًا
To glide away. To lay down. ✱ تَذَعْلَب
Swift she-camel. Ostrich. Hidden affair. Border of a garment. Rag. ذِعْلِب وذِعْلِبَة ج ذَعَالِيب
Kind of leek. Head-strong boy. Small bird. Kind of truffle. Small-mouthed ewe. ذُعْلُوق
To submit to a. o. ✱ ذَعِن a ذَعَنًا, وأَذْعَن ل
To acknowledge a. th. أَذْعَن ب
Submissive, tractable. مِذْعَان
To despatch (a wounded man). ✱ ذَفّ i ذَفًّا وذَفَفًا وذِفَافًا على
To be quick in. — في
To carry off a. o. (plague). — i ذَفًّا ه
To despatch (a wounded man). ذَفَّف وذَافّ وأَذَفّ ه وعلى
To lighten (a burden). ذَفَّف ه
To become possible (affair). إِسْتَذَفّ
Little of. ذَفّ وذِفَاف
Quick. Male hedgehog. Deadly (plague). ذَفِيف
To diffuse itself; to be pungent (odour). To multiply (plant). ✱ ذَفِر a ذَفَرًا
To resolve upon a. th. إِسْتَذْفَر ب

Pungency of odour. ذَفَر وذَفْرَة
Excellent (musk). ذَفِر وأذفَر ج ذُفْر
Army smelling rust. كَتِيبَة ذَفْرَاء
Back of the ear; ear-bone. ذِفْرَى ج ذِفْرَيات وذَفَارَى وذَفَار
Wild rue. ذَفْرَاء
✠ To strike a. o. on the chin. ✠ ذَقَن o ذَقْنًا ه
To lean the chin upon. — وذَقِن على
To have a prominent edge (bucket). ذَقِن a ذَقَنًا
To put a. o. in a strait. ذاقن ه
Chin ✧ Beard. ذَقَن وذَقِن ج أذقان
Wormwood. ✧ ذَقَن الشَيخ
Bearded man. ✧ بو ذَقَن
In spite of thee. ✧ غصبًا عن ذَقَنِك
Long-chinned. أذقَن م ذَقْناء ج ذُقْن
Decrepit old man. ذَقِن
Lower part of the chin. ذاقِنَة
✠ To keep in memory; to remember a. th. To mention a. th. To betroth (a woman). To speak ill or good of. ✠ ذَكَر o ذِكْرًا وتَذكارًا ه
To praise God. — الله
To render (a noun) masculine. To preach. To steel (the edge of a weapon). ✧ To impregnate (a palm-tree). ذَكَّر ه وه
To remind a. o. of. ذَكَّر وأذكَر ه
To discourse with a. o. upon. ذاكَر ه في
To bring forth male children (woman). أذكَرت
To remember a. th. تذكَّر ه
To confer upon. تذاكَر في
To recollect a. th. اذَّكَر وادَّكَر واذدكر ه
To learn a. th. by heart: to remember a. th. إستذكر ه
Remembrance. Memory. Fame, honour; mention. Invocation of God. Book of religious law. Rain. Strong man. ✧ Religious dance of dervishes. ذِكر
Legal deed; written ac' ذِكر الحَقّ
Remembrance. ذُكر
Remembering well. ذَكِر وذَكُر
Male, manly, masculine. Male organ. Good iron. Unproductive (palm-tree). Sharp (sword). ذَكَر ج ذُكُور وذُكُورة وذُكران
Bitter vegetables. ذُكور البَقل

Warning. Mention. ذِكْرَى
Steel (of a sword). Sharpness. Fame. ذُكْرَة
Memory. ذاكِرَة
Stronger, sharper; effective. أذكَر
Having a good memory. ذِكِّير وذَكُور وذِكِّير
Commemoration. تَذكار واستِذكار
Memorandum. Token of friendship.
✧ Ticket, note. تَذكِرَة ج تَذاكِر, ومَذكَرَة
✧ Personal status, certificate. تَذكِرَة نفوس
✧ Passport, way-leave. تذكِرَة مُرور
Bringing forth males (woman). مُذكِر
Virago. Dangerous (desert).
Masculine (gender). Sharp (sword). Terrible (day). مُذَكَّر
Deliberation, conference. مُذاكَرة
The aforesaid. مَذكور وسابِق الذِكر
✠ ذَكَا o ذُكُوًّا وذَكًا وذَكاء . واستذكى
To blaze vehemently (fire). To be hot (war, sun).
To be sagacious. ذَكِيَ a وذَكِيَ a وذَكُو o ذَكاء
To slaughter (a victim). — ذَكَا وذَكاةً ه
To diffuse itself (musk). — ذَكاء
To stir the (fire). To slaughter (a victim). ذَكَّى
To kindle (war, fire). أذكى ه
To send spies against. — العُيُون على
To be intense (fire). إستذكى
Legal slaughter. Live-coal. Sagacity. Age. ذَكا
Sun. ذُكاء
Dawn, daybreak. إبن ذُكاء
Combustible, fuel. ذُكْوَة وذَكِيَّة
Sagacious. Blameworthy. Fragrant (smell). ذَكِيّ ج أذكِياء
Cloud giving much rain. سَحابَة مُذكِيَة
Full-grown (horse). مُذكٍ ومُذكِي ج مَذاكٍ
✠ To be weak, base, obscure (man). ✠ ذَلّ i ذُلًّا وذِلَّة وذَلالَة ومَذَلَّة
To be tractable (beast). — i ذُلًّا وذِلًّا
To abase a. o. ذَلَّل وأذَلّ واستذَلّ ه
To be evenly disposed (branches). ذُلِّل
To become low, vile. To frequent vile companions. أذَلّ
To submit. To be humbled. تذلَّل
To hold a. o. as vile. إستذلّ ه
Humbleness. Weakness. ذُلّ وذَلالَة ومَذَلَّة

Gentleness, mercy. ذِلّ ج أذْلال
Let him remain in his humble state. دَعْهُ على أذْلالِهِ
Vile, weak, contemptible. Submissive. Trodden (road). Short. ذَلِيل ج أذِلّاء وأذِلّة
Good-natured. ذَلُولِيّ
To dangle. ✱ ذَلْذَلَ – تَذَلْذَلَ
Train, skirt of a garment. ذُلْذُل ج ذَلاذِل
Mob, lowest people. ذَلاذِل النّاس
Milk mixed with water. ✱ ذَلَح – ذُلّاح
To eat (food). ✱ ذَلَمَ a ذَلْمًا ه
To be small (nose). ✱ ذَلِفَ a ذَلَفًا
Smallness and evenness of the nose. ذَلَف
Small-nosed. Small (nose). أذْلَف م ذَلْفاء ج ذُلْف
To mute (bird) ✱ ذَلَقَ o ذَلْقًا وأذْلَقَ
To whet (a knife). To weaken a. o. (poison). To light (a lamp). – وأذْلَقَ ه وه
To shine (lamp). To be disquieted (man). ذَلِقَ
To be sharp (spear, tongue). ذَلِقَ a ذَلَقًا وذَلُقَ o ذَلاقَة
To be pointed (branch). إنْذَلَقَ
Point, edge, sharpness. ذَلْق وذَوْلَق
Sharp; eloquent tongue. ذَلَق وذُلُق وذَلِيق
Sharp (tooth, tongue). أذْلَق ج ذُلْق
The lingual letters. الذُّلْق والحُرُوف الذَّوْلَقِيّة
Sharp (spear-head). Milk mixed with water. مُذَلَّق
To blame a. o. ✱ ذَمَّ o ذَمًّا ومَذَمَّة ه
To flow with mucus (nose). ذَمَّ
To reprove a. o. ✧ To swear a. o. upon his conscience. ذَمَّمَ ه
To be content with a scanty (life). ذامَّ ه
To commit a blameworthy action. أذَمَّ
To judge blameworthy. To protect a. o. – ه و ه
To find protection against. – على
To avoid blame. تَذَمَّمَ
To keep aloof from. – من
To blame one another. تَذامَّ
To deserve blame, reproof. إسْتَذَمَّ
✧ To ask protection from a. o. – بِذِمامِهِ

Blame. Vice. ذَمّ ج ذُمُوم
Right, due. Honour. ذِمام ج أذِمّة
Protection enjoyed. Obligation, compact. Responsibility. Safe-conduct. Allied people. Wedding-dinner. ✧ Conscience. ذِمّة ج ذِمَم
✧ Upon my conscience. على ذِمَّتي وفي ذِمَّتي
✧ He owes so much. – على ذِمَّتِهِ كَذا
✧ I discharge my conscience, my debt. أبْرَى ذِمَّتي
✧ To clear a. o. from a charge بَرَّأ ذِمَّتَهُ
Thou art under God's protection. أنت في ذِمّة الله
Christians and Jews under Moslem protection. أهل الذِمّة
Client. Christian under Moslem rule, rayah. ذِمّي
Blameworthy. Pimples on the face. Urine. Dew. Distasteful water. ذَمِيم
Defect. Honour, self-respect. مَذَمّة
To be burdensome to. ✱ ذَمَأ a ذَمْأً على
To be changed and emaciated. ✱ ذَمَتَ i ذَمْتًا
To roar (lion). ✱ ذَمَرَ o ذَمْرًا
To instigate. To threaten a. o. – ه
To appraise a. th. ذَمَّرَ ه
To blame o.'self for neglect. تَذَمَّرَ
To grumble against (God). To threaten a. o. – على
To incite to fight. To blame one another. تَذَمَّرَ وتَذامَرَ
Clever and brave. ذَمِر وذِمْر وذَمِير ج أذْمار
Sacred things; honour, family. ذِمار
✱ ذَمَلَ o i ذَمْلًا وذَمِيلًا وذُمُولًا وذَمَلانًا
To walk gently (camel).
To drive (a camel) gently. ذَمَّلَ ه
Walking slowly. ذَمُول ج ذُمُل
Gentle walk of camels. ذَمِيل
To be intense (heat). ✱ ذَمِهَ a ذَمَهًا
To be exhausted by (heat). – ب
To writhe in agony (slaughtered beast). ✱ ذَمِيَ a وذَماء
To be in the pangs of death (man). ذَمَى i ذَمْيًا
To hasten. ذَمَى i ذَمَيانًا
To beat a. o. to death. أذْمَى ه
To rifle the property of. إسْتَذْمَى ما عِنْدَهُ

Appendix of a book. تَذْنِيب
Torrent. Brook. Long tail. Ladle. مِذْنَب ج مَذَانِب
Guilty, culprit. مُذْنِب
Walking at the rear. مُسْتَذْنِب ومُذَانِب
To depart, to pass along. To die. To be ended (affair). ✲ ذَهَب a ذَهَابًا وذُهُوبًا ومَذْهَبًا
To hold an opinion. To follow the opinion of. – إلى
To hold a belief. To adopt an opinion. ذَهَب مَذْهَب, مَذْهَب إلى, وتَمَذْهَب ب
To accompany a. o. To take away a. th. ذَهَب ب
To forget a. th. – على
To be amazed by the riches of a gold mine. ذَهِب a ذَهَبًا
To gild a. th. ذَهَّب وأَذْهَب ه
To take away a. th. أَذْهَب ه
Gold. Yolk. Measure for corn in Yemen. ذَهَب ج ذُهُوب ذُهْبَان وأَذْهَاب
Ceterach (plant). Golden-leaved vulnerary found in Lebanon. حَشِيشَة الذَّهَب
Ipecacuanha, emetic. عِرق الذَّهَب
Saint John Chrysostome. فَمُ الذَّهَب والذَّهَبِيّ الفَم
Light rain ; heavy rain. ذِهْبَة ج أَذْهَاب وذِهَاب وأَذَاهِيب
Sailing-boat on the Nile. ◻ ذَهَبِيَّة
Atriplex, orache. البَقْلَة الذَّهَبِيَّة
Piece of gold. Gold coin. (*un*.) ذَهَبَة
Golden. ذَهَبِي
Opinion, belief. Rite, sect. Way of acting. Origin. Privy. مَذْهَب ج مَذَاهِب
The four orthodox rites of Islam. مَذَاهِب الإسْلَام
Gilded bay (horse). كُمَيْت مُذْهَب
The Caaba. مُذْهَب
Alyssum, madwort (*plant*). مُذْهِب الكَلْب
To forget a. th. To be diverted from. ✲ ذَهَل a ذَهْلًا وذُهُولًا ه وعن
To be amazed. ذَهِل a ذُهُولًا, وانْذَهَل
To make a. o. to forget a. th. To divert a. o. from. أَذْهَل ه عن
First part of the night. ذَهْل وذُهْل
Amyris opobalsamum, balsam-tree of Mecca. ذُهْل
Horse of good breed. ذُهْلُول ج ذَهَالِيل
Forsaken place. مَذْهَل ج مَذَاهِل

Last remains of life. ذَمَاء
Stench, fetid odour. ذَمَى
To flow (mucus). To be weak, decrepit (man). ✲ ذَنَّ i ذَنِينًا وذَنَنًا
To flow from the nose (mucus). ذَنَّ a ذَنَنًا, وذَنَّن
To ask a. th. from. ذَانَّ ه على
Mucus from the nose. ذُنَان وذَنِين
Want. Small remainder. ذُنَانَة
Whose nose flows with mucus. أَذَنّ م ذَنَّاء ج ذُنّ
To track a. o. ✲ ذَنَب i o ذَنْبًا ه
To become spotted on its stalk (date). ذَنَّب
To make a tail to (a turban). To add an appendix to (a book). – ه
To commit an offence. أَذْنَب
To follow (a path). To make a tail to (a turban). To enter the end of (a valley). تَذَنَّب ه
To attribute (an offense) to. – على
To follow a. o. step by step. To find a. o. guilty. To impute an offense to. To pursue (an affair). إسْتَذْنَب ه
Offense, fault, sin. ذَنْب ج ذُنُوب
Tail. Extremity of a whip. ذَنَب وذَنَبَة ج أَذْنَاب
Sting of a scorpion. – العَقْرَب
Followers, servants. أَذْنَاب وذَنَبَات النَّاس
Species of *reseda*. ذَنَب الخَرُوف
Fox-tail (*plant*). ذَنَب الثَّعْلَب
Aristida (*plant*). ذَنَب الثَّوْر
Equisetum, horse-tail (*pla*.). ذَنَب الخَيْل
Scorpioide, scorpion-grass. ذَنَب العَقْرَب
Plantago, plantain. ذَنَب الفَارَة
Garden-purslain. ذَنَب الفَرَس
Circium, way-thistle. ذَنَب اللَّبْوَة والسَّبُع
To remain steadfast. ضَرَب بِذَنَبِهِ
✧ Comet. نَجم أَبُو ذَنَب
End, extremity. Bed of a stream. ذِنَاب ج ذَنَائِب
Kindred. ذَنَابَة
End of a valley. – وذُنَابَة وذَنَبَة
Following. ذَانِب
Bird's tail. ذُنَابَى وذِنَّبَى وذُنَبَى
Fine-tailed (horse). Tall and evil. Unhappy (day). Lot, portion. ذَنُوب
Kind of millet. (*un*. ذَنَبَانَة) ذَنَبَان
Darnel-grass. ذُنُوبَان وذُنَيْبَاء

✲ ذَهَن a ذَهْنًا To understand a. th.

— وأَذْهَن واسْتَذْهَن ه عن To divert a. o from.

ذَهُن o ذَهَانَة To have a good memory; to be clever.

ذَاهَنَ ه To surpass a. o. in sagacity.

اسْتَذْهَن ه To take away the intelligence (worldly love).

ذِهْن ج أذهان Understanding. Memory. Sagacity. Strength. Grease.

ذَهَن ج أذهان Prudence.

✲ ذَهَا o ذَهْوًا To be proud.

✲ ذُو (ذَوَى for) مث ذَوَان ج ذَوُون

Owner. Endowed with.

ذُو مَالٍ وعَقْلٍ Wealthy. Intelligent.

ذُو أَلْف وَرَقَة *Myriophyllon*, milfoil (*plant*).

ذُو ثَلَاث حَبَّات Medlar-tree.

ذُو ثَلَاث أَلْوَان *Menyanthes trifoliata*, bog-bean.

ذُو خَمْسَة أَجْنِحَة Cinque-foil, five-finger (*plant*).

ذُو خَمْسَة أَصَابِع *Vitex*, chaste-tree.

ذُو مَائَة شَوْكَة *Eryngium*, sea-holly.

ذَوُوهُ His relations. His people.

ذَاوُون وأَذْوَاء Kings of Yemen.

ذُو البَطْن وذَات البَطْن وبَنَات البَطْن The bowels.

ذُو القَرْنَيْن Alexander the Great.

ذَاتُ مث ذَوَاتَان ج ذَوَات (f. of ذُو)

Owner, mistress of. Belonging to.

ذَات الجَنْب والرِّئَة Pneumonia, pleurisy.

جَاء من ذِي ومن ذَات نَفْسِهِ و✧ مِن ذَاتِهِ He came from himself.

كَان ذَا مِن ذِي قَبْل It was in olden times.

ذَات الصُّدُور Hidden thoughts.

ذَات اليَد Wealth.

لَقِيتُهُ أَوَّل ذَات يَدَيْن I met him first of all.

جَلَسْتُ ذَات اليَمِين أو الشِّمَال I sat on the right or left.

ذَات صَبَاحٍ وذَات لَيْلَة A certain morning or night.

✲ ذَاب o ذَوْبًا وذَوَبَانًا To melt. To flow (tear). To become hot (sun). To feed on honey (man). To become foolish. To become emaciated.

ذَاب لِ على To be established with a. o. against another (right).

مَا ذَاب فِي يَدِي مِنْهُ خَيْر I have not got the least good from him.

ذَوَّب ه وه To melt a. th. ✧ To tire out.

أَذَاب ه To settle a business. To obtain (a want). To emaciate a. o. (cares).

— على To make a raid against.

إِسْتَذَاب ه وه To ask honey from. To let a. th. remain. To obtain (a want).

ذَوْب Honey.

ذَوْب الذَّهَب Gold-wash; liquid gold.

هَاجِرَة ذَوَّابَة Very hot noon.

إِذْوَاب وإِذْوَابَة Melted butter.

مِذْوَب Melting-vessel.

مِذْوَبَة ج مَذَاوِب Ladle.

✲ ذَات ج ذَوَات Essence. Substantive noun. One's self. ✧ Influential man.

ذَات الله The essence of God.

بِالذَّات وبِذَاتِهِ ✧ Identical. Personally. Himself; itself.

ذَاتِيّ Essential, personal.

✲ ذَاح o ذَوْحًا To walk firmly.

— ه To gather (flocks).

ذَوَّح ه وه To disperse (camels). To scatter a. th.

مِذْوَح Importune (man).

✲ ذَاد o ذَوْدًا وذِيَادًا , وذَوَّد ه عن To drive away. To dispel (grief) from.

أَذَاد إِذَادَة, وأَذْوَد إِذْوَادًا ه To help a. o. To defend a. th.

ذَائِد ج ذُوَّد وذُوَّاد وذَادَة, وذَوَّاد Defending his rights, honour.

ذَوْد She-camels from 3 to 10. (*s. pl.*)

مَذَاد Pasture-land.

مِذْوَد ج مَذَاوِد Manger. Bull's horn. Tongue (of man).

✲ ذَاذ — ذَاذِيّ *Hypericum*, St John's-wort.

✲ ذَاط o ذَوْطًا ه To strangle a. o. To fill (a vessel).

ذَوْطَة ج أذواط Yellow-backed spider.

✲ ذَاع o ذَوْعًا ه To squander (wealth).

أَذَاع ب To drink the contents of (a tank). To take away a. th.

✲ ذَاف o ذَوْفًا To straddle along.

✲ ذَاق o ذَوْقًا وذَوَاقًا ومَذَاقًا ومَذَاقَة ه

To taste a. th. To try a. o. or a. th. To experience (a trial).

أَذَاق ه ه To make a. o. to taste a. th.

Dung mixed with earth. ذِيَرَة

☆ ذَاعَ i ذَيْعًا وذُيُوعًا وذَيَعَانًا وذَيْعُوعَة
To spread (news, disease).

To reveal (a secret). أَذَاعَ هـ

To manifest a. th. To exhaust (a tank). To take away a. th. — ب

Unable to keep a secret. مِذْيَاع ج مَذَايِيع

To drag (a garment). ☆ ذَالَ i ذَيْلًا

To drag the tail (dove). To strut and drag (his gown : man). To become lean (woman). To be abased. To be lowered (man, state).

To put a long skirt to (a dress). ذَيَّلَ وأَذَالَ إِذَالَةً هـ

To write on the margin of. ذَيَّلَ هـ

To despise a. o. To emaciate (a woman). To use (a horse, a boy) for mean works. To squander (money). To shed (tears). أَذَالَ ه

To let down (her veil; woman). — هـ

To walk proudly. To wag the tail. تَذَيَّلَ

To be low, humble (state). تَذَايَلَ

Extremity. Skirt. Appendix of a book. Tail. Drift of sand. ذَيْل ج ذُيُول وأَذْيَال وأَذْيُل

Rich. طَوِيل الذَّيْل

Refuse of the people. أَذْيَال النَّاس

Long-tailed (horse). Wild bull. ذَيَّال

Appendix of a book. تَذْيِيل

Female-slave. مُذَالَة

Long-skirted (garment). Annotated (book). مُذَيَّل

To blame a. o. ☆ ذَامَ i ذَيْمًا وذَامًا ه

Blame, vice, defect. ذَأْم وذَيْم وذَيْن

To make a. o. to experience a. th.

To taste time after time. تَذَوَّقَ

To hand (spears) to o. a. To taste a. th. تَذَاوَقَ هـ

To try a. o. إِسْتَذَاقَ ه

Taste, relish. ذَوْق وذَائِقَة ومَذَاق

Intellectual relish, good taste. ذَوْق وذَوَاق

✧ Palate, taste; tact. مَذَاق

To write the letter ذ. ☆ ذَالَ — ذَوَّلَ

The letter ذ. Cocks'-crest. ذَال

To become rich and easy. ☆ ذَانَ — تَذَوَّنَ

To be faded (plant). ☆ ذَوَى i وذَوِيَ a ذُوِيًّا

To wither herbage (sun). أَذْوَى إِذْوَاء هـ

Small ewes. ذَوِي

Rind of melons; grape-skins. ذُوَاة

To cook (meat) thoroughly. ذَيَّا هـ تَذْيِيًا

To be thoroughly cooked (meat). To become corrupt (wound). To be worn out (skin). To swell (face). تَذَيَّا

Much water. Fright. Liveliness. ☆ ذِيب — أَذْيَاب

So and so, thus and thus. ☆ ذَيْتَ ذَيْتَ

To pass swiftly. ☆ ذَاحَ i ذَيْحًا

To drink a. th. — هـ

To drink with a. o. ذَايَحَ ه

To abase a. o. ☆ ذَيَّخَ ه

To go round (a place). أَذَاخَ ب

Gold. Wolf. Fine mare. Red star *in Draco*. Proud. Thick-haired male hyena. ذِيخ ج ذُيُوخ وأَذْيَاخ وذِيخَة

To loathe a. th. ☆ ذَارَ a ذَيْرًا

To smear (the teats) with dung. ذَيَّرَ هـ

ر

✱ رَأرَأ To turn the eyes ; to gaze. To glisten (eyes). To look in a mirror. To shine (mirage). To wag the tail.

✱ رَأب a رَأبًا ه To produce trefoil after the crop (field).

— ه To repair (a. th. broken). To settle (a business).

رَأب بَيْنَهُم He made peace between them.

أرْأب ه To arrange, to repair a. th.

رَأب Lusty lord.

— ج رِئاب Herd of seventy camels.

رُؤْبَة ج رِئاب Patch, piece of wood. Part of the night. Want.

رَاب ومِرْأب Repairer, rectifier.

✱ رَأبَل To incline on one side in walk.

رِئبال ج رَآبِل ورَآبِيل Lion, wolf.

✱ رَأد o رُؤُودَة To be supple (branch).

تَرَأّد To incline (branch). To bend (neck). To be unsteady (wind). To tremble in rising (old man).

— وارْتَأد To incline languidly (youth).

رَأد ورَائِد Time after sunrise.

رَأد ورَأدَة ورُؤد ورُؤْدَة Delicate maid.

رُؤد Suppleness of temper.

رِئد ج أرْآد Coeval. Straitness. Offset.

✱ رَأس i رِئاسَة ه To be the chief of (a tribe).

— a رَأسًا ه To strike a. o. on the head.

رَؤُس o رِئاسَة To be a chief.

رُئِسَ To have a complaint of the head.

رَأس و✧ رَيَّس ه على To make a. o. chief; to set a. o. over.

تَرَأّس وارْتَأس و✧ تَرَيَّس To become a chief.

إرْتَأس ه To bend down the head of a. o. To busy a. o.

— ه To seize a. th. by the top.

رَأس ج أرْؤُس ورُؤُوس Head. Head (of cattle); individual. Chief. Uppermost part. Cape, headland. Numerous tribe. Head (of garlic). Upper end of a road. Beginning. ✧ Loaf (of sugar).

رَأس الشَّهر والسَّنَة First day of a month. New year's day.

رَأس العَيْن ورَأس النَّبْع Source, spring.

رَأس القُنْفُذ *Spina alba*, whitethorn.

رَأس الهُدْهُد Kind of orchis.

رَأس الهِرّ *Galeopsis*, hemp-nettle.

رَأس الأفْعَى *Echium* viper's bugloss.

حَبّ الرَّأس Staves-acre, lousewort.

رَأسًا Altogether. Directly.

على الرَّأس والعَيْن With pleasure.

وُلِد على رَأس أخِيهِ He was born next to his brother.

✧ مِن تَحت رَأس On the plea, on account of.

رَأس المال و✧ رَسْمَال Capital-stock.

✧ رَسْمَل To capitalise.

رَئِيس ورَيِّس ج رُؤَساء Chief. ✧ Abbot. Captain of a ship.

الشَّيخ الرَّئِيس Surname of Avicenna.

رَئِيس العُلُوم Science of logics.

الأعضاء الرَّئِيسَة The vital parts of the body.

رَوائِس Upper end of a valley. Foremost clouds

رَآَّس Butcher dealing in heads.

✧ رَأسِيَّة Head-rope, halter.

رِئاسَة Authority, power.

ذُو الرِّيَاسَتَيْن Having both temporal and spiritual authority. Foremost in science and courage.

أرْأس ورُؤاسِيّ Large-headed. Black-headed (ewe).

مَرْؤُوس Subject, subordinate. Big-headed. Hurt in the head.

مِرْآس Horse ahead in a race.

✱ رَأف a رَأفَة , ورَؤُف o رَآفَة, و رَئِف a رَأفًا, ورَأف وتَرَأّف ب To be merciful towards; to pity a. o.

رَأف واسْتَرْأف ه To conciliate a. o.

رَأفَة Mercy, compassion.

رَؤُف ورَأف ورَؤُوف ورَئِف ورائِف Merciful.

✱ رال – إسْتَرْأل To grow (herbage, young ostrich).

رَأل ج أرْؤُل و رِئْلان و رِئال ورِئالَة Ostrich

one year old.

Foam, slaver of beasts. رؤال ورؤول

He passed along quickly. مرّ مُرائلا

To repair a. th. ✱ رأم a رأما ه

To cicatrise (wound). رئم a رأما و رئمانا

To fondle (her young : beast). ه —

To be fond of, to keep to a. th. — a رأما ه

To heal a (wound). To accustom (a she-camel) to a strange young one. To twist (a rope). أرأم ه وه

To compel a. o. to. — ه على

To compassionate a. o ترأم ه

Stuffed skin of a young camel. رأم

White antelope, white gazelle. رئم ج أرآم وآرام

Fondling her young (female). رائم ورائمة ورؤوم

Familiar, licking ewe. شاة رؤوم

Slaver of beasts. رؤام

To see; to think a. th. To hold the opinion of. ✱ رأى يرى رأيا ورؤية وراءة و رئيانا ه

Do, tell me thou, ye. أرأيتك أرأيتكم

Behold! Lo! ألم تر

Most of all. لا ترما ولم ترما واو ترما

I should like to know. Dost thou think that? يا ترى و يا هل ترى و ✧ ياريتني

To judge, to know a. o. or a. th. to *be so*. — ه ه وه ه

To wound a. o. in the lungs. To stick (a flag). — رأيا ه وه

To see a dream, a vision. — رؤيا

To dissemble with. To consult with. To present a mirror to. رآى ه

To act hypocritically with. راءى مراءاة ورئاء ه

To face, to front a. th. — ه

To look in a mirror. To dissemble. To have a complaint of the lungs. To have dreams. To have a good judgment. To show signs of madness. To twinkle. To follow the opinion of lawyers. أرأى إرءاء

To show a. th. To advise a. th. to a. o. أرى إراءة وإراء ✧ أورى وورّى ه ه

To mirror. To show o.'s self. ترأى وتراءى

To see one another. تراءى

To consider a. th. — وارتأى في

To consider a. th. To doubt about. To arrange a. th. إرتأى ه

To consult a. o. To wish to see a. th. إستراى ه

Advice; idea. Skill. رأي ج آراء وأرآء

Schismatics. Prudent men. أهل الرأي

Sardin, pilchard. ◘ راي

Aspect, appearance. رئي وري وزيّ

Sign, symptom. راءة

Dream, vision. رؤيا ج رؤى

The Apocalypse of St John. سفر الرؤيا ورؤيا يوحنا

Sight. Phasis of the moon رؤية و رئية ج رؤى

Hypocrisy. Opposite. رئاء

They seem to be a thousand. هم رئاء ألف

Houses situated opposite. بيوت رئاء

Lung. رئة ج رئون و رئات

✧ Pulmonary, lung-wort. حشيشة الرئة

Beholder; spectator. راء ورآء

Familiar demon. Large snake. رئي

He is fitter, apter to. هو أرأى ب

Beauty of aspect. ترئية ورئي

Mirror. View. مرآة و✧ مراية ج مراء ومرايا

Look, aspect. مرأى ومرآة

He is under my eyes. هو مني مرأى او بمرأى

Hypocrite. مراء ج مراؤون

To collect a. th. To possess a. th. To rule (people). To have authority over. ✱ رب o ربّا ه و ه

To increase a. th. To complete (a benefit). — ه

To perfume (an ointment). — ربّا وربّا ه

— ربّا وربّب تربيبا وتربّة، وتربّب وارتبّ ه

To bring up a child.

To preserve a. th. with rob. ربّب ه

To last (south wind, rain). أربّ

To remain in (a place). أربّ ب

To claim mastership over. تربّب ه

The Lord (God). Master ربّ ج أرباب

✧ Creditors. أرباب الديون

Ministers of state. أرباب الدولة

Lady, mistress. Female idol. Large house. ✧ Scald-head. ربّة

Alexandrian trefoil. Locust-tree. Large crowd. ربّة ج أربة و رباب

رُبّ ج رِبَاب ورُبُوب Rob, inspissated juice of fruits.
رُبَّ ورُبَّةَ ورُبَّمَا ورُبَّتَمَا Often, many a time. Seldom. ✧ Perhaps.
رَابّ Step-father.
رَابَّة Step-mother.
رَبَاب و✧ رَبَابَة Viol. Single-stringed violin. White cloud.
رِبَاب Covenant. Friends. Tithes.
رَبُوب Step-son. Step-father.
رِبَابَة Lordship. Covenant. Government. Collection of arrows.
رَبِّيّ ورَبَّانِيّ ورَبُوبِيّ Lordly. Divine.
رُبَّى ج رُبَاب Ewe after bringing forth. Beneficence. Wealth. Want. Tight knot.
رَبُوبِيَّة Lordship, mastership. ✧ Swelling in the arm-pit.
رَبَّان ورُبَّان The whole : beginning.
رَبِيب ج أَرِبَّة Slave. Step-father ; step-son. Confederate.
رَبِيبَة ج رَبَائِب Foster-mother. Step-daughter. Domesticated ewe.
مَرْبُوب White slave. Reared (child).
مَرَبّ Gatherer. Abode ; meeting-place.
— ومِرْبَاب Ground covered with plants.
مُرَبَّى ج مُرَبَّيَات Preserve, confection.
✱ رَبَأَ a رَبْأً To ascend, to rise. To walk sluggishly.
— ه To take care of. To take away. To remove a. th.
— في To consider (an affair).
— وارْتَبَأ على To look out. To overlook a. th.
إِرْبَأْ بِهِ Do keep it, take cure of it.
مَا رَبَأْتُ رَبْأَهُ I did not know nor desire it.
رَبَأَ ب عن To remove a. o. or a. th. from.
— ه ول, وارْتَبَأ ه To watch, to stand on the look out for.
رَبَأَ تَرْبِئَةً ه To take away a. th.
رَابَأَ ه وه To watch a. o. To caution o.'s self against. To guard a. o.
رَبِيء ورَبِيئَة ج رَبَايَا Watch, scout.
مَرْبَأ ومِرْبَأ ومَرْبَأَة ومُرْتَبَأ Look out ; watch-tower.
✱ رَبَتَ i رَبْتًا ورَبَّتَ ه To rear (a child). To pat (a child).

رَبِتَ a رَبَتًا To be closed, shut.
✱ رَبَثَ o رَبْثًا, ورَبَّثَ ه عن To hold a. o. back from.
تَرَبَّثَ وارْتَبَثَ To be dilatory.
إِرْتَبَثَ To separate (people).
إِرْبَثَ To scatter (sheep).
رَبِيثَة ج رَبَائِث Delusion. Hindrance.
رَبِيث ومَرْبُوث ومُرَبَّث Hindered.
✱ رَبِجَ a o i رَبَاجَة To be rough, silly.
رَبَاجِيّ Rough. Braggart.
✱ رَبِحَ a رِبْحًا ورَبَحًا ورَبَاحًا To gain ; to be lucrative (goods).
رَابَحَ وأَرْبَحَ ه على وب To give a profit to a. o. upon.
أَعْطَاهُ مَالًا مُرَابَحَةً He lent him money for a share in the profit.
تَرَبَّحَ To be astounded. To seek profits.
رِبْح ج أَرْبَاح Profit, gain.
رَبَح Gain at play. Horses for sale.
رَبَاح Profit. Civet-cat.
رَبَاحِيّ Kind of camphor.
رَابِح Lucrative (goods).
رُبَح ورُبَّاح ج رَبَابِيح Male ape. Kid. Weaned camel.
مُرَابَحَة ✧ Agiotage.
✱ رَبَخَ a رَبْخًا في To trudge in (the sand : camel).
✱ رَبَدَ o رُبُودًا ب To stay in (a place).
— ه To confine a. o.
تَرَبَّدَ To become cloudy (sky). To be altered (face). To be stern (face).
إِرْبَدَّ وارْبَادَّ To be ash-coloured.
أَرْبَد م رَبْدَاء ج رُبْد Dust-coloured. Malignant snake. Lion.
رَبْد ورُبَيْدَان *Buphtalmus graveolens*, ox-eye (*plant*).
رَبِيد Dates sprinkled with water.
رُبْدَة ج رُبَد Dust-colour.
مِرْبَد Enclosure. Drying-floor.
✱ رَبِدَ a رَبَدًا ب To be light in (work).
أَرْبَدَ ه To cut a. th.
رَبِد Swift in walk.
رِبْدَة ورَبَذَة ج رِبَاذ Wool for rubbing camels. Rag for cleaning. Knot of a whip.
✱ رَبَسَ o رَبْسًا ه ب To slap a. o. with.
— ه To fill a (water-skin).
إِرْتَبَسَ To be compact. To be mixed.

✧ To engage, to secure a. th. — على
To persevere in. رَابَطَ مُرَابَطَةً ورِبَاطًا ه To be stationed on (the enemy's frontier: army).
To stop in (a place: water). تَرَابَطَ في
✧ To plot with a. o. against. تَرَابَطَ مَعَ To bind o.'s self with.
✧ To bind o'.s self. — وارْتَبَطَ
To take (a horse) for stationing it. إِرْتَبَطَ ه
Tie, bond. Heart. Inn; رِبَاط ج رُبُط station for horses. ✧ Asylum for the poor. Bandage. Suspense of a clergyman.
To die. To recover from illness. قَرَضَ رِبَاطَهُ
✧ Necktie. Nosegay. Plot. رَبْطَة ج رَبَطَات
Monk, ascetic, religious. رَابِط ورَبِيط
Strong-hearted. رَابِط ورَبِيط الجَأْش
Tie. Copula (*in logics*). ✧ Agreement. رَابِطَة
Stationed horses. ✧ Plot. رَبِيطَة
Station for horses. مَرْبَط ج مَرَابِط
Bond, tie, rope. مِرْبَط ومِرْبَطَة
Leagued people; military station. مُرَابَطَة ج مُرَابَطَات
The final ت written ة. التَّاء المَرْبُوطَة
To await. To restrain o'.s self. To drink every fourth day (camels). ✧ To gallop (horse). ✱ رَبَعَ a رَبْعًا
To come on the fourth day (fever). To feel sympathy for. — على
To make a four-stranded rope. رَبَعَ i o a ه
To complete the number four. — ه To be the fourth, fourtieth or forty fourth with. To take the fourth from.
To abstain, to desist from. — عن
To remain quietly in. To pasture freely in (a place: camels). — ب وفي
To have the quartan ague. To have spring-rain, spring-herbage. رُبِعَ
To make a. th. square, four-faced, four-footed. رَبَّعَ ه
✧ To feed (horses) on green food — ه
To lift (a load) with a lever. رَابَعَ ه
To become the farmer of a. o. — ه

To act in o.'s own way. إِرْتَبَسَ في
Misfortune. Much. رَبْس
Great misfortune. رَبْسَاء ج رُبْس
Courageous. Calamity. رَبِيس
Rheum ribes, kind of gooseberry. رِيبَاس
To become bushy (tree). ✱ ربش — أَرْبَشَ
Ground covered with herbs. أَرْض رَبْشَاء
✱ رَبَصَ o رَبْصًا ب، وتَرَبَّصَ ل To await a. o. or a. th. To lay in wait for.
To stick to (a place). تَرَبَّصَ في
To desist from (an affair). — عن
Expectation. Mixed colour. رُبْصَة
✧ رَوْبَصَ ه To refine (silver). ✧ To set a. o. to rights.
Refined silver. ✧ رُوبَاص
✱ رَبَضَ i رَبْضًا ورَبْضَةً ورُبُوضًا To lay down, to cower (beast).
To crouch over (its prey: lion). — على
To alight at. — o i رَبْضًا ورُبُوضًا ه وه
To detain a. o. in. رَبَّضَ ه ب
To become hot (sun). أَرْبَضَ
To park (cattle). To sustain (o.'s people). To render a. o. drowsy (wine). — ه
To cling to a place (cripple). تَرَبَّضَ
Wife, mother or sister. رَبْض ورُبْض ورُبُض ورَبَض
Middle of a thing. Foundation. رُبْض
Wall of a town. Suburbs. Palace. رَبَض ج أَرْبَاض
Intestines. Enclosure for cattle. رُبْضَة ورَبَضَة
The Turks and the Ethiopians. الرَّابِضَان
Heap of corpses. Corpse. Cripple, impotent. رِبْضَة
Large (tree). Populous (village). Big (chain). رَبُوض ج رُبُض
Flocks parked with their shepherds. رَبِيض ج رِبَاض
Safflower. تِرْبَاض
✱ رَبَطَ o i رَبْطًا ه وه To tie, to bind a. th. ✧ To suspend (a clergyman). To lay (anchor).
To be heartened. — جَأْشُهُ رِبَاطَةً
God has strengthened his heart. رَبَطَ الله على قَلْبِهِ
✧ To be a highway robber. — الطَّرِيق
✧ To lay in wait against. — ل

for the fourth of the produce.
To enter its fourth year (sheep); its fifth (horse, oxen); its seventh (camel). To be in the spring. To go to water on the fourth day. To be four in number. أَرْبَعَ
To have the quartan ague. أُرْبِعَ
To sit cross-legged. تَرَبَّعَ فِي الجُلُوسِ
To be fattened. To feed on grass (horse). — وارْتَبَعَ
To spend the spring in (a place). إِرْتَبَعَ و ✧ رَبَّعَ بِ
To heap up (sand). To rise (dust). إِسْتَرْبَعَ
Abode. House. Spring-encampment. Bier. رَبْعٌ ج رُبُوعٌ ورِبَاعٌ وأَرْبُعٌ
Fourth part. Measure of 3. 63 gallons. رُبْعٌ ج أَرْبَاعٌ
Watering of camels every fourth day. رِبْعٌ
Camel born in the spring. رُبَعٌ ج رِبَاعٌ وأَرْبَاعٌ
Quartan ague. حُمَّى الرِبْعِ
Middle-sized (man). رَبْعَةٌ (*m. f.*) ج رَبْعَاتٌ ورَبَعَاتٌ ورِبَعٌ
Gallop. Distance of a race. رَبَعَةٌ
✧ Fourth of a measure. رُبْعِيَّةٌ
Ranunculus, golden-cup (*plant*). ✧ رُبْعِيَّةٌ
Fourth. رَابِعٌ م رَابِعَةٌ ج رَابِعَاتٌ ورَوَابِعُ
✧ Noontide, broad light. رَابِعَةُ النَّهَارِ
Well-being. رَبَاعٌ
Good state. Habit. Authority. رِبَاعَةٌ
رَبَاعٍ ج رُبْعٌ ورُبُعٌ ورِبْعَانٌ م رَبَاعِيَةٌ ج رَبَاعِيَاتٌ Toothless (beast).
Two teeth near the incisors. رَبَاعِيَةٌ ج رَبَاعِيَاتٌ
Composed of four; four and four. رُبَاعَ
Quadriliteral; four cubits high. رُبَاعِيٌّ
Spring. Autumn. رَبِيعٌ ج أَرْبِعَةٌ ورِبَاعٌ
Spring-herbage; spring-rain; water-spring, source. ✧ Farmer, partner.
Share of water. — ج أَرْبِعَاءُ
Fourth part. — ج رُبُعٌ
Luxuriant spring. رَبِيعٌ رَابِعٌ ورَبِيعٌ رَابِغٌ
Name of the third and fourth month of the Arabian year. Autumn and spring. رَبِيعٌ الأَوَّلُ ورَبِيعٌ الآخِرُ
Hoopoe (bird). أَبُو الرَّبِيعِ

Stone lifted for trying strength. Garden. Iron helmet. رَبِيعَةٌ
Pertaining to spring. رَبِيعِيٌّ ورِبْعِيٌّ
Four. أَرْبَعَةٌ م أَرْبَعٌ
Quadrupeds. ذَوَاتُ الأَرْبَعِ
Wednesday. أَرْبِعَاءُ ج أَرْبِعَاءَاتٌ وأَرْبِعَاوَاتٌ
Forty. Fourtieth. أَرْبَعُونَ
Fast of lent. صَوْمُ الأَرْبَعِينَ والصَّوْمُ الأَرْبَعِينِيُّ
Spring-rain. Spring-abode. مَرْبَعٌ ج مَرَابِعُ، ومُرْتَبَعٌ
Lever, crow-bar. مِرْبَعٌ ومِرْبَعَةٌ ج مَرَابِعُ
Bringing forth in the spring (she-camel). Sails of a ship. مُرْبِعٌ
Suffering from quartan fever. مُرْبَعٌ ومَرْبُوعٌ
Square, four-sided, four-footed. ✧ Upper-room. Anchor. Plot of land. مُرَبَّعٌ
✧ Farmer, partner. مُرَابِعٌ
Fourth part of spoils. Full of spring-herbage (land). مِرْبَاعٌ
Of a middling stature. — ومَرْبُوعٌ
Jerboa, fieldrat. يَرْبُوعٌ ج يَرَابِيعُ
To lead a luxuriant life. ✡ رَبَغَ a رَبْغًا
To be luxuriant (life). رَبِغَ a رَبَغًا
To let (camels) drink at pleasure. أَرْبَغَ ه
Luxuriant (life). رَابِغٌ
Plenty, abundance. رَبَاغَةٌ
Plentiful, abundant. أَرْبَغُ
To tie (a kid) by the neck. ✡ رَبَقَ o i رَبْقًا، ورَبَّقَ ه
To throw a. o. into (an affair). — ه فِي
To embellish speech. رَبَّقَ الكَلَامَ
To hang a. th. on the neck. تَرَبَّقَ ه
He was caught in a snare. إِرْتَبَقَ فِي حِبَالَةٍ
To be implicated in a business. — فِي أَمْرٍ
Noose. Snare. رِبْقٌ وتَرْبِيقٌ
Loop of a rope. رِبْقَةٌ ورَبْقَةٌ ج رِبَقٌ وأَرْبَاقٌ ورِبَاقٌ
Beast caught in a noose. رَبِيقَةٌ
Bread and grease. مُرَبَّقَةٌ
To mix a. th. To make (a soup). ✡ رَبَكَ o رَبْكًا ه
To throw a. o. into mire. — ه
To be entangled in an affair. رَبِكَ a رَبَكًا
To be mixed, confused. To be intricate (business). إِرْتَبَكَ وارْبَاكَّ

To struggle in (a snare). To be impeded in (speech). To trudge in (mire). في —

Implicated in an affair. رُبِكَ ورَبِكَ ورَبِيك ومُرتَبِك

Mire. Dates and butter. رَبِيكة

✻ To multiply. To have many children, flocks. رَبَل o i رَبْلًا

To produce autumnal plants (land). رَبَّل وأرْبَل

To be fleshy. To eat, to seek for autumnal plants. To become green in autumn (land). To hunt. تَرَبَّل

To be plentiful (goods). إرتَبَل

Autumnal shrubs, herbage. رَبْل ج رُبُول

Flesh of the thighs. رَبْلَة ورَبَلَة ج رَبَلات

Pulicaria, kind of flea-bane. رَبَل

Audacious thief. رِبْيل م رَبِيلة

Moistness. Fatness. Depression. Comfort. رَبِيلة

Fatness, fleshiness. رَبَالَة ورَبِيلة

Luxurious life. رَبِيلَة العَيش

Daring (brigand). Ferocious (lion). Infirm (old man). Tall and creeping plant. رِيبَال ج رَيَابِيل

Ground abounding with autumnal trees, shrubs. مِربَال

✻ To give a pledge. ربن — أرْبَن ه

To be the captain of a ship. تَرَبَّن

Ship-captain. رُبَّان ورُبَّانِيّ ج رَبَابِنَة

Earnest, pledge. رُبُون وأرْبُون وأرْبَان

✻ To increase (wealth). رَبَا o رِبَاء ورُبُوًّا

To ascend (a hill). ه —

To grow up. To be educated (child). رُبُوًّا ورَبْوًا, ورَبَى رَبَاء ورَبِيًّا —

To swell from fear or running (horse). To be out of breath. o رَبْوًا —

To foster (a child). To make preserves. رَبَّى تَرْبِيَة, وتَرَبَّى ه و ه

To lend to a. o. upon usury. To fondle a. o. رَابَى مُرَابَاة ه

To practice usury. To exceed the measure. أرْبَى

To increase a. th. To give hope to. ه وه —

Usury, unlawful profit. رِبًى

Favour, merit. رَبَاء

Hill. رَبْوَة ج رُبًى ورُبِيّ, ورَابِيَة ج رَوَابٍ

Ten thousand, myriad. رِبْوَة ج رِبْوَات

Hill. رَبَاة ورَبَاوَة

Asthma. Loud breathing. رَبْو ج أرْبَاء

Relations, family. Root of the thigh. أرْبِيَّة

Lobster, prawn, squill. إرْبِيَان

Chrysantemum, corn-marigold. بَهَار إرْبِيَان

Usurer. مُرَابٍ

✧ Preserves, confections. مُرَبَّى ج مُرَبَّيَات

✻ To stammer. رَتَّ a رَتَتًا

To make a. o. to stammer (God). أرَتّ ه

Impediment of speech. رُتَّة

Stammerer. أرَتّ م رَتَّاء ج رُتّ

Chief. Prince. رَتّ ج رِتَّان ورُتُوت

Swine, boar. — ج رُتُوت

✻ To tighten (a knot). رَتَا a رَتْوًا ه

To strangle a. o. ه —

To walk with short steps (camel). — رَتَا ـ

✻ To stammer, to stutter. رَتْرَت

✻ To be fast, fixed. رَتَب o رُتُوبًا وتَرَتَّب

To stand up (in prayer) رَتِب o رَتَبًا ورُتُوبًا

To fasten a. th. To put in order. To organise. ✧ To assign (a pension). رَتَّب ه

To stand up (man). To be reduced to beggary. أرْتَب

To be fast; set in order. تَرَتَّب

✧ It results from it. تَرَتَّب عَلَيْهِ

Difficulty. Prominence of ground; rocks. Measure of the four fingers close together. Space between the third and the little finger extended. رَتَب

Step of stairs. Rank, dignity. ✧ Ritual. Religious service. رُتْبَة ج رُتَب

Earth. Unmovable thing. تُرْتُب وتُرْتَب

Bad slave. Perpetuity. تُرْتَب

They came all together. جَاءُوا تُرْتُبًا

✧ Pension, pay. رَاتِب ج رَوَاتِب ومُرَتَّب

Religious services. Offices. رَوَاتِب

Look out. High rank. ✧ Platform. Bench covered with a mattress. مَرْتَبَة ج مَرَاتِب

✻ To lock (a door). رَتَج o رَتْجًا, وأرْتَج ه

To begin to walk (child) — رَتَجَانًا

To be impeded in speech. رَتِج a رَتَجًا

أرتج To be full of eggs (hen). To overrun (waves). To be good (harvest). To fall incessantly (snow). To be barren (year).

أرتِج وارتُتِج واستُرتِج على To be impeded in (speech).

رِتج Without egress (road). In store (money).

رَتَج ورِتاج Large gate having a wicket.

رِتاجة ج رَتائِج Rock. Narrow-pass.

مَرَاتِج (*pl.*) Narrow roads.

مِرتاج Wooden-bolt.

☆ رَتَخ a رُتوخا To be diluted (flour, mud).

— ب To settle in (a place).

— عن To desist from.

رَتَخة Mire.

☆ رَتَع a رَتْعا ورُتوعا و رِتاعا To have their fill (cattle). To find pasturages. To enjoy a luxuriant life (man).

أرتَع To have good pasture (land). To send forth pasturage (land).

— ه To let (cattle) pasture freely.

رَتْعَة Plenty, abundance.

رَاتِع ج رِتاع ورُتَع ورُتَّع ورُتوع ورَاتِعُون Pasturing freely (cattle). Leading an easy life (man).

أرتاع Crowd of people.

مَرتَع ج مَرَاتِع Place of plenty. Pasturage.

☆ رَتَق o رَتْقا ه (opp to فَتَق) To close up, to sew up (a rent); to reconcile (people).

رَتَق فتقهم He has restored their business.

إرتَتَق To be repaired.

رِتاق Two garments sewed by the borders.

هُوَ الفاتِق والرَّاتِق He is the supreme ruler (*lit* : he rends and mends).

☆ رَتَك o i رَتْكا ورَتَكا ورَتَكانا To run with short steps (camel).

أرتَك ه To drive (a camel) quickly.

— الضَّحِك To laugh coldly.

مَرتَك Litharge.

مرتك ذَهَبيّ Red, gold litharge.

— فِضِّيّ White, silver litharge.

☆ رَتِل a رَتَلا To be set in order. To have white and even teeth.

رَتَّل ه To set (speech) in order. To read correctly. ✧ To sing hymns.

تَرتَّل في الكَلام To speak slowly.

رَتَل Good order. Whiteness of the teeth. Fine speech.

رَتِل Elegant (discourse).

أرتَل Elegant. Stammerer.

تَرتِيل ج تَرَاتِيل ✧ Hymn, sacred song.

رُتَيلاء ج رُتَيلاوات *Phalangium*, venomous spider. Phalangium (*plant*). ✧ Tarentula.

☆ رَتَم i رَتْما ه To break (the nose). To crush a. th.

— في To be brought up (in a tribe).

مَا رَتَم بِكَلِمَة He did not utter a single word.

أرتَم وتَرَتَّم وارتَتَم To twist (a thread) round o.'s finger.

مَا زَال رَاتِما على هٰذا الأمر He is still minding the affair.

رَتَم *Genista*, broom-plant. Esparto, mat-weed. Water-bag filled. Road. Low speaking. Shame.

رَتَمة ج رَتَم , ورَتِيمَة ج رَتَائِم و رِتام Thread tied to a finger for reminding.

P رَاتِنج ورَاتِينَج Pine-resin.

☆ رَتَا o رَتْوا ه To tie up. To loose a. th. To hearten a. o. To draw up (a bucket) gently.

رَتَا To step.

— رَتْوا ورُتُوّا بالرَّأس To make a sign with the head.

— ه إلى To join a. th. to.

✧ رَتَى i ورَتَّى ه To mend a. th.

رَتْوَة Step. Moment. Hill.

☆ رَثَّ i رَثاثة ورُثوثة , وأرَثّ To be threadbare (garment).

أرَثّ ه To wear out (clothes).

أُرثّ To be brought out of a battle wounded.

رَثّ ج رِثاث Old clothes ; rags.

رِثّة ج رِثَث و رِثاث Old furniture. Rabble. Foolish woman.

رَثِيث ج رِثاث Shabby. Wounded man half-dead

☆ رَثَأ a رَثْأ To cool (anger). To have a disease of the shoulder (camel).

— ه وه To curd (milk). To strike a. o.

— ه ب To mix a. th. with.

أرْثَأَ وارتَثَأَ To thicken (milk).
إرتَثَأَ To be confused (man, affair).
— ه To drink (sour milk).
رَثْء Want of intelligence.
رَثْأَة Disease of the shoulder in camels.
رَثِيئَة Sour milk mixed with fresh. Foolishness.
☆ رَثَدَ o رَثْدًا, وارتَثَدَ ه To heap up (furniture).
رَثِدَ a رَثَدًا, وارتَثَدَ To be turbid (water). To be disturbed (man).
أَرْثَدَ To reach moist ground by digging. To stay in a place.
رِثْد و رِثْدَة Party of travellers tarrying.
رَثَد ورَثِيد Old furniture. Rubbish. Weak people.
مَرْثَد Generous man. Lion.
☆ رَثِعَ a رَثَعًا To be very covetous.
رَثِع ج رَثِعُون Covetous man.
☆ إرثَعَنَّ To be continuous (rain). To be loosened (hair). To be weak and flabby.
☆ رَثَمَ i رَثْمًا ه To crush (the nose). To perfume (her nose : woman).
رَثِمَ ـ رَثَمًا, وارثَمَّ To have a white spot on the nose (horse).
رُثْم ورُثْمَة White spot on the nose of a horse.
رَثْمَة ج رِثَام Fine rain.
رَثِم م رَثِمَة, وأرثَم م رَثْماء ج رُثْم White-spotted on the nose (horse).
رَثِيم ومَرْثُوم Bloody. Bleeding (nose).
مَرْثَم ومِرْثَم ج مَرَاثِم Nose.
أرض مُرَثَّمَة Watered land.
☆ رَثَّ — رَثَّان Intermittent drops of rain.
أرض مُرَثَّنَة ومَرْثُونَة Land watered by intermittent rain
☆ رَثَا o رَثْوًا, ورَثَى i رَثْيًا ورِثَاء ورِثَايَة ومَرْثَاة ومَرْثِيَة ه To eulogise (a dead person). To compose an elegy. To keep (a tradition) by heart.
رَثَى i رِثَايَة ه عن To relate a. th. about a. o.
— ل To pity a. o.
شيء يُرْثَى له Deplorable thing.
رَثِيَ a رَثًى To feel pains in the joints.
رَثَّى وتَرَثَّى ه To recite the elegy of a. o.
رَثَّاءَة ورَثَّايَة Hired female mourner.
رَثْيَة Pain in the joints. Wickedness. Foolishness.
مَرْثِيَة ومَرْثَاة و✧ مَرْثَايَة ج مَرَاثٍ Dirge, elegy.
☆ رَجَّ o رَجًّا ه To shake a. th.
— ه عن To hinder a. o. from.
رَجَّ i ورُجَّ رَجًّا, وأرَجَّ وارتَجَّ To quake (earth). To be in commotion (sea). To be confused (speech) To quiver (flesh).
رَجَّة Bustle of (people). Rumbling (thunder). ✧ Shock, trembling.
رَجَاج Lean (sheep). Weak (people).
☆ رَجْرَجَ To be disturbed (man). To quiver (flesh).
تَرَجْرَجَ To waver, to be shaken.
رَجْرَاج A certain medicine.
كَتِيبَة رَجْرَاجَة Numerous army in a state of commotion.
رِجْرِجَة Remainder of foul water. Numerous party in war. Spittle. Foolish.
☆ رَجَأَ — أرْجَأَ To be near to bring forth (she-camel). To be disappointed (hunter).
— ه To put off a (business).
☆ رَجَبَ o رَجْبًا, ورَجِبَ a رَجَبًا من To be ashamed of. To fear a. o.
— رَجْبًا ورُجُوبًا, ورَجِبَ, ورَجَّبَ وأرجَبَ ه To regard with awe ; to honour a. o.
رَجَّبَ ه To prop (a palm-branch).
تَرَجَّبَ To be awed, frightened.
رَجَب ج أرجَاب ورِجَاب ورُجُوب ورَجَبَات Seventh Arabian month.
رُجْبَة Prop for palm-trees. Trap, snare.
رَاجِبَة ج رَوَاجِب Joints of the fingers.
أرجَاب Intestines.
☆ رَجَحَ o a i رُجْحَانًا ورُجُوحًا To weigh down (scale). To preponderate (opinion).
— ه و ه To outweigh a. th.
— ه باليد To weigh a. th. with the hand.
— رَجَاحَة To be grave, sedate.
رَجَّحَ وأرجَحَ ل To give an excess of weight to (a buyer).
— وأرجَحَ ه To weigh down (a scale).
رَجَّحَ ه على To prefer (an opinion) to. To make a. th. to outweigh.

To weigh o.'s self with a. o. To swing with a. o. رَاجَحَ ه

To swing (see-saw). To preponderate (opinion). To waver (man). تَرَجَّحَ

To swing on (a see-saw) إِرْتَجَحَ فِي

Filled (vessels). Heavy (squadrons of cavalry). رُجَّح

Excess of weight. رُجْحَان

Outweighing (scale). Preferable (opinion). رَاجِح

Swing of rope. رُجَاحَة ورُجَّاحَة

أُرْجُوحَة ج أَرَاجِيح, ومَرْجُوحَة ج مَرَاجِيح See-saw.

To incline. To shake. To fade away. ✱ إِرْجَحَنَّ

To carry sheaves to the floor. ✱ رَجَد o رِجَادًا

To quiver, to tremble. رُجِد رَجْدًا, ورُجِّد وأُرْجِد

To recite, to compose verses رَجَز. ✱ رَجَز o رَجْزًا, وارْتَجَز

To rumble (sea, thunder). To move heavily (cloud). تَرَجَّز وارْتَجَز

To vie with a. o. in reciting verses رَجَز. تَرَاجَز

Filth. Idolatry. Punishment. رِجْز ورُجْز

Short metre of poetry. Trembling of the knees in camels. ✧ Wrath. رَجَز

Camel-litter for women. رِجَازَة

Affected with trembling (camel). أَرْجَز م رَجْزَاء

Piece of poetry on a short metre رَجَز. أُرْجُوزَة ج أَرَاجِيز

To groan (camel). To rumble (thunder). ✱ رَجَس o رَجْسًا

To sound the depth of (water). — وأَرْجَس ه

To prevent a. o. from. — i o ه عن

To be filthy. To commit foul deeds. رَجِس a, ورَجُس o رَجَاسَة

To be shaken (building). To thunder (sky). إِرْتَجَس

Crime. Unbelief. Punishment. رِجْس ورَجَاسَة

Filth. رِجْس ورُجْس ورَجِس ج أَرْجَاس

Roaring (sea). Thundering (cloud). رَجَّاس

Stone for sounding a well. مِرْجَاس

Narcissus (flower). P نَرْجِس ونِرْجِس

They are in confusion. هم في مَرْجُوسَة

✱ رَجَع i رُجُوعًا ومَرْجِعًا ومَرْجِعَة ورُجْعَى ورُجْعَانًا إلى To return. To have recourse to.

To return; to retract (a word). — في

To have a beneficial effect upon a. o. (food, advice). — فيهِ

To desist from. To amend for. رَجَع عن

To send back a. o. to. — i رَجْعًا ومَرْجِعًا ه إلى

To give (an answer). To repeat a. th. — ه

To remove a. th. from. — ه عن

To draw back the forefeet in walking (beast). رَجَع i رَجْعًا, ورَجَّع

To repeat (a prayer). رَجَّع في

To send back a. o. To repeat, to retrace a. th. To return a. th. — ه وه

To resort to a. o. To return to. رَاجَع ه وه

To repeat a. th. to. To have a conference with a. o. upon. — ه ه

To stretch the hand backwards. To return to a former condition. أَرْجَع

To bring back a. o. To return a. th. أَرْجَع ه و ه

To give back a. th. bought. To prosper a. o.'s (business: God). — ه

To buy (a she-camel) with the price of another. تَرَجَّع وارْتَجَع ه

To return together (divorced people). To return by degrees. To reply. تَرَاجَع

To claim, to get back a. th. إِسْتَرْجَع ه

Answer, reply. Sound of footsteps. Rain. Pool of water. Profit. ✧ Echo. رَجْع ج رِجَاع ورِجْعَان ورُجْعَان

Return. Resurrection. Reply. ✧ Receipt. Reaction. رَجْعَة ج رِجَع

✧ Second harvest of fruit. رَجْعِي

Answer (to a letter). رُجْعَى ورُجْعَان ورَجْعَة ورَجُوعَة

Return. ✧ Recourse, resort. رُجُوع

Woman returning to her family. ✧ Ship-yard. رَاجِع ج رَوَاجِع

Dung. Repeated (word). Jaded (camel). Repaired (clothes). Sweat. Heated again (dish). Cud. رَجِيع ج رُجُع

paper. Misfortune. Army. Precedence. Time.
Filago, lion's foot (*plant*). ✧ رِجْل الأَسَد
Arum, friar's cowl (*plant*). ✧ — البَقَرة
Atriplex, oroche (*plant*). رِجْل الجَرَاد
Anchusa, pigeon's foot (*plant*). رِجْل الحَمَامَة
Chamemelum, hen's foot (*plant*). رِجْل الدَّجَاجَة
Lagopus, hare's foot (*plant*). رِجْل الأَرْنَب
Lotus ornithopodus, bird's foot trefoil (*plant*). — الزَّاغ والغُرَاب
Ornithopodus, bird's foot (*pla.*). — العُصْفُور
Glechoma, ground-ivy. — القِطّ
Coronopus, crow's foot (*plant*). — القَعْق والزُّرْزُور والعِقَاب
Podophyllum, duck's foot; (dangerous plant). — الوَزّ
Delphinium, lark's spur (*pla.*). — اليَمَامَة
Rigel, fixed star in the left foot of Orio. رِجْل الجَبَّار و رِجْل الجَوْزَاء اليُسْرَى
Star in the right foot of Orio. — الجَوْزَاء اليُمْنَى
Garden purslain. رِجْلَة ج رِجَل
Vigour in walking. Pedestrianism. رِجْلَة ورُجْلَة
Man. (*opp. to woman*). Perfect. Vigorous. Husband. رَجُل و✧ رِجَال ج رِجَال ورَجْلَة
Manlike woman, virago. رَجُلَة
Set free with his mother (suckling). رَجِل ورَجَل
Somewhat curly (hair). — ورَجَل
Having curly hair. رَجِل ج أَرْجَال ورَجَالَى
رَجِل ورَاجِل ج رَجْل ورَجَّالَة ورُجَّال و رِجَال
Pedestrian, on foot. ورُجْلَان
رُجْلَة ورُجُولَة ورُجْلِيَّة ورُجُولِيَّة ورَجُولِيَّة
Manliness.
White-spotted on one foot (beast). Hard ground. رَجْلَى ورَجْلَاء
Foot-passenger. رَجْلَان ج رُجَالَى ورَجَالَى ورَجْلَى
Foot-passenger, pedestrian. رَجِيل ج أَرْجِلَة وأَرَاجِل وأَرَاجِيل
Good walker, tramp. — ج رَجْلَى ورُجَالَى ورَجَالَى
White-spotted on one foot. Large-footed. أَرْجَل م رَجْلَاء ج رُجْل
Hunters. الأَرَاجِيل

Return. Lower part of the shoulder. ✧ Resort. مَرْجِع ج مَرَاجِع
Answer to a letter. مَرْجُوع ومَرْجُوعَة ج مَرَاجِيع
✱ رَجَف o رَجْفًا ورَجَفَانًا ورُجُوفًا ورَجِيفًا To quake (earth). To rumble (thunder). To prepare for war. To tremble (old man). To be restless.
To stir a. th. — ه
To spread alarming news. أَرْجَف
To quake (earth). — وأُرْجِف
To engage in a. th. — في و ب
To be moved. To tremble. إِرْتَجَف
To shake (the head). إِسْتَرْجَف ه
Shock. Earthquake. رَجْفَة
Shivering fever. رَاجِف
First blast of the trumpet on the last day. رَاجِفَة
Rough sea. Day of resurrection. Kind of run. رَجَّاف
Alarming, false news. إِرْجَاف ج أَرَاجِيف
✱ رَجَل o رَجْلًا ه To let (a female) suckle her young. To suck (his mother: young). To tie a. o. by the feet.
To go foot. To have a white-spotted foot (horse). To be curly (hair). To be set free with his mother (young beast). رَجِل a رَجَلًا
To comfort a. o. رَجَّل ه
To comb (the hair). — ه
To let go a. o. on foot. To grant a respite to a. o. To let (a young one) free with his mother. أَرْجَل ه
To alight (rider). To be manlike (woman). To be advanced (day). تَرَجَّل
To go down (a well) without rope. — ه و في
To cook a. th. in a kettle. To go at a middling pace (horse). To extemporise (a speech). إِرْتَجَل ه
To tie (a beast) by the foot: to seize a. o.'s foot. — ه
To follow o.'s own opinion. — برأيه
Walking on foot. Man. رَجْل
Foot. Hind-leg of beasts. رِجْل و✧ إِجر ج أَرْجُل
Sea-gulf. رِجْل البَحْر
Part, portion. Swarm of locusts. Large troop of beasts. Blank — ج أَرْجَال

White spot on a horse's foot. ترجيل
Smallage (herb). تَراجيل
Variegated (garment). Leaving traces of wings on the sand (locusts). Combed. مُرَجَّل
Copper caldron. Comb. مِرْجَل ج مَراجِل
To cast stones at. ✱ رَجَم o رَجْمًا ه
To stone a. o. to death. To curse, to revile a. o. To expel a. o.
To put a stone on a (tomb). — ه
To speak conjecturally. — ورَجَّم بِالغَيْب
✧ To practice magical stoning.
To throw stones at o. a. راجَم ه
To contend with a. o. in (words). — ه في
To protect a. o. — عن
To throw stones at o. another. تَراجَم
To be heaped (stones). إرْتَجَم
Tombstone. Heap of stones. Den of a hyena. رُجْمَة ج رُجَم ورِجام
Missile. Conjecture. Friend. ✧ Magical stoning. رَجْم ج رُجُوم
Grave. Well. Oven. رَجَم ج رِجام
Shooting stars. Tombstones. رُجُم
Stone for cleansing a well. Stone-work around a well. رِجام
The two cross-beams of a pulley. رِجامان
Stoned. The accursed one, Satan. رَجِيم
Strong. Battering (horse). Sling. مِرْجَم
Doubtful (news). مُرَجَّم
Foul speech. مَراجِم
To remain in. To be familiar to (beast). ✱ رَجَن o, ورَجِن a, ورَجُن o رُجُونًا ب
To keep (a beast) in the stable. To be ashamed of. رَجَن o رَجْنًا, ورَجَّن وأَرْجَن ه
To be rancid (butter). إرْتَجَن
To be intricate (business). — على
To abide in. — ب
Deadly poison. رَجِين
Troop, party. رُجَينة
Basket. مَرْجُونة
To be in commotion. ✱ رَجَه i رَجْهًا
To seize with (the teeth). — ب
To put off a. th. أَرْجَه ه
✱ رَجا o رَجاء ورَجْوًا ورَجاة ورَجاءَة ومَرْجاة
To hope for. To fear a. o. ه وه
✧ To beseech a. o.
To remain silent. رَجِيَ a رَجًا

To be unable to speak. رُجِيَ عليه
To hope a. th. رَجَّى وتَرَجَّى وارْتَجَى ه
To put a side to (a well). To miss (game). أَرْجَى ه
To be near to bring forth (female). أَرْجَى
To fear a. o. ✧ To beg a. o. تَرَجَّى ه
Hope. Fear. ✧ Request. رَجاء
Side. Country. رَجا ورَجاء ج أَرْجاء
The two sides of a well. رَجَوا البِئر
What is hoped. رَجِيَّة
What is put off. أُرْجِيَّة
Purple. P أُرْجُوان
Red-purple. أَحْمَر أُرْجُوانِيّ
Width of a hoof. ✱ رَحَح
Wide-hoofed (mule). Flat-soled (man). أَرَحّ
To speak obscurely. ✱ رَحْرَح بالكَلام
To protect a. o. — عَن
Broad (foot). Wide and shallow (vessel). رَحْرَح ورَحْراح ورَحْرَحان
Easy life. عَيْش رَحْراح
✱ رَحِب a رَحَبًا, ورَحُب o رُحْبًا ورَحابَة
To be wide (place).
To enlarge (a house). رَحَّب ه
— ورَحَّب ب, ومَرْحَب ه و✧ اسْتَرْحَب ب
To greet, to welcome a. o.
To be wide, spacious. أَرْحَب
To clear, to enlarge (a place). — ه
Make room, clear the way. أَرْحِبْ وأَرْحِبِي
To become wide, to be easy. تَراحَب
Broad, spacious. رَحْب ورَحِيب ورُحاب
Long-minded; generous, forbearing. رَحْب الصَّدْر
Able, mightx. Generous. رَحْب الذِّراع
Ampleness. رُحْب ورَحابَة
Welcome, be at ease. رُحْبًا بِكَ ومَرْحَبَك
The broadest rib of the breast. رُحْبَى
رَحْبَة ورَحَبَة ج رِحاب ورَحَب ورَحَبات
Wide space. Brands on camels. Cultivated ground. Court. Bed of panic-grass.
Extended borders. رَحائِب
Wider. Name of a tribe, and of a stallion. أَرْحَب
Welcome. رَحابِ
Welcome. Be at ease, at home. أهلًا وسَهلًا ومَرْحَبًا

مَرْحَب Idol in Hadramout.

✡ رَحَض a رَحْضًا , وأَرْحَض ه To wash (clothes).

رُحِض To sweat after fever.

إِرْتَحَض To be disgraced (man).

رُحَضَاء ورُحَاض Abundant sweat of fever.

مِرْحَاض ج مَرَاحِيض Mallet for linen. Washing-tub. Water-closet.

✡ رُحَاق ورَحِيق Strong and pure wine.

✡ رَحَل a رَحْلًا ورَحِيلًا وتَرْحَالًا , و تَرَحَّل وارْتَحَل عن To remove, to depart from.

رَحَل وارْتَحَل ه To saddle, to ride (a camel).

رَحَل ه ب To strike a. o. with (a sword).

رَحَلْتُ لَهُ نَفْسِي I submitted to him patiently.

رَحَّل ه To send, to drive a. o. away.

رَاحَل ه To help a. o. in going away.

أَرْحَل To have beasts for riding. To become strong (camel).

— ه To mount a. o. To train camels for riding.

إِرْتَحَل ه To embark in (an affair).

إِسْتَرْحَل ه To ask a. o. to saddle a beast. To ask a beast for riding.

— ه ه To lower o.'s self before a. o.

رَحْل ج أَرْحُل و رِحَال Camel's saddle. Stage. Dwelling. Luggage.

رُحْلَة Journey. Aim of a journey. ✧ Diary, journey-book.

رِحْلَة ورَحِيل وإِرْتِحَال Emigration.

رَحِيل Camel fit for a journey. Rachel.

رَاحِلَة ج رَوَاحِل Beast for riding.

رِحَالَة ج رَحَائِل Leather horse-saddle.

رَحَّال Saddler. Great traveller.

رَحَّال ج رَحَّالَة Travelling much.

رَحُول ورَحُولَة Fit to be saddled (camel).

أَرْحَل White-backed (horse).

مَرْحَلَة ج مَرَاحِل Stage. One day's journey. ✧ Station of the way of the Cross.

مُرْحِل Trainer, owner of camels.

✡ رَحِم a رَحْمَةً ومَرْحَمَةً ورُحْمًا ورُحُمًا ه To forgive, to have mercy on.

رَحِم , ورَحُم o رَحْمًا ورَحَامَةً , ورُحِم To die after childbirth (woman).

رَحَّم و تَرَحَّم على To express pity for a. o ; to say God have mercy on him!

تَرَاحَم To have mercy upon o. a.

إِسْتَرْحَم ه To implore the mercy of.

رِحْم ورَحِم ج أَرْحَام Womb. Blood-kindred.

رَحْمَة و رُحْم ورُحْمَى Mercy, pity.

أُمّ رُحْم والرُّحْم Mecca.

رُحَام Disease of the womb.

رَحِيم ورَحُوم ج رُحَمَاء Merciful.

الرَّحْمَان الرَّحِيم The All-merciful (God).

رَهَبُوت خَيْر من رَحَمُوت It is better to be feared than to be pitied (*prov.*).

أَرْحَم الرَّاحِمِين The Most Merciful (God).

مَرْحَمَة ج مَرَاحِم Mercy, pity. Favour.

مَرْحُوم ✧ Deceased, late.

مَرْحُومَة *F*. Medina (*town*). Favoured ✧ Deceased.

✡ رَحَا o رَحْوًا , ورَحَى i رَحْيًا , وتَرَحَّى To coil (serpent).

— ه To turn (an arm-mill). ✧ To grind (wheat).

رَحًى ج أَرْحٍ وأَرْحَاء ورُحِيّ وأَرْحِيَة Hand-mill. Thick of a fight. Troop of camels. Chief of a tribe. Spinage. Mollar tooth. Foot of a camel.

✡ رَخّ o رَخًّا ه To tread a. th. under foot.

رَخّ i رَخًّا ه To mix (wine) with water.

أَرَخّ في To excel in.

إِرْتَخّ To be remiss (man) ; soft (dough). To be confused (advice).

رُخّ ج رِخَخَة ج رِخَاخ Castle (at chess). Fabulous bird. ✧ Condor.

رَخَاخ ج رَخَاخِي Easy (life). Soft ground.

✧ تَرَخْرَخ To be weak-hearted, lax (man)

P رَخْت ج رُخُوت Horse's-saddle. ✧ Caparison.

✡ رخش — تَرَخَّش To be stirred.

إِرْتَخَش To be disturbed.

رُخْشَة Bustle, stir.

✡ رَخُص o رُخْصًا To abate (price).

— رَخَاصَة ورُخُوصَة To be tender, supple.

رَخَّص وأَرْخَص ه To lower (the price) of.

رَخَّص وتَرَخَّص ل في To give licence, to allow a. o. to.

أَرْخَص وارْتَخَص ه To purchase a. th. cheap. To find a. th. to be cheap.

إرتخص و استرخص ه وه To find a th. to be cheap. ✧ To ask leave of.

رُخص Cheapness.

رُخصة Indulgence of God. Share of water. ✧ Leave, permission.

رَخص م رَخصَة Fresh, tender. ✧ Plenty.

رَخِيص Cheap. Quick (death).

مُرَخَّص ✧ Proxy. Delegate.

✲ رَخُف o رَخفًا, ورَخِف a رَخفًا, ورَخُف o رَخَافَة ورُخُوفَة To become soft (dough).

أرخف ه To soften (paste).

رَخف ورَخفَة ورُخفَة Softness of the paste.

رَخف ج رِخَاف Soft butter, cream. Soft paste. Dye.

رَخفَة ج رِخَاف Soft butter, soft stone.

✲ رِخل ورَخِل و رِخلَة ج أرخُل و رِخَال ورُخَال و رِخلَان She-lamb.

مُتَرَخِّل Fosterer of she-lambs.

✲ رَخُم o رَخمًا, ورَخَم o رَخَامَة To be sweet, melodious (voice).

رَخُم o رَخَامَة To be gentle, sweet-voiced (girl).

رَخَم o البَيضَ رَخمًا ورَخَمًا ورَخمَة, وأرخم To sit upon her eggs (hen).

رَخِم a o رَخمًا ورَخمَة ه على To pet, to play with (her child : mother). To pity a. o.

رَخَّم ه To curtail (a word). ✧ To marble a. th. To soften (the voice).

— ه To make (a hen) to sit upon her eggs.

رَخَم (un. رَخمَة) Meekness. *Vultur percnopterus*, white carrion-vulture.

رَخَم Thick milk. Sympathy.

رُخَام Marble. Alabaster.

رُخَامَة *Zizyphus lotus*, kind of lote-tree.

رُخَامَى Gentle breeze. Piece of marble.

رَخِيم Melodious (voice). Soft (cushion).

أرخم م رَخمَاء ج رُخم White-headed and black-bodied (horse).

تَرخُوم ويَرخُوم ويَرخَم Male vulture.

✲ رَخِي a رَخًا ورَخوَة . ورَخُو o رَخَاوَة To be soft, remiss.

رَخَا o, ورَخَى a, ورَخِي a, ورَخُو o رَخَاء To lead an easy life.

رَاخَى ه To soften a. th. To loosen (a knot). To remove a. th.

أرخى To run swiftly (horse).

— ه To loose a. th. To let down (a curtain). To let go (a beast) at leisure. To lay (anchor). To let run (sails).

— عِمَامَتَهُ To loosen o.'s turban *i. e.* To lead a quiet life.

— ه ول To loose (the reins) to (a horse).

تَرَاخَى To sprinkle a fine rain (sky). To be slack, lazy.

— عن To remove from.

إرتخى واسترخى To remit; to be remiss.

إسترخى به حالُهُ His circumstances have become easy.

رَخَاء Easiness of life.

رِخوَة وإسترخاء Looseness. Remissness.

رُخَاء Light breeze.

رَاخٍ, ورَخِيّ ورَخو ورِخو ورُخو Soft, lax. Remiss.

رَخِيّ البَال Free from cares.

أُرخِيَّة ج أرَاخِيّ Loosened (curtain).

مِرخَاء ج مَرَاخٍ Running quickly.

✲ رَدّ o رَدًّا ومَرَدًّا وتَردُودًا ه وه عن To drive a. o. back. To avert a. th. from.

رَدّ نَام ✧ He went to sleep again.

— ه وه To refute; to discard a. o. To shut (a door).

— ه على To refuse a. th. to a. o. To restore a. th. to. To return (a salutation) to a. o.

رَدّ جَوَابًا إلى To return an answer to.

— ه إلى To send a. o. back to. To restore a. th. to a former state. ✧ To convert a. o. to (God).

— ه ه وه ه To render a. o. or a. th. *such* or *such*.

لا يَرُدّ عليك شيئًا It will be of no profit to thee.

رَدَّد ه وه To repel forcibly a. o. or a. th.

رَدَّد ه To repeat a. th. To recall to mind, to reciprocate a. th. To re-echo a. th.

رَادّ ه ه To give back a. th. to a. o.

— ه وه To dispute with a. o. To rescind (a sale) with.

أرَدّ To rage (sea). To swell with anger.

Heavily laden (army). Fat رَدَاحٌ ج رُدُحٌ (woman). Overburdened (camel). Fertile (land). Fat-tailed (ram). Serious (riot). Large bowl.
Trap for hyenas. رَدَاحَة ورِدَاحَة
Green-grocer. رَدْحِيّ
To bruise a. th. To fracture (the skull). ✱ رَدَخَ a رَدْخًا ه
To cast stones at a. o. ✱ رَدَسَ o رَدْسًا, ورَادَسَ ه
To beat (the soil). To break (a stone). رَدَسَ o i ه
To take a. th. away. رَدَّسَ ب
To fall from (a place). تَرَدَّسَ مِن
Stone-beater, stone-hammer. Stone for sounding a well. Head. مِرْدَس ومِرْدَاس
Litharge. P مُرْدَاسَنْج
To restrain, to turn away a. o. from. ✱ رَدَعَ a رَدْعًا ه عن
To rivet a nail. — رأس المِسْمَار
To dye, to stain a. th. with. — ه ب
To be altered in colour. رَدِعَ
To break in hitting the butt (arrow). إِرْتَدَعَ
To refrain, to be repelled from. — عن
To be stained, dyed with. — ب
Neck. Saffron. Saffron or blood-stain. رَدْع
Shirt stained with saffron. رَادِعَة
Slime, mire. رِدَاع
Hut for hunting hyenas. رِدَاعَة
Headless (arrow). رَدِيع ومِرْدَع
Balked. Lazy sailor. مِرْدَع
To be muddy (soil). ✱ رَدِغَ — أَرْدَغَ
To sink in mire. إِرْتَدَغَ
Mire, thick mud. رَدَغَة ورَدْغَة ج رَدْغ ورَدَغ ورِدَاغ

✱ رَدَفَ o رَدْفًا, ورَدِفَ a, وارْتَدَفَ ه ول
To follow a. o.
To supply (a king). To bear two (riders: beast). ✧ To be synonymous with another (word). رَادَفَ ه
To mount a. o. behind. أَرْدَفَ ه
To follow o. a. To help o. a. To ride on the same beast. To be synonymous (words). تَرَادَفَ
To attack the rear of (the enemy). إِرْتَدَفَ ه

To be removed. To repeat. تَرَدَّدَ
✧ To go frequently to. — إلى
To falter in (speech). — وتَرَادَّدَ في
They have rescinded the sale تَرَادُّوا البَيْع
He retraced his steps. إرْتَدَّ على عَقِبِهِ
He was converted to God. — إلى رَبِّهِ
To forsake a. th. To apostatise from. — عن
To claim a. th. back from. إِسْتَرَدَّ ه ه
To claim, to take back (a gift). — ه
Restitution. Requital. Answer. Productive land. Impediment in speech. Spurious (coin). رَدّ
Bad thing. رَدٍ ج رُدُود
Stay, refuge.
Deformity. Echo. ✧ Rubbish of bran. Burden of a song. رَدَّة
Profit, usefulness. رَدَّة ومَرَدَّة
Apostasy. رِدَّة
Dislike, aversion. Frequentation of a place. تَرْدَاد وتَرْدَاد
Angry. Swollen (sea). Having swollen udders (ewe). Woman remote from his wife (man). مُرْمَدّ ومُرْتَدّ
Razor. Divorced (woman). [illegible]
To strengthen a. o. To stay (a wall). To take in turn (camels) cleverly. ✱ رَدَأَ a رَدْءًا ه
To be vicious, bad. رَدُؤَ رَدَاءَة
To commit a bad action. أَرْدَأَ
To assist a. o. To quiet a. o. -
To corrupt a. th. To stay (a wall). To let down (a veil). ه -
Help; helper. Matter. Head. رِدْء
Wicked, bad. رَدِيء ج أَرْدِيَاء
To treat a. o. gently. ✱ رَدَبَ
Blind alley. رَدْب
Measure for corn, of about 5 bushels. Canal. إِرْدَبّ ج أَرَادِب
Sink-hole. Baked bricks. إِرْدَبَّة
To walk step by step. ✱ رَدَجَ
Black leather. Black dye. أَرَنْدَج
To be steady in affairs. ✱ رَدَحَ a
To plaster (a house) with mud. To let down (a curtain). ▫ To bully a. o. — ورَدَّحَ
Long space of time. رَدَح
Hinder-curtain of a tent. Spacious square رَدْحَة

استردف ه	To ask a. o. to ride behind him.
ردف ج أرداف	Riding behind. Result. Supplier of a king. Buttocks.
الردفان	The day and the night.
ردف و رداف	Croup of a beast.
ردافة	Temporary vice-royalty.
رديف ج رداف	Riding behind. Bright star in *Cygnus*. In opposition (star). ✧ Reserve army.
ردافى (*s. pl.*)	Riding behind. Auxiliary troops. ✧ Swan.
أردف ج أرادف	Synonymous (word).
مترادف	
✡ ردم i ردما ه	To block (a door). To twang (a bow).
— o ردّ	To flow (liquid).
— وارذم	To be continuous (fever, clouds). To become green again (tree).
ردّم وتردّم ه	To mend (clothes).
تردّم	To be patched (clothes). To be protracted (quarrel).
— ه	To interfere in the affair of.
ردم	Rubbish of buildings. Twang of a bow.
ردم وردام ومردام	Worthless man.
رديم ج ردم	Worn out (garment).
أردم ج أردمون	Skilful sailor.
متردم	Patched place.
✡ ردن i ردنا	To spin (woman). ✧ To purr (cat).
— o ه	To set (furniture) in order.
— i ه	To make (fire) to smoke.
ردن a ردنا	To be wrinkled (skin).
ردّن وأردن ه	To put cuffs to (a shirt).
أردن	To continue (fever).
إرتدن	To make a spindle for o.'s self.
ردن ج أردان	Cuff of a sleeve.
ردن	Clinking of weapons.
ردن	Spun thread. Silk-cloth. Saffron.
أحمر رادني	Yellowish red.
رديني	Spear.
أردن	The Jordan (river). Drowsiness.
مردن ج مرادن	Spindle.
مردن	Obscure. Stinking (sweat).
✡ ردن وردنة	To be weak, tired.
✡ رده a ردها ه ب	To pelt (stones) at a. o.
— ه	To enlarge (a house).
ردّه	To become foremost amongst o.'s people.
رده	Strong, steadfast.
ردهة ج رده و رداه ورده	Hollow in a stony ground. Rock in water. Snow-water. Large building.
✡ ردى i رديا ورديانا	To beat the ground in running (horse). To limp (crow). To hop (child). To increase (flock). To disappear. To fall down.
— ه ه	To break a. th. To knock a. o.
— وأردى على	To exceed (an age).
— ه وه ب	To strike a. th. with (a stone).
— وتردّى في	To fall in (a pit).
ردي a ردى	To perish.
ردّى وأردى ه في	To throw a. o. in (a pit).
رادى ه	To blandish, to entice a. o.
— عن	To protect a. o. with stones.
أردى ه	To destroy a. o. To start (a horse).
تردّى وارتدى	To wrap o.'s self in a cloak.
رداء ج أردية	Cloak. Sword. Bow. Mind. Ignorance. Debt.
غمر الرداء	Bountiful benefactor.
خفيف الرداء	Little burdened by debts or family.
رداة	Wrapper, loose outer-garment.
رداة ج ردى	Rock.
ردٍ م ردية	Lost, ruined.
مرداة ج مرادٍ	Cloak. She-camel.
مردى ج مرادٍ	Stone for battering rocks. Waist-wrapper. *Pl.* Legs of horses, camels, elephants.
مردى الحرب	Dauntless warrior.
مردي و✧ مدري ج مرادي	Pole for propelling a boat.
✡ ردّ o ردّاذا، وأردّ	To drizzle (sky).
أردّ	To leak (bucket). To flow (wound).
ردّاذ	Drizzle. Little wealth.
يوم مردّ	Drizzling day.
أرض مردّة ومردودة	Ground watered by a fine rain.
✡ ردل o، وردل a ردالة ,ردولة	To be corrupt, vile, ignoble.
ردل o ردلا، وأردل ه و ه	To disapprove

(part of his property).
To obtain a. th. from a. o. رَزَأَ a رُزْأً وَمَرْزِئَة ة ه
He has not obtained the least thing from him. مَا رَزَأَهُ زُبَالًا
He is a bountiful man. هُوَ يُرْزَأُ
To diminish, to decrease. إِرْتَزَأَ
Great misfortune. رُزْءٌ ج أَرْزَاء
Wrong, damage. Misfortune. رَزِيئَة ج رَزَايَا و رَزِيَّة
Deprived of her best men (tribe). Generous. مُرَزَّأ ج مُرَزَّأُون
To stick to (a place). ✲ رَزَبَ o رُزُوبًا ه وه
Bulky. Strong. Short. إِرْزَبّ
Iron-bar. إِرْزَبَّة , ومِرْزَبَة ومِرْزَبَّة ج مَرَازِب
Pipe, sewer. Large ship. مِرْزَاب ج مَرَازِيب
Satrap of Persia. P مَرْزُبَان ج مَرَازِبَة
Office of a satrap. P مَرْزُبَة
To fall down from fatigue (she-camel). To fall (grapes). ✲ رَزَحَ a رُزُوحًا ورَزَاحًا
To spear a. o. with. — ه ب
To be in a bad state. — وتَرَازَحَ
To overfatigue (a beast). رَزَّحَ ه
To pick up fallen grapes. أَرْزَحَ
Overfatigue. رُزُوح
Exhausted. رَازِح ج رُزَّح
Overworked, jaded (camels). رَزَاحَى ورَزْحَى ورُزَّح ورَوَازِح
Prop of a vine. مِرْزَح ج مَرَازِح
To thrust a. o. with (a spear). ✲ رَزَخَ a رَزْخًا ه ب
Row of men, trees. P رَزْدَق ورُسْتَق
To set in order. To dispose. ✧ رَزْدَق ه
Blackness. Rural district. P رُزْدَاق ورُسْتَاق ج رُزْدَاقَات ورَزَادِيق
To knock down a. o. ◘ رَزَعَ ه
To be muddy (ground). To be scanty (water). To bring moisture (wind). To reach moist earth by digging. ✲ رَزِغَ — أَرْزَغَ
To delude, to beguile a. o. رَازَغَ ه
To soak (the earth : rain). To despise, to shame a. o. — ه وه
Thin mud. Mire. رَزَغَة ج رَزَغ و رِزَاغ
To groan (camel). ✲ رَزَفَ i رَزِيفًا, ورَزَّفَ وأَرْزَفَ

a. o. To render abject. ✧ To cast off.
To commit impure, foul deeds. To have corrupt companions. أَرْذَلَ
To reject coins. — مِنَ الدَّرَاهِم ه
To say or commit gross words, actions. ✧ تَرَاذَلَ
To look as vile, abject. إِسْتَرْذَلَ ه و ه
Ignoble. Wicked, filthy. رَذْل ج رُذُول وأَرْذَال, ورَذِيل ج رُذَلَاء
Baseness, wickedness, turpitude. wantonness. رَذَالَة
Refuse, waste. رُذَالَة ج رُذَالَات
Vice, abjection. رَذِيلَة ج رَذَائِل
Corrupt, abject. Rubbish. Worse. أَرْذَل ج أَرَاذِل وأَرْذَلُون
To overflow (vessel). ✲ رَذَمَ o i رَذْمًا ورَذَمَانًا, ورَذِمَ a رَذَمًا وأَرْذَمَ
To exceed (a number). أَرْذَمَ على
Rags. Disbanded party. رَذَم
Overflowing (vessel). رَذُوم ج رُذُم ورَذَم
Small troop. رَذَمَان
To be exhausted. ✲ رَذِيَ a رَذَاوَة
Exhausted by disease. Jaded. Weak. رَذِيّ ج رَذَاة
To lay eggs (locust). To resound (rain). ✲ رَزَّ o i رَزًّا, وأَرَزَّ
To stab a. o. — ه
To put a staple to (a lock). — ه
To stick a. th. into. — ه في
To smooth (paper). To facilitate (an affair). رَزَّزَ ه
To stick into a. th. (arrow). إِرْتَزَّ في
To shrink from giving (miser). — عِنْدَ المَسْأَلَة
Rice. رُزّ (*for* أَرُزّ)
Sound from afar. Rumbling of thunder. Gurgling of the belly. Grumbling of a stallion. رِزّ و رِزِيز
Staple, hinge. رَزَّة ج رَزَّات و رِزَاز
Lead. رَزَاز
Rice-merchant. رَزَّاز
Shudder. Stabbing. Small hail. Long-sounding. إِرْزِيز
Food prepared with rice. Glazed (paper). طَعَام مُرَزَّز
To shake a. th. To poise (a load). ✲ رَزْرَزَ ه
✲ رَزَأَ a رَزْأً ورُزْءًا ومَرْزِئَة , ورَزِيَ
To strip a. o. of a رُزْءًا, وارْتَزَأَ ه ه

رَزَفَ To go quickly (she-camel).
— وأَرْزَفَ To be frightened away.
— وأَرْزَفَ إلى To draw near to.
أَرْزَفَ ه To urge on (a she-camel).
✲ رَزَقَ o رِزْقًا ه ه To grant sustenance to a. o. (God).
— ه To thank a. o.
رُزِقَ To be blessed with children.
أُرْزِقُوا They were disbanded, routed.
إِرْتَزَقَ To receive victuals (soldiers).
إِسْتَرْزَقَ ه To ask a livelihood from.
رِزْق ج أَرْزَاق Substance. Gift of God. Allowance of soldiers. Rain. Gain unhoped for.
✧ بَابُ الرِّزْق Livelihood, sustenance.
✧ رِزْقَة ج رِزَقَات Estate, farm.
رِزَقَات *Pl.* Military supplies, stores.
رَزَّاق The Supplier, the Fosterer (God).
رَازِقِيّ Weak. Wine. Long-berried grapes. White lily.
رَازِقِيَّة Garment of white flax. Wine.
مَرْزُوق Lucky, prosperous, blessed.
✲ رَزَمَ o رَزْمًا To die.
— ب To seize a. th. To beget a. o. (woman).
— على To kneel upon (an adversary).
— o i رُزُومًا ورُزَامًا To cleave to the ground (jaded camel).
— رَزْمَةً To be cold (winter).
— رَزْمًا ه To bundle, to pack up a. th.
رَزَّمَ ه To make a bundle of (clothes).
رَازَمَ ه To remain long (in doors). To make purchases (in a market).
— بَيْنَ To pick up (things).
— في المَطَاعِم To eat various sorts of food.
أَرْزَمَ To rumble (thunder). To groan (she-camel). To gurgle (bowels) ✦
إِرْزَامّ To be angered.
رِزْمَة ج رِزَم Parcel, bundle. ✧ Ream of paper.
رَزْمَة Meal sufficient for one day.
رَزَمَة Cry of (a child, she-camel).
رَازِم ج رَزْمَى ورِزَام Exhausted, emaciated (camel).
رِزَام ج رُزَّام Harsh and stubborn man.
رَزَّام Roaring (lion).
مِرْزَم Band of a parcel. *Bellatrix*, star in Orio.
امّ مِرْزَم North wind.

✲ رَزَنَ o رَزْنًا ه To weigh a. th. with the hand.
— ب To stop in (a place).
رَزُنَ o رَزَانَة To be heavy. To be sedate.
رَازَنَ ه To be the companion, friend of a. o.
تَرَزَّنَ في To be cool, staid in (manners).
تَرَازَنَ To be situated opposite (mountains).
رَزْن ج رُزُون ورِزَان Upland retaining water.
رِزْنَة ج رِزَان Swampy ground.
رَزَانَة Sedateness. Sound judgment.
رَزِين Heavy. Grave, sedate.
رَزَان Grave (woman).
أَرْزَن Hard tree used for making sticks.
P رَازِيَانَج Fennel (*plant*).
— شَامِي Anise (*plant*).
P رَوْزَن ورَوْزَنَة Mural aperture, dormer.
P رُوزْنَامَة Year-book, calendar. ✧ Roll of accounts.
✲ رَزِيَ i رَزْيًا ه To receive a gift from.
أَرْزَى ه To repair to; to rely upon a. o.
✲ رَسَّ o رَسًّا ه To sink (a well). To inquire about (news). To scrutinise. To conceal. To bury (the dead).
— بَيْنَ To make peace between. To set (people) at variance.
رَاسَّ ه في To begin (an affair) with a. o.
تَرَاسَّ ه To divulge (secrets) to o. a.
إِرْتَسَّ To spread (news).
رَسّ ج رِسَاس Beginning. First touch of fever. Old well.
رَسَّة Firm (column).
رَسَّة وأَرْسُوسَة Long cap.
رَسِيس Firm. Prudent. Groundless news. Light (wind). Forerunner of love, fever.
□ رِيهْرَاس ✧ سِيرَاس Glue, paste.
✲ رَسَبَ o رُسُوبًا ورَسَبًا To be sunk (eyes). To settle (dregs).
✧ رَسَّبَ To precipitate (substance).
✧ تَرَسَّبَ To settle, to be precipitated (sediment).
رَسَب ورُسَب ورَسُوب Sunk in the wound (sword).
رَاسِب ورَسُوب Sediment, precipitate. Forbearing, steady (man).
رَوْسَب Misfortune.

To use (a word) without restriction. To start (a horse). — ه و ة

To despatch a. o. to. — ة وب إلى

To forsake a. o. — ة عن يَدِه

To empower (a devil) over (man : God). — ة على

He made a proverb of his words. أرسل قولَهُ مَثَلًا

To act gently. To be slow in. ترسَّل في

To correspond together. تراسَل

To hang down ; to be lank (hair). إستَرسَل

To act familiarly, kindly with. — إلى

To speak to great length. — في

Gentle (pace). Gentle-paced (camel). Loose (hair). رَسْل م رَسْلة

Gentle-paced (she-camel). Laziness. Easy (life). Hairy in the legs (she-camel). Lank (hair). رَسْلة

Gentleness. Milk. رِسْل

Foot, leg of a camel. رِسْل ج رِسَال

Company of men. Herd of camels. رَسَل ج أرسَال

The two shoulders. Two veins of the shoulders. رَاسِلَان

Message. Letter. Epistle. Mission. Apostleship. رِسَالة ج رِسَالَات

Female vulture. أمّ رِسالة

✧ The Epistles of the Apostles. الرَسَائل

✧ Sub-deacon. شَمَّاس رَسَائِلي

رَسُول ج رُسُل ورُسْل وأرسُل ورُسَلَاء

Messenger. Envoy. Apostle.

Apostolic. رَسُولي

Messenger. Envoy. Horse started in a race. Wide. Stallion. Sweet water. رَسِيل ج رُسَلَاء ورُسُل وأرسُل

Long necklace of beads. مُرسَلة ج مُرسَلات

Pl. The winds. The angels. The horses. مُرسَلات

Easy-paced (camel). Short arrow. ✧ Messenger. مِرسَال ج مَرَاسِيل

Loosened, pendent (hair). مُستَرسِل

To erase (traces : rain). To leave traces. To write, to sketch a. th. ✧ To establish (a feast). ✡ رَسَم o رَسمًا ه

To assign (a pay) to. — على

To prescribe a. th. to. — ه وب ل

✧ To be well off. ✧ تَرَسْتَق

To be emaciated in the thighs. ✡ رَسِح a رَسَحًا

Wolf. Emaciated in the thighs. أرسَح م رَسحاء ج رُسْح

Hall. Theatre. ✧ مَرسَح ج مَرَاسِح

To be firm. To be rooted (science). To be dessicated (torrent). To be absorbed (rain). ✡ رَسَخ o رُسُوخًا

To fasten a. th. into. ✧ To impress a. th. on the mind. أرسَخ ه في

Deeply versed in science. رَاسِخ في العِلم

Antimony. Native cinnabar. رَاسُخت P

To stick together (eyelids). To be relaxed (limbs). ✡ رَسَع a رَسْعًا

To put upon (a child) amulets against the eye. — ة

To have the eyelids stuck together. رَسِع a رَسَعًا, ورَسَّع

Disease of the eyelids. رَسَع

Plaited thongs of a belt. رَسَاعة ج رَسَائِع

Having diseased eyelids. أرسَع م رَسعاء ج رُسْع

To tie (a beast) by the pastern. ✡ رَسَغ a رَسغًا ة

To soak the earth (rain). رَسَّغ

To render (life) easy. To arrange (a discourse). — ه

To seize a. o. by the ankle (wrestler). رَاسَغ ة

To expend much upon o.'s family. إرتَسَغ على

Pastern-joint. In-step ; carpus of man. رُسْغ ورُسُغ ج أرسَاغ وأرسُغ

Rope tied to the pastern. رِسَاغ

Copious (meal). Easy (life). رَسِيغة

To walk like a shackled man. ✡ رَسَف i o رَسْفًا ورَسِيفًا ورَسَفَانًا

To drive a (beast) in shackles. أرسَف ة

To be slow-paced (camel). To be lank, long (hair). ✡ رَسِل a رَسَلًا ورَسَالة

To read correctly, sedately. رَسَّل في القِرَاءة

To feed (a young beast) with milk. رَسَّل ه

To interchange letters with a. o. To alternate with a. o. in work. رَاسَل ة في وعلى وب

To have numerous flocks ; abundance of milk. أرسَل

✧ To ordain a clergyman. رَسَمَ رِسَامَةً ه

To leave footprints (camel). — o رَسِيمًا

To walk at a vehement pace (camel). — i رَسِيمًا

To stamp (cloth). To drive (a camel) at a quick pace. رَسَّمَ ه و ه

To consider the site (of a house). To plan a. th. To read (verses) attentively. To recollect a. th. تَرَسَّمَ ه

To comply with (an order). ✧ To be ordained (clergyman). إِرْتَسَمَ

To invoke, to praise God. — لله

Trace, impress. Sketch, scheme. Custom. Order. ✧ Ceremony. Tax. رَسْمٌ ج رُسُومٌ وأَرْسُمٌ

To the address of such a person. بِرَسْمِ فُلَانٍ

Heavy tread of a (camel). رَسْمٌ ورَسِيمٌ ومِرْسَمٌ

Leaving traces on the ground. Walking day and night (camel). رَسُومٌ

✧ Custom-house duties. رُسُومَاتٌ

Seal, stamp on clay. رَاسُومٌ

✧ Full uniform. طَاقِمٌ رَسْمِيٌّ

✧ Regularly. Officially. رَسْمِيًّا

Mark, stamp. Misfortune. رَوْسَمٌ ج رَوَاسِمُ

Camels treading heavily. رَوَاسِمُ

Letter. ✧ Order, prescription. مَرْسُومٌ ج مَرَاسِيمُ ومَرَاسِمُ

✱ To make, to put a halter on (a horse). رَسَنَ i o رَسْنًا, وأَرْسَنَ ه

Enula helenium, elecampane. P رَاسِنٌ

Halter, head-rope. رَسَنٌ ج أَرْسُنٌ وأَرْسَانٌ

Nose of a horse; nose of man. مَرْسِنٌ ج مَرَاسِنُ

In spite of him. عَلَى رَغْمِ مَرْسِنِهِ

✱ To be still, firm. To lay at anchor, to moor (ship). رَسَا o رَسْوًا ورُسُوًّا

To relate part of a tradition to a. o. — رَسْوًا ه لهُ من الحَدِيثِ

To retrace a tradition to. — ه عن

To make peace between. — بين

To vie with a. o. in swimming. رَاسَا ه

To be firm, steadfast. أَرْسَى إِرْسَاءً

To anchor (a ship). — ه

Steadfast in good or evil. Pole of a tent. رَسِيٌّ

Motionless; fixed. firm رَاسٍ م رَاسِيَةٌ ج رَاسِيَاتٌ ورَوَاسٍ

Port, anchorage. مَرْسًى ج مَرَاسٍ

He stopped, he remained. أَلْقَى مَرَاسِيَهُ

The cloud stood still and poured down rain. أَلْقَتِ السَّحَابَةُ مَرَاسِيهَا

Anchor. مِرْسَاةٌ و✧ مِرْسَايَةٌ ج مَرَاسٍ

✱ To sprinkle a fine rain (sky). رَشَّ o رَشًّا وتَرْشَاشًا, وأَرَشَّ

To sprinkle (water, blood). To sprinkle (cloth: dyer). To wash a. th. ✧ To sprinkle salt, flour. رَشَّ ه

To spirt blood (wound). أَرَشَّ

To make (a horse) to sweat. To spirtle (ink: pen). — ه وه

To be sprinkled. تَرَشَّشَ

Sprinkling rain. Painful blow رَشٌّ ج رِشَاشٌ

Scattered drops. رَشَاشٌ

Powder for the eye. ✧ رُشُوشٌ

Sprinkler. مِرَشَّةٌ ج مَرَاشُّ

To be loose. ✧ To sprinkle. ✱ رَشْرَشَ

Dry and soft (bread). رَشْرَشٌ ورَشْرَاشٌ

To bring forth (gazelle). ✱ رَشَأَ a رَشْأً

Fawn able to walk. رَشَأٌ ج أَرْشَاءٌ

Dry cocoa-nut used as a ladle. ✱ رُشْبَةٌ

Mud on the upper part of a bucket. مَرَاشِبُ

✱ رَشَحَ a رَشْحًا ورَشَحَانًا, وأَرْشَحَ, وارْتَشَحَ To sweat (body). To ooze (water). To leak (vessel).

To leap briskly (gazelle). — a رُشُوحًا

He has not given him anything. لَمْ يَرْشَحْ لَهُ بِشَيْءٍ

To lick (her young: gazelle). To tend (a flock) well. To foster (a plant: rain). To rear (a child). ✧ To prepare a. o. for an office. رَشَّحَ ه

To bring up (a child). — ه ول

To be able to walk (fawn). To ooze (vessel). To grow (plant). ✧ To have a rheum. تَرَشَّحَ

To be prepared for (an office). — ل

To grow (grass). إِسْتَرْشَحَ

Moisture, sweat. ✧ Rheum. رَشْحٌ

Able to walk (fawn). Reptile. Mountain oozing at its base. رَاشِحٌ — ج رَوَاشِحُ

Swift-shooting (bow). رَشَق
Shooting of an arrow. رِشق ج أرشاق
Scratching of a pen. رَشق و رِشق
Slender (youth). رَشِيق ورَشِيق ج رَشَق
Elegant (style). Swift (arrow).
Slenderness. Elegance of style. رِشَاقَة
To seal (wheat, ✲ رَشَم o رَشمًا, وارتَشَم ه
a vessel). ✧ To make the sign of the Cross.
✧ To christen (a child) privately. ه –
To halter (a horse).
To write. – ورَشَّم
To crave for food at رَشِم a رَشَمًا
its smell.
To flash (lightning). To shoot أرشَم
forth leaves (tree). To see and eat up young shoots (gazelle).
Seal apposed on a store- رَشم ورَشم
room, a vessel.
Ornamented halter. رَشمَة
Young shoot. Black spot on a رَشَم
hyena's face. Mark of rain. ✧ Halter.
Tablet used for sealing. رَاشُوم ورَوشَم
Spotted. Greedy. White-nosed أرشَم
(dog).
To intrude at ✲ رَشَن o رَشنًا ورُشُونًا
dinner (spunger).
To put the head in (a vessel: dog). في –
Share of water. رَشن ورَشَن
Parasite, spunger. Gratuity رَاشِن
given to an apprentice.
Small window, dormer. رَوزَن ج رَوَاشِن P
Centaurea cyanus, blue-bottle تُرشَان
(*plant*).
To give a bribe to a. o. ✲ رَشَا o رَشوًا ه
To bribe a. o. To help a. o. رَاشَى ه
To put a rope to (a أرشَى ه و ه
bucket). To excite (a young beast) to suckle.
To thrust a sword at. أرشَى بالسَّيف في
To blandish a. o. تَرَشَّى ه
To receive bribes (judge). إرتَشَى
To ask for a bribe. إستَرشَى
Bribe. رَشوَة ورِشوَة ورُشوَة ج رُشًى ورِشًى
Bribery.
Rope, bucket-rope. رِشَاء ج أرشِيَة
Pl. Tendrils of plants. Small stars in *Pisces*.
Agallock (*plant*). رَشَاة ج رَشًا

Sweat. رَشِيح
More quick-witted. أرشَح فُؤادًا
Saddle-felt. مِرشَح ومِرشَحَة
Candidate. ✧ Having a rheum. مُرَشَّح
✲ رَشَد o رُشدًا ورَشَادًا, ورَشِد a رَشَدًا
To be well directed; to be orthodox.
To direct a. o. to. رَشَّد وأرشَد ه إلى وعلى ول
✧ To become of age (child). أرشَد
To be in the right way to. إستَرشَد ل
To ask direction from a. o. ه –
Straightforwardness. رُشد ورَشَد
Direction. ✧ Majority of a child.
To become of age. بَلَغ رُشدَهُ
Lawful marriage, رَشدَة و رِشدَة
wedlock.
Nasturtium, cress. حَبّ الرَشَاد
Nasturtium Niloticum. رَشَاد البَحر
Lunaria parviflora or الرَشَاد الجَبَلِيّ –
savignya Ægyptiaca.
Nasturtium deserti. *Ra*- رَشَاد البَرّ –
phanus lyratus or *enarthrocarpus*.
The Director (God). Orthodox رَشِيد
(caliph). Rosetta, town of Egypt.
Female rat. أمّ رَاشِد
Direction. ✧ Spiritual instruc- إرشَاد
tion.
The right ways; the straight مَرَاشِد
paths.
✲ رَشَف i o رَشفًا ورَشِيفًا وتَرشَافًا, ورَشِف a
To sip, to suck a. th. رَشفًا ورَشَفَانًا ه
To empty (a vessel).
To suck رَشَّف وأرشَف وتَرَشَّف وارتَشَف ه
in a. th.
Small quantity of water in a رَشَف
vessel.
Sucker. ✧ *Pl.* Lips. مِرشَف ج مَرَاشِف
To throw (a ✲ رَشَق o رَشقًا ه ب
missile) at.
To cast the looks on a. o. ه بالعَين –
To wound a. o. by words. ه باللِّسان –
To be slender-waisted, رَشُق o رَشَاقَة
elegant, nimble (youth).
To walk with a. o. رَاشَق ه
To throw (missiles) رَاشَق ه, وتَرَاشَق ب
at one another.
To shoot an arrow. To stretch أرشَق
the neck (gazelle).
To cast a glance at. النَّظَر إلى –
To pursue (an affair) sharply. تَرَشَّق في

Complete thy benefits : أَتْمِم الدَّلْوَ رِشَاءَهَا *lit* : add a rope to the bucket (*prov.*).

God لَعَنَ اللهُ الرَّاشِيَ والمُرْتَشِيَ والرَّائِش curse the giver, the receiver and the agent of a bribe!

✲ رَصَّ o رَصًّا, ورَصَّص ه To make (a building) compact. To stack (stones). To set her eggs for brooding (hen). ✧ To dress (a table). To crush (olives). To set (pawns).

رَصَّص ه To overlay (a vessel) with lead. To draw (her veil) up to her eyes (woman).

تَرَصَّص To be compactly set (stones).

تَرَاصَّ To close their ranks (warriors).

رَصَّة ✧ Pier, mole.

رَصَاص و✧ رِصَاص Lead.

رَصَاصَة (*un.*) ✧ Lead-shot, bullet.

رَصَاصِيّ Lead-coloured.

رَصِيص Heap of eggs. Veil drawn up to the eyes.

أَرَصّ م رَصَّاء ج رُصّ Having the teeth close together.

✲ رَصْرَص ه To strengthen (a building). ✧ To fill (a tooth) with lead.

— فِي To remain in (a place).

✲ أَرْصَح م رَصْحَاء ج رُصْح Narrow in the hips.

✲ رَصَدَ o رَصْدًا ورَصَدًا ه وه To lay in wait for. To watch a. th. ✧ To observe (the stars). To enchant (a treasure).

رَصَّد ه To balance (an account).

— وأَرْصَدَ لَهُ خَيْرًا أَو شَرًّا أَو بِالخَيْر He prepared evil or good to him.

رُصِدَ To be soaked by a shower (ground).

رَاصَدَ ه To spy, to watch a. o.

أَرْصَدَ ه To set a. o. on the look out. To requite a. o.

تَرَاصَدَ To watch one another.

تَرَصَّدَ وارْتَصَدَ ه To watch a. th.

رَصَد ورَصِيد ✧ Balance of an account.

رَصْدَة ج رِصَاد Shower.

رُصْدَة Pit-fall for wild beasts. Ring of a sword.

رَصَد ج أَرْصَاد Small quantity of fodder. Rain. Look out. ✧ Talisman, spell.

رَاصِد ج رُصَّد ورَصَد Lion. Lying in wait. Watchman.

رَصُود ورَصِيد Waiting for.

مَرْصَد ج مَرَاصِد Military post. ✧ Observatory.

مِرْصَاد Look out. High road.

✲ رَصَعَ a رَصْعًا ه To slap a. o.

— وأَرْصَعَ ه To wound a. o. with (a spear).

— وارْتَصَعَ ه To grind (grain) between stones.

— رُصُوعًا بِ To stop in (a place).

رَصِعَ a رَصَعًا, وارْتَصَعَ بِ To stick, to adhere to.

رَصِعَ بِ To be fragrant with (perfumes).

رَصَّعَ ه To set (gems). To weave a. th. To build a nest (bird).

— ه بِ To string (pearls) in (a necklace). To inlay a. th. with (gems).

تَرَصَّعَ To be inlaid with gems. To be active.

تَرَاصَعَ To tread, to copulate (sparrows).

إِرْتَصَعَ To be close together (teeth).

رَصِيعَة ج رَصَائِع Knot of a bridle. Ornamental saddle-ring. Wheat ground and cooked with butter.

أَرْصَع م رَصْعَاء ج رُصْع Penetrating (thrust).

✲ رَصَفَ o رَصْفًا ه To make (a pier, a stonework). To join (the feet) in prayer.

لَا يَرْصُفُ بِكَ It does not suit thee.

رَصُفَ o رَصَافَةً To be strong, compact.

أَرْصَفَ To mix (a beverage) with rock-water.

تَرَصَّفَ و تَرَاصَفَ وارْتَصَفَ To stand in compact ranks (army) ; to be compact (stone-work, teeth).

رَصَف ج رِصَاف (*un.* رَصَفَة) Stone-work in a stream. Dam. Sinew fastening an arrow-head.

مَاء الرَّصَف Rock-water.

رَصَافَة ورُصُوفَة Steadfastness ; constancy.

رَصِيف ج رِصَاف Massive (work). Competitor. Tendon of a horse. ✧ Quay. Causeway, embankment.

مِرْصَافَة Hammer.

مُرْتَصِف الأَسْنَان Having compact teeth.

✲ رَصَنَ o رَصْنًا ه To complete a. th. To brand a (beast).

To break and eat (bread). To doubt about (rumours). تَرَضَّخ
To shoot arrows at one another. تَرَاضَخ
He has a foreign accent. يَرتَضِخ لُكنَةً أَعجَمِيَّةً
Doubtful rumours. رَضخ
Paltry gift. — ورَضِيخَة
Stone-crusher. مِرضَاخ ج مَرَاضِيخ
To set things in order. ✡ رَضَد o رَضدًا ه
To be set in order. إِرتَضَد
✡ رَضِم a, ورَضَم i رَضعًا ورَضَعًا ورِضَاعَةً
To suck (the breast). To seek a gift from a. o. ورِضَاعًا ه
To be ignoble. رَضَم a, ورَضُم o رَضَاعَةً
✧ To suckle (a child). رَضَّم ه
To give (a child) to a wet-nurse. To suck with (a foster-brother). رَاضَم مُرَاضَعَةً ورِضَاعًا ه
To suckle (a child). أَرضَم ه
To nurse at the breast (woman). أَرضَعَت
To suck her own teats (goat). إِرتَضَم
To seek (a nurse). إِستَرضَم ه
To ask (a woman) to suckle (a child). — ه ه
Meanness. Small palm-trees. رَضَم
Sucking the breast. Ignoble. Beggar. رَاضِم ج رُضَّم ورُضَّاء
Milk-teeth. رَاضِعَة ج رَوَاضِم
Nursling. Foster-brother. Vile. رَضِيم ورَضِم ج رُضَم
Nurse, nursing woman. مُرضِم و✧ مُرضِمَة ج مُرضِعَات ومَرَاضِم
To roast (meat). ✡ رَضَف i رَضفًا ه
To brand (a beast). To warm (water) with hot stones.
Red hot stone. Knee-bone. رَضف (un. رَضفَة)
He is disquieted, anxious. هُوَ عَلَى الرَّضف
Brand made with hot stones. رَضفَة ج رَضفَات ورَضَف
Surname given to four dauntless Arabian tribes. رَضفَات العَرَب
Hot stone; meat roasted on heated stones. رَضِيف ومَرضُوف
To walk heavily (beast, old man). ✡ رَضَم i رَضمًا
To build (a house) with huge stones. To till (the earth). — ه

To abuse a. o. in words. — ه بِلِسَانِهِ
To be compact (armour). To be sedate (mind). رَصُن o رَصَانَةً
To know a. th. thoroughly. رَصَن ه مَعرِفَةً
To complete; to consolidate. أَرصَن ه
Lycopodium, club-moss (*plant*). رَصَن
Grave, staid in gait, words. رَصَانَة
Grave, sedate. Suffering. رَصِين
Mindful of, serviceable to. رَصِين ب
Iron for branding cattle. مِرصَن
To consolidate a. th. ✡ رَصَا o رَصوًا ه
To settle in (a place). أَرصَى ب
To break a. th. coarsely. To contuse. ✡ رَضَّ o رَضًّا، ورَضَّض، ورَضرَض ه و ه
I am heart-broken. رُضَّت كَبِدِي
To be heavy. To run fast. أَرَضَّ
To make (sweat) to flow (fatigue). — ه
To be broken. To be bruised. تَرَضَّض وتَرَضرَض
To be broken. ارتَضَّ
Dates stoned and soaked in milk. رَضّ ومُرِضَّة ومِرَضَّة
Fragments of broken things. رُضَاض
Beater, mallet. Fleshy man. Pebbly ground. مِرَضَّة
Small pebbles. رَضرَاض
To fall (shower). To lay down (sheep). ✡ رَضَب o رَضبًا
To suck in (saliva). — وتَرَضَّب ه
Kind of lote-tree. Shower. رَاضِب (un. رَاضِبَة)
Sucked saliva. Particle of sugar, musk, snow. Hail. Froth. رُضَاب
To crush (date-stones). ✡ رَضَح a رَضحًا ه
To be broken (fruit-stones). تَرَضَّح
To decline a. th. To excuse o.'s self for. إِرتَضَح مِن
Crushed date-stones. رَضحَة ورَضِيح
Stone for crushing date-stones. مِرضَاح
To crush (the head of a snake). ✡ رَضَخ a i رَضخًا ه
To butt (buck). رَضَخ
To make a paltry gift to. — رَضخَةً ل مِن مَالِهِ
✧ He acknowleged truth. رَضَخ لِلحَقّ
To give a. th. reluctantly. رَاضَخ ه
To cast stones at a. o. — ه

To throw a. o. on the earth. — بِهِ الأرض

Huge stones (*un.* رَضمَة) رَضم ورِضام superposed.

Stacked (building). رَضِيم ومَرضُوم

✲ To supplant a. o. (in favour). رَضَا o رَضوًا ه

To be pleased with. To consent to. رَضِيَ a رِضًى ورُضوانًا ومَرضاةً عَلى وعن

To prefer a. th. To be satisfied with. رَضِيَ ه وب وفي

God be pleased with him! رَضِيَ اللهُ عَنهُ

✧ For the sake of God. الله يَرضَى عَلَيكَ

To be pleasant (life). رُضِيَ

To content a. o. رَضَّى ه

To endeavour to please a. o. To agree with. رَاضَى مُرَاضَاةً ورِضَاءً ه

To satisfy a. o. To content a. o. with a gift. أَرضَى إِرضَاءً ه

To seek to please a. o. تَرَضَّى ه

To be pleased with o. a. ✧ To reconcile. To come to terms. تَرَاضَى

To agree on (a business). — ه

To be pleased with. To approve of. إِرتَضَى ه وه

To seek to please a. o. To ask a. o. to satisfy o.'s self. إِستَرضَى ه

Pleased. رَضٍ ج رَضُون, ورَاضٍ ج رُضَاة

Approval. Consent. رِضًى ورِضَاءٌ ومُرَاضَاة ورُضوَان ومَرضَاة

Man easily (*m. f. s. p.*) pleased. رَجُل رِضًى

Satisfied. Responsible. Lover. Obedient. رَضِيّ ج أَرضِيَاء

Well-being, easy life. عِيشَة رَاضِيَة

Satisfaction. تَرضِيَة

✲ To be foolish. To shout (crowd). رطّ — أَرطّ

To remain still in (a place). — في

To hold a. o. to be foolish. إِسترطّ ه

Foolishness. Shouts. Foolish. رَطِيط ج رِطَاط ورَطَائِط

✲ To be fresh and ripe (dates). رَطُب o رَطَابَة, ورَطَّب وأَرطَب

To feed (cattle) on fresh herbage. رَطَب o رَطبًا ورُطُوبًا ه

To feed a. o. with fresh dates — ورَطَّب ه

To be damp. رَطِب a. ورَطُب o رُطُوبَة ورَطَابَة

To speak o.'s mind right or wrong. رَطَب a رَطبًا

To wet (cloth). رَطَّب وأَرطَب ه

✧ To cool (the blood: drink). رَطَّب ه

To have fresh dates (palm-tree). أَرطَب

To be wetted, moistened. تَرَطَّب

Moist. Tender (branch). Delicate (youth). رَطب ورَطِيب ج رِطَاب

Green plants, fresh herbage. رُطب

Green trefoil. رَطبَة ورُطبَة ج رِطَاب

Fresh and ripe dates. رُطَب (*un.* رُطَبَة) ج أَرطَاب ورِطَاب

Freshness of (a plant, fruit). رَطَابَة

Dampness. Softness of body. رُطُوبَة

Full of green plants (ground). مُرطِب

Well of sweet water among salt wells. رَكِيَّة مَرطَبَة

✧ Refreshments. مُرَطِّبَات

✲ To slap a. o. رَطَس i رَطسًا ه

To be superposed upon a. th. (stones). إِرطَسّ عَلى

✲ To run (man). رَطَل o رَطلًا

To poise in the hand. To anoint and comb (the hair). To let down (the hair). To weigh a. th. — ه

To sell by the *rothl*. رَاطَل ه

Weight of 5 *lbs. in Syria* and of 15 3/4 *oz. in Egypt*. رَطل ورِطل ج أَرطَال

Weak. Remiss (man). Foolish. Justice. رَطل

Light, swift (mare). — ورِطلَة

✲ To put a. o. in a scrape. رَطَم o رَطمًا ه

To be costive (camel). رُطِم

To remain silent. أَرطَم

To be intricate (business). To heap up. إِرتَطَم

To fall in (mire, in a scrape). — في

Intricate business. رُطمَة

✲ To speak in a foreign tongue to. رَطَن o رَطَانَةً ورِطَانَةً ل, ورَاطَن ه

To speak together in a foreign language. تَرَاطَن

Numerous camels with their drivers. رَطَّانَة ورَطُون

Unintelligible language. رُطَينَى

✲ To abate (wind). رَعَّ o رَعًّا

Lowest class of men; ruffians. رَعَاع

To be rippled (water). ✧ To be fresh, refreshed (man). ✲ رَعْرَعَ
To cause (plants) to grow (God). ه —
To ride (a horse) untrained.
To grow (young man). To shake (tooth). تَرَعْرَعَ
Gracious, well-built. رَعْرَعٌ ورُعْرُعٌ ورَعْراعٌ ج رَعارِعُ
Inula arabica (*plant*). رَعْراعُ أَيُّوب
Youth from 10 to 12 years. مُتَرَعْرِعٌ
To tremble with fear. ✲ رَعَبَ a رُعْبًا, وارْتَعَبَ
To coo (pigeon). — ورَعَّبَ
To compose rhyming prose. To threaten. To make spells. — رَعْبًا
To fill (a vessel). To cut up (a camel's hump). — ه
—رَعْبًا ورُعْبًا, ورَعَّبَ تَرْعِيبًا وتَرْعابًا و✧ أَرْعَبَ
To terrify a. o. ه
Threat. Incantation, spell. Rhyming prose. رَعْبٌ
Terror, alarm. رُعْبٌ ورُعُبٌ و✧ رَعْبَةٌ ج رَعَبَةٌ
Coward. رَعِيبٌ ومَرْعُوبُ العَيْنِ
Charmer. Threatener. راعِبٌ ورَعَّابٌ
Coward. Restless (camel). رُعْبُوبٌ ج رَعابِيبُ
Delicate girl. جارِيَةٌ رُعْبُوبٌ ورِعْبِيبٌ ورُعْبُوبَةٌ
Piece of a camel's hump. رُعْبُوبَةٌ ج رَعابِيبُ, وتَرْعِيبَةٌ ج تَراعِيبُ
To cut up (meat). To rend (clothes). ✲ رَعْبَلَ ه
To be in tatters (garment). تَرَعْبَلَ
Clothed in rags. Foolish (woman). رَعْبَلٌ
Unsteady (wind). رَعْبَلَةٌ ورَعْبَلِيلٌ
Ragged garment. رِعْبَلَةٌ ج رَعابِيلُ, وثَوْبٌ رَعابِيلُ
To be white in the wattles (cock). ✲ رَعَثَ a رَعْثًا, ورَعِثَ a رَعَثًا ه
To bite a. th. (snake). رَعَثَ a رَعْثًا ه
To wear ear-rings (woman). تَرَعَّثَ وارْتَعَثَ
Multicoloured tassels over a litter. رَعْثٌ ورَعَثٌ
Pomegranate blossom. رَعْثُ الرُّمَّانِ
Cock's wattle. Hanging lobe. Earring. رَعْثَةٌ ورَعَثَةٌ ج رِعاثٌ
Palm-spathe used for drinking. — ج رَعَثاتٌ

Two-wattled (ewe). Long grapes. رَعْثاءُ
To flash in succession (lightning). ✲ رَعَجَ a رَعْجًا ورَعَجانًا, وأَرْعَجَ
To render a. o. wealthy (God). — ه
To disquiet a. o. — وأَرْعَجَ ه
To increase (wealth). رَعِجَ a رَعَجًا وارْتَعَجَ
To become rich. أَرْعَجَ
To tremble. To run high (torrent). إِرْتَعَجَ
To thunder (sky). ✲ رَعَدَ a o رَعْدًا ورُعُودًا
To threaten, to thunder against a. o. To deck and show herself (woman). رَعَدَ وبَرَقَ
To threaten a. o. To strike a. o. (terror). — وأَرْعَدَ ه
To be assailed by thunder. أُرْعِدَ
To be thunderstruck, frightened. أُرْعِدَ
To quiver (sheep's tail). تَرَعَّدَ
To tremble from age or fear. إِرْتَعَدَ
His muscles quivered. *i. e.* He was terror-stricken. إِرْتَعَدَتْ فَرائِصُهُ
Thunder. رَعْدٌ ج رُعُودٌ
Shudder, fright, fear. رَعْدَةٌ و رِعْدَةٌ
Silurus electricus, torpedo-fish. رَعَّادٌ وسَمَكَةُ الرَّعْدِ
Loquacious. رَعَّادٌ ورَعَّادَةٌ
Thundering (cloud). رَعَّادٌ وراعِدَةٌ ج رَواعِدُ
Calamity. ذاتُ الرَّواعِدِ
To ask importunately. ✲ رَعْدَدَ
Cowardly. Delicate (woman). Food of starch and honey. رِعْدِيدٌ
To contract o.'s self (man). To vituperate. ✲ رعز — راعَزَ
Fine goat's hair. مِرْعِزٌ ومِرْعِزَّى ومِرْعِزَّاءُ
To tremble. To walk sluggishly (from fatigue). ✲ رَعَسَ a رَعْسًا
To nod the head (old man). — رَعَسانًا ه
To cause a shudder to a. o. أَرْعَسَ ه
To shudder. إِرْتَعَسَ
Nodding the head in slumber. رَعُوسٌ
Tottering (camel). رَعِيسٌ
✲ رَعَشَ a رَعْشًا, ورَعِشَ a رَعَشًا, وارْتَعَشَ
To be startled, to shiver.
To inspirit a. o. (war). أَرْعَشَ ه
To tremble from age (head). إِرْتَعَشَ
Startle, panic. رِعْشَةٌ
Startled. Inspirited (warrior). رَعِشٌ

Shaking the head from age (camel). رَعُوش
Coward. رَعِيش اليَدَيْن
Swift (ostrich, she-camel). رَعْشَاء
Raia torpedo, kind of cramp-fish. رَعَّاشَة
White pigeon. مُرَعَّش ومُرَعْش
Marash, town of Syria. مَرْعَش
To drag a. th. To gore and shake (a dog: bull). ✡ رَعَص a رَعْصًا, وأَرْعَص ه
To coil, to roll up (serpent). تَرَعَّص وارْتَعَص
To rise (market). To flash (lightning). To quiver (lance). To be shaken (tree). To bound (kid). إِرْتَعَص
To break the notch of (an arrow). To notch (an arrow). ✡ رَعَظ a رَعْظًا ه
To be broken at its notch (arrow). رَعِظ a رَعَظًا
To slacken a. o. To hurry a. o. To move (the finger). To shake out (a peg). رَعَّظ ه وه
Notch, socket of an arrow-head. رُعْظ ج أَرْعَاظ
To bleed from the nose. ✡ رَعَف o a, ورَعُف رَعْفًا ورُعَافًا
To outrun his competitors (horse). — ه a o
He entered abruptly. — بِهِ البَاب
To bleed (nose). رَعِف a رَعَفًا
To press a. o. To overfill (a water-skin). أَرْعَف ه وه
To be ahead in a race (horse). إِرْتَعَف واسْتَرْعَف
To make (the foot) to bleed (stone). إِسْتَرْعَف ه
Hæmorrhage of the nose. رُعَاف
Bleeding (nose). Ahead in a race (horse). Mountain-peak. Tip of the nose. *Pl.* Spears. رَاعِف ج رَوَاعِف
Stone left in a well for cleansing. رَاعُوف ورَاعُوفَة وأُرْعُوفَة
Fine rains. رُعُوف
Nose and the parts around it. مَرَاعِف
To spear a. o. To widen (a rent). ✡ رَعَل a رَعْلًا ه وه
To thrust a. o. with. وأَرْعَل ه ب

To become mad. رَعِل a رَعَلًا
To sprout forth (vine). رَعَّل
To walk in a file (cattle). To lead the way. إِسْتَرْعَل
Clothes. Peak of a mountain. رَعْل
Male palm-tree. رِعْل
Troop of horses. Palm-tree of bad quality. Ostrich. Family. Sprout. *Melissa perennis*, balm-plant. رَعْلَة ج رِعَال وأَرْعَال وأَرَاعِيل
Mucus from the nose. رُعَال
Bad dates. رَاعِل
First blasts of winds. أَرَاعِيل الرِّيَاح
Advanced party of men, horses. رَعِيل ج رِعَال
Mad. Flaccid — (herbs). أَرْعَل م رَعْلَاء ج رُعْل
Long-eared; lop eared (ewe). رَعْلَاء
Dracunculus, garden tarragon. رُعْلُول
To observe (sunset). To watch a. th. ✡ رَعَم o رَعْمًا ه
To be lean and glandered (ewe). — a رُعَامًا, ورَعُم o رَعَامَة, وأَرْعَم
To wipe the mucus of (a sheep). رَعَّم ه
Mucus of horses, ewes. رُعَام ج أَرْعِمَة
Soul. Glandered ewe. Lean. رَعُوم
✡ رَعَن o رَعْنًا, ورَعِن a رَعَنًا, ورَعُن o رُعُونَة
To be careless, slack, foolish.
To affect the brain of a. o. (sun). رَعَن a رَعْنًا ه
Peak of a mountain. رَعْن ج رُعُون ورِعَان
Darkness of the night. Strong. Restless. رَعُون
Foolish, lax. Numerous (army). Long-nosed. أَرْعَن م رَعْنَاء
Bassorah (town). Renowned grapes. رَعْنَاء
To amend, to revert from error. ✡ رَعَا o رَعْوًا ورَعْوَة ورُعْوَة
To be converted from. إِرْعَوَى إِرْعِوَاء عن
To pasture, to graze (the grass). ✡ رَعَى a رَعْيًا ورِعَايَة ومَرْعًى ه
To tend (flocks). ✧ To itch (body). — ه
To tend (flocks) for a. o. — عن
To observe the setting of (the stars). To be mindful of. To keep (an order). — ورَاعَى ه
To rule (his subjects: chief). رِعَايَة
To show regard to a. o. رَاعَى ه وه

rest o.'s self; to be diligent in.
To turn away from. رَغِبَ عن
To prefer a. th. before. — ب عن
رَغِبَ a رَغْبًا ورُغْبًا ورَغْبَى ورُغْبَى ورَغْبَة ورَغَبَاء
To pray, ورَغَبُوتًا ورَغَبُوتَى ورَغَبَانًا إلى
to ask humbly from a. o.
To be covetous, glut- رَغُبَ o رُغْبًا ورُغُبًا
tonous.
To inspire to a. o. رَغَّبَ وأَرْغَبَ ه في
the desire of.
To expand (valley). تَرَاغَبَ
Wide (road). رَغْب ج رُغُب
Soft, absorbing (ground). رُغُب ورَغَاب
Desire, wish. ✧ Diligence. رَغْبَة
Knot of a sandal thong. رَغْبَانَة
Heavy. Glutto- رَغِيب م رَغِيبَة ج رِغَاب
nous. Wide (valley).
Object of desire. رَغِيبَة ج رَغَائِب
Large gift.
Covetousness. Means of sus- مَرَاغِب
tenance.
To suck (his ✱ رَغَثَ a رَغْثًا, وارْتَغَثَ ه
mother: kid).
To spear a. o. repeatedly. — وأَرْغَثَ ه
To exhaust o.'s wealth by gene- رُغِثَ
rosity. To have a complaint of the
breast.
To suckle (her kid: goat). أَرْغَثَ ه
Pomegranate-blossom. رَغْث
Vein of the breast. رُغْثَاء
Suckling (female). رَغُوث
Place of the ring on the finger. مُرَغَّث
To be ✱ رَغِدَ a رَغَدًا, ورَغُدَ o رَغَادَة
ample and pleasant (life).
To live luxuriantly. أَرْغَدَ
To let (cattle) pasture freely. — ه وه
To render (life) pleasant (God).
To find life to be easy. إِسْتَرْغَدَ العَيْشَ
To be confused. To be mixed إِرْغَادَّ
(milk).
Leading an easy (*m. f. s. pl.*) رَغْد
life.
Easy, luxuriant life. عِيشَة رَغْد ورَغَد
Boiled milk sprinkled with رَغِيدَة
flour.
Darnel-weed. رُغَيْدَاء
Wavering; confused. مُرْغَادّ
To give ✱ رَغَسَ a رَغْسًا, وأَرْغَسَ ه ه
(offspring, wealth) to a. o. (God).

To ponder over a. th. To pasture
together (asses).
✧ He is grateful. رَاعَى الجَمِيل
✧ He shows regard. رَاعَى الخَاطِر
To abound in pasture (land). — وأَرْعَى
To listen to a. o. رَاعَى وأَرْعَى ه السَّمْع
To pasture, to tend (flocks). أَرْعَى ه
To spring up pasturage for — ه ه
(cattle: God).
To spare, to pity a. o. — على
To graze, to browse تَرَعَّى وارْتَعَى
(cattle).
To ask a. o. to tend flocks. إِسْتَرْعَى ه
To call the attention of. — ه السَّمْع
Pasture-lands. رِعْي ج أَرْعَاء
Pastinaca sativa (*plant*). رِعْي الأُيَّل
Verbena, vervain (*plant*). رِعْي الحَمَام
Tended flock. Subjects. رَعِيَّة ج رَعَايَا
✧ Rayahs, non-Moslem subjects. Pa-
rishioners.
Watch. Tending of cattle. رِعْيَة ورَعْيَاء
God keep thee safe! رَعْيًا لَكَ
Mindfulness. رُعْيَا ورُعْوَى ورَعْوَى
Camels pasturing near رَعَاوَى ورُعَاوَى
dwellings.
Shepherd. رَاعٍ ج رُعَاة ورُعْيَان ورُعَاء ورِعَاء
Pastor. Ruler. Tame (beast).
Star in the foot of *Orio*. رَاعِي الجَوْزَاء
Star in *Sagittarius*. رَاعِي النَّعَائِم
Kinds of locusts. رَاعِي البُسْتَان والأُتُن
Scandix, shepherd's needle; إِبْرَة الرَّاعِي
or: Geranium, crane's bill.
Artemisia, mug-wort. حَبَق الرَّاعِي
Shepherd's-rod, kind of عَصَا الرَّاعِي
Polygonum, knot-grass.
Shepherd's purse. كِيس الرَّاعِي
Holly-tree. شَرَّابَة الرَّاعِي
Kind of yellow sparrow. رَاعِيَة الخَيْل
Beginning of رَاعِيَة ورَوَاعِي الشَّيْب
hoariness.
Good تِرْعِيَّة وتِرْعَايَة وتِرْعِي وتُرَاعِيَة
manager of camels.
Pasturage, herbage. مَرْعًى ج مَرَاعٍ
Pasture-land.
Ruled, tended. Regarded. مَرْعِيّ
To live in comfort. To drink ✱ رَغْرَغَ
at leisure (camels).
To ✱ رَغِبَ a رَغْبًا ورَغَبًا ورَغْبَة, وارْتَغَبَ في
wish a. th; to long for. ✧ To inte-

إِسْتَرْغَسَ ه	To find a. th. soft, mellowy.
رَغْس ج أَرْغَاس	Increase. Blessing. Wealth.
مُرْغِس ومُرْغَس	Pleasant life.
✫ رَغَفَ a رَغْفًا ه	To knead (flour, dough).
– ه	To give cakes of flour to (a camel).
أَرْغَفَ	To hurry in walk
– إلى	To fix the looks upon.
رَغِيف ج أَرْغِفَة ورُغْف ورُغُف ورُغْفَان وَرَاغِيف	Round cake, loaf of bread.
✫ رَغَلَ a رَغْلًا ه	To suck (his mother : kid).
أَرْغَلَ	To run to seeds (crops). To sin (man).
– ه	To grow (orache : soil). To suckle (her kid : goat). To displace.
– عن	To stray from (a pasturage : cattle).
– إلى	To lean towards.
رُغْل ج أَرْغَال	*Atriplex hortensis*, garden-orache.
رَغْلَة	Lambkin, kid.
رَغُول	Eating all he can find.
أَرْغَل	Easy, pleasant (life).
✫ رَغَمَ o رَغْمًا, ورَغِمَ a رَغَمًا ه	To dislike.
– ه	To compel a. o. to act reluctantly.
رَغِمَ a, ورَغُمَ o رَغْمًا أَنْفُهُ	His nose clave to the ground *i. e.* he was humbled.
رَاغَمَ ه	To break off in anger from.
أَرْغَمَ الله أَنْفَهُ	God has abased him.
أَرْغَمَ ه	To spite ; to revile ; to compel.
تَرَغَّمَ	To act reluctantly.
تَرَغَّمَ على	To be angry with.
رَغْم ورُغْم و رِغْم ومَرْغَمَة	Reluctance. Dislike.
على رَغْمِ أَنْفِهِ وعلى مَرْغَمَتِهِ و✧ رَغْمًا عَنْهُ	In spite of him.
رَاغِمُ الأَنْف ج رُغْمُ الأُنُوف	Abashed.
رَغَام	Earth, dust. Sand.
رُغَام	Mucus.
رُغَامَة	Thing sought.
رُغَامَى ومَرْغَم و مِرْغَم	Nose.
مُرَاغَم	Place of refuge. Stronghold.
(	Frequented (place).
✫ رَغِنَ a رَغَنًا	To eat and drink with pleasure.
وأَرْغَنَ إلى –	To listen to.
رَغِنَ في	To covet a. th.
أَرْغَنَ ه ه	To make a. o. to covet a. th. To facilitate a. th. to.
رَغْنَة	Even and soft ground.
G أَرْغُن وأَرْغَنُون ج أَرَاغِن	Organ, harmonium.
✫ رَغَا o رُغَاء	To grumble (camel). To shriek (child).
رَغَا o رَغْوًا, ورَغَّى وأَرْغَى	To froth (milk). To rumble (thunder).
رَغَّى ه	✧ To scorify (metals).
أَرْغَى وأَزْبَدَ	To foam with rage ; to threaten.
أَرْغَى ه	To make (a camel) to grumble.
مَا أَثْغَى ومَا أَرْغَى	He has given neither goat nor she-camel.
إِرْتَغَى ه	To drink (the froth of milk).
رَغْوَة ج رُغًى و رِغًى	Rock. Froth of milk.
رَغْوَة القَمَر	Selenite (stone).
رَغْوَة الحَجَّامِين	Sponge.
رُغَاوَة ورُغَايَة	Froth.
مِرْغَاة	Skimmer ; ladle for skimming.
مُرَغّ	Obscure (speech).
✫ رَفَّ o رَفًّا	To eat heartily.
– ه	To drink (milk) daily. To suck.
– ه و ل	To do good to.
– إلى	To rely upon a. o.
– ب	To surround a. o. To honour a. o.
– i رَفًّا ورَفِيفًا, وارْتَفَّ	To flash (lightning). To shine (colour). To twinkle (eye). To be shaken by the wind (plant). ✧ To flutter (bird).
– a رَفَفًا	To be thin (stuff).
– ه	To enlarge the skirt of (a tent, garment). To feed (a beast) with straw.
أَرَفَّ على	To spread the wings over (her eggs : hen).
رَفّ ج رُفُوف و رِفَاف	Shelf ; board on a wall, cornice. Herd of camels, oxen. Flock of sheep. Flight of birds. Enclosure for cattle. Soft garment.
رُفّ ورُفَّة	Broken pieces of straw.
مَا لَهُ حَافٌّ ولَا رَافٌّ	He has no one to take care of him.
رِفًّا	Every day, daily.

To put a saddle-pad on (a beast). — ة وعلى، وأرْفد ل
To do honour; to make a. o. chief. رَفَّد ة
To help one another. ترافد
To gain (wealth). إرتفد
To ask the help of. To ask a gift from. إستَرفد ة
Gift. Help. Share. رِفد ج رُفود وأرفاد
Large cup. رَفد ومِرفَد ج مَرافِد
He is dead أُريق رَفدُهُ
The Tigris and the Euphrates. الرّافِدان
Rafter of a roof. رَافِدة ج رَوافِد
Saddle-pad. Rags for a wound. رِفادة
She-camel filling a large cup at one milking. رَفُود ج رُفُد
To kick. ✡ رَفَس o i رَفسًا و رِفاسًا ه
✧ To thrust (arch).
To kick a. o. in the breast. To tie (a camel's feet). To mince (meat). — ة وه
Kick. ✧ Thrust of an arch. رَفسة
Foot-rope of camels. Habit of kicking. رِفاس
Screw-steamer. ✧ رَفّاس
To eat and drink heartily. ✡ رَفَش o رَفشًا
To pound a. th. To shovel. — ة و ه
To act in a grand style. — رُفُوشًا في
To have large ears. رَفِش a رَفشًا
To comb, to expand (the beard). رَفّش ه
✧ Shoulder-blade. رفش
Shovel. رَفش ومِرفَشة
Shovelling the grain to the meter. رَفّاش
Large-eared. أرفش م رَفشاء ج رُفش
To draw (water) by turns. ✡ رفص — ترافص ه
To rise (price). إرتفص
Turn of drinking. رُفصة
Partner, sharer. رَفِيص
To cast off. To shun a. th. ✧ To recuse (a judge). ✡ رَفَض i o رَفضًا ورَفَضًا ه وة
To let (camels) scatter in a pasture. — وأرفَض ة
To be wide (valley). — وأرفَض واستَرفَض
To pasture freely (camels). o رُفوضًا
To be broken, scattered. ترَفّض
✧ To be bigoted. — في المَذهب
To be scattered. To flow إرفَضّ

Roof. Dewy (plant). Abundance of fodder. Sky-light. Lily. رَفِيف
Pontoon-bridge. ذات رَفِيف
To flutter (bird). To resound. ✡ رَفرَف
To bandage (a limb). — ه
Sky-light; arched window. Tent. Thin brocade. Skirt of a tent. Redundant furniture. Provision. ✧ Splash-board. رَفرَف ج رَفارِف
Male ostrich. Kind of sparrow. ✧ Flight of birds. Pent-roof. رَفراف
To mend (clothes). To bring (a ship) ashore. ✡ رَفَأ a رَفأً ه
To make peace between. — بَين
To allay the fear of; to soothe. — ة
To greet new (spouses). رَفَّأ تَرفِئة وتَرفِيئًا ة
To favour a. o. in a sale. To blandish a. o. رافأ وأرفأ ة
To lean on one side. To comb o.'s hair. To land (ship). أرفأ
To approach. To take refuge to. — إلى
To near a. th. To bring (a ship) ashore. — ه إلى
To agree together. To help o. a. ترافأ
Agreement, union. رِفاء ومُرافاة
Be united and have many children! (*greeting to new spouses*). بالرِفاء والبَنين
Patcher of clothes, darner. رَفّاء
Port: landing-place. مَرفأ ومُرفأ ج مَرافِئ
Frightened. Shepherd. Ostrich flying away. Fawn. يَرفَئِي
To be broken. To be cut (rope). To be crushed (bone). ✡ رَفَت o i رَفتًا، وارفَتّ
To break to pieces; to crumble a. th. ✧ To dismiss (a clerk). رَفَت ه وة
Transit-duty; permit. ✧ رَفتِيّة ج رَفاتِي
Thrashed straw. Pounder, crusher. رُفت
Crumbs. Decayed bones. رُفات
Agrimony (*plant*). رافِت
✡ رَفَث o i رَفثًا ورُفوثًا، ورَفِث a رَفَثًا، وأرفَث
To hold unseemly, obscene speech.
To greet (new spouses). ✡ رفح — رَفّح ة
To rise (dough). ✧ رَفَح
Easy (life). رافِح
To succour a. o. To make a present to. ✡ رَفَد i رَفدًا، ورافَد وأرفَد ة
To stay (a wall). — ه

(tears). To suppurate (wound). To cease (pain).

Scattered herd of gazelles, camels. Little of water. Food. رَفْض ج رُفُوض و رِفَاض

Camels scattered in a pasture. Party of deserters. Sect of Mohammedan heretics. رَافِضَة ج رَوَافِض

Heretic. Fanatic, bigot. رَافِضِيّ ج أَرْفَاض

Fragments, shatters. رُفَاض

Separated parties. Isolated pasturages. ◠ رُفُوض

Cast away. Sweat. Broken spear. رَفِيض

✧ Fanaticism, bigotry. تَرَفُّض

Track of a torrent. مَرْفِض ج مَرَافِض

✱ To extol a. o. To lift a. th. To take away. To urge (a camel). To put a noun in the nominative. To reduce (fractions). To trace back (a tradition). ✧ To raise (a siege, a sitting). To trench (a question). To remit (a tax). رَفَعَ a رَفْعًا ه وه

To make a truce. رَفَعَ السِّلَاح

□ He carried a letter. رَفَعَ جَوَاب

✧ To dispense from. — عن

✧ To withdraw from (an affair). رَفَعَ يَدَهُ عَن

To bring crops to the floor. — رَفْعًا ورَفَاعَة

To honour, to show regard to. — رَأْسًا لِ

To advance speedily (camel). — في السَّيْر

They came to an upland. رَفَعَ القَوْم

To urge on (a horse). — ه في السَّيْر

To arraign a. o. before (a judge). رَفَعَ رَفْعًا ورُفْعَانًا ه إلى

To introduce a. o. to (a king). — رُفْعَانًا ه إلى

To be raised in dignity. رَفُعَ o رِفْعَة ورَفَاعَة

To have a loud voice. — رَفَاعَة

He saw the thing from afar. رُفِعَ لَهُ الشَّيْءُ

To raise, to lift a. th. or a. o. To carry a. o. away (from a battle). ✧ To refine a. th. رَفَّعَ ه و ه

To run inequally (ass). ✧ To hold carnival. رَفَّعَ

To prefer (a case); to summon a. o. before (a judge). رَافَعَ ه وه إلى

To spare the life of. — ب

He endeavoured to circumvent me. رَافَعَنِي وخَافَضَنِي

To become proud. تَرَفَّعَ

To prosecute o. a. before a judge. تَرَافَعَ

To be exalted. To be advanced (day). To rise (price). To disappear (evil). إِرْتَفَعَ

To ask a. th. to be raised, taken away. إِسْتَرْفَعَ ه

It is time to remove the table. — الخِوَانُ

Raising. Removal. Vowel-point of the Nominative. ✧ Tracing of a tradition to its author. Excellent. رَفْع

✧ Withdrawal, replevin. رَفْع يَد

High rank. Honour. رِفْعَة

Land difficult to be watered. أَرْض رَافِعَة الشُّقْيَا

Removal of crops to the floor. ◠ رَفَاع و رِفَاع

Loudness, shrillness of the voice. رَفَاعَة ورُفَاعَة و رِفَاعَة

High rank, dignity. String for raising chains. ✧ Thinness, refinedness. رُفَاعَة

Sect of dervishes. (*un.* رِفَاعِي) Snake-charmers. رِفَاعِيَّة

High in rank. Loud, shrill (voice). ✧ Fine; thin; ingenious. رَفِيع

F. Case preferred to a judge. رَفِيعَة

✧ Carnival. Side-board. مَرْفَع ج مَرَافِع

High. In the nominative (word). Quick step of an ass. Transmitted (tradition). مَرْفُوع

To be luxuriant (life). ✱ رَفُغَ o رَفَاغَة

To be in easy circumstances. تَرَفَّغَ

Ampleness of life. رَفْغ ورَفَاغِيَة ورُفْغُنِيَة

Part of a valley less fruitful. رَفْغ ج أَرْفُغ

Lowest class of people. Side. Straw of maize. — ج أَرْفَاغ

Dirt of the body. Creases of the body; armpit. Abundance. Barren ground. — ج أَرْفَاغ ورُفُوغ

Easy, happy (life). رَافِغ ورَفِيغ وأَرْفَغ

Trailing a garment. Long-tailed رِفَلّ (horse). Fleshy. Wrinkled (camel). Ample clothes. Easy life.
Loose, long (hair). رَفَال
Awkward in dress. ✧ Lop-eared (ass). أرفل م رَفلاء
✫ رفن — إِرْفَأَنَّ To be weak and remiss. To cool (anger). To flee away and rest.
✫ رَفَه a رَفْهًا و رِفْهًا ورُفُوهًا, وتَرَفَّه To enjoy a delicate life.
To go to water daily (camel). رَفَه
To be spent in luxury (life). رَفُه o رَفَاهًا ورَفَاهِيَة
To give well-being to a. o. (God). To let (camels) drink at will. رَفَّه وأَرْفَه ة
To grant a respite to (a debtor). رَفَّه عَن
To live in luxury. To live near water (cattle). أرفه
To rest, to live quietly at a. o.'s. — واسْتَرْفَه عِند
Pity, forbearance, kindness. رَفْهَة
Compassionate towards. رَافِه ب
We are at a distance of an easy night-journey. بَيْنَنَا لَيْلَة رَافِهَة ولِيَالٍ رَوَافِه
Welfare. Comforts of life. رَفَاهَة ورَفَاهِيَة ورُفَهْنِيَة
✫ رَفَا o رَفْوًا ه To darn (a garment).
To allay the fear, to quiet a. o. To maintain a. o. — ة
To agree with. To be gentle towards. رَافَى مُرَافَاةً و رِفَاءً ة
To agree together. ترافى
Agreement, concord. رِفَاء
Long-eared, lop-eared (ass). أَرْفَى م رَفْوَاء ج رفو
Milk of gazelle. أَرْفِيّ
✫ رَقّ i رِقَّة, واسْتَرَقّ To be thin. To be ashamed. To be poor, weakened.
✧ To flatten. To thin (bread). — ه
To have mercy upon, to pity a. o. رَقّ وتَرَقَّق ل
To be or become a slave. رَقّ i رِقًّا
To render a. th. thin. رَقَّق وأَرَقّ ه
✧ To flatten (metals). To move (the heart).
To render (speech) elegant رَقَّق الكَلَام

✫ رَفَق o رَفْقًا, وأَرْفَق ة To be useful, to do service to a. o.
رَفَق ة To strike a. o. on the elbow. To tie (a camel) by the shoulders.
رَفَق, ورَفُق o, ورَفِق a رِفْقًا ومَرْفِقًا ومَرْفَقًا ومِرْفَقًا ب وعلى ول To be gentle to.
رَفُق o رَفَاقَة To be in company.
رَافَق ة To accompany a. o.
أَرْفَق ة, وتَرَفَّق ب To act gently with.
تَرَافَق To journey in company.
تَرَفَّق على To lean upon. ✧ To pity a. o.
إِرْتَفَق To be filled up (vessel). To lean on the elbows.
إِسْتَرْفَق To seek help. To seek a fellow-traveller.
تَمَرْفَق To take an elbow-rest.
رِفْق ورَافِقَة Compassion, pity, gentleness.
رِفْقَة ورَفْقَة ورُفْقَة ج رِفَاق و رِفَق وأَرْفَاق ورُفَق Company.
— ورُفَاقَة Company of travellers.
رَفَق Flowing easily (water). Easy (affair). Disease of the udder.
رِفَاق ج رُفُق Rope for tying camels.
رَفِيق ج رُفَقَاء Companion. comrade, colleague. Gentle.
مِرْفَق ومَرْفِق ج مَرَافِق Elbow. Pillow; elbow-rest.
مَرْفِق ج مَرَافِق Beneficial thing.
مَرَافِق الدَّار Appertenances of a house as kitchen, well, privy.
مِرْفَقَة Elbow-rest. Pillow.
مُرْتَفَق Pillow, resting-place. ✧ Privy.
✫ رَفَل o رَفْلًا ورَفَلَانًا ورُفُولًا, وأَرْفَل To drag o.'s skirt. To trail a garment. To sweep, to strut.
رَفَل o رَفْلًا, ورَفِل a رَفَلًا To be awkward in dress, work.
رَفَّل ه To let (water) collect in a well. To add (a syllable) to (a verse).
— ة To make a. o. chief. To abase.
— وأَرْفَل ه To let loose; to drag (a garment).
تَرَفَّل To have a proud deportment.
رِفْل Train of a garment.
رَفَل Bottom of a pit where water collects.
رَفِلَة Dragging o.'s skirt elegantly. Ugly (woman). Easy (life).

To pronounce softly. رقّق اللفظ

To sow discord between. — ما بَين

To become poor and weak (man). أرَقّ
To ripen (grapes).

To move the heart. — القلب

To enslave a. o., to possess ه واسترَقّ —
a slave.

To become thin. ترقّق

To compassionate a. o. ترقّق ل

To be shallow (water). إسترَقّ

Slavery, slave-trade. ✧ Tambourine. رِقّ

Vellum. Parchment. Sheet رَقّ ج رُقُوق
of paper. Big tortoise. Crocodile.

Broad and soft ground. رَقّ ورِقّ ورَقَق

Weakness. Fineness; thinness. رَقَق

Land regularly flooded رَقّة ج رِقاق
by a river.

Mercy. Bashfulness. Thinness. رِقّة

Easy life. رِقّة العَيش

Weakness. — الجانب

Shallow water. Low sea. رُقاق ورَقّ

Thin bread. (un. رُقاقة) رُقاق ج رِقاق
Easy walk of camels.

Hot (day). Desert; soft place. رَقاق

Slave (m. f.) ج أرِقّاء ورِقاق رَقيق
newly caught. Thin; weak, mean.

Pronouncing softly. — اللفظ

In a poorly state. — الحال

Thin-hoofed (horse). مُرِقّ

The soft parts of the belly. مَراقّ البطن

Rolling-pin. مِرقاق

The two wings of the nose. مَرَقّا الأنف

✧ Spleen; melancholy. مَراقِيّة

✧ Bread in thin sheets. مَرقوق

✱ رَقرَق ه To sprinkle (water, perfumes). To cause (tears) to flow. To mix (wine).

To flow. To flicker (water, ترَقرَق
mirage). To shine in the eyes (tear).

Tear shining in the eye. Glis- رَقراق
tening. Indian melilot. ✧ Shallow (water).

✱ رَقَأ a رَقأ ورُقوءا To stop (blood, tears). To exude (sweat).

To make mischief or peace — رَقأ بَين
between.

To dry (tears, blood). To pro- أرقأ ه
mote (sweat). To prevent bloodshed.

Rags for stopping blood; styptic. رَقُوء

✱ رَقَب o رُقوبا ورَقوبا ورَقابة ورِقبانا ورِقبة ورَقبة ه
To observe (the stars).
To watch over; to wait for.

To tie by the neck. To warn a. o. ه —

To watch over. راقب مُراقبة ورِقابا ه وه
To fear (God). ✧ To control a. th.

To give to a. o. the use of أرقب ه ه
a property for life.

To wait for a. o. ترقّب وارتقب ه و ه
or a. th.

To ascend (a height). إرتقب ه

Thickness of the neck. رَقَب

Life-donation; usufruct for life. رُقبى

Observation. Caution. Fear. رِقبة

He inherited wealth وَرِث مالًا عن رِقبة
from distant relations.

Neck. رَقَبة ج رِقاب ورَقَب وأرقُب ورَقَبات
Nape of the neck. Person, head. Slave.

✧ Thou art responsible هذا في رَقَبَتِك
for it.

Broad-necked. رَقَبان ورَقَبانِيّ

The Watcher (God). رَقيب ج رُقَباء
Watchman. Guardian. In opposition (star). Cousin.

Turnsol, kind of euphor- رَقيب الشمس
bia.

Self-observer, cautious. — نفسِهِ

Venomous snake. — ج رَقيبات ورُقُب

Forlorn woman expecting the رَقوب
death of her husband.

Misfortune. أمّ الرَّقوب

Guardian left in a house. رَقّابة

Broad-necked. Lion. أرقب م رَقباء

Look out; watch- مَرقَب ومَرقَبة ج مَراقِب
tower.

✱ رقح — رَقّح ه To manage a. th. well.

To increase. إرتقح

To earn for o.'s (family) ترقّح ل

Traffic, trade, profit. رَقاحة

Merchant, trader. رَقاحِيّ

✱ رَقَد o رَقدا ورُقودا ورُقادا To sleep.
To lull (heat). To be dull, (market).
To be ragged (garment).

To overlook (an affair). — عن أمر

To put to sleep: to lull a. o. أرقد ه

To sojourn in. — ب

To hurry. إرقدّ

A sleep. A lull. رَقدة

To patch (a garment). ✡ رَقَمَ a رَقْمًا هـ
To repair (a well). ✧ To strike.
To walk quickly (camel). — فِي سَيْرِهِ
To epigrammatise a. o. To overtake a. o. — ه
To hit the target with (an arrow). To strike a. o. with. — هـ ب
To be nonsensical, impudent (man). رَقُمَ o رَقَاعَةً
To patch up (clothes). To manage (property). رَقَّمَ هـ
To be addicted to (wine). رَاقَمَ هـ (عَاقَرَ for)
To show foolishness. أَرْقَمَ
To want repair (garment). — وَاسْتَرْقَمَ
To earn o.'s living. تَرَقَّمَ
To be heedless, unmindful of. مَا ارْتَقَمَ ل وب
Seventh heaven. رَقِم
Sound of an arrow upon the butt. رَقْمَة
Patch. Piece of land. Piece of paper. Shift. Constitutive. Beginning of scab. Target. Letter, note. رُقْعَة ج رِقَاع ورُقَم
Chess-board. رُقْعَة الشِطْرَنْج
White-spotted on the side (ewe). Foolish (woman). Fern. Dwarf-elder. رَقْعَاء
Unsoundness of mind. رَقَاعَة
Firmament. رَقِيع ج أَرْقِعَة
Fool, silly. — وأَرْقَع
Patched (garment). Scabby (man). مُرَقَّع
Object of ridicule. مُرْتَقِع
Silly (. مَرْقَعَان م مَرْقَعَانَة
Violent (hunger). جُوع يَرْقُوع
To go on quickly; to amble. ✡ رَقَلَ — أَرْقَلَ
To cross (a desert). — هـ
Lofty palm-tree. رَقْلَة ج رَقْل و رِقَال
Swift-running (she-camel). مِرْقَال ومُرْقِل ومُرْقِلَة
To write. ✡ رَقَمَ o رَقْمًا
To dot (a book). To stripe (cloth). To brand (a camel). — هـ وه
He streaks water; (*prov. to mean*) a remarkable skill. يَرْقُمُ فِي المَاء
To dot (unpaid items) in a register. To streak (cloth) رَقَّمَ هـ

Great sleeper. رُقَدَة ورَقُود و يَرْقُود
Leap, bound (of a lamb). رَقَدَان
Large jar. Goby, small sea-fish. P رَاقُود ج رَوَاقِيد
Sluggish gait. Brooding of eggs. تَرْقِيد
Soporific. Opium. Distinct road. مُرْقِد ✧ مُرَقِّد
Bed. Sleeping-place. مَرْقَد ج مَرَاقِد
To throb (artery). ✡ رَقَزَ o رَقْزًا
To variegate (cloth). To adorn a. th. ✡ رَقَشَ o رَقْشًا هـ
To embellish (speech). To dot (a writing). To rule (a page). To blame a. o. رَقَّشَ هـ
To adorn himself (man). تَرَقَّشَ
To mix in war (fighters). إِرْتَقَشَ
Speckled viper. رَقَاش
Spotted of white and black. أَرْقَش م رَقْشَاء ج رُقْش
Spotted serpent. Soft palate of camels. Kind of caterpillar. رَقْشَاء
To dance. To flicker (looming). To ferment (wine). ✡ رَقَصَ o رَقْصًا
To amble (camel). ✧ To prance (horse). — رَقَصًا ورَقَصًا ورَقَصَانًا
To dandle a child. To make a. o. to dance. To make (a camel) to amble. رَقَّصَ وأَرْقَصَ ه
To rise and sink (ground). تَرَقَّصَ
Dance. Amble (of camels). رَقْص
Star *in Draco*. رَاقِص
Dancer. ✧ Pendulum, spring of a clock. رَقَّاص
Female dancer. Barren land. Play of the Arabs. رَقَّاصَة
Thrilling, moving verses. مُرَقِّص
To spot a garment with drops. ✡ رَقَطَ عَلَى الثَوْب ونَقَّطَهُ
To be spotted. stained. إِرْقَطَّ وتَرَقَّطَ وارْقَاطَّ
White and black spots. رُقْطَة
Spotted of white and black. Panther. Spotted sheep. أَرْقَط م رَقْطَاء ج رُقْط
Serpentaria, dragon-wort. السَلُوف الأَرْقَط
Riot, sedition. Speckled hen. Oily porridge. رَقْطَاء
Poisonous lizard. السُلَيْسِلَة والسَلْسِلَة الرَقْطَاء

رَقْم ج أَرْقَام ورُقُوم Variegated cloth. Numeral.
رَقْم هِنْدِيّ Arabic numerals.
جَاءَ بِالرَّقِم وبِالرَّقْم He brought much.
رَقِم وبِنْتُ الرَّقِم Misfortune.
رَقْمَة Meadow. Side of a valley. Reservoir. Mallow.
رَقْمَة Plant of the class *pentandria*.
رَقِيم Inscription on a stone, a tablet. ✧ Letter, missive.
أَرْقَم م رَقْشَاء ج أَرَاقِم Speckled snake.
مِرْقَم ج مَرَاقِم Writing-reed. Brand.
مَرْقُومَة Having scanty plants (land). Streaked with brands (beast).
✲ رقن — رَقَّن To write a fair hand.
رَقَّن ه To write a th. in closing the lines. To improve, to adorn a. th. To dot (unpaid items).
— وأَرْقَن ه To dye (the beard) red.
تَرَقَّن To dye herself with henna (woman).
أَرْقَن وارْتَقَن واسْتَرْقَن To be dyed red.
رِقَان ورَقُون وإِرْقَان Saffron, henna.
يَرَقَان ويَرَقَّان Jaundice. Smut, disease in grain.
✲ رَقْو ورَقْوَة Sandy hillock.
✲ رَقِي a رَقْيًا ورُقِيًّا في وإلى To ascend gradually.
رَقَى i رُقْيَةً ورَقْيًا ورُقِيًّا ه وعلى To give a charm to a. o. To enchant a. o.
رَقَّى ه To raise, to exalt a. o.
— كَلَامًا على To bring a charge against.
تَرَقَّى وارْتَقَى ه وإلى وفي To ascend (a mountain).
— في To go up (a ladder). To progress in (science). To be promoted in (rank).
تَرَقَّى بِهِ الأَمْرُ The affair succeeded with him.
إِسْتَرْقَى ه To ask a. o. to enchant.
رُقْيَة و✧ رَقْوَة ج رُقًى ورُقْيَات ورُقْيَات Spell, charm. Amulet.
رَاقٍ ج رُقَاة Sorcerer, magician.
رَاقِيَة ج رَوَاقٍ Witch, sorceress.
رَقَّاء Great and skilful wizard.
مَرْقِيّ Bewitched.
مَرْقًى ومَرْقَاة ومِرْقَاة ج مَرَاقٍ Stair, ladder. Stepping-stone. Ascent.
مُرْتَقًى Place of ascent.

✲ رَكَّ i رَكًّا ورِكَّةً ورَكَاكَةً To be scanty. To be weak, thin. To have little science, a weak judgment.
— o رَكًّا ه في عُنُقِهِ To oblige a. o. to. To put an iron-collar to.
— ه ب To feel a. th. with (the hand).
— ه To compact a. th. ✧ To macadamise (a road).
رَكَّكَ وأَرَكَّ To let down a fine rain (sky).
أُرِكَّ To be watered by a fine rain (earth).
إِرْتَكَّ To quiver.
— في To waver in (an affair). To be indistinct in (speech: drunkard). To be incorrect (in speech).
إِسْتَرَكَّ ه To find a. th. thin, weak.
رَكّ ورِكّ ج أَرْكَاك ورِكَاك Drizzle.
رَكًّا Echo.
شَحْمَة الرَّكَّى Melting fat *said of a useless man.*
رُكَاك ورُكَاكَة (*m. f.*) Shallow-minded. Disregarded.
رَكِيك ج رِكَاك ورَكَكَة Thin, weak. Negligent. Uncompact (cloth).
رَكِيك العِلْم Little learned.
— اللَّفْظ Incorrect in speech.
مُرْتَكّ Confused, indistinct in speech.
مَرْكُوك Repaired (bucket). ✧ Macadamised (road).
✲ رَكْرَكَ To be weak, cowardly.
✲ رَكِب a رُكُوبًا ومَرْكَبًا. وارْتَكَب ه وه To ride (a beast). To voyage on (the sea). To embark (in a ship). To walk in (a road). To embark in (danger). To commit (a fault). To burden a. o. (debts).
رَكِب رَأْسَهُ To act heedlessly, at random. To run away at full speed (horse).
رَكِب هَوَاهُ ورَأْيَهُ He followed his passions, his own opinion.
رَكِب a رَكَبًا To have a big-knee.
رَكَب o رَكْبًا ه To strike a. o. on the knee or with the knee.
رَكَّب ه ه To lend (a camel) to a. o.
— ه To set (jewels). To combine, to compose a. th. To transplant (a palm-shoot). ✧ To set up (a gun, a bed). To forge (news).
✧ رَاكَب ه To distress, to harass a. o.

To be motionless (ship, ✡ رَكَد o رُكُودًا water). To be still (wind, men). To settle (dregs). To turn; to be still (pulley). To reach its midday-height (sun). To poise (balance).
Still, motionless. رَاكِد ج رُكَّد
Full (vessel). Milch-camel. رَكُود
Pl. Resting-places. مَرَاكِد
To bury a. th. ✡ رَكَز o i رَكْزًا, ورَكَّز ه To stick up (a lance). To produce ores (God). To set up a. th.
To contain gold, silver ores (mine). To find ores in a mine. أَرْكَز
To be fixed. To throb (artery). إِرْتَكَز
To lean upon (a bow). — على
Faint noise. Learned; generous man. رِكْز
Firmness, resolution. Palm-shoots. رِكْزَة
✧ Quiet. Sedate, cool-minded. رَاكِز
Gold and silver ore. Buried treasure. رِكَاز ج رِكْزَان وأَرْكِزَة ورَاكِزة
Gold and silver ores. رَكِيزَة ج رَكَائِز
✧ Treasure. Pole of a tent, peg.
Centre of (a circle). مَرْكَز ج مَرَاكِز Head-quarters. Residence. ✧ Seat of government; district. Support.
To reverse, to turn a. th. over. ✡ رَكَس o رَكْسًا ه
To tie (a camel). — ه
To throw a. o. back into a former state. أَرْكَس ه
To be mingled (hair). تَرَاكَس
To relapse into trouble. To be reversed. إِرْتَكَس
Dirt. Crowd. Repair. Bridge. رِكْس
Standing in the middle of the floor (ox). رَاكِس
Pole stuck into the earth. رَكَاسَة و رِكَاسَة
Rope fastening a camel's head to his feet. رِكَاس
To run, to move the feet. To move (stars). ✡ رَكَض o رَكْضًا
To trample in his run (horse). — ب
To fly swiftly (bird). — بِجَنَاحَيْهِ
To urge (a horse) with the feet. — ه بِرِجْلَيْهِ
To escape from. — من

To be fit to be ridden (colt). أَرْكَب
To mount a. o. upon (a beast). — ه
To be set. ✧ To be composed. تَرَكَّب
To heap up (clouds). تَرَاكَب
✧ To be venal. إِرْتَكَب
Party of riders above ten. رَكْب ج أَرْكُب ورُكُوب
Party of riders below ten. رَكَبَة
رُكْبَة ج رُكَب ورُكْبَات ورُكَبَات ورُكُبَات
Knee. Joint of the forelegs.
Influenza, dengue-fever. ✧ ابو الرُّكَب
Star in *Cygnus*. رُكْبَة الدَّجَاجَة
Star in *Sagittarius*. — الرَّامِي
رَاكِب ج رُكَّاب ورُكْبَان ورَكْب ورُكُوب و رَكَبَة
Rider; passenger. Head of (a mountain, of a spike).
Off-shoot of palm-trees. رَاكِبَة ورَاكُوب ورَاكُوبَة ج رَوَاكِب
Imported olive-oil. زَيت رِكَابِيّ
Stirrup of a horse-saddle. رِكَاب ج رُكُب
Camel for riding. — ج رُكُب و رِكَابَات ورَكَائِب
Rider. Skilled in affairs. رَكَّاب ورَكُوب
Camel for riding. رَكُوب ورَكُوبَة ج رَكَائِب
Inserted. Fellow-rider. رَكِيب ج رُكُب
Big-kneed. أَرْكَب م رَكْبَاء
Turn of a sentence. ✧ Frame of the body. Mouth-piece. تَرْكِيب
✧ Vehicle; ship. مَرْكَب ج مَرَاكِب
Beast for riding, nag. ✧ Shoes. مَرْكُوب ج مَرَاكِيب
Constitutive. Compound (word). مُرَكَّب
Gross ignorance of a fop. جَهْل مُرَكَّب
✧ Criminal, culprit. Bribed. مُرْتَكِب
To lean upon a. th. ✡ رَكَح a رَكْحًا, وأَرْكَح وارتَكَح على
To rely upon. To seek refuge towards. — رُكُوحًا إلى
To give refuge to; to stay a. o. أَرْكَح ه
To put o.'s self at ease. To enlarge (o.'s life). تَرَكَّح في
To stay in (a place). — ب
Side of a mountain. رُكْح ج رُكُوح وأَرْكَاح
Area of a house. *Pl.* Foundations. Monk's cells. — ج أَرْكَاح
High and hard ground. رَكْحَاء
Area of a house. رُكْحَة ج رُكَح
Dropping backwards (saddle). مِرْكَاح

To be started (horse). رَكِضَ
To race on horseback with a. o. رَاكَضَ ه
To race together. تَرَاكَضَ
To move the feet (in agony). إِرْتَكَضَ
To be stirred (water). To travel through (a land). To move in the womb (fœtus).
To be disquieted; to stir in (a business). — في
Swift run. رَكْض
Impulse. Temptation (of Satan). رَكْضَة ج رَكَضَات
Good runner; swift-shooting (bow). رَكُوض
Conceited gait. تَرَكُّضَى وَتِرِكِضَاء
Runner. مِرْكَاض
Fire-poker. Side of a bow. مِرْكَض
✡ To bow down in prayer. To be bent (old man). To stoop the head. To become destitute after wealth. ✧ To kneel. رَكَعَ a رَكْعًا ورُكُوعًا
To make a. o. to bow down. ✧ To make a. o. to kneel. رَكَّعَ وأَرْكَعَ ه
Deep hole. رُكْعَة
Prostration in prayer. ✧ Kneeling, genuflection. رَكْعَة ج رَكَعَات
Bent. Prostrate. ✧ Kneeling. رَاكِع ج رُكَّع ورُكُوع ورَاكِعُون
✡ To lay on the ground (snow). رَكَفَ – إِرْتَكَفَ
✡ To kick a. o. رَكَلَ o رَكْلًا ه
— To urge (a beast) with the feet. — ورَكَّلَ ه
To paw (the ground: horse). رَكَّلَ ه
To thrust (a spade) in the ground with (the foot). تَرَكَّلَ ب
To kick one another. تَرَاكَلَ
Leek. رِكْل
Bundle of green vegetables. رِكْلَة
Leek-seller. رَكَّال
Flanks of a beast. مَرْكَل ج مَرَاكِل
Road.
Foot of a rider. مِرْكَل ج مَرَاكِل
✡ To heap up a. th. رَكَمَ o رَكْمًا ه
To be heaped. To be compact (flesh). To become thick (darkness). تَرَاكَمَ وارْتَكَمَ
Heaped clouds. رُكَم ورُكَام

Heap of mud. رُكْمَة
Heap of (sand) Numerous (flocks). رُكَام
High road. مُرْتَكَم الطَّرِيق
✡ To be grave, cool. رَكُنَ o رَكَانَةً ورُكُونَةً
To lean on, to rely upon. ✧ To betake o.'s self to. رَكَنَ o, ورَكِنَ a رُكُونًا, وأَرْكَنَ إلى
To be strong. To be sedate. تَرَكَّنَ
✧ To ground o.'s self upon. إِرْتَكَنَ على
Rat; field-rat. رَكَن
Part, strongest side. Momentous affair. Column. Support. Strength. Substance. رُكْن ج أَرْكَان
The four elements. الأَرْكَان
✧ Staff of an army. أَرْكَان الحَرْب
State ministers. أَرْكَان الدَّوْلَة
Firmness. Sedateness. رُكُونَة ورَكَانَة
Grave, steadfast. Firmly seated (mountain). رَكِين
Prince, chief. Headman. G أَرْكُون ج أَرَاكِنَة
Washing-tub. مِرْكَن ج مَرَاكِن
✡ To dig (the earth). To tighten a. th. To repair a. th. رَكَا o رَكْوًا ه
To double the (load of a camel). — ه على
To sojourn in (a place). — ب
To put off a. th. — وأَرْكَى ه
To speak ill of a. o. — وأَرْكَى على
To seek refuge near. أَرْكَى إلى
To rely upon. تَرَكَّى وارْتَكَى على
Skiff. Leather-bag. ✧ Coffee-kettle. رِكْوَة ورُكْوَة ورَكْوَة ج رَكَوَات ورِكَاء
Well holding water. رَكِيَّة ج رَكَايَا ورُكِيّ
Lasting, steadfast. مُرَاكٍ ومُرْتَكٍ
I rely upon thee. أَنَا مُرْتَكٍ عَلَيْك
Large tank. مَرْكُوّ
✡ To repair (a building). To mend a. th. رَمَّ i o رَمًّا ومَرَمَّةً, ورَمَّمَ وتَرَمَّمَ ه
To browse, to graze (cattle). رَمَّ وارْتَمَّ
— To be decayed (bone). To be silent (people). — i رِمَّةً ورَمًّا ورَمِيمًا, وأَرَمَّ
To be full of marrow (bone). أَرَمَّ
To be prone to. — إلى
To need repairs (wall). إِسْتَرَمَّ
Care, intention. House furniture. رُمّ
Marrow. Herbage. Moist earth. رِمّ
I have no escape from it. مَا لِي مِنْهُ حُمّ ولَا رُمّ

Live bird used as bait for hawks. رَامِح
To spear a. o. To kick a. o. (camel). ✲ رَمَحَ a رَمْحًا ه
To flash faintly (lightning). رَمَحَ
▫ To gallop (horse).
They speared one another. تَرَامَحُوا
Spear. Destitution. رُمْح ج رِمَاح وأَرْمَاح
✧ Four degrees and a half of a circle.
They are at war. كَسَرُوا بَيْنَهُم رُمْحًا
They are united against them. هُم عَلَيْهِم كَرُمْحٍ وَاحِدٍ
Lancer. Two-horned (bull). رَامِح
Arcturus (star). السِّمَاك الرَّامِح
Plague. رِمَاح الجِنّ
To send forth prickles (plant). To become fat (camel). أَخَذَتْ رِمَاحَهَا
Kind of long-legged erboas. ذُو الرُّمَيْح
He leaned upon a staff from old age. أَخَذ رُمَيْحَ أَبِي سَعْد
✧ Circus, racing-field. مَرْمَح
To starve from cold (flock). ✲ رَمَدَ i رَمْدًا ورَمَادَةً
To destroy (a tribe); a flock (hail). — o i ه
To suffer from ophthalmia. رَمِدَ a رَمَدًا, وارْمَدَّ
To put a. th. in the ashes. To mar (a business). رَمَّدَ ه
To have milk before bringing forth (female). رَمَّدَ وأَرْمَدَ
To fall into destitution. To lose flocks. أَرْمَدَ
To afflict a. o. with ophthalmia (God). — ه
✧ To be reduced to ashes. To be blear-eyed. To be covered with ashes. تَرَمَّدَ
To be ash-coloured. To run fast. إِرْمَدَّ
Ophthalmia, blear eyes. رَمَد
Blear-eyed. Dirty (garment). رَمِد وأَرْمَد
Ostrich. رَمْدَاء
Ashes رَمَاد وإِرْمِدَاء ج أَرْمِدَة
Generous, hospitable. كَثِير الرَّمَاد
He exerts himself uselessly, *lit* : he blows upon the ashes. يَنْفُخ في الرَّمَاد
✧ Lye, lixivial water. مَاء الرَّمَاد
Loss, destruction. رَمَادَة

He possesses nothing. مَا لَهُ حَمٌّ ولَا رَمٌّ او حُمٌّ ولَا رُمٌّ
Piece of rope worn out. Whole, totality. ✧ Head-rope. رُمَّة ج رُمَم
He has given the whole of it. أَعْطَاهَا بِرُمَّتِهَا
Celebrated poet. ذُو الرُّمَّة
Decayed bone. Winged ant. رِمَّة ج رِمَم و رِمَام
Clever girl. رَامَّة ج رُمَم
Worn out rope. حَبْل أَرْمَام و رِمَام
Decayed, rotten (bone). رَمِيم ورُمَام
Lip of cloven-hoofed animals. مَرِمَّة ومَرَمَّة
✧ Repairs of decayed houses, streets. تَرْمِيمَات
Calamities. مُرِمَّات
To open the mouth and remain silent. ✲ رَمْرَمَ — تَرَمْرَمَ
Carthamus, wild saffron. رَمْرَام
To stop in (a place: camel). ✲ رَمَأَ a رَمْأً ورُمُوءًا ب
To ascertain (news). — ه
To exceed (a number). — وأَرْمَأَ على
To approach to. أَرْمَأَ إِلى
False rumours. مُرَمَّآت الأَخْبَار
To arrange. To steal a. th. To mix a. th. To wipe a. th. with the hand. ✲ رَمَثَ o رَمْثًا ه
To be disordered (affair). To suffer from the belly (camels). رَمِثَ a رَمَثًا
To exceed (a number). To surpass a. o. رَمَّثَ على
To leave milk in (the udder). — وأَرْمَثَ في
To spare part of o.'s goods. أَرْمَثَ واسْتَرْمَثَ في
To soften a. th. — ه
Species of the bitter plants called حَمْض. Man in tatters. Weak in the back. رِمْث
Raft of timber. Remainder of milk in the udder. Attainment. رَمَث ج أَرْمَاث
Camels afflicted with looseness of the belly. إِبِل رَمِثَة ورَمَاثَى ورَمْثَى
They are in a disordered state. هُم في مَرْمُوثَاء
To mute (bird). ✲ رَمَجَ o رَمْجًا
To spoil (the writing). رَمَّجَ ه

أَرْمَد ورَمَادِيّ Ash-coloured.
مُرْمَد ومُرْمَدّ Blear-eyed.
مُرَمَّد Roast in the ashes (kid).
مُرْمَئِدّ Active, energetic.
رَمَاد رِمْدِد و رِمْدَد و رِمْدِيد Fine and copious ashes.
☆ رَمَز o i رَمْزًا إلى To wink at a. o.
— o ه To commit (a flock) to a new shepherd. To fill up (a skin).
— ه ب To allure a. o. with.
— رَمَزَانًا To jump (gazelle).
رَمُز o رَمَازَة To be restless. To be intelligent; noble. To enjoy authority.
تَرَمَّز To stir (people). To get ready.
إِرْتَمَز To be disturbed. To stir.
إِرْمَأَزّ عن To rise from (a place).
— ه To stick to (a place).
رَمْز ورُمْز ورَمَز ج رُمُوز Sign, wink, hint. Allegory.
رَمِيز Restless. Numerous. Sedate. Intelligent; noble. Respected (man).
رَامُوز ج رَوَامِيز Sea. Origin. Pattern.
رَمَّازَة Large army stirring forward. Harlot.
مَرْمُوز إِلَيْهِ Thing hinted at.
☆ رَمَس o i رَمْسًا ه To cover, to bury a. th.
— وأَرْمَس ه To bury (the dead).
— o رَمْسًا ه To level and conceal (a grave). To conceal (news). To efface (traces: wind).
— ه ب To throw (a stone) at.
إِرْتَمَس في To be dipped into (water).
رَمْس ج رُمُوس وأَرْمَاس ج رَوَامِس Grave. Dust of a grave.
رَامِسَات Winds effacing traces.
رَوَامِس Nocturnal birds
✧ رَمِيس ج رُمْسَان Lambkin.
☆ رَمَش o i رَمْشًا To pasture a while (cattle). ✧ To twinkle (the eyes).
— ه To take a. th. with the fingers.
— ه ب To cast (a stone) at a. o.
أَرْمَش To become leafy (plant). To twinkle.
رَمْش Bunch of odoriferous plants.
رِمْش ج رُمُوش ✧ Eyelids.
رَمَش Crispness of the hair. Blearness. Spots on the nails.
أَرْمَش م رَمْشَاء ج رُمْش Blea-eyed. Fine in body.

أَرْض رَمْشَاء Soil covered with herbs.
☆ رَمَض o رَمْضًا ه To retrieve (an evil: God).
— بَيْن To make peace between.
رَمَّض To dung (hen). To whelp (beast).
رَمِص a ورَمَصًا To have white matter in the eyes.
رَمَص Dry filth of the eyes.
رَمِيص وأَرْمَص م رَمْصَاء ج رُمْص Having dirt in the eye-corners.
الشِّعْرَى الرُّمَيْصَاء Procyon, star in *Canis minor.*
☆ رَمِض a رَمَضًا To be burning (day). To heat the sand (sun). To be scorched by the ground (foot). To be blasted by the sun (flock).
— لِلأَمْر To burn with anger at an affair.
رَمَض o i رَمْضًا ه To sharpen a (spear) between stones.
— i ه To roast (a sheep) on heated stones.
— ورَمَّض وأَرْمَض ه To pasture (sheep) on a burning ground.
رَمَّض ه وه To wait a. o. for a while and go off. To purpose (fasting).
أَرْمَض ه وه To burn a. th. To pain a. o. To affect (the brain: sun). To burn a. o. with anger (affair).
تَرَمَّض To heave (soul); to be in pangs.
— ه To track (game) to a burning ground.
إِرْتَمَض To bound (horse). To be burnt (liver).
إِرْتَمَض من To be distressed by a. th. To be burnt by (heat or grief).
— ل To be disquieted; to be grieved for.
رَمَض Burning of anger. Rain falling on a heated ground.
رَمَضِيّ Summer-rain, clouds.
رَمَضَان ج رَمَضَانَات ورَمَاضِين وأَرْمِضَاء وأَرْمِضَة Ninth Arabian month; Ramadan, fasting-month.
رَمْضَاء Scorching heat. Burning hot (ground).
رَمِيض Sharpened (sword). Flesh of a roasted sheep.

To be lean. To be ash-coloured. إِرْمَكَّ
رَمَكَة ج رَمَك و رِماك ورَمَكات وأَرْماك
Common stud-mare. Weak man.
Ash-colour of camels. رُمْكَة
Black perfume mixed with musk. رَامِك ورَامَك
Ash-coloured. أَرْمَك م رَمْكَاء ج رُمْك
To sprinkle a. th. with sand. To adorn (a couch) with pearls. ☆ رَمَل o رَمْلًا ه
To stain a. th. with blood. — ورَمَّل ه
To weave (a fine tissue). ✧ To sand (a letter).
To walk quickly (man). — o رَمَلًا ورَمَلَان ومَرْمَلًا
To become a widow (woman). — وأَرْمَل وتَرَمَّل
To exhaust provisions. To be exhausted (stores). أَرْمَل
To lengthen (a rope). To adorn a. th. with woven leaves. To weave (a fine tissue). — ه
To be blood-stained. أَرْمَل تَرَمَّل وارْتَمَل
Sand. رَمْل ج رِمَال وأَرْمُل
Geomancy. عِلْم الرَّمْل و✧ضَرْب الرَّمل
Sandy ground. ✧ Sand-pit. رَمْلَة
Black line. رُمْلَة ج رُمَل وأَرْمَال
✧ Sand-glass, sand-clock. ساعَة رَمْلِيَّة
Scanty rain. Excess. Streaks on a wild cow. Musical tune. رَمَل
Sand-seller. ✧ Geomancer. رَمَّال
Destitute. Bachelor. ✧ Widower. أَرْمَل م أَرْمَلَة ج أَرَامِل وأَرَامِلَة
Weak and destitute people. الأَرْمَلَة
Black-footed (white ewe). Barren (year). رَمْلَاء
Stump, stalk of a branch. Needy boy. أُرْمُولَة ج أَرَامِل وأَرَامِيل
Small shackles. مِرْمَل
Texture of palm-leaves. يَرْمُول
Pomegranate. Pomegranate-tree. ☆ رُمَّان (un. رُمَّانَة)
White poppy. رُمَّان السَّعَالي
Androsæmum, all-heal(*pla.*) رُمَّان الأَنْهار
✧ Stomach of ruminant. Woman's breast. Knob of metal. Steelyard. Large shell. رُمَّانَة
✧ Ruby-coloured. رُمَّانِيّ
Pomegranate-grove. مَرْمَنَة

To speak ill of a. o. ☆ رَمَط i رَمْطًا ة
To quiver from anger or age (nose). ☆ رَمَع a رَمَعَانًا
To point at a. th. with (the hand). To issue (tears: eyes). To bring forth (a child). — ب
To shake (the head). — ه
To go on quickly. — رَمْعًا ورَمَعَانًا
To feel a pain in the loins (water-drawer). رُمِع وأُرْمِع
To tremble with anger. تَرَمَّع
Stooping and lifting the head by turns. رَامِع
Pain in the loins. Disease of the bowels. رُمَاع
Soft part of the skull. Buttocks. رَمَّاعَة
Spinning-top. Soft and frail pebble. يَرْمَع ج يَرَامِع
To drivel (infant). To drip (grease). To walk in haste. To shout (man). To be moist (garment, leather). To disperse (camels). To flow (tears). ☆ رمعل — إِرْمَعَلّ
To flow (tears). ☆ إِرْمَعَنّ
To rub (leather) with the hand. ☆ رَمَغ a رَمْغًا ه
To falsify (a speech). To anoint (the head). رَمَّغ ه
To cast a glance at. ☆ رَمَق o رَمْقًا ه و ة
To gaze long at. — ورَمَّق ه و ة
To dispose (a discourse). رَمَّق ه
To make a. th. hastily. — ورَامَق ه
To sip a. th. repeatedly. تَرَمَّق ه
To perish (sheep). To expand (road). إِرْمَاقّ
To be thin, weak. — وارْمَاقّ
Straitened, poorly (life). رَمِق و رِماق
Last breath of life. Flock of sheep. رَمَق ج أَرْمَاق
Bare sustenance. رُمْقَة ورَمَاق و رِماق
Straitened. Invidious. رَامِق ورَمُوق ج رُمُق
Hypocrisy, evil look. رِمَاق
Scanty life. عَيْش مُرَمَّق
Keeping little affection; ill-natured. مُرَامِق
Dim-sighted. يَرْمُوق
To stop in (a place). ☆ رَمَك o رُمُوكًا ب
To keep a. o. in (a place). أَرْمَك ة ب

Armenians. أَرْمَن (أرمَنِيّ .un)
To be vehemently hot (day). ✱ رَمِهَ a رَمَهًا
Indian almond. رَمَه
To throw a. th. To repair to (a place). ✱ رَمَى i رَمْيًا ورِمَايَةً ه وب
To charge a. o. with. To cast (looks) upon. To throw a. o. into (an evil). — ه ب
To speak conjecturally. رَمَى بالغَيْب
May God smite him on his hand! رَمَاهُ اللهُ في يَدِهِ
To give help to a. o. (God). — ل
To shot (an arrow) with a bow. — ه عن وعلى القوس
To exceed (a number). — وأرمى على
رَامَى مُرَامَاةً ورِمَاءً وتِرْمَاءً، وتَرَامَى وارْتَمَى ه
To shoot with a. o. To make a shooting-match with a. o.
To throw, to cast a. th. أرمى ه وب
To cast off. — من اليد
To throw a. o. down from a horse. — ه عن الفرس
To practice usury. To exceed in abuse. — على
To expel a. o. (country). أرمى وترامى ب
To be slack (affair). To heap up (clouds). To shoot o. a. تَرَامَى
To come to (success or failure: affair). — إلى
✧ To fall down at the feet of. — على
To be flung, thrown (missile). إرتمى إرتماء
He went off hunting. خَرَجَ يَرْتَمِي
✧ To fall at the feet of. إرتمى على
Sound of stones thrown. رِمِّي
Excess. Usury. رَمَا
He excels him. عَلَيْهِ الرَّمَا
A throw, a shot. رَمْيَة (.un)
A bad shooter may hit the point (*said of unexpected success*). رُبَّ رَمْيَةٍ من غَيْرِ رَامٍ
Small cloud dropping large drops. رَمِيّ ج أرماء وأرمية ورَمَايَا
Game. ✧ Cartridge. Tax. رَمِيَّة ج رَمَايَا
Sagittarius, (*Zodical sign*). الرَّامِي
The Prophet Jeremiah. إرمياء
Throwing-machine. مِرْمَى ج مَرَامٍ
Small arrow. Cloven foot. مِرْمَاة

Target. Aim; range. مَرْمًى ج مَرَامٍ
Shooting an arrow. Scout. مُرْتَمٍ
To moan. To resound. To twang (bow). To tinkle. ✱ رَنَّ i رَنِينًا، وأَرَنَّ
To listen to. — وأرنّ إلى
To twang (a bow). رَنَّنَ ه
The created beings. الرَّنَى
Moan. Plaintive, ringing sound. Twang. رَنِين ورَنَّة
Bow. Resounding cloud. مُرِنَّة ومِرْنَان
To turn the looks towards. ✱ رَنَا a رَنًا إلى
To have a heavy (deportment) — في
Hare, rabbit. Short-tailed rat. Ornament. ✱ أَرْنَب ج أَرَانِب
She-hare. Tip of the nose. أَرْنَبَة
Cynoglossum, hound's tongue (*plant*). آذَان الأرنب
Furred with hare-hair (garment). مُؤَرْنَب
Full of rabbits, hares (land). مُرْنِب ومُؤَرْنِب ومُؤَرْنَب
Short-tailed field-rat. يَرْنَب
Indian-nut. Smooth date. ✱ رَانِج ج رَوَانِج (رَانِجَة .un)
✧ Madagascar. جَزِيرَة رَانِج
To hum (man). ✱ رنجح — ترنجح
To cause a. o. to reel (wine). ✱ رَنَحَ — رَنَّحَ ه
To faint, to fall in a swoon. رُنِّحَ عَلَيْهِ
To reel (drunkard). تَرَنَّحَ وارْتَنَحَ
Vertigo, giddiness. رُنَح
Reeling. Best aloes-wood. مُرَنَّح
Prow of a ship. مَرَنَّحَة
To be languid. ✱ رَنَخَ o رَنْخًا
To subdue a. o. To render languid. ✧ To drench a. o. (rain). رَنَّخَ ه
✧ To be drenched by rain. تَرَنَّخَ
To cleave to. — ب
Sweet bay. Myrtle. Aloes-wood. رَنْد
The Albanians. ✱ أَرْنَاؤُد وأرناؤط
Plane for wood. P رَنْدَج
To sing. ¤ رَنْدَح
Madder, dyeing plant. ✧ رُنَاس
To be altered (colour). To wag the head against flies (horse). To play. ✱ رَنَعَ a رُنُوعًا
To move (the head) to and fro. رَنَّعَ ه

To be fresh (man). To shine (looming). تَرَهْرَه
Brightness of complexion. رَهْرَهَة
✲ رَهِب a رَهْبَةً ورُهْبًا ورَهْبًا ورَهَبًا ورُهْبَانًا ورَهْبَانًا ه To fear, to dread a. o.
To be jaded (she-camel). رُهِبَت
To ride a lean camel. To wear long sleeves. أَرْهَب
To withhold (camels) from water. — عن
To frighten, to threaten a. o. — وتَرَهَّب واسْتَرْهَب ه
To become a monk. تَرَهَّب و✧ تَرَهْبَن
Emaciated, jaded camel. رَهْب
Thin arrow-head. — ج رِهَاب
Sleeve of a garment. رَهْب
Fright, dread. رَهْبَة ورَهْبَى ورُهْبَى ورَهْبَاء
Religious order; monachism. رَهْبَانِيَّة و✧ رَهْبَنَة
Christian monk. Lion. رَاهِب ج رُهْبَان
Nun. رَاهِبَة ج رَاهِبَات ورَوَاهِب
Dreadful, appalling. رَهِيب ومَرْهُوب
Monastical. رَهْبَانِيّ ورُهْبَانِيّ
Fearful. رَهْبَان ج رَهَابِين ورَهَابِنَة
Monk. رُهْبَان م رُهْبَانَة ج رَهَابِين
Awe, appalment. رَهَبُوت ورَهَبُوتَى
Terrific things. مَرَاهِب
To have a jerking gait. ✲ رَهْبَل — تَرَهْبَل
Unintelligible word. رَهْبَل
Speaking unintelligibly. مُرَهْبِل ومُرَهْبَل
To raise (the dust). To perfume a house. To be about to rain (sky). ✲ رَهَج — أَرْهَج
Dust. Waterless cloud. Riot. رَهْج ورَهَج
Arsenic. رَهْج أَبْيَض
Realgar. red orpiment. رَهْج أَحْمَر
Orpiment, king's yellow. رَهْج أَصْفَر
Gentle walk of a horse. P رَهْوَج ورَهْوَجَة
To pound a. th. ✲ رَهَد a رَهْدًا ه
To make a gross blunder. رَهَّد
Delicacy of life. رَهَادَة
Kindness, gentleness, رَهُودِيَّة
Soft, delicate. رَهِيد م رَهِيدَة
Unsteady, wavering. مَرْهُود
To be slow. To be restricted. ✲ رَهْدَن
To turn round in (walking). — في
To scoff at, to bully. ✧ تَرَهْدَن وتَرَهْدَل على

Shouts of players. Share of food. Well-being. Meadow. مَرْتَعَة
To walk quickly. ✲ رنف — أَرْنَف
To drop the ears (jaded camel). — بِأُذُنَيْهَا
Salix Balchica, wild willow. رَنْف ورَنَف
Border of a sleeve, of the nose. رَانِفَة ج رَوَانِف
✲ رَنِق o رَنْقًا ورُنُوقًا, ورَنِق a رَنَقًا, وتَرَنَّق To be turbid (water).
To render (water) turbid. رَنَّق وأَرْنَق ه
To dispel (an evil: God). رَنَّق ه
To stop in (a place). — ب
To be involved in (an affair). To confuse (the eyes: sleep). — في
To flap the wings (bird). To be dim (sight). To be broken (wing). To be dull (mind). To be weak (body). To look intently. رَنَّق
To wave (standard). أَرْنَق
To wave (a standard). — ه
Turbid (water). رَنْق ورَنِق ورَنَق
Brooding (hen). Barren ground. رَنْقَاء ج رَنْقَاوَات
Muddy water. رَنْقَة ج رِيَانِق
Brightness, splendour. Wavy streacks (of a sword). رَوْنَق
Slime of a river. تُرْنُوق وتُرْنُوق وتُرْنُوقَاء
To sing melodiously; to trill. ✲ رَنِم a رَنَمًا, وتَرَنَّم
To warble (bird). To ring (bow). To trill (man). رَنَّم
Trilling voice; ringing sound. رَنَم ورَنَمَة وتَرْنُومَة
Melodious songstresses. رُنُم
✧ Recitative, hymn. تَرْنِيمَة
To gaze with delight at. ✲ رَنَا o رُنُوًّا ورَنًا, وتَرَنَّى ل وإلى
To overlook, to neglect a. th. — عن
To sing. رَنَّى تَرْنِيَة
To delight; to cheer a. o. (beauty). — وأَرْنَى ه
To equal a. o. in beauty. To blandish a. o. رَانَى ه
Attractive beauty. رَنًا
Sound. Delight. رُنَاء
Looking with delight. رَنَّاء ورَنُوّ
To keep open house; i. e. to be very hospitable. ✲ رَه — رَهْرَه ه

Fool. Coward. رَهْدَن ورُهْدَن و رِهْدَن
رَهْدَن ورَهْدَنَة ورُهْدُنَّة ورُهْدُون ج رَهَادِن
Lark of Mecca.
To stir, to move about. ✱ رَهَز a رَهْزًا ورَهَزَانًا
To stir on behalf of. إِرْتَهَز ل
To tread upon (the ground). ✱ رَهَس a رَهْسًا ه
To be jolted, shaken, stirred. تَرَهَّس
To be flooded (valley). To press together (men). To heap up (locusts). إِرْتَهَس
To become bountiful (man). To yield much milk (she-camel). ✱ رهش – تَرَهَّش ⊙
To be loosened (bow). To shudder (man). To knock together (hoofs). To be in civil war (tribe). إِرْتَهَش
To thrust (the spear) obliquely. – ه
Bountifulness. Share. رُهْشَة ورَهْشُوشِيَّة
Shock of the hoofs. Weak (man). Lean-backed (she-camel). Thin (spear-head). Fine duct. رَهِيش
Two veins in the forefeet of beasts. الرَّاهِشَان
Veins of the palm of the hand, of the forefeet. رَوَاهِش (رَاهِش ورَاهِشَة *un.*)
To hurry a. o. To urge (a debtor). To squeeze a. th. To blame a. o. ✱ رَهَص a رَهْصًا ه و ه
To urge (a debtor). – ورَاهَص ه
To be hurt in the sole (horse). رُهِص, ورَهِص a رَهَصًا
To set the first range (of stones) in a wall. To fasten a. th. أَرْهَص ه
To prosper a. o. (God). To hurt (a horse: stones). أَرْهَص ه
First range of stones in a wall. Bricks of mud. رَهْص
Hurt in the sole of horses. رَهْصَة
Setting the first row of stones. رِهَاص
Wounded on the sole (horse). رَهِيص ومَرْهُوص
Hurting the sole (stones.) Strong rocks. رَوَاهِص
Rank. Office. مَرْهَصَة
To take large (mouthfuls). To glut a. th. ✱ رَهَط a رَهْطًا ,ورَهَّط ه

To remain on horseback. To remain in doors. رَهَّط
To assemble. إِرْتَهَط
رَهْط ورَهَط ج أَرْهُط وأَرْهَاط وجج أَرَاهِط وأَرَاهِيط Kindred, o.'s people. Party of men less than ten. Enemy. (*With a number*) Person, individual.
We are all collected. نَحْنُ ذَوُو رَهْط و إِرْتِهَاط
Leathern flaps used as drawers. رَهْط ج رِهَاط
Mole-hole. رُهْطَة ورُهَطَاء ورَاهِطَاء ج رَهَاطَى
Furniture of a house. رِهَاط
To thin (a sword). ✱ رَهَف a رَهْفًا ه
To be thin (sword). رَهُف o رَهَافَة ورَهَفًا
To whet (a blade). To thin. أَرْهَف ه
To extemporise (a speech). – ب
Thin. Whetted (sword). رَهِيف ومُرْهَف
Slender (horse). مُرْهَف
To be foolish. To lie. To be mischievous, ungodly. To hasten. ✱ رَهِق a رَهَقًا
To near; to overtake a. o. – وأَرْهَق ه
To charge a. o. with evil. رَهَّق ه
To near puberty (youth). رَاهَق
To oppress a. o. أَرْهَق ه طُغْيَانًا
To exact a painful duty from. – ه عُسْرًا
To prevent a. o. by hurry from (performing prayer). – ه ان
To delay prayer to the last minute. أَرْهَق الصَّلَاة
Malice. Tyrannical mind. Imputation. رَهَق
Fast run. رَهَقَى
About one hundred. رِهَاق ورُهَاق مِئَة
Saffron. رَيْهُقَان
Overtaken (by a foe). Reduced to extremity. مُرْهَق
Light-minded. Resorted by guests. Suspected of evil. Wicked. Generous. مُرَهَّق
To pound a. th. between two stones. ✱ رَهَك a رَهْكًا ه
To remain in (a place). – ب
To have a sluggish gait. إِرْتَهَك
Good work. رَهْك
Weakness. رَهْكَة
Weak she-camel. رَهْكَة

Events happen in their fixed time. الأمور مَرْهُونَة بِأوقاتِها
Marine chart. رَهْنامَج ورَاهْنامَج P
To walk gently. To fall calm (sea). To expand the wings. ✲ رَهَا ه رَهْوًا
To part (the legs). — بَيْن
To act gently towards. — وأرْهَى على
To approach towards. To agree with. رَاهَى ه
To come to a broad place. To feed on cranes. أرْهَى
To reconcile with. تَرَاهَى
To mix together. To prepare a porridge. إرْتَهَى
Crane (bird). Crowd of men. رَهْو ج رِهَاء
Depressed or elevated ground. — ورَهْوَة
He has done it easily. فَعَلَهُ رَهْوًا
Porridge of pounded wheat and milk. رَهِيَّة
Orfa, ancient town of Emesa. رُهَا
Easy (life). Continuous hospitality. رَاهٍ
Bee. رَاهِيَة
Amble. Ambler (horse). رَهْوَان
To amble (horse). ✧ رَهْوَن
Fleet (horse). مِرْهَاة ج مَرَاهٍ
To be weak. To be remiss. To droop (load). To issue tears(eye). ✲ رَهْيَأ
To shake. To waver. تَرَهْيَأ
To totter (in walk). To threaten with (rain : cloud). To waver (in). — في
To ponder over (an answer). ✲ روأ — رَوَّأ تَرْوِئَة وتَرْوِيئًا في
Mature examination. رَوِيئَة ورَوِيَّة
Reflection. إرْتِيَاء
The letter ر. Foam of the sea. Kind of acacia-tree. رَاء
To be churned (milk). To be perplexed ; crack-brained (man). To lie. To feel drowsy from satiety or sleep. ✲ رَاب ه رَوْبًا ورُؤُوبًا
He is about to be slain. رَاب دَمُهُ
To be jaded (beast). رَوَّب
To churn, to curdle (milk). — وأرَاب ه
Quantity, amount. رَاب
Curd. رَوْب
Thou art clear from guilt. لَا شَوْب ولَا رَوْب عَلَيْك

Worthless man, cipher. رَهْكَة ورُهَكَة
To quiver. To be flabby ; to be swollen (flesh). ✲ رَهِل a رَهَلًا
To relax a. o. (sleep). رَهَّل وأرْهَل ه
To be flabby ; swollen (horse). تَرَهَّل
Thin cloud. رِهْل
Soft, weak, lax. رَهِل
To drizzle continuously (sky). ✲ رهم — أرْهَم
Drizzle ; fine and lasting rain. رِهْمَة ج رِهَم ورِهَام
Emaciated ewe. رِهَام ورُهُوم
Harmless birds. Large number. رُهَام
More fruitful (land). أرْهَم
Poultice plaster : unguent. مَرْهَم ج مَرَاهِم
Populine, (unguent). مَرْهَم الغَرَب
Watered by a fine rain. مَرْهُوم
To last, to continue. ✲ رَهَن a رَهْنًا
To be settled in a place. — بِالمَكَان
To be emaciated. — رُهُونًا
To pledge a. th. with. To promise a. th. to. — a رَهْنًا ه ه و ه عِند, وأرْهَن ه ه
✧ To mortgage property. — ه
To lay a wager. To race with a. o. for. رَاهَن مُرَاهَنَة ورِهَانًا ه على
To weaken a. o. To pay a. o. in advance. أرْهَن ه
To ask a high price for goods. To pay, to give a. th. in advance. — في
To secure sustenance to (a guest). — ه ل
To give a. o. as hostage. — ه ب
He deposited the corpse in the grave. أرْهَن المَيْتَ القَبْرَ
To lay a wager together. تَرَاهَن
To receive a. th. as a pledge. إرْتَهَن ه
To be bound, obliged to. أرْتَهِن ب
To ask a. th. as a pledge. إسْتَرْهَن ه
Pledge, earnest. ✧ Mortgage. رَهْن ج رِهَان ورُهُون ورَهِين ورُهُن
Manager of cattle. رِهْن مَال
I guarantee it to thee. أنَا لَكَ رَهْن ورَهِينَة بِهِ
Steady. Lasting. Ready (food). Lean. ✧ Strong, fast. رَاهِن م رَاهِنَة
Race-horses for betting. خَيل رِهَان
Pledged. Engaged. رَهِين ومُرْتَهَن ومَرْهُون
Pawn, pledge. رَهِينَة ج رَهَائِن

رَوْبَة ورُوبَة Rennet for milk. Apathy. Livelihood.
رُوبَة Want. Easy life. Part of the night. Piece of meat. *Mespilus Aronia*, medlar-tree. Fertile land.
رَائِب, ورَوْبَان وأَرْوَب ج رَوْبَى Confused, drowsy.
مِرْوَب و✧ مَرْوَبَة Churning-vessel.
✱ رَاثَ o رَوْثًا To dung (horse).
رَوْث (رَوْثَة .*un*) ج أَرْوَاث Dung of hoofed beasts.
رَوْثَة Siftings of wheat. Tip of the nose. Beak of an eagle.
رَاث ومَرْوَث Anus of a horse.
✱ رَاجَ o رَوْجًا ورَوَاجًا To have currency (coin). To sell readily (goods). To be unsteady (wind). To be speedy. To be ready (food).
رَوَّجَ ه To circulate (money). To sell (goods) readily. ✧ To hurry a. th.
— ه وب To hurry a. th.
رَوَّجَ ✧ To hurry; to be speedy.
— على ✧ To get the start of a. o.
تَرَوَّجَ ر To turn around a watering-trough (camel).
رَائِج ومُرَوَّج Current (money). Saleable (goods).
✱ رَاحَ o رَوَاحًا To go, to act in the evening. To go away. ✧ To be lost. To be about, to on the point of.
رَاحَ يَمُوت ✧ He is near death.
— رَوْحًا ورَوَاحًا ه وإلى وعند To go in the evening to.
— i رَيْحًا ه To smell a. th.
رَاحَ a رِيحًا To be windy (day). To be ventilated (house). To become leafy (tree).
— ه To blow upon a. o. (wind).
— رَاحَةً To feel the wind (tree). To become a stallion (horse).
— رَاحَةً ل To be brisk, ready to.
— لِلْمَعْرُوف To do a benefit readily.
— وأَرَاحَ ه من To receive (a favour) from.
— رَوَاحًا ورَاحًا ورَاحَةً ورِيَاحَةً ورُؤُوحًا وأَرْيَحِيَّةً ل To rejoice at a. th.
رِيحَ To be windward (place). To be overtaken by the wind.
رَوِحَ a رَوَحًا To be large, wide.

رَوَّحَ وأَرَاحَ ه To give rest to a. o. To bring back (cattle) in the evening.
رَوَّحَ ه To visit a. o. in the evening. To fan a. o.
— ه To cheer a. o. To perfume (a pomade). ✧ To spoil; to squander a. th. To procure abortion.
رَوَّحَ ✧ To leak (vessel). To miscarry (woman).
رَيَّحَ ✧ To subside (building).
رَيَّحَ ه وه ✧ To allay: to quiet a. o.
رَاوَحَ بَيْن To alternate (two works). To rest on (each foot) in turn. To recline on (each side) in turn.
أَرَاحَ وأَرْوَحَ To stink (water, meat).
أَرَاحَ إِرَاحَةً To be exposed to the wind. To take breath. To die. To take rest. To alight (rider).
— ه على To pay (a debt) to a. o.
— وأَرْوَحَ ه To scent (man: game).
تَرَوَّحَ To grow up (plant). To become leafy (tree). To contract a smell. To act, to depart in the evening.
— ه To go in the evening to a. o.'s.
— ب To fan o.'s self.
تَرَاوَحَ وارْتَوَحَ ه To do a. th. alternatively.
إِرْتَاحَ To be brisk; cheerful. ✧ To take rest.
— ل بِرَحْمَتِهِ To deliver a. o. in his mercy (God).
إِسْتَرَاحَ To take, to find rest.
— ل وإلى To rest upon a. o.
إِسْتَرْوَحَ ه وه To scent a. o. To revive (a tree).
رَاح Wine. Joy, cheerfulness.
يَوْمٌ رَاحٌ و لَيْلَةٌ رَاحَةٌ Windy day, night.
رَاحَة Rest, quiet, ease.
رَاحَة ج رَاحَات ورَاح Palm of the hand. Wife. Even, fruitful land. Court. Fold of a garment. ✧ Racket.
بَيْت الرَّاحَة ✧ Privy.
رَاحَة الأَسَد *Leontis leontopetalum*, lion's leaf (*plant*).
رُوح (*m. and f.*) ج أَرْوَاح Breath of life. Soul. Inspiration. Ghost. ✧ Spirit, essence. Oneself. Charge of a gun.
طَوِيل الرُّوح ✧ Forbearing, long-minded.
الرُّوح القُدُس ✧ The Holy Ghost.

Jesus (for Moslems). رُوح الله
The Angel Gabriel. الرُّوح والرُّوح الأمِين
God, the Supreme Spirit. الروح الأعظم
✧ He feigned to be so. عَمِل رُوحَهُ كَذَا
The devils. الأَرْوَاح الخَبِيثَة والنَجِسَة
Spiritual, incorporeal (being). رُوحَانِيّ ج رُوحَانِيُّون
Agreeable place. مَكَان رُوحَانِيّ
Width between the feet. رَوَح
Rest. Breeze. Joy. Victory. Justice. Mercy. رَوْح
Fine, cheering day, night. يَوْم رَوْح وَلَيْلَة رَوْحَة
Ostrich. Shallow vessel. رَوْحَا
Evening; afternoon. رَوَاح
Rest, quiet. — ورَوَاحَة ورَوِيحَة
رِيح ج رِيَاح وأرْوَاح وأرْيَاح وجج أرَاوِيح وأرَايِيح
Wind: breath. Victory. Strength. Mercy. Smell-scent.
Weather-cock. ✧ أبو رِيَاح
✧ Whitlow. رِيح الشَّوْكَة
Flatulency. Rheumatism. رِيح و✧ رِيحِيَّة
Smell. Wind. رِيحَة
Any aromatic plant. Sweet basil. Livelihood. Offspring. رَيْحَان ج رَيَاحِين
Clinopodium, basil-weed. رَيْحَان بَرِّيّ
Ocimum basilicum, basil-royal. رَيْحَان الحَمَاحِم والمَلِك
Origanum maru, marjoram. رَيْحَان الشُّيُوخ
Kind of wormwood. الرَّيْحَان الأبيَض
Cissus rotundifolia: wild grape. رَيْحَان سُلَيْمَان
Myrtle-tree. رَيْحَان القُبُور
Laurus camphora, camphor-tree. رَيْحَان الكَافُور
Chrysanthemum, corn-marigold. Good woman. رَيْحَانَة
Cooled, pleasant (day). رَيِّح ورَيُوح
✧ Henceforth. مِن اليَوْم ورَائِح
✧ Beyond the river. بالرَّائِح مِن النَّهر
He possesses no flock. مَا لَهُ سَارِحَة وَلَا رَائِحَة
Smell. Evening rain or mist. رَائِحَة ج رَوَائِح
Spacious (place). Part-legged. Shallow (bowl). أرْوَح م رَوْحَاء ج رُوح
Joy. Mercy. إرْتِيَاح
Generous. Brisk. أرْيَحِيّ

Bountifulness. Cheerfulness. أرْيَحِيَّة
Starting-place; place of return. مَرَاح
Stable; station for cattle. مُرَاح
Windy (day); aired. مَرُوح ومَرِيح
Perfumed ointment. دُهْن مُرَوَّح
Fan. مِرْوَح ومِرْوَحَة ج مَرَاوِح
Fifth horse in a race. ✧ At rest. مُرْتَاح
Windward. Desert. مَرْوَحَة ج مَرَاوِح
Resting-place. Grave. Privy. مُسْتَرَاح
To ask a. th. To search for food, fodder. ✫ رَاد o رَوْدًا ورِيَادًا ه
To go to and fro in a pasture. — رِيَادًا
To be restless, sleepless.. رَادَ وِسَادُهُ
To go round about the neighbours, to blow gently (wind). — ورَوْدًا ورَوَدَانًا
To send (a scout) for fodder. رَوَّد ه
رَاوَد مُرَاوَدَةً ورِوَادًا ه عن نَفْسِهِ وعلى نَفْسِهِ
To entice a. o. to sin.
To will. To desire a. th. أرَاد ه
To entice a. o. to. — ه على
To act, to walk gently. أرْوَد إرْوَادًا ومَرْوَدًا ومُرْوَدًا ورُوَيْدًا
To desire, to exact a. th. إرْتَاد ه
To obey. To pasture (cattle). إسْتَرَاد
Scout for fodder. Handle of a hand-mill. Spy. Forerunner. Homeless man. رَائِد ج رَادَة ورُوَّاد ورَائِدُون
Going about the neighbours (woman). رَاد ورَادَة ورَائِدَة ورُوَادَة
Gentle wind. رِيح رَوْد ورُوَاد
Go gently. رُوَيْدًا ورُوَيْدَك
Grant me a delay, thou, ye. رُوَيْدَكِني ورُوَيْدَكُمُونِي
Will, free will. إرَادَة
Decree of the Sultan. إرَادَة سَنِيَّة
Axle of a pulley. Ivory needle for collyrium. Iron of the bit. مِرْوَد ج مَرَاوِد
Willed. Intention. مُرَاد
Pasture ground for camels. Windward place. مَرَاد ومُسْتَرَاد
✧ Candidate, novice. Devotee. مُرِيد
China rhubarb. P رِوَنْد ورَاوَنْد صِينِيّ
Yellow rhubarb. رَاوَنْد خُرَاسَانِيّ و✧ الدَّوَاب
✧ Rhaponticine. رَاوَنْد ذَكَر
Sect of Metempsychosists. الرَّاوَنْدِيَّة
To go to and fro. ✫ رَاذ o رَوْذًا
To weigh (a coin). To test a. o. To ask, to desire a. th. ✫ رَاز o رَوْزًا ه وه

Newly broken and untrained (colt). (*m. f.*) رَيِّض

Pool in a low and hard ground. مَرَاض ج مَرَايِض ومَرَاضَات

To repair to a summit (wild beast). ✲ رَاط o i رَوْطًا ورَيْطًا ب

To be afraid of. ✲ رَاعَ o رَوْعًا, ورِيع من

To return (thing). رَاعَ o i رُوَاعًا

To frighten a. o. — ورَوَّعَ ه

To surprise, to please (beauty). — ه

To be firm in the hand. — في اليد

Thirst-quenching beverage. شَرْبَةٌ رَاعَ بِهَا الفُؤَاد

To be pleasing, sagacious. رَوِعَ a رَوَعًا

To chide sheep. أَرْوَعَ بِالغَنَم

To be frightened at. تَرَوَّعَ وارْتَاعَ من

To be glad, prone to do good. إِرْتَاعَ ل

Fear, fright. War. رَوْع

Heart, mind. رُوع

Surprising beauty, courage. رَوَع ورَوْعَة

Spirited (man). Startled heart. رُوَاع الفُؤَاد

Surprising by beauty, courage. Elegant (word). رَائِع ج رَائِعُون و رُوَّع

F. Admirable or terrible thing. رَائِعَة ج رَوَائِع ورُوَّع

In broad light. في رَائِعَة الضُّحَى والنَّهَار

First white hair. رَائِعَة الشَّيْب

Exciting admiration. أَرْوَع م رَوْعَاء ج أَرْوَاع ورُوع

Frightful, terrible. مُرِيع

Terror-stricken. Perspicacious. مُرَوَّع

To slant, to dodge (thief, fox). ✲ رَاغَ o رَوْغًا ورَوَغَانًا

To deviate from the road. — عن الطَّرِيق

To incline stealthily towards. — إلى

To rush on a. o. with (blows). — على ب

To put grease in (food). رَوَّغَ ه

To delude a. o. To attack a. o. رَاوَغَ ه

To allure a. o. to. — ه على

To seek, to desire a. th. أَرَاغَ وارْتَاغَ ه

To wallow (beast). تَرَوَّغَ

They struggled together. تَرَاوَغُوا

Deviating (road). رَائِغ

Shift, stratagem, slyness. رَوَاغ ورُوَيْغَة

Slant, sly. Fox. رَوَّاغ

Wrestling-place. رَوَاغَة و رِيَاغَة

Abundance of harvest. رِيَاغ

To be still, motionless. ✲ رَافَ o رَوْفًا

To improve (a farm).

To ponder over (a scheme). رَوَّزَ ه

Master-mason. رَازّ ج رَازَة

Watching of masons. رِيَازَة

Weight, amount. مَرَاز ومَرَازَة

Mural aperture, dormer. P رَوْزَن

Annual book, almanac. P رُوزْنَامَة

To have a proud gait. ✲ رَاسَ o رَوْسًا

To eat much.

To wash away a. th. (torrent). — ه

Wicked man. رَوْس سُوء

To eat much. To eat little. ✲ رَاشَ o رَوْشًا

To weaken a. o. (illness). — ه

Hairy on the ears (camel). Weak. رَاش ورَوُوش

✲ رَاضَ o رَوْضًا و رِيَاضًا و رِيَاضَة , ورَوَّض ه

To break, to train (a colt).

To bore (a pearl). — رِيَاضَة ه

To resort to a garden. رَوَّض

To train o.'s body or mind. رَوَّض نَفْسَهُ

To turn (a land) into a garden. — ه

To blandish a. o. To render (a land) verdant (God). رَاوَض ه وه

To quench o.'s thirst. أَرَاض

To quench the thirst of. — ه

To abound in gardens (place). — وأَرْوَض

To stagnate in (a valley, in a pool : water). — واسْتَرَاض

To vie, to contend. تَرَاوَض

To make a spiritual retreat. ✧ To improve in health (sick man). To train o.'s self. ✧ تَرَيَّض

To be trained ; to be broken to poetry. إِرْتَاض

To become spacious (place). To be cheerful (soul). إِسْتَرَاض

Verdant garden, meadow. رَوْض

رَوْضَة ج رَوْض ورَوْضَات و رِيَاض و رِيضَان

Watery meadow. Luxuriant garden. Water in the bottom of a pool. Half a skin of water.

Bodily exercise. Practice of good works and prayer. ✧ Magical performance. Good health. Retreat, mission. رِيَاضَة

Exact science ; mathematics, music. العِلْم الرِيَاضِيّ وعِلْم الرِيَاضِيَّات

Trainer of colts. رَائِض ج رَاضَة ورُوَّاض ورَائِضُون

To wait, to tarry. رَوَّم
To make a. o. to desire a. th. — ب وه ه
To plan various schemes. — رَأْيَهُ
To ridicule a. o. تَرَوَّم بِفُلَانٍ
Pond. Place in the desert. رَامَة
Lobe of the ear. رَوْم ورُوم
Greeks of Byzantium. The Greek church. رُوم ج أَرْوَام
Mediterranean sea. بَحر الرُّوم والبَحر الأَبيَض
Greek ; Byzantine. ◘ Christian. European. رُومِيّ م رُومِيَّة
Turkey in Europe, Roumelia. Ts رُوم إِيلِي
Glue for sticking feathers. رُومَة
✧ Rafter, beam. رُومِيَّة ج رَوَامِي
Rome (town). رُومِيَّة ورُومَة العُظمَى
Desire. Craving. مَرَام ج مَرَامَات
Misfortune, ill-luck. ✲ ران — رُون ج رُؤُون
Main part of a. th. رُونَة
Sound. Critical ; quiet (night, day). أَرْوَنَان
Broken, tamed. مَرُون بو
To be rippled (water). ✲ رَاه o رَوْهًا ورُوَاهًا
To relate (a tradition). To twist (a rope). ✲ رَوَى i رِوَايَةً ه
To carry water for a. o. — ل وعلى
To fasten a. th. on (a camel). — ه على
To draw water for a. o. — ه
To be well watered (cattle, land). To thrive (tree). رَوِي a رَيًّا ورِيًّا ورِوًى, وارْتَوَى مِن المَاء
To ask a. o. to recite (a poem). ✧ To show a. th. to. رَوَّى وأَرْوَى ه ه
To reflect upon a. th. رَوَّى وتَرَوَّى في
To quench the thirst of. To water (plants). أَرْوَى إِرْوَاء ه
To satisfy o.'s thirst. To become compact (limb). تَرَوَّى تَرَوِّيًا
To relate (a fact). — ه
To be twisted (rope). To be strong (limb). إِرْتَوَى
Abundant water. رِوًى
Fruitfulness, abundance رَوٌ
✧ Rain. ◘ Large leathern-bucket. رَيّ
Copious watering. Abundance. رِيّ
Sweet smell. رِيَّا
Abundant water-spring. عَيْن رَيَّة

To be clear (wine). ✲ رَاق o رَوْقًا
To excite wonder in. — ه
To excel, to be superior to. — على
To have long teeth. رَوِق a رَوَقًا
To clarify (wine). To sell (goods) for some better. رَوَّق ه
✧ To recover from illness, anger. رَوَّق
To overcharge a. o. in (a sale). — لَهُ في
Night has spread its darkness. رَوَّق اللَّيل
To have the gallery of o.'s house facing another. رَاوَق ه
To pour (water, blood). أَرَاق ه
To breakfast. ✧ تَرَوَّق وتَرَيَّق
Gallery ; pavilion. Curtain. Horn ; spear held between a horse's ears. Death-rattle. Life. Dauntless man. Self-conceitedness. Pure love. Pure water. Bloom of youth. Beginning of the night. Chief. Body of man. Fine horse. Planning and acting. رَوْق ج أَرْوَاق
He ran vehemently. He remained at rest. أَلقَى أَرْوَاقَهُ
The eyes issued tears. أَسْبَلَت أَرْوَاق العَيْن
Great beauty. رَوْقَة
Handsome, the best (*m. s. pl.*) of men. رُوقَة
Projection of the upper-teeth. رَوَق
Peristyle. Tent. Door-curtain. Eyebrows. رِوَاق ج أَرْوِقَة ورُوق
Strainer. Wine-jar. Cup. رَاوُوق
Bloom of life. Best part ; first part. رَيِّق ورَيْق
Clear, limpid. Comely. رَائِق ج رَوْق ورُوقَة
Breakfast. ✧ تَرْوِيقَة
Horned. Having a projection of the upper-teeth. أَرْوَق م رَوْقَاء ج رُوق
Porticoed (building). Clarified (wine). مُرَوَّق
Common estate ; estate of bankrupts. ◘ مَال الرَّوك
Echo. رَوْكَاء ورَوْكَة
To slaver (cattle). ✲ رَول — رَوَّل
To smear (bread) with grease. — ه
Superfluous tooth in horses. رَائِل
Slaver of horses. رُوَال
To desire a. th. eagerly. ✲ رَام o رَوْمًا ومَرَامًا ه

Slow-sighted. مُرَيِّث العَيْنَيْن

To be vile, remiss. To have parted legs. ✡ رَاخ i رَيْخًا ورَيَخَانًا ورُيُوخًا

To exhaust, to weaken a. o. رَيَّخ ه

Ridge of a mountain. ✡ رَيْد ج رُيُود وأرْيَاد

To become big and fat. ✡ رِيرَ رَيْرًا, ورَيِّر ورُيُور

To render (the marrow) thin (God, fatigue). أَرَار ه

Drivel of a child. رِير

Soft, fluid (marrow). — ورِير ورَار

To walk proudly, to sweep. ✡ رَاس i رَيْسًا ورَيَسَانًا

To take hold of. To overcome a. o. — ه

To collect furniture, flocks. ✡ رَاش i رَيْشًا

To maintain (a friend). To do good, to help a. o. — ه

To feather (an arrow). — وريَّش وأرْتَاش ه

✧ To grow feathers (bird). رَيَّش

To restore o.'s business. تَرَيَّش وارْتَاش و✧ رَيَّش

Feather. Plenty, means of life. رِيش ج رِيَاش وأرْيَاش

Splendid garment. رِيش ورِيَاش

✧ Tuft of feathers, egret. Lancet. Writing-pen. Small stone. رِيشَة

Thick hair on the ears. رَيْش

Leafy (*plant*). رَيْش وريِّش

Kind of *Abrotanum*, southern wood. ذَات الرِّيش

Feathered (arrow). Agent in bribery. رَائِش

Hairy on the ears, cheeks (man). أَرْيَش م رَيْشَاء ج رِيش

Feathered (arrow). مَرِيش ومُرَيَّش

Cloth of one web. Thin covering. ✡ رِيط — رَيْطَة ج رَيْط ورِيَاط

To increase. To thrive (plant). ✡ رَاع i رَيْعًا ورُيُوعًا ورِيَاعًا ورَيَعَانًا

To move about (looming). — رَيْعًا, وتَرَيَّع

To fear a. o. or a. th. رَاع مِن

To come back from. — عَن

To turn back towards. — إلى

To assemble (tribe). To be plentiful, delicious (food). رَيَّع

Sort, species. Lung. رِئَة (*for* رِئَة)

King (at cards). رِئَة Is

Sea-blubber, jelly-fish. رِئَة البحر

Abundant (water). Cloud dropping large drops. Copious drink. Rhyme-letter in (verses). رَوِي

Need. Reflection. Remainder of a debt. رَوِيَّة

✧ Play, drama. Novel. رِوَايَة

رِوَاء ج أَرْوِيَة, ومِروًى ج مَرَاوٍ ومَرَاوَى

Rope for binding a load.

Sweet water. رَوَاء

Brightness of the face. رُوَاء

Relater, narrator. Groom. رَاوٍ ج رُوَاة ورَاوُون

Narrator, reciter. Beast, skin for carrying water. رَاوِيَة ج رَوَايَا

Copiously watered. Green, soft branch. Fleshy. رَيَّان م رَيَّا ج رِوَاء

Female antelope: mountain-goat. أُرْوِيَّة وإرْوِيَّة ج أَرَاوِيّ وأَرْوَى

To plant (a banner). ✡ رَيَى — أَرْيَى ه

Banner. Iron-collar for slaves. رَايَة ج رَايَات ورَايٌ

Comely aspect. رِيّ

To disturb a. o. (thought). To cause doubt, suspicion to. ✡ رَاب i رَيْبًا, وأَرَاب ه

To be suspicious (man). أَرَاب

To doubt, to fear about. تَرَيَّب بِه

To suspect a. o. of (evil). ✧To be sceptical in (belief). — وارْتَاب واسْتَرَاب ب

To doubt about a. th. إرْتَاب مِن

To waver; to have suspicion. إسْتَرَاب

Doubt. Suspicion. Want. Vicissitude. ✧ Scepticism. رَيْب

Anxiety; suspicion; charge. رِيبَة ج رِيَب

Suspicious, perplexing (affair). رَيَّاب ومُرِيب

To be slow; to be late. ✡ رَاث i رَيْثًا, وتَرَيَّث

To be tired. رَيَّث

To soften a. th. — ه

To delay a. o. أَرَاث ه

To find a. th. to be late. إسْتَرَاث ه

Delay, space of time. رَيْث

As long as; while; until رَيْثَمَا

Slow, late (news). رَيِّث

To multiply (flocks, crops). To possess cereals. أرَاء
To flow (water). To meet (people). تَرَيَّم To be late. To stop. To be redundant in a dish (oil).
To be perplexed. – واستَرَام
To bestow a. th. abundantly. – يَدَهُ ب
Abundance of vegetation. رَيْم ورَيَمَان Redundance. Choice part. Moving of the mirage. Fear. Brightness of the day. ✧ Revenue of land.
Elevated hill. Pigeon-tower. Winding mountain-road. Cell of a Christian. رِيم ج رِيَاء
Crowd. Rising ground. رِيمَة
Excellent (horse). فَرَس رَائِم
Register for lands. ◻ تَرِيم
Fruitful soil. أرض مَرِيعَة
Fertilising rain. مَطَر مُرِيع
To put grease in (food). ✲ راغ – رَيَّغ ه
To be greasy (dish). ✧ تَرَيَّغ
Dust, earth. رِيَاغ
Dusty. مُرَيَّغ
To come, to pasture in a fertile country. ✲ رَاف i رَيْفًا, وأَرْيَف إِرْيَافًا, وتَرَيَّف
To be near to suspicion. رَايَف لِلظِّنَّة
To be fertile (land). أَرَاف إِرَافَة, وأَرْيَف إِرْيَافًا
Cultivated, fertile land. Fluvial region. Ampleness of life. ◻ Lower Egypt. رِيف ج أَرْيَاف
Sea-urchin. رِيف البَحْر
Fruitful. رَيِّف م رَيِّفَة
To be rippled (pool). To be poured (water). To quiver. To shine (mirage). ✲ رَاق i رَيْقًا
To give up the ghost. رَاقَ بِنَفْسِهِ رُيُوقًا
To give clear wine to a. o. رَيَّق ه ه
To pour forth (water). أَرَاق ه
To move about (mirage). تَرَيَّق
Falsehood. Glittering (of a sword). Water. Unseasoned bread. رَيْق
Beginning, best of a. th. – ورَيِّق ورَيُّوق
Saliva. Strength. رِيق ج أَرْيَاق (رِيقَة .un)
✧ He made his mouth to water. ✧ أَجْرَى وسَطَّ رِيقَهُ
On fasting; before breakfast. على الرِيق وعلى رِيق نفس
✧ To restrain anger. To take breath. To have a respite. بَلَم وابْتَلَم رِيقَهُ
✧ To breakfast. كَسَر الرِّيق
Pure, clear. Destitute. Fasting (man). Breakfast. رَائِق
Gaping at everything. مُرَيِّق
To slaver (child). ✲ رَال i و✧ رَيَّل رَيْلًا
Slaver. رِيَال و✧ رَيَالَة
✧ Silver coin of about 3 sh. 6 de. رِيَال ج رِيَالَات
Turkish crown (coin). ✧ رِيَال مَجِيدِي
Silver coin with a wreath. ✧ – بُو طَاقَه
Spanish crown (coin). ✧ – بُو مَدْفَع
To droop (load). ✲ رَام i رَيْمًا
To depart from (a place). – ه ومِن وعَن
He has not ceased doing. ما رَامَ يَفْعَل
He was forsaken. رِيمَ بِهِ
To begin to heal (wound). رَام i رَيْمًا ورَيَمَانًا
To stop in (a place). رَيَّم ب
To exceed a. o. or a. th. – على
Redundance. Hillock. Grave. End of the day. White antelope. Step. Long space of time. Bone of a slaughtered beast. رَيْم
◻ Exaggeration. تَرْيِيم
Mary. H مَرْيَم
To feel qualmish. To be dirty (garment). ✲ رَان i رَيْنًا ورُيُونًا
To overcome a. o. To blind a. o. (passion). – ه وعلى و ب
To be involved in a scrape. To be forsaken. رِينَ بِهِ
To experience loss in flocks. أَرَان
Gaiter without sole. رَان
Dirt. Rust. رَيْن
Wine. رَيْنَة ج رَيْنَات
To go and come. ✲ رَاه i رَيْهًا
To make a. o. to go and come. رَيَّه ه
To move about (mirage). تَرَيَّه
Going to and fro (mirage). مُرَيَّه

ز

To frighten a. o. زَأَمَ ه
To force. to constrain a. o. to. أَزْأَمَ ه على
To heal (a wound). — ه
Violent or sudden death. زُؤَام
Eye. Honour. زَئِم
Powerful voice. Provisions. Word. Wind. Gluttony. Want. زَأَمَة
Frightened. زَئِم
Zizania, darnel-grass. ✡ زُأْن — زُؤَان وزُوَان وزِوَان
To be proud, self-conceited. ✡ زَأَى a زَأْيًا
To make a. o. heavy (surfeit). أَزْأَى ه
To be hairy. ✡ زَبَّ a زَبَبًا
To near its setting (sun). — وزَبَّبَ وأَزَبَّ
To fill up (a water-skin). — o زَبًّا ه
To dry (figs, grapes). زَبَّبَ وأَزْبَبَ ه
To spume in speaking. To spume (corners of the mouth). زَبَّبَ وتَزَبَّبَ
To become dry (grapes). تَزَبَّبَ
To be filled up (water-skin). إِزْدَبَّ
Nose. Beard. زُبّ ج أَزْبَاب وأَزُبّ
Celsia orobanche tinctoria (*plant*). زُبّ القِمّ
Bone of cuttle fish used as a medicine. Fistular sea-worm. زُبّ البَحْر
Down. Thick hair in man. Hairiness of the face in camels. زَبَب
Huge deaf rat. Messenger. زَبَاب
Raisins; dry figs. Foam of the mouth. Venom in the mouth of snakes. زَبِيب
A raisin. Ulcer on the hand. Foam of the mouth. زَبِيبَة
Two red spots above the eyes of snakes, dogs. زَبِيبَتَان
Wine made with raisins. زَبِيبِيّ
Seller of raisins. — وزَبَّاب
Hairy. Downy (bird), A certain devil. أَزَبّ م زَبَّاء ج زُبّ
Fruitful year. عَامٌ أَزَبّ
Great misfortune. دَاهِيَة زَبَّاء
To be angry. To fly in war. ✡ زَبْزَبَ
Kind of cat. Ship. زَبْزَب ج زَبَازِب

To walk quickly (ostrich). ✡ زَأْزَأَ
To move a. th. To frighten a. o. — ه و ه
To tremble from fear. To move about in walking. To be moved. — تَزَأْزَأَ
To drink long draughts. ✡ زَأَبَ a زَأْبًا
To bring in (a water-skin) speedily. — وازْدَأَبَ ه
To be nappy, villous (cloth). ✡ زَئِبَ
Nap, villousness of cloth. زِئْبِر وزُؤْبُر وزِوْبَر
To overlay a th. with quick-silver. ✡ زَأْبَقَ ه
Mercury, quick-silver. Fickle man. زِئْبَق وزِئْبِق و✧ زِيبَق
To fill a. o. with anger. ✡ زَأَتَ a زَأْتًا ه غَيْظًا
To sow discord between. ✡ زَأَجَ a زَأْجًا بَيْنَ
To frighten a. o. ✡ زَأَدَ a زَأْدًا وزَأَدًا وزُؤُدًا ه
Fright, fear. زُؤْد وزُؤُد
To roar (lion). ✧ To snort (stallion). ✡ زَأَرَ i o , وزَئِرَ a زَئِيرًا وزَأْرًا وتَزْآرًا , وازْأَرَّ وتَزَأَّرَ
Thicket. Garden. Dense herd of camels. زَأْرَة
Roaring. Angry (man). زَائِر وزَئِر ومُزْئِر
To speak loudly and much. ✡ زَأَطَ a زِئَاطًا
To hurry a. o. ✡ زَأَفَ a زَأْفًا ه
To despatch (a wounded man). أَزْأَفَ على
To cause heaviness to a. o. (surfeit). — ه
Haste. Quick death. زُؤَاف
To walk haughtily. ✡ زَأَكَ a زَأَكَانًا
To die suddenly. ✡ زَأَمَ a زَأْمًا
To glut (food). To strike a. o. with terror. To cause shivering to a. o. (cold). — ه وه
To be terror-stricken. زُئِمَ زَأْمًا , وزَئِمَ a زَأَمًا , وازْدَأَمَ

Book. Psalms of David. زَبُور ج زُبُر
Writing. Misfortune. Mire. Strong. Handsome man. Mount Sina. زِبْير
Broad in the shoulder-blades. Mischievous. أَزْبَر م زَبْرَاء ج زُبْر
Writing-reed. مِزْبَر
Land infested by hornets. أَرْض مَزْبَرَة
Ornament with gems or figures. Gold. Thin cloud. P زِبْرِج ج زَبَارِج
Chrysolithe. Topaz. P زَبَرْجَد ج زَبَارِج وزَبَرْذَج
To dye (cloth) red or yellow. ✱ زَبْرَق ه
Full moon. Scanty-haired. زِبْرِقَان
To quack (duck). ✱ زَبَط i زَبْط وزَبِيط
Mire, mud. ◻ زَبَط
To be in a rage. To be ill-natured. To utter offensive words. ✱ زَبِم — تَزَبَّم
Offensive in anger. زَبِيم
Short; vile. زَوْبَم
Hurricane. Strong. Devil. زَوْبَعَة ج زَوَابِع
Sweet-smelling marum. ✱ زَبْعَر
Ill-natured. Coarse. Hairy on the face. Female crocodile. Rhinoceros. زَبَعْرِيّ
To pluck out (the beard). To break a. th. To open (a lock). ✱ زَبَق i o زَبْقًا ه
To confine. To straiten a. o. — ه
To mix a. th. with. — ه ب
To glide in to (a house). To be ensnared in. إِنْزَبَق في
Corners of a house. زَابُوقَة
To manure (a field). ✱ زَبَل i زَبْلًا, و✧ زَبَّل ه
To bear, to carry a. th. — وازْدَبَل ه
Mote, ant's load. Trifle. زِبَال وزُبَال
Manure, dung of cattle. زِبْل و زِبْلَة
Mouthful; gobbet. زُبْلَة
Sweepings. Anything. زُبَالَة
✧ Sweeper, scavenger. زَبَّال
Basket made of palm-leaves. زَبِيل
Basket. زِبِّيل ج زَبَابِيل و زِنْبِيل ج زَنَابِيل
Dung-heap. مَزْبَلَة ومَزْبُلَة ج مَزَابِل
To sell (dates) on the tree. To prevent her young from sucking (she-camel). ✱ زَبَن i زَبْنًا ه
To knock, to push a. o. — وزَابَن ه
To remove (a tent) from (the road). أَزْبَن ه عن

To churn (milk) in a skin. ✱ زَبَد o زَبْدًا ه
To feed a. o. with fresh butter. — ه
To give a part of property to. — i زَبْدًا ه ول
To foam (sides of the mouth). زَبَّد وتَزَبَّد
To card (wool, cotton). زَبَّد ه
To foam (sea). To be intensely white. To blossom (lote-tree). أَزْبَد
To rage and threaten (man). أَرْغَى وأَزْبَد
To cream (milk). To take the best part of a. th. To swallow a. th. To fulfil (an oath). تَزَبَّد ه
Fresh butter. زُبْد وزُبْدَة ج زُبَد
Gift, present. زَبْد
Scum of water; dross of metals. ✧ Pith, cream. زَبَد ج أَزْبَاد, وزَبَدَة ج زَبَد
✧ Brownish liquor of the cuttle-fish. زَبَد البَحْر
Earthen bowl, dish. زُبْدِيَّة ج زَبَادِيّ
Calendula officinalis (*plant*). زُبَيْدَة
Civet-cat. Fragrant perfume. زَبَاد
Psyllium (plant). زَبَاد وزُبَادَى
Instrument for churning. مِزْبَد ج مَزَابِد
Foaming. Intense white. مُزْبِد
Having fresh butter. مُزْدَبِد
To copy, to transcribe (a book). ✱ زَبَر o i زَبْرًا, وزَبَّر ه
To throw stones at. To repel (a beggar) roughly. زَبَر o زَبْرًا ه
To prohibit a. th.; to prevent from. — ه وه عن
To case (a well) with stones. — ه
To endure, to bear a. th. — على
To become big (ram). زَبِر o زَبَارَة
✧ To trim the vine. زَبَر وزَبَّر الكَرْم
To become stout in body (man). To be brave. أَزْبَر
To bristle up (hair; beast). To prepare to do evil. To shudder. To come forth (hair, plant). إِزْبَأَرّ
Strong. Stone. Understanding. Word. Writing. زَبْر
Book. زِبْر ج زُبُور
Shoulder-blade. Fragment of iron. Mane of lion. Anvil. زُبْرَة ج زُبَر وزُبُر

To withdraw, to retire apart. إنزبن
Side. Curtain of a tent. زبن
Hill at the winding of a valley. زابنة
Rebellious genii. Policemen. زبانية
Angels of divine justice.
Wont to kick زبون ج زبن, و ✧ زباين
(beast). ✧ Simpleton. Dupe. Customer.
Sweet-heart.
Desperate war. حرب زبون
Neck. Haughtiness. زبونة
Horns of a scorpion. Two زبانيا العقرب
stars in *Scorpio*.
Sale of dates on the tree. مزابنة
To carry a. th. ✧ زبا i زبيا, وازدبى ه
To urge on (a beast). — وزبّى وازدبى ه
To draw (evil) upon a. o. زبا ه ب
To lay a snare for a. o. — ل
To dig (a pit-fall). زبّى وتزبّى ه
To become proud : to swell. تزابى
Height unreached by water. زبية ج زبى
Pit-fall for wild beasts.
Speed. Briskness. Kind أزبي ج أزابي
of walk. Evil. Momentous event.
To deck (a bride). ✧ زتّ o زتًّا, وزتّت ه
✧ To cast off, to throw away a. th.
To be adorned (bride). تزتّت
To run (ostrich). To ✧ زجّ o زجًّا
hit a. o. with the butt-end of a
spear.
To shoot arrows at. To strike — ه ب
with (the iron-foot of a spear).
To be thin and arched زجّ a زججًا, وازدجّ —
(eyebrows).
To arch (the eyebrows). To زجّج ه
level (a place).
To put an iron-foot to (a أزجّ ه
spear).
Point of the elbow. زجّ ج زجاج وزججة
Iron-foot of a spear ; arrow-head.
Tush of a stallion.
Glass. زجاج وزجاج وزجاج
Berries. Glass-vessels of the زجاج
clove-tree.
Pellitory, wall-wort (*pla.*). حشيشة الزجاج
Piece of glass ; زجاجة وزجاجة وزجاجة
a glass-vessel ; a lamp.
Glass-seller زجاجي
Manufacturer of glass زجّاج
Having fine and أزجّ م زجّاء ج زجّ

arched brows. Walking with wide-
streched legs (ostrich).
Short lance. مزجّة
Ironed (spear-butt). مزجّج
To chide ✧ زجر o زجرًا, وازدجر ه وب
away (a dog). To cry out to a. o.
To scare a bird away — وازدجر الطير
for drawing auguries.
To abstain, to refrain from. تزاجر عن
To be driven back, إنزجر وازدجر
chidden.
Large fish with زجر وزجر ج زجور
small scales.
Crow. أبو زاجر
I keep him aloof هو مني مزجر الكلب
like a dog.
To start (a pigeon). ✧ زجل o زجلًا ه
To bring forth. To repel ; — ه وب
to spear a. o.
To be cheerful. To raise زجل a زجلًا
the voice. To play.
Play. Shouts. Pleasure. Raising زجل
of the voice. ✧ Vulgar song.
Confused voices, shouts. زجلة ج زجلات
Condition, state. Party زجلة ج زجل
of people. Little quantity.
Rustling (plant). Noisy company. زجل
Thundering (cloud).
Peg of a water-skin. زاجل ج زواجل
Ring on the butt of a spear. Leader
of an army. Loud (song).
Archers. زجّالة
Carrier-pigeons. حمام الزاجل والزجّال
Spear-head. Short spear. مزجل
Wooden arrow. مزجال
To whisper. ✧ زجم o زجمًا
✧ زجا o زجوًا, وزجّى وأزجى وازدجى ه و ه
To urge (a beast) gently.
To succeed easily — زجوًا وزجوًّا وزجاء
(business). To be easily collected
(taxes). To be current (coin). To
cease to laugh.
To be satisfied with. تزجّى ب
Success of an affair. زجاء
Small (gift) ; scanty gain. Slow. مزجى
Weak, feeble. مــزجّى
To snatch a. th. from. ✧ زجّ o زجًّا ه عن
To draw a. th. back quickly. — ه وه
To push a. o.

To slip down (man). ✧ زَحْلَطَ وتَزَحْلَطَ
To roll a. th. along. To fill (a vessel). ✱ زَحْلَفَ ه
God avert thy evil from us! زَحْلَفَ الله شَرَّك عَنَّا
To speak volubly. — في الكلام
To give a. th. to. — ه ل
To be rolled, pushed along. تَزَحْلَفَ
To keep aloof, to retire. إزحَلَفَ وازلَحَفَ
Sloping-place. زُحْلوفَة ج زَحَاليف
Small-footed insects. زَحَالِف
To slide a. th. along. ✱ زَحْلَقَ وزَحْلَكَ
To slip out. To glide. تَزَحْلَقَ وتَزَحْلَكَ
Sliding-place. See-saw. زُحْلوقَة وزُحْلوكَة
To press a. o. (crowd). To put a. o. in a strait. ✱ زَحَمَ a زَحْمًا و زِحَامًا . وزَاحَمَ ه
To approach (a number). ✧ To compete with. زَاحَمَ ه وه
To press together (men). To dash (waves). تَزَاحَمَ وازدَحَمَ
To throng near (water). إزدَحَمَ على
Crowd, pressure, throng. زَحْمٌ وزَحْمَة
Elephant. Bull with a broken horn. First Turkish chief who fought the Arabs. ✧ Competitor. مُزَاحِم
Dodder (plant). ✱ زُحْموك ج زَحَاميك
To be slow, dilatory. ✱ زَحَنَ a زَحْنًا , وتَزَحَّنَ
To remove a. o. from. — ه عن
To drink, to do a. th. reluctantly. تَزَحَّنَ ه وعلى
Of a short stature. زُحَن
Intense heat. Caravan. زَحْنَة
To burn with anger. To jump. To hurry on. ✱ زَخَّ o زَخًّا
To throw into an abyss. To urge (a beast) vehemently. — ه وه
✧ To stoop (beast). To pelt (rain). زَخَّ
To glow (live coal). — i زَخًّا وزَخِيخًا
Anger. ✧ Pelting rain. زَخَّة
Spouse, wife. — ومِزَخَّة ومَزَخَّة
To run high (river). To boil (kettle). To rage (battle). To stir (army). To grow (plant). ✱ زَخَرَ a زَخْرًا وزُخُورًا وتَزْخَارًا
To fill a. th. To adorn. To winnow. To fatten (cattle: herbage). — ه
To cheer a. o. — ه
To boast of. — ب

To snatch a. th. from. ✱ زَحْزَحَ ه عن
To be removed. To retire aside. تَزَحْزَحَ
✱ زَحَرَ a i زَحِيرًا وزُحَارًا وزُحَارَة , وزَحَّرَ وتَزَحَّرَ
To suffer from dysentery. To sigh in travail (woman). To moan.
To be hostile to a. o. زَاحَرَ ه
Dysentery. Sigh, hard breathing. زُحَار وزَحِير وزُحَارَة
Avaricious. زَحِر وزَحَّار وزَحْرَان
To drag himself (child). To creep (reptile). To drag the feet (camel). To fall short (arrow). ✱ زَحَفَ a زَحْفًا وزُحُوفًا وزَحَفَانًا
◻ To dust (a house). زَحَّفَ البَيْتَ
To march off towards (army). — وتَزَحَّفَ وازدَحَفَ إلى
To be tired (camel). To fulfil (an intention). To gather in a body (army). أزحَفَ
To jade (a beast). To shake (a tree: wind). — ه
To come up together (fighters). تَزَاحَفَ
Army moving on slowly. زَحْف ج زُحُوف
Sudden blaze soon subsiding. نَار الزَّحْفَتَيْن
Reptiles. ◻ Palm-branch for dusting. زَحَّافَة
Dragging her feet (she-camel). زَحُوف ج زُحُف , ومُزحِف
To be jaded (beast). ✱ زَحَكَ a زَحْكًا , وأزحَكَ
To stop in (a place). — ب
To approach to. — من
To withdraw from. — عن
To remove a. o. from. زَاحَكَ ه عن
To approach or separate (people). تَزَاحَكَ
To withdraw; to be displaced. ✧ To slip (land); to give way (earth). ✱ زَحَلَ a زُحُولًا , وتَزَحَّلَ
To be jaded; slack (camel). — زَحَلًا
To remove a. th. زَحَّلَ وأزحَلَ ه
To force a. o. into (a place). أزحَلَ ه إلى
Keeping aloof from affairs. زُحَل م زُحَلَة
Saturn (planet). زُحَل
Pellitory, wall-wort. حَشِيشَة الزُّحَل
Narrow place. Slippery stone. زُحْلول
Retired place. مَزحَل

To be garnished with buttons (clothes). To button o.'s clothes. تَزَرَّرَ
Button. Small bone of the heart. Socket of the thigh. Pivot. Edge of a sword. ✧ Bud of a plant. Stud, tassel. زِرّ ج أَزْرَار وزُرُور
Column of religion. زِرّ الدِّين
Good tender of flocks. — المال
Wound made by the teeth, by the edge of a sword. زَرَّة
Mark left by a bite. زِرَّة
Dog-fly, camel-fly. زَارَّة
Quick-witted, lively. زَرِير
A yellow-blossomed dyeing plant. Purslain, blite. P زَرِير (*un.* زَرِيرَة)
Sticking on a wall (missile). زُرَارَة
Biting (ass). مِزَرّ
To sing (starling). ✧ To bud (flower). ✱ زَرْزَرَ
To stir about. تَزَرْزَرَ
Starling (bird). زُرْزُر وزُرْزُور ج زَرَازِر وزَرَازِير
Skilful manager of property. زُرْزُور مال
Of the colour of a starling. زُرْزُورِيّ
Quick-witted. زَرْزَار وزُرَازِر ج زَرَازِر
Greek Patrician. زِرْزَار ج زَرَازِرَة
To pen, to enclose (cattle) in. ✧ To confine a. o. in. ✱ زَرَب o زَرْبًا ه في
To make an enclosure for (cattle). — ل
To flow, to glide (water). زَرِبَ a زَرَبًا
To enter his lurking-place (hunter). إِنْزَرَبَ
To become partly yellow (plant). إِزْرَبَّ
Enclosure for cattle. Hunter's booth. Entrance. زَرْب و زِرْب ج زُرُوب
Water-course. Enclosure. زَرَب
Pillow. Rich carpet. زُرْبِيّ وزِرْبِيَّة ج زَرَابِيّ
Enclosure for cattle. Hunter's booth. Lurking place of wild beasts. زَرِيبَة ج زَرَائِب
Dilution of gold. P زِرْيَاب
Long and strait lane. ✧ زَارُوب ج زَوَارِيب
Water-course. Sewer. ✧ Spout. Pipe. مِزْرَاب ج مَزَارِيب
High-heeled leathern boots. G زُرْبُول ج زَرَابِيل وزَرْبُون

To overcome a. o. in boasting. زَاخَرَ ه
To swell (sea). To come up (tide). To overflow (river). تَزَخَّرَ
Noble. Happy. Bountiful. زَاخِر
Swollen sea. Bountiful man. بَحْر زَاخِر
Tall, dense (plant). زُخَارِيّ
To glory in. ✱ تَزَخْوَرَ ب
To embellish (speech) with lies. To complete a. th. ✱ زَخْرَفَ ه
To deck o.'s self. تَزَخْرَفَ
Gold. Perfection of a work. Bombast, bathos. Hues of plants. *Pl.* Ships. Water-flies. Channels of water. زُخْرُف ج زَخَارِف
Allurements of the world. زَخَارِف الدُّنْيَا
To be proud : to boast. ✱ زَخَفَ a زَخْفًا وزَخِيفًا
To speak much. زَخَفَ في الكلام
To take a. th. from. — ه من
To attire herself (woman). تَزَخَّفَ
Proud, haughty. زَاخِف ومُزَخِّف
To thrust a. o. back. ✱ زَخَمَ a زَخْمًا ه
To stink (meat). زَخِمَ a زَخَمًا, وأَزْخَمَ
To carry away (a load). إِزْدَخَمَ ه
Stinking. زَخِم وأَزْخَم
✧ Plectrum. Whip. Stirrup-strap. زَخْمَة
Stench of meat. زَخَمَة
Part, lot, share. ✱ زِدْب ج أَزْدَاب
The two shoulder-blades. ✱ زِدْر — أَزْدَرَان
He came with empty hands. جَاءَ يَضْرِب أَزْدَرَيْهِ
To play with nuts (child). ✱ زَدَا o زَدْوًا ه و ب
To confer a benefit. أَزْدَى
Hole for playing with nuts. مِزْدَاة
To button (a garment). To heap up a. th. To dust (furniture). To pluck (the hair). To twinkle (the eyes). ✧ To press a. o. ✱ زَرَّ o زَرًّا ه
To drive back. To bite a. o — ه
To spear a. o. with. — ه ب
To glisten (eyes). زَرَّ i زَرِيرًا
To ill-treat an adversary. To be taught by experience (man). زَرَّ a زَرًّا
To bite a. o. زَارَّ ه
To put buttons to (clothing). زَرَّرَ وأَزَرَّ ه

Tiller. Asperser. زَرَّاع ج زَرَّاعة وزرّاعون
Seed-produce. زِرِّيع
Sown field. ◇ Hamlet. مَزْرَعَة ج مَزارِع
Sown (field, wheat). مَزْرُوع ومُزْدَرَع
To leap. ✻ زَرَف o زَرْفًا
To approach towards. — زُرُوفًا وزَرِيفًا إلى
To amplify a speech, to lie. — وزَرَّف في الكلام
To walk slowly. To hurry in walk. زَرَف o زَرِيفًا
To re-open (wound). زَرِف a زَرَفًا, وأَزْرَف
To set aside. To increase a. th. زَرَّف ه
To clear away (a crowd). To thrust a. o. with a spear. — ة
To near (the age) of. — على
To advance. To buy a giraffe. أَزْرَف
To hurry in walk. — في المَشْي
To penetrate, to pass through. To pass away (wind). To go to a pasturage. إِنْزَرَف
Giraffe. زَرَافَة وزُرَافة وزَرَّافة ج زَرَافيّ وزُرَافى وزَرَافى
Liar. زُرَافة
Party of men. زَرَافة وزُرافة ج زَرَافات
Swift (she-camel). زَرُوف وزَرَّاف و مِزْرَاف
To curl (the hair). ✻ زَرْفَن ه
Curl, hair-ringlet. Ring of people. P زُرْفِين و زِرْفِين ج زَرَافين
To mute (bird). ✻ زَرَق o i زَرْقًا
◇ To dart forth.
To shoot (game) with a javelin. — ه
To shift its (load : camel). — وأَزْرَق ه
To ogle, to leer towards a. th. so as to show the white of the eyes. زَرَّقت وازْرَقَّت وازْرَاقَّت عَيْنُهُ نَحْو
To be blue, gray (eye). To become blind. زَرِق a زَرَقًا, وازْرَقّ
To pierce through (arrow). To droop (saddle). To lay on the back. To recoil (man). إِنْزَرَق
To be blue, grayish. إِزْرَقّ وازْرَاقّ
Blue colour. Blindness. Whiteness in the legs of a horse. زَرَق وزُرْقة
White sparrow-hawk. White hair on the forelock. زُرَّق ج زَرَارِيق
Blue, gray. Shining. Falcon. أَزْرَق م زَرْقاء ج زُرْق
Gray, ash-coloured horse. حِصَان أَزْرَق

To burst with anger; to utter foul speech. ◘ إِزْرَأَبّ
Red perch spotted with blue. زَرْبُون
To deceive a. o. ✻ زَرْجَن ة
Vine. Vine-branch. Wine. Pure rain-water. Red dye. P زَرَجُون
To bruise (a limb). ✻ زَرِح a زَرْحًا ة
To be removed. ✻ زَرِح a زَرَحًا
Small sandy hill. زَرْوَح وزَرْوَحَة ج زَرَاوِح
To strangle a. o. with a rope. ✻ زَرَد o زَرْدًا ه
To make (a network, mail). — ه
To swallow (a mouthful). زَرِد a زَرَدًا, وتَزَرَّد وازْدَرَد ه
To take an oath rashly. تَزَرَّد اليمين
To look angrily at. زَرَّد عَيْنَهُ على
Coat of mail. ◇ Mail, ring, mesh. Zebra. زَرَد ج زُرُود
Rope for strangling a camel. زِرَاد ومِزْرَد
Maker of mail. Strangler. زَرَّاد
Marten, kind of weasel. P زَرْدَوا
Throat, gullet. مَزْرَد
Flushed in the face. مَزْرُود
To strangle a. o. ✻ زَرْدَب ة
To strangle a. o. To swallow (food). ✻ زَرْدَم ة وه
Windpipe, air-passage. P زَرْدَمَة
To cast seeds. ✻ زَرَع a زَرْعًا, وازْدَرَع
To sow (a field). To till (the ground). — ه
To cause (plants, children) to grow up (God). زَرَع ه و ة
He rose from destitution to wealth. زُرِع لهُ بَعْد شَقَاوة
To farm out a field to a. o. for a share of the produce. زَارَع ة
To have crops. To grow (seeds). To be able to sow (men). أَزْرَع
To hasten to do mischief. تَزَرَّع إلى الشَرّ
Seeds. Standing corn. Offspring. زَرْع ج زُرُوع
Seed. زُرْعَة
Land fit to be sown. — و زِرْعَة وزُرْعَة وزَرَعَة
Tillage. Agriculture. زِرَاعَة
Field watered by rain. Soft thing. زَرِيع
Seeds; seed-produce. زَرِيعَة
Sower. زَارِع ج زُرَّاع وزَارِعُون

Purchase upon credit.
Water-furrow, rivulet. زُرْنُوق ج زَرَانِيق
The two beams a of shaft. الزُّرْنُوقَان
Coat of mail. زَرَه Pe
✲ زَرَى i زَرْيًا وزُرْيَانًا و زِرَايَةً ومَزْرِيَةً ومَزْرَاةً, وأَزْرَى وتَزَرَّى ه على To upbraid; to blame a. o. for.
أَزْرَى ب To fall short of; to neglect a. th.
— ب To contemn. To disparage a. o.
إِزْدَرَى واسْتَزْرَى ه To undervalue, to scorn at.
زَارٍ ومِزْرَاء Disparager, slanderer.
زَرِيّ Disparaged. Middle-sized (water-skin).
إِزْدِرَاء واسْتِزْرَاء Contempt, scorn.
✲ زَطَّ o زَطًّا To buzz (fly).
زُطّ (زُطِّيّ .un) Indian tribe. ✧ Gipsy.
✲ زَعْزَعَ ه وه To shake a. th. (wind). To urge (camels). ✧ To tickle a. o.
تَزَعْزَعَ To be shaken.
زَعْزَع وزَعْزَاء وزُعَازِع وزَعْزَعَان Violent wind, gale.
زَعْزَعَة ج زَعَازِع Shock, shake. Squadron of horses.
زَعَازِع Storms. Adversities.
✲ زَعَبَ a زَعْبًا ه وه To fill (a water-skin). To carry (a skin) full. ✧ To upbraid a. o.
زَعَّبَ To pour forth its water (skin). To be flooded (ravine).
زَعَبَ وازْدَعَبَ بِحِمْلِهِ To be overburdened in walk (camel).
— وازْدَعَبَ ه To cut off a. th.
زَعَبَ a زَعِيبًا To croak (raven).
تَزَعَّبَ To get angry. To be brisk.
— في To eat or drink to excess.
— ه To divide a. th. together.
زَعْبَة وزُعْبَة و زَعْب Allotment of property.
زَاعِب Flooding (torrent). Good guide.
زَعِيب Croaking of a raven. Humming of bees. ✧ Upbraiding.
زُعْبُوب ✧ Sorb, service-fruit. Azerole.
أَزْعَب م زَعْبَاء ج زُعْب Short and vile.
✧ زَعْبَرَ على To hoax, to cheat a. o.
✧ زَعْبَرَة Imposition, hoax.
✧ مُزَعْبِر ومُزَعْبِرَجِيّ Humbug. Juggler, shuffler.

عدوّ أَزْرَق Desperate foe *lit*: blue-eyed enemy.
موت أَزْرَق Violent death.
الحَجَر الأَزْرَق *Aqua marina*, beryl, precious stone.
زَرْقَاء Sky. Wine.
زَرْقَاء اليَمَامَة Elephantiasis.
الزُّرْق *Pl.* Blind men. Spears. Blades.
زُرَيْق وأَبُو زُرَيْق Crow, jay.
زُرَيْقَاء Dish of milk and oil. Cat.
زَوْرَق Skiff, small boat.
أَزْرَقِيّ ج أَزَارِقَة Sect of heretics.
مِزْرَاق ج مَزَارِيق Short spear, javelin.
✲ زُرْقُم ج زَرَاقِم (.m. f) Intensely blue; gray.
زَرَاقِم Serpents.
✲ زَرَك a زَرْكًا To be naughty (child).
✧ زَرَك o زَرْكًا ه To squeeze, to press against a. o.
✧ زَرَّك ه To harass, to tease a. o.
✧ زَرْكَة Pressure, crowd.
✧ زَرْكَش ه To make brocade.
زَرْكَش P Brocade, embroidered cloth.
✲ زَرَم i زَرْمًا, وزَرَّم وأَزْرَم ه To stop, to cut a. th. short.
زَرِم a زَرَمًا, وازْرَأَمّ To be stopped (tears, dejection, speech). To be annulled (sale).
إِزْدَرَم ه To swallow a. th.
زَرِم Restless. Straitened (man). Scanty. Avaricious.
أَزْرَم Cat.
✲ زَرْنَب Egyptian willow. Locust-tree. Fern. Saffron.
زِرْنِيخ P Arsenic, white arsenic.
زِرْنِيخ أَحْمَر Realgar, sandarac.
زِرْنِيخ أَصْفَر Orpiment, yellow arsenic.
زَرَاوَنْد P Aristolochia, birthwort.
زَرُنْبَد وزَرُنْبَاد P Zodoary (*plant*). Curcuma, kind of turmeric.
✲ زَرْنَق ه To water (the earth) with furrows. To set a shaft on (a well). ✧ To spirt (water) into o.'s mouth.
تَزَرْنَق To buy upon credit. To draw water for hire.
— ه To clothe a. th.
— ب To clothe o.'s self with.
زَرْنَقَة Debt. Excess. Perfect beauty.

Coarse woollen smock. ◘ زَعْبُوط ج زَعَابِيط
Thyme. *See* سَعْتَر. ✧ زَعْتَر
To cry, to yell. ✻ زَعَج a زَعْجًا
To disquiet a. o. To — وأَزْعَج ه وه
expel a. o. To snatch off a. th.
To be disturbed. To be snatched. إِنْزَعَج
Restlessness. Anxiety. زَعَج وانزِعَاج
Restless, disquieted woman. مِزْعَاج
To be scarce ✻ زَعِر a زَعَرًا, وازْعَرّ وازعَارّ
(hair).
To swindle. ✧ زَعَر
Malevolence, ill-nature. زَعَارَّة و✧ زَعَارَة
✧ Fur-tippet for females. زَعَارَة ج زَعَارِر
Scanty-haired. Ha- أَزْعَر م زَعْرَاء ج زُعْر
ving few plants (soil). ✧ Rascal, scoundrel.
Medlar, زُعْرُور و✧ زَعْرُور ج زَعَارِير
three-grained medlar; azarole. Ill-natured (man).
To bray (ass). ✻ زَعَط a زَعْطًا
To strangle a. o. ه —
Quick-killing (death). زَاعِط
To kill ه ✻ زَعَف a زَعْفًا, وأَزْعَف, وازْدَعَف
a. o. on the spot.
Quick (death, poison). زُعَاف ومُزْعِف
Dangerous places. زُعُوف
Snake. مِزْعَافَة
To dye; to season a. th. ✻ زَعْفَر ه
with saffron.
Saffron. زَعْفَرَان ج زَعَافِر
Rust of iron. Tritoxyde زَعْفَرَان الحَدِيد
of iron.
Curcuma, turmeric. الزَّعْفَرَان الشَّعْرِيّ
Dyed, seasoned with saffron. مُزَعْفَر
Sweet porridge. Yellowish (lion).
To shriek. To cry out. ✻ زَعَق a زَعْقًا
To frighten a. o. To drive — ه وب
away, to cry out to (a beast). ✧ To call out a. o.
To raise (the dust: wind). To — ه وه
sting a. o. (scorpion). To salt (food) to excess.
To be bitter, unpotable زَعُق o زَعَاقَة
(water).
To be active. To fear زَعِق a زَعَقًا وزَعِق
by night.
To frighten a. o. To salt أَزْعَق ه وه
(food) to excess. To hasten (the walk).

To reach bitter water by digging. أَزْعَق
To fear by night. To hurry إِنزَعَق
(beast). To move forward (horse).
Cry, call, yell. زَعْقَة ج زَعَقَات
Fearing by night. Brisk yet زَعِق
fearful.
Quick-walking (horse). زَعَّاق
Bitter, salt (water). Scared away. زُعَاق
Bitterness of water. زُعُوقَة
Chicken of the par- زُعْقُوقَة ج زَعَاقِيق
tridge.
Plough. Quick (walk). مِزْعَق
Scared away. مَزْعُوق وزَعِيق
Delay, stay in a place. ✻ زَعْكَة
To be brisk. To prance ✻ زَعِل a زَعَلًا
without rider (horse). To be restless (sick person). ✧ To be sorry, angry.
To discontent, to weary a. o. ✧ زَعَّل ه
To render lively. ✧ To vex a. o. أَزْعَل ه
To remove a. th. from (its — ه مِن
place).
To be brisk, sprightly. تَزَعَّل
Ostrich. ✧ Discontent, weariness. زَعَلَة
Lively. Writhing from زَعِل وزَعْلَان
hunger. ✧ Sorry, grieved.
To assert ✻ زَعَم o زَعْمًا وزِعْمًا وزُعْمًا ه
a. th. true or false. To relate a. th.
To become a — a o زَعْمًا وزَعَامَة ب
surety for.
To covet a. th. زَعِم a زَعْمًا في
He thought so. زَعَم كَذَا
To press, to straiten a. o. زَاعَم ه
✧ To compete with.
To become possible (affair). أَزْعَم
To become excellent (milk). To sprout forth (ground).
To render a. o. covetous. ه —
To make a. o. to guarantee — ه ه
a. th. a. o.
To obey a. o. — إلى
To become the chief of (a party). — على
To pretend falsely. تَزَعَّم
Assertion. ✧ Pretension. Pride. زَعْم
As he pretends. عَلَى زَعْمِهِ
I do not هٰذَا وَلَا زَعْمَتَك, هٰذَا وَلَا زَعَمَاتِك
partake of thy opinion.
Truthful. Mendacious. زُعْمِيّ
Nobility. Chiefdom. Choice زَعَامَة
part. Share of a chief. Weapon. Cow.

Surety, answerable. زَعِيم ج زُعَمَاء
Chief. Spokesman.
Pretension. Object coveted. Object of debate. مَزْعَم ج مَزَاعِم
To deck (a bride). ✲ زَعْنَف ه
Short. Extremities of the body. Refuse. Hem of a vestment Scattered party. Calamity. زَعْنَفَة وزِعْنِفَة ج زَعَانِف
Fins (of fishes). Promiscuous party. زَعَانِف
To speak faintly. ✲ زَغْزَغ الكَلَام
To conceal a. th. ◻ To tickle a. o. — ه وه
To scoff at a. o. — ب
✧ To use foul play. زَغْزَغ بَيْنَهُ
Lively, sprightly. زَغْزَغ
To become downy (boy, chicken). ✲ زَغِب a زَغَبًا , وزَغَّب , وازْغَابّ
To become sappy and leafy (vine). أَزْغَب
Downy hair or feathers. زَغَب
Softest down. زُغَابَة وزُغَابَى
Downy (man, bird). Downy fig, cucumber. Dapple (horse). أَزْغَب م زَغْبَاء ج زُغْب
Fruit of the *Phillyrea*, wild olive-tree. ✲ زَغْبَج
Villousness, nap of cloth. ✲ زِغْبِر وزُغْبُر
Whole. Thin-leaved marum. زَغْبَر
He has taken it altogether. أَخَذَهُ بِزَغْبَرِهِ
To groan loudly (camel). To swell (river). ✲ زَغَد a زَغْدًا
To squeeze (a water-skin). — ه
To squeeze the throat of. — ه
To rouse a. o. by (words). — ه ب
To suckle (a child). أَزْغَد ه
Butter spouting from a skin when squeezed. زَغِيد
To be abundant. To swell (river). ✲ زَغَر a زَغْرًا
To snatch. ◻ To scrutinise a. th. — ه
Abundance, redundance. Excess. زَغْر
Brach-hound, setting-dog. زَغْر وكَلْب زَغَارِيّ
Small. ✧ زَغِير (for صَغِير)
To reciprocate his groans (camel). ✧ To quaver, to sing wedding-songs (woman). ✲ زَغْرَد و◻ زَغْرَط و✧ زَغْلَط وزَلْغَط
زَغْرَدَة ج زَغَارِيد و◻ زَغْرَطَة ج زَغَارِيط
و✧ زَلْغَطَة ج زَلَاغِيط وزَغْلَطَة ج زَغَالِيط

✧ Shrill, trilling cries of joy.
Hiccough. ◻ زَغْطَة وزَغَطَّة
To be plentiful (water). ✲ زَغَف a زَغْفًا
He added lies to his narration. — في حَدِيثِهِ
To spear a. o. with. — ه ب
To take much of a. th. إِزْدَغَف ه
Discharged cloud. Full and long (coat of mail). زَغْف ج أَزْغَاف
Large coat of mail. زَغْفَة وزَغَفَة
Chips of wood. Slender extremities of a tree. زَغَف
Covetous, greedy. مِزْغَف
✧ To squint (man). ✲ زَغِل a زَغَلًا
To pour forth (water). To spirt (a beverage). ✧ To adulterate (money). — وأَزْغَل ه
To suck (his mother : young one). — ه
To feed her chickens (bird). To suckle (a child). أَزْغَل ه
To gush out blood (wound). — بالدَّم
✧ Deception, cheat, adulteration. زَغَل
Mouthful spirted, jet. زُغْلَة
Sucking greedily. زَغُول
Squint-eyed. أَزْغَل
Nimble. Child, baby. ✧ Young pigeon. ◻ Yellow date. ✲ زُغْلُول ج زَغَالِيل
To counterfeit, to cheat a. th. ✧ زَوْغَل
To cheat (man). To be counterfeit. تَزَوْغَل وتَزَاغَل
Counterfeit, cheat, trickery. ✧ زَوْغَلَة
To groan repeatedly (camel). To speak angrily (man). ✲ زَغَم — تَزَغَّم
Stammerer. زُغْموم وزُغْمُوم
To hasten (the walk). To alight ; to expand its wings (male ostrich). To blow gently (wind). ✲ زَفّ i زَفًّا وزَفِيفًا وزُفُوفًا
To conduct (a bride) to her bridegroom. زَفّ o زَفًّا وزِفَافًا , وأَزَفّ , وازْدَفّ ه
To walk quickly. أَزَفّ
To hurry the walk of a. o. — ه
To carry (a load). إِزْدَفّ ه
To carry a. th. away (water). إِسْتَزَفّ ه
Fine feathers of birds. زِفّ
Fine plumage. زِفَف
Troop, band. زُفَّة
One time, one action. زَفَّة
Nuptial procession. زَفَّة وزِفَاف

Ostrich. Swift (she-camel). زَفُوف
Swift. Flight of a bird. زَفِيف وزَفَّان وزِفَاف
Having fine and thick feathers (ostrich). Swift. أَزَفّ
Litter for a bride. مِزَفَّة
To run at full speed (man). ✲ زَفْزَف
To dart down; to expand the wings (bird). To quake. To moan.
To make (plants) to rustle (wind). — ه
Ostrich. Quick. Blowing violently (wind). زَفْزَاف
To fill (a vessel). ✲ زَفَت o زَفْتًا ه وه
To rouse a. o. To expel, to hinder. To anger. To weary a. o.
To tar (a ship). ✧ To defile a. th. زَفَّتْ ه
Pitch, pine-resin. Bitumen used as a remedy. زِفْت
✧ Colophony (resin). زِفْت التَرْمَنْتِين
✧ Cade-oil. زَيْت الزِفْت
Bitumen, liquid pitch. زِفْت رَطِب
Pissasphalt, mineral pitch. — يَابِس
Pitch-oil, coal naphta. دُهْن الزِفْت
Lamp-black. دُخَان الزِفْت
Smeared with pitch. مُزَفَّت
To fill (a vessel). ✲ زَفَد o زَفْدًا ه
To give much barley to (a horse). — ه
To send forth a deep sigh. To begin to bray (ass). To crackle (fire). To send out hot fumes. ✲ زَفَر i زَفْرًا وزَفِيرًا
To carry away. To draw (water). — زَفْرًا ه
✧ To eat fatty food. زَفَّر وتَزَفَّر
✧ To give fatty food; to grease, to soil with greasy food. زَفَّر ه وه
To carry (a burden). إِزْدَفَر ه
Heavy luggage. Water-skin. Party. زِفْر ج أَزْفَار
Tree-prop. ✧ Fatty food. زَفَر
Lion. Brave. Generous. Sea. Large river. Bulky camel. Lord. Considerable gift. Porter. زُفَر
Misfortune. Beginning of the braying of an ass. Deep sigh. زَفِير
✧ Greasy, filthy. Obscene (speech). ✧ زَفِر وزَفْرِيّ
✧ Crystallised alum. شَبَّة زَفِرَة
Deep sigh, moan. زَفْرَة وزُفْرَة ج زَفَرَات
Middle part. ✧ Scum of boiled meat.

Strong-ribbed (horse). أَزْفَر م زَفْرَاء ج زُفْر
Big camel. Great chief. Bow. Tribe. Supporters of a. o. Regiment. زَافِرَة ج زَوَافِر
Female water-carriers. Ribs of horses. زَوَافِر
Deep sigh. مُزْفَر ومُزْدَفَر
Outburst of anger. ✲ زَفَل — أَزْفَل
Party, company. أَزْفَلَة وأَزْفَلَى
To push, to thrust. To dance. To kick. ✲ زَفَن i زَفْنًا
Dancing-girl. Lame (she-camel). زَفُون وزَافِنَة
Booth, tent on a terrace. زِفْن
Swift (camel). ✧ Fruitless sorb-tree. *Tilia*, linden-tree. زَيْزَفُون G
To twang (bow). ✲ زَفَى i زَفْيًا وزَفَيَانًا
To expand the wings (male ostrich).
To raise (figures; looming). To drive (the clouds: wind). To expand (the wings: ostrich). — ه
To carry a. th. أَزْفَى ه
Frightened. مَزْفِيّ ومُنْزَفٍ
To mute (bird). ✧ To slip. ✲ زَقّ o زَقًّا
To feed (her chicks) with the bill (bird). — ه
✧ To push. To extract, to carry (stones). — ه
To skin (an animal). — وزَقَّق ه
To clip (the hair of a skin). زَقَّق ه
Nux vomica, poisonous seed. بُو زَقّ
Wine-skin. زِقّ ج أَزْقَاق و زِقَاق وزُقَّان
Bellows of a hammersmith. — الحَدَّاد
Ascites, dropsy of the belly. إِسْتِسْقَاء زِقِّيّ
Wine. زُقّ ج زَقَقَة
Kind of plungeon. زُقَّة ج زُقّ
Ring-pigeons. زَقَقَة
Drinking with the mouth full. زَقَاق
By-street. Lane. زُقَاق ج أَزِقَّة وزُقَّان
The strait of Gibraltar. الزُقَاق, و بَحْر الزُقَاق
Gold-finch. ✧ زُقَيْقَة وزُقَيْقِيَّة وزُقَاقِيَّة
Shaven (head). Skinned (beast). مُزَقَّق
To chirp at dawn (bird). ✲ زَقْزَق
To mute. To laugh coldly. To be lively (man). ✧ To crackle.
To dandle (a child). — زَقْزَقَة وزِقْزَاقًا ه

To feed (her chicks) with the bill (bird). ◘ To tickle a. o.

مُزَقْزَق Quickly done, despatched (affair).

✧ زَقْزَاقَة Ichneumon.

✱ زَقَبَ o زَقْبًا ه في To frighten (a mole) into (its hole).

— وانزَقَبَ في To enter (its hole : mole).

زَقَّبَ To twitter (sparrow).

زَقَبٌ ج زُقُبٌ Lane, strait road. Neighbourhood, proximity.

✱ زَقَحَ a زَقْحًا وزُقَاحًا To chatter (monkey).

✱ زَقَعَ a زَقْعًا وزُقَاعًا To crow (cock).

✱ زَقَفَ o زَقْفًا, وتَزَقَّفَ, وازدَقَفَ ه To snap up, to snatch a. th. away.

✧ زَقَّفَ وزَقَّفَ (*for* صَفَّقَ) To clap the hands.

✱ زَقَلَ — زُقَّلٌ Robbers, thieves.

◘ زُقْلَةٌ ج زُقَلٌ Cudgel, mace.

زَقِيلَةٌ Lane, narrow road.

✱ زَوْقَلَ To let down the ends of a turban.

رَوَاقِيل Ring of hair around a turban.

✱ زَقَمَ o زَقْمًا, وتَزَقَّمَ, وازدَقَمَ ه To glut, to gobble a. th.

زَقَّمَ ه To give a. o. a deadly food.

أَزْقَمَ ه To make a. o. to gobble.

تَزَقَّمَ To eat cream and dates. To drink to excess.

زَقُّومٌ Infernal tree. Deadly food. Food of cream and dates. Kind of myrobalan.

زَقْمَةٌ A time, one time. Plague.

✱ زَقَنَ o زَقْنًا ه To carry (a burden).

أَزْقَنَ ه To help a. o. to carry (a load).

✱ زَقَا o زَقْوًا وزُقَاءً, وزَقِيَ i زَقْيًا To hoot (owl).

زَاقٍ ج زَوَاقٍ Speaking. *Pl.* Cocks.

زُقْيَةٌ Heap of coins or of any thing.

✱ زَكَّ i زَكًّا وزَكَكًا وزَكِيكًا To totter (old man, child). To run (child, partridge).

أَزَكَّ على To obtain a. th., to persevere in.

تَزَكَّكَ To take up arms.

زُكٌّ Young ring-pigeon.

زِكَّةٌ Weapons, arms.

✱ زَكْزَكَ To totter (old man).

✧ زَكْزَكَ ه To tickle a. o.

تَزَكْزَكَ To take up arms. ✧ To be tickled.

✱ زَكَأَ a زَكْأً ه To strike a. o.

— ه ه To pay (a due) readily to a. o.

— إلى To take refuge to.

إِزْدَكَأَ ه من To collect (a debt) from.

زُكَأٌ وزُكَأَةٌ، وزُكَأَةُ النَّقْدِ Wealthy, paying readily.

✱ زَكَبَ o زَكْبًا ه To fill (a vessel).

إِنْزَكَبَ To be diked (river, sea).

◘ زَكِيبَةٌ ج زَكَائِبُ Sack for grain.

✱ زَكَتَ o زَكْتًا, وزَكَّتَ وأَزْكَتَ ه To fill (a vessel).

زَكَّتَ ه ه To relate a. th. to a. o.

مَزْكُوتٌ Filled. Concerned. Chilled.

✱ زَكَرَ o زَكْرًا, وزَكَّرَ ه To fill (a vessel).

زَكَّرَ وتَزَكَّرَ To become fat (belly). To be filled up (vessel).

زُكْرَةٌ ج زُكَرٌ Small (wine or vinegar-skin. ✧ Navel.

✱ زَكَمَ o زَكْمًا ه, وأَزْكَمَ ه To afflict a. o. with a rheum (God).

— ه To fill (a vessel).

— ب To eject (a liquid). To bring forth (a child).

زُكِمَ To have a rheum.

زُكَامٌ وزُكْمَةٌ Rheum, coryza, cold.

زُكْمَةٌ Harsh man. Last born child.

✱ زَكِنَ a زَكَنًا ه To mind a. th. To understand, to consider a. th. To think of.

زَكَّنَ على To suspect, to doubt, to think about.

زَاكَنَ ه وه To near a. th. or a. o.

أَزْكَنَ ه ه To remind, to inform a. o. of.

— ه To guess a. th. To inform a. o.

زَكَانَةٌ وزَكَانِيَةٌ True estimate.

زَكِنٌ Retentive.

✱ زَكَا o زَكَاءً وزُكُوًّا, وزَكِيَ a زَكًى To grow (plant). To be righteous. To thrive (man).

هٰذَا لَا يَزْكُو بِهِ It does not suit him.

زَكَّى ه وه To make a. th. to grow or thrive. To purify. To improve. ✧ To justify a. o.

— ه To collect poor-rates from.

He gave the tithe on his goods. زَكَّى مَالَهُ
He praised, he justified himself. — نَفْسَهُ
To thrive. أَزْكَى
To give an increase to. — هُ وهُ
To become just. To give alms. To grow. تَزَكَّى
Even number, not odd. زَكًا
Purity. زَكْوَة وزَكَاة ج زَكًا وزَكَوَات Obedience to God. Poor-rates. Legal alms.
Pure from sin. Righteous. Compassionate. زَاكٍ ج زُكَاة, وزَكِيّ ج أَزْكِيَاء
Excellent earth. أَرْض زَكِيَّة
☆ زَلَّ i وزَلَّ a زَلًّا وزَلِيلًا وزُلُولًا ومَزَلَّة وزَلَلًا To slip (foot, tongue). To pass away (life).
To pass quickly. — زَلِيلًا وزُلُولًا
To be deficient (coin). — زُلُولًا
To receive (food). — i هُ
To be thin in the hips. زَلَّ a زَلَلًا
To make a. o. to slip, to err. أَزَلَّ واستَزَلَّ هُ
To grant (a favour) to. — هُ إِلَى
Slippery (ground). زَلّ
Slippery (ground). Deficiency (in weight). Sinfulness. زَلَل
Stones. Smooth stones. (*un* زِلَّة) زِلّ
Slip, sin, error. Nuptials. Banquet. A good deed. Food sent to a friend. زَلَّة ج زَلَّات
Carpet. Woollen blanket. P زُلِّيَّة ج زَلَالِيّ
Deficient in weight (coin). زَالّ ج زَوَالّ وزُلَّل
Pure, sweet, cool, light water. مَاء زُلَال وزُلَازِل وزَلِيل وزَلُول
✧ White of eggs. زُلَال البَيْض
Swift. Lean in the hips. أَزَلّ م زَلَّاء ج زُلّ
Slippery ground. مَزَلَّة ومَزِلَّة
☆ زَلْزَلَ زَلْزَلَةً و زِلْزَالًا وزَلْزَالًا وزُلْزَالًا هُ To quake (the earth : God). To frighten a. o. To urge (camels).
To quake (earth). تَزَلْزَلَ
Earthquake. *Pl.* Calamities. زِلْزَال وزَلْزَلَة ج زَلَازِل
He cleaved to his mother (child). ☆ زَلِبَ a زَلَبًا بِأُمِّهِ

Sweet pancake. زَلَابِيَة
To hasten in walk. ☆ زَلَجَ i زَلْجًا وزَلِيجًا وزَلَجَانًا
He spoke uuconsiderately. زَلَجَ مِن فِيهِ كَلَامٌ
To bolt (a door). — o زَلْجًا, وأَزْلَجَ هُ
To precede a. o. — زَلَجَانًا هُ
To slip, to slide along. زَلِجَ a زُلُوجًا, وتَزَلَّجَ
He lived in a niggardly way. زَلَّجَ العَيْشَ
To render (verses, speech) current. — الكَلَامَ
To addict o.'s self to (wine). تَزَلَّجَ هُ
Slippery place. زَلْج وزَلَج وزَلِيج
Bolt, sliding-latch. زِلَاج ومِزْلَاج
Quick. Slipping (arrow). Long (journey). زَلُوج
Paltry (gift). Intruder. Niggardly. Interested love. Ummanly. مُزَلَّج
To taste a. th. ☆ زَلِجَ a زَلْجًا, وتَزَلَّجَ هُ
To set a. th. apart. ✧ To crawl. ☆ زَلْحَفَ
To retire apart. تَزَلْحَفَ وازْلَحَفَّ
Turtle, turtoise. (*for* سِلَحْفَاة) ✧ زَلْحِفَة
To become fat (cattle). ☆ زَلِخَ a زَلْخًا
To slip (foot); to slide. زَلَخَ i وتَزَلَّخَ
To thrust a. o. with (a spear). — زَلَخَهُ بِ
To advance forward. زَلَخَ o زَلْخَانًا وزَلَخَانًا
To smooth a. th. زَلَّخَ هُ
Slippery place. زَلْخ وزَلِخ
Sliding-place. Pain in the back. زُلَّخَة
To be anxious. ☆ زَلِزَ a زَلَزًا
To walk quickly. ✧ To gobble. ☆ زَلَطَ i زَلْطًا
To strip a. o. of his clothes. ✧ زَلَّطَ هُ
To strip o.'s self of o.'s clothes. ✧ تَزَلَّطَ
✧ Small coin worth 30 paras (about 3 halfpence). Pebble. ✧ زَلَطَة
Nakedness. ✧ زُلْط
Stark-naked. ✧ مُزَلَّط وبِالزُّلْط
To pilfer a. th. To swindle a. th. ✧ To globe, to glut. ☆ زَلِعَ a زَلْعًا, وازْدَلَعَ هُ
To rise (sun). To blaze (fire) زَلَعَ o زُلُوعًا
To burn (o.'s feet) with (fire). — هُ بِ
To be chapped, cracked (skin). To be corrupt (wound). زَلِعَ a زَلَعًا, وتَزَلَّعَ

To inspire a. o. with the desire of. أزلم ه في

To rob a. o. of (a right). To cut (a tree). إزدلم ه

Malignant wound. ✧ Jar. زلمة ج زِلَم

Chapped in the feet. مُزلَّم

Chapped on the heels. زولم

To be dense (cloud). To dash (waves of a torrent). ✱ زلعب – إزلعبّ

To swallow a. th. To throttle a. o. ✧ زلغم ه وه

Throat; gullet, larynx. ✧ زُلقوم ج زلاقيم

To rise (sun). To blaze (fire). ✱ زلغ a زُلوغًا

To grow again (hair). To become covered with feathers (chicken). ✱ زلغب – إزلغبّ

To advance, to draw near. ✱ زلف o زَلفًا وزَلِيفًا، وتزلّف وازدلف

To amplify (a narration). زلّف في

To near a. o. or a. th. To collect a. th. To trouble (people) in every stage of their march (guide). أزلف ه وه

Degree, rank. Nearness. زلف وزلف وزلفى

Garden, meadow. زلف

Dignity. Nearness. Large dish. First part of the night. زُلفة ج زُلَف وزُلَفات وزُلْفات

Filled tank, cistern. Dish. Green urn. Oyster-shell. Smooth rock. Hard ground. Mirror. ✧ Spoon. زلفة ج زلف

Remote (journey). زلوف

Advancing forward. زليف

Village on the confines of the desert *Pl.* Steps of ascent. مزلفة ج مزالف

To slip (foot). To slide. ✱ زلق a وزلق o زلقًا

To loathe and quit (a place). — ب

To cause a. o. to slip. To shave (the head). زلق i زلقًا، وزلّق، وأزلق ه وه

To anoint (the body). To sharpen (iron). To render (a place) slippery. زلّق ه

To become smooth, slippery. To have a glossy, shining face. تزلّق

Slippery place. زلق وزلق وزلاقة

✧ Lapse, slip in words. زلقة

Smooth rock. Mirror. زلقة

Swift (she-camel). Remote (stage). زلوق

Abortive fœtus. زليق

Smooth (*un.* زلّيقة) peach, nectarine. زلّيق ج زلاليق

Glossy and hairless (man). أزلق م زلقاء

Gaiters. Ts توزلوق

Sliding-bolt. Casting her young usually (mare). مزلاق

Slippery, sliding place. مزلق ومزلقة

To gobble a. th. ✱ زلقم

Windpipe. Snout of a dog. زلقوم

To make a mistake. ✱ زلم o زلمًا

To fill (a vessel). — ه

He made him a scanty gift. — وزلّم عطاءه

To cut off (the nose). — وازدلم ه

To pare. To soften a. th. To ill feed. To round (a mill-stone). To spoil (a dish). زلّم ه

To dismount (horseman). ✧ تزلّم

To scamper off. To be set upright. إزلأمّ

Hyrax, rock-badger. Rush-mat. زلم ج أزلام

Cloven hoof. Divining arrow. زلم ج أزلام

Exterior appearance. زلمة وزلمة وزلمة

He looks like a slave. هو العبد زلمة

Wattle of sheep and goats. ✧ Man. Foot-passenger. زلمة ج زلام

Well wrought (arrow-wood). زلم

Having the ear slit and hanging, (camel, ewe). أزلم ومزلّم

Mountain-goat. Calamitous time. الأزلم الجذع

Female hawk. Mountain-goat. زلماء

Spout of a pot. Elephant's trunk. ✧ زلومة

Little lively man. Great and strong (horse). Small-bodied. Lop-eared. Wild cat. Scanty (gift). مزلّم

To be greedy. ✱ زله a زلهًا

Basil-blossom. People. زله

To tighten (sandals) with a. th. To fill up (a skin). To carry away (a lamb: wolf). To outstrip a. o. ✱ زمّ o زمًّا ه وه

To shriek, to make noise. إِزْمَجَرَ
Flute; sound of the flute. Shriek, sound. زَمْجَرَة ج زَمَاجِر وزَمَاجِير
To be proud, haughty. ✲ زَمَخَ a زَمْخًا
Proud. Full (measure). زَامِخ ج زُمَّخ
Hard, long (stage). زَمَخ وزَمُوخ
To roar (tiger). To bud (plant). ✲ زَمْخَر
To grow louder (sound). — وازْمَخَرَّ
Long flute. Dense, entangled (tree). Hollow. Soft. Eminent (man). زَمْخَر
To play upon a reed. ✲ زَمَرَ i o زَمْرًا وزَمِيرًا, وزَمَّرَ
To fill (a skin). — o زَمْرًا, وزَمَّرَ هُ
To divulge (an event). — ب
To stir a. o. against (another). — ه ب
To be scared (gazelle). — o زَمَرَانًا
To cry (ostrich). — i زِمَارًا
To have scanty hair. To be faint-hearted (man). To have little wool (ewe). زَمِرَ a زَمَرًا
To have the eyes blood-shot from anger. إِزْمَأَرَّ
Song, sound. ✧ Flute, pipe. زَمْر ج زُمُور
✧ Bind-weed. زَمْر السُّلْطَان
✧ Bell-flower. زَمْر القَاضِي
Having little hair, wool (man, ewe). Faint-hearted. Nice-looking. زَمِر
Handsome boy. زُمُور وزَمِير وزَوْمَر
Small in stature. Sweet-faced. زَمِير ج زِمَار
Scattered party, gang. زُمْرَة ج زُمَر
Art of a flutist. زِمَارَة
Cry of the ostrich. زِمَار
Flutist, piper. زَامِر وزَمَّار
Flute; double pipe. Iron collar of a dog. زَمَّارَة و✧ زُمَّيْرَة
Alisma plantago, medicinal plant. زَمَّارَة وِمِزْمَار الرَّاعِي
Oats. ◘ زُمَّير
Smyrna (town). إِزْمِير
Musical reed, fife, flute. مِزْمَار ج مَزَامِير
Uvula. لِسَان المِزْمَار
Hymn. Psalm (of David). مَزْمُور ومُزْمُور ج مَزَامِير
Green emerald. P زُمُرُّد وزُمُرُّذ
Stuffed balls of meat and flour. P زَمَاوَرْد وزُمَاوَرْد و✧ بِزْمَاوَرْد

To advance. To speak. To grow (camel's tusk). زَمَّ
He erected the head; he strutted; *lit*: he lifted up the nose. زَمَّ بِأَنْفِهِ, وازْدَمَّ
To bridle (a camel). — وزَمَّمَ ه
To be filled (skin). — o زُمُومًا
To oppose a. o. زَامَّ ه
To fasten (sandals). أَزَمَّ ه
To be fastened, tied. إِنْزَمَّ
To carry away (a lamb: wolf). إِزْدَمَّ ه
Rein, halter. Thong of sandals. ✧ Bonds of friendship. Control. Sincerity. زِمَام ج أَزِمَّة
He is the main spring of the affair. هُوَ زِمَام الأَمْرِ
He is the leader of his tribe. هُوَ زِمَام قَوْمِهِ
He has thrown his affair into his hands. أَلْقَى فِي يَدِهِ زِمَام أَمْرِهِ
My house is near to his. دَارِي زَمَم دَارِهِ
To resound from afar. To peal (thunder). To whinny (horse). To crackle (fire). To hum (singer). To mumble (magician). ✲ زَمْزَمَ
To roar (camel). تَزَمْزَمَ
Abundant (water). Well near the Caaba. زَمْزَم
Roaring of a lion. Clap of thunder. Crackling of fire. زَمْزَمَة ج زَمَازِم
Company of 50 men and camels. زِمْزِمَة ج زَمَازِم
✧ Small water-skin. زَمْزَمِيَّة
To have a grave mien. ✲ زَمُتَ o زَمَاتَةً, وتَزَمَّتَ
To be showy, gaudy (plumage). إِزْمَأَتَّ
Grave in mien. زَمِيت ج زُمَتَاء, وزِمِّيت
To sow discord between. ✲ زَمَجَ o زَمْجًا بَيْنَ
To intrude upon a. o. — على
To be angry. زَمِجَ a زَمَجًا
Angered. زَمِج ومُزْمَنْجِ
Reddish falcon. زُمَّج ج زَمَامِيج
White dun-diver (bird). — المَاء
He took it altogether. أَخَذَهُ بِزَأْمَجِهِ
Root of the tail of a bird. زِمِجِّي
To storm, to make a loud noise. ✲ زَمْجَرَ
To roll his roaring (lion). — وتَزَمْجَرَ

✲ زَمَط o زَمْطًا ✧ To scamper off. To slip (ring).
✲ زَمِع a زَمَعًا To be perplexed, flurried by fear.
زَمَع a زَمَعَانًا To escape swiftly (horse). To go slowly.
زَمَّع وأزمَع ه وعلى وب To keep steadily to. To determine upon.
أزمَع To be uneven, knobbed (plant). To have large knobs (vine-stock).
زَمَع ج أزماع Shudder of fear. Rivulet. Lowest class of people. Knobs, gems of a vine. Scattered plants.
— وزَمَاع Steadiness, perseverance.
زَمَعَة ج زَمَع و زماع Hairs behind the fetlock.
مُزمِع Energetic, resolute.
زَمَعِيّ Hot-brained. Niggardly. Crafty.
زَمِيع ج زُمَعَاء Quick, resolute; of good judgment.
زَمُوع Swift, quick (hare).
زُمَّج Stingless hornet.
أزمَع ج أزامِع Accident, misfortune. Sharp man.
✧ مُزمِع Imminent, impending (event).
✲ زَمَق o i زَمْقًا ه To pluck (the beard). To open (a lock).
ما أغنى عَنهُ زَمقَة It does not avail him anything.
زَمِيقَة ومَزمُوقَة Plucked (beard).
✲ زَمَك o زَمْكًا To fill up (a skin).
— ه على To incite a. o. against.
✧ زَمَّك To be tight (clothes).
إزمَاكّ To be in a rage.
زَمَك Anger.
زَمِكَة Hot-tempered. Short and foolish.
زِمِكّ و زِمِكَّى Root of a bird's tail, rump.
✲ زَمَل o i زَملًا To limp (in running).
— زَمَلًا وزَمَلًا وزَمَلَانًا To run in leaning forward (horse).
ه To carry (a load).
— زُمُولًا ه To follow a. o.
زَمَل زَمْلًا, وزَامَل ه To mount a. o. behind. To counterbalance (a rider) on a camel.
زَمَّل ه في وب To wrap a. th. in o.'s (clothes).

زَمَّل ه او ه To wrap, to conceal a. o. or a. th.
تَزَمَّل وازَّمَّل وازدَمَل ب To wrap o.'s self in (clothes).
زَمِل وزَمَل وزُمَّل Weak, cowardly.
زُملَة Party. Companions.
زَمَلَة Family, household.
زَامِل م زَامِلَة Limping from fieriness (horse).
زَامِلَة و✧ زَمَالَة ج زَوَامِل Beast of burden. Provision-bag.
زَمِيل Fellow-rider. Colleague.
زُمَيل وزُمَيلَة وزُمَّال وزُمَّالَة Weak. Cowardly.
أزمَل ج أزامِل وأزامِيل Confused sound.
— وأزمَلَة The whole. Family.
✧ زَمُّولَة وزَلُّومَة Spout of a cooler.
إزمِيل ج أزامِيل Shoemaker's knife, chisel. Gluttonous. Weak (man).
مُزَمَّلَة Green cooler with a silver spout.
✲ زَوزَمَل ه To drive (camels).
✲ زَمَلَق وزَملُوق Active, brisk.
✲ زَمِن a زَمَنًا وزُمنَة وزَمَانَة To be paralytic, crippled.
أزمَن To last long. To be old.
— ه To afflict a. o. with palsy (God).
— ه عن To delay (a gift) from.
زَمَن وزَمَنَة ج أزمَان Time.
زَمَان ج أزمُن وأزمِنَة Time, long or short.
أزمِنَة *Pl.* Seasons of the year. Tenses of a verb.
زَمَانًا For some time.
زَمَانَة Palsy. Crippleness. Love.
زَمِن وزَمِين ج زَمنَى Cripple. Paralytic.
ساعة زَمَانِيَّة وساعَة زَمَان Indetermined time.
مَرَض مُزمِن Old, chronical disease.
عَامَلَهُ مُزَامَنَة He made a bargain with him for a time.
✲ زَمِه a To become intense (heat).
✲ زَمهَر وازمَهَرّ To be blood-shot from anger (eyes).
إزمَهَرّ To be intensely cold (day). To shine (star). To be contracted (face).
زَمهَرِير Vehement cold. Moon.
مُزمَهِرّ Enraged. Having a smiling face.
✲ زَنّ o زَنًّا To dry up (sinew). ✧ To buzz (insect).

To think evil or good of a. o. To suspect a. o. زَنَّ وأَزَنَّ ه بخَيْرٍ أو شَرٍّ
Kind of chick-pea. Darnel-seed. زِنّ
Baboon, ape. أَبُو زَنَّة
Self-seeking, self-sufficient (man). رَجُل زَنَانِيّ
Narrow, contracted (shade). زَنَان وزَنَاء
Small, scanty. زَنَن
To seek refuge towards. ✲ زَنَا a زَنأً وزُنُوءًا إلى
To ascend (a hill). — في
To contract (shade). To be cheerful. To hurry (man). زَنَّأ
To straiten a. o. زَنَّأ على
To force a. o. towards (a place). To make a. o. to ascend (a hill). أَزْنَأ ه وه
Bulky and short. Narrow. Keeping in urine. زَنَاء
To become fat, plump. ✲ زَنِب a زَنَبًا
Waddling of a duck. زَأْنَبِي
Fearful, faint-hearted. زَيْنَب
To behave proudly. To frown at. ✲ زنبر — تَزَنْبَرَ على
Hornet. Wasp. Quick in answering. Strong ass. Large rat. زُنْبُور ج زَنَابِير
He took the whole of it. أَخَذَهُ بِزُنْبُورِهِ
Wasp. Kind of plane-tree. Sweet fig. زِنْبَار و زِنْبِير
Metal-spring; cock of a gun. زَنْبَرَك Ts
White lily. Oil of jasmine. Wine. ✧ German iris. Night jasmine. Flower-de-luce. ✲ زَنْبَق (un زَنْبَقَة)
✧ Hyacinth (flower). زَنْبَق خُزَامَة
To strut. ✧ To be insolent, peevish. ✲ زنتر — تَزَنْتَر
Distress. ✧ Insolence. زَنْتَرَة
To contract from thirst (bowels). ✲ زَنِج a زَنَجًا
To requite a. o. for evil or good. زَانَج ه
Negroes, Ethiopians. زَنْج و زِنْج ج زُنُوج (un. زِنْجِيّ)
Zanzibar. زِنْجِبَار
Amomum zinziber, ginger. زَنْجَبِيل P
Wine.
Inula, elecampane (*plant*). زَنْجَبِيل الشَّام وزَنْجَبِيل بَلَدِيّ

Polygonum hydropiper, water-pepper (*plant*). زَنْجَبِيل الكِلَاب
Kind of Carline thistle. — العَجَم
To fillip, to snap the thumb. ✲ زَنْجَر
✧ To be covered with verdigris. To be in irons. — وَ✧ تَزَنْجَر
Verdigris, crocus. زِنْجَار
Verdigris green. زِنْجَارِيّ
Fillip. Nail-parings. زِنْجِير ج زَنَاجِير P
Chain. — وَ✧ جِنْزِير
✧ Book-keeping by double entry. حِسَاب الزِنْجِير
White spots on children's nails. زِنْجِير و زِنْجِيرَة
Cinnabar. Vermilion. زُنْجُفْر و زِنْجَفْر P
To praise a. o. To repel a. o. ✲ زَنَح a زَنْحًا ه
To straiten a. o. — وتَزَنَّح ه
To drink (water) repeatedly. زَنَّح وتَزَنَّح ه
To become proud; to speak without restraint. تَزَنَّح
To be rancid (oil). ✲ زَنِخ a زَنَخًا
To cleave, to stick. زَنَخ o i زُنُوخًا
To grow proud. To lift the head (suckling). To speak out o.'s heart. تَزَنَّخ
Rancid, altered (oil). زَنِخ
To snuffle, to snort. ✲ زَنْخَر
To strike (fire). ✲ زَنَد i زَنْدًا, وزَنَّد ه
To fill (a vessel). — o, وزَنَّد
To be thirsty (man). — a زَنَدًا
To punish beyond justice. To lie. زَنَّد
To increase, to exceed. أَزْنَد
To relapse in (a pain). — في
To become angry. To remain speechless. تَزَنَّد
He straitened his family. — على أَهْلِهِ
Fore-arm, wrist. Upper stick of a flint. ✧ Fire-steel. Thorny tree. Maniple of priests. زَنْد ج زِنَاد وأَزْنَاد وأَزْنُد
Two sticks for striking fire. The two bones of the fore-arm. الزَّنْدَان وزَنْدَتَان
Flint-stone. حَجَر الزِّنَاد والنَّار
Baffled. Disappointed. Miser. كَابِي الزِّنَاد
Successful. وَارِي الزِّنَاد
Stingy. Tight (garment). Paltry (gift). مُزَنَّد
Huge elephant. زَنْدَبِيل وزَنْدَفِيل P
To profess dualism, ✲ زَنْدَق — تَزَنْدَق

Manicheism, atheism. To misbelieve.
زَندَقَة Dualism, Manicheism, Magianism. Atheism.
زَندَق وزَندَقِي Miser, niggardly man.
P زِنديق ج زَنادِقَة وزَنادِيق Magian Manichean, dualist. Hypocrite. Atheist.
✱ زَنَر ه زَنرًا ه To put a belt on a. o.
— ه To fill (a vessel).
زَنَّر بِعَينِهِ إلى He looked intently at.
تَزَنَّر To put on a belt. To be thin.
G زُنَّار وزُنَّارَة ج زَنانِير Non-Moslem's girdle. ✧ Waist-belt.
زَنانِير *Pl.* Small pebbles. Little flies.
P زَنزَلخت Azedarac, bead-tree.
✱ زَنِف a زَنَفًا, وتَزَنَّف To be angry.
✱ زَنَق i زَنقًا ه To put a ring to the rein of a horse. To shackle (a mule).
✧ To straiten, to squeeze a. o.
— وزَنَّق وأزنَق على To ill-feed o.'s (people). To be niggardly towards.
زَنقَة Lane, by-street. ✧ Straitness.
زِناق ج زُنُق Halter. Shackles for mules. Necklace.
زِناقَة Ring of a halter under the jaw.
زُنُق Sound intellects.
زَنِيق Firm. Sound (judgment).
✧ زَنقَر في To look angrily at a. o.
✧ زَنقُور ج زَناقِير Recess, corner.
Ts زَنكِين و✧ زَنكِيل Wealthy, rich.
P زَنكاوَة ج زَنكَوات Stirrup.
زَانكِيّ Skilful, clever. ✧ Swindler.
P إزِنكان Ochre, red clay.
✱ زنم — زَنَّم ه إلى To send a competitor to a. o.
زَنَمَة Part of the ear slit and lopping. Wattle of sheep. Sign, token.
زَنِم م زَنِمَة, وأزنَم م زَنماء ج زُنم Having the ear slit and hanging (ewe).
زَنِيم Outsider, adopted. Ignoble.
✱ زَنهَر إلى ب To look intently upon.
P زَنهار Beware. Look out!
✱ زَنَى i زِنًى و زِناء , وزانَى مُزاناة وزِناء To commit adultery, fornication.
زَنَّى ه To charge a. o. with adultery.
زِناء وزِنًى Adultery, fornication.
زانٍ ج زُناة Adulterer, fornicator.
زانِيَة ج زَوانٍ Adulteress. Harlot.

زِنوِيّ و زِنائِيّ Adulterous, adulterine (child).
✱ زِه *Particle of admiration.* Bravo!
✱ زِهِب وزُهبَة Part of goods. ✧ Ammunition.
✱ زَهَد وزَهِد a, وزَهُد o زُهدًا في وعن To abstain, to be free from wordly desires. ✧ To get tired of.
— زُهدًا وزَهادَة, وتَزَهَّد To devote o.'s self to God's service. To be an ascetic.
— a زَهدًا وزَهَّد وأزهَد ه To appraise roughly (a palm-tree).
زَهَّد ه في وعن To make a. o. to shun, to abstain from.
— ه To impute avarice to a. o.
أزهَد To have little property (man).
تَزاهَد ه To despise, to make little of.
إزدَهَد ه To reckon a. th. as little.
خُذ زَهد ما يَكفِيك Take as much as suffices thee.
زُهد وزَهادَة وتَزَهُّد Abstemiousness, asceticism.
زَهد ج زِهاد Legal alms, poor-rate.
زاهِد ج زُهّاد زُهَّد, وزَهِيد Abstemious. Poor (man). Ascetic.
زَهِيد Little, scanty. Poor, niggardly.
— الأكل Abstemious.
— العَين Content with little; disinterested.
مُزهِد Having little property. Poor.
✱ زَهَر a زُهُورًا To shine (moon). To glow (fire). To be glossy (face).
زَهِر a زَهَرًا, وزَهُر o زُهُورَة To have a bright complexion.
أزهَر وازهَرّ To blossom (plant).
— ه To make (the fire) to glow.
إزدَهَر To shine (lamp).
إزدَهَر ب To take care of. To mind.
زَهر وزَهَر ج أزهُر وأزهار وزُهُور جج أزاهِر Blossom, yellow flower. Choice part.
زَهر الكَشاتِبِين ✧ *Digitalis*, fox-glove (*pl*).
— الحَجَر Lichen, rock-moss (*plant*).
— الرَّبِيع ✧ Primrose (*plant*).
— الصَّبّاغ ✧ Chrysanthemum (*flower*).
— العَسَل ✧ Honey-suckle (*plant*).
— العَنكَبُوت ✧ Phalangium (*plant*).
— اللُّؤلُؤ ✧ Daisy (*flower*).
— اللَّيل Marvel of Peru (*plant*).

To be altered (news). To burst in (man). To speak much, loudly. إِزْدَهَف
To carry (a burden). To press a. o. — ه وه
To be compact (marrow). To be marrowy (bone). To disappear (falsehood). ✧ To be disgusted. ✱ زَهَق a زُهُوقًا
To depart (soul). To walk ahead. To overreach the mark (arrow). To perish. — زُهُوقًا وزَهَقًا
To be full of marrow (bone). أَزْهَق
To fill (a vessel). To pierce through (the target). To reduce (error) to nought (God). To shift (the saddle) to its neck (beast). أَزْهَق ه
To hurry (the walk). — في
To take the lead. To spring forward (horse). إِنْزَهَق
Flat ground, plain. زَهَق
Outrunning the others (horse). زَهَقَى
Fat (beast). Lean. Dry. Put to flight. زَاهِق ج زُهُق وزُهُق
Vain, perishing, unsteady. — وزَهُوق
Swift, fast. زَهِق
Deep well. زَاهِقَة وزَهُوق
Nearly one year. زُهَاق سَنَةٍ
Slayer. مُزهِق
Straitened. مُزهَق
To grind a. th. between two stones. To grind. To raise (the dust : wind). ✱ زَهَك a زَهْكًا ه
To shun, to avoid a. th. ✱ زَهَل o زَهْلًا عن
To be white and smooth. زَهِل a زَهَلًا
Quiet, tranquil. زَاهِل
To wash (clothes). To smooth a. th. ✱ زَهْلَق ه
To be washed. To be pure. To be fat. تَزَهْلَق
Light, active. Vehement wind. زِهْلِق
Fat. زُهْلُوق ج زَهَالِق
To be full of marrow (bone). ✱ زَهِم o زَهْمًا, وأَزْهَم
To inveigh against a. o. زَهَم ه
To chide a. o. away. — عَن
To suffer from indigestion (man). To be greasy (hand). زَهِم a زَهَمًا
To be hostile to a. o. To draw near to. To separate from. زَاهَم ه

Impure carbonate of soda. زَهْر المِلْح
Verdigris, crocus. — النحاس
Orange-flower water. مَاء زَهْر
Dice of backgammon. Luck in card-playing. ✧ زَهْر (for زَار)
A flower. Beauty, brightness. زَهْرَة وزَهَرَة
Kidney-vetch. *Acorus*, sweet-flag (*plant*). زَهْرَة
Whiteness, Beauty. زُهْرَة
✧ Pansy, heart's ease (*pl*). زَهْرَة الثَالُوث
Splendour of the world. زَهْرَة الدُّنيا
Aim, purpose, want. زِهْر
Venus (*planet*). زُهَرَة
✧ Venereal diseases. الأَمْرَاض الزُّهَرِيَّة
Strutting, sweeping gait. زَاهِرِيَّة
Flourishing (plant). Bright, fair (complexion). زَاهِر ج زَاهِرُون
Intensely red. أَحْمَر زَاهِر
Bright-faced man. Moon. Friday. Wild bull. White lion. Milk just drawn. أَزْهَر م زَهْرَاء ج زُهْر
✧ Celebrated University of Cairo. الجَامِع الأَزْهَر
Fair woman. Wild cow. زَهْرَاء
The sun and the moon. الأَزْهَرَان
Large silver coin worth about one shilling. ✧ Jolly man. ✧ زَهْرَاوِيّ
Kindling fire for guests ; hospitable. مُزْهِر
Lute, guitar. Large drum. مِزْهَر ج مَزَاهِر
To be vile. To lie. To perish. ✱ زَهَف a زُهُوفًا
To be near to (death). — وازدَهَف إلى
To be nimble in. زَهِف a زَهَفًا ل
To carry a. th. away (wind). — ه
To be ready to mischief. To lie. To slander. أَزْهَف
To revile a. o. — ه
To overthrow a. o. (horse). — وازدَهَف ه
To make a false report to a. o. To thrust a. o. with (a spear). — ه ل
To allure a. o. to (evil). To grant (help) to a. o. — ه ب
To despatch (a wounded man). — على
To amplify (news). To carry away. To destroy a. th. — ه
To go away, to shun. تَزَهَّف وازدَهَف عَن
To be scared away (horse). انزَهَف

White vitriol, sulphate of zinc. زَاجٌ أَبْيَض
Blue vitriol, sulphate of copper. زَاجٌ الأَساكِفَة او الزَّاجِ العِرَاقِيّ
Sulphuric acid. رُوحِ الزَّاجِ
One of زَوج ج أَزْوَاج وزَوجَة جج أَزَاوِيج a pair, a match. Class. Husband, wife; comrade. ✧ Pair, couple.
They form a pair, a couple. هُمَا زَوج وزَوجَان
Wife, spouse. زَوجَة ج زَوجَات
Marriage. Wedlock. زَوَاجٌ وزَوجِيَّة و✧ زِيجَة
To remove, to cease. To depart from. ✻ زَاجَ ٥ زَوجًا عن
To scatter. To collect (cattle). — ه
To displace a. th. To achieve a. th. To take off (an evil: God). أَزَاجَ إِزَاحَةً ه
To be discovered (disease). إِنْزَاجَ
To supply o.'self with provisions. ✻ زَادَ ٥ زَوْدًا، وتَزَوَّد
To supply a. o. with provisions. ✧ To exaggerate a. th. زَوَّد وأَزَاد ه
To provide o.'s self with (a letter) from. To be hit on the head by. تَزَوَّد ه من
To ask, to seek after provisions. ✧ To increase. إِزْدَاد واسْتَزَاد
Travelling-provisions. Stores. زَاد و✧ زُوَّادَة ج أَزْوَاد وأَزْوِدَة
Provision-bag. مزاد ومَزَادَة ومِزْوَد ج مَزَاوِد
✻ زَار ٥ زِيَارَةً وزَوْرًا وزُوَارًا وزُوَارَةً ومَزَارًا، وازْدَار ه وه To visit (a place, a person).
To bind the fore to the hind-girth of a camel. زَار زَوَارًا ه
To incline. To be crook-breasted. زَوِرَ a زَوَرًا
To improve. To set a. th. aright. To embellish a. th. To make void (a testimony). To falsify a. th. ✧ To counterfeit. زَوَّر ه
To show reguard to (a guest). To do good to a. o. — ه
To incite a. o. to pay a visit. أَزَار ه
To address (praise) to a. o. — ه ه
To pay visit to one another. تَزَاوَر
To deviate, to turn aside from. — وازْوَرَّ وازْوَارَّ عن

Bad smell. Grease. Civet, perfume. زُهِم
Stinking fat. زَهِم
Fetid smell of fat meat. زُهْمَة ,زُهُومَة
To blossom. ✻ زَهَا ٥ زَهْوًا وزُهُوًّا وزَهَاء To shine (lamp). To grow, to flourish (plant). To assume colour (date). To grow up (child). To journey after being watered (camels).
To lie. — ٥ زَهْوًا
To despise, to make little of. To shake (a dewy plant: wind). To light (a lamp). To raise (a figure: mirage). To move (a fan). To toss (a ship: waves). — وأَزْهَى ه وه
To render a. o. self-conceited (pride). — ه
To brandish (a stick). To appraise (dates) roughly. زَهَا ب
To be proud, to boast of. زُهِيَ ب
To become reddish (dates). زَهَا وزَهَّى وأَزْهَى
To become proud (man). To grow up (palm-tree). أَزْهَى
To render a. o. self-conceited. إِزْدَهَى ه
To look scornfully at. — ه وب
Amount. Conjecture. زُهَاء
A hundred, about a hundred. زُهَاء مِئَةٍ
Blossom. Splendour. Vanity. Fresh plant. Falsehood, lie. Useless. Coloured date. زَهْو
Splendour, freshness, finery. زُهِيّ
Bright-faced (man). Flowery (plant). زَاهٍ
Self-conceited, proud. إِنْزَهُو ومُزْدَهٍ ومَزْهُوّ
A pair, a couple (*opp. to* تَوّ) of men, ships. Overthrow, ruin. ✻ زَوّ
To sow discord between. ✻ زَاج ٥ زَوْجًا بين
To marry a. o. to. To couple a. th. with. زَوَّج ه ه وب ول
To pair, to be coupled. زَاوَج بَعْضُهَا بَعْضًا
To mingle with a. o. زَاوَج ه
To form a couple with. — وأَزْوَج بين
To marry (a woman). To creep in a. o. (drowsiness). تَزَوَّج ه ،
To marry into (a tribe). — في
To be coupled (expression, rhyme). To be doubled. تَزَاوَج وازْدَوَج
Green vitriol, sulphate of iron. P زَاج ج زَاجَات

Greasy matter of the wool used as a medicine. زُوفَاء رَطْب

Gymnastics. تَزَاوُف

To adorn, to embellish (speech). To gild a. th. To paint. ✲ زَاقَ — زَوَّق ه

Amalgam of gold and quick-silver. Quick-silver. زَاوُوق وزَاوُوق

To move the shoulders in walking. ✲ زَاكَ o زَوْكًا وزَوَكَانًا

Proud demeanour. زَوْك وزَوَكَان

✲ زَالَ o زَوْلًا وزَوَالًا وزُؤُولًا وزَوِيلًا وزَوَلَانًا,

To pass away, to cease. To perish. وازْوَلّ

To retire from (a place). زَالَ o زَوَالًا وزُؤُولًا ه وه عن

May he perish! (*curse*). زَالَ زَوَالُهُ

To displace a. th. from. — o i ه عن

To decline (sun). — زَوَالًا وزُؤُولًا وزَوَلَانًا

To be advanced (day). — زَوَالًا

The shade went away at noon. زَالَ زَائِلُ الظِلّ

To break a journey for a while. — زَيْلُولَة

He shuddered. He was moved by fear. زَالَ و زِيلَ زَوِيلُهُ وزَوَالُهُ

To remove. To suppress a. th. زَوَّلَ وأَزَالَ وازْدَالَ ه

To produce a. th. زَوَّلَ وتَزَوَّلَ ه

To persevere in. To prosecute a. th. زَاوَلَ مُزَاوَلَةً وزِوَالًا ه

To be witty, distinguished (youth). تَزَوَّلَ

To discuss an affair together. تَزَاوَل

To part from. إِنْزَالَ عن

Phantom in sleep. Person. Wonder. Trial. Hawk. Brave. Lively. Bountiful. زَوْل ج أَزْوَال

Sprightly, clever woman. Wonderful. زَوْلَة ج زَوْلَات

End, decay. Declining of the sun. Commotion, motion. زَوَال

Emotion, anxiety. زَوِيل

Falling off, transitory. زَائِل م زَائِلَة

Starless night, long night. لَيْل زَائِل النُجُوم

Animated being. زَائِلَة و✧ زَوَالَة ج زَوَائِل

Hunted game. Women. Stars. زَوَائِل

✧ Sun-dial. مِزْوَلَة ج مَزَاوِل

Fourth part of a. th. ✲ زُوم — زَام

Party of people. زَامَة ج زَامَات

To ask a. o. to pay a visit. إِسْتَزَارَ ه

Bird's crop. زَارَة وزَاوُرَة وزَاوُورَة

Upper part of the breast. Intellect. Phantom in sleep. Resoluteness. (*m. f. s. pl.*) زَوْر

Master, lord. — و زُور و زَوَّر

Falsehood. Calumny. Lie. Idolatry. Idol. Festivals of Jews and Christians. Music-hall. Prudence, strength. Dainty. Softness of a garment. ◻ Threat. Forgery. زُور

✧ Forcibly, by compulsion. بِالزُّور

✧ Perjury, false testimony. شَهَادَة زُور

Flax. Large porous jar. Visitor of women. Use, custom. زِير ج أَزْوَار و زِيَرَة وأَزْيَار

Leaning. Crockedness of the sides. زَوَر

He visited him as a friend. زَارَهُ زِيرَةَ المُحِبّ

Rope binding the fore to the hind-girth. زِوَار وزِيَار ج أَزْوِرَة

Visit. Pilgrimage. زِيَارَة

Visitor. Pilgrim. زَائِر ج زَائِرُون وزَوْر وزُوَّار

A single visit. One time. Slave. زَوْرَة

Wry, oblique. Squint-eyed. أَزْوَر م زَوْرَاء ج زُور

Deep (well). Silver vessel. Bow. Bagdad (town). The Tigris (river). زَوْرَاء

Visit. Place of pilgrimage, shrine. ✧ Tomb of a santon. مَزَار ج مَزَارَات

To urge (a beast) with the bridle. To incline a. th. To remove a. th. ✲ زَاعَ o زَوْعًا ه وه

To cut (a slice of melon) for. — زَوْعَةً ل

To come off (flesh). — وتَزَوَّعَ

To drive (beasts) roughly. زَوَّعَ ه وه

Slice of meat, of a melon. ✧ Wretched. زُوعَة ج زُوع

Policeman. زَائِع ج زَاعَة

To deviate, to swerve from. To decline from truth (in speech). ✧ To be sprained (limb). To become lively, foolish. ✲ زَاغَ o زَوْغًا وزَوَغَانًا

To turn a. o. away from truth. To pull (a camel) with the rein. — ه

To drag o.'s self along. To drag the tail (pigeon). ✲ زَافَ o زَوْفًا

Hyssop (*plant*). زُوفَى وزُوفَاء

✧ زُوم ج أزوام Juice of fruits, meat. Washing.

✱ زَان وزَانَة Indigestion.

زُون Idol. Pagod.

— وزَوَن و زَوَنّ Short man, dwarf.

زوان وزُوَان وزَوَان وزُؤَان ✧ Tares.

✱ زَوَى i زَوِيًا وزَيًّا ه To discard a. th. To conceal (a secret). To seize. To collect a. th.

زَوَّى وتَزَوَّى وانزَوَى To retire in a corner.

زَوَّى ه وه To discard. To carry away.

إنزَوَى To approach one another.

تَزَوَّى وانزَوَى To be contracted, folded.

زَاوِيَة ج زَوَايَا Corner of a house. (*Geom*). Angle. ✧ Square (instrument). Small mosque. Hospital. Asylum.

زَاوِيَة مُثَلَّثَة ✧ Triangle.

— مُنفَرِجَة ✧ Obtuse angle.

✱ زَبِي — زَيًّا تَزيِيَةً ه وه To adorn, to deck. a. th. To write the letter ز.

زَيَّا وتَزَيَّا To adorn o.'s self. To dress in a garb.

زِي و✧ زَيّ ج أزيَاء Appearance, dress. garb. ✧ Harness. Fashion; custom. Like, as. ▫ How?

▫ على زَيّ ▫ In fashion.

▫ زَيّ بَعضُهُ It is exactly the same.

▫ زَيَّك Like thee. How do you do?

✱ زاب — تَزَيَّب To agglomerate, to heap up.

أَزيَب South-easterly wind. Enmity. Briskness. Brisk. Hedge-hog. Vile. Adversity. Devil. Fright. Stranger. Calamity. Copious water.

إزيَبّ Strong.

— البَأس Daring, boisterous.

✱ زَات i زَيتًا ه To put oil in (food). To anoint with oil. To give oil to.

— زَيَّت ه وه To supply a. o. with oil. To put oil in (a lamp).

أزَات To have much oil.

إزدَات To be anointed with oil.

إستَزَات To ask, to seek oil.

زَيت ج زُيُوت Olive-oil. ✧ Any oil, essence.

— حَارّ Linseed-oil.

زَيت الحَارّ Copal, resinous substance.

زَيت حُلو ✧ Olive-oil.

— الخِروَع Castor-oil.

زَيت السُّودَان Oil made with iron-wood seeds.

زَيتُون (un. زَيتُونَة) Olive, olive-tree.

زَيتُون الأرض Widow-wail (*plant*).

— الحَبَش والكَلبَة Wild olive-tree.

— بَني إسرَائيل *Lapis Judaicus* used as collyrium.

زَيتُونِيّ Olive-coloured. Born in autumn (horse).

زَيَّات Dealer in oil.

مُزَيِّت ✧ Oily (blood) as in pleurisy.

مَزِيت ومَزيُوت Seasoned with oil. Oiled.

P زِيج Mason's string. Astronomical tables.

✱ زَاح i زَيحًا وزُيُوحًا وزَيَحَانًا, وانزَاح To be remote, to pass away.

— ه To discard (her veil : woman).

زَيَّح ✧ To the give benediction of the Blessed Sacrament. To rule (paper).

أزَاح ه To remove, to take away.

زِيح ج أزيَاح ✧ Line, streak.

S زَيَّاح ج زَيَّاحَات ✧ Religious benediction, procession.

مَزَاح Place of retirement.

✱ زَاخ i زَيخًا وزَيَخَانًا To do wrong; to be unjust, to stray. To retire.

أزَاخ ه وه To remove, to take away.

تَزَيَّخ To be reviled.

✱ زَاد i زَيدًا وزِيدًا وزَيَدًا وزِيَادَةً ومَزِيدًا وزَيدَانًا To increase, to give in surplus. To exceed a. th.

— في To exaggerate (a narration : liar).

زَادَهُ اللهُ خَيرًا May God load him with blessings!

زَيَّد و✧ زَوَّد ه To increase a. th.

زَايَد ه To outbid another (in an auction).

تَزَيَّد To increase (price). To straddle (she-camel).

— وتَزَايَد في To exaggerate in (speech). To exceed (a price).

تَزَايَدُوا في الثَّمَن وعلى السِّلعَة They bade against o. a. for the commodity.

إزدَاد To increase, to augment.

— ه To take a. th. in excess.

إستَزَاد ه To ask, to seek an increase from. To complain of a. o.

زَيد و✧ زَود Increase; addition. Excess.

هُم زَيد على مِئَة They are more than a hundred.

Spurious, bad coin. دِرْهِم زَيْف وزائِف ج زُيَّف وزُيُوف

Strutting, sweepy. Lion. زَيَّاف

To put a collar to (a shirt). ✻ زاق — زَيَّق ه

To deck herself and daub her eyes with collyrium (woman). زَيَّق وتَزَيَّق

Collar of a shirt. Mason's string. زِيق

To cease, to discontinue. ✻ زال a زَيْلًا

I have not ceased doing it. مَا زِلْتُ أَفْعَلُهُ

Zeyd continues standing. مَا زال زَيْدٌ قائِمًا

I desisted not to urge Zeyd until he did it. مَا زِلْتُ بِزَيْدٍ, ومَا زِلْتُ وزَيْدًا حَتّى فَعَلَهُ

The always Existing (God). الَّذِي لَمْ يَزَل ولَا يَزَال

To remove a. th. from. زال i زَيْلًا, وأَزَال إِزَالَةً ه وه عن

To separate (people). زَيَّل ه وه

To separate, to remove from. زَايَل ه

To disperse, to remain apart. تَزَيَّل وتَزَايَل

To be abashed at. تَزَايَل عن

Width between the thighs. زَيَل

Ingenious, skilful. مِزْيَل ومِزْيَال

To hush a. o. by one word. ✻ زَام a i زَيْمًا ل

To separate (horses). To be compact or dismembered (flesh). تَزَيَّم

Slice of flesh. Dismembered meat. زِيمَة ج زِيَم

Silent, quiet (camel). أَزْيَم م زَيْمَاء

To adorn, to embellish. ✻ زَان i زَيْنًا ه

To adorn, to deck a. th. ✧ To shave a. o. زَيَّن وأَزَان إِزَانَةً ه وه

To be decked, adorned. To be trimmed (speech). To be allured. ✧ To be shaven. تَزَيَّن تَزَيُّنًا, وازَّيَّن وازْدَان ازْدِيَانًا

Beech-tree. زَان وزَيْن

Beauty, ornament. ▫ Beautiful. زَيْن ج أَزْيَان

Cock's comb. زَيْن الدِيك

Ornament. Feast. ▫ Feast of the Nile. ✧ Illumination. زِينَة

Diseases of the hair, nails or skin. أَمْرَاض الزِّينَة

Ornament, attire. زِيَان

Beautiful (moon). زَيَّان

Decorator. Cupper. ✧ Barber. مُزَيِّن

✧ Too much. بِالزِّيَادَة وبِالزَّوْد

Increase; excess. زِيَادَة ج زِيَادَات, وزَائِدَة ج زَوَائِد

Midriff, ligament of the liver. زِيَادَة الكَبِد

The augmentative letters *included in the words* سَأَلْتُمُونِيهَا *and* اليَوْم تَنْسَاهُ حُرُوف الزِيَادَة

Medicinal plant. أَبُو زَيْدَان

✧ Auction, public sale. مَزَاد

Derivative (verb). (*opp. to* مُجَرَّد) مَزِيد

Large water-skin. مَزَادَة ج مَزَاد ومَزَايِد

Yezidees, worshippers of the devil. يَزِيدِيَّة

To twist the lips of (a horse: farrier). ✧ To put a. o. in a strait. ✻ زِير — زَيَّر ه

Porous jar used as strainer. زِير ج أَزْيَار

Horse-twitchers, barnacles. ✧ Strait, perplexity. زِيَار

Squill, sea-onion. ✻ زِيز

Small hills. Feathers. ✻ زِيزَى وزِيزَاء وزَازِيَة ج زَيَازٍ

To yell, to shriek. ✻ زَاط i زَيْطًا وزِيَاطًا

Shouter, shrieker. زَيَّاط

To deviate. To decline (sun). To be troubled (sight). ✧ To be rash. ✻ زَاغ i زَيْغًا وزَيَغَانًا وزَيْغُوغَةً

To redress a. th. (wrong or crooked). زَيَّغ ه

To mislead a. o. To incline. أَزَاغ ه وه

To deck an display herself (woman). تَزَيَّغ

Rook (bird). ▫ Carrion-crow. زَاغ ج زِيغَان

Declination. Doubt. Injustice. زَيْغ

Deviating. زَائِغ ج زَاغَة وزَائِغُون

To be bad, spurious (coin). ✻ زَاف i زُيُوفًا, وتَزَيَّف

To adulterate (money). To leap (a wall). — زَيْفًا ه

To strut, to sweep (man). To waddle (camel). To drag its tail (pigeon). — زَيْفًا وزَيَفَانًا

To make, declare (money) spurious. To dispraise (a speech). To let (bloodshed) unavenged. زَيَّف وتَزَيَّف ه

Cornice of a wall. زَيْف ج زِيَاف وأَزْيَاف وزُيُوف

س

* س Prefixed to the aorist of a verb is the sign of the future.
سَأُسَافِر I will depart.
* سَأْ Cry for chiding an ass.
* سَأْسَأ ب To chide, to urge (an ass).
تَسَأْسَأ To become intricate (business).
* سَأَب a سَأْبًا ه To strangle a. o. to death.
— ه To widen (a skin).
— وسَئِب a سَأْبًا من To gorge o.'s self with (drink).
سَأْب ج سُؤُوب. Large skin. Leather-bag.
سُؤْبَان مَال Good manager of cattle.
مِسْأَب Skin for honey. Leather-skin. Great drinker of water.
* سَأَت a سَأْتًا ه To throttle a. o. to death.
سَأْت Side of the throat.
* سَأَد a سَأْدًا وسَأَدًا ه To strangle a. o.
سُئِد To be ill from the use of salt water.
سَئِد a سَأَدًا. To drink. To reopen (wound).
أَسْأَد To walk day and night.
سُؤَاد Disease from the use of salt water.
* سَأَر a سَأْرًا, وأَسْأَر ه To leave (a remainder of wine) in a vessel.
سَئِر a سَأْرًا. To remain, to be residual.
أَسْأَر من To leave the balance of (an account).
تَسَأَّر ه To drink the remainder of (a beverage).
سُؤْر ج أَسْآر Remainder of water, residue of food.
سُؤْرَة Remainder of youthful vigour.
* سَأَف a سَأْفًا, وسَئِف a سَأَفًا To be chapped around the nails (hand).
سَئِف, وانْسَأَف To chap (lip). To be split (palm-bark).
سَأَف Palm-branch. Hair of the tail.
سَئِف م سَئِفَة Chapped.
سَائِفَة ج سَوَائِف Fine sand at the foot of a hillock.
* سَأَل a سُؤَالًا وسَآلَةً ومَسْأَلَةً وتَسْآلًا ه عن وب To question a. o. on.
سَأَل ه ه To ask a. th. of a. o.
سَاءَل مُسَاءَلَةً, وسَايَل مُسَايَلَةً ه وعن وب To ask a. o. about a. th.
يُسْأَل عن العَهْد He is responsible for the compact.
أَسْأَلَهُ سُؤْلَهُ وسُؤْلَتَهُ ومَسْأَلَتَهُ He granted to him his petition.
◇ تَسَأَّل تَسَؤُّلًا, وتَسَوَّل تَسَوُّلًا To beg alms.
تَسَاءَل وتَسَاوَل To ask o. a. questions.
سُؤْل وسُول وسُؤْلَة وسُولَة وسُؤُول Petition, request.
سَأَّل وسُؤَلَة وسَؤُول. Questioner. Inquisitive.
سُؤَال (opp. to جَوَاب) Question. Interrogation.
سَائِل ج سَائِلُون وسُؤَّل وسَأَلَة Asking, requesting.
— ج سُؤَّال Beggar.
مَسْأَلَة او مَسْئَلَة ج مَسَائِل Want, affair. Problem, question.
مَسْئُول. Asked, questioned. ◇ Responsible.
مَسْئُولِيَّة ◇ Responsibility
* سَئِم a سَأْمَةً وسَأَمًا وسَآمَةً وسَآمًا ه ومن To loathe, to be digusted at.
أَسْأَم إِسْآمًا ه To disgust a. o.
سَؤُوم Loathing, weary.
* سَأَا o سَأْوًا, وسَأَى a سَأْيًا To run.
— ه To purpose a. th. To tear (a garment) by straining.
— بَيْن To excite enmity between.
سَأْو Fatherland. Purpose, aim. Pangs.
بَعِيد السَّأْو Far-reaching aim.
* سَبَّ o سَبًّا وسِبِّيبَى ه To cut, to wound. To hock (a horse).
— في ◇ To slander a. o.
— سَبًّا ه وه To cut a. th. To spear in the anus.
— وسَابَّ ه To abuse grossly, to curse.
سَبَّب ه To find the means of. To occasion a. th.
— ه ل. To prepare furrows for (water).
— ه To abuse a. o
تَسَبَّب To be prepared (means). To be occasioned. ◇ To carry on a petty trade.. To seek a living.

To be the cause of. — ب
To use a. th. as means for. — ب إلى
To revile o. a. To cut o. a. تَسَابَّ
To expose a. o. to reviling. إِسْتَسَبَّ ل
Insult, abuse. سَبّ وسِبَاب ومُسَابَّة
Reviler. Woman's veil. Turban. Peg. Piece of thin stuff. سِبّ ج سُبُوب
Space of time. Period. سَبَّة
Anus. Much reviled (man). Shame, disgrace. سُبَّة
Fore-finger. A week's time. سِبَّة
Rope. Cause, occasion, means. Road. سَبَب ج أَسْبَاب
God has cut his life. قطع الله بِهِ السَّبَب
✧ War ammunition. أَسْبَاب الحَرْب
Means, trade, livelihood. تَعَاطِي الأَسْبَاب
On account of that. بِسَبَب ذٰلِك
Plait of hair. Hair of a horse's mane, forelock, tail. سَبِيب ج سَبَائِب
Piece of cloth. Plait of hair. سَبِيبَة ج سَبَائِب
Sword, *lit* : hamstringer. سَبَّاب العَرَاقِيب
Fore-finger. سَبَّابَة ومِسَبَّة
Abusive language. أُسْبُوبَة
Reviler. Swearer. مِسَبّ ومِسَبَّة وسَابّ وسَبَّاب وسُبَبَة
✧ Gross abuse, curse. مَسَبَّة
Choice camels. إِبِل مُسَبَّبَة
✧ Petty tradesman, pedlar. مُتَسَبِّب
To give vent to (water). To discharge (urine). ✡ سَبْسَب ه
To be poured (water). ✧ To be curled and dependant (hair). تَسَبْسَب
Extensive. سَبْسَب ج سَبَاسِب
Curls of hanging hair. ✧ سَبَاسِيب
Palm-sunday. سَبَاسِب ويوم السَّبَاسِب
To purchase (wine) for personal use. To flay (a skin). To flog a. o. To shake (the hand). To alter (the skin : fire, heat). ✡ سَبَأ a سَبْأً وسِبَاء ومَسْبَأً، واسْتَبَأ ه
To strip off (a skin). سَبَأ ه و ه
To submit to. أَسْبَأ ل
To take a false oath rashly. — على يَمِين كَاذِبَة
To give o.'s self up to (evil). — على
To be flayed (skin). إِنْسَبَأ
Tribe of Yemen. سَبَأ

They dispersed away for ever. تَفَرَّقُوا أَيْدِي سَبَا وأَيَادِي سَبَا
Wine. Purchase of wine. سِبَاء وسَبِيئَة
Wine-merchant. سَبَّاء
Remote journey. سُبْأَة
Slough of serpents. سِبْي الحَيَّة
Mountain-path. مَسْبَأ
To take rest. To cease from work. To enter, to keep the Sabbath (Jew). To be confused. ✡ سَبَتَ o i سَبْت
To cut, to stop a. th. To shave (the head). To behead a. o. To let (the hair) hang down. — ه
To be lethargic ; to swoon. To die. سُبِتَ
To enter upon Saturday. Sabbath day. أَسْبَتَ
To torpify a. o. (drug). أَسْبَتَ و✧سَبَّتَ ه
To be stretched. To be oblong (face). To become ripe (date). إِنْسَبَتَ
To keep the Sabbath. إِسْتَبَتَ
Sabbath-day. Saturday. Week. Excellent horse. Bold child. Artful. Addicted to sleep. سَبْت ج سُبُوت وأَسْبُت
Space of time. سَبْت وسَبْتَة وسَبَنْت وسَبَنْتَة
I remained some time. أَقَمْتُ سَبْتًا وسَبَنْتًا
Kind of marsh-mallow used as a tan. سُبْت
Any tanned skin. سِبْت
Basket. P سَبَت
Anethum graveolens, dill (*pla.*). P سِبِت
Rest. Lethargic slumber. Time. Calamity. سُبَات
The day and the night. ابنا سُبَات
Club (at cards). ✧ سِبَاتِي
Bold. Leopard. Clamorous (woman). سَبَنْتَى ج سَبَانِت
Motionless, lethargic. Entering upon the Sabbath. مُسْبِت
Dead. Shaven. In a swoon. مَسْبُوت
Soft, ripe (dates). رُطَب مُنْسَبِت
To put on a black gown. ✡ سبج — تَسَبَّج
Black globules of jet. Pitch coal. P سَبَج
Black gown without sleeves. سُبْجَة وسَبِيجَة ج سُبَج
Seller of black garments. سَبَّاج
To swim in (a river). ✡ سَبَح a سَبْحًا وسِبَاحَة في و ب
To busy o.'s self in o.'s own سَبَح سَبْحًا

way. To sleep. To be at rest. To spread (tribe). To run (horse).
To dig (the earth). To glide in (the sky : star). To travel far in (a land). To be profuse in (speech). — في
To praise, to glorify God. سَبَّحَ ه و ل
To make a. o. to swim. أَسْبَحَ ه
Leather garment. سَبْحَة
Prayer. Invocation. Moslem beads. سُبْحَة ج سُبَح و سُبُحَات، وتَسْبِيح
The majesty of God. سُبُحَاتُ وَجْهِ الله
Natation, art of swimming. سِبَاحَة
Glory be to God! God is far from *such* imperfection! سُبْحَانَ الله
Swift-running horses. سَوَابِح
Ships. Stars. Souls of the faithful. سَابِحَات
Good swimmer. سَبَّاح ج سَبَّاحُون
Great swimmer. Good runner. سَبُوح ج سُبَحَاء
The All-Glorious (God). السُّبُوح والسَّبُّوح
Hymn, canticle. تَسْبِيحَة ج تَسَابِيح
Strong (garment). مُسَبَّح
Fore-finger. مُسَبِّحَة
✧ Beads used by Christians. مِسْبَحَة ج مَسَابِح
To say: Glory be to God. ✱ سَبْحَلَ وسَبْحَلَى
To be free from work. To sleep deeply. To go off. ✱ سَبَخَ o سَبْخًا، وسَبَّخَ
To be saline (soil). سَبِخَ a سَبَخًا، وأَسْبَخَ
To abate (heat). To cease (throbbing). سَبَّخَ
To allay (heat). To wind (cotton). ✧ To manure. — ه
To dispel (fever, evil) from. — ه عن
To reach a saline soil (by digging). أَسْبَخَ
To cool (heat, anger). To be manured. تَسَبَّخَ
Saline (land). سَبِخ وسَبَخ
Saline. Swampy ground; lagoon. Green water-moss. سَبْخَة وسَبَخَة ج سِبَاخ
Manure. ✧ سِبَاخ
Loosened cotton, hair. Scattered feathers. سَبِيخ (*un.* سَبِيخَة) ج سَبَائِخ
To shave (the hair). ✱ سَبَدَ o سَبْدًا، وأَسْبَدَ ه
To grow feathers (chick). To shoot forth (thistle). To appear (shaven hair). To leave off the anointing of (o.'s hair). سَبَّدَ
To comb and let down (o.'s hair). — ه
Wolf. Misfortune. Black garment. Heads of the thistle نَصِيّ. سِبْد ج أَسْبَاد
He is a sharp thief. هُوَ سِبْدُ أَسْبَادٍ
Little of goat's hair. سَبَد
He does not possess anything. مَا لَهُ سَبَدٌ وَلَا لَبَدٌ
Remains of herbage. سَبَد
Linen-stopper for a tank. Bad omen. Wild swallow. سُبَد ج سِبْدَان
Tall. Daring. Leopard. سَبَنْدَى ج سَبَانِد وسَبَانِدَة
Cuttle-fish; ink-fish. P سَبِيدَاج
To probe (a wound); to sound (a well). To try; to determine a. th. conjecturally. ✱ سَبَرَ o سَبْرًا، واسْتَبَرَ ه
Lion. Brightness of the face. سَبْر
Root. Colour. Beauty; fine appearance. — وسِبْر ج أَسْبَار
Enmity. Likeness. سِبْر
✧ Thou art treated as I am. سِبْرَك بِسِبْرِي
Cool morning. سَبْرَة ج سَبَرَات
سِبَار ج سُبُر، ومِسْبَر ومِسْبَار ج مَسَابِر
Probe for wounds. ومَسَابِير
Fine cloth. Coat of mail of good workmanship. Excellent date. سَابِرِيّ
Writing-tablet, slate. سَبُّورَة
Internal state of a. th. مَسْبَر
Handsome, good looking. مَسْبُور
To beg, to be destitute (man). ✱ سَبْرَتَ
سُبْرُوت وسِبْرِيت وسِبْرَات ج سَبَارِيت
Poor, wretched.
Bare desert. Little. Beardless boy. سُبْرُوت ج سَبَارِيت
✱ سَبِطَ a سَبَطًا وسُبُوطًا، وسَبُطَ o سُبُوطَة
To be loose, lank (hair). وسَبَاطَة
To be abundant (rain). To be liberal (man). سَبُطَ o سَبَاطَة
To suffer from fever. سُبِطَ سَبْطًا
To cast her young ones (ewe). سَبَّطَ
To remain speechless from fear. To fall motionless. To be weak. أَسْبَطَ
To cleave to (the ground). أَسْبَطَ ب
To overlook (an affair). — عن
Grand-son. Jewish tribe. سِبْط ج أَسْبَاط
Lank, not crisp (hair). Abundant rain. سَبْط ج سِبَاط

Bountiful, liberal (man). سَبْط وسَبِط البَنَان او اليَدَيْن

Of a fine stature. سَبْط وسَبِط الجِسْم

Lank, not crisp (hair). Tufted (tree). Thistle نَصِيّ when green. سَبْط

Fever. سَبَاط

February (month). S شُبَاط

Abundance of rain. سَبَاطَة

Loosened hair. Sweepings. Dung-hill. ✧ Cluster of dates. سُبَاطَة

Shoes, boots. ✧ سُبَّاط ج سَبَابِيط

Corridor, vaulted passage. سَابَاط ج سَوَابِيط وسَابَاطَات

Air-cane, pea-shooter. ¤ سَبْطَانَة

To lie down. To be extended. To hurry (camel). ✲ سبطر – اسْبَطَرّ

Daring. Springing forward (lion). Long hanging hair. سِبَطْر ج سِبَطْرَات

Lying on the ground (camels). سِبَطْرَات

Proud, sweeping gait. سِبَطْرَى

Heron. Tall. سَبَيْطَر

To be the seventh of. To revile a. o. To devour (sheep: wolf). To kill; to scare (a wolf). ✧ To frighten a. o. ✲ سَبَعَ a سَبْعًا ه وه

To steal a. th. To make a seven-stranded rope. – ه

To bring forth at the seventh month. To complete 700 men. سَبَّعَ

To reward a. o. sevenfold (God). سَبَّعَ ل

To make a. th. septuple. To divide a. th. To give an heptagonal shape to. To wash (a vessel) 7 times. To reiterate an action seven times. – ه

To revile. To bite a. o. سَابَعَ مُسَابَعَةً وسِبَاعًا ه

To be seven in number. To have flocks attacked by a wild beast. To be infested by wild beasts (road). To water (camels) every seventh day. أَسْبَعَ

To feed a. o. with the flesh of a wild beast. To neglect (a slave). To give (a child) to a nurse. – ه

To steal, to rob a. th. إِسْتَبَعَ ه

To be seven (people). إِسْتَسْبَعَ

Seven. سَبْعَة م سَبْع

Serious (affair). Place of the last judgment. سَبَع

Seventh part. سُبْع ج أَسْبَاع

Beast, bird of prey. Lupus (*constell*). ✧ Lion. سَبُع وسَبْع وسَبَع ج أَسْبُع وسِبَاع

Adiantum, maiden-hair (*pla.*). سَبُع الأَرْض

Cuscuta epithymum, kind of dodder. – الكَتَّان

✧ Dog. – اللَّيْل

Female of a wild beast. Lioness. سَبُعَة وسَبْعَة

Seventy, seventieth. سَبْعُون

The Septuagint. التَّرْجَمَة السَّبْعِينِيَّة

Seventh part. Arabian tribe. سَبِيع

Seventh. سَابِع ج سَبَعَة وسَابِعُون

Seven-lettered. Seven spans high. Enormous (camel). Born at the seventh month. Full-grown (man). سُبَاعِيّ

Wedding-feast. ¤ سُبُوع

Week. أُسْبُوع ج أَسَابِيع

Seven times, sevenfolds. أُسْبُوعًا

Land abounding with beasts of prey. مَسْبَعَة

Forsaken child. Bastard. Slave-born. مُسْبَع

To be full, long (garment). To be abundant (wealth). To extend (rain). ✲ سَبَغَ o سُبُوغًا

To direct o.'s self towards. – إلى

To cast hairless fœtus (beast). سَبَّغَ

To perform the rites of ablution. To enlarge (a garment). أَسْبَغَ ه

To fill a. o. with goods (God). – ه على

Wearing a long coat of mail. سُبَّغ ومُسْبَغ

Abundance. Easiness of life. سُبْغَة

Trailing (clothes). Long (tail). سَابِغ

F. Copious (rain). Ugly (garb). Complete (benefit). Ample (coat of mail). سَابِغَة ج سَابِغَات

Mail of a helmet protecting the neck. Tail. تَسْبِغ وتَسْبِغَة ج تَسَابِغ

To precede, to outstrip a. o. to. ✲ سَبَقَ i o سَبْقًا ه إلى

To overcome. To outstrip a. o. in. – ه وعلى

To cast abortive young (ewe). سَبَّقَ

To receive or to give a wager to a. o. To shackle (a bird). – ه

To race with, compete with a. o. سَابَقَ سِبَاقًا ومُسَابَقَةً ه

To hasten towards. أَسْبَقَ إلى

تَسَابَق واستَبَق To contend together in a race.
✧ أَسْبَق To speak or act hastily.
سُبْقَة وسَبَق ج أَسْبَاق Stake laid in a race.
لهُ سَبْق وسَابِقَة في هٰذَا He has the precedence in it.
سَابِق ج سُبَّاق وسَابِقُون Winner in a race (horse). Previous.
السَّابِقَات The Angels.
سِبَاق Horse-race. Anteriority. Jesses.
سَبَّاق Always ahead, winner (horse).
— غَايَات He has the upper-hand in his designs.
✲ سَبَك i o سَبْكًا, وسَبَّك ه To melt, to mould (a metal).
إِنْسَبَك To be melted, moulded (metal).
سَبِيكَة ج سَبَائِك Ingot.
مَسْبَك ج مَسَابِك Melting-house, foundry.
✲ سَبْكَر To stretch o.'s self. To be tall (girl).
✲ سَبَل o سَبْلًا ه To revile a. o.
سَبَّل ه To allow a. th. To dedicate a. th. to pious uses.
أَسْبَل To put out ears (crops). To drop (rain, tears). To be beaten (road).
— ه To let down (a veil). To shed (tears). To hang down (o'.s hair).
— على To weary a. o. by words.
سَبَلَة ✧ Women's wrapper. Dung.
سَبَل Rain in its fall. Nose. Ear of corn. White of the eye (disease).
سَبَلَة ج سِبَال Mustache. Fore-part of the beard.
سَبَلَة وسُبُولَة وسَبُولَة Spike, ear of corn.
سَبِيل ج سُبُل Road, path. ✧ Means of access. Public fountain.
سَبِيل الله Holy war. Pilgrimage. Desire of learning. Ordinances of God.
لَيْس عَلَيَّ في هٰذَا سَبِيل I have no responsibility on that account.
لَيْس لَك عَلَي سَبِيل Thou hast no plea to allege.
✧ سَبِيلُنَا أن نَفعَل كَذَا We ought to do so.
إِبْنُ السَّبِيل Forlorn traveller.
سَبِيلَة Road, way, path.
سَابِلَة ج سَوَابِل Party of travellers.
Much trodden (road).

أَسْبَل ومُسْبِل ومُسْبَل ومُسَبِّل ومُسَبَّل Having long mustaches.
عَيْن سَبْلَاء Long-lashed eye.
✲ سبن — سَبَنِيَّة Veil of black silk.
أَسْبَن To wear a veil of black silk.
السَّبَنْتَى The leopard.
P إِسْبَانَخ Spinage.
✲ سبه — سُبِه سَبْهًا, وسُبِّه تَسْبِيهًا To dote (old man).
سَبَه Dotage of an old man.
سُبَاه Apoplectic fit.
سَبَاهِي Dotardly (old man).
P سِبَاهِيّ Spahi, cavalry. Sepoy.
✲ سَبَى i سَبْيًا وسِبَاء, واسْتَبَى ه To take a. o. captive.
سَبَى ه وه To captivate (the heart). To estrange a. o. (God). To reach (water) by digging. To carry (wine) to another country.
تَسَابَى To make one another captive.
سَبِيّ وسَبَاء وسَبِيّ Wood carried by a torrent.
سَبْي ج سُبِيّ Captives. Women. Slough of snakes.
سَبِيّ (m. f.) ج سَبَايَا Captive (man or woman).
سَبِيَّة Sea-pearl. Exported wine. Woman taken as captive.
سَابِيَاء ج سَوَابِي Secundine. Numerous flock. Produce of flocks. Camels for breeding. Earth of a mole-hole.
✲ سَتّ Unseemly language. Vice.
سِتَّة م سِتّ Six.
✧ سِتّ ج سِتَّات (for سَيِّدَة) Lady, mistress. Grand-mother.
سِتُّون Sixty. Sixtieth.
سَات Sixth.
✧ سُتَيْتِيَّة Yellowish turtle-dove.
P أُسْتَاذ ج أَسَاتِذَة وأَسَاتِيذ Master, professor. Doctor.
✲ سَتَر o سَتْرًا, وسَتَّر ه وه To veil; to conceal a. th.
تَسَتَّر وانْسَتَر واسْتَتَر To be veiled. To conceal o.'s self.
سِتْر ج سُتُور وأَسْتَار Veil, curtain, screen. Covert. Fear. Modesty.
هَتَك الله سِتْرَهُ God has manifested his shame.
سَتَر Shield.

Track of a road. Measure, size. سُجْح وسُجُح

Natural disposition. سَجْحَة وسَجِيحَة ومَسْجُوح ومَسْجُوحَة

Gentle, meek. Easy (walk). سُجْح وسَجِيح

Opposite. سِجَاح

Fine, well proportioned. أَسْجَح م سَجْحَاء

To bow down; to be lowly. To lower the head (camel). ✱ سَجَد o سُجُودًا

To bow down before a. o. To worship (God). — ل

To be swollen (foot). سَجِد a سَجَدًا

To bow the head. أَسْجَد

To cast down o.'s looks before a. o. — ل

Prostration, adoration. سُجُود

Bowing, stooping. سَاجِد ج سُجَّد وسُجُود

F. Languid (eye). Bent (tree). سَاجِدَة ج سَاجِدَات وسَوَاجِد

Worshipper. سَجَّاد

Prayer-carpet. ✧ Any carpet. سَجَّادَة ومِسْجَدَة

Swollen foot. أَسْجَد

Place of worship; mosque. مَسْجِد ج مَسَاجِد

Forehead. Parts of the body prostrated in prayer. مَسْجَد ج مَسَاجِد

To prolong her groans (she-camel). ✱ سَجَر o سَجْرًا وسُجُورًا

To heat (an oven). To fill (a river; water). To put a collar to (a dog). — ه

To give vent to (water). To heat (an oven). سَجَّر

To swell (sea). سُجِّر

To have friendly intercourse with سَاجَر ه

To follow in a file (camels). To be filled (cup). إِنْسَجَر

Bloodshot colour of the eyes. سَجَر وسُجْرَة

Water filling a river. سُجْرَة ج سُجَر

Fuel. سَجُور ومِسْجَر

True friend. سَجِير ج سُجَرَاء

Place filled by a torrent. سَاجِر

Iron collar for dogs. سَاجُور ج سَوَاجِير

Bloodshot (eye). Clear tank. Lion. أَسْجَر

Heated. Filled. Swollen (sea). مَسْجُور

Covering, screen. سُتْرَة ج سُتَر

✧ Turkish single-breasted coat.

Veil, curtain. سِتَار ج سُتُر, وسِتَارَة ج سَتَائِر

Vespers, evening-service. ✧ صلاة السّتار

Pudical, chaste. سِتِّير

The Concealer (God). سَتَّار

Buffoon, droll. ◻ سُتَارِي وسُوتَارِي

Four. Weight of four *mithcals*. P إِسْتَار ج أَسَاتِير وأَسَاتِر

Covering, veil, curtain. مِسْتَر وإِسْتَارَة

Understood (*pronoun*). مُسْتَتِر

Pudical, (woman). ✧ Not well-off (man). مَسْتُور ج مَسَاتِير ومَسْتُورُون

Oysters. Gs إِسْتِرِيدِيَا

To stow (goods). ✧ سَتَّف ه

Spurious silver. P سَتُّوق وسُتُّوق

To come out in a file. To fall in drops (tears). To escape successively (beads, pearls). ✱ سَتَل o سَتْلًا, وتَسَاتَل

To follow a. o. سَتِل a سَتْلًا, وسَاتَل ه

To follow one another. إِسْتَتَل

Water-spring. Vulture. سَتَل ج سُتْلَان وسِتْلَان

Rubbish of a. th. سَتَالَة

Narrow road. مَسْتَل ج مَسَاتِل

Root of an old tree. ✱ أَسْتَن وأَسْتَان

Constantinople. P الإِسْتَانَة العَلِيَّة

To track a. o. To strike on the buttocks. ✱ سَتِه a سَتَهًا ه

Buttocks. سَتَه وسِتَه وسَتَه, وإِسْت ج أَسْتَاه

To hurry, to hasten. ✱سَتَا o سَتْوًا, وسَتَى i

To lay out the warp of (cloth). سَتَّى وأَسْتَى ه

Warp of cloth. سَتًى وأُسْتِيّ

To plaster, to coat (a wall) with clay. ✱ سَجّ o سَجًّا ه

Milk mixed with water. سَجَّة وسَجَاج

Roofs covered with mud. Virtuous souls. سُجُج

Wooden trowel. مِسَجَّة

Mild (day, air). ✱ سَجْسَج

To coo (dove). ✱ سَجَح a سَجْحًا

To insinuate a. th. to a. o. — وسَجَّح ل بِكَلَام

To be even and soft (cheeks). — سَجِح a سَجَحًا وسَجَاحَة

To be gentle, forbearing. — وأَسْجَح

with water. Bountiful man. Great udder. Gift. Present.

War has various chances. الحَرْب سِجَال

Writing-roll. Deed, writ, judicial record. ✧ Archives. سِجِلّ ج سِجِلَّات

Archivist. أَمِين السِّجِلَّات

Tearful (eye). Abundant (spring). سَجُول

Share. Hard. Large (udder). سَجِيل

Stone of backed clay. P سِجِّيل

Flask-case. سَوْجَل وسَوْجَلَة وسَاجُول

Allowable. مُسْجَل

Mirror. Gold, silver ingots. P سَجَنْجَل ج سَنَاجِل

To flow (tears, water). ✱ سَجَم o سُجُومًا وسِجَامًا، وانْسَجَم

To shed (tears, water). — i o سَجْمًا وسُجُومًا وسَجَمَانًا ه

To be dilatory in. — سَجْمًا وسُجُومًا عن

To shed (tears). سَجَّم وأَسْجَم ه

Water. Tear. Leaf of willow. سَجَم

Shedding tears (eye). عَيْن سَجُوم ج سُجُم

To imprison a. o. To restrain a. o. from speech. To conceal (grief). ✱ سَجَن o سَجْنًا ٥ وه

To split a. th. To dig a (trench) for a palm-tree. سَجَّن ه

Gaol, prison. سِجْن ج سُجُون

Gaoler. سَجَّان

Prisoner. سَجِين ج سُجَنَاء وسَجْنَى

سَجِينَة ج سَجَائِن، وسَاجِنَة ج سَوَاجِن

Stream coming down a hill.

Perpetual. Violent. Hell-fire. Trench for a palm-tree. سِجِّين

To be quiet, calm. To prolong her cry (she-camel). ✱ سَجَا o سُجُوًّا

To shroud (a corpse). سَجَّى تَسْجِيَة ٥

To touch a. th. To treat (an affair). سَاجَى ه

Calm, quiet. سَاجٍ

Gentie wind. Still (she-camel). سَجْوَاء

Natural disposition. سَجِيَّة ج سَجَايَا وسَجِيَّات

To pour forth (water). To flog a. o. ✱ سَحّ o سَحًّا ه و٥

To flow down (water, tears). — o سَحًّا وسُحُوحًا، وتَسَحْسَح

To be very fat (ewe). — i سُحُوحًا وسُحُوحَة

Strung (pearls). Milk mixed with much water.

Loose, hanging (hair). مُسَجَّر ومُنْسَجِر

To be altered, turbid (water). ✧ To be stirred (people). ✱ سَجِس a سَجَسًا

To stink (water). ✧ To rouse (the people). سَجَّس ه و٥

Stir, disturbance. ✧ Riot. سَجَس

Turbid, stinking water. سَجْس وسَجِيس وسَجِس

I will never go to him. لَا آتِيه سَجِيس اللَّيَالِي، وسَجِيس الأَوْجَس وسَجِيس عُجَيْس

To prolong her groans (she-camel); its twang (bow). ✱ سَجَع a سَجْعًا

To pursue (an aim). — ه

To use rhyming prose. To coo (dove). — وسَجَّع

Rhyming, assonant prose. سَجْع ج أَسْجَاع، وتَسْجِيع

Piece of rhyming prose. سَجْعَة، وأُسْجُوعَة ج أَسَاجِيع

Using rhyming prose. Straightforward. Handsome (face). سَاجِع

Aim, pursuit. مَسْجَع

To let down (a curtain). ✱ سَجَف o سَجْفًا، وسَجَّف وأَسْجَف ه

To be thin-waisted. سَجِف a سَجَفًا

To be dark (night). أَسْجَف

سَجْف وسَجِيف وسِجْف ج سُجُوف وأَسْجَاف

Veil, door-curtain.

Portion of the night. سُجْفَة

Curtain. ✧ Fringe of a garment. سِجَاف

Sausage. Ts سُجُوق

To pour out, to spill (a liquid). ✱ سَجَل o سَجْلًا ه

To pour down (a liquid). — وسَجَّل ب

To register a. th. سَجَّل ه

To record a sentence (judge). — على

To vie, to contend with. سَاجَل مُسَاجَلَة وسِجَالًا ٥

To be rich. أَسْجَل

To make large (gifts). To forsake a. o. To fill a vessel. To speak absolutely. — ٥ وه

To leave (an affair) to a. o. — ه ل

To compete, to vie together. تَسَاجَل

To be poured. إِنْسَجَل

Bucket filled سَجْل ج سِجَال وسُجُول

Tough, dry dates. سَحّ وسُحّ
Air, atmosphere. سَحَاح
Giving much water (cloud). سَحُوح
Tearful (eye). سَحَّاحَة
Blood-horse, good runner. فَرَس مِسَحّ
✲ تَسَحْسَح To come down (water).
Court-yard. سَحْسَح وسَحْسَحَة
Vehement rain. سَحْسَح وسَحْسَاح
✲ سَحَب a سَحْبًا ه To trail, to drag a. th. ✧ To draw (a sword, lots, a bill of exchange).
يَسْحَب ذَيْلَهُ He sweeps, he walks proudly.
سَحَب ذَيْلَهُ على مَعَايِبِهِ He overlooked his faults.
تَسَحَّب على To behave familiarly with.
إِنْسَحَب To be dragged, drawn. ✧ To withdraw from partnership.
سُحْبَة Dimness of the sight.
— وسُحَابَة Remains of water.
سَاحِب الحَوَالَة ✧ Drawer of a bill.
سَحَاب ج سُحُب Cloud. (*coll.*)
سَحَابَة ج سَحَائِب A cloud. Space of time.
سِرْنَا سَحَابَةَ يَوْمِنَا We have walked the whole day.
سَحَّابَة ✧ Drawer, chest.
سَحْبَان Name of a man proverbial for his eloquence.
✲ سَحْبَل Wide valley. Large (belly).
✲ سَحَت a سَحْتًا, وسَحَّت, وأَسْحَت To make unlawful profits.
— وسَحَّت وأَسْحَت ه To destroy, to extirpate a. th. To shave utterly.
— ه عن To peel out (the grease) from (the flesh).
أَسْحَت To be unlawful (profit).
أُسْحِت To lose o.'s wealth.
سَحْت Worn out (dress). Unavenged (blood). Punishment. Vehement cold.
سُحْت وسُحُت ج أَسْحَات Unlawful trade.
سُحْت وسَحِيت ومُسْحَت ومَسْحُوت Lost (goods).
سَحْتِيّ Worn out dress.
مَسْحُوت الجَوْف والمِعْدَة Unsatiable (stomach). Suffering indigestion.
✧ سُحْتُوت Ragged garment. Soft desert ✧ Farthing. Little.
✲ سَحَج a سَحْجًا, وسَحَّج ه To scratch a. o. To abrade the skin.

سَحَّج To pare the earth in running (beast).
تَسَحَّج وانْسَحَج To be scratched.
سَحَّاج Running gently (camel).
سَحُوج ومِسْحَاج Wont to swear (woman).
مِسْحَاج Plane. Running gently.
✲ سَحَر a سِحْرًا, وسَحَّر ه To fascinate, to bewitch. To wheedle a. o.
— ه عن To turn a. o. away from.
سَحَّر ه To gild (silver). To spoil (clay: water).
— a سَحْرًا ه To wound a. o. in the lungs.
سَحِر a سَحَرًا To rise, or act at daybreak.
سَحَّر ه To feed a. o. at daybreak.
أَسْحَر واسْتَحَر To be, to depart at daybreak.
تَسَحَّر To eat at daybreak.
إِسْتَحَر To crow at dawn (cock).
سِحْر Witchcraft, sorcery. Eloquence, seduction.
سَحْر وسَحَر وسُحْر ج سُحُور وأَسْحَار وسُحَارَة Lung.
إِنْتَفَخ سَحْرُهُ He has overstrained himself.
سُحْرَة Beginning of dawn.
سَحَر ج أَسْحَار Daybreak. End, edge.
سَحَرِيّ وسَحَرِيَّة Dawn, daybreak.
سَاحِر ج سَحَرَة وسُحَّار وسَاحِرُون Wizard. Learned man. Deluder.
سُوحَر Willow tree.
سَحُور ج سُحُر Meal eaten at daybreak.
سِحَار وإِسْحَار Herb fattening cattle.
سَحَّار Great wizard.
سَحَّارَة ج سَحَاحِير Children's play. ✧ Cupboard, chest.
سَحِير Having a complaint of the belly. Big-bellied (horse).
مَسْحُور Spoiled (food). Wasted (country).
✲ سَحَط a سَحْطًا ومَسْحَطًا ه To slay a. o. To choke a. o. (food).
— ه To put water (in wine).
إِنْسَحَط من To slip down from.
مَسْحَط Gullet, throat.
✲ سَحَف a سَحْفًا ه To peel (grease).

To shave off (the head). To burn a (palm-tree).

To drive the clouds (wind). سَحَف وأَسْحَف ه

To sell (grease). أَسْحَف ه

Grease of the back. سَحْفَة ج سِحَاف وسَحِيفَة ج سَحَائِف

Consumption of the lungs. سُحَاف

Clack of a mill. سَحِيف

Sweeping rain. سَحِيفَة وسَحُوف

Kind of bean used for sciatica. أُسْحُفَان

To pound, to crush a. th. To sweep (the earth: wind). To wear out (clothes). To soften a. th. by rubbing. To crush (an insect). To shave the head. ✡ سَحَق a سَحْقًا, وسَحَّق ه

To destroy a. o. To let down tears (eye). — وأَسْحَق ه وه

To be remote. سَحِق a, وسَحُق o سُحْقًا

To be lofty (tree). سَحَق o سُحُقًا

To be threadbare (clothes). — سُحُوقَة, وأَسْحَق

May God estrange him! أَسْحَقَهُ اللّٰه

To be crushed, brayed. تَسَحَّق وانْسَحَق

To be emptied (bucket). To be widened. ✧ To be contrite (heart). إِنْسَحَق

Shabby vestment. Thin cloud. سَحْق ج سُحُوق

Remoteness, distance. سُحْق وسُحُق

May he be far off! سُحْقًا لَهُ

Tall (ass, palm-tree). سَحُوق ج سُحُق

Remote (place). سَحِيق

F. Heavy rain. سَحِيقَة

Streams of tears. مَسَاحِيق الدُّمُوع

✧ Contrition, sorrow for sin. إِنْسِحَاق القَلْب

To make a single-stranded (rope). To make the warp of (cloth). To peel, to rub off. To file (a metal). To pound a. th. To pick out (coins). To cash (money). ✡ سَحَل a سَحْلًا ه

To pay a. th. cash. To give (100 lashes) to a. o. — ه ه

To revile a. o. — ه

To shed tears (eye). — سَحْلًا وسُحُولًا

To bray (mule). — سَحِيلًا وسُحَالًا

To come to the sea-shore. سَاحَل

To find a. o. reviled. أَسْحَل ه

To be scraped, pared. To be smooth (silver). إِنْسَحَل

To be fluent in speech. — بالكلام

Cash, ready money. سَحْل

Cloth of one thread. String. سَحْل وسَحِيل ج أَسْحَال وسُحُول وسُحُل

Leveret, young hare. سُحَلَة

Sea-shore. Sea-coast. سَاحِل ج سَوَاحِل

Bit of a bridle. سِحَال

Braying of asses, mules. سُحَال وسَحِيل

Filings of gold, silver. Husks of wheat. Refuse of men. سُحَالَة

Single-stranded rope. سَحِيل

Lizard. ¤ سِحْلِيَّة ج سَحَالِي

Tree used for tooth-picks. إِسْحَل

Long-haired (youth). أُسْحُلَان وأُسْحُلَانِيّ ومُسْحُلَان ومُسْحُلَانِيّ

Places watered by a stream. أَسَاحِل

File for wood. Wild ass. Tongue. Brave. Bountifulness. Bridle. Cheek. Copious rain. مِسْحَل ج مَسَاحِل

Salep, dry roots of orchis. ✧ سَحْلَب (*for* خُصَى الثَّعْلَب)

Tortoise. ✧ سَحْلَفَة (*for* سُلَحْفَة) ج سَحَالِف

To become black. ✡ سَحِم a سَحَمًا, وسَحُم o

To blacken (the face). سَحَّم ه

To pour down rain (sky). أَسْحَم

Blackness, black colour. سَحَام وسُحَام وسُحْمَة

Smith's hammers. سُحُم

Black. أَسْحَم م سَحْمَاء ج سُحْم

Horn. Idol. Woman's nipple. Wine-skin. أَسْحَم

To break, to crush (a stone). To rub off (wood). ✡ سَحَن a سَحْنًا

To examine (cattle). سَاحَن وتَسَحَّن ه

To meet a. o. To treat kindly. سَاحَن ه

Appearance, colour. Softness of complexion. سَحْنَة وسَحَنَة وسَحْنَاء وسَحْنَا

Pounding-stone for stones, gold. مِسْحَنَة ج مَسَاحِن

To scrape off; to shovel (mud). To shave (the hair). ✡ سَحَا a i o سَحْيًا ه

To bind (a book) in thin leather. — وسَحَّى وأَسْحَى ه

To shave (the hair). إِسْتَحَى ه

Thin leather for books. سِحَاء ج أَسْحِيَة (*un.* سِحَاءَة)

To be weak-minded. ✡ سَخُف o سَخَافَة
To burst (water-skin). To be thin (cloth).
To act foolishly with. سَاخَف ه
Weak-mindedness. سَخْف وسُخْف وسَخَافَة
Emaciation of hunger. سَخْفَة وسُخْفَة
Weak (mind). Thin (fabric). سَخِيف
To banish a. o. ✡ سَخَل a سَخْلًا ه وه
To take a. th. by deceit.
To find fault with a. o. سَخَّل ه وه
To shake down (dates).
To put off (a business). أَسْخَل ه
Weak, worthless (man). Imperfect thing. سَخْل ج سُخْل وسُخَّال
Lamb. سَخْلَة ج سَخْل وسِخَال وسُخْلَان
Unknown, obscure. مَسْخُول
To blacken, to disgrace a. o. To heat (water). ✡ سخم – سَخَّم ه
To irritate a. o. – بِصَدْرِهِ
To hate a. o. تَسَخَّم علي
Blackness. سَخَم وسُخْمَة
Black colour. Coal; soot. Agreable wine. Black (night). سُخَام
Black. أَسْخَم م سَخْمَاء ج سُخْم
Blackish. سُخَامِيّ
Hatred, malevolence. سَخِيمَة ج سَخَائِم
To be lewd, besmeared. ✧ سَخْمَط
Filth. ✧ سُخْمُط
✡ سَخُن o وسَخِن a وسَخَن o سُخُونَة وسَخَانَة وسَخَنًا وسُخْنَة
To be hot. ✧ To suffer from fever. To be ill.
To be heated (by grief: eye). سَخِن a عَيْنُهُ سَخَنًا وسُخُونًا وسُخْنَة
To warm (water). سَخَّن وأَسْخَن ه وه
✧ To cause fever, to render a. o. ill.
To heat the eyes *i. e.* To afflict a. o. (God). أَسْخَن عَيْنَهُ وبِعَيْنِهِ
سَخْنَة وسُخْنَة وسِخْنَة وسُخُونَة وسَخَانَة
Fever, feverish heat.
سُخْن وسَخْنَان وسُخْنَان وسَخْنَان وسُخَاخِين
Hot. (*opp. to* بَارِد)
Hectic fever. ✧ سُخُونَة رَقِيقَة
Hot. ✧ Feverish, sick. سَاخِن ج سُخَّان
Warm, heated broth. سَخُون
Hot. Inflamed by tears (eye). Painful (blow). سَخِين
Thin gruel of coarse flour. سَخِينَة
Shovel. Butcher's knife. سِخِّين ج سَخَاخِين

Open court. Region. سِحَاءَة ج سَحًى
Thorny tree. Bat.
Scrap of paper. Filings. Meninx. Part of a cloud. Shovel-making. سِحَايَة
Sweeping stream, rain. سَاحِيَة
Shovel-maker. سَحَّاء
Iron shovel, hoe. مِسْحَاة ج مَسَاحٍ
To stick its tail into the ground (locust). ✧ To strike. ✡ سَحّ o سَحًّا
Soft ground. سَخَاخ وسَخْسَاخ
Plain necklace for children. ✡ سِخَاب ج سُخُب
Tree alike to the sweet-rush. سَخْبَر
To be reduced (swelling). ✡ سخت – إِسْخَاتَ
Strong, vehement. سَخْت وسَخِيت
Dung of hoofed animals. سُخْت
Morocco leather. Tanned goat's skin. سِخْتِيَان وسَخْتِيَان P
To agglutinate (leaves). ✡ سخد – سَخَّد
Warm. سَخِد
Yellowness, swelling in the face. سُخْد
✡ سَخِر a سِخْرِيًّا وسُخْرِيًّا, وسَخَّر وتَسَخَّر ه
To constrain a. o. to forced work.
To have a good wind (ship). سَخَر a سَخْرًا
سَخِر a سَخْرًا وسَخَرًا وسُخْرًا وسُخُرًا وسُخْرَة ومَسْخَرًا, وتَسَخَّر واسْتَسْخَر ب ومن To scoff at.
To humble, to abash a. o. ✧ To appoint by law. سَخَّر ه
Forced work, task imposed without pay. Laughing stock. Compelled to work. سُخْرَة
Scoffer, mocker. سُخَرَة
Forced labour without hire. سُخْرِيّ وسِخْرِيّ
Ridicule, scoff, derision. – وسُخْرِيَّة
Kind of *Hyosciamus*, narcotic. سُخَّر
Laughing-stock. ✧ Mask. Buffoon. مَسْخَرَة ج مَسَاخِر
Advocate appointed by law. وَكِيل مُسَخَّر
To be displeased with. ✧ To curse. ✡ سَخِط a سَخَطًا ه وعلى, وتَسَخَّط ه
To discontent, to anger a. o. أَسْخَط ه
To find (a gift) paltry. تَسَخَّط ه
Discontent, anger. سُخْط وسُخُط وسَخَط ومَسْخَط
Hateful. ◻ Idol. مَسْخُوط

To feign; to lie. — وتَسَدَّج
To lay with the face on the ground. إِنْسَدَح
Liar. سَدَّاج
To kill and lay (a beast) on the ground. To prostrate a. o. on the ground. To make (a camel) to kneel. To fill (a skin). ✡ سَدَح a سَدْحًا ه
To kill a. o. — وسَدَّح ه
To be prostrated with parted legs. إِنْسَدَح
Rich. سادِح
Lying prostrate. سَدِيح ومَسْدُوح
To rend (a garment). To loose (o.'s hair). ✡ سَدَر i سَدْرًا وسُدُورًا ه
To be perplexed (man). To be dazzled by the heat (camel). سَدِر a سَدَرًا وسَدَارَة
To go down a declivity. To hurry. To hang down (hair). إِنْسَدَر
Lote-tree. سِدْر ج سُدُور (سِدْرَة .un ج سِدَر)
Vertigo. ✧ سَدَر
Perplexed. Heedless. Sea. سَدِر
Fresh herbage. Castle of king Naman. سَدِير
Two veins of the eye. الأَسْدَرَان
He came back with empty hands. جاء يَضْرِب أَسْدَرَيْهِ
To be the sixth. To make up the number six. ✡ سَدَس i سَدْسًا
To take the sixth part from a. o. — o سَدْسًا ه
To make a. th. hexagonal, six-angled. سَدَّس ه
To be six in number. To water camels every six days. أَسْدَس
سُدْس وسُدُس ج أَسْدَاس, وسَدِيس ج سُدُس
Sixth part, a sixth.
Watering of camels every sixth day. سِدْس
Tooth growing before the بَازِل. سَدَس ج سُدْس وسُدُس
Sixth. سادِس م سادِسَة
Six and six. سُدَاسَ ومَسْدَسَ
Brownish cloak. Lamp-black. سُدُوس وسَدُوس
Six-lettered (word). Six cubits long (veil). سُدَاسِيّ

Boots. Cooking-pots. تَسْخَن وتِسْخَان ج تَسَاخِين
Witty, jolly, facetious. ✧ مَسْخِر
Caldron. مِسْخَنَة ج مَسَاخِن
✡ سَخَا o وسَخِي a سَخَاء وسَخًا وسُخُوًّا وسُخُوَّة
To be liberal, bountiful.
سَخَا o سَخْوًا, وسَخِي a سَخْيًا النَّارَ والقِدْرَ
To give vent to fire beneath a pot.
سَخَتْ نَفْسُهُ, وسَخَا بِنَفْسِهِ, وسَخَّى نَفْسَهُ عن
To withhold o.'s self from.
To show munificence. تَسَخَّى وتَسَاخَى
Munificence, generosity. سَخَاء وسَخَاوَة
Bountiful, liberal. سَخِيّ ج أَسْخِيَاء وسُخَوَاء
Soft plain. سَخْوَاء ج سَخَاوَى وسَخَارٍ
To stop (a flask). To dam (a river). To close up (a breach). To supply (a want). ✧ To balance (a debt). To shut (the mouth). ✡ سَدّ o سَدًّا ه
To hit the right point. To speak, to act rightly in. — i سَدَادًا في
To be rightly disposed, well-directed. — وسَدّ a سَدَدًا, وأَسَدّ
To direct a. o. aright. To point (a spear) at. سَدَّد ه وه
To be set aright. تَسَدَّد
To be stopped, closed up. إِنْسَدّ واسْتَدّ
To be right, well directed. إِسْتَدّ
Barrier, obstacle; dam, a mountain, a screen. سَدّ وسُدّ ج أَسْدَاد
Vice, defect, blindness. — ج أَسِدَّة
Black cloud. Dam. The great wall of China. سُدّ ج سُدُود
Rocky valley retaining water. — ج سَدَدَة
Right, true (word). سَدّ
Rightness, truth. سَدَد وسَدَاد
Milk coagulating in the udder. Stopper. Means of living. سِدَاد (سِدَادَة un)
Obstruction in the nostrils. سُدَاد
✧ Obstruction of the bowels. رِيح السُّدَد
Door, threshold. Seat, dignity. سُدَّة ج سُدَد
The apostolic see. السُّدَّة الرَّسُولِيَّة
Affected with cataract (eye). Old (she-camel). سَادَّة ج سُدُد
Right, just. سَدِيد وأَسَدّ ج سُدّ
He has filled his place. سَدَّ مَسَدَّهُ
To suspect a. o. of. ✡ سَدَج o سَدْجًا ه ب

To be altered from stagnation (water). — وسَدِمَ
To covet a. th. To be addicted to. — ب
Grief, anxiety. سَدَم
Spilt (water). سَدَم وسَدُم وسَدِم وسُدُم ج أسْدَام
Altered waters. مِيَاه سُدُم وأسْدَام
Grieved, repenting. سَادِم وسَدْمَان
Illustrious (man). Mist. سَدِيم ج سُدُم
Sodom (town). سَدُوم
To be door-keeper in a temple of idols. ✱ سَدَنَ o سَدْنًا وسِدَانَةً ه
To let down (a veil, a garment). i o —
Veil, curtain. سِدْن وسَدَن وسَدَان
Keeper of a temple. سَادِن ج سَدَنَة
Fat. Blood. Wool. Veil. سَدِين
Plain, of a single colour. P سَادَه
To stretch forth the hand. ✱ سَدَا o سَدْوًا, وأسْدَى واسْتَدَى بِالْيَد
To play with walnuts (children). — وأسْدَى واسْتَدَى بِالْجَوز
To direct o.'s self towards. سَدَا o سَدًا
To become tender (dates). سَدِي a سَدًى, وأسْدَى
To ascend on. To follow. تَسَدَّى ٥ وه
To sweat (horse). إسْتَدَى
Sixth. سَادِي (for سَادِس)
To make the warp of cloth. ✱ سدى — سَدَّى وأسْدَى وتَسَدَّى ه
To do a benefit to. سَدَّى وأسْدَى إلى
To moisten the earth (dew). سَدَّى ه
To forsake. To get a. th. أسْدَى ه
To make peace between. — بَيْن
Warp of a tissue. Night dew. Honey-comb. Benefit. سَدًى ج أسْدِيَة
Green date. — وسَدَاء
Forsaken, of no avail, useless. سُدًى وسَدًى
Warp of a fabric. أسْدِيّ وأسْدِيّ
Warping mill. مِسْدَاة
Rue (medicinal plant). ✱ سَذَاب
Galega, goat's rue. سَذَاب التَّيْس
Simplicity. ✱ سَذَاجَة
Simple, good-natured; (man). Plain (colour). Unmixed (wine). P سَاذِج وه ✧ سَاذَه
Malabathrum, Indian spikenard. سَادِج هِنْدِيّ

Sixth part. Six years old (beast). Six cubits long (veil). A certain tooth. سَدِيس
To slaughter and throw down a. o. To hurtle a. th. ✱ سَدَع a سَدْعًا ه وه
He was smitten by a calamity. سُدِع سَدْعَةً شَدِيدَةً
God save thee from all misfortune. نَقَذَا لَكَ مِن كُلّ سَدْعَةٍ
Leader, guide. مِسْدَع
To be dark (night). To shine (dawn). To sleep. To be dim (sight). ✱ سدف — أسْدَف
To light (a lamp). To open (a door). To raise (a curtain). To drop (her veil: woman). ه —
To depart from. — عَن
Darkness. Night. Light. Dawn. Ewe. سَدَف
Object seen from afar. Shadow. سَدَف ج سُدُوف
Curtain. سِدَافَة
Blackness of the night. Door-curtain. سُدْفَة
Fat of the hump. سَدِيف
Black. Dark (night). أسْدَف م سَدْفَاء ج سُدْف
To be addicted to. ✱ سَدِكَ a سَدَكًا وسَدْكًا ب
To set (dates) regularly. سَدَّك ه
Addicted to. Dexterous. Spear-thruster. سَدِك
To let down (a curtain). To loose o.'s hair. ✱ سَدَل o i سَدْلًا, وسَدَّل وأسْدَل ه
To rend (a garment). i o سَدْلًا —
To hang down (hair). تَسَدَّل وانْسَدَل
Pearl-necklace hanging on the breast. سِدْل
Veil. — وسُدْل ج أسْدَال وسُدُول وأسْدُل
Inclination. سَدَل
Litter-veil. Door-curtain of a tent. سَدِيل ج سُدُل وسَدَائِل وأسْدَال
Kind of sofa, stuffed bench. P سِدِلِي
To have long mustaches. سُوْدَل
Mustache. سَوْدَل
To shut up, to bolt a door. ✱ سَدَم o سَدْمًا ه
To be grieved, to repent. ✧ To loathe food. سَدِم a سَدَمًا

Armlet. Ring of shackles. Heart. Sparrow hawk. سَوْذَق P

Sparrow-hawk. White falcon. سَذَانِق وسَذَانِيق وسَوذَنِيق وسَوذَانِق وسُوذَانِق P

Sparrow hawk. سَيذَاق وسَيذَقَان وسَيذُقَان P

✲ سَرَّ o سُرُورًا وسُرًّا وسُرَّى وتَسِرَّةً ومَسَرَّةً ه To cheer up, to rejoice a. o.

— سَرًّا ه To cut the navel-string to (a child). To wound a. o. in the navel.

— a سَرًّا To have a complaint of the navel.

سُرَّ سُرُورًا واستَسَرَّ ب To rejoice at, to be glad of.

سَرَّر وأَسَرَّ ه To rejoice, to gladden a. o.

سَارَّ مُسَارَّةً وسِرَارًا في أُذُنِهِ To speak secretly to a. o.

أَسَرَّ ه To conceal (news). To divulge (a secret).

— ه إلى To manifest (a secret) to a. o. To show (love) to.

تَسَرَّر وتَسَرَّى واستَسَرَّ To take a concubine-slave.

تَسَارَّ To reveal secrets to o. a.

— إلى To take delight in.

إِستَسَرَّ عن To hide o.'s self from.

سِرّ ج أَسرَار Secret. Heart, conscience. Marriage. Origin. Choice part. ✧ Mystery, sacrament. Health, toast.

سِرّ تُجَّار Provost of merchants.

سِرّ كَاتِب P First secretary.

أَتعَب سِرَّهُ To weary, to trouble a. o.

بِسِرِّك ✧ To your health.

كَاتِم الأَسرَار Secretary.

سِرًّا وعَلَانِيَةً In secret and openly.

✧ سِرِّيّ Mysterious. Sacramental.

سِرّ وسِرَر ج أَسرَار جج أَسَارِير Lines of the hand, of the forehead.

سَرَر وسُرَر Line of the hand.

سُرّ ج أَسِرَّة, وسَرَر وسِرَر Navel-string.

سُرَّة ج سُرَر وسُرَّات Navel. The best spot of a valley.

سُرَّة الأَرض *Cotyledon*, navel-wort.

سُرُور وسَرُور Joy, delight.

سَرِير ج أَسِرَّة وسُرُر Bedstead. Throne. Royalty, authority. Litter. Base of the head. ✧ Cradle.

سَرِيرَة ج سَرَائِر Secret. Heart.

سُرِّيَّة ج سَرَارِيّ Female slave. Concubine.

السَّرَّاء والضَّرَّاء Happiness and misfortune.

سِرَار ج أَسِرَّة Lines in the forehead.

سَرَار The best part of a race, of a valley.

— وسِرَار Last night of a lunar month.

سَرَارَة ج سَرَار Choice part of a race. Bottom of a valley.

أَسَرّ Worn-out (fire steel). Galled in the breast (camel).

مَسَرَّة Cause of joy, gladness.

— ج مَسَارّ Stems of sweet-smelling plants.

مِسَرَّة ج مَسَارّ Speaking-tube.

✲ سَرسَرَ ه To sharpen (a blade).

سُرسُور المَال Skilled manager of cattle.

✲ سَرَأَ a سَرْأً, وسَرَأً To lay eggs (locust, fish). To be prolific (woman).

أَسرَأَ To be at the time of laying eggs.

سَرْء وسِرْء وسِرْأَة Eggs of locusts, fishes.

سَرُوء ج سُرُوء وسُرَّاء Oviparous.

✲ سَرَبَ o سُرُوبًا To pasture freely (beast). To flow (water).

— في To go at random into (a country).

سَرِبَ a سَرَبًا To overflow (vessel).

سُرِبَ To be injured by the fume of molten silver.

سَرَّبَ To dig the earth on the right and left. ✧ To go back home.

— ه To moisten a new water-skin.

— ه على To send parties of (camels, horsemen) against.

تَسَرَّبَ وانسَرَبَ في To enter (its shelter; beast). ✧ To escape.

سَرْب Camels. Cattle. Road. Breast. Way of acting.

سِرْب ج أَسرَاب Herd (of gazelles); party of women. Collection of palm-trees. Way. Road. Heart.

سَرَب ج أَسرَاب Den of wild beasts. Underground conduit, drain. Flowing water. Frequented (road)

Natural behaviour. سُرْجُوجَة وسِرْجِيجَة
Manure, dung. P سَرْجِين
To go alone, to سَرَحَ a سَرْحًا وسُرُوحًا ✲ pasture on morning (flock).
To drive (a flock) to — سَرْحًا ة وه pasture. To manifest (o.'s thoughts). To send a. o. away.
To attend o'.s business سَرِحَ a سَرَحًا freely
To pasture (a flock) at سَرَّحَ ة وه leisure. To send (away). To repudiate, (a wife). To comb (her hair: woman). To free (a slave). To facilitate (a business).
To send an express to a. o. — ة إلى
To be dispelled (grief). تَسَرَّحَ وانْسَرَحَ
To go at a gentle and quick إنْسَرَحَ pace. To lay on the back in stretching the feet. To undress o.'s self.
Flock pasturing freely. Any سَرْح thornless tree. Plant of the *Pentenaria* class.
Swift-paced horses. خَيْل سُرُح
Divorce. Ease. Haste. سَرَاح
Wolf. سِرْحَان ج سَرَاح وسِرَاح وسَرَاحِين Lion. Middle of a tank.
He does not possess مَا لَهُ سَارِحَة ولا رَائِحَة anything.
Naked horse. Easy. Quickness. سَرِيح Quick. ✧ Vagrant.
Strap. Narrow pas- سَرِيحَة ج سَرَائِح sage in a thicket.
Comb. مِسْرَح ج مَسَارِح
Meadow, pasturage. مَسْرَح ج مَسَارِح
A poetical metre. مُنْسَرِح
Quick-paced (horse). مُنْسَرِح وسِرْيَاح
Jackal. Long- ✲ سُرْحُوب ج سَرَاحِيب bodied (mare). Tall of stature (man).
Rocket, squib. ✧ سَارُوخ ج سَوَارِيخ Cracker.
Fern. ✲ سِرْخِس
To stitch, to ✲ سَرَدَ o i سَرْدًا وسِرَادًا ه sew (leather).
To pierce a. th. To weave — o سَرْدًا (a coat of mail). To coordinate the thread of (a discourse). To read hastily. ✧ To sift (flour).
To continue — الصَّوْمَ وسَرِدَ a سَرَدًا fasting.

Flock of sheep, birds, سُرْبَة ج سُرَب women. Way. Row of vines. Seam of a water-skin. ✧ Great number, many.
Short journey. Seam of a skin. سَرْبَة
Mirage. سَرَاب
Going straight on; heed- سَارِب وسُرُوب lessly.
Drainer of cess pool. سَرَابَاتِي
Black lead. Molten أُسْرُب وأُسْرُبّ P silver.
Road of a beast. Bed مَسْرَب ج مَسَارِب of a stream.
Pasturage. Canal. مَسْرَبَة ج مَسَارِب
Hair of the breast. — ومَسْرُبَة ج مَسَارِب
Long. Swift (stream). مُنْسَرِب
To walk at noon, to walk ✲ سَرْبَخ leisurely. To be sprightly and active.
Far-extending desert. سِرْبَاخ
Straightforward, frank. Ps سِرْبِسْت
To clothe a. o. ✲ سَرْبَلَ ة
To clothe o.'s self ✧ To be تَسَرْبَل confused.
Shirt. Clothing. Breast سِرْبَال ج سَرَابِيل plate.
Strong, sour (taste). Ts سَرْت
✲ سَرَجَ o سَرْجًا, وسَرِجَ a سَرَجًا وتَسَرَّجَ To lie.
To plait (her hair: woman). — ه
To be beautiful (face). سَرِجَ a سَرَجًا
To embellish, to adorn سَرَّجَ ه a. th. To plait o.'s hair. To forge (a story).
✧To whip (clothes). To saddle سَرَّجَ ه (a horse). To register (a letter).
To saddle (a horse). أَسْرَجَ ة
Horse's saddle. سَرْج ج سُرُوج
His business has taken a مَال سَرْجُهُ bad turn.
Lamp; lighted wick. Sun. سِرَاج ج سُرُج
Glow-worm. — اللَّيْل و✧ سِرَاج الغَقْلَة
Mandrake. *Lychnis*, سِرَاج القُطْرُب corn-cockle.
Sesame-oil. سِيرَج وشِيرَج
Saddlery. ✧ Farcy, (horse سِرَاجَة disease).
Liar. سَرَّاج
Saddler. سَرَّاج و✧ سُرُوجِي
Oil-lamp. مِسْرَجَة ومَسْرَجَة ج مَسَارِج

Speed, readiness, quickness. سَرَع وسُرْعَة
Make haste ! السَّرْعِ السَّرْعِ
How quick does he come forth. سَرْعَانَ وسِرعَانَ وسُرْعَانَ ذا خُرُوجًا
Foremost people, horsemen. سَرَعَان
Quick. سَرِيع ج سُرْعَان م سَرِيعَة ج سِرَاع
Ninth poetical metre. السَّرِيع
Prone to good or evil. مِسْرَع ومِسْرَاع ج مَسَارِيع
To feed (a child) well. ✲ سَرْعَف ه
To be well fed (child). تَسَرْعَف
To eat grapes. ✲ سَرِغ a سَرَغًا
Vine-branch. سَرْغ ج سُرُوغ
To eat up (tree-leaves : insect). ✲ سَرَف o سَرْفًا ه
To suckle (a child) to excess. — ه
To be neglectful, ignorant of. سَرِف a سَرَفًا ه
He is addicted to wine. سَرِف بالخَمر
To squander o.'s wealth. أَسْرَف ه
To act immoderately in. — في
Squandering, lavishment. سَرَف وإِسْرَاف
The tank has overflowed. ذَهَب مَاءُ الحَوْض سَرَفًا
Red black-headed caterpillar. سُرْفَة
Negligent, unmindful. سَرِف الفُؤَاد
Ground full of caterpillars. أَرض سَرِفَة
Severe, terrible (day). سَرُوف
Row of vine-stocks. سَرِيف
Lead, pewter. P أُسْرُف
Angel of death for Moslems. إِسْرَافِيل
Seraph. H سَارُوفِيم
✲ سَرَق i سَرَقًا وَسَرِقًا وَسَرَقَةً وسَرِقَة وسَرِقَانًا, واسْتَرَق ه من وه ه
To steal a. th. from.
To be concealed. To become weak (joints). سَرِق a سَرَقًا
He is hoarse. سُرِق صَوْتُهُ
To charge a. o. with robbery. سَرَّق ه
To look stealthily at. سَارَق النَّظر إلى
To steal a.th. little by little. To listen, to look stealthily. تَسَرَّق
To glide away stealthily. إِنْسَرَق
To hear stealthily. إِسْتَرَق السَّمْعَ
To become languid (joints). إِسْتَرَق
Theft, robbery. سَرِقَة وسَرْقَة وسِرْقَة
Agrostis, bent-grass. ◌ سُرَق
Piece of silk-cloth. P سَرَقَة ج سَرَق
Little saw. ✧ سَارُوقَة وسَرَّاقَة

To perforate a. th. To sew (leather). سَرَد ه
To bear green dates (palm-tree). أَسْرَد
To follow uninterruptedly (pearls, tears). تَسَرَّد
To overcome, to get the best of. إِسْرَنْدَى ه
Mailed fabric. Consecutive (stars). سَرْد
Hard green date. سَرَاد
Awl. سِرَاد وسَرِيد ومِسْرَد
✧ Coarse sieve. سَرَد, ومِسْرَد ج مَسَارِد
Coat of mail. مَسْرُود ومَسْرُودَة
Underground vault, tank. ✧ Subterranean passage. P سِرْدَاب ج سَرَادِيب
Tall, strong, blood she-camel. Grove of acacia trees. ✲ سِرْدَاح ج سَرَادِح
Commander-in-chief. P سِرْدَار
To set a pavilion, awning. ✲ سَرْدَق ه
Cloth-tent. Awning. Whirlwind of smoke or dust. سُرَادِق ج سُرَادِقَات
To sprinkle. ✧ سَرْسَب
To hesitate ; to feel scruples. ✧ تَسَرْسَب
Scruple, hesitation. ✧ تَسَرْسُب
Vertigo, brain-disease. P سِرْسَام
✲ سَرَط o i ,وسَرِط a سَرْطًا وسَرَطَانًا ,
To swallow a. th. وتَسَرَّط واسْتَرَط ه
To be swallowed easily (food). إِنْسَرَط
Way, road. سِرَاط وصِرَاط
Sharp, cutting (sword). سُرَاط
Cutting (sword). Swift (horse). سُرَاطِيّ
Great eater. — وسَرَّط وسِرَّاط وسِرْطِيط
Swallowing quickly. سُرَّطَة وسَرَّاط
Crab. Craw-fish. Lobster. Cancer (zodiacal sign). Cancer, canker (disease). سَرَطَان
Gullet. مَسْرَط ومِسْرَط
To be scared away at full speed. ✲ سَرْطَم
Eloquent. Large-gulletted. ✲ سِرَطِم
To hasten, to be quick. ✲ سَرُع o سُرْعَةً وسِرَعًا وسَرَعًا
To hasten towards. سَارَع إلى
To have a swift beast. أَسْرَع
To hurry, to be quick in. — وه في
To bring a. o. speedily. — ب
To hasten to. تَسَرَّع وتَسَارَع إلى وب
Young tender vine-twig. سَرْع وسِرْع
✧ Rein. سُرُع ج أَسْرَاع

Back. Middle of the day, of the road. سَرَاة ج سَرَوَات
The leaders of the people. سَرَوَات القوم
سَرِيّ ج سُرَى وسَرَاة وأَسْرِيَاء وسُرَوَاء
Manly, magnanimous. Choice part. Generous lord.
Generous, of a manly temper (woman). سَرِيَّة ج سَرِيَّات وسَرَايَا
Locust just hatched. سِرْوَاة وسِرْيَة
✻ سَرَى i سُرًى وسَرْيَةً وسُرْيَةً وسِرَايَةً وسَرَيَانًا ومَسْرًى, وأَسْرَى واسْتَرَى To travel during the night.
To make a. o. to travel during the night. — ب وأَسْرَى ه وب
To creep along (roots). To circulate (blood). ✧ To be contagious (disease). سَرَى
To creep in a. o. (poison). — في
To load (a beast) with luggage. — ه
To send forth (a detachment). سَرَّى ه
To free a. o. from cares. — عن قلبهِ
To walk in company with. سَارَى ه
To repair to an upland. أَسْرَى
Night-journey. سُرًى وسَرَيَان وسُرْيَة
Night-traveller. إبن السُرَى
Highest point, summit. سَرَاة ج سَرَوَات
Tree from which bows are made. سَرَاء (un. سَرَاة)
The lion. السَّارِي والمُسَارِي والمُسْتَرِي
Night-cloud. Column. ✧ Mast of a ship. سَارِيَة ج سَوَارٍ
Castle, palace, seraglio. P سَرَايَة وسَرَايَا ج سَرَايَات
Trench for watering palm-trees. سَرِيّ ج أَسْرِيَة وسُرْيَان
Body of troops. Rounded spear-head. سَرِيَّة ج سَرَايَا
Syriac. سِرْيَانِي
Tree for making arrows. ✻ سَاسَب وسَيْسَب
Cassia. Dolichos sesban. ✻ سَيْسَبَان
Ebony. Tree for making bows. ✻ سَاسَم
Long-legged (man). ✻ سِطْط — أَسَطّ
Tow, oakum, stuff. G أُسْطُبَّة
Stone-bench. Blacksmith's anvil. مَسْطَبَة ج مَسَاطِب
✻ سَطَح a سَطْحًا, وسطّح ه To expand (dough). To flatten (a terrace). To spread out dates to dry.

سَرِق وسَرَّاق, وسَارِق ج سُرَّاق وسَرَقَة وسَارِقُون Thief, robber.
Female robber. Neck-fetters. سَارِقَة ج سَوَارِق
Weak. Listening stealthily. مُسْتَرِق
Short-necked — العُنُق
Sour wine. ✻ سُرْقُع
Dung, manure. P سَرْقِين وسِرْقِين
To pine away. ✻ سَرِك a سَرَكًا
To walk sluggishly. ✻ سَرْوَك وتَسَرْوَك
Court of a prince. P سِرْكَار
To exile, to banish a. o. ✧ سَرْكَل ه
To be exiled. ✧ تَسَرْكَل
Money-order. Bill to order. Ts سَرْكِي
To put trousers to. ✻ سَرْوَل ه
To put on trousers. تَسَرْوَل
P سِرْوَال وسِرْوَالَة وسِرْوِيل ج سَرَاوِيل
Full trousers, drawers.
Feathered on the legs (pigeon). Black-legged horse. مسرْوَل
To cut a. th. to pieces. ✻ سرم — سَرَّم ه
To be cut, cut off. تَسَرَّم
Anus, end of the rectum. سُرْم
Pain in the anus. سَرَم
Yellow or black wasp. سُرْمَان
P سَرْمُوج وسَرْمُوجَة وسَرْمُوزَة و✧ سِرْمَايَة
Boots, gaiters.
Long (night). Perpetual. ✻ سَرْمَد
Eternal (God). سَرْمَدِيّ
Atriplex, orache. *Androsæmum*, all-heal (*plant*). [illegible]
Minium, red-lead. [illegible]
To feed (a child) well. To cut (a camel's) hump. ✻ سَرْهَد ه
Fat of a camel's hump. سَرْهَد
Fat (hump), well fed. مُسَرْهَد
To lay eggs (locust). ✻ سَرَا o سَرْوًا
To strip o's clothes. — وسَرَّى ه عن
— وسَرُو, وسَرِي o سَرْوًا وسَرَاوَة وسَرًا وسَرَاء To be magnanimous, manly.
His cares have cleared away. سُرِّي والسُرَى عَنهُ الهَمّ
To show bravery. تَسَرَّى
To choose, to take the best of. إِسْتَرَى ه
Cypress. Merit. Magnanimous. Plant-insect. سَرْو (un. سَرْوَة)
Little arrow. — وسِرْوَة وسُرْوَة ج سِرَاء

To be long-necked. سَطِع a سَطَعًا
To raise (dust). To mark (a camel) on the neck. سَطَع ه وه
Clapping of hands. Sound of a blow, a fall. سَطع
Of a shining white. سَاطِع البَيَاض
Longest pole of a tent. Mark on a camel's neck. Huge camel. سِطَاع
Dawn. Long. سَطِيع
Long-necked. أَسطع
Eloquent, fluent in speech. مِسطَع
Element. إسطَقِس ج إسطَقِسَات G
To intoxicate; to delight a. o. ✲ سَطَل ه
To be intoxicated with hemp. إنسَطَل, واستَطَل
Copper-pail. ◻ Paste of hasheesh. سَطل ج أَسطَال وسُطُول وسَيطَل P
Intoxicated with hemp. ✧ Idiot. مَسطُول
Squadron of men-of-war, fleet. أُسطُول ج أَسَاطِيل G
To shut (a door). ✧ To steel (a sword). ✲ سَطَم o سَطمًا ه
Sharp edge of a sword. سِطَم وسِطَام
Stopper. Fire-poker. سِطَام
Roots, origin. سِطْم
Poker. إسطَام
Abyss of the sea. Origin. أُسطُمّ ج أَسَاطِم
Column; portico. Leg of a beast. Cylinder. أُسطُوَانَة ج أَسَاطِين P
The Stoics. أَهل الأسطُوَانَة
Firm columns. أَسَاطِين مُسَطَّنَة
To be plentiful (water). To step widely; to go headlong (horse). ✲ سَطَا o سَطوًا وسَطوَةً
To assault. To overpower. — على وب
To treat a. o. harshly. سَاطَى ه
Assault. Severity. Might. ✧ Burglary. سَطوَة ج سَطَوَات
Wide-stepping; raising the tail (horse). Tall. ✧ Burglar. سَاط م سَاطِيَة
To rope (liquid). ✲ سعب — تَسَعَّب
To flow in a continuous stream (water). تَسَعَّب
Ropy threads of honey. سَعَابِيب
To call out (goats). ✲ سعم — سَعْسَع ب
To totter (old man). To be broken down. سَعْسَع وتَسَعْسَع

To prostrate a. o. To make (a camel) to kneel. To set free (a suckling). سَطَح ه
To be flattened, levelled. ✧ To stretch o.'s self on the back. تَسَطَّح
To lay on the back; to be spread out. إنسَطَح
Flat top, roof (of a house). Area. Plane. سَطح ج سُطُوح
Lying wounded. Cripple. سَطِيح
Water-skin. — وسَطِيحَة
Creeping plant. Leguminous plant. سُطَّاح (un. سُطَّاحَة)
Level place. Drying-floor. مَسطَح
Pole of a tent. Travelling-mug. مِسطَح ج مَسَاطِح
Roasting-pan. Rolling-pin. — ومِسطَاح
Flattened. Flat nose. Mat of dwarf-palm leaves. مُسَطَّح
Lying dead. Flat-roofed (house). مَسطُوح
To write a. th. ✲ سَطَر o سَطرًا, واستَطَر ه
To throw a. o. down. — ه
To cut a. th. with (a sword). — ه ب
To compose (history). To rule (paper). سَطَّر ه
To tell stories to a. o. — على
To make a slip in reading. أَسطَر
To pass over (a line: reader). — ه
سَطر وسَطَر ج سُطُور وأَسطُر وأَسطَار وجج أَسَاطِير
Row, line. Hand-writing.
Wish, desire. سُطرَة
إسطَار وأُسطَار وأُسطُورَة وإسطِير ج أَسَاطِير
Legends, stories, tales.
Butcher. سَاطِر وسَطَّار
Butcher's knife, cleaver. سَاطُور ج سَوَاطِير
Paper-ruler. ✧ Sample. Black-lines. مِسطَرَة ومِسطَرَة ج مَسَاطِر
Must, new wine. Dust in the air. إِسْطَار ومُسطَارَة
To oversee; to be set over (people). ✲ سَوطَر وسَيطَر وتَسَيطَر على
Inspector, overseer. مُسَيطِر ومُتَسَيطِر
Mason's trowel. ◻ مَسطَارِين
To spread (smell, dust, sunrays). ✲ سَطَع a سطعًا وسُطُوعًا
To clap the hands. — بِالْيَدَين
To be perceived by a. o. (smell). ✧ To touch a. o. — ه

☆ سَعْتَر وزَعْتَر *Origanum*, marjoram. Wild thyme.

☆ سَعَد a سَعْدًا وسُعُودًا To be auspicious (day).

سُعِد وسَعِد a سَعَادَة To be happy. To thrive (man).

سَاعَد وأسْعَد ٥ على To help, to assist a. o. in.

أسْعَد ٥ To render a. o. happy (God). To assist a. o. in weeping (hired mourner).

تَسَعَّد To seek for fodder.

إسْتَسْعَد ب To bode well of.

— ه To ask the help of.

سَعْد ج سُعُود Good (*opp. to* نَحْس) omen. Name of several stars.

السَّعْدَان The two planets Venus and Mercury.

لَبَّيْكَ وسَعْدَيْكَ Mayest thou be happy and aided!

سَعَادَة Happiness, (*opp. to* شَقَاوَة) prosperity.

سَعَادَتَكَ ✧ Your Excellency (title).

سَاعِد ج سَوَاعِد Fore-arm. Chief. ✧Fiddle-stick. (*Dual*) The two wings (of a bird).

سَاعِدَة ج سَوَاعِد Shaft of a pulley. Armlet. Lion. *Pl.* Ducts of milk. marrow. Affluents of a river.

سَعْدَان *Neurada procumbens*, prickled plant much sought for camels. ✧ Monkey.

سَعْدَانَة Pigeon. Callosity of a camel's breast. Areola of the nipple. Knot of the thong of sandals, in the ropes of a scale.

سُبْحَانَه وسَعْدَانَه I praise and obey Him.

سُعَادَى *Cyperus*, sedge, (*un.* سُعْدَة) galingale (*plant*).

سَعِيد ج سُعَدَاء Happy. Canal of irrigation.

☆ سَعَر a سَعْرًا, وسَعَّر وأسْعَر ه To kindle (fire, war).

— ه ب To spread scab to (others: camel).

— ٥ شَرًّا To do general mischief to

— سَعْرَةً في To run about for (an affair).

أسْعَر سَعْرَه I will circumvent as he does.

سُعِر To be blasted by hot wind. To be furious (camel).

سَعِر a سَعَرَانًا To run swiftly (horse).

سَعَّر ه To fix the price of goods.

تَسَعَّر To be lighted (fire). To burn (wood).

إسْتَعَر To begin (scab). To rage (war).

سِعْر ج أسْعَار Rate, current price.

سَعْر Heat. Insanity. Vehement hunger. Contagious scab.

سُعُر Insanity, madness.

سَعِر ج سَعْرَى Insane, mad.

سُعْرَة Beginning. Cough.

سُعْرَة Blackish colour.

سَعِير ج سُعُر Fire, blaze. Kindled fire.

سُعَار Heat. Hunger. Heat of night.

سَاعُور Oven. Fire.

سَاعُورَة Fire.

أسْعَر Thin, emaciated. Blackish.

مِسْعَر ومِسْعَار Fire-brand.

مِسْعَر Mischief-maker. Long (neck). Running with parted feet (horse). Mad (dog).

مَسْعُور Insatiable. Furious (camel).

سِعْرَارَة وسُعْرُور Daybreak. Sun rays entering a loop hole.

☆ سَعَط a o سَعْطًا, وأسْعَط ٥ ه To inject (a medicine) into (the nose).

أسْعَط ٥ ه To spear a. o. in (the nose).

— ٥ عِلْمًا To inculcate a. th. into the (mind).

إسْتَعَط ه To snuff in (a medicine).

سُعَاط وسَعِيط Pungency of odour.

سَعُوط Snuff-medicine, errhine. ✧ Snuff-tobacco.

سَعِيط Dregs of wine. Oil of nutmeg, of mustard-seed. Fragrance.

مِسْعَط ومُسْعُط Snuff-pipe. Nose-syringe.

☆ سَعَف a سَعْفًا, وأسْعَف ٥ ب To manage business of.

سَعِف a سَعَفًا وتَسَعَّف To be cracked around the nails (fingers).

سُعِف To be ulcerated on the face (child)

سَعَّف ه To mix (perfumes).

سَاعَف وأسْعَف ٥ To help, to assist a. o.

أسْعَف To be at hand (affair).

— ل To be within reach (game).

To slander a. o.; to traduce a. o. — سِعَايَةً وسَعْيًا ب عِند

To outpass a. o. — ساعَى ه

To cause a. o. to work, earn. أَسْعَى ه

To seek a. th. — ب

To enable (a slave) to free himself. إِسْتَسْعَى ه

Run. Endeavour. سَعْي

Slander, backbiting. Work imposed upon a slave for getting his freedom. سِعَايَة

Inspector. Chief of Jews and Christians. Messenger, runner. ساعٍ ج سُعَاة

Run. Endeavour. مَسْعًى ج مَسَاعٍ

To shake (a pole). ✡ سَغَر — سَغْسَغَ ه

To season (food) with grease. To anoint (the head).

To roll a. th. along in the dust. — ه في

To enter underground. تَسَغْسَغَ في

To be hungry. ✡ سَغَبَ o وسَغِبَ a سَغْبًا وسُغُوبًا وسَغَبًا وسَغَابَة ومَسْغَبَة

To suffer from hunger. أَسْغَبَ

Starved. سَغِب وسَغْبان م سَغْبَى ج سِغَاب

Lawful, permitted. مُسْغَب

To be swollen. ✡ سغد — سُغِدَ سَغْدًا

Slight rain. سَغْد

To be lean, little, paltry. ✡ سَغِلَ a سَغَلًا

Lean, small, mean. سَغِل

To give a. o. (water) to drink. ✡ سغم — سَغَّمَ ه ه

To be satiated (child). سُغِمَ وأُسْغِمَ

To skim along the ground (bird). ✡ سَفَّ o سَفِيفًا, وأَسَفَّ

To weave (palm-leaves). — سَفًّا, وأَسَفَّ ه

To take dry, parched (food or medicine). سَفَّ a سَفًّا, واسْتَفَّ ه

To drink much without quenching thirst. To eat dry food (camels). سَفَّ الماء

To pursue trifles. To forsake companions. To be near the earth (cloud, bird). أَسَفَّ

To look steadfastly at. To give dry food to (camels). — ه و ه

To bit (a horse). — ه ه

To apply a medicament to (a wound). — ه ه

To come to o.'s house. To be near to. أَسْعَفَ ب

To assist a. o. in. — ه على

Palm-boughs. *Pl.* Drinking cups. House furniture. Natural disposition. سَعَف ج سُعُوف

House furniture. Vile man. سَعَف

Ulcer on the head of children. سَعْفَة

✧ Assistance in money.

White in the forelock (horse). أَسْعَف م سَعْفَاء ج سُعْف

Near, neighbouring. مُسَاعِف

Ulcerated on the head (child). مَسْعُوف

To cough. ✡ سَعَلَ o سُعَالًا وسُعْلَة

To be sprightly. — سَعَلًا

To render a. o. brisk. To cause cough to. أَسْعَلَ ه

To become a termagant (woman). إِسْتَسْعَلَتْ

Cough. سُعَال

Hooping-cough. ✧ سُعَال كَلْبِيّ

Windpipe, bronchial tubes. قَصَب السُّعَال

Ogress, witch. Termagant. سِعْلَاء وسِعْلَى وسِعْلَاة ج سَعَال وسِعْلَيَات

Colt's foot (medical plant). سَعَالِي وحَشِيشَة السُّعَال

Throat. ساعِل ومَسْعَل

To walk quickly (camel). ✡ سَعَمَ a سَعْمًا

Walking quickly (camel). سَعُوم

To erect (a pavilion). ✡ سعن — أَسْعَنَ

To be fat (camel). تَسَعَّنَ

Fat. Pure wine. سَعْن

Skin for drawing water. سُعْن ج سِعَنَة

Of good or bad omen. سَعْنَة

He does not possess a farthing. ما لَهُ سَعْنَة ولا مَعْنَة

Tent, pavilion. سُعْنَة ج سُعَن

Portion, hour of the night. ✡ سعو — سِعْو وسِعْوَة وسِعْواء

Candle, wax. سَعْوَة

Enduring patiently (hardship, sleeplessness). سُعَاوِيّ

To act, to go, to run. ✡ سَعَى a سَعْيًا

To betake o.'s self towards. — الى

To be a tax-gatherer. To prostitute herself (slave). — سِعَايَةً

To busy o.'s self about. — في حاجة

To exert o.'s self in (an affair). — ل

Ceruse, white lead. اسفيذج واسفيذاج P
To set out on a journey. ✡ سَفَر i سُفُورًا
To shine (dawn). To subside (war).
To unveil (her face : woman). — وأسفر من
To dispel the clouds (wind). — سَفرًا ﻫ
To write (a book). To sweep (a house). To sell the best of a flock.
To bridle (a camel). — وسَفَّر وأسفر ﻩ
To settle a difference between. سَفر i o سَفارَةً وسِفارَةً وسَفرًا بَيْن
To send a. o. on a journey. To pasture camels between morning and evening twilight. To kindle (fire). سَفَّر ﻩ
To set off. To travel. To die. سافر مُسافرةً وسِفارًا
To shine (dawn, face). To enter upon daybreak. To be hot (battle). To be stripped of its leaves (tree). To be bald on the forehead. أسفر
To pasture by morning or evening twilight. To come in evening. تَسَفَّر
To ask (a woman) to lift her veil. تَسَفَّر واستسفر
He has got part of his want. — شَيْئًا مِن حاجَتِهِ
To fall off (hair). To clear off (clouds). إنسفر
Mark on the skin. Traveller. سَفر ج سُفُور
Book. Sacred book. سِفر ج أسفار
Departure. Journey. سَفَر ج أسفا
Dawn, twilight.
Travelling-provisions. سُفرَة ج سُفَر
Leather used as a table-cloth. ✧ Table
Nose-bit of camels. سِفار وسِفارَة ج أسفِرَة وسُفر وسفائِر
Without veil (woman). Lean, (horse). سافِر ج أسفار وسفرَة وسُفّار
Writer. سافِر ج سَفَرَة
Travellers. Nomads. قَوم سافِرَة
✧ *Sparganium*, bur-reed (plant). سافِرَة
Falling leaves. سَفِير
Mediator. Ambassador, envoy. — ج سُفَراء
Gold or silver necklace. سَفِيرَة ج سَفائِر
Embassy, mediatorship. سِفارَة وسَفارَة

He could not get anything from him. ما أسفَّ مِنهُ بِتافِهِ
To be altered in countenance. سُفَّ وأسِفَّ وَجهُهُ
Speckled serpent, winged serpent. سِفّ وسُفّ
Basket of palm-leaves. Handful of wheat. Hair-band of women. سُفَّة
Dry medicine. Medical powder. — وسَفُوف
Devil. Skimming of a bird. Saddle-girth. سَفِيف
Plait of palm-leaves. — وسَفِيفَة
To sift (flour). ✡ سَفسَف ﻫ
To patch a work. — العَمَل
Bad (poetry). Bad affair. Incoherent (speaker). ✧ Powder for the eye. سَفساف
Wind raising the dust. مُسَفسِفَة
To drink much without quenching o.'s thirst. ✡ سَفِت a سَفتًا
Unwholesome food. سَفِت
To draw a bill of exchange. ✡ سَفتَج
Bill, draft, check. سُفتَجَة ج سَفاتِج P
To shed (tears). ✡ سَفَح a سُفُوحًا وسَفحًا ﻫ
To spill (blood). — سَفحًا ﻫ
To flow (tears). — سَفحًا وسُفُوحًا وسَفَحانًا
To work without profit. سَفَّح
To give o.'s self up to debauchery. سافَح وتَسافَح
Foot of a mountain. سَفح ج سُفُوح
Do race without wager. أجرُوا سِفاحًا
To take (a woman) unlawfully. تَزَوَّج بِها سِفاحًا
Blood has been shed between them. بَيْنَهُم سِفاح
Generous. Eloquent. Shedder of blood. سَفّاح
Coarse vestment. Large sack. Arrow having no share in the game. سَفِيح
To leap the female (beast). ✡ سَفَد i وسَفِد a سِفادًا ﻩ وعلى وسافَد ﻩ
To put (flesh) upon the spit. سَفَّد ﻫ
To make (an animal) to leap (the female). أسفَد ﻩ على
To mount (a camel) from behind. تَسَفَّد واستَسفَد ﻩ
Wooden or iron spit. سَفُّود ج سَفافِيد

Eaves. ✧ سِفار ج سَفارَات
Sweepings. سُفارَة
Kind of prickly fish. سَفُّور
Writing tablet. سَفُّورَة
Traveller. مُسافِر
Great traveller. Enduring (camel). مِسْفَر ومِسْفار
Broom. مِسْفَرَة ج مَسافِر
Asparagus. P أَسْفَراج
Quince (fruit). ✱ سَفَرْجَل ج سَفارِج وسَفارِل
Anona, custard-apple. سَفَرْجَل هِندِيّ
Broker. Steward. Musician. Skilful blacksmith. G سِفْسِير ج سَفاسِير وسَفاسِرَة
Sophism. G سَفْسَطَة وسِفْسِطَة
Sophistical, sophist. سَفْسَطِيّ
Streaks, glitter of a blade. P سَفْسَقَة وسِفْسِقَة
To be kind, beneficent. ✱ سَفُط o سَفاطَة
To stop up (the chinks of a tank). سَفَّط ه
To exhaust (the contents of a vessel). إِسْتَفَط ه
Basket. Chest for articles of women. Fish-fin. سَفَط ج أَسْفاط
Generous. Lowly. سَفِيط
Furniture of a house. سُفاطَة
Big-headed. مُسَفَّط الرَّأْس
To slap with the wing (bird). To slap the face. To mark. ✱ سَفَع a سَفْعًا ه
To drag a. o. by the hair. — بِناصِيَتِهِ
To parch the face (hot wind). — وسَفَّع ه
To drive back. To slap a. o. To embrace. To fight a. o. [illegible] ه
To warm o.'s self at (a fire). تسفّع ب
To be altered (complexion). أَسْتُفِع
Mark of fire. Dyed garment. سَفْع ج سُفُوع
Blackish spots on the cheeks. سَفَع وسُفْعَة
Colocynth-seeds. سُفْع وسُفْعَة
Damage caused by Satan. سَفْعَة
Falcon. Buffalo. Reddish black. أَسْفَع
F. Black. Brown. Iron-trivet. سَفْعاء ج سُفْع
Stricken by the evil eye. مَسْفُوع
Having sunk eyes. — العَيْن

To shut (a door). ✱ سَفَق o سَفْقًا, وأَسْفَق ه
To slap (the face). To strike hands in a bargain. سَفَق ه
To be coarse (cloth). سَفُق o سَفاقَة
He conclued a bargain with him. أَعطاهُ سَفْقَة يَمِينِهِ
Thick, coarse (cloth). سَفِيق
Impudent. — الوَجْه
Gold or silver leaf. Wooden roller for mats. سَفِيقَة
To pour (tears, blood). To be profuse of (words). ✱ سَفَك i سَفْكًا ه
To be poured (blood, tears). إِنْسَفَك
Little food taken before meal. سُفْكَة
Bloodthirsty, cruel. سَفّاك للدِماء
Great liar. سَفّاك بِالكَلام وسَفُوك
✱ سَفَل o وسَفِل a وسَفُل o سُفُولًا وسَفالًا
To be low, mean, despicable. وتَسَفَّل
سَفُل o سَفالَة وسَفَل o سَفْلًا وسُفْلًا وسِفالًا
To be vile, base, inferior.
To descend to the lowest of. سَفَل o سُفُولًا في
To lower a. o. To put down. سَفَّل ه وه
To be inferior in (science, character). تَسَفَّل واسْتَفَل في
Lower, lowest part of. سِفْل وسُفْل
Vile, lowly, inferior. سِفْل وسَفِيل وسِفْلَة, وسَفِلَة ج سِفَل
Baseness, abjection. Lower part. سَفالَة
Base, humble. سافِل ج سَفَلَة وسافِلُون
Lower part of a spear. Buttocks. سافِلَة
Men of the lowest class. سِفْلَة النّاس وسَفِلَتهُم
Low, inferior. سُفْلِيّ
Low. Lower. أَسْفَل ج أَسافِل
Old age. Perdition. Error. Hell fire. أَسْفَل السّافِلِين
To blow upon the surface of the earth (wind). ✱ سَفَن o وسَفِن a سَفْنًا
To peel, to pare a. th. — i ه سَفْنًا ه
Rough skin. Polishing-stone. Wedge. Adz. سَفَن و✧ سَفِين
Blowing on the surface of the ground (wind). سافِنَة ج سَوافِن, وسَفُون
The saphena vein. سافِين
Ship, G سَفِينَة ج سُفُن وسَفائِن وسَفِين

To be swift in running or flying (animal, bird). ✱ سَفَا o سُفُوًّا
To be scanty-haired on the forelock. To be chapped (hand). سَفِي a سَفًى وسَفَاء
To lose its prickles (grain). To become lean (she-camel). To foolish. أَسْفَى
To render a. o. heedless. — ه
To ill-treat a. o. — ب
Dust. Leanness. Prickly grass. سَفًا
Medicament. سِفَاء
Good walker (mule). أَسْفَى م سَفْوَاء
To raise the dust (wind). ✱ سَفَى i سَفْيًا, وأَسْفَى ه
To be scattered (dust). سَفِيَ a سَفْيًا
To turn the face away. إِسْتَسْفَى الوَجْه
Dust. Wind raising dust. سَافِيَاء
Dust raised by the wind. سَفِيّ
Scanty haired in the forelock (horse). أَسْفَى م سَفْيَاء ج سُفْي
Slanderer, backbiter. مُسْفِ
✱ سَقِب a سَقَبًا وسَقَب o سُقُوبًا وأَسْقَب ل
To be contiguous, near (house).
To near a. th. أَسْقَب ه
To be contiguous. تَسَاقَب
سَقْب ج أَسْقُب وسِقَاب وسُقُوب وسُقْبَان
Young one of camels.
Pole of a tent. — ج سِقْبَان وسَقِيبَة
Neighbourhood. Near. سَقَب
Near. Remote. سَاقِب
To be unhappy. ✱ سَقِت a سَقَتًا وسَقْتًا
Baldness. ✱ سَقَح — سَقْحَة
Bald. أَسْقَح
To emaciate (a horse). ✱ سَقَد — سَقَّد وأَسْقَد ه
Small bird with red feathers. سُقْدَة ج سُقَد وسُقَيْدَة ج سُقَيْدَات
To scorch a. o. (sun). ✱ سَقَر o سَقْرًا ه
To bear sweet dates (palm-tree). أَسْقَر
Hell-fire. سَقَر
Heat of the sun. سَقْرَة ج سَقَرَات, وسَاقُور
Impious. Blasphemer. سَقَّار
Beer of millet. P سُقُرْقَع
To fall, to collapse. ✱ سَقَط o سُقُوطًا ومَسْقَطًا
He was held in contempt. سَقَط مِن عَيْن
To come forth (fœtus). — o سُقُوطًا

boat. Argo (*constellation*). ◇ Oblong book.
◇ Ark of Noah. سَفِينَة نُوح
Ship-building. سِفَانَة
Ship-builder. سَفَّان
Pearl. سَفَانَة
Voracious bird of Egypt. سَيْفَنَة
Polisher (instrument). مِسْفَن
Sponge. ◇ Purificatory. G سَفَنْج وسِفَنْج وسُفُنْج و إِسْفَنْج
Spinage. P إِسْفَانَاخ وإِسْبَانَاخ
Perfumed must, wine. إِسْفِنْد وإِسْفِنْط وإِسْفَنْط
Maple-tree. إِسْفِنْدَان
To overcome a. o. in levity. ✱ سَفَه o سَفْهًا ه
To be foolish, light-witted. To be busy. سَفِه a سَفَهًا
To become unwise; to lose the mind. سَفُه, وسَفِه a نَفْسَهُ
To forget, to be diverted from. To cause a gush of blood (spear). سَفِه ه وه
To drink without quenching thirst. سَفِهَ الشَّرَاب
To be imprudent, ignorant. سَفُه o سَفَاهَةً وسَفَاهًا
To deem a. o. foolish; to stultify a. o. سَفَّهَ وسَفَّه ه
To act foolishly with. To revile a. o. سَافَه ه
To sit by a wine-jar and drink repeatedly. — الدَّنّ
To drink immoderately. — الشَّرَاب
To make a. o. drink without quenching his thirst (God). أَسْفَه ه
To incline (tree-branches: wind). تَسَفَّه ه
To beguile a. o. of (his property). — ه عَن
To revile a. o. ◇ To act imprudently with. — على
To feign ignorance, levity. تَسَافَه
Levity, want of judgment. سَفَه وسَفَاهَة
Foolish. Badly woven. ◇ Unseemly, insolent (word). سَفِيه ج سُفَهَاء وسِفَاه
Women and young children. السُّفَهَاء
Valley filled with water. مُسْفَه
Thirst-giving food. مُسْفِه

Falling-place.   مَسْقَط ومَسْقِط ج مَسَاقِط

Birth-place.   مَسْقَط الرَّأْس

It caused   كَذَا مَسْقَطَة لَه مِن أَعْيُن النَّاس
him disgrace in the regard of men.

Appalling calamity.   مُسْقِطَة الأَحْبَال

Wont to cast off her young ones.   مِسْقَاط

Island of   سُقْطَرَى وسُقْطُرَاء وإِسْقُطْرَى
Socotra.

Native of   سُقْطَرِيّ وسُقْطُرَاوِيّ وسِقِنْطَار
Socotra.

To crow (cock).   ٭ سَقَمَ a سَقْمًا

To knock (a. th. hard). To   — ه وَ
eat the upper part of food. To slap.

I do not know   مَا أَدْرِي أَيْن سَقَم او سَقَمَ
where he is gone to.

To be altered (colour).   أَسْقَم وأُسْتُقِم

Lower part of a well.   سُقْم ج أَسْقَاء
Country. House.

Piece of cloth.   سِقَاء

Part of a veil, or of a turban   سَوْقَعَة
next to the head.

White-headed bird with   أَسْقَع ج أَسَاقِع
green feathers.

To roof (a   ٭ سَقَفَ o سَقْفًا, وسَقَّفَ ه
house).

— o سِيقِينَى وسَقَّف, وسُقِّف, وأَسْقَف وتَسَقَّف
To be made a bishop.

To be tall and bent   سَقِفَ a سَقَفًا
(ostrich).

٭ To ceil (a room).   سَقَّف ه

Roof. Sky.   سَقْف ج سُقُوف وسُقُف وسُقُف
٭ Ceiling.

Tallness and crookedness (of   سَقَف
the ostrich).

Portico, covered   سَقِيفَة ج سَقَائِف
passage. Camel's rib. Plank of a
ship. Splint for wounds.

Tall. Bony. Hairless.   أَسْقَف م سَقْفَاء
Crook-necked (camel).

Bishop.   G   أُسْقُفّ وأُسْقُف ج أَسَاقِفَة وأَسَاقِف
Learned and humble king.

Bishopric, diocese.   أُسْقُفِّيَّة

Wild   G   سِيقِل وسِيقِيل وإِسْقَال وإِسْقِيل
onion, squill.

Kind of snail.   مَسْقَلَة

To throw a. o. down.   ٭ سَقَلَ ه

Slave, Slavonian.   سَقْلَبِيّ ج سَقَالِبَة

To   ٭ سَقِمَ a وسَقُمَ o سَقَمًا وسُقْمًا وسَقَامًا
be diseased.

To set (moon). To come on. To decrease (heat).

To slip in words.   سَقَط فِي الكَلَام

To alight at a. o.'s.   — الى

To stumble upon a. th. lost.   — على

To mistake. To   سُقِط وأُسْقِط فِي يَدِه
repent. To be perplexed.

To make a. th.   سَاقَط مُسَاقَطَة وسِقَاطًا ه
fall gradually.

To speak by turns with.   — ه الحَدِيث

To slacken in a race (horse).   — سِقَاطًا

To drop a. th. To cause   أَسْقَط ه وه
a. o. to fall, to slip. ٭ To subtract
(a number).

To cast her young (female).   — سَقَطَت

He held an   مَا أَسْقَط كَلِمَة ومَا أَسْقَط فِي كَلِمَة
unexceptionable language, did not
commit a mistake.

To learn (news) succes-   تَسَقَّط ه وه
sively. To induce a. o. in to error.

٭ To be worthless, corrupt.   تَسَقَّط

To fall one by one (leaves).   تَسَاقَط واسَّاقَط

To drop upon (a cushion).   تَسَاقَط على
To fall upon the enemy.

Snow. Dew. Worthless (fellow).   سَقَط

— وسَقْط وسُقْط
Cast off fœtus. Sparks
falling from a steel. Extremity of
sand.

Rubbish. Worthless   سَقَط ج أَسْقَاط
stores. Mistake in calculation. Slip
in words. ٭ Cripple. Foundered
(horse). Shameful thing.

Dealer in old stores.   سَقَطِيّ وسَقَّاط

Fall, collapse.   سَقْطَة وسُقُوط

Worthless, vile   سَاقِط وسَاقِطَة وسُقَّاط
(young man).

(Pl. of سَاقِط). Dealers in dates.   سَوَاقِط
Fallen dates.

Sharp sword.   مِسْقَط

Mistake in calculation. Slip in   سِقَاط
words. Wing of bird. Fallen dates.

Rubbish, waste.   سُقَاطَة وسَقَاطَة

٭ Subtraction (arith.).   إِسْقَاط

Door-latch.   سَقَّاطَة وه سَاقُوطَة

٭ Window-shutter.

Bereft of reason. Hail. Ice. Dew.   مُسْقَط

Roots of the Cyperus esculentus,   سُقَّيْط
rush-nut.

Bird's wing.   مَسْقَط

Dropsical, hydropic. مُسْتَسْقٍ
Drinking-place ; cup, tank. مِسْقَاة ومَسْقَاة
To stop ; to clamp (a door). To sink (a well). To cut off (the ears). To void (ordure). ✡ سَكَّ o سَكًّا ه
To be ignoble, mean. — سُكًّا
To have small ears. To be deaf. — a سَكَكًا
✧ To coin money. سَكَّ النُّقُودَ
To be tangled (plant). To be deaf. To be stopped up. إِسْتَكَّ
Nail. peg. Row. سَكٌّ ج سُكُوك وسِكَاك
Narrow well. Narrow-ringed mail. Scorpion's hole. Blocked road. Compound perfume. سُكٌّ
Ploughshare. Die for coining. Stamped coin. Row of tall trees. Post-office. Even road. Street. سِكَّة ج سِكَك
Gold coin. سِكِّيّ
Iron-nail. Post-messenger. سُكِّيّ
Deafness. سَكَك
Atmosphere, air. سُكَاك وسُكَاكَة
Narrow in the ear-hole. Deaf. أَسَكّ م سَكَّاء ج سُكّ
To pour forth (water). ✧ To cast (metals). ✡ سَكَبَ o سَكْبًا وتَسْكَابًا ه
To be poured. ✧ To be cast (metal). — o سُكُوبًا وانْسَكَبَ
Continuous rain. Tall (man). Necessary thing. Blood-horse. Copper, lead. سَكْب
— وسَاكِب وسَكُوب وسَكِيب وأُسْكُوب
Poured out (water).
Aquarius (*constell*). سَاكِب المَاء
Copper, lead. (*un*. سَكَبَة) سَكَب
Anemone (flower).
Large sack. ◘ سَكِيبَة
Threshold (of a door). أُسْكُبَّة
Russian. ✧ مُسْكُوبِيّ
Stew cooked with vinegar. سَكْبَاج P
Sagapenum, medicinal gum. سَكْبِينَج P
✡ سَكَتَ o سَكْتًا وسُكُوتًا وسُكَاتًا وسَاكُوتَة
To break off speech. To pause in singing. To die. To remit (anger).
To be struck with apoplexy. سُكِتَ
To hush. To silence. سَكَّتَ وأَسْكَتَ ه
To keep silent with. سَاكَتَ ه
To remain silent. أَسْكَتَ

To render a. o. diseased. سَقَّمَ وأَسْقَمَ ه
Disease. سَقَم وسُقْم ج أَسْقَام , وسَقَام
Sickly. Languid (eye). Faulty (language). سَقِيم ج سُقَمَاء وسِقَام
Rancorous, malevolent. سَقِيم الصَّدْر
Kind of sycamore. سَوْقَم
Mackerel fish. أُسْقُمْرِي Ts
Valetudinarian. مِسْقَام
Scammony. سَقَمُونِيَا G
To water (a beast, a land). To give to drink to. To find fault with. To traduce a. o. To wish the rain to a. o. ✡ سَقَى i سَقْيًا , وأَسْقَى ه
✧ To temper (iron). — ه
To send rain to a. o. (God). — ه ه
To suffer from dropsy. سَقَى بَطْنُهُ
✧ To poison a. o. سَقَى سَقْوَةً ه
His heart is filled with hatred. سُقِيَ قَلْبُهُ عَدَاوَةً
To give to a. o. to drink. To wish rain to a. o. سَقَّى ه ه
To give drink to a. o. سَاقَى ه
To farm out (a land) in partnership. — ه في
To give water. To water (cattle, fields). ✧ To poison a. o. أَسْقَى ه
To be moistened, watered. تَسَقَّى
To give to drink to o. a. تَسَاقَى
To draw water. To become fat (camel). إِسْتَقَى
To ask rain, water from. إِسْتَقَى واسْتَسْقَى مِن فُلَانٍ
To be dropsical. إِسْتَسْقَى
Watered land. سَقِيّ
God grant him rain ! سَقْيًا وسُقْيًا لَهُ
Yellow serum of dropsy. سَقْي وسِقْي
Drink. Share of water. سِقْي
Milk, or water-skin. سِقَاء ج أَسْقِيَة وأَسْقِيَات وأَسَاقٍ
Drinking place ; cup, tank. سِقَايَة وسُقَايَة
Streamlet. ✧ Water-wheel. سَاقِيَة ج سَوَاقٍ وسَاقِيَات
Cloud letting large drops. Palm-trees irrigated. Papyrus-reed. سَقِيّ ج أَسْقِيَة
Water-carrier. Waterer of fields. Pelican. Vulture. سَقَّاء م سَقَّاوَة وسَقَّايَة ج سَقَّاءُون
Watered by rain or a stream. مَسْقَوِيّ
Dropsy. Prayer for rain. إِسْتِسْقَاء

Silence. سَكْت
◇ In a low tone. على السَّكْت
Apoplexy. Pause. سَكْتة وسُكوت
◇ Coma.
Lullaby. Remains in a vessel. سُكْتة
Continual silence. Silencing (disease). Biting unawares (snake). سُكات
He has reduced him to silence. رَمَاهُ بِسُكَاتِهِ او بِسُكَاتِيهِ
He is at the eve of ending the affair. هُوَ على سُكاتِ الأَمْر
Tenth horse in a race. سُكَيْت وسُكَّيْت
سَكَتَ وسُكوت وساكوت وسِكِّيت وسُكَّيت
Keeping silent. وسُكَّيت
Remains. Temporate summer-days. Refuse of people. أُسْكات
Last arrow of the game. مُسَكِّت
To patch up (a work). ◇ سَكَّج
Provisional patch-work. مُسَكَّج
To fill (a vessel). ✡ سَكَرَ o سَكْرًا ه
To dam (a stream). To shut (a door).
To abate (wind). — سُكورًا وسَكَرانًا
To be dim (sight). سَكِرَ وسُكِّرَ
His eye has been dazzled. سُكِرَت عينُهُ
To be filled (tank). سَكِرَ a سَكَرًا
To rage against. — على
سَكِرَ a سَكْرًا وسَكَرًا وسُكْرًا وسُكُرًا
To become drunk. وسَكَرانًا من
To strangle a. o. ◇ To bolt (a door). سَكَّرَ ه, ه
◇ To candy. To become sugar. تَسَكَّرَ
To intoxicate a. o. (beverage). أَسْكَرَ ه
To feign intoxication. تَساكَرَ
Intoxication, drunkenness. سُكْر
Wine. Date-wine. Vinegar. Food. سَكَر
Dam. ◇ Canal. سِكْر ج سُكور
Pangs of death. Anguish of the soul. سَكْرةُ الموتِ والهَمّ ج سَكَرات
Darnel-weed. سُكَّرة
Still (night, water). ساكِر
Sugar. Sweet grapes. Fresh dates. سُكَّر
◇ Loaf of sugar. قالب سُكَّر
Sugar in powder. سُكَّر هَش
Candy. سُكَّر نَبات
Calotropis gigantea, mudar. سُكَّر العَش

Wine-seller. سَكَّار
سَكْران م سَكْرَى ج سَكْرَى وسُكارَى
Intoxicated. وسَكارَى
Addicted to drink, drunkard. مُسْكِر وسِكِّير وسَكُور ومِسْكِير
Hyoscyamus datora, henbane. شَيْكَران
Cocculus Indicus, Indian-berry. — الحُوت
To insure against loss. To secure a. th. To roll a cigarette. ◇ سَوْكَرَ
Insurance; premium. Is سِيكُورْتا
Saucer, bowl. P سُكُرُّجة وسُكُرَّجة ج سَكارِيج
✡ سَكَمَ وسَكِمَ a سَكْمًا وسَكَمًا, وتَسَكَّمَ
To wander at random. To slumber.
I do not know where he is gone to. ما أدري أين سَكَمَ
Ciliated Sida (*plant*). سُكَّم
To mind trifles. To act recklessly. تَسَكَّمَ
Wanderer. Stranger. ساكِم وسَكِم
Misleading country. مُسْكِمَة
To put (a threshold) to (a door). To tread the threshold of. ✡ سَكَفَ a سَكْفًا, وتَسَكَّفَ ه
To be a shoe-maker. أَسْكَفَ و◇ سَكَّفَ
Shoe-making. سِكافة
Lower eyelids. أُسْكُف
Lintel of a door. ساكِف
Threshold of a door. أُسْكُفَّة
أُسْكَف وإسْكاف وأُسْكوف وسِكاف وسَيْكَف
Shoe-maker. Clever in work.
Port in the East. Is إسْكِلَة ج أساكِل
To totter about. ✡ سَكَمَ o سَكْمًا
Tottering about. سَيْكَم
Monk's hood. S إسْكِيم
Foot-stool. Low table. Ts إسْكَمْلة
To stop. To be still, to subside. To be quiescent (letter). ✡ سَكَنَ o سُكونًا
To dwell in. — سَكَنًا وسُكْنَى ه وفي
◇ To possess a. o. (devil).
To trust to. — الى
To leave a. o. (pain). — عَن
To become destitute, weak. — وسَكُنَ سُكونةً, وأَسْكَنَ
To quiet, to assuage a. o. سَكَّنَ
To render (a letter) quiescent. — ه
To be the fellow-lodger of. ساكَنَ ه وتَساكَنَا في

Daughter; filly. Slice of flesh. سَلِيلَة
Cotton. Wool upon the spindle. Long fish.
Offspring. Essence, pith. سُلَالَة
Bottom of a سَالّ وَسَلِيل ج سُلَّال وسَوَالّ valley. Stream in a valley.
Basket-maker. Thief. ✧ Horse-stealer. سَلَّال
Large needle. مِسَلَّة ج مَسَالّ ومِسَلَّات ✧ Obelisk.
Consumptive, phthisical. مَسْلُول
To chain, to connect a. th. with. ✲ سَلْسَلَ ه ب
To trace a pedigree up to. — ة الى
To pour (water) into a pool. — ه
To fall down in a stream (water). To become thin (garment). تَسَلْسَلَ
Sweet and palatable water. سَلْسَل وسَلْسَال وسُلَاسِل
Iron-chain. Succession. سِلْسِلَة ج سَلَاسِل *Pl.* Lines of a book. Elongated lightnings, clouds, sands.
Back-bone. سِلْسِلَة الظَّهْر
Streaked (fabric). Curly (hair). Glittering (sword). Traced back (tradition). مُسَلْسَل
Andromeda (*const*). المَرْأَة المُسَلْسَلَة
To clarify (butter). To ✲ سَلَأَ سَلْأً a ه extract (sesam-oil). To pluck off the (prickles of a tree).
To pay (money) to a. o. To give *so many* lashes to a. o. — ة ه
To purify (butter). إِسْتَلَأَ ه
Clarified butter. سِلَاء ج أَسْلِئَة
Prickles of palm-trees. Arrow-head. سُلَّاء
To carry ✲ سَلَبَ o سَلْبًا وسَلَبًا واسْتَلَبَ ه off forcibly. To plunder. To bereave a. o. of (reason).
To deprive a. o. of. — واسْتَلَبَ ة ه
To unsheath (a sword). سَلَّبَ ه
To put on mourning clothes سَلِبَ a سَلَبًا
To lose her child (woman). سَلَّبَت وأَسْلَبَت
To lose its leaves (tree). أَسْلَبَ
To mourn for a husband. تَسَلَّبَت
To walk quickly. إِنْسَلَبَ
Theft. Plunder. Negation. Quick سَلْب

To lodge a. o. in. أَسْكَنَ ة ه
To reduce a. o. to destitution (God). — ة
To humble, to lower o.'s self. إِسْتَكَانَ
Inhabitants of a house. (*coll.*) سَكْن
Abode, dwelling. سَكَن وسُكْنَى
Cause of comfort, ease. Fire. Mercy. Blessing. سَكَن
Food, victuals. — ج أَسْكَان
Base of the head. سَكِنَة ج سَكِنَات
Dwelling.
Rest. Sign of quiescence (ْ). سُكُون
Calmness, gentleness. سَكِينَة ج سَكَائِن
Knife. سِكِّين ج سَكَاكِين
Cutler. سَكَّان و✧ سَكَاكِينِي
Rudder. سُكَّان
House, dwelling. مَسْكَن ومَسْكِن ج مَسَاكِن
Poverty, destitution. مَسْكَنَة
(*m. f.*) مِسْكِين ج مَسْكِينُون ومَسَاكِين
Poor. Weak. Humble. ✧ Simple, without guile.
✧ The inhabited world. المَسْكُونَة
✧ Œcumenical (council). مَسْكُونِي
Oxymel. سَكَنْجَبِين P
Alexander the Great. إِسْكَنْدَر ذُو القَرْنَيْن
Alexandria. إِسْكَنْدَرِيَّة
Alexandretta. إِسْكَنْدَرُونَة
Alexandrian. ✧ Light blue colour. إِسْكَنْدَرَانِي
To draw (a sword). ✲ سَلَّ o سَلًّا, واسْتَلَّ ه To extract gently. To steal a. th.
To lose the teeth. — i سَلًّا
To be consumptive. سُلَّ و✧ انْسَلَّ
To afflict a. o. with phthisis (God). أَسَلَّ ة
To steal. To aid in stealing. — ه
To slip, to steal away. To slip out (shackles). تَسَلَّلَ وانْسَلَّ
To spy a. o. — على
Perfume-basket. Toothless. سَلّ ج سِلَال
Consumption, phthisis. سِلّ وسُلّ وسُلَال وداء السِلّ
Secret theft. Rush of a horse. Drawing of a sword. Chink in a tank. ✧ Small basket. Awl. سَلَّة ج سِلَال
Drawn (sword). Son, child. Colt. Spinal cord. Brain of the horse. Pure wine. سَلِيل ج سُلَّال

To take up arms. تَسَلَّحَ
Thin excrement, ordure. سَلْحٌ
Juice of dates for rubbing a butter-skin. سُلَحٌ
Rain-water collected in a tank. سَلَحٌ
Chicken of partridge. سُلَحٌ ج سِلْحَانٌ
Armed. Affected with diarrhea (camel). سَالِحٌ م سَالِحَةٌ
Weapon. Sword. Row. سِلَاحٌ ج أَسْلِحَةٌ
Thin dung, diarrhea. سُلَاحٌ
Arsenal. Garrison. Look out. Armed party. Common nightshade (*plant*). مَسْلَحَةٌ ج مَسَالِحُ
Arcturus (star). ذُو السِّلَاحِ
Glass-bottle. سَلَاحِيَّةٌ
Apostle. S سَلِيحٌ ج سِلِيحُونَ
Reseda luteola, dyer's weed (plant). إِسْلِيحٌ وإِسْلِيخٌ
To expand, to be conspicuous (road). ✡ سلحب — إِسْلَحَبَّ
Equerry. Sword-bearer. P سِلَاحْدَار ج سِلَاحْدَارِيَّةٌ
P سُلَحْفَاةٌ وسِلَحْفَاةٌ وسُلَحْفَاءُ وسُلَحْفَى وسُلَحْفِيَةٌ
Tortoise. Sea-turtle. ج سَلَاحِفُ
Alyssum, madwort. حَشِيشَةُ السُّلَحْفَةِ
Colza. ✡ سَلْجَمٌ
To come to its end (month). To cast its slough (snake). To become green again (plant). ✡ سَلَخَ a o سَلْخًا
To come to the end of (a month). To excoriate (the skin : scab, heat). — هـ
To skin (a sheep). To pull off her shift (woman). ✧ To ransom a. o. — ه وهـ
To separate the day from the night (God). — النَّهَارَ من اللَّيلِ
To strip off (o.'s clothes). To cast its skin (serpent). To follow the day (night). To elapse (month). إِنْسَلَخَ مِن
To recline on the breast. إِسْلَخَّ
End of a month. سَلْخٌ ومُنْسَلَخٌ
Slough of snake. Skin of a slaughtered animal. — وسِلْخٌ
Thread on the spindle. سَلَخٌ
Tastelessness of food. سَلَاخَةٌ
Tasteless (food). ✧ Acanthus (prickly plant). ✧ Treeless (land). سَلِيخٌ
Skinned (sheep). — ومَسْلُوخٌ

step. ✧ Spun silk.
Plough-handle. سِلْبٌ
Booty, plunder. Spoils of a slaughtered animal. Bark of reeds. Tree-fibres. Kind of hyacinth (*plant*). ✧ Moorings. سَلَبٌ ج أَسْلَابٌ
Denuded parts of the body. سَلَبَةٌ
Tall. Light. سَلِبٌ
Light-handed. — اليَدَيْنِ
Swift runner. — القَوَائِمِ
Bereft of a child, a young (female). سَالِبٌ وسُلُبٌ, وسَلُوبٌ وسَلِيبٌ ج سُلُبٌ
Rope-maker. سَلَّابٌ
Thief, robber. (*m. f.*) سَلَّابَةٌ وسَلَبُوتٌ
Mourning clothes of woman. سِلَابٌ ج سُلُبٌ
Bereft of reason. سَلِيبٌ ج سَلْبَى
Road. Manner of acting. Neck of a lion. Turn of a sentence. أُسْلُوبٌ ج أَسَالِيبُ
✧ Cotton-thistle. سَلِيبِينُ الحِمَارِ
Martingale of a horse. سَلَبَنْد
To press forth (the guts). To cut a. th. To shave off (the hair). To rub off. To lash. ✡ سَلَتَ o i سَلْتًا هـ وه
To cleanse a dish (with the hand). — واسْتَلَتَ هـ
To slip away stealthily. إِنْسَلَتَ عن
Thin-husked barley. سُلْتٌ
I have missed it. ذَهَبَ مِنِّي فَلْتَةً وسَلْتَةً
Remainder of food adhering to a vessel. سُلَاتَةٌ
Stripped (bone). مَسْلُوتٌ
Having the nose cut off. أَسْلَتُ ج سُلْتٌ
Abstaining from dyeing (woman). سَلْتَاءُ
Misfortune. Hard year. Toothless camel. ✡ سِلْتِمٌ
To glut a. th. ✡ سَلِجَ a سَلْجًا وسَلَجَانًا هـ
To swallow easily. تَسَلَّجَ هـ
To drink much. — واسْتَلَجَ الشَّرَابَ
Shell-fish. سُلْجَةٌ ج سُلَجٌ
Plant sought by camels. سُلَّجٌ ج سَلَالِيجُ
Gullet. سِلِّجَانٌ
Food easily swallowed. سَلِيجٌ
Rape colza (plant). P سَلْجَمٌ
To void ordure (beast). ✡ سَلَحَ a سَلْحًا
To arm a. o. with (a sword). سَلَّحَ ه هـ
To make a. o. to void ordure. — وأَسْلَحَ ه

Ruler. Sultan. سُلطان ج سَلاطِين
Honey-suckle (*plant*). سُلطان الجَبَل
✧ Garnet-fish. سُلطان إبراهيم
✧ China-aster. سُلطان الزُّهور
✧ Bind-weed. زَهر السُّلطان
Broad-leaved lepidium. حَشِيشَة السُّلطان
Sultana, empress. سُلطانة
Foul-tongued (woman). سَلطانة وسِيلطانة اللِّسان
Highway, public road. طَرِيق سُلطانِيّ
✧ Large hollow bowl. سُلطانِيَّة
Tooth of a key. مِسلاط ج مَسالِيط
To proclaim a. o. sultan. ✧ سَلطن ة
To become a sultan. To assume lordly airs. تَسَلطن
Power, empire. ✧ سَلطَنَة
To expand (valley). ✲ سلطح – إسلَنطح To lay down on (the face).
Lobster, craw-fish. ✧ سَلطَعان سَلطَعُون ج سَلاطِعِين
To cleave (the head). ✲ سَلَم a سَلمًا ه
To be chapped (foot). To be affected with leprosy. سَلِم a سَلمًا
To split a. th. سَلَّم ه
To be cleft on the head. أسلَم
To be cracked, chapped. تَسَلَّم وانسَلَم
Chap on the foot. سَلم ج سُلوء
Slit in a water-skin. Cleft in a mountain. Similar. سِلم ج أسلاء وسُلوء
Two boys of the same age. غُلامان سِلعان وأسلاء
Bitter tree. Kind of aloes. *Sælanthus quadragonus. Cacalia sonchifolia* (*plants*). سَلَم
Senecio badiensis (*plant*). سَلَم أبيَض وسَلَم البَقر
Wound chapping the skin. سَلمة وسَلَمَة ج سَلَمات وسِلاء
Commodity, article of merchandise. ✧Worthless (man, thing). سِلعَة ج سِلَع
Scrofula. Ganglion. Leech. – وسَلعَة وسَلَعَة ج سِلَع
Bitter aloes. سَوْلَم
Leper. Chapped in the foot. Hump-backed. أسلَم م سَلعاء ج سُلم
Guide in the desert. مِسلَم
Strong, deadly poison. سَمّ مُسلَم
Pole set with nails. ✲ سِلغاف
To fracture (the head). ✲ سَلَغ a سَلغًا ه

Nutmeg-oil. Offspring. Bastard cinnamon. ✧ Acacia. سَلِيخَة
Black snake. Scab. سالِخ ج سالِخَة وسَوالِخ وسُلَّخ وسُلخَة
Bald. Red-skinned. Scabby. أسلَخ
Skinning-place; slaughter-house. مَسلَخ ج مَسالِخ
Slough of snakes. Raw leather. Palm-tree dropping its dates when unripe. مِسلاخ
Sea-eel. ✲ سلر – سِلَوز
To lose its lower branches (palm-tree). ✲ سَلِس a سَلَسًا وأسلَس
To be worn out (wood). سَلِس a سَلَسًا
To pay readily (a due) to. – ل ب
To be loose. To be tractable (man). – a سَلَسًا وسَلاسَة وسُلوسًا
To be bereft of reason. سُلِس سُلاسًا وسَلسًا
To set jewels; to string (pearls). سَلَّس ه
To render a. th. easy. أسلَس ه
String for setting pearls. سَلس ج سُلوس
Ear-drop.
Easiness. Mildness. Incontinence of urine. سَلَس
Easiness (of elocution). سَلاسَة
Loose: easy; meek. سَلِس
Tractable (horse). – ومِسلاس القِياد
Want of intellect. سُلاس
Stripped of its stumps (palm-tree). مِسلاس
Easy to swallow. Wine. River of Paradise. ✧ Ornamental waterspout. ✲ سَلسَبِيل
To be hard, sharp. To be eloquent (man). To be foul-tongued (woman). ✲ سَلِط a وسَلُط o سَلاطَة وسُلوطَة
To empower a. o. over. سَلَّط ه على
To prevail over, to subdue. تَسَلَّط على
Power, dominion. سُلطة وتَسَلُّط
Thin and long arrow. Straw-mattress. سِلطة ج سِلَط وسِلاط
Embroidered jacket. ✧ سَلطة
Hard. Sharp-tongued. سَلط وسَلِيط
Eloquent (man). Grain-oil; olive-oil. سَلِيط وسَلِيطَة
Foul-tongued (woman). سَلِيطَة
Authority. Plea, argument. سُلطان

To grow (canine teeth). سَلَغَ a سُلُوغًا
To shed its teeth when 6 years old (ewe, calf).
Raw. Red. Leper. Vile. أَسْلَغ
To be past (event). ✱ سَلَفَ o سَلَفًا
To outgo, to precede. — سَلَفًا وسُلُوفًا
To harrow (the earth). — سَلْفًا ه
To grease (a skin).
To take some food before dinner. سَلَّفَ
To give to a. o. to breakfast. — ه
To lend. To advance a. th. — ه ه
To take the lead. سَالَفَ
To keep pace with a. o. in (a travel). To equal a. o. in. — ه
To advance money to a. o. أَسْلَفَ ه ه
To level; to harrow (the ground). — ه
To borrow a. th. from. تَسَلَّفَ واستَسْلَفَ ه مِن
To marry two sisters. تَسَالَفَ
Leather, provision bag. سَلْف ج أَسْلُف وسُلُوف
Payment in advance. Loan without interest. Good work. سَلَف
Predecessor, ancestor. سَلَف ج أَسْلَاف وسُلَّاف
Partridge. سُلَف ج سُلْفَان وسِلْفَان
Skin. Husband of a wife's sister. ✧ Husband's brother. سِلْف ج أَسْلَاف
Wife of a husband's brother. سِلْفَة
✧ A husband's sister; a brother's wife.
Harrowed field. Leather for lining boots. Breakfast. سُلْفَة ج سُلَف
They came one after another. جَاءُوا سُلْفَةً سُلْفَةً
First juice of grapes. سُلَاف وسُلَافَة ج سُلَافَات
Vanguard of an army. سُلَاف العَسكَر
Best wine. Choice part. — وسُلَافَة ج سُلَافَات
Affinity by marriage. أُسْلُوفَة
Preceding. Past (time). سَالِف ج سَلَف
In former times; in preceding generations. في سَالِف الدَّهر
✧ Amaranth (flower). سَالِف عَرُوس
✧ Locks of hair on the temples. سَوَالِف
Side of the forepart of سَالِفَة ج سَوَالِف

the neck. Past event. ✧ Old tale.
Ahead. سَلِيف
Middle-aged woman, about 45. مُسْلِف
Cylindrical stone-roller. Harrow. Trowel. مِسْلَفَة
To boil a. th. To blast (the plants : cold). To grease a water-skin. To smear (a camel). ✱ سَلَقَ o سَلْقًا ه
To take off (the hair of a skin) with (hot water). — ه ب
To peel off (the flesh) from (a bone). — ه عن
To leave prints on (the soil: foot). — في
To prostrate a. o. To gall (a camel). To excoriate the thighs of (a rider: beast). — ه
To pierce a. o. with (a spear). To hurt a. o. (in words). To flay a. o. with (a whip). — ه ب
To insert (a stick) into (the loop of a sack). — وأَسْلَقَ ه في
To prostrate a. o. on the back. ✧ سَلْقَى سِلْقَاء ه
To shout. To run. To climb a wall. سَلَّقَ
✧ To collect herbs. سَلَّقَ
To hunt wolves. أَسْلَقَ
To scale (a wall). تَسَلَّقَ ه
To fret on o.'s bed (from grief, pain). — على فِرَاشِهِ
To lay prostrate on the back. إِسْتَلْقَى واسْلَنْقَى
White scar on a camel. سَلْق وسَلَق
Even and fertile plain. سَلَق ج أَسْلَاق وسُلْقَان
Garden-beet. Beet-root. Stream of water. سِلْق ج سُلْقَان
Rumex, sour-dock. سِلْق البَرّ
Potamogeton, pond-weed. سِلْق المَاء
Wolf. — ج سُلْقَان وسِلْقَان
She-wolf. Female locust. Foul, lewd woman. سِلْقَة ج سِلَق وسِلَق
Weeping loudly woman. — ج سُلْقَان وسِلْقَان
Weeping, slapping her face (woman). سَالِقَة ج سَوَالِق
Lippitude of the eyelids. Pustules on the tip of the tongue. سُلَاق
Violence of language. سَلَاقَة
Foot-prints on a road. سَلَائِق

To salute, to greet a. o. — ه وعلى
Thou hadst well spoken. ✧ سَلِم ثَمّك
Thank you. God keep thy hands. ✧ سَلِم دَيَاتك
To reconcile with. سَالَم ه
To keep a. o. safe. To betray. أَسْلَم ه
He resigned to the will of God. — أمْرَهُ الى الله
To give up a. th. — عن
To be bitten by a snake. أُسْلِم
To become a Moslem. To submit to. To obey. أَسْلَم وتَسَلَّم
To receive. To manage a. th. تَسَلَّم ه
To be reconciled. To keep pace (horses). تَسَالَم
To touch. To kiss (a stone). إِسْتَلَم ه
To reconcile together. أَسْتَلِم
To submit. To follow the right path. ✧ To threaten to become a Moslem. إِسْتَسْلَم
To call o.'s self a Moslem. تَمَسْلَم
Leathern bucket with a handle. سَلْم ج أَسْلُم وسِلَام
Peace. Peaceful. Islamism. سِلْم
Payment in advance. Prisoner. Captivity. Salutation. Mimosa flava used as tan. سَلَم
Stone. Tender (woman). سَلِمة ج سِلَام
Ladder, stairs, steps : means. سُلَّم ج سَلَالِم وسَلَالِيم
Obedience to God. Greeting. سَلَام
▫ Dear me ! (*Interj. of wonder*). يا سَلَام
Peace be to thee. السَّلَام عَلَيْك
The Heaven. دَار السَّلَام
The City of Peace *i. e.* Bagdad. مَدِينَة السَّلَام
The Tigris. نَهر السَّلَام
A bitter tree. سَلَام وسِلَام
Parlour. Ts سَلَامْلِك
Security. Health. Freedom from defect. سَلَامَة
Phalange of the fingers. South wind. سُلَامَى ج سُلَامَيَات
Black-beetle. أَبُو سَلْمَان
Islamism. Moslems. (*coll*). إِسْلَام
Obedience.
Safer, sounder. Leaves of the Theban palm. أَسْلَم
Solomon, son of David. سُلَيْمَان الحَكِيم

Sword. Greyhound, slaugh hound. سَلُوقِيّ
F. Sitting-place of a pilot. سَلُوقِيَّة
Eloquent (speaker). Sharp. سَلَاق ومِسْلَق ومِسْلَاق
Ascension-day. S السَّلَاق
Falling leaves. Side (of a road). ✧ Pot-herbs. سَلِيق
Boiled (food). Natural disposition. سَلِيقَة ج سَلَائِق
Naturally. بِالسَّلِيقَة
To travel, to go along (a road, a course). ✱ سَلَك o سَلْكًا وسُلُوكًا ه
To be current (coin). To behave. ✧ To succeed (trick). سَلَك
To insert (the hand). — وأَسْلَك ه في
To engage a. o. in a road, a course. — وأَسْلَك ه ه وفي
He acted as a straight-forward man. سَلَك مَسْلَك الصِدْق
To clear (the way). To clean (a pipe). To wind off (thread). سَلَّك ه
To be inserted ; to penetrate. إِنْسَلَك في
String for pearls. سِلْك (*un.* سِلْكَة) ج سُلُوك وأَسْلَاك
Abstruse (speech). دَقِيق السِّلْك
Young of a partridge. سُلَك م سُلَكَة ج سِلْكَان
Walk. Behaviour. Ascetical life. سُلُوك
Spun thread. سِلْكَة ج سِلَك وجج سُلُوك وأَسْلَاك
Straight spear-thrust. سُلْكَى
Their business goes right. أَمْرُهُم سُلْكَى
Road, path. مَسْلَك ج مَسَالِك
Border of a gárment. ✧ Winder. مُسَلِّكة
Slender in body (man). مُسْلَك
Cleanser of pipes. مُسَلِّكَاتي
To be safe. To be free from vice, defect. ✱ سَلِم a سَلَامَة وسَلَامًا
By him who preserves thee. بِيَدي تَسْلَم
To bite a. o. (snake). سَلَم o سَلْمًا ه
To tan (leather). سَلَم i سَلْمًا
To finish (a bucket). To save a. o. from. سَلَّم ه من
To admit (a proposal). To consent to. — ب
To submit to. — ل
To give up, to deliver a. th. to. — وأَسْلَم ه إلى

Weasel. أمّ سُلَيمان
Corrosive sublimate. سُلَيمانِي
Calamine (*mineral*). حَجَر سُلَيمانِي
Safe Regular (verb). سالِم
Bitten by a snake. سَلِيم ج سَلمَى
Mortally wounded.
Safe. Secure. — ج سُلَماء
Sound-hearted. — القَلب
Moslem, musulman. مُسلِم ج مُسلِمُون
✧ Governor of a town. مُتَسَلِّم
Tanned. Bitten by a serpent. مَسلُوم
✱ سلهب — إسلَهَبَّ To stretch himself in running (horse).
Long-bodied (horse). Tall (man). سَلهَب ج سَلاهِب وسَلاهِبَة
✱ سلهم — اسلَهَمّ To be altered (colour).
Tall, slender. سَلهَم
✱ سَلا o سَلوًا وسُلُوًّا وسُلوانًا ه وعن، وسَلِي a سُلَيًّا عن To be diverted from. To console o.'s self for.
✧ He forgot his cares. سَلا هَمَّهُ
سَلّى تَسلِيَةً ل وأسلَى اسلاء ه عن To console a. o. To divert from.
To be safe from wild beasts. أسلَى
To divert, to console o.'s self. تَسَلَّى تَسَلِّيًا
To be dispelled from a. o. (grief). — وانسَلَى انسِلاء عن
To be fat (sheep). إستَلَى استِلاء
Comfort, consolation. سُلوَة وسَلوَة وتَسلِيَة وتَسَلٍّ
He leads a quiet life. هُوَ في سَلوَة مِن العَيش
Quail. (*un.* سَلوَة) سَلوَى ج سَلاوَى
Honey. Consolation.
Solace. Shell used as an amulet. سُلوان
Third horse in a race. مُسَلٍّ
Butter. ✧ مُسَلَّى
Secundine. ✱ سلى — سَلًا ج أسلاء
There is no hope left. إنقطع السَّلَا
✱ سَمّ o سَمًّا ه To poison a. o. ✧ To angry a. o.
To poison (food). To scrutinise a. th. To stop up (a flask). — ه
To conciliate (people). — بَين
To be burning, hot (wind). — o سُمُومًا
I follow thy very design. سَمَت سَمتَك

To be blasted by the simoom (plant, day). سُمّ
To poison (food). سَمَّم ه
To be angry, incensed. ✧ إنسَمّ
Eye of a needle; hole. Poison. سَمّ وسِمّ وسُمّ ج سُمُوم وسِمام
Poison killing on the spot. سَمّ ساعَة
Ratsbane, arsenic. سَمّ الفار
Oleander, rose-bay. سَمّ الحِمار
Cocculus Indicus, Indian-berry. سَمّ السَّمَك والحُوت
Palm-leaves mat. Relationship. سُمَّة ج سُمَم
Holes of the body: mouth, nostrils, ears. سِمام وسُمُوم الإنسان
Simoom, pestilential hot wind. سَمُوم ج سَمائِم
Swift, agile. Mountain-swallow. سَمام
Person. Feather in a horse's neck. Standard. سَمامَة
Gecko, (kind of lizard). سامّ وسَمّ أبرَص
Day of simoom. يَوم سامّ ومُسِمّ ومَسمُوم
Venomous (beast). Death. سامَّة ج سَوامّ
The great and the common people. العامَّة والسّامَّة
Narrow in the nostrils (nose). أسَمّ
Eating to surfeit. مُسِمّ
Holes of the body. ✧ Pores. مَسامّ
Kindred. أهل المَسَمَّة
To run (fox). ✱ سَمسَم
Swift. Fox. Wolf. سُماسِم
Red ant. سُمسُم ج سَماسِم
Sesam. Coriander-seed. (*un.* سِمسِمَة) سِمسِم
Berry of the castor-oil plant. سِمسِم هِندي
Condyle, process on a bone. عَظم سُمسُماني
To pursue a right course. To follow a way by conjecture. ✱ سَمَت o i سَمتًا، وسَمَّت
To dispose speech for. سَمَت i الكَلام ل
To invoke (God) upon. سَمَّت على
To bless (a sneezer). — ل
To front, to be opposite to. سامَت ه
To purpose a. th. سَمَت نَحو، وتَسَمَّت ه
Road. Aim, course. سَمت ج سُمُوت
How fine is his behaviour! ما أحسَن سَمتَهُ

Bountiful ; brave man. Wolf. Sword. ✲ سمذع — سَمَيْذَع ج سَمَاذِع
To spend the night in conversation. ✲ سَمَر o سَمَرًا وسُمُورًا
As long as night-wakers wake. مَا سَمَرَ السَّمِيرُ
To put out (the eye) with hot nails. سَمَر o سَمَارًا وسَمْرًا ه
To mix (milk) with water. To shoot (an arrow). To drink (wine). — وسَمَّر ه
To nail, to rivet. — o i سَمْرًا, وسَمَّره
To be tawny, brownish. سَمِر a وسَمُر o سُمْرَة, واسْمَرّ
To converse with a. o. by night. سَامَر ه
To be dark, brown. أَسْمَر واسْمَارّ
To be nailed. تَسَمَّر
To converse together by night. تَسَامَر
Night-conversation. سَمَر ج أَسْمَار
Night. Shade of the moon. Night-meeting.
Gum-acacia-tree. Mimosa, Egyptian thorn. سَمُر ج أَسْمُر (un. سَمُرَة)
Dusky, brown colour. سُمْرَة
Conversing by night. Place for night-conversation. سَامِر ج سُمَّر وسُمَّار
Company of night-talkers. — وسَامِرَة
The Samaritans. (un. سَامِرِيّ) سَامِرَة
Milk diluted with water. ◻ *Juncus spinosus*, rush for mats. سَمَار
Brown. Spear. Gazelle's milk. أَسْمَر م سَمْرَاء ج سُمْر
Wheat. Flour. السَّمْرَاء
Water and wheat. Water and spear. الأَسْمَرَان
Dark. brownish. ✧ اسْمَرَانِيّ
Diamond. السَّامُور
Swift, noble (camel). سَمُور
Mustella Zibelina, sable. سَمُّور
Night-discourser. سَمِير وسِمِّير
Day and night. إِبْنَا سَمِير
Nail, peg. Good tender of camels. ✧ Corn on the foot مِسْمَار ج مَسَامِير
Strongly built (man). Troubled (life). مُسْمُور
Collection of the poll-tax. ✲ سَمَرَّج وسَمَرَّجَة
Black. Shrill- (un. سَمَرْمَرَة) ✲ سَمَرْمَر

The zenith. سَمْتُ الرَّأْس
The azimuth. السَّمْت
The equinoctial colure. سَمْت الاعْتِدَال
The solstitial colure. سَمْت الانْقِلَاب
To be ugly, foul. ✲ سَمُج o سَمَاجَة
To render a. o. ugly, foul. سَمَّج ه
To find a. o. ugly, hideous. إِسْتَسْمَج ه
سَمْج وسَمِج وسَمِيج ج سِمَاج وسَمِجُون
Ugly. ✧ Foul (talk). وسُمْجَاء وسُمْجَى
Greasy, unpalatable milk. سَمْج وسَمِيج
✲ سَمُح o سَمَاحًا وسُمُوحًا وسَمَاحَة وسُمُوحَة
To be generous. وسَمْحًا وسِمَاحًا, وأَسْمَح
To bestow a. th. bountifully to. سَمَح a سَمَاحًا ل ب
To comply with a. o's wishes. سَمَّح وسَامَح وأَسْمَح
To act, to walk gently. To hurry on. سَمَّح
To forgive, to forbear a. th. to. سَامَح ه ب وفي
To become tractable (beast). أَسْمَح
To permit, to forbear. تَسَمَّح في
To forbear o. a. تَسَامَح
Compliance. Forbearance. سَمَاح وسَمَاحَة
Skin-tents. سِمَاح
Compliant. Smooth (wood). سَمْح وسَمِيح ج سُمَحَاء
Long-backed (ass). Thin in the belly (mare). Long bow. ✲ سَمْحَج
Pericranium ; wound in it. ✲ سِمْحَاق
To grow up (seeds). ✲ سَمَخ o سَمْخًا
To wound a. o. in the ear-hole. ه a —
Hole of the ear. سِمَاخ
Of a fine growth (wheat). حَسَنُ السِّمْخَة
To be perplexed. To raise the head proudly. To divert o.'s self. To sing. ✲ سَمَد o سُمُودًا
To apply o.'s self to. — في
To manure (a land). To divert a. o. سَمَّد ه وه
To swell with anger. إِسْمَد واسْمَادّ
To swell (hand). To vanish. إِسْمَادّ
Unceasingly, continually. سَمْدًا
Composite of manure and ashes. سَمَاد
To feel vertiginous. ✲ سمدر — إِسْمَدَرّ
Cloudiness of the sight ; vertigo. سُمْدُور وسَمَادِير
Salamander. ✲ سَمَنْدَر وسَمَيْدَر
White flour. ✧ Semolina. سَمِيذ P

To listen stealthily to. إستمع لهُ والى
سَمْع (*un.* سَمْعَة) ج أَسْمَاع وأَسْمُع وجج أَسامِع
Sense of hearing. Ear. Report. Fame. وأَساميع
Listen to me. سَمْعَكَ إِلَيَّ
I hear and obey. سَمْعًا وطَاعَةً
He is in a forlorn place. بَيْنَ سَمْعِ الأَرْضِ وبَصَرِهَا
Hearing (man). Report. Good repute. سِمْع
Notorious thing. أَمْر ذو سِمْع او ذُو سَمَاع
May it be heard but not fulfilled! سَمْعًا لا بَلْغًا وسِمْعًا لا بِلْغًا
Do hear, listen! سَمَاعِ
I am an ear-witness of it. هذا سِمْع وسَمْعَة وسَمَاع وسَمَاعَة أُذُنِي
Good fame. سُمْعَة
He has done it for the sake of being heard. فَعَلَهُ سَمْعَةً وسُمْعَةً
Fame. Song, harmony. سَمَاع
Usual not regular (expression). سَمَاعِيّ
Hearer. The Listener (God). Lion. سَمِيع ج سُمَعَاء
The two ears. (*un.* السَّامِعَة) السَّامِعَان
Listening ear. أُذُن سَمْعَة و سَمِعَة وسَمُوع سَمَّاعَة
The brain. أُمّ السَّمْع والسَّمِيع
That thou mayest hear. تَسْمِعَتَك وتَسْمِعَةً لَك
Hearing-place. مَسْمَع
Ear. Handle of a bucket. مِسْمَع ومِسْمَعَة ج مَسَامِع
Shackle, fetter. مُسْمِع
Current reports, rumours. مَسْمُوع ج مَسْمُوعَات
Holes of the body: ears, nostrils, etc. مَسَامِع
To become tall (plant). ✻ سَمَق o سُمُوق
Pure, mere (lie). سُمَاق
Sumach (tree). سُمَّاق وسُمُوق
Yoke. سَمِيق
To raise (a building). ✻ سَمَك o سَمْكًا ه
To ascend. To be lofty, high. سَمَك o سُمُوك
Roof; canopy of heaven. Height. Thickness. سَمْك ✧ وسُمْك
Fish. سَمَك ج سِمَاك وسُمُوك وأَسْمَاك

voiced locust-eating bird.
To be a broker, a mediator. ✻ سَمْسَر
Craft, pay of a broker. سَمْسَرَة
P سِمْسَار ج سَمَاسِر وسَمَاسِير وسَمَاسِرَة
Broker; negotiator.
Jasmine. Marjoram. ✻ سَمْسَق وسِمْسِيق وسُمْسُق
To become sour (milk). ✻ سَمَط o سُمُوطًا
To keep silent (man). سَمَّط وسَمَّط وأَسْمَط
To scald and roast (a kid). سَمَط o i سَمْطًا ه
To hang up a. th. To sharpen (a knife). — ه
To fasten (a bundle) to (a saddle). To put off (a debtor). To keep to a. th. سَمَّط ه وه
To be fastened to. تَسَمَّط ب
String of a necklace. Garment without lining. Sprightly, sharp. Bundle-strap of a saddle. Hanging part of a turban. سِمْط ج سُمُوط
Of a poorly condition. سَمْط وسَمِيط
Woollen garment. سُمْط
Shoes of one piece. Unbranded (she-camel). سُمُط وأَسْمَاط
Table-cloth. Rank (of men). Middle of a valley. سِمَاط ج سُمُط
Range of bricks. سَمِيط وسُمَيْط
Your orders shall be fulfilled. حُكْمُكَ مُسَمَّطًا
Heron (bird). ✻ سَمَيْطَر
✻ سَمِع a سَمْعًا وسِمْعًا وسماعًا وسَمَاعَة وسَمَاعِيَة ه
To hear (a sound). To understand (a meaning).
To listen to (speech). — الى
To obey a. o. To hearken to. — ل ومن
To spread the fame of. سَمَّع ه
To make a. o. to hear. — وأَسْمَع ه ه
To revile a. o. — ه القَبِيح
To disgrace a. o. To divulge. — ب
To tell a. th. to the ears of. To revile a. o. أَسْمَع ه
To put a handle to (a bucket). — ه
Do see and hear! أَبْصِرْ بِهِ وأَسْمِعْ
To listen, to hearken to. تَسَمَّع واسَّمَّع ه والى واسْتَمَع ل والى
To know a. th. by hearsay. تَسَامَع بِهِ

✧ Skate-fish, turbot. سَمَكُ التُّرس
✧ Pike-fish. — الكَرَاكِي
Xiphias, sword-fish. — كَوْسَج
✧ Sole-fish. — مُوسَى
✧ Whale. — يُوسُف
Pisces, the Fishes (*constellation*). السَّمَكَة
✧ He broiled his fish in the fire of a burning house; *i.e.* he derived a profit from a misfortune. شَوَى فِي الحَرِيقِ سَمَكَتَهُ
Upholding or lifting implement. سِمَاك ج سُمُك
السِّمَاكَان, السِّمَاكُ الرَّامِح والسِّمَاكُ الأَعْزَل *Arcturus* and *Spica Virginis* (stars).
Small dried fishes. سُمَيْكَاء
Fishmonger. سَمَّاك
High. Deep. Thick. سَمِيك ومَسْمُوك
Wooden fork upholding a tent. ✧ Vine-prop. مِسْمَاك ج مَسَامِيك
The Heavens. المُسْمَكَات والمَسْمُوكَات
To put out (the eye), with a hot iron. ✱ سَمَل o سَمْلًا, واسْتَمَل ه
To cleanse (a well). — وسَمَّل ه
To yield little water (bucket, tank). سَمَل وسَمَّل
To make peace between. سَمَل وأَسْمَل بَيْن
سَمَل o سُمُولًا وسُمُولَةً وسَمُل o سَمَالَةً, وأَسْمَل To be worn out (clothes).
To speak to a. o. gently. سَمَّل ه بِالقَوْل
To drink. To draw the remains of. To drink (wine) repeatedly. تَسَمَّل
To be lean (man). To contract (shade). إِسْمَالَّ
Shabby clothes. سَمَل ج أَسْمَال
Shabby, worn out. سَمِل وسَمَلَة وسَمُول وسَمِيل
Water-worm. سَمَال
سَمَلَة وسَمْلَة ج سَمَل وأَسْمَال وسِمَال وسُمُول Black mud. Remainder of water.
Remainder (of wine). سُمْلَان
Small cup; saucer. سُوَمْلَة
Bare, even desert. ✱ سَمْلَقَة ج سَمَالِق
To be or become fleshy. ✱ سَمِن a سِمَنًا وسَمَانَةً, وتَسَمَّن
To put butter in (food). To feed a. o. with butter. سَمَن o سَمْنًا, وسَمَّن ه وه
To fatten a. o. To prepare a. th. with butter. To give butter to a. o. سَمَّن ه وه
To be fat naturally. To possess butter, fat flocks. To purchase, to possess a fat beast. أَسْمَن
To ask for fat beasts. إِسْتَسْمَن
To find a. o. fat. — ه
Melted butter. سَمْن ج سُمُون وأَسْمُن وسُمْنَان
Fattening medicine. سُمْنَة
سُمَانَى (سُمَانَاة *un.*) ج سُمَانَيَات, ✧ وسُمُن
Quail. (سُمَّنَة *un.*) ج سَمَامِن
Sect of Indian metempsychosists. السُّمَنِيَّة
Seller of butter. Paint. ✧ Grocer. سَمَّان
Fat (man, land). سَمِين ج سَمِينَة ج سِمَان
Chaste (speech). Numerous (household).
Naturally plump, fat. مُسْمِن
Fattened, become fat. مُسَمَّن
Azure. Blue sapphire (gem). P سَمَنْجُونِيّ وإِسْمَنْجُونِيّ
Salamander. *Asbestos*, amianthus. سَمَنْدَر وسَمَيْدَر
Phenix (fabulous bird). ✱ سَمَنْدَل وسَمَنْد
To run without respite (horse). To be confounded (man). ✱ سَمَه a سُمُوهًا
To let (beasts) pasture. سَمَّه ه
Gossamer. Atmosphere. سُمَّهَى
Lies. Vain things. — وسُمَّيْهَى وسُمَيْهَى وسُمَّيْهَاء وسُمَيْهَاء
To mix up (a story) with lies. To twist (a rope) strongly. ✱ سَمْهَج ه
Falsehood. سِمْهَاج
Fat (boy). Large (country). Misleading desert. ✱ سَمَهْدَر
To bear one year (grain-seed). ✱ سَمْهَر
To be hard (spear, affair). To be thick (darkness). To be dry and tough (thorn). — اسْمَهَرَّ
Hard, strong (spear). سَمْهَرِيّ
To be high, raised. To go hunting. ✱ سَمَا o سُمُوًّا
To aspire to. سَمَت نَفْسُهُ إِلَى
To raise (the eyes). — ب
To be raised to (the eyes). — ل
To name, to call a. o. by his name. — o سُمُوًّا, وسَمَّى وأَسْمَى ه ه او ب

To polish (speech). سَنَّنَ ه
To point a spear. — ه إلى
To grow (teeth of a child). أَسَنَّ
To discharge (water). To make teeth to grow (God). — ه وه
To be aged, old. أَسَنَّ واستسَنَّ
To pick o's teeth. To prance (horse). To move about (mirage). To be discharged (water). To be conspicuous (road). استَنَّ
Tooth (of animals, of a comb, of a saw). Nib of a pen. Horn. Clove of garlic. سِنّ ج أسنان وأسِنَّة وأسُنّ
Age ; lifetime. Coeval. — ج أسنان
Dandelion, lion's-tooth (*plant*). سِنّ الأسد
✧ *Denlaria*, tooth-wort. حُشَيشة الاسنان
He is advanced in age. طَعَن في السِنّ
Road ; conduct ; method. سَنَن وسِنَن وسُنَن وسُنُن
Face. Nature. Behaviour. Religious law, *Sunna*. سُنَّة ج سُنَن
(*un.* سُنّي) أهل السُنَّة والسِنَّة
The Sunnites. (*opp. to* شيعة)
Two-headed axe. سِنَّة ج سِنَن
Spear-head. Whetstone. Flies. سِنان ج أسِنَّة
He manages spears as he likes. هُوَ أطوَع السِنَان
Tooth-brush. Tooth-powder. سَنُون
Whetted. Fallings of a whetstone. Bare (soil). سَنِين
Wind. Heap. Long mound of sand. سَنِينة ج سَنَائِن
More aged, older. أَسَنّ
Whetstone ; grinding-stone. مِسَنّ ج مَسَانّ
Aged, old. مُسِنّ ج مَسَانّ
Polished (marble). Spotted shining face. Stinking (mire). Bright (face). مَسنُون
Beaten (road). مُستَنّ ومُستَسَنّ
Thirst. Head of a pulley. Edge of the vertebra. سِنّين ج سَنَاسِين
Whetstone, emery. سُنباذج P
Small meat pie. سَنبُوسَق وسَنبُوسَك Ts
Boat, skiff. ☆ سُنبُوق
Elder-tree. ✧ سُنبُوقة وسَبُوقة وسُنبُق وإسنبق

To give a name, to name. سَمَّى ه وب
To mention.
To invoke the name of God upon. — في
To vie in glory with. سَامَى ه
To raise a. th. أَسمَى إسمَاء ه
To be called, named. تَسَمَّى تَسَمِّيًا
To claim relationship to. — ب وإلى
To vie together in glory. تَسَامَى تَسَامِيًا
They mounted on horseback. تَسَامَوا على الخَيل
To put on shooting-boots. To hunt gazelles. إِستَمَى
To pay a visit to. To judge well of a. o. — ه
To ask the name of. إِستَسمَى ه وه
Height, highness. سُمُوّ
سَمَاء ج سَمَاوَات أَسمِيَة وسُمِيّ وسِمِيّ
Sky ; canopy of heaven. Cloud. Rain. Roof. Back of a horse.
The Arabs. بَنُو مَاء السَّمَاء
Tent before a house. Figure seen from afar. سَمَاوَة
Good repute, fame. سُمًا
Heavenly. ✧ North wind. سَمَاوِي
✧ Sky-blue colour.
إسم وأُسم ج أسماء وأسامِي وأسماوات
Name. Noun. ✧ Fame.
True name of God supposed to work miracles. الاسم الاعظم واسم الجَلَالة
In the name of God. ✧ Willingly. بِسم الله
High. Equal. Namesake. سَمِيّ م سَمِيَّة
سَامٍ ج سَامُون وسُمَاة م سَامِية ج سَوَام وسَامِيَات
High, lofty, sublime.
Hunters. سُمَاة
Hunter's gaiters. مِسمَاة
Named ; aforesaid. مُسَمًّى
To whet (a knife). To sharpen (the appetite). ☆ سَنّ o سَنًّا وسَنَّنَ ه
To mount a spear-head. To clean (the teeth). To urge on (camels). To spear a. o. To seize with the teeth. To break the teeth of. To facilitate a. th. To undo (a knot). To manage (camels) well. To pour water. To fashion clay. ✧ To indent. سَنّ ه وه
To establish a law upon. To pour (water) upon. سَنّ ه على
To follow a path. سَنّ واستَسَنّ ه

a. o. (science).
To be rancid (oil). سَنِخ a سَنَخًا
To eat to excess. — من الطَّعام
Origin. Socket (of a tooth). Fit of fever. سِنْخ ج أَسْنَاخ
Fetid smell. Dirt. سَنْخَة وسَنَاخَة
To rely, to stay o.'s self on. ✡ سَنَد o سُنُودًا, وتَسَانَد واسْتَنَد إلى
To be near (the age of fifty). — ل
To wear on a streaked garment. سَنَّد
To prop, to strengthen a. th. سَنَّد ه
To back. To assist a. o. سَانَد ه
To reward a. o. for. — ه على
To use dissemblant vowel before the rhyme-letter. — شِعْرَه وفي شِعْرِه سِنَادًا ومُسَانَدَة
To ascend (a mountain). To strive in running. سَنَد وأَسْنَد في
To make a. o. to go up. — ه فى
To stay a. o. upon. أَسْنَد ه الى
To rest a tradition upon. — ه الى
To have recourse to (God). إِسْتَنَد الى
Stay, support. Acclivity; summit of a mountain. سَنَد ج أَسْنَاد
Gnaphalium fruticosum, cotton-weed. سِنْدَة
Kind of streaked clothes. ✧ Receipt, written statement. Title-deed. سِنَاد
The Sind. River Indus (*coll*). سِنْد
Inhabitant of the Sind. سِنْدِي ج سُنَّاد وأَسْنَاد
Strong she-camel. Poetical licence. إِسْنَاد ج أَسَانِيد
Ascription of a tradition. Relation of the attribute to its subject. إِسْنَاد
سَنْدَان ج سَنَادِين و✧ سِدَّان ج سَدَادِين
Anvil.
Holm, evergreen oak. P سِنْدِيَان (*un.* سِنْدِيَانَة)
Time, epoch. Attribute (*in grammar*). Hymiaritic characters. Spurious. مُسْنَد ج مَسَانِد
Couch, pillow. مِسْنَد و✧ مَسْنَد ج مَسَانِد
They went forth under various standards. خَرَجُوا مُتَسَانِدِين
To go fast. ✡ سَنْدَر
Birch (tree). Measure for corn. سَنْدَرَة
Bold. Tall. White (blade). Lion. Big-eyed. Good. Bad. سَنْدَرِي

Kind of run. ✡ سُنْبُك ج سَنَابِك
Forepart of the hoof. Edge of a sword. ✧ Small boat. Punch.
To put forth ears (corn). ✡ سَنْبَل
Ears of corn. ✧ Hyacinth (plant). سُنْبُل (*un.* سُنْبُلَة) ج سَنَابِل
سُنْبُل الطِّيب والعَصَافِير و✧ السُّنْبُل الهِنْدِي
Andropogon nardus, Indian spikenard.
Nardus Cellica, kind of spikenard. سُنْبُل رُومِي
Spica Virginis. (Zodiacal sign). السُّنْبُلَة
To experience drought. ✡ سنت — أَسْنَت
To marry a noble woman (low-born but rich man). تَسَنَّت
Cheese. Honey. Dates. سَنُّوت وسِنُّوت
Anethum graveolens, garden-dill. Cumin.
Barren (land). Destitute (man). سَنِت ومُسْنِت
Year of drought. سَنِيت ومُسْنِت
To spot, to stain. ✡ سَنَج o سَنْجًا ه
Mark of smoke. سِنَاج
Metal weights of a balance. Steel-yard. ✧ Bayonet. P سَنْجَة ج سَنْجَات
White speckled with black. سُنْجَة
Red jujube. P سُنْج
Speckled (garment). مُسَنَّج
Minever; grey squirrel. P سِنْجَاب
Banner. Turkish province. Governor. سَنْجَق ج سَنَاجِق
Greyish, ash-coloured. P سِنْجَابِي
To occur to the mind (thought). To be easy to a. o. (poetry). ✡ سَنَح a سُنْحًا وسُنُوحًا وسُنُحًا ل
To insinuate a. th. — ب
To turn a. o. away from. — ه عن
To smite a. o. with an evil. — ب وعلى
— سُنُوحًا, وسَانَح ومُسَانَحَة وسِنَاحًا وسَانَح
To cross to the right (game).
To shelter o.'s self from (the wind). تَسَنَّح من
To ask a. o. to explain. — ه واسْتَسْنَح عن
Good omen, luck. Middle (of a road) سَنَح
Passing on the right side of a hunter (game). سَانِح ج سَوَانِح
Pearls. Ornament. سَنِيح ج سُنُح
To be rooted in ✡ سَنَخ o سُنُوخًا في

Sandarach ; juniper-resin. سِندَرُوس P
Copal resin. سِندَرُوس بلّوري
Fine silk-brocade. سُندُس P
To be ill-natured. ✻ سَنِرَ a سَنَرًا
Armour. سَنَوَّر
Cat. Prince. Vertebra of the neck. سِنَّور ج سَنَانِير
Musk-cat, civet. سِنَّور الزَّبَاد
To be beardless. ✻ سَنُطَ o سَنَاطَةً وسَنِطَ a سَنَطًا
Acacia Nilotica (plant). سَنط
سِنَاط وسِنَاط وسُنُوط ج سُنُط وأسْنَاط
Beardless.
Blacksmith's hammer. سِنْتَاب
Dulcimer. سِنطِير وسَنطُور G
Length. ✻ سَنطلَة
Sluggish walk. Stooping of the head. سَنطَالَة
✻ سَنَع a o وسَنُع o سَنَاعَةً وسُنُوعًا (ضدّ شَنُع)
To be gracious.
To feel a pain in the wrist. To have fine children. To be gracious (child). أسْنَع
Wrist. Lines in the hand. سِنع ج سِنَعَة وأسنَاع
Tall, fine, gracious. سَنِيع وأسْنَع
The weasel. الشُّنعْبَة
Mountain-road. سَنِيعَة ج سَنَائِع
To precede the (others : camel). ✻ سَنَف o i سَنْفًا, وأسْنَف ة
To gird a camel. — وأسْنَف ة
To blow violently (wind). To raise neck (camel). To appear near (lightnings). أسْنَف
Stripped branch. Leaf. سَنف ج سُنُوف
سِنف (un. سِنفَة) ج سِنف وجج سِنَفَة
Pericarp, pod. Company.
Camel's girth. سِنَاف ج سُنُف وسُنُف
The two pieces of wood on both sides of a pulley. سَنفَتَان وسُنفَتَان
Emery. ✧ سَنفِيرَة
Symphytum, comphrey (*pl*). سَنفِيتُون G
Affected with dearth (soil). مُسْنِفَة
Lean (she-camel).
Camel shifting his saddle forwards or backwards. مِسْنَاف ج مَسَانِيف
To suffer indigestion from milk (young one). ✻ سَنِق a سَنَقًا
To soften a. o. (luxury). أسْنَق

White star. سُنَّيق ج سُنَّيقَات وسَنَائِيق
Whitewashed, plastered house.
Pretty woman. ◻ سُنُّوقَة
To be a tinman. ✧ سَنكَر
✧ To frame (a picture).
Tinman. ✧ سَنكَرِيّ ج سَنَاكِرَة
Martyrology. سِنكِسَار G
To be large in its hump (camel). ✻ سَنِم a سَنَمًا
To fatten (a camel's hump : pasture). سَنَّم وأسنَم ة
To fill (a vessel, a measure). سَنَّم ه
To raise. To make convex (a grave). To ascend upon.
To rise high (blaze, smoke). أسنَم
To mount (a camel). تَسَنَّم ه
To overtake a. o. — ة
Camel's hump, prominence. Chief of a tribe. سَنَام ج أسْنِمَة
Big-humped (camel). In blossom (plant). سَنِم
Fruit of the thistle نَصِيّ when dry. إسْنَام
Blossom. Summit. سَنَمَة
Nectar ; water of Paradise. تَسْنِيم
Moon. Night-robber. ✻ سنمر — سِنِمَّار
Name of a Greek architect.
Anchovy. سَنمُورَة T
To be very old. ✻ سَنِه a سَنَهًا, وتَسَنَّه
To bear every year (tree). سَانَه
To make an agreement with a. o. for one year. — ة
To be old, mouldy (bread). تَسَنَّه
Year. Barrenness. سَنَة ج سَنَهَات
Bearing every two years (tree). سَنهَاء
To irrigate a land (water-wheel, cloud). To flash. ✻ سَنَا o سَنْوًا وسَنَاوَةً ه
To draw water for o.'s self. — ل
To make a contract with a. o. for one year. سَانَى مُسَانَاةً وسِنَاء
Year. Unfruitfulness. Barren land. سَنَة ج سِنُون وسَنَوَات وسَنِين
Year of drought. سَنْوَاء
Yearly. سَنَوِيّ
✧ Anniversary. عِيد سَنَوِيّ
Irrigating water-wheel. سَانِيَة ج سَوَانٍ
Beast for working a wheel.
Watered with a water-engine (ground). مَسْنُوّ ومَسْنِيّ

Wakeful. سُهُد ومُسَهَّد
Strong youth. سَهْوَد
More vigilant than thee. أسهد رَأيًا مِنكَ
To spend the night awake. To flash by night (lightning). * سَهِر a سَهَرًا
To wake in company of. سَاهَر ه
To keep a. o. awake. أسهَر ه
Wakefulness. Sleeplessness. سَهَر وسُهَار
Even-tide. سَهْرَة
Sleepless night. لَيْل سَاهِر
Surface of the earth. Inexhaustible spring. Untrodden desert. Hell. Moon Syria. سَاهِرَة
Wakefulness. Abundance. Halo, sheath of the moon. سَاهُور
The moon has entered its sheath. دَخَل القَمَر في السَّاهُور
Wakeful. سَهَّار وسُهَرَة
To be in the pangs of death. * سَهَف a سَهْفًا
To burn with thirst. To pine away. سَهِف a سَهَفًا
To make little of. إستَهَف ه
Fish scales. سَهَف
Thirst-giving food. طَعَام مَسْهَفَة
Unable to quench his thirst. مَسْهُوف
To blow in a gale (wind). * سَهَك a سَهْكًا
To raise the dust (wind). – ه
To run gently (beast). – سُهُوكًا
To have a foul smell. سَهِك a سَهَكًا
Foul smell of (sweat, fish). سَهَك وسَهْكَة وسُهُوكَة
Stinking. سَهِك
رِيح سَاهِكَة وسَهُوك وسَيْهَك وسَيْهُوك وسَهْكَة
Violent, tempestuous (wind).
Leeward place. مَسْهَك ومَسْهَكَة
To be smooth, even (earth). * سَهُل o سُهُولَة
To be easy (affair). سَهُل o سَهَالَة
To level (the ground). سَهَّل ه
To facilitate a. th. – ه ل وعلى
To be compliant with. سَاهَل ه
To come to a plain. أسهَل
To relax a. o. (medicine). To find a. th. easy. – ه وه
To be relaxed (bowels). أسهِل
To become easy. تَسَهَّل
To show compliance to. تَسَاهَل

Dam. مُسَنَّاة ج مُسَنَّوات ومُسَنَّيَات
To be high in rank. * سَنِيَ a سَنَاء
To loose (a knot). To open (a door). سَنَّى سَنْيًا وسَنَّى ه
To ascend upon. سَنَّى وتَسَنَّى
To treat a. o. kindly. سَانَاهُ مُسَانَاة وسِنَاء
To remain the whole year. To light a house (lightning, fire). أسنَى
To exalt, to raise a. th. – ه
To give a splendid reward. أسنَى لَهُ الجَائِزَة
To be altered by time. To be ready, facilitated. To be open (lock). To be in good circumstances. To be raised. تَسَنَّى
To please a. o. – ه
Lightning. Kind of silk. سَنًى وسَنَا
Common senna. سَنَا وسَنَا مَكِّيّ وحِجَازِيّ
High rank. سَنَاء
Noble, illustrious man. رَجُل سَنَايَا
The whole, the entire thing. السِّنَايَة
Noble. Magnificent (reward). سَنِيّ م سَنِيَّة
Swallow. سُنُونُو
To take a. th. * سَهَب a سَهْبًا ه
To dart forth ahead (horse). To be unsatiable (man). أسهَب
To let (a beast) pasture freely. To suck (his mother: young). – ه وه
To be profuse in speech. – في الكَلَام
To bestow generously. – واستَهَب
To lose the mind from the bite of a snake or from love. To yield no water (well). أُسهِب
Wide desert. Spirited (horse). سَهْب
Far-extending plain. سُهْب ج سُهُوب
Deep (well). سَهْبَة ومُسْهَبَة
To blow violently (wind). * سَهَج a سَهْجًا
To pound (perfumes). To sweep (the soil: wind). – ه
To travel the whole night. – لَيْلَتَهُ
Violent (gale). سَاهِج وسَهُوج وسَيْهَج
Windward. Leeward place. مَسْهَج
To wake, to be sleepless. * سَهِد a سَهَدًا, وتَسَهَّد
To keep a. o. awake (grief). سَهَّد ه
Wake, sleeplessness. سُهْد وسُهَاد وسَهْدَة

To find a. th. easy. إستسهل ه وه
A plain. Easy. Crow. سَهل ج سُهول
Compliant (man). سَهل الخُلق
Little fleshy on the cheeks. سَهل الوجه
Sea-sand brought up. سِهل وسِهلة
Easiness. سُهولة
Diarrhea. إسهال
Easy. Sandy (river-bed). سَهِل
Canopus (*constell*). سُهَيل
Proverbial liar. سُهَيلة
Laxative, purgative. سَهُول مُسهل
To pine away. To frown. ✱ سَهَم a وسَهُم o سُهومًا وسُهومة
To be smitten by simoom. سُهِم
To win a. o. in a game of chance. ساهَم ه
To cast lots between. أسهم بين
To partake a. th. between. تساهم ه
To draw lots. — واستهم
Arrow. Beam of a house. Mast of a ship. Measure of 6 cubits. سَهم ج سِهام
Lot, share. — ج أسهُم وسُهمان وسُهمة
✧ Share of a joint stock. ✧ Ticket in a lottery.
Sagitta (*constell*). سَهم الرامي
Kindred. Portion. Lot. سُهمة
Intense heat. Prudent people. سُهم
Emaciated she-camel. ساهِمة ج سَواهِم
Gossamer. Great heat ; simoon. سَهام
Rocket, squib. ✧ سَهُومة
Leanness. Disease of camels. سُهام
Fellow-player. Share-holder. مُساهِم
Striped garment. مُسَهَّم
Emaciated (camel). مَسهوم ومُسهَّم
To overlook ; to be unmindful of. To be diverted from. ✱ سَها o سَهوًا وسُهوًّا عن وفي
Innumerable flocks. مال لا يُسهَى
To be manageable (camel). سَهُو o سَهارة
To be compliant with. ساهى ه
To construct (a booth). أسهى ه
Dim star in ursa major. سُها وسُهى
Unmindfulness. Cool (water). Gentle (camel). سَهو
Portion of the night. سِهو وسِهواء
Shelf. Closet. Curtain, Booth. Window. سَهوة ج سِهاء
Neglectful. Heedless. ساهٍ وسَهوان

To be bad, wicked. ✱ ساء o سَواء
— سَوءًا وسُوءًا وسَواءة وسَوائية وسَوائة ومَساءة ومَسائية ومَساية ومَساء ومَسائية ه
To wrong. To grieve a. o.
To think ill of a. o. ساء بهِ ظنًّا
To blame, to reprove. سَوَّأ تَسوئة وتَسويئًا ه على
Improve, do not corrupt. سَوِّ ولا تُسَوِّئ
To corrupt, to mar a. th. أساء إساءة ه
To do evil to a. o. — الى
To think ill of. — بهِ الظنَّ
To be ill treated. To be offended. إستاء
Evil, mischief. Leprosy. Wretched. Vice. سُوء ج أسواء ومَساءة ج مَساوئ
Wicked, wretched man. رَجُل سَوء والسُّوء
Foul action. Hell-fire. سُوءى
Bad, evil, shameful. سَيِّئ م سَيِّئة
Sin. Bad action. سَيِّئة ج سَيِّئات
Pudenda. Turpitude. Corpse. سَوءة ج سَوءات
Worse. Ugly, foul. أسوأ م سُوءى
Evil action, word. مَساءة ج مَساوئ
To walk gently. ✱ ساج o سَوجًا وسُواجًا وسَوَجانًا
Round darkish cloak. Teak tree. Indian plantain-tree. ساج ج سِيجان (*un.* ساجة)
✧ Castanets. ساجات
To lead a wandering life. ✧ ساح o
Court-yard. Open-space. Square. ساحة ج ساح وسُوح وساحات
✧ Hermit. Pilgrim. سائح وسَوّاح ج ✧ سُوّاح
✧ Sun-drop (*plant*). حَشيشة السُّوّاح
To sink in the earth (legs). ✱ ساخ o سَوخًا وتَسوَّخ في الطين
To subside (in water). — في الماء
ساخت بهم الأرضُ سُيوخًا وسُؤوخًا وسَوَخانًا
The earth has swallowed them up.
Mire, slime. سُواخ وسُواخي وسُواخِية
To be noble, glorious. ✱ ساد o سِيادة وسَيدودة وسُودَدًا وسُؤدُدًا وسُودَدًا
To rule. To lead (a tribe). To overcome a. o. in glory. — ه
✧ To overtop a. th. ساد على
To be black. سَوِد a سَوَدًا, واسودّ واسوادّ
To be bold. سُوِّد
To make a. o. chief. سَوَّد ه
To blacken a. th. ✧ To make — ه وه

سود

canvass. To manure (a field).

سَوَّد وَجهَهُ وعِزَّهُ To blacken the character. To disgrace a. o.

سَاوَد ه To use deceit with. To speak secretly. To meet a. o. in darkness. To contend with a. o. for mastery.

أَسْوَد وأَسَاد To beget a black boy; or a boy who is a chief.

تَسَوَّد To become a chief. To marry.

✧ To be blackened. ✧ To be manured (field).

إِسْتَاد ه To kill a chief. To ask from (a tribe) a woman in marriage.

سُود وسُوَّد وسُوْدُد Authority of a chief.

سُود Achyranthes polystachia (plant).

سَوْد ج أَسْوَاد (un. سَوْدَة) Valley full of black stones.

سَوَاد Blackness. Numerous flock. Great number. Manure.

– البَلَد Suburbs, villages.

سَوَاد وأَسْوَد العَين The black of the eye.

سَوَاد وأَسْوَد وسَوْدَاء وسُوَيْدَا القَلْب The heart's core.

– ج أَسْوِدَة وجج أَسَاوِد Person.

سُوَاد Secret speaking. Disease of the liver. Sheep disease. Yellowness of the face. Spot on the nails.

سَوَادِيَّة وسُودَانِيَّة والاسْوَد Sparrow.

سُودَان Negroes. Soudan.

سُودُود Ruellia intrusa (plant).

سِيد مـ سِيدَة ج سِيدَان Lion. Wolf.

✧ Chief.

سَيِّد ج أَسْيَاد وسَيَائِد Chief, lord. Husband. A descendant of Mohammed.

السَّيِّدَة ✧ Our blessed Lady.

سَائِد ج سَادَة Chief, prince.

سِيَادَة Authority. ✧ Lordship (title).

أَسْوَد مـ سَوْدَا ج سُود Black. Greater.

أَسْوَد الكَبِد Enemy, foe.

الحَجَر الاسْوَد The black stone of the Caaba.

مـ أَسْوَدَة ج أَسَاوِد Large snake.

سَوْدَا وسُوَيْدَا Spleen. Melancholy.

الأَسْوَدَان Dates and water. The snake and the scorpion.

مُسَوَّدَة ✧ Black bottle. Canvass of a writing.

مُسَوَّدَة ومُسْوَدَّة Bad, severe (days).

سَوَّدَن ه To grieve, to vex a. o.

سوس

✧ تَسَوَّدَن To be peevish, grieved.

٭ سَار ٥ سَوْرًا، وسَوَّر وتَسَوَّر ه to scale, to climb (a wall).

سَار ٥ سَوْرًا وسُؤُورًا الى To assault, to assail.

– في الرَّأْس To rush to the head (wine).

سِرْ شِرْ Forward! Go on.

سَوَّر ه To put bracelets to.

– ه To wall (a town).

سَاوَر مُسَاوَرَةً وسِوَارًا ه To intoxicate a. o. To rush upon.

تَسَوَّر To put on bracelets (woman). To be walled (town).

سُور ج أَسْوَار وسِيرَان Town-wall. Species of fig. Noble camels.

P سَوَارِي ✧ Horsemen. Cavalry.

سَوْرَة Assault of (wine). Paroxysm of fever. Outburst of anger. Strength.

سُورَة ج سُوَر وسُور وسُورَات Rank, dignity. Chapter of the Koran. Sign. Row of stones in a wall.

سِوَار وسُوَار وأَسْوَار ج أَسَاوِر وأَسْوِرَة وسُؤُور وأَسَاوِرَة Bracelet.

سَوَّار Easily intoxicated. Sharp (dog).

أَسْوَار واِسْوَار ج أَسَاوِر وأَسَاوِرَة Clever rider. Archer.

مِسْوَر ومِسْوَرَة ج مَسَاوِر Leathern pillow.

مُسَوَّر Powerful (king). Part of the wrist wearing bracelets.

سَاس ٥ سِيَاسَةً ه To rule (a people). To tend. (A horse). To train. To manage (an affair).

سَاس a سَوْسًا وسَوِس وأَسَاس وأَسْوَاسًا To be attacked by grubs (sheep).

بِيس وسَوَّس وأَسَاس وتَسَوَّس To be worm-eaten (grain, wood).

سَوَّس ه ل To facilitate a. th. to.

سُوِّس To be invested with authority.

✧ سَايَس الامور To manage affairs well.

سُوس ج سِيسَان (un. سُوسَة) Liquorice (plant). Moth-worm; weevil. Nature. Origin.

سُوَاس Disease in the neck of horses.

سِيَاسَة Authority. Politics. Tending of horses.

السِّيَاسَة المَدَنِيَّة Political economy.

سَائِس ج سَاسَة وسُوَّاس Manager. Groom. ✧ Runner.

سَاسَان A celebrated wily beggar.

To give a. th. to a. o. — ه ل
Grant me a respite. أَسِغ لِي غُصَّتِي
To be twin-born with. أَسْوَغَ اسْوَاغًا ه
Twin-born. Twin-brother. A brother. (m. f.) سَوْغ وسَوْغَة
Digestible. سِوَاغ
Easily swallowed. سَائِغ وسَيِّغ وأَسْوَغ ومُسْتَسَاغ
To be smitten by murrain (cattle). ✱ سَاف o a سَوْفًا
To smell a. th. — o سَوْفًا, وأَسْتَاف
To bear a. th. patiently. سَاف على
To put off, to postpone. سَوَّف ه
To give to a. o. full power in. — ه ه
To communicate a secret. To smell at. سَاوَف ه
To lose (a son, cattle). أَسَاف
Particle indicating the future (*longer than* س). سَوْف
Thou shalt see. سَوْف تَرَى
He lives on hope. يَقْتَات السَّوْف
Murrain. Cattle disease. سُوَاف
سَاف ج آسُف وسَافَات وسُوفَة ج سُوف وسُوَف
Row of bricks, clay; soft ground.
Distance. مَسَافَة ج مَسَاوِف وسِيفَة ومَسَاف
Bereft of a son. مُسِيف
Taken from his parents (son). مُسَاف
Nose. مَسَاف
Bereft of her son (mother). مِسْيَاف
✱ سَاق o سَوْقًا وسِيَاقَةً ومَسَاقًا, واسْتَاق
To drive (a beast). To impel, to urge a. o. إِسْتِيَاقًا ه
He treated him like other people. سَاقَهُ مَسَاق غَيْرِهِ
He carries on his narrative. يَسُوق الحَدِيث
To send the dowry to (a woman). — ه إلى وأَسَاق ه ه
To convey a. th. To give up the ghost. — سَوْقًا وسِيَاقًا
He gave up his ghost. — نَفْسَهُ وبِنَفْسِهِ
To hit a. o. on the shank. — ه
To have a stem (plant). سَوِّق
To intrust a. o. with. — ه ه
To contend with a. o. in driving. سَاوَق ه
To give (camels) to drive to. أَسَاق واسْتَسَاق و✧ سَوَّق ه ه
To carry on a trade. تَسَوَّق

Craft of a swindler. طَرِيقَة سَاسَان
P سُوسَان وسُوسَن وسَوْسَن (un. سَوْسَنَة)
Lily. Iris. *Pancratium*.
To whip (a beast). ✱ سَاط o سَوْطًا ه
To mix up (liquids, affairs). To begin (war). — وسَوَّط ه
His soul is oppressed. سَاطَت نَفْسُهُ سَوْطَانًا
To be intricate (affair). إِسْتَوَط
Leathern whip; a lash. Lot. Misfortune. Pond. سَوْط ج سِيَاط وأَسْوَاط
They agree on all points. يَتَعَاطِيَان سَوْطًا وَاحِدًا
Sun-ray penetrating through a hole. سَوْط بَاطِل
Hotch-potch of peas, onions. سُوَيْطَاء
Policeman with a whip. سَوَّاط
Instrument for mixing. مِسْوَط ومِسْوَاط
Horse going only by whip. مِسْوَاط
To pasture freely (cattle). To be lost (thing). ✱ سَاع o سَوْعًا
To bargain, to hire a. o. for the hour. سَاوَع مُسَاوَعَةً وسِوَاعًا ه
To neglect. To lose a. th. أَسَاع إِسَاعَةً ه
To procrastinate. أَسْوَع إِسْوَاعًا
First night-watch. سَوْع وسُوَاع
Hour of 60 minutes. A while. Present time. Distance. Hour of the resurrection. ✧ Clock, watch. سَاعَة ج سَاع وسَاعَات
Sun-dial. — شَمْسِيَّة
Sand-clock; clepsydra. سَاعَة رَمْلِيَّة
Breviary. Book of prayers. ✧ سَوَاعِيَّة
Painful hour. سَاعَة سَوْعَاء
Still, yet, till now. لِلسَّاعَة ✧ لِلسَّا
Watchmaker. ✧ سَاعَاتِي
He has done it on the spot. فَعَلَهُ مِن سَاعَتِهِ
A certain woman. Idol in Ruhat. سُوَاع
✧ Fickle. سُوَيْعَاتِي
Lavisher, spendthrift. مِضْيَاع مِسْيَاع ل
To be easily swallowed. ✱ سَاغ o سَوْغًا وسَوَاغًا وسَوْغَانًا
To be permitted. ✧ To be convenient. — ل
To swallow (food) easily. — o سَوْغًا وسَاغ i سَيْغًا وأَسَاغ ه
The earth has swallowed him up. سَلَقَت بِهِ الارض
To allow, to permit a. th. سَوَّغ ه

Flabbiness of the belly, the limbs. سَوَل وسَوْلة
Annual, official almanac. P سالنامة
Equal, match. سَوِيل
Having a flabby hanging belly. أَسْوَل م سَوْلاء ج سُول
Large bucket. سَوْلاء
To go to pasture (flock). To pass along (wind). ✱ سَام o سَوْمًا وسُوَامًا
To offer (goods) for sale. سَام ه
To ask the price of (goods). — واسْتَام ه وب
To hover over (bird). سَام على
To impose a difficult task upon. — وسَوَّم ه ه
He has wronged him. سَامَهُ خَسْفًا
To send (a beast) to pasture. To mark (a horse). سَوَّم ه
To let a. o. act freely in. — ه ل وفي
To make a raid against. — على
سَاوَم مُسَاوَمَةً وسِوَامًا ب وتَسَاوَم في وإسْتَام
To bargain, To chaffer for (goods). ب وعلى
To send (cattle) to pasture. To dig a hollow by a well. أَسَام ه وه
To cast the eyes upon. — إلى بِبَصَرِهِ
To set a mark upon. تَسَوَّم
Hollow dug in the ground near a pit. Bamboo. Death. She (Noah's son). سَام (un. سَامَة)
Vein in a mine. سَامَة ج سَام
Mark, sign, appearance. سِيمَة وسُومَة وسِيمَاء
Sign. Beauty. Natural magic. سِيمِيَا وسِيمِيَاء
Pasturing cattle. سَائِمَة
Camels pasturing freely. Two hollows beneath a horse's eyes. سَوَام
Quick passage. مَسَام
Wood at the foot of a door-post. مَسَامَة
To be worth. ✱ سَوِي a سَوًى وسَاوَى ه
To be equivalent to.
It is worthless. لا يَسْوَى ولا يُسَاوِي شَيْئًا
To level a. th. To complete, to arrange a. th. سَوَّى تَسْوِيَةً ه
He has been swallowed up. سُوِّيَت عَلَيْهِ الأَرْضُ
To render things equivalent, equal. سَوَّى وسَاوَى ه ب وبَيْن

To walk in a file (camels). To press together (sheep). تَسَاوَق
To be driven (beast). إنْسَاق
Leg, shank; stem of a plant; trunk. Side of a triangle. سَاق ج سُوق وسِيقَان وأَسْوُق
Male ring-dove. سَاق حُرّ
Virgo (Zodiacal sign). سَاق الأَسَد
Stapella (plant). سَاق الغُرَاب
Medicinal plant. — الحُمَام
Capillus Veneris, maiden-hair (*plant*). السَّاق الأَسْوَد
War became fierce. قَامَت الحَرْبُ على سَاقٍ
They strive, they exert themselves diligently. قَام القَوْم على سَاق
He begot 3 sons consecutively. وُلِد لَهُ ثَلاث وَلَدٍ سَاقًا على سَاق
The affair becomes difficult. كَشَف الأَمْرُ عن سَاقِهِ
Rear-guard. Retinue. سَاقَة
Market, mart, fair. سُوق ج أَسْوَاق
The thickest of a battle. سُوق الحَرْب
Subjects of a king. (*m. pl.*) سُوقَة
Waterless cloud driven by wind. سَيِّق
Cattle driven by the enemy. Screen of a hunter. سَيِّقَة ج سَيَائِق وسَيِّقَات
Market-people. ✧ Grocer. Vulgar (man, word). سُوقِيّ
Gruel of parched barley. Wine. سَوِيق ج أَسْوِقَة
Thread of a speech. Dowry. Agony. سِيَاق
Long-legged. سُوَّاق وأَسْوَق
Driver of cattle. Seller of fine flour. سَوَّاق
Servant. Relation (man). Long sloped (mountain). مُنْسَاق
To rub a. th. with. ✱ سَاك o سَوْكًا, وسَوَّك ه ب
To totter in walk. — سِوَاكًا, وتَسَاوَك
To cleanse the teeth. تَسَوَّك واسْتَاك
Tooth-stick made with the *Caparis sodata*. سِوَاك ج سُوك, ومِسْوَاك ج مَسَاوِيك
To ask (a question). To demand. ✱ سَال a سُوَالًا وسَوَالًا
To have a flaccid belly. سَوِل a سَوَلًا
To delude a. o. (Satan). سَوَّل ل
His mind enticed him to. سَوَّلَت لَهُ نَفْسُهُ أَن

Bed of a stream. Apple. سِيب ج سُيُوب
Widower. ✧ سَيِّب
She-camel freed سَائِبَة ج سُيَّب وسَوَائِب from all labour. Emancipated (slave). ✧ Shameless (woman).
Unripe dates. سَيَاب وسَيَّاب وسُيَّاب
An unripe date. Wine. سَيَابَة
To fence. ✱ سَيَّج ه
To be fenced, hedged. ✧ تَسَيَّج
Prickly hedge, fence. سِيَاج ج سِيَاجَات
Scar-fish. سِيجَان
To flow upon ✱ سَاح i سَيْحًا وسَيَحَانًا the surface of the earth (water). To turn, to move (shade).
To travel. To make a pilgrimage. — سِيَاحَة وسُيُوحًا وسَيَحَانًا وسَيْحًا
To let flow (a liquid). سَيَّح وأَسَاح ه
To speak elegantly. سَيَّح تَسْيِيحًا كَثِيرًا
To become large (belly). To be rent (clothes). إِنْسَاح
To open (heart). — بَالُهُ
Flowing water. Striped garment. سَيْح ج سُيُوح وأَسْيَاح
Journey, tour. ✧ Pilgrimage. سِيَاحَة
Implements of a pilgrim. أُهْبَة السِّيَاحَة
Devotee fasting much; wandering ascetic. Pilgrim. ✧ Tourist. Itinerant. سَائِح ج سُيَّاح وسَيَّاح ج سَيَّاحُون
Spreading calumnies about. مِسْيَاح ج مَسَايِيح
Streaked (clothes). Having many tracks (road). Wild ass. مُسَيَّح
Place of travelling. مَسَاح ومَسَاحَة ج مَسَايِح
To sink into mire (foot). To be firm, steady. ✱ سَاخ i سَيْخًا وسَيَخَانًا
Large knife. ✧ Roasting-spit. P سِيخ ج أَسْيَاخ
House of clay. سِيَاخ ج سُيُوخ
To go, to travel. To be current. ✱ سَار i سَيْرًا وتَسْيَارًا ومَسِيرًا ومَسِيرَة
To behave well. سَار سِيرَة حَسَنَة
To establish (a custom, rule). — ه
To bring a. o. — ه وب
Do not mind it. سِر عَنْكَ
To send, to make to go. سَيَّر وأَسَار ه
To render (a proverb) current. سَيَّر ه To relate (ancient stories). To stripe a garment. To take off (a saddle).

To be vile, contemptible. أَسْوَى
To render equal. To level a. th. To omit (a letter) in reading. — ه
He has been swallowed up by the earth. تَسَوَّت واسْتَوَت بِهِ الأَرْضُ
To equal. ✧ To agree together. تَسَاوَى واسْتَوَى فِي
To be mature (man). To be straightened. To be symmetrical, complete, right. To be thoroughly cooked (food.) To be ripe (fruit). إِسْتَوَى
To sit upon. — عَلَى
To direct o.'s self towards. — إِلَى
I had the same design as he. قَصَدْتُ سَوَاهُ
Except, save. سِوَى
سَوَاء مث سَوَاءَان ج أَسْوَاء سِوًى وسُوًى
Equal, like, complete. Equality. Equity. Other, else. Middlepart. ✧ Together.
They are on a par. هُمَا عَلَى حَدٍّ سَوَاء
✧ Whether ... or... سِوَاء .... سَوَا
Right. Even (soil). سَوِيّ م سَوِيَّة ج أَسْوِيَاء
Equality. Vehicle for poor people. Stuffed garment. سَوِيَّة ج سَوَايَا
Equal, alike. سِيّ (m. f.) مث سِيَّان ج أَسْوَاء
Especially. لَا سِيَّمَا ولَاسِيَّمَا
Equinoctial line. Equator. خَطّ الإِسْتِوَاء
Equal. مُسَاوٍ م مُسَاوِيَة
Curved part of a bow. ✱ سِيّ — سِيَة القَوْس ج سِيَات
Milk flowing by itself. ✱ سَيْء وسِيء ج سُيُوء
To draw milk flowing by itself. سَيَّأ ه
To let flow milk (she-camel). تَسَيَّأ
To flow by itself (milk). إِنْسَيَأ
To run (water). To wander at random. To go quickly. To be set free (beast). ✱ سَاب i سَيْبًا
To expatiate at great length. — فِي مَنْطِقِهِ
To set (a beast) free. To free (a slave). To forsake a. th. سَيَّب ه
To walk quickly (man). To glide along (serpent). إِنْسَاب إِنْسِيَابًا
Gift. Hair of the tail. Treasures. Metals. سَيْب ج سُيُوب

To strike a. o. with a sword. — وتَسَيَّف ه
To fight together with a sword. سَايَف وتَسَايَف وَاسْتَاف
To spoil the sewing of (skin). أَسَاف ه
To be stricken with a sword. أُسْتِيف
سَيْف ج سُيُوف وأَسْيَاف وأَسْيُف ومَسْيَفَة
Sword. Sword-fish. Hair of a horse's tail.
Gladiolus, corn-flag. سَيْف الغُرَاب
Three stars in *Orio*. — الجَبَّار
Dolychos polystachium (*plant*). — الرِّبَاح
Sea-shore ; side of a valley. سِيف ج أَسْيَاف
Long and thin (man). سَيْفَان م سَيْفَانَة
Armed parties of men. أَسْيَاف
Armed with a sword. سَايِف ومُسْيَاف
Executioner. سَيَّاف
Unfruitful years. Dearth. مَسَايِف
Plain-sided (coin). مُسَيَّف
To flow (water). ✡ سَال i سَيْلًا وسَيَلَانًا
To spread on a horse's nose (blaze).
To let flow (a liquid). سَيَّل وأَسَال ه
To melt a. th. To lengthen (an iron head of an arrow). أَسَال ه
Squadrons poured in. تَسَايَلَت الكَتَائِب
Torrent. Water-course. سَيْل ج سُيُول
A stream. Shower. ✧ Waistcoat-pocket. سَيْلَة
Flowing of water. سِيلَة
✧ Diarrhea. سَيَلَان البَطْن
Garnet, precious stone. Hilt of a sword. سِيلَان ج سِيَالِين
Fluid, liquid. سَائِل وسَيَّال ج سَوَايِل
✧ There is no harm. Never mind. مَا بِسَايِل
Blaze on a horse's nose. سَائِلَة و✧ سَيَّالَة ج سَوَائِل
Kind of Mimosa. *Cardeus lacteus*, wild artichoke. سَيَالَة ج سَيَال
Pouring, raining heavily (cloud). Kind of large fish. سَيَّال
Water-course. Bed of a stream. مَسِيل ج مَسَايِل ومُسُل وأَمْسِلَة ومُسْلَان
Side of the beard. مُسَال مث مُسَالَان
Mount Sinai. ✡ سِينَاء وسِينَا وطُور سِينَا
Avicenna (celebrated physician). إِبْن سِينَا

To expel a. o. from (a country). سَيَّر ه من
To keep pace with a. o. ✧ To be compliant with. سَايَر ه
To peel off (skin). تَسَيَّر
To travel together. ✧ To keep company together. تَسَايَر
To make travelling-provisions. إِسْتَار
Journey. Leather. Thong. سَيْر ج سُيُور
Course, mode of life. سِيرَة ج سِيَر
Biography. Military expedition. Imported goods. ✧ Matter of speech.
Good conduct. حُسْن السِّيرَة
✧ He began to talk about. فَتَح السِّيرَة على
Garment striped with yellow. سِيَرَاء
Pure gold. Diaphragm. Stripped palm branch. Pellicles of datestones.
The remainder. سَائِر وسَار الشَّيْء
The whole of a thing.
Planets. Caravan. سَيَّارَة ج سَيَّارَات
Distance, journey. مَسِير ومَسِيرَة
Trodden (road). Going his way (man). مَسُور
Striped (tissue). Sweetmeats. مُسَيَّر
Murulus speciosus (*pl.*). Paste made with its roots. ✧ سِيرَاس وسِبْرَاس
Jasmine. ✡ سِيس
Spine of the back. Ass's back. سِيسَاء ج سَيَاسِيّ
Assiout (town of Egypt). أَسْيُوط
To move on the earth (looming, water). ✡ ٥ سَاء i سَيْعًا وسُيُوعًا وتَسَيُّع, وإِنْسَاء
To pasture freely (cattle). سَاء
To plaster a wall with mud and straw. To grease a. th. To tar (a ship). سَيَّع ه
To dry up (plants). تَسَيَّع
To lose a. th. To neglect (camels). أَسَاع ه
Water running on the ground. سَيْع
Mixture of clay and straw. Grease for a skin. سِيَاع
Hour of the night. سِيعَاء وسِيَعَاء
Trowel. مِسْيَعَة وسِيَاع
To be easily swallowed (drink). ✡ سَاغ i سَيْغًا
To be chapped, cracked (skin). ✡ سَاف i سَيْفًا

ش

✱ شَأْب – شُؤْبُوب شَآبِيب Shower. Heat of the sun. Intensity. Blooming of beauty.
✱ شات – شَئِت Wont to stumble (horse).
✱ شَئِز a شَأَزًا وشُؤُوزَةً وشُؤَازًا To be rugged (ground).
شَئِز To fret, to be restless.
أَشْأَز ه To disturb, to startle a. o.
اِشْتَأَز To be frightened away.
شَأْز وشَئِز Rugged, uneven (soil).
✱ شَئِس a شَأَسًا To be hard (soil).
شَأْس وشَئِس Hard and stony (soil).
✱ شَئِف a شَأَفًا وشُئُف To be ulcered (sole of the foot).
– شَأَفًا وشَآفَةً ه ول To hate a. o.
شُئِف To be afraid.
إِسْتَشْأَف To corrupt, to root (ulcer).
شَـأْف Corruptedness of a wound.
شَأْفَة Root. Ulcer on the sole.
إِسْتَأْصَلَ الله شَأْفَتَهُم God extirpated their family.
✱ شَأَم a شَأْمًا ه وعلى To draw ill-luck upon a. o.
شُؤِم o شَآمَةً وشُئِم على To be inauspicious for.
شَأَم ه To send a. o. to Syria.
شَاءَم ب To pass to the left of.
أَشْأَم To go to Syria. To strut.
ما أَشْأَمَهُ How unlucky he is.
تَشَأَّم وتَشَاءَم To pretend to be a Syrian. To go to the left.
تَشَاءَم واشْتَأَم ب To bode ill of a. th.
شُؤْم Bad omen, ill luck. Black (camels).
شَأْم وشَام Syria. ✧ Damascus. Northern region.
◻ بَرّ الشَّام Syria.
شَأْمِيّ وشَامِيّ Syrian. ✧ Damascene. Northern.
شَأْمَة ومَشْأَمَة Left side.
شِئْمَة وشِيمَة ج شِيَم Nature, temper. Character. ✧ Magnanimity.
شَائِم م شَائِمَة Inauspicious, ominous.
أَشْأَم ج أَشَائِم م شُؤْمَى Unlucky, inauspicious.
اليد الشُؤْمَى The left hand.
مَشْؤُوم ومَشُوم و✧ مَيْشُوم ج مَشَائِيم Inauspicious, ominous.
✱ شَأَن a شَأْنًا ه To pursue an aim. To perform a. th. well.
إِشْأَن شَأْنَكَ What thou doest, do it well.
ما شَأَن شَأْنَكَ He did not care about thy concerns.
لأَشْأَنَنَّ شَأْنَهُم I will mar their affair.
اِشْتَأَن شَأْنَهُ وشَان شَأْنَهُ He pursued the same course as he.
شَأْن ج شُؤُون وشِئَان Momentous thing, affair. State. Condition. Dignity.
ما شَأْنُكَ What is the matter with you. What is your business.
مِن شَأْنِهِ أن He has a natural propensity to.
هُوَ سَهِل الشَّأْن He is of easy nature.
مِن شَأن ◻ على شَأن For the sake of, on account of.
✧ مِن شَان خَاطِرِي For my sake.
شَأْن ج أَشْؤُن وشُؤُون Ducts of the tears.
– ج شُؤُون Suture of the skull. Cleft growing palm-trees.
✱ شَأَى o شَأْوًا, وشَاءَى واشْتَأَى ه To precede a. o.
تَشَاءَى To scatter (people).
– ما بَيْنَهُمَا To be distant from o. a.
شَأْو Ambition. Aim. Basketful of earth. Slime.
عَدَا شَأْوًا He ran a heat.
مِشْآة ج مَشَاءٍ Basket. Slime taken from a well.
✱ شَبَّ i شَبَابًا وشَبِيبَةً, وأَشَبَّ To grow up, to become a youth.
– o i شِبَابًا وشَبِيبًا وشُبُوبًا To prance, to leap briskly (horse).
– o شَبًّا وشُبُوبًا, وشُبَّ To grow, to rise.
شَبَّ o وشُبُوبًا ه To kindle (fire). To enhance the beauty of (a lady: hair). To set off (a beast).

Figure. Phantom. ✧ Veronica, speedwell.
Cattle, flocks known by sight. أَشْبَاحِ المَال
Rafter (of a roof). شَبْحَة
Rope of a shackle binding the fore to the hind leg of a horse. شِبْحَة و✧ شَبْحَة
Long. شَبْحَان
Stripped of its bark. Strong garment. ✧ Salt-cod. مُشَبَّح
Addicted to an affair. مَشْبُوح بِأَمْر
To exult. To be insolent (man). ✢ شَبِرَ a شَبَرًا
To measure a. th. by the span. شَبَر o i شَبْرًا
To honour a. o. شَبَّرَ ه
✧ To make gestures. شَبَّر
To give a. th. to a. o. أَشْبَر ه ه
To draw near in a battle. تَشَابَر
Measure. Stature. Marriage. Dowry. Duration of life. شَبْر
Span. Lifetime. شِبْر ج أَشْبَار
Of a small stature. قَصِير الشِّبْر والشِّبْر
Wealth. Gift. Gospel. Consecrated bread. Powers. شَبَر
A thief. شَابِر الميزان
Mist, fog. ✧ شَابُورَة
Horn, bugle. H شَبُّور ج شَبُّورَات وشَبَابِير
Travelling-basket on a camel. ◻ شَبْرِيَّة
To cut a. th. to pieces. To tear its prey (hawk). ✢ شَبْرَق ه
Tattered clothes. ثَوب شَبَارِق وشُبَارِق
✧ Treat. Pocket-money. شَبْرَقَة
To repair a. th. ✢ شبص – ✧ شَبَّص ه
To be intertwisted (trees). تَشَبَّص
Entangled thorns. شَبَص
To draw magical lines on the sand. To strike out (writing). To make cuts on the skin, to scarify. ✢ شَبَط o شَبْطًا ه
To grasp, to cling to. ◻ تَشَبَّط في
February. S شُبَاط وإِشْبَاط
A large carp. شُبُّوط وشَبُّوط ج شَبَابِيط
✧ Broom made of small branches. شَبُّوط
To be satisfied, full (stomach). ✢ شَبِع a شِبَعًا وشَبَعًا ه ومن

To blaze fiercely (fire). شَبَّ i وشُبَّ
To compose amatory verses on a. o. To begin (a book). شَبَّبَ وتَشَبَّبَ ب
To have young sons. To be old (bull). أَشَبَّ
To excite (a horse). To make a. o. to become a youth (God). – ه
It was preordained for him. أُشِبَّ لَهُ
To be kindled (fire, war). تَشَبَّبَ
Alum. Blue stones of vitriol. شَبّ
Sulphate of iron. شَبّ يَمَانِيّ
Marvel of Peru (plant). شَبّ اللَّيل
From youth to old age. مِن شُبَّ إِلى دُبَّ
Youth. Beginning. شَبَاب وشَبِيبَة وشَبُوبِيَّة
The vigour of youth flowed in her. إِستَحَارَ شَبَابُهَا
I came to you in the beginning of the day. جِئتُكَ في شَبَابِ النَّهَار
Fuel. شِبَاب وشَبُوب
Enhancing. Crippled horse. Young or old (bull). شَبُوب
Flute, fife. ✧ شَبَّابَة
شَابّ و✧ شَبّ ج شُبَّان وشَبَاب وشَبَبَة
Young man from 16 to 30.
Young woman from 13 to 30. شَابَّة ج شَوَابّ وشَابَّات وشَبَائِب وشَبَّة
Full-grown (bull). شَبَب ومُشِبّ ومُشَبّ ومِشَبّ
Blazing. Beautiful. مَشْبُوب ج مَشَابِيب
Venus and Mars. المَشْبُوبَتَان
Aneth, garden-dill (*plant*). P شِبِت وشِبَّت
To lay hold upon, to cling. ✢ شَبِث a شَبَثًا, وتَشَبَّث ب
Cleaving to his adversary. شُبَثَة
Spider. Milleped. شَبَث ج شِبْثَان
Flesh-hook. شِبَّاث وشَبُّوث ج شَبَابِيث
To stretch forth the arms in prayer. To extend hands (chameleon). ✢ شَبَح a شَبْحًا
To split a. th. To extend a skin between stakes. To carve, to hew (wood). – ه
To appear. To stand erect before. – ل
To have long arms. شَبُح o شَبَاحَة
To be weak-sighted by age. شَبَّح
To enlarge. To extend a. th. – ه
Gate, large door. شَبْح
Long-armed. – ومَشْبُوح الذِّرَاعَين
Object. Body. شَبَح ج أَشْبَاح وشُبُوح

Network. Mat of reeds. Grating, lattice. ✧ Lattice work of a window. Window.
Hook, paper-fastener. Vice. ¤ مَشبَك ج مَشَابِك
Intricate. ✧ A kind of sweetmeat. ✧ Cripple-legged (horse). مُشَبَّك
Baker's rolling pin. شُوبَك ج شَوَابِك P
To grow up (child). ✡ شَبَل o شُبُولًا
✧ To whip, to sew slightly. شَبَّل
To be inclined to, to aid. To care for her children without marrying (widow). أَشْبَلَ على
Whelp (of a lion). شِبْل ج أَشْبَال وشُبُول وأَشْبُل وشِبَال
Lively, thriving (child). شَابِل
Having whelps (lioness). مُشْبِل
To muzzle a kid. ✡ شَبَمَ o شَبْمًا وشَبَّمَ ه
To be cold. شَبِمَ a شَبَمًا
Cold. Death. شَبَم
Cold (water). Cold and hungry. شَبِم م شَبِمَة
Fat (cow). بَقَرَة شَبِمَة
Muzzle. Fastener of a head-veil. شِبَام
A plant resembling the *henna* in colour. الشَّبَام
Muzzled, having the mouth tied. مُشَبَّم
To be plump, fat (child). ✡ شَبَنَ o شَبْنًا
To be near.
Plump, fat (child). شَابِن
Groom's man. ✧ God-father. ¤ Village, شَبِين وإِشْبِين ج أَشَابِين S
Bride's maid. ✧ God-mother. شَبِينَة وإِشْبِينَة
To liken, to compare a. th. with a. o. To assimilate. ✡ شَبَه – شَبَّه ه ه وب
To render a. th. dubious to a. o. – ه على
To resemble, to be like a. o. or a. th. شَابَه وأَشْبَه ه وه
He is as weak as a woman. أَشْبَه أَمَة
To imitate; to resemble a. o. تَشَبَّه ب
To be alike. To be ambiguous. تَشَابَه واشْتَبَه
To be in doubt about. إِشْتَبَه في
To be dubious to a. o. – على

To loathe a. th. To be disgusted with. شَبِع من
To be perfect, full (intellect). شَبُع عَقْلُهُ o شَبَاعَة
To be nearly satiated (flocks). شَبَّع
To satiate a. o. أَشْبَع
To saturate (cloth) with dye. To increase a. th. – ه
To make (speech) copious – الكلام
To prolong the sound of a vowel. – الحَرَكَة
To be satiated, to be surfeit. To feign satiation. To boast of riches. To satisfy o.'s appetite after dinner. تَشَبَّع
Satiative. شِبْع وشِبَع
Satiety, surfeit. شِبَع
Amount of food sufficient to satiate a. o. شُبْعَة
Full, satisfied. ✧ Rich. شَبْعَان م شَبْعَى ج شَبَاعَى وشِبَاع
Copious. Saturated. شَبِيع
Witty man. شَبِيع ومُشْبَع العَقْل
To become lusty, to be voluptuous. ✡ شَبِق a شَبَقًا
To loathe (meat). – من
Turkish pipe. شُبُوق T
Lusty, lecherous. شَبِق
Oak-tree. ✧ شُبُوق
Baker's rolling pin. شَوْبَق ج شَوَابِق P
To be intricate (business). ✡ شَبَك i شَبْكًا، وتَشَابَك واشْتَبَك
To entangle, to intermix. To knit together. – وشَبَّك ه وشَبَّك بَيْن
To sink wells near one another. أَشْبَك
To be intricate, entangled. To become confused (darkness). تَشَبَّك واشْتَبَك
Net (of hunter, fisherman). Snare. شَبَكَة ج شَبَك وشِبَاك
Wells close each other. Land in which there are numerous wells. شَبَكَة
Family connection. ✧ Intricate affair, difficulty. شُبْكَة
Entangled. Uncertain, dubious (road). شَابِك ج شَوَابِك
The Milky way. أُمّ النُّجُوم الشَّوَابِك
Net. (*un.* شُبَّاكَة) شُبَّاك ج شَبَابِيك

شِبه وشَبَه ج أشباه ومَشابه Likeness. Similitude. Figure.
وَجْهُ الشَّبَه Point of resemblance.
شِبه الجَمْع Collective noun.
شَبَه وشَبَهان وشِبْهان Yellow copper, brass.
شُبْهَة ج شُبَه وشُبُهات Doubt, uncertainty. Equivocal. ✧ Suspicion.
أصحاب الشُّبُهات Persons of suspected character.
تَشْبِيه Comparison. Allegory.
اِشْتِباه Likeness. Ambiguousness. Doubt.
شَبِيه ج شِبَاه Alike.
شَبِيه بِالمُعَيَّن Rhomboid.
— بِالمُنْحَرِف Trapezoid.
مُشَبَّه ومُشْتَبِه Dubious.
مُتَشَابِه Consimilar. Homogeneous.
مُشَابَهَة Resemblance.
✧ مَشْبُوه Suspected, ill-famed.
✧ إمرأة مَشْبُوهَة Courtezan.
✱ شَبَا o شُبُوًّا To be lofty. To shine (face). To rear, to prance (horse).
— ه To kindle brightly (the fire).
أَشْبَى To have distinguished children.
— على To look favourably at.
— ه To give. To honour a. o. To throw a o. into misfortune.
شَبا Water-moss.
شَباة ج شَبًى وشَبَوات Scorpion. Point. Edge of a sword.
— وشَبْوَة Sting of a scorpion.
جارِيَة شَبْوَة Bold young woman.
✱ شَوبَص To be overseer.
شُوباصي (*for* صُوباشي) An overseer of tenantry.
✱ شَتَّ i شَتًّا وشَتَاتًا وشَتِيتًا To be dispersed, to scatter.
— وشَتَّتَ وأَشَتَّ ه وه To scatter, to separate (people).
شُتِّتَ ✧ To be heedless, distract.
تَشَتَّتَ وانْشَتَّ واسْتَشَتَّ To be scattered, set apart.
شَتّ ج أَشْتات Separation, dispersion. Parted, scattered.
أَمر شَتّ وشَتات Disordered business.
جاءوا شَتاتَ شَتاتَ او أَشْتاتًا They came in detached bands.
شَتَّانَ ما هُما او ما بَيْنَهُما How widely different they are!
تَشْتِيت Separation, dispersion.
— الأفكار Heedlessness, distraction.
شَتِيت ج شَتَّى Wide-apart. Scattered.
قَوم شَتَّى وشُتُوت Aggregate of various tribes.
مَسائِل شَتَّى Miscellaneous questions.
مُشَتَّت Distracted (mind).
✱ شَتَر i شَتْرًا ه To cut, to slit a. th.
— ه To offend, to abuse a. o.
شَتِر a شَتَرًا To be cut, dissected.
— وشُتِر والشَّتَر To suffer from an inversion of the eyelids.
شَتِر وشَتَّر ب To revile a. o.
شَتَر Slit. Defect. Inversion of the eyelids.
شُتْرَة Space between two fingers.
شِتِّير Rogue, knave.
أَشْتَر م شَتْراء ج شُتْر Affected with an inversion of the eyelids. Having the lower lip split.
مُشَتَّر Cut, torn off, dissected.
◻ شَتَل i ه To transplant (a plant).
✧ شَتْلَة Nursery-plant.
شَتْلَة القُطْن Cotton plant.
— النِّيل Indigo plant.
✧ مَشْتَل ج مَشَاتِل Seed-plot. Nursery-garden.
✱ شَتَم o i شَتْمًا ومَشْتَمَة ومَشْتُمَة وشاتَم ة To revile, to vilify a. o.
شَتُم o شَتَامَة To have an ugly, hateful face.
تَشَتَّم To expose o.'self to abuse.
شاتَم وتَشَاتَم To revile o. a.
شَتِيمَة ج شَتَائِم Insult. Revilement.
شَتَّام وشَتَّامَة Habitual reviler, insolent.
شَتِيم المُحَيَّا Grim-faced.
— ومُشَتَّم Austere lion.
✱ شَتَن o شَتْنًا ه To weave a stuff.
شَثْن الكَفّ Rough-handed.
✱ شَتَا o شَتْوًا, وشَتَّى وتَشَتَّى ب To pass winter (in a place).
شَتَا To be cold (day, winter).
— وأَشْتَى To enter winter. To suffer from want in winter.
شَتَّى ✧ To rain.
الدُّنيا تُشَتِّي ✧ It is raining.
شاتَى مُشَاتاة وشِتَاء ه To make a

To turn aside a. o. from. ✱ شَجَر o شَجْرًا ة عن
To thrust a. o. with a spear. — ة ب
To tie up a. th. to. — ه إلى
To support, to prop up (a tent). ه —
To open (the mouth). To put o.'s clothes on a tripod.
To be disputed between (affair). — o شُجُورًا بَيْن
To be numerous. شَجِرَ a شَجَرًا
To become a tree (plant). شَجِرَ
To graft (a tree). ◘ شَجَّر ه
To prop (a palm-tree). — ه
To adorn (cloth) with flowers. شاجَر ة
To quarrel with a. o. To graze off.
To feed upon trees from want of herbage (cattle). شاجَر
To produce trees (land). أَشْجَر
To quarrel with, to contend (men). To be intricate, confused (affair). تَشاجَر واشْتَجَر
To withdraw (sleep). اِنْشَجَر واشْتَجَر
To precede, to outstrip. — واشْتَجَر على
To lean the chin upon the hand. اِشْتَجَر
Trees, shrubs. (*un.* شَجَرَة) شَجَر ج أَشْجار
Thuja, tree of life. شَجَر الحَيَاة
Larger *Arum*. — التِّنِّين
Chelidonium, celandine, swallow-wort. — الخَطاطِيف
Ranunculus Asiaticus. — الضَّفادِع
Alyssum, madwort. — الكَلْب
Rosa canina, dog-rose, — مُوسَى
How goodly are the shape and size of her udder مَا أَحْسَن شَجَرَة ضَرْعِهَا
Subject of difference. Discordant affair. شَجْر
Side of the mouth. — ج شُجُور وشِجار
Plantation. Grove. Thicket. Arbour. Orchard. ✧ شَجَرِيَّة
شَجِر وشَجِير وأَشْجَر ومُشْجِر م شَجِرَة وشَجِيرَة الخ
Woody; abounding with trees (land).
Small litter. شِجار وشِجار
Wooden-bar (of a door). Muzzle (for kids). شِجار ج شُجُر
Abounding with trees. Stranger. Bad. Companion. شَجِير
Grove of trees; thicket. مَشْجَر ج مَشاجِر

bargain with a. o. for winter.
To be sufficient for winter (food supply). أَشْتَى ة
Winter. ✧ Rain. شِتاء ج أَشْتِيَة وشُتِيّ
Of winter, wintry. شَتَوِيّ وشَتْوِيّ
Winter-brook. نَهر شَتْوِيّ
Season of winter. شَتَاة وشَتْوَة وشَتْوِيَّة
Cold. ✧ Rainy (weather). شاتٍ
Winter-residence. Winter-quarters. مَشْتًى ومَشْتَاة
Plant used by tanners. Wild nuts. Much, many. ✱ شَثّ ج شِثَاث
Summit of a mountain. ✱ شِثْر ج شُثُور
To be rough (fingers). ✱ شَثِل a شَثَلًا وشَثُل o شُثُولَة
Rough-fingered. شَثِل الأَصَابِع
To be hard, thick (palm of the hand). ✱ شَثِن a شَثَنًا وشَثُن o شُثُونَة
Hard and rough, callous. شَثْن
To cleave (the head). To plough (the sea: ship). To cross a desert. ✱ شَجّ o i شَجًّا ه
To mix with water (wine). — ه ب
To have scurf on the forehead. شَجّ a شَجَجًا
To fracture (the skull). شَجَّج ه
To fight. شاجّ مُشاجَّة وشِجاجًا، وتَشاجّ
Wound. Scar (in the head). شَجَّة ج شِجاج
Wounded in the head. Scarred on the face. أَشَجّ
Split, fractured. — وشَجِيج ومَشْجُوج ومُشَجَّج
To doom to destruction. To afflict. To occupy a. o. ✱ شَجَب o شَجْبًا ة
To stop (a bottle). — ه
To be grieved. To perish. — شُجُوبًا وشَجِب a شَجَبًا، وتَشَجَّب
To be mingled, confused (th.). تَشاجَب
Grief. Want. ✧ Sentence of death. شَجْب
Pole of a tent. — ج شُجُوب
Skin used as a bucket. — ج شُجُوب وأَشْجاب
Loss. Ruin. Misfortune, Grief. Distress. شَجَب
Perished. Sad. شَجِب وشاجِب
Loquacious, talkative. شاجِب
Stopper of a bottle. شِجاب
Clothes-stand. — وشُجُب، ومِشْجَب ج مَشاجِب

To be choked by a. th. شَجِيَ بِ
I made him go away. أَشْجَيْتُهُ عَنِّي
To be deeply moved, grieved. تَشَاجَى على
Bone or any thing obstructing the throat. شَجًا
Grief. Anxiety. Object of want. شَجْو
Desert difficult to travel in. مَفَازَة شَجْوَاء
Sad event. أَمْرٌ شَاجٍ
Anxious. Sorrowful, grieved. شَجٍي م شَجِيَة وشَجِيّ م شَجِيَّة
To be stingy, niggardly of a. th. ✡ شَحَّ a i o شَحًّا وشُحًّا بِ
To be stingy to. — على
✧ To decrease (source). شَحَّ
✧ To wish good to a. o. — في فُلَان
To show o.'self miserly towards. شاحَّ ب على
To quarrel, to grudge o. a. a thing. تَشَاحَّ في
Avarice. ✧ Decrease. شُحّ وشَحّ وشِحّ
Niggardly. Sterile (soil). Giving no fire (steel). شَحَاح
Stingy. ✧ Giving little water (spring). شَحِيح ج شِحَاح وأَشِحَّة وأَشِحَّاء
Giving little milk (she-camel). شَحِيحَة ج شَحَائِح
Years, days in which there is scantiness of rain. أَيَّام او سِنُون شَحَائِح
To fly swiftly (bird). To groan (camel). ✡ شَحْشَح
Avaricious. Croaking much (crow). شَحْشَح
Zealous. Wide (desert). وشَحْشَاح
✡ شَحَب a o وشَحُب o وشُحِب شُحُوبَة وشُحُوبًا
To be changed by fatigue and disfigured by hunger (face).
To scrape the ground. شَحَب a شَحْبًا هُ
Ghastliness of countenance caused by fatigue or hunger. شُحُوب
To drive away a. o. ✧ شَحَت
A pinch (of snuff); a bit, a little. ✡ شَحْتَلَة
Old buck. ✧ Silly fellow. شُحْتُول
To croak (raven). To bray (mule). ✡ شَحَج a i شَحِيجًا وشُحَاجًا وشَحَجَانًا
Croaking (of a raven). Braying (of a mule). شَحِيج وشُحَاج وتَشْحَاج
Wild ass. شَحَّاج ومِشْحَج
Mules. بَنَات شَحَّاج وبَنَات شَاحِج

Wooden trivet. مِشْجَر ج مَشَاجِر
Quarrel, strife, row. مُشَاجَرَة
Figured with forms of trees (cloth). مُشَجَّر
Chinese writing. — الصِّين
To be brave, courageous. ✡ شَجُع o شَجَاعَة
To surpass a. o. in courage. شَجَع o شَجْعًا هُ
To encourage a. o. شَجَّع هُ
To show o.'self brave. To take courage. To feign to be brave. تَشَجَّع
Cowardly. Feeble, crippled by disease. شَجْعَة وشُجَعَة
Courage, bravery. شَجَاعَة
شُجَاع ج شُجْعَان وشِجْعَان, وشُجِيع ج شُجَعَاء وشِجَاع, وأَشْجَع م شَجْعَاء ج شُجْع وشِجَاع
Courageous, brave, bold.
Braver. Lion. Stout. Mad. أَشْجَع م شُجْعَى
Knuckles of the fingers. أَشْجَع وإِشْجَع ج أَشَاجِع
A large snake. — شُجَاع ج شِجْعَان
Brave. Light. أَشْجَع م شَجْعَاء, وشَجِع م شَجِعَة
Raving mad. مُشَجَّع
Perdition, ruin. ✡ شَجَم
Calamities. شُجُم
To be sad. To coo (pigeon). ✡ شَجِن a وشَجُن o شَجَنًا وشُجُونًا
To grieve a. o. To detain a. o. شَجَن o شَجْنًا وشُجُونًا, وشَجَّن وأَشْجَن هُ
To shoot forth (vine). أَشْجَن
To become tangled (trees). تَشَجَّن
To remember a. th. — هُ
Road in a valley. شَجْن ج شُجُون
Grief, sorrow. Need, want. شَجَن ج شُجُون وأَشْجَان
Bough, branch. Tangled, dense trees. Wooded valley. — وشِجْنَة وشَجْنَة وشُجْنَة
The two are closely related. بَيْنَهُمَا شِجْنَة او شُجْنَة الرَّحِم
Road on the side of a valley. شَاجِنَة ج شَوَاجِن
To grieve a. o. deeply. To inspire a. o. with joy. ✡ شَجَا o شَجْوًا, وأَشْجَى هُ
To stir up (discord) between. شَجَا بَيْن
To be grieved, anxious. شَجِيَ a شَجًا

✱ شَحَذَ a شَحْذًا, وأَشْحَذَ ه To sharpen, to whet (a knife).
— المِعدَةَ To sharpen the stomach (hunger).
— ه بِبَصَرِهِ To look fixedly at.
شَحَذ ه في To importune a. o. with sollicitations. ✧ To beg, to ask alms from.
— ه To urge on (a beast).
— وتَشَحَّذ ه To expel; to drive a. o. away.
✧ شِحَاذَة Beggary. Begging.
شَحَّاذ Importunate beggar.
— العَين ✧ Eye-sty.
شَحِيذ ومَشْحُوذ Sharpened (knife).
شَحْذان Hungry. Vehement driver.
مِشْحَذ ومِشْحَذَة وحَجَر الشَّحذ Whetstone.
مَشْحَذَة Incentive to the mind.
✱ شَحَرَ a شَحْرًا ه To open (the mouth).
✧ شَحَّرَ ه To blacken with soot.
شَحْر The middle of a valley.
شِحْرَة Narrow margin of a river, a valley.
✧ شُحَار Blackish earth. Soot ◘ Lung.
✱ شَحْوَر وشُحْرُور ج شَحَارِير Black bird.
✱ شحص — أشحص ه To weary a. o.
— ه من To expel a. o. from.
✱ شَحَطَ a شَحْطًا وشَحَطَان وشُحُوطًا ومَشْحَطًا ه To slaughter (a kid). To outstrip a. o. To sting a. o. (scorpion). ✧ To rub (a match). To drag a. o. on the ground.
— ه To thin (a beverage) with water. To prop (a vine). To fill (a vessel).
— في الأنبوب ✧ To sip with a pipe.
— وشَحِطَ a شَحَطًا To be distant, remote (place).
شَحَّطَ ه To stain a. o. with (blood).
أَشْحَطَ ه To remove a. o. to a great distance.
تَشَحَّطَ ب To flounder in his blood (wounded man).
— في To struggle in the womb (fœtus).
شَحْط Dung of birds. Commotion of the blood.
شَحْط ومِشْحَط Vine-prop.
شَحَّاطَة ج شَحَّاطَات ✧ Phosphoric match. Slippers.
✧ شَاحُوطَة Death-rattle. Toothed hammer for hewing stones.
◘ شَحْطَطَ ه To drag a. o. from place to place.
✱ شَحَفَ a شَحْفًا ه To skin, to flay.
✧ شَحَّفَ ه To cut (a water-melon) into slices. To chip a. th.
✧ شِحْفَة ج شِحَف Chip. Slice.
✱ شَحَكَ a شَحْكًا ه To gag a kid to prevent it from sucking.
شِحَاك Kid's muzzle.
✱ شَحَمَ a شَحْمًا ه To feed a. o. with fat.
شَحُمَ o شَحَامَةً To be very fat.
شَحِمَ a شَحَمًا To be greedy of fat.
✧ شَحَّمَ ه To smear a. th. with grease.
أَشْحَمَ To be fat.
شَحْم ج شُحُوم Suet. Pulp, fleshy part of fruits.
— الخِنزِير Lard.
لَقِيتُهُ بِشَحْمِ كُلَاهُ I found him full of vigour.
شَحْمَة A piece of suet.
— الأرض White worm.
— العَين The ball of the eye.
— الأُذُن Lobe of the ear.
حَجَر شَحْم ✧ Granite.
شَاحِم وشَحَّام Seller of suet.
شَحِم Greedy of fat. Fleshy, pulpy (fruit).
شَحِيم Fat, abounding in fat.
S شَحِيم وشَحِيمَة Syriac breviary.
مُشَحَّم Filled, stuffed with grease. ✧ Mad (dog).
مُشْحِم ومُشَحَّم Possessing much fat. ✧ Very fleshy (fruit).
✱ شَحَنَ a شَحْنًا, وأَشْحَنَ ه ب ⌒ To fill, to garrison (a town) with (troops).
شَحَّنَ ه To lade a (ship).
— ه To drive a. o. away.
شَحَنَ o وشَحِنَ a شَحْنًا ه To chase far without catching any game (hound).
شَحِنَ a شَحْنًا على To bear a grudge against.
شَاحَنَ ه To hate a. o. ✧ To dispute.
أَشْحَنَ To be about to weep (child).
— ه To sheath; to unsheath (a sword).

To hate o. a. تَشاحَن
Cargo, freight. شَحْن
Bill of lading. ✧ بُولِصة الشَّحْن
Deep grudge. Bitter hatred. شَحْناء وشِحْنة ومُشاحَنة
One day's ration. Garrison. Cavalry detachment. شِحْنة ج شِحَن
Prefect of police. — ج شِحَن وشِحان
Full. Freighted. شاحِن م شاحِنة
Filled with malevolence. مُشاحِن
✧ Bill of lading. سَنَدُ المَشْحُونات
To be open (mouth). ✶ شَحا o شَحْوًا، وشَحِيَ a شَحًا
To open (the mouth). شَحا وأَشْحَى ه
To speak freely about a. o. تَشَحَّى على
Broad, spacious. شَحِيّ
Step, stride. شَحْوَة
Having the mouth wide-open (horse). شاحِيَة ج شَواحٍ
To make water. To sound when drawn from the udder (milk). ✶ شَخَّ o شَخًّا
To snore in sleep. — في نَوْمِهِ
To make urine to flow in a stream. — o شَخِيخًا ب
Urine. Excrement. ✧ شَخاخ
Making water (in bed). ✧ شَخّاخ م شَخّاخة
To clash (arms). ✶ شَخْشَخ
Clashing of arms. شَخْشَخة
Sky-light in a court. ◻ شَخْشِيخة
To flow. To stream (milk, blood). ✶ شَخَبَ o a شَخْبًا ومَشْخَبًا، وانْشَخَب
He passed by swiftly upon the ground. مَرَّ يَشْخَب في الأرض
To make (milk) to stream. شَخَب ه
Blood gushing from a wound. شَخْب
Stream of milk from the udder. — وشُخْب، وشُخْبة ج شِخاب
One time right and one time wrong (*lit*): a stream of milk in the vessel and another on the ground (*prov*). شُخْبٌ في الإناء وشُخْبٌ في الأرض
Sound of streaming milk. أُشْخُوب ج أَشاخِيب
To be slender, thin. ✶ شَخُتَ o شُخُوتة
To rip up, to cut open, to slaughter a. o. ✧ شَخَتَ ه وه
To convey a. th. to. شَخَّت ه الى

Thin, slender, lank. Little. شَخْت وشَخَت وشَخِيت ج شِخات
Boat, skiff. ✧ شَخْتُور وشَخْتُورة ج شَخاتِير
To snort. To snore. ✶ شَخَر i شَخِيرًا
To neigh (horse). To bray (ass). — شَخْرًا وشَخِيرًا
To put a coating (to a saddle). To prop up the bunches of a palm-tree. شَخَّر ه
First stage of youth. Space between the fore and the hind part of a saddle. شَخْر
Snoring. Neighing. Mountain-path. شَخِير
Snorer. شِخِّير
To be troubled. To be difficult (affair). ✶ شَخَز a شَخْزًا ه
To put out a. o.'s eye. — عَيْنَهُ
To thrust a. o. (with a lance). — ه ب
To stir up a quarrel between. — بَيْن
To hate o. a. To disagree (people). تَشاخَز
To be disturbed, to be agitated. ✶ شَخَس a شَخْسًا
To open the mouth in gaping (ass). شاخَس وتَشاخَس
To stop (a crack) clumsily. شاخَس ه
To speak in a harsh, unseemly way. أَشْخَس في المَنْطِق
To be irregular (teeth). تَشاخَس
They are on bad terms with one another. تَشاخَس ما بَيْنَهُم
Disorganized, disordered. شَخِيس
To come in view. ✶ شَخَص a شُخُوصًا
To appear. To rise (star). To swell (wound).
To fix the eyes upon, to gaze. — بَصَرَهُ وبِبَصَرِهِ الى
To go from a place to. شَخَص من بَلَدٍ الى
To be disturbed. شُخِص بِهِ
To be stout, big. شَخُص o شَخاصة
To make a. th. distinct. To make the diagnosis of an illness. ✧ To act (a play or drama). شَخَّص ه
To miss the target (arrow). أَشْخَص
To disturb, to frighten a. o. To make to go. — ه
To speak ill of a. o. — ب
To be distinguished, determined. تَشَخَّص
To occur to the (mind). To — ل

present itself to (the eye).
شَخص ج أَشخاص وشُخُوص Person, individual; corporeal form; object seen from afar. ✧ Statue.
شَخصِيّ Personal.
شخصِيًّا Personally.
شَخصِيَّة Personality.
شُخُوص Lethargy.
تَشخِيص ✧ Performance (of a play).
تَشخِيص الأَمرَاض Diagnosis of a disease.
شَخِيص Big, stout. Lord, master. Harsh, bitter (words).
مُتَشَاخِص Disagreeing, discordant.
مُشَخِّص ✧ Actor, stage-player.
◻ شَخَط ه To threaten, to expel a. o.
✲ شَخَل a شَخلًا ه To clarify a beverage.
شَاخَل ه To have a true friendship for a. o.
مِشخَل ومِشخَلَة Filter, strainer.
✲ شَخَم a وشَخِم o وشَخُم a شُخُومًا To be tainted (food).
شَخَّم ه To taint (food),
أَشخَم To be spoiled, to sour (milk).
أَشخَمُ Hoary (hair). Barren (garden).
✲ شَدّ o i شَدًّا To run (man). To be advanced (day). To be intense (fire).
— ه To bind, to fasten tightly (a bundle). To strengthen, to brace a resolution. ✧ To strap; to saddle (a beast).
✧ شِدّ حَيلَك Take courage.
شَدّ الرِّحَال الى To set off towards.
— ظَهرَهُ ✧ To back a. o.
— ه To comfort a. o. (God).
شَدّ o شَدًّا وشَدَّة وشُدُودًا على To attack. To make a raid against.
شَدَّد ه وه To strengthen. To render hard, severe, intense. To double a letter with the sign (ّ).
— على في To be harsh towards a. o. in.
شَادّ ه To contend with. To strive to surpass. To persecute a. o.
أَشَدّ To reach maturity of age, mind. To have a strong riding-beast.
تَشَدَّد واشتَدّ To be strengthened.
— لِلأَمر To exert o.'s self in.
— على To be niggardly to.
اِشتَدّ To be strong, violent. To become intense, to increase (cold, heat, pain). ✧ To thicken.
— في To strain o.'s self for.
— على To be hard upon a. o. (evil).
شَدّ النَّهَار The middle of the day.
شَدَّة Sign (ّ) used for doubling a letter. Assault. ✧ Bundle, parcel. Shoes. Pack of cards. Set of teeth.
شِدَّة ج شِدَد Hardness. Vehemence, intensity.
— ج شَدَائِد Calamity, misfortune, distress.
تَشدِيد Strengthening. Violent pressure. Doubling of a letter.
شَدِيد ج أَشِدَّاء وشِدَاد Violent, hard. Strong. Steady, firm. Tight. Avaricious. Dense.
شَدِيد البَأس Courageous.
أَشَدّ Stronger. Harder. ✧ Thicker. More (*when used to form comparatives*).
أَشَدّ أَحمِرَارًا More intensely red.
أَشُدّ وأَشَدّ Strength. Vigour of life.
بَلَغ أَشُدَّهُ He has attained the vigour of life.
مِشَدّ ✧ Stays.
مُتَشَدِّد Avaricious, severe.
✲ شَدَح a شَدحًا To be fat.
اِنشَدَح To lie down and stretch the legs asunder.
شُدحَة Room, spaciousness. Liberty.
شَادِح وأَشدَح Wide. Ample.
✲ شَدَخ a شَدخًا, وشَدَّخ ه To smash, to crush, to bray a. th.
— ه To strike a. o. on the back of the neck.
— عن To go astray from. To give up a. th.
تَشَدَّخ وانشَدَخ To be crushed, squeezed (fruit). To be smashed (vessel).
شَدَخ Abortive fœtus.
شَدخَة Fresh, soft plant.
شَادِخ Young and tender. Deviating from the aim.
شَادِخَة Blaze on a horse's forehead.
رَكِب a الشَّادِخَة المُحَجَّلَة To perpetrate an atrocity.
أَشدَخ م شَدخَاء ج شُدخ Having a blaze on the forehead (horse).

To urge on (a beast). شَدَا o شَدْوًا ه
To acquire some knowledge of a science. — مِن العِلْمِ شَيْئًا
To compare a. o. to. شَدَا ه ه او ب
To sing well. أَشْدَى
Extremity of a. th. Remnant of strength. Heat. Mange. شَدًا
Little, small quantity. شَدْو
To be alone, isolated. To be exceptional. To be irregular (noun, verb). ✡ شَذَّ o i شَذًّا وشُذُوذًا
To set apart, to isolate a. o. — o شَذًّا, وشَذَّذ وأَشَذَّ ه
To use an irregular expression. أَشَذَّ
Loneliness. Exception to a rule. شُذُوذ
Strangers. People apart from their abode and tribe. شُذَّاذ
Scattered (th.) شَذَّان وشُذَّان
Lotus tree. شِذَّان
Lonely, apart. Irregular, anomalous. شَاذّ ج شَوَاذّ
To bark; to prune (a tree). ✡ شَذَب o i شَذْبًا, وشَذَّب ه
To repel. To defend. — عن
To part away. تَشَذَّب
Branch cut off. Stripped bark. Remainder of fodder. House-furniture. شَذَب ج أَشْذَاب
Branch cut from (a tree). شَذْبَة
Away from his native home. Desperate. شَاذِب
Tall, of fine stature. شَوْذَب
Scythe for trimming trees. مِشْذَب
To get ready for combat. To vent anger. To be scattered. To be lively, alert, nimble. ✡ شذر — تَشَذَّر
Particles of gold. Glass beads. Small pearls. شَذْر ج شُذُور
They dispersed in all directions. ذَهَبُوا شَذَر مَذَر
I could not get a. th. ✡ شَذَف o شَذْفًا, مَا شَذَفْتُ شَيْئًا
Sting (of scorpions, of wasps). ✡ شذم — شَذَام
To smell of musk. ✡ شَذَا o شَذْوًا
To harm a. o. — وأَشْذَى ه
To remove a. o. far off. أَشْذَى ه عن
Musk. Odour of musk. شَذْو
Tree used for making toothpicks. شَذًا

Smashed. Back of the neck. مُشَدَّخ
Fountain, water-spout. P شَادَرْوَان
To cut a. th. to pieces ✡ شَدَف i شَدْفًا ه
To be obscure (night). أَشْدَف
Object seen from afar. Darkness. Cheerfulness. Nobility. شَدَف ج شُدُوف
Tall, great. Ready to rush. شَدِف
Bit, morsel. Portion of the night. شُدْفَة
Bucket for irrigation. ◻ شَادُوف
Left-handed. Great (horse). أَشْدَف م شَدْفَاء ج شُدْف
Curved, bent (bow). مُتَشَادِف
To be wide in the sides of the mouth. ✡ شَدِق a شَدَقًا
To open wide. ✧ شَدَق o شَدْقًا ه
To talk fluently. تَشَدَّق بِالْكَلَام
Side of the mouth. ✧ Jaw. شِدْق ج أَشْدَاق
Edge of a valley. — وشَدِيق ج شُدُق
Wide in the sides of the mouth. Speaking with fluency. أَشْدَق م شَدْقَاء ج شُدْق
Having a large mouth. شَدْقَم وشُدَاقِم
Subdeacon; clergyman. G شِدْيَاق ج شَدَايِقَة
To grow strong, to be able to walk (young of an animal). ✡ شَدَن o شُدُونًا
To have a young strong enough to walk (gazelle). أَشْدَن
Fawn, young one of a gazelle. شَادِن
Having her young one grown up (gazelle). مُشْدِن ج مَشَادِن ومَشَادِين
To break (the head). ✡ شَدَه a شَدْهًا ه
To counfound, to perplex a. o. To charm, to delight a. o. — وأَشْدَه ه
To be perplexed. To be stupefied. شُدِه وانْشَدَه واشْتَدَه
Perplexity, bewilderment, amazement. شَدْه وشَدَه وشُدْه وشُدَاه
Confusing affairs, troubles. مَشَادِه
To sing sweetly (a song). To chant (a poem). ✡ شَدَا o شَدْوًا ه
He sang the same song *i. e.* he imitated him. شَدَا شَدْوَهُ

Pungency of smell. Harm, annoyance. Kind of ship. Salt. Dog-flies.
P شَاذَنَج Blood-stone.
✱ شَرَّ o i شَرًّا وشَرَارَةً وشَرَرًا To be ill-natured, wicked. ✧ To leak out (water).
شَرَّ o شَرًّا, وشَرَّر وأَشَرَّ ﻫ To expose a. th. to the sun.
شَرَّ o شَرًّا ﻩ To find fault with a. o.
شَرَّر وأَشَرَّ ﻩ To defame a. o. To charge with malevolence.
أَشَرَّ ﻫ To make public, to spread abroad.
شَارَّ ﻩ To act boldly towards a. o. To dispute with a. o.
تَشَارَّ To quarrel, to dispute.
شَرّ ج شُرُور (opp. to خَيْر) Evil. Malevolence. Enmity, war. Fault, blemish. ✧ Stalk (of cucumber).
شَرّ م شَرَّة ج أَشْرَار وأَشِرَّاء وشِرَار Bad, wicked. Worse.
هُوَ شَرٌّ مِنكَ He is more wicked than thee.
هِيَ شَرَّة او شُرَّى مِنكَ She is more wicked than thee.
شِرَّة Anger. Ardour, eagerness of youth.
شُرّ Disagreeable thing.
شَرَر وشِرَار (un. شِرَارَة) Sparks of fire.
شَرِير و✧ شَرَّانِيّ ج أَشْرَار وأَشِرَّاء Wicked, vicious. Sea-shore.
شِرِّير ج شِرِّيرُون Very wicked, scoundrel.
✱ شَرْشَر ﻫ To split, to cut a. th. in pieces. To sharpen (a knife). ✧ To let out (water, wheat : vessel, bag). ◻ To cut (grass).
شَرْشَر وشِرْشِر Creeping plant.
شَرَاشِر Soul, the whole individual. Burdens.
أَلقَى عَلَيْهِ شَرَاشِرَهُ He betook himself to him.
شَرْشَرَة ✧ Scattering of wheat, powder.
شُرْشُور ج شَرَاشِير Finch (bird).
◻ شُرْشِير Wild duck.
✱ شَرِب a شَرْبًا وشِرْبًا وشُرْبًا ومَشْرَبًا وتَشْرَابًا ﻫ To drink. To suck ; to absorb (water).

✧ شَرِب الدُّخَان To smoke (tobacco).
شَرِب a شِرْبًا To be thirsty. To quench o.'s thirst.
شَرُب o شَرْبًا To understand, to apprehend (a discourse).
شَرَّب ﻫ To purify (a new skin). To impregnate, to saturate.
— وأَشْرَب ﻩ ﻫ To give a. th. to drink to a. o.
شَارَب ﻩ To drink in company with.
أَشْرَب ﻫ To imbue, to mingle with a. th. (a dye, a colour).
أَشْرَبَنِي مَا لَمْ أَشْرَب He has uttered a false charge against me.
أُشْرِب حُبَّ شَيْءٍ The love of the thing pervaded his heart.
تَشَرَّب To be saturated, imbibed (with a dye).
— فِي To pervade, to imbibe (cloth : dye).
اِسْتَشْرَب To be saturated, fully absorbed (dye, colour).
اِشْرَأَبَّ الى To stretch the neck to look.
شِرْب وشُرْب Drinking.
شِرْب Drinking-time. Time of watering a land.
شَرْبَة A draught. ✧ Purgative. Water-jug (with a long narrow neck).
شُرْبَة Redness on the face. ✧ Soup.
شَرْبَة ج شَرَب وشَرَبَات Copious drink. Ditch dug around a palm-tree for irrigating it.
شَرُوب وشَرِيب Brackish (water).
شَرِيب Fellow-drinker.
شَرَبَّة Grassy plain. Way, manner.
شَرَاب ج أَشْرِبَة Drink. Beverage ; wine.
— ج شَرَابَات ✧ Syrup. Sherbet.
شَرِبَة وشَرُوب وشَرَّاب وشِرِّيب Addicted to drink, great drinker.
شَرَّابَة ج شَرَارِيب ✧ Flake. Tuft, tassel.
✧ شَرَابَاتِيّ Seller of sherbet.
شَارِب ج شَرْب وشُرُوب Drinking, absorbing.
شَارِب ج شَوَارِب Mustaches.
مَشْرَب ج مَشَارِب Drinking-place, watering trough. ✧ Natural disposition, propensity. Opinion.
مَشْرَبَة ج مَشَارِب Soft ground covered

(meat) in slices. ✧ To cut open and spread (figs) in the sun.
To rejoice, شَرَحَ القلبَ والصَّدرَ والخاطِرَ to please a. o. To set at ease.
To be laid open. To be at ease, إِنْشَرَحَ to rejoice.
Exhibition, explanation. شَرْحٌ
Slice of meat. شَرْحَة
Long shred (of meat). شَرِيح وشَرِيحَة
Anatomy; autopsy. عِلْم التَّشْرِيح, تَشْرِيح
Exposed to view (place). ✧ شَرِح
✧ Agreable (place).
Explaining, disclosing. شَارِح ج شُرَّاح
Commentator. Guardian keeping (birds) away from wheat.
Anatomist. مُشَرِّح ج مُشَرِّحُون
To be in the bloom ✲ شَرَخ o شُرُوخًا of life.
Bloom of life. Beginning. شَرْخ ج شُرُوخ
Offspring. Point, top.
They are both alike. هُمَا شَرْخَان
A youth, young man. شَارِخ ج شَرْخ
To run away ✲ شَرَد o شِرَادًا وشُرُودًا at random (horse). ✧ To deviate.
To scare a. o. away. شَرَّدَ وأَشْرَدَ ه
To scatter (people).
✧ To lead astray. — ه
✧ Rain swept against a house. شَرْد
Runaway شَارِد ج شَرَد, وشَرُود ج شُرُد and wandering. Current through a country (poem). ✧ Deviating, astray.
Uncouth expressions, شَوَارِد اللُّغَة words. Exceptions to the rules.
Expelled, scared away. شَرِيد
To cough (from ✧ شردق — تَشَردَق choking).
Party ✲ شِرْذِمَة ج شَرَاذِم وشَرَاذِيم of men. A scout.
Clothes in rags. ثِيَاب شَرَاذِم
To cut a. th. ✲ شَرَز o شَرْزًا ه
To punish, to chastise. To شَرَّز ه revile a. o.
To quarrel with a. o. شَارَز ه
To throw a. o. into mis- أَشْرَز ه fortune.
Roughness, hardness. Rough, hard. شَرْز
Loss, ruin. شَرْزَة
Coagulated P شِيرَاز ج شَرَارِيز وشَوَارِيز milk.

with plants. Watering-trough.
Earthen drinking- مِشْرَبَة ج مَشَارِب vessel. Upper chamber.
Roofed balcony. ◘ مُشْرَبِيَّة
Cherub. H شَارُوبِيم
To entangle a. th. To ✧ شَرْبَك ه confuse.
Intricacy. Complica- شَرْبَكَة وشَرْبُوكَة ted affair.
A kind of cypress. Larch- ✲ شَرْبِين tree.
To become ✲ شَرِث a شَرَثًا, وانْشَرَث thick. To be chapped, cracked (skin, hand).
To be uneven (arrow- شُرِث وشُرِّث wood).
Worn out (shoes). شَرِث وشَرِثَة
Cutting (sword). شَرِث
To put, to set ✲ شَرَج o شَرْجًا ه together. To mix.
To keep company with a o. in. — ه في
To close up شَرَج وشَرَّج وأَشْرَج ه (a bag).
To baste, to stitch شَرَّج و✧ سَرَّج ه (clothes). To weave palm-leaves.
To be like, to resemble a. o. شَارَج ه
To be mixed up. تَشَرَّج
To resemble o. a. To be inter- تَشَارَج mixed.
To be chapped, cracked. إِنْشَرَج
Party, band. Manner, way, kind, شَرْج sort.
They formed two أَصْبَحُوا شَرْجَيْن parties (in the affair).
Those two are one sort. هُمَا شَرْج وَاحِد
Crevice, crack in شَرْج ج شِرَاج وشُرُوج a rock.
Ditch for watering camels. شَرْجَة
Button-hole. Purse. شَرْج ج أَشْرَاج
Alike, similar. Longitudinal half شَرِيج of a piece of wood.
Sack made of palm-leaves. شَرِيجَة
Basting, stitching. تَشْرِيج و✧ تَسْرِيج
Sesame-oil. P شِيرَج و✧ سِيرِج
To enlarge. To ✲ شَرَح a شَرْحًا ه disclose. To carve (the meat). To open (a door). To explain.
To be pleased with. — ب والى
To dissect (a corpse). To carve ه شَرَّح

✡ شَرِس a شَرَاسَةً وشَرَسًا وشَرِيسًا To be quarrelsome, unsociable.
شَرَس o شَرْسًا ه To pull (a beast) by its halter. To offend a. o. with words,
شَارَس مُشَارَسَةً وشِرَاسًا ه To treat a. o. harshly, severely.
تَشَارَس. To behave harshly towards o. a. To be contentious.
شَرْس وشِرْس وشَرَس Small thorny plants.
شَرِس وشَرِيس, وأَشْرَس م شَرْسَاء.
Unsociable, ill natured. Quarrelsome, malicious. Rough, hard (ground).
شَرْسَاء Thin, white (cloud).
شِرَاس و✧ سِرَاس Glue.
✡ شُرْسُوف ج شَرَاسِيف Cartilage of the ribs. Ill-luck.
✧ شِرْس ج شُرُوس Root. Vein.
Ps شرشف ج شَرَاشِف Sheet, bed-clothes. Shroud.
✡ شَرَص o شَرْصًا ه ب To revile a. o. in words.
شَرَص Roughness, hardness.
شِرْص ج شِرَاص وشِرَصَة Temple (of the head).
✡ شَرَط o i شَرْطًا, واشْتَرَط على To impose conditions upon a. o.
— وشَرَّط ه To make incisions on the skin, to scarify a. o.
— ه To tear off a. th.
شَرِط a شَرَطًا To fall into a momentous affair.
شَرَّط ✧ To make chain-work with iron wire.
شَارَط ه To make mutual conditions with.
— وتَشَارَط To stipulate a. th. To enter into an agreement with a. o. ✧ To bet, to lay a wager with.
أَشْرَط ه ل To set apart (a flock) for sale.
— نَفْسَهُ ل To get ready for.
— مَالَهُ في To offer o.'s property for.
— ه الى To hasten, to despatch (a messenger).
تَشَرَّط في To apply o.' self carefully to.
إِشْتَرَط لَهُ ه To grant a. th. under conditions to a. o.

شَرْط ج شُرُوط Condition, stipulation. Term. Incision. Scarification. ✧ Agreement.
شَرَط ج أَشْرَاط Sign. Beginning of a. th.
— وشَرَط ج أَشْرَاط Refuse of a. th.
✧ شِرْطَة Piece of cloth torn off.
شَرْطِيّ Conditional. Stipulated.
شَرْطِيَّة Conditional (proposition). ✧ Written compact.
شُرْطَة Term. Stipulated condition.
— ج شُرَط Guard. Police.
شُرْطِيّ وشُرَطِيّ Watchman. Policeman. Armed attendant.
شَرِيط ج شُرُط Rope made of palm-tree. Scent-box. ✧ String, wire. ◻ Rail of railway.
شَرِيطَة ج شَرَائِط Condition. ✧ Wire. String. Ribbon.
أَشْرَط المَال The refuse of a flock.
مِشْرَط ومِشْرَاط ج مَشَارِط ومَشَارِيط
Lancet, scalpel.
✧ شَرْطُوطَة ج شَرَاطِيط Rag, tatters. ✧ Duster. Rag.
G شَرْطَن ه To ordain (a priest).
✡ شَرَع a شَرْعًا To be seated upon a road (house). To open upon a street (door).
— ل To establish a law for.
— شُرُوعًا ه To begin (a business).
شَرَع يَقُول He began to say.
— في الماء To enter water and drink (cattle).
— في أَمْرٍ To begin (an affair).
— ب To bring (a beast) to the watering-place.
— ه To point a spear.
شَرُع To be pointed (spear).
شَرَّع وأَشْرَع ه في To make a. o. to ford, to wade through (water).
— وأَشْرَع ه To trace (a road). To show (the way).
أَشْرَع البَابَ الى الطَّرِيق To open a door upon the street.
— الرُّمْحَ على وقِبَلَ ه To point a spear at.
إِشْتَرَع ه To establish (a law).
شَرْع Divine law. (among Moslems).
— وشِرْع وشَرَع Equal; equivalent.

All men are equal in this matter. النَّاسُ في هٰذا شَرْعٌ او شِرْعٌ وَاحِدٌ
Bow-string. شِرْعَة وشِرْعَة ج شِرَع وشِرَع وشِرَاع
Awning, roof. Deck of a ship. شَرَعَة ج أشْرَاع
Brave. Fine flax. شَرِيع
Moslem law. Code. Way to water. شَرِيعَة ج شَرَائِع
The Jordan (river). نَهْرُ الشَّرِيعَة
شَارِع م شَارِعَة ج شَوَارِع وشُرَّع وشُرُوع
Lawgiver. Near.
Road, way. ✧ Street. — ج شَوَارِع
House opening into a road. بَيْت شَارِع ودَار شَارِعَة
Inclining to setting (stars). Pointed (spears). شَوَارِع
Sharp (nose). أشْرَع
Legal, lawful. شَرْعِيّ م شَرْعِيَّة
Sail of ships. Bow-string. شِرَاع ج شُرُع وأشْرِعَة
Bravery, courage. شَرَاعَة
Long (lance). شَرَاعِيّ
Long-necked (camel). — وشِرَاعِيّ
Book of the Deuteronomy. تَثْنِيَة الأشْتِرَاع
Way to water. Thoroughfare. Square, market-place. مَشْرَع ومَشْرَعَة ومَشْرُعَة ج مَشَارِع
Legislator. مُشْتَرِع
Small frog. ✱ شِرْغ وشِرْغ
To surpass a. o. in glory, rank. ✱ شَرَفَ o شَرْفًا ه
To embattle, (a wall). — وشَرَّف ه
To be noble, illustrious. شَرُفَ o شَرَافَة
To be raised in dignity. — شَرَفًا
To be over, above. To command over. شَرِفَ a شَرَفًا على
To ennoble a. o. To show regard, honour to a. o. شَرَّف ه
To ascend on a height. — وشَارَف وتَشَرَّف ه
To overlook (a place). شَارَف ه وأشْرَف على
To vie in glory with a. o. شَارَف ه
To be high, lofty. أشْرَف
To be at the point of death. أشْرَف على المَوْت
To compassionate a. o. — على فُلَان

To be ennobled, glorified. To be honoured, regarded. تَشَرَّف
The tribe has lost her best men. تُشُرِّف القَوْمُ
To stand erect. إشْتَرَف واسْتَشْرَف
To rise above, to overtop. إسْتَشْرَف ه
Nobility, dignity. شَرَف وشَرَافَة
High rank, honour. شُرْفَة ج شُرَف
Embattlement (of a wall), merlon. — وشَرَفَة ج شَرَفَات و✧ شُرَّافَة
Choice heads of a flock. شُرْفَة المَال
The nose and ears of man. أشْرَاف الإنْسَان
Regard shown. ✧ Visit. تَشْرِيف
Illustrating himself. شَارِف
Old (she-camel). — ج شُرُف وشُرَّف وشُرُوف وشَوَارِف
Wine-jars. شَوَارِف
Noble, illustrious. Excellent. ✧ Descendant of Mohammed. شَرِيف ج شُرَفَاء وأشْرَاف
More illustrious, nobler. أشْرَف م شُرْفَى
Embattled, indented (building). High, lofty. — م شَرْفَاء ج شُرُف
Master of ceremonies. ✧ تَشْرِيفَاتْجِي
Long ear. أذُن شَرْفَاء
Prominence, eminence. Dungeon. مُشْرَف ج مَشَارِف
Elevated places. مَشَارِف الأرْض
Sword from Yemen. سَيْف مَشْرَفِيّ
Inferior in dignity. Plebeian. مَشْرُوف
To slit (the ear). ✱ شَرَق o شَرْقًا ه
To pluck (fruit). ✧ To sip (broth). — ه
To rise (sun). شَرَق o شَرْقًا وشُرُوقًا
To show ripening dates (palm-tree).
To be bloodshot (eye). شَرِق a شَرَقًا
To have the ear slit (ewe).
To be choked by (spittle, tears). — ب
To be choked.
To go to the East. To have a bright complexion. شَرَّق
To spread (flesh in the sun to dry). To plaster (a wall). ✧ To leave the game half-dead (hunter). — ه
To shine (sun, face). To enter upon the time of sunrise. To become yellow (date). أشْرَق

To shine upon (a place: sun). أشرق ه
To saturate (cloth with dye).
To torment a. o. — ه
To bask in the sun. تشرّق
To split (bow). إنشرق
To be bathed in tears. إشرورق ب
Sunrise, the rising sun. شرق
The East. Levant. — ج أشراق
Light streaming through a chink. — وشرق
Sun. Choking the throat. شرق
Eastern, oriental, easterly. شرقيّ
✧ East wind.
Having the ear slit (ewe). شرقاء
The rising sun. Sunny place in winter. ✧ Violent cough. Pain in the eyes caused by smoke. شرقة
Land not watered by the Nile. ¤ شراقي
Small wood for lighting fire. ✧ شرق واشراق
Sunrise. شروق
Desiccation of meat in the sun. تشريق
Plaster. شارق
Rising and shining (sun, star). شارق م شارقة
Eastern side of a mountain. شارق الجبل ج شرق
East. (opp. to مغرب) مشرق ج مشارق
Eastern countries.
Sunny place. مشرقة ومشرقة ومشراق ومشريق
Whitlow-grass. ✧ جرف مشرقيّ
Roasted. Dyed red. White-washed with plaster. مشرّق
Green wood-pecker. ✱ شرقرق وشرقراق وشرقراق
To sparkle (fire). ✧ شرقط
Spark. ✧ شرقوطة ج شراقيط
To have the strings of the shoes broken. ✱ شرك a شركا
To become the partner of a. o. شرك a شركا وشركة, وشارك ه
To put leather thongs to sandals. شرّك وأشرك ه
✧ To make settlements of money in various places. شرك مالَهُ
To enter into partnership with, to share with a. o. in. To aggregate a. o. in. أشرك ه في
To attribute an equal to God. أشرك ب
To be a polytheist.
To be in partnership. تشارك واشترك
To be aggregated in a (society). ✧ To become a subscriber to (a newspaper). إشترك في
To be homonymous (words). إشترك
Participation, partnership. Duality of gods. Polytheism. شرك
Portion, lot. Partner. — ج أشراك
We desired to share with you. رغبنا في شركِكم
Of a bad standard, deficient (coin). (opp. to صاغ) شرك Ts
Net, snare. شرك ج شرك وأشراك
Track of a road.
Partnership, society. Confraternity. شركة وشركة
Straps of sandals. شراك ج شرك وأشرك
Swift (walk). Repeated (slap). شركيّ وشركيّ
Musical tune. ✧ شاركة
Partnership. Homonymy. ✧ Subscription. إشتراك
Partner. Share-holder. Accomplice. Companion. شريك ج شركاء وأشراك
Polytheist, dualist. مشرك ومشركيّ
Partner. Bondholder. مشارك
Partner. Speaking to himself (man). ✧ Subscriber. مشترك
Common (way, money). Homonymous (word). مشترك
To embroil, to entangle. To trip a. o. ✧ شركل ه
To be involved in. ✧ تشركل في
Entangled, intricate. ✧ مشركل
To split, to rend a. th. To cut off the tip of the nose. ✧ To injure (earthenware). ✱ شرم i شرما
He gave him a part of his wealth. — لهُ من مالِهِ
To have the tip of the nose cut off. شرم a شرما
To escape with a wound (game). شرّم
To split, to tear off a. th. — ه
To be split. To be notched (pot). تشرّم وانشرم

Itching. Eruption of pimples. شَرًى
The refuse or choice of a flock. — وشَرَاة
Side, country. — ج أشْرَاء
Affected with itching, with eruption. شَرٍ م شَرِيَة
Fiery (horse). شَرِيّ م شَرِيَّة
Manner, way. Nature. شَرِيَّة
Alike, similar. شَرْوَى
He has not his like. ما لَهُ شَرْوَى
Artery. شَرْيَان ج شَرَايِين
Purchaser, customer. شارٍ ج شُرَاة
Pl. Heretics, shismatics.
Jupiter (planet). المُشْتَرِي
Purchaser. مُشْتَرٍ
To prune seed-produce. ✱ شَرْيَف
Superfluous leaves. شِرْيَاف
To be barren. ✱ شَزَّ i شَزَازَة
Barren. شَزّ وشَزِيز
Barrenness. شَزَازَة
To be rugged, hard (place). To be lean, slender (animal). ✱ شَزَبَ وشَزُبَ o شَزْبًا وشُزُوبًا
To emaciate (a horse). شَزَّبَ ه
To expect a share in. تَشَازَبَ على
Opportunity. شَزْبَة
Rough, thin, dry. شازِب ج شُزَّب وشَوَازِب
Unwrought tree-branch. شَزِيب ج شُزُوب
Mark, sign. شَوْزَب
To look at a. o. askance. ✱ شَزَرَ i شَزْرًا ه والى
To strike a. o. with (a spear). — ه
To twist (a rope) in the wrong way. — o i واسْتَشْزَرَ ه
To be angry. تَشَزَّرَ
To get ready for (battle). — ل
To look angrily at o. another. تَشَازَرَ
Trial, difficulty. Rope twisted in the wrong way. شَزْر
Redness in the eye. شَزَر وشُزْرَة
Askance (look). Bloodshot with anger (eye). أَشْزَر م شَزْرَاء
To be jolly, lively. ✱ شَزِنَ a شَزَنًا
To be hard. تَشَزَّنَ
To rise for. — ل
To be painful to a. o. (th.) — على
To fell a. o. — ه

Abyss. Bottom of the sea. Sea-gulf. ✧ Breach. شَرْم ج شُرُوم
Having the tip of the nose cut off. أَشْرَم م شَرْمَاء ج شُرْم
To tear a. th. to rags. ✧ شَرْمَط ه
Prostitute, whore. ◻ Duster. ✧ شَرْمُوطَة ج شَرَامِيط
To be cracked (rock). ✱ شَرِنَ a شَرَنًا
Crack in a rock. شَرْن
To cut the superfluous leaves of seed-produce. ✱ شَرْنَف ه
Long and superfluous leaves. شِرْنَاف
To curtail, to cut off a. th. ✱ شَرْنَق ه
✧ To spin its cocoon (silk-worm).
Slough of snake. ✧ Cocoon of silk-worm. شَرْنَقَة ج شَرَانِق
To be greedy, gluttonous. ✱ شَرِهَ a شَرَهًا على او الى
Greediness, gluttony. شَرَه وشَرَاهَة
Glutton, greedy. شَرِه وشَرْهَان
White honey. ✱ شَرْو وشِرْو
Full trousers. ✧ شَرْوَل وشَرْوَال
To purchase. To sell a. th. ✱ شَرَى i شِرَاءً وشِرًى. واشْتَرَى ه
To laugh, to scoff at a. o. — ه
To speak in behalf of a. o. To devote o.'self to. — بِنَفْسِهِ عن
To dry a. th. in the sun. — وشَرَّى ه
To flash time after time (lightning). شَرِيَ a شَرًى. وأَشْرَى
To be angered (man). To run fast (horse). To be affected with eruption (skin). شَرِيَ a شَرًى
To conclude a sale or a purchase with a. o. شَارَى مُشَارَاةً وشِرَاءً ه
To fill up a tank. To shake the bridle. To incline an object. أَشْرَى ه
To set (people) at variance. — بَيْنَ
To be scattered, dispersed. تَشَرَّى
To be impetuous in walk (horse). To apply o.'self to a business (man). إِسْتَشْرَى في
To be serious and difficult (affair). إِسْتَشْرَى
To be disturbed, agitated. إِشْرَوْرَى
Colocynth (*plant*). شَرْي
Purchase, petty trade. شِرَاء وشِرًى ج أَشْرِيَة
Purchase. ✧ شَرْوَة

شَزَن وشِزَن Small bone.
شَزَن Fatigue. Hardship. Hard soil.
شَزَن وشُزُن Side, flank.
☆ شَسَّ i شُسُوسًا To be dry.
شَسّ ج شِسَاس وشُسُوس وشَسِيس Very hard ground.
☆ شَسِبَ a وشَسُب o شَسْبًا وشُسُوبًا To be dry, lean.
شَاسِب ج شُسُب Dry, thin.
☆ شسَع a شَسْعًا وشُسُوعًا To be remote (house).
— شَسْعًا وشَسَّع وأشسَع ه To garnish sandals with thongs.
شُسُوع Remoteness, great distance.
شِسْع ج أَشْسَاع Border, edge. Sandal-thong. Having small flocks. Extremity of a field.
شَاسِع وشَسُوع ج شُسُع Remote.
☆ شَسَف وشَسُف o شُسُوفًا وشَسَافَة To be dry, thin.
شِسْف A piece of dry bread.
شَاسِف Dry, dried up, lean.
شَسِيف Dry, dried up.
شَشْم P Seed used as collyrium.
شَشْمَة Ts Water-closet, privy.
☐ شِشْنَة Sample.
☆ شَصَّ i شُصُوصًا وشِصَاصًا To yield little milk (female). To suffer. To be hard (life). To bite o.'s lips.
— وأشصّ ه عن To repel a. o. from.
ما أدري أين شَصّ I do not know where he is gone to.
شَصّ وشِصّ ج شُصُوص Fishing-hook.
شِصّ ج شُصُوص Sharp thief.
شَصُوص ج شُصُص وشِصَاص Having little milk (female). Unfruitful year.
شَصَاصًا Year of drought. Dearth. Bad saddle-beast.
لَقِيتُهُ على شَصَاصَاء I found him busy.
☆ شَصَب o شُصُوبًا وشَصِب a شَصَبًا To be hard, painful (life).
شَصَب o شَصْبًا ه To scald, to skin (a beast).
أشصَب ه To render (life) painful.
شِصْب ج أشصَاب Barrenness. Hardness.
— وشَصِيب Lot, portion. Luck.
شَصِيبَة ج شَصَائِب Evil fortune, cares. Barrenness. Bottom of a well.
شَاصِب Hard, painful (life).

شَصَّاب Butcher.
☆ شَصَر o شَصْرًا To leap (man). To gore (bull).
— ه To stitch (clothes).
— ه ب To spear a. o.
— i شُصُورًا To become still fixed, (look of a dying man).
شَصَر ج أشصَار Young one of the gazelle.
شَاصِر وشَوْصَر Young one of the gazelle already grown up.
شَاصِرَة ج شَوَاصِر Snare for wild beasts.
☆ شَصَا o شُصُوًّا To look fixedly (dying man). To rise (cloud). To raise its legs (skin filled with water).
— وشَصِي a شُصِيًّا To be stiff (corpse).
أشصَى ه To render (the eyes) fixedly open.
شَصْو Misfortune.
شَاصٍ م شَاصِيَة ج شَاصِيَات وشَوَاصٍ Inflated and stiff.
☆ شَطَّ i o شَطًّا وشُطُوطًا To be far away.
شَطَّ ه وشَطَّط وأشَطّ واشتَطّ عَلَيهِ في To wrong a. o. in a. th.
— شَطَطًا وأشَطّ واشتَطّ في To overrate (the price of goods).
شَاطّ ه To vie with a. o. in overrating.
✧ شَطّط To follow (the bank) of a river. To run on a sand-bank (ship).
— في To penetrate into (the desert).
شَطّ ج شُطُوط وشُطّان Margin of a river.
شَطّ مث شَطّان ج شُطُوط Side or half of a camel's hump.
شِطّة وشَطَاطَة وشَطَاط Distance, remoteness.
شَطَط Exceeding, redundant. Extravagant lie. Excess.
لا وَكس ولا شَطط No more nor less.
شَاطّ م شَاطّة Of a fine stature.
شِطَاط وشَطَاط Tall stature.
بَيْنَهُمَا شِطَاط وشَطَاط There is a great difference between those two.
☆ شَطَأَ a شَطْأً وشُطُوءًا To walk on the bank of a river.
— ب To be able to bear (a burden).
— وأشطَأَ To sprout forth (tree)
شَطَّأَ تَشْطِيئًا To branch off (river).

He has as many daughters as sons. أَوْلَادُهُ شِطْرَةٌ
Half-full (vessel). شَطْرَان م شَطْرَى
Having a teat longer than another (ewe); a skirt longer than the other (garment). شَطُور
Stranger, remote. شَطِير ج شُطَرَاء
Deceit, cunning. ✧ Sharpness شَطَارَة
Deceitful, swindler. Mischievous. Ill-treating his people. ✧ Sharp, cunning. شَاطِر ج شُطَّار
The prodigal son. الِابْنُ الشَّاطِر
Betony (*plant*). شَاطِرَة
Divided, torn in two pieces. مَشْطُور
Contiguous, near. مُشَاطِر
Their houses are contiguous to ours. هُمْ مُشَاطِرُونَا
Game of chess. P شِطْرَنْج
To make a journey. ✡ شَطَس o شَطْسًا في الأرض
Strife. شُطْس وشُطْسَة
Dissenter. شَطُوس
To depart, to go off. ✡ شَطَف o شَطْفًا
To wash, to rince. To chap wood. ✧ شَطَّف
Sharp pointed piece of wood. ✧ شِطْفَة
Missing the aim (arrow). شَاطِف
Protracted journey. نِيَّة شَطُوف
To oppose a. o. ✡ شَطَن o شَطْنًا ه
To enter into the earth. — في
To be far from. — عن
To bind, to hold a. th. with a rope. — ه ب
To remove a. o. or a. th. أَشْطَن ه او ه
Rope. شَطَن ج أَشْطَان
Distant (journey). Deep (well). شَطُون
Wicked, mischievous. شَاطِن
To be wicked, rebellious. ✧ To be noisy, troublesome. ✡ شَيْطَن وتَشَيْطَن
Wickedness, mischief. شَيْطَنَة
The devil. Seducer (man). Wicked. ✧ Noisy, troublesome. شَيْطَان ج شَيَاطِين
To be stiff (corpse). ✡ شَطِي a شُطِيًّا
To skin and cut up (a beast). شَطَّى تَشْطِيَة ه
To be smashed. ✧ تَشَطَّى
To branch off. إِنْشَطَى
✧ Splinter of (bone, wood). شَطْء وشَطِيَّة

To walk with a. o. each on the opposite bank of a river. شَاطَأ ه
Bank, of a river. شَطْء ج شُطُوء
Offshoot. — وشَطْأ ج أَشْطَاء
Bank of a river, sea-shore. شَاطِئ ج شَوَاطِئ وشُطْآن
To be absent. ✡ شَطَب o شَطْبًا
To deflect from. — عن
To cut a. th. lengthwise. To cancel (a sentence). — ه
✧ To make incisions on (the skin). To cross-out (articles). شَطَّب
To make cuts on o.'s skin. تَشَطَّب
To flow (water). — وانْشَطَب
Of a fine stature. Tender and green (bough). شَطْب ج شُطُوب
Green bough. Sword. شَطْبَة ج شُطَب
Of a beautful size (girl). — وشِطْبَة
Streak, ridge of a blade. شُطْبَة وشِطْبَة وشُطْبَة ج شُطَب
Woman cutting out leather in strips. شَاطِبَة ج شَوَاطِب
Quilting-needle. شِطَاب
Ridged (sword). Covered with scars (man). Striped (cloth). Quilted (blanket). مُشَطَّب
To run away. ◻ To rove. ✧ شَطَح a شَطْحًا
To divide a. th. into halves. ✡ شَطَر o شَطْرًا, وشَطَّر ه
To have a teat longer than the others (ewe). — شُطُورًا
To be squint-eyed (man). شَطَر بَصَرَهُ
To withdraw from. — شُطُورًا وشُطُورَة وشَطَارَة عن
To be shrewd, artful. ✧ To be clever, skilful. شَطُر o شَطَارَة
To divide a. th. with a. o. to in halves). شَاطَر ه ه
✧ To swindle, to deceit. To show cleverness. تَشَاطَر
Half. Hemistich of a verse. Side, part. شَطْر ج شُطُور وأَشْطُر
He went towards him. شَطَر شَطْرَهُ
Fortune has two faces. الدَّهْرُ شَطْرَان
He has experienced the two faces of fortune, *i. e.* good and evil. حَلَبَ الدَّهْرَ شَطْرَيْهِ او أَشْطُرَهُ

forth awns (spike). To run to seed (corn).
To dart on (a flock: wolf). إِنْشَمَّ في
Scattered, shattered. شَمّ
Spider's web. شَمّ
Rays of light; beams of the sun. — وشُعَاع ج أَشِعَّة وشُعُم وشِعَاع
Shattering. Light shadow. Milk diluted in water. ✧ Monstrance. شَعَاع
His mind became unsettled. طار فُؤَادُهُ شَعَاعًا
They dispersed away. ذَهَبُوا شَعَاعًا
Corn-husk. شَعَاع وشِعَاع وشُعَاع
✧ To shine (stars). ✻ شَعْشَع
To mix (a beverage). — ه
Light, little dense (shade). شَعْشَع وشَعْشَعَان ومُشَعْشَع
Vine-shoot. ✧ شَعْشَاع
To separate (people). ✻ شَعَب a شَعْبًا
To appear (thing).
To collect *and* to scatter. To repair *and* to impair a. th. — ه
To send a messenger to. — ه الى
To have parted horns, shoulders. شَعِب a شَعَبًا
To part for ever from. شَعَّب وأَشْعَب عن
He departed from this life. شَاعَبَت نَفْسُهُ وأَشْعَب وانْشَعَب
To branch off, to fork (tree). To be arranged (affair). تَشَعَّب وانْشَعَب
To become separated from. — وانْشَعَب عن
Collection. Nation; tribe. Remoteness. Similar. ◻ Coral-reef. شَعْب ج شُعُوب
They congregated after separation. إِلْتَأَم شَعْبُهُم
They are both alike. هُمَا شَعْبَان
Path in a mountain. Numerous tribe. Underground water-course. شِعْب ج شِعَاب
Space between the shoulders. شَعَب
Twig of a tree. Space between two branches. Stream of water in the sand. Chink. Portion. ✧ Branch of a firm. ◻ Bronchiæ. شُعْبَة ج شُعَب وشِعَاب
A portion of goods. شُعْبَة من المَال
Prong of a spit. شُعَب السَّفُّود
Eighth arabian month. شَعْبَان
Death. شَعُوب

✻ شَطّ o شَطَطًا ه To be hard to a. o. (affair).
— وشَطَّط وأَشَطّ ه To scatter, to disperse (people).
Remainder of the day. شَطّ ج أَشْطَاط
Name of a celebrated thief. شِظَاظ
Hooked staff inserted in the loop of a sack. — ج أَشِظَّة
Wood split. Sack fastened. شَظِيظ ج أَشْظَاظ
They dispersed on all sides. طَارُوا أَشْظَاظًا او شَظَاظًا
✻ شَظِف a شَظَفًا To be hard, difficult (life). To lead a life of hardship. To penetrate between the skin and the flesh (arrow). To get coarse (hand).
— وشَظُف o شَظَافَة To wither (tree).
Hardship, bad circumstances. شَظَاف وشَظَف ج شِظَاف
Distance, remoteness. شِظَاف
Splinter of wood. شَظَف
Ankle. Piece of dry bread. شِظَاف ج شِظَافَة
Painful (life). Harsh (man). Rugged (soil). شَظِف
Withering from want of water (tree). شَظِيف
Speaking at random. شِظَف
✻ شَظَم — شَيْظَم م شَيْظَمَة ج شَيَاظِمَة
Big and tall (horse, camel).
✻ شَظِيَ a شَظًى To be split (wood).
— شُظِيًّا To be stiffened (corpse).
شَظَّى تَشْظِيَة ه To divide, to scatter (people).
أَشْظَى ه To wound a. o. on the elbow or knee-bone.
تَشَظَّى To be shattered. To be broken into splinters (wood). To disperse (people).
شَظًى Thin bone of the knees and elbows. Followers.
شَظِيَّة ج شَظَايَا وشَظًى Shank-bone. Splinter of wood. Bow.
✻ شَعّ i شَعَاعًا وشَعًّا To disperse (people). To be spilt (blood, water).
— ه على To send (horsemen) against (the enemy).
— شَعًّا وشَعِيعًا To make haste.
أَشَعّ To spread its rays (sun). To send

شَعِيب ج شُعُب Haversack. Old water-skin.
أَشْعَب ج شُعْب Wide in the horns (buck).
أَشْعَبُ Name of a covetous man.
الشَّاعِبان The two shoulders.
مَشْعَب ج مَشَاعِب Path, way.
مِشْعَب ج مَشَاعِب Drill, perforator.
* شَعْبَذ To practice sleight of hand.
مُشَعْبِذ Juggler.
* شَعِث a شَعَثًا To be disordered (affair).
— شَعَثًا وشُعُوثَة, وتَشَعَّث To be dishevelled (hair).
شَعَّث ه To scatter, to disperse a. th.
شَعَّث To curtail a poetical foot of one syllable.
— عن To defend a. o.
— من To extract, to draw out from.
تَشَعَّث To branch off. To be disordered (hair).
شُعْث Not curried (horses).
شَعِث م شَعِثَة , وأَشْعَث م شَعْثَاء ج شُعْث وشَعْثان Dishevelled (hair).
مُشَعَّث Shortened (poetical foot).
مَشْعُوث ✧ Cracked (vessel).
* شَعَر o وشَعُر o شَعْرًا وشِعْرَى وشُعُورًا وشُعُورَة ومَشْعُورَة ب To remark, to perceive a. th.
— o شِعْرًا وشَعْرًا To make verses. ◘ To be awake.
— وشَعَّر وأَشْعَر ه To line boots with hair.
شَعِر a شَعَرًا, وشَعَّر وأَشْعَر وتَشَعَّر واسْتَشْعَر To be hairy.
شَاعَر ه To vie in poetry with.
— ه To undertake a. th.
أَشْعَر To take a distinctive mark, a password.
— ه ه وب To inform, to warn a. o.
— ه الشِّعَار To cloth a. o. with an undergarment.
أَشْعَرَ الهَمُّ قَلْبَهُ Cares have overtaken him.
تَشَاعَر To pretend to be a poet.
إِسْتَشْعَر الشِّعَار To put on an undergarment.
— خوفًا To be terror-stricken.
شَعْر وشَعَر (*un.* شَعْرَة وشَعَرَة) ج أَشْعَار وشُعُور وشِعَار Hair of the head, of the body.
✧ أُمّ شُعُور Willow-tree.
شَعْر مُسْتَعَار و✧ شَعْر عِيَارَة Wig.
رَأَى الشَّعْرَة His hair begin to become hoary.
شِعْر ج أَشْعَار Knowledge. Feeling. Perception. Poetry, verse.
لَيْتَ شِعْرِي Would that I knew.
شِعْر شَاعِر Fine poetry, poem.
شِعْرَى *Sirius. Procyon* (stars). Time of intense heat. Dog-days.
شَعْرِيَّة ج شَعْرِيَّات ✧ Grate, lattice.
مِيزَان الشَّعْرِيَّة ✧Balance for light weighs.
شَعَار Dnese and tangled trees. Vegetation. Arbour.
شِعَار ج شُعُر وأَشْعِرَة Under-garment. Distinctive sign. Coat of arms. Cry of war. Horse-cloth.
— الحَجّ Rites of pilgrimage.
شُعُور Intelligence. Knowledge.
شَعِير Barley. Fellow, companion.
شَعِيرَة ج شَعِيرَات A grain (weight). Measure of length.
— ج شَعَائِر Silver or brass button. Rite of pilgrimage.
شَعِيرِيّ Seller of barley.
شَعِيرِيَّة ✧ Vermicelli.
أَشْعَر ج شُعْر, وشَعْرَانِيّ ومُشْعِر و✧ مَشْعَرَانِيّ Hairy.
شَعْرَاء ج شُعْر Covered with plants (earth). Hard, rough. Kind of plum. Fur. Camel's fly. Bustle, throng.
دَاهِيَة شَعْرَاء Great calamity.
شَاعِر ج شُعَرَاء Poet.
— مُفْلِق Distinguished poet.
أَشْعَر مِن More cognizant of poetry than.
شُوَيْعِر Having some knowledge of poetry.
شُعْرُور Petty poet, rhymer.
مُتَشَاعِر Pretending to be a poet.
مَشْعَر ج مَشَاعِر One of the five senses (sight, hearing). Bower.
مَشْعُور Garnished with hair. ✧ Cracked (vessel). Crack-brained.
✧ شَعَط a شَعْطًا To be altered by fire (clothes). To burn with rage.
* شَعَف a شَعْفًا ه To busy the mind (affection).

شَعَفَ ه ب To tar (a camel).
شَعِفَ a شَعَفًا بِهِ و بِحُبِّهِ To be enamoured of.
شَعَف Lively affection ; burning love. Upper part of a camel's hump.
شَاعِفَة Light rain.
شَعَفَة ج شَعَف وشُعُوف وشِعَاف وشَعَفَات Summit, top. Lock of hair.
شُعَاف Insanity, madness.
مَشْعُوف Mad. Enslaved by love.
✡ شَعَلَ a شَعْلًا, وشَعَّلَ وأَشْعَلَ ه To light (a fire). To kindle, to stir (war).
شَعَلَ في To be inflamed for.
شَعِلَ a شَعَلًا, وأَشْعَلَ واشْعَالَّ To have a white spot on the tail, or forelock (horse).
أَشْعَلَ To spread everywhere (horsemen). To shed tears (eye). To leak (skin).
— ه To scatter (a flock).
أَشْعَلَ ه في To send (troops) to a country.
تَشَعَّلَ واشْتَعَلَ To blaze up (fire).
إِشْتَعَلَ شَيْبًا To become hoary.
شَعَل Blaze on the tail or forelock of a horse.
رَجُل شَعِل Fiery, ardent man.
شُعْلَة ج شُعَل Firebrand.
شَاعِل وشَعِيل وأَشْعَل م شَعْلَاء White-spotted on the tail or forelock.
شَعِيلَة ج شَعِيل وشُعُل Lighted wick.
شَاعِل ومُشْعِل Kindling.
مِشْعَل ومِشْعَال ج مَشَاعِل ومَشَاعِيل Strainer.
مَشْعَل ومَشْعَلَة ج مَشَاعِل Lamp, firebrand.
مُشْعِل Spreading everywhere (horsemen, locusts).
✡ شَعَمَ a شَعْمًا To reconcile people.
✡ شعن — أَشْعَنَ ه To catch a. o. by the hair.
إِشْعَانَّ To be dishevelled (hair).
شَعَن Scattered bits of herbage, dry plants.
مَشْعُون Disordered (hair).
مُشْعَانّ الرَّأْس Having dishevelled hair.
شَعْنِينَة ج شَعَانِين ✧ Palms, boughs of trees.
✧ عِيد الشَّعَانِين Palm-sunday.
✡ شَعْنَب To have twisted horns (buck).

مُشَعْنَب القَرْن Having the horns turned backwards.
✡ شَغَا o شُغُوًّا To be plucked (hair).
أَشْغَى ه To scatter (soldiers) for a raid.
— ب To watch upon.
غَارَة شَعْوَاء Raid in a hostile country.
شُغَى Plucked, scattered (hair).
شَاءٍ م شَاعِيَة ج شَوَاء Removed. Scattered.
✡ شَعْوَذ To juggle away.
شَعْوَذَة Juggler's trick, legerdemain.
مُشَعْوِذ ومُشَعْوَذ Juggler, conjurer.
✡ شَغْشَغ To turn a sword in the wound. To groan (camel).
— ه To shake the bit (rider).
— في To hurry in.
✡ شَغَبَ شَغْبًا , وشَغِبَ a شَغَبًا , وشَغَّبَ ه او ب او على To excite enmity between.
شَغَبَ a شَغْبًا عن To deviate from.
شَاغَبَ ه To seek to harm a. o.
شَغْب وشَغَب Stir, tumult.
شَغِب وشِغَبّ وشَغَّاب ومِشْغَب ومُشَاغِب Mischief-maker.
✡ شَغَرَ o شُغُورًا To be left defenceless (country). To be remote.
— ه عن To expel from.
— a شَغْرًا To raise the hind leg (dog).
شَغَرَ بِرِجْلِهِ في الغَرِيب To rush to the rescue of a stranger.
شَاغَرَ مُشَاغَرَةً وشِغَارًا ه To marry by compensation. To intermarry. To concert a. th.
أَشْغَرَ To walk in a crowd to.
— واشْتَغَرَ على To perplex a. o. (account).
تَشَغَّرَ في To persevere in (an evil affair).
إِشْتَغَرَ To be entangled (business). To become large (number).
— في To go far into the desert.
تَفَرَّقُوا شَغَرَ بَغَرَ وشِغَرَ بِغَرَ They dispersed in all directions.
شَاغِر Defenceless country. ◘ Camel's saddle.
شَغَّارَة Silex, flint.
شِغِّير Wicked.
✡ شَوْغَر Strong.
شَوْغَرَة Date-basket.
✡ شَغَزَ a شَغْزًا على To behave insolently towards.

To increase. To be deficient. شَفَّ شَفًّا

To emaciate a. o. (cares. disease). — شَفًّا, وشَفَّف ه

To prefer a. th. to another. أَشَفَّ ه على

To drink up (all the contents of a bowl). تشافّ واشتفّ ه

To endeavour to see through a. th. To scrutinize, to fathom a. th. إستشفّ ه

To feel the desire of. — الى

Thin and transparent stuff. Light red veil. Increase. Loss. شَفّ وشِفّ وشُفوف

Transparent, translucent. شفّاف وشَفِيف

Bitter cold. Cold wind. Rain mixed with hail. شفيف

Cold, cold wind. شَفّان

Remainder of water in a vessel. شُفافة

To tremble, to shudder. ✻ شَفشَف

To be mixed with. — ب

To blast (plants : hoar-frost). To dry up. To contract a. th. (heat, cold). — ه

To wear a. o. out (cares). — ه

To sprinkle (a medicinal powder on a wound). — ه على

Cold wind. Rain with hail. Uncompact (tissue). شفشاف

Trembling. Wicked. مُشَفشِف ومُشفشَف

✧ Bigness and prominence of the lips. ✻ شفتَرة و✧ شَفتُورة

✧ Big-lipped. مُشفتَر

To decrease (wealth). ✻ شَفِر a شَفارة

To decrease (wealth). To decline (sun). شَفَّر

To be on the brink of. — على

Place of growth of the eyelash. شَفر وشُفر ج أشفار

There is nobody in the house. ما في الدّار شَفر او شُفر

Border, edge, rim. شُفر وشَفِير

Side of a spear-head, edge of a sword. Broad knife. Shoemaker's knife. شَفرة ج شِفار وشَفر وشَفرات

✧ Scythe, hook, bill. شَفرة

The side of the valley. شَفِير الوادي

Straitened (life). مُشفِر

Camel's lip. مِشفَر ج مَشافِر

To kick a. o. ✻ شَفز i شَفزًا ه

To sow hatred between. شَفزَر بَين

Large needle. شَفِيزة

To trip a. o. ✻ شَفزَب ه

Trip, catch with the leg. شَفزَبيّة

To wound a. o. in the heart. ✻ شَغَف a شَغفًا ه

To feel a passionate love for. شُغِف حُبًّا و✧ انشَغَف

Bottom of the heart. Pericardium. شَغف وشَغَف وشَغاف

Passionate love. شَغف والشِّغاف

Pain in the side. شَغاف وشُغاف

To occupy a. o. in. ✻ شَغَل a شَغلًا وشُغلًا, وأشغَل ه ب

To distract a. o. from. — ه عن

To be busied by. شُغِل وتَشَغَّل واشتَغَل ب

To give much work to. شَغَّل ه

How busy he is ! ما أشغلَهُ

To be diverted from. تَشاغَل عن

✧ To work, (man, machine). إشتَغَل

He felt anxious. إشتَغَل قَلبُهُ

Employment, business. ✧ Work. Natural produce. Make. شَغل وشُغل وشَغَل ج أشغال وشُغول

A work, an employment. ✧ A job. شَغلة ج شَغلات

Thrashing-floor. Heap of wheat. شَغلة ج شَغل

Busied. شَغِل

Penal servitude. أشغال شاقّة

Occupation, employment. إشتِغال

Busying the mind (affair). شاغِل

Main-sail. ◘ شاغُول

Active in work. Labourer. ✧شَغِيل وشَغّال

Business. أشغولة ومَشغَلة ج مَشاغِل

Busy. ✧ Working (machine). مُشتَغِل

Occupied (place). Busy. Anxious (man). مَشغُول

To be unequal (teeth). ✻ شَغا o شُغوًّا وشَغي a شَغًا

To counteract a. o. أشغى ب

Inequality of the teeth. شَغًا

Unequal (tooth). شاغٍ ج شَواغٍ

Having unequal teeth. أشغى م شَغواء وشَغياء ج شُغو

To be thin, transparent (cloth). ✻ شَفّ i شُفوفًا وشَفِيفًا وشَفَفًا

To be emaciated (body). — شُفوفًا

To double (a number.) شَفَنَ a شَفْنًا *
To repeat (a prayer).

To give to a. o. the right of — ب
pre-emption.

To appear double to a. o. شُفِمَ ل
from weak sight (object).

To intercede for a. o. to. شَفَعَ a شَفَاعَةً ، وتَشَفَّعَ لِفُلَانٍ او في فُلَانٍ الى

To join with another — على فُلَانٍ بالعَدَاوَةِ
against.

To welcome a o.'s interces- شَفَّعَ ة في
sion on behalf of.

To double. ♦ To grant to a. o. — ه
the right of pre-emption (judge).

To ask a. o.'s inter- إِسْتَشْفَعَ ة الى فُلَانٍ
cession to.

Pair, couple; one of a شَفْع ج أَشْفَاع
pair.

By pairs, by couples. شَفْعًا

Coupling of two things. Right شُفْعَة
of pre-emption. Madness.

Intercessor. Pre-emptor. شَافِع

Eye seeing double. عَيْن شَافِعَة

Founder of one of the four شَافِعِيّ
Mohammedan rites. Follower of this
rite.

Intercession, mediation. Pro- شَفَاعَة
tection.

Filling two vessels in one milking شُفُوع
(she-camel).

Intercessor, mediator. شَفِيع ج شُفَعَاء
Pre-emptor.

Successful intercessor. مُشَفِّع

To pity a. o. شَفِقَ a شَفَقًا ، وأَشْفَقَ على *
To be anxious about.

To move a. o. to pity for. شَفَّقَ ة على

To weave (a fabric) badly. — ه

To lessen a. th. وأَشْفَقَ ه

To guard against a. o. أَشْفَقَ من

Evening twilight. Fear. شَفَق ج أَشْفَاق
Pity. Shore. Unsubstantial (tissue).
Refuse.

Compassion., pity. Solicitude. شَفَقَة

Compassionate, شَفُوق وشَفِيق ومُشْفِق
tender.

Scanty; insignificant (gift). مُشَفَّق

Gizzard. شَفَل - مِشْفَلَة ج مَشَافِل *

Ceratin-tree. شَفَلَّح *

To look at شَفَن a شَفْنًا وشُفُونًا ة *

a. o. askance or sideways, in wonder
or scorn.

Intelligent. Handsome. شَفِن وشَفِين

Expectation. Looking for an شَفَن
inheritance.

Looking askance. شَافِن وشَفُون

Keen-sighted. شُفُن

Turtle-dove. شَفْنِين ج شَفَانِين *

To strike a. o. on شَفَهَ a شَفَهَهُ ة *
the lips.

To divert a. o. from. — عن

To consume (a. o.'s property : — ة
beggars).

To exhaust (a. o.'s property : — ه
family)

To have many consumers (stores). شُفِهَ

To talk mouth شَافَهَ مُشَافَهَةً وشِفَاهًا ة
to mouth with.

To get near to. — ه

Lip. Edge, rim. شَفَة وشِفَة ج شَفَوَات وشِفَاه

Discreet or importune. خَفِيف الشَّفَة

Word lit : (daughter of the بِنْتُ الشَّفَة
lips).

He his held in لَهُ في النَّاسِ شَفَة حَسَنَة
estimation.

Big-lipped. شُفَاهِيّ

Labial (letter). شَفَهِيّ م شَفَهِيَّة

Conference, intercourse. مُشَافَهَة

Face to face, in immediate مُشَافَهَة
presence.

Impoverished by bounties. مَشْفُوه
Frequented (water-spring). Sought
(dish). Exhausted (wealth).

To near its setting شَفَا o شَفْوًا *
(sun). To appear (new moon).

Extremity, brink. شَفًا م شَفَوَان ج أَشْفَاء
Remainder of life, light.

Having parted lips. أَشْفَى

To cure a. o. from شَفَى i شِفَاء ة من *
(disease). To quench a. o.'s (thirst).

To recover health.

To set (sun). شَفِيَ a شَفًى

To be at the point of أَشْفَى على المَوْت
death

To give (a medicine) to a. o. — ة ه

To cool after anger. تَشَفَّى من غَيْظِهِ

To be restored to تَشَفَّى واشْتَفَى ب
health through.

To be content with. ♦ To إِشْتَفَى ب

Frog-bit. شَقِيق الماء
Glaucium, horn-poppy. — القرن
Corn-poppy. ✧ شُقَّيق
Sister by the same parents. Half of the head. Hemicrany. Fertile valley between two mountains. Abundant rain. شَقِيقة ج شَقائِق
شَقِيقة النُّعمان و✧ (شُقَّيق وشقشقيق) ج
Red anemone, peony. شَقائِق
Etymology, derivation. إشتِقاق
Separation. ✧ Schism. إنشِقاق
Toil; difficulty. مِشقَّة ومَشقَّة ج مَشاقّ
Schist; slate-rock. حَجَر مُشقَّق
Tow from hemp. ✧ مَشاقّ
Schismatic, dissenter. مُشاقّ
To groan (camel). To twitter (bird). ✲ شَقشَق
✧ To rinse (clothes, vessels). — ه
Foam of a camel's mouth. شِقشِقة ج شَقاشِق
Loquacity. شَقشَقة
Speaking fluently. ذُو شَقشَقة
To grow (tooth). ✲ شَقَأ o شَقأ وشُقُوءا
To cleave (the head). To part the hair of the head. — ه
Parting of the hair. مَشقَأ
Comb. مِشقَأ ومِشقَاء ومِشقَأة
✲ شَقب وشِقب ج شِقاب وشُقُوب وشِقَبة
Crack between two rocks. Cleft in a rock where birds build their nests.
To be foul, ugly. ✲ شَقُح o شَقاحة
To break up, to spoil. شَقَح a شَقحا ه
To show redness (dates). To grow (palm-tree). شَقَّح وأشقَح
To revile a. o. شاقَح ه
Date beginning to show redness. شَقحة وشُقحة
What a hideous man! شُقحا وشَقحا لهُ
Ugliness, foulness. Turpitude. شَقاحة
He has committed a foul deed. جاء بالقَباحة والشَّقاحة
Ugly, foul, hideous. شَقِيح
Reddish, ruddy. أشقَح م شَقحاء ج شُقح
Camel-litter. ▫ شَقدَف
To go off, to go away. ✲ شَقَذ i وشَقِذ a شَقذا
To be affected with sleeplessness. To have a piercing, malignant look. شَقِذ a شَقذا

rejoice at an evil befalling an enemy.
✧ His wishes have been fulfilled. — قَلبهُ
To consult (a doctor). إستَشفَى ه
To ask for a remedy. — ب
Recovery. Remedy. شِفاء ج أشفِية
Health-giving. Efficacious. Peremptory (answer). شافٍ م شافِية
More efficacious. أشفَى
Awl. إشفَى ج أشافٍ وأشافِي
Hospital. مُستَشفَى
To spread in the sky (lightning). ✲ شَقّ o شَقّا
To grow (tooth, plant). To gleam (dawn). To look fixedly (dying man). — شُقُوقا
To split (wood). To pass through (a throng). To till (the earth). — شَقّا ه
To part from a company. شَقّ العَصا
To be painful to a. o. (trial). To throw a. o. into distress. — شَقّا ومَشقّة على
✧ To visit a sick person. ✧ شَقّ على المَرِيض
To chip (wood). To articulate (words) distinctly. شَقَّق ه
To disagree with. شاقّ شِقاقا ومُشاقّة ه
To be split, chipped. تَشقَّق
To make a schism, to dissent. تَشاقّ
To be split, furrowed. ✧ To become a schismatic. إنشَقّ
The affair is broken up. — العَصا
To take the half of. إشتَقّ ه
To derive (a word) from. — ه من
To depart from the point in an argument. — في الكلام
Chink, slit. Crack, furrow. شَقّ ج شُقُوق
Daybreak.
Fatigue, pain. — وشِقّ
Part of the whole; half of a. th. Side of the body. Slope of a mountain. شِقّ
Half of a. th. Splinter. Piece of cloth. شِقّة ج شِقَق وشِقاق
Distance. Aim of a journey. Long journey. Oblong piece of cloth. — وشُقّة ج شُقَق
Splitting in half. Hard, painful. شاقّ
Contention. Schism. شِقاق
Uterine brother; brother by the father and mother. Split asunder. Half. شَقِيق

شاقذ ه To oppose a. o.

أشقذ ه To drive away a. o.

ما لهُ شَقَذ ولا نَقَذ He possesses nothing.

ما بهِ شَقَذ ولا نَقَذ There is no defect in him.

شَقِذ وشَقْذان Afflicted with sleeplessness.

شَقَذَى وشَقْذاء Famishing (eagle).

✲ شَقِر a وشَقُر o شَقَرًا وشُقْرة, واشْقَرّ To be sorrel (horse). To have a ruddy, fair complexion.

شُقَر ج شُقور Important business.

شُقْرة Reddish colour.

شُقَر Cock. Lie.

شُقُور Want, necessity.

شَقِر وشُقْران وشُقّار وشَقّارَى Red anemone, peony.

أشْقَر م شَقْراء ج شُقْر Roan, sorrel (horse). Red-haired (man).

✧ أشقراني Red-haired, fair (man).

شَقْراق وشِرِقْرِق Green wood-pecker.

✲ شقص — شقّص ه To cut up (a slaughtered beast).

شِقْص ج أشقاص Portion, share, lot.

شَقِيص Society. Partner, associate.

مِشْقَص ج مَشاقِص Broad iron-head of an arrow.

مُشَقِّص Butcher.

✧ شقطيّة Lock of hair on the top of the head.

✲ شَقَم a شَقْمًا في To near (a vessel) to the lips.

— ه ✧ To heap up (things).

شقّم ل ب ✧ To abuse a. o. by blaspheming against him.

✧ شَقَف o وشقّف ه To cut, to split (stones, wood).

شَقفة و✧ شقفة ج شُقَف Piece of earthenware. Earthenware. Piece, bit.

✧ شَقِيف Huge rock.

◻ شقيقة Coarse salt.

✧ شاقوف Large hammer.

✲ شَقَل o شَقْلًا ه To weigh (a coin). ✧ To measure with a stick. To lift up.

شاقول Iron-shod stick. ✧ Plumb-line.

✧ شقلب ه To upset a. th.

◻ شقلبان Humbug; impostor. Fickle.

✧ شقلبا مقلبا Tupsy turvy.

✲ شَقَن o شَقْنًا, وأشقن ه To make a paltry (gift).

شَقُن o شُقُونة To be paltry (gift).

شَقْن وشَقِن وشَقِين Paltry, scanty.

✲ شَقِي a شَقًا وشَقاء وشَقاوة وشِقاوة وشَقْوة وشِقْوة To be wretched, miserable.

شَقَا o شَقْوًا, وأشقى ه To reduce a. o. to destitution.

شاقى ه To face, to resist a. o. To vie with a. o. in struggling against difficulty.

شَقًا وشقاء وشَقْوة وشقاوة Ill-luck, distress.

شاقٍ ج شَواقٍ High, lofty.

شَقِيّ ج أشقياء Destitute, wretched. Outlaw.

مِشْقَى (for مِشقًا) Comb.

✲ شَكّ o شَكًّا, وتَشَكَّك في To doubt about. ✧ To be scandalised at.

— ه To pitch tents in one row.

— ه ب To transpierce a. o.

— ه وه To penetrate into a. th. (blade).

شَكّ في السِّلاح To be fully armed.

— وشكّك ه ✧ To scandalise a. o.

شكّك ه To throw a. o. into suspicion, doubt.

شَكّ ج شُكوك Doubt, suspicion. Arsenic. Slight fissure in a bone. ✧ Scandal received.

شَكّة Prick with a. th. pointed. Pain in the side. Chain of golden coins.

شِكّة ج شِكَك Weapon.

شاكّ السِّلاح او في السِّلاح Armed at all points.

شاكّة ج شَواكّ Tumour in the throat.

◻ شُكُك On credit.

شِكاك Row of houses.

تشكيك Cause of suspicion. ✧ Scandal given. ◻ Sale, purchase upon credit.

شَكِيكة ج شَكائك وشُكُك Troop, party. Way, wise. Fruit-basket.

مِشَكّ ج مَشاكّ Armour. Instrument for making holes.

مَشكوك فيهِ Dubious, suspected.

◻ شكشوكة Coquettish woman.

Te شكوج Hammer.

✲ شَكَد o i شَكْدًا, وشكّد وأشكد ه ه To give a. th. to.

شُكْد Gift, present.

شاكِد Giver.

Bad augury. شَكِيس

Niggard, ill-natured. ✡ شَكِص وشَكِيص

To moan (sick person). To get angry. To suffer. To be full of seeds (crop). ✡ شَكِم a شَكَمًا

To irritate, to vex a. o. أشكم ة

Avaricious. Suffering pain. شَكِم

Arabic thorn. Prickly artichoke. شُكَاعِي

To be doubtful (affair). To ripen (grapes). ✡ شَكَل o شَكْلًا, وشَكَّل وأشكل

To shackle (a beast). شَكَل وشَكَّل ة

To mark (a writing) with points. ✧ To entangle (a business). شَكَل وشَكَّل ه

To be coquettish (woman). To be red and white. شَكِل a شَكَلًا

To picture, to fashion a. th. To plait two locks of her hair (woman). ✧ To tuck up (clothes). شَكَّل ه

To bear a resemblance to. شاكل ة

To assume a shape, a hue. ✧ To be composed. To adorn herself with flowers (woman). تَشَكَّل

To resemble one another. تَشَاكَل

To be dubious, confused (affair). إشتكل واستشكل

Shape, form, sort. Features. Figure. Convenience. Coquetry. شِكل وشَكل ج أشكال وشُكول

Vowel-point. شَكل وشَكلة

Redness mixed with whiteness. شُكلة

Flirting, coquettish (woman). شَكِلة

Touchy. ✧ شِكلِيّ

Shackle, bond. White spot on a horse's feet. شِكال ج شُكُل

Nosegay. Bouquet. ✧ تَشكِيلة ج تَشَاكِيل

Likeness. شاكِل وشُكلة

He bears a likeness to his father. فِيهِ شُكلة او شاكِل من أبيهِ

Side. Flank. Rule of conduct. Intention. *Pl.* Tracks branching off from a main road. شاكِلة ج شَوَاكِل

Admixture of red on white or of white on red. أشكل م شكلاء ج شُكل

Want, necessity. شَكلاء

Foot-soldiers; footmen. Side, flank. شُوكَلة ج شَوَاكِل

Want. Intricacy. Manner. أشكلة

✡ شَكَر o شُكرًا وشُكورًا وشُكرانًا ة ول وتشكّر ل To thank; to praise a. o.

To fatten (cattle). To become bountiful (man). To yield much milk (female). شَكِر a شَكَرًا

To put forth shoots (palm-tree). وأشكر واشتكر –

To show thankfulness to a. o. شاكر ة

To begin (a discourse) with. ة ه –

To possess milch-camels. أشكر

To be filled with milk (udder). واشتكر –

To shower down rain (sky). To bring rain (wind). To be intense (cold, heat). إشتكر

Thanks, thanksgiving. Praise. شُكر ج شُكور

Thankfulness, gratefulness. شُكران

Small tract of land tilled and sown. ✧ شَكارة ج شَكائر

Grateful. Acknowledging a benefit. شاكِر ج شُكّر وشاكِرون

Hireling. P شاكِرِيّ ج شاكِرِيّة

Pay of a hireling. ✧ Kind of dagger. P شاكِرِيّة

Filled with milk (udder); with tears (eye). شَكرَى ج شَكارَى وشُكارَى

Very grateful. Fattened at small expense. شَكور

Offshoot, sprouts of trees. Fine hair on the temples. Interior bark of a tree. Pith. شَكِير ج شُكُر

Hemlock (*plant*). P شوكران

شَكِرة ج شَكِرات وشَكارَى, ومِشكار

Yielding much milk (female). Milch-cow.

Milky plant. مَشكَرة

To prick a. o. with (a sword, the tongue). ✡ شَكَز o شَكزًا ة

Cross-tempered. شَكِز وشَكِيز

To be cross-tempered. ✡ شَكُس o شَكاسة وشَكِس a شَكَسًا

To treat a. o. harshly. شاكس ة

To quarrel. تشاكس

The day before the new moon. شَكس

Avaricious. Harsh-tempered. شَكِس وشَكْس

Complaint, charge, accusation. شَكَايَة وشَكَارَة وَشَكْوَى
Thing complained of. شَكْوَى ومُشتَكَى مِنْهُ
A complaint. شَكْوَة ج شَكَوَات وشِكَاء
Small water-skin. — وشُكَيَّة
Complaining. Pitiable. Unwell. شَكِي وشَاكٍ م شَكِيَّة وشاكِيَة
Complainant, plaintiff. شاكٍ ومُشتَكٍ ومُتَشَكٍّ
Fully armed. شاكِي السِّلاح
Complained of, culprit. مَشكُوّ ومَشكِيّ ومُشتَكَى عَلَيهِ
He who receives a complaint. مَشكُوّ إليهِ ومَشكِيّ إليهِ
Niche for a lamp in a wall. مِشكَاة
✱ شَلَّ a شَلًّا وشَلَلًا, وشُلَّ وأُشِلَّ To be dried up or disabled (hand).
May thy fingers never be withered. لَا شُلَّ عَشْرُكَ
To drive away (camels). — o شَلًّا وشَلَلًا ه
To stitch (clothes). To shed (tears : eye). — شَلًّا ه
To have the hand dried up. أَشَلَّ
To disable a. o.'s hand (God). — ه
To dash forth (torrent). To fall in large drops (rain). إِنْشَلَّ
Withered hand. شَلَل وشَلَال
Indelible stain. شَلَل
May thy hand never be dried up! لَا شَلَالِ او لَا شَلَلًا
Light-handed. Good companion. شَلَل وشُلُل وشَلُول ومِشَلّ
Scattered (people). شِلَال
Long, distant aim. شَلَّة وشُلَّة
✧ Vine-prop. شَلَّة
✧ Skein. شِلَّة
Disabled, stiff-handed. أَشَلّ م شَلَّاء ج شُلّ
Dried up (hand). يَد شَلَّاء
Wool-cloth. Bed of a stream. شَلِيل ج أَشِلَّة
Cataracts of the Nile. ◻ شَلَّالات
To fall in drops (water). ✱ شَلشَل وتَشَلشَل
To drip (blood, water). شَلشَل ه
To drip (blood : sword). تَشَلشَل ب
Dropping. شَلشَلَة

Every one acts in his own way. كُلٌّ يَعمَلُ على أَشكَلَتِهِ
Likeness. مُشَاكَلَة وتَشَاكُل
Dubious affair, difficulty. مُشكِل ومُشكِلَة ج مَشَاكِل
Solution of dubious things. حَلُّ المَشَاكِل
Shackled. Having a white spot on one or three feet (horse). مَشكُول
✱ شَكَمَ o شَكْمًا, وأَشكَمَ ه To reward, to retribute a. o. ✧ To slap a. o.
To bribe (a judge). To bridle (a horse). شَكَمَ ه
To bite a. o. — o شَكْمًا وشَكِيمًا ه
Gift, bribe. شُكْم وشُكْمَى
Bit. شَكِيمَة ج شَكَائِم وشُكْم وشُكِيم
Incompliance. Repression of injustice.
Untractable, unyielding. ذُو شَكِيمَة او شَدِيد الشَّكِيمَة
Chest, drawers. Te شِكَمجَة
Amble, pace of a horse. Ts أَشكِين
✱ شَكَهَ — شَاكَهَ مُشَاكَهَة وشِكَاهًا ه To be alike to.
To be ambiguous (affair). أَشكَهَ
To be alike. تَشَاكَهَ
✱ شَكَا o شَكْوَى وشَكْوَى وشَكَاة وشَكَاوَة وشِكَايَة وشَكِيَّة ه الى To complain of... to a. o.
To complain of o.'s state to a. o. (sick, destitute person). — ه الى او ل
To affect, to distress a. o. (illness). — شَكْوًا وشَكْوَى وشَكَاة ه
To soothe (a plaintiff). شَكَّى ه
To listen to the complaint of a. o. — وأَشكَى ه
To give to a. o. a cause of complaint. أَشكَى ه
To satisfy the complaint of a. o. by. — ه من
He is accused of. هُوَ يُشكَى ب
To complain to a. o. تَشَكَّى واشتَكَى الى
To be diseased (eye, limb). تَشَكَّى واشتَكَى
To complain of (sickness, pain). — واشتَكَى ه ومن
To complain to one another. تَشَاكَى
Disease ; complaint. شَكَاة وشَكَاء وشَكْو وشَكْوَاء

Fond of sweets. شَوَلْقِي

Sirocco. ✧ شُلُوق (for شُرُوق)

Strawberries. شِلِك TE

Spark. ✱ شَلَم — شِلَم

Darnel-weed. P شِيلَم وشُوَلَم وشالَم

To perplex a. o. ✧ شَلَّم ه

To be perplexed. ✧ إِنْشَلَم

To set off, to depart. ✱ شَلَا o شُلُوًّا

To lift, to take up a. th. — ه

To pour (a hot liquid) for cooling it. ✧ شَلَّى ه

To call a (beast). أَشْلَى إِشْلاء ه

To excite a dog against. — ه على

To call a. o. to help. إِشْتَلَى واسْتَشْلَى ه

To get angry. إِسْتَشْلَى

Remainder, remains. شِلْو ج أَشْلاء
Limb of the body. ✧ Diseased meat.
Pl. Reins of a bridle.

Body of an animal. — وشَلًا

Remains. Piece of meat. شَلِيَّة ج شَلَايَا

✧ Large spoon. مِشْلَى

✱ شَمَّ o a شَمًّا وشَمِيمًا وشِمِّيمَى, وتَشَمَّم

To smell at. واشْتَمَّ ه

✧ To take a walk. شَمَّ الهَوَاء

To have a haughty bearing. — a شَمَمًا
To be lofty (mountain).

To be tried, proved. شُمَّ

To make a. o. to smell. شَمَّم وأَشَمَّ ه ه

To smell at o. a. شَامَّ وتَشَامَّ

To draw near to a. o. or a. th. شَامَّ ه وه

To pass in raising the head. أَشَمَّ

To go astray from. — عن

Give me your hand. أَشِمَّني يَدَك

To smell, to inhale slowly. تَشَمَّم

To scent a. th. To inhale (an odour). إِسْتَشَمَّ ه

Smelling, inhaling of a. th. شَمّ

Smell (sense). — وشَامَّة

▫ Spring-holiday in Egypt. شَمّ النَّسِيم

Tobacco-snuff. ✧ شَمَّة عَطُوس

Fine shape of the nose. Height of a mountain. Proximity. Remoteness. شَمَم

High (saddle). Sweet smell. شَمِيم

Fine-nosed. High. Proud. أَشَمّ م شَمَّاء ج شُمّ

Sweet-smelling streaked melon. شَمَّام (un. شَمَّامَة)

Active, ready to service (man). شَلْشَل وشُلْشُل ومُتَشَلْشِل

Falling in drops (water, blood). شَلْشَل ومُشَلْشِل ومُشَلْشَل

Polite, comely, gentleman. Ts شَلَبِي
✧ Barber.

To shave, to dress a. o.'s hair. ✧ شَلْبَن ه

To be shaven, dressed. ✧ تَشَلْبَن

To kick. To flatten (dough). ✧ شَلَت

Thin mattress. Ts شِلْتَة

To undress o.'self. To change its feathers (bird). To apostatise (monk). ✱ شَلَح a شَلْحًا

To throw off, to reject a. th. ✧ — ه

To strip a. o. of his clothes. شَلَّح ه
To make a. o. strip off his clothes.
✧ To strip a. o. (brigand).

Sharp, cutting sword. شَلْحَاء ج شُلْح

✧ Apostate (monk). شَالِح

✧ Brigandage. تَشْلِيح

Dressing-room (in a bath). مُشَلَّح و✧ مَشْلَح ج مَشَالِح

Mantle cloak. ✧ مَشْلَح

To split a. th. ✱ شَلَخ a o شَلْخًا ه

To despoil a. o. (thief). To plunder, to pilfer. ✧ شَلْدَق وتَشَلْدَق على

To strike deep roots (tree). ✧ شَلَّش

Root. ✧ شِلْش ج شُلُوش

Couch-grass. ✧ شِلْش الإِنْجِيل

Knife. ✱ شَلَط وشَلْطَاء

To burn, to roast. ✧ شَلُوط

To cleave (the head). ✱ شَلَغ a شَلْغًا ه

Iron-rod. ✧ شِلْف

Wallet. ✧ شِلْفَة

Rope of palm-leaves. ✧ مِشْلَاف

Water-fall. ✧ شَلُّوف

To blot (writing), to scrawl. ▫ شَلْفَط

To split a. th. lengthwise. To strike a. o. ✱ شَلَق o شَلْقًا ه وه

✧ To crumble down (wall). شَلَّق

To stand on end (hair). ✧ تَشَلَّق

✧ To perceive stealthily. To have suspicion of. ✧ إِشْتَلَق على

Small fish : eel. شِلْق وشَلِق

Lizard's eggs. شِلْقَة

Knife. شِلْقَاء

Grooms. شَلَقَة

Beggar's bag. شَلَّاق

✧ Wick-holder. شَمّامة ج شَمّامات

Scents, perfumes. شَمّامات

Smell; scent. Musk. Nosegay. مَشْمُوم

✧ To smell a. th. repeatedly. شَمْشَمَ شَمْشَمَةً ه

✱ To rejoice at another's evil. شَمِتَ a شَماتًا وشَماتَةً ب

To greet (a sneezer); to say: God bless you. To disappoint a. o. شَمَّتَ ه

To make a. o. to rejoice at his enemies' evil. أشْمَتَ ه ب

To be balked, disappointed. تَشَمَّتَ

Joy at another's evil. شَماتَة

Rejoicing at an evil. شامِت

Foot, leg. شامِتَة ج شَوامِت

Fulfilling the wish of his enemies. طَوْعَ الشَّوامِت

Disappointed, balked. شِمات وشَماتَى

Uttering wishes. مُشَمِّت

King blessed by his subjects. مَلِك مُشَمَّت

✱ To stitch (clothes). To mix a. th. شَمَجَ o شَمْجًا ه

To urge on, to press a. o. — ه

To go away from. — عن

Small quantity. شَماج

I have not tasted any thing. ما ذُقْتُ شَماجًا

✱ To be lofty (building, mountain). شَمَخَ a شَمْخًا وشُمُوخًا

To magnify o.'s self. — وشَمَخَ أنفَهُ او بأنفِهِ

To lift up, to raise a. th. شَمَّخَ ه

To be lofty. To become proud. تَشامَخَ

Far-extending (desert). شَمُوخ

Height. شُمُوخ

Lofty. Haughty. شامِخ ج شُمَّخ

✱ To walk quickly. شَمَرَ o شَمْرًا، وشَمَّرَ وتَشَمَّرَ وانْشَمَرَ

To pick up a. th. شَمَرَ وشَمَّرَ ه

To tuck up (a garment). To send off (a ship). شَمَّرَ ه

To purpose a. th. — ل

To despatch (a work). — في

To urge on (camels). أشْمَرَ ه

To slay a. o. with (a sword). — ه ب

To prepare for. أشْمَرَ وتَشَمَّرَ وانْشَمَرَ ل

Liberal. Perspicacious: energetic. شِمِّر

✧ Sea-samphire (*plant*). شُمْرَة بَحْرِيّة

Sulphur-wort, hog's fennel (*plant*). ✧ شُمْرَة الخَنازير

Fennel (*plant*). شَمار وشَمْرَة و✧ شُمْر

Acute (pain). شِمِرّ

Diamond. شَمُّور

Expeditious. Swift (she-camel). شِمْرِيّ وشِمِّير ومُشَمِّر

Effective. Exerting himself. شامِر م شامِرَة

Clinging to the teeth (gum). شامِرَة ج شَوامِر، ومُتَشَمِّرَة

✱ To stitch (clothes). شَمْرَجَ ه

To utter confused speech. — في الكلام

Mixed with truth (falsehood). *Pl.* Trifles, vanity. شِمْراج ج شَمارِيج

✱ Palm, vine-branch loaded with fruit. ◻ Branch stripped of its leaves. Stalk of a bunch. شُمْرُوخ وشِمْراخ ج شَمارِيخ

✱ In tatters (clothing). شمرق — شُمارِق وشَمارِيق ومُشْمَرِق

✱ To feel disgust at, to loathe a. th. شَمَزَ o شَمْزًا من، واشْمَأزَّ ه ومن

To contract, to get altered (face). تَشَمَّزَ

Contraction, shrink. Disgust, horror. إشْمِئْزاز وشُمأزِيزَة

Loathing, disgusted. مُشْمَئِزّ

✱ شَمَسَ o i وشَمِسَ a شَمْسًا، وأشْمَسَ

To be bright, glorious, sunny (day).

To be refractory (horse). شَمَسَ o شُمُوسًا وشِماسًا

To show enmity to. شَمَسَ ل

To cast suspicion on a. o. شَمَّسَ ه

To spread a. th. in the sun. شَمَّسَ ه

To worship the sun. ✧ To become a deacon. شَمَّسَ

✧ To assist (a priest) as deacon. شَمَّسَ ل

To be exposed to the sun. To bask in the sun. ✧ To get a sunstroke. تَشَمَّسَ

Sun. Kind of necklace. شَمْس ج شُمُوس

Sunny, solar. شَمْسِيّ

Girasol (*mineral*). حَجَر شَمْسِيّ

✧ Umbrella. ◻ Window-blind. شَمْسِيَّة

✧ Small metallic disk; plate of a lock. شَمْسَة ج شَمَسات

شامِس ج شَوامِس، وشُمُوس ج شُمْس وشُمُس

To shine, to light (lamp). أَشْمَعَ
Wax. Candle. (*un.* شَمْعَة) شَمْع ج شُمُوع
Mirthful, jolly. شَمُوع
Dealer in wax. ◘ Candlestick. Pegs for clothes. شَمَّاع
Wax manufacture. مَشْمَعَة
Waxed. ✧ Oil-cloth, waterproof. مُشَمَّع
P شَمْعَدَان ج شَمْعَدَانَات وشَمَاعِد Candlestick.
To be in a rage. ✱ شمعط – إِشْمَعَطَّ To be scattered.
To disperse. ✱ شَمْعَل وتَشَمْعَل واشْمَعَلَّ
Swift-running (she-camel). شَمْعَل وشَمْعَلَة ومُشْمَعِلّ ومُشْمَعِلَّة
To be merry. ✱ شَمِق a شَمَقًا
To be very lively. تَشَمَّق
To blow (north wind). ✱ شَمَل o شُمُولًا
To expose a. th. to the north wind. – ه شَمْلًا
To wrap the teats of a (ewe) in a bag. – o i شَمْلًا, وأَشْمَل ه
To wrap a. o. in a cloak. شَمِل a شَمْلًا وشُمُولًا, وشَمَّل ه
To be exposed to the north wind. – a شَمَلًا, وشُمِل
To include, to comprehend. شَمَل o شَمْلًا وشُمُولًا وشَمِل a شَمَلًا ه
He has done good or evil to them all. شَمَلَهُم وأَشْمَلَهُم خَيْرًا او شَرًّا
To hasten. شَمَّل وانْشَمَل واشْتَمَل
To be exposed to the north wind. To be wrapped in a cloak. أَشْمَل
To give a cloak to a. o. – ه
To wrap o.'self in clothes. تَشَمَّل واشْتَمَل ب
To wrap o.'self in clothes for sleeping on the ground. إِشْتَمَل الصَّمَّاء
To encompass, to include. To be universal, common to all. إِشْتَمَل على
Meeting. Parting. Things collected. شَمْل
May God unite them, settle their affairs. جَمَعَ اللّٰهُ شَمْلَهُم
May God scatter them, disorder their affairs. فَرَّقَ اللّٰهُ شَمْلَهُم
Small quantity. Small number. شَمَل ج أَشْمَال
Cloak covering the whole body. ✧ Small turban, head-band. شَمْلَة ج شَمَلَات

Sunny (day). Restive (horse). Wicked (man).
Exposed to the sun (field). شَمِيس
Deacon. ✧ Clerk of a priest. S شَمَّاس ج شَمَامِسَة
Basking in the sun. Sturdy. Avaricious. مُتَشَمِّس
To speak fluently. ✱ شَمِص a شَمَصًا
To urge on sharply (a beast). شَمَص o شَمْصًا, وشَمَّص ه
To shudder with fear. إِشْمَصَّ
Very lively (maid). ذَات شِمَاص
Quickness, promptitude. شُمَاص
Strong-headed (horse). شَمُوص
Contracted, shrivelled up. مُتَشَمِّص
To mix up a. th. ✱ شَمَط i شَمْطًا, وشَمَّط وأَشْمَط ه
To have its foliage scattered (tree). شَمَّط
To fill (a vessel). ✧ To rifle, to pluck a. th. – ه
To become hoary. شَمِط a شَمَطًا, واشْمَطَّ واشْمَاطَّ واشْمَأَطَّ
✧ To grow all at once (plant, youth). شَمِط
Hoariness. شَمَط
Aromatics, pickles. – وشَمْط وشِمْط ج شِمَاط وأَشْمَاط
Uproar, disturbance. TE شَمَاطَة
Mixed. Partly green and partly dry (plant). Black and white (wolf). Variegated. شَمِيط
Dawn. الشَّمِيط
Skein, spindleful. ✧ شَمُّوط ج شَمَامِيط
Hoary. أَشْمَط م شَمْطَاء ج شُمْط وشُمْطَان
Party, band. Rent (clothes). ✱ شِمْطَاط ج شَمَاطِيط
The horses came in separate troops. جَاءَت الخَيْل شَمَاطِيط
To detain a. o. ✱ شَمَظ o شَمْظًا ه To urge a. o. gently. To speak to a. o. in a gentle yet severe tone.
To mix up a. th. To take little by little. – ه
To joke, to sport. ✱ شَمَع a شَمْعًا وشُمُوعًا ومَشْمَعًا
To be scattered (th). – شُمُوعًا
To wax a. th. شَمَّع ه
To make a. o. to play. – ه

شمل وشَمال وشَمَل وشِمال وشَميل وشَوْمَل وشَيْمَل North wind.

Bundle of spikes. شِمال و ✧ شَمِيلَة

Sack put upon the udders of a ewe. شِمال

Left hand, left side. Bad omen. شِمال ج أَشْمُل وشَمائِل وشُمُل

Natural disposition. Good qualities. شِمال وشَمِيلَة ج شَمائِل

Northern, northerly. شَمالي

Wine, fresh wine. شَمُول

Mulberry. Raspberry. ✧ شُمُول ج شَمامِيل

General, common. شامِل م شامِلَة

Cloak covering the whole body. مِشْمَل ومِشْمَلَة

Small dagger worn under the clothes. مِشْمَل

Exposed to north wind. Gifted with good qualities. Cooled (wine). مَشْمُول

Cooled wine. مَشْمُولَة

To be smart, sprightly. ✱ شَمْلَل

Brisk (she-camel). شِمْلال وشِمْلِيل

Small quantity. شُمْلُول ج شَمالِيل

◻ Sprightly.

Medlar. ◻ مُشَمْلَة

Scattered on all sides. شَماليل

Beet-root. ◻ Buoy. ✧ شَمَنْدَر وشَمَنْدُور

To mix (wine) with water. ✱ شَنّ o شَنًّا ه على

To start horsemen upon (the enemy). شَنّ وأَشَنّ الغارَة على

✧ To sprinkle with dust. ✧ شَنَّن ه

To be worn out (water-skin). أَشَنّ وتَشَنَّن وتَشانّ واسْتَشَنّ

To be wrinkled, dried up (skin). تَشَنَّن وتَشانّ

✧ To be covered with dust. تَشَنَّن

To become lean. إِسْتَشَنّ

Worn out skin. شَنّ وشَنَّة ج شِنان

Tall. Lean. Starved. شُنُون

Milk thinned with water. شَنِين

Cool water. Poured (water). شُنان

Water flowing from a skin. شُنانَة

Alcali. أُشْنان وإِشْنان

✧ Powder, dust. شَنان

To be cracked (glass). ◻ شَنْشَن

Nature. behaviour. Piece of meat. ✱ شِنْشِنَة ج شَناشِن

✱ شَنَأَ وشَنِئَ a شَنْأً وشِنْأً وشُنْأً وشَنْأَة وشَنْآنًا وشَنَآنًا ومَشْنَأً ومَشْنَأَة ومَشْنُؤَة ه To hate, to loathe a. o.

To confess, to admit a. th. — وشَنِئَ a شَنَأَة ب

To hate o. a. تَشانَأَ

Hatred. شَناءَة ومَشْنَأَة

Hating, loathing. شانِئ ج شُنّاء

Abhorring. شَنْآن م شَنْآنَة وشَنْأَى

Pure. Continence. شَنُؤَة وشُنُوءَة

Flocks liberally given. شَوانِئ المال

Ugly, foul. مَشْنَأ

Hated, hateful. مَشْنُوء ومِشْناء

To have fine teeth. To be cool (day). ✱ شَنِبَ a شَنَبًا

Whiteness of the teeth. ✧ Mustaches. شَنَب

Cold (day). شانِب وشَنِب

Having fine teeth. أَشْنَب وشانِب وشَنِيب م شَنْباء وشانِبَة الخ

Seedless pomegranate. شَنْباء

Circle, flange. ◻ شَنْبَر

Measure holding six or eight mudds. ✧ شُنْبُل ج شَنابِل

Leather-bag, knapsack. T شَنْتَة

Women's ample trousers. ✧ شِنْتِيان ج شَناتِين

To rend (clothing). ✱ شَنْتَر ه

Finger. شُنْتُرَة ج شَناتِر

To be hard (hand-palm). ✱ شَنِثَ a شَنَثًا

To be wrinkled, contracted (skin). ✱ شَنِجَ a شَنَجًا وتَشَنَّجَ وانْشَنَجَ

To wrinkle, to contract (the skin : fire, cold). ✧ To give a stiff neck (cold). شَنَّجَ ه

To suffer from a wry-neck. To be in convulsions. تَشَنَّجَ

Spasmodic contraction. Camel. شَنَج

Convulsion. ✧ Wry-neck. تَشَنُّج

Anchusa tinctoria, orcanet. P شَنْجار

To dishonour a. o. ✱ شَنَحَ -- شَنْحًا على

Tall (camel). شَناحٍ وشَناحِيّ وشُناحِيّ

To take out the thorns of palm-trees. ✱ شَنَخَ -- شَنْخًا عَلَيْهِ نَخْلَةً

✱ شُنْخُوب وشُنْخُوبَة وشِنْخاب ج شَناخِيب Summit of a mountain.

Repast given on the completion of a building, on the return from a journey. ✱ شُنْدُخ وشُنْدُخِيّ وشُنْداخ

peg. ✧ To throttle a. o. To hang (a culprit).
To put a piece of wood into a hive. — وشَنَق ه
To like a. th. — i شَنقًا وشَنِق a شَنقًا
To cut, to divide a. th. شَنَّق ه
To receive the price of blood. or to bind o'self to pay the bloodwite. أشنق
To treat a. o. haughtily. — على
✧ Strangulation. Hanging. شَنق
Blood-money. Surerogatory gift. شَنق
Strap of a water-skin. Long. شِناق
Covetous. شَنِق ج أشناق
Piece of wood for raising honey-comb. شَنِيق
Self-conceited, foppish. شِنِّيق
Carved (meat). مُشَنَّق
Gallows. ✧ مَشنَقة ج مَشانِق
To abstain. ◘ To dress gaudily. ✧ شَنَك
To raise the head. ✧ شَنَّك
To hook a. th. ◘ To trip up a. o. ✧ شَنكَل
Hook. Window-catch. Fishing-hook. Hooked peg. Ts شنكل
To scratch (the skin). ✲ شَنَم o شَنمًا ه
Hard labour. ✲ شَنِي — شانِيَة ج شَوان
✲ شَهِب a وشَهُب o شَهَبًا . واشتَهَب واشهَبَّ واشهابَّ To be grayish.
To alter the complexion (heat, cold). شَهَب a شَهبًا . وشَهَّب ه
To deprive a. o. of his income (drought). أشهَب ه
Mountain covered with snow. شَهب
Gray, gray colour. شَهَب وشُهبَة
Bright blaze. Bright meteor. Star. Brisk, sprightly. شِهاب ج شُهبان وشُهُب وأشهُب
Dauntless warrior, hero. شِهاب الحَرب
Stars shining brightly. الشُّهُب
Gray, grayish. Glossy (armour). Serious affair. أشهَب م شَهباء ج شُهب
Gloomy and cold day. يوم أشهَب
Year of drought. عام أشهَب
Surname of the town of Aleppo. شَهباء
Surname of king Almondher's sons. الأشاهِب
To witness a. th. ✲ شَهِد a شُهودًا ه
To give evidence on. شَهِد a شَهادَةً على

To defame, to disgrace a. o. ✲ شَنَر — شَنَّر على
Disgrace, shame. شَنار
Wicked, ill-natured. شِنِّير وشِنِّيرة
To stamp (a coin). ◘ شَنيَر ه
To tie a. th. ◘ شَنَط o
Now, presently. Tв شِندي
To stick to. ✲ شَنَص o وشَنِص a شُنوصًا ب
Swift running (horse). شَناص وشَناصِيّ وشُناصِيّ
Pieces of roasted meat. ✲ شَنَط — شُنُط
Roast meat. مُشَنَّط
To revile, to disgrace a. o. ✲ شَنظَر ب
Rogue, sly fellow. شِنظِير ج شَناظِير
Summit of a mountain. — وشُنظُورَة
To find a. o. foul. To revile, to dishonour a. o. ✲ شَنِم a شَنعًا ه
To have a loathing for. شَنِع a شُنعًا ب
To be foul, ugly, infamous. شَنُع o شَناعَةً وشَنعًا وشُنعًا وشُنوعًا
To disgrace a. o. شَنَّع ه
To charge with foul deeds. — عَلَيهِ الأمرَ
To be swift in (running). To despatch (business). — وتَشَنَّع في
To ride (a horse). تَشَنَّع ه
To take up (arms). — ه
To find a. th. hateful. إستَشنَع ه
Ugliness. Profligacy. Dastardly act. شُنعَة وشَناعَة وشُنوع
Infamous, hideous. شَنِع وشَنِيع . وأشنَع م شَنعاء . ومُشَنَّع
Spreader of false news. مُشَنِّع
To look at a. o. scornfully. ✲ شَنَف o i شَنفًا الى
To hate, to loathe a. o. شَنِف a شَنَفًا ه ول
To adorn a. o. with earrings. شَنَّف وأشنَف ه
To adorn (speech). شَنَّف ه
To wear earrings. تَشَنَّف
Earring for the upper part of the ear. شَنف ج شُنوف
Net-sack for straw. ◘ شَنِيف
Contemner, scornful. شانِف وشَنِف
He has treated us scornfully. إنَّهُ لَشانِف عَنّا بِأنفِهِ
To pull the bridle (rider). To strap (a water-skin). ✲ شَنَق o i شَنقًا . وأشنَق ه وه
To tie (a beast) to an elevated شَنَّق ه

He swore by God. شهد بالله
To give testimony before a judge against a. o. — على أحد
To bear witness in favour of a. o. — ل
To behold, to witness a. th. شاهد ه
To ask a. o. to bear witness on. أشهد واستشهد ه على
To be slain for God's sake. To suffer martyrdom. أشهد وأستشهد
To say : there is no God but God. تشهّد
To summon a. o. to give evidence on. إستشهد ب
Honey-comb. Honey. شُهد وشَهد ج شِهاد
Testimony, evidence given. Certificate. Act of faith of Moslems. شَهادة ج شَهادات
Martyrdom. Testimony. شَهادة
In testimony of. شَهادةً على
Eye-witness Spectator. Tongue. Angel. Text quoted as a proof. شاهد ج شُهود وشُهَّد
Truthful witness. — ج شَهد وشُهود وأشهاد
Earth. ✧ Fore-finger. شاهِدة ج شَواهِد وشاهِدات
Trustworthy witness. Martyr. Killed in war (moslem). شهيد ج شُهَداء, وشُهَد
Sight, vision. مُشاهَدة
Place of martyrdom. Sight. ✧ Funerals. Shrine. مَشهَد ج مَشاهِد
Meeting-place. — ومَشهَدة ومَشهُدة
The day of Resurrection. المَشهُود
✡ Three to six years old (child). شَهدَر م شَهدَرة
To divulge a. o.'s deeds. ✡ شَهَر a شَهرًا, وشَهَّر ه ب
To draw (a sword). — ه
To hire a. o. by the month. شاهَر مُشاهَرة وشِهارًا ه
To be one month old. أشهَر
To publish, to divulge. — واشتهر ه
To become notorious, illustrious. إشتهر
Month. Moon. New moon. شَهر ج شُهور وأشهُر
Publicity. Fame. شُهرة
Famed, illustrious. شَهِير
Large, broad. شَهيرة

More celebrated. أشهَر
Famous. Divulged. مَشهُور ج مَشاهِير
Monthly wages or pension. مُشاهَرة
To bray (ass). To be lofty (building, mountain). ✡ شَهَق a i شَهِيقًا a وشَهق وتَشهاقًا
To have the death-rattle. To sob. ✧ To hiccough. — شُهاقًا وشَهِيقًا وتَشهاقًا
To bring evil on a. o. (look). — على
Death-rattle. Sobs. hiccough. Final sound of an ass's braying. شَهِيق وتَشهاق
Repeated rattle, sobbing. ✧ Hiccough. شَهقة
High, lofty (mountain). شاهِق
In a rage. ذُو شاهِق
To be of a dark blue colour mixed with red (eye). ✡ شَهِل a شَهَلًا, واشهَلّ
To hurry on a. th. ✧ شَهَّل
To abuse a. o. شاهَل ه
To fade away (brightness of the face). ✧ To be short (garment). To get ready for action. To take a good turn (affair). تَشَهَّل
Dark blue colour. شُهلة وشَهَل
Unavoidable business. شَهلاء
Dark blue mixed with red. أشهَل م شَهلاء ج شُهل
To frighten a. o. ✡ شَهَم a o شَهمًا وشُهومًا ه
To urge on (a horse). — شَهمًا ه
To be sharp-minded, energetic (man). To be full of vigour (horse). شَهُم o شَهامة
Wisdom. Vigour, energy. شَهامة
Sharp-minded, clever. Energetic. شَهم ج شِهام
Chief enjoying authority. — ج شُهوم
Hedge-hog, urchin. شَيهَم
Frightened. Energetic, clever. مَشهُوم
Gerfalcon. Steelyard ; beam of a balance. P شاهِين ج شَواهِين وشَياهِين
Projecting balcony. Tᴇ شَهنِشِين
To bray (ass). ✧ شَهنَق وشَنهَق
Braying (of the ass). ✧ شَهنَقة
✡ شَها o وشَهِيَ a شَهوةً, وتَشَهَّى واشتهى ه
To covet, to long for.
To excite (in a. o.) the desire of. شَهَّى ه

To point out a. th. with (the finger). شَوَّر وأشار الى ب
To consult a. o. شاوَر واستشار ه
To give (advice) to a. o. أشار على ب
To feel ashamed. تَشَوَّر
To consult together. تَشاوَر على
To gather (honey). إشتار واستشار ه
To become fat (cattle). To attire o.'s self. إستشار
Honey taken from the hive. شَور
✧ Advice, counsel.
Shape, figure. Beauty. Ornament. شارَة وشَورَة وشُورَة وشَوار وشِيار
Shame, confusion. ✧ Embroidered handkerchief. ▫ *Avicennia officinalis*, desert-shrub. شَوْرَة
✧ Avenue. شُورَة
Bee-hive. — ومَشار ومِشوارة
Council. Counsel. شُورَى وتَشاوُر
Counsellors. أهل الشُّورَى
Privy council. مَجلِس الشُّورَى
✧ Council of state. شُورَى الدَّولَة
Thurible, censer. ▫ شَورِيَة
Kitchen ustensils; luggage. شَوار وشِوار
Fine horses. خَيل شِيار
Ridge, slope. ✧ شُوار
To stand on a ridge. ✧ شَوَّر
Counsellor, minister. شَيِّر ج شُوَرَاء
Good adviser. خَيِّر شَيِّر
Fine poem. قَصيدة شَيِّرَة
Indication, sign. Hint, allusion. إشارَة
Pronoun demonstrative. إسم الإشارة
✧ Sign of the cross. إشارة الصَّليب
Consultation. إستِشارَة
The aforesaid. مُشار إلَيه
Sown land. مَشارَة ج مَشاوِر ومَشايِر
Adorned, embellished. مَشُور
Counsellor. ✧ Field-marshal. مُشير
Fore-finger. مُشيرَة
Advice given or received. Order. مَشُورَة ومَشْوَرَة ج مَشُورات
The evangelical counsels. ألمشورات الإنجيليّة
Counsellor, adviser. مُستَشار
Horse-show. Good appearance. ✧ Errand. مِشوار ج مَشاوير
Instrument for collecting honey. مِشوَر ومِشوار ج مَشاوِر

To comply with a. o.'s wishes. أشهَى ه
To importune a. o. with requests. تَشَهَّى على
Desire, appetite, lust. شَهوَة ج شَهَوات, واشتِهاء
Longing for. شَهِيّ م شَهِيّة
Appetible (food). Wished. — ومُشتَهًى
Desiring eagerly. Covetous, lewd. شَهوان وشَهوانِيّ
Keen-sighted. رَجُل شاهِي البَصَر
✧ To mix up a. th. with. ✡ شاب ٥ شَوبًا وشِيابًا ه ب
To avert an evil from. — وشَوَّب عن
✧ To be warm (man). شَوَّب
To be mixed, mingled. إنشاب واشتاب
Mixture. Honey. ✧ Warmth, warm. شَوب
He does not possess anything. ما عِندَهُ شَوب ولا رَوب
Deceit, embezzlement. شَوبَة
Stain. Blemish. Ill-luck. شائِبَة ج شَوائِب
Mixture. شِياب
Mixed, mingled. مَشُوب ومَشِيب
Flask case. مُشاوَب ج مَشاوِب
Rural guard, keeper. ✧ شُوباصِي
To appoint a keeper for corn-fields. ✧ شَوبَص ه
To swing (the arms) in running. ✡ شوح — شَوَّح
To deny a. th. شَوَّح ه
Fir-tree. ✧ شُوح
Kind of kite. Vulture. شُوحَة
Joist, plank. ✧ شُوحِيّة ج شَواحِي
To set (sun). ✡ شوذ — شَوَّذ
To cover the sun (cloud). — ه
To put a turban on a. o. — ه
To put on a turban. تَشَوَّذ واشتاذ
Turban. مِشوَذ ومِشواذ ج مَشاوِذ ومَشاوِيذ
To collect honey from the hive. ✡ شار ٥ شَورًا وشِيارًا وشِيارَة ومَشارًا ومَشارَة, وأشار ه
✧ To advise a. o. to. شار على ب
To try (a horse) before buying it. — ٥ شَورًا وشِوارًا, وشَوَّر وأشار ه
To make (fire) to blaze. شَوَّر وأشار وأشوَر ه وب
To show a. th. to. شَوَّر الى ب
To make a. o. ashamed by. — ب

✧ مَشْوَرَ To walk to and fro.
✱ شَاسَ o وشَوِسَ a شَوَسًا, وتَشَاوَسَ To have a scornful look.
شَوِسَ م شَوْسَاء ج شُوس Looking with contempt.
✱ شَوَشَ — شَوَّشَ ه To disorder (a business). ✧ To impair (health). To trouble a. o.
تَشَوَّشَ ✧ To be sick, unwell.
— على To be disordered (affair).
تَشَاوَشَ To be disorderly (mob).
✧ شُوشَة Lock of the scalp, crest.
✧ شَاش Muslin.
شَوَاش Misunderstanding, difference.
Ts شَاوِيش Constable, serjeant.
تَشْوِيش Disorder, disturbance. ✧ Ailment, indisposition.
✱ شَاصَ o a شَوْصًا To rub a. th. with the hand.
— ه To cleanse, to wash a. th.
— وشَوَّصَ وأَشَاصَ ه To pick (the teeth).
شَاصَ To have the tooth-ache; a pain in the bowels. To struggle in his mother's womb (fœtus). To throb (artery).
شَوِصَ a شَوَصًا To be squint-eyed.
شَوْصَة Pain in the belly. Throbbing of an artery. Pleurisy.
شِيَاص Bad temper.
أَشْوَصُ م شَوْصَاء ج شُوص Squint (eye).
✱ شَوَطَ — شَوَّطَ To make a long journey.
— ه To cook (meat). To blast (plants: cold).
تَشَوَّطَ ه To jade (a horse).
شَوْط ج أَشْوَاط Race on horseback.
شَوْط بَاطِل Sunbeam penetrating through a loop-hole.
✱ شَوَظَ — شُوَاظ وشِوَاظ Smokeless blaze. Intenseness of (fire, heat).
✱ شَوِعَ a شَوَعًا To have a blaze on the cheek (horse). To have bristled hair.
شَوَع Blaze on the cheek of a horse.
أَشْوَعُ م شَوْعَاء ج شُوع Having hard and bristly hair; having a blaze on the cheek (horse).
مِشْوَاء Oven-poker.
✱ شَافَ o شَوْفًا ه To polish a. th. ✧ To see a. th.

شَافَ ه بِالقِطْرَان To smear (a camel) with tar.
شِيفَ To be attired.
شَيَّفَ ه To prepare (an eye-wash).
✧ شَوَّفَ ه To show a. th.
أَشَافَ إِشَافَةً على To overlook, to overtop (a place).
— من To fear a. o.
تَشَوَّفَ To attire o.'self.
تَشَوَّفَ من To look from an elevated spot.
— واشْتَافَ الى To behold, to observe.
إِشْتَافَ واسْتَشَافَ To become hardened (wound).
شَوْف Harrow.
✧ شُوفَان Oats.
✧ شَوْفَة Sight, view.
✧ شَوَّافَة Pumice stone.
شِيَاف Eye-wash, eye-powder.
شَيِّفَة وشَيِّفَان Military scout.
مَشُوف Bright, smooth (coin). Smeared with tar (camel).
✱ شَاقَ o شَوْقًا, وشَوَّقَ ه الى To excite a desire in.
شَاقَ ه الى To tie (the ropes of a tent) to (the poles).
تَشَوَّقَ ه والى To show earnest desire for.
إِشْتَاقَ ه والى To long for.
شَوْق ج أَشْوَاق Yearning.
شِيَاق Ropes of a tent.
إِشْتِيَاق Propensity.
شَائِق Inspiring a desire.
شَيِّق ومُشْتَاق Burning with desire.
أَشْوَق ج شُوق Long.
مَشُوقَة Leaned against a wall (a water-skin).
✱ شَاكَ o شَوْكًا To be sharp-pointed. To show his vigour (man).
— ه To prick a. o. (thorn).
شَاكَ وأَشَاكَ ه ه او ب To wound a. o. with a thorn.
شَاكَ a شَاكَةً وشِيكَةً To fall amongst thorns. To walk amidst thistles.
شِيكَ To be covered with red pimples (body).
شَوِكَ وأَشْوَكَ To be thorny (tree).
شَوَّكَ To put forth feathers (chick); new hair (shaven head).

To arm a. th. with thorns. شَوَّكَ ه
To be pricked by thorns. ✧ تَشَوَّكَ
Thorn, prickle, point. شَوْك ج أَشْوَاك
He came with all his people. جَاءَ بِالشَّوْكِ وَالشَّجَرِ
✧ Warrant, proxy, judicial evidence. أَحْرُف الشَّوْك
A prickle, a point. Sting (of insects). Buckle. Tongue. Spur. Weapon. Power, might. Weaver's instrument. Whitlow. ✧ Fork. شَوْكَة
✧ Brank-ursine (*plant*). شَوْكَة اليَهُود
▫ Prickly fig, fruit of the cactus. تِين شَوْكِي
✧ Scrophularia, fig-wort (*pl*). حَشِيشَة الشَّوْكِي
Thorny (tree). شَائِك ج شَاكَة, وَشَوك
Bristling with arms. شَائِك السِّلَاح وشَاكُ السِّلَاح وشَوك السِّلَاح
Ground covered with thorns. أَرْض شَاكَة
Rough to the hand (cloth). أَشْوَك م شَوْكَاء
Thorny (tree). مُشْوِك
Covered with red pimples (body). — وَمَشُوك
To be raised (tail). To be outweighed (scale of a balance). ✱ شَالَ o شَوْلًا وشَوَلَانًا
To raise the tail (she-camel). — بِذَنَبِهَا وأَشَالَتْهُ
He got angry, and then appeased. He is dead. شَالَتْ نَعَامَتُهُ
They went off. — نَعَامَتُهُم
To lift (a stone). To carry (a load). — ب وأَشَالَ ه
To be empty and flaccid (skin, udder). To be scanty (water, milk). شَوَّلَ
To lift (a stone). شَاوَلَ ه
To attack o. a. with (the spear). — وتَشَاوَلَ ب
To be lifted (stone). إِنْشَالَ
To be at enmity with. إِشْتَالَ ل
Remainder of water in a vessel. ✧ Desert, waste land. شَوْل ج أَشْوَال
Sturdy, sprightly man. رَجُل شَوْل
Upper part of a scorpion's sting. Foolish (woman). شَوَّالَة
Large sack. P شُوَال ج شُوَالَات

Raising the tail (she-camel). شَائِل ج شُوَّل وشُوَّال وشُيَّل وشِيَّل
In the seventh month of her pregnancy (she-camel). شَائِلَة ج شَوْل وجج أَشْوَال
Tenth month of the lunar year. شَوَّال ج شَوَّالَات
Scorpion. Foul-mouthed (woman). شَوَّالَة
Left-handed. ▫ أَشْوَل م شَوْلَاء
Small scythe. مِشْوَل
Ash-staff used by donkey-boys. ▫ شُومر
To settle (difficulties). ✱ شَانَ o شَوْنًا الرُّؤُوس
To store up a. th. ▫ شَوَّنَ
To be light-witted. تَشَوَّنَ
Foolish woman. شَوْنَة
Man of war, ship of war. — ج شَوَان
Warehouse; magazine. Barn. ✧ شُونَة ج شُوَن
To be deformed (face). ✱ شَاهَ o شَوْهًا وشَوْهَةً, وشَوِهَ a شَوَهًا
To frighten; to hate a. o. To strike a. o. with the evil eye. شَاهَ ه
To covet, to seek greedily after. شَاهَ الى
To be long or short (neck). شَوِهَ a شَوَهًا
To render a. o. unseemly (God). شَوَّهَ ه
To cast an evil look upon. — على
To be deformed, unseemly. تَشَوَّهَ
To be altered so as to be unknown. — ل
Unseemliness, ugliness. شَوَه
Great distance. شُوهَة
Shah, king of Persia. King (at chess). P شَاه
Check-mate, *lit*: the king is dead. الشَّاه مَات
Chestnut, tree and fruit. P شَاه بَلُّوط
Coryza odora. P شَاهَبَنك
Provost of merchants. P شَاهَبَنْدَر
Hemp. P شَاهدَانِج وشَهْدَانِق
Common fumitory. P شَاهتَرج
Ocimum minimum, sweet basil. P شَاهسفَرَم
Sharp-sighted. شَائِه وشَاه وشَاهِي البَصَر ج شُوَّه
Royal, imperial. P شَاهَانِيّ وشَاهِيّ
Ewe. Wild bovine kind. Goat. Buffalo. Woman. شَاة ج شَاء وشِيَاه وشِوَاه وأَشَاوِه
Evil-eyed. أَشْوَه م شَوْهَاء ج شُوه

Ugly, unseemly. أشْوَه ومُشَوَّه.

Country rich in sheep. أرْض مَشَاعَة

* شَوَى i شَيْأ, وشَوَّى ه To roast (meat).

شَوَّى وأشْوَى ه To feed a. o. with roast meat. To give to a. o. meat to be roasted. To wound a. o. on the skin of the head.

أشْوَى To leave a portion of o.'s supper.

مَا أعْيَاهُ ومَا أشْوَاهُ In what state of exhaustion he is!

إنْشَوَى واشْتَوَى To be roasted, grilled.

شَوًى Low sort of cattle. Thing of little value. Any part of the body that is not vital.

Bone of the skull. شَوَى وشَوَاة

Roast-meat. (un. شِوَاة) شِوَا وشُوَا

شُوَايَة Small piece of meat cut off from a large one.

وشُوَايَة وشِوَايَة Crust of bread. Refuse of a flock.

وشُوَيَّة ج شُوَايَا Remains of flocks or men destroyed.

شَوَّا وشُوَّا Roaster.

Roasted. شُوِيٌّ ومَشْوِيٌّ

Frying-pan. مِشْوَاة ج مَشَاوٍ

* شَاء a شَيْئًا ومَشِيئَة ومَشَائِيَة ه To will a. th.

If God will. Please to God. إنْ شَاء اللّٰه

Bravo! lit: What God willed مَا شَاء اللّٰه is.

To render a. o. ugly (God). شَيَّأ ه

To incite a. o. to. ه على

To cool after anger. تَشَيَّأ

Thing. شَيْء ج أشْيَاء وجج أشَاوَى وأشَايَا Business.

Little thing. شُوَيٌّ وشُوَيَّة

A little.

Little by شُوَيَّة شُوَيَّة وشُوَيَ شُوَيَ little. Gently.

Soon, in a moment. شُوَيَّة أخْرَى

Will (faculty). شِيئَة ومَشِيئَة

Ill-built, shapeless. مُشَيَّأ

* شَاب i شَيْبًا وشَيْبَة ومَشِيبا To become hoary (hair). To grow old.

To render a. o. شَيَّب وأشَاب رَأْسَه وبِرَأْسِه white-haired (cares).

To have children already old. أشَاب

White hair. شَيْب وشَيْبَة

Tree-moss, lichen. شَيْبَة العَجُوز

Hoopoo (bird) شُيْهَب

أشْيَب وشِيبَان مـ شَائِبَة مـ شِيب وشُيَّب جـ شِيب White-haired.

Cold and foggy (day). أشْيَب وشَيْبَان

Calico, chintz. شِيت

* شَاء i شَيْئًا, وأشَاء على To do a. th. carefully.

To render a. o. cautious. To شَيَّخ ه cast a threatening look upon.

To fight with. شَايَح مُشَايَحَة وشِيَاحًا

To apply o.'self to. وأشَاح

To grow wormwood (land). أشَاح

To avert the face from. وَجْهَهُ عن

Kind of wormwood. Cautious, شِيح mindful. Broom-plant; speedwell.

Zeal. Barrenness. شِيَاح

Assiduous. Cautious. شَائِح شَيْحَان ومُشِيح

Zealous. Protector. مُشِيح

* شَاخ i شَيْخًا وشُيُوخَة وشِيخُوخَة وشَيْخُوخَة To become old (man). وشَيْخُوخِيَّة

To be elderly. شَيَّخ

To call a. o. a chief, senior, ه —

To appoint a. o. as chief. ه على —

To insult a. o. ب —

To rebuke a. o. على —

To become old. To pretend to تَشَيَّخ be a chief.

Old age. شَيْخُوخَة وشَيْخُوخِيَّة

Old شَيْخ ج شُيُوخ وأشْيَاخ ومَشَايِخ ومَشْيَخَة man. Elder, cheikh. Chief of a tribe. Mayor. Professor.

Husband. — المَرْأة

Chief, mayor of a village. — البِلَاد

Satan lit: The chief of — النَّار the fire.

The Cheikh-ul-Islam. — الإسْلَام

Matron, elderly woman. شَيْخَة

Republic. مَشْيَخَة

* شَاد i شَيْدًا, وشَيَّد ه To coat (a wall) with plaster. To raise (a building).

To anoint a. th. with. شَيَّد ه ب

To cause a. o. to perish. أشَاد ه

To raise (the voice). To — ه او ب recite (verses).

To cry out for a. th. lost. — بالضَّالَّة

To extol the fame of. بِذِكْرِهِ —

To charge a. o. with — عَلَيْهِ ه او ب foul deeds.

Coating of plaster, gypsum. شِيد

To escort (a funeral). To see a. o. depart. To encourage a. o. شَيَّع ه
To consume a. th. by fire. – ه بالنّار
To call (cattle) lagging behind the flock. شَيَّع وشايَع وأشاع ب
To accompany a. o. for business. To be the partisan of. شايَع ه
May safety follow you. Good speed. أشاعكم اللهُ السّلامَ او بالسّلام
To become a Shiite. تَشَيَّع
To form a party, a sect. تشايَع واشتاع
Quantity. Following. شَيْع
I shall come to thee to-morrow or the next day. آتيك غدًا او شَيْعَهُ
Aromatic plant sought by bees. شَيْعَة
Separate party, sect, dissent. Shiites; sectators of Ali, metualis. شِيعَة ج شِيَع وأشياع (un. شِيعِيّ)
Partner, sharer. شَيِّع ج شُيَعاء
House shared in common. دار شَيِّعَة
Chips of wood for kindling fire. Shepherd's reed pipe; sound of a pipe. شِياع
Notorious (news, secret). Common to many (lot). *Pl.* News spread. Scattered (horsemen). شائع وشاع ج شاعة
Public (building, square). Common, undivided (inheritance). مَشاع ومُشاع
Coal-rake for ovens. مِشياع
Babbler of news. – ومُشَيِّع ومُشِيع
Partisan, follower of. مُشايِع لِ
Partner. Sharer. مُتَشايِع ومُشْتاع
To bind, to tie a. th. to. ✡ شاق i شَيْقًا ه الى
Peak (of a mountain). Cleft between two rocks. Hair of the tail. شِيق وشِيقَة
Aquatic bird. شِيق
To take off a. th. ✧ شال i شَيْلًا ه
To nurse silkworms. ✧ – دُود القزّ
To distill spirits. ✧ – العرق
To raise a. o. To advance a. th. ✧ شَيَّل ه
Porter, carrier of burdens. ✧ شَيَّال
Coins strung into a necklace. ✧ شَيَّالَة
Wholesale, in a lump. ✧ بالمُشايَلَة
To be marked with a mole. ✡ شام i شَيْمًا
To forecast rain from (lightnings). To expect a. th. To sheath or unsheath (a sword). – ه

Plastered (wall). شِيد
Lofty, high (building). – ومُشَيَّد
To fall from a rock. ✧ تَشَيَّر
Rock. ✧ شِير
To make red stripes on (cloth). ✡ شيز – شَيَّز ه
Wood for making bowls. شِيز وشِيزَى
Date with a tender stone. شِيش P
✧ Ramrod. Spit. Window-shutter.
Small-pox. Narghileh. شِيشَة Ts
Breach-loader. شِشخانة Ts
Sample. شِشْنَة Te
To chastise a. o. severely. ✡ شيص – شَيَّص ه
Dates of bad quality. شِيص (un. شِيصَة)
Harshness of temper. شِياص
Enmity. مُشايَصَة
To be burnt. To thicken (oil, butter). To be dealt out (meat). To perish (man). To be unrevenged (bloodshed). ✧ To burn with anger. ✡ شاط i شَيْطًا وشِياطَة وشَيْطُوطَة
To mix (blood) *i. e.* to kill a murderer upon his victim. – الدِّماء
To be quick at work. – في
To expose meat to (the blaze). شَيَّط ه
To consume a. th. by fire. – وأشاط ه
To destroy a. o. To deal out a (slaughtered beast). أشاط ه وه
To spill (blood). To expose a. o. to death. – ه وب
To be burnt. تَشَيَّط
To fly in jerking the wings (pigeon). إستشاط
To burn with anger against. – على
Smell of burnt (meat, cloth); burnt meat. شِياط و✧ شَوِيط
Whirlwind of dust. شَيْطِيّ
Roasting. Meat roasted for a company. تَشْيِيط
Fat, swift (she-camel). مِشْياط ج مَشايِيط
Laughing much. Fat (camel). مُستَشِيط
To spread abroad (news). ✡ شاع i شَيْعًا وشُيُوعًا ومَشاعًا وشَيَعانًا
To accompany a. o. – ه شَياعًا
God speed you. Farewell. شاعكم السّلامُ او شاعكم اللهُ بالسّلام
To spread, to divulge (news). شاع i شَيْعًا ب، وأشاع إشاعَة ه وب

To cover (the feet with dust : road). شام ه

— شَيْمًا وشُيُومًا وشَيِّم وأشام والشام واشتام في To penetrate into.

تَشَيَّم أباهُ To be alike in temper to o.'s father.

إنشام To be watched (person).

شامة ج شام وشامات Mole, spot of beauty. Black she-camel.

ما لهُ شامة ولا زَهراء. He possesses nothing.

شِيمة ج شِيَم Nature, temper, character.

كريم الشِّيَم Gifted with a noble character.

□ شِيمية ج شِيامي Eddy, whirlpool.

شَيام Plain. Dust.

Earth, dust. Rat. شِيام ج شِيَم

أشيم ومَشِيم ومَشُوم ومَشْيُوم ج شِيم وشُوم Marked with a mole.

Placenta, secundine. مَشِيمَة ج مَشِيم ومَشَايِم

To deform a. o. To mar a. th. ✱ شان i شَيْنًا ه وه

To write the letter ش. شَيَّن ه

Ugly, foul. Disgraceful. شَيِّن

Profligacy, shame. مَشَايِن

To look at a. o. with an evil eye. ✱ شاه i شَيْهًا ه

Evil-eyed. شَيُوه وأشْيَه

Sign. Mark. شِيَة ج شِيَات

Tea. شاي

ص

✱ صَأْصَأَ To seek to open the eyes (whelp).

✱ صَأَب — صَئِب a صَأَبًا, وأَصْأَب To swarm with nits (head).

— من To be filled with (drink).

صُؤَابَة ج صُؤَاب وصِئْبَان Nit, louse's egg.

مِصْأَب Having drunk its fill.

✱ صَئِك a صَأَكًا To emit a fetid sweat. To coagulate (blood).

— ب To cleave to.

صَاءَك ه To treat a. o. harshly.

صَئِك Strong, violent.

✱ صَؤُل o صَآلَة To be furious (camel).

صَؤُول Furious.

صَئِيل Groan of camels.

✱ صَأَم a صَأْمًا ه على To lead (troops) against.

صَئِم a صَأْمًا To drink much water.

صَائِم Thirsty.

✱ صَأَى i a صُئِيًّا وصَئِيًّا وصِئِيًّا, وتَصَأَّى To utter its cry (chicken).

يَلْدَغ ويَصْئِي He does harm and complains (*lit.*) the scorpion stings while uttering its cry.

أَصْأَى ه To cause (chickens) to cry out.

✱ صَبَّ o صَبًّا ه To pour forth water. To cast, to mould a. th.

— في To go down into (a valley).

— i صَبًّا, وتَصَبَّب وانصبّ واصطبّ To be poured (liquid).

صُبّ To disappear.

صَبَّ a صَبَابَة الى To love a. o.

أَصَبّ To go down (a declivity).

إنصبّ على To dart on his prey (falcon).

تَصَبَّب To dash forth (torrent).

تَصَابّ واصطبّ ه To drink a remainder of water.

صَبّ Pouring of a liquid. Loving.

صُبّ وصُبَّة What is poured.

صُبَّة Troops of men, cattle.

صَبَب ج أصْبَاب Drainage. Declivity of ground.

صُبَابَة Water in the bottom of a vessel.

صَبَابَة Deep affection.

صَبَّالِيّ Rubican (horse).

صَبِيب ومَصْبُوب Spilt (blood, water).

صَبِيب Blood. Sweat. Frost, ice.

مَصَبّ ج مَصَابّ Mouth of a river.

مِصَبّ Mould for types.

✱ صَبَأَ a وصَبُؤ o صَبْأً وصُبُوءًا To change o.'s religion.

— ه على To lead (a troop) against.

— وأَصْبَأَ To grow (tooth, nail). To rise (star).

قُدِّمَ إليهِ الطعامُ فما صَبَأَ He has not touched the food offered to him.

Large cup.
To bear a. th. patiently. To persevere in. To restrain from. ✲ صَبَرَ i صَبْرًا على
To endure want of. — عن
To bind a. o. To constrain a. o. to. — ه
To withhold a. o. from. — ه عن
To become surety for. صَبَرَ o صَبْرًا وصَبَارَةً ب
To give a surety to. — ه
To exhort a. o. to patience. صَبَّرَ وأَصْبَرَ ه
To embalm (corpses). To stuff (a beast). صَبَّرَ ه
✧ To ballast (a ship). — ه
To act patiently with. صَابَرَ مُصَابَرَةً وصِبَارًا ه
To fall into misfortune. To become bitter (milk). To be bitter, hard. أَصْبَرَ
To feign patience. To show patience. تَصَبَّرَ
To take patience. تَصَبَّرَ واصْطَبَرَ واصَّبَرَ
To be thick. إِسْتَصْبَرَ
Patience. Self-restraint. Bondage. صَبْر
He was killed when in bonds. قُتِلَ صَبْرًا
He was compelled to swear. حَلَفَ صَبْرًا
Obligatory oath. يَمِين الصَّبْر
Edge, side. Denseness. White cloud. صِبْر وصُبْر ج أَصْبَار
He has taken the whole of it. أَخَذَهُ بِأَصْبَارِهِ
He has filled the cup to the brim. مَلَأَ الكَاسَ الى أَصْبَارِهَا
Juice of any bitter plant. Myrrh. Bitterness. Aloes. صَبِر وصَبْر
Ice; frozen water. صَبَر ج أَصْبَار
Ground covered with pebbles. صُبْر وصُبُر
Lump, heap. صُبْرَة ج صِبَار
He has taken it in a lump. أَخَذَهُ صُبْرَةً
Ballast of a ship. صَابُورَة
Intenseness of cold. صَبْرَة وصَبَارَّة
Cork, stopper. صِبَار
Surety. Shatter of rock, iron. صَبَارَة
Stone. صِبَارَة وصُبَارَة
Indian fig, fruit and tree, nopal, cactus. صَبَار وصُبَّار و✧ صُبَّيْر

To rush unexpectedly upon. أَصْبَأَ ه
Apostate, renegade. Sabian. صَابِئ ج صَابِئُون
Sabaoth. Glory, power. H صَبَأُوت وصَبَاؤُوت
Baker's roll. P صَوْبَج وصَوبَج
To visit a. o. in the morning. ✲ صَبَحَ a صَبْحًا، وصَبَّحَ ه
To be comely, gentle. صَبُحَ o صَبَاحَةً
To greet a. o. in the morning. صَبَّحَ ه
To give a. o. to drink in the morning.
To be day-time. To enter upon the morning. To become *such* on the morning. To become. أَصْبَحَ
He became learned. أَصْبَحَ عَالِمًا
I found myself quite alone. أَصْبَحْتُ وَحْدِي
Beware of. أَصْبِحْ ب
To sleep in the morning. تَصَبَّحَ
To eat a. th. in the morning. — ب
✧ To meet a. o. in the morning.
To drink a morning-draught. إِصْطَبَحَ
To light a lamp. — واسْتَصْبَحَ
To take (the advice of). إِسْتَصْبَحَ ب
✧ To sell a. th. in the morning.
Morning, forenoon. صُبْح ج أَصْبَاح، وإِصْبَاح
Morning sleep. صَبْحَة وصُبْحَة
Breakfast. صُبْحَة وتَصْبِيح
Morning-time. صَبَاح وأُصْبُوحَة
At morning. صَبَاحًا
Morning and evening. صَبَاحَ مَسَاءَ
Good morning, happy day. عِمْ صَبَاحًا
Light of a lamp. صُبَاح
صُبَاح وصُبَّاح وصَبِيح ج صِبَاح، وصَبْحَان م
Comely, handsome, gracious. صَبْحَى ج صُبَاحَى
Morning-draught. Milk drawn in the morning. صَبُوح
Fine, fresh (female). صَبِيحَة ج صِبَاح
Morning-hour. صَبِيحَة
Comeliness, beauty. صَبَاحَة وصَبَاحِيَّة
✧ Christmas-box. New year's gift. صَبَاحِيَّة
New year's day. صَبَاح الخَيْر
Fresh (fish, bread). ◻ صَابِح
Lighting. إِسْتِصْبَاح
Daybreak. مَصْبَح ومُصْبَح وإِصْبَاح
Lamp, lantern. مِصْبَاح ج مَصَابِيح

صَبَارَة Barren and elevated ground.
✧ Scouts.
صَابِر, وَصَبِير ج صُبَرَاء Patient. Steady.
صَبُور ج صُبُر, وَصَبَّار Forbearing, meek.
صَبِير وَصَبِيرَة Flat cake of bread upon which food is spread.
صَبِير ج صُبَرَاء Mountain.
— ج صُبُر White or superposed clouds.
أُمّ صَبَّار او صَبُّور Heat. Misfortune. War.
✧ صَابُورِيَّة ج صَابُورِيَّات وَصَوَابِير Basket made of reeds.
✱ صَبَعَ a صَبْعًا ب وعلى To point out a. th. with the finger.
— ه على To show a. th. to.
— ه To stop partly the orifice of a vessel with the finger.
— صَبْعًا وَمَصْبَعَة ه To render a. o. proud.
أِصْبَع وإِصْبِع وأُصْبِع وأَصْبَع وأُصْبِع ج أَصَابِع, وأُصْبُوع ج أَصَابِيع Finger.
على ماشِيَتِهِ إِصْبَع He possesses splendid flocks.
أَصَابِع العَذَارَى وأَصَابِع العَرُوس Black long-grained grapes.
مَصْبَعَة Pride.
مُصْبَع ✧ Prong, spit.
✱ صَبَغَ a o i صِبْغًا وَصَبْغًا ه To dye (cloth). To soak a. th.
— يَدَهُ ب To dip the hand in (water). To set the hand to (an affair).
— ه بالماء ✧ To baptise a. o. by immersion.
صَبَغ o صُبُوغًا To be filled (udder).
صَبَّغ ه To dye deeply (cloth).
— وأَصْبَغ To begin to ripen (dates). To cast off a young one (she-camel).
تَصَبَّغ في To profess (a religion).
اِصْطَبَغ To be dyed. ✧ To be baptised.
صِبْغ وَصِبْغ وَصِبْغَة وَصِبَاغ Dye.
ما أَخَذَهُ بِصِبْغ ثَمَنِهِ He has bought it dearer than its worth.
صِبْغ وَصِبَاغ Seasoning, sauce.
صِبْغَة وَصِبْغَة Religion. Opinion.
✧ Baptism.
صُبْغَة Date beginning to ripen.
صِبَاغَة Craft, art of a dyer.
▫ صَبُوغَة Smoked fish.
صَابِغ Dying.
الصَّابِغ St John the Baptist.
صَبَّاغ Dyer. Liar.

أَصْبَغ Impetuous (torrent).
— م صَبْغَاء ج صُبْغ White-locked (horse).
مَصْبَغَة Dye-house.
✱ صَبَنَ i صَبْنًا ه عن To withhold (a gift) from a. o.
— ه To take (dice) in hand for casting.
إِنْصَبَن واصْطَبَن عن To turn away from.
✧ صَابُون Soap.
✧ صَابُونِيَّة Soap-wort (*plant*).
✧ صَوْبَنَ ه To soap a. th.
مَصْبَنَة Soap-house.
صَبَّان و✧ صَابُونِي Seller of soap.
✱ صَبَا o صَبْوًا وَصُبُوًّا وصِبًا وَصَبَاء To have childlike propensities.
— الى To incline to; to long for.
— o صَبَاء وَصُبُوًّا To blow (east wind).
صُبِيَ وأُصْبِيَ To be blown upon by the east wind.
صَبِيَ a صَبَاء, وتَصَابَى واسْتَصْبَى To behave in a childish way.
صَابَى ه To incline (a spear) for striking. To recite (a verse) in an irregular way. To pronounce (a word) badly.
أَصْبَى To have young children (woman).
أَصْبَى ه To beguile, to captivate a. o.
تَصَبَّى وتَصَابَى ه To deceive, to seduce.
إِسْتَصْبَى ه To treat a. o. as a child.
صِبًى Propensity, inclination.
صَبًا ج أَصْبَاء وصَبَوَات East wind. Breeze.
صَبْوَة Childishness.
صَبِيّ ج صِبْيَان وأَصْبِيَة وصِبْيَة وأَصْب Boy, lad, apprentice.
صُبَيَّة وأُصَيْبِيَة وصِبْوَة Small boys.
صَبِيَّة ج صَبَايَا Girl. ✧ Young woman.
صَابٍ م صَابِيَة Childish.
صَابِيَة North-easterly wind.
مُصْبٍ ومُصْبِيَة Having young children (woman).
✱ صَتَّ o صَتًّا To yell, to shout.
— ه To repel a. o.
صَاتَّ مُصَاتَّةً وصِتَاتًا ه To pick a quarrel with.
تَصَاتَّ To dispute, to quarrel.
صَتّ وصِتّ وصَتِيت Crowd, throng.
صِتّ Contrary.
صَتّ (*for* صَدّ) Subject, topic.
صَتِيت Shrieks. Uproar.

* صَبَّا ـــ صَبًّا ه ول To undertake a. th.
* صَتَع a صَتْعًا ه To overthrow a. o.
تَصَتَّع To stroll idly.
* صتم ـــ صَتْمَ ه To complete a. th.
صَتَم وصُتْم ج صُتم Strong, sturdy, (man). Complete (number).
* صَجَّ o صَجًّا To clang (metallic bodies).
صُجُجُ Clank.
* صَحَّ i صُحًّا وصِحَّةً وصَحَاحًا To be right, proper, sound. To be true (news). To be authentical (deed). To be in good health, to be cured.
صَحَّح ه To cure a. o. ◘ To awake a. o. from sleep.
— ه To make sound, valid. To authenticate (a deed). To verify (an account). To correct (writing).
أَصَحَّ To have (a family or flock) in good state.
— ه To restore a. o. to health (God).
إِسْتَصَحَّ من To recover from (illness).
— ه To find (speech) right, true.
صَحّ ✧ Postcript.
صِحَّة Good health, state. Validity (of a deed).
صَحَاح ج أَصِحَّة Whole. In good health.
صَحِيح ج أَصِحَّاء وصِحَاح وأَصِحَّة وصَحَائِح
Entire, complete, perfect. Sound of body. Free from blemish. Correct. True, genuine. Valid. Authentical. Free from defective letters (verb).
صَحِيح ✧ It is right. Indeed, true.
صَحَاح وصَحِيح الأَدِيم Sound of skin, whose skin is not cut.
✧ إِصْحَاح وأَصْحَاح Chapter of Holy Scripture.
تَصْحِيح Correction. Authentication. Verification of an account.
مَصِحَّة ومَصَحَّة Health-giving (fast, journey).
* صَحْصَح To be clear, obvious.
صَحْصَح وصَحْصَاح وصَحْصَحَان ج صَحَاصِح
Even ground.
تُرَّهَات صَحَاصِح Trifles; false, vain things.
* صَحِب a صُحْبَةً وصَحَابَةً وصِحَابَةً وصَاحَب ه

To be the companion of. ✧ To be the friend of.
أَصْحَب To have a companion. To become submissive (beast).
— ه ه وه To see a. o. attended by.
— ه عن To remove a. o. from.
تَصَحَّب من To be ashamed of.
— ل ✧ To cleave to.
تَصَاحَب مع To live in company with. ✧ To be friendly connected with.
إِصْطَحَب To keep company with o. a.; to live together.
إِسْتَصْحَب ه To choose a. o. as a friend, companion. To keep company with.
صُحْبَة Intercourse, friendly relations. Company. With. ◘ Nosegay.
صُحْبَة فُلان In company with.
صُحْبَة السَّفِينة Of short duration.
صَاحِب ج أَصْحَاب وصَحْب وصَحَابَة وصُحْبَان
Companion; fellow. Endowed with. Owner, master of. Commander. Governor. ✧ Friend.
صَاحِبَة ج صَاحِبَات وصَوَاحِب Wife, mistress.
الصَّحَابَة The companions of Mohammed.
يَا صَاحِ (يَا صَاحِب *for*) O my companion. ✧ O my friend.
مُصْطَحِب Speaking to himself. Mad.
مُصْحِب ومِصْحَاب Submissive, manageable.
مُصَاحِب Intimate companion.
مُصَاحَبَة Intercourse, company.
* صَخَر a صَخْرًا ه To boil (milk).
— ه To strike the brain of (sun).
— a صَخِيرًا وصُحَارًا To bray (ass).
صَخِر a صَخَرًا To be tawny fawn.
أَصْحَر To go forth into the desert. To become blind of one eye. To be broad (place).
— ه وب To manifest a. th.
إِصْحَارّ To assume a tawny colour.
صَحَر وصُحْرَة Fawn-colour.
صَحْرَة وصُحْرَة Openly, in broad light.
صَحِير وصُحَار Braying of the ass.
صَحِيرَة Boiled milk mixed with butter.
أَصْحَر م صَحْرَاء ج صُحْر Fawn coloured.
صَحْرَاء ج صَحَارَى وصَحَارٍ وصَحْرَاوَات Broad desert. Sahara.
* صحف ـــ صَحَّف To make a mistake

Salamander. ◘ أضحايَة
Cause of freedom. مَضحاة
Cup, bowl. مِضحاة
To resound loudly. ✡ صَخّ o صَخًّا وصَخِيخًا
To strike (iron) upon (stones). — o صَخًّا ه على
To deafen (the ears : noise). — ه
He accused him of a great crime. — ه بِعَظِيمَةٍ
Sound produced by the striking of a rock. صَخّ وصَخَّة وصَخِيخ
Sound. Noise. Day of resurrection. Calamity صاخَّة
To shout, to clamour. ✡ صَخِب a صَخَبًا
To raise confused noises (crowd). تَصاخَب
To utter confused cries (birds). إصطَخَب
Uproar, confused noise. صَخَب
Clamorous. صَخِب وصَخّاب وصَخُوب وصَخْبان م صَخِبَة وصَخّابَة وصُخُبّة وصَخُوب وصَخْبَى
Roaring (sea). صَخِب ومُصطَخِب المَوْج
To be burning (day). ✡ صَخِد a صَخَدًا
To utter its cry (woodpecker). صَخَد a صَخْدًا
To scorch a. o. (sun). — a صَخْدًا ه
To give an ear to. — a صُخُودًا الى
To enter upon the hot season. To bask in the sun (lizard). أصخَد
Midday-heat. صاخِدَة ومَصخَدَة
Very hot (day). صَخْدان وصَخَدان
Hard (rock). Intensely hot (midday). صَيْخُود
Intenseness of heat. صَياخِيد الحَرّ
To be rocky (place). ✡ صَخِر — أصخر
✧ To dig (to the rock). To harden as rock. صَخَّر
Rocks, mass of rocks. صَخر وصَخَر ج صُخُور وصُخُورَة
A rock. صَخْرَة وصَخَرَة ج صَخر وصَخَر وصُخُور وصَخَرات
Such a one is like the rock of the valley *i. e.* unshaken. فُلان صَخرَة الوادِي
Clashing of iron. صاخِر
Earthen bowl. صاخِرَة
Rocky (place). صَخِر ومُصخِر
To dig (the ground) with a shovel. ✡ صَخَف a صَخفًا ه

in writing or reading. ◘ To draw back.
To bind the sheets of (a book). أصحَف ه
To be written or read incorrectly (book). تَصَحَّف
To copy or read a writing (incorrectly). — ه
Hollow, large dish. صَحفَة ج صِحاف
Mistaking in reading. صَحّاف وصَحَفِيّ ومُصَحِّف
Surface of the earth. صَحِيف
Sheet of a book, register. صَحِيفَة ج صُحُف وصَحائِف
Slip in writing or reading. تَصحِيف
Book, volume. The Coran. مِصحَف ومُصحَف ج مَصاحِف
To be rough (voice). To be hoarse (man). ✡ صَحِل a صَحَلًا
Having a rough voice. صَحِل وأصحَل
To get erect. ✡ صَحَم — إصطَحَم
To become yellow. To assume a dusty colour (plant). To have withering plants (soil). إصحامّ
Dusty, yellow colour. صُحمَة
Dust-coloured. أصحَم م صَحماء
To strike a. o. To offer a. th. in a dish. ✧ To grind. ✡ صَحَن a صَحنًا ه
To make peace between. — بَيْن
Basin. Plate, dish. صَحن ج صُحُون
Court-yard of a house. صَحن الدّار
Cymbals, castanets. صَحنان
Conch of the ear. صَحناء الأُذُن
Small salt fishes. صَحنَى وصَحناة وصِحناء وصَحناءة
Hollow dish. ◘ Hand-mill. مِصحَنَة
✡ صَحا o صَحوًا وصُحُوًّا, وصَحِي a صَحًا, أصحَى
To be clear, cloudless (sky). To recover from intoxication. To come to o.'self again. ✧ To pay attention.
To awake from sleep. — من النَّوم
To awake a. o. ✧ صَحَّى وأصحَى ه
To become fine (weather). To have fine weather. أصحَى
Brightness of the weather. Lucidness of mind. صَحو
Fine, cloudless (day, sky). — وصاحٍ, ومُصحٍ م مُصحِيَة
Conscious, awake. صاحٍ ج صاحُون وصُحاة

It emanated from his advice. صَدَرَ عن رَأْيِهِ
He has done or said so and so. صَدَرَ مِنْهُ كَذَا وكَذَا
To strike a. o. on the chest. — o i صَدْرًا ه
To feel a pain in the chest. صُدِرَ
To walk ahead (horse). صَدَّرَ
To put a preface, a heading to (a writing). — ه
To commence (speech) with. — ه ب
To give a seat of honour to a. o. — ه
To bring a. o. back from. — وأَصْدَرَ ه عن
To exact a. th. from. To importune a. o. with requests. صَادَرَ ه على وب
To issue (an order). أَصْدَرَ ه
To project the chest. To be placed in the front seat. To walk forward, to be ahead. تَصَدَّرَ
The upper part of. Breast, chest. Seat of honour. Beginning of (day, season). Title of a book. صَدْر ج صُدُور
Chief, president. — القوم
Beginning of a sentence. — الكلام
The higher point of a valley. صُدُور الوادي
The Grand Vizier. Prime minister. الصَّدْر الأَعظم
Return from water, from pilgrimage. صَدَر
Chest or its highest part. صُدْرَة
Waistcoat, bodice. Breast-plate. — و✧ صَدْرِيَّة
Chest-girth of a beast. تَصْدِير و✧ صَدْرِيَّة
Chemisette, bodice. صِدَار
Prominent point of a valley. صَدَارَة, وصَدِيرَة ج صَدَائِر
Premiership. صَدَارَة
Returning from water (cattle). صَادِر م صَادِرَة
He does not possess anything. مَا لَهُ صَادِر ولا وَارِد
Broad-breasted. أَصْدَر ومُصَدَّر
The two veins of the temples. أَصْدَرَان
Result, consequence. Infinitive; root of a word. Origin. مَصْدَر ج مَصَادِر

Iron shovel. مِصْخَفَة ج مَصَاخِف
✱ صَخَمَ o صَخْمًا ه To burn a. o. (sun).
✱ صَدَّ i o صُدُودًا, وصَدًّا عن To shun a. th., to shrink from.
— o صَدًّا, وصَادَّ وأَصَدَّ ه عن To avert a. o. from.
صَدَّ i o صَدِيدًا To shriek, to shout.
صَدَّدَ To clap with the hands, to applaud.
أَصَدَّ To suppurate (wound).
تَصَدَّدَ ل To meet a. o. front to front.
إِصْطَدَّ To veil herself (woman).
صَدّ Removal. Hinderance.
— وصُدّ ج صُدُود وأَصْدَاد Mountain, side of a valley.
صَدَد Neighbourhood. Design. ✧ Topic, point at discussion.
دَارِي صَدَدَ دَارِهِ وعلى صَدَدِهَا My house stands opposite his.
صَدَّاء Name of a water-spring.
صِدَاد ج أَصِدَّة Woman's veil.
صَدِيد Clamour. Matter, pus.
صُدَّاد ج صَدَائِد Path leading to water Serpent. Large lizard.
✱ صَدِئَ a صَدَأً, وصَدُؤَ o صَدَاءَة To stand erect in order to see.
— وصَدُؤَ و✧صَدِّى To become rusty (iron). To be of a rusty colour.
صَدَأَ a صَدْءًا, وصَدَّأَ ه To take off the rust from.
صَدَأ Rust.
رَجُل صَدَأ Slender-bodied man.
صَدِئ م صَدِئَة Covered with rust.
صُدْأَة Rusty colour.
أَصْدَأ م صَدْآء Of a reddish black colour.
كَتِيبَة صَدْأَى Horsemen bearing rusty arms.
✱ صَدَحَ a صَدْحًا وصُدَاحًا To utter a cry (man, bird).
صَدَح Sign. Stony hill.
صَدْحَة وصُدْحَة وصَدَحَة Sea-shell used as an amulet.
صَدَّاح وصَدُوح وصَيْدَح ومِصْدَح Shouter.
✱ صَدَرَ o i صَدْرًا ومَصْدَرًا عن To come back from water (cattle).
— o i صُدُورًا To come to pass, to happen.
— عن ومن To proceed, to emanate from. To result from.

مَصْدُور Feeling a pain in the chest.

✲ صَدَعَ a صَدْعًا, وصَدَّعَ ه وه To split, to cut asunder. To divide flocks To cross (a desert, a river).

صَدَعَ ه To manifest a. th.

— ب To declare the truth. To work a. th. out.

— صُدُوعًا الى To lean towards.

— ه عن To remove a. o. from.

صُدِعَ وصُدِّعَ To have a headache.

✧ صَدَّعَ خاطِر فُلَان To intrust a. o. with an affair.

تَصَدَّعَ وانْصَدَعَ To be split.

تَصَدَّعَ To part (people).

— الأرضُ بِفُلَان Such a one has fled.

صَدْعٌ ج صُدُوع Crack in a hard body.

— وصَدَعٌ Strong and young.

صِدْعٌ Fragment. Party of men.

صَدْعَة ج صَدَعَات Bit, piece. Dissent.

صِدْعَة ج صِدَع, وصَدِيع ج صُدُع Half of a. th. split asunder.

صَدِيع Dawn. Garment under a breast-plate.

صُدَاع Hemicrany, headache.

صَادِع Cleaving. Breaking (dawn). Far-extending (mountain, river).

مَصْدُوع Split. Having a headache.

مَصْدَع ج مَصَادِع Even road in a stony country.

مِصْدَع Eloquent (speaker).

✲ صَدَغَ a صَدْغًا, وصَادَغَ ه To walk along by the side of.

صَدَغَ ه To crush (an ant).

لا يَصْدَغ نَمْلَةً He is a coward: (*lit.*) he could not kill an ant.

— ه عن To deter a. o. from.

— o صَدْغًا وصُدُوغًا الى To incline to.

صَدُغَ o صَدَاغَةً To be weak.

صُدْغ مث صُدْغَان ج أَصْدَاغ Temple. Hair covering the temples. ◻ Door-post.

صَدْغَة ✧ Liquid lime.

صِدَاغ Brand on a camel's temples.

صَدِيغ Weak. Child up to the seventh day of his birth.

الأَصْدَغَان The two veins of the temples.

مِصْدَغَة Pillow, cushion.

مَصْدُوغ ومُصَدَّغ Marked on the temples.

✲ صَدَفَ o صَدْفًا وصُدُوفًا, وتَصَدَّفَ عن To turn away from.

صَدَفَ i صَدْفًا ه عن To keep off a. o. from.

صَادَفَ و✧ صَدَفَ i ه To encounter a. o. by chance.

✧ تَصَدَّفَ To come to pass, to happen.

تَصَادَفَ To meet o. a.

صَدَف و✧ صَدَف ج (*un.* صَدَفَة ✧ صَدْفَة) أَصْدَاف Sea-shell. Mother of pearl.

— وصُدُف وصَدَف وصُدَف Rugged passage in a mountain.

صَدَفَة مث صَدَفَتَان Cavity of the ear.

مُصَادَفَة و✧ صُدْفَة ج صُدَف Chance, occurrence.

✧ صُدْفَة وبالصُّدْفَة At hap-hasard, by chance.

✲ صَدَقَ o صَدْقًا ومَصْدُوقَة في الحَدِيث To speak veraciously.

— ه حَدِيثًا To tell the truth to.

— في To fulfil (a promise).

— في القِتَال To fight gallantly.

صَدَّقَ To run without turning back (game).

— ه To hold a. o. as trustworthy.

صَادَقَ مُصَادَقَةً وصِدَاقًا ه To befriend, to entertain friendly relations with a. o.

✧ — عَلَى To sign (an agreement).

أَصْدَقَ ه To assign a dowry to (a bride).

تَصَدَّقَ To give alms.

— على ب To give a. th. to a. o. for the sake of God.

تَصَادَقَ To rely upon one another. To live like friends.

صَدْق ج صُدُق وصُدْق وصَدْقُون Straight-forward. Steady. Perfect.

صِدْق Truth. Veracity.

صَدَقَة ج صَدَقَات Legal alms. Alms to the poor.

صَدْقَة ج صَدْقَات Perfect (woman).

صَدُقَة وصُدْقَة وصَدْقَة وصُدُقَة ج صَدُقَات وصُدُقَات وصُدْقَات وصَدْقَات Dowry.

صِدَاق ج صُدُق وأَصْدِقَة Dowry.

صَدَاقَة True friendship.

تَصَادُق Good harmony. Friendship.

صَادِق م صَادِقَة Sincere. Trustworthy.

To cry out (man). صَرَّ i صَرًّا وصَرِيرًا
To creak (insect); to squeak (door).
To roar (wind).
To be smitten by cold wind (plant). صُرَّ
To go forward (she-camel). صَرَّر
To constrain a. o. to. صارَّ ه على
To put forth its awns (spike). أَصَرَّ
To hurry in running. — يَعْدو
To resolve upon a. th. To persist in. — على
To be narrow (hoof). إِصْطَرَّ
Intenseness of cold, hoar-frost. صِرّ وصِرَّة
Gale or cold wind. رِيح صِرّ
Intenseness of heat, of fight. Noise. Party. صَرَّة
Purse. Sealed bag of money. صُرَّة ج صُرَر
Ear of corn putting forth awns. صَرَر
Bushy tree. صارّ
Thirst. Want. صارَّة ج صَرائِر وصَوارّ
Bachelor. صَرُور وصَرُورَة وصَرُورِيّ
Bachelor. صَرارَة
Rag for binding a she-camel's teats. Height not reached by water. صِرار ج أَصِرَّة
Boisterous, clamorous. صَرّار م صَرّارَة
Cricket (insect). — اللَّيل
Perseverance, steadiness. إِصْرار
Cry, acute sound. Gnashing of teeth. Grating of a pen. صَرِير
Silver coin. صَرِيرَة ج صَرائِر
Intestines, bowels. مَصارّ
To utter its cry (green wood-pecker). To yell. ✡ صَرْصَر
Cock. Intense (cold). Vehement (wind). صَرْصَر
Cricket, beetle. ✧ Cock-roach. — وصُرْصُر ج صَراصِر
Cricket. Tail (camel). صُرْصُور ج صَراصِير
To cut a. th. To earn. To keep in (urine). To make sour milk. To render a child costive for fattening him. ✡ صَرَبَ i صَرْبًا
To collect in the udder (milk). صَرِبَ a صَرَبًا
To eat gum. To drink sour milk. صَرَّبَ
To prepare (sour milk). إِصْطَرَبَ ه

Perfect, unmingled. Frank.
صَدُوق ج صُدُق وصُدُق, وصِدِّيق ج صِدِّيقون
Trustworthy. Trustful. Just.
Sadduceans. صَدُّوقِيُّون
True friend. صَدِيق ج أَصْدِقاء وصُدْقان
Touchstone. Test, criterion. مِصْداق
Brave fighter. Fiery horse. ذُو مَصْدَق او مِصْدَق
Giving alms. مُصَدِّق ومُتَصَدِّق
Chemistry. ✡ صَيدَلَة
Chemist. صَيدَلانِيّ ج صَيادِلَة
To hurt, to push back a. o. or a. th. ✡ صَدَمَ i صَدْمًا ه او ه
To strike (a stone) against. — ه ب
To overtake a. o. (misfortune). — ه
To knock, to strike a. o. صادَمَ ه
To dash against o. a. To collide (warriors). تَصادَمَ واصْطَدَمَ
Shock, collision. صَدْم (*un.* صَدْمَة)
Patience is to be shown at the first assault of misfortune. الصَّبْر في الصَّدْمَة الأُولى
The two sides of the forehead. الصَّدْمَتان والصَّدِمَتان
Bald. أَصْدَم م صَدْماء
Experienced warrior. رَجُل مُصَدَّم
To clap with the hands: to applaud. ✡ صَدا o صَدْوًا, وصَدَّى
To be thirsty. ✡ صَدِيَ a صَدًى
To dissemble with; to beguile a. o صادَى ه
To reecho (mountain). To die. أَصْدَى إِصْداء
To apply o.'s self to (an affair). To seek a. th. from. تَصَدَّى ل
Thirst. Voice. Echo. Corpse. Brain. Owl. صَدًى ج أَصْداء
He is dead (*lit.*) his echo is silent. صَمَّ صَداهُ
May God destroy him! أَصَمَّ اللهُ صَداهُ
صَدٍ وصادٍ وصَدْيان م صَدْيا وصادِيَة
Thirsting.
Bowels thirsting for. أَحْشاء صَوادٍ الى
To tie up a purse. To put (money) in a purse. ✡ صَرَّ o صَرًّا ه
To bind (a she-camel's) teats. — ه
To erect (the ears: horse). — ه او ب وأَصَرَّ ب

Sky-rocket; cracker. ◘ Ghost. ✧ صَارُوخ ج صَوَارِيخ
Clamorous. Peacock. صَرَّاخ
To feel (the cold). To be galled (horse). To hit or miss the target (arrow). ✱ صَرِدَ a صَرَدًا
To loathe a. th. صَرِدَ قَلْبُهُ عَن
To hit (the target: shooter). صَرَدَ o صَرْدًا, وأَصْرَدَ ه
To give niggardly. صَرَّدَ عَطَاءَهُ
To give to a. o. little to drink. — ه
Pure, unmixed. Elevated point of a mountain. Cold. صَرْد
Cold ground. أَرْض صَرِد ج صُرُود
Cold day. يَوْم صَرْد وصَرِد
Numerous army. جَيْش صَرْد
Cold countries. صُرُود
Large army moving slowly. صَرَد
Sparrow-hawk; green wood-pecker. صُرَد ج صِرْدَان
Two veins beneath the tongue. صُرَدَان
Rainless cloud. صُرَّاد
Wounded by the saddle (horse). صَرِد
Sensible of cold. Enduring cold. — ج صَرْدَى, ومِصْرَاد
Bare, without vegetation (country). Passing through the target (arrow). مِصْرَاد
Having little water (river, vessel). مُصَرَّد
Road, path to heaven. ✱ صِرَاط ج صُرُط
To fell a. o. ✱ صَرَعَ a صَرْعًا وصِرْعًا ومَصْرَعًا ه
To put two valves to a (door); two hemistichs to (a verse). — وصَرَّعَ ه
To be affected with epilepsy. ✧ To have a hemicrany. صُرِعَ
To fling a. o. down. صَرَّعَ ه
To wrestle. To fight a duel with. صَارَعَ مُصَارَعَةً وصِرَاعًا, وتَصَارَعَ واصْطَرَعَ
To humble o'self before. تَضَرَّعَ لِفُلَان
Epilepsy, falling-sickness. Manner, wise. Similar. Corresponding part. ✧ Head-ache. صَرْع ج صُرُوع وأَصْرُع
He has two shapes; he is bi-coloured. هُوَ ذُو صَرْعَيْن
I have visited him morning and evening. أَتَيْتُهُ صَرْعَيِ النَّهَار

To be smooth, glossy. إِصْرَابَّ
Sour milk. Red gum. صَرْب وصَرَب
Small tents of the Arabs. صِرَب
Pasturage becoming green again. صَرْبَة
Seeds, seed-produce. صِرَاب
Sour milk. صَرِيب ج صُرُب
To plaster (a tank) with quick lime. ✱ صَرَّجَ — صَرَّجَ ه
Quick lime. P صَارُوج
To be pure, unmingled (race). ✱ صَرُحَ o صَرَاحَةً وصُرُوحَةً
To explain a. th. صَرَحَ a صَرْحًا, وصَرَّحَ وأَصْرَحَ ه
To be evident (truth). To be clarified (wine). To miss the mark (archer). To be cloudless (sky). صَرَّحَ
To speak plainly. — وصَارَحَ بِمَا فِي نَفْسِهِ مُصَارَحَةً وصِرَاحًا
To be obvious (truth). إِنْصَرَحَ
Castle, tower, lofty building. صَرْح ج صُرُوح
Hard ground. Hall of a house. صَرْحَة
Openly, in broad light. صَرْحَة
Pure, unmingled. صَرْح وصَرَاح وصُرَاح
Genuineness. Obviousness. صَرَاحَة وصُرُوحَة
Pure wine. صُرَاحِيَّة
Large vessel for wine. صُرَاحِيَّة
Pure, unmingled. Obvious, explicit. صَرِيح ج صُرَحَاء وصَرَائِح
Such a tribe came by themselves. جَاءَ بَنُو فُلَان صَرِيحَةً
Plainly. Explicitly. صَرِيحًا
Permission. ◘ Passport. تَصْرِيح
Obvious. ✧ Permitted. مُصَرَّح
Cloudless (sky). مُصَرِّح ومُصَرَّح
To cry out for help. ✱ صَرَخَ o صُرَاخًا وصَرِيخًا, واصْطَرَخَ
✧ To call out to. صَرَخَ ل
To come to the rescue of. أَصْرَخَ ه
To scream repeatedly. تَصَرَّخَ
To cry out one to another. تَصَارَخَ واصْطَرَخَ
To cry for help. إِسْتَصْرَخَ ه
Cry. صُرَاخ وصَرِيخ
Cry, scream. صَرْخَة
Screaming for help. Cock. صَارِخ
Shrieks, alarm. صَارِخَة

Unmixed, pure (wine, beverage). صِرف
The day and the night. الصَّرفان والصَّرفان
Absolutely, in all points. صِرْفًا
Grammarian. صَرْفِيّ
Star called the lion's heart. Amulet. صَرْفَة
Death. Copper. Lead. صَرَفان
Exchange of money. ✧ Brokage. صِرَافَة
Creak of a door, of a pulley. Gnashing of the teeth. Pure silver. Milk freshly drawn. صَرِيف
Palm-bough dried up. — وصَرِيفَة ج صُرُف وصِرَاف
Change. Sale of goods. Freedom of action. Declination, conjugation. (*gram*). تَصرِيف
Changes of time. تَصَارِيف الدَّهر
Free use, free will. ✧ Doings, behaviour. تَصَرُّف ج تَصَرُّفَات
Departure. إِنصِرَاف
صَرَّاف. وصَيْرَف وصَيْرَفِيّ ج صَيَارِفَة وصَيَارِيف Money-changer.
✧ Case, chest, box. صَرَّافَة
Outlet, issue, opening. مَصْرِف ج مَصَارِف
Pure (wine). Exchanged (money). ✧ Expenditure. مَصْرُوف ج مَصَارِيف
Master. ✧ Governor of a province. مُتَصَرِّف
Conjugated (verb). Inflected (noun). مُنصَرِف
Starting-place. Departure. مُنصَرَف
Nouns and verbs that are perfectly inflected and conjugated. مُتَصَرِّفَات
✧ Governorship, province. مُتَصَرِّفِيَّة
To be gallant, hardy. ✧ To be severe, stern. ✡ صَرُم o صَرَامَة
To be broken (rope). صَرَم i صَرْمًا وصُرْمًا
To cut off, to gather (fruit). — وصَرَّم ه
To interrupt a. o. — ه
To stay with a. o. صَرَم عِند
To part from a. o. صَارَم ه
To attain the time of gathering dates (palm-tree). To become destitute. أَصْرَم
To be energetic. To cease (fight). To be at its end (year). تَصَرَّم
To be cut. To be elapsed (winter). — وانصَرَم

Fashion. Similar. Strand of a rope. Wrestler. صِرع ج صُرُوع
State of being. صَرعَة
At all events, in any case. على كلّ صَرعَة
Way of prostrating. صِرعَة
Often prostrated in wrestling. صُرَعَة
صُرَعَة وصَرَّاع وصُرَّاعَة وصِرِّيع. وصَرُوع ج Prostrating his adversaries. صُرُع
Prostrated in wrestling; lying on the ground. صَرِيع ج صَرْعَى
Branch-tree leaning towards the ground. — ج صُرُع
Wrestling-place. مَصْرَع ج مَصَارِع
Valve of a folding-door. Hemistich of a verse. مِصْرَاع ج مَصَارِيع
Wrestler. مُصَارِع
A wrestling. Duelling. مُصَارَعَة
Prostrate. Epileptic. ✧ Suffering from headache. Insane. مَصْرُوع
To send off, to dismiss a. o. ✡ صَرَف i صَرْفًا. وصَرَّف ه
To disregard a. o.; to give up a. th. صَرَف النَّظر عن
To drink wine (unmixed). To decline (a noun). To conjugate (a verb). — وصَرَّف ه
To exchange (money). ✧ To spend (money, time). صَرَف i ه
To deter a. o. from. — ه عن
To squeak (wheel). To gnash the teeth. صَرَف o صَرِيفًا
To spend; to exchange money. To sell (goods). To change the direction (of the wind : God). صَرَّف ه
To intrust a. o. with the management of a business. صَرَّف ه في
To have freedom of action in; to dispose of. تَصَرَّف في
To be declined (noun); conjugated (verb). إِنصَرَف
To depart from. إِنصَرَف عن
To be busy in earning a livelihood. إِصطَرَف
To pray God to avert (misfortunes). إِستَصرَف الله ه
Exchange of money. Accidence (*grammar*). صَرْف
Calamity, misfortune, vicissitude. صَرْف الدَّهر ج صُرُوف

To part from o. another. تَصَارَم
To cut off (fruit). إِصطَرَم ه
Tanned leather. P صَرم
صِرم ج أَصرَام وأَصَارِم وأَصَارِيم وصُرمَان
Crowd, party. Way, manner. Collection of houses.
Shoe. ✧ صِرمَايَة ج صَرَامِي
Troop of camels. Separated portion of a cloud. صِرمَة ج صِرَم
✧ Capital, stock. P صَرمِيَّة
Time of trimming palm-trees. صَرَام وصِرَام
War. صَرَام وصُرَام
Bravery. ✧ Harshness. صَرَامَة
Shoe-maker. ✧ صِرمَاتِيّ وصِرمَايَاتِيّ
Dauntless. صَارِم ج صَوَارِم . وصَرُوم
Cutting (sword). ✧ Stern (man); hard (judge).
Skinner. صَرَّام
Maimed. Dawn. Night صَرِيم
Part of the night. – وصَرِيمَة
Energy, firmness. صَرِيمَة
Mound of sand. – ج صَرَائِم
Poor man having a numerous family. أَصرَم ومُصرِم
Waterless desert. صَرمَاء
Small water-channel. مَصرِم
Curved knife. مِصرَم
The elapsed year. العَام المُنصَرِم
Hautboy. P صُرنَايَة ج صُرنَايَات
To avert an evil from. ✱ صَرَى i صَريًا ه عن
To save a. o. To precede a. o. – ه
To lag behind a. o. – عن
To settle a difference between. – بَين
To stagnate (water). To be altered (milk). صَرِيَ a صَرًى
To let (a ewe) without milking it. صَرَّى ه
To sell a ewe giving much milk. أَصرَى
Altered milk. Residue. صَرًى
Stagnating water. – وصِرًى
Mast, yard. صَارٍ ج صَوَارٍ
Sailor. – ج صُرَّاء وصَرَارِيّ وصَرَارِيُّون
Old well having altered water. صَارِيَة
Unmilked for many days (ewe). صَرَاة ومُصَرًّى ومُصَرَّاة
Stone-bench against a wall. ✱ صطب – مِصطَبَة ج مَصَاطِب ١

Stable. G إِصطَبل ج إِصطَبلَات
Astrolabe. G أُصطُرلَاب
To disperse (a crowd). ✱ صَعصَع ه
To shake a. th. – ه
To be shaken, dispersed. To be lowly, cowardly. تَصَعصَع
Fate has scattered them. – بِهِم الدَّهرُ
Variegated bird. صَعصَع وصُعصُع
To be difficult to. ✱ صَعُب o صُعُوبَةً , وأَصعَب على
To be untractable (beast). To have a refractory beast. – وأَصعَب
To render a. th. difficult. صَعَّب وتَصَعَّب ه
To be harsh towards a. o. صَاعَب ه
To find a. th. difficult. أَصعَب واستَصعَب ه
To be difficult (affair). تَصَعَّب واستَصعَب
To be minute, particular about. To be hard to please in. تَصَاعَب في
Difficulty. صُعُوبَة
Difficult, hard. صَعب ج صِعَاب, وصَعُوب
Difficult things. مَصَاعِب
Stallion. مُصعَب ج مَصَاعِب ومَصَاعِيب
Thyme, origan. ✱ صَعتَر وسَعتَر
Penny-royal, mint. صَعتَر العَرش
To ascend. To go up (a ladder). ✱ صَعِد a صُعُودًا وصَعَدًا وصُعُدًا في
To bring a. o. or a. th. up. – ب
To ascend a mountain. صَعَّد في وعلى الجَبَل
To go down into a valley. – وأَصعَد في الوَادِي
To melt (grease). صَعَّد ه
To make a journey. أَصعَد في الأَرض
To make a. o. to ascend on. – ه في وعلى
To go to Mecca. أَصعَد
To ascend, to rise; to go up. تَصَعَّد وتَصَاعَد واصَّعَّد
To be hard to a. o. (affair). تَصَعَّد وتَصَاعَد ه
The upper part. صُعُد
This plant increases in height. هذا النَّبَات يَنمُو صُعُدًا
Grievous punishment. عَذَاب صَعَد
Ascent. صُعُود
Ascension Thursday. خَمِيس الصُّعُود
Deep sigh صُعَدَاء

Losing its hair (ass). صَعِل م صَعِلَة
— وأَصعَل م صَعلاء ج صُعل Small-headed and thin-necked ostrich.
✲ صَعلَكَ ه To reduce a. o. to beggary.
تَصَعلَكَ To become destitute.
صَعلَكَة وتَصَعلُك Destitution, poverty.
صُعلُوك ج صَعَالِيك وصَعَالِك Beggar.
✲ صعن — أَصعَن To be small-headed and shallow-minded.
إِصعَن To be small, paltry.
✲ صَغَا a صَعْوًا To be thin and paltry.
صَعو ج صَعَوَات وصِعَاء Small sparrow, bull-finch.
✲ صَغِر a وصَغُر o صَغَرًا وصَغَارَةً وصِغَرَةً وصُغرَانًا To be little, small.
صَغُر o صِغَرًا وصُغرًا وصَغَارًا وصَغَارَةً وصُغرَانًا To be vile, despised. To accept contempt.
صَغُر o صِغَرًا ه To be younger than.
مَا صَغُرَنِي إِلَّا بِسَنَة He is only one year younger than I.
صَغَّر وأَصغَر ه To lessen, to diminish a. th.
أَصغَر To bring forth little plants (soil).
— ه To abase a. o.
تَصَاغَرَت إِلَيهِ نَفسُهُ He held himself in little estimation.
إِستَصغَر ه To find a. th. small, little. To make little of. To choose the least.
صِغَر وصَغَارَة Infancy. Smallness.
الصِّغرَة The smallest. The little ones.
أَنَا مِن الصِّغرَة I am one of the smallest.
صُغَار وصُغرَان Paltry, little.
صَغَار وصُغر Contempt, littleness. Weakness.
تَصغِير Diminutive (noun). Decrease.
صَاغِر ج صَغَرَة وصَاغِرُون Bearing ignominy.
صَغِير ج صِغَار وصُغَرَاء Small, mear. Young.
صُغَيِّر وصُغَيِّير Very little thing.
أَصغَر ج أَصَاغِر وأَصَاغِرَة وأَصغَرُون Smaller. Younger (brother).
الأَصغَر The smallest.
الأَصغَرَان The heart and the tongue.
الصُّغرَى The minor of a syllogism.
مُصغِر Producing small plants (soil).
✲ صَغَا o صَغْوًا a وصَغِي a صَغًى وصُغِيًّا To

صَعدَاء Painful task.
صَعدَة ج صِعَاد وصَعَدَات Straight lance.
بَنَات صَعدَة Wild asses.
صَاعِد Rising, ascendant.
مِن الآن فَصَاعِدًا Henceforward, henceforth.
صَعُود ج صُعُد وصَعَائِد Ascent, acclivity.
— ج صَعَائِد, وصَعُودَاء Summit difficult to be reached.
الصَّعِيد Upper Egypt.
صَعِيد ج صُعُد وصُعُدَات Earth, soil. Surface of the earth. Elevated land.
صَعِيدَة ج صَعَائِد ✧ Burnt-offering.
مُصَعَّد Sublimated medicine.
✲ صَعِر a صَعَرًا To be distorted (face, mouth). To be small (head)
صَعَّر وصَاعَر وأَصعَر خَدَّهُ To turn away the face in disdain.
تَصَعَّر To be wry-mouthed.
صَعَر Wryness, distortion of the face.
أَصعَر م صَعرَاء ج صُعر Wry-faced, wry-mouthed.
صَيعَرِيَّة Obliquity in walk.
✲ صَعرَر ه To roll, to sharpe round a. th.
تَصَعرَر To be round-shaped, globulous.
صُعرُر وصُعرُور ج صَعَارِير Concrete gum.
صُعرُورَة Black beetle's ball.
✲ صعف — صُعِف صَعفًا To be seized with shudder.
صَعفَة Shudder.
مَصعُوف Shuddering.
✲ صَعَق a صَاعِقَةً ه To smite a. o. (thunderbolt). To smite a. o. with a thunderbolt (God).
صَعِق a صَعقًا To rumble loudly (thunder).
صَعِق a صَعقًا وصُعِق صَعقًا وصَعقَةً وتَصعَاقًا To faint at the sound of thunder.
أَصعَق ه To cause a fainting fit to.
صَعق Shout, yell. Death.
صَعِق Shrieking loudly. Stunned by a loud noise.
صَعَاق الرَّعد Rumbling of thunder.
صَاعِقَة ج صَوَاعِق Thunderbolt. Deadly punishment. Shrieks of anguish.
حَجَر الصَّاعِقَة Belemnite, thunder-stone.
✲ صَعِل a صَعَلًا, واصعَال To be small-headed and thin-necked.

To examine (people, the pages of a book). صَفَحَ ه وه
To ponder over (an affair). — في
To go off, to turn away from. To forgive to. — عن
To drive away (a beggar). — ه عن حاجَتِهِ
To strike a. o. with the flat of (a sword). — ه ب مَصْفَحًا
To beat (metal) into plates, sheets. صَفَّحَ ه
To clap the hands. صَفَّحَ بِيَدَيْهِ
To plate a. th. — ه
To shake hands with. ✧ To be out of danger (sick people). صافَحَ مُصافَحَةً وصِفاحًا
To drive away (a beggar). أَصْفَحَ ه
To consider a. th. carefully. To seek to recognize (people). تَصَفَّحَ ه او ه
To examine (an affair). تَصَفَّحَ في
To shake hands with. تَصافَحَ
To apologize for. إِستَصْفَحَ ه ه
Flat surface. Flat of a sword. صَفْح وصُفْح ج صِفاح
He kept silent about it. ضَرَبَ عَنْهُ صَفْحًا
Excessive width of the forehead. صَفَح
Excessive width of the cheeks. صِفاح
I met him face to face. لَقِيتُهُ صِفاحًا
Sky, broad side of a. th. صَفِيح
Broad and flat surface. Metallic sheet. Slate. Thin plank. Flat and thin stone. Broad-bladed sword. ✧ Tin. Pie. صَفِيحَة ج صَفائِح
Iron-plate. صَفِيحَة حَدِيد
Side, front-part. Page of a book. صَفْحَة ج صَفَحات
The two cheeks. الصَّفْحانِ والصَّفْحَتانِ
Thin slate. صُفَّاح ج صُفَّاحات وصَفافِيح
Magnanimous, forbearing. صَفَّاح وصَفُوح
Applause. تَصْفِيح
Shake of the hand. مُصافَحَة
Broad. Smooth (face). Reversed (thing). Straight and broad (nose). Inclined. Sixth arrow of the game. مُصْفَح
Plated. Broad. مُصَفَّح
Sword with a broad blade. مُصَفَّحَة ومُصَفِّحَة ج مُصَفِّحات ومُصَفَّحات

incline to setting (sun, star).
To lean, to incline towards. صَغَا الى
To pay attention ; to give ear. To hearken. أَصْغَى الى
To incline (a vessel). To diminish a. th. — ه
Inclination. صَغْو وصِغْو وصَغًى
Hollow of a spoon. Side of a well. صِغْو
Attention, hearkening. إِصْغاء
Dependents, clients. صاغِيَة
To set in order, to array a. th. To set (soldiers) in rank. To spread the wings in flying (bird). ✧ To set up (printing types). ✡ صَفَّ ٥ صَفًّا، وصَفَّفَ ه وه
To put a pad (on a saddle). — وأَصَفَّ ه
To be drawn up in battle array. صافَّ ه
To form a line against. تَصافَّ
To stand in battle order. To be drawn up. إِصْطَفَّ
Order, line, row. Rank of soldiers. صَفّ ج صُفُوف
Lock of hair. Shelf. صَفَّة
Golden coins worn as woman's hair ornament. ✧ صَفِيَّة
Saddle-pad. Stone-bench. صُفَّة ج صُفَف وصُفَّات وصِفاف
Houseless people, vagrants. أَهل الصُّفَّة
Space of time. صُفَّة من الدَّهر
The angels. الصَّافَّات
Yielding many vessels of milk (beast). صَفُوف
Spread in the sun to be dried. Put on the spit to be roasted. صَفِيف
Military station ; battle-field. ✧ Composing-stick. مَصَفّ ج مَصافّ
✧ Sequel of a discourse. — الكَلام
To walk alone in a desert (man). To browse on willow. ✡ صَفْصَفَ
✧ To set in order. — ه
Desert plain. صَفْصَف
Willow ; withy. (*un.* صَفْصافَة) صَفْصاف
Weeping-willow. صَفْصاف مُسْتَحِي
To forgive (*for* صَفَح) (an offence). ✧ صَفَتَ ٥ صَفْتًا
To acquire strength. تَصَفَّتَ
Victory, advantage. صَفْتَة
To flatten, to thin. ✡ صَفَحَ a صَفْحًا ه

Whistling bird. صافِر
There is nobody in the house. ما بِالدار صافِر
Whistle (instrument). ✧ صافُورة وصُوفَيرة
Cholera الهَوَاء الأَصْفَر
Yellow, tawny. Empty. أَصْفَر م صَفْرَاء ج صُفْر
Dark yellow. أَصْفَر فاقِع
Bile. Gold. Herb for dying yellow. Locust without eggs. صَفْرَاء
Gold and saffron. الأَصْفَرَان
Empty-handed, penniless. مُصْفِر
Starving, weakened by hunger. مُصْفَر ومَصْفُور
Kind of nightingale. ✱ صِفْرِد
To tap a. o. on the back of neck. To slap a. o. on the face. ✱ صَفَع a صَفْعًا ه
To tap, to slap one another. صافَع وتَصافَع
Often slapped. صَفْعَان وصَفْعَانِيّ
To clap a. th. ✱ صَفَق o صَفْقًا ه
To avert a. o. from a design. — ه عن مُرادِهِ
To clap its wings (bird). — صَفْقًا وصَفْقَة, وصَفَّق ب
To play on (a musical instrument). To open, to shut (a door). To shake (trees : wind). صَفَق ه
To strike a. o. with a sword. — ه ب
To fill up (a cup). — أَصْفَق ه
صَفَق لَهُ ب او يَدَهُ ب او على يَدِهِ ب وأَصْفَق يَدَهُ ب
To strike hands in (a bargain) with a. o.
To decant (wine). To drive (cattle) from one place to another. — وصَفَّق ه وه
To be compact (cloth). To be shameless (man). صَفُق o صَفَاقَة
To clap the hands ; to applaud. صَفَّق
To change o's place. صافَق بَيْن جَنْبَيْهِ
To strike a bargain. صافَق وتَصافَق عِنْد البَيْع
To repel, to drive back a. o. أَصْفَق ه
To shut (a door). — ه
To agree upon. — على
To feed (a party) to satiety. — لِلقَوم
To be flurried (man). تَصَفَّق
To set to. — ل
To be turned ; put back إنْصَفَق
To dash together (waves). إصْطَفَق

✱ صَفَد i صَفْدًا, وصَفَّد وأَصْفَد ه To bind, to fetter a. o.
أَصْفَد ه To give (flocks, slaves) to a. o.
صَفَد ج أَصْفَاد Gift. Fetter. ✧ Sea-shell, mother of pearl.
صِفَاد Shackle, bond.
✧ أُمّ صُفَيْدَة Wagtail.
✱ صَفَر i صَفِيرًا To whistle (man).
— ب To whistle (a beast).
صُفِر صَفْرًا To be bilious.
صَفِر a صَفَرًا وَصُفُورًا, وأَصْفَر To be empty (house, vessel).
صَفِرَت وِطَابُهُ He is dead.
صَفَّر ه To dye or paint yellow.
— وأَصْفَر ه To void, to empty a. th.
صَفَّر ب ول To whistle up (a beast).
صَفَّر و✧ صَوْفَر To whistle.
أَصْفَر To become poor.
— ه To empty (a vessel).
إصْفَرّ واصْفَارّ To be, to become yellow, pale.
إصْفَرّ To ripen (crop).
صَفْر وصِفْر وصُفْر وصَفِر وصُفُر ج أَصْفَار Void, empty.
— اليَدَيْن Empty-handed.
صِفْر و✧ سِفْر ج أَصْفَار Cipher.
صُفْر Brass. Gold.
صَفَر Second arabian month. Hunger.
صَفَر و✧ صُفَيْرَاء Jaundice.
عُرُوق الصُّفْر *Chelidonium*, celandine.
صَفَر الإِنَاء Loss of flocks.
الصَّفَرَان The two first months of the lunar year.
صَفْرَة Hunger, emptiness of the stomach.
صُفْرَة وإصْفِرَار Yellow colour. Paleness of the face.
صَفَرِيّ وصَفَرِيَّة Autumnal (rain, plant).
صُفَار Whistle. Bile. Worm of the bowels.
— وصِفَار Remainder of food on the teeth of a beast.
صُفَارَة Yellowish and withered plants.
✧ صُفَار البَيْض Yolk.
صَفَّار Worker in brass.
صَفَّارَة Anus. Whistle, fife.
صُفَارِيّة و✧ صَفْرَايَة Oriole, bird with yellow feathers.
صَفِير Sapphire (precious stone).

To be shaken (trees). To vibrate (chord).
صفق ج صُفُوق Side, flank. Face.
— وصَفْقَة Striking of the hands in a bargain.
صَفْقَة Agreement, bargain.
صِفْق Leaf of a door.
صِفَاق ج صُفُق Inner skin. Peritoneum.
صافِقَة People coming together.
صَفَّاق Striker of bargains. Great traveller.
صَفُوق ج صُفُق Steep (mountain).
— ج صُفُق وصَفَائِق Rugged mountain.
صَفِيق Impudent (man). Compact (cloth).
صَوَافِق وصَفَائِق Events.
✲ صَفَن i صُفُونًا To stand upon three legs (horse). To set the feet evenly (man). ✧ To muse.
صَفَّن To make a nest (wasp).
صافَن ه بَيْن To share water among.
تَصافَن ه To share water with o. a.
صَفْن ج أصفان وصُفن وصُفُن وصُفْنان
Leather map; table-cloth.
صُفْن Leathern vessel. Shepherd's bag. Scrotum.
صَفَن ج أصفان Hornet nest. Ear of corn.
صافِن ج صَوَافِن Horse standing on three feet and touching the ground slightly with the fourth. The saphena vein.
✲ صَفَا o صَفْوًا وصَفَاء وصُفُوًّا To be pure, limpid (water). To be clear, cloudless (sky).
صَفَا قَلْبُهُ His heart is free from hatred.
— ه To cream, to take the best of.
— صَفْوًا وصُفُوّ o صَفَاوَةً To be a good milch-camel.
صَفَّى وأصفى ه To clarify; to filter a. th. ✧ To settle (accounts).
صَفَّى الخَمْر To decant (wine).
صافَى ه وأصفى ه ل الوُدّ To have sincere affection for.
أصفى To cease laying eggs (hen). To cease making verses (poet).
— ه ب To distinguish a. o. by a gift.
تَصافَى To live like true friends. ✧ To reconcile.
إصطفى واستصفى ه To choose, to take the best of.

إستصفى ه To find a. th. pure, unadulterated. To take the whole of.
صَفْو و✧ صَفَاوَة Purity. Limpidity.
صَفَاء Purity. Quiet, happy life, pleasure.
صَفْو The choicest. Clear, pure. Sincerity of love.
صَفْوَة وصُفْوَة The choicest, the best.
صِفْوَة Sincere friend.
صَفْوَة ✧ Ashes.
ماء صَفْوَة ✧ Lye.
صَفَاة ج صَفًا وصَفَوَات، وصَفْوَانَة ج صَفْوَان
وصَفَوَان، وصُفْوَاء Rock, stone.
لا تَنْدَى صَفَاتُهُ He never gives a. th.
تَصْفِيَة Filtration. Liquidation.
صافٍ Pure, limpid. Serene (day). ✧ Net profit. Even (colour). Fruitful (palm-tree).
صَفِيّ ج أصفياء Pure. Chosen. True friend.
— وصَفِيَّة True friend (female).
— وصَفِيَّة ج صَفَايَا Booty set apart for a chief. Good milch-camel.
مِصْفَاة و✧ مِصْفَايَة ج مَصَافٍ Strainer, filter.
مُصَفًّى Purified. Cleared.
مُصْطَفًى Chosen. Man's name.
الإناء المُصْطَفَى ✧ The chosen vessel (St. Paul).
✲ صَقِب a صَقَبًا To be near, next to. To be far, remote.
صَقَب o صَقْبًا ه To slap a. o.
— ه To gather a. th. To raise a (building).
صاقَب مُصاقَبَة وصِقَابًا ه وه To be by the side of. ✧ To fit, to suit a. o.
أصْقَب To draw near (game). To be contiguous (house).
— ه To bring a. th. near.
صَقْب ج صِقَاب وصُقْبَان Tall and slender.
— ج صُقُوب Pole of a tent.
صَقَب Proximity. Nearness.
مُصَاقَبَة ✧ Convenience, suitableness.
صَيْقَبانيّ Perfumer, druggist.
✲ صَقَح وصَقَحَة Baldness.
أصْقَح م صَقْحَاء ج صُقْح Bald.
✲ صَقَر o صَقْرًا ه وه ب To strike a. o. with (a stick). To break stones with (a hammer).

Veil. Camel's muzzle. صِقَاع
Crowing of a cock. صُقَاع
Hoar-frost. A kind of wasp. صَقِيع
✧ Coolness of temper.
Loud-voiced. Eloquent. مِصْقَع ج مَصَاقِع
Ready to reply.
Covered with hoar-frost. مَصْقُوع
To polish (a metal). To gloss (cloth). ✫ صَقَل o صَقْلًا وصِقَالًا ه
To strike a. o. with a stick. — ه بِالعَصَا
To throw a. o. down. — بِهِ الأَرْضَ
To be polished, glossy. صَقِل a صَقَلًا
Length of the flanks. صَقَل
Flanks, sides. صُقْل وصُقْلَة
Polishing, burnishing. صِقَال
Tending of horses. — الفَرَس
Slender in the flanks (horse). صَقِل
Scaffold. Frame. ✧ صِقَالَة ج صَقَائِل
Steps.
صَاقِل ج صَقَلَة وصَقَّال, وصَيْقَل ج صَيَاقِل
Polisher, burnisher.
Furbished. Smooth. صَقِيل ومَصْقُول
Sicily (island). صِقِلِّيَّة وصَقِلِّيَّة
Polisher. مِصْقَل ومِصْقَلَة ج مَصَاقِل
Slave, slavonic. ✫ صَقْلَب وصَقْلَبِيّ وصِقْلَابِيّ ج صَقَالِبَة
Beware! Look out! Te صَاقِن
✧ To stagger, to stumble. ✫ صَكّ o صَكًّا
To close (a door). To strike upon a. th. To slap a. o. on (the face). — ه
To be knock-kneed. صَكّ a صَكَكًا
To tremble, to collide (knees). إِصْطَكّ
To come to fight. To collide (armies). — بِالسُّيُوف
Authentical deed, title-deed. Written agreement. صَكّ ج صُكُوك وصِكَاك وأَصُكّ
Intense heat of midday. صَكَّة
Scribe, clerk. صَكَّاك
Knock-kneed. Strong. أَصَكّ م صَكَّاء ج صُكّ
Weak-minded. صَكِيك
Strong. Bolt. مِصَكّ
To smite a. o. (ill-fortune). ✫ صَكَمَ o صَكْمًا ه
To champ the bit (horse). — عَلَى لِجَامِهِ
Blow, shock. صَكْمَة
Ill-luck, misfortune. صَوَاكِم الدَّهْر

To light (the fire). صَقَر وصَقَّر ه
To be very sour (milk). صَقِر واصْقَرّ
To be scorching (sun). — o صَقْرًا وصَقْرَةً, وأَصْقَر
To scorch a. o. (sun). صَقَر ه
To hunt with a hawk. تَصَقَّر
To be lighted (fire). — واصْطَقَر
Kestrel, small falcon. صَقْر ج أَصْقُر وصُقُور وصُقُورَة وصِقَار
Very sour milk. — ج صُقُور وصِقَار
Undeserved curse.
Sharp-sighted hawk. صَقْر صَاقِر
Treacle of dates, grapes. صَقْر وصَقَر ج صُقُور وصِقَار
Sweet (grape, date). صَقِر
He came with lies. جَاءَ بِالصُّقَر والبُقَر او بِالصُّقَارَى والبُقَارَى
Misfortune, calamity. صَاقِرَة
Stone-breaker. صَاقُور
Blasphemer, unbeliever. Seller of treacle. صَقَّار
Sweeter. أَصْقَر
Preserved in treacle. مُصَقَّر
To stray from the right path. ✫ صَقَع a صَقْعًا
I do not know where he is gone to. مَا أَدْرِي أَيْنَ صَقَع
To strike a. o. upon the head. — ه
To fling a. o. down. — بِهِ الأَرْضَ
To crow (cock). — a صَقْعًا وصُقَاعًا وصَقِيعًا
To crumble away (well). صَقِع a صَقَعًا
To have a white spot on the head (bird). To swoon at the sound of thunder.
To be covered with hoar-frost (ground). صُقِع وأُصْقِع
✧ To be cold, frozen, chilled. صَقَّع
To walk on a frozen ground. أَصْقَع
To cover (the soil: hoar-frost). — ه
Shore, country, extent of land. صُقْع ج أَصْقَاع
Uneasiness caused by cold. صَقَع
Affected by cold. صَقِع
✧ Intense cold. صَقْعَة
White spot on the head. صُقْعَة
Having a white spot on the head. أَصْقَع م صَقْعَاء
Sun. صَقْعَاء
Liar. صَاقِع

* صكا o صكوًا ه To cleave to.
* صَلّ i صَليلًا To resound, to clash. To be dried up (water-skin).
صَلّ i صُلولًا, وأَصَلّ To stink, to smell bad (meat, water).
صَلّ o صَلًّا ه To clarify (a beverage). To clear wheat from dust. To line (boots).
— ه To smite a. o. (calamity).
صُلّ Altered (meat).
صَلّ وصِلّ وصَلّة Light and scattered rain.
صِلّ ج أصلال Aspic, basilisk.
— وصِلّ أصلال Wicked man.
صَلّة وصِلّة وصَليل Sound, clank.
صَلّة ج صِلال Leather. Dry earth.
صُلّة Remainder of water. Offensive smell.
صالّة Misfortune, mishap.
صلالة ج أصِلّة Lining of boots.
صُلالة Refuse of wheat.
صَلال ومِصلال Dry mud crackling under the feet.
مِصَلّة Strainer, filter.
مُصِلّ Noble and generous lord. Abundant rain. Cobbler.
* صَلصَل وتَصَلصَل To resound; to rumble (thunder).
صَلصَلة Resounding. Noise.
صُلصُل Horse's forelock. White hair of the mane. Wood pigeon. Good guide.
— وصُلاصِل, ومُصَلصِل Braying (ass).
صَلصال Dry clay.
مُصَلصِل Noisy.
* صَلَب i صَلبًا, وصَلّب ه To crucify a. o.
صَلَب ه To extract marrow from bones. To fry, to roast (meat). To provide (a bucket) with two cross-pieces.
— على To cling to (fever).
صَلُب o وصَلِب a صَلابة To be hard (stone).
صُلِب To be crucified.
صَلّب To get hardened (date). ✧ To make the sign of the cross.
— ه To harden a. th. To give to a. th. the shape of a cross.
تَصَلّب To become hardened, to become firm, stiff.
إصطلب ه To extract marrow from (bones).
صَلب وتَصليب Crucifixion.
صَلب Spine of the back. Marrow. Hard ground.
صُلب ج أصلُب وأصلاب وصِلَبة Spine. Loins.
صَلابة Hardness. Hardening of the heart.
صُلب وصَليب Hard (stone). Hardened (heart).
صُلّب Hard. Whetstone.
صُلّبي Whetstone. Sharpened.
حُمّى صالِب Ague.
صَليب ج صُلبان وصُلُب Cross.
إشارة الصَّليب The sign of the cross.
إسم الصَّليب *Exclam. of wonder.* Great God! *lit* : name of the cross!
حشيشة الصَّليب ✧ Cross-wort.
عود الصَّليب Peony (*plant*).
صَليبي ج صَليبيّة Crusader.
✧ صَلَبوت ✧ Small crucifix.
مُصالَبة Cross-vaulting. Diagonal.
مُصالَبةً ✧ Cross-shaped, cross-wise.
مُصَلَّب Marked with crosses (cloth). Sharpened (spear-head). ✧ Cross-road.
— عليه Marked with a cross.
مَصلوب ج مَصاليب Crucified. ✧ Crucifix.
— عليه Suffering from continuous fever.
* صَلِت o صُلوتة To be prominent, broad (forehead).
صَلَت o صَلتًا ه To start (a horse).
صَلَت i To be watery, clear (milk).
أصلت ه To unsheath (a sword).
إنصلت في سَيرِه To outwalk, to outstrip.
صَلت الجبين Having a (broad forehead).
صَلت ج أصلات Large knife.
صَلت وصَلتان, مِصلت ومِصلات ج مَصاليت Active (man).
إصليت ومُنصَلِت Active. Penetrating (sword).
* صَلَج o صَلجًا ه To melt (silver).
صُلّج Standard money.
صُلَّجة Cocoon.
صَليجة Pure silver ingot.
صَولَجان ج صَوالِجة Short and hooked staff. Crosier, sceptre.
صَولَج وصَولَجة Pure silver.

Hard, barren. Niggardly. صَلد ج أَصلاد
Smooth.
Stingy. أَصلَد م صَلدَاء ج صُلد
Avaricious. Dry. Failing to give fire (steel). Isolated. صَلُود
Lion. Hard. Strong-hoofed (horse). * صِلدِم ج صَلَادِم
Sea eel. * صلر – صِلَّوْر
Broad, spacious. * صلطح – صُلَاطِح ومُصلَطِح
To be bald on the fore-part of the head. * صَلِع a صَلَعًا
To emerge from the clouds (sun). صَلَّع وتَصَلَّع وانصَلَع
Baldness. صَلَع
Part of the head affected with baldness. Forehead. صُلعَة وصَلَعَة
Bald. أَصلَع م صَلعَاء ج صُلع وصُلعَان
Cropped (tree). صَلعَاء
Without herbage (soil). – وصُلَّع وصَلِيع
Misfortune, adversity. الصَّلعَاء والصُّلَيعَاء
Broad and hard rock. صُلَّع وصُلَّاع
May the blessing and mercy of God be upon him. *Shortening of the words.* صَلَّى اللّٰه عَلَيهِ وسَلَّم * صَلعَم
To boast, to brag. * صَلِف a صَلَفًا, وتَصَلَّف
To be innutritive (food). To thunder without giving rain (cloud). صَلِف
To say hard things to. – ل
To breath painfully. To be of little worth (man). أَصلَف
To abhor, to render a. o. hateful. – ه
To come upon a hard soil. To be a flatterer. تَصَلَّف
Boast, brag. Thunder without rain. صَلَف
Boastful, braggart. Rainless (cloud). Tasteless (food). صَلِف ج صَلَافَى وصُلَفَاء وصَلِفُون
Side of the neck. Slope of a hill. صَلِيف
Hard and barren (soil). أَصلَف ج أَصَالِف م صَلفَاء ج صَلَافَى
Hard and barren land. صِلفَاء وصِلفَاءَة
To utter a loud shout. * صَلَق o صَلقًا, وأَصلَق
To attack (a tribe). صَلَق ه وهم
To smite a. o. (sun). – ه

Glabrous. Hard. أَصلَح م صَلحَاء ج صُلح
* صَلُح o وصَلَح a o صَلَاحًا وصُلُوحًا وصَلَاحِيَة
To be sound, (*opp. to* فَسَد) honest, righteous.
To suit, to fit a. o. – ل
That will suit you. هٰذَا يَصلُح لَك
To reconcile, to make peace with. صَالَح مُصَالَحَة وصِلَاحًا ه
To agree with a. o. upon. – ه على
To set a. th. aright. To repair, to reform. أَصلَح ه
To do good to a. o. – الى
To make peace between. – بَين
To reconcile, to make peace. تَصَالَح واصطَلَح واصَّلَح
To agree on. – على
To be arranged (business). إنصَلَح
To adapt o.'s self. To amend, to reconcile. To be corrected, improved. إصطَلَح
To find a. th. proper, good. To judge, to wish a. th. good. إستَصلَح ه
To ask a. o. to make peace. – ه
Peace, reconciliation. صُلح
Goodness, Soundness. Morality. Righteousness. صَلَاح
Technical word, meaning. إصطِلَاح ج إصطِلَاحَات
Technical (word). إصطِلَاحِيّ
Sound, good. proper, honest. ◇ Self-interest. صَالِح ج صَالِحُون وصُلَّاح
He is fit for that. هُوَ صَالِح لِهٰذَا
Goodly, honest. صَلِيح ج صُلَحَاء
Work; self-interest. Advantage. ◇ Calling, employment. مَصلَحَة ج مَصَالِح
Peace, reconciliation. مُصَالَحَة وصِلَاح
Corrector, reformer. ▫ Salt. مُصلِح
Mediator, peacemaker. مُصلِح بَين
To pretend deafness. * صلخ – تَصَالَخ
Great deafness. صَلَخ
Stone-deaf. أَصلَخ م صَلخَاء ج صُلخ
To trample loudly (beast). To grate (teeth). * صَلَد i صُلُودًا
To ascend on. – في
To be hard (soil). To fail to give fire (steel). – وأَصلَد
To be avaricious. صَلَد o صَلَادَة, وصَلَّد
To have a steel giving no fire. أَصلَد
Avarice. صَلَادَة

(meat, a stick) near the fire.
To straighten a stick (in the fire). تَصَلَّى ه
To warm o.'s self at a fire. — واصْطَلَى
Action of the fire. Fire. صِلاء وصَلَى
Forehead. صَلَايَة وصَلَاءَة ج صُلِيّ وصِلِيّ
Stone-pounder for aromatics.
Snare, net for game. مِصْلَاة ج مَصَالِ
Toasted, roasted. مَصْلِيّ
To stop (a flask). ✱ صَمَّ o صَمًّا ه
To be obstructed (ear-hole). صَمَّ a صَمًّا وصَمَمًا
To become deaf. — وأَصَمَّ
He is dead. صَمَّ صَدَاهُ
To determine upon. صَمَّمَ على او في
To persevere in.
To snap a. th. with the teeth. — ه
To penetrate, to pierce into (sword). صَمَّمَ في
To impress a. th. in the mind of. — ه ه
To render a. o. deaf (God). — وأَصَمَّ ه
To find a. o. deaf. أَصَمَّ ه
To stop (a flask). — ه
To feign o.'s self deaf. To turn a deaf ear to. تَصَامَّ
Great misfortune, calamity. صِمّ وصَمَام
Stopper. Male serpent. صِمَّة ج صِمَم
Female hedge-hog. Courageous.
Obstruction of the ear, deafness. صَمَم
Unyielding (man). Fiery (horse). — ومُصَمِّم
Valve, lid. صِمَام ج أَصِمَّة, وصِمَامَة
To remain silent; to feign deafness. صَمَامِ, صَمَامِ
Interior, pith. Bone supporting a limb. Intense (cold, heat). Pure, unmixed. صَمِيم
From the bottom of the heart. من صَمِيم القلب
Deaf. Disregarded (man). أَصَمّ م صَمَّاء ج صُمّ وصُمَّان
Surname of the month Redjeb. الأَصَمّ
Hard soil. Great distress. صَمَّاء
حَجَر أَصَمّ وصَمَّان وصَخْرَة صَمَّاء وصَمَّانَة
Hard stone. Granite, silex.
To apply o.'s self to, to persevere in. ✱ صَمْصَمَ في

To strike a. o. with a stick. صَلَقَ ه ب
To writhe about (sick person). تَصَلَّقَ
To scream in child-birth (woman).
To grate the teeth (stallion). إِصْطَلَقَ
Dirty water. صُلَافَة
Shriek of distress. صَلْق ج أَصْلَاق
Even plain. صَلَق ج أَصْلَاق وجج أَصَالِيق
Even, smooth. صَلِيق م صَلِيقَة
Thin bread. Slice of صَلِيقَة ج صَلَائِق
Eloasted meat.
Eloquent (speaker). مِصْلَق ومِصْلَاق ج مَصَالِيق
✱ صَلَمَ o ؛ صَلْمًا, وصَلَّمَ ه To maim a. o, to cut off the ears, nose.
To uproot a. th. إِصْطَلَمَ ه
Gallant, dauntless men. صَلَم وصَلَمَة
Separated party. صِلَامَة وصُلَامَة ج صِلَامَات وصُلَامَات
Misfortune. Momentous event صَيْلَم
Sword.
أَصْلَم م صَلْمَاء ج صُلْم, ومُصَلَّم الأُذُنَيْن
Having the ears cut off.
To become destitute. ✱ صَلْمَمَ
To pull off a. th. To shave the (head). — ه
He is an unknown man. هُوَ صَلْمَعَة بْنُ قَلْمَعَة
Tall man. ✱ صَلْهَب ومُصَلْهِب
To wound a. o. on the back. ✱ صَلَا o صَلْوًا ه
To pray God. صَلَّى صَلَاةً
To bless, to wish good to. صَلَّى على
✧ To give the nuptial blessing to.
To be the second in a race (horse). — تَصْلِيَةً
Middle of the back, rump. صَلًا ج صَلَوَات وأَصْلَاء,
Prayer. صَلَاة ج صَلَوَات
Oratory, place of worship. مُصَلًّى
✧ Holy water.
The second in a race (horse). مُصَلٍّ
✱ صَلَى i صَلْيًا ه ه او في اوعلى To heat, to roast a. th. at a fire.
To roast (meat). — ه
To lay a snare for. — ل
صَلِيَ a صَلًى وصِلَاء وصُلِيًّا ه او ب To warm o.'self at the fire. To endure the heat of fire.
To put صَلَّى ه على او ب, وأَصْلَى ه ه

house). To deck (a bride). To expose the Blessed Sacrament.
✧ To spare (money). صَمَّد
To come to fight with a.o. صَامَد مُصَامَدَةً وصِمَادًا ه
To rest a. th. upon. أَصْمَد إِلَيْهِ ه وعَلَيْهِ الى
Elevated, hard place. صَمْد ج أَصْمَاد وصِمَاد
✧ Apparel of a bride. — العَرُوس
Lord. Eternal. Enduring hunger and thirst. Craftless people. Solid (body). صَمَد
Prominent rock. ✧ Corporal. Exposition of the blessed Sacrament. صَمْدَة
Stopper. lid. صِمَاد
✧ Net (income). Laid up (money). صَامِد
Massy, solid. مُصْمَد
Place repaired to. مُصَمَّد
To be avaricious. صَمَرًا وصُمُورًا To flow slowly (water). ✱ صَمَر o
To become sour (milk). صَمِر a صَمَرًا, وأَصْمَر i صَمْرًا, — i
To be avaricious. To be, to enter upon the time of sunset. صَمَّر وأَصْمَر
Odour of fresh musk. صَمْر
Brim of a vessel. صُمْر ج أَصْمَار
Place to which water comes slowly. صِمْر
Thin and dry. صَمِير
Sunset. صُمَيْر
Sour milk. صَمْرَة وصَامُورَة
To detain a. o. by persuasion. ✱ صَمَع a صَمْعًا ه
To strike a. o. with a stick. — ه ب
To make a mistake in a speech. صَمِع a صَمَعًا في الكَلَام
To persist in o.'s scheme. صَمَّع على رَأْيِهِ
To keep to. إِنْصَمَع في
Recess in wall, wheat-bin. ◻ صَمْعَة
Small-eared. أَصْمَع م صَمْعَاء ج صُمْع
Slender, not opened (plant).
Overtopping. Cutting sword. أَصْمَع ج صُمْعَان
Penetrating, quick (mind). — وأَصْمَعَان
Sharp-pointed (pie). Sharp-horned (gazelle). مُصَمَّع
To heap up. To give a conical shape to a dish. ✱ صَوْمَع ه

ni

Finely tempered (sword). صَمْصَام وصَمْصَامَة
Fiery horse. صِمْصِم وصُمَاصِم وصُمَاصِمَة
To urge, to incite a. o. to. ✱ صَمَأ a صَمْأً ه على
✱ صَمَت o صَمْتًا وصُمَاتًا وصُمُوتًا, وصَمَّت وأَصْمَت To remain silent.
To hush up, to silence a o. صَمَّت وأَصْمَت ه
To become hardened (ground). أَصْمَت
To render a. th. solid, massive. — ه
Silence. صَمْت وصُمَات وصُمُوت
He has hushed him up. رَمَاهُ بِصُمَاتِهِ
He is on the point of performing the business. هُوَ على صُمَات الأَمْر
Food given for soothing a child. صِمْتَة وصُمْتَة
Silent. Lifeless (*opp. to* نَاطِق) (being). Mute property *as opposed* to flocks. صَامِت
He does not possess mute nor vocal property. مَا لَهُ صَامِت ولَا نَاطِق
Silent, mute. صِمِّيت وصَمُوت
Full (honeycomb). Heavy (breast-plate). Penetrating (thrust). صَمُوت
Wild, savage (country). إِصْمِت وإِصْمِتَة
Solid, sound (wall, vessel). Of one colour (horse, stuff). مُصْمَت
Candle. ✧ صَمْجَة ج صَمْج
To affect the brain (sun). ✱ صَمَح a i صَمْحًا ه
To importune a. o. with questions. — ه
Fetid sweat. Melted grease applied on chaps. صُمَاح
Hard ground. صِمْحَاء وصِمْحَاءَة
Burning (day). صَامِح وصَمُوح
To wound a. o. in the ear-hole. ✱ صَمَخ o صَمْخًا ه
To produce gum (tree). ✧ صَمَّخ وأَصْمَخ
✧ Ear-wax. Arabic gum. صِمْخ
Conduct, hole of the ear; ear. صِمَاخ ج أَصْمِخَة, وأَصْمُوخ
To direct o's self towards. ✱ صَمَد o صَمْدًا ه والى ول, وصَمَّد ه
To strike a. o. with a stick. — ه ب
To set up, to erect a. th. — وصَمَّد ه
To stop (a flask). ✧ To adorn (a

Condiment of mustard and raisins. ✻ صنب – صِناب
Liking that condiment. مِصْنَب
Reddish yellow, chestnut-colour. صِنابِيّ
Old palm-tree. Lonely man, without family. Water-pipe of a tank. ✻ صُنبُور
Pine-cone. جَوْز صُنوبَر
Cold wind. صِنَّبْر ج صَنابِر
Intenseness of cold. صَنابِر الشِّتاء
Pine-tree. صَنَوْبَر
Cone-shaped, conical. صَنَوْبَرِيّ
To fix, to strengthen a. th. ✻ صنت – أَصْنَتَ ه
Small basket. Flask-case. صُنُّوت ج صَنانِيت
To send away (people). ✻ صَنَج o صُنُوجًا ه
To strike a. o. with a stick. – ه ب
To overthrow a. o. صَنَّج بِفُلان
Brass castanets. Cymbals. P صَنج ج صُنُوج
I do not know what sort of man he is. ما أدري أيّ صَنجٍ هو
Player upon the cymbals. صَنَّاج وصَنَّاجة
Surname of an Arabian poet.
Lord, chief. Strong. Hero. Vehement (cold). ✻ صِندِيد ج صَنادِيد
The chiefs of an army. الصَّنادِيد
Box, chest. Safe. ✻ صُندُوق ج صَنادِيق
Public debt office. صُندُوق الدَّيْن
Hump-backed. ◘ أبو صُندُوق
Treasurer. أَمِين الصُّندُوق
Sandal-wood. ◘ Skiff. P صَندَل
Big-headed (ass, camel). – وصُنادِل ج صَنادِل
Chemistry, pharmacy. صَندَلة
Chemist, pharmacist. صَندَلانِيّ ج صَنادِلة
Plane-tree. Kind of palma Christi. P صِنار وصِنّار
Head of a spindle. Fishing hook. Angle. Knitting-needle. صِنّارة ج صَنانِير
Mimosa Nilotica; acacia. ◘ صَنط
Tympanon. ✧ صَنطر
To make, to work a. th. skilfully. To manufacture. To create a. th. (God). ✻ صَنَع a صُنعًا وصُنعًا ه
He has done to him a benefit. – إليه مَعرُوفًا صُنعًا

Upper part of a pie. Monk's cell. صَوْمَع وصَوْمَعة ج صَوامِع
To gum. ✻ صمغ – صَمَّغ ه
To produce gum (tree). To slaver. أَصْمَغ
To extract gum from a tree. إستَصْمَغ ه
Arabic gum. صَمْغ وصَمَغ ج صُمُوغ
✧ Pine-resin. صَمْغ الصَّنَوْبَر
✧ Colophony. صَمْغ البُطْم
Piece of gum. Ulcer. ✧ Biestings. صَمْغة
Ulcered on the nose, lips. صَمْغان وابو صَمْغة
Sides of the mouth. صِمْغان وصامِغان وصِماغان
To become altered (milk, water). ✻ صمق – أَصْمَق
To shut a door. – ه
Altered milk. صَمَقة
Hungry or thirsty. صامِق
To be hard, to become hardened. ✻ صَمَل o صَمْلًا وصُمُولًا
To abstain from food. – عن
To strike a. o. with a stick. – ه ب
To be intertwisted (plant). إصْمَألّ
Strong, hardy. صُمُل
Dry, dried up. صامِل وصَمِيل
Rivet of a screw. ✧ صَمُولة
To rush, to go quickly. ✻ صَمَى i صَمَيانًا، وأَصْمَى
To befall a. o. (accident). صَمَى ه
To urge, to incite a. o. against. – ه على
To kill game on the spot (hunter). أَصْمَى ه
To dart down (bird). إنْصَمَى
To spread on. – على
Impetuous. صَمَيان
To be altered, to stink (water). To emit a fetid smell from the arm-pits. To assume a disdainful look. To get angry. ✻ صنّ – أَصَنّ
To strive to. – على
Basket. Urine of the hyrax. صِنّ
Fetid smell of the arm-pits. Bad odour. صِنّة، وصُنان ج أَصِنّة
Courageous, brave. صَنان
Slothful, neglectful. أَصَنّ
Angry. مُصِنّ غَضَبًا

Manufactured, wrought. مَصْنوع ومُصنَّم
Artificial, fictitious.
To assort, to classify. ✡ صنف — صَنَّف ه
To compose (a book). ✧ To forge a lie.
To put forth leaves (tree). — وتَصَنَّف
To be chapped (lips). To be split (tree). تَصَنَّف
Species, sort, class. صَنف وصِنف ج أَصناف وصُنُوف
Fringe of a vestment. صِنف وصِنفة وصَنِفة
Litterary work. تَصنيف ج تَصانيف ، ومُصَنَّف ج مُصَنَّفات
Galled in the legs (deer). أصنف ج صُنف
Author of a book. مُصَنِّف
Pith, quintessence. ✡ صنفر — صُنافِر
To stink. ✡ صَنِق a صَنَقًا
To take care of. أَصنق في
To exert o.'s self in. — على
Smell of the arm-pits. صُنُق
Stinking. Sturdy. صَانِق ج صَنَقة
To be offensive (smell). ✡ صَنِم a صَنَمًا
To be strong (slave).
To shout (man). To shape out idols for worship. صَنَّم
Strong, robust (slave). صَنِم م صَنِمة
Idol. صَنَم ج أَصنام
Quill of a pen, of a feather. صَنَمة
To be stained with ashes (cook). ✡ صنو — أَصنَى وتَصَنَّى
Ashes. صِناء وصِنًى
Intertwisted trees. صَنو ج صِنو وصُنُوّ
Water, stones between two mountains.
Brother. Son. صِنو ج أَصناء وصِنوان
Uncle. ◻ Nephew.
Sister. Daughter. Aunt. صِنوة
صِنو وصُنو مث صُنوان وصِنيان ج صِنوان
One of a pair or of more than two.
The whole. الصِّنَايَة
Hush! silence! ✡ صَه
✡ صَهِب a صَهَبًا وصُهبَة وصُهُوبة ، واصهَبّ
To be redhaired. To be chestnut (horse). واصهَابّ
A golden, chestnut colour صُهب وصُهبة وصُهُوبة
Reddish, chestnut (colour). أَصهَب م صَهباء ج صُهب
Violent (death). صُهَابِيّ

He has done to him a foul deed. صَنَع بهِ صَنِيعًا قَبِيحًا
To tend, to train (a horse). — صَنعًا وصَنعة ه
To arrange, to embellish a. th. صَنَّع ه
To make the most of his goods (merchant).
To maintain, to support a. o. — وأَصنَع ه
To blandish a. o. صَانَع ه
To strive to seduce a. o. with a bribe. — ه ب
To be affected, assuming. تَصَنَّع
✧ To paint o.'s face.
To prepare (a banquet). ✧ To be artificial. إِصطَنَع
To do good to a. o. — عِند فُلَان صَنِيعة
To choose a. o. as a follower. — فُلانًا لِنَفسِهِ
To order a. th. to be made. — ه وه
To rear (an apprentice).
To ask. a. o. to manufacture a. th. إستَصنَع ه ه
Make, made. صَنع وصُنع
Benefit. صُنع
Skilful workman. صِنع وصَنع اليَدَين
Work. Employment. Workmanship. صَنعة
Art of training horses. — الفَرَس
Art, craft, industry. Skilfulness. صِناعة ج صِناعات وصَنائِع
Arsenal, dockyard. دَار الصِّناعة
Workmen, artisans. أَصحاب الصَّنائِع
Artificial. (*opp. to* طَبِيعِيّ) صِناعِيّ
Work. Deed, benefit. Polished (sword). Trained, skilful. صَنِيع
Handy, dexterous. — وصَناع اليَدَين
Skilful workman. (*m. f.*) صَناع ج صُنع
قَوم صُنعَى وصِنعَى وصُنُعَى وصَنعَى الأَيدِي
Skilful workmen, industrial people.
Action, deed. Work, workmanship. Benefit, favour. صَنِيعة ج صَنائع
He is my disciple. هُوَ صَنِيعِي او صَنِيعَتِي
Affectedness. Artifice. تَصَنُّع
Manufacturing. Creator. Artisan. ✧ Apprentice; servant. صانِع ج صُنَّاع
Cistern. مَصنَع ومَصنَعة ومَصنُعة ج مَصانِع
Constructions, *such as* palaces, strongholds.
Banquet, dinner-party. مَصنعة ج مَصانِع

Excessive heat. Hot day Place burnt by the sun. صَيْهَب
The red liquor *i. e.* wine. الصَّهْبَاء
Tawny beasts. Toasted. مُصَهَّب
✱ صَهَد a صَهْدًا ه To scorch a. o. (sun).
Intenseness of heat. صَهْدَان
Waterless desert. صَيْهَد وصَيْهُود
✱ صَهَر a صَهْرًا, واصْطَهَر ه To melt, to liquefy a. th. To anoint, to grease.
صَاهَر ه وفي, وأَصْهَر ب والى وفي To become related to a tribe by marriage. To become the son or brother-in-law of a. o. in a tribe.
أَصْهَر الجَيْش للجَيْش The army drew near to the other.
إِنْصَهَر To be melted, liquefied.
إِصْطَهَر واصْهَارّ To glisten (chameleon).
صَاهِر Hot, burning.
صِهْر ج أَصْهَار وصُهَرَاء Relationship. Related on the women's side. Kinsman, son-in-law, brother-in-law.
صُهَارَة Molten substance. Marrow.
صَهُور ج صُهُر Roaster. Seller of molten grease.
صَهِير Melted, liquefied.
P صِهْرِيج وصُهَارِج ج صَهَارِيج Cistern.
✱ صَهَل a i صَهِيلًا وصَاهِلَة To neigh (horse).
تَصَاهَل To neigh one to another (horses).
صَاهِل وصَهَّال Neighing.
صَهِيل وصُهَال, وصَاهِلَة ج صَوَاهِل The neighing of horses.
✱ صَهَا a صَهْوًا وصَهِي a صَهًى To have an ulcer.
صَاهَى ه To ride (a horse). To ascend on the top of (a mountain).
صَهْوَة ج صِهَاء وصَهَوَات Back of a beast. Middle of a saddle.
— ج صُهًى Tower on the top of a mountain.
— ج صِهَاء Hollow holding water.
▫ صَوْصَوَة Murmur, squeak.
✱ صَاب o صَوْبًا ومَصَابًا To fall (rain).
— صَوْبًا وصَيْبُوبَةً نَحْوَ, وأَصَاب ه To hit the target (arrow).
— ه To pour (a liquid). To flood the earth (clouds).
صَوَّب ج وه To approve a. o. To find (an advice) to be right.
— ه To stoop, to lower (the head), to raise it. To shoot an arrow straight to the butt. To point (fire-arms).
— ه To start (a horse).
أَصَاب ه To obtain, to attain a. th.
— دَمًا To perpetrate a murder.
أَصَاب في قَوْلِهِ ورَأْيِهِ He is right (in his opinion); he speaks rightly.
— في عَمَلِهِ To act in a straightforward way.
— إِصَابَةً ومُصَابَةً ه To befall, to smite a. o. (misfortune).
— ه ب To smite a. o. (evil eye).
تَصَوَّب To descend, to go downwards.
إِنْصَاب To be shed, poured forth (liquid).
✧ — ب او في To be struck (by an evil).
إِسْتَصَاب اسْتِصَابَةً, واسْتَصْوَب اسْتِصْوَابًا ه To approve, to find a. th. right, good.
صَاب Colocynth.
صَوْب Side, aimed direction. Straight forwardness. ✧ Near, towards.
— وصَيِّب Cloud letting down rain.
صَابَة Misfortune. Weakness of mind.
صُوبَة Heap. ▫ Packsaddle of a camel.
صَوَاب Right, straight forward course. Rightness. convenience. ✧ Judgment. Intellect.
صَوَابِيّ Reasonable, right.
إِصَابَة Successful hit (of an arrow) Acuteness of mind.
صَائِب وصَوِيب ومُصِيب Going straight to the butt (arrow). Straight (mind, judgment).
صُوَّاب وصُوَّابَة وصُيَّابَة القَوْم Choice men of a tribe.
مُصَاب Smitten by a calamity.
— ومُصَابَة ومَصُوبَة Stroke, misfortune.
مُصِيبَة ج مَصَائِب ومُصِيبَات Mishap, blow.
T صُوبَاشِي Rural policeman.
✱ صَات o a صَوْتًا, وصَوَّت وأَصَات To emit a sound, to utter a cry.
صَوَّت وأَصَات بفُلَان To divulge a. th. concerning a. o.
✧ تَصَيَّت تَصَيُّتًا To be renowned, famous.
إِنْصَات To answer to a call. To retrace o's steps. To become erect.

Bag of musk. Small quantity of musk. Sweet odour. صِوَار ج أصْوِرَة
Fine-shaped. صَيِّر
Prone to a. th. أصْوَر ل
Picture, image. تَصْوِيرَة ج تَصَاوِير
Thought, idea. Fancy. Conception of the mind. تَصَوُّر
Photography. تَصْوِير الشَّمْس
Painter. مُصَوِّر
The Creator, God. — الكَائِنَات
Avaricious. ✲ صُوص
Chicken. ✧ صُوص ج صِيصَان
To come successively (bees). ✲ صَاع o صَوْعًا
To measure wheat. — ه
To scatter (people, things). — ه وه
To round a. th. To make a. th. sharp-pointed. To shake plants (wind). To sweep, to prepare a place. صَوَّع ه
To move its wings about (bird). — ب
To disperse (crowd). To be shaken (plant). تَصَوَّع
To retrace o.'s steps. إنْصَاع
صَاع وصَوْع وصُوع ج أصْوُع وأصْوَاع وصِيعَان
Measure for grain.
Flat ground. Play-ground. صَاع وصَاعَة
Gold or silver cup. صُوَاع ج صِيعَان
To shape out, to mould, to fashion. To create a. th. (God). To pattern, to copy a. th. ✲ صَاغ o صَوْغًا ه
To forge (a lie). To form (a tense). — ه
To sink into (the ground: water). صَاغ في
To be fashionned. صِيغَ وتَصَوَّغ وانصَاغ
To silver a. th. ✧ صَيَّغ
Pure, unmixed, standard (money). Honest (man). Sound (body). ✧ صَاغ
Coin having the legal standard. ✧ مُعَامَلَة صَاغ (*opp. to* شُرُك)
Form, shape. Alike, similar. صَوْغ
They are both alike. هُمَا صَوْغَان
He is like his brother. هُوَ صَوْغ وصَوْغَة أخِيهِ
Fashion, shape. Paradigm (*gram*). ✧ Jewels. صِيغَة ج صِيَغ
Arrows of the same workmanship. سِهَام صِيغَة
He is of noble descent. هُوَ من صِيغَة كَرِيمَة

His fame resounded in his time. إنْصَات بِهِ الزَّمَان
Voice, sound. صَوْت ج أصْوَات
Good fame, renown. — وصَات وصِيت وصِيتَة
✧ Good or bad fame. صِيت
Strong-voiced. صَات وصَيِّت
Resounding. مِصْوَات
There is not in the house a. o. raising his voice *i. e.* nobody. مَا بِالدَّار مِصْوَات
Metallic sheet for baking. ✧ صَاج
To split a. th. ✲ صَاح o صَوْحًا ه
To dry up a. th. (sun, wind). صَوَّح ه
To become split. To become dried up. تَصَوَّح
To be cloven. To shine (moon). إنْصَاح
Bank of a river. Foot of a mountain. صَوْح وصُوح
Barren land. صَاحَة
Plaster. Sweat of a horse. Shoot of the palm-tree. صُوَاح
Dishevelled hair. صُوَّاحَة
To listen to a. o. ✲ صَاخ — أصَاخ ل
Cyst of the bones. Misfortune. صَاخَة ج صَاخَات وصَاخ
To incline a. th. towards. ✲ صَار o صَوْرًا , وأصَار ه الى
To cut, to divide a. th. صَار ه
To decide a point (judge). — الحُكْم
To lean, to incline. صَوِر a صَوَرًا
To shape out a. th. To paint, to picture. صَوَّر ه
I fancied. صُوِّر لِي
To demolish, to break a. th. أصَار ه
To be shaped. To be painted. تَصَوَّر
To imagine, to fancy. — ه
To be bent. To be demolished. إنْصَار
Bank of a river. صَوْر ج صِيرَان
Grove of palm-trees. صَوْر ج صِيرَان وأصْوَار
Horn, hunting-horn. Tyre (town). صُور
Summit of a mountain. Musk-rat. صَارَة
Itching of the head. صَوْرَة
Shape. Exterior appearance. Copy. Picture, image. Manner. ✧ Picture. Formula. صُورَة ج صُوَر وصِوَر
Draught of a letter. صُورَة كِتَاب
Apparently, obviously. صُورَةً
Herd of oxen. صُوَار وصِيَار ج صِيرَان

Craft, art of a goldsmith. صِيَاغَة

Goldsmith, jeweller. صَائِغ ج صُيَّاغ وصَاغَة وصُوَّاغ

Liar. صَوَّاغ وصَيِّغ

Gold or silver jewels. ✧ مَصَاغ ج مَصَاغَات

✱ صَاف o صَوْفًا وصُؤُوفًا, وصَوِف a صَوَفًا To be laniferous (beast).

To deviate, to miss the butt (arrow). To turn away from (face). صَاف o صَوْفًا عن

To speak the language of the soofies. صَوَّف كَلَامَهُ

To avert (a misfortune : God). أَصَاف ه عن

To become a soofi. تَصَوَّف

Wool. صُوف ج أَصْوَاف

He has given it for nothing. أَعْطَاهُ بِصُوفِ رَقَبَتِهِ

Flock of wool. صُوفَة

Seller of wool. صَوَّاف

Soofi (musulman devotee). صُوفِيّ ج صُوفِيَّة

Woolly. صَافٍ وصَافٍ وصَائِف وأَصْوَف

Woolly. صَوِف وصُوفَانِيّ

Tinder. ✧ صُوفَان (*un.* صُوفَانَة)

Middle of the head. Turban. Battle-field. ✱ صَوْقَعَة

To stick to (smell). ✱ صَاك o صَوْكًا

He is motionless. مَا بِهِ صَوْك وَلَا بَوْك

To dart furiously upon a. o. (wild beast). ✱ صَال o صَوْلًا وصَوْلَةً على

To assault, to overpower a. o. — صَوْلًا وصِيَالًا وصُؤُولًا وصَيَالًا ومَصَالَة

It has been decreed by God. صِيلَ ل

To soak, to dilute (gypsum). To wash (corn). To clear a thrashing-floor from rubbish. صَوَّل ه

To assault. صَاوَل مُصَاوَلَةً وصِيَالًا وصِيَالَةً ه

To attack one another. تَصَاوَل

Rush, violence. Authority. Sudden attack. Strength. صَوْلَة

Wheat washed in water. صُولَة الحِنْطَة

Rubbish of wheat. Sweepings of a thrashing-floor. صُوَالَة

Vessel for soaking. مِصْوَل ج مَصَاوِل

Broom for a thrashing-floor مِصْوَلَة

To fast. ✱ صَام o صَوْمًا وصِيَامًا, واصْطَام

To reach its mid point (day). To abate (wind).

To cause a. o. to fast. صَوَّم ه

Fast. صَوْم وصِيَام

Fasting, faster. صَائِم ج صَائِمُون وصُوَّام وصُيَّام وصُوَّم وصُيَّم وصِيَام

Bulky and strong. صَيِّم

Fasting. صَوْمَان ج صَيَامَى

Faster. صَوُوم

Waterless and barren (land). صَوَّام

Standing-place of a horse. مَصَام ومَصَامَة

✱ صَان o صَوْنًا وصِيَانًا وصِيَانَةً, واصْطَان ه وه To preserve, to keep a. o. or a. th.

To surround a. th. with walls, to enclose. ✧ صَوَّن ه

To guard o.'s self from. تَصَوَّن وتَصَاوَن من وعن

Preservation, keeping. صَوْن

Censer for perfumes. صَوْنَة

Ward-robe. صِوَان وصُوَان وصِيَان ج أَصْوِنَة

Keeping. Chastity, modesty. صِيَانَة

Flint-stone, quartz, silex. صَوَّانَة ج صَوَّان

Town on the Nile. Quarry. أَصْوَان

Guarded. مَصُون ومَصْوُون

Chaste (woman). مَصُونَة

Echo. ✱ صَوّ – صُوَّة ج صُوًى وجج أَصْوَاء Mound, hillock. Road. Stones set up for guidance.

Tombs. صُوًى وأَصْوَاء

He has taken it entirely. أَخَذَهُ بِصُوَاهُ

✱ صَوَى i صُوِيًّا, وصَوِيَ a صَوًى, وصَوَّى وأَصْوَى To dry up (tree).

To be strong, sturdy. صَوِيَ a صَوًى

Dried up. صَوِيّ وصَاوٍ

To wash a. th. imperfectly. ✱ صِيأ – صَيَّأ ه

Imperfect washing. صِيئَة

To crow, to cry loudly. ✱ صَاح i صَيْحًا وصَيْحَةً وصِيَاحًا وصَيَحَانًا

To call out to a. o. — بِفُلَان

To exclaim against a. o. — على فُلَان

They have been frightened. صِيحَ بِهِم

They have been destroyed. صِيحَ فِيهِم

To shout, to utter a shrill cry. صَيَّح

To call out to one another. صَايَح وتَصَايَح

To be cracked, broken. تَصَيَّح وانْصَاح

To break (dawn). انْصَاح

Cry. Crowing of the cock. صَيْح وصِيَاح

Fortress. ✲ صِيصَة وصِيصِيَة ج صَيَاصٍ
Cock's spur. Horn of bulls, gazelles.
To incite (people) ✲ صَاء i صَيْئًا ه one against another. To separate (sheep).
To go astray. ✧ صَيَّع عن الطَّرِيق
To be stirred (water). ✧ To be تَصَيَّع perplexed, led astray.
To season (a dish). ✲ صاغ – صَيَّغ ه ✧ To give a legal standard to money.
✲ صَاف i صَيْفًا, وصَيَّف وتَصَيَّف واصطاف ب
To spend summer in a place.
To deviate صَاف i صَيْفًا وصَيْفُوفَة عن from the mark (arrow).
To receive a summer rain. صِيف
To be sufficient to a. o. for صَيَّف ه summer. ✧ To glean.
To make a صَايَف مُصَايَفَة وصِيَافًا ه contract for summer.
To enter upon the season of أَصَاف summer. To beget a child in old age.
Summer. صَيْف ج أَصْيَاف, وصَيْفَة ج صِيَف
Belonging to summer. Summer صَيْفِيّ rain. Born in summer.
Summer rain. صَيِّف
Warm (weather). صَائِف وصَاف
Summer expedition. صَائِفَة ج صَوَائِف
Summer-place, مَصِيف ومُتَصَيَّف ومُصْطَاف country.
Watered by a summer مَصِيفَة ومَصْيُوفَة rain (country).
Often watered by summer مِصْيَاف rains (land). Marrying when old (man).
Dust raised. ✲ صِيق, وصِيقَة ج صِيَق
Sound, noise, offensive smell.
Sparrow. صِيق ج صِيقَان
To cling to (smell). ✲ صَاك i صَيْكًا ب
Short and strong. ✲ صيم – صِيَّم
China. ✲ صين – الصِّين
Chinese. China earthenware. صِينِيّ
Tray, plate. ✧ صِينِيَّة و✧ صَانِيَّة ج صَوَانِي
✧ Patine.
Cloth-tent. صيون – ✧ صِيوَان
Conch of the ear. صِيوَان الأُذُن

I met him before لَقِيتُهُ قَبْلَ كُلّ صَيْحٍ ونَفْرٍ dawn.
Shout, yell. Punishment from صَيْحَة Heaven. Sudden attack.
Shouter, shouting. صَائِح م صَائِحَة
Wailing of women at a الصَّائِحَة funeral.
Shouter ; clamorous. صَيَّاح م صَيَّاحَة
To hunt, ✲ صَاد i a وتَصَيَّد واصْطَاد ه to chase, to fish.
To hunt, to fish for a. o. صَاد ه صَيْدًا
To have the neck erected. صَيِد a صَيَدًا To be glandered (camel).
Copper. Camel's glanders. صَاد
Hunting. Fishing. Shooting. صَيْد Fish or game caught, prey.
صَائِد وصَيَّاد ج صَيَّادُون, وصَيُود ج صُيُد
Hunter. Fisherman. Sportsman. وصِيد
Erecting the neck. أَصْيَد م صَيْدَاء ج صِيد Prince. Glandered (camel).
Hard ground. Saida, town of صَيْدَاء Syria.
Copper. Gold. صَيْدَان
Termagant. صَيْدَانَة
Net, مِصْيَد ومِصْيَدَة ومَصِيدَة ج مَصَايِد snare. Trap. Pitfall.
Caught in chase. مَصِيد
Hunter. Lion. مُصْطَاد
To ✲ صَار i صَيْرًا وصَيْرُورَة ومَصِيرًا become. To go back to the encampment. ✧ To happen, to come to pass (event).
To befall a. o. – مَصِيرًا الى
To render a. o. صَيَّر وأَصَار إِصَارَة ه وه a. th. *such*.
To have a likeness to. تَصَيَّر ه
Result of an affair, issue. Great- صِير priest of the Jews. Little salt-fishes. Crevice of a door.
He is on the point of هُوَ على صِيرِ الأَمْر finishing the affair.
Sound of castanets. صِيَار
Enclosure for صِيَارَة, وصِيرَة ج صِيَر وصِير cattle.
A becoming such or such. صَيْرُورَة
Dry fodder, straw. صَائِرَة
Place of arrival. Result, issue. مَصِير

ض

* ضِبْ Pearl. Fish.
* ضَئِد ضُؤَادًا To have a rheum.
أَضْأَد ه To cause a rheum to a. o.
ضُؤْد وضُؤْدَة Rheum in the head.
* ضَأَز a ضَأْزًا وضَأَزًا ه To be injust towards a. o.
ضُوزَى وضِئْزَى Defective (lot).
* ضَأْضَاء وضَوْضَاء وضَوْضَى Noise, bustle, uproar.
ضُؤْضُؤ وضِئْضِئ Root, stock. Offspring.
* ضُئِك To have a rheum in the head.
ضُؤَاك Cold, rheum.
* ضَؤُل o ضَآلَة وضُؤُولَة To be lean, thin, little, mean.
ضَأَل a ضَأْلًا, وضَاءَل شَخْصَهُ To cower, to crouch.
تَضَاءَل To be little. To make o's self small. To conceal o.'s self.
ضَئِيل ج ضُؤَلَاء وضِئَال وضَئِيلُون Lean, thin, small.
— الرَّأْي Weak-minded.
ضُئَيْلَة Thin snake.
* ضَأَن أَضْأَن To have numerous sheep.
ضَائِن ج ضَأْن وضَأَن وضَئِين Sheep.
ضَائِنَة ج ضَوَائِن Ewe.
✧ ضَانِي Mutton (meat).
* ضَبَّ i ضَبًّا To flow (water). To be fixed in the ground (th). To become silent (person).
— ه ✧ To gather (children).
— وضَبَّب وأَضَبَّ على To keep a. th. carefully. ✧ To watch (school-children).
ضَبَّ i ضَبًّا وضُبُوبًا To be affected with a tumour (lip).
ضَبُب o ضَبَابَة, وأَضَبَّ To abound in lizards (land).
ضَبَّب ه وه To feed a. o. with butter and rob. To put a bolt to a door.
أَضَبَّ To be misty (day). To be numerous. To remain silent. To speak; to scream.
— ه To cleave to a. o.
— ه To pour, to spill water.
أَضَبَّ على ما في نفسه To conceal o's mind.
✧ إِنْضَبَّ To be tucked (skirts). To be guarded, watched (child).
ضَبّ وضِبّ Hatred, anger.
ضَبّ Tumour on the lips.
ضَبّ ج ضِبَاب وأَضُبّ وضُبَّان Lizard.
ضَبَّة ج ضِبَاب Door-latch. ✧ Wooden lock.
ضَبِيب و✧ ضَبَاب Point of a sword.
ضَبَابَة ج ضَبَاب Fog, mist.
ضَبِيبَة Food for children.
ضَبِب ومَضَبَّة ج مَضَابّ Abounding with lizards (place).
مُضَبِّب Hunting lizards.
✧ ضَبْضَب To be misty (weather).
* ضَبَأ a ضَبْأً وضُبُوءًا To crouch (hunter).
— على To overtake a. o.
— الى To seek refuge towards.
أَضْبَأ ه وعلى To conceal, to hide a. th.
إِضْطَبَأ To be concealed, hidden.
مَضْبَأ ج مَضَابِئ Hiding place.
* ضَبَث i ضَبْثًا, واضْطَبَث ب To grasp, to clasp a. th.
ضَبْثَة ج أَضْبَاث Grasp.
مِضْبَث ج مَضَابِث Claws, nails.
* ضَبَح a ضَبْحًا ه To blacken a. th. (fire).
ضَبَح a ضَبْحًا وضُبَاحًا To snore (horse).
— ضُبَاحًا To yelp (fox).
ضَابَح ه To abuse a. o. by words.
إِنْضَبَح To be blackened (by fire).
ضِبْح Ashes.
* ضَبَر o ضَبْرًا ه To pile up (stones). To stitch (the leaves of a book).
— ضَبْرًا وضَبَرَانًا To leap (horse).
ضَبْر ج ضُبُور Besieging machine; testudo.
— وضِبْر Wild nut-tree.
ضِبَار وضُبَار Books, pamphlets.
ضَبَارَة Strength, good constitution.
ضِبَارَة وضُبَارَة ج ضَبَائِر, وإِضْبَارَة ج أَضَابِير Bundle of books.
ضَبْر Leaping.

Lion. صِبرّ وضَبُور
Strong, hard, vehement. ضَبِير
To be wicked, prone to evil. ✲ ضَبِس a ضَبَسًا
Mischievous, prone to evil. ضِبْس وضَبِس وضَبِيس
To hold fast, to gripe. To maintain. To keep order in a country. To render (an account) accurate. To correct; to dot (a writing). ✧ To confiscate, to sequester (goods). To arrest a. o. To draw up (a report). To point (a gun). ✲ ضَبَط o i ضَبْطًا وضَبَاطَة ه وه
He does not his work accurately. لَا يَضْبِط عَمَلَهُ
He does not read correctly. لَا يَضْبِط قِرَاءَتَهُ
To be ambidextrous. ضَبِط a ضَبَطًا
To take hold of a. o. forcibly. تَضَبَّط ه
To be strengthened. To be kept in due order. إِنضَبَط
Accuracy, organization. Arrest. Strengthening. Police. ضَبْط
Strong, hardy. Firm. Lion. ✧ Officer in the army. ضَابِط ج ضُبَّاط
Almighty (God). ضَابِط الكُلّ
✧ Policeman, constable. ضَابِطِي ج ضَابِطِيَّة
General rule, law. ضَابِطَة ج ضَوَابِط
✧ Report, official document; decision of a court. مَضْبَطَة ج مَضَابِط
Tenacious, more tenacious. Ambidextrous. أَضْبَط م ضَبْطَاء ج ضُبْط
Firm. Accurate (account). ✧ Well made. مَضْبُوط و✧ مَظْبُوط
To run (horse). ✲ ضَبَع a ضَبْعًا وضُبُوعًا وضَبَعَانًا, وضَبَّع
To throw the hands for striking. — ضَبْعًا ه وعلى
To wrap o'self in a cloak in covering the left shoulder and leaving the right uncovered. إِضطَبَع
Arm, upper part of the arm. Quick pace of a horse. ضَبْع ج أَضْبَاع
Unfruitful year. ضَبُع
Hyena. ضَبُع
Male hyena. ضَبْع وضَبُع ج ضِبَاع وأَضْبُع وضُبُع

Species of truffles. Kind of poppy. فَسْوَة الضَّبُع
Male hyena. ضِبْعَان ج ضَبَاعِين
To be narrow (place). ✲ ضَبَن o ضَبْنًا
To hold a. th. under the arm-pits. أَضْبَن واضطَبَن ه
Arm-pit. ضَبْن وضِبن
Hard ground. ضِبْن
Narrow (place). ضَبِن
Family. ضُبْنَة وضِبْنَة وضُبُنَة وضَبِنَة
To alter; to burn a. th. (fire). ✲ ضَبَا o ضَبْوًا ه
To seek refuge at. — الى
To overtake a. o. أَضْبَى على
To prevent a. th.. — ه
Ashes. ضَاب
Bread baked in ashes. مُضْبَاة
To clamour, to make noise. ✲ ضَجَّ i ضَجًّا وضَجِيجًا وضَجَاجًا, وأَضَجَّ
To quarrel, to contend with a. o. ضَاجَّ مُضَاجَّةً وضِجَاجًا ه
Bustle, confused voices, uproar. ضَجَّة وضَجَاج وضُجَاج وضَجِيج
Ivory. Sea-shell. ضَجَاج
Grumbling much when milked (she-camel). ضَجُوج
To be annoyed, disgusted with. ✲ ضَجِر a ضَجَرًا, وتَضَجَّر من وب
To tease, to vex a. o. أَضْجَر ه
Annoyance; disgust. ضَجَر وضُجْرَة
Vexed, grieved (man). ضَجِر
Disgusted, disquieted. ضَجُور
Annoying. مُضْجِر ج مَضَاجِر ومَضَاجِير
To recline. ✲ ضَجَع a ضَجْعًا وضُجُوعًا, وانضَجَع واضَّجَع واضطَجَع
To incline to setting (star). ضَجَع وضَجَّع
To act slowly in (an affair). ضَجَّع وتَضَجَّع في
To lie by the side of. ضَاجَع ه
To lay a. o. on the side. To take a. th. down. أَضْجَع ه وه
To neglect (a business). تَضَاجَع عن
Species of glasswort used as soap; detersive. ضَجَع
Inclination to a party. ضِجْع
A slumber. A piece of soap. ضَجْعَة
Weakness of mind. — وضُجْعَة

(pond). To be in small quantity (water).
To dwindle away, to disappear. To clear off (cloud). إِضْمَحَلَّ
Shallow (water). ضَحْل ج أضحال وضُحُول وضِحَال
Shallow place. مَضْحَل
To bask in the sun. * ضَحَا o ضَحْوًا وضُحُوًّا وضُحِيًّا
To appear, to be exposed to the sun. — ضَحْوًا وضُحِيًّا
He is dead. ضَحَا ظِلُّهُ
To be smitten by the sun-beams. ضَحِيَ a ضَحًى
To become uncovered, to be revealed. — ضَحَاء
To go forth into sunshine. — لِلشَّمْسِ
To pasture (cattle) in the forenoon. To give a. th. to eat in the forenoon. ضَحَّى ه
To slaughter (a victim) in the forenoon. — ب
Go slowly, gently! ضَحِّ رُوَيْدًا
To go to a. o. in the forenoon. ضَاحَى مُضَاحَاةً ه
To enter upon the time of forenoon. أَضْحَى
He has done it in broad light. — يَفْعَلُ كَذَا
To reveal, to manifest a. th. — ه
May God keep you in safety. لَا أَضْحَى اللهُ ظِلَّكَ
To eat in the forenoon. To go into the sunshine. تَضَحَّى
Forenoon. Forenoon-meal. ضَحَاء
Early part of the forenoon. ضَحْو وضَحْوَة
Part of the forenoon when the sun is already high. ضُحًى
His discourse is rather confused. مَا لِكَلَامِهِ ضُحًى
Mornings and evenings. الضُّحَى والأَصَائِل
Ewe offered up as victim, victim, burnt-offering. ضَحِيَّة ج ضَحَايَا
Ewe offered up in sacrifice. أَضْحَاة ج أَضْحًى
Victim. أُضْحِيَّة ج أَضَاحِيّ
Feast of the sacrifices; Korban Bairam. يَوْم الأَضْحَى
Exposed to the sun. Outlying. ضَاحٍ

Laziness, sloth. Way of reclining. ضِجْعَة
ضُجْعَة وضُجَعَة وضُجْعِيّ وضُجْعِيَّة وضِجْعِيَّة
Slothful, sluggish.
Slothful. Foolish. ضَاجِع ج ضَوَاجِع
Declivity of a valley. Setting (star).
Mouth of a river. ضَاجِعَة
Numerous sheep. ضَاجِعَة وضَجْعَاء
Foolish, silly. ضَجُوع ومَضْجُوع
Bed-fellow. ضَجِيع
Sleeping-room, bed. مَضْجَع ج مَضَاجِع. ومُضْطَجَع
Places much rained upon. مَضَاجِع الغَيْث
To be distorted (mouth, nose). * ضَجِمَ a ضَجَمًا
To be at issue (affair). تَضَاجَمَ بَيْن
Distorted, wry (mouth, nose). أَضْجَم م ضَجْمَاء
Wry-mouthed. مُتَضَاجِم
Sun; light of the sun. * ضَحّ — ضِحّ
Land exposed to the sun.
To move about (looming). * ضَحْضَحَ وتَضَحْضَحَ
Small quantity of water. ضَحْضَاح
To laugh. * ضَحِكَ a ضَحْكًا وضِحِكًا
To laugh at, to ridicule a. o. ضَحِكَ على ومن وب
To grin (monkey). ضَحِكَ a ضَحْكًا
To send forth lightnings (cloud).
To display its flowers (garden); to become covered with plants (soil). — عن
To sport, to joke with. ضَاحَكَ ه
To make a. o. to laugh. أَضْحَكَ ه
To laugh. تَضَحَّكَ وتَضَاحَكَ واسْتَضْحَكَ
To mock. — من وعلى وب
To laugh, to joke (people). تَضَاحَكَ
A laugh, laughter. ضَحْكَة
Laughing-stock, droll. ضُحْكَة
Joke, sport, comical thing. أُضْحُوكَة ج أَضَاحِيك
Laughing. Sending forth (lightnings: cloud). ضَاحِك
Tooth displayed in laughing. ضَاحِكَة ج ضَوَاحِك
ضَحَكَة وضُحُكَة وضَحَّاك وضَحُوك ومِضْحَاك
Laughing much, laugher.
Joking, sporting, funny. مُضْحِك
Jokes, sports. مُضْحِكَات
To have little water * ضَحَلَ a ضَحْلًا

Wrong, hurt, injury. ضَرَر ج أضرار
Necessity; distress. Natural want. ضَرُورة ج ضَرُورَات
Blindness. Loss. ضَرَارة
Need. Compulsion. إضطرار
Harmful, unwholesome. ضَارّ
Blind. ضَرِير ج أضِرَّاء وأضرار
Plant. *Pl.* Necessaries. ضَرِيرَة ج ضَرَائِر
Necessary, essential. ضَرُورِيّ
Bad state. تَضُرَّة وتَضُرَّة
Loss, damage, wrong. مَضَرَّة ج مَضَرَّات ومَضَارّ
Harmful, unwholesome. Polygamous. مُضِرّ
Polygamy. مُضَارَّة
Constrained, compelled. مُضطَرّ
To be hidden. ✱ ضَرَأ a ضَرْأً
To dry (plant). إنضَرَأ
To strike a. o. with. ✱ ضَرَب i ضَرْبًا ه ب
To mix a. th. with. — ه ب
To smite a. o. (scourge). To sting a. o. (scorpion). — ه
To strike money. — السِّكَّة
To propound a proverb. — مَثَلًا
To play on musical instruments. ضَرَب آلات الطَّرَب
To pass over in silence. ضَرَب عَنْهُ صَفحًا
To pitch a tent. — خَيمَة
To impose (a tax) on. — ه على
To fix (a term) to. — ه ل
To perform prayer. — الصَّلاة
To divide, to separate. — بَين
To seize the goods of. — على يَدَي فُلَان
To prevent a. o. from hearing. — على أُذُنِهِ
To multiply (a number) by. — كَذَا في كَذَا
To lean. To incline towards. — الى
To swim. — في المَاء
To make a journey. — في الأرض ضَرْبًا وضَرَبَانًا
To be blasted by hoar frost (land). ضُرِب
To be set up as an example. ضُرِب مَثَلًا
To be blasted by cold (plant). ضَرِب a ضَرَبًا
To strike strongly (hand). ضَرُب o ضَرَابَة
To strike, to beat ضَرَّب ه وه

Side. Outskirts. ضَاحِيَة ج ضَوَاحٍ
He has done it publicly. فَعَلَهُ ضَاحِيَةً
Cloudless (day, night). إضحِيَان م إضحِيَانَة
Exposed to the sun (land). مَضحَاة
To shed tears (eye). ✱ ضَخّ o ضَخًّا ه
To pour water, — ه
Squirt. مِضَخَّة
To be fat, bulky. ✱ ضَخُم o ضَخَامَة وضِخَمًا
Bulk, stoutness. ضَخَامَة
Corpulent, stout, bulky. ضَخِم ج ضِخَام
To overcome a. o. ✱ ضَدّ o ضَدًّا ه
To remove gently a. o. from. — ه عن
To contravene, to thwart a. o. To contrast with. ضَادّ ه
To contradict. To get angry. أضَدّ
To oppose one another. تَضَادّ
Contrary, repugnant. Similar. ضِدّ وضَدِيد
Antagonist. Contradictory meaning. — ج أضداد وضِدّ
Contradictory expressions. لُغَات الأضداد
Contrarily, in opposition to. ضِدًّا و بالضِّدّ
Contrast. Contradiction. Opposition. تَضَادّ ومُضَادَّة
Nonsenses. ✱ ضَدِي — ضَوَادٍ
To harm, to injure a. o. ✱ ضَرّ o ضَرًّا وضُرًّا, وضَارّ ه
To oppose, to contend with a. o. ضَارّ مُضَارَّة وضِرَارًا ه
To be a polygamist. أضَرّ
To do harm to a. o. أضَرّ ب وه
To compel a. o. to. — ه على
To sustain damage from. تَضَرَّر و✧ وانضَرّ من
To compel a. o. to. إضطَرّ ه الى
To be compelled to. To be in need of. إضطُرّ الى
Damage, harm. ضُرّ وضَرّ
Polygamy. ضِرّ
Damage, harm. Thicket. ضَرَّاء ج أضُرّ
Distress, poverty, hardship. ضُرَّة ج ضَرَائِر
Necessity, need. Flesh of the udder, flesh beneath the thumb. ضَرَّة
Fellow-wife (amongst Moslems). ضَرَّة المَرْأة ج ضَرَائِر وضَرَّات

striking. Origin, descent.
Edge of a sword. — ومَضرَب ج مَضارِب
Bone full of marrow. مَضرِب ومَضرَب ج مَضارِب
Mallet. Plectrum. مِضرَب ومِضرَاب ج مَضارِب
Pavilion, large tent. مِضرَب ج مَضارِب
Motionless (serpent). مُضرِب ومُضرِبَة
Edge of a sword. مَضرَبَة ومَضرِبَة
✧ Clapper of a bell. مِضرَبَة الجَرَس
Limited partnership (*commandite*). مُضارَبَة
Moved, disturbed, startled. مُضطَرِب
Mixed up (treacle). ✧ Crack-brained. مَضرُوب
To split a. th. ✡ ضَرَح o ضَرحًا ه
To smear, to stain (clothes) with blood. — ه بِدَم
To dye red (cloth). To embellish, to dispose (a discourse). ضَرَّج ه
To make (the nose) to bleed. — ه بالدَّم
To be stained (with blood). To be dyed red (cloth). To become red (cheek). To spread (lightning). To deck herself (woman). تَضَرَّج
To be split; to be broad (road). To open (plant). إِنضَرَج
They parted. — ما بَيْنَهُم
To dart on (hawk). — على
Dyed red. Quick (walk, run). ضَرِيج
Red dye, red silk. Good runner (horse). إِضرِيج
Besmeared with blood. Dyed red. مُضَرَّج
Rags. مِضرَج ج مَضارِج
Large, wide (eye). مَضرُوجَة
To dig a grave. ✡ ضَرَح a ضَرحًا ل
To throw off, to remove a. th. — ه
— o ضَرحًا وضِرَاحًا. وضَرَح o ضِرَاحًا بِرِجلها To kick (beast).
To be dull (market). — o ضُرُوحًا
To revile a. o. To get near to. ضارَح ه وه
To keep off customers from (the market). To spoil a. th. أَضرَح ه
To remove a. o. from. — ه عن
They parted. إِنضَرَح ما بَيْنَهُم
Skin. ضَرح
Corrupt. Distant (journey). ضَرَح

violently. To quilt (clothes).
To mix. ضَرَّب ه ب
To excite a strife amongst. — بَيْن
To fight, to come to blows with a. o. ضارَب مُضارَبَة وضِرَابًا ه
To traffic with a. o.'s property for a share in the profit. — ه ولهُ في المَال وبهِ
To be covered with hoar-frost. أَضرَب
To be well baked (bread).
To leave, to forsake a. th. — عن
To halt, to stay in a place. — في
To dry up (water : hot wind). — ه
To be in commotion, to dash together (waves). تَضَرَّب واضطَرَب
To come to blows (people). تَضارَب واضطَرَب
To be moved, troubled, anxious. إِضطَرَب
Blow. Throbbing. Multiplication. ضَرب
Mint. دَار الضَّرب و✧ ضربخانَة
Kind. Manner. Last foot of a verse. Coined (money). Lean, thin. ضَرب ج ضُرُوب وأَضرَاب وأَضرُب
Similar, alike. — ج أَضرَاب
A stroke. Chastisement, scourge. ضَربَة ج ضَرَبَات
The ten plagues of Egypt. ضَرَبَات مِصر
Thick and white honey. ضَرَب
The strokes of time. ضَرَبَان الدَّهر
Striking. ضارِب وضَرُوب
Shuffling arrows before drawing them. Spreading darkness (night). Depressed ground planted with trees. Hard ground in a plain. ضارِب
Sandy valley. — ج ضَوَارِب
Striker. ضَرِيب ج ضُرَبَاء
Struck, beaten. — ج ضَربَى
Species Similar. Shape. Lot. Snow, ice, hoar-frost, rime. — ج ضَرَائِب
Nature, temper. Sword; point, edge (of a sword). Skein of cotton. Wounded by a sword. Rate, tax. ◻ Measure of 8 ardebs. ضَرِيبَة ج ضَرَائِب
Digression, retraction in speech. إِضرَاب
Corrective particle. حَرف الإِضرَاب
Trouble, disturbance. إِضطِرَاب
Time and place of مَضرَب ج مَضارِب

Prone to kick. ضَرُوح

Tomb. ضَرِيح ج ضَرَائِح

Removed, remote. ضَرِيح

To bite a. th. or a. o. strongly. ✱ ضَرَسَ i ضَرْسًا, وضَرَّس ه وه

To remain silent the whole day. ضَرَّس

To be hard on a o. (lot). — وضَرَّس ه

To wall up a well. — i o ضَرْسًا ه

To be set on edge (teeth). ضَرِسَ a ضَرَسًا

To try, to train a. o. (war). ضَرَّس ه

To come to fight. ضَارَس وتَضَارَس

He set his teeth on edge. أَضْرَس أَسْنَانَهُ

To move, to trouble a. o. — ه

To silence a. o. — ه بِالْكَلَام

Molar tooth. ضِرْس ج أَضْرَاس وضُرُوس

Steep hill. Scattered rain. Stone for casing a well. — ج ضُرُوس

Polypody (plant). أَضْرَاس الكَلْب

Setting on edge of the (teeth). ضَرَس

Of evil disposition, ungovernable. ضَرِس

Prone to bite (she-camel). Vehement (war). ضَرُوس

Well cased with stones. Vertebræ of the back. Starved. Biscuit. Date. ضَرِيس ج ضَرَاسَى

Mute. أَخْرَس أَضْرَس

Tooth-shaped (cloth). مُضَرَّس

Cased with stones (well). Stony tract. مَضْرُوسَة

✱ ضَرَطَ i ضَرْطًا وضَرِطًا وضُرَاطًا وضَرِيطًا
To break wind.

To have a scanty beard and faint eyebrows. ضَرِط a ضَرَطًا

To scoff at. ضَرَّط وأَضْرَط بِهِ

Emission of wind. ضُرَاط وضَرِيط

Breaking wind frequently. ضَرَّاط وضَرُوط

Little-haired in the beard and eyebrows. أَضْرَط م ضَرْطَاء ج ضُرْط

To draw near stealthily. ✱ ضَرَعَ o ضُرُوعًا, وضَرَّع وتَضَرَّع من

To set (sun). ضَرَعَت وضَرَّعَت

ضَرِعَ a ضَرَاعَةً وضَرِعَ a ضَرَعًا وضَرُعَ o ضَرَاعَة
To humble, to lower o.'s self.

To resemble a. o.; to be like. ضَارَع ه وه

To lower, to humble a. o. أَضْرَع ه

To give a. th. to a. o. — ه ل

To beseech, to make humble entreaties to a. o. تَضَرَّع الى واسْتَضْرَع ل

Breast. Cow's udder. ضَرْع ج ضُرُوع

Like. ضِرْع ج ضُرُوع

Weak, little, a young one. ضَرَع ج ضَرَع

Humility, submissiveness. ضَرَاعَة

Humility in prayer. Prayer. Entreaty. تَضَرُّع ج تَضَرُّعَات

Submissive, humble. ضَارِع ج ضَرَعَة, وضَرِع وأَضْرَع

Having big udders (cow). Large-breasted (woman). ضَرِعًا وضَرُوع وضَرِيع وضَرِيعَة

White grapes with large berries. ضُرُوع

Similar. Aorist tense. مُضَارِع

Lion. ✱ ضِرْغَم وضِرْغَام ج ضَرَاغِم

Lion. Gallant, energetic man. Strong stallion. ضِرْغَامَة

To fight like a lion. ضَرْغَم وتَضَرْغَم

Skin for milk. ✧ ضَرْف ج ضُرُوف

To be broken down by old age. To be poor, destitute. ✱ ضَرُكَ o ضَرَاكَة

Broken down by old age. Poor, unhappy. ضَرِيك ج ضُرَكَاء وضَرَائِك

To burn (fire). To burn with passion (man). ✱ ضَرِم a ضَرَمًا

To rage against. — على

To eat greedily. — في الطَّعَام

To light, to stir up the fire. ضَرَّم وأَضْرَم واسْتَضْرَم ه

To be kindled, to blaze (fire). تَضَرَّم واضْطَرَم

To glisten (white hair). إِضْطَرَم

Stœchas, French lavender. ضُرْم وضِرْم

Starved. Vehement in running. Young one of the eagle. ضَرِم

Brand; live coal; fire. ضَرَمَة ج ضَرَم

There is nobody in the house. مَا بِالدَّار نَافِخ ضَرَمَة

To spend time and exertions uselessly. نَفَخ في غَيْر ضَرَم

Light fuel. ضِرَام

Kindled wood. ضِرَامَة

Burnt in fire. ضَرِيم

Kind of gum. ضِرْيَم

To bleed (artery, wound). ✱ ضَرَا o ضُرُوًّا

ضَرِيَ a ضَرَاوَة وضَرًى وضَرْيًا وضَرَاءَة ب
To be greedy, fond of.

Weakness of mind. Defective construction of a sentence. ضَعف
Weakness of body. ✧ Illness. ضُعف
Double, manifold. Interline. ضِعف ج أضعاف
Weak, feeble. ضَعفان ج ضَعافى, وضَعُوف
ضَعِيف ج ضُعَفاء وضِعاف وضَعَفة وضَعفى
Weak. Blind. Defective (discourse). ✧ Ill. Lean.
Double, treble, multiple. تَضعِيف و إضعاف
✧ Lily of the valley. مَضعَف
Land watered by a weak rain. أرض مُضعَّفة
Doubled, increased manifold. مُضاعَف
Held as weak. مُتضعَّف
To have an abundant harvest. ✱ ضفّ – أضفّ
Abundant harvest. ضَفِيف
Verdant garden. Lump of dough. ضَفِيفة
To speak confusedly. ✱ ضَفضَف
To masticate (meat) imperfectly ه – from want of teeth. To multiply (words).
To imitate the voice of a wolf, a hare. ✱ ضَغَب a ضَغبًا
Howl of a wolf. Noise, rustling. ضَغِيب وضُغاب
To mix a. th. To confuse (discourse). To wash imperfectly (clothes). ✱ ضَغَث a ضَغثًا ه
To relate a. th. confusedly. أضغَث ه
To collect (herbs). إضطغَث ه
Bundle of dry and green herbs mixed together. ضِغث ج أضغاث
Nightmares. أضغاث أحلام
To push, to press, to squeeze a. o. against. ✱ ضَغَط a ضَغطًا, وأضغط ه
To press a. o. in a crowd. ضاغَط مُضاغَطة وضِغاطًا ه
To squeeze one another. تضاغَط
Pressure, compression, squeezing. ضَغط
Pressure. Narrow space of a grave. ضَغطة
Pression, uneasiness, straitness. Distress. Compulsion. ضُغطة
Pressure of a crowd. ضِغاط
Keeper, watcher of. ضاغِط على

To be trained for the chase (hound). ضرِي a ضَرًى وضِراء وضَراء ب
To train (a hound) to (the chase). To excite in a. o. the desire of. ضرّى وأضرى ه ب
To overtake (game : hunter). إستضرى ه
Thicket in a valley. Bushy country. ضَراء
Horrors of war. ضَرَى
Hound. ضِرو م ضِروة ج ضِراء وأضرٍ
Terebinth (tree). ضِرو وضرو
Trained to the chase. Carnivorous (beast). ضارٍ م ضارِية ج ضَوارٍ
Bleeding continually (artery). Juice of unripe dates. ضَرِي
To bleed (artery). ✱ ضرى i ضَرْيًا بالدم
To have the jaws contracted. ✱ ضَزّ a ضَزَزًا
To champ the bit (horse). To be stingy towards a o. أضزّ على
Having the jaws contracted. أضزّ م ضَزّاء ج ضُزّ
Wicked, hot-tempered. – ج ضُزّاز
To snatch a. th. from a. o. ✱ ضَزَن o i ضَزنًا ه
To contend about the possession of a. th. تضازن
Ill-natured son. ضَيزَن
To trample a. th. under foot. ✱ ضَعَز a ضَعزًا ه
To pull down (a building). ✧ To scatter a. th. ✱ ضَعضَع ه
To be humbled. ✧ To be scattered. To be concealed. To be out of mind (sick man). تضعضع
To be feeble, weak. ✱ ضَعُف o ضَعفًا وضُعفًا, وضَعُف o ضَعافة وضَعافية
To exceed a. o. or a. th. twofold, manifold. ضَعَف a ضَعفًا ه وه
To find a. o. weak. ضعّف وتضعّف واستضعف ه وه
To double, to treble, to multiply manifold. – وضاعف وأضعف ه
To weaken a. o. (illness). أضعف ه
To ride on a weak beast. أضعَف
To receive the double. أضعِف
To be doubled, to be increased manifold. تضاعف

Camel's girth. ضَفْر وضِفَار ج ضُفُر
Heap of sand. — ج ضُفُور وضَفِرَة ج ضَفِر
Side, shore. Plait of hair. Strap of a girth. ضَفِير
Lock of hair. Dam. ضَفِيرَة ج ضَفَائِر
To leap. ✱ ضَفَز o ضَفْزًا
To strike and repel a. o. To put the bit to (a horse). — ه
To force a morsel into the mouth. — واضطفز ه
Pounded barley; oat-meal. ضَفْز
Slanderer, backbiter. ضَفَّاز
Large mouthful. ضَفِيزَة ج ضَفَائِز
To bind a. th. tightly with ropes. ✱ ضَفَط o ضَفْطًا ه ب
To be big-bellied. To be foolish. ضَفُط o ضَفَاطَةً
Stupidity, silliness. ضَفْطَة
Transport camels. ضَافِطَة وضَفَّاطَة
Camel-driver. ضَفَّاط
Large caravan. ضَفَّاطَة
To come to a. o.'s house. ✱ ضَفَن i ضَفْنًا الى
To kick a. o. — ه
To overthrow a. o. on the ground. — بِهِ الأَرْضَ
To perform a business. — بِحَاجَتِهِ
To relieve the bowels. — بِغَائِطِهِ
To help o. another. تَضَافَنُوا
Of a small stature. Foolish. ضِفَنّ وضِفِنّ
To abound (th). To overflow (tank). ✱ ضَفَا o ضُفُوًّا
Side. ضَفًا مث ضَفَوَان
Plenty of goods. ضَفْوَة من العَيْش
To stray from the right path, to deviate. To be misled. To disappear; to die. ✧ To remain. ✱ ضَلّ i ضَلًّا وضَلَالَة
To stray from the road. — الطَّرِيق وعَنْهُ
To lose a. th. To forget a. th. — ه وه
He has lost the fruit of his toil. — سَعْيُهُ
To mislead a. o. — بِفُلَان
To lead a. o. astray. To lose, to miss a. th. To find a. o. mistaken. ضَلَّل تَضْلِيلًا وتَضْلَالًا, وأَضَلّ ه وه
To feign to be straying. تَضَالّ
To try to mislead a. o. إِسْتَضَلّ ه

Nightmare. ضَاغُوط
Weak of mind. ضَغِيط ج ضَغْطَى
F. Weak (*plant*). ضَغِيطَة
Depressed ground reached by water. مَضْغَط ج مَضَاغِط
To bite a. th. ✱ ضَغِم a ضَغْمًا ه وب
What is caught with the teeth. ضُغَامَة
Lion. ضَيْغَم وضَيْغَمِيّ
To brood rancour against a. o. ✱ ضَغِن a ضَغَنًا على
To incline to. — الى
To hate o. another. تَضَاغَن واضطغن
To take a. th. beneath the arm-pit. إِضْطَغَن ه
Side. Propensity. Hatred. ضِغْن ج أَضْغَان
Slack, remiss (horse). ضَاغِن
Curved, rancorous. ضَغِن م ضَغِنَة
Rancour, malice. ضَغِينَة ج ضَغَائِن
To cheat at play. ✱ ضَغَا o ضَغْوًا
To mew (cat). — ضَغْوًا وضُغَاء
To cry out together. تَضَاغَى
To writhe from hunger. — من الجُوع
To hurry towards. ✱ ضَفّ o ضَفًّا وضَفَفًا على
To pick up, to collect a. th. — ضَفًّا ه
To throng in a point (crowd). تَضَافّ
Straitened. ضَفّ الحَال
Greyish tick. ضُفّ ج ضِفَفَة
Crowd of people. ضَفَّة
Side of a valley. Bank of a river. — وضِفَّة
Party thronging at a repast. Numerous family. Destitution, straitened circumstances. Haste, readiness. ضَفَف
Good milk-camel. ضَفُوف
Frequented (place). مَضْفُوف
To be full of frogs (pond). ✱ ضَفْدَع
Frog. ضَفْدَع وضِفْدِع ج ضَفَادِع
A frog. ضَفْدَعَة وضِفْدِعَة
To plait her hair (woman). To twist (a rope). To tress a. th. ✱ ضَفَر i ضَفْرًا, وضَفَّر ه
To assist, to help a. o. in. ضَافَر ه على
To help one another in. تَضَافَر على
To be plaited (hair), twisted (rope). إِنْضَفَر
Plait of hair. ضَفْر ج ضُفُور

ضَلَّ وضلّ ضَلَال وضَلَالَة Confusion, mistake. Loss, doom.
هُوَ ضُلّ بْنُ ضُلّ وضِلّ أضْلَالٍ He is an unknown man.
ضَلَّة Uncertainty, anxiety. Absence. Speech on the absent.
ضِلَّة Error.
ذَهَبَ دَمُهُ ضِلَّةً His blood has been unrevenged.
ضَالّ ج ضَالُّون وضُلَّال Misled. Erring.
ضَالَّة ج ضَوَالّ A stray; a lost beast.
ضَلُول وضِلِّيل Straying, wandering.
ضَلَال Error. Water never reached by sun.
أُضْلُولَة ج أضَالِيل Mistake.
وَادِي تُضُلِّلَ وَوَادِي تُضَلِّلَ وضِلّ تَضْلَالٍ Vanity, delusive things.
مَضَلَّة ومَضِلَّة Error, confusion. Misleading country.
مُضِلّ Misleading. Seducer, deluder. Looming.
مُضَلَّل Strayed, lost. Obstinate in error.
✱ ضَلُع o ضَلَاعَة, واضطلع To be sturdy.
ضَلِع a ضَلَعًا, وتَضَلَّع To be filled with food or drink.
— على To incline towards. To act wrongfully.
— ه To strike a. o. upon the ribs.
ضَلِع a ضَلَعًا وضَلْعًا To be crooked.
ضَلَّع ه To bend, to incline a. th. To deviate a. th. To make rib-shaped figures on cloth.
أضْلَع ه To incline a. th.
تَضَلَّع من عِلْمٍ To possess a science thorougly.
إضْطَلَع ب To be able to carry a burden.
ضَلْع مع Inclination, liking for.
ضَلَاعَة وضَلَاعَة Strength, vigour.
ضَلَع الدَّيْن Weight of a debt.
ضِلْع وضِلَع ج ضُلُوع وأضْلَاع وأضْلُع Rib. Side of a triangle. A square root.
ضِلَع Slope, ascent. Trap. Bough.
ضِلَعَة Side.
ضَالِع Acting wrongfully.
ضَلِع Crooked by nature.
ضَلِيع ج ضُلُع Sturdy, strong. Bending (bow).
ضَلِيع الفَمِ Large-mouthed.
أضْلَع ج ضُلْع Sturdy. Large-toothed.
مُضْلِع ومُضْطَلِع ل Able to.
حِمْل مُضْلِع Overburdening load.
دَابَّة مُضْلِع Unable to carry its load (beast).
مُضَلَّع Figured with stripes, ribs (cloth).
✱ ضَمَّ o ضَمًّا ه To draw together, to collect the parts of a. th. To mark a letter with a damma.
— ه To grasp, to put a. o. in a strait.
— ه الى صَدْرِهِ To embrace a. o.
— على To get hold of.
— وضَامَّ ه الى To unite a. th. to.
ضَامَّ ه على أمْرٍ To conjoin with a. o. in business.
تَضَامَّ To gather, to unite together.
إنْضَمَّ الى To be united, joined; to be annexed to.
إضْطَمَّ ه To draw a. th. to o.'self.
— على To take possession of.
ضَمّ Union, connection.
ضَمّ وضَمَّة Sign of the damma.
ضَامّ Collecting, uniting.
ضِمَام Means of union.
ضَمُوم River flowing between two hills.
ضَمِيم وضَمِيمَة Companion.
إضْمَامَة ج أضَامِيم Company of men. Writing-book. Bundle of writings.
مَضْمُوم Collected, united. Marked with a damma.
✱ ضَمْضَمَ To encourage o.'s self. To snarl (lion).
— على To take a. th. altogether.
ضَمْضَم وضُمَاضِم Angry lion. Courageous.
✱ ضَمَخ o ضَمْخًا, وضَمَّخ ه To anoint (the body) with aromatics.
ضَمَخ Bug.
ضَمَخ Calamity, misfortune.
✱ ضمحل — إضْمَحَلَّ To dwindle away. To clear off (cloud). *See* ضحل.
✱ ضَمَخ o ضَمْخًا, وضَمَّخ ه To anoint (the body) with unguents.
تَضَمَّخ وانضمخ واضطمخ ب To be daubed with perfumes (body).
✱ ضَمَد o i ضَمْدًا, وضَمَّد ه To dress a ·

Silent. ضَامِز وضَمُوز

To eat a. th. stealthily. ✡ ضَمَسَ i ضَمْسًا ه

To be verdant (plant). ✡ ضمك – إِضْمَأَكَّ. To become covered with plants (land). To swell with anger (man).

To warrant, to guarantee a. th. To bail out a. o. ✧ To farm, to rent a. th. ✡ ضَمِنَ a ضَمْنًا وضَمَانًا ه او ب

To be affected with a chronical disease. ضُمِنَ a ضَمَنًا وضَمَانَةً

To render a. o. responsible, a surety for. ضَمَّنَ ه ه

To include in, to insert a. th. into. To insert (another's verses) in a poem. ✧ To farm out (taxes, revenues). – ه ه

To guarantee, to become responsible for. To contain, to include. تَضَمَّنَ ه

✧ To be farmed out (land, taxes). – وانْضَمَنَ

Chronical disease. ضَمَن وضُمْنَة وضَمَان وضَمَانَة

Contents, inside of a. th. ✧ Here inclosed. ضِمْن

Suretiship, bail. ✧ Farming out, letting out. ضَمَان

Suffering from chronical disease. ضَمِن

Guarantee, accountable, bailer. ضَامِن وضَمِين ج ضُمَنَى

✧ Farming, renting. ضَامِن

Palm-trees included within a village. ضَامِنَة

Damages (*law*). تَضْمِينَات

Incomplete (sentence). Implied (word). Incidental (sentence). مُضَمَّن

Thing waranted. Contents of a writing. مَضْمُون ج مَضَامِين

✡ ضَنَّ a i ضِنًّا وضِنَّةً وضَنَانَةً واضْطَنَّ ب
To be tenacious, niggardly of a. th.

To be niggardly of a. th. to a. o. To grudge a. o. – ب على

Special, proper to. ضِنّ

Brave, courageous. ضَنَن

Tenacious, niggardly of. ضَنِين

Things held in estimation that one appropriates and keeps tenaciously. ضَنَائِن

Thing of which مَضَنَّة ومَضِنَّة ج مَضَانّ

wound. To anoint and bind (the head).

To strike a. o. with a stick. ضَمَدَ ه ب

To dry up; to be dry. ضَمِدَ a ضَمَدًا

To hate a. o. – على فُلَان

To gather people. أَضْمَدَ ه

To be bandaged. تَضَمَّدَ

Dry or tender. The best or the worse of a flock. ضَمَد

Friend. ضِمْد

Bandage, fillet. ضِمَاد وضِمَادَة

I am on the eve of. أَنَا على ضِمَادَةٍ من

Bandaged (wound). مُضَمَّد ومَضْمُود

To be thin, lean. ✡ ضَمَرَ وضَمُرَ o ضُمُورًا

To emaciate (a horse). ضَمَّرَ وأَضْمَرَ ه

To conceive a. th. To conceal a. th. To determine upon a. th. To suppress (a word understood). أَضْمَرَ ه وه

To conceal a. th. in the mind. To think of; to apply o.'self to. – ه في نَفْسِهِ

To be thin, contracted (face). تَضَمَّرَ

To dry up (bough). إِنْضَمَرَ

To be slender. إِضْطَمَرَ

Slender, thin. ضَمْر م ضَمْرَة

Leanness. ضُمْر وضُمُر

Secret thought; conscience. Hidden. Pronoun. ضَمِير ج ضَمَائِر

Doubtful, undetermined (promise, debt). ضِمَار

Atrophy. ◻ ضُمُور

Female fortune-teller. ◻ ضَمَّارَة

Thought, idea, mind. إِضْمَار

Slender (man, camel). Dried up (bough). ضَامِر ج ضُمَّر وضَوَامِر

Wild mint, basil. ضَوْمَرَان وضَيْمُرَان

Concealed in the mind. Understood. مُضْمَر

Recesses, secrets of the heart. مُضْمَرَات

Dried up (bough). مُنْضَمِر

Hippodrome. Training-place for horses. مِضْمَار

To keep silent. ✡ ضَمَزَ o i ضَمْزًا

To watch over. To be sparing of. – على

Stony and isolated hill. ضَمْز وضَمُوز

Blackener, discreditor. ضَامِز

To do wrong ✲ ضَهَد a ضَهْدًا, وأَضْهَد ه to.
To ill-treat, أَضْهَد ه وب واضطهَد ه to persecute a. o.
Ill treatment. إضطِهَاد ج اضطِهَادَات Persecution.
Persecutor, oppressor. مُضطَهِد
Persecuted, oppressed. مُضطَهَد
Summit of a mountain, ✲ ضَهْر وضَاهِر peak.
To bite a. o. ✲ ضَهِس a ضَهْسًا
To be collected ✲ ضَهَل a ضَهْلًا وضُهُولًا (milk). To yield little milk (ewe). To be in small quantity (beverage).
To curtail a. o. of his due. — ه حَقَّهُ
To begin to ripen (palm-tree). أَضْهَل
Collected (milk). Small quantity ضَهْل of water.
He has given him little. أعطاهُ ضَهْلَةً
Yielding little water (spring). ضَاهِلَة
Giving little milk (ewe) ضَهُول ج ضُهُل little water (well).
To be barren (ground). ✲ ضَهِي a ضَهًى To have no milk (woman).
To resemble a. o. ضَاهَى ه
Barren ground. Having no milk ضَهْيَاء (woman).
Similar, alike. ضَهِيّ م ضَهِيَّة
Likeness, conformity. مُضَاهَاة
To shine, ✲ ضَاء o ضَوْءًا وضُوءًا وضِيَاءً to be bright (fire, light).
To make a. th. to shine ضَوَّأ تَضوِئَةً ه brightly. To light a lamp. To light up a house.
To turn away from. — عن
To shine, to be bright. أَضَاء إِضَاءَةً
To illuminate, to light up a — ه place.
Help me and I will أَضِئ لي أَقْدَحْ لَكَ help thee.
To look from the dark at people تَضَوَّأ by the light of their fire. ✧ To be lighted.
To obtain light by means إِسْتَضَاء ب of.
To take information, to seek — من advice from.
Light, brightness. ضِيَاء وضَوْء ج أَضْوَاء
Moonshine. ضَوْء القَمَر

one is tenacious; precious thing.
To conceal o.'self ✲ ضَنَأ a ضَنْأً في in (a country).
To be numerous (flock). — ضَنْأً وضُنُوءًا
To have many — وضَنِئ a ضَنْأً, وأَضْنَأ children (woman).
To have many flocks. أَضْنَأ
To be ashamed of. إِضطَنَأ ل ومن
Numerous offspring. ضَنْء ج ضُنُوء
Destitution, straitness ضُنَاءَة وضُنَاءَة of life.
Prolific (woman). ضَانِئ وضَانِئَة ج ضَوَانِئ
To strike the ✲ ضَنَب o ضَنْبًا ه ب earth with.
To seize a. th. — ب
To be plump, ✲ ضَنِط a ضَنَطًا من compact in flesh.
To press together (crowd). إِنْضَنَط
Distress. ضَنَط
Feeble; weak- ✲ ضَنُك o ضَنَاكَةً tempered.
To be narrow — ضَنْكًا وضَنَاكَةً وضُنُوكَةً (place).
To be affected with rheum. ضُنِك ضَنْكًا
Strait, narrow. ضَنْك
Straitened circumstances. عِيشَة ضَنْك
Of a strong constitution. ضِنَاك
Rheum. ضُنَاك وضُنكَة
Weakness of temper. ضَنَاكَة
Straitness, distress. — وضَنِيك
Weak of mind and ضَنِيك ج ضُنُك body. Hireling.
To be sickly. ✲ ضَنِي a ضَنًى
To wear out, to disable ضَانَى وأَضْنَى ه a. o. (latent disease).
To languish, to pine away. إِنْضَنَى
Weakness, languor. ضَنًى
Sickly, diseased. — وضَنٍ
Little children. ضَنْو ضِنْو
To alter a. th. ✲ ضَهَب a ضَهْبًا ه ب by means of fire.
To be weak, unmanly. — ضُهُوبًا
To roast (meat). To strai- ضَهَّب ه ghten, to supple a bow over a fire.
To treat a. o. shockingly. ضَاهَب ه
Rabble. ضَهْب القوم
Straightened by fire (bow). ضَهْبَاء
Roasted but not thoroughly مُضَهَّب cooked (meat).

Coming by night. ضَارٍ م ضَارِيَة
Slender-bodied. ضَارِيّ م ضَارِيَّة
To incline towards. ✡ ضَاجَ i ضُيُوجًا وضَيَجَانًا الى
To be waste (country). ✡ ضَاحَ i ضَيْحًا
To mix milk wih water. — وضَيَّحَ ه
To give to a. o. milk mixed with water. ضَيَّحَ ة
To be mixed with water (milk). تَضَيَّحَ
Milk mixed with water. ضَيْحٌ وضَيَاحٌ
To harm, to injure a. o. ✡ ضَارَ i ضَيْرًا ة
Harmful, hurtful. ضَائِرٌ
To act wrongfully. ✡ ضَازَ i ضَيْزًا
To wrong a. o. in his rights. — ة حَقَّهُ
Unjust allotment. قِسْمَة ضِيزَى
To walk in shaking the shoulders (fat person). ✡ ضَاطَ i ضَيْطًا وضَيَطَانًا
Walking in shaking the shoulders. ضَيْطَان وضَيَّاط
To perish, to be lost, led astray (th). ✡ ضَاعَ i ضَيْعًا وضِيعًا وضَيْعَةً وضَيَاعًا
To lose, to miss (a. th.) ضَيَّعَ وأَضَاعَ ه
To squander, to waste away (o.'s goods).
To possess an estate, a land. أَضَاعَ
To miss a. th.
Loss. Dereliction. ضَيْعٌ وضَيَاعٌ و✧ ضِيعَانٌ
He died uncared for. مَاتَ ضِيعًا وضِيَعًا وضَيَاعًا
To no avail. ضَيَاعًا
What a loss! ✧ يَا ضِيعَانَهُ
Village. ضَيْعَة ج ضِيَعٌ وضِيَاعٌ وضَيْعَاتٌ
Profession. Funded property. Estate.
He minds what is not of his concern. فَشَتْ عَلَيْهِ الضَّيْعَةُ
Small village; small property. ضُيَيْعَةٌ
Lost, misled. ضَائِعٌ ج ضُيَّعٌ وضِيَاعٌ
He has eaten after fasting. أَكَلَ في مَعًى ضَائِعٍ
More forlorn. أَضْيَعُ
Lavisher, prodigal. مِضْيَاعٌ ومُضَيِّعٌ
Loss, ruin. مَضْيَعَة ومَضِيعَة
To become the guest of; to alight at the abode of. ✡ ضَافَ i ضَيْفًا وضِيَافَةً
To incline to. — i ضَيْفًا الى
To deviate from the butt (arrow). — عن
To near its setting (sun). — وضَيَّفَ وتَضَيَّفَ

Sunshine. ضَوْءُ الشَّمْسِ
Lighting, illumination. إِضَاءَةٌ
Bright. ضَوِيءٌ ومُضِيءٌ
To make noise. ✡ ضَاضَا — ضَوْضَى ضَوْضَاةً
Noise, uproar. ضَوْضَى وضَوْضَاءٌ
Clamorous. مُضَوْضٍ
To pass by the butt (arrow). ✧ To be wearied. ✡ ضَاجَ o ضَوْجًا عن
To be spacious. — وانْضَاجَ
To wind (river). تَضَوَّجَ
Winding of a river. ضَوْجٌ ج أَضْوَاجٌ
To mix milk with water. ✡ ضَوَحَ — ضَوَّحَ ه
To give to a. o. diluted milk. — ة
To be starving. ✡ ضَارَ o ضَوْرًا
To harm a. o. to damage. — ة
To writhe from hunger or pain. تَضَوَّرَ
To howl in hunger (wild beast).
Vehement hunger. ضِوَرٌ
Black cloud. ضُورٌ
Poor, wretched, despised. ضُورَةٌ
To eat up (a fruit). ✡ ضَازَ o ضَوْزًا ه
Splinter of a tooth-pick. ضَوْزٌ وضُوَازَةٌ
Tooth-pick. مِضْوَازٌ
To collect (things). ✡ ضَاطَ — ضَوَّطَ ه
Distortion of the jaw. ضَوَطٌ
Having a small jaw. أَضْوَطُ
Liquid dough. Slime, mud. ضَوِيطَةٌ
To shake, to agitate a. th. ✡ ضَاعَ o ضَوْعًا ه
To diffuse itself (odour). To writhe in crying (child). — وتَضَوَّعَ
To spread the wings to its mother that he might be fed (young bird). تَضَوَّعَ وانْضَاعَ
Night bird, male owl. ضُوَعٌ وضِوَعٌ
To have many children. ✡ ضَانَ o ضَوْنَةً, وتَضَوَّنَ
Runnet used for coagulating milk. ضَوْنٌ
Little girl. ضَوْنَةٌ
Male cat. ضَيْوَنٌ ج ضَيَاوِنُ
To be slender, mean. ✡ ضَوِيَ a ضَوًى, وأَضْوَى
To take refuge towards. To come nightly to. ضَوَى i ضَيًّا وضُوِيًّا الى
To weaken a. o. To defraud a. o. of his right. أَضْوَى ة
To perform a. th. imperfectly. — ه —
To unite to. انْضَوَى الى

ضَافَ ه عن To turn away a. o. from.
ضَيَّفَ وأَضَافَ ه To entertain a. o. as a guest.
أَضَافَ الى To seek refuge in.
أَضَافَ ه الى To annex, to adjoin a. th. To put (a noun) in the genitive case.
– ه على To urge a. o. to alight at a. o.'s.
إِنْضَافَ الى To be adjoined, annexed to.
تَضَايَفَ To stand side by side.
إِسْتَضَافَ ب To ask hospitality from.
ضِيَافَة Hospitality.
دار الضِّيَافَة ومَضِيف Hospice. Strangers' home.
إِضَافَة Adjunction. Grammatical relation ; genitive.
إِضَافِيّ Correlative (noun).
تَضَايُف Relation, connection.
ضَيْف ج ضُيُوف وأَضْيَاف وضِيفَان Guest, visiter, parasite.
ضَيْفَن Intruder.
مُضِيف Hospitable man ; host.
مُضَاف Adjunct. Encompassed (in war). Having a correlative (noun).
مُضَاف إِلَيْهِ Correlative noun.
مِضْيَاف Hospitable.
مَضِيفَة ومُضِيفَة Care, trouble.
مَضِيفَة Khan, guests'room.
* ضَاقَ ِ ضِيقًا وضَيْقًا To be narrow, strait, to be straitened. To be tenacious (man).

ضَيَّقَ وأَضَاقَ ه To straiten, to contract a. th.
ضَيَّقَ على To act severely towards a. o. to put in a strait.
ضَايَقَ ه To treat a. o. harshly.
أَضَاقَ To lose wealth. To be reduced to destitution.
تَضَيَّقَ وتَضَايَقَ To be straitened (place).
تَضَايَقَ To feel uneasy (in a place). To feel uncomfortable.
ضِيق وضَيْق Sorrow, anguish.
ضَيْقَة وضِيقَة ج ضِيَق Straitness. Mansion of the moon.
ضَيِّق وضَائِق وضَيْق Narrow, straitened.
أَضْيَق م ضِيقَى وضُوقَى Narrower.
مَضِيق ج مَضَايِق Narrow place ; glen, mountain-pass. Difficulty, perplexity.
* ضَامَ ِ ضَيْمًا ه To oppress, to damage a. o. ✧ To cause pain to a. o. (disease).
– واسْتَضَامَ ه حَقَّهُ To wrong a. o. in his rights.
✧ إِنْضَامَ To be seriously ill.
ضَيْم ج ضُيُوم Injustice, oppression, damage.
ضِيم Side of a mountain.
ضَائِم Wrong-doer.
مَضِيم Wronged, oppressed.
✧ مُنْضَام Seriously ill.
✧ ضَايَنَ To wear well (clothes).
Ts ضَيَاه Strong (man). Wearing well (clothes).

ط

To lower, to stoop (the head). To urge (a horse). ✡ طَأْطَأَ ه وه
To loose the rein to a horse. — يَدَهُ بِالعِنَانِ
To be abased. تَطَأْطَأَ
Depressed ground. طَأْطَاء
Cuckoo (bird). ✧ طَاطُوي
There is nobody in the house. طار — مَا بِالدَّار طُوْرِيٌّ
To practice medicine. To act kindly, mildly. ✡ طَبَّ o i طَبًّا
To patch a water-skin. — وطَبَّب ه
✧ To put a vessel upside down. طَبَّ الوِعَاء
To be wounded in the lungs. طُبَّ
To patch up (clothing). To hang up and shake a skin. طَبَّب ه
To treat a sick person medically. طَبَّب وطَابَّ ه
To practice medicine. To become a medical man. To be under treatment. تَطَبَّبَ
To ask medicines from a. o. To consult a physician. إِسْتَطَبَّ ه
Skilful practitioner. طَبٌّ م طَبَّة
Will. Habit. طِبٌّ
Medicine. Kindness, mildness. طَبٌّ وطِبٌّ وطُبٌّ
Medical, medicinal. طِبِّيٌّ
Oblong piece of land, cloth or cloud. طِبَّة ج طِبَب وطِبَابَة ج طِبَاب
Leather band at the lower part of a skin. ✧ Wad for gun. طَبَّة
Sunbeams at sunrise. طِبَب الشَّمْس
Physician. Medical man. Clever, learned. طَبِيب ج أَطِبَّاء وأَطِبَّة
Practitioner, medical man. مُتَطَبِّب
To murmur (water). ✧ To pat (a child). ✡ طَبْطَب
Murmur of flowing water. طَبْطَبَة
To cook (meat). To boil the (contents of a cooking-pot). To affect a. o. (fever, heat). ✡ طَبَخ o a طَبْخًا, وطَبَّخ ه وه

To grow up (child). طَبَّخ
To be nicely cooked, boiled. إِنْطَبَخ واطَّبَخ
Cooking of a dish. طَبْخ
Cooked food. — وطِبْخ
Froth of the kettle. طُبَاخَة
Kitchen, culinary art. طِبَاخَة
Cooked. Cooked food. Baked brick. Gypsum. طَبِيخ ج أَطْبِخَة
Hot wind. طَبِيخَة ج طَبَائِخ
Cooking. Devil tormenting the damned. Hot-fever. طَابِخ ج طُبَّخ
The hottest hour of the day. طَابِخَة
Very foolish. طَبِخَة وأَطْبَخ
Cook. طَبَّاخ
Kitchen. مَطْبَخ ج مَطَابِخ
Cooking-pot; kitchen implement. مِطْبَخ ج مَطَابِخ
Cooked, dressed (dish). ✧ Mature (man). Calender. مَطْبُوخ
To leap. To conceal o.'s self. ✡ طَبَر o طَبْرًا
Axe. P طَبَر
Pillar. طِبْر
Misfortunes, calamities. بَنَاتُ طَبَار
Regiment. Tv طَابُور
Tiberias (town). طَبَرِيَّة
Hardened white sugar. Sugar-candy. P طَبَرْزَد
Axe. ✡ طَبَرْزِين
To fill (a vessel). ✡ طَبَر o طَبْرًا ه
Rock. Two-humped camel. طِبْز
To sink the foot into mud, water. ✧ طَبَس o طَبْسًا ب
To smear with mud. ✧ To play in the mud (child). طَبَّس ه
Saucer, tray. Te طِبْسِي
Mankind. ✡ طَبْش
Chalk. ✡ طَبَاشِير
To imprint a. th. on. To coin (money). ✡ طَبَع a طَبْعًا ه وعلى
To print (a book). To stamp. To seal, to impress, to brand. To fashion, to make (a sword). — ه

To be fashioned, shaped. طُبِع على
To be dirty. To be rusted. طَبِع a طَبَعًا
To impress a. th. strongly. طَبَّع ه
 To fill up a measure. To stain, to soil a. th. ✧ To break, to train (a horse).
To be filled up (measure). ✧ To be broken, trained (beast). تطبّع
To get an habit. To be affected, unnatural. To assume (a temper). تَطَبَّع ب
To be imprinted, stamped, (seal). إِنطبع
Imprint. Stamp, seal, impress. Temper, nature. Shape, mould, pattern. طَبْع ج طباع
Drawing (of a printing proof). طَبْعَة
Filling of a measure, vessel. River. طِبْع ج أطْباع
Rust, dirtiness. — وطَبَع ج أطْبَاع
Dirty, rusty. Vicious. طَبِع
Temper, natural dispositions, habit assumed. طِبَاع وطَابِع
Printing-house, printing-press. طِبَاعَة
Temper, nature. Habit. طَبِيعَة
Seal, signet, ring, stamp. ✧ Postage-stamp. طَابَع وطَابِع ج طَوَابِع
Manufacturer of swords. Potter. Printer, typographer. طَبَّاع
Nature. Temper, constitution. طَبِيعَة ج طَبَائِع
Natural, inborn. طَبِيعِيّ
Physical science. عِلْم الطّبِيعِيَّات
Filthy, greasy. أَطْبَع
Potter's clay. طُبْعَان
Printing-house. مَطْبَعَة ج مَطَابِع
Printing-press. مِطْبَعَة ج مَطَابِع
✧ Trained (horse). مُطَبَّع
Gifted with poetical talent. Natural, unaffected. مَطْبُوع
Pl. Publications. مَطْبُوعَات
To be stuck to the side (arm). To be shut (hand). ✶ طَبِق a طَبَقًا وطَبَقًا يَدُهُ
To coincide, to fit. طَبَق
To set to. — يَفْعَل
✧ To cover, to overwhelm a. o. (falling house). طَبَق o على
To cover a. th. To cover the whole of the earth (water); the whole sky (cloud). To sever the joints (sword). ✧ To conform, to adapt a. th. To shut (a book). To shoe (a horse). ✧ To join the fingers, the eyelids. طَبَّق ه وه
To leap in running (horse). طَبَّق
To agree with a. o. To comply with o.'s desire. To be fitted, matched to. طَابَق مُطَابَقَة وطِبَاقًا ه وه
To match two things. To wear two shirts. — بَيْن
To walk with short steps (shackled-man). To put the hind feet in the prints of the forefeet (horse). طَابَق
To get accustomed to. — على
To cover, to encompass, to wrap a. th. To fold (a cloth), to shut (a book). أَطْبَق ه
To appear in geat numbers (stars). أَطْبَق
To agree upon. To seize a. o. (fever). — على
How clever he is! مَا أَطْبَقَهُ
To agree. تَطَابَق
To be covered. To be shut (book). تَطَبَّق وانطَبَق
Convenience, conformity. Bird-lime. Hour, moment of the day. Numerous party. طِبْق
He came at last. جَاء طِبْقًا
In conformity with the law. طِبْقًا لِلقَانُون
Cover. Round tray. Large dish. Surface of the earth. Numerous party. Period of time. Layer. ✧ Pincers. طَبَق ج أطْبَاق
Snare, trap. طِبْقَة ج طِبَق وطِبَق
Misfortunes, calamities. بَنَات طَبَق
Layer. Story of a building. Series, class. طَبَقَة ج طَبَقَات وطِبَاق
Closed hand. يَد طَبِقَة
Hour of the night. طَبِيق ج طُبُق
Adapting, fitting. طِبَاق وتَطْبِيق
It suits, it resembles it. هٰذَا طِبْقُهُ وطَبَقُهُ وطِبَاقُهُ وطَبِيقُهُ
✧ Plot. طَبِيقَة
Frying pan. Half of a sheep. ✧ Story of a building. طَابِق وطَابَق ج طَوَابِق وطَوَابِيق
Cover, lid. ✧ Story. طَابِق
Covering, overwhelming. مُطْبِق م مُطْبِقَة
Underground cell, gaol. مُطْبَق

Concert. ✲ طَأْن
To fry, to broil a. th. ✲ طَجَن o طَجْنًا ه
To speak vulgarly. ◘ طَجِن و طَجْرَم
Frying pan, saucepan. G طَاجِن و طَيْجَن ج طَوَاجِن و طَيَاجِن
To spread a. th. ✲ طَحَّ o طَحًّا ه
To scrape the ground with. — ه ب
To let fall, to hurl down a. th. أَطَحَّ ه
To be extended, spread. إِنْطَحَّ
Scrapings. طُحَّة
To break, to scatter a. th. ✲ طَحْطَح ه
To scatter, to destroy (a tribe). — ة وب
To repel a. o. with the hand. ✲ طَحَث a طَحْثًا ة
To draw a sigh. ✲ طَحَر i طَحْرًا وطَحِيرًا
To bring out (dirt : eye, a spring). — a طَحْرًا ه
Little clear cloud. طَحْر وطَحَر وطَحَرَة
The sky is cloudless. مَا في السَّمَاء طَحَر
Sigh. طَحِير وطُحَار
Shooting an arrow far away (bow). Flying swiftly (arrow). مِطْحَر
Desperate war. مِطْحَرَة
Isolated cloud. ✲ طحرر — طُحْرُور ج طَحَارِير
To wound a. o. in the spleen. ✲ طَحَل a طَحْلًا وطَحَلًا ة
To have a complaint of the spleen. طُحِل طَحْلًا
To have the spleen enlarged. To smell bad (water). To be of a blackish colour (beast). طَحِل a طَحَلًا وطَحَلًا
Spleen. طِحَال ج طُحُل وأَطْحِلَة وطِحَالَات
Disease of the spleen. طُحَال
✧ Ceterach. حَشِيشَة الطُّحَال
A grey blackish colour. طُحْلَة
Having his spleen enlarged. Ill-humoured. Covered with moss (water). Black. طَحِل
Of a dingy, ash colour. Turbid (beverage). أَطْحَل م طَحْلَاء ج طُحْل
Having a complaint of the spleen. مَطْحُول
To be overspread with green moss (stagnating water). ✲ طَحْلَب
Green moss. ✧ Sea-moss. طِحْلِب وطُحْلُب
Overspread with moss. مُطَحْلَب ومُطَحْلِب
To dart upon. ✧ طَحَم a طَحْمًا على

Madness. Continuous fever. جنون مُطبِق وحُمَّى مُطبِقة
The letters ظ ط ض ص. حُرُوف مُطبَقة
Of a sound judgment, accurate. مُطَبِّق
Cloud covering the sky. سَحَابَة مُطبِقة
Adaptation, conformity. Symmetry. مُطَابَقَة
Corresponding, matched, correlative, conformable. مُطَابِق
To beat the drum. ✲ طَبَل o طَبْلًا , وطَبَّل
Drum. Kettle drum. طَبْل ج طُبُول وأَطْبَال
Art of beating the drum. طِبَالَة
Drummer. Kettle-drummer. طَبَّال
Poll-tax. ✧ Drum of the ear. Small table. Platter, dish. طَبْلِيَّة ج طَبْلِيَّات
Ewe. طُوبَالَة ج طُوبَالَات
To cover the fire. ✲ طَبَن i طَبْنًا ه
To be clever, experienced in. — وطَبِن a طَبْنًا وطَبَانَة وطَبَانِيَة وطُبُونَة ل وه
To deepen a hollow in the ground. طَابَن ه
To agree with a. o. — ة
Large crowd. طَبْن وطَبَن
Guitar. Lute. طُبْن
Game of the Arabs. Dead beast used as a bait. — وطِبْن وطَبْن وطُبَن
Cleverness, skilfulness. طِبْنَة ج طِبَن
Intelligent. طَابِن وطَبِن
Hollow in the earth for covering the fire. طَابُون
Oven. ✧ طَابُونَة
Pistol. Ts طَبَنْجَة ج طَبَنْجَات
Persian dish. P طَبَاهِجَة
To call, to invite a. o. ✲ طَبَا o طَبْوًا واطَّبَى , وطَبَى i طَبْيًا وأَطْبَى ة
Teats of wild beasts and of solid or cloven-hoofed animals. طِبْي وطُبْي ج أَطْبَاء
Head-covering of the Maronite priests. ✧ طَبِيَّة
Fort, redoubt. Ts طَابِيَة
Game of quoits. ✲ طَثّ
Quoit. مِطَثَّة
To be creamy (milk). ✲ طَثَر o طَثْرًا وطُثُورًا , وطَثَّر
To increase a. th. أَطْثَر ه
Cream. Mud. Luxurious life. Greasy-wool. Green moss. طَثْرَة
Creamy (milk). طَاثِر
Musquito, gnat. طَثْيَار وطَيْثَار

Crowd, multitude of people. Impetus of a torrent. Falling of darkness. طَحْمَة وطِحْمَة وطُحْمَة

Violent, impetuous (river). طَحُوم

To grind, to mill (wheat). To bruize, to pound a. th. ✱ طَحَن a طَحْنًا. وطَحَّن ه

To be milled, to be pounded. تَطَحَّن

Grinding. طَحْن

Flour. طِحْن وطَحِين

✧ Corn milled at one time. طَحْنَة

Dregs of sesame-oil. طَحِينَة

Standing in the middle of the floor (ox). طَاحِن

Pl. Molar teeth. طَاحِنَة ج طَوَاحِن

Miller. طَحَّان

Millery. طِحَانَة

Mill. Mill-stone. طَاحُون وطَاحُونَة ج طَوَاحِين، وطَحَّانَة

Numerous flocks. Desperate struggle. طَحُون وطَحَّانَة

Mill, mill-stone. مِطْحَنَة ج مَطَاحِن

Mill, grinding place. مَطْحَنَة ج مَطَاحِن

Coiled up (snake). مِطْحَان

To go off, to start. To perish. ✱ طَحَا o طَحْوًا

To throw a. o. down. — ه

To stretch o.'self. طَحَا a طَحْوًا

To spread a. th. on the ground. — ه

To render a. o. restless (cares). طَحَا ب

To throw a ball. — بِالكُرَة

Flat ground. طَحًا

Overspreading (crowd). طَاحٍ

Large umbrella, canopy. مِظَلَّة طَاحِيَة ومَطْحُوَّة ومَطْحِيَّة

Overspreading everywhere (weeds). مُطْحِيَة

To be peevish, unsociable. ✱ طَخَّ o طُخُوخًا

Harsh and unsociable temper. طُخُوخ

To be dull, veiled (eye). ✱ طَخِش a طَخْشًا وطَخَشًا

Cares, grief. Sour milk. ✱ طِخْف — طَخْف

Light, translucid cloud. طَخَاف

To be proud. ✱ طَخِم a طَخْمًا وطَخُم o طَخَامَة

To become black (meat). اطْخَمَّ

Flock of goats. طَخْمَة

Black spot on the tip of the nose. طُخْمَة

Dried meat becoming black. طَخِيم

To be obscure (night). ✱ طَخَا o طُخُوًّا

Lofty cloud. Cares. طَخَاء

Darkness. طَخْيَة وطِخْيَة وطُخْيَة

Thick, intense (darkness). طَاخِيَة

Obscure night. Unintelligible (speech). طَخْيَاء

To collect and drive (cattle). ✱ طَرَّ o طَرًّا ه

To restore, to whitewash a building. To ravish, to snatch a. th. To cut (a piece of cloth). — ه

To fall from a terrace. To grow forth (plant, mustache). — وطَرَّ i o طَرًّا

To whet a knife. — o طَرًّا وطُرُورًا ه

To throw a. o. down. أَطَرَّ ه

To incite a. o. to. — ه على

To cut, to curtail a. th. — ه

All of them are come. جَاءُوا طُرًّا

Flank. طَرَّة

Bank of a river. Side, edge. Streak, stripe. Lock of hair, forelock. Signet, stamp. طُرَّة ج طُرَر وطِرَار وطُرَّات وأَطْرَار

Borders of a country. أَطْرَار البِلَاد

Youth whose mustaches grow forth. طَارّ وطَرِير

Pickpocket. طَرَّار

Dinner-tray. طِرِّيَان

Of goodly appearance. طَرِير

Sharpened, cutting. — ومَطْرُور

Anger without motive. غَضَب مُطِرّ

To boast. To speak much. ✧ To crack (glace). ✱ طَرْطَر

Sediment, dregs, tartar. ✧ طَرْطِير

Long and pointed cap of the Arabs. طُرْطُور

✧ A kind of sauce. طَرْطُور

To happen, to fall unexpectedly upon a. o. ✱ طَرَأَ a طَرْءًا وطُرُوءًا على

To be fresh, juicy. طَرُؤَ o طَرَاءَة وطَرَاء

To commend a. o. highly. أَطْرَأَ ه

Recent, fresh. طَرِيء م طَرِيئَة

Unexpected, unforeseen. طَارِئ ج طُرَّاء وطُرَاء

Misfortune. طَارِئَة ج طَارِئَات وطَوَارِئ

Extravagant praise. Hyperbole. إِطْرَاء

Sheet of paper. ✧ طَرْحِيَّة ج طَرَاحِي
Lying prostrate on the ground. طَرِيح ج طَرْحى
Forsaken, cast off. — ومَطْرُوح
Conversation. مُطارَحَة
Throwing place. مَطْرَح ج مَطارِح
✧ Place, spot.
Long (spear). Piercing (sight). مِطْرَح
Prince, chief. T طَرْخَان ج طَرَاخِنَة
Artemisia dracunculus, tarragon. S طَرْخُون
To persecute, to drive back a. o. To collect (scattered flocks). ✲ طَرَد o طَرْدًا وطَرَدًا ه وه
To pursue, to track a beast. طَرِد a طَرَدًا ه
To raise (a whip). طَرَّد ه
To charge upon, to drive off the enemy. طَارَد مُطارَدَةً وطِرَادًا
To banish a. o. To make a wager with a. o. أَطْرَد ه
To attack, to pursue one another. تَطارَد
To be banished, driven off. إِنْطَرَد واطَّرَد
To follow a right course (affair). To be consistent (proof). To flow (river). إِطَّرَد
To make a digression. To simulate flight and come back to the charge. إِسْتَطْرَد
Removal. expulsion. Hunting. Tracking of wild beasts. طَرْد
To read a. th. in the sequel or the reverse. قَرَأ طَرْدًا او عَكْسًا
✧ Package, parcel. طَرْد ج طُرُودَة
Repeller. Driving people away by the length of his reading. Light boat. Long (day). ✧ Breakwater. Dyke. طَرَّاد
✧ Bolt. طَرَّادَة
Banishment. Mention of a. o.'s ancestors. إِطِّرَاد
Digression. إِسْتِطْرَاد
Expelled. Tracked beast. Long (day). Born before or after another. طَرِيد
The day and the night. الطَّرِيدَان
Tracked beast, game. Stolen flocks. Piece of land. Oblong piece of cloth. طَرِيدَة ج طَرَائِد

Coming from an unknown place (pigeon). Strange (event). طُرْآنِيّ
To be moved with joy or sadness. ✲ طَرِب a طَرَبًا
To sing, to make music. To be cheerful. طَرَّب و✧ تَطَرَّب
To excite a. o. to joy or sadness. طَرَّب وأَطْرَب وتَطَرَّب ه
To desire a. o. to sing. إِسْتَطْرَب
Emotion of joy or sadness. Delight. طَرَب
Moved; cheerful; sad. طَرِب م طَرِبَة
Affected with emotion. طَرُوب ومِطْرَاب و مِطْرَابَة
By-road, narrow road. *Pl.* Roads branching off. مَطْرَب ومَطْرَبَة ج مَطارِب
Musician, singer. مُطْرِب
Musical instruments. آلَات مُطْرِبَة
✧ Railing; long table. Gs طَرَابِيزُون
Turkish red cap. ✧ طَرْبُوش ج طَرَابِيش
Portion of a wall; stone-building. Prominent rock used as a sign. ✲ طربل — طِرْبَال ج طَرَابِيل
Thrashing-machine. طِرْبِيل ج طَرَابِيل
Tripoli of Syria. طَرَابُلُس الشَّام
Tripoli of Barbary. طَرَابُلُس الغَرْب
Medicinal plant. ✲ طُرْثُوث ج طَرَاثِيث
To fling, to cast away a th. ✲ طَرَح a طَرْحًا ه وب. واطَّرَح ه
✧ To miscarry (woman). طَرَحَت
To subtract (a number). — ه
To cast off. — ه عن
To put a. th. upon. To make (a question) to a. o. — ه على
✧ To raise a cry of alarm. طَرَح الصَّوْت
To live in luxury. طَرِح a طَرَحًا
To fling away. To raise a building high. طَرَّح ه
To discourse with a. o. طَارَح ه الكَلَام
To dissert on science. تَطارَحَا العِلْمَ
To be thrown off. To rush forth. ✧ إِنْطَرَح
Fling, subtraction. طَرْح
✧ Cry of alarm. طَرْح الصَّوْت
Thrown aside, cast off. طِرْح
Remote place. طَرَح وطَرُوح وطَرَاح
A throw. Persian mantle. ✧ Woman's head-veil. طَرْحَة
Square mattress. ✧ طَرَّاحَة ج طَرَارِيح

To hurt (the eye) and make it water. طَرَفَ هـ
There is no one left amongst them. مَا بَقِيَتْ مِنْهُمْ عَيْنٌ تَطْرِفُ
To be hurt and to water (eye). طُرِفَ
To be newly acquired (property). To descend from an ancient family (man). طَرُفَ o طَرَافَةً
To walk on the side of, the bank of. To attack the extremity of the enemy's lines. To lose the teeth. طَرَّفَ
To choose a. th. To drive back the foremost (horses) to the rear. ه —
To dye the tips of her fingers (woman). هـ —
To close the eyes. أَطْرَفَ
To present a. o. with a. th. new. ه —
To walk on the brink. To become sharp pointed. تَطَرَّفَ
To buy a. th. new. إِطَّرَفَ هـ
To find a. th. to be new. To esteem a. th. new. إِسْتَطْرَفَ هـ
Side, part. Bank, extremity, edge, fringe. End, tip. طَرَفٌ ج أَطْرَافٌ وَأَطَارِيفُ
The extremities of the body. أَطْرَافُ الْبَدَنِ
The low people. أَطْرَافُ النَّاسِ
The near relations of a. o. — فُلَانٍ
Two stinged serpent. ذُو الطَّرَفَيْنِ
Twinkling of the eye. طَرْفٌ وَطَرْفَةٌ
Sight. Glance.
Noble from both parents. طِرْفٌ ج أَطْرَافٌ
Horse of high breed. Noble. Newly acquired (property). طِرْفٌ ج طُرُوفٌ وَأَطْرَافٌ
New, just known (man). طِرْفٌ
Changing, unsteady. — وَطَرِفٌ
Reckoning many ancestors. طَرِفٌ وَطَرِيفٌ
Blood spot in a wounded eye. طَرْفَةٌ
Hurt causing the eye to water. Novelty. A thing new, novel, curious. طُرْفَةٌ ج طُرَفٌ
Tamarisk. (*un.* طَرْفَاءَةٌ وَطَرَفَةٌ) طَرْفَاءُ
Newly acquired, recent, novel, rare. طَارِفٌ وَطَرِيفٌ ج طُرُفٌ
Plenty of goods. طَارِفَةُ عَيْنٍ
The eyes. The sides of a tent. الطَّوَارِفُ

Short spear. Pole. طِرَادٌ, وَمِطْرَدٌ ج مَطَارِدُ
Charge of horsemen. مُطَارَدَةٌ وَطِرَادٌ
Long (day). مُطَّرِدٌ
General rule. مُطَّرِدٌ
High road. مِطْرَدَةٌ وَمَطْرَدَةٌ
To embellish o. self. To amend. ✱ طَرِزَ a طَرَزًا
To clothe o.'self luxuriously. طَرِزَ فِي الْمَلْبِسِ
To embroider (cloth). طَرَّزَ هـ
To be embroidered (cloth). تَطَرَّزَ
Shape, figure. طَرْزٌ
Embroidery, embroidered garment. Fashion, use, shape. P طِرَازٌ ج طُرُزٌ
Art of embroidering. طِرَازَةٌ
Embroiderer. طَرَّازٌ وَمُطَرِّزٌ
To obliterate a. th. ✱ طَرَسَ i طَرْسًا هـ
To restore a manuscript. To collate writings. To paint a door black. طَرَّسَ هـ
To be particular about o.'s food. تَطَرَّسَ فِي الْمَطْعَمِ
To disdain a. th. — عَنْ
Leaf of paper. Palimpsest. طِرْسٌ ج أَطْرَاسٌ وَطُرُوسٌ
To retreat, to draw off. ✱ طَرْسَمَ عَنْ
To be or become deaf. ✱ طَرِشَ a طَرَشًا
To whitewash (a wall). To vomit. ✧ طَرَشَ o طَرْشًا هـ
To deafen a. o. ✧ طَرَّشَ ه
To feign deafness. تَطَارَشَ
Deafness. طَرَشٌ وَطُرْشَةٌ
Whitewash. ✧ طَرْشٌ
Cattle, flocks. ✧ طَرْشٌ ج طُرُوشٌ
Deaf. أَطْرَشُ م طَرْشَاءُ ج طُرْشٌ, وَأَطَارِيشُ
Pickles. Te طُرْشُو وَطُرْشِيٌّ
To be foolish. To have scanty hair on the eyelashes. ✱ طَرِطَ a طَرَطًا
Stupid, fool. طَارِطٌ وَطَرِطٌ
Thin in the eyebrows. طَارِطٌ وَطَرِطُ الْحَاجِبَيْنِ وَأَطْرَطُ م طَرْطَاءُ
To splash a. o. ✧ طَرْطَشَ ه
✧ To stammer. طَرْطَلَ
End, crest. Ground-artichoke. طُرْطُوفَةٌ
To twinkle (eyes). ✱ طَرَفَ i طَرْفًا
To slape a. o. on the face. ه —
To twinkle the eyes. — بِبَصَرِهِ وَبِعَيْنِهِ

Water defiled by beasts.
Snare, net. — وطِرق وطِرْقة ج طِرَق
Fold of a water skin. طِرق ج أطراق
Way, road. Method; habit. طُرْقة ج طُرَق
Leather lining. Round iron plate. طِراق ج طُرق
طَرِيق ج طُرُق وطُرُقات وأطرق وأطرِقة وأطرقاء
Way, road, path.
Lofty palm-tree. طَرِيقة ج طَرِيق
Way, road. State, course. Rule of life. Line, streak. Chief of a tribe. ✧ Means. Order of dervishes. طَرِيقة ج طَرائق
Worn out clothing. ثوب طرائق
The changes of time. طرائق الدهر
Knocking at a door. Divining by means of pebbles. Coming by night. Morning-star. طارِق ج طُرّاق
Gibraltar. جبل طارق
F. Misfortune, distress. Small seat. Family, tribe. طارِقة ج طَوارِق وطارِقات
Having the head and eyes lowered. Humble. طِرّيق ومُطرِق ومِطراق
Mallet. Blacksmith's hammer. Beating rod. مِطرَق ومِطرَقة ج مَطارِق
File, line. مِطراق ج مَطارِيق
Trodden (ground). Frequented (road). Pelted by rain (meadow). مَطرُوق
Malleable substance. مُتطرِّق
To be filled with honey (hive). ✱ طَرِم a طَرَمًا
To flow from the hive (honey). — a طَرْمًا
To become covered with tartar (tooth). أطرم
To remain speechless. To be puzzled. تطرّم
Honeycomb. Honey. طَرم وطِرم
Liver. طَرَمة
Dimple of the upper lip. — وطِرمة وطُرمة
Tartar of the teeth. طُرامة
Cabin, wooden house. P طارمة ج طارمات
Silly, stupid. ✧ مَطرُوم
Fire-engine; pump. Syringe. ✧ طُرنبة وطُلمبة
To boast falsely. ✱ طَرمَذ

A. th. novel rare, strange. طَرِيفة ج طَرائف وأطروفة
Wonderful thing. Illustriousness of descent. طِراف
Leather tent. — ج طُرُف
Newly acquired. مُطرف
A square silk gown, adorned with figures. مُطرَف ومِطرَف ج مَطارِف
Unsteady, changing. مِطراف
Hurt so as to water (eye). مَطرُوف
✧ Olive-press. — ج مَطارِيف
To blink, to wink. To wear many clothes. To be dark (night). ✱ طَرفَس
Darkness. طِرفِسان
Dark (night). طِرفِساء
To blink. ✱ طَرفَش
To come to a. o. by night. ✱ طَرَق o طُرُوقًا وطَرقًا ه
To knock at a door. To beat (wool). To ring (a bell). To play upon (a musical instrument). — o طَرقًا ه
To cast pebbles (wizard). طَرق
To be light-minded. طُرِق
To drink turbid water. طَرِق a طَرَقًا
To open the way to. طَرّق ل
To acknowledge (a debt) after denial. — ب
To expand, to render a. th. malleable. — ه
To line (clothes). To sheath (boots). To wear (double garment). طارق بين
To remain silent with cast down eyes. To follow o. another (camels). أطرق
To busy o.'self about (trifles). — الى
To aim at, to wish, to draw near to. تطرّق الى
To walk in a file. تطارق
To be spread (wings of a bird). To part away and leave the main road. To follow each other (day and night). إطّرق
To consult (wizards). إستطرق ه
To get into an habit, to follow a course. — ه
Stroke, time. طَرق وطُرق وطَرقة
I went to him two or three times. أتيته طَرقًا او طَرقَين
Sound of a musical instrument. طَرق

طرمذة وطرماذ وطرمذان ومطرمذ
Boastful, glorying vainly.

✱ طرو o وطري a طراوة وطراءة وطراء وطراة To be quite fresh, freshly plucked (fruit).

طرا o طروا To come, to arrive from afar.

طرّى ه To cool, to moisten (a. th.) To season (a dish).

أطرى ه To lavish praises on a. o.

إطرورى To have the belly swollen.

طرا Spiritual being. Numberless.

طراوة Freshness, ripeness of a fruit, tenderness, moisture.

طري م طرية Fresh, recent, moist; tender bread.

إطرية Vermicelli. Macaroni.

أطروان Freshness; first beginning of a. th.

مطرى Perfumed, mixed with aromatics.

✱ طري a طرى الى To run up. To come, to pass near.

✱ طزر o طزرا ه To repel a. o. by boxing.

✱ طس o طسا ه To quarrel with. To silence a. o. To beat.

— ه في To plunge a. o. into water.

— الى To go far off, towards.

طسّس To make a journey.

— في To penetrate into (a country).

ما أدري أين طس او أين طسّس I do not know where he is gone to.

طس ج طسوس وطساس وطسيس, وطسّة ج طسّات وطسّات Wooden cup.

طسّاس Cup manufacturer.

طساسة Art of manufacturing cups.

✱ طسأ a طسأ وطسيء a طسأ To suffer from indigestion.

أطسأ ه To cause indigestion to a. o.

P طست ج طسوت Brass basin.

✱ طسع a طسعا في To penetrate into a country.

طسِم a طسما To be short of victuals.

طسِم وطسيم Short of provisions.

✱ طسل o طسلا To gleam, to move about (mirage).

طسل Water flowing on the surface of the soil.

✱ طسم o طسما ه To obliterate a. th.

— i طسوما To be obliterated.

طسِم a طسما To suffer from indigestion.

طسم Dust. Darkness.

طسام وطسام وطسّام Heap of dust.

✱ طش o i طشا, وأطش To let fall a fine rain (sky). ✧ To produce a bubbling (hot iron steeped into water).

طُش To have a cold, rheum.

طش وطشيش Fine and gentle rain.

طشة وطشاش Rheum.

طشاش Weakness of sight.

مطشوش Watered by a fine rain (ground).

P طشت A brass wash-basin.

P طشت دار Keeper of the vestry.

P طشتخان Marble, gold or silver tray.

✧ طص To see.

✱ طعم a طعما وطعما, وتطعّم ه To taste a. th.

— طعما وطعاما To eat a. th.

— طعما To be grafted (tree). ✧ To be baited (fishing hook). To be vaccinated (child).

طعّم وأطعم ه وه To graft a tree. ✧ To vaccinate a. o. To bait a fishing-hook.

طاعم وتطاعم To bill (pigeons).

أطعم To bear fruit (tree).

— ه To feed a. o.

تطعّم ✧ To be vaccinated, grafted.

إطّعم To have a good taste; to be ripe (fruit).

لا يطّعم There is no improvement in it.

إستطعم ه To taste a. th. To find it palatable.

— ه To ask food.

طعم ج طعوم Taste, flavour.

طعم Food. ✧ Bait, lure. Poison.

طِعمة Manner of eating. Livelihood.

طعمة ج طعم Food, eatable. Taste, flavour. Invitation to dinner.

طعمية Balls of minced meat.

طعام ج أطعمة وجج أطعمات Food, eatable, dish. Wheat.

طعام وطعم Satiating food.

طاعم وطعيم Feeding well, satiated.

أنا طاعم عن طعامكم I can do without your food.

Injustice, infidelity. طَغوَى وطُغيان
Rebellion against God.
Steep mountain. طَغيَة
Rebel. طَاغٍ ج طُغاة وطَاغُون م طَاغِيَة
Impious. Cruel.
Insolent. Tyrant. King of the — وطَاغِيَة
Greeks.
Thunderbolt. طَاغِيَة
Idol. Devil. Rebellious. طَاغُوت ج طَوَاغِيت
Seducer.
To be near to : ✲ طَفَّ o i طَفًّا مِن
within reach of.
Take what is within خُذ مَا طَفَّ لَكَ
thy reach.
To raise a. th. طَفَّ ه ب
To expand the wings (bird). طَفَّف
To leap (horse).
To give a deficient (measure). — ه
To fill up (a measure). أطَفَّ ه
To look down from above upon — على
a. th. To get possession of. To hit.
To be skilful in a. th. To lay — ل
snares for a. o.
To be within reach of. — واسْتَطَفَّ على
Bank, side, limit. طَفّ
Redundance of — وطَفَف وطِفَاف وطُفَافَة
a measure.
Incomplete, deficient. Unimportant. طَفِيف
The sourrouding part of. Tract طَافَّة
between a desert and mountains.
Sprightly, brisk, swift. طَفَّاف
Filled to the brim (vessel). طَفَّان
To be weak, soft. To spread ✲ طَفطَف
the wings (bird). To burn out
(wick).
Flank, side. طَفطَفَة ج طَفَاطِف
Bank, brink, edge. طَفطَاف
To go out (fire). ✲ طَفِئَ a طُفُوءًا, وانطَفَأ
To extinguish (fire). ✧ To أطفَأَ و✧ طَفَّأ
slake (lime).
Extinction of the blaze. طُفُوء وانطِفَاء
Extinguishing. مُطفِئ
One of the coldest days. مُطفِئ الجَمر
Great misfortune. مُطفِئ الرَّضف
Extinguisher. مِطفَأة و✧ مِطفَايَة
To be overfull. ✲ طَفَح a طَفحًا وطُفُوحًا
To overflow (vessel).
Go off, get away. إطفَح عَنِّي

Ewe for butchery. طُعُومَة
Inoculation ; vaccination ; تَطعِيم
grafting.
Food, dish. Dining- مَطعَم ج مَطَاعِم
room, refectory.
Eating greedily. مِطعَم
Hospitable. مِطعَام
Having a livelihood. مُطعَم
Food. ✧ Graft. Vaccination. مَطعُوم ج مَطَاعِيم
To spear a. o. ✲ طَعَن a o طَعنًا ه ب
To wound a. o. by words. To calumniate. طَعَن طَعنًا وطَعَنَانًا في او على . . . بِالقَول
To penetrate into a land. طَعَن في
To be advanced in age. طَعَن في السِّنّ
To be stabbed. To be smitten by طُعِن
the plague.
To fight together with the lance. تَطَاعَن تَطَاعُنًا وطِعَانًا وطَعَنَانًا, واطَّعَن
A thrust with the lance. Stinging word. طَعنَة
Plague, pestilence. طَاعُون ج طَوَاعِين
طَعَّان ومِطعَن و مِطعَان ج مَطَاعِن ومَطَاعِين
Wont to thrust the enemy.
Backbiter, disparager. طَعَّان
Pierced with a lance. طَعِين ومَطعُون
Smitten by the plague.
To dart upon a. o. ✲ طَغَر a طَغرًا على
Straight. Straight forward. T طُوغرِي
Imperial monogram T طُغرَاء ج طُغرَاءات
of the Sultan.
Silliness. ✲ طَغم — طُغُومَة وطُغُومِيَّة
To feign ignorance. تَطَغَّم
Mass of water. Ocean. طَغم
Low people. Mean game. Vile طَغَام
words.
Foolish. طَغَامَة
Choir, hierarchy of ✧ طَغمَة ج طَغمَات
Angels.
✲ طَغَا o طُغُوًّا وطُغوَانًا, وطَغِي وطَغَى a طَغيًا
To exceed the bounds. To be وطُغيَانًا
iniquitous, mischievous. To overflow
(river). To rage (sea). To be roused
(blood).
To be impi- طَغَى a وطَغِي a طَغيًا وطُغيَانًا
ous, tyrannical. To bellow (wild ox).
To render a. o. mischiev- طَغَّى وأطغَى ه
ous, unjust.

To overfill a (vessel). طَفَّح وأطفح ه
To scum a cooking pot. إطّفح ه
Fullness. ✧ Eruption of the skin. طِفَاح
Redundance, excess. طُفاحَة
Overfull, overflowing. طَافِح م طَافِحَة, وطفحان م طَفحى
Dry, arid. طَافِحَة
Skimmer. مِطفَحَة
✧ Trap, snare. مَطفَحَة
☆ To bury (the dead). طَفَذ i طَفذًا ه
Tomb. طَفذ وطَفَذ ج أطفاذ
☆ To leap (horse). طَفر i طَفرًا وطُفورًا
To be overspread with cream (milk). طَفَّر
To drive a. o. away. ✧ To ruin a. o.; to render a. o. wretched. طَفَّر ه
— وأطفر ه ه To make a horse to leap over a stream.
Leap. Cream of milk. ✧ Offshoots of trees. Eruption of pustules. طَفرَة
✧ Penniless. طَفران
☆ To be dirty, filthy. طَفِس a طَفَسًا وطَفَاسَة
Dirty, greasy. طَفِس
✧ To glide away, to escape. طَفَش
☆ To begin, to set to. طَفِق i وطَفِق a طَفقًا وطُفوقًا في
He set doing. طَفِق يَفعَل
He has fulfilled his wishes. طَفِق بِمُرادِهِ
To help a. o. to attain a. th. أطفَق ه ب
☆ To be in infancy, delicate. طَفُل o طُفولَة وطَفالَة
To rise; to be near setting (sun). طَفَل o طُفولًا
To be soiled by dust (plant). طَفِل a طَفَلًا, وطُفِل
To intrude at a feast. To come on (night). To be near setting (sun). طَفَّل
To drive a beast gently. — ه
To meditate upon (a discourse). — ه
To have an infant child, a young one. To be about setting (sun). To be upon the time preceding sunset. أطفَل
To be a parasite. To be childish. تطفَّل
Time before sunset. طَفَل
Tender, soft. طَفل م طَفلَة ج طِفال وطُفول
Tiny. Baby. طِفل م طِفلَة ج أطفال
Dry mud. طَفال وطُفال
Infancy. طَفالَة وطُفولَة وطُفولِيَّة

Turbid water in the bottom of a tank. طَفِيل
Intruder, parasite. طُفَيلِيّ
Having a little child. Blasting plants (cold night). مُطفِل ج مَطافِيل ومَطافِل
☆ To die. طَفَن o طَفنًا
— ه To tie, to confine a. o.
Lie; humbug. طَفَانِين
☆ To float upon water. To run (gazelle). طَفا o طَفوًا وطُفُوًّا
— فوق To appear above.
— في To undertake a. th.
Floating (dead fish). طَافٍ م طَافِيَة
Halo around the sun or moon. Froth of a cooking-pot. طُفاوَة
Leaf of the Theban-palm. Malignant streaked serpent. طُفيَة ج طُفًى
☆ ✧ To burst, to crack. طَقّ o طَقًّا
Burst, crack. طَقّ
☆ To resound loudly. طقطق
— ه To crack the joints.
Trampling of horses. Cracking of the knuckles. طَقطَقَة
✧ Weather. G طَقس
✧ Rite, liturgy. — ج طُقوس
Set of clothes, of tools. Uniform. Harness. T طَقم وطاقِم ج طُقومَة
✧ To dress up. To be richly harnessed (horse). تطقَّم
✧ Full-dressed. Harnessed. مُطقَّم
Yataghan, turkish dagger. T يَطقَان
☆ To moisten slightly the soil (dew). طَلّ o طَلًّا
— ه To put off (a debtor).
— ه حَقَّهُ To offend a. o. in his rights.
To shed blood without retaliation. طَلّ o طَلًّا وطُلولًا ه
✧ To overlook, to look out. — على
To be unavenged (bloodshed). طَلّ i وطُلّ a طَلًّا وأطِلّ
To overlook, to see from above. To overtop. أطَلّ واستطَلّ على
To let blood unavenged. أطَلّ ه
To strech out the neck or to stand on the toes for looking. تَطالّ
Slight dew or rain. طَلّ ج طِلال وطِلَل
Milk. Blood. طُلّ
Serpent. طِلّ
Sweet smell. Sweet wine. Cool طَلَّة

garden. Easy life. Wife. ◊ View.

Dilution of milk. Neck. طُلَّة ج طُلَل

Remains of a ruined house. Deck of a ship. طَلَل ج طُلُول وأَطْلَال

Remains of a ruined house طَلَالَة

Exterior shape. Grace, beauty. Cheerfulness.

Mat of palm-leaves. طَلِيل ج أَطِلَّة وطُلُل وطِلَّة

Unretaliated (bloodshed). طَلِيل وطُلَّاء ومَطْلُول ومُطِلّ

Elevated place; look out. مُطَلّ ج مُطَالّ

Uvula. طُلْطُل و◊ طُلْطُلَة

Death. Hopeless disease. — وطُلَاطِل

Misfortune. — طُلَاطِلَة

Toledo (town). طُلَيْطِلَة

Moistened by dew (place). مَطْلُول

To seek, to pursue a. th. ✻ طَلَب o طَلَبًا, وتَطَلَّب واطَّلَب ه

◊ To provoke a. o. To ask a. o. in marriage. — ه

◊ To seek to avenge a bloodshed. — ب

To beseech a. o. طَلَب الى فُلَانٍ أَنْ

To ask, to sue, to demand a. th. instantly. طَلَّب وتَطَلَّب ه

To claim, to ask from a. o. the payment of. طَالَب مُطَالَبَةً وطِلَابًا ه ب

To be distant (water). أَطْلَب

To grant a. o.'s petition. To incite a. o. to ask a. th. — ه

To be wished, sought for, asked. ◊ إنطَلَب

Petition, claim. Request. طَلَب وطِلْبَة

Object sought for, desired. طَلَب وطِلْبَة وطَلِبَة

Betrothed. طِلْب م طِلْبَة

Looking for a. o. طِلْب ج أَطْلَاب وطِلَبَة

◊ Prayer, litany. طِلْبَة

Far extending journey. طُلْبَة

Asking in marriage. Student. طَالِب ج طُلَّاب وطُلَّب وطَلَبَة وطَلَب

طَلَّاب وطَلُوب وطَلِيب ج طُلُب وطُلَبَاء
Requester, demander.

◊ Affianced, betrothed. طَلِيب م طَلِيبَة

Question, claim. Query. Problem. مَطْلَب ج مَطَالِب

Remote, distant (water). مُطْلِب

Intention, aim. ◊ Claimed debt. مَطْلُوب ج مَطَالِيب

To flow (water). ✻ طَلَث o طُلُوث

To exceed the measure. طَلَث على

To be jaded, tired (beast). ✻ طَلَح a طَلْحًا وطَلَاحَة

To jade, to tire (a beast). — وطَلَّح وأَطْلَح ه

To be wicked. طَلَح o طَلَاحًا

To be empty-bellied. طَلِح a طَلَحًا وطُلْحًا

To importune a. o. طَلَّح على

Easy life. طَلْح

Acacia. طَلْح وطِلَاح

Jaded, tired. — وطَلِح وطَلِيح

Abounding in acacias (place). طَلِح

Bad state, wickedness, corruptness. طَلَاح (*opp to.* صَلَاح)

Sheet of paper. طَلْحِيَّة ج طَلَاحِيّ

Wicked, mischievous. طَالِح ج طَالِحُون وطُلَّح

To soil, to blacken a. th. To mar (writing). ✻ طَلَخ o طَلْخًا ه

To disperse. To flow. إطْلَخَّ

Muddy water. طُلَخ

Old thaler of Maria Theresa worth about 4 sh. ◘ طَلَرِي

To erase (writing). ✻ طَلَس i طَلْسًا, وطَلَّس ه

To be lost (eye-sight). طُلِس

To be thrown into prison. طُلِس بِهِ في السِّجن

To be of an ash colour. طَلِس a طَلَسًا وطَلَس o طُلْسَة

To be effaced (writing). To wrap o.'self in a persian mantle. تَطَلَّس

To be concealed, involved in mystery (affair). إنطَلَس

Written paper. Obliterated writing. Old, shabby (clothes). Glabrous wolf. طِلْس ج أَطْلَاس

A blackish, dust colour. طُلْسَة

Rags for wiping. طَلَّاسَة

Blind. طَلِيس وطِلِّيس

P طَيْلَسَان وطَيْلِسَان وطَيْلُسَان ج طَيَالِسَة
Persian mantle, hood.

Glabrous, smooth. Blackish. Suspicious character. ◊ Satin. أَطْلَس م طَلْسَاء

◊ Geographical map. أَطْلَس

Obliterated. Dark, black. Clad in a persian mantle. مُتَطَلِّس

To cast down the eyes, and ✻ طَلْسَم

assume an austere countenance. To draw magical lines (wizard).
G طِلَسْم وطِلَّسْم ج طَلَاسِم وطِلَّسْمَات Talisman, charm, spell. وطِلَّسْمَات
☆ طلع o طُلُوعًا ومَطْلِعًا ومَطْلَعًا To rise (sun). To grow (tooth, plant). ✧ To become, to turn out well or ill. To go out. To go up.
— طُلُوعًا على الأمر To learn a. th.
— على فُلانٍ To come on, to come towards a. o.
— عن To start from. To disappear.
— a o وطَلِع a طُلُوعًا ه To climb upon (a mountain).
✧ ما يطلع بيدي It is not in my power.
طلع ه To reach (a country).
— من To go out from, to emerge.
طلع على بالِهِ It occurred to his mind.
طلع خُلقُهُ ✧ He got out of temper.
✧ طَيلَع ٥ To expel, to put a. o. out.
طلّع To sprout forth (palm-tree).
— ه To fill up (a measure). ✧ To raise, to take up.
— على ✧ To look at. To seek for.
طالع مُطالَعةً وطِلَاعًا ه To examine a. th. carefully.
— ٥ ب To expose, to explain a. th. to a. o.
أطلع To appear (star). To grow (plant). To vomit.
— ٥ على To inform, to acquaint a. o. with a. th.
— إليهِ مَعرُوفًا He granted him a favour.
— واطّلع على To occur, to come suddenly upon a. o.
تطلّع To be filled up (measure).
— الى To direct o's looks towards a. th.
— في To consider a. th. attentively.
— واطّلع ه To learn, to know a. th.
إطّلع على To examine, to study a. th.
— طِلع فُلان To be acquainted with a. o's affairs.
إستطلع ه و٥ To take information about a. th. To seek to know a. o.
طَلْع Quantity. Spathe of a palm-tree; pollen.
— وطِلْع Look out, elevated spot.

طِلْع Shore, extent of land within sight.
طَلْعَة Face, countenance, mien. ✧ Ascent, acclivity.
حيّا الله طَلْعَتَهُ May God rejoice him.
طِلَاع ج طُلْع Fullness.
طُلُوع ج طُلُوعات Going up. ✧ Boil, furuncle.
✧ طُلُوع وطَلْعَة الخُلق Outburst of passion.
طَلَّاع الثَّنايا والأَنْجُد Able man; experienced manager.
طُلَعاء وطُوَلِع Vomit.
تطلُّع و✧ تَطْلِيعة Glance, wink.
طَلِيعة ج طَلَائِع Vanguard. Skirmishers.
طالِع ج طَوالِع Rising (star). New moon. Arrow overpassing the butt. Morning twilight. Horoscope. ✧ Water-works.
مَطلَع ومَطلِع ج مَطالِع East. Place of rising of the sun and stars. Look-out. Tower. Ladder. Beginning of a poem, of an ode.
مُطَّلَع Elevated place, easy of ascent.
☆ طَلَغ a طَلْغًا وطَلَغَانًا To be feeble or tired.
☆ طلف — طَلَّف على To add to.
أطلف ٥ ه To give a. th. to a. o.
— ه To permit, to let a. o. do a. th.
طَلَف وطَلْف Impunity.
طَلَف Gift, present. Easy.
☆ طَلَق i طَلْقًا ٥ ه To give, to deliver a. th. to.
— وأطلق يَدَهُ بِخَيرٍ To open the hand for giving alms.
طَلَق o وطَلُق o طَلَاقًا To be repudiated (woman).
طَلِق a طَلَقًا To be remote, to be off.
طَلُق o طُلُوقَةً وطَلَاقَةً To have a cheerful countenance. To be temperate (night, day).
طَلَّق وأطلق ٥ To divorce (wife).
أطلق ٥ وه To set free (prisoners, flocks). To fire (a gun).
أطلق الكلامَ To express a. th. in an absolute way.
أُطلِقَتْ الكلمةُ على This word is only used to mean such a. th.
تَطَلَّق وانطلق To cheer up, to brighten (face).

sign of the way.
To restrain (an animal), to tie (a kid) by the leg. ✲ طَلَا ﮦ طَلْوًا ﮦ
Brightness, gleam of dawn. طُلْوَة
Beauty, elegance. طِلَاوَة وطُلَاوَة
Saliva drying on the lips. — وطَلًا
طَلًا وطَلْو ج أَطْلَاء وطِلَاء وطُلِيّ وطُلْيَان
Young one of a gazelle.
To anoint, to coat, to varnish, to overlay a. th. with (any fluid). ✲ طَلَى i طَلْيًا, وطَلَّى ﮦ وﮪ ب
To gild a. th. طَلَى ﮪ بِذَهَب
To have yellow teeth. طَلِيَ a طَلًى
To incline the head from weakness. To indulge in o.'s passions. أَطْلَى
To give o.'self up to pleasure. تَطَلَّى
To be anointed, smeared, overspread with. تَطَلَّى واطَّلَى ب
Person. Seriously ill. Desire. طِلًى ج أَطْلَاء
Pleasure, delight. طِلَى
Oil, tar, varnish, fluid pitch. Thickenned juice of grapes. Wine. طِلَاء
Tegument over coagulated blood. طُلَاء
Draught of milk. طُلَّى
Neck, base of the neck. طُلْيَة وطُلَاة ج طُلًى
Lambkin. طَلِيّ ج طُلْيَان
Tartar of the teeth. — وطِلْيَان
Dark (night). Having yellow teeth. طَالٍ
Anointed, smeared, varnished. Tied by the foot. طَلِيّ ومَطْلِيّ
Depressed ground. مِطْلًى ومِطْلَاء ج مَطَالٍ
Dangerously ill. Prisoner for life. مُطْلًى
To overwhelm, to swallow up a. th. (sea). ✲ طَمَّ o طَمًّا وطُمُومًا ﮪ
He has been swallowed up by the sea. طُمَّ بهِ البَحْر
To fill (a vessel) to the brim. To shave (the head, the hair). — ﮪ
To fill up a vessel with earth. — o i طَمًّا ﮪ
To become serious (affair). طَمَّ
To alight on a tree (bird). طَمَّ الشَّجَرة وطَمَّم وتَطَمَّم
To run quickly (man, horse). طَمَّ o طَمًّا وطَمِيمًا

To pass swiftly (gazelle). تَطَلَّق
To be discharged, set free. To start. To be fluent (tongue). To be eloquent. إِنْطَلَق
To be brought away. أُنْطُلِق بِهِ
To be cheerful, glad. إِطَّلَق
To be loosened (bowels). إِسْتَطْلَق
To set (she-camels) free. — ﮦ
Shackle, leather bond. Bowels. Run of a (horse). طَلَق ج أَطْلَاق
Parturition. Eloquence. Amianthus. طَلْق ج أَطْلَاق
Free, set loose. — وطُلُق وطُلْق وطَلِيق
Temperate (night, day). طَلْق م طَلْقَة
Portion. Lawful, allowable. طِلْق
That is allowed to you. هُوَ لكَ طِلْقًا
You are free from suspicion. أَنتَ طِلْق مِنْهُ
To be confined unfettered in a prison. حُبِسَ طَلْقًا وطُلُقًا
طَلْق وطِلْق وطُلُق وطَلِيق الوَجْه
Having a bright, open face.
Generous, bountiful. — م طَلْقَة اليَدَيْن
Speaking fluently, eloquent. — وطِلْق اللِّسَان
Voluble, eloquent, free from impediment (tongue). لِسَان طُلُق وطَلِق وطَلِيق
Divorce. طَلَاق
Brightness of the face. طَلَاقَة وطُلُوقَة الوَجْه
General or absolute acception of a word. إِطْلَاق
Absolutely, generally. على الإطْلَاق او مُطْلَقًا
Departure, removal. إِنْطِلَاق
Repudiated, dismissed (woman). طَالِق ج طُلَّق, وطَالِقَة ج طَوَالِق
Loose, unrestricted, set free. Absolute (sense). General (opinion). مُطْلَق
To even (a cake of bread) before baking it. ✲ طَلَم o طَلْمًا, وطَلَّم ﮦ
Board for expanding dough. طُلْم
Small round cake of bread. طُلْمَة ج طُلَم و✧ طَلَامِيّ
Rolling pin. مِطْلَمَة
To assume a severe mien. ✲ طَلْمَس
✧ To be obscured (mind). — و✧ تَطَلْمَس
Darkness. Desert without طِلْحِسَاء

He mounted his mare from behind. إطَّمر على فرسِهِ
Shabby clothes. Poor, destitute. طِمر ج أطمار
Full-blood horse. طِمرّ وطِمِرّ وطمرِد
Curry-comb, brush. ▫ طُمّار
Lofty place. طمّار
Misfortunes. بنات طمّار
Flea. طامِر
Flea. Unknown (person). طامِر بنُ طامِر
Scroll of paper or papyrus. Volume, tome. طامور وطومار ج طوامير
Builder's string. In rags. مِطمَر ومِطمار
He resembles his father. هو على مِطمار أبيهِ
Underground cellar, magazine. ✧ Buried treasure. مَطمُورة ج مَطامير
To be effaced, to disappear (traces). ✧ To sink into water. ✱ طمَس i o طُمُوسًا، وتطمَّس وانطمَس
To lose its brightness (star, eye). To be remote. طمَس
To look from afar. — بِعَينِهِ
To destroy, to blot out the trace of. — i طمسًا وأطمَس على
To conjecture, to guess. طَمَس i طَماسَة
To disappear altogether. طُمِس
Obliterated. Remote. طامِس ج طوامِس
Blind. طَميس ومَطمُوس
To be cupid of. To covet eagerly (property). To yearn after. ✧ To impose on a. o. ✱ طمِع a طمعًا وطَماعًا وطَماعِيَةً في وب
To be covetous, insatiable. طمُع o طَماعَة
To render a. o. covetous of a. th. أطمَع وه ✧ طمّع ه
✧ To embolden a. o. against a. o. — ه في
Covetousness. Greediness Ambition. طمع وطَماعَة وطَماعِيَة
Thing coveted. Soldiers' pay. طمع ج أطماع
Covetous, ambitious. طامِع وطمِع وطمُع ج طمِعون وطُمَعاء وطَماعَى وأطماع
Most covetous. طمّاع ومِطماع
Thing exciting desire. مَطمَع ج مَطامِع
Incentive. مَطمَعَة
Thing coveted. مَطمُوع فيهِ
To drive (a beast). ✱ طمَل o طملًا ه وه

To attain to the time for being cut (hair). أطمّ واستطمّ
To be covered up. ✧ To be swallowed up, engulfed. إنطمّ
Mass of water. Sea. Great number. طِمّ
Courser, swift horse. — وطِمِيم
Great wealth. الطِّمّ والرِّمّ
Catastrophe. Last judgment. طامَّة
To stammer. ▫ طمطم
Having a bad arabic pronuntiation. ✱ طِمطِم وطِمطِمِيّ وطُمطُمانِيّ
Defect of pronunciation. طُمطُمانِيَّة
High sea. طمطام
Tomatoes. ▫ طُماطِم
To menstruate (woman). ✱ طمَث o وطمِث a طمثًا
Menses Filth, dirt. طمث
To be raised towards (look). ✱ طمَح a طمحًا وطِماحًا وطُموحًا الى
To rise in order to see. — بِبَصَرِهِ الى
To be proud, haughty. — بأنفِهِ
To take, to bring a. th. away. — ب
To be disobedient (woman, beast). To run away with (his rider : horse). — a طِماحًا وطُموحًا على
To raise the feet (horse). طمّح
To raise (the eyes) towards a. th. أطمَح ه الى
Misfortunes. طمحات وطمَحات
Restive. Covetous (look). طَمُوح
Swollen (sea). طَمُوح المَوج
High, lofty. طامِح
Unsubmissive (beast). — ج طوامِح
Covetous, cupid. طمّاح
To leap, to bound. ✱ طمَر i طمرًا وطُمورًا وطِمارًا
To travel. — طُمورًا
To bury, to conceal a. th. beneath (the earth). — طمرًا ه
To become swollen (wound). طمَر o طمرًا
To fill (a ditch). ▫ To curry (a horse). — ه وه
To have the toothache. طمِر
To be swollen (hand). طمِر a طمَرًا
To fold, to roll up a. th. To let down (a curtain). طمّر ه

To ring, to tinkle (metal). To buzz (insect). ✡ طَنطَن
Tinkling. Buzz. Sound of a mandoline. ✧ Fuss, pomp. طَنطَنة
To be ashamed; to remain speechless. ✡ طَنَأ a طَنأً, وطَنِئَ a طَنَأ
To stoop towards a. th. أَطنَأَ الى
Deadly serpent. حَيَّة لا تُطنِئ
Remains of life. Evil propensity. طِنء
To be crook-backed. To be long in the back and weak in the hind-legs (horse). ✡ طَنِبَ a طَنَبًا
To pitch (a tent). To shake (a skin). طَنَّبَ ه
✧ To be proud, self-conceited. طَنَّبَ
To stop in a place. — ب
To have o.'s tent contiguous to another's. طَانَبَ ه
To raise the dust (wind). To extend far away (river). To follow in a file (camels). أَطنَبَ
To be profuse, immoderate in speech. — في الكلام
Rope of a tent. String of a bow. Sinew of the body. Root of a tree. طُنُب ج أَطنَاب وطِنَبَة
Tall (lance, horse). أَطنَب م طَنبَاء
Tent. إِطنَابَة ج أَطانِيب
Profuseness of speech. إِطنَاب
Shoulder. مَطنَب ج مَطَانِب
Numerous (army). مِطنَاب
Prolix, profuse (in speech). مُطنِب
✧ Self-glorifying. مُطَنِّب
Fastened with ropes (tent). مُطَنَّب
Neighbour next to a tent. مُطَانِب
Lute. Kind of mandoline. P طُنبُور وطِنبَار ج طَنَابِير
Classes, species. P طنج — طُنُوج
Copper-pot. ✧ Saucepan. Ts طَنجَرة
To eat to excess. ✡ طَنِخَ a طَنَخًا
To cause indigestion to a. o. طَنَّخَ وأَطنَخَ ه
To scoff at. ✡ طَنَزَ o طَنزًا ب
To mock a. o. طَانَزَ ه
They mocked at one another. تَطَانَزَ
Mocker, scoffer. طَنَّاز
To remain silent, still. ✧ طَنَّش
Women's horn-shaped cap. ✧ طَنطُور
Uvula. ✧ طُنطُلَة

To expand, to flatten (dough). To weave (a mat). To stain a. o. (blood).
To be impregnated with (blood, oil). طُمِلَ وطَمِلَ a طَمَلًا
To erase (writing). أَطمَلَ ه
To join with thieves. إِنطَمَلَ
To be exhausted (water). أُطمِلَ ه
Creatures. الطَّمَل
Thief. Scoundrel. Black garment. Worn out clothes. Necklace. طِمل
Shameless. — ج طُمُول, وطَامِل وطُمُول
Mud. طِمل وطَملَة وطُملَة وطَمَلَة
Stained with blood (arrow). Kid. Mat. Necklace. Mire. طَمِيل
Pond, reservoir. طَمِيلَة
Pastry-cook's roller. مِطمَلَة
To act zealously, cunningly. ✡ طَملَس
Hatred. طَملَسَة
To rest from, to rely upon. ✡ طمن — طَأمَنَ من
To bend down (the back). To still a. th. طَأمَنَ ه
To quiet, to tranquillise. ✧ طَمَّنَ ه
To stoop (man). To be depressed (ground). تَطَأمَنَ
To enjoy tranquillity, quietness. إِطمَأَنَّ
To rest upon, to trust to. — الى
Quietness, tranquillity. إِطمِئنَان وطُمَأنِينَة
Quiet, enjoying rest. طَمِن ج طُمُون, ومُطمَئِنّ
Confident and relying upon a. o. — الى
Flat. depressed (ground). مُتَطَأمِن ومُطمَئِنّ
To run high, to be swollen (sea). To overflow (river). To become tall (plant). To be lofty (thought). ✡ طَمَا o طُمُوًّا وطَمَى i طَميًا
Swollen, overflowing. طَامٍ
Silt, deposit of the Nile. ¤ طَمْي
To ring (silver plate). To buzz (insect). ✧ To tingle (ears). ✡ طَنَّ i طَنِينًا, وطَنَّن
To cause (metal) to tinkle. To cut off (a limb) quickly. أَطَنَّ ه
Tinkle. Buzzing. Ringing. ✧ Tingling of the ears. طَنِين
Resounding. طَنَّان
Renowned poem. قَصِيدَة طَنَّانَة

He has spoken fluently. ✱ طهف — أطْهَف في كَلامِهِ
To give to a. o. a part of o.'s property. أطْهَف لِفُلان طَهْفَة من
Fresh cream. زُبْدَة طَهْفَة
To walk quickly. ◻ To be disgusted. ✱ طَهَق a طَهْقًا
To be stinking (water). ✱ طَهَل وطَهِل a طَهْلًا وطَهَلًا, وتَطَهَّل
Fetid (water). طَهِل وطاهِل
Little provender. Tender vegetable. Remainder. طُهْلَة
Small cloud. طِهْلِئَة
To be big, thick. ✱ طهر — طَهُر
To shun, to avoid a. o. or a. th. — من
To be disgusted with a. o. تَطهَّر عن
To loathe (food). — ه
Brownish colour. طُهْمَة
Complete, perfect, well done. Fat, thin (horse). مُطهَّم
To ramble in a country. ✱ طَهَا o طَهْوًا
To cook, to roast (meat). — a o طَهْوًا وطُهُوًّا وطُهيًا وطَهايَةً ه
To be skilled in an art. أطْهَى
Work. طَهْو
Bit of straw. طاهِي
Cooked food. طُهْي
Cook, roaster, baker. طاهٍ ج طُهاة وطُهِيّ
Female cook. طاهِيَة ج طَواهٍ وطاهِيات
Pellicle on the surface of milk, blood. طُهاوَة
Craft, art of a cook. طِهايَة
To go and come. ✱ طاء o طَوْءًا
To be off, to depart. — a طَوْءًا
To rise (price of goods). تَطاءَ تَطايُؤًا
Hump. طاءَة
To register (a house). To beatify (a saint). ✧ طَوَّب ه وه
Baked brick. ✧ Cannon, artillery. طُوب (un. طُوبَة)
Land-tax. Official survey. Ts طابُو
Stopper. Playing ball. ✧ طابَة
First Coptic month. C طُوبَة
✧ Baker of bricks. طَوَّاب
✧ Artillery-man, gunner. Ts طُوبجي
Arsenal. Ts طُوبخانَة
To threaten ruin. To perish. To go away. To wander. To fall. To miss the aim (arrow). ✱ طاح o طَوْحًا

To be suspicious. ✱ طَنِف a طَنَفًا
To have a depraved heart. — طَنافَة وطُنُوفَة وطَنَفًا
To suspect a. o. To put thorns above (a wall). طَنَّف ه وه
To covet a. th. — نَفْسُهُ الى
How self-possessed he is. ما أطْنَفَهُ
To overtake a. o. تَطنَّف ه
To feel a propensity to. — الى
Projection. Peak of a mountain. Roof. Cornice of a wall. طَنف وطُنف وطَنَف وطُنُف ج طُنُوف وأطْناف
Suspicious. Abstemious. Corrupt. طَنِف
Ascending upon a mountain. مُطنِّف
Carpet. P طِنفِسَة وطَنفَسَة وطُنفُسَة ج طَنافِس
To sell or buy the fruit of a palm-tree. To have a complaint of the lungs, spleen. ✱ طَنِي a طَنًى وأطْنَى
To live in profligacy. — في وأطْنَى
To treat a. o. for the spleen. To cauterize (a camel) in the side. طَنَّى ه
To be prone to suspicion. أطْنَى
Disease of the spleen or lungs. Suspicion. Ashes. طَنًى
Having a complaint of (the spleen or lungs). — وطَنٍ
To be pure, clean; to be chaste, righteous. ✱ طَهَر وطَهُر o طُهْرًا وطُهُورًا وطَهارَةً
To discard a. th. طَهَر a طَهْرًا ه
To purify a. o. or a. th. To circumcise a. o. طَهَّر ه وه
To be purified. تَطهَّر تَطهُّرًا واطَّهَّر اطِّهَّرًا
Cleanliness, purity. طُهْر وطُهْرَة وطَهارَة
Purification. Circumcision. تَطْهِير
Pure, undefiled. ✧ Holy, chaste. طاهِر ج أطْهار, وطَهِر ج طَهِرُون, وطَهِير ج طَهارَى
Purifying. طَهُور
✧ Purgatory. مَطْهَر
Vessel for ablutions. Washing-room. مِطْهَرَة ج مَطاهِر
To enter into (the earth). ✱ طَهَس a طَهْسًا في
I do not know what has become of him. ما أدْرِي أيْنَ طُهِسَ بِهِ
To mar (a work). ✱ طَهَش a طَهْشًا ه

Moon. Brightness of the face after illness. طَوْس
▫ Fuss, noise. طُوسَة
Peacock. Silver. Verdant land. طَاوُوس ج طَوَاوِيس وأَطْوَاس
Finery; showy ornaments. تَطْوِيس وتَطَوُّس
Adorned, decked. Fine. مُطَوَّس
✧ To abash, to stun a. o. To castrate. ✲ طوش – طَوَّش
✧ Disturbance, tumult. Revolution. Heedlessness. طَوْشَة
Eunuch. T طَوَاشِي ج طَوَاشِيَة
To obey a. o. ✲ طَاعَ o a طَوْعًا ل, وأَطَاعَ ه وانْطَاعَ ل
The pasturage is at his disposal. طَاعَ وأَطَاعَ لَهُ المَرْتَع
To render a. o. obedient, submissive. طَوَّعَ ه
To facilitate a. th. to a. o. To incite a. o. to a. th. – ه ل
To agree with a. o. upon. طَاوَعَ ه على او في
To obey willingly. تَطَوَّعَ
To do a. th. willingly. – ب
To devote o.'self to. تَطَاوَعَ ل
To be able to. إِسْتَطَاعَ واسْطَاعَ ه
Obedience, submissiveness. طَاعَة وطَوَاعِيَة وإِطَاعَة
Obedient, submissive. طَاعٍ وطَوْع وطَيِّع وطَائِع ومُطِيع
Manageable (horse). طَوْع العِنَان
Spontaneously, willingly. طَوْعًا
Power, ability of doing a. th. إِسْتِطَاعَة
Obedience. Compliance. Passiveness of a verb. مُطَاوَعَة
Obedient. مِطْوَاع م مِطْوَاء
Obeyed (king, law). مُطَاع
Sordid avarice. شُحّ مُطَاع
Passive (verb). مُطَاوِع
Volunteer (soldier). مُتَطَوِّع ومُطَّوِّع
Horse-tail (plant). ✧ حَشِيشَة الطَّوْع
✲ طَافَ o طَوْفًا وطَوَافًا وطَوَفَانًا حَوْل وب
To walk around a. th. To patrol.
To ramble in a country. – في البِلَاد
To appear to a. o. in sleep (phantom). – بِهِ طَوْفًا
To overflow (river). – طَوْفًا
طَوَّفَ تَطْوِيفًا وتَطَوَّفَ تَطَوُّفًا , وتَطَوَّف واسْتَطَاف

To lead a. o. astray. To strike a. o. with a stick. طَوَّحَ ه
To induce a. o. To engage into a perilous desert. To fling a. th. away. – ب
To cast missiles at a. o. طَاوَحَ ه ب
To cause a. o. to perish. أَطَاحَ ه
To err at random. تَطَوَّحَ
To make a long journey in various countries. تَطَاوَحَت بِهِ النَّوَى
Distant aim. نِيَّة طَوْح
Astray, misled. طَائِح م طَائِحَة
Accidents of fortune. طَوَائِح
Perilous place. مَطَاوِح
To be firm, steadfast. ✲ طَادَ o طَوْدًا
To go through (a country). طَوَّدَ وتَطَوَّدَ في
To rise in the air. إِنْطَاد
Lofty mountain. طَوْد ج أَطْوَاد وطِوَدَة
Dangerous desert. مَطَادَة
Dangerous place. مَطَاوِد
✧ Balloon. مُنْطَاد ج مَنَاطِيد
To approach. ✲ طَارَ o طَوْرًا وطَوَرَانًا ب
Hoop. ▫ Tambourine. ✧ طَار وطَارَة
Manner, way of acting. Kind, class. Limit. Time (repeated action). طَوْر ج أَطْوَار
Men are of various sorts. النَّاس أَطْوَار
One time, once. طَوْرًا
Time after time. طَوْرًا بَعْدَ طَوْر
Now ... then. طَوْرًا.. طَوْرًا
Mountain. Mount Sina. طُور
Equal, correspondant (part). طَوَار
Area, yard of a house. – وطِوَار
Savage, wild. Stranger. طُورِيّ وَطُورَانِيّ
There is nobody in the house. مَا بِالدَّار طُورِيّ
Seven-branched candlestick. ▫ Pick-axe. طُورِيَّة
He has reached the utmost limits. بَلَغ الأَطْوَرَيْن
To recover brightness after illness (face). ✲ طَاسَ o طَوْسًا
To tread a. th. under foot. – ه
I do not know where he is gone to. مَا أَدْرِي أَيْن طَوَّس
To deck herself (woman). To ruffle its feathers (pigeon). تَطَوَّس
Drinking-cup, bowl. طَاس ج طَاسَات

To circuit around a. th. حَوْل وب
To conduct a. o. round (the Caaba). طَوَّف ه
To turn around. To approach. أَطَاف ب
Turn, circuit. Patrol, night-watch. طَوْف
Raft of water-skins. — ج أَطْوَاف
Flood, deluge, typhoon. طُوفَان (un. طُوفَانَة)
Patrol. Night-watch. طَائِف
Diabolical suggestion. طَائِف من الشَّيطان
Portion. Corporation. Nation, rite, family. طَائِفَة ج طَوَائِف
Devoted servant. طَوَّاف م طَوَّافَة
✧ Cork-wood. Float-light.
Place of circuiting. مَطَاف
✲ طَاق o طَوْقًا وطَاقَةً, وأَطَاق ه وعلى To be able of doing a. th.
To put a neck-ring on. طَوَّق ه ه
To impose a difficult task on a. o.
To enable a. o. to do a. th.
To be enabled to do a. th. طُوِّق على
To believe o.'self able to. طَوَّقَت لَهُ نَفْسُهُ
To adorn o.'self with a necklace. تَطَوَّق واطَّوَّق
Arch; vault. P طَاق ج طَاقَات وطِيقَان
Layer, stratum; a single sole.
Ledge of a mountain. — وطَائِق
Power, ability. طَوْق وطَاقَة وإطَاقَة
Necklace. Circle, hoop. طَوْق أَطْوَاق
✧ Collar.
Bunch of odoriferous herbs. طَاقَة
Handful of hair. Grating. ✧ Loop-hole. Window; air-hole.
Cotton under-cap. ✧ طَاقِيَّة
Ring-dove. مُطَوَّق
To last long, to be protracted. ✲ طَال o طُولًا
There is a long time since. As long as. طَالَمَا
To do good, service to. طَال وتَطَوَّل على
To protract, to lengthen, a. th. To expand, to spread. طَوَّل وأَطَال وأَطْوَل ه
To remain long doing. طَوَّل
To weary a. o. with delays. — على
To grant a delay to (a debtor.) طَوَّل ل
To slacken the rein to (a horse).
✧ Take patience. طَوِّل رُوحَك

To procrastinate with a. o. طَاوَل ه في
To put off (the payment of a debt).
To vie with a. o. in greatness or excellence.
To spread, to be lengthened. تَطَاوَل
To trespass upon a. o.'s rights. — على
To treat a. o. arrogantly.
To be long, tall, high. To become long, elongated. إِسْتَطَال
To overcome a. o. — على
To find a. o. late. ✧ إِسْتَطْوَل ه وه
Power. Superiority. Wealth. طَوْل
Length, tallness. Duration. Longitude. طُول ج أَطْوَال
Circles of longitude. خُطُوط او دَوَائِر الطُّول
Forbearance, patience. طُول الرُّوح
Life, life-time. طِيلَة
An aquatic long-legged bird. طُوَل
Tether. طِوَل وطِيَل
Long absence. — وطِيَل وطُوَل
Long time. Life. طِوَل وطِيَل وطُوَال وطِيَال
Arrogance; high-handed proceedings. تَطَاوُل و✧ مُطَاوَلَة
Profit, advantage. Power, wealth. Superiority. طَائِل وطَائِلَة ج طَوَائِل
Enmity, rancour. طَائِلَة
There is no profit in it; it is of no avail. لَا طَائِل فِيهِ
Table, backgammon. Is طَاوِلَة
▫ Trough, manger.
Tall, long. Lasting long. (Poetical) metre. طَوِيل ج طِوَال وطِيَال
Bountiful. Powerful. طَوِيل البَاع
✧ Forbearing, long-minded. طَوِيل الرُّوح
Taller, longer. أَطْوَل ج أَطَاوِل م طُولَى ج طُوَل
Exceedingly tall. طُوَّال وطُوَال
Rein, halter. مِطْوَل ج مَطَاوِل
Oblong. مُتَطَاوِل و✧ طُولَانِيّ
Late, slack, backward. مُطَوَّل
Long, oblong, a metre (in poetry). ✧ Parallelogram. مُسْتَطِيل
To roll up, to fold up, (paper, linen). ✲ طَوَى i طَيًّا ه
He has turned away from me. — كَشْحَهُ عَنِّي
To conceal (an affair). — ه او كَشْحَهُ على

To go through a country, or stages. طوَى البِلاد او المَنازِل
God has closed his life. — الله عُمْرَهُ
May God grant us to meet again. — الله البُعْد لنا
To remain the whole day fasting. — نَهارَهُ صائِمًا
To plaster (a well). — ه بِحِجارةٍ
To remain one day without.... — يَوْمًا عن...
To be folded, rolled up, concealed. طُوِي
To suffer from hunger. طوِي a طوًى, وأطوَى
To coil up (serpent). تَطوَّى
To be folded, rolled, wound. إِنطوَى واطَّوَى
To gather round a. o. إِنطوَى على فُلان
Hunger. Water-skin. طَوًى
A thing folded ; roll. طوًى وطِوًى
Folding. Casing of a well with bricks. Curtailment of a letter (in poetry). طَي
✧ Here enclosed. في طَيِّهِ
Way of folding. Stage, distance. طِيَّة
Intention, design. Conscience. طِيَّة وطَويَّة
طاوٍ وطَاوٍ وطَيَّان م طاوِية وطَوِية وطَيًّا
Hungry.
Thin-bellied. طاوِي البطن والحَشَا
Terrace, flat top of a house. Floor for drying dates. Rock in the sand. طايَة
Frying-pan. Tᴇ طاوا وطُوَّة
Bundle, parcel. Hour of the night. طَوِيّ ج أطواء
Well cased with stones. — وطَوِيَّة
Roll, scroll. Fold. Spiral. مَطوًى ج مَطاوٍ
✧ Penknife.
The folds of the intestines. مَطاوِي الأَمعاء
The coils of a snake. مَطاوِي الحَيَّة
To be good, delightful, pure. ✧ To be in good health. ✡ طاب i طابًا وطِيبًا وطِيبةً وتَطيابًا
He was delighted at it. طابَت نَفسُهُ بِهِ
To be bettered (life). طاب العَيشُ ل
To give up a. th. willingly. — نَفسًا عن
To render a. th. good, agreable. To better a. th. To find a. th. pleasing, sweet. طَيَّب وأطابَ ه

To embalm, to perfume. طَيَّب ه وه
✧ To cure.
To soothe a. o.'s mind. ✧ — خاطِرَهُ
To jest, to sport with a. o. طايَب ه
To have good things. To speak gently, kindly. أطاب
To offer relishes to a. o. — ل
How good it is. ما أطيَبَهُ
To be perfumed, embalmed. تَطيَّب
To find good, agreable, palatable. To seek for good (things). إستطاب واستطيَب ه
To ask a. o. for sweet water. إستطاب ه
Palatable thing. طاب
Odorous. Perfume, fragrant smell. طيب ج أطياب وطُيُوب
Nutmeg. جَوز طِيب
Wine. *Surname* of Medinah. طابَة
✧ Ball.
The choicest of (herbage). Clear (wine). The well of Zemzem. طِيبَة
I have done it willingly. فَعَلتُهُ بِطِيبةٍ
Better, more agreable. The choicest of a. th. أطيَب ج أطايِب
Happiness. طُوبَى ج طُوبَيات
Be happy! Blessed art thou! طُوباكَ وطُوبَى لكَ
Blessed, happy. ✧ Beatified. طُوبانِيّ وطُوباوِيّ
Good, sweet. Perfumed. Perfect (God). Honest. In good health. طَيِّب
North wind. ◻ طَيَاب
✧ Beatification. Beatitude. تَطوِيب ج تَطوِيبات
The choicest things. الأطايِب والمَطايِب
Perfumed, sweet-scented. مُطيَّب
To go astray, to perish. ✡ طاح i طَيحًا
To lose, to destroy a. th. طَيَّح
To perplex, to confound a. o. — ه
To reject, to cast off a. th. — ب
To squander (wealth). أطاح ه
To be scattered. تَطايَح
To defile, to be foul. To be proud. To be frivolous. ✡ طاخ i طَيخًا
To charge a. o. with foul action or speech. — وطَيَّخ ه
To be reviled, disgraced. To be tarred (camel). تَطيَّخ

Ignorance. Pride طَيْخ

To fly (bird). ✡ طار i طَيْرًا وطَيَرَانًا وطَيْرُورَةً ومَطَارًا

To hasten to do a. th. — ب

To go, to fly towards. — الى

His fame has spread far and wide. — لَهُ صِيتٌ في النَّاسِ

His reason fled away. طار عَقْلُهُ

To get out of temper. طار طَائِرُهُ

To let fly (a bird). طَيَّرَ هُ وب وطايَرَ وأَطارَ هُ

To draw a bad omen from. تطيَّر واطَّيَّر ب ومن

✧ To fly in the air (balloon). To explode. تطيَّر

To be shattered. تطايَرَ واستطار

To be cleft. إنطار

To rise (market). To be cracked (wall). To spread (dawn). إستطار

To draw a sword quickly from the scabbard. — هُ

To be started at full speed (horse). To be made to fly (bird). To be astounded. أُستُطِير

Bird; fowl. طَيْر وطائِر ج طُيُور وأَطْيَار

◻ Butterfly. طَيْر الجَنَّة

Kind of small plum. قَلْب الطَّيْر

He remains motionless *lit.* as if he had a bird upon his (head). كأنَّ على رأسِهِ الطَّيْرَ

Sedate man. ساكِن الطَّائِر

Carrier-pigeon. Cygnus (*constell*). Omen. طائِر

Flight of a bird. طَيَرَان

Bad omen, ill-luck Augury. طِيَرَة وطِيْرَة

Levity, unsteadiness. طَيْر وطَيْرَة وطَيْرُورَة

Spirited (horse). ✧ Assay-balance for gold. Tongue of a balance. Pedlar. Volatile (substance). Stream. طَيَّار

✧ Child's kite. طَيَّارَة

Seller of birds. طُيُورِي

Swift running (horse). مُطَار

Large-mouthed (well). Abounding in birds (land). مَطَارَة

Garment figured with birds. Split aloes-wood. مُطَيَّر

Spreading (dust, hoariness). مُسْتَطِير

Launched at full speed (horse). مُسْتَطَار

Swarm of (insects). ✡ طاس — طايس

To be light-headed, fickle. To be bereft of intellect. To miss the target (arrow). ✡ طاش i طَيْشًا

To make (an arrow) to deviate. أطاش هُ

Levity, unsteadiness. طَيْش وطَيْشَان و✧ طِيَاشَة

Light, heedless, unsteady. طائِش وطيَّاش م طائِشَة وطيَّاشَة

To appear (in sleep) phantom. ✡ طاف i طَيْفًا ومَطَافًا

To circuit, to go round about. طَيَّف

Phantom, spectre. Anger. Madness. طَيْف

✧ Solar spectre. — شَمْسِيّ

Going round about. Patrol. طائِف

To fashion, to do a. th. accurately. ✡ طام i طَيْمًا

God has created him good. طامَهُ اللهُ على الخَيْر

To plaster a. th. with clay or mud. ✡ طان i طَيْنًا, وطَيَّنَ هُ

To seal a letter. طان كِتَابًا

God has created him upright. طانَهُ اللهُ على الخَيْر

To be plastered with mud. تَطَيَّن

Mud, clay. طِين وطِينَة

Nile mud, slime. طِينُ إبْلِيز وطين مِصْر

Armenian bole. — الأَرْمَنِيّ

Terra sigillata, Lemnian earth. — المَخْتُوم

Handful of clay, mud. Nature, inborn dispositions. طِينَة

Muddy (place). طَان

Worker in clay; labourer, plasterer with mud. طَيَّان ومُطَيِّن

Hone, whet-stone. طَيُّون

Linula viscosa (plant). طَيُّون

Plastered with clay. مَطِين

ظ

To cry out. To marry. ✱ ظَأَب a ظَأْبًا
To marry a. o.'s sister-in-law. ظَاءَب ه
They have married two sisters. تَزَوَّجَا بِالْمُظَاءَبَة
Married to a. o.'s sister-in-law. Clamour, bustle. ظَأْب ج أَظْؤُب وظُؤُوب
To feel tenderness for. ✱ ظَأَر a ظَأْرًا وظِئَارًا , واظَّأَر على
To inspire a. o. with affection for. — وظَاءَر وأَظْأَر ه على
To nurse an other's child. ظَاءَر ه
To take a nurse for a child. إِظَّأَر ه ل
Fondling a stranger child. Nurse. Foster-father. Column. ظِئْر ج أَظْؤُر وأَظْآر وظُؤُور
Fond of a young stranger. ظَؤُور وظُؤْورَة ومَظْؤُورَة
To marry a. o.'s sister-in-law. ✱ ظَأَم — ظَاءَم ه
To cry out. To marry. ظَأْم
Edge of a sword; point of an arrow. ✱ ظُبَة ج ظُبَات وظُبًى
To suffer from fever. ✱ ظَبْظَب
Clamours, shouts. ظَبْظَاب وظَبَاظِب
Fawn, antelope. ✱ ظَبْي ج ظِبَاء وأَظْبٍ وظُبِيّ وظَبَيَات
She-gazelle. Young maid. ظَبْيَة ج ظِبَاء وظَبَيَات
Abounding in gazelles (land). مَظْبَاة
To sharpen (a stone). ✱ ظَرَّ مَظَرَّةً ه
To slaughter (a beast) with a sharp-edged stone. — ه
To walk upon sharp pebbles. أَظَرَّ
Sharp-edged stone. ظِرّ وظُرَر وظُرَرَة ج ظِرَّان وأَظِرَّة
Spread with sharp pebbles (ground). ظَرِير
Guide-post. ظَرِير ج ظِرَار وأَظِرَّة وظُرَّان
Land full of flint-stones. مَظَرَّة
Silex, flint. مِظَرَّة ج مَظَارّ
To cleave, to stick to. ✱ ظَرِب a ظَرَبًا
To become hard (hoof). ظُرِّب
Projecting stone. Knoll. ظَرِب ج ظِرَاب

Pole-cat. ظَرِبَان ج ظِرْبَى وظَرَابِين وظَرَابِي
They became disunited. فَسَا بَيْنَهُم الظَّرِبَان
To be comely, fine, elegant. To be intelligent, clever. ✱ ظَرُف o ظَرْفًا وظَرَافَة
To embellish, to adorn a. th. ✧ ظَرَّف ه وه
To have fine, gracious children. أَظْرَف
To pretend skilfulness. To pretend beauty, grace. تَظَرَّف وتَظَارَف
✧ To be embellished, adorned. تَظَرَّف
To find a. o. handsome, gracious, elegant. To seek for a. th. gracious, fine. إِسْتَظْرَف ه وه
Vessel. Space of time. Circumstance. Adverb. ✧ Metal coffee-holder. ظَرْف ج ظُرُوف
He is faithful, trustworthy. هُوَ نَقِيّ الظَّرْف
I saw him personnally. رَأَيْتُهُ بِظَرْفِهِ
Beauty, elegance, grace. Wit, sharpness. ظَرْف وظَرَافَة
ظَرِيف ج ظِرَاف وظُرَفَاء وظُرُف وظُرُوف
Fine, graceful. Intelligent, witty. Skilful.
To flow (water). ✱ ظَرَى i ظَرْيًا
To suffer from diarrhea. — بَطْنُهُ
To be sharp, clever. ظَرِي a ظَرًى
Biting, pungent. ظَارٍ م ظَارِيَة
Skilful, clever. ظَرَوْرَى
To be off, to depart. ✱ ظَعَن a ظَعْنًا وظَعَنًا وظُعُونًا ومَظْعَنًا
To leave o's country. — عن الدِّيَار
To make a. o. to journey. أَظْعَن ه
To travel in a litter (woman). إِظَّعَن ه
Rope for fastening a woman's litter. ظِعَان
Camel carrying a litter. ظَعُون ج ظُعُن
ظَعِينَة ج ظَعَائِن وظُعْن وظُعُن وجج أَظْعَان
Litter set on a camel's back. Woman travelling in a litter. وظُعُنَات
To scratch a. o. with the nails. ✱ ظَفَر i ظَفْرًا , وظَفَّر وأَظْفَر ه

ظَفِر a ظَفَرًا To have a pellicle over the eye.
ظُفِر To have the cataract.
ظَفِر واظّفر ه وب وعلى To get posession of.
— ب وعلى To overcome, to gain the mastery over. To conquer.
ظَفّر وأظفر ه ب To render a. o. victorious of.
ظَفّر ه To wish a. o. to be victorious.
إظّفر ه To clutch its prey (hawk).
ظِفر وُظفر وُظفر ج أظفار وأظافير Finger-nail. Clutch, claw, talon, spur.
ظُفر الطِّيب وُظفر العفريت *Unguis odoratus*; odoriferous substance added to incense.
كلّ ذي ظُفر Any clutched or clawed animal.
✧ ظُفر الحَجَر Sard, cornelian (stone).
رَجُل مُقلّم الظُفر Feeble man.
ما بالدّار ظُفر There is nobody in the house.
ظُفر القِط Lion's foot (*plant*).
ظُفر وظَفَرة Disease of the eye. Pellicle growing on the eyes; cataract.
ظَفَر Success, victory.
ظَفِر وظِفّير وظَفِير Successful.
أظفر Long-nailed
مُظفّر ومِظفار Victorious.
☆ ظَلّ a ظَلًّا وظُلولًا To remain. To last (day, night).
ظَلّ يَفعَل To continue doing a. th.
ظَلْتُ وظِلْتُ أفعَل I went on doing.
ظَلّل وأظَلّ ه وه To shade, to give shade over.
ظَلّل ب To brandish (a whip).
أظَلّ To be shady (day). To draw near (affair).
تظلّل ب To be shadowed by, to remain under the protection of.
إستظلّ ب To seek the shade. To shade o.'self with.
— ب ومن To be shaded by.
ظِلّ ج أظلال وظِلال وظُلول Shade, shadow, shelter.
بقيتُ عِندهُ ظِلَّ النّهار I remained with him the whole day.
ظَلَل Water always in the shade.

ظَلّة Abode. Health.
ظُلّة ج ظِلال وظُلَل Awning. Shed. Bench in the shade. Booth. Covering.
ظَلال وظِلال وظِلالة Anything shading. Cloud. Screen.
ظَليل ومُظِلّ Shady (place).
ظِلّ ظَليل Thick umbrage.
ظَليلة ج ظَلائِل Meadow covered with trees.
مِظلّة ومَظلّة ج مَظالّ Large tent. Umbrella. Canopy, screen.
☆ ظَلَع a ظَلَعًا To limp, to halt (beast).
— بهم الأرض The earth would not contain them.
ظَلْع Defect.
قِ على ظَلْعِك Conceal thy defects.
إرْقَ على ظَلْعِك Do thy best.
ظالِع ج ظُلَّع Suspicious.
☆ ظَلَف i نَفْسَهُ ظَلْفًا وظَلِف a ظَلَفًا عن To refrain from.
— ه To hit (a cloven-footed beast) on the hoof.
— ه i ظَلْفًا, وظالف ه To render its track unapparent (beast).
ظالَف ه To follow a. o.'s track.
ظَلِف a ظَلَفًا To be hard (soil). To be painful (life).
— عن To abstain from.
ظالف على To increase.
أظلف To walk upon a stony ground.
ظِلْف ج ظُلوف وأظلاف Cloven hoof. Foot-print.
جاءوا على ظِلْفِهِ They came on his track.
وَجَد ظِلْفَهُ He has found what he desired.
ظَلْف Useless, vain. Lawful.
ذَهَب دَمُهُ ظَلْفًا وظَلَفًا وظَليفًا His blood has not been avenged.
ظَلَف وظَلِف Height unreached by water.
أرض ظَلْفَة وظَلِفَة وظالَفة Hard soil.
أظلوفة ج أظاليف Hard ground.
ظَليف ج ظُلَف وظُلَف Hard (soil). Painful (affair). Wicked, vile (man). Adversity.
ظَلِف وظَليف النّفس Abstaining from indecorous things.
أخذهُ بِظَلْفِهِ وبِظَلِفِهِ وبِظَليفَتِهِ He has taken the whole of it.
☆ ظَلَم i ظَلْمًا وظُلْمًا ومَظْلِمة To misuse

a. th. To act wrongfully. To overflow (river).
To wrong, to harm a. o. To act tyrannically towards. — ه
To deprive a. o. of a right. — ه حقّه
To misplace, to misuse a. th. — ه
To dig the ground in a wrong place. To drink (the milk) of a skin before it thickens. — ه
To be dark, obscure. ظَلِمَ a ظَلَمًا ، وأظلم
To complain of a. o.'s ill-doings. ظلّم ه
To enter upon; to be in darkness. أظلم
How dark it is! How mischievous he is! ما أظلمه
To act wrongly. تظلّم
To trespass upon a o.'s rights. — ه حقّه
To complain of a o.'s wrong-doings. — من
To do wrong one to another. تظالم
To bear injustice. إنظلم واظّلم
Whiteness of the teeth. Snow. ظَلْم
Misuse of a. th. Wickedness, oppression, tyranny. ظُلْم
ظُلْمَة وظُلُمَة ج ظُلَم وظُلَمَات وظُلْمَات وظُلُمَات Obscurity, darkness.
The three last nights of a lunar month. الظُّلَم
The Atlantic Ocean. بحر الظُّلُمات
Wrong, injustice. ظُلامة ومَظْلِمَة ج مظالِم
Unjust, tyrannical. ظالِم ج ظالمون وظُلّام وظَلَمة
Obscurity. ظَلام وظَلْماء
Tyrant, oppressor. ظَلّام وظَلُوم
Vexed, oppressed, wronged. ظَلِيم ومَظْلُوم
Male ostrich. ظَلِيم ج ظِلْمان
Property unjustly ravished. Milk drunk before it coagulates. ظَلِيمة
Dark. Nefarious. Bad (day). Dark green (plant). مُظْلِم
To be thirsty. ✱ ظَمِئَ a ظَمَأً وظَمَاء وظَمَاءة
To desire a. th. earnestly. — الى
To alter a. th. (heat). To jade (a horse). ظمّأ وأظمأ ه
Thirst. Earnest desire. ظِمْء ج أظماء ، وظَمَاء
Life-time. ظِمْء الحياة
ظَمِئ وظامِئ وظَمْآن م ظَمِئة وظامِئة وظَمْأى

Thirsty. Longing for. وظَمْآنة ج ظِماء
Burning with thirst, often thirsty. مِظْماء
Thirsty place. مَظْمَأ
To be brown. ✱ ظَمِيَ a ظَمًى
Brown. Withered. Pining away. أظْمى م ظَمْياء ج ظُمْي
To think, to suppose. To conjecture a. th. ✱ ظَنّ o ظَنًّا ه
To suspect, to think evil of. — وأظنّ واظّنّ ه
To think, to form an opinion. تظنّن وتظنّى
Opinion. Conjecture. Probability. ظَنّ ج ظُنُون وأظانين
Suspicion. ظِنّة ج ظِنَن وظَنائن
Simple, ingenuous. Suspecting much, mistrustful. Well having little water. ظَنُون
Suspected, suspicious. ظَنِين
Mark, indication of a thing or quality. مَظِنّة ج مَظانّ
Probable opinions. مَظْنُونات
Shank, shin-bone. ✱ ظُنْبُوب ج ظَنابِيب
He has facilitated the affair. قرع ظنابيب الأمر
To be obvious, clear. To appear, to come forth. To go out. ◇ To shoot forth (tree). To have relief of the bowels. ✱ ظَهَر a ظُهُورًا
To know (a secret). — على سِرّ
To have the upper hand over. — ظَهْرًا وظُهُورًا ب وعلى
To wound a. o. on the back. — a ظَهْرًا ه
To neglect (an affair). — ب
To have a complaint of the back. ظَهِر a ظَهَرًا
To be strong-backed. ظَهُر o ظَهارة
To enter upon the time of midday. ظهّر وأظهر
To be careless, unmindful of. — وأظهر ه
To help, to back a. o. ظاهر مُظاهرة وظِهارًا ه
To put on two garments. — بين ثوبين
To show, to manifest a. th. To proclaim, to declare. أظهر ه
To render a. o. victorious of. To divulge a secret to a. o. — ه على
To appear. تظاهر

To show a. th. To boast, to تَظَاهَر ب
make a show of.

They backed o. another. تَظَاهَرَ القَوْمُ

To ask succour, help. إِسْتَظْهَر ب

To be ready, disposed to. — ل

To gain mastery over. — على

To prepare (a beast) for — ه وه
riding. To know (a book) by heart.

Back. Upper, ظَهْر ج ظُهُور وأَظْهُر وظُهْرَان
outward part of a. th. Back of a
beast. Deck (of a ship) Litteral
meaning of (a book).

Having a numerous ثَقِيل الظَّهْر
household.

Do not forget my لَا تَجْعَل حَاجَتِي بِظَهْر
business.

He has given boun- أَعْطَى عَن ظَهْر يَد
tifully.

He is on the eve of his هُوَ عَلَى ظَهْر
departure.

He has recited it by قَرَأَهُ مِن ظَهْر قَلْبِهِ
heart.

Rear (of an army). أَقْرَان الظَّهْر

Top of a mountain. ظَهْر الجَبَل

Back of the hand. ظَهْر الكَفّ

◊ He is well backed. لَهُ ظَهْر

◊ He wearied him. كَسَّر ظَهْرَهُ

◊ He lost courage. إِنْقَطَم ظَهْرُهُ

◊ Look out! Out of the way! ظَهْرَك

بَيْن ظَهْرَيْهِم وبَيْن ظَهْرَانَيْهِم وبَيْن أَظْهُرِهِمْ
In their midst, amongst them.

Narrow side of a feather. ظُهْر ج ظُهْرَان

Midday, noontide. ظُهْر ج أَظْهَار

Having a pain in the back. ظَهِر

Help, assistance, backing. ظَهْرَة

Backing, assisting. Family. — وظُهْرَة

Furniture. Family, tribe. ظَاهِرَة

He came جَاءَنَا بِظَهْرِتِهِ وبِظُهْرِتِهِ وبِظَهَرَتِهِ
to us with his family, his followers.

Saddle-camel. ظَهْرِيّ ج ظَهَارِيّ
Neglected.

Auxiliary, protector. Broad- ظَهِير
backed. Having a pain in the back.

Midday, noontide. ظَهِيرَة وظُهْرِيَّة

Party, company. Narrow side ظُهَار
of a feather.

Saddle-cloth, housings. ◊ ظِهَارَة

Outside of (a garment). ظِهَارَة
◊ Carrier's pad.

Apparition, outburst. ظُهُور

◊ Feast of the Epiphany. عِيد الظُّهُور

Declaration, manifestation. إِظْهَار

External, outward. Conspicuous. ظَاهِر
Appearance, outside.

Family, tribe. ظَاهِرَة ج ظَاهِرَات وظَوَاهِر
Prominent eye. Pl Heights, mountains.

Apparently. فِي الظَّاهِر

Outwardly, manifestly. ظَاهِرًا وظَاهِرَةً

He has recited it by heart. قَرَأَهُ ظَاهِرًا

Look out, looking-place. مَظْهَر

Possessing saddle-beasts. مُظْهِر

Coming at the point of — ومُظْهِر
midday.

Big and strong-backed. مُظَهَّر

To repel, to drive ظاف o ظُوف ه
a. o. away.

He grasped أَخَذَهُ بِظُوف رَقَبَتِهِ وبِظَافِهَا
him by the skin of his neck.

Corpse in putrefaction. ظِيَّة

Honey. ظَيّ وظَيَّان

Wild jasmine; virgin's bower. ظَيَّان

Full of wild jasmine (ground). مَظْيَاة

ع

To gurgle (filled bucket). عَبَّ o عَبًّا
To gulp, to swallow water in one draught. — ه و✧ غَبَّ
To rise and swell (sea). — عُبابًا
To be addicted to (wine). تَعَبَّبَ ه
Light of the sun. عَبّ وعَبُ الشَّمْس
Neck of a sleeve. عُبّ ج عِباب ✧Waistcoat-pocket. Arm-pit, breast.
Berries of the common cherry. *Croton villosum.* Alkekengi. عُبَب
The drinking of water without vessel. عَباب و✧ غَبّ
Swollen waves, billows. عُباب
To break out into words. عَبّ عُبابَهُ
Pride, haughtiness. Glorying. عُبِّيَّة
Blood-horse. Rivulet. يَعْبُوب ج يَعابِيب
To fly (army). ✠ عَبْعَبَ
Cloak of camel's hair. Freshness of youth. عَبْعَب
To prepare (perfumes). To set in order (furniture, troops). ✠ عَبَأَ a عَبْأً, وعَبَّأَ ه
He does not care about it. ما يَعْبَأُ بِ
Burden, load. Bag. عِبْء ج أَعْباء
Like, equal. — وعَبْء ج أَعْباء
Hair or woollen striped cloak. عَباء وعَباءَة و✧ عَبايَة ج أَعْبِئَة و✧ عُبِي
Way, road, path. مَعْبَأ
To busy o.'s self about trifles. ✠ عَبِثَ a عَبَثًا
To laugh, to scoff at. — بِ
To prepare a dish made with dried curd. عَبَثَ i عَبْثًا
To mingle, to mix a. th. with. — ه بِ
Sport, play. ✧ To no avail, nonsense. عَبَث
Uselessly, to no avail. عَبَثًا
Dish made of dried curd. عَبِيثَة ج عَبائِث
Rabble. عَبِيثَة النَّاس
To worship, to serve (God). ✠ عَبَدَ o عِبادَةً وعُبُودَةً وعُبُودِيَّةً ه
To enslave; to render submissive. عَبَّدَ وأَعْبَدَ ه

To open (a road). عَبَّدَ ه
To give a slave to a. o. أَعْبَدَ ه ه
To apply to. To devote o.'s self to (the worship of God). تَعَبَّدَ لِ
To enslave, to treat a. o. like a slave. To invite a. o. to God's obedience. — ه
To use, to take a. o. as a slave. إِعْتَبَدَ واسْتَعْبَدَ ه
Man. ⌒ Slave, servant. ✧ Negro. عَبْد ج عَبِيد وعِباد وعُبْدان وأَعْبُد
Heliotrope, turnsol. عَبْد وعَبَّاد الشَّمْس
Kind of melon. ◻ عَبْد اللاوي وعَبْدَلِّي
✧ Actæa, baneberry. حَشِيشَة عَبْد المَسِيح
Slave-born. عَبْد قِنٌّ وقِنٌّ
Strength. Perseverance. عَبَدَة
Relating (*opp. to* رَبَّانِي) to men, to slaves. عَبْدِيّ م عَبْدِيَّة
Servitude, slavery. Devotion, godliness. عَبْدِيَّة وعُبُودَة وعُبُودِيَّة
Old standard coins. دَراهِم عَبْدِيَّة
Tribes of christian Arabs. عِباد
Belonging to a christian tribe. عِبادِيّ
Obedience. Worship, piety, godliness. عِبادَة
Parties of men, animals, going at random. عَبابِيد وعَبادِيد
Enslavement. تَعْبِيد واسْتِعْباد
Piety, godliness, devotion. تَعَبُّد
Worshipper. Pious, godly. عابِد ج عَبَدَة وعُبَّاد وعابِدُون
Place of worship, temple, sanctuary. مَعْبَد ج مَعابِد
Beaten, trodden (road). Honoured. مُعَبَّد
Enslaved, reduced to slavery. — ومُسْتَعْبَد
Worshipped. Idol. مَعْبُود
To elapse (time). To dwindle away (generation). ✠ عَبَرَ o عَبْرًا وعُبُورًا
To cross, to pass over (a river). — ه

Explanation. Style, interpretation of the thoughts. Trope. تَعْبِير
Wayfarer ; passenger. Elapsed (time). عَابِر م عَابِرَة
Weeping man, woman. رَجُل او إمرأة عَابِر
Wayfarer ; passer along. عَابِر سَبِيل
Ewe or goat one year old. عَبُور ج عَبَائِر
Compound perfume. Numerous. عَبِير
مَعْبَر (و ✧ مَعْبُور) ج مَعَابِر ومَعَابِير
Crossing of a river ; ford, passage.
Means of crossing, as bridge, ferry. مِعْبَر و✧ عَبَّارَة
Thick-woolled (sheep). مُعْبَر
Considered. ✧ Regarded. مُعْتَبَر
To look sternly, to frown. ✠ عَبَس i عَبْسًا وعُبُوسًا . وعَبَّس
To contract (the face). — وعَبَّس ه
To assume a stern countenance. To be cross-faced. تَعَبَّس
Dried dirt. عَبَس
Frowning, sternness, of the face. عُبُوس
Stern. Grim-faced. عَابِس وعَبُوس
Looking sternly. عَبَّاس
Lion. العَابِس والعَبَّاس والعَبُوس
Strong lion. عَنْبَس ج عَنَابِس
To better, to arrange a. th. ✠ عَبَش o عَبْشًا ه
Conveniency. عَبْش
To spoil a. th. ✠ عَبَط i عَبْطًا ه وه
To raise (the dust). To befall a. o. (mishap).
To rush into fight. — نَفْسَهُ في الحَرْب
To slaughter (a young and fat beast). To slander a. o. To slay wrongfully. عَبَط واعْتَبَط ه
To dig (a ground) yet untilled. — ه
To forge a lie against. — واعْتَبَط ه على
To ravish a. o. in the bloom of life (death). أَعْبَط واعتبط ه
Mere lie. عَبْط
He is dead in the prime of life. مَاتَ عَبْطَةً
Slaughtered when young (animal). Fresh (blood, meat, saffron). ✧ Foolish. عَبِيط ج عُبُط وعِبَاط
To cling to a. th. (perfume). To remain in (a place). To be greedy of (man). To become impregnated with (place). ✠ عَبِق a عَبَقًا وعَبَاقَةً وعَبَاقِيَةً ب

To read (a book) mentally. عَبَر وعَبَّر ه
To try (money).
To interpret (a dream). — عِبَارَةً وعَبْرًا, وعَبَّر ه
To shed tears. — عَبْرًا وعَبِر a عَبَرًا
To convey a. o. across a river. عَبَّر ه
He expressed his mind. عَبَّر عَمَّا في نَفْسِهِ
To explain a. o.'s mind. — عن فُلَان
The affair has been above his strength, ability. — بِهِ الأَمْرُ
To consider, to ponder over. To watch a. o. or a. th. To take into account. ✧ To show regard, honour to. إعْتَبَر ه وه
To get experience from, to take warning by. — ب
To be astonished at. — من
To shed tears. إسْتَعْبَر
To relate to a. o. (a dream) ; to ask a. o. to explain (a dream). — ه
To weigh (coins). — ه
Shore, bank, margin. عَبْر وعِبْر
Beyond the river. — النَّهر
Trifles, falsehood, vanity. بَنَات عِبْر
Numerous gathering. مَجْلِس عَبْرٌ وعِبْرٌ
Great number, crowd. عُبْر
Heat in the eyes causing tears. — وعَبَر
Sturdy, strong. عِبْر وعُبْر
Fit to every work. — لِكُلّ عَمَل
Bold traveller. Strong to journey (camel). — أَسْفَار
Tears. عَبْرَة ج عَبَرَات وعِبَر
Regard, consideration. Warning, example. عِبْرَة ج عِبَر
Passage, crossing. عُبُور
Explanation of the (meaning of a word). Passage of a book ; phrase. Style. عِبَارَة
That means. هٰذَا عِبَارَة عن
عَبْر م عَبْرَة, وعَبْرَان م عَبْرَى ج عَبَارَى
Shedding tears, tearful.
Hebraic. Hebrew. عِبْرَانِيّ وعِبْرِيّ
The Hebraic language. العِبْرَانِيّ والعِبْرِيّ والعِبْرَانِيَّة
Consideration, reflection. Relation, connection. ✧ Regard shown. إعْتِبَار
Relating, relative. إعْتِبَارِيّ
Relatively to. إعْتِبَارِيًّا

Jasmine. Narcissus.
To reprove a. o. To let (camels) pasture freely. ✡ عَبْهَلَ ه
Pasturing by themselves (cattle). عَبَاهِل
To have a bright, fair complexion. ✡ عَبَا o عَبْوًا
To set in order; to put up (th). — وعَبَّى ه
To set (troops) in order. ✧ To fill (a sack). To thread (a needle). To load (a gun). ✡ عبى — عَبَّى تَعْبِيَة ه
To fill up (a bag). To plant closely. ✧ أعْبَى ه
To be set in order. ✧ To be filled (skin, bag). تَعَبَّى
To help o. a. in preparing a repast (men of two parties). تَعَابَى
Share, portion. ✧ Thick (crops, forest). عَبِيّ
Wide striped garment. عَبَايَة
See عَبَا.
To trouble, to annoy a. o. with questions. ✡ عَتَّ o عَتًّا ه
To importune a. o. by requests. — ه ب
To quarrel with a. o. عَاتَّ ه
To insist upon (a question). To repeat (the same words). تَعَتَّتَ في
Hardness, roughness of language. عَتّ
Moth, tick, mite. ✧ عُتّ
✡ عَتَبَ o i عَتْبًا وعَتَبَانًا وعِتَابًا ومَعْتَبًا ومَعْتِبَة
To be discontented, angry with a. o. ومَعْتِبَة على
To blame, to reprove a. o. — عَتْبًا وعِتَابًا وعِتِّيبَى ه
To limp, to hop. — عَتْبًا وعَتَبَانًا وتَعْتَابًا
I have not trodden upon the threshold of such a one. مَا عَتَبْتُ بَابَ فُلَان
To put a threshold or lintel (to a door). To draw together the tucks of trousers. عَتَّبَ ه
To remonstrate with a. o. on. عَاتَبَ مُعَاتَبَةً وعِتَابًا ه على
To satisfy a. o. أعْتَبَ ه
To go far from. أعْتَبَ عن
To accuse a. o. of a blameworthy action. تَعَتَّبَ على
No blame upon him in respect of anything. لَا يُتَعَتَّبُ بِشَيْءٍ

To spread out (a perfume). ✧ To saturate (a room: smoke, smell). عَبِقَ ه
To be saturated with (atmosphere). ✧ تَعَبَّقَ
To be oppressed (chest). ✧ — وانْعَبَقَ
Effluvium, exhalation. عَبَق
✧ Oppression of the chest. عَبْقَة
Remainder of butter adhering to a skin. عَبِقَة
Sending out a perfume. عَبِق م عَبِقَة
Crafty. Scar on the face. Clever thief. عَبَاقِيَة
✧ Saturated. Heavy (head); oppressed (chest). مُعَبَّق ومَعْبُوق
To gleam and move about (mirage). ✡ عَبْقَرَ
Desert full of genii. عَبْقَر
Gleam of looming. عَبْقَرَة
Beautiful, excellent. Great, strong. Rich carpet. Mere lie. عَبْقَرِيّ
Garments splendidly manufactured. عَبْقَرِيَّة
To mix a. th. with. ✡ عَبَكَ o عَبْكًا ه ب
Morsel, parsel. عَبَكَة
I have tasted nothing at all. مَا ذُقْتُ عَبَكَةً
To strip (a tree) of its leaves. To repel; to hold back; to cut off a. th. ✡ عَبَلَ i عَبْلًا ه
To bring a. th. away. — ب
To be large, thick. عَبِلَ a عَبَلًا وعَبَلَ o وعَبُلَ o عَبَالَة
To become bulky. To become white. To put forth (leaves) not-expanded; to drop its (leaves: tree). أعْبَلَ
Thick, bulky. Tamarisk. عَبْل وعَبِل ج عِبَال
Slender or fallen leaves. عَبَل ج أعْبَال
Mountain with white rocks. Granite. أعْبَل
Broad and long arrow-head. مِعْبَلَة ج مَعَابِل
To be silly and rude. ✡ عَبُمَ o عَبَامَة
Weak, tired. عَبَام
Stupid and rude. عَبَامَاء
To be thick, big. ✡ عَبُنَ o عَبْنًا
Big (hawk). عَبَنّ وعَبَنَّى
Well proportioned; graceful. ✡ عَبْهَر

To remonstrate o. with another. تَعَاتَب
To pursue a right course. إِعْتَتَب
To withdraw from (an affair). — عن ومن
To leave an even road for a rugged one. — ه
To please a. o. To request a favour from. إِسْتَعْتَب ه
Prone to censure. عِتَب
Disagreeable thing. Defect. Hardship. عَتَب وعَتَبَة
Hold of a door. Stair, step of a ladder. عَتَبَة ج عَتَب وعَتَبَات
Ascent of a hill. عُتْبَة
Favour granted. عُتْبَى
Blame, reproof. Complaint, charge. عِتَاب، ومَعْتَبَة ومَعْتِبَة ج مَعَاتِب
Subject of reproof or quarrel. أُعْتُوبَة ج أَعَاتِيب
Mutual reproof. تَعَاتُب
Reproved. Blameworthy. مَعْتُوب
To be at hand, prepared. ✲ عَتُد o عَتَادًا وعَتَادَةً
To provide, to prepare a. th. for the future. عَتَّد وأَعْتَد ه
To perform (a work) carefully. تَعَتَّد في
Implements, apparatus. Wooden drinking bowl. عَتَاد ج أَعْتُد وأَعْتِدَة وعُتُد
Ready for a race (horse). Strong, sturdy. عَتُد وعَتِد
At hand, ready. ✧ Future, to come. عَتِيد
Scent-box. عَتِيدَة
To quiver (lance). To sacrifice (sheep). ✲ عَتَر i عَتْرًا وعَتَرَانًا
To get strong, sturdy. — عَتْرًا
Origin. Slaughtered beast. Species of marjoram. عِتْر
He came back to his natural disposition. عاد الى عِتْرِهِ
Family, relations. Necklace of aromatic beads. Particle of musk. Stock of a tree. عِتْرَة
Strong. Courageous. Wild (place). عَتَّار
Ewe offered in sacrifice to idols. عَتِيرَة
To lay violent hands on, to take away forcibly. ✲ عَتْرَس ه

Hot-tempered. Male ogre. Mishap. عِتْرِيس
To be harsh towards a. o. ✲ عَتْرَف ل
Strong. Dauntless. Wicked. عِتْرِيف وعُتْرُوف
To bend, to fold a. th. ✲ عَتَش i عَتْشًا ه
To pluck (the hair). ✲ عَتَف i عَتْفًا ه
Portion of the night. عِتْف من اللَّيْل
To be freed (slave). ✲ عَتَق i عِتْقًا وعَتَاقَة وعَتَاقًا
To reassume brightness; to thrive. To outrun the others (horse). To be old (wine). To grow old. — عِتْقًا وعَتَق o وعَتُق o عِتَاقَةً
To be binding on a. o. (oath). — على
To render (wine) old. To free (a slave). To set (a prisoner) free. عَتَّق وأَعْتَق ه وه
To start (a horse). To better (flocks). أَعْتَق ه
To dig and case (a well) with stones. — ه
To become old; to be worn out. ✧ تَعَتَّق
Freedom, emancipation. عِتْق وعَتَاق وعَتَاقَة
Oldness, antiquity. عِتْق وعُتْق
Beauty. Excellence. Liberty, freedom. عِتْق
Freed, free. Old man. Young girl. Young bird. عَاتِق ج عَوَاتِق
Old bow. — وعَاتِقَة
Shoulder. — ج عَوَاتِق وعُتُق
Antiquated, old. Excellent. Noble. Freed (slave). Old and good (wine). عَتِيق ج عُتَقَاء
Hunting-vulture. Excellent horse. عَتِيق ج عِتَاق
Old and exquisite (wine, perfume). مُعَتَّق
Antiquities. ✧ مُعَتَّقَات
To attack the enemy. To rush for biting (horse). ✲ عَتَك i عَتْكًا
He rushed for striking him. — عَلَيْهِ يَضْرِبُهُ
To rush upon him for doing mischief. — عَلَيْهِ بِشَرٍّ
To persevere in a design. — بِنِيَّتِهِ
To become sour (wine, milk). To become old (bow). — i عَتْكًا وعُتُوكًا

Slothful, slow. مِعْتام
Obscure, dark ; dull. مُعْتِمٌ ومُعْتِم
To urge a. o. vehemently towards. ✡ عَتَنَ o عَتْنًا ه الى
To importune (a debtor). أَعْتَنَ على
Harsh, pitiless. عاتِنٌ وعَتُون ج عُتُن
✡ عته — عُتِهَ عَتْهًا وعُتْهًا وعُتاهًا وعَتاهَةً وعَتاهِيَةً To become mad, idiotic. To be confused in mind, bewildered.
To addict o.'self to. عُتِهَ في
To annoy a. o. incessantly. — في فُلانٍ
To lose the head. To spend recklessly. To affect refinement in dress. تَعَتَّهَ
To feign ignorance. — عن
Madness, insanity. عَتاهَةٌ وعَتاهِيَةٌ وعُتاهِيَةٌ
Idiot, mad. مَعْتُوه وعَتاهِيَة ومُعَتَّه
To be proud, haughty. To be strong (gale). ✡ عَتا o عُتُوًّا وعِتِيًّا
To assume insolent airs. تَعَتَّى
Insolence, pride. عُتُوٌّ وعُتِيٌّ وعِتِيٌّ
Insolent, haughty. عاتٍ ج عُتاة وعُتِيٌّ
Rebellious, immoderate. عَتِيٌّ ج أَعْتاء
To freat (wool : moth). ✡ عَثَّ o عَثًّا ه
To importune, to vex a. o. — ه
To sing in a trilling way. عَثَّثَ تَعْثِيثًا وعاثَّ مُعاثَّةً وعِثاءً في الغِناء
To pretend a. th. ; to produce pretexts. تَعاثَّ
To deter a. o. from virtue. إِعْتَثَّ ه عِرْقُ سُوءٍ
Snake. عَثّاء
Viper. عِثٌّ ج عِثاث
Moth-worm ; grub. عُثَّةٌ ج عُثٌّ وعُثَث
To drink often by small draughts. ✡ عَثَجَ i عَثْجًا
✡ عَثَرَ o i وعَثِرَ a وعَثُرَ o عَثْرًا وعَثِيرًا وعِثارًا
To stumble, to trip.
To obtain knowledge of (a secret). عَثَرَ o عَثْرًا وعُثُورًا على
Fortune has forsaken him ; he has perished. عَثَرَ جَدُّهُ
To cause a. o. to stumble. To decoy, to debauch, to revile a. o. To render a. o. unhappy عَثَّرَ وأَعْثَرَ ه
To complain of a. o. to. أَعْثَرَ بِفُلانٍ عِند
To make a. th. known to. — ه على
To stumble. To falter (tongue). ✧ To become poor, wicked. تَعَثَّرَ
To be involved in a. th. — في

To stick to a. o. (perfume). — ب
Time, space of time. عَتْك
Noble, generous. Unsteady. Pure, clear, (wine). عاتِك
Old (bow). عاتِكة ج عَواتِك
To draw along ; to pull, to carry a. o. away forcibly. ✡ عَتَلَ o i عَتْلًا ه
To carry a (burden). — ه
To be quick to do evil. عَتِلَ a عَتَلًا الى الشَّرّ
✧ We have shared your anxiety. عَتَلْنا هَمَّك
To exercise the craft of a porter. عَتَّلَ
To remain still in a place. تَعَتَّلَ وانْعَتَلَ
To be pulled, drawn away. إِنْعَتَلَ
I will not make a single step to follow you. لا أَنْعَتِلُ مَعَك ولا أَتَعَتَّلُ مَعَك
Clod of earth. Iron-rod for lifting stones. Carpenter's gimlet. ✧ Crowbar. عَتَلَة ج عَتَل
Prone to evil. عَتِل
Glutton. Rough, wicked. عُتُلّ
Porter. عَتّال ج عَتّالة
Porterage. عِتالة
Hired man ; labourer. عَتِيل ج عُتَلاء وعُتُل
Serious disease. داء عَتِيل
To tarry, to delay a. th. ✡ عَتَمَ i عَتْمًا, وعَتَّمَ ه
To withdraw from (an affair). — وعَتَّمَ عن
He has not been long without acting. ما عَتَمَ أن يَفْعَل
A third of the night is elapsed. عَتَمَ وأَعْتَمَ اللَّيْلُ
To walk, to arrive during the first third of the night. عَتَّمَ وأَعْتَمَ
To be milked at nightfall (flock). عَتَمَ o i عَتْمًا, وأَعْتَمَ وتَعَتَّمَ واسْتَعْتَمَ
Wild olive-tree. عُتْم وعُتُم
Darkness. ✧ عُتْم وعَتْمَة
The first third of the night. Time of nightfall-prayer. Darkness of night. Return of flocks in the evening. عَتَمَة
Tardy, late. عاتِم وعَتُوم
Stars veiled by dust or mist. نُجُوم عاتِمات
Yielding milk in the evening only (she-camel). عَتُوم

عَثْرَة ج عَثَرَات A stumble, a slip, a mistake. Holy war.
حَجَرُ عَثْرَةٍ Stumbling-block.
عَاثِرٌ Stumbling, staggering.
عَثُورٌ Wont to stumble.
عَاثُور ج عَوَاثِر Place of perdition. Pit for wild beasts. Snare.
— وعِثَار Distress, difficulty.
عَثَرِيّ Careless, unmindful of the world.
عِثْيَر Dust, earth.
— وعَثْيَر وعَيْثَر Obscure trace.
✧ مُعَثَّر Wretched, corrupt. Destitute.
✱ عَثْكَل — تَعَثْكَل To be loaded with bunches (vine, palm-tree).
عِثْكَال وعُثْكُول وعُثْكُولَة ج عَثَاكِيل Bough loaded with clusters.
✱ عَثِل a عَثَلًا To be abundant. To be thick, bulky.
عَثِل وعَثْل Plentiful. Thick, bulky.
عَثُول ج عُثُل Foolish, stupid.
عِثْيَل Male hyena.
✱ عَثَم o عَثْمًا To be imperfectly set (broken bone). To become callous (wound).
— ه To set (a bone) imperfectly.
— واعْتَثَم ه To stitch (clothes).
إِعْتَثَم ب To seek help from.
عُثْمَان Young of bustard, of snake.
أَبُو عُثْمَان Serpent.
عُثْمَانِيّ Ottoman.
Ts عُثْمَانْلِيّ Turkish horseman.
الدَّوْلَة العُثْمَانِيَّة The Ottoman Empire.
✱ عَثَن o عَثْنًا وعُثَانًا وعُثُونًا , وعَثَّن To smoke (fire).
عَثَن فِي To ascend (a hill).
عَثِن a عَثَنًا To smell smoke. To be perfumed.
عَثَّن ه To fumigate. To perfume a. th.
— على ، To excite evil amongst.
تَعَثَّن To be perfumed, fumigated.
عَثَن , وعُثَان ج عَوَاثِن Smoke.
— ج أَعْثَان , وعِثَن Small idol.
عِثْن Manager of property.
عَثِن Infected with smoke (food).
✱ عُثْنُون ج عَثَانِين Long beard. Length of the beard.
✱ عَثَا o عُثُوًّا وعَثَا a i وعَثِي a عُثِيًّا وعَثَيَانًا To perpetrate crimes.
عِثْوَة ج عُثًى Plait of hair. *Pl.* Plants.

عَاثٍ ج عُثَاة وعُثِيّ Rascal, mischief-maker.
✱ عَجَّ a i عَجًّا وعَجِيجًا To cry out, to raise the voice. To grumble; to bellow (bull). To rumble (thunder).
— وأَعَجَّ To raise the dust (wind).
عَجَّج ه من الدُّخان To fill (a house) with smoke.
تَعَجَّج من الدُّخان To be filled with smoke.
عَجّ وعَجِيج Cry, clamour; bellow, groan.
✧ عُجَّة Omelet, egg-fritter.
عَجَاج Dust, smoke. Foolish. Low people.
عَجَاجَة Dust. Troop of camels.
لَفَّ عَجَاجَتَهُ عَلَيْهِم He made a raid against them.
لَبَّدَ عَجَاجَتَهُ He gave up his work.
عَجَّاج Boisterous, clamorous.
عَجْعَج To utter a cry, to vociferate.
عَجْعَاج Vociferous, clamorous.
عَجْعَجَة Clamour, confused noise.
✱ عَجِب a عَجَبًا من او ل To wonder at.
عَجَّب وأَعْجَب ه To excite wonder to.
أُعْجِب ب To admire, to be pleased with.
أُعْجِب بِنَفْسِهِ To be self-admirer.
مَا أَعْجَبَهُ بِرَأْيِهِ How conceited he is in his judgment.
تَعَجَّب واسْتَعْجَب من To admire, to wonder at.
عَجْب ج عُجُوب Rump, root of the tail.
عُجْب ج أَعْجَاب Pride, self-admiration.
عَجَب ج أَعْجَاب Wonder, astonishment.
عَجَب عُجَاب Astoundment.
— وعُجَاب وعُجَّاب وعَجِيب Wonderful, extraordinary.
عَجِيبَة ج عَجَائِب Wonder, miracle.
أُعْجُوبَة ج أَعَاجِيب Miracle.
أَعْجَب More wonderful.
تَعَجُّب Astonishment. Admiration.
مُعْجِب Charming, admirable.
مُعْجَب بِنَفْسِهِ Self-admiring.
✱ عَجَد وعُجْد A grape.
عَنْجَد وعُنْجَد وعُنْجُد Raisin, currant.
عَجَدَة ج عَجَد Raven.
✱ عَجَر i عَجْرًا على To importune a. o. To prohibit a. o. (judge).

To assault a. o. with (a sword). عجر على فُلَان ب
To bend the (neck). — ه
To start quickly. — عَجْرًا وعَجَرَانًا, وعاجَر
To be thick, bulky. To be knotted (wood). عَجِر a عَجَرًا
To be wrinkled from fatness (belly). تَعَجَّر
To veil her head (woman). إعتجر
Protuberance, projection. عَجَر
Species of cucumber. عَجُور
Knot in wood. Knob, vice. عُجْرَة ج عُجَر
His external and hidden defects. عُجَرُهُ وبُجَرُهُ
✧ Pumpkin. عَجُّور
Fat, thick. Knotted. Filled. ✧ Sour, unripe (fruit). أعجر م عجراء ج عُجر
Woman's veil. مِعْجَر
To strip a. o. naked. ✱ عَجْرَد ه
To be naked. تَعَجْرَد
Naked. مُعَجْرِد ومُتَعَجْرِد
Streak on the sand. ✱ عُجْرُوز ج عَجَارِيز
To be awkward, rude to. To show pride towards. ✱ عجرف — تَعَجْرَف على
Roughness in speech, behaviour. Self-magnification. Rashness. عَجْرَفَة
Rest-harrow (*plant*). عُجْرُم وعِجْرِم
To become old (woman). ✱ عَجَز o وعَجُز عُجُوزًا, وعَجَّز
◻ To be deficient (account). عَجِز
To be unable to. To lack strength for. عَجَز i وعَجِز a عَجْزًا ومَعْجِزًا ومَعْجَزَة ومَعْجِزَة وعَجَزَانًا وعُجُوزًا عن
To refrain from. To find, to judge a. o. weak. ✧ To weary, to trouble, to baffle. عَجَّز وأعجز ه
To lean towards. عاجَز الى
To weaken, to disable a. o. أعجز ه
He was unable to obtain the thing. أعجزه الشيء
To be wonderfully eloquent. أعجز بالفصاحة
Inability, impotence. Hilt of a sword. ◻ Deficit. عَجْز
Hinder part of the body, buttocks. Last word of a verse. — وعُجْز وعَجُز ج أعجاز
He is the last child of his father. هو عِجْزَة أبيه

Ornament of a sword-hilt. عِجاز وعِجازة
Impotent, disabled. عاجز ج عَوَاجِز
Old woman. عَجُوز ج عُجُز وعَجَائِز
Seven days in the latter part of winter. أيّام العَجُوز
Having large posteriors. أعجز م عجزاء
Eloquence of a discourse. إعجاز
Always backward; impotent. Road. مِعْجاز
Wonder, miracle. مُعْجِزَة ج مُعْجِزات
Importuned by requests. مَعْجُوز
To withhold a. o. from. ✱ عَجَس i عَجْسًا ه عن
To procrastinate. تَعَجَّس
To follow, to pursue (a business). — ه
To detain a. o. — ب
Middle part of a. th. عَجْس
Handle of a bow. — وعِجْس
✱ عَجَف o عُجُوفًا, وعَجِف i عَجْفًا وعُجُوفًا
To abstain from food. وعَجَّف نفسه عن الطعام
To nurse patiently (the sick). To bear a. o. — نفسه وأعجف بنفسه على
To emaciate (a beast). عَجَف o i وأعجف ه
To become lean (animal). عَجِف a وعَجُف o عَجَفًا
To eat little by reason of dearth. عَجَّف
To possess emaciated cattle. أعجف
Leanness. عَجَف
Colocynth. عِجاف
Emaciated. عَجِف (*m. f.*), وأعجف م عجفاء ج عِجاف
Dry, lean. Contracted in body. عَنْجَف وعُنْجُف
To perplex, to inconvenience a. o. ✧ عَجَّق ه
To intricate, to confuse a. th. عَجَّق ه
Press, hindrance. ✧ عَجْقَة
To make speed, haste. ✱ عَجِل a عَجَلًا وعَجَلَة, وعَجَّل وتعجّل
To forward a. th. speedily to. عَجِل ب . . . الى
To outgo, to precede a. o. To urge, to press a. o. عَجَّل وأعجل واستعجل ه
To have a. th. done speedily. عَجَّل ه
To offer to a. o. food hastily prepared. عَجَّل ل

Barbarian. Any people foreign to Arabs.
Date-stone. عَجَم وعُجام
Palm-tree. عَجَمَة وعَجَمَــة ج عَجَمَات
Rock.
Defective speaking in Arabic. عُجْمَة
Foreign origin of an Arabic word.
Large bat. Swallow. عَجَّام
Speaking أعْجَم ج أعْجَمُون وأعَاجِم Arabic incorrectly. Foreigner.
Speechless animal, عَجْمَاء ج عَجْمَاوَات brute. Tract of sand without trees.
Mute. Silent (waves). (s. pl.) أعْجَم
Foreign to the Arabs. عَجَمِيّ وأعْجَمِيّ
✧ Persian.
Dotted (writing). Obscure مُعْجَم (speech). Locked (door).
The letters of the حُرُوف المُعْجَم alphabet.
To knead ✱ عَجَن o i عَجْنًا, واعْتَجَن ه (flour). To press into a mass.
To lean for rising. عَجَّن
To lean on a (stick). — على
To be kneaded (flour). تَعَجَّن وانْعَجَن
Dough-paste. عَجِين ج عُجُن
Piece of dough. Crowd. عَجِينَة
Kneader; عَاجِن وعَجَّان م عَاجِنَة وعَجَّانَة kneading dough.
Leaning for rising. عَاجِن
Perinœum. عِجَان
Fool, silly. عَجَّان
The middle of a. th. عَاجِنَة الشيء
Very fat (she-camel). عَجَنَاء
Kneading-trough. مِعْجَن ومِعْجَنَة ج مَعَاجِن
Various dishes made with flour. مُعَجَّنَات
Electuary, inspissated مَعْجُون ج مَعَاجِين juice. Unguent. Hashish paste.
To saw discord ✱ عجه — عَجَّه بَيْن between.
To be entangled (business). تَعَجَّه
Servant. Bride- ✱ عُجَاهِن ج عَجَاهِنَة groom. Cook. Hedge-hog.
To put out (a ✱ عَجَا o عَجْوًا, وعَاجَى ه child) to nurse.
To groan (camel). عَجَا o عُجُوًّا
To grin (face). عَجَا وعَجَّى ه
Date-paste; stuffed عُجَاوَة وعَجْوَة وعَجَايَة dates.
Fruit-stone. ✧ Dates in lump. عَجْوَة

He punished, he عَاجَل بِذَنْبِهِ او بِضَرْبَتِهِ struck him without respite.
To urge, to preclude أعْجَل ه عن a. o. from.
To accelerate (an تَعَجَّل واسْتَعْجَل في affair).
To despatch (business). تَعَجَّل ه
Haste, hurry, عَجَل وعَجَلَة واسْتِعْجَال readiness.
Calf. عِجْل ج عُجُول وعِجَال وعِجْلَة
Heifer. عِجْلَة ج عِجَل وعِجَال
Thing hastily done. عَجَلَة وعُجْلَة وعُجَالَة Food hastily prepared. Clay.
Cart, car. عَجَلَة ج عَجَل وعِجَال وأعْجَال Wheel, pulley. Kind of ladder.
Transitory. (opp. to آجِل) العَاجِل Ready, present.
Hasty, expeditious. عَاجِل وعَجِل وعَجُل
عَجْلَان م عَجْلَى ج عَجَالَى , وعَجُول ج عُجُــل.
Speedy, diligent. وعَجِيل ج عِجَال
Bereft of her عَجُول ج عُجُل وعَجَائِل child (mother); of her young (she-camel).
Premature death. العَجُول
Speedy walk. عُجَيْلَة وعَجِيلَى
More expeditious, quicker. أعْجَل
Urging. مُعَجِّل ومُعْجِل ومِعْجَال ج مَعَاجِيل Precocious (palm-tree).
Premature (fruit). مُعَجَّل
Hastened, hurried. مُعَجَّل
Plant for fattening women. مُسْتَعْجِلَة
To chew. To ✱ عَجَم o عَجْمًا وعُجُومًا ه bite a. th. for trying it. To test (a sword).
To try a. o. — وعَاجَم ه
My eyes have not مَا عَجَمَتْهُ عَيْنِيّ مُنْذ beheld him since.
He has tried, proved him. عَجَم عُودَهُ
To dot (a عَجَم o عَجْمًا, وعَجَّم وأعْجَم ه writing).
To speak Arabic incor- أعْجَم الكَلَام rectly.
To be obscure, إنْعَجَم واسْتَعْجَم على abstruse (language).
To be unable to answer. إسْتَعْجَم
To mutter. To be impeded in — ه reading.
Persia. العَجَم وبِلَاد العَجَم
Persian people. عُجْم وعَجَم ج أعْجَام

Time, season. Beginning or best time of. عِدَّان

Calculation, account, census. تَعْدَاد وتَعْدِيد

Readiness. Ability, aptitude. إِسْتِعْدَاد

Number, numerous. Reckoned amongst. Equal, like. عَدِيد

Portion, lot. عَدِيدَة ج عَدَائِد

Computed days. أَيَّام عَدِيدَة

Ready to set off. مُعِدّ

Ready, prepared. مُعَدّ

Female mourner. مُعَدِّدَة

Prepared, ready. Able. مُسْتَعِدّ

Fine sand. ✡ عدب – عَذَاب

Heap of sand. عَدُوب

To be bold. ✧ To dig with a pickaxe. ✡ عَدَر o عَدْرًا

To be well watered (place). عَدِر a عَدَرًا, واعتَدَر

Abundant rain. عَدْر وعُدْر

✧ Pickaxe, mattock. مَعْدُور

To serve a. o. ✡ عَدَس i عَدْسًا ه وهـ

To toil. To tend (a flock). To tread a. th.

– عَدْسًا وعَدَسَانًا وعِدَاسًا وعُدُوسًا في الأَرْض

To journey.

To have red pimples. عُدِس

Lentils. عَدَس

Orobanche, broom-rape (*plant*). أَسَد العَدَس

A lentil grain. Red pimple; small pustule. ✧ Lens. Concrete of pebbles and cement. عَدَسَة

Lenticular. عَدَسِيّ

Aromatized soup of lentils. Bat's dung used as a medicine. عَدَسِيَّة

To eat little. ✡ عَدَف i عَدْفًا, وتَعَدَّف

Small quantity of fodder. عَدْف وعَدَف وعُدَاف, وعَدُوف ج عُدُف

I have not tasted the least thing. مَا ذُقْتُ عَدْفًا او عَدَفًا او عُدَافًا

Portion of the night. Company of ten to fifty men. عِدْف

Bit of straw in the eye. عَدَف

Portion. Party of men. Gathering. عِدْفَة ج عِدَف

Root of a tree. – وعَدَفَة ج عَدَف

✡ عَدَق i عَدْقًا وعَدِق a عَدَقًا وعَدَّق بِظَنِّهِ

To conjecture.

Milk for suckling an orphan. عُجْوَة وعُجَاوَة وعِجَايَة

Child fed by a foster-mother. Orphan. عَجِيّ وعُجِيّ م عَجِيَّة وعُجِيَّة ج عَجَايَا

Sinew of the hands, feet. عَجَايَة ج عُجًى وعَجَايَا

To reckon, to count, to number. To make the census of. ✡ عَدّ o عَدًّا, وعَدَّد ه

To believe, to think a. o. to be such. – ه وه ه

I thought he was sincere. عَدَدْتُهُ صَادِقًا

To eulogise (a dead person). عَدَّد ه

To prepare, to dispose a. th. for. عَدَّد وأَعَدّ ه ل

To draw lots; to share a. th. with. عَادّ مُعَادَّة وعِدَادًا ه

The pain of the sting was felt anew after one year. عَادَّتْهُ اللَّسْعَة

To be prepared, disposed. تَعَدَّد

To multiply, to increase. – وتَعَادّ

To exceed the number of. – وتَعَادّ على

To be reckoned. To be prepared. To rely upon ✧ To be self-conceited, haughty. إِعْتَدّ

That is not to be taken into account. هٰذَا شَيْءٌ لَا يُعْتَدُّ بِهِ

To prepare, to be ready to. إِسْتَعَدّ ل

Number, quantity. عَدَد ج أَعْدَاد

Age of man. – الإِنْسَان

Computation; number. Census. Fit of madness. عِدَاد

He belongs to such a tribe. هوَ في عِدَاد بَنِي فُلَان

Pain of a sting felt anew after one year. عِدَاد وعِدَّد

Great number, abundance. Spring; well-water. Equal. match. عِدّ ج أَعْدَاد

Number; a certain number, many. Legal period of retirement assigned to a widow or divorced woman before she may marry again. عِدَّة ج عِدَد

Pustules on a beautiful face. عُدّ وعُدَّة

Apparatus; provision Military equipment; supplies, implements. ✧ Set of tools. Horse's saddle, harness. عُدَّة ج عُدَد

Be ready. كُونُوا على عُدَّةٍ

عَدَق وعَدِق وأعدَق يَدَهُ To plunge the hand into (a basin) for searching.

عَادِق الرَّأي Acting at hap-hazard, at random.

عَدَقَة ج عَدَق Grapnel, harpoon.

عَوذَق وعَوذَقَة ج عُدُق Grapnel.

✡ عَدَكَ o عَدكًا ه To beat (wool) with a mallet.

✡ عَدَل i عَدلًا وعَدَالَةً وعُدُولَةً ومَعْدِلَةً To act equitably.

— عَدلًا ه To straighten.

— ه بِغَيرِهِ To treat a. o. equally with.

— عَدلًا وعُدُولًا عن To turn aside from.

— عُدُولًا الى To come back to.

— ه To equal, to be like to.

— وعَادَل ه في المَحْمَل To counterbalance a. o. in a litter.

عَدُل o عَدَالَةً To be straightforward, upright.

عَدَّل وأعدَل ه To make straight, equal, right. To equilibrate, to counterpoise a. th.

عَدَّل ه To direct a. o. in the right course. To judge, to declare (a witness) to be trustworthy.

— الحُكمَ To redress a sentence.

— المِيزَان To equilibrate the two scales of a balance.

عَادَل مُعَادَلَةً وعِدَالًا ه وه To be like, equal to. To counterpoise.

— بَينَ To arrange, to adjust two things.

عَادَل بَين أمرَينِ عِدَالًا To hesitate between two affairs.

إنعَدَل عن To deviate, to stray from.

إعتَدَل To be equiponderant. To be moderate, temperate. To be symmetrical, proportionate.

— و✧ استَعدَل ✧ To be lusty, stout.

عَدل Justice, equity. Justness. Accuracy. Derivation (of a word).

— Upright, just, (*m. f. s. pl*). straightforward.

— ج أعدَال Like, equal, intermediate; average. Requital. Ransom.

عِدل ج أعدَال وعُدُول Like, equal (in weight, size, value). Half a load.

— ر✧ عَدِيلَة Bundle, bag, sack.

عَدَل Counterbalance of two bags.

عَدلَة وعُدلَة Trustworthy, veracious (witness).

عَدَالَة Justice, equity.

إعتِدَال Uniformity. Equilibrium. Temperateness of weather. Symmetry, proportion. Equinox. Tropic.

الإعتِدَال الرَّبِيعِي Vernal equinox.

إعتِدَالِي Equinoctial.

تَعدِيل Equalisation; equivalence, equal division. Levelling. ✧ Average.

عَدِل, وعَادِل ج عُدُول Just, upright.

عَدِيل ج عُدَلَاء Equivalent, equiponderant. ✧ Brother in law.

العَدِيلَان ✧ The two husbands of two sisters.

العَدِيلَتَان The two burdens of a beast. Saddle-bags.

مُعَدِّل النَّهَار Equator.

مُعَادِل Equal, average.

مُعَادَلَة Proportion, symmetry, equilibrium.

مَعدِل ومَعدُول Outlet. Manner of acting.

مَعدُول Redressed. Derivate (word).

مُعَدَّل ومُعتَدِل Proportionate, symmetrical; counterpoised.

مُعتَدِل Temperate, moderate. ✧ Stout.

مُعَدَّلَات البَيت The corners of a house.

✧ مُستَعدِل In good health, lusty.

✡ عَدِم a عُدمًا وعَدَمًا To be wanted, lost. To exist not. To be deficient.

عَدُمَ عَدَامَةً To be foolish, destitute of intellect.

— ه To lack, to miss a. th.

أعدَمَ ه To be lacking to a. o. ✧ To put to death.

— ه ه To deprive a. o. of a. th.

— إعدَامًا وعُدمًا To render a. o. destitute (God).

✧ إنعَدَم To come to nought. To be lost, annihilated.

عَدَم وعُدم وعُدُم Nought, non-existence, loss, lack. Total absence.

عَدِيم ج عُدَمَاء, وعَدِم ومُعدِم Poor, destitute.

✧ عَدِيم الـ... Deprived, bereft of; without.

✧ عَدِيم الشَّبِيه والنَّظِير Pairless, without equal.

To exceed the bounds. أَعْدَى فِي
To trespass, to transgress. To be or become transitive (verb). تَعَدَّى
To pass towards. تَعَدَّى الى
To encroach upon the rights of. — على
To receive (a dowry) from a wife. — ه
To be at enmity. To spread a contagious disease. To race on foot. To be remote; to go off. To be uneven (ground). تَعَادَى
To show hostility to. إِعْتَدَى على
To implore the protection of a. o. against. إِسْتَعْدَى ه على
To make (a horse) to run. — ه
Heat, run. عَدْو
Like, similar. Heat. عَدَاء وعِدَاء
Tombstone. Stone covering of a well. عِدْو وعِدَاء وعِدَى
Side, shore, country. عِدًى وعَدًى ج أَعْدَاء
Hostile party. قَوْم عِدًى وعُدًى
Enmity. hostility. عَدَاوَة
Injustice, oppression. — وعُدْوَى وعُدْوَان
Save, except (*adv*). عَدَا ومَا عَدَا
Complaint deferred to a judge. Contagious disease. عَدْوَى
Alike, equal. عُدْوَة وعِدْوَة
Elevated spot. Margin, brink (of a river). — وعِدْوَة ج عِدَاء
Barren soil. Unevenness of a saddle, seat. Remoteness. Hindrance. عُدَوَاء
I came on riding uncomfortably. جِئْتُ على مَرْكَبٍ ذِي عُدَوَاء
Hardship. عُدَوَاء الشُّغْل
Swift-running. عَدَوَان
Runner. عَدَّاء
Troops beginning the attack. *Name of an Arab tribe.* عَدِيّ
Foe, enemy. عَدُوّ م عَدُوَّة ج أَعْدَاء وأَعَادٍ
The greatest foe. أَعْدَى عَدُوّ
Running. Enemy. عَادٍ ج عُدَاة
The lion. العَادِي
Sides of (a tablet). عَادِيَان
Hostile party. Distance. Hinderance. Injustice. عَادِيَة ج عَوَادٍ
The changes of time, its hardships. عَوَادِي الدَّهْر
Trespass, transgression, offence. تَعَدٍّ واعْتِدَاء

The things preserved, and the lost ones. السَّالِم والعَادِم
Lost, annihilated. مَعْدُوم
✲ عَدَن o i عَدْنًا وعُدُونًا ب وه To abide, to stay in (a place).
To manure (a land). To pull out (a rock). — عَدْنًا ه
To manure (a land). To dig (the ground). To work (a mine). عَدَّن ه
Aden in Yemen. عَدَن
Sojourn. Eden. عَدْن
Paradise; gardens of eternal abode. جَنَّات عَدْن
Keeping to the same pasturage (camel). عَادِن ج عَوَادِن
Shore of the sea. Bank of a river. Space of seven years. عَدَان
Numerous party. عَدَانَة ج عَدَانَات
Patch on a leathern bucket. — وعَدِينَة ج عَدَائِن
Mine, ore. Metal, mineral. Native place, place of production. ¤ Excellent. مَعْدِن ج مَعَادِن
Metallic (substance), metal. Mineral (kingdom); mineralogical. مَعْدَنِيّ
Pickaxe. مِعْدَن
Miner, worker of a mine. مُعَدِّن
✲ عَدَا o عَدْوًا وعَدَوَانًا وتَعْدَاءً وعَدًا To run.
To turn a. th. away, a. o. from. — عَدْوًا وعُدْوَانًا ه عن
To transgress, to trespass upon. To neglect a. th. — ه وعن
To run, to rush on. — على
To act wrongfully towards. — عَدْوًا وعُدُوًّا وعَدَاءً وعِدْوَانًا وعُدْوَى على
To be hostile to. عَدِي a عَدًا ل
To make a. o. to cross, to pass. To render (a verb) transitive. ✧ To cross (a river). عَدَّى ه وه
To deter a. o. from. — ه عن
Do not mind him. عَدِّ عَنْهُ
To treat a. o. as an enemy. عَادَى مُعَادَاةً وعِدَاءً ه
To hit successively two animals of the chase. — بَيْن صَيْدَيْن
To start (a horse). أَعْدَى ه
To infect a. o. with (disease). — ه من
To act wrongfully towards. — على
To help, to assist a. o. against. — ه على

تَعْدِيَة Use of a verb in a transitive sense. Transitiveness of a verb.
التَّعَادِي Rugged, uneven places.
مُعْدٍ Contagious (disease).
مَعْدًى Passage ; shelter.
مَعْدُوّ عَلَيْهِ ومَعْدِيّ عَلَيْهِ Oppressed.
مُتَعَدٍّ Transitive (verb).
مُتَعَدٍّ ومُعْتَدٍ على Unjust : tyrannical.
مَعْدِيَّة ج مَعَادِي ¤ Ferry-boat.
مُتَعَادٍ Uneven : stony (ground).
✱ عَذَبَ i عَذْبًا To abstain from eating, through excess of thirst.
— وأَعْذَبَ واسْتَعْذَبَ عن To neglect (a business).
عَذَبَ i وعَذَّبَ وأَعْذَبَ ه عن To hinder a. o. from.
عَذُبَ o عُذُوبَة To be sweet, palatable.
عَذِبَ a عَذَبًا To be overspread with green moss (water).
عَذَّبَ ه To chastise, to torment, to torture a. o.
أَعْذَبَ To have, to find sweet water.
— ه To clean a (water-pond).
أَعْذِبْ نَفْسَكَ عن To get rid of.
✧ تَعَذَّبَ To be punished. To suffer.
إِعْتَذَبَ To hang down the ends of a turban.
إِسْتَعْذَبَ To draw sweet water.
— ل To give sweet water to a. o.
— ه To find a. th. sweet, palatable.
عَذْب ج عِذَاب Palatable.
عَذَب وعَذَبَة Motes, particles. Tree-branch. Rag used by women-mourners. Ends of a turban.
عَذِب Covered with motes, green moss (water).
عَذْبَة وعَذِبَة وعَذَبَة ج عَذَبَات Green moss, duckweed.
عَذَبَة ج عَذَبَات Tip of the tongue. Strap of (a whip), string of (a balance). End of a turban.
عَذَاب ج أَعْذِبَة Chastisement. Pain, supplice.
عَاذِب وعَذُوب Abstaining from eating through excessive thirst.
عُذُوبَة Sweetness of water.
أَعْذَب More palatable (water).
✱ عَذَرَ i عُذْرًا وعُذُرًا ومَعْذِرَة, وأَعْذَرَ ه في وعلى To excuse ; to free a. o. from blame.

عَذَرَ عَذْرًا ه To circumcise (a child).
— o i عَذْرًا وعُذْرًا ه ب To bridle (a horse).
عُذِرَ To have a complaint of the throat (child).
عَذَّرَ وعَاذَرَ To allege bad excuses.
عَذَّرَ To grow on the cheeks (of a boy : down).
— ه To efface the traces (of a house). To defile a. o.
— وأَعْذَرَ في To be inexcusable. To be excusable.
أَعْذَرَ ه To circumcise (a child). To put the cheek-strap to a horse.
تَعَذَّرَ واعْتَذَرَ عن To draw back. To excuse o.'s self, to apologise for.
— واعْتَذَرَ To be effaced (design, trace).
تَعَذَّرَ على To be impossible to a. o. (affair).
إِعْتَذَرَ To complain. To be excusable.
إِسْتَعْذَرَ من To apologise for.
عُذْر ج أَعْذَار Excuse. Plea. Virginity. Menses of women.
أَبُو عُذْرِ هٰذَا الكَلَام The first utterer of this sentence.
عِذَار ج عُذُر Cheek. Down covering the cheeks. Cheek-strap of a bridle. Brand on a camel.
خَلَعَ العِذَار He has thrown off all shame.
عِذْرَة ج عِذَر Excuse.
عُذْرَة ج عُذَر Lock of hair ; horse's forelock. Prepuce. Circumcision. Virginity.
عَذِرَة ج عَذِرَات Human excrement. Refuse of wheat. Court-yard. Dunghill.
عَذِير ج عُذُر Apologising for ; advocate.
— وإِعْذَار Feast for the circumcision of a child.
تَعَذُّر Difficulty, impossibility.
عَاذِر وعَاذِرَة Excrements.
عَاذُور ج عَوَاذِير Pain in the throat.
عَذْرَاء ج عَذَارَى وعَذَارٍ Virgin. Scavenger's daughter. *Virgo* (*Zodiacal sign*). Unbored pearl. Untrodden sand.
العَذْرَاء The Blessed Virgin Mary.
عُذْرَى ومَعْذُرَة ج مَعَاذِر, ومِعْذَار ج مَعَاذِير Excuse.

To be scabby (camel). ✡ عرّ i o عَرًّا, وعُرَّ
To afflict, to disgrace a. o. — ه , وعَرَّ بِشَرٍّ
To manure (a field). — وعَرَّر ه
To utter a cry (ostrich). ✧ To low. عَرَّ i عِرَارًا, وعَارَّ مُعَارَّةً وعِرَارًا
To be defiled (dwelling). أَعَرَّ
To be restless in bed. تَعَارَّ
To address a. o. humbly. إعترّ واعترّ ب
To spread (scab). إِسْتَعَرَّ
Mange. Vice. Madness. Dung. Dirt. Scabby. عَرّ
Dung of birds. Scab of camels. عُرّ وعُرَّة
Scab, mange. عَرَر .وعُرُور
Scabby. Small-humped (camel). أَعَرّ م عَرَّاء ج عُرّ
Prostitute, harlot. عُرِّيّ
Retaliation. *Buphthalmum*, ox-eye (plant). عَرَار
Prematurely weaned (child). — م عَرَارَة
Crime. Shame. عُرَار
Ill-nature. Might. Root. عَرَارَة
Stranger (to a tribe). ✧ Bellowing. عَرِير
Disgracing his family. عَارُور وعَارُورَة
Crime. Annoyance. Fine. Blood-price. Treachery. مَعَرَّة ج مَعَرَّات
Scabby; defiled. مَعْرُور
Beggar addressing humbly. مُعْتَرّ
Juniper-tree. ✡ عَرْعَر
Summit, top of a mountain. Mountain-cypress. Partition of the nose. عُرْعُرَة ج عَرَاعِر
Stopper of a bottle. — وعَرْعَرَة
Fat (camel). Noble, chief. عُرَاعِر ج عَرَاعِر
To be in good Arabic (language). To be a true Arab (man). ✡ عَرُب o عُرُوبَة وعُرُوبِيَّة
To be disordered (stomach). To be swollen, to leave a scar (wound). To swell (river). عَرِب a عَرَبًا
To point out to a. o. the unseemliness of. عَرَّب ه على
To speak out on behalf of. — عن
To Arabicise (a word). — وأَعْرَب ه
To use good Arabic style. To prune (a palm-tree). To scarify (a horse).

Excused. Circumcised. Affected with angina. مَعْذُور
To taste (food). ✡ عَذَف i عَذْفًا من
To eat a. th. تَعَذَّف ه
I have not tasted anything. مَا ذُقْتُ عَذْفًا ولَا عَذُوفًا ولَا عُذَافًا
Food, drink of men and beasts. عَذُوف
Tall, strong (camel). ✡ عذفر — عُذَافِر ج عَذَافِرَة
To trim (a palm-tree). ✡ عَذَق i عَذْقًا, وعَذَّق ه
To mark (a ewe) with red wool. — وأَعْذَق ه
To stigmatise a. o. عَذَق ه بِشَرٍّ
Palm-tree loaded with dates. عَذْق ج أَعْذُق وعِذَاق
Raceme of dates: bunch of grapes. عِذْق ج أَعْذَاق وعُذُوق
Mark made with red wool. عَذْقَة وعِذْقَة
To find fault with, to upbraid a. o. ✡ عَذَل i o عَذْلًا, وعَذَّل ه
To be blamed. To blame o.'s self. تَعَذَّل واعتذل
Blame, reproof. عَذْل وعَذَل وتَعْذَال
Days of intense heat. أَيَّام عُذْل وأَيَّام مُعْتَذِلَات
Reprover. عَاذِل ج عُذَّل وعُذَّال وعَذَلَة
Severe censor. عُذَلَة وعَذُول وعَذَّال وعَذَّالَة
Anus. عَذَّالَة
Blamed. مَعْذُول ومُعَذَّل
Bountiful, lavisher. مُعَذَّل
To chew (horse). To defend o.'s self. ✡ عَذَم i عَذْمًا
To blame a. o. — ه
Wont to bite (horse). Biting in words (man). عَذُوم ج عُذُم
Biting. Flea. عَذَّام
Blame, reproof. عَذِيمَة ج عَذَائِم
To be wholesome (air, country). ✡ عَذَا o عَذْوًا
To be healthy, remote from water (land). عَذِيَ a عَذًى وعَذُوَ o عَذَاوَةً
To hold (a country) as healthy. إِسْتَعْذَى ه
Healthy, wholesome (climate). عَاذٍ وعَذِيّ
Salubrious country. أَرْض عَذَاة وعَذِيَّة وعَذِيَة

To give an earnest. عَرَّبَ وأَعْرَبَ

To afford (clear arguments). أَعْرَبَ ب

To express o.'s mind clearly. — ه To pronounce the final accents of a word.

To adopt the customs of Arabs. To become a naturalized Arab. تَعَرَّبَ واستَعْرَبَ

Arabs of the desert. Bedouins. عُرْب وعَرَب ج أَعْرُب وعُرُوب وعُرْبَان

The genuine Arabs. عَرَب عَرْبَاء وعَارِبَة

People of foreign or mixed descent, naturalized amongst the Arabs. عَرَب مُتَعَرِّبَة ومُسْتَعْرِبَة

Disordered (stomach). Yielding much water (well). عَرِبَة

Arab; of true Arabian blood. White barley. عَرَبِيّ ج عَرَب

Arabic, Arabic language. لُغَة عَرَبِيَّة

The science of the Arabic tongue. عِلْم العَرَبِيَّة

Unsettled Arabs of the desert. Bedouins. أَعْرَابِيّ ج أَعْرَاب وجج أَعَارِيب

Swollen, overflowing (river). عَارِب وعَارِبَة

Desinential syntax. Grammatical analyses. إِعْرَاب

Swift river. Soul, mind. عَرَبَة ج عَرَب وعَرَبَات

Carriage, car, wagon. عَرَبَة و✧ عَرَبِيَّة

Coachman, carter. ✧ عَرَبَجِيّ

✧ Godfather. عَرَّاب

✧ Godmother. عَرَّابَة

State, qualities of a genuine Arab. عُرُوبَة وعُرُوبِيَّة

Full blood Arabian horses. خَيْل عِرَاب وأَعْرُب

There is nobody at home. مَا بالدَّار عَرِيب او مُعْرِب

Declinable (word). مُعْرَب

Expressing his mind (clearly). Possessing true Arabian horses. مُعْرِب

Arabicised (word). مُعَرَّب

To be unsociable, quarrelsome. ✱ عَرْبَدَ

Quarrelsome, ill-natured. عِرْبِيد ومُعَرْبِد

Male viper; red serpent. Custom, use. عِرْبَدّ

To entangle; to disturb a. o. ✧ عَرْبَسَ ه

To be perplexed, confused (man). ✧ تَعَرْبَسَ

To climb up (a tree, wall). ✧ عَرْبَشَ وتَعَرْبَشَ

To give an earnest to. ✱ عَرْبَنَ ه

عُرْبُون وعَرَبُون وعُرْبَان و✧ رَعْبُون ج عَرَابِين

Earnest-money. Pledge. و✧ رَعَابِين

To tan a hide with a plant. ✱ عَرْتَنَ

Plant for tanning red. عَرْتَن

To ascend (a ladder). ✱ عَرَجَ o عُرُوجًا ومَعْرَجًا في

To be carried up. عُرِجَ ب

To limp. To be lame. عَرَجَ وعَرِجَ a عَرَجًا

To incline towards setting (sun). عَرَجَ a وعَرُجَ o عَرَجًا

To lean on one side (building). عَرَّجَ وتَعَرَّجَ

To make (a building) to incline. عَرَّجَ ه

To halt, to stop in (a place). To undertake (a work). — وتَعَرَّجَ

To turn from; to leave a. th. عَرَّجَ عن

To render a. o. lame (God). أَعْرَجَ ه

To feign lameness. تَعَارَجَ

To be inclined on one side; to deviate. إِنْعَرَجَ

To stray from; to forsake. — عن

Lameness. عَرَج وعَرَجَان

How great is his lameness! مَا أَشَدَّ عَرَجَهُ

Lame. أَعْرَج م عَرْجَاء ج عُرْج وعُرْجَان Crow. ✧ Knave (at cards).

Female hyena. عَرْجَاء

Straying. عَرْجَة وعُرْجَة وتَعَرُّج وتَعْرِيج Declivity.

Bad affair. أَمْر عَرِيج

Midday. Eating but once a day. عُرَيْجَاء

Noxious snake. أُعَيْرِج ج أُعَيْرِجَات

Place of ascent. Ladder, stairs. مَعْرَج ومِعْرَاج ج مَعَارِج ومَعَارِيج

Night of the Ascent amongst Moslems. لَيْلَة المِعْرَاج

Sloping (land). Bending (of a river). مُنْعَرَج

Crooked palm-bough. ✱ عُرْجُد وعُرْجُود

To strike with a stick. ✱ عَرْجَنَ ه To imprint figures (on cloth). To dye with saffron, henna.

Bough of a palm-tree. عُرْجُون ج عَرَاجِين

To grow (tooth, plant). ✱ عَرَدَ o عُرُودًا

Halting place. مُعْرَس ومُعَرَّس
To make a vine-stalk. ✻ عَرَش o i عَرْشًا وعَرَّش وأَعْرَش ل
To roof (a house). To raise (a hut). — ه
To prop the stalks of a vine upon a trellis. — عَرْشًا وعُرُوشًا ه
To case in stones the lowest part of (a well). — عَرْشًا ه
To settle in (a place). — i عُرُوشًا ب
To be astonished, puzzled. عَرِش a عَرْشًا وعَرَشًا
To press (a debtor). — عَرَشًا ب
To prop a wine on a shed or cane-hut. To roof (a house). عَرَّش ه
To stick to ; to give o.'s self up to a. th. To settle in a country. تَعَرَّش ب
To hang from an arbour (grapes). إِعْتَرَش
عَرْش ج أَعْرَاش وعُرُوش وعُرُش وعِرَشَة
Throne of God, of a king. Arbour ; pavilion. Nest on a tree. Might, power.
Bier for the dead. Wood for casing the upper part of a well. عَرْش
Side of the neck. عُرْش ج عِرَشَة وأَعْرَاش
Instep. Ear.
Trellis, shed. ✧ Carriage-shaft. عَرِيش ج عُرُش
Litter for women. — وعَرِيشَة ج عَرَائِش
✧ Vine-arbour. عَرِيشَة
Sheltered by an arbour. مُعَرَّش ومَعْرُوش
Upheld by a trellis (vine). ✧ Vine-clad (wall).
To be restless (camel). ✻ عَرَص i عَرْصًا
To be brisk, lively (child). To thunder and send forth lightnings (sky).
To flash (lightning). عَرِص a عَرَصًا
To be glad, sprightly (man).
To spread a. th. in the sun. عَرَّص ه
To be tossed, shaken. أَعْرَص
To stay in (a place). تَعَرَّص ب
To play, to sport (child). To quiver (skin). To flash (lightning). إِعْتَرَص
Flashing (lightining). عَرَص وعَرِص
Court, area, square. عَرْصَة ج عَرَصَات وعِرَاص وأَعْرَاص
Cloud sending forth lightnings عَرَّاص

To cast (stones) far away. عَرَد عَرْدًا ه
To take flight, to draw back in fear. عَرِد a عَرَدًا, وعَرَّد
To rise, to set (star). To stray from (a road). عَرَّد
To turn aside, to go far from. — عن
To pierce (an animal) through (arrow). — في
Hard, stiff, thick. عَرْد وعَرِد وعُرُدّ
Ballista, stone-throwing machine. عَرَّادَة
Tamarind (tree). ▫ عِرْدِيب
To be hard, contracted. ✻ عَرَز i عَرْزًا, وعَرِز a عَرَزًا
To pull a. th. strongly. عَرَز ه
To show to a. o. the end of. — ل
To conceal a. th. عَرَّز ه
To be contracted. — وعَارَز وتَعَارَز
To counteract, to importune a. o عَارَز ه
To spoil a. th. أَعْرَز ه
To be difficult to a. o. (affair). تَعَرَّز واسْتَعْرَز على
Hut on a tree for a rural guard. Den of lion. ✻ عرزل — عِرْزَال ج عَرَازِيل
Band of thieves. قَوْم عَرَازِيل
To be cheerful. ✻ عَرَس o عَرْسًا
To be merry. To cleave to. To be weak, tired. عَرِس a عَرَسًا
To alight for rest during the night. عَرَّس وأَعْرَس
To give a wedding-dinner. أَعْرَس
To have the bride brought to his house (bridegroom). — بِأَهْلِهِ
Partition between two apartments. Pole of a tent. عَرْس ج أَعْرَاس
Bridegroom, husband. عِرْس ج أَعْرَاس
The two spouses ; husband and wife. العِرْسَان
Weasel. إِبْن عِرْس ج بَنَات عِرْس و✧ عَرْسَة
Wedding. Wedding-party. عُرْس وعُرُس ج أَعْرَاس وعُرُسَات
Flowers of nenuphar. ▫ عَرَائِس الفِيل
Weasel-coloured. عِرْسِيّ
Bridegroom, spouse. عَرُوس وعَرِيس ج عُرُس
Bride. عَرُوس وعَرُوسَة ج عَرَائِس
Kind of fish. عَرُوسَة البَحْر
Retreat of lion ; thicket. عِرِّيس وعِرِّيسَة

To join (funerals) on the way. عارَض ه
To present (a petition). أعرَض ه
To widen a. th.
To shun. To oppose. — عن
To be munificent. — في المَكارِم
To come within reach (game). — ل
To be possible to a. o.
He was able to do good. أعرَضَ لهُ الخَيْرُ
To be exhibited, displayed. تَعرَّض
To happen, to occur to a. o. — لِفُلان
To thwart, to counteract a. o.
To interfere in (an affair). — لِلأمر
To become within reach. تعرَّض ه ول
To emulate o. a. To oppose o. a. To be contradictory (news). تَعارَض
To happen. To be across (a road, a stream). إعترَض
To be strong-headed (horse). — في رَسَنِهِ
To present o.'s self to. To oppose; to cause obstruction to. — ل
To lay across. To form an obstacle. — الشيء دُون
To point out the faults of. To object to. — على فُلان
To review (troops). To face a. o. To ride a restive (horse). — ه
To shoot (an arrow) and kill a. o. — لِفُلانٍ بِسَهمٍ
To seek a. th. broad. إستَعرَض
To question a. o. To ask a. o. to show. — ه
To slay people indiscriminately. — القوم
Ask any one among the Arabs. إستَعرِض العَرَب
Unforeseen event. Compensation. Exhibition (of goods). Review of an army. عَرَض
Goods, movables (except gold and silver). Side of a mountain. Breadth. Width. Latitude (*geogr*). — ج عُرُوض
The day of the Judgment. يَوم العَرض
عَرضُ حال وعَرضُحال ج عَرضُحالات
✧ Written account, request.
Cloud. Hour of the night. — ج عُرُوض وأعراض وعِراض
Tops of the trees. أعراض الشَّجَر
Good repute. Honour, عِرض ج أعراض

Thundering. Quivering (lance).
To slit a. th. by pulling. ✲ عَرصَف ه
Chamæpitys, ground-pine, medicinal plant. عَرصَف
Wooden peg of a saddle. Flexible bone of the proboscis. Whip of sinews. عُرصاف ج عَراصِيف
Lion. ✲ عِرصام
Glutton. عَرَصَم
Miser. عُرضُوم
To happen (accident). ✲ عَرَض i عَرضًا
✧ To expose, to send a petition.
An accident happened to him. عَرَض لهُ عارِضٌ من
He was seized with a fit of fever. عَرَضَهُ عارِضٌ من الحُمَّى
To review (troops). — ه وه
To present a. o. with a. th. عَرَض ه ل
To expose a. th. to view. To prepare a. th. to.
He gave him a suit of clothes as a payment of his debt. — لهُ من حقِّهِ ثَوبًا
To put (a sword) upon. — ه على
To offer a. th. for (sale).
To slay, to flog a. o. — ه على السَّيف او السَّوط
To follow the traces of a. o. عَرَض عَرضَ فُلان وعُرضَهُ
To appear to; to be within sight, in the power of. — وعَرِض a عَرَضًا وأعرَض ل
To be seized with madness. عُرِض
(opp. to طال) عَرُض o عِرَضًا وعَراضَةً
To be broad, to be widened.
To place a. th. opposite to. To explain; to apprise a. o. of a. th. To propose a. th. to. عَرَّض ه ل
To widen, to make broad. — ه
To hint, to suggest a. th. To write indistinctly. To barter. To become energetic. عَرَّض
To speak equivocally. To make hints, to allude to. عَرَّض ب او ل
To avoid a. o. To thwart, to oppose a. o. To requite a. o. عارَض ه
To keep up with a. o. in walking. — ه في السَّير
To imitate a. o. — ه بِعَمَلِهِ
To collate (a writing) with. — ه ب

pearing in laughter.
Broad. Full. Plentiful. عَرِيض ج عِرَاض
Yearling kid. — ج عُرْضَان
Wealthy, *lit.* big-bellied. — البِطَان
✧ Petition. Letter ; brief. عَرِيضَة
Show-place. Exhibition. مَعْرِض ج مَعَارِض
Apparel of a girl. مِعْرَض
Opposition, obliquity. مُعَارَضَة
Bastard. Brazen-faced man. إِبْن المُعَارَضَة
Featherless arrow. Equivocal speech. مِعْرَاض
Abstruse (speech). مُعَرَّض ج مَعَارِض ومَعَارِيض
Petition. ◻ Crack-brained. مَعْرُوض
Laying across. Objector. Unforeseen. مُعْتَرِض
Timbal, lute. ✱ عَرْطَبَة وعُرْطُبَة
✱ عَرَف i عِرْفَة وعِرْفَانًا وعِرِفَّانًا ومَعْرِفَة ه
To know, to perceive by the senses or mind.
To bear a. th. patiently. — ل
To acknowledge (a fault). — بِذَنْبِهِ ل
To manage (business) skilfully ; to govern. — o عِرَافَة على
To have an ulcer in the palm of the hand. عُرِف عَرْفَة
To be set over people. عَرُف o عَرَافَة
To use perfumes. عَرِف a عَرَفًا
To acquaint a. o. with ; to inform of. عَرَّف ٥ ه او ب
To let know the name of a. o. To introduce a. o. to. — ٥ بِفُلَان
To point out a. o.'s (defects). — ٥ فُلَانًا
To perfume a. o. or a. th. — ٥ وه
✧ To hear the confession of a. o. (priest). — ٥
To prefix the article to (a noun) ; to define a. th. — ه
To have a fine crest (cock) ; fine mane (horse). أَعْرَف ٥
To be determined (noun). تَعَرَّف
To inquire, to take information about. — ه
To be known by such a one. — بِفُلَان
To be acquainted together ; to recognize one another. تَعَارَف
To be humble and submissive. إِعْتَرَف
To become aware of. — ه

soul ; one's self. Body. Valley. Smell. Army.
Infamy, violation. هَتْك العِرْض
His honour is untouched. هُوَ نَقِيّ العِرْض
He is a sweet-smelling man. هُوَ طَيِّب العِرْض
Side, lateral part. Slope (of a mountain). Main part. عُرْض ج عِرَاض
He is from common descent. هُوَ من عُرْض النَّاس
He looked at him sidelong. نظر إِلَيْهِ عن عُرْضٍ او عن عُرُضٍ
Accident (*opposed to* substance). Movables. Furniture. Hazard, luck. Accident. Profit acquired by chance. عَرَض ج أَعْرَاض
He was hit by a random arrow. أَصَابَهُ سَهْم عَرَضٍ
At random ; unintentionally. عَرَضًا
Intention. Target. Purpose عُرْضَة
He is a match for him. هُوَ عُرْضَةٌ لِذٰلِك
I have exposed him to. جَعَلْتُهُ عُرْضَةً ل
Corner of a house. عَرْضِيّ
Accidental. (*opp. to* جَوْهَرِيّ) عَرَضِيّ
✧ Venial (sin).
Unsteady on horseback. Restive (camel). ✧ Army-corps. عُرْضِيّ
Restiveness of a beast. عُرْضِيَّة
Mark on a camel's thigh. Main part of a tradition. عِرَاض ج عُرُض
She brought a child out of wedlock. جَاءَت بِوَلَدٍ عن عِرَاضٍ
Broad, wide. عُرَاض
Gift, present. ✧ Discharge of fire-arms as a rejoicing. عُرَاضَة
Foot of a verse. Metre (in poetry). Prosody. عَرُوض ج أَعَارِيض
Shore ; road. Meaning of (speech). — ج عُرُض
Science of prosody. عِلْم العَرُوض
Prosodist. عَرُوضِيّ
Opposition. Objection. إِعْتِرَاض
Fit, crisis of an illness. Obstacle, hindrance. Cheek. عَارِض ج عَوَارِض
The two cheeks. العَارِضَان
Thin-bearded. خَفِيف العَارِضَيْن
Rafter, cross-beam. عَارِضَة ج عَوَارِض
Tooth in the side of the mouth. Side of the cheek. Part of the face ap-

To question a. o. إعتَرَفَ ه
To confess the (faith). To acknowledge (a fault). ✧ To confess (sins). — ب
He bore the affair patiently. — لِلأَمرِ
To know a. th. إستَعرَفَ ه
To ask to be introduced to a. o. — الى
To be swollen (sea). To have a fine mane (horse). إعرَورَفَ
To prepare to mischief. — لِلشَّرّ
Smell (specially good). عَرْف
Acknowledgement. Crest of a cock. Mane of a horse. Beneficence, goodness. Elevated place. Waves. Known. Common-language. عُرْف ج أعْرَاف
Common law. عُرف الشَّرع
They came one after another. جاءَ القَومُ عُرُفاً
I acknowledge that I owe him a thousand benefits. لَهُ عَلَيَّ أَلفٌ عُرفاً
Patience. عِرف وعُرف
Elevated sands, places. عُرُف
Wind. Ulcer in the palm of the hand. عُرْفَة
Question, asking. — وعِرفَة
Prominence. Limit between two things. عُرْفَة ج عُرَف
Arafa, mountain near Mecca. عَرَفَة
Witchcraft. Divination. عِرَافَة
Diviner, sorcerer. عَرَّاف ج عَرَّافون
Common use or (*opp. to* شَرعيّ) speech. عُرْفِيّ
Aphorism. عُرفِيَّة
Arbitrary (custom). Private. عَرَفِيّ
✧ Arbitration. حُكم عُرفِيّ
Limbus. ✧ الأَعراف
Acknowledgment, thankfulness. ✧ Sacramental confession. إعتِرَاف
Knowledge. Benefit; boon. عِرفان
Definition of a. th. Tariff. تَعرِيف ج تعاريف وتعريفات
The Book of definitions. كِتَاب التَّعرِيفات
The definite article ال حَرف التَّعرِيف
Patient. Known. عَارِف ج عَرَفَة
Benefit, gift. عَارِفَة ج عَوَارِف
Patient, steadfast. عَرُوف ج عُرُف
Knowing, learned. عَرُوفَة
Chief of a corporation. Appraiser. School-master. Known. عَرِيف ج عُرَفَاء

Crested (cock). Full-maned (horse). أعرَف مو عَرفاء ج عُرف
Knowledge, science. مَعرِفَة ج مَعَارِف
Gratefulness. مَعرِفَة الجَمِيل
Face. مَعرَف ومَعرِف ج مَعَارِف
(*Pl*). Friends, acquaintances.
May God vivify your faces. حَيَّا الله مَعَارِفَكُم
The friends of such a one. مَعَارِفُ فُلان
Place where the mane grows. مَعرَفَة ج مَعَارِف
Definite. Determinate. مُعَرَّف
✧ Confessor (priest). مُعَرِّف
Good, suitable. Benefit, service, favour. Active voice (of a verb). Fragrant. Having an ulcer in the hand. مَعرُوف
✧ Beneficent, serviceable. صَاحِب مَعرُوف
✧ Confessor of the faith. مُعتَرِف
Thorny tree ✧ Kind of brank-ursine. ✡ عَرفَج
Gummiferous tree. Species of mimosa. ✡ عُرفُط
To strip (a bone) of the flesh. ✡ عَرَقَ o عَرقاً ومَعرَقاً. وتَعَرَّقَ ه
To penetrate into a country. — o عَرَقاً وعُرُوقاً في الأَرض
To line a (leathern bag). — ه
To be lean, emaciated. عُرِقَ
To sweat. عَرِقَ a عَرَقاً
To make a. o. to sweat. عَرَّقَ ه
To add little water to (a beverage). — وأعرَقَ ه
✧ To boil (figs). عَرَّقَ ه
To fill half (a bucket). — وأعرَقَ في
To come into Irak. أعرَقَ
To strike deep roots (tree). — واعتَرَقَ واستَعرَقَ
To promote sweat. إستَعرَقَ
Bone stripped from its flesh. Beaten path. عَرق ج عِرَاق
Sweat of the body. Moisture of walls. Milk. Row of bricks, animals. Foot-prints of animals walking in a file. Plait of palm-leaves. ✧ Spirit; any distillated liquor. عَرَق
Weariness, fatigue. — القِربَة
Token of friendship, reward. — الخِلال
Vein, artery. عِرق ج عِرَاق وأعرَاق وعُرُوق

Sweating, exuding water. ✧ عَرِقَان
Iron instrument for stripping a bone. مِعْرَق
Mixed with little water (drink). مُعْرَق ومُعَرَّق ومَعْرُوق
Lean, emaciated. مَعْرُوق ومُعَرَّق
Sudorific, promoting sweat. مُعَرِّق
To hamstring (a beast). ✱ عَرْقَب ه
To help (a beast) in rising.
To journey through mountain-paths. ✧ To be intricate (business). تَعَرْقَب
Tendo Achillis. Hock. عُرْقُوب ج عَرَاقِيب
Winding roads (in a mountain).
Entanglement, complication of business. عَرَاقِيب الأُمُور
To skip (child). To creep (snake). ✱ عَرْقَص
To stray from the right course. ✱ عَرْقَل
To involve a. o. in difficulties. — على
To entangle (business). To use shifts in (speech). — ه
To be entangled, intricate (business). To be full of artifices (speech). ✧ To be crippled; to be taken with a cramp. تَعَرْقَل
Crafty, shuffling. عِرْقَال
Misfortunes. عَرَاقِيل
Difficult, intricate affairs. — الأُمُور
Perplexity. ✧ Palsy. Cramp. تَعَرْقُل
To scrape; to rub out. To wear out (clothes). To devour (plants: cattle). ✧ To knead (dough); to mix up a. th. ✱ عَرَكَ ٥ عَرْكًا ه
To train; to render a. o. experienced (time). — ه
To endure vexation. — الأَذَى بِجَنْبِهِ
War has crushed them. عَرَكَتْهُم الحَرْب
✧ He spoke at random. عَرَكَ فِي حَدِيثِهِ
To menstruate (woman). عَرَكَ ٥ عَرْكًا وعُرَاكًا وعُرُوكًا, وأَعْرَكَ
To be a strong fighter. عَرِكَ a عَرَكًا
To contend with a. o. عَارَكَ مُعَارَكَة وعِرَاكًا ه
To be scraped, rubbed away. تَعَرَّكَ
To fight with a. o. تَعَارَكَ واعْتَرَكَ
Rubbing. Experience. (*un.* عَرْكَة) عَرْك
✧ Kneading.

Ore (in a mine). Origin of a man. Thread, root of a tree. Fresh milk. Sandy hill. Rugged and isolated mountain. Streamlet of water. Saline ground. عِرْق ج عُرُوق
✧ Tormentil (*plant*). عِرْق الإِنْجِبَار
✧ Dragoon's blood (*plant*). — الحَمْرَة
✧ Liquorice-root. — السُّوس
✧ Ipecacuanha. Long pepper. — الذَّهَب
Rumex, patience (*plant*). — المُسْهِل
Mother-of-pearl. — لُؤْلُؤ
Sciatica, hip-gout. — النَّسَا
Timber, beams. ◻ عُرُوق الشَّام
Chelidonium, yellow-wood (dye). العُرُوق الصُّفْر
Madder (dye). العُرُوق الحُمْر
Plant for fattening women. العُرُوق البِيض
There is a little water in the drink. فِي الشَّرَاب عِرْق مِن المَاء
The pulsative arteries. العُرُوق الضَّوَارِب
The veins, blood-vessels. العُرُوق السَّوَاكِن
Sweating much. عُرَق وعُرَقَة
Road in a highland. عَرِقَة
Root, fibre of a tree. عِرْقَة ج عِرْقَات وعِرَق
Stock, source of wealth. عِرْقَاة
Row, file. Whip. عَرَقَة ج عَرَق وعَرَقَات
Sandy hillock. Piece of wood for carrying a bucket. عَرْقُوَة ج عَرَاقٍ
Misfortunes. ذَات العَرَاقِي
Generous; of noble descent (man). Full-blood (horse). عَرِيق ومُعْرِق
Rooted. — وأَعْرَق
Lining of a bag. Sea-shore. Flesh around the nails. Edge of the ears. Seam of a table-cloth. Court-yard. عِرَاق ج أَعْرِقَة وعُرْق وعُرُق
Cotton cap worn under a turban. عِرَاقِيَّة و✧ عَرَقِيَّة ج عَرَاقٍ
Irak. Mesopotamia. بِلَاد العِرَاق
Basrah and Koofah (towns). العِرَاقَان
Drop of water. Abundant rain. عُرَاق وعُرَاقَة
Plants springing up after the rain. عُرَاق الغَيْث
Molar teeth. Years. عَوَارِق

Harsh, violent. Numerous army. ✧ Vehement rain. ✻ عَرَمْرَم
To become hardened (body). ✻ عَرْمَس
Stone. Hard (she-camel). عِرْمِس
✧ Bunch stripped of its grapes. عَرْمُوش ج عَرَامِيش
To become overspread with green moss (water). ✻ عَرْمَض
Green substance upon water. Thorny tree. عَرْمَض
To become accustomed to a. th. ✻ عَرَن o عَرْنًا على
To put a piece of wood into (a camel's) nose. — o i ه
To have a disease of the legs (beast). عَرِن a عَرَنًا
To live on meat. أَعْرَن
Smell of cooked meat. عِرن
Disease of the legs, amongst beasts. Ulcer on the neck of camels. عَرَن وعِرَان
Ulcered on the legs. عَرُون
Forest, thicket. Strength. Flesh. عَرِين ج عُرُن
Covert (of lions). — وعَرِينَة ج عَرَائِن
Wooden bit inserted into a camel's nose. عِرَان
Waves, billows. High sea. عُرَانِيَة
Upper part of the nose. Chief. First part of a. th. عِرْنِين ج عَرَانِين
Prominent part of a mountain. Spindle. ✧ Tendril of (a vine). Head of Indian corn. ✻ عِرنس — عِرْنَاس ج عَرَانِيس
To befall a. o. (accident). To repair to a. o. ✻ عَرَا o عَرْوًا ه
To shudder, to shiver from fear or fever. — وعُرِي
To regret a. th. sold. عُرِي إلى
To put a handle to (a leather-bag). To make button-holes in (a garment). عَرَّى وأَعْرَى ه
To overwhelm a. o. (sorrows). To repair to a. o. إِعْتَرَى ه
Region, vicinage. Free from trouble. عِرو ج أَعْرَاء
Befalling of a misfortune. عَرْو واعتِرَاء
Shivering fever. The North. عُرَوَا
Handle. Loop used as a button-hole. Suburbs of a town. عُرْوَة ج عُرى

Time (repeated action). War. عَرْكَة ج عَرَكَات
Sound, voice, noise. عَرْك وعِرك
Strong wrestler; antagonist. Heap of sand. عَرِك ج عَرِكُون
Fisherman. عَرَكِيّ ج عَرَك وجج عُرُوك
Crowding at water. عِرَاك
He brought all his camels together to water. أَوْرَدَ إِبِلَهُ العِرَاك
Drudge; bearing annoyance. عُرَكَة
Small-humped camels. عَرُوك
Nature, temper. Camel's hump. عَرِيكَة ج عَرَائِك
Mild-tempered. لَيِّن العَرِيكَة
Menstruating (woman). عَارِك ج عَوَارِك, ومُعْرِك
Battle-ground. مَعْرَك ج مَعَارِك, ومُعْتَرَك
Battle-field. مَعْرَكَة ومَعْرُكَة ج مَعَارِك
Altercation, wrestling, fight, conflict. — ومُعَارَكَة
Fighter. Wrestler. مُعَارِك
Trodden upon by cattle (ground). Heaped up (sand). Intermingled at water (cattle). مَعْرُوك
To gnaw (a bone). To crop (a tree : beast). ✧ To bind (a book). ✻ عَرَم o i عَرْمًا ه
To treat a. o. harshly. — ه
To treat a. o. perversely. — عُرَامًا على
To be ill-natured. عَرِم a وعَرُم o عَرَامَة
To mix up. ✧ To heap up. عَرَّم ه
To be gnawed (bone). ✧ To be heaped up. To swell (river). تَعَرَّم
To gnaw (a bone). To crop (a tree : beast). — ه
To be strong-headed (horse). إِعْتَرَم
Mixture of white and black. عَرَم وعُرْمَة
Impetuosity of an army. Ill-nature. Ignorance. عُرَام
Heap of corn, of sand, or dung. Iron-helmet. عُرْمَة وعَرَمَة ج عَرَم
Hard, wicked. عَرِم
Dam. Vehement rain. عَرِمَة ج عَرِم
Wicked, violent (man). Bitterly cold (day). عَارِم
Book-binder. ✧ عَرَّام
Calamity. Ditch. عَرِيم ج عُرْمَان
Speckled, white and black. أَعْرَم م عَرْمَاء ج عُرْم

God! to him belongs glory and power. اللهُ عَزَّ وجَلَّ
To be hard to a. o. (affair). عَزَّ a عَلَيْهِ
It would be very hard to him to do so. — أن يَفعَل كَذا
To overcome, to gain mastery over. عَزَّ o عَزًّا ه في
To render a. o. mighty, strong; illustrious, noble. عَزَّزَ وأَعَزَّ ه
To strive to overcome a. o. عازَّ ه
To love a. o. أَعَزَّ ه
I am distressed by what has befallen thee. أَعْزِزْتُ بِمَا أَصابكَ
To obtain power, consideration. To become scarce and dear (goods). To behave with pride. تَعَزَّزَ
To become mighty, illustrious. إِعْتَزَّ
To be proud of, to glory in. — ب
To overcome a. o. — على
To agglutinate (sand). إِسْتَعَزَّ
To overpower a. o. إِسْتَعَزَّ على
God has caused him to die. — اللهُ بِهِ
To overcome a. o. (disease). أُسْتُعِزَّ بِالعَلِيلِ
Power. Nobility. Conquest. Impossibility. Intensity. عِزّ
Of course; necessarily. عَزًّا بَزًّا
Fawn of a gazelle. عَزَّة
Power, glory. Scarcity. Abstruseness. عِزَّة
Mighty. Honoured. Proud. Impossible. Difficult. Scarce, precious. عَزِيز ج عِزاز وأَعِزَّة وَأَعِزَّاء
Cyperus esculentus (*plant*). حَبّ العَزِيز
Ruler of Egypt. عَزِيز مِصْر
Magnanimous. (*opp. to* ذليل) عَزِيز النَّفْس
More powerful. Dearer. More honoured. أَعَزّ م عُزَّى
Goddess of the pagan Arabs. العُزَّى
Powerful and glorious by the help of God. مُعْتَزّ بِالله
Overcome by illness. مِعْزاز المَرَض
To live in celibacy. ☆ عَزَب o عُزْبَةً وعُزُوبَةً, وتَعَزَّب
To be, to go far away from. عَزَب o i عُزُوبًا عن
To be desert (country). عَزَّب
To protract (an absence). To put off (business). عَزَّب

Thicket. Company of men. Valuable property. Lion.
I am free from it. أنا عُرْوَة مِنْهُ
Seized with an access of fever. عارٍ ج عُرَاة
Smitten by misfortune. مُعْتَرًى
To become naked, bare of clothes. To be free, exempted from. ☆ عَرِي a عُرْيَةً وعُرْيًا من
To strip a. o. of (his clothes). عَرَّى وأَعْرَى ه ها او من
To free a. o. from. عَرَّى ه من
To ride a horse unsaddled. عارَى
To encamp; to travel in a desert. To be exposed to the cold of night. أَعْرَى
To withdraw. To denude a. o. أَعْرَى ه
To give to a. o. the fruit of a palm-tree for one year. — ه ها النَّخلَة
To be divested of clothes. تَعَرَّى من
To journey alone. إِعْرَوْرَى
To commit a shameful action. — أَمْرًا قَبِيحًا
To ride (a horse) without saddle. — فَرَسًا
Wall, enclosure. Open field. عَرًى
Desert, waste. Nakedness. عَرَاء ج أَعْرَاء
Nakedness. عُرْي وعُرْيَة
Shore, spot. Intenseness of cold. عَرَاة
Unsaddled horse. فَرَس عُرْي
Cold wind. عَرِيّ وعَرِيَّة
Cotton smock-frock with full sleeves. ◘ عَرِي
Palm-tree stripped of its fruit. عَرِيَّة
Naked. Free, destitute. عارٍ ج عُرَاة
Naked. Active (horse). عُرْيَان ج عُرْيَانُون
Uncovered part of the body. مَعْرًى ومَعْرَاة ج مَعارٍ
The hands, feet and face. المَعارِي
Stripped; denuded. مُعَرًّى
To be powerful, strong. To strengthen o.'s self. To become weak. To be dear, rare, precious. To be insuperable (difficulty). ☆ عَزَّ i عِزًّا وعِزَّة وعَزَازَة
To become illustrious, exalted. — i عِزًّا
The worth of a thing is enhanced by its contrary. كُلّ يَعِزّ من ضِدِّهِ

Musical instrument, mandoline, lute. مِعْزَف ومِعْزَفَة ج مَعَازِف
To dig the earth (with a spade). To eat. ※ عَزَق i عَزْقًا ه
To defeat, to crush a. o. — o فُلَانًا ضَرْبًا
Unsociable, untractable. عَزِق ج عُزُق
Vessel, censer. عَزْقِيّ
Swing. ✧ عُنْزُوقَة
Elegance in dress. ▫ عَزْقَلَة
Spade, hoe. مِعْزَق ومِعْزَقَة ج مَعَازِق
To remove, to set apart; to discharge a. o. from (office). ※ عَزَل i عَزْلًا، وعَزَّل ه وه عن
To be discharged, dismissed. عُزِل
✧ To cleanse a. th. عَزَّل ه
To withdraw, to retire from. تَعَزَّل وانْعَزَل واعْتَزَل عن
To resign (an office). To withdraw from (business). تَعَزَّل واعْتَزَل ه
To part from o. another. تَعَازَل
To be discharged, removed from office. تَعَزَّل واعْتَزَل و✧ انْعَزَل
Discharge from office. عَزْل
State of being unarmed. عَزَل
Weakness. عُزْل
Unarmed. عُزْل ج أَعْزَال
Life in retirement. Solitary life. عُزْلَة
Cleansing. تَعْزِيل
Having no weapon. Isolated tract of sand. Unable to fly (bird). Cloud without rain. Portion of meat set apart for an absent man. أَعْزَل ج عُزْل وأَعْزَال وعُزَّل وعُزْلَان
Anus. Mouth of a water-skin. عَزْلَاء ج عَزَالِي وعَزَالَى
✧ Insulating stool. عَازِل
Secluded spot. Place of retirement. مَعْزِل
Far away from. بِمَعْزِل عن
The Seceders (musulman dissenters). مُعْتَزِلَة
Traveller remaining apart. Weak. Disarmed. مِعْزَال ج مَعَازِيل
※ عَزَم i عَزْمًا وعُزْمًا ومَعْزَمًا وعَزِيمًا وعَزِيمَة وعَزَامَة وعُزْمَانًا على وه
To resolve upon.
To carry out a resolution. To be resolved upon (affair). عَزَم
To beseech a. o. to. عَزَم على فُلَان ل او أن

To be remote, distant. To send camels to a remote pasturage. أَعْزَب
To send a. o. far away. — ه
To remain unmarried. تَعَزَّب
Hamlet, farm. ▫ عَزْبَة ج عِزَاب
Celibacy. عُزْبَة وعُزُوبَة
Remote pasturage. عَازِب
▫ Widower, divorced woman. عَازِب م عَازِبَة
Bachelor, spinster, single. عَزَب (m. f.) ج عُزَّاب وأَعْزَاب
Bachelor. ▫ Widower عَزِيب, وأَعْزَب م عَزْبَاء ج عُزْب
Female slave. Wife. مِعْزَبَة
Pasturing camels far away. مِعْزَاب ومِعْزَابَة
To blame, to reprove a. o. ※ عَزَر i عَزْرًا ه
To prevent a. o. from. — ه عن
To constrain a. o. To teach (religion) to a. o. — ه على
To correct, to punish severely. To flog a. o. To assist. To honour a. o. ✧ To insult a. o. عَزَّر ه
Reproof. Punishment. عَزْر وتَعْزِير
Punishment less than prescribed by law. تَعْزِير
Reproved. مُعَزَّر
Ezrail (the Angel of death). ※ عِزْرَائِيل
To turn away from; to be disgusted with a. th. ※ عَزَف o i عَزْفًا وعُزُوفًا عن
To hum in the desert (genii). — عَزِيفًا
To play upon a musical instrument. — i عَزْفًا وعَزِيفًا
To utter a faint, confused sound. عَزَّف
To hear the rustling of the wind. أَعْزَف
Rustling of the wind. Confused sound. ✧ Music. عَزْف
Wild pigeon. عُزْف
Musician, player upon musical instruments. عَازِف
Displeased with. Inconstant friend. عَزُوف وعَزُوفَة ج عِزَاف
Humming, faint sound in the desert. Rumbling of thunder. عَزِيف
Thundering cloud. عَزَّاف

To console o.'s self, to take patience. تَعَزَّى عن
To console, to condole one another. تَعَازَى
Patient. عَزٍ م عَزِيَة وعَزِيّ م عَزِيَّة
Patience; endurance. ✧ Wailing of the dead; visit of condolence. عَزَاء
Relationship; original connection. عِزْيَة
Consolation afforded; condolence. تَعْزِيَة
Consoled. مُعَزًّى
Consolator, comforter. مُعَزٍّ
To patrol, to go the rounds by night. To come late (news). ✡ عَسَّ o عَسًّا وعَسَسًا
To give to a. o. little to eat. — ه
To go roundabout by night. إِعْتَسَّ
To search for a. th. during the night. To follow traces (dog). — ه
Patrol, night-watch. عَسّ وعَسَس
Glass, tumbler. عُسّ ج عِسَاس وعِسَسَة
The she-camel has yielded milk unwillingly. دَرَّت النَّاقَةُ عِسَاسًا
Going round-about, patrolling by night. عَاسّ ج عَسَس وعُسِيس, وعَسَّاس
Wolf. Night-watch. العَسَّاس
Grumbling when milked (she-camel). Yielding little milk. Seeking for prey, game, by night (man, lion). عَسُوس
Petition, request. مَعَسّ
To fall in; to dissipate (darkness of night). To near the earth (cloud). ✡ عَسْعَسَ
To prowl about (wolf). — وتَعَسْعَسَ
Wolf. Beast of prey. Mirage. عَسْعَس وعَسْعَاس
Hedgehogs. عَسَاعِس
To hire a (stallion). ✡ عَسَبَ i عَسْبًا ه
To run away (wolf). أَعْسَبَ
To feel a dislike for. إِسْتَعْسَبَ من
Offspring. عَسْب
Bone of the tail. Instep. Shaft-feather. Cleft in a mountain. Leafless palm-branch. عَسِيب ج عُسُب وعُسْب وعُسْبَان
King of the bees. Prince, chief. Gold. Kind of partridge. Blaze on a horse's forehead. يَعْسُوب ج يَعَاسِيب
Panther. ✡ عُسْبُر ج عَسَابِر
To stretch out ✡ عَسَجَ o i عَسْجًا وعَسَجَانًا

✧ To urge a. o. to. To invite a. o. to dinner. عَزَم ه على
To make a spell (wizard). ✧ To exorcise. — وعَزَّم
To determine upon. To be firmly resolved to. تَعَزَّم واعْتَزَم ه وعلى
To carry out a resolution. To betake o.'s self to. إِعْتَزَم
Resolution, firm purpose. عَزْم ج عُزُوم
People endowed with resolution, constancy. أُولُوا العَزْم
Dregs of pressed raisins. عَزْم ج عُزُم
Kindred. Tribe. عُزْمَة ج عُزَم
Intention. Resolution. Duty imposed by God. عَزْمَة ج عَزَمَات
Steadiness. Swift run. عَزِيم
Steadiness, firmness of resolution. Duty imposed by God. ✧ Invitation to dinner, party. عَزِيمَة ج عَزَائِم
He is an unsteady man. مَا لَهُ عَزْمَة ولَا عَزِيمَة
Fulfilling a promise. Seller of dregs of raisins. عَزْمِيّ
Acting resolutely. Faithful friend. عَازِم م عَزَمَة وعَازِمُون
Affair decided upon. أَمْرٌ عَازِم
Sincere friends. عَزَمَة
Resolute in his designs. عَزُوم
Snake-charmer. Reciting spells. عَزَّام ومُعَزِّم
The lion. العَزَّام والمُعْتَزِم
✧ Exorcism. تَعْزِيم
Resolutely undertaken. مَعْزُوم
✧ Invited, guest.
Determined upon. Resolute. مُعْتَزِم على
✡ عِزْه وعِزِه وعِزْهِيّ وعِزْهَاة ج عِزَاه وعِزَاهِيّ وعِزْهُون Abstemious. Vile.
To trace back the origin of a. o. to. ✡ عَزَا o عَزْوًا ه وه الى
To assert to be the son of a. o. — وتَعَزَّى واعْتَزَى الى ول
Party of men. عِزَة ج عِزًى وعِزُون
Connection, lineage, descent. عِزْوَة
To trace back a. o. to. ✡ عَزَى i عَزْيًا ه ه الى
To bear patiently; to console o.'s self. To receive comfort, condolence. عَزِيَ a عَزَاء على
To console, to condole a. o. عَزَّى ه

More difficult, more unlucky. أَعْسَر م عُسْرَى ج عُسْر
Left-handed. —ج عُسْراء ج عُسْر و ✧ عِسْرَاوِي
Ambidextrous. أَعْسَر يَسَر
Pressing a debtor importunately. مُعْسَر
Poor, destitute. مُعْسِر
Critical (state). Insolvent (debtor). مَعْسُور
To act wrongfully (prince). To be at the point of death. ✱ عَسَف i عَسْفًا
To take a. o. as servant. — ه
To seize a. th. forcibly. — ه
To act, to speak recklessly. — في الأمر او الكَلَام
To work for a. o. — على ول
To stray from (the road). To go at random. — ه وعن وتَعَسَّف واعْتَسَف عن
✧ To wipe off a. th. عَسَّف ه
To overwork a. o. عَسَّف وأَعْسَف ه
To lose the way by night. أَعْسَف
To treat a. o. wrongfully. تَعَسَّف ه
To treat (an affair) inconsiderately. — واعْتَسَف ه
To be bent. إِنْعَسَف
To compel, to constrain a. o. to. إِعْتَسَف ه ب
Wrong-doing, oppression. Death. عَسْف
Unjustly, violently, forcibly. عَسْفًا
Disease of the windpipe. عُسَاف
Suffering from convulsion of the windpipe. عَاسِف (*m. f.*) ج عَوَاسِف
Unjust, oppressor, tyrant. عَسُوف وعَسَّاف ومِعْسَف
Labourer, hired workman. عَسِيف ج عُسَفَاء
To stick to. ✱ عَسِق a عَسَقًا, وتَعَسَّق
To prosecute a. th. eagerly. — على
Ill-nature. Injustice. عَسَق
Hard towards his debtors. عُسُق
Wine mixed with much water. عَسِيقَة
To move about, to shine (looming). ✱ عَسْقَل
Looming. عَسْقَل ج عَسَاقِل وعَسَاقِيل
To form an encampment (soldiers). To gather. To become dark (night). ✱ عَسْكَر
To levy (troops); to collect an army. — ه

the neck in walking. To limp, to halt (camel).
To be bent, crooked (old man). إِعْسَنْجَ
Thorny tree. Box-thorn. عَوْسَج
Gold. Gems. Large camel. ✱ عَسْجَد
Horses wearing rich trappings. عَسْجَدِيَّة
To twist (a rope). ✱ عَسَد i عَسْدًا ه
Strong. Big snake. عِسْوَد
Long worm. عِسْوَدَّة
To be difficult, adverse (time). ✱ عَسَر o i عَسْرًا وعُسْرًا على
To oppose. — وعَسَّر على
To press (a debtor); to compel a. o. — وأَعْسَر ه
To be left-handed. To be ambidextrous. عَسِر a عَسَرًا
عَسِر a عُسْرًا وعُسُرًا وعَسَرًا ومَعْسُورًا, وعَسُر o عُسْرًا وعَسَارَةً
To be difficult to a. o. (affair). To be harsh, ill-tempered.
To render a. th. (difficult). عَسَّر ه
To meet a. o. on the left side. — ه
To treat a. o. harshly. عَاسَر ه
To be reduced to destitution. أَعْسَر
To have a laborious childbirth (woman).
To be abstruse (speech). To be hard to bear. تَعَسَّر
To behave harshly, to disagree one with the other. تَعَاسَر
To extort a. th. from, to embezzle: إِعْتَسَر من مال فُلَان
To constrain, to compel a. o. — ه
To ride an untrained camel.
To be difficult to a. o. (affair). إِسْتَعْسَر على
To find a. th. difficult, painful. — ه
Hardship. Strait circumstances. عُسْر وعُسُر
Retention of urine. عُسْر البَوْل
Critical circumstances. Destitution. عُسْرَة وعُسْرَى ومَعْسَرَة ومَعْسُرَة
White feather on the wing of a bird. عَسْرَة وعَسْرَاء
They came one after another. جَاءُوا عُسَارَيَات وعُسَارَى
They scattered on all sides. ذَهَبُوا عُسَارَيَات
Difficult. Critical (time). Ill-tempered (person). عَسِر وعَسِير

To give to a. o. his want. إعْتَسَم ه
To wear old (shoes). — ه
Rigidity of the arm or leg. عَسَم
A mouthful. عَسْمَة
Piece of dry bread. عَسَمَة
Having the arm or leg dried up. أَعْسَم م عَسْمَاء ج عُسْم
Being in good or bad business. عَسْمِيّ
Earning for his family. عَسُوم ج عُسُم
Piece of dry bread. Small draught. عُسُوم
To fatten (beasts : fodder). ✱ عَسِن a عَسَنًا في
To produce few plants (ground). أَعْسَن وتَعَسَّن
To seek the traces of a. o. تَعَسَّن ه
Length and fineness of the hair. Fatness. عَسَن
Similar, alike. عِسْن
Fatness. — وعُسْن
Traces of a thing. أَعْسَان الشَّيْء
To become hard and dry (wood). To become intensely dark (night). ✱ عَسَا o عُسُوًّا وعَسَاء، وعَسِيَ a عَسًى
To become coarse and rough (hand). عَسَا o عُسُوًّا
To become advanced in age (man). عَسَا o عَسْوًا وعُسُوًّا وعُسِيًّا وعَسَاء وعَسْوَة
Wax. عَسْوٌ
Fading of a plant. Thick. Coarse. عُسُوّ
Withering (plant). عَاسٍ م عَاسِيَة
To be near, (*defective verb*). about to. To be on the eve of. عَسَى
It might be that... May be that... Perhaps. عَسَى أن
I might understand. عَسَى أن أَفْهَم
He may become better. عَسَاهُ أن يَنْصَلِح
What a clever man! How suited he is! أَعْسِ بِهِ
Able, fit, suited to. عَسٍ وعَسِيّ ومَعْسَاة ب
It becomes thee to do so. بِالعَسِيّ او بِالعَسَى أن تَفْعَل كَذَا
Girl near to attain puberty. مِعْسَاء
To keep to its nest (bird). ✱ عَشّ o عَشًّا
To acquire a. th. To repair (clothes). — ه
To dislodge (people). — وأَعَشّ ه
To be slender, lean (body). — o عُشُوشَة وعَشَاشَة وعَشَشًا

Army, troops. Large number. عَسْكَر ج عَسَاكِر
Distress, anxiety. Dearth. عَسْكَرَة
Soldier, military. عَسْكَرِيّ ج عَسْكَرِيَّة
Military service. عَسْكَرِيَّة
Camp. مُعَسْكَر
To season (food) with honey, ✱ عَسَل o i عَسْلًا، وعَسَّل ه
To supply a. o. with a provision of honey. — وعَسَّل ه
To quiver (lance). عَسَل i عَسْلًا وعُسُولًا وعَسَلَانًا
To be rippled by the wind (water). — o عَسْلًا وعَسَلَانًا
To run in (the desert). — ب
To ask for honey. إِسْتَعْسَل
عَسَل ج عُسُل وعُسُول وعُسْل وأَعْسَال وَعُسْلَان
Honey. Flowers. Gum of trees. Juice of fresh dates.
✧ Honeysuckle (*plant*). زَهْر العَسَل
Honeycomb. Origin of a man. عَسَلَة
Honey-coloured, honey-like. عَسَلِيّ
Straightforward, righteous man. عَاسِل وعَسُول ج عُسُل
Collecting honey in the hives. Quivering (lance). عَاسِل وعَسَّال
Quivering (lance). عَاسِلَة ج عَوَاسِل
Hive. Bees. عَسَّالَة
Perfumer's broom. عَسِيل ج عُسُل
Manufactured or natural hive. مَعْسَلَة وَمَعْسُلَة
Prepared with honey. مُعَسَّل ومَعْسُول
To shoot forth green and tender boughs (tree). ✱ عَسْلَج
Young and tender twig. Heedless (boy). عُسْلُج ج عَسَالِج، وعُسْلُوج ج عَسَالِيج
To desire earnestly, to covet a. th. ✱ عَسَم i عَسْمًا في
It is a thing which nobody wishes to take forcibly. هٰذَا أَمْرٌ لا يُعْسَمُ فيهِ
To gain; to earn a living. — i عَسْمًا وعُسُومًا
To toil, to exert o.'s self in. — في
To shed tears. To have the eyelids closed (eye). — وأَعْسَم
To be distorted (foot, hand). عَسِم a عَسَمًا، وأَعْسَم
To stiffen, to render (the arms, legs) rigid. أَعْسَم ه

Watering of cattle every ten days. عِشْر

Tenth part; a tenth; tithe. عُشْر ج عُشُور وأَعْشَار

Broken heart. قَلْبٌ أَعْشَار

Large cooking-pot broken in pieces. قِدْر أَعْشَار

Asclepias gigantea (*plant*). ◘ عُشَر

Ten. عَشَرَة م عَشْر

Ten. عَشَرَة ج عَشَرَات

Friendship, social intercourse. عِشْرَة

Tenth. Gathering the tithe. Watered on the tenth day (camel). عَاشِر ج عُشَّر

Ninth or tenth day of Moharram. ✧ New year's day (among Moslems). Kind of pudding. عَشُورَى وعَاشُور وعَاشُورَاء وعَاشُورَى

✧ Sociable, liking society. عَشُور

Gatherer of tithes. Publican. Farmer of taxes. عَشَّار ج عَشَّارُون

She-camel in the tenth month of her pregnancy. عُشَرَاء

They came by parties of ten, ten and ten. جَاءُوا عُشَارَ او مَعْشَرَ

The tenth part of. عُشَارَة

Ten cubits long (garment). Boat on the Nile. عُشَارِيّ

Decimal numbers. أَعْشَارِيّ

Friend, associate. Husband; wife. عَشِير ج عُشَرَاء

The tenth. — ج أَعْشِرَاء

Cognation, kindred. Kinsfolk on the father's side. Tribe. عَشِيرَة ج عَشَائِر

Collective body of men. مَعْشَر ج مَعَاشِر

Tenth part. مِعْشَار

Friend, companion. مُعَاشِر

Social intercourse, friendly relations. مُعَاشَرَة

Pregnant (mare). ✧ مُعَشِّرَة

To become green (plant). ✱ عَشْرَق

Circœa, enchanter's nightshade (*plant*). Species of cassia. عِشْرِق

To make up the number twenty. عَشْرَنَ

Twenty. Twentieth. عِشْرُون, عِشْرِين

To totter, to hobble. ✱ عَشَز i عَشَزَانًا

To walk in leaning upon (a stick). — على

To loathe a. th. ✱ عشف — أَعْشَفَ ه وعن

To nest (bird). عَشَّش واعْتَشّ

To emaciate (the body: God). أَعَشّ واعْتَشّ ه

To be repaired (garment). إِنْعَشّ

To take scanty provisions. إِعْتَشّ

Unimportant gift. Slender. عَشّ

Bird-nest upon a tree. عَشّ وعُشّ ج عِشَاش وأَعْشَاش وعِشَشَة

Slender tree. عَشَّة

Thatch-hut. ✧ عُشَّة ج عُشَش

Question, petition. مَعَشّ

Nesting-place of birds. مُعَشِّش

Making its nest (bird). مُعَشِّش

To become dry, to wither (herbage). ✱ عَشِب a عَشَبًا

To produce green herbs (ground). — وعَشُب o عَشَابَةً, وعَشَّب وأَعْشَب

To gather green herbs, to herborize. ✧ To scrape. عَشَّب

To find pasture-lands. أَعْشَب

To feed on herbage and become fattened (cattle). — وتَعَشَّب

To become covered with luxuriant herbage (ground). إِعْشَوْشَب

Green, fresh herbs, pasturage. عُشْب ج أَعْشَاب

Families composed only of adults. عِيَال عَشَب

Vegetation. Verdiness of a field. عَشَابَة

Broken and bent with age. (*m. f.*) عَشَبَة

Covered with green herbs (field). عَاشِب وعَشِب وعَشِيب ومُعْشِب, ومِعْشَاب ج مَعَاشِيب

To tithe a. th. ✱ عَشَر o عَشْرًا وعُشُورًا, وعَشَّر ه وه

To make up the number ten; to be the tenth. — i عَشْرًا

He became the tenth of them. — هم

To repeat 10 times the same cry (ass, crow). عَشَّر

To be in the tenth month of pregnancy (mare, she-camel). — وأَعْشَر

To court the society of; to haunt a. o. عَاشَر ه

To be ten in number. أَعْشَر

To have friendly intercourse with o. a. To become intimate with, to frequent o. a. تَعَاشَر

Weakness of the sight. عَشَاء وعَشَارَة
Blindness. Night-blindness.
Supper, evening meal. عَشَاء ج أعْشِيَة
The Lord's supper. العَشَاء السِّرّيّ
Nigthfall, dusk. عِشَاء وعَشِيّ
Nigthfall, evening. عَشِيَّة ج عَشَايَا وعَشِيَّات
Yesterday evening. عَشِيَّة أمس
Sunset (مَغرِب) and dusk (عَتَمَة). العِشَاءَان
Belonging to the evening. عَشَوِيّ
Dusk, darkness of the night. عَشْوَة
Fire-brand. Fire seen from afar during the night. عُشْوَة وعِشْوَة
Pasturing by night (cattle). عَاشِيَة ج عَوَاشٍ
Night-blind. عَشٍ م عَشِيَة, وأعْشَى م عَشْوَاء
Blind (she-camel). Darkness of night. عَشْوَاء
He acts inconsiderately. يَخْبِط خَبْط عَشْوَاء
Cook. Ts عَشِّي وعَشِّجِي
Place of supper. مُتَعَشَّى
To become hard. ✱ عَصَّ a عَصًّا وعَصَصًا
✧ To press, to squeeze a. th. – على
To press (a debtor). عَصَّص على
Tail-bone. عُصْص وعُصُص
✱ عَصْعَص وعُصْعُص ج عَصَاعِص , وعُصْعُوص
Mean (man). Tail-bone. Coccyx. ج عَصَاعِيص
To bind (a limb). To put on a turban. To tighten. ✱ عَصَب i عَصْبًا, وعَصَّب ه
To surround (a water-trough : cattle). – عَصْبًا وعَصِب a عَصَبًا ب
To combine with a. o, – بِفُلَان
To dry in the mouth (saliva). – ه وب
To become unclean (teeth). To become red (horizon). – عَصْبًا وعُصُوبًا
To take a. th. by force. – عَصْبًا وعِصَابًا على
To have sinews (flesh). عَصِب a عَصَبًا
To choose (a leader : party). To starve (people : dearth). عَصَّب ه
To walk at a quick pace (camel). أعْصَب
To put on a turban, a bandage. تَعَصَّب
To be satisfied with. – ب

No foul deed will be imputed to me. مَا يُعْشَفُ لِي أمْرٌ قَبِيحٌ
To love a. o. passionately. ✱ عَشِق a عِشْقًا وعَشَقًا ومَعْشَقًا ه
To cleave, to stick to. عَشِق ب
✧ To fit in. عَشِق وتَعَشَّق
To show love to. تَعَشَّق
To love o. another passionately. تَعَاشَق
Passionate, excessive love. عِشْق
Bind-weed. عَشَقَة ج عَشَق
Loving passionately. عَاشِق (m. f.) ج عُشَّاق وعَاشِقُون وعَوَاشِق
Sweetheart, lover. عَشَّاق وعِشِّيق
To be dried up (tree). ✱ عَشِم a عَشَمًا وعُشُومًا, وتَعَشَّم
✧ To give hope to. To hope for. i عَشَم
✧ To resolve upon. تَعَشَّم ب
Covetousness, eagerness. عَشَم وعَشَمَة
Dry and sour bread. خُبْز عَشِم
Mixture of two colours. Dried up (tree). أعْشَم م عَشْمَاء
To give an opinion, to conjecture. ✱ عَشَن o عَشْنًا, وعَشَّن واعْتَشَن
To attack a. o. without motive. إعْتَشَن ه
Dates of bad quality. عُشَان وعُشَانَة
To go by night. ✱ عَشَا o عَشْوًا ه
To give supper to. – عَشْوًا وعَشْيًا ه
To pasture (cattle) by night. – عَشْوًا ه
To turn away from. عَشَا عن
To direct o.'s self towards (the fire) by night. – عَشْوًا وعُشُوًّا ه والى
To be weak-sighted. To be night-blind. – o عَشْوًا وعَشِي a عَشًا
To wrong a. o. عَشِيَ على
To eat supper. To feed (cattle) during the night. عَشِي a وتَعَشَّى
To give supper to a. o. عَشَّى وأعْشَى ه
To pasture (cattle) by night. To catch (night-birds) with a light. عَشَّى ه
To blind a. o. أعْشَى ه
To eat the evening-meal. تَعَشَّى
To feign blindness, ignorance. تَعَاشَى
To set off at nightfall. إعْتَشَى
To repair towards the fire by night. – ه او ب
To be guided during the night by the light of a fire. المُتَعَشَّى نارًا

To defend a. th. desperately. تعصّب في
To be obstinate in.
To be bigoted, a zealot. — في دينهِ
To form a league with. — ل ومع
To struggle desperately against. — على
To become difficult (affair). إِنعصب واعصوصب
To wind a turban round (the head). إعتصب ب
To coalesce, to league together. — واعصوصب
Turban. Kind of garment. Sharp boy. Saliva drying in the mouth. عَصْب
Bind-weed. — وعُصْب وعَصَب
Sinew. Choice men of a tribe. عَصَب ج أعصاب
Sinewy, muscular. عَصَبِيّ
Sinew, nerve. League, coalition. Relations on the father's side. Distant relation having no legal claim. ✧ Black head-kerchief worn yb women. عَصَبَة ج عَصَبات
Manner of binding a turban. عِصْبَة
Troop, band of men, of cattle, of birds. ✧ Faction, gang. عُصْبَة ج عُصَب
We form a party; we are in number. نحنُ عُصْبَةٌ
Rope for tying a camel's thigh. عِصاب
Thread-maker or seller. عَصَّاب
Bandage. Head-band. Turban. Red mist seen in a time of drought. عِصابة ج عَصائِب
Ugly and lean (woman). عَصُوب
Bound with a rope (she-camel). Lights and guts of sheep bound and roasted together. عَصِيب ج أعصِبَة وعُصُب
Vehemently hot (day). يَوم عَصِيب
Party-spirit. Patriotism. Relationship on the father's side. عَصَبِيَّة
Obstinacy, stubbornness. Fanaticism, zealotry, bigotry. — وتعصُّب
Wearing a turban: crowned. Lord, master. Reduced to straitness by dearth. مُعَصَّب
Bandaged (wound). Starved. Thin (sword). مَعْصُوب
To bend, to ✱ عَصَد i عَصْدًا, وأعصد ه

twist a. th. To prepare a gruel. To deviate (arrow).
To constrain a. o. to. عَصَد i عَصْدًا ه على
To stiffen (thread) with starch. ✧ عَصَّد ه
To be starched (thread). ✧ تعصَّد
To raise a clamour in fight. عَصْوَد عَصْوَدَة
Gruel of flour with butter and honey. ✧ Starch-paste. عَصِيدَة
To press, to squeeze (grapes). To wring (linen). ✱ عَصَر i عَصْرًا, واعتصر ه
To withdraw a. th. from; to prevent a. o. from. — ه وه عن
To have rain. أعصر
To put forth husks (corn-crops). عَصَّر
To express the juice of grapes. — ه
To attain puberty (girl). — وأعصر
To be contemporary with. عاصر ه
To enter upon the afternoon. أعصر
To be squeezed, expressed (fruit). To become difficult (affair). تعصَّر وانعصر واعتصر
To take refuge towards. تعصَّر واعتصر ب
To draw, to extort a. th. from. To take back (a gift) from. إعتصر ه من
Afternoon. عَصْر ج أعصُر وعُصُور
Afternoon-prayer. صَلاة العَصْر
The morning and evening. العَصْران
He came late. جاءَ عَصْرًا
عَصْر وعِصْر وعُصْر ج أعصار وأعصُر وعُصُور
Time. Age, century, epoch.
He is matchless in his time. هوَ فَرِيد عَصْرِهِ
Of illustrious descent. كَرِيم العَصْر والعَصِير
He came untimely. لَم يَجِئْ لِعُصْرٍ
Asylum, refuge. عُصْر وعَصَر وعُصْرَة ومُعتَصَر
Expressed juice (of a fruit). ✧ Must. عَصِير وعَصِيرَة وعُصار وعُصارَة
Pl. Three stones for pressing grapes. عاصِرَة ج عَواصِر
Dust swept by the wind. عِصار
In a moment. على عِصار من الزَّمان
Whirlwind, hurricane. إعصار ج أعاصِر وأعاصِير
Presser. عَصَّار
Origin, family. Element, constituent. عُنصُر وعُنصَر ج عَناصِر

Sparrow. ✧ عُصْفُور دُورِي
Female sparrow. ✧ Bundle of ropes. عُصْفُورَة
To be distorted, crooked (wood). To urine. ✳ عَصِل a عَصَلًا
To bend, to twist a. th. عَصَل o عصلًا ه
To be late. عَصَّل
To twist a. th. — ه
Crookedness, distortion. Twisting tracts of sand. عَصَل
Bowels. عِصْل وعَصَل ج أَعْصَال
عَصِل م عَصِلَة ج عِصَال , وأَعْصَل م عَصْلَاء
Distorted, crooked. ج عُصْل
Intricate affair. أَمْرٌ أَعْصَل
Wild onion, squill. عُنْصُل وعُنْصَل ج عَنَاصِل
Harsh towards a debtor. مِعْصَل
Crooked staff. مِعْصَال ج مَعَاصِيل
To be strong, hardy. ✳ عَصْلَب
Strong, hardy. عَصْلَب وعُصْلُب وعُصْلُبِيّ
To preserve, to protect a. o. ✳ عَصَم i عَصْمًا ه وه
To keep a. o. safe from evil. — ه من المَكْرُوه
To seek refuge towards. — الى
To strap the head of (a skin). — وأَعْصَمَ ه
To be white-footed (horse, goat). عَصِم a عَصَمًا
To strengthen a. o. upon a saddle. أَعْصَمَ ه
To hold fast by. To lay hold upon a. th. — واعْتَصَم ب
To protect o.'s self. — وانْعَصَم واعْتَصَم من
To abstain from sin; to protect o.'s self from evil. أَعْصَم واعْتَصَم واسْتَعْصَم من الشَّرّ
To have recourse to. إِعْتَصَم واسْتَعْصَم ب
Remains, traces. عُصْم وعُصُم وعَصِيم
White spot on a beast's foot. عَصَم
Strap of a water-skin. Collyrium. Handle of a vessel. عِصَام ج أَعْصِمَة وعُصُم وعِصَام
Virtuous, self-ennobled. عِصَامِيّ
Protection. Prevention. Immunity from sin, error. Virtue, chastity. عِصْمَة
— ج عِصَم وأَعْصُم وعِصَمَة وجج أَعْصَام
Dog's collar.

The four elements. [illegible] الأَرْبَعَة
Whitsunday. Pentecost. [illegible]ـرَة
Simple, uncompound (substance). [illegible]ـرِي
Pressing-place. [illegible] ومَعْصَرَة ج مَعَاصِر
Generous, giving freely. كَرِيم العُصَارَة والمَعْصَر والمُعْتَصَر
Wine-press; olive-press. مِعْصَر ومِعْصَرَة ج مَعَاصِر
Adult, marriageable (girl). مُعْصِر ج مَعَاصِر ومَعَاصِير
Rain-clouds. مُعْصِرَات
Contemporary, contemporaneous. مُعَاصِر
To lunch. ✧ تَعَصْرَن
Lunch. ✧ عَصْرُونِيَّة
To blow in a gale (wind). To be quick. ✳ عَصَف i عَصْفًا وعُصُوفًا , وأَعْصَف
To earn for (o.'s family). — واعْتَصَف ه
War has blasted them. عَصَفَت وأَعْصَفَت الحَرْبُ بِهِم
To cut corn when green. عَصَف o عَصْفًا ه
To put forth blades (corn). To go astray. To perish (man). أَعْصَف
Blades, dry leaves of corn-produce. عَصْف
Smell of wine. عَصْف
Violent, blowing in a gale, stormy (wind). عَاصِف وعَاصِفَة ومُعْصِف ومُعْصِفَة
Storm, whirlwind, hurricane. عَاصِفَة ج عَوَاصِف
Blowing violently (wind). عَصُوف ج عُصُف , وعَصِيف
Swift-running (gazelle, she-camel). عَصُوف
Dry leaves. Heads of the ears of corn. عَصِيفَة
Particles falling off from the corn-ears. عُصَافَة
To dye yellow. ✳ عَصْفَر ه
To be dyed yellow. تَعَصْفَر
Carthamus tinctorius, bastard safflower (yellow dye). عُصْفُر
Sparrow; any small bird. King. Blaze on a horse's head. عُصْفُور ج عَصَافِير
He is hungry. نَقَّتْ عَصَافِيرُ بَطْنِهِ
High breed camels. عَصَافِير المُنْذِر
Gillyflower. عُصَيْفِرَة و✧ عُصَيْفِيرَة

To be intricate (affair). تعصّى واعتصى
To become hard (fruit-stone). إعتصى
Rebellion, disobedience. عِصيان ومَعصِيَة
Rebel, disobedient. عاصٍ ج عُصاة
Bleeding unceasingly (vein). — ج عَوَاصٍ
عَصِيّ ج عَصِيُّون وأعصياء, وعَصّاء ج عَصّاؤون
Rebellious. Apostate.
The Orontes (river). نهر العاصي
To seize with the teeth, to bite a. th. ✻ عَضّ a عَضًّا وعَضِيضًا ه وب وعلى
He spoke evil of him. عَضَّهُ بِلِسانِهِ
Fortune has been severe for him. عَضَّهُ الزَّمانُ
To cling, to stick to. عَضّ a عَضِيضًا ب
To bite strongly. عَضَّض ه
To bite o. a. (cattle). عاضّ مُعاضَّة وعِضاضًا
To make a. o. to seize a. th. with the teeth. أعضّ ه ه
I wounded him with my sword. أعضضتُهُ سَيفي
To bite one another. تعاضّ
Bite; seizure with the teeth. عَضّ وعَضِيض (un. عَضَّة)
The strokes of fortune and war. عَضّ الزَّمان والحَرْب
Niggardly. Wicked. Cunning. Resolute and strong. عِضّ ج عُضُوض وأعضاض
Good walker. — سَفَر
Barley, fodder for cattle. عُض
Morsel, bit. عَضاض
Patient under trial. عِضاض عَيْش
Prone to bite. Tyrant. Severe time. Bit of bread. Deep well. عَضُوض
Bone, cartilage. عُضاض وعُضّاض
To cut off a. th. ✻ عَضَب i عَضْبًا ه
To disable a. o. (disease). — ه
To revile a. o. — ه بِلِسانِهِ
To pierce a. o. with a spear. — ه ب
To prevent a. o. from. — ه عن
Having a broken horn, a slit ear (sheep). عَضِب a عَضَبًا, وأعضَب
To deter, to cut off a. o. from. عاضَب ه
Sharp sword. Sharp tongue. Heedless (child). عَضْب
Reviler. عَضّاب

Dog's collar. White-footed. عُصْمَة
Gluttonous, voracious. عَصُوم وعَيْصُوم
Prohibited; well defended. عاصِم
Meal of parched barley. أبو عاصِم
Chaste (woman). Well defended; *surname of* Medinah. Capital town, metropolis. عاصِمَة ج عَواصِم
The province of Antioch. العَواصِم
White-footed (horse, wild goat). أعصَم م عَصْماء ج عُصْم
Wrist; upper part of the hand. مِعصَم ج مَعاصِم
Shelter. Place of refuge. مُعتَصَم
Having recourse to God for protection. مُعتَصِم بالله
Impeccable, infallible. مَعصُوم
To strike a. o. with a stick. To bind (a wound). ✻ عَصا o عَصْوًا ه وه
To take (a stick). عَصِي a عَصًا
To use a sword as a staff. — واعتصى بالسَّيف
To give a stick to a. o. عَصَّى ه
To strike o. a. with a staff. عاصَى ه
To put forth fruitless shoots (vine). أعصَى
To lean upon (a staff). إعتصى على
To cut (a stick) from a tree. — ه
Staff, stick. Stay. Support. Handle of an axe. Leg-bone. Tongue. عَصا ج عُصِيّ وأعصٍ
Polygonum, knot-grass. عَصا الرَّاعي
Mild-tempered man. لَيِّن العَصا
Weak-tempered man. ضَعِيف العَصا
He split the staff *i. e.* he made a schism. شَقّ العَصا
He threw the staff *i. e.* he broke his journey. ألقى العَصا
The staff is broken *i. e.* they are disunited. إنشقّت العَصا
He has peeled the staff *i. e.* he has opened his mind to him. قَشَر لهُ العَصا
He has admonished him severely. قَرَع لهُ العَصا
Small staff, rod. عُصَيَّة
To rebel against; to disobey. To baffle all means (hemorrhage). ✻ عَصَى i عَصْيًا ومَعصِيَة
To rebel against. — ه وعلى تَعاصَى واستَعصَى على

أعضب م عضباء ج عُضب Having a broken horn, a slit ear. Brotherless. Weak, helpless.
مَعضوب Feeble, sickly, crippled.
✱ عَضَد o عَضدًا ه To help, to assist a.o. To wound a. o. on the arm.
عُضِد To have a pain in the arm.
عَضَد i عَضدًا, واستعضد ه To lop (a tree) with a hook.
عَضَّد وأعضد To deviate (arrow).
عاضد ه To help, to succour a. o.
تعاضد To help one another.
إعتضد To become strong.
— ه To take a. th. upon the arm.
— ب To ask assistance from a. o.
إستعضد ه To pluck (fruit).
عَضُد ج أعضاد Side. Stay, support; helper, assistant.
هُوَ عَضُدِي He is my help, my support.
عَضُد وعُضُد وعَضِد ج أعضاد وأعضُد Upper arm of man; arm of a beast. Strength.
عَضَد Disease in the arm of a camel.
عاضدان Two rows of palm-trees bordering a stream.
عَضاد (m. f.) Short (man, woman).
عِضاد Large bracelet. Iron reaping-hook. Brand on a camel's arm.
عِضادة الطَّرِيق Side of a road.
هُوَ عِضادته He is his inseparable companion.
عِضادتا الباب The two posts of a door.
عَضادِيّ وعُضادِيّ Large in the upper-arm.
عَضِيد ج عِضدان Row of palm-trees. Short palm-tree.
أعضد Having slender arms or an arm shorter than the other.
مِعضد ج معاضد Reaping-hook.
مِعضد ومِعضاد Armlet, amulet.
مِعضاد Large butcher's knife.
مَعضود Lopped, trimmed (tree).
✱ عَضرَس Intense cold. Hail, snow.
✱ عَضرَط The perinæum.
عُضرُط وعُضرُوط وعُضارِط ج عَضارِط وعَضارِيط وعَضارِيطة Hired man. Low; base. *Pl.* Attendants, followers. Thieves, rogues.
عُضرُط ج عَضارِيط Gullet, œsophagus.
✱ عَضَل o عَضلًا, وعَضَّل على To act harshly towards; to weary a. o.
— ب To straiten a. o. (affair).
— a i o عَضلًا وعِضلًا وعِضلانًا, وعَضَّل ه To prevent (a woman) from marrying.
عَضِل a عَضَلًا To have a muscular body.
عَضَّل بأهلهِ To become strait with people (land).
أعضل ه وب To be difficult to a. o. (affair).
— وتعضَّل ه To baffle the skill of physicians (disease).
عِضل Foul, crafty man.
عَضَل ج عِضلان Large rat.
عَضِل وعَضَلِيّ Musculous, muscular.
عَضَلة ج عَضَل وعَضَلات, وعَضِيلة ج عَضائِل Muscle.
عُضلة ج عُضل وعُضَل Misfortune, calamity.
عُضال (*m. f.*) ومُعضِل Momentous (affair). Chronical, incurable (disease).
مُعضِلة ج مُعضِلات Distressing event. Misfortune. Intricate question.
✱ عَضم ج عِضام Handle of a bow. Root of the tail.
— ج أعضِمة وعُضُم Winnowing-fork.
✱ عَضَه a عَضهًا وعَضِيهة وعِضهة To lie. To utter magic words.
— ه To slander, to revile a. o.
— ه To browse on acacia-trees (camel).
عَضِه a عَضَهًا, وأعضه To lie, to calumniate.
عِضَه ج عِضُون Lie. Calumny. Witchcraft.
— وعِضاهة ج عِضاه Any thorny tree. Species of acacia-tree. ✧ Hawthorn.
عَضِيهة ج عَضائِه Calumny. Falsehood.
عَضِه م عَضِهة Abounding with acacia-trees (ground).
— وعاضِه (*m. f.*) Depasturing thorny trees.
عاضِه Wizard.
عاضِهة ج عَواضِه Deadly (snake). Lie.
✱ عَضا o عَضوًا, وعَضَّى ه وه To share a. th. To skin (sheep).
عَضَّى ه To divide a. th. into classes, parts.
عُضو وعِضو ج أعضاء Limb of the body. ✧ Member of a society.
عِضة ج عِضون Portion. Party, sect. Lie.
رَجُل عاضٍ Man in good circumstances.

✲ عطّ o عطًّا, وعطّط ه To slit (a piece of cloth).
– ة To master a. o.
– ة الى الأرض To fell a. o. on the ground.
تعطّط وانعطّ To be split, chopped (wood).
إنعطّ To bend (wood).
عُطط Pieces of cloth slit lengthwise.
✲ عطعط To shout, to yell (fighters).
✲ عطِب a عطبًا, واعتطب To perish. To be exhausted (beast). ◻ To be rotten.
– على To lose o.'s temper with.
عطُب o عَطبًا وعُطوبًا To be mellowy, soft (cotton).
عطّب To put forth gems (vine).
– ه To brew (wine) for bettering it. ✧ To spoil, to injure a. th.
أعطب ة To cause the loss of a. o.
إعتطب ه To carry (fire) in a rag.
عَطَب Softness of cotton.
عُطب وعُطُب Cotton. Wool.
عُطبة Flake of cotton. Rag.
مُعطِب Destitute, poor.
مَعطب ج معاطِب Dangerous place.
✲ عطد Hardship, severity.
عطوّد Hard, distant (journey). High (mountain). Long (day). Liberal (man).
✲ عطِر a عطرًا To send out sweet odours.
عطّر ة وه To perfume a. o. or a. th.
تعطّر واستعطر To be perfumed, to smell good. To remain unmarried (woman).
عِطر Sweet odour, perfume.
عِطر ج عُطور Sweet-smelling, aromatic. Essence.
عِطر الوَرد Essence of rose.
عِطريّ Aromatic, fragrant.
عِطارة Trade of a perfumer, a druggist.
عطِر م عطِرة, وعطّار م عطّارة, ومِعطار م مِعطارة (m. f.) Sweet-smelling. Perfuming himself. Valuable (she-camel).
عاطر ج عُطر Liking perfumes.
عطّار Perfumer, druggist.
مُعطّر Perfumed.
معطير (m. f.) Fragrant with perfumes.

✲ عطرّد High (mountain). Tall (man). Long (day). Generous.
عُطارِد Mercury (planet).
✲ عطَس i o عَطسًا وعُطاسًا To sneeze. To break (daylight).
عطست بِهِ اللُّجَم Ill luck befell him. He died.
عطّس ة To cause a. o. to sneeze.
عُطاس وعَطسة Sneezing, sneeze.
هو عَطسةُ فلانٍ He bears a likeness to him.
عاطِس Sneezing. Daybreak.
عاطوس و ✧ عَطوس Snuffing-tobacco, snuff.
اللُّجَمُ العَطوس Death.
مَعطس ج مَعاطِس Nose.
مُعطِس Sternutatory.
✲ عطِش a عَطشًا To be thirsty.
– الى To thirst for a. th.
عطّش وأعطش ة To cause intense thirst to a. o.
عاطش ة To vie with a. o. in bearing thirst.
تعطّش To bear thirst.
عَطش Thirst.
عَطشة Paroxysm of thirst.
عطِش وعطش م عَطِشة وعَطشة Thirsty (person, place).
عُطاش Thirst-giving disease; insatiable thirst.
عطشان ج عَطاشَى وعِطاش وعَطشَى Thirsting. Dried up (soil). Longing for.
مُعطّش Withheld from water (beast).
مَعطش ج مَعاطِش Appointed time of thirst for camels.
مَعطشة ج مَعاطِش Thirsty ground.
مِعطاش (m. f.) Often thirsty.
✲ عطف i عَطفًا وعُطوفًا الى To incline, to lean towards.
– ه To turn aside (a beast) by pulling the rein.
– وعطّف ه To bend, to incline (wood). To fold (a pad).
عطف كلمةً على أُخرى To connect (a word) to another with a conjunction.
– عن To turn away from.
– ة عن To remove a. o. from.
– وتعطّف على To feel sympathy for.
عطِف a عطفًا To have long eyelash.

To neglect a. th. To render (a country) unoccupied, uncultivated. ✧ To impair, to injure. a. th.
To wear no jewel (woman). تَعَطَّل
To be unemployed (labourer). ✧ To be impaired.
Destitute of good, learning. عُطْل وعُطُل ج أعْطَال
Without bridle nor halter (horse). Unarmed (man). Without string (bow). عُطُل ج أعطَال
✧ Damage, loss. عُطْل
✧ Interest of money. عُطْل المال
Want of ornament. Neck. Body, person. Denuded parts of the body. عَطَل
Idleness, worklessness. عُطْلَة
عَاطِل ج عَوَاطِل وعُطْل, وعُطُل ج أعطَال
Wearing no ornament (woman). Undotted (verse).
Destitute of goods, ornaments, qualities. ✧ Damaged. Worthless. Bad. عَاطِل
Stalk of a male palm-tree. عَطِيل وعَيْطَل
Tall, fine (she-camel). عَيْطَل
✧ Cripple. عَطِيلَة
Worthless, damaged. عَطْلَان
✧ Workmen's strike. Damage. Holyday. Delay. تَعْطِيل
Sect denying the divine attributes. مُعَطِّلَة
Unemployed. Untended (flock). Not used (well). Uncultivated (land). ✧ Damaged. Unproductive (money). مُعَطَّل م مُعَطَّلَة
Desert leading to Hedjaz. ◻ عَطْمُور
To macerate (hides). ✡ عطَن o i عَطْنًا, وعَطَّن
To lay near water (cattle). — عُطُونًا
To stink (hide in the tan). ✧ To become mouldy. عَطِن a عَطَنًا, وانْعَطَن
To let cattle rest near water. عَطَّن وأعْطَن ه
Fatherland. عَطَن ج أعْطَان
Resting-place for cattle near water. — ومَعْطِن ومَعْطَن ج مَعَاطِن
Rich and generous. رَحْب العَطَن
Stink. ✧ Mouldiness. عَطَن و✧ عَطْنَة
Macerated and stinking (hide). ✧ Mouldy. عَطِن م عَطِنَة, ومُعَطَّن م مُعَطَّنَة

To inspire sympathy to a. o. for. عطّف ه على
To wrap a. o. in a cloak. — ه ثَوْبَهُ
To wrap o.'s self in a cloak. تَعَطَّف واعْتَطَف ب
To be affectionate, favourable to a. o. تَعَاطَف
To have a proud gait. — في مِشْيَتِهِ
To be inclined. To be bent, folded. إنْعَطَف
✧ To be benevolent towards. — نَحْوَ
To try to conciliate a. o. To implore the mercy of. إسْتَعْطَف ه
Propensity, sympathy. Bend of a road. Conjunction (*gram.*). عَطْف
Conjunctive particle, like ثُمَّ, ف, و. حَرْف العَطْف
Side of the body. Arm-pit. Shoulder. عِطْف ج أعْطَاف وعِطَاف وعُطُوف
He is a self-admirer. يَنظُرُ في عِطْفَيْهِ
Turn, by-street. Vine-prop. عَطْفَة
Tendrils of a vine. عِطْفَة
Creeping plant. عَطَف
Ample garment. Waist-wrapper. Sword. عِطَاف ج عُطُف وأعْطِفَة
Affectionate. Cloak. Conjunction. عَاطِف ج عُطُف
Mercy, kind feeling. Relationship. Bias. عَاطِفَة ج عَوَاطِف وعَاطِفَات
Snare, trap for game. عَاطُوف ج عَوَاطِيف
Trap. Of good disposition. عَطُوف
Bow. عَطِيفَة ج عَطَائِف, وعِطَافَة
Connected to another (word). مَعْطُوف
Word to which another is connected. مَعْطُوف عَلَيْهِ
Curved bow. مَعْطُوفَة
Neck. Bending of the body. Fold of a garment. مَعْطِف ج مَعَاطِف
Cloak. Sword. مِعْطَف ج مَعَاطِف
Bending of a valley. مُنْعَطَف الوَادِي
✡ عَطَل o وعَطِل a عَطَلًا وعُطُولًا, واسْتَعطَل
To wear no jewel (woman).
To be destitute of (wealth, learning). — عَطَلًا من
To be workless (workman). عَطَل o عَطَالَة
To divest (a woman) of her ornaments. To strip a. o. of his goods. To leave a. o. unemployed. عَطَّل ه وه

عَطِين وعَطِينَة Stinking (person).
— ومَعطُون Put into the tan (hide).
عَاطِن ج عُطَّان وعُطُون وعَطَنَة Lying down near water (camel).
عِطَان Tan for hides.
* عَطَا o عَطْوًا ه والى To receive; to give a. th.
— رَأْسَهُ ويَدَيهِ الى To raise the head and the hands towards.
عَطَّى ه To minister to a. o. To urge a. o.
عَاطَى مُعَاطَاةً وعِطَاءً, وأَعطَى ه ه To offer a present to a. o.
عَاطَى ه To serve a. o.
أَعطَى To be tractable (beast).
مَا أَعطَاهُ لِلمَالِ How bountiful he is!
تَعَطَّى وَاسْتَعطَى To ask for a. th.
تَعَطَّى To hurry on.
— ه To exercise (a profession).
تَعَاطَى ه To hand a. th. to o. a. To quarrel about a. th. To engage in. To exert o.'s self in.
تَعَاطَى الشِّعرَ To be addicted to poetry.
عَطًا وعَطَاء ج أَعطِيَة, وعَطِيَّة ج عَطَايَا وعَطِيَّات Gift, present. Soldiers' pay, allowance.
أَعطَى من More bountiful than.
مُعطٍ Giving, granting.
هَل أَنتَ مُعطِيَّه Wilt thou give it to me?
مِعطَاء (m. f.) ج مَعَاطٍ ومَعَاطِي Munificent, generous.
* عَظَّ o عَظًّا ه To try a. o. (war).
— ه بِالأَرضِ To fell a. o. on the ground.
عَاظَّ مُعَاظَّةً وعِظَاظًا ه To ill-treat o. a. To fight desperately with o. a.
عَظَّة Rigour, trials of war.
* عَظَب i عَظْبًا وعُظُوبًا To dry up (hide). To become hard (hand).
— على To take care of a. th.
— وعَظِب a عَظَبًا على To bear a. th. patiently.
عَظَّب ه عن To delay, to hinder a. o. from.
عِظْيَبُ الخُلُق Wicked.
* عُنظُب وعُنظُبَان Kind of locust.
* عَظِر a عَظَرًا ه To feel disgust at a. th.
أَعظَر ه To disorder the stomach (drink).
عِظَارَة Indigestion of drink.

عَظُور ج عُظُر Indisposed through excess of drink.
* عَظَل o وعَظِل a عَظْلًا, وتَعَاظَل واعتَظَل To couple (dogs, locusts).
عَظَّل وتَعَظَّل على To collect together against. To press upon.
عَاظَل مُعَاظَلَةً وعِظَالًا To overlay a. th.
— في القَافِيَة عِظَالًا To insert (in poetry) verses of another poet.
— الكَلَامَ او بِهِ To make repetitions in a discourse.
عَاظِل وعَظلَى Coupled (locusts).
يَوم العُظَالَى The day of conflict amongst the Arabs.
تَعَظلَم To become of a dark blue.
* عِظلِم Indigo, woad; plant dyeing blue. Dark (night).
* عَظُم o عِظَمًا وعَظَامَةً, وأَعظَم To be great, big. To be momentous, grievous (affair, misfortune).
عَظُم على To become momentous, distressing (affair, misfortune).
عَظَم o عَظْمًا, وأَعظَم ه To give a bone to (a dog).
— عَظْمَةً ه To strike a. o. on the bones.
عَظَّم ه To dismember a (sheep).
— وأَعظَم ه وه To hold a. o. as great; to regard, to honour, to exalt a. o. To exaggerate a. th.
تَعَظَّم To be exalted. To grow tall. To be looked upon as great.
— وتَعَاظَم واستَعظَم To magnify o.'s self; to be proud.
تَعَاظَم To be held as great. To become important, grievous.
إستَعظَم ه وه To judge a. o. great. To wonder at the magnitude of. To take the greatest part of.
عَظْم ج أَعظُم وعِظَام Bone.
عَظْم وعُظْم الشَّيء ج أَعظَام Main part.
عِظَم وعِظْم وعُظْم Hugeness; magnitude, importance.
عَظْم الطَّرِيق The middle of the road.
عَظَمَة وعَظَمُوت وعَظَامَة Greatness, grandeur. Pride.
عَظَمَة The thick part of the arm, of the tongue.
عَظَمَات القَوم The chiefs of the people.
عَظِيم ج عُظَمَاء وعِظَام Great. Big, tall,

To shut o.'s self up for dying from starvation. إعتَفَد
To roll a. o. in (the dust). To rub (a vessel) with (earth). To soil with (dust). ✲ عَفَر i عَفْرًا , وعَفَّر ه في
To water (corn-crops) for the first time. To fecundate (a palm-tree). — ه
To be dusty. To be ash-coloured. عَفِر a عَفَرًا , واستعفر
To roast (meat) in the sun, in hot sand. To throw a. o. down in the dust. To render a. th. white. To wean (her young) gradually (female). عَفَّر ه وه
✧ To glean (in a field). — ه
To fall into destitution, contempt. عُفِر
To be soiled with dust. ✧ To be gleaned (ears, olives). تَعَفَّر وانْعَفَر واعتَفَر
To cast its prey upon the ground (lion). إعتَفَر ه
To drag (o.'s clothes) in the dust. — ه
Dust. عَفْر وعَفَر ج أعفار
Obvious speech. كَلام لَا عَفْرَ فِيهِ
Boar, swine, young pig. عِفْر وعُفْر ج أعفار وعِفار
Tremendous lion. أَسَدٌ عِفِر
Dull market. عُفْر
Wicked, mischievous man. رَجُل عِفر وعِفِرّ
Dust-colour. Shudder. عُفْرَة
Hair of a lion's mane. Feathers of a cock's crest. Hair of the forelock of a horse. — وعُفْرَى
Intenseness of heat, cold. Rabble. عُفُرَّة
Wheat boiled without grease. Bread without seasoning. Tree used for striking fire. عَفار
Malignance. ✧ Gleaning. عَفَارَة
Misfortune. Wicked and crafty. عِفْرِيَة
Hair on the top of the head. — وعِفْرَاة
Torrefied in the sun. Dry Unseasoned (bread). عَفِير
Scarabee. عُفَيْرَة
Lion. Blackbeetle. Firm-minded. Full-grown man. عِفْرِيْن وعِفر
White, untrodden land. عَفْرَاء
Reddish-white (gazelle). أعفَر م عَفْرَاء ج عُفْر
Reddish sand. Gazelle. Portion of the night. Active ass. يَعفُور ج يَعافِير

grand. Serious, important. Terrific (event).
Enormous; portentous. عُظام وعُظّام
✧ Good. Very well, all right. عَظِيم
Tke noblemen of the kingdom. عُظَمَاء المَمْلَكَة
Portentous event; important affair. Frightful (crime). عَظِيمَة ج عَظَائِم
Greater. More serious. أعظَم م عُظْمَى
Greyish pigeon. عَظَمِيّ
Glorying in decayed bones *i. e.*: having no other glory than that of his ancestors. عِظَامِيّ
The main part of. مُعظَم
Momentous event. مُعظَمَة
Exalted. مُعَظَّم
To harm, to poison a. o. unawares. To deter a. o. from good. To calumniate a. o. ✲ عَظَا o عَظْوًا ه
Large lizard. ✲ عظي – عِظَايَة وعِظَاءة ج عَظَاء وعِظَاء وعَظَايا وعِظَايَات
To refrain from unlawful pleasure To be chaste. ✲ عَفّ i عَفًّا وعِفَّة وعَفَافًا وعَفَافَة , وتَعَفَّف
To abstain from. — واستَعَفّ عن
To render a. o. chaste (God). أعَفّ ه
To take medicines. تَعَافّ
To graze on (dry herbage : cattle). إعتَفّ واستَعَفّ
Continence. Self-restraint. Chastity; abstemiousness. عِفَّة وعَفَاف
Chaste, continent. Temperate. Abstemious. عَفّ وعَفِيف ج عُفُون وأعِفَّاء وأعِفَّة
Desinterested, incorruptible. عَفِيف النَّفس
Remainder of milk in the udder. عُفَّة وعُفَافَة
He came at the proper time. جاء على عِفَّانِهِ
To twist a. th. ✲ عَفَت i عَفْتًا ه
To speak Arabic barbarously. — كَلامَهُ وفيهِ
Kind of gruel. عَفِيتَة
To strike a. o. with (a stick). ✲ عَفَج i عَفْجًا ه ب
Intestines, guts. عِفْج وعَفَج وعَفِج ج أعفاج
Mallet. مِعفَجَة ومِعفَاج
To jump on both feet. ✲ عَفَد i عَفْدًا وعَفَدَانًا

Following a caravan and living on their provisions. مُعافِر
✧ Gleaner. مُعْفِر
Dusty. ✧ Gleaned. مُعَفَّر
✲ عِفْرِيت ج عَفارِيت Cunning. Bold. Demon. Powerful and malignant genius.
To be crafty, to become wicked. تَعَفرَت
Ts عفارِم وعَفارِم عَلَيْك Bravo!
✲ عَفَس i عَفْسًا ه To roll a. o. in the dust. To detain a. o.
عافَس ه To wrestle with a. o.
تَعافَس واعتَفَس To wrestle together.
إنعَفَس في To be rolled in the dust.
✲ عَفَش i عَفْشًا ه To heap up (things).
✧ عَفَّش To pick up things of no value. To eat much of various dishes.
✧ عَفش وعَفْشة Rubbish. Luggage.
عُفاشة من النَّاس Worthless people.
✲ عَفَص i عَفْصًا ه To wring a. th. To bend a. th.
— ه To overcome a. o. in wrestling.
— وأعفَص ه To stop (a bottle).
عَفَّص ه To dye a. th. with gall-nuts
عافَص ه To wrestle with a. o.
إعتَفَص حَقَّهُ من To recover a debt from.
عَفص Gall-nut. Oak-tree producing galls.
عَفَص Distortion of the nose.
عَفِص Bitter, pungent.
عِفاص Purse. Leather-stopper.
عُفوصة Bitterness, acridity.
✲ عَفَط i عَفْطًا وعَفِيطًا وعَفَطانًا To break wind (goat).
— عَفْطًا وعَفِيطًا To sneeze (sheep).
— عَفْطًا To smack the lips (shepherd).
عَفط وعَفِيط Flatulence. Sneezing.
ما لَهُ عافِطَة ولا نافِطة He does not possess a farthing.
✲ عَفَق i عَفْقًا To go and come often. To awake after a short sleep.
— ه To patch up, to botch a. th. To catch, to seize a. th.
عَفَق الغنم بَعضًا على بَعض To drive (sheep) together.
عافَق مُعافَقة وعِفاقًا ه To blandish a. o.
أعفَق To go and come to no purpose.
تَعَفَّق ب To seek a shelter in.

إنعَفَق في To be expeditious in (work).
إعتَفَق ه To dart on (its prey: lion).
— ب To fight with (the sword).
عُفاقة Rump of animals.
مِعفاق الزِّيارة Visitor.
✲ عَفَك i عَفْكًا الكَلامَ To speak at random.
عَفِك a عَفكًا وعَفَكًا To be foolish.
أعفَك م عَفكاء ج عُفك Foolish.
عَفِك وعَفِيك Light-witted.
✲ عَفَن i عَفنًا, وعَفَّن ه To alter (the meat: air).
عَفِن a عَفنًا وعُفونة, وتَعَفَّن ✧ وعَفَّ To be mouldy, corrupt, putrid.
عَفَن وعُفُونة Mouldiness, putrefaction. Malaria.
عَفِن ومَعفُون ومُعَفَّن Mouldy, putrid, stinking.
مُتَعَفِّن Miasmatic (air).
✲ عَفا o عَفْوًا To be dense, tufty. To be scarce, scanty (hair, herbage). To be clear (water). To be erased (trace). To be redundant.
عَفا o عَفْوًا, وعَفَى i عَفْيًا ه وه To let (hair) grow. To give bountifully to a. o.
عَفا وعَفَّى ه To erase (a trace).
عَفا عن فلانٍ وله ذَنْبَهُ He forgave him his fault.
عُفِي عنهُ May God forgive him.
عَفَّى على ما كان He mended his previous conduct.
عَفَّى عَلَيْهِم الخِبالُ Perdition, destruction effaced them *i. e.* they died.
عافَى مُعافاةً وعِفاءً, وأعفَى ه من To preserve a. o. from. To restore a. o. to health.
عافاكَ الله May God keep thee in good health!
✧ عافاك وعَفاك Bravo! Well done!
أعفَى To give liberally.
— ه To let grow (the hair, beard).
أعفَى ه بِحَقِّهِ He has paid up his debt to him.
تَعَفَّى To be effaced (trace).
تَعافَى To recover from illness, to be cured.
إعتَفَى ه To go to a. o. for asking a. th.
إستَعفَى من To seek to be freed,

Pregnant or thought such (mare). عَقُوق ج عُقُق
Tender fruit-stones. نَوَى العَقُوق
Red shell. Ravine worn by a torrent. Red chalcedony; carnelian. عَقِيق ج أَعِقَّة
Flash of lightning spreading in the clouds. River. Soft date-stone. Hair of a young just born. Wool of a young sheep. عَقِيقَة ج عَقَائِق
The agate. العَقِيق اليَمَانِي
Stems (of vines, palm-trees). عِقَّان
Disobedient, refractory. عَقّ, وعَاقّ ج عَقَقَة وأَعِقَّة
Disobedient. عُقَق وأَعَقّ وعَقُوق
To chatter (magpie). ✡ عَقْعَق
Magpie, bird of evil omen. Chattering of a magpie. عَقْعَق ج عَقَاعِق و✧ قَعْعَق ج قَعَقَان
Rustling of a new garment, of paper. عَقْعَقَة
To strike a. o. on the heel. To come at the heel of. ✡ عَقَب o عَقْبًا ه
To bind (an arrow) with a sinew. — ه
To succeed, to take the place of. — عَقْبًا وعُقُوبًا وعَاقِبَةً فُلَانًا ومَكَانَهُ
To follow a. o. closely. To barter a. th. — وعَقَّب وعَاقَب مُعَاقَبَةً ه وه
To endeavour repeatedly to. To reiterate (a raid) in the same year. To sit on the heels and make a supererogatory (prayer). عَقَّب في
He fled away and did not return. وَلَّى مُدْبِرًا ولَمْ يُعَقِّب
To ride by turns with a. o. in (a journey). To alternate a. th. with. عَاقَب مُعَاقَبَةً ه في
To punish, to requite. — مُعَاقَبَةً وعِقَابًا ه
To die. To leave offspring. To give in exchange. أَعْقَب
To return to a. o. (fever). To ride (a horse) by turns. To succeed to a. o. — ه
To occasion (a disease). — ه
To requite a. o. for. — ه ب
To take careful information about. تَعَقَّب عن
To follow step by step. To be at — ه

exempted from a. th. To resign (an office).
Dust. Rain. White spot on the pupil of the eye. عَفَاء
Ostridge feathers. Long hair of an ass. عِفَاء
The ass. أَبُو العِفَاء
Erasure. The best part of. Excess, redundance. Pardon, amnesty. Favour, benefit. Excuse, plea. Untrodden, uncultivated land. عَفْو
He granted it spontaneously, as a favour. أَعْطَاهُ عَفْوًا
Foal of an ass. عَفًا وعَفْو وعِفْو وعُفْو ج عِفْوَة ج وعِفَاء
Pardon. Blood-price. عَفْوَة
Froth of a cooking pot. First and best broth. Hair of the head. عُفْوَة وعَفْوَة وعِفَاوَة وعُفَاوَة
Remainder in a cooking-pot. عُفَاوَة وعِفَاوَة
Demand of exemption; resignation of office. إِسْتِعْفَاء
The merciful. (God). عَفُوّ
✧ Thick, strong (bough). عَفِيّ
Forgiver. Demander of a favour. Comer to water. Guest. عَافٍ ج عُفَاة وعُفِيّ وعَافِيَة
Seeker of herbage, of means of subsistence. Good health. عَافِيَة ج عَوَافٍ وعَافِيَات
Receiving many guests and petitioners *i. e.* generous. كَثِير العَافِيَة
Pardon. Exemption Recovery. مُعَافَاة
Convalescent. مُتَعَافٍ
To rend, to split a. th. ✡ عَقّ o عَقًّا ه
To disobey, to be refractory to (his father: son). — o عُقُوقًا ومَعَقَّةً ه
To be pregnant (mare). — i عَقَقًا وعَقَاقًا وعِقَاقًا
To be rent, ripped. — a عَقَقًا, وانْعَقّ
To shoot forth (palm-tree). To become pregnant (mare). أَعَقّ
To be tightened (knot). إِنْعَقّ
To burst (cloud). — واعْتَقّ
To draw (the sword). إِعْتَقّ ه
Bitter (water). عَقّ وعُقَاق
Deep hollow. عَقَّة
Hair of a fœtus. عِقَّة ج عِقَق

Copaiva, resinous juice. بَلَسِر التَّعْقِيبَة
Procrastinating (debtor). مُعَقِّب
Substitute. Skilful driver of (cattle). Head-covering of a woman. Ear-ring. مِعْقَب
Bringing forth a male and a female alternately (woman, beast). مِعْقَاب
The angels of the day and the night. Praises of God repeated a hundred times at the end of prayer. المُعَقِّبَات
Follower. Avenger. مُعَاقِب
Jacob, James. يَعْقُوب
Male partridge. يَعْقُوب ج يَعَاقِيب
The Jacobites (Syrian heretics). اليَعَاقِبَة وَاليَعْقُوبِيَّة
Remainder of illness. Pimples on the lips after fever. *Pl.* Misfortunes. ✡ عُقْبُول وعُقْبُولَة ج عَقَابِيل
To make a knot; to tie (a rope). To contract, to conclude (a bargain). To arch (a vault). ✡ عَقَد i عَقْدًا , وعَقَّد هـ
To cement a building. عَقَد البِنَاء بِالجِصّ
To thicken (liquid). ✧ To bud (pla.). عَقَد
To vouch a. th. to a. o. عَقَد هـ ل او الى
To have recourse to a. o. for protection. — عُنُقَهُ الى
To reckon with the fingers. عَقَد الحِسَاب
To intrust a. o. with the government of. عَقَد لِفُلَان على
To oblige a. o. to enter an agreement upon. — وعَقَّد ه على
To be tongue-tied. To become impeded (tongue). عَقِد a عَقَدًا
To thicken (a liquid). عَقَّد وأَعْقَد هـ
He used obscure speech. عَقَّد الكَلَامَ وفِيهِ
To enter a compact, to make a treaty with. عَاقَد ه
To become entangled (business). To be heaped up (sand, clouds). تَعَقَّد
To be knit, complicated (thread). To be confirmed (bargain). — وانْعَقَد واعْتَقَد
To thicken, to coagulate (liquid). — وانْعَقَد
To conclude a compact together. تَعَاقَد
To be vaulted, arched. ✧ To be performed (marriage). To gather (meeting). إِنْعَقَد
Power was secured to his son. — الأَمْر لِابْنِهِ

the heels of. To find fault with.
To alternate with each other (day and night). تَعَاقَب
To perform a. th. alternately. — في
To detain a. o. To withhold a. th. To experience a. th. as the result of. إِعْتَقَب ه وهـ
It ended for him in repentance. — مِنْهُ نَدَامَةً
To follow the foot-steps of. إِسْتَعْقَب ه
Race, run. عَقْب ج عِقَاب
Heel. Son; grand-son, offspring. Following immediately. Pivot, axis. عَقِب ج أَعْقَاب , وعَقْب ج أَعْقَاب
He came close after him. جَاءَ في عَقِبِهِ او في عَقْبِهِ
Result, consequence. عُقْب وعُقُب ج أَعْقَاب
Sinew, tendon used as string. عَقَب ج أَعْقَاب
Turn, in succession. Stage of a journey. Remainder. Substitute. عُقْبَة ج عُقَب
Mark, outward sign. Variegated cloth. عِقْبَة ج عِقَب
Remainder of beauty. عُقْبَة وعِقْبَة الجَمَال
He only does it once a month. مَا يَفْعَل ذٰلِكَ إِلَّا عِقْبَةَ القَمَر
Mountain-road; ascent, acclivity. عَقَبَة ج عِقَاب
Issue, result of a. th. Retribution; reward or punishment. عُقْبَى
Requital, punishment. عِقَاب ومُعَاقَبَة , وعُقُوبَة ج عُقُوبَات
Eagle, ospray. عُقَاب ج أَعْقُب وعِقْبَان
Elevated spot. Projecting rock. Standard, banner.
Terrible eagle having sharp talons. عُقَاب وعَقَنْبَاة وعَبَنْقَاة وبَعَنْقَاة
Aetites, eagle-stone. حَجَر العُقَاب والنَّسْر
Aquila (constellation). العُقَاب
Follower, successor. عَقِيب ومُعْقِب ومُعَاقِب
In consequence of that. — ذٰلِكَ
Worthy successor. عَقُوب
Punishment. Imprisonment. عُقُوبَة
Successor, the last (in a succession). Vicar, lieutenant. عَاقِب
Result. Consequence, sequel. Offspring. عَاقِبَة ج عَوَاقِب
The results of the event. عَوَاقِب الأَمْر
End. عُقْبَان

(thread). Abstruse (discourse).
Entered (compact). Vaulted (building). مَعْقُود
He has no settled opinion. مَا لَهُ مَعْقُود
Honey thickened by fire. Food prepared with honey. يَعْقِيد
To put forth bunches (vine). ✲ عَنْقَد
Cluster. bunch of grapes. عُنْقُود ج عَنَاقِيد
To hock (a beast). To wound a. o. To slay a. o. To mark (a beast) on the legs. To cut off the head of (a palm-tree). ✲ عَقَر i عَقْرًا ه وهـ
To hit (game). To detain a. o. — ب
— عَقْرًا وعُقْرًا وعَقَارًا ، وعُقِر ، وعَقُر o عُقْرًا
To be barren (woman). وعَقَارَةً
To have no issue (affair). عَقُرَ عُقْرًا
To become stupefied through fear. عَقِر a عَقَرًا
To slaughter (a camel). عَقَّر ه
To vie with a. o. in generosity. To contend with a. o. in reviling. عَاقَر ه
To apply o.'s self to. To cling, to keep to. To be addicted to (drink). — هـ
To render (a woman) barren (God) To stupefy a. o. أَعْقَر ه
To possess an extensive estate. To last (rain). To grow (plant). تَعَقَّر
To be galled (on the back: beast). — وانْعَقَر واعْتَقَر
To be hamstrung (beast). إِنْعَقَر
To be unable to draw an augury. إِعْتَقَر ه
Constitutive part of. Wound. Interstice. Main part of a house. عَقْر
Ruined palace. Palace. — وعُقْر
Childless man. Compensation, dowry given to woman. عُقْر
First or last egg of a hen. Cock's egg; Godsend. بَيْضَة العُقْر
Hearth. عُقْر وعُقُر
Barrenness, sterility. عُقْر وعَقْرَة وعُقْرَة وعَقَارَة
Sandy hill. عَقْرَاء
Landed property, estate. عَقَار ج عَقَارَات
Wine. Rich furniture. عُقَار
Exhausting his beasts. عُقَر وعُقَرَة ومِعْقَر

To become compactly formed (fruit-stone). To become firmly established (bonds of fraternity). إِعْتَقَد
To believe a. th. firmly. إِعْتَقَد هـ
To acquire (goods). — مَالًا
Knot. Contract, compact. Responsibility, coherence. عَقْد
The supreme ruler *lit*: he who binds and looses. صَاحِب العَقْد والحَلّ
Arch, vault. Compound number from ten to twenty. عَقْد ج عُقُود
Necklace. String of pearls. عِقْد ج عُقُود
Tongue-tied. عَقِد
Heap of sand. Strong. (*un*. عَقَدَة وعَقِدَة) عَقَد وعَقِد
Impediment of speech. Rottenness of the teeth. عَقَد وعُقْدَة
Root of the tongue. عَقْدَة
Knot. Moral bond, obligation. Ganglion. Joint, articulation of the bones, fingers. Gem, bud of (plants). Government of a province. Funded property acquired. Place abounding with trees. Pasturages. عُقْدَة ج عُقَد
His anger has subsided. تَحَلَّلَتْ عُقْدَتُهُ
Tie, bond. Cohesion. Contract of (marriage). Conclusion of an agreement. إِنْعِقَاد
Faith, belief, tenet. إِعْتِقَاد
Article of faith; dogma. — ومُعْتَقَد
Obscurity of speech. تَعْقِيد الكَلَام
Witches. العَاقِدَات
Haberdasher. عَقَّاد
Haberdashery. عِقَادَة
Tongue-tied; impeded in speech. أَعْقَد م عَقْدَاء ج عُقْد
Knit. Congealed. Female slave. Bound by a treaty; ally. عَقِيد
A man of mean or generous disposition. — الكَرَم او اللُّؤْم
✧ Leader of an army. — العَسْكَر
Belief, religious tenet. عَقِيدَة ج عَقَائِد ، ومُعْتَقَد
String of beads, amulets. مِعْقَاد ج مَعَاقِيد
Binding-place. Joint, articulation. Meeting-place for a compact. مَعْقِد ج مَعَاقِد
Enchanter, charmer. مُعَقِّد
Knotty (wood). Complicated مُعَقَّد

عَقَّار ج عَقَاقِير Drugs, aromatics. Simples.
حَدِيد جَيِّد العَقَاقِير Finely-tempered iron.
عَقَاقِيرِيّ Chemist, druggist, herbalist.
عَقُور ج عُقُر Wounding, biting (beast of prey).
عُقَرَة وعَاقُور و مِعْقَر و مِعْقَار ومُعَقِّر Galling the back (saddle).
عَقِير ج عَقْرَى , ومَعْقُور Wounded, stabbed, hocked.
عَقِير Terror-stricken. Childless.
عَقِيرَة ج عَقَائِر Wounded (beast). Cut in the legs. Voice of a singer, a weeper, a reader. Slain nobleman.
عَاقِر ج عُقَّر وعَوَاقِر Barren (woman); unfruitful (land).
— ج عُقَّر Childless (man).
عَاقِر قَرحَا *Anthemis pyrethrum*, pellitory of Spain.
أَعْقَر م عَقْرَاء ج عُقْر Having the teeth broken (camel).
مُعْقِر Possessing much property.
✲ عَقْرَب To twist, to curl, to bend a. th.
تَعَقْرَب To be crisp, curled (lock of hair). To be unfaithful to a promise.
عَقْرَب ج عَقَارِب Scorpion. Strap, thong. ✧ Hand of (a watch, clock). *Pl.* Slanders. Calamities. Curls of hair.
عَقَارِب الشِّتَاء Intenseness of cold, hardships of winter.
العَقْرَب *Scorpio (Zodiacal sign).*
حَشِيشَة العَقْرَب *Heliotropum Europæum*, heliotrope.
عَقْرَبَة Female scorpion. Clever female slave. Hook of a saddle.
عُقْرُبَان Male scorpion. Earwig. ✧ Peg.
مُعَقْرِب م مُعَقْرِبَة Full of scorpions (place).
مُعَقْرَب م مُعَقْرَبَة Curved, twisted. Strong.
✧ عُقْرُق Frog.
✲ عَقَش o عَقْشًا ه وه To bend (wood). To gather (cattle).
عَقَش وعَقَش Fruit of a thorny tree. Top of a vine.
✲ عَقَص i عَقْصًا ه To twist her hair (woman).
— ه ✧ To sting a. o. (wasp).

عَقِص a عَقَصًا To have the horns twisted back (buck). To be ill-tempered; niggardly. To be restive (beast).
عَقَّص To entangle (an affair). ✧ To prick, to itch; to sting (insect).
عَقص وعَقصَة ✧ Sting.
عَقِص Accumulated sand. Niggardly.
عُقْصَة ج عُقَص Knob, knot.
عِقْصَة ج عِقَص وعِقَاص , وعَقِيصَة ج عَقَائِص Lock, plait of hair.
وعِقَاص
عِقَاص ج عُقُص Red silk, string for making hair-tresses.
عَاقُوص ✧ Sting of insects.
أَعْقَص م عَقْصَاء ج عُقْص Having the horns twisted backwards. Having distorted fingers. Having crooked teeth.
مُعَقِّص ✧ Stinging, itching.
مَعْقُوص ✧ Stung. Sting of insects.
مُعَاقَصَة Struggle, contention.
مِعْقَص ج مَعَاقِص Crooked or broken in the head (arrow).
✲ عَقَف i عَقْفًا , وعَقَّف ه To fold, to bend (wire); to crook a. th.
تَعَقَّف واعْتَقَف To be bent, folded, twisted.
عُقَف Fox.
عُقْفَة Bending, crookedness.
أَعْقَف Contorted. Rude, churlish (Arab).
عَقْفَاء Iron hook.
— وعُقَيْفَاء Plant alike to the rue.
عُقَاف Disease distorting the legs of sheep.
عَاقِف ج عَوَاقِف Attacked with distortion of the legs.
عُقَّافَة Crooked stick. ✧ Hook.
مَعْقُوف Crook-backed (old man).
✲ عَقْفَر ه وعلى To destroy, to overwhelm a. o. (calamity).
تَعَقْفَر To perish (man). To be crushed by misfortune.
عَنْقَفِير ج عَقَافِير A termagant. A scorpion. Old she-camel. Crafty (ogre).
✲ عَقَل i عَقْلًا , وعَقَّل واعْتَقَل ه To bind the folded legs of (a camel) to his thighs.
— i o عَقْلًا ه To confine (the bowels).
عَقَل i عَقْلًا ومَعْقُولًا , وعَقَّل وتَعَقَّل To be intelligent; to become wise.
— ه To trip a. o. in wrestling.

Intellectual, rational, mental, abstract. عَقْلِيّ
Shackle, tether; halter. عِقَال ج عُقُل
✧ Head-band.
Poor-rate, tax paid in sheep or camels. — ج عُقُل وعُقُل
Man of rank whose ransom is quoted high. عِقَال المِئِين
عَاقِل (*m. f.*) ج عُقَّال وعُقَلَاء وعَاقِلُون
Intelligent, wise. Initiated Druse.
Payer of a blood-wit for manslaughter. Wild goat. عَاقِل ج عَاقِلَة
Understanding. Female hair-dresser. عَاقِلَة ج عَاقِلَات وعَوَاقِل
Initiated Druses. ◻ Cramp in the leg. عُقَّال
Relations on the father's side. عَاقِلَة الرَّجُل
Bending of a valley. عَاقُول ج عَوَاقِيل
Hardship, hindrance. Wayless country. High sea; billows.
Large valley. Long sandy hill. Sword. Intestines. عَنْقَل وعَقَنْقَل ج عَقَاقِل وعَقَاقِيل
Intelligent. Astringent (medicine). عَقُول
Secluded, keeping in doors (woman). The best part. عَقِيلَة ج عَقَائِل
Pearl. عَقِيلَة البَحْر
Crook-legged. أَعْقَل م عَقْلَاء ج عُقْل
Wiser. أَعْقَل م عُقْلَى ج أَعَاقِل وعُقَل
Stronghold, refuge. Lofty mountain. مَعْقِل ج مَعَاقِل
Moral bond. Ransom, blood-money. مَعْقُلَة
His tribe is bound to pay the blood-price. دَمُهُ مَعْقُلَةٌ على قَوْمِهِ
Hooked staff. ✧ مِعْقَايَة
Power of understanding, intellect. Intelligible; reasonable. Constipated (bowels). ◻ Well. مَعْقُول
Metaphysics. عِلْم المَعْقُولَات
☆ عَقَم o عَقْمًا, وعَقِم o عُقْمًا, وعَقِمَ a عَقَمًا
To be barren (womb). To become dry (joints). وعَقْمًا, وعَقِم
To remain silent. عَقِم a عَقَمًا
To render (the womb) barren (God). عَقَم i عَقْمًا, وعَقَّم وأَعْقَم ه
To hush a. o. عَقَّم ه

To outwit a. o. عَقَل o ه
To render a. o. costive (medecine). — o i ه عَقْلًا
To understand a. th. To comb (her hair: woman). — i عَقْلًا ه
To pay the blood-price to. — القَتِيل
To pay the blood-price for a. o. — عن فُلَان
To accept the blood-price and give up retaliation. — لَهُ دَمَ فُلَان
To ascend on the summit of a mountain (wild goat). To contract at midday (shade). — i عَقْلًا وعُقُولًا
To take refuge towards. — الى
To have contorted legs. عَقِل a عَقَلًا
To produce bunches (vine). عَقَّل
To render a. o. intelligent, prudent. — ه
To vie in intelligence with. عَاقَل ه
To be on a par with a. o. for the blood-price.
To find a. o. intelligent. أَعْقَل ه
To show intelligence. To conceive a. th. abstractedly in the mind. To be conceivable (thing). To become entangled in (a net: game). تَعَقَّل
To cross the legs upon the saddle. — واعْتَقَل ه
To intersert the fingers under a. o.'s foot for helping him to ride. تَعَقَّل لِفُلَانٍ بِكَفَّيْهِ
To pretend intelligence, cleverness. تَعَاقَل
To pay the blood-price conjointly with a. o. — دَمَ فُلَانٍ
To bind and confine a. o. as a prisoner. To bind the feet of a ewe for milking her. إِعْتَقَل ه
To receive the blood-price from a. o. — من دَمِ فُلَان
To be tied, impeded (tongue). أُعْتُقِل
To hold a. o. to be intelligent. إِسْتَعْقَل ه
Reason, intelligence, mind. Knowledge. Blood-money. Stronghold. عَقْل ج عُقُول
Impediment in speech. عُقْلَة واعْتِقَال
Shackle, bond. A unit. ✧ Knot in wood. عُقْلَة ج عُقَل

To litigate with a. o. To contend with a. o. for superiority. عاقَم ه مُعاقَمة وعِقامًا
Red cloth. عَقْم وعَقَمة وعِقْمة
Barrenness. عُقْم وعَقْمة
Barren (*m. f.*) (woman). Unproductive (land, mind). Gloomy (day). عَقِيم ج عَقائِم وعُقُم
Distressing, grievous (illness, war). — وعَقام وعُقام
Childless. Ill-natured (man). عُقام
Childless (man). عَقِيم ج عُقَماء وعِقام وعَقْمَى
Of noble descent (man). عُقْمِيّ
Abstruse (discourse). — وعُقْمِيّ
Joint in a horse. *Pl.* Vertebræ of the horse. مَعْقِم ج مَعاقِم
To sink (a well). ✲ عَقا o عَقْوًا, واعتقى
To be hoisted (flag). عَقا
To hate a. th. To hinder a. o. — ه وه
Surroundings of a town. Court of a house. عَقْوة ج عِقاء
To dislike a. th. ✲ عَقِيَ i عَقْيًا ه
To suckle (a new-born child) for the first time. To void ordure for the first time (infant). — وعَقَّى ه
To circle aloft in the air (bird). عَقَّى
Whence art thou coming? مِن أَيْنَ عَقَّيْتَ او أَعْتَقَيْتَ
To become bitter. أَعْقَى
To reject from the mouth (bitter food). — ه
Excrement of a new born child. عِقْي ج أَعْقاء
Native gold. عِقْيان
To be sultry (day). To remain at home (man). To put off a. o. To ask a. o. to repeat (a narrative). To explain a. th. ✲ عَكَّ o i عَكًّا
To oppress a. o. unremittingly (fever).
To confound a. o. (by arguments). To assault a. o. with (a whip). To weary a. o. by repeating the same words. — ه ب
To prevent, to turn a. o. back from. — ه عن
✧ To beat, to open (a road). — ه
Burning day. يَوْم عَكّ

Sultriness. عَكَّة وعُكَّة ج عِكاك
Violent access of fever. Burning sand. Butter-skin. عَكَّة وعُكَّة ج عِكاك
Butter-skin. عُكَّة ج عُكَك وعِكاك
Acre, *town of Syria*. عَكَّة وعَكَّاء
Intenseness of heat. Hot windless day. عَكِيك ج عِكاك
To gather, to throng (camels). To boil (cooking pot). To remain standing, to stand still. ✲ عَكَب o عُكُوبًا
To be thick in the lips, in the chin. عَكِب a عَكَبًا
To crush a. o. (cares). تَعَكَّب ه
To be raised (dust). إِعْتَكَب
To raise (the dust). — ه
Dust. عَكَب وعُكاب
Echinops, globe-thistle. عُكُوب
Numerous crowd. عاكِب ج عُكُوب
Ill-conformed. أَعْكَب م عَكْباء
Spider. عَنْكَب وعَنْكَبُوت ج عَناكِب وعَناكِيب
Spider's web. نَسْج العَنْكَبُوت
Phalangium (*plant*). زَهْر العَنْكَبُوت
To seek refuge, to repair to. ✲ عَكَد i عَكْدًا, وأَعْكَد الى
To be or become possible to a. o. (affair). — ه
To become fat (camel, lizard). عَكِد a عَكَدًا
To cleave to. — ب واعتكد ه
To cower down in fear of hawks (bird). إِسْتَعْكَد
Middle of a thing. عَكْد
Dry (tree). Fat (camel). عَكِد
Lizard's hole. Rump-bone. عُكْدة ج عُكَد
Root of the tongue. Base of the heart. عُكْدة
Place of refuge. مَعْكِد
To return upon a. o. ✲ عَكَر o i عَكْرًا وعُكُورًا, واعتكر على
To turn back with the spear upon (the enemy). — بالرُّمح على
To be turbid (water). عَكِر a عَكَرًا و✧ تَعَكَّر و✧ تَعَوْكَر
To render (water) foul, turbid. عَكَّر وأَعْكَر و✧ عَوْكَر ه
✧ To disturb, to grieve a. o. عَكَّر خاطِرَه
To be intensely dark أَعْكَر واعتكر

(night). To be thick (darkness).

To return to the charge (fighters). تعاكر واعتكر

To fall thick (rain). To raise the dust (wind). To last (youth). إعتكر

Sediment, dregs. Rust of a sword. عَكَر

Starting-point, origin. Custom, habit. عِكْر

They came back to their original state. عادوا الى عِكْرِهم

Charge, new onset. عَكْرَة ومَعْكَر

Troop of camels. Root of the tongue. عَكَرَة ج عَكَر

Turbid, dreggy (water). عَكِر ومُعْكَر و✧ مُعَكَّر

Attacking persistingly. عَكَّار

To lean upon (a staff). ✱ عَكَز o عَكْزًا, وتعكّز على

To stick (a spear) into the ground. عَكَز ه

To guide o.'s self by means of. – ب

To be wrinkled, shrivelled. عَكِز a عَكَزًا

To put an iron-head (to a spear). عَكَّز ه

Wicked, wretch. عِكْز

Iron-footed stick, crutch. Shepherd's staff. ✧ Crosier. عُكّاز وعُكّازة ج عكاكيز وعُكّازات

To reverse a. th. ✱ عَكَس i عَكْسًا ه To invert (a word, a sentence). To pour sour milk upon (a dish).

To changed the turn of his affair. – على فلانٍ أمرَهُ

He avert a. o. from an affair. To counteract a. o.'s design. – ه عن أمرِهِ

To check (a camel) with a rope. – ه

To render a. o. unhappy, wicked. To prevent a. o. ✧ عَكَّس ه

To come to blows with a. o. ✧ To cross a. o.'s designs. عاكس معاكسةً وعِكاسًا ه

To crawl. تعكّس

To be inverted, reversed. To be reflected (light). تعاكس وانعكس واعتكس

Inversion, reversal. Reflection, refraction of (light). عَكْس وانعكاس

On the contrary. Vice-versa. بالعكس

Rope for checking a camel. عِكاس البعير

Sour milk poured upon broth. Layer, slip. عَكِيس

There shall be much contention before the business is ended. دون الأمر عِكاس ومِكاس

Inversion of a sentence. مُعاكسة

Reversed, upset, inverted. ✧ Unlucky (lot). Unhealthy (climate). مَعْكوس

To be intermingled (herbs); dishevelled (hair). ✱ عَكِش a عَكَشًا, وتعكّش

To pick up, to make things together. عَكَش i عَكْشًا ه

To return to the charge. – على

To be complicated, intricate (business). To weave its web (spider). تعكّش

Dishevelled (hair). Worthless (man). ✧ Awkward, clumsy. عَكِش

Spider, spider's web. عُكّاش وعُكّاشة وعُكاش وعُكاشة

Clumsiness, awkwardness. عَكاشة

To be crabbed (man). To be unmanageable (beast). ✱ عَكِص a عَكَصًا

To push a. o. back. عَكَص i عَكْصًا ه

To be niggardly of a. th. تعكّص بشيءٍ على

Unsociable (man). Hindering the walk (sand). عَكِص

To hinder a. o. ✱ عَكَظ i عَكْظًا ه

To turn a. o. away from. عكّظ ه عن

To put off (a debtor). عاكظ ه

To be complicated (business). To become difficult to a. o. تعكّظ على

To vie, to contend with. تعاكظ

Short, little. عَكِيظ

Frequented fair near Mecca. عُكاظ

To arrange, to set a. th. in order. ✱ عَكَف o i عَكْفًا ه

To confine, to withhold a. o. in. – ه على

To debar a. o. from. – ه عن

To apply o.'s self assiduously to. – o i عَكْفًا وعُكوفًا, و✧ انعكف على

To turn round. عَكَف حَوْلَ وب

To be strung (pearls). – في النظم

To stay (in a place). – وتعكّف واعتكف في

To curl, to plait (her hair: woman). To string (pearls). عكّف ه

To cleave, to keep to. عاكف ه وه

To pray in seclusion (Moslem). إعتكف
Curly, crisp (hair). عَكِف
Persevering. عاكِف ج عُكوف وعُكَّف وعاكِفون علي
Prayer in seclusion. إعتكاف
Plaited, dressed (hair). مَعكوف
☆ عَكَل o i عَكلا ه وه To tie (a beast). To make up (things).
To detain a. o. in prison. — ه
To exert o.'s self in. — في
To express an opinion upon a matter. — في الأمرِ او برأيهِ
To be doubtful (affair). — وأعكل واعتكل على
To shun society. إعتكل
Base, vile. عُكل وعِكل ج أعكال
Of small size. Avaricious. عاكِل ج عُكل
Rope; shackles. عِكال
Sandy hillock. عَوكَل وعَوكَلة
Prison; gaol. مَعكَل
Shepherd's crooked staff. مِعكَل ج مَعاكِل
☆ عَكَم i عَكما ه To wrap, to pack up (luggage).
To bind (luggage) for a. o. To bind (goods) upon (a camel). — ه ه
To be prevented from. عُكِم عن
To help a. o. in packing. أعكم ه
To be heaped up To poise the two burdens of a camel. إعتكم
Corner of the belly. عَكمة البطن
Bundle, burden. Rope for binding goods. عِكم ج أعكام, وعِكام ج عُكم
Camel-driver, muleteer. عَكّام
☆ عكن — تعكّن To be wrinkled (belly).
Wrinkle of the belly. عُكنة ج عُكَن وأعكان
Numerous party; numerous camels (above 200). عُكنان وعَكّنان
☆ عَكا o عَكوًا ه To tie up (a horse's tail).
To gird o.'s self (with a waist-wrapper). — ب
To show kindness. — على
Root of the tail, of the tongue. Main part. Twisted sinew used as a whip. عَكوة وعُكوة ج عُكا وعِكاء
Big, thick-sided. أعكى م عَكواء
☆ عَكي i عَكيا, وعكّى وأعكى To die.

To gird o.'s self (with a veil). عكّي ب
To bind a. th. tightly. أعكى ه
Seller of sinews. Dead, late, deceased. عاكٍ ج عُكاة
☆ عَلّ o i عَلّا وعَلَلا وتَعِلّة To drink a second draught.
To give to drink a second time. To repeat a. th. — وعلّل ه
To beat a. o. for the second time. علّ المضروب وعلّه ضربًا
To be sick, ill. عُلّ
To gather (fruit) a second time. علّل ه
To divert, to busy a. o. by. — ه ب
To disclose, to manifest the causes of. — ه
To decline a noun. — وأعلّ الكلمة
To afflict a. o. with a disease (God). To give to drink a second time. أعلّ ه
To adduce pleas, excuses. تعلّل واعتلّ
To stick to a. th. To occupy o.'s self with. — واعتلّ ب
To recover from confinement, to be churched (woman). تعلّل وتعالّ
To be ill, sick. To have a blemish. To have a defective letter (word). إعتلّ
To avert a. o. from a design. — ه
Lean and small, paltry. علّ ج أعلال
Diversion. Fellow-wife. Second draught. Misfortune. Need. علّة ج عَلّات
The sons of the same father by various mothers. بنو العلّات
Perhaps, may be. علّ ولعلّ
Perhaps thou mayest do it. علّك تفعل
Plea, excuse, allegation. Efficient cause. Illness, sickness. Diversion. Accident. Defectiveness (of a word, verb). عِلّة ج عِلَل وعِلّات
Cause and effect. العِلّة والمعلول
The defective letters ا. و. ي. حروف العِلّة
Distraction, amusement. عُلالة وتعِلّة
Second draught or drinking. عَلَل
Upper-room. عِلّيّة وعُلّيّة ج عَلاليّ
هو من عِلّيّة قومهِ او من عُلّيّتهم او من عِلّيّتهم He is one of the foremost men of his tribe.
The highest of the seven heavens; its inhabitants. عِلّيّون

To cleave, to cling to a. th. تَعَلَّث ب
To patch (a work). — ه
To select a. th. at hazard. إِعْتَلَث
Steady, persevering. عِلْث
Mess, mixture of two things; olive-oil or butter mixed with curd. عُلَاثَة
Unselected travelling-provisions. أَعْلَاث الزَّاد
To become strong (man). ✱ عَلِج عَلَجًا
To exert o.'s self in. To tend (a sick person). To dress (a wound). To treat (a business). To manipulate, to exercise o.'s skill upon. To manufacture, to work (iron). To prepare (food. medicines). عَالَج مُعَالَجَة وعِلَاجًا ه وه
✧ To quarrel, to contend with. — ه
To prescribe a medical treatment. تَعَالَج
To wrestle, to contend together. — واعْتَلَج
To dash together (waves). To collect together (sand). إِعْتَلَج
To become bulky, strong (body). To grow forth (beard). إِسْتَعْلَج
Ass. Wild ass. Foreign to the Arabian race. Unbeliever. Strong and stout. Hairy, thick-bearded. عِلْج ج عُلُوج وأَعْلَاج
Sandy hills in Arabia. رَمْل عَالِج
Treatment of a disease. Efficacious medicine. عِلَاج ومُعَالَجَة
✧ Strife. مُعَالَجَة و✧ عِلَاجَة
Strong and big. مُسْتَعْلِج الخَلْق
Male ostridge. Male frog. Duck. Buck. Orchard of palm-trees. Wave of the sea. Darkness of night. عُلْجُوم ج عَلَاجِيم
Strong (she-camel). Careless (woman). ✱ عَلْجَن
Dust collected at the root of a tree. عَلْجَان
To be hard, strong, unmanageable, (man). ✱ عَلِد a عَلَدًا
To become thick, strong (man). إِعْلَنْدَى
Hardness. Hard sinew of the neck. Refusing to move. عَلْد ج أَعْلَاد
Thick, big. عَلَنْدَى ج عَلَانِد, وعُلَادَى
I have no escape from مَا لِي عَنْهُ مُعْلَنْدَد

Permutation of a defective letter إِعْلَال وتَعْلِيل واعْتِلَال
Allegation, plea. تَعِلَّة
Sick, ill. عَلِيل ج أَعِلَّاء, ومُعَلّ ومَعْلُول
Repeatedly perfumed (woman). عَلِيلَة ج عَلِيلَات وعَلَائِل
Ill. Defective (word) مُعْتَلّ
Caused, effected; effect. مُعَلَّل
Pool left by a torrent. Dyed twice (cloth). Superposed clouds. Rain after rain. يَعْلُول ج يَعَالِيل
To be unsteady, loose. ✱ عَلْعَل وتَعَلْعَل
Male lark. عَلْعَل وعُلْعَال
Disturbance, riot, mischief. عُلْعُول
To become rough (hand). To become tough, hard (flesh). To be broken (edge of a sword). ✱ عَلِب o عَلْبًا وعَلِب a عَلَبًا
To become tainted (meat). To mark a. th. To notch, to cut. — o عَلْبًا وعَلَّب ه
To bind a sinew round the hilt of a sword. — o, i عَلْبًا وعَلَّب ه
To stink (flesh). To be thick, coarse. إِسْتَعْلَب
To stretch o.'s self. To be ready to mischief. To bristle up his hair (cat). إِعْلَنْبَى إِعْلِنْبَاء
Brand. Impression. Scar. عَلْب
Hard and barren ground. Place of growth of the *Spina Christi*, kind of lote-tree. — وعِلْب ج عُلُوب
Hard to the touch; coarse. Old (buck). عَلِب
Leathern vessel for milking. ✧ Snuff-box. Casket. عُلْبَة ج عُلَب وعِلَاب
Knob of a tree, knot of wood. عِلْبَة ج عِلَب
The choice men of the party. عِلْبُوبَة القَوْم
Lead. عَلَابِيّ
Muscle on the side of the neck. عِلْبَاء ج عَلَابِيّ
He has become advanced in age, decrepit. تَشَنَّج عِلْبَاؤُهُ
To give no fire (flint). ✱ عَلَث i عَلْثًا
To mix a. th. with. — ه ب
To fight desperately. عَلِث a عَلَثًا
To lay snares for a. o. تَعَلَّث ل

To put forth pods (acacia-tree). عَلَّف وأعلف
To seek fodder. تعلّف
To eat fodder. إعتلف
To seek fodder by neighing (horse). إستعلف
Fodder, provender. عَلَف ج أعلاف وعِلاف وعُلوفة
Fruit of a species of acacia. عُلَّف
Seller of fodder. عَلّاف ج علّافة
Provender, forage. عَلوفة ج عُلُف
Wages. Victuals. Pay of soldiers. Pension. عُلوفة ج علائف
Fed in the stable (beast). عَلوفة وعَليف ومَعلوف
Rude, churlish old man. Fleshy, hairy (man). High-bred (horse). Bulky (stallion). عُلفوف
Fattened (cattle). مُعلّف
Manger. Stable. Nose-bag. مَعلَف ج مَعالِف
Cochlearia, scurvy-grass. حَشيشة المَعالِف
To crop (plants : beast). ✱ عَلَق o عَلقًا وعُلوقًا من
To blame a. o — ه بلسانِه
To have leeches applied to the throat. To have leeches cleaving to the throat in drinking. عُلِق
To hang, to be suspended. To catch, to cling, to hold fast to. To concern, to pertain to. عَلِق a عَلَقًا ب
To be caught in (a net : game). — عُلوقًا ب
To become pregnant (woman). — بولد
To become attached by love to. — عُلوقًا وعِلقًا وعَلَقًا وعَلاقةً ه وب
He began doing. عَلِق يَفعَلُ
To hang up, to suspend a. th. to. علّق ه ب وعلى
✧ To catch fire. To be kindled (war). علّق
✧ To set fire to. — ه
✧ To give fodder to (a beast). علّق ل
To close (a door). — ه
To make an extract from. — ه من
To be captivated by. عُلِّق ه
To catch (game) in a net. To apply leeches. أعلق

it. I have no means of attaining it.
To stick to a place and refuse to move (camel). ✱ عَلوَد
To become sedate, grave (man). إعلوّد
Full-grown (camel). Thick (neck). Bulky (lezard). Sedate, calm (chief). عِلوَدّ وعَلوَدّ وعِلوَد
To be disquieted, restless (sick person). ✱ علز a عَلَزًا
To weaken, to disturb a. o. أعلز ه
Restless, disquieted. عَلِز
Colic. Rage. Sudden death. عِلّوز
To drink (water). ✱ عَلَس i عَلسًا ه
To grow worse (disease). عَلّس
They have not given him the least food. ما عَلّسوه تَعليسًا
Food, eatable. عَلس وعُلاس وعَلوس
We have not tasted any thing. ما عَلَسنا عَلوسًا
Kind of wheat. Lentils. عَلَس
Experienced. مُعلّس
To disorder (the stomach : food). ✱ علص — عَلّص في
To wrestle with a. o. عالص ه
He took little of it. إعتلص مِنهُ شَيئًا
Indigestion, colic. عِلّوص
To brand (a camel) on the neck. ✱ عَلَط o i عَلطًا, وعَلّط ه
To stigmatise a. o. عَلَط ه بالقول
To brand, to disgrace a. o. — وعلّط ه بِشَرّ
To unbridle (a beast). علّط ه
To quarrel with a. o. إعتلط ه وب
To cling to (a camel's) neck and mount it; to ride a camel without saddle. To pursue a heedless course; to rush inconsiderately into. إعلوّط ه وه
Bare (she-camel). عُلُط ج أعلاط
Necklace. Ring on the dove's neck. Black collyrium. عُلطة ج عُلَط
Forepart of the neck. Rope on a camel's neck. Contention, strife. عِلاط ج أعلِطة وعُلُط
Brand on a camel's neck. — وإعليط
Stars that have no names. أعلاط الكواكب
To give fodder, to feed (cattle). ✱ عَلَف i عَلفًا, وعَلّف وأعلف ه

To fasten a. th. to. أَعْلَقَ ه ب
To put a suspensory strap (to a ه –
bow).
To be suspended, fastened to. تَعَلَّقَ ب
To cleave, to cling to.
To stick to; to love a. o. – واعتلَقَ ٥ وب
Hole in a garment. عَلَق
Precious thing. – وعِلق ج أعلاق وعُلوق
Bag. Rich garment.
Fond of learning. عِلق عِلمٍ
Prone to evil. Mischief-maker. عِلق شَرٍّ
Pulley, well-rope. Suspensory عَلَق
of a water-skin, of a bow.
Leech. عَلَقَة ج عَلَقَات وعَلَق
□ Bastinado, flogging. عَلقة ج عَلَق
Boy's garment. Rich garment. عِلقة
Property, goods. Attach- عُلقة ج عُلَق
ment.
There remained لَمْ يَبْقَ عِندَهُ عُلقة
nothing with him.
I have interest in it. لِي في هٰذا عُلقة
A little of; remainder (of milk, عَلاق
food).
Stick to it. عَلاقِ
Attachment, true love. عَلاقَة ج عَلائِق
Contention. Obligation; blood-price.
Sufficiency, living. Trade. Craft,
means of subsistence. Dowry ✧ Nose-
bag.
Affection, love. Handle, عِلاقة ج عَلائِق
suspensory, thong of a whip, of a
shield. By-name. Stalk of a fruit.
Misfortune, death. She-camel عَلوق
yielding no milk.
He has treated us عامَلَنا مُعامَلة العَلوق
like a she-camel who yields no milk.
i. e. He has frustrated our expecta-
tion.
Barley, fodder for beasts. عَليق
Camels sent for عَليقة ج عَليقات وعَلائِق
bringing corn.
Thorny shrub. Field bind- عُلّيق وعُلَّيقَى
weed. Common bramble. Any clim-
bing plant. Rapsberry-tree.
Eglantine, sweet-brier. عُلّيق الكَلب
Demon, goblin. Wolf. Tail. عَوْلَق
Hunger.
Dependence, attachment. تَعَلُّق
Persian hand-writing. Special تَعليق
construction of verbs like ظَنَّ, عَلِمَ etc.
Marginal note. Appendix تَعليقة ج تَعاليق
to a book. ✧ String of coins worn
as an ornament.
Man clinging to every رَجُل ذُو مَعلَقة
thing; plunderer.
Milking-vessel. مِعلَق ج مَعالِق
Spoon. (*for* مَلعَقة) ✧ مَعلَقة
Suspended. Attached by love. مُعَلَّق
✧ Having a leech (beast).
Name of selected Arabic poems مُعَلَّقات
that were suspended in the Caaba.
Suspensory. Pendant مِعلاق ج مَعالِيق
of an earring. Stirrup-leather. The
vital parts; heart, spleen, liver,
lungs.
Litigator. – وذُو مِعلاق
Belonging to, dependent on. مُتَعَلِّق ب
Concerns of a man. تَعَلُّقات وتَعَلُّقات
Colocynth. Wild cucum- ✲ عَلقَم ج عَلاقِم
ber. Anything bitter.
To chew a. th. To ✲ عَلَكَ i o عَلكًا ه
knead (dough). To champ (the bit:
horse). To grind (the teeth).
To tan (a skin). To tend عَلَّكَ ه
(cattle). To manage (property). ✧ To
talk nonsense.
The hair has become إعلَنكَكَ الشَّعر
very black, thick.
Resin for chewing. عِلك ج عُلوك وأعلاك
Piece of resin. ✧ Trifle. عِلكة
Viscous, cohesive. Tough عَلِك
(food).
The molar teeth. العَلِكات
Resin-seller. ✧ Humbug. عَلّاك
Impediment in speech. عَوْلَك
To mark a. th. ✲ عَلَمَ o i عَلمًا ه
To slit (the lip).
To surpass a. o. in science. – o ٥
To know; to possess عَلِمَ a عِلمًا
learning.
To learn, to be informed of. – ه وب
To be aware of.
To have the upper-lip slit. عَلِمَ a عَلَمًا
To teach a. th. عَلَّمَ وأعلَمَ ه وب
to a. o.
To assume a distinctive – وأعلَمَ نَفسَهُ
mark at war (horseman).
✧ To sign (a deed). عَلَّمَ على

a. th. is supposed to be found. Way-mark.
Marked (cloth, coin). مُعْلَم
Teacher, master. ✧ Learned man. Master-mason. مُعَلِّم
Mistress of a school. مُعَلِّمَة
Known, notorious. Active (verb). ✧ No doubt, indeed. مَعْلُوم
✧ Fees, payment for professional services. مَعْلُوم ج مَعَالِيم ومَعْلُومَات
✡ عِلْمَاد وعِلْمَادَة ج عَلَامِيد وعَلَامِدَة Distaff.
✡ عَلَن i o وعَلُن o وعَلِن a عُلُونًا وعَلَنًا وعَلَانِيَة. واعْتَلَن واسْتَعْلَن To become known, notorious.
عَالَن مُعَالَنَة وعِلَانًا ه, وأَعْلَن ه ب To manifest a. th. To act openly with; to show open (enmity) to.
عَالَن ه ه, وأَعْلَن ه وب ل To publish; to reveal a. th. to a. o.
To promulgate a. th. أَعْلَن ه
Divulging secrets. عُلَنَة
Publicity, notoriousness. عَلَانِيَة
Acting openly. عَلَانِيَة ج عَلَانُون, وعَلَانِيّ ج عَلَانِيُّون
Publicly, openly. عَلَانِيَة
Manifestation, declaration. Advertisement, post-bill. إِعْلَان
✡ عَلْوَن عَلْوَنَة وعُلْوَانًا ه To put a title to (a book), an address to (a letter).
Title, heading of a book. Address of a letter. عُلْوَان
✡ عَلِه a عَلَهًا To be disturbed, stupefied. To be confused by drink. To go to and fro. To be fiery (horse).
Stupefied. عَلْهَان م عَلْهَى ج عِلَاه وعَلَاهَى
✡ عَلَا o عُلُوًّا, وعَلِي a عَلَاء, واعْتَلَى To become high, lofty; to go up. To rise in rank, dignity.
To be advanced (day). عَلَا واعْتَلَى
To raise, to take a. o. or a. th. up. عَلَا ب
To mount (a beast). To overcome, to overtop a. o. عَلَا ه وه
To strike a. o. with (a sword): to assail. — ه ب
He ascended upon the place. — المَكَان وبهِ
He became proud. — في الأَرْض
He was raised in dignity. — في المَكَارِم

To vie in learning with a. o. عَالَم ه
To suspend a mark upon (a horse) in war. To make a mark upon cloth (manufacturer). أَعْلَم ه وه
To become learned. To learn; to be learned. تَعَلَّم ب
To learn (a science, an art). — ه
To learn a. th. together. تَعَالَم ه
To know a. th.; to get information about. To flow upon the ground (water). To shine (lightning). إِعْتَلَم ه
To wish to know; to take information about a. th. from a. o. إِسْتَعْلَم ه ه
Sign, mark, limit-stone. Way-mark. Elevated mountain. Fissure in the upper lip. عَلَم ج أَعْلَام وعِلَام
Ornamented border in cloth. Standard, flag. Chief of a tribe. ج أَعْلَام
Proper noun (*gram*). إِسْم عَلَم
Science, learning. Firm belief. عِلْم ج عُلُوم
The learned men. أُولُو العِلْم
Scientific. عِلْمِيّ
Book-marker. Target. Aim. ✧ عَلَّام
On what? عَلَامَ (for عَلَى مَا)
Mark, sign, token, symptom. Guide-post. Mile-stone. عَلَامَة ج عَلَام وعَلَامَات
Information. Post-bill; hand-bill. إِعْلَام
Teaching, instruction. ✧ Catechism. تَعْلِيم ج تَعَالِيم
World, universe. عَالَم ج عَوَالِم وعَالَمُون
Worldly, lay. عَالَمِيّ
Layman, secular. ✧ عَلْمَانِيّ
Knowing, aware; learned. عَالِم ج عُلَمَاء وعُلَّام وعَالِمُون
Singer, dancer woman. ◻ عَالِمَة ج عَوَالِم
Thoroughly learned. Hawk. Skilful in genealogies. عَلَّام وعَلَّامَة وتِعْلِمَة وتِعْلَامَة
Learned. Doctor in law. The Omniscient (God). عَلِيم ج عُلَمَاء
The Ulemas, Musulman divines. العُلَمَاء
Sea. Well yielding much water. Male hyena. Frog. Plump, delicate. عَيْلَم ج عَيَالِم
More learned. أَعْلَم ج أَعَالِم
Harelipped. أَعْلَم م عَلْمَاء ج عُلْم
Guide-post. Place where مَعْلَم ج مَعَالِم

Native from the Arabian uplands. عَالِيّ
The Sublime Porte. البَابُ العَالِي
Elevated place; mountain; sky. عَلْيَاء
High.
Higher, loftier; أَعْلَى م عُلْيَا ج أَعَالٍ وعُلًى
nobler.
I was upon the ter- كُنْتُ أَعْلَى السَّطْحِ
race.
Tall, bulky. Male Hyena. عِلْيَان وعَلْيَان
House-furniture.
Superiority, high place, rank. إِسْتِعْلَاء
Nobility acquired; merit, مَعْلَاة ج مَعَالٍ
dignity.
The seventh and best arrow in المُعَلَّى
the game.
Lofty, high, most high. مُتَعَالٍ
The Supreme King, God. المَلِكُ المُتَعَالِي
The emphatic الحُرُوف المُسْتَعْلِيَة
letters خ, ص, ض, ط, ظ, ق, غ
✡ عَلَى *Preposition meaning: elevation, opposition, debt, duty, obligation, time, conformity, dependence.* Upon, on, at, against, according to, above.
On horseback. عَلَى ظَهْرِ الدَّابَّةِ
He entered upon him. دَخَلَ عَلَيْهِ
We have raised فَضَّلْنَا بَعْضًا عَلَى بَعْضٍ
some people above others.
Thou must do. It is عَلَيْكَ أَنْ تَفْعَلَ
incumbent upon thee.
He is indebted. عَلَيْهِ دَيْنٌ
I have acted according عَمِلْتُ عَلَى أَمْرِكَ
to thy order.
He has done it in عَمِلَهُ عَلَى كِبَرِ سِنِّهِ
spite of his advanced age.
In his time. عَلَى عَهْدِهِ
During a time of inadver- عَلَى حِينِ غَفْلَةٍ
tence.
We sat down near the جَلَسْنَا عَلَى النَّارِ
fire.
He went out against him. خَرَجَ عَلَيْهِ
Fortune turned كَانَتِ الدَّائِرَةُ عَلَيْهِمْ
against them.
For the sake of God. عَلَى وَجْهِ اللهِ
Through, by means of عَلَى يَدِ فُلَانٍ
such a one.
I will relate it to أُحَدِّثُكَ عَلَى أَنْ تَسْتُرَهُ
thee, provided thou keepest it secret.
To be universal, general, ✡ عَمَّ o عُمُومًا
common.

To raise, to elevate عَلَّى وعَالَى وأَعْلَى ه وه
a. o. or a. th.
To take off (a burden from عَلَّى ه عن
a beast).
To compete with a. o. for supe- عَالَى وأَعْلَى
riority. To ascend in upper Arabia.
To ascend, to climb on a. th. عَالَى ه وب
Be off, clear off. عَالِ عَنِّي
To rise, to go up by steps. تَعَلَّى
To be lofty. To be proud. — وتَعَالَى
To recover (confined — وتَعَالَى من
woman).
God, may He be exalted! اللهُ تَعَالَى
Come on. تَعَالَ
To be advanced (day). To rise, إِسْتَعْلَى
to ascend higher.
To find a. th. high, too high. — ه
To mount upon (a thing). — واعْلَوْلَى ه
Upper part. عَلُ
مِن عَلُ ومن عَلٍ ومن عَلَا ومن عَلْوٍ ومن عَالٍ
From above, from the top; above.
They are the leaders of هُمْ عِلْيُ القَوْمِ
the tribe.
Grandeur, nobility, high rank. عَلَاء وعُلًى
High place, height. عَلِي وعَلَايَة
The highest part, عَلْو وعُلْو وعِلْو الـ...
the top of.
He took him forcibly. أَخَذَهُ عَلْوًا
Upper part of عِلَاوَة ج عَلَاوَى وعَلَاوِيّ
the head, of the neck. Burden. Super-addition.
The upper part of. عُلَاوَة الـ...
Elevation, height, highness. عُلُوّ
Anvil. Tall she-camel. عَلَاة ج عَلًا وعَلَوَات
High, lofty. Noble, عَلِيّ ج عَلِيُّون وعِلْيَة
illustrious. Eminent (rank, man).
The most High (God).
The headmen, the leaders عِلْيَةُ النَّاسِ
of the people.
Upper-room. عِلِّيَّة ج عَلَالِيّ
The seventh Heaven; paradise; عِلِّيُّون
highest place in Heaven. The Angels, the Blessed.
High, lofty. Sublime. ✧ First عَالٍ
rate (goods).
Illustrious, noble. عَالِي الكَعْبِ
The highest part عَالِيَة ج عَالِيَات وعَوَالٍ
of a thing. The point of a lance. Spear. Uplands of Nejd in Arabia.

The generality of men. The common people. عَامَّة النَّاس

The whole of the tribe came. جَاءَ القَوْمُ عَامَّةً

The laymen, (*opp. to* الخَوَاصّ) the common people. العَوَامّ

✧ Coalition. عَامِّيَّة

General, universal. عَمِيم م عَمِيمَة ج عُمُم

Of tall stature (woman). Lofty (palm-tree).

General, universal, common. عُمُومِيّ

More general, universal. Great number. أَعَمّ

Having many paternal uncles. مُعِمّ ومُعَمّ ومِعَمّ

Including all in his bounty. مِعَمّ

Wearing a turban. Made a chief. مُعَمَّم ومُتَعَمِّم

To collect a numerous army. ✠ عَمْعَمَ عَمْعَمَةً

Scattered parties of men. عَمَاعِم

To beat with a stick. To subdue a. o. To wind (wool) for spinning. ✠ عَمَتَ i عَمْتًا, وعَمَّتَ ه وه

Flake of wool. عَمِيتَة ج عُمُت وأَعْمِتَة وعَمِيت وعَمَائِت

Careful keeper. Intoxicated. Ignorant and feeble; unable to act by himself. عِمِّيت ج عَمَامِيت

To walk quickly, to hasten in walk. ✠ عَمَجَ i عَمْجًا في سَيْرِهِ

To swim. — في المَاء

To wind about in walk. To wind (valley). عَمَّجَ وتَعَمَّجَ

Reptile, serpent. عَمْج وعُمَّج وعَوْمَج

To prop up, to stay a. th. upon columns. ✠ عَمَدَ i عَمْدًا, وعَمَّدَ وأَعْمَدَ ه

To resolve upon, to intend. To aim at. عَمَدَ ل والى

To direct o.'s self towards. — الى

To oppress a. o. (disease); to grieve. To throw down a. o. or a. th. — ه وه

✧ To baptise a. o. عَمَدَ i وعَمَّدَ ه

To be or become astonished, angry. To become moistened (earth). عَمِدَ a عَمَدًا

To cleave to. — ب

To stop, to obstruct (a stream). عَمَّدَ ه

To include, to comprehend the whole of. عَمَّ ه

To include all persons in. — عَمًّا القَوْمَ ب

He bestowed his favours upon all. — الجَمِيعَ بِالعَطِيَّة

He wound a turban round his head. عَمَّ رَأْسَهُ عَمًّا, وعُمِّمَ

To become a paternal uncle. عَمَّ o عُمُومَة

To attire a. o. with a turban. عَمَّمَ ه

To render a. th. general, universal. — ه

To be attired with a turban. To blossom; to become luxuriant (plant). تَعَمَّمَ واعْتَمَّ واسْتَعَمَّ

To call a. o. a paternal uncle. تَعَمَّمَ ه

To take a. o. as a paternal uncle. إسْتَعَمَّ ه

Crowd. Numerous party. Dense (palm-trees, herbs). عَمّ

Paternal uncle. ✧ (*for* حَمٌ) Father-in-law. Step-father. عَمّ ج عُمُومَة وأَعْمَام وأَعُمّ

Paternal aunt. عَمَّة ج عَمَّات

Cousin. ✧ Husband. Brother-in-law. إبْنُ العَمّ

Female cousin. ✧ Wife. Sister-in-law. بِنْتُ العَمّ

✧ Step-mother, mother-in-law. إمْرَأَة العَمّ

Way of wearing a turban. عِمَّة

He wears his turban well. هُوَ حَسَنُ العِمَّة

One of the common people; vulgar. عِمِّيّ

Completeness. Largeness of body. عُمَم

Whole, complete, full-grown. Crowd. عَمَم

Totality, universality. عُمُوم

Generally, in the whole. عُمُومًا وبِوَجْه العُمُوم

Uncleship. عُمُومَة

Belonging to an uncle. عَمَوِيّ

Turban, head-band. عِمَامَة ج عَمَائِم وعِمَام

He loosened his turban *i. e.* He is in easy circumstances. أَرْخَى عِمَامَتَهُ

General, universal, unrestricted. عَامّ

Vulgar, popular. عَامِّيّ

Delegate; trustworthy. مُعْتَمَد عَلَيْهِ
To inhabit, to dwell ✱ عَمَرَ o عَمْرًا ه in; to repair frequently to (a place). To build (a house). To promote (good). To worship (God).
To be frequented, inhabited (by – ب people : market, place).
To preserve a. o. alive (God). – وعَمَّرَ ه
To render (a – عِمَارَة, وعَمَّرَ وأَعْمَرَ ه house) prosperous.
To keep to (a عَمَرَ o i عِمَارَةً وعُمُورًا ه house, a property).
عَمَرَ o i عُمْرًا وعَمْرًا وعَمَارَةً, وعَمِرَ a عَمْرًا
To live long. وعَمْرًا وعَمَارَةً
To thrive, عَمَرَ i o وعَمُرَ o وعَمِرَ a عَمَارَةً to be in a prosperous state.
To keep (a country) in عَمَّرَ وأَعْمَرَ ه a prosperous state. To furnish (a house). ✧ To build (a house).
To give a. th. to a. o. عَمَّرَ وأَعْمَرَ ه ه for life.
✧ To fill a lamp with oil. To عَمَّرَ ه load (a gun). To wind up (a watch).
I adjure thee by thy أَعْمَرَكَ ٱللّٰهَ أَنْ life to.
To find (a country) inhabited, أَعْمَرَ ه flourishing.
To people. To colonise (a – ه ه country) with.
I gave him the house for أَعْمَرْتُهُ الدَّارَ life.
To wind a turban round o.'s إِعْتَمَرَ head.
To frequent, to resort to (a – ه place). To perform the ceremonies of the pilgrimage at Mecca.
To colonise (a place), to إِسْتَعْمَرَ ه في stock it with (people).
Life. Lifetime. Religion. عَمْرٌ ج أَعْمَار
I swear by my religion. لَعَمْرِي
In the عَمْرَ ٱللّٰهِ وعَمْرَكَ ٱللّٰهَ ولَعَمْرُ ٱللّٰهِ name of God.
Gum of the jaw. Earring. عَمْر ج عُمُور
The two wattles of the uvula. العَمْرَان
Life. Life-time. عُمْر وعُمُر ج أَعْمَار Generation of man.
Two generations *i. e.* 80 years. أَلْعُمْرَان
Religion. Head-covering for عَمْر women.

To purpose a. th. To commit تَعَمَّدَ ه (a sin) intentionally.
✧ To be baptised. – وإِعْتَمَدَ
To be propped, stayed. إِنْعَمَدَ
To lean upon a. th. To rely إِعْتَمَدَ على upon a. o. To undertake (a journey) at a gentle pace.
To trust in, to rely upon – ه وعَلَيْهِ في a. o. in (business).
Resolution, determination. عَمْد وتَعَمُّد
Premeditately, عَمْدًا وتَعَمُّدًا و✧ بالعَمْد on purpose.
He has done it فَعَلَهُ عَمْدًا او عن عَمْدٍ intentionally.
He has فَعَلَ ذٰلِكَ عَمْدَ عَيْنٍ وعَمْدًا على عَيْنٍ done it knowingly and willingly.
Moistened by rain (place). عَمِد
He is a bountiful man. هُوَ عَمِدُ الثَّرَى
Stay, support; scout. Flag of عُمْدَة truce. ▫ Chief of a village. ✧ Trustee, proxy.
Pole of a tent. Column, عِمَاد ج عَمَد pillar. Flag of truce.
Receiving many guests. طَوِيل العِمَاد
Noble. رَفِيع العِمَاد
Migratory أَهْل العِمَاد والعَمُود والعُمُد tribes.
✧ Baptism. عِمَاد وعِمَادَة وإِعْتِمَاد
عَمُود و✧ عَامُود ج أَعْمِدَة وعَمَد وعُمُد
Prop, support, column, base. Chief of a party; head of the family. Vertical and perpendicular line. Mace, club.
The back. عَمُود البَطْن
The upright timber of عَمُود الصَّلِيب the cross.
The gleam of dawn. – الصُّبْح
Shaft of a balance. – المِيزَان
Vertical, perpendicular خَطّ عَمُودِيّ line.
Distressed, diseased; عَمِيد م عَمِيدَة broken by love.
The chief, the support of a – القَوْم tribe.
Propping. ✧ Baptising. مُعَمِّد
Propped, supported. مَعْمُود ومُعَمَّد Passionate. ✧ Baptised.
Baptism. ✧ مَعْمُودِيَّة
The Baptist (St John). ✧مَعْمَدَان ومَعْمَدَانِيّ

Hard (day). Dark (night). عَمَّاس ج عُمُس وعُمْس
Perplex. عَمُوس وعُمَامِس
He perjured himself. حَلَفَ عَلَى ٱلْعَمِيسَةِ وعَلَى ٱلْعُمَيْسِيَّةِ
Difficult, obscure (business). مُعَمَّس
To be weak-sighted; blear-eyed. ✲ عَمِش a عَمَشًا
To make impression upon a. o. (discourse). — في
To cure a. o. of blearedness (God). عَمَّش ه
To restore, to repair a. th. أَعْمَش ه
To neglect a. th. تَعَامَش عن
Weakness of sight, blearedness. عَمَش
Dirt, serosity of the eyes. ✧ — وعَمَاش
Bunch of grapes stripped of its berries. عُمْشُوش ج عَمَاشِيش و✧ عُمْلُوش
Dim-sighted, blear-eyed. أَعْمَش م عَمْشَاء ج عُمْش
To be deep (well). ✲ عَمُق o عَمَاقَةً وعُمْقًا
To be long, far-extending (place). — وعَمِق a عَمَاقَةً وعُمْقًا
To deepen (a well). عَمَّق وأَعْمَق واعْتَمَق ه
To deepen, to scrutinise a. th. عَمَّق النَّظَرَ في وتَعَمَّق في
To be profuse in speech. تَعَمَّق في كَلَامِهِ
To go deep into science. تَعَمَّق في الدَّرْس
Depth (of a well); bottom, distance. عُمْق وعَمْق وعُمُق ج أَعْمَاق
Extremity of the desert. عَمْق وعُمُق ج أَعْمَاق
Depth, abyss of the sea. عُمْق البَحْر
Sediment of butter in a vessel. عَمَقَة
Depth. عَمَاقَة
Deep. Long, far-extending (valley). عَمِيق ج عِمْق وعُمُق وعِمَاق وعَمَائِق
To work. To manufacture a. th. To practise a handicraft. To work, to be efficacious (medicine). ✧ To do, to make. ✲ عَمِل a عَمَلًا
To be made governor over (a province). To be appointed to (an office of the government). — لِفُلَانٍ على
To apply o.'s self to. — على
To act upon a. o. To make impression upon a. o. To govern (a word) *gram.* — في

Greeting to mean: Long live thou! Flowers, green adorning a feast-room. عَمَار
Head-ornament; crown, turban. عَمْرَة، وعَمَارَة ج عَمَار
Visit to a place; to the Caaba. عُمْرَة ج عُمَر وعُمُرَات
Greeting. ✧ Squadron, fleet. عَمَارَة
Cultivation. Breast of man. Small tribe. Great tribe. Structure, building. عِمَارَة
Gift for life. Cultivation (of a country). عُمْرَى
Inhabited. Cultivated (land). Prosperous. عَامِر ج عُمَّار م عَامِرَة ج عَوَامِر
Cultivated, frequented (place). عَمِير ومَعْمُور
Hive. Numerous tribe. عَمِيرَة ج عَمَائِر
More cultivated, more populated. أَعْمَر
Flourishing state, prosperity. Civilisation. عُمْرَان
Cultivator. Mason, architect. Righteous. Steady. Calm and meek in speech. عَمَّار
Inhabited, flourishing country. مَعْمَر
Architect, mason. مِعْمَار و✧ مِعْمَارِيّ ج مِعْمَارِيَّة
Visitor. Wearing a turban. مُعْتَمِر
Colony. مُسْتَعْمَرَة ج مُسْتَعْمَرَات
Kid, lamb. يَعْمُور ج يَعَامِير
✲ عمرد وعمرط — عَمَرَّد وعَمَرَّط و✧ عُرْمُوط
Long road. Mischievous (man). Noxious (wolf). Excellent (camel). ج عَمَارِد وعَمَارِط وعَمَارِيط
To be effaced, unreadable (writing). ✲ عَمَس o عَمْسًا
To feign ignorance of. عَمَّس ه
To hide, to conceal a. th. — وأَعْمَس ه
To be gloomy, dull (day). عَمِس a وعَمُس o عَمْسًا وعُمُوسًا وعَمَسًا وعَمَاسَة
To reveal a secret to a. o. To dissimulate with. عَامَس ه
To overlook a. th., to take no notice of. تَعَامَس عن
To leave a. o. in uncertainty. — على
Difficult (affair). عَمْس وعَمَاس وعَمُوس وعَمِيس
Hard (war). عَمَاس وعَمِيس

عَمِلَ To be purulent (wound).
— ه على To appoint a. o. governor of (a province).
عُمِّلَ على To be set over (a province).
عَامَلَ ه To treat, to transact business with a. o. To deal with a. o.
أَعْمَلَ ه To make a. o. to work, to manufacture. To hasten (a camel).
— ه To work (a machine).
تَعَمَّلَ ل وفي To apply o.'s self to ; to strive for.
تَعَامَلَ To transact business one with another.
✧ إنعَمَلَ To be wrought, performed.
إعْتَمَلَ To be employed. To work for o.'s self.
إسْتَعْمَلَ ه To employ a. o. to a. th. To require a. o. to work.
— ه To make use of, to employ a. th. To feign a. th.
عَمَل ج أعْمَال Work, employment. Action, deed, labour. The governing of a word. (*gram.*) ✧ Manufactured work. Pus, matter.
بَنُو العَمَل Foot-passengers.
أعْمَال البَلَد The offices, provinces of a country.
عَمِل Able workman. Quick (camel). Continual (lightning).
عَمِلَة Action, work, deed.
عَمْلَة Theft ; treachery, unfaithfulness.
عِمْلَة Manner of working, doing. Workmanship, make of.
— وعُمْلَة Wages, hire of a workman.
✧ Current money, cash. عُمْلَة
عَمَلِيّ Practical. Artificial, factitious.
عَمَلِيَّة Practice, use, experience. ✧ Surgical operation.
عَامِل ج عُمَّال وعَمَلَة وعَامِلُون Working, acting. Labourer. Governor of a province ; public officer.
عَامِل ج عَوَامِل Governing another (word).
عَامِل وعَامِلَة ج عَوَامِل Part of the spear next to the iron-head.
عَوَامِل Feet, legs. Beasts of burden.
عَمَّال Great worker ; labourer.
عَمَّال وعمّ يكتب ✧ He is writing presently.
عِمَالَة وعُمَالَة وعُمُولَة Workman's wages. Brokerage.
عَمُول Workman, able workman.
عَمِيل ج عُمَلَاء Agent, commissioner, broker.
إسْتِعْمَال Use, employment, service.
مَعْمَل ج مَعَامِل Manufacture, works, factory.
مُعَامَلَة ج مُعَامَلَات Commercial transaction. Proceedings. ✧ Money.
مُسْتَعْمَلَة ✧ Second-hand. Chamber-pot. ◻ Boatswain.
مَعْمُول Manufactured. Artificial. Governed (word). ✧ Almond-cake.
يَعْمَل ويَعْمَلَة Excellent camel and she-camel
✲ عملق — عِمْلَاق ج عَمَالِقَة وعَمَالِيق Fascinating with (the eyes). Tall (man). The Amalekites.
✲ عَمَن i وعَمِن a عَمْنًا ب To dwell in (a place).
عَمَّن وأعْمَن To go to, or to dwell in the country of Oman.
✲ عَمِهَ وعَمِه a عَمَهًا وعُمُوهًا وعَمَهَانًا, وتَعَامَهَ To be confounded, bewildered.
عَمِه a عَمَهًا To have no sign of the way (desert).
عَمَّهُ في ظُلْمِهِ He wronged him without motive.
عَمِه ج عَمِهُون. وعَامِه ج عُمَّه Confused, perplex.
أعْمَه م عَمْهَاء ج عُمْه Without signs of the way (desert).
✲ عَمِيَ a عَمًى, وتَعَمَّى To be or become blind, ignorant.
— عن To swerve from (duty). To stray from (the right course).
— على To be obscure, dubious to a. o. (affair).
عَمَى i عَمْيًا To flow (water). To foam (water).
عَمَّى وأعْمَى ه To blind a. o. To deprive of the sight.
عَمَّى ه To render (speech) abstruse, obscure.
مَا أعْمَاهُ How great his blindness, his error is !

They were killed to the last. قُتِلُوا عَن آخِرِهِم

God is above all description. تَعَالَى اللهُ عَمَّا يَصِفُون

He has related it on the authority of such a one. حَدَّث عَن فُلَان

From what? From that which. عَمَّا وعَمَّ (for عن ما)

From whom? From him who. عَمَّن (for عن من)

To appear. To occur to. ✱ عَنَّ i o عَنًّا وعَنَنًا وعُنُونًا, واعْتَنَّ ل

To turn aside from. عَنَّ عَن

To put a title to a book. — وعَنَّن وعَنْوَن عُنْوَانًا ه

To revile a. o. To confine (a camel). To manage (a horse) with reins. — وأَعَنَّ ه

To put reins to (a bit). — وعَنَّن وأَعَنَّ ه

To moan, to sigh frequently. ✧ عَنْ عَنِينًا (for أَنَّ)

To meet face to face. To oppose a. o. عَانَّ مُعَانَّةً وعِنَانًا ه

First apparition of an object. عَنَن وعِنَان

Enclosure for camels. عُنَّة ج عُنَن

I have seen him just now. رَأَيْتُهُ عَيْنَ عُنَّة

I gave it to him exclusively of others. أَعْطَيْتُهُ عَيْنَ عُنَّةٍ وعُنَّةٍ

Rain-cloud. عَنَان

Visible part of the sky; horizon. — السَّمَاء

Surroundings of a house. — الدَّار

Rein, bridle. عِنَان ج عُنُن وأَعِنَّة

Light, nimble. طَرِف العِنَان

Impotent (man). عِنِّين

Slow to do good. عَنَّان عن الخَيْر

Summit of (the trees). Horizon (of the sky). Natural dispositions (of the devils). أَعْنَان

The utmost of thy power is to do so. عُنَانَاكَ أَن تَفْعَل كَذَا

Title of a book. Heading. عُنْوَان وعُنْيَان

Appearing. Cloud. عَانّ م عَانَّة

Interfering in every thing. Fine speaker. مِعَنّ

Mad, insane. مَعْنُون

To trace back (a tradi- ✱ عَنْعَن عَنْعَنَة

To sham blindness, to feign ignorance. تَعَامَى

To direct o.'s self towards. To choose, to prefer a. th. اِعْتَمَى وه

To be blind. إِعْمَايَ واعْمَايَ

Blindness; thoughtlessness, inconsiderateness. عَمًى

Dark clouds. Contention. عَمَاء

Error, obstinacy. عَمَاءَة وعَمَايَة وعَمِيَّة

Blindness; error. عَمِيَّة وعُمِيَّة وعَمَايَة وعَمَاءَة و✧ عَمَاوَة

We left them at the point of death. تَرَكْنَاهُم عُمًى

His slayer is unknown. قُتِيلَ عِمِّيًّا

Trial, war, riot. عِمِّيًّا

Pride, haughtiness. Error. عِمِّيَّة

Blind. Obscure (night). عَمٍ ج عَمُون م عَمِيَة ج عَمِيَات, وأَعْمَى و✧ عَمْيَان م عَمْيَاء ج عُمْي وعُمْيَان وأَعْمَاء وعُمَاة

Ignorant, blind-minded. عَمِي القَلْب

The two blind things *i. e.* a torrent, and the fire of a burning house. الأَعْمَيَان

The foolish, the blind. Waste and desert countries. الأَعْمَاء

Foolish, blind (people). أَعْمَاء عَامِيَة

Relating to a blind, an insane man. أَعْمَوِيّ وعَمَوِيّ

Obscure, wayless desert; place of wandering. مَعْمَاة ج مَعَامٍ

Abstruse (meaning). Enigma. مُعَمًّى

✱ عَن *Preposition meaning: Separation, compensation, transition, superiority, succession, remoteness.* From, instead of, for.

He journeyed from his country. سَافَر عَن بَلَدِهِ

He parted with us. ذَهَب عَنَّا

After a while. عَن قَلِيل وعَمَّا قَلِيل

God reward thee in my stead! جَزَاكَ اللهُ عَنِّي خَيْرًا

He died leaving a child. مَات عَن وَلَد

He died when 60 years old. مَات عَن سِتِّين سَنَة

Impotent, unable to. عَاجِز عَن

Willingly, with pleasure. عَن رِضًى

What is hidden to the mind. مَا يَخْفَى عَن الأَفْهَام

To buzz (fly). To face dangers; ✱ عَنْتَر to be gallant at war.
To spear a. o. — ه ب
Fly; blue fly. عَنْتَر وعَنْتَر وعُنْتُر
Buzzing. Bravery, dauntlessness. عَنْتَرَة
Name of a celebrated hero ✧ و — عَنْتَر and poet.
Bodice, long-sleeved jacket. ✧ عَنْتَرِي
Dried ✱ عنث — عَنْثة وعُنْثة وعَنْثُوة وعُنْثُوة herbage.
To bend; to ✱ عَنَج o عَنْجًا وأَعْنَج ه draw a. th. To break in (a camel). To stop (a beast) by pulling the rein up.
To tie (a bucket) with a rope. — ه
To feel a pain in the loins. أَعْنَج
To set a. th. in order. — ه
Rope of a bucket. عِنَاج ج أَعْنِجَة وعُنُج Pain in the back-bone.
His case depends on such a one. عِنَاجُهُ إلى فُلَان
Thy affair depends on him. هُوَ عِنَاجُ أَمْرِك
Long-bodied; long-necked (camels) *Pl.* Fine, swift (horses, camels). عَنْجُوج ج عَنَاجِيج
Raisin. ✱ عَنْجَد وعِنْجَد وعُنْجُد
To smack the lips. ✱ عَنْجَر
Smacking of the lips. عَنْجَرَة
To transgress the bounds of. To deviate, to part from. To oppose (the truth). To resist obstinately. ✱ عَنَد o i وعَنِد a وعَنُد o عُنُودًا عن
To bleed unceasingly (vein). — وأَعْنَد
To thwart, to contend stubbornly with; to rebel against. To cleave to. عَانَد عِنَادًا ومُعَانَدَة ه
To oppose; to follow a. o. obstinately. أَعْنَد ه
To thwart o. a., to contend obstinately with o. a. تَعَانَد
To resist the rider; to run off (horse). إِسْتَعْنَد
To prosecute a. o. obstinately. To overcome a. o. (vomiting). — ه
Preposition of time and place. At. Near. By. At the point of; about. عِنْد
I came from his house. جِئْتُ من عِنْدِهِ
I possess wealth. عِنْدِي مَال
I think so; it is my opinion. عِنْدِي كَذَا

tion) to a. o. To substitute the ع to the أ. ✧ To sigh, to moan.
To produce grapes (vine). ✱ عنب — عَنَّب
Grapes. عِنَب ج أَعْنَاب
Berry of grapes. Wine. Pustule. عِنَبَة ج عِنَبَات
Solanum nigrum, garden night-shade. عِنَب الثَّعْلَب او عِنَب الذِّيب
Bear's grape. — الدُّبّ
Vine-stock. عَقْلَة عِنَب
Large-nosed. أَعْنَب
Seller of grapes. عَنَّاب ج عَنَّابُون
Rhamnus zizyphus, (*un.* عُنَّابَة) jujube (tree and fruit). عُنَّاب
Abundance of water. عُنْبَب
Ambergris. Shield. Spermaceti-whale. Saffron. *Gamphrena globosa* (plant). ✧ Storehouse. Cabin, hold of a ship. ✱ عَنْبَر ج عَنَابِر
Bitter cold of winter. Nobility of a tribe. عَنْبَرَة
Perfumed with ambergris. عَنْبَرِي
✧ Aromatic liquor, ratafia. عَرَق عَنْبَرِي
Perfumed with ambergris. مُعَنْبَر
Calico, cotton-cloth. ✧ عَنْبَرْكِيس
To fall into distress. To commit a crime. To commit fornication. To break anew (set bone). To be spoiled. ✱ عَنِت a عَنَتًا
To constrain a. o. to do a th. difficult. To treat harshly. To cause a. o. to perish. عَنَّت ه
To throw a. o. into difficulty. To break (a bone) anew. To treat (a sick man, a beast) roughly. أَعْنَت ه وه
To cause annoyance to; to point out the defects of. To confuse a. o. by questions. تَعَنَّت ه
Sin, crime, mistake. عَنَت
Broken anew (bone). عَنِت ومُعْنَت
Steep, difficult of ascent (hill). عَنُوت
Difficulty, distress, annoyance. Insertion of a letter before the rhyme. إِعْنَات
To shun, to avoid a. o. عَنْشَط عن
Mountain. Beginning. Notch of a bone. عَنْشُوت

He sat down by the side of such a one. جلس عِند فُلَانٍ
He came at sunrise. جاء عند طُلوع الشَّمس
Margin, side. عَند
He walks in the middle, not on the side. يَمشِي وَسطًا لا عَندًا
Rebellion. Stubbornness, obstinacy. عِناد ومُعانَدة
Swerving from duty; rebellious. Stubborn, obstinate. عانِد ج عُنَّد وعَوانِد
Deviating from the right course. عَنُود ج عُنُد
Strong-headed, obstinate. عَنِيد ج عُنُد
Rebellious, disobedient. Opponent. مُعانِد
Philosophical sect affirming the objective existence of ideas or mental images. العِنديَّة
Sect denying the objective existence of ideas. العِناديَّة
Bold, daring. * عندأ – عِنداو وعِنداوَة
Wickedness, deceit. Hardship, disaster. عِنداوَة
Nightingale. * عَندَليب ج عَنادِل
Tarragon (*plant*). Brazil-wood dyeing red. * عَندَم
Intensely red. عَندَمِي
To turn aside, to retire apart from. * عَنَز o عَنزًا, واعتَنَز واستَعنَز عن
To strike a. o. with a javelin. عَنَّز ة
To discard a. th. أعنَز ه
Goat. Female of the eagle, of the bustard, of the vulture and of the hawk. Rock in water. Black hillock. عَنز ج عِناز وعُنُوز وأعنُز
A she-goat, she-gazelle. عَنزَة
Javelin. Staff with a pointed iron. عَنَزَة ج عَنَز وعَنَزات
Tried by misfortunes. عَنُوز وعَنِيز
To bend (wood). * عَنَس i عَنسًا ه
To remain without marrying (man, girl). – o i وعَنِس a عُنُوسًا وعِناسًا
To admire o.'s self incessantly in a looking-glass. عَنِس a عَنَسًا
To keep (a girl) unmarried till middle age. عَنَّس ة
To become advanced in age without marrying (girl). عَنَّسَت وعَنِسَت وأعنَسَت

To alter (the face : age). أعنَس ه
To become long in hair (tail). إعنَونَس إعنِيناسًا
Strong she-camel. Eagle. Rock. عَنس ج عِناس وعُنُوس
Bachelor, spinster. عانِس ج عَوانِس وعُنس وعُنَّس وعُنُوس
Looking-glass. عِنّاس ج عُنُس
To bend (wood). * عَنَش o عَنشًا ه
To trouble, to annoy a. o. – ة
To seize a. o. by the neck. عانَش مُعانَشَة وعِناشًا, واعتَنَش ة
To catch o. a. by the neck. تَعانَش
Six-fingered. أعنَش
To have scanty hair. * عنص – أعنَص
Scattered remains. عُنصُوَة وعِنصاة وعِنصوَة وعُنصُوَة ج عَناص
Dishevelled hair. عَناص
He had very little left of his wealth. ما بَقِيَ من مالِهِ إلَّا عَناص
To treat a. o. harshly, rudely. * عَنُف o عُنفًا وعَنافَةً ب وعلى, وعَنَّف وأعنَف ه
To upbraid, to blame a. o. rudely. عَنَّف ة
To take a. th. violently. To undertake (an affair) inconsiderately. To dislike a. th. إعتَنَف ه
To displease a. o. To disagree with. To be unsuitable to a. o. – ة
Roughness, violence. عَنف وعِنف وعُنف
They went out one after the other. خَرَجُوا عَنفًا عَنفًا
Beginning (of an affair). عَنفَة وعُنفَة
Anew, again. عُنفَة وعُنُفَة
Violent, harsh, rough. عَنِيف ج عُنُف
Bloom of youth. عُنفُوان الشَّباب
To show arrogance, insolence. * عنفص – تَعَنفَص و ◊ عَنفَص
Tuft of hair between the lower lip and the chin. * عنفق – عَنفَقَة ج عَنافِق
To be long-necked. To become thin in the neck. * عَنِق a عَنَقًا
To begin to ripen (dates). عَنَّق
To seize by the neck; to squeeze the throat. To disappoint, to distress a. o. – ة
To embrace a. o. عانَق مُعانَقة وعِناقًا ة
To become tall; to put forth ears أعنَق

fruit. Vine-tendrils.
Fissure in the lips. عَنِمَة
Male frog. عَيْنُوم
Red, beautiful (face). عَنْجِي
To be, to become submissive, obedient. ✡ عَنَا o عُنُوًّا وعَنَاء
To put forth (plants : earth). — ب
To befall a. o. (affair). — بِفُلَان
To distress a. o. (business). — عَلَى فُلَان
To take a. th. peaceably *or* forcibly. — فُلَان عَنْوَةً
To become a captive amongst. — وعَنِيَ a عَنَا فِي
To detain a. o. as a captive. عَنَّى وأَعْنَى ه
To abase, to humble a. o. أَعْنَى ه
To produce (plants : ground). — ه
Side, shore. Crowd. عَنَا وعِنْو ج أَعْنَاء
Violence, strength. Love. Submission. Captivity. عَنْوَة
Forcibly, violently. عَنْوَةً
Captive. عَانٍ ج عُنَاة، وعَنِيّ م عَنِيَّة
Moslem women. Captive women. Workers. Captives or like captives. العَوَانِي
Detained as a captive. مُعَنًّى
To mean, to intend ; to hint at a. th. ✡ عَنَى i عَنْيًا وعِنَايَةً بِالقَوْل كَذَا
To belong to ; to concern a. o. — ه
To happen to a. o. — عَنْيًا ل
To produce (plants : ground). — ب
To be beneficial to a. o. (food). — فِي
To trouble, to disquiet a. o. (affair). — عِنَايَةً وعُنِيًّا ه
To be anxious about. To mind, to be occupied by. عُنِيَ عِنَايَةً وعُنِيًّا ب
Keep in mind my business. لِتُعْنَ بِحَاجَتِي
To be beneficial to a. o. (food). عَنِيَ a عَنًى فِي
To be tired, wearied. — a عَنَاء
To disquiet, to trouble a. o. عَنَّى وأَعْنَى ه
To take care of. To contend with. To struggle against (difficulty). To endure a. th. To treat a. o. medically. عَانَى ه وه
To be tried, tired. تَعَنَّى ه
To bear (cares, troubles). — ه
To take care of. to be anxious about : to attend to. إِعْتَنَى ب

(corn-crops). To walk quickly with wide steps (horse). To set (Pleiades). To disperse (the dust : wind).
To put a collar to (a dog). — ه
To enter into its hole (jerboa). تَعَنَّق
To embrace o. a. تَعَانَق
To seize o. a. by the neck (fighters) ; to embrace o. a. إِعْتَنَق
To undertake a. th. in earnest. — ه
Neck. Company of men. ✧ Trunk (of a tree) : stalk (of a leaf, of a fruit). عُنْق وعُنُق وعَنَق ج أَعْنَاق
They long for thee. هُمْ عُنُق إِلَيْك
Formerly, of old. عَلَى عُنُق الدَّهْر
A company of men came to me. أَتَانِي عُنُق مِن النَّاس
The people came in by parties. جَاء القَوْم عُنُقًا عُنُقًا
Length of the neck. Quick pace (of a beast). عَنَق
Embrace. Badger. عِنَاق ومُعَانَقَة
She-kid. Lynx. Disappointement. عَنَاق ج أَعْنُق وعُنُوق
Ursus meles, badger. عَنَاق وعَنَاق الأَرْض
The she-goats after the she-camels *i. e.* straitness after ampleness (*proverb*). العُنُوق بَعْد النُّوق
Long-necked. أَعْنَق م عَنْقَاء ج عُنْق
Phenix ; griffin (fabulous birds). Calamity. عَنْقَا، وعَنْقَاء مُغْرِبٌ ومُغْرِبَةٌ، وعَنْقَاء مُغْرِب
Burrow of a jerboa. عَانِقَاء
Embracer. Neck. عَنِيق
Hard and elevated ground. مُعْنِق ج مَعَانِيق
Fine-necked. مُعَنَّق ومِعْنَاق ج مَعَانِيق
Curved rocks. مَعْنُقَة
Necklace. Hill in front of a tract of sand. مِعْنَقَة ج مَعَانِق
Elevated mountains. مُعَنِّقَات
To be heaped up (sand). ✡ عَنَكَ o عَنْكًا وعُنُوكًا، وتَعَنَّك
To enter the sands. عَنَّكَ وأَعْنَكَ واعْتَنَك
To close (a door). عَنَّك وأَعْنَك ه
Root, origin. Portion of the night. Door. Main part. عَنْك وعُنْك
Heaped up (sand). Assiduous. عَانِك
Sand heaped up. عَنِيك ج عُنُك
Spider. (*See* عكب). ✡ عَنْكَبُوت
Tree of Hedjaz bearing a red ✡ عَنَم

Hardship, distress. عَناء وعَنِيَّة
Crushing toil. عَناءٌ عانٍ ومُعْنٍ
Kindness, care. عِنَايَة وإعْتِناء
Divine Providence. العِنَايَة الإلهيَّة
Full of solicitude. عَنٍ وعانٍ ومُعْتَنٍ
Meaning; hidden sense. مَعْنًى ج مَعانٍ
It means that. هٰذا مَعْنَاهُ
Rhetorics. عِلْم المَعَاني
Endowed with good qualities. حَسَن المَعَاني
Spiritualists. أهل المَعَاني
Virtual, abstract. Mental, allegorical. مَعْنَوِيّ
Long-necked (gazelle, ostrich). Serpent. ✱ عهج — عَوْهَج
To meet, to behold, to visit a. o. (in a place). ✱ عهد a عَهْدًا ه ب
To be acquainted with a. o. — ه
To observe a. th. carefully. To fulfil (a promise). — ه
To enter (an agreement) with. To impose a condition, to enjoin a. th. to. To make a bequest to a. o. عهد الى
To hold o.'s self responsible towards a. o. for. — الى فُلانٍ في
To make a compact with. To swear to a. o. عاهَد ه
To exact (a promise) from. — ه الى
To guarantee a. th. to a. o. أعْهَد ه من
To take care of; to inspect a. th. To frequent a. o. To renew acquaintance with. تَعَهَّد وتعاهد واعتهد ه
To make a mutual compact. تعاهد
To exact (a promise) from. إستعهد من
To hold o.'s self responsible for a. th. — ه من نَفْسِهِ
Oath, bond, compact. Order. Responsibility. Promise. Treaty, agreement. Time, epoch. First rain of the ear. Acquaintance. True friendship, affection. Diploma of appointment to an office. عَهْد ج عُهُود
The Old Testament. ألعَهْدُ ألعَتِيق
The New Testament. ألعَهْدُ الجَدِيد
Crown-prince, heir-apparent. وَلِيّ ألعَهْد
In the time of such a one. على عَهْدِ فُلان
I have known him insolent. عَهْدِي بِهِ سَفِيهًا
Rain in the beginning of the spring. عَهْد وعَهْدَة ج عِهَاد
Spring-rain. عِهْدَة وعِهَادَة
Written statement of a compact; sale-deed. Weakness of mind. Defective writing. Responsibility. عُهْدَة
He is responsible for it. عُهْدَتُهُ عَلَيْهِ
Utmost care. تَعَهُّد
Applied to affairs. عَهِد
Guarantee, security. عِهْدَان
Confederate. Party of a compact. Old, ancient. عَهِيد
Ally, confederate. Client. مُعاهِد
Alliance, covenant. Compact, treaty. مُعاهَدَة
The contracting parties. ألمُتَعاهِدُون
Meeting-place, rendezvous. مَعْهَد ج مَعاهِد
Stipulated, warranted by a compact. Known. Rained upon (ground). مَعْهُود
✱ عَهَر a عَهْرًا وعَهَارَةً وعُهُورًا وعُهُورَةً
To lead a dissolute life. To be a debauchee, a libertine. وعَهِر a عَهَرًا
To commit fornication, adultery with. — إلى, وعاهر ه
Debauchery, ribaldry. عِهْر وعَهارة
Debauchee, profligate. عاهِر ج عُهَّار
Strong (camel). Ogre, goblin. عَيْهَر
To leave (camels) pasture by themselves. ✱ عهل — عَيْهَل
Emperor, mighty sovereign. Independent (woman). عاهِل ج عَوَاهِل
Tall, swift, excellent (she-camel). Tall, strong, unsteady (woman). Strong (wind). عَيْهَل وعَيْهُول وعَيْهال
To dry up (palm-branch). ✱ عَهَن i o عُهُونًا
To remain in (a place). — عَهْنًا ب
To go forth from (a place). — مِن
To show zeal in. — في
To be broken or bent (branch). — i عَهْنًا
Wool; dyed wool. عِهْن ج عُهُون
Tuft of wool. عِهْنَة
He is a good manager. هُوَ عِهْن مَال
Palm-branch. Limb of the human body. Destitute. Strengthless, sluggish. عاهِن ج عَوَاهِن
Bending of a broken branch. عُهْنَة

a (sick person) time after time. To turn away (a beggar).
To do a. th. a second time; to repeat. To be wont to. — عَوْدًا وعِيادًا ه
To train, to accustom a. o. to. عَوَّدَ ه ه
To observe a feast. ✧ عَيَّدَ
To greet a. o. on a feast-day. — و✧ عايَدَ ه
To come back to a. th. عاوَدَ مُعاوَدَة وعِوادًا ه
To return to a. o. time after time (fever). To hold a conference with. — ه
To reiterate (a question) to. — ه ب
To have the habit of. — وأعادَ ه
To repeat (a word). أعادَ ه
To restore a. o. to a former state. — ه الى
To become accustomed to. تعوَّدَ واعتادَ واستعادَ ه
To visit (a sick person) often. تعوَّدَ ه
To return to fight. To do a work by turns. تعاوَدَ
To ask from a. o. to repeat a. th. إستعادَ ه ه وه من
To ask a. o. to return. — ه
Ancient Arabian tribe. عاد
(1) *Indeclinable particle having the sense of* إنَّ. عادِ
I slept while thy father remained awake. رَقَدْتُ وعادِ أباكَ ساهِر
(2) *Interrog. part. in the sense of* هَل. عادِ
Is thy father abiding. عادِ أبوك مُقِيم
(3) *Negative answer to a question.*
Has Zeyd gone forth? He has not. عادِ خرَجَ زَيد — عادِهِ
Habitual. Old. Old building; ruins. عادِيّ
Return. Repetition. Old (animal). Ancient (road). عَوْد ج عِيَدَة وعِوَدَة
Thou hast to return. لكَ العَوْدُ والعَوْدَة
He came back on the spot. رَجَع عَوْدًا على بَدْءٍ او عَوْدَهُ على بَدْئِهِ
Wood, rod. Aloes-wood. Seven-chorded lute. عُود ج أعواد وعِيدان
Aloes-wood. عُود البَخُور — القاقُليّ — القَماريّ — النَّدّ

Long possessed and newly acquired goods. عاهِن المال
He blurted out speech inconsiderately. رَمَى الكلامَ على عَواهِنِهِ
✲ عاثَ o عَوْثًا, وعَوَّثَ ه عن To avert a. o. from (an affair). To disturb a. o.
تَعَوَّثَ To lose the mind; to be perplexed.
مَعاث Way, road; course.
أخذنا مَعاثًا مُستقيمًا We have taken the right path.
ما لي عن الأمرِ مَعاث I have no escape from it.
✲ عاجَ o عَوْجًا ومَعاجًا ه To turn aside (a beast, with the rein).
— عن To give up (a design).
— ب او على To stop in (a place). To call at, to alight at a. o.'s.
— ه ب To make a. o. to stop in (a place).
عَوِجَ a عَوَجًا To be or become crooked, bent, distorted. To be ill-natured.
عَوَّجَ ه To crook, to bend, to distort (a. th.) To set (a. th). with ivory.
تعوَّجَ واعوَجَّ و✧ انعوَجَ To be or become crooked, contorted.
إنعاجَ على To incline towards.
عاج Ivory, elephant's tusk. Tortoise-shell. Any bone. Submissive (camel).
عاجة Piece of ivory.
عِوَج Deviation from rectitude, insincerity.
عَوَج وإعوِجاج Distortion, wryness; unevenness of ground.
عوّاج Seller of ivory.
▫ ذُرَا عُوَيجَة Sorgo, drooping millet.
أعوَج م عَوجاء ج عُوج Curved. Disloyal.
أعوَج Name of a celebrated stallion.
أعوَجِيّ Issued from that stallion.
إعوِجاج العِظام Rickets.
مَعاج Secluded halting-place.
مُعوَج Crooked. Insincere.
✲ عادَ o عَوْدًا وعَوْدَةً ومَعادًا الى ول To return, to come back to.
— ل To become beneficial to.
— عَلَيهِ To become noxious to.
عادَ عَوْدًا To become. To happen.
— عَوْدًا وعِيادَةً وعِيادًا وعُوادَةً To visit

Aloes-wood. عُود الهِنديّ
Ptarmic, a sternutatory. — العُطاس
Pellitory. — القُرح
Wood of the true Cross. — الصَّليب
Peony (flower).
Periodical feast-day. Anniversary. عِيد ج أعياد
Feast of Bairam (amongst Moslems). Feast of Easter (amongst Christians). العيد الكبير
Present given on a feast-day. عِيديَّة
Custom, habit. Manners, morals. ✧ Menses. عَادَة ج عَاد وعِيد وعَادَات وعَوَائِد
Player upon the lute. عَوَّاد
Lofty palm-trees. عَيْدَان
More useful. أَعوَد
Repetition. إعادة
Use, habit. إعتياد
Usual, habitual. إعتياديّ
Usually. إعتياديًّا
Visitor (of a sick person). عائد ج عُود وعُوَّد وعُوَّاد
Return; profit, advantage, benefit. Income. عائدة ج عَوائد
Custom-duties, returns. ✧ عَوائد الكُمرك
Return. Food brought agai nfor a new guest. عُوادة
Return. Place of return. Meeting-place. مَعاد
The life to come. The pilgrimage to Mecca. Place of wailing for a dead person. المَعاد
Coming back often. The lion. Experienced in business. مُعِيد
Trained mare. فَرَس مُبدِئ مُعِيد
The Creator and the Raiser of the dead (God). المُبدِئ المُعِيد
Visited (sick people). مَعُود ومَعْوُود
Accustomed, trained. مُعَوَّد ومُتَعَوِّد ومُعتاد
Wont to. مُعاوِد
Return. Wont, habit. مُعاوَدة
✱ عاذ o عَوذًا وعِيَاذًا ومَعاذًا ومَعاذة , وتَعَوَّذ واستعاذ بفلان من To have recourse to a. o. from (danger).
To cleave to (the bone : flesh). عاذ ب
May God protect us! نعوذ بالله
To invoke the protection (of God upon). عَوَّذ وأعاذ وأعوَذ ه

To hang an amulet upon (a child). عَوَّذ ه
To induce a. o. to have recourse to a. o. in danger. — ه بفلان من
To seek refuge o. with another. To rely o. upon another in a danger. تعاوَذ
To say : I seek the protection of God against. إستعاذ بالله من
Refuge, protection. عَوذ وعِياذ
Recourse for shelter, protection. عَوذ وعِياذ
Recourse to God. — بالله
عُوذة ج عُوَذ , وتَعوِيذ ج تعاويذ . ومَعاذة ج مَعاذات Amulet, charm.
Dislike. عَواذ
Unwillingly. عَواذًا
Taking refuge. عائذ ج عُوَّذ
Having just brought forth (she-camel, mare). — ج عُوذ وعُوذان
Four stars forming a quadrilateral figure. العَوائذ
Refuge, protection, shelter. مَعاذ ومَعاذة
God forbid! مَعاذ الله ومَعاذ وَجهِ الله
Place of the collar on a horse. مُعَوَّذ
✱ عار o عَورًا , وعَوَّر وأعوَر ه To render a. o. blind of one eye.
To mar off; to injure a. th. To spoil (a well). عار ه
To become blind of one eye. To be dried up (one of the eyes). عَوِر a عَوَرًا , واعوَرّ
To send, to drive a. o. back. To jeopardise (flocks). عَوَّر ه
To deprive a. o. of. To debar a. o. from. — عن الأمر
To gauge (weights, measures). عَوَّر وعاوَر ه
To lend a. th. to. عاوَر وأعار ه ه
To do a. th. by turns with. عاوَر ه ه
To become within reach (game). To show o.'s self to. To expose o.'s self (at war). أعوَر ه ول
To receive a. th. for temporary use. تعوَّر ه
To take, to do a. th. by turns. To interchange, to lend a. th. one to another. — وتعاوَر واعتوَر ه
To ask a loan from a. o. To use (an expression) metaphorically. إستعار ه

Loss of one eye. Weakness. Unsoundness. Disgrace. عَوَر

Pudenda. Woman. Breach, gap (in a frontier). Cleft (in a mountain). عَوْرَة ج عَوْرَات

Sunrise and sunset. — الشَّمْس

Hurting the eye (foul matter). Ophtalmia. عَائِر

Great quantity. عَائِرَة

عَارَة وعَارِيَة وعَارِيَّة و✧ عِيَارَة ج عَوَارِيّ وعَوَارٍ Loan; borrowed or lent thing.

Rent, hole; burn in a garment. Vice, defect. عَوَار وعُوَار وعِوَار

Of corrupt morals. عَوِر م عَوِرَة

Straw, mote; matter collected in the eye. عُوَّار ج عَوَاوِير وعَوَاوِر

Lending; loan. إِعَارَة

Borrowing. Metaphor. إِسْتِعَارَة

Artificial, false. Metaphorical. إِسْتِعَارِيّ

One-eyed. Crow. Without way-mark (road). أَعْوَر م عَوْرَاء ج عُور وعُورَان

One-eyed (woman). Bad, foul (word, deed). Waterless (desert). عَوْرَاء

Lent. Lank (horse). مُعَار

Dangerous (place). Depraved (man). مُعْوِر

Borrowed. Metaphorical. مُسْتَعَار

False, not genuine. Rag on a camel's rump. Tree for making tooth-picks. يَسْتَعُور

To be lacking wanting to a. o. To want, to require a. th. ✲ عَازَ o عَوْزًا, وأَعْوَزَ ة وهـ

To be scarce, wanting. عَوِزَ a عَوَزًا

To be destitute. To become difficult (affair). عَوَّزَ وأَعْوَزَ

To reduce a. o. to destitution. أَعْوَزَ ة

Berry of grapes. (*un.* عَوْزَة) عَوْز

Destitution, want, need. عَوَز و✧ عَازَة

Poor, destitute. عَوِز وعَائِز وأَعْوَز ومُعْوِز

Worn out clothes. مِعْوَز ومِعْوَزَة ج مَعَاوِز

Necessities, wants. مَعَاوِز

To prowl about by night (man, wolf). ✲ عَاسَ o عَوْسًا وعَوَسَانًا

To manage (goods, flocks) skilfully. — عَوْسًا وعِيَاسَة هـ

To laugh grinningly. عَوِسَ a عَوَسًا

Manager of property. عَائِس

Polisher of knives. Grin-faced in laughing. أَعْوَس م عَوْسَاء ج عُوس

Knife, pen-knife. ✧ عُوَيْسِيَّة

To be obscure (speech). ✲ عَاصَ a وعَوِصَ a عِيَاصًا وعَوَصًا

To become impossible to a. o. (affair). — واعْتَاصَ عَلَى

To utter uncouth (speech). To compose abstruse (verses). عَوَّصَ وأَعْوَصَ

To wrestle with a. o. عَاوَصَ ة

To perplex (an antagonist). أَعْوَصَ عَوَصًا وعِيَاصًا بِ

To perplex a. o. by arguments. — عَلَى

Barren (female). عَائِص ج عُوص

Abstruse, (poetry). Uncouth, strange (expression). Difficult (affair). Rugged (place). عَوِيص, وأَعْوَص م عَوْصَاء

He embarks in a difficult undertaking. يَرْكَب العَوْصَاء

✲ عَاضَ o عَوْضًا وعِوَضًا وعِيَاضًا, وعَوَّضَ وعَاوَضَ وأَعَاضَ ة مِن To give to a. o. a. th. in exchange for. To indemnify for.

May God restore it to thee! عَاضَكَ اللهُ مِنْهُ

To compensate. تَعَوَّضَ واعْتَاضَ

To take or receive a. th. in exchange for. إِعْتَاضَ هـ عَن او مِن

To ask from a. o. compensation for. To substitute a. th. — واسْتَعَاضَ ة هـ

Thou wilt never see his like. لَن تَرَى مِثْلَهُ عَوَضُ

I shall never part from thee. لَا أُفَارِقُكَ عَوَضَ العَائِضِينَ

Compensation, exchange; damages, indemnity. عِوَض وتَعْوِيض ومُعَاوَضَة

In exchange, instead of. عِوَضًا عَن او مِن

Substitute, thing given in exchange. عِوَض ج أَعْوَاض, وعَائِض ومَعُوضَة

Punch, stage-puppet. ✧ عِيوَاظ

To circle over a. th. (bird). ✲ عَافَ o عَوْفًا عَلَى

To free, to exempt a. o. ✧ عَوَّفَ ة

To prowl about by night (lion). تَعَوَّفَ

State, condition. Fortune; omen. Cock. Wolf. عَوْف

Good speed! Good luck! نَعِمَ عَوْفُكَ

Prey which a lion carries عُوَاف وعُوَافَة

To neglect o.'s family. عَيَّلَ ه
To wail, to weep loudly. عَوَّلَ ه وأَعوَلَ واعتَوَلَ
To rely upon a. o. To ask assistance from. To impose a burden upon. ✧ To determine upon. عَوَّلَ عَلَى وب
To become poor. ✧ أَعَالَ إِعَالَةً
To exceed the bounds of justice (tax-gatherer). — ه
To twang (bow). To be greedy of. أَعوَلَ
He possesses nothing of his own. مَا لَهُ عَالٌ وَلَا مَالٌ
Painful affair. Helper (man). عَوْلٌ
Sustenance of a family.
Woe to him! عَوْلَ فُلَانٍ
Weeping, lamentation. عَوْلٌ وعَوْلَةٌ وعَوِيلٌ وتَعوِيلٌ
Reliance. Cry for help. Stay, support (man). عِوَلٌ
Shelter against rain. عَالَةٌ
Household, family, children. عَيِّلٌ ج عِيَالٌ وعَيَايِلُ وعَالَةٌ
Destitution. Care of a large family. إِعَالَةٌ
Wrongful course. Declining (balance). عَائِلٌ
✧ Family, wife. عَائِلَةٌ ج عَائِلَاتٌ
Lamented, bewailed. مُعْوَلٌ عَلَيْهِ
Pickaxe, iron-bar. مِعْوَلٌ ومِعْوَالٌ ج مَعَاوِلُ
He is not to be relied upon. لَيْسَ عَلَيْهِ مُعَوَّلٌ
To swim. To float along (ship). ✱ عَامَ o عَوْمًا
To bear fruit every second year (palm-tree). عَوَّمَ وعَاوَمَ
To make up (corn-crops) into sheaves. عَوَّمَ
✧ To launch (a ship). ✧ To fill up (a measure). — ه
✧ To row. — ب
To enter a contract with. To hire a. o. for one year. عَاوَمَ ه
Year. عَامٌ ج أَعْوَامٌ
Annual (plant). عَامِيٌّ
Sheaves, handfuls of reaped corn. Float, raft. Twist of a turban. Head of a rider seen from afar. عَامَةٌ ج عَامٌ
Flotation. Not fordable (river). عَوْمٌ وعَوْمَةٌ

away by night. Profit, windfall.
✱ عَاقَ o i عَوْقًا وعَيْقًا, وعَوَّقَ وأَعَاقَ إِعَاقَةً, واعتَاقَ ه عَن
To impede, to delay, to hinder a. o. from.
I was disappointed by the failing of my provisions. أُعوِقَ بِي الزَّادُ
To be hindered, delayed. To loiter. تَعَوَّقَ
Hindrance, obstacle. عَوْقٌ وعُوقٌ ج أَعْوَاقٌ
Hinderer; diverting people from doing good. عَوْقٌ وعَوَقَةٌ
Slow. Cowardly. عُوَقٌ وعَوِقٌ وعِوَقٌ وعَيِّقٌ وعُوَّقٌ وعُوَقَةٌ
Hunger. عَوْقٌ
Delay. ✧ عَاقَةٌ
Retardation, impediment. إِعَاقَةٌ وتَعوِيقٌ
✧ Skill, cleverness. عَيَاقَةٌ
Capella (star). ✧ Handsome, polite, gentlemanlike. عَيُّوقٌ
Hinderer. ✧ Skilful. عَائِقٌ ج عُوَّقٌ وعَوَائِقُ
Obstacle, hindrance. عَائِقَةٌ ج عَوَائِقُ
To attack a. o. ✱ عَاكَ o عَوْكًا على
To fight together. تَعَاوَكَ
To press together. إِعتَوَكَ
No motion is perceived in it. مَا بِهِ عَوْكٌ
At first. أَوَّلُ عَوْكٍ وبَوْكٍ
Fight. عَوِيكَةٌ ومَعْوَكَةٌ
To deviate from the right course. ✱ عَالَ o عَوْلًا
To rule wrongfully, to stray from justice. — فِي الحُكْمِ
To incline on one side (balance). — o عَوْلًا وعَالَ i عَيْلًا
To exceed the bounds in. — فِي
To distress, to disquiet a. o. (affair). — ه
عَالَ o عَوْلًا وعِيَالَةً, وأَعَالَ إِعَالَةً وأَعْوَلَ إِعْوَالًا وأَعْيَلَ إِعْيَالًا
To have a numerous family.
عَالَ o عَوْلًا وعِيَالَةً وعُؤُولًا, وعَيَّلَ وأَعَالَ ه
To provide for (o.'s family). To feed (poor orphans).
His mother lamented his death. عَالَ وعِيلَ عَوْلَهُ
His patience has been overcome; he lost patience. عَالَ وعِيلَ صَبْرُهُ
To be reduced to destitution. To be overcome. عِيلَ

Smitten by a scourge مَعْيُوه ومَعِيه ومَعُوه (flock).

✡ عوَى i عَيًّا وعُوَاء وعَوَّة وعَوِيَّة و ✧ عَوّى

To howl, to yelp. To attain mature age (wolf, dog, fox).

To twist (the hair). — وعَوّى واعتَوَى ه To bend a. th.

To reply against a. o. — وعَوَى عن فُلَانٍ To confute a. o.

To stir up (dogs) by howling. عاوَى الكِلَاب

To collect and howl against a. o. (dogs). تَعاوَى على

To be bent. إنعَوَى

To incite (dogs) to howl. To ask help against. To stir (people) to rebellion. إستَعوَى ه

Rebellious clamour, tumult. عَوَّة

Howl, yelp. عُوَاء و ✧ عَوِيّ

Howling much. Dog. عَوَّاء

Bitch. Fox's cub. Lynch. مُعاوِيَة

To be ✡ عَيَّ وعَيِي a عَيًّا وعَيَاء ب او عن unable to; to lack power, ability for. ✧ To be ill.

To falter in speech. عَيِي عِيًّا في المَنْطِق

To be unable to express o.'s mind. عَيَا تَعْيِيَة وعايَا مُعايَاة

To speak to a. o. enigmatically. عايَاه

To be tired, jaded. أعيَا

To tire a. o. (walk). To disable a. o. To baffle (the physicians' skill: disease). — ه

To be impracticable to a. o. (business). — وتَعايَا على

To be unable to, disabled from. تَعيًّا وتَعايَا وإستَعْيَا ب

Incurable disease. عَيَاء

Unable, impotent. Stammering. عَيّ ج أعيَاء وعَيِيّ ج أعيِيَاء وأعيِيَة

Impotent. ✧ Sick, ill. عَيَّان

Enigmatical, obscure speech. أعيِيَّة

Wearied, tired. مُعْيِي

To chide sheep by the cry عَا عَز. ✡ عَيْعَى وعَوْعَى وعاعَى مُعاعَاة وعاعَاة

To have a blemish, a defect. To be unsound, defective (goods). ✡ عاب i عَيْبًا

To alter (goods). — وعَيَّب وتَعَيَّب ه

To charge a. o. with a عاب وعَيَّب ه

Swimming insect. Serpent. عُومَة ج عُوَم

Floating (ship). Swimming. عائِم م عائِمَة

By swimming. عائِمًا وعَوْمًا

Good swimmer. عَوَّام

Contract for one year. مُعاوَمَة

Boat, ship. مُستَعام

To be of middle age (woman). ✡ عان o عَوْنًا, وعَوَّن

عَوَّن تَعوِينًا وعاوَن مُعاوَنَة وعِوَانًا , وأعان

To help, to assist a. o. against. إعانة على

To help o. another. تَعاوَن واعتَوَن

To ask the help of. إستَعان ه وب

Help, assistance, succour. عَوْن

With the help of God. بِعَوْن الله

Helper, servant. Armed attendant, guard. عَوْن ج أعوَان

She-ass. Herd of wild asses. Pubes. عانَة ج عُون وعانات

Succour, help. إعانَة ومُعاوَنَة

Of middle age. Married woman. Repeated fighting. Ground watered by rain. عَوَان ج عُون

Lofty palm-tree. Worm living in the sands. عَوانَة

Traducer, spy, police-spy. عَوَانِي ج عَوَانِيَّة

Help, assistance. مَعانَة ومَعُونَة ومَعُون

Police-officer. صاحِب المَعُونَة

Barge. ✧ مَعُونَة

Helper, substitute, coadjutor. مُعاوِن

Helping much and often. مِعْوَان ج مَعاوِين

To be smitten by a plague, a bane (flock, crops). ✡ عاه o i عُوهًا, وعَيْهًا

To alight during the night for rest. To confine o.'s self in (a place). To have (cattle, crops) smitten by disease, scourge. عَوَّه وأعاه وأعوَه وتَعَوَّه

To bring a calamity upon a. o. ✧ To maim, to cripple a. o. عَوَّه ه

Scourge, disease, bane. ✧ Deformity. عاهَة ج عاهات

Men exposed to sufferings, to hardships. أهل العاهات

Tried by misfortunes. ✧ Sickly, deformed, crippled. مُعَوَّه ومُتَعَوِّه

Caravan, file of camels. عِير ج عِيرَات وعِيَرَات

عَيْر ج أعْيَار وعِيَار وعُيُور وعُيُورَة وعِيَارَات

Domestic *and* wild ass. Pupil of the eye. Prominent line on a map, a leaf. Mountain. Projecting bone of the hand, or the body. King, chief. Wooden peg. Drum.

It is as empty as the belly of an ass *i. e.* there is no good in it. هُوَ كَجَوْفِ عَيْرٍ

Kind of pigeon. عَيْر السَّرَاة

Young ass. عُيَيْر

Self-admirer. Shunning society. عُيَيْر وَحْدِهِ

Random arrow. Current (poem). عَائِر م عَائِرَة

Legal standard for money, weights and measures. ✧ Caliber. عِيَار ج عِيَارَات

Currency of (a poem). عِيَارَة

✧ Wig, false hair. عِيَارَة الشَّعْر

Sharp, sprightly. Idle (man). Rogue, vagrant. ✧ Crane for weights. عَيَّار

Legal standard for measures, weights. مِعْيَار ج مَعَايِير

Difficulties, defects. مَعَايِر

To wither (corn-crops). ✱ عَاس – أَعْيَس

To be grayish (camel). تَعَيَّس

Grey hair. عَيَس

Of a reddish white (camel). أَعْيَس م عَيْسَاء ج عِيس

Female locust. عَيْسَاء

Name of Jesus (for Moslems). عِيسَى

Relating to Jesus; Christian. عِيسَوِيّ وعِيسِيّ

Order of dervishes. العِيسَوِيَّة

✱ عَاشَ i عَيْشًا وعِيشَةً ومَعَاشًا ومَعِيشًا ومَعِيشَةً وعَيْشُوشَةً

To live. To spend life.

To give means of subsistence to; to keep a. o. alive. عَيَّش وأَعَاش ه

To live with a. o. عَايَش ه

To seek means of subsistence. To substain life scantily. تَعَيَّش

They lived in society. تَعَايَشُوا بِأُلْفَةٍ

Life, living عَيْش وعِيشَة

Food, wheat. ▫ Bread. عَيْش

▫ Roll of bread. رَغِيف عَيْش

▫ Kind of mince-pie. عَيْش بِلَحْمٍ

▫ Beech-nut. عَيْش السَّرَايَا

vice To shame, to stigmatise a. o.

Vice, defect, unsoundness. عَيْب رعَاب ج عُيُوب

✧ What a shame. يا عَيْب الشُّوم

Leather-bag. Vice, defect. Confidant. Family. Comb for cotton. عَيْبَة ج عِيَب وعِيَاب وعِيَبَات

Censor. Given to fault-finding. عُيَبَة وعَيَّاب وعَيَّابَة

Altered: defective, unsound. عَائِب

Defect. Disgrace. Stain. مَعَاب ومَعَابَة ج مَعَايِب

Full of defects, vices. مَعِيب ومَعْيُوب

Bag-manufacturer. مُعَيِّب

✱ عَاثَ i عَيْثًا وعُيُوثًا وعَيَثَانًا ه To do mischief amongst. To damage a. th. (animal).

To squander wealth. – فِي مَالِهِ

To grope for a. th. in the dark. عَيَّث

Causing damage. Lion. عَائِث وعَيُوث وعَيَّاث

Prodigal. Mischief-maker. عَيْثَان م عَيْثَى

✱ عَاجَ i عَيْجًا Verb *only employed with a negation.* To heed. To profit.

I am not satisfied with it. مَا عِجْتُ بِهِ

I do not care about his words. مَا أَعِيجُ مِن كَلَامِهِ بِشَيْءٍ

Profit, advantage. عَيْج

✱ عِيد Feast. *See* عود

✱ عَارَ i عَيْرًا To wander (man); to go at random (beast). To spread (news). To become celebrated (poem).

To do mischief amongst. To upbraid, to revile. a. o. عَيَّر ه

To weigh, to assay (coins). – ه

To be overspread with green moss (water). عَيَّر

To equalize (a weight). To gauge (measures, weights). To assay (gold). عَايَر مُعَايَرَةً وعِيَارًا ه

To lend a. th. To set (a horse) free. To fatten (a horse). To pluck out (the hair of the tail). أَعَار إِعَارَةً ه وه

To reproach, to abuse o. a. in words. تَعَايَر

Shame, disgrace, vice. عَار ج أَعْيَار

□ Mushroom. عَيْش الغُرَاب
□ Seller of bread. عَيَّاش
Easy life. عِيشَة رَاضِيَة او رَغْد
Living, alive. Leading an easy life. عَائِش ج عَائِشُون
Means of life. ✧ Wages; pension. مَعَاش ومَعِيشَة ج مَعَايِش
Having a livelihood. مُتَعَيِّش
Wood of tangled trees. Stock, race. ✡ عيص — عِيص ج عِيصَان وأعْيَاص
Thicket of trees. مَعِيص
Difficult to be obtained. مِعْيَاص
To be long (neck). ✡ عَاط i عَيْطًا, وتَعَيَّط
To be long-necked. عَيِط a عَيَطًا
To shout (player, drunkard). To yell, to scream. ✧ عَيَّط
✧ To cry out to, to upbraid a. o. عَيَّط على
✧ To call out a. o. عَيَّط ل
To quarrel (players). تَعَيَّط
Loud cries of boys at play. عِيط
Cry, clamour, uproar. عِيَاط
Noise, bustle. Loud rebuke. ✧ عَيْطَة
Long-necked. أعْيَط م عَيْطَا ج عِيط
✡ عَاف a i عَيْفًا وعِيَافًا وعَيَفَانًا وعِيَافَة ه
To loathe a. o. ✧ To cast off a. th.
Let me alone. ✧ عِيفْنِي
To augur from the flight of (birds). عَاف i عِيَافَة ه
To circle over (bird). — عَيْفًا على
To have a beast loathing water. أعَاف إعَافَة
To furnish o.'s self with travelling-provisions. إعْتَاف
Flight of birds. عَيْفَة
Loathing, disliking. عَائِف
Diviner, augur. — ومُتَعَيِّف
To hinder; to turn away. ✡ عَاق i عَيْقًا
To call out, to vociferate. — عَيَّق
Sea-shore. Yard of a house. عَيْقَة
To walk in a proud gait. ✡ عَاك i عَيَكَانًا
To become destitute, poor. ✡ عَال i عَيْلًا وعَيْلَة وعُيُولًا ومَعِيلًا
To reduce a. o. to destitution. — i عَيْلًا ومَعِيلًا ه
To lead a. o. astray. — ه
To have a proud gait. — وتَعَيَّل في المَشْي
To be in quest of prey (wild beast). عَيَّل
To feed (o.'s family) scantily. — ه

To let (a horse) pasture freely.
To have a numerous family. — وأعَال ه وأعْيَل إعْيَالًا
Destitute, poor. عَائِل ج عَالَة وعُيَّل وعِيل وعَيْلَى
Household, family. عَيِّل و✧ عَائِلَة ج عِيَال
Poverty, want. ✧ Family. عَيْلَة
Having a proud gait. عَيَّال
Fodder, straw. عِيَالَة ومَعَالَة
Having a numerous family. Seeking after prey (lion). مُعِيل م مُعِيلَة
To long for milk. ✡ عَام a i عَيْمًا وعَيْمَة
To lack milk (people). أعَام
To deprive a. o. of milk. — ه
To select the best. To tend towards. إعْتَام
Longing for milk. Thirst. عَيْمَة
Selection, choice. عِيمَة
Day. عَيَام
Longing for milk. عَيْمَان م عَيْمَى ج عَيَامَى
Bereft (of a wife, of flocks). عَيْمَان أيْمَان ج عَيَامَى
To hurt a. o. in the eye. To smite a. o. with the evil eye. ✡ عَان i عَيْنًا ه
To flow (water, tears). — i عَيْنًا وعَيَنَانًا
To bring (news) to a. o. — i عِيَانَة, واعْتَان ه
To become (a spy) for. — على واعْتَان ل
He dug till he found a spring. حفر حَتَّى عَانَ او أعَانَ
To be wide in the eyes. عَيِن a عَيْنًا وعِينَة
To specify, to particularise a. th. To single out a. o. To bore (a pearl). To stir (war). To appoint a. o. عَيَّن ه وه
To assign property to. — المَالَ ل
To sell or buy a. th. upon credit. To sell a. th. upon credit to a. o. on the condition of buying it back at a lower price. To blossom (trees). عَيَّن
To view, to face a. o. عَايَن مُعَايَنَة وعِيَانًا ه
How evil-eyed he is! مَا أعْيَنَهُ
To be perplexed. To be blistered (water-skin, camels' feet). To see, to look at a. th. تَعَيَّن ه وه
To be clear, distinct, obvious. تَعَيَّن

To be appointed, assigned to. تعيّن على
To be imposed upon a. o. (affair).

✧ To be enlisted in the army. تعيّن في الجنديّة

To buy upon credit. To take the best of. إعتان ه ا

Eye. Look. عَيْن ج أعيُن وعُيُون وأعيان
Hole; eye of a needle; eyelet. Bud of a tree. Small opening. Defect. Aspect, countenance. Spy, watcher. Stroke of the evil eye. Party of men. Direction. Human being; self, substance. One of the two saddle-bags. One scale of a balance. Middle letter of a triliteral word. Sun. Money; cash.

Water-spring. — أعيُن وعُيُون

Great star in the eye of *Taurus*. عين الثور

Buphtalmum, ox-eye (plant). عين البقر

Cat's eye, kind of quartz. عين الهرّ

Willingly, with pleasure. على الرّأس والعَيْن

As far as the eye can reach. مَدَى العَيْن

Within sight. بُعْد العَيْن

He is the very man; it is the very thing. هُوَ هُوَ عَيْنُهُ او بِعَيْنِهِ

There is no one in the house. ما بالدّار عَيْنٌ او عائِن

He left the reality for the shadow. طَلَب أثرًا بَعْد عَيْنٍ

I bought it with ready money. إشْتَرَيْتُهُ بِالعَيْن

Hypocritical friend *lit*: as long as he is seen. صَدِيق عَيْنٍ

The land put forth buds of plants. نَظَرَتِ البِلادُ بِعَيْنٍ او بِعَيْنَيْن

I have much regard for thee. أنْتَ عَلَى عَيْنِي

He has done it carefully. فَعَلَ ذٰلِكَ عَلَى عَيْنٍ او عَيْنَيْن

The chief men, the personages of a place. ألأعْيان

Eyelet. ✧ Eye-glass. عُيَيْنَة و✧ عُوَيْنَة

✧ Spectacles, eye-glasses. Sea-shells. ✧ عُوَيْنات

✧ Sample. عَيِّنِيَّة

Choice, selection. عِينَة

Fine clothes. ثَوب عِينَة

Sale upon credit. Buying back at a lower price of a. th. already sold. بَيْع عِينَة

Ocular view. Clear, evident. عِيان ومُعايَنَة

I faced him, I saw him personally. لَقِيتُهُ عِيانًا

Ploughshare. عِيان ج أعْيِنَة وعُيُن

Eye-witness. عِيانِيّ

Black grapes with large berries. Black plums. عُيُون البَقَر

Spectacles. ◻ عُيُون قِزاز

Evil-eyed. عَيُون ج عِين وعُيُن

Brotherhood. مُعايَنَة

Wide-eyed, black-eyed. أعْيَن م عَيْناء ج عِين

Verdant (soil). عَيْناء

Determination, appointment. ✧ Quota, share assigned to each. تَعْيِين

Place where one is seen. Abode. Halting-place. مَعان

Smitten by the evil-eye. Running upon the surface of the earth (spring). مَعِين ومَعْيُون

Figured with eyes, with lozenge-shaped designs (cloth). مُعَيَّن

Determined. ✧ Enlisted (soldier). مُتَعَيِّن

غ

✻ غَبَّ o غِبًّا على To attack a. o. every second day (fever).
— عن To go away at intervals from.
زار ه غِبًّا To visit a. o. from time to time.
غَبَّ i غِبًّا وغُبُوبًا To drink every two days (cattle). ✧ To gulp, to sip (man).
— وأَغَبَّ عِند To spend the night at.
— غِبًّا وأَغَبَّ To be altered (meat).
غَبَّبَ في To be remiss in. To make havock among (the sheep : wolf).
— عن فُلَان To repel an evil from.
أَغَبَّ ه وهم To visit a. o. every two days. To water (cattle) every two days. To yield (milk) every two days (she-camels).
— ه وعلى To seize a. o. every two days (fever).
تَغَبَّبَ To look for the issue of.
غِبّ End, result. Journey of two days. ✧ After.
غِبًّا Seldom, from time to time.
زُرْ غِبًّا تَزْدَدْ حُبًّا *Prov.* Visit seldom, thou shalt find more love.
حُمَّى الغِبّ Tertian ague.
غَبّ ج أَغْبَاب وغُبُوب Depressed land. Wave dashing on the shore. Gulf.
غُبَّة Small supply of food.
غُبَّة ✧ Draught, gulp.
غَبَب ج أَغْبَاب Dew-lap of an ox. Gills of a cock.
غَبِيبَة Milk drawn in the morning mixed with other in the evening.
مَغَبَّة End, issue.
✻ غَبْغَبَ To cheat in trade.
غَبْغَب ج غَبَاغِب Dew-laps of oxen. Gills of cocks. Place of sacrifice in Mina.
✻ غَبَثَ غَبْثًا To prepare curd.
— إِغْبَثَّ To be dust-coloured.
غُبْثَة Grayish, ashy colour.
أَغْبَث Grayish.
غَبِيثَة Food made of curd and butter.
✻ غَبِجَ a غَبْجًا ه To drink by draughts.
غُبْجَة Draught.
✻ غَبَرَ o غُبُورًا, وأَغْبَرَ واغْبَرَّ To be dusty, dust-coloured.
غَبَّرَ To go away, to pass. To remain, to stay; to continue.
غَبِرَ a غَبَرًا To become corrupt, ulcerous (wound). To bear rancour.
غَبَّرَ ه To sprinkle, to soil a. o. with (dust).
— وأَغْبَرَ To raise (the dust). To outstrip a. o.
أَغْبَرَ To be rainy (weather).
أَغْبَرَ في To exert o.'s self zealously in.
أَغْبَرَّ To be dusty (day). To be sprinkled with dust (man).
اِغْبَرَّ إِغْبِرَار To become dust-coloured.
غِبْر Rancour, secret hatred.
غُبْر ج أَغْبَار وغُبَّر ج غُبَّرَات Remainder of milk; remains of a. th.
غَبَرَة وغُبْرَة وغُبَار Dust.
غُبْرَة Dust-colour.
دَاهِيَة الغَبَر Distress, misfortune.
غَبِر Corrupt, ulcerous (wound).
غَابِر ج غُبَّر وغَابِرُون Going, passing away. Remaining behind. (*Gram*): the future tense.
أَغْبَر م غَبْرَاء ج غُبْر Dust-coloured.
الغَبْرَاء The earth. Female partridge.
بَنُو الغَبْرَاء The strangers, the poor.
غُبَيْرَاء (*dim. of* غَبْرَاء) Intoxicating drink made with millet. Sorb. Service-tree.
جَاءَ على غُبَيْرَاء الظَّهْر He has not obtained anything.
تَرَكَهُ على غُبَيْرَاء الظَّهْر He left him completely destitute, deprived of every thing.
غُبْرُور Dust-coloured sparrow.
مُغْبَرّ Dusty, covered with dust.
مُغَبِّرَة Godly people repeating incessantly their prayers.
✻ غَبَسَ o غَبْسًا وأَغْبَسَ واغْبَسَّ واغْبَاسَّ To be obscure, dark (night).
أَغْبَس To be ash-coloured (wolf).

Darkness. Gray colour. غُبْسَة وغَبَس

Gray. Greedy (wolf). Bay (horse). أَغْبَس ج غُبْس

To deceive a. o. To draw to its close (night). ✱ غَبِش a غَبَشًا ه, وأَغْبَش

To see indistinctly (eye). ✧ غَبَّش ه

To deceive, to wrong a. o. تَغَبَّش ه

Intense darkness before dawn. غَبَش ج أَغْبَاش, وغُبْشَة

Weakness of sight. ✧ غَبَاشَة

Dark (night). Black (beast). غَبِش م غَبِشَة, وأَغْبَش م غَبْشَاء ج غُبْش

To feel (an animal) with the hand. ✱ غَبَط i غَبْطًا ه

To emulate a. o. without envy. غَبَط وغَبِط a غَبْطًا وغِبْطَة ه

To excite emulation. غَبَّط ه

To give a continuous rain (sky). To cover the soil (plant). أَغْبَط

To grasp a. o. unremittingly (fever). — على فُلَان

To keep (a saddle) upon (a beast's) back. — ه على

To rejoice at. تَغَبَّط

✧ To be angry, irritated. — وانْغَبَط

To be content, satisfied with o.'s happiness. إِغْتَبَط

Prosperous state, well-being. غَبْط

Sheaves of reaped corn. — وغَبَط ج غُبُوط

Beatitude, happiness. Wish, desire for the happiness of another without envy. ✧ *Title given to Oriental Patriarchs*: His Beatitude. غِبْطَة

Stream of water engulfed. Camel-saddle. Depressed land elevated on the extremities. غَبِيط ج غُبُط

Vortex, whirlpool of a river. Slough. ✧ غَبِّيط

Rainy sky. سَمَاء غَبْطَى

Emulating without grudge. غَابِط ج غُبَّط

Covered with verdure (ground). ✧ Full of eddies (river). مَغْبَطَة

✧ Full of mire (road). Angry. مُغْبِط

Envied. Blessed. مَغْبُوط

To give to a. o. the evening draught. ✱ غَبَق o غَبْقًا ه

To milk (a beast) in the evening. تَغَبَّق ه

To drink in the evening. إِغْتَبَق

To drink a. th. in the evening. — ه

Evening draught. Milk drawn in the evening. غَبُوق

Drinking in the evening. غَبْقَان م غَبْقَى

To deceive, to cheat, to defraud a. o. (in a bargain). ✱ غَبَن o غَبْنًا وغَبَنًا ه في

To conceal a. th. غَبَن ه

To fold and hem (the edge of a garment, a skin). غَبَن o غَبْنًا ه

To forget, to neglect a. th. غَبِن a غَبْنًا وغَبَنًا ه وفي

To be of a weak judgment, easily deceived. To be mistaken. غَبِن a غَبَانَة وغَبَنًا

He is weak-minded. — رَأْيَهُ

They were unaware of the thing. غَبِنُوا خَبَرَ الشَّيْءِ

To cheat o. a. تَغَابَن

To hide a. th. under the arm-pit. إِغْتَبَن ه

Deceit, cheating, imposition, swindling. غَبْن وغَبَن ج غُبُون

Foul play, gross fraud. — فَاحِش

Shortening, hemming in of a dress. غُبْنَة

Weakness of mind. غَبَانَة

Swindler. Cowardly. Slothful. غَابِن

Cashmere cloth. ✧ غُبَانِي

Knavish, fool. غَبِين ومَغْبُون

Deceit, imposition. غَبِينَة

Day of the last judgment. يَوْم التَّغَابُن

Arm-pit. مَغْبِن ج مَغَابِن

Cheated in a bargain. مَغْبُون

Mutual cheating in trade. مُغَابَنَة

To have no intelligence of; to understand not, to be unintelligent. ✱ غبو – غبي a غَبًا وغَبَاوَة ه وعَن

To be ignorant of (news). — عن

To be hidden, unknown to a. o. غَبِيَ عَلَى او مِن

To be unmindful of, to take no account of. To show ignorance of. تَغَابَى عَن

To feign unmindfulness. تَغَابَى

Hidden thing Earth concealing an object. غَبَاء

Unmindfulness. Inadvertence, neglect. غَبْوَة وغُبْوَة

To find herbage and become fat (horse). إغثّث
To extract purulent matter from (a wound). إستغثّ ه
Leanness of (a beast). غثاثة
Lean. Worthless, meagre (speech). غثّ وغثيث
Pus, matter. غثيث وغثيثة
Disordered state of mind. غثيثة
To dwell, to remain. ✡ غثغث غثغثة
To wash (clothes) without beater
To undulate (herbage). ✡ غثر o غثرًا بالنّبات
To exude (gum : plant). أغثر ه
To be villous (cloth). إغثارّ
Nap of cloth. غثر
Refuse of mankind ; rabble. غثر وغثرة وغثراء وغيثرة
Reddish brown colour. غثرة
Villous, velvety. أغثر م غثراء ج غثر
Dingy. Ignorant (man).
Gum of some plants. مغثر ومغثار ومغثور ج مغاثير
To give at once to a. o. the best. ✡ غثم o غثمًا لفلان
Ash-colour. غثمة
Ash-coloured. أغثم
Mixed, mingled. مغثوم
✡ غثا o غثوًا وغثوًّا, وغثى i غثيًا, وأغثى ه
To carry (rubbish : torrent).
To mix (language). To confuse. غثى i ه وه
To be disturbed, stirred (mind, heart). — i غثيًا وغثيانًا, وتغثّى
Scum and rubbish swept by a torrent. غثاء, غثّاء
Gipsy, buffoon. ¤ غجري ج أغجار
To be covered with pestilential buboes (camel). ✡ غدّ a غدًّا, وغدّ
To be affected with a swelling, a ganglion, a lump. — وغدّد, وأغدّ وأغدّ
To take o.'s (lot, share). غدّد ه
To be angry with. أغدّ على
Cattle-plague. Camel-plague. غدد ج غداد
Pestilential bubo. غدّة وغددة ج غدد
Wen, goitre. Lump, ganglion; king's evil.
Part, share, lot. غدّة ج غدائد

✧ Thin mist. غثو
Ignorance. Stupidity. غباوة
Simple, stupid, unintelligent. غبيّ ج أغبياء
✡ غبي — ✧ غبي على (for غمي) To swoon, to faint.
To conceal, to cover a. th. To shorten (the hair). غبّى ه
To pour down a shower (sky). أغبى
Shower. Dust in the sky. غبية ج غبيات
He came at sunset. جاء على غبية الشّمس
Dense, tangled (tree). أغبى م غبياء
Pitfall covered with earth. مغباة
To plunge a. o. forcibly into (water). ✡ غتّ o غتًّا ه في
To grieve, to weary a. o. — ه
To upbraid, to silence a. o. — ه بالكلام
To drink successive draughts of. — ه
To conceal (laughter).
To be covered with trees (place). ✡ غتل a غتلًا
Bushy (place). غتل
To be impeded in speech. ✡ غتم i غتمًا
To speak Arabic in an indistinct, barbarous way.
To weary a. o. by repeated visits. — أغتم ه
To suffer from indigestion. إغتشم
Suffocating heat. غتم
Incorrect, barbarous language. غتمة
Impediment of speech.
Speaking incorrectly, indistinctly. أغتم م غتماء ج غتم
Thick (milk). Oppressed. غتمي
Death. حياض غتيم وحياض غتيم
To be lean, weak (beast). To be corrupt (language). ✡ غثّ a i غثاثة وغثوثة, وأغثّ
To secrete purulent matter (wound). — i غثًّا وغثيثًا, وأغثّ
To become unpleasing to a. o. (country). To put a. o. to trouble. غثّ i غثًّا على
There is nothing bad in his opinion. لا يغثّ عليه شيء
He asks the opinion of every one. لا يغثّ عليه أحد
He held bad talks. أغثّ في الكلام

Having a wen, a ganglion. غَادٍ ومُغِدّ
Hot-tempered. (m. f.) مِغْدَاد
Covered with pestilential buboes مَغْدُود (camel).
✱ غَدَر i o غَدْرًا وغَدَرَانًا ه وب To betray, to deceive a. o. To neglect (a duty).
غَدِر a غَدَرًا To be full of rocky tracts (land). To drink rain-water.
— وأَغْدَر To become dark (night).
غَادَر مُغَادَرَة وغِدَارًا ه To act treacherously with a. o. To betray.
— وأَغْدَر ه To cast, to leave, to omit a. th.
إِسْتَغْدَر To become full of pools (country).
غَدْر, وغَدْرَة ج غَدَرَات Treachery, faithlessness, fraud.
غَدْرًا Treacherously, perfidiously.
غَدَر وغَدْرَة وغَدَارَة, وغُدْرَة ج غُدَرَات Remainder; portion.
غَدَر Uneven, hard (ground).
ثَبْت الغَدَر Steadfast (in fight, speech, action).
غَدِير ج غُدُر وغُدْرَان وأَغْدِرَة Pool left by the rain. ✧ River, torrent.
غَدِيرَة ج غَدَائِر Lock, plait of hair.
— ج غُدْرَان Piece of land covered with plants.
غَادِر ج غَادِرُون وغُدَّار وغَدَرَة Deceiver.
غُدَر وغُدَرَة وغِدِّير Treacherous, unfaithful.
غَدَّار وغَدُور (m. f.) Perfidious, faithless.
غَدَّارَة ج غَدَّارَات ✧ Small pistol.
▫ غَدَارِيف Vertebræ.
✱ غَدَف o غَدْفًا, وغَدَّف في العَطَاء To be generous.
✧ غَدَّف (for جَدَّف) To blaspheme, to swear. To curse.
أَغْدَف To cast a veil of darkness upon the earth (night).
— ه على To let (a veil) down on her face (woman). To let fall a net on (the game: hunter).
غَادِف Rower; seaman.
غُدَاف ج غِدْفَان Crow. Thick-feathered vulture. Black and long hair. Black wing.
غُدَافِيّ Black.
غَادُوف, ومِغْدَف ج مَغَادِف Oar.

✱ غَدِق a غَدَقًا To flow abundantly (spring).
— وأَغْدَق واغْدَوْدَق وغَيْدَق To be copious (rain). To have much saliva.
غَدِق a غَدَقًا To be soaked by the rain (ground).
غَدَق Abundant water.
غَدِق Soaked by the rain (soil).
غَيْدَق Abundant (rain). Fruitful (year).
غَيْدَق وغَيْدَاق وغَيْدَقَان Delicate, soft (man, woman).
غَيْدَاق ج غَيَادِيق Vehement (running). Ample (means of life). Liberal (man). Long-bodied (horse).
✱ غدن — تَغَدَّن To lean, to incline down (bough).
إِغْدَوْدَن To be long, luxuriant (head of hair). To be fresh, verdant (plant).
غَدَن Doze, slumber.
— وغُدْنَة Delicacy. Softness.
غُدَانِيّ Delicate, soft,
✱ غَدَا o غُدُوًّا To go, to come, to journey early in the morning. To enter upon the morning.
— غُدُوًّا وغُدْوَة واغْتَدَى على To come at a. o.'s very early.
غَدِي a غَدًا, وتَغَدَّى To eat (the morning-meal).
غَدَّى ه To give to a.o. (the morning-meal).
غَادَى ه To come at a. o.'s early.
غَدٌ (for غَدْو) Morrow, next day.
غَدًا وفي الغَدِ To-morrow.
✧ غَدِي To-morrow, soon, later on.
غُدْوَة ج غُـدًى وغُدُوّ, وغَدَاة ج غَدَوَات, وغَدِيَّة ج غَدَايَا وغَدِيَّات Morning, time between daybreak and sunrise.
بالغُدُوّ والآصَال In the mornings and evenings.
أَتَيْتُهُ العَشَايَا والغَدَايَا I went to him in the mornings and evenings.
غَدِيَة وغُدْوَة Very early in the morning.
غُدَيَّة Rather early.
غَدَاء ج أَغْدِيَة Morning-meal. Breakfast. ✧ Dinner.
غَدِيّ وغَدَوِيّ Of the morrow.
غَادٍ Early comer.
الغَادِي والرَّائِح Coming and going.
غَادِيَة ج غَوَادٍ وغَادِيَات Morning-cloud, morning-rain.

Eating the morning-meal. غديان م غديا
Place repaired to in the morning. مَغْدَى ومَغدَاة
✻ غذّ o i غذًّا, وأغذّ To flow with foul matter (wound): with blood (vein). To lag behind.
أغذّ ه او في To hasten (the walk).
غاذّ Purulent. Lachrymal vein.
غَذِيذَة Pus, matter.
غذغذ ه To diminish a. th.
تَغَذْغَذ To leap, to spring.
✻ غذر — اغتذر To prepare a dish made of flour and milk.
غذيرة Food made of flour and milk.
✻ غذم o غذمًا لِفُلَان من To give at once to a. o. the best of a. th.
— وغذِم a غذمًا, وتغذّم واغتذم ه To eat, to swallow a. th. greedily.
غُذمة ج غُذم Herd of cattle.
— وغذمة ج غذم Abundance of milk.
غذيمة ج غذائم Wide (well)
وقعوا في غُذمةٍ او غذيمةٍ They fell in a distressing case.
غذم ومتغذّم Gluttonous.
✻ غذمر ه To mix up, to jumble things together.
— الكلام To speak volubly, scornfully. To utter threats.
تغذمر To shout, to yell.
غذمرة ج غذامير Clamours. Anger, confused words.
مُغذمِر Whimsical, freakish.
✻ غذا o غذوًا ه To feed a. o. To benefit a. o. (food).
— ه ب To feed a. o. with.
غذا To walk quickly. To flow (blood, urine). To be interrupted (urine).
غذّى ه To feed, to bring up (a child).
تغذّى واغتذى To feed o.'s self. To be fed.
إستغذى ه To throw a. o. down violently on the ground.
غذاء ج أغذية Food, whether solid or liquid; aliment; sustenance of the body.
غاذٍ ج غُذاة وغاذون Fosterer, rearer.
غاذي مال Manager of cattle.
القوّة الغاذية The nutritious and digestive organs.

غذيّ م غذيّة Abundant (pasture).
غذيّ ج غِذاء, وغذويّ Fœtus. Lamb, kid, youngling.
غذوان م غذونة Swift (horse). Foul-tongued.
مُغذٍّ Feeder. Comforting, wholesome (food).
✻ غرّ o غرًّا وغِرّة وغرورًا ه To deceive, to allure a. o.
— غرًّا وغِرارًا ه To feed its chickens with (the bill: bird).
غُرّ من العلم He is well instructed.
غرّ وغرِر a غرارة To be inexperienced.
— i غرًّا وغرارة To act in a childlike way.
غرّ a غررًا وغرارة وغُرّة To have a blaze on the forehead (horse). To be white (complexion). To be eminent, generous.
غرّر تغريرًا وتغرّة To cut, to come forth (fore-teeth). To expand its wings (bird).
— ه To fill (a skin).
غرّر بنفسه To undertake a. th. blindly. To risk (o.'s self). To rush headlong into a peril.
غارّ غِرارًا To be dull (market). To yield little milk (she-camel).
إغترّ To be heedless, deceived, unprepared.
— واستغرّ ب To be deceived, seduced by.
— واستغرّ ه To overtake a. o. unawares.
غرّ ج غرور Fold, wrinkle, crease, furrow. Gap, cleft in the earth.
طويته على غرّه I left him in his previous state.
غرّ وغرار Edge of a sword.
غُرّة ج غرر Blaze upon the forehead of a horse. Gleam of dawn. New moon. Whiteness of complexion, of the teeth. Best, choice part. Face, forehead. First day of the month. Eminent (man). Good behaviour.
غِرّ (m. f.) ج أغرار Inexperienced, heedless.
غِرّة ج غِرر Heedlessness, neglect.
غرر Risk, peril
غِرار Deficiency, paucity; inconsideration. Dullness of a market.

In haste. عَلَى غِرَار

On the same pattern, course, manner. عَلَى غِرَارٍ وَاحِدٍ

Delusion. Vanities. غُرُور

Seducing, blinding (the mind). Vain, delusive. غَارّ ج غُرَّار

Allurer, seducer. Heedless, inconsiderate. غَرَّار وغَرُور

The deceitful one *i. e.* the world. الغَرُور

Deceived; dupe. Cautioner, surety. Easy (life). غَرِير ج غُرَّان

Inexperienced. Good nature. — ج أَغِرَّاء وأَغِرَّة

More negligent. أَغَرّ م غَرَّاء ج غُرّ وغُرَّان Bright (complexion). Fine. Having a blaze on the forehead (horse). Brilliant. shining from afar. Noble, eminent. Beautiful, hot (day).

Carelessness, neglect. غَرَارَة

Sack for straw. غِرَارَة ج غَرَائِر

Niggardly. مُغَارّ الكَفّ ج مَغَارّ

Deluded. ◻ Self-conceited. مَغْرُور

To gargle. To bubble up (cooking-pot). To crepitate (broiled meat). To cut the throat. ☆ غَرْغَرَ

To gargle o.'s throat with. To drop (tears : eye). تَغَرْغَرَ ب

Guinea fowl. غِرْغِر

Gizzard. Blaze upon a horse's forehead. غُرْغُرَة

Gargling. Bubbling of a pot; rattling sound in the throat: guttural sound. غَرْغَرَة

To go away, to depart. ☆ غَرَبَ o غَرْبًا

To be affected with a tumour (eye).

To set (star, sun). To be absent, remote (person). — غُرُوبًا

غَرَبَ o غُرْبَةً وغُرْبًا, وغَرَّبَ وتَغَرَّبَ واغْتَرَبَ To forsake o.'s country. To emigrate. To live in a foreign country.

To be obscure, inunderstood (word). To become a foreigner. غَرُبَ o غَرَابَةً

To be black. غَرِبَ a غَرَبًا

To go towards the west. غَرَّبَ وأَغْرَبَ To bring forth black and white children. To remove, to put away.

To pasture cattle in a remote land. غَرَّبَ

To cause a. o. to emigrate. To banish a. o. غَرَّبَ ه

To go to the west. To do or say a. th. strange, extraordinary. To laugh immoderately. To run swiftly. To go far into a country. أَغْرَبَ

To make (a horse) to run to exhaustion. To fill (a skin). — ه وه

To come from the west. To go abroad. To become a stranger. تَغَرَّبَ

To marry a stranger, a foreign woman. إِغْتَرَبَ

To find a. th. extraordinary, strange. إِسْتَغْرَبَ ه

To laugh to excess. — واسْتُغْرِبَ

West, place of sunset. غَرْب ج غُرُوب Edge of (a sword). Tears. Flow of wine, tears. Large bucket. Lachrymal vein. Inner and outer angle of the eye. Tumour in the eyes. Distance. Sharpness of a sword, of the tongue, of temper.

Western, occidental. Westerly (wind). غَرْبِيّ

Remote country. نَوًى غَرْبَة

Silver cup. Willow. Gold. Wine. غَرَب

Journey abroad. State of a stranger, of a foreigner. Emigration. غُرْب وغُرْبَة وتَغَرُّب واغْتِرَاب

Crow (quite black). Edge (of a sword). غُرَاب ج أَغْرُب وغُرُب وغِرْبَان وأَغْرِبَة

Rook, Noachian crow. غُرَاب نُوحِيّ

Crow's foot (*plant*). رِجْل الغُرَاب

Mushroom, toad's stool (*pl.*). عُشّ الغُرَاب

Very fruitful land. أَرْضٌ لَا يَطِيرُ غُرَابُهَا

Bird of bad omen. غُرَاب البَيْن

The affair became intricate. صُرَّ عَلَيْهِ رِجْل الغُرَاب

Corvet. غُرَاب ج غِرْبَان وأَغْرِبَة

Arabs of black complexion. أَغْرِبَة العَرَب

Strangeness of a word, of an expression. غَرَابَة

Sunset. غُرُوب

Western side (of a mountain). Setting (sun). Withers (of a camel). Upper part of a. th. غَارِب ج غَوَارِب

Stranger. Traveller. Strange, uncouth, extraordinary. غَرِيب ج غُرَبَاء

Strange, wonderful event. Hand-mill. غَرِيبَة ج غَرَائِب
Dawn. Snow, hail. White or fringed with white (eyelids). مُغرَب
West, place of sunset. مَغرِب ج مَغَارِب
The west. Northern Africa. المَغرِب
The hour of sunset. مَغرِب الشَّمس
Western. مَغرِبِيّ
Algerian. Moor. — ج مَغَارِبَة
Going towards the west. مُغَرِّب
Have you received any news from a foreign country? هل جاءكم من مُغَرِّبَة خَبَر
Excellent grapes. Black-haired (old man). ✻ غِربِيب
To sift (wheat). To scatter, to crush (a party of men). ✻ غَربَل ه
Siftings. غُربَلَة
Sieve. Tambourine. غِربَال ج غَرَابِيل
Sparrow. غِربِيل
Sifted, scattered. Refuse of mankind. In decay (empire). مُغَربَل
To be slightly or extremely hungry. ✻ غَرِث a غَرَثًا
To render (a beast) hungry. غَرَّث ه
Slightly or vehemently (hungry). Slender. غَرثَان ج غَرثَى وغَرَاثَى وغِرَاث
To warble, to sing (bird). To hum (insect). ✻ غَرِد a غَرَدًا, وغَرَّد وأَغرَد وتَغَرَّد
To excite (birds) to sing (meadow). إِستَغرَد ه
The meadow excites the flies to buzz. — الرَّوضُ الذُّبَابَ
To assail a. o. violently. To overcome a. o. إِغرَندَى ه وعلى
Warbling, song of birds. أُغرُود وأُغرُودَة ج أَغَارِيد
Singing (bird). غِرد وغَرِد. وغِرِّيد ومُغَرِّد
Truffles. Booth of reeds. غِرد وغَرد (un. غِردَة وغَردَة)
To prick a. th. with (a needle). To plant (a tree). ✻ غَرَز i غَرزًا ه
To put (the foot) into (the stirrup). — ه في
To stick her eggs into the earth (locust). — وغَرَّز

To prick (a needle) into a. th. غَرَّز وغَرَّز ه في
To fix (a stick) into (the ground). — وأَغرَز ه ب
To submit (rebel). غَرِز a غَرَزًا
To sink, to penetrate into. تَغَرَّز واغتَرَز في
To put (the foot) into (the stirrup). إِغتَرَز
To be on the eve of departure. — السَّيرَ
Ingrafted sprigs. Leathern stirrup. غَرز ج غُرُوز
Keep to his stirrup *i. e.* Follow, obey him. إِلزَم غَرزَهُ
A puncture, a stitch. غُرزَة ج غُرَز
Nature, native disposition. Natural gift. Spontaneity. Instinct غَرِيزَة ج غَرَائِز
Inborn, natural. Spontaneous. Instinctive. غَرِيزِيّ
Plunging, sinking. غَارِز م غَارِزَة ج غُرَّز
Off-set, cutting of trees. تَغرِيز ج تَغَارِيز
Grove. Place of growth. Base of a tooth, of the neck. مَغرِز
Sunk, stuck into. Inborn, natural. مَغرُوز
To plant (a tree). To confer (a benefit). ✻ غَرَس i غَرسًا, وأَغرَس ه
To be planted (tree). إِنغَرَس
Plant. Shoot, offset, slip. غَرس ج أَغرَاس وغِرَاس
Crow. Membrane enclosing the fœtus. Set of trees. غِرس ج أَغرَاس
✧ To layer. غَرَس العَقل
Planted shoot. Female slave. غَرِيسَة ج غَرَائِس وغِرَاس
Act, time of planting. غِرَاس
Place of planting. Woman. مَغرِس ج مَغَارِس
Planted (tree). مَغرُوس
Piastre, Turkish coin equal to 2 1/2 d. ✧ غِرش ج غُرُوش
To long for a. th. ✻ غَرِض a غَرَضًا الى
To be grieved by. To fear a. th. To feel disgust at. — من
To wean (a kid) before the time. غَرَض i غَرضًا, وغَرَّض ه
To fill (a vessel); to fill (a غَرَض ه

vessel) partly. To despatch (a business).
To give to a. o. fresh milk, fresh food. غَرَضَ لهُ غَرِيضًا
To pluck fresh fruit. — وغَرَّضَ هُ
To bind (a camel's girth). — وأغْرَضَ هُ
To be fresh, juicy. غَرُضَ o غِرَضًا
To eat fresh meat, fruits. غَرَّضَ
He is an inexhaustible sea. هُوَ بَحْرٌ لَا يُغَرَّضُ
To bring (camels) to water in the morning. غَارَضَ هُ
To vex, to grieve a. o. أغْرَضَ هُ
To fill (a skin). To hit (the butt). — هُ
To be broken (bough) without being separated. تَغَرَّضَ وانْغَرَضَ
✧ To side with a. o.; to bias. تَغَرَّضَ لِ
To be plucked fresh (fruit). إغْتَرَضَ
To aim at. — هُ
✧ To charge a. o. with unfairness, bias. ✧ إسْتَغْرَضَ هُ
Rent. fold. غَرْض ج غُرْضَان
— ج غُرُوض وأغْرَاض. وغُرْضَة ج غُرَض وغُرُض
Girth of a camel-saddle. Fold.
Target, mark. Aim. Scope, pursuit. Selfish aim. ✧ Bias, prejudice. غَرَض ج أغْرَاض
Fresh (meat, dates). A. th. white, fresh, tender. New song. Good singer. غَرِيض ج أغَارِيض
✧ Self-interest. Selfishness. Bias. Partiality. غَرَضِيَّة ج غَرَضِيَّات
Place of the girth (on an animal). مَغْرِض ج مَغَارِض
Cartilage. ✡ غُرْضُوف
Piece of wood on the side of a camel-saddle. — مث غُرْضُوفَان ج غَرَاضِيف
✡ To take (water) with the hand or a ladle. ✡ غَرَفَ o i غَرْفًا, واغْتَرَفَ هُ
To tan (a skin). To put (a rope) upon (a camel's head). To cut off a. th. To clip (the hair). — o غَرْفًا هُ
To take a. th. altogether. تَغَرَّفَ هُ
To be cut off, bent, broken off. إنْغَرَفَ
Plant for tanning leather غَرْف وغَرَف
Sole, sandal. غِرْفَة ج غِرَف
Spoonful, handful. غُرْفَة ج غِرَاف, وغُرَافَة
Upper- غُرْفَة ج غُرَف وغُرُفَات وغُرَفَات وغُرْفَات

chamber. The seventh heaven. Lock of hair. Rope put on a camel's head.
Lading (water) with the hand. غَارِف
Swift (she-camel). Hair clipped upon the forehead. غَارِفَة ج غَوَارِف
Measure for grain. غِرَاف
Wide-stepping (horse). Having much water (river). ✧ Water-wheel. غَرَّاف
Bed of reeds. Thicket of trees. غَرِيف
Thicket. Sole; worn out sandal. غَرِيفَة
Ladle; large spoon. مِغْرَفَة ج مَغَارِف
Laded. Cut, clipped. مَغْرُوف
✡ To sink into water; to be submerged. To be drowned, shipwrecked. ✡ غَرِقَ a غَرَقًا في الماء
To drink a draught of. غَرَقَ o غَرْقًا من
To drown, to submerge a. o. غَرَّقَ وأغْرَقَ هُ في الماء
To ornament (a bit, a scabbard) with (gold, silver). غَرَّقَ وأغْرَقَ هُ بِ
To brace a bow-string to the utmost. — وأغْرَقَ في القَوْس
To come near to a. o. To be at hand (death). غَارَقَ هُ
To exceed (the bounds), to exaggerate a. th. أغْرَقَ في
To overtake and outstrip the other horses. إغْتَرَقَ
To attract (the looks). — هُ
To gasp for breath. — النَّفَسَ
To take up a. th. altogether; to comprise the (whole). To overshoot (the mark). إسْتَغْرَقَ هُ
To exaggerate, to be immoderate in. To exceed (the bounds) in. — في
To be drowned in tears (eye). إغْرَوْرَقَ
Drowning, submersion, shipwreck. غَرَق و✧ غَرِيق
Submersion. غَرْقَة
Draught. غُرْقَة ج غُرَق
Emphyteusis, form of mortgage. غَرُوقَة
Submersion. Hyperbole. Excess, exaggeration. إغْرَاق
Inclusion. Exaggeration. إسْتِغْرَاق
Sunk, submerged, drowned. Shipwrecked. Flooded (land). غَارِق وغَرِق
Breathless, terror-stricken. غَرِق الصَّوْت

☆ غَرَا o غَرْوًا ه To glue a. th. To adhere to (the heart: fatness). To wonder at.

غَرِيَ a غَرَاء وغَرًى، وغُرِيَ وغُرِّيَ وأُغرِيَ ب To desire earnestly, to cling, to adhere to. To persevere in.

غَرَّى ه To smear a. th. To stick a. th. with glue.

غَارَى مُغَارَاةً وغِرَاءً ه To quarrel with.

— بَيْن To join, to unite (two things).

أَغْرَى ه ب To incite desire. To tempt, to seduce, to allure a. o. by. To render a. o. desirous, fond of. To set a. o. as a chief over.

— العَدَاوَة بَيْن To excite hatred between.

تَغَرَّى To adhere, to stick to.

غِرَاء وغَرًا ج أَغْرَاء Glue; paste. Youngling. Lean. Beauty.

بِهِ غَرًا He is comely.

غَرَاء وغَرْوَى Eager desire, fondness.

لَا غَرْوَ ولَا غَرْوَى No wonder, no wondering at.

غَرِيّ م غَرِيَّة Comely. Adherent. Red dye.

غَرِيَّان Two celebrated buildings in Koofah.

تَغْرِيَة Adherency.

إِغْرَاء Instigation, incitement.

مُغْرِي Inciting, urging.

مُغْرَى Incited, urged.

مَغْرُوّ ومَغْرِيّ Gluey; glued.

✧ مِغْرَاة Instrument for gluing.

☆ غَزَر o غَزْرًا، واغْتَرَّ ب To become attached to a. o.; to cleave to.

✧ — غَزًّا ه في To prick (a needle) into.

غَازَّ ه To wrestle, to contend with.

أَغَزَّ To be thorny (tree).

✧ إِنْغَزَّ في To penetrate, to sink into.

تَغَازَّ ه To quarrel (about a. th).

غَزَّة Gaza (town of Palestine).

غُزَّاز Philanthropists.

☆ غَزُر o غَزْرًا وغَزَارَة وغُزْرًا To be abundant. To abound in milk (ewe); in water (spring).

غَازَر واسْتَغْزَر To give a little in order to obtain more in return.

أَغْزَر To possess numerous milch-camels (tribe). To have much rain.

— ه To be munificent to; to lavish (favours, gifts).

غَرِيق ج غَرْقَى Submerged. Drowned. Overwhelmed. ◘ Deep.

G غَارِيقُون وأَغَارِيقُون Agaric (*medicinal plant*); antidote.

مُغَرَّق ومُغْرَق Richly adorned (bit).

☆ غَرْقَأ To lay eggs without shells (hen).

غِرْقِئ Interior pellicle of eggs. White of eggs.

☆ غَرْقَد White of eggs. Box-thorn.

☆ غَرْقَل To become rotten (egg, melon). To pour water on o.'s head.

☆ غَرِل a غَرَلًا To be uncircumcised.

غُرْلَة ج غُرَل Prepuce.

أَغْرَل م غَرْلَاء ج غُرْل Uncircumcised. Fruitful (year). Easy (life).

☆ غَرِم a غُرْمًا وغَرَامَة ومَغْرَمًا ه To pay (a debt, a tax, a fine). To pay a. th. (instead of another).

— في التِّجَارَة To lose in trade.

غَرَّم وأَغْرَم ه ه To compel a. o. to pay (a fine, a debt). To fine a. o.

أُغْرِم ب To be fond, eagerly desirous of.

تَغَرَّم To take an obligation upon o.'s self.

✧ إِنْغَرَم To become enamoured, inflamed with love.

إِغْتَرَم To take upon o.'s self the payment of a debt.

غُرْم وغَرَامَة ج غَرَامَات Payment of a. th. obligatory. Tax, damage, debt, duty, fine. Indemnity.

غَرَام Passion, earnest desire. Punishment, affliction. Hardship. Obligation.

غَرِيم ج غُرَمَاء Creditor. Debtor. Antagonist. Competitor, litigant.

مَغْرَم ج مَغَارِم Debt, obligation.

مُغْرَم Longing, passionate for. Burdened by debts.

مَغْرُوم ✧ Enamoured.

☆ غَرِن a غَرَنًا To be dry (dough).

غَرِين وغِرْيَن Slime, mud.

✧ غُرْنَة Trough, tub.

☆ غَرْنَق — غُرْنُوق وغُرْنَيْق وغِرْنِيق Stork, crane. Tender plant. Forelock.

غُرْنُوق وغُرَانِق ج غَرَانِق وغَرَانِيق وغَرَانِقَة Comely youth. Fair girl.

غَزَر ج غُزر Basket made of palm-leaves, or halfa-grass.
غَزْر وغَزَارَة Abundance (of milk, water).
✧ غَزّار Reeds, canes.
غَزِير م غَزِيرَة ج غِزَار Copious, abounding in milk (flock); in tears (eye); in water (spring); in leaves (plant).
مُغَازِر ومُسْتَغْزِر Giving a little in order to receive more in return.
مَغْزُور Well watered by rain (ground).
✱ غَزَل i غَزْلًا, واغْتَزَل ه To spin (flax, cotton, wool).
غَزِل a غَزَلًا ب وغَازَل ه وتَغَزَّل ب To flirt, to court a. o.; to ogle.
غَزِل To stop at the gazelle's cry (hound).
أَغْزَل To spin, to twirl (a spindle). To have a young one (gazelle).
✧ إِنْغَزَل To be spun (cotton).
تَغَازَل To sport, to dally; to hold amorous talks with o. a. (lovers).
غَزْل Spun thread, or yarn. Spider's web.
غَزَل وتَغَزُّل Amorous talk. Erotic verses.
غَزَال ج غِزْلَان وغِزْلَة Male gazelle; young gazelle.
دَم الغَزَال Dragon's blood, resinous juice.
غَزَالَة She-gazelle. Rising sun.
غَزِل Courting women, gallant.
✧ غَزَالِيَّة Stuff of silk and cotton.
غَازِلَة ج غَوَازِل وغُزَّل Spinning (woman).
غَزَّال م غَزَّالَة Spinner.
أَغْزَل من الحُمَّى More frequent visitor than the fever.
مَغْزَل ومِغْزَل ج مَغَازِل Spindle.
◘ أَبو مَغَازِل Crane. Stork.
مَغْزُول Spun (silk, cotton, yarn).
✱ غَزَا o غَزْوًا, واغْتَزَى ه وه To direct o.'s self towards. To wish, to purpose a. th.; to aim at.
— غَزْوًا وغَزَوَانًا وغَزَاوَة ه To go forth to fight with. To make a raid.
غَزَّى وأَغْزَى ه To send (troops) in a military expedition. To grant a delay to (a debtor).
أَغْزَى To have her husband at war (woman).

إِغْتَزَى ب To cleave to a. o. as a special friend.
غَزْو Wish, intention, aim.
غَزْو وغَزَوَان وغَزَاوَة Military expedition. Razzia. Raid, attack.
غَزْوَة ج غَزَوَات A raid, a warring.
غَزَوِيّ Relating to a campaign.
غَازٍ ج غُزَاة وغُزًّى وغُزِيّ وغُزَّاء Waging war. Victorious, champion of Islam.
الغَازِي Title of the Sultans.
غَزَاة ج غَزَوَات Expedition, raid.
◘ غَازِيَة ج غَوَازِي Dancing-girl.
◘ غَزِيَّة War-tax.
مَغْزًى ج مَغَازٍ War, campaign. Seat of a war.
— الكَلَام Moral of a discourse; intended meaning.
المَغَازِي Records of exploits; feats of war.
✱ غَسَّ o غَسًّا في To go deep into (a country).
— ه في To plunge a. o. into (water).
إِنْغَسَّ في To be plunged into (water). To be under (water).
غُسّ (s. pl.) ج أَغْسَاس وغِسَاس وغُسُوس Feeble, despicable.
غَسَّان Name of the leader of a tribe.
مُلُوك غَسَّان Chiefs of an Arabian tribe.
✱ غَسَر To drive out (a cat).
غَسَر o غَسْرًا على To urge (a debtor).
تَغَسَّر To be entangled (thread). To be intricate (business).
غَسَر Rubbish swept by the wind into a pond.
غَسِير Complicate, confused (business).
✱ غَسَف Darkness.
أَغْسَف To walk in the dark.
✱ غَسَق i غَسْقًا وغَسَقَانًا وغَسَقًا, وأَغْسَق To be obscure (night).
— غَسْقًا وغَسَقَانًا To let down a fine rain (sky).
— غُسُوقًا, وغَسِق a غَسَقَانًا To be confused by tears (eye).
غَسَق وغَاسِق Duskiness at nightfall.
غَسَق Refuse of wheat.
غَاسِق Moon. Night.
غَسَاق وغَسَّاق Bitter cold. Stinking. Purulent matter.
✱ غَسَل i غَسْلًا وغُسْلًا, وغَسَّل ه To wash

(linen). To wash, to cleanse (the body). To cleanse (from sins: God).

To beat a. o. with a whip. ه بِالسَّوْط —
To flog.

To be washed, cleansed. إِنْغَسَلَ

To wash o.'s self. To perform ablutions. إِغْتَسَلَ

To anoint o.'s self with perfumes. ب —

Washing (of the body, of the dead); ablution. غَسْل وَغُسْل

Wash, perfume for the head. Water used for ablution. Marsh-mallow. Geranium. غِسْل وَغُسْل وَغِسْلَة وَغَسُول وَغَسُّول

Wash-water, lye. غُسَالَة

Washed. ✧ Washing, clothes for the wash. غَسِيل ج غَسْلَى وَغُسَلَاء

Purulent matter. Washing. غِسْلِين

Washer of linen, of the dead. غَاسِل م غَاسِلَة

Soap, herbs used in washing. Potash, glasswort. غَاسُول

Washerman. Laundress. غَسَّال م غَسَّالَة

مَغْسَل وَمَغْسِل ج مَغَاسِل. وَمُغْتَسَل ج مُغْتَسَلَات
Laundry. Wash-house. Bath.

Wash-stand; wash-pot. مِغْسَل و✧ مَغْسَلَة

To be dark (night). ✱ غَسَمَ o غَسْمًا, وَأَغْسَمَ

Black colour. Darkness. Dust. غَسَم

To chew a. th. ✱ غَسَنَ o غَسْنًا ه

Recesses of the heart. غُسَان الْقَلْب

Vigour, fieriness of youth. غَسَّان وَغَيْسَان

Thou art not a match for him. مَا أَنْتَ مِن غَسَّانِهِ او غَيْسَانِهِ

Very handsome. غَسَّانِيّ وَغَيْسَانِيّ

غُسْنَة ج غُسَن . وَغُسْنَاة ج غُسْنَات وَغُسُنَات
Lock of hair.

To be obscure (night). ✱ غَسَا o غَسْوًا, وَغَسِيَ a غَسًى , وَأَغْسَى

Unripe date. غِسَاة ج غَسًى وَغَسَوَات

To cheat, to act dishonestly with. ✱ غَشَّ o غِشًّا, وَغَشَّش ه

To counterfeit, to adulterate (goods). غَشَّ ه

To allow o.'s self to be deceived. إِغْتَشَّ و✧ انْغَشَّ

To suspect a. o. to be a deceiver, a dissembler. إِغْتَشَّ وَاسْتَغَشَّ ه

False pretence, fraud, dishonest conduct. Counterfeit coin. Defect. Rancour; duplicity. غِشّ

Deceiver, dissembler. غُشّ ج غُشُون, وَغَاشّ ج غُشَّاش وَغَشَشَة

Turbid, muddy (water). Counterfeit (coin). غَشَش

Beginning or end of the night. Little in quantity (water). غِشَاش

Speedily, hastily. غِشَاشًا وعلى غِشَاش

Deceiver, impostor. غَشَّاش

Counterfeited. Adulterated. مَغْشُوش

Deceiver. ✱ غَشْقَاش

To do a. th. inconsiderately. To cut wood by night indiscrimanetely. ✱ غَشِمَ i غَشْمًا

To deal unjustly, wrongfully with; to tyrannise. To smear (a camel) entirely with tar. غَشَمَ o غَشْمًا ه —

To feign simplicity, inexperience. ✧ تَغَاشَمَ

To judge a. o. to be simple, ignorant. ✧ إِسْتَغْشَمَ

Injustice, tyranny. غَشْم

Ignorance, simplicity. ✧ غُشْم

✧ Awkward, inexperienced. Rough (stone). غَشِيم ج غُشَمَاء

Tyrannical. Violent. غَاشِم وَغَشُوم

Courageous, energetic. مِغْشَم

Indomitable, energetic. Bold. ✱ غَشَمْشَم

Boldness. غَشْمَشَة وَغَشْمَشِيَّة

To follow o.'s own mind. To be self-confident. To rush forth (torrent). ✱ غَشْمَرَ

To do a. th. speedily, hastily. ه —

To treat a. o. unjustly. ه —

To take a. th. forcibly. تَغَشْمَرَ ه

To become irritated with. على —

Injustice. غَشْمَرَة وَغَشْمَرِيَّة

To come to a. o. ✱ غَشَا o غَشْوًا ه

To strike a. o with (a stick). غَشِيَ a غَشَيَانًا ه ب

To come towards a. o. ه —

To engage blindly (in an affair). To cover a. o. To surprise. غِشَاوَة ه وه —

Veil, covering, wrapper. غِشْوَة وَغُشْوَة وَغِشَاوَة وَغُشَاوَة

A veil is spread over his heart *i. e.* he does not understand. على قَلْبِهِ غُشَاوَة

White-headed (horse). أَغْشَى م غَشْوَاء

In spite of thee. ✧ غَضبًا عن رَقَبَتِك
Violence, open force, tyranny. إِغْتِصَاب
Rape.
Oppressor, ravisher. غَاصِب ج غَاصِبُون وغُصَّاب, ومُغْتَصِب
Compelled, violated. مَغْصُوب ومُغْتَصَب
Snatched.
To draw (a branch) ✱ غَصَن i غَصْنًا ه to o.'s self. To snatch, to pull off a. th.
To avert a. o. from. — ٥ عن
To be laden with غَصَّن وأَغْصَن grapes (bunch).
To put forth branches (tree). أَغْصَن
Branch, غُصْن ج غُصُون وغِصَنَة وأَغْصَان bough, shoot.
Golden-rod (*plant*). غُصْن الذَّهَب
A bough, a branchlet. غُصْنَة
To ✱ غَضَّ o غَضًّا وَغِضَاضًا وَغَضَاضَة ه ومن lower (the eyes, the voice). To blink. To lessen a. th. To shorten (hair). To deprive a. o. of.
To avert (the eyes) from. غَضَّ ه عن
To bear (the sight) of. — ه ل
To lower, غَضَّ o غَضًّا وَغَضَاضَة من فُلَانٍ to lessen the estimation of a. o. To look scornfully at.
To become غَضَّ a i غَضَاضَة وغُضُوضَة sappy, fresh (plant). To be bright, thin-skinned (woman).
To become soft, tender. To eat غَضَّض fresh things.
To be contracted, to blink. إِنْغَضَّ (eye).
غَضّ ج غِضَاض, وغَضِيض ج أَغِضَّة وأَغِضَّاء
Fresh, tender, sappy, thin-skinned (plant, woman).
Upper part of the face. غِضَاض وغُضَاض
Decrease, lowering. Defect, غَضَاضَة vice. Languor.
غُضَّة ج غُضَض , وَغَضِيضَة ج غَضَائِض, ومَغَضَّة
Decrease, falling off. ج مَغَاض
Tangled, luxuriant (tree). ✧ مُغِضّ
To decrease, to become ✱ غَضْغَض ه scanty (water).
To diminish, to sink — وتَغَضْغَض (water).
To be angry ✱ غَضِب a غَضَبًا ومَغْضَبَة على with.

To cover, to ✱ غَشِي a غَشْيًا وغِشَايَة ٥ ه conceal a. th.
To be dark (night). To غَشِي وأَغْشَى surprise a. o. (event).
To swoon, to غُشِي عَلَيْهِ غَشْيًا وغُشْيًا وغَشَيَانًا faint.
To put a covering غَشَّى وأَغْشَى ٥ وعلى over.
To have a. th. covered — وأَغْشَى ٥ ه by a. o.
God has put a veil أَغْشَى الله على بَصَرِهِ over his eyes (*lest he should see*) *i. e.* God has hardened his heart.
To cover o.'s self تَغَشَّى واستَغْشَى ب with (a garment).
Covering, case. Skin of غِشَاء ج أَغْشِيَة the eye. Pericardium. Scabbard of a sword.
Veil, cover. غِشَايَة وغُشَايَة
Swoon, fainting. غَشْيَة وغَشْي وغُشْي وغَشَيَان
Covering, veiling. غَاشٍ م غَاشِيَة
Veil, cover, case. غَاشِيَة ج غَوَاشٍ Housing. Followers, servants, guests. The resurrection. Calamity.
Swooning, fainting. مَغْشِيّ عَلَيْهِ
Covered, wrapped. مُغْشًى ومُغَشًّى
To be choked by ✱ غَصَّ a غَصَصًا ب a. th. To be overwhelmed by (sorrow). To be crammed (room).
To choke. To put a. o. in a أَغَصَّ ٥ strait. To grieve a. o.
He has reduced us to — عَلَيْنَا الأَرْضَ straits.
To be in anguish. إِغْتَصَّ
Obstructing the throat; غُصَّة ج غُصَص stopping the breath (food, anger, grief).
Choked, obstructed. غَاصّ وغَصَّان
To compel a. o. ✱ غَصَب i غَصْبًا ٥ على to do a. th.
To snatch — ٥ ه او ه من واغْتَصَب ه a. th. forcibly; to violate a. o.
To act wrongfully, غَاصَب ٥ و✧ تَغَاصَب violently o. with another.
To be constrained, compelled. ✧ إِنْغَصَب
Violence, constraint. Thing غَصْب taken forcibly.
Against his will, in spite of غَصْبًا عَنْهُ him.

To become dark (night). – وأغضف
To break a. th. To let a. th. hang down. غضّف ه
To become cloudy; to prepare to rain (weather). To be laden with fruit (palm-trees). أغضف
To coil itself (serpent). To be broken, folded. تغضّف
To favour a. o. (fortune). To cover a. o. (night). – على
To collapse, to be decayed (well). – وانغضف
Easy (life); enjoying an easy (life). غاضف م غاضفة
Lop-eared (dog). *Pl.* Hounds. – وأغضف م غضفاء ج غضف
Dark (night). Easy (life). Fruitful (year). أغضف
To be sluggish, jaded (hackney). ✻ غضفر
Rude, coarse, thick (man). Fleshy ear. Big, old lion. غضنفر وغضفر
To withhold, to prevent a. o. from. ✻ غضن o i غضنًا ه عن
To wrinkle, to fold a. th. غضّن ه
To pour a continuous drizzle (sky). – وأغضن
To continue unremittingly upon a. o. (fever). – على
To be wrinkled, folded. تغضّن
Wrinkle (of the skin); crease, fold (of a garment). Trouble, weariness. غضن وغضن ج غضون
Sclerotic tunic of the eye. غضن العين
The folds of the ear. غضون الأذن
In the midst of, meanwhile. في غضون ذلك
Patch of small-pox. غضنة وغضنة
Having the eyes contracted. أغضن
To be dark (night). ✻ غضا o غضوًا
To be whole, in good state. – غضوًّا
To be dark (night). ✻ غضى – أغضى
To contract (the eyelids). To close (the eyes).
To look over a. th.; to refrain wilfully from. To bear patiently. أغضى على
To feel disgust, dislike for. – ل
To avert (the eyes) from. – ه عن
To feign to take no notice of. To shut (the eyes) upon. تغاضى عن

To be angry with a. o. for the sake of (a living person). غضب ل
To be angry with a. o. for the sake of (a dead person). – ب
To rouse a. o. to anger. غاضب
To rouse a. o. to anger. أغضب ه
To be angry To boil fiercely (cooking-pot). تغضّب واستغضب على
Anger, wrath, passion. غضب ومغضبة
Intensely red. Lion. Bull. Hard stone. Shield, garment of skin. Skin of the skull. Fish. Patch of small-pox. غضب وغضبة
Angered; prone to anger. غضب وغضب
Hot-tempered. (*m. f.*) غضوب
Hot-tempered. غضبان م غضبى وغضبانة ج غضبى وغضابى وغضاب، ومغضب
Nervous, peevish, angry. غضابيّ
Object of anger. مغضوب عليه
To give abundance of goods, an ample life to a. o. (God). ✻ غضر o غضرًا ه
To turn away from. غضر i غضرًا وتغضّر عن
To hinder a. o. To cut off a. th. To tan (a skin). – ه وه
To give to a. o. a portion of o.'s property. – لفلان من ماله
To be soft, tender. – غضرة وغضارة
To acquire (wealth), to become rich. غضر a غضرًا
To die young. أغتضر
Prosperity, easiness of life, well-being. غضر وغضارة وغضراء
Cohesive green clay. غضار وغضارة
Large dish, bowl. غضارة ج غضائر
Thriving; easy (life). غضر م غضرة
Fertile ground. Greenish clay. غضراء ج غضارى
Green, soft, fresh. غضير م غضيرة
Happy, comfortable. مغضر ومغضور
Cartilage. ✻ غضروف ج غضاريف
To break a branch (not thoroughly). To fold (a pillow). To relax (the ears: dog). ✻ غضف i غضفًا ه
To slacken its run (ass). غضف
To be relaxed (ear). To be lop-eared (dog). To be easy, comfortable (life). غضف a غضفًا وغضوفًا

غضًا Euphorbia, tamarisk. Thicket of trees.

غضياء Ground full of tamarisks. Rugged (land).

غاضٍ م غاضية ج غواض. ومُغضٍ Dark (night). Excellent, plentiful (thing). Wealthy (man).

✡ غطّ o i غطًّا, وأغطّ ه وه في To plunge, to dip a. o. or a. th. into (water).

غطّ i غطيطًا To snore, to snort. To bray. To rattle (slaughtered beast. To gurgle cooking-pot).

— غطّ To perch (bird).

تغاطّ To contend in diving, plunging.

إنغطّ To be immerged (in water).

غطّ Immersion.

غطاط Sand-grouse.

— وغُطاط Last remains of darkness before dawn.

غطيط Snoring. Rattle.

✧ غطيطة Fog, mist.

✡ غطغط To boil audibly (cooking-pot).

— وتغطغط To rage, to roar (sea). To be dispersed, shattered.

غطغطة Boiling of a cooking-pot. Roaring of the sea. Cry of the sand-grouse.

✡ غطرس وتغطرس To be self-conceited, a self-admirer.

غطرس ه To irritate a. o. ◻ To overlook, to connive at.

— على To despise: to look at a. o. scornfully.

تغطرس ل To get angry with.

تغطرس في مشيته To have a haughty gait.

غطرسة Haughtiness.

غِطرِس ج غطارس, و غِطريس ج غطاريس Haughty.

✡ غطرف ه To make a. o. to be a chief (God). To treat a. o. arrogantly.

— تغطرف To have a haughty gait. To be ambitious, self-conceited. To desire power, superiority.

غطرفة Ambition. Haughtiness. Proud gait. Sport, play.

غِطراف Illustrious man. Chief.

غِطريف وغُطرُوف وغِطرُوف ج غطارفة وغطاريف Hawk. Noble (lord). Generous (man.) Comely, elegant (youth). Fly. Wide (neck).

✡ غطس i غطسًا ه وه في To immerge a. o. into (water).

— في To dive, to be immerged in (water).

— بِهِ اللُّجَّ Death has swallowed him up.

غطّس ه وه في To plunge a. o. or a. th. into (water). ✧ To baptise by immersion.

✧ تغطّس To bathe, to dive (into water).

تغاطس To contend in diving, plunging. To feign o.'s self heedless, inconsiderate.

✧ غِطاس Baptism by immersion.

✧ عيد الغطاس Baptism of J. B. Epiphany.

تغطيس Immersion. ✧ Baptism.

غاطس م غاطسة Diving, plunged. ✧ Senseless, swooning.

غطّاس Plungeon (bird). Diver.

غطوس Diver. Bold man.

مِغطس ج مغاطس Bath, washing-basin.

G مغنطيس ومغناطيس Magnet. Loadstone. ✧ Magnetism.

✡ غطش i غطشًا, وأغطش To be dark (night).

— غطشًا وغطشانًا To crawl along (old-man, cripple).

غطِش a غطشًا ب To be dim-sighted.

غطّش ه ل To advise a. o. to.

أغطش ه To render (the night) obscure (God).

تغطّش To be dim, weak (sight).

تغاطش To feign o.'s self blind, unmindful.

غطش Weakness of sight. Darkness of night.

أغطش م غطشاء ج غطش Weak-sighted.

غطشاء Obscure (night).

فلاة غطشاء Misleading desert. Wayless, waterless.

✡ غطف Welfare, well-being. Abundance of the eyebrows. Length of the eyelashes.

أغطف م غطفاء Having long eyelashes, thick eyebrows. Easy (life).

غطفان Name of an Arabian tribe.

☆ عطل o غطلًا To be overcast (sky).
غطِل a غطلًا To be dark (night).
غَطْيَل To have abundance of cattle, large property.
غَيْطل To traffic on cattle. To press on, to raise a clamour (crowd).
إغطال To be heaped up.
غَيْطَلَة Confused voices. Darkness. Throng.
غَيْطَلَة وغَيْطل Dense, tangled trees. Collection of men, cattle. Bulls, cows; antelopes. Cat. Darkness. Confusion, uproar.
☆ غطم — غِطمٌ و غِطَيْم وغَطْمَطم Great sea. Large (crowd). Generous (man).
☆ غطمط وتغطمط To rage (sea). To dash together (waves). To boil fiercely (cooking-pot).
غُطامِط وغَطْمَطِيط Rough sound. Roaring (of the sea).
☆ غطا o غطوًا وغُطوًّا, وغطّى وأغطى ه To cover, to conceal a. th.
غطا To spread its darkness (night). To rise, to overflow (water).
أغطى To spread its branches (tree). To be sappy and to cover the ground (vine).
غِطاء ج أغطِيَة Cover, lid, covering. Ignorance.
غِطايَة Tunic.
☆ غطى i غطيًا وغُطيًا To be obscure (night). To be flourishing (youth).
— ه وعلى, وغطّى ه To veil, to cover a. th.
— وأغطى To spread its branches (tree).
تغطّى واغتطى To be covered.
☆ غف — ✧ غفّ o To take what is sufficient for sustenance. To throng around.
تغفّف واغتفّ To become fattened on green fodder (cattle).
غفّ Dry leaves or herbage.
غُفّة Sufficiency of green fodder. Mouse.
— من العَيْش Portion, sufficiency of food.
☆ غفر i غفرًا, وغفّر وأغفر ه To cover, to hide a. th.

غفر الشَّيْب ب To conceal (hoary hair) with (a dye).
غَفَر i غَفرًا وغِفيرًا وغَفِيرَة وغُفرانًا ومَغفِرَة وغُفُورًا ه ل To forgive (a sin) to a. o. (God).
— وغفِر a غَفرًا, وغُفِر To relapse (into a disease). To become villous (cloth). To heal. To reopen (wound).
غفر الجَلَبُ السُّوق Import has lowered the prices of the market.
غفّر ه وه To say: May God forgive thee! ✧ To attach an indulgence to (a rosary).
أغفر To exude gum (plant). To produce herbs (land).
تغفّر To collect gum. ✧ To have an indulgence attached to it (rosary).
تغافر To forgive o. to a.
إغتفر ه ل To forgive (a fault) to a. o.
✧ إنغفر To be forgiven (sin).
إستغفر ه من ه ه To beg pardon for sins from (God). To apologise for.
أستغفرُ اللّٰهَ I beg pardon from God! God forbid!
غفر وغفر Villousness of cloth. Belly.
غَفر وغُفار Down of the neck. Small herbage.
غُفر وغَفر ج أغفار وغِفرَة وغُفُور Young of the mountain-goat.
غِفر Calf. Insect.
غَفر وغَفارَة (for خفر) ✧ Escort; guard. Night-watch.
غفِر الوَجه او القَفا Hairy on the face or the back of the neck.
غُفرَة Covering, cover.
غفَر الأمر بِغُفرَتِهِ He has settled the affair in a becoming way.
غُفران Pardon. Indulgence.
سَنَة الغُفران ✧ Jubilee.
غِفارَة ج غَفائِر Hair-covering.
غفّارة ✧ Cope.
إستِغفار Apology, begging of pardon.
غافِر ج غفرَة وغافِرُون Forgiving.
غَفُور وغفّار The Pardoner (God).
غَفِير Hair of the neck. Covering. ✧ Watchman.
الجَمَّاء الغَفِير Large crowd.
جاءوا جمٌّ الغَفِير او جمًّا غَفِيرًا او الجمّ الغَفِير They came in a crowd.

Cover. Patch. Surplus. غفِيرة
He is unforgiving. ما فِيهِ غفِيرة
Water-melon. غزفَر
Helmet; head-covering worn under the helmet. مِغفَر ومِغفَرة ج مَغافِر
Manna, gum of some plants. — ومُغفُور ومُغفُور ج مَغافِر ومَغافِير
Pardon, forgiveness. مَغفِرة
✱ غفص — غافَص مُغافَصة وغِفاصًا ه To come upon a. o. unexpectedly.
Unforeseen misfortune. غافِصة ج غَوافِص
May God preserve us from unforeseen calamities! وَقانَا اللهُ من الغَوافِص
✱ غفق i غَفقًا To come back of a sudden.
— على To dart upon a. o.
— ه بالسَّوط To flog, to lash a. o. with a whip.
— غفقة To have a short sleep.
تَغفَّق To nap, to doze.
تَغفَّق الشَّراب To drink the whole day.
إغتفَق ب To encompass a. o.
غَفق Slight rain.
غَفقة Nap, doze.
مَغفِق Place of return.
مُنغفَق Starting-place.
✱ غفل o غُفُولًا وغَفلةً وغَفَلًا To be unmindful, careless, heedless.
— وتَغافَل عن To overlook, to neglect.
غفَّل وأغفَل ه To render a. o. careless.
تغفَّل ه To cover, to veil a. th.
غافَل وتَغفَّل واغتفَل واستَغفَل ه To overtake a. o. unawares. To watch a. o. for profiting by his inadvertence.
أغفَل ه To neglect; to forget. To overlook a. th.
تَغافَل To feign o.'s self inadvertent.
غَفَل Easiness of life.
— وغُفُول وغَفلة Neglect, forgetfulness. Carelessness.
غُفل ج أغفَال Without way-mark; without cultivation (land). Unbranded (beast). Cipher (man). Anonymous (book, poem).
غَفلان وتَغافُل Heedlessness, carelessness.
غَفلةً وعلى الغَفلة Of a sudden, unawares.
✧ مَوت الغَفلة Sudden death.
غافِل ج غافِلون وغُفُول وغُفَّل, وغَفلان Neglectful, careless.
مُغفَّل Heedless. Apathetic, inadvertent. Dupe. ◘ Absurd.
مِغفَلة Hair beneath the lower lip.
✱ غفا o غَفوًا وغُفُوًّا, وغَفِي a غَفيَة , وأغفَى To float (upon the water) th. To sleep lightly; to feel drowsy.
غَفو وغَفوة Light sleep, nap. Drowsiness.
غافٍ م غافِيَة Height unreached by water Sleepy, drowsy.
✱ غفى i غَفيًا, وأغفَى ه To clear (the wheat) of its refuse.
أغفَى To be mixed with weeds (wheat).
غُفاء وغَفَى Bits of straw; weeds. Refuse of wheat.
غَفيَة Height unreached by water.
غُفاءة White spot on the iris of the eye.
✱ غَقّ i غَقًّا وغَقيقًا To bubble up (pitch). To screech (eagle).
غَق Cry of the eagle.
غَق وغَقيق Gurgling of a vortex.
✱ غَلّ o غَلًّا ه في To insert a. th. into another.
— في To be inserted, introduced into.
— بَصَرُهُ To become insane.
— المَفازة To penetrate into a desert.
— بَين To flow amid (trees: water).
— وغَلَّل ه To put manacles, an iron-collar to a. o.
— وغَلَّل ه To clothe o.'s self with (a tunic).
— o غُلُولًا , وأغَلّ To act unfaithfully, to defraud.
— i غِلًّا وغَلِيلًا صَدرُهُ To thirst for revenge; to be filled with hatred.
غُلّ غُلًّا وغُلّة To be vehemently thirsty.
غَلَّل ه ب To perfume the (beard) with (balm).
أغَلّ و✧ غَلّ To yield a good crop (land). To put on a coat of mail. To make a raid.
— البَصَر To fix the looks.
— ه To charge a. o. with treachery.
أغَلّ على To bring provisions for (o.'s family).
تَغلّل وانغَلّ في To enter, to penetrate into.
إغتَلّ ب To perfume o.'s self (with balm).

To be thick-necked. غَلِب a غَلَبًا
To make a. o. to gain mastery over. To declare a. o. to be the winner. غَلَّب ه على
To contend with a. o. for superiority. غَالَب مُغَالَبَةً وغِلَابًا ه
To get the mastery over (a country); to overpower. تَغَلَّب عَلَى
To be overcome. ✧ إِنْغَلَب
To be tangled (plant). إِغْلَوْلَب
Victory, conquest; superiority. Antonomasia (*figure of rhet.*). غَلَبَة
Often victorious. ✧ Inquisitive, jabberer. كَثِير أَلغَلَبَة
Speedily victorious. غَلَّاب
Winner, conqueror. غَالِب ج غَلَبَة
Pl. Insuperable difficulties. غَالِبَة ج غَوَالِب
Crowd. Te غَلَبَه لق
Disorderly fellow, jabberer. ◘ غَلَبَاوِيّ
Generally, for the most part, most probably. غَالِبًا وفِي ٱلغَالِب وفِي ٱلأَغْلَب
More powerful, more frequent, more probable. أَغْلَب
Thick-necked. Lion. أَغْلَب م غَلْبَاء ج غُلْب
Thicket of tangled trees. Large (tribe). غَلْبَاء
✧ Majority (of votes); greater number. أَغْلَبِيَّة
Overcome. Declared the winner. مُغَلَّب
Overcome. ✧ Unable to earn livelihood for his family. مَغْلُوب
Victory. Place of victory. مَغْلَبَة
To rescind (a sale). ✶ غَلَت o غَلْتًا ه
To make a mistake (in calculation). غَلِت a غَلَتًا
To take a. o. unawares. تَغَلَّت واغْتَلَت ه
Nightfall. غَلَتَة
Error in calculation. غُلْتَة
To mix a. th. ✶ غَلَث i غَلْثًا ه
To fail to give fire (steel). غَلِث a غَلَثًا, واغْتَلَث
To fight desperately. غَلِث a غَلَثًا
Mixture. غَلَث
Fighting desperately. غَلِث ومُغَالِث
Bitter plant. غَلْثَى
Wheat mixed with barley or darnel weeds. غَلِيث ومَغْلُوث

To gather (crops). To enjoy (a right). إِسْتَغَلّ ه
To ask a. o. to supply provisions. — ه
Rancour, secret hatred. غِلّ
Manacles. Wife. Collar of iron. غُلّ ج أَغْلَال
Burning thirst. غُلّ وغُلَّة وغَلَل
Crops, income, seed-produce. Income from the rent of a house. Cost of workmanship. غَلَّة ج غَلَّات وغِلَال
Water flowing amid trees. Strainer. غَلَل ج أَغْلَال
Tunic. Pin fastening two rings of a coat of mail. غِلَالَة ج غَلَائِل
Light food. غَلُول
Vehement thirst. Thirst for revenge. Violent love, hatred. غَلِيل
Coat of mail. Under-garment. Garment worn beneath a coat of mail. غَلِيلَة ج غَلَائِل
Deceit, unfaithfulness. إِغْلَال
There shall be no deceit nor bribe. لَا إِغْلَال ولَا إِسْلَال
Thirsty. غَلِيل م غَلِيلَة, وغَلَّال ومُغْتَلّ ومَغْلُول
Yielding a good crop (field). مُغِلّ ومِغْلَال
Fettered, handcuffed. مُغَلَّل
Crops, proceeds of the year. مُغَلَّات ومُسْتَغَلَّات
In bonds, fettered, manacled. مَغْلُول
To hurry in walk. ✶ غَلْغَل وتَغَلْغَل فِي
To ooze through (water). To break o.'s way into.
To anoint o.'s self with perfume. تَغَلْغَل بِالغَالِيَة
Conveyance of a message. رِسَالَة مُغَلْغَلَة
Confused clamours. غُلْغُلَة
✶ غَلَب i غَلْبًا وغَلَبًا وغَلَبَةً ومَغْلَبًا ومَغْلَبَةً ه وعلى
To overcome, to get the upper hand over a. o.
To predominate in a. o. (quality). — على فُلَانٍ
To deprive a. o. from a. th. by victory. — ه على شَيْءٍ
It was taken away from us forcibly. غُلِبْنَا عَلَيْهِ
✧ We have been baffled *i. e.* we have been unable to persuade him. غُلِبْنَا فِيهِ

* غَلَظَ i وغَلُظَ o غِلَاظَةً وغِلْظَةً وغُلْظَةً وغِلَظًا To be or become thick, bulky (man). To be rough, brutal incompliant.
واستغلظ – To become thick (body, liquid). To be coarse (cloth). To be deep (colour). To be rugged, uneven (ground). To produce seeds (ear of corn).
غَلَّظَ ه وه To render thick, coarse, rough, difficult. To make a strong (oath).
– ه على To impose hard conditions upon a. o. To render a. th. difficult to.
أغلظ لِفُلَانٍ في القول To hold gross, harsh language to.
– ه To find, to buy coarse (cloth).
إستغلظ ه To find a. th. too coarse, to abstain from buying it.
غَلَظ Uneven, rugged ground.
غِلَظ وغِلظة Thickness, unevenness, roughness. Opacity.
غِلْظة وغِلَاظة Coarseness, roughness, rudeness in speech, manners. Difficulty. Strength. Endurance.
بَيْنَهُمَا غِلْظة They two are at enmity.
غليظ ج غِلَاظ Thick, coarse (man, cloth). Rude, rough in manners. Hard-hearted. Severe (pain). Deep (colour). ✧ Obtuse, dull (mind).
– ومُغلَظ Forcible (oath).
مُغَلَّظ Exacted on hard conditions (blood-price).
مُغَالَظَة Hatred, enmity.
* غَلَفَ o غَلْفًا وأغلف ه To provide a. th. with a case. To put (a flask, a knife) into (a case). To put a covering to (a saddle).
غَلِفَ a غَلَفًا To be uncircumcised.
غَلَّفَ ه To put a. th. in a case; ✧ To wrap (a letter) in an envelope.
تغلف واغتلف To be put into a case, a scabbard; in an envelope (letter).
غَلَف Tree for tanning leather.
غُلْفة Prepuce.
أغلف م غلفاء ج غُلف Enclosed in a case (flask); in a scabbard (sword). Uncircumcised. Hardened (heart).

* غَلَج i غَلْجًا وغَلَجَانًا To run at an even pace (horse).
تَغَلَّج على To deal unjustly with a. o.
غَلج Bloom of life.
أغلوج ج أغاليج Bending, tender bough.
* غلس – غَلَّس وأغلس To journey or do a. th. before dawn.
غَلَّس في الصَّلَاة To perform the prayer before daybreak.
– الماء To go to the water before daybreak.
أغلس To enter upon the last part of the night.
غَلَس ج أغلاس Darkness at the end of the night.
غَلَسًا Very early, before dawn.
غِليس وغُلَس Wild ass.
وقع في وادي تُغُلِّسَ He fell into a great misfortune.
* غَلَص o غَلْصًا, وغَلْصَمَ ه To cut the throat of.
▫ غِلص وغِلس Errand-boy. Shop-boy, snob.
* غَلْصَمَة ج غَلَاصِم Back of the neck. Epiglottis, larynx. Root of the tongue. Throat. Chief man; chief of a tribe.
هُوَ في غَلْصَمَة من قومهِ He is one of the chief men of his tribe.
* غَلِط a غَلَطًا و✧ تَغَلَّط To commit a mistake, a slip (in writing, speaking).
غَلَّط ه To attribute (a mistake) to a. o.
غالط مُغَالَطَةً وغِلَاطًا, وأغلط ه To cause a. o. to commit a mistake. To seek, to induce a. o. into error.
غالط ✧ To fail (fire-arm). To trick (in play).
غَلَط Slip, mistake, lapse in speech or writing, *lapsus linguæ, calami*.
غَلْطة A mistake, a slip.
غالط و✧ غلطان Wrong, mistaken.
مُغَالَطَة Sophism.
غَلُوطَة, ومَغلطة ج مَغَالِط, وأغلوطة ج أغلوطات وأغاليط Sophistical language. Captious question. Faulty language.
مِغلاط Wont to make mistakes.
مُغلَط و✧ مَغلوط Faulty.
مُغالِط Sophistical, beguiling.

ıad. young slave. Page.
Young girl. Female slave. غُلَامَة
Youth, puberty. غُلَامِيَّة وغُلُومِيَّة وغُلُومَة
Male tortoise. Big-headed and thick-haired young man. غَيْلَم
To attain its strength (youth). ✱ غَلَن o غَلْنًا
To abate, to become still (sea, wind, evil). ✧ غَلَّن
✧ Lull. Dead, flat calm (on sea). غَلِينَة
To exceed the bounds. ✱ غَلَا o غُلُوًّا
To be excessive. To grow (plant).
To be bigoted, a zealot. — بِالدِّين
— o غَلْوًا وغُلُوًّا بِالسَّهْمِ وغَالَى مُغَالَاةً وغِلَاءً
To exceed the usual distance in shooting an arrow. السَّهْمَ او بِالسَّهْمِ
To increase in price (goods). غَلَا o غَلَاءً
To overcharge (for goods). غَلَّى هُ
To exert o.'s self strenuously in. To exceed the bounds in. غَالَى مُغَالَاةً وغِلَاءً فِي
To sell or buy (goods) at an excessive price. — مُغَالَاةً ب وه
To ask too high a price for (goods). To cause (things) to become dear (God). أَغْلَى هُ
To buy (goods) too high. — ب
To strip (a vine) of its leaves. — هُ
To grow, to become tufted, tangled (plant). — وتَغَالَى واغْلَوْلَى
To walk quickly (camel). إِغْتَلَى
To find a. th. high-priced. إِسْتَغْلَى هُ
High price, dearness of goods. غَلَاء
Exaggeration, hyperbole. غُلُوّ وغُلْوَاء وغُلَوَاء
Liveliness of youth. Excess. غُلْوَاء وغُلَوَاء وغُلْوَان
Distance of a bow-shot. *Stadium* about (400 cubits). غَلْوَة ج غَلَوَات وغِلَاء
Dear (goods). Precious. غَالٍ م غَالِيَة ج غَوَالٍ
I sold it at a high price. بِعْتُهُ بِالغَالِي
Arrow shot too high. مِغْلَى ومِغْلَاة ج مَغَالٍ
To boil (cooking-pot). To ferment (wine). ✱ غَلَى i غَلْيًا وغَلَيَانًا، و✧ انْغَلَى
To boil cocoons for breaking their stiffness. ✧ غَلَى الشَّرَانِق

Scabbard, case, sheath, covering. Envelope of a letter. غِلَاف ج غُلُف وغُلْف
✧ Enveloppe. Bundle of letters. Pericardium. Pellicle of (an egg). مُغَلَّف ج مُغَلَّفَات
Green moss growing upon water. ✱ غَلْفَق
To go away. ✱ غَلَق i غَلْقًا
To be forfeited (pledge). غَلِق a غَلَقًا
To be unredeemed (slave). To be grieved, annoyed. To have incurable galls (cmael's back).
To close (a door, an outlet). غَلَّق وأَغْلَق و✧ غَلَق غَلْقًا
✧ To conclude (a bargain). غَلَّق
To bet with a. o. غَالَق هُ
To constrain a. o. to. أَغْلَق هُ عَلَى
To be surrendered in the hands of justice (culprit). أُغْلِق فِي يَدِ الوَالِي
To make bets with o. a. تَغَالَق
To be locked, bolted (door). إِنْغَلَق
To be difficult to a. o. (speech). To remain speechless. To be definitive (sale). إِسْتَغْلَق عَلَى
Wooden lock. Great door. ▫ Basket. غَلَق ج أَغْلَاق وجج أَغَالِيق
Confused (speech). Bolted (door). Forfeited (pledge). Ill-natured (man). Galled (camel). غَلِق
Poisonous plant of Arabia. Tree used as tan, *Peganum harmala*. غِلْقَة وغَلْقَى
Remainder, end, closing. ✧ غِلَاقَة
Balance of an account. ✧ غِلَاقَة حِسَاب
Closed, bolted (door). غُلُق ومُغْلَق ومَغْلُوق
✧ Source of income (as a mill). مَغْلَق ج مَغَالِق
Winning arrow. مِغْلَق ج مَغَالِق ومَغَالِيق
Wooden lock. Key. — ومِغْلَاق ومَغْلُوق ج مَغَالِيق
To be excited by lust. ✱ غَلِم a غَلَمًا وغُلْمَة، واغْتَلَم
To attain puberty (boy). To fly to the head (beverage). To be stirred (waves). إِغْتَلَم
Lust. غَلَم وغُلْمَة
Lustful. غَلِم وغِلِّيم ومُغْتَلِم
Young man, غُلَام ج غِلْمَان وغِلْمَة وأَغْلِمَة

grieved afflicted; affected with a cold, a rheum.
To low (bull). To shout (warriors). ✱غَمْغَمَ
To speak confusedly. تَغَمْغَمَ
Bellowing (of bulls). غَمْغَمَة ج غَمَاغِم
Shouts (of varriors). Confused speech.
To render a. o. heavy (digestion). To cover a. th. ✱غَمَتَ i غَمْتًا ه وه
To become heavy through bad digestion. غَمِتَ a غَمَتًا
To drink water in long draughts. ✱غَمَجَ i غَمْجًا وغَمِجَ a غَمَجًا ه
Draught. غَمْجَة وغُمْجَة ج غُمَج
To anoint (a bow). ✱غَمْجَرَ ه
Viscous matter. غِمْجَار
To put (a sword) in the scabbard. ✱غَمَدَ o i غَمْدًا, وأَغْمَدَ ه
To cover, to repair a. th. غَمَّدَ ه
To conceal a. o.'s faults. غَمَّدَ وتَغَمَّدَ ه
To insert a. th. into another. أَغْمَدَ ه
To put (a sword) in the scabbard. To fill (a vessel). تَغَمَّدَ ه
To forgive; to cover a. o. with its mercy (God). — ه ب
To enter into, to be involved in darkness. إِغْتَمَدَ ه
Scabbard, case, sheath. غِمْد ج أَغْمَاد وغُمُود
Laden (ship). غَامِد (m. f.)
Filled up with earth (well). غَامِدَة ج غَوَامِد
Celebrated castle in Yemen. غُمْدَان
Scabbard. مَغْمَد ج مَغَامِد
To overflow, to cover a. th. or a. o. (water). To overwhelm a. th. (sea). ✱غَمَرَ o غَمْرًا ه وه
To surpass. ✧ To clasp a. o. — ه
To load a. o. (with favours). — ه ب
His heart is filled with hatred for. غَمِرَ a صَدْرُهُ غِمْرًا وغَمَرًا على
To be unlearned, inexperienced. To be abundant (water). غَمُرَ o غَمَارَةً وغُمُورَةً
To water (a horse) in a vessel. غَمَّرَ ه
✧ To heap up (sheaves). To seduce a. o. To clasp a. o.
To smear her face with cosmetic (woman). — وتَغَمَّرَ واغْتَمَرَ

To boil (water). غلى وأغلى ه
To perfume o.'s self with musk and ambergris. تَغَلَّى
Bubbling, boiling of water. غَلْي وغَلَيَان
Kettle. Copper-boiler. ✧ غَلَّايَة
Nargileh, Persian pipe. Ship of war. ✧ غَلْيُون ج غَلَايِين وغَلَاوِين
Perfume composed of musk and ambergris. غَالِيَة ج غَوَالٍ
Boiled (wine). Decoction. مَغْلِيّ ومُغْلَى
To cover, to conceal a. th. ✱غَمَّ o غَمًّا ✧ غَمَّمَ ه
To grieve, to afflict a. o. غَمَّ وأَغَمَّ ه
We had a sultry day. غُمَّ وأُغِمَّ يَوْمُنَا
To be veiled (new moon). To be confused to a. o. (news). غُمَّ على
To have long and thick hair. غَمَّ a غَمَمًا
To grieve o. a. غَامَّ ه
To be overcast (sky). أَغْمَّ
What a grief thou hast caused to me! ما أَغَمَّكَ لِي او إِلَيَّ او عَلَيَّ
To assume a stern look. تَغَامَّ
To be veiled, covered. إِنْغَمَّ
To be grieved, saddened. — واغْتَمَّ
Grief, sadness, perplexity. غَمّ ج غُمُوم, وغُمَّة ج غُمَم
Suffocating, sultry day. يَوْم غَمّ
Dark, sultry night. لَيْلَة غَمّ وغَمَّة وغُمَّى
Difficult case. أَمْر غُمَّة
✧ The head and feet of (a slaughtered sheep). غَمَّة
Of a sudden, unexpectedly. ✧ طَمَّة غَمَّة
Distress. Darkness. Dust. غُمَّى
Hard, grievous affair. غُمَّى
Long and abundant hair. غَمَم
Thin, whitish clouds. غَمَام وغَمَامَة ج غَمَائِم
Cold in the head, coryza. غُمَام
Camel's muzzle. غِمَامَة ج غَمَائِم
Covering. Dull, sultry (day, night). غَامّ م غَامَّة
Long, thick-haired. أَغَمّ م غَمَّاء
Without interstice (cloud).
Sadness. Mishap, cloudy (night). غَمَّاء
Heated and thickened (milk). غَمِيم
Overcast (sky). Grievous, afflicting. مُغِمّ
Overcast, cloudy (sky). Sad, مَغْمُوم

rage a. o. To find a. o. weak.
The heat abated and allowed me to set out. أَغمَزَني الحَرُّ
To wink at one another. تَغامَز
To blame a. o. or a. th. إِغتَمَز ه وه
Wink, sign with the eye. غَمز
A wink ; a hint. غَمزَة
Weak man. Worthless cattle. غَمز ج غَمز وأَغماز
Trigger. ✧ غَمّاز
Dimple. ✧ غَمّازَة
Vice, defect, weakness. غَمِيزَة
There is nothing in him to be coveted. No fault is to be found in him. مَا فِيهِ غَمِيزَة او مَغمَز
Defects, vices. مَغامِز
Suspected, blameworthy. مَغمُوز
To set (star). ☆ غَمَس i غُمُوسًا
To plunge, to dip a. th. into (dye, water). — غَمسًا, وغَمَّس ه في
To water (beasts) scantily. غَمَّس ه
✧ To set bricks, stones in cement.
To rush into perils. غَامَس
To contend with o. a. in diving. — ه
To be plunged, dipped into. To penetrate into. إِنغَمَس واغتَمَس في
✧ To be cemented (brick). إِنغَمَس
Penetrating (spear-thrust). Momentous, distressful (affair). غَمُوس
Perjury made purposely. أَليَمِين أَلغَمُوس
Dark (night). Darkness. Hidden, mysterious. Not yet known (verses). غَمِيس
Thicket of shrubs, reeds. — وغَمِيسَة
Plungeon, diver (bird). غَمّاسَة ج غَمّاس
Plunged, dipped into. ✧ Cemented (stone). مَغمُوس
Rushing headlong into (dangers, war). مُغامِس
To be dim-sighted. ☆ غَمِش a غَمَشًا
✧ To scratch a. o. — ه
Dim-sighted. أَغمَش
To despise, to blame a. o. or a. th. ☆ غَمَص i وغَمِص a غَمصًا ه وه
To be ungrateful for a benefit — النِعمَة
To calumniate ; to impute evil to a. o. — على فُلان قَولًا
Do not charge me falsely. لا تَغمِص عَلَيَّ

To engage in a desperate struggle with a. o. غامَر ه
To drink in a small vessel (man). To drink little (cattle). تَغَمَّر
To embrace, to clasp o. a. ✧ تَغامَر
To plunge, to be plunged into water. To be drowned. إِنغَمَر واغتَمَر
To submerge, to ingulf, to overflow a. th. (water). إِغتَمَر ه
Deep of water. Main of the sea. Generous (man). Fiery (horse). Full (garment). غَمر ج غِمار وغُمُور
Rabble. — مِن النَّاس
Bountiful, liberal man. — الخُلق والرِّداء
Inexperienced, ignorant. — وغِمر وغُمر ج أَغمار
Rancour, secret hatred. Thirst. غِمر ج أَغمار
Hatred. Inexperienced. غَمَر ج غُمور
Mixed party of people. — النَّاس
Saffron. ✧ Sheaf, armful. Bosom. غُمر وغُمرَة ج أَغمار
Small drinking-cup. غُمَر ج غِمار وأَغمار
Deep water, abyss; great quantity. Distress, overwhelming misfortune. غَمرَة ج غَمَرات وغِمار وغُمَر
The pangs of death. غَمَرات المَوت
Saffron. Gypsum. Cosmetic made with saffron. غُمرَة
Ignorance; coarseness; inexperience. غَمارَة
Thick crowd, throng. غُمار وغَمار وغُمارَة وغمارَة
Overflowing, overwhelming (water). Waste (land). ✧ Embracing, clasping. غامِر
Depth of water, abyss. غَمِير
Rushing blindly into danger. مُغامِر ومُغَمِّر
Watered (tree). Covered with dry ears (wheat). Drunken (man). مُغتَمِر
Obscure, unknown. مَغمُور
To wink, to make a sign with (the eyes, eyebrows). ☆ غَمَز i غَمزًا ه ب
To feel a. th. (with the hand). — ه ب
To calumniate a. o. غَمَز ب وعلى
To break out (disease). To appear (defect). غَمَز
To find fault with ; to dispa- أَغمَز في

To be blear (eye). غمِص a غَمَصًا
To contemn a. o. إِغْتَمَص ه
Blearedness. غَمَص
Liar. أَغْمُوص الحَنجَرَة
Perjury. يَمِين غَمُوص
Constellation of Procyon. الغَمُوص والغُمَيصاء
Blear-eyed. أَغْمَص م غَمْصاء ج غُمْص
Wounded in o.'s belief, honour. مَغْمُوص عَلَيْهِ
To be hidden, concealed. To be abstruse (discourse). ✱ غَمَض o غُمُوضًا, وغَمُض o غُمُوضَة
To be compliant with a. o. in (a bargain). غَمَض i غَمْضًا, وغَمَّض وأَغْمَض عن فلان في
To penetrate into. غَمَض i o غَمْضًا في
To be depressed (land). غَمِض a وغَمُض o غُمُوضَة وغَمَاضَة
To shut (the eyes). غَمَّض وأَغْمَض ه
To render (speech) ambiguous, obscure. غَمَّض ه
To close (the eyes) upon. To forbear a. th. — وأَغْمَض على
To look scornfully at a. o. أَغْمَضَت العَيْنُ فلانًا
To be closed (eye). إِنْغَمَض
I have not shut my eyes. مَا أَغْتَمَضَتْ عَيْنايَ
Lowland. غَمْض ج أَغْماض وغُمُوض
Despised, unknown (man). ذُو غَمْض
Twinkling of the eyes. Sleep. غُمْض وغِمَاض وغَمَاض وتَغْمِيض وإِغْمَاض وتَغْمَاض
I have not shut my eyes; *i. e.* I remained sleepless. مَا أَكْتَحَلَت عَيْنِي غُمْضًا او غِمَاضًا الخ
I got that without trouble. أَتَانِي ذٰلِكَ على أَغْتِمَاضٍ
Obscure (discourse). Low, depressed (ground). Base, despised (man). Unknown (nobility). غَامِض ج غَوَامِض
Abstruse question. Secret, mystery. غَامِضَة ج غَوَامِض وغَامِضَات
Vice, defect. غَمِيضَة
Blind-man (children's play). ✧ غُمَّيْضَة
Much depressed land. مَغْمَض ج مَغَامِض
Premeditated sins. مُغْمِضَات
Closed (eye). Obscure, equivocal (word). مُغْمَض
To despise a. o. ✱ غَمَط i وغَمِط a غَمْطًا ه

To disacknowledge (a right). To be ungrateful for (benefits). To drink (water) greedily. غَمَط ه
To cleave to a. o. (fever). أَغْمَط على
To conceal a. o. (earth). تَغَمَّط على
To get the best over a. o. after having been overcome by him. إِغْتَمَط ه
To overcome a. o. (in speech). — ه ب
Depressed ground. غَمْط
To be damp (soil). ✱ غَمَق o غَمْقًا a وغَمِق o وغَمُق
To be deep. ✧ غَمِيق (for عَمُق)
To dig deeply. ✧ غَمَّق (for عَمَّق)
Damp (ground); watery (plant). غَمِق م غَمِقَة
Disease of the loins. غَمَقَة
Depth. ✧ غُمْق (for عُمْق)
Deep. ✧ غَمِيق ج غِمَاق
Having a complaint of the loins. مَغْمُوق
To cover a. o. (with clothes) for promoting sweat. ✱ غَمَل o غَمْلًا ه
To cover, to bury a. th. To heap up (grapes). To put a. th. in a right state. To fold and bury (hides). — ه
To overlay one another and wither (plants). — وتَغَمَّل
To become corrupt by reason of bandages (wound). غَمِل a غَمَلًا
To lose its hair in the sand (hide). إِنْغَمَل
Buried in the sand. غَمِل ومَغْمُول
Valley covered with trees. ✱ غُمْلُول ج غَمَالِيل
Fameless, unknown (man). مَغْمُول
✱ غَمْلَج — غَمَلَّج وغُمْلُج (*m. f.*) وغُمْلَاج وغُمْلُوج وغَمْلِيج م غُمْلُوجَة وغَمْلِيجَة
Fickle, unsteady.
To bury (a skin). To accumulate (grapes). ✱ غَمَن o غَمْنًا
To be buried in (the earth). — غُمِن وانْغَمَن في
To roof a house with wood and earth. To cover a. th. ✱ غَمَا o غَمْوًا, وغَمَى i غَمْيًا, وغَمَّى
The sick man fell into a swoon. غُمِيَ وأُغْمِيَ على المَرِيض
We had a gloomy day, a dark night. غُمِيَ وأُغْمِيَ يَوْمُنَا او لَيْلَتُنَا

To suffer from oppression of the chest. ☆ غنص a غنصًا
To be at the point of death. ☆ غنظ i غنظًا
To distress, to grieve, to counteract a. o. — ه
Grief, anxiety. غنظ وغنظ وغناظ وغِناظ
☆ غنم a غُنمًا وغَنمًا وغَنمًا وغَنيمة وغُنمانًا
To take a. th. as spoil.
To earn a. th. without trouble. — غنمًا ه
To give to a. o. a share of booty. To give a. th. as a free gift. غنّم ه
To plunder a. th.; to lay hands on a. th. as spoil. تغنّم واغتنم ه
To seize an opportunity. إغتنم واستغنم الفُرصة
Earning obtained without work. غُنم وغُنيم ومَغنَم ج مَغانِم
Prey, booty, spoil. غنيمة ج غنائم
Sheep, ewes, goats. غَنَم ج أغنام وغُنوم
Numerous flock. غنم مُغَنَّمة ومُغنَمة
The utmost of thy ability is to do so. غُنامَاك أن تفعل كذا
Shepherd; owner of sheep. غنّام
Taking spoil. Succeeding without trouble. غانِم م غانِمة
To stay (in a place). ☆ غني غِنًى ومَغنًى ب
To be constant in love with a. o. — لهُ بالمَودّة
To marry. To be satisfied with her husband (wife). غني a غِنًى
To be free from want, wealthy. غني a غِنًى وغَناء
To be satisfied with. — ب
To do without a. th. — عن
To coo (pigeon). غنّى
To render a. o. wealthy. غنّى وأغنى ه
To sing; to recite verses. غنّى ه وه وتغنّى ب
To praise, to blame a. o. — وتغنّى ب
To do instead of, to satisfy a. o. أغنى عن
That will be of no use to thee. هذا ما يُغني عنك شيئًا
He filled for him the place of such a one. أغنى عنهُ غَناء فلانٍ
This man has been useless. ما أغنى فلانٌ شيئًا

To be hidden. To be dubious to a. o. (news, affair). أُغمي على
Swoon, fainting. غَمي وإغماء
Roof made with reeds and earth. غِماء وغَمى ج أغمية وأغماء
In a swoon. غَمى (s. pl.) ج أغماء
Fainting. مُغمًى عليهِ
The sky is overcast. في السّماء غَمي او غمى
☆ غنّ a غَنّة To speak through the nose, to snuffle.
To be bushy, lively (with insects, birds: valley). — وأغنّ
To render (a garden) verdant. غنّن ه
To sing with a melodious voice. To buzz (insect). To hum (man). To be filled (skin). أغنّ
To render (a branch) flowery (God). — ه
Nasal voice; twang. Gentle voice. Sound of a stone. غُنّة
Humming of insects. غُنان
Speaking through the nose. Very populous (village). Luxuriant (garden). أغنّ م غنّاء
☆ سب — غُنبة ج غُنَب Round lines of the corners of the mouth.
☆ غنث a غنثًا To drink in taking breath at each draught. To be prone to evil (soul).
☆ غنج a غنجًا, وتغنّج To coquet; to flirt. ✧ To be over-affected, lackadaisical.
✧ غنّج ه To spoil, to fondle (a child).
غُنج وغُنُج وغِناج Flirtation. Coquetry. ✧ Grimace, simper.
غَنِج م غَنِجة, ومِغناج Coquettish (m. f.) flirt. ✧ Foppish, simperer.
غُنجة Hedge-hog.
✧ مُغنّج Lackadaisical, mincing.
☆ غُنجُل ج غناجل Badger.
☆ غندر — غُندَر وغُندُر Fat, soft (child).
✧ تغندر To be over-affected in dress, in deportement. To be foppish, to flirt.
✧ غَندَرة Affectation in dress.
✧ غندور ج غنادِرة Fop. Coxcomb. Dandy
. غندقجي ج غندقجيّة Gunsmith

towards the ground (branch).
Supple, lithe. Swift (horse). غوج
Broad (camel).
To go down to (a low country). ✱ غار o غوزًا, وَغوَّر وأغار وتَغوَّر في
To penetrate into. — o غوزًا وغُؤورًا وغِيارًا في
To deepen, to scrutinise a. th. carefully. — في أمرٍ
To sink, to be lost in the earth (water). To be intensely hot (day). To halt; to alight at noon for rest (traveller). غار o غوزًا , وغوَّر
To sink in its socket (eye). — غوزًا وغُؤورًا
To set (star). — غِيارًا وغُؤورًا , وَغوَّر
To bestow benfits upon a. o. (God). غار o غِيارًا ه بِخيرٍ
To succour, to aid a. o. (God). — ه ول
To defeat, to throw back (the enemy). غوَّر ه
To conceal a. th. To cause (springs of water) to disappear. — ه
غاوَر مُغاوَرَةً ه, وأغار إغارَةً وغارَةً ومَغارًا
To make a raid to in (the enemy's country). واستَغار على
To come to a. o. for seeking help. أغار ب او إلى
To run swiftly, to gallop (horse). أغار
To make reciprocal raids. To urge horses against o. another. تَغاوَر
To settle in a low country. To become fat (cattle). To become swollen (wound). إستَغار استَغارَة
To ask (God) to render a country fruitful. إستَغوَر إستِغوارًا ه
Hole, cavern, cave. Lowland. Bottom of the palate. Pit of the chin. Zeal. Laurel-tree. Numerous army. غار ج أغوار وغِيران
The two armies dashed together. إلتقى الغاران
Raid on horseback, inroad, predatory incursion, razzia. Navel. Gallop, quick run of a horse. غارَة ج غارات
To pour horsemen for a hostile incursion. شَنّ الغارة
Bottom of a. th. Low ground. غوْر

To be, to become rich. تَغنّى وتَغانى واغتَنى واستَغنى
To be self-sufficient.; to be in no need of a. o else. تَغانى
To do without a. th., to want no... To dispense with. إستَغنى عن
To ask God to grant wealth. — ألله
Sufficiency, adequacy. غِنى و غُنية وغُنيان
He cannot do without it. ما لهُ عَنهُ غِنى او غُنية
Wealth, sufficiency. غِنى وغَناء
Song, tune. غِناء, وأُغنيَّة وإِغنيَة ج أغانيّ وأغانٍ
Rich, wealthy. غنيّ ج أغنياء وغانٍ
Needing no ornaments, modest, chaste (woman). غانِيَة ج غَوانٍ وغانِيات
Place of abode. مَغنى ج مَغانٍ
He cannot do without it. ما لهُ عَنهُ مَغنى
That place is fit for such a one. مَكانُ كذا مَغنى من فُلانٍ
He filled the place of such a one. أغنى عَنهُ مَغنى فُلان او مُغناهُ ومَغناتَهُ ومُغناتَهُ
Singer. مُغنٍ
Songstress. مُغنِّيَة
To overlook, to be unmindful of a. th. ✱ غهب a غَهبًا عن
To journey in darkness. إغتَهب
Unintentionnally, at hap hazard. غَهبًا
Intense darkness. Dark (night). Of a deep black (horse). Unmindful, heedless. Weak. غَيهَب ج غَياهِب
Bustle of a fight. غَيهَبَة
Crowd, press. ✱ غو — غاغة وغَوغاء
Locusts beginning to fly. Rabble. Riot, quarrel, confusion. غَوغاء
To help, to assist a. o. To rescue a. o. ✱ غاث o غَوثًا, وأغاث إغاثَةً ومَغوثَةً ه
To cry for help. غَوَّث
God has relieved us in his mercy. أغاثَنا اللهُ بِرَحمَتِهِ
To ask the succour of a. o. إستَغاث ه وب
Cry for help. غوث وغُواث وغَواث
Rescue, help, succour. غَوث وغِياث وإغاثَة وغَويث
Call for help. إستِغاثَة
To bend the body in walking (man, horse). To incline ✱ غاج o غَوجًا, وتَغوَّج

Invidious. Deep in knowledge ; able. بَعِيد الغَوْر

Sinking into the earth (water). غَوْر و غائِر

Noon. Mid-day sleep, siesta. غائِرة

Sun. Mid-day nap. غَوْرة

Cavern, cave, grotto. مَغار ومُغار ومَغارة ومُغارة ج مَغاوِر ومَغارات

Making frequent raids ; predatory. مُغاوِر ومِغوار ج مَغاوير

To purpose a. th. ✱ غاز o غَوْزًا ه

✧ Gaz. Petroleum. F غاز ج غازات

To talk nonsense. ◘ غَوَّش

Locust-eating bird. ✧ بو غَوْش

Discordant sound. Bustle, uproar. — ✧ غَوْشة

Glass bracelets. ◘ غُوَيْشات

✱ غاص o غَوْصًا ومَغاصًا وغِياصة وغِياصًا في To dive, to plunge, to sink into (water).

To deepen, to examine a. th. minutely. To come suddenly upon a. th. — على

To dip, to plunge a. o. into (water.) غَوَّص ه في

Diving, plunging. Artful. غائِص ج غاصة وغُوّاص

Going deep in (sin). — في

Diver (bird). Pearl-diver. غَوّاص

Diving-place. مَغاص

Abstruse, deep (for عَوِيص) (speech). ✧ غَوِيص

To sink in (the sand : foot). To be concealed, depressed. ✱ غاط o غَوْطًا

To sink, to deepen (a well). — وغَوَّط ه وأغاط ه

To enter into. غاط في

To swallow (food) in large mouthfuls. غَوَّط

To relieve the bowels. تَغَوَّط

To vie with a. o. in plunging. تَغاوَط

To be bent (wood). إنغاط

غَوْط وغاط ج غُوط وأغْواط وغِيطان وغِياط Depression of land.

Young camel. ◘ غاوِط

Depressed land. Garden. Privy. Human excrement, fæces. غائِط

Surroundings of Damascus. Fruitful valley. غُوطة

Deep. ◘ غَوِيط

Marjoram (*plant*). P غاغ

To take a. th. away unexpectedly. To cause a. o. to perish (waterless land). To intoxicate a. o. (wine). ✱ غال o غَوْلًا , واغتال ه وه

To eat voraciously. ✧ غَوَّل

To hurry in (an affair). غاوَل في

To assume various colours, shapes. To be confused (affair). To be wayless (desert). تَغَوَّل

To destroy a. o. (ogre). — ه

Lock of a door. ✧ غَال

Headache. Intoxication. Perplexity, anxiety. Extensive desert. غَوْل

He fell in a perplexing case. ألَى غَوْلًا غائِلةً

Unforeseen misfortune, accident. Demon. Ogre. Genius assuming various shapes. ◘ Snake. غُول ج أغوال وغِيلان

Alkanet (*plant*). حَنّا الغُول

Secret murder. غِيلة

Unforeseen (misfortune). غائِل

Destructive (desert). Misfortune. Wickedness, mischief. غائِلة ج غَوائِل

Sword-stick, dagger. مِغْوَل

Loss, ruin. مَغالة

To allure to evil, to seduce, to mislead a. o. ✱غَوَى i غَيًّا , وغَوَّى وأغوَى ه

To be seduced, misled : to err. To be disappointed. غَوَى i غَيًّا وغَوِي a غَوَايَة

To suffer indigestion (young camel). ✧ To be covetous. غَوِي a غَوًى

To curdle (milk). غَوَّى ه

To coalesce against. تَغاوَى على

To be seduced, misled. ✧ To incline towards. To be allured by. إنغوَى

To deceive, to lead astray. To seduce a. o. إستغوَى ه

I spent the night hungry. بِتُّ غَوًى

Error, wrong course. غَيّ وغَوَايَة

Error. ✧ Thing coveted. غَيّة وغِيّة ج غِيّات

Natural, unlawful child. وَلَد غَيّة وغِيّة

Allurement, deceit. أَغْواء

Seducer. Satan. غاوٍ ج غُواة وغاوُون

Small head. رأس غاوٍ

Water-skin. غاوِيَة

غاوٍ وغوٍ وغويّ وغيّان Led into error, disappointed. Following his passions.

أغويّة أغاوِي , ومَغواة ج مَغاوٍ , ومُغَوّاة ج مُغَوّيات Snare, pitfall, trap. Dangerous place.

مُغوٍ ومُغوٍ Misleading, deceiving.

بِتُّ مُغوِيًا ومَغوِيًّا I spent the night hungry.

✱ غيي — غَيًّا وأغيا ه To set up (a flag, a limit).

غايا ب To brandish (a sword).

أغيا To be motionless (clouds). To attain the utmost degree in a. th.

غاية ج غايات وغايٍ Aim, purpose. Flag, standard. Utmost limit, maximum.

✧ للغاية و ه بغاية Exceedingly.

غايتك أن تفعل كذا The utmost of thy ability is to do so.

غيايَة Light of the sun-rays. Cloud. Shadow.

مُغيًّا A. th. to which a limit is set.

✱ غاب i غَيبًا وغِيابًا وغَيبة وغُيُوبًا ومَغيبًا عن To be absent, remote, hidden from.

— غِيابًا وغَيبُوبة To set, to disappear (sun, moon).

غاب عن الصَّواب He lost his mind.

— i غِيابة وغُيُوبة وغِيابًا وغيبة في To be hidden, concealed in.

— غِيبة واغتاب ه To backbite a. o.

غَيَّب ه وه To render unapparent; to remove, to conceal a. o. or a. th.

— ه ✧ To learn a. th. by heart.

غَيَّبَهُ غَيابُهُ May he be buried in his grave!

غايَب ه To address a. o. absent.

أغاب To have her husband absent: (woman).

تغيَّب عن To absent o.'s self, to go away from.

تغايب To glide away, to escape.

غيب وغَيبة وغِياب ومَغيب Absence, removal from a place.

غيب ج غِياب وغُيوب Hidden things; fate.

وَقَعنا في غيبة او غيابة We fell in a depressed ground.

غيبًا ومَشهدًا In the presence and absence.

عالِم الغَيب The Knower of secret and hidden things *i. e.* God.

عالَم الغيب The invisible world.

غائب ج غَيب وغُيَّب وغُيّاب وغائبون Absent. Third person (*gram.*).

✧ غيبًا وعلى الغائب By heart, by memory.

غابة ج غاب وغابات Depressed, low ground. Thicket. Forest. Spear.

غِيبة Backbiting, slander.

غَيَاب Grave.

— وغَيَّاب الشَّجَر The roots of the trees.

غَيابة ج غيابات Covert. Screen.

غَيابة البِئر The bottom of a pit.

غِيابيّ By default (sentence).

مَغيب الشَّمس Sunset.

مُغيب ومُغيبة Whose husband is absent (woman).

✱ غاث i غَيثًا ه To water the earth (rain, God).

غِيث To be watered by rain (earth).

تغيَّث To become fat (camel).

غَيث ج غُيُوث Abundant rain. Herbage springing up after rain. Cloud.

ذُباب الغَيث Bees.

غَيِّث Pouring abundant rain (cloud).

ذو غَيِّث Swift-running (horse).

ذاتُ غَيِّث Yielding much water (well).

مَغيث ومَغيُوث Watered by rain (ground).

✱ غَيِد a غَيَدًا To be thin, pliant (bough). To bend the neck from fatigue or softness.

تغايد في مِشيَتِهِ To bend the body in walking.

غَيَد Softness, suppleness. Bending of the neck.

غِيد غِيد Come on! Make haste.

غادة ج غادات Young, tender and pliant bough. Soft young woman.

أغيد م غيداء ج غِيد Young, tender, pliant (bough). Young and slender (youth).

غَيدان الشَّباب Bloom of youth.

✱ غار a غَيرة وغَيرًا وغارًا على To be jealous of.

— مِن To grudge a. o.

— i غَيرًا , وغَيَّر ه To pay the bloodwit to. To supply a. o. with provisions.

To haunt thickets (lion). غَيَّض
Small quantity, decrease, falling off. Fœtus not yet complete. غَيْض
Covert of lions. Swamp covered with trees. Thicket. غَيْضَة ج غِيَاض وأَغْيَاض وغَيْضَات
Pool. مَغِيض ج مَغَايِض
To enter, to hide o.'s self in. ☆ غَاط i غَيْطًا في
Garden, lowland. غَيْط
Dispute. مُغَايَطَة
To distress, to enrage a. o. ☆ غَاظ i غَيْظًا, وغَيَّظ وغَايَظ وأَغَاظ ه
To become intensely hot (day). تَغَيَّظ
To become angry, enraged. تَغَيَّظ وانْغَاظ واغْتَاظ
Outbreak of anger. Rage. Offence. غَيْظ وغِيَاظ
Anger, irritation. إِغْتِيَاظ
Angered, enraged. مَغِيظ ومُنْغَاظ ومُغْتَاظ
To have branches dependent to the right and left (tree). ☆ غَاف i غَيَفَانًا, وأَغْيَف وتَغَيَّف
To act in cowardly at war. غَيَّف
To incline (a bough). أَغَاف ه
To bend the body in walking (man, horse). To be wrinkled. تَغَيَّف
Sweet-fruited tree. غَاف
Flight of birds. غَيْف
Bending, soft (plant, youth). Soft (life). أَغْيَف
Long-bearded. غَيَّاف
To squander (goods) away. ☆ غَاق – غَيَّق ه
To change o.'s mind. To be unsteady. – في رَأْيِهِ
Aquatic bird. غَاق وغَاقَة
Crow. غَاق
To suckle (a child : pregnant woman). ☆ غَال i غَيْلًا, وأَغَال إِغَالَةً وأَغْيَل إِغْيَالًا
To be dense (tree). To bring forth twice a year (ewe). أَغْيَل
To be tangled (tree). تَغَيَّل واسْتَغْيَل
To deceive a. o. treacherously. To do mischief to a. o. unawares. إِغْتَال ه
Lock. ✧ غَال ج غَالَات
Milk of a pregnant woman. غَيْل ولَبَن غَيْل
Streamlet running on the غَيْل غُيُول

To bestow (rain, wealth) upon a. o. (God). غَار i غِيَارًا ه ب
To change, to barter, to exchange. To alter, to corrupt a. th. غَيَّر ه
To barter a. th. with a. o. غَايَر مُغَايَرَة وغِيَارًا ه
To excite the jealousy of a. o. أَغَار ه
To be altered; to undergo a change. ✧ To be emaciated, altered in health. تَغَيَّر
To be jealous of o. a. To be different, unlike (things). تَغَايَر
Difference, change. غَيْر ج أَغْيَار
Other, else, different. Lie. Not at all. Except. Without. غَيْر
And so on, et cœtera. غَيْر ذَلِك
Another than thou came to me. جَاءَنِي غَيْرُكَ
Adultered, altered. غَيْرُ خَالِص
There is but one man in my house, and nobody else. عِنْدِي رَجُلٌ لَا غَيْرُ
I took no more than ten of them. قَبَضْتُ عَشَرَةً لَا غَيْرُهَا او لَا غَيْرُ
They came all but one. جَاءَ القَوْمُ غَيْرَ فُلَانٍ
Without that. بِغَيْرِ او مِن غَيْرِ ذَلِك
But, yet, still, nevertheless. غَيْرَ أَنَّ
Changes of fortune. غِيَر
Jealousy. Zeal, emulation. غَيْرَة
Blood-price. Provision of wheat. غِيرَة ج غِيَر
Barter. Exchange. Mark in dress distinguishing non-Moslems. ✧ Emaciation, alteration in health. غِيَار
Emulation. تَغَايُر
غَيُور (*m. f.*) وغَيْرَان م غَيْرَى ج غَيَارَى
Zealous, jealous.
✧ Ticklish. غَيَّار
Intermittent (fever). Digestive (power). مُغَيِّرَة
Altered. ✧ Pale, emaciated. مُتَغَيِّر
Watered by rain (land). مَغِير ومَغْيُور
Very jealous. ✧ Unwholesome (climate, water). مِغْيَار ج مَغَايِير
To decrease; to be scanty (water). To abate (price). ☆ غَاض i غَيْضًا ومَغَاضًا, وتَغَيَّض وانْغَاض
To lessen, to diminish a. th. غَاض وغَيَّض, وأَغَاض ه

surface of the earth. Valley full of springs.

Tangled tree. Bed of reeds, thicket. Covert of a lion. Valley watered by a stream. غِيل ج أغْيَال وغُيُول

Shift, craft, treason. غِيلَة

He has slain him treacherously. قَتَلَهُ غِيلَةً

Suckling in pregancy (woman). غَائِلَة ومُغِيل ومُغْيِل

Secret hatred. Evil. غَائِلَة ج غَوَائِل, ومَغَالَة

Haunting a thicket.-Lion. غَيَّال

Sweet lote-tree. P أُمّ غَيْلَان

Suckled in pregnancy. مُغَال ومُغْيَل

Haunting a thicket (lion). مُغْيِل ومُتَغَيِّل

Tangled (tree). مِغْيَال

* غَامَ i غَيْماً, وغَيَّمَ وأَغَامَ إغَامَةً وأَغْيَمَ

To be clouded (sky). إغْيَاماً, وتَغَيَّمَ

To be affected with a burning thirst (camel). غَامَ وغِيمَ

Cloud. Anger. Thirst. Dense (tree). غَيْم ج غُيُوم

Vehemently thirsty (camel). غَيْمَان م غَيْمَى

To be thirsty. To be oppressed (mind). * غَانَ i غَيْنًا

To feel a lively emotion. غِينَ وأُغِينَ على قَلْبِهِ

To cover (the sky: cloud). أغَانَ ه

غ The 19th letter of the alphabet. Cloud darkening the sky. غَيْن

Dense trees. غَيْنَة

Matter flowing from a corpse. غِينَة

Long. Green. أغْيَن م غَيْنَاء ج غِين

Green and tufty (tree). غَيْنَاء

ف

ف *Prefixed particle expressing* :

1° *Order, uninterrupted succession.* And then, after :

He confined him in prison, and then killed him. حَبَسَهُ فَقَتَلَهُ

Zeyd came first, then Amrou. جَاءَ زَيْدٌ فَعَمْرُو

Day by day, year after year. يَوْمًا فَيَوْمًا, سَنَةً فَسَنَةً

2° *Change of subject.* And then :

He questioned him, and the latter answered. سَأَلَهُ فَقَالَ

3° *Causality, result of an action* :

If you love me, you must consequently follow me. إنْ كُنْتُمْ تُحِبُّونِي فَاتَّبِعُونِي

4° In order to :

Pay me a visit, that I may honour thee. زُرْنِي فَأُكْرِمَكَ

Where is thy house, that I may visit thee. أَيْنَ بَيْتُكَ فَأَزُورَكَ

5° Therefore *after the interrogative* أ :

Thou hast then seen him. أفَرَأَيْتَهُ

6° *When following* أمَّا *it is expletive*:

As to the dead, they shall rise. أمَّا الْمَوْتَى فَيَقُومُونَ

He has forged a calumny against me. * فَأَتَ – إفْتَأَتَ عَلَيَّ البَاطِلَ

He is lonely in his opinion. إفْتَأَتَ بِرَأْيِهِ

To hit a. o. in the heart. To affect a. o. (heart-disease). To dishearten a. o. (fear). * فَأَدَ a فَأْدًا ه

To bake (bread) in hot ashes. — ه

To roast (meat) in the fire. — وافْتَأَدَ ه في النَّار

To be affected with heart-disease. To be struck in the heart. فُئِدَ فَأْدًا, وفَئِدَ a فَئَدًا

To be moved (heart). To blaze (fire). تَفَأَّدَ

To light (a fire). إفْتَأَدَ

Appendages of the œsophagus as the lungs, liver. Heart. Mind, soul. فُؤَاد ج أفْئِدَة

Bread baked in hot ashes. أُفْؤُود ج أفَائِيد

Fire-place for roasting, baking. مُفْتَأَد

مِفْأَد ومِفْآد ومِفْأَدَة ج مَفَائِد ومَفَائِيد
Wooden poker. Roasting-spit.

Wounded in the heart. Having a heart-disease. Baked, toasted, roasted (in the fire). Faint-hearted. مَفْؤُود

To dig the earth. * فَأَرَ a فَأْرًا ه

To bruise, to crush, to crumble a. th. with the fingers. ✲ فَتَّ o فَتًّا, وفَتَّتَ هـ
It is a heart-rending event. أمر يفتّ الكبد
It weakened him. فتّ في ساعِدِهِ
To be brayed, crushed. To be crumbled. تَفَتَّتَ وانفتّ
Crumbling. Fissure, cleft in a rock. فتّ
Dispersed (family, tribe). فتّ وفِتّ وفُتّ
Dry dung used as fuel. Lump of dates. فَتَّة وفُتَّة
Crumbs of bread; particles (of wool). فُتَات, وفَتِيتَة ج فَتَائِت
Crumbled bread; crushed. فَتُوت وفَتِيت ومَفْتُوت
To prevent (camels) from quenching their thirst. ✧ To bray, to crumble a. th. ✲ فَتْفَتَ هـ
To be bruised, crumbled. تَفَتْفَتَ
Whispers. فَتَافِت
To put out (the fire). To put a stop to a. th. ✲ فَثَأَ a فَثْأً هـ
To forget a. th. فَتِيَ a فَتْأً عن
He has not ceased doing it. ما فَتِئَ وما فَتَأَ وما أَفْتَأَ يَفعَل
Penny-royal (*aromatic plant*) ✲ فتج – فُوتَنْج
To open (a door, an outlet). To give vent to water. ✲ فَتَحَ a فَتْحًا, وفَتَّح هـ
To conquer (a country). To take (a stronghold). To begin, to undertake (a conversation, an affair). To part (the legs). To mark a letter with a *fatha*. To explain (a difficulty). فَتَحَ هـ
To judge between (two parties). – بَيْن
✧ To open a bargain. To offer a price. فَتَحَ السِّعْر
To draw an omen. – الفَأل
To reveal a. th. to. To inform a. o. of. To favour a. o. To facilitate a. th. To give victory over a. o. (God). – على
To help a. o. (God). – فَتْحًا وفُتَاحَةً على
✧To open (the bowels: medicine). فَتَّحَ هـ
To begin a dispute with a. o. To send summons to. To address a. o. first. To bargain with a.o. without فَاتَحَ ة وهـ

To bury a. th. under ground.
To be full of rats (place). فَئِرَ a فَأَرًا
Rat, mouse. Musk. فَأْر ج فِئْرَان وفِئَرَة وفُؤُور
Pilosella, mouse-ear (*plant*). آذان الفأر
Musk-vesicle. فَأْر وفَأْرَة
Mouse. ✧ Carpenter's plane. فَأْرَة
Spoiled by rats (milk, food). فَئِر م. فَئِرَة
Abounding with rats (land). فَئِرَة ومَفْأَرَة
Fenugreek cooked with dates. فَئِرَة وفُؤَارَة وفِئْرَة
To strike, to cut (wood) with a pick-axe. ✲ فَأَسَ a فَأْسًا هـ
To strike a. o. with an axe. To strike a. o. on the back of the head. – ة
Pick-axe. Hoe. Constellation of *Ursa minor*. Town of Fez in Morocco. فَأْس ج فُؤُوس وأَفْؤُس
Projecting part of the back of the head. – الرَّأس
To sob. ✲ فَأَقَ a فُؤَاقًا
Sobbing. فُؤَاق
To make a. o. to augur, to divine a. th. ✲ فأل – فَأَّلَ و✧ فَوَّلَ ة ب
To draw a good omen from. To bode well of a. th. ✧ To be superstitious. تَفَأَّلَ وتَفَاءَلَ وافْتَأَلَ و ✧ اسْتَفْوَلَ ب
Good omen, augury. ✧ Superstition. فَأْل ج فُؤُول وأَفْؤُل, وتَفَاؤُل
May no evil fortune befall thee. لا فَأْلَ عَلَيْكَ
Game of children, puzzle. فِئَال
To fill its mouth with herbs (camel). ✲ فَأَمَ وفَئِمَ a فَأْمًا, وتَفَأَّمَ من
To quench thirst with (water). فَأَمَ من
To widen (a pack-saddle. a bucket). To fill (a vessel). فَأَّمَ وأَفْأَمَ هـ
Numerous party. فِئَام
They have cut it in pieces. قَطَّعُوهُ فُؤَامًا
To strike, to cleave a. th. To split (the head) with a sword. ✧ To lance (an abscess). ✲ فَأَى a فَأْوًا وفَأْيًا هـ
To alight upon a depressed ground. To wound the head so as to lay the bone bare. أَفْأَى
To be split, cracked (vessel). To be opened, uncovered. اِنْفَأَى
Cleft, chink, gap. Narrow-pass. فَأْو
Party of men. فِئَة ج فِئَات وفِئُون

buying. To undertake (an affair) with. To know (o.'s wife).

تَفَتَّحَ وانفتح To open (blossom). To be opened. ✧ To be opened (mind).

تفتّح في الكلام To open o.'s heart, to pour out o.'s sentiments. To make a show, a display of science.

تفاتحوا كلامًا بينهم To speak secretly o. to a.

إنفتح To be opened.

إفتتح ه To conquer (a country).

— واستفتح ه To open (a door). To commence a. th.

— واستفتح ه ب To open (an assembly). To inaugurate. To undertake, to begin (an affair) with.

إستفتح ب To open the sale with (merchant).

إستفتح ه To ask the explanation of (a text).

— ه To ask the help of a. o.

فتح وتفتيح Opening, beginning.

فتح Fatha, vowel-sound *equal to a short a*; vowel-sign.

فتح ج فتوح Victory, conquest of a country. First rain. Help of God. Watercourse.

فتوحات Conquered countries. Victories.

فتحة Sign of a fatha (ـَ).

فتاحة Succour. Victory.

فِتاحة وفُتاحة Sentence of a judge. Litigation.

بينهما فتاحات They are at law; they dissent.

فُتُح Large orifice; wide-mouthed (flask). Open (door).

فتحة ج فُتح Display, show of science.

فاتح ✧ Of a light colour.

فاتحة ج فواتح Beginning, exord.

الفاتحة وفاتحة الكتاب First chapter of the Coran.

فتوح First rain in the spring.

— ج فُتُح Having a wide orifice to the teats (she-camel).

فتّاح Opener. Conquerer, victorious. Judge. Wide (tent).

الفتّاح God.

إفتتاح ومُفتتح Opening, inauguration. Preamble, introduction.

حرف الاستفتاح The opening letter *i. e.* ألا indeed.

إستفتاح ✧ Opening of a market; first sale of the day.

مَفْتَح ج مَفاتِح Magazine, treasury.

مِفْتَح ج مَفاتِح , ومِفْتاح ج مَفاتِيح Key.

مَفْتوح Opened. Conquered (country). Marked with fatha (letter). ✧ Light (colour).

مُتَفَتِّح وفتيح ✧ Open-minded (child).

✱ فَتِخَ a فَتَخًا To have weak, relaxed, supple (limbs): weak knees (camel).

فتخ a فتخًا , وفَتَّخ ه To bend and stretch (the fingers, the toes).

أفتخ To be fatigued.

تفتّخ To put ringlets on the fingers, on the toes (woman).

فتخ Weakness of the legs. Anklet. Abscess, swelling.

فَتْخة وفَتَخة ج فَتخ وفُتُوخ وفَتَخات Finger-ring; toe-ring. Ring without a stone.

فتوخ الأسد Claws of a lion.

أفتخ م فتخاء ج فُتْخ Having supple, weak, relaxed (limbs). To be crook-footed.

✱ فتر i o فتورًا وفُتارًا , وتفتّر To become remiss after vigour. To become tepid, lukewarm (water).

— عن To be remiss (in work).

— فتورًا وفترة To abate, to cool (heat).

— فتورًا وفترًا To become languid (body, look).

فتّر ه To render (water) lukewarm. To cause (the heat) to abate (God).

فتّر وأفتر ه To render a. o. weak, remiss, languid.

أفتر To be weak-sighted.

إستفتر To become submissive (horse).

فتر وفتور Langour, weakness, remissness. Tepidity.

فِتر Half a span, space between the thumb and the fore-finger.

فُتر Mat made of palm-leaves.

فترة ج فترات Langour, faintness. Interval between two fits of fever, between the missions of two prophets. Interregnum. Truce.

— وفِتّر Torpedo-fish.

embark rashly (in an affair). To act rashly.
To rush blindly into. To persevere in. To be skilful in (a craft). فَتَكَ فِي
To murder a. o. treacherously. To wound, to kill by surprise. — بِ
To card (cotton). فَتَّكَ هـ
To embark rashly in (an affair). فَاتَكَ هـ
To compete with a. o. in skill. To assault a. o. openly. To keep constantly to a. o. To pay to a. o. the price agreed upon. — ﻫ
He followed his own way in the affair. تَفَتَّكَ بِأَمْرِهِ
Rashness. Unruliness. Violence. فَتْك
Treacherous murderer. Felon. فَاتِك ج فُتَّاك
To twist (a rope, a thread). ✱ فَتَلَ i فَتْلًا, وفَتَّلَ هـ
He has caused him to change his mind. فَتَلَ ذُؤَابَتَهُ
To avert (the face) from. — هـ عن
✧ To turn a. o.'s brain. فَتَلَ عَقْلَهُ
To be twisted. تَفَتَّلَ وانْفَتَلَ
He turned away from his prayer. إِنْفَتَلَ عن صَلَاتِهِ
Parting of a camel's legs. فَتَل
Thread. ▫ فُتْلَة
Seed-vessel, blossom of the mimosa سَلَم and سَمُر. فَتْلَة ج فَتَل
Fruit of the mimosa عُرْفُط. فَتْلَة
It will be of no avail to thee. هٰذَا مَا يُغْنِي عَنْكَ فَتْلَةً او فَتَلَةً او فَتِيلًا
✧ Crookedness, unstraightforwardness. إِنْفِتَال
Twisted (thread). فَتِيل ومَفْتُول
Rope of palm-fibres. Pellicle of a date-stone. Wick. Dirt of the skin rolled between the fingers. ▫ Flask. فَتِيل وفَتِيلَة ج فَتَائِل وفَتِيلَات
▫ Amianthus. حَجَر الفَتِيلَة
Rope-weaver. Nightingale. فَتَّال
Having parted legs (camel). أَفْتَل م فَتْلَاء ج فُتْل
Instrument for twisting ropes. مِفْتَل
Strongly twisted (thread, wick). مُفَتَّل
Strong in make (man). مَفْتُول الخَلْق
✧ Semolina. مُفَتَّلَة

Weak. Remiss, languid. Lukewarm (water). فَاتِر م فَاتِرَة
Lukewarm (water). فَاتُور
To inspect, to scrutinise a. th. To inquire about. ✧ To search for. ✱ فَتَشَ i فَتْشًا, وفَتَّشَ هـ وعن
Search, inspection. تَفْتِيش
Investigator, scrutiniser. فَتَّاش
Rocket, fusee. ✧ فُتَيْشَة
Inspector. مُفَتِّش
To tread upon. To grind a. th. ✱ فَتَغَ a فَتْغًا هـ
To be ground between the molar teeth. تَفَتَّغَ
To break, to slit. To disjoin, to disunite. To unsolder. To unsew (a garment). To put leaven in (dough). ✱ فَتَقَ o فَتْقًا, وفَتَّقَ هـ (opp. to رَتَقَ)
To set people at variance. فَتَقَ بَيْنَ
To yield a good crop (land). فَتِقَ a فَتَقًا
To correct, to render (language) clear. فَتَّقَ الكَلَام
To have fat (cattle). To have a fine weather. To pierce the clouds (sun). To reach a place not rained upon. أَفْتَقَ
To be swollen in the flanks (cattle). To be slit, unsewed, disjoined. To be cracked (hand). To clear away (clouds). تَفَتَّقَ وانْفَتَقَ
Slit, rent. Disunion. فَتْق
Place spared by the rain. — ج فُتُوق
Rupture, hernia. — و✧ فِتَاق
Daybreak, dawn. — وفَتَق
Calamity; drought, scarcity. فُتُوق
Year of little rain. عَامٌ ذُو فُتُوق
Great lump of leaven. Sun piercing the clouds. Mixture of perfumes, medicines. فِتَاق
Shining (dawn). Sharp (sword). Swollen (camel). فَتِيق
Sharp-tongued. — اللِّسَان
Sharp-tongued (woman). فُتُق ومُتَفَتِّقَة
He is the supreme ruler (*lit.* splitting and repairing). هُوَ الفَاتِقُ والرَّاتِقُ
Pierced, split. Ruptured. مَفْتُوق
King. Blacksmith. Door-keeper. Carpenter. فَيْتَق
To ✱ فَتَكَ o i فَتْكًا, وفُتُوكًا, وأَفْتَكَ

Youth. Generosity. Manly qualities. فَتَاء وفُتُوَّة
فُتْوَى وفَتْوَى وفُتْيا وفَتْيا ج فَتَاوٍ وفَتَاوَى Decision of sacred law.
Consultation on a point of law. إِسْتِفْتَاء
فَتًى مث فَتَيَان وفَتَوَان ج فِتْيَان وفِتْيَة وفُتُوَّة وفُتُوّ وفِتِيّ وفُتِيّ Young slave. Youth. Youthful. Brave, generous.
Morning and evening. الفَتَيَان
Full-grown girl. ✧ Maid-servant. فَتَاة مث فَتَاتَانِ ج فَتَيَات وفَتَوَات
◘ Prostitute, strumpet. فَاتِيَة ج فَوَاتِي
Young (camel). Youthful. فَتِيّ م فَتِيَّة ج فِتَاء وأَفْتَاء
Cadet, younger. More generous. أَفْتَى
Mufti, doctor, expounder of the law of the Koran. مُفْتٍ
To scatter (dates) from a basket. ✱ فَتَّ o فَتًّا ه
To be broken-hearted (man). اِنْفَتَّ
They have been beaten, subdued. أُفْتِتُوا
Millet-bread. Colocynth-seeds. فَتّ
Scattered dates. تَمْر فَتّ
Multitude, abundance. مَفَتَّة
To cool (anger). ✱ فَثَأَ a فَثْأً ه
To temperate (cold). To allay the boiling of a cooking-pot with cold water. — فَثْأً وفُثُوءًا ه
To remove, to avert a. o. from. — ه عن
To be tired, jaded. أَفْثَأَ
To alight, to abide in a place. — ب
To abate (heat). — وانْفَثَأَ
To diminish a. th. To allay the heat of (water.) ✱ فَثَجَ o فَثْجًا ه
To be overburdened, fatigued. — وفَثِجَ وأَفْثَجَ وأُفْثِجَ
Inexhaustible sea. بَحْرٌ لَا يُفْثَجُ
Pregnant (she-camel). فَاثِج ج فَوَاثِج
Golden, silver, or metal tray. Marble-table. Disk of the sun. Carpet. ✱ فَثْر — فَاثُور
To break (the head). ✱ فَثَغَ a فَثْغًا ه
To part the legs. ✱ فَجَّ o فَجًّا, وأَفَجَّ مَا بَيْنَ رِجْلَيْهِ
To strain (a bow-string). فَجَّ ه
To have the knees, hocks wide apart (man, beast). فَجِجَ a فَجَجًا
To walk in parting the legs. To أَفَجَّ

To burn a. th. To melt, to assay (gold, silver). ✱ فَتَنَ i فَتْنًا ه
To rouse a. o. to rebellion. To decoy, to seduce, to allure, to enamour a. o. فَتَنَ i فَتْنًا وفُتُونًا, وفَتَّنَ وأَفْتَنَ ه
To put to the test, to try a. o. To deceive a. o. — فِتْنَة ومَفْتُونًا ه وه
To be tried by misfortunes. فُتِنَ
To be seduced, enamoured. — وأُفْتِنَ وافْتَتَنَ
To rouse a. o. to rebellion. إِفْتَتَنَ ه
To be seduced, enamoured. To join in a riot. To be excited to revolt. إِفْتَتَنَ
State. Species. فَتْن
Life is two-sided. العَيْش فَتْنَان
Assaying of metals; trial, test. Allurement, seduction. Discord, riot, disturbance. Civil war. Women. Impiety, unbelief. Sin. Chastisement. Madness. A kind of Mimosa. فِتْنَة ج فِتَن
✧ Acacia-flower. فَتْنَة
Misleading. Disturber. Tempter, seducer. Alluring, captivating. فَاتِن ج فُتَّان, وفَتَّان
Goldsmith; silversmith. فَتَّان
The devil. الفَتَّان
Gold and silver coins. الفَتَّانَان
Touch-stone. فَتَّانَة
Burnt (silver). Black stones. فَتِين
Ground burnt by the sun. — ج فُتُن
Trial, temptation. Excited to revolt. Tried by misfortunes. Tempted, seduced. Mad. مَفْتُون
To surpass a. o. in generosity. ✱ فَتَا o فَتْوًا ه
To be youthful, full-grown. To be brave, generous. فَتِيَ a فَتًى, وتَفَتَّى وتَفَاتَى
To be kept apart from boys (girl). To attain puberty. فُتِّيَتْ تَفْتِيَة, وتَفَتَّتْ تَفَتِّيًا
To give to a. o. a decision of sacred law (mufti). أَفْتَى ه في
To assume the air of a young man (girl, old man). To make a show of generosity. تَفَتَّى وتَفَاتَى
They appealed to (the mufti) for decision. تَفَاتَوْا الى
To ask (a judge) to give a decision of sacred law. إِسْتَفْتَى ه

every side (misfortune).
✧ To burst out, to be blown up (machine, powder). إِنْفَجَر
To dissipate before (dawn: night). عن —
To forge speech. إِفْتَجَر الكَلَامَ وفي الكَلَام
Bountifulness. Benefit. Wealth. فَجَر
Daybreak, dawn. Dawn-prayer. فَجْر
Morning-star, Lucifer. كَوْكَب الفَجْر
Lie. Vice; sin. فَجْرَة
He has forged a lie. رَكِبَ فَجْرَةً
Wide part of a valley into which water flows. فُجْرَة ج فُجَر
Outlet for water. — ومَفْجَر ومَنْفَجَرَة ج مَفَاجِر , ومُنْفَجَر
Wickedness, dissoluteness, debauchery, impiety. فُجُور وفَجَار
Paths, ways. فِجَار
Four days of the sacred months in which the Arabs waged war. أَيَّام الفِجَار
فَاجِر ج فَجَرَة وفُجَّار , وفَجُور ج فُجُر , وفَاجُور
Declining. Libertine, profligate. Liar. Adulterer. Wicked. Sorcerer, wizard.
✧ Ill-natured, foul-mouthed. فَاجِر م فَاجِرَة
To act proudly, to assume a haughty mien. ✲ فَجَس o فَجْسًا وتَفَجَّس
To overcome a. o. ه —
To boast falsely. أَفْجَس
To show haughtiness towards a. o. تَفَجَّس على
To distress, to afflict a. o. (loss in goods, family). ✲ فَجَم a فَجْمًا, وفَجَّم ه
To be distressed by a loss in (goods or family). فُجِم ب وفي
To be painfully affected, distressed. تَفَجَّم
To compassionate a. o.'s sufferings. لِفُلَانٍ —
To be greedy, glutton. ✧ إِنْفَجَم
Gluttony. ✧ فَجْمَة
Misfortune, loss of property, of dear ones. فَجِيعَة ج فَجَائِع
Terrible and unexpected death. مَوت فَاجِع وفَجُوع
Woman crushed by misfortunes. إِمرَأَة فَاجِع
Calamity. فَاجِعَة ج فَوَاجِع
To become soft, fleshy. ✲ فَجَل o فَجْلًا وفَجِل a فَجَلًا

mute (ostrich). To travel in a narrow-pass.
To tear (the earth with the ploughshare). أَفَجَّ ه ب
To walk with parted legs. تَفَاجَّ
To be strained (bowstring). إِنْفَجَّ
Mountain-road; ravine. فَجّ ج فِجَاج, وفُجَاج
Water-melon. فِجّ
Crude, unripe (fruit). ✧ Peevish. فِجّ وفَجَاجَة و✧ فَجّ
Parting of the legs. فَجَج
Straddling. أَفَجّ م فَجَّاء ج فُجّ
Intervening space, interstice. فُجَّة
He straddles. يَمْشِي مُفَاجًّا
To answer peevishly. To be talkative. ✲ فَجْفَج
Talking disorderly, clamorous. فِجْفَاج
To fall upon a. o. unexpectedly, to surprise a. o. ✲ فَجَأَ وفَجِئ a فَجْأً وفُجَاءَةً وفُجْأَةً , وفَاجَأَ وافْتَجَأَ ه
To be surprised by sudden death. فُوجِئ
To take a. o. in the very fact. أَفْجَأَ ه
Surprise, unexpected event. Sudden (death). فُجَاءَة
Of a sudden, unawares. فُجَاءَةً وفَجْأَةً
Surprising (lion). فَاجِئ ومُفَاجِئ
To cut, to cleave. To give vent to (water). ✲ فَجَر o فَجْرًا, وفَجَّر ه
To open (a channel) to. To make dawn to gleam (God). فَجَّر ه
To deviate from justice. فَجَر o فُجُورًا عن الحَقّ
To lie. To act immorally. To commit unlawful actions. To be weak-sighted. — فَجْرًا وفُجُورًا
To oppose, to rise against, to contradict a. o. To disbelieve a. th. To commit adultery with. ه —
To show generosity. فَجِر a فَجَرًا
To enter upon the time of daybreak. To be or become dissolute. أَفْجَر
To find a. o. to be vicious, profligate, rebellious. ه —
To open its way and flow freely (water). To break (dawn). تَفَجَّر وانْفَجَر
To act bountifully. — وانْفَجَر بِالكَرَم
To come upon a. o. from تَفَجَّر على

To sit in-parting the legs. تَفَحَّج
To be wide apart (legs). إِنْفَحَج
Parting of the heels. فَحَج
Walking in أَفْحَج م فَحْجَاء ج فُحْج turning the toes in.
To emit (an opinion) ✱ فحر — إِفْتَحَر ه rejected by all.
To lick up, to lap ✱ فَحَس a فَحْسًا ه (water) from the hand. To rub off (the awn) of barley.
To become ✱ فَحُش o فُحْشًا, وتَفَاحَش immoderate, excessive, enormous (thing). To be or become atrocious, abominable, foul, obscene. To become ugly (woman).
To hold gross language with. فَاحَش ة
To commit atrocities. أَفْحَش وتَفَاحَش
To hold أَفْحَش وتَفَحَّش في الكَلَام على unseemly, obscene talks against.
To find a. th. foul, تَفَحَّش ب واسْتَفْحَش ة evil, excessive.
Excess. Turpitude. فُحْش وفَحْشَاء Shocking language.
Dissolute in words or فَحَّاش م فَحَّاشَة actions.
Immoral, gross, foul. فَاحِش م فَاحِشَة Exorbitant, excessive. Atrocious. Stingy.
Turpitude. Excess, فَاحِشَة ج فَوَاحِش enormity. Abomination. Adultery. ✧ Prostitute.
Shameless, profligate. مُتَفَحِّش
To scrutinise, to ✱ فَحَص a فَحْصًا عن examine a. th. To inquire after, to search for.
To drench (the ground : rain). — ه To dig the (ground). To disclose, to lay out a. th. To scrap (the ground) for laying eggs (sand-grouse).
To scrap (the ground) with. — ب
To search فَاحَص مُفَاحَصَة وفِحَاصًا ة after the defects or the secrets of o. a.
To scrutinise, to تَفَحَّص وافْتَحَص عن examine a. th. minutely.
Search, inquiry. Even ground. فَحْص Inhabited land.
Dimple of the chin. فَحْصَة

To enlarge a. th. فَحَّل ه
To contrive, to invent a. th. إِفْتَجَل ه
Radish, turnip. (*un.* فُجْلَة) فُجْل وفُجُل
◻ Seller of radishes. Greengrocer. فَجَّال
Having parted legs; splay-footed. أَفْجَل
To indent, to ✧ فَجَم o فَجْمًا, وفَجَّم ه blunt (a knife).
To be notched, blunted ✧ تَفَجَّم وانْفَجَم (knife).
Notch, indenture. ✧ فَجْم
Thick in the corners of the mouth. أَفْجَم
Rue (plant). ✱ فجن — فَيْجَن
To raise (the string ✱ فَجَا o فَجْوًا ه of a bow). To open (a door). To part the legs.
To have the legs wide فَجِيَ a فَجًا apart.
To disclose, to lay a. th. bare. فَجَّى ه
To remove a. o. from. — ه عن
To make large family expenses. أَفْجَى
To have an intervening space. تَفَاجَى
To open (door). إِنْفَجَى
Parting of the legs. فَجًا
Space, gap, interstice. Court-yard. فَجْوَة ج فَجَوَات وفِجَاء
Extensive tract of land. — وفَجْوَاء
Having the legs, knees أَفْجَى م فَجْوَاء wide apart.
To hiss ✱ فَحَّ o i فَحًّا وفَحِيحًا وتَفْحَاحًا (viper). ✧ To spread (perfume).
To snore in sleep. — i فَحِيحًا
Hissing of serpents. فَحّ وفَحِيح وتَفْحَاح
Pungency of pepper. فَحَّة الفُلْفُل
Hissing snakes. فُحُح
To be true in love. To blow in ✱ فَحْفَح sleep. To be hoarse.
Hoarseness. فَحْفَحَة
Talkative, speaker. فَحْفَاح
To search ✱ فَحَث a فَحْثًا, وافْتَحَث عن a. th.
To be ✱ فَحَج a فَحْجًا وفَحِج a فَحَجًا proud, haughty.
To فَحَّج وفَحَج وتَفَحَّج وانْفَحَج في مِشْيَتِه walk in turning the toes in.
To desist, to turn back from. أَفْحَج عن
To part the hind-legs (of a — ة milch-camel).

A piece of charcoal. فَحْمَة ج فَحَمَات
First and darkest part of the night. — ج فِحَام وفُحُوم
Coal-black. فَحْمِي
Blackness. فُحُومَة
Coal-man. ✧ Carbonaro, freemason. فَحَّام ج فَحَّامَة
Stagnating (water). فَاحِم
Black (hair). Still (water). Silent (man). فَاحِم وفَحِيم
Speechless, unable to answer. مُفْحَم
Carbonised. مُفَحَّم
To hint at. ✱ فَحَا o فَحْوًا, وفَحَّى بِكَلَامِهِ إِلَى
To season (food) in the cooking-pot. فَحَّى ه
To hold a conversation with. To elicit the intention of a. o. فَاحَا ه
Seasoning, seeds. Onions. فَحًا وفِحًا ج أَفْحَاء
Honey-comb. فَحْوَة
Meaning (of a discourse). فَحْوَى وفَحْوَاء وفُحْوَاء ج فَحَاوٍ
To breath heavily; to snore in sleep. To hiss (snake). To diffuse itself (smell). ✱ فَخَّ i فَخًّا وفَخِيخًا, وافْتَخَّ
To be weakened (legs). فَخَّ i فَخًّا وفَخَّةً وفَخَخًا
Trap, snare, net. فَخّ ج فِخَاخ وفُخُوخ
Snoring. Morning-sleep. Slut. فَخَّة
Hiss of snakes. فَخِيخ
To brag, to boast. ✱ فَخْفَخَ
Rustling of paper, of new clothes. ✧ Show, pomp, luxury. فَخْفَخَة
To coo (pigeon). To lie. ✱ فَخَتَ a فَخْتًا
To make a hole in (a roof). To open (a vessel). To cut off a. th. — ه
To backbite a. o. ✧ فَخَت فِي
To walk proudly. To strut (woman). To wonder. To have the habit of lying. تَفَخَّتَ
To be perforated (roof, ceiling). إِنْفَخَتَ
Hole (in a roof). Moonlight. Hunter's snare. فَخْت
Ring-dove. فَاخِتَة ج فَوَاخِت
To become proud. ✱ فَخَجَ a فَخَجًا
To hit a. o. in the thigh. ✱ فَخَذَ a فَخْذًا ه
To be wounded in the thigh; to have the thigh broken. فَخِذَ

Searcher, inquirer. فَحِيص
Searcher after the vices. فَحِيص ومُفَاحِص
Hollow dug by a sand-grouse for laying eggs. مَفْحَص ج مَفَاحِص وأُفْحُوص ج أَفَاحِيص
To split, to cut (melons) open. ✱ فَحَضَ a فَحْضًا ه
To send to a. o. (a stallion). To choose (a stallion) for (a flock). ✱ فَحَلَ a فَحْلًا, وافْتَحَلَ ل ه
To lend, to give a stallion to a. o. أَفْحَلَ ه
To be manly, masculine. To become barren (tree). To affect coarseness (in dress, food). تَفَحَّلَ
To become tall, strong (male palm-tree). To become momentous (affair). إِسْتَفْحَلَ
Quality of a stallion. Virility. Manliness. فِحْلَة وفُحُولَة وفِحَالَة
فَحْل ج فُحُول وأَفْحُل وفِحَال وفِحَالَة وفُحُولَة
Stallion, male. Energetic man.
Reciter of poetry, traditions. — ج فُحُول
Male palm-tree. Mat of palm-leaves. فُحَّل, وفُحَّال ج فَحَاحِيل
Virago, masculine woman. فَحْلَة
Barren (tree). مُتَفَحِّل
To be exhausted (well). ✱ فَحَمَ o فُحُومًا
To be unable to answer. To drink in intense darkness. فَحَمَ a فَحْمًا
فَحَمَ o وفَحِمَ a وفَحُمَ فَحْمًا وفَحَامًا وفُحُومًا, وأُفْحِمَ
To be choked by (sobs: child). To bleat until he becomes hoarse (ram).
To be intensely black. فَحُمَ o فُحُومًا وفُحُومَة
To blacken (the face) with charcoal. فَحَّمَ ه وه
To silence (a weeping child). To hush up a. o. To prevent (a poet) from uttering verses (anxiety). To enter upon the darkest part of the night. أَفْحَمَ ه
Do not set off in the darkest part of the night. فَحِّمُوا وأَفْحِمُوا عَنْكُم مِن اللَّيل
To drink an evening-draught. إِفْتَحَمَ
Charcoal. فَحْم وفَحَم وفَحِيم
Mineral, pit-coal. فَحْم الحَجَر وحَجَرِي

To show staidness, forbearance. To dress splendidly. To be a fop. ✡ فخل – تفخّل
Affecting staidness. Fop. مُتفخِّل
To be corpulent, stout. To be great in estimation. ✡ فَخُم o فَخَامَة
To enjoy public consideration – في عُيون النّاس
To read or pronounce emphatically. فَخَّم الحُرُوف
To magnify, to show regard to a. o. ه –
To magnify o.'s self. تَفَخَّم
High in rank, estimation. Bulky, thick. Strong (discourse). فَخْم
Pride, haughtiness. Swelling. فُخْمِيَّة
Consideration, regard. Emphasis, pathos. تَفْخِيم
Most honoured. أَفْخَم
Magnified, honoured. مُفَخَّم
To flap the wings (bird). To shout out. To run (man). To tread heavily upon the ground (flock). ✡ فَدّ i فَدِيدًا
He threatens me. هُوَ يَفُدّ لِي وَيَمُدّ لِي
To walk with a haughty gait. To cry out in a sale (men). فَدَّد
Shouter. Proud. Treading heavily *Pl.* Husbandmen, neatherds, ox-drivers, camel-drivers. Nomads. فَدَّاد ج فَدَّادُون
Frog. Cowardly. فَدَّادَة
To shout out. To escape from danger. ✡ فَدْفَد
Hard and even ground. Desert. فَدْفَد
Screamer. Harsh-voiced. فُدْفُد
To crush a. o. (debt, weight). ✡ فَدَح a فَدْحًا ه
To judge, to find a. th. painful, burdensome. أَفْدَح واسْتَفْدَح ه
Crushing (debt, weight). فَادِح
Calamity. فَادِحَة ج فَوَادِح
To fracture (the skull) of. ✡ فَدَخ a فَدْخًا ه
To take refuge on the summit of a mountain (wild goat). To become cold (cooked meat). ✡ فَدَر i فَدْرًا وفُدُورًا
To become foolish. فَدِر a فَدَرًا
To break (stones). فَدَّر ه
To be broken (stones). تَفَدَّر

To call (a tribe) by small parties. فَخَّذ ه
To disperse (people). To separate a. o. from. – ه عن وبَيْن
To rout and scatter (people). فَاخَذ ه
To draw back, to retire. To be late. تَفَخَّذ
To submit. إِسْتَفْخَذ
Thigh. ✧ Leg (of mutton). فَخِذ وفَخْذ (*f.*) ج أَفْخَاذ
Portion of a tribe. فَخْذ ج أَفْخَاذ
✡ فَخَر a فَخْرًا وفَخَرًا وفَخَارًا وفَخَارَةً وفِخِّيرَى وفِخِّيرًا، وافْتَخَر
To boast of. To glory in.
To surpass a. o. in nobility, glory. فَخَر o ه
To judge a. o. to surpass another in excellence. فَخَر a وفَخَّر وأَفْخَر ه على
To scorn a. o. فَخِر a فَخَرًا من
To vie in glory with, to surpass a. o. in excellence. فَاخَر مُفَاخَرَةً وفِخَارًا ه
To vie in boasting with o. a. تَفَاخَر
To bring forth noble children (woman). أَفْخَر
To magnify o.'s self. تَفَخَّر
To buy a splendid (thing). To find a. th. excellent, grand. إِسْتَفْخَر ه
Glory, illustration, nobleness, excellence. فَخْر وفَخَر
Boasting, glorying. Glory, honour. إِفْتِخَار
Glorying in; boastful. Excellent, splendid, precious. Stoneless date. فَاخِر
Boastful. فَخُور وفَخِير وفِخِّير
Boasting; vying in glory. Surpassed in glory. فَخِير
Hole, hollow. ◻ فَخِيرَة
Pottery, earthenware. Baked clay. Potter's clay. فَخَّار
Aromatic plant. Marjoram. فَاخُور ج فَيَاخِير •
Potter. فَخَّارِيّ او ✧ فَاخُورِيّ
Pottery. فَاخُورَة
Cause of glorying. Generous deed. مَفْخَرَة ومَفْخُرَة ج مَفَاخِر
To boast falsely. To magnify o.'s self. ✡ فَخَز a فَخْزًا، وفَخِز فَخَزًا، وتَفَخَّز
Merit, self-glorification. فَخْز
To miss, to lose a. th. ✡ فَخَش a فَخْشًا ه

High building. فَدَن ج أَفْدَان
Pair of فَدَان وفَدَّان ج فَدَادِين وأَفْدِنَة وفُدُن bulls for ploughing. Plough. ✧ Bull.
Acre; area, one day's labour. فَدَّان
Sown field.
Plumb-line. ✧ فَادِن ج فَوَادِن
✧ With weight and measure. على القِدَّةِ والفادِنِ
✱ فدى i فَدَى وفِدَى وفِدَاء , وفادَى مُفَادَاةً
To free (herself) in giving a sum for divorcing (woman). وفِدَاء ه من
To give a ransom for (a captive).
To free (a slave); to redeem a. o. from.
To say to a. o.: فَدَى ه بِنَفْسِهِ وفَدَّى ه
May I be thy ransom!
To divorce (her husband) in giving a sum (woman). فَادَى ه
To accept from a. o. the ransom of a slave. أَفْدَى ه الأَسِيرَ
To make a barn for dates. To dandle (a child). — ه وه
To redeem o. another. تَفَادَى
To guard against, to abstain from. — وافْتَدَى من
To be redeemed, freed, ransomed. إِنْفَدَى
To free a. o. in paying a ransom. To free herself from her husband (woman). إِفْتَدَى بِفُلَان
فِدًى وفَدًى وفِدَاء وفِدْيَة ج فِدًى وفِدْيَات
Ransom, price given for freeing a captive.
May my father be thy ransom! فِدَاكَ أَبِي وفَدًى لكَ أَبِي
Barn. Heap of dates, barley. Bulk. فَدَاء ج أَفْدِيَة
The Redeemer; Our Lord Jesus-Christ. الفَادِي
Brave, chivalrous. ✧ فِدَاوِيّ ج فِدَاوِيَّة
Pl. Sect of the Assassins.
To be alone, apart from. ✱ فذّ o فَذًّا عن
To thrust a. o. back vehemently. — ه
To bring forth one only (ewe). أَفَذَّ
To become alone, independent. تَفَذَّذ واسْتَفَذَّ
Alone, single. Scattered (date). فَذّ ج أَفْذَاذ وفُذُود
Featherless (arrow). أَفَذّ

فَدَر ج فُدُور, وفَادِر ج فَوَادِر, وفَدُور ج فُدُر
Wild goat.
Piece of meat, of rock. فِدْرَة ج فِدَر
Lump of dates.
Silver. Fat boy. فُدُرّ
Walking alone. فُدَرَة
Mass of rock upon the top of a mountain. فَادِرَة وفِنْدِيرَة
Abounding in chamois (land). مَفْدَرَة
Retreat of the chamois.
To have spiders in a house. ✱ فدس — أَفْدَس
Spider. فُدْس ج فِدَسَة
Large jar. فَيْدَس
Holyday, recreation. ✧ فَيْدُوس
To break (the head) of a. o. ✱ فَدَش o فَدْشًا ه
To have the wrist or ankle distorted. To be distorted (joint). ✱ فَدِع a فَدَعًا
To distort a. o. فَدَّع ه
Distorsion of the ankle or wrist. فَدَع
Distorted (man). أَفْدَع م فَدْعَاء ج فُدْع
Distorted part (of the joints). فَدَعَة
To break, to crush a. th. hollow. To season (food) with grease, butter. ✱ فَدَغ a فَدْغًا ه
✧ To wound a. o. in the head. — رَأْسَهُ
To be broken. To be softened. إِنْفَدَغ
Instrument for breaking. مِفْدَغ ج مَفَادِغ
To comb out (cotton). ✱ فدك — فَدَّك ه
To have (cotton) carded.
To be impeded in speech; to be heavy, silly. ✱ فَدُم o فُدُومَة وفَدَامَة
To cover the mouth of (a man, of a vessel) with. فَدَم i فَدْمًا ه وعلى ب وفَدَّم وأَفْدَم ه
Plumb-line. ✧ فادِم ج فَوَادِم
Impeded in speech. Heavy, dull, silly. فَدْم ج فِدَام
Strainer for a ewer. Piece of cloth for wiping the mouth. فِدَام ج فُدُم , وفِدَّام وفِدَّامة وفِدُّوم
Having a strainer (jug), having the mouth covered (vessel). مُفْدَم ومُفَدَّم
Saturated with red dye (cloth). مُفْدَم
Ewers, pots. المُفَدَّمَات
To fatten (cattle). To raise (a building). ✱ فدن — فَدَّن ه
Red dye. فَدَن

Strange thing. أَمْرٌ فَرِيٌّ
To lead a dissolute life. ✱ فَرَتَ o فَرْتًا
To be weak-minded. فَرِتَ a فَرَتًا
To be sweet (water). فَرُتَ o فُرُوتَةً
Sweet (water). فُرَاتٌ
The Euphrates. الفُرَاتُ
The Tigris and the Euphrates. الفُرَاتَانِ
Sweet water. ماء ومِيَاه فُرَاتٌ
To jabber. ✧ To be angry. ✱ فَرْتَنَ
To walk with short steps.
To feel a heaving of the stomach (pregnant woman). ✱ فَرَثَ o فَرْثًا, وتَفَرَّثَ وانفَرَثَ
To wound a. o. in the liver. — i فَرْثًا وفَرَّثَ ه
To scatter and give out to a.-o. (a basket of dates). — o i ه ل
To be scattered (tribe). فَرِثَ a فَرَثًا, وتَفَرَّثَ
To rip up (an animal) and empty the contents of its stomach. أَفْرَثَ ه
To expose a. o. to blame; to vilify a. o. أَفْرَثَ ه
Contents of a ruminant's stomach. فَرْثٌ ج فُرُوثٌ, وفَرَاثَةٌ
To open (a door, the mouth). To enlarge a. th. To part (the legs). ✱ فَرَجَ i فَرْجًا, وفَرَّجَ ه
To let a space between. — بَيْنَ
To make room for. فَرَجَ ل
To dispel cares from. To comfort a. o. in. — وفَرَّجَ ه عن
✧ To show a. th. to. To show a sight to. فَرَّجَ ه على
To have chickens (hen). To clear away (dust) أَفْرَجَ
To clear the way, to remove from. — عن
To be dispelled (cares). ✧ To take a walk, to amuse o.'s self. تَفَرَّجَ
✧ To look with pleasure at. تَفَرَّجَ على
To be opened, disclosed, parted. To be dispelled (grief). To be comforted (man). إِنْفَرَجَ
He has been comforted. — عَنْهُ الغَمُّ
Gap, interstice. Space between the legs. Pudenda. Womb. Open place. فَرْجٌ ج فُرُوجٌ
Unable to keep a secret. فِرْجٌ وفُرُجٌ وفُرْجَةٌ

Separately, singly. فَذَاذًا وفُذَاذًا وفَذَاذَى
To contract o.'s self for leaping unexpectedly. ✱ فَذْفَذَ
To settle (an account). ✱ فَذْلَكَ ه
Sum total. Recapitulation. فَذْلَكَةٌ
To fly, to escape. ✱ فَرَّ i فَرًّا وفِرَارًا ومَفَرًّا ومَفِرًّا
To examine the teeth of a horse to know his age. To inquire about, to investigate a. th. — i فَرًّا وفِرَارًا وفُرَارًا عن
The affair came back to its former state. فُرَّ الأَمْرُ جَذَعًا
To put a. o. to flight. أَفَرَّ ه
To laugh at. تَفَرَّرَ ب
To fly on every side. تَفَارَّ
To show the teeth in smiling. To flash (lightning). إِفْتَرَّ
Flying, fugitive. (*m. f. s. pl.*) فَرٌّ
Flight. فَرٌّ وفِرَارٌ
He is the best of his tribe. هُوَ فُرُّ او فُرَّةُ القَوْمِ
Way of laughing. ✧ Quail. فِرَّةٌ
Confusion. Evil. Intensity (of heat). فُرَّةٌ وأَفُرَّةٌ
Fugitive. فَرُورَةٌ وفَرَّارٌ وفَرُورٌ وفَرُورَةٌ
Quick-silver. فَرَّارٌ
Lambkin, kid; wild calf. فُرَارٌ وفُرُرٌ وفُرُورٌ
Refuge, shift. مَفَرٌّ ج مَفَارُّ
Good runner in a flight (horse). مِفَرٌّ
To flap the wings (bird). To be unsteady, fickle. To hurry on at a quick pace. To come out from its cocoon (moth). ✱ فَرْفَرَ
To cut, to break a. th. To mangle a. o. To champ the bit and shake the head (horse). — ه وه
To be confused in speech. — في الكَلَامِ
Unsteadiness, fickleness. فَرْفَرَةٌ
Sparrow. Fat (young man). فُرْفُرٌ وفِرْفِرٌ
Lamb, kid. — وفُرَافِرٌ وفُرْفُورٌ
✧ Butterfly, moth. فَرْفُورٌ ج فَرَافِيرُ
China-ware. ✧ فَرْفُورِيٌّ
Unsteady, fickle. Lion. Mar-all. فُرَافِرٌ م فُرَافِرَةٌ
Purple. Violet. G فِرْفِيرٌ
Wild ass. ✱ فرأ — فَرَأٌ وفَرَاءٌ ج أَفْرَاءٌ وفِرَاءٌ

To be dispelled (fear). — وأفْرَخَ

To clear away (affair). أفْرَخَ

To dispel (fear). أفْرَخَ هـ

They disclosed their أفْرَخُوا بَيْضَهُم
secret *lit* : they hatched their egg.

To take pigeons for bree- إسْتَفْرَخَ ه
ding.

فَرْخ ج أفْرُخ وأفْراخ وفِراخ وفُرُوخ وأفْرِخَة وفِرْخان

Chick, young bird. Offset
of a plant. Base, faint-hearted man.

Shoots of a tree. فَرْخ الشَّجَرَة

Sheet of paper. ة فَرْخ وَرَق

Female chicken. Off-shoot, فَرْخَة ج فِراخ
sprout.

Poultry-house. مَفْرَخ ج مَفارِخ

Incubator, مُسْتَفْرَخ وة مَعْمَل الفِراخ
hatcher.

To فَرَدَ o وفَرِدَ a وفَرُدَ o فُرُودًا وانْفَرَدَ
be alone, single, sole. To be simple,
uncompound.

To secede, to isolate o.'s self فَرَدَ عن
from.

To فَرَدَ وأفْرَدَ وتَفَرَّدَ وانْفَرَدَ واسْتَفْرَدَ ب
busy o.'s self solely about a. th.

To seclude o.'s self from the world فَرَدَ

To bring forth a single one أفْرَدَتْ
(female).

To isolate, to set أفْرَدَ واسْتَفْرَدَ هـ
a. th. apart.

He despatched a messen- أفْرَدَ رَسُولًا إلى
ger to.

To be pairless, تَفَرَّدَ وانْفَرَدَ واسْتَفْرَدَ في
unique in.

To seek solitude. إسْتَفْرَدَ

To encounter a. o. alone. To هـ و ه
single out a. th.

One. single : one فَرْد ج فِراد وأفْراد
individual. Odd.

Odd and even. فَرْد وزَوْج

Unique in his kind, — ج أفْراد وفُرادَى
pairless.

One fellow of a match, of a — ج فِراد
pair.

I met him when we were لَقِيتُهُ فَرْدَيْن
alone.

◆ Pistol. فَرْد ج فُرُدَة وفُرُود

One by one, separately. فَرْدًا فَرْدًا

Stars shining here أفْراد وفُرُود النُّجُوم
and there

Joy after sadness; relief, فَرَج وإنْفِراج
comfort.

Pudding-pie. أمّ الفَرَج

Relief, freedom from cares. فُرْجَة وفَرْجَة

Interstice, gap. فُرْجَة ج فُرَج

◆ Pleasant sight. فُرْجَة

Children's shirt. فُرُّوج ج فَرارِيج

Chicken. فَرُّوج وفُرُّوج ج فَرارِيج

Interstice bet- فُرْجَة ج تَفارِيج وتَقارِج
ween the fingers, the bars of a railing. ◆ Thing pleasant to behold

Weak, cowardly man. — وتَفْراجَة

Fur-mantle, ample gown. فَرَجِيَّة

Dispelling cares. Glad- فارِج ومُفَرِّج
dening the heart.

Turkish lady's cloak. TE فَراجَة

Hen having chickens. مُفْرِج

Isolated; man slain in the مُفْرَج
desert.

Having the elbow parted from مُفْرَج
the arm-pit. Comb.

Obtuse angle. زاوِيَة مُنْفَرِجَة

Comforted. Opened (door). مَفْرُوج

Compasses. P فِرْجار

To curry (a horse). فَرْجَنَ ه

Curry-comb. فِرْجَوْن

To be glad, cheerful, فَرِحَ a فَرَحًا
pleased.

To rejoice at. — ب

To cheer, to rejoice a. o. فَرَّحَ وأفْرَحَ ه

To crush a. o. (debt). أفْرَحَ ه

Joy. cheerfulness. ◆ Wedding, فَرَح
feast.

Joy, merriness. Cause of فَرْحَة وفُرْحَة
joy. Present given to a messenger
of good news.

Glad, فارِح ج فارِحُون، وفَرِح ج فَرِحُون
joyful, lively.

فَرْحان م فَرْحَى. وفَرْحانَة ج فَراحَى وفَرْحَى وفُرُوح ج فُرُح

Merry, cheerful,
content.

Cheering, gladdening. مُفَرِّح ومُفْرِح

Destitute; crushed by (debts). مُفْرَح

Merry, exulting. (*m. f.*) مِفْراح

To live in happiness. فَرُخَ a فَرَخًا

To have chickens (hen). فَرَّخَ وأفْرَخَ

To be hatched (egg).

To sprout(plant). To swarm. فَرَّخَ

To shoot forth (cut tree)

فَرِد وفَرَد Alone, lonely. Pairless, matchless.

فَرْدَة ج فُرَد ◻ Poll-tax. Bag. ✧ Bale; half a beast's load.

فُرْدَة Going alone, solitary.

جاءُوا فُرَادَ وفَرَادَ وفُرْدَى وفِرادًا وفُرَادَى They came one by one.

اِنْفِرَاد Loneliness, seclusion.

عَلَى انْفِرَادٍ Lonely, apart from men.

فَارِد Sole, alone. Refined, white sugar.

فَرُودِيَّة ✧ Turban for women.

فَرِيد م فَرِيدَة Apart from others, alone unparalleled, unique; excellent.

فَرِيدَة ج فَرَائِد Precious pearl. ◻ Quire of paper.

فَرَّاد Seller of pearls.

أَفْرَد ◻ Smooth.

مُفْرَد Isolated, apart, (*Gram*). Singular. Simple, uncompound.

مُفْرَدَة ج مُفْرَدَات Medicinal simple.

مُفَرِّد Secluded from the world.

مُفَرَّد Isolated, apart. Enriched with pearls (necklace).

مُتَفَرِّد ومُنْفَرِد Solitary. Separated.

✱ فَرْدَس To throw a. o. down violently on the ground.

فَرْدَسَة Width, broadness.

فِرْدَوْس ج فَرَادِيس Garden, fruitful valley. Paradise.

✱ فَرَز i فَرْزًا, وأَفْرَز ه To separate, to set a. th. apart. To divide a. th.

فَرَّز عَلَيَّ بِرَأْيِهِ He decided against me according to his opinion.

فَارَز ه To separate from (a partner).

أَفْرَز ه To come within the reach of (a hunter : game).

— ه ب To distinguish a. o. by a special gift.

اِفْتَرَز ه دُون أَهْل بَيْتِهِ He decided it without consulting his people.

فَرَوز To die (man).

فَرْز وإِفْرَاز Separation. Distinction.

فَرْز Plain between two hills.

فِرْز Path on a hill. Turn, time.

— أَفْرَاز وفُرُوز Share set apart for its owner.

فِرْزَة ج أَفْرَاز وفُرُوز Share, lot.

سِنّ الإِفْرَاز ✧ Age of discretion.

F إِفْرِيز ج أَفَارِيز Cornice, covering course of a wall.

فَارِز Clear, distinct (discourse).

فَارِزَة Road in the sands.

P فَرْوَز Fringe.

فَيْرُوز وفِيرُوز وفَيْرُوزَج Turquoise. A dye.

مُفَرْوَز Separated. Distinguished. Adorned with a fringe (cloth, garment).

✱ فَرْزَدَق ج فَرَازِق وفَرَازِد Piece of bread.

✱ فِرْزِع — فُرْزُعَة ج فَرَازِع Bundle, armful of fodder.

✱ فِرْزِل Fetters, shackles. Shears for cutting iron.

P فِرْزَان ج فَرَازِين Queen (in chess).

✧ فَرْزَن فِي To observe, to look at.

تَفَرْزَن To become queen (in chess : pawn).

✱ فَرَس i فَرْسًا, وافْتَرَس ه To break the neck, to crush, to kill (its prey : wild beast). To beat a. o. unmercifully.

— i بِالعَيْن فِرَاسَةً To be a good physiognomist; to perceive intuitively.

فَرُس o فَرَاسَةً وفُرُوسَةً وفُرُوسِيَّةً To be skilled in horsemanship or in any work.

فَرَّس ه To train (a rider). ✧ To encourage, to excite a. o.

— ه ه To expose (a sheep) to be devoured by wild beasts.

— ه ✧ To plaster a terrace with white clay.

أَفْرَس To have a goat seized by a wolf (inadvertent shepherd).

— الأَسَد حِمَارَهُ He let a lion devour his ass *i. e.* he made a sacrifice for escaping safe.

— عن To leave (a remainder of property) as a prey.

تَفَرَّس فِي To look steadfastly at.

— فِيهِ ه To discover, to perceive a. th. in a. o. from outward signs.

فُرْس The Persians. ✧ White clay for terraces.

بِلَاد الفُرْس وبِلَاد فَارِس Persia.

فَارِسِيّ Persian.

الفَارِسِيَّة The Persian language.

فِرْس The kali-plant.

(bird). To spread branches (tree). ✧ To come out from the cocoon (silkworm).
To be furnished with carpets (house). أفرَش
To backbite a. o. To fell a beast before slaughtering it. أفرَش ه
To flutter (bird). تفرّش
To tread upon. To spread out the arms on the ground To give unrestrained liberty to o.'s tongue. To take (a wife). To make little of. To follow the steps of a. o. إفترَش ه وه
To throw a. o. down on the ground — ه
Mat, carpet, mattress. Furniture. Field, plain. Corn-produce. Young camels. فَرْش ج فُرُوش
✧ Bed, mat, mattress. فَرْشة
He has a fine appearance. هو حسن الفِرْشة
Brush. Ts فُرْشَة وفُرْشاة وفُرْشاية
Bubbles on the surface of wine. Dry mud on the surface of the ground. ✧ Wheel of a mill. Moth, butterfly. Tire of (a wheel). فَرَاش
Bed, mat, carpet, mattress. Wife. فِرَاش ج فُرُش وأفرِشَة
✧ The catches of a wooden lock. فَرَاش قُفل
✧ Waiter. Upholsterer. فَرَّاش
Butterfly. Thin bone of the head. Iron-pin. Little water. Nimble, light (man). فَرَاشَة ج فَرَاش
Mare seven days after having brought forth. Creeping plant). فَرِيش ج فَرَائِش
Mat, carpet. مِفرَش ج مَفارِش
Housing, saddle-cloth. مِفرَشة ج مَفارِش
Spread like a carpet. Covered with carpets. Paved, spread. مَفرُوش
Spreading far away (corn-crops). مُفَرِّش
Without hump (camel). مُفَرَّش
To set the legs apart. ✶ فَرشح فَرشحة وفَرشحى
Broad plain. Tall and fat (woman, she-camel). Rainless cloud. فِرشاح
✧ Knave (at cards). ✧ فِرشاة

Horse, mare. فَرَس (m. f.) ج أفراس Name of various stars. Pegasus.
Race-horse. فرس الرِّهان
They are both like two race-horses i. e. they are on the same level. هُما كفَرَسَي الرِّهان
Hippopotamus. فرس البحر
▫ Mantis (insect). Grasshopper. فرس النبي
Mare. فَرَسة
Cold wind. Swelling, ulcer on the neck. فَرْسة
Horsemanship. ✧ Bravery. فَرَاسة وفُرُوسة وفُرُوسيّة
Diagnostics. Physiognomy. Penetration of mind; insight. فِراسة
Physigonomist صاحب فِراسة
Killed, devoured (prey). فَرِيس ج فَرْسَى
Prey seized by a wild beast; spoil. فَرِيسة ج فَرائِس
Rider, horseman. The lion. فارِس ج فُرسان وفَوارِس
More skilled in horsemanship. More penetrative. أفرَس
Pharisian. H فَرِّيسِيّ
Lion. أبو فِراس وفَرّاس
Overtaken by cold wind. Having the back broken; humpbacked. مفروس
Parasang (measure of three miles). Measure of time. P فَرسَخ ج فَراسِخ
Malum Persicum, peach. P فِرسِق وفِرسِك
Camel's or man's foot. ✶ فرسن — فِرسِن ج فَراسِن
The lion. الفُرَاسِن
Wild leek (*plant*). ▫ Eye-bright (plant). فَرَاسِيُون
Water-horehound (*plant*). فَرَاسِيُون الماء
Mother-wort (*plant*). فَرَاسِيُون القلب
To spread (a carpet, a bed); to furnish (a house). ✶ فَرَش o i فَرشًا وفِراشًا، وافترَش ه
To facilitate (an affair) for. فَرَش ه ه
To spread (a carpet) for a. o. — فَرَّش وأفرَش ه ه
To pave, to furnish (a house). To spread a carpet in (a room). فَرَّش و✧ أفرَش ه
To expand the wings, to flutter فَرَّش

To cut, to slit, to pierce a. th. ✶ فَرَضَ o فَرْضًا ه

To wound (a horse) on the cartilage-of the shoulder. ة —

To ornament (leather). فَرَّض ه

To alternate with a. o. in. فَارَض ة في

To offer itself to a. o. (opportunity). أَفْرَض ة

To use a. th. by turns. تَفَارَض ه

To seize (the opportunity). إِفْتَرَض ✧ اسْتَفْرَض ه

Opportunity, seasonable time. Turn, succession. ✧ Holyday. فُرْصَة ج فُرَص

It is thy turn to. جَاءَت فُرْصَتُكَ من

Acting by turns with. فَرِيص

Part of a horse between the shoulder and the ribs. فَرِيصَة ج فَرَائِص

Jugular vein. — ج فَرِيص

He trembled with fear. *lit* : his muscles quivered. إِرْتَعَدَت فَرِيصَتُهُ او فَرَائِصُهُ

مِفْرَص ج مَفَارِص, ومِفْرَاص ج مَفَارِيص

Punch, iron instrument for cutting.

Grape-stone. ✶ فِرْصِد و فِرْصَاد

Red dye. Mulberry-tree. فِرْصَاد

To notch (wood). ✶ فَرَض i فَرْضًا. وفَرَّض ه

To suppose that, to make an hypothesis. فَرَض ه وأن

To impose laws to a. o. (God). To prescribe a. th. to a. o. (man). — وأَفْرَض وافْتَرَض ه على

To assign (the rate of a tax, of a pension) to a. o. To present a. o. with a. th. To give an appointment to a. o. — وأَفْرَض ه ل

To be old (animal). To be wide. فَرَض i وفَرُض o فُرُوضًا وفَرَاضَة

To know Divine law. To become skilled in the law of inheritance. فَرُض o فَرَاضَة

To digest divine precepts. To explain points of law clearly. فَرَّض ه

To receive their pay (soldiers). To dwindle away, to be destroyed (tribe, family). ✧ To suppose, to make an hypothesis. إِفْتَرَض

Notch, incision. فَرْض ج فِرَاض

Precept, divine law. Ordinance. Duty. Share of an inheritance. Fees, soldier's pay. فَرْض ج فُرُوض

✧ Breviary, divine office. كِتَاب ٱلفَرْض

Notch at the extremity of a bow. Opening in a wall. Sea-port. Gap in the bank of a river. Cavity of an inkstand. Piece of wood in which the pin of a door turns. فُرْضَة ج فُرَض و فِرَاض

Mouth of (a river). Garment, clothing. فِرَاض

Bulky, thick. فَارِض ج فُرَّض

Skilled in divine law, in the science of inheritance. — وفَرِيض وفَرَضِيّ

✧ Supposition, hypothesis. إِفْتِرَاض

Divine precept, ordinance of God. فَرِيضَة ج فَرَائِض

Part of jurisprudence treating of inheritance. عِلم الفَرَائِض

Punch, intstrument for notching. مِفْرَض ومِفْرَاض

Notched. Prescribed, imposed. Granted, supposed. مَفْرُوض

By-rules, statutes. مَفْرُوضَات

To precede (people). ✶ فَرَط o فُرُوطًا ة

✧ To shake off (nuts) from a tree. ه —

To precede a. o. to the water in order to prepare the buckets. — o فَرْطًا i وفَرَاطَة ة

To neglect, to be remiss in. — o فَرْطًا في وفَرَّط ه وفي

He hastened to speak before him. فَرَط عَلَيهِ في القَول

To escape, to be said, done hastily, unintentionally (word, action). فَرَط من

To overcome a. o. — فُلَانًا

To despatch a messenger to. وفَرَّط ة إلى وأَفْرَط

He lost a child in infancy. فَرَط وافْتَرَط وَلَدًا

To praise or censure a. o. to excess. To forsake a. o. To precede a. o. فَرَّط ة

To disperse, to dispel a. th. ه —

To avert (a misfortune) from a. o. (God). — ه عن

To ascend (a mountain). To go down (a valley). ✱ فَرَعَ a فَرْعًا ه
To overtop, to surpass a. o. in tallness or rank. a – فَرْعًا وفُرُوعًا ه
To conciliate (people). – بَيْنَ
To check (a horse) with (the bridle). – ه ب
To have abundant hair. فَرِعَ a فَرَعًا
To slaughter a firstling. فَرَّعَ وأَفْرَعَ
To go down (a valley). فَرَّعَ ه وفي
To deduce (a consequence) from (a principle). – ه من
✧ To send forth sprouts, boughs. To divide, to allot. – وأَفْرَعَ
To go down (a mountain). أَفْرَعَ في ومن
To alight at a o.'s house. – ب
To take care of a. o To wound (a horse's mouth : bit). – ه
To assail (a flock : wild beast). – ه
To explore (a country).
To begin (a narrative). To undertake (a journey). – وإِسْتَفْرَعَ ه
To branch off (tree). تَفَرَّعَ
To derive from (a principle : consequence). – من
To marry the chief woman of a tribe. تَفَرَّعَ القَوْمَ او في بَنِي فُلَان
To deflour (a virgin). إِفْتَرَعَ
Summit, upper part. Branch, bough, sprout. Woman's hair. Consequence of a principle. فَرْع ج فُرُوع
Chief of a tribe. – القَوْم
The principles and the consequences. الأُصُول والفُرُوع
Ravine. فَرْع ج فِرَاع
Firstling, first-born camel. Distribution. Lice. فَرَع ج فُرْع
Summit of a mountain. فَرْعَة ج فِرَاع
Vamp, upper-leather of a shoe. فَرْعَة و✧ فَرَعَة
Deduced, derived. فَرْعِيّ
Development. Ramification. ✧ Distribution, allotment. تَفْرِيع
Axe, hatchet. فَرَّاعَة
Lofty (mountain). Comely. Vile. فَارِع
Life-guard. – ج فَرَعَة
Summit of a mountain فَارِعَة ج فَوَارِع

To encounter, to outpass a. o. فَارَطَ مُفَارَطَةً وفِرَاطًا ه
To hurry, to hasten in a. th. أَفْرَطَ ب
He drew his sword. – بِيَدِهِ إِلى سَيْفِهِ
To transgress. To exceed the bounds in. – في
To overfill (a basin). To forget; to leave off a. th. – ه
To overburden a. o. – على
To outrun the others (horse). تَفَرَّطَ ه
To vie in speediness with. To hurry. To come too late (affair). تَفَارَطَ
To overwhelm a. o. suddenly (grief). – ه
To be dissolved. ✧ To be beaten down (fruit). إِنْفَرَطَ
His benefits shall not be lost لا يُفْتَرَطُ إِحْسَانُهُ
Excess, exaggeration. Neglect. Missed opportunity. Space of time. Way-mark. فَرْط
Beware not to be remiss in it! إِيَّاكَ والفَرْطَ في
I went to him after a delay of few days. أَتَيْتُهُ فَرْطًا
I went to him one day after. أَتَيْتُهُ فَرْطَ يَوْمٍ
Hill, summit of a hill. فَرْط ج أَفْرُط وأَفْرَاط
First gleam of dawn. أَفْرَاط الصَّبَاحِ
✧ Small money. فَرْط وفُرَاطَة
Arriving first. (s. pl.) فَرَط
Injustice. Excess. Horse outstripping the others. فُرُط
Affair given up. أَمْرٌ فُرُطٌ
Precedence in a race. فَرْطَة وفُرْطَة
Journey. فُرْطَة في البِلَاد
Exaggeration, excess. إِفْرَاط
Neglect. ✧ Prodigality. تَفْرِيط
✧ Cheapness of an article. Cheap. فِرْط
Arriving first. Lost (goods). Uttered hastily (word). فَارِط ج فُرَّاط
Spendthrift, squanderer. ✧ فِرِّيط
Exceeding the bounds. Excessive, exaggerate. مُفْرِط
Forsaken, given up. Overflowing (tank). مُفْرَط
To widen a. th. ✱ فَرْطَحَ ه
◘ Storm, tempest. I فَرْطُونَة

Thick-haired أفرَغ م فَرْعَاء ج فُرْع وفَرْعَان (man).
Peace-maker. مِفْرَع ج مَفارِع
Broad-shouldered. مُفرِع الكَتِف
To be proud, tyrannical. ✲ فَرْعَن
Pharaoh, name of the فِرْعَون ج فَرَاعِنَة ancient kings of Egypt. Proud, unbelieving man, tyrant. Crocodile.
To be ✲ فَرَغ o a وفَرِغ فُرُوغًا وفَرَاغًا empty, unoccupied (place).
To be unemployed. To be — من الشيء free from work. To finish a. th.
To apply o.'s self entirely — لـ وإلى to; to intend doing a. th.
To die. — فُرُوغًا
To be poured forth (water). فَرِغ a فَرَغًا
To walk at an easy pace فَرُغ o فَرَاغَة (beast). To produce a large wound (blow). To be anxious.
To empty (a place, a vessel). فَرَّغ ه To pour (a liquid).
To give to a. o. leisure to. — ه ل
To shed (water, blood). To أفْرَغ ه cast (metal) in a mould.
To pour, to empty a. th. أفْرَغ ه على upon.
To infuse patience. — عَلَى فُلَانٍ الصَّبْرَ to a. o. (God).
To be free from work. تَفَرَّغ
To busy o.'s self exclusively — لـ about.
To pour (water) upon o.'s self. إفْتَرَغ ه
To vomit. إسْتَفْرَغ
To exhaust (a vessel). — ه
To exhaust o.'s — جُهْدَهُ ومَجْهُودَهُ ل self in endeavours for.
Mouth of a فَرْغ ج فُرُوغ, و فِرَاغ ج أفْرِغَة bucket, of a jug.
Large vessel, udder. فِرَاغ ج أفْرِغَة
Free time, leisure; holyday. فِرْغ وفَرَاغ
Privy. ✧ بَيْت الفَرَاغ
His blood has been ذَهَب دَمُهُ فَرْغًا وفِرْغًا shed to no purpose.
Broad and flat (land). فَرِيغ ج فِرَاغ Wide-stepping (horse). Broad (way). Sharp (tongue, knife).
Large water-skin. Wide (wound). فَرِيغَة
Gemini (constellation). فُرُوغ
Casting of metals. إفْرَاغ

Vomit. إسْتِفْرَاغ
Empty, void. Free فَرِغ, وفَارِغ ج فُرَّاغ from employment. Workless.
Opening a large wound أفْرَغ م فَرْغَاء (spear).
Metal-founder. مُفْرِغ
Molten (metal). مُفْرَّغ ومُفْرَغ
The pneumatic machine. الآلَة المُفَرِّغَة
Running briskly (horse). مُسْتَفْرِغ
✧ To open (plant, heart). ✲ فَرْفَح
Garden فَرْفَخ وفَرْفَخَة و ✧ فَرْفَحِين P purslane.
To separate, to ✲ فَرَق o i فَرْقًا وفُرْقَانًا ه make a distinction, to set apart a. th. To decide a. th. To explain a. th. distinctly.
To distinguish (truth) from فَرَق بَيْن (falsehood).
To part (the hair). — ه فَرْقًا
To branch off (road). فَرَق o فُرُوقًا
To be obvious, clear to a. o. — لِفُلَان (affair).
To give a soup to a — وأفْرَق ه woman after childbirth.
The she-camel went apart فَرَّقَت النَّاقَة for bringing forth.
To fear, to be frightened. فَرِق a فَرَقًا To plunge in the waves.
To share, to فَرَّق تَفْرِيقًا وتَفْرِقَة ه distribute. To give away a. th. in parts. To disorder, to confuse (an affair). To pour out (words).
To frighten a. o. — ه
To separate, to divide a. th. فَرَّق مَا بَيْن between.
To forsake, to فَارَق مُفَارَقَة و فِرَاقًا ه abandon a. o. ✧ To be freshly dead.
To recover from small-pox. أفْرَق من
To frighten a. o. To let (camels) ه — pasture by themselves. To neglect (flocks).
To be disordered تَفَرَّق تَفَرُّقًا وتِفِرَّاقًا (business). To be at variance. To scatter (company). To branch off (tree).
To separate, to إنْفَرَق وتَفَارَق وافْتَرَق disperse away.
Separation. Difference. Parting فَرْق of the hair. Cock's crest. Flax.

Synonym. فَرْق ج فُرُوق
Measure used in Medina. فَرَق ج فُرْقَان, وفَرَق ج أَفْرَاق
Parting of the hair, of the beard, of the teeth. فَرْق
First gleam of dawn. فَرَق (for فَلَق) وفُرْقَان
Flock of sheep. Portion. Party of boys. Mountain. Wave. فِرْق
Distinction between good and evil. Any sacred book; the Koran. فُرْق وفُرْقَان
Sect, body, party of men. Military, naval division. فِرْقَة ج فِرَق
Separation (of friends). فُرْقَة وفَرَاق و فِرَاق وافْتِرَاق ومُفَارَقَة
Faint-hearted. فَرِق م فَرِقَة, وفَرِق م فَرِقَة, وفَارُوق وفَرُوق وفَرُّوق
Cowardly (man, woman). (*m. f.*) فَارُوقَة وفَرُوقَة وفَرُّوقَة
Distribution. تَفْرِيق وتَفْرِقَة
Retail: in parts. بِالتَّفْرِيق
Large party of men. Part. Company. ✧ General in chief, Major-general. فَرِيق ج أَفْرِقَاء وأَفْرِقَة وفُرُوق
Soup of dates, rice and milk. Stray ewe. فَرِيقَة
Having parted teeth, hair, or a parted beard. White cock. أَفْرَق م فَرْقَاء ج فُرْق
Separation, division. إِفْتِرَاق
Separating, distinguishing. Isolated (cloud). فَارِق ج فُرَّاق
Going apart for bringing forth (she-camel). – ج فُرَّق وفُرُق ج فَوَارِق
Surname of the Caliph Omar. الفَارُوق
Africa. G أَفْرِيقِيَة
Branching of a road. Parting of the hair. مَفْرِق ج مَفَارِق
✲ Two stars near the pole. الفَرْقَد مث الفَرْقَدَان ج الفَرَاقِد
✲ To run at full speed. ✧ To burst, to explode. فَرْقَع
To crack (the fingers). – ه
To crack (joints). تَفَرْقَع
Cracking of the fingers. ✧ Explosion. فَرْقَعَة
▫ Whip of cords. فِرْقِلَّة
✲ To pick out, to husk (grain, corn) between the fingers. To rub a. th. with the hand. ✧ To rub (the body). فَرَك o فَرْكًا, وفَرَّك ه
To hate o. a. (husband and wife). فَرِك وفَرُك a فِرْكًا وفُرُوكًا وفِرِكَّانًا ه
To be flaccid (ear). فَرِك a فَرَكًا
To forsake, to abandon a. o. فَارَك ه
To be easily shelled (corn). To begin to ripen. أَفْرَك
To falter in speech; to stumble. To commit a mistake in speech. تَفَرَّك
To be rubbed betwen the fingers. To be shelled, husked (ear of corn). – وانْفَرَك
To become hard and full (grain). إِسْتَفْرَك
Conjugal hatred. فِرْك
Easy to be shelled (nut) فَرِك
Flaccid (ear). فَرِكَة وفَرْكَاء
Hating her husband (woman). فَارِك وفَرُوك
Wheat cooked with butter. فَرِيك
Easily shelled, husked. – م فَرِيكَة
✧ Turnscrew. مِفْرَك ج مَفَارِك
Hated, loathed. مُفَرَّك
To make a. o. to stumble, to totter. To entangle, to perplex. ✧ فَرْكَش ه
To stumble, to totter; to be entangled. ✧ تَفَرْكَش
To mince, to chop (tobacco). ✧ فَرَم i فَرْمًا, وفَرَّم ه
To shed his teeth (child). ✧ فَرَّم أَسْنَانَهُ
To be chopped, minced. ✧ تَفَرَّم
Piece of meat, of cheese. فَرْمَة
✧ Diplome, patent, decree, firman. P فَرْمَان ج فَرَامِين
Chopper of tobacco. ✧ فَرَّام
Shedding his teeth (child); toothless. أَفْرَم
Oven. ✲ فُرْن ج أَفْرَان
Baker. ✧ فَرَّان
Round cake. Baker. فُرْنِيّ
Baking woman. فَارِنَة
Rat. ✲ فِرْنِب
Franks. Europeans. P إِفْرَنْج وإِفْرَنْجَة
Frank, European. – فِرَنْجِيّ وإِفْرَنْجِيّ
To assume the manners of Europeans. ✧ تَفَرْنَج
Sword of fine work- P فِرِنْد ج فَرَانِد

To be astonished, amazed. فَرِيَ a فَرًى
To blame a. o. To repair a. th. To open (a vein). أَفْرَى ه وه
To be cut, rent (garment). To burst forth (water-spring). تَفَرَّى وانفرى
The night was over. تَفَرَّى اللَّيلُ
To forge (a lie) against. إِفْتَرَى ه على
✧ To calumniate a. o. — ب وعلى
Bustle, confusion. فَرِيَّة
Lie, imposture. فِرْيَة ج فِرًى
Lie. ✧ Hostility. إِفْتِرَاء
Wonderful, remarkable thing. Large (bucket). فَرِيّ م فَرِيَّة
✱ To be scared away from her retreat (gazelle). فَزَّ o فَزًّا
To turn away from. — عن
To startle, to frighten a. o. away. — ه عن
To suppurate (wound). — i فَزِيزًا
To ooze (sweat, water).
To be startled, excited. — i فَزَازَة وفُزُوزَة
✧ To leap.
To scare, to frighten a. o. away. ◻ To provoke a. o. أَفَزَّ واستفزّ ه
To come to fight. تَفَازَّ
To disturb, to startle a. o. (fear, joy). إِستفزّ ه
Young one of the antelope. Fearful. Active (man). فَزّ ج أَفْزَاز
Leap, bound, startle from fear. فَزَّة
✱ To rend (a garment). To split a. th. فَزَر o فَزْرًا ه
To strike a. o. upon the back with (a stick). — ه ب
To burst (a skin) open. ✧ To rip up (an animal). فَزَر وفَزَّر ه وه
To be rent (clothes). — o فُزُورًا
To have a hump on the back or chest. فَزِر a فَزَرًا
To be rent (garment). To be burst (skin). ✧ To be ripped up (beast). تَفَزَّر وانفزر
Small flock of sheep. Kid. Root, origin. فِزْر
Slits, rents. فِزَر
Hump on the chest or back. Broad way. فُزْرَة ج فُزَر
Hump-backed or أَفْزَر م فَزْرَاء ج فُزْر

manship. Red rose. Silk-cloth. Pomegranate seed.
✱ فِرْنَاس ج فَرَانِسَة Brave. Chief of a village. Lion.
فَرْنَسَة المَرْأَة Good management of a housewife.
فَرَنْسا France.
فَرَنْسِيّ و✧ فَرَنْسَوِيّ وفَرَنْسَاوِيّ و◻ فِرَنْسِيس French, Frenchman.
✱ فرنق — تَفَرْنَق To become bad, corrupt. To be erect (camel's ear).
فُرَانِق Guide of an army, messenger. Jackal, lion's provider.
✱ فَرِه a فَرَهًا To be lively, fiery (horse).
فَرُه o فَرَهَة وفَرَاهِيَة وفُرُوهَة To be skilful, clever (man).
أَفْرَه To take a lively, a comely slave. To bring forth fine children (woman).
إِستفره ه To seek for fiery horses.
فَرِه ج فَرِهُون م فَرِهَة, وفَارِه م فَارِهَة, وأَفْرَه م فَرْهَاء ج فُرْه Clever, skilful; nimble, lively, joyful (man).
فَارِه ج فُرَّه وفَرَهَة وفُرْه وفُرْهَة Brisk (ass, mule). Beautiful (youth, girl).
فَرَاهَة وفَرَاهِيَة وفُرُوهَة Liveliness. Skilfulness. Beauty.
✱ فَرْهَد To become fat (boy).
◻ فَرْهَد ه To confound; to jade a. o.
فُرْهُد Fat, plump (youth). Lion's cub.
✱ فرا — فَرَى ه To fur, to line (a gown) with fur.
إِفْتَرَى ه To put on a fur.
فَرْو وفَرْوَة ج فِرَاء Fur, furred garment.
فَرْوَة Skin of the head. Garment of camel-hair. King's crown. Abundance.
◻ أَبُو فَرْوَة The chestnut.
◻ فَرْوِيَّة Fur.
فَرَّاء Furrier.
مُفَرَّاة Furred (gown), pelisse.
✱ فَرَى i فَرْيًا ه على To forge (a lie) against a. o.
— ه To go over a country.
فَرَى الفَرِيَّ He has accomplished a feat.
— وفَرَّى وأَفْرَى ه To slit to cut out or to rip off (a skin).

To deliver to a. o. (a safe-conduct). — ل في

To make room for a. o. — وفسّح وافسح وتفسّح ل

To be wide, broad (place). فَسُح o فَسَاحَة, وأفسح

To enlarge (a place). فسّح ه

✧ To dispense a. o. with an ecclesiastical law. فسّح ل

To be enlarged, broad (place). ✧ To stroll about; to enjoy o.'s self. تفسّح وانفسح

To take o.'s ease in (a place). تفسّح وتفاسح في

To be at ease; to divert o.'s self. إنفسح

Enlarging. Safe-conduct. ✧ Dispensation. فسح

Broad-breasted. فُسُح وفُسْحُم

Open space, square. ✧ Holyday, respite. Dispensation from fasting. فُسْحَة ج فُسَح

Ample scope. — وفَسَاحَة

Roomy, broad (place). فَسِيح وفُسَاح وفُسُح وفُسْحُم

Width of the steps. فَيْسَحَى

✡ To disjoin, to dissunder a. th. To annul (a deed). To abrogate (a law). To rescind a bargain). To corrupt (an opinion). To dislocate (the hand). فسخ a فسخا, وفسّخ ه

To be weak in body and mind. فسخ a فسخا

To be corrupt (advice). ✧ To be corrupted, spoiled. — وفسخ a فسخا

✧ To be corrupted, altered. To be cracked, split, full of crevices. فسّخ

To annul (a deed, a compact) by mutual consent. فاسخ ه ه وتفاسخ ه

To forget a. th. أفسخ ه

To be disjointed, dislocated, dissundered. To fall off (hair of a corpse). ✧ To be full of crevices, cracked. تفسّخ

To be spoiled, disordered. To be annulled (compact). إنفسخ

Disjunction, separation. Abrogation. Annulling, abolition. Weakness in body, in mind. فسخ

hump-breasted. Fleshy woman.

Wide road. Blackish ant. فازر

Way in the sand. فازرة

Panther. فزارة

✡ To fear, to be frightened at. فزع a فزعا وفزعا, وفزع a فزعا من

To seek refuge in fear towards a. o. فزع إلى ومن

To succour a. o. — وأفزع ه

◘ To attack, to rush against. فزع على

To frighten a. o. فزّع وأفزع ه

He has been delivered from fear. فُزّع عن فلان

To awake a. o. from sleep. أفزع ه من النوم

To dispel fear from a. o. — عن فلان

Fear, fright. Succour given in distress. فزع ج أفزاع

Dreaded, feared. فُزْعَة

Very cowardly. فُزَعَة و✧ فزيع

Fearful, timid. فازع ج فزعة, وفزع ومُفازع

Frightening. فزّاعة

Refuge, shelter. مفزع ومفزعة

Gallant. Coward. مُفزّع

Red Turkish cap. فَس TE

✡ Bug. فَسّ – فسفس وفسفاس ج فسافس

✧ Small pustule. فسفوسة ج فسافيس

✧ Mosaic-work. فُسَيْفِسَاء وفُسَيْفِسَة

✡ To slit, to rent a. th. فسأ a فسأ, وفسّأ تفسئة وتفسيئا ه

To strike a. o. on the back with (a stick). فسأ وتفسّأ ه

To turn a. o. away from. فسأ ه عن

To have a prominent chest. فسِئ a فسأ

To be rent, slit. تفسّأ

To spread out (disease). — في وبين

Hollow-backed and hump-breasted. أفسأ

Pistachio. Pistachio-tree. فُسْتُق وفُسْتَق و✧ فِسْتُق P

Of a pistachio-colour (garment). فستقي

✧ Basin with an ornamental water-spout. فسقية

Ts فستن – فُسْتَان ج فساتين وفسطان

Woman's dress, petticoat.

✡ To part the legs. فسج – فسّج

He turned away from me. أفسج عني

✡ To make long strides. فسح a فسحا

Weak in body and mind. فسح وفسخة
Portion, share, bit. فسخة
Unable to manage his business. فسيح
▫ Small dried fishes.
▫ Sardines, herrings, salt-fish. فسيح فرنجي
Dissundering, abolishing. Void (contract). ✧ Faded (garment). فاسح
✲ To be corrupt, vicious, disordered. فسد o i وفسد o فسادًا وفسودًا
To corrupt, to mar a. th. To pervert. to deprave a. o. فسّد وأفسد ه وه
He ill-treated his people. فاسد رهطه
To rouse (a country) against. أفسد ه على
To set people at variance. – بين
✧ To misrepresent, to traduce a. o. – على
To do mischief between. أفسد واستفسد في
To be at variance, to disagree. تفاسد
✧ To be corrupted, altered. إنفسد
To ill-treat and provoke a. o. استفسد ه
To endeavour to mar a. th. – ه
✧ Instigation to discord. فسد
Corruption, mischief, disturbance. Dissension. Damage. ✧ Discord. فساد
Instigation to rebellion, to disorder. إفساد
Corrupt. wicked. Worthless, vicious. فاسد وفسيد ج فسدى
Seducer, mischief-maker. مفسد
Mischief-maker. مفسد و✧ فسدي
Cause of corruption, mischief. مفسدة ج مفاسد
✲ To disclose (a. th. hidden). To explain a. th. clearly. فسر o i فسرًا, وفسّر ه
To examine the urine of a sick person (physician). فسر o i فسرًا وتفسرة
To explain, to comment (a text). فسّر ه
To ask from a. o. the explanation of a text. تفسّر واستفسر ه عن
Explanation, commentary, glose. تفسير ج تفاسير
Urine of a sick person. تفسرة
✲ فسط – فسّاط و فسطاط ج فساطيط
Large tent of coarse cloth.

Camp, city; meeting-place of a tribe. Name of old Cairo. فسطاط ج فساطيط
✲ To go astray from justice. To transgress divine commandments. To live in profligacy, disorder. To become ungodly, wicked. profligate. فسق i o وفسق o فسقًا وفسوقًا
To commit lewdness, crime against nature with. فسق ب
To come out from its skin (ripe date). – وانفسق
To pervert, to corrupt a. o. To declare a. o. to be an unbeliever, sinful (judge). فسّق ه
Prevarication. Disobedience. Immoral life. فسق وفسوق
L Fountain, jet-d'eau. فسقية ج فسقيات
Libertine, trangressor, sinful. فاسق ج فسقة وفسّاق وفاسقون
Scoundrel. rascal. adulterer. فسق وفسّاق وفسّيق
O wicked woman! O adulteress! يا فساق
✧ Tick, insect. فاسوق
Way of wearing a turban. فاسقية
Mouse. فويسقة
✲ To make little of a. o. فسكل ه
Last in a race (horse). Vile, mean. فسكل
✲ To be vile, inferior, of low origin. فسل a وفسل o فسالة وفسولة, وفسيل
To wean (a child). فسل o فسلًا ه
To adulterate (money), to declare (coins) to be adulterated. To declare (goods) to be of bad quality. فسّل وأفسل ه
To cut and plant the offset of a palm-tree. أفسل ه
Rubbish. Filings of iron. فسالة
فسل ج فسلاء وأفسال وفسول وفسولة وفسال
Base, ignoble, low. Base (coin). Vine-cuttings for planting. وفسل
Foolish. فسل
I ✧ French beans. فسوليه
Offset of a palm-tree. فسيلة ج فسيل وفسائل وجج فسلان
P ▫ Exorcism. أفسون
✲ To emit a noiseless wind. فسا o فسوًا وفساء

Noiseless wind, flatulence. فُسَاء
Truffles. فَسَوَات الضِّبَاع
Black-beetle. فَاسِيَة وفَاسِيَاء ج فَوَاسٍ
✲ فَشَّ o فَشًّا To belch. To pilfer. To boast vainly. ✧ To subside (wound).
— ه To open a door (without key). To squeeze out the air from (a water-skin).
— ه فَشَّ الوَطْبَ To cool (an angry man). To exhaust (the udder of a she-camel).
— بَيْنَ To scatter slanders amongst.
✧ فَشَّ خُلْقَهُ He gave vent to anger.
إِنْفَشَّ To come forth from a skin (wind). To be reduced (swelling).
— عن To be remiss in a. th.
فَشٌّ Subsiding of a wound. Carob-tree.
— وفَشُوش Coarse garment.
فَشَّاش Pickpocket, opening doors without keys.
فَاشُوش Weak-minded, irresolute.
✲ فَشْفَشَ To be weak-minded. To lie much. ✧ To grumble.
✲ فَشَا a فَشْوًا To boast.
تَفَشَّا ب وفي To spread amongst (people : disease).
✲ فَشَجَ i فَشْجًا, وفَشَّجَ To open the legs, to keep them apart.
تَفَشَّجَ To sit with parted legs.
✧ فَشَحَ a فَشْحًا To stray from the right path. To part the legs. ✧ To apostatise.
✲ فَشَخَ a فَشْخًا ه To treat a. o. wrongfully. ◘ To open the legs.
— في اللعِب To cheat at play.
— وفَشَّخَ To be wearied. ✧ To make wide strides.
— على ✧ To stride over a. o.
فَشْخَة ✧ Step, stride.
✧ فَشَرَ o وفَشَّرَ To dot. To boast vainly.
✧ فَشَار Humbug. Dotage. Idle boast.
✧ فَشَّار Boaster, humbug, braggart.
فَاشِرَى Bryony (plant).
✲ فَشَطَ — ✧ فَشَطَ o فَشْطًا To boast vainly.
إِنْفَشَطَ To split, to crack (damp wood).
✧ فَشَّاط Humbugger, boaster,
✲ فَشَغَ a فَشْغًا To be dried up at the top (maize).
✲ فَشَغَ a فَشْغًا, وفَشَّغَ ه To cover a. th.
فَشَغَ وأَفْشَغَ ه ب To assail a. o. with (a whip).
فَشَّغَ ه To overcome a. o. (sleep).
فَاشَغَ بَيْنَ وفُوشِغَ بِالنَّاقَةِ To accustom a she-camel to a young that is not her own.
أَفْشَغَ To be worthless, good for nothing.
تَفَشَّغَ To be slow, slothful. To wear a coarse garment.
— في To cover the head (hoary hair). To pervade the body (blood).
— ه وفي To glide in and conceal o.'s self amongst the tents.
إِنْفَشَغَ To appear, to increase.
فَشْغَة Convolvulus. Interior substance of a reed.
فَاشِغَة وفَشْغَاء Hanging down on the forehead (forelock).
فُشَاغ وفَشَّاغ Smilax, sarsaparilla (medicinal plant).
فِشَاغ Sloth, sluggishness.
أَفْشَغ Having the teeth disparted Having irregular horns (ram).
مِفْشَغ Checking a horse. Thwarting.
✧ فِشْك Dung of horses.
TE فَشَكَة وفَشَنْك ج فَشَك Cartridge, rocket, fusee.
بَيْت الفَشَك Cartridge-box.
✲ فَشِلَ a فَشَلًا To become cowardly, remiss, weak.
— وانْفَشَلَ ✧ To fall short of.
فَشَّلَ وأَفْشَلَ ه ✧ To frustrate a. o. To confound a. o.
فَشَّلَ وأَفْشَلَ وتَفَشَّلَ وافْتَشَلَ To put a curtain to her litter (woman).
تَفَشَّلَ To flow (water). To marry (man).
فَشَل Sluggishness, remissness. ✧ Disappointment, failing.
فَشِل ج فُشْل وأَفْشَال, وفَشِيل وفَشِيل Remiss, cowardly, apathetic.
فِشْل ج فُشُول, ومِفْشَل ج مَفَاشِل Curtain on a camel-vehicle.
أَفْشَل م فَشْلَاء ج فُشْل ✧ Left-handed.
أَليَد الفَشْلَاء ✧ Left hand.
P مِفْشَلَة Gizzard of a bird.

To scatter, to run away. تَفَصْفَص
Green, fresh clover. فِصْفِصَة ج فَصَافِص
Brisk, energetic (man). فُصَافِص
The lion. الفُصَافِصَة
To appear in all its splendour (dawn). ✱ فَصَح a فَصْحًا ه
To be pure, without froth (milk). فَصُح o فَصَاحَةً, وفَصُح وأَفْصَح
To use good, clear language. To be eloquent. فَصُح o فَصَاحَةً, وأَفْصَح
To appear (dawn). To be clear, evident. To yield pure milk (ewe). To celebrate the feast of Easter. أَفْصَح
To be delivered from. — مِن
He manifested his desire. — عن مُرَادِهِ
To speak clearly, eloquently. تَفَصَّح
He made a show of eloquence. — وتَفَاصَح في كَلَامِهِ
Pure, without froth (milk). فَصْح وفَصِيح
Easter-tide. Easter. Passover. فِصْح
Easter, paschal (time). فِصْحِيّ
Eloquence. Chasteness of speech. فَصَاحَة
Chaste in speech, eloquent (man). فَصْح, وفَصِيح ج فُصَحَاء وفِصَاح وفُصُح
Clear, evident, cloudless (day). مُفْصِح
To take no heed of. ✱ فَصَخ a فَصْخًا عن
To luxate (the hand). — ه
Weak-minded. فَصِيخ وفَصِيخَة وفَاصِخَة
To bleed a. o. (surgeon). ✱ فَصَد i فَصْدًا وفِصَادًا ه
To cut (a vein) open. — وافْتَصَد ه
To moisten a. th. for softening it. فَصَّد ه
To open its gems (tree). أَفْصَد وانْفَصَد
To flow (blood). تَفَصَّد وانْفَصَد
Drawing of blood, bleeding. فَصْد وفِصَاد
Dates mixed with blood. فُصْدَة وفَصِيدَة
Bleeding. ✧ فِصَادَة ج فَصَائِد
Wagtail (bird). ◻ أَبُو فِصَادَة
Bleeder, phlebotomist. فَصَّاد
Kind of black-pudding. فَصِيد
Bled. فَصِيد م فَصِيدَة, ومَفْصُود م مَفْصُودَة
Crevice, fissure, split. تَفْصِيد
Lancet. مِفْصَد
To squeeze (dates) out of their skin. To pull out, to take off a. th. ✱ فَصَع a فَصْعًا ه
To give a. th. to a. o. — وفَصَّع ب ل
To force a. th. out from. فَصَّع ه مِن

✧ Prayer (in the Greek liturgy). ◻ أَفْشِين ج افَاشِين
✱ To spread (news). To be disclosed (secret). To become known (fame). To scatter in a pasturage (cattle). ✱ فَشَا o فَشْوًا وفُشُوًّا وفُشِيًّا
He knew not how to manage his affairs *lit* : his property became too extensive. فَشَت عَلَيهِ الضَّيعَة
To have numerous flocks. أَفْشَى
To spread (news). To divulge (a secret). — ه
To become wide (ulcer); to spread (ink). تَفَشَّى
To spread out amongst (disease). — ه وب
Revelation of a secret. Spreading of news, of a disease. إِفْشَاء
Increase in cattle. فَشَاء
Swoon. فَشْيَان
Spreading (evil, secret). فَاشٍ
Scattered flock. فَاشِيَة ج فَوَاشٍ
To pull out a. th. from. ✱ فَصَّ i فَصًّا, وافْتَصَّ ه مِن
To suppurate (wound). To weep slightly (child). To produce a noise (locust). — i فَصِيصًا
Nothing remained in my hand therefrom. ما فَصَّ في يَدِي مِنهُ شَيْءٌ
He glared at. فَصَّص بِعَيْنَيهِ
To set a gem in (a ring). — ه
He gave him part of his due. أَفَصَّ إِلَيهِ شَيْئًا مِن حَقِّهِ
To get rid of, to part away from. إِنْفَصَّ مِن
To get a. th. from a. o. إِسْتَفَصَّ ه مِن
Stone of a ring. Joint of two bones. Pupil of the eye. Head of garlic. Origin, true state of a. th. ◻ Axle of a wheel. فِصّ وفَصّ ج فُصُوص وأَفُصّ
Trefoil, lucern. فَصَّة
Marsh-trefoil. فَصَّة المَاء
Seller, setter of ring-stones. فَصَّاص
Fruit-stone. فَصِيص
Set with (a gem). مُفَصَّص ب
To speak quickly. ✱ فَصْفَص الكَلَام
To bring (accurate news). To feed (a beast) with clover. ✧ To strip (a bone) from the flesh. — ه

To go out from. إنفصم من
He exacted his due from. إقتصم حقّهُ من
Having the head uncovered. فَصْمَان
Mouse. قَصْعَاء
To set apart, to separate a. th. ✲ فَصَل i فَصْلاً ه
To distinguish (a. th.) from (another). — ه عن
To set a limit between. — بَيْن
To settle questions (judge). — الخُصُومات
✧ To determine the price of (goods). — البِضَاعَة
To wean (a child). فَصَل i فِصَالاً , وافتَصَل ٥ عن الرَّضَاع
To sprout (vine). فَصَل o فُصُولاً
To go forth from (a country) — من
To intercalate (golden beads and pearls) in a necklace. To allot a. th. To cut out (a garment). To narrate a. th. with all its particulars. To analyse (speech). فَصَّل ه
To cut up (a sheep). — ٥
To break with, to dissolve society with a. o. ✧ To dismiss a. o. To make a bargain with a. o. فَاصَل ٥
To attain the time of being weaned (child). ✧ To depart from life (sick person). أفصَل
To be separated, divided, decided. ✧ To be dismissed (official). إنفَصَل
To part from, to abandon a. o. or a. th. — عن
To transplant (a palm-tree). ه إفتَصَل
Separation, disjunction. Joint of a limb. Chapter, section of (a book.) Decision, sentence. Season of (the year). Plague. ✧ Trick, question. فَصل ج فُصُول
The day of the last judgment. يَوم الفَصل
Offset of palm-tree. فَصلَة
The words أمَّا بَعدُ *following the preliminary compliments in a discourse.* فَصل الخِطَاب
Young camel. Wall of enclosure in front of the main wall of a city. فَصِيل ج فُصلان وفِصَال
Young camel weaned. Family, kinsfolk. Piece of meat. فَصِيلة ج فَصَائِل

They came with all their relatives. جاءوا بِفَصِيلَتِهِم
Weaning of a young one. فِصَال
Cut of (a garment). Particular of a narrative. تَفصِيل
In retail. With all particulars. بالتَّفصِيل
Piece of cloth cut out for a garment. Cut of a garment. تفصِيلَة ج تَفَاصِيل
Interested eulogist. Cutting (sword). فَصَّال
Separation, division. إنفِصَال
Decisive (sentence). فَاصِل
Line of demarcation. خَطّ فَاصِل
Set of beads alternating with pearls in a necklace. Rhyme of a verse; last word of rhyming prose. فَاصِلَة ج فَوَاصِل
Decisive sentence. Arbitration. Sharp-edged sword. Violent thrust of (a sword). فَيصَل ج فَيَاصِل
Judge, arbitrator. — وفَيصَلِيّ
Joint of a limb. مَفصِل ج مَفَاصِل
Arthritis, pain of the joints. وَجَع المَفَاصِل
Tongue. مِفصَل
Separated, disjoined. With full particulars. Strung with beads and pearls intercalated (necklace). Cut out (garment). مُفَصَّل
✧ Hinge. مُفَصَّلَة ج مُفَصَّلات
To crack (a vessel). To cut off, to sever a. th. ✲ فَصَم i فَصْماً ه
To be ruined (house). فُصِم
To abate (fever, rain). أفصَم
To depart from a. o. (fever). — عَنهُ
To be cracked. تَفَصَّم وانفَصَم
To be cut off, separated. إنفَصَم
Cracked; broken. فَصِيم وأفصَم ومَفصُوم
To separate a. th. from. ✲ فَصَى i فَصْياً ه مِن
To free a. o. or a. th. from. فَصَّى ٥ وه مِن وعَن
To separate from. فَاصَى ٥ وه
To cease (rain, heat). أفصَى عَن
The shooter has caught nothing. أفصَى الصَّائِدُ
To be cleared from, deprived of. أفصَى وتَفَصَّى وانفَصَى مِن

Raisin-seed. Date-stone. ـتْ
Mildness of weather. فَضْيَة
Mild day. يَوْم فَضْيَة أو فَضِيَة
Release, deliverance. فَضْيَة, وفَصِيَّة ج فَصَايَا
☆ فَضّ o فَضّاً ه To break (a seal). To deflour (a virgin). To shed (tears). To resolve (a difficulty). To bore (a pearl).
لَا يَفْضُض ٱللّٰهُ فَاكَ May God not break thy teeth!
— ه To dismiss, to clear (a crowd).
— ه على To share a. th. between.
فَضَّض ه To silver a. th.
تَفَضَّض وانفضّ To break up, to disperse (meeting).
إنفضّ To break up, to be scattered. To flow (tears).
إفتضّ ه To pour (water) little by little.
فَضّ Scattered people, things.
فَضَض وفِضَاض وفُضَاضَة وفَضِيض Particles, fragments.
فَضَض وفَضِيض Sprinkle of water in an ablution.
فِضَّة Silver. ✧ One para.
— وفَضَّة ج فِضَاض Rocky ground.
فِضِّي Of silver, silvery.
فَاضَّة ج فَوَاضّ Misfortune, calamity.
مِفْضَاض ومِفَضّ ومِفَضَّة Harrow.
☆ فَضْفَض To be ample (garment). To be easy (life).
فَضْفَاض Ample (coat of mail). Easy (life). Generous (man).
☆ فضج — تَفَضَّج وانفَضَج عَرَقاً To be moist with sweat.
فَضِيج Sweat.
☆ فَضَح a فَضْحاً ه To disgrace a. o. To make misdoings to be known. ✧ To dishonour (women).
— ه To resolve (a puzzle). To outshine (the stars: moon).
فَضَح وأفضح To appear (dawn).
فَضِح a فَضَحاً To be whitish (object).
فَاضَح ه وتَفَاضَح To disgrace, to revile o. a.
أفضح To bear ripening dates (palm-tree).
إنفضح وافتضح To be put to shame, disgraced. To be constuprated (woman).
إفتضح To be disclosed, revealed (shame).
فَضَح Disgraceful. Dawn.
أفضح م فَضْحاء ج فُضْح Whitish.
فَضَّاح Revealer of a secret. Defamer.
فُضُوح وفُضُوحَة وفَضَاحَة وفِضَاح Shame, disgrace.
فَضُوح Disgracing.
فَضِيح Covered with shame, disgraced, atrocious.
— في المال Bad manager of cattle.
فَضِيحَة ج فَضَائِح Shame, disgrace, ignominy. Shameful action.
مَفْضَحَة ج مَفَاضِح Shame. Shocking behaviour.
☆ فَضَخ a فَضْخاً, وافتضخ ه To break (a. th. hollow).
أفضخ To ripen (grapes).
إنفضخ To be broken, split.
فَضُوخ Intoxicating drink.
فَضِيخ Juice of grapes. Date-wine.
☆ فَضَل o وفَضِل a فَضْلًا To be redundant, in excess.
— ه To surpass a. o. in eminence.
فَضَّل ه على To hold a. o. to excel another in merit. To prefer a. th. or a. o. to.
فَاضَل مُفَاضَلَة وفِضَالًا ه To vie with a. o. in excellence.
أفضل في To exceed, to excel in a. th. To make profit in (trade).
— على To do good, to bestow a favour upon.
— على . . . في To surpass a. o. in.
— واستفضل مِن To leave a remainder of.
تَفَضَّل To wear a single garment.
تَفَضَّل على To judge o.'s self to be superior to. ✧ To grant a favour to, to honour a. o.
✧ تَفَضَّل Please come in. Take a seat. Help yourself.
تَفَاضَل To contend for superiority.
فَضْل ج فُضُول Excess, redundance, remainder. Excellence, superiority. Benefit, favour, grace. *Arith.* Rest of a subtraction.

Water flowing upon the surface of the earth. فِضَاء
Promiscuous mass, mixture. فَضًى وفَوْضَى
Mess, mixed food. طَعَام فَضًى
They are without chief. They are in anarchy. أَمْرُهُم فَضًى
I remained quite alone. بَقِيتُ فَضًى
Leisure, worklessness. ✧ فَضْوَة وفَضَاوَة وتَفَضٍّ
✧ Free, idle, workless. Empty (place). فَاضٍ م فَاضِيَة
To break a. th. ✲ فَطَأَ a فَطْأً ه
To grieve, to distress a. o. To throw down and strike a. o. — ه
To have a depressed back and a prominent chest. فَطِئَ a فَطَأً
To prostrate a. o. on the ground. فَاطَأَ بِهِ الأَرْضَ
To become ill-tempered, peevish. أَفْطَأَ
To lag behind a. o.; to retreat from. تَفَاطَأَ عن
Prominence of the chest and hollowness of the back. فَطْأَة وفَطَأ
Prominent in the chest. أَفْطَأ م فَطْآء ج فُطْء
To enlarge, to flatten a. th. ✲ فَطَحَ a فَطْحًا, وفَطَّحَ ه
To strike a. o. with (a stick). — ه ب
To be broad, flat (head, nose). فَطِحَ a فَطَحًا
Broad-headed, broad-nosed. Chameleon. أَفْطَح ومُفَطَّح
Prehistoric age. Time of plenty. Bulky, stout. ✲ فِطَحْل
✧ Scholars; heroes. فَطَاحِل
To cleave, to split a. th. To find out, to begin a. th. To create a. th. (God). ✲ فَطَرَ o فَطْرًا ه
To bake unleavened bread. — العَجِين
To milk a ewe with the thumb and forefinger. — ه
To breakfast, to break the fast. — فِطْرًا وفُطُورًا
To make a. o. to breakfast. To give the breakfast to a. o. فَطَّرَ وأَفْطَرَ ه
To be unleavened (dough). فَطُرَ وتَفَطَّرَ
To enter upon breakfast-time. أَفْطَرَ
To be cracked, split. To spread its leaves (plant). تَفَطَّرَ وانْفَطَرَ
issure, crack. فَطْر ج فُطُور

Moreover, besides, much less. A fortiori. فَضْلًا عن
By the grace of God. بِفَضْل الله
Exceeding, redundant. Remainder, rest. Wine. ▫ Excrement. فَضْلَة ج فَضَلَات وفِضَال
Work-clothes; night-clothes. — وفُضُل
Wearing of a simple garment. فِضْلَة
Redundant, superfluous part. Remainder, residue. فُضَالَة ج فُضَالَات
Bountiful, فَضَّال
Attainment. Merit. Virtue. فَضِيلَة ج فَضَائِل
Eminence, superiority. Superlative (*gram*). تَفْضِيل
Superabundant. Superior. Virtuous. Redundant. ✧ Learned man. فَاضِل ج فُضَلَاء
Excess, increase. Benefit, favour. فَاضِلَة ج فَوَاضِل وفَاضِلَات
Increase in flocks. — المَال
Exceeding all measure. فَضُول
Useless thing. Intrusion. فُضُول
Intruder, inquisitive. Tailor. فُضُولِيّ
Distinguished man. فَضِيل ج فُضَلَاء
More distinguished. Better. أَفْضَل ج أَفْضَلُون وأَفَاضِل
Excellent in merit, superior. مِفْضَل ومُفَضَّل
Single garment; every-day-clothes مِفْضَل ومِفْضَلَة ج مَفَاضِل
Very generous. مِفْضَال م مِفْضَالَة
To be broad, wide (place). ✲ فَضَا o فَضَاء وفُضُوًّا
✧ To be empty, void (place). ✧ فَضِيَ a فَضَاوَة
✧ To be unemployed. To have leisure. ✧ — وتَفَضَّى
To empty, to clear (a place). ✧ فَضَّى ه
To go forth to the desert. أَفْضَى
To reach, to arrive to. — إلى
To bring a. o. to (a place: road). To result for a. o. (affair). To communicate (a secret) to. — بِهِ إلى
✧ He had leisure to consider the affair. تَفَضَّى لِلأَمْر
Large plain. Court, enclosure. Unoccupied (place). فَضَاء
Private. بَيت الفَضَاء ومُفْضًى

Grape. فِطر وفُطر
Breaking of the fast. Breaking his fast (man). فِطر
Feast at the breaking of the fast of Ramadhan. عيد الفِطر
Alms given at the end of Ramadhan. زكاة وصَدَقة الفِطر
Poisonous mushroom. Toad-stool. فُطر وفُطُر
Natural disposition. Religious feeling. Religion of Islam. فِطرة ج فِطَر
Breakfast. فَطور وفَطوريّ و ✧ فُطور
□ Sample. Bill of sale. I فُطورة
Azym, unleavened (*opp. to* خمير) (bread). Unpremeditate, hasty. فَطير
Pan-cake, fritter. فطيرة ج فطائر
Blunt (sword). فُطار
Cipher, worthless man. فُطاريّ
Pastry-cook. □ فَطاطِريّ ج فَطاطِريّة
Chap on the face, nose. أُفطور ج أَفاطير
The Creator. فاطِر
To be flat-nosed. ✱ فَطِس a فَطَسًا
To die without disease. فطس i فُطوسًا ✧ To be smothered, choked.
To flatten (iron : blacksmith). — ه
To utter a. th. in o.'s face. — وفطّس ه بالكلمة
To cause a. o. to perish, to kill a. o. ✧ To smother, to suffocate. فطّس ه
Berry of the myrtle-tree. فَطس
A myrtle-berry. Bead worn as an amulet. ✧ Smother. فَطسة
Flattening of the nose. فَطسة وفنطيسة
✧ Dead beast. Carrion, carcass. فَطيس وفَطيسة ج فطائس
Large hammer. فِطّيس ج فَطاطيس
Pig's snout. فِطّيسة
Flat-nosed. أفطس م فطساء ج فُطس
To wean (a young one). ✱ فطم i فطمًا ه ~
To disaccustom a. o. from. فطم ه عن
To cut (a rope). ✧ To dip (cloth) in dye. — ه
To become barren (tree, female). ✧ فطّم
To reach the time of being weaned. أفطم
To be weaned. إنفطم
To abstain from. — عن

Weaning of a child. فِطام
Weaned (young one). فَطيم ج فُطُم
A sea-fowl. فَطيمة
Having her young one weaned (female). فاطِم وفاطِمة ج فواطِم
Weaned lamb. سخلة فاطِم
Fatimah, Mohammed's daughter. فاطِمة
✱ فَطَن وفَطُن o وفَطِن a فِطنًا وفُطنًا وفَطَنًا وفُطُنًا وفِطنة وفُطونة وفَطانة وفَطانِيَة ب وإلى ول
To seize, to understand a. th. To be intelligent, penetrative.
To explain a. th. to a. o. ✧ To remind a. o. of. فطّن ه ب او إلى او ل
To draw a. o.'s attention to. فاطَن ه في
✧ To reflect, to remember. تفطّن
Intelligence, prudence. sagacity. فِطنة ج فِطَن
فاطِن وفَطِن وفَطِين وفَطون وفَطُن وفَطن ج
Intelligent, open-minded. Prudent. فُطن وفُطُن
To urge (a beast) vehemently. ✱ فطا o فطوًا ه
To be rough, harsh, unmanly. ✱ فظّ a فظاظة وفظظ وفِظاظ
To press out (the water) of a ruminant's stomach. — o فظًّا, وافتظّ ه
Unmanly, harsh, churlish. فظّ ج أفظاظ
Water in the stomach of a ruminant. فظّ ج فِظاظ وفُظوظ
Harshness, unmanliness. Roughness. فظاظة وفَظَظ وفِظاظ
To be foul, unseemly, difficult. To be critical (affair). ✱ فظع o فظاعة, وأفظع
To be filled to the brim (vessel). فظِع a فظعًا
To reckon (an affair) hard, difficult. — ه وب ومن وأفظع ه
To be in critical circumstances. أُفظِع
To find a. th. hideous, shocking; difficult, critical. تفظّع واستفظع ه
Difficulty. ✧ Hideousness. فظاعة
Abominable; difficult. Excessive. ✧ Ugly, hideous. فظيع ومُفظِع
✧ To upbraid loudly, to bully a. o. ✱ فَعَر ه a صَوتًا
To do; to act. To perform a. th. ✱ فَعَل a فعلًا ه

Foaming with rage. فاءِ
Flower of the Egyptian privet فاعِيَة
Wont to calumniate (woman).
Viper. أَفْعَى ج أَفَاعٍ
Country full of vipers. أَرض مَفْعَاة
Branded in the shape of a viper مُفْعَاة
(camel).
To diffuse itself (odour). ✱ فَغَ o فَغْمَة
To open (the mouth). ✱ فَغَر a o فَغْرًا وأَفْغَر ه
To be half-opened (mouth, flower). — وانْفَغَر
Rising of the Pleiades. الفَغْرَة
Mouth of a river. فُغْرَة ج فُغَر
Wide (spear-thrust). طَعْنَة فَغَار
Perfume. Cubeb. Lotus of India. فَاغِرَة
Broad plain. Hollow in a mountain. مَفْغَرَة
Emperor of China. ✱ فَغْفُور
Kind of China-ware. ¤فَغْفُورِيّ و✧ فَرْفُورِيّ
To fill the nose (odour). ✱ فَغَم a فَغْمًا وفُغُومًا ه
To kiss a. o. — وفَاغَم ه
To open (rose). فَغِم a فُغُومًا, وتَفَغَّم
To become accustomed to. فَغِم فَغَمًا ب
To be fond of, busy about.
To abide in a place. — بِمَكَان
To fill (a place : odour) ; to fill (a vessel). أَفْغَم ه
To be filled up. To be dispelled (rheum). إِنْفَغَم
Food remaining between the teeth. فَغْم
Mouth. Chin. فُغْم وفُغُم
He, it depressed him *lit* : he took hold of his chin. أَخَذ بِفُغْمِهِ
Eager, fond of. فَغِم على ومُفْغَم ب
To spread (news). To fade (plant). ✱ فَغَا o فَغْوًا
To become bad, corrupt (palm-tree). To become ugly. To become rebellious. To fall into destitution. To blossom (saffron). أَفْغَى
To irritate a. o. — ه
Disease of palm-trees. Dates of bad quality. Refuse. فَغًا
Blossom of henna. فَغْو وفَاغِيَة
To bark from fear (dog). ✱ فَقْفَق
To speak volubly, to jabber. — في الكَلَام
Dotage, doter. فَقْفَاق

To act upon a. o. فَعَل وافْتَعَل ب
N. B. This verb and its derivates are used as paradigms upon which all verbs and grammatical forms are measured.
To be done. To be impressed. إِنْفَعَل
✧ To be vexed, to spite.
To intrigue, to forge a lie against a. o. إِفْتَعَل عَلَيهِ كَذِبًا وزُورًا
To forge (hand-writing). — ه
Action, work, deed. Verb. فِعْل ج فِعَال وأَفْعَال وجج أَفَاعِيل
Actually, virtually. بالفِعْل (opp. to بِالقُوَّة)
Custom, use. فِعْلَة
Good or bad action done by a single agent. فَعَال
Good or bad action done by two or many agents. فِعَال
He has performed good actions. هُوَ حَسَنُ الفَعَال
They do good actions. هُم حِسَان الفِعَال
Handle of a tool. فِعَال ج فُعُل
Imper. Do thou. فَعَالِ
Impression. ✧ Spite. إِنْفِعَال
Acting, active, doer. (*Gr.*) Agent. ✧ Efficacious. Workman, labourer, digger. فَاعِل ج فَاعِلُون وفَعَلَة
Gr. Subject, noun agent. Present participle. إِسْمُ الفَاعِل
✧ Efficacity. فَاعِلِيَّة
Foot of a verse. أَفَاعِيل وتَفَاعِيل
Made, done. Passive. Result, effect. مَفْعُول ج مَفَاعِيل
Gr. Object, regimen. مَفْعُول بِهِ
Gr. Past participle ; noun patient. إِسْمُ المَفْعُول
It produced a distressing effect (wound). جَاء بِالمُفْتَعَل
Falsified, altered (book). كِتَاب مُفْتَعَل
To fill (a vessel) to the brim. ✱ فَعَم a فَعْمًا, وفَعَّم وأَفْعَم ه
To be filled up (vessel). To become fat (arm, leg). فَعُم o فَعَامَة وفُعُومَة
To fill (a house : perfume). أَفْعَم ه
To fill (a. o.) with anger. — ه
To be filled (vessel). إِفْعَوْعَم
Full, filled with people. فَعْم ومُفْعَم
To be wicked like a viper. ✱ فَعَا — تَفَعَّى

Foolish. فَقْفَاقَة

✧ To slit (a pimple). To put out (an eye). فَقَأَ a فَقْأً , وفَقَّأَ تَفْقِئَةً ه

To burst (a pomegranate) open. To hull (a nut, an almond). فَقَّأَ ه

To burst (cloud, pustule). To be pulled out (eye). ✧ To husked (fruit). تَفَقَّأَ وانفقأ

Membrane enveloping the head of the fœtus. فَقْأَة وفَاقِيَاء

Hollow in a rock, or stony ground. — وفَقِيّ

Lanced, put out. ✧ Hulled (nut). مَفْقُوء ومَفْقِيّ

Ravine, channel of a torrent. مُفَقِّئَة

✧ To open the eyes (whelp). To blossom (tree). فَقَحَ a فَقْحًا , وفَقَّحَ

To open (rose). تَفَقَّحَ

To set, to prepare to. — ب ول

To lean against o. a.'s back. تَفَاقَحَ

Orifice of the anus. Blossom. فَقْحَة ج فِقَاح

Palm of the hand. — وفَقَاحَة

Blossom of plants. Tall, handsome woman. فُقَّاح

Prone to do mischief. مُتَفَقِّح لِلشَّرّ

✧ To lose a. th. To miss a. th; to want a. th. To be deprived of. فَقَدَ i فَقْدًا و فِقْدَانًا وفُقُودًا ه وه

To cause to a. o. the loss of a. o. or a. th. أفقد ه ه او ه

To search out a. th. lost, missed. تَفَقَّدَ وافتقد ه

To miss, to regret the absence of o. a. تَفَاقَدَ

To seek for, to miss a. o. absent. إفتقد و✧ استفقد ه

✧ To visit (a sick person). إفتقد و✧ استفقد ه

Absence, loss of a person, of a thing. فَقْد و فِقْدَان وفُقُود

Vitex, chaste-tree. فَقْد وفَقَد

Wanting, missing. Bereft of her husband, of her children (woman). فَاقِد

Lost, absent, lamented. فَقِيد ومَفْقُود

He died unlamented. مَاتَ غَيْرَ فَقِيد

✧ To dig the earth. To incise. فَقَرَ o فَقْرًا, وفَقَّرَ

To bore (a pearl). ✧ To put out (an eye). To press (grapes). — وفقر ه

To overwhelm a. o. (evil). فَقَرَ ه

To feel a pain in the vertebræ. فَقِرَ a فَقَرًا

To be poor, destitute. فَقُرَ o فَقَارَةً , وافتقر

To dig a hollow for (a young palm-tree). فَقَّرَ ل

To impoverish a. o. أفقر ه

To lend to a. o. (a beast) for riding; (a land) for sowing. — ه ه

What a poor man! مَا أفقرَهُ

To feign poverty. تَفَاقَرَ

To burst open (abscess, fruit). ✧ إنفقر

To want, to be in need of. إفتقر إلى

Poverty, destitution. فَقْر ج فُقُور ومَفَاقِر

Poverty, side. فُقْر ج فُقَر

فَقْرَة ج فَقْر, وفِقْرَة ج فِقَر وفِقَرَات و فِقْرَات ,

Vertebræ, spine of the back. وفَقَارَة ج فَقَار

Three stars in Orion. فَقَار الجَوْزَاء

Celebrated sword of Ali. ذُو الفَقَار

Mark, butt. Hillock. Choice verse or passage of an author. فِقْرَة ج فِقَر

Proximity. Ditch. Gore of a shirt. فُقْرَة ج فُقَر

Vertebral. فَقَارِيّ

Misfortune. فَاقِرَة ج فَوَاقِر

Having the vertebræ broken. فَقِر وفَقِير ومَفْقُور

Poor, destitute, needy. فَقِير ج فُقَرَاء

Canal, aqueduct. Mouth of a canal. Hollow dug for planting or watering palm-trees. فَقِير ج فُقُر

Strong. Fit to be ridden (colt). مُفْقِر

Able to, fit for. — ل

Resolute man. Damaskeened (sword). مُفَقَّر

✧ To die. فَقَسَ i فُقُوسًا

To break, to burst (her eggs: bird). ✧ To relax (a spring). To discharge (a gun). فَقَسَ i فَقْسًا ه

To kill (a beast). To pull the hair of. ✧ To spite, to vex a. o. — ه

To repel a. o. violently from. — ه عن

✧ To be relaxed (spring); discharged (gun). To lose patience. فَقَسَ وانفقس

To melt (butter) for clarifying it. ✧ فَقَّسَ ه

To play with Easter eggs (children). ✧ فَاقَسَ وتَفَاقَسَ

Crushing (poverty). مُفْقِم
Dry and hard (plant). مُتَفَقِّم
To winnow (corn). ✡ فَقَل o فَقْلًا ه
To be luxuriant (land). أَفْقَل
Luxuriant (land). أرض كثيرة الفقل
Winnowing-basket, fan. مِفْقَلَة ج مَفَاقِل

✡ فَقِم a فَقَمًا وفَقْمًا وفُقُومًا, وفَقُم o فَقَامَة,
To be grave, important, momentous (affair). وتَفَاقَم
To have inequal jaws. فَقِم a فَقَمًا وفَقْمًا
To have an indigestion. To be full (vessel). To become abundant. To be consumed (wealth).
To seize (a beast) by its muzzle. فَقَم o فَقْمًا, وتَفَقَّم ه
Jaw. Dog's muzzle. فُقْم وفَقْم
Mouth. فُقْم
Having irregular incisors, unequal jaws. Crooked (affair). أَفْقَم م فَقْمَاء ج فُقْم

To be learned, skilled in divine law. To be endowed with penetration. ✡ فَقِه a فَقَهًا, وفَقُه o فَقَاهَة
To understand a. th. فَقِه a فِقْهًا, وتَفَقَّه ه
To overcome a. o. in science. فَقَه o فَقْهًا ه
To teach a. o. To render intelligent, skilled. فَقَّه وأَفْقَه ه
To vie with a. o. in knowledge of divine law. فَاقَه ه
To study jurisprudence thoroughly. تَفَقَّه
Learning. Knowledge of jurisprudence. فِقْه
Science of divine law. فَقَاهَة
Skilled in jurisprudence. Lawyer. Intelligent. ▫ Schoolmaster فَقِه وفَقِيه وفَقُه ج فُقَهَاء
Companion of a mourner woman. مُسْتَفْقِهَة

To follow the trace of. ✡ فَقَا o فَقْوًا (for فَقَأ) ه
Notch of an arrow. فُقْوَة ج فُقًى

To loose, to disjoin. To separate a. th. To luxate (a limb). To break (a seal). To resolve (a difficulty). To open (the hand). To open (the jaw.) ✡ فَكَّ o فَكًّا ه

To be upset, overthrown. تَفَقَّس وانْفَقَس
To be melted, purified (butter) ✧ تَفَقَّس
To pull o. a. by the hair. تَفَاقَس
Relaxing of a spring. Discharge of a gun. Fit of passion. ✧ فَقْسَة
Pain in the joints. فُقَاس
Spring of a trap. مِفْقَاس

To crack (nuts, eggs) with the hand. ✡ فَقَش i فَقْشًا ه
✧ To burst, to split (wood). To break (waves). فَقَّش
✧ To break, to crush (fruit). فَقَّش ه

To break (an egg). ✡ فَقَص i فَقْصًا ه
Melon. ▫ Large cucumber. فَقُّوص
Iron-ring in a plough. فَقِيص
Iron-mace for breaking. مِفْقَاص

Only, but. ✡ فَقَط
To write down in words the total of a sum. ✧ فَقَّط ه

To be intensely yellow. To die from heat. To grow up (child). ✡ فَقَع o a فَقْعًا وفُقُوعًا
To crush a. o. (misfortune). — ه
✧ To burst, to explode. To be grieved to death. فَقَع
To be intensely red. فَقِع a فَقَعًا
To crack the fingers. To burst (a flower). To dye (a hide) red. فَقَّع ه
To speak inconsiderately. To utter idle words. — في الكلام
✧ To despite a. o. to death. — ه
To be reduced to destitution. أَفْقَع
To become white (eyes). تَفَاقَع
To be cleft, to crack, to burst. إِنْفَقَع
Fungus, truffles of bad quality. Intense whiteness, yellowness. فَقْع وفِقْع ج فِقَعَة وأَفْقُع وفُقُوع
Clear (colour). فَاقِع
Pure yellow colour. أَصْفَر فَاقِع
Calamity. فَاقِعَة ج فَوَاقِع
Red-faced (man). فُقَّاع وفُقَاع وفَقِيع
Wicked, perverse. فُقَّاع
Beer, drink made with fruits. فُقَّاع
Bubbles upon the surface of water. فُقَّاعَة ج فَقَاقِيع
Pure (colour). Intensely white, red, yellow. White pigeon. فَقِيع, وأَفْقَع م فَقْعَاء ج فُقْع
Unripe (fig). ـ فَقِيع

To release, to set free (a captive, a slave). فكّ فكًّا وفكاكًا ه
To recover (a pledge). — فكًّا وفُكوكًا, وافتكّ ه
To be broken down (old man). — فكًّا وفُكوكًا
To be out of joint, luxated (limb). — a فكّكًا, وانفكّ
To be foolish. — a o فكًّا وفكّة
To disjoin, to undo, to dissolder, to separate a. th. ✧ To disentangle, to unravel, to undo a. th. فكّك ه
To lose o's temper; to have no self-control. تفكّك
To be disjoined, undone, separated. To be parted (fingers). To be set free (slave). انفكّ
✧ To extricate o.'s self from. — من
He has not ceased standing up. ما انفكّ فلانٌ قائمًا
He has not ceased to. ما انفكّ أن
To endeavour, to disjoin, to loose a. th. إستفكّ ه
Disjunction, luxation, separation. فكّ
Jaw. ◻ Bit of a horse. فكّ ج فُكوك
Silliness. *Corona Borealis* (*constell*). فكّة
Money for redeeming a pledge. فِكاك وفَكاك
Disjoining. Decrepit. Foolish. فاكّ ج فكّكة وفِكاك
Disjoining much. فكّاك
Speaking inconsiderately, incoherently. — بالكلام
Resolving difficulties. — للمُشكِلات
Having the shoulder-blade out of joint. Part in which the jaws meet. أفكّ م فكّاء ج فُكّ
✱ فكر i فِكرًا وفَكرًا, وفكّر وأفكر
To reflect, to think on, to ponder over. وتفكّر وافتكر في
To recall a. th. to the mind. To remind a. o. of. فكّر ه ه
Thought, idea. فِكر ج أفكار
Reflection. Cares. Want. فكرى و فِكرة ج فِكر
I do not care for it. ما لي فيه فِكر او فَكر
I have no need of it. لا فكر لي في هذا

Lock, fastener of a window. ✧ فاكورة ج فواكير
Thinker, thoughtful. فِكّير وفَيكر
To sprain, to put (a limb out of joint). ✧ فكش o فكشًا ه
To be dislocated, sprained. ✧ إنفكش
Luxation, sprain. ✧ فِكش
To lower the head in grief or spite. ✱ فكع a فكعًا وفُكوعًا
No one knows where he was this morning. لا يُدرَى أين فكع
To apply o.'s self to. ✱ فكل — افتكل في
Shudder, shiver. Crowd. Wood-pecker. أفكل
They came all together. جاء القومُ بأفكلهم او بأفاكيلهم
Terror-stricken. مَفكول
To persist in. ✱ فكن o فكنًا في
To be astonished, thoughtful. To repent, to regret. تفكّن
Repentance, regret. فُكنة
To be merry, lively, jolly. ✱ فكه a فكهًا وفكاهةً, وتفكّه
To bring fruit to a. o. To enliven a. o. with facetious talks. فكّه ه
To joke with a. o. فاكه ه
To eat fruit. To abstain from it. تفكّه
To enjoy a. th. To slander a. o. jestingly. — ب
To joke, to jest together. تفاكه
Joke, merriment. فُكاهة وفكيهة
Wonderful thing, witticism. أُفكوهة ج أفاكيه
Witty, jovial. فكه وفاكه
Jolly, jocose. فكه م فكهة
Asperser. فكه بأعراض الناس
Having much fruit (tree). فاكه
Fruit. Sweetmeat. فاكهة ج فواكه
The fire. فاكهة الشتاء
Fruit-seller. فاكهانيّ
To notch (a sword). To rout (an army). ✱ فلّ o فلًّا, وفلّل ه وه
He is out of mind. فلّ i فلًّا عنهُ عقلُهُ
✧ To escape, to run away. To be off. To go back home (workman, pupil). فلّ
✧ To make a. o. to escape, to go back. فلّل ه

To lose flocks. To be in a barren land. أفلّ

To be defeated, routed (army). تَفَلَّلَ وانفلّ

To be notched (sword); broken (tooth). — وانفلّ وافتلّ

To take the tenth of. إستفلّ ه

Routed, in flight (army). فَلّ ج فُلول وأفلال وفُلّال (s. pl.)

Rout, army put to flight. كتيبة فَلّ

Notch on the edge of a sword. Spark. Filings of iron. فَلّ ج فُلول وفِلال

Waterless desert. — ج فلّ وأفلال, وفِلّ وفِلّيّة ج فَلَالِيّ

Devoid of all good. — من الخير

Jasmine. ✧ فُلّ وفِلّ

Break in a sword. فَلَل

Notch in a sword. ✧ Flight. Return from work. فَلّة

Notched (sword). Broken (tooth). فليل وأفلّ ومَفلول ومُنفلّ

Rolled up (hair). فليل وفليلة

Areca, betel-nut. ✲ فَوْفَل وفُوفُل

To sweep, to walk with a proud gait. To pick the teeth. ✲ فَلْفَل وتَفَلْفَل

✧ To go back one by one (party). فَلْفَل

To season (a dish) with pepper. To curl (the hair). فَلْفَل ه

Pepper, pepper-corn, allspice. P فُلْفُل وفِلْفِل

Long-pepper. مُفَلْفَل

Pungent, peppered. Crisp, curly (hair). P دار فُلفُل

To loose, to set free a. o. ✲ فَلَت i فَلْتًا, وأفلت ه

To escape, to slip away. فلت وأفلت وتَفَلَّت وانفلت

◻ To smuggle a. th. فلّت ه

To overtake a. o. فالت مُفالتةً وفِلاتًا ه

To glide away from a. o. (thing, person). أفلت ه

To escape from a. o. (thing). تَفَلَّت من

To long after. تَفَلَّت إلى

To rush upon. — على

He spoke unpremeditately, he extemporised. إفتلت الكلامَ

To do, to take a. th. of a sudden. — ه

To die suddenly. أُفتُلِت

To be surprised by. — ب

Flight, escape. فَلْت

Thou hast no escape from it. ما لك منهُ فلت

Swift (horse). فَلْت وفَلَتان وفِلِتّان وفَلَتان

Unexpected event. Inconsiderate action. Last night of a lunar month. فَلْتة

The event happened unexpectedly. حدث الأمرُ فلتةً

Blunders, mistakes. فَلَتات

Rascal, rogue. ✧ فَلْتيّ وفلاتي

Free, escaped. ✧ Profligate, libertine. فالت

✧ Offensive, unbecoming talk. كلام فالت

Tight garment. كِساء فَلوت

To split a. th. asunder. To till (the earth) ✲ فَلَج o i فَلْجًا وفُلوجًا, وفَلَّج ه

To share, to allot a. th. amongst. — وفَلَّج ه بين او على

To succeed well. فلج وأفلج

To overcome (an antagonist). — وأفلج على

He has afforded his proofs. فلج بحُجّتِهِ

To ravish the heart of a. o. — بقلب فلان

To have the half of the body paralysed. فُلِج و✧ انفلج

To have the (teeth, legs) apart. فلِج a فَلَجًا

To contend for superiority with. فالج ه

To make a. o. to gain the mastery over (God). أفلج ه على

To adduce clear (proofs). — ه

To be chapped (feet). تَفَلَّج

To break (day). ✧ To become paralysed (man). إنفلج

Success, victory; good luck at play. فَلْج وفُلْج وفُلْجة

Half. Division. فِلْج ج فُلوج

Measure for grain. فِلْج, وفالج ج فَوالِج

Width between the teeth or the thighs. Daybreak. فَلَج

Streamlet. — ج أفلاج

Small cup, coffee-cup. P فِنجان ج فَناجين

Dividing in two halves. Hemiplegia, palsy. Two-humped camel. Winning at the game (arrow). فالج

Cocoon of silkworm. P فَيْلَج ج فَيالج

Having أفلج م فلجاء, ومُفَلَّج الأسنان
the teeth apart.
Disordered (affair). مُفلَّج
Paralysed. مفلوج ج مَفَالِيج
To cleave a. th. To ✱ فَلَح a فَلحًا ه
till the ground.
To deceive a. o. — ه وب
To be chapped (under-lip). فَلِح فَلَحًا
To laugh at a. o.; to beguile فَلَّح ب
him.
To be successful, lucky. أفلح واستفلح
To live on. أفلح ب
Slit, chap, crack. فلح ج فُلُوح
Chap on the under-lip. فَلَح وفَلَحَة
Prosperity; success. Safety. — وفَلَاح
Cultivated ground. فَلَحَة
Tillage, agriculture. فِلاحة وفَلاحة
Husbandman, فَلَّاح ج فَلَّاحُون وفَلَّاحة
peasant. Sailor. ✧ Ruffian, rough
man.
Having the under- أفلح م فَلحاء ج فُلح
lip chapped.
Crack-lipped, chap- مُتفلِّح الشَّفَة واليَدَيْن
handed.
To slit a. th. ✱ فَلَخ a فَلخًا ه
To strike a. o. فلّخ ه
Stone of a water-mill. فَيلخ ج فَيَالِخ
To cut a slice of ✱ فَلَذ i فَلذًا لِفُلان من
(meat) to a. o. To give part of a. th.
to.
To cut a. th. into pieces. فلّذ ه
To take the part of a. th. إفتلذ ه ه
from.
Liver of camels. فِلذ ج أفلاذ
Piece of meat, or فِلذة ج فِلَذ وأفلاذ
metal.
Treasures buried in the أفلاذ الأرض
earth.
Sweet- P فَالُوذ وفَالُوذَج ج وفَالُوذَق وفَالُوذَج
meat made of starch, water and
honey.
Steel; pure iron. P فُولاذ و✧ بُولاد
Cut. Made of steel (sword). مَفلُوذ
Bronze. Brass. Rough ✱ فِلِزّ وفِلِزّ وفُلُزّ
(man).
To declare a. o. to be ✱ فلس — فَلَّس ه
bankrupt (judge). ✧ To reduce a. o.
to destitution.
To be penniless, destitute. To أفلس
become poor. ✧ To become bank-
rupt.
Atome; rubbish, scale of fish. فَلس
Destitution. فَلس
Farthing, small G فَلس ج فُلوس وأفلُس
copper coin *Pl.* ▫ Money (in gene-
ral).
Scales of a fish. فُلوس السَّمَك
Money-changer. فَلَّاس
✧ Bankruptcy. إفلاس
Having round spots (horse). مُفلَّس
Covered with scales.
Insolvent, penniless. مُفلِس ج مَفَالِيس
✧ Bankrupt.
Palestine. ✱ فَلَسطُون وفِلَسطِين
A Philistine. فِلَسطِيّ وفِلَسطِينِيّ
To become a phi- ✱ فلسف — وتَفَلسَف
losopher. To philosophise.
Philosophy. G فَلسَفَة
Philosophic. فَلسَفِيّ
Philosopher. G فَيلَسُوف ج فَلاسِفَة
The Philosopher, surname of الفَيلَسُوف
Aristotle.
To unfold (a piece of cloth). ✧ فَلَش o ه
To escape from (a cala- ✱ فَلَص o من
mity).
To deliver, to save a. o. فَلَّص ه
To be saved. أفلص وتَفَلَّص وانفلص
To overlook, to be ✱ فلط o فَلطًا عن
inadvertent to a. th.
To overtake, to meet a. o. فالط ه
unexpectedly.
To surprise a. o. (affair). أفلط ه
To be surprised by. أفتُلِط ب
Unexpected event. فَلَط
Surprise. فِلاط
Plato (Greek philosopher). G أفلاطُون
To expand, to flatten a. th. ✱ فَلطح ه
Broad and flat (bread). فِلطاح ومُفَلطَح
To split, to cut ✱ فَلَع a فَلعًا, وفَلَّع ه
a. th.
To be split, cut asunder. تَفَلَّع وانفلع
Crack, crevice, cleft; chap فِلع ج فُلُوع
on the feet.
Piece of a camel's hump. فِلعة ج فِلَع
Distress, calamity. فَالِعة ج فَوَالِع
Cutting (sword). فَلُوع ج فُلُع, ومِفلَع
Made of many pieces مُفَلَّعة
of leather (bag).

✧ To foretell events, to soothsay. فلّك وتفلّك
Globe, spherical body. Celestial sphere, sky. Weather. فَلَك ج أفلاك وفُلك وفُلُك
Hillock, mound. — ج فِلاك
Astronomy. عِلم الفلك
Astronomic, celestial. فَلَكِي
Astronomer, astrologer. فَلَكِي ج فلكيّة وفلكيّون
Any spherical object. Whirl of a spindle. فِلكة ج فلك
Felucca, sailing ship. Ark of Noah. فُلك ✧ فلوكة ج فلائك
Round-breasted (girl). Soothsayer, astrologer. مُفلِك
The two tonsils. ألإفليكان
☆ To cut off the nose of. فلم — إفتلم ه
Man of a tall size. Wide-mouthed well. Comb. Numerous (army). فيلم
✧ Belgium. Holland. Dutch, Belgian, Flemish. فلمنك Ts
☆ Such a one. فلن — فُلان م فُلانة
Such (a place), such (a thing). فُلانيّ م فُلانيّة
✧ Cork, stopper. فلينة
✧ God-child. فليون
☆ To journey. To acquire experience. فلا o فلوًا وفلاء
To strike a. o. with (a sword). — ه ب
To wean (a young one). To bring up (a child). — وأفلى وافتلى ه
To have a colt fit to be weaned. To engage in a desert. أفلى
فِلو ج أفلاء, وفَلُوّ وفُلُوّ م فِلوة وفَلُوّة وفُلُوّة
Colt. Filly. ج أفلاء وفَلاوى
Desert, waterless plain. فَلاة ج فَلا وفلوات وفُلِيّ و فِلِيّ وأفلاء
✧ Open space, atmosphere. فلا ✧
☆ To louse (the head). فلى i فَليًا, وفلّى ه
To scrutinise (an affair). To study the meaning of (a poem). فلى ه
To strike a. o. with (a sword). — ه ب
To examine (people). — وافتلى ه
To clear o.'s self from lice. تفلّى
To ask to be loused. تفالى واستفلى
They seek for herbage in the desert. يفتلون الفلاة
Lousing of the head. فِلاية وتفلية
Black-beetle spotted with white فالية

☆ To split, to cut a. th. in two halves. فلق i فلقًا, وفلّق ه
(God) made the dawn to break. فلق الصُّبح
To produce a. th. wonderful, a master-piece. أفلق وافتلق
To be cracked, chapped, split. تفلّق
To run swiftly. — وافتلق في العدو
To be cracked, split. إنفلق
Crack, split, fissure. فَلق ج فُلوق
Wood split in two, splint. Wonderful thing. Misfortune. فِلق
He has spoken to me personally *lit*: with his own mouth. كلّمني من فِلق فيهِ
Dawn. Ravine between two mountains. ✧ Stocks, bastinado. فَلَق ج أفلاق
Valley between two hills. — ج فُلقان
He has brought evil. جاء بعُلَق فُلَق او بعُلَقٍ فُلَقٍ
Brand on the ear of a camel. فلقة
Splint, fragment, half of a. th. فِلقة ج فِلق, وفِلاقة ج فِلاق
Wonderful thing. فليق وفليقة وفَلَقى
Misfortune, calamity. — وفليقة ومَفلقة
Splitting asunder. Depressed ground. فالِق م فالقة
Causing seeds and fruit-stones to germinate (God). فالِق الحَبّ والنّوى
Army, body of 5000 men. Calamity, distress. Cocoon. فيلق ج فيالِق
Curded (milk). فِلاق وفلوق
The eggs have been broken. صار البيض فُلاقًا وفِلاقًا وأفلاقًا
Of great genius (poet). مُفلِق
Kind of peach split in the drupe. فُلّيق
The same peach when dried. مُفلّق
Split. Branded on the ear (camel). مَفلوق
☆ To swallow (the contents of a vessel). فلقح ه
✧ To become supercilious, overbearing. تفلقح
To show a smiling face. — إلى النّاس
Cavalier, overbearing. فلقحي و✧ مُفلقح
☆ To have rounded breasts (girl). فلك o فلكًا, وفلّك وأفلك
To be rounded (breast). — وتفلّك واستفلك
To apply o.'s self assiduously to. فلّك وأفلك في

✧ Rejoicing, parade. I فَنْتَازِيَّة
To stare. ◘ To be generous. ✧ فَنْجَر
Skilful horsemen. فَنَاجِرَة
Coffee-cup. P فِنْجَان ج فَنَاجِين
To bruise (a bone). ✱ فَنَخ a فَنْخًا ه
◘ To cancel a. th.
To get mastery over, to — وفَنَّخ ه
overcome a. o.
Weak, subdued (man). فَنِيخ
Overpowering the enemy. مِفْنَخ
To swell the nostrils. To be ✱ فَنْخَر.
proud; to assume a haughty gait.
Colossal, enormous. فُنْخُر وفُنَاخِر
To become weak- ✱ فَنِد a فَنَدًا , وأَفْنَد
minded (old, sick man). To lie. To commit a mistake.
To sit on the top of a hill. فَنَّد
To ridicule a. o. To be weak- فَنَّد ه
minded, liar. To contradict a. o. To point out the faults of.
✧ To classify, to diversify a. th. ه —
To give the particulars of an account. To lop a vine.
To ask a. th. from. — وفَانَد وتَفَنَّد ه على
To weaken the mind of (old age) أَفْنَد ه
To repent of. تَفَنَّد مِن
Large mountain. فَنْد وفِنْد
Species, sort. Branch, فِنْد ج أَفْنَاد وفُنُود
bough. Numerous company.
The divisions of the night. أَفْنَاد اللَّيل
By parties. أَفْنَادًا أَفْنَادًا
✧ Wax-candle. فِنْد الشَّمْع ج فُنُود
Dotage. Weakness, blunder. فَنَد ج أَفْنَاد
Lie. Unthankfulness.
They form one separate هُمْ فِنْدٌ على حِدَةٍ
party.
Turkish title. Sir. T أَفَنْدِيّ ج أَفَنْدِيَّة
Effendi. Master.
Lump of ✱ فِنْدِير و فِنْدِيرَة ج فَنَادِير
dates. Large rock detached from a mountain.
Inn, caravansary. ✱ فُنْدُق ج فَنَادِق
Nux avellana, hazel-nut.
Landlord of an inn. G فُنْدُقَانِيّ
Register for receipts فُنْدَاق ج فَنَادِق
and expenditure.
Paper-lantern. Light- ✧ فَنَار ج فَنَارَات
house.
Great destitution. ✱ فَنْس — فَنَس

and black. ✧ Vent-hole of a gun.
Forerunners of an evil. بِلْيَة الأَفَاعِي
Mouth. Orifice, ✱ فَم وفُم وفِم ج أَفْوَاه
opening. Mouth of a river.
Point of a sword. — السَّيف
Two stars in *Cancer*. فَم الأَسَد
Fomelhaut, bright star in — الحُوت
Pisces.
Star in *Pegasus*. — الفَرَس
Belonging to the mouth. فَمِيّ وفَمَوِيّ
Two mouths. فَمَانِ وفَمَوَانِ
To adorn, to beautify a. th. ✱ فَنّ o فَنًّا ه
To put off the payment of a — دَيْنَهُ
debt.
To drive on (camels). — ه
To deceive a. o. in. — ه في
To ask or offer various things. فَنَّن ه
To mix various things; to sort. To change (o.'s mind).
To classify (things). To gather — ه وه
(men) from various tribes.
To be diversified, variously mixed. تَفَنَّن
◘ To be crafty.
To give variety to — وافْتَنّ في الحَدِيث
a narrative.
To urge (a horse) to go at إِسْتَفَنّ ه
different paces.
Kind, species, فَنّ ج فُنُون وأَفْنَان وجج أَفَانِين
sort. Mood, manner. Art, branch of knowledge.
Academy. دَار الفُنُون
The various branches of فُنُون العُلُوم
science.
The turns, modes of speech. أَفَانِين الكَلَام
Branch of a tree. فَنَن ج أَفْنَان وجج أَفَانِين
Space of time. فَنَّة
Abundant pasture. فَنَّة
Branchy (tree). فَنَّاء وفَنْوَاء
Luxuriant (hair). Thick-haired. فَيْنَان
Species, sort; way. Inter- أُفْنُون ج أَفَانِين
wisted bough. Obscure discourse.
Miscellany. Unevenness in a تَفْنِين
texture. Ornament, decoration.
Industrious, inventive. مِفَنّ م مِفَنَّة
Skilled in various branches of مُتَفَنِّن
learning.
Old and wicked (woman). مُفَنَّنَة
Party. ✱ فَنْء
Crowd. فَنَأ

Lantern. Slanderer. فانوس ج فوانيس
To be remiss in action. ✱ فنش – فَنْش
Well-room; ✱ فنطس – فِنطاس ج فَناطِيس tank of sweet water in a ship. Bowl for the crew.
Dog or wolf's muzzle; فِنطِيسة ج فَناطِيس pig's snout.
To become rich. ✱ فنم a فنمًا
Wealth, good. Nobleness of mind, فَنَم generosity. Good repute. Strong (perfume).
Enriched; become rich. فَنِم وفَنِيم
To make a. o. to ✱ فنق – فَنَّق وفانَق ه lead a soft, delicate life.
To enjoy a delicate life after أفنَق destitution.
To live in luxury. تَفَنَّق
Young and fat (she-camel). فُنُق
Brought up delicately – ومِفناق (girl).
Excellent stallion- فَنِيق ج فُنُق وأفناق camel.
Sack, large bag. فَنِيقة ج فَنائِق
To stay in (a place). ✱ فَنَك o فُنُوكًا ب
To apply o.'s self to. – وأفنَك على
To persist in. – وأفنَك في
To eat regulary فَنَك o وفَنِك a فُنُوكًا في with good appetite.
To embark in (an affair). فَنَك وفانَك في To continue doing a. th.
Wonderful thing. Assiduity. فَنَك وفَنْك
Kind of fox; marten. P فَنَك
Hour of the night. فِنْك وفُنْك
Junction of the two jaws. فَنِيك
Root of a bird's tail. إفنِيك
Foolish (woman). مُتَفَنِّكة
Morel (*plant*). ✱ فنو – فَناة ج فَنًا
Cow, bull. – ج فَنَوات
Thick-haired (woman). Branchy فَنواء (tree).
To pass away, to ✱ فَنِيَ وفَنَى a فَناء disappear. To be transitory, perishable. To be worn out; to pine, to fade away.
To coax, to blandish a. o. فانَى ه
To destroy, to annihilate a. th. أفنَى ه
To destroy o. a. تَفانَى
Perishableness. Nought. فَناء
The transient world. دار الفَناء

Court-yard, enclosure. فِناء ج أفنِيَة وفُنِيّ
Transient, perishable. فانٍ م فانِيَة Worn out.
From an unknown مِن أفناء النّاس origin.
Night-shade (*plant*). أفانِيّ
To be weak, disabled. ✱ فَهّ وفَهِه a فَهاهة
To forget a. th. – فَهًّا ه وعَنهُ
To disable a. o. فَهَّه وأفَهَّ ه
To cause a. o. to forget. – ه ه وعن
Weak, unable. فَهّ وفَهِيه م فَهَّة وفَهِيهة
Weakness, incapacity. فَهّة وفَهاهة Fault, mistake.
I have not noticed any مَا رَأيتُ مِنهُ فَهّة fault in him.
Wine-measure. Clear wine. P فَيهَج
To be sleepful, neglectful. ✱ فَهِد a فَهَدًا
To manage carefully فَهَد a فَهْدًا لِفُلان a. o.'s business during his absence.
Lynx, hunting-panther. فَهْد ج فُهُود وأفهُد
Neglectful, sluggish. فَهِد م فَهِدة
Full-grown and فَرْهَد، وأفهُود ج أفاهِيد fat youth.
To be exhausted, out of ✱ فهر – فَهِر breath (horse).
To become rich. تَفَهَّر في المال
Stone-pestle. فِهر و فِهرة ج أفهار وفُهُور
Pure milk boiled with heated فَهِيرة stones and sprinkled with flour.
To put an index to a book. ✱ فَهرَس ه To make a catalogue.
Index, table P فِهرِس وفِهرِست ج فَهارِس of contents; catalogue.
To break a. th. ✱ فَهَض a فَهضًا ه
To wound a. o. on the ✱ فَهَق a فَهقًا ه neck.
To overflow فَهِق a فَهقًا وفَهَقًا، وتَفَهَّق (vessel).
To fill up (a vessel). أفهَق ه
To spread in the sky – وتَفَهَّق وانفَهَق (lightning).
First vertebra of the neck. فَهقة ج فِهاق
Wound on the neck. فاهِقة
Broad, wide. مُنفَهِق
He was pro- ✱ فيهق – تَفَيهَق في كَلامِهِ fuse in speech.
Broad, ample. فَيهَق ج فَياهِق
✱ فَهِم a فَهمًا وفَهَمًا و فَهامة وفَهامِيَة

Although he see it, هُوَ فَوْتَ فِيهِ او يَدِهِ it is beyond the reach of his mouth or hand; *i. e.* he shall not attain it.
Sudden death. مَوْتَ الفَوَات
Distance, interval. Irregularity. تَفَاوُت
Acting in his own way. (*m. f.*) فُوَيْت
To spread its perfume ✱ فَاحَ o فَوْحًا (musk). To be cool (day).
To take the fresh air. To cool o.'s self. فَوَّحَ
To run (horse). To hurry on (man). To send flocks to water by droves. أَفَاحَ
To be hurried, urged. أُسْتُفِيحَ
فَوْحٌ ج أَفْوَاحٌ وفُؤُوحٌ وجج أَفَاوِيحُ وأَفَاوِحُ
Collection of men, of animals. Party, troop.
In separate bodies, by parties. أَفْوَاجًا أَفْوَاجًا
Upland. Party, band. فَائِجَة
To boil ✱ فَاحَ o فَوْحًا وفُؤُوحًا وفَوَحَانًا (cooking-pot). To bleed (wound).
To diffuse its perfume — وتَفَاوَحَ (flower). To become intense (heat).
To shed (blood). To make a أَفَاحَ ه (cooking-pot) to boil.
Diffusion of an odour. فَوْحٌ وفَوَحَان
An exhalation of odour. فَوْحَة
To blow (wind). To ✱ فَاخَ o فَوَاخَانًا abate (heat).
Do avoid midday-heat. أَفِخْ عنك من الظَّهِيرَة
To break wind. — وأَفَاخَ
To die. To remain in the ✱ فَادَ o فَوْدًا possession of its owner (property).
To mix a. th. with. — ه ب
To cause the loss of a. o. أَفَادَ ٥
To give (goods) to a. o. — ٥ ه
Tuft of hair on فَوْد مث فَوْدَانِ ج أَفْوَاد the temples. Temple of the head. Large bag.
Hoariness appeared بَدَا الشَّيْب بِفَوْدَيْهِ on his temples.
Side of the tent, or فَوْدُ الخِبَاء او الوَادِي the valley.
Spendthrift, prodigal. مِفْوَاد
To boil ✱ فَارَ o فَوْرًا وفُؤُورًا وفَوَرَانًا fiercely (cooking-pot). To be roused

To understand, to perceive a. th. إِفْتَهَمَ ه
To make a. o. to understand a. th. فَهَّمَ وأَفْهَمَ ٥ ه
To understand by degrees. To try to understand a. th. تَفَهَّمَ ه
✧ To be understood. إِنْفَهَمَ
To understand each other. تَفَاهَمَ
To question a. o. about. إِسْتَفْهَمَ ٥ ه
Intelligence, understanding, conception of the mind. فَهْم
Interrogation, question. إِسْتِفْهَام
The interrogative particle. (هَلْ) حَرْف الاِسْتِفْهَام
Intelligent, sharp. فَهِم رح فَهِيم
To forget, to overlook ✱ فَهَا o فَهْوًا عن a. th.
To be a man of weak judgment. أَفْهَى
Valerian (plant). ✱ فُو
To elapse ✱ فَاتَ o فَوْتًا وفَوَاتًا (time).
He died. فَاتَ وأُفْتِيتَ
To miss (an opportunity). — وافْتَاتَ ٥ To fail to attain a. th.
The time of prayer is فَاتَتِ الصَّلَاة elapsed.
To outgo, to outstrip a. o. فَاتَ ٥ ب in.
✧ To enter (a house). ◻ To pass. فَاتَ في
✧ To fade away (flower). فَوَّتَ
✧ To insert, to introduce a. th. — ه into.
To cause a. o. to miss a. th. أَفَاتَ ٥ ه ◻ To let a. o. pass.
To outstrip a. o. To do, تَفَوَّتَ عَلَيهِ في to decide a. th. without consulting another.
To follow at inter- تَفَاوَتَ تَفَاوُتًا وتَفَاوَتًا vals. To contrast with o. another. To be distinct, unlike.
He found out a locution. إِفْتَاتَ كَلَامًا
To exercise authority — على فُلَانٍ في upon a. o. in.
He followed his own — عَلَيهِم بِرَأْيِهِ advice without consulting them.
Nothing can be done لَا يُفْتَات عَلَيهِ without his consent.
Space between two fingers. فَوْت ج أَفْوَات

(anger). To ferment (wine). To throb (artery). To spurt forth (water).
To diffuse itself (perfume). — فَوَرًا وفَوَرَانًا
To make a (cooking-pot) to boil. — فَوْرًا, وأَفَارَ و✧ فَوَّرَ هـ
Ebullition. Fit of passion; hurry. فَوْر
He came back instantly. رَجَعَ مِنْ فَوْرِهِ
Immediately, in a hurry. عَلَى الفَوْر
Vehemence of heat, of anger. فَوْرَة
The hour following nightfall. — العِشَاء
Food given to a woman after childbirth. Fenugreek. فِيرَة
Irons of the tongue (of a balance). فِيَارَان
Boiling. Anger, passion. *Pl.* Gazelles. فَائِر ج فُور
His anger was excited. فَارَ فَائِرُهُ
Foam of boiling water. فُوَارَة
Boiling fiercely. فَوَّار
Hot-tempered (man). فَيُّور
Spring. ✧ Water-spout, jet d'eau. ◻ Typhoon. فَوَّارَة
To acquire, to obtain a. th. ✲ فَازَ o فَوْزًا بِ
To escape from. — مِن
To save o.'s life. فَازَ بِنَفْسِهِ
To die, to perish. — وفَوَّزَ
To flee, to run away. To go into a desert. فَوَّزَ
To get a. th. for a. o. To enable a. o. to obtain a. th. أَفَازَ ه بِ
Victory, success. Safety, deliverance. فَوْز
A victory, a success. فَوْزَة
Tent with two poles. فَازَة
Refuge. Desert. مَفَازَة ج مَفَاوِز ومَفَازَات
To float on the surface of water. ✧ فَاشَ o فَوْشًا
To set a. th. afloat. ✧ فَوَّشَ هـ
To explain (words). ✲ فوص — فَاوَصَ هـ
To intrust a. o. with an affair. To give jurisdiction to. ✲ فاض — فَوَّضَ هـ إِلَى
To give (a woman) in marriage without receiving a dowry. — ه
To be equal, copartner of فَاوَضَ ه فِي
a. o. in. To hold a conference with a. o.
To be copartners in (an affair). To consult, to converse with o. a. upon. تَفَاوَضُوا فِي
People without chief. قَوْمٌ فَوْضَى
أَمْرُهُمْ فَوْضَى بَيْنَهُمْ وفَوْضُوضَى وفَوْضُوضَاء
They are all equal. They have no chief. They live in anarchy.
They hold property in common. أَمْوَالُهُمْ فَوْضَى بَيْنَهُمْ
✧ Communist, socialist. فَوْضَوِيّ
Delegation, power of attorney; jurisdiction. تَفْوِيض
Conversation, conference. مُفَاوَضَة
Property held in common. Communism. شَرِكَة مُفَاوَضَة ومُفَاوَضَة
Waist-wrapper. ✧ Napkin, towel, apron. Kerchief. ✲ فوط — فُوطَة ج فُوَط
To put a waist-wrapper on a. o. فَوَّطَ ه
To die. ✲ فَاظَ o فَوْظًا وفَوَاظًا
Aroma of a perfume. Strength of a poison. ✲ فوع — فَوْعَة
Insects swarmed in. ✧ فَاعَتِ الحَشَرَاتُ فِي
To vomit (sick person). ✧ تَفَوَّعَ
To diffuse itself (odour). ✲ فَاغَ o فَوْغًا
Exhalation of a perfume. فَوْغَة
Suffocating (smell). فَائِغَة
To put the thumb-nail upon the nail of the forefinger to mean: I will not give or I have not received so little as that. ✲ فَافَ o فَوْفًا
Bull's bladder. Whiteness of the nails. فَوْف وفُوف ج أَفْوَاف
Pellicle of a stone-fruit. فُوف وفُوفَة
He has not tasted anything. مَا ذَاقَ فُوفًا
Having white stripes (garment). أَفْوَاف ومُفَوَّف
To overcome, to surpass a. o. ✲ فَاقَ o فَوْقًا وفَوَاقًا ه
To be above a. o. — هـ
To sob. ✧ To awake from sleep. To recollect a. th. — فُوَاقًا
To gasp (dying man); to die. فَاقَ بِنَفْسِهِ فُؤُوقًا وفُوَاقًا
To break (an arrow) on the notch. فَاقَ فَوْقًا هـ
To be broken at the notch (arrow). فَاقَ a وفَوِقَ a فَاقًا وفَوْقًا

To make a notch to (an arrow). فوّق ه

To make (a young one) to drink (milk) by intervals. ✧ To awake a. o. To remind a. o. of. — ه

To prefer a. th. to. فوّق ه على

To put the notch of (an arrow) on the bowstring. أفاق إفاقة وأفوق إفواقًا ه

To recover o.'s senses after (a swoon). To awake from (sleep, intoxication). To recover from (a disease). أفاق واستفاق من

✧ To remember; to recollect. تفوّق

To rise, to raise o.'s self above. — على

To drink by draughts. To waste away o.'s goods. تفوّق ه

To milk a (she-camel) by intervals. — واستفاق ه

To be broken at the notch (arrow). إنفاق

To fall into destitution. To gasp and sob (dying man). إفتاق

Large bowl filled with food. Cooked olive-oil. فاق

Destitution, poverty. فاقة

Particle. On, upon, (*opp. to* تحت) above, over, more, on high. فوق

From above, towards the upper part. من فوقُ، إلى فوقُ

We remained more than a month. لبثنا فوق شهر

Superior, upper. (*opp. to* تحتاني) فوقاني

Tip of the tongue. Notch of an arrow. First way; manner, direction. فوق ج فُوَق وأفواق

He went away and did not come back. ما ارتدّ على فوقه

May such a one die! رجع فلان الى فوقه

Notch of an arrow. فُوَق

Notch of an arrow. فوقة ج فوق

Milk collected in the udder between two milkings. فيقة ج فِيق وفيقات وأفواق وجج أفاويق

Recovery from a disease, from intoxication. Rest, intermittence. إفاقة

Superior, excellent. Superfine. ✧ Awake, remembering. فائق ج فوقة

Supernatural. فائق الطبيعة

Time between two successive milkings, two milkings. فَواق وفُواق

He remained in my house but a short time. ما أقام عندي إلّا فواقًا

Gasp, death-rattle. فُواق ج أفوقة وآفقة وجج أفوقات

Broken at the notch (arrow). أفوق

He has partially succeeded. رجع بأفوق ناصل

Excellent (poet). مُفيق

Broad beans. ✠ فول

Thyme, mint. ◻ فولية

Seller of broad beans. فوّال

To make bread. ✠ فام — فوْمًا

Bread; wheat; any grain used for bread. ✧ Chick-peas. فوم

Ear of corn. Pinch of a. th. فومة ج فوم

Swan. ◻ فون

To pronounce (a word, a discourse). ✠ فاه ٥ فوهًا، وتفوّه ب

To be wide-mouthed. فوه a فوهًا

To create a. o. with a great mouth (God). فوّه ه

To have a private conversation with a. o. فاوه مفاوهة ه وفاهى مفاهاة ه

To enter into the orifice of. تفوّه ه

To hold a conference together. تفاوه

To eat and drink much after dearth. إستفاه استفاهًا واستفاهة

Mouth, orifice. فوه وفاه وفيه ج أفواه

My mouth. (*for all cases*) فيّ

Perfume. Species, kind. *Pl.* Aromatics فوه ج افواه وافاويه

Small mouth. فويه

He fell dead on his face. مات لفيه

I spoke to him in private, mouth to mouth. كلّمته فاه إلى فيّ

Width of the mouth. فوه

Madder, plant used for dyeing. فوه وفوّة

Mouth, orifice, entrance. فوهة ج فوهات

Crater of a volcano, فوهة البركان

Eloquent. Glutton. فيه ومفوه

Talk. Backbiting. فوّهة

Entrance of a valley. Crater of a volcano. — ج فوّهات وأفواه وفوائه

Wide-mouthed. أفوه م فوهاء ج فوه

Opening a large wound (spear-thrust); large-mouthed (well). فوهاء

Aromatised (drink). مفوّه

Dyed with madder (cloth). — ومفوّى

To hasten, to hurry on.   أَقَامَ إِقَاجَةً ✳

To bleed (wound).   فَاحَ i فَيْحًا وفَيَحَانًا ✳

   To boil (cooking-pot).

To be verdant (spring).   — فَيْحًا وفُيُوحًا

To spread themselves for   وفَرَ a فَيْحً

   a raid : (horsemen). To be broad

   (place).

To squander a. th. away ; to   فَيَّحَ هـ

   give a. th. with profusion.

Abundance of herbage in a   فَيْحٌ وفُيُوحٌ

   plain.

Spreading for a raid (horsemen).   فَيَّاحٌ

Spread out (o horsemen).   رِفِيحِي فَيَاحِ

Immense (sea). Generous.   فَيَّاحٌ

Extensive (land) ;   أَفْيَحُ م فَيْحَاءُ ج فِيحٌ

   large (house).

To spread (perfume).   فَاخَ i فَيْخًا وفَيَخَانًا ✳

To turn aside from.   أَفَاخَ مِن

Saucer, cup. Abundant pasturage.   فَيْخَةٌ

   Vehement heat.

To continue, to last. To   فَادَ i فَيْدًا ✳

   pass away.

To accrue to a. o. (benefit).   — لـ

To have a haughty gait.   — وفَيَّدَ

✦ To lend a. th. upon interest.   فَيَّدَ هـ

To do service ; to give   أَفَادَ إِفَادَةً هـ ه ه

   (property) to. To acquaint a. o. with.

To derive profit from.   — واسْتَفَادَ مِن

To impart knowledge o. to a.   تَفَايَدَ

   To do service o. to a.

Saffron.   فَيْد

Utility, advantage,   فَائِدَة ج فَوَائِد

   profit. ✦ Interest on money.

Owl. Lion. Walking elegantly.   فَيَّاد

Having a proud demeanour.   وفَيَّادَة

Advantage. profit. Wealth.   إِفَادَة

   Knowledge.

Useful, profitable. Having a   مُفِيد

   complete meaning (word).

To seclude o.'s self.   فَازَ — إِنْفَاز ✳

Nervous, muscular.   فَيَّز

To boast falsely.   فَاشَ i فَيْشًا ✳

To vie with. a. o.   فَايَش مُفَايَشَةً وفِيَاشًا ه

   in boasting : to utter vain threats

   against.

To boast falsely of.   تَفَيَّش هـ

To give up a. th.   — عن

Boastful, humbug.   فَائِش وفَيَّاش وفَيُوش

Distinguished chief.   فَيَّاش

Preposition meaning : In, into,   فِي ✳

   amongst, during. With, in company

   of. For, for the sake of. Upon. By (in

   multiplication, proportion). Concer-

   ning. In comparison with.

In the house   فِي الْبَيْت

Amongst people.   فِي النَّاس

In such a year.   فِي سَنَة كَذَا

During few years.   فِي بِضْع سِنِين

He came with his retinue.   جَاءَ فِي مَرْكَبِهِ

He has spent his   بَذَل مَالَهُ فِي سَبِيلِ اللّٰه

   wealth for the sake of God.

Chapter the first :   الْبَاب الْأَوَّل فِي التَّقْوَى

   On the fear of God.

What is the present   مَا الدُّنْيَا فِي الْآخِرَة

   world in comparison with the life

   to come.

Five multiplied by three.   خَمْسَة فِي ثَلَاثَة

Its length   طُولُه خَمْسُون ذِرَاعًا فِي تِسْعَة أَذْرُع

   is of 50 cubits by nine in breadth.

There is.   فِيه ✦

There is not.   مَا فِيه ومَا فِيش ✦

To turn, to change   فَاءَ i فَيْئًا وتَفَيُّأً ✳

   (shade).

To return, to come back to.   — إِلَى

To take a. th. as booty.   — واسْتَفَاءَ هـ

To give much shade (tree).   فَيَّأَ تَفْيِئَة

To turn round (shadow).   أَفَاءَ

To give back a. th. to.   — هـ عَلَى فُلَان

To shade o.'s self in.   تَفَيَّأ هـ وفِي

To seek protection   تَفَيَّأ فُلَان

   towards a. o.

Shade. Booty made   فَيْء ج أَفْيَاء وفُيُوء

   by Moslems.

Expression   يَا فَيْء ويَا كَمْيَ ويَا شَيْءَ مَالِي

   of wonder or grief. Oh! Alas! for

   my wealth! O my wonder! what a

   wealth !

Return.   فِيئَة وفِيئَة

Detachment, party   فِئَة ج فِئَات وفِئُون

   of soldiers.

Shade. Booty.   تَفِيئَة

He came at the   دَخَل عَلَى تَفِيئَة فُلَان

   heels of such a one.

Submitted to Moslems (country,   مُفَاء

   person).

Shaded place.   مَفْيَأَة ومَفْيُؤَة

Courier. Party of men.   فَيْج ج فُيُوج P

   Messenger.

* فاص i فيصًا في To penetrate into (a country).
ما فِصتُ أفعَل I have not ceased doing it.
أفاص To have the fingers parted.
— عن To slip from (the hand).
— الكلام To pronounce distinctly.
ما عَنهُ مَفيص It is unavoidable.
* فاض i فَيضًا وفَيَضانًا وفُيُوضًا وفَيضُوضَةً
To be abundant. To overflow. To flow (blood, water). To spread out (news).
— فَيضًا To be filled up, to overflow (vessel).
— صَدرُهُ بالسِّرّ He revealed his secret.
فاض مِن To come out from.
— فَيضًا وفُيُوضًا To die.
فاضت نفسُهُ His soul has departed.
أفاض ه To pour (a liquid). To fill (a vessel) to the brim.
أفاض To go from a place to another in a crowd (pilgrims). To ruminate (camel).
— في To engage in (a conversation).
— على فُلان To win a. o.
— بكلمة To pronounce (a word) distinctly.
تفيّض To shed tears (eyes).
إستفاض To spread about (news).
— الوادي شجرًا The valley is covered with trees.
— فُلانًا To ask a. o. to pour water.
فَيض ج فُيُوض River. Abundance, profusion. Generosity.
غَيض مِن فَيض Little from much; a drop from a sea.
أرض ذات فُيُوض Land profusely watered.
إفاضة Press, movement of a crowd.
فَيَضان وفائِض Abundance, redundance.
فَيَضان النيل ◘ Flood-season of the Nile.
فائِض ◘ Interest (on money).
فيّاض Overflowing (torrent). Bountiful (man).
مُفاض ومُستفيض ومُستفاض فيه Spread, divulged (news).
مُفاضة Ample (coat of mail). Extensive land.
* فاظ i فَيظًا وفَيظانًا وفُيُوظًا وفَيظُوظَةً
To die.
أفاظ ه To cause a. o. to die (God).
* فَيفى وفَيفاء، وفَيف ج فياف وأفياف وفُيُوف
Desert, waterless land.
* فاق i فَيقًا بنفسِهِ He gave up the ghost.
✧ فيّق ه To awake a. o. To remind a. o.
أفيَق To compose excellent verses.
فَيق Clucking of a cock.
فِيق Man of tall stature.
* فال i فَيلةً وفُيُولةً وفَيلُولةً، وتفيّل To be weak, unsound (judgment).
فيّل ه To judge (an opinion) to be erroneous.
تفيّل To grow up (plant, youth).
P فيل م فيلة ج أفيال وفُيُول وفِيَلة Elephant. ✧ Bishop (at chess).
سِنّ الفيل Ivory.
داء الفيل Barbadoes leg (disease).
آذان الفيل Cuckoo-pint (*plant*).
فيّال ج فيّالة Elephant-driver.
فال وفائل وفيل وفيّل الرأي Of weak judgment (man).
فَيالة Unsoudness of judgment.
فيّل اللحم Bulky, fleshy.
مَفيُولاء Young ones of the elephant.
* فان i فَينًا To come, to arrive.
✧ To be stingy.
فَينة Time, moment. ✧ Avarice.

ق

To croak (raven). ✱ قَأْقَأ
Croak of a raven. قَأْقَاء
White of eggs. قِئْقِئ
To eat, to drink a. th. ✱ قَأَب a قَأْبًا ه
To drink to excess. قَئِب a قَأْبًا وقَأَبًا مِن
Great drinker. قَؤُوب ومِقْأَب
Large vessel. قَوْأَب وقَوْأَبِيّ
To dry up (herbage). ✱ قَبَّ o i قَبًّا
To cut off, to sever the hand). ✧ To lift (a stone). — i قَبًّا واقْتَبَّ ه
✧ He rose and went out from the place. قَبَّ عَنِ المَوْضِع
To be disorderly (crowd). To become dry (fruit). To heal (wound). — i قُبُوبًا
To gnash the teeth (animal). — i قَبًّا وقَبِيبًا
To be emaciated (belly). قَبِب a قَبَبًا
To wither (plant). To build a cupola. قَبَّب
To render a. th. convex. — ه
To be surmounted by a dome (building). To bulge. To stoop (man). تَقَبَّب
To enter (a dome). — ه
Head; chief, king. Stallion. Piece inserted in the opening of a shirt. Sheave of a pivot. ✧ Shaft of a balance. قَبّ
Chief of a tribe. Sacrum. قِبّ
Lankness of the belly. قَبَب
Aloe arborea (*plant*). قُبَّب
Dome. Pavilion. Leathern tent. Palankeen. Vaulted building. ✧ Steeple. قُبَّة ج قُبَب وقِبَاب
The Tabernacle (amongst the Israelites). قُبَّة الشَّهَادَة او الزَّمَان
The dome of Islam *i. e.* Basrah. قُبَّة الإسلام
✧ Collar of a garment. قُبَّة الثَّوب
The year after the next. القَابّ
Thunder. Rain-drop. قَابَّة
Cutting (sword). Thick (nose). قُبَاب
Slender in the waist. أَقَبّ م قَبَّاء ج قُبّ
Emaciated by fasting. قُبِّيّ
Surmounted with a copula, vaulted. ✧ Convex. مُقَبَّب

To bray (ass). To roar (lion). To dote (man). To emit a sound. ✧ To swell out (skin). ✱ قَبْقَب
Cowry, sea-shell. قِبْقِب
Garrulous, liar. Rough. قُبَاقِب وقَبْقَاب
Wooden clog. قَبْقَاب ج قَبَاقِيب
Partridge ✧ Snipe. P قَبْج
✱ قَبُح o قُبْحًا وقُبُحًا وقَبَاحَة وقُبَاحًا وقُبُوحًا وقُبُوحَة To be hideous, ugly. To be foul, abominable (deed).
To render a. o. or a. th. ugly, hideous, foul (God). To disapprove a. th. قَبَح a قَبْحًا, وقَبَّح ه وه
He showed the foulness of such a one's doings. قَبَّح على فُلان فِعْلَهُ
To outrage a. o. قَابَح ه
To commit a foul deed. أَقْبَح
To find a. th. abominable, hideous. To disapprove, to loathe a. th. إستَقْبَح ه
Deformity, ugliness, turpitude. قُبْح وقُبُح وقَبَاحَة
Shame to him! قُبْحًا لَهُ .
Joint of the shank and the thigh. قَبَاح وقَبِيح
Ugly, shameful, abominable. قَبِيح ج قِبَاح وقَبْحَى وقَبَاحَى
Shameful action, turpitude. قَبِيحَة ج قَبَائِح وقِبَاح
To bury (the dead). ✱ قَبَر o i قَبْرًا ومَقْبَرًا ه
To have a grave dug for (the dead). To have a. o. buried. To permit to a. o. to bury a dead person. أَقْبَر ه
Grave. tomb. قَبْر ج قُبُور
قُبَرَة وقُبَّرَة وقُنبَرَة وقُنْبُرَة وقُنْبَرَاء وقُنْبُرَاء Lark (bird). ج قَنَابِر
Long and white raisin. قُبَّر
Lantern of a bat-fowler. *Pl.* Beaters insnaring (game) into a net. قُبَّار
Bean-caper (*plant*). قُبَّار البَقْلَة
Depressed (ground). قَبُور
مَقْبَرَة ومَقْبِرَة ومَقْبُرَة ومِقْبَرَة ج مَقَابِر Burial-ground, cemetery.
Sepulchral. Keeper of a cemetery. مَقْبَرِيّ ومَقْبُرِيّ

Cyprus (island). Pure copper. قُبْرُس ✲
Bagpipe. قُبُز T
To ask قَبَس i قَبْسًا , واقْتَبَس ه مِن ✲ or take fire from a. o. To learn a. th. from.
To teach a. o. To catch واقْبَس ه عِلمًا — (a disease).
To give fire to a. o. أقْبَس ه
To borrow passages from a book. إقْتَبَس
Origin, source. قِبْس
Firebrand; lighted fire-wood taken from a fire. قَبَس و مِقْبَاس
Hastiness. Loan received. قَبْسَة
Acquisition of knowledge. إقْتِبَاس العِلْم
Handsome-faced. قَابُوس
Live coals. Firebrand. Lighted fire-wood. مَقْبِس ج مَقَابِس
Hasty; seeking fire. مُقْتَبِس نَارٍ
Hook and eye. Buckle. قُبْشَة TE
To take a. th. with the end of the fingers. To take a pinch of. قَبَص i قَبْصًا , وقَبَّص ه ✲
To hinder a. o. from quenching his thirst. قَبَّص ه
To run at full gallop (horse). قَبَص i قَبْصًا
To be big-headed. قَبِص a قَبَصًا
To swarm on (a tree: locusts). — وتَقَبَّص على
To take a pinch of. إقْتَبَص قُبْصَة مِن
Heap of sand. Crowd of people. قِبْص
Pain in the liver. Bigness of the head. قَبَص
Pinch, handful of food. قَبْصَة وقُبْصَة وقَبِيصَة
Nimble, lively. قَبِص
Swift (horse). قَبُوص
Big-headed. Fleet (horse). أقْبَص م قَبْصَاء ج قُبْص
Earth heaped up. قَبِيص وقَبِيصَة
Vehement run. قِبِصَّى
Shackles for race-horses. مِقْبَص ج مَقَابِص
I took it according to the measure. أخَذْتُهُ على المِقْبَص
To seize with the hand, to grasp a. th. قَبَض i قَبْضًا ه ب او على ب ✲
To discharge, to remove a. o. from. — ه عن
To constipate (the bowels: food). — ه

To contract, to restrain a. th.
To receive money. قَبَض واقْتَبَض ه
He abstained from grasping. قَبَض يَدَهُ عن
To take a. o.'s soul (God). — ه
To dart forth (bird, horse). — وانقَبَض
He was taken by death. قُبِض
To give to a. o. (money) in the hand. قَبَّض ه ه
To pick up and set th. apart. — ه
To restrain a. th.
To grasp the hand of a. o. قَابَض ه
To make a handle for (a sword). أقْبَض ه
To be wrinkled (skin). To be costive (belly). تَقَبَّض
To shrink from. — عن
To rush towards. — إلى
To deliver (goods) and money to a. o. تَقَابَض
To be contracted; to shrink. إنْقَبَض
To crouch before leaping (lion). To be taken, grasped. To be distressed.
To hasten in. إنْقَبَض في
To receive money from. إقْتَبَض ه مِن
To take a handful of. إقْتَبَض قَبْضَةً مِن
Grasp. Seizure. Receiving of money. قَبْض
Property taken in possession. Hastiness, quickness. قَبَض
Death. قَبْضَة
The thing came into his possession. صار الشَّيْء في قَبْضَتِهِ
Handful. قَبْضَة وقُبْضَة
Able manager of flocks. قُبَضَة
Quickness. Rush. قَبَاض وقَبَاضَة
Grasping strongly. قُبَّاض وقُبَّاضَة
Contraction. Aversion. إنْقِبَاض
Grasping. Tax-gatherer. Astringent (food). قَابِض
The taker of the souls *e. i.* the Angel of death. قَابِض الأَرْوَاح
Lively, quick. Assiduous, attentive. قَبِيض
Swift run. قِبِضَّى
Handle, hilt of a sword. مِقْبَض ومَقْبِض ج مَقَابِض
Crouching before leaping (lion). مُتَقَبِّض
To grasp a. th. To mix, to collect th. قَبَط o قَبْطًا ه ✲

To be responsible for. قَبِل وقَبُل o i قَبَالَةً ب
To be affected with convergent strabismus. قَبِل o قَبَلًا , وقَبِل a قَبَلًا
To give a kiss to. قَبَّل ه وه
To make a. o. to guarantee a. th. To hold a. o. responsible for. — ه ه
To be seated opposite, to face a. o. To be in opposition (stars). To correspond to. قَابَل ه وه
To collate (a writing) with. To compensate a. th. with another. — ه ب
To welcome, to receive a. o. kindly. To advance against a. o. — ه وأَقْبَل على
To become intelligent. ✧ To thrive: to be abundant (harvest). أَقْبَل
To be covered with plants (soil). — بِالنَّبَات
To come forth. أَقْبَل إِلى وعَلَى
To bring a. o. in the presence of. أَقْبَل ه ه
To go southward. تَقَبَّل
To receive, to take a. th. To hear (a prayer: God). To become a surety for. To assume (an obligation). — ه
To meet together face to face. To front o. a. To be in opposition (stars). تَقَابَل
To extemporise (a speech). To begin (an affair) anew. إِقْتَبَل ه
To come forward; to encounter a. o. To come in the presence . in front of. To anticipate a. th. إِسْتَقْبَل ه وه
To recover from (illness). — مِن
To be future, to be about to come. إِسْتَقْبَل
To be squint-eyed. إِقْبَلَّ وإِقْبَالَ
Before, (*opp. to* بَعْد) beforehand. قَبْلُ وقَبْلًا ومِن قَبْلُ
Before that. قَبْلَ ذٰلِكَ او مِن قَبْلِ ذٰلِكَ
Before (*with a verb*). قَبْلَ أَن
Forepart, front side. قُبْل وقُبُل
I go towards thee. أَقْبِل قُبُلَكَ
رَأَيْتُهُ قُبُلًا وقَبَلًا وقُبُلًا وقِبَلًا وقَبِيلًا وقَبَلِيًّا
I saw him in front, face to face.
Summit of an opposite hill. Convergent strabismus. First appearance of an object. Extemporisation. قَبَل
Henceforward. مِن ذِي قَبَل وقِبَل

✧ To shudder with fear. قَبَط و✧ تَقَبَّط
✧ To make a. o. to shudder. ✧ قَبَّط ه
✧ Shudder. قَبْطَة
Copts. قِبْط وأَقْبَاط
A Copt. Coptic. قِبْطِي وقُبْطِيّ ج قَبَاطِيّ
Fine Egyptian linen. قُبْطِيَّة ج قَبَاطِيّ
Preserve, sweetmeat. قُبَّاط وقُبَّيْط وقُبَّيْطَى وقُبَّيْطَاء
Woollen cloak. Small locust. ✧ قَبُوط
Captain of a ship. ✧ قَبْطَان ون قَابُودَان
✱ To conceal the head in its skin (hedge-hog); in his clothes (man). ✱ قَبَع a قُبُوعًا
To be out of breath, to pant. — قَبْعًا
☐ To drink eagerly.
To grunt (pig). To roar (elephant). — قَبْعًا قِبَاعًا وقُبَاعًا
To ramble in (a country). — قُبُوعًا في
✧ To pull out a. th. — قَبْعًا, وقَبَّع ه
To drink from (a skin). — واقْتَبَع ه
To enter (its nest: bird). إِنْقَبَع في
Bugle. ✧ Small cup. قُبْع
Hedge-hog. قُبَع
Calyx of a flower. قُبْعَة
Variegated bird. Veiled (woman). قُبَعَة
Cap; conical bonnet. ✧ قُبَّعَة
✧ Woollen cap. Conical hood. قُبُوعَة ج قَبَابِيع
Fearful. قُبَاع
Hedge-hog. Stupid. Measure of capacity. قُبَاع
Silver or iron pommel of a sword. قَبِيعَة ج قَبَائِع
Grunt of a pig. قِبِيعَة وقِنْبِيعَة
Horses late in a race. قَوَابِع
✱ Huge, enormous (man, animal). ✱ قَبَعْثَرَى ج قَبَاعِث
☐ War-ship. Pontoon. T قَبَاق
✱ To receive, to meet a. o. To accept (a proposition). ✱ قَبِل a قُبُولًا وقَبُولًا ه وه
To blow from the south (wind). قَبَل o قَبْلًا وقَبُولًا قُبُولًا
To busy o.'s self about. To undertake a. th. — o قَبْلًا , وأَقْبَل على
To put thongs to (a sandal). — a قَبْلًا , وقَابَل وأَقْبَل ه
To come, to draw near (time). قَبِل a قَبَلًا , وأَقْبَل
To receive a child at his birth (midwife). قَبِل a قِبَالَةً

قَبَل Power, influence.
مَا لِي بِهِ قِبَل I have no authority for that.
قِبَلًا In front, in the presence of.
قِبَلَهُ In his hands, next to him.
مِن قِبَلِهِ On his behalf.
قِبْلَة Opposite side of the horizon. Direction to Mecca. ✧ South.
مَا لَهُ فِي هٰذَا قِبْلَةٌ وَلَا دِبْرَةٌ He cannot distinguish the front from the back *i. e.* he knows not what to do.
اِجْعَلُوا بُيُوتَكُم قِبْلَةً Seat your houses opposite.
قِبْلِيّ ◻ Southern. South-wind. Upper Egypt.
قَبْلَة وقُبْلَة Love-philter. Amulet.
قُبْلَة ج قُبَل , وتَقْبِيل Kiss. ◻ Track of a beast.
قِبَال Thong of a sandal.
حَشِيشَة القِبَال Campion (*plant*).
لَا يَعْرِف قِبَالًا مِن دِبَار He is unable to distinguish anything.
قَبَالَة Suretyship, warrant. Obligation assumed.
قُبَالَتَهُ و✧ قِبَالَهُ Opposite, in front of him.
قَبُول وقُبُول Welcome, kindness, approbation. Acceptance.
قَبُول وقَبِيل Midwife.
قَبِيل Surety, warrantor. Consort.
— ج قُبُل وقُبَلَاء Class of men.
مِن هٰذَا القَبِيل From this side, from this point of view.
لَا يَعْرِف قَبِيلًا مِن دَبِير He cannot distinguish a comer from a goer.
قُبَيْلًا A little before, a while ago.
قَبِيلَة ج قَبَائِل Nomadic (tribe). Stone covering a well. Bone of the skull.
إِقْبَال Coming, arrival. Thriving.
إِسْتِقْبَال Opposition of two stars. Time to come, the future.
أَقْبَل م قَبْلَاء ج قُبْل Afflicted with a convergent squinting.
قَابِل Receiving, meeting. Next (year). Receiving the bucket from the water-drawer.
— ل Liable to.
قَابِل لِلْمَوْت Subject to death, mortal.
قَابِلَة ج قَوَابِل Midwife. *Pl.* Beginnings of.
قَابِلِيَّة Ability, liability to. ✧ Appetite.

مُقَابِل Seated opposite. Noble-born.
مُقَابَل ومُدَابَر Noble by both parents.
مُقَابَلَة وتَقَابُل Confrontation. Collation of two texts. Opposition of two stars.
مُقْبِل Coming. Next (year). Auspicious.
مُقَبَّل Patched (garment).
مُقْتَبَل الشَّبَاب Still young.
مُسْتَقْبِل Opposite. Encountering. Future (time).
☆ قَبَن i قُبُونًا To penetrate into (a country).
قَبَّن ه To weigh a. th. with a steelyard. ✧ To weigh a. th. in the hand
أَقْبَن To flee away at full speed.
إِقْبَأَنّ وإِقْبَانّ To be wrinkled, contracted.
قُبْنَة Hurry, haste.
قَبَّان Steelyard.
حِمَار وعَيْر قَبَّان Wood-louse (insect). Blackbeetle.
قَبَّانِيّ Weigher.
✧ قُبُونَة Weighing of.
قِبَانَة Craft of a weigher.
☆ قَبَا o قَبْوًا ه To pluck, ta take off a. th. with the fingers. To raise a (building. To collect (saffron).
— قَبَّأ ه To bend, to fold a. th.
قَبَّى ه To put th. in order. To cut out (a gown). ✧ To render a. th. convex.
— على To wrong a. o.
تَقَبَّى To have the shape of a cupola. To clothe o.'s self in a gown. To bulge out.
— ه To follow a. o. step by step.
إِنْقَبَى عن فُلَان To hide o.'s self from.
إِقْتَبَى ه To set things in order.
قَبْو ج ✧ أَقْبِيَة Testudo, besieging machine. ✧ Vault, cave, underground room.
قَبَاء ج أَقْبِيَة Man's gown with full sleeves.
قِبَاء Interval, space.
بَنُو قَابِيَاء Wine-drinkers.
قَابِيَة Collecting saffron (woman).
مَقْبُوّ Contracted, thick-set.
مَقْبِيّ Fat.
☆ قَبِي — قَبِي Space, interval.
قَبَايَة Desert.

To deceive o. a. تَقَاتَر

Stinginess. Scanty food. قَتْر وتَقْتِير
Bare sufficiency.

Dust. قَتْر وقَتَرة وقُتْرة

Side, region. قَتَر وقُتْر ج أقْتَار

Hut of a hunter. قُتْرة ج قُتَر

Short arrow. قِتْرة ج قِتَر

The lurking one, the devil. — وأبُو قِتْرة

Smell of cooked meat, of aloes- قُتَار
wood

First appearance of hoariness. قَتِير

Head of the nails of a coat of mail.

Light, comfortable (saddle, قَاتِر ومُقْتِر
shield).

Stingy. قَاتِر وقَتُور وأقْتَر ومُقَتِّر

Guitar. قِيتَار ج قَيَاتِير وقِيثَار ج قَيَاثِير

Dust-coloured. أقْتَر

To be vile. * قَتُم a قُتُوعًا

Hive in a rock. قَتْم

Wood-fretter. قَتْم

To kill, to put * قَتَل o قَتْلًا وتَقْتَالًا ة
a. o. to death. ✧ To beat a. o. unmercifully.

He slew him for avenging his قَتَلَه بأخِيه
brother's murder.

To commit suicide. نَفْسَه

To allay (hunger, cold). To mix ه —
(wine) with water.

To know a. th. thoroughly. — ه خُبْرًا

To perpetrate slaughter قَتَّل ة
amongst.

To wage war ' قَاتَل مُقَاتَلَة وقِتَالًا وقِيتَالًا ة
with a. o.

May God curse him! ة الله

God bless him! What قَاتَلَه الله مَا أفْصَحَه
an eloquent man !

To expose a. o. to death. أقْتَل ة

To apply o.'s self strenuously to. تَقَتَّل ل

To walk in inclining the — في المِشْيَة
body (woman).

To fight with one another. تَقَاتَل واقْتَتَل

To die from madness. أقْتَتَل

To risk, to jeopardise o.'s اسْتَقْتَل
life.

Violent death ; murder, slaughter, قَتْل
manslaughter. Capital punishment.
✧ Thrashing, drub.

Enemy, foe, fighter. قِتْل ج أقْتَال
Gallant. Similar, alike.

To lie ; to slander. * قَتَّ o قَتًّا

To falsify (a conversation). ه — وقَتَّت

To follow the footsteps of a. o. قَتَّ إلى
(spy).

To collect little by little. To ه —
arrange a. th.

To gather ; to cook aro- ه — قَتَّت
matics.

To extirpate, to snatch a. th. ه — اقْتَتَّ

Lie. Luzern ; fodder. قَتّ

Mimosa (plant). قَتَّات

Backbiter, calumniator. قَتَّات وقَتُوت

False reports. أقَاوِيل مَقْتُوت ومُقَتَّت

To feed a. o. with * قَتِب o قَتْبًا ة
roasted tripes.

To saddle (a beast). أقْتَب ة

To impose a severe أقْتَب فُلَانًا يَمِينًا
oath upon a. o.

Intestines, guts. قِتْب وقِتْبَة ج أقْتَاب

Pack-saddle. — وقَتَب ج أقْتَاب

Hump, hunch. ✧ قَتَب

Hump-back. ه أبُو قَتَب

Saddled beast. قَتُوبَة

Thorny tree used as * قَتَاد — قَتَاد
fodder for camels. Tragacanth-tree.

To prepare fodder for (a camel). ة قَتَّد

Frame of a قَتَد وقَتِد ج أقْتَاد وقُتُود وأقْتُد
camel's saddle.

To live scantily. * قَتَر i o قَتْرًا وقُتُورًا
To be barely sufficient (sustenance).

To give bare suste- قَتَّر وقَتَر وأقْتَر على
nance to (o.'s family).

To exhale its odour — وقَتَّر a قَتْرًا، وقَتَر
(cooked meat).

To cleave to a. th. قَتَّر وأقْتَر ه

To emit its smell (cooked meat). قَتَّر

To fumigate o.'s self in order —
not to be scented by wild beasts
(hunter).

To bring things together. — بين

To lie in wait (hunter). To be أقْتَر
reduced to destitution. To perfume
o.'s self.

To be angry. تَقَتَّر

To prepare to (fight). — ل

To lurk in wait for game — للصَّيْد
(hunter).

To try to deceive a. o. — ة

To depart from. — عن

To abound in cucumbers (land). * قَثَّا – أَقَثَّا
Cucumis sativus, cucumber. قِثَّاء وقُثَّاء وه قَثَّا و ✧ مُقَثِّي
Elaterium, squirting cucumber. قِثَّاء الحِمَار
Virginia snakeroot. قِثَّاء الحَيَّة
Cucumber-bed. مَقْثَأَة ومَقْثُوَة
To craunch cucumbers. * قَثَد o قَثْدًا
To cut cucumbers. إِقْتَثَد
Yellow cucumber; gherkin. قَثَد
To provide o.'s self with furniture, utensils. * قَثَر – اقْتَثَر ه
House-furniture, utensils. قُثْرَة وقُثْرُدَة
To acquire wealth. * قَثَم i قَثْمًا, واقْتَثَم ه
To soil a. o. with dejection. قَثَم ه
To give to a. o. the best of. قَثَم o قَثْمًا لَهُ مِن
To be defiled with dejection قَثِم a وقَثَم o قُثْمَة وقَثْمًا
To be dusty. قَثِم o قَثْمًا وقَثَامَة
Acquiring wealth. Very liberal. قُثَم
Dust-colour. قُثْمَة
Collecting wealth for doing good. قَثُوم
To acquire (wealth). * قَثَا o قَثْوًا, وقَثَى i قَثْيًا, واقْتَثَى ه
To be pure, unmixed. ✧ To cough. * قَحَّ o قُحُوحَة وقَحَاحَة
✧ Violent cough. قَحَّة
Pure, unmixed. Unripe (melon). قُحّ ج أَقْحَاح, وقُحَاح
True born Arab. أَعْرَابِيّ قُحّ وقُحَاح
Miser. لَئِيم قُحّ وقُحَاح
To burst out into laughter. * قَحْقَح
To cough (camel). ✧ To lead a profligate life. * قَحَب o قَحْبًا وقُحَابًا, وقَحَّب
To prostitute herself (woman). قَاحَب وتَقَحَّب
Coughing. Aged. قَحْب
Prostitute, strumpet. قَحْبَة ج قِحَاب
Cough. قُحَاب
Violent (cough). قَاحِب
To have the hump fully developed (camel). * قَحِد a قَحَدًا, وأَقْحَد
Camel's hump. قَحَدَة ج قِحَاد وأَقْحُد
Base of the hump. – ومَقْحَدَة
Lonely, without kindred. قَحَاد
Sturdy old man. * قَحْر ج أَقْحُر وقُحُور
Strong old age. قَحَارَة وقُحُورَة

A murder. ✧ A thrashing, a drub. قَتْلَة
Way of killing. قِتْلَة
Horrible way of killing. قِتْلَة سُوء
Weapon. Strength. Remainder. قَتَال
War, fight. ✧ Quarrel. قِتَال ومُقَاتَلَة
Killing, murderer. Deadly (poison). قَاتِل ج قُتَّال وقَتَلَة
Wolf's bane, kind of aconit. – الذِّئْب
Apocymum, dog's bane. – الكَلْب
Murderer. Slayer. قَتُول (m. f.) ج قُتُل وقُتَّل
Murdered. Slain. قَتِيل (m. f.) ج قَتْلَى وقُتَلَاء وقَتَالَى, ومَقْتُول
Vital part of the body. Murder. مَقْتَل ج مَقَاتِل
Experienced, tried. مُقَتَّل
Battle-field. مُقْتَتَل
To rise in the air (dust). * قَتَم o قُتُومًا, وقَتِم a قَتَمًا
To be brown. اِقْتَمّ
Brown, dusky colour. قُتْمَة وقَتَام وقُتْمَة
Darkness. قَتَام
Dust. قَتَام وقَتَمَة
Abyss of death. حِيَاض قُتَيْم
Brown. Blackish, dark, obscure. قَاتِم ج قَوَاتِم, وأَقْتَم
Remote and dark (place). قَاتِم الأَعْمَاق
To dry up (fish). * قَتَن o قُتُونًا
To become consumptive. To have a bare sustenance. قَتُن o قَتَانَة, وأَقْتَن
To destroy (ticks). أَقْتَن ه
Dark brown colour. قَتَان وقُتْنَان
Dark brown. قَاتِن
Starved. Vile. Thin (spear-head). قَتِين (m. f.)
To serve a. o. well. * قَتَا o قَتْوًا وقَتًا و قِتًى ومَقْتًى ه
To take a. o. as a servant. إِقْتَوَى ه
Backbiting. قَتْوَة
Servant. قَاتٍ, ومَقْتَى ومَقْتَوِيّ
To drag, to draw a. o. along. * قَثَّ o قَثًّا ه
To drive (cattle). – ه
To uproot (a tree), to pull out a. th. – واقْتَثَّ ه
To acquire property. قَثَّ o قَثًّا وقَثِيثَى
Utensils. قُثَاث
Numerous company, crowd. قَثَاثَة وقَثِيثَة ومَقَثَّة

Washing away (river). قُحاف, وقَاحِف ج قحف

Shovel. Scraper. Dust-pan. ✧ قَاحُوف وقَاحُوفة

Winnow. Dust-pan. مِقْحَفَة ج مَقَاحِف

Taken away. Having a fracture on the skull. مَقْحُوف

✱ قَحَل a قُحُولًا, وقَحِل وقَحِل a قَحْلًا وقَحَلًا,

To be raw-boned (old man). To be advanced in age. وتَقَحَّل

To become dry, to dry up. قَحِل

To dessicate a. th. أَقْحَل ه

To emaciate a. o (fasting). ٥ —

Tabes of sheep. قُحَال

Dryness, aridity. قُحُولة

Dry, raw-boned (old man). قَاحِل وقَحْل وقَحِل وإنقَحْل ومُتَقَحِّل

To rush blindly into. ✱ قَحَم o قُحُومًا فِي

To enter (a desert). a قَحْمًا ه —

To come near to. إلى —

To embark a. o. inconsiderately in an affair. قَحَّم وأَقْحَم ٥ فِي

To throw off (his rider) with the face on the ground (horse). قَحَّم ٥

To impel (a horse into a river : rider). أَقْحَم ٥ ه

To insert (a word) between the subject and its regimen as : قطع يَدَ ورِجلَ زَيدٍ *instead of* قطع يَدَ زَيدٍ وَرِجلَهُ ه —

To be driven away from a land by drought (tribe). أُقْحِم

To enter (a river : horse). تَقَحَّم ه

To throw (its rider) on the face (horse). ب —

To rush blindly into. وانقَحَم فِي واقتَحَم ه —

To despise a. o. إِقْتَحَم ٥

Old, broken. قَحْر أَم قَحْمَة ج قِحَام

Rash undertaking. Unfruitful year. قُحْمَة ج قُحَم

The hardships of the road. قُحَم الطَّرِيق

Decrepitude. قَحَامَة وقُحُومَة

Intensely black. أَسْوَد قَاحِم

Decrepit. Revolving rapidly (wheel). قَحُوم

Rushing rashly into perils. مِقْحَام ج مَقَاحِيم

Dangerous places. مَقَاحِم

To jump. To stir about. ✱ قَحَز a قَحْزًا

To strike a. o. with (a stick). وقَحَز ٥ ب —

To throw a. o. down. قَحْزًا وقُحُوزًا بِفُلَانٍ —

To scatter (urine : dog). قَحْزًا وقُحُوزًا وقَحَزَانًا ب —

To fall like a dead man. قُحُوزًا —

To be thrust back. قُحِز

To speak harshly to a. o. قَحَّز وتَقَحَّز الكَلَامَ إِلَى فُلَانٍ

Misfortunes. قَاحِزَات

Bramble-net for birds. قُحَازَة

To lead a hard and painful life. ✱ قَحِش — ✧ قَاحَش

To pass swiftly. ✱ قَحَص a قَحْصًا

To discard, to remove a. o. from. قَحَص وأَقْحَص ٥ عَن

He has outstripped him in running. سَبَقَهُ قَحْصًا

To strike a. o. violently. ✧ To take away (dirt). ✱ قَحَط a قَحْطًا ٥ وه

To fail (rain). وقَحِط a قَحْطًا —

قَحَط وقَحِط a قَحْطًا وقَحَطًا وقُحُوطًا, وقُحِط

To be rainless (year). وأَقْحَط

To be afflicted with drought (land, tribe). قُحِط وقَحِط قَحْطًا, وأَقْحَط

To fecundate (a palm-tree). ✧ To scrape the bottom of (a cooking-pot) in emptying it. قَحَّط ه

To smite (a land) with drought (God). أَقْحَط ه

Droughtiness, rainless year. ✧ Dearth. قَحْط

Unfruitful year. Barren, droughty (land). قَاحِط ج قَوَاحِط, وقَحِط وقَحِيط ومَقْحُوط

To wash, to sweep away a. th. (torrent, rain). ✱ قَحَف a قَحْفًا, واقتَحَف ه

To fracture the skull of. قَحَف ٥

To winnow (corn). ه —

Skull. Lesion of the skull. Glass or wooden bowl. قِحْف ج أَقْحَاف وقُحُوف وقِحَفَة

He possesses nothing. مَا لَهُ قِدّ ولَا قِحْف

He has brought a disaster upon him. رَمَاهُ بِأَقْحَاف رَأْسِهِ

Large draught. قِحَاف

Refuse, rubbish. قُحَافَة

Drift-wind, sand-pillars. عَجَاجَة قَحْفَاء

How much, how many. ✧ قَدْ أَيْش ◘ قَدْ إِيْ
It is equal to it, it is of the same size. عَلَى قَدِّهِ
Leathern cup. Strap. Whip. قِدّ
Thong, strip. Party, sect. Paper-ruler. قِدَّة ج قِدَد وأَقِدَّة
Urchin. Jerboa. قَدَاد
Pain in the bowels, gripe. قُدَاد
Meat cut in slices and dessicated in the sun. قَدِيد ولَحْم مُقَدَّد
Garment in rags. قَدِيد
Followers of an army as blacksmiths. قَدِيدِيُّون
Road, way. Even soil. مَقَدّ
Iron paring-knife. مِقَدّ ومِقَدَّة
Cut in slices. ✧ Thin, emaciated. مَقْدُود
To strike fire with (a steel). ✱ قَدَحَ ٥ قَدْحًا, واقْتَدَحَ ب
To make a hole in (the wood of an arrow). To perforate (a tree: worm). قَدَحَ في
To speak ill of. To impugn, to impair a. o. — في فلانٍ
To contest the lineage of a. o. قَدَحَ في نَسَبِهِ
To couch the cataract (oculist). ه — To lade out soup from the pot. ✧ To perforate (wood).
To be sunk in its socket (eye). — وقَدِحَ
To weaken, to emaciate (a horse). قَدَّحَ ٥.
To revile o. another. قادَحَ ٥ وتَقادَحَ
To settle (an affair). إِقْتَدَحَ ه
Canker of wood, of the teeth. قَدْح
قِدْح ج أَقْدَاح وقِدَاح وأَقْدُح وجج أَقَادِيح
Featherless arrow. Divinatory arrow. Portion allotted. ✧ Hole.
Drinking-cup, bowl. ◘ Measure of capacity. قَدَح ج أَقْدَاح
Management of an affair. قِدْحَة
A striking of fire. قَدْحَة وقِدْحَة
Ladleful of soup. قُدْحَة
Art of making cups. قِدَاحَة
Fly. قُدُوح وأَقْدَح
Remainder of broth in a vessel. قَدِيح
Striking fire. Reviler, slanderer. قادِح

Weak. Arab born in the country. مُقْحَم
To snatch, to take the whole of. ✱ قَحَا ٥ قَحْوًا, واقْتَحَى ه
Chamomil (medicinal plant). قُحْوَان وأُقْحُوَان ج أَقَاحٍ وأَقَاحِيّ
✧ Marigold (flower). ✧ قُوقَحَان
1° *Corroborative particle added to a verb. When preceding the past, it means that an event has truly or recently happened, and when preceding the aorist it means that an event is expected to be shortly performed.* Indeed. Surely. Already. ✱ قَدْ
Zeyd has just risen. قَدْ قَامَ زَيْدٌ
Thy father is expected to come to-day. قَدْ يَقْدَمُ أَبُوكَ ٱلْيَوْمَ
The Messiah is already come. قَدْ جَاءَ ٱلْمَسِيحُ
2° *It means also prossibility.* It may.
A liar may sometimes say the truth. قَدْ يَصْدُقُ ٱلْكَذُوبُ
3° *Used as a noun it means sufficiency.* Enough.
A silver coin will do for me. قَدْنِي دِرْهَمٌ
A silver coin is sufficient for Zeyd. قَدْ زَيْدًا دِرْهَمٌ
To cut a. th. lengthwise. To dilacerate (leather, cloth). To cut off a. th. into shreds. ✱ قَدَّ ٥ قَدًّا, وقَدَّدَ واقْتَدَّ ه
To cross (a desert). To cut a. o. short (in speech). قَدَّ ه و٥
To suffer from colic. قُدَّ
To cut meat into strips and dessicate it in the sun. قَدَّدَ ه
To be cut into shreds. To be dried in the sun (meat). To be torn off (garment). To be lean. To make up parties. To part away (people). تَقَدَّدَ
To be cut into shreds. إِنْقَدَّ
To settle (affairs). إِقْتَدَّ ه .
To be even, smooth. To follow the same course. To walk in a line (camels). إِسْتَقَدَّ
Lamb's skin. Size of the body. Amount, measure, proportion, size. Whip. قَدّ ج أَقُدّ وقِدَاد وقُدُود
Musical tune. ✧ Popular tune, song. — ج قُدُود .

Earthen-pot urn. قِدْر و✧ قِدْرَة ج قُدُور
Fate, lot. Irreversible decree of God, predetermination. Power, might. Quantity, measure. Intrinsic value. ✧ Personal worth, rank. About. قَدْر ج أَقْدَار
The night of the decree, 27 th of Ramadhan. لَيْلَة القَدْر
Measure of a garment. قَدْرَة
Power, ability, wealth. قُدْرَة ومَقْدِرَة ومَقْدُرَة
Small flask. Space between two palm-trees. قَدْرَة
Power. ✧ Appraisement, valuation. قِدَار وقِدَار
Small cooking-pot. قُدَيْر وقُدَيْرَة
Power, might, strength. Opulence. قَدَارَة وقُدُورَة واقْتِدَار
Fatalism, predestination. Valuation Virtual sense of a word. ✧ Supposition. تَقْدِير ج تَقَادِير
Virtually. تَقْدِيرًا
Cooked in a pot. قَادِر وقَدِير
Powerful. Able to. قَادِر
Short-necked. More powerful. أَقْدَر م قَدْرَاء
Musulman (*opp. to* جَبْرِيَّة) sect opposed to the Fatalists. قَدَرِيَّة
Amount, measure. ✧ Space of time. مِقْدَار
As much, in as much as. بِمِقْدَار مَا
Predetermined. Fatalism. Fate, destiny. مُقَدَّر, ومَقْدُور ج مَقَادِير
✧ Appraiser of (crops). مُقَدِّر
Powerful. Becoming. مُقْتَدِر
To be pure, spotless ; to be holy. ✡ قَدُس o قُدْسًا وقُدُسًا
To purify, to sanctify a. o. (God). To hallow, to bless (God). قَدَّس ه
To go to Jerusalem. ✧ To say mass. To hear mass. To consecrate (bread, wine). قَدَّس
To be sanctified. ✧ To be consecrated (bread, wine). تَقَدَّس
Holiness, sanctity. ✧Reverence, *title used in addressing a priest.* قُدْس وقُدُس وقَدَاسَة
The Holy of Holies. — الأَقْدَاس
Jerusalem. أَلقُدْس

Hot (fever). Canker-worm. قَادِحَة ج قَوَادِح
Striking fire. Manufacturer of cups. قَدَّاح
Flint, stone of a steel. — وقَدَّاحَة
Iron or stone of a steel. قَدَّاح وقَدَّاحَة
Iron for striking fire. مِقْدَح ج مَقَادِح ومِقْدَاح ج مَقَادِيح
Ladle. Couching needle. ✧ Drill, gimlet. مِقْدَح ومِقْدَحَة
✧ Mischief-maker. مِقْدَاح
✡ قَدَر i o وقَدِر a قُدْرًا وقُدْرَة ومَقْدِرَة ومَقْدَرَة ومَقْدُرَة على To be able, to have strength for. To gain mastery over a. o.
To arrange, to prepare a. th. قَدَر i قَدْرًا ه
To measure a. th. by. — وقَدَّر ه ب
To value the amount of. قَدَر o i قَدْرًا وقَدَرًا ه وه
They have not realised what God is. مَا قَدَرُوا اللهَ حَقَّ قَدْرِهِ
To cook (meat). To prepare a. th. — o i قَدْرًا ه
To determine a. th. for a. o. To decree a. th. to a. o. (God). — قَدْرًا وقَدَرًا, وقَدَّر ه على
To allot a. th. to. — وقَدَّر ه ل
To be short-necked. قَدِر a قَدَرًا
To enable a. o. to. قَدَّر وأَقْدَر ه على
To assign (allowances). To ponder over (an affair). To predetermine a. th. ✧ To appraise, to value a. th. To suppose, to conjecture a. th. قَدَّر ه
To commensurate a. th. to. قَادَر ه
To be prepared, determined, decreed. تَقَدَّر
The garment is made according to his measure. تَقَدَّر الثَّوبُ عَلَيْهِ
To comprise a. th. virtually. — ب
To be made according to measure (garment). إِنْقَدَر
To be powerful, able. إِقْتَدَر
To be enabled, empowered to. — على
To ask (God) to decree a. th. إِسْتَقْدَر ه ه
Determined quantity, amount. Fate. Power, ability Wealth. Convenient. قَدَر ج أَقْدَار

The archangel Gabriel (for Moslems). ✧ The Holy Ghost (for Christians). رُوح ٱلقُدُس و✧ الرُّوح القُدُس

Small cup. Small plate. قُدُس وقُدَس

Large ship. قَادِس ج قَوَادِس

✧ Trough of a water-wheel. Mill-course. قَادُوس ج قَوَادِيس

Silver trinkets. Stone-trough. قُدَاس

High rank. شَرَف قُدَاس

Precious stone. قَدِيس

Rushing with the sword in hand. قَدُوس بِٱلسَّيف

Holy Mass. قُدَّاس ج قَدَادِيس

Sanctification. Blessing. ✧ Eucharistical consecration. تَقدِيس

Very holy. قَدُّوس وقُدُّوس

Holy. قِدِّيس ج قِدِّيسُون

Holy place. مَقدِس

Jerusalem. بَيت ٱلمَقدِس والبَيت المُقَدَّس

Holy scripture. The Bible. الكِتَاب ٱلمُقَدَّس

Relating to Jerusalem. مَقدِسِيّ ومُقَدَّسِيّ

Pilgrim to Jerusalem. ✧ مُقَدِّسِيّ ج مَقَادِسَة

To withhold a. o. To check (a horse). To strike (a horse) on the muzzle. ✠ قَدَع a قَدعًا ة

He is not to be reviled. لا يُقدَع أنفُهُ

To have (an affair) performed. قَدَّع ه

To drink by small draughts from. — من

To restrain, to remove a. o. from. — وأقدَع ة عن

To be weakened (eyes). قَدِع a قَدَعًا

I have nearly reached the age of fifty. قَدِعَت لِي ٱلخَمسُون

To overpower his rider (horse). قَادَع ة

To prepare mischief to a. o. تَقَدَّع بِالشَّرّ ل

To flutter around a lamp (moths). To die one after the other. To counteract, to check o. a. تَقَادَع

To spear o. a. — بِالرِّمَاح

To be restrained, repelled from. إِنقَدَع عَن

Weakening of the sight. قَدَع

Timid. Salt (water). Weeper. قَدِع

Modest (woman). قَدِعَة وقَدُوع

Fiery (horse). Vile, despised. Fond of. قَدُوع

Wrinkled, crumpled. مُقَدَّع

Stick, staff. مِقدَعَة

To exhaust (water). ✠ قَدَف o قَدفًا ه

Earthen jug, earthen bowl. قُدَاف

✠ قَدَم o قَدمًا وقُدُومًا , وقَدَّم وتَقَدَّم واستَقدَم ة To precede a. o. To lead the way to.

To advance boldly against. To venture upon. قَدَم o وقَدِم a وأقدَم على

To be back from (a journey). قَدِم a قُدُومًا وقِدمَانًا ومَقدَمًا من

To arrive at (a place). To meet a. o. — ه وة

To be previous. To be old, ancient. قَدُم o قَدَامَة وقِدَمًا, وتَقَادَم

To make a. o. to precede, to put a. o. foremost, ahead. To set a. o. over, to promote. قَدَّم وأقدَم ة

To prefer a. o. or a. th. to. قَدَّم ة وه على

To present a. th. to. To pay a. th. beforehand to. — ه ل

To give an oath. — وأقدَم ٱليَمِين

To introduce o.'s self to. — وتَقَدَّم بَين يَدَيه

To go forward. To be promoted. To be in progress. تَقَدَّم

To advance towards. — إلى

To order a. o. to. — إلى في

To be preferred to. To surpass a. o. To outstrip a. o. To be previously (done or said). — على

To advance boldly. To lead the way in war. إستَقدَم

To ask the promotion of a. o. — ة

Precedence, pre-existence. قِدَم

By-gone times. Antiquity. قِدم

Of old, in olden times. قِدمًا وقِدَمًا

Precedency. High rank. Bravery. Foot (measure). قَدَم

Human foot, step. قَدَم ج أقدَام

Nadir سَمت ٱلقَدَم

Brave, bold. قَدَم (*m. f. s. pl.*) وقَدِيم (*m. f.*) , وقُدُم وقُدُم

He walked straight on. مَضَى قُدُمًا

He was foremost in war. مَشَى ٱلقُدُمَ والقُدُمِيَّة

Rugged, stony (ground). قَدِم م قَدِمَة
Precedence, priority. قُدْمَة وقِدْمَة
Courage, boldness. قُدُمَـة
Proud deportment. قُدْمِيَّة وقُدُمِيَّة
He is يَمْشِي ٱلْقُدْمِيَّة والتَّقْدُمَة والتَّقْدُمِيَّة
 always foremost at war.
Gallant, dauntless. قَدُوم ج قُدُم
Carpen- قَدُوم و✧ قَدُّوم ج قَدَائِم وقُدُم
 ter's axe.
Forepart. Before, in front. قُدَّام
Before thee. قُدَّامَكَ
By-way. ✧ قَدُّومِيَّة
Bravery, perseverance. إِقْدَام
Present, offering. Intro- تَقْدِمَة ج تَقَادِم
 duction.
Preeminence, preference. Pri- تَقَدُّم
 macy. ✧ Progress.
Antiquity, oldness. تَقَادُم
Arriving. Foremost. قَادِم ج قُدُوم وقُدَّام
 Future, next (year).
Head. — ج قَوَادِم
Foremost part. Forepart قَادِمَة ج قَوَادِم
 of a saddle. Vanguard.
Fore-feathers of the — ج قَوَادِم وقُدَامَى
 wings.
Old, قُدَام . وقَدِيم ج قُدَمَاء وقُدَامَى وقَدَائِم
 ancient.
The Ancient (God). ٱلْقَدِيم
Of old, previously. قَدِيمًا وفي ٱلْقَدِيم
Since a long time. مِنَ ٱلْقَدِيم
Chief, leader, first قُدَّام وقُدَّام وقَيْدَم
 in rank.
Forepart, prominent part. قَيْدُوم وقَيْدَام
The Ancients, *opp. to* the ٱلأَقْدَمُون
 Moderns.
Interior angle مُقْدِم ومُقْدَم ج مَقَادِيم
 of the eye. Forepart of a saddle.
Forepart of a. th. — ومُقَدَّم و✧ مَقْدَم
 Prow of a ship.
Put forward, chief. Premiss of a مُقَدَّم
 syllogism.
Forepart of a. th. Van- مُقَدِّمَة ومُقَدَّمَة
 guard. Preface of a book. Premiss
 of a syllogism.
Forward. Chief. Leader. مُتَقَدِّم
Above-mentioned, afore- مُتَقَدِّم ذِكْرُهُ
 said.
Brave, foremost مِقْدَام ومِقْدَامَة ج مَقَادِيم
 in fight.

✧ Feet of sheep. مَقَادِم
Turkish lady. (*for* خاتون) Te قَادِن
To be ☆ قَدَا o قَدْوًا, وقَدِي a قَدًى وقَدَاوَة
 palatable (food).
To draw near. قَدَا o قَدْوًا
To arrive from a journey. — وأَقْدَى
What a dainty food! مَا أَقْدَى هٰذَا الطَّعَامَ
To walk straight on. تَقَدَّى
To imitate a. o. إِقْتَدَى ب
Good smell. قَدًا
Palatable (dish). قَدٍ وقَدِيّ
Trunk, root. قِدْو ج أَقْدَاء
Straightforwardness. قِدْوَى
Pattern, model, قِدْوَة و قُدْوَة وقُدْوَة
 example
To emigrate by reason ☆ قَدَى i قَدْيًا
 of dearth.
To walk quickly (horse). — قَدَيَانًا
To suffice to a. o. (thing). ✧ قَدَّى ه
To resist a. o. قَادَى ه
To walk gravely. تَقَدَّى
Kind of snake. قِدَة ج قِدَات
Measure, amount. قَـدًى
Behaviour. قِدْيَة
Emigrant coming in. قَادِيَة ج قَوَادٍ
To feather ☆ قَذَّ o قَذًّا, وقَذَّذ وأَقَذَّ ه
 (an arrow). To cut (the feathers of
 an arrow) evenly.
To cut (the hair). — وقَذَّذ ه
To trim, to adorn a. th. قَذَّذ ه
Feather of an arrow. قُذَّة ج قُذَذ وقِذَاذ
 Man or horse's ear.
Flea. — وقُذَذ ج قِذَّان
Clippings. قُذَاذَة ج قُذَاذَات
Feathered or أَقَذّ ج قُذّ وجج قِذَاذ
 featherless arrow.
He possesses nothing. مَا لَهُ أَقَذّ وَلَا مَرِيش
Back of the head. مَقَذّ
Knife. مِقَذّ ومِقَذَّة
To revile a. o. ☆ قَذَى — قَاذَى ه
To treat a. o. harshly. تَقَذَّى لِفُلَان
To be ☆ قَذَر وقَذُر o, وقَذِر a قَذَرًا وقَذَارَة
 filthy, defiled.
To قَذَر o قَذْرًا, وقَذِر a قَذَرًا, وقَذَّر ه وه
 soil, to defile a. o. or a. th.
To loathe, to قَذِر a ه وتَقَذَّر ه وه
 dislike a. th.
To find a. th. أَقْذَر وتَقَذَّر واسْتَقْذَر ه
 filthy, loathsome

Dirt, filth, foul matter. قَذَر ج أَقْذَار
Foul action, offence. قَاذُورَة ج قَاذُورَات
Avoiding society. Dainty. قَاذُور وقَاذُورَة وقَذُور وذُو قَاذُورَة
Shunning men (woman). قَذُور
Filthy, unclean. قَذِر وقَذَر وقَذُر وقَذِر
Avoiding foul actions. قُذَرَة
Sloven. مَقْذَر ج مَقَاذِر, ومُتَقَذِّر
To revile a. o. ✠ قَذَع a قَذْعًا, وقَاذَعَ وأَقْذَعَ ه
To endeavour to harm a. o. تَقَذَّعَ ل بِالشَّرّ
Dirt. Foul speech. قَذَع
Dirty, unseemly. قَذِع
Offensive talk. Obscenity. قَذِيعَة
To vomit. To row. ✠ قَذَف i قَذْفًا
To throw a. o. into (the fire). — ه في
To cast (a stone). — ه وب
To throw (stones) at. To charge a. o. with (foul actions). — واسْتَقْذَفَ ه ب
To throw stones at. قَذَّفَ وقَاذَفَ
To hurry in running (horse). تَقَاذَفَ
To throw stones at o. a. To revile o. a. — ب
Rowing. Foul accusation. قَذْف
Side, margin of a valley. قُذَف وقَذَف وقُذُف وقُذْفَة
Slippery place. قَذَف وقُذُف
Remote (distance); far away (desert). — وقُذُف وقَذُوف وقَذِيف
Summit of a mountain. قُذْفَة ج قِذَاف وقُذَف وقُذُف وقُذُفَات
Missile. ✧ Shell. قِذَاف, وقَذِيفَة ج قَذَائِف
Ballista; projectile. Slinger. Balance. Rower. Vehicle. قَذَّاف
Fleshy. Gallant warrior. مُقَذَّف
Oar. مِقْذَف ج مَقَاذِف, ومِقْذَاف ج مَقَاذِيف
Missile, projectile. مَقْذُوف ج مَقَاذِيف
To strike a. o. on the back of the head. To slander a. o. ✠ قَذَل o قَذْلًا ه
To apply o.'s self to. — في
Defect, vice. قَذَل
Back of the head. قَذَال ج قُذُل وأَقْذِلَة
He gave him a part of his goods. ✠ قَذَم o قَذْمًا ل من مالِهِ
To sip a. th. قَذِم a قَذَمًا ه
To hurry on. اِنْقَذَمَ
Generous master. قُذَم
Draught of water. قُذْمَة

To have many defects. ✠ قَذِن — أَقْذَن
To be pained by a mote (eye). ✠ قَذِيَ a قَذًى وقَذَيَانًا
To discharge white matter (eye). قَذَى i قَذْيًا وقَذًى وقُذِيًّا وقَذَيَانًا
To throw in or take out a mote from (the eye). قَذَّى وأَقْذَى ه
To reward a. o. قَاذَى ه
Mote, any matter falling into the eye. قَذًى وقَذَاة
Fine dust. قِذًى ج أَقْذَاء وقُذِيّ
Pained by a mote (eye). قَذِيَة وقَذِيَّة ومَقْذِيَّة
He bears annoyance patiently. يُغْضِي عَلَى القَذَى
✠ قَرَّ i قَرَارًا وقُرُورًا وقَرًّا وتَقْرَارًا وتَقِرَّةً في
To settle in (a place).
To keep to, to persevere in. — على
To pour cold water in (a cooking-pot). To allay the boiling of (a cooking-pot) with cold water. — a i o قَرًّا ه
To cool any one with (water). — ه على
✧ To confess, to acknowledge a. th. قَرَّ ب او في
To be refreshed (eye). To be consoled, rejoiced after grief. قَرَّ a i قُرَّةً وقَرَّةً وقُرُورَةً
To be cool (day). — a i o قَرًّا
To hiss (snake). — o قَرِيرًا
To cease cackling (hen). — o قَرًّا وقَرِيرًا
To be smitten by the cold, to be seized with cold. قُرَّ قِرًّا
To compel a. o. to acknowledge a. th. قَرَّرَ ه ب وعلى
To ascertain. ✧ To write down (a fact, a statement). — ه
To compel a. o. to remain in (a state, a place). — وأَقَرَّ ه في
To agree with a. o. To live in company with. قَارَّ ه
To suffer from cold. أَقَرَّ
To make a. o. to suffer from cold (God). — ه
To console, to cool the eyes of a. o. (God). — عَيْنَهُ وبِعَيْنِهِ
To let a. o. act freely in (a work). أَقَرَّ ه على او في
To acknowledge a. th. — ب

Small watering-trough. Small jug. مَقَرَّة
Refreshed. Cool (day). Suffering from cold (man). مَقْرُور
To coo (pigeon); to grumble (camel); to rumble (belly). ✧ To be hollow (tree). To complain (man). ✱ قَرْقَرَ
To laugh loudly. — في الضَّحِكِ
Even, soft ground. قَرْقَر وقَرْقَرَة
Cooing of a dove. Features. ✧ Complaint. *Pl.* Borborygmus. قَرْقَرَة ج قَرَاقِر
Grumbling of a camel. Grumbling loudly (camel). قَرْقَار
Be quiet! (*said to a woman*). قَرْقَارِ
Having a loud voice (camel-driver). قُرَاقِر وقُرَاقِرِيّ
Loquacious (woman). قُرَاقِرَة
Foam of a camel. ✧ Hollow of a tree. قَرْقَارَة
Long ship. ✧ Lamb. قُرْقُور ج قَرَاقِير
✧ Hollow (tree). قَرْقَارَة ومُقَرْقَر
✱ قَرَأَ a o قَرْأً وقِرَاءَة وقُرْآنًا, واقْتَرَأَ ه
To read (a book).
To study under (a master). — على فُلَان
To transmit salutation to a. o. — قِرَاءَة عَلَيْهِ السَّلَام
To make up (things). — قَرْءا وقُرْآنًا ه
To study, to read with. قَارَأَ ه مُقَارَأَة وقِرَاء
To give a. th. to read; to teach reading to. أَقْرَأَ ه
To send compliments to a. o. — ه السَّلَامَ
To blow periodically (wind). To lag behind. To set (star). To be at hand (event). To menstruate (woman). أَقْرَأَ
To return from (a journey). — مِن
To devote o.'s self to the reading of the Koran. تَقَرَّأَ
To ask a. o. to read. إِسْتَقْرَأَ ه
Reading. Way of reading. قِرَاءَة ج قِرَاءَات
Moment. Measure, rhythm of verses. قَرْء ج أَقْرَاء وقُرُوء وأَقْرُؤ
The various sorts of verses. أَقْرَاء الشِّعْر
Reading. The Koran. قُرْآن
Reader. قَارِئ ج قُرَّاء وقَرَأَة وقَارِئُون
Clever reader. قَرَّاء ج قَرَّاؤُون

He acknowledged the rights of. أَقَرَّ لِ بِحَقِّهِ
To be strongly established (thing). To be ascertained (fact). تَقَرَّرَ
To be settled in (a place). تَقَارَّ في
To be quiet, to be at rest. إِسْتَقَرَّ
To settle in (a place). — في
Rest. Litter for camels. Cold. Chicken. قَرّ
The next day after the feast of Sacrifice. يَوْم القَرّ
Cold day, cold night. يَوْم قَرّ ولَيْلَة قَرّ وقَرَّة
Morning and evening. أَلقَرَّتَان
Fold of a garment. قَرّ الثَّوْب
Coolness, chill, winter-cold. Insect swimming upon water. قُرّ
He has found rest. وَقَعَ بِقُرِّهِ
Abode. Quiet, rest. Plain. Bottom (of the sea). Flocks. قَرَار وقَرَارَة
The lasting abode. Everlasting life. دَار القَرَار
Tailor. Butcher. Mechanic. قَرَارِيّ
Coolness. قِرَّة
Frog. قِرَّة وقُرَّة وقَرَّة
Refreshment. ✧ Water-cress. قُرَّة
Species of cress. — العَيْن
He is my consolation *lit*: he cools my eye. هُوَ قُرَّة عَيْنِي
Remainder of food in a pot. قُرَّة وقَرُورَة وقُرَارَة وقُرَارَة
Unavoidable calamity. قُرَى
Cold water thrown into a cooking-pot. قَرَرَة وقَرَارَة وقُرَارَة وقُرُورَة
Glass bottle, phial. Apple of the eye. Urinal. قَارُورَة ج قَوَارِير
Acknowledgment of a duty. إِقْرَار
Consoled, refreshed. قَرِير العَيْن
Compulsion. ✧ Written statement. تَقْرِير
✧ Letters patent; document. Deposition of a witness. تَقْرِير ج تَقَارِير
✧ Written (proof). تَقْرِيرِيّ
Stability. تَقْرَار وتِقِرَّة
Remaining. Cold (day). ✧ Acknowledging. قَارّ
Continent, inland. قَارَّة
Abode. Bottom. مَقَرّ ج مَقَارّ ومُسْتَقَرّ
Bottom of a well. مَقَرّ البِئْر

قُرَّاء ج قُرَّاؤُون وقَرَارِيّ Ascetic.
مَقْرُوء ومَقْرِيّ ومَقْرُوّ Read.
مِقْرَأ و ✧ قَرَّايَة Pulpit.

✡ قَرُبَ a ة ، وقَرُبَ o قُرْبًا وقُرْبَانًا وقِرْبَانًا
من وإلى To be near in rank, relationship to. To draw near to.
قَرِبَ وقَرُبَ To be at hand (event).
قَرَبَ o قَرْبًا ، وقَرَّبَ وأَقْرَبَ ه To put (a sword) into the scabbard.
قَرِبَ a قَرَبًا To have a complaint of the flanks.
قَرَّبَ ة وه To bring a. o. or a. th. near. To show favour to. To present an offering to (God). ✧ To offer a. th. To give Holy Communion.
قَرَّبَ To gallop (horse).
قَارَبَ ة وه To be the neighbour of.
— ة To speak kindly to.
— في To act wisely.
— أن To be near to.
أَقْرَبَ To be about to bring forth.
— ه To fill (a vessel) nearly to the brim.
تَقَرَّبَ تَقَرُّبًا وتِقِرَّابًا إلى To approach to. To seek to advance o.'s self in the favour of. To court the friendship of.
تَقَرَّبَ ✧ To receive Holy Communion.
تَقَارَبَ To draw near to o. a. To be nearly ripe (corn-crops).
اِقْتَرَبَ To draw nearer. To be near to fulfill a promise.
اِسْتَقْرَبَ ه To find a. th. to be near.
قُرْب وقُرَاب Proximity.
عَن قُرْب Soon. From a short distance.
قُرْب وقُرُب ج أَقْرَاب Side, flank.
قَرَب Well in the vicinity.
— وقِرَابَة Night-journey to the water.
قُرْبَة وقُرُبَة ج قُرَب وقُرُبَات Good work. Kindred, relationship.
قَرَبَة State of a vessel nearly filled.
قِرْبَة ج قِرْبَات وقِرَب وقِرِبَات Water-skin.
✧ قُرْبَاتِي ج قُرْبَات Gipsy.
قِرَاب ج قُرُب وأَقْرِبَة Scabbard, case.
قِرَاب وقُرَاب الشيء Tantamount, equivalent.
قَرَابَة وقُرْبَى Kindred, relationship.
هُوَ قَرَابَتِي (for هُوَ ذُو قَرَابَتِي) He is akin to me.

قُرْبَان ج قَرَابِين Offering to God. ✧ Holy Eucharist.
عِيد القُرْبَان ✧ The feast of Corpus Christi.
قُرْبَان بَيْرَام Ts Feast of Sacrifices (amongst Moslems).
قُرْبَان وقُرْبَان (s. pl.) Favourite of a prince.
قَرْبَان م قَرْبَى ج قِرَاب Nearly full (vessel).
تَقْرِيب Approximation. Gallop.
تَقْرِيبًا وبِالتَّقْرِيب Approximatively, nearly.
قَارِب ج قَوَارِب Seeker of water by night. Skiff, boat.
قَرِيب (s. pl.) ج أَقْرِبَاء Near. Neighbour. *Pl.* Relations.
عَن قَرِيب Proximately, soon.
قَرِيب Fish salted when fresh.
جَاءُوا قُرَابَى They came within a short time.
أَقْرَب ج أَقَارِب وأَقْرَبُون Nearer. More likely. *Pl.* Near relations.
قَرْنَبَى Long-footed dung-beetle.
مُقْرِب Blood-mare. Saddled (beast).
مَقْرَب ومَقْرَبَة By-way, nearest road.
مُقْرِب ج مَقَارِب ومَقَارِيب Near to bring forth (female).
مَقْرَبَة ومَقْرِبَة ومَقْرُبَة Near relationship.
مُقَرِّب Approaching. Offering. Sacrificator.
مُقَارِب Average, mean.
مُقَارَب Average price; of a middling sort.
مُتَقَارِب Close to. Poetical metre.

✡ قَرَبُس — قَرَبُوس و ✧ قُرْبُوس ج قَرَابِيس Saddle-bow.
◻ قُرْبَيْضَة Large back.
✡ قَرَتَ o ، وقَرِتَ a قُرُوتًا To become livid (contused skin).
قَرِتَ a قَرَتًا To be altered (complexion).
قَارِت ومُقْتَرِت Ransacking.
— وقَرَّات Excellent musk.
✡ قَرَثَ a قَرْثًا To toil (man). To earn.
قَرَثَ o قَرْثًا ة To grieve a. o. (event).
✡ قَرَحَ a قَرْحًا ، وقَرَّحَ ة To wound a. o.
قَرَحَ ة ب To show regard to.
— واقْتَرَحَ ه To sink (a well) in a

To be worm-eaten (hide). ✡ قَرِد a قَرَدًا
To be crisped (hair). — وتَقَرَّد
To remain silent. قَرِد وقَرَّد وأقرَد
To collect (milk, butter) in (a vessel). قَرَّد i قَرْدًا ه في
To take off the ticks of (a camel). To deceive a. o. ✧ To curse, to wish the devil to harm a. o. قَرَّد ه
Stout and short. قَرْد
Tick of camels. قُرْد ج قِرْدَان
قِرْد ج قُرُود وأقراد وقِرَدَة وقِرَدَة
Baboon. Ape. ✧ The devil.
She-monkey. قِرْدَة ج قِرَد
Refuse of wool falling off from sheep. قَرَد
Tick of camels. قُرَاد ج قِرْدَان
Scabby (camel). Heaped up (cloud). قَرِد م قَرِدَة
Trainer of monkeys. قَرَّاد
Ibis (bird). ○ ابو قِرْدَان
Rocky hill. ✡ قَرْدَد ج قَرَادِد, وقُرْدُود ج قَرَادِيد
Rocky hill. Upper part of the back. Severity of winter. قُرْدُودَة
To acknowledge a. th. To humble o.'s self. ✧ To be an armourer. To become live (coal). ✡ قَرْدَح
Armourer. ✧ قَرْدَاحِيّ وقَرْدَحْجِيّ ج قَرَادِحَة
To take a. th. with the tip of the fingers. To pinch (the flesh). ✡ قَرَز o قَرْزًا ه
To take offence at. ✧ إنقَرَز مِن
Pinch. قُرْزَة
Quarrel. ✧ مُقَارَزَة
Kind of shrub. ✡ قُرْزُح وقُرْزُحَة
To collect and tie up her hair on the top of the head (woman). ✡ قَرْزَل
Hair tied up on the head. قُرْزُل
To compose wretched verses. ✡ قَرْزَم ه
Wretched poet. قِرْزَام
To be congealed (water). ✡ قَرِس i قَرْسًا
To be severe (winter). — وقَرِس a قَرَسًا
To freeze (water). To benumb (the fingers : cold). قَرَّس وأقرَس ه
To be congealed (branch). أقرَس
Severe cold. قَرْس وقَرَس وقَرِيس
Small gnat. قِرْس
Frozen. قَرِس وقَرِيس

place where water was not found.
To have all its teeth *i. e.* to be 5 years old (horse). قَرَح a قُرُوحًا وقَرِح a قَرَحًا, وأقرَح
To be covered with ulcers. قَرِح a قَرَحًا, وتَقَرَّح
✧ To incite a. o. to. قَرَّح ه
To stare at a. o. قَارَح ه
To have ulcered camels. أقرَح
To affect a. o. with ulcers (God). — ه
To prepare to do evil. تَقَرَّح ل
To extemporise (verses). To choose a. o. To invent a. ✧ To vote for. إقتَرَح ه وه
To ask a. th. importunately from. — ه وب على
To ask a poet to recite (verses). — ه على شَاعِر
Wound, ulcer. قَرْح ج قُرُوح
First water of a well. Beginning of a. th. قُرْح
Soundness, freedom from ulcers. قَرَح
Wound, ulcer. ✧ Cough. (*un.*) قَرْحَة
Blaze on a horse's forehead. Beginning of spring. قُرْحَة
Ulcerated, scabby. قَرِح
Clear and pure water. Land fit to be sown. قَرَاح ج أقرِحَة
Not yet attacked by, clear from small-pox (child). Wild truffle. قُرْحَان
Sedentary. Who has never witnessed war. قُرْحَان وقُرَاحِيّ
Irresponsible for. قُرَاحِيّ وقُرْحَان مِن
Extempore speaking. Invention. ✧ Vote. إقتِرَاح
قَارِح (*m. f.*) ج قَوَارِح وقُرَّح ومَقَارِيح
Full-grown (camel). Pregnant (she-camel). ✧ Experienced.
Wounded, ulcerated. Pure (water). قَرِيح ج قَرْحَى وقَرَاحَى
Inborn disposition, temper. قَرِيحَة ج قَرَائِح
Having a blaze on the forehead (horse). أقرَح م قَرْحَاء ج قُرْح
Garden adorned with white flowers. رَوْضَة قَرْحَاء
Ulcerated. مُقَرَّح ومَقْرُوح
Trodden (road). مُقَرَّح

Intensely cold, glacial. Frozen (water). قارِس م قارِسة
Big and strong. قُراس وقُرَاسِيَة
To curtail a. th. ✧ To craunch (a fruit). ✲ قَرَش o قَرْشًا i ه
To earn for (o.'s family). قَرَش وقَرَّش واقترش ل
To sow discord between. قَرَّش بَيْن
To curd (milk). قَرَّش
To haunt a. o. To meddle in. ✧ قارَش ه وه
To injure a bone (wound). To become rich. أقْرَش
To slander a. o. — ب
To gather (people). تَقَرَّش
To realise (profits). — ه
To be intermingled in a fight (spears). تَقارَش واقترش
Turkish piastre equal to 2d Shark. قِرْش ج قُرُوش Ge
✧ Sour cheese. قَرِيش وقَرِيشة
Tribe of Koreysh. قُرَيْش
Koreyshite. قُرَشِيّ
✧ Rich, wealthy. مُقَرِّش
To pinch a. o. To sting a. o. (gnat). ✲ قَرَص o قَرْصًا ه وه
To prick off a. o. in (words). — ه ب
To wash (clothes) with the ends of the fingers. — ه
To spread out (the dough) into round cakes. — وقَرَّص ه
To pinch a. o. To harm a. o. قارَص ه
To become sour (milk). قَرِص a قَرَصًا
To pinch; to dislike, to defame o. another. تقارصا
قُرْص ج أقراص وقِرَصة وقِراص (قُرْصة *un*)
Round cake of bread. Disk of the sun. Globule of perfume. ✧ Disk of metal used as a head-ornament for women. ج قُرَص
Nettle. قُرَّاص وقُرَيْص و✧ وقُرَّيص
Pincers. □ قَرَّاصة
Anchor of a ship. قُرَيْص
Intensely red. أحمر قُرَّاص
Sour (milk). Stinging insect. قارِص
Biting (word). قارِصة ج قَوارِص
Cornelian cherry. ✧ Prune. قَراصِيَة G
Rounded. مُقَرَّص
Curved knife, pincers. مِقْراص

To privateer. ✧ قَرْصَن
Privateer, corsair. قُرْصان ج قَرَاصِين Sp
Grain remaining in the ear after the thrashing. ✲ قرصد — قَرْصَدٌ
To contract; to hide o.'s self. ✲ قَرْصَم
To write closely. — الكِتاب
Eryngium, thorny plant; sea-holly. قِرْصِعْنة وقَرْصَعْنة
To cut a. th.; to sever (a bond). To gnaw (cloth: mouse). ✲ قَرَض i قَرْضًا, وقَرَّض ه
✧ To lend money to. — ه
To recite (a poem). قَرَّض ه
He died. — رِباطَهُ
To incline in walk to the right and left. — في سَيْرِه
To cross a river. — الوادِي
To pass by a place. — المَكان
To requite a. o. for good or evil. — وقارَض مُقارَضةً وقِراضًا ه
To die. To pass from one thing to another. قَرِض a قَرَضًا
To praise or blame a. o. قَرَّض ه
To lend money to a. o. for a share in the profit. قارَض ه في المال مُقارَضةً وقِراضًا
To lend money to. أقْرَض ه
To requite o. a. (in good or evil). To make a poetical contest. تَقارَض
To vie in (praise). — ه
To be cut off (dynasty). To elapse (time). إنْقَرَض
To borrow from. إقْتَرَض مِن
To impair the reputation of. — عِرْض فُلان
To ask a loan from إسْتَقْرَض مِن
Requital in good or evil. Loan received. قَرْض ج قُرُوض
Loan. ✧ قُرْضة
Clippings, cuttings. قُراضة
Poetry. Cud. قَرِيض
Borrower. مُقْرِض
Shears, scissors. *Fig.* Biting tongue. مِقْراض ج مَقارِيض
Weasel. إبن مِقْراض
Thin-sown places. Wine-jars. مَقارِض
Tree of the desert having a yellow blossom. ✲ قرضا — قَرَضِيّ
To cut off, to separate a. th. ✲ قَرْضَب ه

Scroll of paper, writing, book. Skin used as a target *Pl.* Documents, stocks. قِرْطَاس وقُرْطَاس ج قَرَاطِيس
Red garment. ✲ قَرْطَف وقَرْطَفَة
To clothe a. o. with a tunic. ✲ قَرْطَق
To put on a tunic. تَقَرْطَق
Tunic. قُرْطَق G
✲ قرطل — قِرْطَلَّة و✧ قَرْطَل ج قَرَاطِل
Basket, bag.
Pack-saddle. قِرْطَالَة ج قِرْطَال
To cut off, to sever a. th. ✲ قَرْطَم ه
Cartham-seed. Saffron. قِرْطِم وقُرْطُم
Oats. قُرْطُمَان
Leprosy. ✧ قِرْطَام
To pluck (leaves) of mimosa flava. To tan (leather). ✲ قَرَظ i قَرْظًا ه
To become a man of rank. قَرِظ a قَرَظًا
To eulogise (a living man). قَرَّظ ه
To praise o. a. تَقَارَظ المَدْح
Leaves of mimosa flava used as tan. قَرَظ
Seller of tan. قَرَّاظ
Panegyric of a living man. قَرِيظ وتَقْرِيظ
Ram of Yemen. قَرَظِيّ وقُرَظِيّ
To knock at (a door). To beat (the drum). To hit the butt (arrow). ✲ قَـرَع a قَرْعًا ه
To strike a. o. on the head with (a stick). — رَأْسَهُ بِ
To gnash the teeth in despair. — سِنَّهُ
To empty a cup (drinker). — جَبْهَتَهُ بالإِنَاء
To win a. o. in a game of chance. قَرَع o قَرْعًا ه
He lost in a game of chance. قُرِع عَلَيْهِ قَرْعًا
To be bald. To receive an advice. To be beaten at play. قَرِع a قَرَعًا
To be empty (house, fold). To be little kept (holiday). To be scurfy. — a قَرْعًا وقَرَعًا
To disturb, to disquiet a. o. To upbraid a. o. To cure (a pustulous camel). قَرَّع ه
To come to fight. To gamble; to cast dice. قَارَع مُقَارَعَة وقِرَاعًا
To cast lots among. أَقْرَع بَيْن

To collect (meat) in the pot. To eat (meat) entirely.
To eat dry things. قَرْضَب
Refuse left in a sieve. قِرْضِب
Eating tough food. قِرْضَاب ج قَرَاضِبَة
Thief. Poor. Sharp (sword). — وقُرْضُوب ج قَرَاضِبَة
To cut a. th. To take away a. th. ✲ قَرْضَم ه
To chop (leeks). ✲ قَرَط o قَرْطًا, وقَرَّط ه
✧ To pronounce the letter *r* thickly. قَرَط o بِالرَّاء
To curtail a. o. of a due. — وقَرَّط على
To be lop-eared (ram). قَرِط a قَرَطًا
To bridle (a horse). To adorn (a girl) with earrings. قَرَّط ه
To snuff (a candle). To incite (a horse). ✧ To rub out, to clip (coins). — ه
To give little to. ✧ To check (a horse). To tighten a. o. قَرَّط على
To wear on earrings. تَقَرَّط
To be curtailed (due). ✧ إِنْقَرَط
Leek. قِرْط
قُرْط ج أَقْرَاط وقِرَاط وقُرُوط و قِرَطَة
Earrings, ear-drop. Pendant of gold. Blaze of fire. Trefoil.
✧ Thick pronunciation. Log of wood. قَرْطَة
Lighted wick قِرَاط
Candle-snuff. قُرَاطَة
Grain of carob-tree. Carat, weight equal to 4 grains. The 24 th part of a deenar or of any thing. ✧ Inch. ◘ Half a gill. قِرَاط وقِيرَاط ج قَرَارِيط G
Tamarisk-seeds. قَارِيط وقَرَارِيط
Miller. ✧ قَارُوط الطَّاحُون
Ointment of ceruse. قَيْرُوطِيّ G
Lop-eared (ram). أَقْرَط
Wearing earrings. مُقَرَّط
A trifle. ✲ قِرْطِيط وقِرْطِيطَة
To cut the bones of (a slaughtered beast). To overthrow a. o. ✧ To overpower a. o. ✲ قَرْطَب ه
To be powerless. ✧ تَقَرْطَب
Cutting (sword). قُرَاطِب
✧ Blackberry-tree. Brier. قُرْطُب
Cordova, town of Spain. قُرْطُبَة
Sheet of paper. ✲ قَرْطَس

Choice (stallion). Master, chief. ✧ Scald-headed. مَقْرُوع

He paved the house with bricks. أَقْرَع دارًا آجُرًّا
To give to a. o. the best of. — ه و ه
To check (a horse) with (the reins). — ه ب
To come back to righteousness. — إلى الحقّ
I spent the night restless. بِتُّ أَتَقَرَّع وأَنْقَرِع
To turn over, to be restless. تَقَرَّع
To cast dice. To draw lots together. ✧ To quarrel. تَقَارَع
✧ To be scald-headed. إِنْقَرَع
To abstain from. إِنْقَرَع عن
To cast lots for. إِقْتَرَع في وعلى
To select a. th. To kindle (the fire). To compose (verses). — ه
Vegetable marrow. Pumpkin. قَرْع
A pumpkin. Brand on a camel's thigh. ✧ Skull. Scald-head. قَرْعَة
Bet, wager. White pustule. قَرَع
Baldness. Pustule. قَرَع وقَرَعَة
Lot, sortilege. Leathern bag. ✧ Conscription. Vote قُرْعَة ج قُرَع
They drew lots. رَمَوا القُرْعَة
He has won. أَلْقُرْعَة لَهُ
He has lost. — عَلَيْهِ
The best part of. قُرْعَة وقَرِيعَة
Sleepless. Injured (nail). قَرِع
Day of the judgment. Abuse. قَارِعَة
Calamity. Upper part of a road. — ج قَوَارِع
Wood-pecker (bird). قَرَّاع
Despised. Choice (stallion). قَرِيع ج قَرْعَى
Hero of his time. قَرِيع الدَّهْر
Chief, hero. قِرِّيع
Bald. Scald-headed. Without bark (tree). Hard (place). Complete (number). Bare (mountain). ✧ Hornless (beast). أَقْرَع م قَرْعَاء ج قُرْع وقُرْعَان
Bare meadow, garden. Misfortune. Court-yard. قَرْعَاء
Dyer's broom. حَشِيشَة القُرْعَان
Bag for collecting dates. مِقْرَع
Erecting the head (horse). مُقْرِع
Knocker, whip, rod. Cudgel. مِقْرَعَة ج مَقَارِع
Mallet. مِقْرَاع

To suspect a. o. of. To charge a. o. with. ✱ قَرَف i قَرْفًا, وقَرَّف ه ب
To ill-treat a. o. قَرَف على
To mix up a. th. قَرَف ه
To earn for (o.'s family). — ل
To peel off (fruit). To pare off the scarf of (a wound). — وقَرَّف ه
To be on the point of contracting a disease. ✧ To loathe a. th. قَرِف a قَرَفًا
To be loathsome (food). قَرُف وأَقْرَف
To draw near to. To commit (a fault). قَارَف مُقَارَفَةً وقِرَافًا ه وه
To charge a. o. To infect a. o. with, to communicate (a disease) to. ✧ To cause disgust. أَقْرَف ه
To render a. o. liable to suspicion. — ب
To become connected with. — ل
To be pared off (scarf of a wound). تَقَرَّف
To earn. إِقْتَرَف
To commit (a crime). — ه
To be suspected of. — ب
To loathe a. th., to be disgusted with. ✧ إِسْتَقْرَف من
Larder for meat. قَرْف ج قُرُوف وقِرَاف
Bark of pomegranate. Crust of bread sticking to the oven. Dry excretion of the nose. قِرْف
Mixture. Contagion. Relapse. ✧ Disgust. قَرَف
Able to. — وقَرِف وقَرِيف ب
Suspicion. Shocking action. Bark. Earnings. Clove-bark. Cinnammon. قِرْفَة ج قِرَف
Bastard cinnamon. قِرْفَة خطِيَّة
He is the object of my suspicion. هُو قِرْفَتِي
I think I can find my want in such a tribe. بَنُو فُلانٍ قِرْفَتِي
Cemetery, grave. ◻ قَرَافَة
Harsh, unjust. قَرُوف ج قُرُف
Man of dark complexion. قَرْفِي ومُقْرِف
Intensely red. أَقْرَف
Place on a tree stripped of its bark. مَقْرَف

To begin to eat dry things (young beast).
✧ To crop (herbage : lamb). قَرَم ه
To gnaw, to eat up a. th. ه o قَرْمًا —
To bark a. th.
To insult a. o. grossly. To make ﻩ —
an incision on (a camel's) nose.
To long for (meat). قَرِم a قَرَمًا إلى
To teach a. o. to eat. قَرَّم ﻩ
To keep (a stallion) in the أَقْرَم ﻩ
stable.
To become a stallion إِسْتَقْرَم
Stallion kept in the قَرْم ج قُرُوم
stable. Chief of a tribe. Incision on a camel's nose.
Crimea (peninsula of). أَلقِرِم والقِرِيم
Greediness for meat. قَرَم
Skin taken off from قَرْمَة وقُرْمَة وقُرَامَة
a camel's nose.
✧ Stump of a tree. قِرْمِيَّة ج قَرَامِيّ
Remainder of bread in the oven. قُرَامَة
Vice, defect.
Kept in the أَقْرَم ج قَرْمَاء ج قُرْم, ومُقْرَم
stable (stallion).
Marked with an incision on the قَرْمَاء
nose.
Figured curtain قِرَام ومِقْرَم ومِقْرَمَة
of red wool.
To preserve (meat) in its ✧ قَوْرَم
grease.
Stewed meat. ✧ قَاوَرْمَة
To plaster with mud. To ✲ قَرْمَد ه
build, to pave (a house) with bricks.
Male mountain-goat. قُرْمُود ج قَرَامِيد
Baked brick. قِرْمِيد ج قَرَامِيد G
Gypsum. Female mountain-goat.
Built with bricks. Plastered. مُقَرْمَد
Coccus, kermes (insect) yiel- قِرْمِز P
ding a red, crimson dye.
Dyed red with kermes; قِرْمِزِيّ
crimson.
◘ Scarlet-fever. قِرْمِزِيَّة
To collect a. th. ✧ To ✲ قَرْمَش ه
grind, to eat (anything) dry.
Rabble of people. قِرْمِش مِن النَّاس
To enter its hole ✲ قَرْمَص وتَقَرْمَص
(pigeon).
قِرْمِص وقِرْمَاص وقُرْمُوص ج قَرَامِيص
Pigeon-nest. Hollow dug as a shelter

Born from a slave مُقْرِف ج مَقَارِف
father (man); from a common horse (nag). ✧ Loathsome.
To squat in putting the hands ✲ قَرْفَص
around the legs.
To bind a. o.'s hands under his legs. ﻩ —
Squatting. قِرْفِصَى وقُرْفُصَى وقُرْفُصَاء
Thieves. قَرَافِصَة
To cluck (hen). ✲ قَرَق o قَرْقًا
To deceive a. o. ب —
To walk in a plain. قَرِق a قَرَقًا
To make (a hen) to brood. ✧ قَرَّق
To brood her eggs (hen).
To have a rupture. ✧ إِنْقَرَق
Vile origin. Game played with قِرْق
pebbles.
Even soil, plain. قَرَق وقَرِق
Hernia, rupture. ✧ قُرْق
Brood-hen. قُرْقَة
Rake. Hard labour. ◘ قَرَاقَة
To become dry (bread). ✧ قَرْقَد
To dry (bread). ✧ قَرْقَد ه
Squirrel. ✧ قرقد — قَرْقَدَان وقَرْقَدُون
To call up (a puppy). ✲ قَرْقَس وقَرْقَص ب
Small flea. قِرْقِس
Puppy, little dog. قُرْقُوس وقُرْقُوص
To gnaw hard (bread). ✧ قَرْقَش ه
Crisp bread, ✧ قَرْقُوشَة ج قَرَاقِيش
biscuit.
To cut into small pieces. ✧ قَرْقَط ه
To gnaw a. th. (mouse).
Small bit. ✧ قَرْقُوطَة
To rumble (carriage). ✧ قَرْقَع
To crash, to clatter. ✧ تَقَرْقَع
Clatter, crash, rumbling. ✧ قَرْقَعَة
To coo (pigeon). To laugh ✲ قَرْقَف
loudly (man). To grumble (camel).
To frighten a. o. ﻩ —
To shiver from cold. قُرْقِف وتَقَرْقَف
Wine. قَرْقَف وقُرْقُوف
Prolonged cooing. Peal of قَرْقَفَة
laughter.
Shrill-voiced cock. قُرَاقِف
Gown ✲ قرقل — قَرْقَلٌ وقِرْقِلٌ ج قَرَاقِل
without sleeves.
To ill-feed (a child). ✲ قَرْقَم ﻩ
Ill-fed (child). مُقَرْقَم
Kind of plungeon, diver. ✲ قِرِلَّى
✲ قَرَم i قَرْمًا وقُرُومًا ومَقْرَمًا وقَرَمَانًا, وتَقَرَّم

from cold. Baking-place.
He walked with short steps. ✲ قَرْمَطَ في المَشْيِ
To write closely, to close the lines. — الكِتَابَ
✧ To crop a. th. (cattle). — ه
To be contracted, shrivelled. إِقْرَمَّطَ
Close writing. ✧ Stinginess. قَرْمَطة
Barbel (fish). ✧ Dwarf. قُرْمُوط
Musulman sect, Karmathian. قَرْمَطِيّ ج قَرَامِطة
Short thornless shrub. Worthless man. ✲ قَرْمَل (*un.* قَرْمَلة)
Two-humped camel. Hair-pin. Small and hairy camel. قِرْمِل ج قَرَامِل
To conjoin a. th. with. ✲ قَرَنَ i قَرْنًا ه ب
To couple two (horses). — ه
To gallop (horse). قَرَنَ o قِرَانًا
To perform two (affairs) at the same time. To eat two (fruits) together. To unite two (qualities). — o قِرَانًا, وأَقْرَنَ بَيْنَ
To have the eyebrows joined. قَرِنَ a قَرَنًا
To unite (many things) together. To bind (captives) together. ✧ To give a triangular or conical shape to. قَرَّنَ ه وه
To enter society with. ✧ To be the companion of. قَارَنَ مُقَارَنَةً و قِرَانًا ه
To be in conjunction with (star). — ه
To compare a. th. with. — ه ب
To shoot two arrows at the same time. To eat two dates in one mouthful. To bring two captives bound with one rope. أَقْرَنَ
To be near to open (boil). To rush and swell (a vein : blood). — واستقرن
To be able to. — واستقرن ل
To be unable to. To stray from (a path). أَقْرَنَ عن
To be angulous, prominent. ✧ تَقَرَّنَ
To be associated. تَقَارَنَ
To be joined, united to. إِقْتَرَنَ ب
Horn. Insect's antenna. Side of the head. First rays of the sun. Point of a blade. Prominent angle. Entrance of the desert. Best part قَرْن ج قُرُون
of a pasturage. Time, age, generation. Equal in age.
Lock of hair. Summit of a mountain. Plait of hair. Rope of fibres. — ج قِرَان وقُرُون
The two-horned, *surname of* Alexander the great. ذُو القَرْنَيْن
Rhinoceros. ◻ قَرْن خَرْتِيت
Cyclamen, sowbread. قَرْنُ الغَزَال
Rhinoceros. ◻ أُمّ القَرْن
Unicorn. Rhinoceros. وَحِيد القَرْن
Imp of Hell. قَرْن او قَرْنَا الشَّيْطَان
Equal in (age, merit), match. Competitor. قِرْن ج أَقْرَان
Quiver. Coupled with another (camel). Rope binding two camels. قَرَن ج أَقْرَان
Sword. Arrow. — ج قِرَان
Corner. Projecting angle. Tip of the tongue. قُرْنَة ج قُرَن
Conjunction of two stars, of two things Coincidence. قِرَان ومُقَارَنَة
Cornelian-tree, dogwood. G قَرَانِيَا
Armed with a sword and arrows. قَارِن
Name of a wealthy man. قَارُون
Joined. Companion, comrade. Spouse, consort. Coeval. Accomplice. قَرِين وقُرَانَى ج قُرَنَاء
Soul. Wife. Context. Female devil harassing women. قَرِينَة ج قَرَائِن
Houses facing one another. دُور قَرَائِن
Flask, bottle. قَرَّان
Eating two fruits at the same time. Galloping (horse). Kneeling on both knees together. قَرُون
Soul. — وقَرُونَة
Horned. Having the eyebrows joined. أَقْرَن م قَرْنَاء
Horned snake. حَيَّة قَرْنَاء
Having numerous flocks and no shepherd. مُقْرِن
Yoke or oxen. مِقْرَن
Joined. Angulous. Horned. مُقَرَّن
Sticking to a. o. continually (devil). مَقْرُون ب
Chain of mountains. مُقَرَّنَة
Caravan. قَيْرَوَان ج قَيْرَوَانَات
Moslem town in North Africa. قَيْرُوَان
Rat, jerboa. ✲ قَرْنَب

To live in a village. أَقْرَى
Entertainment of a guest. Water collected in a tank. قِرًى
Borough. village. قَرْيَة ج قُرًى و✧ قَرَايَا
Ant-hill. — النَّمْل
Coagulated (milk). Canal, water-course. قَرِيّ ج أَقْرِيَة وأَقْرَاء وقُرْيَان
Stick. Ant-hill. ◘ Yard of a ship. قَرِيَّة و✧ قَرْيَة ج قَرَايَا
Villager. (opp. to بَادٍ) قَارٍ
House full of people. Point of a spear. قَارِيَة
Short-legged and long-beaked green bird. — وقَارِيَّة ج قَوَارٍ وقَوَارِيّ
Villager. قَرَوِيّ
Basin. مَقْرًى ومَقْرَاة
Very hospitable. مِقْرًى ومَقْرَاء م مِقْرَاة ومِقْرَاء
Bowl for serving guests. *Pl.* Furniture of a kitchen. مِقْرًى ومِقْرَاة ج مَقَارٍ
To jump. ✲ قَزَّ o i قَزًّا
To loathe a. th. — عن وه
To shrink from impurity. — قَزًّا, وتَقَزَّزَ مِن الدَّنَس
Silk. ✧ Raw silk. P قَزّ ج قُزُوز
Silkworm. دُود القَزّ
Shunning impurity. قَزّ وقِزّ وقُزّ وقَزَز وقُزَّاز ومُتَقَزِّز
Dragon. Short snake. قَزَاز وه خَزَّاز
✧ Glass. Window-glass. (for زُجَاج) قَزَاز
Drinking-glass. قَازُوزَة
Dealer in silk. ✧ Glass-seller. قَزَّاز
To season a. th. with aromatics. ✲ قَزَحَ a قَزْحًا, وقَزَّحَ ه
To bubble up (cooking-pot). To become high (tree). — قَزْحًا وقَزَحَانًا
To eject (urine : dog). — وقَزَحَ a قَزْحًا وقُزُوحًا, وقَزَّحَ ب
To adorn (speech). قَزَّحَ ه
To branch forth (tree). تَقَزَّحَ
Urine of a dog. قَزْح
The devil. Angel set over the clouds. قُزَح
Rainbow. قَوْس قُزَح
Iris of the eye. قُزَحِيَّة
Onion-seed. Aromatics. ✧ Offshoot of mulberries. قِزْح ج أَقْزَاح
Streak of yellow, red, green. قُزْحَة ج قُزَح

Species of beetle. قَرَنْبَى
Cauliflower. (for قُنَّبِيط) ✧ قَرْنَبِيط
To mew (bird of prey). ◘ To be chilled. ✲ قَرْنَس
Projecting part of a mountain. قِرْنَاس
Head of Indian corn. ✧ قَرْنُوس ج قَرَانِيس
Ridged roof. مُقَرْنَس
Forepart of a boot. ✲ قَرْنَص — قُرْنُوص ج قَرَانِيص
Butt-end of a rifle. ◘ قُرْنَافَة
Clove-tree. ✲ قَرَنْفُل وقَرَنْفُول
Clove. كَبْش القَرَنْفُل
Pink (flower). Carnation. قَرَنْفُلَة
Aromatised with cloves. مُقَرْفَل
To be affected with jaundice. To be swollen with blows. ✲ قَرِهَ a قَرَهًا
Jaundiced. أَقْرَه م قَرْهَاء ج قُرْه, ومُتَقَرِّه
To direct o.'s self towards. ✲ قَرَا o قَرْوًا إِلَى
To follow, to pursue a. th. — واقْتَرَى واسْتَقْرَى ه
To have a complaint of the back. أَقْرَى
To collect purulent matter (abscess). إِسْتَقْرَى
Back. Pumpkin. قَرًا
Watering-trough. قَرْو ج قُرُوّ
Outfall of a press. Wooden-cup. — ج أَقْرَاء وأَقْرٍ وقُرِيّ
I saw them pursuing the same way. رَأَيْتُهُم على قَرْوٍ واحِدٍ
Testicular hernia. قَرْو وقَرْوَة
Custom. Buttocks. قَرْوَاء
Back, middle of the back. قَرْوَان
Affected with testicular hernia. قَرْوَانِيّ
Summit of a hill. مَقْرًى ج مَقَارٍ
Sentry. Guard. Ts قَرَاقُول
Punch and Judy, puppet-show. Ts قَرَاكُوز
To receive a. o. as a guest. ✲ قَرَى i قِرًى وقَرَاء, واقْتَرَى ه
To offer (food) to (a guest). — ه ه
To collect (water) in (a tank). — i قَرْيًا وقِرًى ه في
To explore, to cross (a country). — وتَقَرَّى واقْتَرَى واسْتَقْرَى ه
To ask hospitality from. أَقْرَى واقْتَرَى واسْتَقْرَى ه

To pasture (cattle) cleverly. قَسَّ وقَسَّس ه
To become a priest. قَسَّ قُسُوسَةً وقِسِّيسَة
Good herdsman. Christian priest. ✧ Monk, priest. قَسّ ج قُسُوس
Hamlet. قَسَّة
Backbiter. قَسَّاس
Priest, clergyman. قِسِّيس ج قِسِّيسُون وقُسَّان وأَقِسَّة وقَسَاوِسَة و✧ قَسَاقِسَة
Spurious (money). Egyptian (cloth). قَسِّي
Priesthood. قُسُوسَة وقِسِّيسِيَّة و✧ قُسُوسِيَّة
Ivy. ✧ قِسُّوس
To flow (water). To incline towards its setting (sun). ✱ قَسَبَ i قَسْبًا
To be hard, tough. قَسُبَ o قُسُوبَةً وقُسُوبًا
Very hard. Tough date. قَسْب
Murmuring sound of water. قَسِيب
To be hard. ✱ قَسَحَ a قَسَاحَةً وقُسُوحَةً
To treat a. o. harshly. قَاسَحَ ه
Hard, tough. قَاسِح وقُسَاح ومَقْسُوح
To force a. o. to. ✱ قَسَرَ i قَسْرًا, واقْتَسَرَ ه عَلَى
Constraint, compulsion. قَسْر
By force, by constraint. قَسْرًا
Lion. Sturdy. قَسْوَر وقَسْوَرَة ج قَسَاوِر وقَسَاوِرَة
Herbs of the shore. قَسْوَرَة ج قَسْوَر
Great, tall. قَيْسَرِيّ ج قَيَاسِر وقَيَاسِرَة
Street around a mosque. قَيْسَرِيَّة
To act wrongfully ✱ قَسَطَ i قَسْطًا وقُسُوطًا
To distribute, to disperse a. th. To assess (a tax). — ه
To act justly. قَسَطَ o i قِسْطًا, وأَقْسَطَ
To have the sinews of feet dried up. قَسِطَ a قَسَطًا
To pay (a debt) by instalments. To set (plants) regularly (gardener). To cry by intervals (cock). قَسَّطَ ه
To be stingy in. قَسَّطَ فِي
To be niggardly towards. — عَلَى
To assess a. th.; to allot. — واقْتَسَطَ ه
They divided it between themselves. تَقَسَّطُوهُ بَيْنَهُم
Equity. Just. (s. pl.) قِسْط
Measure for grain, قِسْط ج أَقْسَاط

Seller of seeds. قَزَّاح
Water-bubbles. قَوَازِح
Aromatics, seasoning. تَقَازِيح
To run swiftly (gazelle). ✱ قَزَعَ a قُزُوعًا
To run (horse). قَزَّعَ
To shave the head in leaving tufts of hair. — ه
To despatch (a messenger). To start (a horse). — ه
To apply a. o. exclusively to. — ه ل
To burst in high words against a. o. أَقْزَعَ ل فِي القَوْل
To be ready to start (horse). تَقَزَّعَ
To be shaven (head). To be scattered (clouds).
Scattered portions of clouds. Flax. Rufuse of wool. قَزَع
Lock of hair on the top of the head. — وقُزْعَة وقَزِيعَة
Portion of a cloud. Spurious child. ◻ Dwarf. قَزَعَة
Rag, portion of a garment. قَزَعَة وقِزَاع
Loosing the hair (buck). أَقْزَع
Nimble. Having little hair on the forelock (horse). مُقَزَّع
To halt. ✱ قَزَلَ i قَزْلًا وقَزَلَانًا
To halt, to limp. قَزِلَ a قَزَلًا
Lame, cripple. أَقْزَل م قَزْلَاء ج قُزْل
To blame a. o. ✱ قَزَمَ i قَزْمًا ه
To be mean, paltry. قَزِمَ a قَزَمًا
Mean appearance. Inferiority. قَزَم
(m. f. s. pl.) قَزَم ج قُزُم وأَقْزَام قَزَامَى م قَزَمَة ج قَزَمَات, قَزْم وقَزِم وقُزُم م قَزْمَة وقَزِمَة وقُزُمَة
Vile, mean, paltry.
Vile, contemptible. قِزَام
Sudden death. Insuperable. قُزَام
T ◻ Pick-axe. قَزْمَة ج قِزَم
T ◻ Copper-boiler. قَزَان
To shun impurity. To play at a certain game of the Arabs. ✱ قَزَا o قَزْوًا
To become impure, defiled. أَقْزَى
Snake. A certain game. قُزَة ج قُزَات
Te Lamb. قُوزِي
To fell and kill a. o. ✱ قَزَى — قَزَّى ه
Nickname. قِزْي
To slander a. o. ✱ قَسَّ o قَسًّا وقُسًّا ه
To seek after a. th. — وتَقَسَّسَ ه
To take out the marrow of (a bone). قَسَّ ه

Repartition, allotment. (*Arith.*) قِسْمَة Division.
Share, portion قِسْمَة ج قِسَم
Quotient (*arith*). خَارِج ٱلقِسْمَة
Beauty. Face. قَسِمَة وقَسَمَة ج قَسِمَات وقَسَمَات
Oath. Truce. Swearers. قَسَامَة ج قَسَامَات
Beauty, elegance. — وقَسَام
Alms. Portion of the allotter. قُسَامَة
Cloth-folder. Middling, average. قَسَامِيّ
Distribution. ✧ Exorcism. تَقْسِيم
Repartition of inheritance. قِسَام
Co-partaker. قَسِيم ج أَقْسِمَاء وقُسَمَاء, ومُقَاسِم
Portion, lot. قَسِيم ج أَقْسِمَاء
Fine, elegant. — ج قُسُم
Perfume-box. Market. قَسِيمَة ج قَسَائِم
▫ Receipt-foil torn out from a register.
أُقْسُومَة ج أَقَاسِيم, ومَقْسَم ومَقْسِم ج مَقَاسِم
Portion, lot.
Water-works. مَقْسِم
✧ Exorcised. مُقَسَّم عَلَيْهِ
Partaking. ✧ Exorcist. مُقَسِّم
Distributed. ✧ (*Arith.*) Dividend. مَقْسُوم
(*Arith*). Divisor. — عَلَيْهِ
To have horny hands. ✱ قسن — أَقْسَن
To be hard, dry (wood). To be dry, old (man). To be dark (night). إِقْسَأَنَّ إِقْسِئْنَانًا وقُسَأْنِينَة
To be pitiless, hard (heart). To be bad (money). ✱ قَسَا o قَسْوًا وقَسْوَةً وقَسَاوَةً وقَسَاءً
To harden (the heart). قَسَّى وأَقْسَى ه
To be hard, pitiless for. — قَلْبُهُ على
To undergo, to endure (hardships). قَاسَى ه
✧ To treat a. o. harshly. — ه
Hardness of heart. قَسَاوَة
Of a bad standard (money). قَسِيّ ج قِسْيَان وقَسِيَّات
Hard (heart, stone). Difficult. — ج قَسِيُّون, وقَاسٍ ج قُسَاة
Pot. ▫ قَاسِيَة
Hardening of the heart. مَقْسَاة لِلقَلْب
To recover after emaciation. ✱ قَشّ o قُشُوشًا
To pick up. To collect things. To rub a. th. with the hand. قَشّ o i قَشًّا ه

bushel. Balance. Portion, lot. Just weight, measure.
Costus, aromatic plant. Perfume. قُسْط
Stiff-legged. قُسْط وقَسِيط الرِّجل
Stiff (leg, neck). أَقْسَط م قَسْطَاء ج قُسْط
Rainbow. قُسْطَان وقُسْطَانِيّ وقُسْطَانِيَّة
Just. مُقْسِط ج مُقْسِطُون
To sort (money). ✱ قَسْطَر ه
✧ Earthen-pipe. قَسْطَر ج قَسَاطِر
Clever man. قَسْطَر وقَسْطَار
Money-changer. قَسْطَرِيّ ج قَسَاطِرَة
✱ قسطس — قُسْطَاس وقِسْطَاس ج قَسَاطِيس
Balance. Steelyard.
Dust. ✱ قَسْطَل وقَسْطَال وقُسْطُول ج قَسَاطِل
✧ Discharge-pipe.
Murmuring of a stream. قَسْطَلَة
Constantinople. قُسْطَنْطِينِيَّة العَلِيَّة G
To divide, to distribute a. th. To separate (friends: time). ✱ قَسَم i قَسْمًا. وقَسَّم ه وه
To dispose a. th. methodically. To hesitate (in an affair). قَسَم ه
To be handsome-faced. قَسُم o قَسَامَةً
To partake a. th. between many. قَسَّم ه بَيْن
✧ To exorcise a possessed man. قَسَّم على
To partake a. th. with a. o. قَاسَم ه ه
To bind o.'s self by oath to a. o. for. — ه على
He swore by God. أَقْسَم بِاللّٰه
To swear to. — أن
To adjure a. o. not to. أَقْسَم على أن
To be divided (men). تَقَسَّم
To divide (men : time). — ه
To share a. th. together. تَقَاسَم واقْتَسَم ه
To swear to o. a. تَقَاسَم
To be shared into, to branch off into. إِنْقَسَم الى
To ask a. th. to be partaken. إِسْتَقْسَم ه
To exact an oath from. — ه
Allotment, division. Gift, share. Doubt. قَسْم
Temper, nature. Use, custom. — وقِسْم
Portion. Share. Section (of a book). قِسْم ج أَقْسَام وجج أَقَاسِيم
Oath. Asseveration. قَسَم ج أَقْسَام, ومُقْسَم

To pick up chips of wood. ✧ قَشْبَرَ قَشْبَرَةً
Long-bearded. ✱ قِشْبار وقُشابِر اللّحية
▫ Scurf of the head. قُشْبُر
Milky plant. Dregs of butter when cooked with flour and dates. ✱ قشد — قِشدة
To peel off (a fruit). ✱ قَشَرَ o i قَشْرًا, وقَشَّر ه
To be barked, peeled. تَقَشَّر وانقشر
To strip o.'s clothes. إقتشر
Rind, peel of fruit. قِشْر ج قُشُور
Husk. Skin. Shell of an egg. Crust of a wound. Garment.
Fish one palm long. — وقُشْر
Intensely red colour. قَشَر
Covered with a thick bark. قَشِر
Wings of locusts. القَشْران
Washing the ground (rain). قَشْرَة وقُشْرَة
Bark, shell, crust. Piece of bark, skin. Clothes. قِشْرَة
Excoriating the skin (blow). Last in a race (horse). قَاشِر م قَاشِرَة
Disastrous year. قَاشُور وقَاشُورَة
Removed skin, bark, rind. قُشَارَة
Barked, shelled. أَقْشَر م قَشْرَاء ج قُشْر
Having the nose excoriated. Intensely red.
Naked. مُقَشَّر ومُقْتَشِر
Clear answer. جواب مُقَشَّر
Importune beggar. مِقْشَر
To take off (a covering) from. ✱ قَشَط o i قَشْطًا ه عن
✧ To slide (saddle). قَشَط
✧ To slip from the finger (ring). — مِن الخنصر
To plunder a. o. (robber). To ravish a. th. ✧ قَشَط ٥ وه
To become clear (sky). To be plundered by a brigand. تَقَشَّط وانقشط
✧ Cream. قَشْطَة
Stitching. تَقْشِيط
✧ Leather strap. Counter (at cards). Fish. قِشَاط
Penknife. ✧ مِقْشَط ج مَقَاشِط
To disperse (a party). ✱ قَشَع a قَشْعًا ٥
To clear off (the clouds: wind). — وأَقْشَع ه

✧ To sweep (a house). To scum (a pot).
To pick up a. th. To be dry (plant) قَشّ
To escape, to glide away. قَشّ وأَقَشّ وانقشّ
To pick up (refuse). قَشّ وقَشَّش
✧ To weed (a field). قَشَّش ه
To be barren (soil). أَقَشّ
To recover from small-pox. — مِن
Bad palm-tree. Large bucket. قَشّ
✧ Stubble, straw, rush.
✧ Sea-weed. قَشّ البحر
✧ A bit of straw. A bit. (*un.*) قَشَّة
✧ Nest, small house. قُشّ ج قُشُوش
Rubbish, refuse. قُشَاش وقَشِيش
Picking up refuse. قَشَّاش
Raffling. ✧ قَاشُوش
Rustling of a serpent. قَشِيش
Wicker-broom. ✧ مِقَشَّة
Demijohn, carboy. ✧ مُقَشْقَة
To cure a. o. from the mange. ✱ قَشْقَش ٥ من
To pick up (wood) here and there for proper use. — ه
To be cured from (the scab). تَقَشْقَش من
To mix poison with (the food). ✱ قَشَب i قَشْبًا, وقَشَّب ه ب
To poison a. o. قَشَب ٥ السُّمّ
To corrupt, to vitiate a. th. — ه
To do harm to a. o. — وقَشَّب ٥
To defile a. o. with. — ٥ ب
To be polished (sword). To be new, clean. قَشُب o قَشَابَة
✧ To be chapped, cracked (skin). قَشَّب وتَقَشَّب
To become rusty (sword). تَقَشَّب
To be praised or blamed. إِقْتَشَب
Filthiness. قَشْب
Poison. Rust. Refuse of food. قِشْب ج أَقْشَاب
Vile, worthless man. رَجُل قِشْب خِشْب وقِشْبَة
Poison. ✧ Chaps on the skin. قَشَب ج أَقْشَاب
New. Clean. Worn out. Polished or rusted (sword). قَشِيب ج قُشُب وقُشْب
Worn out garments. قُشَانِيَّة
Mixed (descent). مُقَشَّب
Of mixed race. — النَّسَب

To be light. ✧ To see. قَشِعَ a قَشَعًا

To be cleared away (cloud). أَقْشَعَ وتَقَشَّعَ وانْقَشَعَ

To be over (cold, darkness). ✧ To be seen. إِنْقَشَعَ

To be dispersed (people). — وتَقَشَّعَ

To start from (people). — عَن

To be dispelled (anxiety). — عَن القَلْب

Dry skin. Skin-garment worn out. قَشْع ج قِشَع

Tent made of skins. — ج قُشُوع

Cloud clearing away. قَشْع وقِشْع

Sweepings of a bath. — وقِشْع وقُشْع

Scattered clouds. Piece of dry skin. قَشَعَة ج قِشَاع, وقِشْعَة ج قِشَع

Dry. Unsteady. قَشِع

Rag, tatter. قِشَاع

Pituite. قُشَاعَة

Scattered (fodder). قَشِيع

Kid forsaken by its mother. ✧ قَشُوع

To be distrustful, suspicious. ◻ تَقَوْشَع

To shudder; to have the goose-skin. To be unfruitful (year). ✲ قَشْعَر — إِقْشَعَرَّ

Shudder, horripilation, goose-flesh. قُشَعْرِيرَة

Shuddering. مُقْشَعِرّ ج قَشَاعِر

Old (man, vulture). Lion. ✲ قَشْعَم ج قَشَاعِم

War. Calamities. Hyena. Ant-hill. Spider. أُمّ قَشْعَم

✲ قَشِفَ a قَشَفًا, وقَشُفَ o قَشَافَة, وتَقَشَّفَ

To be neglectful of cleanliness. To lead a painful, a squalid life.

To render life hard to a. o. (God). قَشَّفَ عَيْشَهُ

✧ To mortify o.'s self. تَقَشَّفَ

To wear shabby, filthy clothes. — في لِبَاسِهِ

Painful life. ✧ Austere life. قَشَف وتَقَشُّف

Mortification. تَقَشُّف ج تَقَشُّفَات

Austere-looking; sun-burnt; slovenly. قَشِف وقَشْف وقَشِيف

Hard year. عَام أَقْشَف

✧ Barracks. ◻ Hospital. Ts قُشْلَة و◻ قِشْلَاق

To eat much. To eat the best dishes. To split (palm-leaves). ✲ قَشَمَ o قَشْمًا ه

Bed of a stream. قَشَم وقِشَم ج قُشُوم

Unripe dates. قَشَم وقِشَم

Woollen garment, fur. قَشَام

Remainder of a meal. قُشَام وقُشَامَة

Dry vegetable. قَشِيم ج قُشُم

China-ware. ✧ قَشَن — قِيشَانِي

To bark (wood). To skin (a snake). ✧ To cream (milk). ✲ قَشَا o قَشْوًا, وقَشَّى ه

To wipe (the face). — ه

To fall into destitution. أَقْشَى

Basket of palm-leaves. قَشْوَة ج قَشَوَات وقِشَاء

✧ Cream. Foam. قَشْوَة

Straw-basket. ✧ قَشْوِيَّة

Adulterated money. قَاش

Slender (man). قَشْوَان م قَشْوَانَة

Barked, peeled. مَقْشُوّ ومَقْشِيّ ومُقَشًّى

To cut off, to clip (the nails, hair). ✲ قَصَّ o قَصًّا, وقَصَّصَ ه

To seem pregnant (female). — وأَقَصَّ

To come upon a. o. (death). — وأَقَصَّ ٥

To relate a. th. to. قَصَّ o قَصَصًا ه على

To follow (the footsteps) of. قَصَّ o قَصًّا وقَصَصًا, وتَقَصَّصَ واقْتَصَّ ه

To show the way to. قَصَّ لِفُلَان الطَّرِيقَ

To plaster (a wall). قَصَّصَ ه

To be quit with a. o. To retaliate upon a. o. To settle an account with. To punish a. o. قَاصَّ مُقَاصَّةً وقِصَاصًا ٥

To be wasted, worn out (beast). أَقَصَّ هُزَالًا

To retaliate for a. th. upon a. o. أَقَصَّ ٥ مِن

To allow a. o. to revenge himself. — مِن نَفْسِهِ

To keep in memory (the words) of a. o. تَقَصَّصَ ه

To requite o. a. تَقَاصَّ

To be clipped, cut off. إِنْقَصَّ

To relate (a fact) accurately. إِقْتَصَّ ه

To retaliate upon. — مِن

To seek retaliation from a. o. To ask a. o. to relate a. th. إِسْتَقَصَّ ٥

Cuttings, clippings. قَصّ

Breast. Middle of the breast. — وقَصَص

قَصّ وقَصَّة (for جِصّ وجِصَّة) ج قِصَاص

Gypsum.

Narration, story. Records. قِصَّة ج قِصَص وأَقَاصِيص

Lock of hair. قُصَّة ج قُصَص و قِصَاص

Retaliation. Punishment. قِصَاص

Euphorbia Canarica, plant sought by bees. Cytisus (shrub). قُصَاص

Back of the head. Sternum. قُصَاص

Clippings of nails. قُصَاصَة

Hairy part of the breast. قَصِيص

Plant used for cleansing. — وقَصِيصَة ج قَصَائِص

He knows where to get what he wants. عَالِمٌ بِمَنْبَت القَصِيص

Narrator, story-teller. قَاصّ وقَصَّاص

Clipped in the forelock (horse). مُقَصَّص

Trace. مَقَصّ

Scissors. مِقَصّ ج مَقَاصّ

Ear-wig. ✧ أَبُو مَقَصّ

To break a. th. To clip (the hair). ✱ قَصْقَصَ

Malignant and hideous snake. قَصْقَاص وقُصَاقِص

Strong and big (lion, camel). قُصَاقِص ج قَصَاقِص وقُصَاقِصَات

To cut off a. th. ✱ قَصَبَ ـِ قَصْبًا, واقْتَصَبَ ه

To cut up (a sheep : butcher). قَصَبَ ه

To refuse drink (camel). — ـِ قَصْبًا وقُصُوبًا

To prevent (a beast) from drinking. — ه

To revile a. o. — وقَصَّبَ ه

To send forth stalks (plant). قَصَّبَ

To curl (the hair). ✧ To cut (stones). To embroider (cloth). قَصَّبَ ه

To produce reeds (place). To have (beasts) abstaining from drinking. أَقْصَبَ

Back. Gut. قُصْب ج أَقْصَاب

Reeds. Any plant having a jointed stem. Bones of the fingers and toes. Pipe, channel. Cane. Musical reed. The bronchia. Ducts of the lungs. ✧ Gold or silver thread. قَصَب

Sugar-cane. قَصَبُ السُّكَّر و✧ قَصَبُ المَصّ

He has outstripped the others *lit* : He won the cane of victory. أَحْرَزَ قَصَبَ السَّبَق

Well recently dug. Bone of the nose. Main part of a country. Pole, measure of about 12 feet and a half. Seat of government, chief city. قَصَبَة

Windpipe. قَصَبَة الرِّئَة

Œsophagus, the gullet. قَصَبَة المَرِي

Fine linen. قَصَبِيّ ج قَصَب

Player on the pipe. قَاصِب ج قُصَّاب

Abstaining from drinking. قَاصِب وقَصِيب

Dam. قِصَاب

Butcher. Flute-player. ▫ Land-surveyor. قَصَّاب

Pipe. Flute. Reviler. قَصَّابَة

Lock of curled hair. قُصَّابَة ج قُصَّاب, وتَقْصِبَة وتَقْصِيبَة ج تَقَاصِب وتَقَاصِيب

Pipe, tube. قَصِيبَة ج قَصَائِب

Art of playing upon the flute. Craft of a butcher. قِصَابَة

Twisted, curled, (hair). ✧ Brocaded (cloth). مُقَصَّب

Cane-brake. مَقْصَبَة

To repair to. To purpose, to intend a. th ✱ قَصَدَ ـِ قَصْدًا ه او ل او إِلَى

To betake o.'s self to a place. — قَصَدَهُ

To break a. th. asunder. — وقَصَّدَ ه

To act moderately in. قَصَدَ واقْتَصَدَ في

To spare money. إِقْتَصَدَ في النَّفَقَة

To compose poems. قَصَدَ وقَصَّدَ وأَقْصَدَ

To compose and trim verses. قَصَّدَ القَصَائِد

To hit and kill on the spot (arrow). To bite and kill a. o. (snake). أَقْصَدَ ه

To be killed, to die (dog). تَقَصَّدَ

To be broken in halves (spear). — وانْقَصَدَ

Aim, intention. Resolution. Straight (road). Just, middle course. قَصْد

On purpose ; deliberately. بِقَصْدٍ

I direct myself towards thee. إِلَيْكَ قَصْدِي

He is before thee. هُوَ قَصْدَكَ

Thistle. Tamarisk-branch. قَصَد

Broken asunder (spear-staff). قَصِد وقَصِيد وأَقْصَاد

Fragment, bit. قِصْدَة ج قِصَد

Poem of 3 or 6 verses and more. Marrow-bone. Full of marrow. قَصِيد

Poem of 7 or 10 verses upwards. قَصِيدَة ج قَصَائِد وقَصِيد

Easy, short (journey). قَاصِد ج قُصَّاد

✧ Apostolic delegate. قَاصِد رَسُولِي

To confine o.'s self to. إِقْتَصَر عَلَى
To find a. th. to be short. إِسْتَقْصَر ه
Shortness. قِصَر وقِصْر
Neglect, shortcoming, inability. قَصْر وقَصَر وقُصْرَة وقَصَار وقُصُور
Use of a restrictive particle as إِلَّا. قَصْر
Palace, castle. قَصْر ج قُصُور
Utmost limit. قَصْر وقَصَار وقُصَار وقُصَارَى
قَصْرُكَ وقَصَارُكَ وقُصَارُكَ وقُصَارَاكَ أَنْ تَفْعَلَ هٰذَا
The utmost of thy power is to do so.
هُوَ ٱبْنُ عَمِّي قُصْرَةً وقِصْرَةً وقَصِيرَةً ومَقْصُورَةً
He is my first cousin on my father's side.
Pain in the neck; stiff-neck. قَصَر
Rubbish left in the sieve. — وقَصَرَة وقِصْرَى وقُصَارَة
Grain left in the ears. قَصَرَة وقُصَارَة وقُصْرِيّ
Base of the neck. Fragment of wood, of iron. قَصَرَة ج قَصَر وأَقْصَار وقَصَرَات
Closet. Private apartment. قُصَارَة
Piece of excellent ground. — الأَرْض
Craft of a fuller. قِصَارَة
Date-basket. قَوْصَرَة وقَوْصَرَّة
Chamber-pot. ✧ قَصْرِيَّة
Cesar. Emperor. L قَيْصَر ج قَيَاصِرَة
Great. قَيْصَرِيّ ج قَيَاصِر وقَيَاصِرَة
Cesarea, (name of 3 towns). L قَيْصَرِيَّة
✧ Bazaar; building surrounded with porticoes or shops.
Shortening. Shortcoming. Laziness. تَقْصِير
Necklace. تِقْصَار وتِقْصَارَة ج تَقَاصِير
Minor, pupil. Remote (water). قَاصِر م قَاصِرَة
Powerless. Stingy. قَاصِر وقَصِير اليَد
Pudical in her looks (woman). — الطَّرْف
Short, of short stature. قَصِير ج قِصَار وقُصَرَاء
Having a short pedigree. — النَّسَب
Kept within the house (girl). قَصِيرَة ج قِصَار وقَصِيرَات وقَصَائِر
Kept indoor (woman). Nuptial chamber. قَصُورَة
Fuller. قَصَّار
أَقْصَر ج أَقَاصِر وأَقْصَرُون م قُصْرَى ج قُصَر
Shorter.
◻ The temple of Luxor. الأَقْصُر

Tax-gatherer. قَاصِد الدَّفْتَر
Easy (road). قَاصِد ج قَوَاصِد
Between us and the water there is a short night-journey. بَيْنَنَا وبَيْنَ المَاء لَيْلَةٌ قَاصِدَة
Just, moderate course. Political economy. اقْتِصَاد
Sparing of money. — فِي النَّفَقَة
Dying suddenly. مُقْصَد
مَقْصَد ومَقْصِد ومَقْصُود ج مَقَاصِد ج مَقَاصِيد
Design, thing aimed at.
Of middle size (man). مُقْصَد ومُقْتَصِد
Tin, pewter. ✱ قَصْدِر — قَصْدِير
To fail. To be dear (price).) ✱ قَصَر o قُصُورًا
To miss the (but: arrow). — عَنْ
To be unable to perform a. th. To fall short of. To quit a. o. (pain). — وقَصَّر عَنْ
To shorten, to curtail a. th. To bleach, to whiten (cloth). ✧ To whiten (wax) in the sun and dew. قَصَر i قَصْرًا, وقَصَّر ه
To shorten (a prayer). قَصَر ه ومِن, وأَقْصَر مِن
He confined him in his house. قَصَرَهُ فِي بَيْتِهِ
He entrusted him exclusively with the affair. — ه عَلَى أَمْرٍ
To restrict a. th. to. — ه عَلَى كَذَا
I confined myself to that. قَصَرْتُ نَفْسِي عَلَى كَذَا
To feel a pain in the neck; to have a stiff-neck. قَصِر a قَصَرًا
To be short. قَصُر o قِصَرًا وقَصَرًا وقَصَارَة
He has been unable. He has been stingy. قَصُرَتْ يَدُهُ
To be remiss in work. قَصَّر فِي
To give stingily. — العَطِيَّة
✧ To lag behind. قَصَّر
To punish a. o. ✧ قَاصَر ه
To be upon the evening. To be old (beast). To beget short children. أَقْصَر
To neglect, to fall short of performing (an affair). — وتَقَاصَر عَنْ
To contract, to shorten o.'s self. تَقَصَّر
To confine o.'s self exclusively to. — ب
To feign to be short. تَقَاصَر
To be unable to. — عَنْ

To rumble (thunder). قَصَفَ i قَصْفًا وقَصِيفًا
To grumble (camel).
To be tender, weak (wood). To break in halves (arrow, tooth). To hang down (plant). قَصِفَ a قَصَفًا
To meet. To play, to joke. تَقَصَّفَ
To be broken. تَقَصَّفَ وانقصف
To dash together (crowd). تَقَاصَفَ
To rush (upon). — وانقصف على
To be pushed, dashed. إِنْقَصَفَ
To forsake a. o. إِنْقَصَفَ عَنْ
Revelling, good cheer. قَصْف وقُصُوف
Rushing of a crowd. قَصْفَة
Stair, degree. Isolated tract of sand. — ج قَصَف وقُصْفَان
Sweeping (wind). Rumbling (thunder). قَاصِف م قَاصِفَة
Easily shaken. قَصِف
Unable to bear hunger. قَصِف البَطْن
Broken asunder. قَصِف وقَصِيف
Having the teeth broken. أَقْصَف م قَصْفَاء ج قُصْف
Gambling-house. مَقْصَف ج مَقَاصِف
To reap (green fodder). ✱ قَصَلَ i قَصْلًا ه, واقتصل ه
To thrash (wheat). To cut (the neck). قَصَّلَ ه
To give green fodder to (cattle). — ه وعلى
To be reaped. تَقَصَّلَ وانقصل واقتصل
Stoppage. قَصْل
Refuse of wheat, of barley. — وقِصْل وقَصَل وقُصَالَة
Weak. قِصْل
Herd of camels. قَصْلَة وقِصْلَة
Sharp (sword). قَاصِل وقَصَّال ومِقْصَل
Barley, wheat reaped when green. قَصِيل
Biting (tongue). Breaking every thing (camel). مِقْصَل
To break a. th. ✱ قَصَمَ i قَصْمًا ه
(God) punishes the wrongdoer. — ظَهْرَ الظَّالِم
To be broken. تَقَصَّمَ وانقصم
Breaking of the foreteeth. قَصَم
Locusts' eggs.
Bit, fragment. قِصْم ج أَقْصَام, وقِصْمَة وقُصْمَة
Step of a staircase. قَصْمَة

Having a complaint of the neck. اقْصَر م قَصْرَاء ج قُصْر
Mallet of fuller. مِقْصَر ومِقْصَرَة
Evening. مَقْصِر ومَقْصَر ومَقْصَرَة
It cannot be avoided. لَيْسَ عَنْهُ مِن مَقْصَر
The last moments of evening. المَقَاصِر والمَقَاصِير
His palace is opposite mine. هُوَ مُقَاصِري
Shortened. Bleached. Ended by a short alef (noun). ✧ Whitened (wax). White cloth. مَقْصُور
Closet. Kept indoor (woman). مَقْصُورَة ج مَقَاصِير
To swallow (water). ✱ قَصَعَ a قَصْعًا ه
To bruise (the grain : mill).
To crush (a louse). To strike (a child) on the head. To stunt (a child : God). To despise a. o. — ه
To swell with blood (wound). — ب
He is perverted. — الشَّيْطَان في قَفَاهُ
To keep at (home). — وقصّع ه
To allay (the thirst : water). — وقصّع ه
To be stunted (child). قَصِعَ a قَصَعًا, وقَصُعَ o قَصَاعَةً
To germinate (seed). To furrow the earth (mole). قَصَّعَ
To wrap o.'s self in clothes. — في
To come out from (a pass). — مِن
To become purulent (boil). تَقَصَّعَ ب
Wooden bowl for 10 persons. ✧ Filling of a terrace. قَصْعَة ج قَصَعَات و قِصَع و قِصَاع
Burrow of a mole. قُصَعَة ج قُصَع, وقُصَعَة وقُصَعَاء وقُصَاعَة وقَاصِعَاء وقُصَيْعَاء ج قَوَاصِع
Short, stunted, puny (child). قَصِع وقَصِيع ومَقْصُوع
Sharp (sword). مِقْصَع
The sun has reached its middle course. ✱ قصعل — إِقْصَعَلَّتِ الشَّمْسُ
Garden-sage. ✧ قَصْعِين
To break (wood). ✱ قَصَفَ i قَصْفًا, وقَصَّفَ ه
To be broken. قَصِفَ
✧ May God break thy life in the middle! يَقْصِف عُمْرَك
To revel, to make good cheer. قَصَفَ o قَصْفًا وقُصُوفًا, وأقصف

The extremities of the world. أقاصي الأرض
Docked in the ears (cattle). مَقصُوّ ومَقصِيّ ومَقصًى
Remote. مُقصًى
☆ قضّ i قَضِيضًا To crackle (thong).
— o قضًّا ه To bore (a pearl). To pierce (wood). To bray a. th. To destroy (a wall). To pull out (a peg).
— ه على To launch (horsemen) against.
— وأقضّ ه To sprinkle (food) with sugar.
قضّ a قضضًا, وأقضّ واستقضّ To be full of gravel (place, food).
— من الطعام To be mixed with gravel (food).
أقضّ To pick up (refuse). To be hard (resting-place).
— ه To render (a place) hard (God).
تقضّض وانقضّ To dart down (bird).
إنقضّ To be broken. To be thrown down. To threaten to fall (wall). To shoot down (star).
— على To dash upon (the enemy: horsemen).
إستقضّ ه To find (a bed) hard.
قضّ Cracking of the knee.
قضّ وقضض Pebble.
قضّ وقضيض Full of pebbles (place).
جاء القوم قِضُّهم و قَضَّهم وقَضَضُهم وقَضِيضُهم وبِقَضِيضِهِم They came all of them.
قضّة و قِضّة Small pebbles.
قضّة ج قِضاض Rocks superposed.
قِضّة Genus, species. Virginity.
— ج قِضّات Place full of pebbles.
قُضّة وقُضّة Vice, defect.
أقضّ م قضّاء Hard, full of pebbles (soil). Hard, compact (coat of mail).
☆ قضقض ه To mangle its prey (lion).
تقضقض To be broken, smashed.
قضقضة Breaking of a bow.
القضقاض القُضقاض ج القُضاقِض Lion.
☆ قَضِئ a قَضأ To be worn out (skin). To become red (eye).
— قضأ وقضاءة To be blackened (character).
— قَضأ To eat.
أقضأ ه To feed a. o.
تقضأ من To hold a. o. to be low born.

قَصِم وقَصِيم Frail.
قُصَم Breaking all.
قَصِيمة ج قَصِيم وقُصُم وقَصائِم Sandy ground abounding in tamarisks.
أقصم م قصماء ج قُصم Having the fore-teeth broken.
قَيصُوم ذَكَر Southern-wood (*plant*).
قَيصُوم أُنثى Santonin (*plant*).
☆ قصمل ه To eat a. th. greedily. To cut a. th.
قَصمَل وقصمول وقُصمُل Strong, sturdy.
قصمَلة Worm in the molar teeth.
☆ قصا o قَصوًا وقُصُوًّا وقَصًا وقَصاء, وقَصِي a To be remote, far away (place)
— وتقصّى عن To be far away from.
قصا o قَصوًا, وقصّى تقصية ه To dock the ears.
قصّى ه To cut (the nails).
قاصى ه To be far off from.
أقصى ه وه To remove a. o. far away. To bring a. th. to its utmost limit.
أقصى To protect the wing of an army.
تقصّى واستقصى ه وفي To fathom (a question). To study a. th. thoroughly. To exhaust (a subject). To manage (a business) carefully.
إستقصى To inquire after, to investigate.
قصًا Maiming of the ear. Remote relationship. Land, country.
قصًا وقصاء Remoteness. Inside of (a house).
هو في قَصاه He is in his country.
حُطني القصا Be off from me!
قَصوة Notch on the ear of a beast.
إستقصاء Inquiring, deep study.
قَصِي ج أقصاء م قصيّة ج قصايا Remote (place, man).
قاصٍ ج أقصاء وقاصُون Far off.
قاصية ج قَواصٍ Old (ewe). Land, country.
☆ بُو قيصا Elm-tree.
أقصى م قصواء The farthest. Docked in the ear.
الجامع الأقصى Mosque upon the site of the temple of Jerusalem.
أقصى ج أقاص م قُصوى وقُصيا ج قُصى Farther.
الغاية القُصوى The last end.

قَضِي م قَضِئَة Rotten.
قَضَأَة وقُضْأَة Vice. Shame. Corruption.
✻ قَضَب i قَضْبًا ة To strike a. o. with a rod.
— واقْتَضَب ة To ride an untrained (beast).
قَضَب وقَضَّب واقْتَضَب ه To cut off (a branch).
قَضَّب ه To prune (the vine).
— وتَقَضَّب To spread its rays (sun).
أَقْضَب To bring forth nutritious plants (land).
تَقَضَّب وانْقَضَب To be lopped, pruned.
إِنْقَضَب To move on (star).
إِقْتَضَب ه To extemporise (a speech).
قَضْب Branchy tree. Nutritious plant. Clover.
قَضْبَة ج قَضَبَات Bow. Arrow. Rod.
— ج قَضْب Nutritious plant.
قَضْبَة Flock, herd.
قَضِيب ج قُضْبَان Rod, stick.
— ج قُضُب Sharp (sword). Bow made of one branch.
قُضَابَة Cuttings. Splinters.
قَاضِب ج قَوَاضِب ,وقَضَّاب وقَضَّابَة ومِقْضَب Cutting (sword).
قَضَّابَة Active (man).
مِقْضَب ومِقْضَاب Scythe.
مِقْضَاب Abounding with nutritious plants (land).
مَقْضَبَة Place abounding with nutritious plants.
مُقْتَضَب Untrained. Extemporaneous (discourse). Poetical metre.
✻ قَضَم a قَضْمًا ة To subdue, to tame a. o.
تَقَضَّم وانْقَضَم To be chopped and scattered.
إِنْقَضَم عن To be separated, remote from.
قَضْم وقُضَاء وتَقْضِيم Pain in the belly.
قُضَاء وقُضَاعَة Flour-dust. Rubbish falling from a wall.
✻ قَضُف a قَضَافَة وقَضَفًا و قِضَفًا To be thin, lean.
قَضَف Small stones.
قَضَفَة Bird.
— ج قَضَف وقِضَاف و قُضْفَان Sandy hillock.

قَضَفَة Isolated tract of sand.
قَضِيف ج قِضَاف وقُضْفَان Thin; slender.
✻ قَضِم a وقَضَم i قَضْمًا ه To crunch a. th. dry.
قَضِم a قَضَمًا To have the teeth broken and black. To be broken (tooth). To be blunted (sword).
قَاضَم مُقَاضَمَة To buy a. th. in retail.
أَقْضَم ة To feed (a beast) with grain.
— واسْتَقْضَم To make little provision (in time of dearth).
قَضَم Notch in a blade. Sword.
قُضْمَة وقَضَام وقَضِيم ومَقْضَم Anything dry crackling under the teeth.
مَا ذُقْتُ قُضْمَةً او قَضَامًا او مَقْضَمًا I have not tasted the least food.
✧ قَضَامِيّ Toasted chick-peas.
قَضِم وقَضِيم ,وأَقْضَم م قَضْمَاء ج قُضْم Blunted (sword, tooth).
قَضِيم ج قَضَم Parchment. Leathern mat. Barley. Silver.
✻ قَضَى i قَضَاء ه To decide, to determine a. th. To fulfil (a duty). To satisfy (a want). To execute (an order).
— ه ل To settle (an affair) for a. o.
— ه على To prescribe a. th. to a. o.
— ة ه To pay (a debt) to.
قَضَى وقَضَى أَجَلَهُ او نَحْبَهُ He died.
— ه إلى To relate, to explain a. th. to.
ضَرَبَهُ فَقَضَى عَلَيْهِ He struck him dead.
قُضِيَ مِنْهُ العَجَب He was struck with wonder.
قَضَى i قَضْيًا وقَضَاء وقَضِيَّة بَيْن To judge between.
قَضَى على To condemn a. o.
قَضَى ل To discharge a. o. (judge).
قَضَّى تَقْضِيَة و قِضَّاء ه To finish, to perform a. th.
قَضَّى ة To appoint a. o. as a judge.
— ه بَيْن To send down (calamities) to (God).
قَاضَى ة To summon a. o. before a judge
تَقَضَّى To be performed, finished. To be fulfilled, consumed.
تَقَضَّي (for تَقَضَّض) To stoop (bird).
تَقَاضَيَا To be at law.

To exact from a. o. the payment of (a debt). تقاضى واقتضى ه ه
To come to nought. To be accomplished, to pass away. إنقضى
He died. إنقضى نَحْبُهُ
It required, it necessitated. إقتضى
To render a. th. necessary. ه —
To ask a. o. to decide a. th. إستقضى ه ه
To be appointed judge. أستُقضِيَ
Sentence, judgment. قَضَى وقَضَاء ج أقضِيَة
Irreversible decree of God. Fate, lot. Accomplishment.
Deciding. Death. قَضِيّ
Sentence. Event. Thing, matter. Case of law. Proposition, thesis. قَضِيَّة ج قَضَايَا
Bitter plant of the kind حَمْض. قِضَة ج قِضَى و قِضَات
End, consummation. إنقِضَاء
Exigence. Convenience. إقتِضَاء
Judge, cadi, magistrate. قَاضٍ ج قُضَاة
Chief justice. قَاضِي القُضَاة
Deadly poison. سَمٌّ قَاضٍ
Death. قَاضِيَة
Decider, arbitrator. قَضَّاء
Performed. Fulfilled. مَقْضِيّ
Necessitated. مُقتَضًى
According to; in consequence of. بِمُقتَضَى ال...
As reason requires. بِمُقتَضَى العَقل
To be high (price). ✡ قَطَّ o i قَطًّا وقُطُوطًا, وقَطَّ
To nib (a pen). To pare (the hoof of a horse). قَطَّ ه قَطًّا, واقتطّ ه
✧ To desist from. قَطَّ عَن
To be short, crisp, curly (hair). قَطَّ وقَطِطَ a قَطَطًا وقَطَاطَة
To turn, to carve (wood). قَطَّطَ ه
Only, solely. قَط وقَطَاطِ
It suffices me. قَطْنِي وقَطِي
Not at all, not ever (*after the preterite*). قَطُّ
I have never seen him. مَا رَأَيْتُهُ قَطُّ
Male cat. قِطٌّ ج قِطَاط و قِطَطَة
Civet, musk-cat. قِطُّ الزَّبَاد
✧ Cat-mint. حَشِيشَة القِطّ
Portion. Register. قِطٌّ ج قُطُوط
Female cat. Nibbing of a pen. قِطَّة

Dear (price). قَطٌّ وقَاطٌّ
Crisp and short (hair). قَطٌّ وقَطِطٌ
قَطٌّ ج قَطُّون و قِطَاط وأقطَاط, وقَطِط ج قَطِطُون
Crisp, short-haired.
Circumference of a hoof. Pattern. Top of a mountain. قَطَاط ج أقِطَّة
Circuit of a grotto. — وقُطَيطَة ج قَطَائِط
The horses came by troops. جَاءَت الخَيل قَطَائِط
Turner. قَطَّاط
Bone upon which a pen is nibbed. مِقَطٌّ ومِقَطَّة
To drizzle. To cluck (hen). ✡ قَطقَط
Drizzle. قِطقِط
Cry of the partridge. قَطقَطَة
To frown (the face). ✡ قَطَب i قَطبًا وقُطُوبًا, وقَطَّب
To collect a. th. To fill (a vessel). To close (a bag). قَطَب i قَطبًا ه
✧ To spread across a house (beam). قَطَب
To anger a. o. ه —
To stitch (clothes). — وقَطَّب ه
To assemble (crowd). — وأقطَب
To mix (wine). قَطَب وقَطَّب وأقطَب ه
✧ To frown (the face). To be stitched (garment). To fail (food). ✧ إنقَطَب
To precede others in (walking, speaking). ✧ قَوْطَب على في
قَطب و قِطب وقُطب وقُطُب ج أقطَاب وقُطبَة
Axis. Axle-tree of a wheel. ج قُطب
Pole. Pivot. Pole-star. Chief. Main supporter (in an affair). قُطب ج قُطُوب وأقطَاب و قِطَبَة
The polar star. نَجمَةُ القُطب
Polar (circle). قُطبِيّ
Fibrous plant for making ropes. قِطبِيّ
A pole of the terrestrial sphere. قُطبَة
✧ Stitch.
Arrow hitting the target. Caltrop, star-thistle, (*plants*). قُطبَة ج قُطَب
He has taken it in a lump. أخَذ البَاقِي قَطبًا
Mixture. Lowest part of the opening of a gown. قِطَاب
Piece of meat. قُطَابَة
Mixture of two kinds of milk. قَطِيب وقَطِيبَة

Mixed (wine). قَطِيب ومَقطُوب
Frowning. Lion. قَاطِب وقَطُوب
All. The whole. قَاطِبَة
They came all together. جاء القوم قاطِبَةً
☩ قطر ه قطرًا وقُطُورًا وقَطَرَانًا, وتَقطَر To drop (water). To drip.
قطر قطرًا ه To overthrow a. o. violently. To smear (a camel) with tar.
— ه To sew (a garment).
— قُطُورًا To run away.
ما أدري مَن قَطَرَهُ او مَن قَطر بِهِ I do not know who has taken it.
قطر ه قطرًا, وقطَّر, وأقطر ه To drip (a liquid). ✧ To distil a. th.
— ه To tie (beasts) in a file.
قطر ه To perfume (clothes) with aloes-wood.
— ه على فَرَسِهِ He threw him down from his horse.
أقطر To be near to drop.
طعَنَهُ فأقطَرَهُ He thrusted him with the spear and dashed him down.
تقطَّر To perfume o.'s self with aloes-wood. To fall on the side. To throw o.'s self down from an elevated place.
— عن To lag behind.
تقاطر To walk side by side. To come by parties.
إقطَرَّ واقطارّ To begin to dry (plant).
إستقطر ه To distil a. th. To drop (a liquid) drop by drop.
قطر وقَطَرَان Distillation.
قطر ج قِطار Rain. Dropping liquid. Drop.
✧ قطر مَكَّة والقاطِر المَكِّيّ Resinous juice of the dragon's blood.
قطر Brass. Copper. Striped stuff.
قُطر ج أقطار Side, flank. Celestial or terrestrial zone.
القُطر المِصريّ Egypt.
✧ قُطر الدَّائِرَة Diameter of a circle.
أربعة أقطار العالم The four parts of the world.
قُطر وقُطُر Aloes-wood.
أخذ الباقي قطرًا He took the rest in a lump.
قَطرَة ج قَطَرات A drop. ✧ Drops of eye-water.
قَطرَةً قَطرَةً Drop by drop.

قُطرَة وقُطَيرَة Trifle, paltry thing.
قُطار وقَطُور ومِقطار Letting fall drops (cloud).
قُطارَة Dropping liquid; small quantity of water.
قِطار ج قُطُر وقُطُرات File of camels.
✧ File of carriages. Railway-train.
قُطارِيّ وقُطارِيَّة Blackish and venomous snake.
▫ قُطيرَة ج قَطائِر Sailing-boat.
✧ قطرِيَّة Calamint (*plant*).
تَقطِير Distillation.
قاطِر Dripping. Gum.
القاطِر المَكِّيّ Dragon's blood.
مِقطَر ومِقطَرَة ج مَقاطِر Censer.
مِقطَرَة Chains, stocks.
مَقطُور Rained upon (land). Smeared with tar (camel).
☩ قَطرَب To hurry on.
تَقطرَب To stir about.
قُطرُب Demon, genius. Puppy. Light, lively. Restless insect. Melancholia.
✧ قِطرِيب Plough-peg.
✧ قَطرَمِيز Jar, glass-jar.
☩ قَطرَن To smear (a beast) with tar.
قِطرَان وقَطِرَان Tar extracted from the juniper or savin-tree.
مُقطرَن Smeared with tar.
▫ قَيطَاس L Whale.
☩ قطع a قطعًا ومَقطعًا وتِقِطَّاعًا ه To cut, to suppress, to curtail a. th.
— ه ل To put a. th. apart. To cut out (a garment) for.
قطع ه To intercept (a road: thief). To abolish (an habit); to stop a. th.
— ه عن To prevent a. o. from.
— قطعًا وقُطُوعًا ه To cross (a river) on a bridge or in swimming. To cross (a country).
— وأقطع ه بالحُجَّة He convinced him.
قطع لِسانَهُ He silenced him with benefits
— بَين To settle a difference between.
قطع رَحِمَهُ قطعًا وقَطِيعَة He broke with his people.
قطعَنِي وقطَّعَنِي وأقطعَنِي الثَّوبُ قَطعًا The garment fits my size.
قطع فُلانٌ الحَبلَ Such a one hanged himself.

He has sold his horse. قطع عُنُقَ دَابَّتِهِ
To fill a tank to the half. — الحَوضَ
To consume (food). — ه
✧ To lose its strength (medicine). To digest (stomach). قَطِعَ
To be exhausted (well). — قُطوعًا وقِطاعًا To dry (spring). To fly to a hot country (bird). ✧ To abstain from meat.
✧ He is not convinced. هذا لا يَقطع عقلَهُ
It is unlikely, incredible. هذا لا يَقطع العقلَ
✧ To overlook a. th.: to make abstraction of. قطع نَظَرَهُ عن
He stopped short; he was unable to answer. قطع a وقطِع o قَطاعَةً, وقَطِع لِسانُهُ
To be cut (breathing). قُطِع
He was stopped in the way. — بِهِ
He was hindered from attaining his want.
To cut in small pieces. To put a. th. to rags. To scan (a verse). ✧ To wear out (a garment). قطّع ه
To inflict a punishment upon a. o. (God). — ه على
To outrun the others (horse). — ه
To mix wine with (water). — ه ب
✧ He trifled time away. قطّع الزّمان
To break with a. o. ✧ To cut a. o. short. قاطع ه
✧ To fix the price of a work, or of a salary. — ه على كذا من الأُجرَة او العَمَل
To make a. o. to cross (a river). To make or let a. o. cut (wood). To assign to a. o. a (land) as fee. أقطع ه ه
To cease laying eggs (hen). To be exhausted (well). To be silenced. To be in need of water (tribe). To be nearly ripe (palm-tree). أقطعَ
To be severed from o.'s people. — عن أهلِهِ
To be cut, broken. To be ragged (garment). To be mixed with water (wine, milk). تَقطَّع
To sever the bonds of friendship. To cease (relationship). تَقاطع
To break (rope). To be interrupted. To finish. To be severed (tie). To be disused (habit). To be dried (spring). إنقطع
To be attached, devoted to. إنقطع إلى
To divide a flock. إقتَطع قِطعَةً من مالِهِ
To be worm-eaten (fruit). ✧ تَقَرطَم
Cutting. Breaking, stopping. Pause in reading. قطع
Undoubtedly. Absolutely. قطعًا
Spear-head short and broad. Piece cut off. قِطع ج أقطاع وأقطُع و قِطاع
Horse-cloth. — ج أقطاع وقُطوع
Portion of the night. — و قِطع
Scarcity of water. قُطع وقُطعَة
Asthma. Colics. قُطع
Breaking off with o.'s folk. قَطَع وقُطعَة
Loosing the voice. قَطِع
Fragment, piece, slice. قِطعَة ج قِطَع
Piece of land. Piece cut. قُطعَة ج قُطَع وقُطُعات
Stump of the hand. Amputated part of a limb. — وقَطَعَة ج قَطَع وقَطَعات
✧ Decisive (answer). قَطعِيّ
Shears. قِطاع ج قِطَعَة
Season of gathering dates. زَمان القِطاع
Fragment. Piece cut. قُطاعَة
Abstinence from milk, food. ✧ قِطاعَة ج قَطائِع
✧ Mishap, danger, adversity. قُطُوع
✧ He escaped from danger. فاتَهُ قُطُوع
Piece of mat; worn out mat. ✧ قُطُوع وقُطُوعَة
قَطِيع ج قُطعان وأقطاع و قِطاع وجج أقاطِيع
Flock, herd.
Similar, alike. — ج قُطعاء
— ج قُطعان وأقطِعَة و قِطاع وأقطُع وأقاطِع وقُطُع
Rod. Branch. Cut from a tree. وقُطُعات
Unable to rise. قَطِيع القِيام
Short in speech. قَطِيع الكَلام
Beware of discord! إتّقوا القُطَيعاء
Forsaking of relations. Land held in fee. Tax. قَطِيعَة ج قَطائِع
Garment in rags. ثَوب أقطاع
Fee assigned to soldiers. إقطاعَة ج إقطاعات
Colics. Pain in the belly. تَقطِيع
Stature, shape. Cut of a verse. Features. — ج تَقاطِيع
Shears, scissors. Cutting (sword). Peremptory (proof). Sour (milk). ✧ Blunted (mustard). Strengthless قاطِع

(medicine). Abstaining from milk-food. Side of a river.
Brigand. قاطِع الطَّرِيق ج قُطَّاع وقُطَّع Highway-robber.
Migratory birds. قاطِعة ج قَواطِع
✧ قاطوع Fruit-eating worm.
قطّاع Cutter. ✧ Stone-cutter.
قطّاعة Pickaxe. Beam for crossing a stream.
قطوع Yielding no more milk (she-camel).
— لإخوانهِ Breaking off with his brothers.
✧ قطيع Digesting well (stomach). - Digestive, light (water).
أقطع م قطعاء ج قُطْع وقُطعان One-handed. Dumb. Sharper (sword). ✧ Worse, more wretched.
رَحِم قطعاء Breaking off with o.'s family.
تقطيع Pain in the bowels.
مُقطع، ومُقطع بالحُجَّة Reduced to silence.
مُقطَع Stranger, remote.
— النهر Ford of a river.
مَقطَع ج مَقاطِع Place of cutting. Syllable. Stone-quarry. ✧ Piece of cloth.
مَقاطِع الأوديَة The ends of the valleys.
— الأنهار The fords of the rivers.
مقطع الحقّ Point of a debate; test for knowing truth from falsehood.
مِقطع Any cutting instrument. Cutting (sword).
مِقطاع Unsteady. Soon exhausted (well).
مَقطعة Preventive.
بالمُقاطعة By the job; at a price agreed upon (work).
✧ مُقاطَعة ج مُقاطَعات Province, district.
مُقطَّع Cut to pieces. ✧ Ragged (clothes).
مُقطَّعة ومُقطَّعات Short (garment verses).
مُنقطِع القرين Pairless.
— ل Devoted to.
أنفس المُنقطِعين ✧ The forlorn souls of Purgatory.
مُنقطَع الوادي End of a valley.
مَقطوع ✧ Forlorn (man). Broken-winded (horse).

مَقطوع بهِ Cut off from. Asthmatic.
✧ قطف i قَطفًا، وقطّف واقتطف ه To gather (grapes); to pluck (fruit). To snatch away a. th.
— وقطّف ه To scratch a. o. with the nails.
قطف o i قِطافًا وقُطوفًا To walk at a quick pace (horse).
قطّف ه To sift (flour).
أقطف To have ripe grapes (vine). To have a slow-paced horse.
قطف Gathering. Scar. Curtailment of (a verse).
قِطف و✧ قَطف *Atriplex herba*, hypericum androsœnum.
قطف ج قُطوف (*un.* قطفة) Scar, trace. Orach. wild spinach.
قِطف ج قُطوف و قِطاف Bunch of grapes. Plucked fruit.
قطفة Species of thistle.
قِطاف وقَطاف Vintage.
قُطافة Grapes falling during the vintage.
قطّاف Vintager.
قَطوف ج قُطُف Walking at a slow pace.
قطيف ومقطوف Plucked (fruit).
قطيفة ج قطائف وقُطُف Velvet. Villous garment. *Pl.* Sweetmeats. Fine, reddish dates.
أقطف More greedy. More speedy.
مِقطف ج مَقاطِف Scythe. ✧ Bolter.
مِقطف و✧ مَقطف ج مَقاطِف Basket.
مُقطأنة Of small size (man).
✧ قطل o i قطلًا، وقطّل ه To cut a. th.
— عُنقهُ To cut the neck to.
قطّل ه To throw down a. o.
تقطّل To be cut at the root.
قُطل وقطيل Cut off (tree).
قطيلة Rag used as a sponge.
✧ قطلب Arbute, strawberry-tree.
✧ قطم i قَطمًا ه To cut off a. th. To seize a. th. with the teeth.
قَطِم a قَطَمًا To be fond of meat.
✧ قَطمة وقطيمة Bit, fragment.
قَطِم Greedy of meat.
قطام وقَطامِيّ وقُطامِيّ Sparrow-hawk.
مِقطم ج مَقاطِم Clutch, claw.
✧ قِطمِر — قِطمِير وقِطمار Integument of a date-stone.

Clash of arms. Shivering fever. Dry dates. Hard road. قَعْقَاء
Claps of thunder. قَعَاقِم
To be of a conical shape. ✡ قَعِبَ – قَعَّبَ
To speak gutturally, abstrusely. – الكَلَامَ وفِيهِ
Wooden cup. قَعْب ج أَقْعُب و قِعَاب و قِعَبَة
Depth of speech. – الكَلَامِ
Hollow in a mountain. قُعْبَة
Cup-shaped. مُقَعَّب
Goat's beard, salsify. ✧ قَعْبَرِيس
Squill. Pancratium (plants). ✡ قَعْبَل وقَعْبِل
Goat's beard, salsify. قُعْبُول
To give to a. o. little of. ✡ قَعَثَ a قَعْثًا وقَعْثَةً لِفُلَان مِن
To root out a. th. قَعَّثَ ه
To squander (goods). أَقْعَثَ في
To bestow bountifully upon. – واقْتَعَثَ العَطِيَّةَ ل
To be uprooted. To crumble down (wall). إِنْقَعَثَ
To extract much earth from a well. إِقْتَعَثَ
Abundant rain. Sweeping torrent. قَعِيث
To sit down. To lay upon the breast (bird). To give fruit every second year (palm-tree). To have no husband (woman). ✧ To remain idle. ✡ قَعَدَ o قُعُودًا ومَقْعَدًا
To give up, to neglect a. th. قَعَدَ عَن
To make a. o. to sit down. – بِ
To prevent a. o. from – بِفُلَان عَن
He prepared for war. – لِلْحَرْب
He began to revile. – يَشْتُم
To serve a. o. To be sufficient to a. o. قَعَّدَ وأَقْعَدَ ه
To sit down with a. o. قَاعَدَ ه
To make a. o. to sit down. To give a seat to a. o. To cripple a. o. (God). أَقْعَدَ ه
To hinder a. o. from. أَقْعَدَ وتَقَعَّدَ ه عَن
To be crippled. أُقْعِدَ
To put off (an affair). تَقَعَّدَ وتَقَاعَدَ عَن
To ride (a beast). إِقْتَعَدَ ه
May God preserve thee! قَعْدَكَ اللهَ
People remaining at home in time of war. Soldiers without pay. قَعَد
Sitting of a man. قِعْدَة

Name of the dog of the 7 sleepers. قِطْمِير
To reside in a place. ✡ قَطَنَ o قُطُونًا في وب
To serve a. o. – ه
To be bent (back). قَطِنَ a قَطَنًا
To become mealy (vine). ✧ To become musty (food). قَطَّنَ
To settle a. o. in a place. – ه بِمَكَان
Root of a bird's tail. Part between the two hips. قَطَن ج أَقْطَان
Cotton. قُطْن وقُطُن ج أَقْطَان
Flake of cotton. قُطْنَة
Third stomach of a ruminant. قِطْنَة وقَطِنَة
Frame of a camel-saddle. قِطَان ج قُطُن
Any pulse like peas, beans, lentils. Cotton-garment. قُطْنِيَّة وقِطْنِيَّة ج قَطَانِيّ
Inhabitant. قَاطِن ج قُطَّان وقَاطِنَة وقَطِين
Resident slaves, servants. قَطِين ج قُطُن (s. pl.)
Large cavern. ✧ قِطِّين ج قَطَاطِين
Bent (back). أَقْطَن
Cotton (un. قِيطَانَة) or silk lace, string. ✧ قِيطَان ج قَيَاطِين
Cellar; closet. قَيْطُون
Cotton-plantation. مَقْطَنَة
Gourd-plant. Any plant without stem. يَقْطِين و ✧ أَقْطِين
To walk slowly. To walk with short steps. To cry (sand-grouse). ✡ قَطَا o قَطْوًا
To procrastinate. To be late. تَقَطَّى
To sit on the croup of a horse. – ه
Croup of a horse. قَطَاة
Sand-grouse. – ج قَطًا وقَطَوَات
They dispersed in various places. ذَهَبُوا في الأَرْضِ بِقَطَا
Walking with short steps. قَطَوَان وقَطْوَان
Thick and bitter water. ✡ قَعَّ – قُعّ وقُعَاع
To crackle, to rattle, to clash. ✡ قَعْقَعَ
To clatter, to shake a. th. – ه
To overrun the earth. – في الأَرْض
To produce a clattering sound. تَقَعْقَعَ
They are gone. قَعْقَعَتْ وتَقَعْقَعَتْ عُمُدُهُم
Magpie. Raven. قَعْقَع وقُعْقُع
Clash of arms. Gnashing of the teeth. قَعْقَعَة

ذو القِعْدة وذو القَعْدة The 11 th month of the Arabian year.
قِعْدَة Manner of sitting. Last born (child).
قُعْدَة ج قُعْدَات Ass. Saddle.
قَعْدَة Litter for women. Carpet.
قُعَدَة Sedentary.
إقعاد وقُعَاد Lameness. Impotence.
قِعَاد Spouse, wife.
قاعِد ج قُعُود Sitting. ✧ Idle.
— ج قَوَاعِد Full of grain (sack). Having ceased to bear children (woman). Young palm-tree.
قَعَد The Abstainers, Musulman (*pl.*) schismatics.
قاعِدَة ج قَوَاعِد وقاعِدات Basis (of a column). Foundation of (a building). Pedestal. Rule, pattern.
قاعِدَة المُلك Capital town of a kingdom.
قُعْدِيّ وقُعْدِيَّة Impotent. Sedentary.
قَعُود ج أَقْعِدَة وقُعُد وقِعْدان وقعائد Young camel fit for riding.
قَعِيد Companion. Keeper. (*s. pl.*) Coming from behind (beast).
قَعِيدَكَ الله I adjure thee by the name of God.
قَعِيدَة ج قَعَائِد Wife. Female companion. Sack.
مَعَاش تَقَاعُد ✧ Pension.
مَقْعَد ج مَقَاعِد Sitting-place. ✧ Parlour.
مَقْعَدَة و✧ قَعْدَة A seat. ✧ Posteriors.
مُقْعَد Crippled.
مُقْعَد النَّسَب Man of short lineage.
— الحَسَب Man without nobility.
— الأَنْف Big-nosed.
مُقْعَدَة Basket of palm-leaves. Waterless well.
المُقْعَدات Frogs.
✡ قَعَر a قَعْرًا ه To sink (a well). To reach the bottom of (a well). To empty (a cup). To cut (a tree) from the root.
— ه To fell, to crush a. o.
قَعُر o قَعَارَة To be deep, hollow.
قَعَّر وأَقْعَر ه To deepen a. th.
قَعَّر وتَقَعَّر في كَلامِهِ He spoke gutturally.
أَقْعَر To reach the zenith (star).
تَقَعَّر To be deep, hollow. To be cut down (tree). To be felled.

إنْقَعَر To be uprooted (tree).
قَعْر ج قُعُور Bottom (of anything). Hollow in the earth. Bowl. Town.
قَعْر Intelligence, sagacity.
بَعِيد القَعْر Deep-minded.
قَعْرَة وقُعْرَة Hollow in the earth.
قَعْرَان ومِقْعَار Deep (cup).
قَعُور وقَعِير Very deep.
قَيْعَر وقَيْعَار ومِقْعَار Speaking gutturally.
مُقَعَّر Hollow. Concave.
✡ قَعِس a قَعَسًا, وتَقَاعَس واقْعَنْسَس To have a protuberant breast and a hollow back.
قَعَس a o قَعْسًا To walk in protruding the breast.
أَقْعَس To become wealthy.
تَقَاعَس To protrude the chest and hollow the back. *i. e.* To be refractory.
تَقَاعَس عَن To hold back from. To give up a. th.
قَعِس ج قَعْسَان, وأَقْعَس م قَعْسَاء ج قُعْس Having a protuberant chest and a hollow back.
مُقْعَنْسِس ج مَقَاعِس ومَقَاعِيس Strong.
قَرْعَس Strong-backed and big-necked.
✡ قَعْوَس — تَقَعْوَس To be broken (old man). To be ruined (house).
قَعْوَس Broken old man.
✡ قَعَش a قَعْشًا ه To gather a. th. To pull down a (wall). To fold a. th.
إنْقَعَش To be destroyed (wall). To go away.
✡ قَعَص a قَعْصًا, وأَقْعَص ه To kill a. o. on the spot.
قُعِص To be seized with murrain (sheep).
إنْقَعَص To die on the spot. To be folded.
قَعْص Violent death.
مَات قَعْصًا He died on the spot.
قُعَاص Murrain, cattle-plague.
✡ قَعَض o قَعْضًا ه To bend (a branch).
قَعْض ومَقْعُوض Bent.
✡ قَعَط a قَعْطًا To cry. To be a coward. To be dry.
— ه To drive a. o. back.
— وقَعَّط ه To urge (a beast).

قعط على — To urge (a debtor). To be angry with.
— واقتعط ه — To bind (a turban).
قعط a قعطًا — To be humbled, abashed.
قعّط وأقعط في القول — To hold obscene talk.
أقعط — To shout.
— ه — To despise a. o.
— عن — To recede from.
قعط — Large flock of sheep.
مِقعط ومِقعطة — Turban.
✱ قعطر ه — To fell a. o.
— ه — To fasten a. th.
✱ قعطل ه — To throw a. o. down.
— في الكلام — To be profuse in speech.
— على غريمه — To urge a debtor.
✱ قعف a قعفًا ه — To uproot (a tree). To exhaust (a vessel). To sweep away (the earth : rain). To raise (dust) in walking.
قعِف a قعفًا, وتقعّف وانقعف واقتعف — To crumble down (wall).
تقعّف وانقعف واقتعف — To be pulled out. To die.
إقتعف ه — To seize a. th. greedily.
قعف — Range of hillocks.
قاعِف — Sweeping rain.
قُعاف — Sweeping (torrent).
✧ قعق ج قُعقان — Crow, raven.
✧ قعقر — To heap stones in a conical shape.
✧ قعقور (*for* قهقور) — Conical heap of stones.
✱ قعل — أقعل واقعالّ — To open (vine-blossom).
إقتعل ه — To pluck (a flower).
قُعال — Vine-blossom.
قاعِلة ج قواعِل — Oblong mountain.
قعيل — Male hare.
قوعلة — Hillock, hill.
قيعل — عُقاب قيعلة وقيعلة — Eagle having its nest on the summit of a mountain.
✱ قعِم a قعمًا, وأُقعِم — To be seized with a deadly disease.
أقعم ه — To sting and kill a. o. (snake).
قعمة المال — Choice part of a flock.
✱ قعِن a قعنًا — To be short (nose).
قعن — Kneading-trough.
أقعن م قعناء ج قُعن — Short-nosed.

✱ قعِي a قعًا — To have the nose turned up.
أقعى — To sit on its tail (dog). To squat. To be turned up (nose). To rise high (star).
— ه — To force (a horse) to back.
قعو مث قعوان ج أقعٍ — Iron-chape of a pulley.
أقعى م قعواء — Having the nose turned up.
✱ قفّ o قفوفًا — To dry (linen, plant). To stand on end (hair). To steal a coin (money-changer). To contract. ✧ To crouch, to cower.
أقفّ — To cease laying eggs (hen). To dry up (tears).
إستقفّ — To contract, to become wrinkled (old man).
قفّ وقفيف — Leguminous plants.
قُفّ ج قِفاف وأقفاف, وقُفّة — Height, hill.
قُفّ — Rocky place. Cloud like a mountain.
قفّ من الناس — Rabble.
قَفّة وقُفّة — Short man.
قَفّة وقِفّة وقُفّة — Shiver of fever.
قُفّة ج قُفَف — Basket.
قفّاف — Pilfering money.
قفّان — Trustee.
على قفّان ذلك — In consequence of that.
هذا قفّانه — This is the time.
✱ قفقف وتقفقف — To shiver from cold.
✱ قفِي a قفًا — To be spoiled by rain (plant).
✱ قفح a قفحًا ه — To loathe a. th.
— عن — To abstain from.
قفيحة — Cream upon which milk is added.
✱ قفخ a قفخًا وقِفاخًا ه — To strike a. th. hard or hollow.
قفيخة — Food of dates and grease.
✱ قفد i قفدًا ه — To slap a. o. on the neck.
قفِد a قفدًا — To have stiffness in the pastern. To have a big, flaccid neck.
ما زلتُ أقفِدُ لك — I have not ceased to act for thee.
قفد — Stiffness in the pastern.
أقفد م قفداء — Wearing the shoe at the toe (horse). Big-necked.
إعتمّ القفداء — He wound the turban upon the top of his head.

P قفدان وقفدانة Leather-case for perfumes.
✱ قفر o قفرًا, وتقفّر واقتفر ه To track a. o. ◊ To verify a. th.
قفِر a قفرًا To be scarce (flock). To be unseasoned (food).
قفّر ه To pick up (things).
أقفر To be depopulated (country). To be vacant (house). To come to the desert, to be lonely. To have no provision.
— ه To find (a country) desert.
اقتفر ه To pick (a bone).
أقفر وقفار Unseasoned (bread).
قفر ج قفار وقفور, وقفرة Bare and waterless desert. Wild land.
القفر اليهودي Asphaltum.
قفير ج قفران Bee-hive. Unseasoned (bread).
قافور وقفّور وقفّورة Integument of the palm-blossom.
قفّورة ج قفافير ◊ Large basket.
مقفار Desolate land.
✱ قفز i قفزًا وقفزانًا وقفازًا وقفوزًا To spring (gazelle).
قفز To die.
قفّز ة To make a. o. to spring.
تقفّز ب To dye her hands and feet with henna (woman).
تقافز To compete in leaping.
قفزة ج قفزات, وقفزى Bound, leap.
قافز وقفّاز Springing.
خيل قافزة ج قوافز Bounding horses.
القوافز The frogs.
قفيز ج أقفزة وقفزان Measure for grain. ◊ Miller's fee payed in kind. Hasp of a lock.
أقفز ومقفّز White-footed (horse).
قفّاز ج قفافيز Long felt-gloves.
✱ قفس i o قفسًا وقفوسًا To die.
— ه To grasp a. th.
— ة To take hold of a. o. by the hair.
قفِس a قفسًا To have the tip of the nose large.
تقفّس To bound (gazelle).
تقافس ب To seize o. a. by (the hair).
قفاس وقفساء Vile (slave).
أقفس م قفساء ج قفس Born from a slave father. Anything long and folded.

قفساء Intestines, guts.
✱ قفش o i قفشًا ه To eat a. th. greedily. To take, to gather a. th.
— ة To milk (a she-camel) quickly.
— ة ب To strike a. o. with a stick.
انقفش واقتفش To crouch down.
قفش Short boot.
قفش Thieves, robbers.
✱ قفص i قفصًا ة وه To tie the legs of (a gazelle) together. To put things together. To torment a. o.
قفِص a قفصًا To be lively, light, nimble. To be benumbed by cold.
قفّص ة To tie (a gazelle) by the feet. ◊ To put (a bird) in a cage.
أقفص To have bird-cages.
تقفّص To roll o.'s self up. To conglobulate.
تقافص To be intertwisted. To be complicated.
قفص وقفص وقفص Lace-work, lattice-work.
قفص ج أقفاص Cage. Lattice, wicker-work. ▫ Basket of palm-leaves.
قفِص Benumbed by cold; contracted.
قافصة ج قوافص Lofty (hill).
مقفّص Tied by the foot. Checkered (cloth). ◊ Caged (bird).
P قفطان ج قفاطين Ample upper-gown.
✱ قفع a قفعًا ة ب To strike (the fingers) with (a rod). To ferule a. o.
— ة عن To keep a. o. aloof from.
قفِع a قفعًا To be contracted, to shrivel (foot, ear). To be short-tailed (sheep).
قفّع ه To preserve, to store up a. th. To contract (the fingers : cold).
تقفّع To be contracted, shrivelled.
انقفع To dry up and harden (plant).
— عن To be prevented, to refrain from.
قفع Testudo (besieging machine).
قفع Sorrow, grief.
قفعة ج قفاع وقفعات Basket of palm-leaves.
قفاع وقفّاع Disease distorting the feet of sheep.
قفاع لماله Sparing of his goods.
قفاعة Bramble-net.
أقفع م سمعاء ج قفع Having shrivelled

To charge a. o. with foul deeds.

To attribute a. th. قَفَا وأَقْفَى واقْتَفَى ه ب particularly to.

◊ To hide o.'s self behind a. th. قَفَا

To have a. o. قَفَّى ه ب او عَلَى أَثَرِه ب tracked. To follow the footsteps of. To rhyme two verses.

To avail o.'s self of ◊ قَافَى واسْتَقْفَى ه the absence of a. o.

To prefer a. o. or a. th. to. أَقْفَى ه وه على

To follow, to imitate a. o. تَقَفَّى واقْتَفَى

To strike a. o. on تَقَفَّى واسْتَقْفَى ه ب the neck with.

To charge a. o. falsely with. تَقَافَى ه

To select a. th. اقْتَفَى ه

قَفَا وقَفًا ج أَقْفِيَة وأَقْفٍ وقُفِيّ وقِفِيّ Nape of the neck. ◊ Back of the hand, of a knife.

I shall never do it. لا أَفْعَلُه قَفَا الدَّهْر

He is broken down, رُدَّ قَفًا او على قَفَاهُ decrepit.

◊ Behind, from behind. مِن قَفَا

Behind his back and بالقَفَا وبالوَجْه before his face. On the right and the wrong side.

Dust raised by the rain. قَفْو

Selection. ◊ Silk tresses worn قَفْوَة by women on the back.

Thou hast made a بِئْس القَفْوَةُ قَفْوَتُكَ bad choice.

Reproach. Abuse. Fault. قِفْوَة

Liberality shown to a guest. قَفَاوَة

◊ In the absence of. Without قَفَاوَة عن the knowledge of.

Imitation. Preference. اقْتِفَاء

Pit dug by a hunter. قَفِيَّة

Attainment, superiority. قَفِيَّة

Coming in a file. قَفِي وقَفِيَّة وقَاف

Honoured guest. Food served to قَفِيّ a guest.

Back of the neck. Rhyme. قَافِيَة ج قَوَافٍ Verse. Ode.

Rhymed prose, poetry. الكَلَام المُقَفَّى

Cardamom (odoriferous ✻ قَفَل – قَافِلَة plant).

Salsola fruticosa, saltwort (plant). قَافِل ◊ Ermine. قَافُو وقَافُوم T

To be few in num- ✻ قَلَّ i قِلًّا وقُلًّا ورِقْلَة ber, small in quantity. To be rare.

---

ears, distorted toes. Short-tailed. Stooping the head.

A drooping herb. Turned up قَفْعَاء (toe). Shrivelled (ear)

Stooping the head. مُقْنَعِم

Rod, ferule. مِقْفَعَة

To come back ✻ قَفَل o i قُفُولًا وقَفْلًا from a journey.

To preserve, to store – i قَفْلًا وقُفُولًا up a. th.

To be dry (skin). – o قُفُولًا، وقَفِل a قَفَلًا

To lock up (a door). قَفَّل ه وأَقْفَل ه وعلى

◊ To cut off the قَفَل (قَفَن for) ه top of (a tree).

To shrivel, to dry (the أَقْفَل ه وه skin : thirst).

To follow a. o. with the eyes. – ه

To bring a. o. back from. – ه عن

To assemble (people) for. – ه على

He gave at once the – المَال فُلَان whole property to.

To be locked, تَقَفَّل وانْقَفَل واقْتَفَل واسْتَقْفَل padlocked (door).

To be niggardly. اسْتَقْفَل

Dry tree. قَفْل وقَفْلَة

He has given him a أَعْطَاهُ أَلْفًا قَفْلَة thousand at one time.

Lock, padlock. قُفْل ج أَقْفَال وأَقْفُل وقُفُول Bolt. ◊ Skein of thread.

Travellers coming back. قَفْل

Having a good memory. قَفْلَة

Coming back قَافِل ج قَافِلَة وقُفَّل وقُفْل from a journey. Slender (horse).

Caravan. Party of tra- قَافِلَة ج قَوَافِل vellers.

Dessicated. Whip. Narrow pass. قَفِيل

Locksmith. قَفَّال

Vein of the arm. قِيفَال G

Stingy. مُقْفِل ومُتَقَفِّل ومُقْفِيل اليَدَيْن

To strike a. o. on the ✻ قَفَن o قَفْن ه back of the head.

To behead (a ewe). – وأَقْفَن واقْتَفَن ه

To die. قَفَن i قُفُونًا

To behead a. o. قَفَّن ه

Back of the head. قَفَن وقَفَّن

To follow the foot- ✻ قَفَا قَفْوًا وقُفُوًّا ه steps of. To efface the traces of (God).

To strike a. o. on the neck. ✻ قَفَا

Thou camest seldom. قَلَّ مَا جِئْتَ
At least, minimum. قَلَّمَا
To lift, to raise قَلَّ قَلًّا . وأَقَلَّ واسْتَقَلَّ ه a. th. To uphold, to maintain a. th.
To lessen, to diminish. قَلَّلَ ه وه
To lessen a. o. in the eyes of. — ه فِي عَيْنِهِ
He gave him very little. قَالَّ لَهُ العَطَاء
To possess little. أَقَلَّ
To diminish a. th. To find a. th. little. To give little. أَقَلَّ ه
To seize a. o. (fear). — واسْتَقَلَّ ه
To rise high (sun). تَقَالَّ
To find a. th. small, little, few. — ه
To make little of. إِسْتَقَلَّ ه وه
To grow (plant). To raise himself (man). To rise in its flight (bird). To become angry. إِسْتَقَلَّ
To go away from (the tents : people). — عن
To be independent, absolute (governor). — بالوِلَايَة
He is alone in his opinion. — بِرَأْيِهِ
Low wall. Shudder. قِلّ
Exiguity, small number. Poverty. قِلّ وقُلّ
Lonely, helpless man. رَجُل قِلّ
No one but Zeyd says so. قَلَّ وأَقَلّ رَجُلٍ يَقُولُ ذٰلِكَ إِلَّا زَيْد
He is an unknown man. هُوَ قُلُّ بْنُ قُلّ
Recovery of health, wealth. قَلَّة
Earthenware bottle. Top of the head. Summit of a mountain. Stud of a hilt. قُلَّة ج قُلَل وقِلَال
Paucity, smallness, rarity. قِلَّة ج قِلَل
Plural of paucity (from 3 to 10). جَمْع القِلَّة
They started all of them. إِرْتَحَلُوا بِقِلِّيَّتِهِم
He took it altogether. أَخَذَهُ بِقِلِّيَّتِهِ وبِقِلِّيلَتِهِ او بِقِلِّيلَاهُ
Cell, closet. قِلِّيَّة ج قَلَالِيّ ✧ قِلَّايَة ج قَلَّايَات
Independence, absolutism. إِسْتِقْلَال ✧ اسْتِقْلَالِيَّة
Few. Small. Rare. Destitute of. Short of stature. قَلِيل ج قُلُل وقَلِيلُون وأَقِلَّاء ، وقَلَال وقُلَّال ج قُلُل
Seldom. Little. قَلِيلًا
Little by little. قَلِيلًا قَلِيلًا

Scattered people from various tribes. قُلَل
People gathered from various places. قُلَّل
Less. أَقَلّ
The least, the minimum. الأَقَلّ
Poor. أَقَلّ ومُقِلّ
Who has left few verses (poet). مُقِلّ
Adorned with a stud (sword). مُقَلَّل
Independent (sovereign). مُسْتَقِلّ
To move, to agitate a. th. ✲ قَلْقَلَ قَلْقَلَةً وقِلْقَالًا ه
✧ To trouble, to disquiet a. o. — ه
To be shaken. ✧ To be disquieted. ◻ To tremble. تَقَلْقَلَ
Cassia. قِلْقِل وقُلْقُلَاق
Trouble, anxiety. قَلْقَلَة
Clod of earth. ◻ قُلَيْقِلَة
To turn a. th. upside down, to change a. th. To till (the ground). To reverse a. th. ✲ قَلَبَ i قَلْبًا ، وقَلَّبَ ه
To extract the marrow of (a palm-tree). قَلَبَ ه
To cause a. o. to die (God). — وأَقْلَبَ ه إِلَيْهِ
To become red (dates). قَلَّبَ
To hit a. o. in the heart. قَلَبَ o i قَلْبًا ه
To be turned over. To be flabby (lip). To have contorted lips. قَلِبَ a قَلَبًا
To be affected with heart-disease. قُلِبَ
To handle (substances). To ponder over (a business). قَلَّبَ ه
To be baked on one side (bread). To be dry externally (grapes). أَقْلَبَ
To be turned over, changed. To be restless in bed (sick man). ✧ To be unsteady, fickle. تَقَلَّبَ
To act in o.'s own way in. — في
To be inverted, reversed. To be upset. إِنْقَلَبَ
His circumstances have changed. — ظَهْرًا لِبَطْن
To come back to. To turn towards. — إلى
Reversal. Inversion. Wrong side, reverse. قَلْب و✧ قُلْب

(*Gram.*) Inversion, transposition of words, letters. قَلْب
Heart. Mind, soul; intimate thought. Middle part. Center of an army. Kernel. Marrow, pith; best part. قَلْب ج قُلُوب
(*Gram.*) verbs of heart like عَلِمَ, ظَنَّ. أَفْعَال القُلُوب
(*m. f. s. pl.*) وم قَلْبَة, وقُلْب م قُلْبَة قَلْب
Genuine, of true race (man).
Bracelet. White serpent. قُلْب ج قُلْب
Marrow of palm-trees. قُلْب وقَلْب ج أَقْلَاب وقُلُوب وقِلَبَة
Disease. Toil. قَلَبَة
There is no disease in him. مَا بِهِ قَلَبَة
Cordial. Intimate. قَلْبِي
Solstice. إِنْقِلَاب الشَّمْس
Changes of fortune. تَقَلُّبَات الأُمُور
Heart-disease. Disease of camels. قُلَاب
Inverting. Date becoming red. قَالِب
Mould. Model of (a boot). Clog. Wooden frame of an arch. ◘ Model. قَالَب ج قَوَالِب
Loaf of sugar. قَالَب سُكَّر
Artful; clever in business. حُوَّل قُلَّب وحُوَلِيّ قُلَّبِيّ وحُوَّلِيّ قُلَّب
Unsteady. Wolf. قُلُوب
Ancient well. Ditch. قَلِيب ج أَقْلِبَة, وقُلُب وقُلْب
✧ Latch-key. قَلَّابَة
Reversed (lip). Having a reversed lip. أَقْلَب م قَلْبَاء
Turned up. Affected with heart-disease. مَقْلُوب
On the reverse, on the wrong side. بِالمَقْلُوب
Hoe. ✧ Hammer of a gun. مِقْلَب ج مَقَالِب
Inversion. Field open to action; free scope. The future life. مُنْقَلَب
To cast, to mould a. th. ✧ قَوْلَب
To perish. ✱ قَلِتَ a قَلَتًا
To be left childless (mother). أَقْلَتَ
To destroy a. o. — ه
Hollow in a rock, in the ground. Cavity of the eye. قَلْت ج قِلَات
Dangerous place. مَقْلَتَة ج مَقَالِت
Mother bereft of all her children. مِقْلَات ج مَقَالِيت
To be yellow (tooth). To have yellow teeth. ✱ قَلِحَ a قَلَحًا

To clean the teeth of. قَلَّحَ ه
To be in quest of (sustenance) in time of dearth. تَقَلَّحَ ه
Yellowness of the teeth. قَلَح وقُلَاح
Dirty garment. قَلِح
Having yellow teeth. قَلِح م قَلِحَة, وأَقْلَح م قَلْحَاء ج قُلْح
Black-beetle. Cantharis. أَقْلَح
To uproot (a tree). ✱ قَلَخَ a قَلْخًا ه
To low (camel). قَلَخَ a قَلْخًا وقَلِيخًا
To lash a. o. with (a whip). قَلَخَ ه ب
Wild ass. قَلَّاخ
To wind a. th. upon. To put a necklace upon. ✱ قَلَدَ i قَلْدًا ه على
To twist (a rope). To water (corn-produce). To twist (a wire). — ه
To seize a. o. every day (fever). — ه
To collect (milk) in. — ه في
To gird a. o. with a sword. — وقَلَّدَ ه السَّيْف
To put (a rope) on the neck of (a beast). To follow the opinion of. ✧ To mimic a. o. To counterfeit a. th. قَلَّدَ ه وه
He follows nobody's advice. لَمْ يُقَلِّد أَحَدًا
To put (a necklace) upon (a woman). To invest a. o. with (an office, a dignity). — ه ه
To swallow up a. o. (sea). أَقْلَدَ على
To put on (a necklace). تَقَلَّدَ ه
To take (an affair) upon o.'s self. — الأَمْر
To gird on a sword. — السَّيْف
To come to water by turn. تَقَالَدَ المَاء
To draw (water). إِقْتَلَدَ المَاء
To overcome a. o. (sleep). إِقْلَوَّدَ ه
Filigreed (bracelet). قَلْد
Day in which fever returns. Quartan ague. Portion of water. Party. Cup. قِلْد
The sky has given us rain every week. سَقَتْنَا السَّمَاء قِلْدًا في كُلّ أُسْبُوعٍ
He has intrusted me with his affair. أَعْطَانِي قَلْدَ أَمْرِهِ
Copper-thread rolled around a ring. قِلَاد وإِقْلِيد
Necklace. Collar. *Name* قِلَادَة ج قَلَائِد

of 7 stars *called also* قَوْس.

Celebrated verses. قَلَائِد ومُقَلَّدَات الشِّعْر

String. Twisted (rope). قَلِيد ومَقْلُود

Magazine, cellar. قِلِيد, ومِقْلَاد ج مَقَالِيد, ومِقْلَدَة

Imitation. Appointment. Diploma. ✧ Counterfeiting. Mimicry. تَقْلِيد ج تَقَالِيد وتَقْلِيدَات

✧ Oral tradition. التَّقْلِيدَات

Neck. إِقْلِيد ج أَقْلَاد

Key. G إِقْلِيد ج أَقَالِيد, ومِقْلَد ج مَقَالِد, ومِقْلَاد ج مَقَالِيد

Fodder-bag. Purse. Crooked staff. مِقْلَد ج مَقَالِد

He is in strait circumstances. ضَاقَتْ مَقَالِدُهُ او مَقَالِيدُهُ

He entrusted him with the management of the affairs. أَلْقَى إِلَيْهِ مَقَالِيد الأُمُور

Wearing a necklace. Invested with a dignity. مُقَلَّد

To jump. To limp. To suck in. ✱ قَلَز o i قَلْزًا

To shoot (arrows). — ب

To give to a. o. a cup of. — ة ه

To lay eggs in the ground (locust). — وقَلَّز وأَقْلَز

To be swift. To run. تَقَلَّز

To empty (a cup). اِقْتَلَز ه

Light-footed, lively, nimble. قُلُز

Brass, bronze. قُلْز وقِلِزّ

Pilot. Screw-nail. Te قَلَاوُوز

To swallow a. th. ✱ قَلْزَم وتَقَلْزَم ه

Town in Arabia. قُلْزُم

The Red Sea. بَحْر القُلْزُم

To have a heaving of the stomach. To dance in singing. To sing sweetly. To drink much wine. ✱ قَلَس i قَلْسًا وقَلَسَانًا

To overflow (vessel). — ب

To overrun (sea). — بِالمَاء

To welcome a. o. To beat the kettle-drum. قَلَّس

To humble o.'s self before. — لِفُلَان

To put on a cap. تَقَلَّس

Cable. Undigested food, phlegm rejected by the mouth. قَلْس ج قُلُوس

Cloud. قَلْس البَحْر

Raging (sea). Cap-seller. قَلَّاس

To put a cap on a. o. ✱ قَلْسَى وقَلْنَس ة

To put on a cap. تَقَلْسَى وتَقَلْنَس

Rounded cap worn by Greek priests. قَلَنْسُوَة و✧ قَلُوسَة

Eel. P أَنْقَلِيس وإِنْقِلِيس وأَنْكَلِيس

To take off the crust of (a wound). ✱ قَلَش o قَلْشًا ه

Short and stout, small and bulky. قَلَّاش

Smallness of body. قَلَاشَة

Artful, cunning. P قَلَّاش وأَقْلَش

Stock, stocking. ✧ قَلْشِين ج قَلَاشِين

To rise in a well (water). To contract (shade); to shrink after washing (cloth). To be contracted (lip). ✱ قَلَص i قُلُوصًا

To depart (party). — عن الدَّار

To heave (stomach). To feel qualmish. — وقَلِص a قَلَصًا

To be tucked up (clothes). قُلِّص

To tuck up (a garment). قَلَّص ه

To be contracted, wrinkled. تَقَلَّص

Water rising in a well. قَلْصَة ج قَلَصَات

Young (she-camel). Young female ostrich. قَلُوص وقَلَائِص وقُلُص وقِلَاص

Rising (water). قَلَّاص وقَلِيص

Cloud bringing snow. قَلَّاص الثَّلْج

✧ To empty, to cleanse (a tank). To scrape (the mud). ✱ قَلَط o قَلْطًا ه

✧ To buy a. th. unconditionally. بَاع ه قَلْطًا

Wicked, insolent man. قَلَطِيّ

Dwarf; puny child, dog or cat. — وقُلَاط

Scrotal hernia. قِيلِيط

✧ Heap of dung. قُلَيْط

To pluck, to snatch off a. th. ✧ To dismiss (a servant). To drive a. o. away. ✱ قَلَع a قَلْعًا, وقَلَّع واقْتَلَع واسْتَقْلَع ه وة

To root out (a tree). To extract (stones). قَلَّع ه

To dismiss, to discharge a. o. — ة

To take off (o.'s clothes). — ه

To be removed from office. قُلِع

To be unsteady on horseback. To totter (wrestler). قَلِع a قَلَعًا وقَلَعَة

To build a fortress. أَقْلَع

To sail a ship. — ه

To leave off (a place, an affair). To leave a. o. (fever). أَقْلَع عن

To be snatched, uprooted. To be removed from office. To fall off. تَقَلَّع وانْقَلَع واقْتَلَع

To snatch a. th. away. اِقْتَلَع ه
Architect's axe. Mine of lead. قَلْع
Shepherd's bag. — ج قُلُوع وأَقْلُع
Intermittence of fever. قَلْع و قِلْع
Remittance of fever. Crust of scab. قَلَع
Sail of a ship. قِلْع ج قُلُوع و قِلَاع
Fortress. Shepherd's bag. Off-shoot pulled off from a palm-trunk. قَلْعَة ج قِلَاع وقِلَع وقُلُوع
Piece split lengthwise. قِلْعَة ج قِلَع
Unsteadiness. Temporary goods. قُلْعَة
He is on a journey. هُوَ عَلَى قُلْعَةٍ
Temporary stay. مَـنْزِل قُلْعَةٍ
Sitting-place in which one must incessantly rise. مَجْلِس قُلْعَةٍ
Rock, heap of rocks. قَلَعَة ج قَلَع و قِلَاع
Large cloud. Large she-camel. — ج قَلَع
White lead. قَلْعِيّ
Cracked clay. Pustules on the lips. قُلَاع
Sail of a ship. قِلَاعَة
Isolated rock in a plain. Uprooted stone. قُلَاعَة
Intermittence of fever. إِقْلَاع ومُقْلَع
Blaze on the back of a horse. دَائِرَة القَالِع
Stone-quarry. مَقْلَع ج مَقَالِع
✧ Sling. مِقْلَاع ج مَقَالِيع
✲ Crispness of the hair. قَلْعَطَة
To be crisp (hair). اِقْلَعَطَّ
✧ To stain a. th. To disgrace a. o. ✧ قَلْعَط ٥ وه
To be defiled. To be affected with elephantiasis. ✧ تَقَلْعَط
Dirt, filth. Elephantiasis. ✧ قِلْعَاط
To bark (a tree). To turn a. th. upside down. ✲ قَلَف i قَلْفًا ه
To pull out (a nail). — واقتلف ه
To circumcise (a boy). قَلَف o قَلْفًا قَلْفَـةً ٥
To open (a vessel). قَلَف i قَلْفًا وقَلْفَةً ه
To calk (a ship). — وقَلَّف ه
To be uncircumcised. قَلِف a قَلَفًا
To take (dates) without measuring. اِقْـتَلَف ه
Tree-bark. Rind of pomegranate. قِلْف (un. قِلْفَة)
Finger-nail pulled out. قِلْفَة

Foreman, architect. Female housekeeper in a harem. ◻ قَلْفَة
Prepuce. قَلْفَة وقُلْفَة ج قُلَف
Bark. قُلَافَة
Art of calking ships. قِلَافَة
Uncircumcised. Soft (life). Plentiful (year). أَقْلَف م قَلْفَاء ج قُلْف
Having an uncircumcised heart. — القَلْب
Uncircumcised hearts. قُلُوب قُلْف وقُلُف
Date-basket. قَلِيف ج قُلُف, وقَلِيفَة ج قَلِيف
Opened (vessel). قَلِيف ومَقْلُوف
To calk (a ship). ✓ Ts قَلْفَط (for جَلْفَط) ه
To be restless, disquieted, flurried. ✲ قَلِق a قَلَقًا
To disturb, to disquiet a. o. أَقْلَق و✧ قَلَّق ٥
Anxiety, restlessness. ✧ Sleeplessness. قَلَق
قَلِق م قَلِقَة. ومِقْـلَاق (m. f.) و✧ مُقَلَّق
Anxious. Loose.
Restless, flurried, sleepless. — و✧ قَلْقَان
Vitriol. ✲ قَلْقَدِيس
Potato, colocasia. G قُلْقَاس
Potato ✧ قُلْقَـاس إِفْرَنْجِي
To prick the tongue with colocasia. ✧ قَلْقَس
To cut a. th. To pare (the nails). ✲ قَلَم i قَلْمًا, وقَلَّم ه
Reed, pen. Hand-writing. Style. Divinatory arrow. ✧ Streak in cloth. Order of numerals. Office in the government. ◻ Slap. قَلَم ج أَقْلَام وقِلَام
Bachelor. قَالِم ج قَلَمَة
Parings of nails. A trifle. قُلَامَة
Province. District, climate. One of the 7 climates of the Ancients. G إِقْلِيم ج أَقَالِيم
Stuff shot of different colours. *Hence*: Fickle, changing (man). ✧ Chameleon. أَبُو قَلَمُون
Pen. مِقْلَمَة ج مَقَالِم
Knots on the wood of a spear. مَقَالِم الرُّمْح
Cut, pared. ✧ Striped (cloth). مُقَلَّم
Without husband (woman). مُقَلَّمَة
Troop of 1000 warriors. أَلْف مُقَلَّمَة

مَقَاوِم ومُقَامِ الظِّفر Weak, vile.
ه أَبُو قَلَمْبُو Crab-fish.
* قلمس — قَلَمَّس Having much water (well). Generous (man). Clever (man).
G قُولَنج Colic.
P قَلَنْدَار Dervish, calender.
ه قِيلُون Lock of a door.
* قَلْنَس ة To put a cap on a. o.
تَقَلْنَس To put on a cap.
قَلَنْسُوَة وقُلَنْسِيَة ج قَلَانِس وقَلَاسٍ وقَلَانِيس, و✧ قَلُوسَة ج قَلَالِيس وقَلُوسَات Cap, hat.
قُلَيْنِسَة وقُلَيْسِيَة Small cap.
* قَلَا o قَلْوًا, وقَلَى i قَلْيًا ه To fry (meat) in a pan.
قَلَا o قِلًا وقَلَاء, وقَلَى i وقَلِي a قِلًى وقَلَاء ومَقْلِيَة ة To hate, to dislike a. o.
تَقَلَّى إلى To feel hatred for.
— على فِرَاشِهِ To be restless in bed.
تَقَالَى To have a mutual hatred.
اِقْلَوْلَى To be restless. To depart. To rise in the air (bird).
قِلْو Light. Lively young ass.
قِلْوَة Swift beast.
قُلَة ج قُلَات وقُلُون, ومِقْلَى ومِقْلَاء Pieces of wood with which children play.
قِلْى وقِلَى Potash.
قُلَّى Summits of mountains. Tops of men's heads.
قَلَّاء Manufacturer of frying-pans.
قَلِيَّة ج قَلَايَا A frying, a fritter.
قَلِيَّة ج قَلَالِي Monk's cell. Closet.
مِقْلَى ومِقْلَاة ج مَقَالٍ Frying-pan.
مَقْلَاة Manufactory of frying-pans.
مَقْلِيّ ومَقْلِيّ Fried.
* قَمَّ o قَمًّا, واقْتَمَّ ه To devour (dishes).
قَمَّ ه To sweep (a house).
تَقَمَّم ه To rummage amongst (sweepings). To be on the summit of.
قِمَّة ج قِمَم Top of the head. Summit. Body.
هُوَ حَسَن القِمَّة He has a fine stature.
قُمَّة Mouthful of a lion.
قُمَامَة ج قُمَام Sweepings. Troop of men.
مِقَمّ ومُقْتَمّ Voracious.
مِقَمَّة ج مَقَامّ Broom.
مِقَمَّة Lip of cloven-hoofed animal
* قَمْقَم ه To pick up (remains).

تَقَمْقَم To be submerged, drowned.
✧ To grumble, to murmur.
P قُمْقُم وقُمْقُمَة وقَمَاقِم Copper-boiler. Scent-flask. Sprinkler.
قَمْقَام وقُمْقَام Important business. Great number. Tick, ring-worm; vermin.
— وقُمْقَام وقَمَاقِم Extensive sea. Generous lord.
* قَمَا a وقَمُو o قَمَاءَة وقُمَاءَة وقَمَاءَة To be vile, contemptible.
قَمَا a قَمْأً, وقَامَأ وأَقْمَأ وتَقَمَّأ ة To suit a. o. (place). To stay in (a place).
— a وقَمُؤ o قُمُوءًا وقُمُوءَة وقَمْأً وقَمَاء وقَمَاءَة, وأَقْمَأ To become fat (cattle).
أَقْمَأ ة To render a. o. contemptible. To please a. o.
تَقَمَّأ ه To collect a. th. little by little. To take the best of.
قَمِيء ج قِمَاء Small, abject, paltry.
قَمْأَة ومَقْمَأَة ومَقْمُؤَة Shaded place.
قَمْأَة وقُمَاءَة Abundance of herbage. Easiness of life.
* قَمَح o قُمُوحًا, وقَامَح وتَقَمَّح واقْمَحّ To refuse to drink (camel).
قَمِح a قَمْحًا, واقْتَمَح ه To take into the mouth (parched food). To swallow a dry (medicine). To drink (milk, wine).
قَمَّح ة To send a. o. away with a paltry gift.
أَقْمَح To become feculent (ear of corn). To ear (corn). To raise the head in lowering the eyes.
— واقْتَمَح To become mature (wheat).
أَقْمَح بِأَنْفِهِ To become proud. To raise the head.
قَمْح Wheat.
قَمْحَة A grain (weight). A grain of wheat.
قُمْحَة Mouthful of dry food.
— وقُمْحَان وقُمَّحَان Scum upon the surface of old wine. Turmeric (Indian aromatic). Saffron.
شَهْرَا قِمَاحٍ The months of December and January.
قَامِح ج قُمَّح وقِمَاح Abstaining from drinking (camel).
* قَمَد i قُمُودًا To refrain, to abstain.

To become valuable (worthless thing). أقمز ه
Worthless thing. قمز
A bound, a leap. ✧ قَمْزَة
Handful of dates. قُمْزَة ج قُمَز
To plunge a. o. into (water). ☆ قَمَس o i قَمْسًا، وأقمس ه في
To dive into (water). قَمَس وانقمس في
To vie with a. o. in plunging. قَامَس مُقَامَسَة وقِمَاسًا ه
He vies in plunging with a fish *i. e.* he contends with one stronger than he. يُقَامِس حُوتًا
To plunge together. تَقَامَس
To set (star). إِنْقَمَس
Plunger, diver. قَامِس وقَمَّاس
The Ocean, sea. ✧ Dictionary. قَامُوس ج قَوَامِيس
Distinguished chief. L قُمُس ج قَمَامِس وقَمَامِسَة
Chief. Abyss of the sea. *Pl.* Misfortunes. قَوْمَس ج قَوَامِس
To pick up (refuse). ☆ قَمَش o i قَمْشًا، وقَمَّش ه
To eat refuse. ▫ To put on fine garments. تَقَمَّش
Refuse. ✧ Cotton, linen-cloth. قُمَاش ج أَقْمِشَة
Furniture of a house. — البَيْت
The dregs of the people. — النَّاس
✧ Leathern whip. Ts قَمْشَة
Cloth-merchant. قَمَّاش
To bound, to take fright (ass). ☆ قَمَص o i قِمَاصًا
To gallop (horse). — قَمْصًا و قُمَاصًا
To roll (a ship : sea). وقَمَّص ب
To clothe a. o. with a shirt. قَمَّص ه
To put on a shirt. تَقَمَّص
Insects upon water. Newly hatched locusts. قَمَص
The ass has become strengthless. مَا بِالعَيْر مِن قِمَاص
Anxiety, restlessness. قِمَاص و قِمِصَّى
Long shirt, gown. ✧ Alb. قَمِيص ج قُمُص وأَقْمِصَة وقُمْصَان
Pericardium. قَمِيص القَلْب
Restless (beast). — وقَمُوص
Coptic priest. C قُمُّص
Metempsychosis. تَقَمُّص وتَقْمِيص

To be long-necked. قَمِد a قَمَدًا
Strong, stout. قُمُدّ م قُمُدَّة
Long-necked. أَقْمَد م قَمْدَاء
To gamble. ☆ قَمَر i قَمْرًا
To win a. o. in a game. ✧ To overcome a. o. in a dispute. — o i وتَقَمَّر ه
To lose at play. قُمِر
To be white. To be burst (skin). To be dazzled by snow. To wake in the moonlight. قَمِر a قَمَرًا
✧ To toast (bread). قَمَّر ه
To gamble. To play a game of hazard with. ✧ To quarrel with. قَامَر مُقَامَرَة وقِمَارًا ه
To journey by moonshine (traveller). To wait for the rising of the moon. To be moonlit (night). أَقْمَر
To come forth by moon-light (lion). تَقَمَّر
To hunt or visit a. o. by moonlight. To pursue (birds) with a light. — ه
To gamble together. ✧ To quarrel. تَقَامَر
To be white, moonlit. إِقْمَارّ
Moon. قَمَر ج أَقْمَار
Selenite. حَجَر القَمَر
✧ Apricot-paste. قَمَر الدِّين
The sun and the moon. القَمَرَان
Greenish white colour. قُمْرَة
Moonlit (night). قَمِرَة
Lunar. ✧ Small silver coin. قَمَرِيّ
Lunar letters. حُرُوف قَمَرِيَّة
Ring-dove. Canary (bird). قُمْرِيّ ج قَمَارِيّ
Loop-hole. Garret-window. ✧ قَمَرِيَّة
Turtle-dove. Female pigeon. قُمْرِيَّة ج قَمَارِيّ وقُمْر
Game of hazard. Gambling. قِمَار
Partner or antagonist in a game. قَمِير ج أَقْمَار، ومُقَامِر
Moon-coloured. Bright. Dull white. أَقْمَر م قَمْرَاء ج قُمْر
Moonlit (night). — ومُقْمِر ومُقْمِرَة
Moonshine. Little bird. قَمْرَاء
To eat almonds. ☆ قَمْرَص
To pick a. th. with the fingers. ☆ قَمَز o i قَمْزًا ه
✧ To jump. قَمَّز } (*for* قَمَّص
✧ To make a. o. to jump. قَمَّز ه

Hooked staff. Iron column. مِقْمَعَة ج مَقَامِع
Subdued. Sorted (flock). Suffering from indigestion. مَقْمُوع
To sprout (plant). To be the chief of a tribe. ✲ قَمْعَل
Big-bellied pot, cup. قُمْعُل
Chief of a tribe; head-shepherd. قِمْعَال
Large cup. قُمْعُول ج قَمَاعِيل
Sprout, bud. Knobbiness. قُمْعُولَة ج قَمَاعِيل
To swarm with lice (head). ✲ قَمِل a قَمَلًا, وقَمَّل
To be black-spotted (plant). To multiply (people). قَمِل
To become lusty. — وتَقَمَّل
To bud out. أَقْمَل
Lice. قَمْل (un. قَمْلَة)
Covered with vermin. قَمِل ومُقَمَّل
Tick. Ring-worm. Small ants. Red-winged insect. قُمَّل
To purpose a. th. ✲ قمن — تَقَمَّن ﻫ
Manner, wise. قَمَن
Fit, able to. قَمَن (m. f. s. pl.) وقَمِن م قَمِنَة ل
Abler. أَقْمَن ب
Convenient to. مَقْمَن ومَقْمَنَة ل
Fit to. Bath-stove. ✧ Oven. قَمِين ج قُمَنَاء
To go at random. ✲ قمه — تَقَمَّه
Camel going at random. قَامِه ج قُمَّه
To observe a. th. To scrutinise (news). ✲ قَنَّ o قَنًّا ﻫ
To remain quiet. To acquire a slave. إِقْتَنَّ
To stand upright. — واقْتَنَأَنَّ
To undertake a. th. personally. إِسْتَقَنَّ ب
Hillock. Sleeve of a shirt. ✧ Hen-coop. قُنّ
Slave. قِنّ (m. f. s. pl.) ج أَقْنَان وأَقِنَّة
Hillock. Top of a mountain. قُنَّة ج قُنَن وقِنَان وقُنَّات
Strand of a rope. ✧ Galbanum (resinous plant). قِنَّة ج قِنَن
Way, mood. قَنَن
Glass-bottle, flask. قِنِّينَة ج قَنَانِيّ وقِنَان
Rule, law. Custom. G قَانُون ج قَوَانِين

✲ قَمَط o i قَمْطًا, وقَمَّط ﻫ To swaddle (a child). To shackle, to pinion a. o. To put (camels) in a file.
— ﻫ ✧ To bind (a wound); to put a (head-band).
قِمَاط ج قُمُط Swaddling-clothes.
— وقِمْط Ropes, bonds, shackles.
وَقَعْتُ عَلَى قِمَاطِهِ I have found out his stratagems.
✧ قَمْطَة Head-band. Small turban.
حَوْل قَمِيط Full year.
✲ قَمْطَر ﻫ To fasten (a skin).
إِقْمَطَرَّ To become distressful (day).
قِمَطْر ج قَمَاطِر Book-case. Fetters, bonds. Strong camel. Short man.
قُمَاطِر وقَمْطَرِير Unauspicious (day).
✲ قَمَع a قَمْعًا, وأَقْمَع ﻫ To subdue a. o.
قَمَع ﻫ To strike a. o. on the head.
— وأَقْمَع ﻫ عن To prevent a. o. from.
قَمَع ﻫ To empty (a skin). To blast (the plants: cold).
— في To penetrate into.
— وأَقْمَع To be easily swallowed (beverage).
قَمِع a قَمَعًا To be weak-sighted. To have a sore eye, a pain in the knee.
قَمَّع ﻫ To apply a funnel into. To pluck (a date-stalk).
تَقَمَّع To shake the head (ass). To be bewildered. To remain apart.
— واقْتَمَع ﻫ To select the best of.
إِنْقَمَع To be subdued, overpowered. To glide stealthily into a house.
إِقْتَمَع ﻫ To empty (a skin).
قِمَع وقَمْع وقِمْع ج أَقْمَاع Funnel.
قِمَع وقِمْع ج قُمُوع Stalk of a fruit, of a flower.
— الخَيَّاط Thimble.
قَمَع Red tumour on the eyelid. Swelling of a horse's knee. Weakness of the sight.
قَمِع, وأَقْمَع م قَمْعَاء ج قُمْع Weak-sighted. Swollen in the knee.
قَمَعَة وقُمْعَة وقِمَعَة ج قِمَع The choice part.
قَمَعَة ج قَمَع Top of a camel's hump.
— ج مَقَامِع Large fly.
✧ قَامُوع ج قَوَامِيع Cone-shaped column.
قَامِعَة ج قَوَامِع Subduing the passions (God's grace).

Children's garment. قُنْبُعَة
Grunt of pigs. قَنِيبِعَة
Party of horse-men. ✫ قَنْبَل وقَنْبَلَة ج قَنَابِل
To stand long in prayer. To prolong warring. To be obedient to God. ✫ قَنَت o قُنُوت, وأَقْنَت
To humble o.'s self to (God). — ه ول
To eat little. قَنَت o قَنَاتَة
Obedient to God. Assiduous to prayer. قَانِت م قَانِتَة
Invocation. Steadfastness in religion. قُنُوت
Abstemious (woman). قَنِيت
Retaining water (skin). قَنِيت
◘ Small boat on the Nile. gondol. T قُنْجَة ج قِنَاج
To bend (wood). ✫ قَنَح a قَنْحًا ه
To lift (a door) with a piece of wood. — وأَقْنَح ه
To have thirst satisfied. — وتَقَنَّح
To put a wooden peg to (a door). قَنَّح ه
Wooden peg, lever for opening a door. قُنَّاحَة
Sugar-candy. Honey of the sugar-cane. P قَنْد ج قُنُود
Sweetened with sugar-candy. مُقَنَّد ومَقْنُود
Sugar-candy. Perfumed must of wine. Ambergris. Camphor. Musk. Condition of a man. L قَنْد — قِنْدِيد ج قَنَادِيد
Sexton. G قَنْدَلَفْت
To amend. ✫ قَنْدَس
To go through (a country). — في
Castor, beaver. قُنْدُس
Stock of a gun. Butt's end. Ts قُنْدَق ج قَنَادِق
Ritual, mass-book of the Greeks. G قِنْدَاق
Big-humped. ✫ قَنْدَل وقَنَادِل وقَنْدَوِيل
Aspalathus, thorny shrub the flowers of which yield an excellent oil. *Calycotome spinosa*, prickled broom. قُنْدُول
Lamp, branched candlestick. قِنْدِيل ج قَنَادِيل
Shop. Butcher's hook. ✫ قَنَر — قِنَار وقِنَارَة ج قَنَايِر

Psaltery, harp. ✧ Penance. ◘ *Pl.* Taxes, duties.
Canonical. Regular. قَانُونِي
To impose a penance upon. ✧ قَوْنَن ه
To receive a penance. ✧ تَقَوْنَن
Large rat. Mole. Sea-shell. ✫ قِنْقِن
Guide skilled for finding water. — قُنَاقِن
To be intensely red. ✫ قَنَا a قُنُوءًا
To be dyed red (beard).
To mix (milk) with water. — قَنَأ ه
To dye a. th. red. — وقَنَّأ تَقْنِئَة وتَقْنِيئًا ه
To dye (the beard) black.
To kill a. o. To incite a. o. to kill. قَنَأ a قَنْأ, وأَقْنَأ ه
To die. To be spoiled (hide). قَنِئَ a قُنُوءًا
The thing has become possible to me. أَقْنَأَنِي الشَّيْءُ
Dark red. أَحْمَر قَانِئ
Shaded place. مَقْنَأَة ومَقْنُؤَة
To set (sun). ✫ قَنَب o قُنُوبًا
To trim (a vine). قَنَب ه
To enter into. — وتَقَنَّب في
To open (blossom). — o قَنْبًا
To send forth leaves (corn-crops). قَنَّب
To form a squadron (horsemen). — وأَقْنَب وتَقَنَّب
To glide away (debtor). أَقْنَب
Calyx of a flower. قُنْب ج قُنُوب
Sail of a ship. Sheath. قُنْب
Lion's claw. String of a bow. — وقِنَاب
Ears of corn. قُنَاب وقُنَابَة
Cannabis Indica, hemp. Flax. قُنَّب وقِنَّب وكَنَّب
Troop of men. Dense clouds. قَنِيب
Troop of horsemen. مِقْنَب ج مَقَانِب
Lion's claw. Hunter's bag. — ومِقْنَاب
Lark. ✫ قُنْبُر وقُنْبُرَاء (قُنْبُرَة وقُنْبَرَة .un) ج قَنَابِر
Bomb, shell. P قُنْبُرَة ج قَنَابِر, وقُنْبُل ج قَنَابِل
Tuft of feathers. قُنْبُرَة
✧ Hunchback. ◘ أَبُو قُنْبُور
Crested hen. دَجَاجَة قُنْبُرَانِيَّة
To swell. ✧ تَقَنْبَر
Man's full gown. ✫ قُنْبَاز ج قَنَابِيز
Cauliflower. ✫ قُنَّبِيط و✧ قَرْنَبِيط
Envelope of a grain. ✫ قَنْبَع — قُنْبُع

✣ قِنَّار Small onions.
✣ قَنَّرٌ و إِقْنِيز Goblet.
أَقْنَرَ To drink in a goblet.
✣ قُنْزُعَة وقَنْزَعَة وقِنْزِعَة ج قَنَازِع وقُنْزُعَات Hair around the head. Lock of hair. Tuft. Pebbles.
✣ قنس – قِنْس ج قُنُوس, وقَوْنَس ج قَوَانِس Summit of the head.
P قَنَس *Enula*, elecampane (*plant*).
قَوْنَس وقَوْنُوس ج قَوَانِيس Tapering top of a helmet.
✣ قَنْسَر ه To make a. o. grow old (trials).
تَقَنْسَر To be broken by age.
قَنْسَر وقِنَّسْرِيّ Broken by age.
✣ قَنَص i قَنْصًا وتَقَنَّص واقْتَنَص ه To hunt, to catch (the game).
قَنْص واقْتِنَاص Hunting, chase.
قَنَص, وقَنِيص ومَقْنُوص Game, prey.
قَانِص وقَنَّاص وقَنِيص Hunter.
قَانِصَة ج قَوَانِص Gizzard. Pole upholding a roof.
L قُنْصُل ج قَنَاصِل ✧ Consul.
✧ قُنْصُلِيَّة وقُنْصُلَاتُو Consulate.
✣ قَنِط a قَنَطًا, وقَنَط o i قُنُوطًا, وقَنُط o قَنَاطَة To despair.
قَنَّط وأَقْنَط ه To drive a. o. to despair.
قَنَط وقُنُوط Despair.
قَنِط وقَانِط وقَنُوط م قَنِطَة الخ Despairing.
✣ قَنْطَر To give up nomadic life. To possess hundredweights of money. ✧ To break down (horse). To canter (horse). To be thrown off (rider).
– ه To arch, to vault a. th.
تَقَنْطَر ✧ To gallop, to prance. To break down (horse).
قِنْطِر Wood-pigeon.. Misfortune.
قَنْطَرَة ج قَنَاطِر Vaulted bridge. Large building. ✧ Center, bow, vaulted passage.
قِنْطَار ج قَنَاطِير Standard of weight; weight of 100 rothls.
G قِنْطَارِيُون Centaury (plant).
مُقَنْطَر Completed, aggregated.
مُقَنْطَرَة Parallel of latitude. Sun-dial.
✣ قَنِع a قَنَعًا وقَنَاعَةً وقُنْعَانًا ب To content with. ✧ To be convinced of.

قَنَع a قُنُوعًا To beg, to beseech earnestly.
– ب To be contented with.
– قُنُوعًا To go to water, to the stable (flock).
– وأَقْنَع واسْتَقْنَع To have a full udder (ewe).
قَنَّع وأَقْنَع ه To satisfy a. o. ✧ To convince a. o.
قَنَّع ه To put a veil to (a woman).
– ه ب To lash (the head) with (a whip).
أَقْنَع ه To incline (a vessel). To raise (the head).
– ه To pasture (cattle).
– بِيَدَيْهِ في الصَّلَاة وفي القُنُوت To raise the hands in prayer.
تَقَنَّع To show content. To veil herself (woman). To wrap o.'s self in a garment.
اِقْتَنَع ب To be contented with.
قَنَع وقَنَاعَة Satisfaction, content. Abstemiousness.
قِنْع ج أَقْنَاع, وقِنَاع ج قُنُع Weapons.
قِنْعَة ج قِنَع وجج قِنْعَان Upland.
قُنْعَة وقُنُوع Mendicity.
قَنَعَة Top of a mountain.
قُنُوع Lowliness of a beseecher. Content.
قِنَاع Woman's head-veil. Pericardium.
قِنَاع ج أَقْنَاع وأَقْنِعَة Tray made of palm-sprays.
قَنِع ج قَنِعُون Contented. Abstemious, temperate.
قَنُوع ج قُنُع, وقَنِيع ج قُنَعَاء, وقَانِع ج قُنَّع
Beseecher. Abstemious, sober.
قُنْعَان, ومَقْنَع ج مَقَانِع Sufficient.
شَاهِدٌ قُنْعَان او مَقْنَع Witness whose testimony is sufficient.
مِقْنَع ومِقْنَعَة Woman's veil.
مُقَنَّع Wearing an iron-helmet.
✣ قَنِف a قَنَفًا To be covered with dry slime (ground).
قَنِف و✧ تَقَنَّف مِن To loathe a. o. or a. th.
قَنَّف ه ب To slash a. th. with (a sword).
أَقْنَف To have dependent ears. To have a large army.
– واسْتَقْنَف To maintain order in his dominions: (king).

To acquire a. th. ✫ قَنَى i قَنْيًا و قُنْيَانًا ه
To mix a. th. قَانَى ه
To suit a. o. — ه
To satisfy, to please a. o. أَقْنَى ه
To bring (game) within the reach of. — ه ه ول ل
Property. قُنْيَة وقِـنْيَة ج قِنًى
To burst out laughing. ✫ قَهْقَه
Peal, burst of laughter. قَهْقَهَة
To be grayish. ✫ قَهِب a قَهَبًا
Grayish colour, dusky white. قُهْبَة
Grayish. قَهْب م قَهِبَة, وأَقْهَب م قَهْبَاء
Dust-coloured partridge. قُهَيْبَة
The elephant and the buffalo. الأَقْهَبَان
To walk with short steps. ✫ قَهَد a قَهْدًا في مِشْيَتِهِ
White, Kind of sheep. Unopened narcissus. قَهْد ج قِهَاد
To subdue, to get mastery over. To oppress a. o. ✫ قَهَر a قَهْرًا ه وه
To constrain, to compel a. o. to. — ه على
To become soft by cooking (meat). قُهِر
To treat a. o. harshly. To thwart a. o. قَاهَر ه
To have o.'s people subdued. أَقْهَر
To find a. o. overpowered, subdued. أَقْهَر ه
Constraint. Ill-treatment. ✧ Despite. قَهْر
Force, violence. قُهْرَة
Forcibly. قَهْرًا وقُهْرَةً
He is humbled by all men. هُوَ قُهْرَةٌ لِلنَّاس
Wicked (woman). قُهْرَة
Constraining. Victorious. Mars (planet). قَاهِر م قَاهِرَة
Lofty mountains. جِبَال قَوَاهِر
Cairo in Egypt. القَاهِرَة ومِصْر القَاهِرَة
The Subduer (God). القَهَّار
Management. P قَهْرَمَة
Steward. Surveyor. P قَهْرَمَان م قَهْرَمَانَة ج قَهَارِمَة
Cloth of wool and silk. ✫ قُهْز وقِهْزِيّ
To walk backwards, to retrograde. ✫ قَهْقَر
✧ To revile a. o. To render life painful to. — ه
To go backwards. To be despi- تَقَهْقَر

Smallness and flatness of ears. قَنَف
Slime of a dried river. قِنْف
Big-nosed. قُنَاف وقِنَاف
Party of men. Abstemious. قَنِيف ج قُنُف
Rain-cloud.
Thick and flat-eared. أَقْنَف م قَنْفَاء ج قُنْف
✫ قُنْفُذ ج قَنَافِذ, وقُنْفَذ وقُنْفُد ج قَنَافِذ
Hedgehog. Rat. Sandy mound.
Beaver. Otter. Sea-urchin. قُنْفُذ بَحْرِيّ
Slanderer. — لَيْل
To be wrinkled, shrivelled. ✫ قَنْفَش
To be untidy. — في اللِّبَاس
Unkempt, untidy; scorched on the nose. قُنَافِش
Untidy, squalid. مُقَنْفِش في اللِّبَاس
To halt in a place. ✧ قَنَق
Stage, halt. Residence of an official; quarters. Ts قُنَاق ج قُنَاقَات
To be rancid (nut). To stink (greasy hands). To be dusty. ✫ قَنِم a قَنَمًا
Odour of rancid oil. قَنَمَة
Smelling rancid oil (hand). قَنِمَة
Person, hypostasis. G أُقْنُوم ج أَقَانِيم
✫ قَنَا o قَنْوًا وقُنْوَانًا وقُنُوًّا وقِنْوَة, واقْتَنَى ه
To acquire, to appropriate a. th.
To create a. th. (God). — قَنْوًا ه
To preserve modesty. — i وقَنِيَ a قَنْوًا, وقَنَّى وأَقْنَى ه واقْتَنَى ه
To be hooked (nose). قَنِيَ a قَنًا
To be kept indoor (girl). قُنِيَت قِنْيَةً
To dig (a channel). قَنَّى ه
To render a. o. wealthy (God). أَقْنَى ه
To spare (money). تَقَنَّى
Bunch of dates. قَنَا وقِنًى وقِنْو ج أَقْنَاء وقُنْيَان وقِنْوَان
Sheep possessed. قُنْوَة وقِنْوَة
Property. Earnings. — وقُنْوَة ج قُنًى
Reward. قِنَاوَة
Conduit for water, canal. Pipe. قَنَاة ج قُنِيّ وقِنَاء وقَنَوَات
Spear. Spout of a mug. قَنَاة ج قُنًى وقَنَوَات وقُنِيّ وقَنَيَات
Spine of the back. — الظَّهْر
Owner, acquirer. قَانٍ م قَانِيَة
Intensely red. أَحْمَر قَانٍ
Armed with a spear. قَنَّاء ومُقْنٍ
Hook-nosed. أَقْنَى م قَنْوَاء
Shady place. مَقْنَاة ومَقْنُوَة

sed, reviled. ◊ To lead a painful life.

Conical heap of stones. قَهْقُور

Retrogradation. ◊ Wretched life. قَهْقَرَى وقَهْقَرَة

To return backwards, to retrograde. رَجَع القَهْقَرَى

✱ قَهَل a قَهْلًا وقُهُولًا ,وقَهِل a قَهَلًا ,وتَقَهَّل

To be dry (hide).

To be ungrateful towards. قَهَل ة

To be slovenly, unclean (man). قَهِل a قَهَلًا ,وتَقَهَّل

To defile o.'s self. To meddle into another's concern. أَقْهَل

To be feeble, broken. إِنْقَهَل

Face, countenance. قَيْهَل وقَيْهَلَة

To have little appetite. ✱ قَهِم a قَهَمًا

To become serene (sky). أَقْهَم

To connive at. – في

To loathe or to desire (food). – عن او إلى

To drink much wine. ✱ قهو – أَقْهَى

Wine. ◊ Coffee (beverage). قَهْوَة

Coffee-house. قَهْوَة ◊ ج قَهَاوٍ

Waiter, coffee-seller. ◊ قَهْوَجِي

To have little appetite. ✱ قَهِي a قَهًى ,وأَقْهَى عن الطَّعام

Furnished with travelling provisions. Lively, fiery. قَاهٍ م قَاهِيَة

To dig (the ground). ✱ قاب o قَوْبًا ,وقَوَّب ه

To draw near. To fly away. To break its egg (chicken). قاب

To uproot a. th. To leave traces upon (the earth). قَوَّب ه

To be uprooted. To be excoriated (skin). تَقَوَّب

To break asunder (egg). تَقَوَّب وإِنْقَاب

To be hollowed (earth). إِنْقَاب

Their secret has been disclosed. إِنْقَابَتْ بَيْضَتُهُم

To choose a. th. إِقْتَاب ه

Space between the middle and the end of a bow. Space. قَاب

They are at a bow's length. بَيْنَهُمَا قَابُ او قِيبُ قَوْسٍ

Distance between two stars. قَابُ قَوْسٍ

Empty egg, Chicken. قَابَة وقَائِبَة

Shells of broken eggs. Hollow. قُوب

Chicken. ◘ Epidemic skin-disease. قُوب ج أَقْوَاب

Tetter, *dartre* (eruption). قُوبَاءُ وقُوبَا ج قُوَب ,وقُوبَة وقُوَبَة

Peeled off. Having shed his slough (snake). مُتَقَوِّب

To feed, to nourish a. o. ✱ قات o قَوْتًا وقُوتًا وقِيَاتَةً ,وأَقَات ة

To be able to. أَقَات ه وعلى

To be sustained, fed on. To feed on. تَقَوَّت واقْتَات ب

Put fuel in thy fire. إِقْتَتْ لِنَارِك قِيتَةً

To ask food from. إِسْتَقَات ة

Celastrus edulis, tree of Yemen. قات

Lactuca inermis, kind of lettuce. قات الرُّغْيان

Food. Victuals. قُوت ج أَقْوَات

Aliment. قَائِت وقِيت وقِيتَة وقُوَات

Keeper, witness. The Feeder (God). مُقِيت

To suppurate (wound). ✱ قاح o قَوْحًا ,وتَقَوَّح

To sweep (a house). قَوَّح ه

To refrain from giving. أَقَاح

Space. Middle of a court-yard. قَاحَة ج قُوح

To be disordered (intestines). ✱ قاخ o قَوْخًا

Dark night. لَيْلَة قَاخٍ

✱ قَاد o قَوْدًا وقِيَادَة وقِيَادًا ومَقَادَة وقَيْدُودَة ,وقَوَّد واقْتَاد ة (*opp. to* ساق)

To lead (a horse) with a halter. To lead (a murderer) to death.

To lead (an army). قَاد o قِيَادَة ة

To be led. To become compact (flour). قِيد

To be long-necked (horse). قَوِد o قَوَدًا

To take the lead. أَقَاد

To give to a. o. horses to lead. – ة خَيْلًا

To retaliate for a. o. by (killing the murderer). – ة ب

He allowed him to retaliate upon the murderer. أَقَادَهُ الدَّمَ او مِن القَاتِل

To be tractable (beast). إِنْقَاد واقْتَاد

To obey a. o. To become conspicuous (road). إِنْقَاد ل

To follow the lead of. إِسْتَقَاد ل

To ask a. o. to retaliate upon. – ة من

Distance. قَاد وقِيد

Horses, led-horses. قَوْد

Retaliation, punishment. قَوَد
Halter. قِيَاد, ومِقْوَد ج مَقَاوِد
Tractable. سَلِس القِيَاد
Manageable (horse). قَيِّد وقَيِّد وقَوُود
Strong-necked. أَقْوَد م قَوْدَاء ج قُود
Avaricious. Broad-necked (horse). Lofty (mountain).
Oblong mountain. — ومُقْوَد
Leader قَائِد ج قُوَّد وقُوَّاد وقَادَة وجج قَادَات of horses. Commander-in-chief. Star in *Ursa major*.
Prominence. قَائِد
Oblong hill. قَائِدَة
He submitted to him. أَعطاهُ قِيَادَهُ ومَقَادَتَهُ
To walk on the tiptoes. ✱ قَار o قَوْرًا
To catch (game) by guile. — ه
To cut a hole in (cloth). To cut (a melon) in round slices. — وقَوَّر, واقْتَار اقْتِيَارًا واقْتَوَر اقْتِيَارًا ه
To coil (snake). To be nearly elapsed (night). To separate in round portions (cloud). تَقَوَّر
To fall. To crumble down (wall). إِنْقَار
To be destitute. إِقْتَار
To examine (a narration). إِقْتَار ه
To be wrinkled (skin). To be lean (horse). To fade away (plant). إِقْوَرَّ
Liquid pitch, tar. Large herd of camels. قَار
New cotton. Cotton-rope. قَوْر
Knoll of a mountain. Black hillock, ground covered with black stones. Isolated hill. Name of a tribe. She-bear. قَارَة ج قَارَات وقَار وقُور وقِيرَان
Round hole cut in (a shirt, in a wall). قُوَارَة
Wide, spacious. أَقْوَر م قَوْرَاء
Calamities. أَقْوَرِيَّات وأَقْوَرُون
✧ Scoop (medical instrument). قَوَّارَة
Cut in round pieces. Besmeared with tar. Lean (camel). مُقَوَّر
To precede a. o. ✱ قَاس o قَوْسًا ه
To measure a. th. — واقْتَاس ه ب او على
To be crook-backed. قَوِس a قَوَسًا, وقَوَّس وتَقَوَّس واسْتَقْوَس
✧ To fire (a gun). قَوَّس ه
✧ To shoot a. o. — ه
To compare o.'s self with. قَايَس ه

To be bent, bowed. ✧ To be shot. تَقَوَّس
To mark the head with white (hoariness). تَقَوَّس ه
To arm o.'s self with (a bow). — ه
To imitate a. o. إِقْتَاس ب
Bow. Carder. قَوْس ج قِسِيّ وأَقْوَاس وقِيَاس
Bow of a violin. Fore-arm. Cubit, measure.
Sagittarius (Zodiacal sign). القَوْس
Rain-bow. قَوْس قُزَح
Hermitage. Hunter's booth. قُوس
Hard (time). قَوِس وقُوسِيّ وأَقْوَس
Bow-maker. Bow-man. ✧ Consular guard, cawass. قَوَّاس وقَوَّاص ج قَوَّاسَة
Starting race-horses. قِيَاس ومَقَاوِس
Gun-shot. ✧ قُوَاس
Small bow. قُوَيس وقُوَيسَة
هُوَ مِن خَيْرِ قُوَيْسٍ سَهْمًا او صار خَيْرَ قُوَيْس
From antagonist he became friend. سَهْمًا
Sage (*plant*). قُوَيْسَة وقُوَيْسَة العَيْن
Crook-backed. Elevated (heap of sand). أَقْوَس
Bow-case. Race-ground. Hippodrome. مِقْوَس ج مَقَاوِس
To put a crupper on (a horse). ✧ قَوَّش ه
✧ Crupper. T قُوش ج أَقْوَاش
Asparagus. Te قوش قنماز
To destroy (a house). To pull off (a tent). ✱ قَاض o قَوْضًا, وقَوَّض ه
To be destroyed, to collapse (house). To be routed (army). To be restless (bird). تَقَوَّض وانْقَاض
Flock of sheep. ✱ قَاط — قَوْط ج أَقْوَاط
Date-basket. قَوْطَة
✧ Dates in paste. ◻ Tomato. ✧ قُوطَة
Shepherd. قَوَّاط
To lag behind (man). To limp (dog). ✱ قَاع o قَوْعًا
To walk cautiously. تَقَوَّع
To climb upon (a tree: chameleon). — ه
Even place. Soft land. Depressed plain. قَاع ج قِيعَان وأَقْوَاع وأَقْوُع وقِيع
Floor for drying dates. قَوْع ج أَقْوَاع
Paved court. ✧ Parlour, sitting-room. قَاعَة ج قَاعَات
To track a. o. ✱ قَاف o قَوْفًا, واقْتَاف ه

To prognosticate a. th. قاف
To correct a. o. تَقوَّف ه
Able prognosticator. Physiognomist. قائف ج قافة
The letter ق. Imaginary mountain around the earth. ✧ Mount Caucasus. قاف
Upper border of the ear. قُوف
Thou hadst a narrow escape. نَجَوتَ بقُوفِ نَفسِكَ
Black mill-stone. ✧ قُوقًا
To cluck (hen). ✲ قاق قَوقًا ه ✧ قاقَ
Light-minded. قاق
Very tall man. — وقُوق وقِيق
✧ Raven. — ج قِيقان
Cormorant. قاق الماء
Pelican, aquatic bird. قُوق
Cap of judges. Ts قاوُوق ج قَوَاوِيق
Snail. Cowry, sea-shell. ¤ قَوقَة وقَوقَمَة
To cluck (hen). ✲ قَوقَا قَوقَاة, وقَوقَى قَوقَاة وقِيقَاء
To squat down. ¤ قَوقَر
✲ قال ο قَولًا وقالًا و قِيلًا وقَولَة ومَقالًا ومَقالَة ه
To say a. th.
To speak to. — ل
To profess (a doctrine). — ب
To grasp a. th. — بِيَدِهِ
To beckon (with the head). — بِرأسِهِ
To relate (the words of). To say a. th. on the account of. — عن
To speak against a. o. — على
To emit an opinion upon. — في
Dost thou think that Zeyd is ill? أَتَقُولُ زَيدًا مَرِيضًا
It is said. They say. قِيل
To attribute false reports to. قَوَّل وأَقال إقالة وأَقوَل إقوالًا ه
To discourse with. To confer with. To dispute with. ✧ To conclude a bargain with. قاوَل ه
To forge out reports upon. تَقوَّل على
To confer together upon. تَقاوَل في
To exercise authority upon. إِقتال على
To choose a. th. — ه
Tittle-tattle. Sayings of men. قال وقِيل
Public talk, town-talk. القالُ والقِيلُ
King of the Himyarites. Kinglet. قَيل ج أَقوال وأَقيال وقُيُول
قَول ج أَقوال وجج أَقاوِيل, وقالَة وقَولَة ومَقال
Saying, speech. ومَقالَة
Wing of an army. Te قُول
Watch-house, patrol. Ts قَرَاقُول
Adjutant-major. Ts قُول آغاسِي
قُوَلَة وقَوّال وقَوّالَة وقَوُول وقُوُول وتِقوَلَة وتِقوالَة, ومِقوَل ومِقوال (m. f.) ج مَقاوِل
Loquacious. Eloquent.
Speaking, saying. قائِل ج قُوَّل وقُيَّل وقالَة وقُوُول
Treatise. Chapter. مَقالَة
Conference. ✧ Bargain. مُقاوَلَة
Tongue. مِقوَل ج مَقاوِل
Said. Word. مَقُول ومَقوُول
The 10 categories. المَقُولات العَشر
(1) Substance. الجَوهَر
(2) Quantity. ألكَمّ
(3) Quality. ألكَيف
(4) Relation. ألإضافَة
(5) Place. ألأَين
(6) Time. ألمَتَى
(7) Collocation. ألوَضع
(8) Possession. ألمِلك
(9) Action. ألفِعل
(10) Passion. ألإنفِعال
To rise, to stand up. To stop (jaded beast). To be lively (walk). To appear in broad light (truth). To come back to life. ✲ قام ο قَومًا وقَومَة وقِيامًا وقامَة
The time of prayer is come. قامَت الصَّلاة
The commodity is worth so much. قام المَتاعُ بِكَذا
To rise against. To superintend a. o. To persevere in. — على
To rise for honouring a. o. — ل
To stand in the place of; to fill the charge of. — مَقامَهُ
To sustain a. o. — ه وعلى
He undertook an affair. — بأَمرٍ
He fulfilled his promise. — بِوَعدِهِ
I have a pain in the back. قام بي ظَهري
She began to weep. قامَت تَنوح
To erect, to set up; to set aright. To rectify. To make accurate. To value. ✧ To awake, to rouse a. o. قَوَّم ه وه
To be drawn (game). ✧ قُوِّم اللَّعِب
To rise against, to قاوَم مُقاوَمَة وقِوامًا ه

It is worthless. He is unsteady. ما لهُ قِيمَة
Provisions for soldiers. إِقَامَة ج إِقَامَات
Straightforwardness. Normal state. ✧ Pregnancy. إِسْتِقَامَة
✧ Almanach. تَقْوِيم ج تَقَاوِيم
Survey of a land. — البلاد
Manager. Upright. قَيِّم م قَيِّمَة
The husband. قَيِّم المَرْأَة
◘ Guardian. Juggler. قَيِّم ج قَيِّمِين
The true religion. القَيِّمَة
Upright, conspicuous. Vertical. Steady. قَائِم ج قُوَّم وقُيَّم وقُوَّام وقُيَّام
Hilt of a sword. — السَّيف
Waterworks. — الماء
قَائِم مَقَام وقَيِّم مَقَام و✧ قَائِمَقَام وقَيِّمَقَام
Lieutenant. Vice-roy. Turkish governor.
Rebellious. Perpendicular to. قَائِم على
Rectangle. قَائِم الزَّاوِيَة
Bill of sale. Leg of a table. ✧ List. Register. Invoice. Paper-money. ◘ Telegraphic post. قَائِمَة ج قَائِمَات وقَوَائِم
Foot of a quadruped. Hilt of a sword. — ج قَوَائِم
Right angle. زَاوِيَة قَائِمَة
Chief. Of fine stature. قَوَّام ج قَوَّامُون
Right, upright. Fast. قَوِيم ج قِيَام
Lark. قُومِيَّة
Self-existing (God). قَيُّوم وقَيَّام
✧ Drawn (game). قَيُّوم
Abode. Place, time of abode. مَقَام ومُقَام
Standing-place. Residence. Rank, dignity. مَقَام ج مَقَامَات
Seating. Meeting. Speech in a meeting. مَقَامَة ومُقَامَة ج مَقَامَات
Handle of the plough. مِقْوَم
Resistance, opposition. مُقَاوَمَة
Right. ✧ Straightforward. مُسْتَقِيم
✧ Pregnant woman. مُسْتَقِيمَة
Copper or iron handle of a vessel. ☆ قون — قَوْنَة ج قُوَن
Tree for making bows. قَان
✧ Medal, picture. G قُونَة ج قُوَن
✧ Melon. T قَاوُون
To shriek. ☆ قَاه — قَوَّه
To track (the game). — ه
To cry out to one another. تَقَاوَه

oppose a o. To assist a. o. To be equal to.
To set up a. th. To establish (a proof). To perform (prayer). أَقَام إِقَامَة وقَامَة ه
To raise (the dead). To make a. o. to stand up. — ه
To continue a. th., to keep to. — على
To remain in (a place). — ب
He stood in his stead. أَقَام بِهِ قَام مَقَامَهُ
To perform (prayer). To straighten a. th. To render (a market) brisk. — ه
To set a. o. over. To appoint a. o. to. — ه على
To begin a law-suit against. — دَعْوَى على
To be straightened. To subsist. تَقَوَّم
To rise one against the other. To oppose o. a. تَقَاوَم
To cut (the nose) to. إِقْتَام ه
To get up. To rise. To be upright, in good state. To be straightforward. ✧ To be pregnant (woman). إِسْتَقَام
To return to (God : sinner). — إلى
Abode, dwelling. قَوْم وقُوم وإِقَامَة
قَوْم (*m. f.*) ج أَقْوَام وأَقَاوِم وأَقَاوِيم وأَقَائِم
Tribe, nation. Party of men; some people.
Station. Pause in prayer. Revolution. ✧ Nocturn, night-service. قَوْمَة
What is right. ✧ Speedily. قَوَام
قَوَام وقَوْمَة وقَوْمِيَّة, وقَامَة ج قَامَات وقِيَم
Stature.
Livelihood. Sustenance. قَوَام وقِوَام وقَوْمِيَّة
Normal state. Main stay. قِوَام وقِيَام
He is the sustainer of his family. هُوَ قِوَام وقِيَام أَهْلِهِ
The worship of God. القِيَام بِاللهِ
Return to God. القِيَام للهِ
Stature of man. Height. Sheave of a water-wheel. قَامَة ج قِيَم
Resurrection. قِيَامَة
Day of the last judgment. يَوْم القِيَامَة
✧ He raised an uproar. قَام القِيَامَة
Value, price. Stature of man. قِيمَة ج قِيَم

Obedience. Power. Comfortable (life). قاه

Leading an easy life. قاهٍ م قاهِيَة

To be, to become strong. ✱ قَوِيَ a قُوَّة

To prevail upon a. o. To be able to do a. th. قَوِيَ على ه وه

To be equal to a. o. — ب

To be vacant (house). — قِيًا وقَوَايَة

To be hungry. To be withheld (rain). — قَوَى

To overcome a. o. in strength, to overpower. قَوَى قُوَّة ه

To strengthen a. o.; to hearten a. o. قَوَّى ه

To vie in strength with. To wrestle with. قَاوَى مُقَاوَاة ه

To inhabit a desert. To be empty (house). To be rich. To be destitute. To have a strong horse. أَقْوَى إِقْوَاء

To diversify the rhymes of (a poem). To weave (a rope) with many strands. — ه

To acquire strength. تَقَوَّى واقْتَوَى واسْتَقْوَى

To bid against o. a. تَقَاوَى واقْتَوَى

To spend the night hungry. تَقَاوَى

To appropriate, to claim the property of. إِقْتَوَى ه

Desert. قِيّ وقَوَاء وقِوَاء

Hunger. قَوَاء وقَوَى

He spent the night in hunger. بَاتَ القَوَاء او القَوَى

Strength. Power. Vigour. Faculty. قُوَّة ج قُوَّات وقُوًى

Strand of a rope. قُوَّة ج قُوًى

✧ Seeds given to poor husbandmen. تَقْوِيَة ج تَقَاوٍ

Grasping. Empty (house). Rainless (year). قَاوٍ م قَاوِيَة

Many-stranded (rope). قَوٍ م قَوِيَة

Strong. Mighty. ✧ Much. قَوِيّ ج أَقْوِيَاء

Diversification in the rhymes of a poem. إِقْوَاء

Virtually. (*opp. to* بالفِعل) بالقُوَّة

Stronger. Richer. أَقْوَى

Strengthening. Comfortable. مُقَوٍّ م مُقَوِّيَة

Riding a strong beast. مُقْوٍ م مُقْوِيَة

Strong (horse). Empty (house).

To vomit. ✱ قَاءَ i قَيْأً ه

Stuff saturated with dye. ثَوْب يَقِيءُ الصِّبغ

The thrust has caused blood to spout. قَاءَت الطَّعْنَةُ الدَّمَ

To provoke vomiting (medicine). قَيَّأَ تَقْيِئَة, وأَقَاءَ إِقَاءَة ه

To excite o.'s self to vomit. تَقَيَّأَ تَقَيُّؤًا, واسْتَقَاءَ اسْتِقَاءَة

To endeavour, to desire to vomit. إِسْتَقَاءَ

Vomit. Vomited food. قُيَاء وقَيْء

Vomiting much. قَيُوء وقَيَّوء

Emetic. دَوَاء مُقَيِّئ

Pheasant (fowl). ◻ قِيج

To suppurate (wound). ✱ قَاحَ i قَيْحًا, وقَيَّحَ وأَقَاحَ وتَقَيَّحَ

Purulent matter. قَيْح ج قُيُوح

To be fettered. ✱ قَادَ — قِيد

To shackle (a beast). To bind a. o. قَيَّدَ ه

To dot (letters). To register a. th. To prohibit (a. th: religion). To restrain (the meaning of a word). — ه

To bind a. o. with (benefits). — ه ب

To be in irons. To be registered. To be restrained. تَقَيَّدَ

To be detained in (a work). تَقَيَّدَ ب

Fetters, shackles. قَيْد ج قُيُود وأَقْيَاد

Gum of the teeth. — الأَسْنَان

Brand upon a horse's neck. — الفَرَس

Measure. — وقِيد وقَاد

There is between them the length of a spear. بَيْنَهُمَا قَيْد وقِيد وقَاد رُمْح

Halter. قِيَاد

Charm, spell. Book-binding. تَقْيِيد

Registered. Ankle (of a woman). Pastern of (a horse). مُقَيَّد ج مَقَايِيد

To tar (a camel, a ship). ✱ قَيَّرَ ه وه

Pitch, tar. قِير وقَار

To scrutinise a. th. إِقْتَارَ ه

Pitch-seller. قَيَّار

Of low origin. قَيُّور

To take the measure of. ✱ قَاسَ i قَيْسًا وقِيَاسًا, واقْتَاسَ ه

To compare a. th. with. To take a. th. as a pattern. — ه ب وعلى

To strut, to walk haughtily. — قَيْس

Alike, equal to. قَيْض وقِيَاض ل
They are equal. هُمَا قَيْضَانِ
Fragment of a bone. قِيضَة ج قِيض
✧ Crafty man.
Stone heated in the fire. قَيْض وقَيْضَة
Barter.
Barter. قِيَاض وقِيَاضَة ومُقَايَضَة ومُقَارَضَة
Holding much water (well). مُقِيضَة
To be hot, burning (day). ☆ قَاظ i قَيْظًا
To spend the summer at (a place). — وقَيَّظ ب وتَقَيَّظ ب وه
To suffice a. o. (for summer). قَيَّظ ة
To make a bargain with a. o. for summer. قَايَظ مُقَايَظَةً وقِيَاظًا ة
Heat of summer. Midsummer. ✧ Drought, want of rain. قَيْظ ج أَقْيَاظ وقُيُوظ
Intense heat. Born in summer (sheep). قَيْظ قَائِظ
Summer-residence. مَقَاظ ومَقِيظ
Plants remaining green till midsummer. مَقِيظَة
To grunt (pig). ☆ قَاء i قَيْعًا
To track a. o. To scrutinise a. th. ☆ قيف — قَيَّف وتَقَيَّف ه
✧ To criticise a. o. قَيَّف ة
To go through (a country). تَقَيَّف ه
Tracking. ◘ Fashion, form of dress. قِيَافَة
Importune beggar. ✧ Criticiser. مُقَيِّف
To cluck (hen). ☆ قَاق i قَيْقًا
Unsteady, fickle. قِيق
Pellicle of an egg. Spadix of the palm-tree. قِيقَة ج قِيَق
Uneven and hard ground. قِيقَاة وقِيقَاءَة ج قَوَاقٍ وقِيَاقٍ وقِيق
To make a siesta. ☆ قَال i قَيْلًا وقَائِلَةً وقَيْلُولَةً ومَقَالًا ومَقِيلًا
To milk, to drink at midday. — قَيْلًا
To discourse together at leisure (men). To make a siesta. قَيَّل
To make a. o. to drink at midday. — ة
To give a. th. in exchange to a. o. قَايَل ة ه
To rescind (a sale) with. أَقَال إِقَالَةً ة ه
To make (a beast) to drink at midday. — ة

To verify the measure of. ✧ To adjust (the beams of a roof). قَايَس مُقَايَسَةً وقِيَاسًا ه
To compare (things) together. To deduce a. th. by analogy with. — بَيْن ... وه ب وإلى
To belong to the tribe of Kais. تَقَيَّس
To be measured, compared, confronted. إِنْقَاس
He imitates his father. يَقْتَاس بِأَبِيهِ
Measure, distance. قَاس وقِيس
There is a spear's length between them. بَيْنَهُمَا قَاس او قِيس رُمْحٍ
Name of a tribe. قَيْس
Measurement. Comparison. Analogy. Model, pattern. Syllogism. Rule. قِيَاس ج أَقْيِسَة
Regularly. Conformably to the pattern. على القِيَاس
Regular. قِيَاسِيّ
Proportion. Appraisement by analogy. مُقَايَسَة
Quantity. Instrument for measuring. Regulator. مِقْيَاس ج مَقَايِيس
◘ Nilometer. مِقْيَاس النِّيل
To fall (tooth). ☆ قَاص i قَيْصًا, وانقاص
To collapse (well). تَقَيَّص وانْقَاص
Crumbled down (well). قَيَّاصَة الجُول
To be broken, split. ☆ قَاض i قَيْضًا
To break a. th. To hollow (a well). To assimilate a. th. — ه
To barter a. th. with. To assimilate a. th. to. — ه ب
To be abundant in a well (water). قِيضَ
To decree a. th. for a. o. (God). قَيَّض ة ل
To brand (a beast) with a heated stone. — ة
To barter with. قَايَض مُقَايَضَةً وقِيَاضًا ة
To be broken (egg). تَقَيَّض
To be appointed to a. o. (fate). — ل
To be like (o.'s father). — ة
To fall to pieces (wall). تَقَيَّض وانْقَاض
To make barters. تَقَايَض و✧ تَقَارَض
To be cracked (egg, flask, tooth). To collapse (well). إِنْقَاض
To destroy, to extirpate a. th. أَقْتَاض ه
Egg-shell. Compensation, substitute. قَيْض

أقال الله عثرته May God forgive his fault, his lapse !

تقيّل To nap. To collect (water).

— ه To resemble o.'s father.

تقايل To rescind (a sale).

إقتال ه ب To barter a. th.

✧ إستقال To give in o.'s resignation.

— ه البيع To ask a. o. to rescind a sale.

— ه عثرته To ask from a. o. forgiveness for a fault.

قيل ج أقيال Kinglet of Arabia.

قيل وقيول Milk drunk before a siesta.

قيلة وقيولة She-camel milked at midday.

قائل ج قيّل وقيّال وقيل Napping.

قائلة Mid-day.

— وقيلولة Siesta.

إقالة Rescission of a sale.

مقيل Resting-place.

☆ قان i قيناً ه To beat (iron). To set a. th. in order. To repair (a vessel).

— ه على To give (inborn qualities) to a. o. (God).

قيّن ه وه To adorn a. th.

تقيّن To be adorned.

إقتان واقتانّ To be luxuriant (plant, garden).

قان Tree used for making bows.

قين ج قيون وأقيان Blacksmith ; locksmith : any smith.

— ج قيان Slave.

قينة ج قيان Songstress, female slave.

— ومقيّنة House-maid, hair-dresser.

H قايين Cain, Adam's son.

ك

* كَأْس ج كَأْسَة ج أَكْؤُس وكُؤُوس وكَأْسَات وكِئَاس Cup, drinking-cup.
✧ Chalice. Cymbal.

* كَأَل a كَأْلًا وكَأْلَةً وكُؤُولًا To purchase or sell a. th. in compensation of a debt.
إِكْوَأَلَّ To be short, stunted.
* كَأَنَ a كَأْنًا To become strong in make.
* كَبَّ o كَبًّا ه على ول To prostrate a. o. on (the face).
ه — To turn a. th. upside down. To wind (thread) into a ball. ✧ To pour (a liquid).
كَبَّبَ To roast meat. ✧ To make meat-balls.
أَكَبَّ To be overturned, turned upside down.
ه — To throw down a. o. on the face.
أَكَبَّ على To bend down towards. To busy o.'s self about. To keep to (a work).
ل — To lean on.
ه — ✧ To spill (a liquid).
تَكَبَّبَ To be contracted, to become compact (sand, tree). To fall down (camel). To wrap o.'s self in a garment.
إِنْكَبَّ To be inverted, overturned.
✧ To be spilt (liquid).
على — To apply o.'s self assiduously to.
كَبّ Plant of the kind حَمْض.
كَبَّة وكُبَّة Charge, attack in a fight.
Dash, collision. Intenseness of cold.
كُبَّة ج كُبَب Ball of thread. Troop of men, horses. ✧ Force-meat balls.
Trump; heart (at cards). ◻ Plague, bubo.
كُبَايَة ✧ Tumbler, drinking-glass.
كَبَاب Roast-meat.
كُبَابَة Cubeb (a medicine).
كُبَاب Flock of sheep. Glomerated (sand). Moist and compact (earth).

* كَ وكِ وكُم وكُنَّ Affixed pronoun of the 2^p^ person.
ضَرَبَكَ He has struck thee.
كِتَابُكَ, كُتُبُكَ, وكِتَابُكُم وكِتَابُكُنَّ Thy book; your books.
كَ *Particle*, as, like.
كَأَنَّ وكَأَنْ (for كَ و أَنَّ) As if it were, like.
كَأَنَّ وكَأَنْ زَيْدًا أَسَدٌ Indeed Zeyd is like a lion.
كَأَنَّكُم خَرَجْتُم الى لِصٍّ You came forth as it it were against a thief.
كَأَيِّن وكَأَيٍّ How many.
كَمِثْلِهِ Like him.
كَذَلِكَ So, much.
كَمَا As, like, when.
كَالأَسَد Like a lion.
* كَأْكَأَ وتَكَأْكَأَ To draw back. To run away (thief). To be weak, cowardly.
تَكَأْكَأَ To gather (people).
تَكَأْكَأَ في الكَلَام To falter in speech.
كَأْكَأ Fear. Faint-heartedness. Escape of a thief.
* كَئِبَ a كَأْبًا وكَأْبَةً وكَآبَةً, وأَكْأَب واكْتَأَب To be broken-hearted, distressed.
أَكْأَبَ ه To distress a. o.
إِكْتَأَبَ To be blackish (ground).
كَأْب وكَأْبَة وكَآبَة وكَأْبَاء Sorrow, intense grief.
كُؤْبَة Cause of sorrow.
كَئِب وكَئِيب ومُكْتَئِب Broken-hearted, sorrowful.
مَا أَكْأَبَهُ How sad he is!
مُكْتَئِب Blackish (ashes).
* كَأَدَ a كَأْدًا To be sad, grieved.
تَكَأَّدَ وتَكَاءَدَ ه وهِ To distress a. o. (event). To assume a painful (duty).
إِكْوَأَدَّ To tremble (old man).
كَأْدَاء Adversity. Sadness. Dark night.
كَؤُود Steep, difficult (hill, ascent).
كُؤَدَاء Deep sigh.
كَار ج كَارَات P ✧Calling, profession, work.
كَاز P Shears for leather. ✧ Petroleum, mineral oil. Gas.

✧ Ball, pin-cushion. كُبَابَة
✧ Hedgehog. كُبَابَة الشَّوْك
Dandelion (*plant*). كُبَيْبَات الشِّتَاء
Having down cast eyes. مِكَبّ ومِكْبَاب
Ball of spun thread. مِكَبّ ج مِكَبَّات ومَكَابّ
✡ كَبْكَبَ ه وه To upset, to turn upside down. To hurl a. th. down into an abyss. To bring (a flock) together. ✧ To wind a. th. into a ball. To scatter here and there. To make force-meat (balls).
تَكَبْكَبَ To gather (throng). To be wound up, glomerated. To be spilt.
— في ثِيَابِهِ He wrapped himself in his clothes.
Game on horse-back. كَبْكَب وكَبْكَب
Crowd, press. كَبْكَبَة وكُبْكُبَة وكُبْكُوب وكُبْكُوبَة
✧ Ball of spun thread, of wool. كُبْكُوب
✧ Force-meat ball. كُبْكُوبَة
✡ كَبَتَ i كَبْتًا ه To prostrate, to humble.
— ه لِوَجْهِهِ He prostrated him on his face.
— غَيْظَهُ في جَوْفِهِ He concealed his anger in his bosom.
Very sad. مَكْبُوت
✧ كَبُّوت ج كَبَابِيت Overcoat. Woollen cloak.
✧ كَبَّلَ ه To round, to form a. th. into balls.
✧ كَبَّلَ ل To hold foul, abusive language to.
✧ تَكَبَّلَ To be rounded.
✧ كَبُّولَة Small ball, pill.
✡ كَبِثَ a كَبَثًا To be altered, to stink (meat).
Altered (meat). كَبِيث ومَكْبُوث
Fruit of the أَرَاك when ripe. كَبَاث
✡ كَبَحَ a كَبْحًا, وأَكْبَحَ ه ب To check, to pull up (a horse) with (the bridle).
كَبَحَ ه عَن To hinder a. o. from.
— ه ب To strike a. o. with (a sword).
— ه To send back (an arrow : wall).
كَابَحَ ه To insult a. o.
أَكْبَحَ To be elevated (place).
Of bad omen. كَابِح ج كَوَابِح
Elevated (place). مُكْبِح ومُكَبَّح
✡ كَبَدَ o كَبْدًا ه To wound a. o. in the liver. To affect a. o. painfully (cold).
To purpose a. th. كَبَدَ وتَكَبَّدَ ه
To have a complaint of the liver. كَبِدَ a كَبَدًا, وكُبِدَ
To culminate, to reach the meridian (star). كَبَّدَ وتَكَبَّدَ
To endure (hardships). To struggle against (difficulties). كَابَدَ مُكَابَدَةً وكِبَادًا ه
To thicken (milk). تَكَبَّدَ
To reach the middle of (a desert). — ه
Midst of the sky. كَبْد وكَبَد وكَبْدَاء وكُبَيْدَاء وكُبَيْدَاة
Liver. كَبِد وكِبْد ج أَكْبَاد وكُبُود
Enemies, *lit* : black-livered. سُود الأَكْبَاد
Middle of a bow. Cavity of the belly. Inside. Center, middle-part. كَبِد
Gold and silver mines. Inside of the earth. — الأَرْض
Atmosphere. Meridian. Middle part of a tract of sand. Distress, trouble. كَبَد
Concha Veneris, shell of Venus. كَبْدَة
Disease of the liver. كُبَاد
Cedrat (bitter orange). ✧ كَبَّاد
Arm-mill. كَبْدَاء
Big-bellied. Walking slowly. أَكْبَد م كَبْدَاء ج كُبْد
Cause of suffering. كَابِد
Suffering, enduring. كَابِد ومُكَابِد
✡ كَبِرَ a كِبَرًا ومَكْبِرًا To be advanced in years.
To exceed a. o. in (age). كَبَرَ o كُبْرًا ه ب
To become stout, tall. To grow big. To become great, illustrious. To become momentous (affair). كَبُرَ o كِبَرًا وكُبْرًا وكَبَارَةً
To increase a. th. To extol, to magnify a. o. كَبَّرَ تَكْبِيرًا وكِبَّارًا ه وه
To treat a. o. scornfully. To strive to overcome a. o. كَابَرَ ه
To deem a. o. or a. th. great, momentous. أَكْبَرَ واسْتَكْبَرَ ه وه
To become haughty, to magnify o.'s self. تَكَبَّرَ وتَكَابَرَ واسْتَكْبَرَ
Insolence. Haughtiness. Heinous crime. كِبْر
Greatness (moral and physi- كِبْر وكُبْر

✧ To be broken to work (beast). تَكَبَّس
To be filled up with earth (well). انْكَبَس —
Invasion. Sudden attack. Pressure. كَبْسَة
Earth for filling a well. House of clay. Cave at the foot of a mountain. Origin. كِبْس
Unexpected attack, surprise. كَبْسَة
Large cluster of dates. كِبَاسَة ج كَبَائِس
Steep mountains. جِبَال كُبْس وكُبُس
Night-mare. ✧ Arm of a plough. كَابُوس ج كَوَابِيس
Covering his head in sleeping. كُبَاس
He came by surprise. جَاءَ كَابِسًا
Aquiline (nose). كَابِسَة
Excellent dates. Roll of perfume worn by women as an ornament. ✧ Pickles. كَبِيس
Intercalary, leap year. سَنَة كَبِيسَة
Having a prominent forehead. أَكْبَس م كَبْسَاء ج كُبْس
مِكْبَس ج مَكَابِس و مِكْبَاس ج مَكَابِيس
Hand-press, hydraulic press, piston.
Casting down his looks. Attacking suddenly. مُكَبِّس
✧ Broken, trained (young beast). Double (flower). مُكَبَّس
Surrounded. Invaded. Filled with earth. ✧ Pressed. Pickled. مَكْبُوس
To take a handful of. ✩ كَبَش o كَبْشًا ه
✧ To scoop up a. th. with both hands.
Ram. Chief, leader. Battering-ram. ✧ Wild sheep. كَبْش ج كِبَاش وأَكْبُش وأَكْبَاش
Buttress on a wall. ✧ Mulberry. — ج كُبُوش
Pillar, column. كَبْش ج كُبُوش و✧ أَكْبَاش
✧ Spoonful, handful. Scummer. كَبْشَة
✧ Clove. كَبْش القَرَنْفُل
To cut a. th. ✩ كَبَع a كَبْعًا, وكَبَّع ه
To reckon and sort (money). كَبَّع ه
To prevent a. o. from. — ه عن
To submit, to humble o.'s self. — كُبُوعًا
Sea-monster. ✧ كَبْع
Barge, pontoon. ✧ كَبَك
Kitchen-board. ✧ كَبَكَة
Ranunculus Asiaticus (*plant*). P كَبِيكَج
To put irons ✩ كَبَل i كَبْلًا, وكَبَّل واكْتَبَل ه

cal). Nobility. Main part of an affair.
Advanced age, oldness. كِبَر وكَبْرَة وكِبْرَة
He is هُوَ كِبْرُ هُمْ وكِبْرَتُهُمْ او كُبْرُ هُمْ وكُبْرُ تُهُمْ the greatest or the oldest amongst them.
Stoutness, greatness. كِبَار
Drum. Caper-tree, capers. P كَبَر ج كِبَار وأَكْبَار
Pride. Grandeur, magnificence. كِبْرِيَاء
Augmentative form of a word. تَكْبِير
Cry of الله أَكْبَر God is greater.
Pride, arrogance. تَكَبُّر
Great كُبَار وكُبَّار وكَابِر, وكَبِير ج كِبَار وكُبَرَاء (in body, rank). Old, elder, eldest. Important (thing).
Of high rank. كَبِير وكَابِر
Asa fœtida, gum-resin. ◻ أَبُو كَبِير
They have تَوَارَثُوا المَجْدَ كَابِرًا عَن كَابِر inherited glory from father to son.
Enormity, heinous crime. كَبِيرَة ج كَبَائِر وكَبِيرَات
Wine *i. e.* (the mother of crimes). أُمُّ الكَبَائِر
Older, greater. أَكْبَر ج أَكَابِر وأَكْبَرُون
The chief men, the leaders, the nobility. الأَكَابِر
Major term of a syllogism. كُبْرَى
Advanced years. مَكْبِر ومَكْبَرَة ومَكْبُرَة
Self-magnifying (God). ✧ Proud. مُتَكَبِّر
Bridge. Tʀ كُوبْرِى
Sulphur. Brimstone. ✧ Lucifer matches. ✩ كِبْرِيت
Red gold. ذَهَب كِبْرِيت
To sulphurate a. th. كَبْرَت ه
Sulphurated. مُكَبْرَت
To besiege, to surround (a town). To take a. o. by surprise. To fill up (a well) with earth. ✧ To cure, to pickle (fruit). ✩ كَبَس i كَبْسًا ه
To muffle o.'s head with (a garment). — رَأْسَهُ فِي
To add an intercalary day to a leap-year. — السَّنَة بِيَوْم
To press upon, to squeeze a. th. — على
To have the upper part of the head prominent. كَبِس a كَبَسًا
✧ To break (a beast) to work. كَبَّس ه
To shampoo; to rub the body at bath.

to (a captive). To confine a. o. in prison.
To put off the payment of (a debt) to. كبّل وكابل ه ٥
To hinder the purchase of (a property) for availing o.'s self of the right of preemption. كابل ه
To be fettered. To be confined in prison. تكبّل
To bind (a purse). To keep (property) for o.'s self. إكتبل ه
Shackles, fetters, irons. كِبْل ج كُبُول
Short (dress). كَبْل وكابِلِيّ
¤ Mahogany (wood). كابُلِيّ
Hunter's net. كابُول
Fettered (prisoner). مُكبَّل ومَكْبُول
✱ To hem (a garment). كَبَن o كَبْنًا ه
To conceal a. th.
To turn (a gift) from. — ه
To turn aside from. — عن
To go quietly (horse). — i كَبْنًا وكُبُونًا
To be quiet. — كُبُونًا
He refrained his tongue from. أكبَن لِسانَهُ عَن
To be contracted. إكبأنّ
Fold of a leathern bucket. كِبْن وكُبْن
Niggardly. كُبُنّ وكُبُنَّة
Disease of camels. كُبان
Strong. مُكْبَن
Attacked with a disease (camel). مَكْبُون
✧ Housings, horse-cloth. كُوبان
✱ To fall prostrate on the face. كَبَا o كَبْوًا وكُبُوًّا لِوَجْهِهِ
To smoulder in the ashes (fire). كَبَا
To fade away (plant). To rise (dust). To stumble; to run without sweating (horse).
To empty (a flask). To sweep off (refuse). — ه
To perfume (a garment). To cover up (fire). كَبَّى ه
To fail (steel). أكْبَى
To fail to strike (fire: man). To alter (o.'s countenance). — ه
To fumigate a garment with (incense). To perfume o.'s self. تكبّى على واكتبى ب
To lay prostrate on the earth. إنكبى

✧ To totter.
Sweepings. كِبًا وكِبًى ج أكْباء , وكِبَة ج كُبُون
Sort of frankincense. كِباء ج كُبًى
Oozing water. Moon-rays. كُباء
Stumble. Dust. Fall on the face. كَبْوَة
Censer. كُبْوَة
¤ Pale, wan, dull (colour). كابِي
Hospitable. كابِي الرَّماد
Drinking-glass, tumbler. ✧ كُبّايَة
To whisper a. th. in (the ear). ✱ كَتّ o كَتًّا, وأكَتّ واكْتَتّ الكلامَ في
To reckon, to number a. th. كَتّ ه ٥
Innumerable army. جَيْش لا يُكَتّ
To walk slowly, with short steps. كَتّ o كَتِيتًا
To boil (cooking-pot). To groan (camel). كَتّ i كَتًّا
To vex, to thwart a. o. — ٥
✧ To pour out (a liquid). — ه
To listen to (a narration). إكتتّ ه
Lean. (*m. f.*) كَتّ
Green, verdure. كُتَّة
Refuse of a flock. كُتَّة
Sound of boiling. Grumbling of camels. ✧ Lint, tow. كَتِيت
Thick pudding. كَتِيتَة
To laugh gently. ✱ كَتْكَتَ
¤ Floss-silk; coarse silk, tow. كَتْكَتْ
Chicken newly hatched. كَتْكُوت ج كَتاكِيت
To write. ✱ كَتَب o كَتْبًا وكِتابًا وكِتْبَة وكِتابَة
To be a public writer.
To decree, to ordain a. th. (God). — كِتابًا ه
To write to a. o. on. — إلى ب
To write (a book). — وكَتَّب واكتَتَب ه
To bequeath a. th. to. To inscribe a. o. for (an office). — ل ه
To prescribe a. th. to. — ه على
To write a. th. dictated by, or heard from a. o. — عن
To sew (a water-skin). كَتَب كَتْبًا, واكتَتَب ه
To teach calligraphy to. كَتَّب وأكتَب ٥
To form squadrons. كَتَّب ٥
To correspond by letters with. To write with a. o. كاتَب ٥
To dictate (a poem) to. أكْتَب ٥ ه

أكتب ه To close (a bag).
تكتّب To form into squadrons. To gird o.'s self.
تكاتب To correspond by letter with o. a.
إكتتب To write down o.'s name in a public register. To be inscribed. ✧ To become a subscriber to (a paper).
— ه لنفسه To take a copy of a. th.
— واستكتب ه ه To ask a. o. to write a. th. To ask a. o. to dictate a. th.
كِتْبَة Transcription of a book.
كُتْبَة ج كُتَب Thongs for sewing a sack.
كِتاب ج كُتُب وكُتْب Writing, handwriting. Marriage-contract. Letter. Book. Register. Predestination.
الكِتاب Any sacred book. Scripture.
أهل الكِتاب Jews and Christians. People of Scripture.
✧ كُتُبي ٥ كتابجي Book-seller.
Te كتابخانه Library.
كِتابة Writing, writ, deed. Letter. Register. Inscription (on a monument). ✧ Spell, charm, amulet.
كَتيبة ج كَتائِب Squadron, detachment of cavalry. ✧Writ. Diploma, patent. Decree, ordinance.
كاتِب ج كاتِبون وكُتّاب وكَتَبَة Writer, scribe, clerk, secretary. Learned man.
كُتّاب ج كَتاتِيب Boys-school.
مَكْتَب ج مَكاتِب Elementary school. ✧ Office of a merchant.
مَكْتَبة ج مَكاتِب Library. ✧ Book-selling. Writing-desk.
مُكْتِب Writing-master.
مُكاتِب Correspondent.
مُكاتَبة Correspondence.
مَكْتُوب ج مَكاتِيب Letter. Writing.
مُكْتَتَب Registered, written down.
✲ كَتَح a كَتْحًا على To cover a. o. with dust (wind).
— ه To eat a. th. to surfeit. To strip (a land : locusts).
P كَتْخُود ✧ Steward, manager.
✲ كَتَد وكَتِد ج أكتاد وكُتُود Part of the back between the shoulders.

أكتد Having the upper part of the back prominent.
هُمْ أكتاد They follow or they resemble one another.
G كاتِدرا وكَنِيسَة كاتِدرائيّة ✧ Cathedral.
✲ كَتِر – أكْتَر To be big-humped (camel).
كَتْر Rank, dignity. Middle-part.
— كِتْر وكَتَر ج أكتار High camel's hump.
كَتْرَة Hump. Part of the hump.
كِتْر Dome-like structure.
✲ كَتِع a كَتَعًا To be contracted. ✧ To be crippled.
— وكَتَع a كَتْعًا في To do (a work) speedily.
كَتَع a كُتُوعًا في To penetrate into (a land).
كَتَّع ه To mince (meat).
كاتَع ه To make a. o. to perish (God).
تَكاتَع To follow one another.
— ه To do a. th. connectedly.
كُتَع ج كِتْعان ، وكُتَيع Vile, despicable.
كُتْعَة ج كِتاع ، وكُتْعَة ج كُتَع ، وكِتْعَة ج كِتَع Small bucket.
أكْتَع ج كُتْع Crook-fingered. ✧ Cripple, one-handed.
كَتْعاء ج كُتْع Maid-servant.
إشْتَرَيْتُها جَمْعاء كَتْعاء I have bought it altogether.
رَأَيْتُ إخوتَك أجمَعين أكْتَعِين I saw all thy brothers.
مَكْتُوع ✧ Cripple, one-handed.
✲ كَتَف i كَتْفًا To walk slowly in shaking the shoulders.
كَتَف i كَتْفًا وكِتافًا ه To hit a. o. on the shoulder. To gall (a beast) on the shoulder (saddle).
— وكَتَّف ه To handcuff a. o. behind his back.
كَتَف i كَتْفًا وكَتَفانًا To flutter (bird).
كَتِف a كَتَفًا To be broad-shouldered (man). To have the shoulders wide apart (horse).
كَتَّف To walk in shaking the shoulders (horse).
— ه To repair (a vessel) with a leaf of metal. To mince (meat).
تَكَتَّف To raise the shoulders in

To hold (water : skin). ✧ To be costive. كَتَمَ كُتُومًا وكِتَامًا ه
To conceal a. th. from. كَاتَمَ ه ه
To conceal a. th. from o. another. تَكَاتَمَ ه
To be concealed, hidden. إِنْكَتَمَ –
To commit (a secret) to a. o. إِسْتَكْتَمَ ه ه
Concealment, discretion. كَتْمٌ وكِتْمَانٌ
Concealing of a secret. كِتْمَةٌ
Plant for dyeing the hair black. كَتَمٌ وكُتْمَانٌ
Costiveness. ✧ كُتَامٌ
Concealing. Carefully kept (secret). Whole, sound (bow). ✧ Costive. كَاتِمٌ م كَاتِمَةٌ
Secretary. كَاتِمُ الأَسْرَارِ
Discreet. كُتَمَةٌ وكَتُومٌ وكَتَّامٌ
Keeper of a secret. كَتُومٌ ج كُتُمٌ
Unbroken, whole (bow). – وكَتِيمٌ
Silent (camel). كَتِيمٌ
Big-bellied. Surfeited. أَكْتَمُ
Kept (secret). مَكْتُومٌ ومُكْتَتَمٌ
To be blackened by smoke (walls). To be filthy (clothes). To be dyed green by herbage (lips of cattle). To be viscous and dirty (water-skin). ✱ كَتِنَ a كَتَنًا
To glue, to agglutinate. كَتَّنَ وأَكْتَنَ ه
Black of smoke. Blackness on the lips. Dirt. كَتَنٌ
Dirty, unclean. كَتِنٌ
Divinatory arrow. كَتِنٌ وكَتِينٌ
Flax. Linen. كَتَّانٌ
Green moss. – وكَتَّانَةٌ
Alb. Surplice. ✧ كَتُّونَةٌ
To walk with short steps. ✱ كَتَا o كَتْوًا
To overcome an adversary. أَكْتَى
To be thick ; to be short and crisp (beard). ✱ كَثَّ i كَثَاثَةً وكُثُوثَةً , وكَثَّ a كَثَثًا
To have a thick beard. أَكَثَّ
Thick (beard). كَثٌّ وكَثِيثٌ
Thick-bearded. – وكَثُّ اللِّحْيَةِ , وأَكَثُّ م كَثَّاءُ ج كُثٌّ
To foam (milk). To froth (cooking-pot). To be thick (beard). ✱ كَثَأَ a كَثْأً , وكَثَّأَ
To skim (a pot). – ه
To be tangled (plant). – وكَثَأَ

walking (horse). To walk by starts (locust).
To cross the arms in prayer. تَكَتَّفَ فِي الصَّلَاةِ
Shoulder-blade. Shoulder. كَتِفٌ وكِتْفٌ ج أَكْتَافٌ وكِتَفَةٌ
Broadness of the shoulders. Lameness, limp. كَتَفٌ
Pain in the shoulder-blade. كُتَافٌ
Manacle, handcuff. كِتَافٌ ج كُتُفٌ
Leaf, plate of metal. Broad (sword). كَتِيفٌ ج كُتُفٌ
Bolt. Hatred. Smith's tongs. كَتِيفَةٌ ج كَتَائِفُ
Locust beginning to fly. كُتْفَانٌ وكِتْفَانٌ
Broad-shouldered. Having parted shoulders (horse). أَكْتَفُ م كَتْفَاءُ ج كُتْفٌ
Galled on the shoulders (beast). مِكْتَافٌ
To fetter, to confine a. o. in prison. ✱ كَتَلَ o كَتْلًا ه
To press a. th. into a lump. – وكَتَّلَ ه
To adhere, to stick together. كَتِلَ a كَتَلًا
To be compact ; to be pressed into a lump. تَكَتَّلَ
Lump of dates, of clay ; bunch. Piece of meat. كُتْلَةٌ ج كُتَلٌ
✧ Scabious (*plant*). كُتْلَةٌ
✧ Everlasting flower. الكُتْلَةُ الصَّفْرَاءُ
Bulkiness, thickness. كَتَلٌ وكُتَالٌ
Soul. Want. Provision. كُتَالٌ
He relied upon me. أَلْقَى عَلَيَّ كُتَالَهُ
Palm-tree unreached by the hand. كَتِيلَةٌ ج كَتَائِلُ
Hard, difficult. Misfortune. أَكْتَلُ
Date-basket made of palm-leaves and holding 15 صَاع. مِكْتَلٌ ومِكْتَلَةٌ ج مَكَاتِلُ
Round and compact. Stout and short (man). مُكَتَّلٌ
To become a Greek Catholic. ✧ كَوْتَلَ وتَكَوْتَلَ
Greek Catholic. ✧ كُوتَالِي ج كَوَاتِلَةٌ
✧ Roman Catholic. G كَاثُولِيكِيّ ج كَاثُولِيكِيُّون
✧ The Greek Catholics. G كَاثُولِيك
To become a Catholic. ✧ كَثْلَكَ
To conceal (a secret). To restrain (anger). ✱ كَتَمَ o كَتْمًا وكِتْمَانًا , وكَتَّمَ واكْتَتَمَ ه
To breathe painfully (horse). – الرَّبْوَ

To multiply (words).   أَكْثَرَ القَوْل

To multiply; to be or   تَكَثَّر و♦ كَوْثَر
become many, numerous. To swarm.
To make a false show of wealth.

To speak much, to be   تَكَثَّر بالكَلَام
loquacious.

To vie in number. To increase,   تَكَاثَر
to become numerous.

To find a. th. numerous,   إِسْتَكْثَر ه وه
excessive.

To ask much of.   — مِن

♦ To thank a. o.   — بِخَيْرِو

Great number, abundance.   كِثْر وكَثْر

Main part, redundance.   كُثْر الشَّيْء

Spadix of palm-trees.   كِثْر وكَثَر

Great number, abundance.   كَثْرَة وكِثْرَة
Much. Plurality. Frequency.

Excess, redundance.   كُثْرَى

Increase, frequency.   تَكَاثُر

Often, frequently.   بِتَكَاثُر

Numerous. Frequent. ♦ Much.   كَثِير
Very. Often.

Numerous, many   رِجَال كَثِير وكَثِيرَة وكَثِيرُون
men.

Many women.   نِسَاء كَثِير وكَثِيرَة وكَثِيرَات

Crowd.   كِثَار وكُثَار

Much. Often.   كَثِيرًا

Liberal man.   كَيْثُر

More numerous. Oftener.   أَكْثَر

More than.   — مِن

The greatest part of men;   أَكْثَر النَّاس
most of people.

Rich, wealthy.   مُكْثِر

Loquacious,   (m. f.) مِكْثَار ومِكْثِير
babbler.

Crushed by debts.   مَكْثُور عَلَيْهِ

To be thick (dust).   ✷ كَوْثَر – تَكَوْثَر

Numerous, plentiful. Generous   كَوْثَر
man. River of Paradise.

To be overspread   ✷ كَثَم a كَثْمًا وكَثَم
with cream (milk).

To be affected with   – كُثُوعًا وكَثَع
diarrhea (sheep).

To be red and   – كَثَعًا وكُثُوعًا وكَثِعَ a كَثَعًا
swollen with blood (lip).

To cast forth scum (cooking-   – كَثَّع
pot). To be covered with herbage
(ground). To cicatrise (wound). To
grow (beard).

Seed of water-cress.   كَثْأَة

Scum. Cream of milk. Leek.   كَثْأَة وكَثَاة
Rocket.

To make up, to   ✷ كَثَب i o كَثْبًا ه
collect (things). To pour out (a
liquid).

To dart on.   كَثَب o كَثْبًا على

To come within reach   – وأَكْثَب ه
(game).

To be in small quantity.   كَثُب

To approach,   كَاثَب , وأَكْثَب ه ول ومِن
to draw near to a. o.

To give to a. o. a cupful   أَكْثَب ه
of milk.

To be heaped up. To be poured   إِنْكَثَب
out.

Proximity.   كَثَب

He shot the game   رَمَاهُ مِن كَثَب وعَن كَثَب
within reach.

Cupful of milk.   كُثْبَة ج كُثَب

Withers of a horse.   كَاثِبَة ج أَكْثَاب

Heaps of   كَثِيب ج أَكْثِبَة وكُثُب وكُثْبَان
sand.

To collect. To   ✷ كَثَح a كَثْحًا ه
scatter th.

To drive away the dust upon   – ه على
a. o. (wind).

To take off a. th. from.   – مِن

To lay a. th. bare, to   – وكَثَّحَه عَن
disclose.

To fight with (the sword).   تَكَاثَح ب

Small troop.   كَثْحَة

To be numerous, to   ✷ كَثُر o كَثْرَة
swarm. To happen often (event).

He did it frequently.   كَثُر ذَاكَ مِنْهُ

To exceed a. th.   كَثَر o كَثْرًا ه وه
in number.

To multiply, to increase   كَثَّر وأَكْثَر ه
a. th. To do a. th. often.

♦ Thank   كَثَّر خَيْرَك والله يُكَثِّر خَيْرَك
thee, thanks. lit : May God increase
thy property!

To vie with a. o. in number.   كَاثَر ه

To exceed a. o. in number.

To ask much water   – واسْتَكْثَر ه المَاء
from.

To bring much. To grow, to   أَكْثَر
put forth its spadix (palm-tree).
To be rich.

Scum, cream. كَشْفَة وكُشْفَة
Slime, mud. كَثْفَة
Lip red and swollen with blood. شَفَة كاثِعَة
Red-lipped. أَكْثَم
✱ كَثُف o كَثَافَة , وتَكَاثَف واسْتَكْثَف To thicken (liquid). To be coarse. To be tufty and thick (plants).
To thicken a. th. كَثَّف ه
To come within the reach of. أَكْثَف من
To find a. th. thick. إِسْتَكْثَف ه
Troop. كَثْف
Thickness, coarseness. كَثَافَة
Thick. Rough (man). كَثِيف
✱ كَثَل o كَثْلاً ه To make up (things).
Heap of corn. كُثْل
Tiller, anchor of a ship. كَوْثَل وكَوْثَلّ
✱ كَثَم o كَثْماً ه To pick up a. th. To follow the traces of. To craunch (a cucumber).
— ه عن To turn a. o. back from.
كَثِم a كَثَماً To draw near. To tarry.
كاثَم ه To accost, to haunt a. o.
أَكْثَم ه To be within reach (game).
— ه To fill up (a skin).
— في To retire in.
تَكَثَّم To be stupefied. To retire.
كَثِم وكاثِم Thick.
أَكْثَم Broad (road). Big-bellied. Surfeited.
✱ كَثَن — كُثْنَة Flower-basket.
✱ كَجَّ o كَجًّا To play.
كُجَّة Children's play.
✱ كُحّ — عَرَبِيّ كُحّ ج أَعْرَاب أَكْحَاح Genuine (Arab).
✱ كحب — كَحَّب To produce sour grapes (vine).
كَحْب Sour grapes. Podex.
كاحِب م كاحِبَة Numerous. Blazing (fire).
✱ كَحَص a كُحُوصاً To be effaced.
— وكَحَّص ه To efface a. th.
✧ كَحَف a كَحْفاً ه To tread down the heel of (a shoe).
✧ إِنْكَحَف To be trod down at the heel (shoes).
كُحُوف Limbs of the body.
✱ كَحَل o a كَحْلاً , وكَحَّل ه وه To anoint (the eyes) with collyrium.
كَحَل السُّهَادُ عَيْنَه Sleeplessness anointed his eye, i. e. he spent the night sleepless.
كَحِل a كَحَلاً To be barren (year).
— وأَكْحَل ه وه To smite (a tribe: drought).
— وأَكْحَل وتَكَحَّل واكْتَحَل واكْحَالّ بالنَّبات To become verdant (ground).
كَحِل a كَحَلاً To have black eyelids.
✧ كَحَّل ه To cement (a wall).
تَكَحَّل واكْتَحَل To anoint o.'s eyes with collyrium.
كَحْل Hard year.
كَحَل Brown colour of the eyelids.
كَحْلُ وكُحْلُ وكَحْلَة Sky, firmament.
صَرَّحَت كَحْلُ او الكُحْلُ او الكَحْلَة The sky is cloudless.
كُحْل Antimony. Collyrium. Great wealth.
كِحْل وكِحَال وكَحْلَة Amulet.
كِحَال Antimony-powder.
✧ كاحِل ج كَوَاحِل Ankle.
✧ كَحَّال Oculist. Cementer.
كَحِيل وكَحِيل (m. f.) م كَحِيلَة ج كَحَلَى Anointed with collyrium (eye). وكَحَائِل
كَحِيل ج كَحَائِل , وكَحْلَى Black-eyed. ✧ High-bred (horse).
كُحَيْل Pitch.
✧ كُحْلِيّ Azure-coloured.
أَكْحَل م كَحْلَاء ج كُحْل Black-eyed. Having brown eyelids; having painted eyelids.
الأَكْحَل Median vein of the arm.
كَحْلَاء White-bodied and black-eyed (ewe). Bugloss, echium (plant).
كُحَيْلَاء *Calendula arvensis*, marigold (*plant*).
مِكْحَل ومِكْحَال Pencil for collyrium.
مُكْحُلَة ومِكْحَلَة ج مَكَاحِل Collyrium-case, ▫ Rifle, gun.
▫ كَحْيَ وكَحْيا (for كَتْخُودَا) Steward.
✱ كَدّ وكَدّ o كَدًّا To toil, to exert o.'s self assiduously.
— ه To jade (a beast). ✧ To urge (a beast).
— ه To comb (the hair). To extract a. th. with the hand.
— ه ب To beckon to a. o. with (the fingers).
— واكْتَدّ واسْتَكَدّ ه To require much exertion from a. o. (work).

Dusty-coloured partridge. كُدْرِيّ وكُدَرِيّ
Dusky. أَكْدَر م كَدْرَاء ج كُدْر
Torrent. أَكْدَر
Dates mashed in milk. كُدَيْرَاء
To sneeze (beast). ✲ كَدَس i كَدْسًا وكُدَاسًا
To urge (a beast). — ه
To heap up (spikes). — وكَدَّس ه
To press together (horses). كَدَّس وتَكَدَّس
To walk quickly. To walk heavily in moving the shoulders (beasts). تَكَدَّس
Sneezing of beasts. كَدْسَة وكُدَاس
كُدْس ج أَكْدَاس, وكُدَّاس ج كَدَادِيس, وكُدَاسَة
Heap of herbage. و✧ كَدِيس ومَكْدَس
Sneezing (beast). كَادِس ج كَوَادِس
To scratch a. o. To strike a. o. with a sword. ✧ To bite a. o. (horse, mule). ✲ كَدَش i كَدْشًا ه
To seek to earn for (o.'s family). — ل
To obtain (a gift from). — وأَكْدَش ه من
To degenerate (horse). To lose beauty, freshness. ✧ كَدَّش
Bite of a horse. كَدْشَة
Nag, hackney, jade. ✧ كَدِيش ج كُدْش
To drive a. o. or a. th. back. ✲ كَدَع a كَدْعًا ه وه
Trampling of cattle. ✲ كَدْفَة
To trample upon the ground (cattle). أَكْدَف
To bite with the edge of the teeth. To pursue (game). ✲ كَدَم o i كَدْمًا ه وه
He searched the thing in the wrong place. — في غير مَكْدَم
To crop (herbage : cattle). كَادَم ه
To be in bonds (captive). أُكْدِم
Bite. Mark. كَدْمَة
Remainder of food in a vessel. كُدَامَة
Place, mark of a bite. مَكْدَم
✧ To couple (oxen) to a plough. ✲ كَدَن o كَدْنًا ه
To wrap o.'s self in (clothes). — ب
Woman-litter. Camel-saddle. Curtain of a tent. كِدْن وكِدْن ج كُدُون
Camel-rope. كِدَان
Grease. Camel's hump. كِدْنَة
✧ One day's work. كَدْنَة
Mixed breed of men and beasts. كَدَانَة

To repel a. o. violently. كَدَّ ه
To be avaricious. أَكَدَّ واكْتَدَّ
To be wearied, harassed. تَكَدَّد
Toil, exertion. Mortar. كَدّ
Rugged soil. كِدَّة وكَدِيد
Remainder of food in a vessel. كُدَادَة
Laborious. Toilsome (work). كَدُود
Ground trodden upon. Pounded salt. Rugged land. كَدِيد
Remains of a pasturage. أَكِدَّة
Separate parties. قوم أَكْدَاد وأَكَادِيد
Comb. مِكَدّ
To be blasted by cold (plant). ✲ كَدَأَ وكَدِئَ a كَدْأً وكُدُوءًا
To blast (the plants : cold). كَدَأَ وكَدَّأَ ه
Slow, unproductive ground. كَادِئَة
White spot on the nails. ✲ كَذَب وكَدِب وكَدَب وكُدُب
To toil, to exert o.'s self in. ✧ To walk painfully. ✲ كَدَح a كَدْحًا في
To scratch (the face). To dress (the hair). — وكَدَّح ه
To earn for (o.'s family). كَدَح واكْتَدَح ل
To be scratched (skin). تَكَدَّح
Scratch. كَدْح ج كُدُوح
✲ كَدُر o كَدَارَةً وكَدِر a كَدَرًا وكَدَارَةً وكُدُورًا وكُدُورَةً وكُدْرَةً
To be turbid (liquid). To be dead (colour).
To pour out (water). كَدَر o كَدْرًا ه
To trouble a. o. — على فُلان
To be distressful (life) كَدِر
To render a. th. turbid. كَدَّر ه
To trouble a. o. — ه وعَيْشَهُ
To be troubled. To fade away. تَكَدَّر واكْدَرّ
To experience trials. To be wearied. تَكَدَّر وتَكَدَّر عَيْشُهُ
To alight (bird). To be scattered (stars). إِنْكَدَر
To hurry in (walk). — في
To dart upon. — على
Turbidness. Trouble, weariness. كَدَر
Dead colour. كُدْرَة
Slime ; green moss. كُدْرَة
Sheaf of corn-crops. كُدْرَة ج كُدَر
Light cloud. — وكُدْرِيّ وكُدَارِيّ
Troublesome. Turbid. كَدْر وكَدِر وكَدِير

كَدِين م كَدِينَة Fleshy, plump.
* كَوْدَن وكَوْدَنِيّ ج كَوَادِن Hackney, of mixed breed (horse).
* كَدَه a كَدْهًا, وكَدَّه ة وه To bruise a. o. To break a. th. To part (the hair). To crush a. o. (cares).
كَدَه عَلَى فُلَانٍ To overcome a. o.
تَكَدَّه To be broken.
كَده ج كُدُوه Contusion.
مَكْدُوه Sad.
* كَدَا o كَدْوًا وكُدُوًّا To be unproductive (ground). To be unpromising (corn-crops).
— كِدَاء ه To cut off a. th.
كَدِيَ a كَدًى ب To be choked by (a bone).
كَدِيَ To have an indigestion of milk (young camel). To turn round and vomit (dog).
* كَدَى i كَدْيًا ة To detain a. o.
— وأَكْدَى To give little.
كَدَّى تَكْدِيَة To beg alms.
أَكْدَى To be exhausted (mine). To reach a hard ground by digging.
سَأَلَهُ فَأَكْدَى He has not answered his request.
أَكْدَى ة عن To prevent a. o. from.
تَكَدَّى To beg alms.
كَدٍ وكَدِيّ Inodorous (musk).
كُدْيَة ج كُدًى Tuff. Large rock.
— وكَدَاة وكَدَايَة Heap of earth, of wheat.
كُدْيَة Beggary.
كُدْيَة وكَادٍ Adversity.
مُكَدٍّ م مُكَدِّيَة Beggar.
* كَذَّ o كَذًّا To be rough to the hand.
أَكَذَّ To walk upon pumice-stones.
كَذَّان Soft stone; tufa-stone, pumice-stone.
* كَذَا ر كَذِي So, such.
كَذَاكَ وهٰكَذَا Thus, in such a wise.
بِمَكَانِ كَذَا وكَذَا In such a place.
قَبَضْتُ كَذَا وكَذَا دِرْهَمًا I have cashed so many coins.
* كَذَبَ i كَذِبًا وكَذْبًا و كِذْبَةً وكِذَابًا و كِذَّابًا To lie, to say a falsehood. To be wrong (senses, opinion). To be cut off (milk).
— ة To deceive a. o. (sight). To disappoint the expectation of.
كُذِبَ To be falsely accused.
كَذَّبَ وأَكْذَبَ ة To accuse a. o. of lying. To find a. o. a liar.
— تَكْذِيبًا وكِذَّابًا ب To deny a. th.
كَذَّبَ وأَكْذَبَ نَفْسَهُ To bespeak o.'s self.
مَا كَذَّبَ أَنْ يَفْعَل He has not desisted from doing.
كَذَّبَ عَنِ القِتَال He shrank from fight.
كَذَّبَ عَنَّا الحَرّ Heat has abated.
— وكَاذَبَ مُكَاذَبَةً وكِذَابًا ة To give the lie to a. o.; to contradict a. o.
أَكْذَبَ ة To make a. o. to lie. To manifest the lie of.
تَكَذَّبَ To affect lying.
— ة To esteem a. o. to be a liar.
تَكَاذَبَ To lie to o. another.
إِسْتَكْذَبَ ة To accuse a. o. of lying, to deem a. o. a liar.
كِذْب وكَذِب وكِذَاب وكَذْبَى وكِذْبَان, وأُكْذُوبَة
ج أَكَاذِيب Lie, falsehood.
كَاذِب ج كُذْب وكُذَّاب وكَذَبَة, وكَذُوب ج
كُذُب, وكَذْبَان وكَيْذَبَان وكَيْذُبَان Liar; false, vain (news).
كَذُوب وكَذُوبَة The soul. Liar.
كَاذِبَة ج كَاذِبَات وكَوَاذِب Lie, falsehood.
كَذَّاب وكِذْبَة وكَذُوبَة وتِكِذَّاب Impostor, wont to lie.
مَكْذَبَة ومَكْذُبَة ج مَكَاذِب, ومَكْذُوب
ومَكْذُوبَة ج مَكَاذِيب Lie.
تَكَاذِيب Lies.
* كَرَّ o كُرُورًا To come back. To follow by turns (night and day). ✧ To be wound (thread).
— o كَرًّا ة To bring back (a horse).
— o كَرًّا وكُرُورًا وتَكْرَارًا على To return to the charge upon.
يَفِرّ ويَكِرّ كَرًّا He wheels round in battle.
كَرَّ a كَرِيرًا To rattle (chest).
كَرَّرَ تَكْرِيرًا وتَكْرَارًا وتَكِرَّة ه To repeat a. th. ✧ To refine a. th.
تَكَرَّرَ To be repeated. ✧ To be refined.
كَرّ وكَرَّة Attack, charge.
كَرّ ج كُرُور وكِرَار Rope used as a ladder. Cable.
— وكُرّ ج كِرَار Well.
كُرّ ج أَكْرَار وكُرُور Carpet, mat.
كُرّ ج كِرَار Measure equal to 6 ass-loads. ✧ Ass.
كَرَّة ج كَرَّات Charge in war. Time,

repetition of an action. ✧ One hundred thousand.
Globe, sphere, ball. ✧ كُرَة (for كُرّة) ج كُرَات
✧ Cellar, pantry. كِرَار وكِلَار
Cowry used as an amulet. كِرَار
Returning to fight. كَرَّار ومِكَرّ
▫ Bobbin, reel. كَرَّارِيَّة
Succession of ages. كُرُور الدُّهُور
Rattle; sound in the throat. كَرِير
Repetition. ✧ Refinement of sugar. تَكْرَار وتَكْرِير
At repeated times. تَكْرَارًا
Place of attack. مَكَرّ
To laugh loudly and repeatedly. ✧ To murmur (water). To rumble (intestines). ✻ كَرْكَرَ
To pile up (things) To heap up and drive the clouds (wind). To repeat a. th. To turn (the mill-stone). — ه
To detain, to withhold a. o. — ه
To remove a. th. from. — ه عن
To call (hens). — ب
To hover (bird, cloud). تَكَرْكَرَ
To bestir o.'s self in (an affair). — في
Callosity on the breast of camels. كِرْكِرَة ج كَرَاكِر
✧ Borborigmus. كَرْكَرَة
To twist (a rope). ✻ كَرَبَ o كَرْبًا ه
To tighten (the shackles) of. — ه على
To distress, to grieve a. o. (affair). To load (a beast). ✧ To overwork a. o. — ه
To put a rope to (a bucket). — وكَرَّبَ وأَكْرَبَ ه
To be near setting (sun). To die away (fire). كَرَبَ o كُرُوبًا
To be near doing. كَرَبَ يَفْعَل
To expand (dough) with a rolling-pin. To eat dates. — وكَرَّبَ
To plough (the ground) before (sowing). — كَرْبًا و كِرَابًا ه ل
To draw near to. كَارَبَ ه
To hurry in. أَكْرَبَ في
To fill up (a skin). — ه
To pick (dates) nearest to the stem. تَكَرَّبَ ه
To be surfeited. ✧ إِنْكَرَبَ
To be sad. إِكْتَرَبَ

Stump of a palm-branch. Rope of a bucket. كَرَب
Anxiety, grief. كَرْب ج كُرُوب، وكُرْبَة ج كُرَب
✧ Indigestion. كُرْبَة
Beam in which the head of a tent-pole is inserted. كَرَبَة ج كَرَب
Adversity. كَرَابَة ، وكَرِيبَة ج كَرَائِب
Dates nearest to the stem of a palm-tree. كُرَابَة وكُرَابَة ج أَكْرِبَة
Cherubim; Archangels. H كَرُوب وكَارُوبِيم
Rolling-pin. كَرِيب
Sad. كَرِيب ومَكْرُوب
Promptitude, haste. إِكْرَاب
Tight. Sinewy (joint). Strong (horse). مُكْرَب
To shackle, to fetter a. o. ✧ كَرْبَجَ ه
✧ To contract (joints). ✧ كَرْبَجَ وتَكَرْبَجَ
Greengrocer-shop. P كُرْبَج ج كَرَابِج
Horse-whip, bastinado. P كِرْبَاج ج كَرَابِيج
Cotton-cloth. ✻ كِرْبَاس ج كَرَابِيس
To be impeded in walk. ✻ كَرْبَشَ
To be contracted, wrinkled. تَكَرْبَشَ
To walk in the mud. ✻ كَرْبَلَ
To mix a. th. with. — ه ب
To cleanse (wheat). — ه
Carder for cotton. ✧ Raft-frame. كِرْبَال ج كَرَابِيل
He came on sluggishly. جاء يَمْشِي مُكَرْبَلًا
Complete year. ✻ كَرِت — سَنَة كَرِيت
To decant. To transfuse a. th. ✧ كَرَّتَ ه (for كَلَّتَ ه)
To be involved in another's business. ✻ كَرْتَمَ
To be contracted (hand). ✧ تَكَرْتَمَ
Contraction. ✧ كِرْتَاء
To make quarantine. ✧ كَرْتَنَ
Quarantine. Is كَرَنْتِينَة
Pasteboard. Fs كَرْتُون ج كَرَاتِين
Candia (Island of). ✻ كِرِيت او كِرِيد
To oppress a. o. (grief). ✻ كَرَثَ i o كَرْثًا، وأَكْرَثَ ه
To break (rope). إِنْكَرَثَ
To mind a. th. إِكْتَرَثَ ل
I do not mind him. ما أَكْتَرِثُ لَهُ
Leek. كُرَّاث وكَرَّاث (un. كُرَّاثَة وكَرَّاثَة)

كَارِثٌ م كَارِثَةٌ ج كَوَارِثُ Grievous. Grief. Calamity.
كَرِيثٌ Hard (affair).
إِنَّهُ لَكَرِيثُ الأَمْرِ He shrinks from the affair.
✻ كَرِجَ a كَرَجًا, وكَرِجَ وأَكْرَجَ وتَكَرَّجَ To become musty (bread).
✧ كَرِجَ o كَرْجًا To whirl round a bridge (water). To trot, to roll down. To read readily (child).
✧ كَرْجٌ Reading without spelling.
كَرْجٌ (un. كُرْجِيٌّ) The Georgians.
كُرَّجٌ Colt.
— ج كَرَارِجُ Wooden horse.
✻ كِرْجٌ ج أَكْرَاجٌ Monk's cell.
✻ كَرَخَ a كَرْخًا ه إلى و To bring (water) to.
P كَرْخَانَةٌ ج كَرَاخِين Manufactory.
✧ Silk-manufactory.
✻ كَرَدَ o كَرْدًا ه To urge (a beast). To drive away (the enemy).
— ه To cut a. th.
كَارَدَ ه To expel a. o.
كَرْدٌ Base of the neck.
كُرْدٌ وأَكْرَادٌ (un. كُرْدِيٌّ) The Kurds (people of Asia).
P كَرْدَانٌ ✧ Necklace.
✻ كَرْدَحَ To run with short steps.
تَكَرْدَحَ To run fast. To roll down.
كَرْدَحَةٌ Quick run with short steps.
كَرْدَاحٌ Running swiftly.
P كَرْدَارٌ Construction, plantation on the ground of a neighbour.
✻ كَرْدَسَ To shuffle off.
— ه To divide (horsemen) into squadrons.
— ه To tie up a. th. ✧ To heap up (sheaves).
كُرْدِسَ To be shackled.
تَكَرْدَسَ To be short and stout.
كُرْدُوسَةٌ ج كَرَادِيسُ وكَرَادِسُ Squadron of cavalry. Bone covered with meat. ✧ Heap of spikes.
✻ كَرْدَمَ To run like a dwarf.
تَكَرْدَمَ To run away from fear.
كَرْدَمٌ, وكُرْدُومٌ ج كَرَادِيمُ Dwarf.
✻ كَرَزَ i كُرُوزًا إلى To seek refuge at. To hide o.'s self in. To lean towards.
كَرَزَ i ✧ كَرْزًا To preach the Gospel.
كَرَّزَ To mew (falcon).
كَارَزَ إلى To repair to and conceal o.'s self in.
— عن فلان To escape from.
كُرْزٌ ج كِرَزَةٌ Shepherd's bag.
✧ كَرْزٌ وكِرَازَةٌ Sermon.
T كَرَزٌ (un. كَرَزَةٌ) Cherry. Cherry-tree.
كُرَّزٌ ج كَرَارِزَةٌ Hawk, falcon.
كُرَّزٌ في صِنَاعَتِهِ Skilled in his work.
كُرَّزٌ وكُرَّزِيٌّ ومُكَرَّزٌ Vile, contemptible.
كُرَازٌ ج كِرْزَانٌ, وكُرَازٌ Bottle, flask.
كُرَازٌ ج كَرَارِيزُ Ram carrying the shepherd's bag Ram carrying the bell.
كَرِيزٌ Sour cheese.
✧ كَارِزٌ وكَارُوزٌ Preacher.
✧ كَرَسَ i كَرْسًا To cleanse (a stable).
✻ كَرَّسَ ه To found (a building). ✧ To consecrate (a church).
أَكْرَسَ To be defiled with urine and dung.
أَكْرَسَ ه To impark, to inclose (kids).
تَكَرَّسَ To be strongly laid (foundation). ✧ To be consecrated (church).
إِنْكَرَسَ على To lean upon.
— في To enter and conceal in.
كِرْسٌ ج أَكْرَاسٌ وجج أَكَارِسُ وأَكَارِيسُ Dry dung mixed with urine. Contiguous houses. Enclosure for kids. Origin.
كُرَّاسَةٌ ج كُرَّاسٌ وكَرَارِيسُ Quire. Pamphlet.
كُرْسِيٌّ ج كَرَاسِيُّ وكَرَاسٍ Chair, throne. Learning. Power of God.
— المَلِكِ Throne of a king. Capital-town.
— الأُسْقُفِ Episcopal seat.
هُوَ من أهل الكُرْسِيِّ He is a learned man.
كِرْيَاسٌ ج كَرَايِيسُ Privy on the upper-floor.
كُرَّوسٌ Big-headed.
كُرُّوسَةٌ ج كُرُّوسَاتٌ Carriage, coach.
مُكَرَّسٌ ومُكَرْكَسٌ Formed of gems intercalated with larger beads (necklace).
P كَرَسْتَةٌ Materials.
✧ كَرْسَحَ ه To cripple a. o.
✧ تَكَرْسَحَ To be crippled.
✻ كُرْسُوعٌ ج كَرَاسِيعُ Bone of the wrist.

To find rain-water. أَكْرَع
To offer the side to the (hunter : ة — game).
To perform ablutions. تَكَرَّع
Rain-water. Thinness of the shank. كَرَع
Vile, contemptible. (s. pl.) —
Trotters of sheep, oxen. Shank. كُرَاع ج أَكْرُع وجج أَكَارِع
Extremity; top of a mountain. — ج كِرْعَان
Horses, mules. الكُرَاع
The farthest limits of the world. أَكَارِع الأَرْض
Seller of trotters. كُرَاعِيّ
Leaning on water (tree). كَارِع وكَرِيع
Palm-treen upowater. كَارِعَة ج كَارِعَات
Having thin shanks. أَكْرَع
Strong-legged (horse) مُكْرَع القَوَائِم
To sniff and raise the head (ass). ✲ كَرَف ٥ كَرْفًا, وأَكْرَف
To froth forth (pot). ✲ كَرْفَا
Lofty clouds heaped up. كِرْفِئ
Ceratin-tree. كِرْفِئَة
To blaspheme religion. ✧ كَرَفَت بِالدِّين
To drop; to upset. To roll a. th. along. — ة وه
To roll down. ✧ تَكَرْفَت
To be impeded in walk. ✲ كَرْفَس
To be deformed. تَكَرْفَس
Celery (kitchen vegetable). كَرَفْس
Water-parsnip. كَرَفْس المَاء
Alambic. ▫ Calico. ✧ كَرَكَة ج كَرَكَات
▫ Fur-coat, pelisse. كُرْك T
Ardea virgo, Numidian crane. ✲ كُرْكِيّ ج كَرَاكِيّ
Pike-fish. كَرَاكِيّ
Dredging-machine. ▫ كَرَاكَة
✧ Hard labour, galleys. ▫ Shovel. كُورَك وكُرِيك T
✧ To disturb, to disorder a. th. ✧ كَرْكَب ه وة
To be disturbed, disordered. تَكَرْكَب
Disturbance, disorder. Imbroglio. ✧ كَرْكَبَة
Rhinoceros. كَرْكَدَّن وكَرْكَدَن P
Sea-unicorn, narwhal. كَرْكَدَان بَحْرِي
To repel a. o. ✲ كَرْكَس ه
To tie (a beast). — ة

To strike a. o. on the wrist-bone. كَرْسَم ة
To put cotton into (an inkstand). ✲ كَرْسَف ه
To tie. To hock (a beast). — ة
Cotton. كُرْسُف وكُرْسُوف
Flake of cotton for inkstands. كُرْسُفَة وكُرْسُوفَة
Bitter vetch. Sort of chick-peas. ✲ كرسن — كِرْسِنَّة و✧ كِرْسِنَّة
To be wrinkled (skin). ✲ كَرِش a كَرَشًا
To contract the face. To prepare a haggis. كَرَّش
To become big-bellied. كَرِش و✧ أَكْرَش
To be wrinkled, contracted (face). تَكَرَّش
To become large in the stomach (kid). To begin to eat (kid). إِسْتَكْرَش
Stomach of ruminants. ✧ Paunch. كِرْش وكَرِش ج كُرُوش
Household, companions of a man. — الرَّجُل
Astragalus, milk-vetch. — الأَرْنَب
Vesicle, receptacle for ambergris. — العَنْبَر
Plant of the class *Pentandria*. كِرْش وكَرْش
✧ Stuff of thin silk; crape. كَرِيشَة
✧ Beam, joist of a floor. كَرِيشَة ج كَرِيشَات
Kind of haggis. Tripe. مُكَرَّشَة
Big-bellied. مُكَرِّش ومَكْرُوش
Arabic written with Syriac characters. كَرْشُونِيّ S
To pound (cheese). ✲ كَرَص i كَرْصًا ه
To mix (cheese) with. — ه ب
To eat cheese. كَرَّص
To heap up a. th. إِكْتَرَص ه
Sour cheese mixed with herbs. كَرِيص
Milking-vessel. مِكْرَص
To discredit a. o. ✲ كَرَظ o كَرْظًا في
To lean upon a (vessel) for drinking. To sip in. ✲ كَرَع وكَرِع a كَرْعًا وكُرُوعًا في
To wound a. o. on the shank. كَرَع a كَرْعًا ة
To be thin in the shank. To be thin (shank). To be of low condition. To be fond of trotters. كَرِع a كَرَعًا

The two noble things *i. e.*: war and the pilgrimage to Mecca. الكَرِيمَان
Precious thing. Any noble part of the body. Noble-born lady. ✧ Daughter. كَرِيمَة ج كِرَام وكَرَائِم وكَرِيمَات
The two eyes. الكَرِيمَتَان
◘ Yellow amber. كَارِم
Noble, generous. كُرَّام ج كُرَّامُون
Very generous. كُرَّام وكُرَّامَة ومِكْرَام
O bountiful man! يا مَكْرُمَان
Vine-dresser. كَرَّام
Noble, generous qualities. مَكْرَم ومَكْرُمَة ج مَكَارِم
Noble action. مَكْرُم ومَكْرُمَة ج مَكَارِم
Fertile land. أَرْض مَكْرَمَة
Moire, kind of watered silk. ✧ كَرَمْسُوت
Cabbage, beet. Dates with milk. ✱ كُرُنْب وكَرَنْب
Gourd used as a vessel. كِرْنِيب ج كَرَانِيب
✧ Skeleton; emaciated man. كَرْنِيبَة
Food made with cabbage. كُرُنْبِيَّة
To be wrinkled (skin). ✧ كَرْنَش (*for* كَرِش)
To cut off the stump of a branch. ✱ كَرْنَف ﻫ
Stump of a branch. كُرْنَاف ج كَرَانِيف
Big (nose). مُكَرْنِف
✱ كَرِه a كَرْهًا وكُرْهًا وكَرَاهَة وكَرَاهِيَة
To disprove, to dislike a. th. ومَكْرَهَة ﻫ
To be loathsome. كَرُه o كَرَاهَة وكَرَاهِيَة
To disgust a. o. with. كَرَّه ﻫ ه وه الى
To compel a. o. to. أَكْرَه ه على
To express dislike at. تَكَرَّه وتَكَارَه ﻫ
To find a. th. loathsome. إِسْتَكْرَه ﻫ
Aversion, disgust. كَرْه وكُرْه وكَرَاهَة وكَرَاهِيَة
كَرْهًا وعلى كُرْهٍ وإِكْرَاهًا وعلى إِكْرَاهٍ وعلى
Unwillingly; in spite of. كَرَاهِيَة
Hateful, disliked. كَرِه وكَرِيه
Disagreeable thing. War, adversity. كَرِيهَة ج كَرَائِه
Cutting sword. ذُو الكَرِيهَة
The horrors of war. الكَرَائِه
Dislike; disliked things. Calamities. مَكْرَهَة ومَكْرُهَة ج مَكَارِه
Adversity. مَكْرُوهَة

Curcuma, Indian saffron. ✱ كُرْكُم
P Spinel ruby. كَرْكَند
To be productive (earth). To be generous (man). To be precious, valuable. To yield rain (clouds). ✱ كَرُم o كَرَمًا وكَرَامَة وكَرَمَة
To overcome a. o. in generosity. كَرَم o كَرْمًا ه
To prize (a horse). كَرَّم تَكْرِيمًا وتَكْرِمَة، وأَكْرَم ه
To declare a. o. to be generous. To show regard to. كَرَّم ه
To show greater regard to a. o. than. — ه على
How generous he is to me! ما أَكْرَمَهُ لي
To vie in generosity with. كَارَم ه
To have generous children. To entertain guests bountifully. أَكْرَم
To show regard to. — ه
✧ Willingly, for your sake. تُكْرَم
To be bountiful. أَكْرَم وتَكَرَّم
To keep aloof from (disgraceful actions). تَكَرَّم وتَكَارَم عن
To seek a. th. noble, precious. إِسْتَكْرَم
Nobleness of character. Generosity. كَرَم
Generous. Fertile (land). Good quality of a horse. (*m. f. s. pl.*) كَرَم
Vine. (*un.* كَرْمَة) كَرْم ج كُرُوم
✧ Orpine, roseplant. بَقْلَة الكَرْم
Bryony (*plant*). الكَرْمَة البَيْضَاء
Regard, consideration. Thaumaturgy. كَرَامَة
For the love and regard due to. Willingly. حُبًّا وكَرَامَة ل
For thy sake. كَرْمًا وكُرْمَة وكُرْمَى وكُرْمَانًا لك
Regard shown. Hearty welcome to a guest. إِكْرَام
For thy sake. إِكْرَامًا لك و✧ كِرْمًا لك
Noble action. أُكْرُومَة
Pillow of honor. تَكْرِمَة
كَرِيم (*opp. to* لَئِيم) ج كِرَام وكُرَمَاء
Noble. Generous. The Generous (God). Thorough-bred (horse). Excellent (ground). Valuable. Precious (store). Kind (face). ✧ Turtle-dove.
The glorious face of God. وَجْهُ اللهِ الكَرِيم

Niggardly, uncompliant. كَزّ اليَدَيْن
Avarice. كُزَز
Shivering from cold. كُزاز وكُزّاز
Coriander (*plant*). ✲ كُزْبَرَة وكُزْبُرَة وكَزْبَرَة وكُسْبُرَة
Capillary (*plant*). — البِئْر
Fumitory (*plant*). — الحَمام
✧ Chervil (*plant*). — خَضْراء
✧ Hair-moss, golden maiden-hair (*plant*). — الصَّخْر
✧ Eye-glass, quizzing-glass. كُوزْلُك T_E
To craunch (a fruit). ✲ كَزَم o كَزْمًا ه
To be short-handed. كَزِم a كَزَمًا
To contract (the fingers: cold). كَزَّم ه
To be contracted. أَكْزَم
To be satiated with. — عن
To craunch (fruits). تَكَزَّم ه
Avarice. Gluttony. Smallness of the nose, of the fingers. كَزَم
Fearful, shy. كَزِم م كَزِمَة
Short-nosed. Short (hand). أَكْزَم م كَزْماء ج كُزْم
Avaricious. أَكْزَم البَنان
To bray, to grind a. th. ✲ كَسَّ o كَسًّا ه
To have small teeth. — a كَسَسًا
To take the utmost care in. تَكَسَّس في
Date-wine. Dry and beaten meat. كَسِيس
Bruised, pounded. — ومَكْسُوس
Having small teeth. أَكَسّ م كَسّاء ج كُسّ
To pound, to bray a. th. ✲ كَسْكَس ه
✧ To mumble. ◘ To recoil.
Gruel of coarse semolina. كُسْكُس
To pursue a. o. closely. ✲ كَسَأ a كَسْأً ه
To urge (a beast) in the track of others. To overcome a. o. in a quarrel.
Portion of the night. كِسْءٌ مِن اللَّيل
Hinder part; latter part *Pl.* Traces. كُسْء وكُسُوء ج أَكْساء
He fell down on the back of his neck. رَكِبَ كُسْأَهُ
To earn, to gain a. th. To acquire (knowledge). ✲ كَسَب i كَسْبًا, وتَكَسَّب, واكْتَسَب ه
To make a. o. to acquire a. th. — وكَسَّب وأَكْسَب ه ه
To seek to earn. ✧ To progress. تَكَسَّب

To round a. th. To repeat a. th. To line (a well) with wood. To dig (the earth). ✲ كَرَا o كَرْوًا ه
To run swiftly. — وكَرَى i كَرْيًا
To play at (ball). — وكَرَى i كَرْيًا ب
To dig (a canal). كَرَى i كَرْيًا ه
To nap. To have thin and parted legs. كَرِيَ a كَرًى
To hire (a beast, a house) to. كَارَى مُكاراة وكِراء, وأَكْرَى ه ه وه
✧ To be an ass-hirer. كَارَى
To increase. To decrease. To keep sacred vigils. أَكْرَى إِكْراء
To postpone (an action). To prolong (a discourse). To let (a house). — ه
To sleep. تَكَرَّى
To hire (a beast, a house). تَكارَى واكْتَرَى واسْتَكْرَى ه
Drowsiness. Leanness of the legs. كَرًى
Hire. كَرْو وكُرُو وكَرْوَة
Rent. Wages. Hire. كِراء وكِرْوَة
✧ Mule's load.
Sphere, ball. كُرَة ج كُرات وكُرًى وكُرِين وكِرِين
The celestial sphere. — الكَواكِب
The terrestrial globe. — الأَرض
Hirer. كَرِيّ ج أَكْرِياء
Slumbering. — وكَرٍ وكَرْيان
Spherical, globular. كُرِيّ وكُرَوِيّ
Thin (leg). Thin-legged. أَكْرَى م كَرْواء
Kind of partridge. كَرَوان م كَرَوانة ج كِرْوان وكَرَاوِين
Caraway-seed. G كَرَوْيا وكَرَوْياء وكَراوِيا ✧
Muleteer. Hirer of asses. مُكارٍ ج مُكارُون و✧ مُكارِيّة
Walking slowly (camel). المُكْرِي
To become dried, tough. ✲ كَزَّ o كَزازَة وكُزُوزَة, واكْتَزّ
✧ To dislike a. th. — مِن
✧ To gnash the teeth. — على أَسْنانِهِ
To contract a. th. كَزَّ o كَزًّا ه
To shrink from cold. كُزَّ
To afflict a. o. with cold (God). أَكَزَّ ه
To be niggardly. إِكْتَزّ
Dry, tough. Ugly (face). Hard (gold). كَزّ ج كُزّ
Stiff (bow). كَزَّة

To fold (a pillow). To inflect (a letter) with kasra. To annul (a will). To allay (thirst).
✧ To break a journey. كَسَرَ في السَّفَر
✧ To break fast. — الصَّفْرَة
He hindered him from his design. — ه عَن مُرَادِهِ
He contracted the eyes. — مِن طَرْفِهِ
To alight in folding the wings (bird). كَسَرَ i كَسْرًا وكُسُورًا
The wind has abated. كَسَرَت الرِّيحُ
To break to pieces. To crease a. th. (*Gram*). To use an irregular (plural). كَسَّرَ ه
✧ To break, to humble. a. o. كَسَّرَ ه
To have a defective pronunciation. كَسَّرَ في الكَلَام
To bargain in a sale. ✧ كَاسَرَ في البَيْع
To be broken to pieces. To be crumbed (pie). To be wrinkled, folded. ✧ To be broken, civilised. تَكَسَّرَ
To be broken. To be routed (army). To abate (heat). ✧ To be bankrupt. إِنْكَسَرَ
To break a. th. إِكْتَسَرَ ه
كَسْر (*un.* كَسْرَة) ج كُسُور وكُسُورَات
Fraction (of a number). Fold.
un. كِسْر وكَسْر ج كُسُور وأَكْسَار (كِسْرَة
Limb. Piece (of bread). ج كِسْرَات)
Skirt of a tent.
Windings, ravines of the valleys. كُسُور الأَوْدِيَة
Broken ground. أَرْض ذَات كُسُور
Kosroes, surname of the Persian kings. P كِسْرَى ج أَكَاسِرَة وأَكَاسِر
Fragments, particles. كُسَار وكُسَارَة
✧ Ground freshly tilled. كُسَارَة
Broken. Having a foot broken (camel). كَسِير ج كَسْرَى وكَسَارَى
Elixir. Alchimia. إِكْسِير
Rout. ✧ Bankruptcy. إِنْكِسَار
Area of a circle. تَكْسِير
Irregular plural. جَمْعُ التَّكْسِير وجَمْع مُكَسَّر
Eagle. Saxifrage (*plant*). كَاسِر ج كُسَّر
Camels breaking their saddles. Flesh-eating beasts. الكَوَاسِر
Place of fracture. Intrinsic state. مَكْسِر ج مَكَاسِر

To make (a slave) to earn. ه أَسْتَكْسَبَ
Earning, benefit. كَسْب
Sustenance, earning. كِسْبَة
Dregs of oil. كُسْب
Acquired (science). إِكْتِسَابِيّ
Earning, winner. كَاسِب و✧ كَسْبَان
Pl. Limbs of the body. كَاسِبَة ج كَوَاسِب
Wolf. Hunting-bitch. كَسَاب
Gaining much. كَسُوب
Plant alike to the carthamus. كَشُوب
Hound. كُسَيْب
Gain, profit. مَكْسَب ومَكْسِب ومَكْسِبَة ج مَكَاسِب
✲ Coriander. (*for* كُزْبَرَة) كُسْبُرَة
✧ Thimble. P كُسْتُبَان
✧ Watch-chain. T كُسْتَك ج كَسَاتِك
Chestnut. ✧ كَسْتَنَا
Scanty-bearded. ✲ كَسَج — كَوْسَج
Xyphias, sword-fish. To have a scarce beard. P كَوْسَج
To sweep (a house). To sweep a. th. away (wind). To carry away. ✧ To lop (a tree). ✲ كَسَحَ a كَسْحًا ه
To be crippled in the legs. كَسِحَ a كَسَحًا
To ill-treat a. o. كَاسَحَ ه
What an untractable man! مَا أَكْسَحَهُ
To be swept. إِنْكَسَحَ
To sweep off (property). إِكْتَسَحَ ه
Impotence of the limbs; lameness. كَسَح
✧ Rachitis, rickets. كُسَاح
Sweepings. Crippleness. كُسَاحَة
Disappointing man. كُسَح
Weak-handed. Impotent. كَسِيح وكَسِيح وكَسْحَان
Cripple. Lame. أَكْسَح ج كُسْحَان
Broom. مِكْسَحَة
To be unsaleable (goods). ✲ كَسَدَ وكَسُدَ o كَسَادًا وكُسُودًا
To be dull (market). — وأَكْسَدَ
To have unsaleable goods. أَكْسَدَ
Dullness of a market. كَسَاد وكُسُود
Dull (market). كَاسِد وأَكْسَد
Unsaleable (goods). Worthless (thing). كَاسِد وكَسِيد
To loiter. ✧ كَسْدَر
To break off a. th. To rout (an army). To retail (goods). ✲ كَسَرَ i كَسْرًا ه

كَيْسُوم ج أَكَايِسِم, وأَكْسُوم ج أَكَايِسِم
Luxuriant (garden).
Numerous horses. خَيْل أَكَايِسِم
To walk with short steps. ✱ كَسْمَل
To clothe a. o. with. ✱ كَسَا o كَسْوًا, وأَكْسَى ه ه
To clothe o.'s self in. كَسِيَ a وكَسِيَ كَسًا, وتَكَسَّى ب
To vie in glory with. كَاسَى ه
To be clothed. إِكْتَسَى
To be clad with (plants: ground). — ب
To ask clothes from. إِسْتَكْسَى ه
Glory. كَسَاء
Garment. كِسَاء ج أَكْسِيَة
Set of clothes. ✧ Carpet covering the Caaba. كِسْوَة ج كُسًى وكِسًى وكِسَاوِر
Clothed better. Giving more clothes. أَكْسَى
To produce a rustling (serpent). ✧ To be stern-looking. ▫ To shrink. To be wrinkled. ✱ كَشَّ i كَشِيشًا
✧ To drive away (flies, hens). — ه
✧ He met him sternly. كَشَّ في وَجْهِهِ
✧ Peddlery, hawking. كَشَّة
Pollen of palm-trees. كُشّ
Lock of hair. Curl of hair. كُشَّة
▫ Tree-moss, lichen. كُشَّة العَجُوز
▫ Sea-moss. كُشَّة العَرُوس
Rustling of a snake. Crackling of fire. Sparkling of wine. كَشِيش
▫ Fly-flap. مِكَشَّة
To rustle (snake, cloth). To flee. ✧ To behave peevishly. ✱ كَشْكَش
Inexhaustible sea. بَحْر لا يُكَشْكَش
Rustling. Escape. كَشْكَشَة
✧ Border of cloth, lace, festoon. كَشْكَش ج كَشَاكِش
To craunch; to peel a. th. ✱ كَشَأ a كَشْأً ه
To wound a. o. with (a sword). — ه ب
To roast, to dry up (meat). — وأَكْشَأ ه
To be chapped (hand). كَشِئَ a كَشْأً وكَشَاء
To be surfeited with. — وتَكَشَّأ من
To be scraped off, pared (skin). تَكَشَّأ
Surfeited. كَشِئ وكَشِيء
Roasted and dried (meat). كَشِيء

He is valued when put to trial. هُوَ طَيِّبُ المَكْسِرِ
He is my nearest neighbour. هُوَ جَارِي مُكَاسِرِي
Routed (army). Marked with kasra (letter). ✧ Bankrupt. مَكْسُور
To put (the tail) between the legs (dog). ✱ كَسَمَ a كَسْمًا, واكْتَسَمَ ب
To strike a. o. on the buttocks. — ه
▫ To go down (the Nile). كَسَم
He pursued them the sword in their backs. أَتْبَعَ أَدْبَارَهُم يَكْسَعُهُم بالسَّيْف
He threw water upon the she-camel's udder. كَسَعَ النَّاقَةَ بِغُبْرِهَا
White hair on the forelock. كُسْعَة
White spot of the forelock of beasts. White feathers under the tail. Beasts of burden. Slaves. كُسْعَة ج كُسَع
White in the forelock (horse). White-spotted (dove). أَكْسَع
To cut out (cloth). To hock (a beast). ✧ To rebuke a. o. ✱ كَسَفَ i كَسْفًا ه
To eclipse (the sun: God). To lower (the eyes). كَسَفَ i كُسُوفًا ه
To be eclipsed (sun). كَسَفَ و✧ انْكَسَفَ
To assume a stern look, to be frowned (face). كَسَفَ
His affairs are disordered. — حَالُهُ
To cut a. th. to pieces. ▫ To disappoint a. o. كَسَّفَ ه وه
Sternly and niggardly. كَسْفًا وإِمْسَاكًا
Eclipse of the sun. كُسُوف و✧ انْكِسَاف
كِسْفَة ج كِسْف وكِسَف وجج أَكْسَاف وكُسُوف
Fragment, bit.
Eclipsed (sun, moon). Unlucky (day). كَاسِف م كَاسِفَة
Stern-faced, frowning. كَاسِفُ الوَجْهِ
Grieved. — البَالِ
To be lazy, slothful, sluggish. ✱ كَسِلَ a كَسَلًا, وتَكَاسَلَ
To render a. o. lazy. أَكْسَلَ ه
Sloth, neglect, laziness. كَسَل وتَكَاسُل
كَسِل وكَسْلَان ج كَسَالَى وكُسَالَى وكَسْلَى وكَسَالِي
Slothful, lazy.
Slothful. Delicate (girl). كَسُول
Sluggish. Soft (woman). (*m. f.*) مِكْسَال
To pound a. th. dry. ✱ كَسَمَ i كَسْمًا ه
To earn for (o.'s family). — على
✧ Manner; shape. Costume. كِسْم

To eat a. th. greedily. To glut.	✱ كَشَبَ i كَشْبًا, وكَشَّبَ ه
Thimble.	P كَشْتُبَان ج كَشَاتِبِين
Cuscuta. Dodder (clinging plant).	✱ كَشُوث — كُشُوث وكَشُوثَى وكَشُوثَا.
To brood hatred against.	✱ كَشَحَ a كَشْحًا ل, وكَاشَحَ ه بالعَدَاوَة
To scatter (people).	كَشَحَ ه
To sweep (a house).	— ه
To bark (wood).	— وكَشَّحَ ه
To brand, to cauterise (a beast) on the flanks.	— وكَشَّحَ ه
To scatter away from.	— وانكَشَحَ عن
To have a complaint of the flanks.	كَشِحَ
✧ To clear away (clouds) ; to become serene (sky).	كَشَّحَ
Disease of the flank.	كَشَح
Flanks. *Concha Veneris*, shell.	كَشْح ج كُشُوح,
He broke off with him.	طَوَى كَشْحَهُ عن فُلان
He resolved secretly upon the thing.	طَوَى كَشْحَهُ على الأمرِ
Brand on the flank.	كِشَاح
Secret hatred.	كُشَاحَة
Blade of a sword.	مِكْشَح ومِكْشَاح
Axe.	مِكْشَاح
✧ Serene (sky).	مُكَشِّح
Having a complaint of the flanks.	مَكْشُوح
To cut a. th. with the teeth.	✱ كَشَدَ i كَشْدًا ه
To purify (butter).	أكْشَدَ ه
Earning for o.'s people.	كَشَد وكَاشِد وكَشُود ج كُشُد
To show the teeth (beast), to grin.	✱ كَشَرَ i كَشْرًا, وكَشَّرَ عن نابه
To smile to a. o.	كَشَرَ إلى
To show the teeth to. To smile to.	كَاشَرَ ه
To threaten a. o.	أكْشَرَ لهُ عن أنيابه
Showing of the teeth.	كِشْرَة
Food made of lentils and rice.	◻ كَشَرِي
He is my front-neighbour.	هُوَ جَارِي مُكَاشِرِي
To take off (a covering) from.	✱ كَشَطَ i كَشْطًا, وانشَكَطَ ه عن
To skin (a camel).	— ه
To be taken off. To be dispelled (fear).	كَشِطَ وانكَشَطَ
Skin of a camel.	كِشَاط
To go away from.	✱ كَشَمَ a كَشْمًا عن
To be anxious.	كَشِمَ a كَشَمًا
To uncover, to unveil, to disclose a. th. To discover, to explore (a country).	✱ كَشَفَ i كَشْفًا وكَاشِفَة, وكَشَّفَ ه
To uncover a. th. To examine a. th.	— عن
His misdoings have laid bare his shame.	كَشَفَتْهُ الكَوَاشِف
To visit a sick person.	✧ كَشَفَ عَلَى مَرِيض.
To be put to flight.	كَشِفَ a كَشَفًا
To compel a. o. to disclose a. th.	كَشَّفَ ه عن
To reveal a. th. to.	كَاشَفَ ه ب
To show open enmity to.	— ه بالعَدَاوَة
To show the gums in laughing.	أكْشَفَ
To be laid bare, disclosed ; to uncover o.'s self.	تَكَشَّفَ وانكَشَفَ
To spread in the sky (lightning).	تَكَشَّفَ
To manifest mutual defects.	تَكَاشَفَ
To ask a. o. to reveal a. th.	إستَكْشَفَ ه عن
Inspection, inquest. Survey, appraisement. Discovery. ✧ Customhouse report.	كَشْف
Twisting of the hair.	كَشَف
Gift offered to a sick person.	✧ كَشْفَانِيَّة
Discoverer. Inspector. ✧ Probe for wounds.	كَاشِف ج كَشَفَة
Shameful action.	كَاشِفَة ج كَوَاشِف
Pioneer, explorer. ✧ Customhouse officer.	كَشَّاف
Unarmed (warrior). Having curled locks.	أكْشَف م كَشْفَاء
Unveiled, disclosed. Explained.	كَشِيف ومَكْشُوف
Bareheaded.	مَكْشُوف الرَّأس
Kiosk, pavilion.	P كُشْك
Groats mixed with sour milk and dried in the sun.	كِشْك ج كُشُوكَة
To cut off the (nose).	✱ كَشَمَ o كَشْمًا, واكْتَشَمَ ه
To have a corporal or moral defect.	كَشِمَ a كَشَمًا
Having a defect.	أكْشَم

أكشر وكشّر Lynx.

P كِشْمِش Small stoneless raisin, currant.

✧ كوشن ج كواشين Receipt for taxes.

✧ كشني Vetch (*plant*).

✱ كصّ i كصًّا وكصيصًا To be weak (voice).

— كصًّا To be gathered (people).

— كصيصًا بالنّاس To be frequented (water).

أكصّ To flee away.

تكاصّ واكتصّ To throng, to press (crowd).

كصيص Fright. Shudder. Emotion. Contortion. Hum of locusts.

كصيصة ج كصائص Crowd. Net for catching gazelles.

✱ كصم o كصومًا To meet with a repulse.

— كصمًا ه To repel a. o.

✱ كصى i كصيًا To lose consideration.

✱ كظّ o كظًّا ه To oppress a. o. (food).

— كظاظًا وكظاظة ه To grieve a. o. (affair).

كاظّ مكاظّة وكظاظًا ه To struggle desperately with a. o.

تكاظّ To hate o. a. To fight desperately together.

إكتظّ مِن To be oppressed by (surfeit).

— ب To be overfilled (canal).

كظّة Surfeit, heaviness of the stomach.

كِظاظ Hardship, difficulty, grief.

كظّ Harsh, untractable (man).

— وكظيظ ومُكتظّ ومكظوظ Overworked. Overbusy.

كظيظ ومكظوظ Surfeited.

✱ كظب o كظوبًا To be fat.

✱ كظر o كظرًا ه To notch (a bow, a flint).

كظر Notch on a bow. Fat of the reins.

كِظر Sinew fastening the notch of a bow.

✱ كظم i كظمًا ه To close (a door). To stop, to obstruct a. th.

— i كظمًا وكظومًا ه To repress (anger).

— كظومًا To interrupt rumination (camel).

— على جرّته وكظم كظومًا To break off speaking.

كظم وكظم ج كظام وأكظام Throat, bronchi, fauces.

كِظام Stopper, bond.

أخذ بكظام الأمر He has undertaken the affair steadily.

كِظامة Mouth of a river.

— وكظيمة ج كظائم Subterranean conduit of a well.

كظيمة ج كظائم Large water-skin.

كظيم ومكظوم Choked with anger.

✱ كظا o كظوًّا To be compact (flesh).

تكظّى سِمَنًا To be full of fat.

✱ كعّ i o كعًّا وكعوعًا وكعاعة وكيعوعة To be faint-hearted.

أكعّ ه To render a. o. faint-hearted.

كعّ وكاعّ Weak and shy.

كعّ وكاعّ الوجه Sweet-faced.

✱ كعكع To prevent, to withhold a. o.

تكعكع To be withheld. To be alarmed.

كعكع Weak and cowardly.

✱ كعب o i كعوبًا وكعابة وكعوبة, وكعّب To have the breasts formed (girl).

كعب a كعوبًا To swell (breasts).

— كعبًا, وكعّب ه To fill up (a vessel).

كعّب ه To render a. th. cubical. To fold (cloth) in squares.

أكعب To hurry away.

كعب ج كعاب وكعوب وأكعب Joint of the bones. Ankle-bone.

— ج كعب وكعاب Die; ossicle. Cube.

— ج كعوب Knot of reeds. Glory.

ذهب كعبهم Their glory has vanished.

كعب Woman's breast.

كعبة ج كعبات Die for playing. Square house.

الكعبة The Black stone, the Caaba.

كعبة Virginity.

كعاب وكاعب ومكعّب Having rounded breasts (girl).

كاعب ج كواعب, ومكعّب Swollen (breast).

مكعّب Cubical. Cube.

✱ كعبر ه ب To trench off a. th. with (a sword).

كعبرة وكعبورة ج كعابر Knot, knob. Prominent bone. Pod of a radish. *Pl.* Heads of the bones.

✱ كعت — إكعتّ To hurry away. To sit down.

كَعت م كَعتة Short-sized.
كَعتة Cover of a flask.
كُعَيت ج كِعتان Nightingale.
* كَعتَر في مِشيَتِهِ He reeled in walking.
* كَعِر a كَعَرًا To be big-bellied (child).
— وكَعِرَ To be fat-humped (camel).
كَعَر a كَعرًا ه ✧ To drive a. o. into a corner. To urge on (a beast).
كَعرة Ganglion.
كَعِر Big-bellied.
* كَعَز a كَعزًا ه To pick a. th. with the fingers.
* كَعَس – كَعس ج كِعاس Bone of the finger-joints.
P كَعك (un. كَعكة) Cake, biscuit.
* كَعَل – تَكَعَّل To stick, to agglutinate.
كَعَل Dung (of beasts). Dates in lump.
* كَعَم a كَعمًا ه وه To muzzle (a camel). To stop (a vessel).
— وكاعَم ه ✧ To thwart a. o.
كِعَم ج كِعام Sheath, case.
كِعام وكِعامة Camel's muzzle.
كُعوم الطَّرِيق The openings of the road.
كَعِيم ومَكعُوم Muzzled. ✧ Vexed.
* كَعَن – أكعَن To lose liveliness.
* كَعا o كَعوًا To be cowardly, sluggish.
✧ كَعِي a عن To be unable to.
✧ كَعَّى ه To weary out a. o.
كاعٍ م كاعِيَة ج أكعاء Coward. Fugitive.
P كاغِد وكاغَد ج كَواغِد Paper.
كاغِدِيّ Seller of paper.
* كَفَّ o كَفًّا ه To hem, to fell (a garment). To overfill (a vessel). To wrap (the foot) in a rag. To collect (things).
كَفَّ ه عن To drive a. o. away from.
كَفَّ وتَكافَّ عن To desist; to refrain from. To withdraw from (a place).
كُفَّ او كُفِّ Leave it off.
كُفَّ وكَفَّ بَصَرُهُ He has been blinded.
تَكَفَّف واستَكَفَّ ه To ask (beggar).
إنكَفَّ To hold out the hand (beggar).
إنكَفَّ عن To refrain from. To set out from.
إستَكَفَّ To roll up (snake). To be luxuriant (hair).

إستَكَفَّ ه To shade o.'s eyes with the hand for looking at a. th.
— النَّاسُ حَولَهُ The people stood round for examining it.
— ه عن To seek to remove a. th. from.
— بالصَّدَقة To ask alms.
كَفّ ج كُفوف وأكُفّ وكُفّ Palm of the hand. Hand (to the wrist). Scale of a balance. Purslane (*plant*). Hemp-seed. Paw of a beast. Handful. ✧ Glove. Slap. Quire of paper.
كَفّ مَريَم *Anastatica Hierochuntina*, rose of Jericho.
— الأسَد Leontopetalon, lion's-leaf. *Cyclamen Europæum.*
— الكَلب Leaves of the *Celastrus edulis* when dry.
— الأجذَم او الجُذَماء *Vitex*, chaste-tree.
— الدُّبّ *Helleborus fetidus*, bear's foot.
— الهِرّ Variety of Ranunculus, crow-foot.
— الضَّبُع او السَّبُع Ranunculus (*plant*).
— الذِئب Gentian, fell-wort (*plant*).
الكَفّ الخَضِيب Star in *Cassiopeia.*
✧ ضَرَبَهُ كَفًّا He gave him a slap.
كَفَّةَ كَفَّةَ وكَفَّةً لِكَفَّةٍ وكَفَّةً عن كَفَّةٍ In front, opposite.
كِفَّة ج كِفَف وكِفاف Palm of the hand. Bezel of a ring. Plate of a balance. Frame of a drum. Hollow full of water. Anything round. Libra (*constell.*).
كِفَّة وكُفَّة Hunter's net.
كُفَّة ج كُفَف وكِفاف Border of a garment. Selvage. Crowd.
✧ كُفِّيَّة (*for* كوفِيَّة) Head-shawl.
كَفَف Beggary.
— وكَفاف Sufficiency, livelihood.
كِفَف Cavity of the eyes.
كِفاف The like of. Sufficient (food).
دَعنِي كَفافِ Let me alone, and I shall leave thee.
كِفاف ج أكِفَّة The choice part of. Selvage (of a garment). Circuit, rim. Blade (of a sword). Side of a cloud.
كَفّاف ج كَفَفَة Stitching. Having the teeth worn out (camel).

To race with. كَافَتَ مُكَافَتَةً وكِفَاتًا ه
To contract. To be compact. إِنْكَفَتَ
To be lean (horse). To be altered (colour).
To be turned away from. — عن
To take the whole of. إِكْتَفَتَ ه
Dead. Unseasoned (bread). كَفْتٌ
Quick, light (man).
Small pot. — وكِفْتٌ
Leaves of the *Celastrus edulis* when *green*. كَفْتَةٌ
Fiery (horse). كَفْت وكَفْتَة
✧ Balls of minced meat. T كَفْتَة
He died suddenly. مَاتَ كِفَاتًا ومُكَافَتَةً
Sound provision-bag. Sufficiency. كَفِيت
✻ كَفَحَ a كَفْحًا, وكَافَحَ. مُكَافَحَةً وكِفَاحًا ه
To kiss. To meet a. o. face to face.
To strike a. o. with (a stick). — ه ب
To take off (a covering). كَفَحَ ه
He pulled the bridle and checked the horse. — لِجَامَ الفَرَسِ وأَكْفَحَ الفَرَسَ
To be ashamed, frightened. كَفِحَ a كَفَحًا
He manages his own business. كَافَحَ أُمُورَهُ
To repel a. o. from. أَكْفَحَ ه عن
To front o. a. (fighters). To dash together (waves). تَكَافَحَ
Struggle. War. كِفَاح ومُكَافَحَة
I met him face to face. لَقِيتُهُ كِفَاحًا
He has given him every sort of goods. أَعْطَاهُ كِفَاحًا
Equal. Unexpected guest. Husband. كَفِيح
Rough (sea). مُتَكَافِح الأَمْوَاجِ
To strike a. o. with (a stick). ✻ كَفَخَ a كَفْخًا ه ب
To cover, to conceal a. th. ✻ كَفَرَ o كَفْرًا وكُفْرًا, وكَفَّرَ ه
To become an unbeliever; to be ungrateful. ✧ To blaspheme, to curse. — o كُفْرًا وكَفْرًا وكُفُورًا وكُفْرَانًا
To deny (the faith). كَفَرَ ب
To deny (a benefit). — كُفُورًا وكُفْرَانًا ه وب
To make an unbeliever of. كَفَّرَ ه
To accuse a. o. of unbelief. ✧ To make a. o. to curse.
To forgive (a sin) to a. o. (God). — ه ل

They came all of them. جَاءَ النَّاسُ كَافَّةً
Truce. مُكَافَّة
Blind. مَكْفُوف ج مَكَافِيف, وكَفِيف
The eyes. المُسْتَكِفَّات
To repel, to prevent a. o. from. ✻ كَفْكَفَ ه عن
✧ To wrap a. o. or a. th. — ه او ه
To be withheld, prevented. تَكَفْكَفَ
✧ To wrap o.'s self in clothes.
To fly away. ✻ كَفَأَ a كَفْأً
To follow, to repel a. o. — ه
To give up (a design). — عن
To turn upside-down; to reverse, to upset (a vessel). — وكَفَّأَ وأَكْفَأَ واكْتَفَأَ ه
To requite a. o. كَافَأَ مُكَافَأَةً وكِفَاءً ه وه
To resist a. o. To watch a. th. To equal a. o.
He has pierced them both with his spear. — بَيْنَهُمَا بِرُمْحِهِ
To be inclined. To be prolific (she-camel). To intervert the accents of a rhyme. أَكْفَأَ
To incline a. th. — ه
To give to a. o. the produce of (camels). — ه ه
He swaggers in walk. تَكَفَّأَ فِي المِشْيَةِ
To be equal to a. o. تَكَافَأَ
To turn away. To be defeated. To be altered (colour). إِنْكَفَأَ
To ask from a. o. the produce of (camels) for one year. إِسْتَكْفَأَ ه ه
Equality, likeness. كَفَاء وكَفَاءَة
Match, equal. Tent-curtain. كِفَاء
Equal. كِفْؤ وكَفْؤ وكُفُؤ ج أَكْفَاء وكِفَاء
✧ Match, able.
Equal, sufficient. كُفُوء وكَفِيء وكَفِيئَة
Annual produce (of camels, palm-trees). كَفْأَة وكُفْأَة
Interior of a valley. كِفْء وكَفِيء
Dissonance in a rhyme. إِكْفَاء
Coeval. Equivalent. مُكَافِئ م مُكَافِئَة
To tuck (the skirts). To draw a. th. to o.'s self. ✻ كَفَتَ i كَفْتًا, وكَفَّتَ ه
God has taken him. — اللهُ فُلَانًا
To withhold, to turn a. o. away from. — ه عن
✧ To pour out a. th. at once كَفَتَ ه
To fly or run swiftly. كَفَتَ i كَفْتًا وكِفَاتًا وكَفِيتًا وكَفَتَانًا, وتَكَفَّتَ

He redeemed his oath. كَفَّر عن يَمِينِهِ
To pay honour, to (a prince) in bowing down. كَفَّر ل
The king has been crowned. كُفِّر لِلْمَلِكِ
To deny (a debt) to. كَافَر ه ه
To inhabit (a village). أَكْفَر واكْتَفَر
To call a. o. an unbeliever ; to make of a. o. an unbeliever. To charge a. o. with blasphemy. أَكْفَر ه
Homage of Persians to their king. كَفْر
Village, remote village. Grave. كَفْر ج كُفُور
Darkness of the night. — وكَفْر وكَفْرَة
Ingratitude. Unbelief. Tar for ships. ✧ Blasphemy. كُفْر وكُفْرَان
Integument of a palm-blossom. كَفَر وكَفَرَّى وكُفُرَّى وكِفِرَّى وكَافِر
High (mountain). كَفِر
Atonement. Crown. تَكْفِير
Ungrateful. Infidel. Renegade. Disbeliever. كَافِر (opp. to مُؤْمِن) ج كُفَّار وكَفَرَة وكِفَار وكَافِرُون , وكَفُور ج كُفُر
Dark cloud, night. Sea. Armed from head to foot. Coat of mail. كَافِر
Amphoras, jars. كَوَافِر
Camphor. Camphor-tree. كَافُور
Camphorata Monspeliensis (plant). حَشِيشَةُ الكَافُور
Ungrateful to God. Impious. كَفَّار م كَفَّارَة
Atonement. Alms, fasting. كَفَّارَة
Clad in armour. مُكَفِّر ومُتَكَفِّر
Treated with ingratitude. Fettered ; shackled. مُكَفَّر
To be crook-footed (child). ✻ كَفِس a كَفَسًا
To be distorted (foot). إِنْكَفَس
Crook-footed. أَكْفَس م كَفْسَاء ج كُفْس
Swaddling-clothes. كِفَاس
To nurse a. o. ✻ كَفَل o كَفْلًا وكَفَالَةً , وكَفَّل ه
To guarantee ; to make o.'s self responsible for. كَفَل o i وكَفِل a وكَفُل o كَفْلًا وكُفُولًا وكَفَالَةً ب
To assume (a duty). — ب وعن
He became surety for him to his creditor. كَفَل عَنْهُ لِغَرِيمِهِ
To appoint a. o. as surety for. To ask a. o. to be surety for. كَفَّل وأَكْفَل ه ه

To conclude an agreement with. كَافَل ه
He became answerable to him for. تَكَفَّل لَهُ ب
He put a pad upon the camel and sat upon it. — واكْتَفَل البَعِيرَ
To place a. o. behind o.'s self. إِكْتَفَل ب
We have passed over the mountain. إِكْتَفَلْنَا بِالجَبَل
Posteriors, buttocks. كَفَل ج أَكْفَال
Double requital. Portion, part. Riding behind ; standing at the rear (soldier). Camel-saddle, pad. كِفْل ج أَكْفَال
Fosterer. Surety. كَافِل ج كُفَّل
God. الكَافِل
Bail, surety, warrant. كَفَالَة
Surety. responsible. Similar. كَفِيل (m. f. s. pl.) وج كُفَلَاء
Neighbour. Companion, ally. مُكَافِل
Secured (debt). مَكْفُول بِهِ
Debtor whose debt is warranted. — عَنْهُ
Warrantee. — لَهُ
To spin (wool). To cover (bread) with hot ashes. ✻ كَفَن i كَفْنًا ه
To shroud (the dead). — وكَفَّن ه
To wrap o.'s self in. تَكَفَّن ب
Without salt (food). كَفْن
Shroud. كَفَن ج أَكْفَان
The Holy Shroud. الكَفَن المُقَدَّس
To shine in darkness (star). To be intensely dark (night). To be stern-looking. ✻ كَفْهَر — إِكْفَهَرَّ
Shining of stars. Darkness. إِكْفِهْرَار
Thick and black (cloud). Stern (look). Rugged (mountain). مُكْفَهِرّ
Equal, alike. ✻ كَفُو وكُفُوّ
Able. ✧ كَفُو
To suffice, to satisfy a. o. ✻ كَفَى i كِفَايَةً ه
God is a sufficient witness. كَفَى بِاللّٰهِ شَهِيدًا
To do instead of. كَفَى ه مِن وعن
To give sufficient provision to. كَفَى ه مَؤُونَةً
To protect a. o. against. كَفَى ه عَدُوَّهُ او شَرَّ عَدُوِّهِ
To suffice a. o. كَافَى مُكَافَاةً وكِفَاءً و✧ كَفَّى ه
To requite a. o. with. — ه ب
To grow (plant). تَكَفَّى

illumed by lightnings (cloud).

To smile. To flash faintly   إنْكَلَّ
(lightning). To be blunted (sword).

Fatigue, weariness.   كَلّ وَكَلال وَكَلاَلَة

Burden. Family. Orphan.   (s. pl.) كَلّ
Single (man). Back of (a sword).

All, the whole.   كُلّ

The whole.   الكُلّ

Any one.   كُلّ مَن

Every soul.   كُلّ نَفْس

Every one, each.   كُلّ أَحَدٍ

He has killed them all.   وَقَتَلَهُمْ كُلَّهُمْ

The whole affair is in   إِنَّ الأَمْرَ كُلَّهُ لله
the hand of God.

Whatever. Whenever.   كُلَّمَا

✧ Whoever.   كُلَّمَن

Not at all.   كَلاَّ

Blunt sword.   كَلَّة

Delay.   كَلَّة

✧ Ball, marble. Bomb,   كُلَّة ج كُلَل Ts
shell.

Veil. Musquito-curtain.   كِلَّة ج كِلَل وكِلاَت

State, condition.   وَكَلاَل

Remote relationship ; cousins.   كَلاَلَة

He is a remote relation.   هُوَ ابْنُ عَمِّ الكَلاَلَةِ

Universal.   كُلِّيّ م كُلِّيَّة

The whole. ✧ University,   الكُلِّيَّة
college.

The genera, universas, the   الكُلِّيَّات
five predicates.

Crown. Flesh   إكْلِيل ج أَكَالِيل وأَكِلَّة
around the nails. Umbel of a plant.
Three stars in Scorpio. ✧ Clerical
tonsure.

Melilot, honey-lotus.   المَلَك

Rosemary (shrub).   الجَبَل

Blunt (sword).   كَلّ وكَلِيل م كَلَّة وكَلِيلَة
Weakened (sight). Faint (lightning).
Dull (man).

Jaded. Languid.   كَالّ

Crowned. Flowery (meadow).   مُكَلَّل
✧ Married.

To become callous   ✧ كَلْكَل وتَكَلْكَل
(skin).

Callousness, blister.   ✧ كَلْكَلَة

Chest.   ✻ كَلْكَل ج كَلاَكِل

Short and nimble (man).   كَلْكَل ج كَلاَكِل

To keep a. o.   ✻ كَلأَ a كَلْأً وكِلاَءَةً
safe, to guard a. o. (God).

To content with. To do with-   إِكْتَفَى بِ
out a. th.

To ask a. o. to do for.   إِسْتَكْفَى ه ه

To rely on, to trust to a. o.   — بِ

Suffi-   (m. s. f. pl.) كِفَايَة وكِفْي وكُفِي
ciency. Enough.

This man   هذَا رَجُلٌ يَكْفِيكَ وكَافِيكَ مِن رَجُل
will do for thee.

✧ Sufficiently.   بِالكِفَايَة

Food, sufficiency.   كِفْيَة ج كُفًى

Sufficient.   كَفِيّ وكَاف ج كُفَاة

Requital, reward.   مُكَافَأَة

✻ To shine, to glisten   كَكَبَ – كَوْكَبَ
(iron).

Star ; constellation. White-   — ج كَوَاكِب
ness in the eye. Dew-drops. Water.
Source of a well. Brightness of iron.
Sword. Main part. Youth in the
prime of life. Chief of horsemen.
Garden-flower. Toadstool.

Mushroom. Talc.

Siderite (mineral).   حَجَرُ الكَوْكَبِ

Gloomy, calamitous(day).   يَوْمٌ ذُو كَوَاكِب

They dispersed in   ذَهَبُوا تَحْتَ كُلِّ كَوْكَب
every direction.

Un. A star. Crowd. ✧ Detach-   كَوْكَبَة
ment of cavalry, squadron.

Starred, star-lit (sky).   مُكَوْكَب

✻ كَلَّ i كَلاًّ وكِلَّة و كَلاَلاً وكُلُولاً وكَلاَلَةً وكُلُورَةً
To be tired, weary, weak. To have
only remote relations.

To become dim (sight). To be   — وكَلَّ
blunted (sword). To be on edge
(teeth).

To forsake o.'s people.   كَلَّ

To crown a. o. ✧ To marry (a   ه
couple : priest).

To act zealously in.   فِي

To rush upon.   عَلَى

To be frightened away from.   عَنْ

To have jaded beasts.   أَكَلَّ

To jade (beasts)   ه

To weaken (the sight : tears).   ه

To be crowned. ✧ To receive the   تَكَلَّلَ
nuptial blessing.

To surround a. o.   — بِ

To be a remote rela-   ✻ وبِهِ النَّسَبُ
tion to a. o.

To be faintly   — وانْكَلَّ واكْتَلَّ عَنِ البَرْقِ

To be postponed (payment). كَلَأَ كُلُوءَةً
To fix (the eyes) on. — وكَلَّأَ وأَكْلَأَ هـ في
To eat herbage (camel). كَلَّأَ وأَكْلَأَ
To abound with herbage (country). كَلَأَ ، وكَلِئَ a كَلَأً ، وأَكْلَأَ واسْتَكْلَأَ
To bring (a ship) ashore. كَلَّأَ تَكْلِيئًا وتَكْلِئَةً هـ
To buy upon credit. To receive (an earnest). — وتَكَلَّأَ واكْتَلَأَ واسْتَكْلَأَ هـ
He ended his life. أَكْلَأَ عُمْرَهُ
To be sleepless (eye). إِكْتَلَأَ
To be on the watch against. — مِن
Fresh herbage. كَلَأٌ ج أَكْلَاءٌ
Safe-keeping. كِلَاءَةٌ
Sheltered haven. Bank of a river. كَلَّاءٌ ومُكَلَّأٌ
Postponed debt. Earnest. كَالِئٌ وكَالٍ ج كَوَالِئُ وكَوَالٍ ، وكُلَأَةٌ
Abounding in herbage (ground). كَلِئٌ م كَلِئَةٌ ، ومُكْلِئٌ ومَكْلَأَةٌ
May God lengthen thy life to the utmost limit! بَلَغَ اللّٰهُ بِكَ أَكْلَأَ العُمْرِ
Sleepless (man). كَلُوءُ العَيْنِ
To spur (a horse). To double (a leather-bag). ✱ كَلَبَ o كَلْبًا ه وهـ
To bark for stirring dogs (man). كَلَبَ i كَلْبًا ، واسْتَكْلَبَ
To become rabid, mad (dog). To be foolish (man). To be enraged. To be hard (winter). To eat voraciously. كَلِبَ a كَلَبًا
To desire a. th. eagerly. — على
To suffer from canine madness. كُلِبَ كَلَبًا
✧ To cohere (parts of a whole). كَلَّبَ
To train (a hound). — ه
To torment a. o. To show enmity to. كَالَبَ مُكَالَبَةً وكِلَابًا ه
To feed upon (thorns : camel). — هـ
To have rabid camels. أَكْلَبَ
To show mutual hatred. تَكَالَبَ
To rush together upon. تَكَالَبَ على
Dog ; any animal of prey. Iron on the axis of a mill. Iron-hook, peg. Pawn (in a game). كَلْبٌ ج كِلَابٌ وأَكْلُبٌ وجج أَكَالِبُ
The constellation *Canis major*. *Sirius*, dog's star. الكَلْبُ الأَكْبَرُ
The constellation *Canis minor*. *Procyon* star. — الأَصْغَرُ والمُتَقَدِّمُ

Cynoglossum, dog's tongue. لِسَانُ الكَلْبِ
Sea-dog. ✧ Shark. كَلْبُ البَحْرِ
Beaver. — المَاءِ
The wolf. — البَرِّ
Fetid and yellow-leaved thorny shrub. أُمُّ الكَلْبِ
Horehound (*plant*). حَشِيشَةُ الكَلْبِ
Empalement. مَقْتَلَةُ الكِلَابِ
✧ *Term of contempt*. Rascal, doggish man. إِبْنُ كَلْبٍ
Hook of a saddle. كَلْبٌ وكَلَّابٌ
Canine madness, hydrophobia, Canine hunger. Severity of cold. كَلَبٌ
Rabid (dog). ✧ كَلْبَانُ
Bitch. Wicked woman. كَلْبَةٌ
The fever. أُمُّ كَلْبَةٍ
Thorny tree without branches. كَلْبَةٌ وكَلِبَةٌ
Pincers, forceps. كَلْبَتَانِ وكُلَّابَةٌ ج كُلَّابَاتٌ
Straitness. Dearth. Intensity of cold. Rope of palm-fibres for sewing skins. كُلْبَةٌ
Delirium, paroxysm of rabies. كَلَابٌ
Bitter-stoned (apricot). كَلَابِيٌّ
Spear. Prong. Hooked iron, hooked peg. Spur of a hawk. *Pl*. Thorns of a tree. كُلَّابٌ وكَلُّوبٌ ج كَلَالِيبُ
Having hounds. كَالِبٌ وكَلَّابٌ
Pack of hounds. كَالِبٌ وكَلِيبٌ
كَلِبٌ ج كَلِبُونَ ، وكَلِيبٌ ج كَلْبَى ومَكْلُوبٌ
Rabid, hydrophobic. Severe (time).
Eager of. كَلِبٌ على
Training hounds. مُكَلِّبٌ
Trained (hound). Fettered (captive). مُكَلَّبٌ
Handcuffs, manacles. ☐ كَلَبْشٌ
To start (a horse). To throw or to collect a. th. ✱ كَلَتَ i كَلْتًا ه وهـ
To pour a. th. into. — هـ في
To be poured. To shrink (man). إِنْكَلَتَ
To drink up a. th. إِكْتَلَتَ هـ
Portion of food. كُلْتَةٌ
Brave, generous. ✱ كَلِجٌ — كَالِجٌ
Strong men. كُلُجٌ
To be stern-looking, grin (face). ✱ كَلَحَ a كُلُوحًا وكُلَاحًا ، وأَكْلَحَ وتَكَلَّحَ
To contract (the face). كَلَّحَ وأَكْلَحَ هـ
To meet a. o. with a stern face. كَالَحَ ه

✧ To cost a. o. *so much* (goods). كلّف ه
✧ He took the trouble, he took pains. — خاطِرَهُ
To inspire a. o. with; to enamour a. o. of. أكلف ه ب
To undertake (a painful task). تكلّف ه
To pretend a. th. ✧ To spend (money). To constrain o.'s self.
✧ To spend for. — على
To assume a reddish hue (wine). إكلافّ
Brown reddish colour. كَلَف وكُلْفة
Love, attachment. كَلَف وكَلَافة
Red spots on the face. ✧ Freckles. كَلَف
Expense, cost. — وكُلْفة ج أكلاف
Constraint, trouble, inconvenience. ✧ Expenditure. كُلْفة ج كُلَف
In love with. كَلِف م كَلِفة ب
Painful task. كَلُوف، وتكليفة ج تكاليف
✧ Trouble, fuss, ceremony, *Pl.* Taxes, duties; expenses; legal summons. تكليف ج تكاليف
✧ Without ceremony. بِلا تكليف
Brown, tawny. أكلف م كلفاء ج كُلْف
Wine. الكَلْفاء
Intruder. Dissembler. مُتكلِّف
✧ Raft on the Tigris. كَلَك ج كَلَكات P
To wound a. o. ✡ كَلَم o i كَلْمًا، وكلّم تكليمًا ه
To speak to, to address a. o. كلّم تكليمًا وكِلّامًا ه
To converse with a. o. كالم ه
To converse together. تكالم
To utter (words). تكلّم تكلّمًا وتِكِلّامًا ه وب
To speak on behalf of. To speak of a. o. — عن
Wound. كَلْم ج كُلُوم وكِلام
Word. Discourse; poem. كَلِمة ج كَلِمات وكَلِم
Word, expression, sentence. كَلْمة ج كَلْمات، وكِلْمة ج كِلَم
The ten Commandments. العَشْر الكَلِمات
The Verb of God. الكَلِمة الإلهيّة
Language, speech. Saying. Talk. Sentence. كَلام
Dogmatic theology. عِلْم الكَلام
Defective sentence. كَلِم
◘ Large carpet, rug. كِلِيم ج أكلِمة
Eloquent. كَلْمانيّ وكَلَمانيّ وكِلِّمانيّ

To smile. To flash repeatedly (lightning). تكلّح
Stern look. كَلاحة
Barren year. كَلاحِ وكُلاح
Mouth and its surrounding parts. كَلْحة
Stern, peevish. Severe (winter). كالِح
Ugly, foul (man). كَوْلَح
To heap up (things). ✡ كَلَد i كَلْدًا، وكلّد ه
To be thick, compact. تكلّد
Rugged and stoneless ground. Hills. كَلَد
Hard and uneven ground. كَلَدة
Chaldean, from Chaldea. كَلْدان وكلْدانيّ
✧ Cellar. كَلَار
✧ Keeper of a cellar. كلارجي
✧ Clergy. أكليرُس G
✧ Clergyman, clerical student. أكليريكيّ
To make up th. ✡ كَلَز i كَلْزًا، وكلّز ه
To dart upon its prey (falcon). إكلأزّ
✧ England. (*un.* إنكليزيّ) إنكليز
Englishmen. Protestants.
To plaster (a house). — كلس — كلّس ه
To calcine (a body).
To be calcined (lime). — وتكلّس
To quench thirst. — وتكلّس من الماء
Quick lime. كِلْس
Grayish colour. كُلْسة
✧ Socks, stockings. كَلْسة ج كَلْسات
✧ Lime-kiln. كَلّاسة
Grayish (wolf). (*for* أطلس) أكلس
Chyle. كيلوس G
Lime-burner. Seller of lime. كَلّاس ومُكلِّس
✧ Eel. أنكليس T
To dry (scurf). ✡ كَلِع a كَلَعًا، وكَلِع a كَلْعًا
To be dirty, chapped (foot). كلِع a كَلَعًا
To defile a. o. (dirt). أكلع ه
To ally, to unite together. تكالع
Ill-natured. كِلْع ج كِلَعة
Dirt, chaps on the feet. كَلَع
Filthy (vessel, skin). كَلِع
Part of a flock. كَلْعة
Strength. كَلَاع
To become red (face). ✡ كَلِف a كَلَفًا
To be addicted to, to be in love with. — ب
To impose (a difficult task) upon. كلّف ه ه

To wrap o.'s self in (clothes). تكمّم ب
To be wrapped. تكمّم
Quantity, amount, quantum. كمّ وكمّيّة ج كمّيّات
Sleeve. كُمّ ج أكمام وكِمَمة
Round cap. كُمّة
كِمّ ج أكمام وكِمام وأكِمّة وأكاميم وكِمامة
Calyx of a flower. Envelope of the palm-blossom.
Muzzle. — وكِمام
Harrow. Muzzle for asses. مِكَمّة
To wrap o.'s self in clothes. To put on a round cap. ✱ كمكم — تكمكم
Camcamum-tree; mastic-tree and its resin. كمكام
To walk barefoot. To be chapped (foot), ✱ كمِيَ a كمَأ
To be mindless, heedless of. — عن
To feed a. o. with truffles. كمَأ a كمأ , وأكمأ ه
To abound in truffles (place). أكمأ
To pick up truffles. تكمّأ
To loathe a. th. — ه
To hide (the dead) in the earth. — على فلانٍ
Blackish truffle. Mushroom. كمْء ج أكمؤ وكمأة
Seller of truffles. كمّاء
Bed of truffles. مَكمأة ومَكمُؤة
✧ Bill of exchange. I كمبيالة ج كمبيالات
To be dark bay (horse). ✱ كمُت o كمتا وكمتة وكماتة
To repress (anger). كمَت o كمتا ه
To dye (cloth) dark red. كمّت ه
To become dark red (horse, wine). كمّت
To be dark bay. أكمت واكمتّ واكماتّ
Yellow bay colour. كمتة حمراء
Chestnut-bay colour. — صفراء
Dark bay (horse). كميت (m. f.) ج كمت
Reddish wine. Nightingale.
Brown bay horses. خيل كماتي
To walk with short steps. ✱ كمثر
Pear. (un. كمثراة كمثريات) ✱ كمّثرى
✧ White unleavened bread. P كماج
Flour of first quality.
To pull in, to check (a horse). ✱ كمح a كمحا , وأكمح ه
To put forth its gems (vine). أكمح

Orator, eloquent. تكلام وتِكلام وتكلامة وتِكلامة
Interlocutor. *Surname of* Moses. كليم ج كلماء
Wounded. — ج كلمى , ومكلوم
Speaking. Musulman theologian. First person (*in grammar*). متكلّم
Crab-fish. ع أبو كلمبو
To wound a. o. in the kidneys ✱ كلى i كليا ه
To have a complaint of the kidneys. كلِي a كلى , واكتلى
To come to a hidden place. كلّى تكلية
To keep on the rear. تكلّى
كلية وكلوة مث كليتان وكلوتان ج كلى وكلوات وكليات
Loin. Kidney. Under part of a cloud.
The sides of the valley. كلى الوادي
Emaciated ewes. غنم حمراء الكلى
Both, the two (ones). كِلا م كِلتا
I saw the two men (them both). رأيت كِلا الرجلين والرجلين كِليهما
I saw the two women. رأيت كِلتا المرأتين والمرأتين كِلتيهما
Four feathers of a bird's wing. كلى الطير
Having a complaint of the kidneys. مكلي
Particle of admiration and interrogation. How much? how many? how long! ✱ كم
How many gold coins we have spent! كم دينارٍ أنفقنا
How many gold coins hast thou? كم درهما عندك
✧ Some, few. كم واحد
✧ How much, much more. كم بالحري
Suffix of the 2[d] *person of the personal and possessive pronoun masculine plural.* You. Your. كم
As. كما
Suffix of the 2[d] *masc. and fem. pers of the dual.* You both. Your two. كما
To cover a. th. To stop a (vessel). ✱ كمّ o كمّا ه
To muzzle (a bull). — ه
To put forth the integument of its blossom (palm-tree). كمّ كمّا وكموما , وكمّم وأكمّ
To put sleeves to (a gown). كمّم وأكمّ ه

To come to blows. ✧ تَكَامَشَ
Nimble. كَمْش وكَمِيش وكَمِيش
Laborious (man). كَمِيش الإِزَار
✧ Handful. كَمْشَة
Having small udders (ewe). كَمُوش وكَمِشَة وكَمِيشَة
✧ Pincers. كَمَّاشَة
Purblind. Short-footed. أَكْمَش م كَمْشَاء ج كُمْش
To cut (the legs). ✻ كَمَع a كَمْعًا ه
To put the head in (a vessel). — في
To wade through (water : horse).
To lie besides, to sleep with a. o. كَامَع ه
To drink from the mouth of (a skin). إِكْتَمَع ه
Bed-fellow. كِمْع وكَمِيع
Man's garment. Dwelling. كِمْع
He is at home. هُوَ في كِمْعِي
✻ كَمَل وكَمُل o وكَمِل a كَمَالًا وكُمُولًا وتَكَمَّلَ
To be whole, perfect, complete. To be achieved. وتَكَامَلَ واكْتَمَلَ
To perfect, to perform a. th. كَمَّلَ وأَكْمَلَ واسْتَكْمَلَ ه
✧ To recover the remainder of (a debt). إِسْتَكْمَلَ ه
The whole. كَمَل
I gave him the whole of the property. أَعْطَيْتُهُ المَالَ كَمَلًا
Perfection. كَمَال ج كَمَالَات
Complement. تَكْمِلَة و✧ كَمَالَة
Perfect. Whole. كَمِيل
Perfect. Poetical metre. كَامِل ج كَمَلَة
Finished (well or ill). مِكْمَل
Supererogatory works. مُكَمِّلَات
To lay hid. ✻ كَمَن o وكَمِن a كُمُونًا , واكْتَمَن
To lurk in wait of. — لِفُلَان
To be concealed (hatred). — في الصَّدْر
To have red eyes. كَمِن a وكُمِن كُمُونًا
To conceal a. th. To brood (hatred). أَكْمَن ه
To lay in wait. تَكَمَّن
Too, also. ✧ كَمَان
Ambush. كَمْنَة ج كِمَان
Amaurosis, the drop serene. كُمْنَة
Hidden. Latent. Unawares. كَمِين ج كُمَنَاء
It is a hidden affair. هذا أَمْرٌ فِيهِ كَمِينٌ

Checking (his horse). كَامِخ
To be haughty. ✻ كَمَخ a كَمْخًا بِأَنْفِهِ
To check (a horse) with (the bridle). — ه ب
Pride, self-magnification. كُمَاخ
Vinegar-sauce, seasoning. P كَامَخ ج كَوَامِخ
Damask stuff, silk. ✧ كَمْخَا
✧ Dirt, dregs, sediment. كَمْخَة
✻ كَمِد a كَمَدًا
To be sad, grieved. To be worn out (garment). To fade (colour).
To beat (cloth : fuller). كَمَد o كَمْدًا وكُمُودًا ه
To foment (a limb). ✧ To level (a terrace). كَمَّد ه
To distress a. o. (sorrow). أَكْمَد ه
To cleanse (a stuff) imperfectly. — ه
Paleness, alteration of complexion. Change of colour. كُمْد وكَمَد وكُمْدَة
Sorrowful countenance, sadness. كَمَد وكُمْدَة
Beating of a garment. Fomentation. كِمَاد
Bandages. — وكِمَادَة
Altered in complexion ; sorrowful. كَامِد وكَمِد وكَمِيد
✧ To cover, to wrap a. th. ✻ كَمَر o كَمْرًا ه
To be covered. ✧ إِنْكَمَر
Waist-purse. moneybelt. P كَمَر ج أَكْمَار
✧ Custom-house. Ts كُمْرُك و ☐ جُمْرُك
To round a. th. with the hand. ✻ كَمَز i كَمْزًا ه
Round heap of dates. Sand-mound. كُمْزَة ج كُمَز
To be stern-looking. ✻ كَمَس o كُمُوسًا
Purblind. أَكْمَس م كَمْسَاء
To bind the teats of (a she-camel). ✻ كَمَش o كَمْشًا ه
To maim a. o. with (the sword). — ه ب
To clasp a. th. كَمَش o كَمْشًا , وكَمَّش ب
كَمِش a كَمْشًا , وكَمُش o كَمَاشَة , وأَكْمَش
To be nimble, quick. وتَكَمَّش وانْكَمَش
To urge a. o. كَمَّش ه
To tuck up (the skirts). — ه
To be wrinkled (face). To shrink (cloth). تَكَمَّش وانْكَمَش

Latent, lurking. كَمِين وكَامِن ومُتَكَمِّن
Cumin (*plant*). كَمُّون
Light brown. ✧ كَمُّونِي
Careum, Armenian cumin. كَمُّون أرمَنِي
Pigella, black cumin. — بَرِّي
Anise (*plant*). — حُلو
Concealment, lurking. كُمُون
Philosohical sect asserting أهل الكُمُون
that souls were created at the same time.
Lurking-place. مَكْمَن ج مَكَامِن
Hidden (sorrow). مُكْتَمِن و✧ مُتَكَمِّن
Two-chorded violoncella, P كَمَنْجَة
fiddle.
To be blind. To be dim ✱ كَمِه a كَمَهًا
(eye). To be dark (day).
To wander at random. تَكَمَّه
Blindness from birth. كَمَه
Wandering at random. كَامِه ومُتَكَمِّه
Born blind. أكْمَه م كَمْهَاء ج كُمْه
He is gone at random. ذهب كُمَيْهِي
Blind. مُكَمَّه العَيْنَيْن
To tuck up (o.'s clothes). To ✱ كَمْهَل
set on.
To be collected (things). تَكَمْهَل
To contract from cold. إكْمَهَلَّ
To ✱ كَمَى i كَمْيًا, وكَمَّى وأكْمَى وتَكَمَّى ه
conceal a. th.
He put on a breast- كَمَى وكَمَّى نَفْسَهُ
plate and a helmet.
To kill (a warrior). أكْمَى
To conceal (a house) from — ه عن
(sight).
He was clad in armour. تَكَمَّى في السِّلَاح
To crush a. o. (calamity). تَكَمَّى ه
The army had its chief تُكُمِّيَ الجَيْشُ
killed.
To be concealed. إنْكَمَى
Iron-clad. Brave. كَمِيّ ج كُمَاة وأكْمَاء
Armed. مُتَكَمٍّ
Postfix of the personal and possessive pronoun of the 2^d^ person feminine plural. You. Your ✱ كُنَّ
To كَنَّ o كَنًّا وكُنُونًا, وكَنَّن وأكَنَّ واكْتَنَّ ه
conceal, to keep (a girl) from sight.
To keep (a secret). — وكَنَّن وأكَنَّ ه في
✧ To be soothed (grief). كَنَّ واسْتَكَنَّ
To abate (wind).
✧ To soothe, to quiet a. o. كَنَّن ه
To be concealed from إكْتَنَّ واسْتَكَنَّ
sight (girl).
To go back home. إسْتَكَنَّ
Veil. House. Covert. كِنّ ج أكْنَان وأكِنَّة
Place of concealment.
Blanket, wrapper. كِنَّة
Daughter-in-law. Sister- كَنَّة ج كَنَائِن
in-law.
✧ Quiet, rest. كَنَّة
Ridged roof. Shade. كُنَّة ج كُنَان وكُنَّات
Veil, covering. كِنَان ج أكِنَّة
Quiver. كِنَانَة ج كَنَائِن وكِنَانَات
Fire-pot ; warmer. كَانُون وكَانُونَة ج كَوَانِين
December. كَانُون الأوَّل
January. كَانُون الثَّانِي
Hidden. Carefully kept. كَنِين ومَكْنُون
Hidden. Secret hatred. مُسْتَكِنَّة
To be sedentary, cowardly. ✱ كَنْكَن
To be coarse, ✱ كَتَب o كُتُوبًا, وأكْتَب
rough. To become rich.
To stow a. th. in كَنَب i كَنْبًا ه في
(a bag).
To be callous كَنِب a كَنَبًا, وأكْنَب
(hand).
To be impeded (tongue). أكْنَب
He feels a pain in the — عَلَيْهِ بَطْنُهُ
belly.
Callousness. كَنَب
Raceme of a palm-tree. كِنَاب
Barren, dry (tree). كَنِيب
Coarse (camel's foot). مِكْنَب ومُكْنِب
Horse-housing. ✱ كَنبَش — كَنْبُوش
To be strong, ✱ كَنَت o كَنْتًا في خَلْقِهِ
well-built.
To be rough (skin). كَنِت a كَنَتًا
To submit to. إكْتَنَت إلى
Strong (skin). كَنِيت
Alkekengi, winter-cherry. ✱ كَاكَنج
To disacknowledge ✱ كَنَد o كُنُودًا ه
(benefits). To cut a. th.
Part of a mountain. كِنْدَة
Unthankfulness. كُنُود
Unthankful. كُنُد وكَنُود (*m. f.*) وكَنَّاد
Rebellious. Ungodly. Avaricious, كَنُود
pitiless. Barren (soil).
Frankincense. G كُنْدُر
High and hard ground. ✱ كَنْدَرَة
Perch, roost for falcons.
✧ European boots. T كُنْدُرَة

✧ Bootmaker. — T كُنْدُرْجِي

Hellebore; ptarmic. — P كُنْدُس

Magpie. — ✱ كُنْدُش

Border of cloth. — Ps كُنَار

Fruit of the lote-tree. — ✱ كُنَار

Canary (bird). — ✧ كَنَارِي

Piece of linen. — كِتَّارَة

Kind of guitar. — كِنَّارَة وكَنَّارَة ج كَنَّارَات وكَنَانِير

To bury (a treasure). To press a. th. in a bag. To stick (a spear). — ✱ كَنَز i كَنْزًا ه

To be compact (flesh). To be pressed together (dates). — إِكْتَنَز

Buried treasure. Gold. — كَنْز ج كُنُوز

Fleshy. — كِنَاز (m. f.) ج كُنُز وكِنَاز, وكَنِيزُ اللَّحْم وكَنِيزَةٌ

Season of storing dates, storage. — كَنَاز

Stored dates. — كَنِيز

Compact and hard. — — ومُكْتَنِز

Treasure. Depository. — مَكْنَز ج مَكَانِز

To sweep (a house). — ✱ كَنَس o كَنْسًا, وكَنَّس ه

To enter her covert (gazelle). — كَنَس i كُنُوسًا, وتَكَنَّس واكْتَنَس

To retire in a tent. — تَكَنَّس

Sweepings. — كُنَاسَة

Nose-bag. ✧ Jewish synagogue. — كَنِيس

Retired, shy girl. Christian church; synagogue, temple. — كَنِيسَة ج كَنَائِس

Ecclesiastical. — ✧ كَنَائِسِي

Covert of gazelles. — كِنَاس ج كُنُس وأَكْنِسَة

Repairing to its covert (gazelle). — كَانِس ج كُنُوس وكُنَّس وكَوَانِس

The stars. The angels. — الجَوَارِي الكُنَّس

Sweeper. — كَنَّاس

Broom. — مِكْنَسَة ج مَكَانِس

Remaining in its covert (gazelle). — مُكَانِس

To twist the skirts of (a garment). To blunt (a toothpick). — ✱ كَنَش o كَنْشًا ه

To urge a. o. to complete a. th. — أَكْنَش ه عن

Stump, stub. — كُنَاشَة ج كُنَاشَات

To move the nose in scoffing. — ✱ كَنَص — كَنَّص

Sturdy (ass). — كُنَاص

To grieve a. o. (affair). — ✱ كَنَظ o i كَنْظًا, وتَكَنَّظ ه

Anxiety. — كُنْظَة

To fold the wings for alighting (bird). — ✱ كَنَع a كُنُوعًا, وأَكْنَع

To draw to its setting (sun). To be at hand (affair). — كَنَع

To desire a. th. — — في

To submit to. — — الى

To cleave to a. o. (scent). — — ب

He swore by God. — — بالله تعالى

To retire from. — — وكَنَّع عن

To shrivel. — كَنَع a كُنُوعًا وكَنِع a كَنَعًا

To contract a. th. — كَنَّع ه

To humble o.'s self. — أَكْنَع

To assemble. — — واكْتَنَع

To be bound with (fetters: captive). — تَكَنَّع في

To be addicted to. — تَكَنَّع ب

To draw near (night). — إِكْتَنَع

To compassionate a. o. — — على

Wrinkled, broken (old man). — كَنِيع

Camous (nose). Fettered (captive). — كَانِع

Having a broken hand. Vehement (hunger). — كَنِيع

Dry-handed. — أَكْنَع م كَنْعَاء ج كُنْع, ومُكَنَّع ومُكْتَنِع ومَكْنُوع

Canaan, son of Ham. — كَنْعَان

The Canaanites. — الكَنْعَانِيُّون

To keep, to preserve a. th. To hoard, to press (a measure). — ✱ كَنَف o كَنْفًا ه

To stray from. — — عن

To fence a. th. — — وكَنَّف ه

To help a. o. — كَنَف وكَانَف وأَكْنَف ه

To build an enclosure for (cattle). — — o i كَنْفًا ه

To surround, to encompass a. o. — تَكَنَّف واكْتَنَف ه

To make an enclosure for cattle. — إِكْتَنَف

Shepherd's bag. — كِنْف

Wing of birds. Shelter, protection. — كَنَف ج أَكْنَاف

Side, flank. Country, neighbourhood. — — وكَنَفَة

Retired place. Privy. Enclosure. Veil. Shield. — كَنِيف ج كُنُف وكُنْف

Shelter. — كَانِفَة

Pastry made of sweet vermicelli. — ✧ كِنَافَة وكَنِيفَة ج كِنَافَات

Help, succour. — مُكَانَفَة

Thick-bearded. — مُكَنَّف اللِّحْيَة

To electrise a. th. ✧ كَهْرَبَ هـ
Yellow amber. كَهْرَبَا وكَهْرَبَاء
Electrical. P كَهْرَبَائِيّ وكَهْرَبِيّ
Electricity. كَهْرَبَائِيَّة وكَهْرَبِيَّة
Ambergris. ◘ كَهْرَمَان
To be full of caves (mountain). ✱ كهف — تَكَهَّفَ
To enter (a grotto). إِكْتَهَفَ هـ
Grotto, cavern. Shelter. كَهْف ج كُهُوف
The seven sleepers. أَصْحَاب الكَهْف
Egg-plant, *aubergine*. ✱ كَهْكَب وكَهْكَم
Fourth Coptic month; December. C كِيهَك
✱ كَهَلَ a كُهُولًا, وكَهُلَ o كُهُولَةً, وكَاهَلَ واكْتَهَلَ
To reach mature age.
To marry. كَاهَلَ
To be full-grown (plant). تَكَهَّلَ واكْتَهَلَ
Mature age. كُهُولَة وكُهُولِيَّة
Of mature age (man). Full-grown (pla.). كَهْل ج كَهْلُون وكُهُول وكِهَال وكُهْلَان وكُهَّل
Withers of a horse; base of the neck. كَاهِل ج كَوَاهِل
Spider. كَهُول
To crush a. o. (adversity). ✱ كَهَمَ a كَهْمًا ه
To be blunted, weakened, كَهِمَ a وكَهُمَ o كَهَامَةً وكُهُومًا
To be weakened (eye-sight). أَكْهَمَ
Blunt (sword). Slow-pacing (horse). Impeded (tongue). كَهَام
Decrepit and miserable (man). — وكَهِيم
To pretend to be a diviner. ✱ كَهَنَ a o كَهَانَةً وتَكَهَّنَ
To foretell a. th. to. — ل
To become a diviner. كَهُنَ o كَهَانَةً
✧ To be a priest. كَهَّنَ
Divination. كِهَانَة
✧ Priesthood. S كَهْنُوت
Diviner. Steward. ✧ Priest. كَاهِن ج كَهَنَة وكُهَّان
To be red-faced and foul-breathed. ✱ كَهِيَ a كَهًى
To vie in pride with. كَاهَى ه
To warm the fingers with the breath. أَكْهَى
To abstain from. — عن
To respect to regard a. o. إِكْتَهَى ه
I am ashamed to explain it verbally to thee. أَكْتَهِيكَ أَنْ أُشَافِهَكَ بِهِ

Acanthus, bear's breech (*plant*). P كَنْكَر
Coffee-kettle, metal boiler. ◘ كَنَكَة
To reach the farthest limit of. ✱ كنه — أَكْنَهَ واكْتَنَهَ هـ
Bottom, farthest end. Entity. Way, manner. Quantity. Opportunity. كُنْه
He knows it perfectly well. يَعْرِفُهُ كُنْهَ المَعْرِفَةِ
Improper speech. كَلَام فِي غَيْرِ كُنْهِهِ
Portions of clouds like mountains. ✱ كَنَهْوَر
To allude to. To speak allusively of. ✱ كَنَا o وكَنَى i كِنَايَةً عَن ب
To by-name, to surname a. o. كَنَى i كُنْيَةً وكِنْيَةً, وكَنَّى وأَكْنَى ه هـ وب
To be by-named. تَكَنَّى واكْتَنَى ب
By-name. كُنْوَة وكُنْيَة ج كُنًى وكِنًى
Metonimy. Allusion. كِنَايَة
Instead of. كِنَايَةً عَن
Hinting. Speaking metaphorically. كَانٍ ج كَانُون وكُنَاة
Hinted at. مَكْنِيّ عَنْهُ
Surnamed. مُكَنًّى
To warm the hands with the breath. To roar (lion). To groan (camel). ✱ كه — كَهْكَهَ
Roaring of lions; groan of camels. كَهْكَهَة
Weak, timid. كَهْكَاه وكَهْكَاهَة
To be dark gray (camel).. ✱ كَهِبَ a وكَهُبَ o كَهَبًا وكُهُوبًا
To be altered (colour). إِكْهَابَّ
Dark gray colour (of camels). كُهْبَة
كَاهِب م كَاهِبَة, وأَكْهَب م كَهْبَاء ج كُهْب
Dark gray.
To run (ass). ✱ كَهَدَ a كَهْدًا وكَهَدَانًا
To start (an ass). — ه
To importune with requests. — فِي الطَّلَب
To be weary, tired. أَكْهَدَ
To tire, to weary a. o. — ه
Toil, weariness. كَهْد
Swift-running (ass). كَهُود اليَدَيْن
To be advanced (day). To be intense (heat). ✱ كَهَرَ a كَهْرًا
To meet a. o. with a stern face. To oppress a. o. — ه
Stern-looking. كَهْرُور وكَهْرُورَة

To hasten. كار واكتار واستكار
To carry a bundle on the back. — واستكار
To thrust down a. o. with a spear. كوّر ه
To pack up (luggage). — ه
To make (the night) to alternate with (the day : God). — ه على
To despise a. o. أكار على
To fall down. To be prostrate. تكوّر
To wind on a turban. To be in readiness. To raise the tail in running (horse). إكتار
Ship laden with corn. كار ج كارت
✧ Craft, profession.
Nature. Plenty of goods. كوْر
Twist of a turban. Large flock. — ج أكوار
Blacksmith's furnace. Bellows. Hornet's nest. كور ج أكوار وأكوُر وكيران
Camel-saddle. — ومكوَر
Bundle. ✧ Round pad for expanding dough. كارة ج كارات
Province, district, town. ◻ Forehead. G كوره ج كوَر
Bee-hive of clay. ✧ Recess in a wall for storing food. كُوارة وكوّارة ج كوائر
Turban. مِكْوَر ومِكْوَرة
✧ In a lump, in a lot. ◻ مكوَرجة بالكورجة
To drink from a mug. ✱ كاز o كوزًا
To collect (things). — ه
To gather (tribe). تكوّز
To ladle (water) with a mug. إكتاز ه
Earthen jug with a handle. P كوز ج أكواز وكوزة وكيزان
Oblong-headed. مُكوّز الرأس
To walk on 3 feet (hamstrung camel). To coil itself up (snake). ✱ كاس o كوسًا
He walked slowly. — في السَّير
He abated the price in the sale. — في البيع
He was pitched on the head. — على رأسِهِ
To prostrate a. o. — وأكاس ه
To be thrown upside-down. تكوّس
To be tufty (plant). تكاوس
To hinder a. o. from. إكتاس ه عن
Drinking-cup. ✧ Chalice. كاس ج كاسات
Contrary wind. كوْس

Red-faced and foul-breathed. Stone without crack. أكهى
Men of talent. ألأكهاء
✱ كوّ وكوّة وكُوّة ج كوّات وكوًى وكواء Garret-window; mural aperture.
To drink from a cup. ✱ كاب o كوبًا, واكتاب
To pound a. th. كوّب ه
Cup without handle. كوب ج أكواب
Sigh. كوبة
Stone pestle. Drum. Chess. Backgammon. كوبة
To have few leaves (corn-crops). ✱ كوث — كوّث
Good crop. كوثة
To overpower a. o. ✱ كاح o كوحًا, وكوّح وكاوح وأكاح ه
To do harm to o. a. تكاوح
Foot of a mountain. كاح وكيح ج أكياح وكيوح
Clever manager of cattle. كِواح مال
Reed-hut, pavilion. Cell. P كوخ — كوخ وكاخ ج أكواخ وكوخان وكيخان وكوخة
Steward of a prince. P كاخية (كتخودا for) ج كواخ
To stop, to detain a. o. ✱ كاد o كوْدًا ه
To be about to. To intend, to wish. كاد a كودًا ومكادًا ومكادة
He was near to do. كاد وكيد يفعل
I was on the point of departing. كِدتُ أذهبُ
He has not seen her. لم يكد يراها
I scarcely see. ما أكاد أبصر
I wish to conceal it. أكاد أخفيها
To heap up, to hoard (things). كوّد ه
To tremble (old man). إكواد
I will not do it at all. لا أفعله ولا كودًا
I have no wish nor intention. لا مهمّة لي ولا مكادة
Scarcely. ✧ بالكاد
Heap. كودة ج أكواد
Inner side of the thighs. ✱ كوذ — كاذة مث كاذتان
To fall down to the thighs (waist-wrapper). كوّذ
Cowry used as money. كوذة
Pandanus odoratissimus (tree). كاذي
To wind (a turban) round (the head). ✱ كار o كورًا, وكوّر ه على

To walk on tiptoe. إكتام

Herd of camels. كوم ج أكوام

Heap of (earth, corn). كومة وكومة ج كوم وأكوام

High. Prominent. Big-humped (camel). أكوم م كوماء ج كوم

To be, to exist. To happen. To be *such* or *so*. ✱ كان o كونًا وكيانًا وكينونة

Nothing happens but what God wills. ما شاء الله كان

There was in the town. كان في المدينة

Zeyd was standing. كان زيدٌ قائمًا

He is dead. صار إلى كان

They are dead. صاروا إلى كانوا

To belong to. كان لِ

It was thy duty to do. كان لك أن تفعل

He used to do so. كان يفعل كذا

✧ When. متى كان

Whenever. إذا كان

✧ If. إن كان

✧ Whatever may be; in any case. كان ما كان

Would that it had never existed! لا كان ولا استكان

✧ Whoever, whosoever. Whatever person. أي من كان

✧ Whatsoever, whatever. Anything. أيش ما كان

To become surety for. كان o كونًا وكيانًا على

To create, to produce a. th. كوّن ه وه

To come into existence, to originate. تكوّن

To answer for. إكتان على وب

To become humble, lowly. إستكان

Existence, state, being. كون

Because, on account of. لِكون و✧ من كون

Being, existence. كون ج أكوان

State. Nature. كِيان

Warrant, surety. كِيانة

Saturn (planet). P كيوان

The book of Genesis. سِفر التكوين

The created beings. الكائنات

Place, spot. Instead of. مكان ج أمكنة وأماكن

Place. State, Erudition. Rank. مكانة ج مكانات

To be astonished. ✱ كوه a كوهًا

To press upon a. o. (business). تكوّه على

Kettle-drum. Square (carpenter's instrument). P كوس ج كوسات

✧ Small gourd, cucumber. Small vegetable marrow. ✧ كوسا (*un.* كوساة)

Thin-bearded, beardless. كوسى (*for* كوسج)

Dense (plant). Heaped up (sand). كوساء ج كوس

Chisel for stones. مِكوس ج مكاوس

✧ To be active in (work). ✱ كاش o كوشًا في

✧ To make up (things). كوّش ه

✧ Diligence, activity. كوشة

✧ Detachment, troop. كاشة وكوشة

To have a prominent wrist-bone. ✱ كوع a كوعًا

To luxate the cubitus with (a blow). كوّع ه ب

✧ To stop the bleeding of (a wound) with hot oil. — ه

To have the cubitus luxated. ✧ To be fomented with oil. تكوّع

Extremity of the radius, cubitus, wrist-bone. ✧ Elbow. كاع وكوع ج أكواع

Prominence, distortion of the cubitus. كوع

Having a prominent or luxated wrist. أكوع م كوعاء ج كوع

To sew up (leather). ✱ كاف o كوفًا ه

To shear (leather). To form the letter ك. To go to Cufa. كوّف ه

To assemble (people). تكوّف تكوّفًا وكوفانًا

The letter ك. الكاف

Cufa (town in the province of Bagdad). كوفة

Mound of sand. — وكوفان وكوفان وكوّفان

Thicket of reeds, trees. كوفان وكوفان

Cufic writing. كوفيّ

The grammarians of Cufa. الكوفيّون

Head-shawl. كوفيّة

Star. *See* كب. ✱ كوكب

To throng (people). ✱ كال — تكوّل

To assault, to crush a. o. — وانكال على

Papyrus (*plant*). كولان وكولان

✧ Queen (at cards). ✧ كول

To heap up (earth, stones). ✱ كوم — كوّم ه

✱ كَوَى i كَيًّا ه To cauterise a. o. To sting a. o. (scorpion).

— ه بِعَيْنِهِ He gazed at him.

— ه ✧ To iron (linen).

كَاوَى ه To insult a. o.

تَكَوَّى To feel a burning pain.

إِكْتَوَى To be cauterised.

إِسْتَكْوَى To ask to be cauterised.

كَيّ و✧ كَوِي Cauterisation. ✧ Ironing.

✧ حَجَر الكَيّ Lunar-caustic.

كَوَّاء Insolent.

✧ كَوَّايَة Female ironer of linen.

كَاوِيَاء, ومِكْوَاة ج مَكَاوٍ Hot iron for branding. ✧ Iron for linen.

✱ كَيَا – كَاء i كَيًّا وكَيْئَةً وكَآء o كَوْءًا وكَآء عن To shy from.

أَكَاء To deter a. o.

كَآء وكَآءَة وكَيّء وكَيْئَة Faint-hearted, cowardly.

✱ كَيْ ولِكَيْ In order that.

كَيْ لَا ولِكَيْ لَا Lest.

كَيْمَا ولِكَيْمَا In order that.

✱ كَيت – كَيَّت ه To cram (a bag). To pack a. th.

كَيتَ وكَيتَ So and so, thus and thus.

✱ كَاحَ i كَيْحًا, وأَكَاحَ في To penetrate into a. th. (sword).

أَكَاحَ ه To destroy a. o.

✱ كَادَ i كَيْدًا To exert o.'s self, to strive. To shift, to plot, to be artful. To vomit. To yield fire (flint).

— وكَايَدَ ه To circumvent, to ensnare a. o.

✧ كَيَّد To be obstinate, rancorous.

تَكَايَد To lay snares to o. a.

إِكْتَاد To be ensnared.

كَيْد ج كِيَاد Deceit, shift. War. Vomit. ✧ Rancour.

مَكِيدَة ج مَكَايِد Stratagem, wile, shift.

✱ كَارَ i كَيَارًا To raise the tail in running (horse).

كِير ج أَكْيَار وكِيَرَة وكِيرَان Blacksmith's bellows.

G كِير His lordship (title of a Greek bishop).

✱ كَاسَ i كَيْسًا وكِيَاسَة To be intelligent, shrewd (child).

— ه To outwit a. o.

كَيَّس ه To render a. o. clever, shrewd.

✧ كَيَّس ه To bag a. th.

كَايَس ه To vie in sagacity with.

أَكَاس إِكَاسَةً وأَكْيَس إِكْيَاسًا To beget sagacious children.

تَكَيَّس To affect shrewdness.

كَيْس وكِيَاسَة Intelligence, skill.

كِيس ج أَكْيَاس وكِيَسَة Purse, membrane of the fœtus. Bag. ✧ Hair-glove for rubbing in a bath.

✧ على كِيس ان In order to, under the plea of.

✧ عَلَى كِيسِهِ At his own expense.

كَيِّس ج أَكْيَاس وكَيْسَى, ومُكَيَّس Sagacious. Shrewd.

✧ كُوَيِّس Pretty, nice.

كَيْسَان Treachery.

أَكْيَس م كِيسَى وكُوسَى ج كِيس More clever, shrewder.

✧ أَكْوَس Prettier, nicer.

مِكْيَاس ج مَكَايِيس, ومَكْيَسَة Begetting acute sons (woman).

✧ مُكَيِّس ومُكَيِّسَاتِي Waiter, rubber in a bath.

✱ كَاصَ i كَيْصًا وكَيَصَانًا وكُيُوصًا To walk quickly.

— الطَّعَام To eat alone. To eat much.

— عَن To be deterred from.

كَايَص ه To treat (an affair).

كَيْص Avarice, sordidness.

✱ كَاعَ i كَيْعًا وكَيْعُوعَةً عَن To be deterred from.

كَائِع وكَاعٍ ج كَاعَة Faint-hearted.

✱ كَافَ i كَيْفًا, وكَيَّف ه To cut a. th.

كَيَّف ه To give a shape to.

✧ كَيَّف ه To enliven, to divert a. o.

تَكَيَّف To assume a shape. ✧ To make merriment.

كَيْفَ How? Like, as.

كَيْفَ حَالُكَ How dost thou do?

كَيْفَ تَصْنَع أَصْنَع I shall act as thou.

✧ كَيْف Well-being, enjoyment. Caprice, humour.

✧ عَلَى كَيْفِهِ As it pleases him.

كَيْفَمَا كَان Howsoever.

كَيْفِيَّة ج كَيْفِيَّات Qualification, mode of entity. ✧ Pleasure-party.

كِيفَة ج كِيَف Piece of cloth.

✱ كَيك – كَيْكَة ج كَيَاكِي Egg.

كُيَيْكَة وكُيَيْعَة Small egg.

✲ كَالَ ¡ كَيْلًا وَمَكَالًا وَمَكِيلًا, وكَيَّلَ هُ To measure (grain). To weigh (coins).
— هُ هُ وَلِ To measure a. th. for a. o.
— هُ بِ To compare a. th. with.
هٰذَا الطَّعَامُ لَا يَكِيلُنِي This food is not sufficient for me.
كَالَ ¡ كَيْلًا To give no fire (steel).
كَايَلَ هُ To measure for a. o. To requite a. o.
تَكَيَّلَ To keep on the rear (soldier).
تَكَايَلَ To quarrel together. To partake a. th. together.
إِكْتَالَ من وعلى To receive measured corn from.
كَيْل ج أَكْيَال Measure for grain about 3 $^1/_2$ gallons. Fragments of a flint. ✧ Contents of a measure. Measure of 6 mudds.
كَيْلَة ج كَيْلَات ✧ Vessel for measuring. Measure of two mudds.
كِيَالَة Measuring. Fee of a measurer.
كَيِّل وكَيُّول Rubbish, waste.
كَيُّول Rear-rank of fighters. Coward.
كَيَّال Grain-measurer.
مِكْيَل ومِكْيَال ومِكْيَلَة ج مَكَايِل ومَكَايِيل Measure for grain.
G كِيمِيَاء وكِيمِيَا Alchemy. Chemistry.
كِيمِيّ وكِيمَاوِيّ Alchemist. Chemist. Chemical.
✲ كَانَ ¡ كَيْنًا واسْتَكَانَ لِ To submit to.
أَكَانَ هُ To humble a. o.
إِكْتَانَ To be sad, grieved.
كِينَة Adversity. State, condition.
✧ كِينَا Quina, quinine.
✲ كَاهَ ¡ كَيْهًا هُ To smell the breath of.
كَـيِّه Unskilful, awkward.

ل

Particle used as a corroborative. لَ ✲
Indeed the Lord hearkens to my prayer. إِنَّ رَبِّي لَسَمِيعُ الدُّعَاءِ
As thou livest! لَعَمْرُكَ
Had he not repented, he would have surely perished. لَوْلَا تَابَ لَهَلَكَ
Used instead of لِ *with the affixed pronouns.*
To me, to us, to thee, to him, to you. لِي لَنَا لَكَ لَهُ لَكُم
Preposition expressing possession, attribution, design. To, for. لِ ✲
Glory be to God! أَلْمَجْدُ لِلّٰهِ
It is to thee to decide the affair. لَكَ الأَمْرُ
I have no gold coin. مَا لِي دِينَارٌ
He came up to our rescue. قَامَ لِمُعَاوَنَتِنَا
Before the Aorist لِ *is used as a conjunction, to express the aim, intention, order.* That, in order to.
I have come in order to show thee regard. جِئْتُكَ لِأُكْرِمَكَ او لِأَنْ أُكْرِمَكَ
He must write. لِيَكْتُبْ فَلْيَكْتُبْ وَلْيَكْتُبْ
Because. لِأَجْلِ
Because. لِأَنَّ
Why? لِأَيِّ شَيْءٍ ✧ لَيْش ◻ لَي
Lest; lest he, that he may not. لِئَلَّا (*for* لِأَنْ لَا)
Till now, not yet. لِلسَّاعَة و✧ لِسَّة
Why? On what account? لِمَا
Why? لِمَاذَا
Adverb of negation: no, not at all. Not (*with nouns and verbs*). لَا ✲
Zeyd is come, not Amr. جَاءَ زَيْدٌ لَا عَمْرٌو
Is used instead of لَيْسَ.
There is no good in him. لَا خَيْرَ فِيهِ
Do not do it. لَا تَفْعَلْ ذٰلِكَ
He came without speaking. جَاءَ لَا يَتَكَلَّمُ
He shall not depart to day. لَا يُسَافِرُ اليَوْمَ
He came to me, but did not ask me anything. جَاءَنِي وَلَا سَأَلَنِي شَيْئًا
Be always happy! لَا زِلْتَ سَعِيدًا
Even not, nor. وَلَا

Especially, above all. لَاسِيَّمَا
To shine, to be bright (star). To blaze (fire). To undulate (mirage). ✲ لَأْلَأَ وَتَلَأْلَأَ
Pearl. لُؤْلُؤ
A pearl. A wild cow. لُؤْلُؤَة ج لَآلِئ
Pearl-like colour. لُؤْلُؤِيّ وَلُؤْلُؤَان
Art of setting pearls. لِئَالَة
Exultation, complete joy. Light of a lamp. لَأْلَاء
Seller of pearls. — وَلَآل وَلَأَّاء
Standing up, upright. ✲ لَأَبَ — مُلْتَئِب
To urge, to importune a. o. ✲ لَأَطَ a لَأْطًا ه
To sadden, to discard a. o. ✲ لَأَظَ a لَأْظًا ه
To eat becomingly. ✲ لَأَفَ a لَأْفًا الطَّعَامَ
To send a. o. towards. ✲ لَأَكَ — أَلْأَكَ ه إِلَى
Message, mission. مَلْأَك وَمَلْأَكَة
Messenger. Angel. مَلْأَك وَمَلَك و✧ مَلَاك ج مَلَائِكَة وَمَلَائِك
To dress (a wound). To solder, to close up (a rent, a hole). To furnish (an arrow) with feathers. ✲ لَأَمَ a لَأْمًا ه
To accuse a. o. of villainies. — ه
To repair a. th. To better, to consolidate a. th. لَأَّمَ وَلَاءَمَ وَلِئَامًا وَأَلْأَمَ ه وه
To be low-born. To be avaricious. لَؤُمَ لُؤْمًا وَمَلْأَمَةً وَلَآمَةً
To suit a. o. (food, climate). To be adapted to. To agree with a. o. لَاءَمَ ه
To make peace between. — بَيْنَ
To have low-born sons. To act meanly. أَلْأَمَ
To be mended, soldered. To be corrected, bettered. تَلَأَّمَ وَتَلَاءَمَ وَالْتَأَمَ
To heal (wound). To stick together; to coalesce, to unite together. إِلْتَأَمَ
To put on a breast-plate. إِسْتَلْأَمَ
To have an ungenerous father. — ه

To betake ungenerous sons-in-law.
لأم Repaired, arranged. Feathered (arrow).
لِئم Peace, concord, agreement.
— ج آلآم ولئام Equal, alike.
لُمة (m. f.) Equal.
لُؤم Meanness of temper. Avarice.
لُوَام Need, want, thing necessary.
رِيش لُؤَام Feathers of an arrow.
لأمة ج لأم ولُؤَم Breast-plate.
لُؤمة Agricultural implements. Plough. Furniture of a house. Tale-bearer.
لَئِيم ج لِئام ولُؤَماء ولُؤمان Vile, ignoble. Avaricious.
مَلأم ومَلأمَ Excusing base people.
يَا لَأمَان ويَا لُؤمَان ويَا مَلأم O villain!
مُلأّم Wearing a coat of mail.
مُلائِم Becoming, convenient. Fit, suitable.
مُلاءَمة Convenience.
مُلتئِم Repaired. United, collected.
✲ لأى a لأيًا, والتأى To be slow.
ألأى إلآء To fall into distress.
إلتأى اِلتِئاء To be distressed.
لأي ولأي ولأواء Hardship, trouble.
✲ لَبّ o لَبًّا, وألَبّ ب To stop in (a place).
لَبّ ة To wound a. o. in the breast.
— ه To shell (a nut).
— وألَبّ ة To put a breast-strap to (a horse).
لَبّ o a لَبًّا ولَبابة To be gifted with a penetrative mind. To be kind-hearted.
لَبّب To become pulpy (grain).
— ة To tuck up o.'s clothes. and grapple a. o. by the collar. To strike a. o. on the upper part of the chest.
ألَبّ To have pulpy grain (corn).
ألَبّ ل To happen to a. o. (event).
تَلَبّب To tuck up o.'s clothes.
تَلَبّب ل To gird o.'s self for (fight).
لَبّ على Assiduous to.
لُبّ ج لُبُوب Heart; middlepart. Fruit-stone. Core, pulp of a fruit. Crum of bread. Fecula.
— ج ألباب وألُبّ Heart, mind, intelligence.
— ولُباب Pith, quintessence, choice part.

لَبّة ج لَبّات Upper part of the breast. Loving her husband (woman).
لَبَب ج ألباب Upper part of the breast. Breast-girth of a horse. Fine sand scattered on the ground.
هُوَ في لَبَب رَخِيّ He is in easy circumstances.
لَباب Small quantity of fodder.
لَبابِ لَبابِ There is no harm.
لُباب Pure, stainless (nobility).
لِبابة Fine flour. Garb of a warrior.
بَنات ألبُب Veins of the heart.
لَبِيب ج ألِبّاء Gifted with a sound judgment. Assiduous, persevering.
تَلبِيب ج تَلابِيب Collar. Garment covering the upper part of the breast.
مُلَبّ ومُلَبَّب Having a breast-girth (horse).
مَلبُوب Gifted with a sound judgment.
✲ لَبلَب ب To fondle (her child: mother). To lick (her young one: ewe).
لَبلَب To scatter (people). ✧ To prate.
لَبلَب ولَبلُب Kind, meek.
لَبلاب *Dolichos lablab*, bindweed. Convolvulus.
✧ Speedwell (plant). لَبلاب المَجُوس
Te لَبلَبِي Toasted chickpeas.
P لَولَب ج لَوالِب Pipe, conduit. Sink-hole. ✧ Stairs in spiral. Screw; pegs. Tap, spout. Metal-spring.
لَولَبِيّ Spiral.
✲ لَبَأ a لَبأً ة To milk (a ewe) for the first time.
— وألبَأ ه To boil (biestings).
— وألبَأ ة To give to a. o. (biestings).
إلتبَأ واستَلبَأ ة To suck (his mother: lamb).
لِبَأ Biestings.
لَبُأة ولَباءة ولَبوَة ج لَبُوات Lioness.
✲ لَبِيتة ج لَبِيت Carp-fish; gold-fish.
✲ لَبِث a لَبثًا ولُبثًا ولَبَثًا ولَباثًا ولَباثة ولَبِيثة, وتَلَبّث ب To abide, to tarry in (a place).
مَا لَبِث أن فَعَل He was not long before doing it.
لَبّث وألبَث ة ب To delay a. o. in.
إستَلبَث ة To find a. o. slow.

be leafy (plant). ✧ To be pressed, crammed (bag).
Wool. لَبْد
He possesses nothing مَالَهُ سَبَدٌ ولَا لَبَدٌ
lit : he has no hair nor wool.
Matted (hair). لَبِد
Sedentary, remaining at home. — ولُبَد ولُبَّد
Last of Lokman's seven eagles. لُبَد
Wool, hair pressed and rolled together. Felt. لِبْد ج لُبود وأَلْباد, ولِبْدَة ج لِبَد
Mane of a horse, of a lion. لِبْدَة ج لِبَد ✧ Felt-cap.
Pad, saddle-felt. لِبْد ولِبَادَة و✧ لُبَّاد
He never stays at home. لَا يَجِفّ لِبْدُهُ
Numerous flocks, extensive property. مَالٌ لُبَد وأَبْد ولَابِد
Felt-cap. لُبَّادَة
Lurking. Lion. لَابِد
Manufacturer of felt. لَبَّاد
Tick, worm. لَبُود
Fodder-bag. Small bag. لَبِيد
Quail (bird). — ولُبَادَى ولُبَّادَى
Sticking to (his horse). مُلْبِد على
To strike, to revile a. o. ✱ لَبَزَ i لَبْزًا ه
To eat greedily. — ه
To confuse a. th. To render a. th. dubious. ✱ لَبَس i لَبْسًا, ولَبَّس ه على
To put on (a garment). لَبِس a لُبْسًا ه To clothe o.'s self. ✧ To attire o.'s self.
To enjoy a long time the society of. — ه دَهْرًا
To conceal a. th. To confuse a. th. To dress a. o. لَبَّس ه
To interfere in (a business). لَابَس ه
To know a. o. intimately. — ه
To cover a. th. أَلْبَس ه
To clothe a. o. with (a garment). — ه ه
To clothe o.'s self with. To interfere in (an affair). تَلَبَّس ب
To be confused, dubious, ambiguous to a. o. (affair). إِلْتَبَس على
Confusion, dubiousness, ambiguousness. لَبْس ولُبْس ولُبْسَة والْتِبَاس
Clothes, garment. لِبْس ج لُبُوس
Dress. Confusion. لِبَاس ج أَلْبِسَة ولُبُس
✧ Tight drawers.

Delay. Tarrying, sojourning. لَبْث ولَبْث ولَبَاث
Tarrying, staying. لَبِث ولَابِث
Delay. Short stay. لُبْثَة
Promiscuous company. لَبِيثَة ج لَبَائِث
He felled him on the ground. ✱ لَبَج لَبْجًا بِهِ الأَرْضَ
To strike a. o. with (a stick). — ه ب
He was prostrated on the earth. لُبِج بِهِ
Grappling iron. لَبْجَة ولَبَجَة ج لَبْج ولَبَج
To become old. ✱ لَبِخ a لَبْخًا, ولَبَّخ وأَلْبَخ
Decrepit old man. لَبِخ
To beat, to strike a. o. ✱ لَبَخ a لَبْخًا ه
To be fleshy (body). — a لُبُوخًا
✧ To bruise a. o. with blows. ✧ لَبَّخ To apply a poultice.
To slap a. o. on the face. لَابَخ مُلَابَخَة ولِبَاخًا ه
To perfume o.'s self. ✧ To be bruised with blows. تَلَبَّخ
✧ Poultice, cataplasm. لَبْخَة ج لَبَخَات
Acacia mimosa : acacia of Egypt. لَبْخَة و ◻ لَبَخ
Fleshy. لَبِيخ
Vesicle of musk. لَبِيخَة
To stick to (the ground). To squat on the ground (man). ✱ لَبَد o لُبُودًا, وأَلْبَد ب
To dwell in (a place). — ولَبِد a لَبَدًا, وأَلْبَد ب
To pad, to felt the opening of a sword-sheath. لَبَد i لَبْدًا, ولَبَّد ه
To mat, to felter (hair, wool). To felt a. th. ✧ To cram a. th. To ram (the earth). To spy a. o. — ولَبَّد ه وه
To cleave to (the earth : dew). To lay (dust : rain). لَبَّد ه
To patch, to mend a. th. — وأَلْبَد ه
To wad (a saddle). أَلْبَد ه
To put a felt-cloth on (a horse). — ه
To stick a. th. to. — ه ب
To put forth soft hair (camel). أَلْبَد
To become compact (earth). To be entangled (wool, hair). To be felted (wool). ✧ To lurk. تَلَبَّد
To be commingled (leaves). To إِلْتَبَد

Modesty, honest shame. لباس التَّقوى
Way of dressing. Costume, dress. لِبسة
Clothing. Breast-plate. لَبُوس
Threadbare (garment). Alike, equal. لَبِيس
Ambiguousness. ✧ Coat, layer. تلبيس
Hypocrite, dissembler.
He came feigning to be heedless. جاء لَابِسًا أُذُنَيْهِ
Having or wearing many clothes. لَبَّاس
Clothing. مَلْبَس ج مَلَابِس
He has no pride. إِنَّ فِيهِ لَمَلْبَسًا
Clothes, clothing. مَلْبُوس ج مَلَابِيس
◘ Mad, bigot.
Ambiguous, confused (case). مُلَبَّس
✧ Sweetmeats, comfits.
Equivocal, confused, dubious. مُلْبِس ومُلْتَبِس
✧ To pick up a. th. To pack off. ◘ To make a dam. ✧ لَبَّش ه
Clothes, luggage. People of various tribes. ✧ لَبْش
Brushwood bundles of reeds for a dam. ◘ لِبْش
He threw him on the ground. ✱ لَبَط o لَبْطًا بِهِ الأَرْضَ
To be overthrown. لُبِطَ بِهِ
✧ To kick. لَبَطَ i و✧ لَبَّط
To gallop (camel). لَبَطَ i لَبْطًا، وتَلَبَّطَ والتَبَطَ
To be confounded. تَلَبَّطَ والتَبَطَ
Gallop. لَبْطة
A kick. لَبْطة
Wont to kick. لَبَّاط
To soften a. th. ✱ لَبَقَ o لَبْقًا، ولَبَّقَ ه
To be intelligent, sagacious, skilful, able. لَبِقَ a لَبَقًا، ولَبُقَ o لَبَاقَةً
To suit a. o. (clothes). — ب ول
✧ To adorn, to embellish a. th. لَبَّقَ ه
Elegance in dress. Skilfulness. skill, dexterity. لَبَق ولَبَاقة
Skilful, dexterous, able. لَبِق ولَبِيق
Softened. ✧ Embellished. مُلَبَّق
To mix a. th. ✱ لَبَكَ o لَبْكًا، ولَبَّكَ ه
To confuse, to entangle (an affair).
✧ To involve, to entangle a. o. in. لَبَّكَ ه ب
To hold unbecoming talks. أَلْبَكَ
To be entangled (affair). تَلَبَّكَ والتَبَكَ

Imbroglio, complicated (case). لَبْك ولَبَكة
Entangled (affair). لَبِك
Mouthful. ✧ Perplexity. لُبْكة
Party of men. لُبَاكة ولَبِيكة
Food made of dates and butter or of flour and fresh cheese. لَبِيكة
Entangled. ✧ Busy, anxious. مُلْتَبِك ومَلْبُوك
To have the udders filled with milk (ewe). ✱ لَبِنَ a لَبَنًا، وأَلْبَنَ
To give to a. o. milk to drink. لَبَنَ o i لَبْنًا ه
To strike a. o. with. — ه ب
To make bricks with clay and straw. لَبَّنَ
He treated the affair in council. — المَجْلِسَ
To have much milk. To prepare a porridge of bran, milk and honey. أَلْبَنَ
To be slow, to be late. تَلَبَّنَ
To suck milk. اِلْتَبَنَ
To ask for milk. اِسْتَلْبَنَ
Milk. Sour milk. Curd. لَبَن ج أَلْبَان
Raw bricks of clay and straw. ✧ Unburnt bricks. لَبِن ولِبْن ولِبِن (un لَبِنَة)
Galactite. حَجَر اللَّبَن
White clay. لَبَن العَذْرَاء
Cream-cheese. لَبْنَة
Meat-balls prepared with sour milk. ✧ لَبَنِيَّة
Breast; middle of the breast. لَبَان
Sucking of milk. ◘ Rope for towing. لِبَان
Olibanum, gum-resin used as frankincense. لُبَان
Pitch-resin; depilatory. لُبَان شَامِي
✧ Magnesia, Epsom salt. لُبَان العَذْرَاء
Affair, business, cares. لُبَانَة ج لُبَانَات ولُبَان
Mount Lebanon. لُبْنَان
Lebanese, from Lebanon. لُبْنَانِي
Rich in milk. لَابِن ج لَابِنُون
Udder, teats. لَوَابِن
Fond of milk. لَبِن ولَبُون
لَبِنَة ولَبِينَة , ولَبُون ولَبُونَة ج لِبَان ولُبُن ولُبْن
Milch-ewe. ولَبَّان
Storax لُبْنَى
Benzoin-gum. عَسَل اللُّبْنَى

Fed on milk (horse). لَبِين
Bricklayer. لَبَّان وَمُلَبِّن
✧ Seller of sour milk. لَبَّان
Food made of bran, milk and honey. تَلْبِين وتَلْبِينَة
Milking-vessel. Mould for bricks. مِلْبَن ج مَلَابِن
✧ Frame of a door, of a window. مَلْبَن
Food of starch and sugar.
Lioness. ✲ لَبُوَة ج لَبَوَات
To answer a call. ✲ لبى – لَبَّى تَلْبِيَةً
He undertook the pilgrimage with zeal. – بِالْحَجّ
Here I am. At thy service. لَبَّيْكَ
They are in perfect harmony. بَيْنَهُم مُلْتَبِيَة
To bray, to crumble a. th. To tighten, to bind a. o. ✲ لَتَّ o لَتًّا ه
To stir a. th. with. – ه ب
✧ To jabber, to tattle. لَتَّ
To cleave to. لُتَّ ب
To conceal the head under the wings (bird). أَلَتَّ
✧ Gossip; tittle-tattle. لَتّ
✧ Trifle; nonsense. لَتَّة
Goddess of the ancient Arabs. لَات ولَاتّ
✧ Jabberer. لَتَّات
Mixture. Tree-bark crumbled with the fingers. لُتَات
✧ To prate. ✲ اَسْتَلَتَ
Perjury, false oath. ✧ Tattle, nonsense. لَتْلَتَة
To hurt a. o. with. ✲ لَتَأَ a لَتْأً ه ب
He struck him on the chest. – ه في صَدْرِهِ
To look steadfastly at. – بِعَيْنِهِ إلى
To cleave to. ✲ لَتِبَ o لَتْبًا ولُتُوبًا ب
To be steady, steadfast in. – في
To fasten (a housing) upon (a horse). – و لَتَّبَ ه على
To impose (an affair) upon a. o. أَلْتَبَ ه على
To come to blows. تَلَاتَبَ
To clothe o.'s self in. إِلْتَتَبَ ه
Adhering. Steadfast. لَاتِب
Keeping to his house. مِلْتَب
Old clothes. مَلَاتِب
To strike. a. o. ✲ لَتَحَ a لَتْحًا ه

To cast fierce looks at. لَتَحَ ه بِبَصَرِهِ
To be hungry. لَتِحَ a لَتَحًا
Intelligent. لَتِح ولَاتِح ولُتَاح ولُتَحَة
Starved. لَتْحَان م لَتْحَى
To strike a. o. with the fist. ✲ لَتَدَ i لَتْدًا ه
To cuff, to box a. o. ✲ لَتَرَ لَتْرًا ه
To strike a. o. ✲ لَتَمَ o لَتْمًا ه
To shoot (an arrow). – ه
Wound. لَتْم
Hedge-hog. ✲ لتن – أُتْنَة
The Latin church (*opp. to* the Eastern). The Latins. L لَاتِين (*un.* لَاتِينِي)
✲ لتي – أَلَّتِي م اللَّتَانِ ج اللَّوَاتِي والَّلَاءِي واللَّاتِي
F. of أَلَّذِي. Who.
Diminutive of الَّتِي. أَللَّتَيَّا واللُّتَيَّا
Misfortune. أَلَّتِي واللُّتَيَّا
To be continuous (rain). ✲ لَثَّ o لَثًّا, وأَلَثَّ
To remain in (a place). – وأَلَثَّ ب
To importune a. o. – وأَلَثَّ على
Dew. لَثّ
To be weak, feeble. ✲ لَثْلَثَ
To speak indistinctly. – كَلَامَهُ
To roll a. o. along in (the dust). – ه في
To urge upon. – على
To waver in. – وتَلَثْلَثَ في
Let us quiet. اَلْثِثُوا بِنَا
To roll o.'s self in (the dust). تَلَثْلَثَ في
Weak, irresolute. لَثْلَاث ولَثْلَاثَة
To lap a. th. (dog). ✲ لَثَا لَثْأً ه
To set (furniture) in order. ✲ لَثَدَ i لَثْدًا ه
Travellers at rest. لِثْدَة
To tap a. o. slightly. ✲ لَثَطَ i لَثْطًا ه
Inner part of the lips near the roots of the teeth. ✲ لِثَة
To pronounce ر thickly. To mispronounce letters. ✲ لَثِغَ a لَثَغًا
Mispronunciation of the letter ر. لَثْغ ولُثْغَة
Mouth. لَثْغَة
Mispronouncing the letter ر. أَلْثَغ م لَثْغَاء ج لُثْغ
To be windless and damp (day). To be moist. To be muddy (ground). ✲ لَثِقَ a لَثَقًا
To moisten, to wet a. th. لَثَّقَ وأَلْثَقَ ه
To be moistened. تَلَثَّقَ والْتَثَقَ

لَثَق Moisture. Mud.
لَثِق Moist, wet. Muddy (ground).
✱ لَثَم i ولَثِم a لَثماً ه To kiss (the hands, the mouth).
لَثَم i لَثماً ه To pound (pebbles) in walking (camels). To wound (a camel's feet : pebbles).
لَثَم i ولَثِم a والتَثَم وتلَثَّم To muffle o.'s self.
لِثمَة Way of putting a muffler.
لَثمَة A kiss.
لِثَام Muffler.
لَاثِم ج لُثَّم Bruising, breaking.
مَلثُوم Hurt by pebbles (foot).
مُلثَم ومُتَلَثِّم Muffled.
✱ لَثِيَ a لَثًى وأَلثَى To exude gum, resin (tree).
تلَثَّى والتَثَى To collect gum.
لَثًى Gum, resin of various trees. Dew.
— الثَّوب Uncleanliness of clothes.
لَثٍ م لَثِيَة Moist. Gummy, resinous (tree).
لِثَة ج لِثَات ولِثًى Gum of the teeth.
لَثَاة Uvula.
الحُرُوف اللِّثَوِيَّة The gingival letters ث, ذ and ظ.
✱ لَجَّ a i لَجَجاً ولَجَاجاً ولَجَاجَةً في To insist upon a. th. To quarrel obstinately about. To persevere in.
— على To importune, to urge a. o.
— بِهِ To cleave to a. o. (cares).
لَجَّج To enter the main sea (ship).
لَاجَّ ه To quarrel obstinately.
تلَجَّج واستَلَجَّ ه To claim a. th. importunately.
إِلتَجَّ To be confused (voices). To be rough, swollen (sea).
إِستَلَجَّ ب To keep (an oath).
لُجّ, ولُجَّة ج لُجَج ولُجَاج Crowd, large quantity. Main sea, fathomless sea. Depth.
لُجَّة Silver. Mirror.
لَجَّة Confused voices.
لَجَاج ولَجَاجَة Instance, obstinacy. Importunity.
لَاجّ ولَجُوج ولَجُوجَة ولُجَجَة Quarreller, pertinacious. Importune.
لُجِّيّ Expanded and fathomless (sea).
مَلجُوج عليه Importuned, urged.

✱ لَجلَج وتلَجلَج لِسانُهُ بِالكَلام To repeat the same words ; to stutter.
— في فِيهِ To chew a. th., to turn (a morsel) in the mouth.
لَجلَاج Stammerer.
✱ لَجَأَ a لَجأً, ولَجِئ a لَجَأً, والتَجَأَ إلى To seek the protection of, to take refuge with.
لَجَّأ ه To bequeath (property) exclusively to one heir.
لَجَّأ وأَلجَأ ه إلى To force to oblige a. o. to.
أَلجَأ ه To defend, to protect a. o.
— أَمرَهُ إلى He committed his affair to.
لَجَأ, ومَلجَأ ج مَلاجِئ Shelter, refuge, protection.
تَلجِئَة Compulsion, force.
لَاجِئ ومُلتَجِئ Repairing to ; asking protection.
✱ لَجِب a لَجَباً To be disorderly (mob). To roar (sea).
لَجُب o لُجُوبَة, ولَجَّب To yield little or much milk (ewe).
لَجَب Uproar, clamour. Agitation of the sea.
لَجِب Clamorous (army).
لَجبَة ولَجَبَة ولَجِبَة ج لِجَاب ولَجَبَات Yielding little or much milk (ewe).
✱ لَجَذ o ولَجِذ a لَجذاً To graze (cattle). To eat (man).
— من To take little of.
— ه To importune a. o. with requests.
— ه على To incite, to urge a. o. to.
— لَجذاً ولَجَذاً ه To lick up (a vessel : dog).
✱ لَجَف o لَجفاً في To furrow (its retreat : gazelle).
لَجِف a لَجَفاً, وتلَجَّف To be enlarged (sides of a well).
لَجَّف وتلَجَّف ه To enlarge the sides of (a well).
لَجَف ج أَلجَاف Hole in the sides of a well. Middle part of a valley.
لِجَاف ج لُجُف وأَلجِفَة Threshold of a door.
لَجِيفَة Side of a door.
✱ لَجَم o لَجماً ه To sew (a garment).
لَجَّم وأَلجَم ه To reach the mouth of (a swimmer : water).

To be emaciated by old age. لَجِبَ a لَجَبًا
Conspicuous road. لَحْب, ولاحِب ج لَوَاحِب
Lean she-camel. لَحِيب
Instrument for barking. Sharpened iron. Slanderer. Holding indecent language. مِلْحَب
Opened (road). مُلْحَب ومَلْحُوب
To bark (a stick). ✡ لَحَتَ a لَحْتًا ه
To strip a. o. لَحَتَ ة
To strike a. o. with (a stick). — ة ب
Bark peeled off. لُحَاتَة
To betake o.'s self towards. ✡ لَحَجَ a لَحْجًا والتَحَجَ إلى
He smote him with the evil eye لَحَجَ ة بِعَيْنِهِ
To stick fast in (the scabbard: sword); to the finger (ring). لَحِجَ a لَحَجًا
To misrepresent (news) to. لَحَّجَ ه على
To compel a. o. to seek shelter towards. أَلْحَجَ والتَحَجَ ة إلى
To seek shelter towards. اِلْتَحَجَ إلى
To be closed (door). اِسْتَلْحَجَ
Orbit of the eye. لَحْج
Socket of the eye. Corner of a house. لُحْج ج أَلْحَاج
Narrow (place). لَحِج
Refuge, shelter. مَلْحَج ومُلْتَحَج ج مَلَاحِج
Pl. Narrow places, circumstances.
To falsify (an event) to a. o. ✡ لَحْوَجَ ه على
To make a niche in the side of a tomb. ✡ لَحَدَ a لَحْدًا, ولَحَّدَ وأَلْحَدَ ه
To bury (a corpse). لَحَدَ ة
To dig a grave for. — وأَلْحَدَ ل
To deviate, to stray from the right line. — وأَلْحَدَ
To act unfairly with. لَاحَدَ ة
To defame a. o. أَلْحَدَ ب
He swerved from the true religion; he became a heretic. — والتَحَدَ عن دِينِ الله
To deviate towards. اِلْتَحَدَ الى
لَحْد ولُحْد ج أَلْحَاد ولُحُود, ومُلْحَد ومَلْحُود
Niche in the side of a tomb. Tomb.
Deviation. Heterodoxy. إِلْحَاد
Sloping, slanting (well). لَحُود
Atheist, naturalist, impugner of religion. مُلْحِد ج مُلْحِدُون ومَلَاحِدَة
Dug in the side of a grave (tomb). مُلْحَد ومَلْحُود

To bridle (a horse). أَلْجَمَ و✧ لَجَّمَ ة
To be bridled (horse). اِلْتَجَمَ
To ask a. o. to bridle a horse. اِسْتَلْجَمَ ة فَرَسًا
Average ground. لَجَم ج أَلْجَام
Bit, bridle. لِجَام ج أَلْجِمَة ولُجُم
Place of the bit. Horse's mouth. لَجْمَة ومُلَجَّم
Bridled, checked. مُلْجَم و✧ مَلْجُوم
To mix, to prepare food for (camels). ✡ لَجَنَ o لَجْنًا, ولَجَّنَ ه
To stop (camel). لَجَنَ o لِجَانًا ولُجُونًا
To walk slowly. — في المَشْي
To adhere to. لَجِنَ a لَجَنًا ب
To stick, to agglutinate. تَلَجَّنَ
Leaves made into a paste for camels. لَجَن ولَجِين
Party, committee. Commission لَجْنَة
Slow (camel). (*m. f.*) لَجُون
Silver. لُجَيْن
To be close (relationship). ✡ لَحَّ i لَحًّا
To stick together (eyelids). — a لَحًّا ولَحَحًا
To be restive, slack (beast). To give a continuous rain (cloud). أَلَحَّ
To press (a debtor); to harrass a. o. with requests. To gall (the back of a beast: saddle). — على
He beseeched instantly. — في السُّؤَال
Close (relationship). لَحّ
Instance, pertinacity. إِلْحَاح
Narrow (place). لَاحّ ولَحِح
Asking importunately. Pouring down a continuous rain (cloud). مُلِحّ
Galling, wounding (saddle). مِلْحَاح
To remain motionless in a place. To start, to depart. ✡ لَحْلَحَ وتَلَحْلَحَ
Milk-thistle, lady's thistle. لَحْلَاح
Chief of a tribe. مُلَحْلِح
To follow a highway. ✡ لَحَبَ a لَحْبًا, والتَحَبَ ه
To open (a road). To bark (a stick). To strip (a bone) from its flesh. — ه
To strike a. o. with (the sword). — ة ب
To leave a mark upon. — ولَحَّبَ ه
To be opened, conspicuous (road). — لُحُوبًا

Refuge, shelter. مُلْتَحَد

To be avaricious. ✱ لَحِزَ a لَحَزًا, وتَلَحَّزَ

To secrete abundant saliva caused by acidity. تَلَحَّزَ

To swerve from. To give up a. th. — عن

To contend together in declaiming. تَلَاحَزَ

Avaricious. لِحْز ولَحِز

Entanglement, perplexity. مَلْحَز ج مَلَاحِز

To eat (the wool : worm). To devour (the plants : locusts). ✱ لَحَسَ a لَحْسًا ة

To lick a. th. ✧ To excoriate (a beast) by rubbing (saddle). لَحِسَ a لَحْسًا ومَلْحَسًا ولَحْسَةً ولُحْسَةً ه

To give a. th. to lick to a. o. لَحَّسَ ة ه

To send forth sprouts (ground). أَلْحَسَ

To receive (a due) from. إِلْتَحَسَ ه مِن

□ Caterpillar. لَحْس ج أَلْحَاس

Unfruitful (year). لَاحِسَة ج لَوَاحِس

Greedy, eat-all. لَحُوس

Inauspicious. Avaricious. لُحُوس

Bare, stripped ground. مَلْحَس ج مَلَاحِس

Greedy. Brave. مِلْحَس

Licked. Bared. Lank. مَلْحُوس

To undertake (an affair). ✱ لَحَصَ a لَحْصًا في

To give the particulars of (an affair). — ولَحَّصَ ه

To put a. o. in (a strait). لَحَّصَ ة في

To be stopped, closed up (needle-eye). إِلْتَحَصَ

To compel a. o. to. — ة إلى

To stick to. — ة وه

Mishap, ill-luck, perplexity. لَحَاص

Straitened, narrow. لَحِيص

Shelter, refuge. مَلْحَص

To look sideways at a. o. ✱ لَحَظَ a لَحْظًا ولَحَظَانًا ة او إلى

To consider, to observe a. o. or a. th. attentively. To watch o. another. لَاحَظَ مُلَاحَظَةً ولِحَاظًا ة وه

To be adherent to. تَلَحَّظَ

To have a mutual relation (things). تَلَاحَظَ

Look from the angle of the eye, side-glance. لَحْظ ج أَلْحَاظ ولِحَاظ

A glance ; twinkling of the eye ; moment. لَحْظَة ج لَحَظَات

Outer angle of the eye. لَحَاظ ج لُحُظ

Mark under a beast's eye. لِحَاظ وتَلْحِيظ

Upper feathers of an arrow. لِحَاظ

Pl. Eyes. لَاحِظَة ج لَوَاحِظ

Alike, similar. لَحِيظ

Inspector. □ Police-officer. مُلَاحِظ

Consideration, remark, observation. مُلَاحَظَة

To wrap a. o. in a garment. ✱ لَحَفَ a لَحْفًا, وأَلْحَفَ ة

To trail a veil, a cloak. To walk haughtily. لَحَّفَ

To help, to protect a. o. لَاحَفَ ة

To wrap a. o. in (bed-sheets). — ة ه

To accompany a. o. or a. th. — ة وه

To be importune (beggar). To reach the foot of a mountain. أَلْحَفَ

To wrap o.'s self in (a cloak). ✧ To be confined to bed. تَلَحَّفَ

To wrap o.'s self in (a garment, a sheet). إِلْتَحَفَ ب

Foot of a hill. Covering. لِحْف

Way of wrapping. لِحْفَة

Sheet, wrapper, cloth. لِحَاف ج لُحُف

Wife. ✧ Blanket.

Waist-wrapper. مِلْحَف ومِلْحَفَة ج مَلَاحِف

Bed-sheet, blanket.

✧ Bed-sheet sewed to a blanket. مِلْحَفَة

To overtake, to reach a. o. or a. th. ✱ لَحِقَ a لَحْقًا ولَحَاقًا ة وب

To cleave to a. o. — إلى

To be slender (horse). — لُحُوقًا

✧ To dole out a. th. لَحَّقَ على

To follow a. o. ✧ To intrude upon a. o. لَاحَقَ ة

To overtake, to join with a. o. أَلْحَقَ ة

To annex, to add a. th. to. — ه ب

To overtake o. another. To come up together. To be adjunct (things). تَلَاحَقَ

To come up and stick to. إِلْتَحَقَ ب

To sow an alluvial ground. إِسْتَلْحَقَ

To claim a. th. as a right. — ه

To become affiliated to. — ة

Sequel. Dates of second quality. Alluvial soil. لَحَق ج أَلْحَاق

Sheath of a bow. لِحَاق

Annexion, adjunction, affiliation. إِلْحَاق

Connected, adjoined. لَاحِق

Butcher. Meat-seller. لَحَّام
Union, alliance, connexion. إِلْتِحَام
Having, giving meat. لَاحِم ج أَوَاحِم
Carnivorous, flesh-eating (animal). — وَاحِم
Fleshy, pulpous. Slaughtered. لَحِيم
Fed upon meat. Sort of cloth. Allied to a tribe. Captive. مُلْحَم
Slaughter ; fight. ✧ Slaughter-house. مَلْحَم ج مَلَاحِم
Well twisted (rope). مُلَاحَم
Affecting the flesh only (wound). مُتَلَاحِمَة
To speak Arabic incorrectly. ✱ لَحَن a لَحْنًا ولَحَنًا ولُحُونًا ولَحَانَةً ولَحَانِيَةً
To incline to. — لَحْنًا إلى
To speak to a. o. unintelligibly. — لِفُلَان
To be intelligent. لَحِن a لَحَنًا
To understand (a word). — ه
To point out barbarisms to a. o. لَحَّن ه
He modulates his voice in reading. — في القِرَاءَة
To repeat a. th. to a. o. لَاحَن ه
To make a. o. to understand a. th. أَلْحَن ه
Sound, melody. Musical note ; accent, tone of the voice. Tune, modulation. Way of speaking. Value, import of words. Incorrect speaking, barbarism. لَحْن ج أَلْحَان ولُحُون
Art of music, harmony. صِنَاعَة الأَلْحَان
Intelligence. لَحَن
Intelligent. لَحِن
Speaking incorrectly. لُحَنَة
Mispronouncing, canting. Pointing out incorrect speaking. لُحَنَة
More intelligent. أَلْحَن
Modulated sound. تَلْحِين
Speaking incorrectly. لَاحِن ولَحَّان ولَحَّانَة
To peel off the inner bark of (a tree). ✱ لَحَا o لَحْوًا, ولَحَى a لَحْيًا, والْتَحَى ه
To revile a. o. To cover a. o. with shame (God). لَحَا o لَحْوًا, ولَحَى a لَحْيًا ه
To quarrel, to contend with. لَاحَى مُلَاحَاةً ولِحَاءً ه
To commit a blameworthy action. أَلْحَى

Date of second quality. لَاحِقَة ج لَوَاحِق
Overtaking, joining. مُلْحِق
Additional. Appendix, supplement. Postscript. مُلْحَق
To stick, to cleave to. ✱ لَحَكَ a لَحْكًا, ولَاحَكَ وتَلَاحَكَ ب
To joint into each other (vertebræ). لَوْحَكَ
To lick (honey). لَحِكَ a لَحْكًا ه
Kind of lizard. لُحَكَاء ولُحَكَة
Narrow-passes. مَلَاحِك
To close up ; to consolidate a. th. To solder (metal). ✱ لَحَمَ o لَحْمًا ه
To smite a. o. with (the sword). — ه ب
To feed a. o. on meat. To butcher (a man). لَحَمَ a لَحْمًا ه
To be fleshy. To be fond of meat. لَحِمَ a لَحَمًا , ولَحُمَ o لَحَامَةً
To be killed, slaughtered. لُحِمَ لَحْمًا
To stick to (a place). لَحِمَ ب
To join, to solder a. th with. لَاحَمَ وأَلْحَمَ ه ب
To ally together through marriage. لَاحَمَ
To have much meat. To be rich in grain (corn-crops). To be slack (beast). أَلْحَمَ
He allowed him to blacken the character of. — ه عِرْضَ فُلَانٍ
To weave (a stuff). To compose (a poem). أَلْحَمَ ه
Do perform what thou hast begun. أَلْحِمْ مَا أَسْدَيْتَهُ
To kill one another. تَلَاحَمَ
To coalesce. To be repaired. To cicatrise (wound). — والْتَحَمَ
To be desperate (fight). إِلْتَحَمَ
To be broad (way). إِسْتَلْحَمَ
To follow (a high road). — ه
To be surrounded by fighters. إِسْتُلْحِمَ
Flesh, meat ; pulp of a tree. لَحْم ولَحَم ج لِحَام ولُحُوم ولُحْمَان وأَلْحُم
Beef, pork, mutton. لَحْم البَقَر والخِنْزِير والضَّأن
Piece of meat, of flesh. لَحْمَة
Warp, woof of cloth. Hawk's portion of the game. — ولُحْمَة ج لُحَم
Kindred. لُحْمَة ج لُحَم
Soldering. لِحَام

To stink (person). To be rotten (walnut). ✱ لَخِنَ a لَخَنًا
Uncircumcised. Stinking. أَلْخَن م لَخْنَاء ج لُخْن
To inject a medicine through the nostrils of. ✱ لَخَا o لَخْوًا, ولَخَى i لَخْيًا, وأَلْخَى ه
To chatter. لَخِيَ a لَخًى
To befriend, to court a. o. لَاخَى ه
To backbite a. o. — ب
To incite a. o. to. — ه على
To eat sops. إِلْتَخَى
Sop. لِخَاء
Snuff-medicine. لَخًا ولَخَاء ومِلْخَى
Jabberer. Having the mouth distorted. أَلْخَى م لَخْوَاء
Having one knee bigger than the other (camel). — ولَخٍ م لَخِيَة
To quarrel, to contend violently with. ✱ لَدَّ o لَدًّا, ولَادَّ مُلَادَّةً ولِدَادًا ه
To withhold, to hinder a. o. from. لَدَّ ه عن
To administer (a medicine) to (a child) through the corner of the mouth. — لَدًّا ولُدُودًا, وأَلَدَّ ه ه
To prepare (a draught). — ه
To contend, to cavil. لَدَّ a لَدَدًا
To defame, to confound a. o. لَدَّد ب
To defend a. o. لَادَّ مُلَادَّةً عن
To turn the head to the right and left in amazement. To be slow. تَلَدَّد
To swallow a draught through the corner of the mouth. إِلْتَدَّ
Sack. لَدّ
Quarrel, violent dispute. لَدَد
لَادّ ولَدُود ولَدِيد , وأَلْتَدَد ويَلَنْدَد , وأَلَدّ م
Quarrelsome, caviller. لَدَّاء ج لُدّ ولِدَاد
Medicine absorbed through the corner of the mouth. لَدُود ولَدِيد ج أَلِدَّة
Sides of the neck, of a valley. لَدِيدَان
I have no escape from it. مَا لِي عَنْهُ مُلْتَدّ
To throw (a stone) at. To slap a. o. with (the hand). ✱ لَدَسَ o لَدْسًا ه ب
To shoe (a camel). To repair (a camel's) shoes. لَدَّس ه وه
Fat. لَدِيس ج أَلْدَاس
Stone for breaking fruit-stones. مِلْدَس ج مَلَادِس

To wind the part of a turban under the chin. تَلَحَّى
To revile o. a. تَلَاحَى
To begin to grow (beard). To let grow the beard. إِلْتَحَى
Chin, under-jaw. Part on which the beard grows. لَحْي مث لَحْيَان ج أَلْحٍ ولُحِيّ
Inner bark of a tree. Pulp of a fruit. لِحَاء
Beard. لِحْيَة ج لِحًى ولُحًى
Goat's beard (culinary plant). Salsify. لِحْيَةُ التَّيْس
Maiden-hair. Fern. — الحِمَار
Jupiter's beard (*plant*). — الرَّاعِي
Meadow-sweet (*plant*). — المِعْزى
Water-furrow. لِحْيَان
Long-bearded. أَلْحَى ولِحْيَانِيّ
Relating to the beard. لِحَوِيّ
Reviled. مَلْحِيّ
To speak confusedly, to gabble. ✱ لَخَّ o لَخًّا في كَلَامِهِ
To be entangled (business). إِلْتَخَّ
Mazy, full of thickets and intricate passes (valley). لَاخّ
Disordered in mind (drunkard). مُلْتَخّ
To shake a. th. ✱ لَخْلَخَ ه
Kind of perfume. لَخْلَخَة ولَخَالِخ
To disorder, to confuse a. th. ✧ لَخْبَطَ ه
To have fleshy eyelids. To be swollen (eye). ✱ لَخِصَ a لَخَصًا
To extract the pith of. To abridge, to sum up (a question). لَخَّص ه
Flesh around the eye. لَخْصَة ج لِخَاص
Fleshy, swollen (udder, breast). لَخِص
Summing up, short report. تَلْخِيص
Having fleshy eyelids. أَلْخَص م لَخْصَاء ج لُخْص
Resume, summary. مُلَخَّص
To strike a. o. violently. ✱ لَخَفَ a لَخْفًا ه
Thin and white stone. لَخْفَة ج لِخَاف
To cut a. th. ✱ لَخَمَ o لَخْمًا ه
To slap a. o. — ولَاخَمَ مُلَاخَمَةً ولِخَامًا ه
□ To be entangled in. تَلَخَّم
Slap. لِخَام
Languidness, remissness. Intricacy. لَخْمَة
Sluggish, remiss. لَخْمَة ولَخِمَة

In thy presence, before thee. لَدَيْكَ
To be sweet, pleasing, delightful. ✻ لَذَّ a لَذَاذًا ولَذَاذَةً
To find a. th. delightful; to delight in. — وتَلَذَّذَ و إِلْتَذَّ ه وب واستَلَذَّ ه
To delight a. o. لَذَّذَ ه
Sweet, agreeable, delightful. Speaking sweetly. Sleep. لَذّ
Pleasure, delight. لَذَّة ج لَذَّات
Sweet, agreeable, delightful. لَذِيذ ج لُذّ و لِذَاذ
More pleasing, more delightful. أَلَذّ
Delight, pleasure. مَلَذَّة ج مَلَاذّ
To be lively, nimble, quick. ✻ لَذْلَذَ
Lively, sprightly, speedy. لَذْلَاذ
To sip a. th. ✻ لَذَجَ o لَذْجًا ه
To press, to importune a. o. — ه
To burn a. th. (fire). To burn (the heart: love). ✻ لَذَعَ a لَذْعًا ه
He wounded him with the tongue. — ه بِلِسَانِهِ
To turn about (person). To blaze (fire). تَلَذَّعَ
To experience a sharp pain. إِلْتَذَعَ
Burn. لَذْعَة
Offensive talk. لَاذِعَة ج لَوَاذِع
Sarcastic, sharp-tongued. لَذَّاع
Sagacious, quick-minded. Eloquent, disert. لَوْذَع ولَوْذَعِيّ
Lattakieh (Syrian town). ✻ اللَّاذِقِيَّة
To please a. o. ✻ لَذِمَ a لَذَمًا ه
To stay in (a place). — ب
To attach a. o. to. أَلْذَمَ ه ب
To be addicted to. أُلْذِمَ ب
Keeping at home. لُذَمَة
Laudanum. P لَاذَن ولَاذَنَة
To stick to. ✻ لَذِيَ a لَذًى ب
Who. (*s. and pl.*) أَلَّذِي مث أَللَّذَانِ ج أَلَّذِين
To stick, to fasten a. th. with; to bolt (a door) with. ✻ لَزَّ o لَزًّا ولَزَزًا ولِزَازًا, وأَلَزَّ ه وه ب
To be fastened, joined to. لُزَّ ب
To constrain a. o. to repair to. — ه إِلى
To spear a. o. — ه ب
To press, to importune a. o. لَزَّ على
To give to a. o. a strong constitution (God). لَزَّزَ ه
To cleave to a. o. (antagonist). لَازَّ مُلَازَّةً ولِزَازًا ه

To sting a. o. (scorpion). ✻ لَدَغَ a لَدْغًا وتَلْدَاغًا ه
He pricked him to the quick with words. — ه بِكَلِمَةٍ
He caused him to be stung by a scorpion. أَلْدَغَهُ العَقْرَبَ
Sting, prick, bite. لَدْغَة
Thorn; prick. لُدَّاغ
Sarcastical, carper. Biting words. لُدَّاغَة
Stung (by a scorpion). لَدِيغ ج لَدْغَى ولُدَغَاء, ومَلْدُوغ
Sarcastic people, revilers. قَوْم لَدْغَى ولُدَغَاء
To slap a. o. on the face. ✻ لَدَمَ i لَدْمًا ه
To patch (a garment). — وأَلْدَمَ وتَلَدَّمَ ه
To grasp a. o. unremittingly (fever). أَلْدَمَ عَلَى
To be rent, worn out (clothes). تَلَدَّمَ
To be restless, anxious. To beat her face in grief (woman). إِلْتَدَمَ
Sound of the falling of a stone. لَدْم
Honourable relationship. لَدَم
Patchwork. لِدَام
Patcher. لَدَّام
Worn out, patched up (garment). لَدِيم
Stone for cracking date-stones. مِلْدَم ومِلْدَام
Foolish. مِلْدَم
The fever. أُمّ مِلْدَم
To be soft, tender, pliable. ✻ لَدُنَ o لَدَانَةً ولُدُونَةً
To soften a. th. To moisten (a garment). لَدَّنَ ه
To procrastinate, to linger in. تَلَدَّنَ في
To apologise to a. o. for (a delay). To delay (his rider: horse). — على
At; in the presence of. لَدُنْ ولُدْنُ ولَدْنِ ولَدَنْ ولُدُنْ ولَدِن
He possesses wealth. لَدُنْهُ مَالٌ
He came in his name. جَاء مِن لَدُنْهُ
At our place; at our hands. لَدُنَّا
For our part. مِن لَدُنَّا
Softness, suppleness of the body. لَدَانَة ولُدُونَة
Limber, supple, pliant. لَدْن ج لُدْن ولِدَان
To be coeval, contemporaneous. ✻ لدى — أَلْدَى إِلْدَاءً
At, in the presence of. لَدَى

إلتزّ ب To adhere, to be stuck to.
لِزّ Catch, ring of a door.
لزز ولِزاز Bar of a door.
لِزاز خصمٍ ومِلَزّ Contentious; pertinacious, caviller.
لَزّ ولَزِيز شرٍّ Incorrigible.
عَجُوز لَزُوز Wrinkled old woman.
مُلَزَّز Of a strong constitution (man).
✱ لزأ a لَزْءا, وألزأ ه To fill (a vessel). To bring forth (a child: woman).
لزّأ ولزّأ وألزأ ه To tend, to feed (cattle) well.
تلزّأ To be filled (vessel). To be satiated (man).
✱ لزب o لُزُوبا To be fixed, fast. To be barren (year).
— ب To stick, to cling to.
— ه To sting a. o. (scorpion).
لزِب a لَزَبا, ولزُب o لَزَبا ولُزُوبا To be contracted. To be hardened (mud).
لِزْب Narrow-pass.
لَزْبَة ج لِزَب ولَزَبات Dearth. Calamity. Barren year.
لازِب Sticky. Necessary,
ما هذا بِضَرْبَة لازِب It is not indispensable.
لَزِب ج لِزاب Exiguous.
✧ هُوَ ابن عَمّي لَزْب He is my cousin closely related.
عَزَب لَزَب Bachelor.
مِلزاب ج مَلازِيب Stingy, avaricious.
✱ لزِج a لَزَجا ولُزُوجا To be ductible. To be viscous, slimy.
— ب To stick, to glue to.
تلزّج To clog (leaves). To be viscous dirty (hair).
لُزُوجة Viscosity.
لَزِج م لَزِجَة Stretching. Viscous, gluey.
لزجة ولزجة ولزيجة Keeping at home.
P لازَوَرد ولازُوَرد ولازَوَرْد Lapis lazuli (precious stone).
لازَوَرديّ ولازُوَرديّ Azure-blue.
✱ لزق a لُزُوقا, والتزق ب To stick, to cleave to.
لازق مُلازَقة ولِزاقا ه To cleave to.
ألزق و✧ لزّق ه To stick, to glue a. th.
لزّق ه To botch (a work).
لِزْق Side. Companion.

هُوَ لِزْقي ولِزْقي He cleaves to me; he is my companion.
لِزاق Glue, paste.
— الذَّهَب Chrysocolla, carbonate of copper.
— الرُّخام والحَجَر Lithocolla, cement.
لَزُوق ولازُوق و✧ لَزْقة Poultice, plaster.
لَزِيق Intimate companion.
لَزِيقاء ولُزَّيقى و✧ لَزَّيق Mucilaginousness.
في كَلامِهِ لُزَّيقى His discourse is attaching.
✱ لزِم a لُزُوما ولَزْما ولِزاما ولَزامَة ولُزْمة ولُزْمانا ه وب To remain (in-door, in bed). To cleave to a. th.
— ه وب To stick to a. o.
— ه To be incumbent upon a. o. (duty).
لازَم مُلازَمة ولِزاما ه وه To follow a. o. closely. To continue a. th.
ألزم إلزاما ه ه To make a. th. to cleave to a. o.
— ه وب To compel a. o. to.
إلتزم ه وب To be obliged to. To take a. th. upon o.'s self. ✧ To contract for collecting (the tithes). To undertake (a work) at a stated price.
— ه To grasp a. o.
إستلزم ه To necessitate a. th.; to judge a. th. necessary.
لَزام Continuous, unceasing.
لِزام Judgment. Assiduous.
لُزَمَة Assiduous.
لُزُوم Necessity, want.
— ولُزُوميّة ومُلازَمَة والتِزام Necessary consequence.
إلتزام ج إلتزامات Obligation, duty. ✧ Farming of tithes.
لازِم Necessary. *Gr.* Intransitive (verb).
لَوازِم *Pl.* Articles of want. Set of tools; stores.
صار الشَّيْء ضَرْبَة لازِم The thing has become necessary.
مِلْزَمة ومِلزم ج مَلازِم Press; vice.
مُلازِم ✧ Helper. Adjudant-major.
مُلْتَزِم ✧ Contractor, farmer of tithes.
✱ لزَن o لَزْنا, ولزِن a لَزَنا, وتلازن To press (crowd).

Obstructed, narrow (place). لَزِن ولَزِن ومَلزُون
Year of dearth. Strait, critical circumstances. — ولَزِنَة ج لِزَن
Distressful (night). لَزِنَة ولِزِنَة ولَزِنَة
Calamitous (time). أَلزَن
✧ Broom (shrub). لَزّان
To eat a. th. To lick (a vessel). To graze (cattle). ✱ لَسّ o لَسًّا ه
To sprout forth (land). أَلَسّ
Sprouts of plants. لُسَاس
Still, yet, till now. (*for* لِلسَّاعَة) لِسَّا ✧
To sting a. o. (bee, scorpion). ✱ لَسَب i a لَسْبًا ه
To lash a. o. with (a whip). لَسَب ه ب
To revile a. o. — ه بِلِسَانِهِ
To lick (honey). لَسِب a لَسْبًا ه
To stick to. — ب
He caused him to be stung by a snake. أَلسَبَهُ حَيَّةً
He bites with his tongue. هُوَ لَسَّابَة لِلنَّاس
A trifle. لَسُوب وأَسْوب
To exhaust the (udder : milking). ✱ لَسَد i لَسْدًا, ولَسِد a لَسَدًا ه
To lick (honey, a vessel). — ه
To sting a. o. (scorpion). ✱ لَسَع a لَسْعًا ه
To sting a. o. in words. — ه بِلِسَانِهِ
To penetrate into (a country). — في
To set (people) at variance. أَلسَع بَيْن
He caused him to be stung by a snake. أَلسَعَهُ حَيَّةً
Backbiter. لُسَعَة ولَسَّاع
Stung by a scorpion. لَسِيع ج لَسْعَى ولُسَعَاء, ومَلسُوع
To stick to. ✱ لَسِق a لُسُوقًا, والتَسَق ب
To have the lungs parched by thirst (camel). لَسِق a لَسَقًا
To stick a. th. to. أَلسَق ه ب
To compel a. o. to cleave to. — ه
Intimate companion. لِسْق ولَسِيق
To taste a. th. ✱ لَسَم o لَسْمًا ه
To be unable to speak. لَسِم a لَسَمًا
To make a. o. to taste a. th. To make a. o. to understand a. th. أَلسَم ه ه
To ask for a. th. — واستَلسَم ه
To be eloquent. ✱ لَسِن a لَسَنًا
To bite a. o. in words. لَسَن o لَسْنًا ه

To make a. th. sharp-pointed. لَسَّن ولَسَّن وأَلسَن ه
To contend in words with. لَاسَن ه
To relate to a. o. (the words) of. أَلسَن ه ه
He lent him a suckling. — ه الفَصِيل
To blaze (fire). تَلَسَّن
لِسَان (*m. f.*) ج أَلسُن وأَلسِنَة ولُسْن ولُسُن
Language. Tongue. Epistle, letter.
Tongue of a balance. — المِيزَان
Spokesman of a tribe. — القَوْم
Tongue-shaped flame. — النَّار
Language in action. State speaking by itself. — الحَال
Wild bugloss. Borage (*plants*). — الثَّوْر
Plantago major, *arnoglossum*, larger plantain. — الحَمَل
Lion's tail (*plant*). — السَّبُع
Plantain (*plant*). — الثَّمَل
Honey-wort (*plant*). — العُصْفُور
Seed of the ash-tree. — العَصَافِير
Cynoglossum, hound's tongue (*plant*). — الكَلْب
Hart's tongue (*plant*). — الإِيَّل
✧ On behalf, in the name of. على وعن لِسَان فُلان
Every language is a man *i. e.* One stands for as many men as he knows languages. كُلّ لِسَانٍ بِإِنسَان
Double-tongued, dissembler. Bilinguous. ذُو لِسَانَيْن
Lingual (letter). لِسَانِيّ
Eloquent. لَسِن ج لُسُون, وأَلسَن م لَسْنَاء ج لُسْن
Tongue-shaped (sandal). لَسِين ومُلَسَّن
Stone at the entrance of a trap. مِلْسَن
Liar. مَلسُون
To eat greedily. ✱ لَسَا o لَسْوًا
To push, to repel a. o. ✱ لَشّ o لَشًّا ه
To be flurried by fear. ✱ لَشلَش
Flurried, restless. لَشْلَاش
To become vile. ✱ لَشَا o لَشْوًا
To destroy, to annihilate a. th. لَاشَى ه
To be abolished, sacrificed, reduced to nought. تَلَاشَى
Destruction, abolition, annihilation. مُلَاشَاة وتَلَاشٍ
✱ لَصّ a لَصًّا ولَصَاصًا ولُصُوصِيَّة ولَصُوصِيَّة,
To be a thief, to practice robbery. وتَلَصَّص

لَصَّ o لَصًّا ه — To do a. th. stealthily. To close (a door). To steal a. th.
لَصَّصَ ه — To compact (a building).
تَلَصَّصَ — To become a thief.
✧ — على — To spy a. o. in secret.
إلتَصَّ ب — To stick, to adhere to.
لِصّ ولُصّ ج لُصُوص وألصاص ولِصَصَة — Thief, brigand.
لِصَّة ولُصَّة ج لِصَّات ولُصَّات ولَصَائِص — Female thief.
لَصَص — Nearness of the shoulders, of the teeth.
ألَصّ م لَصَّاء ج لُصّ — Having narrow shoulders. Close-teethed.
لَصَّاء — Narrow forehead.
لُصُوصِيَّة ولُصُوصِيَّة — Thievishness, brigandage, robbery.
مَلَصَّة — Infested by thieves (country).
✱ لَصِبَ a لَصَبًا في — To stick to (the scabbard : sword); upon (the finger : ring).
— ب — To stick to (the bones : skin).
إلتَصَبَ — To be narrow.
لِصْب ج لِصَاب ولُصُوب — Narrow-pass, strait.
لَصِب — Avaricious.
لَوَاصِب — Deep and narrow wells.
مُلتَصِب — Strait (road).
مِلْصَاب — Sticking to the scabbard (sword).
✱ لَصَعَ a لُصُوعًا — To dry upon the bones (skin).
✱ لَصِفَ a لَصَفًا — To dry up (skin).
لَصَفَ o لَصْفًا ه — To set (stones) compactly.
— لَصَفًا ولَصِيفًا ولُصُوفًا — To be bright (colour).
✱ لَصِقَ a لَصَقًا ولُصُوقًا, والتَصَقَ ب — To stick, to glue to.
لاصَقَ ه وه — To adhere, to be contiguous to. To associate with.
ألصَقَ ه ب — To glue a. th. with.
لِصْق ولَصِيق — Adherent, companion.
هُوَ لِصْقِي و بِلِصْقِي ولَصِيقِي — He is always sticking to me.
لَصُوق — Plaster, poultice.
مُلصَق — Adhering. Ally. Adoptive son.
✱ لَصَا o لَصْوًا ه — To insult (a woman).
— ولَصَى i لَصْيًا, ولَصِيَ a لَصًى إلى — To dog, to spy a. o.

✱ لَضِمَ i لَضْمًا ه — To oppress, to do violence to a. o.
✧ — ه ب — To join a. th; to string (beads) with.
✱ لَطَّ i لَطًّا ب — To apply o.'s self to.
— ه — To lower (a veil). To close a (door).
لَطَّ ه عن — To conceal a. th. from.
— ه وه عن — To deny (a right) to.
— وألَطَّ على — To conceal a. th.
ألَطَّ — To be violent in a quarrel.
ألَطَّ وتَلَطَّطَ ه — To deny (a debt).
إلتَطَّ — To veil o.'s self.
— ب — To be impregnated with.
لِطّ ج لِطَاط — Necklace of beads.
لَطَط — Denial of a debt.
لَطَاط ومِلْطَاط — Prominent rock.
لاطّ ومُلِطّ — Rogue, rascal.
ألَطّ — Toothless.
مِلْطَاط — Hand-mill. Rolling-pin. Bank of a river. Wound on the pericranium.
✱ لَطَأَ a لُطُوءًا, ولَطِئَ a لَطْأً ب — To cleave to (the ground). To beat a. o. on the back.
لاطِئَة — Scarcely curable abscess. Scalp-wound.
مِلْطَا ومِلْطَاة — Pericranium.
✱ لَطَثَ o لَطْثًا ه — To clap, to slap a. o. To trouble a. o. (affair). To collect a. th.
تَلاطَثَ — To dash together (waves). To clap, to slap o. a.
مَلاطِث — Bruised parts.
✱ لَطَحَ a لَطْحًا ه — To slap a. o. on the back.
— بِهِ — He prostrated him.
✱ لَطَخَ a لَطْخًا, ولَطَّخَ ه ب — To defile, to splash, to smear a. o. with.
— ه بِشَرٍّ — To sully, to charge a. o. with evil.
تَلَطَّخَ ب — To be defiled, smeared with.
لَطْخ — Small portion.
لُطُوخ — Dirt, filth.
لَطِخَة ج لَطِخَات, ولِطِّيخ — Stupid, foolish.
✱ لَطَسَ o لَطْسًا ه وه — To knock a. o. or a. th. To trample heavily upon.
— ه ب — To cast (a stone) at.
لاطَسَ ه — To be defiled by.
تَلاطَسَ — To dash together (waves).

✧ Slight indisposition. حَرَكَة لُطف
Thinness, gracefulness. Kindness in words. لَطَافَة
Compliance, agreeable intercourse. Fondness. تَلَطُّف
Thin, delicate. لَطِيف ج لِطَاف ولُطَفَاء Gentle, kind. Witty (word). ✧ Slight (disease).
The Kind One (God). اللَّطِيف
F. Witticism; nicety of language. لَطِيفَة ج لَطَائِف
Parts of the ribs adjacent to the chest. لَوَاطِف
Amiable, kind. مُلَاطِف ولَطْفَان
To slap a. o. ✱ لَطَم i لَطْمًا, ولَطَّم ه
To be slapped. To have a blaze on the cheek (horse). لَطِم
To seal (a letter). لَطَّم ه
To slap, to knock a. o. لَاطَم مُلَاطَمَة ولِطَامًا ه
To slap o. a. تَلَاطَم
To dash together (waves). To come into collision. — والتَطَم
Slap. Shock. لَطْمَة ج لَطَمَات
Slapped. لَطِيم ومَلْطُوم ومُلَطَّم
Orphan of both parents. Ninth horse in a race. Perfume. لَطِيم
Having a blaze on the cheek (horse). لَطِيم (*m. f.*) ج لُطْم, ومُلَطَّم
Musk, perfume. Beasts loaded with perfumes. Scent-box. لَطِيمَة ج لَطَائِم
Cheek. مَلْطِم هث مَلْطَمَان
To shelter o.'s self in a cave. ✧ To shelter o.'s self anywhere. ✱ لَطَا o لَطْوًا, و✧ لَطَى i لَطْيًا
To settle in (a place). لَطِي a لَطْيًا ب
To suspect a. o. of keeping a. th. in his house. لَطِيَ a لَطًى ب
To oppress, to crush a. o. — ه
To lay wait for (the enemy), to lurk for watching a. o. تَلَطَّى على
To shelter o.'s self. تَلَطَّى
Place. Forehead. لَطَاة
Blaze on a horse's forehead. دَائِرَة اللَّطَاة
Shelter. ✧ لَطْوَة ومَلْطَى
Veil of Greek Bishops. ✧ لَاطِيَة ج لَاطِيَات
To pursue, to track a. o. ✱ لَظَّ o لَظًّا ولَظِيظًا ه

Pick-axe. مِلْطَاس ج مَلَاطِيس
Stone for breaking fruit-stones. — ومِلْطَس ج مَلَاطِس
To slap a. o. on the face. ✧ لَطَش o لَطْشًا (*for* لطس) ه
To have a slight knowledge of. To hew (stones) roughly. To do, to know a. th. imperfectly. ✧ لَطَّش تَلْطِيشًا ب
To slap o. a. ✧ تَلَاطَش
Fancy, mania, hobby-horse. A slap; a shock. Staggers. ✧ لَطْشَة
Crack-brained, freakish. ✧ مَلْطُوش
To kick a. o. ✱ لَطَع a ولَطِع a لَطْعًا ه
To lick a. th. لَطَع ولَطِع ه بِلِسَانِهِ, والتَطَع ه
To strike a. o. with (a stick). لَطَع ه ب
To hit a. o. on (the eye). To erase (a name). To hit (the target). ✧ To set a. th. on fire. — ه
He is dead. — إِصْبَعَهُ
To be toothless. لَطِع a لَطَعًا
To shed its teeth (camel). تَلَطَّع
To drink up (a beverage). إِلْتَطَع
Fall of the teeth. White spot on the inside of the Negroes' lips. لَطَع
Palate. لَطْع ج أَلْطَاع
✧ Oil-cloth put under a child. لَطْعَة ج لَطَعَات
Licking his fingers. لَطَّاع
Toothless. أَلْطَع م لَطْعَاء ج لُطْع
To be kind with a. o. ✱ لَطَف o لُطْفًا ب ول
To be thin, graceful. To be elegant, gentle. لَطُف o لُطْفًا ولَطَافَة
To render a. th. fine, elegant. ✧ To mitigate (an evil). لَطَّف ه
To treat a. o. gently; to fondle a. o. لَاطَف ه
To favour a. o. with. أَلْطَف ه ب
To show kindness to a. o. in. To present a. o. with. — وتَلَطَّف وتَلَاطَف بِهِ ولَهُ في
To treat o. a. kindly. تَلَاطَف
To find a. th. delicate, gracious. إِسْتَلْطَف ه
Benefit, gift, favour.. لُطْف ج أَلْطَاف
Gift, present. لَطْفَة
Kindness, courtesy. لُطْف ج أَلْطَاف

To drive a. o. away. لَظَّ o لَظًّا ه
To fall uninterruptedly (rain). أَلَظَّ
To remain in (a place). To cleave to a. o. — بِ
To keep to, to persevere in. — وفي
To pursue one another (warriors). تَلَاظَّ مُلَاظَّةً ولِظَاظًا
Harsh, untractable man. لَظّ
Assiduous. مُلِظّ
Importuner. مِلَظّ ومِلظاظ
To blaze fiercely (fire). ✻ لَظِيَ a لَظًى, وتَلَظَّى والتَظَى
To stir (the fire). لَظَّى ه
To burn with (anger). تَلَظَّى والتَظَى
Blazing fire. لَظًى
Hell-fire, hell. لَظَى
To produce tender herbs (ground). ✻ لعّ — أَلَعَّ
To collect tender herbs. (*for* تَلَعَّى (تَلَعَّعَ
Cry uttered to a. o. who stumbles. لَعْ ولَعًا ولَعْلَع
Incurable evil, *lit* : helpless stumble. عَثْرَة لا لَعًا لَهَا
Tender herbs. Succory. لُعَاع
Herb. Draught. لُعَاعَة
The world and its pleasures are short. الدُّنْيَا ومُتَاعُهَا لُعَاعَة
To break (the bones). ✻ لَعْلَعَ
To flicker (looming). — وتَلَعْلَعَ
To be broken, crushed. To be exhausted, jaded. To loll out its tongue (dog). تَلَعْلَعَ
Flickering of mirage. لَعْلَع ج لَعَالِع
Exhaustion, overfatigue. لَعْلَعَة
Cowardly, fearful. لَعْلَاع
To drivel (baby). ✻ لَعَبَ ولَعِبَ a لَعْبًا, وأَلْعَبَ
لَعِبَ a لَعْبًا ولَعِبًا وتَلْعَابًا , ولَعَّبَ وأَلْعَبَ وتَلَعَّبَ وتَلَاعَبَ To play, to sport.
To play at (a game). ✧ To play upon (a musical instrument). لَعِبَ بِ
He practiced fencing. لَعِبَ بالسَّيْفِ وَالتُّرْس
He is the sport of cares. لَعِبَ بِهِ الهُمُومُ
The houses are the play of the winds. — الرِّيَاحُ بالدِّيَار
To dally, to joke with a. o. لَاعَبَ ه
To make a. o. to play, to sport. أَلْعَبَ ه
To play a trick to a. o. ; to scoff at. تَلَاعَبَ بِ

Play, sport, joke. Game. لَعْب ولِعْب (*un.* لَعْبَة (
Colchicum autumnale (*plant*) ; remedy for rheumatism. اللَّعْبَة البَرْبَرِيَّة
Plaything, toy. Dice. Game. Laughing-stock. Puppet. لُعْبَة ج لُعَب
Play, sport. Laughing-stock. أُلْعُوبَة و✧ لَعُوبَة
Drivel of a child. Mucilage of plants. لُعَاب
Honey. لُعَاب النَّحْل
Gossamer. — الشَّمْس
Mucilaginous. لُعَابِيّ
Juice of some fruits. لُعَابِيَّة
لَعِب ولَعُوب (*m. f.*) , ولُعَبَة و لِعِّيب ولَعَّاب Jolly, sportive, playful.
Great joker, player. تِلْعَاب وتِلْعَابَة وتِلِعَّاب وتِلِعَّابَة وتِلْعِيبَة
Place of entertainment. Theatre. Just, tournament. مَلْعَب ج مَلَاعِب
A sleeveless play-corslet. مُلْعِبَة ومِلْعَبَة
Puppet. مَلْعَبَة
Fellow-player, partner. مُلَاعِب
Brandisher of spears. (*Surname of many warriors*). — الأَسِنَّة
A short-necked, white-bellied and long-winged green bird of the desert. — ظِلِّهِ
Drivelling (child). ✧ Trick. مَلْعُوب ج مَلَاعِيب
To be dilatory, slow. ✻ لَعِثَ a لَعَثًا
Dilatory, slow. أَلْعَث م لَعْثَاء ج لُعْث
To tarry, to waver in. To ponder on a. th. ✻ لَعْثَمَ وتَلَعْثَمَ في
To cause a smart pain to a. o. (blow). ✻ لَعَجَ a لَعْجًا ه وه
To waste a. o. (grief). — فُؤَادَهُ
To distress a. o. (affair). لَاعَجَ ه
To stir (the fire). أَلْعَجَ ه
To be sad, grieved. إِلْتَعَجَ
Smart (blow). Burning (love). لَاعِج ج لَوَاعِج
✧ Lagopus, hare-foot (bird). ✧ لَاعَرِين
To lick (her young : she camel). ✻ لَعَزَ a لَعْزًا ه
To bite a. th. ✧ To chew. ✻ لَعَسَ لَعْسًا, و✧لَعْوَسَ ه
To have dark-red lips. لَعِسَ a لَعَسًا
Deep red of the lips. لَعَس ولُعْسَة

Accursed. ✧ Iliac passion in horses. مَلْعُون ج مَلَاعِين
To collect odorous plants. To thicken (honey). ✻ لعو – تَلَعَّى
I felt qualmish. ✧ لَعَت نَفْسِي
Covetous ; wicked. لَعُو م لَعْوَة ج لِعَاء
Vehemence of hunger. لَعْوَة
Hunting bitch. – ولَعَاة ج لَعَوَات
Aristolochia sempervirens (*plant*). لَعِيَّة
Fearful. لَاعٍ
Euphorbia triaculeata ; tithymal. لَاعِيَة ج لَوَاعِي
To hurry. ✻ لَعْوَق
Weak-minded, foolish. لَعْوَق
✻ لَغَب a o ولَغِب o لَغْبًا ولَغُوبًا ولُغُوبًا . ولَغِب
To be weary, overfatigued. To lap (dog). لَغَبًا a
To sow dissension in (a tribe). لَغَب a لَغْبًا عَلَى
To make false reports to. – ه
To fatigue, a. o. To jade (a beast). لَغَّب وأَلْغَب وتَلَغَّب ه
To track (the game). To pursue a. o. closely. تَلَغَّب ه
Weak-minded. Vicious (speech). Gum of the front teeth. لَغْب ولَغُوب
Ill-trimmed arrow. لَغْب ولُغَاب
Bad pen. لَغْب ولَغَب ولَغِب ولَغِيب
He has overtaken him. أَخَذَ بِلَغَبِ رَقَبَتِهِ
Weak-mindedness. لَغَابَة ولَغُوبَة
Tired, weary. لَاغِب ج لُغَّب
Languid, gentle winds. رِيَاح لَوَاغِب
To bring (camels) together. ✻ لَغَد a لَغْدًا ه
To erect (the ears). – ه
To clasp the hand of. لَاغَد والتَغَد ه
Lobe of the ear. Flesh of the palate. لُغْد ج أَلْغَاد, ولُغْدُود ولِغْدِيد ج لَغَادِيد
Angered. مُتَلَغِّد
To distort a. th. ✻ لَغَز o لَغْزًا ه
To make (its burrow) to wind (jerboa). – وأَلْغَز ه
He spoke enigmatically, equivocally. – ولَاغَز فِي الكَلَام وأَلْغَز الكَلَام
Tortuous burrow ; winding road, maze. لُغْز ولَغْز ولُغَز
Riddle, enigma ; ambiguous speech. لُغْز ولُغُز ولَغَز ولُغَز ج أَلْغَاز

Red-lipped. Tangled (plant). أَلْعَس م لَعْسَاء ج لُعْس
I have not tasted a mouthful. مَا ذُقْتُ لَعُوسًا
Greedy of food. لَعْوَس ج لَعَاوِس
To be difficult (affair). ✻ لَعِص a لَعَصًا
To show harshness towards. تَلَعَّص عَلَى
To brand (a beast) on the neck. To tattoo a. o. ✻ لَعَط a لَعْطًا ه
To harm, to wound a. o. with. – ه ب
✧ To deprive a. o. of his favours (God). – ه
To pasture near dwellings (cattle). To go along a wall. لَعَط
Tattooing, streaks. لَعْط ج أَلْعَاط
Side of a wall, of a mountain. لَعْط
Evil look. Black spot on the neck of sheep. لَعْطَة
Black-spotted on the neck (ewe). لَعْطَاء
Pasturage near dwellings. مَلْعَط ج مَلَاعِط
To crouch (lion). ✻ لعف – أَلْعَف وتَلَعَّف
To lick a. th. ✻ لَعِق a لَعْقًا ولَعْقَة ولُعْقَة ه
He is dead. – إِصْبَعَهُ
To give to a. o. a. th. to lick. أَلْعَق ه ه
To be altered (colour). أَلْتَعِق
Remainder of green pasture. لَعْقَة
Spoonful. لُعْقَة
Avaricious, greedy. لَعِق وَعِق
Linctus, electuary. لَعُوق
Spoon. ✧ Trowel. مِلْعَقَة و✧ مَعْلَقَة ج مَلَاعِق
Garnet, rubis. لَعْل P
Perhaps, it may be that. ✻ لَعَلّ
Perhaps thou mayest. لَعَلَّك
To curse a. o. ✻ لَعَن a لَعْنًا ه
To curse a. o. لَاعَن مُلَاعَنَة ولِعَانًا ه
To curse o. a. تَلَاعَن والتَعَن
To curse o.'s self. إِلْتَعَن
Curse, imprecation. لَعْن, ولَعْنَة ج لَعَنَات ولِعَان
Curse. لَعَان ولَعَانِيَة
Curser. لَعَّان
Cursing often. لُعَنَة ج لُعَن
Accursed, loathed. (*m. f.*) لُعْنَة ولَعِين
Manikin used as scarecrow. لَعِين
The accursed one *i. e.* Satan. أَللَّعِين
Object of curse. Privy in a public place. مَلْعَنَة ج مَلَاعِن

Sound, voice. Slip, mistake. لغا
Word, expression. لُغَة ج لُغًى ولُغات
Classical language. Dialect.
Philology. عِلم اللُّغَة
Philologists. أهل اللُّغَة
Trifle, vanity. Slip of language. Useless word. لَغْو ولاغِيَة
Rash oath. يمين لَغو
Idiomatic. Lexicographist, philologist. لُغَوِيّ ✧ لُغَوِيّ
Subject, topic. Idioma, slang. ✧ لَغوة
Idle word, action. لَغوَى
Weak, tender (plant). Soft-fleshed ✱ لَغوَس
Groundless rumours. لَغوَسَة مِن الخَبَر
To roll up, to wrap a. th. ✱ لفّ o لَفًّا, ولَفَّف ه
To wrap (a corpse) in. لفّ ه في
✧ To twist a turban round. — اللَّفَّة
To conjoin a. th. with. لفّ ه ب
He mixes all sorts of food. — في الأكل
To be tangled (plants). — والتفّ
To hide (the head) under the wing (bird). ألفّ ه
To wrap o.'s self in (a cloak). تَلَفَّف والتفّ في
To gather against. تلفّف والتفّ على
To mix together (fighters). تلافّوا
They came with people from various tribes. جاءوا بِلَفِّهم وبِلَفِيفِهم
Involution and evolution (*in rhetoric*). لفّ ونَشْر
Mixed crowd. لِفّ ج لُفوف وألفاف
They came with their own people. جاءوا ومَن لَفّ لِفَّهم
Grove. حديقة لَفّ ولِفّ ولَفَّة ولِفَّة ولَفّاء
✧ Turban, head-band. لَفَّة ج لَفّات
Wrapper, glume, envelope. Swaddling-clothes. لِفافَة ج لَفائِف
Distortion of a muscle. لَفَف
Complicated. Rabble. Friend. *Gr.* Verb having two weak letters. لَفِيف
Skein, roll. Lock of hair. لَفِيفَة ج لَفائِف
Bushy. Impeded in speech. Perplexed. أ لَفّ م لَفّاء ج لُفّ
Tufty trees. ألفاف
Tufty plants. تَلافِيف
Blanket, wrapper. مِلَفّ ومِلْفاف

Riddle, equivocation. لُغَيزاء ولُغَيزَى وأُلْغوزَة
Slanderer, backbiter. لَغّاز
✱ To clamour, to utter confuse sounds. لغط a لَغطاً ولِغاطاً, والغط وألغط
To coo (pigeon, grouse). لغط a لَغطاً ولَغيطاً
To throw heated stones into (milk). ألغط ه
Confused noise. clamour. لغط ولَغَط ج ألغاط
✱ To round up (a moufthul). لغف a لَغفاً ه
To meet. To kiss a. o. لاغف ه
To associate with thieves. ألغف
To give balls of food to a. o. To ill-treat a. o. ألغف ه
Mouthful. لُغفَة
Accomplice of thieves. لَغِيف ج لُغَفاء
Gang of robbers. مُلغفَة
✱ To foam (camel). To spread false rumours. لغم a لَغماً
✧ To mine (a building). لغّم ه
To anoint the corners of the mouth with. تلغّم ب
He moved the corners of the mouth in speaking. — بالكلام
To recall a. th. to memory. — بذِكر
Ointment. Nerves and veins of the tongue. لَغم
✧ Blasting mine. Ts لُغم ج لُغوم ولُغومَة
Foam of camels. لُغام
✦ Miner. Ts لُغمجي
Corners of the mouth. مَلاغِم
▫ To be defiled, smeared. ▫ لَغمط
✱ To be tangled (plant). ✱ لغن — إلغانّ
✱ To speak. ✱ لغا o لَغواً
— o لَغواً, ولغا a ولَغِي a لَغاً ولَغاية ولاغِيَة وملغاة في القول To utter nonsenses. To commit blunders in speech
To be addicted to. To drink (water) without quenching thirst. لَغِي a لَغًى ب
To sport, to joke with. لاغى ه
To exclude, to eliminate, to suppress a. th. ألغى ه
To disappoint a. o. — ه
To study the idiotisms of a. o.'s language. إستلغى ه

Wrapped. ✧ Cabbage. ملفوف
To eat greedily. To totter. ✱ لفلف
To wrap, to cover a. th. — ه
To wrap o.'s self in. تلفلف ب
Weak, infirm. لفلف و لفلاف وملفلف
Bindweed. ✧ لفلاف
To bark (a tree). To traduce a. o. ✱ لفأ a لفأ ولفاء, والتفأ ه
To strip (the flesh) from (a bone). — ه عن
To turn a. o. back from. — ه عن
The wind swept (the clouds) away from the sky. — ه عن وجه السماء
To strike a. o. with (a staff). لفأ ه ب
To remain; to be redundant. لفي a لفأ
Remainder of a due. Dust. A little. لفاء
Boneless piece of flesh. لفئة
To wring, to twist a. th. about. ✱ لفت i لفتًا
He spoke inconsiderately. — الكلام
To strip (a tree) from (its bark). To avert (the face) from. — ه عن
To ill-treat (cattle). — ه
To avert a. o. from. — ه عن
To turn towards. To take care of. To show regard to. تلفت والتفت إلى
He looked about to the right and left. تلفت بوجهه يمنة ويسرة
Do not mind him. لا تلتفت لفته
Turnip. Half of a. thing Cow. ✧ Rape (*plant*). لفت
Left-handedness. لفت
A turn. A glance to the right or left. لفتة ج لفتات
Cross-tempered. لفات ولفوت
Ill-treating cattle. لفتة
Gruel of colocynth and flour. لفيتة
Left-handed. Twist-horned (ram). Squint-eyed. Foolish. Awkward. ألفت م لفتاء ج لفت
Heed. Regard, care. *Gram.* Abrupt transition. إلتفات
To exhaust (a pasturage). To conceal (news). To fulfil (a design). ✱ لفث — إستلفث ه
To become destitute, bankrupt. ✱ لفج — ألفج
To constrain a. o. to beg a. th. لفج ه
Abjectedness. لفج
Bankrupt. ملفج ومستلفج
To burn a. th. (fire, wind). ✱ لفح a لفحًا ولفحانًا
To strike a. o. slightly with (a sword). — a لفحًا ه ب
Burning (heat, wind). لفوح ولافح ج لوافح
Mandrake, sweet smelling egg-plant (شمام). لفاح (*un.* لفاحة)
To cast forth (venom); to eject (spittle) from (the mouth). ✱ لفظ i ولفظ a لفظًا ه وب
To cast a. th. on the shore (sea). To reject a. o. (tribe). — ه إلى
He died. لفظ ولفظ نفسه
He pronounced, he uttered words. لفظ وتلفظ بالكلام
Utterance, pronunciation, accent. Word, expression. لفظ ج ألفاظ, ولفظة ج لفظات
Literally, verbally. لفظيًّا
Feeding her chickens with the beak (bird). لافظة
The sea. Ewe. Mill. The present world. اللافظة
Particles ejected from the mouth. Refuse, remainder. لفاظة ج لفاظات ولفاظ
Expectorated. Uttered. لفيظ وملفوظ
To cover the head (hoariness). ✱ لفم a لفمًا, ولفّم ه
To eat much. ألفم
To be hoary (man). تلفّم
To wrap o.'s self in (clothes). To be clothed with (verdure: land). — والتفم ب
He surrounded the enemy. — على العدو
To be altered (colour). التفم
Cloak. لفاع
Patch on a shirt. لفاعة ولفيعة
To fell (a seam). ✧ To stitch (a garment). ✱ لفق i لفقًا, ولفّق ه
To obtain a. th. لفق a لفقًا ه
He set doing. — يفعل
To embellish (a narration) with lies. To forge up (a story). ✧ To patch up (a work). لفّق ه
To overtake a. o. تلفّق ب

To restore her affairs (tribe). تلافق
Skirt. لِفْق
Double-skirted garment. مُلاءة ذات لِفقَين
They are inseparable. هُمَا لِفقَان
Piece of cloth sewed with another. لِفَاق وتِلفَاق
✧ Sewing. Falsehood. False story. تلفيقة ج تلفيقات
✧ Selvage. مَلفقة
✧ To humbug, to make up stories. لَوْفَق لَوفَقَة
✱ Left-handed. Foolish. لفك – لَفِيك وأَلْفَك
✱ To veil her face (woman). لَفَم i لَفمًا, وتَلَفَّم, والتفم
Woman's face-veil, muffler. لِفَام
S Doctor in divinity. مِلفَان و✧ مُلفَان ج مَلافِنة
✱ To wrong a. o. لَفَا o لَفوًا حَقَّهُ
✧ To come back (home). To frequent (a house). لَفَى i إلى
✧ To attract a. o. to o.'s house. أَلْفَى ه
To find a. th. or a. o. أَلفَى ه وه
I found him at the last gasp. أَلفَيتُهُ يَمُوتُ
To mend, to repair a. th. تَلافَى ه
Dust, earth, rubbish. لَفَاء
✧ Strangers. لِفَايَة
✧ Meeting-place, rendezvous. مَلفَى
✧ To lap. To be loose (horse-shoe). To rumble (belly). لَقّ o لَقًّا
To strike (the eye) with the hand. – ه
Furrow, crevice. لَقّ
Ditches narrower on the upper part. لَقَقَة
✧ Bat, racket. مِلَقّ
✱ To clap its beak (crane). To move its tongue and jaws (snake). لَقلَق
To agitate a. th. – ه
To be moved, clapped. تَلَقلَق
Crane, stork. لَقلَق ولَقلَاق ج لَقَالِق
Clapping of the crane's bill. لَقلَقَة
The clashing letters *i. e.* ب, ج, د, ط, ق حُرُوف القَلقَلَة
Still and piercing (look). مُلَقلَق
✱ To nickname a. o. لقب – لَقَّب ه ب
To receive the nickname of. تَلَقَّب ب
Nickname, by-name. لَقَب ج أَلقَاب
✱ To impregnate (a palm-tree). To vaccinate a. o. To graft a tree). لقح a لَقحًا, ولَقَّح وأَلقح ه
✧ To throw a. th. لَقَح ولَقَّح ه
To conceive (female). To be impregnated (palm-tree). لَقِح a لَقحًا ولَقَحًا ولَقَاحًا, وتَلَقَّح
To impregnate (trees : wind). To swell (the clouds : wind). أَلقَح ه
He caused evil between them. أَلقَح بَينَهُم شَرًّا
To charge a. o. with a false crime. تَلَقَّح على
To feign to be pregnant (she-camel). تَلَقَّح
✧ To stretch o.'s self on the ground. – والتَقَح
To be fecundated (palm-tree). إِلتَقَح
To be fit to be fecundated (palm-tree). إِستَلقَح
Pollen of male palm-trees. Fecundation. لَقح ولَقَاح
Wet-nurse. Eagle. Raven. لِقحَة ج لِقَح ولِقَاح
Milch-camel. لِقحَة ولَقحَة ج لِقَح ولِقَاح, ولَقُوح ج لِقَاح ولَقَائِح
Full of dangers (war). Pregnant. لَاقِح ج لَوَاقِح
Pregnant (she-camel). – ولَقُوح ج لُقُح
Fecundating trees; rain-bringing (winds). لَوَاقِح ومَلَاقِح
Pregnant (she-camel). مُلقَحَة ج مَلَاقِح
Fœtus. Mother. Source of fecundation. مَلقُوحَة ج مَلَاقِيح
✱ To strike, to punch a. o. لَقَز o لَقزًا ه
✱ To find fault with; to abuse a. o. لَقَس o i لَقسًا ه
He was prone to (evil). لَقِسَت نَفسُهُ a لَقَسًا إلى
He felt a loathing for. لَقِسَت وتَلَقَّسَت نَفسُهُ مِن
✧ To detain, to delay a. o. لَقَّس ه
To nickname a. o. لَاقَس مُلَاقَسَة ولِقَاسًا ه
✧ To be detained, delayed. تَلَقَّس
To abuse o. a. تَلَاقَس
Mange, scab. لَقَس ولَاقِس
Reviler. Sower of discord. لَقِس

To be altered (colour).	أُلتُقِع
Flies.	لَقّاء ولَقّاء
Humbugger.	لُقَعَة, ولَقّاعَة ج لَقّاعات
Humbugger, braggart.	لَقّاء وتِلِقّاء وتِلِقّاعَة
To catch (a ball).	✱ لَقِف a لَقْفًا ولَقَفانًا, وتَلَقَّف والتَقَف ه
To crumble down (tank).	لَقِف a لَقْفًا, وتَلَقَّف
To swallow up (a dish).	أَلقَف وتَلَقَّف ه
Side of a tank.	لَقَف ج أَلقاف
Nimble, dexterous.	ثَقِف ولَقِف ولَقِيف
Crumbling (tank).	لَقِف ولَقِيف
◘ Sky-light.	مَلقَف
To obstruct, to stop (a road).	✱ لَقَم o لَقْمًا ه
To gobble (a mouthful).	— ولَقِم a لَقْمًا, وتَلَقَّم والتَقَم ه
To feed a. o. by mouthfuls. To feed (a bird) with the beak.	لَقَم وأَلقَم ه ه
✧ To cut (bread) into mouthfuls. To put (coffee) in boiling water.	لَقَّم ه
He has silenced him.	أَلقَمَهُ الحَجَرَ
✧ To be cut into pieces (bread).	تَلَقَّم
Middle of a road.	لَقَم ولُقَم
Morcel, gobblet. Mouthful.	لُقمَة ج لُقَم, ولَقِيم
Lokman, celebrated philosopher and fabulist.	لُقمان الحَكِيم
Glutton, voracious.	تِلقام وتِلقامَة
To be quick-minded.	✱ لَقُن o لَقانَة
To perceive, to understand a. th. sharply.	لَقِن a لَقْنًا ولَقَنَة ولَقانَة ولَقانِيَة, وتَلَقَّن ه
To make a. o. to understand a. th. ✧ To suggest, to dictate a. th. to a. o.	لَقَّن ه ه
To learn a. th. easily.	أَلقَن ه
To receive (advice) from.	تَلَقَّن ه
Support, help.	لِقن
Keen intelligence.	لَقانَة ولَقانِيَة
Mastic, cement.	✧ لاقُونَة
Keen-minded.	لَقِن
To afflict a. o. with facial paralysis (God).	✱ لَقا o لَقوًا ه
To have the mouth distorted by palsy.	لُقِيَ لَقوًا
Palsy, distortion of the mouth.	لَقوَة
Swift eagle. Female eagle.	— ولِقوَة ج لِقاء وأَلقاء

Late, tardy.	✧ لَقِيس
To converse with a. o.	✧ لَقَش — لاقَش ه
Word, talk.	✧ لَقش
Pine-wood used as fuel.	✧ لِقش
To burn (the skin).	✱ لَقَص a لَقصًا ه
To be narrow.	لَقِص a لَقَصًا
He was distressed, painfully affected.	لَقِصَت نَفسُهُ
To take, to seize a. th.	إِلتَقَص ه
Garrulous. Prone to mischief.	لَقِص
To pick up a. th. To glean. To mend (a garment).	✱ لَقَط o لَقطًا ه
To acquire (knowledge) from (a book).	— ه مِن
✧ To overtake a. o. in running. To catch (a bird, a thief).	— ه
To be opposite to, to face a. th.	لاقَط مُلاقَطَة ولِقاطًا ه
To pick up (fruit).	تَلَقَّط والتَقَط ه
To fall upon a. th. by chance. To collect a. th.	إِلتَقَط ه
Pickings. (*un.* لَقطَة ولُقطَة ولُقاطَة) Gleanings. Treasure-trove. ✧ Foundling.	لَقَط
Gold-ore ; mine-ore.	— المَعدِن
Gleanings.	لُقاط ولِقاط
He lives from gleanings.	يَتَعَيَّش بِاللُّقاط عَن الإِلتِقاط
Gleaner. Patcher. Freed slave.	لاقِط م لاقِطَة
Gizzard.	لاقِطَة الحَصَى
Picked up. Foundling (child).	لَقِيط ج لُقَطاء, ومَلقُوط
Vile.	لَقِيطَة ج لَقائِط
People of the lowest class.	أَلقاط
Pincers, tongs.	مِلقَط ج مَلاقِط
Nippers. Writing-reed. Spider.	مِلقاط ج مَلاقِيط
To throw a. th. away. To pick, to peck a. th. (fly).	✱ لَقَع a لَقعًا ه
To sting a. o. (snake).	— ه
He overcame him in words.	— ه بِالكَلام
He smote him with the evil eye.	لَقَع ه بِعَينِهِ
To pass swiftly.	— لَقَعانًا
To quarrel with a. o.	لاقَع ه
He broke forth into idle words.	تَلَقَّع بِالكَلام

✱ لَقِيَ a لِقَاءً ولِقَاءَةً ولَقَايَةً ولُقْيَانًا ولِقْيَانَةً ولِقْيًا ولُقْيَةً ولُقًى ه وه To meet a. o. To find out a. th.

لَقِيَ ✧ To last long (garment).

— على ✧ To lean upon.

لَقَّى ه ه To procure a. th. for.

لُقِّيَ ه مِن To receive a. th. from.

لَاقَى مُلَاقَاةً ولِقَاءً ه To encounter a. o. face to face.

أَلْقَى ه إلى To throw a. th. on the ground. To forward a. th. to.

— إلَيْهِ السَّمْعَ He listened to him.

— ه مِن To displace a. th. To cast a. th. away from.

— ه على To bestow (mercy) upon a. o. To inspire a. th. to a. o. (God). To charge a. o. with. To propose (a riddle) to.

أُلْقِيَ To be thrown, flung.

تَلَقَّى والتَقَى ه وه To meet a. th. or a. o.

تَلَاقَى والتَقَى To meet together.

إسْتَلْقَى على قَفَاهُ He laid on the back.

— ه مِنَ الهَوَاءِ ✧ He caught it in the air.

لَقًى ج أَلْقَاء Cast off refuse.

لَقِيَّة ج لُقًى Encounter; finding.

لِقَاء ولُقْيًا وتِلْقَاء Facing. Encounter.

لِقَايَة و✧ لَقِيَّة Thing found by chance.

لَقَاة Middle of a road.

تِلْقَاءَهُ Over against; towards, opposite.

مِن تِلْقَاءِ نَفْسِهِ Spontaneously.

لَقِيّ م لَقِيَّة Coming in front.

هُمَا لَقِيَّانِ They both face one another.

أُلْقِيَّة ج أَلَاقِيّ Riddle. *Pl.* Accidents, mishaps.

مُلْقًى على Leaning upon.

مَلْقًى ومُلْتَقًى Meeting-place, rendezvous, Branching of two roads. Confluent of two streams.

يَوْمُ التَّلَاقِي The day of the last judgment.

مُلَقًّى Tried by misfortunes. Cast.

— ومُلْقًى ومَلْقِيّ Inauspicious.

✱ لَكَّ o لَكًّا ه To cuff, to thump a. o. on the neck.

— ه To strip (a bone) from the flesh. To mix a. th.

إلْتَكَّ To be compressed, squeezed. To be compact (crowd).

إلْتَكَّ في To speak incorrectly. To linger in (an affair).

لَكّ Flesh. Banyan-tree, producing gum-lac.

لَكّ ج أَلْكَاك ولُكُوك Lac, 100000 (rupees). ✧ Ten billions.

لُكّ Lac, resin.

لَكَّة ج لِكَاك Box, blow, punch.

لُكِّيَّة Compact-fleshed (she-camel).

لَكَّاء Leather varnished with gum-lac.

لَكِيك ج لِكَاك Compact (army). Liquid pitch. Compact flesh.

— ومُلَكَّك Firm-fleshed.

✧ لَكْلَكَ To strike a. o. repeatedly with the fist.

✧ لَكْلَك Trot.

✱ لَكَأَ a لَكْأً ه وبِهِ الأَرْضَ He prostrated him on the ground.

— ه To lash a. o. To give to a. o. his due.

لَكِئَ a لَكَأً ب To keep to (a place). To cling to a. o.

تَلَكَّأَ على To apologise to a. o.

— عن To give up a. th.

✱ لَكَثَ o لَكْثًا ه To overburden a. o. To strike a. o.

لَكِثَ a لَكَثًا To have an ulcer on the mouth (camel).

لَكَث ولُكَاث Pustules on a camel's mouth.

لُكَاث Whitish, glistening stones mica.

لُكَّاث Plasterers.

✱ لَكَحَ a لَكْحًا ه To box, to strike a. o. with the fist.

✱ لَكَدَ o لَكْدًا ه To strike a. o. with the hand, to repel a. o.

لَكِدَ a لَكَدًا عَلَى To adhere to a. th. (dirt).

— وتَلَكَّدَ ب To stick together (dirt). To become fleshy.

لَكِد Avaricious. Ill-tempered.

مِلْكَد Mallet, pestle.

مُلَاكِد Setting his bonds so as to find relief (captive).

✱ لَكَزَ o لَكْزًا To strike a. o. upon the breast with the fist.

لَاكَزَ ه وتَلَاكَزَا To box together.

✧ تَلَكَّزَ على ✧ To criticise, to scoff at a. o.

age of discretion (boy). To draw near.
He is on the point of doing. أَلَمَّ يَفعَل
To catch, to overtake a. o. — على
He caught the meaning. — بالمَعنى
He committed a fault. — بالذَّنب
To visit a. o. إلتَمَّ ه
To be collected (people). إلتَمَّ
✧ Numerous crowd. لَمّ ج لُمُوم
Visit. Collection. Misfortune. ✧ Meeting. لَمَّة ج لِمَام
Touch of insanity. لَمَّة ولَمَام
Fellow-traveller. Party of women. (s. pl.) لُمَّة
Lock of hair falling on the lobe of the ear. لِمَّة ج لِمَم ولِمَام
Evil eye. Dread. لامَّة
Seldom, at times. لِمَامًا
Meeting-house. دار لَمُومَة
Experience, knowledge. إلمَام
Gatherer. ✧ Alms-collector. لَمَّام
Momentous (affair). Gathering his people. مِلَمّ
Visitor. Reaching maturity. مُلِمّ
Accident. Stroke of fortune. مُلِمَّة ج مُلِمَّات
Gathered. Crack-brained. مَلمُوم
1° *Negative particle*. Not yet. But. Only, since, because. ✱ لَمَّا
They have not yet experienced sorrow. لَمَّا يَذُوقُوا العَذَاب
(2°) *Conjunction preceding the perfect*. When. Since.
When he came, I honoured him. لَمَّا جاءَ أكرَمتُهُ
To tuck up (the skirts). To heap up (stones). To round (a stone). ✱ لَملَم ه
To be collected, rolled up. تَلَملَم
Numerous and compact army. لَملَم ومُلَملَم
Crowd. لَملُوم
Elephant's proboscis. مُلَملَمَة
To lay hands upon. To appropriate a. th. ✱ لَمَا a لَمْوًا ه وعَلَى, والْمَا عَلَى
To get possession of. To take away a. th. stealthily. To deny (a right). أَلمَى عَلَى
To take a. th. away. — وتَلَمَّا, وإلتَمَا ب
To enclose a. o. (earth). — على
To be altered (complexion). ألتَمِي

Avaricious. لَكِز
To tap a. o. slightly. To prick (a beast). ✱ لَكَش i لَكشًا ه
To strike a. o. with the fist. ✱ لَكَض o لَكضًا ه
To eat and drink. To bump the head against its mother's udder (suckling). ✱ لَكَع a لَكعًا
To chide a. o. publicly. To sting a. o. (scorpion). — ه
To be contemptible. لَكِع a لَكَعًا ولَكَاعَة
To agglutinate on (the body: dirt). — لَكَعًا على
Vile, infamous. لَكَع, لَكُوع ولَكِيع, وأ لكَع
To dwell, to insist upon (a matter). ✧ لَكَّف في
To punch, to cuff a. o. ✱ لَكَم o لَكمًا ه
To box together. لاكَم ه
✧ Fisticuffs, punch, box. لَكمَة
Hard (hoof). لَكَّام ومِلكَم ومُلَكَّم
To be impeded in speech. ✱ لَكِن a لَكَنًا ولُكنَة ولُكُونَة ولُكنُونَة
But (*after a negation*). But not (*after an affirmation*). (for لاكِن ولاكِنَّ) لٰكِن ولٰكِنَّ
Brass basin. P لَكَن ج أَلكَان
Impediment in speech, barbarous speaking. لُكنَة
Stammerer. أَلكَن م لَكنَاء ج لُكن
✧ Inn, hotel. Is لُوكَندَة
To stick to. ✱ لَكِي a لَكًى ب
Given, addicted to. لَكِيّ
In order that. لِكَي ولِكَيمَا
Lest. لِكَيلا
Negative particle giving to the present the sense of the perfect. Not. ✱ لَم
He did not eat. لَم يَأكُل
Why? For what reason? لِمَ
Is it not? أَلَم, وأَفَلَم, وأَوَلَم
To pick up, to collect (things). ✱ لَمَّ o لَمًّا ه
May God repair the disorder of his affairs! لَمَّ اللّهُ شَعثَهُ
To alight at a. o.'s. — وأَلَمَّ وإلتَمَّ ب
To be seized with madness. لُمَّ
To commit slight faults. To near maturity (palm-tree). To near the أَلَمَّ

Place in which a. th. is taken. Net of hunters. مَلْمُوءَة

To eat with the extremity of the mouth. ✱ لَمَجَ o لَمْجًا ه

To give (little food) to a. o. before a meal. لَمَّجَ ه ب

To take a little food. تَلَمَّجَ

Little food taken before a meal. لَمَاج, ولُمْجَة ج لُمَج

I have not tasted anything. مَا ذُقْتُ لَمَاجًا

Ugly, hideous Eating much. لَمِج ولَمِج ولَمِيج

Corners of the mouth. مَلَامِج

Glossy, smooth. مُلَمَّج

To glance stealthily at. ✱ لَمَحَ a لَمْحًا ه وه وإلى, وأَلْمَحَ إلى ه وه والتَمَحَ ه وه

To shine, to glisten. لَمَحَ a لَمْحًا ولَمَحَانًا وتَلْمَاحًا

To hint at. لَمَّحَ إلى

To show (her face) stealthily (woman). أَلْمَحَ ه

His sight was lost. أُلْتُمِحَ بَصَرُهُ

Evidence. لَمْح

I will show thee the thing clearly. لَأُرِيَنَّكَ لَمْحًا بَاصِرًا

Glance, glimpse. Likeness of features. لَمْحَة

Shining (star). لَامِح ولَمُوح ولَمَّاح

Sharp-sighted falcon. لُمَّاح

Hint, allusion. تَلْمِيح ج تَلَامِيح

Features. مَلَامِح

He has the features of his father. فِيهِ لَمْحَة او مَلَامِح مِن أَبِيهِ

To humble o.'s self before. ✱ لَمَدَ o لَمْدًا ه

Lowered, humbled. لَمْدَان

To wink to a. o. To make a sign with the eye. To reproach, to speak ill of. To strike, to repel a. o. ✱ لَمَزَ o i لَمْزًا ه

Backbiter. لُمَّاز ولُمَزَة

To touch, to feel a. th. with the hand. ✱ لَمَسَ o i لَمْسًا, ولَامَسَ ه

To seek or ask for a. th. لَمَّسَ ه

To help a. o. to attain a. th. أَلْمَسَ ه ه

To ask, to beg, to request a. th. تَلَمَّسَ ه

To seek, to request a. th. from. إِلْتَمَسَ ه مِن

Touch, contact, palpation. لَمْس

Diamond. G أَلْمَاس

Of suspected origin, or character. لَمُوس ج لُمُس

Soft, delicate woman. لَمِيس

Road. لَمُوسَة

He touched him on the diseased part. كَوَاهُ لَمَاسِ او المُتَلَمِّسَة

Unable to defend himself (man). لَا يَرُدُّ يَدَ لَامِس

Bargain concluded by touching the commodity. بَيْع المُلَامَسَة

Place felt with the hand. مَلْمَس

Felt. Smooth, polished (saddle). مَلْمُوس

To eat starch. ✱ لَمَصَ o لَمْصًا

To take and lick a. th. on the finger. To pinch a. o. — ه وه

To be within reach (tree). أَلْمَصَ

Starch. لَمَص

To be flurried, to fret. ✱ لَمَطَ o لَمْطًا

To take away a. th. إِلْتَمَطَ ب

To taste. To wipe o.'s lips with the tongue. ✱ لَمَظَ o لَمْظًا, وتَلَمَّظَ

He gave him a part of his due. لَمَظَ ولَمَّظَ ه مِن حَقِّهِ

To enrage a. o. أَلْمَظَ على

To move about his tongue (snake). تَلَمَّظَ

I have not tasted anything. مَا تَلَمَّظْتُ بِشَيْءٍ

To snap a. th. إِلْتَمَظَ ه

To smack (the lips). To steal, to take off a. th. To wrap o.'s self in. إِلْتَمَظَ ب

To have a white spot on the lower lip (horse). إِلْمَظَّ

White spot on the lower lip of a horse. لَمَظ ولُمْظَة

He has nothing to taste. مَا لَهُ لَمَاظٌ

White-spotted on the lip (horse). أَلْمَظ

Circuit of the lips. مَلَامِظ

To flash (lightning). To glisten (colour). ✱ لَمَعَ a لَمْعًا ولَمَعَانًا, وتَلَمَّعَ والتَمَعَ

To make a sign with (the hand). To flap (its wings: bird). To snatch a. th. — وأَلْمَعَ ب

To variegate (cloth). لَمَّعَ ه

To have withering plants (land). أَلْمَعَ

To carry off a. th. تلمّع والتمع ه
To be altered (colour). إلتمع
Brightness, shining. لمع ولمعان
Withered part of a لُمعة ج لُمَع ولِماع plant. Part of the body unwashed in the ablution. Crowd of people. Brightness of complexion.
He has enough to live on. معهُ لُمعة من العيش
Spot on a horse's skin. تلميع ج تلاميع
Looming.
Fluttering light. لامعة ج لوامع
Upper part of a child's skull. — ولمّاعة
Desert subject to mirage. Vulture. لمّاعة
Sharp-minded. ألمع وألمعيّ ويلمعيّ
Liar. يلمع
Mirage. Lightning not followed by rain *Pl.* Glittering weapons. يلمع ج يلامع
Wings of a bird. ملمعا الطائر
Soil where mirage is produced. أرض مُلمِعة ومُلمِعة ومُلمّعة
Piebald (horse). Speech mixed of Turkish and Arabic. مُلمّع
To write. To erase a. th. To slap a. o. on the eye. ✱ لمق o لمقا ولموقا ه
To look at. — إلى
To fix (the eyes) on. — ه ب
To patch up, to botch (a work). ✧ لمّق (*for* رمّق) ه
To take little (food). تلمّق ب
Middle part of a road. لمق الطريق
Small quantity of food or drink. لماق
To knead (dough). ✱ لمك o لمكا ه
He has not taken the least food. ما تلمّك بلماك
Eye-water. لمك ولُماك
Anointed with collyrium. لميك
Strong youth. يلمك
✧ Galleys, penal servitude. لومان G
To sentence a. o. to the galleys. ✧ لوّمن ه
✧ Harbour. إيمان T
Lemon. ليمون (*un.* ليمونة)
To eat up a. th. ✱ لما o لموا ه
Party from three to ten. Equal, coeval. Wife. Mate. One of a pair. لُمة

To have the lips of a deep red. ✱ لمى a لمًى ولمياً, ولميَ a لمّى
To steal a. th. ألمى ب
To be altered (colour). ألتمى
Deep red of the lips. لمى ولِمى ولُمى
Red-lipped. Thick (shade). Tufty (tree). ألمى م لمياء ج لُمى
Negative particle used before the future. He, she, it will not. ✱ لن
Thou shalt not see me. لن تراني
Anchor. P لنجر
To weave (a fine textile). ✱ لهله ه
Weak (poetry, speech). لهله
Looming desert. لهله لهلهة ج لهاله
To blaze fiercely (fire). ✱ لهب a لهباً ولهَباً ولهيباً ولهابا ولهبانا
To burn with thirst. لهب a لهباً ولهبانا
To make (the fire) to blaze. لهّب وألهب ه
To be fiery, to raise dust in his run (horse). To flash time after time (lightning). ألهب
To incite a. o. to. — ه ل
To blaze up (fire). تلهّب والتهب
He was burnt by hunger. — والتهب جوعاً
To burn with anger. To be inflamed (limb). إلتهب
Cleft, ravine between two rocks; defile in a mountain. لِهب ج ألهاب ولُهوب ولِهاب ولِهابة
Blaze, ardour of fire. لهب ولهيب و ✧ لهلوبة
Burning thirst. لُهبة ولهبان ولُهاب
Burning heat. Hot day. لهبان
Fieriness of a horse. ألهوب
Inflammation (disease). إلتهاب ج إلتهابات
Burnt by thirst. لهبان م لهبى ج لِهاب
Saturated with red dye (cloth). مُلهب
Divinity, divine nature. ✱ لهت — لاهوت (*opp. to* ناسوت)
Theologian, theological. لاهوتيّ
Theology. عِلم اللاهوت
Dogmatic theology. اللاهوت النظريّ
Moral theology. اللاهوت الأدبيّ
To loll the tongue (dog). ✱ لهث a لهثا ولُهاثا, والتهث
To be thirsty. لهث a لهثا ولهثانا ولهاثا
Fatigue, thirst. لهثة
Ardour of thirst. Pangs of لُهاث

death. Red spots on palm-leaves.
Thirsty. لَهْثَان م لَهْثَى
To be addicted, accustomed to. لَهِج a لَهَجًا, وأَلْهَج ب *
To give little food to a. o. before dinner. لَهَّج ة
To be intricate (affair). To curdle (milk). To close from drowsiness (eyes). إِلْهَاجَّ
Tongue. Dialect, accent, language. لَهْجَة
Little food taken before dinner. لُهْجَة
Addicted to, craving for. لَهِج ولَاهِج ب
Drowsy, slumbering. مُلَهَّج
Intricate (affair). مُلْهَاجّ
To cook (meat) imperfectly. To do a. th. precipitately. لَهْوَج وتَلَهْوَج ه *
Broad and beaten road. لَهْجَم *
To be beaten, traced out (road). تَلَهْجَم
To jade a. o. To overburden (a beast : load). لَهَد a لَهْدًا ة *
To lick, to eat up a. th. — ه
To repel a. o. in striking. To press a. o. — ولَهَّد ة
To injure, to wrong a. o. أَلْهَد ة
To treat a. o. scornfully, harshly. — ب
To help a. o. against. — بِرَجُل على
Weakening of the legs. Tumour on the chest of camels. لَهَد
Sigh, sob. لُهَاد
Overburdened, jaded (beast). لَهِيد
Sort of pudding. لَهِيدَة
To cut a. th. لَهْذَم وتَلَهْذَم ه *
Sharp pointed. لَهْذَم ج لَهَاذِم ولَهَاذِمَة
To become hoary. لَهَز a لَهْزًا ة القَتِيرُ *
To strike a. o. on the chest. — ولَهَّز ة
He bumped its head against its mother's udder (young camel). لَهَز ضَرْعَ أُمِّهِ
Rugged hill. لَاهِز
Star of hair on a horse's jaw. دَائِرَة اللَّاهِز
Protuberant bone of the jaw. لَهْزَة
Hoary. مَلْهُوز
To appear on (the cheeks : hoariness). لَهْزَم ه *
Protuberant bone beneath the ear. لِهْزِمَة مث لِهْزِمَتَان ج لَهَازِم
To lick a. th. لَهَس a لَهْسًا ه *
To rush upon (food). لَهَس ولَاهَس على
To hurry towards. لَاهَس إلى
A licking, a trifle. لُهْسَة ولُهَاس ولُهَاسَة
Sprightly. لَاهِس ج لَوَاهِس
To slap a. o. with the flat of the hand. لَهَط a لَهْطًا ة *
To hit a. o. with (an arrow). — ة ب
✧ To gobble. (for رَهَط) — ه
To prostrate a. o. — بِهِ الأَرْضَ
To bring forth a child (woman). — بِوَلَدِهَا
Rumours, reports. لَهْطَة من الخَبَر
To be compliant. لَهِع a لَهَعًا ولَهَاعَة *
To speak from the corner of the mouth. لَهِع a لَهَعًا
Compliant. لَهِع ولَهِيع وأَهْيَع
To regret a. th. missed. لَهِف a لَهَفًا, وتَلَهَّف عَلَى *
To grieve for a. o. لَهَّف ة
To be greedy of. أَلْهَف إلى
To be heart-broken. To blaze (fire). إِلْتَهَف
Regret, sorrow. لَهْف
How do I pity thee! يَا لَهْفِي عَلَيْكَ
What a pity for him! يَا لَهْفَ فُلَان
How unhappy I am! What a loss! يَا لَهْفَ وِيَا لَهْفَا وِيَا لَهْفَاهُ
Alas! What a loss! يَا لَهْفَتَهْ وِيَا لَهْفَتَاهُ
Sad. Disquieted. لَهْفَان م لَهْفَى ج لُهْف ولَهَافَى
Heart-broken. لَاهِف ولَهِيف القَلْب ج لُهَاف
To be snow-white. لَهِق ولَهَق a لَهَقًا ولَهَقًا, وتَلَهَّق *
White bull. لَهَق ولَهِق ولِهَاق
White cow. لَهَقَة ولَهِقَة ولِهَاق
Snow-white. لَهَق ولَهِق م لَهَقَة ولَهِقَة ج لِهَاق
Whitened. مُلَهَّق
To brag, to boast falsely. لَهْوَق وتَلَهْوَق *
To patch up, to botch (a work). لَهْوَق العَمَل وتَلَهْوَق في
لَهِم a لَهْمًا ولَهَمًا, وتَلَهَّم والتَهَم ه *
To glut, to gulp a. th.
To inspire a. o. with (God). أَلْهَم ة ه
It exhausted the udder (young camel). إِلْتَهَم مَا في الضَّرْع
To be altered, faded (colour). أُلْتُهِم
To ask inspiration from (God). إِسْتَلْهَم ة

Pl. Those who sin inadvertently; careless children. لاهٍ ج لاهُون
Plaything; sport, toy. مِلهًى ج مَلاهٍ
Instruments of music. مَلاهٍ
Place of entertainment. مَلهًى ج مَلاهٍ
Amusing (man). Musician. مُلهٍ
✱ لو ولو أنَّ *Conditional, optative particle*: If, though.
Had he come, I would have honoured him. لو جاءَني لأكرمتُهُ
He would like to live a thousand years. يَوَدّ لو يُعمَّرُ ألفَ سَنَةٍ
If not; unless. لو لا ولو لم ولو ما
If not the Lord, we should have perished. لو لا الربُّ لَهَلَكنا
Even if, altough. ✧ *Exclamation of wonder.* Indeed! is it possible! ولو
Give alms, were it but little. تَصَدَّقوا ولو بِقَليل
✱ لاب ٥ لَوبًا ولُوابًا ولَوَبانًا To be thirsty. To wander around the water.
To anoint a. th. or a. o. لَوَّب ٤ وه
To have thirsty cattle. ألاب
Thirsty (cattle). لائِب ج لُؤُوب ولُوب
Lybians. Negroes. لاب
Numerous flocks. نَعَم لابٌ
Collection of black camels. لابَة
Rocky ground. — ج لابات, ولُوبَة ج لُوب
Tract of black stones. لابَة ولُوبَة
People kept apart. Negroes. لُوبَة
Lybian. لُوبِيّ
Dolichas lubia, French beans; kidney beans. لُوبِياء ولوبيا ولُوباء
Perfume. Saffron. مَلاب
✱ لات ٥ لَوتًا To shift, to shun a question.
To conceal (news). — ه
To prevent a. o. from. — وألات ٤ عن
It is not the time for. لات حِين
Idol, goddess of the pagan Arabs. لات
✱ لاث ٥ لَوثًا ه To twist (a turban) round. To mix a. th. To chew a. th.
To soak a. th. To remain at (home). — ه
To stick to. To seek refuge towards. — ب
To be dilatory, slow in (work). — ولوث a لَوَّث وألاث في

Aged. لِهِم ج لُهُوم
Gluttonous, ravenous. لَهِم ولُهَم ولَهُوم ولَهيم وتِلهَم
Divine inspiration. Animal instinct. إلهام ج إلهامات
Numerous army. لُهام
Large cooking-pot. لُهَيم
Misfortune. Fever. Death. اللُّهَيم وأمُّ اللُّهَيم
✱ لهن — لَهَّن ٤ ول To give to a. o. a morsel before dinner.
To make a present to a. o. after a journey. — وألهن ٤
Present given by a traveller. Food taken before a meal. لُهنَة ج لُهَن
✱ لَها ٥ لَهوًا ب To divert o.'s self with. To forget a. th. by.
To delight in. — ٥ لَهوًا ولُهُوًّا إلى
To turn away from. — لُهِيًّا ولِهيانًا عن
To love, to cling to. لَهِي a لَهًا ب
To divert o.'s self from, to forget a. th. — وتَلَهَّى والتهى عن
To divert a. o. from. لَهَّى ٤ عن
To amuse a. o. with. — ٤ ب
To draw near to. لاهى ٤ وه
To quarrel with. — ٤
To reach the time of being weaned (child). — الفِطامَ
To divert o.'s self with music. ألهى
To divert a. o. from a. th. (play). ألهى ٤ عن
To throw grain in the mill-hole. — الرَّحى وفي الرَّحى
To entertain o.'s self with. تَلَهَّى وتلاهى والتهى ب
Play, entertainment, pastime. Woman. لَهو
Instrument of music. آلة لَهو
Quantity, evaluation. لُهاء
About a hundred. — مِئَة
Uvula. لَهاة ج لَهَوات ولَهَيات ولُهِيّ ولَهًا ولِهاء
Fruit of the alkekengi. حبّ اللَّهو
Grain thrown in the mill-hole. لَهوَة ولُهوَة ج لُهًى
Gift. — ولُهيَة ج لُهًى
Bountiful. مِعطاء اللُّهَى
Entertainment, pastime, sport. تَلهِيَة وأُلهُوّة وأُلهِيَّة

To defile (clothes) with (mud). لَاثَ ولَوَّثَ ه ب
To make (water) turbid. لَوَّثَ ه
To mix (straw) with. — ه ب
He entrusted his flocks to such a one. أَلَاثَ مَالَهُ بِفُلَانٍ
To have green herbage mixed with dry (land). أَلْوَثَ
To defile o.'s self with (mud, or dirt). To be soiled with. تَلَوَّثَ ب
To be wound round. To be strong. To become fat. To have self-restraint. To be entangled (business). إِلْتَاثَ
He became confused in speech. — في الكَلَامِ
He was stained with blood. — بالدَّمِ
To stick to a pen (hair). — بالقَلَمِ
Twist of a turban. Strength. Wounds. Weak proof. Evil, malevolence. لَوْثٌ
Weakness. لَوْثٌ ولُوثَةٌ
Intertwisted plant. لِيثٌ
Tangled (plants). Hoary (beard). لَيِّثٌ م لَيِّثَةٌ
Intertwisted (plants). لَاثٌ ولَائِثٌ
Flabby. Slow. Weak. Strong. أَلْوَثُ م لَوْثَاءُ ج لُوثٌ
مَلَاثٌ ومِلْوَثٌ ج مَلَاوِثُ ومَلَاوِثَةٌ ومَلَاوِيثُ
Center, pivot; refuge. Influential man or tribe.
To mumble; to turn a. th. in the mouth. ✱ لَاجَ o لَوْجًا ه
He has led us by a winding road. لَوَّجَ بِنَا الطَّرِيقَ
Need, want. لَوْجَاءُ
To appear, to shine (star). To flash (lightning). ✱ لَاحَ o لَوْحًا وأَلَاحَ
To look at a. o. or a. th. لَاحَ إِلى وه
To alter the complexion (journey, thirst). — ولَوَّحَ ه
لَاحَ o لَوْحًا ولُوحًا ولُوَاحًا ولُؤُوحًا ولَوَحَانًا
To thirst.
To make a hint. ✧ To ripen (grapes). ▫ To become sick, exhausted. لَوَّحَ
To wave a. th. about. لَوَّحَ وأَلَاحَ ب
To render a. o. hoary (age). لَوَّحَ ه
He raised the stick upon him. — ه بالعَصَا

He heated it in the fire. لَوَّحَ ه بالنَّارِ
To feed a child. To hold up (eggs) to the light. — ه وه
To cause the loss of. أَلَاحَ ه
To carry away a. th. — بِحَقِّهِ
To fear a. o. To guard against. To blush at (a word). — مِنْ
To be parched by thirst. إِلْتَاحَ
To examine a. th. إِسْتَلَاحَ في
Tablet. Board, plank; plate of metal, pane. Glance. Wide and flat bone. لَوْحٌ ج أَلْوَاحٌ وأَلَاوِيحُ
✧ Sheet-iron, latten. لَوْحُ حَدِيدٍ
Flashing weapons. أَلْوَاحُ السِّلَاحِ
Air, atmosphere. Thirst. لُوحٌ
Outward appearance, feature. ✧ Register. Diplomatic note. لَائِحَةٌ ج لَوَائِحُ
Intensely white. Dawn. Wild bull. لِيَاحٌ و لَيَاحٌ
Metonimy. *Pl.* Notes, remarks. تَلْوِيحٌ ج تَلْوِيحَاتٌ
✧ Fruit beginning to ripen. تَلَاوِيحُ
Soon thirsty. Tall. Slender. مِلْوَحٌ ومِلْوَاحٌ ومِلْيَاحٌ
Lean. Owl used as a bait, decoy-bird. مِلْوَاحٌ
Parched, altered by thirst. مُلْتَاحٌ
To mix a. th. ✱ لَاخَ o لَوْخًا
To be mixed. To rise (dough). إِلْتَاخَ
To be rebellious, wrongful. ✱ لَوِدَ a لَوَدًا
Rebellious. أَلْوَدُ
✱ لَاذَ لَوْذًا ولِوَاذًا ولُوَاذًا ولِيَاذًا , ولَاوَذَ مُلَاوَذَةً , وأَلَاذَ ب
To take refuge at. To seek shelter in.
The road encompassed the house. لَاذَ وأَلَاذَ الطَّرِيقُ بِالدَّارِ
To circumvent a. o. To thwart a. o. لَاوَذَ ه
To elude, to shift, to shun a. o. — عَنْ
Winding of a valley, circuit of a mountain. لَوْذٌ ج أَلْوَاذٌ
Red silk-cloth. لَاذَةٌ ج لَاذٌ
Shore. Country. لَوْذَانُ
Shelter. Stronghold. Place of refuge. مَلَاذٌ ومَلْوَذَةٌ ج مَلَاوِذُ
To seek (*for* لَاذَ ومَلَاذَ) a shelter. ✱ لَازَ o ومَلَازٌ

To stuff a. th. with almonds. ه
Almond, tree (*un.* لَوْزَة ج لَوْزَات) and fruit. لَوْز
The two tonsils. لَوْزَتَان
Poor, destitute. عَوِز لَوِز
Almond-shaped. لَوْزِيّ
Almond-cake. لَوْزِيَّة و P لَوْزِينَج
Seller of almonds. لَوَّاز
Rich in almond-trees (land). مَلَازَة
To be fond of (sweetmeats). To taste a. th. ✱ لَاسَ o لَوْسًا ه
Mouthful. لُوَاسَة
Morsel for tasting. لَوَاس ولَوُوس
Fond of sweetmeats. لَائِس ولَوُوس ولَوَّاس وأَلْوَس
To be jaded, over-fatigued. ✧ لَاشَ o لَوْشًا, ولَوَّشَ
To jade a. o. ✧ لَوَّشَ ه
Nothing. ✧ لَاش (*for* لَا شَيْء)
To look stealthily through the chink of a door. ✱ لَاصَ o لَوْصًا, ولَاوَصَ
To shun. To desist from. لَاصَ عَنْ
✧ To be annoyed. To fret. — مِنْ
✧ To press a. o. importunately. لَوَّصَ ه
To eat starch and honey. لَوَّصَ
To look intently on. لَاوَصَ ه وإلى
To seek to circumvent or to decoy a. o. in — ه عن
To enable a. o. to. أَلَاصَ ه على
To be terror-stricken. أُلِيصَ
To coil up, to fold up. تَلَوَّصَ
Pain in the throat. Sore ear. لَوْص
Pain in the back. ✧ Weariness, fretfulness. لَوْصَة
Food made of starch and honey. لَوَاص ومُلَوَّص
To cleave to (the mind: thought). To take away a. th. ✱ لَاطَ o لَوْطًا, والْتَاطَ ب
Te sin unnaturally. لَاطَ وتَلَوَّطَ
To plaster (a tank) with clay. To hide a. th. — والْتَاطَ ه
To conjoin a. th. with. لَاطَ ه ب
To him a. o. with (an arrow). To smite with (the evil eye). — ه ب
To insist upon. — o لَاطًا فِي
The patriarch Lot. لُوط
Sympathy, bond. Cloak. Active and nimble. لَوْط

Joist, beam. لَاطَة ج لَاطَات
Usury. لِيَاط
More sympathetic. أَلْوَط بِالقَلْب
To affect a. o. deeply (love). ✱ لَاعَ o لَوْعًا ✧ لَوَّعَ ه
To scorch a. o. (sun). لَاعَ ه
To be anxious, faint-hearted. To be sick. To be wicked. — لَوْعًا ولُؤُوعًا, ولَاعَ a o لَوْعَةً
To be broken, affected (heart). إِلْتَاعَ
Moral pain; pangs of love. لَوْعَة
Anxious, faint-hearted. Diseased. Wicked. لَاعٍ ج لَاعُون ولَاعَة وأَلْوَاع ولَائِع
Coquettish woman. لَاعَة ج لَاعَات
To eat dry fodder (cattle). ✱ لَافَ o لَوْفًا
To chew a. th. — ه
Unpalatable fodder, food. لَوْف
Serpentaria. *Momordica luffa* (*plants*). لُوف
Arum Dracunculus, dragon's wort. لُوف الأَرْقَط ولُوف الحَيَّة
Lion's foot (*plant*). — السَّبُع ولُوف الجُعْدِي
Cotyledon (*plant*). لُوفِي
Wet, moist (fodder). مَلُوف
To soften a. th. To put cotton in (an inkstand). ✱ لَاقَ o لَوْقًا ه
He shall not remain at. لَا يَلُوق عِنْد
To twist, to crook a. th. ✧ لَوَقَ ه
To butter (a dish). ▫ To sow in a soft ground. لَوَّقَ ه
To be contorted, twisted. ✧ إِنْلَوَقَ والْتَوَقَ
He has not tasted the least food. مَا ذَاقَ لَوَاقًا
Stupidity. لَوَق
An instant, a moment. لَوْقَة
Fresh butter. Dates mixed with butter. لُوقَة وأَلُوقَة
Foolish. ✧ Contorted, twisted. أَلْوَق م لَوْقَاء
Spatula. ✧ مِلْوَق
To chew a. th. To champ (the bit: horse). To impair the reputation of. ✱ لَاكَ o لَوْكًا ه
To transmit a message to. أَلَاكَ ه إلى
Chewed morsel. لَوَاك
Pipe. *See* (لب). ✱ لَوْلَب ج لَوَالِب
✱ لَامَ o لَوْمًا ومَلَامًا ومَلَامَة, ولَوَّمَ وأَلَامَ

To blame, to criticise a. o. for. ‏لَامَهُ ه على او في‏

It has been cut off, curtailed. ‏لِيمَ بِهِ‏

To write the letter ل. ‏لَوَّمَ لَامًا‏

To rebuke o. a. ‏لَاوَمَ مُلَاوَمَةً ولِوَامًا ه‏

To commit blameworthy actions. ‏أَلَامَ‏

To linger in. ‏تَلَوَّمَ في‏

To reprove o. a. ‏تَلَاوَمَ‏

To be blamed, rebuked. ‏إِلْتَامَ و♢ انْلَامَ‏

To deserve reproof. ‏إِسْتَلَامَ‏

To incur reproof from a. o. ‏— إِلَى‏

Terror. Person, individual. Kindred. The letter ل. ‏لَامٌ ج لَامَاتٌ‏

Blame, reproof. ‏لَوْمٌ‏

Blameworthy (action). ‏لَوْمَةٌ ولَائِمَةٌ‏

Blame, reproach. ‏لَوْمَى ولَوْمَاءُ‏

Blamed, reproved. ‏لُومَةٌ ومَلِيمٌ ومَلُومٌ‏

Expectation, delay. ‏لُومَةٌ وتَلَوُّمٌ‏

Blame, reproof. ‏لَائِمَةٌ ج لَوَائِمُ‏

Censor, criticiser. ‏لُوَمَةٌ ولَوَّامٌ‏

Two celebrated poems rhyming in ل. ‏لَامِيَّةُ العَجَمِ ولَامِيَّةُ العَرَبِ‏

Blame, reproval. ‏مَلَامٌ ومَلَامَةٌ ج مَلَاوِمُ‏

Blameworthy (man). ‏مُلِيمٌ‏

✲ To assume its colour (date). ‏لون — لَوَّنَ‏

To colour a. th. ♢ To illuminate (a book). ‏— ه‏

To be coloured, painted. To be variegated. To be variable. ♢ To be illuminated (book). ‏تَلَوَّنَ و إِلْوَنَّ‏

To change o.'s mind. ‏تَلَوَّنَ‏

Colour, hue. Appearance. Date. Kind, sort. ♢ State. Dish, sort of food. ‏لَوْنٌ ج أَلْوَانٌ‏

Date of bad quality. ‏لَوْنَةٌ ,ولِينَةٌ ج لِينٌ وجج لِيَانٌ‏

♢ How? What sort? ‏إِيش لَوْن وأَيْشْلَوْن‏

Changing, unsteady. ‏مُتَلَوِّنٌ‏

✲ To gleam (mirage). ‏لَاهَ ٥ لَوْهًا ولَوَهَانًا ,وتَلَوَّهَ‏

To create (the world : God). ‏لَاهَ ه وه‏

Shining of mirage. ‏لَوْهٌ ولَوْهَةٌ ولُؤُوهَةٌ‏

♢ Pole, Polish. ‏T لَاه‏

Poland. ‏بِلَادُ اللَّاه‏

✲ To twist (a rope). To bend a. th. ‏لَوَى i لَيًّا ولَوِيًّا ه‏

To give up a. th. ‏— والتَوَى عن‏

To put off (the payment of a debt) to. ‏— لَيًّا ولِيَّانًا ه ه او ب‏

To deny (a debt) to a. o. ‏لَوَى ه بِحَقِّهِ‏

To avert (the face) from. To conceal a. th. from. ‏— لَيًّا ولِيَّانًا ه عَن‏

He turned his head. ‏— رَأْسَهُ او بِرَأْسِهِ‏

To lean towards. To feel an inclination for. To stick to. ‏— على‏

To be curved (arrow). To wind (sand). To be distorted (herb, plant). To writhe (stomach). To coil up (snake). To deviate, to become wry. ‏لَوِيَ a لَوًى‏

To incline (the head, the neck). ‏لَوَّى ه‏

To coil up (snake). ‏لَاوَى لِوَاءً ومُلَاوَاةً‏

To reach the winding of a sandy tract. To have withered plants. ‏أَلْوَى إِلْوَاءً‏

To turn or lean (the head). To beckon with. To snatch. To destroy a. o. (fortune). To deny (a due). To shift in (speech). ‏— ب‏

To hoist (a flag). ‏— ه‏

To be twisted (rope). To writhe. To wind (river, sand). ‏تَلَوَّى والتَوَى‏

To coil (serpent). To flash in zigzag (lightning). To writhe in agony. ‏تَلَوَّى‏

To agree upon (a business). ‏تَلَاوَى على‏

To set apart (a portion of food). ‏إِلْتَوَى ه‏

To be intricate for a. o. (affair). ‏إِلْتَوَى على‏

Winding of sand. ‏لِوًى ج أَلْوَاءٌ وأَلْوِيَةٌ‏

Flag, standard. ♢ Turkish province. ‏لِوَاءٌ ج أَلْوِيَةٌ وأَلْوِيَاتٌ‏

♢ Brigadier-general. ‏مِير لِوَا‏

Mast for a flag. ♢ Head-pad. ‏لِوَايَةٌ‏

They sent out for help. ‏بَعَثُوا بِالسِّوَاءِ واللِّوَاءِ‏

Complaint of the stomach, of the back. ‏لَوًى‏

Having a complaint of the stomach, of the back. Curved. ‏لَوٍ م لَوِيَةٌ‏

Trifles, vanities. ‏لَوًى‏

Withered (herbage). ‏لَوِيٌّ م لَوِيَّةٌ‏

Portion of a meal set apart. ‏لَوِيَّةٌ ج لَوَايَا‏

Twist, coil. Winding. Contortion. Spiral, volute. ☐ Snake. Coiling tube of a nargile. ‏لَيَّةٌ ج لِوًى‏

To plaster a. th. ✧ لَيَّس ه
To stick, to cleave to. ✧ لَيَّس ب
To pass a. th. over. تَلَايَس عَن
Brave. أَلْيَس م لَيْسَاء ج لِيس
✧ Plastered. مُلَيَّس
Tardy, late. مُلَايِس
To incline. ✱ لَاص i لَيْصًا
To displace a. th. — وأَلَاص ه
To suit a. o. ✱ لَاط i لَيْطًا ب
To join, to stick a. th. to. لَيَّط ه ب
Colour. Natural disposition. لِيط
Skin. Bark, rind. — ولِيطَة ج لِيط ولِيَاط
Gypsum. Lime. Human excrement. لِيَاط
Satan. شَيْطَان لَيْطَان
To be wearied. To be flurried. ✱ لَاعَ i لَيْعَانًا
Ravenous hunger. لَيْعَة الجُوع
Strong gale. رِيح لِيَاع
To be stupid. ✱ لَيغ — تَلَيَّغ
Stupidity. لَيغ
Mispronouncing. أَلْيَغ م لَيْغَاء ج لِيغ
Stupid. — ولِيَاغَة
To be fibrous (palm-tree). ✱ لِيف — لَيَّف
To rub (the body) with palm-fibres. To use (palm-fibres) as ropes. — ه
Fibres of palm-trees used as ropes. Spongious substance of trees. لِيف
Tuft of palm-tree fibres. لِيفَة
Fibrous, spongious. لِيفَانِيّ
To befit, to suit a. o. ✱ لَاق i لَيْقًا و✧ لِيَاقَةً ب
This affair does not befit us. هٰذَا الأَمْرُ لَا يَلِيق بِنَا
It is not suitable for thee to do so. لا يَلِيق أَن تَفْعَل كَذَا
To suit a. o. (clothes). To adhere to. لَاق i لَيْقًا ب
To put cotton into (the inkstand). — لَيْقًا ولَيْقَةً, وأَلَاق ه
He attached him to his own person. أَلَاقَهُ بِنَفْسِهِ
He does not save a penny. مَا يُلِيق دِرْهَمًا
To be attached, devoted to a. o. إِلْتَاق ل
To act sincerely with. إِلْتَاق ب
Scattered portions of clouds. لِيَق
Flake of cotton or silk لِيقَة ج لِيَق

✧ لِيَة ج لِيَات (for أَلْيَة) Fat tail of merino sheep.
Levite, from the tribe of Levi. لَاوِيّ ج لَاوِيُّون
Branding-iron. لَاوِيَاء
Curved, crooked, contorted. Solitary. Quareller. أَلْوَى م لَيَّاء ج لُيّ
Land remote from water. لَيَّاء
Bracelets of twisted filigree. Peg of musical instruments. ✧ Windlass ; capstan. مَلْوَى ج مَلَاوَى
Curved, contorted. مُلْتَوٍ
The windings of the road. مَلَاوِي الطَّرِيق
A sea-fish. ✱ لِيّ — لِيَاء
To withhold, to prevent a. o. from. ✱ لَات i لَيْتًا, وأَلَات ه عَن
He has not wronged him in any way مَا أَلَاتَهُ شَيْئًا
Side of the neck. لِيت مث لِيتَان ج أَلْيَات
✱ لَيْتَ ويَا لَيْتَ *Particle expressing a wish impossible to be realised and used with the accusative*: May it be that! Would that!
Please to God that youth might come back! لَيْتَ الشَّبَابَ يَعُودُ
It has sometimes the sense of وَجَدْتُ I found.
I found Zeyd returning. لَيْتَ زَيْدًا شَاخِصًا
Would that! يَا لَيْتَ شِعْرِي ويَا لَيْتَنِي و✧ يَا رَيْتَنِي
To be brave like a lion. ✱ لَاث — لَيَّث ولَيِّث وتَلَيَّث واسْتَلْيَث
To vie in courage with a. o. لَايَث ه
Lion. Kind of spider. Strength. Eloquent. لَيْث ج لُيُوث
Lioness. Strong (she-camel). لَيْثَة ج لَيْثَات
Dauntless, brave. أَلْيَث م لَيْثَاء ج لِيث, ومِلْيَث
✱ لَيْس ولَيْس ب (1°) *Negative and defective verb having no aorist*: To be not.
Zeyd is not standing. لَيْسَ زَيْدٌ قَائِمًا
Am I not your Lord? أَلَسْتُ بِرَبِّكُم
(2°) *Means* : save, except.
Except thee. لَيْسَكَ ولَيْسَ إِيَّاكَ
To be brave. لَيِس a لَيَسًا

To لَيَّنَ تَلْيِينًا, وأَلَانَ إِلَانَةً, وأَلْيَنَ إِلْيَانًا ه soften, to make a. th. supple.

To be kind, لَايَنَ مُلَايَنَةً ولِيَانًا ه, وتَلَيَّنَ ل gentle with. To soothe, to blandish a. o.

To polish, to smooth (a sword). لَايَنَ ه

To be softened. ◻ To make gymnastics. تَلَيَّنَ

To find a. th. soft, tender supple, pliant. إِسْتَلَانَ ه

Softness. لِين ولِينَة ولَيَان و✧ لُيُونَة
Meekness, tenderness.

The soft letters *i. e* : ا , و and ي حُرُوف اللِّين

Easiness, softness of life. لَيَان العَيْش

Arched (*for* إِيوَان) ✧ لِيوَان ج لَوَاوِين hall, gallery.

Soft, limber, supple, easy. لَيِّن ج لَيِّنُون وأَلْيِنَاء, ولَيْن ج لَيْنُون

✧ Mercury (*plant*). حَشِيشَة اللِّين

Purslain (*plant*). البَقْلَة اللَّيِّنَة

Cushion. لِينَة

◻ Gymnastics. تَلْيِين

Meekness, kindness. مُلَايَنَة

Emollient, laxative (medicine). مُلَيِّن

To be hidden, concealed. ✻ لَاهَ i لَيْهًا
To be lofty, high.

put in an inkstand. Clay for smearing walls.

Pasture-land. Steadiness. لَيَاق

Blaze. لِيَاق

Becomingness. propriety. لِيَاقَة
✧ Elegance.

Becoming, seemly. لَائِق

More becoming. أَلْيَق

Supplied with silk or cotton (inkstand). مَلِيق

To hire a. o. for the night. ✻ ليل — لَايَلَ ه

To be overtaken by the night. أَلَالَ إِلَالًا, وأَلْيَلَ إِلْيَالًا

Night. Bustard, young bustard. لَيْل

A night ; one night's journey. لَيْلَة ج لَيْلَات ولَيَالٍ ولَيَائِل

Long and dark night. لَيْل لَائِل وأَلْيَل ومُلَيَّل ولَيْلَة لَيْلَاء

By night. لَيْلًا

Nightly, nocturnal. لَيْلِيّ

Lest. *See* لِ. (*for* لِأَنْ لَا) لِئَلَّا

✧ Lilac (flower). P لَيْلَك

Peace, concord. Likeness. لِيم

Lemon, citron. (*un*. لَيْمُونَة) ✻ لَيْمُون

To be soft, tender, smooth. To be mild, kind. To be relaxed (belly). ✻ لَانَ i لِينًا ولَيَانًا ولِينَةً

م

✲ ما (1) *Interrogative pronoun*: What ?

ما فعل What has he done ?

ما جزاؤهُ What does he deserve ?

ما *interrogative* loses its ا after *a preposition, for inst*: حتّى مَ, إلى مَ, لِمَ, بِمَ (*for* حتّى ما, إلى ما, لِما, بِما).

ما أنتَ What art thou ?

ما لكَ What is the matter with thee ?

ما لي بهِ What do I care about it ?

ما عليكَ ✧ Never mind. What to thee ?

(2) *Relative pronoun*. What.

علمتُ ما صنع زيدٌ I knew what Zeyd had done.

Is used sometimes as meaning: شيء thing.

أحسنُ ما يكون The best thing that may be.

قليل ما هم They are very few or of little worth.

(3) *Added to a noun, it means indetermination*: some, a certain.

جاء لِأمرٍ ما He came for some business.

يوماً ما A certain day.

(4) *Adverb of time*: As long as.

ما دمتُ حيّاً As long as I shall live.

(5) *Postponed to an adverb*, ما *forms a conjunction and gives a general meaning*.

بينما Whilst.

حالما As soon as.

حيثما Wheresoever, whenever.

حينما When, whenever.

طالما As long as.

عندما When.

كيفما Howsoever.

كلّما Whensoever, whenever.

أينما Wheresoever.

(6) *Is expletive in compound words such as*. أنّما, إنّما, عمّا, رُبّما, لكنّما, كأنّما, كيما, إمّا (*for* إن ما) متى ما إذا ما, أيّ ما

(7) *Particle of wonder*. What a... ! How... he is !

ما أعذبَهُ وما أحلاهُ What a sweet and charming (thing or man) !

(8) *Negative particle*: not.

ما أدري I do not know.

ما رأيتُهُ I have not seen him.

ماذا How ? What (*interrog.*) ?

ماذا تفعلُ What art thou doing ?

لِماذا جئتَ Why art thou come ?

ما بين Between, among. ✧ Ante-chamber.

ماهيّة Essence, constitutive part. ✧ Wages.

✲ مأمأ مأمأة To bleet (ewe).

✲ مُؤتة Town of Syria renowned for its swords.

✲ مَؤُج ٥ مُؤُوجة To be salt, bitter (water).

مأج Salt (water).

✲ مأد a مأداً To be tender, supple (plant).

أمأد ه To render (a plant) fresh, soft.

إمتأد ه To acquire (wealth).

مأد ويمؤود Tender (plant).

✲ مأر a مأراً ه To fill up (a skin).

– وماءر ومُماءرة ومِئاراً بين To sow discord between.

مئر a مأراً To reopen (wound)

– وامتأر على To feel hatred for.

ماءر ه To compete with a. o.

تماءر To compete together.

مئر ومئر Mischief-maker.

مئر Difficult (affair).

مِئرة ج مِئر Hatred, rancour. Slander.

أمرٌ مئير Critical affair.

✲ مأس a مأساً على To be angered with.

مأس بين To sow discord between.

– ومئس a مأساً To be widened (wound).

مائس ومؤوس ومِمأس ومِمآس Slanderer.

✲ مئق a مأقاً, وامتأق To sob (child).

أمأق To sob.

إمتأق To be vehement (anger).

مأق مث مأقان, ومُؤق ومُوق ج آماق وأمآق ومَواق ومآق, ومُؤق ومَوق ومأقي ج مآقي Interior angle of the eye.

Sob. مَأْقَة
Sobbing. مَئِق
To be lusty. ✲ مَأَل ومَئِل a مُؤُولَة ومَآلَة
He was unprepared for. مَا مَأَل مَأْلًا لِ
Lusty. مَأْل ومَئِل
Garden. Hand-mill. مَأْلَة ج مِئَال
To sustain, to supply a. o. with provisions. To wound a. o. on the navel. ✲ مَأَن a مَأْنًا ه
He was taken unawares. He has not minded it. مَا مَأَن لَهُ ومَا مَأَن مَأْنَهُ
To prepare a. th. مَأَّن ه
To reflect upon. — ومَاءَن في
Navel and its surrounding parts. مَأْنَة ج مَأَنَات ومُؤُون
Mouth-provisions. Weight. Trouble. مَؤُونَة ومُؤْنَة ج مُؤَن
Mark. Becoming, proper thing. مَئِنَّة
Convenience. مَمْأَنَة
To mew (cat). ✲ مَأَا o مُوَاء
To stretch (a skin). — مَأْوًا ه
To be stretched, dilated. تَمَأَّى
To spread amongst (evil). — بَيْن
To become the hundredth. ✲ مَأَى a مَأْيًا
To be covered with leaves (tree).
To sow discord between. مَأَى بَيْن
To engage zealously in. — في
To be one hundred in number. أَمْأَى إِمْآءً
One hundred. مِئَة ج مِئَات ومِئُون ومُؤُون ومِاءٍ
Hundredth. مِئَوِيّ
To draw up water from a well. ✲ مَتَّ o مَتًّا
To spread a. th. — ه
To seek to get access, favour to. To seek alliance with a. o. by (marriage). مَتَّ o مَتًّا ومَتْمَتَ إلى ب
To remind a. o. of the bonds of kindred. مَاتَّ ه
Inviolable bonds. Relationship, affinity. مَتَات, ومَاتَّة ج مَوَاتّ
To pull out (a bucket). To draw (water). ✲ مَتَح a مَتْحًا ه
To snatch off a. th. — وامْتَتَح ه
To lay eggs (locust). — ومَتَّح وأَمْتَح
Water-drawer. مَاتِح ومَتُوح
Prolonged (day, night). مَتَّاح
Well provided with a pulley. مَتُوح
To cut off, to snatch. ✲ مَتَخ a o مَتْخًا
To persist in, to cleave to. مَتَخ في
To snatch a. th. أَمْتَخ وإمْتَتَخ ه
Long and supple wood. عُود مِتِّيخ
Rod. مِتِّيخَة
To remain in (a place). ✲ مَتَد o مُتُودًا ب
To pull (a rope). To cut a. th. ✲ مَتَر o مَتْرًا ه
To be scattered (sparkles). تَمَاتَر
To pull a. th. together. تَمَاتَر ه
To be stretched (rope). إِمْتَتَر وامَّتَر
✧ Metre (measure). F مِتْر ج أَمْتَار
To twist a. th. ✲ مَتَس i مَتْسًا ه
To scatter a. th. with the fingers. ✲ مَتَش i مَتْشًا
His eye became dim-sighted through hunger. مَتِشَتْ a عَيْنُهُ مَتَشًا
White spot on the nails. مَتْش ومَتَش
Weakening of the sight. مَتَش
Weak-sighted. أَمْتَش م مَتْشَاء ج مُتْش
To carry a. th. away. ✲ مَتَع a مَتْعًا ومُتْعَة ب
To be advanced (day). To rise (mirage). To be strong (rope). To be intensely red (wine). To be at its apogee (sun). — a مُتُوعًا
To give (a dowry) to (a divorced woman). To let a. o. enjoy a. th. long (God). مَتَّع وأَمْتَع ه ب
To do without a. th. أَمْتَع عَن
To enjoy the use of. — ب
To enjoy a. th. long. تَمَتَّع وامْتَتَع واسْتَمْتَع ب ومِن
Enjoyment, use. Small quantity of food. مُتْعَة ومِتْعَة ج مُتَع ومِتَع
Dowry given to a divorced woman. مُتْعَة الطَّلَاق
Furnitures, goods. Provisions. ◘ Belonging to. مَتَاع ج أَمْتِعَة, و◘ بِتَاع
Long. Well twisted (rope). Intensely red (wine). Excellent. مَاتِع
Enjoyment. ✧ License to carry on a trade. تَمَتُّع واسْتِمْتَاع
To curtail a. th. ✲ مَتَك o مَتْكًا ه
To circumvent a. o. in (a sale). مَاتَك ه في
Insect's trunk. مَتْك ومُتْك ومُتُك
Cedrat, citron. — ومُتْك
To be strong. To be steadfast. ✲ مَتُن o مَتَانَة
To remain in (a place). مَتَن o مُتُونًا ب

compare a. o. with.

To punish a. o. as an example. To mutilate (a sheep). مَثَلَ o مَثْلًا ومُثْلَةً, ومَثَّلَ تَمْثِيلًا

He remained standing before him. مَثَلَ ومَثُلَ o مُثُولًا بَيْنَ يَدَيْهِ

To be excellent, eminent. مَثُلَ o مَثَالَةً

To show (a pattern) to a. o. مَثَّلَ ه ل

To liken a. th. to. To copy (a pattern). — ه ب

To relate (a fact). To use (parables). — وتَمَثَّلَ وامْتَثَلَ ه وب

To retaliate upon a. o. (king). To set up a. th. أَمْثَلَ ه

To avenge a. o. by retaliating upon a. o. — ه مِن

To become alike to, to imitate. تَمَثَّلَ ه وب

To fancy a. th. To use a. th. as a proverb. — ه

To relate upon the authority of. — مِن

To be alike. تَمَاثَلَ

To recover from (illness). — مِن

He obtemperated to the order of such a one. إِمْتَثَلَ أَمْرَ فُلَانٍ

He followed his custom. — طَرِيقَتَهُ

To avenge o.'s self on. — مِن

Likeness. Like. Similar, match. Requital, equivalent. مِثْلٌ (m. f. s. dual, pl.). وج أَمْثَال

He or she is like him. هُوَ او هِيَ مِثْلُهُ

They are like him. هُمْ او هُمَا او هُنَّ مِثْلُهُ

As, like. مِثْلَ وكَمِثْلِ

Like thee. مِثْلُكَ و♦ مِثْل حِكَايَتِك

As well as. مِثْلَمَا

Argument. Narration. Maxim, comparison. Proverb. Parable. Similar. مَثَلٌ ج أَمْثَال

He cited a proverb, an allegory. ضَرَبَ مَثَلًا

Pattern. مُثْلَة

Exemplary punishment. — ومَثُلَة ج مَثُلَات

Pattern, type. Example. Amount. Form (of a noun). Defective in its first radical (verb). مِثَال ج أَمْثِلَة ومُثُل ومُثْل

Excellence. مَثَالَة

To walk the whole day with. مَتَّنَ بِفُلَانٍ

To spread a. th. — ه

To strike a. o. on the back. — o i مَتْنًا, وأَمْتَنَ ه

To strengthen (a skin, a tent). To season (food). مَتَّنَ ه

To give the start to a. o. in a race. — لِفُلَانٍ

To grant a delay to (a debtor). To part with a. o. To vie in cleverness with. مَاتَنَ ه

To vie together in cleverness. تَمَاتَنَ فِي

Side of the back. Muscle of the back. Middle part of a road. Back. Broad side of a sword. Main part (of a speech). Text. مَتْن ج مِتَان ومُتُون

Hard and rugged ground. — ومَتْنَة

Strength, steadfastness. مَتَانَة

Ropes of a tent. تَمْتِين وتِمْتَان ج تَمَاتِين

Dispute. مُمَاتَنَة

Genuine author of (a work). مَاتِن

Strong, solid. مَتْن ومَتِين

✱ To mind trifles. مَتِهَ a مَتْهًا

To boast unseasonably. To be confused. To act foolishly. تَمَتَّهَ

✱ To spread (a rope). مَتَا o مَتْوًا, ومَتَى i مَتْيًا ه

To lean forward in (shooting). تَمَتَّى فِي

When? at what time? مَتَى

How long? حَتَّى مَتَى

When, as soon as. مَتَى مَا ومَتَى مَن

✱ To wipe (o.'s hands). To cleanse (a wound). To grease (the mustaches). To divulge (news). مَثَّ o مَثًّا ه

To exude butter (skin). To sweat from fatness. مَثَّ

✱ To exude butter (skin). مَثْمَثَ مَثْمَثَةً ومِثْمَاثًا

To shake a. th. To mix. — ه

✱ To mix a. th. To empty (a well). مَثَجَ o مَثْجًا ه

✱ To lay in wait, to lurk. مَثَدَ o مَثْدًا

To lay a. o. in wait. — ه

✱ To have an ungraceful gait. مَثَعَ a o ومَثِعَ a مَثْعًا

Hyena. مَثْعَاء

✱ To resemble, to imitate a. o. مَثَلَ o مُثُولًا, وماثَلَ ه

To مَثَلَ ومَثَّلَ تَمْثِيلًا وتِمْثَالًا, وماثَلَ ه ب

مَثَالَة ج مَثَالَات ومَثَائِل و✧ مَثِيلَة ج مَثِيلَات
✧ Task, lesson of a pupil.
Example. أُمْثُولَة ج أُمْثُولَات وأَمَاثِيل
Image, statue, likeness. تِمْثَال ج تَمَاثِيل
Likeness. تَمَاثُل ومُمَاثَلَة
Similar. Excellent, first rate. مَثِيل ج مُثُل
Effaced (trace). مَاثِل
Stramonium, thorn-apple. Stacte, myrrh-oil. جَوْز مَاثِل
Celebrated example. مِثْل مَاثِل
Lamp. مَاثِلَة
More alike. More perfect. أَمْثَل م مُثْلَى ج أَمَاثِل
The leading men. الأَمَاثِل
To have a complaint of the bladder. ✱ مَثِنَ a مَثَنًا
To wound a. o. in the bladder. مَثَنَ i o مَثْنًا ة
Bladder. Womb. مَثَانَة ج مَثَانَات
Having a complaint of the bladder. أَمْثَن م مَثْنَاء, ومَثِن ومَمْثُون
To spittle, to eject (water). ✱ مَجَّ o مَجًّا ه مِن فِيهِ
✧ To sip in a. th. — ه
He rendered him suspected. مَجَّجَ بِفُلَانٍ
To start (horse). To be sappy (wood). To ramble in a country. أَمَجَّ
To spit from (the pen : ink). إِنْمَجَّ مِن
Flow of slaver. Seed of Indian peas. مَجَج
Slaverer (old man). Old she-camel. مَاجّ
Stupid. أَحْمَق مَاجّ
Spittle. Expressed juice. مُجَاج ومُجَاجَة
Honey. مُجَاج النَّحْل
Rain. — المُزْن
Wine. — العِنَب
Juice, sap. مُجَاجَة
Flaccidity of the muscles of the mouth. Maturity of grapes. مَجَج
To scrawl (a writing). ✱ مَجْمَجَ ه
To relate (news) confusedly. To write indistinctly. — في
Flabby, flaccid. مَجْمَاج
To be proud. ✱ مَجَحَ ومَجِحَ a مَجْحًا ومَجَحًا, وتَمَجَّحَ
Proud, haughty. مَجَّاح
To be great, glorious, noble. ✱ مَجَدَ o مَجْدًا, ومَجُدَ o مَجَادَة

To surpass a. o. in greatness. مَجَدَ ة
To pasture in a fat land (cattle). مَجِدَ o مَجْدًا ومُجُودًا, وأَمْجَدَ
To satiate (cattle) with green herbage. — o مَجْدًا, ومَجَّدَ وأَمْجَدَ ة
To glorify, to praise a. o. مَجَّدَ وأَمْجَدَ ة
To give a considerable (gift) to. مَجَّدَ ه
To vie in glory with. مَاجَدَ مُمَاجَدَة ومِجَادًا ة
To multiply (favours) to. أَمْجَدَ ة ه
To be glorified, praised. تَمَجَّدَ
To boast. To vie together in glory. تَمَاجَدَ
To yield more fire (wood). *i. e.* To be more generous. إِسْتَمْجَدَ
Glory, nobility. Dignity. Generosity. Elevated ground. مَجْد ج أَمْجَاد
The Glorious (God). المَجِيد
Noble, glorious. Generous. Sublime. Much, copious. مَاجِد م مَاجِدَة ج مَوَاجِد
Nobler, more glorious. أَمْجَد ج أَمَاجِد
✧ Turkish silver crown worth 3^{sh}. and 6^{d}. مَجِيدِيّ
▫ Turkish (pound). ✧ Turkish decoration. مَجِيدِيَّة
To be gravid and emaciated (sheep). ✱ مَجِرَ a مَجَرًا, وأَمْجَرَ
To practice usury with. مَاجَرَ مُمَاجَرَة ومِجَارًا وأَمْجَرَ ة
To sell or buy (a beast) in (the womb). — وأَمْجَرَ ة في
Fœtus of sheep. Sale or purchase of a fœtus. Usury. Game of hazard. Large army. Prudence, intelligence. مَجْر
Emaciated sheep. شَاة مَجِرَة
Hungarian. Leanness of a pregnant sheep. مَجَر
Hungary. بِلَاد المَجَر
Shackle, bond. مِجَار
Bringing forth twins (woman). مُمْجِر ج مَمَاجِر
To follow the religion of the Magians. ✱ مجس — مَجَّسَ ة
To make a. o. a magian. — تَمَجَّسَ
Magians. Parsees, fire-worshippers. (*coll.*) مَجُوس
A magian. Relating to the Magians. مَجُوسِيّ

To scorch (the skin : fire). ✱ مَحَشَ a مَحْشًا, وأَمْحَشَ ه
To skin a. th. To wash a. th. away (torrent). ✧ To obliterate (a word). مَحَشَ ه
To be burned. إِمْتَحَشَ
To burn with anger. — غَضَبًا
House-furniture. مَحَاش
Gathering round a fire for making a covenant. مِحَاش
Burnt, toasted. مُحَاش
To run (gazelle). ✱ مَحَصَ a مَحْصًا
To struggle (slaughtered beast). To flash (lightning).
To refine gold with (fire). To polish (a blade). — ه ب
To take off a. th. To forgive (sins : God). To dress (meat). مَحَّصَ ه
To try a. o. — ه
To reappear (eclipsed sun). أَمْحَصَ وانْمَحَصَ
To recover from (illness). أَمْحَصَ مِن
To be forgiven (fault). To clear away (darkness). تَمَحَّصَ
To be reduced (swelling). إِنْمَحَصَ
Softened, smoothed (rope). مَحِص
Polished (sword). مَحِيص ﻫ مَحِيصَة
Strong (horse). مَحِص ومُمَحَّص ومَمْحُوص
Flashing (lightning). مَحَّاص
Indulgent, forbearing. أَمْحَص
To be of pure race. ✱ مَحُضَ o مُحُوضَة
To be unmixed.
To drink pure (milk). مَحِضَ a مَحْضًا, وامْتَحَضَ
To give pure milk to. مَحَضَ a مَحْضًا, وأَمْحَضَ ه
He bore him sincere affection. — ومَاحَضَ وأَمْحَضَ ه الوُدَّ
He was truthful in his narration. أَمْحَضَ الحَدِيثَ
Pure milk. Unmixed, unalloyed. مَحْض ج مِحَاض, ومَمْحُوض
Pure, genuine (Arab). مَحْض
Fond of pure milk. مَحِض
Sincere advice. أُمْحُوضَة
Of pure race. مَمْحُوض النَّسَب
To soften (a bowstring) with the fingers. ✱ مَحَطَ a مَحْطًا, ومَحَّطَ ه

Magianism, Parseeism. مَجُوسِيَّة
To speak and act inconsiderately. ✱ مَجِمَ a ومَجُمَ o مَجَاجَة
To eat dates and milk. مَجَمَ a مَجْمًا ومَجَمَة, وتَمَجَّمَ
To hold bad talks. مَاجَمَ وتَمَاجَمَ
Shameless (woman). مَجِمَة ومُجَمَة
Dish of dates and milk. مَجِيم
Fond of dates and milk. Brazen-faced, barefaced. مَجَّاء ومَجَّاعَة ومُجَّاعَة
✱ مَجَلَ o مَجْلًا ومُجُولًا, ومَجِلَ a مَجَلًا, وأَمْجَلَ
To be blistered (hand).
To blister (the hands : work). أَمْجَلَ ه
Blister. مَجْلَة ج مِجَال ومَجْل
To be thick and hard. ✱ مَجَنَ o مُجُونًا
To be shameless, careless. To hold unseemly talks. To wanton. To joke. — مُجُونًا ومُجْنًا ومَجَانَة, وتَمَجَّنَ
To joke together. تَمَاجَنَ
Boldness, wantonness. Joke, sport. مَجَانَة
Gratuitous. Jolly. مَجَّان
Free of charge, gratis. مَجَّانًا
Shameless. Wanton. Ludicrous. مَاجِن ج مُجَّان
✱ مَحَّ i o a مَحًّا ومَحَحًا ومُحُوحًا ومُحُوحَة وأَمَحَّ
To be worn out (garment).
To be effaced (trace). أَمَحَّ
Worn out, shabby (clothes). مَحّ ومَاحّ
Pith, choice part. مُحّ
Yolk of eggs. — ومُحَّة
Deceiver, liar. مَحَّاح
To be intensely hot (day). ✱ مَحُتَ o مَحَاتَة
To irritate a. o. مَحَتَ a مَحْتًا ه
Hot day. Difficult. Unmixed, pure. مَحْت ج مُحُوت ومُحَتَاء
To flay, to skin a. th. To soften (a rope, leather). To sweep away (the dust : wind). To churn (milk). ✱ مَحَجَ a مَحْجًا ه
To grant a respite to. مَاحَجَ مُمَاحَجَة ومِحَاجًا ه
To repel a. o. with the wrist. ✱ مَحَزَ a مَحْزًا ه
Marum (aquatic plant). مَرُو مَاحُوز ومَاحُوزِيّ
To rub (leather). ✱ مَحَسَ a مَحْسًا
Skilful leather-dresser. أَمْحَس

Barren (soil). مَاحِل ومَحُول ومُمْحِل ومِمْحَال
Extended. Sour milk mixed with fresh. مُمَحَّل
Extensive (desert). Lasting (affair). مُتَمَاحِل
✲ مَحَن a مَحْنًا, وامْتَحَن ه To prove a. th. To examine (a student).
مَحَّن ه وه To strike a. o. To wear out (a garment). To clean out (a well).
— ومَحَّن ه To soften (the skin).
✧ مَاحَن ه To thwart a. o.
إِمْتَحَن ه To examine (a word).
مَحْن Supple. Work, craft.
مِحْنَة ج مِحَن Trial. Suffering.
إِمْتِحَان Trial. Temptation. Examination.
✲ مَحَا o a مَحْوًا, وتَمَحَّى وامْتَحَى وامَّحَى To be effaced.
مَحَا o a مَحْوًا, ومَحَى a i مَحْيًا, ومَحَّى ه To erase a. th. To cancel (sins: God).
تَمَحَّى مِن To ask a. o. to erase, to forgive.
مَحْو Erasure. Abolition. Black spots in the moon.
مَحْوَة Disgrace. Rain. Moment.
مَحْوَة West wind, North wind clearing the clouds.
مِمْحَاة Rag for wiping; towel.
مَمْحُوّ ومَمْحِيّ Erased, cancelled.
✲ مَخّ — مَخَّخ وتَمَخَّخ وامْتَخّ ه To extract (marrow).
أَمَخّ To be marrowy (bone). To be fat (sheep). To be farinaceous (grain).
مُخّ ج مِخَاخ ومِخَخَة Marrow. Brain. Pith.
مُخَاخَة Marrow sucked from a bone.
مَخِيخ Marrowy (bone).
مَخِيخَة ج مَخَائِخ Fat (sheep).
✲ مَخْمَخ ه To extract the marrow from (a bone).
✲ مَخَج a مَخْجًا, وتَمَخَّج ه To shake about (a bucket) for filling it.
✲ مَخَر a o مَخْرًا ومُخُورًا To cleave the water (ship). To be watered ground).
— ه To widen (the pulley) by rubbing (axle-tree). To irrigate (a land). To plough (the ground).

إِمْتَحَط ه To draw (the sword). To snatch (a spear).
عَامٌ مَاحِط Rainless year.
✲ مَحَق a مَحْقًا, ومَحَّق ه To efface, to erase, To annihilate a. th.
مَحَق ه To deny blessings to (an undertaking: God).
مَحَّق ه وه To blast (the plants: heat). To destroy a. o.
أَمْحَق To be at the end of a month (moon). To perish (cattle).
تَمَحَّق وانْمَحَق وامْتَحَق وامَّحَق To be blotted out, destroyed.
مَحَاق ومُحَاق ومِحَاق Absence of moonlight in the three last nights of a lunar month.
مَحِيق Sharpened (spear-head).
مَاحِق الصَّيْف The middle of summer.
— الحَرّ Very hot (day).
أَمْحَق Unprosperous.
✲ مَحَك a مَحْكًا, ومَحِك a مَحَكًا, وأَمْحَك وتَمَحَّك To be quarrelsome, contentious.
مَاحَك ه To quarrel with.
تَمَاحَك To quarrel together.
مَحِك ومَاحِك ومَحْكَان ومُمْتَحِك Quarrelsome.
✲ مَحَل a ومَحِل a مَحْلًا ومُحُولًا, ومَحُل o مَحَالَة To be barren (land, year).
— ومَحِل a ومَحُل o مَحْلًا ومِحَالًا بِفُلَانٍ إِلى To traduce a. o. to.
مَحَّل ه To strenghten a. o.
مَاحَل مُمَاحَلَة ومِحَالًا ه To act cunningly, hostilely towards.
أَمْحَل To be smitten by dearth (people). To be barren (ground).
— ه To render (a land) barren (God).
تَمَحَّل ه To intrigue for.
— لِفُلَان حَقَّهُ He contrived to obtain a right for him.
تَمَاحَل To act cunningly with o. a.
مَحْل Dearth. Drought. Craft.
أَرْض مَحْل ومَحْلَة Barren land.
مِحَال Skilfulness. Craft. Quarrel. Enmity. Calamity.
مَحَالَة ج مَحَال Large pulley.
مَحَّال Artful. The Devil.
مَاحِل ومَحُول Artful. Intriguer.
مَاحِل Barren (year).

To wipe (a child's) nose. مَخَطَ ة
To shoot a penetrating (arrow). أَمْخَطَ هـ
To wipe o.'s nose. تَمَخَّطَ وامْتَخَطَ
To snatch off a. th. To draw (the sword). إِمْتَخَطَ هـ
Mucus, discharge from the nose. مُخَاط
Gossamer. مُخَاط الشَّيْطَان ومُخَاط الشَّمْس
Cordia myxa Assyrian, sebesten plum. مُخَاطَة ومُخَيِّط
Lever, crow-bar. ✧ مُخْل ج أَمْخَال ومُخُول
He rinceed o.'s mouth. ✧ مَخْمَضَ فَاهُ وتَمَخْمَضَ
To shed tears. ✻ مَخَنَ o مَخْنًا
To draw water from (a well). To bark (wood). To polish (leather). — هـ
Short and light. Long. مَخِن م مَخِنَة
◻ Public-house; wine-shop. P مَيْخَانَة
To remove a. o. from. ✻ مخى — مَخَّى ة عن
To apologise to. أَمْخَى وتَمَخَّى إلى
To abstain from. تَمَخَّى وامْتَخَى مِن
Mocha, town of Arabia celebrated for its coffee. مَخَا
To be advanced (day). To rise (ebb). ✻ مَدَّ o مَدًّا
To spread (a carpet). To stretch (the arm). To put (oil) in a lamp. — ومَدَّد ومَادَّ مُمَادَّة ومِدَادًا هـ
To lengthen a. o.'s life (God). مَدَّ عُمْرَ فُلَان
To strain (a rope). مَدَّ هـ وب
To take ink from (an inkstand). — واسْتَمَدَّ مِن
To grant a delay to. — ومَادَّ وأَمَدَّ ة
To give barley-water to (camels). — وأَمَدَّ ة
To supply (an inkstand) with ink. مَدَّ وأَمَدَّ هـ
To manure (a land). — هـ وهـ بالدِّمَال
To supply a. o. with (stores, troops). — وأَمَدَّ ة ب
To pull a. th. together. مَادَّ ة هـ وتَمَادًّا هـ
To be sappy (plant). To suppurate (wound). أَمَدَّ
To dip a. o.'s pen in the ink. — ة
To spread; to be protracted. تَمَدَّد وامْتَدَّ
To expand a. th. تَمَدَّد هـ
To be stretched. To be prolonged. ✧ To strut, to waddle. إِمْتَدَّ

To extract (marrow). To take the best of. مَخَر a مَخْرًا هـ
To face (the wind). To inhale (the wind : horse). تَمَخَّر واسْتَمْخَر وامْتَخَر هـ
To extract (marrow). To choose the best of. إِمْتَخَر هـ
Light whitish clouds; cirri. بَنَات مَخْر
Clearing of water. Flatulence. مَخْرَة
Choice article. مَخْرَة ومِخْرَة ومُخْرَة
Axle of a pulley. مِخْوَر
Tavern. Suspicious house. P مَاخُور ج مَوَاخِر ومَوَاخِير
To utter lies, stories. ✻ مَخْرَق
Story. Humbug. مَخْرَقَة
Plaything. مِخْرَاق ج مَخَارِيق
To fret, to be restless. ✻ مخش — تَمَخَّش
To cream (the milk), to churn (the milk). To shake a. th. ✻ مَخَض a o i مَخْضًا هـ
He dashed the bucket (in the well). مَخَض بالدَّلْو
He drew much water. — المَاءَ بالدَّلْو
He pondered over the advice. — الرَّأْيَ
To be seized with the pangs of childbirth (female). مَخِضَت a مَخَاضًا , ومُخِضَت ومَخَّضَت وتَمَخَّضَت
To be overspread with cream (milk). To have she-camels near to bring forth. أَمْخَض
To be creamed (milk). To be shaken, churned. To struggle in the womb (fœtus). تَمَخَّض وامْتَخَض
Time has brought disturbances. تَمَخَّض الدَّهْرُ بالفِتْنَة
Pangs of parturition. She-camels near to bring forth. مَخَاض
Churned (milk). Milk after butter has been extracted. مَخِيض ومَخُوض ومَمْخُوض
Seized with the pangs of parturition (female). مَاخِض ج مَوَاخِض , ومُمَخِّض , ومُتَمَخِّض
Milk while in the skin. إِمْخَاض ج أَمَاخِيض
Churn. مِمْخَض ومِمْخَضَة ج مَمَاخِض
To pierce through (arrow). ✻ مَخَط a o مَخْطًا ومُخُوطًا
To blow (o.'s nose). — هـ مِن
He drew (the sword). — السَّيْفَ
To pull off a. th. — مَخْطًا هـ

To ask aid, succour from. إستمدّ ه
Ebb. Rising of water. مَدّ ج مُدُود
Reach of the sight. *Gr.* Lengthening of the vowels ا و ى State of a word ended by أ as رِدآء وسَمآء . Prolongation of the voice on a vowel instead of two hamzas as آمَن for أأمَن
Sign of the medda (~). — ومَدّة
Measure of various standards. Bushel, two pints. مُدّ ج أمْداد و مِددة ومِداد
Dip of ink. Length. Space of time. مُدّة ج مُدَد
Succour; assistance in (troops, food). مَدَد وإمْداد
Ink. Manure. Oil of a lamp. مِداد
On the same pattern. عَلَى مداد وَاحِد
Continuous increase. Substance (*opp. to form*). Humour of the body. مَادّة ج مَادّات ومَوَادّ
Material. مَادِّي
Threads of the warp, of a web. أمِدّة و ✧ مَدّة
Salt water. مِدان وإمِدّان
Custom, habit. أمْدُود
Auxiliary troops. إمْدادِي
Long, protracted. مَدِيد م مَدِيدة ج مُدُد
Barley or flour-water for camels. Poetical metre. مَدِيد
Short space of time. مُدَيْدة
Pitched (tent). مُمَدّد
Poetical metre. مُمْتَدّ
Spread. Lengthened (vowel). مَمْدُود
✱ مَدَح a مَدْحًا ومِدْحَة ومَدّح وتَمَدّح
To commend, to praise a. o. وامْتَدَح ه
To be commended. To glory. تَمَدّح
To be spacious (ground). To be distended (flank). — وامْتَدَح وامّدح
To praise o. a. تَمادَحُوا
Praise. مَدْح
Ficus religiosa, species of fig-tree. مُدْح
Praise. Praiseworthy action. مِدْحَة ج مِدَح
Panegyric, eulogy. مَدِيح ج مَدائِح ,وأُمدُوحة ج أمادِيح
Panegyrist. مَادِح ومَدّاح
To be powerful, mighty. ✱ مَدَخ a مَدْخًا
To be self-conceited. تَمَدّخ
To wrong a. o. تَمادَخ وامْتَدَخ على

Mighty, great. مَادِخ ومَدِيخ ومِدِّيخ
To plaster (a tank) with clay. ✱ مَدَر o مَدْرًا , ومَدّر ه
To be plastered with clay. تَمَدّر
To take (clay). إمْتَدَر ه
Clods of clay, dry mud. Villages, boroughs. مَدَر (*un.* مَدَرة)
Villager. مَدَرِي
Big-bellied. Uncircumcised. أمْدَر م مَدْرَاء ج مُدْر
Hyena. المَدْرَاء
Bed of clay. مَمْدَرة
To rub (leather). ✱ مَدَس o مَدْسًا ه
To become dim, sunken through hunger or heat (eye). ✱ مَدِش a مَدَشًا
To give to a. o. scantily of. مَدَش o مَدْشًا ه ولَهُ مِن
He has not given him anything. مَا مَدَش ومَا مَدّش ومَا أمْدَش ه شَيْئًا
Squint. مَدَش
Suppleness of a limb. مَدَش ومَدْشَة
Having supple limbs. أمْدَش م مَدْشَاء ج مُدْش
Thief. مَدّاش اليَد
To veil o.'s self. ✱ مدل — تَمَدّل
To come to (a town). ✱ مَدَن o مُدُونًا ه
To settle in (a place). — ب
To build towns. ✧ To civilise. مَدّن
To become civilised. ✧ تَمَدّن
To enjoy the comforts of life. تَمَدّن
Town, city. مَدِينَة ج مُدُن ومُدْن ومَدائِن
Medinah (town of Arabia). ألْمَدِينَة
The city of the peace, *i. e.* Bagdad. مَدِينَة السَّلَام
He knows it thoroughly; *lit*: he is a citizen of the town. هُوَ أبْنُ المَدِينَة
Social state. Civilisation. ✧ تَمَدّن
From Medina. Citizen. Civil, (law, tribunal). مَدَنِي
Midianite. مَدْيَنِي
To grant (a delay) to. ✱ مدى — مَادَى وأمْدَى ه
To be advanced in age. أمْدَى
To last long. تَمادَى
To procrastinate, to persevere in. — في
Term, limit. Space. مَدَى ومُدْيَة ومِيداء
Reach of the sight. مَدَى البَصَر
Measure for corn. Bushel. مُدْي ج أمْدَاء

مُدْيَة ومِدْيَة ج مُدًى ومُدْيَات ومُدَيَات Long knife; dagger, poniard.
مَدِيّ ج أمْدِيَة Tank without stone-work.
مِيدَاء البَيْت Opposite the house.
أمْدَى العَرَب The most illustrious of the Arabs.
* مُذْ Since. (*See* مُنْذ)
* مَذْمَذِيّ Elegant, clever.
مَذْمَاذ Liar.
* مَذِح a مَذَحًا To rub o.'s thighs in walking.
أمْذَح م مَذْحَاء Wounded on the thighs. Stinking.
مَا أمْذَح رِيحَهُ How foul-breathed he is!
* مَذِر a مَذَرًا, وتَمَذَّر و✧ مَوْذَر To be rotten (egg). To feel quaimish.
مَذَّر ه To scatter (things).
أمْذَر ه To addle (her eggs : hen).
تَمَذَّر To disperse (crowd). To coagulate (milk).
شَذَر مَذَر Here and there, on every side.
مَذِر م مَذِرَة و✧ مُمَوْذَر Rotten (egg). Dirty.
* مَذَع a مَذْعًا ومَذَعَة To ooze (spring).
— ه ل To hint, to insinuate a. th. to.
مَذَّاع Liar. Indiscreet. Changing.
* مَذَق o مَذْقًا ه To adulterate (milk).
— الوُدّ ومَاذَقَهُ في الوُدّ مِذَاقًا He was insincere in love.
إمْتَذَق وامَّذَق To be adulterated (milk).
سَقَانِي مَذْقًا ومَذْقَةً He gave me adulterated milk.
مَذِيق ومَذُوق Adulterated (milk).
مَذَّاق ومُمَاذِق Insincere, hypocrite.
وُدّ مَمْذُوق Insincere friendship.
* مَذِل a مَذَلًا To be restless, anxious.
— وأمْذَل وامْذَلَّ To be benumbed (foot).
مَذِل a ومَذَل o مَذْلًا ومَذَالًا, ومَذُل o مَذَالَة
ب To let out (a secret).
مَذِلَت ومَذَلَت نَفْسُهُ ب He was generous of.
أمْذَل ه To weary a. o.
إمْذَل To be apathetic.
مَذَل Torpor. Benumbness.
— النَّفْس واليَد Forbearing, generous.
مِذْل Of small size.
مَاذِل ومَذِل Generous.
مَذِل Anxious. Intruder.
مَذِيل Indiscreet. Restless (sick person).
رِجَال مَذْلَى Anxious, nervous men.
* مَذَى i مَذْيًا, ومَذَّى وأمْذَى ه To set (a horse) free in a pasturage.
أمْذَى ه To dilute (wine) with water.
مَاذِيّ The honey.
مَاذِيَة Wine. Woman.
* مَرَّ o مَرًّا ومُرُورًا ومَمَرًّا, واسْتَمَرَّ To elapse (time). To pass, to cross.
— وامْتَرَّ ب وعلى To pass by, along, across.
مُرَّ يُمَرُّ مَرًّا ومِرَّةً بِهِ To be bilious.
مَرَّ a o مَرَارَةً, وأمَرَّ To be bitter.
مَرَّر وأمَرَّ ه To render a. th. bitter.
مَارَّ مُمَارَّةً ومِرَارًا To be dragged along.
— ه To pass with a. o.
— وأمَرَّ ه To struggle with a. o.
أمَرَّ To become bitter.
أمَرَّ ه ب To let a. o. pass by.
— ه على To make a. o. to cross (a bridge).
— ه To twist (a rope) strongly.
مَا أمَرَّ ومَا أحْلَى He has not uttered any bitter nor sweet word.
مَا يُمِرُّ ومَا يُحْلِي He does neither evil nor good.
تَمَارُّوا مَا بَيْنَهُم They wrestled together.
إسْتَمَرَّ To continue on, to persevere. To be steady, firm.
إسْتَمَرَّ مَرِيرُهُ His steadiness lasted to the end.
— ه To find a. th. bitter.
— بِفُلَان على To maintain a. o. in (an office).
مَرّ Passage. Iron-shovel. Spade. Rope.
مَرّ ومُرُور Course, succession of days.
مُرّ ج أمْرَار Bitter. Myrrh. High-spirited (man). ✧ Sturdy (horseman).
خَشَب مُرّ ✧ *Quassia amara* (bitter bark).
مُرّ صَافٍ ومُرّ مَكَّة Myrrh.
مَرَّة ج مِرَار ومَرَّات Once, one time, one turn.
بِالمَرَّة Altogether. At once. ✧ Entirely.
مِرَارًا وذَات المِرَار Sometimes, often.
مِرَّة ج مِرَر وجج أمْرَار Strength. Firmness. Intellect.

The angel Gabriel. ذُو مِرَّة
Gall, bile. مِرَّة ج مِرَر
The yellow and the black bile. Absinth and colocynth. أَلْمِرَّتَان
Satan. أَبُو مُرَّة
Centaurea calcitrapa (*plant*). مُرَار
Bitterness. Gall-vesicle. مَرَارَة ج مَرَارَات ومَرَائِر
Vinegar-sauce. مُرِّيّ
Course of time. مُرُور الزَّمَان
Strong. Steady. مَرِير ج مَرَائِر
Small rope. Steadiness, resolution. — ومَرِيرَة ج مَرَائِر
Scorzonera, viper's-grass. Hieracium. Gallingale, sedge (*plants*). مُرَيْر
Delicate maid. مَارُورَة ومُرَيْرَاء
More bitter. More steady. أَمَرّ م مُرَّى
Old age and destitution. Aloes and mustard. Wormwood and colocynth; *lit*: the two bitterest things. أَلْأَمَرَّان
Passage. Space of time. مَمَرّ
Strongly woven (rope). مُمَرّ
Bilious. مَمْرُور
To get angry. To be bitter. ✲ مَرْمَر
To give vent to (water). To grieve a. o. — ه وه
To shift (sand). To quiver (flesh). ✧ To murmur. تَمَرْمَر
Marble, alabaster. مَرْمَر
Soft in flesh. Juicy pomegranate. — ومَرْمَار
To be wholesome (food). ✲ مَرَأَ ومَرِئَ a ومَرُؤَ o مَرَاءَة
To eat (food). To give (food). مَرَأَ ه
To be beneficial to a. o. (food). مَرَأَ وأَمْرَأَ ه
To have womanly features. مَرِئَ a مَرَأً
To be manly. مَرُؤَ o مُرُوءَة
To be wholesome (climate). — o مَرَاءَة
To wish a good health to a. o. مَرَّأَ ه
To show manliness. تَمَرَّأَ
To find (food) wholesome. إِسْتَمْرَأَ ه
Man. Human being. مُرْء ومَرْء ومِرْء وأَمْرُؤ وأَمْرَأ
Woman. Wife. مَرْأَة وأَمْرَأَة ومَرَة
Small man. Small woman. مُرَيْءٌ م مُرَيْئَة
Manliness. Manly qualities. مُرُوءَة ومُرُوَّة

Manly. Wholesome (food, climate). مَرِيء م مَرِيئَة
To thy health! May it profit thee! مَرِيئًا هَنِيئًا
Gullet. مَرِيء ج أَمْرِئَة ومُرُوء
Wholesome (food). مُمْرِئ
To smooth a. th. ✲ مَرَتَ i مَرْتًا ه
Barren (land). Without eyebrows (man). مَرْت ج أَمْرَات ومُرُوت وأَمَارِيت
Without eyelashes. مَرْت الحَاجِبَيْن
Hairless (beast). — الجَسَد
Bare, stripped land. — ومَرُوت وأَرْض مَمْرُوتَة
Barrenness of a land. مُرُوتَة
To moisten (dates). To suck (his finger: child). To soften a. th. ✲ مَرَثَ o مَرْثًا ه
To soak a. th. in (water). — ه في
To be contentious, to cavil. To be meek, forbearing in a dispute. مَرِثَ a مَرَثًا
To crumb a. th. مَرَّثَ ه
Contentious. Meek. مَرِث ومِمْرَث ج مَمَارِث
To be disordered (affair). To be spoilt. To be loose (finger-ring). ✲ مَرِجَ a مَرَجًا
To pasture freely. مَرَجَ o مَرْجًا
To pasture (a horse). — وأَمْرَجَ ه
To speak freely of. — ه في
To mix a. th. with. — ه ب
To let two seas unconnected (God). — وأَمْرَجَ ه
To break (a compact). أَمْرَجَ ه
Meadow. مَرْج ج مُرُوج
Disturbance. مَرَج
Pasturing freely. (s. pl.) مُرُج
They are in confusion. بَيْنَهُم هَرْج ومَرْج
Smokeless fire. مَارِج
Liar. مَرَّاج
Coral. Pearls. Leguminous plant. مَرْجَان و✧ مُرْجَان
Disordered, confused (affair). مَرِيج
✧ Pimpernel (*plant*). مَرِيجَانَة
Blunderhead, mar-all. مِمْرَاج
Harrow. مَوْرَج
To roll (boat). ◻ إِتْمَرْجَى
To provoke, to threaten a. o. ✧ تَمَرْجَل على
To be lively, cheerful. ✲ مَرِحَ a مَرَحًا

To water (eye). مرِح مَرَحَانًا

To plaster (a house) with clay. ✤ مَرَح a مَرْحًا ه

To anoint (a skin) with oil. مَرَّح ه To sweep (wheat). To fill up (a new skin).

To enliven, to cheer a. o. أمْرَح ة

Liveliness. مَرَح ومَرَحَان

Cheerful, exulting. مَرِح جـ مَرْحَى ومَرَاحَى, ومِرِّيح

Exclamation in hitting the target. (*opp. to* بَرْحَى) مَرْحَى ومَرَحِيًّا

Excellent (bow, wine). مَرْوَح

Fiery (horse). – ومِمْرَح ومِمْرَاح

Tearful (eye). Productive (land). مِمْرَاح

To anoint (the body). ☆ مَرَخ a مَرْخًا, ومَرَّخ ه

To soften (dough) with water. أمْرَخ ه

To anoint o.'s self with. تَمَرَّخ ب

Cynanchum vinimale, tree used for striking fire. مَرْخ

Ointment. مَرُوخ

Flowing (water). Venting. مَارِخ

Tender (wood). Anointed. مَرِخ ومِرِّيخ

Mars (*planet*). Long arrow. مِرِّيخ

To be audacious, rebellious. ☆ مَرَد o مُرُودًا, ومَرُد o مَرَادَة ومُرُودَة

To be accustomed, inured to. مَرَد على

To soak and mash (bread). To cut a. th. To drive (a beast) vehemently. To propel (a boat) with a pole. To suck (the breast : child). مَرَد o مَرْدًا ه

To be beardless (youth). مَرِد a مَرَدًا ومُرُودَة

To coat (a building). To strip (a branch) of its leaves. مَرَّد ه

To prepare a nest for (pigeons). – تَمْرِيدًا وتَمْرَادًا ل

To rebel. To remain long beardless. تَمَرَّد

To rebel against. – على

Neck. مَرَاد, ومَرَّاد جـ مَرَارِيد

Rebellion. مُرُود وتَمَرُّد

Wooden pole ; oar for boats. مُرْدِيّ جـ مَرَادِيّ

Rebellious, unbeliever. مَارِد جـ مَرَدَة ومُرَّاد ومَارِدُون

Rebellious. Diluted milk. Soaked in milk (date). مَرِيد جـ مُرَدَاء

Lofty building. بَنَاء مَارِد

Beardless (youth). أمْرَد جـ مُرْد

Without fetlock (horse). – م مَرْدَاء جـ مُرْد

Barren (sand) ; leafless (tree). مَرْدَاء

Pigeon's nest. تِمْرَاد جـ تَمَارِيد

Audacious in rebellion. مِرِّيد

Litharge, protoxyde of lead. P مُرْدَاسِنج ومُرْدَاسِنك

Sweet marjoram. Pomade. P مَرْدَقُوش وِمْ بَرْدَقُوش

To pinch a. o. slightly. To slander a. o. ☆ مَرَز o مَرْزًا ة

To cut off a piece of. – مَرْزَة مِن

To impair (the character). إمْتَرَز ه

To receive (the part) of a. th. – ه مِن

To deprive (a partner) of his share. – ة

Piece cut off. Sweet marjoram (*plant*). مَرْزَة ومِرْزَة

Prince. P مِرْزَا

Persian governor. P مَرْزُبَان جـ مَرَازِبَة

Sweet marjoram (*plant*). P مَرْزَجُوش ومَرْزَنْجُوش

To dilute and mash (a medicine). To suck (his fingers : child). ☆ مَرَس o مَرْسًا ه

To wipe o.'s (hands) with. – ه ب

To fall from the pulley (rope). – ومَرِس a مَرَسًا

His affairs were unsettled. مَرِسَتْ حِبَالُهُ

To exert o.'s self in (an affair). To practise (a craft, a virtue). مَارَس مِرَاسًا ومُمَارَسَة ه

To set aright (a rope) in the gear. أمْرَس ه

To rub o.'s self against. تَمَرَّس وامْتَرَس ب

To struggle against (trials). تَمَرَّس ب

To struggle, to contend together. تَمَارَس

To exert itself in (a quarrel) (tongue). إمْتَرَس في

✤ Raffle (at play). مَرس

Broken to affairs. مَرِس جـ أمْرَاس

They are of the same sort. هُمْ على مَرِس وَاحِد

To be hairless, scanty-haired.	مَرِطَ a مَرَطًا
To tuck up (the sleeves).	مَرَّطَ ه
To be fit to be plucked (hair).	أَمْرَطَ
To drop its dates (palm-tree). To hurry in her walk (she-camel).	
To fall off (hair).	تَمَرَّطَ وامَّرَطَ
To be plucked (hair).	إِنْمَرَطَ
To collect, to take a. th. hastily.	إِمْتَرَطَ ه
Woollen or silk garment.	مِرْطٌ ج مُرُوط
Portulaca linifolia, species of purslain.	مُرْطَة
Hairless, scanty-haired. Thief.	أَمْرَطُ م مَرْطَاء ج مُرْط
Featherless (arrow).	— ومَرِيط ومِرَاط ج مُرُط
To anoint (the head).	✡ مَرَءَ a مَرْءًا, وأَمْرَءَ ه
To abound with herbage (valley).	مَرِءَ a مَرَعًا, ومَرُءَ o مَرَاعَةً, وأَمْرَءَ
To have (flocks) in a fertile land.	أَمْرَءَ
To find (a valley) full of pasturage.	أَمْرَءَ ه
To hurry. To seek a good pasturage.	تَمَرَّءَ
To penetrate into (a country).	إِنْمَرَءَ في
Pasturage.	مَرْءٌ ج أَمْرُء وأَمْرَاء
Grease.	مُرْعَة ومِرَاء
Kind of partridge.	مُرَعَة ومُرْعَة ج مُرَء ومِرْعَان
	مَرِيع ج أَمْرُء وأَمْرَاء, وأَمْرُوعَة ج أَمَارِيع ✡
Rich in pasturage (man).	مُمْرِءٌ
To graze (horse).	✡ مَرَغَ a مَرْغًا العُشْبَ وفِيهِ
✧ To roll a. o. in the dust.	— ه وه
To grease (food).	
To slaver (camel).	— وتَمَرَّغَ
To be stained (reputation).	مَرِغَ a مَرَغًا
To let (a beast) wallow.	مَرَّغَ تَمْرِيغًا وتَمْرَاغًا ه
To stain the character of.	— وأَمْرَغَ ه
To slaver. To chat.	أَمْرَغَ
To dilute (dough) in water.	— ه
To anoint o.'s self with (oil).	تَمَرَّغَ ب و✧ تَمَرْمَغَ
To wallow in the dust (mule).	— في التُّرَاب و✧ تَمَرْمَغَ
He wavered in the affair.	تَمَرَّغَ في أَمْرِهِ
Rope.	مَرَسَة ج مَرَس وجج أَمْرَاس
✧ String, thin rope	
Strength, vigour.	مِرَاس ومَرَاسَة
Compliant (man).	سَهْلُ المِرَاس
Uncompliant (man).	صَعْبُ المِرَاس
Dates soaked in water or milk.	مَرِيس
Date-wine.	◻ مَرِيسَة
Hot South-wind.	◻ مَرِيسِيّ
Strong, powerful (stallion).	مَرَّاس
Experience, practice.	مُمَارَسَة
Myrtle-tree. Rose of Jericho.	✧ مَرْسِين
Hospital. Lunatic asylum.	P مَارَسْتَان ج مَارَسْتَانَات
To scratch (the face).	✡ مَرَشَ o مَرْشًا ه
To bite a. o. with the tongue.	— ه
To take off a. th.	إِمْتَرَشَ ه مِن
To earn for (o.'s family).	— ل
Earth washed away by rain.	مَرْش ج مُرُوش وأَمْرَاش
Outstanding debt.	مُرَاشَة
Wicked, biting.	أَمْرَشُ م مَرْشَاء ج مُرْش
To strip (a tree) of its leaves.	✧ مَرْشَقَ ه
To press (the teat) with the fingers.	✡ مَرَصَ o مَرْصًا ه
To outstrip.	مَرِصَ a مَرَصًا
To fall off (bark).	تَمَرَّصَ
To be diseased.	✡ مَرِضَ a مَرَضًا ومَرْضًا
To tend, to nurse (the sick).	مَرَّضَ ه
To be remiss in (work).	— وتَمَرَّضَ في
To render a. o. ill.	مَرَّضَ وأَمْرَضَ ه
To have diseased cattle.	أَمْرَضَ
To find a. o. ill.	— ه
To feign illness.	تَمَارَضَ و✧ اسْتَمْرَضَ
Disease.	مَرَض ومَرْض ومَرْضَة ج أَمْرَاض
Hypocrisy, doubt.	
Blight, mildew.	مُرَاض
	مَارِض ومَرِض ج مِرَاض, ومَرِيض ج مَرْضَى
Diseased. Weak, languid.	ومَرَاضَى
Pale (sun).	مَرِيضَة ج مِرَاض ومَرْضَى
Languid (eye).	
Slight wind.	رِيح مَرِيضَة
Valetudinarian, sickly.	مِمْرَاض و✧ مَمْرُوض
To pluck out (the hair).	✡ مَرَطَ o مَرْطًا, ومَرَّطَ ومَارَطَ ه
✧ To gnaw, to craunch a. th.	خَرْطَ ه
To tear off.	

Soft and hard. Trained, accustomed. Nature. State. مَرِن
They are of the same temper. هُمْ عَلَى مَرِنٍ وَاحِدٍ
Softness, suppleness (of the body). مَرَانَة ومُرُونَة
Cornus mascula, dog-wood-tree used for making spears. Hard and pliant spear. مُرَّانَة ج مُرَّان
Cartilage of the nose. Hard and smooth (spear). مَارِن ج مَوَارِن
Holy chrism. Sacrament of confirmation. S مَيْرُون
Muscles of the arm. أَمْرَان
Exercise, training. تَمْرِين
Maronite, of mount Lebanon. مَارُونِي و ✧ مُورَانِي ج مَوَارِنَة
To become a Maronite. ✧ مَوْرَن وتَمَوْرَن
To be weakened (eye). ✲ مَرِهَ a مَرَهًا
Affected with heart-disease. مَرِهُ الفُؤَاد
Pure white. Pool of stagnating water. مُرْهَة
Weak-sighted. White (mirage). أَمْرَه م مَرْهَاء ج مُرْه
Sore eye. عَيْن مَرْهَاء
To anoint (a wound). ✲ مَرْهَم مَرْهَمَة ه
Poultice. مَرْهَم ج مَرَاهِم
Silex. Marum (aromatic plant). ✲ مَرْو (un. مَرْوَة)
From Merw in Khorassan. مَرْوِيّ
Marrubium, hoarhound. مَرُّوِيَّة
To stamp the ground (horse). ✲ مَرَى i مَرْيًا
To press (a she camel's) teats. To urge (a beast). — ه
To extract a. th. — وامْتَرَى ه
To draw (rain) from the clouds (wind). — وامْتَرَى واسْتَمْرَى ه
To oppose a. o. stubbornly. مَارَى مُمَارَاة ومِرَاء ه
To let flow her milk (she-camel). أَمْرَى
To attire o.'s self in. تَمَرَّى ب
To quarrel together. تَمَارَى
To doubt about. تَمَارَى وامْتَرَى في
Quarrel. Contradiction. مِرَاء
Run of a lashed horse. Gush of milk. مِرْيَة
Doubt. Quarrel. مِرْيَة ومُرْيَة
Milch-camel. مَرِيّ ج مَرَايَا

Slaver. Meadow. مَرْغ
Wallowing-place. مَرَاغ ومَرَاغَة ومُتَمَرَّغ
Mad. مَارِغ
Profligate. أَمْرَغ م مَرْغَاء ج مُرْغ
Cœcum. مِمْرَغَة
✲ مَرَق o مُرُوقًا, وانْمَرَق وامَّرَق مِن الرَّمِيَّة
To pierce through (the game: arrow).
He strayed from the true religion. مَرَق مِن الدِّين
He was disobedient. — مِن الطَّاعَة
✧ To cross, to pass by. مَرَق
To fill (a pot) with broth. مَرَق o i مَرْقًا, وأَمْرَق ه
To pierce a. o. quickly with. مَرَق ه ب
To pluck the hair of a hide. To draw (a sword). — ه
To drop its dates (palm-tree). مَرِق a مَرَقًا
To sing (maid). مَرَّق
✧ To let a. o. pass. مَرَّق ه
To fall off (hair). تَمَرَّق وانْمَرَق
To go out quickly from. إِمْتَرَق مِن
Stinking hide or wool. مَرْق ومِرْق, ومَرْقَة ج مَرْقَات
Ear of corn. مَرْق ج مُرُوق ومِرْق ج أَمْرَاق
Gravy, broth. مَرَق ومَرَقَة
✧ Hypocondria. Hypocondriasis. مَرَاق
Wool plucked from a skin. مُرَاقَة
Heretics. مَارِقَة
Insolent, shameless. ✧ مَرِق
Sky-light, window. مَمْرَق ج مَمَارِق
Eyes of butter. مُمَرَّق
Marum (*plant*). ✲ مَرْمَاحُوز
To weary, to annoy a. o. ✧ مَرْمَس ه
To be wearied, troubled. ✧ تَمَرْمَس
Rhinoceros. ✲ مِرْمِيس
To spoil a. th. ◻ مَرْمَط
To become smooth and hard. ✲ مَرَن o مَرَانَة ومُرُونَة ومُرُونًا
To become hardened by (work) (hand). — على
To get accustomed to. — o مُرُونًا ومَرَانَة على
To soften a. th. — o مَرْنًا, ومَرَّن ه
To train, to inure a. o. to. مَرَّن ه على
To be trained, inured to. تَمَرَّن على
Garment. Soft leather. Fur. Side. مَرْن ج أَمْرَان

White smooth-haired calf. Shabby clothes. ✧ Saint. مَارِيّ م مَارِيَّة
Smooth-feathered partridge. Woman of fair complexion. White antelope. مَارِيَّة
Maria, woman's name. مَارِيَّة
Mary, the Blessed Virgin. H مَرْيَم
Cyclamen, sow-bread (*pla.*). بَخُور مَرْيَم
✧ Sage (*plant*). مَرْيَمِيَّة
To be sour (beverage). ✧ To be tasteless. ✱ مَزَّ a مَزَازَة
To overcome a. o. — على
To suck a. th. مَزَّ o مَزًّا ه
To set a. th. apart. مَازَّ مُمَازَّة بَيْن
To suck, to taste a. th. تَمَزَّزَ ه
To be remote. تَمَازَّ
Difficult business. أَمْرٌ مَزٌّ ومُزٌّ ومَزِيزٌ
Leisure. ✧ Sourish. مَزَز
I shall do it at leisure. أَفْعَلُهُ على مَزَزٍ
Sour taste. ✧ Tastelessness. مَزَازَة
Sour. ✧ Tasteless. مُزٌّ م مُزَّة
Palatable wine. — ومُزَّاء
Excellence. مِزٌّ
He has the mastery over thee. لَهُ مِزٌّ عَلَيْكَ
A sucking. Palatable wine. مَزَّة
Excellent. عَزِيز مَزِيز
Difficult, more difficult. Better. أَمَزّ م مَزَّاء ج مُزّ
✧ To become sour, acrid. ✱ مَزْمَزَ
To shake about a. th. — ه
To be shaken. تَمَزْمَزَ
To rise. — لِلْقِيَام
Yellow slippers. ◘ مِزْمِزِي
To mingle (a liquid) with. ✱ مَزَجَ o مَزْجًا ومِزَاجًا ه ب
To incite a. o. against. — ة على
To assume a yellow hue (corn-crops). مَزَّجَ
To intermingle with. To contend with a. o. مَازَجَ ة
To be mixed. To frequent o. a. تَمَازَجَ
To be mixed with. إِمْتَزَجَ ب
Bitter almond. مَزَج ومِزَج ومَزِيج
Honey. مِزَج ومَزَج
Mixture of a liquid. Constitution. Complexion of the body. مِزَاج ج أَمْزِجَة
Mixed. مَزِيج ومَمْزُوج ومُمْتَزِج

Woman's boots. P مُوزَج ج مَوَازِج ومَوَازِجَة
To joke, to jest. ✱ مَزَحَ a مَزْحًا
To assume colour (grapes). مَزَّحَ
To jest with. مَازَحَ مِزَاحًا ومُمَازَحَة ة
To joke together. تَمَازَحَ
Spike, ear of corn. مَزْح
Joke, jest. مُزَاح ومُزَاحَة
Cold. Yellow slippers. ✱ مَزد ج مَزَد
To sip a. th. ✱ مَزَرَ o مَزْرًا ه
To fill up (a skin). — ومَزَّرَ ه
To be energetic (man). To become hard (fruit). مَزُرَ o مَزَارَة
To drink (a draught). تَمَزَّرَ ه
Abyssinian beer; beverage made of millet, barley or grain. مِزْر
Of noble origin. كَرِيم المِزْر
Energetic. مَزِير ج أَمَازِر
To bound swiftly (gazelle). ✱ مَزَعَ a مَزْعًا ومَزَعَة
To pick (cotton) with the fingers. — ومَزَّعَ ه
To divide a. th. مَزَّعَ ه
He trembled with anger. تَمَزَّعَ غَيْظًا
Flake of cotton. مِزْعَة ج مِزَع
Piece of meat. Draught of water. — ومُزْعَة ج مِزَع ومُزَع
Hedge-hog. مِزَّاع
To tear off (a garment). ✱ مَزَقَ i مَزْقًا ومَزْقَةً, ومَزَّقَ ه
To impair (the character) of. — ه
To mute (bird). مَزَقَ o i مَزْقًا
To scatter (a tribe). مَزَّقَ تَمْزِيقًا ومُمَزَّقًا ة
To destroy (a kingdom). مَزَّقَ ه
To vie in swiftness with. مَازَقَ ة
To be scattered (tribe). تَمَزَّقَ
To be torn to pieces. — وانْمَزَقَ
Rag, tatter. مِزْقَة ج مِزَق
Ragged garment. ثَوْب مِزَق
Swift-running (horse). مِزَاق
To go away. To fly away. ✱ مَزَنَ o مَزْنًا ومُزُونًا, وتَمَزَّنَ
To fill up (a skin). مَزَنَ ومَزَّنَ ه
To praise a. o. — ومَزَّنَ ة
To seek to commend o.'s self. تَمَزَّنَ
To outstrip a. o. To get accustomed to. — على
Rain-cloud. مُزْن

He soothed him by words. مَسَأَ ه بِالقَوْل
To set (people) at variance. — وأَمْسَأَ بَيْن
Middle part of a road. مَسْءٌ
Jolly. Impudent. مَاسِئٌ م مَاسِئَة
✱ To wipe a. th. with the hand. To comb (the hair). مَسَحَ a مَسْحًا ه
He curried his horse. — عَن فَرَسِهِ
He washed his hands. — يَدَيْهِ بِالْمَاء
To anoint a. th. with. — ه ب
To dispel (an evil : God). To coax a. o. — ه
To beguile a. o. — او رَأْسَهُ
To strike a. o. with (the sword). — ه ب
To survey (a land). مَسَحَ مَسْحًا ومِسَاحَة ه
To lie. — مَسْحًا وتَمْسَاحًا
To have the thighs rubbed by a coarse garment. مَسِحَ a مَسَحًا
To beguile, to wheedle a. o. مَسَّحَ ومَاسَحَ ه
To wipe a. th. مَسَّحَ وتَمَسَّحَ ه
To anoint a. o. with. مَسَّحَ وتَمَسَّحَ ه ب
He washed himself. تَمَسَّحَ بِالْمَاء
Such a one is penniless. فُلَان يَتَمَسَّحُ
To agree upon. To strike a bargain with. تَمَاسَحَ على
To unsheath (a sword). إِمْتَسَحَ ه
Anointing. ✧ Land-surveying. مَسْح
Saddle-felter. Hair-cloth. مِسْح ج مُسُوح وأَمْسَاح
High road. — ج مُسُوح
Friction. Impression of a wet hand. Mark, sign. مَسْحَة
He has some traits of beauty. عَلَيْهِ مَسْحَة مِن الجَمَال
✧ Extreme-Unction. مَسْحَة المَرْضَى
Mensuration of land. مِسَاحَة
Geometry. عِلْم المِسَاحَة
Smooth. Piece of gold or silver. Sweat. Anointed, wiped. مَسِيح ج مُسَحَاء ومَسْحَى
Christ, the Messiah. أَلْمَسِيح
The Antichrist ; the false Christ. — الدَّجَّال
Christian. مَسِيحِيّ ج مَسِيحِيُّون ومَسِيحِيَّة
Christianity. أَلْمَسِيحِيَّة
Lock of hair. Bow. Temple of the head. مَسِيحَة ج مَسَائِح

Hail-stone. حَبُّ المُزْن
Habit. State. مَزْن
Ant's eggs. مَازِن
Ant. إِبْن مَازِن
✱ To joke, to jest with. مَزَه a مَزْهًا, ومَازَه
✱ To become proud. مَزَى i مَزْيًا
To praise, to commend a. o. مَزَّى ه
Remote. مَازٍ ومُتَمَازٍ
Attainment, privilege. مَازِيَة ج مَازِيَات, ومَزِيَّة ج مَزَايَا
He sat far from me. قَعَد عَنِّي مَازِيًا ومُتَمَازِيًا
The great, the mighty (men). مُزَاة
Distinguished, elegant. مَزِيّ م مَزِيَّة
✱ To touch a. th. with the hand. To smite a. o. (misfortune). To strike a. o. مَسَّ a مَسًّا ومَسِيسًا ومِسِّيسَى ه وه
He was somewhat drunk. مَسَّهُ السُّكْر
Necessity compelled to. مَسَّتِ الحَاجَة إلى
To have a touch of madness. مُسَّ
To touch a. o. مَاسَّ مُمَاسَّة ومِسَاسًا ه
To be in contact with, contiguous to. — ه
To make a. o. to touch a. th. أَمَسَّ ه ه
To come in contact. تَمَاسَّ
Contact. Stroke of madness. مَسّ
First fit of fever ; contact of fire. — الحُمَّى او النَّار
Contiguousness, contact. مُمَاسَّة
Touching. مَاسّ م مَاسَّة
Pressing need. حَاجَة مَاسَّة
The sense of touch. القُوَّة المَاسَّة
There is a close relationship between them. بَيْنَهُم رَحِم مَاسَّة
Do not touch. لا مَسَاس
Touch. Contact. مِسَاس
Salt water. Undrinkable, or wholesome water. Bezoar-stone. مَسُوس
Touching much. ✧ Goad. مَسَّاس
Crazy ; whimsical. مَمْسُوس
✱ To be intricate, confused (business). مَسْمَسَ مَسْمَسَة ومِسْمَاسًا
✱ To joke. To beguile. To be slow. To be rude. مَسَأَ a مَسْأً ومُسُوءًا
To follow the middle of (a road). To delay (a payment). To allay the boiling of (a pot). — ه

Surveyor; measurer of land. مَسَّاح ج مَسَّاحَة
Liar. Having the breast chafed by rubbing (camel). مَاسِح
Female hair-dresser. مَاسِحَة ج مَوَاسِح
Having the thighs inflamed by rubbing. Having a flat sole (man). أَمْسَح م مَسْحَاء ج مُسْح
Even, bare (soil). — ج أَمَاسِح
Even and pebbly soil. Unseemly (woman). مَسْحَاء
Long piece of wood in a ship. أُمْسُوح ج أَمَاسِيح
Impostor, dissembler. تِمْسَح ج تَمَاسِح, و مِمْسَح
Crocodile. — وتِمْسَاح ج تَمَاسِيح
Rag, duster. مِمْسَح ومِمْسَحَة
To transform, to metamorphose a. o. To adulterate (a book). To emaciate (a horse). To render (food) tasteless. ✱ مَسَخ a مَسْخًا ه وه
To scoff at, to vilify a. o. — ومَسَّخ ه
To be dissolved (tumour). أَمْسَخ
To become emaciated (arm). إِمَّسَخ
To unsheath (a sword). إِمْتَسَخ ه
Metamorphosis. Plagiarism. مَسْخ
Metamorphosed, deformed. ✧ Monster (person). مَسْخ ج مُسُوخ
✧ Deformity. Abuse. مَسْخَة
Metamorphosed. Hideous. Tasteless. Stupid. مَسِيخ
Horse-tail (*plant*). أُمْسُوخ
Lean in the rump (horse). ✧ Deformed. مَمْسُوخ
To ridicule a. o. ✧ مَسْخَر ه وتَمَسْخَر على
Laughing-stock. مَسْخَرَة ج مَسَاخِر
To twist (a rope). ✱ مَسَد o مَسْدًا ه
To emaciate (a horse) for a race. — ه
To shampoo (the joints). ✧ مَسَّد ه او على
Strong woman. إِمْرَأَة حَسَنَة المَسْد
Fibres of palm-trees; rope of fibres or leather. Iron axle-tree of a pulley. مَسَد ج مِسَاد وأَمْسَاد
Skin for butter or honey. مِسَاد
Strong, sturdy. مَمْسُود
◻ Coptic month of August. C مِسْرَى

To squeeze (a skin, the bowels, linen). ✱ مَسَط o مَسْطًا ه
Purgative plant. مَاسِط
Muddy water. مَسِيط ومَسِيطَة
River, valley having little water. مَسِيطَة
Trowel. ✧ مَسْطَارِين
✱ مَسَك i o مَسْكًا, ومَسَّك وأَمْسَك وتَمَسَّك وتَمَاسَك وامْتَسَك واسْتَمْسَك ب To take hold of.
To grasp a. th. مَسَك وأَمْسَك ه بِيَدِهِ
To be tenacious. مَسُك o مَسَاكَة
To perfume a. th. with musk. مَسَّك ه
To give an earnest to. — ه
To withhold, to keep back. To astringe (the bowels: medicine). أَمْسَك ه وه
To refrain from. — واسْتَمْسَك عن
He did not abstain from. مَا تَمَاسَك أن
Freshly flayed skin. Catch, grip. مَسْك ج مُسُوك
They are afraid. هُمْ في مُسُوك الثَّعَالِب
Dam. Horn or ivory-armlets. Tortoise-shell. مَسَك
Child's caul. مَسْكَة ومَاسِكَة
Musk (perfume). مِسْك
Chenopodium Botrys goose-foot (*plant*). مِسْك الجِنّ
✧ Musky, musk-fruit. مِسْكِيّ
Musk-deer. غَزَال المِسْك
Particle of musk. مِسْكَة ج مِسَك
Handle. Well dug in a hard ground. Sustenance. Sound judgment. مُسْكَة ج مُسَك
There is no intelligence in him. مَا فِيهِ مُسْكَة او مِسَاك او مَسِيك
Avarice. مُسْكَة ومُسُكَة ومِسَاك ومَسَاكَة
Dam. مَسَاك ومَسِيك
Reservoir. Water-works. مَسَّاكَات
Avarice. Abstemiousness. إِمْسَاك
Earnest, pledge. مُسْكَان
Tongues; forceps. مَاسِك و مَاشِك
Avaricious, niggardly. مُسُك ومَسِيك ومَسَّاك ومِسِّيك ومُمْسِك ومُسْكَة ج مُسَك
Hard ground. مَسِيكَة وأَرْض مَسِيكَة
Burnet (*plant*). — ومِسْكِيَّة
Stechas (*plant*). مُمْسِك الأَرْوَاح
White-spotted (horse's foot). مُمْسَكَة
Impregnated with musk, musky. مُمَسَّك
To flow (water). ✱ مَسَل o مَسْلًا
To draw (a sword). إِمْتَسَل ه

He is one of the best men of his tribe. هُوَ فِي مُشَاشَةِ القَوْمِ
Towel, napkin. مَشُوش
Apricot. (*un.* مِشْمِشَة) ✡ مِشْمِش
Apricot-tree.
Bitter-kernelled apricot. ✧ — كَلَبِيّ
Sweet-kernelled apricot. ✧ — لَوزِيّ
To mix, to confuse a. th. ✡ مَشَجَ o مَشْجًا ه
Mixed; confused. مَشَج وَمَشِيج وَمَشْج ج أَمْشَاج
To have the thighs chafed by a coarse garment. ✡ مَشِحَ a مَشَحًا
To anoint (the sick) with holy oil. ✧ مَشَحَ a مَشْحًا (for مَسَحَ)
To clear away (sky). أَمْشَحَ
✧ Extreme-Unction. S مَشْحَة
To be cheerful. ✡ مَشِرَ a مَشَرًا
To sprout (tree). — وَمَشَّرَ وأَمْشَرَ وتَمَشَّرَ
To clothe a. o. مَشَّرَ ه
To dress up. To appear rich. تَمَشَّرَ
Leaf coming out. مَشَرَة
Fine-shaped ear. أُذُن حَشْرَة مَشْرَة
Vegetation of the earth. مَشَرَة وَمَشْرَة الأَرْض
What a luxuriant land! مَا أَحْسَنَ مَشَرَةَ هٰذِهِ الأَرْض
Soil covered with green. أَرْض مَاشِرَة
To dress (the hair). ✡ مَشَطَ o i مَشْطًا, ومَشَّطَ ه
To be chapped (hand). مَشِطَ a مَشَطًا
To have the sides comb-shaped (she-camel). — ومَشَّطَ
To dress o.'s hair. إِمْتَشَطَ
Blandisher, coaxer. دَائِم المَشْط
Comb. Weaver's loom. Shoulder-blade. Comb-shaped brand on a camel. Curry-comb. مُشْط
Metatarsal bone, instep. — الرِّجْل
✧ Bridge of a fiddle. — الكَمَنْجَة
Comb. مُشْط وَمِشْط وَمَشِط ومُشُط ومُشْطٌ ج مِشَاط وأَمْشَاط, و مِمْشَط
Manner of combing. مِشْطَة
Craft of a hair-dresser. مِشَاطَة
Combings. مُشَاطَة
Comber, hair-dresser. مَاشِط م مَاشِطَة
Combed. مَشِيط وَمَمْشُوط
To have a splinter in the hand. To be muscular (horse). ✡ مَشِظَ a مَشَظًا

River-bed. مَسَل ج أَمْسِلَة ومُسُل ومُسْلَان ومَسَايِل
Beauty of an oval face. مَسَالَة
To wish a good evening to. To come in the evening to. ✡ مسي – مَسَّى ه
Good evening. مَسَّاكَ الله بِالخَيْر
To enter upon the evening. أَمْسَى إِمْسَاءً ومُمْسًى
He became ill in the evening. فُلَان مَرِيضًا —
He came late. مَسَّى بِهِ اللَّيْلُ و✧ تَمَسَّى
Afternoon; evening. مَسَاء وأَمْسِيَّة
Good evening. مَسَاء الخَيْر
Yesterday evening. — وأَمْسِيَّة ومُسْيِي و مِسْي أَمْسِ
Runnet. ✧ مَسْوَة
Beginning of the evening. مُسَيّ ومُسَيَّان
✧ Yesterday. أَمْس
Night-cell. مُمْسًى
To extract a. th. ✡ مَسَى i مَسْيًا ه
To emaciate (the cattle: heat). ه —
To be torn off. تَمَسَّى وتَمَاسَى
To be thirsty. إِمْتَسَى
Deaf to advice. مَاسٍ م مَاسِيَة
Misfortunes. تَمَاسٍ
To dilute a. th. To wipe o.'s hands. To suck (a bone). ✡ مَشَّ o مَشًّا ه
He took little by little the property of. — مَالَ فُلَانٍ
To quarrel with. To milk (a she-camel). × —
To have a callosity on the foot (beast). مَشِشَ a مَشَشًا
To extract the marrow of (a bone). مَشَّشَ وتَمَشَّشَ ه
To be marrowy (bone). أَمَشَّ
To befall a. o. (lot). إِنْمَشَّ ل
To obtain a share of. إِمْتَشَّ مِن
To exhaust (the udder). To take off (her ornaments: woman). ه —
To purify o.'s self with (a stone). إِمْتَشَّ ب
Soft earth. Soul; natural disposition. مُشَاش
He is of a generous character. هُوَ طَيِّب المُشَاش
Cartilage of a bone. Soft bone. Stony tract. مُشَاشَة ج مُشَاش

Splinter of a bone. مَشَظ ومِشْظة
Uncertain rumours. مَشْظة
To steal a. th. away. To earn a. th. To card (cotton). ✡ مَشَع a مَشْعًا ه
To milk (ewes). — ه
To clean out (a dish). — ومَشَّع ه
To cleanse o.'s self. تَمَشَّع
To snatch (a garment). To exhaust (the udder). To draw (the sword). إمْتَشَع ه
Flake of carded cotton. مِشْعَة ومَشِيعَة
To craunch (a cucumber) slowly. ✡ مَشَغ a مَشْغًا ه
To strike; to revile a. o. — ه
To blacken (the character) of. To dye (cloth) with red clay. مَشَّغ ه
Red clay. مِشْغ
Worn out rag. Dry mud mixed with thorns for cleansing flax. مِشْغَة
To act speedily. ✡ مَشَق o مَشْقًا
To unfurl, to spread a. th. To dye (the hair). To tear up (a garment). To chafe (the thighs : coarse garment). To eat the best of a pasturage (cattle). ✧ To strip (a tree) of his leaves. — ه
To write in large letters. — في الكِتَابة
To flog a. o. — ه
To eat little of a meal. — من الطَّعام
To be tall and slender. مُشِق
To wound o.'s thighs by rubbing. مَشِق a مَشَقًا
To revile a. o. مَاشَق ه
To flog a. o. أمْشَق ه
To dye a. th. with red clay. — ه
To be over (night). To be rent (garment). To be barked (branch). ✧ To be stripped of its leaves (tree). تَمَشَّق
To pull along a. th. تَمَاشَق ه
To pull off, to snatch a. th. إمْتَشَق ه
Tall and fine stature. مَشْق
Red clay. مِشْق ومَشَق
Rent garment, tatters, rags. Flake of cotton. مِشْقَة ج مِشَق
Rubbish of carded wool. Floss-silk. Tow, oakum. — ومُشَاقَة
Having little flesh, slender. مِشْق ومَشِيق ومَمْشُوق
Shabby, worn out clothes. مَشِيق

Having the thighs wounded by rubbing. Chafed (skin). أمْشَق م مَشْقَاء ج مُشْق
Dyed with red clay. مُمَشَّق
Slender (waist). Lean (horse). Long and thin (bough). ✧ Stripped of its leaves (tree). مَمْشُوق
To decrease (flesh). ✡ مَشَل o مُشُولًا
To draw little (milk). — ه
To draw (the sword). — وامْتَشَل ه
To yield little milk (she-camel). مَشَّل
Little fleshy. مَاشِل ومَمْشُول
Sweet-kernelled apricot tree. ✡ مِشْلَوز
✧ Medlar, tree and fruit. T مُشْمُلًا
To scratch (the skin). To excoriate a. o. To pare (a skin). ✡ مَشَن i مَشْنًا ه وه
To exhaust the milk of (a she-camel). — وامْتَشَن ه
To take off a. th. To draw (the sword). إمْتَشَن ه
Scratch, excoriation. مَشْنَة
Fresh dates. ◻ Mortar. مِشَان ومُشَان
To relax a. o. (medicine). ✡ مشو — أمْشَى ه
✧ He went to stool. مَشَى بَطْنُهُ
To use a. th. as a laxative. إسْتَمْشَى ب
Purgation. مَشْو ومَشُوّ ومَشِيّ ومَشَا
Walk, errand. ✧ مِشْوَار
To walk. ✡ مَشَى i مَشْيًا وتِمْشَاء، ومَشَّى وتَمَشَّى
He was a backbiter. مَشَى بِالنَّمِيمَة
To traduce a. o. to. مَشَى بِهِ إلى
To make a. o. to walk, to go on. To promote (an affair). مَشَّى تَمْشِيَة. وأَمْشَى إمْشَاء ه
To walk with a. o. مَاشَى ه
To have numerous flocks. أمْشَى
To walk along. To take a walk. تَمَشَّى
To act upon a. o. (wine). تَمَشَّى في
To walk together. تَمَاشَيَا
To have cattle for breeding. إمْتَشَى
Walk. مَشْي
Gait, deportment. مِشْيَة
Walker. Foot-passenger, foot-soldier. مَاشٍ ج مُشَاة ومَاشُون
Slanderers. ✧ Foot-soldiers; infantry. مُشَاة

To suck (the breast). ✡ مَصَد o مَصْدًا ه
To suck a. th.
To render a. o. submissive. — ه
To be intense (cold, heat). — مَصُدَ
Thunder. Shower. مَصْد
Intenseness of cold, heat. مَصْد ومَصَد
High — ومَصَد. ومَصَاد ج أمْصِدَة ومُصْدَان
and red hill. Top of a mountain.
Shower, rain. مَصْدَة
Place of refuge, shelter. مَصَاد
To ✡ مَصَر o مَصْرًا, وتَمَصَّر وامْتَصَر ه
milk (a ewe) with the tip of the fingers.
To yield little milk (ewe). مَصَّر
To build (towns). To choose (a ه —
town) for a capital.
He has given him little. — عَلَيْهِ العَطَاء
To become a metropolis (town). تَمَصَّر
To be unimportant (gift). To disperse away (people).
Egypt. Cairo. مِصْر
Chief town of a مِصْر ج أمْصَار ومُصُور
kingdom. Country. Boundaries of two countries.
Cufa and Basra (towns). أَلمِصْرَان
Egyptian. مِصْرِيّ م مِصْرِيَّة ج مِصْرِيُّون
✧ A para, a farthing. مِصْرِيَّة ج مَصَارِيّ
Pl. Wealth, money.
Yielding little مَصُور ج مِصَار ومَصَائِر
milk (female).
مَصِير ج أمْصِرَة ومُصْرَان وجج مَصَارِين
Intestine, gut.
Mastic, ✡ مُصْطَكَى ومَصْطَكَاء ومَصْطَكَى
gum of the lentisk-tree. ▫ Spirits perfumed with mastic.
To flash (lightning). ✡ مَصَع a مَصْعًا
To start (horse).
To strike a. o. with (a stick). — ه ب
To miscarry (woman). — وأمْصَعَت بِالوَلَد
To be exhausted (milk). — مُصُوعًا
To quarrel مَاصَع مُمَاصَعَة ومِصَاعًا, وتَمَاصَع
together.
To go deep into (a إِنْمَصَع وامْتَصَع في
land).
Warlike. مَصَع ومَصِع
Yielding little milk. مَاصِع ومَاصِعَة
Berry of the مُصْعَة ومُصَعَة ج مُصَع ومُصَع
thistle عَوْسَج. Green bird.
To drop (water). ✡ مَصَل o مَصْلًا ومُصُولًا

مَاشِيَة ج مَاشِيَات ومَوَاش Quadruped.
Cattle. *Pl.* Flocks.
مَشَّاء ج مَشَّاؤُون Good walker. Slanderer.
مَمْشًى ج مَمَاش Walking-place. ✧ Gallery, passage, corridor. Foot-path.
✡ مَصّ o a مَصًّا, وتَمَصَّص وامْتَصّ ه To
suck a. th., to sip in.
مَصّ ✧ To lose its juice (fruit).
أَمَصّ ه ه To give to a. o. a. th.; to
suck.
مَصّ (un. مَصَّة) Sucking, suction.
قَصَب المَصّ Sugar cane.
مُصَّة ومُصَاص Choice part, pith.
هُوَ مُصَاص قَوْمِهِ He is the best of his
tribe.
✧ مُصَاصَة What is sucked.
مَاصّ م مَاصَّة Sucker.
مَصَّاص Sucker. Cupper. ▫ Cement.
✧ مَصَّاصَة ✧ Spout of a mug. Pipe of a
syringe. Owl. Vampire.
مَصَّان م مَصَّانَة Sucking his ewes
through avarice.
مَصُوص ج مَصَائِص Meat cooked with
vinegar.
مَصِيص Wet, damp (sand).
مَصِيصَة Bowl.
مِصِّيص ✧ String, thread.
مِمَصّ Sucker. ✧ Syphon.
مَمْصُوص Emaciated by disease.
✡ مَصْمَص المَاء He rinsed his mouth.
To rinse (a glass). ✧ To suck a. th. ه —
مُصَامِص Of pure race, genuine.
✡ مَصَح a مَصْحًا ومُصُوحًا To disappear,
to cease. To be worn out (clothes).
To fade (blossom). To be exhausted (milk). To be effaced (house). To be obliterated (writing).
— ومَصِح a مَصَحًا To decrease (shade).
مَصَح ب To carry off a. th.
مَصَح اللّٰهُ ومَصَّح وأَمْصَح مَرَضَك May God
cure thy disease!
أَمْصَح Thin (shade).
✡ مَصَخ a مَصْخًا ه To pull away a. th.
To pull out (panic-grass).
تَمَصَّخ وامْتَصَخ ه To take hold of a. th.
إِمَّصَخ To be weaned (child).
امْتَصَخ عن To be separated from.
أُمْصُوخَة ج أُمْصُوخ وأَمَاصِيخ Sheath of
panic-grass. White pith of papyrus.

His ذَهَب دَمُهُ خِضرًا مَضِرًا وخِضرًا مِضرًا blood is still unrevenged.
Mudar, ancestor of the Mudarees. مُضَر
Tribe of the Mudarees. مُضَرِيَّة
Meat cooked with sour milk. مَضِيرَة
Whey. مُضَارَة
To masticate a. th. ✱ مَضَغ a o مَضغًا ه
He chewed his brother's flesh *i. e.* He disgraced him. — لَحْمَ أَخِيهِ
To fight desperately with. مَاضَغ ه
To be eatable (meat). To bring forth ripe dates (palm-tree). To ripen (date). أَمْضَغ
Mastication. مَضْغ ومَضَاغ
What is chewed. مَضَاغ ومُضَاغَة
Masticatory. Clot of blood. مُضْغَة ج مُضَغ
Unimportant affairs; trifles. مُضَغ الأُمُور
Flesh adhering to the bones. مَضِيغَة ج مَضِيغ ومَضَائِغ
Mad, insane. مَضَّاغَة
The two jaws, mandibles. أَلْمَاضِغَان
Desperate struggle. مُمَاضِغَة
To pass away (event); to elapse (time). To go on. ✱ مَضَى i o مُضِيًّا ومُضُوًّا
To penetrate into; to advance further on. — i o مَضَاء ومُضُوًّا في
To execute (an affair). To conclude (a bargain). — على
He died — سَبِيلَهُ ولِسَبِيلِهِ مُضُوًّا
To take a. th. away. مَضَى ب
To cut, to be sharp (sword). مَضَى مَضَاء
To promote, to advance (an affair). To execute (an order). To conclude (a sale). ✧ To sign (a deed). أَمْضَى إِمْضَاء ه
To be successfully performed (affair). To be executed (order). تَمَضَّى
Carrying out of a decree. ✧ Signature. إِمْضَاء
Progress, furthering. مُضْوَاء
Past (time). Sharp (sword). Efficacious (discourse). مَاضٍ م مَاضِيَة
The preterite tense. أَلْمَاضِي
Sharper; more efficacious. أَمْضَى
Executed, fulfilled (order). أَمْرٌ مَمْضُوٌّ عَلَيْهِ

To be put on a sieve for draining (fresh cheese). To suppurate (wound). To percolate. مَصَل مَصْلًا
To make (fresh cheese). مَصَّل ه
To give an instalment to a. o. — ل من
To waste (wealth) away. To exhaust (ewes) by milking. — وأَمْصَل ه وه
To make curd. — مُصُولًا
Whey. مَصْل ومَصَالَة
Drippings. مَصَالَة ومُصَالَة
Oozing (skin). Small quantity of milk. Paltry gift. مَاصِل
To pain, to distress a.o. (wound, grief). To grieve a. o. ✱ مَضّ o مَضًّا ومَضِيضًا, وأَمَضّ ه
To burn (the eyes, the tongue: collyrium, vinegar). — وأَمَضّ ه
To experience pain from. مَضّ a مَضَضًا من
To be distressed, pained. — a مَضَضًا ومَضِيضًا ومَضَاضَة
To itch (skin). أَمَضّ ه
To quarrel together. تَمَاضّ
Itching, burning. Sour (milk). مَضّ م مَضَّة
Pain, grief. Sour milk. مَضَض
Salt water. Pure, unmixed. Pain, burning in the eye. مُضَاض
Burning. مُضَاضَة
He rinsed his mouth. ✱ مَضْمَض المَاء في فِيهِ مَضْمَضَة ومِضْمَاضًا
I have not closed my eyes. مَا مَضْمَضْتُ عَيْنِي بِنَوْم
Drowsiness crept into his eyes. مَضْمَض وتَمَضْمَض ٱلنُّعَاس في عَيْنَيْهِ
To impair (the reputation) of. To disgrace a. o. ✱ مَضَح a مَضْحًا, وأَمْضَح ه
To ooze (skin). To dart its rays (sun). مَضَح
✱ مَضَر ومَضُر o ومَضِر a مَضْرًا ومَضَرًا ومُضُورًا
To become sour (milk).
To destroy a. o. To reckon a. o. amongst the Mudarees. مَضَّر ه
To be numbered among the Mudarees. تَمَضَّر
Fresh, soft. مَضِر
Sour (milk). مَضِر ومَاضِر ومَضِير
Soft life. عَيْش مَضِر

Watered by rain. مَطِير ومَمْطُور
Swift-paced (horse). مَطَّار
Mug. Town of Heliopolis. مَطَـرِيَّة
Waterproof garment. مِمْطَر ومِمْطَرَة ج مَمَاطِر
Swift (horse). مُتَمَطِّر
Intermittent (rain). مُتَمَاطِر
Asking for rain. Seeking bounty. Silent. مُسْتَمْطِر
Rained upon (man, place). مُسْتَمْطَر
Bishop, metropolitan. G مَطْرَان ج مَطَارِين ومَطَارِنَة
To taste a. th. in smacking the lips. ✲ مطق – تَمَطَّق ه
Sweetness. مَطْقَة
To stretch (a rope). To flatten (tin). To work (iron). ✲ مَطَل o مَطْلًا ه
To put off the payment of (a debt). – ومَاطَل وامْتَطَل ه
To delay the payment of a. th. to. – ومَاطَل مُمَاطَلَةً ومِطَالًا ه ب
To grow tall and tangled (plant). إمْتَطَل
Putting off (of a promise). مَطْل ومُمَاطَلَة ومِطَال
Remainder of water in a basin. مُطْلَة ومَطْلَة
Craft of a tinman, ironmongery. مِطَـالَة
Ironmonger, tinman. مَطَّال
Dilatory (debtor). مَطَّال ومَطُول ومُمَاطِل
Beaten iron, tin. مَطِيلَة ج مَطَائِل
Elongated (iron). Delayed (payment). مَمْطُول
To hasten; to hurry the walk. To join a friend. ✲ مَطَا o مَطْوًا
To urge a beast (rider). To pull (a rope). – ه وه
To render the way long to. – ب
To be lengthened (day). مَطِي a مَطًا
To ride (a beast). أَمْطَى وامْتَطَى ه
To mount a. o. upon (a beast). أَمْطَى ه ه
To become long (day). To spread, to stretch the arms in walk. تَمَطَّى
Back of a beast. مَطًى ج أَمْطَاء
Alike; fellow. مِطْو ج مِطَاء
Length, extent. مُطَوَاء

To strain, to stretch a. th. ✲ مَطَّ o مَطًّا, ومَطَّط ه
To stretch (the eyebrows). To assume a proud (mien). To extend (the fingers). To draw (a bucket). مَطَّ ه
To be proud, haughty. – خَدَّهُ
To revile a. o. مَطَّط ه
To waddle, to sweep in walk. To rope (milk). تَمَطَّط
To adorn (a narrative). تَمَطَّط في
Proud deportment. مَطِيطَاء ومُطَيْطَاء ومُطَيْطَى
Slime in the bottom of a trough. Place hollowed by the feet of cattle. مَطِيطَة ج مَطَائِط
To be unmindful of. ✲ مَطْمَط في
To slap a. o. ✲ مَطَح a مَطْحًا ه
To be swollen (river). تَمَطَّح وامْتَطَح
To eat much. ✲ مَطَخ a مَطْخًا
Foolish. Proud. Dissolute. مَطَّاخ ج مَطَاطِخ
To yield rain (sky). ✲ مَطَر o مَطْرًا ومَطَرًا, وأَمْطَر
The sky rained upon them. مَطَرَتْهُم السَّمَاء
It rains. أَلسَّمَاء تَمْطُر
He has not received the least benefit from him. مَا مُطِر مِنْهُ خَيْرًا او بِخَيْرٍ
To run quickly (horse). To light quickly (bird). – مَطْرًا ومُطُورًا
To go through (a country). – مُطُورًا وتَمَطَّر في
To bring a. th. away. مَطَر ب
To send down rain (God). To sweat. أَمْطَر
To expose o.'s self to the rain. To go fast (horse). To fly swiftly (bird). تَمَطَّر
To ask rain from (God). – واسْتَمْطَر ه
To expect silently; to lower the eyes. إسْتَمْطَر
To seek the beneficence of. – مِن
Shower, heavy rain. مَطَر ج أَمْطَار
Use, custom. مُطْر ومَطْرَة ومَطِرَة
Water-skin. Wooden or leathern vessel. مَطَرَة
Rainy (weather). مَطِر ومَاطِر ومَطِير ومُمْطِير
Wide-mouthed (well). مَطَار ومَطَارَة

Hour, instant, moment. مَطْوَةٌ
Nag, riding-beast. مَطِيَّةٌ ج مَطَايَا ومَطِيّ
To blame, to find fault with. ✱ مَظَّ o مَظًّا ك
To resist; to treat a. o. harshly. مَاظَّ مُمَاظَّةً ومِظَاظًا ك
To revile o. a. تَمَاظَّ
Wild pomegranate-tree. Dragon's blood (resinous juice). مَظٌّ
Roughness, harshness of temper. مَظَاظَةٌ
To soften (a thong). ✱ مَظَمَ a مَظْمًا, ومَظَّمَ ه
To lick up a. th. تَمَظَّمَ ه
To be dilatory in. — في
With. At the time of. Notwithstanding. ✱ مَعَ ومَعْ
With thee. مَعَكَ
In the evening. مَعَ العَشِيَّةِ
With all that, nevertheless. Notwithstanding. مَعَ ذَلِكَ
Although, though. مَعَ أَنَّ
Though he may be rich. مَعَ كَوْنِهِ غَنِيًّا
Together, at the same time. مَعًا
Concomitance. Simultaneousness, connexion. ✧ Private household of a prince. مَعِيَّةٌ
To melt (grease). ✱ مَعَّ o مَعًّا
To walk by intense heat. To fight (people). To repeat. ✱ مَعْمَعَ
To pour a vehement (rain: sky). ه —
Crepitation of fire in the reeds. Uproar, bustle of fighters. *Pl.* Wars. مَعْمَعَةٌ ج مَعَامِعُ
They agreed together. صَارُوا مَعَامِعًا
Partaking the opinion of every one. مَعْمَعِيٌّ
Intense heat. Intensely hot or cold (night, day). مَعْمَعَانٌ ومَعْمَعَانِيٌّ
To rub (a skin). ✱ مَعَتَ i مَعْتًا
To rush forth. To go swiftly or gently (she-camel). To blow gently (wind). ✱ مَعَجَ a مَعْجًا
To strike (its mother's udder: young camel). ه —
To shake the plants (wind). في النَّبَاتِ —
To stir (a pencil) in. ه في —
To curvet (ass). تَمَعَّجَ
Bloom of life. مَعْجَةٌ

Swift-running horse. مَعُوجٌ
To seize, to snatch a. th. unawares. To draw (the sword). To pull up (a bucket). ✱ مَعَدَ a مَعْدًا, وامْتَعَدَ ه
To injure the stomach of. ه —
To journey through (a country). مَعَدَ في
To snatch a. th. away. — مَعْدًا ومُعُودًا ب
To have a disease of the stomach. مُعِدَ
Tender; fresh (fruit). Swift (camel). Bulky, coarse. مَعْدٌ م مَعْدَةٌ
Side of man. مَعَدٌ
Stomach. مَعِدَةٌ ومِعْدَةٌ ج مَعِدٌ ومِعَدٌ
Fresh, juicy (dates). مُتَمَعِّدَةٌ
To fall out (finger-nail). To lose its hair (lock). ✱ مَعِرَ a مَعَرًا
To be scarce (feathers, hair). — وأَمْعَرَ
To alter (the countenance: anger). مَعَّرَ ه
To have travelling-provisions exhausted. To become poor. — وأَمْعَرَ
To be destitute of plants (land). أَمْعَرَ
To fall off (hair). To be altered by anger (face). تَمَعَّرَ
Ill-nature. مَعَارَةٌ
Hairless. Scanty (hair). Bare (soil). Falling (nail). Niggardly. مَعِرٌ م مَعِرَةٌ, وأَمْعَرُ م مَعْرَاءُ ج مُعْرٌ
Having the forehead convulsed by anger. مَمْعُورٌ
To be rich in goats. ✱ مَعِزَ a مَعَزًا, وأَمْعَزَ
To become hard (ground). مَعِزَ
What a hard, a strong man! مَا أَمْعَزَهُ
What an energetic man! مَا أَمْعَزَ رَأْيَهُ
To be frowned (face). تَمَعَّزَ
To be diligent in. إِسْتَمْعَزَ في
Hardness of the ground. مَعَزٌ
مَعْزٌ ومَعَزٌ ج أَمْعُزٌ ومَعِيزٌ, ومِعْزَاءُ ومِعْزَى
Bucks and goats. Kind of goats.
Goats. Herd of mountain goats from 30 upwards. أُمْعُوزٌ ج أَمَاعِزُ وأَمَاعِيزُ
Goat, buck. Goat-skin. مَاعِزٌ ج مَوَاعِزُ
Energetic. مَاعِزٌ ومَعِيزٌ ومُسْتَمْعِزٌ
Hard, stony ground. أَمْعَزُ م مَعْزَاءُ ج مُعْزٌ وأَمَاعِزُ
Owner of goats, goat-herd. مَعَّازٌ

Putting off the payment of a debt. مَعِك, وِمِمِيك ومُمَاعِك
Silly; quarreller. مَعِك
Numerous (camels). مَعْكَى
Big and fat (camels). (s. pl.) مَعْكَاء
Warm bread overlaid with sugar and butter. ✧ مَعِيكَة
To pluck, to snatch away a. th. To damage a. th. ✡ مَعَل a مَعْلًا ه
To backbite a. o. — ب
To avert a. o. briskly from. — وأمْعَل ه عن
Acting dexterously; sharp. مَعِل
Evil, mischief. مَعَالَة
To acknowledge or to disown a. th. ✡ مَعَن o مَعْنًا. وأمْعَن ب
To flow (water). To be started (horse). مَعَن a مَعْنًا, ومَعُن a مُعُونًا, وأمْعَن
To be well watered; to grow (plant). مَعِن a مَعَنًا
To be well watered (ground). To run fast (horse). To be rich. To be poor. أمْعَن
To be assiduous; to ponder over. أمْعَن
To look intently at a. th. — النَّظر في و✧ تَمَعَّن في
Useful. Easy (thing). Numerous. Scarce. مَعْن
He possesses nothing. مَا لَهُ سَعْنَة ولا مَعْنَة
Inn. Spa. مَعَان
Travelling apparatus, house-utensils. Legal alms. Good work. ✧ Quire of paper. ◻ Caldron. مَاعُون ج مَوَاعِين
Barge, mahone. ✧ مَعُونَة
Water flowing upon the surface of the earth. مَعِين ج مُعُن ومُعُنَات
To mew (cat). ✡ مَعَا o مُعَاء
To bear ripening dates (palm-tree). أمْعَى
To spread (evil). تَمَعَّى
Ripening date. مَعْو
Intestines, guts. ✡ مَعْي ومِعًى ومِعَاء ج أمْعَاء
To mix up, to embroil a. th. To chew (meat). ✡ مَغْمَغ ه
To shake a. th. in (water). — ه في
He spoke confusedly. مَغْمَغ الكَلام
He did his work clumsily. He patched his work. مَغْمَغ في عَمَلِهِ

To rub (leather) strongly. ✡ مَعَس a مَعْسًا ه
To revile, to strike a. o. — ه
✧ To crush down a. th. — ومَعَّس ه
Dauntless, brave. مَعَّاس ومُتَمَعِّس
To have the nerves of the feet sprained. To be distorted (finger). To ache (belly). To limp. ✡ مَعِص a مَعَصًا
To be in a rage. تَمَعَّص وامْتَعَص
Pain in the sides. مَعَص
Feeling a pain in the feet from overfatigue. مَعِص ومَعِيص
To be vexed by. ✡ مَعِض a مَعَضًا, وامْتَعَض مِن
To anger a. o. مَعَّض وأمْعَض ه
Moved, exasperated. مَاعِض ومَعِض
To distend a. th. To pluck (hair, feathers). ✧ To scald off (hair) with boiling water. ✡ مَعَط a مَعْطًا ه
To put off (a payment). — ب
To draw (the sword). — وامْتَعَط ه
To have scanty hair (wolf). مَعِط a مَعَطًا, وتَمَعَّط
To fall off gradually (hair). تَمَعَّط وامَّعَط وانْمَعَط وامْتَعَط
To become worn, smooth (rope). إمْعَط وامْتَعَط
Hairless (wolf). Bare (sand, soil). مَعِط وأمْعَط م مَعْطَاء ج مُعْط
To wash (the earth) away (torrent). To drink a. th. greedily. ✡ مَعَق a مَعْقًا ه
To be deep (well). To be far distant (place). مَعُق o مَعْقًا ومَعَاقَة
To deepen (a well). أمْعَق ه
To be deep. To be wicked. تَمَعَّق
Depth; distance. Pl. Remote parts of the desert. مَعْق ومَعَق ومُعْق ج أمْعَاق وأمَاعِق وأمَاعِيق
Deep. مَعِيق
To rub a. th. ✡ مَعَك a مَعْكًا ه
To overcome a. o. in (wrestling). — ه في
He put off the payment of his debt to. مَعَك دَيْنَهُ وبِدَيْنِهِ ومَاعَك ه بِدَيْنِهِ
To be insane. مَعُك o مَعَاكَة
To drag a. o. along on the ground. مَعَّك ه
To be rolled on the ground. تَمَعَّك

To be stretched, distended. تَمَغَّط وامَّغط وامتغط
To be advanced (day). إمتغط
To draw (the sword). — ه
To feel the gripes ✲ مَغَل ومَغِل a مَغْلًا (beast).
To calumniate — a مَغْلًا ومَغَالَة بِفُلانٍ a. o.
To be corrupt (eye). مَغِل a مَغَلًا
To have cattle seized with colic. أَمْغَل To bring forth a child every year (woman).
Milk of a pregnant female. مَغْل ومَغَل
Colic caused by herbs مَغْلَة ج مِغَال mixed with earth. Ewe, goat bringing forth every year.
Treachery, perfidy. مَغَالَة
Eating earth. مِمْغَل
Magnet. G مغناطيس ومَغْنَطِيس
✧ Magnetic. مغنطيسيّ
To mew (cat). ✲ مَغَا o مغوًا
To pronounce a. th. ✲ مَغَى a مَغْيًا
To be softened (leather). تَمَغَّى
Slanderer. Suspicious. مَاغِيَة
To impregnate (a ✲ مَقّ o مَقًّا ه female palm-tree). ✧ To suck grapes and cast out the skin. To suck (the breast : child).
To bill (her chickens : bird). مَقَّق ه
To ill-feed a. o. — على
To drink little by little. تَمَقَّق
To exhaust (his mother's — وامتَقّ ه milk : suckling).
Length of the body. مَقَق
Sucking kids. Foolish people. مَقَقَة
Long-bodied (horse). أَمَقّ م مَقَّاء ج مُقّ Long (tract of land).
To hate ✲ مَقَت o مَقْتًا, ومَقِّت ومَاقِت ه a. o.
To be hateful. مَقُت o مَقَاتَة
To render a. o. hateful to. مَقَّت ه إلى
How hateful he is to me! مَا أَمْقَتَهُ عِنْدِي
How do I hate him! مَا أَمْقَتَنِي لَهُ
To be hateful to. تَمَقَّت إلى
To bear a mutual hatred. تَمَاقَت
Hatred. مَقْت
Hateful marriage, *i. e.* زَوَاج المَقْت with a father's divorced wife.
Married with his father's wife. مَقْتِيّ

To be confused, intricate مَغْمَغ ومُغْمِغ (affair).
To steep and mash ✲ مَغَث o مَغْثًا ه في (a medicine) in.
To beat a. o. lightly. — ه
To impair (the reputation) of. — ه
To struggle with ماغَث مُمَاغَثَة ومِغَاثًا ه a. o.
Wrestler, athlet. مَغِث
Struggle. Conflict. Play. مَغْث ج مِغَاث
Laid prostrate by rain مَغِيث ومَمْغُوث (corn-crops).
Wild pomegranate. Aromatic مُغَاث root from India.
To suck (its ✲ مَغَد a مَغْدًا ه وه mother : young one). To suck in, to sip a. th.
To thrive (plant). — مَغْدًا
He led a soft life. — في عَيْش ناعِم
To be fat, plump — ومَغِد a مَغَدًا (body).
To suckle (a child). أَمْغَد ه
Soft, tender. Bulky, tall. مَغْد
Egg-plant ; mandrake. Gum مَغْد ومَغَد of the lote-tree.
To pass swiftly. ✲ مَغَر a مَغْرًا
To fall upon (the ground : — في shower).
To dye a. th. with red ochre. مَغَّر ه
To yield reddish milk (ewe). أَمْغَر
To pierce a. o. with (an — ه ب arrow).
Light shower. مَغْرَة
Red clay, red ochre. — ومَغَرَة
Reddish colour. مَغَر ومُغْرَة
Ruddy man. Sorrel (horse). أَمْغَر
Reddish (milk). مُغَيْر
To pierce a. o. ✲ مَغَس a مَغْسًا ه ب with (a spear).
✲ مُغِص مَغْصًا . ومَغِص a مَغَصًا ; وتَمَغَّص بَطْنُهُ و✧ انمغص
To suffer from colic.
Colic, pain in مَغْص ومَغَص و✧ مَغِيص the belly.
Seized with colic. مَمْغُوص
To strain ; ✲ مَغَط a مَغْطًا, ومَغَّط ه to stretch a. th.
He braced the bow vehe- مَغَط في القَوْس mently.
To run (camel, horse). تَمَغَّط

Bottom of a well; pebbles, earth in a well. مَقْل

Bdellium, Theban palm; kind of gum. مُقْل

Fruit of the wild palm-tree. مُقْل مَكِّيّ

Stone for measuring water. Bottom of a well. مَقْلَة

¤ Large turban of the ulemas. مُقْلَة ج مُقَل

Eye; eyeball. مُقْلَة ج مُقَل

Azure, pale blue colour. Weak sight. ☆ مقه — مَقَه

Azured. Having sore eyes, red eyelids. أَمْقَه م مَقْهَاء ج مُقْه

To furbish (a blade). ☆ مَقَا o مَقْوًا, مَقَى i مَقْيًا ه

Care, preservation. مَقْو ومَقْوَة ومُقَاوَة

أَمْقِه وإمْقِهِ مَقْوَك ومَقْوَتَك ومُقَاوَتَك مَالَك Keep it as thy own property.

To suck up (marrow). ☆ مَكَّ o مَكًّا, وتَمَكَّك وامْتَكّ ه

To press (a debtor). — ه وتَمَكَّك ه وعلى

Mecca. مَكَّة

From Mecca. مَكِّيّ و✧ مَكَّاوِيّ

What is sucked. Marrow. مُكَاك ومُكَاكَة

Measure for grain. Drinking-cup. ✧ Weaver's loom. مَكُّوك ج مَكَاكِيك ومَكَاكِيّ

Sucking his ewes through avarice. مَكَّان

To abide, to dwell in (a place). ☆ مَكَتَ o مَكْتًا ب

☆ مَكَثَ o مَكْثًا ومُكْثًا ومَكَثًا ومُكُوثًا ومُكْثَانًا ومِكِّيثَى ومِكِّيثَاء, وتَمَكَّث ب To tarry, to stay in (a place).

To be patient, grave. مَكُثَ o مَكَاثَة

To loiter; to pause, to expect. تَمَكَّث في

Expectation, abode. مَكْث ومُكُوث ومَكْثَان

Expecting. مَاكِث ومَكِيث

Staid, sedate, slow. مَكِيث

To remain in (a place). ☆ مَكَدَ o مَكْدًا ومُكُودًا ب

Comb. مِكَد

Unexhaustible (well). مَاكِد م مَاكِدَة

مَاكِدَة ومَكْدَاء, ومَكُود ج مُكُد ومَكَائِد Abounding with milk (she-camel

Hated, abominable, loathsome. مَقِيت ومَمْقُوت

Parsley (plant). G مَقْدُونِس و✧ بَقْدُونِس

To break (the neck) of a. o. ☆ مَقَرَ o مَقْرًا ه

To macerate (salt fish). — وأَمْقَر ه

To be bitter, acid, sour. مَقِرَ a مَقَرًا

To become bitter, sour (milk). أَمْقَر

Bitterness, acridness, sourness. مَقَر

Aloes. Poison. مَقْر ومَقِر

Bitter, sour, acrid. مَقِر ومُمْقِر

Pickled fish. سَمَك مَمْقُور

To fill (a skin). To smash a. th. ☆ مَقَسَ o مَقْسًا ه

To plunge a. th. into (water). — ه في

To feel dizzy. مَقِسَ a مَقَسًا, وتَمَقَّس

To pour much (water). مَقَّس ه

To vie in diving with o. a. مَاقَس ه

He vies in diving with a fish (prov.). i. e. he contends with one more clever than he. يُمَاقِس حُوتًا

To break (the neck) of a. o. ☆ مَقَطَ o i مَقْطًا ه

To anger a. o. — ه

To bind a. o. by (oath). To strike a. o. with (a stick). — ه ب

To tie a. o. with a rope. —

To fell a. o. — ه وب ومَقَّط ه

Auguring from the casting of pebbles. Violent (blow). Exhausted (camel). Slave freed by a freedman. مَاقِط

Well twisted rope. مِقَاط ج مُقُط

To drink a. th. greedily. ☆ مَقِمَ a مَقْمًا ه

To suck (its mother: young one). — ه

To be suspected of. مُقِمَ ب

To have the complexion altered through grief. أَمْتَقِم

Stagnating water. مَقْم ج أَمْقُم

He pursues his design unremittingly. هُوَ شَرَّاب بِأَمْقُم

To look at a. o. ☆ مَقَلَ o مَقْلًا ه

To plunge a. th. into water. — ه

To plunge o. a. into water. مَاقَل ه وتَمَاقَل

To plunge repeatedly. إِمْتَقَل

أمكود ج أماكيد Remainder of bloodwit.

☆ مَكَرَ o مَكْرًا ه وب, وماكر ه To beguile, to circumvent a. o.

— وأمكر ه To punish (a deceiver: God).

مَكَر ه To dye a. th. red. To water (a field).

مَكِر a مَكَرًا To be red.

مَكَّر To store up (grain).

أمكر ه To beguile a. o.

تماكر To seek to circumvent o. a.

إمتكر وأمْكر To be dyed red; to be red-coloured.

مَكْر Artifice, craft, shift. Stratagem. Red clay.

مَكْرَة Craft, stratagem, shift.

— ج مَكْر ومُكور *Herniaria lenticulosa*, plant used as fodder for cattle.

ماكِر ج ماكِرون ومَكَرَة Crafty, deceitful.

مَكُور ومَكَّار Deceiver, trickster.

مُمْتَكِر ومَمْكُور Dyed red.

☆ مَكَس i مَكْسًا ه في البَيْع To defraud, to cheat a. o. in a sale.

— ومَكَّس To collect taxes.

ماكس مُماكَسة ومِكاسًا ه في البَيْع He contended with him in the sale.

مَكْس ج مُكُوس Market-tax. Custom-duty.

صاحِب المَكْس وماكِس ومَكَّاس Tax-gatherer.

☆ مَكَل o مُكُولًا To hold little water and much slime (well).

مَكْلَة ومُكْلَة Slime in a well.

مَكُول ج مُكُل Slimy (well).

مِمْكَل Having little water (tank). Having much water (well).

مُمْكَلَة ومَمْكُولة Old waterless well.

☆ مَكُن o مَكَانَة, وتَمَكَّن عِند To have credit with.

مَكُن o ✧ To be fast, strong.

مَكِن a مَكْنًا, وأمْكَن To have eggs (lizard).

مَكَّن ه To strengthen a. th.

— وأمْكَن ه من To enable, to empower a. o. to.

أمْكَن ه To become possible, easy to a. o. (affair).

يُمْكِن أن It may be that.

ما يُمْكِنُهُ النُّهوض او أن يَنْهَض He is unable to get up.

تَمَكَّن To be strengthened.

— ه وب To have a firm footing in (a place).

— واستَمْكَن من To get the mastery over; to get hold of. To be enabled to.

مَكْن ومَكِن Locusts, lizards' eggs. (*coll.*) مَكْنَة مَكِنَة *un.* ج مَكْنات ومَكِنات

Locust's egg. Bird's nest.

مَكِنَة ومُكْنَة Vigour. Power, ability.

✧ مَكِنَة ومَاكِنَة ج ماكِنات Machine, engine, instrument.

إمْكان Possibility, likeliness.

✧ عَلَى قَدَر الإمْكان As much as possible.

مَكان ج أمْكِنَة وأماكِن Place, spot. Rank, degree.

كان من العِلمِ والعقل بِمَكانٍ He had a great deal of knowledge, and cleverness.

مَكانَة Influence, credit. Power, high rank. ✧ Strength.

ذُو مَكانَة In good order.

مَكِينَة Slowliness.

ماكِن, ومَكِين ج مُكَناء Steady, fast, strong.

مُمْكِن Possible, likely.

مُتَمَكِّن Strengthened, fastened.

مُتَمَكِّن أمْكَن Declinable in all cases (noun).

مُتَمَكِّن غير أمْكَن Declinable in two cases (noun).

غير مُتَمَكِّن Indeclinable.

☆ مَكَا o مَكْوًا ومُكاء To whistle through the fingers. To chirp (bird).

مَكِي a مَكًا To be blistered (hand).

مَكًى ومَكْو ج أمْكاء Den, lair.

مُكاء ومُكًا Whistle; chirp of birds.

مُكّاء ج مَكاكِيّ Whistling bird.

☆ مَلّ o مَلًّا ه To stitch, to tack (a garment).

— وامْتَلّ ه To put (bread, meat) into embers.

مَلّ ه بالنّار To straighten (a bow) in the fire.

— وأمَلّ على To be tedious (journey).

— وتَمَلّل وإمْتَلّ في المَشْي He hastened the walk.

To help, to conspire with a. o. for. مَالَأَ ه على

To afflict a. o. with a rheum (God). أَمْلَأَ ه

He was filled with anger. تَمَلَّأَ وامتلأ غَيْظًا

To help o. another in. تَمَالَأَ على

He has wealthy, solvent debtors. إِسْتَمْلَأَ في الدَّيْن

Quantity, full measure, vessel. مِلْء ج أَمْلَاء

As much as the hand can hold. Handful. مِلْء الكَفّ

He sleeps soundly. يَنَام مِلْء الجَفْن

Crowd. The chief men, princes. Deliberation. Character. Manners. مَلَأ ج أَمْلَاء

Rheum, defluxion. مُلَاء ومُلَاءَة

Woman's plaid. Bed-sheet. مُلَاءَة ج مُلَاء و❖ مِلَايَة

Surfeit, repletion. مِلْأَة وإمْتِلَاء

Way of filling. مِلْأَة

Full. مَلْآن م مَلْأَى ومَلْآنَة ج مِلَاء

▫ Egyptian measure of about a gallon. مَلْوَة

Rich, wealthy; solvent man. مَلِيء ومَلِيّ ج مِلَاء ومُلَآء وأَمْلِيَاء

Water-carrier. ❖ مَلَّا

He is the richest man of his tribe. هُوَ أَمْلَأُ القَوْم

Filled. مَمْلُوء ومُمْتَلِيء

☆ To coax, to soothe a. o. with false promises. مَلَث o مَلْثًا ه وه بالكَلَام

To beat a. o. slightly. — ه

To adulate, to dissemble with. مَالَث ه

Dusk, nightfall. مَلْث ومَلَث

☆ To suck (his mother: child). مَلَج o ومَلِج a مَلْجًا ه

To suckle (a child). أَمْلَج ه

To exhaust (its mother's milk: suckling). إِمْتَلَج ه

Foster-brother. Illustrious (man). مَلِيج

Yellowish, brown. Barren desert. أَمْلَج

Sucking his she-camels out of avarice. مَلْجَان

Sugar-candy. Wild أُمْلُوج ج أَمَالِيج

To be disgusted with, weary of. مَلّ a مَلَلًا ومَلَالَة ومَلَالًا ه ومن

— To be restless, to fret (sick person). — وتَمَلَّل

To weary a. o. أَمَلّ ه وعَلَيْهِ

To dictate a. th. to. — إِمْلَالًا ه على

To embrace (a religion). تَمَلَّل وامْتَلّ ه

To be pulled. إِنْمَلّ

To be wearied of. إِسْتَمَلّ ه

Wearied. مَلّ

Hot ashes. Feverish sweat. Weariness. مَلَّة

Bread baked under the ashes. خُبْز المَلَّة

Religion. Belief. Nation, rite. مِلَّة ج مِلَل

Stitch. مُلَّة ج مُلَل

Bread well baked. مُلَّى

Weariness. مَلَل ومَلَال ومَلَالَة

Feverish sweat. Pain in the back. Restlessness of a sick person. مُلَال

Wearied, disgusted. (*m. f.*) مَلُول ومَلُولَة

Baked, cooked in embers (meat, bread). مَلِيل ومَمْلُول

Trodden (path). مَلِيل ومُمَلّ

Feverish heat. Intense thirst. مَلِيلَة

Annoyance. مَمْلُول

☆ To hurry on. مَلْمَل

To trouble a. o. (accident). — ه

To be restless in bed, to fret. تَمَلْمَل

Swiftness. Elephant's trunk. مَلْمَلَة

Needle for collyrium. Stiletto, style. مَلْمُول

Swift (ass). مُلَامِل

Swift-running (she-camel). مَلْمَلَى

☆ To fill a. th. To satisfy a. o. with. مَلَأ a مَلْأً ومِلْأَة ه ه ومن وب

— To help a. o. in. — ه على

He spread his fame in the whole earth. — مِنْهُ الأَرْض

He put him to strait. — عَلَيْهِ الأَرْض

To be rich, wealthy. — ومَلُؤَ o مَلَاءَة ومَلَاء

To be full of. مَلِئَ a مَلْأً وتَمَلَّأَ وامْتَلَأَ مِن

To have a rheum. مُلِئَ ومَلُؤَ o مَلَاءَة

To fill a. th. مَلَّأَ تَمْلِئَة ه

To brace (a bow) to the utmost. — وأَمْلَأَ في

To draw water. ❖ مَلَا

date. Foliage of a wild cypress growing in the desert.
Mason's trowel. مَالِج و✧ مَالَش ج مَوَالِج P
To put salt in (a dish). To salt (fish). ✱ مَلَح a i مَلْحًا ه
To suckle (a child). — a مَلْحًا ه ول
To backbite a. o. — ه وعِرْضَهُ
To become salt (water). مَلَحَ a o ومَلُحَ o مُلُوحَةً ومَلَاحَةً ومُلُوحًا
To become beautiful, pretty. To be good, fine. To become fat (camel). مَلُحَ o مَلَاحَةً ومُلُوحَةً
To be dusty, grayish. مَلِحَ a مَلَحًا
To compose excellent poetry. مَلَّحَ
To put much salt in (a dish). To rub (a camel's palate) with salt. مَلَّحَ وأَمْلَحَ ه
To be the commensal of. To be the foster-brother of. مَالَحَ مُمَالَحَةً ومِلَاحًا ه
To become brackish (sweet water). أَمْلَحَ
To give salt water to (the cattle). — ه
He commended him. — ه بِنَفْسِهِ
What a goodly man! مَا أَمْلَحَهُ ومَا أُمَيْلِحَهُ!
To become fat (beast). To affect cleverness. تَمَلَّحَ
✧ To threaten a. o. تَمَلَّحَ ل
To mix truth with falsehood. إِمْتَلَحَ
To be intermixed of white and black (ram). إِمْلَحَّ
To find a. th. fine, goodly. إِسْتَمْلَحَ ه
Salt. Facetious speech. Knowledge. Learned men. Beauty. Goodliness. Inviolable compact. مِلْح ج مِلَاح
Nitre. مِلْح بَلْمُوت
Rock-salt. مِلْح مَخْتُوم
Saltish, brackish water. مِلْح ج أَمْلَاح ومِلَاح ومِلَح ومِلْحَة
Compact, bond. مِلْح ومِلْحَة
There is a sacred bond between them two. بَيْنَهُمَا مِلْح او مِلْحَة
Saltish, salt. مِلْح و✧ مَالِح
Grayish. Bluish. مَلَح ومُلْحَة
Main body of the sea. مَلْحَة
Witticism. Prosperity. مُلْحَة ج مُلَح
Wind propelling a ship. Bag. Veil. مِلَاح

Beauty of the face. Kindness. Sentence. Witticism. مَلَاحَة
Navigation. Salt-trade. مِلَاحَة
Salt-mine. مَلَّاحَة ومَمْلَحَة
Saltiness. Stock-fish. مُلُوحَة
Witticism, witty. أُمْلُوح ج أَمَالِيح
Sailor, seaman. Trader in salt. ✧ Hoary frost. مَلَّاح
Salt (fish, water). Good, handsome, facetious. مَلِيح ج مِلَاح وأَمْلَاح
Good, pretty. مُلَاح ج مُلَاحُون
Suæda baccata; acid leguminous plants. مُلَّاح
✧ All right, well! مَلِيح
Mixed of white and black (ram). Dusty. أَمْلَح م مَلْحَاء ج مُلْح
Grey-haired, grey-bearded. — الشَّعْر واللِّحْيَة
Blue-eyed. — العَيْن
More beautiful, finer. أَمْلَح م مُلْحَى ج أَمَالِح ومُلَح
Kind of long-shaped grapes. مُلَاحِيّ
Salted fish. مُمَلَّح ومَمْلُوح ومَلِيح ومِلْح
Salt-vessel. Saline. مِمْلَحَة ج مَمَالِح
Possessor of or trader in salt. مُتَمَلِّح
To journey at a vehement pace. To go away. ✱ مَلَخَ a مَلْخًا
He occupies himself with trifles. — في البَاطِل
To pull out. To draw forth a. th. — وامْتَلَخَ ه
To become corrupt, tasteless (meat). مَلُخَ o مَلَاخَةً
To blandish, to fondle a. o. مَالَخَ ه
To put out (an eye: hawk). تَمَلَّخَ وامْتَلَخَ ه
To pull out (a tooth). To draw (the sword). To pull off (the bridle). إِمْتَلَخَ ه
Fugitive slave. Blandisher. مَلَّاخ
Corchorus olitorius. Jew's mallow. Garden mallow. مُلُوخِيَّة ومُلُوخِيَا G
Deprived of reason (man). مُمْتَلَخ العَقْل
To stretch a. th. ✱ مَلَدَ o مَلْدًا ه
To be soft, tender. To quiver (bough). مَلِدَ a مَلَدًا
To soften (a hide). مَلَّدَ ه
Softness, delicateness; youthfulness. مَلَد ومَلَدَان
Tender. مَلْد, وأَمْلَد م مَلْدَاء ج مُلْد

delicate (youth). Soft (bough).
Soft, tender, (youth). أملد وأملود وإمليد
Bare, waste (desert). إمليد
To lie. To run swiftly (horse). ✲ مَلَدَ o مَلْدًا
To smite a. o. with (the sword). — ه ب
To become confused (darkness). To be insincere. مَلِدَ a مَلَدًا
To receive a. th. from. إمتلد ه من
Insincere, hypocritical, liar. أملذ ومَلّاذ ومَلَذان ومَلوذ
To lag behind. ✲ ملز o مَلزًا عن
To take a. th. away. — ب
To deliver a. o. from. ملّز ه عن
To bring a. th. away. أملز وتملّز وامتلز ه
To be delivered from. تملّز عن
To escape from, إنملز وامّلز من
Muscular. مَلِز
Ravisher. Wolf. مَلّاز
To urge (a beast). To castrate (a ram). ✲ مَلَسَ o مَلسًا ه
To fawn, to blandish a. o. — ه بلسانه
To be smooth, even. مَلِسَ a ومَلُسَ o مَلاسة ومُلوسة
To smoothe a. th. To level (the ground). ملّس ه
To deliver a. o. from. — ه من
To overspread (darkness). To lose its wool (ewe). أملس
To become smooth. تملّس
To slip forth from (the hand). To escape from. — وانملس وامّلس من
To be taken away (sight). أُمتُلِس
To be smooth. إملاسّ
Thin upper garment. ◘ مَلَس
Confusedness of darkness. مَلَس الظلام
Swift (she-camel). Unfaithful (man). مَلَسَى
He sold it unconditionally. باعه الملسى لا عُهدة
Polish, smoothness. مَلاسة
Kind of rake, harrow. مَلّاسة
Smooth, sleek. Having no crack (bow). Sound (beast's back). أملس م ملساء ج مُلس
Easy to swallow (beverage). مَلساء

Unfruitful year. سنة مَلساء
Midday. Sour milk mixed with sweet. مُلَيساء
Barren desert. إمليس وإمليسة ج أماليس وأماليس
Roller for the ground. مِملسة
To rummage. ✧ To pluck off (the hair, feathers). ✲ مَلَشَ o مَلشًا ه
Mole-cricket (insect). ✧ مالوش ج مواليش
To slip, to get loose (rope). To escape. ✲ مَلِصَ a مَلَصًا, وتملّص
To miscarry (woman). أملصت بولدها وأملصت
To be delivered from. To escape from. تملّص وانملص وامّلص من
Slippery, smooth (bow-string). مَلِص ومَليص
Abortion. مَليص
Smooth-headed (man). أملص
Bald. أملص الرأس
Wont to miscarry (woman). مِملاص
To smear (a wall) with clay. ✧ To putty (a vessel). ✲ مَلَطَ o مَلطًا, ومَلّط ه
Stark-naked. ◘ عريان مَلط
To shave (the hair). مَلَطَ ه
✧ To scald (a beast) for removing the hair. — ه
To be of mixed race. مَلَطَ ومَلُطَ o مُلوطًا
To have no hair on the body. مَلِطَ a مَلَطًا ومُلطة
To recite the half of a verse alternately with (another). مَلَّطَ ومالط ه
To cast off her fœtus (she-camel). أملط
To be polished, smooth, unfeathered (arrow). تملّط
To snatch a. th. unawares. إمتلط ه
Knave; of mixed origin. مِلط ج أملاط ومُلوط
Gypsum. Cement. Putty. مِلاط ج مُلط
Wound on the head. مِلطى ومِلطاء ومِلطاة
Kind of swift run. مَلَطى
Hairless on the body. Featherless (arrow). أملط ج مُلط
Featherless (arrow). Hairless (abortive fœtus). مَليط

Malta (island). ✧ مَالِطَة
Maltese. مَالِطِي
Wont to cast her fætus (she-camel). مِمْلَاط
To skin (a sheep). ✧ To tear off (clothes). ✱ مَلَم a مَلْمًا, وامتَلَم ه وه
To run swiftly (she-camel). مَلَم وأَمْلَم وانمَلَم وامتَلَم
They are all united against him. هُمْ عَلَيْهِ مَلْمٌ وَاحِدٌ
Barren desert. مَلَاء ومَلِيم ج مُلْم
Swift-running (she-camel). مَلِيم ومَيْلَم
To dally, to wanton with. ✱ ملغ — مَالَغ ه
To show foolishness. تَمَلَّغ
To mock a. o. تَمَالَغ ب
Foolish. Churlish. Wanton. مِلْغ ج أَمْلَاغ
Libertine, wanton. مَالِغ ج مُلَّاغ
Churlish, unseemly. أَمْلَغ م مَلْغَاء ج مُلْغ
To flatter a. o. ✱ مَلِق a مَلَقًا ه ول, ومَالَق ه
To erase a. th. To flog a. o. مَلَق o مَلْقًا ه، وه
To suck (his mother : child). مَلَق ه
To wash (a garment). — وأَمْلَق ه
To level (the ground). مَلَّق ه
✧ To blandish a. o. مَلَّق ه
To fall into destitution. To stumble (horse). أَمْلَق
To impoverish a. o. (fate). — مَالَهُ
To blandish, to flatter a. o. تَمَلَّق تَمَلُّقًا وتِمِلَّاقًا ه ول
To be smooth, polished. إِنْمَلَق وامَّلَق
To escape from a. o. إِنْمَلَق مِن
To draw out, to extract a. th. إِمْتَلَق ه
Flattery, blandishment. مَلَق وتَمْلِيق وتَمَلُّق
Fawner, flatterer. مَلِق ومَلَّاق
Gentle-paced and swift-running (horse). — ومَيْلَق
Flat and smooth stone. مَلَقَة ج مَلَقَات
▫ League of distance. Open space.
Mason's trowel. ✧ مَالَق
Stone-roller. — ومِمْلَق ومِمْلَقَة
✱ مَلَك i مِلْكًا ومُلْكًا ومَلَكَة ومَمْلَكَة,
To possess a. th. وتَمَلَّك وامتَلَك ه
To become the owner of.
To conquer (a country) over. مَلَك ه مِن
To have self-control. مَلَك نَفْسَهُ
To rule over. — على
To take (a wife). — i مِلْكًا ومُلْكًا ه
To knead (dough) well. — مَلْكًا, ومَلَّك وأَمْلَك ه
To give to a. o. the possession of. ✧ To transfer property to. مَلَّك وأَمْلَك ه ه
To make a. o. to reign over. — وأَمْلَك ه على
To give (a wife) to. — وأَمْلَك ه ه
✧ To give a support to (a cross-bar). مَلَّك ه
To take a wife, to marry. أَمْلَك إِمْرَأَةً
To act as a sovereign. To appropriate. To become a landlord. تَمَلَّك
✧ To be rooted in a. o. (habit). — ه
To restrain o.'s self from. تَمَالَك عَن
He could not restrain from. مَا تَمَالَك أَنْ او عَن أَنْ
To become the owner of ; to buy (an estate). To win (the heart). ✧ إِسْتَمْلَك
Right of property. مِلْك
Funded property ; real estate. ✧ Freehold (land). مِلْك ومُلْك ج أَمْلَاك
Sovereignty, ownership, possession. مُلْك
Common of pasture. Water, well. مَلْك ومُلْك ومَلَك
Foot of a beast. مِلَاك ج مُلُك
Prop, support. — ومِلَاك
He is not self-possessed. مَا لَهُ مَلَاك
Angel. مَلَك ومَلَاك (*for* مَلْأَك)
King. مَلِك ومَلْك ج مُلُوك وأَمْلَاك
Fumitoria officinalis, common fumitory. بَقْلَة المَلِك
Castor-oil. حَبّ المُلُوك
Queen. مَلِكَة
Property. مَلْكَة ومُلْكَة ومَمْلَكَة
Royalty. ✧ Queen. Habit, faculty. مَلَكَة
He treats his subjects well. هُوَ حَسَن المَلَكَة
Custom, habit. مَلَكَة ج مَلَكَات
Possessor, owner. مَالِك ج مُلَّاك ومُلَّك
One of the four orthodox imams. مَالِك
Heron (bird). — الحَزِين
Moslem belonging to the مَالِكِي

orthodox rite of Abdelmalek.

Royal. مَلَكِيّ م مَلَكِيَّة و✧ مُلُوكِيّ

✧ Melchite (Greek). — ومَلِكِيّ

✧ Officer in the civil service. مُلْكِيّ

Property, right of property. مِلَاكَة ومُلْكِيَّة

Garden-mallow. مُلُوكِيَّة

Marriage-contract. إِمْلَاك

Kingdom; empire. Royalty. Heaven. The invisible world. مَلَكُوت

Royalty. Kingdom; country. مَمْلَكَة ومَمْلُكَة ج مَمَالِك

Bond-man. عَبْدُ مَمْلَكَةٍ او مَمْلِكَةٍ او مَمْلُكَةٍ

Owner, possessor. Sovereign. مَلِيك ج مُلَكَاء

Mother-bee. — النَّحْل

Property, possession. ✧ White slave. Well kneaded (dough). مَمْلُوك

Slave. Mameluke. ✧ Apron. مَمْلُوك ج مَمَالِيك

✧ Spleen. Melancholy. G مَالَنْخُولِيَا

To advance at a quick pace. ✱ مَلَا o مَلْوًا

To make a. o. to enjoy a. th. long (God). مَلَّى وأَمْلَى ه ه وه

To enjoy a. th. long. مَلِيَ وتَمَلَّى ه وه وب

To forbear long (a sinner: God). أَمْلَى ه ول إِمْلَاء

To loose the bridle to (a camel). — ل

To dictate (a letter) to. أَمْلَى ه على

To ask a. o. to dictate a. th. To beseech the forbearance of a. o. إِسْتَمْلَى ه

Desert. مَلَا ج أَمْلَاء

The day and the night. أَلْمَلَوَان

Looming desert. مَلَاة ج مَلَوَات ومَلًا

مَلْوَة ومُلْوَة ومِلْوَة, ومَلَاوَة ومِلَاوَة ومُلَاوَة Space of time.

Dictation. ✧ Correct writing. إِمْلَا ج أَمَالِيّ وأَمَالٍ

Long, prolonged. مَلِيّ

Long space of time. — مِنَ الدَّهْر

A long time; a while. مَلِيًّا

Continually. ✧ تَمَلِّي

Billion. ✧ Million. F مَلْيُون ج مَلَايِين

From what? Of what (*interrogative*)? ✱ مِمَّ (*for* مِن مَا)

From that which (*relative*). مِمَّا

(1°) *Interrogative (m. f. s. pl.)* ✱ مَنْ *pronoun*. Who? Whom? Whoever.

Who is he? Who is she? مَن هُوَ، مَن هِيَ

Who is thy Lord? مَن رَبُّكَ

(2°) *Relative pronoun*. He who, she who. مَن

He who does good, shall be rewarded for it. مَن يَعْمَل خَيْرًا يُجزَ بِهِ

There are men who do not believe in God. مِنَ النَّاس مَن لَا يُؤْمِنُ بِاللهِ

I passed by one whom thou likest. مَرَرْتُ بِمَن مُعْجِب لَكَ

Preposition used (1°) *for expressing a starting point, part of a whole, origin*. From, of. Some. Amongst. مِن

I started from Bagdad. سِرْتُ مِن بَغْدَاد

Composed of body and soul. مُرَكَّب مِن نَفْس وجَسَدٍ

Some men say, there are men who say. مِنَ النَّاس مَن قَالَ

He has taken some golden coins. أَخَذ مِن الدَّنَانِير

(2°) *for determining time, mood of action*. On, upon. From, of.

He died the very same day, on the same hour. مَات مِن يَوْمِهِ ومِن سَاعَتِهِ

What has been lost of money. مَا ذَهَب مِن المَال

Shun the abomination of idols. إِجْتَنِبُوا الرِّجْس مِنَ الأَوْثَان

He went out from the door. خَرَج مِن البَاب

He has crossed the river upon the bridge. عَبَر النَّهْرَ مِن جِسْرِهِ

(3°) *Means separation, distinction*.

He knows the wicked from the righteous man. يَعْلَم المُفْسِد مِنَ المُصْلِح

He escaped from. أَفْلَتَ مِن

(4°) *Means sometimes* instead of.

You have preferred the present world above the future. إِرْتَضَيْتُم الدُّنْيَا مِنَ الآخِرَة

(5°) *Is expletive before the subject of a negative or interrogative verb*.

No man came to me. مَا جَاءَنِي مِن رَجُل

No one can. مَا مِن أَحَدٍ يَقْدِر

Has any ship left? هَل سَافَر مِن مَرْكَب

(6°) *It means* : than.

He is stronger than I. هُوَ أَقْوَى مِنِّي

(7°) *Means : relation, likeness.* Between.
There is no relation between him and me. لَسْتُ مِنهُ ولَيْسَ مِنِّي
There is no comparison between thee and this man. أَيْنَ أَنتَ مِن هٰذَا الرَّجُل
Whereas. مِن حَيْث
To bestow (a favour) upon. ✱ مَنَّ o مَنًّا و مِنِّيقَى , وامْتَنَّ عَلَى ب
To recall (benefits); to reproach a. o. for (a gift). مَنَّ o مَنًّا ومِنَّةً , وامْتَنَّ عَلَى وَ ✧ مَنَّنَ ه
To weary a. o. (journey). مَنَّ o مَنًّا , وأَمَنَّ وتَمَنَّنَ ه
To break (a rope). — ه
To co-operate with a. o. مَانَّ ه
To request the benevolence of. إِسْتَمَنَّ ه
Gift, favour, benefit. Manna, viscous substance collected from the ash-tree. مَنّ
By the grace of God. بِمَنِّهِ تَعَالَى
Weight of 2 rothls. مَنّ ج أَمْنَان
Strength. Weakness. مُنَّة ج مُنَن
Grace, kindness, favour. Reproachful of benefits. مِنَّة ج مِنَن , وامْتِنَان
Female hedge-hog. Spider. مِنَنَة
Death. Time. مَنُون
He has experienced many changes of fortune. دَارَ عَلَيْهِ المَنُون
Recalling benefits. مَنُون وَمَنُونَة
Benevolent, bountiful. مَنَّان م مَنَّانَة
The Benefactor (God). أَلْمَنَّان
Weak. Strong. Fine dust. Weak rope. مَنِين ج أَمِنَّة ومُنُن
More bountiful than. أَمَنُّ مِن
Cut, broken. Strong. Weak. Attainable. مَمْنُون
He has done his best. بَلَغ مَمْنُونَهُ
Uninterrupted reward. أَجْرٌ غَيْرُ مَمْنُون
✧ Much obliged! مَمْنُون
✧ Obligation, acknowledgment of a benefit. مَمْنُونِيَّة
To soak (a hide) in ooze. ✱ مَنَا a مَنْأً ه
Hide in the tan. Tanning-place. مَنِيئَة
Ballista *See* جَنَق . مَنْجَلِيق ومَنْجَنِيق G
Water-engine. Water-wheel. مَنْجَنُون ج مَنَاجِين G

To grant, to give a. th. to a. o. To give to a. o. the usufruct of (a flock). ✱ مَنَح a ; i مَنْحًا ه ه
To shed continuous tears (eye). مَانَح مُمَانَحَةً ومِنَاحًا
To present a. o. with a gift. — ه
To be near to bring-forth (beast). أَمْنَح
To receive (a gift). إِمْتَنَح وامْتَنَح ه
To ask for (a gift, for a loan) from. إِسْتَمْنَح ه
Gift. Loan of money. مِنْحَة ج مِنَح
Ewe the milk of which is let out. — ومَنِيحَة ج مَنَائِح
Bountiful, beneficent. مَنَّاح
Milch-camel, sheep. مَنُوح
Third arrow of the game to which no lot is assigned. مَنِيح
Since. ✱ مُنْذُ ومُذ
I have not seen him since Friday. مَا رَأَيْتُهُ مُنْذُ او مُذ يَوْمُ الجُمْعَة
I have not seen him this whole month. مَا رَأَيْتُهُ مُنْذُ او مُذ شَهْرُنَا هٰذَا
To deny a. th. to. To hinder a. o. from. ✱ مَنَع a مَنْعًا ه عن وعن وه
To defend, to protect a. o. or a. th. against. — ه وه مِن
To be inaccessible, unapproachable (man, place). مَنُع o مَنَاعَةً ومَنَاعًا
To debar a. o. ✧ To prevent (a calf) from sucking. مَنَّع ه
To deny a. th. to a. o. To seek to hinder a. o. from. مَانَع ه ه
To be unapproachable, inaccessible (place). تَمَنَّع وامْتَنَع
To intrench o.'s self in. تَمَنَّع ب
To abstain, to refrain from. — وامْتَنَع عَن
To hinder o. a. from. تَمَانَعَا ه
Prohibition, refusal, hindrance. ✧ Interdict. مَنْع
Power of resistance; unapproachableness. مَنَعَة ومَنْعَة
He is well defended. هُوَ فِي مَنَعَةٍ
Strength of a position. مَنَاع ومَنَاعَة
Imperative form. Do hinder. مَنَاعِ
Abstemiousness. مَنْعَى وامْتِنَاع
Hindrance, obstacle. Impossibility. إِمْتِنَاع

To abstain from. تَمَهْمَهَ عن
Waste land. Far-extending desert. مَهْمَه ومَهْمَهَة ج مَهَامِه
Prince. P مَهْتَر ومِهْتَار
To swoon. ✡ مهج — أمْتُهِجَ
Blood of the heart. Soul. Life. مُهْجَة ج مُهَج ومُهَجَات
His soul departed. خَرَجَتْ مُهْجَتُهُ
Clear, thin (milk). أمْهَج وأمْهُوج وأمْهُجَان
✡ مَهَد a مَهْدًا, ومَهَّد وتَمَهَّد واسْتَمْهَد ه
To spread out (a carpet). To smooth.
To earn sustenance. مَهَد وَامْتَهَد
He presented excuses to. مَهَّد لِفُلَان العُذْرَ
He admitted his excuses. — لَهُ عُذْرَهُ
To arrange (an affair). To facilitate a. th. مَهَّد ه
To become powerful (man). To be arranged, facilitated (affair). تَمَهَّد
To be high (camel's hump). إمْتَهَد
He has not prepared the way for that. مَا امْتَهَد مَهْدَ ذَلِكَ
He has not conferred any benefit upon me. مَا امْتَهَد عِنْدِي يَدًا
Bed. Cradle. Ground. مَهْد ج مُهُود
Elevated ground, depressed ground. مُهْد ج مِهَدَة وأمْهَاد, ومُهْدَة ج مُهَد
Bed. Smooth ground. مِهَاد ج أمْهِدَة ومُهُد
Pure butter. مَهِيد
Spread (carpet). Arranged (affair). Lukewarm (water). مُمَهَّد
✡ مَهَر a o مَهْرًا ومُهُورًا ومَهَارًا ومَهَارَة ه
To become skilled in (an art); to be experienced in. وفي وب
To assign a dowry to (a woman). مَهَر a o مَهْرًا, وأمْهَر ه
To ask, to procure a colt. مَهَّر
To vie in skill with. مَاهَر ه
To assign a dowry to (a wife). أمْهَر ه
To acquire skill. تَمَهَّر
Dowry, nuptial gift. مَهْر ج مُهُور ومُهُورَة
Colt. Firstling. مُهْر ج مِهَار وأمْهَار و مِهَارَة
Filly. مُهْرَة ج مُهَر ومُهْرَات ومُهَرَات
Seal, signet, stamp. P مُهْر
◘ Review of troops. P مَهْرَان
Skill in (a science). مَهَارَة
Having a rich dowry, dowager, lady. مَهِيرَة ج مَهَائِر
Skilful. Experienced. مَاهِر ج مَهَرَة

Defender, defensive. مَانِع ج مَنَعَة ومَانِعُون
Hindrance. What prevents (a noun) from being declinable. — ج مَوَانِع
Hindering, debarring. مَنُوع ومَنَّاع
Inapproachable, inaccessible. Well fortified (place). Powerful, strong. مَنِيع ج مُنَعَاء
Impossible, unattainable. مُمْتَنِع
Prohibited. Indeclinable (noun). مَمْنُوع
Memphis town in Egypt. C مَنْفَ
Who? (*masc.*). ✡ مَنُو مث مَنَان ج مَنُون
Who? مَنِي مث مَنَيْن ج مَنِين
Who? (*fem.*). مَنَة مث مَنْتَان ج مَنَات
To try a. o. with. ✡ مَنَا o مَنْوًا ه ب
مَنًا مث مَنَوَان ومَنَيَان ج أمْنَاء وأمْنٍ ومُنِيّ
Weight equal to 2 rothls.
My house is opposite to his. دَارِي مَنَا دَارِهِ
Idol of the ancient Arabs. مَنَاة
Thing desired. مُنْوَة
To determine upon a. th. To experience a. th. ✡ مَنَى i مَنْيًا
To test a. o. with (God). — ه ب
To be tried by. مُنِي ب
To be favoured in. مُنِي ل
To inspire a. o. with (the desire) of. مَنَّى تَمْنِيَة ه ه وب
To put off a. th. مَانَى مُمَانَاة ه
To grant a delay to. To reward. To blandish a. o. — ه
To shed (blood). أمْنَى ه
To reach Mina (pilgrim). — وامْتَنَى
To desire, to wish a. th. To alter (a narrative). تَمَنَّى و✧ اسْتَمْنَى ه
Death. Fate. مَنًى ومَنِيَّة ج مَنَايَا
Mina, station of pilgrims near Mecca. مِنًى
◘ Town, place. Minia, town in Upper-Egypt. مِنْيَا
Desire, object of desire. مُنْيَة ج مُنًى, وأمْنِيَّة ج أمَانِيّ وأمَانٍ
Wish, desire. تَمَنٍّ ج تَمَنِّيَات
Things sought after. مُتَمَنَّيَات
To treat (cattle) gently. ✡ مَهَّ ه
To be gentle. مَهْمَه
Gently! Stand still. مَهْ ومَهْ مَهْ
Gentle walk. Easy thing. مَهَه ومَهَاه
Beauty, brightness. Comely. ⌒ مَهَاه
To prevent a. o. from. ✡ مَهْمَهَ ه عن

Pus of a corpse. مَهْل ومُهْل ومَهْلَة ومُهْلَة
Mineral. Molten copper. Fish. مُهْل
Liquid pitch. مُهْل ومُهْلَة
Preparation. Delay. مُهْلَة
He has made all his preparations. أَخَذَ مُهْلَتَهُ
He has surpassed him. أَخَذَ عَلَيْهِ المُهْلَة
Whatever. Whenever. ✲ مَهْمَا
Whatever thou shalt do, I will do it. مَهْمَا تَفْعَلْ أَفْعَلْ
Whenever Zeyd will visit me, I shall show him regard. مَهْمَا يَزُرْنِي زَيْدٌ أُكْرِمْهُ
To serve a. o. as a servant. ✲ مَهَن a o مَهْنًا ومَهْنَة ة
To treat a. o. harshly. — مَهْنًا ة
To be despised, weak. مَهُن o مَهَانَة
To handle a. th. مَاهَن ه
To weaken a. o. To employ a. o. أَمْهَن ة
To be a servant. إِمْتَهَن
To take a. o. into service. — ة
To make a daily use of. To wear out (clothes). — ه
To overwork (a servant). — ة
Service, office. ✧ Craft, profession. مَهْنَة ومِهْنَة ج مِهَن ومُهَن
Skill in work. مَهْنَة ومِهْنَة ومَهِنَة ج مِهَن ومُهَن
Domestic, servant. مَاهِن ج مُهَّان
Maid-servant. مَاهِنَة ج مَوَاهِن
Reviled. Weak. مَهِين ج مُهَنَاء
To strike a. o. violently. ✲ مَهَا o مَهْوًا ة
To be white-haired (beast). مَهَا o مَهْوًا
To silver or gild a. th. مَهَا a i مَهْيًا ه
To be watery (milk). مَهُو o مَهَاوَة
To dilute a. th. To whet (a blade). أَمْهَى ه
To urge (a horse). — ة
He sunk (*for* أماه) the well till he found water. حَفَرَ البِئْرَ حَتَّى أَمْهَى
Pearls. White pebbles. Sword with a narrow blade. Clear milk. Hailstone. Fresh dates. مَهْو
Rock-crystal. مَهًى
Wild cow. Piece of crystal. Sun. مَهَاة ج مَهًا ومَهَوَات ومَهَيَات
Berry of the *Bassia latifolia*, equatorial tree. مَهْوَا

Kind of red wheat. مَهْرِيَّة
Fleet camels, dromedaries. — مَهَارَى ومَهَارِيّ ومَهَارٍ
Having a colt (mare). مُمْهِر
Dowered (woman). مَمْهُورَة
Autumnal equinox. Festival. مَهْرَجَان P
To repel a. o. with the hand. ✲ مَهَز a مَهْزًا ة
To burn a. th. To tear a. th. with the nails. ✲ مَهَش a مَهْشًا ه وة
To be burnt. إِمْتَهَش
To wash (a garment). ✲ مَهَص — مَهْص ه
To be dipped into (water). تَمَهَّص في
To be bare (soil). إِمْهَاص
Barren (soil). مَهْصَاء
Sudden flush of the face. ✲ مَهَم
To be of a dull white. ✲ مَهِق a مَهَقًا
To drink a. th. at intervals. تَمَهَّق ه
Greenish colour of water. مَهَق
Dead white. أَمْهَق م مَهْقَاء ج مُهْق
Beaten track. Remote land. مَهْيَق
To pound, to bruise a. th. ✲ مَهَك a مَهْكًا, ومَهَّك ه
To soften a. th. مَهَّك ه
To be sterile (stallion). مَهَك a صُلْبُهُ ومُهِك مَهْكًا
He performed the work becomingly. تَمَهَّك في العَمَل
To quarrel together. تَمَاهَك
Youth; sappiness of youth. مَهْكَة ومُهْكَة
Full of vigour (youth). مُمَهَّك ومُمْتَهِك
Impotent (stallion). مَهِيك
To act at leisure, without haste. ✲ مَهَل a مَهْلًا ومُهْلَة, وتَمَهَّل في
To be foremost. مَهِل a مَهَلًا
To grant a delay to a. o. To show forbearance to. مَهَّل وأَمْهَل ة
To ask a. o. for a delay. إِسْتَمْهَل ة
Gentleness of proceedings, slowness. Leisure. مَهْل ومَهَل ومُهْلَة
Used as an imperative. Gently. مَهْلًا
No respite. لَا مَهَل
Slowly, gently. عَلَى مَهَل
Do it gently. عَلَى مَهْلِكَ
He had a respite granted to him (for repenting). رُزِقَ فُلَانٌ مَهَلًا

To whet (a blade). ✱ مَهَى i مَهْيًا, وأَمْهَى وامْتَهَى ه

To rout (the enemy). إِسْتَمْهَى

To launch (a horse) at full speed. — ه

What is the matter? ✱ مَهْيَم

To mew (cat). ✱ مَاء o مُوَاء, وأَمْوَأ

To mew like a cat (man). أَمْوَأ

Cat. مَائِيَة ومَائِنَة ومَائِيَّة

To die. To die away (fire). To be worn out (garment). ✱ مَات o مَوْتًا

To be forlorn (place); to be untrodden (road). To become still (wind). — مَوَتَانًا ومُوَاتًا

To put to death, to kill. مَوَّت وأَمَات ه

To vie in patience with a. o. مَاوَت ه

To lose (children, cattle: man). To lose (her offspring: beast). أَمَات

To soften (meat) by cooking. To cool (anger). To mortify (a limb). — ه

He mortified his passions. أَمَات نَفْسَهُ

What an apathetic man! مَا أَمْوَتَهُ او مَا أَمْوَت قَلْبَهُ

To be obsolete (word). أُمِيت

To feign o.'s self dead تَمَاوَت

To face, to seek death. إِسْتَمَات اسْتِمَاتَةً واسْتِمَاتًا

To exert o.'s self to the utmost for. — ل

Death. مَوْت ومَوْتَة

Natural death. Sudden death. مَوْت أَبْيَض

Death by the sword. — أَحْمَر

Death by strangulation. — أَسْوَد

Swoon. Madness. مُوتَة

Kind of death. مِيتَة

Death. مَيْتُوتَة

The putting to death. Mortification. إِمَاتَة

Rinder-pest, murrain. مَوْتَان ومُوتَان

Apathetic. مَوْتَان م مَوْتَانَة الفُؤَاد

Death. Inanimate goods. Uninhabited (place). مَوَتَان

Dying, at the point of death. مَائِت ج مَائِتُون, و✧ مَوَّات

Terrific death. مَوْت مَائِت

Dead, lifeless (man). مَيْت ج أَمْوَات ومَوْتَى ومَيْتُون, ومَيِّت ج مَيِّتُون

Dead (female). مَيْت ومَيْتَة ج مَيْتَات, ومَيِّتَة ج مَيِّتَات

Carrion. مَيْتَة

Dead, dying. مَيِّت

Inanimate thing. Unoccupied land. مَوَات

Decease, death. مَمَات

Mortified. Disused (word). مُمَات

Deadly. مُمِيت

Mortal sin. خَطِيئَة مُمِيتَة

Facing death. Dauntless. مُسْتَمِيت

To mix a. th. with. ✱ مَاث o مَوْثًا ومَوَثَانًا ه ب

To steep a. th. into (water). — ه في

To be mixed, diluted. إِنْمَاث

To rage (sea). To be disorderly (crowd). ✱ مَاج o مَوْجًا ومَوَجَانًا, وتَمَوَّج

To decline, to swerve from. مَاج عن

Wave, billow. (*un.* مَوْجَة) مَوْج ج أَمْوَاج

Fieriness of youth. مَوْجَة الشَّبَاب

Good-natured, merry. ✱ موذ — مَاذٌ

White and excellent honey. Weapon. مَاذِيّ

Light coat of mail. — ومَاذِيَّة

Light wine. مَاذِيَّة

To be in commotion (sea). To move to and fro. ✱ مَار o مَوْرًا

To flow upon (the ground: blood). — عَلَى

(The spear) was moved in the wounded man. — في المَطْعُون

To shed (blood). — وأَمَار ه

To raise (the dust: wind). أَمَار ه

He moved (the sword) in the wounded man. — ه في المَطْعُون

To go and come (man). تَمَوَّر

To fall off (hair). — وانْمَار

To draw (the sword). إِمْتَار ه

Saint. S مَار ومَارِي

Commotion, tossing of the waves. Beaten track. مَوْر

Dust raised by the wind; dust-drift. مُور

✧ Kind of merino-sheep. مُور وغَنَم مُور

The Morea (in Greece). مُورَة

Hair falling off. — ومُوَارَة

Penetrating (arrow). مَائِر

Stream of blood. مَائِرَات

Set in motion, swinging. مَوَّار

Soft and swift-running (camel). مَوَّار اليَد

Banana, tree and fruit. ✲ مَوز (*un.* مَوزة)
Seller of bananas. مَوّاز
To shave (the head). ✲ مَاس o مَوسًا هـ
Diamond. Light, fickle. مَاس
Razor. ✧ Pen-knife. مُوسَى (و✧ مُوس) ج مَوَاسٍ ومُوسَيَات
The prophet Moses. مُوسَى
Sole-fish. سَمَك مُوسَى
✧ To form sand-beds (river). ✲ مَاش o مَوشًا
To glean (grapes). — هـ
Indian peas. Mean furniture. مَاش
Little is better than nothing. أَلْمَاش خَيرٌ مِن لَاشَ
To wash, to cleanse (a garment). ✲ مَاص o مَوصًا, ومَوَّص هـ
To pick (the teeth). مَاص هـ
To be a dealer in straw. مَوَّص
Straw. مَوص
Lye. مُوَاصة
Fieriness of youth. ✲ ماع — مَوعَة الشَّبَاب
To mew (cat). ✲ مَاغ o مُوَاغًا
To be cheap (commodity). ✲ مَاق o مَوقًا
To be foolish. — o مَوَاقة ومُؤُوقًا ومَوقًا
To perish. — o مَوقًا ومُوقًا ومُؤُوقًا ومُوَاقة . وانماق
To feign madness. تَمَاوَق
To act foolishly. إِستمَاق
Foolishness. مُوق
Dust. Winged ant. Leather-boots. مُوق ج أَموَاق
Foolish, stupid. مَائِق ج مَوقَى
Great fool. أَحمَق مَائِق
To be rich in flocks. ✲ مَال a o مَولًا ومُؤُولًا
To give flocks to. مَال o مَولًا , وأَمَال ه
To render a. o. wealthy. مَوَّل ه
To become wealthy. تَمَوَّل واستمَال
To lay aside (money) تَمَوَّل هـ
Flocks. Wealth, personal property. مَال ج أَموَال
Rich, wealthy (man). مَال ج مَالَة ومَالُون
Taxes. Treasury. ✧ مَال مِيرِي
Capital, stock. ✧ رَأس مَال
Wealthy (woman). مَالَة ج مَالَة ومَالَات
Monetary, financial. مَالِيّ
Wealth, finance. ✧ Public treasury. مَالِيَّة

✧ Ministry of Finance. نَظَارَة ووزَارَة المَالِيَّة
Very rich. مَوِّل ومَيِّل
A little wealth. مُوَيل
Song of camel-drivers. ✧ مَوَّال ج مَوَاوِيل
To be affected with pleurisy. ✲ موم — مِيمَ مَومًا
Wax. Pleurisy. Weaver's or cobbler's tool. Malignant small-pox. P مُوم
Pleuritic. مَمُوم
Desert. ✲ مومي — مَومَاء ومَومَاة ج مَوَامٍ
Pissasphalt. P مُومِيَا
✧ Egyptian mummy. P مُومِيَة
To provide a. o. with victuals. ✲ مَان o مَونًا ومُؤُونَة, ومَوَّن ه
✧ He acted on his behalf in. مَان على فُلَانٍ في
✧ To give food to (a workman). مَوَّن ه
To store provisions for o.'s family. تَمَوَّن
Victuals, stores, provisions. ✧ Cement of lime and pounded bricks, mortar. مُونَة
Cupboard. Store-house. بَيت المُونَة
Provider, purveyor. مَوَّان
To hold much water (well). To draw water (ship). ✲ مَاه a o مَوهًا ومُؤُوهًا ومَاهَة
To give water to. — وأَمَاه ه
To mix a. th. with. مَاه o مَوهًا هـ ب
To abound with water (place). مَوَّه
To gild or silver (a metal). To put water into (a kettle). To puzzle, to confuse a. o. — هـ وه
To embellish (a narrative) to. — هـ على
Do not delude thyself. لَا تُمَوِّه بِكَ
✧ He dispelled (cares) from his mind. مَوَّه عن بَالِهِ هـ
To come upon water (digger). To yield much rain (clouds). To be full of water-springs (land). أَمَاه إِمَاهَة وأَموَه إِموَاهًا
To water (cattle). — ه
To put water into (an inkstand). To whet (a knife). — هـ
To be sappy (tree). تَمَوَّه و✧ تَمَاوَى
Water. Juice, sap of plants. مَاء ج أَموَاه ومِيَاه

Brightness of the face. Pudency. مَاءُ الوَجْهِ
Sap. Water of a sword. — ومُوهَة ومُوَاهَة
Gold-wash. — الذَّهَب
Rose-water. — وَرْد
Cranes, storks. بَنَات المَاء
Water. مَاه ومَاءَة
Middle of a town; seat of a government. مَاه
Faint-hearted. Stupid. — الفُؤَاد ومَاهِي الفُؤَاد
Watery, aquatic. مَاءِيّ ومَاهِيّ ومَاوِيّ
Looking-glass, mirror. مَاوِيَّة ج مَاوِيّ
A little water. مُوَيه ومُوَيْهَة و ✧ مُوَيّ
✧ Water.
Sap. مَائِيَّة ومَاوِيَّة
Better supplied with water. أَمْوَه
Adulterated (narrative). مُمَوَّه
Name of women. ✲ مَيّ ومَيَّة ومَيَّا
Juice of quinces prepared into a medicine. P مَيبَة
To steep; to dissolve a. th. in (water). ✲ مَاثَ i مَيثًا, ومَيَّثَ ه في
To be softened by rain (ground). تَمَيَّثَ
To be dissolved in (water : salt). إِنْمَاثَ في
To obtain riches, the comforts of life. إِمْتَاثَ
Soft, gentle. Easy life. مَيْث
Soft (ground). مَيثَاء ج مِيث
To be mingled. ✧ مَاجَ i مَيجًا
To waddle. ✲ مَاحَ i مَيحًا ومَيحُوحَة, وتَمَيَّحَ
To descend into a well for drawing water. مَاحَ
To draw (water) with the hand. — وامْتَاحَ ه
He cleaned his teeth with (a tooth-pick). مَاحَ فَاهُ ب
To intercede for a. o. to. — ه عِنْد
To make a gift to a. o. — i مَيحًا ومِيَاحَة, وامْتَاحَ ه
To have intercourse with. مَايَحَ ه
To swing (bough). To reel (drunken man). تَمَيَّحَ وتَمَايَحَ
To ask for a gift from. To ask the intercession of. اسْتَمَاحَ ه
Water-drawer. مَائِح ج مَاحَة, ومُيَّاح

Intercessor. مُسْتَمِيح
To abate (heat, fever). To die away (fire, anger). ✲ مَاخَ i مَيخًا
To be convulsed. To oscillate (bough). To quiver (mirage). To be amazed. To feel giddy. ✲ مَادَ i مَيدًا ومَيَدَانًا
To waddle, to incline in walking. — وتَمَايَدَ
To visit a. o. مَادَ ه
To furnish a. o. with travelling-provisions. To ask a. o. for food. إِمْتَادَ ه
Sea-sick, giddy, heaving. مَائِد م مَائِدَة ج مَيدَى
Table; fare, food. مَائِدَة ج مَائِدَات ومَوَائِد
Because, unless. (for وبَيدَ أن) مَيدَ أن
On account of. مَيدَى
He has done it on that account. فَعَلَهُ مَيدَى ذٰلِكَ
Measure, amount. Length of a road. مِيدَاء
In front of him. بِمِيدَاهُ وبِمِيدَائِهِ
Race-ground; field. Ample (life). مَيدَان و مِيدَان ج مَيَادِين
Shaken, tossed. مَيَّاد م مَيَّادَة
Asking, asked for a gift. مُمْتَاد
To gallop in a race-field (horse). ✧ مَيْدَنَ
To make (a horse) to gallop. — ه
To convey (stores) to o.'s family. ✲ مَارَ i مَيرًا, ومَايَرَ وأَمَارَ ه
To comb (wool). مَارَ ه
To macerate (saffron) in water. مَارَ وأَمَارَ ه
He mimicked him. سَايَرَهُ ومَايَرَهُ
To liquefy a. th. أَمَارَ ه
A disturbance took place amongst them. تَمَايَرَ مَا بَيْنَهُم
To supply a. o. with provisions. إِمْتَارَ ل
Stores, provisions, wheat, corn. مِيرَة ج مِيَر
Purveyor, conveyer. مَائِر ج مُيَّار ومَيَّارَة ومُمْتَار
To set a. th. apart from. To discern between. ✲ مَازَ i مَيزًا, ومَيَّزَ وأَمَازَ ه مِن
To distinguish a. th. — ومَيَّزَ وأَمَازَ ه
To be distinguished, set apart. تَمَيَّزَ وانْمَازَ وامْتَازَ واسْتَمَازَ

He burst with rage. تَمَيَّز مِن الغيظ
To withdraw, to retire apart. إِستماز
Muscular. مَيِز ومَيِّز
Distinction. Discrimination. *Gr.* Distinctive term. تَمييز
Age of discrimination. سِنّ ألتَّمييز
✧ Court of cassation. مَحكَمَة التَّمييز
✧ Privilege, patent-letters. إِمتياز ج امتيازات
✧ Civil dignity (in Turkey). مُتَمَيِّز
✱ To swagger, to sweep. مَاس i مَيسًا ومَيَسانًا, وتَمَيَّس
— To spread (a disease) in a tribe (God). وأَمَاس ه في القوم
To fringe, to border (a garment). مَيَّس ه
Tree used for making saddles. Kind of lote-tree, celtis tree. Erect grape-vine. مَيس
Libration of the moon. مَيس ومَيَسان القمر
Strutting. مَائِس ومَيَّاس ومَيُوس ومَيسان
Bright star. مَيسان ج مَيَاسِين
✱ To mix a. th. with. مَاش i مَيشًا ه ب
— To garble (news). ه
— To milk (a female) partially. ه
— To cross (a field). i مَيشَة ه
✱ To deviate, to remove from. مَاطَ i مَيطًا ومَيَطانًا, وأَمَاط عن
To act wrongfully in. مَاط i مَيطًا في
— To remove a. o. وأَماط ه
To separate in confusion (people). تَمَايَط
He possesses nothing. مَا عِندَهُ مَيط
Repulsion, shunning. مِيَاط
They are in confusion. هُمْ في هِيَاط ومِيَاط
✱ To flow (liquid). To run (horse). مَاع i مَيعًا
— To melt (grease). وتَمَيَّع وانماع
To make (a liquid) to flow. To liquefy (grease). أَمَاع إِمَاعَة وإِمَاعًا ه
Frankincense. Storax. Prime (of youth). First part of (a race). مَيعَة
Fluid. مَائِع
Long forelock. مَائِعَة ج مَوَائِع
✱ To lean, to incline to. To repair to (a place). To feel sympathy for. مَال i مَيلًا ومَمَالًا ومَمِيلًا ومَيَلانًا وتَمْيَالًا ومَيلُولَة إِلى
To deviate from (truth, a path). To be unfair for a. o. مَال عَن
To try a. o. (fortune). مَال على فُلانٍ
He judged unfairly. مَال في حُكْمِهِ
To incline to setting (sun). To draw towards its end (night, day). مَال i مُيُولًا
The road has been long for us. مَال بِنَا الطَّرِيقُ
To be inclined, to lean. To overtop (wall). مَيِل a مَيَلًا
To incline a. th. مَيَّل وأَمَال ه
He hesitated between two affairs *a.* مَيَّل بَين أَمرَين
✧ To call at a. o. مَيَّل عِند
To hold, to side with a. o. To attack, to fight a. o. To incline towards. مَايَل ه
To pronounce a fatha like an English *a.* أَمَال إِمَالَةً
To swagger, to sway from one side to another. تَمَيَّل وتَمَايَل
They are at variance. بَينَهُم تَمَايُل
To lean, to incline. إِستمال
To conciliate, to win the heart. — ه وبِقَلبِهِ
To measure a. th. with both hands or with extended arms. — ه
Inclination. Propensity, partiality, bias. Sympathy *Geom.* Obliquity. مَيل ج أَميَال
Ecliptic (*astron*). دَائِرَة المَيل
Probe for wounds. Pencil, style for collyrium. Mile of 4000 cubits. Range of the sight. Mile-stone. مِيل ج أَميَال وأَمْيُل ومُيُول
Time, moment. مِيلَة ج مِيَل
Inflection of a fatha to a kasra. إِمَالَة
More inclined, more sympathetic. Overtopping (wall). Swaying on horseback. Without weapon. أَميَل ج مِيل
Tufty tree. Mound of sand. Manner of wearing a turban. مَيلَاء
Inclined. Unfair. Prone. مَيَّال
✱ To lie. مَان i مَينًا
— To till (the ground). ه
To dissemble with o. a. تَمَايَن ه

To hold much water (well). ✫ ماه i مَيْهًا ومَيَهَةً
To gild (a sword). — ه
To give water to a. o. — ه

Ploughshare. مان
Lie. مَيْن ج مُيُون
Liar. مَائِن ومَيَّان ومَيُون
False friend. مُتَمَايِن الوُدّ

ن

Postfix of the 1st person of the plural: We, us. Our. نا
Like us. مِثْلُنا
Our book. كِتَابُنَا
To be weak, remiss in a. th. ✫ نَأْنَأَ نَأْنَأَةً ومُنَأْنَأَةً, وتَنَأْنَأَ في
To be unable to. — عن
Weak, feeble. Cowardly. نَأْنَأ ونَأْنَاء ونُؤْنُؤ ومُنَأْنَأ
To moan. ✫ نَأَت a i نَأْتًا ونَئِيتًا
To grudge a. o. — ه
The lion. النَّـأْآت
To be removed from. ✫ نَأَث a نَأْثًا ومَنْأَثًا عن
To remove a. o. أَنْأَث ه
To go through (a country). ✫ نَأَج a نُؤُوجًا في
To blow (wind). To low (bull). To hoot (owl). نَأَج a نَئِيجًا
He cried unto God. — إلى الله
To be overtaken by a violent wind. نُئِج
Humming (insect). Hissing (wind). نَائِجَة ج نَائِجَات
Whistling sound of the wind. نَئِيج
Blowing with a shrill sound (wind). نَؤُوج ج نَوَائِج
To abound with springs (land). ✫ نَأَد a نَأْدًا
To crush a. o. (misfortune). To grudge a. o. — ه
Calamity. نَأْد ونَآدَى ونُؤُود
To catch a. th. To put off, to delay a. th. ✫ نَأَش a نَأْشًا, وتَنَاءَش ه
To be postponed, delayed. تَنَاءَش وانْتَأَش
He came very late. جاء نَئِيشًا
He overtook us at night-fall. لَحِقَنَا نَئِيشًا مِن النَّهَار
To apply o.'s self to. ✫ نَأَف a نَأْفًا في
He quenched his thirst. نَئِف a نَأْفًا ونَأَفًا مِن الشَّرَاب

To loathe a. o. نَئِف ه
To have a jerking deportment. ✫ نَأَل a نَأْلًا ونَأَلَانًا ونَئِيلًا
Having a jerking deportment. نَؤُول
To sigh, to moan (man). To twang (bow). To snarl (lion). ✫ نَأَم a i نَئِيمًا
Noise, sound. نَأْمَة
May God silence him by death! أَسْكَتَ اللهُ نَأْمَتَهُ
To remove, to be remote from. ✫ نَأَى a نَأْيًا ه او عَن
To dig (a trench) around a tent. نَأَى وأَنْأَى وانْتَأَى ه
Imp. Do dig the trench. نَ النُّؤْيَ ونَهْ
To keep a. o. aloof. نَاءَى ه
To avert (an evil) from. — ه عن
To remove a. o. from. أَنْأَى إِنْآءً ه عن
To remove, to be far from. تَنَاءَى تَنَائِيًا, وانْتَأَى انْتِئَاءً عَن
To be remote from o. another. تَنَاءَوْا
Trench around a tent. نَأْي ونُؤْي ونِئْي ونُؤَى ج آنْآء وأَنْـآء, ونُؤِيّ ونِـئِيّ
Single fife, pipe. ✧ نَاي ج نَايَات
Remote from his people. نَاءٍ م نَائِيَة
Distant place. مُنْتَأًى
To be excited (ram). ✫ نَبّ i نَبًّا ونَبِيبًا ونَبَابًا
To have a knotted stem (plant). نَبَّب
To have vent (water). تَنَبَّب
Knot of a stem. Track, way. Tube. Pipe. Row of trees. Siphon. أُنْبُوب ج أَنَابِيب
Jointed stem of a reed. أُنْبُوبَة ج أُنْبُوب وأَنَابِيب
Bronchiæ, air-passages. أَنَابِيب الرِّئَة
To be high, lofty. ✫ نَبَأ a نَبْأً ونُبُوءًا
To overtake, to come upon a. o. — عَلَى
To pass from (a place) to (another). — مِن . . . إلى

To bark faintly (dog). نَبَأَ a نَبْأً
My sight recoils from it. نَبَأَ بَصَرِي عَنْ ذٰلِكَ
To announce (news) to a. o. نَبَّأَ تَنْبِيئًا, وأَنْبَأَ ه ه او ب
I was informed that a slave had reviled me. نُبِّئْتُ عَبْدًا سَبَّنِي
To inform o. a. of. نَابَأَ ه ○
To pretend prophecy, to prophesy. تَنَبَّأَ تَنَبُّؤًا
To ask for (news). إِسْتَنْبَأَ ه
To inquire about (news) from. — ه
News, information. نَبَأٌ ج أَنْبَاء
Faint voice. Barking of dogs. نَبْأَة
Prophecy. نُبُوءَة ونُبُوَّة
Prophetic. نَبَوِيّ
Wanderer; wayfarer. Eminence. Well traced road. نَبِيء
Prophet. نَبِيء ونَبِيّ ج أَنْبِيَاء ونَبِيُّون
Prophetess. نَبِيئَة ونَبِيَّة ج نَبِيئَات ونَبِيَّات
Prominent (place). High, lofty. Crossing a country (man, stream). نَابِئ م نَابِئَة
Minor prophet. نُبَيِّئ ونُبَيّ
Surname of a celebrated poet. المُتَنَبِّي
To grow, to sprout (plant). To produce plants (land). * نَبَتَ o نَبْتًا ونَبَاتًا, وأَنْبَتَ
To grow up (child). — o نَبَاتًا ونَبْتَة, وأَنْبَتَ
To plant (a tree). To sow (grain). ✧ To quilt (a garment). نَبَّتَ ه
To rear (a child). — ه
To make plants to grow (God). أَنْبَتَ ه
Plant, vegetation. نَبْت (*un.* نَبْتَة)
Plant, vegetable. نَبَات ج نَبَاتَات
✧ Sugar-candy. — وسُكَّر نَبَات
Botanist. Vegetal. نَبَاتِيّ
Botany. عِلْم النَّبَات
Offspring of men or cattle. *Pl.* Inexperienced young men. نَابِتَة ج نَوَابِت
Their offspring grew up. نَبَتَتْ لَهُمْ نَابِتَة
Bough. ✧ Mace. ◘ Stick, pole. نَبُّوت ج نَبَابِيت
Canal of irrigation. نَبِيتَة ج نَبَائِت
Trees, plants. تَنْبِيت ج تَنَابِيت
Growing-place. Origin. مَنْبِت ومَنْبَت ج مَنَابِت

Ground rich in plants. مَنْبَات
Thorny carob. Poppy (plant). يَنْبُوت ج يَنَابِيت
To clean out (a well). * نَبَثَ o نَبْثًا ه
To take away (earth). — وانْتَبَثَ ه
To discover (a hidden thing). نَبَثَ عَنْ
To investigate a. th. تَنَابَثَ واسْتَنْبَثَ عَنْ
To swell (dough). إِنْتَبَثَ
Trace. نَبَث ج أَنْبَاث
Wicked. Malignant. خَبِيث نَبِيث
Slime of a well. Secret. نَبِيثَة ج نَبَائِث
Children's game. أُنْبُوثَة
To have a strong and harsh voice. * نَبَجَ i نَبِيجًا
To come out from its covert (partridge). To ooze (water). — o نُبُوجًا
To falter in speech. To sit upon a hillock. أَنْبَجَ
To swell (bone). تَنَبَّجَ وانْتَبَجَ
Hillock. نَبَجَة ج نِبَاج
Howling, barking. نَبَّاج
Buttocks. نَبَّاجَة
Sweetmeats, confections. أَنْبِجَات
Oozing of water. مَنْبَج
Making void promises. مِنْبَج
* نَبَحَ i a نَبْحًا ونَبِيحًا ونُبَاحًا ونِبَاحًا وتَنْبَاحًا
To bark (dog). To hiss (serpent). ◘ To pulsate (wound).
To bark at a. o. (dog). — ه وعلى ونَابَحَ ه
To coo (old hoopoe). — نُبَاحًا
To make (dogs) to bark. أَنْبَحَ واسْتَنْبَحَ ه
Barking of dogs. نُبَاح ونِبَاح
Clamour and barking. نُبُوح
Barker. Shell from Mecca used as an amulet. نَبَّاح
Cooing hoopoe. Barking dog. نُبَاح
Night-comer *lit.* rouser of the dogs. المُسْتَنْبِح
To leaven (dough). * نَبَخَ i o نُبُوخًا
To knead leavened dough. أَنْبَخَ
Blister. Small-pox. نَبْخ ونَبَخ
Oakum for calking ships. Sulphur matches. نَبْخَة ونَبَخَة
Speaking emphatically. Remote land. نَابِخَة ج نَوَابِخ
Hillock, mound. نَبْخَاء ج نَبَاخَى
Sour bough. نَبَّاخ وأُنْبَخَان
To fling a. th. * نَبَذَ i نَبْذًا, ونَبَّذَ ه

To cast off; to neglect a. th.
To throw a. th. to. To dissolve (a covenant) with. — ه إلى
He steeped the dates, the grapes. نبذ التمر او العنب
To make date or grape-wine. نبذ ونبّذ وأنبذ وا نتبذ النبيذ
To pulsate (artery). نبذ نبذًا ونبذانًا
To part with. To thwart a. o. نابذ منابذة ونباذًا ه
To throw a piece of cloth to a. o. in a sale *i. e.* to set a bargain. — ه في البيع
To declare war to. — ه الحرب
To withdraw from o. a. (fighters). — وتنابذ وانتبذ
To retire apart. إنتبذ
A little; small number, small quantity. نبذ ج أنباذ
The refuse of the people. أنباذ الناس
Side, shore. نبذة ونُبذة
Fragment; article of a treaty. Exemplary of a book. — ونبذة ج نُبَذ
He sat apart. جلس نبذة ونُبذة
Intoxicating beverage made of dates or raisins. ✧ Wine. نبيذ ج أنبذة و ✧ نبيد
Flung. — ومنبوذ
Wine-merchant. نبّاذ
Foundling, bastard. منبوذ
Pillow. مِنبذة ج منابذ
To grow (boy) To raise the voice to a high pitch (singer). ✱ نبر i نبرًا
To raise a. th. To mark a letter with a hamza. — ه
To drive a. o. away in shouting. — ه
To calumniate a. o. — ه بلسانه
✧ To speak imperiously to. ✧ تنبّر على
To swell (hand). To ascend the pulpit. إنتبر
Sudden (thrust). Shameless. ✧ Harsh, imperious (word). نَبر
Tick. Camel's fly. نِبر ج أنبار ونِبار
Magazine, barn, granary. نِبر وأنبار ج أنابر وأنابير
✧ Storehouse. Hold of a ship. أنبار وعنبر
Dimple on the upper lip. Hamza. Swelling. Raising of the voice. Prominence. نبرة

Large mouthful. نبرة ج نُبَر
Shouter. Eloquent. نبّار
Platform. Pulpit. مِنبر ج منابر
Lamp, lantern. Spear-head. Bold. نِبراس ج نباريس
To nickname a. o. ✱ نبز i نبزًا ونبّز ه
To give nicknames to one another. To revile o. a. تنابز
Nickname, name of reproach. نبز ج أنباز
Vile, ignoble. نِبز
Nicknamer. نُبزة
To speak in a meeting. ✱ نبس i نبسًا ونبسة ونبّس
He has not uttered a single word. ما نبس وما نبّس بكلمة
Speakers. Hasteners. نُبس
أنبس الوجه م نبساء الوجه ج نُبس الوجه
Austere-looking.
To take a. th. out. To disclose (a secret). To dig up, to exhume (a corpse). To ransack (a grave). ✱ نبش o نبشًا ه
He dug up a treasure. — كنزًا عن الأرض
To earn sustenance for (o.'s family). — ل
✧ To search for; to rummage a. th. — ونبّش في
To pull out a. th. إنتبش ه
Species of hard pine. نَبش ا
Earth extracted from a well. نبيشة
Grave-digger. نبّاش
Occupation of a grave-digger. نِباشة
Plucked root of a plant. أنبوش ج أنابيش
Uprooted tree. — وأنبوشة
✧ Confusion. ◻ منابشة
To speak out. ✱ نبص i نبصًا
To chirp (bird). — i نبيصًا
Sprout of a plant. نَبص
Word. نبصة
To throb. To flash faintly (lightning). ✱ نبض i نبضًا ونبضانًا
To flow (water). — o نبوضًا
نبض في القوس وأنبض القوس وعنه وأنبض الوتر وبه
He twanged the bowstring.
Throbbing of an artery, pulse. نبض ونبَض ج أنباض
Fiery (heart). نبض ونبَض ونبِض
He is motionless. ما به حبض ولا نبض

Single pulsation, throbbing. نَبْضَة ونَبَضَة
Nerve. Anger. نَابِض
He was roused to anger. نَبَضَ نَابِضُهُ
Place of pulsation. مَنْبِض
Mallet for carding cotton. مِنْبَض
To gush forth (spring). ◘ To result. ✲ نَبَطَ o i نَبْطًا ونُبُوطًا
To draw (water). نَبَطَ i o نَبْطًا هـ
To reach water by digging (a well). — ونَبَّطَ وأَنْبَطَ وتَنَبَّطَ واسْتَنْبَطَ هـ
◘ To scoff at a. o. نَبَطَ ه
To bring a. th. to light. To deduce a. th. أَنْبَطَ واسْتَنْبَطَ هـ
To appear. أُنْبِطَ واسْتُنْبِطَ
To pretend to be a Nabathean. تَنَبَّطَ
To compose (a discourse). ◘ To speak imperiously. إِنْتَبَطَ هـ
To find out, to elicit a. th. To elucidate (a question : lawyer). إِسْتَنْبَطَ هـ
Internal state of a man. نَبْط
Nobody knows his intimate thoughts. لا يُدرَك نَبْطُهُ
First water of a well. White hair on a horse's flank. نَبَط ونُبْطَة
Nabatheans. نَبَط ج أَنْبَاط ونَبِيط
Belonging to the Nabatheans. نَبَطِيّ ونُبَاطِيّ
Discovery, invention, contrivance. إِسْتِنْبَاط
White-spotted on the side (horse). أَنْبَط م نَبْطَاء ج نُبْط
To issue forth (water). ✲ نَبَعَ a i o نَبْعًا ونُبُوعًا ونَبَعَانًا
To emerge from. — مِنْ
To cause (springs) to ooze (God). أَنْبَعَ هـ
To ooze (water). تَنَبَّعَ
Chadara tenax, tree for making bows, arrows. ✧ Spring. نَبْع
Bow made with *chadara tenax*. نَبْعِيَّة
Hard, steady. صَلِيب النَّبْع
Origin. نَبْعَة
He his of a noble race. هُوَ مِن نَبْعَة كَرِيمَة
Sweating limbs of the camel. نَوَابِع البَعِير
Spring. Origin. مَنْبَع ج مَنَابِع
Water-spring. Streamlet. يَنْبُوع ج يَنَابِيع
To appear. To gush forth (water). To become a good poet. To be scurfy (head). To spread (evil). ✲ نَبَغَ a o i نَبْغًا ونُبُوغًا
To rise against a. o. (heretic). نَبَغَ على
He led an easy life. — في الدُّنيا
To let out flour (bag). — بالدَّقِيق
To sift flour. أَنْبَغَ
To haunt (a place). — هـ
Dust of a mill. نَبَغ ونُبَاغ
The choice of the tribe. نَبَغَة القَوْم
Remarkable, distinguished man. نَابِغَة ج نَوَابِغ، ونَبِيغ ج أَنْبِغَاء
Surname of 8 celebrated poets. أَلنَّوَابِغ
Relating to those poets. نَابِغِيّ
Scurf of the head. نُبَاغ ونَبَّاغَة ونُبَاغَة ونُبَّاغَة
Heretics, novators. نَبَّاغَة
Dusty high road. مَحَجَّة نَبَّاغَة
To write. To come out. ✧ To gush forth (blood, pus). ✲ نَبَقَ o نَبْقًا، ونَبَّقَ
To rule and arrange (a blank book). ✧ To forge, to falsify a. th. نَبَّقَ هـ
To elicit (a discourse). إِنْتَبَقَ هـ
Mealy matter of the palm-pith. نَبَق
Zizyphus spina Christi, lote-tree and its fruit. ◘ Wild-apple, crab-apple. نَبْق و نِبْق ونَبِق ونَبَق
Large vine-knob. Drupe. نُبَيقَة ج نَبَابِق
Alembic. أَنْبِيق ج أَنَابِيق
Planted in a row (palm-trees). مُنَبَّق
To be elevated (place). ✲ نَبَكَ o نُبُوكًا، وانْتَبَكَ
Peakish hill. نَبَكَة ونَبْكَة ج نَبَك ونِبَك ونِبَاك ونُبُوك
High (ground). نَابِك م نَابِكَة ج نَوَابِك
To shoot at. To give arrows to a. o. To surpass a. o. in skill. ✲ نَبَلَ o نَبْلًا ه
To pick up arrows for a. o. — على
To treat a. o. kindly. — ب
To soothe a. o. with (food). — ه ب
To be clever, noble. نَبُلَ o نَبَالَة
To give arrows to a. o. نَبَّلَ وأَنْبَلَ ه
To vie in skill with a. o. نَابَلَ ه
To have ripe dates (palm-tree). أَنْبَلَ
To make rough (arrows). — هـ
To show sagacity; to be skilful. To die (camel). تَنَبَّلَ
To purify o.'s self with pebbles. — ب

To take the best of. تَنَبَّلَ مِن
To vie with a. o. in shooting, in making arrows. تَنَابَلَ
To die, to be killed. إِنْتَبَلَ
To carry away a. th. — ه
To take heed of. To prepare to. — ل
He has taken no notice of it. مَا إِنْتَبَلَ نَبْلَهُ او نُبْلَتَهُ او نَبَالَهُ او نَبَالَتَهُ
To ask for arrows from. إِسْتَنْبَلَ ه
To take the best of. — ه
(*fem.*) نَبْل ج نِبَال وأَنْبَال ونُبْلَان (*un.* نَبْلَة)
Arrow.
Nobility. Sagacity. نُبْل
Small pebbles. نَبَل ونُبَل
Reward. Gift. Mouthful. Choice part. Merit. Nobility. نُبْلَة ج نُبَل ونُبْلَات
Arrow-making. نِبَالَة
Ability, merit. Personal accomplishment. نَبَالَة
Preparation. نُبَالَة
He got ready for the thing. أَخَذَ لِلأَمْرِ نُبْلَهُ او نُبَالَتَهُ
Endowed with superior merit. Generous, noble. نَبْل م نَبْلَة, ونَبِيل ج نِبَال
Corpse, carcass. ◘ Silver armlets. نَبِيلَة ج نَبَائِل
Shooter. Arrow-maker. نَابِل ج نُبَّل, ونَبَّال ج نَبَّالَة
Clever, skilful. نَابِل م نَابِلَة
More clever. Better shooter. أَنْبَل
Lazy, slothful. تِنْبَال وتِنْبَالَة
Constantinople. G إِسْتَنْبُول
✠ نَبِهَ a نَبَهًا, وانْتَبَهَ ل To be mindful of. To heed a. th.
To awake from sleep. — نَبَهًا, وتَنَبَّهَ وانْتَبَهَ مِنَ النَّوْمِ
To be renowned, celebrated. نَبَهَ o ونَبِهَ a ونَبُهَ o نَبَاهَةً
To rouse, to remind a. o. of. To notify a. th. to. نَبَّهَ ه على او إلى
He called him by his name. — ه بِاسْمِهِ
He roused him from sleep. نَبَّهَ وأَنْبَهَ ه مِنَ النَّوْمِ
To forget a. th. أَنْبَهَ ه
To be mindful. To have notice of. تَنَبَّهَ على ول
✧ To be wary, to guard against. إِنْتَبَهَ
Awakening. Sagacity. نُبْه
Stray-beast found by chance. نَبَه

I chanced to find it. وَجَدْتُهَا نَبَهًا
Renown, illustriousness. Nobility. نَبَاهَة
Heed, awakening. Wariness. إِنْتِبَاه
The fox. أَبُو نَبْهَان
Remark, notice, summons. تَنْبِيه
Noble, celebrated, illustrious. نَابِه ونَبَه ونَبِه, ونَبِيه ج نُبَهَاء
Important affair. أَمْرٌ نَابِهٌ
High, eminent. نَبَاه
✧ Alarm-clock. مُنَبِّه
Incentive to. Memorandum. مُنَبِّهَة على
Forgotten affair. حَاجَة مُنْبَهَة
Wakeful, heedful. مُتَنَبِّه ومُنْتَبِه
To glance off, to take no effect (sword). ✠ نَبَا o نَبْوًا ونُبُوَّةً عَنِ الضَّرِيبَةِ
He was restless in bed. — جَنْبُهُ عَنِ الفِرَاشِ
To disagree with, to unfit a. o. (place). نَبَا ب
To be remote, opposed. To become dim (sight). نَبَا o نُبُوًّا ونُبِيًّا ونَبْوَةً
To shrink from. To miss the butt (arrow). — عَن
To blunt (a sword). أَنْبَى ه
Scorn, harshness of manners. نَبْوَة
Height. — ونَبَاوَة
Remote (thing). Blunt (sword). نَابٍ
Strongly cambered (bow). نَابِيَة
To boil (cooking-pot). ✠ نَتَّ i نَتِيتًا
His nostrils swelled from anger. — o مَنْخِرُهُ نَتًّا ونَتِيتًا
To divulge (news). نَتَّتَ ه
To swell up (wound). To be prominent. To protrude. To be marriageable (girl). ✠ نَتَأَ a نَتْأً ونُتُوءًا
To overtake a. o. To exalt o.'s self about. — على
To encounter. To be high, prominent. إِنْتَتَأَ
Hillock. Ascent. ◘ Tumour. نَتَأَة ونُتُوء
To swell, to grow. ✠ نَتَبَ o نُتُوبًا
To assist (a beast) in bringing forth. ✠ نَتَجَ i نَتْجًا ه
The wind has drawn forth rain from the clouds. نُتِجَتِ الرِّيحُ السَّحَابَ
To bring forth (female). نَتَجَتْ ونُتِجَتْ نِتَاجًا وَلَدًا, وأَنْتَجَتْ
✧ To improve (child). نَتَّجَ
To result from. — مِن

نَتَجَ وأَنْتَجَ ه مِن To deduce (a conclusion) from. To infer a. th. from.
أَنْتَجَ To be near to bring forth. To have pregnant females.
تَنَتَّجَ To be in parturition (female).
تَنَاتَجَ وانْتَتَجَ To breed (cattle).
إِسْتَنْتَجَ ه To deduce, to conclude a. th.
نِتَاج Parturition of beasts.
نَتِيجَة ج نَتَائِج Young beasts of the same year; brood. Conclusion of a syllogism. Result, consequence, fruit.
هُمَا نَتِيجَةٌ They are of the same year.
غَنَمِي نَتَائِج My ewes are of the same age.
بِالنَّتِيجَة ✦ Consequently therefore, in short.
نَاتِج Assisting a female in bringing forth. ✦ Growing.
نَتُوج On the point of bringing forth.
مَنْتِج Time of parturition
مِنْتَجَة Rump of animals.
✲ نَتَحَ a نَتْحًا ونُتُوحًا To exude (sweat). To become moist (skin).
— ه To make a. o. to sweat (heat).
نَتْح Sweat.
نُتُوح *Pl.* Tree-resin.
مَنْتَح ج مَنَاتِح Pores of the skin.
مِنْتَحَة Rump (of beasts).
✲ نَتَخَ i نَتْخًا ه To pull off. To pluck (the hair).
— بِبَصَرِهِ إلى To gaze at.
مِنْتَاخ Tweezers, pincers.
✲ نَتَرَ o نَتْرًا ه To snatch a. th. To pull a. th. violently. To rend (a garment). To brace (a bow).
نَتَرَ ه بِ To spear a. o.
— الكَلَامَ To utter violent language.
نَتِرَ a نَتَرًا To be damaged: to perish.
إِنْتَتَرَ To be pulled.
نَتْر Weakness. Harshness.
قَابَلَهُ بِنَتْرٍ He received him harshly.
نَتْرَة ج نَتَرَات Penetrative thrust.
نَاتِرَة ج نَوَاتِر Bow breaking its string.
✲ نَتَشَ i نَتْشًا ه To pull out (a thorn). To extract a. th. To pluck out (hair). To pinch and pull (meat) with the beak (hawk).
— لِ To earn for (o.'s family).
مَا نَتَشَ مِنْهُ شَيْئًا He has not obtained the least thing from him.

يَنْتِشُ مِن كُلِّ عِلْمٍ He acquires knowledge in every branch.
بِئْرٌ لَا تُنْتَش Inexhaustible well.
نَتَشَ i نَتْشًا وتَنْتَاشًا ه To backbite a. o.
أَنْتَشَ To germinate (seed); to sprout (plant).
نَتْش Germ, sprout.
مِنْتَاش Tweezers.
✲ نَتَعَ o نُتُوعًا To exude (sweat, blood). ◻ To carry away.
أَنْتَعَ To sweat much.
✲ نَتَغَ o i نَتْغًا ه To slander a. o.
أَنْتَغَ To scoff, to mock.
مِنْتَغ Calumniator.
✲ نَتَفَ i نَتْفًا ونَتَّفَ ه To pluck out (hair, feathers).
تَنَتَّفَ وتَنَاتَفَ وانْتَتَفَ To be plucked (hair, feathers).
نَتْف Plucking of the hair.
نُتْفَة ج نُتَف What is plucked with the hand, pinch. A little of.
أَعْطَاهُ نُتْفَةً مِن He has given him a little of.
نُتَاف ونُتَافَة Falling hair, feathers.
نُتَفَة Shallow, superficial (man).
نَتِيف Depilated (camel).
مِنْتَاف Tweezers.
✲ نَتَقَ o i نَتْقًا To be prolific (woman). ✦ To vomit.
— o نُتُوقًا To become fat.
نَتَقَ i نَتْقًا ونُتُوقًا ه To jolt (his rider horse).
— ه To shake a. th. To draw up (a bucket). To strike (fire). To shake (a sack).
أَنْتَقَ To build a house opposite to another's. To marry a woman having many children.
نَتْق ونِتَاق ✦ Vomit.
دَارُهُ نِتَاقُ دَارِي His house is opposite to mine.
نَاتِق Yielding fire (flint). Jolting his rider (beast). The month of Ramadhan.
— ومِنْتَاق Prolific (woman).
مُنْتِق ✦ Emetic.
✲ نَتَلَ i نَتْلًا ه To drag a. o. To empty (a bag).
— ه To revile a. o.

To rush forth from the lines (soldier). نتل i نتلا ونتولا ونتلانا, واستنتل من
To become tangled (herbage). تناتل
To become ready for fight. — واستنتل
Ostrich's egg filled with water and buried in the sand. نتل ونتل
Near relationship. نتيلة
✱ نتن i ونتن a نتنا, ونتن o نتونة ونتانة وأنتن
To stink (meat).
To infect, to taint a. th. نتّن ه
Stench, fetor. نتن ونتانة
نتن ونتين ومُنتِن ومِنتِن, ومِنتين ج مَناتين
Stinking.
Fetid tree. *Mercurialis annua* (plant). نيتون ونتين
Vest, jacket, waistcoat with sleeves. ✧ مِنتِيان
Bean-trefoil. Hemp-nettle (*plants*). مِنتِنة
To swell (limb). ✱ نتا o نتوًّا
To lag behind; to retire backward. أنتى
To resemble a. o. — ه
To assault a. o. تنتّى على
To break (abscess). استنتى
Swollen (limb). Prominent, jutting. ناتٍ م ناتية
To divulge (news). To anoint (a wound). ✱ نثّ o i نثًّا ه
To ooze (oil). — i ه نثيثا ونثًّا
To communicate news to o. a. تناثّ
Moist, damp (wall). نثّ
Ointment. نثاث
Moisture exuded by a skin. نثيثة
Piece of wool for anointing. مِنثّة ج مَناثّ ومنثّات
To rip up (the belly). ✱ نثج i نثجا ه
He relieved his bowels. — ما في بطنه
To hang down; to be unsteady (load). إستنثج
Cipher, coward. نثج
Buttocks. نثج ومنثجة
To stand still. To grow (truffle). ✱ نثد a نثودًا
To scatter, to sprinkle, to disperse a. th. ✱ نثر o i نثرًا ونثارًا, ونثّر ه
He spoke much. — الكلام
He had numerous children. — الولد
He bore much fruit (tree). — الثمار
He took off (the coat of mail). — ه عنه

✧ To fall off (tree-leaves). نثر
To sneeze (beast). — i نثيرا
To blow o.'s nose. To snuff up water. أنثر
To throw a. o. down upon the nose. To make the nose to bleed. — ه
To be scattered, strewn. To fall off (hair, leaves). تنثّر وتناثر وانتثر
To fall sick and die (people). تناثر
To snuff up (water) and reject it. إنتثر واستنثر
Prose; rhyming (*opp. to* نظم) prose. ✧ Embroidery on cloth. نثر
Interstice between the mustaches. Cartilage of the nose. Ample coat of mail. Sneeze (of a beast). نثرة
Falling particles. Loquacity. نثر
Loquacious, divulger. نثِر ونيثران ومنثار
Good milch-ewes. Prolific. نثور
Scattered. Shedding its leaves (rose). نثير
Scattered particles. Crumbs of a table. نثار ونثارة
Money, fruit scattered at a feast. نِثار
Prosaist. Sneezing (ewe). ناثر
Scattered, dispersed. Cipher (man). ✧ Embroidered (cloth). مُنتثر
Palm-tree shaking off its dates. مِنثار
Prose. *Papaver erraticum*, kind of poppy. Gilliflower. منثور
To press a. o. upon the ground for silencing him. ✱ نثط o نثطا ه
To overburden a. o. — نثطا ونثوطا ه
To quiet, to appease a. o. نثّط ه
To vomit much. To bleed (nose). ✱ نثع — أنثع
To dung (horse). ✱ نثل o نثلا
To cleanse (a well). — o i وانتثل ه
To empty (a quiver). نثّل واستنثل ه
To take off (a coat of mail). — ه عنه
To put (a coat of mail) upon. — ه على فلان
To rush together against. تناثل إلى
Cleansed (ditch). نثيل
Large coat of mail. Dimple between the mustaches. نثلة
Horse's dung. نثيل
Earth taken from a well. نثالة ونثيلة
Remains, rubbish. نثيلة

* نَثَمَ i نَثْمًا, وانتثم — To hold unseemly talks.

* نَثَا o نَثْوًا ه — To divulge (news). To scatter a. th.

تَنَاثَى — To remind o. a. of.

نَثًا — Anecdote, mention.

* نَثَى i نَثْيًا ه — To divulge (news).

أَنْثَى ٥ — To backbite a. o.

— مِن — To be ashamed of.

* نَجَّ i نَجًّا ونَجِيجًا — To hasten. To flow with purulent matter (abscess).

نَجُوج — Swift.

* نَجْنَجَ ه — To move, to stir a. th.

— أمرًا — To ponder over (an affair) without undertaking it.

تَنَجْنَجَ — To be agitated, perplexed.

* نَجَأَ a نَجْأً, وتَنَجَّأَ وانتجأ ٥ — To smite a. o. with the evil eye.

نَجُؤٌ ونَجِيءٌ ونَجُوءُ ونَجِيءُ العَيْن — Evil-eyed.

نُجْأَة السَّائِل — Evil eye of a beggar.

* نَجُبَ o نَجَابَةً, وأَنْجَبَ — To be noble-born (man). To be generous.

نَجَبَ o i نَجْبًا, ونَجَّبَ وانتجب ه — To bark (a tree).

أَنْجَبَ — To beget generous sons. To beget a cowardly son.

تَنَجَّبَ — To perform a generous deed.

إِنْتَجَبَ واستنجب ه — To choose, to select a. th.

نَجْب ونُجَبَة — Noble, generous.

نَجَب — Bark of a root or of a tree.

نَجَابَة — Nobility of race. Generosity.

نَجِيب ج نُجُب ونُجَبَاء وأنجاب — Noble-born. Generous. Excellent, good-breed (beast).

نَجَائِب ونَوَاجِب — The best parts.

مِنْجَاب (*m. f.*) ج مَنَاجِيب, ومُنْجِب م مُنْجِبَة ج مُنْجِبَات ومَنَاجِب — Having noble sons.

* نَجَثَ o نَجْثًا, وتَنَجَّثَ عن — To scrutinise.

نَجَثَ ٥ — To cry out to a. o. for help.

تَنَاجَثَ — To reveal secrets o. to a.

إِنْتَجَثَ واستنجث ه — To draw out, to extract a. th.

نَجْث ونُجُث — Coat of mail. Pericardium.

— ج أنجاث — House.

نَجِيث ونَجَّاث — Searcher, inquirer.

نَجِيث — Hidden secret. Mound used as a butt for shooters.

نَجِيثَة — Bad news divulged. Endeavour.

بَلَغَت نَجِيثَتُهُ — He has exerted himself to the utmost.

* نَجَحَ a نَجْحًا ونُجْحًا ونَجَاحًا, وأنجح — To be accomplished (affair).

— في — To succeed in; to attain (a want).

نَجَّحَ ه و٥ — To help a.o. to attain a. th.

مَا أَنْجَحَ فُلَانٌ — Such a one did not succeed.

أَنْجَحَ ه ل — To make a. o. to prosper (God).

— ب — To overcome a. o.

تَنَجَّحَ واستنجح ه — To accomplish (an affair) successfully.

تَنَاجَحَ — To become true (dream).

إِسْتَنْجَحَ ٥ ه — To beg of (God) the success of.

نُجْح ونَجَاح — Success; attainment of a want.

نَجَاحَة — Patience.

نَاجِح م نَاجِحَة — Successful (affair). Thriving.

— ونَجِيح — Vehement (walk), quick pace.

نَجِيح م نَجِيحَة — Patient (mind).

— ومُنْجِح ج مَنَاجِح ومَنَاجِيح — Successful, attaining a want.

رَأْي نَجِيح — Right counsel.

* نَجَخَ a نَجْخًا — To boast, to glory. To eat away its margin (river). To arise (disturbance).

تَنَاجَخَ — To boast together. To dash together (waves).

نَاجِخ ونَجُوخ — Roaring (sea).

نَاجِخ — Roaring of the sea.

* نَجَدَ o نَجْدًا, وأنجد ٥ — To overcome, to prevail over a. o.

نَجَدَ o نُجُودًا — To become manifest (affair).

نَجِدَ a نَجَدًا — To sweat. To become stupid, dull.

— ونُجِدَ نَجْدًا — To be oppressed by grief.

نَجُدَ o نَجَادَةً ونَجْدَة — To be courageous.

نَجَّدَ ه — To furnish (a house). To trim, to stuff (beds, pillows).

نَجَّدَ ٥ — To render a. o. experienced (time).

نَاجَدَ ٥ — To assist a. o. To come forth to fight a. o.

He has attained the عضَّ على ناجِذِه
age of puberty.

War has been أَبْدَت الحَرْبُ ناجِذَيْهَا
vehement.

Silphium (plant). أَنْجَدان

Mole-rats. (*pl. of* جُلَذ *and of* خُلَذ) مَناجِذ

٭ نَجَرَ o نَجْرًا To be hot (summer-
day). To prepare a food of milk and
butter.

To hew, to fashion (wood : car- ه —
penter). To determine upon, to undertake a. th. To warm (water) with
heated stones.

To fillip a. o. To urge (camels) ة —
vehemently.

To suffer from thirst. نَجِرَ a نَجَرًا

To feed a. o. with milk and flour. ة أَنْجَرَ

Origin. Shape of a beast. Per- نَجْر
sonal attainment. Nobility. Territory
of Mecca or of Medinah.

Violent access of thirst. نَجَر

Origin, root. Colour. نِجَار ونُجَار

Carpentry. نِجَارَة

Chips, parings of wood. نُجَارَة

Hot summer-month. ناجِر

Carpenter. نَجَّار ج نَجَّارُون

Milk mixed with flour or butter. نَجِيرَة

لَأَنْجُرَنَّ نَجِيرَتَكَ I will reward thee according to thy merit.

Hook of a door. Town in Arabia نَجْران
and in Hauran.

Seized with intense thirst نَجِر ونَجِرِي
(camel).

Anchor. P أَنْجَر وأَنْجَرَة ج أَناجِر

Nettle (*plant*). أَنْجَرَة

Point aimed at. مَنْجَر

Heated stone for warming مِنْجَرَة
water.

Hewn wood. Water-pulley. مَنْجُور
✧ Wainscoting of a house.

٭ نَجَزَ o نَجْزًا, ونَجُرَ وأَنْجَزَ ه To achieve,
to perform (an affair).

To come to end, to ونَجِزَ a نَجَزًا
perish. To be accomplished (affair).
To be fulfilled (promise).

To come forth against a. o. ناجَزَ ة

To fulfil (a promise). أَنْجَزَ ه

To give the last stroke to (a على —
wounded man).

To go to Nejd. To sweat from أَنْجَدَ
grief. To become high (building).
To become serene (sky).

To assist, to help a. o. ه وه
To answer (a call).

To become high, lofty. تَنَجَّدَ

To recover strength. إِسْتَنْجَدَ

To ask for assistance from. ة وب —

To be emboldened against. على —

Skilful guide. Nejd. highland of نَجْد
Arabia.

— ج أَنْجُد وأَنْجَاد ونِجَاد ونُجُود ونِجَاد وجج
Stony table-land. Elevated أَنْجِدَة
road.

He can هُوَ طَلَّاع أَنْجُد ونِجَاد وأَنْجِدَة
manage affairs thoroughly.

House-furniture (as نَجَد ج نُجُود ونِجَاد
carpets, beds, curtains).

Sweat from sorrow. Impediment نَجَد
in speech.

Courage, vigour. Fight. نَجْدَة ج نَجَدَات
Adversity. Fright. Aid.

From Nejd (horse). نَجْدِي

Suspensory of a sword. نِجَاد

Of high stature رَجُل طَوِيل النِّجَاد
(man).

Gallantry, courage, bravery. نَجَادَة

Mattress-maker. نَجَّادَة

Brave, coura- نَجُد ونَجِد ونُجُد ج أَنْجَاد
geous.

Brave. Grieved. نَجِيد ج نُجُد ونُجَدَاء

Long-necked, spirited (camel). نُجُود

Tall and intelligent woman. — ج نُجُد

Stupid, dull, ناجِد م ناجِدَة ج نَواجِد
weary.

Stuffer of mattresses. نَجَّاد ومُنَجِّد

Wine. Saffron. Blood. ناجُود ج نَواجِيد
Wine-vessel.

Small mountain. Neck- مِنْجَد ج مَناجِد
lace of pearls and gold.

Rod for urging a beast. مِنْجَدَة ج مَناجِد
Wooden instrument for wool.

Aid. Fighter. مُناجِد

Afflicted. Subdued. مَنْجُود

٭ نَجَذَ i نَجْذًا To bite, to catch a. th.
with the molar teeth.

To importune a. o. ة —

To try a. o. (fortune). نَجَّذَ ة

Molar tooth. ناجِذ ج نَواجِذ

تَنَجَّزَ الشَّرابَ He addicted himself to drink.
تَنَجَّزَ واستَنجَزَ ه To achieve a. th. successfully. To ask the fulfilment of (a promise).
تَناجَزَ To contend, to fight together.
نَجْز ونَجاز Achievement, fulfilment.
هُوَ عَلَى نَجْزِ حاجَتِهِ He is on the eve of accomplishing his affair.
ناجِز ونَجِيز م ناجِزَة ونَجِيزَة Present, ready (money).
بِعْتُهُ ناجِزًا بِناجِزٍ I sold it for ready money.
مُناجَزَة وتَناجُز Fight.
✻ نَجِسَ a نَجَسًا ونَجُسَ o نَجاسَة To be unclean, impure, filthy.
نَجَّسَ وأَنجَسَ ه وه To defile. To contaminate. To render a. o. impure.
تَنَجَّسَ To become defiled, impure. To purify o.'s self.
نَجاسَة Filthiness. Legal impurity.
نَجْس ونَجَس ونَجِس ونَجُس ج أَنجاس Filthy, impure, unclean.
ناجِس ونَجِس ونَجِيس Incurable (disease).
تَنجِيس Amulet made of unclean things.
مُنَجِّس Maker of unclean amulets.
✻ نَجَشَ o نَجْشًا في To connive for ensnaring another in (a sale).
— ه To rouse, to track (the game). To search after a. th. To collect. To draw forth. To kindle (the fire).
— o نَجْشًا ونِجاشَةً To hurry. to press on.
تَناجَشَ في To outbid a. o. at (a sale).
إِستَنجَشَ ه To extract a. th. To start (game).
نَجْش Connivance for ensnaring another in a sale.
ناجِش ونَجاشِيّ ونَجّاش ومِنجاش Beater of the chase; hunter.
نَجِيش ونَجّاش Huntsman, starter.
نِجاش ونَجاشِيّ Negus, king of the Abyssinians.
✻ نَجَعَ a نَجْعًا ونُجُوعًا, وأَنجَعَ To be wholesome, beneficial (food).
— نَجَعَ في To be efficacious (medicine, speech). To act upon.
نَجَعَ وتَنَجَّعَ وانتَجَعَ واستَنجَعَ To seek for pasturages.
نَجَعَ ه او ب To give to (camels) water and flour to drink.
نُجِعَ ب To be fattened by. To benefit of.
أَنجَعَ To thrive.
— ه To give milk to (a youngling: shepherd).
تَنَجَّعَ وانتَجَعَ ه To ask a favour from.
طَعامٌ يُنجَعُ او يُستَنجَعُ بِهِ او عَنهُ Wholesome food.
نُجعَة ج نُجَع Foraging.
ناجِع ج ناجِعَة ونَواجِع Beating about for pasturages, forager.
شُجاع نُجاع Very courageous.
نَجُوع Water mixed with flour or grain. Wholesome (water).
— الصَّبِيّ Milk.
نَجِيع Wholesome (food). Efficacious (speech). Blackish (blood). Leaves shaken off and made into paste for cattle.
مَنجَع Pasturage.
مُنتَجَع ومُستَنجَع Place in which pasturages are searched.
مُنتَجَع Station in pasturage.
✻ نَجَفَ o نَجْفًا ه To fashion (an arrow). To cut (a tree) at the root.
— وانتَجَفَ ه To milk out (a ewe).
نَجَّفَ ه To drift (sand-hills: wind).
— إِفُلانٍ نُجفَة مِن He gave away to a. o. a little of.
إِنتَجَفَ واستَنجَفَ ه To shake (the clouds), to cause (rain: wind).
نَجَف ج نِجاف Mound, sand-hill. Place spared by a flood. Dam.
نَجَفَة Sand-drift. ◘ Chandelier, lustre.
نَجَفَة الكَثِيب Sand-drifts, dunes.
نُجفَة Small quantity, little of.
نِجاف Threshold; lintel.
نَجِيف ج نُجُف, ومَنجُوف Broad-headed (spear).
مِنجَف ج مَناجِف Basket.
◊ T أَنجاق Scarcely, hardly.
✻ نَجَلَ o نَجْلًا To become verdant (soil).
— ه وب To beget (a son: father).
— ه To kick a. o. on the buttocks. To ill-treat a. o.
— ه To rip up, to skin (a beast) from the hocks. To till (the ground).

I allowed him to pay his debt by instalments. جعلتُ مالي عليهِ نجوماً
This information is groundless. ليس لهذا الحديث نَجمٌ
Graminaceous plant. A star. ✧ Blaze on a beast. Asterisk. نَجمة
Stalkless plant. Word. نَجمة
Dactylis repens, species of dog-grass. نَجَمة
The Pleiads. النَّجم
Astronomy. Astrology. عِلم النُّجوم
Ass. ذو النَّجمة
Astrologer. Astronomer. نَجّام ومُنَجِّم ومُتَنَجِّم
Well traced road. Mine. Source, origin. مَنجَم ج مَناجِم
Iron-beam of a balance. مِنجَم
Ankle. — ومَنجِم
To drive back a. o. ✡ نَجه a نَجهاً, وتَنَجَّه وانتجه ة
To be saved, to escape from. ✡ نَجا o نَجواً ونَجاء ونَجاة ونَجاية مِن
He saved his life. نَجا برأسِهِ
To rush forth. — نَجاء
To trim (a tree). — نَجواً, وأنجى واستنجى ه
To skin (a beast). — نَجواً ونَجا, وأنجى ه
To whisper (a secret) to. — نَجواً ونَجوَى, وناجَى مُناجاةً ونِجاءً ة
To rescue a. o. (from danger). نَجَّى وأنجى ة مِن
To raise (a field) against flooding. نَجَّى ه
To clear away (clouds). To have ripe dates (palm-tree). أنجى
To disclose, to lay a. th. bare. — ه
To bring a. o. to a prominent place. — ة
To search for a raised ground. تَنَجَّى
To whisper in the ear to. تَناجَى وانتجى
To take a. o. as a confidant. إنتجى ة
To quicken the walk. To purify o.'s self after excretion. إستنجى
To be delivered from. — مِن
To obtain a. th. from. — ه مِن فلان
To draw (a bowstring). — ه
Hide. Frame of a camel-litter. نَجا

To disclose. To manifest a. th.
To strike off pebbles (camel). To throw a. th. نَجَل i نَجلاً ه وب
To erase (a writing). — ه
To pierce a. o. with (a spear). — ة ب
To have large eyes. نَجِل a نَجَلاً
To pasture (cattle) on herbage. أنجَل ة
To come to fight together. To have numerous offspring. تَناجَل
To appear and disappear. To remove water from the foot of a wall. إنتجل
To become swampy (ground). إستنجل
Offspring. Child. Father. Water oozing from the ground. Flowing water. Crowd. نَجل ج أنجال
Father. Thorough bred (horse). ناجل
Wide-eyed. أنجَل م نَجلاء ج نُجل ونِجال
Wide (eye). Opening a large wound (spear-thrust). نَجلاء
Bitter plant sought by camels. Bastard dittany. نَجيل ج نُجُل
Reaping-hook. Opening a wide wound (spear). Luxuriant (crops). Clever camel-driver. مِنجَل ج مَناجِل
The Gospel. The New Testament. إنجيل ج أناجيل G
Evangelist. إنجيليّ
Couch-grass. ✧ شِلْـش الإنجيل
To appear. To rise (star). ✡ نَجَم o نُجوماً, وأنجم
To ooze (water). To grow (tooth). To come out (heretic). To result. نَجَم
To accomplish a. th. To pay (a debt) by instalments. — نُجوماً, ونَجَّم ه
To astrologise. نَجَّم وتَنَجَّم
To be over (cold, rain). To clear away (weather). أنجم وانتجم
To observe the stars (astronomer). تَنَجَّم
Star. Appointed time. Grass; germinaceous plant. True origin. نَجم ج أنجُم وأنجام ونُجوم ونُجُم
May thy star rise *i. e.* be happy! علا نَجمُك
He ponders over what he has to do. ينظر في النُّجوم

Delivery, salvation. نجو ونجا ونجاة ونجاء

Make thy escape. النَّجاكَ النَّجاكَ والنَّجاءَكَ النَّجاءَكَ

Cloud that has discharged rain. Excrement. Secret confided. نَجْو ج نِجاء

Secret confided. Confidants. نَجْوَى ج نَجاوَى

Elevated ground. Swift (camel). نَجاة ج نَجًى, ونَجْوَة ج نِجاء

He is free from evil. هُوَ بِنَجْوَةٍ مِنَ الشَّرّ

Large tract of land. نَجاوَة

Secret. Confidant. نَجِيّ ج أَنْجِيَة

Swift (camel). ناجٍ

Shelter, place of refuge. Elevated ground. مَنْجًى ج مَناجٍ

Means of salvation. مَنْجاة ج مَناجٍ

Truth is the means of salvation. أَلصِّدْقُ مَنْجاة

Confidential intercourse. مُناجاة

✱ To reciprocate a sound, a humming in the throat. نَحَّ i نَحِيحًا

Avarice. Bountifulness. نَحاحَة

Avaricious. شَحِيح نَحِيح

✱ To reiterate a pectoral sound. نَحْنَح وتَنَحْنَح

To repel (a beggar) shockingly. ه —

✱ To weep, to wail loudly. نَحَب a i نَحْبًا ونَحِيبًا

To cough (camel). — i نَحْبًا ونُحابًا

To bet. — a نَحْبًا

To bind o.'s self by vow. — o نَحْبًا, ونَحَّب

To travel at a quick pace. نَحَب ونَحَّب في السَّيْر

To work strenuously. To go hastily to water. نَحَّب

To apply o.'s self to. — على

To cite a. o. to (a judge). To bet with a. o. ناحَب ه

To appoint a time for fighting. تَناحَب

To wail, to sob. إِنْتَحَب

Weeping. Quick journey. Exertion. Gentle or rapid walk. Dixed time. Vow. Wager. A necessity. Game of hazard. Death. نَحْب

He is dead. قَضَى نَحْبَهُ

Lots. Sortilege. نُحْبَة

Wail, weeping. نَحِيب

Weeping. ناحِب ومُنْتَحِب

Rapid walk. سَيْر مُنَحِّب

✱ To cut, to sculpture (stones). To hew (wood). نَحَت o i ونَحِت a نَحْتًا ه

He cut out a house in the mountain. — بَيْتًا في الجَبَل ومِن الجَبَل

To emaciate (a beast : journey) to prostrate a. o. — ه

To blame, to revile a. o. — ه بِلِسانِهِ

He impaired his reputation. — عِرْضَهُ

He was made generous by nature. نُحِتَ على الكَرَم

He hewed off wood. إِنْتَحَت مِن الخَشَبَة

Cutting, sculpture. نَحْت

Nature, constitution. — ونَحات ونَحِيتَة

Chips, parings of wood. نُحاتَة

Stone-cutter. Sculpter. نَحّات

Wail. Abraded (hoof). Stranger to a tribe. نَحِيت

Cut out, polished (stone). Sculptured. نَحِيت ومَنْحُوت

Adz ; sculptor's chisel. مِنْحَت ومِنْحات ج مَناحِت ومَناحِيت

✱ To stab in the throat ; to slaughter (a beast). نَحَر a نَحْرًا وتَنْحارًا ه

He has a deep knowledge in science. نَحَر الأُمُورَ عِلْمًا

My house is seated opposite to his. — دارِي دارَهُ

To wound a. o. in the throat. ناحَرَ ه

To seize o. a. by the throat. تَناحَر وانْتَحَر على

To face o. a. (houses). تَناحَر

To commit suicide. إِنْتَحَر

The day of sacrifice, the 10 th of the month Zu-elhidge. يَوْم النَّحْر

Upper part of the chest, of the throat. Beginning of a day, of a month. نَحْر ج نُحُور

I met him openly. لَقِيتُهُ صَحْرَةً بَحْرَةً نَحْرَةً

Slaughterer, stabber. ناحِر ونَحُور

ناحِرَة ج ناحِرات ونَواحِر ونَحِيرَة ج نَحائِر

First or last day, first or last night of a month.

The two jugular veins. أَلنّاحِرانِ والنّاحِرَتانِ

Skilful, experienced. نِحْر, ونِحْرِير ج نَحارِير

Slaughtered (camel). نَحِير ج نَحْرَى ونُحَراء ونَحائِر, ومَنْحُور

Part in which a beast is stabbed. Place of sacrifice. مَنْحَر

To be corpulent (she-camel). ✻ نَحَص a نُحُوصًا
He paid him his due. – لِفُلَانٍ بِحَقِّهِ نَحصًا
Foot of a mountain. نَحص
Yielding no milk from fatness (she-ass). نَحُوص ج نَحَائِص ونُحُص
Corpulent, bulky (she-camel). نَحُوص ونَحِيص
To strip (a bone). ✻ نَحَض a i نَحضًا, وانتَحَض ه
To sharpen (a spear-head). To importune a. o. with requests. نَحَض ه وه
To become emaciated. نَحَض a نُحُوضًا, ونُحِض وأُنتُحِض
To have compact flesh. نَحُض o نَحَاضَةً
Compact flesh. نَحض ج نُحُوض ونِحَاض
Piece of compact flesh. نَحضَة ج نِحَاض ونَحَضَات
Fleshy. Emaciated. Thin (spear-head). نَحِيض ومَنحُوض
To sigh, to moan. ✻ نَحَط i نَحِيطًا
To pant, to be out of breath. – نَحطًا ونَحِيطًا
Stifled sob. نَحط ونُحَاط ونَحِيط
Seized with violent cough. نَاحِط
Proud, haughty. نَحَّاط
To be naturally lank, meagre. ✻ نَحِف a ونَحُف o نَحَافَةً
To emaciate a. o. أَنحَف ه
Emaciation, lankness. نَحَافَة
Thin and lean. نَحِف ج نَحِفُون, ونَحِيف ج نِحَاف ونُحَفَاء, ومَنحُوف
To become emaciated from fatigue or disease. ✻ نَحِل a ونَحَل a o ونَحُل o نُحُولًا
To give a wedding-present to (a bride); to give a.th. freely to a. o. نَحَل a نُحلًا ه
To revile a. o. To attribute falsely (words, verses) to a. o. – نَحلًا ه ه
✧ To warm rooms for nursing silkworms. نَحَّل
To give to a. o. part of o.'s property. – وأَنحَل ه ه
✧ To swarm (bees). أَنحَل
To emaciate, to exhaust a. o. (fatigue, disease). أَنحَل ه
He boasted falsely تَنَحَّل وانتَحَل شِعرَ غَيرِهِ

Slaughterer. Hospitable. مِنحَار
To pound a. th. in a mortar. ✻ نَحَز a نَحزًا ه
To kick back a. o. – ه ب
He boxed him on the chest. – ه فِي صَدرِهِ
To have a disease of the lungs (camel). نَحِز, ونُحِز a نَحزًا
To have diseased camels. أَنحَز
Disease of the lungs among (camels). نُحَاز
Root, source, origin. – ونِحَاز
Nature ; condition, state. نَحِيزَة ج نَحَائِز
Uneven and hard ground. Long tract of land.
Diseased in the lungs (camel). نَحِز ونَاحِز ونَحِيز ومَنحُوز
Mortar. مِنحَاز
✻ نَحِس a نَحسًا, ونَحُس o نُحُوسَةً ونَحَاسَةً
To be inauspicious, unlucky.
To harass a. o. نَحَس a نَحسًا ه
To overlay a. th. with copper. نَحَّس ه
To inquire minutely about. – وتَنَحَّس واستَنحَس ه
To fast before taking a medicine. To abstain from flesh-meat (Christian). تَنَحَّس
To fall headlong. To relapse (sick man). تَنَاحَس وانتَحَس
Ill-luck. (opp. to سَعد) نَحس ج نُحُوس
Distress. Unprosperous (day).
The two inauspicious planets i. e. Saturn and Mars. النَّحسَان
The three last nights of a lunar month. النُّحَس
Copper. Brass. Sparks, shatters of iron when beaten. Nature, temper. نُحَاس ونِحَاس
He is naturally generous. هُوَ كَرِيم النُّحَاس
Piece of copper. نُحَاسَة
نَحس ونَحِس ونَاحِس ونَحِيس م نَحسَة ونَحِسَة ونَاحِسَة ونَحِيسَة
Inauspicious, fatal.
Year of drought, of dearth. عَام نَاحِس ونَحِيس
Coppersmith. نَحَّاس
Inauspicious events. مَنَاحِس
Unprosperous, unlucky. مَنحُوس م مَنحُوسَة

نْحْوِيٌّ وَ نَحَوِيٌّ جِ نَحْوِيُّون وَنَحَوِيُّون، وَنَاسٍ
جِ نَحَاة Grammarian. ◊ Pedantic.

Side. نَاحَاة وَنَاحِيَة جِ نَوَاحٍ وَنَاحِيَات
Region. District, limit.

Towards, in the direc- نَاحِيَة وَفِي نَاحِيَة
tion of.

To churn (milk). نَحَى a i نَحْيًا ه ✱
He directed his looks نَحَى بَصَرَهُ إِلَى
towards.

To displace, to take a. th. – وَنَحَى ه
away.

To point at, to strike a. o. أَنْحَى ل ه
with (a weapon).

He lashed him with a – عَلَيْهِ بِالسَّوْطِ
whip.

To be discarded. تَنَحَّى

To lean upon. To apply o.'s اِنْتَحَى فِي
self to.

Milk-skin; churning-vessel. نَحْى جِ أَنْحَاء

Churn. Broad- نِحْى جِ أَنْحَاء وَنُحِيّ وَنِحَاء
headed arrow.

Aim, object in aim. نَجِيَّة

He is the butt of the هُوَ نَجِيَّة الْقَوَارِع
strokes of fortune.

Distance. Winding مَنْحَاة جِ مَنَاحٍ
stream.

The absent; those who أَهْل الْمَنْحَاة
are remote.

To walk strenuously. نَخَّ o نَخًّا ✱

◊ To stoop; to lower the head.

To urge (a beast) vehemently. ه –

To utter a grunt نَخَّ ه وَب وَ نَخَّة ه
for making (a camel) to kneel.

Oblong carpet. نَخَّة جِ أَنْخَاخ

Working beasts. Slave-drivers. نُخَّة
◊ Stoop.

Beasts of burden. Shepherds. نُخَّة

Ammi, bishop's P نَانَخَة وَنُوَنْخَة وَنَانُخَة
wort.

To make (a camel) to نَخْنَخ ه وه ✱
kneel. To discard a. th.

To lay upon the breast (camel). تَنَخْنَخ

To bite (ant, louse). نَخَب o نُخْبًا ✱
To tear out (the game : hawk).

To take forth a. th. To take the ه –
best of.

To be cowardly. نَخِب a نَخَبًا

To beget a cowardly son. To أَنْخَب
beget a brave son.

of verses made by another; he pla-
giarised.

To profess, to adopt (a re- اِنْتَحَل ه
ligion).

Bees A bee. (un. نَحْلَة) (coll). نَحْل
Gift, present. نَحَل وَنُحْل وَنُحْلَى وَنُحْلَان

Gift. Dowry. نِحْلَة وَنُحْلَة جِ نِحَل وَنُحَل
wedding-present. False pretention.
Lawsuit. Religious sect.

Emaciation. نُحُول

Plagiarism, literary theft. اِنْتِحَال

Exhausted. Lean, thin. نَاحِل جِ نَحْلَى وَنُحَّل

Thinned by use (sword). نَاحِلَة جِ نَوَاحِل

Exhausted, emaciated. نَحِيل جِ نَحْلَى

◊ Warmed room for silkworms. مَنْحَل

To heave, to نَحَم i نَحْمًا وَنَحِيمًا وَنَحَمَانًا ✱
pant (horse).

Kind of flamingo. نُحَام

Panting. Avaricious. نَحَّام

Pronoun of the نَحْنُ وَ ◊ نِحْن وَنَحْنَا ✱
first person of the dual and plural.
We.

To direct نَحَا a o نَحْوًا، وَانْتَحَى ه وه ✱
o.'s self towards.

He followed the same course نَحَا نَحْوَهُ
as he; he had the same design.

He directed his looks نَحَا بَصَرَهُ إِلَى
towards.

To stoop, to lean. نَحَا o نَحْوًا

To discard a. o. from. – ه عَن

To put a. th. aside from. نَحَى ه عَن
To ward off a. th. from.

To lean on one side in أَنْحَى وَانْتَحَى
walking (camel).

He averted the looks from. أَنْحَى بَصَرَهُ عَن

To advance towards a. o. أَنْحَى عَلَى

To accost a. o. obliquely. ل – وَانْتَحَى

To go aside, apart. تَنَحَّى

To turn away from. عَن –

To lean upon a. th. تَنَحَّى وَانْتَحَى ل

Towards, near. About, the like. نَحْو

He went Eastwards. ذَهَب نَحْوَ الشَّرْق

As thou wouldst say; for نَحْو قَوْلِك
instance.

About ten thousand. نَحْو عَشَرَة آلَاف

Side, tract, country. Inten- نَحْو جِ أَنْحَاء
tion, design. Way, road.

Syntax of gram- – جِ أَنْحَاء وَلَحُوز وَنَحِيَّة
mar.

إِنْتَخَبَ ه To choose, to select a. th.
— ه To elect a. o. ✧ To predestinate a. o. (God).
نَخْب Cowardice. Large draught of wine for drinking healths; toast.
نُخْبَة ونُخَبَة ج نُخَب Choice part. Selected company.
نَخْب ونَخِب ونَخِبٌ ونُخَبٌ ونَخِيب ج نُخُب.
وأَنْخَب Cowardly, faint-hearted.
إِنْتِخَاب Choice, election. ✧ Predestination.
مُنْتَخَب ومَنْخُوب ويَنْخُوب Cowardly, faint-hearted.
مَنْخُوب Emaciated, lean.
مِنْخَاب Weak man; cipher.
✲ نَخَتَ o نَخْتًا To peck (bird).
✲ نَخَجَ a نَخْجًا ه وب To agitate (a bucket) in a well.
نَخَّجَ To dash against its banks (torrent).
نَخِيج Fine butter oozing from the skin.
P نَاخُذَاة ج نَوَاخِذ Ship-captain.
تَنَخَّذ To be the captain of a ship.
✲ نَخَرَ o i نَخْرًا ونَخِيرًا To snore; to snort.
— ه ✧ To eat a. th. away (worm).
نَخِرَ a نَخَرًا To be worm-eaten, wasted (wood). To crumble (bone).
نُخَرَة Hurricane.
— ونُخْرَة ج نُخَر Snout, forepart of the nose.
نَخِير Snoring.
مَا بِالدَّار نَاخِرٌ There is nobody in the house.
نَاخِر ج نُخُر Pig, wild boar.
نَاخِر ونَخِر م نَاخِرَة ونَخِرَة Decayed, crumbling (bone, wood).
نَخَّار Snorer. Pig.
نِخْوَار ج نَخَاوِرَة Noble, haughty. Weak.
مِنْخَر ومَنْخِر ومُنْخُر ومُنْخُر ومَنْخُور و✧ مِنْخَار ج
مَنَاخِر ومَنَاخِير Nostrils. Nose.
✲ نَخْرَبَ ه To eat away (a tree: worm).
نُخْرُوب ج نَخَارِيب Fissure; hole. Bee-cells.
✲ نَخَزَ a نَخْزًا ه ب To prick, to stab a. o. To sting a. o. in (words).
نَخْزَة Prick; thrust.

✲ نَخَسَ o a نَخْسًا ه To prick, to goad (a beast).
— ه وب To disturb, to arouse a. o.
— o a نَخْسًا To insert (a piece of wood) in a pulley.
نُخِسَ To waste away (flesh). To be scabby on the tail.
تَنَاخَسَ To mingle their waters (tanks).
نِخَاس ونِخَاسَة Wood inserted in the hole of a pulley.
نَخَاسَة ونِخَاسَة Slave-trade; cattle-trade.
نَخَّاس Goader. Seller of beasts. Seller of slaves.
نَاخِس Scab on a camel's tail.
— ونَخُوس Young antelope.
نَخِيس Loosened pulley provided with a piece of wood.
نَخِيسَة Ewe and goat's milk mixed together.
مِنْخَس ج مَنَاخِس Goad. Spur.
مَنْخُوس Goaded. Scabby on the tail (camel)
✲ نَخَشَ a نَخْشًا ونُخِشَ To become lean.
نَخِشَ a نَخَشًا To be worn out in the lower part (thing).
نَخَشَ o نَخْشًا ه وه To urge (a beast). To incite a. o. To shake a. th. To bark (wood). To harm a. o.
تَنَخَّشَ إلى To direct o.'s self towards.
✧ نَخْشُوش ج نَخَاشِيش Gill of fishes.
✲ نَخَصَ o a نَخْصًا ه To become emaciated through old age.
— وأَنْخَصَ ه To emaciate a. o. (old age)
نَخِصَ a نَخَصًا, وانْتَخَصَ To waste away (flesh).
✲ نَخَطَ o نَخْطًا, وانْتَخَطَ ه To blow o.'s nose.
نَخَطَ o نَخِيطًا ب To backbite a. o.
— على To treat a. o. scornfully.
إِنْتَخَطَ ه To be like a. o.
نَخْط ونَخَط Men, race of men.
مَا أَدْرِي أَيُّ النَّخْطِ هُوَ I do not know what sort of man he is.
✲ نَخَعَ a نَخْعًا ه To slaughter (a beast). To kill, to slay a. o. To bear sincere friendship to. —

نَخَم ه ه To give sincere advice to a. o.

— لِفُلانٍ بِحَقِّهِ He acknowledged his right.

— ه عِلمًا To master (a science).

نَخِم a نَخَمًا To be sappy (plant).

تَنَخَّم To expectorate.

— وانتَخَم To pour down rain (cloud).

إنتَخَم عن To be thrown far away from (o.'s country).

نَخاع ونِخاع ونُخاع ج نُخُع Spinal cord. ✧ Brains.

نُخاعَة Phlegm, pituite.

✧ نَوخَعَة Back of the neck, nape.

أَنخَع More contemptible (name).

مَنخَع The first vertebra jointing the neck to the head.

✡ نَخَف a o نَخفًا To snort (goat), to snuffle.

أَنخَف To sniff.

نَخفَة Cleft of a mountain.

نِخاف ج أَنخِفَة Boots.

نَخِيف Snorting, snuffle.

✡ نَخَل o نَخلًا ه To sift (flour).

— ونَخَّل ه To send down (snow, drizzle: cloud).

نَخَّل وتَنَخَّل وانتَخَل ه To select, to pick out the best of.

نَخَل لهُ النَّصِيحَة To give disinterested advice to.

نَخَلَت السَّماءُ الثَّلجَ او الوَدَق It snows; it drizzles.

نَخل ونَخِيل Palm-tree. (*un.* نَخلَة ونَخِيلَة) Palm.

نُخالَة Bran; rubbish remaining in the sieve.

نُخَيلَة Small palm-tree. Nature. Advice.

ناخِل الصَّدر Disinterested adviser.

نَصِيحَة ناخِلَة Sincere advice.

نَخائِل القَلب Straightforward design.

نَخّال Rag-gatherer.

مُنخُل ومُنخَل ج مَناخِل Sieve.

✡ نَخَم o نَخمًا To sing, to play.

نَخِم a نَخَمًا ونَخمًا, وتَنَخَّم To expectorate; to wipe o.'s nose.

نُخامَة Phlegm, mucus.

✡ نَخا o نَخوَة, ونُخِي وانتَخَى To swell with pride.

نَخا ٪ To extol a. o.

✧ نَخَى وأَنخَى واستَنخَى ه To incite, to enhearten a. o.

أَنخَى To increase in pride.

تَنَخَّى وانتَخَى على To behave haughtily towards.

نَخوَة Pride, point of honour. ✧ Courage.

✡ نَدّ i نَدًّا ونَدِيدًا ونَدَدًا ونُدُودًا ونِدادًا To run away (camel).

نَدَّد ب To defame a. o. To divulge (a secret). To revile a. o.

— وأَنَدّ ه To disperse (camels).

نادّ ه To oppose a. o.

تَنادّ To disagree and disperse (party of men).

نَدّ Hill, mound.

نَدّ ونِدّ Ambergris, compound perfume.

نِدّ ج أَنداد Idol.

— ونَدِيد ج نُدَداء A like; an opponent.

ما لهُ نِدٌّ او نَدِيدَة He is unequalled.

ذَهَبُوا أَنادِيد وتَنادِيد They dispersed on all sides.

✡ نَدَأ a نَدْأً ه To cook (meat) in hot ashes.

— ه To frighten a. o.

نَدِيء Flesh buried in hot ashes.

نَدًى ونِدأَة ونُدأَة Rain-bow. Halo. Redness in the clouds at sunrise or sunset.

نَدأَة ونُدأَة Abundance of cattle, of wealth.

✡ نَدَب o نَدبًا ه To bewail, to eulogise (a dead person).

نَدَب ه ل وإلى, وانتَدَب ه ل To invite, to urge a. o. to.

نَدِب a نَدَبًا ونُدُوبَة ونُدُوبًا To be covered with scars.

— a نَدَبًا, وأَندَب To leave a scar (wound).

نَدُب o نَدابَة To be clever, active.

أَندَب نَفسَهُ وبِنَفسِهِ He jeopardised his life.

إنتَدَب ل To answer (a call, summons). To contradict a. o.

— ه ✧ To depute a. o.

خُذ ما انتَدَب Take thou what is offered.

نَدب ج نُدُوب Shooting of an arrow. Scar of a wound.

— ج أَنداب Wager, stake in a race.

نَدَب ج نُدُوب ونُدَباء م نَدَبَة ج نَدَبات

Active, clever, sharp-minded (man). Spirited (horse).
Scar. نَدَبَة ج نَدَب وجج نُدُوب وأَنْدَاب
Elegy. Lamenting of the dead. نُدْبَة
Call, invitation. — وانتِدَاب
Eloquent Arab. عَرَبِيّ نُدْبَة
Wailing for the dead. Elegist. نَادِب
Wailing-woman. نَادِبَة ج نَوَادِب
Hired wailing woman. نَدَّابَة
Wailing of the dead. Funeral meeting. مَنْدَب ج مَنَادِب
Strait of Bab el-Mandeb : *lit* : strait of the wail. بَاب المَنْدَب
Bewailed. Approved (thing). ✧ Deputy, envoy. مَنْدُوب
To enlarge (a place). ✱ نَدَح a نَدْحًا ه
To be distended by repletion (cattle). تَنَدَّح
To disperse in a pasturage (sheep). — وانتَدَح
Multitude. Width, spaciousness. نَدْح ونُدْح
Spacious place. — ج أَنْدَاح , ونَدْحَة ونُدْحَة
Broad plain. Disengagement, freedom. مُنْتَدَح ومَنْدُوحَة
I am disengaged from that affair. لِي عَن هٰذَا الأَمْرِ مُنْتَدَح ومَنْدُوحَة
Broad and bare plains, deserts. مَنَادِح
To land, to come ashore (ship). ✱ نَدَخ a نَدْخًا ه
To bring (a ship) ashore to. أَنْدَخ ه
To brag, to boast. تَنَدَّخ
Fool. أَنْدَخ
Indifferent to abuse given or received. مِنْدَخ
To fall out, to drop out (thing). To be prominent, to jut out. To be rare, extraordinary. ✱ نَدَر o نَدْرًا ونُدُورًا
To go forth from. — مِن
To be dislocated (bone). — مِن مَوْضِعِهِ
To outgo others in (science, excellence). — فِي
To experience a. th. — ه
To be good. To be eloquent; to be strange (word). نَدُر o نَدَارَة
To beat a. th. down. To take forth a. th. أَنْدَر ه
He has told us strange things. أَنْدَر وتَنَادَر عَلَيْنَا

Rare. Uncouth (word). نَدْر ونَادِر
Piece of gold or silver in a mine. نَدْرَة
Rareness. نَدْرَة ونُدْرَة
Once, rarely. نَادِرًا وفي النَّادِر, ونَدْرَةً وفي النَّدْرَة
Rare thing. Scarcity. Curiosities, witticisms. نَادِرَة ج نَوَادِر
Quaint, uncouth expressions. النَّوَادِر مِن الكَلَام
He is the marvel of his time. هُوَ نَادِرَة الزَّمَان
لَقِيتُهُ نَدَرَى وفي نَدَرَى, والنَّدَرَى وفي النَّدَرَى I met him once.
I gave him a hundred coins out of my own property. نَقَدْتُهُ مِئَةً نَدَرَى
Thrashing-floor. Heap of wheat. أَنْدَر ج أَنَادِر
Syrian village celebrated for its wine. أَنْدَر
Wide (sack). أَنْدَرَانِيّ
Ground-flour, hall. ✧ مَنْدَرَة ج مَنَادِر
To be sagacious (child). ✱ نَدِس a نَدَسًا
He threw him down on the ground. نَدَس o بِهِ الأَرْضَ نَدْسًا
To thrust a. o. with (a spear). — ه ب
To turn a. o. away from the right way. — ه عن
He had a vague opinion on. — الظَّنَّ على
To curse and revile a. o. To spear a. o. نَادَس ه
To be thrown down. To ooze through the sides of a well (water). تَنَدَّس
To be upon the watch for (news). — ه وعن
To revile o. a. تَنَادَس
Sharp-minded, sagacious. نَدْس ونَدِس ونَدُس
Piercing spears. رِمَاح نَوَادِس
Nimble, active (woman). مِنْدَاس
Lace, tuft, tassel. ✧ أُنْدُوشَة ج أَنَادِيش
To protrude (eye). ✱ نَدَص o نُدُوصًا
To emerge from. — نَدْصًا ونُدُوصًا مِن
To let out purulent matter (abscess). — ونَدِص a نَدَصًا
To recover (a debt) from a. o. أَنْدَص واستَنْدَص مِن
Importuner. Foolish woman. مِنْدَاص ج مَنَادِيص

To keep low company. ندء – أندء ✱
To poke a. o. wlth the finger. To sting a. o. (scorpion). To tickle a. o. ✱ ندغ a ندغا ه وه
To spear a. o. To sting a. o. in (words). To fell a. o. — ه ب
To sprinkle (dough) with flour. ندّغ ه
To coax, to soothe a. o. نادغ ه
To harm, to injure a. o. أندغ ب
To smile. إنتدغ
Kind of marjoram. ندغ ونِدغ
White spot on the nails. نُدغة ومِندغة
Wicked ; disparager. مِندغ
Rolling-pin. مِندغة
To tease (cotton). ✱ ندف i ندفا
To send down (rain : cloud). — ب
He played the lute. — بالعُود
To drive (a beast) vehemently. — وأندف ه
To run swiftly (horse). — ندفا ونديفا وندفانا
Drop of milk. ✧ A little. نُدفة
Craft of a teaser. نِدافة
Teaser. ندّاف
Carder's bow. قوس النّدّاف
Carded (cotton). نديف ومندوف
Carder's mallet. مِندف ومِندفة
To take out a. th. to (a place). To pull out (a bucket). To snatch a. th. away. ✱ ندل o ندلا ه
To pick (dates) out of (a basket). — ه من
To be defiled (hand). ندل a ندلا
To wipe o.'s self with a towel. To wind (a towel) round o.'s head. تندّل بالمِنديل وتمندل
Dirt. ✧ Vile, coward. ندل
Waiters at table ; butlers. نُدُل
Root. Odoriferous wood. ✧ Witchcraft. مَندل ج مَنادِل
Towel, napkin. Veil. Head-band. مِندَل ومَنديل ج مَنادِل ومَنادِيل
To totter (old man). ✱ نودل
Tottering from old age. مُنودِل
Andalusia. Spain. ✱ أندلس
To repent of, to regret a. th. ✱ ندِم a ندما وندامة, وتندّم على
To drink with ; to be the fellow-drinker of. نادم مُنادمة ونِداما
To incite a. o. to repentance. أندم ه
They kept company for drinking. تنادموا على الشراب
To be easy, within reach. إنتدم
Repentance, regret, contrition. ندم وندامة وتندّم ومَندم
Contrite, repenting. نادم ج نُدّام, وندمان ج ندامى
ندمان ج ندامى وندمان, ونديم ج نُدماء ونِدام
Fellow-drinker, commensal, convivialist.
Object of repentance. مَندمة
✧ Corporal (of the Greeks). G أندميس
To urge (a beast). To repel a. o. ✧ To call out a. o. ✱ نده a ندها ه
Go away, I do not want thee. إذهب فلا أنده سربك
To go on well (affair). إنتده واستنده
Herd of cattle. ندهة ونُدهة
To assist at a meeting. To be generous. ✱ ندا o ندوا
To call a. o. To convoke (a meeting). — ه
The meeting-place cannot hold them. ما يندوهم النادي
To be wet, dewy. To reecho (voice). ندي a ندى ونداوة ونُدوّة
I have not obtained anything from him. ما نديت وما انتديت منه
To wet, to moisten a. th. ندّى تندية وأندى إنداء ه
To call a. o. To summon a. o. نادى مُناداة ونداء ه وب
To attend a meeting with. To vie in glory with. — ه
To divulge (a secret). — ب
To proclaim a. th. to. — على
To be generous. To be fine-voiced. أندى
To show liberality. To be wetted. To quench thirst. تندّى
To call out o. a. تنادى
To meet on convocation. تنادى وانتدى
Moisture ; dew. Green fodder. Grease. Generosity. Perfume. ندى ج أنداء وأندية
Voice, call. نِداء ونُداء
Vocative (*gram*). نِداء
Assembly of people. Meeting-place. ندوة ونادٍ ونديّ ج أندية, ومُنتدى

Water-trough for horses. نَدْوَة

Wet, moist. نَدٍ م نَدِيَة , ونَدِيّ م نَدِيَّة

Liberal. نَدِي ونَدِيّ الكَفّ

Having a resounding voice. نَدِيّ الصَّوت

Palm-trees remote from water. نَخْل نَادِيَة

Runaway camels. إِبِل نَوَادٍ

Calamities. أَلنَّوَادِي

Shattered fragments of date-stones. نَوَادِي النَّوَى

More generous than. أَنْدَى مِن

He has a stronger voice than. هُوَ أَنْدَى صَوتًا مِن فُلَانٍ

Day of the last judgment. يَوْمُ التَّنَادِي

Public caller, herald. مُنَادٍ

Dewy. Pasture near water. مُنْدًى

Calamity. مُنْدِيَة

Shameful (action, word). — ج مُنْدِيَات

To discharge urine. * نَدَّ o نَدِيدًا

Saliva, mucus. نَدِيد

To vow a. th. to God. * نَذَرَ o i نَذْرًا ونُذُورًا ه لِلّهِ

To devote (a child) by vow to God's service. To put a. o. in the vanguard. — ه

He promised it by vow. — وانْتَذَرَ على نَفْسِهِ ه

To be aware, cautious of. نَذِرَ a نَذَرًا ب

أَنْذَرَ إِنْذَارًا ونُذْرًا ونُذُرًا ونَذِيرًا ه ب

To warn, to caution a. o. against.

To warn o. another. تَنَاذَرَ

To caution one another against. — ه وه

Vow. Votive offering. نَذْر ج نُذُور

Warning, caution. إِنْذَار ونُذْرَى ونُذْر ونَذَارَة

Consecrated to God. Nazarite (amongst the Jews). Preacher, apostle, prophet. Hoariness. Spy. نَذِير ج نُذُر

Votive gift. Child consecrated to God. Front line of fighters. نَذِيرَة

Warning, exhorting. مُنْذِر ج مُنْذِرُون

The cock. أَبُو المُنْذِر

Almanzor, an Arab king. أَلْمُنْذِر

Arab kings issued from Almanzor. مَنَاذِرَة

Devoted to God. مَنْذُور

The lion. مُتَنَاذِر

To ooze (sweat, water). * نَدَعَ a نَدْعًا

To beevile, contemptible. * نَذُلَ o نَذَالَةً ونُذُولَةً

نَذْل ج أَنْذَال ونُذُول , ونَذِيل ج نُذَلَاء ونِذَال

Vile, despised.

Mischief. Strong man. * نَرْب — نَيْرَب

P نَرْبِيج ج نَرَابِيج , و ✦ نَرْبِيش ج نَرَابِيش

Winding tube of a nargile.

Thrashing-machine. Drag. Ploughshare. * نَوْرَج ونَيْرَج ج نَوَارِج

Narcissus (flower). P نَرْجِس ونِرْجِس

Cocoa-nut. P نَارَجِيل ونَارْجِيل

Nargile, Persian pipe. P نَارَجِيلَة و ✦ أَرْكِيلَة ج نَارَجِيلَات

Backgammon ; tables. P نَرْد — نَرْدَ

Sack made of palm-leaves.

Nard, spikenard. G نَارَدِين ونَرْدِين

To conceal o.'s self in fear. * نَرَزَ o نَرْزًا

New year's day. P نَيْرُوز

Orange. P نَارَنْج

To abound with water-springs (land). * نَزَّ i نَزًّا ونَزِيزًا , وأَنَزَّ

To twang (bowstring). To leap (gazelle). To ooze (water). نَزَّ i نَزِيزًا

To part with a. o. — عن

To foster (her young : gazelle). نَزَّزَ ه

To remove a. o. from. — ه عن

To vie in glory with. نَازَّ ه

Water oozing from the ground. نَزّ ونِزّ و✦ نَزَازَة و نَزَز ج نُزُوز

Active. Clever. Light ; fickle. Much. نَزّ

Eager desire. نِزَّة

Prone to evil. نِزَاز ونَزِيز بِشَرّ

Unsteady, fickle. نَزِيز ومُسْتَنَزّ

Cradle. مِنَزّ

To shake the (head). * نَزْنَزَ

To dandle (a child). — ه

To excite discord between. * نَزَأَ a نَزْأً بَيْن

To incite a. o. against. نَزَأَ ه على

To turn a. o. back from. — ه عن

To be addicted to. نُزِئَ ب

Prone to, desirous of. مَنْزُوءٌ ب

To bell (deer). * نَزَبَ i نَزْبًا ونُزَابًا ونَزِيبًا

To revile o. a. تَنَازَبَ

Nickname. نَزَب ج أَنْزَاب

Buck-antelope. نَيْزَب

To gambol (child). * نَزَجَ o نَزْجًا

* نزح a i نزحا ونزوحا To be remote (abode). To have her wells exhausted (tribe). To be exhausted (well).
— وأنزح ه To exhaust (a pool). ✧ To dredge (a river).
نزح بهِ وانتزح To be absent from home.
نزح ج أنزاح Exhausted well. Turbid water.
نازح ونزوح ج نُزُح Exhausted (well).
— ونزوح ونزيح Remote, far away.
مُنتزح Far distant.
بمُنتزح من كذا Far removed from such a thing.
قوم منازيح Remote tribe.
مِنزحة ج مَنازح Bucket.
* نزر o نزرا ه To importune a. o., to press a. o. with questions.
لا يُعطي حتى يُنزر He does not give unless pressed.
نزر نزرا ه وهـ To make little of.
نزُر o نزرا ونزرة ونزارة ونزورة ونزورا To be small, mean, little in number.
نزّر وأنزر ه To make a paltry (gift).
تنزّر To dwindle away.
نزر ونزير ج نزر, ومنزور Exiguous, scanty; mean.
نزرة ونزور Having few children (woman).
نزار Name of a tribe and of her chief.
نزور ج نُزُر Exiguous, having little milk or few children (woman).
* نزع i نزعا, ونزّع وانتزع ه من To pull off, to take out (garments) from.
نزع ه وهـ To discharge a. o. from office. To draw (a bucket). To take out (the hand) from the bosom. ✧ To spoil a. th.
— ونازع نِزاعا To be in the pangs of death (man).
نزع نزوعا ه وإلى To resemble a. o.
— عن وانتزع ه To abstain from, to shun a. th.
نزع i نزاعة ونزاعا ونزوعا, ونازع نِزاعا إلى أهله He yearned towards his family.
نزع نِزاعا إلى To desire a. th.
نزع a نزعا To be bald over the temples.

نازع منازعة ونزاعا ه To litigate, to contend with.
— ه To be adjoining to (a land).
أنزع To have the temples bare.
تنازع إلى To run quickly to.
تنازع في To disagree, to litigate upon.
— ه To discourse, to recise (verses) with o. another.
إنتزع To be wrung, snatched. ✧ To be spoilt, disordered.
— ه وب To cite (a verse). To wrest a. th. from.
نزع ونزاع ومنازعة Pangs of death.
نزعة مث نزعتان ج نزعات Temples bare of hair.
نِزاع ونزاعة ومنازعة Litigation, dispute.
النَّزَعة Shooters.
عاد السهم إلى النزعة The arrow came back to the shooters *i. e.* the property came back to its owner.
صار الأمر إلى النزعة The affair came into competent hands.
نزيع ج نزاع Stranger, remote. Gathered (fruit).
— ونزوع ج نزاع Shallow (well).
نزيعة ج نزائع Woman married out of her tribe.
أنزع م نزعاء Bald over the temples.
مَنزع Aim. Butt.
مِنزع Arrow shot afar.
مَنزعة Aim in view.
— ومَنزعة Care, anxiety.
* نزغ a نزغا ه To blacken a. o.'s character.
— ه ب To wound a. o. in (words).
— بين To set (people) at variance.
— ه إلى To incite a. o. to (evil).
نزغة ج نزغات Incitement to evil.
نزّاغ ومِنزغ ومِنزغة Slanderer.
* نزف i نزفا, وأنزف ه To exhaust (a well).
— دم فلان To draw blood from a. o.
نُزف ه To flow abundantly (blood).
— ونُزِف To be exhausted (well).
نُزِف To be weakened by a loss of blood. To be drunk. To be out of mind. To be unable to reply.
نزف a نزفا To be dried (tears).

To menstruate (woman). نَزَف
To be exhausted (well). To have (wells, wine, tears) exhausted. To be drunk. أَنزَف
To dry (the tears). — واستنزف ه
To lose the senses. أنزف
To drain (water). إنتزف ه
Flow, loss of blood; menses. نَزف الدم
Exhaustion of a well. نُزف
Dried, exhausted (veins). نُزُف
Small quantity of water. نُزفة ج نُزَف
Imper. Do drain, exhaust. نَزَافِ
Exhausted (well). نَزُوف
Weakened by fever. Drunk. نَزِيف
Weakened by a flow of blood. نَزِيف ومُنزَف ومَنزُوف

✻ نزق o i نزقًا, ونزق a نَزَقًا ونزوقًا
To be swift, to rush forth (horse).
To have a hasty temper and cool quickly. نَزَق i نزقًا, ونزق a نَزَقًا ونُزُوقًا
To be filled (basin). نزق a
To make (a horse) to leap. نَزَّق وأنزق ة
To meet a. o. with abuse. نَازَق مُنَازَقة ونِزَاقًا ة
To laugh immoderately. أنزق في الضحك
To revile o. a. in words. تَنَازَق
Light-mindedness, fickleness, hastiness. نَزَق
Adjacent place. مَكان نَزَق
Start in a run. نَزقة
Fickle, unsteady. Running and stopping soon. نَزِق م نَزِقة
Refractory (she-camel). ناقة نِزَاق
✻ نزك o نزكًا ة To spear a. o. To slander a. o.
Slanderer. نُزَك ونزّاك
Rascals, rogues. Worthless goats. نُزيكات
P نَيْزَك ج نَيَازِك Short spear. *Pl.* ✧ Shooting stars.
✻ نزل i نُزُولًا To go down. To abate (price).
To bring a. o. down. — بفلان
To happen to a. o. (accident). — بهِ
To alight at (a place). — ه وفي
To alight at a. o.'s (guest). — نُزولًا ومَنزَلًا ة وب وعلى
He gave up his right. — نُزولًا وتنزّل عن الحق

To have a rheum. نُزِل a نَزْلَة
To grow (crops). — a نَزَلًا
نَزَّل تنزيلًا, وأنزل إنزالًا ومُنزَلًا, واستنزل ة
To give hospitality to; to lodge, to entertain (a guest).
To bring or send a. o. or a. th. down. — وأنزل ة وه
To insert a. th. ✧ To deduct a. th. To write down a. th. نزّل ه
To send down (revelation) to (a prophet: God). نزّل وأنزل ه على
To come down upon, to take the field against. نَازَل مُنَازَلة ونِزَالًا ة في الحرب
To come down gradually. تَنَزَّل
To dismount from camels for riding horses (fighters). تَنَازَل
✧ To condescend to. تنازل إلى
To abdicate, to resign (an office). To desist from. ✧ To endorse (a bill). To deliver up a. th. — عن
To ask to bring down a. o. or a. th.; to ask a. o. to come down. To claim (the payment) of. إستنزل ة وه
To be discharged from office. أُستُنزِل
Food offered to a guest. نُزْل ونُزُل ج أنزال
Growth of crops. — ونُزُل ونَزَل
Rheum. Fluxion, congestion. نَزلة ج نَزَلات
Influenza. نزلة صَدرية
Another time. نزلة أخرى
Good corn-field. أرض نَزِلة
I left them in a good state. تركتهم على نَزَلاتهم
Hospitality. Journey. نِزَالة
He treats his guests well. هو حسن النزالة
Imper. (*m. f. s. pl.*) Come thou, ye down. نَزَالِ
Accident; divine scourge. Stroke. نَازِلة ج نَوَازِل ونازلات
Stranger. Guest. Copious (meal). Suit of clothes. نَزِيل ج نُزَلَاء
Stage. Inn, lodgings. Mansion (of the moon). مَنزِل ج مَنَازِل
Inn. Degree, rank. Dignity. مَنزِلة
Arithm. Order of the numerals. — ج مَنَازِل
To drive (camels) away from water. ✻ نزه o نزهًا ة

نَزِهَ a ونَزُهَ o نَزَاهَةً ونَزَاهِيَةً To be pure, free from evil. To be wholesome (climate).
نَزَّهَ ه عَنِ السُّوء To declare (God) free from imperfection.
— نَفْسَهُ عَنِ القَبِيحِ He kept aloof from sin.
— ه ✧ To entertain, to cheer a. o.
تَنَزَّهَ To be remote from water. ✧ To take a walk. To divert o.'s self.
— عَن To keep aloof from (shame).
تَنَزَّهُوا بِحُرَمِكُم عَنِ القَوْمِ Set your wives apart from the tribe.
إِسْتَنْزَهَ مِن To abstain, to keep away from.
نَزِهٌ, ونَزِهٌ ج نُزَهُونَ, ونَزِيهٌ ج نُزَهَاءُ ونِزَاهٌ Pure, free from blame (man). Wholesome, well seated (country).
نُزْهَةٌ ج نُزَهٌ Pleasure. Distance.
هُوَ يَتَنَزَّهُ عَنِ المَاءِ او عَنْهُ He is remote from water.
أَرْضٌ ذَاتُ نُزْهَةٍ Pleasant country.
نَزَهٌ ونَزَاهَةٌ Purity, guiltlessness, continence.
تَنْزِيهٌ ✧ Recreation, party.
نَازِهُ النَّفْسِ ج نُزَهَاءُ ونِزَاهٌ Aloof from sin, pure : solitary.
مَنْزَهَةٌ و✧ مُتَنَزَّهٌ Pleasant place, promenade.
✲ نَزَا o نَزْوًا ونُزُوًّا ونَزَوَانًا To leap. To frisk (ass).
نَزَا عَلَى To leap (the female : cloven-footed beast).
نَزَا بِهِ قَلْبُهُ إِلَى His heart yearns for.
نَزَا o نَزَوَانًا عَن To escape from.
نُزِيَ نَزْوًا To lose all the blood.
نَزَّى وأَنْزَى ه To make a. o. to leap.
تَنَزَّى To leap, to bound.
تَنَزَّى إِلَى الشَّرِّ He was prone to evil.
نَزَاءٌ ونُزَاءٌ (un. نَزْوَةٌ) Leap, bound.
نُزَاءٌ Staggers, disease of sheep.
نَزَوَانٌ Violence, fit, crisis.
نَازِيَةٌ Impetus.
نَزِيٌّ ونَزَّاءٌ ومُنْتَزٍ إِلَى الشَّرِّ Mischief-maker.
نَزِيَّةٌ Cloud. Deep (bowl).
أَنْزَى Leaping better.
✲ نَسَّ o i نَسًّا, ونَسَّسَ ه To urge (a beast) vehemently.
— نَسًّا ونُسُوسًا To be dry (bread, meat). To go at a gentle pace (man).
نَسَّ نَسًّا وتَنَسَّاسًا To go to water.
تَنَسَّسَ ه To be on the watch for (news).
نَاسٌّ Spy. Dry (bread).
أَلنَّاسَّةُ والنَّسَّاسَةُ *Surname* of Mecca.
نَسِيسٌ ج نُسُسٌ Vehement exertion. Nature. Violent hunger.
— ونَسِيسَةٌ Last breath of life.
بَلَغَ مِنْهُ نَسِيسُهُ او نَسِيسَتُهُ He was about to die.
نَسِيسَةٌ Slander.
تَنْسَاسٌ Rapid walk.
مِنَسَّةٌ Stick.
مِنْسَاسٌ Neat-herd's staff.
✲ نَسْنَسَ To fly swiftly (bird). To blow (cold wind).
نِسْنَاسٌ ج نَسَانِسُ Fabulous single-footed dwarf. ✧ Pigmy. Ape.
✲ نَسَأَ a نَسْأً, ونَسَّأَ تَنْسِئَةً ه To drive (a beast) along.
— ه عَن To keep back (a beast) from (water).
— ه ب To mix (milk) with (water).
نَسَأَ ه To give to a. o. milk and water.
— a نَسْأً ومَنْسَأَةً To become fat (cattle).
— وأَنْسَأَ ه To postpone a. th. To prolong (the life : God).
— نَسَاءً, وأَنْسَأَ ه البَيْعَ وفِيهِ He sold it to him upon credit.
— عَن فُلَانٍ دَيْنَهُ He granted a delay to his debtor.
إِنْتَسَأَ عَن To go back, to deviate from.
— فِي To wander in (a pasturage : beast).
إِسْتَنْسَأَ ه To ask a delay from (a creditor).
نَسَاءٌ Length of life.
نِسَاءٌ (نَسْوٌ) *Pl.* Woman.
نَسْءٌ Intoxicating drink. Watery milk. Fatness.
نُسْأَةٌ ونَسِيئَةٌ Delay granted to a debtor.
بَاعَهُ بِنُسْأَةٍ وبِنَسِيئَةٍ He sold it upon credit.
نَسِيءٌ Delay. Postponed (month of truce among the Arabs). Thin milk.
مِنْسَأَةٌ ومَنْسَاةٌ Stick ; shepherd's staff.

ber forming a proportion *as* 5 *to* 10 or 4 *to* 8.
Poem including erotic verses. (*Gram*) of relative noun ended by يّ. مَنسُوب ج مَنَاسِيب
Relating to. مَنسُوب إلى
Ants in a file ; track of ants. ✱ نَيْسَب
Straight, conspicuous road. — وَنَيْسَبَان
Mankind. (*from* إِنس) ✱ نَاسُوت
To draw a. th. together. To weave (cloth). To plait. To compose (verses). To forge (a narration). To streak (the sand : wind). To ripple (the water : wind). ✱ نَسَج o i نَسْجًا ه
To be woven (stuff). To be streaked (sand). To be rippled (water). إِنتَسَج
Weaving. نَسْج
Spider's web. نَسْج ونَسِيج العَنكَبُوت
Weaver's art. نِسَاجَة
Weaver. Liar. نَسَّاج
Woven. Web. Texture. *Pl.* Prayer-carpets. نَسِيج ج نُسُج
He is unequalled in. هُوَ نَسِيج وَحْدِهِ ب
Textile fabric, tissue. نَسِيجَة ج نَسَائِج
Weaver's shop. مَنسَج ومَنسِج
Weaver's loom. مِنسَج ومِنسَاج
Woven. Coordinate (narration). مَنسُوج
To disperse (dust). To rake. To covet a. th. ✱ نَسَح a نَسْحًا ه
Rubbish of dates. نُسْح ونُسَاح
Instrument for removing dust ; rake. مِنسَح
To obliterate, to conceal a. th. ✱ نَسَخ a نَسْخًا، وانتَسَخ ه
To abolish (a law). To transfer a. th. To copy (a book). To substitute a. th. to ; to metamorphose. نَسَخ ه
To abrogate (a verse of the Coran). أَنسَخ ه
To succeed to o. a. To transmigrate (souls). تَنَاسَخ
To hand down a. th. successively. ه —
To copy (a book). إِنتَسَخ واستَنسَخ ه
To ask a. o. to copy a. th. إِستَنسَخ ه ة
Obliteration, abrogation of a law. Transcription. نَسْخ
✧ Usual style of writing. ▫ Quack druggist. نَسْخِي
Copy. Transcript نُسْخَة ج نُسَخ

To mention the genealogy of. To ask the pedigree of. ✱ نَسَب o i نَسَبًا ونِسْبَةً ة
To trace back (a pedigree) to. To attribute a. th. to. To accuse a. o. of. ه إلى —
To mention a. o. in erotic verses. — نَسَبًا ونَسِيبًا ومَنسَبَةً ب
✧ To adapt a. th. ✧ نَسَّب ه
To be of the same stock as. To be akin to. To resemble a. o. To befit o. a. To be sorted, analogous to. To be symmetrical, proportionate to. نَاسَب ة وه
To pretend to be issued from. تَنَسَّب وانتَسَب إلى
To correspond ; to agree together. تَنَاسَب
To trace back o.'s lineage. إِنتَسَب واستَنسَب
To claim descent from. إِنتَسَب إلى
To ask the pedigree of. ✧ To judge a. th. fit, convenient. إِستَنسَب ة وه
Lineage. Kindred on the father's side. نَسَب ج أَنسَاب
Relationship. Arithmetical or geometrical proportion. ✧ Relationship by marriage. نِسبَة ونُسبَة
In relation, in proportion to. بِالنِّسبَة الى
Relation. Relative adjective ending in يّ, *as* أرضيّ *from* أرض. Resemblance, conformity. نِسبَة ج نِسَب
Having a known pedigree. Erotic poem. Related by marriage, kinsman. ✧ Brother-in-law. نَسِيب ج أَنسِبَاء
Skilful genealogist. نَسَّاب ونَسَّابَة
More fitted. More skilful genealogist. ✧ More convenient. أَنسَب
More elegant amatory poem. شِعر أَنسَب
✧ Arithmetical proportion. Symmetry. تَنَاسُب
Relation, analogy. Convenience. Proportion. مُنَاسَبَة وتَمَنَاسُب
Akin. Sorted, homogeneous, analogous. مُنَاسِب
Proportionate. (*Arithm*). Num- مُنَاسِب

Particle or verb effecting a change in grammatical forms. (as لا, إنّ, أ) or (as ظنّ, كان, كاد). ناسِخ ج نَوَاسِخ
Verse of the Coran superseding another. آية ناسِخة
Transmigration of souls. Succession of ages. تَنَاسُخ
Uninterrupted transmission of an estate. مُنَاسَخة
Sect of metempsychosists. تَنَاسُخيَّة
Abolished. Transcribed. مُنتَسَخ ومَنسُوخ
✱ To take off a. th. from. To scrape, to rub out a. th. نَسَر o نَسْرًا ه عن
To lance (an abscess). — ه
To backbite a. o. — ه
To peck (flesh : vulture). — i نَسْرًا ه
To be untwisted (rope). To break (abscess). To be torn off (clothes). تَنَسَّر
To forsake a. o. (happiness). — عن
To be worn into rags (rope). إنتَسَر
The ignoble bird became a vulture i. e. the weak one became strong. إستَنسَر البَغاث
Vulture. Eagle. Idol of the Arabs. نَسر ج أَنسُر ونُسُور
Three stars in *Aquila*. النَّسر الطائر
Bright star in *Lyra*. النَّسر الواقِع
Frog of a horse's hoof. نَسر ج نُسُور
Ulcer, incessant defluxion, fistula. ناسُور ج نَوَاسِير
✧ To become cancerous (wound). نَوسَر
Beak of a bird of prey. Vanguard of an army. Troop of 30 to 200 horses. مِنسَر ومَنسِر ج مَنَاسِر
Wild rose, eglantine. نِسرِين
Nestorian (Syrian sect). G نَسطُوريّ ج نَسَاطِرة
✱ To be loose and bare (tooth). نَسَع a نَسْعًا ونُسُوعًا, ونَسَّع
He went over the country. — في الأرض
To be exposed to the North wind. أَنسَع
To disperse in a pasturage (cattle). إنتَسَع
Thong of a camel's girth. نِسع ج نُسع ونِسَع وأَنسَاع ونُسُوع
Outlines of a road. أنساع الطَّرِيق
North wind. نِسع وريح نِسعيّة, ومِنسَع
✱ To tattoo (the hand). نَسَغ a نَسْغًا ه
To lash a. o. with (a whip). To throw out a sarcasm upon. — ه ب
He went through the country. — في الأرض
To be bare and loose (tooth). نَسَّغ ونَسَّع
To shoot forth (tree). أَنسَغ
To lash a. o. with a whip. — ه
To disperse in a pasturage (cattle). إنتَسَغ
Sap flowing from a cut down tree. نُسغ
Sweat. نَسِيغ
Pastry cook's prick. مِنسَغة
✱ To shatter, to smash a. th. To winnow (grain). To pluck (plants : cattle). ✧ To pare (the hoof : farrier). نَسَف i نَسْفًا ه
To scatter (dust : wind). — وأَنسَف ه
To pull down (a building). To pluck (grass : beast). — وانتَسَف ه
To bite a. o. نَسَف o نَسْفًا ونُسُوفًا ه
To throw down a. o. (wrestler). تَنَسَّف
To whisper, to speak secretly to o. a. تَنَاسَف الكَلامَ
To whisper, to speak secretly to. إنتَسَف الكَلامَ
To be altered (colour). أُنتُسِف
نَسفة ونَسِيفة ونِسفة ونُسفة ونَسَفة ج نِساف
Black pumice-stone. ونِسف ونُسَف
Rubbish of wheat. Froth of milk. نُسافة
Mark of a bite. Whisper, secret conversation. Footprints on a race-field. نَسِيف
Kind of swallow. نَسَّاف ج نَسَاسِيف
Torpedo-boats. ✧ مَرَاكِب نَسَّافة
Full to overflowing (vessel). نَسفان
Winnowing-basket. مِنسَف ج مَنَاسِف
Muzzle of the ass. — ومُنسِف ج مَنَاسِف
Instrument for demolishing. Sieve. ✧ Butteris. Shelf, board. مِنسَفة
✱ To string, to set (pearls). To compose (a discourse). نَسَق o نَسْقًا ه
To arrange symmetrically. To set a. th. in order. نَسَّق ه
To follow in (a file). نَاسَق بَين
To speak in rhyming prose. أَنسَق
To be set in order. تَنَسَّق وتَنَاسَق وانتَسَق
Order, symmetry, rhythm. نَسَق

Loose threads, hair. Lint. ✧ نُسَالَة
Honey flowing from the honeycomb. نَسِيل ونَسِيلَة
Wick. Feathers, hair shed. ✧ Rag. نَسِيلَة
Camels for breeding. نَسُولَة
Swift runner. نَسَّال
Successive generation, progeny. تَنَاسُل
To blow gently (breeze). To diffuse itself (aroma). ✱ نَسَم i نَسْمًا ونَسِيمًا ونَسَمَانًا
To stamp the earth (camel). i نَسْمًا —
To be altered, corrupted. a ونَسِم نَسَمًا —
To abound in springs (land). نَسُم o نَسَامَةً
To invigorate, to inspirit a. o. نَسَّم ه
To free (a slave). ه —
To begin (an affair). في —
To smell a. o. or a. th. To whisper a. th. نَاسَم مُنَاسَمَةً ونِسَامًا ه وه
To respire; to breath. To become alive. تَنَسَّم
To inhale (the air). To apply o.'s self to (study). To inquire about (news). ه —
To exhale (a perfume: place). ب —
Breeze, breath of life. Effaced road. Smell, odour. نَسَم ج أَنْسَام, ونَسِيم
Breath. Breath of life. Man. Asthma. Living being. Slave (male or female). نَسَمَة ج نَسَم ونَسَمَات
Men, mankind. (Pl. of أَنْسَام) أَنَاسِم
Dying man. نَاسِم
Gentle breeze, zephyr. نَسِيم ج نِسَام
Sole of a camel. Foot of the ostrich. Mark, trace. Way, manner. مَنْسِم ج مَنَاسِم
To give up (a work). ✱ نَسَا o نَسْوَةً
Tendon of the heel. نَسًا مث نَسَوَان ونَسَيَان ج أَنْسَاء
Sciatic nerve. ✧ Sciatica. عِرْق النَّسَا
Draught of milk. نَسْوَة
Women. نِسْوَة ونُسْوَة ونِسَاء ونِسْوَان
Small, feeble woman. نُسَيَّة
Womanly, womanish. نِسْوِيّ ونُسْوِيّ
To feel a pain in the tendon of a heel. ✱ نَسِيَ a نَسًى
To wound a. o. in the tendon of the heel. نَسَى i نَسْيًا ه

Copulative particles (*gram*). حروف النَّسَق والنَّسْق
Well set (teeth, pearls, discourse). نَسَق ونَسِيق ومَنْسُوق
Regularly, serially. نَسَقًا
Rhet. Enumeration of attributes in a sequel. تَنْسِيق
To be godly, to worship (God). ✱ نَسَك o نَسْكًا ونُسْكًا ونُسُكًا ونَسِيكَة ومَنْسَكًا, وتَنَسَّك
He devote himself to God. لله —
To give o.'s self up to asceticism. الى —
To become an ascetic. نَسُك o نَسَاكَةً
To wash (a garment). To better a (saline ground). نَسَك o نَسْكًا ه
Devotion, godliness. Asceticism. نِسْك ونُسْك ونُسُك
Victim offered up. نُسْك ونُسُك
Gold or silver ingot. نَسِيك
Sacrifice offered to God. Nugget of gold or silver. نَسِيكَة ج نَسَائِك
Pious, godly. Ascetic. نَاسِك ج نُسَّاك
Place of pilgrimage, of sacrifice. Rites of sacrifice. مَنْسَك ومَنْسِك ج مَنَاسِك
The rites of pilgrimage. مَنَاسِك الحجّ
Short-haired (horse). Fattened (land). مَنْسُوك
To beget (sons). ✱ نَسَل o نَسْلًا ه وب وأَنْسَل ه
To moult (bird, beast). وأَنْسَل ه —
✧ To ravel out (cloth). و✧ نَسَّل ه —
To fall off (feather, hair). نَسَل o نُسُولًا, وأَنْسَل
To slip off (garment). أَنْسَل عَن
He hurried the walk. نَسَل o i نَسْلًا ونَسَلًا ونَسَلَانًا في مَشْيِه
✧ To fall into rags (garment) To be ravelled out (cloth). ✧ نَسَّل
To be at moulting-time (beast, bird). أَنْسَل
To outrun a. o. ه —
T multiply by generation (men, beasts). تَنَاسَل
Offspring, posterity, descendants. نَسْل ج أَنْسَال
Milk flowing from the udder. Milky juice of a green fig. نَسَل
Moulting of animals. نُسَال ونَسِيل

نَسِي م نَسِيَة, والنَّسِي م نَسْياء Hurt in the nerve of the leg.

الأَنْسَى Nerve in the lower part of the leg.

مَنْسُوّ ومَنْسِيّ Wounded on the nerve of the leg.

* نَسِي a نَسْيًا ونِسْيانًا ونِسَايَة ونَسْوَة ه To forget, to forsake a. th.

نَسَّى وأَنْسَى ٥ ه To make a. o. to forget a. th.

تَنَاسَى To pretend forgetfulness.

نَسْي ونِسْي ج أَنْسَاء Oblivion; forgetfulness. Small things left by a traveller.

نَسْوَة ونِسْيان Oblivion.

نَسْيان Forgetful.

نَسِيّ م نَسِيَّة Forgetful. Overlooked.

نَسِيّ Intercalary days of the Coptic year.

مَنْسِيّ Forgotten.

مِنْسَاة Staff, stick.

* نَشَّ o نَشًّا ٥ To urge (a beast) gently.

— ه To mix up a. th. ◘ To whisk away (flies).

نَشَّ i نَشًّا ونَشِيشًا To sink into the earth (water). To gurgle (water). To bubble up (cooking-pot). To ferment (wine). To ooze (water-skin).

نَشّ Weight of 20 dirhems, half an ounce.

نَشَّاش Absorbing water (salt ground). ✧ Blotting-paper.

نَشَّاشَة Absorbing water without producing (land).

نَشُوش *Inula odora* (*plant*).

نَشِيش Gurgling, bubbling of water.

◘ مِنَشَّة Fly-whisk.

* نَشْنَش To bubble up (boiling pot). To rustle (coat of mail). To be nimble.

— ه To take off o.'s clothes quickly. To pluck and disperse its feathers (bird). To devour (flesh).

✧ تَنَشْنَش To be in the way of recovery (sick person).

نَشْنَاش ونَشْنَشِيّ Alert, nimble.

* نَشَأَ a ونَشُوَ o نَشْأً ونُشُوءًا ونَشْأَةً ونَشَاءً To grow up (child). To happen. To be produced. To live. To rise (cloud).

نَشَّأَ وأَنْشَأَ ٥ To rear (a child).

— ه To raise (the clouds : God).

نُشِئَ وأُنْشِئَ To be grown up, reared (youth).

أَنْشَأَ ه To create a. th. (God). To find out, to produce a. th. To compose (a discourse). To set up a. th. To begin (a building). To forge a. th.

أَنْشَأَ يَقُول He began to say.

تَنَشَّأَ ل To set to (work).

إِسْتَنْشَأَ ه To seek after (news).

— ه في To set up (a sign) in (the desert).

— ٥ ه في To ask from a. o. a poem upon.

نَشْء Risen cloud. Race of men.

هُوَ مِن نَشْءِ سُوء He is of bad race.

نَشْء ج نَشَأ Young camels newly born.

نَشَاء ونُشُوء ونَشْأَة Growth, production.

نَشِيء Part of a cloud appearing.

نَشْأَة ونَشِيئَة Sprouts of plants.

نَشِيئَة Stone set in the bottom of a tank.

إِنْشَاء Creation, contrivance. Style. Epistolography.

دِيوَان الإِنْشَاء Seal-office.

نَاشِئ (*m. f.*) ج نَشْء ونَشَأ Young man, young girl.

— ج نَاشِئَة Appearing in the night.

نَاشِئَة ج نَوَاشِئ Beginning of the day, of the night. Young maid.

مَنْشَأ Place of origin, source.

مُنْشِئ Redactor of a writing. Tutor.

مُنْشَأ ومُسْتَنْشَأ Set up (flag).

مُسْتَنْشِئَة Divineress.

* نَشِبَ a نَشَبًا ونُشُوبًا ونُشْبَة في To stick to, to be caught in a. th.

— نُشُوبًا بَيْن To become intricate between (war). ✧ To gush forth.

— ٥ To be incumbent upon a. o. (affair).

نَشِبَ مَنْشَب سُوء He engaged into an intricate case.

مَا نَشِبَ او لَمْ يَنْشَب أَن فَعَل He delayed not to do so.

مَا نَشِبَ يَقُول He has not ceased saying.

To fix, to insert a. th. into. نَشِبَ وأَنْشَبَ ه في

To begin, to set about. نَشَبَ في

He waged open war with. نَاشَبَ ه الحَرْبَ

To plunge, to fix a. o. into. أَنْشَبَ ه في

He ensnared (the game) in a net. أَنْشَبَ ه بِحِبَالَتِهِ

To be caught, entangled. To cling to (the heart: love). To be fixed into. تَنَشَّبَ وانْتَشَبَ في

To cleave together. تَنَاشَبَ

To collect (wood). إِنْتَشَبَ ه

Moveable or unmoveable property. Land and live stock. نَشَبٌ ونَشَبَة

They possess no fixed property. مَا لَهُمْ نَشَبٌ

Involved in an affair. Sticking fast. The wolf. نُشْبَة

Arrows. (*coll*). نُشَّاب ج نَشَاشِيب

A wooden arrow. ✧ Pole of a carriage. نُشَّابَة

Belemnite, arrow-head (stone). حَجَر النُّشَّاب

Possessing arrows. Shooting. نَاشِب م نَاشِبَة

Stuck, fixed, caught. — ونَشِب م نَشِبَة

Shooter, arrow-maker. نَشَّاب

Archers. قَوْم نَشَّابَة

Inextricable difficulty. مَنْشَب سُوءٍ

Unripe date. مِنْشَب ج مَنَاشِب

✱ نَشَجَ i نَشِيجًا To be choked with tears; to sob (man). To produce a gurgling (pot). To reciprocate its braying (ass); its croaking (frog).

Stream of water; bed of a stream. نَشَج ج أَنْشَاج

✱ نَشَحَ a نَشْحًا ونُشُوحًا To drink without quenching thirst. To drink o.'s fill.

✧ نَشِحَ To be altered, corrupt (meat, water).

Small quantity of water. نَشُوح

Drunken (man). — ج نُشَ،

Skin filled to overflowing. سِقَاء نَشَّاح

✱ نَشَدَ o نَشْدًا ونِشْدَةً ونِشْدَانًا, وأَنْشَدَ ه To seek after, to cry for (a stray beast). To give information of a. th. lost.

To be acquainted with. ه —

To remind a. o. of (a promise). نَشَدَ ه ه

To adjure a. o. by God. — نَشَدًا ه

To say: I beseech thee by God. نَشَدْتُكَ اللهَ

To conjure, to beg a. o. by God. — ه اللهَ وبِاللهِ

To ask a. o. to swear by God. نَاشَدَ مُنَاشَدَةً ونِشَادًا ه

To recite (verses) to. أَنْشَدَ ه ه

To satirise a. o. — ب

To take information about (news). تَنَشَّدَ ه

To recite poetry o. to the other. تَنَاشَدَ ه

To ask a. o. to recite (verses). إِسْتَنْشَدَ ه ه

I adjure thee by God to do. نِشْدَكَ اللهَ إِلَّا فَعَلْتَ

Voice, sound. Search. نِشْدَة

Elevation of the voice. نَشِيد

— ونَشِيدَة ج نَشَائِد, وأُنْشُودَة ج أَنَاشِيد Poem recited in a meeting. Declamation.

The Canticle of Canticles. نَشِيد الأَنَاشِيد

Sal ammoniac. P نُشَادِر ونُوشَادِر

✱ نَشَرَ o نَشْرًا, ونَشَّرَ ه To expand, to spread (cloth, carpets). To display (a flag).

He desired that thing earnestly, *lit*: he spread out his ears to it. نَشَرَ لِذٰلِكَ الأَمْرِ أُذُنَيْهِ

To saw (wood). To scatter a. th. To propagate a. th. نَشَرَ ه

To publish (news). — o i نَشْرًا ه

He charmed away sickness. نَشَرَ ونَشَّرَ عَنِ المَرِيضِ

To become verdant after rain (land). To become green again (plant). To put forth (leaves). To spread (foliage). نَشَرَ o نُشُورًا

To recall to life, to rise (the dead). نَشَرَ o نَشْرًا ونُشُورًا, وأَنْشَرَ ه

To be quickened (dead). نَشَرَ ونُشِرَ

To disperse by night in a pasture (cattle). نَشِرَ a نَشَرًا

To be spread, unfolded, expanded. تَنَشَّرَ وانْتَشَرَ

To become long (day). To be swollen (sinew). To spread (news). إِنْتَشَرَ

To become dispersed (camels). To be spread.
إستنشر ه To ask from a. o. to publish, to spread a. th,
نَشْر Sweet odour. Dry herbage becoming green after rain. Life.
نَشَر Scattered (people, sheep). Disorganised (affair).
جاء القوم نَشْرًا ونَشَرًا The people came in a scattered state.
يوم النُّشُور Day of the resurrection.
نَشْرَة ج نَشَرَات ✧ Review, periodical.
نُشْرَة ج نُشَر Charm, amulet for curing the sick.
نُشَارَة Saw-dust.
إنتِشَار Publication.
— الإيمان ✧ Propagation of the faith.
نَاشِرَة ج نَوَاشِر Sinew of the arm.
نَشُور ج نُشُر Shaking the clouds (wind).
نَشِير Heaped up corn.
تَنَاشِير Scrawls of children.
مَنْشُور ج مَنَاشِير Letters patent. ✧ Prism (*in geom*). Encyclical; prospectus. Circular.
مِنْشَار ج مَنَاشِير Saw. Pitchfork for wheat. Saw-fish.
✲ نَشَز o i نَشْزًا في To overtop, to be prominent.
— في To raise o.'s self in (a place).
— i نَشْزًا بِقِرْنِهِ He lifted up and threw down his antagonist.
— o i مِن To heave from (fear : soul).
— نُشُوزًا على ومِن To be disobedient to (her husband : wife). To ill-treat (his wife : husband).
أنشز ه To displace a. th. To raise and set together (the bones of the dead : God).
نَشَاز, ونَشْز ج نُشُوز ونِشَاز, ونَشَز ج أنْشَاز Elevated place.
نَاشِز Rising from a place. Protruding. Throbbing (vein).
— الجَبْهَة Having a prominent forehead.
نَاشِزَة ج نَوَاشِز Rebellious (wife).
✲ نَشَص o i نُشُوصًا To be lofty (cloud). To stick out (tooth).
— مِن وعلى To be rebellious, to hate (her husband : wife).
— عَن To be expelled from.
أنشص ه To expel a. o. from.
إنتشص ه To root out (a tree).
نَشَاص ج نُشُص ونَشَائِص Lofty cloud.
نَاشِص ج نَوَاشِص Rebellious, termagant (woman).
✲ نَشِط a نَشَاطًا, وتَنَشَّط To be sprightly, lively, nimble, cheerful. To become fat (beast).
نَشَط o نَشْطًا ه To make a slip-knot to (a rope).
نَشَط i نَشْطًا ه To draw out (the bucket) from a well without a pulley.
— مِن بَلَدٍ إلى بَلَدٍ He passed from a country to another.
نَشَّط وأنشط ه وه To knot, to tie; to unknot, to untie (a rope). To cheer, to inspirit, to encourage a. o.
— ه إلى وفي To incite a. o. to.
أنشط To have sprightly, lively (people, beasts).
— ه To fatten (cattle : pasturage).
— ه مِن To loose (a beast) from.
تَنَشَّطَت في سَيْرِهَا She hurried in walk (she-camel).
— ل To set zealously to (work).
— ه To cross (a desert) swiftly.
إنتشط To be untied (rope).
إنتشط ه To strain (a rope) for untying it. To scale (a fish). To pluck (herbage : cattle).
إستنشط To be wrinkled (skin).
نَشَاط Cheerfulness, liveliness. Fieriness.
نَاشِط Roving along (wild bull). Path deviating from the main road.
نَاشِط, ونَشِيط ج نِشَاط ونَشَاط Cheerful; active, lively.
نَاشِطَات Shooting-stars. Departing souls of the faithful.
نَوَاشِط Digressions, departure from the main subject.
بِئر نَشُوط Deep well requiring much exertion for pulling the bucket.
بِئر أنشاط وإنشاط Shallow well from which the bucket comes forth by a single pull.
نَشِيط ومُنشِط Having brisk people, beasts.
أنشوطة Booty made by the leader of a raid, during the march.

أُنْشُوطَة و✧ شُوطَة. وشَاْنُوطَة و□ شُنَيْطَة ج
أَنَاشِيط Silp-knot, tie easily undone.
مِنْشَط Sprightly, lively.
✱ نَشَظ o نُشُوظًا To grow, to shoot forth (plant).
✱ نَشَم a نَشْمًا ومَنْشَمًا, وأَنْشَم ة To inject a medicine to a. o. through the nose or mouth.
— وأَنْشَم ة ه To suggest a. th. to.
— وانْتَشَم ه To snatch a. th. away.
نَشَم a نَشْمًا To hiccup.
— a نُشُوعًا To have a narrow escape from death.
نُشِم ب To be addicted to, fond of.
أَنْشَم ة ب To help, to assist a. o. with.
إِنْتَشَم ه To snuff (a medicine).
نَشُوع Sternutatory powder.
مَنْشُوع ب Addicted to, fond of.
مِنْشَم Snuff-pipe for injection.
✱ نَشَغ a نَشْغًا To flow (water). To hiccup from desire or grief.
نُشِغ ب To be enamoured with.
نَشُوغ Sternutatory powder.
مِنْشَغَة Snuff-tube.
✱ نَشِف a ونَشَف o نَشْفًا, وتَنَشَّف ه To absorb (water : tank). To drink in (sweat : garment).
— ونَشَف في To be absorbed by (the ground: water).
نَشَف مَالُهُ His wealth has been exhausted.
نَشَف ونَشَّف ه To imbibe (water) with a sponge. To dry (clothes). To wipe.
نَشِف a و✧ نَشَّف To be exhausted (spring). To dry (garment).
أَنْشَف ة To give to a. o. frothing milk to drink.
تَنَشَّف ه To wipe (o.'s body).
إِنْتَشَف To drink frothing milk.
— ه To wipe off (dirt).
أَنْتَشِف To fade (colour).
نَشْف Absorption of water.
نِشْفَة ونُشْفَة Residue at the bottom of a vessel.
— ونَشْفَة ونُشْفَة ونَشَفَة ج نَشَف ونُشَف ونِشَف
ونَشَف ونِشَاف Black pumice-stone.
نَشْفَة ونَشَّافَة Towel, sponge, for wiping.
نُشْفَة ونُشَافَة Froth of fresh milk.
نَشِفَة Water-absorbing (earth).

✧ نَشْفَان Consumption, marasmus.
نَشَّاف ج نَشَّافَة Soaking bread in the soup before dinner. Dryer.
نَشَّاف ✧ Blotting-paper.
✧ نُشُوفَات Dried fruits (as raisins, figs).
نَاشِف ✧ Exhausted (spring). Dry. Severe (man). Unseasoned (bread).
مِنْشَفَة ج مَنَاشِف Towel. Napkin.
✱ نَشِق a نَشْقًا ونَشَقًا, وتَنَشَّق واسْتَنْشَق ه To smell (an odour). To snuff, to inhale a. th. ✧ To snuff (tobacco).
نَشِق في To be caught in (a net : gazelle). To be ensnared (man).
أَنْشَق ة ه To give a. th. to smell to. To inject (a medicine) through the nose of.
— ة في To catch (a gazelle) in (a net).
تَنَشَّق وانْتَشَق واسْتَنْشَق ه To snuff a. th.
تَنَشَّق واسْتَنْشَق ه ✧ To be on the watch for (news).
نُشْقَة Running-knot.
نَشْقَة ✧ Snuff of tobacco.
نَشُوق Any snuff-medicine. ✧ Snuffing-tobacco.
نَشَاقَى Entangled in a net (game).
مَنْشَق ج مَنَاشِق Smelling power. Nose, nostrils.
✱ نَشَل o نُشُولًا To be little fleshy (thigh). To be emaciated (man).
— o نَشْلًا ه To snatch away, to pilfer.
— i o نَشْلًا, وانْتَشَل ه To carry off and devour (a piece of meat) from the pot.
نَشَل ه To cook (meat) without condiment.
نَشَّل ة To offer food (to a guest) at his arrival.
فَخِذ نَاشِلَة Emaciated thigh.
نَشَّال Wont to snatch meat from the pot. ✧ Dodger, swindler.
نَشِيل Snatched from the pot (meat). Unseasoned (food). Thin-bladed (sword). Just drawn (water).
مَنْشَلَة Part of the little finger covered by the ring.
مِنْشَل ومِنْشَال ج مَنَاشِل Kitchen-fork.
✱ نَشِم a نَشَمًا To be variegated, spotted of white and black.
نَشَّم To be altered (meat).

نَشِر في فلان He impaired the reputation of such a one.
— وتَنَشَّر في الشرّ He began to do mischief.
نَشَّر الله ذِكرَهُ May God render his memory illustrious!
تَنَشَّر في أمرٍ He undertook an affair.
تَنَشَّر ه To endeavour to acquire (knowledge).
نَشَم Tree for making bows; celtis, nettle-tree.
نَشِم Spotted white and black.
مَنْشَم ومَنْشِم Black stinking fruit.
Female perfumer whose perfumes brought ill luck.
دقّوا بينهم عِطر مَنْشِم They are at war; *lit.* they have pounded the perfumes of Mensham.
✧ نَيْشَن To take aim.
P نِيشان ج نَيَاشِين Insignia of an order, badge. Aim, target. Mark.
✱ نَشِي a نِشْوَة ونُشْوَة , وتَنَشَّى وانتَشى
واستَنشَى ه To smell (an odour).
— a نَشْواً ونَشْوَة ونُشْوَة ,ونَشَّى وانتَشى To feel dizzy (from wine).
نَشِيَ واستَنشَى ه To get wind of, to inquire about (news).
نَشِيَ ب To resume (an affair).
نَشَّى ✧ To starch (linen).
نَشَا Sweet scent. Sweet-scenting trees.
نَشَا ونَشَاء Starch.
نِشْيَة ج نَشَايَا Sweet odour.
نَشْوَة Dizziness caused by wine. Smell.
✧ نَشَاوِيَّة Food made of starch and milk.
نَشْيَان بالأخبار ولِلأخبار Watching for news.
نَشْوَان م نَشْوَى ج نَشَاوَى Dizzy, intoxicated.
C مَنشِيَّة Village, place.
✱ نَصّ o نَصّاً ه To display (a bride). To raise, to show a. th.
نَصّ ه إلى To manifest, to reveal a. th. to. To trace back (a tradition) to.
— ه ل وعلى ✧ To dictate (a letter) to.
— ه على To specify a. th.; to make a statement about.
— ه To importune a. o. with questions. To seat, to display (a bride) on her throne.
نَصّ ه To heap up (furniture). To raise (the neck: gazelle). To move, to shake a. th.
يَنُصّ أنفَهُ غضباً He moves about his nose from anger.
نَصّ i نَصِيصاً To hiss (fried meat). To boil (kettle).
نَصَّص ونَاصّ ه To press (a debtor) to the utmost.
إنتَصّ To stand up. To be lofty. To be seated upon her throne (bride).
نَصّ ج نُصُوص Text (of a book). Ordinance. End, utmost limit. Quotation. Technical term.
نَصَّة Female sparrow.
نُصَّة ج نُصَص Forelock of hair.
نَصّ ونَصِيص Vehement (walk).
نَصِيص القوم Number of people.
نَصَّاص الأنف Moving about the nose.
مَنَصَّة Pavilion for a bride
مِنَصَّة ج مَنَاصّ Throne, seat of honour for a bride.
وُضِع على المِنَصَّة He has been exposed to disgrace.
مَنصُوص عَلَيهِ Determined. Sentenced.
✱ نَصَب o نَصْباً, وأنصَب ه To set. To set up, to raise. To put down a. th.
نَصَب i نَصْباً, وأنصَب ه To pain, to distress a. o. (disease, cares).
— ونَصَّب ه To set up (a stone) as a sign. To hoist (a flag). To plant (a tree).
نَصَب To hurry in walk; to walk the whole day.
— ه To pronounce, to mark the final letter of (a word) with fatha ´ or ً.
— لهُ ونَاصَب ه He showed hatred to him.
— لهُ الحَرب He declard war to him.
— ه ل To modulate a song (Arab).
— ل وعلى ✧ To lay a snare to, to decoy a. o.
— ونَصَّب ه To raise a.o. to dignity.
نَصِب a نَصَباً To be tired
— في To exert o.'s self to the utmost in.
نَصَّب ه To erect (the ears: horse).
نَاصَب ه الشرّ He waged an open war; he showed open enmity to him.

Origin. Rank, dignity. مَنصِب ج مَنَاصِب Office, function.
Functionaries, magistrates. أهل وأرباب المَنَاصِب
Iron-trivet. مِنصَب ج مَناصِب
Fatigue, hardship. مَنصَبة
Erect, superposed (stones). Regular (teeth). مُنَصَّب
Adversary. Archer. مُنَاصِب
Rising high (dust). مُنتَصِب
Having the horns standing out (ram). مُنتَصِب القَرنَين
Set up (snare). In the accusative (noun); in the subjunctive (verb). مَنصُوب
✲ نَصَت i نَصتًا, وأنصَت وانتَصَت To be silent, to listen.
نَصَت ل وأنصَت ل وه To listen silently to.
أنصَت ه وه To silence a. o.
تَنَصَّت To be on the watch for listening.
إستَنصَت To stand up for listening.
إستَنصَت ه To ask a. o. to be silent.
نُصتَة Silence.
✲ نَصَح a نَصحًا ونُصحًا ونَصَاحَة ونَصِيحَة ونَصَاحِيَة ه ول To give advice to. To counsel a. o. earnestly.
— a نَصحًا ونُصُوحًا To be pure, genuine. To be sincere (friend).
— نُصُوحًا To be sincere (repentance).
— الرِيّ To drink its fill (beast).
— ه To perform a. th. earnestly. To sew (a garment) well. To water abundantly (the ground: rain).
✧ نَصِح a نَصَاحَة To become fat, fleshy.
✧ نَصَّح ه To fatten a. o.
نَاصَح ه To give sincere advice to a. o.
أنصَح ه To water (cattle) to their fill.
تَنَصَّح To be prodigal of good advice.
— ه To sew (a garment).
— لِفُلَان To act as a good adviser, a good friend to.
إنتَصَح To accept sincere advice.
— واستَنصَح ه To deem a. o. a faithful adviser.
إستَنصَح ه To ask good counsel from.
نَصح ونُصح Advice, counsel.
نِصَاح ج نُصُح ونَصَاحَة Thread for sewing.

أنصَب ه To assign a part to. To weary a. o.
— ه To put a handle to (a knife). To trace back (a tradition).
تَنَصَّب وانتَصَب To rise up. To be raised. To be hoisted (flag).
تَنَصَّب To rise in the air (dust).
إنتَصَب To be marked, pronounced with fatha (final letter). To be vertical.
— لِلحُكم He rose for pronouncing the sentence (judge).
نَصب Mark set up. Pole. Limit. Idol. Disease. Misfortune. Modulate dsong. Word marked with fatha on the last letter *i. e.* accusative or subjunctive. ✧ Plants (*coll.*).
نِصب Lot, portion.
نُصب, ونُصُب ج أنصَاب Idol. Sign set up. Pole. Disease. Affliction.
هٰذَا نُصبُ عَينَيّ It is always set before my eyes.
نَصَب Fatigue, toil.
— ج أنصَاب Standard, sign set up.
نَصبَة ج نَصَبَات ✧ A plant. Trick, foul play.
نِصبَة Way of standing up.
نِصَاب ج نُصُب Origin. Handle of a knife. Amount of property liable to be taxed.
نَصِيب ج أنصِبَة ونُصُب Portion, lot. Cistern. Luck. Snare.
✧ يا نَصِيب Lottery.
ضَرَب بِنَصِيب He was lucky (at play).
نَصِيبَة ج نَصَائِب Stones set up around a tank. Pole.
نَاصِب Crushing (grief). Troublesome (life).
نَاصِبَة ج نَوَاصِب Particles governing the subjunctive as إذَن, أن, كَي, لَن.
✧ نَصَّاب Swindler, tricker.
النَّوَاصِب والنَّاصِبِيَّة وأهل النَّصب Dissenters bearing a violent hatred to Ali.
أنَاصِيب وتَنَاصِيب Signs of the way, as set up stones, poles.
نَصِيبِين Nisibin in Mesopotamia.
أنصَب م نَصبَاء ج نُصب Having erect horns (ram). Having a prominent breast (she-camel).

نِصَاحَات Skins. Snares, loops, nooses.
نَصَاحَة Warning. ✧ Fleshiness.
نَاصِح ج نُصَّاح ونُصَّح Sincere adviser.
نَاصِح م نَاصِحَة Unmixed, pure (honey). ✧ Fat, corpulent.
— الجَيْب Pure-hearted, sincere (man).
نَاصِح ونَاصِحِيّ ونَصَّاح Tailor, sewer.
نَصِيح ج نُصَحَاء Sincere, disinterested (adviser).
نَصُوح True, sincere (repentance).
نَصِيحَة ج نَصَائِح Sincere advice, faithful counsel.
مِنْصَح ومِنْصَحَة Needle for sewing.
مُتَنَصَّح Sewed (garment).
مَنْصُوحَة Watered by rain and luxuriant (land).

✱ نَصَرَ o نَصْرًا ونُصُورًا ه To assist, to succour a. o. To render a. o. victorious (God).
— ه على ومِن To aid a. o. against (his enemies). To preserve a. o. from.
— ه To water (the ground) copiously (rain).
نَصَّر ه To make a. o. a Christian.
تَنَصَّر و✧ تَنَصْرَن To become a Christian.
— ل To endeavour to assist a. o.
تَنَاصَر To assist one another. To verify one another (accounts).
إِنْتَصَر على To overcome (the enemy). To conquer (a country).
— مِن To revenge one's self upon.
إِسْتَنْصَر ه على To ask the assistance of a. o. against.
— بِفُلَانٍ على To take a. o. as a defender against.
نَصْر ونُصْرَة Aid, assistance. Victory.
نَصْرَان ونَصْرَانِيّ ج نَصَارَى Christian.
نَصْرَانَة ونَصْرَانِيَّة ج نَصَارَى Christian woman.
النَّصْرَانِيَّة Christianity.
إِنْتِصَار Victory, conquest.
نَاصِر ج نُصَّار ونَصْر وأَنْصَار ونَاصِرُون Auxiliary, assistant.
نَصِير ج نُصَرَاء وأَنْصَار, ونَصْر ونُصُور Defender, auxiliary.
نُصَيْرِيَّة (نُصَيْرِيّ un) The Ansarees, sect of Gnostics in Syria.
الأَنْصَار (أَنْصَرِيّ un) The assistants of Mohammed.

أَنْصَر Uncircumcised.
نَاصِرَة Nazareth (in Galilea).
نَاصِرِيّ Nazarene, from Nazareth.
نَصَّار Powerful defender.
◻ مَنْصَر ج مَنَاصِر Gang of thieves.
مُنْتَصِر Victorious.
مَنْصُور م مَنْصُورَة Defended by God. Victorious.
أَرْض مَنْصُورَة Land watered by rain.
✧ تَنَصْرَن To be converted to christianity.
بُخْتَ نَصَّر Nabuchodonosor.

✱ نَصَع a نُصُوعًا ونَصَاعَة To be pure unmixed.
— نُصُوعًا To be snow-white (colour). To be clear, manifest (affair). To quench o.'s thirst.
— ب To beget (a child).
— وأَنْصَع ب To acknowledge (a debt).
أَنْصَع To betray o.'s sentiments.
نَصْع ونِصْع ونُصْع White leather. White cloth.
نِصْع Leather-map for playing, or sitting.
نَاصِع ونَصِيع Pure, unmixed (colour).
نَاصِع البَيَاض Snow-white.
مَنْصَع ج مَنَاصِع Privy.

✱ نَصَفَ o i نَصْفًا, وأَنْصَفَ To reach its midst (day, month).
— o نَصْفًا ه To read the half of (a book : reader). To reach (mid-legs : garment). To cover the half of (the head : hoary hair).
— o نَصْفًا ونَصَافَةً ه To receive, to take a half from a. o.
— ه To drink half (a vessel).
— وأَنْصَفَ ه To take the half of a. th.
نَصَّفَ ه بَيْن To divide a. th. in halves between.
— o نُصُوفًا, ونَصَّفَ To have dates half-ripe (palm-tree).
— o نَصْفًا ونَصَافًا ونَصَافَةً, وأَنْصَفَ ه To serve a. o.
نَصَّفَ To be half-white and half-black (head, beard).
— ه To divide a. th. by the midlle.
— ه To veil (a girl).
نَاصَفَ ه ه To partake the half of a. th. with

To stick in a. th. (arrow), نَصَلَ فِي
To fix (an arrow-head). – ﻫ
To come out from (a place). – مِن
To escape, to free o.'s self from.
To put an iron-head to (an arrow). نَصَّلَ ﻫ
To stick (an arrow) into. – ﻫ في
To take off (an arrow-head). أَنصَلَ ﻫ
To extract, to pull out a. th. from. أَنصَلَ وتَنَصَّلَ ﻫ مِن
To get out from (a scrape). تَنَصَّلَ مِن
To justify, to clear o.'s self from a. th. to. تَنَصَّلَ إِلى فُلَانٍ مِن
To select a. th. – ﻫ
To slip, to come out (arrow-head). إِنتَصَلَ
To extract a. th. To lay down (thistle-blossoms : heat). To uproot (dry plants : wind). إِستَنصَلَ ﻫ
نَصْل ج نِصَال وأَنصُل ونُصُول (un نَصْلَة) Iron-head of a spear, of an arrow. Blade of a sword. Spun thread of a spindle. Head.
Iron-head of a spear. Javelin. نَصْلَان
Joint of the neck and head. Hulled wheat. Jaw. Summit of the head. Axe. نَصِيل ج نُصُل
– ومِنصَال ج مَنَاصِيل, ومِنصَل ج مَنَاصِل Stone pestle.
Small body of cavalry. مَنصَال
Sword. مُنصُل ومُنصَل ج مَنَاصِل
المُنصِل ومُنصِل ومَنصَل الأَسِنَّة والإِلَال والأَلّ Name of the month Rejeb.
To seize a. o. by the forelock. ✱ نَصَا ٥ نَصْوًا, وأَنصَى ٥
To dress the hair of the forelock to. – ٥
To seize o. another by the forelock (wrestlers). نَاصَى مُنَاصَاةً ونِصَاءً ٥
To catch o. a. by the forelock. تَنَاصَى
Throes, gripes in the bowels. نَصْو
Forelock ; hair of the forehead. نَاصِيَة ج نَوَاصٍ ونَاصِيَات
The chief men of a tribe. نَوَاصِي النَّاس
Junction of two valleys at their upper part. مُنتَصًى
To abound with thistles (ground). ✱ نَصِيَ – أَنصَى
To curl o.'s locks. تَنَصَّى

To be fair, impartial, to act equitably. To journey at midday. أَنصَفَ
To treat a. o. equitably, to do justice. – ٥
To obtain justice from. – مِن فُلَان
To exact justice for a. o. from. – ٥ مِن
To be a servant, a slave. تَنَصَّفَ
To submit to a. o. To take a. o. as a servant ; to claim part of a. o.'s property. To appeal to the justice of (a prince). – ٥
To veil her head (girl) ; to put on a muffler. – وانتَصَفَ
To obtain a due from. تَنَصَّفَ وانتَصَفَ واستَنصَفَ مِن
To act equitably with o. a. تَنَاصَفَ
To reach its middle (day). إِنتَصَفَ
To act equitably.
To pierce (the game : arrow). – ٥
Half. Justice. نِصْف ونُصْف و✧ نُصّ ج أَنصَاف
Justice. نَصَف ونَصَفَة وإِنصَاف
Middle-aged, middle-sized, equidistant. (m. f. s. pl.) نِصْف
Middle-aged (man). نَصَف ج أَنصَاف ونَصَفُون
Middle-aged (woman). نَصَف ج أَنصَاف ونُصُف ونُصْف
Half. Bicoloured cloth. Veil, muffler. Measure for grain. نَصِيف
Domestic servant. نَاصِف ج نُصَّاف ونَصَف ونَصَفَة
The middle of a stream-bed. نَاصِفَة ج نَوَاصِف
Half-filled (vessel). نَصْفَان م نَصْفَى
Servant, maid-servant. ✧ Trick. مِنْصَف م مِنْصَفَة ج مَنَاصِف
Middle of a road. مَنصَف ومَنصِف
Muffled. مُنَصَّف
Expressed juice reduced to the half by cooking. مُنَصَّف
Middle of a month, of a year. مُنتَصَف
To come off (beard, hair-dye). ✱ نَصَلَ ٥ a نُصُولًا, وتَنَصَّلَ
To come out, to be harmless (venom, sting). To fall off (hoof). نَصَلَ
To be fixed to its head (arrow). To slip (arrow-head). – ٥ نَصْلًا

To be contiguous to. تَنَضَّى ب
To ally o.'s self by marriage to the chief men of a tribe. ه –
To be long (hair). To be high (upland). إِنْتَضَى
To obtain a. th. ه –
Young and tender thistle. (*un.* نَصِيَّة) (*coll*.) نَصِيّ
Remainder. Choice part of a tribe, of a flock. نَصِيَّة ج نَصِيّ وأَنصاء وأَناصٍ
☆ نَضَّ i نَضًّا ونَضِيضًا To flow gently. To ooze forth (water). To burst (water-skin).
To move (the wings : bird). ه –
To manifest, to show a. th. ه –
To become possible (affair). i نَضِيضًا –
Take what thou art enabled to obtain. خُذْ مَا نَضَّ لَكَ مِن
To disturb, to move a. th. نَضَّض ه
To accomplish (an affair). أَنَضَّ وتَنَضَّض ه
He received his due little by little. تَنَضَّض واسْتَنَضَّ حَقَّهُ مِن
He sought a benefit little by little. إِسْتَنَضَّ مَعْرُوفًا
Gold and silver money. نَضّ
Disagreeable thing. أَمْر نَضّ
Possible, within reach. Coins received at a sale. نَاضّ
Small benefits. نِضَاض
Remainder of water. Last born (child). نُضَاضَة
In small quantity (water). Trifling, exiguous. نَضِيض ج نِضَاض
Little fleshy (man). نَضِيض اللَّحْم
Small quantity of milk. نَضِيض مِن اللَّبَن
Slight rain ; gentle wind. نَضِيضَة ج أَنِضَّة ونَضَائِض
Hissing of meat roasted upon heated stones. – ج نَضَائِض
They came all together. جَاء القَوْم بِأَقْصَى نَضِيضِهِم ونَضِيضَتِهِم
Thirsty camels. إِبِل ذَاتُ نَضِيضَةٍ ونَضَائِض
☆ نَضْنَض ه To dart out (its tongue : snake).
Darting its tongue : restless, malignant (serpent). نَضْنَاض ونَضْنَاضَة
☆ نَضَب o نُضُوبًا To flow : to run.
نَضَب o i نُضُوبًا To sink in its socket (eye). To become scanty (harvest). To be exiguous (wealth). To be far-extending (desert). To die. To be remote (people).
To sink into the earth (water). To have little milk (she-camel). نَضَّب ونَضَّب
To twang (a bow). أَنْضَب ه
Far-extending (desert). Dried up (tank). نَاضِب ج نُضَّب
Thorny tree for making arrows. تَنْضُب ج تَنَاضِب
☆ نَضِج a نَضْجًا To be thorougly cooked (meat). To become ripe (fruit). To suppurate (ulcer).
She exceeded the year without bringing forth (pregnant she-camel). – ونَضَّجَت بِوَلَدِهَا
To ripen (fruit). To cook (meat) thoroughly. أَنْضَج ه
Maturity of fruit. Cooking of meat. نُضْج ونَضْج
Thoroughly cooked (meat). Ripe (fruit). نَاضِج ونَضِيج
Of sound judgment (man). نَضِيج الرَّأْي
Suppurative medicine. مُنْضِج و ✧ مَنْضَج ج مَنَاضِج
Spit for roasting. مِنْضَاج
☆ نَضَح i a نَضْحًا, وأَنْضَح To bud forth (tree). To form its grain (corn-crops).
To sprinkle (a house) with (water). نَضَح ه ب
To moisten a. th. ه على –
To allay (thirst). To water (palm-trees) by means of a beast. ه –
To shoot (arrows) at. ه ب –
He defended himself with arguments. نَضَح عَن نَفْسِهِ
To defend a. o. – ونَاضَح عَن
To exude water (skin). To sweat (horse). نَضَح a نَضْحًا وتَنَضَّاحًا
To shed tears (eye). – وتَنَضَّح وانْتَضَح
To asperse the honour of. أَنْضَح ه
To clear o.'s self from (a charge). تَنَضَّح مِن
To excuse o.'s self from. – وانْتَضَح مِن
To be sprinkled (water). إِنْتَضَح

To be fresh, bright (face). To be green (foliage). وَنَضَرًا وَنَضَارَةً, وأَنْضَرَ

To grant an easy life to a. o. (God). نَضَرَ o نَضْرًا, وَنَضَّرَ وأَنْضَرَ ه وه

To find a. th. bright, pleasant. إِسْتَنْضَرَ ه

Splendour; brightness and beauty. Plentiful life. نَضْر وَنَضْرَة وَنَضَارَة

نَضْر ج نِضَار وأَنْضُر, وَنُضَار وَنَضِير وأَنْضَر Pure gold or silver.

Pure, unmixed. Board, joist. نُضَار

Tamarisk for making bowls. — وَنِضَار

Bright. Green, prosperous. نَضِر وَنَضِير وأَنْضَر

Beautiful and bright. Intense (colour). Green water-moss. نَاضِر

Intense red. أَحْمَر نَاضِر

☆ نَضَفَ o i نَضْفًا, وَنَضِفَ a نَضَفًا, وانْتَضَفَ ه To exhaust (the udder: young camel).

To amble (she-camel). أَنْضَفَ

To make (a she-camel) to amble. ه —

Wild marjoram. نَضَف

Purity, cleanliness. ✧ نَضَافَة (for نَظَافَة)

Easy trot, amble of camels. نَضَفَان

Impure, foul, defiled. نَضِف ج نَضِفُون

Impure. ✧ Pure, clean. نَضِيف

To overcome a. o. in shooting. ☆ نَضَلَ o نَضْلًا ه

To be exhausted, emaciated (camel). نَضِلَ a نَضَلًا

To defend. نَاضَلَ مُنَاضَلَةً وَنِضَالًا وَنِيضَالًا عَن

To contend in shooting with. ه —

To exhaust, to emaciate (a beast). أَنْضَلَ ه

To drive. To take away a. th. from. تَنَضَّلَ ه وه

To compete in a shooting-match. تَنَاضَلَ وانْتَضَلَ

To vie in glory with o. a. إِنْتَضَلَ

To select (an arrow). To single out (a man) from the crowd. — ه وه

Winner in a shooting-match. نَاضِل ج نُضَّال

To draw (the sword). ☆ نَضَا o نَضْوًا, وانْتَضَى السَّيْفَ ه

To cross (a desert) quickly. نَضَا ه

He stripped him of his clothes. — ه مِن ثَوْبِهِ

To sprinkle water upon the body after ablution. إِنْتَضَحَ واسْتَنْضَحَ

Aspersion of water. Water sprinkled in ablution. نَضَح

نَضَح ج نُضُوح وأَنْضَاح, وَنَضِيح ج نُضُح Watering-trough near to a well.

Beast carrying water for watering. نَاضِح م نَاضِحَة ج نَوَاضِح

Driver of a camel carrying water; waterer. نَضَّاح

Kind of perfume. Any medicine injected into the mouth. نَضُوح

Shooting many arrows (bow). — وَنَضَّاحَة وَنُضَحِيَّة

To wet, to sprinkle a. o. or a. th. ☆ نَضَحَ a نَضْحًا ه وه

To boil forth (water-spring). — نَضْحًا وَنَضَحَانًا

To shoot (arrows) at. — ه فِي

To sprinkle o. another. نَاضَحَ مُنَاضَحَةً وَنِضَاحًا ه

To be poured upon (water). إِنْضَحَ عَلَى

To be sprinkled (water). إِنْتَضَحَ

Aspersion (of water). Mark of perfumes upon clothes. نَضْح

A shower. نَضْحَة

Abundant (rain, spring). نَضَّاخ م نَضَّاخَة

Sprinkling-bottle. Holy water-sprinkler. مِنْضَحَة ج مَنَاضِح, و✧ نَضَّاحَة

To pile up (furniture). To set in order. ☆ نَضَدَ i نَضْدًا, وَنَضَّدَ ه

To be disposed regularly (teeth). تَنَضَّدَ

To assemble, to remain in (a place). إِنْتَضَدَ ب

Goods piled up, set in order. Couch-frame. Glory. Nobility. Noble. نَضَد ج أَنْضَاد

Illustrious paternal and maternal uncles. أَنْضَاد الرَّجُل

Body of men. Auxiliaries, company. — القَوْم

Superposed (rocks). Piled up (clouds). — الجِبَال والسَّحَاب

Fat (she-camel). نَضَد وَنَضُود ج نُضُد

Set in order; compact. Piled up. نَضِيد وَمَنْضُود وَمُنَضَّد

Pillow, stuffed articles. نَضِيدَة ج نَضَائِد

☆ نَضَرَ o وَنَضِرَ a وَنَضُرَ o نَضْرَةً وَنُضُورًا

نضا ونضّى الثوبَ عنه He took off his clothes.

— o نضوًا ونُضِيًّا ه To outrun (the others : horse).

— o نضوًا ونُضُوًّا To come out (hair-dye).

— o نضوًا To be reduced (wound). To be absorbed (water).

أنضى ه To lend to a. o. an exhausted camel.

أنضى وتنضّى ه To exhaust, to emaciate (a beast).

أنضى وانتضى الثوبَ To wear out (clothes).

نِضو ج أنضاء Part of the bit upon which the bridle is tied. Impaired arrow-wood. Worn out garment.

نِضو م نِضوة ج أنضاء , ونَضِيّ م نَضِيَّة Jaded, emaciated (beast).

✧ نَضوة Horseshoe.

✱ نضى i نضيًا السيفَ He drew (the sword) *See* o نضا.

✱ نطّ i نطًّا To dote. ✧ To jump, to frolic.

— في الأرض To go away.

— نطيطًا To escape, to run away.

نطّ (*un.* نطّة) ✧ Leap, bound.

نطّاط Dotard. ✧ Jumper, frolicsome.

نطيط م نطيطة Remote (place).

✱ نطنط ✧ To hop, to frisk ; to trot (horse).

— ه To stretch (the hand).

نطنط ونُطانِط ج نطانِط Of tall stature.

✱ نطب o نطبًا, وأنطب ه To fillip a. o. on the ear.

ناطب ه To incite a. o. against.

ناطِب ج نواطِب, ومِنطب ومِنطبة Strainer, cullender.

✱ نطح a i نطحًا ه, وناطح مناطحة ونطاحًا ه To gore a. o. (bull). To strike a. o. with the horns.

تناطح وانتطح To butt togethers (rams).

تناطح To dash together (waves).

النَّطح The star in the horn of *Aries*.

نطحة Butt, gore. Blow, shock.

ما لهُ ناطح ولا خابط He has neither camel nor sheep.

ناطح ج نواطح Difficulty, stroke of fortune.

نطّاح Butting vehemently.

نَطوح ونطيح Unfortunate (man).

نطيح Coming full butt against a. o. (wild beast). Having two curls of hair on the forehead (horse).

نطيح ومنطوح Gored to death.

نَطيحة ج نطائح ونطحى Sheep killed or wounded with the horns.

✱ نطر o نطرًا ونِطارة ه To watch (a vine, a fruit-garden).

— ه ✧ To wait for a. o.

نطر Watching, look out.

نِطارة Salary, employ of a watchman.

ناطِر وناطور ج نُطّار ونطَرة ونُطَراء ونَواطِير Watchman, keeper of vines. Look-out, sailor.

نُطّار Scarecrow set up in a field.

✧ مَنطَرة ج مَناطِر Look-out, watching-place.

✧ نطرون Egyptian natron.

✱ نطِس a نطسًا To become learned, skilful in an art.

تنطّس في To be refined in (cleanliness), in (speech).

— ه وعن To examine a. th. carefully.

نَطِس ونَطُس ونِطّيس ونِطاسيّ Learned, skilful. Exact in affairs.

G نِطاسيّ ونِطّيس Student in physic.

نُطُس Skilful physicians.

نُطَسة Exact, scrupulous in manners.

ناطِس Spy, searcher for news.

✱ نُطِع نطعًا وانتطع To be altered (colour).

تنطّع في To be deep, extravagant in (speech).

نِطع ونَطع ونِطَع ج نُطوع وأنطاع Leather-cloth for playing, working, or beheading a culprit.

نِطع ونِطَع ج نُطوع Forepart of the palate.

الحروف النِطعيّة The palatal letters ت, د, ط.

نِطاع Territory occupied by a tribe.

نطّاع Wont to put aside part of his food.

✱ نطف o i نطفًا وتَنطافًا ونطَفانًا ونِطافة To flow gently (water). To ooze (water-skin). To exude (venom).

— ه To pour (water). ✧ To snuff (a candle).

Belt of *Orio* (*const.*). نِطَاق ومِنطقة الجَوزَاء

Gifted with speech. Endowed with reason. Cattle. نَاطِق

Flank. Rationable, human (soul). نَاطِقَة

He has no cattle nor property. مَا لَهُ نَاطِق وَلَا صَامِت

Expression of ideas in language. Diction. Logics. مَنطِق

Logician. مَنطِقِيّ

Girdle, belt, zone. مِنطَق ومِنطَقَة ج مَنَاطِق

The Zodiac. مِنطَقَة البُرُوج

✧ Torrid zone. المِنطَقَة الحارَّة

Eloquent. مِنطِيق

Influential, of high rank. مُنتَطِق

Girded. Surrounded with clouds (mountain). Waist. مُنَطَّق

Uttered. Proper meaning (of a word). مَنطُوق

To foment (the head). ✲ نَطَل o نَطلًا. ونَطَّل ه

To express (wine) from grapes. نَطَل ه

To pour a little water from (a skin). إِنتَطَل مِن

Grapes-skin. نَطَل

Remainder of wine. Wine flowing from the press. نِطَل

Draught of water, of milk. نُطلَة ونَاطِل

I could not obtain anything. مَا ظَفِرتُ بِنَاطِل

Vessel for measuring wine. نَاطَل ونَأطَل ونَيطَل ج نَيَاطِل

Calamity, distress. نَيطَلَاء ونَيطَل

He threw him into evils. رَمَاهُ بِالأَنطَلَة

Method of irrigation used in Egypt. ◻ نَطَّالَة

Aromatic bath. نَطُول

✧ Turkey in Asia, Anatolia. أَنَاطُول

◻ Bag of rushes for irrigating. مِنطَال

Wine-press. مَنَاطِل

To be remote (dwelling). ✧ To be damp (place). ✲ نَطَا o نَطوًا

To stretch a. th. To weave (a fabric). — ه

To vie in length with a. o. To warp (a fabric) conjointly with a. o. (woman). نَاطَى ه

To give a. th. to. ه ه (*for* أَعطَى) أَنطَى

✲ نَطِف ونَطُف وأَنطَف ه To impute a vice to a. o.

نَطِف a ونُطِف نَطفًا ونَطَافَة ونُطُوفَة To be stained, accused of a vice.

نَطِف To be altered (thing). To be ulcerated (camel). To have an indigestion (man).

نَطَّف ه To put earrings to (a girl).

تَنَطَّف To be stained. To put on earrings (girl).

— مِن To loathe a. th.

إِستَنطَف ه To waste away (wealth).

نُطفَة ج نُطَف Semen.

نَطَف Corruption, evil, defect.

نُطفَة ج نُطَف و نِطَاف Small or great quantity of pure water.

— ونُطَافَة Drop of water, remainder of water in a bucket.

أَلنُّطفَتَان The two seas *i. e.* the Mediterranean and the Red Sea.

نُطفَة ونُطَفَة ج نُطَف Earring. Small pearl.

نَطِف Impure. Wounded in the brain.

نَاطِف Sweetmeat prepared with trickle.

نَطُوف Rainy (night).

✲ نَطَق i نُطقًا ومَنطِقًا ونُطُوقًا To speak, to articulate sounds.

نَطَّق ه To gird a. o.

— ه To reach the middle of (a mountain : water). To endow a. o. with (speech : God).

نَاطَق واستَنطَق ه To talk with a. o.

أَنطَق واستَنطَق ه To make a. o. to speak.

تَنَطَّق وانتَطَق وتَمَنطَق To gird o.'s self. To put on a belt.

انتَطَق To put on a flounced petticoat (woman).

— ب To be surrounded by (hills : country). To be surrounded by o.'s people.

إِستَنطَق ه To question a. o. (judge).

نُطق Speech, articulate language, utterance.

نِطَاق ج نُطُق Belt. Flounced petticoat. Double range of rocks on a mountain Water-ripple.

تناطى To struggle together ; to strive to outstrip o. a.
— الكلام To discuss, to dispute.
نطيّ م نطيّة Remote, distant.
نطاة ج أنطاء Stalk of unripe dates.
نطاوة ✧ Dampness.
ناطٍ م ناطية ✧ Damp.
✱ نظر o ونظر a نظرًا ومنظرًا ونظرانًا وتنظارة وتنظارًا ه وه وإلى To look at a. o. or a. th. To consider a. th. To face a. o. To oversee, to inspect a. th.
— ل To compassionate, to aid a. o.
— بين To judge between.
— ه نظرًا في To take care of. To inspect a. th. To reflect upon a. th.
—، أنظر ه To look for a. th. To sell a. th. upon credit.
— وأنظر وتنظّر ه To grant a respite to.
— ونظّر ه To sell a. th. upon credit.
داري تنظر إلى داره وتناظر داره My house faces his.
نُظِر To be smitten by the evil eye.
ناظر مناظرة ه وه To be alike, equal to. To discuss with.
— وأنظر ه وه ب To compare a. o. or a. th. to.
أنظر ب To resemble a. o.
تنظّر ه وه To consider, to watch a. o. or a. th.
تناظر To face o. a. To contend together.
انتظر واستنظر ه وه To look for a. th. To await a. o.
استنظر ه To ask a delay from.
نظر ج أنظار Glance. Look. ✧ Regard shown, kindness.
في هذا نظر This is to be examined.
حيّ نظر Tribe whose tents front o. another.
✧ هو تحت نظر فلان He is under the care of such a one.
نظرًا إلى وبالنظر إلى With regard to ; in respect of.
نِظر Similar, alike.
نظرة A look, a glance. Vice, defect. Evil look. Benevolence.
نظِرة Delay.
نظريّ Speculative (science).
نِظار ونظارة Countenance, outward appearance. Perspicacity.
✧ Financial administration. Ministry. نظارة
Imp. Wait thou! نظارِ
ناظر ج نظّار Guardian, keeper. Vine-keeper. Eye. ✧ Manager. Minister of state.
سديد الناظر Free from suspicion.
الناظران The two veins on the sides of the nostrils.
ناظرة ج نواظر Eye. *Pl.* Veins, nerves of the eyes.
نظّار Fiery (horse). Seer.
نظّارة Beholders.
نظّارة وناظور ✧ Spectacles, telescope.
ناظور وناظورة (*m. f. s. pl.*) Keeper of a vine ; chief of a tribe.
سمعنّة نظرنّة وسمعنة نظرنة Intrusive and inquisitive (woman).
نظور ونظورة (*m. f. s. pl.*) ج نظائر ,
وناظورة (*m. f. s. pl.*) ج نواظير Leader man of a tribe.
نظير ج نظراء م نظيرة ج نظائر Facing, corresponding to. Like, equal, match, correspondent.
النظير The Nadir *opp. to the Zenith.*
نظيرة (*m. f. s. pl.*) Leader man of a tribe. Vanguard of an army.
منظر ج مناظر Sight, point of view. Appearance. ✧ Theater.
— ومنظرة ج مناظر Look-out. Belvedere.
منظريّ ومنظرانيّ Fine-looking.
منظار ج مناظير Mirror. Telescope.
منظورة Vicious (woman).
✱ نظف o نظافة To be clean, neat, pure.
نظّف ه To render a. th. clean, pure.
تنظّف To be purified, to cleanse o.'s self.
انتظف ه To exhaust (its mother's milk : youngling).
استنظف To choose, to select a. th. clean.
— ه To take the whole of a. th. To pay the whole (tribute : viceroy).
نظافة Cleanliness. Purity.
نظيف ج نظفاء Clean, pure.
◻ نظليّ Delicate, effeminate.
✱ نظم i نظمًا ه إلى To join a. th. to.

To string (pearls). To set things in order. To trim (verses). نَظَمَ نَظْمًا ونِظَامًا, ونَظَّمَ هـ

To be striped (fish, lizard). نَظِمَ ونَظَّمَ وأَنظَمَ

To repair. To reform. To set a. th. in order. نَظَّمَ هـ

To be full of eggs (hen). أَنظَمَ

To be set in order. تَنَظَّمَ وتَنَاظَمَ وانتَظَمَ

To be rightly arranged (affair). تَنَظَّمَ وانتَظَمَ

To pierce a. o. with (a spear). إِنتَظَمَ ه ب

Order. String of pearls. Poetry, poetical style. The Pleiads. نَظْم

Swarm of locusts. — ونِظَامٌ مِن جَرَادٍ

Rule of conduct, custom, use. Standard. Order, harmony. ✧ Regular troops. Uniform. نِظَام

String of pearls. — ج نُظُم

Public order; civil laws. — ج نُظُم وأَنظِمَة وأَنَاظِيم

They act in the same way. هُم عَلَى نِظَامٍ وَاحِدٍ

He is the support of his affair. هُوَ نِظَامُ أَمْرِهِ

His affair is not in good order. لَيسَ لِأَمْرِهِ نِظَامٌ

Two white streaks (in lizards, fishes). نِظَامَانِ وإِنظَامَانِ وأُنظُومَتَانِ

Row of sandy hills. Set of eggs in the ovary. أَنظَام

✧ A private, a common soldier. نِظَامِي

Setting in order. Poet. Streaked (fish, lizard). نَاظِم

Row of wells. Mountain-path provided with water-holes. نَظِيم

Set in order. نَظِيم ومَنظُوم

✧ Reforms, new regulations set by Sultan Mahmoud. تَنظِيمَات

Set in order. Poem, verses. ✧ Splendid. Comfortable (house). مَنظُوم

New and tender plant. ✡ نعع – نُعَاعَة ج نُعَاع

Mint. ✡ نَعنَع ونُعنُع

✧ Penny-royal mint. — المَاء

Things appended to the belt. نَعَانِع المِنطَقَة

To ✡ نَعَبَ a i نَعْبًا ونَعِيبًا ونُعَابًا وتَنْعَابًا ونَعَبَانًا croak (raven). To crow in stretching the neck (cock). To cry out (crier).

To walk quickly in stretching the neck (camel). — a نَعْبًا

Swift (wind). نَعْب

Swift (she-camel). نَاعِبَة ج نَوَاعِب, ونَعَّابَة, ونَعُوب ج نُعُب

Raven, young raven. نَعَّاب

Swift-running (horse). — ومِنعَب

To describe a. o., to characterise, to commend a. th. or a. o. ✡ نَعَتَ a نَعْتًا, وانتَعَتَ هـ وه

To add an epithet to a (substantive). نَعَتَ هـ

To show good qualities. نَعِتَ a نَعَتًا

To be endowed with good qualities. To be light-footed (horse). نَعُتَ o نَعَاتَةً

To be handsome-faced. أَنعَتَ

To be described by. أُنتُعِتَ ب

To ask a. o. to describe. إِستَنعَتَ ه هـ

Description. Qualification. نَعْت

Epithet. نَعْت ج نُعُوت

Horse winner in a race. نَعْت ونَعْتَة ونَعِيت ونَعِيتَة ومُنعِت

To take a. th. ✡ نَعَثَ a وأَنعَثَ هـ

To scatter (o.'s wealth). أَنعَثَ في

Male hyena. ✡ نعثل – نَعثَل

Deportment of an old man. نَعثَلَة

To be intensely white (colour). ✡ نَعَجَ o نَعْجًا ونُعُوجًا

To be fat (camel). To have an indigestion of mutton. نَعِجَ a نَعَجًا

Ewe. Woman. نَعْجَة ج نِعَاج ونَعَجَات

Even (ground). Swift (she-camel). نَاعِج م نَاعِجَة ج نَوَاعِج

Having an indigestion of mutton. نَعِج ج نَعِجُون

To snort (beast). To gush forth (blood). ✡ نَعَرَ i a نَعِيرًا ونُعَارًا

He clamoured in the riot. — في الفِتنَة

To throng (crowd). ✧ To pick with a spear. To cuff a. o. — a نَعْرًا

To set to (work) carefully. To overrun (a country). نَعَرَ فِي

To resist a. o. — ه

To go towards a. o. — إلى

To be harassed by flies (beast). نَعِرَ a نَعَرًا

To wheel (an arrow) on the nail. نَعَر ه
To produce its first fruit (أَرَاك tree). أَنْعَر
Harassed by flies (beast). Restless. نَعِر م نَعِرَة
Snorting, snurl. ✧ Boxing. Knife-thrust. نَعْرَة ج نَعَرَات
Blast of wind and heat at the rising of the Pleiads. نَعْرَة النَّجْم
Pride. Difficult affair. نُعَرَة, نُعَرَة
Cartilage of the nose. نُعْرَة ونُعَرَة
Blue fly harassing horses. نُعَرَة ج نُعَر ونُعَرَات
Shouts, bustle. نَعِير
Brooding his designs beforehand. ـ أَنْفِهِ
Rebellious ; clamorous. Firebrand. Wound gushing with blood. نَعَّار م نَعَّارَة
Vein spurting with blood. ـ ونَعُور ونَاعُور
Far-away journey. نِيَّة نَعُور
✧ Two-handled earthenware mug. نَعَّارَة و✧ نَعَارَة ج نَعَاير
Water-wheel. Bucket for raising water. نَاعُور ونَاعُورَة ج نَوَاعِير
To drowse, to doze. ✱ نَعَس a o نَعْسًا
To be weak (in mind and body). To be dull (market). ـ a نَعْسًا
To have sluggish sons. أَنْعَس
To lull, to make a. o. asleep. ـ ه
To feign dozing. تَنَاعَس
Sleepiness, drowsiness. Languidness of the limbs. نُعَاس
Drowsy, dozing. نَاعِس ج نُعُس, ونَعْسَان
To raise, to comfort a. o. (God). ✧ To quicken. ✱ نَعَش a نَعْشًا, ونَعَّش وأَنْعَش ه
To raise a. o. (from a fall). To restore a. o. to wealth. To put (the dead) on a litter. To eulogise (the dead). نَعَش ه
To be carried on a litter (dead man). To be raised after a fall. To be comforted, recalled to life. نُعِش
To say to a. o. May God raise thee. نَعَّش ه
To rise after a fall. To become lively after languidness. To be quickened, reinvigorated. إِنْتَعَش

Bier for the dead. Ostrich-trap. نَعْش
The constellation of *Ursa*. بَنَات نَعْش
Name of the stars in the tail of *Ursa*. إِبْن نَعْش
Cheering. ✧ نَعَاشَة
To waste (a land ; locusts). ✱ نَعَص a نَعْصًا ه
✧ To yelp (dog). نَعَص و✧ ونَعْوَص
To totter. نَعِص a نَعَصًا
To become angry, to bear rancour. To rise after a fall. إِنْتَعَص
✧ Swamp. نَعْص
Helpers نَاعِصَة
To get a. th. from. ✱ نَعَض a نَعْضًا ه مِن
Thorny tree used for tanning or making tooth-picks. نُعْض
Leaving morsels half-eaten (eater). Uudertaking a long journey. ✱ نعط — نَاعِط ج نُعُط
To run slowly, to walk in swaying. ✱ نَعْظَل
To intercept the way to ; to debar a. o. from. ✱ نعف — نَاعَف ه وانْتَعَف ل
To live in the hills. أَنْعَف
To ascend a hill (rider). To appear. إِنْتَعَف
To leave a. th. to a. o. ـ ه إلى
Elevated ground in a valley, depressed ground in a mountain. نَعْف ج نِعَاف
Dependent thong of a sandal. نَعْفَة
Saddle strap, housings trappings. نَعَفَة
Dependent ear. أُذُن نَاعِفَة ونَعُوف
Soft, flaccid. ضَعِيف نَعِيف
Steep eminence. مَنَاعِف
To cry out to (sheep). ✱ نَعَق a i نَعْقًا ونَعِيقًا ونُعَاقًا ونَعَقَانًا ب
To croak (raven). ✧ To bleat (sheep). ـ نَعِيقًا ونُعَاقًا
Cry of the muezzin. نَعْقَة المُؤَذِّن
Two stars in *Orio*. النَّاعِقَان
To give sandals to a. o. ✧ To curse. ✱ نَعَل a نَعْلًا ه
To shoe(a horse, a camel). ـ ونَعَّل وأَنْعَل ه
To wear boots. نَعِل a نَعَلًا
To put on boots. Tohave many boots. أَنْعَل
To be shod. تَنَعَّل وانْتَعَل

Yes, certainly. So. نَعَمْ

Bravo! All right! Go on! نِعِمَّا و نِعْمَتْ

Prosperity, happiness. نُعْم ج أَنْعُم

Camels, sheep. Cattle. نَعَم ج أَنْعَام ونُعْمَان وجج أَنَاعِيم

Well-being. Delicate life. Wealth. Cattle. نَعْمَة ونُعْمَى

Rich, wealthy. وَاسِع ٱلنِّعْمَة

نِعْمَة ج نِعَم وأَنْعُم ونِعْمَات ونِعِمَات, ونُعْمَى, ونَعْمَاء ج أَنْعُم Benefit, grace, favour. ✧ Privilege.

The Benefactor ; *title applied to a sovereign*. وَلِيّ ٱلنِّعَم

The grace of God. نِعْمَة ٱللّٰه

For the sake of; with pleasure. نُعْم ونُعْمَ ونَعْمَة ونُعْمَة عَيْنٍ

Ostrich. Desert. نَعَام (un. نَعَامَة)

Name of the stars in *Sagittarius*. — ٱلصَّادِر وٱلوَارِد

With pleasure ; for the sake of. نُعْمَى ونُعِيم ونَعَامَ ونُعَامَ ونَعَامَى عَيْنٍ

South wind. نُعَامَى ج نَعَائِم

Stone projecting in a well. Sign of the way. Road. Pavilion on a mountain. Joy. Membrane of the brain. نَعَامَة ج نَعَائِم ونَعَامَات

Name of various stars in *Pegasus*. The 20th mansion of the moon. ٱلنَّعَائِم

Mellowness, softness. نُعُومَة

Blood. Surname of the kings of Hira. نُعْمَان

Anemone (*plant*). شَقَائِق ٱلنُّعْمَان

Beneficence, favour, grace. إِنْعَام ج إِنْعَامَات (un. إِنْعَامَة)

Well-being, content. Joy, delight. تَنَعُّم

Thorny tree with fleshy leaves. تَنْعِيمَة

Soft (garment); mellowy. Soft to the touch. Tender (plant). Easy, life; leading an easy life. ✧ Pounded fine (sugar). نَاعِم م نَاعِمَة

✧ Sage, (aromatic herb). ٱلنَّاعِمَة

Delight. Pleasure. Bliss. Heaven. نَعِيم

Favours of God. نَعِيم ٱللّٰه

Bool-minded, good-nature.d — ٱلبَالِ

Sountiful. مِنْعَام

Cweet language. كَلَام مُنَعَّم

Tender (plant). مُنَاعِم ومُتَنَاعِم

Leading a soft life مَنْعَم ومُنَاعِم, ومُتَنَعِّم ومُتَنَاعِم

He journeyed on foot. He sew a hard ground. إِنْتَعَلَ ٱلأَرْضَ

Sole. Sandal, horse-shoe. Metallic end of a scabbard Hard and barren land. نَعْل ج نِعَال وأَنْعُل

✧ Farrier. نَعْلَبَنْد P

Pair of shoes. نَعْلَان

A sole. A shoe, sandal. نَعْلَة

White spot on a horse's instep. إِنْعَال

Shod (man, horse). Hard (hoof). نَاعِل ومُنْعَل ومُنَعَّل

Hard ground. مَنْعَل وأَرْض مَنْعَل ومَنْعَلَة

Hard-hoofed (horse). White-spotted on the instep (horse). Furnished with a leathern sole (stocking). مُنَعَّل

✱ نَعِمَ a o نَعُمَ a نَعْمَة ومَنْعَمًا To lead an easy life. To be soft (life).

— ه To suit a. o. (abode).

نَعِمَ بِ . . . عَيْنًا To rejoice at.

نَعِمَ ٱللّٰهُ بِكَ عَيْنًا ونَعِمَكَ ٱللّٰهُ عَيْنًا May God favour thee!

نَعِمَ a نَعْمًا To be green and tende (bough).

نَعُمَ a نُعُومَة To be soft, mellowy.

نِعْمَ ونِعِمَّا م نِعْمَتْ *Verb of praise* (*defective*). How excellent is...!

نِعْمَ ٱلرَّجُلُ زَيْدٌ و نِعْمَ رَجُلًا زَيْدٌ What an excellent man Zeyd is!

نَعَّمَ ونَاعَمَ ه To procure well-being to.

نَعَّمَ ه وأَنْعَمَ ل To answer affirmatively to.

نَعَّمَ ه To soften, to render mellowy, comfortable, pleasing. ✧ To pulverise.

نَاعَمَ وتَنَعَّمَ وتَنَاعَمَ To lead a soft life.

نَاعَمَ ه To fasten (a rope).

أَنْعَمَ وتَنَعَّمَ To be suitable, salubrious (place).

أَنْعَمَ ه عَلَى او ه بِ To grant (a favour) to.

— فِي To apply o.'s self to.

— ٱلنَّظَرَ فِي To look carefully at.

— ه To render a. th. comfortable, pleasing.

أَنْعَمَ ٱللّٰهُ بِكَ عَيْنًا May God bless thee!

أَنْعَمَ ٱللّٰهُ صَبَاحَكَ May God give thee a happy morning!

أَنْعَمَ ه To go barefoot to.

تَنَعَّمَ To walk barefoot. To enjoy a pleasant life.

To mew (cat). ✯ نَغَا o نُغَاء

Chap on a camel's lip; on a horse's hoof. Fresh dates. نَغْو

To announce the death of a. o. to. ✯ نَعَى a نَعْيًا ونَعِيًّا ونُعْيَانًا ه ل

To invite a. o. to bewail a dead person. — ه

To reproach a. o. with (faults). — ه عَلَى

✧ To moan, to lament. نَعَى i

To receive the news of a. o.'s death. نُعِيَ إِلى

To convey a death-message to. تَنَاعَى

His fame has been spread. إِسْتَنْعَى ذِكْرُهُ

To strike a. o. repeatedly (misfortune). — بِفُلَان

Announcement of a decease. نَعِيَّة ج نَعِيَّات, ونَعِيّ ونَعْي ✧ نَعْوَة

Announcing the death. نَعِيّ وناعٍ ج نُعَاة ونَاعُون

Imperat. Announce the death of. نَعَاءِ

Death-message. مَنْعًى ومَنْعَاة ج مَنَاعٍ

Part of the throat near the uvula. ✯ نَغ — نُغْنُغ ج نَغَانِغ

To have the throat diseased. نُغْنِغ

To swallow (saliva). ✯ نَغَبَ a o i نَغْبًا ه
To sip (water: bird).

To gulp water (man). — فِي الشُّرْب

Draught, gulp. نَغْبَة ونُغْبَة ج نُغَب

Evil action. نُغْبَة

To pull out (the hair). ✯ نَغَتَ a نَغْتًا ه

To boil (pot). ✯ نَغَرَ i ونَغِرَ a نَغَرًا ونَغَرَانًا

To tickle (a child). نَغَّرَ ه

To call out (a she-camel). — ب

To boil with anger. — وتَنَغَّرَ

To be angered with. — وتَنَغَّرَ عَلَى

To be rotten (egg). To yield milk besmeared with blood (ewe). أَنْغَرَ

To dissemble. تَنَاغَرَ

Spring of salt water. نَغْر

Boiliug with anger. Jealous. نَغِر م نَغِرَة

Red-beaked nightingale. نُغَر ج نِغْرَان
Young sparrow.

Fretful, nervous, hot-tempered. نَغَّار

Wound bleeding abundantly. جُرْح نَغَّار

To tickle (a child). To tease a. o. (slanderer). ✯ نَغَزَ a نَغْزًا ه

✧ To prick a. o. with (a needle). — ه ب

To excite dissension between. — بَيْن

Intriguer. نَاغِز ج نُغَّاز

Backbiter. نَغَّاز

To be shaken, to waver. ✯ نَغَشَ a نَغْشًا ونَغَشَانًا, وتَنَغَّشَ وانْتَغَشَ

To feel a leaning toward. نَغَشَ إِلَى

To coax, to wheedle a. o. ✧ نَاغَشَ ه
To converse with a. o. upon an affair.

To pretend kindness. ✧ تَنَاغَشَ

To swarm with. إِنْتَغَشَ ب

Shaking, motion. نَغْشَة ج نَغَشَات

Short-sized. نُغَاش ونُغَاشِيّ

To fail to carry out a design. To be disturbed (affair). To be interrupted (watering). ✯ نَغِصَ a نَغَصًا

To interrupt the watering of (camels). — ونَغَصَ a نَغْصًا, وأَنْغَصَ ه

To render (life) troublesome (God, cares). نَغَّصَ وأَنْغَصَ ه عَلَى

To be perturbed, troublesome (life). تَنَغَّصَ

To press together (camels). تَنَاغَصَ

To be moved with pity for. ✧ إِسْتَنْغَصَ ل

Hindrance. ✧ Thing moving to pity. نُغْصَة

✯ نَغَضَ o i نَغْضًا ونُغُوضًا ونَغَضَانًا ونَغَضًا

To shake about, to be convulsed, to wag. وأَنْغَضَ وتَنَغَّضَ

To wag (the head). To shake, to jog a. th. — ه وب ونَغَّضَ وأَنْغَضَ ه

To be numerous. To heap up (clouds). — نَغَضًا

Trembling; having a jerking gait. نَغِض

Cartilage of the shoulder-blade. نَغْض ونُغْض ونَاغِض

Male ostrich. نَغْض و نِغْض
Lusty.

Heaped up (clouds). نَاغِض ج نُغَّض

Wrinkled in the belly. نَغَّاض ٱلْبَطْن

Worm found in date-stones, in the nostrils of sheep. ✯ نغف — نَغَف

Ends of the upper-jaw. النَّغَفَتَانِ

To croak (raven). ✯ نَغَقَ i نَغِيقًا ونُغَاقًا

To be spoilt in tanning (hide). To be malevolent (intention). ✯ نَغِلَ a نَغَلًا
To be ulcered (wound).

He was angered with. — قَلْبُهُ عَلَى
He bore rancour to.

Surroundings of a house. نفانف الدّار
Sprig of plants. ✲ نفا – نُفَاة ج نُفًا
To boil with anger. ✲ نَفَت i نَفْتًا ونَفَتَانًا ونَفِيتًا
To boil fiercely (kettle). – ونافَت
Boiling fiercely (pot). نَفُوت
Flour diluted with water or milk. نَفِيتَة
To puff, to blow upon a. o. (wizard). ✲ نَفَث o i نَفْثًا فِي وعلى
To enchant a. o. – ه
To sputter, to expectorate. To eject (its venom : snake). To emit (blood : wound). – ه
To whisper a. th. to. نافَث ه
Puff, spittle. نَفْث ونَفْثَة ج نَفَثات
Erotic verses. نَفْث الشَّيْطان
Spittle. نُفَاثَة
Enchanter. نافِث ونفّاث
Issuing from a wound (blood). نَفِيث
To spring up (hare). To come forth (chicken). ✲ نَفَج o نَفْجًا ونَفَجانًا ونُفُوجًا
To blow strongly (wind). – نَفْجًا
To fill (a skin). To heave up (the shift : breast). – ه
To magnify o.'s self, to boast vainly. – وتَنَفَّج وانتفج
To start (a hare). أنفج ه
To show (anger). إستنفج ه
Harsh (voice). نافِج
Vesicle of musk. Gush of wind. Rain-cloud. Daughter. The last rib. Vessel full of perfumes. نافِجَة ج نَوافِج
Proud, boastful. نفّاج
Patch under the sleeves of a garment. نِفاجَة
Bow. نَفِيجَة ج نَفائِج
Stranger to a tribe. نَفِيج ج نُفُج
Exaggerating in speech. أنفجاني
To diffuse itself (perfume). To blow (wind). To spurt forth blood (vein). ✲ نَفَح a نَفْحًا ونَفَحانًا ونُفاحًا
To strike a. o. slightly with (a sword). – ه ب
To shake (o.'s hair). – ه
To struggle with a. o. نافح ه
To protect a. o. – عن فلان
To oppose, to resist a. o. إنتفح ب
To come back to. – إلى

To sow discord between. نَغِل بَيْن
To be spurious (child). نَغَل o نُغُولَة
To spoil (leather) in tanning. أنغل ه
Dissension. نَغَل
Illegitimate, bastard (child). نَغْل ونَغِل ونَغِيل م نَغْلَة الخ
Spoilt in tanning (hide). نَغِل م نَغِلَة
Tick found in leather. نُغَيْلَة
✲ نَغَم o i ونَغِم a نَغْمًا، ونَغَّم وتَنَغَّم فِي الغِناء
To speak in a thrilling tone, to hum.
He remained silent without uttering a single word. سَكَت فَمَا نَغَم بحَرْف او مَا تَنَغَّم بِشَيْء
He gulped, he sipped the beverage. نَغَم فِي الشَّراب
To whisper to a. o. ناغَم ه
Whisper. Hum. Thrilling song. Sweet melody. نَغْم ونَغَم ج أنغام
Melody. Melodious voice. نَغْمَة ونَغَمَة ج نَغَمات
Draught, gulp. نَغْمَة ج نُغَم
To speak clearly to a. o. ✲ نَغَا o نَغْوًا، ونَغَى i نَغْيًا، وأنغى إلى
He remained silent without uttering a single syllable. سَكَت فَمَا نَغَا او مَا نَغَى بِحَرْف
◇ To twitter (bird). ناغَى
To cheer up, to soothe (a child). To fondle, to blandish a. o. – ه
To rise towards. To draw near to. – ه
The billow raised towards the clouds. – المَوْجُ السَّحاب
This moutain rises to the sky. هٰذا الجَبَل يُناغِي السَّماء
To struggle. To vie. تناغى
◇ Twittering of birds. مُناغاة
Low and sweet voice, gentle whisper. Rumour, report. نَغْوَة ونَغْيَة
To sow (the earth). ✲ نَفّ o نَفًّا ه
To eat dry (flour). ◻ To blow o.'s nose. – a نَفًّا ه
Flies. ◻ نِفَّ
Bolting-table. نُفّي ج نَفافي
Air. Abrupt side of a mountain. Slope of a hill. Desert. ✲ نَفْنَف ج نَفانِف
Abyss between two mountains. – ونَفْنَاف
◇ Flake of snow ; drizzle. نفناف

Blast, gust of wind. نَفْحَة ج نَفَحَات
Aroma, strong odour. Gift.
He does not cease bestowing favours. لَا تَزَال لَهُ نَفَحَات مِنَ ٱلْمَعْرُوف
Design long brooded over. نِيَّة نَفَح
Letting flow her milk (she-camel). Far-shooting (bow). نَفُوح
Beneficent, bountiful. نَفَّاح
Meddlesome, intruder. نَفِيح ومِنْفَح
Lamb's stomach, rennet. إِنْفَحَة وإِنْفِحَة وإِنْفَحَّة ج أَنَافِح
✱ نَفَخ o نَفْخًا ونَفَّخ بِفَمِهِ فِي وه To blow into a th. To blow (the fire, a trumpet).
To fill a. o. (food). نَفَخ ه
— بِشِدْقَيْهِ وانْتَفَخ و ✧ نَفَخ رُوحَهُ To be swollen with pride.
To be swollen, inflated. تَنَفَّخ وانْتَفَخ
To be advanced (day). To be ambitious. إِنْتَفَخ
Blast; breath. Pride. نَفْخ
Breath. ✧ Flatulence. نَفْخَة
Swelling, inflation. — ونُفَاخ
There is nobody in the house. مَا بِٱلدَّارِ نَافِخ ضَرَمَة
Water-bubble. Air-bladder of a fish. نُفَّاخَة
Summit of the head. ✧ نَافُوخ (*for* يَافُوخ)
Blower of fire. نَفِيخ
Big-bellied, plump. أَنْفَخَان وإِنْفِخَان وأُنْفُخَانِيّ وإِنْفِخَانِيّ م أَنْفُخَانَة الخ
Bellows. مِنْفَاخ ومِنْفَخ ج مَنَافِيخ ومَنَافِخ
Ambitious, swell. مُنْتَفِخ
✱ نَفِد a نَفَدًا ونَفَادًا To be consumed, exhausted (stores, wealth). To fail, to cease.
✧ نَفَّد ه To give the particulars of (an account).
To prosecute a. o. in justice. نَافَد ه
To spend away, to consume (stores). To be exhausted (well). أَنْفَد
— وانْتَفَد واسْتَنْفَد ه To spend a. th.
To plead a suit before (a judge). تَنَافَد إِلَى
To exact and receive the whole of (a debt). To draw (milk). إِنْتَقَد ه
Litigator. مُنَافِد
He remained apart. قَعَد مُنْتَفِدًا

Broad place. Scene of a riot. مُنْتَفَد
✱ نَفَذ o نُفُوذًا ونَفَاذًا ه To pierce a. th. through (arrow, spear).
— نَفْذًا ونَفَاذًا ه ومِن وفي To transpierce (the game: arrow).
— وأَنْفَذ ه To pass through (a crowd).
— نُفُوذًا ونَفَاذًا To be effective, to be carried out (order). To be a thoroughfare (road).
— فِي To carry out (business) skilfully.
— إِلَى To reach a. o. (letter).
نَفَّذ وأَنْفَذ ه To transmit a. th. To carry out (an order). To transpierce with (an arrow). To join (a party).
تَنَافَذ إِلَى To defer a case to (a judge).
نَفَذ ج أَنْفَاذ Execution. Penetration.
أَمَرَ بِتَنْفِيذِهِ He has ordered to execute it.
طَعْنَة لَهَا نَفَذ Penetrative thrust.
نَفَاذ ونُفُوذ Execution. Efficacity. ✧ Influence.
نَافِذ Penetrative. Effectual, clever in business. Thoroughfare.
نَوَافِذ ومَنَافِذ ٱلْإِنْسَان Holes of the body as nose, mouth etc.
نَفِيذ Effective (order).
نَافِذَة ج نَوَافِذ Window, loop-hole.
نَفَاذ ونُفُوذ Carrying out his designs.
مَنْفَذ ج مَنَافِذ Egress, passage. Loop-hole.
✱ نَفَر o i نُفُورًا ونِفَارًا مِن To be scared away, to break loose (beast).
— i نَفْرًا To disperse away (people).
— مِن To shun a. o. To shy at.
— عَن To go away from.
— إِلَى To hurry, to rush towards.
— نِفَارًا ونُفُورًا ونَفِيرًا لِ To busy o.'s self with.
— نَفْرًا ه To overcome a. o.
— نَفْرًا ونُفُورًا مِن مِنًى To come back from Mina (pilgrim).
— نُفُورًا To be swollen (eye). ✧ To jut out.
— نَفْرًا ونَفَرَانًا, واسْتَنْفَر To be scared away (gazelle).
نَفَّر وأَنْفَر ه عَلَى To declare a. o. winner over.
— وأَنْفَر واسْتَنْفَر ه To scare (a beast) away.
نَفَّر عَن فُلَان To give a nickname to.

To make (a gazelle) to bound. نَفَّز ه To dandle (a child).
To twirl (an arrow) upon the nail for trying it. — أنفز ه
To leap, to frolic together (children). تنافز
Bounding antelope. نَفُوز ونَيفُوز
To smite a. o. with (the evil eye). ✱ نَفَس o نَفسًا ه ب
To be tenacious of. نَفِس a نَفسًا ب
He envies the good of. — عَلَى فُلَان بِخَيرٍ
To judge a. o. to be unworthy of. نَفِس نَفَاسَةً ه عَلَى فُلَانٍ
To be confined (woman). نَفَس a ونُفِس غُلَامًا نَفسًا ونَفَاسَةً ونِفَاسًا
To be precious, to be in request. نَفُس o نَفَاسَةً و نِفَاسًا ونَفَسًا, وأنفس
To console, to cheer a. o. نَفَّس ه
To dispel (grief) from. — ه عَن
To sigh for, to aspire to a. th. نَافَس مُنَافَسَةً ونِفَاسًا فِي
To vie with a. o. in (the pursuit of). — ه فِي
To please a. o. أنفس ه
To inspire a. o. with the desire of. — ه فِي
To breathe, to respire. To become long (day). To shine (dawn). To be cracked (bow). تَنَفَّس
To sprinkle (water : wave). — ه
He drew a deep sigh. — ٱلصُّعَدَاء
To desire a. th. eagerly. To quarrel about a. th. تَنَافَس فِي
Soul, vital principle. Blood. Evil eye. Spirit. Person, individual. Self of a man or thing. Intention, desire. Pride. Scorn. Appetite. ✧ Stomach. نَفس ج نُفُوس وأنفُس
✧ He committed suicide, he killed himself. قَتَل نَفسَهُ
✧ He felt qualmish. لَعِبَت نَفسُهُ
✧ He had a heaving of the stomach. غَثَت نَفسُهُ
He came by himself. جَاءَنِي هُوَ نَفسُهُ او بِنَفسِهِ
He came with three persons. جَاءَ مَعَهُ ثَلَاثَة أنفُس
The essence, the constituent of the affair. نَفس ٱلأمر

To contend for nobility with. ✧ To dislike a. o., to shun. نَافَر نِفَارًا ومُنَافَرَةً ه
To help, to assist a. o. أنفر ه
To contend before an umpire for glory. To contest together. ✧ To shun o. a. To be discordant (things). تَنَافَر
To give o.'s self up to. — ل
To convoke (a tribe) to war. إستَنفَر ه
Secession, separation. نَفر
Party of warriors, of fugitives. — ونَفرَة ونَفِير
Before all, first. قَبلَ كُلِّ صَيحٍ ونَفر
Flight, secession. نَفرَة
Wicked man. عِفر نِفر و عِفرّ نِفرّ
Party from 3 to ten men. Aversion. ✧ Private, soldier, individual. نَفر ونَفَر ج أنفَار
Three persons. ثَلَاثَة نَفَر او أنفَار
Day of the departure from Mina to Mecca. يَوم ٱلنَّفر او ٱلنَّفَر او ٱلنَّفِير او ٱلنُّفُور
Sentence of a judge. Award. نُفرَة
Amulet against the evil eye. نُفرَة ونُفَرَة
Flight. Aversion. نِفَار ونُفُور
Rising in a body. ٱلنَّفِير العَامّ
Shyness of (a beast). نِفَار
Sentence of a judge ; costs of a lawsuit. نُفَارَة
Dispute, quarrel. *Gr.* Assemblage of unharmonious words in a sentence. تَنَافُر
Scared away (beast). ✧ Jutting. نَافِر (m. f.) ج نُفر
Winner. — ج نُفَّر
Familiars, kindred. نَافِرَة
He came with all his people. جَاءَ فِي نَافِرَتِهِ او فِي نَفرَتِهِ او فِي نُفُورَتِهِ
✧ Pall, cover of the chalice. Liturgy. Consecrated bread. S نَافُور
Shy (beast). نَافِر ونَفُور وينفُور ومُستَنفِر
Nenuphar, water-lily. نَوفَر ولَوفَر ونَيلُوفَر ونَينُوفَر
Jet d'eau, water-spout. ✧ نَوفَرَة
Signal of an attack. Brass-bugle. نَفِير
Scared away. مُستَنفَر
Overcome. مَنفُور
To bound, to leap (gazelle). ✱ نَفَز i نَفزًا ونَفَزَانًا

نفس ٱلشيء The very thing; the thing itself.
◆ ليس لي نفس للأكل I have no appetite.
◆ نفسهُ كبيرة He is haughty.
◆ عفيف النفس He is a disinterested man.
سالت نفسهُ His blood flowed.
قال لنفسهِ He said to himself.
نفس المتكلّم The first person of the singular.
نفس ج أنفاس Breathing. Breath, gust. Freedom of action. Long discourse. Draught. ◆ Style, wit. Sweet voice. Nargile.
شراب ذو نفس Agreeable beverage.
هو في نفس من أمورهِ He acts at his own will.
◆ إشرب نفس Do smoke a nargile.
نفسة Delay.
نفاس Childbirth, delivery.
تنفّس Breath.
نافس Evil-eyed. Fourth arrow of the game.
نفيس م نفيسة ج نفائس Precious, much sought.
نفيس ومنفس Numerous (goods).
أنفس More precious, dearer.
نفساء ونفساء ونفساء ج نفاس ونفس ونفس ونوافس ونفساوات Confined (woman).
◆ نفساني Selfish, sensual.
◆ نفسانيّة Egotism, ill-will.
متنفس Breathing (animal),
متنفّس Passage of the breath.
منفوس م منفوسة Just born. Precious (thing).
✡ نفش o نفشًا, ونفّش ه To pick (cotton) with the fingers.
◆ نفش روحه He was puffed up.
◆ نفش ه To puff up a. o.
— i o ونفِش a نفشًا, وتنفّش To pasture by themselves during the night (cattle). ◆ To swell in water (wood, grain).
أنفش ه To send (cattle) to pasture alone by night.
تنفّش وانتفش To bristle up (cat). To ruffle its feathers (bird). ◆ To be swollen (wood).
نفش Wool. Produce of the earth.
نفش ونفيش ... Old furniture.

بقر وغنم نفش ونوافش ونفّاش Cattle pasturing by night without shepherd.
◆ نفشيّة ◆ Almond-cake.
نفّاش Proud, puffed up. *Citrus spon-ginus rugosus*, large citron.
متنفّش ومنتفش Swollen and soft.
متنفّش, منتفش ٱلشعر Dishevelled, bristled (hair).
أنف منتفش Flat nose, snub-nose.
✡ نفض i نفضًا, وأنفض ب To utter (a word) quickly.
أنفض في الضحك He laughed loudly.
— بشفتيهِ He smacked the lips.
نُفاض Diabetes of sheep.
منفاض Laugher
✡ نفض o نفضًا To be consumed (victuals). To produce its last stalks (corn-crops); its last bunches (vine). To fade away (colour).
— ونفّض ه To shake off (leaves, fruit) from a tree. To shake off the dust of (a garment).
نفض ه To make a. o. to shiver (fever).
نفض وتنفّض واستنفض ه To explore (a country).
إذا تكلّمت نهارًا فأنفض Whenever thou speakest by day-time, look about.
نفض وأنفض To bring forth (she-camel). To be prolific (female).
نفض o نفوضًا من To recover from (disease)
أنفض To be consumed, exhausted (stores). To perish (flocks).
— ه عن To discard a. o. from.
إنتفض To be shaken (tree). To be dusted (clothes). To be verdant (vine). To fret, to be restless.
إستنفض To send scouts. To cleanse o.'s self.
— ه To elicit a. th.
نفض ونفاض ونفاض ونفاضة Shaken off (leaves, fruit).
نفضة ونفضة ونفاض ونفضاء Shivering caused by fever.
نفضة Circumscribed rain.
نفضة ونفيضة ج نفائض Party of scouts.
نفضى Shaking, shiver, trembling.
نفاض ونفاض Exhaustion of victuals: dearth

Boy's garment. Mat for receiving leaves beaten off. نِفَاض ج نُفُض
He is without any garment. مَا عَلَيْهِ نِفَاض
Shivering fever. Faded (clothes). ✧ Penniless. Mad. نَافِض
أَخَذَتْهُ حُمَّى نَافِضٍ وحُمَّى نَافِضٌ وحُمَّى بِنَافِضٍ
He was seized with a shivering fever.
Prolific (woman). نَفُوض
Leaves beaten off. أَنَافِيض
Winnowing-basket. Fan. Duster. مِنْفَض
✧ Ashes-plate. مِنْفَضَة ج مَنَافِض
Cloth for receiving leaves beaten off. مِنْفَاض
☆ نَفِطَ a نَفْطًا ونَفَطًا ونَفِيطًا, وتَنَفَّط To be blistered (hand).
نَفَطَ i نَفْطًا, وتَنَفَّط To boil (cooking-pot). To become angry (man). To speak confusedly.
— i نَفِيطًا To sneeze (goat).
— ب To scatter (urine) about (goat).
أَنْفَطَ ه To blister (the hands : work).
تَنَافَطَ To froth forth (pot).
نَفْط ونِفْط Tar. ✧ Naphtha, petroleum.
نَفْط ✧ Lucifer-matches.
نَفْطَة ونِفْطَة Small-pox. Pustule, blister.
نَفْطَة Prone to anger.
نَافِطَة Blistered (hand). Goat.
نَفَّاط ج نَفَّاطَة Machine for throwing naphtha.
نَفَّاطَة ونِفَّاطَة Naphtha-well. Lamp. Blister.
نَفِيط ومَنْفُوط م نَفِيطَة الخ Covered with ulcers.
✧ مُنَفِّط Vesicatory.
☆ نَفَعَ a نَفْعًا ه ب To profit, to be useful to a. o.
نَفَعَ مِن To be beneficial, to serve as an antidote to.
نَفَعَ ه To be profitable to.
إِنْتَفَعَ ب ومِن To profit by. To enjoy.
إِسْتَنْفَعَ ه To seek the advantage of, to be useful to.
نَفْع ونَفَاع ونَفِيعَة Usefulness, profit, means of success.
نِفْعَة ج نِفَع ونِفَع Leather-band sewn on a travelling-bag.
نَافِع م نَافِعَة Useful, beneficial.

نَفَّاع, ونَفُوع ج نُفُع Useful, serviceable (man).
مَنْفَعَة ج مَنَافِع Advantage, utility. Profit, use.
مَنَافِع الدَّار Requisites of a house, as (a well, washing-trough).
☆ نَفَقَ o نَفَاقًا To be saleable (goods). To be brisk (market).
— ونَفِقَ a نَفَقًا To be exhausted (stores).
نَفَقَ o نُفُوقًا To perish (cattle, people). To be excoriated (wound).
— o ونَفِقَ a نَفَقًا, ونَفَّق To come out of its hole (mole).
نَفَّقَ وأَنْفَقَ ه To find a market for (goods).
نَافَقَ مُنَافَقَة ونِفَاقًا To enter its hole (mole).
— في الدِّين He played the hypocrite in religion.
أَنْفَقَ To be impoverished by almsgiving.
— ه To sell (goods) readily.
أَنْفَقَ واسْتَنْفَقَ ه على To expend money over.
تَنَفَّقَ على To present itself to a. o. (opportunity).
— ه To drive out (a mole).
إِنْتَفَقَ To go into or out of its burrow (mole).
نَفَق ج أَنْفَاق Burrow of a mole ; underground.
نِفَاق ومُنَافَقَة Hypocrisy. ✧ Sacrilege.
لَا إِنْفَاق على نِفَاق No expenses for doing evil.
نَفَقَة ج نَفَقَات ونِفَاق Expenses, expenditure.
نَافِق Saleable (goods). Brisk (market).
نَافِقَة Vesicle of musk.
نُفَقَة, ونَافِقَاء ج نَوَافِق Burrow of a mole.
أَنْفَق More saleable.
نَيْفَق Waist-band of trousers ; tuck.
مِنْفَاق Spendthrift.
مُنَافِق Hypocrite.
☆ نَفَلَ o نَفْلًا To swear, to take an oath
— ه To present a. o. with (a gift). To divide spoils amongst (soldiers).
— ونَفَّل وأَنْفَلَ ه النَّفَل To give booty to.
نَفَّلَ ه To give an oath to.

تَفَّل عن فلانٍ To defend, to protect a. o.
تَنَفَّل، وانتفل To make supererogatory prayers, works.
تَنَفَّل على To defraud a. o. of his share of booty.
إنتفل مِن To escape from. To be freed, delivered from.
— ه مِن To ask a. th. from.
نَفَل Supererogatory work.
نَفَل ج أنفال و نِفال Booty. Gift, gratuity. *Trifolium melitotus Indica*, odoriferous trefoil.
نَافِلَة ج نَوَافِل Supererogatory work or prayer. Booty. Voluntary gift. Grandson.
نُفَل The 4th, 5th and 6th nights of a lunar month.
✡ نَفِه a نُفُوهًا To be cowardly.
نَفِه a نَفهًا To be wearied (mind).
نَفَّه وأنفه ه To jade (a beast).
أنفَهَ لَهُ مِن He has given him little of.
نَافِه ج نُفَّه, ومَنفُوه Faint-hearted.
— ومُنَفَّه Jaded (beast).
✡ نَفَا o نَفوًا, ونَفَى i نَفيًا, ونَفَّى ه وه عن To expel, to drive away, to remove a. o. or a. th. from.
نَفَا ه مِن بَلَدِهِ To banish, to exile a. o.
— ه To deny, to disacknowledge, to refuse a. th. To sweep away (rubbish : torrent).
— i نَفيًا ونَفَيَانًا ه To raise (the dust : wind). To pour out (coins) for trying them (banker).
نُفِيَ i نَفيًا, وانتَفَى To be exiled, driven away.
نَافَى ه To repel, to remove a. o.
— ه To be inconsistent with, repugnant to. To preclude a. th. else.
هٰذَا يُنَافِي ذَاك This is inconsistent with that.
تَنَافَى To be incompatible, inconsistent (things).
نَفي Expulsion. Disacknowledgement. *Gram*. Negation.
حَرف النَّفي Negative particle.
نَفَاء ونَفَاة ونَفيَة ونَفَاوَة ونُفَايَة ونَفَايَة Rubbish, refuse.
نَفيَة ونَفِيَّة ج نَفَيَات Mat of palm-leaves.
نَفَيَان Foliage, fallen leaves.

نَافٍ م نَافِيَة *Gr*. Negative (particle).
نَفِيّ Rubbish. Froth cast forth by a pot. Drops falling on a water-drawer. Rubbish scattered by the feet of horses. Followers of an army.
نَفِيّ ومَنفِيّ Cast off. Expelled, exiled.
مَنفِيّ *Gr*. Negative (verb, sentence).
تَنَافٍ ومُنَافَاة Inconsistency, incompatibility of two things.
مَنفَى ج مَنَافٍ Exile, place of exile.
✡ نَقَّ i نَقِيقًا To croak (frog). To cluck (hen). To mew (cat).
— ✧ نَقًّا ✧ To grumble.
نَقّ ✧ Mumbling, complaint.
نَقَّاق م نَقَّاقَة Frog. ✧ Grumbler.
✡ نَقنَق To croak incessantly (frog). To cluck (hen, ostrich). ✧ To grumble, to scold incessantly.
نَقنَق في الأكل ✧ He protracts eating.
نِقنِق م نِقنِقَة ج نَقَانِق Ostrich.
نَقَانِق و✧ مَقَانِق Sausages. Stuffed tripes.
✡ نَقَب o نَقبًا ه To pierce (a wall). To bore a. th. To tap (the navel). To patch (boots). To make (a vest). ✧ To clear, to dig up (a ground). To couch (the cataract).
— ونَقَّب وأنقب في To go through (a country).
نَقَّب عَن To ascertain, to spread (news).
— ه To befall a. o. (misfortune).
— على القوم نِقَابَة He was the chief of his tribe.
نَقِب a نَقَبًا To be worn out in the soles (boots). To have the feet worn out (camel).
— ونَقُب o نِقَابَة To be elected chief of a tribe.
نَقَّب وتَنَقَّب عَن To scrutinise (an affair).
نَاقَب ه نِقَابًا To meet a. o. unexpectedly.
وَرَدتُ الماء نِقَابًا I came to water, unexpectedly.
أنقب To become the chief of a tribe. To have its feet worn out (camel).
تَنَقَّب وانتَقَب To veil her face (woman).
نَقب Perforation. ✧ Digging of a land.
نَقب ج أنقاب ونِقَاب Hole in a wall, breach; tunnel. Ulcer in the side
— ونُقب ج نِقَاب ونِقَاب Mountain-path.

Scab. نَقَب ونُقْب ونَقِب
Hole. ✧ Land newly broken. نَقْبة
Way of veiling the face. نِقْبة
Hole, breach. Scurf of the scab. Rust. Face. Colour. Vest worn by women. نُقْبة ج نُقَب
The ears. ألأنقاب
Woman's veil. Learned man. Road in a hard ground. نِقاب ج نُقُب
Boring a wall. Ulcer in the side. ناقِب م ناقِبة
Miner. نَقَّاب
Flute. Tongue of a balance. Chief of a tribe; intendant. headman. Having the windpipe perforated (dog). نَقِيب ج نُقَباء
✧ Chief of the nobles. نَقِيب الأشراف
Soul, mind. Nature, temper, advice. نَقِيبة ج نَقائب
Mouth-piece. ◻ تَنْقِيبة
Lancet. مِنقَب ومِنقَبة
Narrow-pass, defile. – ومَنقِب ج مَناقِب
Narrow-pass. Attainment, merit, virtue. مَنقَبة ج مَناقِب
To extract (marrow) from a bone. ✲ نَقَت o نَقْتًا ه
To extract (marrow). ✲ نَقَث o نَقْثًا وانتَقَث ه
To entangle (a speech). نَقَّث ه
To dig up (the ground). – وانتَقَث ه
To bark a. th. ✲ نَقَح a نَقْحًا ونَقَّح ه
To pare off the knots of a (palm-trunk). To strip off the ornaments of (a sword).
To trim (verses). To read over (a book) carefully. نَقَّح وأنقَح ه
To quarrel with. ناقَح ه
To melt away (fat of a she camel). To be corrected. تَنَقَّح
To extract (marrow). إنتَقَح ه
White summer-cloud. نَقَح
✧ Stain on a garment. نَقْحة
To strike a. o. on the skull. ✲ نَقَخ a نَقْخًا ه وه
Fresh, clear water. نُقاخ
Pith, cream, choice part. نُقاخ
To look stealthily at. ✲ نَقَد o نَقْدًا ونُقُودًا ه وإلى
He glared at. – بِعَينِهِ إليه

To pay a. th. in ready money. نَقَد نَقْدًا وتَنقادًا ه ه ول
To crack (a nut) with the fingers. To peck (a grain : bird). – ه
To pick out (coins). – وتَنَقَّد وانتَقَد ه
To criticise (a writing). نَقَد وانتَقَد ه
To be broken, rotten (tooth). To be abraded (hoof). نَقِد a نَقَدًا
To ask a severe account from. ناقَد ه
To become leafy (tree). أنقَد
To grow up (boy). إنتَقَد
To receive cash, ready (money). – ه
To pick out the faults of. – على
Cash, ready money. نَقْد
✧ Dowry, wedding-present for a bride. – العَرُوس ج نُقُود
Standard money. دِرْهَم نَقْد ج نُقُود
✧ Good money. نَقدِيَّة
Little fleshy. نَقْد ونَقَد
Stunted, puny (boy). نَقَد ونَقِد
Inferior breed of sheep. نَقَد ج نِقاد ونِقادة
Anthemis, kind of plant. Caraway. نَقْد ونُقْد ونَقَد
Hedge-hog. أنقَد والأنقَد
Tortoise. – وإنقِدان
Assayer of money. Fault-finding, censor. نَقَّاد
Bill of a bird. مِنقاد ج مَناقِيد
Nut-cracker. مِنقَدة ج مَناقِد
To rescue a. o. from. ✲ نَقَذ o نَقْذًا ونَقَّذ وأنقَذ ه مِن
To save a. o. from. تَنَقَّذ واستَنقَذ ه مِن
To escape, to be safe. نَقِذ a نَقَذًا
Rescue, deliverance. نَقَذ
Safety to thee! نَقَذًا لك
Delivered, rescued. نَقَذ ونَقِيذ
He possesses nothing. ما لهُ سَبَدٌ ولا نَقَذٌ
Horse taken as booty. Breast-plate. نَقِيذة ج نَقائذ
To fillip, to snap the fingers. To smack the tongue against the palate ✲ نَقَر o نَقْرًا
To call a. o. apart. – بِفُلان
To strike, to revile a. o. – ه
To engrave (stone, wood). To play (the lute). To beat (the drum). To hit (the butt : arrow). – ه
To hollow out (a stone). – في

نقر في النّاقور To sound, to blow the bugle.
— البَيْضة عن الفرخ The (hen) pierced the egg for letting out its chicken.
نقر عن ونقّر ه وعن وتنقّر وانتقر ه To scrutinise, to fathom a. th.
— ونقّر ه To peck (a grain : bird).
نَقِر a نَقَرًا To get out of temper. To be seized with staggers (sheep).
نقّر ه بإسمِهِ He called him out by his name.
— في To level (a place) for making its nest (bird).
ناقر مُناقرةً ونقارًا ه To quarrel with. To thwart a. o.
أنقر عن To abstain from.
✧ تناقر To dispute, to quarrel together.
إنتقر ه To hollow out (the earth : torrent).
— ه ب To hollow (the earth) with (the hoofs : horse).
— ه وب To call, to invite a. o. apart.
— ه To choose. To write a. th.
نقر (*un.* نقرة Hollow. Excavation. Fillip, snap ; smack.
ما أثابهُ نقرة He has not given him the least reward.
نَقَر Loss of property.
نَقِر م نَقِرة Angered.
نقر ونقرة ونقير Little spot on a date-stone.
ليسوا في نقير They are worthless, mean.
نِقرة ونِقار Dispute, quarrel.
نُقرة ج نُقَر ونِقار Pit of the nape, of the stomach. Small hollow in the earth. Socket of the eye. Bird's nest. ✧ Dimple.
نُقرة ج نِقار Molten gold or silver ingot.
نقرى Defamation.
بنات النقرى Slanderous women.
دعوتهم نقرى I sent them a special invitation.
يُصلّي النقرى He hurries in prayer.
نُقَرة Disease of the feet amongst sheep.
ناقور ج نواقير Bugle.
نُقارة Beak full.

ما ترك نُقارة إلّا انتقرها He has left nothing without writing it.
ناقر ج نواقر Hitting the target (arrow).
ناقرة ج نواقر Misfortune. Conclusive evidence.
نقّار Pecking (bird). Engraver. Scrutiniser.
نقّار الخشب ✧ Wood-pecker.
▫ نقّارة Large drum.
نقير ج نُقُر Palm-trunk hollowed into a trough or steps. ▫ Boat on the Upper Nile.
— ج نِقران ✧ Trough for cement.
— ج أنقرة Hollow in the ground, in a stone. Origin, stock.
كريم النقير Noble-born.
✧ نُقيرة ونقّارة Small drum. Cymbal.
مِنقار ج مناقير Bird's bill. Pick for hollowing mill-stones.
مِنقر ج مناقر Pick-axe. ✧ Chisel.
مُنقر ومِنقر ج مناقير Wooden cup. Narrow-mouthed well, tank.
منقّر العين ومُنتقِرها Hollow-eyed.
☆ نِقرِس Gout, podagra.
— ونِقرِيس Experienced and clever (physician).
☆ نقز o i نقزًا ونِقازًا ونقزانًا To leap, to bound (gazelle). ✧ To shudder from fear (man).
نقّز ه To dandle (a child). To make (a gazelle) to leap. ✧ To cause a shudder to.
أنقز To drink continually pure water. To acquire ill-conditioned cattle.
إنتقز To be struck by murrain (beast).
— لفلان من To give to a. o. the refuse of.
نَقز ونَقَز Ill-conditioned sheep.
نَقز Pure, sweet water.
— ونقز Nickname, byname.
نقزة Leap, bound. ✧ Shudder.
داء النُقاز Murrain ; staggers of sheep.
✧ نقيز Sharp pain.
عطاء ناقز وذو ناقز Paltry gift.
نواقز الدابّة Feet of a horse.
☆ نقس o نقسًا وانتقس ه To strike, to ring (a sheet of iron).

To lessen the right نَقَص وانتَقَص ة حَقَّهُ
of. To wrong a. o.

To speak ill of. ة تَنَقَّص وانتَقَص

To diminish a. th. gradually. ه تَنَقَّص

To dwindle away. تَنَاقَص

To diminish, to decrease. إنتَقَص

To ask for an abatement ه إِسْتَنْقَص
of (price).

Loss, decrease. نَقْص ونُقْصَان ومَنْقَصَة
Waste.

Want (of judgment, of piety). نَقْص

He wants so much. نَقْصَانُهُ كَذَا

Defect, vice. Detraction. نَقِيصَة ج نَقَائِص
□ Sack.

Imperfect. Defective نَاقِص ج نُقَّص
(coin). Gr. Defective (verb).

✦ Tender, public auction. مُنَاقَصَة

٭ نَقَض o نَقْضًا ه To pull down (a
house). To break (a compact). To
reverse (a sentence : judge). To untwist (a rope). To undo a. th.

To crack (joint). نَقْضًا o i —

To be contradictory to. ه نَاقَض

His second نَاقَض قَوْلُهُ الثَّانِي قَوْلَهُ الأَوَّل
utterance contradicted the first.

To squeak (eagle). أَنْقَض

To crack (the fingers). To ex- ه —
tract (truffles). To overburden (a
beast).

To smack the lips for calling. ب —
(goats); for urging (a beast).

To crumble down loudly (house). تَنَقَّض
To crack (bone). To drip (blood).
To be unwoven (rope).

To burst (the earth : truffles). عَن —

To be contradictory, repugnant تَنَاقَض
(words).

To be cracked (building). وانتَقَض
To be untwisted (rope).

To be unsound (wound, affair). إنتَقَض
To be broken (compact).

To rebel against. عَلى —

To be cracked (wall). إِنْقَاضّ

Destruction. Refutation of an نَقْض
argument. Suppression of the seventh letter in the metre مُفَاعَلَتن
(prosody).

Disjoined, disordered. نَقَض مِ نَقَضَة
Emaciated by walk (beast).

To ring (sheet of iron). نَقَس

To revile, to ة نَقْسًا، ونَقَّس a نَقَس
scoff at.

To fill (an inkstand). ه نَقَس

To revile o. a. ة نَاقَس

Scab. نَقْس

Ink. نِقْس ج أَنْقُس وأَنْقَاس

Iron-sheet struck نَاقُوس ج نَوَاقِيس
with a clapper; gong. ✦ Bell.

Irony, scoffing. مُنَاقَسَة

٭ نَقَش o نَقْشًا وﭐ نَقَّش ه To
variegate a. th., to paint a. th. To
chisel, to engrave a. th.

To strike date-clusters with نَقَش ه
thorns for ripening them. To clear
a cattle-enclosure from thorns. To
pluck (the hair).

— ﭐنْتَقَش ه مِن To extract (a thorn)
from (the foot).

To be at variance with. ة نَاقَش

نَاقَش ة الحِسَاب أَو فِيهِ He exacted from
him the particulars of the ac-
count.

أَنْقَش عَلى غَرِيمِهِ He harassed, he pressed
his debtor.

To strike the earth with the إِنْتَقَش
foot for beating out a thorn (camel).

To have a. th. engraved عَلى القَصّ
on a signet-ring.

— ه To extract, to pull out a. th.

— حَقَّهُ مِن He collected the whole of
his debt from.

— ة وه To choose a. th. or a. o.

Variegated work, engra- نَقْش ج نُقُوش
ving. Picture. Trace. Piece of gum.
Embroidery.

Picture (art). Sculpture. نِقَاشَة

Painter. Sculpter. Chiseler, نَقَّاش
engraver.

Pain- مِنْقَاش ج مَنَاقِيش، ومِنْقَش ج مَنَاقِش
ter's brush; pencil. Chisel. Tweezers
for extracting thorns.

Wound in the head شَجَّة مُنَقِّشَة ومَنْقُوشَة
from which a splinter is to be extracted.

٭ نَقَص o نَقْصًا ونُقْصَانًا وتَنَقَاصَا To decrease, to fall short. To abate.

— ونَقَص وأَنْقَص وانتَقَص ه To diminish,
to waste a. th.

نَقض ج أنقاض ونُقوض Crust of earth broken by truffles.

— ونِقض Untwisted part of a fabric.

نُقض ج أنقاض ونُقوض. Crack in a building.

نَقضَة ج نُقض ✧ Beam, joist.

نُقاضة Unwoven part of a fabric; unravelled threads of a rope.

نَقيض Voice, sound, crackling. Cracking of the joints.

— م نَقيضة. Contradictory. Contradictor.

طَرَفَا نَقيض The two extreme parts.

نَقيضان Two inconsistent things.

نَقيضَة ج نَقائِض Mountain-road. Poem contradictory to another.

☆ نَقَط o نَقطًا, ونَقَّط ه To dot (a letter).

نَقَط ✧ To drip (liquid).

نَقَّط ه To spot, to speck (a garment).

— ه وب على ✧ To throw (coins) at.

نَقَّط ه وه ✧ To collect coins for (a bride). To drip (a liquid).

تَنَقَّط. To have spots of pasturage (land).

— ه To break (news). To eat (bread) little by little.

نُقطة ج نُقَط ونِقاط Diacritical point. Geometrical point. Spot, speckle. Full stop. ✧ A drop (of water, of blood).

ما اختلفوا في نُقطةٍ They agreed on all points.

نُقَط ونِقاط من الكلأ Separate tracts of pasturage.

ذاء النُّقطة. ✧ Falling-sickness, epilepsy. Apoplexy.

نَاقِط ونَقِيط Slave of a slave.

نَقّاط Dotting the Coran.

✧ نُقوط Wedding-present collected for a bride

☆ نَقَع a نَقعًا To raise the voice. To shout. To increase (mortality).

— ب To quench thirst with. To be informed of (news).

— ه ب To break out into (high words) against.

— وأنقع وانتقع ه ل To slaughter (a camel) for (guests).

— وأنقع ه في To macerate (a medicine) in (water).

— وأنقع ب To protract (shouts).

— واستنقع To be raised (voice).

نَقَع a نَقعًا ونُقوعًا, واستنقع To stagnate (water).

— ه To quench (the thirst).

أنقع واستنقع To become altered and yellow (water).

أنقع ه To quench the thirst of a. o.

— فُلانًا To fillip a. o. on the nose.

— شرًّا ل To prepare mischief for.

أُنتُقِع واستُنقِع To be altered (colour).

إستنقع في To collect in (a tank: water). To bathe in (a pool).

نَقع ج نِقاع ونُقوع Dust raised by the wind, by a beast.

— ج نِقاع وأنقُع, ونُقعان. Swampy ground.

— ج أنقُع Swamp.

إنَّهُ لشرَّاب بأنقُع He is inured to hardship.

نُقاعة Dilution.

نَاقِع Deadly (venom). Fresh (blood). Quenching (water).

نَقّاع Arrogant, haughty.

نُقوع ونَقيع Fresh and wholesome water.

نُقوع ومَنقوع Dilution.

نُقوع ✧ Dried apricot.

رَجُلٌ نُقوع أذنٍ Credulous man.

نَقِيع Infusion, mash.

— ج أنقِعَة Well holding much water.

نَقيعة ج نَقائع Animal slaughtered for a guest.

أنقع More thirst-quenching.

مِنقع ج مَناقِع, ومِنقعة Vessel for diluting a medicine.

مَنقع ج مَناقِع Swamp. Sea. Thirst-quenching.

مَنقع الدَّم Place of capital punishment, block.

سَمٌّ مُنقع Poison made into a confection.

مُنقَع Dilution. Pure milk. Stone-cup.

مُنقع ومُنقعة Bowl for mashing dates in milk.

مُستنقع Pool of stagnating water. Washing-tank.

☆ نَقَف o نَقفًا ه To break (the skull). To split (an egg). To break its egg (chicken). To strain (a beverage). To dilute a. th. To bark (a pomegranate).

— To examine a. th.

To cut open (a colocynth). نقف وأنقف وانتقف ه

✧ To fillip a. o. نقف نقفة ه

To break the skull of a. o. ناقف مُناقفة ونقافاً ه

To fill (a valley) with eggs (locusts). أنقف ه

To give (a bone) to a. o. for extracting its marrow. – ه ه

To strike o. a. with the sword. تناقفا

To draw, to extract a. th. إنتقف ه

Chicken coming forth from its egg. نُقف ونِقف

Depressed tract on the summit of a mountain. نَقفة

Prudent (man). نِقاف

In the same way. في نِقاف وَاحِد

Prudent, wary ; inquisitive (man). نقّاف

Worm-eaten (tree-stem). نقيف ج نُقف

Bird's beak. Cowry used as a polisher. مِنقاف

Pale, wan (complexion). Rotten (tree-stock). مَنقُوف

✶ To convey, to transmit, to transfer a. th. To transplant (a tree). To transcribe (a book). نقل o نقلاً, ونقّل ه

To relate, to quote a. th. from. نقل ه عن

✧ To remove o.'s lodgings. To scamper off. نقل

To mend (clothes) : to patch (shoes). – ونقّل وأنقل ه

To shatter (a bone : blow). نقّل ه

✧ To have a. th. carried. To remove.

To bring dessert to (a guest). – ه

✧ To give weapons to. – ه الأسلحة

To walk warily. To gallop (horse). ناقل مُناقلة ونقالاً, وانتقل

To relate (events) o. to a. – ه ه

To hand (cups : drinkers). – مُناقلة ه

To be carried, copied ; to come down by tradition. تنقّل وانتقل

To be transported. To be served as dessert. To shift. To amuse o.'s self. تنقّل

What is generally brought with the wine. ما يُتنقّل بهِ على الشَّراب

To relate (news) to o. a. تناقل ه

✧ To do a. th. by turns.

To emigrate from (a country) to. إنتقل مِن . . . إلى

He died. – إلى رَحمةِ الله

Translation, transfer. Narration. نقل (un. نقلة)

Worn out, patched (shoes). – ونقل ونقل ج أنقال ونقال

Dessert ; preserves, dried fruit served with wine. نقل ونُقل ج نقول وأنقال ونقولات

Reply, answer. Stones of a ruined house. نقل

Rocky (ground). Prone to reply (man). نقِل

Short and broad (spear-head). نقلة ج نِقال

Detraction. نُقلة ج نُقل

Emigration. – وانتقال

Spinster unasked in marriage. نِقلة ج نِقل

Feast of the Assumption of the Virgin. عِيدُ انتقال العَذراء

Traditional. (opp. to مَعقُول) نقليّ ومَنقول

◻ Freight. ناقِلية

Narrator. ✧ Pregnant (woman). ناقِل ج ناقِلون ونقلة

Change of fortune. Migratory tribe. ناقِلة ج نواقِل

Nomad, stranger. Torrent (m. f.) coming from a land rained upon. نقيل

Swift-running horse. فَرَس ذُو نقيل

Stranger (woman). نقيلة

Patch on shoes. نقيلة ج نقائل ونقيل

Syrian dates. أنقِلاء

Swift-running horse. فَرَس نقّال ومِنقل ومُناقِل

Mountain-path. Worn out sole, shoe. ✧ Copper-brazier. مَنقل ج مَناقِل

Shattering the bone (wound in the head). مُنقّلة

Means of transport. Locomotion. ✧ Kind of draughts. مِنقلة ج مَناقِل

A day's journey. مَنقلة

Chattels, moveable (goods) (opp. to real property). مُنتقل ج مُنتقِلات

✶ نقم i ونقِم a نقماً ونقَماً وتِنقّاماً ; وانتقم مِن

To avenge o.'s self of, to punish a. o.

To reprove a. o. for. نَقِمَ ه مِن وعلى
To distress, to harass a. o. ✧ نَاقَمَ ه
To take revenge upon. ✧ إِسْتَنْقَمَ
Middle of a road. نَقْم
Revenge, penal punishment. Heaven-inflicted blow. نِقْمَة ونَقِمَة ج نِقَم ونِقَم ونَقِمَات
To be in the way of recovery from. ✲ نَقِهَ a نَقَهًا ونَقَهَ a نُقُوهًا, وانْتَقَهَ مِن
To catch (the meaning) of. نَقِهَ a نَقْهًا ونُقُوهًا ونَقَاهَةً ونَقَهَانًا, واسْتَنْقَهَ ه
To cure a.o. from (a disease). أَنْقَهَ ه مِن
To make a. o. to understand (a discourse). — ه ه
Listen to me! Lend me thy ear! أَنْقِهْ لِي سَمْعَكَ
To be soothed; consoled by. إِنْتَقَهَ مِن
To question a. o. إِسْتَنْقَهَ ه
Recovery. نَقَه ونُقُوه (un. نَقْهَة)
Recovering. نَاقِه ج نُقَّه
Catching the meaning of a speech. — ونَقِه
To extract marrow from (a bone). ✲ نَقَا o نَقْوًا, ونَقَى i نَقْيًا, وانْتَقَى ه
To be pure, unmixed, spotless. نَقِيَ a نَقَاء ونَقَاوَة ونَقَاءَة ونُقَاوَة ونَقَايَة
To cleanse a. th. To cull a. th. To weed (a field). To prune (a vine). نَقَّى وأَنْقَى ه
To be full of fecula (wheat). To be fat (camel). أَنْقَى
To select, to sort a. th. تَنَقَّى وانْتَقَى ه
Sandy hillock. نَقًا مث نَقَوَان ونَقَيَان ج أَنْقَاء ونُقِيّ
Bone of the arm. Bone full of marrow. نَقًا ونَقْو ونِقْو ج أَنْقَاء
Marrow of a bone. Fat of the eye. نِقْي ج أَنْقَاء
Purity, cleanliness. نَقَاء ونَقَاوَة
Marrow, pith of a. th. نُقَايَة ج نَقَايَا ونُقَاء, ونُقَاوَة ج نُقًا ونُقَاء
The choice part. نَقْوَة ونُقَاوَة ونُقَاة
Refuse, siftings of wheat. نُقَاة ونُقَاة ونُقَايَة ونُقَايَة
Choice part. *Pl.* Alkaline-plants used for washing. نُقَاوَة ج نَقَاوَى
Pure, clean, pious. نَقِيّ ج نِقَاء وأَنْقِيَاء
Word. نَقِيَّة ج نَقَايَا
Steadily. نِقَةً نِقَةً

Thin-fingered. أَنْقَى م نَقْوَاء
Road, path. المُنَقِّي
To urge (a debtor). ✲ نَكَّ o نَكًّا على
To take off the scab of (a wound). ✲ نَكَأَ a نَكْأً ه
To kill or wound a. o. — ه وفيه
To pay to a. o. his due. — ه حَقَّهُ
He recovered his due from. إِنْتَكَأَ حَقَّهُ مِن
Paying readily. زُكَأَة نُكَأَة
To render a. o. unhappy (circumstances). ✲ نَكَبَ o نَكْبًا ونَكَبًا ه
To blow obliquely (wind). — نُكُوبًا
To defend, to protect a. o. — نِكَابَةً ونُكُوبًا على
To incline (a vessel, a bow) for emptying its contents. To bruise, to hurt (the foot: stone). — نَكْبًا ه
To throw a. th. away. — ه او ب
To deviate from (a road). — نَكْبًا ونُكُوبًا, ونَكِبَ a نَكَبًا, ونَكَّبَ عَن
To feel a pain in the shoulder. نَكِبَ a نَكَبًا
To be overtaken by a misfortune. نُكِبَ
To put aside, to remove a. o. نَكَّبَ ه
To put a. o. out of (the way). — ه وبهِ عَن
To shun, to avoid a. o. To deviate from. تَنَكَّبَ عَن
To carry (a bow) upon the shoulders. — وانْتَكَبَ ه
Misfortune, disaster. نَكْب ج نُكُوب
Inclination. Pain in the shoulder amongst camels. نَكَب
Wounded at the foot (beast). نَكِب م نَكِبَة
Misfortune, disgrace. نَكْبَة ج نَكَبَات
Heap of grain not measured. نُكْبَة ج نُكَب
Circuit of a hoof. نَكِيب
Feeling a pain in the shoulder (beast). Without bow (man). Having one shoulder higher han the other. أَنْكَب
Deviating from truth. أَنْكَب ومِنْكَاب عَن الحَقّ
Side wind. نَكْبَاء ج نُكْب
North-east wind. نُكَيْبَاء
Shoulder of men and beasts. Side. Helper, protecter. Elevated land. مَنْكِب ج مَنَاكِب

To overcome a. o. (sleep). نَكَحَ نِكَاحًا ه
✧ To run away (beaten beast). نَكَحَ
To marry a. o. to. أَنكَحَ ه ه
To ally by marriage. تَنَاكَحَ
Marriage-contract; formula of marriage. نُكْحٌ ونِكْحٌ
Marriage. Marriage-contract. Conjugal intercourse. نِكَاحٌ
Polygamist. نُكَحٌ ونُكَحَةٌ
Married (woman). نَاكِحٌ ونَاكِحَةٌ
Women, wives. مَنَاكِحُ
To withhold a. o. ✱ نَكَدَ o نَكَدًا ه
To deny a. th.; To give little to a. o. To trouble a. o. with requests. — ه
To ask much and receive little. To be troubled with requests. نُكِدَ
To be hard (life). To lead a painful life. To hold little water (well). نَكِدَ a نَكَدًا
To render (life) painful and hard. To waste away (wealth). نَكَّدَ ه
To trouble, to intrude upon a. o. — ونَاكَدَ ه
To be vexed, troubled. تَنَكَّدَ
To treat o. a. harshly, to disturb o. a. تَنَاكَدَ
Harshness; troublesomeness. نَكَدٌ وتَنْكِيدٌ
Unserviceable. نَكْدٌ ونَكَدٌ ونَكِدٌ ج أَنكَادٌ ومَنَاكِيدُ
Harsh, troublesome, teasing. — وأَنكَدُ م نَكْدَاءُ ج نُكْدٌ
Paltry, trifling (gift). نَكَدٌ ولُكَدٌ ومُنَكَّدٌ ومَنكُودٌ
Bereft of her children (woman). Yielding little milk (she-camel). نَاكِدٌ ج نُكُدٌ
Yielding little or much milk (she-camel). نَكْدَاءُ ج نُكُدٌ
Troubled with requests. Asking much and receiving little. مَنكُودٌ
Receiving little. ✧ Unlucky, accursed. مَنكُودُ الحَظِّ
Cares, troubles. مُنَكِّدَاتٌ
✱ نَكِرَ a نَكَرًا ونُكْرًا ونُكُورًا ونَكِيرًا،
To be ignorant of; unacquainted with. To disown a. o. وأَنكَرَ ه وه
To disavow, to deny. To disapprove a. o. or a. th. — ه وه

Secondary feathers of a vulture. أَلمَنَاكِبُ
Star in *Pegasus*. مَنكِبُ الفَرَسِ
Star in *Orio*. مَنكِبُ الجَوْزَاءِ
Such a one always shuns me. فُلَانٌ مَعِي عَلَى حَدِّ مَنكِبٍ
Experiencing misfortunes. Hurt at the foot. Oblique road. مَنكُوبٌ
To leap, to bound in running (horse). ✱ نَكَتَ o نَكْتًا
To leave (a mark) upon (the ground). — ه ب
To throw a. o. head down. — ه
To empty (a bone, a pipe, a bow). — ه
He uttered witticisms. نَكَّتَ فِي كَلَامِهِ
✧ To criticise, to harass a. o. نَكَّتَ عَلَى
To be thrown down headlong. إِنْتَكَتَ
Witticism; witty allusion. ✧ Quaint, odd man. نُكْتَةٌ ج نُكَتٌ
Speck, spot of different colours. Spot in a mirror. Mark left by a stick or a finger upon the ground. — ج نُكَتٌ ونِكَاتٌ
Epigrammatist, mocker. ✧ Censor, troublesome. نَكَّاتٌ
Dates beginning to ripen. رُطَبَةٌ مُنَكِّتَةٌ
To break (a compact). To untwist (a rope). To split the end of (a tooth-pick). ✱ نَكَثَ o i نَكْثًا ه
To break a mutual (promise). تَنَاكَثَ ه
To be broken (compact). To be undone (rope). To be split (tooth-pick). إِنْتَكَثَ
To turn from (an affair) to (another). — مِن . . . إِلَى
Untwisted threads. نِكْثٌ ج أَنكَاثٌ
Unwoven part of a rope; splint of a tooth-pick. نُكَاثَةٌ
✧ Rogue, rascal. رَجُلٌ نَاكِثٌ
Soul, mind. Difficult affair. Utmost endeavour. Breach of promise. Nature. Strength of soul. نَكِيثَةٌ ج نَكَائِثُ
Unwoven (rope). حَبْلٌ مَنكُوثٌ وأَنكَاثٌ
To marry (woman). ✱ نَكَحَ i o نِكَاحًا
To marry (a woman). — واستَنكَحَ ه

نَكُرَ o نَكَارَةً To be hard, difficult (affair).

نَكَّرَ ه وه To change the appearance of. To disguise, to alter a. o. or a. th. (*Gram*). To render (a noun) indeterminate.

نَاكَرَ ه To struggle against a. o. To dispute with, to contradict a. o.

أَنْكَرَ ه وه To deny, to disown a. o. or a. th.

— ه عَلَى To disapprove, to find fault with a. o. in.

تَنَكَّرَ To change for the worse. To assume an unknown appearance. To disguise o.'s self.

— لِ To feel a dislike for.

تَنَاكَرَ To feign ignorance. To behave together like strangers or foes.

تَنَاكَرَ واسْتَنْكَرَ ه To disacknowledge a. th., to be ignorant of.

إِسْتَنْكَرَ ه To ask of a. o. what he is ignorant of.

✧ — ه To disapprove, to abhor a. th.

نَكْر ونُكْر ونَكَارَة ونَكْرَاء Acuteness of mind. Art, deceit.

مَا أَشَدَّ نُكْرَهُ What a cunny man!

نُكْر ونُكُر ونَكْرَاء ومُنْكَر Difficult affair.

نَكِر ونَكُر ونُكُر (*m. f.*) ج أَنْكَار Shrewd, sharp.

نُكْر ومُنْكَر Unknown.

نَكْرَاء Mishap, misfortune.

نَكْرَة ونَكِير وإِنْكَار Negation. Refusal. Disavowal, denial. Disapprobation.

أَمْرٌ نَكِير Difficult business.

نَكِير ومُنْكَر The two Angels of death.

نَكِرَة ج نَكِرَات Indeterminate noun.

تَنَكُّر Disguise, change for the worse. Incognito.

نَاكِر الجَمِيل Ungrateful, unthankful.

مُنْكَر ج مُنْكَرَات ومَنَاكِر Unknown. Denied. Disapproved by God (action).

— ج مُنْكَرُون ومَنَاكِير Cunny, perspicacious. Unheard of, extraordinary (event).

مُنْكَرَات Abominable, hateful actions.

مُنَكَّر *Gram*. Indeterminate (noun).

مَنْكُور ويَنْكُور Unknown (road).

✱ نَكَزَ o نَكْزًا ه To strike, to urge; to goad (a beast).

نَكَزَ ه To prick a. th.

— ه To sting a. o. (serpent). ✧ To elbow (a sleeper).

— ونَكِزَ a نَكْزًا To be exhausted (well).

نَكَزَ o نُكُوزًا To sink into the earth (water).

أَنْكَزَ ه To exhaust (a well).

نِكْز Refuse. Marrow remaining in the bone.

نَاكِز ج نَوَاكِز, ونَكُوز ج نُكُز Exhausted well.

✧ نَاكُوزَة Goad, sting.

نَكَّاز ج نَكَاكِيز ونَكَّازَات Small-headed and venomous snake.

✱ نَكَسَ o نَكْسًا, ونَكَّسَ ه وه To reverse, to invert a. th. To throw upside down. To make a. th. in the wrong way. To lower (a flag). To lower (the head) carelessly.

— ه To cause a relapse to a. o. (food).

نُكِسَ To relapse (sick person).

نَكِسَ a نَكْسًا عَنْ To be inferior to (o.'s companions).

تَنَكَّسَ To be inverted, overthrown. ✧ To lower the head carelessly.

إِنْتَكَسَ To fall headlong. To have a relapse (sick person).

نُكْس ونُكَاس وانْتِكَاس Relapse.

تَعْسًا لَهُ ونُكْسًا او تَعْسًا لَهُ ونَكْسًا May misfortunes befall him!

نِكْس ج أَنْكَاس Arrow with a broken head. Weak; cipher (man).

— ومَنْكُوس Born the feet foremost (child).

نُكْس Old man bent by age.

نَاكِس ج نَوَاكِس Lowering the head.

مُنَكَّس Spiritless horse.

قَرَأَ الكِتَابَ مَنْكُوسًا He read the book by the end.

مَنْكُوس ومُنْتَكِس Relapsing (sick man).

✱ نَكَشَ i a نَكْشًا, وإِنْتَكَشَ ه To empty, to clean out (a well).

بَحْرٌ لَا يُنْكَشُ Inexhaustible sea.

نَكَّشَ ه To destroy a. th. To examine a. th. minutely. ✧ To dig up (the ground).

لَمَّة مَا تُنْكَش Part of a plant that cannot be plucked out.

To be free from. نَكِفَ a نَكَفًا مِن
To tease, to despite a. o. ✧ نَاكَفَ ه
To exchange words with a. o. — الكَلَامَ
To remove, to free a. o. from a. th. أَنْكَفَ ه
To discuss, to dispute together. تَنَاكَفَ
To decline, to fall away. إِنْتَكَفَ
To be proud, haughty. إِسْتَنْكَفَ
To find (the trace) of. — ه
To scorn, to refuse a. th. To loathe a. th. — مِن
Two projecting bones of the jaw of a camel. نَكَفَتَانِ ونُكْفَتَانِ ونَكِفَتَانِ ج نَكَفَات
Ganglion at the root of the jaw. نَكَف
Tumour on a camel's jaw. نُكَاف
Affected with a tumour on the jaw. مَنْكُوف
✡ نَكَلَ o i نُكُولًا, ونَكِلَ a نَكَلًا عَن و مِن
To shrink, to abstain from.
He inflicted an exemplary punishment upon him. نَكَّلَ نَكْلَةً, ونَكَّلَ بِهِ
To be punished as a warning to others. نَكِلَ a نَكَلًا
To avert a. o. from. نَكَّلَ وأَنْكَلَ ه عَن
Fetters, bonds. Curb for race-horses. نِكْل ج أَنْكَال ونُكُول
He is the scourge of the wicked. إِنَّهُ لَنِكْل شَرّ
Striking punishment, warning. نَكَال ونُكْلَة ومَنْكَل
God has chastised him in a striking manner. رَمَاهُ اللهُ بِنُكْلَةٍ
Experienced man. Strong horse. نَكَل
Weak, cowardly. نَاكِل ج نُكَّل
Engine of torture, rack. Torture. مِنْكَل ج مَنَاكِل
Machine for cutting tobacco. ✧ مِنْكَلَة ج مَنَاكِل
To puff, to breathe into the face of. ✡ نَكَهَ a i نَكْهًا لَهُ وعَلَيْهِ
To smell the breath of a. o. — ونَكِهَ a نَكْهًا, واِسْتَنْكَهَ ه
To be foul-breathed. نُكِهَ
Foul breath of the mouth. نَكْهَة
To wound, to hurt a. o. ✧ To tease, to vex a. o. ✡ نَكَى i نِكَايَةً, وأَنْكَى ه او فِي
Mayest thou be free from evil! لَا تُنْكَى
To be vexed, to despite. ✧ إِنْتَكَى

To finish, to perform a. th. نَكَشَ ه ومِن
✧ Digger. نَكَّاش
Scrutiniser. مِنْكَش
Hoe, rake. مِنْكَاش و✧ مَنْكُوش ج مَنَاكِش
✡ نَكَصَ o i نَكْصًا ونُكُوصًا ومَنْكَصًا عَن
To withdraw from.
He turned back from the path of justice. نَكَصَ على عَقِبَيْهِ
To return, back. إِنْتَكَصَ
To urge a. o. to desist from. ✡ نَكَظَ o نَكْظًا, ونَكَّظَ وأَنْكَظَ ه
To dissuade from. — ونَكَّظَ وأَنْكَظَ ه عَن
To hurry. نَكِظَ a نَكَظًا
His case became difficult. تَنَكَّظَ عَلَيْهِ أَمْرُهُ
Striving, endeavour. نَكْظ ونَكَظ ونَكْظَة ومَنْكَظَة
To repel, to hurry a. o. away from. To make a. o. to desist from. ✡ نَكَعَ a نَكْعًا, ونَكَّعَ وأَنْكَعَ ه عَن
To rebuke a. o. — ه
He paid or withheld his due. — ه حَقَّهُ
To abstain, to shrink from. — عَن
He has not ceased doing it. مَا نَكَعَ يَفْعَلُهُ
I do not know where he has gone to. مَا أَدْرِي أَيْنَ نَكَعَ
To milk (a beast) in striking her udder. — a نَكْعًا وتَنْكَاعًا ه
To be red-nosed. نَكِعَ a نَكَعًا
Rebuke, kick, cuff, box. Plant alike to the طُرْثُوث. Head of any plant. نَكْعَة
Reddish brown complexion. نَكَع ونَكَعَة
Red blossom of the plant طُرْثُوث used as dye. Amaranth. Tragacanth gum. نُكَعَة ونُكَعَة
Red (woman, lip). نَكِعَة
Red-faced, snub-nosed. نَكِعَة وأَنْكَع
Walking backwards. Flat (nose). مَنْكَع
To stop a. th. ✡ نَكَفَ o نَكْفًا, وانْتَكَفَ ه
Rain falling uninterruptedly. غَيْثٌ لَا يُنْكَفُ
Inexhaustible sea. Innumerable army. بَحْرٌ او جَيْشٌ لَا يُنْكَفُ
To find (the trace) of a. th. نَكَفَ ه
To wipe (tears) with the finger.
To refuse, to reject a. th. To abstain from. نَكَفَ o نَكْفًا, ونَكِفَ a نَكَفًا عَن

✧ Teasing, spite. نِكَايَة ج نِكَايَات
✧ Bitter word. كَلَامٌ مُنْكٍ
Indigo-pigment. P نِيلَج
Smoke-black for tattooing. نِيلَنْج
Nenuphar, aquatic plant. ✱ نِيلُوفَر و نِينُوفَر
Azarole, medlar-tree. Plane-tree. ✱ نَلْك ونُلْك
To diffuse its perfume (musk). To spread an odour (wind). ✱ نَمَّ o i نَمًّا
To relate (talks) malevolently. To fill (speech) with lies. — ه
To sow discord between. نَمَّ بَيْنَ
نَمٌّ م نَمَّة ونَمُوم ومِنَمٌّ ج نَمُّون وأَنِمَّاء ونُمٌّ
Slanderer, malevolent reporter.
Ant, louse. نَمَّة ونِمّ ونِمَاء
Vice, defect. Counterfeit (coin). Cheating. Enmity. Nature. Essence. نُمِّيّ ج نَمَامِيّ
There is nobody in the house. مَا فِي الدَّار نُمِّيّ
Ring-dove. نُمِّيَّة
Movement, life. نَامَّة
God has reduced him to silence, *i. e.* he is dead. أَسْكَتَ اللهُ نَامَّتَهُ
Wild thyme. نَمَّام
Slander, malignant report. Grating of a pen. نَمِيم ونَمِيمَة ج نَمَائِم
To streak the ground (wind). To embellish a. th. ◻ To mutter a. th. ✱ نَمْنَمَ ه
Streaks made by the wind on the earth. نِمْنِم ونَمْنِيم
Wren (bird). نُمْنُمَة
✧ Water-cress. نَمْنَام
White spot on the nails. نُمْنُم ونِمْنِم
Streaked (garment). مُنَمْنَم
P نَمُوذَج وأُنْمُوذَج ونَمُوذَجَات وأُنْمُوذَجَات
Model, pattern, sample.
To be spotted, streaked (cloud). ✱ نَمِرَ a نَمَرًا
To become angry. To be angry, wicked. — ونَمَّرَ وتَنَمَّرَ
To frown (the face). ✧ To mark, to number a. th. نَمَّرَ ه
To find clear water. أَنْمَرَ
To be like a panther, to be spotted. To burst into threats. ✧ To be numbered. تَنَمَّرَ
To wish, to prepare evil to. — ل

نَمِر و نِمْر ج نُمْر ونُمُر وأَنْمُر وأَنْمَار و نِمَار و نِمَارَة ونُمُور ونُمُورَة
Leopard, tiger, panther.
She-panther, tigress. نَمِرَة ج نَمِر
Streaked or wollen garment. نَمِرَة ج نِمَار
Iron hook for catching a wild beast. — نَمِرَة ونَامُورَة
Spot, speck. ✧ Number. نُمْرَة ج نُمَر
Spotted, striped, streaked. أَنْمَر م نَمْرَاء ج نُمْر
Wholesome, salubrious (water). Unimpaired (honour). نَمِر ونَمِير
Tiger-like, striped, spotted. Angry. مُتَنَمِّر
✱ نُمْرُق و نِمْرِق ونُمْرُقَة ونِمْرِقَة و نِمْرِقْعَة ونُمْرُقَّة ج نَمَارِق
Saddle-cushion.
To hide, to conceal (a secret). ✱ نَمَسَ i نَمْسًا ه
To slander a. o. — ب
To sow discord between. — بَيْنَ
To comunicate a secret to. — ونَامَسَ ه
To be rancid (butter). نَمِسَ a نَمَسًا
To conceal a. th. from a. o. نَمَّسَ ه على
To lay in a lurking-place (hunter). نَامَسَ وتَنَمَّسَ
To sow discord between. أَنْمَسَ بَيْنَ
To be hidden, concealed (affair). تَنَمَّسَ
To conceal o.'s self. إِنْمَسَ
Ichneumon, Egyptian rat. Ferret. Weasel. نِمْس ج نُمُوس
✧ Hen-louse. نَمَس
Backbiter, intriguer. نَمَّاس ونَامُوس
Confidant. Lion's den. Lurking-place, net of hunters. Dissembling, deceit. Law of God. ✧ Honour, character. Gnat. نَامُوس ج نَوَامِيس
The Angel Gabriel. أَلنَّامُوس والنَّامُوس الأَكْبَر
To increase the credit of a. o. ✧ نَوْمَسَ ه
To acquire credit, repute. ✧ تَنَوْمَسَ
Den of a lion. ✧ Gnat. نَامُوسَة
✧ Mosquito-curtain. نَامُوسِيَّة
Dull, of a dusky-colour. أَنْمَس م نَمْسَاء ج نُمْس
Confidant. مُنَامِس
✧ Austria. T نَمْسَة
Austrian. نَمْسَاوِيّ

☆ نَمَش o نَمْشًا، وأَنْمَش To misrepresent, to traduce a. o.
نَمَش ه To strip (a land) bare (locusts).
— ونَمَش الكَلامَ To lie.
نَمِش a نَمَشًا To have the skin spotted, freckled.
نَمَّش في أُذْنِهِ To whispered in his ear.
— ه ✧ To moisten (the wheat).
نَمَش (un. نَمَشَة) Freckles, specks on the skin. Streaks in a picture.
✧ نَمْشَة Sword, dagger.
نَمِش م نَمِشَة، وأَنْمَش م نَمْشَاء ج نُمْش
Freckled. Variegated. Waved (blade).
مِنْمَش Slanderer, intriguer.
☆ نَمَص o نَمْصًا، ونَمَّص تَنْمِيصًا وتَنَمَّاصًا ه To pull out (the hair).
أَنْمَص To sprout (plant).
تَنَمَّص To depilate herself (woman). To pasture on the first herbage (cattle).
نَمَص Down, small feathers.
نِمَاص Needleful.
نُمَاص ج نُمُص وأَنْمِصَة Month.
نَمِيص Plucked (hair, plant).
مِنْمَص ومِنْمَاص Depilatory ; tweezers.
☆ نمط — نَمَّط ل على To show a. th. to.
نَمَط ج نِمَاط وأَنْمَاط Manner, way, Carpet, saddle-cloth.
على هٰذَا النَّمَط In this manner.
هُمْ على نَمَط وَاحِد They are of the same sort.
☆ نمغ — نَمَغَة Summit of a mountain. Choice part of a tribe. Abundance of goods.
☆ نَمَق o نَمْقًا ه To slap a. o. on (the eye). To write (a book).
نَمَّق ه To write (a book) elegantly ; to adorn, to embellish (a book).
أَنْمَق To produce stoneless dates (palm-tree).
نَمَق Middle part of a road. Book.
نَمَقَة Offensive smell.
نَمِيقَة ج نَمَائِق Letter elegantly written.
مُنْمِق Stoneless date.
مُنَمَّق Affected (speech).
☆ نَمَل o ونَمِل a نَمْلًا، وأَنْمَل To slander ; to disclose a. th. maliciously.
نَمَل ونَمِل في To climb (a tree).
نَمِل a نَمَلًا To feel a formication, a tingling (limb).
نَامَل To walk like a shackled man.
تَنَمَّل To be disorderly (mob).
نَمْل وأَنْمُل ج نِمَال (un. نَمْلَة ونَمَلَة) Ant.
نَمْل Small pustules.
نَمْلَة Lie. Crack on a horse's hoof. Ant-hill.
نِمْلَة ونُمْلَة ونَمِيلَة Slander, backbiting.
نُمْلَة Remainder of water in a basin.
نَمِل م نَمِلَة Swarming with ants (place). Fiery (horse).
— الأَصَابِع Dexterous, light-handed.
نَمِل ونَامِل ونَمَّال ومِنْمَل ومُنْمِل Slanderer, malevolent reporter.
نَامِلَة Party of travellers.
إِمْرَأَة نَمِلَى ومُنَمِّلَة Boisterous (woman).
أَنْمُلَة وأَنْمَلَة وإِنْمِلَة ج أَنَامِل وأَنْمُلات Tip of the fingers.
مُنَمَّل ومُتَنَمِّل Written closely.
مَنْمُول Damaged by ants. Tongue.
☆ نَمِه a نَمَهًا To be amazed, astonished.
☆ نَمَا o نُمُوًّا To grow. To be saturated with dye (colour). ✧ To progress, to thrive.
— ه إلى To attribute (talks) to. To report a. th. to.
نُمُوّ Growth, increase. ✧ Progress.
☆ نَمَى i نَمْيًا ونُمِيًّا ونَمَاء ونَمِيَّة To grow ; to increase (goods). To rise (water, price). To be saturated (dye). To fly away (game).
— ه على To raise a. th. on.
— ونَمَّى ه To stir (the fire).
نُمِي إلى To be related to a. o. (event).
— ونَمَّى ه إلى To relate (an event) to.
نَمَّى تَنْمِيَة، وأَنْمَى إِنْمَاء To increase, to grow
أَنْمَى ه To give growth, increase to. ✧ To promote, to further a. th.
أَنْمَى ه و ه To spread (malignant reports). To hit and wound (the game).
تَنَمَّى To grow, to rise.
تَنَمَّى وانْتَمَى To rise in the air (hawk).
إِنْتَمَى الى To trace back o.'s origin to.
نَمَاة ج نَمًى Small ant. Louse.
نَمِيَّة Double thread rolled up into a ball.
نَامٍ Growing. ✧ Progressing.

ناميَة ج نوامٍ Faculty of growing, growth. Created beings.
— الكرْم Vine-shoot laden with grapes.
✲ نَعْنَه ة عن To frighten away (a beast) from. ✧ To overtire a. o. To deaden a. o. with blows.
تَنَهْنَه To refrain, to turn away. ✧ To be half-dead from fatigue, blows.
✲ نَهِئَ a ونَهُوَ o نَهْأً ونَهَاءَةً ونُهُوءَةً ونُهُوءًا ونَهَاوَةً To be insufficiently cooked (meat).
أَنْهَأ ه To cook (meat) insufficiently. To do (a work) imperfectly.
نَهِيء Insufficiently cooked (meat).
✲ نَهَب o a ونَهِب a نَهْبًا, وناهَب وانْتَهَب ه To plunder, to carry off (spoils).
نَهَب ة To bite a. o. on the heel (dog).
— وناهَب ة To carp at, to bite a. o. in words.
ناهَب ة To race with (another horse).
أَنْهَب ه To give a. th. as booty.
تَنَاهَب ه To make long (strides). To quarrel about (a spoil).
إنْتَهَبَ الشَّوطَ The (horse) won the race.
نَهْب Plunder, booty.
هٰذا زَمَانُ النَّهْب This is the time of plundering.
نَهْب ج نِهَاب Prey, booty. Way of running.
نُهْبَة ونُهْبَى ونُهَيْبَى ونُهَّيْبَى Booty, plunder, spoil. Raid.
نَهَّاب Plunderer, ravisher.
مِنْهَب Winner in a race(horse).
مُنْتَهَب Plundered. Place of plunder.
✲ نُهْبُرَة ج نَهَابِر, ونُهْبُور ونُهْبُورَة ج نَهَابِير Abyss. Hell. Abyss of hell.
✲ نَهْبَل م نَهْبَلَة Old.
✲ نَهَت i نَهِيتًا ونُهَاتًا To growl (lion). To bray (ass). To moan (man).
نُهَات ونَهِيت Growl of a lion.
نَاهِت Growling, braying. The throat.
النَّهَات والمِنْهَت والمُنْهِت The lion.
✲ نَهَج a نَهْجًا ونُهُوجًا, واسْتَنْهَج To be opened, trodden (road).
نَهَج a نَهْجًا ه To open (a road). To follow (a track). To clear (an affair).

نَهِج i ونَهَج a نَهَجًا To be out of breath, to pant.
نَهِج i a ونَهَج a نَهْجًا To be worn out (clothes).
أَنْهَج To be traced (road). To be clear (affair). To be worn out (clothes).
— ه To trace (a road). To elucidate (an affair). To wear out (a garment).
— ة To put (a horse) out of breath.
إنْتَهَج To follow a track.
إسْتَنْهَجَ سَبِيلَ فُلَانٍ He followed the course of, he imitated such a one.
نَهْج Plain road.
نَهَج ونَهِيج Painful breathing, panting.
مَنْهَج ومِنْهَج ومِنْهَاج ج مَنَاهِج ومَنَاهِيج Well traced road. Manner of action.
✲ نَهَد a o نُهُودًا To become swollen and rounded (breasts). To be filled (water-skin).
— ونَهَّد To have rounded breasts.
نَهَد a o نَهْدًا ونَهَدًا ل وإلى To rush upon (the enemy).
— وأَنْهَد ه To increase (a gift).
نَهُد o نُهُودَةً To be fine and strong (horse).
نَاهَد ة To come to blows with a. o. To draw lots with a. o. in shutting the hand
أَنْهَد ه To fill (a vessel).
تَنَهَّد To sigh; to heave (breast).
تَنَاهَد To share together the expenses of a journey.
— في الحَرْبِ They assaulted o. a. at war.
إسْتَنْهَد ة To provoke a. o. to fight.
نَهْد ج نُهُود Woman's breast. Strong and fine horse. Dauntless, gallant man. Lion. Name of a tribe.
نَهْد ونِهْد Share of common expenses.
نَاهِد ونَاهِدَة ج نَوَاهِد, ومُنَهِّد Round-breasted (girl).
نَهْدَاء Elevated sand-hill.
نِهَاد Quantity, measure.
— مِئَة About one hundred.
نَهَّاد Rushing upon.
نَهْدَان Full (basin, vessel).
نَهِيد Cream, fresh butter.

To seize (an opportunity). إِنْتَهَزَ ه
To seize a. th. hastily.
He laughed immoderately. — في الضَّحِكِ
Quantity, measure. نَهز ونِهاز و نِهاز
Opportunity. نُهزة ج نُهَز
Seasonably, opportunely. عَلَى نُهزَةٍ
Chief of a tribe. نَاهِز القَوْمِ
Raising the chest in walk (ass). نَهَّاز
Surroundings of a well. مُنْهَز البِئْر
To bite a. o. ✱ نَهَس ونَهِس a نَهْسًا (snake).
To snap a. th. — وانْتَهَس ه
To outrage a. o. إِنْتَهَس ة
Hawk. نُهَس أو نَهَس
Wont to bite. Lion. نَهَّاس ونَهُوس ومِنْهَس
Wolf.
Lean, emaciated. نَهِيس ومَنْهُوس
Place of biting, bite. مَنْهَس
To bite a. th. ✱ نَهَش a i نَهْشًا ة وه with the front teeth. To sting a. o. (serpent). To tear (her face) from grief (woman). To reduce a. o. to destitution (fate). To distress a. o.
✧ To be out of breath, (*for* نَهَج) نَهِش to pant.
To be thin (arm, shank). نُهِش وانْتَهَش
To bite o. a. تَنَاهَش
Bite. نَهْش (*un.* نَهْشَة)
Light-handed, نَهْش اليَدَيْن والقَوَائِم light-footed.
Acts of violence, iniquitous نَهَاوِش behaviour.
Distressed. Emaciated. مَنْهُوش
Thin-legged. — القَدَمَيْن
Tearing her face with her مُنْتَهِشَة nails (woman).
To bite a. o. ✱ نَهْشَل ة
To eat a. th. greedily. — ه
Lion. Hawk. نَهْشَل
To rise from ✱ نَهَض a نَهْضًا ونُهُوضًا عَن sitting; to stand up.
To rise for. To set to (work). نَهَض ل
To rise, to stand against. — على
To rush upon (the enemy). — إلى
To stand erect (plant). To ex- نَهَض pand the wings for flying (bird).
To resist a. o., to struggle نَاهَض ة against.
To stir, to set a. o. on foot. أَنْهَض ة

Dish made of colocynth-seeds نَهِيدَة cooked with flour.
Sigh, moan. تَنَهُّد
To flow abundantly ✱ نَهَر a نَهْرًا (blood, river). To make a raid in the day-time.
To dig (a channel) for a river. نَهَر ه
To drive a. o. back. ✧ To call — ة out a. o.
To reach water — ونَهِر a نَهَرًا، وأَنْهَر by digging.
To flow (blood). To be, to do أَنْهَر a. th. in the day-time. To be unsuccessful.
To bleed incessantly (vein). — وانْتَهَر
To make (a river, blood) to أَنْهَر ه flow. To widen (a wound).
To drive a. o. away roughly. إِنْتَهَر ة
✧ To upbraid, to carp at a. o.
To flow abundantly, to become إِسْتَنْهَر wide (river).
River. نَهْر ج أَنْهُر وأَنْهَار ونُهُر ونُهُور
Fluvial, river-(fish). نَهْرِيّ
Day, نَهَار ج أَنْهُر ونُهُر و✧ نَهَارَات day-time.
Young bustard. — ج أَنْهِرَة ونُهُر
By day and night. لَيْلًا ونَهَارًا
Making a raid in the day-time. نَهِر
Wide (river). Clear, bright (day).
White grapes. — ونَاهِر
Abundant thing; much. شَيْءٌ نَهِير
Glorious, splendid day. نَهَار أَنْهَر
Bed of a river. Channel of water. مَنْهَر
Dung-hill. مَنْهَرَة
To be at hand, to draw ✱ نَهَز a نَهْزًا near (event). To rise for taking a. th.
To raise the chest in walk — بِصَدْرِهَا (beast).
To raise the head for pro- — بِرَأْسِهَا tecting itself (beast).
To shake (the head). To — ه وة strike the udder of its mother (youngling). To drive a. o. back.
He shook the bucket — بِالدَّلْوِ في البِئْر in the well.
To draw near to a. o. To نَاهَز ه seize (an opportunity). To overtake (the game: hunter).
To compete together. تَنَاهَزَا

To drive the clouds along (wind). أنهض ه

They rushed one upon the other in (the fight). تناهضوا في

To be roused, set on foot. إنتهض

To rise for. — ل

To arouse, to stir a. o. to. To incite a. o. to. إستنهض ه ل

Injustice. Hard (ground). نهض

Standing, getting up, rise. نهوض

Power, ability. نهضة

Rush towards. نهضة إلى

Incitement, rousing. إنهاض

Ready to fly (chicken). Active (workman). ناهض

Pl. Strong and tall camels. ناهضة ج نواهض

Helpers of a man, as brothers, servants. ناهضة الرجل

Rising often. نهّاض

Difficult roads. نهاض الطُرُق

✲ نَهَق i a o ونَهِق a نهقًا ونهاقًا ونهيقًا وتنهاقًا

To bray (ass).

Wild rocket (*plant*). نهق ونهق

Throat of an ass. نواهق

Two projecting bones in the jaw of hoofed animals. — وناهقتان

To win a. o. ✲ نهك a نهاكة ه

To wear threadbare (clothes). — ه

He ate to excess. — من الطعام وفيه

He blackened his character. — عرضه

To enervate a. o. (wine). To weaken a. o. (fever). — a نهكا ه

To exhaust (a pond, the udder). — ه

Do charge the enemy energetically. إنهكوا وجوه القوم

To exhaust (wine). نهك a نهكا ه

To emaciate and exhaust a. o. (fever). نهك a نهكا ونهكة ونهاكة, وانتهك ه

To punish a. o. severely نهك a نهكا ونهكة, وأنهك ه

To be weakened, exhausted by disease. نُهك نهكا

To be brave, dauntless. To be strong. نهك o نهاكة

To lessen the character of. To violate the honour of. إنتهك ه

To be undone, dissundered- To be parted (fingers). To be freed (slave). إنهك

Curtailment of a poetical metre. نهك

Weakening, consumption. نهكة

Energetic, brave, fearless. ناهك ونهيك

Strong (camel); sharp (sword). نهيك

Cause of weakness, of exhaustion. منهكة

Weakened by disease. منهوك

To drink a first draught. To qnench (thirst). To be thirsty. ✧ To be jaded, exhausted. ✲ نهل a نهلا ومنهلا

It is enough for the present. إنهل تلان

To water (camels) for the first time. To irritate a. o. أنهل ه

To water (a seed-plot) for the first time. — ه

A draught, a gulp. نهلة

First watering, first drinking. نهل

Thirsty. Quenching his thirst. ناهل ج نهال ونهل ونهول ونهلة ونهلى

Going to the water (men, beasts). ناهلة ج نهال ونواهل

Drinking, quenching his thirst. Thirsty. ✧ Exhausted, jaded. نهلان ج نهلى

Watering-place. Halting-place in the desert. منهل ج مناهل

Tomb. Grave. Bounty. منهل ومنهال

To chide (camels). ✲ نهم i a نهما ونهيما ونهمة ه

To roar (lion). To sigh, to moan (man). — i نهما

To cast (stones) at a. o. — a نهما ه ب

To be greedy of (food). To be eager for. نهم a ونُهم نهما ونهامة في

To sigh, to moan with a. o. ناهم ه

Inordinate appetite. Gluttony. نهم

Insatiable desire. Need, want. نهمة

Greedy; insatiable. Glutton. نهم ونهيم

Blacksmith. Carpenter. نهام ونهام ونهامي ونهامي ونهامي

Owl. Monk. نهام ج نهم

Insatiable. منهوم

Fond, enamoured of. — ب

Submissive (she-camel). منهام ج مناهيم

Carpenter's workshop. منهمة

✲ نها o نهوا, ونهى a و✧ i نهيا, ونهى ه عن

To prohibit, to forbid a. o. from.

To desist from (a design). نهي a نهى, وأنهى عن

To be intelligent, prudent. نهو o نهاوة

Infinite, boundless. غَيْر مُتَنَاهٍ
Issue, end, utmost degree. مُنْتَهًى
Gram. Last forms of plural. – الجُمُوع
To rise painfully. ☆ نَاءَ o نَوْءًا وتَنْوَاءً
To fall down from fatigue.
He groaned under the burden. – بِالحِمْل
To rise against a. o. – إِلَى
To crush a. o. (burden). – بِهِ
To set at the rising of another (star). – نَوْءًا، واسْتَنَاءَ
To oppose a. o. نَاوَأَ مُنَاوَأَةً ونِوَاءً ه
To overwhelm a. o. (burden). أَنَاءَ إِنَاءَةً ه
To ask a gift from a. o. إِسْتَنَاءَ ه
Star setting at the rising of another. Star foreboding rain. Rain. ✧ Storm. نَوْءٌ ج أَنْوَاءٌ ونُوآن وأَنْوُءٌ
More clever in astronomy. أَنْوَأُ
To supply, to fill the place of a. o. To act as lieutenant, agent in. ☆ نَابَ o نَوْبًا ومَنَابًا ونِيَابَةً عَن فُلَان فِي
To come back consecutively to. – وأَنَابَ إِلَى
To come back to (God : sinner). نَابَ وأَنَابَ إِلَى
To overtake a. o. (misfortune). نَابَ o نَوْبَةً ونَوْبًا، وانْتَابَ ه
To act by turns with a. o. نَاوَبَ ه
He appointed him in the place of such a one. أَنَابَ ه عَن فُلَان
To do a. th. by turns. To relieve o. a. To alternate with. تَنَاوَبَ عَلَى وفِي
To act by turns in. إِنْتَابَ فِي
To come back consecutively to a. o. To happen to a. o. (event). – ه
To appoint a. o. as a substitute, agent. To ask a. o. to be a substitute, lieutenant. إِسْتَنَابَ ه
Stage in the desert. A day and a night's journey. Strength. Vicinage. نَوْب
By turns. نَوْبًا وبِنَوْب
✧ Altogether, entirely. بِنَوْب وبِالنَّوْب
The Nubians. (*un.* نُوبِيّ) نُوب ونُوبَة
Turn, time. Space of time. Opportunity.. Troop of men. Fit of fever. ✧ Release of a watch. نَوْبَة ج نُوَب
Body of soldiers keeping watch by turns. أَهْل وأَصْحَاب النَّوْبَة

To come to, to reach (a place). نَهِيَ وأَنْهِيَ وانْتَهَى إِلَى
That man, those men are sufficient for thee. نَهَاكَ مِن رَجُلٍ ونَهُوكَ مِن رِجَالٍ
That woman suffices to thee. نَهَتْكَ مِن أَمْرَأَةٍ
To attain the utmost degree. نَهَّى وتَنَاهَى
To come to (a pond). أَنْهَى
To perform, to accomplish a. th. ✧ To hint at, to warn a. o. – ه وه
To transmit, to deliver a. th. to. – ه إِلَى
To be performed, finished تَنَاهَى وانْتَهَى
To stagnate in a pond (water). تَنَاهَى
To abstain, to refrain from. – وانْتَهَى عَن
To desist mutually from. تَنَاهَوْا عَن
To bring, to lead a. o. to. إِنْتَهَى ب إِلَى
Prohibition, interdiction. نَهْي
Influential men. أَهْل النَّهْي
Pond of stagnating water. نَهْي ونِهْي ج أَنْهٍ وأَنْهَاء ونُهِيّ ونِهَا
Prohibition. Understanding, wariness. نُهْيَة ج نُهًى
Extreme limit, utmost degree. – ونِهَاء ونِهَايَة ج ونِهَايَات
Wisdom, prudence. نُهًى
Quantity, measure. Highest level of water. نِهَاء ونُهَاء
They are about one hundred. هُمْ نِهَاء مِئَة
Glass-flask. نِهَاء ونُهَاء ونِهًى
End, term. Completion. إِنْتِهَاء
Sufficient, replacing another. نَاهٍ
That man suffices to thee. هٰذَا رَجُلٌ نَهْيُكَ ونَاهِيكَ مِن رَجُلٍ
Conscience. نَاهِيَة ج نَوَاهٍ
He is a man without conscience. مَا لَهُ نَاهِيَة
Wary, cautious. نَهٍ ونَهِيٌ ج نَهُون، ونَهِيّ ج أَنْهِيَاء
Bottom of a valley retaining water. تَنْهَاة وتَنْهِيَة ج تَنَاهٍ
Obstruction ; wooden dam. تِنْهَاة
End, limit. مَنْهَاة
Wary, prudent man. رَجُل مَنْهَاة
What is forbidden. مَنْهِيّ عَنْهُ
Prohibited things. مَنَاهٍ
High-minded. مُتَنَاهِي العَقْل

نَوْبَة ج نَوْبَات ♦ Music. Concert, orchestra. Musical-box.

بِالنَّوْبَة By turns.

نَوْبَة ج نُوَب Misfortune, distress, accident.

نَوْبَاتِيّ ونَوْبَتْجِيّ ♦ Musician. □ Sentinel.

نَوْبَتِيَّة ♦ Band, body of musicians.

نِيَابَة Lieutenancy, vice-royalty; delegation.

نِيَابَة عَنْ Instead of, in lieu of.

نَائِب ج نُوَب ونُوَّاب Lieutenant, delegate, substitute, vice-gerent. ♦ Member (of parliament).

مَجْلِس النُّوَّاب ♦ Parliament. Chamber of deputies.

نَائِبَة ج نَوَائِب ونَائِبَات Quotidian (ague). Misfortune.

مَنَاب Lieutenancy, vicariate. Road leading to the water.

مُنِيب Abundant spring-rain.

مُنِيب إلى الله Coming back to God, penitent.

مُنْتَاب Coming on morning and evening.

‡ نَاتَ o نَوْتًا To totter, to reel in walking.

نُوتِيّ ج نَوَاتِيّ ونُوتِيَّة L Sailor, boatman.

♦ Stingy.

‡ نَاجَ o نَوْجًا To dissemble.

نَوْجَة ج نُوَج Hurricane, storm.

‡ نَاحَ o نَوْحًا ونُوَاحًا ونِيَاحَةً ومَنَاحًا To coo (dove).

— ه وعلى To wail for, to bewail the death of.

نَاوَحَ بَعْضُهَا بَعْضًا To face one another (wailing women).

تَنَوَّحَ To dangle.

تَنَاوَحَ To be seated opposite (mountains). To blow from opposite sides (winds).

اِسْتَنَاحَ To wail, to lament. To howl (wolf).

— ه To make a. o. to weep.

نَوْح ونِيَاح (un. نَوْحَة) Weeping, wailing for the dead.

نِسَاء نَوْح Mourner-women.

نُوح The Patriarch Noah.

نِيَاحَة Wailing of the dead. Funeral ceremony.

نَائِحَة ج نُوح وأَنْوَاح ونُوَّح ونَوَائِح ونَائِحَات Hired wailing-women.

نَوَّاح م نَوَّاحَة Weeping much.

نَوَّاح Turtle-dove.

نَيِّحَة Wind blowing contrarily to another.

مَنَاحَة Funeral house. Mourning-place.

‡ نَاخَ – نَوَّخَ الأَرْض تَنْوِيخًا To level (the earth : God).

أَنَاخَ إِنَاخَةً ه To make (a camel) to kneel.

— ب To halt in (a place).

— بِفُلَان To befall a. o. (misfortune).

— ب وعلى To besiege (a town).

تَنَوَّخَ واسْتَنَاخَ To kneel.

نَوْخَة Halting-place, station, stage.

نَائِخَة Remote land.

مَنَاخ ج مُنَاخَات Kneeling-place of camels, station, stage. ♦ Climate; hence: almanac.

‡ نَادَ o نَوْدًا ونُوَادًا ونَوَدَانًا To nod the head from sleepiness,

تَنَوَّدَ To swing (bough).

‡ نَارَ o نَوْرًا ونِيَارًا. ونُوْر وأَنَار وتَنَوَّر واسْتَنَار To shine, to glow.

نَارَ وتَنَوَّرَ To escape; to take flight.

— وتَنَوَّرَ ه مِنْ بَعِيد To perceive (a fire) from afar.

نَارَ ونُوْرَ ه To brand (a camel) with a hot iron.

— نَوْرًا ونُوَارًا ونِوَارًا To give no ground to suspicion (woman).

نَوَّرَ تَنْوِيرًا. وأَنَارَ إِنَارَةً To blossom (plant).

نَوَّرَ To have its stone formed (date). To gleam (dawn). To ripen (corn-crops).

— ه وهـ او ل To give light, to illumine a. th.; to enlighten a. o.

— على فُلَان To fascinate a. o. (wizard).

نَوَّرَ ه To tattoo (the arm).

نَاوَرَ ه To abuse a. o.

أَنَارَ إِنَارَةً، وأَنْوَرَ إِنْوَارًا To appear.

أَنَارَ إِنَارَةً ه To light up, to illumine (a house). To elucidate (a question).

تَنَوَّرَ وانْتَارَ وانْتَوَرَ To anoint o.'s self with depilatory paste.

تَنَوَّرَ واسْتَنَارَ To be lighted up (house). ♦ To be enlightened (man).

اِسْتَنَارَ ب To ask light from.

— على To overcome a. o.

Fire. Heat of war. Brand. Advice. نَار ج نِيرَان ونِيرَة ونُور ونِيَار وأَنوَار
Erysipelas (disease). النَّار الفَارِسِيَّة
Volcano. جَبَل نَار
◘ Steamer. مَركَب نَار
Fiery. ✧ Burning. نَارِيّ و✧ نِيرَانِيّ
Flower, blossom. نَوْر ج أَنوَار (un. نَوْرَة)
Light. Luminous body. Manifestation of truth. نُور ج أَنوَار ونِيرَان
Daze; Cologne-earth. حَجَر النُّور
✧ The Virgin Mary *lit*: Mother of light. أُمّ النُّور
✧ Holy Saturday in Holy week. سَبْت النُّور
Luminous. ◘ White dun-diver. نُورِيّ
Gipsy; rogue. نَوَرِيّ ج نَوَر
✧ Diocese. Church-rate paid to a Greek bishop. Self-heal (*plant*). ✧ نُورِيَّة
Depilatory paste. Tattooing-powder. Tar, liquid pitch. Brand made with a hot iron. نُورَة
Cautious, unsuspected woman. نَوَار ج نُور
WLite flower. Blossom. نُوَّار ج نَوَاوِير
✧ Month of may. نُوَّار
Lamp-black. Indigo. Antimony-powder. نَؤُور ونُؤُور
Illumination. Lighting. إِنَارَة وتَنوِير
Illumination. إِستِنَارَة
Bright, brilliant. Lighting. نَيِّر م نَيِّرَة
Luminous star in *Corona Borealis*. أَلنَّيِّر والمُنِير مِن الفَكَّة
Striking punishment. نَيِّرَة وذَاتُ مَنوَر
✧ Such a one is gifted with prudence. فُلَان ذُو نَيِّرَة
Hatred. نَائِرَة ج نَوَائِر
Small fire. نُوَيرَة
Brighter. Fine. أَنوَر
Lighting. Glowing. مُنِير
Lighted place. Way-mark. Landmark. مَنَار
Surname of an Ethiopian prince. ذُو المَنَار
Light-stand. Lantern. Light-house. Minaret of a mosque. مَنَارَة ج مَنَاوِر ومَنَائِر
Lighted gallery; sky-light. ◘ مِنوَار
First day of the Persian year; new year's day. ◘ Autumnal equinox. P نَوْرُوز ونَيرُوز

To dangle, to swing (thing). ✲ نَاس o نَوْسًا ونَوَسَانًا
To drive (the cattle). — نَوْسًا ه
To halt in (a place). نَوَّس ب
To move, to toss a. th. أَنَاس ه
To be set in motion by the wind (bough). تَنَوَّس
Men. نَاس (for أُنَاس)
Humanity, human nature. ✧ نَاسُوت (opp. to لَاهُوت)
Dependent lock of hair. نُوَاس
Cobweb. — العَنكَبُوت
Excellent white grapes. نُوَاسِيّ
Dangling, tossed. نَوَّاس
Sepulchral vault; funeral crypt. Sarcophagus. G نَاوُوس ونَاؤُوس ج نَوَاوِيس
Lighted wick. ✧ نُوَيسَة
To seize, to catch a. th. ✲ نَاش o نَوْشًا، وتَنَاوَش وانتَاش ه
To catch a. o. by the head or beard. — ه
He has helped him in obtaining a benefit. نَاش ه خَيرًا
To attack, to charge (the enemy) in (a fight). نَاوَش ه فِي وب
To wipe (the hands) with (a towel). تَنَوَّش ه ب
To attack o. a. with (the spear). تَنَاوَش ب
To drive, to take out from. إِنتَاش ه وه
To rescue a. o. from (danger). — ه مِن
Strong man. رَجُل نَؤُوش
Fever. ◘ نَوْشَة
Skirmish. Quarrel. مُنَاوَشَة
Dark purple, violet-colour. ◘ مَنَاوِيش ومَنَاوِيشِي
To lag behind. ✲ نَاص o نَوْصًا
To rise towards. — إِلَى
To escape from, to shun a. o. — نَوْصًا ومَنَاصًا ومَنِيصًا عَن
— نَوْصًا ومَنَاصًا ونَوِيصًا ونِيَاصًا ونِيَاصَة ونَوَصَانًا To move on.
To set to (work); to undertake (an affair). نَاوَص ه
To wish a. th. أَنَاص ه
To spring up (horse). إِستَنَاص

To move a. o. or a. th. إستناص ه وه
Wild ass. نَوْص
Start. Movement. Strength. نَوِيص
Refuge, shelter. مَنَاص
To flash (lightning). To dangle, to swing. ✱ ناص o نَوْصًا
To go through (a country). — في
To shake off (a stake). To give vent to (water). — ه
To dip (cloth) in (the dye). نوّص ه ب
To show zeal in one's looks. To have ripe dates (palm-tree). أناص
Sink-hole. *Sacrum*, rump. *Pl.* Elevated places. Outlet for water. نَوْص ج أنواص وأناويص
Shelter, refuge. مُناص
To hang, to suspend a. th. ✱ ناط o نَوْطًا ونياطًا ه ب
✧ To belong to a. o. — ب
To be distant (house). — وانتاط
To treat (an affair) without consulting. — وانتاط ه
To be attached, annexed to. To be connected with. نيط وانتاط ب
To suspend a. th. to a load. نوّط ه
To lend (a beast) to a. o. for carrying provisions. إستناط ه ه
Hung up. Additional weight hung to a load. نَوْط
Date-basket. — ج أنواط ونياط
Gizzard. Thicket of tamarisks or any thorny trees. Tumour on the breast or neck of a beast. Ground unreached by water. نَوْطَة
Well filled by the oozing of the sides. نَيِّط
Aorta-vein. نِيط
Extent of a desert. Two stars in *Scorpio*. نِيَاط
Suspensory of a skin, of an urn or bow. Handle. — ج أنوِطة ونُوط
Vein of the loins. نائط
✧ Lean meat. لحم نائط
Saddle-ornament. تَنْوَاط
Yellow bird of the passerine kind suspending its nest on tree-boughs. تَنَوُّط وتُنَوِّط
Far distance. مَناط
It is as far from me as the Pleiads. هذا مِنّي مَناطَ الثُّرَيَّا
Suspended, hung up. Intrusted to. Adventitious people mixing in (a tribe). ✧ Dependent upon. مَنُوط ب
To be dependent (bough). ✱ ناع o نَوْعًا وناع i نَيْعًا
To expand the wings for darting on its prey (falcon). To be thirsty. ناع o نَوْعًا
To divide, to classify a. th. To shake (a bough : wind). نوّع ه
To be shaken (bough). تنوّع واستناع
To branch off in species, to ramify. To be of various kinds. تنوّع
To walk ahead. تنوّع واستناع في
Class. Species, kind. Way, manner. نَوْع ج أنواع
Fruit freshly plucked. نَوْعَة
Thirst. نُوع
Specific. نَوْعِيّ
Jaw, mandible. ✧ نِيع ج نِياع
Burned with thirst. نائع ج نِياع
Bent (branch). نائع ج نوائع
Exhausted by hunger and thirst. جائع نائع ج جِياع نِياع
Manner, wise. مِنواع
Remote place. Branching off. Sorted. مُتنوّع
To be tall and high (camel). To be high, eminent. ✧ To exceed, to overtop a. th. ✱ ناف o نَوْفًا
To overlook, to overtop a. th. — i وأناف على
To exceed, to surpass. نيّف وأناف على
Top of the hump. Cry of the hyena. نَوْف ج أنواف
Excess, redundance. Benefit, favour. نَيْف ونَيِّف
Ten and more. عَشَرَةٌ ونَيِّف
Tall and high (camels). نِياف
Excellency, eminence (*titles*). ✧ نِيَافَة
Eminent, high, noble. Exceeding (a number). نائف
Tall and big (camel). نَيَّاف
Overtopping (mountain). مُنِيف م مُنِيفَة
Idol of the Arabs. مَناف
To remove the fat from flesh. ✱ ناق o نَوْقًا
To train, to break in (a camel). نوّق ه

Thou must do so. نَوَالُكَ وَنَوَالُكَ أَنْ تَفْعَلَ كَذَا
That is not convenient. لَيْسَ ذٰلِكَ بِنَوَالٍ
Gift, present. Kiss. نَوْلَة
Gift. Grace, favour. (un. نَائِلَة) نَائِل
Idol of the Arabs. نَائِلَة
Receipt, acquisition. ✧ Holy Communion. تَنَاوُل
Earrings. مُنَال
Weaving-loom. مِنْوَل وَمِنْوَال
Way, manner. مِنْوَال
In this wise. عَلَى هٰذَا ٱلْمِنْوَال
They are of the same sort هُمْ عَلَى مِنْوَالٍ وَاحِدٍ
Thou must do so. مِنْوَالُكَ أَنْ تَفْعَلَ كَذَا
Authoritative interpretation. ✧ Holy Communion. مُنَاوَلَة
✧ Shipping, freight. G نَاوُلُون
To sleep. To abate (wind, sea). To be dull (market). To be extinguished (fire). To be benumbed (limb). To stop (artery) To. die. ✧ To lay down. ✱ نَامَ o نَوْمًا وَنِيَامًا
To be unmindful of. — عَن
To rely upon a. o., to trust in. — وَتَنَاوَمَ وَاسْتَنَامَ إِلَى
To sleep more than (another). نَامَ o نَوْمًا ه
To make asleep, to lull a. o. نَوَّمَ وَأَنَامَ ه
To vie in sleep with. نَاوَمَ ه
To kill a. o. To find a. o. asleep. To crush, to straiten (people : dearth). أَنَامَ ه
To attain puberty. تَنَوَّمَ
To feign sleep. To try to sleep. تَنَاوَمَ وَاسْتَنَامَ
Sleep. نَوْم وَنُوَام
Poppy. أَبُو ٱلنَّوْم
A nap, a doze. نَوْمَة ج نَوْمَات
Night-dress. blanket. Great beneficence. Trustworthy. Well-being. Supple, mellowy (cloth). Streaks left on the sand by the wind. Wood for making arrows. نِيم
I have trust in him. هُوَ نِيمِي
sleeping. Way of sleeping. نِيمَة
His provisions will not suffice for one night. مَا لَهُ نِيمَةُ لَيْلَةٍ
نَائِم ج نِيَام وَنُوَّم وَنُيَّم وَنُوَّام وَنُيَّام وَنَوْم

To fecundate (a palm-tree). To set a. th. in order. نَوَّقَ ه
To do a. th. carefully. To be refined in (dress, food). تَنَوَّقَ وَتَنَيَّقَ فِي
To choose a. th. إِنْتَاقَ ه
To be like a she-camel (camel). إِسْتَنْوَقَ
Top of a mountain. نِيق ج نِيَاق وَأَنْيَاق وَنُيُوق
Reddish white. نَوَق
Zeal, skill. Foppishness. Daintiness. نِيقَة
She-camel. نَاقَة ج نَاق وَنُوق وَنِيَاق وَأَنْوُق وَأَنْوَق وَأَوْنُق وَأَيْنُق وَنَاقَات وَنِيَاقَات وَأَنْوَاق وَأَيَانِق
Young she-camels. أَيْنُقَات
Clever manager. نَوَّاق
Refined in dress, food. نَيِّق وَمُتَنَيِّق وَمُتَنَوِّق
Trained, broken in (camel). Fecundated (palm-tree). Set in order. مُنَوَّق
To be foolish. ✱ نَوِكَ a نَوَكًا وَنَوَاكًا وَنَوَاكَة
To find a. o. foolish. أَنْوَكَ ه
What a foolish man! مَا أَنْوَكَهُ
To be foolish. إِسْتَنْوَكَ
To deem a. o. foolish. — ه
Foolishness. نُوك وَنُوك
Foolish. أَنْوَك ج نَوْكَى وَنُوك
To give a. th. to a. o. ✱ نَالَ o نَوْلًا ه وَلَهُ او ه ب
To apply o.'s self to. — ب
This is for him the time of acting. نَالَ لَهُ أَنْ يَفْعَلَ
To be generous. نَالَ a نَيْلًا وَنَائِلًا
To bestow a. th. upon. نَوَّلَ ه ه وَعَلَى وَل
To offer, to hand over a. th. to. نَاوَلَ ه ه
✧ To give Holy Communion. — ه
To procure a. th. for a. o. أَنَالَ ه ه
What a bountiful man! مَا أَنْوَلَهُ
To take, to reach a. th. with the hand. تَنَوَّلَ وَتَنَاوَلَ ه
✧ To receive Holy Communion. تَنَاوَلَ و✧ اِسْتَنَاوَلَ
He reached such a place. — مَكَانَ كَذَا
Generous giver. نَال ج أَنْوَال
Gift. Grace, favour. نَال وَنَوَال
Gift. Manner, wise. Loom. نَوْل ج أَنْوَال

Sleeping. ✧ Confined to bed; laying down.

Night of sound sleep. لَيْل نَائِم

Vile, base. Ignorant. نُومَة ونُوَمَة ونُوَمِيّ

Great sleeper. نَؤُوم (m. f.) ونُوَم ونُوَّام ونُوَّمَة

O sleeper! يَا نَوْمَان

Sleep. مَنَام

Dream. — ج مَنَامَات

Dormitory, sleeping-place. مَنَام ومَنَامَة

Shop. Public-house. Night-dress. ◻ Grave. مَنَامَة

Soporific. مُنَوِّم

Depressed land. مُسْتَنَام

To mark a noun with tanwin ـٌ ـٍ ـً To write the letter ن To pronounce (a nunnation). ✱ نون — نَوَّن تَنْوِينًا ه

The letter ن. نُون ج نُونَات

Large fish. Blade of a sword. Inkstand. *Fig.* Science. نُون ج نِينَان وأَنْوَان

Jonah the prophet. Celebrated sword. ذُو النُّون

Large fish. Dimple in a child's chin. نُونَة

Piece of verses rhymed in ن. نُونِيَّة

Nunnation (*grammar*). تَنْوِين

To grow (plant). To hoot (owl). ✱ نَاه i o نَوْهًا ونَيْهًا

To abstain from a. th. To scorn at, to refuse a. th. — a o نَوْهًا عَنْ

To fill (cattle) without satiating them (herbs). — ه

To raise, to push a. th. نَوَّه ه

To extol, to render a. o. famous. نَوَّه ه وبِهِ وبِاسْمِهِ

To call a. o. about. — بِهِ

To be praised. To be raised. تَنَوَّه

Abstinence. نَوْه ونُوه

Praise. Honourable mention. تَنْوِيه

More illustrious than. أَنْوَه مِن

To intend, to purpose a. th. ✱ نَوَى i نَوَاةً ونِيَّةً ه

To keep, to preserve a. o. (God). — ه

To emigrate from (a place) to (another). — i نَوَى مِن . . . إِلَى

To cast (date)-stones. — ونَوَّى وأَنْوَى واسْتَنْوَى ه

To go off, to be remote from. نَوَى i نِيَّةً ونَوًى عَن

To become fat (she-camel). نَوَى i نَيًّا ونَوَايَة

To have its stone fromed (date). نَوَّى وأَنْوَى

To perform (a business). — وأَنْوَى ه

✧ To mew (cat). نَوَّى

To let a. o. carry out his designs. — ه

To rise against, to resist. نَاوَى مُنَاوَاةً ه

To be remote. To be in a journey. أَنْوَى

To purpose a. th. تَنَوَّى وانْتَوَى ه

To carry out (a design). To stop in (a place). إِنْتَوَى ب

Absence, remoteness. Intention. Course, direction, end of a journey. نَوًى

They have stopped. إِسْتَقَرَّ نَوَاهُم

Fat, grease. نِيّ

Fatness of a beast. نَيّ

Date-stone. Weight of five dirhems. نَوَاة ج نَوًى ونَوَيَات وجج أَنْوَاء ونُوِيّ

Intention, purpose, resolution. Scheme. Aim of a traveller. نِيَّة ج نِيَّات ✧ نَوَايَا

Sympathetic friend. ✧ Mew (of a cat). نَوِيّ

Camels fed on dates. إِبِل نَوَوِيَّة

Fat (she-camel). نَاوٍ م نَاوِيَة ج نِوَاء

Intention, aim intended. مَنْوًى ج مَنَاوٍ

To be raw, uncooked (meat). ✱ نَاءَ i نَيْأً ونُيُوءًا ونُيُوءَة

To do a. th. imperfectly. نَيَّأَ ه

To cook (meat) insufficiently. — وأَنْيَأَ ه

Rawness of food. نُيُوءَة

Raw, uncooked (meat). Imperfect (action). Pure (milk). نِيْء ونِيّ و✧ نَيّ

Postfix of the 1st person of the singular. Me. ✱ ـنِي

He struck me. ضَرَبَنِي

To hit a. o. on a canine tooth. ✱ نَابَ i نَيْبًا ه

To bite with the canine teeth. To be old (she-camel). نَيَّب

To bite the wood of (an arrow) for trying it. — ه

To sprout (plant). — وتَنَيَّب

Canine tooth, tusk, fang. نَاب و✧ نِيب ج أَنْيُب وأَنْيَاب ونُيُوب وأَنَايِيب

Old she-camel. — ج أَنْيَاب ونُيُوب ونِيب

rent track of a road.
Double-threaded (textile). ذُو نِيرَيْن
Strong (man). Big, fleshy (camel).
Cane-roll of a loom. ✧ Gum of the teeth. نِيرَة
Clearer, more distinct. أَنْيَر
Double-threaded (cloth). مُنَيَّر
They are at variance. بَيْنَهُم مُنَايَرَة
To throb (artery). ✱ نَاضَ i نَيْضًا
To obtain, to procure a. th. ✱ نَالَ a i نَيْلًا ونَالًا ونَالَة ومَنَالًا ه
He has impaired his reputation. نَالَ مِنْ عِرْض فُلَان
To get a. th. for. — وأَنَالَ إِنَالَة ه وه ل
Attainment. نَيْل ونَالَة
Grace, favour obtained. نَيْل ونَائِل ونَيْلَة
Indigo-plant. The Nile. The Indus (rivers). نِيل
Indigo-dye. نِيل ونِيلَة
Attainment. مَنَال
Difficult to be obtained. بَعِيد ٱلْمَنَال
What is obtained. مُنِيل

Chief of a tribe. نَاب ج أَنْيَاب
Old she-camel. نَيُوب
Having long canine teeth. أَنْيَب م نَيْبَاء ج نِيب
To totter from weakness. ✱ نَاتَ i نَيْتًا
To incline, to be shaken (bough). ✱ نَاحَ i نَيْحًا ونَيَحَانًا
To become hard (bone). — نَيْحًا
To harden (the bones); to break (them: God). نَيَّحَ ه
✧ To make (the dead) rest in peace (God). To give rest to a. o. — ه
I have not procured any good to him. مَا نَيَّحْتُهُ بِخَيْرٍ
✧ To rest; to die. تَنَيَّحَ
Hardened (bone). نَيِّح
✧ Eternal rest, death. نِيَاحَ
To border (cloth). To weave (a fabric). ✱ نَارَ i نَيْرًا, ونَيَّرَ وأَنَارَ ه
To call a. o. أَنَارَ ب
Warp, woof, border of cloth. نِير ج أَنْيَار
Yoke for oxen. Appa- — ج أَنْيَار ونِيرَان

ه

Here he his. هَا هُوَ
Here I am. هَاءَنَذَا
Here, hither. هَاهُنَا
7° *Is used as a particle for swearing.*
By God. هَا ٱللّٰه
8° *Means.* To take. هَاءِ او هَا
(*dual*) هَاؤُمَا (*fém*) وهَاءِ (*masc*) هَاءَ
Take, thou, ye. وهَاؤُم وهَاؤُنَّ (*pl.*)
One may say also. (*f.*) وهَاكِ (*m.*) هَاكَ
Take, (*pl.*) وهَاكُم وهَاكُنَّ (*dual.*) وهَاكُمَا thou, ye.
The letter ه. ✱ هَاء ج هَاءَات
The ه of pause (*added after an alef;*) *as* وا أَسَفَاهْ . هَاء ٱلسُّكُوت وهَاء ٱلْوَقْف
To burst out laughing. ✱ هَأْهَأَ
To call, to chide (dogs, camels). — ب
Noisy laughter. هَأْهَا وهَأْهَاء
Imperative of وَهَب Give. ✱ هَبْ
To blow (wind). To rise (star, dawn). ✱ هَبَّ o هَبًّا وهُبُوبًا وهَبِيبًا

1° *Is added to exclamatory sentences preceded by* يَا *or* وَا. ✱
What a pity! O my father! وَا حَسْرَتَاهْ, يَا أَبَتَاهْ
2° *Postfix of the possessive pronoun*: His, her, theirs. ✱ ه وهَا وهُم
3° *Prefix of the personal pronoun of the 3d person.* He, him, she, her, it. both, them, they. هُوَ, هِيَ مث هُمَا ج هُم, وهُنَّ
4° *Pronoun postfixed to nouns and verbs.* His, her, it, them. ه. هَا, هُم, هُنَّ
His wealth is great. مَالُهُ كَثِير
He took her. أَخَذَهَا
He separated them. فَرَّقَ شَمْلَهُم
5° *Demonstrative prefixed to pronouns.* ✱ هَا
This, that. هٰذَا, هٰذِه, هٰذَاك *pl.* هٰذَان
These, those. هٰؤُلَاء, هٰؤُلَائِك
6° *Is used as a demonstrative,* Lo. look!

To awake a. o. from sleep. — من
To quiver (sword). — هَبًّا وهُبُوبًا
To be brisk, quick-paced (man, beast). — هَبًّا وهُبُوبًا وهَبِيبًا وهِبابًا
Whence hast thou come? مِن أَيْنَ هَبَبْتَ
To cut, to sever a. th. (sword). هَبَّ o هَبًّا وهَبَّةً وهِبَّةً ه
To be put to flight. To be absent, unperceived. — هِبابًا
He set about doing. هَبَّ يَفعَلُ
To be absent, remote from. هَبَّ a هِبابًا عَن
To rend (a garment). هَبَّبَ ه
To brandish (a sword). To cause (the wind) to blow (God). أَهَبَّ ه
To arouse a. o. from (sleep). — ه مِن
To be worn out (garment). تَهَبَّبَ
To cut, to split a. th. إِهتَبَّ ه
To cause (the wind) to blow (God). To ask for the blowing of (the wind). إِستَهَبَّ ه
Blowing of the wind. هُبُوب
Atoms, motes, fine dust in the air. هَباب
Once, one time. A blowing. هَبَّة
Short space of time; long time. Last remains of morning-twilight. — وهِبَّة
I saw him once. رَأَيْتُهُ هَبَّةً
Penetration of (a sword). State, condition. هِبَّة
Piece of a garment. هِبَّة ج هِبَب
Ragged garment. ثَوب أَهباب وهَبابِب وهِبَب
Violent wind. هَبُوب وهَبُوبَة وهَبِيب
Windward. مَهَبّ ج مَهابّ
To be quick. To chide (a beast). To quiver (looming). ✧ To bark (dog). ✫ هَبْهَبَ
To slaughter (a beast). — ه
To move about; to be shaken. تَهَبْهَبَ
Dawn. Mirage. Game of children. Clamorous. هَبْهاب
To strike down, to lower, to abase a. o. ✫ هَبَتَ i هَبْتًا ه
To be cowardly. To be disquieted. To faint (heart). هُبِتَ
Weakness. Faint heartedness. هَبْتَة

Shrinking from fear. Bewildered. Lowered. هَبِيت ومَهْبُوت
To squander (wealth). ✫ هَبَثَ o هَبْثًا
To strike a. o. with (a stick). ✫ هَبَجَ a هَبْجًا ه ب
To cause (a limb) to swell. To kill (a dog) ✧ To scratch a. o. (cat). هَبَّجَ ه
To be swollen (body). ✧ To scratch o.'s self to blood. تَهَبَّجَ
Tumour on a she-camel's udder. هَبَج
Striped (gazelle). هَبِيج
Peevish. Dull (man). ✧ Scratched. مُهَبَّج
Having a swollen face. — ومُتَهَبِّج الوَجه
Coffee-pestle. ✧ مِهباج ج مَهابِيج
Drain for collecting water. Depressed land. End of a valley. ✫ هَوْبَجَة ج هَوابِج
Gardens in Yemen. الهَوابِج
To strut, to have a self-conceited gait. ✫ هبخ — إِهبَيَّخ إِهبِياخًا
Soft boy, girl. Stupid man. Large river. هَبَيَّخ م هَبَيَّخَة
To collect and cook (colocynth-seeds). ✫ هَبَدَ i هَبْدًا, وتَهَبَّدَ واهتَبَدَ ه
To feed a. o. with (colocynth-seeds). — ه ه
Colocynth and its seeds. هَبد وهَبِيد
To be quick, brisk. ✫ هَبَدَ i هَبْدًا, وهابَدَ وأَهبَدَ واهتَبَدَ
Swift (she-camel). هابِدَة ج هَوابِد
To be fleshy (camel). ✫ هَبِرَ a هَبَرًا
To cut (meat) in large pieces. هَبَرَ o هَبْرًا
To carve a slice of (meat) to a. o. — لِفُلانٍ هَبْرَةً مِن
To be strong and healthy. أَهبَرَ
To become thin. إِهتَبَرَ
To cut off (a limb) with (the sword). — ه ب
Boneless piece of meat. هُبر
Large piece of meat without bones. Shell worn as an amulet. هَبْرَة
Depressed land, sand-tract. هَبر ج هُبُور وهُبُر
Depressed land. هَبِير ج هُبُر وأَهبِرَة
Huge (camel). هَبِر م هَبِرَة
Hairy (ape). Cutting (sword). هَبّار
Wind raising the dust. رِيح هُبارِيَّة
Flakes of cotton. Particles of هِبرِيَة

degrade a. o. To abate the price of (goods).
To emaciate a. o. (disease). هَبَطَ ه
To collapse, to give way. إِنْهَبَطَ
Lowering, decrease, falling off. Declivity. هَبْط وهُبُوط
Fall, abatement of price. هُبُوط السِّعْر
O God, grant us an increase not a decrease in our condition. أَللّٰهُمَّ غَبْطًا لَا هَبْطًا
Descent, lowering. Collapse. Depressed ground. هَبْطَة
Declivous (ground). هَبُوط
Emaciated. هَبِيط ومَهْبُوط
Declivity. مَهْبِط ج مَهَابِط
To walk in stretching the neck (ass). To encompass. ✡ هَبَعَ a هُبُوعًا هَبَعَانًا
Ass just born. Born at the end of breeding-time. هُبَع ج هِبَاع وهُبَعَان
To sleep. ✡ هَبَغَ a هَبْغًا هُبُوغًا
To squat down like the Persians. ✡ هبقع – إِهْبَنْقَع
Bulky and strong-bodied. هَبْقَع وهُبَاقِع
Proud, foolish. Beggar leaning on a stick. Visitor of women. هَبَنْقَع
To give way under the pressure of the feet (earth). ✡ هبك – إِنْهَبَكَ ب
Foolish. Soft earth. هَبَنْكَة
To be deprived of (a son) by death (mother). ✡ هَبِلَ a هَبَلًا ه
✧ To dote, to rave. هَبِلَ
To say to a. o: May thy mother be deprived of thee by death *i. e.* to curse a. o. هَبَّلَ ه
To earn for (o.'s people). هَبَّلَ وتَهَبَّلَ واهْتَبَلَ ل
To crush a. o. (excessive fatness). هَبَّلَ وأَهْبَلَ ه
✧ To give a vapour-bath to a. o. To foment (a diseased limb). هَبَّلَ ه
To bereave (a mother) of her son. أَهْبَلَ ه
✧ To take a vapour-bath. To be fomented (limb). تَهَبَّلَ
To scheme evil designs. To intrigue. إِهْتَبَلَ
To catch (the game). – ه وه
Mind thy business. إِهْتَبِلْ هَبَلَكَ
State, condition. هَبَل

feathers, reeds. Scurf of the head. Spider. هَبُور
Small ant. Atom. Growing barley. هَبُّور
Thick-haired monkey. Lynx. Kind of lily. هَوْبَرَة
To sing at a wedding. ✧ هَوْبَرَ
Fleshy. أَهْبَر م هَبْرَاء ج هُبْر
To jerk in walking. ✡ هَبْرَجَ
To adorn (cloth) with figures. – ه
Quick walk. Jerking gait. Figured cloth. هَبْرَج
Persian horseman. Elegant, fine. New gold coin. ✡ هبرز – هِبْرِزِيّ
Goldsmith. Blacksmith. Wild bull. ✡ هَبْرِقِيّ
Grown up (child). ✡ هبرك – هَبْرَك وهُبَارِك
To speak much. To eat much. ✡ هَبْرَمَ هَبْرَمَة
To die suddenly. ✡ هَبَزَ i هُبُوزًا هَبَزَانًا
White violet (flower). Gilliflower. Slanderer. ✡ هَبَس
To gather (flocks). ✡ هَبَشَ i وهَبِشَ a هَبْشًا, وهَبَّشَ ه
To earn a. th. for (o.'s family). To exercise (a craft). هَبَشَ وتَهَبَّشَ ل
To be collected (people, army). تَهَبَّشَ واهْتَبَشَ
Rabble. Company of men. هُبَاشَة
Earnings. هُبَاشَات
To be brisk, lively. ✡ هَبِصَ a هَبَصًا, وهَبَصَ i هَبْصًا
To be eager after. – على
He laughed immoderately. إِنْهَبَصَ واهْتَبَصَ لِلضَّحِك
He did the work speedily. إِهْتَبَصَ فِي العَمَل
To abate (price). To light (bird). To become abject, mean, lowly. ✧ To collapse (wall). ✡ هَبَطَ o هُبُوطًا
To go down (a declivity). – o i هُبُوطًا مِن
He descended into the valley. – الوَادِي
To go from (a place) to (another). – مِن . . . إِلَى
He fell from his rank. – مِن مَنْزِلَتِهِ
To bring, to send a. th. down. To beat a. o. To هَبَطَ o هَبْطًا, وأَهْبَطَ ه وه

✧ Vapour. هَبلَة
Lurking for a prey (wolf). هَبل
Name of an idol, of the chief of a tribe. هُبل
Request, petition, importunity. هَبالة
Striving to make earnings. هَبال
Hunter.
Bereaved of her children (mother). هَابل وهَبُول
✧ Fool, silly. هَبل ومَهبُول
Abel, Adam's son. هبيل وهابيل
Vapour-bath, fomentation. تَهبيل
Womb, place of gestation. مَهبِل ج مَهابِل
Elegant gait. هبلي
Christian monk. هبيلي
Swift-running. مِهبــل
Accursed. مُهَبَّل
Taken away by death (child). مَهبُول
✧ Stupid, foolish.
Greyhound. Glutton. ✲ هبلَع
Foolish. Intriguer. ✲ هَبنَك
To rise in the air (smoke, dust). To run away (horse). To die (man). To be turned into ashes (embers). ✲ هَبا o هُبوًّا
To raise (the dust : horse). أهبَى ه
To jog o.'s hands. تَهبَّى
Dust rising in the air. هَباء ج أهباء
Motes seen in the sun-rays.
Mote, particle of dust. هَباءة
Whirlwind. Dust-colour. هَبوَة ج هَبَوات
Bark of a tree ; sap-wood. هُبايَة الشَّجر
Rising in the air (dust). هَابٍ ج هُبًى
Stars clouded by the dust. نُجوم هُبًى
Dusty, windward place. مَوضع هَابِي التُّراب
The dust of the grave. الهابِي
✲ To rend (a garment). هَتَّ o هَتًّا ه
To strip (a tree) of (its leaves). To spin uninterruptedly (woman). To shatter a. th. To pour forth (a liquid).
To speak fluently, to utter (speech) volubly. — الكلام
To undervalue, to disparage a. o. — ه
✧ To threaten, to scold (a child). — عَلَى
In pieces, in shatters. هَتًّا بَتًّا
Tattler. هَتَّات وهَتهَت
To shatter, to smash a. th. ✲ هَتهَت

To urge (a camel). To drink. To speak volubly.
To strike a. o. with. ✲ هَتأ a هَتأً ه ب
To eat a. th. — ه
To be bent, crooked. هَتِئَ a هَتأً
To be rent, worn out (clothes). تَهتَّأ
Rent. Swelling. هَتاء وهُتُوء
Moment. Portion. هَتء وهَتِيء وهِتاء وهَتأة
Crooked. hump-backed. أهتأ
To disorder the mind of a. o. (old age, grief). ✲ هَتَر i هَترًا ه
To rave, to be delirious. ◘ هَتَر وهَترَس
To disparage a. o — وهَتَّر ه
To revile a. o. هاتَر ه
To dote, to become disordered in mind. أهتَر وأُهتِر
To rave on the same subject. أهتِر
To recriminate with o. a. To be contradictory (testimonies). تَهاتَر
To be addicted to ; to dote on a. th. To follow blindly o.'s desire. إستَهتَر وأُستُهتِر
✧ To overlook (an affair). — ب
To be passionately fond of. أُستُهتِر ب
Lie. Nonsense. Error in speech. Misfortune. Absurdity. هِتر ج أهتار
First portion of the night. هِتر مِنَ اللَّيل
Cheat, knave. هِترٌ أهتار
Nonsense. هِتر هاتِر
Insanity. Disorder of mind. هُتر وهُترَة
Nonsense, doting, stupidity. تَهتُّر وتَهتار
Contradictory testimonies. Mutual recriminations. تَهاتُر
Disordered in mind. مُهتَر
Fond of doting on. مُستَهتَر ب
Following blindly his desires. مُستَهتِر
3d Coptic month. November. هَاتُور Ce
To rouse (a dog). ✲ هَتَش
To be roused, stirred (dog, wild beast). هُتِش واهتَتَش
To hurry towards a. o. ✲ هَتَم هَتمًا الى
To coo (pigeon). ✲ هَتَف i هَتفًا
To cry out to a. o. هَتَف i هُتافًا ب
To praise a. o. — ه وب
Her beauty is praised. يُهتَف بِها
Call, cry. هُتاف
Unseen man whose voice is heard. هاتِف
Twanging (bow). هَتُوف وهَتَّافَة وهَتفَى
Thundering cloud. سَحابَة هَتُوف

To rend, to discard ☆ هَتَكَ i هَتْكًا ه (a veil), To divulge, to unveil a. th. To rend (clothes). To violate (the honour).
He disgraced him; he brought — سِتْرَهُ him to shame.
To tear a. th. to rags. هَتَّكَ ه
To journey by a dark هاتَكَ ٱلْهُتْكَة night.
To be rent (veil). تَهَتَّكَ وانهَتَكَ
To be dishonoured, covered with تَهَتَّكَ shame.
He laid idle. — في البَطالَة
Middle of the night. هُتْكٌ
✧ Criminal assault. هَتْك العرض
Defamation. Hour of the night. هُتْكَة
Dishonour, shame, disgrace. هَتِيكَة
Shameless, مُتَهَتِّك ومُنهَتِك ومُسْتَهتِك unchaste.
To pour ☆ هَتَل i هَتْلًا وهُتُولًا وتَهتالًا وهَتَلانًا a continuous rain (sky).
Continuous rain, drizzle. هَتَلان
Clouds giving a continuous سَحائِب هُتَّل rain.
To break the ☆ هَتَم i هَتْمًا, وأهتَمَ ه (front-teeth). To strike a. o. upon (the mouth).
To have the front-teeth هَتِم a هَتَمًا broken.
He beat him unmerci- هَتَّمَ ه بالضَرب fully.
To be broken (tooth). تَهَتَّم
Contradictory evidence; illegal تَهاتُم proofs.
Fragment, broken piece. هُتامَة
Having the front- أهتَم م هَتْماء ج هُتْم teeth broken at the root.
To be garrulous. ☆ هَتمَرَ هَتمَرَة
To speak obscurely. ☆ هَتمَلَ هَتمَلَة
☆ هَتَنَ i هَتْنًا وهُتُونًا وهَتَنانًا وتَهتانًا, وتَهاتَنَ
To pour down intermittent showers (sky). To flow continually (rain, tears).
Showery (cloud). هاتِن وهَتُون ج هُتُن وهُتَّن
To trample down a. th. ☆ هَتا o هَتْوًا ه
To give a. th. to a. o. هاتَى ه ه
Give thou! هاتِ م هاتِي
To lie. To mix a. th. ☆ هَتَّ o i هَتًّا
Liar. هَتّات

To be disordered (affair). ☆ هَتهَتَ
To tread a. th. under foot. — ه
To treat (people) tyrannically. — ه
To pour down a heavy (rain: — ب cloud).
Confused noise, voices. هَتهَتَة وهَتهات
Quick, hasty. Slanderer. Dusty هَتهات place. Confused.
To bray, to pound a. th. ☆ هَتَم i هَتْمًا ه
To give to a. o. a great — لِفُلانٍ مِن part of.
Eagle; young vulture. Hill of red هَيثَم sand; even hill.
They fell in a ☆ هثمل — وقَعوا في هَثمَلَة scrape.
To be sunken in its ☆ هَجَّ o هَجِيجًا orbit through hunger (eye). To burn fiercely (fire).
To pull down (a — هَجًّا وهَجِيجًا ه house).
✧ He emigrated. هجّ مِن الجَور
To make the fire to blaze. هَجهَج ه
✧ To constrain a. o. to emigrate. — ه
To protract (a business). إهتَجَّ في
To be self-willed. إستَهجَّ
To urge (a party of travellers). — ه
Yoke of a bull. هُجّ
✧ Emigration. هُجَّة
Sunken in its socket هاجّة ومُهجَجّة (eye).
Quick walk. هَجاج
He followed his own judg- رَكِب هَجاجَ ment. He went at random.
Do abstain! هَجاجَيك
Dust spreading everywhere. هَجاجَة Foolish man.
Long and even shore. هَجِيج ج هُجّان
Deep valley. — وإهجِيج
Magic lines. هَجِيج ج هُجّان
To grumble (camel). ☆ هَجهَج
To scare away (a lion) by shou- — ب ting.
Grumbling of a camel. Tall. هَجهاج Easily scared away.
To be appeased ☆ هَجَأَ a هَجأً وهُجُوءًا (hunger).
To eat a. th.; to fill (the stomach). — ه
To be vehemently hungry. هَجِئ a هَجَأً
To appease (hunger). أهجَأ ه

To give a. th. to eat to. أهجأ ه ه
He paid him his due. — ه حقّه
To spell (in reading). تهجّأ
To drive (a beast) along. ✲ هجب i هجبًا ه
Inconsiderate, wrongful (man). ✲ هَيْجَبُوس
To sleep by night or in the day. To remain awake. ✲ هجد o هُجُودًا، وتهجّد
To awake from sleep. To pray in the night. هجّد وتهجّد
To awake from sleep or to cause a. o. to sleep. هجّد ه
To sleep. To lay the neck upon the ground (camel). أهجد
To cause a. o. to sleep. To find a. o. asleep. — ه
Sleeping, praying in the night. هاجد ج هُجُود وهُجّد
Praying in the night. هَجُود ج هُجُود وهُجّد
Night-prayers. تهجّد
Watching for prayer. مُتهجّد
To break with a. o. To forsake, to abstain from, to shun a. th. ✲ هجر o هجرًا وهِجرانًا، وأهجر ه وه
To talk deliriously in (sleep). — هُجْرًا وهِجّيرى وإهجيرى في
To be intensely hot (day). هجّر
To journey in the middle of the day. هجّر وأهجر وتهجّر
To perform (prayer) before the time (Moslem). هجّر إلى
To emigrate. To leave nomadic life. — من
To dote, to speak nonsense. أهجر إهجارًا وهجرًا في منطقه
To use unseemly speech. To laugh, to scoff at a. o. — بفلان
To pretend to be an emigrant. تهجّر
To forsake, to cut o. a. تهاجرًا واهتجرًا
Forsaking, parting. Hottest hour of the day. هَجْر
Midday, noon. هجر النهار
I met him some time after we parted. لقيته عن هجر
The tree shot forth and expanded. ذهبت الشجرة هجرًا
Unseemly, foul language. هجر ومهاجر
Excellent. Wayworn. — هِجْر

Name of the town and province of Bahrein. هَجَر
Estrangement. Removal from the desert to a town. هِجْرة
Emigration. — وهُجْرة
The Hegira, beginning of the Mohammedan era A. D. 622 ألهجرة
Unseemly talk. Sufficiency. هجراء
He is not adequate to the work. ما عنده غناء ذلك ولا هجراؤه
Bow-string. Rope for tying a camel's foot, tether. هِجار
Hagar, Ishmael's mother. هاجر
Excellent. هاجر
Foolish talk, nonsense. هاجرة ج هاجرات وهواجر
Midday-hour; hottest hour of the day. — وهجير وهجيرة
He charged him with disgraceful actions. رماه بالهاجرات وبالمُهجِرات
Large watering-trough. Large cup. هجير ج هُجْر
Better, nobler. Longer, thicker. أهجر
Of the Hegira (year). هِجْري
Excellent, distinguished. هاجري
Townsman of Bahrein. — وهجري
Custom, use, habit. Speech, language. هِجّير وهِجّيرى وهِجّيرة وهجريّا
Midday-meal. هجوري
Fine, distinguished. Lofty (palm-tree). مُهجِر م مُهجِرة
Emigrant. مُهاجر
He held obscene talks. تكلّم بالمهاجر
Forsaken (house). Uncouth (word). Absurd (speech). مهجور
The Companions of Mohammed during his flight to Medina; the emigrants. ألمهاجرون
Fox, fox's cub. Monkey. Bear. ✲ هِجرِس ج هجارس
More learned than a monkey. أعلم من هِجرِس
Foolish, mad. Greyhound. ✲ هِجْرَع
To whisper in the ear to. ✲ هجز — هاجز
Whisper. هجز
To occur suddenly to (the mind: thought). To speak to o.'s self. ✲ هجس o i هجسًا في

To deter a. o. from. هَجَسَ ه

To refrain from. إِنْهَجَسَ عَن

Whisper: mutter. هَجْس

Suggestion, thought. — وهاجِس ج هَوَاجِس

The Lion. الهَجَّاس

Azymous, unleavened (bread). مُتَهَجِّس

They got into a scrape. وَقَعُوا فِي مَهْجُوس مِنَ الأَمْرِ

To drive (a beast) gently. ✻ هَجَش o هَجْشًا ه

To point out a. th. — إلى

To set (people) at variance. — بَيْنَ

He has longed for it. هَجَشَتْ لَهُ نَفْسُهُ

Standing up, rise. هَجْشَة

Crowd of people. هاجِشَة ج هَوَاجِش

To slumber in the night. To set (star). ✻ هَجَعَ a هُجُوعًا وتَهْجَاعًا

To be appeased (hunger). — هُجُوعًا

To appease (hunger). — هَجْعًا, وأَهْجَعَ ه

To let a. o. sleep. هَجَّعَ ه

هِجَع وهُجَع وهَجِيع و هِجْعَة وهُجَعَة و مِهْجَع Neglectful. Foolish.

Slumber, light sleep in the first part of the night. Portion, watch of the night. هَجْعَة

Way of sleeping. هِجْعَة

Watch of the night. هَجِيع مِنَ اللَّيْل

Slumbering. هاجِع ج هُجَّع وهُجُوع

Sleeping-room, dormitory. مَهْجَع

To be flabby in the belly. To be disordered (country). ✻ هَجِفَ a هَجَفًا

To be flabby in the belly. To be hungry. إِنْهَجَفَ

Old (ostrich). Sluggish (man). Big-bellied. هِجَفّ

To throw (a stick). To wink at, to ogle (woman). ✻ هَجَلَ o هَجْلًا ب

To impair (the reputation) of. هَجَّلَ ه وفي

To revile a. o. in (words). — ه وب

To follow a plain. هاجَلَ

To vie with a. o. — ه

To set (cattle) free. To enlarge a. th. To lose (wealth). أَهْجَلَ ه وه

To find out a. th. إِهْتَجَلَ ه

Depressed plain between two mountains. هَجْل ج أَهْجَال وهِجَال وهُجُول

Depressed plain. هَجْلَة ج هَجَلَات, وهَجِيل

Shameless woman. هَجُول ج هَجَائِل

Slow; sluggish. Stupid. هَوْجَل ج هَوَاجِل Small anchor. Wayless, misleading desert. Clever guide. Long night.

To assail, to assault a. o. To storm (a place). To intrude upon, to come upon a. o. unawares. ✻ هَجَمَ o هُجُومًا على

To make a. o. to break in at; to urge a. o. to. — وهَجَّمَ وأَهْجَمَ ه على

To set in unexpectedly (cold, heat). هَجَّمَ

To overthrow (a building). — ه

To collapse (building). — وانْهَجَمَ

To be sunken in its socket (eye). هَجَمَ o هَجْمًا وهُجُومًا

To draw (milk) to the last drop. — ه

To pounce upon, to attack a. o. هاجَمَ ه

To avert (a disease) from. أَهْجَمَ ه عَن

To give rest to (camels). — ه

To draw (milk) to the last drop. — واهْتَجَمَ ه

To rush blindly into. ✧ تَهَجَّمَ على

To venture upon. ✧ تَهَجَّمَ ب

They rushed one upon another. تَهَاجَمَا

To shed tears (eye). إِنْهَجَمَ

Sweat. هَجْم

Large drinking-cup. — ج أَهْجَام

Assault, charge, storming. Coup-de-main. Third of the five divisions of the night. Sudden setting in of (cold, heat). Herd from 40 to 100 camels. هَجْمَة

He came at nightfall. جَاءَ بَعْدَ هَجْمَةٍ مِنَ اللَّيْل

Sudden attack. هُجُوم

Rushing impetuously. Blasting (wind). هَجُوم

Milk put into a skin. هَجِيمَة

To be base-born. To be born of a slave-woman. To be half-blooded. To be incorrect (speech). To fail to give fire at the first stroke (flint). ✻ هَجُنَ o هُجْنَة وهَجَانَة وهُجُونَة

To be married before puberty (girl). هَجَنَ o i هَجْنًا

To insult, to outrage a. o. هَجَّنَ ه وه

To treat a. o. scornfully. To abhor, to detest a. th.

To possess full-blood camels. أهجن
To marry (a girl) before puberty. — ة
To judge (an action) vile, disgraceful. إستهجن ه
Defect, vice. Incorrect language. هُجنة ج هُجَن
Noble extraction. هِجانة
Of good breed (*m. f. s. pl.*) (camel). White blood-camel. هِجان
هجين ج هُجُن وهُجناء وهُجنان ومَهاجين ومَهاجنة
Vile, low. Mongrel; born of a slave-mother. Half-bred. Low born.
✧ Dromedary.
▫ Dromedarist. هَجّان
Female dromedary. هَجينة ج هُجُن وهَجائن وهجان
Steel failing to give fire at the first stroke. Girl married before puberty. هاجن
Precocious palm-tree. هاجنة
Young people married together before puberty. غِلمة أهيجنة
Worthless, common people. مَهجنة ومَهجنى ومَهجنى ومَهجناء
Fecundated by a blood-stallion (she-camel). مُهَجَّنة
✶ هجا o هَجوًا وهِجاء وتَهجاء ة To satirise, to censure a. o. (poet). To scoff, to rail at a. o.
— هَجوًا وهِجاء, وهجّى وتَهَجّى ه To form syllables, to spell a. th.
To be hot (day). هَجوَ o هَجاوة
To satirise o. a. هاجى ة
To find (a poem) satirical. أهجى ه
To satirise o. a. (poets). تَهاجى واهتجى
Epigram. Dispraise. هِجاء
Spelling. — وتَهجية وتَهَجٍّ
Alphabet, letters of the alphabet. حُروف الهجاء والتهجية والتَّهَجي
In this manner, on this pattern. على هِجاء هذا
Epigram, satirical poem; libel. أُهجوّة وأُهجيّة ج أَهاجيّ
Satiric poet, railer. هاجٍ
Laughing-stock, satirised. مَهجوّ
✶ هدّ o هَدًّا وهُدودًا ة وه To break, to crush a. th. To overthrow, to pull down (a building). To crush, to overwhelm a. o. (misfortune). To be weak in body, advanced in age.
To crash, to crumble down (building). هَدّ i هَديدًا
He is a an excellent man. إنّهُ لهَدّ الرَّجل
مَرَرتُ بِرَجلٍ هَدِّكَ مِن رَجُلٍ او بامرأةٍ هَدِّكِ مِن امرأةٍ
I passed by a man, by a woman stronger, hardier than thee.
He is a dauntless man. فُلانٌ يُهَدّ
To threaten, to frighten a. o. هَدَّد وتَهَدَّد ة
To follow o. a. تَهادّ
To fall down. To be demolished. إنهَدّ
Demolition, destruction. Strong, generous man. هَدّ
Weak man. Harsh voice. — وهِدّ ج هُدُون
Truly I am not weak, I am not a coward. إنّي غيرُ هِدٍّ
Loud crash of a falling building. هَدّة وهَديد
Threat. Frightening. تَهديد وتَهَدُّد
Rumbling of the sea. Underground rumbling. هادّ
Thunder هادّة
Cowardly, weak. هَدادة وأهَدّ
Go gently. هَدادَيك
Declivity. هُدود
Pick-hammer. ✧ مِهَدّة
To coo (pigeon). To grumble (camel). ✶ هَدهَد
To dandle (a child). — ة
To lower; to throw a. th. down. — ه
I fancy. يُهَدهَد إليَّ
هُدهُد وهُدهِد وهُداهِد ج هَداهِد وهَداهيد
Any cooing bird. Hoopoe (bird). Wild pigeon.
Murmuring sound. Cooing of a dove هَدهَدة
Patience, meekness. هَداهِد
Do have patience. عَلَيكَ بالهَداهِد
To take rest. ✶ هَدَأ a هَدأ وهُدوءًا To be appeased (pain). To be still, motionless (wind, storm). To stop.
To stay in (a place). — ب
To die. — هُدوءًا
People were at rest. هَدأتِ الرِّجلُ والعَينُ *lit.* the eye and the foot were still.
To be crook-backed (man). هَدِئ a هَدأً

To have the hump depressed by overloading (water : camel).

هَدَّأَ تَهْدِئَةً وأَهْدَأَ إِهْدَاءً ة To still, to quiet, to calm a. o. To assuage, to allay (passions).

✧ هَدَأَ ة To restrain, to check a. o.

✧ — ه To hold (water : vessel).

أَهْدَأَ ة To pat, to lull (a child). To bend a. o. (old age). To wear out (clothes).

لا أَهْدَأَهُ اللهُ May God leave him in his distress!

تَهَدَّأَ To take rest. ✧ To be soothed; to be calm (sick person). To be stilled, lulled. To be dull (price).

هَدْءٌ Behaviour, temper.

— وهُدْءٌ وهَدْأَةٌ مِنَ اللَّيْلِ Portion of the night.

هُدُوٌّ وهَدِيءٌ ومَهْدَأٌ Part of the night.

ما لهُ هِدَأَةُ لَيْلَةٍ His provisions will not last for a night.

أَتَانَا هُدُوءًا He came to us after a short rest.

هُدُوءٌ و✧ هَدَاوَةٌ Rest. Stillness, silence, quiet, calm.

هَدْءَاءُ Having the hump depressed by overloading (she-camel).

أَهْدَأُ (*m. f.*) Bent, hump-backed.

مَهْدَأَةٌ ومُهَيْدِئَةٌ State, condition.

✠ هَدِبَ a هَدَبًا To have long lashes (eye).

— وأَهْدَبَ To have long branches (tree).

هَدَبَ i هَدْبًا ة وه To milk (a she-camel). To pluck (a fruit). To cut off a. th.

تَهَدَّبَ To be pendulous (branches). To hang down (part of a cloud).

هُدْبٌ وهُدُبٌ ج أَهْدَابٌ (*un.* هُدْبَةٌ وهُدُبَةٌ) Eyelash. Fringe, border of a garment.

هَدَبٌ ج أَهْدَابٌ (*un.* هَدَبَةٌ) Leafless twigs. Foliage of the cypress, tamarisk.

هَيْدَبٌ Cloud hanging towards the earth. Filaments of a flower. Continuous tears.

— وهُدَبٌ وهُدَّابٌ Stupid, heavy, dull.

هُدَّابٌ Cypress-leaves; permanent foliage. Fringe of a garment.

هَدِبٌ م هَدِبَةٌ, وأَهْدَبُ م هَدْبَاءُ Having long eyelashes; a long forelock (horse); long-branches (tree); a long nap (cloth). Lion.

هِنْدَبٌ وهِنْدَبَى وهِنْدِبَاءُ Succory, endive.

✠ هُدَبِدٌ وهُدَابِدٌ Sour and thick milk. Weakness of the sight. Weak-sighted. Black gum.

✠ هَدَجَ i هَدْجًا وهَدَجَانًا وهُدَاجًا To walk with short steps (old man). To walk gently, to tot about.

هَدَّجَ واسْتَهْدَجَ To run in a tremulous manner (ostrich).

هَدَجَ i هَدَجَانًا To boil vehemently (cooking-pot).

— هَدَجًا To whizz (wind).

— هَدَجَةً, وتَهَدَّجَ To fondle her young one (she-camel).

تَهَدَّجَ To be tremulous (voice).

— على To manifest the good actions of.

هَدَّاجٌ Running, walking in a tremulous manner.

هَوْدَجٌ ج هَوَادِجُ Domed woman-litter upon a camel.

هَدُوجٌ Boiling quickly (cooking-pot).

مِهْدَاجٌ Yearning towards her young one (she-camel, ostrich). Whizzing (wind).

مُسْتَهْدِجٌ Hasty.

✠ هَدَرَ o i هَدْرًا وهَدَرًا To be spent to no avail (goods, toil). To be shed without retaliation (blood).

— ه To spend a. th. uselessly. To go for nothing; to be unavenged (blood).

هَدَرَ i هَدْرًا وهَدِيرًا To rumble (waves, thunder). To low (calf). To grumble (camel). To roar (lion). To bray (ass). To be sonorous (voice).

— هَدْرًا وهَدِيرًا وتَهْدَارًا To coo (pigeon). To ferment (wine).

— هُدُورًا To shoot forth (palm-tree).

— هُدُورًا وهَدِيرًا To be luxuriant (plant, herbage).

هَدَّرَ To grumble repeatedly (camel).

أَهْدَرَ ه To let (bloodshed) unavenged (prince).

تَهَادَرَ To shed the blood of o. a. without retaliation.

Worthless (man). هَدر وهَدَر
His endeavours were useless. ذَهَبَ سَعْيُهُ هَدرًا وهَدَرًا
Sluggish, dull. هِدر
Worthless, low (man). هَادِر ج هَدَرَة
Milk thickening on the surface.
Land covered with vegetation. هَادِرَة ج هَوَادِر
Worthless man, woman. Mean people. هَدَرَة وهِدَرَة وهُدَرَة
Rumbling (of the waves). Grumbling of camels. Roaring (of lions). Fermentation (of wine). هَدِير
Swollen. أَهْدَر م هَدْرَاء ج هُدر
Shed unavenged (blood). Spent to no avail (wealth). مَهْدُور
Like the brayer in the enclosure *i. e.* making a great ado for nothing. كَالْمُهْدِرِ فِي الْعُنَّةِ
To drive (a beast) along. ✧ To think of. To be uneasy about a. th. ✱ هَدَسَ i هَدْسًا ه
Myrtle. هَدَس (*un.* هَدَسَة)
✧ Busying thought. هَادِس
To be disquieted. ✧ تَهَوْدَس
To break a. th. (hollow). ✱ هَدَغَ a هَدْغًا ه
To be crushed, broken. إِنْهَدَغ
To enter at, to come to. ✱ هَدَفَ o هَدْفًا إِلَى
Is any one newly come to you? هَلْ هَدَفَ إِلَيْكُمْ هَادِف
He approaches the age of 50. هَدَفَ وأَهْدَفَ لِلْخَمْسِين
To be weak, slothful. هَدِفَ i هَدْفًا
To overtop, to overlook a. th. أَهْدَفَ على
To seek refuge towards. — إِلَى
To happen to a. o. (affair). — لِ
To rise up, to stand erect (man). To be high, projecting. — واسْتَهْدَفَ
To become the butt of a company; to be much spoken of. إِسْتَهْدَفَ
Bulky. هِدف
Prominence, lofty building, hill. Butt, aim. Tall man. هَدَف ج أَهْدَاف
Party of men. Block of isolated houses. هِدفَة ج هِدَف
New comer arriving unexpectedly. هَادِف م هَادِفَة

Crowd, party of people. هَادِفَة
Wide (basis). مُسْتَهْدِف
To pull down (a building). ✱ هَدَكَ i هَدْكًا ه
Obese (man). هَوْدَك
To rush upon a. o. (people). ✱ هدكر — تَهَدْكَرَ على
Thick milk. هُدَكِر وهَيْدَكُور
House supported by massy pillars. بَيْت هَيْدَكُور الأَسَاطِين
To coo (dove). ✱ هَدَلَ i هَدِيلًا
To dangle a. th. — هَدْلًا ه
To have an ulcerated and hanging lip (camel). هَدِلَ a هَدَلًا
To hang loosely (branch). تَهَدَّلَ
Having a hanging lip (camel). هَدِل وهَادِل
Hanging branches. هَدَال
Party, crowd. هَدَالَة
Cooing of a dove. Young pigeon. هَدِيل
Pendulous (lip). أَهْدَل م هَدْلَاء ج هُدْل
To throw, to pull down (a building). ✱ هَدَمَ i هَدْمًا ه
To break a. o.'s back. — ه
To be sea-sick. هُدِمَ
To overthrow (a building). هَدَّمَ ه
To be demolished, to fall to pieces. تَهَدَّمَ وانْهَدَمَ
To be worn out (clothes). تَهَدَّمَ
He threatened him. تَهَدَّمَ غضبًا عليه
Shed without retaliation (blood). هَدْم وهَدَم
Destruction, demolition. هَدْم
Patched garment. Decrepit old man. Old boot. Worn out apparel. ✧ Clothes, underclothing. هِدْم ج أَهْدَام وهِدَم و✧ هُدُوم
Well crumbling down. Ruin. هَدَم
Part of a flock. Slight rain. هَدْمَة
Refuse, remains of plants from the preceding year. هَدِيم
Sea-sickness, giddiness. هُدَام
Destroyed. Coagulated (milk). مَهْدُوم
Watered by a sligh train (earth). مَهْدُومَة
To rend (clothes). ✱ هَدْمَل
Ragged (clothes). Dishevelled (man).. هِدْمِل
Food and drink. Former age. Gathering of men. Sandy land abounding in trees. هِدْمِلَة

Way, manner, direction. هَدْي
He acted in his own way. هَدَى هَدْيَهُ
Victim to be slaughtered in Mecca. هَدْي وهَدِيّ وهَدِيَّة
Direction, right course; true religion. The Coran. هُدًى وهِدَايَة
He follows the right way, the true religion. هُوَ عَلَى هُدًى
Behaviour. هَدْيَة وهِدْيَة
What a fine behaviour! مَا أَحْسَنَ هِدْيَتَهُ
Persevere in the same course. خُذْ فِي هِدْيَتِكَ
Course, manner. هِدْيَة وهُدْيَة
Ponder over the course to be followed in thy affair. أُنْظُرْ هُدْيَةَ وهِدْيَةَ أَمْرِكَ
Entitled to respect or protection. هَدِيّ
Bride. هَدِيّ وهَدِيَّة
The same thing, the same manner. هُدَيًّا
Gift, present, offering. هَدِيَّة ج هَدَايَا
Offering, presentation. إِهْدَاء
Leader. Guide. هَادٍ ج هَادُون وهُدَاة
Point of an arrow, of a spear.
Neck of a horse. Handle. Beginning of the night. Camels walking ahead. — ج هَوَادٍ
Stick. Rock projecting over the water. Neck of a horse. هَادِيَة ج هَادِيَات وهَوَادٍ
Beasts walking ahead. أَلْهَادِيَات
Bountiful. مِهْدَاء
Vessel, tray for offering a gift. مِهْدَى
The Mahdi, leader and reformer of Islam, expected to come at the end of the world. المَهْدِيّ
Bride conducted to the bridegroom. مُهْدَاة ومَهْدِيَّة
He is in the same state as before. هُوَ عَلَى مُهَيْدِيَتِهِ
To read (a book), to recite (a narrative) quickly. ✧ To meditate, to reflect upon. ✡ هَذَّ o هَذًّا وهَذَذًا وهُذَاذًا ه
To cut off a. th. quickly. — واهْتَذَّ ه
Sharp (sword). هِذّ وهَذَاذ وهَذُوذ
Quickly and repeatedly. هَذَاذَيْكَ
Cutting quickly. Painful journey. ✡ هَذْهَاذ وهُذَاهِذ

To be appeased, quieted. ✡ هَدَنَ i هُدُونًا
To kill a. o. — ه
To bury a. th. — هَدْنًا ه
To soothe, to calm a. o. To quiet (a child). — وهَدَّنَ ه
To conclude a truce, to make peace with a. o. هَادَنَ ه
To emaciate (a horse). أَهْدَنَ
To be arranged, to take a good turn (business). To conclude a truce (armies). تَهَادَنَ
To swerve from (a resolution). إِنْهَدَنَ عَنْ
Fruitfulness. هِدْن
Slight rain. هَدْنَة
Reconciliation. Truce, peace, armistice. هُدْنَة ومُهَادَنَة
Quiet, stillness. هُدْنَة وهُدُون ومَهْدَنَة
Conclusion of peace. هِدَانَة
Slow, slothful; foolish. هِدَان ج هُدُن
To direct a. o. to the way. To show the right way or course to. ✡ هَدَى i هُدًى وهَدْيًا وهِدَايَةً وهِدْيَةً ه
To direct a. o. towards. — ه ل و إِلَى
To go in the right way. To follow the true religion. هَدَى واهْتَدَى
هَدَى i هِدَاء, وهَدَّى وأَهْدَى واهْتَدَى ه إِلَى
To bring (the bride) to (the bridegroom).
To lead the way to (others: horse). هَدَى واهْتَدَى ه
To present a. o. with (a gift); to offer (a present) to. To guide, to bring a. o. or a. th. to. هَدَّى وأَهْدَى إِهْدَاءً ه ل وإِلَى
To offer presents o. to a. هَادَى مُهَادَاةً ه
To make a picnic. — هِدَاء ه
He came swaggering between. جَاء يُهَادِي بَيْنَ
To send (a victim) to Mecca. أَهْدَى ه إِلَى
To make presents o. to a. To waddle, to totter. تَهَادَى
He has followed the true course for obtaining his want. إِهْتَدَى لِأَمْرِهِ
To ask to be guided, directed aright. إِسْتَهْدَى
To ask for (a present). — ه

Demonstrative pronoun. This. See ذا. (for هَاذَا) هذا ✲
To cut, to trench a. th. To put (the enemy) to flight. To hurt a. o. in words. ✲ هَذَأَ a هَذْأً ه وه
To die of (cold). هَذِئَ a هَذَأً مِن
To burst (tumour). تَهَذَّأَ
Showel. هَذَاة
To crop, to trim (a tree). To trim, to dress (wood). To cleanse, to repair. To polish (the style). ✲ هَذَبَ i هَذْبًا, وهَذَّبَ ه
To go quickly, to run, to flow. — i هَذْبًا وهَذَابَةً, وهَذَّبَ وهَاذَبَ وأَهْذَبَ
To rear, to bring up (a child). هَذَّبَ ه
To pour down (rain) quickly (cloud). أَهْذَبَ ه
To be arranged, improved (affair). To be well brought up, amended (child). تَهَذَّبَ
Integrity, sincerity. هَذَبَ
There is no sincerity in his love. ما فِي مَوَدَّتِهِ هَذَبٌ
Swift (horse). هَبِيب
Amble, easy pace of a horse. هَيْذَبِي
Education of a child. تَهْذِيب
Swift (camels). مَهَاذِيب
Upright, honest (man). مُهَذَّب
Polished, trimmed. Well bred (child). — ومُتَهَذِّب
To have a haughty gait (woman). ✲ هَذْخَر هَذْخَرَة
To be intensely hot (day). ✲ هَذَر o i هَذْرًا
He babbled, he talked nonsense. — هَذْرًا وتَهْذَارًا, وأَهْذَر فِي مَنْطِقِهِ
To be incoherent, foolish (speech). سَرِ a هَذَرًا
Dotage. Delirium. Loquacity. هَذَر
Babbler, raver. هَذِر وهَذُر وهُذَرَة وهُذُرَّة وهَذَّار وهِذْرِيَان
Babbler, dotard. هَيْذَار وهَيْذَارَة ومِهْذَر ومِهْذَار ومِهْذَارَة
Doting (woman). هَذِرَة وهَيْذَرَة ومِهْذَار
Speaking quickly. Nimble. هِذْرِيَان
To talk volubly. ✲ هَذْرَبَ
Custom, use. هُذْبِرِي
Quick in acting, in speaking. هُذْرُبَان
To be sprightly; to hurry on. ✲ هَذْرَفَ

Swift, sprightly. هُذْرُوف ج هَذَارِيف
To speak, to read quickly. ✲ هَذْرَمَ
Speaking, reading quickly. هُذَارِم وهُذَارِمَة
To be brisk; to hasten. ✲ هَذَفَ i هُذُوفًا
Hasty, brisk. هَذِف وهَذَّاف ومُهْذِف
Prominence of ground. Cloud. Beginning or end of the night. Rain seen from afar. ✲ هذل — هُذْلُول ج هَذَالِيل
To be shaken, tossed about (bucket). To walk in tottering. ✲ هَوْذَلَ
To be light, active. ✲ هَذْلَمَ
To eat quickly. ✲ هَذَمَ i هَذْمًا
To cut a. th. speedily. — ه
Gallant, courageous. هُذَام وهَيْذَام
Cutting (sword). هُذَام و مِهْذَم
To walk with short steps. ✲ هَذْمَلَ
To rave, to speak deliriously. ✲ هَذَا o هَذْوًا فِي الكَلَام
To cut a. th. with (the sword). — ه ب
To rave, to talk nonsense. ✲ هَذَى i هَذْيًا وهَذَيَانًا
To talk nonsense with a. o. هَاذَى ه
To boil (meat) to rags. أَهْذَى ه
To talk nonsense together. تَهَاذَى
Dotage, delirium, raving. هُذَاء وهَذَيَان
Raver. هَذَّاء, هَذَّاءَة
To have a subcutaneous tumour (camel). To suffer from diarrhea. ✧ To flow (sand, seeds). To fall off (leaves, fruit). ✲ هَرَّ i هَرًّا وهُرَارًا
He suffered and died from diarrhea (camel). هَرَّ سَلْحَهُ
To be ill-natured. — a هَرًّا
✧ To pour out (sand). — o ه
To twang (bow). — o i هَرًّا وهَرِيرًا
To feel disgust at. — ه
He grinned in the face of the beggar. — فِي وَجْه السَّائِل
To howl, to whine from cold (dog). هَرَّ i هَرِيرًا إِلى
To cause (a dog) to whine (cold). — وأَهَرَّ ه
To become dry and stiff (thorns). هَرَّ i o هَرًّا
To be seized with diarrhea. هُرَّ

To rout, to put to flight. هَرَّبَ وأَهْرَبَ ه
✧ He smuggled it. هَرَّبَ ه مِنَ الكُمْرُك
To be frightened away (horse). To travel far into a land. أَهْرَبَ
To raise (the dust : wind). To constrain a. o. to run away. — ه
They fled from one another. تَهَارَبُوا
Escape, flight, emigration. هَرَب و✧ هَرِيبَة
Fugitive. هَارِب و✧ هَرْبَان
Nobody cares about him. He possesses nothing. *lit* : he has no friends nor enemies. مَا لَهُ قَارِب وَلَا هَارِب
Place of refuge. مَهْرَب ج مَهَارِب
✧ Escape. Shift, subterfuge.
To rend (clothes). ◻ هَرْبَدَ ه
Servants of a fire-temple. Doctors of the Magians, of the Parsees. هِرْبِذ ج هَرَابِذَة
Slow amble. ✲ هَرْبَدَة
Proud gait, stately deportment. هِرْبِذِيّ
Swift-footed (wolf). Light-fingered (thief). ✲ هُرْبُع
To spear a. o. ✲ هَرَتَ o i هَرْتًا ه ب
To slit, to widen (a garment). To impair (the reputation). — ه
To boil (meat) to rags. — وأَهْرَتَ ه
To have a wide mouth. هَرِتَ a هَرَتًا
He opened the mouth. هَرَّتَ شِدْقَهُ
Lion. هَرِت وهَرَّات وهَرُوت وهَرِيت
Impaired (character). Wide-mouthed. Rent (garment). هَرِيت وأَهْرَت
Wide in the sides of the mouth. مُهَرَّت ومَهْرُوت الفَم
Luggage, clothes. Kitchen-implements. ✧ هَرْتَك ج هَرَاتِك
Ragged (clothes). ✲ هِرْث
Lion. ✲ هَرْثَم وهُرَاثِم
To riot, to make a faction, a disturbance (people). To run much (horse). To exert o.'s self strenuously. ✲ هَرَجَ i هَرْجًا
To be profuse, incoherent in (speech). — في
✧ To sport, to dally. — وهَرَّج
To be dazzled, excited by heat or tar (camel). هَرِجَ a هَرَجًا

To show the teeth like a dog (woman). To snarl at. هَارَّ ه
To call (sheep) to water. أَهَرَّ ب
Male cat. هِرّ ج هِرَرَة
She-cat. هِرَّة ج هِرَر
Subcutaneous tumour attacking camels. Diarrhea. هُرَار
The star α in *Lyra* and another in *Scorpio*. December and January. الهَرَّارَان
Grapes fallen on the ground. هَرُور
Snarl of a dog. Ill-temper. Dislike. هَرِير
Celebrated battle between two tribes. يَوْم الهَرِير
Suffering from diarrhea. مَهْرُور
To move, to shake a. th. ✲ هَرْهَرَ ه
To call, to bring (sheep) to water. — ب
Murmur of running water. هَرْهَر
Bleating of sheep. هَرْهَرَة
Abundance of milk, of water. هَرْهَار وهُرَاهِر وهُرْهُور
To utter foul, incorrect speech. ✲ هَرَأَ a هَرْأً في مَنْطِقِهِ
To be intensely cold (wind). — هَرْأً وهَرَاءَةً
To debilitate, to kill (a beast) : to affect a. o. severely (cold). — وأَهْرَأَ ه
To boil (meat) to rags. هَرَأَ وهَرَّأَ وأَهْرَأَ ه
To be done to rags (meat). هَرِئَ a هَرْأً وهُرْءًا وهُرُوءًا, وتَهَرَّأَ
To starve with cold (beast, man). هُرِئَ
To take the fresh air in the evening. أَهْرَأَ
To kill a. o. — ه
He multiplied idle words. — الكَلَامَ وفِيهِ
Off-shoot of palm-trees. هِرَاء
Indecent, foul speech. Garrulous. هُرَاء
Done to rags (meat). Severe, destructive (cold). هَرِيء
Time of intense cold. هَرِيئَة
Blasted by the cold. مَهْرُوء
To fly away, to escape. ✲ هَرَبَ o هَرَبًا وهُرُوبًا ومَهْرَبًا وهَرَبَانًا
To escape towards. — مِن... إلى
To be old, decrepit. هَرِبَ a هَرَبًا

To scare away (a wild beast). هَرَّجَ بِ
To affect a. o. (wine). — ه
To distress (a camel) by overfatigue during hot weather. — وأَهْرَجَ ه
To be disorderly, factious (crowd). ✧ To wanton, to dally together. تَهَارَجَ
He became excited by wine. إِهْتَرَجَ مِنَ النَّبِيذ
Riot, confusion. Slaughter, civil war. ✧ Sport, wantonness. هَرْج
Disturbance, faction, conflict. هَرْج وهَرَج
Foolish. Weak. هِرْج
✧ Wanton, dallier. هَارِج ومُهَارِج
Good runner (horse). هَرَّاج وهِمْرِج ومِهْرَاج
Disorderly meeting. هَرَّاجَة
Wantonness, dalliance. مُهَارَجَة
To be quick. ✫ هَرْجَبَ هَرْجَبَة
Tall, bulky camel. هِرْجَاب وهِرْجَب
Lame. ✫ هَرْجَم
To tot about. ✫ هِرْجَل هَرْجَلَة
Tall, long-bodied (man). هِرْجَال ج هَرَاجِيل
To tear, to injure (a garment). To impair (the reputation) of. To dye a. th. yellow. ✫ هَرَدَ i هَرْدًا ه
To boil (meat) to rags. — وهَرَّدَ ه
To fall to pieces (cooked meat). هَرِدَ a هَرَدًا
Disturbance, riot, faction. هَرْد
Female ostrich. Vile man. هِرْد
Turmeric, yellow dye. هُرْد
Dyed yellow. هُرْدِيّ ومَهْرُود
To run heavily with short steps. ✫ هَرْدَبَ
✧ To threaten, to frighten a. o. — بِ
In disorder (people). ◘ هَرْدَبَشْت
Old woman. Cowardly. Big-bellied. هِرْدَبَّة
To walk slowly. ✫ هَرْدَجَ
To strike a. o. To beckon at. ✫ هَرَزَ i هَرْزًا ه
To perish. ✫ هَرِزَ a هَرَزًا
To perish. ✫ هَرْوَزَ وتَهَرْوَزَ
To eat a. th. greedily. To bruise, to bray a. th. To crush a. th. down. ✫ هَرَسَ o هَرْسًا ه
To be gluttonous. هَرِسَ a هَرَسًا
Pounding, pulverisation. هَرْس
Cat. — وهِرْس
Ragged garment. Lion. هَرِس
Abounding with thorny trees (land). — م هَرِسَة
Kind of thorny tree. هَرَاس
Lion. Pounding cooked meat and flour into a paste. هَرَّاس
Pounded, brayed (grain). هَرِيس م هَرِيسَة
Cooked meat and wheat pounded together. — وهَرِيسَة
Mortar. Wash-stand for ablutions. Big and heavy (camel). Dauntless (man). ◘ Howitzer. مِهْرَاس ج مَهَارِيس
To be ill-tempered. ✫ هَرِشَ a هَرَشًا
To be hard, inauspicious (fate). هَرُشَ o i هَرْشًا
To set (people, dogs) against o. a. هَرَّشَ بَيْنَ
✧ To become old. هَرَّشَ
To stir (dogs) against o. a. هَارَشَ مُهَارَشَةً وهِرَاشًا ه على
To quarrel with. ✧ To wanton with. — ه
✧ To dally, to wanton together. تَهَارَشَ
To assail o. another (dogs, men). — واهْتَرَشَ
✧ Old, broken down (man). هِرْش
Uproar, bustle, riot; fight. ✧ Wantonness, horse-play. هِرَاش ومُهَارَشَة
Manageable (horse). مُهَارِش العِنَان
To dry up (cotton in the inkstand). ✫ هَرْشَفَ
Cotton put in the inkstand. Towel, rag. Worn out woman. هِرْشَفَّة وهِرْشَبَّة
To be mangy. ✫ هَرِصَ a هَرَصًا
Mange. Tetters. Worms. (*coll*). هَرَص
Pool of stagnant water. هَرِيصَة
To rend (clothes). ✫ هَرَضَ o هَرْضًا ه
To be affected with dry mange. هَرِضَ a هَرَضًا
To be affected with tetters on the body. هَرَّضَ
Mange. Tetters. هَرَض
To impure the reputation of a. o. ✫ هَرَطَ o هَرْطًا ه وفي
He held idle talks. — في الكَلَام
To have a flabby flesh. هَرِطَ a هَرَطًا

Heraclius (Byzantine emperor). هِرَقْلُ وهِرَقِلُ G
To sweep, to strut. ✧ To become old, decrepit. ✱ هَرْكَل
Stately gait. ✧ Decrepitude. هَرْكَلَة
Large fishes; seals, cetacea. Surge-beaten place. هَرَاكِلَة
Fine, good-looking woman. هَرْكَلَة وهِرْكَلَة وهِرْكَوْلَة وهُرْكُلَة
To tear a. th. to pieces. ◘ هَرْكَن ه
To hurry in walk; to go a kind of amble. ✱ هرل — هَرْوَل
To become decrepit by age. ✱ هَرِم a هَرَمًا ومَهْرَمًا ومَهْرَمَة
To chop (herbs). ✧ هَرَم i هَرْمًا ه
To mince (meat). هَرَّم ه
To praise, to extol a. o. or a. th. ه ٥ —
To render a. o. decrepit (God, age). هَرَّم وأَهْرَم ٥
To pretend to be old. تهارم
To judge, to find a. o. old, broken down. إِسْتَهْرَم ٥
Mincing, chopping. Acrid plant; kind of euphorbia. هَرْم
Advanced age, decrepitude. هَرَم ومَهْرَمَة
Pyramid of Egypt. هَرَم ج أهرام وهِرَام
Understanding. Soul. هِرِم
Very old, decrepit. هَرِمَات وهَرْمَى
Feeding on acrid plants. هَارِم م هَارِمَة ج هَوَارِم
Dry wood. Dry (wood). هَرْمَى
Wicked woman. هَرُوم
Understanding, mind. هُرْمَان
Ancient wells. ✱ هَرَامِيت
To chew a. th. To be put out (fire). ✱ هَرْمَز
The great. King of Persia. P الهُرْمُز الهُرْمُزان الهَارْمُوز
To be frowned, cross (face). ✱ هَرْمَس
Mercury. Egyptian god. Egyptian king under whom the Septuagint was made. هِرْمِس G
Man-eater lion. Panther's cub. هِرْمَاس
Lion. Rhinoceros. Buffalo. هِرْمِيس
◘ Hieroglyphics. هِجَايَة هَرْمَسِيَّة
Uproar, bustle. هَرْمَسَة
To pull out (the hair); to depilate a. o. ✱ هَرْمَل ه و٥

To revile o. a. تَهَارَط
Flaccid flesh. Old ewe. Braggart. هِرْط وهِرْطَة
To become a heretic, a heresiarch. ✧ هَرْطَق وتَهَرْطَق
Heresy. ✧ هَرْطَقَة
✧ Heretic. هَرْطُوقِيّ ج هَرَاطِقَة G
Tall. Long-bodied (man). ✱ هِرْطَال
Oats. ✱ هرطم — هُرْطُمَان
To flow quickly (blood). ✱ هَرِع a هَرَعًا
To run, to hurry towards. هَرِع a هَرَعًا إلى
To point (a spear). هَرَّع وأَهْرَع ه
To hasten. أَهْرَع
To hurry in walk. To tremble from anger; to shiver from fear. هُرِع وأُهْرِع
To be pointed (spear). تَهَرَّع
Quick and tremulous pace. هَرَع وهُرَاع
Flowing quickly (blood). هَرِع
Easily moved to tears. — م هَرِعَة
Louse. هَرَعَة وهَرِعَة
Seized with a nervous trembling. مُهْرَع ومُهْرُوع
The Lion. المُهْرِع والمِهْرَاع
To praise a. o. or a. th. to excess or without reason. ✱ هَرَف i هَرْفًا ه و٥
He hurried to perform prayer. هَرَّف إلى الصَّلاة
To give fruit precociously (palm-tree). هَرَّف وأَهْرَف
To become wealthy. أَهْرَف
To pour (a liquid). ✱ هَرَق a هَرْقًا, وهَرَّق ه
Cool thy anger! هَرِّق على جَمْرِك
To pour (water, tears). هَرَاق (for أراق) يُهَرِيق هِرَاقَة, وأَهْرَق
To rush upon a. o. (fighters). — على
Imperative. Dismount, take rest ye! هَرِيقُوا عَنكُم
To flow abundantly (tears, rain). إِهْرَوْرَق إِهْرِيرَاقًا
To be poured. هُرِيق وأُهْرِق
Effusion of blood, tears. إِهْرَاق
Glazed paper. Bare desert. Parchment. Papyrus. مُهْرَق ج مَهَارِق
Poured. مُهْرَق و مُهْرَاق ومُهَرَاق
Pouring. مُهْرِق ومُهْرِيق
Poured (rain). مُهْرَوْرِق

To be broken down by age (woman). ✻ هَرمَلَت

Old woman. هِرمِل

Hair remainig on the sides of the head. هُرمُول ج هَرَامِيل

To pervade (a tree : worm). ✻ هَرنَص ه

Tree-worm ; canker-worm. هِرنِصَانَة

Big or small louse. ✻ هُرنُع وهُرنُوع ج هَرَانِع

To grin, to sneer. ✻ هَرنَف

Fruit of the *Agallochum*-tree. ✻ هَرنُوِيّ وهَرنُوَة وهَرنُوِيّ

To beat a. o. with a stick. ✻ هَرَا o هَروًا, وتَهَرَّى ه

Herat, town of Khorassan. هَرَاة

To thrash a. o. ✻ هَرِي a هَرِيَة

✧ To wear out (clothes). To alter a. th. (dampness). — هَرَّى ه

To dye (cloth) yellow. هَرَّى ه

To ridicule a. o. هَارَى ه

✧ To be worn out (clothes). To be rotten (fruit). ✧ تَهَرَّى وانهَرَى

Stick. هِرَاوَة ج هَرَاوَى

Sceptre, staff. — أَلمُلك

Granary, store-house for corn. هُرِيّ ج أهرَاء

Rottenness. ✧ هَرَيَان

Weak (man). Overthrown (building). هَار م هَارِيَة

To quiver, to brandish (a lance). To shake (the trees : wind). ✻ هَزَّ o هَزًّا وهَزهَز ه وب

It set me in good spirits. هَزَّ مِن عِطفِي

✧ To rock (a child). هَزَّ ه

To urge (beasts) by singing. — هَزِيزًا ه

To be shaken, to vibrate. تَهَزَّز واهتَزَّ و✧ هَزَّ وانهَزَّ

To walk briskly by the singing of his driver (camel). To become tall (plant). To shoot (star). إهتَزَّ

To rejoice in (good actions). — ل

Shock, shake, vibration. ✧ Earthquake. هَزَّة

Briskness : good spirits, liberal disposition. Bubbling of a pot. هِزَّة

Rumbling of thunder. — وهَزِيز

Murmuring of the wind. هَزِيز

Shock, shake, commotion. مَهَزّ ومَهَزَّة

Shaken (tree). ✧ Stupid. مَهزُوز

To shake, to quiver ✻ هَزهَز ه وه

a. th. To subdue a. o.

To move along. To vibrate, to oscillate. To become submissive. To leap for joy (heart). تَهَزهَز

To bound joyfully towards. — إلى

Vibration, oscillation. هَزهَزَة

Commotion, Disturbance, shock ; affliction. Sedition. War. هَزهَزَة ج هَزَاهِز

Flowing abundantly (water). هُزهُز وهَزهَاز وهُزَاهِز

Shining, glittering (sword). هَزهَار

To excite (a beast : rider). ✻ هَزَأ a هَزأً ه

To let (camels) die of cold. — وأهزَأ ه

To scoff at ; to deride a. o. هَزَأ وهَزِئ a هُزءًا وهُزُؤًا وهَزأً وهُزُوءًا ومَهزَأَة ب ومِن

To die suddenly. هَزِئ a هَزأً

To be severely affected by cold. أهزَأ

To laugh, to scoff at. تَهَزَّأ وتَهَازَأ واستَهزَأ ب

Scoff, rail, sneer. هُزء وهُزُؤ واستِهزَاء

Cold (morning). Difficult to be crossed (desert). هَازِئَة

Laughing-stock, ridiculous. هُزأَة

Scoffer, mocker, sneerer. هُزَأَة

Strong camel. Vulture. ✻ هزب – هَوزَب

Fierce, lion. هَيزَب

To cut off a. th. ✻ هَزبَر ه

Bulky lion. Sturdy camel هِزبَر وهِزَبر ج هَزَابِر

To be reduced to extreme destitution. ✻ هَزبَل

To hum, to sing in undertone. To recite verses on a trilling rhythm. ✻ هَزِج a هَزَجًا, وهَزَّج وتَهَزَّج

To compose verses of 4 feet. أهزَج

To twang (bow). To rumble (thunder). تَهَزَّج

Quavering, trilling of the voice. Rumbling of thunder. Rhythm. Trilling song. Poetical metre of 4 feet. هَزَج

Humming (man). Buzzing (fly). Merry, lively. هَزِج

Portion of the night. هَزِيج مِنَ ألَّيل

Trilling song. أُهزُوجَة ج أهَازِيج

To despatch work. ✻ هَزَر i هَزرًا

To defame a. o. To banish a. o. — ه

To bastinade a. o. هَزَر ه ب
He threw him down. — بِهِ الأرض
To load a. o. with presents. — بِفُلان
Deceived. Stupid. هِزر
Beating, bastinado. Laziness. هَزرَة ج هَزَرات
Light earth. — وهَزرَة ج هَزَرات
Sluggishness. — وهُزَيرَة
He is a lazy fellow. هُوَ هَزَرات
Simpleton, dupe. ذُو هَزَرات ومُهزَر
Nightingale. P هَزار ج هَزَارات
Sturdy (boy). Weak (old man). هَزوَّر
Banished, expelled. هَزِير ومَهزُور
Wearing shabby clothes. ✧ مُهزَّر
Bryonia dioica (plant). P هَزَرجشان
To be quick. ✱ هَزرَف
Quick ostrich. هِزرَاف وهُزَارِف وهِزرَوف وهُزرُوف
To break, to smash a. th. ✱ هَزَع a هَزعًا، وهَزَّع ه
To hurry, to go quickly. هَزَع وتَهَزَّع واهتَزَع
To have a frowning look. تَهَزَّع
To assume a false appearance before a. o. — ل
To swagger, to incline in walk (woman). — في مِشيَتِها
To be broken, smashed. إنهَزَع
To quiver, to vibrate (sword). إهتَزَع
Mangling his prey (lion). هُزَع وهُزَاع ومِهزَع
Alone, single, unique. هِزَاع
There is but one arrow in his quiver. ما في الجَعبَة إلّا سَهمٌ هِزاع
Portion of the night. هَزِيع مِنَ اللَّيل
Last arrow of a quiver. أهزَع
There is no one in the house. ما في الدار أهزَع
To riot, to raise a disturbance. ✧ هَيزَع
To riot. ✧ — وتَهَيزَع
Fear. Bustle of war. ✧ Disturbance, riot. هَيزَعَة
To carry away a. th. (wind). ✱ هَزَف i هَزفًا ه
To be lively, brisk. ✱ هَزِق a هَزَقًا
He laughed immoderately. — وأهزَق في الضَّحِك
Briskness, sprightliness. هَزَق

Laughing loudly. (m; f.) مِهزَاق
To jest, to joke in (words or actions). ✱ هَزَل i هَزلًا، وهَازَل في
To exhaust, to emaciate (a beast). — هَزلًا، وهَزَّل ه
To have exhausted, emaciated cattle. — وأهزَل
هَزَل o هَزلًا وهُـزَالًا، وهَزِل a هَزَلًا، وهُزِل هُزالًا
To be exhausted, emaciated.
To find a. o. sportive, not in earnest. أهزَل ه
✧ To make little account of; to look scornfully at. — و✧ استَهزَل
Jest, joke. هَزل وهُزَالَة
Leanness, emaciation. هُزَال
Jester, joker. هَزِل وهَزَّال وهِزِّيل
Lean and thin, exhausted. هَزِيل ج هَزلَى، ومَهزُول ج مَهَازِيل
Unfruitful years. مَهَازِل
To run swiftly (ostrich). ✱ هَزلَج هَزلَجَة
Quick, ostrich. هَزلَج
Quick, light wolf. هِزلَاج
Quick, swift. ✱ هَزلَم
To twang (bow). ✱ هَزَم i هَزمًا
To hollow out (wax) with the hand. To sink (a well). — ه
He lessened his right. — لَهُ حَقَّهُ
To put to flight, to rout (the enemy). هَزَم وهَزَّم ه
To feel a propensity to. هُزِم على
To twang (bew). To rumble (thunder). To burst (skin). تَهَزَّم
To be broken short (stick). To fall to pieces (building). — وانهَزَم
It broke forth and poured its rain (cloud). تَهَزَّم واهتَزَم بالماء
To be put to flight, routed (army). إنهَزَم
To trample on the ground (horse). إهتَزَم
To set quickly to (work). — ه
To slaughter (a ewe). — ه
Flight, rout. هَزم وهَزِيمَة وانهِزَام
Waterless cloud. Depressed ground. — ج هُزُوم
Twang of a bow. هَزَم
Tractable horse. Heavy (rain). هَزِم
Hollow impressed in a soft body, in wax. هَزمَة ج هَزَم وهُزُوم وهَزَمَات

Misfortune, disgrace. هَازِمَة ج هَوَازِم
Twanging (bow). هَزُوم
Thunder, rumbling of thunder. Vehement (rain). هَزِيم
Inexhaustible well-spring. Rout. هَزِيمَة ج هَزَائِم
To speak uninterruptedly. ✱ هَزْمَجَ
Confusion of sounds, uninterrupted speech. هَزْمَجَة
Confused (sound, voice). هُزَامِج
Dust. ✱ هزن — هَوْزَن
To depart, to be off. ✱ هَزَا o
To crumble a. th. ✱ هَسَّ o هَسًّا ه
To speak to o.'s self. — i هَسًّا
Broken, crumbled. Whisper. هَسِيس
To clink (jewels); to rustle (coat of mail). ✱ هَسْهَسَ وتَهَسْهَسَ
To conceal (news). هَسْهَسَ ه
Clang, din. هَسْهَسَة
Whisper. هَسَاهِس
To hurry on, to be quick. ✱ هَسَمَ
To become languid, weak (man). To be broken (wood). ✱ هَشَّ o i هَشًّا
To beat off (tree-leaves) for (cattle). — ه على
▫ To drive away (flies). هَشَّ ه
To be soft, tender (bread). — i هُشُوشَة
To be tender, brittle. هَشَّ a هَشَاشَة
To be ready to. To be cheerful, well disposed towards. هَشَّ i o هَشَاشَة وهَشَاشًا، واهْتَشَّ ل
He rejoiced at it. أَهَشَّ بِهِ
To cheer, to enliven a. o. هَشَّشَ ه
To find a. o. weak, languid; to find a. o. cheerful, kind. إِسْتَهَشَّ ه
Tender, brittle, soft. Sweating much (horse). ✧ In powder (sugar). هَشّ
Tender (bread). — وهَشَاش
Pumice stone. حَجَر هَشّ
Kind. هَشُّ المَكْسَر
Kind, gracious. هَشُّ الوَجْه
I am glad of it. أَنَا بِهِ هَشٌّ بَشٌّ
▫ Round long-necked jug. هَشَّة
Kindness, compliance. هَشًا وهَشَاشَة
Soft. Compliant, kind. Dry herbage. هَشِيش
To move, to agitate. ✱ هَشْهَشَ
Commotion. هَشْهَشَة

Liberal, bountiful. هَشْهَاش
To exhaust the milk of (a she-camel). ✱ هَشَرَ o هَشْرًا ه
Thinness, lightness. هَشْر
Liveliness, merriness. هَشْرَة
Tree losing its leaves early. شَجَرَة هَشِرَة وهَشُور
Flaccid. Kind of artichoke. هَيْشَر
✧ To emigrate. To ramble, to rove. ✧ هَشَلَ o هَشْلًا
To yield little milk (she-camel). هَشَّلَ
✧ To banish, to expel a. o. — ه
To lend (a beast) to a. o. without the leave of its owner. أَهْشَلَ
To use (a beast) without permission. إِهْتَشَلَ ه
✧ Vagrancy. هَشْلَة
Beast used without permission. هَشِيلَة
✧ Vagrant, vagabond. هَاشِل
To crush, to bruise a. th. ✱ هَشَمَ i هَشْمًا، وهَشَّمَ وتَهَشَّمَ ه
To honour a. o. ✧ To cover a. o. with wounds. هَشَّمَ ه
To conciliate a. o. تَهَشَّمَ ه
He showed kindness towards. — على فُلَان
To be broken (dry tree). ✧ To be covered with wounds. تَهَشَّمَ وانْهَشَمَ
I worked for him unwillingly. إِهْتَشَمْتُ نَفْسِي لَهُ
Generous, bountiful. هَشِم
Bounty, generosity. هِشَام
Mountain-goat. هَشَمَة ج هَشَمَات
Wound in the head. Blow shattering the bones. هَاشِمَة
Broken, crushed. Dry and broken plant. Weak. هَشِيم
Arid land. هَشِيمَة
He is a bountiful man. مَا هُوَ إِلَّا هَشِيمَةُ كَرَمٍ
To wrestle sportively with a. o. ✱ هَشَا — هَاشَا ه
To crush, to tread a. th. under foot. To pierce a. th. To impress a. th. with the hand. ✱ هَصَّ o هَصًّا ه
To have sparkling eyes. هَصْهَصَ
Eye of the elephant. هَاصَّة
Crushed, trodden under foot. هَصِيص ومَهْصُوص
Spark, crackling of fire. هَصِيص النَّار

mountain formed of one mass of rocks.
Shower. أَهْضُوبَة ج أَهَاضِيب
Sturdy, strong. Sweating much (horse). هِضَبّ
To feed (sheep) abundantly. ✲ هضج – هَضَّج
Small boys. صِبْيَان هَضِيج
To pour forth (verses, words). ✲ هَضَل o هَضْلًا ب
To rain (sky). أَهْضَل
Numerous army. هَيْضَل
Armed party. – وَهَيْضَلَة
Confused voices. هَيْضَلَة
To break a. th. To digest (food : stomach). To facilitate digestion (medicine). ✲ هَضَم i هَضْمًا ه
To wrong, to oppress a. o. – وتَهَضَّم واهْتَضَم ه
He wronged, him he lessened his right. هَضَم حَقَّهُ
He remitted to him a part of his due. – لَهُ مِن حَقِّهِ طَائِفَةً
To be slender (horse). هَضِم a هَضَمًا
To shed its front-teeth (beast). أَهْضَم
To yield to (the enemy). تَهَضَّم ل
To be easy of digestion (food). To be dissolved, melted. To break, to be crushed (fruit). إِنْهَضَم
Depressed ground. Bottom of a valley. هَضْم وهِضْم ج هُضُوم وأَهْضَام
Beware of walking by night and in the bottoms of the valleys. أَللَّيْلَ وأَهْضَامَ ٱلْوَادِي
Digestion. هَضْم وانْهِضَام
Digestible, easy of digestion. سَرِيع ٱلِانْهِضَام
Undigestible. بَطِيء ٱلِانْهِضَام
Digestible (medicine). هَاضِم
Digestible. هَضُوم وهَضَّام وهَاضُوم
Digestive power. قُوَّة هَاضِمَة
Open-handed. يَد هَضُوم ج هُضُم
Wronged in his rights. هَضِيم
– م هَضِيمَة, وأَهْضَم م هَضْمَاء ج هُضْم
Slender, thin-bodied.
Pipe, fife. قَصَبَة هَضِيم ومُهَضَّمَة ومَهْضُومَة
Injustice, oppression. Funeral dinner. هَضِيمَة ج هَضَائِم

To impress a. th. with the hand on a soft body. ✲ هَضْهَص ه
Strong (man, lion). Black. هُضْهُص وهُضَاهِص
Having sparkling eyes. هَضْهَاص
To run away, to flee. ✲ هَضَب
To draw (a bough) to o.'s self. To pull, to incline a. th. ✲ هَصَر i هَصْرًا ه وب, واهْتَصَر ه
To incline, to break a. th. without separating it. To squeeze, to take hold of. هَصَّر ه
To be pulled, bent, inclined. إِنْهَصَر واهْتَصَر
To straighten (the racemes of a palm-tree). To crush the head of (his prey : lion). إِهْتَصَر ه
Sea-shell worn as an amulet. هِصْرَة وهَصَرَة
هَصِر وهَاصِر وهُصَر وهَصَّار وهَيْصَر وهَصُور
Lion. Squeezing. Declining (fortune). ومِهْصَر ومِهْصَار الخ
To break, to smash a. th. ✲ هَصَم i هَصْمًا ه
Lion. هُصَم وهَصَّام وهَيْصَم ومِهْصَم
Strong, sturdy man. هَيْصَم
To become old. ✲ هَصَا o هَصْوًا
To break a. o.'s back. هَاصَى ه
Sturdy man. أَهْصَاء
To walk quickly (camel). ✲ هَضّ o هَضًّا وهَضْهَض
He had a graceful gait. – المَشْيَ
To break gently, to bruise a. th. – ه واهْتَضّ ه
To be broken, crushed. إِنْهَضّ
I fell short of my duty towards him. إِهْتَضَضْتُ نَفْسِي ل
Party of people. هَضَّاء
Furious (stallion). هَضَّاض وهَضْهَاض
Broken, crushed. هَضِيض ومَهْضُوض
To rain continuously (sky). ✲ هَضَب i هَضْبًا
To wet a. o. (rain). – ه
To be profuse in (speech). – واهْتَضَب فِي
To be oblong (hill). إِسْتَهْضَب
هَضْبَة ج هِضَاب وهِضَب وهَضَب وهَضَبَات
Shower of rain. Run, heat. Isolated and depressed hill; وجج أَهَاضِيب

✻ هضى – هاضى ه To despise, to make little of.
هضاة Lock of hair. She-ass.
أهضاء Party of men.
✻ هطّ – أهطّ م هطّاء ج هُطّ Good walker (camel).
✻ هَطهَطَ To neigh (horse).
– في To be quick in (work).
هُطاهِط Horse.
✻ هطر i هَطرًا ه To beat, to fell (a dog).
تهطّر To fall down, to collapse (well).
هَطرة Humble appearance of a poor man.
✻ هطرس – تهطرس To waddle, to sweep.
✻ هطع a هَطعًا وهُطوعًا To go along fearfully in looking fixedly at a point (beast).
أهطع واستهطع في السّير To walk fast in stretching the neck (camel).
أهطع في العَدو He quickened the pace.
هَطِيع Broad way, large road.
✻ هطف i هَطفًا To yield rain (cloud).
– ه To milk (the females : shepherd).
هطِف Shower.
✻ هطل i هَطلًا وهَطلانًا وتهطالًا، وتهطّل To rain fast. To send forth showers (cloud).
هَطل ه وه To cause (a horse) to sweat (run, heat). To pour (water).
هَطل Thin and continuous rain.
دِيمة هُطل وهَطلاء Rain falling in large drops.
مطر هُطِل وهطّال Heavy rain.
سحاب هاطِل وهَطِل وهطّال Cloud pouring down large drops.
سحائب هُطل Clouds pouring rain in large drops.
هَطلى Walking slowly (beast).
هَيطل ج هَياطِلة وهَياطِل Fox. Party engaged on a raid, marauders. *Pl.* Turkish or Indian tribe famed for its strength and gallantry.
✻ هَطلَم Numerous army. Crowd. Mighty man.
✻ هطا o هَطوًا ب To throw a. th.
وقع بينهم هُطًى A struggle was engaged between them.

✻ هَمهَمَة To vomit.
✻ هَيعَر To be restless, boisterous (woman).
هَيعَرة Boisterous woman, hag. Vampire.
✻ هفّ i هفًّا وهَفِيفًا To whizz, to hiss (wind).
– i هَفِيفًا To walk quickly (man). To glitter, to shine.
✧ هَفّت نفسي إلى I felt an inclination to.
إهتفّ To glitter (mirage). To tingle (ear).
هَفّ وهِفّ Small fishes.
هِفّ Empty. Rainless (cloud). Empty (honey-comb).
هَفّاف م هفّافة Light, swift (bird). Breeze.
هَفّان Trace, mark.
جاء على هَفّانه He followed his steps.
مُهفّف م مُهفّفة Thin, translucid (cloth). Glistening (mirage).
✻ هَفهَف وتَهَفهَف To have a slender body.
هَفهاف ومُهَفهَف Slender (body). Thirsty. Light (wing). Thin (garment).
✻ هَفت i هَفتًا وهُفاتًا To hover, to fly about. To crumble down. To speak much inconsiderately. To be fine, slender.
– وانهفت To fall to pieces, to crumble down.
تهافت To fall in pieces (garment). To be continuous, successive. To fall quickly (snow).
– على To rush, to press upon. To fall into (the fire : moth). To crowd to (the water) continuously (people).
هَفت Depressed soil. Inconsiderate (word). Continuous, falling quickly (rain). Stupidity. ◻ Annoyance.
هَفات Foolish.
هَفِيتة Emigrants driven away by drought.
مَهفُوت Stupefied.
✻ هفا o هَفوًا وهَفوة وهَفوانًا To run swiftly. To flutter and take its flight (bird). To tumble, to slip. To commit a fault. To be hungry.

هفا هَفْوًا وهُفُوًّا ✡ To whirl about (wool). To palpitate (heart).
— ب To raise (a flake of wool : wind).
هفا الفُؤَادُ The heart yearned towards.
هَافَى ه To entice a. o.
✧ هَفِيَ a هَفًى To starve.
✧ هَفَّى ه To starve a. o.
هَفًا Transient rain. ✧ Ravenous hunger.
هَفَاة Gentle rain.
هَفْوَة ج هَفَوَات Fault, slip, error.
هَافٍ م هَافِيَة ج هَوَافٍ Destitute. Starving.
أَهْفَاء Foolish people.
✡ هَقْب Width, breadth.
هِقَب وهِقِط *Cries for exciting horses.*
هَقَبْقَب Sturdy, strong.
✡ هقر – هَقَوَّر Long-bodied man.
✡ هَقَمَ a هَقْمًا ه To cauterise (a horse).
تَهَقَّم To be proud, impudent.
تَهَقَّمُوا وِرْدًا They thronged at the water.
إِنْهَقَم To suffer from hunger.
إِهْتَقَم ه To divert a. o. from (virtue : passion). To exhaust a. o. (ague).
أَهْتُقِم To be altered (colour).
هَقِم م هَقِمَة Insatiable.
هَقْعَة Star of hair on the upper part of a horse's breast. Three stars in *Orio.* Fifth mansion of the moon.
هُقَعَة Wont to recline on the elbow in a gathering.
هَيْقَعَة Clash of swords. Clatter.
مَهْقُوع Having a tuft of hair on (the breast (horse).
✡ هقل – هِقْل م هِقْلَة Ostrich.
هَاقِل Male rat.
✡ هَقْلَس ج هَقَالِس Male ostrich. Ill-natured. Fox. Wolf.
✡ هَقِم a هَقَمًا To have a ravenous hunger.
تَهَقَّم ه To subdue, to overcome a. o.
— ه To swallow up a. th. in large mouthfuls.
هَقِم م هَقِمَة Ravenous, voracious.
هِقَمّ Glutton. Sea. Male ostrich.
هَيْقَم Roaring of the sea. Gurgling noise in swallowing. Extensive sea.

✡ هَقِيَ i هَقْيًا To be delirious.
— وأَهْقَى ه To bully a. o. To seduce a. o.
✡ هَكَّ o هَكًّا ه To crumble down (well).
— ه To pulverise a. th. by rubbing. To draw (milk) to the last drop.
— ه ب To spear a. o. time after time.
— ه To intoxicate a. o. (wine). To injure the reputation of.
هُكَّ To be thrown down.
إِنْهَكَّ To be intoxicated.
هَكّ ج هَكَكَة وأَهْكَاك Disease of the mind.
هَكِيك ومَهْكُوك Pounded.
✡ هَكَبَ هَكْبًا To scoff at a. o.
✡ هكد – هُكِّدَ على To press (a debtor).
✡ هٰكَذَا So, thus, in the same manner ; in that way.
✡ هَكَرَ i وهَكِرَ a هِكْرًا وهَكَرًا, وتَهَكَّرَ To be astounded.
هَكِرَ a هَكْرًا وهَكَرًا To be sleepy or to sleep deeply.
هَكِر وهَكِر Sleeping. Wandering.
مَا فِيهِ مَهْكَر ومَهْكَرَة No wonder at it.
✡ هَكَارِس *Pl.* Frogs.
✡ هَكَعَ a هُكُوعًا To be quiet, to take rest. To halt. To cough (camel). To spread its darkness (night).
مَا يُدْرَى أَيْنَ سَكَعَ وأَيْنَ هَكَعَ Nobody knows where he is gone to, nor where he stopped.
هَكِعَ a هَكَعًا , واهْتَكَعَ To be lowly, submissive. To be grieved, angry.
هُكَاع Sleep, exhaustion. Cough.
هُكَعَة Foolish.
✡ هَكَفَ a هَكْفًا To walk and run swiftly.
✡ هكل – تَهَاكَلُوا They came to fight.
هَيْكَل To be big and tall.
هَيْكَل ج هَيَاكِل Huge (beast). Tall and arborescent plant. Lofty building. Altar, temple. Statue.
✡ هكم – تَهَكَّم To crumble down (well). To rain fast.
تَهَكَّمَ على فُلَانٍ To threaten, to be angered with.
— على أَمْرٍ To be sorry for.
— ه وب To rail, to scoff, to mock at
هَكِم Wicked. Intruder.

Mockery, scoff, derision. تَهَكُّم وأُهْكُومَة
Proud. مُسْتَهْكِم
✱ هكن – تَهَكَّن To repent.
✱ هَل *Interrog. particle.* Is.. he, she, it...? Did.. he, she, it?
هَلْ زَيْدٌ قَائِمٌ Is Zeid standing?
هَلا Halloo, *cry* for urging horses.
حَيَّ هَلَ وحَيَّ هَلا على الصَّلاة Come on, come ye to prayer.
هَلّا Why not?
✱ هَلّ i هَلا To fall heavily (rain). To appear (new moon). To begin (lunar month). To rejoice. ✧ To lose their gloss, to become shabby (clothes).
– ه ✧ To expand (the dough: woman).
هَلّل وهيلل هَيْلَلة To be frightened, to fly away. To praise God, by repeating لا إله إلّا الله, (there is no God but God).
– عن To abstain from.
هَالّ مُهالّة وهِلالاً ه To hire (a workman) for a lunar month.
أَهَلّ إهلالاً, وأُهِلّ To appear (new moon). To raise the voice in saying لَبَّيك (Here I am).
أَهَلّ واستهلّ To begin to cry (new-born child).
أَهَلّ عن لَيْلَة كذا He perceived the new moon on such a night.
– بِفُلان To make a cut upon a. o. (sword).
– بِذِكر الله He invocated the name of God.
أُهِلّ لِلّهِ بِ To say: In the name of God before slaughtering (a victim).
تَهَلَّل واهتلّ To be bright (face, cloud). To exult.
تَهَلَّل To have a smiling, open face.
– وانْهَلّ واستهلّ To shed tears (eye).
إنهلّ واهتلّ واستهلّ To fall heavily and loudly (rain).
إستهلّ To give the first rain (sky). To raise, to lower the voice.
أستهلّ To begin to shine (new moon).
هَلّ To be drawn; to glitter (sword).
هِلّ وهَلّة ج هِلة Beginning of a lunar month.
ما أصاب هَلّة He has not obtained the least thing.
هَلّة ج هَلل Rain.
هَلَل Fear.
هَلَكَ هَلَلا He died with fear.
هَلل وهَلال وهِلال First rain.
هِلال ج أَهِلّة وأَهَالِيل New moon. Crescent of the moon. The two first or two last days of a lunar month. Anything crescent-shaped. Grapnel. Double-pointed spear-head. ✧ Parenthesis.
هُلى Joy after sadness.
ذَهَب بِهِلِّيَان بِذي هِلّيان He went nobody knows whereto.
هَلِيلة Land in which rain is circumscribed.
إهلال واستهلال First night of a lunar month.
إستهلال Exordium of a speech.
أهاليل Rains.
تَهَلّل Exultation.
ذَهَب دَمُهُ في تَهَلّل His blood has been shed to no avail.
مُهَلّل Crescent shaped. Lean and bent (camel).
H هَلِلُويَا Halleluiah.
✱ هَلْهَل ه To weave (a stuff) thin. To sift (flour) with a fine tissue. To repeat (a sound).
– الشِعر To refine poetry.
– في To procrastinate in (an affair).
هَلهَل يُدرِكُهُ He was on the point of overtaking him.
هَلهَل ✧ To bewail (the dead: Druse). To pronounce the Mohammedan formula of faith. To threaten to become a Moslem (angry Christian).
هَلهَل وهَلهَال وهُلاهِل ومُهَلهَل Light (tissue).
هُلاهِل Refined, elegant (poetry).
▫ هَلهُولَة Rag.
✱ هَلَب i هَلْبًا, وأَهلَب To keep on running (horse).
هَلَب ه To drench a. o. (dew).
– وهَلَّب ه To pluck (the hair). To clip (a horse's tail).
هَلَب وهَلَّب ه بِلِسانِهِ To satirise, to revile.
هَلِب a هَلَبًا To be hairy (man).
تَهَلَّب وانهلب To have the hair plucked, the tail shorn.

He confided a secret to him. هَالَس فُلَانًا وأَهْلَس إِلَيْهِ
To smile. To whisper. أَهْلَس
Thinness, leanness. ✧ Nonsense, idle words. هَلْس
Consumption, hectic fever. — وهُلَاس
Weak, convalescent people. هُلْس
Hallucination. ◻ هَلْوَسَة
Weak-bodied. هَالِس ج هَوَالِس
Exhausted. Consumptive, hectic. ✧ Pounded fine. مَهْلُوس
Insane. مُخْتَلَس ٱلْعَقْل
Having a flaccid belly. ✲ هلط — هَالِط
Tangled, luxuriant (herbage).
To be anxious, fretful. ✲ هَلِع a هَلَعًا
Restless, anxious. هَلِع وهَلُوع
Greedy. هُلَع وهَالُوع
He possesses nothing. مَا لَهُ هِلْع ولَا هِلَّعَة
Fearful, fretful. Impatient. هُلَعَة
Swift (ostrich). هَالِع م هَالِعَة, هِلْوَاع
Hirsute, thick-bearded; thick (beard). ✲ هلف — هِلْوَف
To hurry on. ✲ هَلِق i هَلْقًا, وتَهَلَّق
Now, (for هٰذَا الوَقْت) on the spot, immediately. ✧ هَلَّق وهَلَّقْتِيَّة
Vehement (hunger). ✲ هِلَقْت وهِلَّقْس وهِلَّقْف
To glut a. th. ✲ هَلْقَم ه
Big and tall. Lion. هِلْقَام
Gluttonous, voracious. — وهِلْقَامَة وهِلَّقَامَة
✲ هَلَك i وهَلِك a هَلْكًا وهَلَاكًا وهُلْكًا وتَهْلُوكًا وهُلُوكًا ومَهْلَكًا ومَهْلِكًا ومَهْلُكًا وتَهْلَكَةً وتَهْلِكَةً وتَهْلُكَةً
To perish, to die miserably. To pass away. To be reduced to nought. ✧ To be damned
— i هُلْكًا وهَلَاكًا , وهَلَّك وأَهْلَك واسْتَهْلَك
To destroy. To lose a. o. or a. th. ه وه
To sell (property). أَهْلَك ه
✧ To damn a. o. (God). — ه
He swaggered gracefully. تَهَلَّك وتَهَالَك فِي مَشْيِهِ
To sink exhausted upon (a bed). To covet a. th. eagerly. تَهَالَك عَلَى
To strive in. — فِي
To rush into danger. To strive after. إِنْهَلَك واهْتَلَك
To spend away (wealth). ✧ To sink (a debt). إِسْتَهْلَك ه

To unsheath (a sword). إِهْتَلَب ه
Horse-hair, coarse hair; pig's bristle. Eyelash. Continual rain. هُلْب (un. هُلْبَة)
Hairy (man). هَلِب
Severity of winter. هُلْبَة وهُلَّبَة ٱلشِّتَاء
Vehemently cold day. هَالِب الشَّعَر
Rainy night. لَيْلَة هَالِبَة
Cold wind with rain. Rainy, plentiful (year). هَلَّاب وهَلَّابَة
Cold winter-day. هَلَّاب وهَلِيب ومُهَلِّب
Hairless or clipped (tail). Hairy, coarse-haired (man). Rainy, fruitful (year). أَهْلَب م هَلْبَاء ج هُلْب
Shorn-haired. مَهْلُوب
Kind of dates. ✲ هلبث — هِلْبَاث
Stupid, dull. هِلْبُوث
Thick milk. ✲ هلبج — هُلَبِج وهُلَابِج
Idiotic, foolish man. Great eater. هِلْبَاجَة
Intimate friend. A little. Garment. ✲ هَلْبَس وهَلْبَسِيس
To peel off, to scrape off, to bark. To scratch (the skin). ✲ هَلَت o هَلْتًا ه
To be peeled, barked. To glide away. إِنْهَلَت
Rabble, mob. ✲ هلث — هَلْثَاء وهِلْثَاءَة وهُلْثَة
Languor in man. هُلَات
To relate incredible, strange things. ✲ هَلَج i هَلْجًا
To conceal a. th. أَهْلَج ه
Nightmares, incoherent dreams. هَلْج
Thorny tree. هُلَج
Prune-shaped fruit. Myrobalan-tree. ✧ Ellipsis (*géo.*) P إِهْلِيلَج وإِهْلِيلِج وهَلِيلَج
Yellow myrobalan. — أَصْفَر
Black myrobalan from Cabul. — كَابُلِي
Large cooking-pot. ✲ هلجب — هِلْجَاب
To seize a. o. (fever). ✲ هَلَد
Patched garment. Coarse cloth. ✲ هِلْدِم
✧ To tattle, to talk nonsense. ✲ هَلَس i هَلْسًا
To emaciate a. o. (disease). — ه
✧ To pound a. th. fine. — ه
To be consumptive. To lose the mind. هُلِس
To become lean. هَلُس

To creep (worm, insect). هَمَّ i هَمًّا وَهَمِيمًا
To become old, infirm. هَمَّ o هُمُومَةً وَهَمَامَةً, وأَهَمَّ وانْهَمَّ
The woman hummed for lulling the boy. هَمْهَمَتِ المَرْأَةُ في رأس الصَبِيّ
To be anxious about, to search a. th. carefully. To louse (the head). تَهَمَّمَ ه
To be melted (grease). ✧ To be troubled, anxious. إِنْهَمَّ
To mind a. th. To take care of. إِهْتَمَّ ب
He took great pains for the management of his affair. — لَهُ بأَمْرِهِ
He concerned himself in the interests of his people. إِسْتَهَمَّ
To draw the attention, to excite the zeal of a. o. in behalf of. — ه ب
Intention, purpose. Care, anxiety, concern. Important matter. هَمّ ج هُمُوم
Ambitious, high-minded. رَجُلٌ هَمٌّ
This is the man thou standest in want of. هٰذَا رَجُلٌ هَمُّكَ وهِمَّتُكَ مِن رَجُلٍ
Decrepit old man. هِمّ ج أَهْمَام
Broken down (old man, woman). هِمَّة ج هِمَّات وهَمَائِم
Ambition. Mind, aspiration, aim, scheme. Zeal. هِمَّة ج هِمَم
Ambitious. رَجُلٌ بَعِيد الهِمَّة
Venomous reptile (as scorpions, serpents, worms, lice). ✧ *Pl.* Insects, vermin. هَامَّة ج هَوَامّ
More momentous. أَهَمّ
Care, concern. Solicitude. إِهْتِمَام ج اهْتِمَامَات
I do not care abont it. لَا هَمَامِ ولَا مَهَمَّةَ لِي
He came low-spirited. جَاء هِمَامِ
Hero, magnanimous man. Melting (hail). هُمَام ج هِمَام
Slanderer. Energetic, effective man. هَمَّام
Yielding much water (well, cloud). Swift-paced (she-camel). Reed shaken by the wind. هَمُوم
Thin rain. هَمِيم وهَمِيمَة ج هَمَائِم
Distressing busying. Important, matter. مُهِمّ م مُهِمَّة ج مُهِمَّات

Ruin, perdition. Death. Damnation. هَلْك وهُلْك وهَلَاك
Destruction. هَلَكَة وهَلَكَاء وتَهْلُكَة
Heavy loss; disaster. هَلَكَة هَلْكَاء
Unfruitful year. هَلَكَة ج هَلْك وهَلَكَات
Do it at any rate. إِفْعَل ذٰلِكَ إِمَّا هَلَكَتْ هُلْكُ أو هُلْكُهُ
Vile, lowly. هِلْكَة ج هِلَك
Barren, unwatered land. أَرْض هَلَكُون وهَلِكُون
Perishing, dead; perishable. ✧ Damned. هَالِك ج هَلْكَى وهُلَّك وهُلَّاك وهَوَالِك
Exhausted, jaded. ✧ هَلْكَان
Covetous soul. هَالِكَة
Mole. Dormouse. Broom-rape. هُالُوك
Beggars. Strayers (seeking fodder or water). هُلَّاك
Blacksmith. هَالِكِيّ
Loss. Cause of death, danger. تَهْلُكَة
The valley of perdition. *i. e.* the world; its vanities. وَادِي تُهُلِّكَ
Perilous place. Desert. مَهْلَكَة ومَهْلِكَة ومَهْلُكَة ج مَهَالِك
Parasite. مُهْتَلِك
Straying foragers. مُهْتَلِكُون
✧ Sinking-fund. إِسْتِهْلَاك
To call out a. o. ✱ هلم — أَهْلَمَ بفُلَانٍ
To carry a. th. away. إِهْتَلَمَ ب
هَلُمَّ م هَلُمِّي مث هَلُمَّا ج هَلُمُّوا وهَلْمُمْنَ
Come on, come to me.
Bring it here, bring the thing. — الشَّيْءَ
And so forth; and so on. *Et cetera.* هَلُمَّ جَرًّا
Veal served with the skin. Kind of animal jelly. هُلَام
Adhesive, sticky. هَلِيم
Flaccid, soft. هِلَّم م هِلَّمَة
Asparagus. ✧ هَلْيُون
They, them, their. (*Pl. of* هُوَ) ✱ هُم
To intend, to purpose a. th. To meditate, to determine upon a. th. To be anxious about. ✱ هَمَّ o هَمًّا ب
To threaten to fall (wall). هَمَّ بالسُّقُوط
To busy (the mind). To disquiet; to cause anxiety to a. o. (affair). هَمَّ o هَمًّا ومَهَمَّةً, وأَهَمَّ ه
To waste (the body: disease). To melt (grease). To draw (milk). هَمَّ ه

To be worn out in the folds (cloth). هَمَدَ o هَمْدًا وهُمُودًا
To extinguish (the fire). To allay; to soothe (grief). هَمَّدَ وأَهْمَدَ هِ
To abate (wind). To remain silent in a trial. أَهْمَدَ
To stay in (a place). — بِ
He hurried the walk. — فِي السَّيْرِ
He rushed on food. — فِي الطَّعَامِ
To soothe (anger: gift). — هِ
Apoplexy. Trance. هَمْدَةٌ
Going out (fire). Worn out, ragged. Ripe, yellow date. Barren land. هَامِدٌ
Sheep-tax registered on the rolls. هَمِيدٌ
Hamadan, tribe in Yemen. هَمْدَانُ
Swift camel or she-camel. Exertion, quickness. Intensity of rain, of heat. ✡ همذ — هَمَاذِيُّ
Hamazan, town in Arabia. هَمَذَانُ
Relating to Hamazan. Loquacious. هَمَذَانِيٌّ
To be poured forth (water, tears). ✧ To snort, to neigh (horse). To snarl (wild beast). ✡ هَمَرَ o i هَمْرًا
To pour forth (water). To draw forth (milk) to the last drop. To multiply (words). To pull down (a building). — هِ
To give to a. o. a part of. — لِفُلَانٍ مِنْ
To stamp the ground (horse). — واهْتَمَرَ هِ
To take, to bring a. th. away. هَامَرَ ة
To charm, to bewitch a. o. أَهْمَرَ ة
To run vehemently (horse). أَهْتَمَرَ
To be poured (water). To be pulled down (building). To have its leaves beaten down (tree). إِنْهَمَرَ
✧ Neighing of a horse. هَمْرٌ
Fat and bulky. Heaped up (sand). هَمُورٌ
Shower. Angry speech. Shell used as an amulet. هَمْرَةٌ
Boisterous woman. هَمَرَى
Cloud pouring down showers. هَامِرٌ وهَمَّارٌ
Babbler. هَمَّارٌ ومِهْمَرٌ ومِهْمَارٌ ويَهْمُورٌ
To give confused news. To speak confusedly. To utter idle words. ✡ هَمْرَجَ

✧ War-ammunitions, stores, materials. مُهِمَّاتٌ
Important duties. مَهَامٌّ
Over-anxious; grieved. مَهْمُومٌ
To mutter, to grumble (man). To snarl (beast). To hum for lulling a child. ✡ هَمْهَمَ وتَهَمْهَمَ
Hoarse voice. Snort, snarl of a beast. هَمْهَمَةٌ ج هَمَاهِمُ
Dauntless chief. Lion. Wild crow. هَمْهَامٌ
Nothing is left. هَمْهَامِ
Personal pronoun and affix of the possessive pronoun (in the dual). They two, both. Them two. Their two. ◻ They, them (*for the plural*). ✡ هُمَا
To rend, to wear out (a garment). ✡ هَمَأَ a هَمْأً, وأَهْمَأَ هِ
To be rent (garment). To become ragged, worn out. تَهَمَّأَ وانْهَمَأَ
Threadbare, ragged garment. هِمْءٌ ج أَهْمَاءٌ
To be overspread with grease (dish). ✡ هَمَتَ o
He laughed and spoke in a low tone. هَمَتَ الْكَلَامَ والضَّحِكَ
To be hungry. ✡ هَمِجَ a هَمَجًا
To patch up (an affair). هَمَجَ o هَمْجًا هِ
To quench thirst in one draught (camel). — مِنَ الْمَاءِ
To run at full speed (horse). أَهْمَجَ
To conceal a. th. — هِ
To be exhausted by heat (man). To be pale, wan (face). إِهْتَمَجَ
Gnats, grubs. Foolish people. Rabble, ruffians. Scarce food. Hunger. Lean ewes. Mismanagement. هَمَجٌ ج أَهْمَاجٌ (هَمَجَةٌ *un*)
Ruffian, man of a low class. هَمَجِيٌّ
Whitout chief (army). Without shepherd (flock). هَامِجٌ
Violent hunger. Scared by flies (gazelle). هَمَجٌ هَامِجٌ
Young, slender-bodied gazelle. هَمِيجٌ
To die away (fire). To cool (anger); to become still (wind). To die, to perish. To be barren (ground). ✡ هَمَدَ o هُمُودًا

Swiftness. State of confusion. هَمْرَجة
Trifle.
✻ هَمْرَجل Swift, generous (horse). Bulky (camel).
✻ همرش – تَهَمْرَش To riot, to be in confusion (people).
هَمْرَشَة Riot, disturbance.
هَمْرَش Yielding much milk (she-camel). Old woman.
✻ هَمَز o i هَمْزًا ة وهـ To pinch; to repel a. o. To nip (a mouse : cat). To spur (a horse). To backbite, to find fault with. To suggest evil to a. o. (Satan). To bite a. o. To break a. th. To mark, to pronounce (a vowel) with a hamza.
– بِهِ الأرض He threw him on the ground.
✧ هَمَّز على To threaten, to frighten a. o.
إِنْهَمَز To be marked with hamza (letter).
هَمْز الشَّيْطان Madness; diabolical possession.
هَمْزَة ج هَمَزَات Hamza. ء
– الوَصْل Silent hamza marked thus (ٱ).
– القَطْع Hamza pronounced separately.
هَمَزَات الشَّيْطان Evil suggestions of Satan.
هَمَزَى Violent (wind). Far-shooting (bow).
هَامِز وهَمَّاز Slanderer.
هُمَزَة Backbiter.
رَجُل هَمِيز الفُؤَاد Sagacious, active man.
مِهْمَزَة Whip. Goad for asses.
مِهْمَز ج مَهَامِز, ومِهْمَاز ج مَهَامِيز Stick. Spur, iron-shod staff.
مَهْمُوز Spurred, nipped. Marked with hamza. (*Gram.*) having a hamza in its radical (verb).
✻ هَمَس i هَمْسًا To walk day and night unremittingly.
– هـ To chew, to mumble a. th. To press (grapes). To break a. th. To mumble, to utter inaudible (words).
– بِالقَدَم To tread the ground softly.
– إلى فُلَان بِحَدِيثِهِ He whispered news to him.
– في قَلْبِهِ بِوَسْوَسَتِهِ He suggested evil to him (devil).
✧ هَمَّس ة To thrash a. o.
هَامَس ة To speak inaudibly.
تَهَامَسَا To converse secretly with.
هَمْس Faint sound, voice; soft tread of camels.
يَتَكَلَّم هَمْسًا He speaks with a faint voice.
هَمَّاس وهَمُوس Walking softly. Crushing his prey (lion).
هَمِيس Faint sound of a camel's steps.
مَهْمُوس Uttered inaudibly. Softly articulated (word).
أَلْحُرُوف المَهْمُوسَة *The soft letters comprised in the* 3 *following words* حَثَّهُ شَخْصٌ فَسَكَتَ
✻ هَمَيْسَم Insuperable, strong (man). Tall.
✻ هَمَش o هَمْشًا هـ To collect, to pick up (things).
– ة To bite a. o.
– i وهَمِش a هَمَشًا To speak much.
هَامَش ة To urge, to excite a. o.
تَهَمَّش To give little water (spring).
تَهَامَش واهْتَمَش To be intermingled (crowd).
إِهْتَمَش To creep (reptile). To go quickly. To be intermingled.
هَمْشَة Confusion, medley.
✧ هَامِش Margin of a book.
هَمَشَى Babbler (woman).
✻ هَمَط i هَمْطًا هـ To lay hands upon a. th.
– وتَهَمَّط واهْتَمَط هـ To take a. th. forcibly.
هَمَط واهْتَمَط ة To wrong a. o.
إِهْتَمَط هـ To impair the reputation of
هَمَّاط Wrong-doer.
✻ هَمَع o a هَمْعًا وهُمُوعًا وهَمَعَانًا وتَهْمَاعًا To shed tears.
– على To fall upon (a tree : dew).
تَهَمَّع To sham weeping.
أَهْتُوع To be altered (colour).
هَمِع Pouring down rain (cloud).
هَامِعَة ج هَوَامِع Flowing (tears).
هَمُوع Liquid, fluid.
هَيْمَع وهَمَيْمَع Quick death.
✻ هَمَغ a هَمْغًا هـ To break (the skull).

Thin rain. هَمِيَة
Pasturing at random (camels). هَامِيَة ج هَوَامٍ
Purse of a girdle, waist-band, sash. P هِمْيَان ج هَمَايِين
✧ Royal, imperial. P هُمَايُون وهُمَايُونِيّ
To weep, to moan. ✱ هَنَّ i هَنًّا وهَنِينًا
To sigh after a. th. — إلى
To create (a camel) strong (God). أَهَنَّ ه
Fat under the pupil of the eye. Remainder of marrow. Strength of a camel. هَانَّة وهُنَانَة
Weeping woman, female mourner. هَنَّانَة
Strong مَهْنُون
Personal and possessive pronoun of the 3d person of the plural feminine. They, them. Their, theirs. ✱ هُنَّ
Pronoun of the 3d person of the plural (m. and f.) They, them. ✧ هِنَّهْ
To be beneficial, pleasant to a. o. (food). ✱ هَنَأَ a i o هَنْأً وهِنْأً وهَنَاءً ه ول
Health made it pleasant to me. هَنَأَتْنِيهِ ٱلْعَافِيَةُ
May it give thee joy! لِيَهْنِئْكَ
To say to a. o.: May it give thee joy! هَنَأَ a هَنْأً, وهَنَّأَ ه ب
To smear (a camel) with tar. — o i a هَنَأَ ه
To feed, to maintain, to help a. o — o i هَنَأَ ه
To find insufficient herbage (cattle). هَنِئَ a هَنَأً وهَنْأً
To rejoice at. هَنِئَ ب
To enjoy (food). — ه
هَنِئَ a هَنَأً وهَنْأً, وهَنُؤَ o هَنَاءَةً وهَنَاءَةً وهَنَأً
To be pleasant (thing). To happen without trouble (affair). To be wholesome, beneficial (food).
To greet, to congratulate a. o. on. هَنَّأَ تَهْنِيئًا وتَهْنِئَةً ه ب
To give a. th. to a. o. أَهْنَأَ ه
To be benefited by (food). To pride o.'s self in. To rejoice at. تَهَنَّأَ تَهَنُّؤًا ب
To be glad, happy. تَهَنَّأَ
To ask a. o. for help, for a gift. To grant a. th. to a. o. إِسْتَهْنَأَ ه
Smearing with tar. Part of the night. Gift. هِنْء

✱ هَوْق Luxuriant herbage. Dry herbage.
هَوَق Crack-brained.
✱ هُمَقِع وهُمَّقِع Stupid, foolish.
✱ هَمَكَ o هَمْكًا ه في To urge a. o. in (an affair).
تَهَمَّكَ وانْهَمَكَ في To exert o.'s self perseveringly. To persist obstinately in.
إِهْمَاكَ To be angry.
✱ هَمَلَ o i هَمْلًا وهَمَلَانًا وهُمُولًا, وانْهَمَلَ
To bathe in tears (eye). To flow abundantly (tears). To overflow (water).
هَمَّلَ To give continuous rain (sky).
— i هَمْلًا To pasture freely day and night (camels).
أَهْمَلَ و✧ هَمَّلَ ه To forsake, to leave off a. th. To overlook, to neglect.
أَهْمَلَ ه To let (a letter) without dots.
✧ تَهَامَلَ To be neglectful of.
هِمْل Coarse garment of the Arabs. Ragged hair-tent.
هَمَل Flocks pasturing freely day and night. Water flowing freely.
تَرَكَهَا هَمَلًا He set them free, day and night.
هَامِل ج هَوَامِل وهَمُولَة وهَامِلَة وهَمَل وهُمَّل
وهُمَّال وهَمَلَى Set free day and night (camel).
هُمَّال Soft, flaccid. Waste land.
هَمَالِيل Remainder of fodder. Weak birds. Threadbare garment.
✧ تَهَامُل Sloth. Neglect.
مُهْمَل Obsolete, disused (word). Without diacritical points (letter).
— و✧ مَهْمُول Neglected. Overlooked.
✱ هَمْلَج هَمْلَجَة To walk at a gentle pace (hackney).
هِمْلَاج ج هَمَالِيج Beast walking at a gentle pace. Lean (sheep).
✱ همن — هَمَّنَ ه To put a. th. in a purse.
هَيْمَن To say Amen.
— على To oversee, to watch over. To expand the wings over (her chickens: hen).
المُهَيْمِن والمُهَيْمِن The Watcher (God).
✱ هَمَا o هَمْوًا وهَمَى i هَمْيًا وهَمَيَانًا To flow (water, tears). To pasture here and there (cattle). To shed tears (eye).

هَنَاء Congratulation. ✧ Enjoyment, good health.
هِنَاء Tar, liquid pitch.
هَنِيءٌ م هَنِيئَة Wholesome, pleasant (food). Easy (affair).
هَنِيئًا لَكَ *Good wish*. Mayest thou enjoy it!
هَنِيئًا مَرِيئًا With enjoyment and health; to your health!
هَانِئ Servant.
هُنَيْئَة A little. Short space of time.
تَهْنِئَة Greeting, congratulation.
مَهْنَأ Anything succeeding without trouble.
مَهْنُوء Smeared with tar.
مُهَنَّأ Greeted.
✱ هنب — هَنْبَاء وهَنْبَى Inconsiderate, insane (woman).
مِهْنَب Exceedingly foolish.
✱ هَنْبَت وهَنْتَب To act slowly; to be remiss.
✱ هَنْبَثَة ج هَنَابِث Momentous, arduous affair. *Pl.* Confused news, affairs. Calamities.
✱ هَنْبَذَة ج هَنَابِذ Difficult affair.
✱ هِنْبِر وهِنَّبْر وأُم هِنَّبْر The hyena.
✱ هَنْبَس وتَهَنْبَس To be in quest of news.
✱ هَنْبَص To titter.
هِنْبِص Despised, weak.
✱ هَنْبَغ To suffer from hunger.
هُنْبُغ وهِنْبَاغ وهُنْبُوغ Vehement (hunger).
✱ هَنْبَل هَنْبَلَة To limp (wild beast).
✱ هنج — تَهَنَّج To move about (fœtus).
✱ هند — هَنَّد ه To blandish, to flirt with a. o. (woman). To abuse a. o.
— ه To sharpen (a sword).
— في To be unable to. To be slow in.
هِنْد India. The Indians.
— ج هِنْدَات وهُنُود Woman's name.
— ج أَهْنُد وأَهْنَاد وهُنُود Herd of 100 to 200 camels.
هِنْدِيّ ج هُنُود Indian, Hindu. Aloes-wood.
✧ سُنْبُلَة هِنْدِيَّة Indian spikenard.
سَيْف هُنْدُوَانِيّ Indian sword.
هُنَيْدَة *Dimin. of* هند Flock of 100 heads. Century.
عَاش ٱلْهُنَيْدَة He lived 100 years.
مُهَنَّد Made of Indian iron (sword).
هِنْدَب وهِنْدِبَى وهِنْدِبَاء Wild or garden-succory, endive.
✧ هِنْدِبَاء بَرِّيّ Dandelion (*plant*).
P هِنْدَاز Measure. Limit.
هِنْدَازَة ٱلْخَيَّاط Standard-cubit (25 inches).
✱ هَنْدَس ه To trace (a road); to sketch (a building).
هَنْدَسَة Measure. Geometry. Architecture.
هِنْدِس Dauntless. Skilful.
هَنْدَسِيّ Geometrical.
مُهَنْدِس Geometrician. Architect. Engineer.
✱ هَنْدَم To arrange, to dispose a. th. symmetrically. To shape, to pare (wood).
P هِنْدَام Symmetry, harmony of parts; modesty.
مُهَنْدَم Symmetrical.
✱ هنر — هَنَرَة Hollow of the ear.
✱ هَنَم a هَنْمًا ه To fold, to bend a. th.
— ه To brand (a camel) on the neck.
— ل To submit to.
هَنِم a هَنَمًا To have a crooked and prominent neck (camel).
إِسْتَهْنَم To be unable to answer.
هَنَم Crookedness of a camel's neck.
هَنْعَة Brand on a camel's neck. Three stars of *Gemini*. Two stars of *Orio*. Sixth mansion of the moon.
هَانِع ج هُنَّع Submissive.
أَهْنَع م هَنْعَاء ج هُنْع Having a contorted neck.
هَنْعَاء Low and compact (hill).
✱ هنف — هَنَّف وأَهْنَف To hasten, to hurry on.
هَانَفَتْ مُهَانَفَةً وهِنَافًا, وأَهْنَفَتْ وتَهَانَفَتْ To sneer (woman).
T هَانِم (for خَانِم) ✧ Turkish lady. Title in addressing her.
✱ هَنْقَب وهِنْقَب Short.
✱ هَيْنَم ه To conceal, to keep a. th. secret.
هَيْنَمَة Low voice; faint noise.
هَيْنُوم Inunderstood (word).

Tall and fickle (man). Courageous. أَهْوَجُ م هَوْجَاء ج هُوجٌ
Swift (she-camel). Violent (wind). هَوْجَاء ج هُوجٌ
To repent, to rteurn to good. ✡ هَادَ o هَوْدًا, وتَهَوَّدَ
To be or become a Jew. — وتَهَوَّدَ
To sing, to speak gently. هَوَّدَ تَهْوِيدًا وتَهْوَادًا
He spoke in a low tone. — وتَهَوَّدَ فِي مَنْطِقِهِ
To walk slowly. To be still, at rest. To sleep. To act gently. To fall in (night). ✧ To descend a valley. هَوَّدَ
To intoxicate a. o. (wine). To turn a. o. to Judaism. — ه
To return to. To make peace with. To feel sympathy towards. هَاوَدَ ه وه
✧ He was compliant in the sale. — فِي ٱلْبَيْعِ
To be allied by sacred bonds, (marriage or patronage). To become a Jew. تَهَوَّدَ
To use gentle speech. — فِي ٱلْمَنْطِقِ
He abated the price. ✧ تَهَاوَدَ فِي ٱلثَّمَنِ
Man's name. هُودٌ
Jews. — ويَهُودُ
Hump of a camel. هَوْدَةٌ ج هَوَدٌ
Forbearance. gentleness. Peace, favour; sacred bond. هَوَادَةٌ
Sweet voice. تَهْوِيدٌ وتَهْوَادٌ
Repenting, coming back to truth. هَائِدٌ ج هُودٌ
Jew. يَهُودِيٌّ
Jewess. Judœa. Judaism. يَهُودِيَّةٌ
Asphaltum. قَفْرُ ٱلْيَهُودِ
Sonchus, sow-thistle. ٱلْبَقْلَةُ ٱلْيَهُودِيَّةُ
Lapis Judaicus, Jew's stone. حَجَرٌ يَهُودِيٌّ
Sand-grouse. ✡ هوذ — هَاذَةٌ ج هَاذٌ
Kind of partridge. هُوذَةٌ ج هُوَذٌ
Behold! Here is. (*for* هُوَ *and* ذَا) ✡ هُوَذَا
To fall to pieces, to crumble down (building). ✡ هَارَ o هَوْرًا وهُؤُورًا
To crush down (people). To deceive a. o. — هَوْرًا ه
To avert a. o. from. — ه عَنْ
To incite a. o. to. — ه عَلَى
To conjecture a. th. — ه
To suspect a. o. of. — ه ب
To overthrow; to prostrate a. o. To pull down (a building). هَارَ وهَوَّرَ ه وه

Time. ✡ هنو — هِنْو
A thing. هَنٌ وهُنٌ مث هَنَانِ وهَنَوَانِ ج هَنُونَ
A little thing, somewhat. هَنَةٌ ج هَنَوَاتٌ وهَنَاتٌ
That belongs to thee. هٰذَا هَنُكَ
To say: come here, thou, man, woman! يَا هَنُ أَقْبِلْ ويَا هَنَةُ أَقْبِلِي
He has some defects. بِهِ هَنَاتٌ
A little, a while; somewhat هُنَيَّةٌ وهُنَيْهَةٌ
Stay a while. أُمْكُثْ هُنَيْهَةً
Disaster, misfortune. هَنَاةٌ ج هَنَوَاتٌ
Here, from here. ✡ هُنَا وهٰهُنَا
There, thither. هُنَاكَ وهُنَالِكَ
Interj. No doubt. Surely. Woe! ✡ هِهِ
To stammer, to be impeded in speech. ✡ هَهَّ a هَهًّا وهَهَّةً
Pronoun of the 3[d] *person of the singular masculine.* He. ✡ هُوَ مث هُمَا
It is I; it is he. أَنَا هُوَ, هُوَ هُوَ
Foolish; faint-hearted. ✡ هَوْهَاءٌ وهُوهَاءٌ وهَوْهَاءَةٌ
To rejoice in. ✡ هَاءَ o هَوْءًا ب
To think well or ill of. — ه بِخَيْرٍ او بِشَرٍّ او بِهِ خَيْرًا او شَرًّا
He aspired to great things. هَاءَ بِنَفْسِهِ إِلَى ٱلْمَعَالِي
Here I am. هَاءَ وهَاءَنَذَا
Take thou, ye. Here thou art, here you are. هَاءَ وهَاءِ (*sing.*) هَاؤُمَا (*dual.*) هَاؤُمْ وهَاؤُنَّ (*plur.*)
Take thou, ye. هَاكَ هَاكِ هَاكُمْ هَاكُنَّ هَاكُمَا
Here, from here. هَا هُنَا
No, by God! لَا هَاءَ ٱللّٰهِ
Here is a gold coin. هَاءَ دِينَارًا
Intention, scheme, aim. Penetrating mind. هَوْءٌ
It occurred to my mind. وَقَعَ فِي هَوْئِي وفِي هُوئِي
Ambitious, brooding high designs. بَعِيدُ ٱلْهَوْءِ
Garrulous, foolish. Distance, remoteness. Heat of fire. ✡ هَوْبٌ
To go down a ravine. ✡ هوت — هَوَّتَ
To call after a. o. — ب
Deep valley, ravine. ✧ Precipice. Abyss, chasm. هُوتَةٌ وهُوَتَةٌ ج هُوَتٌ
Thirst. ✡ هُوتَةٌ
To be tall and foolish. ✡ هَوِجَ a هَوَجًا

✧ To hurl down a. o. or a. th. ◻ To annoy a. o.

To crumble down (building). تَهَوَّر وتَهَيَّر وانهار

To rush heedlessly into (an affair). To be nearly elapsed (night, winter). تَهَوَّر

To attack a. o. (disease). — ه

To collapse (sand-hill). إِنهار

To perish. إِهْتَوَر

Weak, feeble. Perishable. هَارٌ وهارٍ وهَيَّار

Lake. Flock of sheep. هَــوْر ج أَهْوَار

Peril, danger. هَوْرَة ج هَوْرَات

Suspicion. هُورَة

Loss, ruin. هَوَارَة

Ruined (building). هَائِر وهَائِر

Rash, heedless. هَيِّر

Volunteer, irregular (soldier). ✧ هَوَّارِي ج هَوَّارَة

Rashness, boldness. ✧ Tumble. تَهَوُّر

Sinking sand. Depressed land. Barren plain. تَيْهُور

To die. ✱ هوز — هَوْز

Creatures. Men. هُوز

To smash, to break a. th. To eat a. th. voraciously. ✱ هاس o هَوْسًا ه

He prowled about by night. — بِٱللَّيْل

He roved around the thing. — حَوْل ٱلشَّيْء

To drive (cattle) along. — ه

To do havoc among (sheep: wolf). — فِي

To be light-headed, crack-brained. هوِس a هَوَسًا

To render a. o. crack-brained, giddy (disease). هَوَّس ه

To become foolish. ✧ To desire earnestly. To rejoice. تَهَوَّس

Light-headedness, giddiness, insanity. ◻ Dock for ships. ✧ Violent desire, passion. Hope. هَوَس

Intimate thought. ✧ Toasted wheat. ◻ Canal-lock. هَوِيس

The lion. الهَوَّاس والهَوَّاسَة

Voracious. All-destroying. أَهْوَس م هَوْسَى

Time consumes every thing. الزَّمَان أَهْوَس

Crack-brained. Extravagant. ✧ Over-excited. مُهَوَّس

To make a disturbance, to be excited (crowd). To take fright, to run away (horse). ✧ To bark (dog). ✱ هَاش o هَوْشًا

To collect (wealth) unlawfully. — وهَوَّش

To fret, to be restless. هَوِش a هَوَشًا

To mix up. To confound (things). هَوَّش ه

To throw disorder, dissension amongst. — ه وبَيْن

✧ To set dogs against a. o. — ه

To mix o.'s self among (a (crowd) ✧ To make mischief. هَاوَش ه

To be mingled, confused. تَهَوَّش وتَهَاوَش

To assemble against. تَهَوَّش على

Multitude of men, beasts. هَوْش

Confusion. Commotion, disturbance. هَوْشَة ج هَوْشَات وهَوَشَات

Mesentery, membrane in the abdomen. ◻ هُوشَة وهُشَة

Rabble; confused company. هَوِيشَة

Multitude of men, camels mixed together. هُوَاشَات

Wealth unjustly acquired. — وتَهَاوِش ومَهَاوِش

To be fretful, restless. ✱ هَاعَ a هَوَعًا

They were ready to attack one another. — بَعْضُهُم إِلى بَعْض

To vomit. هَاعَ a o هَوْعًا

To make a. o. to vomit. هَوَّع ه مَا أَكَل

To excite vomiting. تَهَوَّع القَيْء

Vomiting. هَوْع وهُوَاع وهَيْعُوعَة

Eagerness. هَوْع

Enmity. — وهُوع

Greedy. هَاعٌ وهَاعٍ

Herald, crier in a battle. مِهْوَع ومِهْوَاع

Cold wind; hot wind. ✱ هَوْف

To be foolish. ✱ هَوِك a هَوَكًا

To be stupefied, astounded. To be involved recklessly in a scrape. تَهَوَّك وانهاك

Stroke of madness. هَوْك

Crack-brained. هَوِك ويَهْكُوك

Ditch, hole in the ground. هُوكَة

Stupefied, amazed. هَوَّاك ومُتَهَوِّك

To awe, to strike a. o. with fear. ✱ هَال o هَوْلًا, وهَوَّل ه

To see frightful dreams (drunkard). هِيلَ

To sprinkle a sacred fire with salt. To deck herself (woman). هَوَّل

To frighten, to threaten a. o. with (a stick). — عَلَيْهِ ب

To deform, to render a. o. hideous. — ة وهـ

To be awful. تَهَوَّل

To assume the appearance of a wild beast for rendering (a she-camel) submissive. — ل

To be awed, terror-stricken. إِهتال

Poplar (tree). Cardamom (Indian spice). هال

Awe, dread. Swell of the sea. هَوْل ج أَهْوال وهُؤُول

Awful thing. — وهِيلَة

Halo of the sun or moon. هالَة ج هالات

Sacred fire sprinkled with salt for taking oaths. هُولَة

Cause of dread. Scarecrow. تَهْوِيل

Mixture of colours; motley. Variegated garment. — ج تَهاوِيل

Awful, dreadful. هائِل م هائِلَة

Awe, dread. هَوْل هائِل ومَهُول

More terrible, more awful. أَهْوَل

Dreadful, terrific (place). مَهال ومَهُول ومَهِيل

Administering oaths at a sacred fire. مُهَوِّل

To nod the head in sleep. To sleep. ☆ هوم — هَوَّم وتَهَوَّم

Depressed tracts of land. هَوم

Medicinal plant, kind of jasmine used against calculus. — أَلمَجُوس

Head. Top of the head. Corpse. Headman, chief of a tribe. Owl. هامَة ج هامات وهام

Extensive plain. هَوْمَة وهَوْماة

The lion. الهَوَّام

Big-headed. أَهْوَم

To become easy to a. o. (affair). ☆ هان o هَوْنًا على

To become weak, contemptible, base. هان o هُونًا وهَوَانًا ومَهانَةً

To become quiet, gentle. — o هَوْنًا

To facilitate a. th. to a. o. هَوَّن هـ على

To despise, to contemn a. th. — هـ

Do not grieve for it; take patience. هوِّن عَلَيْكَ

He has self-indulgence. هاوَن نَفْسَهُ

To despise a. o. or a. th. أَهَان ة وهـ

To scorn at. تَهاوَن واسْتَهان ب

To neglect; to take no account of. تَهاوَن هـ

To be outraged, reviled. ✧ إِنهان

To be broad (desert). إِهْوَأَنَّ

Tranquillity, quiet. Modesty, staidness, gentleness. هَوْن

He walks gently. يَمْشِي هَوْنًا

Here, there. ✧ هَوْن وهَوْنِيك

Abjection, lowliness. هُون وهُوَان ومَهانَة

Creature. هُون

I do not know what sort of man he is. مَا أَدْرِي أَيُّ ٱلْهُونِ هُوَ

Walking gently (woman). هَوْنَة وهُونَة

Easiness, quiet. هِينَة

Do walk gently, at thy ease. إِمْشِ على هَوْنِكَ وعلى هِينَتِكَ

Staidness, slowness, forbearance. هُوَيْنًا

Scorn, contempt. ✧ Offence, injury. إهانَة ج إهانات

Light. Easy to be done or borne. Staid, quiet. هَيْن ج هَيْنُون, هَيِّن ج أَهْوِناء وهَيِّنُون

Mortar, vessel for pounding. P هاوَن وهاوُن وهاوُون ج هَوَاوِين

Easy, light. Easier, lighter. أَهْوَن م هَوْناء

Neglect. Sloth. تَهاوُن

Contemned. ✧ Offended. مُهان

Remote place; depressed land. مُهْوَئِنّ ومُهْوَأَنّ

To be wide (wound). ☆ هَوَى i هُوِيًّا
To be hurled down. To die (man). To dart on a prey (falcon). To blow (wind).

To advance quickly with its rider (beast). — بِرَاكِبِها

To be raised and stretched out towards a. th. (hand). — ل

To advance quickly in. — في

To rise (star). To tingle (ear). — هُوِيًّا

To go down. To set (star). To be bereft of her children (mother). — هُوِيًّا وهَوَيانًا

To go up, to ascend (a hill). هَوَى هُوِيًّا ه
To love, to desire a. o. or a. th. هَوِيَ a هَوًى ه وه
✧ To blow (wind). هَوَّى تَهْوِيَةً
— To expose a. th. to the wind, to air; to aerate. ه
To walk at a quick pace. هَاوَى مُهَاوَاةً وهِوَاءً
— To be fond of. To blandish a. o. ه
To fall down from a high place. أَهْوَى وانْهَوَى
To be stretched forth towards a. th. (hand). أَهْوَى ل
— He stretched forth his hand towards it. إِلَيْهِ بِيَدِهِ
— He rushed upon him with the sword. لَهُ بِٱلسَّيْفِ
To be hurled down into (an abyss) one upon another. تَهَاوَى فِي
To captivate, to seduce a. o. إِسْتَهْوَى ه
✧ To catch cold. إِسْتَهْوَى
Inclination, passion, desire. Object of love. Love, fondness. هَوًى ج أَهْوَاء
Sybarites. أَهْلُ ٱلأَهْوَاءِ
Air; asmosphere. Empty space. Cowardly. ✧ Weather, climate. Tune. Wind. هَوَاء ج أَهْوِيَة
Cholera. الهَوَاء الأَصْفَر
Atmospheric. هَوَائِيّ
He has treated him now with kindness and then with harshness. عَامَلَهُ بِٱلْهِوَاءِ وٱللِّوَاءِ
Abyss, deep valley. هُوَّة وهُوَّاة
Deep valley. Abyss, gulf. Atmosphere. أُهْوِيَّة
He likes it better than. It is dearer to him than. هٰذَا أَهْوَى إِلَيْهِ مِن
Enamoured. هَوٍ م هَوِيَة
Falling. Rising or setting (star). هَاوٍ م هَاوِيَة
Abyss, depth. Atmosphere. Bereft of her children (mother). هَاوِيَة
The abyss of Hell. أَلْهَاوِيَة
Ascension of a star. Tingling in the ear. هَوِيّ
— Part of the night. وهُوِيّ وتَهْوَاء مِن ٱللَّيْل
Very deep well. هَوِيَّة ج هَوَايَا
Fan. ✧ هَوَّايَة

Chasm, ravine. Atmosphere. مَهْوًى ومَهْوَاة ج مَهَاوٍ
✡ *Feminine pronoun of the third person*. She. هِيَ مث هُمَا ج هُنَّ
✡ To be fine-shaped (man). هَاءَ i a وهَيُؤَ o هَيَاءَةً وهَيَاءَةً
— To desire, to long for. a هِيَاءَةً إِلَى
— To prepare, to get ready for. a i هِيَاءَةً ل
To prepare, to arrange a. th. هَيَّأَ تَهْيِئَةً وتَهْيِيئًا ه
To agree with a. o. upon. هَايَأَ مُهَايَأَةً, وهَايَا مُهَايَاةً ه في
To be prepared, disposed to. To be about to. تَهَيَّأَ ل
The thing has become attainable to him. تَهَيَّأَ لِفُلَان ٱلشَّيْءُ
They agreed together upon. تَهَايَأُوا على
Cry for calling camels to water. هِيْءْ وهِيءِ
Interj. expressive of wonder or regret. Oh! O. يَا هَيْءَ
Shape, appearance. Goodly aspect. Mien, countenance, gait, garb. هَيْئَة وهِيئَة ج هَيْئَات وهَيَآت
Astronomy. عِلْم الهَيْئَة
Good-looking. هَيِّئٌ وهَيِيء
Preparation, apparatus. تَهْيِئَة
Thing agreed upon. مُهَايَأَة ومُهَايَاة
✡ *Interj*. Eh. هَيَا
Unknown man whose father is unknown. هَيُّ بْنُ بَيّ وهَيَّانُ بْنُ بَيَّانَ
Come on. Let us go. هَيًّا هَيًّا
✡ هَابَ a هَيْبًا وهَيْبَةً ومَهَابَةً, وتَهَيَّبَ واهْتَابَ ه
To dread; to regard a. o. with awe, caution.
Imperative. Do, fear. هَبْ
To make a. th. to be feared by. هَيَّبَ ه إِلَى
To call out, to urge (camels) by the cry هَبِي, هَبْ, هَابْ. أَهَابَ ب
— To incite a. o. to. بِفُلَان إِلَى
To awe, to fear, to reverence a. o. تَهَيَّبَ ه
Snake. Chiding of camels. هَاب
Awe, reverential fear. ✧ Modesty, dignity. Countenance, bearing. هَيْبَة
✧ Shameless; without feeling. قَلِيل الهَيْبَة

Male goat. Shepherd. هَيْبَان وَهَيَبَان
Dust, earth.

هَيِّبَان وَهَيْبَان وَهَائِب وَهَيِّب وَهَيُوب وَهَيُوبَة وَهَيَّاب وَهَيَّابَة Very timid. Very respectful.

Dreadful. Venerable, awing. هَيُوب وَمَهِيب وَمَهُوب

More respected, dreaded. أَهْيَب

Fear. Awe, respect. مَهَابَة

Dangerous, dreadful (place). مَهَاب وَمَهُوب

Cause of fear. مَهْيَبَة

☆ هَاتِ م هَاتِي مث هَاتِيَا ج هَاتُوا وَهَاتِينَ Give, bring.

هَيْتَ وَهِيتَ لَكَ وَلَكُمَا وَلَكُم وَلَكُنَّ Come here, come on, thou, ye!

To call a. o. هَيَّتَ بِ

Clamorous. هَيَّات

☆ هَاتَ i هَيْتًا To be excited, confused (crowd).

— وَهَيْتَانًا لِ To give little to a. o.

— مِن المَال He obtained a sufficiency.

— فِي , وَاسْتَهَاتَ ه To do havoc among (cattle).

هَايَتَ ه To vie with a. o. in wealth, in number of followers.

تَهَيَّتَ ه لِ To give a. th. to a. o.

إِسْتَهَاتَ ه To ask much. To deem (a gift) considerable.

— المَال To squander the property of.

هَيْتَة Party of men.

☆ هَاجَ i هَيْجًا وَهَيَجَانًا وَهِيَاجًا To be raised (dust). To be swollen (sea). To be inflamed (eye). To be stirred (blood). To be roused (anger). To be disturbed, disquieted (man). To dash, to rush forth. To wither (plant). To have dried plants (land). To be thirsty (camel).

— ه وب وَهَيَّجَ ه To raise (the dust).

هَيَّجَ ه بَيْنَ To stir (war). To excite (evil, discord) between.

هَايَجَ مُهَايَجَة وَهِيَاجًا ه To raise a contest; to engage in (a fight) with.

يَوْم الهِيَاج Day of battle.

أَهَاجَ إِهَاجَة ه To blast (the plants: wind).

أَهْيَجَ إِهْيَاجًا ه To find (a land) covered with withered plants.

تَهَيَّجَ وَاهْتَاجَ To be raised (dust). To be excited (man).

تَهَايَجَ To rush upon, to fight with o. a.

هَيْج Agitation, discord, disturbance. Civil war. Excitement of blood. Fieriness. Yellowness of a plant.

يَوْمٌ هَيْجٌ Cloudy, rainy, windy day.

هِيجِ وَهجِ *Cry for rousing camels.*

هَيَجَان Bustle, commotion. Fieriness.

✧ مَجْنُون هَيَجَانِي Dangerous madman.

هَاجَة ج هَاجَات Female frog. Ostrich.

هَيْجَاء وَهَيْجَى Battle, conflict, war.

هَائِج Outburst of anger.

هَاجَ هَائِجُهُ His anger has been roused.

هَائِجَة Land having withered plants.

☆ هِيخ *Cry for making camels to kneel.*

☆ هَادَ i هَيْدًا وَهَادًا, وَهَيَّدَ ه To put in motion. To distress, to frighten a. o.

— وَهَيَّدَ ه To repair, to put a. th. in order. To chide a. o. To frighten, to deter a. o.

هَيَّدَ To walk at a quick pace.

مَا يَهِيدُنِي ذَلِكَ I do not care for it. It does not disturb me.

مَا لَهُ هَادٌ وَمَا لَهُ هَيْدٌ He is motionless, he cannot be roused.

أَيَّام هَيْد Unhappy days.

هَيْد وَهِيد وَهَاد *Cry for urging camels.*

هَيْدَان Cowardly, dastardly.

يُعْطِي الهَيْدَان وَالزَّيْدَان He gives to any comer.

☆ هِير — هَيَّرَ ه To destroy, to pull down a. th. ✧ To prepare materials.

تَهَيَّرَ To crumble down. To hurry.

هَيْر وَهِير وَهَيِّر North wind.

هَيْرَة Even, flat land.

هَيَار Ruins. rubbish. ✧ Materials for work.

يَهْيَر Hard stone. Tree-gum. Mist, mirage. Lie; contest. Poison. Kind of dormouse.

يَهْيَرِي Abundant water. Trifle, tinsel.

☆ هَيْرَع Faint-hearted, weak.

رِيح هَيْرَعَة Wind raising the dust.

☆ هَاسَ i هَيْسًا To walk.

— ه To take much of.

— ه To put (the enemy) to flight.

هَيْس Implement of labour, plough.

هَيْسِ هَيْسِ *Interj.* Bravo! Go on!

أهيس Courageous, hardy.

✱ هاش i هَيْشًا To be excited, disorderly (crowd). To collect (mob). To utter foul language.

— ه To destroy, to damage a. th.

✧ هَيَّش To be dense, tangled (foliage).

هَيْشَة ج هَيْشَات Mixed company, rabble. Conflict, discord.

✧ هِيشَة وهِيش Shrub, thicket.

✧ هِيش *Cry for stopping asses.*

✧ مُهَيِّش Thick, tangled.

✱ هاص i هَيْصًا To mute (bird).

— ه To break (the neck) of a. o. To ill-treat a. o.

مَهِيص ج مَهَايِص Place on which mute falls.

✱ هاض i هَيْضًا To mute (bird).

— وإهتاض ه To break (a bone) anew.

هَيْص Bird's mute.

هاض ه To cause a relapse to a. o. To grieve a. o.

— الحُزْنُ قَلْبَهُ He fell back into his former grief.

تَهَيَّض وانهاض To be broken anew (bone).

هَيْض Bird's mute.

هَيْضَة Relapse in a disease, in grief. Cholera, diarrhea. Languor.

هَيْضَاء Crowd, press.

مَهِيض Broken anew (bone).

✱ هاط i هَيْطًا, وهايط مُهَايَطَة وهِيَاطًا To cry out, to raise an uproar.

تَهَايَطُوا They met for settling their business.

ما زال في هَيْط ومَيْط He does not cease to do mischief and to vociferate.

هُم في هِيَاط ومِيَاط They are in confusion, restless.

✱ هاع i a هَيْعًا وهَيْعَة وهُيُوعًا وهَيَعَانًا To fuse (lead). To be faint-hearted. To be hungry.

— i a هَيْعًا إلى To thirst, to yearn after (water : camels).

— a هَيْعَة وهَاعًا To be slothful, indolent.

— a هَيَعَانًا مِن To be wearied by.

— a i هَيْعًا To be spread, expanded. To fuse (molten lead). To vomit.

تَهَيَّع To be spread, expanded.

— وانهاع To spread in the air (mist ; mirage).

هاع وهَيْعَة Indolence, sloth.

هاع لاع وهائِع لائِع Weak, cowardly.

هَيْعَة Fusion of lead.

هائِع Obscure (night).

هِيَاع لِيَاع Violent (wind).

هائِعَة Noise, uproar.

مَهْيَع ج مَهَايِع Beaten, broad (road).

مُتَهَيِّع ومُنْهَاع Wrong-doer, prone to evil.

✱ هيغ — هَيَّغ ه To drench (the earth : rain). To grease (a dish).

أهْيَغ Easy, pleasant (life). Plentiful (water). Fruitful (year).

✱ هَيِف وهاف a هَيَفًا وهَيْفًا To be slender, thin-bellied.

هاف i هَيْفًا, واهتاف To be vehemently thirsty.

هاف a هَيْفًا To escape (slave).

— هِيَافًا وهُيَافًا To inhale the wind (thirsty beast).

أهْيَف To have thirsty cattle.

هَيْف Thirst. Hot South-westerly wind.

ذَهَبَتْ هَيْفُ لِأَدْيَانِهَا They fell back into their former practice. They followed their old track.

هائِف وهَيْفَان وهَيُوف و مِهْيَاف ومُهْتَاف Vehemently or soon thirsty.

هافَة Soon thirsty (she-camel).

أهْيَف م هَيْفَاء ج هِيف Thin-bellied, slender.

✱ هَيْق ج أهْيَاق وهُيُوق Tall and thin. Male ostrich.

✧ هِيق Tall and thin ; stupid, knave.

هَيَّق To become a knave. ✧ To stand idle.

أهْيَق To be long-necked.

✧ هَيْكَ (for هٰكَذَا) So, thus.

✱ هال i هَيْلًا, وهَيَّل وأهال ه على To pour (flour, sand) upon a. th. without measure.

تَهَيَّل وانهال To be poured (flour, sand)

إنْهَال على فُلَان To assault, to beat, to revile a. o. (party).

هال وهَيْل وهَيَلَان وهَيَال Poured sand.

هال وأهْيَل Poured (sand).

هَيْل وهَيْلَمَان (coll.) Numerous flocks. The sand and the wind.

هَيْل وحَبُّ الهَال Cardamom-seed.

Waterless desert. هَيْمَاء
Bewildered, stupefied. هَائِم ج هُيَّم وهُيَّام
Desperate lovers, people crazed by love. هُيَّام
Affected with unquenchable thirst (camel). أَهْيَم م هَيْمَاء ج هِيم
Vehemently thirsty. Loving passionately. هَيْمَان م هَيْمَى ج هِيَام وهَيْمَى
Starless night. لَيْل أَهْيَم ولَيْلَة هَيْمَاء
Heart bewildered by love. قَلْب مُسْتَهَام
To affront a. o. ✧ هَان i ه
Get off! Be gone! Again, once more! ✡ هِيهِ هِيهِ
How far! Very far is... What a difference between. ▫ Indeed! Not in the least. I wish it would. هَيْهَاتَ وَهَيْهَاتِ
How far! هَيْهَاهُ وَهَيْهَاهَ وَهَيْهَاهٍ
How far! هَائِهَاتَ وَهَايْهَانَ وَهَيْهَان وَتَهَايْهَات

Overflowing (sand, flour). مَهِيل ومُهَيَّل ومُهَال
✧ Mote, atom. G هَيُول
✧ Matter (*opp. to* form *in logics*). Raw material. هَيُولَى وهَيُولَى ج هَيُولِيَّات
Material. هَيُولِيّ وهَيُولَانِيّ
✡ هَام i هَيْمًا وهُيُومًا وهِيَامًا وهَيَمَانًا
To love a. o. desperately. وتَهْيَامًا ب
Mind thy own business! هِمْ لِنَفْسِكَ
He wandered about like a mad man. هَامَ عَلَى وَجْهِهِ
To be thirsty. — i هُيَامًا وَهِيَامًا
To bewilder a. o. (love). هَيَّم وتَهَيَّم ه
He took care of himself. اِهْتَامَ لِنَفْسِهِ
His heart was maddened by love. اُسْتُهِيمَ فُؤَادُهُ
Quick-sand, drift-sand. هُيَام ج هُيُم
Passionate love. Vehement thirst. هَيَام وهِيَام
Thirst-giving disease among camels. هُيَام

و

1° *Conjunction*. And, also. ✡ وَ
Zeyd and Amru are come. جَاءَ زَيْدٌ وعَمْرٌو
2° *Is expressive of concomitance*. Together with, whilst; at.
Do not eat fish whilst drinking milk. لَا تَأْكُل السَّمَكَ وَتَشْرَبَ اللَّبَنَ
He came at sunrise. جَاءَ وَالشَّمْسُ طَالِعَةٌ
3° *Particle used for swearing, often followed by the genitive*. By.
By God! وَاللهِ
4° *When followed by the accusative, it means sometimes* : With.
What have I to do with Zeyd? مَا لِي وَزَيْدًا
I travelled together with Zeyd. سَافَرْتُ وَزَيْدًا
✧ With me, with him. وَإِيَّاهُ وَإِيَّايَ
5° *When following the interrogative particle* أ (أَوَ) *it means*. Then.
Are you then astonished? أَوَ عَجِبْتُم
6° *When used in poetry with an indeteminate noun governed by* رُبَّ *at the beginning of a verse, it means*. Oftentimes *or* scarcely.
The night is often as dreadful as the waves of the sea. وَلَيْلٍ كَمَوْجِ البَحْرِ
I have scarcely seen a generous man. وَرَجُلٍ كَرِيمٍ رَأَيْتُهُ
If not, otherwise. وَإِلَّا
Exclamation. Indeed; is it possible! ✧ وَلَو
Interj. expressive of grief and wonder. Alas! Halloo! ✡ وَا
Alas for Zeyd! وَازَيْدُ ووَازَيْدًا ووَازَيْدَاه
What a wonderful thing! وَا عَجَبَاهُ
What an eloquent man thou art! وَا أَنْتَ فَصِيحٌ
To bark (dog); to yelp (jackal). ✡ وَأْوَأَ وَأْوَأَةً
To be ashamed, to shrink from. ✡ وَأَب i وَأْبًا وإِبَةً من
To be contracted in the edges (hoof). — a وَأْبَةً
To become angry. وَئِبَ a وَأَبًا
To disgrace, to angry a. o. أَوْأَبَ وأَتْأَبَ ه

إتأب من To be ashamed of.
ابة وتؤبة وموئبة Disgrace, shame, ignominy.
وأب Wide cup. Great camel. Strong. Cup-shaped (hoof).
وأبة Hollow in a rock. Short and stout (woman).
— ووائبة Deep and wide (well).
موئبات Shameful, disgraceful things.
✱ وأج Severe and protracted dearth.
◻ واح ج واحات Oasis.
✱ وأد يئد وأدًا ه To bury (a daughter) alive (Arab).
تؤاد واتّأد في To act slowly in.
تؤادت عليه الأرض He has been concealed in the land.
وأد ووئيد Loud voice, crash. Braying of camels.
وئيد وتؤدة وتؤاد Gravity, staidness, gentleness.
وئيد ووئيدة وموؤودة Buried alive (girl).
✱ وأر يئر وأرًا، وأوأر ه To frighten a. o. away.
وأر وأرًا وإرة ه ول To prepare a place for (fire).
وأر ووأّر ه في To throw a. o. into (distress).
إستوأر To be frightened away (cattle). To hurry in darkness.
إرة ج إرات وإرون Hearth, fire-place.
وؤرة ج وأر وأور Fire-place.
وئار Clay-bed. Bog.
وئر Burning, hot (ground).
✱ وأص يئص وأصًا به الأرض To throw a. o. down on the ground.
توأّص To gather and press round the water.
وئيصة Troop of men.
✱ وأط يئط وأطًا ه To visit a. o.
وأطة Rising ground. Abyss of the sea.
✱ وأل يئل وألًا ووؤولًا ووئيلًا، وواءل مواءلة
وءولًا إلى To seek shelter, refuge at.
— وواءل من To shun a. th.
أوأل في To defile (fodder(with dung (cattle).
وأل ومؤئل وموألة Shelter, refuge.
وألة Dung of cattle.
✱ وأم — وأم توئيمًا ه To create, to render a. o. ugly, deformed (God).
واءم مواءمة ووئامًا ه To agree, to live peacefully with.
وأم Warmed room.
وأمة Imitative (man).
مـوأم Big-headed; ugly.
متوائم Harmonious, congruous.
✱ وأى يئي وأيًا To promise, to threaten.
— ه To bind o.'s self; to answer for.
تواءى To assemble (people).
إتّأى To accept a promise.
إستوأى To exact a promise.
وأي Number of people. Opinion.
وأى م وأاة ووآة Strong beast. Wild ass.
وأية ووئية Large cooking-pot. Large bowl.
وئية Sack. Good house-wife. Pearl.
✧ واوي ج واوية Jackal.
✱ وبّ o وبًّا To prepare for fight.
✱ وبأ a وبأً، ووبّأ ه To set (furniture) in order.
وبأ وأوبأ إلى To point out, to indicate a. th. To beckon at.
وبئ a وبأً، ووبؤ o وباء ووباءة، ووبئ وبأً، وأوبأ To yearn towards her young one (camel). To be plague-stricken (country).
أوبئ To suffer from indigestion (beast).
إستوبأ ه To find (a country) smitten by an epidemic.
وبأ ج أوباء، ووباء ج أوبئة Plague, contagious disease, epidemic.
وبائي Epidemical, pestilential, contagious.
وبئ ووبيء وموبوء Plague-stricken (country). Tainted (water). Sick (person).
✱ وبت i وبتًا ب To remain in (a place).
✱ وبخ — وبّخ ه To blame, to upbraid a. o.
وبخة Blame, reproof, reproach.
✱ وبد a وبدًا To be poor, to be burdened by a large family (man). To be worn out (clothes). To be hot (day).
وبد على To get angry with.

Spotted with scabs (camel). وَبِش
To flash (lightning); to shine. ✱ وَبَص يَبِص وَبْصًا ووَبِيصًا ووَبِيصَةً
To become luxuriant (soil). — وأَوْبَص
To open the eyes (whelp). وَبَص ووَبَّص
To be brisk, active. وَبِص a وَبَصًا
He has given me little. وَبَّص لي بِيَسِير
To make (fire) to blaze. أَوْبَص
Nimble, lively. وَبِص م وَبِصَة
Shining, gleaming. وَابِص م وَابِصَة
Fire, live coal, flash of lightning. وَابِصَة ووَبِيصَة
He believes every thing he hears. إِنَّهُ لَوَابِصَةُ سَمْعٍ
The moon. Shining (cloud, moon). وَبَّاص
✱ وَبَط يَبِط ووَبِط a وَبُط o وَبْطًا ووَبَاطَةً
To be weak, paltry, cowardly. ووَبْطًا ووُبُوطًا
To revile, to abase a. o. ة وَبَط يَبِط وَبْطًا
To open, to widen (a wound). ه —
To hinder a. o. from. ة عن —
To disable. To debilitate a. o. ة أَوْبَط
To abuse, to upbraid a. o. i ✱ وَبَغ
Scurf of the head. Skin-disease of camels. وَبَغ
✱ وَبَق يَبِق ووَبِق a i وُبُوقًا ومَوْبِقًا ووَبَقًا
To perish. واسْتَوْبَق
To cause a. o. to perish. To confine in prison. ة أَوْبَق
Place of perdition. Prison. Valley of Hell. Interval; appointed term. مَوْبِق
Pernicious, noxious. مُوبِق
He faced many dangers. رَكِب المُوبِقَات
To pour down an abundant rain (sky). To run vehemently (horse). ✱ وَبَل يَبِل وَبْلًا
To pursue (the game). ه —
To strike a. o. with (a stick). ة ب —
To be unhealthy, unwholesome (land, pasture). وَبُل o وَبَالًا ووَبَالَةً ووُبُولًا ووَبْلًا
To be assiduous to. وَابَل ه
To find (a land) unhealthy. إِسْتَوْبَل ه
Heavy rain. Avaricious. وَبْل ووَابِل
Upper part of the thigh, of the arm or shoulder Patella of the knee. Young camels, lambs. وَابِلَة

To isolate, to separate a. o. or a. th. أَوْبَد ة وه
Hollow in a rock; cleft in a mountain. وَبْد
Destitution. Vice. وَبَد
Poor man burdened by a large family. وَبَد (s. and pl.) ج أَوْبَاد
Destitute. Evil-eyed. وَبِد
Destitute. Ignorant. مُسْتَوْبِد
Magian priest. P مَوْبَذ ومَوْبَذَان ج مَوَابِذَة
To have soft hair (camel). ✱ وَبِر a وَبَرًا، وأَوْبَر
To be fecundated (palm-tree). وَبِر
To stay in (a place). وَبَر يَبِر وَبْرًا ب
To become downy (young ostrich). To lead a secluded life. To walk without leaving traces (fox). وَبَّر
Kind of weasel. Syrian hyrax. وَبْر ج وُبُور و وِبَار وَوِبَارَة
Soft hair, fur of camels, hares, goats. وَبَر ج أَوْبَار
The inhabitants of hair-tents. i. e. the nomads. أَهْلُ الوَبَر
Hairy, furry. وَابِر
There is no one in the house. مَا بِالدَّار وَابِرٌ
Covered with downy hair. وَبِر م وَبِرَة، وأَوْبَر م وَبْرَاء
Small and bad truffles. بَنَات أَوْبَر وبَنَات الأَوْبَر
I have experienced many a disappointement from his part. لَقِيتُ مِنْهُ بَنَات أَوْبَر
✧ Steamer. Locomotive. Railway train. Steam-engine. Stove. Lamp. I وَابُور وَبَابُور
▫ Camel-hair cloth. وَبُورِدِيّ
To be white-spotted (nails, skin). ✱ وَبِش a وَبَشًا
To throng and form a promiscuous crowd. To be revived by blowing (coals). وَبَّش
To produce variegated plants (earth). أَوْبَش
White spot on the nails. Spots of scab. وَبْش ووَبَش
Rabble, medley, refuse of men. وَبْش ج أَوْبَاش
Scarce and scattered plants. الأَوْبَاش من النَّبَات

وَبَال Unhealthiness of climate; Mischief done. Evil result.

وَبَلَة وأَبَلَة Unhealthiness of climate; unwholesomeness of food.

وَبَلَى Yielding much milk.

وَبِيل Unhealthy, unwholesome (climate, food). Hard, heavy (blow). Mallet, beetle.

— ووَبِيلَة Large stick. Bundle of wood.

مَوْبَل ومِيبَل Thick staff.

أَبِيل على وَبِيل Old man leaning upon a stick.

مِيبَلَة Leathern whip.

☆ وبن — ما بالدّار وَابِن There is no one in the house.

وَبْنَة Mischief. Hunger.

☆ وَبِه a وَبْهًا To become proud.

وَبَه ووَبِه a وَبْهًا, وأَوْبَه ل وب To take into account, to mind a. th.

لا يُوبَهُ بِهِ ولَهُ Nobody cares about him.

☆ وَتّ Coo of the male dove.

وَتَاوِت Evil suggestions.

وَتَا يَتَأ وَتأً في مِشْيَتِهِ He has a sluggish gait.

☆ وَتَب i وَتْبًا To remain fast in a place.

☆ وَتُح o وَتَاحَةً ووُتُوحَةً ووَتِحَةً To be paltry, mean (gift).

وَتَح يَتِحُ وَتْحًا وتِحَةً, وأَوْتَح ه To give a paltry (gift).

أَوْتَح To have little wealth.

— ه To distress a. o.

تَوَتَّح ه To drink little (wine).

وَتْح ووَتَح ووَتِح ووَتِيح Paltry, small (gift). Vile (man). Scanty (food).

ما أَغْنَى عَنّي وَتْحَةً He, it has been of no use to me.

☆ وَتَخ يَتِخ وَتْخًا ه ب To strike a. o. with (a stick).

وَتَخَة Mud.

مِيتَخَة Stick.

☆ وَتَد يَتِد وَتْدًا وَتِدَةً, ووَتَّد وأَوْتَد ه To fix (a stake) into the ground.

وَتَد ووَتَّد To become fixed fast (peg, stake). To fix a. th. firmly. To put forth stalks (corn).

وَتْد ووَتَد ووَتِد ج أَوْتَاد Stake, tent-peg. Erect and prominent thing. Poetical measure. ◻ Off-shoot.

أَوْتَاد الأَرض Mountains *lit*: pegs of the earth.

— البِلاد Chief men of a country.

— الفَم The teeth.

مِيتَد ومِيتَدَة Mallet for fixing pegs.

☆ وَتَر يَتِر وَتْرًا وتِرَةً, ووَتَّر وأَوْتَر ه To put a string to; to brace (a bow-string).

— وأَوْتَر ه To pray at intervals. To render (a number) odd.

وَتَر ه To hate a. o. To irritate a. o.

— ه ه To harass a. o.; to do mischief. to. To defraud, to make a. o. to suffer loss. To render a. o. solitary by killing his relatives. To frighten a. o. To retaliate (bloodshed) wrongfully.

وَاتَر مُوَاتَرَةً ووِتَارًا ه, وأَوْتَر بَيْن To act at intervals. To send (letters) consecutively.

تَوَتَّر To become stretched (sinew).

تَوَاتَر To follow one another at intervals, to be consecutive.

وَتْر ووِتْر ج أَوْتَار Single, unique; (The) One (God). Odd (number). *Geom.* Arc of a circle.

وِتْرًا وِتْرًا One by one, separately.

وِتْر وتِرَة Revenge, retaliation of a murder.

وَتَر ج أَوْتَار Bow-string, chord of musical instruments. Sinew. Row.

وَتَرَة ج وَتَر ووَتَرَات, ووَتِيرَة ج وَتَائِر ووَتِيرَات Pellicle between the fingers. Cartilage of the upper ear. Partition between the nostrils.

وَتَرَة Nerve of the tongue, of the back.

وَتِيرَة Uniform road. Natural disposition, conduct. Delay, remissness. Restraint. Rose-blossom; white, red, rose. Blaze on a horse.

تَتْرَى (*for* وَتْرَى) One by one; consecutively.

تَوَاتُر Succession at short intervals. Tradition related by successive witnesses.

مُوَاتَرَة الصَّوْم Fasting at intervals.

مُتَوَاتِر Consecutive, at short intervals. Tradition related by consecutive tes-

To make a. o. to sit on (a cushion). وَثَّبَ ة هـ
To assault, to leap upon a. o. وَاثَبَ ة
To make a. o. to leap, to bound. أَوْثَبَ ة
He took possession of his estate unjustly. تَوَثَّبَ فِي أَرْضِهِ
He took hold of his land unjustly. — عَلَيْهِ فِي أَرْضِهِ
To rush upon o. a. تَوَاثَبَ
Abrupt exordium in poetry. وَثْب
Leap, bound, assault. وَثْبَة
Seat, throne, bed. وِثَاب
Bounding (mare, antelope). وَثَبَى
Jumper, leaper. وَثَّاب م وَثَّابَة
✧ Contraction of the nerves, neuralgia. وَثَّاب
Antelope. أَبُو وَثَّاب
Even ground; elevated ground. Jumper. Sitter. Rivulet. مِيثَب
Peaceful (prince). مَوْثَبَان
To become thick, dense, corpulent. ✯ وَثُجَ o وَثَاجَة
To give much of a. th. أَوْثَجَ هـ
To become numerous (flocks). To be dense, intertwisted (plants). إِسْتَوْثَجَ
Stoutness, bulkiness. وَثَاجَة
Thick, corpulent (man). Dense (herbage). Compact (texture). وَثِيج
Luxuriant (land). مُوتَثِجَة
Uncompact (cloth). مَوْثُوجَة
Remainder of water in a pond. Dampness. Slime, mire. ✯ وثخ — وَثْخَة
Muddy, slimy (soil). Thick (milk). وَثِيخَة
Of weak constitution. مَوْثُوخ الخَلْق وَمَوْثُوخُهُ
To become smooth, soft (bed, carpet). To be fleshy, fat. ✯ وَثُرَ o وَثَارَة
To beat a. th. soft, smooth. وَثَرَ يَثِرُ وَثْرًا, وَوَثَّرَ هـ
To ask much of. إِسْتَوْثَرَ مِن
To find (a bed) soft. — هـ
Leather-garment for girls. وَثْر
Smoothness, softness of a carpet, a bed. وِثْر وَوَثِير وِثَار
Housings of a horse. Covering for clothes. Skins of beasts of prey. — وَمِيثَرَة ج مَوَاثِر وَمَيَاثِر

timonies. Poetical metre in which a movent letter is inserted between two quiescents.
Consecutively, at short intervals. بِتَوَاتُرٍ وَمُتَوَاتِرًا
Braced (bow). Wronged (man) unable to retaliate a murder. مَوْتُور
Pros. Rhyme ending by a moving letter between two quiescents as مَفَاعِيلُنْ. مُتَوَاتِر
✯ وَتِغَ a وَتَغًا To commit crimes; to be guilty. To perish. To utter foolish speech. To be ill-natured (child).
To destroy a. o. (God). To imprison a. o. To throw a. o. into misfortunes (God). أَوْتَغَ ة
To disgrace religion by (a crime). — هـ ب
To flow continuously (water). ✯ وَتَنَ يَتِنُ وُتُونًا وَتِنَة
To remain long in (a place). — ب
To wound a. o. in the aorta. — وَتْنًا وَوَتِينًا
To be wounded in the aorta. وُتِنَ
To persevere in. وَاتَنَ هـ
To become fat (cattle). إِسْتَوْتَنَ
Strife, dissension. وَتْنَة
Fast in a place. Flowing continuously (water). وَاتِن
The aorta, artery of the heart. وَتِين ج وُتُن وَأَوْتِنَة
To deaden (the flesh: blow). ✯ وَتَأَ a وَتْأً هـ
To bruise, to contuse (a limb). To luxate (a bone). — وَأَوْتَأَ هـ
To be bruised, contused (limb); to be luxated (bone). وَتِئَ a وَتْأً وَوُتُوءًا, وَوُتِئَ
Bruise, contusion, dislocation. وَتْء وَوَتَاءَة
Bruised, contused, dislocated (limb). وَتِئٌ وَوَتِيٌّ وَمَوْتُوءٌ
Mallet for striking pegs. مِيتَأَة
To leap, to bound, to spring. To stand up. To sit down. ✯ وَثَبَ يَثِبُ وَثْبًا وَوُثُوبًا وَوَثَبَانًا وَوِثَابًا وَوَثِيبًا وَثِبَة
He attained illustriousness in one start. وَثَبَ إِلَى الشَّرَفِ وَثْبَةً
To seat a. o. upon a cushion. وَثَّبَ ة

Softness, smoothness ; abundance of flesh. وَثَارَة
Smooth, level, soft. وَثِير م وَثِيرَة
Fat, fleshy (woman).
To break the head of. ✱ وَثَغ يَثَغ وَثْغًا ه
Small quantity of (rain). وَثْغَة ووَثِيغَة مِن
Intertwisted spring-herbage. وَثِيغَة
Thick porridge, mess. ثَرِيدَة وَثِيغَة و ثَرِيدَة مَوْثُوغَة
To put (a pot) on a trivet. ✱ وَثَف يَثِف وَثْفًا, و وَثَّف وأَوْثَف ه
To trust, to rely upon. ✱ وَثِق يَثِق ثِقَة ووُثُوقًا ومَوْثِقًا ب
To be fast, firm. To be steadfast ; to be sanguine. وَثُق o وَثَاقَة
To strengthen, to fasten a. th. وَثَّق ه
To judge a. o. trustworthy. — ه
To bind a. o. by a compact. وَاثَق مُوَاثَقَة ووِثَاقًا ه
To reinforce (a garrison). أَوْثَق ه
He bound him tightly, he tied him fast. — ه بِالْوِثَاق
To be sanguine, hopeful. To be tight (knot). تَوَثَّق
To act confidently in a. th. — في
To secure to o.'s self (the property, or use) of a. th. — واسْتَوْثَق مِن
They bound themselves by contract to. تَوَاثَقُوا على
To close (a door). إِسْتَوْثَق ب
To secure o.'s self against a. o. ; to bind a. o. by an agreement. — مِن فُلَان
He secured his property by. — مِن أَمْوَالِهِ ب
Trust, confidence. ثِقَة
Trustworthy, honest. ثِقَة (m. f. s. pl.) ج ثِقَات
Band, bond, rope. Moral bond. وَثَاق ووِثَاق ج وُثُق
Confident, steady. وَاثِق م وَاثِقَة
Firm (compact). Steady, resolute. وَثِيق ج وِثَاق
Trust. Bond. Written agreement ; security. Pledge. Full of herbs (land). ✧ Compact ; contract. Bill, billet. Certificate. وَثِيقَة ج وَثَائِق
Stronger, faster. أَوْثَق م وُثْقَى
مَوْثِق ومِيثَاق ج مَوَاثِق ومَيَاثِق ومَوَاثِيق
Compact, bond, promise. Will, bequest.
Strongly built (man). مُوَثَّق الْخَلْق
To strengthen a. th. To collect (wealth). ✱ وَثَل — وَثَّل ه
Rope of palm-fibres. وَثَل
Palm-fibres. Hempen-rope. Weak rope. وَثِيل
To run swiftly (horse). To paw the ground (horse). To beat the ground (rain). ✱ وَثَم يَثِم وَثْمًا
To break, to pound a. th. — ه
To wound, to make (the foot of a horse) to bleed (stone). — وَثْمًا ووِثَامًا ه
To have scanty plants (land). وَثِم a وَثَمًا
To be compact in flesh. وَثُم o وَثَامَة
The (horse) started off. وَاثَم في الْعَدْو
What an unproductive land ! مَا أَوْثَمَهَا
Small quantity. وَثْم
Compact in flesh. وَثِيم م وَثِيمَة
Heap of wheat, straw. Pebbles, broken stones. وَثِيمَة
Pawing (horse). خُفّ مِيثَم
Wooden, or stone idol. ✱ وَثَن ج وُثْن ووُثُن وأَوْثَان
To be extensive (property). أَوْثَن
To load a. o. with gifts. — ه
To remain. To survive. To be strong, sturdy. To be fattened (flock). To shoot forth (palm-trees). إِسْتَوْثَن
To ask much of. — مِن
Steadfast. Flowing in a stream (water). وَاثِن
Gentile, heathen, pagan. وَثَنِيّ ج وَثَنِيُّون
To be bruised (limb) ; dislocated (hand). ✱ وُثِيَ وَثْيًا
To have a beast wounded ; a ship wrecked (traveller). أَوْثَى
Sufferings. وَثْي
Hammer, mallet. مِيثَاءَة
Contused (limb). مَوْثِيّ
To be swift, to hasten. ✧ To blaze (fire). ✱ وَجّ o وَجًّا
Medicinal plant. Galangal. Sweet-cane. Ostrich. Sand-grouse. وَجّ

binding. To deserve: to have a claim to.
Cowardly. Stupid. وَجْب ووَجَّاب ووَجَّابَة
Large water-skin. وَجْب ج وِجَاب
Stake at a race.
Place in which water stagnates. وِجَاب
Crash, loud noise. One meal a day. وَجْبَة ج وَجَبَات
✧ A set, a suit of. — مِن
Necessity, unavoidableness. وُجُوب
Obligatory (*opposed to* إمتِنَانِي *optional*). وُجُوبِي
Palpitation of the heart. وَجِيب ووَجَبَان
Allowance of food. Adjudication. وَجِيبَة
Affirmation. (*opp. to* سَلْب) إيجَاب
Affirmative. Positive. إيجَابِي
Binding, unavoidable. Slain, killed. وَاجِب م وَاجِبَة
Duty, obligation. وَاجِب ج وَاجِبَات فِي ٱلعَمَل
Existing necessarily; self-existent (God). وَاجِب ٱلوُجُود وٱلوَاجِب لِذَاتِهِ
Cause. مُوجِب
The first cause, God. المُوجِب
Necessary cause. المُوجِب بِالذَّات
Affirmative (sentence). Result, effect. مُوجَب
Treat him as he deserves. عَامِلْهُ بِمُوجَب فِعْلِهِ
✧ Upon my conscience. بِمُوجَب ذِمَّتِي
Affirmative proposition. مُوجَبَة ج مُوجَبَات
Momentous action (good or bad). مُوجِبَة ج مُوجِبَات
The time of my death is at hand. حَانَ مَوْجِبِي
Wrestling-place. مَوَاجِب
Eating once a day. مُوَجِّب
Deserving, worthy of. مُسْتَوْجِب ب
✯ وجح — وَجَح وأَوْجَح To appear, to be conspicuous.
To glow (fire). To reach the rock (digger). أَوْجَح
To let down the curtain of (a tent) ه —
To be painfully ejected (urine). ه —
To compel a. o. to fly towards. ه إلى —
Smooth rock. وَجَاح
Veil, curtain, covering. — ووِجَاح ووُجَاح

✯ وَجَأَ a وَجْأً, وتَوَجَّأ ه ب To stab a. o. with (a knife).
وَجَّأ ه To find (a well) exhausted. To compress (dates) together.
أَوْجَأ To be exhausted (well). To come back with empty hands (shooter).
— ه عَن To repel a. o. from.
إتَّجَأ To be compact (bunches).
وَجْء ووَجَأ ووَجَاء Of bad quality (water).
وَجَاة ووَجَأة ووَجَاءة Exhausted or yielding bad water (well).
وَجِيئة Dish of locusts or dates in powder beaten up with butter or oil. Cow.
✯ وَجَب يَجِب وُجُوبًا وجِبَة To become binding, obligatory; to be due. To exist necessarily (God).
— على فُلَان To take effect; to be incumbent, binding upon a. o.
— وَجْبَة To fall down with a loud crash (wall).
— وَجْبًا ووُجُوبًا To set (sun). To be sunken in the socket (eye). To fall dead.
— ه عَن To repel a. o. from.
— وَجْبًا ووَجِيبًا ووَجَبَانًا To throb (heart).
وَجُب o وُجُوبَة To be cowardly.
وَجَّب To coagulate in the udder (biestings). To be tired (camel).
— وأَوْجَب وتَوَجَّب To eat one meal a day.
وَجَّب ه على, وأَوْجَب ه ل وعلى To render a. th. obligatory to.
وَجَّب ه To accustom a. o. to eat once a day. To milk (a she-camel) once a day. ✧ To show due regard to (a guest).
— بِهِ ٱلأَرْضَ He threw him down upon the ground.
وَاجَب مُوَاجَبَة ووِجَابًا, وأَوْجَب ه ل To adjuge a. th. to a. o. (auctioneer).
أَوْجَب To do actions deserving reward or punishment.
— ه To affirm, to ascertain a. th. To cause (the heart) to palpitate (God).
— لِفُلَانٍ حَقَّهُ He declared the right of such a one.
إسْتَوْجَب ه To deem a. th. necessary,

Closely woven (cloth). وَجِيحِ ومُوجَح
Shelter, refuge. Smooth skin. مُوجَح
Closed or curtained (door). مَوْجُوح
✻ وَجَد ووَجِد يَجِد وَجْدًا وجِدَةً ووُجْدًا ووُجُودًا ووِجْدَانًا وإِجْدَانًا ه To find, to obtain; to find out a. th. lost. To perceive, to know by experience.
To find a. o. or a. th. (such and such). — ه ه وه ه
To be moderately rich; to earn wealth. — يَجِد وَجْدًا ووُجْدًا وجِدَةً ه
To become angry with a. o. — i o وَجْدًا وَجِدَةً ومَوْجِدَةً ووِجْدَانًا على
To love a. o. passionately. — وَجْدًا, وتوجَّد ب
To grieve for. وَجِد a وَجْدًا ب
To be found, discovered. وُجِد وُجُودًا
To be created; to come into existence, to exist. — مِنَ ٱلْعَدَم
To create a. th. (God). To bring into existence. ✧ To invent, to discover a. th. أَوْجَد إِيجَادًا ه
To enrich a. o. (God). To comfort, to strengthen a. o. — ه
To procure a. th. for; to make a. o. to find a. th. أَوْجَد ه ه
To complain of a. th. تَوَجَّد ه
To be sorry for a. o. — ل
To make a show of love, of sadness. تَوَاجَد
To be found. ✧ إِنوَجَد
Wealth, power, ability. جِدَة
Excitement, passion, rapture. وَجْد
Pond of stagnating water. وَجْد ج وِجَاد
Wealth. Joy. Love. Power. وَجْد ووِجْد ووُجْد
Conscience; emotion of joy; grief. وِجْدَان
Internal perceptions; supernatural things. وِجْدَانِيَّات
Existence. Invention, discovery. وُجُود
Existence, being. وُجُودِيَّة
✧ He fainted; he lost consciousness. غَابَ عن الوُجُود
Creation. ✧ Invention. إِيجَاد
Finder. Rich, solvent. Angry. وَاجِد
Able to. — ل
In love with. — ب

Level ground. وَجِيد ج وُجْدَان
Outbreak of anger. مَوْجِدَة
Found. Existing. Present. مَوْجُود
The existing beings, the universe. أَلْمَوْجُودَات
To constrain a. o. to. ✻ وجد – أَوْجَدَ ه إلى وعلى
Hollow full of water in a mountain. Pool, cistern. وَجْذ ج وِجْذَان ووِجَاذ
To dread, to caution o.'s self against. ✻ وَجِر a وَجَرًا مِن
To pour a medicine into a. o.'s mouth. To say to a. o. unpleasant things. وَجَر يَجِر وَجْرًا, وأَوْجَر ه
He speared him in the mouth. أَوْجَر ه الرُّمْحَ
To swallow (a medicine) by draughts. To drink a. th. reluctantly. تَوَجَّر ه
To swallow (a medicine). إِتَّجَر ه
Cavern, grotto. وَجْر ج أَوْجَار
Fear. وَجَر
Cautious, wary. وَجِر وأَوْجَر
Cautious, wary. وَجِرَة ووَجْرَاء f.
Pitfall, trap for wild beasts. وَجْرَة ووَجَرَة ج أَوْجَار
Den of wild beasts. Side of a valley worn away by a torrent. وِجَار ووَجَار ج أَوْجِرَة ووُجُر
Medicine poured into the mouth. وَجُور ووُجُور
Unpleasant words. وَجُور
Instrument for pouring a medicine into the mouth. مِيجَر ومِيجَرَة
Tennis-racket. مِيجَار
✻ وَجَز يَجِز ووَجُز a وَجْزًا ووَجَازَةً ووُجُوزًا
To be brief, concise (speech). في
To be concise, brief in (speech). وَجَز يَجِز وَجْزًا ه
To be concise (speech). وَجُز o وَجَازَةً, وأَوْجَز إِيجَازًا
To abridge (a speech). To epitomise (a book). أَوْجَز ه وفي
To give a. th. readily. — ه
To ask the accomplishment of a. th.; to despatch (an affair). تَوَجَّز ه
Expeditious, speedy. Prompt (speech). Giving readily. وَجْز
Concise (speech); epitomised (book). — ووَجِيز ووَاجِز ومُوجَز ومُوجِز

Concision. (*opp. to* إطناب) إيجاز
Abridgment.
In short, in few words. بالإيجاز
Laconic, concise. مِيجاز
☆ وَجَس يَيجِس وَجْساً ووَجَسَاناً To feel an apprehension about, to dread a. th.
— يَيجِس وَجْساً To be hidden, unperceived.
أَوْجَس وتَوَجَّس في نفسِهِ He conceived a thought in his mind.
تَوَجَّس ب ول To listen fearfully to (a sound).
— ه To taste (food).
وَجْس Throbbing of fear. Faint sound. Apprehension.
وَاجِس Busying thought.
أَوْجَس Trifle, little. Time.
ما ذُقْتُ عِنْدَهُ أَوْجَس I have not tasted the least thing at his house.
لا أفعلهُ سَجِيسَ الأَوْجَس والأَوْجُس I will never do it.
☆ وَجِع a يَوْجَع ويَيْجَع ويَاجَع وَجَعاً To feel a pain. To ache.
يَوْجَعُهُ رَأْسُهُ ويَوْجَعُ رَأْسَهُ He has the head-ache.
أَوْجَع ه To pain, to hurt a. o.
تَوَجَّع To manifest pain, sorrow. To complain, to moan.
— لِفُلَانٍ مِن He was pained for. He compassionated his (sufferings).
◊ إتوَجَّع To feel a pain.
جِعَة Kind of beer; barley-wine.
وَجَع ج أَوْجَاع ووِجَاع. Pain, suffering. Disease.
وَجِع ج وَجِعُون ووَجْعَى ووَجَاعَى, ومُوجَع Ill, suffering.
وَجْعَاء Posteriors.
وَجِيع م وَجِيعَة, ومُوجِع م مُوجِعَة Painful.
مَوْجُوع Infirm, aching.
☆ وَجَف يَجِف وَجْفاً ووَجِيفاً ووُجُوفاً To be moved.
— وَجِيفاً To throb, to palpitate (heart).
— وَجْفاً ووَجِيفاً To run.
أَوْجَف ه To make (a beast) to run.
إِسْتَوْجَف ه To ravish; to distress (the heart : love).
وَجْف ووَجِيف Run.
وَاجِف Throbbing (heart).
وَاجِفَة Earthquake.

T أُوجاق وُوجاق ج وُجاقات ◊ Hearth, fire-place. Household. Stove. Body of Turkish troops. Training-place.
☆ وَجِل a وَجَلاً ومَوْجَلاً To be fearful, cowardly.
وَجَل o وَجْلاً ه To surpass a. o. in fear.
وَجُل o وَجَالَةً To be advanced in age.
أَوْجَل ه To frighten a. o.
وَجَل ج أَوْجَال Fear, wariness.
وَجِل ج وَجِلُون ووِجَال, وأَوْجَل وَجِلَة
ج وَجِلات Fearful, cautious.
أَوْجَل مِن More fearful than.
وُجُول Old people.
وَجِيل ومَوْجِل Pool of water.
☆ وَجَم يَجِم وَجْماً ووُجُوماً To remain silent with downcast eyes, in grief or anger.
— ه ومِن To dislike, to shun a. th.
— عَن To remain silent by fear of.
— وَجْماً ه To cuff, to fist a. o.
— وُجُوماً To be hot (day).
وَجْم Wicked. Way, manner.
وَجْمُ سَوْء Wicked man.
وَجْم ووَجَم ج أَوْجَام ووُجُوم Heap of stones used as a way-mark in the desert.
وَجْم Avaricious.
وَجِم ووَاجِم Downcast.
وَجْمَة Shame, disgrace.
وَجِيم Intensely hot (day).
وَجِيمَة Blasted (corn-crops).
أَوْجَمُ الرَّمْل Larger extent of sand.
مِيجَمَة Wooden mallet.
☆ وَجَن يَجِن وَجْناً, ووَجَّن ه To full (cloth).
وَجَن ب To throw, to cast a. th.
— بِهِ الأَرْضَ He prostrated him on the ground.
وَجَّن ه To beat (a hide : tanner).
ما أَدْرِي أَيُّ مَن وَجَّن الجِلْدَ هُوَ I do not know what sort of man he is.
تَوَجَّن To humble o.'s self.
وَجْنَة ووُجْنَة ووَجَنَة وأُجْنَة وإِجْنَة وأَجْنَة ج
وَجَنات Prominent part of the cheeks.
وَجْنَاء Strong; having prominent cheeks (she-camel).
وَجِين Bank of a river; rugged margin.
أَوْجَن ومُوَجَّن Having prominent cheeks.
الأَوْجَن Huge mountain.

مِيجَنَة ج مَوَاجِن ومَيَاجِن Mallet, beetle.

مَوْجُونَة Shy, fearful (woman).

✱ وَجِه يَوجَه وَجهًا ه To surpass a. o. in rank, estimation. To strike a. o. on the face.

وَجُه ه وَجَاهَة To enjoy consideration, regard.

وَجَّه إلى To aim at, to direct o.'s self.

— ه إلى . . في حَاجَةٍ He sent him to (a place) for an affair.

— وَجْهَهُ لله He converted himself to God. He became a Moslem.

— ه To give a good turn to (an affair). To fall evenly upon the ground (rain).

وَجِّه الحَجَرَ وِجهَةً مَا لَهُ Give a good turn to the affair, *lit*: turn the stone on the right side.

وَجَّه وأَوجَه ه To raise a. o. to dignity.

وَاجَه مُوَاجَهَةً ووِجَاهًا ه To encounter, to face a. o.

لَقِيَهُ مُوَاجَهَةً او وِجَاهًا To meet a. o. face to face.

أَوْجَه ه To find a. o. honoured. To show regard to. To discard (a beggar).

تَوَجَّه To repair, to direct o.'s self. To become old.

— نحو وإلى To direct o.'s steps towards.

تَوَاجَهَا To face, to front o. a. ✧ To have an interview with o. a.

اِتَّجَه إلى To direct o.'s self towards.

— لَهُ رَأْيٌ A thought occurred to his mind.

وَجْه ج أَوْجُه ووُجُوه وأُجُوه Face, front-side. Surface. Front of a house. Side of cloth. Face, countenance. Beginning of a day, a century. Reason, way, manner. Point of view. Object of speech. Surface. Side. Honour, regard, dignity. Purpose, course. Lucidity (of mind). Good fortune. Aim. End, result. Chief (of a party). ✧Page (of a book). ◘ Unit.

اِبْيَضَّ وَجْهُهُ He has illustrated himself.

اِسْوَدَّ وَجْهُهُ He has blackened his character.

عَمِلَهُ لِوَجْهِ اللهِ He has done it for the sake of God.

ضَرَبَ وَجْهَ الأَمْرِ وعَيْنَهُ He has hit the point in the affair.

أَخَذَ وَجْهًا ✧ He acquired credit. regard.

أَخَذَ وَجْهًا على ✧ He became accustomed to.

مَضَى على وَجْهِهِ He went away headlong, recklessly.

بِوَجْهٍ In any way.

على وَجْهِهِ Heedlessly, at random, headlong.

لِوَجْهِ اللهِ وإِبْتِغَاءَ لِوَجْهِ اللهِ For the sake of God. To please God.

كَلَام ذُو وَجْهَيْنِ Ambiguous speech; double-faced.

على الوَجْهَيْنِ In both cases, in the two points of view.

وَجْه ج وُجُوه Chief man; leading man, headman.

وِجْه ووُجْه Side, shore.

وَجُه ووَجِه Regarded, enjoying consideration.

جِهَة ووُجْهَة ج جِهَات ووُجهَات ووُجْهَة Front-side. Side, aspect. Respect, reference. Country, shore. Manner, way.

مِن جِهَتِهِ In respect, on account of him.

مِن كُلِّ جِهَةٍ From every side.

وَجَاهَة Regard, authority, consideration.

وِجَاهَ أَلْفٍ About one thousand.

وِجَاهَهُ ووُجَاهَهُ وتِجَاهَهُ وتُجَاهَهُ Opposite to him.

وَاجِهَة ✧ Front of a house.

وَجِيه ج وُجَهَاء Chief man, prince. Regarded, deserving. Worthy of respect.

وَجِيه م وَجِيهَة Born the feet foremost (colt, child).

وَجِيه م وَجِيهَة، ومُوَجَّه م مُوَجَّهَة Two-sided (garment).

وَجِيهَة ج وَجِيهَات ووَجَائِه Amulet against the evil eye.

وَجِيهِيّ Of high breed (horse).

أَوْجَه More regarded, more remarkable.

نَظَرَ إِلَيَّ بِأُوَيجِهِ سُوءٍ He looked at me with an evil eye.

To forsake, to leave a. o. alone before (the enemy). أَوْحَد ه ل
God has made him lonely *i. e.* has deprived him of his dear ones. أَوْحَد اللهُ جَانِبَهُ
To remain alone, unique. To withdraw, to retire apart. تَوَحَّد
He was singular, alone in his opinion. — بِرَأْيِهِ
God is the only one Lord. تَوَحَّد اللهُ بِالرُّبُوبِيَّة
God has protected him alone in a peculiar way. تَوَحَّدَهُ اللهُ بِعِصْمَتِهِ
To be united, conjoined. To become one. To be identified. To coalesce, to unite, to be unanimous (people). إِتَّحَد
To become, to be united to. — ب
Unification, oneness. حِدَة وَوَحْدَة وَوَحد
Separately, by o.'s self. عَلَى حِدَتِهِ
He has made it of himself, without the help of any one. فَعَلَهُ عَلَى ذَاتِ حِدَتِهِ وَمِنْ ذَاتِ حِدَتِهِ وَمِن ذِي حِدَتِهِ
By himself; he alone. وَحْدَهُ وَعَلَى وَحْدِهِ
He came alone. جَاءَ وَحْدَهُ وَعَلَى وَحْدِهِ
They sat by themselves. جَلَسُوا وَحْدَهُمْ وَعَلَى وَحْدِهِمْ
He is unequalled. هُوَ نَسِيجُ وَحْدِهِ
Alone, unique. Isolated, apart. وَحْد وَوَحِد م وَحْدَة وَوَحِدَة
Unity of God. وَحْدَانِيَّة
Singular in opinion. وَحْدَانِيّ
Singularity. Solitude. وَحْدَة
One ('single number), a single one, singular, sole. ✧ Same. وَاحِد م وَاحِدَة مث وَاحِدَان ج وَاحِدُون
They are one tribe. هُمْ حَيٌّ وَاحِد وَوَاحِدُون
Pairless, matchless, unequalled. وَاحِد ج وُحْدَان وَأُحْدَان
The only One, the Sole (God). أَلْوَاحِد
One by one, one and one. وَاحِدًا وَاحِدًا
Lonely, apart. Unique, only one (son). وَحِيد م وَحِيدَة
Unique, pairless. أَوْحَد ج أُحْدَان
He is unparalleled in his time. هُوَ أَوْحَدُ أَهْلِ زَمَانِهِ
I am not alone to have done such a thing. لَسْتُ فِي هٰذَا ٱلْأَمْرِ بِأَوْحَدَ

Ambilogy in speech. Distortion of a horse's legs. (*Prosody*). Vowel-accent preceding the quiescent rhyme-letter of a verse (*called* الرَّوِيّ المُقَيَّد). تَوْجِيه
Direction towards. تَوَجُّه وَاتِّجَاه إِلَى
✧ Promotions. تَوْجِيهَات
Regarded, distinguished. Two-humped, on the back and chest. مُوَجَّه
Struck on the face. مَوْجُوه
Interview. ✧ Adulation. مُوَاجَهَة
✱ To have the hoofs injured by walk; to feel a pain in the hoofs (horse). وَجِيَ a وَجًى, وَتَوَجَّى
To find a. o. worthless. وَجَى يَجِي وَجْيًا, وَأَوْجَى ه
To come back with empty hands (hunter). أَوْجَى
To chafe the feet, hoofs (walk). ه — To render a. o. useless, worthless.
To abstain from. أَوْجَى عن
To remove a. o. from. — ه عن
Having a lesion in the hoofs. وَجٍ وَوَجِيّ م وَجِيَة وَوَجِيَّة وَوَجْيَاء
Hurt in the hoofs. وَجِيّ
Bundle. وِجَاء ج أَوْجِيَة
Worthless. وَجِيّ ج أَوْجِيَاء
✱ Stake, peg. Name of a destitute man. وَحّ
✱ To emit a hoarse voice. To warm the fingers with the breath. وَحْوَح
Nimble, expeditious (man). Fiery, impetuous. Barking dog. وَحْوَح وَوَحْوَاح
✱ Disease of camels. وُحَاب
✱ To seek refuge, shelter. وَحِجَ وَحْجًا
Depressed land. وَحَجَة ج أَوْحَاج
✱ To be unique, alone, unparalleled. To remain lowly, apart. To be identical. وَحَد يَحِد حِدَةً وَوَحْدًا وَحْدَةً وَوُحُودًا, وَوَحُد يَحِد وَحَادَةً وَوُحُودَةً
To unify; to make one. To identify, to render alike, similar. To judge a. o. or a. th. to be unequalled. وَحَّد ه وه
He asserted the belief in the unity of God. — الله
To bring forth one lamb only (ewe). أَوْحَد

تَوْحِيد Unitarianism, belief in the unity of God, worship of the true God.
تَوَحُّد Seclusion, solitude.
إِتِّحاد Union, agreement, concord: intimate connection.
أُحادَ ومَوْحَدَ One after another, one and one.
جاءُوا أُحادَ او مَوْحَدَ They came one by one.
مُوَحَّد (*Gram.*) Marked with one point (letter). ✧ Unified (debt).
مُتَوَحِّد Isolated, secluded, single, one, unique, alone.
✲ وَحِرَ يَوْحَرُ وَحَرًا To be poisoned by lizards (food). To eat food infected by lizards.
وحِرَ يَحِرُ ويَوْحَرُ ويَيْحَرُ وَحَرًا صَدْرُهُ His heart was filled with hatred.
أَوْحَرَهُ مِن حَسَدٍ He filled him with hatred.
أَوْحَرَ ه To poison (food: reptile).
وَحَر Rancour.
وَحِرٌ م وَحِرَةٌ Rancorous.
وَحَرَة ج وَحَر A white venomous lizard spotted with red. Short (camel). Dark and ugly (woman).
✲ وَحُشَ o وُحُوشَةً ووَحَاشَةً To abound with wild beasts (land).
وَحَشَ يَحِشُ وَحْشًا, ووَحَّشَ بِ To throw away (arms and clothes) for escaping.
وَحَّشَ ه وه ✧ To desolate, to depopulate (a land). To brutify a. o.
أَوْحَشَ وتَوَحَّشَ To become desolate, wild, uninhabited (land). To be hungry.
أَوْحَشَ ه To find (a country) waste, lonely.
— ه To trouble a. o.; to make a. o. to feel loneliness.
تَوَحَّشَ To become savage, wild, unsociable.
— ل To fast before taking (a medecine).
إِسْتَوْحَشَ To experience loneliness. To be sad, afraid (man). To be deserted, desolate (place).
— مِن To feel a dislike for a. o. To mistrust a. o.
إِسْتَوْحَشَ ل To miss, to regret a. o.
وَحْش Desert, waste (place). Shy (girl). Lone, solitary.
لَقِيتُهُ بِوَحْشِ إِصْمِتَ أَو إِصْمِتَةَ I met him in a deserted country.
وَحْش ج وُحُوش ووُحْشان, ووَحِيش Beast of prey, wild beast.
حِمار وَحْش وحِمار وَحْشِيّ Wild ass.
هُوَ مِن وَحْشِ النَّاسِ He is of the refuse of the people.
وَحْشَة Loneliness, solitude. Shyness, wildness. Sadness, disquietude. Fear, unsociableness. Waste, desert.
وَحْشِيّ A wild beast. Barbarous (man). Wild (beast). Uncouth (word). Exterior side. Wild fig. Back of the hand or foot.
وَحْشِيَّة Blasting wind.
تَوَحُّش Wildness, savageness, unsociableness.
وَحْشان ج وَحاشَى Sad. Sorrowful.
✧ وَحِيش Ugly, bad.
مُتَوَحِّش Become wild (beast). Peevish, savage, uncivilized (man).
مَوْحُوشَة Haunted by wild beasts (land).
مُسْتَوْحِشَة Waste and desert (land).
✲ وَحَصَ i ه To drag a. th. on the ground.
وَحْصَة Cold, coolness.
✲ وَحَفَ يَحِفُ وَحْفًا, ووَحَفَ To throw o.'s self down (man, camel).
وَحَفَ إِلى To hurry towards.
وَحِفَ a وَحَفًا, ووَحُفَ o وَحافَةً ووُحُوفَةً To be luxuriant (plant, hair).
وَحَّفَ وأَوْحَفَ To hasten.
وَحَّفَ ه ب To strike a. o. with (a stick).
وَحْف ووَاحِف Luxuriant (plant). Thick-feathered (wing).
وَحْف ووَحَف Black and luxuriant hair.
وَحْفَة Sound.
— ج وِحاف Black stone.
وَحْفاء ج وَحافَى Land full of black stones. Red (earth).
مَوْحِف ج مَوَاحِف Resting-place for camels.
مُوَحَّف Emaciated, exhausted (camel).

To urge a. o.; to call (a messenger). إِسْتَوْحَى ه
To take information about a. th. — ه
To inquire from a. o. about. — ه ه
Letter, writing. Revelation, thing revealed by God. وَحْي
Voice. وَحْي, وَوَحًى ج وُحِيّ, ووحاة
Angel. Chief of a tribe. Speediness, haste. وَحًى
Make haste; go speedily. أَلْوَحَى أَلْوَحَى
Quick death. وَحِيّ م وَحِيَّة
Quicker. أَوْحَى
Pain. Wish, intention. ✲ وَخْ
To become flabby (belly). ✲ وَخْوَخَ
Coward, weak. Impotent. Slothful. Fleshy. Soft date. وَخْوَاخ
To make long strides. ✲ وَخَدَ يَخِدُ وَخْدًا ووَخَدَانًا ووَخِيدًا
Wide stride. وَخْد ج وُخُود
Making wide strides. وَاخِد ووَخُود ووَخَّاد
(for آخَذَ) وخذ — وَاخَذَ مُوَاخَذَةً ه ✧
To upbraid, to reprove a. o.
Late. (from آخِر) وَخْرِيّ ◻
To prick a. o. with a needle. To lance, to scarify. To appear on (the head: hoary hair). ✲ وَخَزَ يَخِزُ وَخْزًا ه
Small quantity. Plague. Pricking pain. وَخْز
They came four and four. جَاءُوا وَخْزًا وَخْزًا
Cake made with honey. وَخِيز
To be cheap (goods). To be base, low (man). ✲ وَخُشَ o وَخَاشَةً ووُخُوشَةً
To revile, to debase a. th. To give little of. وَخَّشَ ه
He made him a paltry gift. أَوْخَشَ لَهُ بِعَطِيَّةٍ
He impaired his reputation. — فِي عِرْضِهِ
To mix up a. th. — ه
وَخْش (m. f. s. pl.) ج أَوْخَاش و وِخَاش
Vile, base, mean, contemptible (man).
Refuse of mankind. — أَلنَّاس
To oscillate, to quiver. ✲ وَخَصَ — يَخِصُ وُخُوصًا, وأَوْخَصَ
He gave little him. أَوْخَصَ لَهُ بِعَطِيَّةٍ
Oscillation. وُخُوص
To prick, to ✲ وَخَضَ يَخِضُ وَخْضًا ه ب

To sink into mire. ✲ وَحِلَ a وَحَلًا ومَوْحَلًا, وتَوَحَّلَ
To become muddy (soil). ✧ وَحَّلَ
To render (the ground) muddy. ✧ وَحَّلَ ه
To throw a. o. into mire. أَوْحَلَ ه
He afflicted him with an evil. — ه شَرًّا
To be muddy, slimy (place). تَوَحَّلَ واسْتَوْحَلَ
He made a conditional oath. إِتَّحَلَ فِي يَمِينِهِ
Slime, thin mud. وَحْل ووَحَل ج وُحُول وأَوْحَال
Muddy, slimy. وَحِل م وَحِلَة
Mire. Fall in the mire. مَوْحِل
To be incompliant (female). To have a longing, a craving (pregnant woman). ✲ وَحِمَتْ تَحِمُ وتَوْحَمُ وَحَمًا, وتَوَحَّمَتْ
To satisfy the craving of (a pregnant woman). وَحَّمَ ه
To slaughter (a beast) for satisfying the craving of (a pregnant woman). وَحَّمَ ل
Longing of a pregnant woman. وَحَم ووِحَام و وَحَام
Longing, craving. Lust. وَحَم
Longing for a. th. (pregnant woman). وَحْمَى ج وِحَام ووَحَامَى
He asks for what he does not want. وَحْمَى وَلَا حَبَل
✲ وَحَنَ ووَحِنَ يَحِنُ ويَوْحَنُ وَحْنًا وحِنَةً عَلَى
To be angry with, to hate a. o.
To be big-bellied. To be vile. To perish. تَوَحَّنَ
Sticky mud. وَحْنَة
To suggest, to point out a. th. to. To put a. th. into (the mind). ✲ وَحَى يَحِي وَحْيًا, وأَوْحَى إِلَى ب
He despatched a messenger to such a one. وَحَى وأَوْحَى إِلَى فُلَانٍ
To write (a letter). وَحَى ه
God inspired his heart. — فِي قَلْبِهِ
He spoke secretly, he revealed a. th. to him. — إِلَيْهِ الكَلَامَ
To hasten. — وَحْيًا ووَحًى ووَحَاءً, وتَوَحَّى
To urge, to rouse a. o. وَحَّى ه
To reveal a. th. to a. o. أَوْحَى ه ه
To beckon to o. another. تَوَاحَوْا

To purpose a. th. ✡ وخن – توخّن
Corruption. وَخْنَة
To purpose, to aim at. ✡ وَخَى يَخِي وَخْيًا ه
I had the same design as thou. وَخَيْتُ وَخْيَكَ
I do not know where he is gone to. ما أدري أيْنَ وَخَى
He endeavoured to please such a one. وَخَّى وتوخّى رِضَى فُلَانٍ
He sent him on an errand. وَخَّى ه لِأَمْر
To become the brother of. To fraternise with. وَاخَى مُوَاخَاةً (for آخى مُؤَاخَاةً)
To purpose, to aim at. To prefer a. th. to. تَوَخَّى ه
To question, to inquire of a. o. about. إسْتَوْخَى ه
Aim, straight course; direct road. وَخْيٌ ج وُخِيٌّ ووخي
✡ وَدّ a وِدًّا وُدًّا و وَدَادًا ووُدَادًا ووِدَادَةً
To love, to be fond of a. o. To will, to wish for a. th. و مَوَدَّةً ومَوْدِدَةً ومَوْدُودَةً ه وه
I wished it to be so. وَدِدْتُ لَوْ كَانَ كَذَا
To love a. o. وَادَّ مُوَادَّةً و وِدَادًا ه
To show love to a. o. تَوَدَّدَ إِلى
To court, to attract the love of. – ه
To love o. a. تَوَادُّوا
Love, attachment. Wish, desire. وَدّ ووُدّ و وِدّ و وَدَاد وُدَاد
I wish it to be so يُودِّي و ◇ بِدّي أنْ يَكُونَ كَذَا
Pole, stake. Wooden peg. Idol in the time of Noah. وَدّ (for وَتِد)
وَدّ و وِدّ وُدّ ج أوْدَاد وأوُدّ وأَوِدّ و مُوَدّ
Affectionate, friendly. Beloved.
Affectionate. (m. f.) وَدُود
The Beloved (God). الوَدُود
Friendly, loving. وَدِيد ج أودّة وأوِدّاء
Friends, beloved ones. (coll.) وَدّ و وِدّ ووُدّ وَوَدِيد
Fonder of. أوَدّ
Friendship, love. مَوَدَّة
Mutual love. مُوَادَّة وتَوَادّ
To level (the soil). ✡ وَدَأ يَدَأ وَدْأ ه
To ill-treat a. o. – ب
To be kept from a. o. (news). وَدِئَ a وَدَاء، وتَوَدَّأ عن

wound a. o. slightly with (a spear).
Hoariness has appeared upon his head. وَخَطَهُ الشَّيْبُ
Slightly wounded. وَخِيض
To whiten a. o. (hoary hair). ✡ وَخَط يَخِط وَخْطًا ه
To spear a. o. – ه ب
He underwent various chances in trade. – فِي أَلْبِنَه
To become hoary. وُخِط
Penetrating, piercing through. مِيخَط
Hoary (man). Speared. مَوْخُوط
To thicken, to be solidified (mallow). ✡ وَخَف يَخِف وَخْفًا
To backbite, to abuse a. o. – ه
To beat up (mallow) for thickening it. – وأوْخَف ه
To slip (foot). إتَّخَف
Leather-bag. وَخْفَة
Thickened (mallow). Dish of dates and cream. Liquid mud. وَخِيفَة
Foolish. مُوخِف
To be unhealthy (place); to be indigestible (food). ✡ وَخُم o وَخَامَةً ووُخُومَةً ووُخُومًا
To suffer from indigestion. وَخِم a وَخَمًا، واتَّخَم مِن وعَن
To render unhealthy. To soil, to taint a. th. وَخَّم ه
To cause indigestion to a. o. أتْخَم ه (for أوْخَم)
To find (a place, food) tainted, unwholesome. تَوَخَّم واسْتَوْخَم ه
Indigestion. تُخَمَة ج تُخَمَات وتُخَم
Unhealthiness of (a place, food). ◻ Danger. وَخَامَة ووُخُومَة
Piles of camels. ◇ Filthiness, dirt. وَخَم ج أوْخَام
◇ Filthy, dirty. وَخِم ووَخِيم
Dull, heavy, rough (man). وَخْم أو وَخِم ج أوْخَام
Unhealthy (climate). وَخِيم ووَخُوم ج وَخَامَى و وِخَام
Indigestible (food). Noxious. وَخِيم
أرض وَخْمَة ووَخِمَة ووَخَام ووَخُوم ووَخِيمَة
Land having insalubrious pastures.
Insalubrious pasturages. أرض مَوْخَمَة ومُوخِمَة

To level (the وَدَّأ تَوْدِيئًا وتَوْدِئَةً ه على earth) over a. o. *i. e.* to bury a. o.
He caused the loss وَدَّأ على فُلَانٍ وبِفُلَان of such a one.
He destroyed him. تَوَدَّأ على فُلَان
He took his property. تَوَدَّأ على مَالِهِ
The earth has been تَوَدَّأَت عَلَيهِ ٱلأَرضُ levelled upon him; he is dead.
The news have been تَوَدَّأَت عَنهُ الأَخبار cut off from him.
Loss, destruction. وَدأ
Dangerous place. Waterless مُودَّأَة desert.
He is in a very ✡ وَدب — هُوَ على وَدْبٍ bad state.
To cut the ✡ وَدَج يَدِج وَدْجًا. ووَدَّج ه jugular vein to (a beast).
To set in order. To settle a وَدَج بَيْن difference between.
To make peace, to act gently وَادَج ه with a. o.
Jugular vein. Cause, وَدَج ج أَوْدَاج motive. Means of attaining.
They are two brothers. هُمَا وَدَجَان
Jugular vein. وِدَاج مث وِدَاجَانِ
To become fat (camel). ✡ وَدِج — أَوْدَج
To submit to. أَوْدَج ل
Ficus religiosa, species of fig- وَدَج tree.
He has been useless مَا أَغنَى عَنِي وَدَجَة to me.
To be dead-drunk. ✡ وَدَر يَدِر وَدْرًا
To discard, to repel a. th. — ه
Avert thy face from me. دِرْ وَجْهَكَ عَنِّي
To beguile a. o. To send (a وَدَّر ن messenger).
To ward off (an evil). To squan- — ه der (wealth).
Avert thy face from وَدِّر وَجهكَ عَنِّي me.
To throw a. o. into dan- وَدَّر وتَوَدَّر ه ger.
To be spent away (wealth). تَوَدَّر
To embark in (a danger). — في
To be hidden ✡ وَدَس يَدِس وَدْسًا على to a. o.
I do not know where مَا أَدرِي أَيْنَ وَدَس he is gone to.
To conceal a. th. وَدَس ب

He did not relate وَدَّس إِلَيهِ بِكَلَام everything to him.
To shoot وَدَس ووَدَّس وأَوْدَس وتَوَدَّس forth (ground).
To be hidden. وَدَّس
Off-shoots, sprouts. وَدْس و وِدَاس
How fine its vegeta- مَا أَحسَن وَدَسَهَا tion is!
Sprouting (plant). وَادِس ووَدِيس
Covered with sprouts, buds مُوَدَّوسَة (land).
He did ✡ وَدَص يَدِص وَدصًا إِلَيهِ بِكَلَام not complete his narration to him.
To let, to permit (*chiefly used in the aorist and imperative*). ✡ وَدَع يَدَع
Let me do. دَعنِي أَفعَل
To bid farewell وَدَع يَدَع وَدْعًا, ووَدَّع ه to; to take leave of.
To be quiet, وَدَع يَدَع ووَدُع يَوْدُع وَدَاعَةً calm; meek, sedate. To become wealthy.
To deposit (clo- وَدَع a وَدْعًا, ووَدَّع ه في thes) in (a ward-robe).
To be reconciled to. وَادَع ه
To intrust a. o. with. To أَوْدَع ه وه deposit a. th.
To confide (a letter) to. — ه ه
To receive (a deposit). — ه
To lay, to keep a. th. in (a تَوَدَّع ه chest).
To employ a. o. — ه
I was bidden farewell. تُوُدِّع مِنِّي
To make peace with. To take تَوَادَع leave from o. a.
To act gently, sedately. إِتَّدَع
To recommend a. th. to. إِستَوْدَع ه ه To deposit a. th. in the hands of.
Grave; railing, enclosure وَدَع ج وُدُوع around a grave.
Mole, field-rat. وَدْع ووَدَع وأَوْدَع
Sea-shell used as an amulet. Cowry. وَدْعَة ووَدَعَة ج وَدْع ووَدَع ووَدَعَات
Noah's ark. The Caaba, the black stone of Mecca. Idols. ذَاتُ الوَدْع او الوَدَع,
Farewell. Alkali. وَدَاع
✧ Octava of a feast. وَدَاع عِيد
Meekness, forbearance. Mild, quiet temper. وَدَاعَة

Misfortune. ذَاتُ وَدْقَيْنِ
Red spots on the eyes, وَدْق ووَدَق
Swelling of the eyes, ears.
Bloodshot (eye); swollen (eye, ear). وَدِقَة
Intenseness of heat. وَدِيقَة
Lawn, meadow. — ج وَدَائِق
In heat (she-ass). وَادِق ووَدُوق ووَدِيق
Vicinage. مَوْدُوق
To be fat (meat). ✱ وَدَك a وَدَكًا
To season (food) with grease. وَدَّك ه
Grease. Gravy. وَدَك
Fatness. دِكَة
وَادِك ووَدِك م وَادِكَة ووَدِكَة , ووَدِيك
Fat, obese (man). (*m. f.*) ووَدُوك
Porridge of flour mixed with fat. وَدِيكَة
Calamities. بَنَات أَوْدَك
To churn (milk). ✱ وَدَل يَدِل وَدْلًا ه
To moisten, to soak; to wet a. th. ✱ وَدَن يَدِن وَدْنًا و وِدَانًا, ووَدَّن واتَّدَن ه
To deck (a bride). وَدَن ه
To shorten, to curtail a. th. — وَدْنًا , ووَدَّن وأَوْدَن
To strike a. o. or a. th. with (a stick). وَدَن ه وه ب
To bring forth weak children (woman). وَدِنَتْ a وَدْنًا, وأَوْدَنَتْ
To be soft (skin). تَوَدَّن
To be wetted, soaked. إِتَّدَن
Wetted, soaked. وَدِين ومَوْدُون
Soft, supple. أَوْدَن
Sickly (child). مُودَن ومَوْدُون
Short-necked, having distorted shoulders. مَوْدُون
To prevent, to remove a. o. from. ✱ وَدَه يَدِه وَدْهًا ه عَن
To flock (camels). To be overcome, to submit (antagonist). إِسْتَوْدَه
To be well managed (affair). To despise a. o. — ه
To pay the blood-price. ✱ وَدَى يَدِي وَدْيًا وَدِيَةً ه
Give the blood-price of the slain man. دِ , دِيَا , دُوا القَتِيلَ
To flow. وَدَى i وَدْيًا
To draw near to. — ه
✧ To send a. o. وَدَّى تَوْدِيَةً ه
✧ To lead to (a place: road). — إِلى

Rest, ease; meekness. Ampleness of life. دَعَة وتُدْعَة وتَدْعَة وتَدَاعَة
Peaceful, quiet. وَادِع
He has obtained dignities without trouble. نَال المَكَارِمَ وَادِعًا
Quiet, easy of temper. Tractable (horse). وَدِيع ج وُدَعَاء
Compact, alliance. — ج وَدَائِع
Deposit, trust. وَدِيعَة ج وَدَائِع
More quiet. Having a white throat (pigeon). أَوْدَع
Meek; quiet; having a limb diseased. مُتَّدِع
Nest-egg for brooding. ✧ مَوْدَعَة
Repose, ease. مَوْدُوع
Submissive (horse). — ومُودَع
Deposited. مَوْدُوع ومُسْتَوْدَع
Depositor. مُسْتَوْدِع
Depositary. Womb. مُسْتَوْدَع
Wardrobe. Dayly clothes. مِيدَع ومِيدَعَة ومِيدَاعَة ج مَوَادِع
Hard language. كَلَام مِيدَع
He has no helper, nobody to take care of his affair. مَا لَهُ مِيدَع
To melt (grease). To leak (vessel). ✱ وَدَف يَدِف وَدْفًا
He gave little to him. — لَهُ العَطِيَّة
To stop on the summit a mountain (antelope). تَوَدَّف فَوْق الجَبَل
To ascertain (news). تَوَدَّف واسْتَوْدَف ه
To be luxuriant (plant). إِسْتَوْدَف
To melt (grease). — ه
To pour milk into (a vessel). — فِي
Green meadow, verdant garden. وَدْفَة ووَدِيفَة
Species of thistle *called also* نَصِيّ. وَدْفَة
To drop (rain). ✱ وَدَق يَدِق وَدْقًا
To approach to. To become possible to a. o. (affair). — وَدْقًا ووُدُوقًا إِلى
To become familiar with. — ب
To be sharp (sword). To be flabby (belly). To have an umbilical hernia. وَدَق
To yield rain (sky). — وأَوْدَق
وَدَق i ووَدِق a ووَدُق o وَدْقًا ووِدَاقًا ووَدَقَانًا
To be in heat (she-ass, mare).
To have the eyes bloodshot by disease. وَدِقَتْ تِيدَق وَدَقًا
Drizzle. وَدْق

To strut, to swagger. وَذَفَ وتَوَذَّفَ
Beginning, origin. وَذَفَان
To receive a piece of meat from (a butcher). ✡ وذل – تَوَذَّلَ مِن
Nimble, brisk (maid-servant). وَذَالَة ووَذْلَة
Piece of meat kept apart. وَذَالَة
Polished piece of silver. Metallic (mirror). Piece of fat of the hump, of the tail. Cheerful, brisk. وَذِيلَة ج وَذِيل ووَذَائِل
To be broken (bucket-strap). ✡ وَذِمَ a وَذَمًا
To put a collar on (a dog). To cure (a she-camel) from warts. وَذَّمَ ه
To cut up a. th. – ه
To exceed the age of (fifty : man). – على
To impose upon o.'s self (a pilgrimage to Mecca). To put (a strap) to a bucket. أَوْذَمَ ه
Redundance, excess. Warts in a she-camel's womb. وَذَمٌ
Strap of a bucket. – ج أَوْذَام
Ventricle with the bowels. وَذَمَة ج وِذَام
Victim offered at Mecca. Votive offering. وَذِيمَة ج وَذَائِم
To admire a. th. To change, to turn over. ✡ وَذَنَ – تَوَذَّنَ ه
To scratch (the face) with the nails. ✡ وَذَى يَذِي وَذْيًا ه
Harm, damage. وَذَاة
Pain. Disease. Defect. Cold. وَذِيَّة
He is spotless, without defect. مَا بِهِ وَذِيَّة
To throw, to reject a. th. ✧ وَرَّ o وَرًّا ه
Haunch-bone. وَرّ و وَرَّة
Ditch in the earth. وَرَّة
To look fixedly at. ✡ وَرْوَرَ النَّظَر
He spoke volubly. وَرْوَرَ في الكَلَام
Bird of the species *Merops*, bee-eater. ✧ وَرْوَار ج وَرَاوِير
Weak-sighted. وَرْوَرِيّ
To repel a. o. or a. th. ✡ وَرَأَ يَرَأُ وَيَوْرَأُ وَرْأً ه وه
To be surfeited. – مِن
I was not aware of the thing. مَا وُرِئْتُ ومَا وُرِئْتُ بِهِ
Beyond, behind. In front. وَرَاءَ

To perish. To be fully armed. أَوْدَى إِيدَاءً
To take a. o. away (death). – ب
To receive blood-money. إِتَّدَى
To acknowledge (a debt, a right). إِستَوْدَى ب
Bloodwit equal to 500 camels. دِيَة ج دِيَات
Ruin, loss. وَدَى
Valley. River-bed. Road, way. Oasis. وَادٍ ج أَوْدِيَة وأَوْدَايَة وأَوْدَاء وأَوْدَاة ✧ وِدْيَان
Goletta, port of Tunis. حَلْق الوَادِ
The two (words) have the same meaning and the same sound. هُمَا مِن وَادٍ وَاحِدٍ
We have not the same design as thou. أَنتَ فِي وَادٍ ونَحْنُ فِي وَادٍ
Palm-shoots. وَدِيّ (*un.* وَدِيَّة)
To hasten, to hurry on. ✡ وَذْوَذَ
To despise, to find fault with. To drive away a. o. ✡ وَذَأَ يَذَأُ وَذْءًا ه
To be blamed, charged with a fault. إِتَّذَأَ
Harsh, hateful language. وَذْء
Disease ; defect. وَذْأَة
Stomach of a ruminant (*pl.*) eaten with milk. Punctures, loops made in sewing. ✡ وِذَاب
To be chafed on the thighs (man). ✡ وَذِحَ a وَذَحًا
Dry dung sticking to the wool, to the tail of sheep. وَذَحٌ ج وُذُحٌ
He has been of no use to me. مَا أَغْنَى عَنِّي وَذْحَة
Vile, contemptible. أَوْذَحُ
To cut (meat) in slices. To wound a. o. ✡ وَذَرَ يَذِرُ وَذْرًا، ووَذَّرَ ه
To let, to leave, to desist. (*Only used in this sense in the present and imperative*). يَذَرُ
Let, cease. ذَرْ م ذَرِي
Boneless meat. وَذْرَة ج وَذْر ووِذَر
The two lips. أَلْوَذْرَتَان
Piece of cloth cut off from a garment. وُذَارَة
To flow (water). ✡ وَذَعَ يَذَعُ وَذْعًا
Spring ; flowing water. وَاذِع
To melt (grease). ✡ وَذَفَ يَذِفُ وَذْفًا
To waddle, to sweep. – وَذَفَ وَذَفَانًا

وَرَاءَهُم Behind or before them.
وَرَاء Grand-son.
✻ وَرِبَ a وَرَبًا To become corrupt (man, root).
✧ وَرَّبَ i ه To slant, to crook a. th.
وَرَّبَ عَن To express a. th. equivocally.
وَارَبَ مُوَارَبَةً و وِرَابًا ه To try to beguile, to circumvent a. o.
✧ إِنْوَرَبَ To slant, to slope, to be oblique.
وَرْب ج أَوْرَاب Den of wild beasts. Space between two ribs. Span. Limb of the body. Mouse-hole. ✧ Obliquity. Diagonal.
وِرْب Limb. Deceit, crookedness.
بِٱلْوَرْب ✧ Aslant, obliquely. Diagonally. Athwart.
بِٱلوِرْب Craftily, cunningly.
وَرَبَة Buttocks. ✧ Small turban.
أُورُوبَا وَأُرُبَّا Europe.
أُورُوبَاوِيّ وأُورُبِّي European.
وَارِب وَمَوْرُوب ✧ Aslant, oblique.
وَرِب Corrupt (root, man).
مُوَارَبَة و وِرَاب Shift, equivocation.
✻ وَرِثَ يَرِثُ وِرْثًا وإِرْثًا و إِرْثَةً ووِرَاثَةً و رِثَةً وتُرَاثًا ه To inherit a. th. of. To become the heir of a. o.
— ه او ه مِن To inherit a. th. from.
وَرَّثَ وأَوْرَثَ ه To appoint a. o. as the heir of.
— وأَوْرَثَ ه ه To bequeath a. th. to a. o.
وَرَّثَ ه To stir (the fire).
أَوْرَثَ ه ه To occasion (evil, sorrow) to a. o.
تَوَارَثَ ه To inherit a. th. To be transmitted by inheritance (property).
تَوَارَثُوا ٱلْمَجْدَ كَابِرًا عَن كَابِرٍ They inherited nobility from their ancestors.
إِرْث و وِرْث و وِرَاثَة Inheritance.
تُرَاث Inheritance, hereditary estate.
وَارِث ج وَرَثَة ووُرَّاث Heir. Survivor.
اللّٰهُمَّ إِجْعَلْهُ ٱلْوَارِثَ مِنِّي Let him alive, to my God, that he may be my heir.
مِيرَاث ج مَوَارِيث Inheritance, heritage.
مَوْرُوث Inherited (property). Bequeather, devisor.
✻ ورج — وَارِجَة ج أَوَارِجَة وأَوَارِجَات Account-book for receipt and expenditure. Register. Roll.
✻ وَرِخَ a وَرَخًا، وتَوَرَّخَ To become soft, thin (dough).
وَرَّخَ ه (See أَرَّخَ) To put the date on (a writing). To record a. th. (chronicler).
أَوْرَخَ ه To soften (dough) with water.
تَوَرَّخَ واستَوْرَخَ To be moistened (soil).
وَرِخ م وَرِخَة Luxuriant (ground).
وَرِيخَة ج وَرَائِخ Moist (earth). Soft (dough).
✻ وَرَدَ يَرِدُ وُرُودًا ه To come to (the water). To arrive, to be present at. To draw near to (a place).
— واستَوْرَدَ ه To draw (a doctrine, an error).
وَرَدَ ه To seize a. o. (fever).
— على To reach a. o. (letter). To present o.'s self before. To object to, to oppose a. o. To attack a. o. ✧ To give a good (produce) to a. o. (land).
وَرَدَ ووَرَّدَ To blossom (tree).
وُرِدَ To have an intermittent fever.
وَرُدَ o وُرُودَةً، واِيرَادَّ To be red, bay (horse).
وَرَّدَت To paint her cheeks red (woman).
— ه To dye (cloth) red.
وَارَدَ ه To come to water with a. o. To compose verses coincident with another poet's.
أَوْرَدَ إِيرَادًا، واستَوْرَدَ ه To bring (cattle) to water. To offer, to present a. o. with. To bring a. o., to make a. o. to come.
أَوْرَدَ ه To adduce, to mention, to cite (a proof). To bring (news). ✧ To give a good (produce: land).
تَوَرَّدَ To seek the way to water. To become rose-coloured (cheeks).
— ٱلْبَلْدَةَ They entered the town by small detachments (cavalry).
— واستَوْرَدَ ٱلْمَاءَ He came to water.
تَوَارَدَ ه To arrive together to (water).
— إِلى To arrive successively at (a place).
تَوَارَدَ ٱلشَّاعِرَان The two poets chanced to compose coincident verses.
وَرْد Saffron. Lion. Brave.
وَرْد ج وُرْد و وِرَاد وأَوْرَاد Reddish bay (horse).

◆ Returns, revenue; income. وَارِدَات و إيرادات
◆ Guardian, watchman. Is وَرْدِيَان
Coincidence between two pieces of verses. ◆ Index of the Bible. تَوَارُد ومُوَارَدَة
Road leading to water. Watering-trough. مَوْرِد ج مَوَارِد
Watering-trough. High road. مَوْرِدَة
Dyed red or rose (cloth). Dyed with saffron. Reddened (cheek). مُوَرَّد
Lion. مُتَوَرِّد
Seized with a fit of fever. مَوْرُود
◻ Camp, tents of an army. Ts أُورْدِي وأُورْدُو
To be overspread with green moss (water). To become green (plant). ✱ وَرِس a وَرَسًا
To dye (a stuff) yellow, red. وَرَّس ه
To produce turmeric (land). To put forth leaves (tree). To become yellow (thistle). أَوْرَس
Memecylon tinctorium, plant of Yemen used as a liniment and yellow dye. Turmeric, Indian saffron. وَرْس
Red (garment). Putting forth leaves (tree). Bright (saffron). وَارِس ووَرِيس
Reddish yellow. Bowl made of yellow wood. Yellow pigeon. وَرْسِيّ
Dyed red, yellow (cloth). وَرْسِيَّة ووَرِيسة ومُوَرَّسة
To eat greedily. To covet, to seek to obtain. ✱ وَرِش يَرِش وَرْشًا ووُرُوشًا
To take food with the hand and swallow it greedily. وَرَش ه
To come to (a dinner-party) uninvited. To be a parasite. — على
To incite a. o. against. — ه بِفُلَان
To be swift (beast). وَرِش a وَرَشًا
To sow discord between. وَرَّش بَيْن
Milk-food. وَرْش
Colic, gripes. وَرَش
◆ Factory, work-shop. Distressing affair. وَرْشَة
Intruder, sponger. وَارِش م وَارِشَة
Brisk, lively (camel). وَرِش م وَرِشَة
◆ Noisy (child).
Wild dove. Ring turtle-dove. وَرَشَان ج وِرشان ووَرَاشِين

وَرْد ج وُرُود Blossom. Rose. (*un.* وَرْدَة)
— جُورِيّ ونصيبيّ Damask-rose.
— جَبَلِيّ ◆ Wild rose, sweet brier.
— الحُبّ *Ranunculus Asiaticus*, crow-foot (*plant*).
— الحَمِير Peony (*plant*).
— الحِمَار او الفَخَّار Chrysanthemum (*plant*).
— دَفْرَاء Wind-flower, anemone (*pl.*).
— الزِّينَة و◆ الزَّوَانِي Althea, marsh-mallow (*plant*).
— السِّيَاج Sweet brier, hawthorn (*pl.*).
— اللَّيْل Marvel of Peru (*plant*).
— مُلَمَّم *Astur palumbarius*, goshawk.
مَاء وَرْد Rose-water.
وِرْد ج أَوْرَاد Coming to water. Periodical fever; fit-day. Section of the Coran recited privately. Army. Share of water. Flight of birds. Herd of camels. Party of travellers coming to water.
وِرْد الطَّرِيقَة ◻ Watchword of dervishes.
بِنْت وَرْدَان ج بَنَات وَرْدَان Wood-louse.
وَرْدَة Rose. Bay (mare). ◻ Look out!
عَشِيَّة وَرْدَة Evening in which the horizon assumes a reddish hue.
وُرْدَة Reddish colour.
وَرْدِيّ Reddish, rose-coloured.
وَرْدِيَّة ◆ Rosary, beads.
وَرِيد وحَبْل ج أَوْرِدَة ووُرُود ووُرْد ج وِرْدَان ج أَوْرِيد هث وَرِيد Jugular vein.
مُنْتَفِخ الوَرِيد Hot-tempered, prone to anger.
وَارِد ج وَارِدُون ووُرَّاد ووَارِدَة ووُرُود Coming to water; comer; arriver.
وَارِد Go-ahead, hardy. Long (hair). Road. Sudden inspiration. ◆ Income. Import.
وَارِد الأَرْنَبَة Long-nosed.
ألصَّادِرُون والوَارِدُون The comers and goers.
وَارِدَة Way, path.
وَارِدَة وقَوْم وَارِدَة Party going to water.
وَارِدَة الأَغْصَان With dependent branches (tree).
وَارِدَات Hills celebrated by a battle between two Arab tribes. ◆ Import goods.

✱ وَرَصَت تَرِص وَرْصًا . ووَرَّصَت وأَوْرَصَت
To lay eggs (hen).

✱ وَرَضَت تَرِض وَرْضًا, ووَرَّضَت To lay eggs (hen).

وَرَّض To seek for pasturages. To intend fasting.

✱ ورط — وَرَّط وأَوْرَط ه To hurl a. o. down into an abyss. ✧ To entice a. o. to (a crime).

وَرَّط وأَوْرَط ه في To hide (camels) amongst (others). To involve a. o. in (a difficult case).

وَارَط ه مُوَارَطَة و وِرَاطًا ه To circumvent a. o.

تَوَرَّط To be hurled down, to roll down.

— واسْتَوْرَط في To embark in (a difficult affair).

وَرْطَة ج وَرَطَات و وِرَاط Precipice, abyss. Hollow. Distressing case. Scrape. Slime. Well. Wayless plain; perdition. Anus.

وِرَاط Cheating; concealment of camels in order to avoid the poor-rate.

شَرّ مُوَرِّط Misfortune.

أُورْطَة TE Battalion.

✱ وَرِعَ يَرِع ويَوْرَع وَرَعًا و وَرْعًا و وُرُوعًا و وُرُوعًا و وَرْعَة, ووَرُعَ o وَرَاعَة To be pious, to be godly. To abstain from unlawful things.

وَرُعَ يَرْعُ ووَرُعَ o وَرَاعَة ووَرَاعًا ووَرْعَة ووُرْعَة ووُرُوعًا ووُرْعًا To be faint-hearted, weak.

وَرِعَ يَرِع وَرَاعَة عَن To abstain from.

وَرَّعَ ه عَن To compel a. o. to abstain from.

— وأَوْرَعَ بَيْن To interpose, to intervene between.

وَارَعَ ه To consult a. o.

تَوَرَّعَ مِن وعَن To abstain from (sin).

وَرَع Godliness.

— و رِعَة و رِيعَة Self-restraint, continence.

رِعَة Good or bad behaviour. State, condition.

وَرِع ج أَوْرَاع Godly. Self-controlled. Weak. Timid.

مَالُهُ أَوْرَاع His cattle are ill-conditioned.

◘ أُورْغُول Flute, fife.

✱ وَرَف يَرِف وَرْفًا وَوَرِيفًا وَوُرُوفًا و رِفَة To spread afar (shadow). To become luxuriant (plant).

وَرَّف وأَوْرَف To spread afar (shadow).

وَرَّف ه To suck (a plant). To allot (a land).

وَرْف Thin parts of the liver.

رِفَة Verdant plant.

✱ وَرَق يَرِق وَرْقًا, ووَرَّق وأَوْرَق To put forth leaves (tree).

وَرَق ووَرَّق ه To strip (a branch) of its leaves.

وَرَّق ه ✧ To parget (a wall).

أَوْرَق To become rich. To come back with empty hands (hunter).

تَوَرَّق To eat tree-leaves. To feed on leaves (beast).

إِيرَاق To become yellow (grapes).

وَرِق ووُرْق ووِرْق ووَرَق ج أَوْرَاق و وِرَاق Silver, coined silver.

رِقَة ج رِقُون Land becoming green after rain.

وَرَق ج أَوْرَاق Leaves, foliage. Sheet of paper; plate of metal. Clot of blood.

لَعِب ٱلْوَرَق ✧ Play at cards.

وَرْقَة Defect in a bow.

وُرْقَة Ash-colour.

وَرَقَة ج وَرَقَات Tree-leaf, sheet of paper. ✧ Card, playing-card.

وَرَقَة (*m. f.*) Vile or noble. ✧ Coating, layer, pargeting.

وَرَاق Luxuriance of a land.

وِرَاق Growth-season of leaves.

وِرَاقَة Paper-manufacture.

وَرَّاق Paper-maker. Stationer. Clerk, copyist. Rich.

وَارِقَة ووَرِقَة ووَرِيقَة Leafy (tree).

أَوْرَق م وَرْقَاء ج وُرْق Dusky, ash-coloured (camel). Ashes. Year of drought. Milk mixed with two thirds of water.

زَمَان أَوْرَق Drought.

وَرْقَاء ج وَرَاقِي ووَرَاقٍ Dove. She-wolf.

أَلتِّجَارَةُ مَوْرَقَةٌ أَلْمَال Trade is a means of increasing wealth.

مُوَرِّق Paper-seller. ✧ Pargeter.

مَا زِلْتُ مِنكَ مُوَارِقًا I have not ceased remaining by thy side.

To lean, to recline on the hip-bone. ✲ وَرَكَ يَرِكُ وَرْكًا, وتَوَرَّكَ وتَوَارَكَ

To put a. o. on the hip-bone. — ووَرَّكَ هُ

To wound a. o. on the haunch. وَرَكَ ه

To remain in (a place). وَرَكَ وُرُوكًا, وتَوَرَّكَ ب

To lean one thigh only on the saddle. — ووَرَّكَ

To fold a leg for alighting (rider). وَرَكَ وتَوَرَّكَ

To be able to do. وَرَكَ ووَرَّكَ وتَوَرَّكَ على

To recline on the side. وَرِكَ يَرِكُ وُرُوكًا

To be prominent (haunch). وَرِكَ a وَرَكًا

To render a. th. necessary. وَرَّكَ هُ

To stray from (a place). — في

To charge a. o. with (misdoings). — على

To cross (a mountain). وَارَكَ هُ

To carry (a child) on the hip-bone. تَوَرَّكَ ه

To rest on the thighs in (prayer). — في

To procrastinate in. — عَن

Haunch, hip-bone. وَرْكٌ و وِرْكٌ ووَرِكٌ ج أَوْرَاكٌ

Side of a bow; place where the string is tied to the bow. وِرْكٌ

They are all united against me. هُم عَلَيَّ وُرْكٌ ووَرِكٌ وَاحِدٌ

Part of the saddle adhering to the thigh. وَارِكٌ و وِرَاكٌ ومَوْرِكٌ ومَوْرِكَةٌ

Piece of cloth adorning the forepart of a saddle. وِرَاكٌ ج وُرُكٌ

Source of news. وَرَكِي و وِرْكِي

Land-tax, duties. Ts وِيرْكُو ووِيرْكِي

Having prominent haunches. أَوْرَكُ م وَرْكَاءُ ج وُرْكٌ

He has no share in these goods. هُوَ مُورِكٌ فِي هٰذَا ٱلْمَالِ

He has no responsibility in that affair. إِنَّهُ لَمُوَرَّكٌ فِي هٰذَا ٱلأَمْرِ

Forepart of a saddle. مِوْرَاكٌ ومِوْرَكَةٌ

Saddle-cushion. مِوْرَكَةٌ

✲ ورل — وَرَلٌ ج وِرْلَانٌ وأَوْرَالٌ وأَوْرُلٌ

Large venomous lizard, monitor.

Skink, species of lizards. وَرَلٌ مَائِيٌّ

Crocodile. وَرَلٌ نِيلِيٌّ

To be swollen (skin). ✲ وَرِمَ يَرِمُ وَرَمًا, وتَوَرَّمَ

To become tall (plant). وَرِمَ

He was inflamed with anger *lit*: his nose swelled. وَرِمَ أَنْفُهُ

To cause a swelling on (the skin). وَرَّمَ هُ

He was swollen with pride. — بِأَنْفِهِ

To have the udders swollen (she-camel). أَوْرَمَ

To enrage a. o. — ه وبِهِ

Swelling, tumour. وَرَمٌ ج أَوْرَامٌ

Scirrhus, cancerous growth. وَرَمٌ مُتَحَجِّرٌ

Swollen. وَارِمٌ م وَارِمَةٌ

Party of men. أَوْرَمٌ

I do not know what a man he is. مَا أَدْرِي أَيُّ ٱلأَوْرَمِ هُوَ

Gum of the teeth. مَوْرِمٌ

Swollen. Stout, big. مُوَرَّمٌ

To correspond to, to match a. th. ✲ ورن — وَارَنَ هُ

To be oiled, softened. تَوَرَّنَ

Chameleon. ◻ وَرَنٌ ووَرَنَةٌ

◻ Sample. T أُورْنِك ج أَرَانِيك

To be clumsy, unskilful, awkard. To be violent (wind). ✲ وَرِهَ a وَرَهًا

To be fat (woman). وَرِهَتْ تَرِهُ وَرَهًا

He was unskilled in business. تَوَرَّهَ فِي ٱلْعَمَلِ

Heavy with rain (cloud). وَرِهٌ م وَرِهَةٌ, وأَوْرَهُ م وَرْهَاءُ

Very fat (woman). وَرِهَةٌ

Broad (house). وَارِهٌ

Foolish, clumsy, awkward. أَوْرَهُ م وَرْهَاءُ

Gale, strong wind. رِيحٌ وَرْهَاءُ

To wound a. o. in the lungs. ✲ وَرَى يَرِي وَرْيًا ه

To corrode (the flesh : pus). — هُ

To be kindled (fire). — وَرْيًا و رِيَةً

To be fat (camel).

To yield fire (steel). وَرَى ووَرِيَ يَرِي وَرْيًا ووُرِيًّا و رِيَةً

To be compact (marrow, flesh). وَرِيَ يَرِي وَرْيًا

(*f.*) رِ, رِيَا, رِينَ : (*m.*) رِ, رِيَا, رُوا

Imper. of ورى. Wound him in the lungs.

To conceal, to hide, to dissemble, to disguise a. th. ✧ To show a. th. وَرَّى تَوْرِيَةً هُ

Sewer, pipe. Water-spout. P مِيزَاب ج مَيَازِيب
To bear. to carry (a burden). ✱ وَزَرَ يَزِرُ وِزْرًا هـ
To fill up (a fissure). — وَزْرًا هـ
To overcome a. o. — ه
وَزَرَ يَزِرُ ووَزِرَ يَوْزَرُ ووُزِرَ وَزْرًا وِزْرًا و وِزْرَة
To perpetrate (a crime).
To be suspected of (a crime). وُزِرَ
To be a vizier a minister. وَزَرَ يَزِرُ وِزَارَةً, وتَوَزَّرَ ل ووَازَرَ ه
To help, to assist a. o. in. وَازَرَ ه على
To preserve, to store up a. th. أَوْزَرَ هـ
To bring away, to strengthen. To conceal a. th.
To give shelter to. — ه
To be appointed vizier. تَوَزَّرَ
To commit a crime. To put on a short dress. إِتَّزَرَ
He dressed up. — بِثَوْبِهِ
To choose a. o. as minister of State. إِسْتَوْزَرَ ه
To bring away a. th. — هـ
Heavy load, burden. Crime, fault, sin. Polytheism. وِزْر ج أَوْزَار
Weapons, war-apparatus. أَوْزَار الحَرْب
Lofty mountain; stronghold, shelter, refuge. وَزَر
Short garment. ✧ Apron. وِزْرَة ج وِزْرَات و وِزَرَات
Dignity, office of a vizier, ministry. وِزَارَة ووَزَارَة
Vizier, minister of State. Helper. ◻ Queen (at chess). وَزِير ج وُزَرَاء وأَوْزَار
Helper. Vizier. مُوَازِر
Guilty, or charged with a crime. مَوْزُور
Crime. مَوْزُورَة
To withhold, to refrain a. o. To keep (an army) in battle-order. ✱ وَزَعَ يَزَعُ وَزْعًا ه
To excite, to urge a. o. to. — وَزُوعًا, وأَوْزَعَ ه ب
To share, to allot a. th. between. وَزَّعَ وأَوْزَعَ هـ بَيْن
To divide (a task) between. وَزَّعَ هـ على
To reveal a. th. to a. o. (God). أَوْزَعَ ه هـ

To shift, to allude ambiguously to, to equivocate on. وَرَّى عَن
To cause a. o. irritation in the lungs (wound). — ه
He averted the eyes from. — بَصَرَهُ عن
To produce (fire: flint). — وأَوْرَى وا سْتَوْرَى هـ
To conceal, to hide a. th. وَارَى مُوَارَاةً هـ
To show, to expose a. th. to view. ✧ أَوْرَى (for أَرَاى) هـ
To conceal o.'s self from (sight). تَوَرَّى وتَوَارَى عَن
To ask (an advice) from. إِسْتَوْرَى ه هـ
Pus, matter. Purulent ulcer. وَرْي
Creature. Man, mankind, men. Disease of the lungs. وَرَى
I do not know what a man he is. ما أَدْرِي أَيُّ ٱلْوَرَى هُوَ
Yielding fire (steel). Lusty. وَارٍ ووَرِيّ
Extemporiser. وَارِي الزَّنْد في الإِقْتِرَاح
Musk of good quality. مِسْك وَارٍ
Disease of the lungs. وَارِيَة
Tinder, tow, dung for striking fire. رِيَة ووَرِيَّة ٱلنَّار
Dissimulation. Ambilogy. Equivocation. تَوْرِيَة
Duck, goose (for إِوَزّ) (See أَوز). ✱ وَزّ ووَزِين
Wall goose-foot (plant). رِجل الوَزّ
To incite a. o. against. ✧ وَزَّ o وَزًّا ه على
Abounding in geese (land). مُوَزَّة
To waddle; to toddle. ✱ وَزْوَزَ
Death. وَزْوَز
Light-mindedness. وَزْوَزَة
Fickle, unsteady man. وَزْوَاز
To dessicate (meat). ✱ وَزَأَ a وَزْءًا هـ
To separate (people) ready to fight. — ه
To tie up (a bag). To fill (a skin). وَزَّأَ تَوْزِئَة وتَوْزِيئًا هـ
To bind a. o. by an oath. — ه
To throw off (his rider: horse). — ب
To be filled (skin). To drink his fill (man). تَوَزَّأَ
Strong, stout, sturdy. وَزَأ
To flow (water). ✱ وَزَبَ يَزِبُ وُزُوبًا
To go through (a country). أَوْزَبَ فِي
Sharp thief. وَزَّاب

أُوزِعَ ب To be incited to.
تَوَزَّعَ To be shared, divided, allotted.
— ه To be shared, distributed amongst.
إِتَّزَعَ To be withheld, checked, contined. To refrain.
إِسْتَوْزَعَ ه ه To ask (God) to inspire a. th.
وَازِع ج وَزَعَة ووُزَّاع ووَازِعُون Coercitive. Leader of an army. Shepherd's dog.
وَزَعَة Life-guard.
وَزُوع Incitement, instigation.
أَوْزَاع Separated bodies, parties of men.
مُتَّزِع Resolute, steadfast.
✱ وَزَغَتْ تَزِغُ وَزْغًا, وأَوْزَغَتْ بِـ To scatter (urine : she-camel).
أَلطَّعْنَةُ تُوزِغُ بِالدَّمِ The spear-thrust has caused blood to gush.
وَزَغ Trembling, convulsion. Coward.
— ج أَوْزَاغ Weak.
أَلأَوْزَاغ Weak people.
وَزَغَة ج وَزَغ وأَوْزَاغ وَوِزْغَان وَإِزْغَان وَوِزَاغ Large lizard, gecko.
✱ وَزَفَ يَزِفُ وَزْفًا ووَزِيفًا, ووَزَّفَ وأَوْزَفَ To hurry on.
وَازَفَ وتَوَازَفَ To share the expenses of a. th. together.
✧ وَزَل Broom (*plant*).
✱ وَزَمَ يَزِمُ وَزْمًا ه To settle (a debt). To break a. th.
— وَزَمَ نَفْسَهُ He ate once a day.
وُزِمَ وَزْمَةً فِي مَالِهِ He experienced a loss in goods.
وَزِمَ ✧ To be contracted and reddened by cold (limb).
وَزْم ووَزْمَة Quantity.
وَزْم ووَزِيم ووَزِيمَة Bundle of vegetables.
وَزْمَة Meal taken once a day.
وِزَام Speediness, swiftness.
وَزِيم Piece of meat.
وَزِيم ووُزَّام Flesh.
مُتَوَزِّم Trampling heavily.
✱ وَزَنَ يَزِنُ وَزْنًا وَزِنَةً To weigh a. th. To be equal in value or weight to.
هٰذَا يَزِنُ دِرْهَمًا It is worth one dirhem.
— ه ه ول To weigh (money) for a. o.
— الشِّعْرَ He composeed verses according to the rules.

وَزُنَ ه وَزَانَةً To be weighty, heavy. To have a sound judgment.
✧ وَزَّنَ ه To have a. th. weighed.
— وأَوْزَنَ نَفْسَهُ عَلَى He applied his mind to.
وَازَنَ مُوَازَنَةً ووِزَانًا ه To poise, to balance a. th. To front a. th.
— ه To requite a. o.
— بَيْنَ To compare (things).
تَوَازَنَ To be equal in value or weight.
إِتَّزَنَ To be weighed. To be regularly composed (verses). To be equal, alike.
— ه To weigh (coins). To receive weighed (coins).
وَزْن وزِنَة Weighing.
وَزْن ج أَوْزَان Weight. Standard-measure, standard-weight. Measure of a verse. Paradigm of a verb.
— ج وُزُون Load of dates hardly carried by a man.
وَزْنَ وزِنَةَ الجَبَل Opposite, in front of the mountain.
هُوَ وَزْنَهُ ووِزَانَهُ وزِنَتَهُ وبِوِزَانِهِ وبِوِزَانَتِهِ He is opposite to him.
لَيْسَ لَهُ وَزْنٌ He, it is worthless.
هٰذَا دِرْهَمٌ وَزْنٌ This coin has the legal standard.
رَاجِحُ الوَزْنِ Very intelligent.
وَزْنَة ج وَزَنَات Weight. ✧ Gold or silver talent *equal to* 396 *English pounds*.
وِزْنَة Way of weighing.
إِنَّهُ لَحَسَنُ الوِزْنَةِ It is weighed accurately.
وَازِن Weighing. Having full weight (money).
وَزِين Colocynth in powder. Weighty.
وَزِينُ الرَّأْيِ Prudent, weighty man.
أَوْزَن Outweighing. Man of great weight.
— القَوْمِ Chief of a tribe.
مُوَازَنَة Equilibrium, balance. Parallelism in words.
مُوَازِن Equivalent, equiponderant.
مَوْزُون Weighed. Regular (verb, verse).
مَوْزُونَة Short and intelligent (woman).
مِيزَان ج مَوَازِين Balance. Pair of scales. Accuracy. Quantity, measure.

Paradigm of a verb; measure of a verse. *Libra (Zodiacal sign)*.
✧ Barometer. مِيزَان الجَوّ او الهَوَاء
✧ Thermometer. — الحَرّ والبَرد
✧ Hygrometer. — الرُّطُوبَة واليُبُوسَة
The day has reached its midst. قَامَ او اسْتَقَامَ مِيزَانُ ٱلنَّهَار
✧ Budget of a State. المِيزَانِيَّة المَالِيَّة
✱ To be collected, heaped up. وَزَى يَزِي وَزْيًا
To be opposite to. To match a. th. To be parallel to. وَازَى ه
To lean the back against. أَوْزَى إِيزَاء ه إِلى
To smear (a house) with clay. — ل
To be opposite, equal. To be parallel (line). تَوَازَى
To ascend (a mountain). إِسْتَوْزَى في
Short and bulky (man). Strong (ass). وَزَى
Equivalence. Parallelism. مُوَازَاة
Parallel (line). مُتَوَازٍ
Standing erect. Strong-headed (man). مُسْتَوْزٍ
✱ To speak indistinctly. To prompt, to suggest evil, false things to a. o. (devil, passion). ✧ To render a. o. scrupulous (conscience). وَسْوَسَ وَسْوَسَةً وَوِسْوَاسًا ل وإِلى
He whispered to himself; he mumbled. — إِلَيهِ نَفْسُهُ
✧ To be perplexed, to have scruples. تَوَسْوَسَ
The suggester, Satan. أَلْوَسْوَاس
Suggestion of Satan. Indistinct speech. Temptation, evil thought. Clinking of trinkets. Faint sound of hunters, dogs. Melancholia. ✧ Scruple, perplexity. وَسْوَاس ج وَسَاوِس
✱ To abound with herbs (ground). وَسَبَ يَسِبُ وَسْبًا، وأَوْسَبَ إِيسَابًا
To be dirty, defiled (garment). وَسِبَ يَوْسَبُ وَسَبًا
Plants, herbs. وِسْب
Dirtiness, uncleanliness. وَسَب
Woolly (ram). مُوسِب
Half ripe (dates). مِيسَب
✱ To walk at a quick pace (camel). وَسَجَ يَسِجُ وَسْجًا وَوَسِيجًا وَوَسَجَانًا

To drive (a camel) at a quick pace. أَوْسَجَ ه
Swift (camel). وَسَّاج وَوَسُوج
✱ To be defiled, soiled, dirty (garment, body). وَسِخَ يَوْسَخُ وَسَخًا
To dirty, to defile a. th. وَسَّخ وأَوْسَخ ه
To be filthy, defiled, soiled. تَوَسَّخ واتَّسَخ واسْتَوْسَخ
Dirtiness, filthiness. وَسَخ ج أَوْسَاخ
Dirty, filthy, defiled. وَسِخ
✱ To place (a pillow) beneath the head of. وسد — وَسَّدَ ه ه
To rely upon a. o. in (an affair). — ه إلى
He hastened the walk. أَوْسَدَ فِي ٱلسَّيْر
To incite (a hound) to (the chase). أَوْسَدَ ه ب
To use a. th. as a pillow. To rest the head upon a. th. تَوَسَّدَ ه
Pillow, cushion. وِسَاد وَوُسَاد ج وُسُد
Cushion, pillow. وِسَادَة وَوُسَادَة ج وَسَائِد وَوِسَادَات،
Great sleeper. Foolish. عَرِيض الوِسَاد
✱ وَسَطَ يَسِطُ وَسْطًا وَسِطَةً، وتَوَسَّطَ ه وه
To be, to seat in the middle, midst of. To be equally distant from (the extremes).
He occupies a good rank amongst his people. وَسَطَ قَوْمَهُ وفِيهِم وَسَاطَةً
To become noble, distinguished. وَسُطَ ٥ وَسَاطَةً
To put a. th. in the middle. To cut a. th. by the middle. وَسَّطَ ه
To choose a. o. as arbitrator. — ه بَيْن
To take a middling, average thing. To be of a middling sort. تَوَسَّطَ
To intervene, to mediate between. — بَيْن
Midst, middle. وَسْط وَوَسَط
He sat in the midst of the people. جَلَسَ فِي وَسْطِ ٱلقَوْم
He sat in the middle of the house. قَعَدَ فِي وَسَط ٱلدَّار
Middling, average. Just, equitable. Intermediate, equidistant. وَسَط (*m. f.*) ج أَوْسَاط
✧ Intermediate, average; central. وَسْطَانِيّ
Door. وَاسِط

to render a. th. spacious, capacious.
To enrich a. o. (God). وَسَّع وأَوْسَع على
To be rich, wealthy. أَوْسَع
He made large expenses. – ٱلنَّفَقَة
To be comfortable in (a place). To be profuse in; to take a wide range in. To stride in (walking); to expatiate in. تَوَسَّع فِي
He increased his expenses. – فِي ٱلنَّفَقَة
To be ample, broad. To be expanded, enlarged; to spread out. إِتَّسَع وإِسْتَوْسَع
To be in easy circumstances. To increase (thing). To be enabled. إِتَّسَع
Width, extent. Ability. Wealth. وَسْع ووُسْع وسَعَة
It is within his power. هٰذَا فِي وَسْعِهِ او وُسْعِهِ او سَعَتِهِ
Capacity, width, extent. Ampleness of life. سَعَة ووُسْعَة وٱتِّسَاع وتَوْسِعَة
Court-yard. Public square. Plain. ✧ وُسْعَة
Extent. Extension of the meaning of a word. إِتِّسَاع
Broad, spacious. Liberal. Capacious. وَسِيع ووَاسِع ومُتَّسِع
The Comprehensive (God). ٱلْوَاسِع
Wide-stepping (horse). وَسِيع ووَسَّاع
Brisk, nimble (man). وَسَّاع
Broader, more capacious. أَوْسَع
Wealthy. مُوسِع
Enriched. مُوَسَّع عَلَيْهِ
To store, to heap up (things). To contain a. th. To wrap everything in (darkness: night). ✱ وَسَق يَسِق وَسْقًا ﻫ
I shall not do it as long as my eyes are wet *i. e.* never. لَا أَفْعَلُهُ مَا وَسَقَتْ عَيْنِي ٱلْمَاء
To load (a camel). – ه
✧ To load, to stow (a ship). – ﻫ ﻫ
To drive (camels) along. – وَسِيقًا ه
To be pregnant (she-camel). وَسَقَتْ وَسْقًا
To divide (wheat) in loads, bags. وَسَّق ﻫ
To be the equal of a. o. To oppose, to contend with a. o. وَاسَق ه
To be laden with fruit (palm-tree). أَوْسَق

Forepart of a camel-saddle. وَاسِط ووَاسِطَة
Mediator, go-between. Means. Arbitration. *Arith.* Middle terms. وَاسِطَة ج ✧ وَسَائِط
The best, the central pearl of a necklace. – ٱلْقِلَادَة
He is one of the best men of his tribe. هُوَ فِي وَاسِطَةِ قَوْمِهِ
Because, for the reason that. ✧ By means of, by the help of. بِوَاسِطَة
Mediator, arbitrator, intercessor. وَسِيط ج وُسَطَاء
He is the more conspicuous man of his people. هُوَ وَسِيطٌ فِيهِم
There is more water than mud. صَار ٱلْمَاءُ وَسِيطَةً
Mean, middling. Medium of a syllogism. أَوْسَط ج أَوَاسِط م وُسْطَى ج وُسَط
Middle-finger. وُسْطَى
Middle of a. th. أَوْسَط ٱلشَّيْء
Mediation, arbitration. وَسَاطَة وتَوَسُّط
Middle, inside of a house. مُوسَط ٱلْبَيْت
Middling, mean, average; mediator. مُتَوَسِّط
The Mediterranean Sea. ٱلْبَحْر ٱلْمُتَوَسِّط
✱ وَسِع يَسَع ويَسِع سَعَة وسِعَة،ووَسُع يَوْسُع وَسَاعَة
To be broad, ample, wide (place).
To hold, to be capacious (place, vessel). وَسِع يَسَع سِعَة وسَعَة ﻫ
هٰذَا ٱلْإِنَاء يَسَعُ عِشْرِينَ كَيْلًا او يَتَّسِع فِيهِ عِشْرُون كَيْلًا
This vessel can hold 20 measures.
Keep to thy house. لِيَسَعْكَ بَيْتُكَ
وَسِعَتْ رَحْمَةُ ٱللهِ كُلَّ شَيْءٍ وعلى وبِكُلِّ شَيْءٍ
The mercy of God encompasses every thing.
I am unable to do it. مَا أَسَعُ ذٰلِكَ
It is not allowable for thee to do. لَا يَسَعُكَ أَنْ تَفْعَل
To enrich a. o. (God). وَسَع يَوْسَع وَسْعًا على
O my God, pour thy favours upon us! أَللّٰهُمَّ سَعْ عَلَيْنَا
To be active, sturdy (boy). To be a good walker (horse). وَسُع ο وَسَاعَة وسَعَة
To enlarge, to expand, وَسَّع وأَوْسَع ﻫ

أَوْسَقَ ه To put a load on (a camel).

إِتَّسَقَ To be collected, gathered. To be settled, composed (affair). To be full (moon).

إِسْتَوْسَقَ To flock in (camels).

— لَهُ الأَمْرُ The affair has become practicable to him.

وَسْق ج وُسُوق وأَوْسَاق Camel's load equal to 60 صَاعٍ. ✧ Cargo, lading of a ship.

وَسْقَة ✧ Cargo of a ship.

وَسِيق Rain.

وَسِيقَة ج وَسَائِق Herd of camels.

وَاسِق ج وَاسِقَات ووِسَاق Pregnant (she-camel).

مَوَاسِق ومَوَاسِيق (pl. of وَاسِق) Pregnant (she-camels).

مَوْسُوق ✧ Laden (ship).

مُتَّسِق Stowed. A poetical metre.

مِيسَاق ج مَيَاسِيق ومَآسِيق Bird fluttering in his flight.

✱ وَسَلَ يَسِلُ وَسِيلَةً, ووَسَّلَ وتَوَسَّلَ إِلَى اللّٰهِ بِ He made entreaties to (God) for.

تَوَسَّلَ ه To bring (camels) away stealthily.

وَاسِل Seeking the favour of God.

وَاسِلَة ووَسِيلَة ج وَسَائِل Affinity. Relationship. Connexion. Means of access, of gaining favour. Credit, honourable station.

أَخَذَ إِبِلِي تَوَسُّلًا He has taken my camels away stealthily.

✱ وَسَمَ يَسِمُ وَسْمًا وسِمَةً ه وه To brand (a beast); to stigmatise (a culprit). To stamp, to mark a. th. ✧ To impress an indelible character (sacrament).

— ه ب To describe, to depict a. th.

— وَسْمًا ه To surpass a. o. in beauty.

وَسُمَ يَوْسُمُ وَسَامَةً ووَسَامًا To bear the impress of beauty (face).

وَسَّمَ To be in Mecca at the meeting of pilgrims.

وَاسَمَ ه To vie in beauty with.

تَوَسَّمَ To search for spring-grass.

تَوَسَّمَ ه To try to prognosticate a. th.

تَوَسَّمْتُ فِيهِ الخَيْرَ I perceived kindness impressed in his features.

تَوَسَّمَ ب To be dyed with woad-leaves.

إِتَّسَمَ To be branded. stigmatised, distinguished.

وَسْم ✧ Indelible character of a sacrament.

وَسْم ج وُسُوم, وسِمَة ج سِمَات, ووِسَام Brand impressed with a hot iron.

وِسَام ج أَوْسِمَة ✧ Mark, symptom. Title of a book. Badge. Insignia of an order. Order of knighthood.

وَسْمِيّ Spring-rain. Spring-grass.

وَسْمَة ووَسِمَة Woad-leaves used for dyeing.

وَسَامَة Beauty of the face.

وَسِيم ج وُسَمَاء ووِسَام Comely.

مَوْسِم ج مَوَاسِم Place, time of meeting of the pilgrims in Mecca. Periodical fair. ✧ Harvest-time. Fair, mart. Disease attacking once in life. □ Straw.

مِيسَم ج مَيَاسِم ومَوَاسِم Iron-tool for branding a beast. Stamp. Impress of beauty.

مَوْسُوم Branded, cauterised.

— بِالخَيْرِ Having a goodly face.

✱ وَسِنَ يَوْسَنُ وَسَنًا ووَسْنَةً وسِنَةً, واسْتَوْسَنَ To sleep deeply. To slumber.

وَسِنَ To be stifled by the exhalations of a well.

أَوْسَنَ ه To stifle a. o. (effluvia of a well)

رُزِقَ مَا لَمْ يُوسَنْ بِهِ فِي نَوْمِهِ He got into possession of things he would not have dreamt of.

وَسَن وسِنَة ووَسْنَة Slumber, deep sleep. Sloth.

وَسَن ج أَوْسَان Want.

مَا هُوَ مِنْ هَمِّي وَلَا مِنْ وَسَنِي I do not want it nor do I care for it.

وَسِن ووَسْنَان م وَسِنَة ووَسْنَى Slumbering. Sleeping.

مِيسَان (m. f.) Sleepy, sleeping.

مَوْسُونَة Slothful woman.

✱ وَسِي — وَاسَى ه ب (for آسَى) To soothe a. o. with (soft words).

أَوْسَى ه To shave (the head).

□ وَسِيَّة ج أَوَاسِي Large estate, common.

مُوسَى ج مَوَاسٍ Razor. See مُوس.

Moses. مُوسَى
Mosaical (law). ✧ Israelite. مُوسَوِيّ
Face. (for وَجه) ¤ وَشّ ج وُشُوش
To speak faintly, confusedly (people). To give quickly. ✡ وَشْوَش
To whisper to a. o. ه —
Confused speech, whisper. Lightness. وَشْوَشَة
Light. Nimble. وَشْوَاش ووَشْوَشِيّ ووِشْوَاش
Thick, coarse. ✡ وَشِب — وَشْب
Thick skin of a date. وَشْبَة
Mob, medley. وِشْب ج أَوْشَاب
To be entangled (roots, branches). To be complicate (pedigree, relationship). To become entangled, intermixed. ✡ وَشَج يَشِج وَشْجًا
My cares are manifold. وَشَجَتْ في قَلْبِي هُمُوم
To lace (a basket) with a thong. وَشَج ووَشَّج ه
To render (relationship) complicated (God). وَشَّج ه ب
God has mixed people together *i. e.* He has complicated their relationship by marriage. — الله بَيْن القَوْم
To be intricate, entangled. تَوَشَّج وتَوَاشَج
Complicated relationship. وَاشِجَة
Intricacy of relationship. Ash-wood used for spears. Spears. وَشِيج
Root of a tree. Twisted fibres. وَشِيجَة ج وَشَائِج
They are of the common people. هُم وَشِيجَة القَوْم
To gird a. o. with an ornamented belt. To adorn a. o. To strike a. o. on the waist. ✡ وشح — وَشَّح ه
To adorn, to embellish a. th. ✧ To paraphrase (a text). ه —
To deck herself with a sash (woman). تَوَشَّحَتْ واتَّشَحَتْ
To wrap o.'s self in (a garment). To throw (part of a garment) upon the left shoulder. — واتَّشَح ب
To gird (the sword). تَوَشَّح ب
Various ornaments of a woman. Woman's belt engrossed with gems, gold or silver. Double necklace of gems. Scarf. Sash. وِشَاح ج وُشُح وأَوْشِحَة ووَشَائِح
Sword of the Caliph Omar. الوِشَاح
Sword. وِشَاحَة
Striped with white (goat). وَشْحَاء
Double rhyme in verses. تَوْشِيح
Double-rhymed (poem). مُوَشَّحَة ج مُوَشَّحَات
To saw (wood). To sharpen (her teeth : woman). ✡ وَشَر يَشِر وَشْرًا ه
To have her teeth sharpened (woman). إتَّشَرَتْ واسْتَوْشَرَتْ
Saw, blunt knife. مِيشَار
Prism. مَوْشُور ج مَوَاشِير
To hasten. ✡ وَشِز يَشِز وَشْزًا
To prepare for (mischief). تَوَشَّز ل
Elevated place, height. Misfortune. Haste. Support. وَشْز ووَشَز ج أَوْشَاز
I found him in a hurry. لَقِيتُهُ على وَشَزٍ او أَوْشَازٍ
Helpers, protectors. Misfortunes. أَوْشَاز
Stuffed cushion. وَشِيزَة ج وَشَائِز
To break (a bone). To fix (an axe) on its handle. ✡ وَشَظ يَشِظ وَشْظًا ه
To join a party of (travellers). إلى —
Servants, followers. Rabble. Intruders. وَشِيظ ج أَوْشَاظ
Piece added to a wooden bowl. وَشِيظَة ج وَشَائِظ
They are people of a low class. هُمْ وَشِيظَة القَوْم
To mix a. th. ✡ وَشَع يَشَع وَشْعًا ه
To climb (a hill). — وَشْعًا ووُشُوعًا ه وفي
To make up (thread, cotton) into a ball. To print (cloth). وَشَّع ه
To appear on the head (hoariness). ه —
To blossom (tree). أَوْشَع
To swarm with. تَوَشَّع ب
To go up (a mountain) in grazing (flock). — في
Blossom of vegetables. Egyptian willow. وَشْع
Cobweb. وُشْع
Medicine injected through the nose. وَشُوع
Layer of palm-leaves under the coating of a flat roof. Quick-set hedge around a garden. Weaver's وَشِيع

tool. Variegated tent of a chief.
وَشِيعَة ج وَشَائِع Trail of dust. Weaver's bobbin. Ball of spun cotton. Strips on a stuff.
☆ وشغ – وَشَّغ ه To stain (clothes) with (blood).
تَوَشَّغ بِالسُّوء He committed a foul deed.
☆ وَشَق يَشِق وَشْقًا, واتَّشَق ه To cut (meat) in slices.
وَشَق ه ب To spear a. o.
وَشَّق ه To cut off a. th.
أَوْشَق في To stick, to adhere to.
تَوَاشَق واتَّشَق ه To cut in pieces; to rip up (the body).
وَشْق Scattered pasturage.
وَاشِق ووَشَّاق Going and coming.
وُشَّق (for أُشَّق) Gum ammoniac.
وَشِيق ووَشِيقَة ج وَشَائِق Meat cut in pieces and dried.
مِيشَاق ج مَوَاشِيق Tooth of a key.
☆ وَشُك يَوْشُك وَشْكًا ووَشَاكَة ووَشْك
To be quick, expeditious (affair).
وَشُك ذَا خُرُوجًا He hastened out.
وَاشَك وأَوْشَك To walk quickly, to hasten the pace.
أَوْشَك أَن To be on the eve, on the point of; to be about to.
يُوشِك الأَمْرُ أَن يَكُونَ او يُوشِك أَن يَكُونَ الأَمْرُ The thing is about to happen; it will soon happen.
وَشْك ووُشْك و وَشْكَان ووُشْكَان Quickness.
وَشْكَان ووُشْكَان مَا يَكُون How quickly done!
وِشَاك Swiftness.
وَشِيك (m. f.) Expeditious, speedy.
مُوَاشِكَة Swift (she-camel).
☆ وَشَل يَشِل وَشْلًا ووَشَلَانًا To fall by drops, to drip (water).
– وُشُولًا To be helpless, destitute (man).
– إِلى To assume an humble appearance before a. o.
أَوْشَل ه To find (water) in small quantity. To lessen (the portion) of.
وَشَل ج أَوْشَال Water trickling from a mountain. Small or great quantity of water. Abundant or few tears. Awe.

جَاءُوا أَوْشَالًا They came one after another.
هُوَ من أَوْشَال القَوْم He is from a common class.
وَاشِل Oozing water (mountain).
– الحَظّ Unlucky.
مَوَاشِل Places, spots.
☆ وَشَم يَشِم وَشْمًا, ووَشَّم ه To tattoo (the hand).
أَوْشَم To shoot forth plants (soil). To flash (lightning). To have ripening grapes (vine).
– في فُلَان To increase upon a. o. (hoariness).
– في To attack (th character) of a. o. To observe a. th. carefully.
إِسْتَوْشَم To ask to be tattooed.
وَشْم ج وِشَام ووُشُوم Tattooing. First sprout, off-shoot.
وَشْمَة Rain-drop.
مَا عَصَيْتُهُ وَشْمَةً I have not opposed him by a single word.
وَشِيمَة Evil, enmity, malevolent language.
وَاشِمَة Female tattooer.
P وَشْنَة ◻ *Griot*, kind of bitter cherry.
☆ وَشَى يَشِي وَشْيًا وشِيَةً, ووَشَّى ه To variegate, to imprint figures on (cloth). To embroider (a garment). To adorn, to embellish a. th.
وَشَّى الكَلَام He adorned the narrative with lies.
وَشَى يَشِي وَشْيًا و وِشَايَةً To increase (tribe).
مَا وَشَت هٰذِهِ المَاشِيَة عِنْدِي بِشَيْء This beast has not produced to me any young one.
وَشَى وَشْيًا و وِشَايَةً بِفُلَان إِلى To misrepresent, to accuse a. o. falsely to.
أَوْشَى إِيشَاء To shoot forth plants (earth). To produce its first fruit (palm-tree). To become rich. To give a brief account of a speech. To contain a vein of gold (mine).
– ه To extract a. th. gently.
– في To take little of.
– ه To heal a. o. (medicine).
– واسْتَوْشَى ه To spur, to launch (a horse).
تَوَشَّى في فُلَان Hoariness appeared upon him.

To be fast, firm. ✱ وَصَد يَصِد وَصْدًا
To remain in (a place). — ب
To weave (cloth). — وَصْدًا, ووَصَّد ه
To warn; to incite a. o. وَصَّد ه
To build a stone-enclosure for sheep. أَوْصَد واستَوْصَد
To incite (a dog) to the chase. أَوْصَد ه
To close (a door). To stop a. th. — ه
To oppress a. o.; to put a. o. to it. — على
Weaver. وَصَّاد
Threshold of a door. Entrance. Court-yard. Short-stemmed (plant). Cavern of the 7 sleepers. Straitened. وَصِيد ج وُصُد
Stone-enclosure for cattle. — ووَصِيدَة ج وَصَائِد
Closed (door). مُوصَد
Veil, curtain. مُوَصَّد
Registered agreement. ✱ وصر — وِصْر ووَصَرَّة ووَصِيرَة
Small bird. ✱ وصع — وَصْع ج وِصْعَان
Chirping of small birds. Small birds. وَصِيع
To walk gracefully (colt). ✱ وَصَف يَصِف وُصُوفًا
To describe, to narrate, to characterise a. th. — وَصْفًا وصِفَةً ه وه
Indescriptible thing. شَيْءٌ لَا يُوصَف
To prescribe (a medicine) for a. o. — وَصْفَةً ه ل
To become fit for service (boy). وَصُف ٥ وَصَافَةً
To conclude a bargain with a. o. on description of the article. وَاصَف ه
To be fit for service. أَوْصَف
To take a. o. as a servant. تَوَصَّف ه
To describe a. th. to o. a. ✧ To abuse o. a. تَوَاصَف ه
To be described. إِتَّصَف
To be distinguished, to be characterised by good qualities. — ب
To ask a. o. to describe. إِسْتَوْصَف ه ه
He consulted the physician upon his disease. — الطَّبِيبَ لِدَائِهِ
Description, characteristic. Quality, adjective. Epithet; attribute. وَصْف ج أَوْصَاف
Medical prescription. وَصْفَة

To be set (broken bone). إِيتَشَى
To call, to rouse a. o. To urge (a horse) for trying his strength. إِسْتَوْشَى ه
Figured work on cloth. Silk brocade adorned with figures. Glitter of a sword. Gold-ore. وَشْي ج وِشَاء
Wealth. وَشَاء
Calumniator. Prolific. Weaver. وَاشٍ م وَاشِيَة ج وُشَاة ووَاشُون
Gold stampers. وُشَاة
Traducer. Merchant of brocade. وَشَّاء
Mark, sign. Mixture of colours. شِيَة ج شِيَات
Spotted (bull). أَشْيَه
Variegated (cloth). Embroidered. Adorned. مُوَشًّى ومَوْشِيٌّ
To build, to make a. th. strongly. ✱ وَصَّ ٥ وَصًّا ه
To close her face-veil (woman). وَصَّصَت
To peep through the hole of a veil (girl). To open the eyes (whelp). ✱ وَصْوَص
Hole for the eyes in a veil. وَصْوَص ووَصْوَاص ج وَصَاوِص
Veil of a girl. وَصْوَاص ج وَصَاوِص
Big stones on the soil. وَصَاوِص
To be defiled (garment). ✱ وصأ — وَصِئَ ه
To last, to continue; to be firm, settled. To be incumbent (debt). ✱ وَصَب يَصِب وُصُوبًا
To apply o.'s self to. To manage (an affair) skilfully. — على
وَصِب يَوْصَب وَصَبًا, ووَصَّب وأَوْصَب وتَوَصَّب
To be ill, diseased.
To beget diseased children. أَوْصَب
To afflict a. o. with a disease (God). — ه
To keep perseveringly to. — على
Space between the fore and the fourth finger. وَصْب
Disease, illness. Emaciation of the body. وَصَب ج أَوْصَاب
Ill, diseased. وَصِب ج وَصَابَى و وِصَاب
Continual (punishment). Incumbent (debt). وَاصِب
Far-extending (desert). وَاصِبَة
Suffering unremittingly. مُوَصَّب

Quality. Qualification, adjective. صِفَة ج صِفَات

Essential attributes. صِفَات ذَاتِيَّة

Qualificative. Adjectival, attributive. وَصْفِيّ

Qualification of a noun. State of an adjective. وَصْفِيَّة

Fitness for service. وَصَافَة و إِيصَاف

Sect denying the attributes of God. صِفَاتِيَّة (un. صِفَاتِيّ)

Young lad, servant. ✧ Negro slave. وَصِيف ج وُصَفَاء

Maid-servant. ✧ Negress slave. وَصِيفَة ج وَصَائِف

Good describer. Experienced physician. وَصَّاف

Described. Qualified. Qualifiable (noun). مَوْصُوف

Purchase or sale on description. مُوَاصَفَة

Dispensary. مُسْتَوْصَف

✱ وَصَل يَصِل وَصْلًا وصِلَةً وُصْلَةً ه ب To unite, to connect a. th. with.

— ه ب To give a. th. to a. o.

— رَحِمَهُ He did good to his people.

— وُصُولًا ووُصْلَةً وصِلَةً ه وإلى To arrive at, to reach (a place).

— ه وإلى To be delivered to a. o. (letter). To reach a. o. (news).

— وَصْلًا وصِلَةً, ووَاصَل مُوَاصَلَةً و وِصَالًا ه To be friendly connected with.

وَاصَل ه To be contiguous to.

وَصَّل ه ب To unite a. th. closely with.

— وأَوْصَل ه وه إلى To deliver a. th. to a. o. To bring a. o. to (a place).

وَاصَل مُوَاصَلَةً و وِصَالًا ه وفي To continue a. th. uninterruptedly. To keep persistingly to.

تَوَصَّل إلى To reach (a place). To be connected with. To obtain access to. To bribe a. o.

تَوَاصَل To be friendly connected.

إِتَّصَل To be continuous, uninterrupted.

— إلى To reach, to arrive at.

— ب To be connected with a. o., to communicate to. To be contiguous, adjoining to.

Union of friends. Connection of sentences. Conjunction. Match, fellow of a pair. ✧ Receipt. وَصْل

It is its match. هُوَ وَصْلُهُ

Conjunctive letter *i. e.* ا, و, ه *or* ي added to the last movent letter of a verse (الرَّوِيّ المُتَحَرِّك). حَرْف الوَصْل

Last night of a lunar month. لَيْلَةُ الوَصْل

Quiescent alef marked thus (ٮ). وَصْل ووَصْلَة

Limb, member. *Pl.* Joints of the body. وُصْل و وِصْل ج أَوْصَال

Junction, union. وُصْلَة واتِّصَال

✧ Stop-plank, joist. وَصْلَة

Means of connection, bond, tie. وُصْلَة ج وُصَل

Free gift, favour. صِلَة ج صِلَات

Woman wearing false hair. وَاصِلَة

Junction, union. Connective. Connection of a verb with its complement. وِصَال

Arrival. وُصُول

✧ Receipt. وُصُول ج وُصُولَات

Unitive. Bountiful. وَصُول

Intimate friend. ✧ Continuous thing. وَصِيل

Bond. She-camel bringing forth consecutively for 10 years. Ewe that has brought forth two females yearly for seven years. Abundance of produce. Cultivation. Striped cloth from Yemen. Sword. Coil of thread. Extensive country. وَصِيلَة ج وَصَائِل

Contiguousness. ✧ Relationship. إِتِّصَال و✧ اتِّصَالِيَّة

Continuity, communication. Union of two friends. مُوَاصَلَة

Junction. Juncture of a rope. مَوْصِل

The town and province of Mosul. أَلْمَوْصِل و✧ المُوصِل

Mesopotamia, and the province of Mosul. أَلْمَوْصِلَان

From Mosul. Muslin. مَوْصِلِيّ و✧ مُوصَلِّيّ

Written with letters united together (poem). مُوَصَّل (*opp. to* مُقَطَّع)

Contiguous, adhering. Continual. مُتَّصِل

✧ Recommendation, notice, letter of introduction. تَوْصِيَة
Prescribing. Testator. (*m. f.*) وَصِيّ
Legatee. Trustee. Commissioned agent. Executor
Testator. مُوصٍ ومُوصٍ
Testamentary bequest. مُوصًى بِهِ
Legatee. مُوصًى لَهُ
Trustee, executor of a will. مُوصًى إِلَيهِ
To be destitute (man). ✱ وَضَ وَضًا
To be clean, neat, fair. ✱ وَضُوَ o وُضُوءًا ووَضَاءَة
To surpass a. o. in fairness. وَضَأَ a وَضْأً ه
To vie in brightness with. وَاضَأَ ه
He performed ablutions before prayer. تَوَضَّأَ بِالمَاء لِلصَّلَاة
To attain to puberty. To make o.'s self clean, neat. To wash o.'s self. تَوَضَّأَ
Brightness, whiteness, cleanliness. وَضَاءَة
Ablutions performed before prayer. تَوَضُّؤ
Water for ablution. وَضُوء
Clean, bright. وَضِيء ج أَوْضِيَاء ووِضَاء
وَاضِئ ج وَضَأَة, ووُضَّاء ج وُضَّاؤُون ووَضَاضِئ
Clean, neat.
Tank, vessel for ablutions. مِيضَأَة ومِيضَاءَة
Place of ablution. Privy. مُتَوَضَّأ
To be clear, obvious, conspicuous. ✱ وَضَحَ يَضِحُ وُضُوحًا ووَضِحَة, وأَوْضَحَ
To explain, to disclose. To render a. th. clear, perspicuous. وَضَّحَ وأَوْضَحَ ه
To bring forth white children (woman). أَوْضَحَت
The wound has laid the bone bare. أَوْضَحَت الشَّجَّة
Whence art thou come? مِن أَيْنَ أَوْضَحْتَ
To be clear. To be white (sheep). تَوَضَّحَ واتَّضَحَ
To ask from a. o. explanations about. إِسْتَوْضَحَ ه ه
To shadow the eye with the hand for (seeing a. th. distinctly) — ه وعَن
Gleam of dawn. Moon. Leprosy. Star of white hair on a وَضَح ج أَوْضَاح

United, connected. Kind of hornet, wasp. مَوْصُول
Conjunct. — ج مَوْصُولَات
Conjunctive particle as أَن, مَا. مَوْصُول حَرْفِيّ
Relative pronoun, as الَّذِي, مَن. — إِسْمِيّ
Adding false hair to hers (woman). مُسْتَوْصِلَة
To spoil, to mar a. th. To crack (a vessel). To bind, to tie a. th. hastily. ✱ وَصَمَ يَصِمُ وَصْمًا ه
To languish, to be exhausted. وُصِّمَ
To exhaust, to weaken a. o. (fever). — ه
To be exhausted, ailing. تَوَصَّمَ
Disease. وَصْمٌ
Crack. fissure. Knot in wood. وَصْم ج وُصُوم
Defect, blemish. Dishonour, stain — وَصْمَة
Torpor, exhaustion. وَصْمَة وتَوْصِيم
Space betwen the ring-finger and the little one. وَصِيم
To be contiguous, adjoined to. ✱ وَصَى يَصِي وَصْيًا ب
To connect, to join a. th. to (another). — ه ب
To have a dense vegetation (land). وَصَى وَصْيًا ووُصِيًّا ووَصَاءَة
To bequeath a. th. to. وَصَّى تَوْصِيَة, وأَوْصَى إِيصَاء لِفُلَانٍ ب
To recommend a. th. To appoint a. o. as a tutor to (children). — ه وإِلى فُلَانٍ ب
To appoint a. o. as executor, trustee by will. — وأَوْصَى إِلى فُلَانٍ
To be contiguous to (country). وَاصَى ه
To order, to enjoin a. th. upon a. o. (God). أَوْصَى ه
To order, to command a. th. to. أَوْصَى ه ب وفي
To make mutual recommendations. تَوَاصَى
He received with kindness the recommendation given to him. إِسْتَوْصَى بِهِ خَيْرًا
Injunction, command. Will. Request. وَصِيَّة ج وَصَايَا
Recommendation, admonition. وصاة ووَصَايَة

To feed on acrid plants near water (camel). وَضِمَ وَضِيمَةً, وأَوْضَمَ

He humbled himself. — نَفْسَهُ وَضْعًا ووُضُوعًا وَضِعَةً

To remit (a debt, a sin) to a. o. — وَضْعًا ه عن

To bring forth (a child) woman. — حَمْلَهَا وُضْعًا ووَضْعًا وتُضْعًا

To forge (an account). To compose (a book). To let down (her veil : woman). — وَضْعًا ه

He stopped. وَضَعَ عَصَاهُ

He put (the enemy) to the edge of the sword. — السَّيْفَ في

To suffer losses in (trade). وَضِعَ يَوْضَعُ ووُضِعَ ضِعَةً ووَضِيعَةً في

To be vile, humbled. وَضُعَ o ضِعَةً ووَضَاعَةً

To be an adoptive or illegitimate son. — وَضَاعَةً

To humble, to lower a. o. وَضَّعَ ه

To wad (a garment). وَضَّعَ ه

To bet with a. o. واضَعَ مُوَاضَعَةً ووِضَاعًا ه

To deliver (goods) to the buyer. — ه

To agree with a. o. upon. — ه في

Come here that I may give thee an advice. هَلُمَّ أُوَاضِعْكَ الرَّأْيَ

To walk at a gentle and swift pace. أَوْضَعَ

To drive (a beast) at a gentle pace. — ه

To experience losses in (trade). أُوضِعَ في

To be humble, modest. To lower o.'s self. تَوَاضَعَ واتَّضَعَ

There is a great distance between us. تَوَاضَعَ مَا بَيْنَنَا

To agree about (an affair). — على

To be humbled. To sink into contempt. To lower (a camel's head) in order to ride. إِتَّضَعَ

To ask for an abatement of price ; to ask for relief. إِسْتَوْضَعَ

Situation, site. Posture. Conformation. Manner. وَضْع ج أَوْضَاع

Abasement, lowliness. ضَعَة وضِعَة

Situation, location, position. وِضْعَة

Set the brick otherwise. ضَعِ اللَّبِنَةَ غَيْرَ هٰذِهِ الوِضْعَةِ

horse's forehead or forefeet. Hoariness. High road. Anklet, silver trinkets. Milk. Whiteness. Standard money.

She-ass. وَضَحَة

Obviousness. وُضُوح واتِّضَاح

Clear explanation. إِيضَاح وتَوْضِيح

Clear, obvious, perspicuous. White (camel). Bright (star). وَاضِح

Spotless (man). — الحَسَبِ

Tooth displayed in laughter. واضِحَة ج وَاضِحَات وأَوَاضِح

Moonlit nights. أَوَاضِح

Obvious, evident. Bright, fine. Day. وَضَّاح

Spotless. حَسَب وَضَّاح

White bone for playing by night. عَظْم وَضَّاح

Daybreak-prayer. بِكْرُ الوَضَّاحِ

Ewes, camels. وَضِيحَة ج وَضَائِح

Bringing forth white children (woman). Wound laying a bone bare. مُوضِحَة ج مَوَاضِح

Keeping to a high-road. Whitish (camel). مُتَوَضِّح

Obvious. مُتَّضِح

To fill (a bucket) to the half. ✡ وَضَحَ يَضِحُ وَضْحًا, وأَوْضَحَ ه

To race together (horses). To vie with a. o. in drawing water. وَاضَحَ مُوَاضَحَةً و وِضَاحًا ه, وتَوَاضَحَ

To draw water for a. o. أَوْضَحَ ل

Water filling half a bucket. وَضُوح

To be dirty, greasy. ✡ وَضِرَ a وَضَرًا

Filthiness, greasiness. Washings of a milk-skin. Smell of altered food. Foulness. وَضَر ج أَوْضَار

Greasy. وَضِر م وَضِرَة ووَضْرَى

Of bad morals. — الأَخْلَاقِ وذُو أَوْضَار

Anus. وَضْرَى

Dates in a lump. Large rock. — ووَضْرَاء

To put, to put down, to place. ✡ وَضَعَ يَضَعُ وَضْعًا ومَوْضِعًا ومَوْضُوعًا ه

To lessen the power of. — مِن

To remit (part of a debt, of a tax). — عَن

To impose (a fine, a tax) upon. — ه على

He beheaded him. — عُنُقَهُ وَضْعًا

He humbled him. — وَضْعًا فُلَانًا ومِن فُلَانٍ

plait (a hair-strap). To set (bricks) close together.
To humble o.'s self to. تَوَضَّن ل
To be joined, connected to. إِتَّضَن ب
Hair or leathern girth. وَضِين ج وُضُن
Its girth is loose i. e. the beast is lean. قَلِقَ وَضِينُهَا
Folded, woven. وَضِين ومَوْضُون
Coat of mail compactly woven and adorned with gems. مَوْضُونَة
Bag of palm-leaves. مِيضَنَة ج مَوَاضِين
To creak (load). To cry out (child). To screech (bat). ✱ وَطَّ o وَطّ
To be weak. To speak quickly. ✱ وَطْوَط
Large bat. Mountain-swallow. Faint-hearted and weak. Clamorous. وَطْوَاط ج وَطَاوِيط ووَطَاوِط
✱ وَطِئَ يَطَأُ وَطْأً, ووَطَّأَ وتَوَطَّأَ ه بِرِجْلِهِ
To tread a. th. under foot. و ✧ وَطِئَ a تَوَطَّى
To ride (a horse). وَطِئَ ه
To ramble in (a country). — ه
To ill-treat, to plunder (a country : enemy). — ه
To level, to make a. th. plain. وَطَّأَ a وَطَأَ ه
To be well trodden, even, level (ground). To be soft (bed). وَطُؤَ o وُطُوءَة ووَطَاءَة
To level the ground. To soften (a bed). To facilitate (an affair). ✧ To lower a. th. وَطَّأَ تَوْطِئَة ه و ✧ وطّى
To repeat the same (rhyme : poet). — ووَاطَأَ في, وأَوْطَأَ ه وفي
To agree with a. o. upon. وَاطَأَ وأَوْطَأَ وتَوَطَّأَ وتَوَاطَأَ ه على
To make a. o. to trample upon. أَوْطَأَ إِيطَاء ه ه وب
To help a. o. to mount (a horse). — ه ه
To humble, to tread down a. o. — ه
He compelled him to act recklessly. — ه عَشْوَةَ والعَشْوَةَ
To agree upon. تَوَاطَأُوا على
To be levelled (ground). To be prepared, facilitated (affair). To be elapsed, complete (month). إِتَّطَأَ إِتِّطَاء وايتَطَأَ ايتِطَاء

Lowering. Abasement. وَضَاعَة
Positive, legal (prescription). وَضْعِيّ م وَضْعِيَّة
Putting, laying down. Unveiled (woman). وَاضِع
Humble, low, vile, mean. وَضِيع ج وُضَعَاء
Fresh dates laid in jars. Depository. وَضِيع
Luggage of travellers. Duty, tax. Trust, deposit. Fresh flour mixed with butter. Adoptive son. Abatement of price. Moral book. وَضِيعَة ج وَضَائِع
Hostages. Taxes. Troops in garrison. وَضَائِع
Hostages taken by Khosroes. وَضَائِع كِسْرَى
Humility, modesty. تَوَاضُع واتِّضَاع
Place, spot. Proper place of a. th. Proper application of a word. مَوْضِع ج مَوَاضِع, ومَوْضِعَة
He is a kind-hearted man. في قَلْبِهِ مَوْضِعَة ومَوْقِعَة
Broken. Of weak constitution. مُوَضَّع
Humble, lowering himself. مُتَّضِع ومُتَوَاضِع
Put, laid. Apocryphal (tradition). Losing in trade. مَوْضُوع م مَوْضُوعَة
Object of a science. Subject of a book ; topic. Substance (opp. to accident). Duty, task. مَوْضُوع ج مَوَاضِيع ومَوْضُوعَات
To amble (camel). ✱ وَضَف يَضِف وَضْفًا, وأَوْضَف
To make (a she-camel) to amble. أَوْضَف ه
Sling. وَضَف ج أَوْضَاف
Slinger. وَضَّاف ج وَضَّافَة
To place (meat) on a plank for desiccating it. ✱ وَضَم يَضِم وَضْمًا ه, وأَوْضَم ه ول
To revile a. o. إِسْتَوْضَم ه
Plank or mat for drying meat. وَضَم ج أَوْضَام وأَوْضِمَة
He crushed them under blows ; he abased them. تَرَكَهُم لَحْمًا على وَضَم
Body of 200 or 300 men. وَضْمَة ووَضِيمَة
Funeral dinner. Heap of fodder. وَضِيمَة
To fold a. th. To ✱ وَضَن يَضِن وَضْنًا ه

To find a. th. smooth, soft. إستوطأ ه
Trampling, tread. وَطْءٌ
Depressed land. — ووَطَاء
Carpet, seat. وَطَاء و وِطَاء
A treading. Violence, oppression, pressure. Punishment. Footstep. وَطْأَة
Party of travellers. (*coll.*) وَطْأَة
Softness of a bed; evenness of the ground. طَأَة وطِئَة ووَطَاءة ووُطُوءة
Comfortableness, comfort. طَأَة وطِئَة
Comfortably, softly. على طَأَةٍ او طِئَةٍ
Repetition of the same word as a rhyme (*prosody*). إيطاء
Introduction, preliminary explanation. تَوْطِئَة
Even, soft. وَاطِئ
Party of travellers. Dates dropped by a tree. وَاطِئَة
Even, smooth, soft. Lowered, humbled. وَطِيءٌ و ✧ وَطِيّ
Mild-tempered. — الخُلُق والجانب
Dates and milk. Biscuit, cake. Bag of dried meat. وَطِيئَة
Footstep. Step, stool. مَوْطَأ ومَوْطِئ ج مَوَاطِئ
Depressed ground. مِيطَأ
Levelled. Facilitated. مُوَطَّأ
Easy, sociable (man). مُوَطَّأ الأكناف
Having numerous partisans. — العَقِب
Accord, agreement. مُوَاطَأَة
✡ وطب — وَطْب ج أَوْطُب و وِطَاب وأوطاب
Milk-skin. وجمع أَوَاطِب
He has been killed; he is dead *lit*: his skin has been emptied. صَفِرَتْ وِطَابُهُ
Harsh man. Protuberant woman's breast. وَطْب
Big-breasted (woman). وَطْبَاء
To thrust a. o. back violently. ✡ وَطَح يَطِح وَطْحًا وطِحَةً ه
To hurt, to harm o. a. To crowd around the water (cattle). تَوَاطَحُوا
Dirt sticking to the claws, hoofs. وَطَح
To treat (an affair). ✡ وطخ — تَوَاطَخ ه
To be made fast, lasting. ✡ وَطَد يَطِد وَطْدًا
To press; to strengthen. — ووَطَّد ه
To flatten (the ground). وَطَد ه
To prepare (a place) for a. o. — ه ل

To press, to keep a. th. close to. وَطَد ه إلى
To keep up (stones) at the entrance of (a cavern). — ه على
To be strengthened, fastened. تَوَطَّد
Violent blow, thrust. وَطْدَة
Mountains. أوطاد
Firm, steadfast. وَاطِد ووَطِيد ومَوْطُود
Bases of a building. Supports of a cooking-pot. وَطَائِد
Wooden mallet for beating the ground. Handle of a gimlet. مِيطَدَة
Steadfast, firm. Hard. مُتَوَاطِد
Want, object wanted. Aim in view. ✡ وَطَر ج أوطار
He has attained his aim: he has obtained what he wanted. قَضَى وَطَرَهُ وأوطارَهُ
To stamp, to beat (the ground). To crush, to smash a. th. ✡ وَطَس يَطِس وَطْسًا ه
To knock a. th. — ه وب
To dash together (waves). تَوَاطَس
To assault a. o. (people). — على
Oven, furnace. وَطِيس
War has been kindled. حَمِيَ الوَطِيسُ
Battle, affray. وَطِيس ج أَوْطِسَة ووُطُس
Seriousness (of an affair). وَطِيسَة
To relate part of (news) to a. o. ✡ وَطَش يَطِش وَطْشًا, ووَطَّش ه ل
To speak obscurely. — الكلامَ
To strike a. o. وَطَش ه
To remove a. o. from. — ه عن
To give little to. — ووَطَّش ه
To prepare (a speech, an affair) for. وَطَّش لِفُلَانٍ
They struck him and he did not oppose them. ضَرَبُوهُ فَمَا وَطَّش إليهم
To have thick eyebrows. To fall (rain). ✡ وَطِف يَوْطَف وَطَفًا
Thickness of the eyebrows. Train of a garment. End of a cloud. وَطَف
He has scanty hair. عَلَيْهِ وَطْفَةٌ مِنَ الشَّعَر
Having thick eyebrows. Thick (darkness). Easy (life). Heavy with rain and nearing the earth (cloud). أَوْطَف م وَطْفَاء ج وُطْف
✧ Tent, pavilion. وِطَاق ج وِطَاقَات
To ✡ وَطَن يَطِن وَطْنًا, وأَوْطَن إيطانًا ب

The world has many changes. للدُّنيا وَظَائِف

✧ The functions of the limbs, of the organs. وَظَائِف الأَعْضَاء

✧ Functionary, official of the Government. مُتَوَظِّف

Suspicion. ✱ وظِر — وَظْمَة

To shout, to be disorderly (crowd). To howl, to bark (dog). To yelp (fox). ✱ وَعْوَعَ وَعْوَعَةً ووَعْوَاعًا

Fox, jackal. وَعْوَع ج وَعَاوِع

Bustle of an excited crowd, disturbance. Disorderly (mob). Yelping of dogs, jackals. وَعْوَاع

✱ وَعَبَ يَعِبُ وَعْبًا, وأَوْعَبَ واسْتَوْعَبَ هـ To take a. th. altogether.

To collect a. th. To achieve (a work). أَوْعَبَ إِيعَابًا هـ

To uproot (a tree). To cut off (the nose). — واسْتَوْعَبَ هـ

To insert a. th. into. أَوْعَبَ هـ في

The whole tribe has emigrated. أَوْعَبَ بَنُو فُلَانٍ جَلَاءً

All the men went out for a raid. أَوْعَبَ القَوْمُ

They came as numerous as possible. جَاءُوا مُوعِبِينَ

He cut off his nose altogether. إِسْتَوْعَبَ جَدْعَهُ

To contain a. th. (place, vessel). To be equivalent to. To conceive (a discourse). To study, to exhaust (a subject). إِسْتَوْعَبَ هـ

High road. وَعْب ج وِعَاب

Extensive tracts of land. وِعَاب

Broad, wide (house). وَعِيب

He came running with all his might. جَاءَ بِرَكْضٍ وَعِيبٍ

Better fitted to contain a. th. أَوْعَبُ لِ

✱ وَعِثَ يَوْعَثُ وَعْثًا ووَعَثًا , ووَعُثَ يَوْعُثُ وُعُوثَةً To be rugged, difficult to walk upon (road). To be hard (affair). To be soft (ground).

To be broken (hand). وَعِثَ يَوْعَثُ وَعَثًا

To withhold, to hinder a. o. وَعَّثَ ه

To walk on a rugged road. To be unable to speak. أَوْعَثَ

To mar (an affair). — هـ

He squandered his wealth away. — في مَالِهِ

settle, to dwell in, to inhabit (a place).

To choose (a country) as an abode. To settle in (a country). وَطَّنَ وأَوْطَنَ وتَوَطَّنَ واتَّطَنَ واسْتَوْطَنَ هـ

He accustomed himself to. He disposed himself for. وَطَّنَ وأَوْطَنَ وتَوَطَّنَ نَفْسَهُ على

To agree with a. o. upon. وَاطَنَ ه على

Dwelling. Fatherland. Stable for cattle. وَطَن ج أَوْطَان

Abode, dwelling. Fatherland, home. Battle-field. مَوْطِن ج مَوَاطِن

Enclosure for race-horses. End, purpose. مِيطَان

✱ وَظَبَ يَظِبُ وُظُوبًا هـ وعلى, ووَاظَبَ على To apply o.'s self assiduously to. To persevere in.

To trample upon (the ground). وَظَبَ يَظِبُ وَظْبًا هـ

Perseverance, steadfastness, application. مُوَاظَبَة

Knife made with a flint-stone. مِيظَب

Deprived of his flocks (man). Exhausted by cattle (herbage). مَوْظُوب م مَوْظُوبَة

To be fat, plump. ✱ وَظِرَ a وَظَرًا

Fat, plump. وَظِر

To shorten (a camel's) halter. To wound (a camel) on the shank. To follow a. o. ✱ وَظَفَ يَظِفُ وَظْفًا ه

To assign an allowance to. ✧ To give employment to. وَظَّفَ ه

To impose (a task) upon a. o. To assess a tax upon a. o. — هـ على

To become attached to; to agree with, to assist a. o. وَاظَفَ ه

To be raised to dignity, to office. To get an employment. ✧ تَوَظَّفَ

To take a. th. altogether. إِسْتَوْظَفَ هـ

Slender part of a beast's foreleg. وَظِيف ج أَوْظِفَة ووُظُف

The camels arrived in a file. جَاءَتِ الإِبِلُ على وَظِيفٍ وَاحِدٍ

Daily allowance. Instalment (of a debt). Rate of a duty. Compact. Task. ✧ Office employment. وَظِيفَة ج وَظَائِف

They have entered a compact. بَيْنَهُمَا وَظِيفَةٌ

To withhold, وَعَرَ يَعِرُ وَعْرًا, ووَعَّرَ ه عن to prevent a. o. from.
To render (a place) rugged, وَعَّرَ ه uneven. To render (an affair) hard, difficult.
To interrupt a. o. وَعَّرَ ه
To come to a rugged tract. To أَوْعَرَ have little wealth.
To be uneven, hard for a. o. — بِفُلَانٍ (road).
To lessen a. th. — ه
To find (a road) hard, — واستوْعَرَ ه rugged.
To become uneven (road). To تَوَعَّرَ be difficult (affair). To be harsh, unsociable (man).
To be confused in (speech). — في
Ruggedness, roughness of a وَعْر ووُعُور place.
Steep, وَعْر ج وُعُور وأَوْعُر وأَوْعَار ووُعُورَة rugged, uneven (road). Arduous (question).
Little generous. — ٱلمَعْرُوف
Very little. قَلِيلٌ وَعْر
Rugged, steep, وَعِر ووَاعِر ووَعِير وأَوْعَر arduous (road). Difficult of access (place).
Scanty (hair). مَعِر وَعِر
Uncouth (word). وَعْرِيّ
To suggest, to recommend a. th. to a. o. ✻ وَعَزَ يَعِزُ وَعْزًا, ووَعَّزَ وأَوْعَزَ إِلَيْهِ في
To command a. th. أَوْعَزَ ب
To tread a. th. under foot. ✻ وَعَسَ يَعِسُ وَعْسًا ه
To stride along in stretching the neck (camel). وَاعَسَ وأَوْعَسَ
To vie in quickness with a. o. by night. وَاعَسَ ه
To walk upon a sandy ground.. أَوْعَسَ
Tree used for making lutes. Foot-prints. Soft sand. وَعْس ج أَوْعَاس
He has left traces. بَقِيَ لَهُ وَعْسٌ
Sandy (ground). أَوْعَس م وَعْسَاء ج وُعْس وجج أَوَاعِس
Sandy hill producing vegetables. وَعْسَاء
Sandy ground; soft, untrodden soil. مِيعَاس ج مَوَاعِيس
To exhort ✻ وَعَظَ يَعِظُ وَعْظًا و عِظَةً ه

Broken bone. Flat and soft ground. Emaciation. Difficult affair. وَعْث ج وُعُوث
Road difficult to walk upon. — ووَعِث ومُوْعَث
Fat and bulky (woman). وَعْثَة
Hardship, toil. Bad quality. وَعْثَاء
Hardship of a journey. وَعْثَاء السَّفَر
He committed sin. رَكِبَ الوَعْثَاء
Misfortune, distress. وُعُوث
Contemned, unregarded. مَوْعُوث
To make a promise to. ✻ وَعَدَ يَعِدُ وَعْدًا وعِدَةً ومَوْعِدًا ومَوْعِدَةً ومَوْعُودًا ومَوْعُودَةً ه
To promise (good) to. To threaten a. o. with (an evil). — ه ه وب وأَوْعَدَ إِيعَادًا ه ه
The earth promised to yield good produce. وَعَدَتِ ٱلأَرْضُ
To appoint (a time, a place) to a. o. for the fulfilment of a promise. وَاعَدَ ه ه
To make mutual promises. — ه وتَوَاعَدَ
To threaten a. o. with. أَوْعَدَ ه ب
To threaten a. o. تَوَعَّدَ ه
To accept a promise. To utter reciprocal threats. إِتَّعَدَ اتِّعَادًا وايتَعَدَ يَأْتَعِدُ ايتِعَادًا
Promise. عِدَة ج عِدَات, ووَعْد ج وُعُود (un. وَعْدَة)
Promissory. عِدِيّ وعِدَوِيّ
Threats. وَعِيد
Foreboding rain (cloud). Announcing a hot or cold day (morning). Promising (horse). وَاعِد
Promising (land). وَاعِدَة
Moslem sect holding very severe tenets. وَعِيدِيَّة
Time or place of a promise. Alliance. مَوْعِد ج مَوَاعِد
Time of promise. Appointment. Meeting-place. مِيعَاد ج مَوَاعِيد
The land of promise; Palestine. أَرْض ٱلمِيعَاد والمَوْعِد
Promise, thing promised. مَوْعُود ج مَوَاعِيد
To be hard, rugged, uneven (soil). ✻ وَعَرَ يَعِرُ وَعْرًا ووُعُورًا, ووَعِرَ يَوْعَرُ و يَعِرُ وَعَرًا, ووَعُرَ يَوْعُرُ وَعَارَةً ووُعُورَةً

To overtop. ✡ وَعَل يَعِل وَعْلًا
To climb (a mountain). تَوَعَّل ه
To fly to a mountain (antelope). إِسْتَوْعَل
To seek refuge towards. إِسْتَوْعَل إلى
وَعْل وَوَعِل ج أَوْعَال ووُعُول ووُعْل ووَعِلَة
Antelope, mountain-goat. ومَوْعَلَة
Refuge, shelter. وَعْل ج أَوْعَال ووُعُول
Eminent man.
Thou hast no escape from it. مَا لَكَ عَنْهُ وَعْلٌ
They are all united against us. هُمْ عَلَيْنَا وَعْلٌ وَاحِدٌ
Button-hole. Handle of a jug. وَعْلَة
Steep part of a mountain. Prominent rock.
Wild she-goat, antelope. وَعِلَة ج وَعِلَات ووِعَال
Retreat of an antelope. مُسْتَوْعَل ج مُسْتَوْعَلَات
To hail ✡ وَعَم وَوَعِم يَعِم وَعْمًا ه (the tents of a tribe) by saying: أَنْعِمِي Be prosperous.
Good morning, good evening, good night. عِمْ صَبَاحًا وَمَسَاءً وظَلَامًا
Path, sign seen from afar on the side of a mountain. وَعْم ج وِعَام
To become fat (cattle). ✡ وعن – تَوَعَّن
To take a. th. altogether. – ه
Whitish hard and barren ground. وَعْن ج وِعَان، وَوَعْنَة ج وِعَان
To heal (shattered bone). To flow (pus). To cicatrise over the pus (wound). ✡ وَعَى يَعِي وَعْيًا
To accumulate in (a wound: pus). – في
To gather, to keep a. th. To understand, to learn a. th. from. – ه
✧ To awake from sleep. To pay attention. To recover o.'s senses. ✧ وَعِي يَوْعَى
To remember a. th. ✧ وَعِي ل
To awake a. o. ✧ وَعَّى ه
To store up (victuals) in a vessel. To keep a. th. in mind. أَوْعَى إِيعَاء ه
✧ Look out, beware! وَعْي وأَوْعَى
To be stingy towards. أَوْعَى ه وعلى
To uproot (a – وإِسْتَوْعَى اسْتِيعَاء ه

a. o. To warn a. o. of (reward or punishment). To preach.
To accept, to follow an advice. To be warned, exhorted. إِتَّعَظ
Exhortation, sermon. Warning. وَعْظَة، وعِظَة ج عِظَات
Sermon. Warning. وَعْظ ج وَعْظَات، مَوْعِظَة ج مَوَاعِظ
Homily. وَعْظَة ومَوْعِظَة في الأَنَاجِيل
Warning, exhorting. وَاعِظ ج وُعَّاظ ووَاعِظُون
Preacher. – ووَعَّاظ
✧ Catechumens. مَوْعُوظُون
To be weakened (sight). ✡ وَعُف يَوْعُف وُعُوفًا
Hard ground retaining water. وَعْف ج وِعَاف
To have a rumbling in the bowels (horse). ✡ وَعَق يَعِق وَعْقًا ووَعِيقًا ووُعَاقًا
To hurry, to go quickly. وَعِق يَعِق وَعْقًا على
To be ill-tempered. وَعُق يَوْعُق وَعَقَة، وتَوَعَّق واسْتَوْعَق
To withhold, to counteract a. o. To judge a. o. to be unsociable. وَعَّق ه
How speedy he is! مَا أَوْعَقَهُ
Unsociable, ill-tempered. وَعْق ووَعِق ووَعْقَة ووَعِقَة
Greedy, avaricious. وَعِق لَعِق
Quarrelsomeness, unsociable temper. وَعْقَة
To be intense (heat). To be jaded, overfatigued. ✡ وَعَك يَعِك وَعْكًا ووَعْكَة
To weaken, to enervate a. o. (fever). – ه
To break a. th. in small pieces. – وَعْكًا ه
To roll a. o. or a. th. in (the dust). – وأَوْعَك ه وه في
To press together (to the water: camels). أَوْعَك
To be unwell, dejected. تَوَعَّك
Collapse, prostration, exhaustion. وَعْك
Intensity of fever, of a disease. Collapse. Exhaustion. Fall in a race. Battle-field. وَعْكَة
Exhausted by fever, or disease. وَعِك ووَعِك ومَوْعُوك

tree). To recover the whole of (a debt).

✧ توغّى توغّياً واستوعى في To make a. th. carefully. To be long-minded, forbearing in (an affair).

وغي Pus. Clamours.

ما لي عنهُ وغيّ I must do it necessarily.

لا وغيَ عن ذلك الأمر I cannot avoid that affair.

وغى Shouts, clamours.

وعاء ووُعاء ج أوعية وجج أواعٍ Vessel, jar, bag for storing provisions. Heart of man.

واعٍ ✧ Awake ; cautious.

واعي اليتيم واليهِ Guardian of an orphan.

واعية Cry, sound. Attentive (ear).

أوعى من More intelligent, more mindful than.

موعي الرُّسغ Strong-wristed.

✱ وغب يوغب وُغوبة ووغابة To be big (camel).

وغب ج أوغاب ووغاب Sack. House-furniture. Utensils. Foolish, weak. Huge camel.

✱ وغد يغد وغدًا ه To serve a. o. as a servant.

وغد يوغد وغادة To be weak of body and mind ; to be low, foolish, mean.

واغد ه To imitate a. o.

— ه في السير He vied in swiftness with him.

وغد م وغدة ج أوغاد ووغدان Servant, slave. Foolish, weak in body or mind, low, mean. Arrow having no share in the game. Egg plant.

✱ وغر يغر وغرًا To be intensely hot (summer-noon).

— ووغر يوغر وييغر وغرًا صدرُهُ على To burn with anger against.

وغر وأوغر ه او صدرَهُ He irritated him.

وغّر ه To warm (milk) with heated stones. To make (water) to boil.

أوغر To enter upon the heat of noon.

— ه To scald (a pig).

— ه To collect (taxes).

— ه إلى To constrain a. o. to.

— ه ه To grant to a. o. (an estate) free of taxes (prince).

أوغروا بينهم ميغرًا They agreed together upon the time of the meeting.

توغّر To become angry.

وغر ووغر Hatred, anger, rancour. Clamours of an army.

وغرة Excessive heat of midday.

وغير Roasted (meat). Boiled (milk).

— ووغيرة Milk warmed with heated stones.

ميغر Appointment, time agreed upon.

✱ وغف يغف وغفًا ووُغوفًا To be weakened (sight).

— وأوغف To hasten, to run up.

✱ وغل يغل وُغولًا في To enter, to conceal o.'s self in.

— وغلا ووُغولًا ووغلانًا على To come to (a feast) uninvited (parasite).

أوغل إيغالًا في السير He hastened the walk.

أوغلتهُ الحاجةُ في ذلك Necessity compelled him to do so.

أوغل وتوغّل في To penetrate far into (a country). To go deep into (science). ✧ To give o.'s self up to (sin).

وغل Wine drunk without invitation. Vile man. Parasite. Boasting falsely of his origin. Dense tree.

— ووغِل Ill-fed.

ما لي عنهُ وغل I must do it. I have no escape from it.

وغالسعر Asking too high a price, overcharging.

إيغال *Rhet.* Pathos, hyperbole emphatic words adding no meaning.

✱ وغم يغم وغمًا ب To relate false (news).

وغم يوغم وغمًا على To brood hatred against.

توغّم على To become angry with.

تواغم To come to fight ; to look fiercely at o. a. (fighters).

وغم ج أوغام Hatred, enmity, war. Ruffian, knave.

✱ وغن — توغّن Ta be dauntless.

✱ وغى — وغى ووني Clamour, uproar. War

واغية ج أواغٍ Ditch dug as a limit.

✱ وفد يفد وفدًا ووُفودًا ووفادة وإفادة على او إلى To come to, to reach (a

quantity. Fulness.
وَفر ج وُفُور Wealth, sufficiency. Comprehensive. Numerous, complete (property, furniture).
✧ وَفر Savings.
وَفرَة ج وِفَار Thick and long hair.
✧ تَوفِير Savings, economy.
وَافِر Poetical metre consisting of six feet (مُفَاعِلَن).
— ومُتَوَافِر ~ Abundant, copious, complete, rich.
وَافِرَة Fat tail of a ram. The present world.
أَوفَر م وُفرَى More abundant, more complete.
أَوفَر م وَفرَاء ج وُفر Large (water-skin). Full (bowl). Big (ear). Abounding with plants (land).
مُوَفَّر الشَّعر Thick-haired.
مُوَفَّر ومَوفُور Full, unshortened (metre).
قَوم مُتَوَافِرُون Numerous tribe.
✲ وفز — أَوفَز ه To urge, to incite a. o.
تَوَفَّز ل To prepare for (mischief).
إِستَوفَز فِي قِعدَتِهِ He sat so as to be ready to rise.
إِستَوفَز ل To be on the watch, on the look-out for.
وَفز ووَفَز ج أَوفَاز و وِفَاز Haste, hurry.
على أَوفَاز و وِفَاز ووَفَزٍ Ready to depart, in haste.
مَكَان وَفز Elevated place.
مُتَوَفِّز Anxious, restless.
✲ وَفَض يَفِض وَفضًا ووَفَضًا, وأَوفَض واستَوفَض To hasten, to go quickly.
أَوفَض ه To set (cattle) apart. To expel a. o.
— لِفُلَانٍ To spread a carpet for a. o.
إِستَوفَض To disperse in pasturing (camels).
— ه To urge to, hurry a. o.; to drive a. o. away.
وَفض ووَفَض ج أَوفَاض Haste, hurry.
وَفَض ج أَوفَاض Board for carving meat.
وَفضَة ج وِفَاض Leathern quiver. Shepherd's bag. Dimple in the upper lip.
أَوفَاض Parties of men coming from various tribes.
نَاقَة مِيفَاض Quick-stepping she-camel.

place). To be deputated to (a king: ambassador).
وَفَّد وأَوفَد واستَوفَد ه على او إلى To send a. o. anywhere. To despatch (an envoy) to.
وَافَد ه على To come together to.
أَوفَد To rise, to be overtopping. To hasten. To erect the head and ears (gazelle).
مَا أَحسَن مَا أَوفَد حَارِكَهُ How fine is the prominence of his withers!
أَوفَد وتَوَفَّد على To overtop, to overlook a. th.
تَوَافَد To arrive together at.
إِستَوفَد فِي قِعدَتِهِ He sat so as to be able to rise quickly.
وَفد ج وُفُود وأَوفَاد Company of men sent for a common purpose. Deputation. Envoy, embassy. Summit of a sandy tract.
لَقِيَ وَفدَيِ الخَيرِ والشَّرِّ He has experienced ill and good fortune.
هُم على أَوفَادٍ They are on the eve of their departure.
وَافِد ج وُفُود ووَفد وأَوفَاد ووُفَّاد ووُفَّد Arriving, coming (envoy). Walking ahead (camel).
وَافِد مث وَافِدَان Prominent part of the cheek.
✲ وَفَر يَفِر وَفرًا ووُفُورًا و فِرَةً, ووَفُر o وَفَارَة To be plentiful, copious. To be numerous (flock).
وَفَر يَفِر وَفرًا و فِرَةً ه ل To increase a. o.'s (wealth).
— ه ه To return (a gift) to a. o.
— عِرضَ فُلَانٍ ووَفَر فُلَانًا عِرضَهُ ووَفَر لَهُ عِرضَهُ He preserved, he kept his honour safe.
وَفَّر وأَوفَر ه To increase (property).
وَفَّر ه To render a. th. complete, copious. To cut out a large piece of (cloth). ✧ To save (money).
— وَاستَوفَر عَلَيهِ حَقَّهُ واستَوفَر حَقَّهُ He gave him the whole of his due.
تَوَفَّر ✧ To be saved (money).
— على To show regard to. To show zeal for.
تَوَافَر واتَّفَر To increase, to multiply (goods).
وَفر ووَفِرَة ووُفُور ووَفرَة Abundance, great

Lofty building. ✲ وفم — وَفَم ج أَوْفَاء
Cloud foreboding rain.
Grown up youth. غُلَام وَفَم ج وِفْمَان وغُلَام وَفْمَة وأَفْمَة
Cork, stopper. وَفْمَة ووَفِيمَة ج وِفَاء
Basket of palm-leaves. وَفْمَة ووَفِيمَة
Pen-wiper. وَفِيمَة
To come seasonably; to suit a. o.'s wishes (affair). ✲ وَفِق يَفِق وَفْقًا
To find, to meet with a. th. fit, suitable. — ه
To render a. th. fit, suitable. To adapt (an affair). وَفَّق ه
To help, to direct a. o. (God). — ه
To conciliate (two persons). To match (two things). — ووَافَق بَيْن
To meet a. o. To concur with. To fit, to suit a. o. وَافَق مُوَافَقَة ووِفَاقًا ه
To agree with a. o. upon. — ه فِي او على
To walk in a file (camels). أَوْفَق
To agree, to comply with a. o. on a point. — لِفُلَانٍ
To adapt (an arrow) to the bow-string. — ه وب
He met us unexpectedly. أُوفِق لَهُ لِقَاؤُنَا
To be helped, favoured by God. To succeed in an undertaking. تَوَفَّق
To agree upon a. th. تَوَافَق فِي
They succoured o. a. تَوَافَقُوا
They agreed upon a. th. إِتَّفَقَا على او فِي
To happen to a. o. (event). إِتَّفَق ل
To ask (God's) assistance. إِسْتَوْفَق ه
Sufficiency. Opportunity, seasonable time. وَفْق
The people came in perfect agreement. جَاءَ ٱلْقَوْمُ وَفْقًا
His milch-camel yields sufficient milk for the whole family. حَلُوبَتُهُ وَفْقُ عِيَالِهِ
I went to him on the very moment of the affair. أَتَيْتُهُ لِوَفْقِ ٱلْأَمْرِ ولِتُوفَاقِهِ وتِيفَاقِهِ
Good order. Succour given by God. Success; good luck. تَوْفِيق
First appearance of the new moon. تَوْفِيق ٱلْهِلَال وتُوفَاقُهُ وتِيفَاقُهُ وتَوَفُّقُهُ ومِيفَاقُهُ
Chance, coincidence, unexpected event. Union, harmony, agreement. إِتِّفَاق
Accidental, casual. إِتِّفَاقِيّ
Coming seasonably. Suitable. وَافِق م وَافِقَة
Companion, fellow, friend. وَفِيق
Convenience, conformity. Coincidence. وِفَاق ومُوَافَقَة
Agreement, union, accord. (*Arith.*) Divisibility of two numbers by a common divisor. — وتَوَافُق
Fit, suitable. مُوَافِق
(*Arith.*). Having a common divisor (numbers). مُوَافِقَانِ
Wont to speak seasonably. Successful. مُتَوَفِّق
To peel, to skin a. th. ✲ وَفَل يَفِل وَفْلًا ه
A little, a trifle. وَفْل
Full-grown. Complete. وَافِل
To be a churchwarden. To manage church-property. ✲ وَفَه يَفِه وَفْهًا
Churchwarden. وَافِه
Office of a churchwarden. وِفَاهَة
Church-guardianship. وَفْهِيَّة
To fulfil (a promise); to pay (a debt). ✲ وَفَى يَفِي وَفَاءً, وأَوْفَى إِيفَاءً ه وب
He atoned for his fault. وَفَى عَنْ ذَنْبِهِ
To be plentiful, complete. — وُفِيًّا
The coin has a legal standard. — الدِرْهَمُ ٱلْمِثْقَالَ
What wealth cannot procure. مَا لَا يَفِي بِهِ ٱلْمَال
He paid to him the whole of his due. وَفَّى ووَافَى وأَوْفَى ه حَقَّهُ
To come to, to encounter a. o. وَافَى وأَوْفَى ه
To accomplish (a vow). أَوْفَى ه
To rise above, to overlook a. o. — على
He received the whole amount of his due. تَوَفَّى تَوَفِّيًا واسْتَوْفَى اسْتِيفَاءً حَقَّهُ
God caused him to die. تَوَفَّاهُ ٱللّٰه
To die. تُوُفِّيَ و✧ تَوَفَّى
The whole of the tribe came in. تَوَافَى ٱلْقَوْم
✧ To exact the whole of. To make up for. To complete (years of age). إِسْتَوْفَى ه
Lengthening of life. وَفَاء
Such a one is dead, mayest thou live long! مَاتَ فُلَانٌ وأَنْتَ بِوَفَاهُ
Accomplishment of a vow, وَفَاء وإِيفَاء

To have a time assigned for acting. وُقِّتَ ووُقِتَ
Time, hour, moment, season. وَقْت ج أَوْقَات
Now. (for هٰذَا الوَقْت) ◘ دِلْوَقْت ودِلْوَقْتِي
At that time. وَقْتَئِذٍ
On the spot, immediately. لِلْوَقْتِ ولِوَقْتِهِ
Unseasonably. فِي غَيْرِ وَقْتِهِ
Temporary, transient. ✧ Precarious, provisional. وَقْتِيّ
Determined, fixed (action). مُوَقَّت ومَوْقُوت
Appointment: rendez-vous. ◘ Time-tables. مَوْقِت, ومِيقَات ج مَوَاقِيت
Meeting-place of the pilgrims to Mecca. مَوَاقِيت الحَجّ او الحَاجّ
✱ وَقِح يَقِح قِحَة, ووَقُح يَوْقُح وَقَحًا, ووَقُحَ
To be impudent, shameless, barefaced (man). To be hard (hoof). يَوْقُح وَقَاحَة ووُقُوحَة
To harden (the hoof) with fat. To repair (a trough). وَقَّح ﻫ
To be hard (hoof). أَوْقَح واسْتَوْقَح
To be shameless, barefaced. تَوَقَّح واتَّقَح
To show impudence. تَوَاقَح
Insolence, barefacedness. قِحَة ووَقَح ووَقَاحَة ووُقُوحَة
Impudent, brazen-faced. وَقِح م وَقِحَة, ووَقَاح (m. f.) ج وُقُح
Man remaining long on horseback. رَجُل وَقَاح الذَّنَب
Barefaced woman. إِمْرَأَة وَقَاح الوَجْه
Tried by misfortunes. مُوَقَّح
✱ وَقَد يَقِد وَقْدًا ووَقَدًا ووُقُودًا وقِدَة ووَقَدَانًا
To be lighted, kindled. To blaze (fire). وتَوَقَّد واتَّقَد واسْتَوْقَد
To light (a lamp, a fire). وَقَّد وأَوْقَد وتَوَقَّد واسْتَوْقَد ﻫ
He has kindled war. أَوْقَد نَار الحَرْب
He has given over the fooliness of youth. — لِلصِّبَا نَارًا
To be excited. To be sharp, clever. تَوَقَّد
Fire. (un. وَقْدَة وَوَقِدَة) وَقْد ووَقَد
Burning, combustion. وَقْد وقِدَة واتِّقَاد
Heat of fire, of summer. ◘ Illumination. وَقْدَة
Fuel, combustible. وِقَاد ووَقِيد ووَقُود
✧ Burnt-offerings. وَقُود
✧ Fire, ardour of fire. وَقِيد

fulfilment of a promise. Payment of a debt.
◘ Highest water of the Nile. وَفَاء النِّيل
Prominence of ground. وَفِي ومِيفَى ومِيفَاة
Death. وَفَاة ج وَفَيَات
Faithful to a promise. Perfect, complete. وَفِيّ ج أَوْفِيَاء
Fulfilling a promise. Copious. Complete. وَافٍ م وَافِيَة
The first chapter of the Koran. سُورَة الوَافِيَة
Coming, arriving. مُوَافٍ
Shutter of an oven. Brick-kiln. Bake-house. مِيفَى
Rising above (a place: bird). مِيفَاء على
To bark (dog). To squeak (bird). ✱ وَقْوَق
Tree used for making inkstands. Faint-hearted, cowardly. Cuckoo (bird). وَقْوَاق
Prater, babbler. (m. f.) وَقْوَاق
To set (sun). To be hidden (thing). ✱ وَقَب يَقِب وَقْبًا ووُقُوبًا
To enter a grotto. To be eclipsed (moon). To be sunken in its socket (eye). — وَقْبًا
To overspread a. o. (darkness, misfortune). — على
To be hungered, empty-bellied. أَوْقَب إِيقَابًا
To place a. th. in a cavity. — ﻫ
Cavity of a rock in which water collects. Cavity of the eyes, shoulders. Cavity under a horse's eyes. Pl. House-furniture. وَقْب ج أَوْقَاب
Stupid, foolish. — م وَقْبَة, ووَقْبَان م وَقْبَى
Hollow in a rock. Large loophole. Skylight. Hollow in the upper part of a pie. وَقْبَة
Ventricle of a lamb. قِبَة ج قِبَات
Sea-shell. مِيقَب
Drinking much water. Foolish (woman). مِيقَاب
Journey continued by day and night. سَيْر المِيقَاب
To fix, to appoint the time of (an action). ✱ وَقَت يَقِت وَقْتًا, ووَقَّت ﻫ
To determine (a time) for. وَقَّت ﻫ ل
To give an appointment to a. o. — ووَاقَت ﮦ

□ Lighting, matches. وَقِيدَة
Stoker. وَقَّاد ج وَقَّادُون
Lively, fiery. Penetrative, acute (mind). وَقَّاد ومُتَوَقِّد
Kind of fat goats with reddish hair. وَقِيدِيَّة
Hearth, fire-place. مَوْقِد ج مَوَاقِد, ومُسْتَوْقِد
✧ Furnace, stove. ✧ مَوْقِدَة ج مَوَاقِد
Yielding fire at once (flint). مِيقَاد
Kindled, lighted. مَوْقُود ومُتَّقِد
To strike a. o. mortally. To fell, to beat a. o. to death. To overcome a. o. (sleep). To soothe a. o. (meekness). ✡ وَقَذَ i وَقْذًا ه
To leave a. o. ill, lying on the ground. — وأَوْقَذَ ه
Sluggish, slow. Ready. وَقِيذ
Sick person at the point of death. — ومَوْقُوذ
Pl. Stone-pavement. وَقِيذَة ج وَقَائِذ
Prominent bone or limb, as the shoulder, the elbow. مَوْقِذ ج مَوَاقِذ
Beaten to death (ewe). مَوْقُوذَة
To render (the ear) deaf (God). To split (a bone). ✡ وَقَرَ يَقِرُ وَقْرًا ه
To sit gravely at home. — وَقْرًا ووُقُورَةً فِي
To be dignified, sedate, staid. To be forbearing, patient. — قِرَةً, ووَقُرَ يَوْقُرُ وَقَارَةً وقِرَةً وَوَقَارًا
To be affected with deafness (ear). وَقِرَتْ تَقِرُ, ووَقِرَتْ تَوْقَرُ وَقْرًا ووُقِرَتْ
Ta have a cracked hoof (beast). وَقِرَ يَوْقَرُ وَقْرًا
To be split (bone). وُقِرَ
To honour, to regard a. o. To extol, to praise a. o. To render a. o. grave, sedate. To wound a. o. To quiet (a beast). وَقَّرَ ه
To leave traces upon. — ل
To crush a. o. (debts). To load (a beast). To cause (the hoof) to be chapped (God). أَوْقَرَ إِيقَارًا وقِرَةً ه
To be laden with fruit (palm-tree). أَوْقَرَ وأُوقِرَ
To be sedate, grave. To be patient, still. تَوَقَّرَ واتَّقَرَ
To become fleshy (camel, woman). إِسْتَوْقَرَ
To take a load of. — وِقْرَهُ ه
Dullness of the ear, deafness. Crack in the hoof; lesion in the bone of the leg. Cavity of the eye, of a rock. وَقْر ج وُقُور
There is hatred in his heart. فِي صَدْرِهِ او فِي قَلْبِهِ وَقْرٌ
Burden, heavy load. Load of an ass, a mule. وِقْر ج أَوْقَار
Pl. Lesion in a bone. Crack in a rock. *Pl.* Traces. وَقْرَة ج وَقَرَات
Weight, heaviness. Decrepit old man. Time of illness. Family قِرَة ج قِرَات
Flock of about 500 sheep. — ووَقِير
Shepherd. Owner of sheep, asses. وَقَرِيّ
Gravity of conduct, of deportment. Staid behaviour, dignity, meekness, forbearance. وَقَار وتَيْقُور
Sedate, staid; calm and patient (man). وَقُر ووَقَار
Grave. وَقُور (*m. f.*) ج وُقُر
Hollow in a rock. وَقِير ووَقِيرَة
Very destitute. فَقِير وَقِير
Cracked, split (bone). وَقِير ومَوْقُور
Laden (beast). وَقْرَى ومُوقَرَة
Burdened (man). مُوقَر
Laden with fruit (palm-tree). مُوقِر ومُوقِرَة ومُوَقَّرَة ومِيقَا
Regarded, honoured. Intelligent, experienced (man). مُوَقَّر
Plain at the foot of a mountain. مَوْقِر
To spread on (the body: scab). ✡ وَقَسَ يَقِسُ وَقْسًا فِي
To take off (the skin). To mention (a foul action). — ه
To communicate the scab to (camels). وَقَّسَ ه
Scab, mange. وَقْس
Mean people of a tribe. أَوْقَاس
To be effaced (trace). ✡ وَقَشَ يَقِشُ وَقْشًا
To move on. تَوَقَّشَ
Movement, commotion. وَقْش ووَقْشَة ووَقَشَة
Chips of wood. وَقَش
To be broken (neck). ✡ وَقَصَ يَقِصُ وَقْصًا
To break a. o.'s (neck). To tread heavily (the rising grounds: horse). — ه

It became incumbent upon him to speak. وَقَعَ ٱلْقَوْلُ عَلَيْهِ
An accident befell him. وَقَعَ لَهُ وَاقِعٌ
To light upon (a tree: bird). — على
To stand instead of; to do for. وَقَعَ مَوْقِعًا
To slander, to dishonour a. o. — وُقُوعًا ووَقِيعَةً فِي فُلَانٍ
A thought occurred to his mind. — فِي نَفْسِهِ
The discourse made impression upon him. — ٱلْكَلَامُ فِي نَفْسِهِ
He was moved by the speech. — الْكَلَامُ مِنْهُ مَوْقِعًا
He approved of it. — عِنْدَهُ مَوْقِعُ ٱلرِّضَى
He took it to heart. He laid it to heart. — مِن قَلْبِهِ فِي مَكَان
To hurry towards. — وَقْعًا إِلى
To sharpen (a sword) with a hone. — ووَقَّعَ هُ
To abrade (the hoofs: stony ground). وَقَعَ ووَقَّعَ هُ
To rush upon (the enemy). وَقَعَ وَقْعًا ووَقْعَةً, وأَوْقَعَ ب
To deviate, to stray from. وَقَعَ مِن او عَن
He repented. وُقِعَ فِي يَدِهِ
To go barefoot. To have the feet chafed by a hard ground. وَقِعَ يَوْقَعُ وَقَعًا
To halt during the night (traveller). To be at rest (camel). وَقَّعَ
To gall (a camel's back: saddle). To sprinkle the (earth: rain). To register (a decree); to sign a decree. ◘ To impose (a tax). وَقَّعَ هُ
He formed an opinion upon. — على فُلَان
He furbished the sword. — على ٱلسَّيْف
To experience, to fall into a. th. To attack (the enemy). وَاقَعَ مُوَاقَعَةً ووِقَاعًا ه وهُ
To retain (water: lawn). To tune (instruments, voices: musician). أَوْقَعَ
To execute a. th. To ensnare a. o. To let fall a. th. — ه وهُ
To rush upon, to charge (the enemy). — ب
To punish, to grieve a. o. by. — ب ه
To expect, to be in wait for. تَوَقَّعَ واسْتَوْقَعَ هُ
✧ To find out, to meet with. تَوَ... لِ

His riding-beast threw him off and broke his neck. وَقَصَت بِهِ رَاحِلَتُهُ
To have the neck broken. وُقِصَ
To be short-necked. وَقِصَ يَوْقَصُ وَقَصًا
✧ To devour a carrion (dog). وَقَّصَ
To break a. o.'s (neck). وَقَصَ هُ
He threw chips of wood on the fire. — على ٱلنَّار
To create a. o. short-necked (God). أَوْقَصَ هُ
To walk strenuously, to trot (beast). تَوَقَّصَ
He passed by at the trot of his mare. مَرَّ يَتَوَقَّصُ بِهِ فَرَسُهُ
Defect, vice. وَقْص
(*Pros.*) Suppression of the second movent letter of a foot. — ووَقَص
Chip of wood. *Pl.* Mixed rabble. وَقَص ج أَوْقَاص
They are dispersed. صَارُوا أَوْقَاصًا
Vertebræ of the neck. ✧ Carrion, carcass. وَقِيصَة ج وَقَائِص
Short-necked. أَوْقَص م وَقْصَاء ج وُقْص
The shortest of the two roads. أَوْقَص ٱلطَّرِيقَيْنِ
Broken. Curtailed of one letter (poetical foot). مَوْقُوص
✱ To beat a. o. unmercifully. To render a. o. heavy (milk). وَقَطَ يَقِطُ وَقْطًا هُ
He felled him on the ground. — بِهِ ٱلأَرْضَ
To contain a cavity (rock). وَقَّطَ
Hollow in which water collects. وَقْط ج أَوْقَاط, ووَقِيط ج وِقَاط و وِقْطَان
Dejected by grief, sleeplessness. وَقِيط ج وَقْطَى ووَقَاطَى
Unmercifully beaten. وَقِيط ومَوْقُوط
✱ To beat a. o. violently; to bruise a. o. وَقَظَ يَقِظُ وَقْظًا هُ
To persevere in. — على
Exhausted, unable to rise up. وَقِيظ
✱ To fall (rain). To happen, to take place (event). To kneel (camel). وَقَعَ يَقَعُ وُقُوعًا
Dissension took place between them. وَقَعَ بَيْنَهُم
The right has been ascertained. وَقَعَ ٱلْحَقُّ

To rush against, to assault o. a. To come to fight. تَوَقَّع
✧ To beseech a. o. — على
To want to be sharpened (sword). إِسْتَوْقَع
To fear, to dread a. o. — ه
Fall. وَقْع ووُقُوع
Blow, sound of a blow. Elevated part (of a mountain). وَقْع
Foreboding rain (cloud). وَقْع ووَقِع
Barefooted. Having the feet chafed by a hard ground. وَقِع
Rocks. وَقْع (*un.* وَقْعَة)
A fall, a blow. Conflict of fighters وَقْعَة
✧ Quantity of food eaten at one time. Meal. وَقْعَة ج وَقَعَات
Lighting of birds. وِقْعَة
Round brand on a horse. وِقَاع
Signature, seal put on a decree. Opinion. ✧ Levying of a tax. تَوْقِيع
Decree of a prince. — ج تَوَاقِيع
Harmony of voices. إِيقَاع
Expectation, prospect. تَوَقُّع
Accident, event. Necessary. Transitive (verb). وَاقِع ج وُقَّع ووُقُوع
✧ In fact, in truth. فِي الوَاقِع
Star in *Lyra*. أَلنَّسْر الوَاقِع
Occurrence, event, accident. Onslaught, shock, fight. وَاقِعَة
The Resurrection. أَلْوَاقِعَة
✧Official report, statement. صُورَة الوَاقِعَة
Sharpened (sword). Abraded by a hard ground (hoof). Hard soil in which water stagnates. ✧ Refugee. وَقِيع ج وُقَّع
Shock, onslaught, attack. Slander, ill-speaking. Hollow. Hard ground retaining water. وَقِيعَة ج وَقَائِع ووِقَاع
Slanderer. وَقَّاع ووَقَّاعَة
Falling-place. Place of an event. مَوْقِع ج مَوَاقِع
Places rained upon. مَوَاقِع أَلْمَطَر
Battle-fields. — أَلْحَرْب
Lighting-place of a bird. مَوْقَعَة أَلطَّائِر ج مَوَاقِع
Rubbing-board for linen. Beetle, mallet, hammer. Hone. مِيقَعَة ج مَوَاقِع
Light-footed. Sealer, seal-keeper. مُوَقِّع

Tried by misfortunes. Sharpened (sword). مُوَقَّع
Abraded by a hard ground (hoof). مَوْقُوع
To stand up. ✱ وَقَف يَقِف وَقْفًا ووُقُوفًا
To stand still, to stop (man, beast).
To pause in reading. — على الكَلِمَة
To wait for a. o. ✧ To rise up at the entering of a. o. وَقَف لِفُلَان
To stop (a beast). To allay the boiling of (a cooking-pot). — وَقْفًا ه وه
Who has detained thee? مَن وَقَفَكَ
To bequeath (a mortmain) to. وَقَف و✧ أَوْقَف ه ل وعلى
To busy o.'s self about. وَقَف وُقُوفًا على
To become aware of. To take information about a. th.
To acquaint a. o. with. — وَقْفًا ه على
He put off (the affair) till the arrival of such a one. — ه على حُضُور فُلَان
To withhold, to prevent a. o. from. — ه عَن
To put upright, to raise a. o. To stop (a beast). وَقَّف و✧ أَوْقَف ه
He taught the reader to pause. وَقَّف القَارِئ
To dye (her hands) with (henna : woman). وَقَّف ه ب
To repair (a saddle). To explain (a tradition). — ه
The army was stationed by detachments. وَقَّف الجَيْش
He performed the stations of the pilgrimage to Mecca. — فِي أَلْحَجّ
To stand in battle by the side of. وَاقَف مُوَاقَفَة ووِقَافًا ه في
To make a. o. to persevere in. To stand by a. o. for (help). To stand against a. o. for. — ه على
To stand still, speechless. أَوْقَف إِيقَافًا
What has detained thee here? مَا أَوْقَفَكَ هٰهُنَا
To put off (an affair). To refrain from. أَوْقَف وتَوَقَّف عَن
To hesitate, to defer a. th. تَوَقَّف فِي
To be steadfast, to persevere in. ✧ To consist in, to rest on. تَوَقَّف على
To stand against o. a. (figh- تَوَاقَف

a. o. harshly, to grieve, to humble, to repel a. o.
To check (a horse) with the bridle. وَقَمَ ه
To still (the boiling of a pot). — ه
To be stripped of its herbage by cattle (land). وُقِمَ
To threaten a. o. تَوَقَّمَ ه
To kill (the game). To remember (a word). To purpose a. th. — ه
To keep to, to persevere in. — فِي
Sword. Staff. Whip. Rope. وِقَام
To catch doves in their nests. ✱ وقن — أَوْقَنَ إِيقَانًا ه
To climb (a mountain). تَوَقَّنَ فِي
Bird's nest. Hollow in the earth. وَقْنَة وأُقْنَة ج وُقُنَات وأُقُنَات
Kept in-doors (girl). مَوْقُونَة
The Ocean. G أُوقِيَانُوس
To obey a. o. ✱ وَقِهَ يَقِهُ وَقْهًا, وأَيْقَهَ واتَّقَهَ واسْتَيْقَهَ ل
Obedience, submission. وَقْهَة
To keep, to preserve a. o. or a. th. ✱ وَقَى يَقِي وِقَايَةً ووَقْيًا ووَاقِيَةً, ووَقَّى ه
To repair, to arrange. وَقَى وَقْيًا ووُقِيًّا ه
Do mind thy concerns. قِ على ظَلْعِكَ
To dread, to guard against a. o. or a. th. تَوَقَّى واتَّقَى ه وه
To fear, to honour (God). To be pious, godly. إِتَّقَى, وتَقَى يَتْقِي تُقًى وتَقِيَّة وتِقَاء ه
Do fear God. تَقِ (*m.*) وتَقِي (*f.*)
Keeping, watch, caution. وَقْي ووِقَايَة ووَاقِيَة
Preservative, preventive. وِقَاء و وَقَاء ووِقَايَة ووُقَايَة
The augmentative ن *as in* نُونُ الوِقَايَة ضَرَبَنِي, لَيْتَنِي.
Fear of God. تُقًى وتَقْوَى, وتُقَاة ج تُقًى
Godly, pious. تَقِيّ ج أَتْقِيَاء
Cautioning, preservative. Comfortable (saddle). وَقِيّ ووَاقٍ
Green wood-pecker. الوَاقِي والوَاق
An ounce, twelfth part of a rothl, weighing about 1 1/2 English ounce. G أُوقِيَّة ج أَوَاقِيّ وأَوَاقٍ
Kept, guarded. مَوْقِيّ
Preserved. Brave. مُوَقًّى
Fearing God, godly. مُتَّقٍ

ters). ✧ To appear in a court (parties).
To ask a. o. to stand up, to stand still. إِسْتَوْقَفَ ه
Bracelet of ivory. Ring of metal or horn around a shield. Pause in reading. (*Prosody*). Quiescence of a letter at the end of a foot. وَقْف
Pious bequest; mortmain. وَقْف ج أَوْقَاف ووُقُوف
Station, stoppage. Flattened sinew surrounding a bow. وَقْفَة
Antelope driven to strait. وَقِيفَة
Stop, halt, standing. وُقُوف
Delay, respite. Mark on an arrow of the game. تَوْقِيف
Standing still. Bequeathing a pious bequest. وَاقِف ج وُقُوف ووُقَّف
Informed, aware of. — على
Protracted. Drawing back in fight. وَقَّاف ووَقَّافَة
✧ Connection, dependence. تَوَقُّف
Stopping-place. Station. Cavity in a horse's flanks. The face, eyes and hands of a woman. مَوْقِف ج مَوَاقِف
Taught by experience (man). White-spotted in the upper part of the ears (horse). Red-haired on the forefeet (ox). مُوَقَّف
Piece of wood for quashing ebullition. مِيقَف و مِيقَاف
Stopped. Bequeathed (mortmain). Traced back to the companions of Mohammed (tradition). (*Pros.*) Quiescent at its end (verse). مَوْقُوف
To stand on one leg. ✱ وَقَلَ يَقِلُ وَقْلًا
To climb (a mountain). — وتَوَقَّلَ فِي
Wild palm-tree, its fruit. وَقْل ج أَوْقَال
Rocks, stones. Palm-roots shooting off at the foot of the trunk. وَقَل
Going up a hill (horse). — ووَقِل ووَقُل
Fruit-stone of the wild palm-tree. وَقْلَة ج وُقُول
More skilled in ascending. أَوْقَل
Caravansary, inn. ◻ أَوْقَلَة
Ascending a hill easily (horse). تَوَقْلَة
To treat ✱ وَقَمَ يَقِمُ وَقْمًا, ووَقَّمَ وأَوْقَمَ ه

✱ وكأ – أوكأ إيكاء, وتوكّأ واتّكأ على To lean the back upon.
أوكأ ه To give to a. o. a pillow to recline upon.
آتكأ ه To make a. o. to lean.
ضربه فأتكأه He struck and threw him upon his side.
إتّكأ To sit in leaning the back; to recline upon the side.
– عند فلان To eat at a. o.'s house.
تُكأة Walking-stick. Dull (person).
إتّكاء Leaning, reclination. (*Pros.*) Redundance.
مُتّكأ ج مُتّكآت Sofa-bed, couch. Table-bed. Sitting-room. Repast.
رئيس المُتّكأ Butler; steward.
مُتّكئ Leaning, reclining.
✱ وكب يكب وكبًا ووكوبًا ووكبانًا To walk slowly.
– وكبًا To stand erect.
– وواكب على To apply o.'s self perseveringly to.
وكب a وكبًا, ووكّب To become black (date).
واكب ه To walk in (a procession).
أوكب To keep with a retinue. To flap the wings before flying, or lighting (bird).
واكبة Foot of a beast.
وكّاب Dejected by grief.
وكوب ومُواكبة Stretching the neck in walking (gazelle).
موكب ج مواكب Retinue of a prince. Train of attendants, cortege.
✱ وكت يكت وكتًا في المشي To walk with short steps.
– في To imprint a mark upon.
– ووكّت ه To fill (a vessel).
وكّت To become spotted (ripening date).
وكت Small quantity.
وكتة Spot, speck. Slight trace.
وكيت Slander, intrigue.
موكوت Anxious and restless.
✱ وكث – وُكاث Food prepared in haste.
إستوكث To take some food before the morning-meal.
✱ وكح يكح وكحًا ه ب To trample upon.
أوكح To be weary.
– ه To interrupt, to discontinue a. th.
– عن To cease, to abstain from.
– في حفره He reached the rock in digging.
إستوكح To refrain from giving. To become big (chicken).
أوكح Stony ground, rock.
✱ وكد يكد وكودًا ب To stay, to dwell in (a place).
– وكدًا ه To purpose a. th., to aim at. To hit (the point), to attain (an aim).
وكد وكده He had the same design as he.
– ووكّد وأكّد وأوكد ه To fasten (a saddle). To tighten (a knot). To confirm (a compact). ✧ To affirm.
توكّد وتأكّد To be confirmed, fastened.
وكد Aim in view. Care, anxiety.
وُكد Exertion, endeavour.
وِكاد وإكاد ج وكائد Tether of a beast.
وكيد وأكيد ومؤكّد وموكّد Strengthened.
✧ أكيد Certain, sure.
أوكد وآكد More steady.
توكيد وتأكيد Strengthening. Strain of a discourse. Pleonasm. ✧ Assertion, affirmation.
تواكيد وتآكيد ومياكيد Leathern wither-band.
مؤكّد Corroborative.
✧ مؤكّد Sure, certain.
متوكّد Ready for action.
✱ وكر يكر وكرًا ووكورًا To enter its nest (bird). To leap (gazelle). To have a jerking run (horse, camel).
– وكرًا, ووكّر وأوكر ه To fill (a vessel).
وكّر وكرًا, ووكّر To prepare a banquet at the completion of a building.
توكّر To be surfeited (child, bird).
إتّكر To nest (bird).
وكر ج أوكار وأوكر ووكور Bird's nest. Shelter, covert.
وكر ووكر ووكرى Jerking run.
وكرى Swift runner (she-camel). Stamping the ground in walk (woman).
وكرة ج وكر Bird's nest.
– ووكرة ووكير ووكيرة Feast given at the completion of a building.

Strong water-skin. مِيكَع

Ploughshare. مِيكَعَة ج مِيكَع

✱ وَكَف يَكِف وَكْفًا وَوَكَفَانًا وَوُكُوفًا وَوَكِيفًا

To drop (water, tears). To let out water (bucket). وتَوْكَافًا. وأَوْكَف

To gutter (flat roof). — وأَوْكَف وتَوَكَّف

To have a defect, a vice. To be unjust, wrongful. To commit an offence. وَكِف يَوْكَف وَكَفًا

To put a pack-saddle upon (an ass). وَكَّف وأَكَّف وَآكَف ه

He attacked him at war. وَاكَف ه في الحَرْب

To lead a. o. into crime. أَوْكَف ه

To expect (news). تَوَكَّف ه

To counteract a. o. — ل

To decline, to deviate. تَوَاكَف

To make (water) to drip, to give vent to (water). إِسْتَوْكَف ه

Vice, defect. Foot of a mountain. Weakness. Corruption. Heaviness. Sweat. Awning. وَكَف ج أَوْكَاف

Pack-saddle for asses. وِكَاف وإِكَاف ج وُكُف

To slacken the pace (beast). ✱ وَكَل يَكِل وَكْلًا وَوُكُولًا

To intrust a. o. with (an affair). — ه إِلى

To put confidence in (God). — وَكْلًا, وأَوْكَل بِ

To appoint a. o. as an agent, a trustee, a proxy. وَكَّل ه

✧ To feed a. o. (*for* أكل) وَكَّل

To intrust a. o. with. To delegate, to set a. o. over (an affair). — ه ب

To walk sluggishly (beast). وَاكَل وِكَالًا

To trust in o. a. — مُوَاكَلَةً ووِكَالًا ه

To be appointed as a trustee. تَوَكَّل

To hold o.'s self responsible for. To assume an affair upon o.'s self. تَوَكَّل بِأَمرٍ

To trust in, to rely upon. — واتَّكَل على

To rely upon o. another. تَوَاكَل

To leave, to forsake a. th. — ه

Impotent, disqualified man appointing a trustee. وَكَل وَوُكَلَة وتُكَلَة ومُوَاكِل

Slow pace of a beast. وِكَال

Trusteeship. Power وَكَالَة ج وِكَالَات

✱ وَكَز يَكِز وَكْزًا ه To fist, to drive a. o. back.

To thrust a. o. with (a lance). — ه ب

To stick (a spear) into the ground. — ه في

To be ready for (mischief). تَوَكَّز ل

To lean on (a staff). — على

To be gorged with (food). — مِن

To decrease, to become deficient. ✱ وَكَس يَكِس وَكْسًا, وأَوْكَس

To diminish, to lessen a. th. وَكَس ووَكَّس ه

To experience losses in (trade). وُكِس وأُوكِس في

To upbraid, to blame a. o. وَكَّس ه

He inflicted a loss upon him. — مَال فُلَان

Loss, damage. Decrease. Falling off. Mansion in which the moon is eclipsed. Splinter of bone remaining in the wound. وَكْس

He sold at a loss. بَاع بِالوَكْس

The wound of his head is cicatrised without being perfectly cured. بَرَأَت الشَّجَّة على وَكْس

Neither more nor less. لا وَكْسَ ولا شَطَط

Contemptible, vile, mean. أَوْكَس

To apply o.'s self unremittingly to. ✱ وَكَظ يَكِظ وَكْظًا, ووَاكَظ على

To bump the head against (his mother's udder: lamb). To sting a. o. (scorpion). ✱ وَكَم يَكِم وَكْمًا ه

To strike a. o. on (the nose). — ه

To reprehend a. o. on. — ه ب

To have a distorted toe. وَكِم يَوْكَم وَكَمًا

To be vile (man). To be strong (horse). To be rough (skin). وَكُم يَوْكُم وَكَاعَة

To tread (the hen: cock). وَاكَم ه

To become hardened (foot). To be deprived of good qualities. To cause inconvenience. أَوْكَم

To be fast, firm (thing). — واتَّكَم واسْتَوْكَم

Distortion of the toe. وَكَم

Vile, contemptible. وَكُوع لَكُوع ووَكِيع لَكِيع

Strong (horse). Strongly sewed (water-skin). وَكِيع

Resolute, steady heart. قَلْب وَكِيع

Having distorted toes. Foolish. أَوْكَم م وَكْعَاء ج وُكْم

To strike a. o. with (a stick). ✻ وَلَثَ يَلِثُ وَلْثًا ه ب

To conclude a precarious agreement with. — عَقْدًا لِ

Small quantity of rain. Compact — Precarious promise. Remainder of wine, water. Flour. وَلْث

Lasting (evil). Crushing (debt). وَالِث م وَالِثَة

To penetrate into. ✻ وَلَجَ يَلِجُ وُلُوجًا ولِجَةً ه وإلى

To feel a pain. وُلِجَ

He disposed of his property during his lifetime. وَلَّجَ مَا لَهُ

He intrusted him with the affair. — ه وإليهِ الأَمْرَ

To insert, to introduce a. th. into (another). أَوْلَجَ إِيلاجًا, وأَتْلَجَ إِتْلاجًا ه في

To penetrate into. تَوَلَّجَ إلى واتَّلَجَ ه

✧ To take (an affair) upon o.'s self. تَوَلَّجَ ه

Road in the sand. وَلَج

An entering, a passing in. وُلُوج ولِجَة

Thoroughfares. Inland countries. Spoons for honey. وُلُج

Cave, cavern. Winding of a valley. Passage. وَلَجَة ج وَلَج وأَوْلاج ووَلَجَات

Going in and out incessantly. Restless, unquiet. وُلَجَة خُرَجَة

Misfortune. Pain in the belly. Pain, suffering. وَالِجَة

Suffering (man). — ومَوْلُوج

Going in and out incessantly, bustler. خَرُوج وَلُوج

Familiar; follower, partisan. وَلِيجَة

Meddlesome, artful, intriguer. خَرَّاج وَلَّاج

Covert of a wild beast. تَوْلَج

Entrance, way in. مَوْلَج ج مَوَالِج

To overload (a beast). ✻ وَلَحَ يَلِحُ وَلْحًا ه

Large sack, date-basket. وَلِيحَة ج وَلِيح ووَلَائِح

✻ وَلَدَ يَلِدُ وِلَادَةً ووِلَادًا وإِلَادَةً ولِدَةً ومَوْلِدًا

To bring forth (female). To beget sons (man).

To give birth to (a child). To produce (a plant: land). — ه وه

To assist (a woman) in child-birth (midwife). To assist (a female) وَلَّدَ ه وه

of attorney. Management, agency.

✧ Factory. وَكَالَة تِجَارِيَّة

Reliance upon another. تُكْلَان

Delegation, procuration. تَوْكِيل

Reliance, trust. إِتِّكَال

Slack, wanting the spur (horse). وَاكِل م وَاكِلَة

Trustee, manager, agent, proxy, attorney. ✧ Representative of a firm. Station-master. وَكِيل ج وُكَلَاء

Intrusted to a.o. (affair). مَوْكُول إلى

To grieve a. o.; to subdue a. o. ✻ وَكَمَ يَكِمُ وَكْمًا ه

To be grieved, sad. وَكِمَ يَكِمُ كِمَةً

To be stripped of its plants (land). وُكِمَتْ

Forest haunted by wild beasts. وَكْمَة

To sit down. To run vehemently. ✻ وَكَنَ يَكِنُ وَكْنًا

To brood (hen). — وَكْنًا ووُكُونًا ه وعلى

To be strengthened, firm. To enjoy authority. تَوَكَّنَ

Bird's nest; hole, shelter of a bird. وَكْن ج أَوْكُن ووُكُن ووُكُون ومَوْكِن

Nest. وَكْنَة ووُكُنَة ج وُكُنَات ووُكْنَات ووُكَن

Sitting. وَاكِن م وَاكِنَة

To tie the head of (a skin). ✻ وَكَى يَكِي وَكْيًا ه, وأَوْكَى ه وعلى

He gave sparingly to. أَوْكَى على فُلَانٍ

He became silent. — على فِيهِ, وأَوْكَى حَلْقَهُ

To be filled (skin). To be laden with fat (camel). To be costive (bowels). إِسْتَوْكَى

Leather-strap of a skin. وِكَاء ج أَوْكِيَة

Closed skin. مُوكًى

To wail, to shriek (woman). To howl (wolf). ✻ وَلْوَلَ وَلْوَلَةً ووَلْوَالًا

Wailing. Cries of pain, grief; cries of wailing-women. Howl. وَلْوَلَة ووَلْوَال

To hasten, to go quickly. ✻ وَلَبَ يَلِبُ وُلُوبًا

To penetrate into. — في

To reach so far as. — إلى

▫ Kind of *Euphorbia*. وَلَب

Off-shoot. Off-spring. وَالِبَة

To impair (the right) of a. o. ✻ وَلَتَ يَلِتُ وَلْتًا, وأَوْلَتَ ه

Born from an Arab father and a foreign mother. Post-classical (word). Apocryphal (book). مُوَلَّد
Inconclusive argument. بَيِّنَة مُوَلَّدَة
Midwife. مُوَلِّدَة
Born. Child. مَوْلُود ج مَوَالِيد
✧ Next born, younger than his brother (child). مَوْلُود على رَأْس أخِيهِ
☆ To walk quickly in stretching the neck (she-camel). وَلَس يَلِس وَلْسًا وَوَلَسَانًا
— To deceive, to act perfidiously with. وَلْسًا, وَوَالَس ه
To misrepresent (facts). وَالَس وأَوْلَس ب
To conspire together against. تَوَالَسُوا على
Deceit, treachery. وَلْس ومُوَالَسَة
Walking quickly in stretching the neck (camel). وَلُوس
☆ To lie. وَلَع يَلَع وَلْعًا ووَلَعَانًا
— He wronged others in their right; he carried away their property. وَلَعًا بِحَقّ الغَيْر
— To stop, to detain a. o. ه
I do not know what has hindered him. مَا أَدْرِي مَا وَلَعَهُ
وَلِع يَوْلَع ويَلَع وَلَعًا وَوَلُوعًا, وأُولِع وَلُوعًا و إِيلاعًا
To be fond of; to covet a. th. وتَوَلَّع ب
To be streaked (bull). وَلَّع
✧ To kindle (the fire). — ه
To render a. o. eagerly desirous of. To urge, to excite a. o. to. وَلَّع وأَوْلَع إِيلاعًا ه ب
I do not know what has become of him. إِتَلَع فُلَانًا وَالِعَةٌ
Lie. وَلْع
Great lie. وَلْع وَالِع
Violent love, fondness. وَلَع ووَلُوع
✧ Live coal; match. وَلْعَة
Liar. وَالِع ج وَلَعَة
Hindrance. وَالِعَة
Inquisitive (man). وُلَعَة
Palm-blossom involved in its envelope. وَلِيع
In love with, eagerly desirous of. مُولَع ب
Streaked (bull, horse). مُوَلَّع
Heart-wounded; raptured; passionately fond. مُوتَلَع ومُتَلَّع القَلْب

in parturition. To rear (a child). To produce a. th.
To derive, to originate a. th. from. وَلَّد ه مِن
To bring forth (ewe). To be at the time of delivery (woman). أَوْلَدَتْ إِيلادًا
He begot a child from her. أَوْلَدَهَا وَلَدًا
To be born, to emanate, to be produced, to derive from. تَوَلَّد مِن
They multiplied by generation. تَوَالَدُوا
To ask a child (from God). إِسْتَوْلَد
Child, son, offspring, youngling. وَلَد و وُلْد ووِلْد (m. f. s. pl.) ج أَوْلَاد وِولْدَة و إِلْدَة ووُلْد
I do not know from which origin he is. مَا أَدْرِي أَيُّ وَلَدِ الرَّجُلِ هُو
Infant child. وُلَيْد
Child-birth. Birth-time. لِدَة
Born at the same time, coeval, coetaneous. لِدَة هث لِدَات ج لِدُون ولِدَات
Childbirth, delivery, birth. وِلَادَة
Ætites, eagle-stone. حَجَر الوِلَادَة
Parent, father, mother. وَالِد هر وَالِدَة ج وَالِدُون ووَالِدَات
Bringing forth (female). وَالِد ووَالِدَة ج وَالِدَات
Pregnant. Prolific (ewe). — ووَلُود ج وُلْد
Both parents, father and mother. أَلْوَالِدَان
Infancy, childhood. Harshness of temper. وُلُودِيَّة ووَلُودِيَّة
Childishness. — و✧ وَلْدَنَة
✧ To be childish; to dally, to wanton. تَوَلْدَن
Effect produced by an instrument. (*Prosody*). First use of a comparison or description. تَوْلِيد
Birth. تَوَلُّد
Born. Son, boy · slave-born. وَلِيد ج وِلْدَة ووِلْدَان
Girl; slave-born female. وَلِيدَة ج وَلَائِد
Momentous affair. أَمْر لَا يُنَادَى وَلِيدُهُ
Birth-time, birth-place. Birth-day, feast. مَوْلِد ج مَوَالِد
Birth-time. مِيلَاد ج مَوَالِيد
Feast of Christmas. عِيدُ المِيلَاد
Having brought forth (ewe). مُوْلِد ج مَوَالِد ومَوَالِيد

☆ وَلَغ يَلَغ ويَالَغ ووَلِغ يَلِغ ويُولَغ وَلْغًا ووَلَغَانًا وُوُلُوغًا ووَلَغَانًا في وبـ ومن To lap (dog).
مَا وَلَغ وَلُوغًا He has not tasted anything.
أَوْلَغ ه To give to (a dog) a. th. to lap.
وَلْغَة Small bucket.
وَلُوغ Lick, draught, morsel.
مِيلَغ ومِيلَغَة Drinking-vessel for a dog.
مُسْتَوْلِغ Regardless of his honour.
☆ وَلَف يَلِف وَلْفًا ووِلَافًا وإِلَافًا ووَلِيفًا To flash successively (lightnings).
— وَلِيفًا To come together in a file (men).
✧ وَلَف لـ To pack up things for (departure).
وَالَف مُوَالَفَة ووِلَافًا ه To have familiar intercourse with; to be attached to.
✧ وَلْف *Cyclamen*, sow-bread (*plant*).
وِلْف Friend.
وِلَاف ووَلِيف Gallop of a horse.
وَلِيف ووُلُوف Continuous lightning.
مُوَالَفَة Familiar intercourse.
مُوَالِف و✧ وَلِيف Familiar, intimate friend.
☆ وَلَق يَلِق وَلْقًا To walk quickly.
— ه بـ To strike a. o. with (a sword). To thrust a. o. slightly with (a spear).
— في To persevere in.
أُلِق أَلْقًا وأُولِق إِيلَاقًا To be seized with madness.
وَلَقَى Run of a she-camel. Swift (she-camel).
وَلِيقَة Dish made of flour, butter and milk.
أَوْلَق Madness.
مَأْلُوق ومُؤَوْلَق Insane.
☆ ولم — أَوْلَم To give a feast, a dinner-party.
وَلْم ووَلَم Saddle-strap.
وَلْمَة The whole (of a thing).
وَلِيمَة ج وَلَائِم Feast, dinner-party.
☆ وَلَه يَلِه ووَلِه يَلِه ويُولَه وَلَهًا, وتَوَلَّه واتَّلَه To be sad. To be dejected, depressed by grief.
وَلِه ووُلِه مِن To fear a. th.
وَلِه إِلى أُمِّهِ He ran up in fear to his mother (child).
وَلِهَت على وَلَدِها She yearned after her child.

وَلَّه ه To bereave (a mother) of (her child).
— وأَوْلَه ه To confound, to perplex a. o. (grief).
إِتَّلَه ه To intoxicate a. o. (wine).
إِسْتَوْلَه To be disturbed in mind.
وَلَه Grief. Consternation. Fear.
وَالِه (*m. f.*) ووَلْهَان Bereft of a dear one. Dejected.
وَالِهَة ووَلْهَى Desponding, dejected (woman).
أَلْوَلْهَان Satan
وَقَع فِي وَلِهِي تُوَلِّه He was destroyed.
مُولَه ومُوَلَّه Water absorbed in the sand.
مِيلَه Perplexing desert.
مِيلَاه ج مَوَالِيه Grieved by the loss of her child (mother). Strong (wind).
☆ وَلَى ووَلِي يَلِي وَلْيًا ه وه To be adjacent, contiguous to. To follow a. o. or a. th. immediately.
كُلْ مِمَّا يَلِيكَ Do eat what is within thy reach.
وَلِي وِلَايَةً ه وعلى To be set over (a province), to have charge of.
وَلِي ه وعلى To rule a. o.
— وَلَايَةً ووَلَاء ه To be the friend of.
وُلِي To be watered by spring-rain (ground).
وَلَّى تَوْلِيَةً, وأَوْلَى إِيلَاء ه ه To set a. o. over. To intrust a. o. with the government of (a province), the management of (an affair).
وَلَّى ه وعَن To turn away from; to shun a. o. or a. th.
وَلَّى وتَوَلَّى هَارِبًا He turned back, he made his escape.
وَلَّى ه ظَهْرَهُ He turned the back upon him.
— وتَوَالَى To begin to dry (dates).
وَالَى مُوَالَاةً ووِلَاء ه To be the friend, helper, auxiliary of; to unite with.
— ه وبَيْن To continue, to pursue a. th. To combine (two affairs).
— ه To set (sheep) apart.
أَوْلَى إِيلَاء ه وه To bring a. o. or a. th. near.
— ه ه To intrust a. o. with the care of (an orphan).

▫ *Polite term for calling* a Moslem woman. وَلِيَّة
Saddle-cloth. Food set apart for a guest. — ج وَلِيَّات وَوَلَايَا
Contiguous house. دَار وَلِيَّة
Showery. وَلْوِيّ
Appointment to an office. Transfer of a purchase. تَوْلِيَة
Jurisdiction, dominion. Proximity. تَوَلٍّ
Uninterrupted succession. تَوَالٍ
Vali, governor of a Turkish province. وَالٍ ج وُلَاة
Abler, fitter for, worther more of, entitled to. أَوْلَى مث أَوْلَيَان ج أَوْلَوْن وأَوَالٍ ب
F. Abler, worthier (woman). وُولْيا مث وُلْيَيَانِ ج وُلَى وَوُلْيَيَات
Expression of curse or threat. Woe to him! Woe to thee! أَوْلَى لَهُ, أَوْلَى لَكَ
Relative adject. of أَوْلَى theirs. أَوْلَوِيّ
Master, lord. Freed slave. Helper, auxiliary. Friend, companion. Son-in-law; uncle, nephew, cousin; near relation. Ally, follower. Mollah, Moslem judge. مَوْلَى ج مَوَالٍ
Kind of short poem. مَوَالِيَا
Camel-drivers song, romance, cantata. ✧ مَوَّال ج مَوَاوِيل
Ward, minor. مَوْلِيّ م مَوْلِيَّة
Order of dervishes Mevlevis. مَوْلَوِيَّة (un. مَوْلَوِيّ)
Suzerainty. مَوْلَوِيَّة
Invested with authority. مُتَوَلٍّ
Following uninterruptedly, successive. مُتَوَالٍ
Name (*for* مَتَاع عَلِيّ) *of the* sectators of Ali (*in Syria*). Metualis. مُتَوَالٍ ج مَتَاوِلَة
✱ وَمَأَ يَمَأُ وَمْأً, وَوَمَّأَ تَوْمِئَةً, وأَوْمَأَ إِيمَاءً إِلَى
To make a sign with the head to.
To agree with a. o. وَامَأَ مُوَامَأَةً ه
Sign with the head. وَمْء وإِيمَاء
Accident, mishap. وَامِئَة
Above-mentioned, aforesaid. مُومَأ إِلَيْهِ
Mark of a sun-stroke. ✱ ومح — وَمْحَة
To be hot, sultry (night). ✱ وَمِدَ يَوْمَدُ وَمَدًا
To get angry with. — عَلَى
Intense heat in the night. وَمَد وَوَمْدَة
Sultry night. لَيْلَة وَمِد وَوَمِدَة

He conferred a benefit upon him. أَوْلَى ه مَعْرُوفًا
What a bountiful man! مَا أَوْلَاهُ لِلْمَعْرُوف
To take a. o. as a friend. تَوَلَّى تَوَلِّيًا ه
To be invested with (a dignity). To take a. th. upon o.'s self. To be intrusted with (an affair). — ه
They subdued him by the sword. تَوَلَّوْهُ بِالْحَدِيد
To turn the back to. تَوَلَّى عَن
To come consecutively. تَوَالَى تَوَالِيًا
To conquer, to overpower. To get the mastery over. To reach (the aim in view). إِسْتَوْلَى اسْتِيلَاءً عَلَى
Vicinage, neighbourhood. وَلْي وَوَلَاء
We became parted after union. تَبَاعَدْنَا بَعْدَ وَلْيٍ
His house adjoins mine. دَارُهُ وَلْيُ دَارِي
Second rain in the spring. وَلْيٌ وَوَلِيٌّ ج أَوْلِيَة
Government, management. Kindred. Friendship. Relationship. Help, succour. وَلَاء
They are the relations of such a one. هُمْ وَلَاءُ فُلَانٍ
Right of succession to the property of a freed man. وَلَاء وَوَلَايَة
Continuity. وِلَاء
If not; or. ✧ وِلَّا (for وَإِلَّا)
They came one after another. جَاءُوا وِلَاءً او عَلَى وِلَاء
Government, management of a province. Supremacy, dominion. وِلَايَة
Blood-kindred. وَلَايَة ووِلَايَة
State. Vilayet, Turkish province. وَلَايَة ووِلَايَة ج وِلَايَات
The United States. الوِلَايَات المُتَّحِدَة
They are all leagued against me. هُمْ عَلَيَّ وَلَايَة وَاحِدَة
They give help to one another. هُمْ عَلَى وَلَايَةٍ وَاحِدَةٍ
Friend, beloved. Lord, master. Benefactor, partner, companion. Heir. Tutor, guardian. Saint (amongst Moslems). وَلِيّ ج أَوْلِيَاء
The friend of God. وَلِيّ الله
Crown-prince. وَلِيّ العَهْد
✧ Master of favours (*surname of* the Sultan). وَلِيّ النِّعَم

* وَمَز يَمِز وَمْزًا ب To move (the nose : excited man).
تَوَمَّز To prepare to rise up (man).
يَتَوَمَّز في المَشي He walks hoppingly.
* وَمَس يَمِس وَمْسًا ه ب To rub, to polish a. th. with.
أَوْمَسَت To prostitute herself (woman).
مُومِس ومُومِسَة Prostitute, strumpet.
* وَمَض يَمِض وَمْضًا ووَمِيضًا ووَمَضَانًا, وأَوْمَض إِيمَاضًا To shine faintly (lightning).
أَوْمَض To look stealthily, to glance at.
— بِعَيْنِهِ He smiled.
— ه بِعَيْنِهِ He made a sign to.
وَمِيض ووَمَضَان Flash of lightning.
* ومط — وَمْطَة Weariness, over-fatigue.
* وَمِق يَمِق وَمْقًا ومِقَة ه To love a. o. tenderly.
وَامَق مُوَامَقَة ووِمَاقًا ه, وتَوَامَق To love one another.
تَوَمَّق ه To court the affection of a. o.
وَامِق In love of, lover.
وَمِيق ومَوْمُوق Loved, cherished.
* ومك — وَمْكَة Fullness, broadness.
* ومن — تَوَمَّن To have a numerous progeny.
* وَمِه يَوْمَه وَمَهًا To be vehemently hot (day).
* ومى — مَوْمَاة ومَوْمَاء ج مَوَامٍ Desert. (*See* ومأ).
* ون — وَنّ Weakness. Kind of cymbal.
✧ وَنّ To hum, to buzz (fly). To grumble, to complain.
* ونب — وَنَّب ه To upbraid, to rebuke a. o.
* وَنَج Kind of guitar.
* وَنَك يَنِك وَنْكًا في To settle in (a place).
* وَنَم يَنِم وَنْمًا ووَنِيمًا To leave dirt (fly).
وَنْمَة ووَنِيم Dirt of flies.
* وَنَى يَنِي ووَنِيَ يَوْنَى وَنْيًا ووُنِيًّا ووِنَاء ووِنْيَة ونِيَّة ووَنًى في To be weak, remiss, slow in.
— ه To forsake a. o.
— ه To tuck up (the sleeves).
— عَن To give up a. th.
لَا يَنِي يَفْعَل He does not cease doing.

وَنَّى تَوْنِيَة To be slow in acting.
أَوْنَى إِيناء ه To weaken, to enervate a. o.
تَوَانَى تَوَانِيًا في To be remiss in (work). To be dilatory in.
وَنًى ووَنَاء Fatigue, weariness. Slowness, remissness.
وَنَاة وأَنَاة وأَنِيَّة Languid in her deportment (woman).
وَنَاة ووَنِيَّة Pearl.
وَانٍ ج وَانِيَة Weak; slow, remiss. Weary.
تَوَانٍ Slowness, delay. Remissness, languidness.
مُتَوَانٍ Lazy, remiss, languid, dilatory.
مِينَا ومِينَاء Glass-bead. Enamel.
— ومِينَاء ج مَوَانٍ ومَوَانِيّ Port, harbour.
* وَهْوَه وَهْوَهَة To snarl, to grumble, to snort (lion, dog). To weep (woman).
وَهْوَاه Snarling (lion).
* وَهَب يَهَب وَهْبًا ووَهَبًا وهِبَةً ه ل To give, to bestow a. th. upon.
وَهَبَنِي ٱللّٰهُ فِدَاءَك May God give me for thy ransom!
هَبْنِي (*m.*) هَبِينِي (*f.*) فَعَلْتُ كَذَا Suppose I have done so.
هَبَا (*dual*) هَبُوا, هَبْنَ (*pl.*) Suppose, you both.
— يَهَب ووَهِب يَهِب ه To surpass a. o. in liberality.
وَاهَب ه To vie in liberality with.
أَوْهَب لِفُلَان To remain with, in the possession of: to come within the reach of a. o. (thing).
— ه لِفُلَان To prepare a. th. for a. o. To facilitate a. th. for a. o.
تَوَاهَب To reciprocate gifts.
إِتَّهَب اِتِّهَابًا ه To receive a. th. as a gift.
إِسْتَوْهَب ه To ask a. th. as a gift.
— ه ه او مِن To ask a. o. for (a gift).
هِبَة ج هِبَات Free gift, present.
— ومَوْهِب ومَوْهِبَة ج مَوَاهِب Grant, favour, benefit.
وَاهِب ووَهَّاب ووَهَّابَة ووَهُوب Giving. Giver. Generous.
وَهْبِيّ Infused (grace). Inborn (gift).
وَهَّابِيَّة Fanatical sect of Arabia, the Wahabees.
مَوْهِب ومَوْهِبَة ج مَوَاهِب Gift, present.

To excite a. o. to. وَهَز ه على
To tread heavily (beast of burden). To walk sluggishly (man). تَوَهَّز
He rushed upon him from behind. — خَلْفَهُ
Short and sturdy man. وَهْز
Deportment of a modest woman. وَهَازَة
Having a fine gait. أَوْهَز
Trampling heavily. مُوَهِّز ومُوَهَّز ومُتَوَهِّز
✲ To tread under foot. To break, to smash a. th. وَهَس يَهِس وَهْسًا ه
He acted cunningly in the affair. — في أمر
To act wrongfully towards (o.'s people). — على
To walk at a quick pace (camel, man). — ووَاهَس وتَوَهَّس وتَوَاهَس
To act cunningly and wrongfully with a. o. وَاهَس ه
To walk sluggishly. تَوَهَّس
Evil. Slander. وَهْس
Dish made of locusts and grease. وَهِيسَة
✲ To walk barefoot. To walk heavily. وهش — تَوَهَّش
✲ To break a. th. soft. To throw a. o. down. To tread a. th. heavily under foot. وَهَص يَهِص وَهْصًا ه
Tract of depressed land. وَهْصَة
Depressed place. مَوْهِص ج مَوَاهِص
Stout (man). مَوْهُوص ومُوَهَّص الخَلْق
✲ Round and depressed tract. وهض — وَهْضَة
✲ To be languid, weak. وَهَط يَهِط وَهْطًا
To break; to tread a. th. under foot. — ه
To pierce a. o. with a spear. — ه
To weaken; to throw a. o. down. To throw a. o. into misfortune. To wound; to kill a. o. أَوْهَط ه
To be broken, trodden under foot. تَوَهَّط
To sink into (mire). تَوَهَّط في
To spread (a mattress). — ه
Emaciation. Party of men. وَهْط
Grove, thicket of *mimosa*. — مِن
Deep ditch. Gulf, abyss. وَهْطَة ج وَهْط ووِهَاط

Small tank, pool. Hollow in a mountain holding water. مَوْهَبَة
Preparing. Powerful. مُوهِب
Prepared, ready (food). مُوهَب
Bestowed. Son, child. مَوْهُوب
Donee. — لَهُ
✲ To squeeze, to compress a. th. وَهَت يَهِت وَهْتًا ه
To stink (meat). أَوْهَت
Depressed ground. وَهْتَة ج وَهْت
✲ To apply o.'s self carefully to. وَهَث يَهِث وَهْثًا، وتَوَهَّث في
✲ To blaze fiercely (fire). وَهَج يَهِج وَهْجًا ووَهَجَانًا
To kindle (the fire). أَوْهَج ه
To be kindled (fire). To be vehemently hot (day, sun). To be strong (perfume). To shine (gem). تَوَهَّج
Heat of (the sun, of fire). وَهَج
Ardour, heat. Diffusion of an odour. وَهِيج
Ardent, intense (fire). وَهَّاج
✲ To prepare (a bed) for a. o. وهد — وَهَّد ه ل
To recline down. تَوَهَّد
Depressed, low ground. وَهْد ج أَوْهُد ووُهْدَان
Abyss, deep cavity. وَهْدَة ج وَهْد ووِهَاد
Depressed (ground). أَوْهَد
First days of a lunar month, of a week. أَوَاهِد
✲ To throw a. o. into an inextricable difficulty. ✧ To frighten a. o. وَهَر يَهِر وَهْرًا، ووَهَّر ه
To pass away (night). To be over (winter). To collapse (sand-hill). تَوَهَّر
He disturbed him in speech. — ه في الكَلَام
To know a. th. to certainty. إِسْتَوْهَر واسْتَيْهَر ب
Heat and mirage produced by the reflection of the solar rays. وَهْر
✧ Fright, fear. Dignified mien. وَهْرَة
Dignified, sedate. ✧ صَاحِب وَهْرَة
Oran, town of Algeria. وَهْرَان
✲ To tread a. th. under foot. To strike and repel a. o. To crush (a louse). وَهَز يَهِز وَهْزًا ه وه

He omitted (a prostration) in (prayers). أَوْهَم رَكْعَةً مِن

To suspect a. o. of. أَوْهَم وأَتْهَم واتَّهَم ه ب

To suppose, to imagine, to conjecture, to suspect a. th. تَوَهَّم ه

To be scared, perplexed. To be afraid (child). ✧ إنوَهَم واستوهَم

To be suspected of. إتَّهَم ب

Opinion, thought, surmise, presumption. Imaginitive power. Instinct. High road. ✧ Fright, fear. وَهْم ج أَوهَام

There is no escape from it. لا وَهْمَ مِن هٰذَا

Strong and well trained (camel). وَهِم م وَهِمَة ج أَوهَام ووُهُوم ووُهْم

Suspicion, doubt. وَهْمَة

Imagination, representative power. وَاهِمَة وقُوَّة وَهمِيَّة

Imaginary, conjectural, hypothetic. False, groundless. وَهمِيّ

Groundless opinion; chimera, fancy, hypothesis. وَهمِيَّة ج وَهمِيَّات

Amphibology; ambiguousness. إيهَام

Suspicion; charge. Imputation Calumny. تُهَمَة ج تُهَم وتُهَمَات

Suspected. تَهِيم ومُتَّهَم

Suspecting, suspected. مُتَّهِم

Opinion, supposition, fancy. تَوَهُّم

Imagined, fancied, supposed. مَوْهُوم

To be, to enter upon the middle of the night. ✡ وَهَن يَهِن وَهْنًا, وأَوْهَن

To weaken, to disable a. o. وَهَن ووَهَّن وأَوْهَن ه

وَهَن ووَهِن يَهِن, ووَهُن يَوْهُن وَهْنًا ووَهَنًا

To be weak, unable to work. ووَهِن يَوْهَن ووَهْنًا

To be unable to fly (surfeited hawk). تَوَهَّن

Weakness, languidness in work. وَهْن ووَهَن

Short and bulky (man). Big and strong (camel). وَهْن

Middle of the night. — ومَوْهِن مِن اللَّيل

Foreman. وَهِين

Weak, disabled. وَاهِن ج وُهُن

The shortest rib. Rheumatism in the arms, shoulders. وَاهِنَة

Riots, quarrels. أَوهَاط

To become verdant (plant). To be shaken (plant). To draw near (man). ✡ وَهَف يَهِف وَهْفًا ووَهِيفًا

To come within the reach of. — وأَوْهَف ل

To be a sacristan. وَهَف يَهِف وَهْفًا ووَهَافَةً

Sacristan. وَاهِف

Church-keeping, vestry. وِهَافَة ووُهْفِيَّة وهِفِّيَّة

To catch, to hold a. o. in a lasso. ✡ وَهَق يَهِق وَهْقًا ه

To withhold a. o. from. — ه عَن

To stretch the neck in walk. وَاهَق

To vie in quickness with (another: camel). — ه

To throw a lasso to (a beast). أَوْهَق ه

He confused him in speech. تَوَهَّق ه في الكَلَام

To do the very same thing; to keep pace together. تَوَاهَق

Lasso, noose. وَهْق ووَهَق ج أَوهَاق

To conjecture, to form opinions concerning a th. ✡ وَهَل يَوْهَل و يَهِل وَهْلًا إلى

To be frightened, scared. To be weak. وَهِل يَوْهَل وَهَلًا, واستَوْهَل

To be scared away towards. وَهِل إلى

To commit a mistake in. To overlook a. th. — في وعَن

To frighten a. o. وَهَّل ه

To lead a. o. into error. تَوَهَّل ه

Fright, fear. وَهَل ووَهْلَة

Since the first instant, first of all. أَوَّلَ وَهْلَةٍ ووَهَلَةٍ ووَاهِلَةٍ

Weak. fearful. وَاهِل ومُستَوْهِل

To imagine, to fancy a. th. To occur to the mind (thought). ✡ وَهَم يَهِم وَهْمًا ه

To form a wrong opinion about, to think of. — في

To make a mistake in (calculation). وَهِم يَوْهَم وَهَمًا, وأَوْهَم في

To make a. o. to form an opinion about, to make a. o. to suspect a. th. وَهَّم وأَوْهَم ه

✧ He scared such a one. وَهَّم على فُلَان

He left out (such a sum) in (the account). أَوْهَم كَذَا مِن

Slothful (woman). وَهْنَانَة
Weak, feeble. مَوْهُونٌ م مَوْهُونَة
✡ To be weak, frail. To be foolish (man). To threaten to fall (wall). To be rent (clothes). To break asunder (skin, rope). To burst (cloud). وَهَى وَوَهِيَ يَهِي وَهْيًا
His business are in a bad state *lit*: his water-skin has burst. وَهَى سِقَاؤُهُ
To spoil, to injure a. th. أَوْهَى إِيهَاءً ه
To chap the hands (cold, work). — يَدَهُ
Chap, gap, chink. (*un.* وَهْيَة) وَهْيٌ ج وُهِيٌّ وَأَوْهِيَة
Weak, flaccid. Rent. وَاهٍ ج وَاهُونَ وَوُهَاةٌ
✧ Considerable thing. شَيْءٌ وَاهٍ
Small rent. وُهَيَّة
Pearl. Fat beast fit to be slaughtered. وَهِيَّة
Abyss, chasm between two mountains. أُوهِيَّة
✡ *Interject. expressive* (1) *of admiration with* ب *or* ل. وَوَه — وَاهٍ وَوَاهًا وَوَاهَا
Oh! What a fine thing! وَاهًا لَهُ وَبِهِ
(2) *of sorrow with* على Alas!
Alas! We have missed it. وَاهًا عَلَى مَا فَاتَ
✡ *Interject. expressive of admiration, pity.* Fie! Bravo. وَيْ ل وَوَيْ كَأَنَّ وَكَأَنَّ
How despicable or admirable is Zeyd! وَيْ لِزَيْدٍ
Alas! rich people are loved and poor people are despised. وَيْ كَأَنْ مَنْ يَكُنْ لَهُ نَشَبٌ يُحْبَبْ وَمَنِ افْتَقَرَ يُحْتَقَرْ
✡ Woe! وَيْبٌ
Woe to thee! وَيْبَكَ وَوَيْبٌ لَكَ
Woe to him! وَيْبٌ وَوَيْبًا وَوَيْبٍ وَوَيْبَ ل

What a wonderful thing! وَيْبًا لِهٰذَا
Measure for grain (22 to 24 medds. *about* 5 *bushels*). وَيْبَة ج وَيْبَات
✡ *Interject. of pity or threat.* Oh! Woe? وَيْحَ وَوَيْحٌ
Oh! how unhappy is Zeyd! وَيْحٌ وَوَيْحًا لِزَيْدٍ, وَوَيْحَ زَيْدٍ وَوَيْحَهُ
Woe to thee! وَيْحَكَ
✡ *Word of praise or tenderness used chiefly in addressing a child.* Dear me! وَيْس
Dear me! How beautiful he is! وَيْسَهُ
Alas, poor child! Mercy on him! وَيْسٌ وَوَيْسًا لَهُ
Destitution, poverty. Thing coveted. وَيْس
He has found the object of his desire. لَقِيَ وَيْسًا
✡ Woe to thee! (*for* وَيْلَكَ) وَيْكَ
✡ Calamity, mishap. Valley of hell. *Word of threat or dispraise*: Woe! Alas! وَيْلٌ
Woe to me, woe to thee! Woe to him! وَيْلِي, وَيْلَكَ, وَيْلَهُ
Woe to Zeyd! وَيْلٌ وَوَيْلًا لِزَيْدٍ
Terrific disaster. وَيْلٌ وَائِلٌ وَوَيْلٌ وَوَيْلِيل
To wish evil to a. o. وَيَّلَ ه ول
To wail in saying: Woe to me! تَوَيَّلَ
To wish evil one to another. تَوَايَلَ
Disgrace, dishonour. وَيْلَة ج وَيْلَات
✡ Cunning, artful. وَيْلِم — وَيْلِمَّة
Said of a gallant man jeopardising his life: *lit*: Woe to his mother? (*for* وَيْ او وَيْلٌ لِأُمِّهِ) وَيْلُمِّهِ
✡ Slander, backbiting. وَيْم — وَيْمَة
✡ Black grapes. وَيْن — وَيْن
✧ Where? (*for* أَيْن) وَيْن
✡ *Word of incitement or complaint.* Go on! Alas! وَيْه — وَيْهَ وَوَيْهًا

ي

✲ ي *Postfix and pronoun of the first person masc. and feminine.* My.
كِتَابِي, دَارِي, غَنَمِي My book, my house, my sheep.
When preceded by ا , و . ي *it takes fatha* ـَ.
عَصَايَ, بَنِيَّ My stick. My sons.
أُكْتُبِي *Sign of the feminine in the imperative* : Write thou, woman!
✲ يَا *Vocative particle* Holloa, O! Oh!
يَا زَيْدُ أَقْبِلْ O Zeyd, come on!
It is also used with لِ *for expressing admiration.*
يَا لَهُ رَجُلًا او مِن رَجُلٍ! O! What a man!
✧ يَا أَللهُ *Exclamation of incitement.* Come on, cheer up!
✧ يَا تُرَى *Exclamation of wonder or wish.* May it be! Would God!
يَا مَا How. How much, how often! (*in an exclamative sentence*).
✧ يَمَّا . . يَمَّا Whether... or.
يَا هُوَ *Invocation or call.* O God! I say, hear!
✲ يَايَا يَأْيَاةً وَيَايَاءً ه To show kindness to, to flatter a. o.
— ب ول To call out a. o.
يُؤْيُؤٌ ج يَآيِي Kind of hawk.
T يَاي ج يَايَات ◻ Spring, elastic force.
✲ يَئِسَ يَيْأَسُ وَيَيْئِسُ يَأْسًا وَيَآسَةً مِن To despair of.
يَئِسَ يَيْأَسُ يَأْسًا To know, to be acquainted with.
يَئِسَتْ إِيَاسًا To be or become barren (woman).
أَيْأَسَ إِيَاسًا ه To drive a. o. to despair. To render (a woman) barren (God).
إِتَّأَسَ إِتِّئَاسًا, وَاسْتَيْأَسَ اسْتِيآسًا مِن To despair of.
يَأْس وَيَآسَة Despair.
يَأْس Consumption, phtysis.
يَائِس Barren, (woman).
يَائِس وَيَئُوس وَيَؤُوس Desponding, hopeless.

✲ يَبَّ — يَبَّبَ ه To waste, to ruin (a land).
يَبَاب Waste, desolate (land). Ruin.
✲ يَبِد — أَيْبَد Kind of barley.
S يَبْرُوح Root of the mandrake. *See* بَرَح.
✲ يَبِسَ يَيْبَسُ وَيَيْبِسُ يَبْسًا وَيُبْسًا, وَإِيْتَبَسَ To become dry. To wither (plant). To be stiff, tough, hard. To languish (friendship).
يَبَّسَ وَأَيْبَسَ ه To dry, to desiccate a. th.
أَيْبَسَ To have withered plants (land). To walk on a dry ground.
أَيْبِس *Imper.* Hush. Be silent!
يَبْس وَيُبْس Desiccation. Drought, barrenness.
يَبْس وَيَبِس وَيَابِس وَيَبُوس وَيَبِيس وَأَيْبَس Desiccated, barren, stiff, tough hard, costive.
يَبَس Dried (road). Worthless (man, woman). Having no milk (ewe, woman).
أَلْيَبَس The dry land (*opp. to* the sea).
يُبُوسَة Dryness, drought. Stiffness, hardness.
تَيْبِيس Desiccation.
يَبِيس Withered plant.
— المَاء Sweat, dry sweat.
أَلْأَيْبَسَان The two shank-bones.
أَيَابِيس Hard bodies for trying swords.
بَيْنَهُمْ ثَدْيٌ أَيْبَس They are disunited.
مِيبَاس Blasting (wind).
✲ يَتَع — يَتُوع وَيَتُّوع *Euphorbia*, tithymal (*plant*).
✲ يَتِمَ يَيْتِمُ, وَيَتِمَ يَيْتَمُ, وَيَتُمَ يَيْتُمُ يُتْمًا وَيَتْمًا مِن أَبِيهِ, وَتَيَتَّمَ To be or become an orphan.
يَتِمَ يَيْتِمُ يَتْمًا To be weary, jaded.
يَتَّمَ وَأَيْتَمَ ه To bereave (a child) of his father.
أَيْتَمَتْ إِيتَامًا She was left with orphan children (widow).
يُتْم وَيَتْم وَيَتَم Orphanage; dereliction.

What a handy woman! مَا أَيدَى فُلَانَةَ
يَدٌ مث يَدَانِ ج أَيدٍ ويُدِيّ وجج أَيَادٍ
Hand. Arm. Foreleg of a beast. Handle of a tool. Wing of a bird. Sleeve of a garment. Fulness of a garment. Might, power, authority, upper hand. Influence, ability. Help, assitance.
Benefit, favour. — ج يَدِيّ ويُدِيّ وأَيدٍ Generosity.
Powerful, influential. Owner. ذُو اليَد
That is in my hands; it belongs to me. هٰذَا فِي يَدِي
I have no hand in it. مَا لِي بِذَالِكَ يَدَانِ
They go hand in hand against me. هُم يَدٌ وَاحِدَةٌ عَلَيَّ
He gave it to him as a free gift. أَعطَاهُ عَن ظَهرِ يَدٍ
Before him, at hand. ✧ Under his obedience. بَينَ يَدَيهِ
Before the hour. بَينَ يَدَيِ السَّاعَةِ
He sold his sheep at two different prices. بَاعَ الغَنَمَ بِيَدَينِ
I owe him a benefit. I acknowledge his beneficence. لِفُلَانٍ عِندِي يَدٌ او يَدَى
I shall never do it. لَا أَفعَلُهُ يَدَ الدَّهرِ
He has the upper hand in that affair. لَهُ يَدٌ بَيضَاءُ فِي هٰذَا الأَمرِ
He is a thief; *lit*: long-handed. يَدُهُ طَوِيلَةٌ
He is unable to do it; *lit*: short-handed. يَدُهُ قَصِيرَةٌ
He repented. سُقِطَ او أُسقِطَ فِي يَدَيهِ
He has a great fund of science. لَهُ اليَدُ الطُّولَى فِي العِلمِ
They dispersed on all sides. ذَهَبُوا أَيدِي او أَيَادِي سَبَا
That is what thou hast deserved. هٰذَا مَا قَدَّمَت يَدَاكَ
Bright star in *Orio*. يَدُ الجَوزَاءِ
Manual (work). يَدِيّ و يَدَوِيّ
Dexterous, handy (man). Full (garment). Easy (life). يَدِيٌّ م يَدِيَّةٌ
Handy, light-handed (woman). يَدِيَّةٌ
Helper, bearing a hand. يَدَّاءٌ
Helped, aided. مُودٍ
Wounded on the hand. مُودًى إِلَيهِ
Entrapped by the forelegs (gazelle). مَيدِيٌّ
To be hard. To be hot (stone). ✱ يَرَّ يَيَرُّ يَرَارًا

Weakness, weariness. يَتَمٌ
He walks sluggishly. فِي سَيرِهِ يَتَمٌ
يَتِيمٌ ج يَتَامَى وأَيتَامٌ ويَتَمَةٌ ومَيتَمَةٌ
Orphan child; fatherless (child). Motherless (beast). Unique, pairless, the only one.
Pairless pearl. دُرَّةٌ يَتِيمَةٌ
The wonder of his time. يَتِيمَةُ الدَّهرِ
Isolated tracts of sand. يَتَائِمُ
Woman left with orphan children. مُوتِمٌ ج مَيَاتِمُ
War renders children orphans and their mothers widows. الحَربُ مَيتَمَةٌ مَأيَمَةٌ
She brought forth a child the feet foremost. ✱ يَتَنَ — يَتَنَت وأَيتَنَت وَلَدًا
Birth of a young the feet foremost. يَتنٌ
Born the feet foremost. مَيتُونٌ
Having brought forth a young one the feet foremost. مُوتِنٌ ومُوتِنَةٌ
Original name of Medinah. ✱ يَثرِبُ
Gog and Magog, Northern nations. يَأجُوجُ ومَأجُوجُ H
Crooked mall for playing. ✱ مِيحَارٌ (*See* حار)
Red. Onager ✱ يَحمُورٌ (*See* حمر)
Anything black. Beast of burden. Smoke. ✱ يَحمُومٌ (*See* حم)
Moslem name of S[t] John the Baptist. ✱ يَحيَى
✧ Stewed meat, ragout. يَخنِي و يَخنَةٌ P
To dye (cloth) red. ✱ يَدَءَ — يَدءٌ ه
He imposed upon himself (a pilgrimage). أَيدَءَ ه على نَفسِهِ
Saffron. Brazil wood. Tarragon. Kind of red gum. أَيدَءٌ
Hackney. Led-horse. يَدَكٌ Ts
To wound a. o. on the hand. To maim a. o.'s hand. ✱ يَدَى يَدِي يَديًا ه
To aid, to be beneficent, to do good to. — ه
To receive a benefit. يُدِيَ
He lost one hand. يَدِيَ مِن يَدِهِ
To hand down a. th. to; to requite a. o. يَادَى مُيَادَاةً ه
He deserved well of him. He lent a hand to such a one. أَيدَى إِيدَاءً عِندَ فُلَانٍ او إِلَيهِ

يَرّ Evil, calamity; enmity; war.
يَارّ ويَرّان Hot, burning (day).
✡ يَرْبُوع Gerboa (*See* ربع).
P يَرَج — يَارَج ج يَرَارِج Bracelet, armlet.
G أَيَارَجَة وإِيَارَجَة ج أَيَارِج Laxative, electuary.
✡ يَرِع يَرَعًا To be faint-hearted, cowardly.
يَرْع Young calf.
يَرَع Faint-heartedness, cowardice. Gnat.
يَرَاع (*un.* يَرَاعَة) *Cicindela*, firefly. Reed. Pipe. Writing-reed. Mosquito.
يَرَاعَة A firefly. A writing-reed. Reed-bank. Ostrich.
يَرَاع ويَرَاعَة Cowardly, faint-hearted.
✡ يرق — يَرَقَان ويُرَقَان Jaundice. Smut, blight (disease in grain).
مَيْرُوق ومَأْرُوق Jaundiced (man). Smutty.
✡ يرقع — جُوع يَرْقُوع Vehement hunger.
☐ يَرَك Chrysoprase, kind of massive quartz.
P يَرْمَقَان و✡ أَرْمَقَان Fine silk tissue.
✡ يَرَنَأ ه To dye a. th. with henna.
يُرَنَّاء ويَرَنَّاء ويَرَنَّا Henna, plant and dye.
✡ يَزِيدِيَّة (*un.* يَزِيدِيّ) The Yezidees, Pagan sect on the Euphrates.
P يَزَك (*un.* يَزَكِيّ) Watchman, spy, sentinel.
✡ يَازُول *Allium roseum*, species of wild garlic.
✡ يَسّ i يَسًّا To journey, to go on (man).
✡ يَسَر يَيْسِر يَسْرًا ويَسَرًا To become gentle, tractable (man, beast).
يَسَرَتْ وأَيْسَرَتْ To have an easy confinement (woman).
يَسَر يَيْسِر To draw lots with arrows.
— ويَاسَر وتَيَاسَر ه To occur to a. o. on the left-side.
يَسِر يَيْسَر يَسَرًا To be easy to a. o. (affair).
يَسُر يَيْسُر يُسْرًا To become scanty.
يَسَّر To multiply, and prosper (flocks). To possess prosperous flocks.
— ه ل To facilitate, to prepare a. th. for.

يَسَّر وأَيْسَر ه ل To render a. o. prosperous. To smooth the way to.
يَاسَر ه To behave gently, easily towards.
أَيْسَر إِيسَارًا ويُسْرًا To be wealthy, in easy circumstances.
أَيْسَر إِيسَارًا To pass to the left-hand side.
تَيَسَّر واسْتَيْسَر To become easy (thing).
تَيَسَّر ل To get ready for (fight). To treat a. o. gently.
تَيَاسَر واتَّسَر وايْتَسَر ه To draw lots for allotting (a slaughtered beast).
يُسْر ويُسُر ويَسَار ويَسَارَة Gentleness. Easiness of life. Readiness to act.
يَسَر ج أَيْسَار Party of gamblers.
— ويَاسِر ج أَيْسَار Easy, gentle, tractable. Superintendant at the game of arrows.
يَاسِر Occurring on the left-hand side.
يَسَار ج يُسُر ويُسْر Left hand; left-hand side.
يُسْرَى مث يُسْرَيَان ج يُسْرَيَات، ويَسْرَة Left side.
يَسَارًا او عَن ٱلْيَسَار On the left side.
أَعْسَر يَسَر Ambidexter, using both hands alike.
يَسَرَة ج أَيْسَار ويَسَرَات Broken lines of the palm of the hand. Brand on a beast's thighs.
أَيْسَر Easier. Left handed. Left side; seated on the left.
يَسُور ج يُسُر Winner at the game in arrows.
يَسِير Easy, possible. Small in quantity, trifling.
يَسِيرًا A little, in small quantity.
تَيْسِير Prosperity, increase in (flocks).
حَسَن ٱلتَّيْسِير والتَّيْسُور Walking gracefully (horse).
مَيْسِر Game of arrows, of hazard. Slaughtered camel staked for the game.
مَيْسَرَة ومَيْسِرَة ومَيْسُرَة Easiness of temper, gentleness. Easiness of circumstances.
مَيْسَرَة ج مَيَاسِر Left side. Left wing of an army.
مُيَاسَرَة Gentleness.

the top of the head.
Summit of the head. Vertex. يَافُوخ ويأْفوخ ج يَوَافِيخ
He has overcome him. رَكِب يافوخَهُ
To be grown up, adult (youth). ☆ يَفَع يَيفَع يَفعًا, وأَيفَع
He climbed the mountain. — جبلًا وتَيَفَّع
Hill. Adult, young man. يَفَع و يَفَاع ج يُفُوع
Adult. (*m f. s. pl.*) يَفَع ج أَيفاع, و يَفَعَة
Of full age, adult, young man. يَافِع ج يَفَعَة ويُفْعَان
Pl. Difficult (affairs). Lofty (mountains). يَافِعَة ج يَافِعَات
Elevated ground. مَيفَعَة ج مَيَافِع
Broken by age (old man). Four years old (bull). ☆ يَفَن ج يُفُن
Cow in calf. يَفَنَة ج يَفَنَات
To be white. ☆ يَقّ a يُقُوقَة
Spadix of palm-trees. Cotton. يَقَق
Snowy-white. أَبيَض يَقَق و يَقِق ج يَقَائِق
Co- (*un.* يَاقُوتَة) يَاقُوت ج يَوَاقِيت P rundum, sapphire. Various gems of the East.
Carbuncle, ruby; red sapphire, red hyacinth. يَاقُوت بِهرَمَانِي وأَحمَر
Blue sapphire, azure hyacinth. — أَزرَق
Green corundum, Oriental emerald. — أَخضَر
Topaz; yellow sapphire, gold hyacinth. — أَصفَر
To wake, to be awake. To be cautious, wary. ☆ يَقِظ يَيقَظ يَقَظًا, ويَقُظ يَيقُظ يَقَاظَة
To awaken a. o. from sleep. يَقَّظ وأَيقَظ ه
To raise (the dust). To excite (hatred). To caution a. o. — وأَيقَظ ه
To awake, to be awakened. To be roused (attention). To become cautious, vigilant. تَيَقَّظ واستَيقَظ
To tinkle (anklets). إستَيقَظ
Waking, sleeplessness. يَقَظَة
Waking, awake. Cautious, watchful. يَقِظ ويَقُظ ويَقظَان ج أَيقَاظ
Wakeful. Cautious (woman). يَقظَى ج يَقَاظَى
More wary than. أَيقَظ مِن
Cock. أَبُو اليَقظَان

Wealthy, in easy circumstances. مُوسِر ج مَيَاسِير, ومُيَسَّر
The Bestower, the Disposer of all things *i. e.* God. المُيَسِّر H
Successfully accomplished (affair). Easy, practicable. مَيسُور ج مَيَاسِير
Do take what is easy, and leave what is difficult in it. خُذ مَيسُورَهُ ودَع مَعسُورَهُ
Christian name of Jesus Our Lord. يَسُوع H
Jesuit. ✧ يَسُوعِيّ ج يَسُوعِيَّة
Joseph. يُوسُف H
▫ Kind of mandarin-orange. يُوسُف أَفَندِي
✧ Sequestration. Prohibited. Contraband. يَسَق Ts
✧ To prohibit; to sequester, to confiscate. ✧ يَسَّق على
✧ To be sequestered, confiscated. ✧ تَيَسَّق عَلَيهِ
✧ Sequestration, confiscation. ✧ تَيسِيق
✧ Cavass, attendant escorting consuls, bishops in the East. يَسَقِيّ و يَسَقجِيّ Ts
Jasmine (flower). يَاسَمِين ويَاسَمُون P
✧ Long live the Sultan! يَاشا — بَادِشَاهِمِز جُوق يَاشَا Ts
Jasper, precious stone. ☆ يَشب ويَصب
Jasper, precious stone of various colours. ☆ يَشف ويَصف
Jade, dark green stone; agate. يَشم P
✧ Face-veil of women. يَاشمَق Ts
Dry herbage; fodder. ☆ يَصر — أَيصَر ج أَيَاصِر
To bleat (ewe, goat). ☆ يَعَر يَيعِر و يَيعَر يُعَارًا
Kid tied in a pitfall for alluring lions. يَعر ويَعرَة ج يِعَار
Bleating of sheep. يُعَار
Bleating often. يَعُور
Squall *uttered for frightening a wolf, for warning a man.* Hideous. Ugly. ☆ يعط — يَعَاطِ ويُعَاط يَاعَاط
To squall for frightening (wolves). يَعَّط ويَاعَط وأَيعَط ب
Gazelle. *See* عفر. ☆ يَعفُور
▫ Echo. يَاغِي ج يَوَاغِي G
▫ Label, post-bill. يَافتَة ويَافطَة T
To strike a. o. on ☆ يَفَخ يَيفَخ يَفخًا ه

To be certain, obvious. ✻ يَقِنَ يَيْقَنُ يَقْنًا ويَقَنًا
— To know a. th. to a certainty, to be convinced of. يَقْنًا ه وب, وتَيَقَّنَ ه
To be sure, certain of. To believe a. th. firmly. أَيقَنَ واسْتَيْقَنَ ه وب
True knowledge. يَقَن
— Credulous, too easy of belief. و يَقِن ويَقُن ويَقِنَة
Certainty. Persuasion. Settled conviction. Firm, unwavering belief. يَقِين
True knowledge. عِلْمُ ٱلْيَقِينِ وعِلْمٌ يَقِينٌ
Unquestionable truth. حَقُّ ٱلْيَقِينِ
Certainly, undoubtedly. يَقِينًا
He knows it for a certainty. عَلِمَهُ يَقِينًا
G أَيقُونَة ج أَيقُونَات و✧ قُونِيَة ج قَوَانٍ Picture, medal.
Knowing to a certainty. مُوقِن
Credulous. مِيقَان م مِيقَانَة
Collar of a coat. يَقَا ويَاقَه Te
✧ One. Ace (at cards, dice). يَكْ P
From one to another. مِنْ يَكٍّ لِيَكٍّ
Nephew. يَكُن Te
The New World, America. يِكِي دُنْيَا Te
Janissary, guard of a consul. يَكِيشَرِيّ و✧ يَنكِشَرِيّ Te
Unevenness of the foreteeth. ✻ يلل — يَلَل
Having short or uneven foreteeth. Short (hoof). Even, smooth (rock). أَيَلّ م يَلَّا
Leathern shields. Skin. Steel. ✻ يَلَب
White. ✻ يَلَق وأَبْيَض يَلَق
White goat. يَلَقَة
✧ Sack of (for جَوَالِق) straw put under a load. يَالِق ج يَوَالِيق
▫ Waistcoat. يَلَك Te
Boatswain. يَلْكَنْجِي Te
Furred coat of the Tartars. يَلْمَق ج يَلَامِق P
Aloes-wood. يَلَنْجُوج ويَلَنْجَج وأَلَنْجَج P
To be thrown into the sea. To be overrun by the sea (shore). ✻ يمم — يُمَّ يُيَمُّ يَمًّا
To purpose a. th. يَمَّمَ وتَيَمَّمَ ه
He cleansed (the sick man's) face and hands with sand before prayer. يَمَّمَهُ لِلصَّلَاة
To aim at a. o. with (a spear). يَمَّمَ ه ب
To perform ablutions with sand. تَيَمَّمَ
Sea. ✧ Side, part. يَمّ ج يُمُوم
✧ As to me; for my part. مِنْ يَمِّي
✧ Completely. Not at all. ✧ يَمّ
Wild pigeon. يَمَام (un. يَمَامَة)
Turtle-dove. يَمَام يَتِيمِيَّة
Young one of the pigeon, of the ostrich. يَأْمُوم
Successful, lucky. مُيَمَّم
Thrown into the sea. Swept by the sea. مَيْمُوم
✧ Homily, sermon. S مِيمَار ج مَيَامِر
Centaura eriophora (plant). ✻ يَمْرَارَة ويَمْرُور
▫ Scullion, helper. يَمَاق Te
To meet a. o. on the right side. ✻ يَمَنَ و يَمِنَ يَيْمَنُ يَمْنًا ه
To bless, to render a. o. prosperous (God). يَمَنَ يَيْمُنُ يَمْنًا ويُمْنًا ه
To lead a. o. to the right. يَمَنَ يَيْمِنُ يَمْنًا, ويَمَّنَ ويَامَنَ وتَيَامَنَ ب
To be happy, lucky. يَمَنَ يَيْمُنُ, و يَمِنَ يَيْمَنُ, ويَمُنَ يَيْمُنُ, ويُمِنَ يُمْنًا ومَيْمَنَةً
He was a cause of blessing for his people. يَمَنَ ويَمِنَ يَيْمَنُ ويَمُنَ يَيْمُنُ ويُمِنَ يُمْنًا ومَيْمَنَةً على قَوْمِهِ او لِقَوْمِهِ
He blessed him. يَمَّنَ على فُلَانٍ
To go to the right side. يَمَّنَ ويَامَنَ وأَيْمَنَ وتَيَامَنَ
— To go to Yemen. و يَامَنَ وأَيْمَنَ
To belong, to relate to Yemen. تَيَمَّنَ
— To augur well of. ب
— He made the dead man to recline on his right side in the grave. بِالْمَيِّتِ
He foreboded a good issue of the affair. تَيَمَّنَ فِي الأَمْرِ
To swear, to administer an oath to. إِسْتَيْمَنَ ه
— To draw a good omen from. ب
Happiness, auspicious, success. يُمْن
Felix Arabia, Yemen. يَمَن ويَمَنَة
The Yemen. أَلْيَمَن
From Yemen. يَمَنِيّ, ويَمَانٍ م يَمَانِيَة ج يَمَانُون, ويَمَانِيّ م يَمَانِيَّة ج يَمَانِيُّون
Right-hand, right side. يَمِين
On the right side; to the right. يَمْنًا ويَمْنَةً ويَمِينًا وعَن اليَمِين

Troublesomeness.
Mirage. يهير
Madness, insanity. ✡ يهم — يهم
Mad, stupid. Rugged mountain. Mute. Dauntless. أيهم م يهماء
Wayless desert. Starless (night). أيهم ويهماء
The two mad things *i. e.* a torrent and the fire ; *or* a torrent and a rabid camel. ألأيهمان
The Jews *See* هود. (*un.* يَهُودِيّ) ✡ اليَهُود
The sun. ✡ يُوح ويُوحى
✧ Officer in waiting, aid-de-camp. P ياور ج ياورِيّة
Joppe, Jaffa (town). ✡ يافا
✧ Captain in the army. T يُوزبَاشِي
Bedstead, bedstick. ✧ يُوك ج يُوكَات
To spend, to last a day. ✡ يَوم — يَام
To hire a. o. by the day. يَاوَم مُيَاوَمَة ويِوَامًا ه
Civil day of 24 hours. Time. Day of a battle. يَوْم ج أيّام وأيَاوِيم
From day to day, day by day. يَوْمًا فيَوْمًا
The very same day. مِن يَوْمِهِ
On a day to come, once, one day. يَوْمًا مَا
On a certain day. يَوْم مِن الأيّام
To-day, this day. أليَوْم
Experienced man. إبنُ الأيّام
Distressing day. يَومٌ أيوَمُ ويَوِمٌ
Distressing, long day. The last day of the month. يَوم ذُو أيّام وذُو أيَاوِيم
The days of God (in which He manifested His justice or mercy). أيّام الله
The days *i. e.* the wars of the Arabs. أيّام العَرَب
Dayly, diurnal. يَوْمِيّ
Dayly, every day, day by day. يَوْمِيًّا
✧ A day's pay ; labour's daily hire. ✧ Journal, register. يَوْمِيّة
Then, at that time, on that day. يَوْمَئذٍ
✧ Newspaper, review. مُيَاوَمَة ج مُيَاوَمَات
Jonas. Greece, the Greeks. G يون — يُونَان
Greek, Hellen. Greek language. يُونَانِيّ ج يُونَانِيُّون
Moslem name of the prophet Jonas. ✡ يُونِس
To form a beautiful ✡ يبي — يَيَّايَاء تَيْيِئَة ي

Compact confirmed by an oath. Oath. يمين ج أيمُن وأيمَان
— ج أيمُن وأيمَان وأيَامِن وأيَامِين The right hand, the right side.
Happiness, prosperity. Power, success. — ج أيمَان
I swear by God. أيمُنُ وإيْمُنُ وأيمَنُ وأيمِنُ الله
I swear by God. إيمُ وإيمِ وامُ وأمِ الله
They have deceived us. أتَوْنَا عَن اليَمِين
Much regard is shown to him amongst us. فُلانٌ عِندَنَا بِاليَمِين
Perjury. يَمِينُ الصَّبْر
Right hand. Right side. يُمنَى مث يُمنَيَان ج يُمنَيَات
Striped cloth from Yemen. يُمنَة
Fortunate, auspicious. يَامِن ويَمِين وأيمَن
Agate, hyacinth (stone). حَجَر يَمَانِيّ
Blite (culinary plant). البَقْلَة اليَمَانِيَّة
Right (side, limb). Dexterous, right-handed. أيمَن م يُمنَاء ج أيَامِن ويُمن
Auspiciously and successfully. عَلَى أيمَن اليَمِين
The South. South wind. ألتَّيمَن
Horizon of Yemen. ألتَّيمَنِيّ
Right side. Prosperity, happiness. Right wing of an army. مَيمَنَة ج مَيَامِن
Happy, successful. مُيمَّن
Fortunate. Auspicious. ✧ Monkey. مَيمُون ج مَيَامِن
Thorny carob. *See* نبت. ✡ يَنبُوت
Water-spring *See* نبع. ✡ يَنبُوع
✧ Trefoil. T يُونجَة
Aniseed. (*for* أنِيسُون) ✧ يَانِسُون
✡ يَنَع يَينِع ويَينَع يَنعًا ويُنعًا ويُنُوعًا، وأينَع To ripen (fruit). To be practicable (thing).
A lofty tree. يُنع
Red beads, red shells. (*un.* يَنَعَة) Cornelian (stone). يَنَع
Ripe (fruit). Red colour. يَانِع ج يَنع، ويَنِيع
Redness of the blood. يُنُوع
Vulnerary. Psyllium seed. ✡ يَنم
Helmet. يَلْمَقِيَّة
To lose the mind. To ascertain a. th. ✡ يهر — استَيهَر
To persist in. إستَيهَر في
To exchange a. th. for another. — ب
Broad place. Persistency. يَهر ويَهَر

Appendix

ETYMOLOGICAL TABLE

LIST OF ARABIC WORDS DERIVED FROM FOREIGN LANGUAGES

FOREIGN LANGUAGES.

FRENCH

Carton	كَرْتُون	Boucle	بُكْلَة
Mètre	مِتْر	Police	بُولِيس
Million	مِلْيُون	Terme	تِرْم
		Gaz	غَاز

GERMAN

		Groschen	قِرْش وغِرْش

GREEK

θηριακή	تِرْيَاق	ἔχιον	أَخْيُون
θέρμος	تُرْمُس	ἀψίνθιον	إِفْسِنْتِين
καθολικός	جَثْلِيق	οὐγκία	أُوقَة , أُوقِيَّة
μαγγάνικος	مَنْجَلِيق ومَنْجَنُون	βάρβιτος	بَرْبَط
χαλκεῖον	خَلْقِين	ὄβρυζον	إِبْرِيز
κανθαρίτης	خَنْدَرِيس	ἐπαρχία	أَبْرَشِيَّة
ἱερευς	خُورِي	πορφύρα	بِرْفِير وفِرْفِير
τραπέζιον	دَرَابْزِين	παραμονή	بَرَمُون
ῥοδάκιον	دُرَاق	βασιλική	بَاسِلِيق
δραχμή	دِرْهَم	πε(ρι)τραχήλιον	بَطْرَشِيل
δελφίν	دُلْفِين	πατρίκιος	بِطْرِيق
δάφνη	دِفْلَى	πατριάρχης	بَطْرِيَرْك
ὄργανον	أُرْغُن	πιττάκιον	بِطَاقَة
ἄρχων	أَرْكُون	μακεδονίσιον	بَقْدُونِس , مَقْدُونِس
σερβούλη (Byzantine)	زَرْبُول	πύξος	بَقْس
ζωνάριον	زُنَّار	βούγλωσσον	بَلَغَصُون
ζίζυφον	زَيْزَفُون	μβάμια (Modern)	بَامِيَا
ὄστρίδια (ὄστρεον)	إِسْتِرِيدِيَا	ἔβενος	أَبْنُوس

κήρωτός	قيروطي	στυππεῖον	أسطب
κεραμίς	قرميد	στοιχεῖον	إسطقس
κρανεία	قرانيا	στόλος	أسطول
κισσος	قسوس	σοφιστής	سفسطة
Κωνσταντινοπολις	قسطنطينية	σπόγγος	إسفنج
κέφαλος	قيفال	ἐπίσκοπος	أسقف
κολοκάσιον	قلقاس	σκίλλα	سيقل
κλίμα	إقليم	σκαμμωνία	سقمونيا
κυλική	قولنج	ψαλτήριον	سنطور
ὠκεανός	قاموس	σύμφυτον	سنفيتوس
κανών	قانون	συναξάριον	سنكسار
κανδηλάπτης	قندلفت	ὑποδιάκονος	شدياق
κοντάκιον	قنداق	χειροτονῶ	شرطن
κενταύρειον	قنطاريون	σάπων	صابون
γνώμη	أقنوم	σταῦλος	إسطبل
εἰκών	قونية و إيقونة	ἀστρολάβον	أسطرلاب
καθέδρα	كاتدرا	τήγανον	طاجن
καθολικός	كاثوليكي	τραπέζιον	طرابزون
χέρνιψ	كرنيب	τάξις	طقس
κάρον	كرويا	τέλεσμα	طلسم
κλῆρος	إكليروس	ἀγαρικόν	غاريقون
χυλος	كيلوس	μάγνης (ητος)	مغنطيس
χόνδρος	كندر	εὐχή	أفشين
χώρα	كورة	ὀβολός	فلس
Κύρ(ιος)	كير	φιλοσοφία	فلسفة
χημεία	كيميا	φιλόσοφος	فيلسوف
ἀδάμας	ألماس	Πλάτων	أفلاطون
λιμήν	لومان	πανδοχεῖον	فندق
μητροπολίτης	مطران	περσικόν	فرسق
μαστίχη	مصطكي	κιθάρα	قيثار
μολόχη	ملوخيا	κερατίον	قيراط

مَلَنخُولِيَا	μελαγχολία	نَاوُلُون	ναῦλον
أنبيق	ἄμβιξ	نَاووس	ναός
إستنبول	εἰς τὴν πόλιν	هَرْطُوقي	αἱρετικός
أَنْدَمِيس	αντίμηνσιον	هِرَقْل	Ἡράκλειος
إنجيل	Εὐαγγέλιον	هِرمِس	Ἑρμῆς
نَارِدِين	νάρδος	هَيُول	ὕλη
نَسطُوري	Νέστωρ	أَيَارِجَة	ἱερά
أنقليس وأنكليس	ἔγχελυς	يَاغِي	ἠχὴ
نُوتِيّ	ναύτης	يُونَان	Ἴων

HEBREW

يَأجوج	גוג	سَوسَن	שושן
مَأجوج	מגוג	شَبُّور	שופר
إسرائيل	ישראל	شاروبيم وكروب	כרבים
إسمعيل	ישמעאל	صَبَأُوت	צבאוה
إيل	איל	عَنْصَرَة	עצרה
تِشْرِين	תשרי (Syro-chaldaic)	فَرِّيسي	פרשי (Syro-chaldaic)
تَوْرَاة	תורה	قَايِن	קין
جِبرَائِيل	גבראיל	لاوِيّ	לוי
جَالُوت	גלה	مُوسَى	מושי
جَهَنَّم	גיהנם	هللويا	הללויה
سَارُوفِيم	שרופים	يَسُوع	ישוע

ITALIAN

بَسابُورْط	Passaportc	بَطَّارِيَّة	Batteria
بَادري	Padre	بَقَّلا	Baccalà
بُرْكَان	Vulcano	بُولِيصَة	Polizza
بِرْنَيطة وبَرّيطة	Borreta	بَنْتُو	Venti
بُوسطَة	Posta	بَنْدَيرَة	Bandiera
بِسِلَّة	Piselli	بَنَادُورَة	Pomo d'oro
بَطَاطَا	Patata	بَنْك	Banca

Fagioli	فَسُولِيَة	Balla	بَالَة
Fattura	فَطُورَة	Birra	بِيرة
Cappotto	كَبُّوت	Dozzina	دُزِّينَة
Carrozza	كَرّوسَة	Damigiana	دَامجَانَة
Quarantina	كَرَنْتِينَة	Re	رَيَّة
Cambiale	كَمْبِيَالَة	Scala	إِسْكلَة
Locanda	لوكَنْدَة	Sicurta	سِكُورْتَا
Vapore	وابُور	Scala	صِقَالة
Europa	أُورُبَّا	Tavola	طَاولَة
Guardiano	وَرْدَيَان	Fortuna	فُرْطُونَة

LATIN

Comes	قُمُّس	Balneum	بِلَّان
Conus	قَوْنَس	Domesticus	دُمُسْتُق
Conditum (vinum)	قِنْدِيد	Denarius	دِينَار
Consul	قُنْصُل	Piscina	فِسْقِيَّة
Latinus	لَاتِين	Cesar	قَيْصَر
		Cetus	قِيطَاس

PERSIAN

نِيمْبِرِشْت	بِرِشْت	آزَادْ دِرَخْت	أَزْدَرَخْت
بُورَه	بَوْرَق	بَبَر	بَبْر
پِرْگَار	بِرْكَار	بَابُونَه	بَابُونَج
بَرْنَامَا	بَرْنَامَج	پَابُوش	بَابُوج
پِشْكِير	بِشْكِير	بَادَه	بَاذَق
بَافْتَه	بَفْتَه	پِيَادَه	بَيْذَق
پِرْگَار	بِيكَار	بَادِنْگَان	بَاذِنْجَان
بَنْك	بَنْج	بَرْدَه	بَرْذَج
فُنْدُق	بُنْدُق	أَبْرِيشَم	أَبْرِيسَم
بَنَفْسَه	بَنَفْسَج	بَرْزَغَه	بَرْذَعَة
پَنْگَان	بَنْگَام	بَرْزُون	بَرْذَون

گوهر	جوهر	بوته	بوتقة وبوطة
خپ or خنب	حب	بوریا	بوریة
خدیو	خدیوي	بوسه	باس
خوش آب	خشاف	پیله	باله
کند	خندق	پیاده	پیادي
خونکار	خنکار	تنبان	تبان
جیکل	جیهل	ترازو	ترازي
خود	خوذة	ترنگبین	ترنجبین
خیار چنبه	خیار شنبه	تنباکو	تنبك وتبغ
دیباه	دیباج	گداد	جداد
تخت دا	دخدار	گورب	جورب
تیریز	دخریص	گرده‌بان	جردبان
دیده‌بان	دیدب	گرده	جردق
دوربین	دربین	گوارش	جوارش
[illegible]	دمق	سرموزه	جرموق
دویتدار	دوادار	گزر	جزر
طشتخوان	دیسق	گل	جل
دوره	دوراق	گل اب	جلاب
درگاه	درقاعه	چوال	جوالق
دستکره	دسکرة	گلشان	جلسان
دول آب	دولاب	گل انگبین	جلنجبین
[illegible]	دلق	گلنار	جلنار
دانگ	دانق	گل نسرین	جلنسرین
ده خان	دهقان	جامگی	جامکیة
دالیز or دالیج	دهلیز	گاومیش	جاموس
دهنه	دهنج	گمان	جمان
راتیناج	راتینج	جان باز	جنباز
نرگس	نرجس	زنگار	جنزار
ارغوان	ارجوان	چنگ	جنك
رزه	رزدق	گهبد	جهبد
روه	رزداق ورستاق	جوخا	جوخ

رِزْيانج	رَازيانه	سَرْجين وسَرقين	سَرْگين
رَنْدَج	رَنْدَه	سِرْدَاب	سَرد آب
رَهَوج	رَهْوا	أُسْرُفِ	سِرْب وأُسْرُب
رَهْنامِج	رَهْنامَه	سَرِقَة	سَرَه
زِرْيَاب	زَرْ آب	سِرْوال	شَلْوار
زَرَجون	زَرْگون	سُرْموج	سَرْمُوزه
زَرْدَمَة	زَرْدَمَن	سَرْمَق	سَرْمه
زَرْدَوا	زَرْدَاوه	سَرَايَه	سَرَاى
زُرُنْباد	زَرُنبَه	أُسْطُوَانه	أُسْتُون
زِرْنِيخ	زَرْنَه	إِسْفِيدَاج	سُفِيدَه
زَمَاوَرْد	بزْمَاوَرْد	سَقَرْقَع	سُكُرْكَه
زُمُرُّد	زُمُرُّد	سَكْبَاج	سِك بَاهَا
زِنْجفَار	سَنْجُرَف	سَكْبِينَج	سَكْبِينَه
زَنْجبِيل	زَنْجفِيل	سُكُرَّجه	سُكُرَّچه
زَنْزَلَخْت	ازَاد دَرَخت	سَلْجَم	شَلْغَم
زِنْدِيق	زَنْدِيك	سِلْحَفَاة	سَوَلاخ پاي
زَنْكَاة	أُوزَنْكى	سَمَانْجُونِي	أَسْمَان گُون
زَاج	زَاك	سَنْبَاذَج	سَنْبَادَه
زِيج	زَه	سَنْج	سَنْجِيد
إِسْفَانج		سَنْجَة	سَنْك
إِسْبَانَخ	اسْبَانَج	سِنْدِيَان	سَنْدَى
سِبَاهِي	سِپَاهِي	سِوَارَى	سِوَار
أُسْتَاذ	أُسْتَاد	شِبِث	شِبِت
إِسْتَار	جِهَار	شَوبَق	شَوبَج
سَتُّوق	سِه تُو	شَاذَنْج	شَادَنَه
سِجِّيل	سَنْك گِل	شَشَم	چِشَم
سِدِلِّيّ	سِه دِلَه	سِشْمَة	چشْمَه
سَاذَج	سَادَه	شَاكِرِي	چَاكِر
سُوذَق		شِنْجَار	شِنْكَار
سِيذَق	سَدَانَك	شَاهَتَرَج	شَاهَتَرَه
سِيذَانِق		شِيلَم	شِيلَه

شِيرَج	شِيرَه	فَالُوذ	پَالُودَه
شِيرَاز	شِيرَازَه	فُولاذ	پولاد
شَاهَانِي	شَاهَانَه	قَبْج	كَبْك
صَوْبَج	چُوپَه	قُرطَق	كُرْتَه
صَارُوج	چارو	قَيرَوَان	كارْوَان
صَرْم	چَرْم	قَفْطَان	خَفْتَان
صَرمِيَّة	سَرمَايَة	قَلَنْدَر	قَرَنْدَل
صُرْنَايَة	صُور نَاي	قُمْقُم	كُمْكُم
صَنْج	سِنْج	قَهْرَمَة	قَهْرَمَان
صَنْدَل	سَنْدَل	كَتْخُودَا	كَتْخُدَا
صِنَار	چِنَار	كُرْبَج	كُرْبَه
صِهْرِيج	صَرنَج وصَرنِيج	كَرْخَانَة	كَار خَانَه
طَبَر	تَبَر	كَرْكَدَّان	كَرْكَدَان
طَبَاهِجَة	تَبَاهَة	كُشْتُبَان	أَنْكُشْتَبَانَه وأَنْكُشْتَوَانَه
طَسْت	طَشْت	كَوْسَج	كُوسَه
طُنْبُورَة	دُنْبَه بَرَه	كِسْرَى	خُوسْرو
طَنَج	تَنَك	كُشْك	كُوشْك
طَنفَسَة	تَنْبَسَه	كَعْك	كَاك
غَلْيُون	قَلْيُون	كَامِخ	كَامَه
فِرْجَار	بِرْكَار	كَمَنْجَة	كَمَانْچه
فَرُوز	پِرْوَاز	كُنْدُس	كُنْدُش
فِرِيز		كَهْرَبَا	كَارْبَا
فَرْزَن	فَرْزِين	كَوْخ	كَاخ
فَرْسَخ	فَرْسَنْك	كُوز	كُوزَه
فَرْفَخ	پَرْپَهِين	لاَزُورْد	لاَژُورْد
إِفْرَنْج	فَرَنْك	لَنْجَر وانْجَر	لَنْكَر
فِرِنْد	پَرَنْد	لَوْلاَب	لُولَه
فُسْتُق	پِسْتَه	لَيْلاَك	لَيْلَنْك
فِلْجَان.	فِنْجَان	مَرْزَنْجُوش ومَرْدَقُوش	مَرْزَنْكُوش
فِيل	پِيل	مَوْزَج	مُوزَه
فَيْلَج	پِيلَه	مَالَج	مَالَه

Goodword English Publications

The Holy Quran: Text,Translation and Commentary (HB), Tr. Abdullah Yusuf Ali

The Holy Quran (PB), Tr. Abdullah Yusuf Ali

The Holy Quran (Laminated Board), Tr. Abdullah Yusuf Ali

The Holy Quran (HB), Tr. Abdullah Yusuf Ali

Holy Quran (Small Size), Tr. Abdullah Yusuf Ali

The Quran, Tr. T.B. Irving

The Koran, Tr. M.H. Shakir

The Glorious Quran, Tr. M.M. Pickthall

Allah is Known Through Reason, Harun Yahya

The Basic Concepts in the Quran, Harun Yahya

Crude Understanding of Disbelief, Harun Yahya

Darwinism Refuted, Harun Yahya

Death Resurrection Hell, Harun Yahya

Devoted to Allah, Harun Yahya

Eternity Has Already Begun, Harun Yahya

Ever Thought About the Truth?, Harun Yahya

The Mercy of Believers, Harun Yahya

The Miracle in the Ant, Harun Yahya

The Miracle in the Immune System, Harun Yahya

The Miracle of Man's Creation, Harun Yahya

The Miracle of Hormones, Harun Yahya

The Miracle in the Spider, Harun Yahya

The Miracle of Creation in DNA, Harun Yahya

The Miracle of Creation in Plants, Harun Yahya

The Moral Values of the Quran, Harun Yahya

The Nightmare of Disbelief, Harun Yahya

Perfected Faith, Harun Yahya

Quick Grasp of Faith, Harun Yahya

Timelessness and the Reality of Fate, Harun Yahya

In Search of God, Maulana Wahiduddin Khan

Islam and Peace, Maulana Wahiduddin Khan

An Islamic Treasury of Virtues, Maulana Wahiduddin Khan

The Moral Vision, Maulana Wahiduddin Khan

Muhammad: A Prophet for All Humanity, Maulana Wahiduddin Khan

Principles of Islam, Maulana Wahiduddin Khan

Prophet Muhammad : A Simple Guide to His Life, Maulana Wahiduddin Khan

The Quran for All Humanity, Maulana Wahiduddin Khan

The Quran: An Abiding Wonder, Maulana Wahiduddin Khan

Religion and Science, Maulana Wahiduddin Khan

Simple Wisdom (HB), Maulana Wahiduddin Khan

Simple Wisdom (PB), Maulana Wahiduddin Khan

The True Jihad, Maulana Wahiduddin Khan

Tabligh Movement, Maulana Wahiduddin Khan

A Treasury of the Quran, Maulana Wahiduddin Khan

Woman Between Islam and Western Society, Maulana Wahiduddin Khan

Woman in Islamic Shari'ah, Maulana Wahiduddin Khan

The Ideology of Peace, Maulana Wahiduddin Khan

Indian Muslims, Maulana Wahiduddin Khan

Introducing Islam, Maulana Wahiduddin Khan

Islam: Creator of the Modern Age, Maulana Wahiduddin Khan

Islam: The Voice of Human Nature, Maulana Wahiduddin Khan

Islam Rediscovered, Maulana Wahiduddin Khan

Words of the Prophet Muhammad, Maulana Wahiduddin Khan

God Arises, Maulana Wahiduddin Khan

The Call of the Qur'an, Maulana Wahiduddin Khan

Building a Strong and Prosperous India and Role of Muslims, Maulana Wahiduddin Khan

Islam As It Is, Maulana Wahiduddin Khan

Sermons of the Prophet Muhammad, Assad Nimer Busool

Bouquet of the Noble Hadith, Assad Nimer Busool

Forty Hadith, Assad Nimer Busool

Hijrah in Islam, Dr. Zafarul Islam Khan

Palestine Documents, Dr. Zafarul Islam Khan

At the Threshold of New Millennium, Dr. Zafarul Islam Khan

Islamic Sciences, Waqar Husaini

Islamic Thought..., Waqar Husaini

The Qur'an for Astronomy, Waqar Husaini

A Dictionary of Muslim Names, Prof. S.A. Rahman

Let's Speak Arabic, Prof. S.A. Rahman

Teach Yourself Arabic, Prof. S.A. Rahman

Islamic Medicine, Edward G. Browne

Literary History of Persia (Vol.1 & 2), Edward G. Browne

Literary History of Persia (Vol.3 & 4), Edward G. Browne

The Soul of the Quran, Saniyasnain Khan

Presenting the Quran, Saniyasnain Khan

The Wonderful Universe of Allah, Saniyasnain Khan

A-Z Ready Reference of the Quran (Based on the Translation by Abdullah Yusuf Ali), Mohammad Imran Erfani

The Alhambra, Washington Irving

The Encyclopaedic Index of the Quran, Dr. Syed Muhammad Osama

The Essentials of Islam, Al-Haj Saeed Bin Ahmed Al Lootah

Glossary of the Quran, Aurang Zeb Azmi

Introducing Arabic, Michael Mumisa

Arabic-English Dictionary, J.G. Hava

The Arabs in History, Prof. Bernard Lewis

A Basic Reader for the Holy Quran, Syed Mahmood Hasan

The Beauty of Makkah and Madinah, Mohamed Amin

A Brief Illustrated Guide to Understanding Islam, I.A. Ibrahim

The Concept of Society in Islam and Prayersin Islam, Dr. Syed Abdul Latif

Decisive Moments in the History of Islam, Muhammad Abdullah Enan

The Handy Concordance of the Quran, Aurang Zeb Azmi

The Hadith for Beginners, Dr. Muhammad Zubayr Siddiqui
A Handbook of Muslim Belief, Dr. Ahmad A Galwash
Heart of the Koran, Lex Hixon
A History of Arabian Music, Henry George Farmer
A History of Arabic Literature, Clément Huart
How Greek Science Passed to Arabs, De Lacy O' Leary
Humayun Nama, Gulbadan Bano
Islam and the Divine Comedy, Miguel Asin
Islam and Ahmadism, Muhammad Iqbal
The Islamic Art and Architecture, Prof. T.W. Arnold
The Islamic Art of Persia, Ed. A.J. Arberry
Islamic Economics, Sabahuddin Azmi
Islamic Thought and its Place in History, De Lacy O' Leary
The Life of the Prophet Muhammad, Mohd. Marmaduke Pickthall
Life of the Prophet Muhammad, B. Salem Foad
The Most Beautiful Names of Allah (HB), Samira Fayyad Khawaldeh
The Most Beautiful Names of Allah (PB), Samira Fayyad Khawaldeh
The Moriscos of Spain, Henry Charles Lea
Muhammad: The Hero As Prophet, Thomas Carlyle
Muhammad: A Mercy to All the Nations, Qassim Ali Jairazbhoy
The Muslims in Spain, Stanley Lane-Poole
One Religion, Zaheer U. Ahmed
The Pilgrimage to Makkah, Sir Richard F. Burton
Principles of Islamic Culture, Dr. Syed Abdul Latif
The Sayings of Muhammad, Sir Abdullah Suhrwardy
Selections from the Noble Reading, Tr. T.B. Irving
A Simple Guide to Islam, Farida Khanam
A Simple Guide to Islam's Contribution to Science, Maulvi Abdul Karim
A Simple Guide to Muslim Prayer, Muhammad Mahmud Al-Sawwat
Spanish Islam (A History of the Muslims in Spain), Reinhart Dozy
The Spread of Islam in France, Michel Reeber
The Spread of Islam in the World, Prof. T.W. Arnold